THE NEW YALE BOOK OF QUOTATIONS

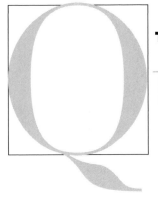

THE NEW YALE BOOK OF

Quotations

Edited by Fred R. Shapiro

Foreword by Louis Menand

Yale

UNIVERSITY PRESS

New Haven and London

First published in 2006 as *The Yale Book of Quotations*. This revised edition published 2021.

Yale University Press books may be purchased in quantity for educational, business, or promotional use. For information, please e-mail sales.press@yale.edu (U.S. office) or sales@yaleup.co.uk (U.K. office).

Designed by Nancy Ovedovitz and set in Scala, Didot, and Syntax types by Newgen North America.

Printed in the United States of America.

Library of Congress Control Number: 2020946412

ISBN 978-0-300-20597-8 (hardcover : alk. paper)

A catalogue record for this book is available from the British Library.

This paper meets the requirements of ANSI/NISO Z39.48-1992 (Permanence of Paper).

10 9 8 7 6 5 4 3 2 1

*To Murray Shapiro, who brought home a quotation dictionary
from the Strand bookstore more than fifty years ago;
and
To Robert K. Merton, who stood on the shoulders of giants
and whose own shoulders were very broad indeed*

CONTENTS

FOREWORD

Louis Menand

The New Yale Book of Quotations is a fun book to browse, and there are not many reference books we can say that about. Maybe the old print version of the *Oxford English Dictionary (OED)*, the pages of which W. H. Auden is supposed to have worn out in his copy.

Like the *OED*, the *Yale Book* is fun in a scholarly way (if that is not oxymoronic). It does what scholarship is supposed to do, which is to set the record straight and throw light into dark corners. There is a distinct pleasure just in knowing that Winston Churchill did not invent the term "iron curtain," and that Marie Antoinette never said "Let them eat cake." It feels good to be a person who knows that "The buck stops here" originated not with Harry Truman but on a card above an army lieutenant's desk in 1929, and that "You're either part of the solution or you're part of the problem," ascribed to Eldridge Cleaver, derives from a prayer by a Congressional chaplain, Peter Marshall, that appears in the Congressional Record for January 1947. And it's cool to find out that phrases that seem to have come out of nowhere—"Shit happens," "Get a life"—actually came from somewhere.

But the pleasure in knowing that a lot of conventional quotation wisdom, of the *Bartlett's Familiar* variety, is often mistaken is not only academic, or fun in the Trivial Pursuit sense. This knowledge is also demystifying. In the quotation universe, as in our mundane material world, the rich get richer, and not always because they earned it. The bigger the name, the more likely the misattribution. Churchill gets the credit for "iron curtain" because he is already the owner of a major reputation for colorful phrases. Meanwhile, the lowly wordsmiths, language's burger flippers, labor in obscurity.

The *Yale Book*'s recovery of these names is a valuable service in the cause of social justice. For it somehow does not shock us to have it revealed, especially in this revised edition, that the distribution of credit for famous sayings maps onto the structure of social relations. Women, it turns out, have often come up with memorable words and phrases standardly attached to men. There is a sociology of quotation.

So "I disapprove of what you say, but I will defend to the death your right to say it," everybody's favorite Voltaire quotation, was actually written by his biographer Evelyn Beatrice Hall, as the sort of thing Voltaire might have said. And "The only difference between the rich and other people is that the rich have more money" was a remark made to Hemingway by the critic Mary Colum. Hemingway liked it so much he borrowed it for his (probably fictional) conversation with F. Scott Fitzgerald.

The *OED* shows us that words have histories, that their meanings have evolved (or, really, shifted in the wind of circumstance) over time. And the *Yale Book* shows us that quotations evolve, as well. They are embellished ("Play it, Sam" morphs into "Play it again, Sam"), punched up ("If you build it, they will come"), and bumper-stickered ("What would Jesus do?"). And, to a greater or lesser degree of significance, quotations are always—it is the very nature of the genre—taken out of context. "We the people of the United States," "It is a truth universally acknowledged," "April is the cruelest month," "It was the best of times," "Mistah Kurtz—he dead": they are the pith of much larger texts, convenient handles on the enormous trunk of speech. Their permanence—for, unlike memes, which are shooting stars, quotations are like the planets, quasi-immortal—gives the comforting illusion of comprehensibility to the limitless expanse of recorded utterance. We will never read, let alone grasp, all of the work of Martin Heidegger, but knowing the phrase "Language is the house of being" allows us to pretend we have. That's our handle on Heidegger.

As with the *OED*, browsing the *Yale Book* is also fun in the fun-house sense. A trip through these pages can induce a sensation of vertigo. What is not, potentially, a quotation? If "Where's the beef?" and "He's dead, Jim" can achieve immortality, so might any phrase, given enough circulation. "You can get a happy quotation anywhere if you have the eye," as Oliver Wendell Holmes, Jr. (a veritable quotation mint) put it.

Boiled way down, a quotation is just a string of words that latches on. Every family has its own stock, found verbal objects that get picked up, mimicked, transformed by repetition into mottos or refrains. So does every person. Song lyrics, lines of poetry, bits remembered from children's books. It's strange how precious these are. They are amulets, charms against chaos, secret mantras for dark times. The *Yale Book* tells us where these little bits of ourselves came from.

ACKNOWLEDGMENTS

The editor has been extremely fortunate to receive outstanding support from staff at Yale University Press. Excellent editorial support and sound judgment came from Sarah Miller, former editor for literature and the performing arts; Ash Lago, language manager; and Adina Berk, senior editor for history. Others at the Press who provided important help included John Donatich, director; Jessie Dolch, copy editor; Nancy Ovedovitz, former design manager; Jeffrey Schier, senior manuscript editor; Sonia Shannon, senior designer; Eva Skewes, editorial assistant; Karen Stickler, assistant designer; and Jenya Weinreb, director of publishing operations.

This book benefited greatly from the help of readers and researchers from throughout the world. An enormous debt is owed to Garson O'Toole, who was inspired by the first edition of *The Yale Book of Quotations* to create the magnificent website quoteinvestigator.com. His contributions are described in the Introduction to this volume. Another person who furnished superb research about quotations was Barry Popik, whose website barrypopik. com contains an enormous amount of material about quotations and phrases. Charles Clay Doyle was the principal editor of *The Dictionary of Modern Proverbs* (the other editors were Wolfgang Mieder and Fred R. Shapiro), a landmark achievement that furnished much information for *The New Yale Book of Quotations*.

The first edition of *The Yale Book of Quotations* noted other reference works that were indispensable, namely the *Oxford Dictionary of Quotations*, *Bartlett's Familiar Quotations*, the *Oxford Dictionary of Proverbs*, *The Oxford Dictionary of Nursery Rhymes*, *The Columbia Granger Dictionary of Poetry Quotations*, and the outstanding books of Ralph Keyes, Nigel Rees, Suzy Platt, and Robert Andrews. The *Oxford Dictionary of Quotations* provides marvelously precise citations for quotations, and many of its pre-1800 citations were silently accepted for this book. (This is comparable to the practice of *The Oxford English Dictionary* in silently accepting citations from other scholarly lexical dictionaries.) Post-1800 quotations here have generally been verified from the original publications or standard editions. Other very helpful quotation compilations published since the first edition of *The Yale Book of Quotations* came out in 2006 included the following:

Bartlett's Familiar Black Quotations, edited by Retha Powers

Brewer's Famous Quotations, edited by Nigel Rees

The New Penguin Dictionary of Quotations, edited by Robert Andrews

The Oxford Dictionary of American Quotations, edited by Hugh Rawson and Margaret Miner

The Quote Verifier, edited by Ralph Keyes

Perhaps the most gratifying consequence of the publication of the original *Yale Book of Quotations* was the response it inspired from individuals—scholars, journalists, and people who just love quotations—in the United States and indeed around the globe. Suggestions about quotations that should be added and improved information about quotation origins have continually poured in to the editor, and *The New Yale Book of Quotations* is much the better as a result. The foremost contributors were Murray Biggs, Edward K. Conklin, Jordan Jefferson, Gary Saul Morson, and Benjamin Zimmer. Others who were significantly helpful included Garry Apgar, John M. Baker, Joel S. Berson, Sam Clements, S. M. Colowick, Tom Dalzell, Bob Dies, Jay Dillon, William FitzGerald, William Flesch, Thomas Fuller, Bryan Garner, Jane Garry, Aaron Gertler, Dan Goncharoff, Stephen Goranson, Jonathon Green, Donna Halper, Katherine Harper, Peter Harvey, John R. Henderson, Ken Hirsch, Laurence Horn, Eric M. Jones, Rik Kabel, Sue Kamm, David Klumpp, Richard Langworth, Jeffry Larson, Dennis Lien, Jonathan E. Lighter, Michael J. "Orange Mike" Lowrey, Rosalie Maggio, Wolfgang Mieder, Sylvia Milne, Denise L. Montgomery, Peter Morris, Bill Mullins, Erick Ramalho, Willis Regier, Peter Reitan, D. G. Rogers, Andrew Shapiro, James Shapiro, Jesse Sheidlower, Max Siegel, Andrew Steinberg, Victor Steinbok, Paul Tankard, Bonnie Taylor-Blake, Suzanne Watkins, Kerry Webb, Peter Weisman, Mary Whisner, Douglas C. Wilson, and Kevin W. Woodruff.

The editor's colleagues at the Yale Law Library have been unfailingly patient with his obsession with quotations. Teresa Miguel-Stearns, the director of the library, and her predecessor, Blair Kauffman, have been extraordinary in their encouragement and support. Alison Burke obtained many books and articles through interlibrary loan for the project. Other Yale Law librarians who suggested quotations or answered a wide variety of questions included Julian Aiken, Bonnie Collier, Jason Eiseman, Lisa Goodman, Ryan Harrington, Shana Jackson, Jordan Jefferson, Craig Kirkland, Julie Krishnaswami, Scott Matheson, John Nann, Lucie Olejnikova, Dawn Smith, Camilla Tubbs, Daniel Wade, Michael Widener, and Cesar Zapata. The editor's wife, Jane Garry, and children, Andrew Shapiro and James Shapiro, were even more patient in dealing with a husband and father once again "caught in the web of quotations."

Generous financial support for the first edition of *The Yale Book of Quotations* was provided by grants from the Andrew W. Mellon Foundation. Harriet Zuckerman, former senior vice president of the foundation, was the sponsor of the grants, which focused on exploring the usefulness of the JSTOR database for research into quotations and word origins. Ms. Zuckerman's sponsorship reflected her own interest in the sociology of knowledge and also the strong interest of her late husband, the great sociologist Robert K. Merton, in quotations. Merton coedited *Social Science Quotations* and wrote a classic book devoted to a single quotation, *On the Shoulders of Giants: A Shandean Postscript*. The spirit of these two books, at the intersection of literature, history, and sociological issues of innovation and diffusion, has been a major inspiration for both the Yale and the New Yale books of quotations.

INTRODUCTION

The Yale Book of Quotations was published in 2006, with two principal ambitions: to capture the most famous quotations more comprehensively than other compilations, and to use pioneering research methods to trace quotations to their true origins. The response by reviewers and readers was overwhelmingly positive—for example, an article in the *Wall Street Journal* named the *Yale Book of Quotations* as the second most essential of all reference books. Yet in hindsight the first edition may be seen as a pathbreaking starting point. Subsequently, with much help from many talented researchers from around the world who were inspired by that edition, the editor has been able to fully revolutionize our knowledge of the history of famous quotations. In addition, his investigations have revealed the striking fact that many familiar sayings were authored by women whose role has been forgotten, and who have often had their verbal inventions credited to prominent men.

The extensive quotation discoveries and improvements that have been made since 2006 are now presented in *The New Yale Book of Quotations.* At a time when the values of accuracy and truth are increasingly under siege, this volume presents documented true sources for the words of insight, wit, eloquence, and history that are beloved or remembered by so many of us. Also unveiled here are the most notable quotations from the culture and politics of recent years, the products of a frenetic and turbulent era.

The Art and Science of the Quotation Dictionary

Quotations are a fundamental mechanism for the transmission of art and thought. Ralph Waldo Emerson wrote, "By necessity, by proclivity, and by delight, we all quote." The delight is our natural response to the monuments of creativity and wisdom kept alive by quotations, a communal bond uniting us with past culture and with other lovers of words and ideas in our own time. A dictionary of quotations supports the communal bond.

The Yale Book of Quotations was the first major quotation book geared to the needs of the contemporary reader. This new edition continues to provide ample coverage of modern and American materials, encompassing such areas as popular culture, children's literature, sports, computers, politics, law, and the social sciences, as well as presenting the best-known quotations from older literary and historical sources and from worldwide cultures. Many hundreds of very famous and popular quotations omitted from other quotation dictionaries will be found in these pages.

The *Yale Book* was also the first quotation book to be compiled using state-of-the-art research methods to seek out quotations and to trace quotation sources to their authentic origins or earliest discoverable occurrences. Essentially, the approach used was the same as that of historical dictionaries, such as *The Oxford English Dictionary*, that try to trace words back to their oldest findable uses. *The New Yale Book of Quotations*, like its predecessor, may be viewed as a historical dictionary of quotations.

Both art and science come into play in compiling a quotation dictionary. The art requires the dictionary compiler to be sufficiently attuned to the intensity and impact of words so that he (or she) "knows" a great quotation "when he sees it," to paraphrase Supreme Court Justice Potter Stewart on pornography. Like Emily Dickinson recognizing poetry, the quotation anthologist responds to the verbal quarry with the sense that "it makes my whole body so cold no fire ever can warm me. . . . I feel physically as if the top of my head were taken off."

The ideal quotation for inclusion should sparkle, like Anatole France's comment on the "majestic equality of the law, which forbids the rich as well as the poor to sleep under bridges, to beg in the streets, and to steal bread." In that respect it might resemble the people who, according to Jack Kerouac, "never yawn or say a commonplace thing, but burn, burn, burn like fabulous yellow roman candles exploding like spiders across the stars." Or it should be famous enough that it is part of the conversation of arts and ideas in a culture, like Lord Acton's observation, "Power tends to corrupt and absolute power corrupts absolutely."

The science of compiling a quotation dictionary consists in exhaustively identifying the most famous quotations, tracing them to their original sources as far as possible, and recording those sources precisely and accurately. For this book, novel techniques were used in pursuit of those standards, highlighted by extensive computer-aided research. An enormous number of historical texts are now available in electronic form. By searching online databases one can often find earlier or more exact information about famous quotations. The very well-known maxim "Justice delayed is justice denied" was until recently listed in the *Oxford Dictionary of Quotations* as a "late 20th century saying." When British newspaper databases are searched, however, it becomes abundantly clear that the great prime minister William Gladstone used "justice delayed is justice denied" in an important speech about Ireland on March 16, 1868. Other searching for *The New Yale Book of Quotations* unearthed usage of these words in the *Weekly Mississippian* (Jackson, Miss.), November 23, 1838. Moreover, Edward K. Conklin of Honolulu emailed the *New Yale Book*'s editor with the results of his own online sleuthing: the formulation "Justice delayed is little better than justice denied" was used in an 1815 book, and in 1646 a pamphlet was published with the title *Another Word to the Wise, Shewing that the Delay of Justice, Is Great Injustice.*

Like the "justice delayed" example, many famous and interesting quotations have no definite original source. Other quotation dictionaries may give vague citations such as "Remark" for these; *The New Yale Book of Quotations*, however, attempts to give the earliest findable occurrence. Usually the citation takes the form "Quoted in," followed by the oldest known book or article or other publication in which the words in question appear:

Is that a gun in your pocket, or are you just glad to see me?
Quoted in *The Wit and Wisdom of Mae West*, ed. Joseph Weintraub (1967) [listed in this book under *Mae West*]

If there is substantial reason to doubt the validity of the attribution by the oldest source, the form "Attributed in" is used:

640K [of computer memory] ought to be enough for anyone.
Attributed in *InfoWorld*, 1 Jan. 1990 [listed in this book under *Bill Gates*]

Powerful online and other research methods make it possible to trace quotations to the most accurate sources. Some notable quotations misattributed by earlier quotation dictionaries include the following: "The opera ain't over until the fat lady sings" (actually by Ralph Carpenter, not Dan Cook); "Put all your eggs in one basket, and then watch that basket" (Andrew Carnegie, not Mark Twain); "Go West, young man" (Horace Greeley, not John Soule); "War is hell" (Napoleon, not William Tecumseh Sherman); "There ain't no such thing as free lunch" (Walter Morrow, not Milton Friedman); "Winning isn't everything—it's the only thing" (Red Sanders, not Vince Lombardi); "If you can't stand the heat, get out of the kitchen" (Buck Purcell, not Harry Truman).

The following were some of the most helpful of the electronic tools, presenting images and searchable text of billions of pages of publications that were searched regularly to help determine quotation sources, wording, and frequency:

- ProQuest (newspapers, periodicals, and other materials from the eighteenth century to the present)
- Newspapers.com (newspapers from the eighteenth century to the present)
- NewspaperArchive.com (newspapers from the seventeenth century to the present)
- America's Historical Newspapers (U.S. newspapers from the seventeenth to twentieth centuries)
- Nineteenth Century U.S. Newspapers (U.S. newspapers from the nineteenth century)
- LexisNexis (newspapers and periodicals from the twentieth and twenty-first centuries)
- JSTOR (scholarly journals in the humanities, social sciences, and natural sciences, 1665 to the present)
- Early English Books Online (primarily British books, 1473–1700)
- Eighteenth Century Collections Online (primarily British and U.S. books from the eighteenth century)
- America's Historical Imprints (U.S. books, 1639–1820)
- Google Books (tens of millions of books scanned from large libraries)
- HathiTrust (millions of books scanned from large libraries)

The publication of *The Yale Book of Quotations* triggered a remarkable "crowd-sourcing" response by quotation lovers and researchers spanning the globe. Employing printed books, online searching, and their own memories, many readers emailed, or communicated by other avenues, outstanding contributions of quotations for inclusion or of improvements in information about quotes in the *Yale Book*. The names of the more active such contributors are given in the Acknowledgments, but special credit needs to be elaborated here for Garson O'Toole.

In 2007 O'Toole became curious about the genesis of the supposed Chinese curse "May you live in interesting times," which

Wikipedia had traced back to 1950. He then was able to find the curse in a 1944 book and posted his discovery on a blog. This posting was noticed by the *Yale Book of Quotations* editor, who added a comment pointing out that the *Yale Book* had a 1939 citation. O'Toole later wrote that he "purchased a copy of *The Yale Book of Quotations* and began purposefully scanning its entries." The rest is history, as he was inspired by the Yale volume to create, three years later, a website he titled Quote Investigator (quoteinvestigator.com). Quote Investigator has grown to include well over a million words of authoritative quotation-sleuthing. O'Toole's brilliant researches have greatly aided *The New Yale Book of Quotations*, which has many dozens of entries reflecting Quote Investigator findings.

The compilation of the present book has also benefited from extensive use of the electronic mailing list of the American Dialect Society and the Project Wombat network of reference librarians and researchers, both of which bring together very skilled people dedicated to answering sophisticated questions. Specific contributors are listed in the Acknowledgments. Finally, traditional methods of library research, utilizing the resources of the Yale University Library and Yale Law Library as well as interlibrary borrowing from other institutions, were pursued to verify quotations and to find their origins.

The research efforts outlined above were devoted not only to tracing and verifying quotation origins, but also to ensuring that all of the most famous quotations were included in this book. As a result, many important quotations not found in prior quotation dictionaries appear here, such as Willard Motley's 1947 suggestion to "Live fast, die young, and have a good-looking corpse!"; the famous sentence

from Lou Gehrig's farewell speech at Yankee Stadium in 1939: "Today I consider myself the luckiest man on the face of the earth"; and Friedrich Nietzsche's 1888 epigram, "Whatever does not kill me makes me stronger." More than a thousand previous quotation collections and other types of anthologies were canvassed; many Internet resources were perused; and experts on specific authors and types of literature were consulted.

As a result of the unique approaches and methods employed, *The New Yale Book of Quotations* has a Janus-like duality. As noted above, the *New Yale Book* serves a very traditional function of gathering the monuments of literary expression and other forms of enduring culture. It also, however, captures the most celebrated items of contemporary discourse and public life. Thus William Shakespeare and Donald Trump coexist in these pages. One of them is far less eloquent than the other, but, for better or worse, both are now part of our verbal heritage, with Mr. Trump's most remarkable utterances and tweets carefully recorded here. Other recent individuals whose quotes have been introduced or supplemented in this edition include, among many others, Warren Buffett, Hillary Clinton, Pope Francis, Jonathan Franzen, Alan Greenspan, Steven Jobs, Cormac McCarthy, Lin-Manuel Miranda, Toni Morrison, Barack Obama, Sarah Palin, David Foster Wallace, and Warren Zevon.

"Anonymous Was a Woman" and the Serenity Prayer

Virginia Woolf, in *A Room of One's Own*, wrote, "I would venture to guess that Anon, who wrote so many poems without signing them, was often a woman." She was referring to literary creation as a whole, not the special subset called "quotations," but the editor of *The New Yale Book of Quotations* has discovered, time and again, that in the realm of famous lines Anonymous was often a woman. Many of the great quotesmiths have been women who are now forgotten or whose wit and wisdom are erroneously credited to more-famous men.

The researches that went into *The New Yale Book of Quotations* and its predecessor edition supply the proof of the unrecognized role of women in creating iconic sayings. Here is a list of some of the most glaring female-to-male misattributions:

I will not follow where the path may lead, but I will go where there is no path, and I will leave a trail.
Muriel Strode, but usually attributed to Ralph Waldo Emerson

He has achieved success who has lived well, laughed often, and loved much.
Bessie A. Stanley, but usually attributed to Ralph Waldo Emerson

I disapprove of what you say, but I will defend to the death your right to say it.
Evelyn Beatrice Hall, but usually attributed to Voltaire

Truth is the first casualty in war.
Ethel Snowden, but usually attributed to Hiram Johnson

Iron Curtain.
Ethel Snowden, but usually attributed to Winston Churchill

Live a fast life, die young, and be a beautiful corpse.
Irene L. Luce, but usually attributed to Willard Motley

The only difference between the rich and other people is that the rich have more money.
Mary Colum, but usually attributed to Ernest Hemingway

Now I know why nobody ever comes here; it's too crowded.
Suzanne Ridgeway, but usually attributed to Yogi Berra

We will overcome.
Lucille Simmons, but usually attributed to Pete Seeger

Just say the lines and don't trip over the furniture.
Lynn Fontanne, but usually attributed to Noël Coward

If you make it here, you make it anywhere.
Julie Newmar, but usually attributed to Fred Ebb

We are a nation of communities . . . like a thousand points of light.
Peggy Noonan, but usually attributed to George H. W. Bush

Read my lips: no new taxes.
Peggy Noonan, but usually attributed to George H. W. Bush

Twenty years from now you will be more disappointed by the things you didn't do than by the ones you did do. So throw off the bowlines. Sail away from the safe harbor. Catch the trade winds in your sails.
Sarah Frances Brown, but usually attributed to Mark Twain

Our deepest fear is not that we are inadequate. Our deepest fear is that we are powerful beyond measure. It is our light, not our darkness, that most frightens us.

Marianne Williamson, but usually attributed to Nelson Mandela

Ladies and gentlemen of the class of '97: Wear sunscreen.
Mary Schmich, but usually attributed to Kurt Vonnegut

There are other renowned quotations that are not necessarily misattributed to men but have had their origination by a woman forgotten:

No time like the present.
Originated by Mary de la Rivière Manley

No man is a hero to his valet.
Originated by Anne-Marie Bigot de Cornuel

Twinkle, twinkle, little star,
How I wonder what you are!
Up above the world so high,
Like a diamond in the sky!
Originated by Jane Taylor

Mary had a little lamb,
Its fleece was white as snow,
And everywhere that Mary went
The lamb was sure to go.
Originated by Sarah Josepha Hale

Laugh and the world laughs with you;
Weep, and you weep alone.
Originated by Ella Wheeler Wilcox

See Spot run.
Originated by Clara Murray

What does it matter so long as they don't do it in the street and frighten the horses.
Originated by Beatrice Campbell

Oh, no. It wasn't the airplanes. It was Beauty killed the Beast.
Originated by Ruth Rose

The wave of the future.
Originated by Anne Morrow Lindbergh

War is not healthy for children and other living things.
Originated by Lorraine Schneider

It takes a village to raise a child.
Originated by Toni Morrison

E.T. phone home.
Originated by Melissa Mathison

Black Lives Matter.
Originated by Alicia Garza

Women, long denied full participation in cultural and public spheres, have nonetheless contributed a wealth of eloquence and insight in their writings, songs, and political discourse. *The New Yale Book of Quotations* has striven to give them substantial representation. The same holds true for African Americans and other historically marginalized groups. Among nationalities, the *New Yale Book* continues to have the largest number of quotations from U.S. authors, but it has an increased number of quotes from countries on every continent.

One very famous quotation that appears to be the invention of a woman but is not listed above has a special story that can be related for the first time here. This is the "Serenity Prayer," the most renowned and beloved prayer of modern times. The most common version is "God grant me the serenity to accept the things I cannot change, courage to change the things I can, and wisdom to know the difference." There has been considerable misinformation about this prayer's origins, whose attribution has usually been assigned to the great theologian and political philosopher

Reinhold Niebuhr and dated 1943. *The Yale Book of Quotations* listed Niebuhr as the author. In 2008, the *New York Times* reported in a front-page story that the *Yale Book* editor had made discoveries casting doubt on Niebuhr's origination, launching a controversy that included a second front-page story in the *Times* citing the editor's partial retraction of those doubts. Research for the *New Yale Book* then continued to generate new evidence bearing on the authorship question.

The ultimate *New Yale Book of Quotations* findings tracing the "Serenity Prayer" back in time proved that this prayer was used in 1933. An official with the Young Women's Christian Association named Winnifred Crane Wygal was the author of the earliest known occurrence. Wygal was an associate of Niebuhr's, and it is possible that she took the prayer in some unpublished form from him. However, Professor William FitzGerald of Rutgers University, in an upcoming book, puts forth a new interpretation, that Winnifred Wygal was the coiner who combined some pieces apparently drawn from Niebuhr with important other pieces of her own devising to create a most memorable prayer. The findings and interpretation are explained further in the entry in this book under Wygal's name.

What This Book Includes

This book takes a broad view of what constitutes a quotation, from passages of writing or speech that range in length from a sentence to a paragraph or longer; to lines or stanzas of poetry; to short phrases, slogans, and proverbs.

Most of the quotations were selected because they are "famous," that is, they are often quoted or anthologized. Online search engines and databases such as Google and LexisNexis were regularly utilized to determine frequency of use. In some instances, fame was defined in terms of a specialized area; for example, scientific quotations that are not familiar to the general public were included because of their familiarity to scientists.

Familiarity or fame was not the sole criterion for inclusion, however. Some items were included because of their wit, eloquence, or insight, others because of their historical importance. F. Scott Fitzgerald, for example, wrote eloquently, in *Tender Is the Night,* of "scars healed, a loose parallel to the pathology of the skin, but there is no such thing in the life of an individual. There are open wounds, shrunk sometimes to the size of a pin-prick but wounds still. The marks of suffering are more comparable to the loss of a finger, or of the sight of an eye. We may not miss them, either, for one minute in a year, but if we should there is nothing to be done about it." And Abraham Lincoln added his words to history in the Emancipation Proclamation of 1863: "I do order and declare that all persons held as slaves within said designated States, and part of States, are, and henceforward shall be free."

Special attention has been paid to certain modern giants of quotability. In this book, Mark Twain, Ambrose Bierce, Oscar Wilde, George Bernard Shaw, Winston Churchill, F. Scott Fitzgerald, George Orwell, and Dorothy Parker loom as large as names like John Milton, Alfred Lord Tennyson, Lord Byron, Alexander Pope, and John Keats do in traditional quotation compilations. Readers will find other, more recent authors here who do not appear at all in previous collections.

Quotations are drawn from poetry, drama, essays, and fiction; from philosophical, historical, and social-scientific writings, as well as the literature of mathematics and the natural sciences; from commentaries on music, the visual arts, the business world, and military affairs. Quotations from the Bible, which provides more entries than any other source after Shakespeare, are supplemented by Christian sources such as the Book of Common Prayer and non-Christian scriptures and religious texts such as the Koran, the Talmud, and the Bhagavadgita.

Many well-known or historically important lines from politicians' speeches and other remarks are found in this book, especially emphasizing U.S. politics and history, from Thomas Jefferson and John Adams to Barack Obama and Donald Trump. The U.S. political heritage is also represented by important legal quotations, from landmark judicial opinions, the U.S. Constitution, and various commentaries on the law.

This book also gathers an abundance of memorable lines from song lyrics and motion pictures. Famous "film lines" are listed in a special section under that name; however, true to this book's emphasis on presenting the earliest sources, those lines that can be traced to earlier books or plays are listed under the author of the book or play. Thus, for instance, readers will find "There is no place like home" under L. Frank Baum because this line appeared first in his 1900 book *The Wonderful Wizard of Oz* rather than in the 1939 movie.

A particularly prominent special class of quotation is the proverb, defined by John Simpson in *The Concise Oxford Dictionary of Proverbs* as "a traditional saying which offers advice or presents a moral in a short and pithy manner." In most cases proverbs have no known originator, and no amount of research is likely to uncover one. Reference works deal with this anonymity in several ways. Proverbs may be listed under the name of the earliest known user, or they may be listed with information about the century of origin. They also may be listed with detailed citation to the earliest known use. The research behind those first uses, however, has been limited, based on haphazard reading programs. Now, however, online searching of vast collections of historical texts makes it possible to research proverb origins systematically. Such research was pioneered to some extent in *The Yale Book of Quotations* and further developed in *The Dictionary of Modern Proverbs,* edited by Charles Clay Doyle, Wolfgang Mieder, and Fred R. Shapiro and published in 2012. Employing the same methods, *The New Yale Book of Quotations* presents evidence that may be close to the true first appearance in print for many proverbs, resulting in a much more accurate picture of their histories.

The transformations wrought by the state-of-the-art research techniques applied to proverbs can be quite stunning. The celebrated saying "If anything can go wrong it will," known as "Murphy's Law," is attributed by standard reference books to U.S. Air Force engineer Edward A. Murphy, Jr., in 1949. However, diligent online searching by Stephen Goranson, Bill Mullins, and the editor of this volume has demonstrated that "Murphy's Law," with that name, was discussed in print as a humorous maxim of science and technology before the supposed 1949 Air Force incident, which must be deemed apocryphal. Incidences of the proverb itself have now been retrieved from as far back as 1908 in magicians' literature.

Before *The Yale Book of Quotations* and *The Dictionary of Modern Proverbs,* proverb dictionaries included very few proverbs that originated after 1900, leaving the user to conclude that proverbs were purely antiquarian sayings that were no longer coined in modern times. But nothing could be further from the truth. Modern proverbs proliferate constantly and are among our most colorful and popular expressions. In *The New Yale Book of Quotations,* a special section of "Modern Proverbs" includes such familiar items as "Different strokes for different folks," "Never criticize anybody until you have walked a mile in his shoes," "The customer is always right," and "Shit happens."

How to Use This Book

Arrangement of Quotations

Quotations are ordered alphabetically by author (or speaker) name. Where the author is best known by a pseudonym, such as Mark Twain, he or she is listed under the pseudonymous name, with the birth name in parentheses. A few collective works, such as the Bible, the Koran, and the Constitution of the United States, are listed alphabetically among the author entries. In addition, several special sections that highlight specific categories of quotations are also placed in alphabetical order among the author entries:

Advertising Slogans
Anonymous (quotations that have known origins but unknown or corporate authors and that do not fit into other well-defined categories)
Anonymous (Latin)
Ballads
Film Lines

Folk and Anonymous Songs
Modern Proverbs
Nursery Rhymes
Political Slogans
Proverbs
Radio Catchphrases
Sayings (expressions that have origins probably impossible to trace and that are not strictly proverbs)
Television Catchphrases

Within each author section, quotations are arranged chronologically, and alphabetically by source title within the same year. Quotations with a source beginning "Quoted in," "Reported in," or "Attributed in" are listed at the end, in that order. "Attributed in" is used where there is substantial reason to doubt that the putative author actually wrote or said the item in question.

Quotations within the special sections, which share the characteristics of having anonymous or collective authorship or presenting difficulties in tracing authorship, are listed by first keyword, title, product name, television or radio program name, or other description, rather than by author.

Authors

Author names are followed by the author's nationality, occupation, and birth and death years. If exact years are not known, the abbreviation "ca." (*circa*) indicates approximate years; "fl." (*floruit*) is included if all that is known is the year or years in which an author worked (or "flourished"). In some instances, an author annotation explains additional information about the author's identity or works, the assignment of quotations to that author, or cross-references to related author entries. A few author entries are joint entries, such

as Mick Jagger and Keith Richards; where
the pairing is less established, quotations
with multiple authors are listed under the
more prominent author, with a note crediting
coauthors.

Quotations from song lyrics are listed under
the lyricist's name. Lines from motion pictures
are listed in the section "Film Lines" under the
name of the movie, with additional identification of the character uttering the line, the
actor playing the character, and the screenwriter or screenwriters. (Exceptions are made
for Woody Allen, Mel Brooks, W. C. Fields,
George Lucas, Groucho Marx, Monty Python's
Flying Circus, Mario Puzo, and Mae West,
whose film lines are collected under their
own names as authors rather than in the Film
Lines section.) Quotations from politicians'
speeches are credited to the politician rather
than to speechwriters, whose identity is often
impossible to verify. Similarly, no attempt has
been made to trace television and radio catchphrases to individual writers.

Text of Quotations

The texts of the quotations have been taken
verbatim from the original sources or, for
many of the older items, from standard editions. For items that are "Quoted in," "Reported in," or "Attributed in," unless otherwise
noted, the text given is exactly that found in
the secondary source referred to. Quotations
are capitalized at the beginning and end with a
period even if they begin or end in the middle
of a sentence. Omissions in the middle of a
quotation are indicated by an ellipsis. Spell-
ings and capitalization of older quotations have
been modernized, with some exceptions, such
as Geoffrey Chaucer, where custom retains the

original form. A few British spelling conventions, such as words ending in "-our," have
been Americanized. Complex indentation of
poetry has generally been simplified to a left-
justified format.

Quotations from foreign languages have
been translated into English. Where the quotation is somewhat familiar to English speakers
in the original language (usually from Latin
or French sources), the original is included in
italics before the translation.

Sources of Quotations

Even the most scholarly prior quotation
dictionaries include many vague source references, such as "Remark" or "Last words." *The
New Yale Book of Quotations,* however, provides
precise sources; even those quotations whose
exact provenance is untraceable are identified
as "Quoted in," "Attributed in," or "Reported
in" followed by a precise secondary source.

The usual source citations take the following
forms:

Books: Title, chapter number, year of
publication.

Plays: Title, act/scene number, year of publication or first performance.

Poems: Title, beginning line number or (for
longer poems) stanza number, year of
publication in book form.

Short Stories, Essays, Articles: Title, year of
publication. For literary authors, usually
only the title of the story or essay is given;
for other authors, the book or periodical in
which the publication was included may be
given if helpful.

Speeches: Description of speech, place of
delivery, date of delivery (place of delivery
is not indicated for broadcast speeches).

Annotations and Cross-References

In many instances, annotations after the quotation source help clarify the meaning, context, significance, or history of the quotation. They range in length from a few words to mini-essays on key quotations such as "There ain't no such thing as free lunch" or "Lies, damned lies, and statistics." The annotations are the product of intensive research and are perhaps the most distinctive feature of this book. In addition, in some entries clarifying information is provided in brackets before the text of the quotation.

Often a quotation was inspired by or refers to an earlier one, and sometimes the same thought is expressed by two or more authors, each of whose versions is memorable and merits inclusion. These connections are brought to the reader's attention through cross-references that identify author name and quotation number. For example, Yogi Berra's comment "It ain't over 'til it's over" is linked to Ralph Carpenter's analogous "The opera ain't over until the fat lady sings." Interested readers will find that some of the cross-references constitute important discoveries about the precursors of famous quotations.

Keyword Index

The Keyword Index is an important means of access to partially remembered quotations or quotations about a particular topic and serves as a form of subject index. Significant words from a quotation are listed in the index. A reader wanting to find quotations about money, for instance, will be able to do so by looking up "money" in the Keyword Index. Keywords and context excerpts (in which the keyword is abbreviated, such as "m." for "money") are listed alphabetically. Plural nouns are treated as separate keywords from the corresponding singular nouns; for example, "computer" and "computers" are listed separately. As with cross-references, the Keyword Index points the reader to the indexed quotation by identifying the author name and quotation number within that author section.

To help improve future editions of *The New Yale Book of Quotations,* suggestions from readers are most welcome. These could be new quotations or improvements on information in this edition. Please submit such contributions to fred.shapiro@yale.edu.

THE NEW YALE BOOK OF QUOTATIONS

Jacques Abbadie

French clergyman and author, 1654–1727

1 *Ont pû tromper quelques hommes, ou les tromper tous dans certains lieux & en certains tems, mais non pas tous les hommes, dans tous les lieux & dans tous les siècles.*

One can fool some men, or fool all men in some places and times, but one cannot fool all men in all places and ages.
Traité de la Vérité de la Religion Chrétienne pt. 1, sec. 1, ch. 2 (1684)
See Lincoln 66

Edward Abbey

U.S. environmentalist and writer, 1927–1989

1 Growth for the sake of growth is the ideology of the cancer cell.
Quoted in *Reader's Digest,* Jan. 1970

William "Bud" Abbott 1895–1974 and Lou Costello (Louis Cristillo) 1906–1959

U.S. comedians

1 [*Explaining the unusually named players on a baseball team:*] Who's on first, What's on second, I Don't Know is on third.
The Naughty Nineties (motion picture) (1945). According to Chris Costello, *Lou's on First* (1981), this Abbott and Costello baseball routine was developed during their burlesque years, then first heard on the *Kate Smith Radio Hour* in 1938.

Bella Abzug

U.S. politician, 1920–1998

1 We don't want so much to see a female Einstein become an assistant professor. We want a woman schlemiel to get promoted as quickly as a male schlemiel.
Quoted in *U.S. News and World Report,* 25 Apr. 1977

Chinua Achebe (Albert Chinualumogu)

Nigerian novelist, 1930–2013

1 Among the Igbo the art of conversation is regarded very highly, and proverbs are the palm-oil with which words are eaten.
Things Fall Apart ch. 1 (1958)

2 He had already chosen the title of the book, after much thought: The Pacification of the Primitive Tribes of the Lower Niger.
Things Fall Apart ch. 25 (1958)

3 In such a régime [the government of Chief Nanga in Nigeria], I say, you died a good death if your life had inspired someone to come forward and shoot your murderer in the chest—without asking to be paid.
A Man of the People ch. 13 (1966)

Dean Acheson

U.S. statesman, 1893–1971

1 Great Britain has lost an empire and has not yet found a role.
Speech at U.S. Military Academy, West Point, N.Y., 5 Dec. 1962

2 A memorandum is written not to inform the reader but to protect the writer.
Quoted in *Wall Street Journal,* 8 Sept. 1977

John Emerich Edward Dalberg-Acton, First Baron Acton

English historian, 1834–1902

1 Liberty is not a means to a higher political end. It is itself the highest political end.
"The History of Freedom in Antiquity" (1877)

2 There is no error so monstrous that it fails to find defenders among the ablest men. Imagine a congress of eminent celebrities, such as More, Bacon, Grotius, Pascal, Cromwell, Bossuet, Montesquieu, Jefferson, Napoleon, Pitt, &c. The result would be an Encyclopedia of Error.
Letter to Mary Gladstone, 24 Apr. 1881

3 Power tends to corrupt and absolute power corrupts absolutely. Great men are almost always bad men.
Letter to Mandell Creighton, 3 Apr. 1887
See William Pitt, Earl of Chatham 3

4 Writers the most learned, the most accurate in details, and the soundest in tendency, frequently fall into a habit which can neither be cured nor pardoned,—the habit of making history into the proof of their theories.
The History of Freedom and Other Essays ch. 8 (1907)

Abigail Adams
U.S. First Lady, 1744–1818

1 In the new Code of Laws which I suppose it will be necessary for you to make I desire you would Remember the Ladies, and be more generous and favorable to them than your ancestors. Do not put such unlimited power into the hands of the Husbands. Remember all Men would be tyrants if they could. If perticular care and attention is not paid to the Ladies we are determined to foment a Rebellion, and will not hold ourselves bound by any Laws in which we have no voice, or Representation.
Letter to John Adams, 31 Mar. 1776
See Defoe 2

2 I can not say that I think you are very generous to the Ladies, for whilst you are proclaiming peace and good will to Men, Emancipating all Nations, you insist upon retaining an absolute power over Wives. But you must remember that Arbitrary power is like most other things which are very hard, very liable to be broken— and notwithstanding all your wise Laws and Maxims we have it in our power not only to free ourselves but to subdue our Masters, and without violence throw both your natural and legal authority at our feet—"Charm by accepting, by submitting sway Yet have our Humor most when we obey."
Letter to John Adams, 7 May 1776

3 It is really mortifying, sir, when a woman possessed of a common share of understanding considers the difference of education between the male and female sex, even in those families where education is attended to. . . . Nay why should your sex wish for such a disparity in those whom they one day intend for companions and associates. Pardon me, sir, if I cannot help sometimes suspecting that

this neglect arises in some measure from an ungenerous jealousy of rivals near the throne.
Letter to John Thaxter, 15 Feb. 1778

4 These are times in which a genius would wish to live. It is not in the still calm of life, or the repose of a pacific station, that great characters are formed. . . . Great necessities call out great virtues.
Letter to John Quincy Adams, 19 Jan. 1780

5 Patriotism in the female sex is the most disinterested of all virtues. Excluded from honors and from offices, we cannot attach ourselves to the State or Government from having held a place of eminence. . . . Yet all history and every age exhibit instances of patriotic virtue in the female sex; which considering our situation equals the most heroic of yours.
Letter to John Adams, 17 June 1782

Charles Francis Adams
U.S. lawyer and diplomat, 1807–1886

1 It would be superfluous in me to point out to your lordship that this is war.
Dispatch to Lord John Russell, 5 Sept. 1863

Douglas Adams
English science fiction writer, 1952–2001

1 This is the story of The Hitchhiker's Guide to the Galaxy, perhaps the most remarkable, certainly the most successful book ever to come out of the great publishing corporations of Ursa Minor. . . . It has the words "DON'T PANIC" inscribed in large, friendly letters on the cover.
The Hitchhiker's Guide to the Galaxy "Fit the First" (radio program) (1978)

2 Man had always assumed that he was more intelligent than dolphins because he had achieved so much . . . the wheel, New York, wars, and so on, whilst all the dolphins had ever done was muck about in the water having a good time. But conversely the dolphins believed themselves to be more intelligent than man for precisely the same reasons.
The Hitchhiker's Guide to the Galaxy "Fit the Third" (radio program) (1978)

3 [*Answer to the "Ultimate Question of Life, the Universe and Everything":*] Forty two.
The Hitchhiker's Guide to the Galaxy "Fit the Fourth" (radio program) (1978)

4 In the beginning the Universe was created. This has made a lot of people very angry and been widely regarded as a bad move.
The Hitchhiker's Guide to the Galaxy "Fit the Fifth" (radio program) (1978)

5 The first ten million years were the worst. And the second ten million, they were the worst too. The third ten million I didn't enjoy at all. After that I went into a bit of a decline.
The Hitchhiker's Guide to the Galaxy "Fit the Fifth" (radio program) (1978)

6 There is a theory which states that if ever anyone discovered exactly what the Universe is for and why it is here, it will instantly disappear and be replaced by something even more bizarrely inexplicable. There is another theory which states that this has already happened.
The Hitchhiker's Guide to the Galaxy "Fit the Seventh" (radio program) (1978)

7 Anyone who is capable of getting themselves made President should on no account be allowed to do the job.
The Hitchhiker's Guide to the Galaxy "Fit the Twelfth" (radio program) (1980)
See Twain 14

8 It was none the less a perfectly ordinary horse, such as convergent evolution has produced in many of the places that life is to be found. They have always understood a great deal more than they let on. It is difficult to be sat on all day, every day, by some other creature, without forming an opinion about them.
Dirk Gently's Holistic Detective Agency ch. 2 (1987)

9 It can hardly be a coincidence that no language on Earth has ever produced the expression "as pretty as an airport."
The Long Dark Tea-Time of the Soul ch. 1 (1988)

10 What god would be hanging around Terminal Two of Heathrow Airport trying to catch the 15.37 flight to Oslo?
The Long Dark Tea-Time of the Soul ch. 6 (1988)

11 Now we have the World Wide Web (the only thing I know of whose shortened form— www—takes three times longer to say than what it's short for).
The Salmon of Doubt (2002)

12 I love deadlines. I like the whooshing sound they make as they fly by.
Quoted in Harley Hahn and Rick Stout, *The Internet Yellow Pages* (1994)

Franklin P. Adams
U.S. journalist and humorist, 1881–1960

1 These are the saddest of possible words:
"Tinker to Evers to Chance."
Trio of bear cubs, and fleeter than birds,
Tinker and Evers and Chance.
Ruthlessly pricking our gonfalon bubble,
Making a Giant hit into a double—
Words that are heavy with nothing but trouble:
"Tinker to Evers to Chance."
"Baseball's Sad Lexicon" l. 1 (1910). Joe Tinker, Johnny Evers, and Frank Chance were the double-play combination for the Chicago Cubs.

2 Years ago we discovered the exact point, the dead center of middle age. It occurs when you are too young to take up golf and too old to rush up to the net.
Nods and Becks (1944)

3 Elections are won by men and women chiefly because most people vote against somebody, rather than for somebody.
Nods and Becks (1944)
See W. C. Fields 21

Henry Brooks Adams
U.S. historian and writer, 1838–1918

1 Politics, as a practice, whatever its professions, has always been the systematic organization of hatreds.
The Education of Henry Adams ch. 1 (1907)

2 Accident counts for as much in companionship as in marriage.
The Education of Henry Adams ch. 4 (1907)

3 All experience is an arch, to build upon.
The Education of Henry Adams ch. 6 (1907)

4 Only on the edge of the grave can man conclude anything.
The Education of Henry Adams ch. 6 (1907)

5 A friend in power is a friend lost.
The Education of Henry Adams ch. 7 (1907)

6 Friends are born, not made.
The Education of Henry Adams ch. 7 (1907). These same words had appeared earlier in Blanche Howard, *Aulnay Tower* (1885).

7 [Charles] Sumner's mind had reached the calm of water which receives and reflects images without absorbing them; it contained nothing but itself.
The Education of Henry Adams ch. 16 (1907)

8 Chaos often breeds life, when order breeds habit.
The Education of Henry Adams ch. 16 (1907)

9 The difference is slight, to the influence of an author, whether he is read by five hundred readers, or by five hundred thousand; if he can select the five hundred, he reaches the five hundred thousand.
The Education of Henry Adams ch. 17 (1907)

10 The progress of evolution from President Washington to President Grant was alone evidence enough to upset Darwin.
The Education of Henry Adams ch. 17 (1907)

11 A teacher affects eternity; he can never tell where his influence stops.
The Education of Henry Adams ch. 20 (1907)

12 One friend in a life-time is much; two are many; three are hardly possible. Friendship needs a certain parallelism of life, a community of thought, a rivalry of aim.
The Education of Henry Adams ch. 20 (1907)

13 What one knows is, in youth, of little moment; they know enough who know how to learn.
The Education of Henry Adams ch. 21 (1907)

14 He had often noticed that six months' oblivion amounts to newspaper death, and that resurrection is rare. Nothing is easier, if a man wants it, than rest, profound as the grave.
The Education of Henry Adams ch. 22 (1907)

15 Practical politics consists in ignoring facts.
The Education of Henry Adams ch. 24 (1907)

16 All the steam in the world could not, like the Virgin, build Chartres.
The Education of Henry Adams ch. 25 (1907)

17 Modern politics is, at bottom, a struggle not of men but of forces.
The Education of Henry Adams ch. 28 (1907)

18 No one means all he says, and yet very few say all they mean, for words are slippery and thought is viscous.
The Education of Henry Adams ch. 31 (1907)

John Adams
U.S. president, 1735–1826

1 A Pen is certainly an excellent Instrument, to fix a Mans Attention and to inflame his Ambition.
Diary and Autobiography, 14 Nov. 1760

2 The jaws of power are always opened to devour, and her arm is always stretched out, if possible, to destroy the freedom of thinking, speaking, and writing.
A Dissertation on the Canon and the Feudal Law (1765)

3 The law, in all vicissitudes of government, fluctuations of the passions, or flights of enthusiasm, will preserve a steady undeviating course; it will not bend to the uncertain wishes, imaginations, and wanton tempers of men. . . . On the one hand it is inexorable to the cries and lamentations of the prisoners; on the other it is deaf, deaf as an adder to the clamors of the populace.
Argument in defense of the British soldiers in the Boston Massacre Trials, 4 Dec. 1770
See Bible 114; Algernon Sidney 1

4 A government of laws, and not of men.
"Novanglus Papers" no. 7 (1774). Almost certainly derived from James Harrington, but Adams's use of the phrase gave it wide circulation in the United States. He also used "government of laws, and not of men" in the Declaration of Rights drafted for the Massachusetts Constitution in 1780.
See Archibald Cox 1; Gerald Ford 3; James Harrington 1

5 The judicial power ought to be distinct from both the legislative and executive, and independent upon both, that so it may be a check upon both, as both should be checks upon that.
"Thoughts on Government" (1776)

6 I agree with you, that in Politicks the Middle Way is none at all.
Letter to Horatio Gates, 23 Mar. 1776

7 The Second Day of July 1776, will be the most memorable Epocha, in the History of America.—I am apt to believe that it will be celebrated, by succeeding Generations, as the great anniversary Festival. It ought to be commemorated, as the Day of Deliverance by solemn Acts of Devotion to God Almighty. It ought to be solemnized with Pomp and Parade, with Shews, Games, Sports, Guns, Bells, Bonfires, and Illuminations from one End of this Continent to the other from this Time forward forever more.
Letter to Abigail Adams, 3 July 1776

8 I am but an ordinary Man. The Times alone have destined me to Fame—and even these have not been able to give me, much. . . . Yet some great Events, some cutting Expressions, some mean Hypocrisies, have at Times, thrown this Assemblage of Sloth, Sleep, and littleness into Rage a little like a Lion.
Diary and Autobiography, 26 Apr. 1779

9 I must study Politicks and War that my sons may have liberty to study Mathematicks and Philosophy. My sons ought to study Mathematicks and Philosophy, Geography, natural History, Naval Architecture, navigation, Commerce and Agriculture, in order to give their Children a right to study Painting, Poetry, Musick, Architecture, Statuary, Tapestry, and Porcelaine.
Letter to Abigail Adams, 12 May 1780

10 Amidst your Ardor for Greek and Latin I hope you will not forget your mother Tongue. Read Somewhat in the English Poets every day. . . . You will never be alone, with a Poet in your Poket. You will never have an idle Hour.
Letter to John Quincy Adams, 14 May 1781

11 You are afraid of the one—I, of the few. We agree perfectly that the many should have a full fair and perfect Representation.—You are Apprehensive of Monarchy; I, of Aristocracy. I would therefore have given more Power to the President and less to the Senate.
Letter to Thomas Jefferson, 6 Dec. 1787

12 But my Country has in its Wisdom contrived for me the most insignificant Office [the vice-presidency] that ever the invention of Man

contrived or his Imagination conceived: and as I can do neither good nor Evil, I must be borne away by Others and meet the common Fate.
Letter to Abigail Adams, 19 Dec. 1793

13 [*Upon moving into the new White House:*] I pray Heaven to bestow the best of Blessings on this House and all that shall hereafter inhabit it. May none but honest and wise Men ever rule under this roof.
Letter to Abigail Adams, 2 Nov. 1800

14 You and I ought not to die, before We have explained ourselves to each other.
Letter to Thomas Jefferson, 15 July 1813

15 Remember, democracy never lasts long. It soon wastes, exhausts, and murders itself. There never was a democracy yet that did not commit suicide.
Letter to John Taylor, 15 Apr. 1814

16 When People talk of the Freedom of Writing, Speaking or thinking, I cannot choose but laugh. No such thing ever existed. No such thing now exists: but I hope it will exist. But it must be hundreds of years after you and I shall write and speak no more.
Letter to Thomas Jefferson, 15 July 1817

17 The Revolution was effected before the war commenced. The Revolution was in the minds and hearts of the people.
Letter to Hezekiah Niles, 13 Feb. 1818

18 No man who ever held the office of President would congratulate a friend on obtaining it. He will make one man ungrateful, and a hundred men his enemies, for every office he can bestow.
Letter to Josiah Quincy, 14 Feb. 1825

19 A boy of fifteen who is not a democrat is good for nothing, and he is no better who is a democrat at twenty.
Quoted in Thomas Jefferson, Journal, Jan. 1799
See Batbie 1; Clemenceau 5; George Bernard Shaw 48

20 [*Statement made to Jonathan Sewall, 1774:*] Sink or swim, live or die, survive or perish with my country.
Quoted in Preface to *Novanglus and Massachusetts* (1819). "Live or die, sink or swim" appears in George Peele, *Edward I* (ca. 1584).

21 [*"Last words":*] Thomas Jefferson survives.

Quoted in Susan Boylston Adams Clark, Letter to Abigail Louisa Smith Adams Johnson, 9 July 1826. In fact, Jefferson had died a few hours earlier on this, the fiftieth anniversary of the Declaration of Independence. Eliza Quincy, in her 1861 memoirs, wrote that the last words Adams spoke distinctly were "Thomas Jefferson"; the rest of the sentence, she noted, was inarticulate.
See Jefferson 55

John Quincy Adams
U.S. President, 1767–1848

1 America . . . well knows that by once enlisting under other banners than her own, were they even the banners of foreign independence, she would involve herself beyond the power of extraction, in all the wars of interest and intrigue, of individual avarice, envy, and ambition, which assume the colors and usurp the standard of freedom. The fundamental maxims of her policy would insensibly change from liberty to force. . . . She might become dictatress of the world. She would be no longer the ruler of her own spirit.

Address, Washington, D.C., 4 July 1821

2 In charity to all mankind, bearing no malice or ill will to any human being, and even compassionating those who hold in bondage their fellow men, not knowing what they do.

Letter to Bronson Alcott, 30 July 1838
See Lincoln 51

3 [*Upon collapsing in U.S. Senate, 21 Feb. 1848, two days before his death:*] This is the last of earth. I am content.

Quoted in William H. Seward, Eulogy of John Quincy Adams Before Legislature of New York (1848)

Samuel Adams
U.S. revolutionary leader, 1722–1803

1 Men who content themselves with the semblance of Truth and a display of Words, talk much of our Obligations to Great Britain for Protection: Had she a single Eye to our Advantage? A Nation of shop keepers are very seldom so disinterested.

An Oration Delivered at the State-House, in Philadelphia (1776)
See Napoleon 5; Adam Smith 7; Josiah Tucker 1

2 [*Upon hearing gunfire at Lexington, Mass., 19 Apr. 1775:*] What a glorious morning is this!

Quoted in William Gordon, *This History of the Rise, Progress, and Establishment of the Independence of the United States of America* (1788)

Sarah Flower Adams
English hymnwriter, 1805–1848

1 Nearer, My God, to Thee.
Title of hymn (1841)

Scott Adams
U.S. cartoonist, 1957–

1 The basic concept of the Dilbert Principle is that the most ineffective workers are systematically moved to the place where they can do the least damage: management.
Wall Street Journal, 22 May 1995
See Peter 1

Harold Adamson
U.S. songwriter, 1906–1980

1 Comin' in on a Wing and a Pray'r.
Title of song (1943). Based on an alleged remark by a real pilot landing a crippled plane.

Jane Addams
U.S. social worker, 1860–1935

1 The cure for the ills of Democracy is more Democracy.
Democracy and Social Ethics introduction (1902)

Joseph Addison
English man of letters, 1672–1719

1 Sir Roger . . . told them, with the air of a man who would not give his judgement rashly, that *much might be said on both sides.*
The Spectator no. 122, 20 July 1711

2 Our disputants put me in mind of the cuttle-fish, that when he is unable to extricate himself, blackens all the water about him till he becomes invisible.
The Spectator no. 476, 5 Sept. 1712

3 What pity is it
That we can die but once to serve our country!
Cato act 4, sc. 4 (1713)
See Nathan Hale 1

4 "We are always doing," says he, "something for Posterity, but I would fain see Posterity do something for us."
The Spectator no. 583, 20 Aug. 1714

5 [*"Last words":*] See in what peace a Christian can die.

Quoted in Thomas Foxton, *Serino* (ca. 1721)

6 [*On the superiority of his writing to his conversation:*] I have but ninepence in ready money, but I can draw for a thousand pounds.

Quoted in James Boswell, *The Life of Samuel Johnson* (1791) (entry for 7 May 1773)

George Ade
U.S. humorist and playwright, 1866–1944

1 "Whom are you?" he asked, for he had attended business college.

Chicago Record, 16 Mar. 1898

2 Anybody can win, unless there happens to be a second entry.

Fables in Slang, "The Fable of the Brash Drummer and the Peach Who Learned That There Were Others" (1899)

Konrad Adenauer
German chancellor, 1876–1967

1 History is the sum total of all the things that could have been avoided.

Quoted in *Washington Times,* 2 May 1998

Alfred Adler
Austrian psychiatrist, 1870–1937

1 All our institutions, our traditional attitudes, our laws, our morals, our customs, give evidence of the fact that they are determined and maintained by privileged males for the glory of male domination. These institutions reach out into the very nurseries and have a great influence upon the child's soul.

Understanding Human Nature (1927)

2 Every neurotic is partly in the right.

Problems of Neurosis (1930)

Polly Adler
Russian-born U.S. madam and writer, 1900–1962

1 A House Is Not a Home.

Title of book (1953)

2 The women who take husbands not out of love but out of greed, to get their bills paid, to get a fine house and clothes and jewels . . . these are whores in everything but name. The only difference between them and my girls is that my girls gave a man his money's worth.

A House Is Not a Home ch. 10 (1953)

Theodor Adorno
German philosopher, sociologist, and musicologist, 1903–1969

1 To write poetry after Auschwitz is barbaric.

"Kulturkritik und Gesellschaft" (1951)

Advertising Slogans

1 Friends don't let friends drive drunk.

Advertising Council

2 Just say no.

Advertising Council antidrug campaign. Became closely identified with Nancy Reagan but was originated by the advertising agency Needham, Harper & Steers.

3 Stronger than dirt.

Ajax laundry detergent

4 In space no one can hear you scream.

Alien motion picture promotional slogan

5 I can't believe I ate the whole thing.

Alka-Seltzer antacid

6 Mama Mia, that's a spicy meatball.

Alka-Seltzer antacid

7 Plop, plop, fizz, fizz. Oh what a relief it is.

Alka-Seltzer antacid

8 You're in good hands with Allstate.

Allstate insurance

9 Sometimes you feel like a nut, sometimes you don't.

Almond Joy/Mounds candy bars

10 Got milk?

American Dairy Association/National Dairy Council

11 Don't leave home without it.

American Express credit card

12 Garbo Talks!

Anna Christie motion picture promotional slogan

13 Here's to the crazy ones. The misfits. The rebels. The troublemakers.

Apple computers

14 Think different.

Apple computers

15 There's an app for that.
Apple iPhone

16 There's something about an Aqua Velva man.
Aqua Velva aftershave

17 We're Number Two. We try harder.
Avis car rentals

18 Reach out and touch someone.
Bell System

19 Let your fingers do the walking.
Bell System Yellow Pages telephone directory

20 The ultimate driving machine.
BMW automobiles

21 This Bud's for you.
Budweiser beer

22 Whassup?
Budweiser beer

23 Have it your way.
Burger King restaurants

24 Nothing comes between me and my Calvins.
Calvin Klein jeans

25 I'd walk a mile for a Camel.
Camel cigarettes

26 M'm, M'm good.
Campbell's soup

27 What's in your wallet?
Capital One credit card

28 See the USA in a Chevrolet.
Chevrolet automobiles

29 It's not nice to fool Mother Nature!
Chiffon margarine

30 Is it true blondes have more fun?
Clairol hair coloring

31 Does she . . . or doesn't she? . . . Only her hairdresser knows for sure.
Clairol hair coloring

32 If I've only one life, let me live it as a blonde.
Clairol hair coloring

33 I'd like to teach the world to sing in perfect harmony,
I'd like to buy the world a Coke and keep it company.
Coca-Cola soda

34 It's the real thing.
Coca-Cola soda

35 The pause that refreshes.
Coca-Cola soda

36 Things go better with Coke.
Coca-Cola soda

37 Look Ma! No cavities!
Crest toothpaste

38 A diamond is forever.
De Beers mining
See Loos 2; Robin 2

39 But wait, there's more!
Dial Media products

40 Every picture tells a story.
Doan's kidney pills

41 The most interesting man in the world.
Dos Equis beer

42 Time to make the donuts.
Dunkin' Donuts

43 Better Things for Better Living . . . Through Chemistry.
Du Pont

44 When E. F. Hutton talks, people listen.
E. F. Hutton brokerage

45 It keeps going, and going, and going . . .
Energizer batteries

46 All my men wear English Leather, or they wear nothing at all.
English Leather cologne

47 Put a tiger in your tank!
Esso gasoline. Muddy Waters recorded the song "(I Want to Put a) Tiger in Your Tank," written by Willie Dixon, in 1960.

48 When it absolutely, positively has to be there overnight.
Federal Express delivery service

49 Have you driven a Ford lately?
Ford automobiles

50 Who's that behind those Foster Grants?
Foster Grant sunglasses

51 Fair and balanced.
Fox News

52 15 minutes could save you 15 percent or more on car insurance.
GEICO auto insurance

53 Progress is our most important product.
General Electric

54 We bring good things to life.
General Electric

55 Babies are our business, our only business.
Gerber baby food

56 The best a man can get.
Gillette razors

57 Leave the driving to us!
Greyhound Bus Lines

58 When you care enough to send the very best!
Hallmark greeting cards

59 The man in the Hathaway shirt.
Hathaway shirts

60 57 Varieties.
Heinz ketchup

61 Intel inside.
Intel computer chips

62 Look for the union label.
International Ladies' Garment Workers' Union

63 99–44/100% Pure: It floats.
Ivory soap

64 Just when you thought it was safe to go back in the water.
Jaws 2 motion picture promotional slogan

65 This time . . . It's personal.
Jaws: The Revenge motion picture promotional slogan

66 They're GR-R-REAT!
Kellogg's Frosted Flakes cereal

67 Snap! Crackle! and Pop!
Kellogg's Rice Krispies cereal

68 It's finger lickin' good.
Kentucky Fried Chicken

69 Never underestimate the power of a woman.
Ladies' Home Journal magazine

70 What happens in Vegas, stays in Vegas.
Las Vegas Convention and Visitors Authority

71 Betcha can't eat just one.
Lay's potato chips

72 You don't have to be Jewish to love Levy's Rye Bread.
Levy's rye bread

73 I've fallen, and I can't get up.
LifeCall emergency alert devices

74 Because I'm worth it!
L'Oreal beauty products

75 LS/MFT—Lucky Strike Means Fine Tobacco.
Lucky Strike cigarettes

76 The milk chocolate melts in your mouth, not in your hand.
M&M's candies

77 There are some things money can't buy. For everything else there's MasterCard.
MasterCard credit card

78 Good to the last drop!
Maxwell House coffee

79 I'm lovin' it.
McDonald's restaurants

80 You deserve a break today.
McDonald's restaurants

81 Is it live, or is it Memorex?
Memorex audiotape

82 Merrill Lynch is bullish on America.
Merrill Lynch brokerage

83 Because so much is riding on your tires.
Michelin tires

84 It's Miller time.
Miller beer

85 Tastes great, less filling.
Miller beer

86 We'll leave a light on for you.
Motel 6

87 I want my MTV!
MTV television network

88 I'm [*stewardess name*] . . . Fly me.
National Airlines

89 Take a bite out of crime.
National Crime Prevention Council

90 Enquiring minds want to know.
National Enquirer newspaper

91 Nestle's makes the very best chocolate.
Nestle's chocolate

92 I love New York.
New York City tourism

93 Just do it.
Nike athletic shoes

94 Take it off, take it all off.
Noxzema shaving cream

95 This is not your father's Oldsmobile.
Oldsmobile automobiles

96 Oh I wish I were an Oscar Mayer wiener.
Oscar Mayer frankfurters

97 Keep that schoolgirl complexion.
Palmolive soap

98 This is your brain. This is your brain on drugs. Any questions?
Partnership for a Drug-Free America

99 At Paul Masson, we will sell no wine before its time.
Paul Masson wines

100 Come Alive! You're in the Pepsi Generation.
Pepsi-Cola soda

101 It takes a tough man to make a tender chicken.
Perdue chicken

102 Get a piece of the rock.
Prudential insurance

103 The Greatest Show on Earth.
P. T. Barnum Circus

104 It's ten p.m. Do you know where your children are?
Public service announcement

105 I liked it so much, I bought the company.
Remington shavers

106 Roaches check in . . . but they don't check out.
Roach Motel insect traps

107 How do you spell relief? R-O-L-A-I-D-S.
Rolaids antacid

108 At 60 miles an hour the loudest noise in this new Rolls-Royce comes from the electric clock.
Rolls-Royce automobiles

109 We make money the old-fashioned way. We earn it.
Smith Barney brokerage

110 With a name like Smucker's, it has to be good!
Smucker's fruit spreads

111 Say it with flowers.
Society of American Florists

112 Like a good neighbor, State Farm is there.
State Farm insurance

113 Eat fresh.
Subway restaurants

114 Think outside the bun.
Taco Bell restaurants

115 We'd rather fight than switch!
Tareyton cigarettes

116 You can trust your car to the man who wears the star.
Texaco gasoline

117 Four out of five dentists recommend sugarless gum for their patients who chew gum.
Trident chewing gum

118 Silly rabbit, Trix are for kids.
Trix cereal

119 Fly the friendly skies of United.
United Airlines

120 A mind is a terrible thing to waste.
United Negro College Fund
See Quayle 2

121 The Few. The Proud. The Marines.
United States Marines

122 Be all that you can be.
United States Army recruiting slogan

123 Only you can prevent forest fires.
United States Forest Service

124 They Laughed When I Sat Down at the Piano.
United States School of Music

125 It slices! It dices!
Veg-O-Matic food-processing appliance

126 Can you hear me now? Good.
Verizon Wireless cell service

127 I'm not a doctor, but I play one on TV.
Vicks cough syrup

128 His Master's Voice.
Victor phonographs

129 You've come a long way baby.
Virginia Slims cigarettes

130 It's everywhere you want to be.
Visa credit card

131 Drivers wanted.
Volkswagen automobiles

132 Where's the beef?
Wendy's restaurants
See Mondale 1

133 It's the only way to fly.
Western Airlines

134 The Breakfast of Champions.
Wheaties cereal

135 Winston tastes good like a cigarette should.
Winston cigarettes

136 Ring around the collar.
Wisk laundry detergent

137 Builds Strong Bodies 12 Ways.
Wonder Bread

138 Your King and Country need you.
World War I recruitment slogan (Great Britain)

139 Loose lips sink ships.
World War II public service slogan

140 Double your pleasure, double your fun
with . . . Doublemint, Doublemint,
Doublemint gum.
Wrigley Doublemint gum

Aeschylus
Greek playwright, ca. 525 B.C.–ca. 456 B.C.

1 In our sleep, pain which cannot forget falls
drop by drop upon the heart until, in our
own despair, against our will, comes wisdom
through the awful grace of God.
Agamemnon l. 176

Aesop
Greek fabulist, Sixth cent. B.C.

1 Then one day there really was a wolf, but when
the boy shouted they didn't believe him.
"The Boy Who Cried Wolf"

2 Oh, you aren't even ripe yet! I don't need any
sour grapes.
"The Fox and the Bunch of Grapes"

3 The Wolf in Sheep's Clothing.
Title of story

Jean Louis Rodolphe Agassiz
Swiss-born U.S. naturalist, 1807–1873

1 The eye of the trilobite tells us that the sun shone
on the old beach where he lived; for there is
nothing in nature without a purpose, and when
so complicated an organ was made to receive the
light, there must have been light to enter it.
Geological Sketches ch. 2 (1866)

2 The world has arisen in some way or another.
How it originated is the great question, and

Darwin's theory, like all other attempts to
explain the origin of life, is thus far merely
conjectural. I believe he has not even made the
best conjecture possible in the present state of
our knowledge.
"Evolution and Permanence of Type" (1874)

James Agee
U.S. writer and critic, 1909–1955

1 We are talking now of summer evenings in
Knoxville, Tennessee, in the time that I lived
there so successfully disguised to myself as a
child.
"Knoxville: Summer of 1915" (1947)

2 Sleep, soft smiling, draws me unto her: and
those receive me, who quietly treat me, as one
familiar and well-beloved in that home: but will
not, oh, will not, not now, not ever, but will not
ever tell me who I am.
"Knoxville: Summer of 1915" (1947)

3 But he did not ask, and his uncle did not speak
except to say, after a few minutes, "It's time to
go home," and all the way home they walked in
silence.
A Death in the Family ch. 20 (1957)

Spiro T. Agnew
U.S. politician, 1918–1996

1 I've been in many of them [ghetto areas] and to
some extent I would have to say this: If you've
seen one city slum you've seen them all.
Campaign speech, Detroit, Mich., 18 Oct. 1968
See Robert Burton 4

2 A spirit of national masochism prevails,
encouraged by an effete corps of impudent
snobs who characterize themselves as
intellectuals.
Speech at Republican fund-raising dinner, New
Orleans, La., 19 Oct. 1969

3 Ultraliberalism today translates into a
whimpering isolationism in foreign policy, a
mulish obstructionism in domestic policy, and
a pusillanimous pussyfooting on the critical
issue of law and order.
Speech at Illinois Republican meeting, Springfield,
Ill., 10 Sept. 1970

4 In the United States today, we have more than
our share of the nattering nabobs of negativism.

Address to California Republican state convention, San Diego, Calif., 11 Sept. 1970

George Aiken
U.S. politician, 1892–1984

1 The United States could well declare unilaterally that this stage of the Vietnam War is over—that we have "won" in the sense that our Armed Forces are in control of most of the field and no potential enemy is in a position to establish its authority over South Vietnam.
Speech in U.S. Senate, 19 Oct. 1966. Often paraphrased as "claim victory and retreat" or "declare victory and retreat."

Howard H. Aiken
U.S. computer scientist, 1900–1973

1 At the present time there exist problems beyond our ability to solve, not because of theoretical difficulties, but because of insufficient means of mechanical computation.
"Proposed Automatic Calculating Machine" (1937)

Catherine Aird (Kinn Hamilton McIntosh)
English detective fiction writer, 1930–

1 If you can't be a good example, then you'll just have to be a horrible warning.
Quoted in *St. Louis Post-Dispatch*, 1 Nov. 1989

Anna Akhmatova
Russian poet, 1889–1966

1 In those years only the dead smiled, glad to be at rest.
Requiem "Prologue" (1935–1940) (translation by D. M. Thomas)

2 In the fearful years of the Yezhov terror I spent seventeen months in prison queues in Leningrad. One day somebody "identified" me . . . and whispered in my ear . . . "Can you describe this?" And I said: "Yes, I can."
Requiem preface (written 1957) (translation by D. M. Thomas)

Todd Akin
U.S. politician, 1947–

1 If it's a legitimate rape, the female body has ways to try to shut that whole thing down.
KTVI-TV interview, 19 Aug. 2012

Zoë Akins
U.S. playwright, 1886–1958

1 The Greeks Had a Word for It.
Title of play (1930)

Ryūnosuke Akutagawa
Japanese writer, 1892–1927

1 When *I* kill a man, I do it with my sword, but people like you don't use swords. You gentlemen kill with your power, with your money, and sometimes just with your words: you tell people you're doing them a favor. True, no blood flows, the man is still alive, but you've killed him all the same. I don't know whose sin is greater—yours or mine.
"In a Bamboo Grove" (1922) (translation by Jay Rubin)

Alain (Émile-Auguste Chartier)
French poet and philosopher, 1868–1951

1 Nothing is more dangerous than an idea, when you have only one idea.
Propos sur le Religion no. 74 (1938)

Edward Albee
U.S. playwright, 1928–2016

1 When you're a kid you use the [pornographic playing] cards as a substitute for a real experience, and when you're older you use real experience as a substitute for the fantasy.
The Zoo Story (1959)

2 Who's afraid of Virginia Woolf.
Who's Afraid of Virginia Woolf? act 1 (1962). Found by Albee as graffiti on a restroom wall.
See Frank Churchill 1

3 I swear . . . if you existed I'd divorce you.
Who's Afraid of Virginia Woolf? act 1 (1962)

Alcaeus
Greek poet, ca. 625 B.C.–ca. 575 B.C.

1 Wine, dear boy, and truth.
Fragment 366

Amos Bronson Alcott
U.S. educator, 1799–1888

1 To be ignorant of one's ignorance is the malady of the ignorant.
Table Talk "Conversation" (1877)

Louisa May Alcott

U.S. novelist, 1832–1888

1 "Christmas won't be Christmas without any presents," grumbled Jo, lying on the rug.
Little Women ch. 1 (1868–1869)

2 I am angry nearly every day of my life, Jo, but I have learned not to show it; and I still hope to learn not to feel it, though it may take me another forty years to do so.
Little Women ch. 8 (1868–1869)

3 Housekeeping ain't no joke.
Little Women ch. 11 (1868–1869)

4 I'm not afraid of storms, for I'm learning how to sail my ship.
Little Women ch. 44 (1868–1869)

5 What *do* girls do who haven't any mothers to help them through their troubles?
Little Women ch. 46 (1868–1869)

6 Women have been called queens a long time, but the kingdom given them isn't worth ruling.
An Old-Fashioned Girl ch. 13 (1870)

Alcuin

English scholar and theologian, ca. 735–804

1 *Vox populi, vox Dei.*
The voice of the people is the voice of God.
Letter 164

Priscilla Mullins Alden

English-born colonial settler, ca. 1602–ca. 1684

1 [*To John Alden, who was importuning her on behalf of Miles Standish:*] Prithee, John, why do you not speak for yourself?
Attributed in Timothy Alden, *A Collection of American Epitaphs and Inscriptions, with Occasional Notes* (1814). Henry Wadsworth Longfellow popularized Alden's question when he used it in his poem "The Courtship of Miles Standish" (1858): "Why don't you speak for yourself, John?"

Edwin E. "Buzz" Aldrin

U.S. astronaut, 1930–

1 [*Remark during first moon walk, 20 July 1969:*] Magnificent desolation.
Quoted in *N.Y. Times*, 21 July 1969

Alexander the Great

Macedonian king, 356 B.C.–323 B.C.

1 If I were not Alexander, I would be Diogenes.
Quoted in Plutarch, *Parallel Lives*

Alexander II

Russian tsar, 1818–1881

1 Better to abolish serfdom from above than to wait till it begins to abolish itself from below.
Speech, Moscow, 30 Mar. 1856

Cecil Frances Alexander

Irish poet and hymnwriter, 1818–1895

1 All things bright and beautiful,
All creatures great and small,
All things wise and wonderful,
The Lord God made them all.
"All Things Bright and Beautiful" (hymn) (1848)

2 The rich man in his castle,
The poor man at his gate,
God made them, high or lowly,
And order'd their estate.
"All Things Bright and Beautiful" (hymn) (1848)

Elizabeth Alexander

U.S. writer, 1962–

1 In today's sharp sparkle, this winter air,
any thing can be made, any sentence begun.
On the brink, on the brim, on the cusp,
praise song for walking forward in that light.
"Praise Song for the Day" l. 40 (2009)

Michelle Alexander

U.S. lawyer and author, 1967–

1 Rather than rely on race, we use our criminal justice system to label people of color "criminals" and then engage in all the practices we supposedly left behind. . . . We have not ended racial caste in America; we have merely redesigned it.
The New Jim Crow introduction (2010)

Alexandra

German-born Russian tsarina, 1872–1918

1 Be Peter the Great, Ivan the Terrible, Emperor Paul—crush them all under you . . . be the Master, & all will bow down to you.
Letter to Tsar Nicholas II, 14 Dec. 1916

Alfonso the Wise

Castilian king, 1221–1284

1 Had I been present at the Creation, I would have given some useful hints for the better ordering of the universe.

Attributed in Thomas Carlyle, *History of Frederick the Great* (1858–1865). According to Diego Catalán, *La Estoria de España de Alfonso X: creación y evolución* (1992), the earliest known version of this legendary remark occurs in a fourteenth-century Portuguese manuscript by Count Pedro de Barcelos, *Crónica Geral de Espanha de 1344*.

Nelson Algren

U.S. writer, 1909–1981

1 A Walk on the Wild Side.

Title of book (1956)
See Lou Reed 3

2 Never play cards with a man called Doc. Never eat at a place called Mom's. Never sleep with a woman whose troubles are greater than your own.

A Walk on the Wild Side pt. 3 (1956). Ralph Keyes, in his book *The Quote Verifier*, presents strong evidence that Algren took these rules from Algren's friend Dave Peltz.

Choudhry Rahmat Ali

Pakistani nationalist, 1895–1951

1 At this solemn hour in the history of India, when British and Indian statesmen are laying the foundations of a Federal Constitution for that land, we address this appeal to you, in the name of our common heritage, on behalf of our *thirty million Muslim* brethren who live in **PAKSTAN**—by which we mean the five Northern units of India, Viz: **P**unjab, North-West Frontier Province (**A**fghan Province), **K**ashmir, **S**indh and Baluchis**tan**.

Now or Never: Are We to Live or Perish Forever (1933). The acronym was later slightly modified from "Pakstan" to "Pakistan."

Muhammad Ali (Cassius Clay)

U.S. boxer, 1942–2016

1 I am the greatest.

Quoted in *Wash. Post*, 14 Oct. 1962. Ali was preceded by wrestler "Gorgeous" George Wagner in using this phrase. In Ali's autobiography he says that he first used it before a Las Vegas bout in June 1961.

2 Not only do I knock 'em out, I pick the round.

Quoted in *N.Y. Times*, 9 Dec. 1962

3 [*Description of his boxing strategy:*] Float like a butterfly, sting like a bee.

Quoted in *N.Y. Times*, 19 Feb. 1964. Probably coined by Ali's adviser, Drew "Bundini" Brown, who says these words in the *New York Times* article of 19 Feb. 1964.

4 [*Responding to having his draft status reclassified:*] I ain't got no quarrel with them Viet Cong.

Press conference, Miami, Fla., 17 Feb. 1966

5 It's hard to be humble when you are as great as I am.

Quoted in *N.Y. Times*, 30 Nov. 1974

6 My new style on the ropes is called the "Rope-A-Dope."

Quoted in *Chicago Tribune*, 16 May 1975

7 [*Description of upcoming fight against Joe Frazier in the Philippines, at a press conference announcing the fight, New York:*] A thriller in Manila.

Quoted in *N.Y. Times*, 18 July 1975

8 It's just a job. Grass grows, birds fly, waves pound the sand. I beat people up.

Quoted in *N.Y. Times*, 6 Apr. 1977

9 No Viet Cong ever called me "nigger."

Attributed in Russel B. Nye, *Crises on Campus* (1971). According to Ralph Keyes, *"Nice Guys Finish Seventh"* (1992), "Ali never made this comment. . . . Despite extensive searching by himself and others, [Ali biographer Thomas] Hauser has never found the source of 'No Viet Cong ever called me nigger.' He concluded that it was just one of those sayings that got picked up and passed around in the sixties." The earliest known recorded version appeared in the *New York Times*, 24 Feb. 1966: "One Negro demonstrator carried a sign that said 'The Viet Cong Never Called Me Nigger.'"

Saul Alinsky

U.S. political activist, 1909–1972

1 A racially integrated community is a chronological term timed from the entrance of the first black family to the exit of the last white family.

Quoted in Jonathon Green, *Morrow's International Dictionary of Contemporary Quotations* (1982)

Abbé Léonor Soulas d'Allainval
French playwright, ca. 1695–1753

1 *L'Embarras des Richesses.*
  The Embarrassment of Riches.
  Title of play (1726)

Lewis Allan (Abel Meeropol)
U.S. songwriter, 1903–1986

1 Southern trees bear a strange fruit,
  (Blood on the leaves and blood at the root,)
  Black body swinging in the southern breeze,
  Strange fruit hanging from the poplar trees.
  "Strange Fruit" l. 1 (1937). Originally titled "Bitter Fruit"; later made into a song.

Elizabeth Akers Allen
U.S. poet, 1832–1911

1 Backward, turn backward, O Time, in your flight,
  Make me a child again just for to-night!
  "Rock Me to Sleep" l. 1 (1860)

Ethan Allen
U.S. soldier, 1738–1789

1 [*Reply to Captain Delaplace, commander at Fort Ticonderoga, N.Y., 10 May 1775, who exclaimed, "By whose authority do you act?":*] In the name of the Lord Jehovah and the Continental Congress.
  Quoted in *Memoirs of the Late Dr. Benjamin Franklin* (1790)

Fred Allen (John Florence Sullivan)
U.S. comedian, 1894–1956

1 [*Catchphrase of character Senator Claghorn:*] That's a joke, son!
  Fred Allen Show (radio series) (1932–1949)

2 A conference is a gathering of important people who singly can do nothing but together can decide that nothing can be done.
  Letter to William McChesney Martin, Jr., 25 Jan. 1940

3 California is a fine place to live—if you happen to be an orange.
  American Magazine, Dec. 1945

4 I have just returned from Boston. It is the only sane thing to do if you find yourself up there.
  Letter to Groucho Marx, 12 June 1953

5 A molehill man is a pseudo-busy executive who comes to work at 9 A.M. and finds a molehill on his desk. He has until 5 P.M. to make this molehill into a mountain. An accomplished molehill man will often have his mountain finished even before lunch.
  Treadmill to Oblivion pt. 2 (1954)

6 Hollywood is a place where people from Iowa mistake each other for movie stars.
  Quoted in Evan Esar, *The Dictionary of Humorous Quotations* (1949)

7 A celebrity is a person who works hard all his life to become well known, then wears dark glasses to avoid being recognized.
  Quoted in James B. Simpson, *Best Quotes of '54, '55, '56* (1957)

8 All the sincerity in Hollywood you could stuff in a flea's navel and still have room left to conceal eight carroway seeds and an agent's heart.
  Quoted in *Long Beach* (Calif.) *Press-Telegram,* 6 May 1959

9 Imitation is the sincerest form of television.
  Quoted in *Newsweek,* 14 Jan. 1980

Steve Allen
U.S. entertainer, 1921–2000

1 Tragedy plus time equals comedy.
  Cosmopolitan, Feb. 1957. Usually quoted as "Comedy equals tragedy plus time."

Woody Allen (Allen Stewart Konigsberg)
U.S. comedian and filmmaker, 1935–

1 Some guy hit my fender the other day, and I said unto him, "Be fruitful, and multiply." But not in those words.
  Private Life (record album) (1964)
  See Bible 6

2 A fast word about oral contraception. I asked a girl to go to bed with me and she said "no."
  Woody Allen Volume Two (record album) (1965). Originally used in a nightclub performance, Chicago, Ill., Mar. 1964.

3 Not only is there no God, but try getting a plumber on weekends.

New Yorker, 27 Dec. 1969

4 Play it again, Sam!

Play It Again, Sam act 2 (1969)
See Film Lines 42

5 [*Virgil Starkwell, played by Woody Allen, speaking:*] I was so touched by her that, after fifteen minutes, I wanted to marry her and, after half an hour, I completely gave up the idea of snatching her purse.

Take the Money and Run (motion picture) (1969). Cowritten with Mickey Rose.

6 [*Virgil Starkwell, played by Woody Allen, speaking:*] He [the psychiatrist] said, well, do I think that sex is dirty and I said: "It is if you're doing it right."

Take the Money and Run (motion picture) (1969). Cowritten with Mickey Rose.

7 [*Louise, played by Janet Margolin, speaking:*] He never made the ten-most-wanted list. It's very unfair voting. It's who you know.

Take the Money and Run (motion picture) (1969). Cowritten with Mickey Rose.

8 [*Fielding Mellish, played by Woody Allen, choosing between freedom and death:*] Well, freedom is wonderful. On the other hand, if you're dead, it's a tremendous drawback to your sex life.

Bananas (motion picture) (1971). Cowritten with Mickey Rose.

9 [*Fielding Mellish, played by Woody Allen, speaking:*] I object, your honor! This trial is a travesty. It's a travesty of a mockery of a sham of a mockery of a travesty of two mockeries of a sham.

Bananas (motion picture) (1971). Cowritten with Mickey Rose.

10 [*Allan Felix, played by Woody Allen, speaking:*] I hate the beach. I hate the sun. I'm pale and I'm redheaded. I don't tan—I stroke.

Play It Again, Sam (motion picture) (1972)

11 If only God would give me some clear sign! Like making a large deposit in my name at a Swiss bank.

New Yorker, 5 Nov. 1973

12 [*Miles Monroe, played by Woody Allen, responding to the comment "It's hard to believe that you haven't had sex for two hundred years":*] Two hundred and four if you count my marriage.

Sleeper (motion picture) (1973). Cowritten with Marshall Brickman.

13 [*Miles Monroe, played by Woody Allen, speaking:*] My brain? It's my second favorite organ.

Sleeper (motion picture) (1973). Cowritten with Marshall Brickman.

14 [*Miles Monroe, played by Woody Allen, speaking about what he believes in:*] Sex and death. Two things that come once in a lifetime. But at least after death you're not nauseous.

Sleeper (motion picture) (1973). Cowritten with Marshall Brickman.

15 [*Boris Grushenko, played by Woody Allen, speaking:*] Some men are heterosexual and some men are bisexual and some men don't think about sex at all, you know, they become lawyers.

Love and Death (motion picture) (1975)

16 [*Boris Grushenko, played by Woody Allen, responding to "Sex without love is an empty experience":*] Yes, but—as empty experiences go—it's one of the best!

Love and Death (motion picture) (1975)

17 [*Boris Grushenko, played by Woody Allen, speaking:*] It's not the quantity of your sexual relations that count, it's the quality. On the other hand, if the quantity drops below once every eight months, I would definitely look into it.

Love and Death (motion picture) (1975)

18 [*Boris Grushenko, played by Woody Allen, speaking:*] If it turns out that there *is* a God, I don't think that he's evil. I think that the worst you can say about him is that basically he's an underachiever.
Love and Death (motion picture) (1975)

19 It's not that I'm afraid to die. I just don't want to be there when it happens.
Without Feathers "Death (A Play)" (1975)

20 How wrong Emily Dickinson was! Hope is not "the thing with feathers." The thing with feathers has turned out to be my nephew. I must take him to a specialist in Zurich.
Without Feathers "Selections from the Allen Notebooks" (1975)
See Emily Dickinson 10

21 Why does man kill? He kills for food. And not only food: frequently there must be a beverage.
Without Feathers "Selections from the Allen Notebooks" (1975)

22 On the plus side, death is one of the few things that can be done as easily lying down.
Without Feathers "The Early Essays" (1975)

23 Money is better than poverty, if only for financial reasons.
Without Feathers "The Early Essays" (1975)

24 The chief problem about death, incidentally, is the fear that there may be no afterlife—a depressing thought, particularly for those who have bothered to shave. Also, there is the fear that there is an afterlife but no one will know where it's being held.
Without Feathers "The Early Essays" (1975)

25 The lion and the calf shall lie down together but the calf won't get much sleep.
Without Feathers "The Scrolls" (1975)
See Bible 167

26 [*Alvy Singer, played by Woody Allen, speaking:*] That's essentially how I feel about life. Full of loneliness and misery and suffering and unhappiness, and it's all over much too quickly.
Annie Hall (motion picture) (1977). Cowritten with Marshall Brickman.

27 [*Alvy Singer, played by Woody Allen, on Los Angeles:*] I don't want to live in a city where the only cultural advantage is that you can make a right turn on a red light.

Annie Hall (motion picture) (1977). Cowritten with Marshall Brickman.

28 [*Alvy Singer, played by Woody Allen, after having sex:*] That was the most fun I ever had without laughing.
Annie Hall (motion picture) (1977). Cowritten with Marshall Brickman.
See Mencken 41

29 [*Alvy Singer, played by Woody Allen, speaking:*] I was thrown out of N.Y.U. my freshman year for cheating on my metaphysics final, you know. I looked within the soul of the boy sitting next to me.
Annie Hall (motion picture) (1977). Cowritten with Marshall Brickman. The same joke appeared in a monologue recorded live in March 1964 and included in the 1964 record album *Woody Allen*.

30 [*Alvy Singer, played by Woody Allen, speaking:*] I was suicidal as a matter of fact and would have killed myself, but I was in analysis with a strict Freudian, and, if you kill yourself, they make you pay for the sessions you miss.
Annie Hall (motion picture) (1977). Cowritten with Marshall Brickman. This joke appeared in a monologue recorded live in August 1968 and released on *The Third Woody Allen Album*.

31 [*Alvy Singer, played by Woody Allen, speaking:*] Hey, don't knock masturbation. It's sex with someone I love.
Annie Hall (motion picture) (1977). Cowritten with Marshall Brickman.

32 [*Alvy Singer, played by Woody Allen, speaking:*] A relationship, I think, is, is like a shark, you know, it has to constantly move forward or it dies, and I think what we got on our hands is a dead shark.
Annie Hall (motion picture) (1977). Cowritten with Marshall Brickman.

33 It seemed the world was divided into good and bad people. The good ones slept better . . . while the bad ones seemed to enjoy the waking hours much more.
New Yorker, 21 Nov. 1977

34 More than any other time in history, mankind faces a crossroads. One path leads to despair and utter hopelessness. The other, to total extinction. Let us pray we have the wisdom to choose correctly.
Side Effects "My Speech to the Graduates" (1980)

35 [*Sandy Bates, played by Woody Allen, speaking:*]
You can't control life. It doesn't wind up
perfectly. Only . . . only art you can control. Art
and masturbation. Two areas in which I am an
absolute expert.
Stardust Memories (motion picture) (1980)

36 [*Danny Rose, played by Woody Allen, speaking:*]
The man has an axe. There's two of us. There'll
be four of us in no time.
Broadway Danny Rose (motion picture) (1984)

37 [*Harry Block, played by Woody Allen, speaking:*]
The most beautiful words in the English
language are not "I love you," but "It's benign."
Deconstructing Harry (motion picture) (1997). Garson
O'Toole has discovered the following much earlier
version: "'I have always maintained (and always
will) that the most beautiful word in English is
"benign" and the ugliest word is "malignant,"' writes
a San Francisco girl named Erna" (*The Robesonian*
[Lumberton, N.C.], 12 Nov. 1968).

38 Love is the answer but while you're waiting for
the answer, sex raises some good questions.
Quoted in *Time,* 15 Sept. 1975

39 [*Of bisexuality:*] It immediately doubles your
chances for a date on Saturday night.
Quoted in *N.Y. Times,* 1 Dec. 1975

40 I don't want to achieve immortality through
my work. . . . I want to achieve it through not
dying.
Quoted in Eric Lax, *Woody Allen and His Comedy* (1975)

41 Showing up is 80 percent of life.
Quoted in *N.Y. Times,* 21 Aug. 1977

42 [*Of his love for his adoptive stepdaughter, Soon-Yi
Farrow:*] The heart wants what it wants. There's
no logic.
Quoted in *USA Today,* 24 Aug. 1992. "The Heart
wants what it wants" appeared in a letter from Emily
Dickinson to Mary Bowles in spring 1862.
See Pascal 14

Margery Allingham
English mystery writer, 1904–1966

1 Once sex rears its ugly 'ead it's time to steer
clear.
Flowers for the Judge ch. 4 (1936)

2 It's crackers to slip a rozzer the dropsy in snide.
The Fashion in Shrouds ch. 6 (1938). Slang for
"It's crazy to give a policeman an illegal payoff in
counterfeit money."

3 It's pitch, sex is. Once you touch it, it clings
to you.
The Fashion in Shrouds ch. 6 (1938)

Pedro Almodóvar
Spanish film director, 1951–

1 *Mujeres al Borde de un Ataque de Nervios.*
Women on the Verge of a Nervous Breakdown.
Title of motion picture (1988)

Joseph Alsop
U.S. journalist, 1910–1989

1 [*On the progress of the Vietnam War:*] At last
there is light at the end of the tunnel.
Syndicated newspaper column, 13 Sept. 1965
See Dickson 1; John Kennedy 29; Navarre 1

Luis Walter Alvarez
U.S. physicist, 1911–1988

1 There is no democracy in physics. We can't say
that some second-rate guy has as much right to
opinion as Fermi.
Quoted in D. S. Greenberg, *The Politics of Pure
Science* (1967)

Kathie Amatniek
U.S. feminist, 1943–

1 Sisterhood is powerful.
New York Radical Women leaflet, 15 Jan. 1968

Eric Ambler
English novelist, 1909–1998

1 The important thing to know about an
assassination or an attempted assassination is
not who fired the shot, but who paid for the
bullet.
A Coffin for Dimitrios ch. 2 (1939)

St. Ambrose
French-born Italian bishop, ca. 339–397

1 When I go to Rome, I fast on Saturday, but here
[Milan] I do not. Do you also follow the custom
of whatever church you attend.
Quoted in St. Augustine, "Letter 54 to Januarius"
(ca. 400) (translation by Sister W. Parsons). Source of
the proverb "When in Rome, do as the Romans do."
See Proverbs 258

Oscar Ameringer

U.S. socialist and writer, 1870–1943

1 The Democrats solicit votes from the poor and contributions from the rich on the pretext of protecting each from the other.

Quoted in Paul H. Douglas, *The Coming of a New Party* (1932). This is now usually quoted with the beginning "Politics is the gentle art of getting votes from the poor," etc.

Fisher Ames

U.S. political leader, 1758–1808

1 I have heard it remarked, that men are not to be reasoned out of an opinion that they have not reasoned themselves into.

Independent Chronicle (Boston), 12 Oct. 1786

2 [*Of biennial elections:*] The sober, second thought of the people shall be law.

Speech at Massachusetts Convention, 9 Jan. 1788

Kingsley Amis

English writer, 1922–1995

1 Consciousness was upon him before he could get out of the way.

Lucky Jim ch. 6 (1953)

2 His mouth had been used as a latrine by some small creature of the night, and then as its mausoleum.

Lucky Jim ch. 6 (1953)

A. R. (Archie Randolph) Ammons

U.S. poet, 1926–2001

1 In nature there are few sharp lines.

"Corson's Inlet" l. 31 (1972)

2 No humbling of reality to precept.

"Corson's Inlet" l. 116 (1972)

Roald Amundsen

Norwegian explorer, 1872–1928

1 Beg leave to inform you proceeding Antarctica. Amundsen.

Cable to Robert Falcon Scott, 12 Oct. 1910

Anacharsis

Scythian prince, Sixth cent. B.C.

1 Written laws are like spiders' webs; they will

catch, it is true, the weak and poor, but would be torn in pieces by the rich and powerful.

Quoted in Plutarch, *Parallel Lives*
See Jonathan Swift 3

Hans Christian Andersen

Danish children's book writer, 1805–1875

1 Then they knew that the lady they had lodged was a real Princess, since she had felt the one small pea through twenty mattresses and twenty feather-beds, for it was quite impossible for any one but a true Princess to be so tender.

"The Princess on the Pea" (1835)

2 *Keiserens nye Klæder.*
The Emperor's New Clothes.

Title of story (1837)

3 "But the emperor has nothing at all on!" a little child declared.

"The Emperor's New Clothes" (1837)

4 *Den grimme Ælling.*
The Ugly Duckling.

Title of story (1843)

5 But what did he see in the clear stream below? His own image; no longer a dark, gray bird, ugly and disagreeable to look at, but a graceful and beautiful swan. To be born in a duck's nest, in a farmyard, is of no consequence to a bird, if it is hatched from a swan's egg.

"The Ugly Duckling" (1843)

Marian Anderson

U.S. opera singer, 1902–1993

1 [*Of prejudice:*] Sometimes, it's like a hair across your cheek. You can't see it, you can't find it with your fingers, but you keep brushing at it because the feel of it is irritating.

Quoted in *Ladies' Home Journal,* Sept. 1960

Maxwell Anderson

U.S. playwright, 1888–1959

1 And since six o'clock there's been a wounded sniper in the tree by that orchard angle crying "Kamerad! Kamerad!" Just like a big crippled whippoorwill. What price glory now?

What Price Glory? act 2 (1924). Coauthored with Laurence Stallings.

Poul Anderson
U.S. science fiction writer, 1926–2001

1 I've yet to see any problem, however complicated, which when you looked at it the right way didn't become still more complicated.
"Call Me Joe," *Astounding Science Fiction*, Apr. 1957

Robert Anderson
U.S. playwright, 1917–2009

1 [*On the duties of the headmaster's wife:*] All you're supposed to do is every once in a while give the boys a little tea and sympathy.
Tea and Sympathy, act 1 (1953)

2 Years from now . . . when you talk about this . . . and you will . . . be kind.
Tea and Sympathy act 3 (1953). Ellipses in original text.

3 Death ends a life, but it does not end a relationship, which struggles on in the survivor's mind toward some resolution, which it never finds.
I Never Sang for My Father act 2 (1968)

Warner Anderson
U.S. actor, 1911–1976

1 [*Of San Francisco:*] The wonderful thing about this city is when you get tired you can always lean against it.
Quoted in *Wash. Post*, 25 Jan. 1959. Often erroneously attributed to Mark Twain.

Kristen Anderson-Lopez
U.S. songwriter, 1972–

1 Here I stand in the light of day
Let the storm rage on
The cold never bothered me anyway.
"Let It Go" (song) (2013). Cowritten with Robert Lopez.

André 3000 (André Lauren Benjamin)
U.S. hip hop musician, 1975–

1 Shake it like a Polaroid picture.
"Hey Ya!" (song) (2003)

Lancelot Andrewes
English bishop and sermon-writer, 1555–1626

1 It was no summer progress. A cold coming they had of it, at this time of the year; just, the worst time of the year, to take a journey, and specially a long journey, in. The ways deep, the weather sharp, the days short, the sun farthest off *in solstitio brumali,* the very dead of Winter.
Of the Nativity sermon 15 (1622)
See T. S. Eliot 68

Julie Andrews
English singer and actress, 1935–

1 I'd like to thank all those who made this award possible—especially Jack Warner.
Speech at Academy Awards, 5 Apr. 1965. Andrews had won the Best Actress award for the film *Mary Poppins,* a role she had taken after Warner passed her over for repeating her stage role of Eliza Doolittle in the motion picture version of *My Fair Lady.*

Norman Angell (Ralph Norman Angell Lane)
English pacifist, 1872–1967

1 The Great Illusion.
Title of book (1910)

Maya Angelou (Marguerite Johnson)
U.S. writer, 1928–2014

1 It's in the reach of my arms,
The span of my hips,
The stride of my step,
The curl of my lips.
I'm a woman
Phenomenally.
Phenomenal woman,
That's me.
"Phenomenal Woman" l. 6 (1978)

2 You may write me down in history
With your bitter, twisted lies,
You may trod me in the very dirt
But still, like dust, I'll rise.
"Still I Rise" l. 1 (1978)

3 Blacks should be used to play whites. For centuries we had probed their faces, the angles of their bodies, the sounds of their voices, and even their odors. Often our survival had depended on the accurate reading of a white man's chuckle or the disdainful wave of a white woman's hand.
The Heart of a Woman ch. 12 (1981)

Kenneth Anger

U.S. author and film director, 1927–

1 Hollywood Babylon.
Title of book (1975)

Joan Walsh Anglund

U.S. writer, 1926–

1 A bird does not sing
because he has an answer.
He sings
because he has a song.
A Cup of Sun (1967). These words, with "doesn't"
instead of "does not" and "it" instead of "he," are
frequently misattributed to Maya Angelou.

Paul Anka

Canadian singer and songwriter, 1941–

1 I've lived a life that's full, I traveled each and
    ev'ry highway,
And more, much more than this, I did it
    my way.
"My Way" (song) (1969). Translation of a French
song by Claude François and Jacques Revaux.

Kofi Annan

Ghanaian secretary-general of the United
Nations, 1938–2018

1 When states decide to use force to deal with
broader threats to international peace and
security, there is no substitute for the unique
legitimacy provided by the United Nations.
Opening speech to United Nations General
Assembly, New York, N.Y., 12 Sept. 2002

Anne, Princess Royal

British princess, 1950–

1 [*Of her "horsey" image:*] When I appear in public
people expect me to neigh, grind my teeth, paw
the ground, and swish my tail—none of which
is easy.
Quoted in *Observer* (London), 22 May 1977

Anonymous

See also Advertising Slogans, Anonymous (Latin),
Ballads, Folk and Anonymous Songs, Modern Proverbs,
Nursery Rhymes, Political Slogans, Proverbs, Radio
Catchphrases, Sayings, *and* Television Catchphrases.

1 [*Describing the founding of Harvard College:*]
After God had carried us safe to *New-England*,

and wee had builded our houses, provided
necessaries for our livelihood, rear'd convenient
places for Gods worship, and setled the Civill
Government: One of the next things we longed
for, and looked after was to advance Learning
and perpetuate it to Posterity; dreading to leave
an illiterate Ministery to the Churches, when
our present Ministers shall lie in the Dust.
New Englands First Fruits (1643)

2 All human beings are born free and equal in
dignity and rights.
Universal Declaration of Human Rights article 1
(1948)

3 *Arbeit macht frei.*
Work liberates.
Inscription on gates of Dachau and Auschwitz
concentration camps (1933–1945). First appeared
as the title of a short novel by Lorenz Diefenbach in
1872.

4 [*Supposed British newspaper headline announcing
storm in the English Channel holding up
shipping:*] Continent isolated.
Quoted in *Yorkshire Post*, 31 Dec. 1930. This was
alluded to as a headline from the *Times* (London), but
a search of the Times Digital Archive does not turn
up any such headline. Presumably the story is an
apocryphal chestnut.

5 [*Premature and erroneous headline about U.S.
presidential election:*] Dewey Defeats Truman.
Chicago Tribune, 3 Nov. 1948

6 Don't tread on me.
Motto on first U.S. flag (1775)

7 Equality of rights under the law shall not be
denied or abridged by the United States or by
any State on account of sex.
Equal Rights Amendment (proposed amendment to
Constitution of United States) (1972). Passed by
the U.S. Congress but never ratified by the requisite
number of states.

8 Equal Justice Under Law.
Inscription on West Portico of U.S. Supreme Court
Building, Washington, D.C.

9 [*Headline:*] Ford to City: Drop Dead.
N.Y. Daily News, 30 Oct. 1975. Described President
Gerald Ford's promise to veto any bill providing
money to bail out New York City from bankruptcy;
probably alienated enough New Yorkers to swing the
results of the 1976 national presidential election.

10 Form is emptiness and the very emptiness is
form; emptiness does not differ from form, nor

does form differ from emptiness; whatever is form, that is emptiness, whatever is emptiness, that is form.

Heart Sutra v. 3 (fourth century)

11 From Ghoulies and Ghosties
And Long Leggetty Beasties
And things that go bump in the night
Good Lord, deliver us.

"The Cornish or West Country Litany." Earliest printed record occurs in F. T. Nettleinghame, *Polperro Proverbs and Others* (1926), but it certainly predates that printing.

12 Here men from the planet Earth first set foot on the moon, July 1969 A.D. We came in peace for all mankind.

National Aeronautics and Space Administration plaque left on moon by astronauts (1969)

13 It became necessary to destroy the town to save it.

Unnamed U.S. Army major quoted in *N.Y. Times*, 8 Feb. 1968. The major was referring to the decision to bomb and shell the town of Bentre, Vietnam. Accusations have arisen in recent years that Associated Press reporter Peter Arnett fabricated the quotation.

14 It was resolved, That England was too pure an Air for Slaves to breathe in.

"In the 11th of Elizabeth" (1568–1569). Printed in John Rushworth, *Historical Collections* vol. 2 (1680–1722).

15 Lies, damned lies, and statistics.

Leeds Mercury, 29 June 1892. The earliest known occurrence of the precise phrase "lies, damned lies, and statistics" was in a speech by future British prime minister Arthur Balfour, quoted in the Leeds newspaper in 1892. Earlier, a letter published in the *National Observer*, 13 June 1891 (discovered by Stephen Goranson), stated: "It has been wittily remarked that there are three kinds of falsehood: the first is a 'fib,' the second is a downright lie, and the third and most aggravated is statistics." Goranson believes that English politician Charles Dilke (1843–1911) was the most likely originator of the quip about statistics. He also, however, has found a precursor nonstatistical saying: "A well-known lawyer, now a judge, once grouped witnesses into three classes: simple liars, damned liars, and experts" (*Nature*, 26 Nov. 1885).

16 Justice the Guardian of Liberty.

Inscription on East Portico of U.S. Supreme Court Building, Washington, D.C.

17 Know thyself.

Inscription on temple of Apollo at Delphi, Greece

18 Lizzie Borden took an ax
And gave her mother forty whacks;
And when she saw what she had done
She gave her father forty-one.

Verse about trial of Lizzie Borden for murdering her parents (1892)

19 May the road rise to meet you.
May the wind be ever at your back.

"An Irish Wish"

20 Next year in Jerusalem!

Haggadah

21 Nothing in excess.

Inscription on temple of Apollo at Delphi, Greece
See Horace 19; Horace 26; Proverbs 195

22 Now is the time for all good men to come to the aid of the party.

Sentence devised to test speed of first typewriter (1867). According to *Respectfully Quoted*, ed. Suzy Platt, "Author unknown. . . . Other sources credit [Charles E.] Weller as author of the famous sentence, but he does not claim the credit in his book. The sentence is still in use, though it is often written as 'their' party."

23 The quick brown fox jumps over the lazy dog.

Sentence used to test letters of keyboard, quoted in *N.Y. Times*, 22 Feb. 1885

24 Remember Pearl Harbor.

World War II slogan, quoted in *Oregonian* (Portland), 9 Dec. 1941

25 The Roman Pontiff, when he speaks *ex cathedra*, that is, when . . . he defines a doctrine regarding faith or morals to be held by the universal church is, by the divine assistance promised to him in Blessed Peter, possessed of that infallibility with which the divine Redeemer [Jesus] wills that His church should be endowed.

Dogma of papal infallibility issued by Vatican Council, Rome, 13 July 1870

26 [*Alleged entreaty by young baseball fan to "Shoeless Joe" Jackson after his arrest in the "Black Sox" bribery scandal, 28 Sept. 1920:*] Say it ain't so, Joe.

Quoted in *Pittsburgh Post-Gazette*, 7 Apr. 1921. This appears to be a later paraphrase of "Tell us, Joe, that it ain't so," reported by the *Los Angeles Times*, 30 Sept. 1920, as being said by a youngster to Jackson as the latter stepped out of the court building. Jackson later denied that any such encounter had taken place. James T. Farrell, in *My Baseball Diary* (1957), recalled fans calling out "It ain't true, Joe" to Jackson after the game of 27 Sept. 1920.

27 The sky is falling! The sky is falling!
"Chicken-licken" (nursery story)

28 Something old, something new, something
borrowed, something blue.
Wedding rhyme

29 Speak Truth to Power.
Title of pamphlet by American Friends Service
Committee (1955). Bayard Rustin, one of the
pamphlet's authors, had written in a 15 Aug. 1942
letter: "The primary function of a religious society is
to 'speak the truth to power.'" The phrase "speaking
truth to power" has been found by Barry Popik as
early as 1748, in the pamphlet *A Free Briton's Advice
to the Free Citizens of Dublin.* Popik also has found
that the English painter and writer Benjamin Robert
Haydon frequently wrote of "telling truth to power"
beginning in 1846.

30 That no man of what estate or condition, shall
be put out of land or tenement, nor taken
nor imprisoned, nor disinherited, nor put to
death, without being brought in answer by due
process of law.
Statute of Westminster (1354)

31 [*On the failed assassination attempt on British
Prime Minister Margaret Thatcher by the
Provisional IRA at the Grand Hotel, Brighton,
England:*] Today we were unlucky. But
remember, we have only to be lucky once. You
will have to be lucky always.
Statement by Irish Republican Army, Oct. 1984

32 Warning: The Surgeon General Has
Determined That Cigarette Smoking Is
Dangerous to Your Health.
Statement required by law to appear on cigarette
packaging and advertisements (1965)

33 Western wind, when will thou blow,
The small rain down can rain?
Christ, if my love were in my arms
And I in my bed again!
"Western Wind" (1790)

34 [*Comment of U.S. soldier about French village,
1944:*] We sure liberated the hell out of this
place.
Quoted in Max Miller, *The Far Shore* (1945)

35 We, the peoples of the United Nations
Determined to save succeeding generations
from the scourge of war, which twice in
our lifetime has brought untold sorrow to
mankind, and

To reaffirm faith in fundamental human rights,
in the dignity and worth of the human person,
in the equal right of men and women and of
nations large and small, and . . . for these ends

To practice tolerance and live together in peace
with one another as good neighbors, and

To unite our strength to maintain international
peace and security . . .

Have resolved to combine our efforts to
accomplish these aims.
Charter of the United Nations preamble (1945)

Anonymous (Latin)

1 *Ad majorem Dei gloriam.*
To the greater glory of God.
Motto of the Society of Jesus

2 [*Salutation by gladiators:*] *Ave Caesar, morituri te
salutant.*
Hail Caesar, those who are about to die salute
you.
Quoted in Suetonius, *Lives of the Caesars*

3 *Ave Maria, gratia plena, Dominus tecum:
Benedicta tu in mulieribus, et benedictus fructus
ventris tui, Jesus.*
Hail Mary, full of grace, the Lord is with thee:
Blessed art thou among women, and blessed
is the fruit of thy womb, Jesus.
"Ave Maria" (Hail Mary) (eleventh cent.)
See Bible 282

4 *Cave ab homine unius libri.*
Beware the man of one book.
Quoted in Isaac D'Israeli, *Curiosities of Literature*
(1791–1793)

5 *De minimis non curat lex.*
The law is not concerned with trifles.
Legal maxim

6 *Divide et impera.*
Divide and rule.
Political maxim

7 *Et in Arcadia ego.*
And I too in Arcadia.
Tomb inscription often depicted in classical paintings

8 *Gaudeamus igitur,
Juvenes dum sumus.*
Let us then rejoice,
While we are young.
Medieval students' song

9 *Habeas corpus.*
You should produce the body.
Legal phrase

10 *Post coitum omne animal triste.*
After coitus every animal is sad.
Post-classical saying. The *Oxford English Dictionary* states, "The phrase as such does not occur in classical Latin, but cf. [pseudo-Aristotle] *Problems* . . . 'Why do young men, on first having sexual intercourse, afterwards hate those with whom they have just been associated?'; Pliny *Nat. Hist.* . . . 'man alone experiences regret after first having intercourse.'"

11 *Requiescat in pace.*
May he rest in peace.
Saying. Frequently abbreviated R.I.P.

12 *Sic semper tyrannis.*
Thus ever to tyrants.
State motto of Virginia. Recommended by George Mason.
See John Wilkes Booth 1

13 *Sic transit gloria mundi.*
So passes away the glory of the world.
Pronouncement during papal coronations

Jean Anouilh
French playwright, 1910–1987

1 Saintliness is a temptation too.
Becket act 3 (1959)

St. Anselm
Italian-born English clergyman and philosopher, 1033–1109

1 And assuredly that, than which nothing greater can be conceived, cannot exist in the understanding alone. For, suppose it exists in the understanding alone: then it can be conceived to exist in reality; which is greater.
Proslogium ch. 2 (1078) (translation by Sidney Norton Deane). This is the "ontological argument" for the existence of God.

John Anster
Irish poet, 1793–1867

1 What you can do, or dream you can, begin it. Boldness has genius, power, and magic in it.
Faustus, a Dramatic Mystery (1835). This is widely attributed to Goethe but is in fact at best a paraphrase of a line from Goethe's *Faust:* "Now at last let me see some deeds!"

Susan B. Anthony
U.S. women's rights leader, 1820–1906

1 Men, their rights and nothing more; women, their rights and nothing less.
Motto of *The Revolution* (newspaper), 8 Jan. 1868

2 Join the union, girls, and together say *Equal Pay for Equal Work.*
The Revolution, 18 Mar. 1869

3 It was we, the people, not we, the white male citizens, nor yet we, the male citizens, but we, the whole people, who formed this Union. And we formed it, not to give the blessings of liberty, but to secure them; not to the half of ourselves and the half of our posterity, but to the whole people—women as well as men.
Statement in court after conviction for attempting to vote, Rochester, N.Y., 17 June 1873

4 Failure is impossible.
Speech to National Woman Suffrage Association celebration of Anthony's eighty-sixth birthday, Washington, D.C., Feb. 1906

5 It is urged that the use of the masculine pronouns he, his, and him in all the constitutions and laws, is proof that only men were meant to be included in their provisions. If you insist on this version of the letter of the law, we shall insist that you be consistent and accept the other horn of the dilemma, which would compel you to exempt women from taxation for the support of the government and from penalties for the violation of laws. There is no she or her or hers in the tax laws, and this is equally true of all the criminal laws.
Quoted in Ida Husted Harper, *The Life and Work of Susan B. Anthony* (1899)

Apelles
Greek painter, Fourth cent. B.C.

1 Not a day without a line.
Attributed in Pliny the Elder, *Historia Naturalis*

Guillaume Apollinaire (Guglielmo Apollinaris de Kostrowitzky)
Italian-born French poet, 1880–1918

1 *Les souvenirs sont cors de chasse
Dont meurt le bruit parmi le vent.*
Memories are hunting horns

Whose sound dies on the wind.
"Cors de Chasse" (1912)

2 *Sous le pont Mirabeau coule la Seine.*
Under Mirabeau Bridge flows the Seine.
"Le Pont Mirabeau" (1912)

3 *Vienne la nuit, sonne l'heure,*
Les jours s'en vont, je demeure.
Come night, strike the hour.
Days go, I endure.
"Le Pont Mirabeau" (1912)

4 This new union—for up until now stage
sets and costumes on the one hand and
choreography on the other were only
superficially linked—has given rise in [the
ballet] *Parade* to a kind of *"sur-realisme."*
Excelsior, 11 May 1917. First appearance of the word
surrealisme or *surrealiste.*

Kwame Anthony Appiah
English-born Ghanaian-U.S. philosopher,
1954–

1 The truth is that there are no races: there is
nothing in the world that can do all we ask race
to do for us.
*In My Father's House: Africa in the Philosophy of
Culture* ch. 2 (1992)

St. Thomas Aquinas
Italian theologian, ca. 1225–1274

1 *Ergo necesse est devenire ad aliquod primum*
movens, quod a nullo movetur; et hoc omnes
intelligunt Deum.
Therefore it is necessary to arrive at a prime
mover, put in motion by no other; and this
everyone understands to be God.
Summa Theologicae pt. 1 (ca. 1265)

The Arabian Nights

1 Who will change old lamps for new ones? . . .
new lamps for old ones?
"The History of Aladdin"

2 Open Sesame!
"The History of Ali Baba"

Yassir Arafat (Muhammad 'Abd ar Ra'uf
al-Qudwa al-Husayni)
Palestinian president, 1929–2004

1 The Palestine National Council, in the name of
God, and in the name of the Palestinian Arab
people, proclaims the establishment of the
state of Palestine on our Palestinian land, with
Jerusalem as its capital.
Declaration of Independence, 15 Nov. 1988

Louis Aragon
French poet, 1897–1982

1 We know that the nature of genius is to provide
idiots with ideas twenty years later.
Treatise on Style pt. 1 (1928)

Diane Arbus
U.S. photographer, 1923–1971

1 Most people go through life dreading they'll
have a traumatic experience. Freaks were born
with their trauma. They've already passed their
test in life. They're aristocrats.
Diane Arbus (1972)

2 I really believe there are things which nobody
would see unless I photographed them.
Diane Arbus (1972)

John Arbuthnot
Scottish physician and pamphleteer, 1667–1735

1 Curle (who is one of the new terrors of Death)
has been writing letters to every body for
memoirs of his life.
Letter to Jonathan Swift, 13 Jan. 1733

Archilochus
Greek poet, Seventh cent. B.C.

1 The fox knows many things—the hedgehog one
big one.
Fragment 103
See Isaiah Berlin 1

Archimedes
Greek mathematician, ca. 287 B.C.–212 B.C.

1 [*On the principle of the lever:*] Give me but one
firm spot on which to stand, and I will move
the earth.
Quoted in Pappus, *Synagoge*

2 [*After thinking of a method to test the purity of
gold:*] Eureka!

I've got it!
Quoted in Vitruvius Pollio, *De Architectura*

Elizabeth Arden (Florence Nightingale Graham)

U.S. business executive, ca. 1880–1966

1 Nothing that costs only a dollar is worth having.
Quoted in *Chicago Tribune*, 25 June 1978

Hannah Arendt

German-born U.S. political philosopher, 1906–1975

1 Power can be thought of as the never-ending, self-feeding motor of all political action that corresponds to the legendary unending accumulation of money that begets money.
Origins of Totalitarianism ch. 5 (1951)

2 Bureaucracy, the rule of nobody.
The Human Condition ch. 6 (1958)

3 Thought . . . is still possible, and no doubt actual, wherever men live under the conditions of political freedom. Unfortunately . . . no other human capacity is so vulnerable, and it is in fact far easier to act under conditions of tyranny than it is to think.
The Human Condition ch. 45 (1958)

4 To abolish the fences of laws between men— as tyranny does—means to take away man's liberties and destroy freedom as a living political reality; for the space between men as it is hedged in by laws, is the living space of freedom.
The Origins of Totalitarianism, 2d ed., ch. 13 (1958)

5 It was as though in those last minutes he [Adolf Eichmann] was summing up the lessons that this long course in human wickedness had taught us—the lesson of the fearsome, word-and-thought-defying *banality of evil*.
Eichmann in Jerusalem: A Report on the Banality of Evil ch. 15 (1963)

6 No punishment has ever possessed enough power of deterrence to prevent the commission of crimes. On the contrary, once a specific crime has appeared for the first time, its reappearance is more likely than its initial emergence could have been.
Eichmann in Jerusalem: A Report on the Banality of Evil epilogue (1963)

7 Where all, or almost all, are guilty, nobody is.
Eichmann in Jerusalem: A Report on the Banality of Evil epilogue (1963)

8 The hypocrite's crime is that he bears false witness against himself. What makes it so plausible to assume that hypocrisy is the vice of vices is that integrity can indeed exist under the cover of all other vices except this one. Only crime and the criminal, it is true, confront us with the perplexity of radical evil; but only the hypocrite is really rotten to the core.
On Revolution ch. 2 (1963)

9 It is well known that the most radical revolutionary will become a conservative on the day after the revolution.
New Yorker, 12 Sept. 1970

10 The practice of violence, like all action, changes the world, but the most probable change is to a more violent world.
Crises of the Republic "On Violence" (1972)

11 The sad truth of the matter is that most evil is done by people who never made up their minds to be or do either evil or good.
The Life of the Mind vol. 1, ch. 18 (1978)

Ludovico Ariosto

Italian poet, 1474–1533

1 Nature made him and then broke the mold.
Orlando Furioso canto 10 (1532)

Aristophanes

Greek playwright, ca. 450 B.C.–ca. 388 B.C.

1 To make the worse appear the better reason.
The Clouds l. 114 (423 B.C.)
See Milton 27

2 The old are in a second childhood.
The Clouds l. 1417 (423 B.C.)

3 [*Suggesting a name for the city of the Birds:*] Cloudcuckooland.
The Birds l. 819 (414 B.C.) (translation by William Arrowsmith)

4 You Birds have a great deal to gain from a kindlier Olympos. . . . A perpetual run, say, of halcyon days.
The Birds l. 1594 (414 B.C.) (translation by William Arrowsmith)

5 These impossible women! How they do get around us!

The poet was right: can't live with them, or
　　without them!

Lysistrata l. 1038 (411 B.C.) (translation by Dudley
Fitts)
See Martial 2

6 Under every stone lurks a politician.

Festival Time l. 530 (410 B.C.)

7 [*The cry of the frogs:*] Brekekekex, koax, koax.

The Frogs l. 209 (405 B.C.) (translation by Kenneth
McLeish)

8 Oftentimes have we reflected on a similar abuse
In the choice of men for office, and of coins for
　　common use;
For your old and standard pieces, valued and
　　approved and tried,
Here among the Grecian nations, and in all the
　　world beside,
Recognized in every realm for trusty stamp and
　　pure assay,
Are rejected and abandoned for the trash of
　　yesterday;
For a vile, adulterate issue, drossy, counterfeit
　　and base,
Which the traffic of the city passes current in
　　their place!

The Frogs l. 891 (405 B.C.) (translation by Kenneth
McLeish). Considered to be the earliest expression
of the economic principle later known as
"Gresham's Law."
See Gresham 1; Henry Macleod 1; Henry Macleod 2

Aristotle

Greek philosopher, 384 B.C.–322 B.C.

Translations and citation information are from The
Complete Works of Aristotle: The Revised Oxford
Translation, *ed. Jonathan Barnes (1984).*

1 The whole is not, as it were, a mere heap, but
the totality is something besides the parts.

Metaphysics bk. 8, 1045a. More commonly rendered
as "the whole is more (or greater) than the sum of its
parts."

2 One swallow does not make a summer.

Nicomachean Ethics bk. 1, 1098a

3 We must as a second best, as people say, take
the least of the evils.

Nicomachean Ethics bk. 2, 1109a

4 We . . . make war that we may live in peace.

Nicomachean Ethics bk. 10, 1177b
See Vegetius 1

5 A tragedy, then, is the imitation of an action
that is serious and also, as having magnitude,
complete in itself; in language with pleasurable
accessories, each kind brought in separately
in the parts of the work; in a dramatic, not in
a narrative form; with incidents arousing pity
and fear, wherewith to accomplish its catharsis
of such emotions.

Poetics ch. 6, 1449b

6 A whole is that which has beginning, middle,
and end.

Poetics ch. 7, 1450b

7 A likely impossibility is always preferable to an
unconvincing possibility.

Poetics ch. 24, 1460a

8 It is evident that the state is a creation of
nature, and that man is by nature a political
animal.

Politics bk. 1, 1253a

9 That man is more of a political animal than
bees or any other gregarious animals is evident.
Nature, as we often say, makes nothing in vain,
and man is the only animal who has the gift of
speech.

Politics bk. 1, 1253a

10 He who is unable to live in society, or who has
no need because he is sufficient for himself,
must be either a beast or a god.

Politics bk. 1, 1253a

11 Nature makes nothing incomplete, and nothing
in vain.

Politics bk. 1, 1256b

12 We should behave to our friends as we would
wish our friends to behave to us.

Quoted in Diogenes Laertius, *Lives of the Philosophers.*
The positive version of "The Golden Rule."
See Bible 225; Chesterfield 4; Confucius 9; Hillel 2

13 When he [Aristotle] was asked "What is a
friend?" he said "One soul inhabiting two
bodies."

Reported in Diogenes Laertius, *Lives of the
Philosophers*

Richard Armour

U.S. humorist, 1906–1989

1 Shake and shake
The catsup bottle.

None will come,
And then a lot'll.
"Going to Extremes" l. 1 (1949)

Louis Armstrong

U.S. jazz musician and singer, 1901–1971

1 All music is folk music. I ain't never heard no
horse sing a song.
Quoted in *N.Y. Times,* 7 July 1971

Neil A. Armstrong

U.S. astronaut, 1930–2012

1 Contact light. Okay, engine stop. ACA out
of detent. Modes control both auto, descent
engine command override, off. Engine arm off.
413 is in.
Quoted in *IEEE Spectrum,* July 1994. Actual first
words said upon *landing* on the moon, 20 July 1969.

2 Houston. Tranquility Base here. The Eagle has
landed.
Radio message announcing first landing on moon,
20 July 1969

3 That's one small step for a man, one giant leap
for mankind.
Message upon first stepping on surface of moon,
20 July 1969. The original transmission was heard
as "one small step for man," and this erroneous or
misspoken version was initially reported widely.

Robert Armstrong

English government official, 1927–

1 [A misleading impression] is perhaps being
economical with the truth.
Testimony in *Spycatcher* trial, Sydney, Australia,
18 Nov. 1986
See Edmund Burke 25; Twain 86

Arnauld-Amaury

French clergyman, fl. 1200

1 [*Response when asked how true Catholics could be
distinguished from heretics at massacre of Béziers,
1209:*] Kill them all. God will recognize his own.
Quoted in Caesarius of Heisterbach, *Dialogus
Miraculorum* (ca. 1233) (translation by Jonathon
Sumption). Usually quoted as "Kill them all, and let
God sort them out."

Ernst Moritz Arndt

German poet and political writer, 1789–1860

1 This is the German's fatherland,
Where wrath pursues the foreign band,—
Where every Frank is held a foe,
And Germans all as brothers glow,—
That is the land,—
All Germany's thy fatherland.
"What Is the German's Fatherland" (1813)

Peter Arno (Curtis Arnoux Peters)

U.S. cartoonist, 1904–1968

1 I consider your conduct unethical and lousy.
Cartoon caption, *Peter Arno's Parade* (1929)

2 [*Spoken by a man with a rolled-up engineering
plan under his arm walking away from a crashed
airplane:*] Well, back to the old drawing board.
Cartoon caption, *New Yorker,* 1 Mar. 1941

Matthew Arnold

English poet and essayist, 1822–1888

1 Who ordered, that their longing's fire
Should be, as soon as kindled, cooled?
Who renders vain their deep desire?—
A God, a God their severance ruled!
And bade betwixt their shores to be
The unplumbed, salt, estranging sea.
"Switzerland: To Marguerite—Continued" l. 19 (1852)

2 Wandering between two worlds, one dead,
The other powerless to be born.
"Stanzas from the Grande Chartreuse" l. 85 (1855)

3 Nations are not truly great solely because the
individuals composing them are numerous,
free, and active; but they are great when these
numbers, this freedom, and this activity are
employed in the service of an ideal higher than
that of an ordinary man, taken by himself.
"Democracy" (1861)

4 It is a very great thing to be able to think as
you like; but, after all, an important question
remains: *what* you think.
"Democracy" (1861)

5 Of these two literatures [French and German],
as of the intellect of Europe in general, the
main effort, for now many years, has been a
critical effort; the endeavor, in all branches of
knowledge—theology, philosophy, history, art,
science—to see the object as in itself it really is.
On Translating Homer Lecture 2 (1861)

6 He [the translator] will find one English book
and one only, where, as in the *Iliad* itself,
perfect plainness of speech is allied with
perfect nobleness; and that book is the Bible.
On Translating Homer Lecture 3 (1861)

7 The grand style arises in poetry, *when a noble
nature, poetically gifted, treats with simplicity or
with severity a serious subject.*
On Translating Homer: Last Words (1862)

8 [*Of Oxford:*] Whispering from her towers the
last enchantments of the Middle Age. . . .
Home of lost causes, and forsaken beliefs, and
unpopular names, and impossible loyalties!
Essays in Criticism First Series, preface (1865)

9 For the creation of a master-work of literature
two powers must concur, the power of the man
and the power of the moment, and the man is
not enough without the moment.
Essays in Criticism First Series, "The Function of
Criticism at the Present Time" (1865)

10 [Edmund] Burke is so great because, almost
alone in England, he brings thought to bear
upon politics, he saturates politics with
thought.
Essays in Criticism First Series, "The Function of
Criticism at the Present Time" (1865)

11 The notion of the free play of the mind upon
all subjects being a pleasure in itself, being an
object of desire, being an essential provider
of elements without which a nation's spirit,
whatever compensations it may have for them,
must, in the long run, die of inanition, hardly
enters into an Englishman's thoughts.
Essays in Criticism First Series, "The Function of
Criticism at the Present Time" (1865)

12 I am bound by my own definition of criticism:
*a disinterested endeavor to learn and propagate the
best that is known and thought in the world.*
Essays in Criticism First Series, "The Function of
Criticism at the Present Time" (1865)

13 Philistinism!—We have not the expression in
English. Perhaps we have not the word because
we have so much of the thing.
Essays in Criticism First Series, "Heinrich Heine"
(1865)

14 *Philistine* must have originally meant, in the
mind of those who invented the nickname, a
strong, dogged, unenlightened opponent of the
chosen people, of the children of the light.
Essays in Criticism First Series, "Heinrich Heine"
(1865)

15 [*Of Oxford:*] That sweet City with her dreaming
spires.
"Thyrsis" l. 19 (1866)

16 Listen! you hear the grating roar
Of pebbles which the waves draw back, and
fling,
At their return, up the high strand,
Begin, and cease, and then again begin,
With tremulous cadence slow, and bring
The eternal note of sadness in.

Sophocles long ago
Heard it on the Aegean.
"Dover Beach" l. 9 (1867)

17 The Sea of Faith
Was once, too, at the full, and round earth's
shore
Lay like the folds of a bright girdle furl'd.
But now I only hear
Its melancholy, long, withdrawing roar,
Retreating, to the breath
Of the night-wind, down the vast edges drear
And naked shingles of the world.
"Dover Beach" l. 21 (1867)

18 Ah, love, let us be true
   To one another! for the world, which seems
   To lie before us like a land of dreams,
   So various, so beautiful, so new,
   Hath really neither joy, nor love, nor light,
   Nor certitude, nor peace, nor help for pain.
   "Dover Beach" l. 29 (1867)

19 And we are here as on a darkling plain
   Swept with confused alarms of struggle and
      flight,
   Where ignorant armies clash by night.
   "Dover Beach" l. 35 (1867)

20 This something is *style*, and the Celts certainly
   have it in a wonderful measure.
   On the Study of Celtic Literature sec. 6 (1867)

21 The power of the Latin classic is in *character*,
   that of the Greek is in *beauty*. Now character is
   capable of being taught, learnt, and assimilated:
   beauty hardly.
   Schools and Universities on the Continent (1868)

22 The whole scope of the essay is to recommend
   culture as the great help out of our present
   difficulties; culture being a pursuit of our total
   perfection by means of getting to know, on all
   the matters which most concern us, the best
   which has been thought and said in the world.
   Culture and Anarchy preface (1869)

23 Our society distributes itself into Barbarians,
   Philistines, and Populace; and America is just
   ourselves, with the Barbarians quite left out,
   and the Populace nearly.
   Culture and Anarchy preface (1869)

24 I am a Liberal, yet I am a Liberal tempered by
   experience, reflection, and renouncement, and
   I am, above all, a believer in culture.
   Culture and Anarchy introduction (1869)

25 Culture is then properly described not as
   having its origin in curiosity, but as having its
   origin in the love of perfection; it is *a study of
   perfection*.
   Culture and Anarchy ch. 1 (1869)

26 Not a having and a resting, but a growing and
   a becoming is the character of perfection as
   culture conceives it.
   Culture and Anarchy ch. 1 (1869)

27 The pursuit of perfection, then, is the pursuit
   of sweetness and light. . . . He who works for

sweetness and light united, works to make
reason and the will of God prevail.
Culture and Anarchy ch. 1 (1869)
See Jonathan Swift 1

28 I often, therefore, when I want to distinguish
   clearly the aristocratic class from the Philistines
   proper, or middle class, name the former, in
   my own mind, *the Barbarians.*
   Culture and Anarchy ch. 3 (1869)

29 The freethinking of one age is the common
   sense of the next.
   *God and the Bible: A Review of Objections to Literature
   and Dogma* (1875)

30 [*Of Percy Shelley:*] Beautiful and ineffectual angel,
   beating in the void his luminous wings in vain.
   Poetry of Byron preface (1881)

31 That which in England we call the middle class
   is in America virtually the nation.
   A Word About America (1882)

32 The best poetry will be found to have a power
   of forming, sustaining, and delighting us, as
   nothing else can.
   Essays in Criticism Second Series, "The Study of
   Poetry" (1888)

33 The difference between genuine poetry and the
   poetry of Dryden, Pope, and all their school,
   is briefly this: their poetry is conceived and
   composed in their wits, genuine poetry is
   conceived and composed in the soul.
   Essays in Criticism Second Series, "Thomas Gray" (1888)

34 Poetry is at bottom a criticism of life.
   Essays in Criticism Second Series, "Wordsworth" (1888)

35 Have something to say, and say it as clearly as
   you can. That is the only secret of style.
   Quoted in G. W. E. Russell, *Collections and
   Recollections* (1898)

George Asaf (George Henry Powell)
English songwriter, 1880–1951

1 Pack up your troubles in your old kit-bag,
   And smile, smile, smile.
   "Pack Up Your Troubles" (song) (1915)

Roger Ascham
English scholar and courtier, 1515–1568

1 Mark all mathematical heads, which be only
   and wholly bent to those sciences, how solitary

they be themselves, how unfit to live with others, and how unapt to serve in the world.
The Schoolmaster bk. 1 (1570)

John Ashbery
U.S. poet, 1927–2017

1 As I sit looking out of a window of the building
   I wish I did not have to write the instructional
      manual on the uses of a new metal.
   I look down into the street and see people, each
      walking with an inner peace,
   And envy them—they are so far away from me!
   Not one of them has to worry about getting out
      this manual on schedule.
   "The Instruction Manual" l. 1 (1956)

2 There is the rich quarter, with its houses of
      pink and white, and its crumbling, leafy
      terraces.
   There is the poorer quarter, its homes a deep
      blue.
   There is the market, where men are selling hats
      and swatting flies.
   "The Instruction Manual" l. 60 (1956)

3 I turn my gaze
   Back to the instruction manual which has made
      me dream of Guadalajara.
   "The Instruction Manual" l. 73 (1956)

Howard Ashman
U.S. songwriter, 1951–1991

1 Tale as old as time
   True as it can be
   Barely even friends
   Then somebody bends
   Unexpectedly.
   "Beauty and the Beast" (song) (1991)

2 Tale as old as time
   Song as old as rhyme
   Beauty and the Beast.
   "Beauty and the Beast" (song) (1991)

Isaac Asimov
Russian-born U.S. science fiction writer,
1920–1992

1 The fundamental law impressed upon the
   positronic brains of all robots.... On no
   conditions is a human being to be injured in
   any way, even when such injury is directly
   ordered by another human.
   "Liar!" (1941). The first explicit statement of the First
   Law of Robotics.
   See John Campbell 1

2 The three fundamental Rules of
   Robotics.... One, a robot may not injure a
   human being under any conditions—and, as a
   corollary, must not permit a human being to
   be injured because of inaction on his part....
   Two ... a robot must follow all orders given by
   qualified human beings as long as they do not
   conflict with Rule 1.... Three: a robot must
   protect its own existence as long as that does
   not conflict with Rules 1 and 2.
   "Runaround" (1942). In later reprints of this story,
   such as the one in *I, Robot* (1950), Asimov used the
   following wording: "One, a robot must not injure a
   human being, or, through inaction, allow a human
   being to come to harm.... Two ... a robot must
   obey the orders given it by human beings except
   where such orders would conflict with the First Law.
   And three, a robot must protect its own existence
   as long as such protection does not conflict with the
   First or Second Laws." The rules were first suggested
   to Asimov by editor John W. Campbell, Jr.
   See John Campbell 1

3 [*"Zeroth Law of Robotics":*] No Machine may
   harm Humanity; nor, through inaction, may he
   allow Humanity to come to harm.
   "The Evitable Conflict" (1950)
   See John Campbell 1

4 There is a cult of ignorance in the United
   States, and there has always been. The strain of
   anti-intellectualism has been a constant thread
   winding its way through our political and
   cultural life, nurtured by the false notion that
   democracy means that "my ignorance is just as
   good as your knowledge."
   Newsweek, 21 Jan. 1980

Herbert Asquith
British prime minister, 1852–1928

1 [*Of the possibility that the House of Lords would be
   flooded with new Liberal peers to guarantee passage
   of the Finance Bill:*] We shall wait and see.
   Quoted in *Times* (London), 21 Jan. 1910

Margot Asquith (Emma Alice Margaret Tennant)

British society figure, 1864–1945

1 If not a great soldier, he [Lord Kitchener] is at least a great poster.

More Memories ch. 6 (1933)

2 [*Of David Lloyd George:*] He can't see a belt without hitting below it.

Quoted in *Listener*, 11 June 1953

3 [*To actress Jean Harlow, who had been mispronouncing Asquith's first name:*] The final "t" in my Christian name is silent, unlike your family name.

Quoted in Lewis Einstein, Letter to Oliver Wendell Holmes, Jr., 4 Oct. 1934

Mary Astell

English religious writer, 1668–1731

1 If Absolute Sovereignty be not necessary in a State, how comes it to be so in a Family? or if in a Family why not in a State; since no Reason can be alledg'd for the one that will not hold more strongly for the other? . . . If *all Men are born free,* how is it that all Women are born Slaves? As they must be if the being subjected to the *inconstant, uncertain, unknown, arbitrary Will* of Men, be the *perfect Condition of Slavery?*

Reflections upon Marriage, 3rd ed., preface (1706)

Mary Astor (Lucile Langhanke)

U.S. actress, 1906–1987

1 Five stages in the life of an actor. . . . 1. Who's Mary Astor? 2. Get me Mary Astor. 3. Get me a Mary Astor type. 4. Get me a young Mary Astor. 5. Who's Mary Astor?

A Life on Film ch. 14 (1967). A very similar quotation by the actor Hugh O'Brian appeared in the *Pasadena Independent*, 23 Sept. 1960.

Nancy Astor

U.S.-born British politician, 1879–1964

1 The first time Adam had a chance he laid the blame on woman.

My Two Countries ch. 1 (1923)

2 One reason why I don't drink is because I wish to know when I am having a good time.

Quoted in *Christian Herald*, June 1960. This was a condensation of remarks made by Astor at the Edinburgh World's Christian Temperance Union Convention in 1926.

3 The penalty of success is to be bored by people who used to snub you.

Quoted in *Reno Evening Gazette*, 4 May 1964

4 [*Speech, Oldham, England, 1951:*] I married beneath me, all women do.

Quoted in *Dictionary of National Biography 1961–1970* (1981)

Mustapha Kemal Atatürk

Turkish statesman, 1880–1938

1 It was necessary to abolish the fez, emblem of ignorance, negligence, fanaticism, and hatred of progress and civilization, to accept in its place the hat—the headgear worn by the whole civilized world.

Speech to Turkish Assembly, Oct. 1927

Ti-Grace Atkinson

U.S. feminist and writer, 1938–

1 Love is the victim's response to the rapist.

Quoted in *Sunday Times Magazine* (London), 14 Sept. 1969

2 Feminism is a theory, lesbianism is a practice.

Quoted in Sidney Abbott and Barbara Love, *Sappho Was a Right-On Woman* (1972). This saying, from a 1970 speech, is usually quoted, "Feminism is the theory, lesbianism is the practice."

Margaret Atwood

Canadian writer, 1939–

1 This above all, to refuse to be a victim.

Surfacing ch. 27 (1972)

2 I would like to be the air
that inhabits you for a moment
only. I would like to be that unnoticed
and that necessary.

"Variation on the Word *Sleep*" l. 27 (1981)

3 We were the people who were not in the papers. We lived in the blank white spaces at the edges of print. It gave us more freedom. We lived in the gaps between the stories.

The Handmaid's Tale ch. 10 (1986)

4 Nobody dies from lack of sex. It's lack of love we die from.

The Handmaid's Tale ch. 18 (1986)

5 A divorce is like an amputation; you survive,
but there's less of you.
Quoted in *Time*, 19 Mar. 1973

John Aubrey
English antiquarian, 1616–1697

1 Oval face. His eye a dark grey. He had auburn
hair. His complexion exceeding fair—he was
so fair that they called him *the lady of* Christ's
College.
Brief Lives "John Milton" (1690)

2 He had read much, if one considers his long
life; but his contemplation was more than his
reading. He was wont to say that if he had read
as much as other men, he should have known
no more than other men.
Brief Lives "Thomas Hobbes" (1690)

W. H. Auden
English-born U.S. poet, 1907–1973

1 Stop all the clocks, cut off the telephone,
Prevent the dog from barking with a juicy bone,
Silence the pianos and with muffled drum
Bring out the coffin, let the mourners come.
"Funeral Blues" l. 1 (1936)

2 He was my North, my South, my East and West,
My working week and my Sunday rest,
My noon, my midnight, my talk, my song;
I thought that love would last for ever: I was
wrong.
"Funeral Blues" l. 9 (1936)

3 History to the defeated
May say Alas but cannot help or pardon.
"Spain, 1937" l. 90 (1937)

4 Evil is unspectacular and always human,
And shares our bed and eats at our own table.
"Herman Melville" l. 17 (1939)

5 The Godhead is broken like bread. We are the
pieces.
"Herman Melville" l. 40 (1939)

6 An important Jew who died in exile.
"In Memory of Sigmund Freud" l. 24 (1939)

7 To us he is no more a person
now but a whole climate of opinion.
"In Memory of Sigmund Freud" l. 67 (1939)
See Glanvill 1

8 One rational voice is dumb: over a grave
The household of Impulse mourns one dearly
loved.
Sad is Eros, builder of cities,
And weeping anarchic Aphrodite.
"In Memory of Sigmund Freud" l. 109 (1939)

9 Like love we don't know where or why
Like love we can't compel or fly
Like love we often weep
Like love we seldom keep.
"Law like Love" l. 57 (1939)

10 I sit in one of the dives
On Fifty-second Street
Uncertain and afraid
As the clever hopes expire
Of a low dishonest decade.
"September 1, 1939" l. 1 (1939)

11 I and the public know
What all schoolchildren learn,
Those to whom evil is done
Do evil in return.
"September 1, 1939" l. 19 (1939)

12 What mad Nijinsky wrote
About Diaghilev
Is true of the normal heart;
For the error bred in the bone
Of each woman and each man
Craves what it cannot have,
Not universal love
But to be loved alone.
"September 1, 1939" l. 59 (1939)

13 We must love one another or die.
"September 1, 1939" l. 88 (1939). In a 1955 printing
of the poem Auden changed this to "love one another
and die."

14 Ironic points of light
Flash out wherever the Just
Exchange their messages:
May I, composed like them
Of Eros and of dust,
Beleaguered by the same
Negation and despair,
Show an affirming flame.
"September 1, 1939" l. 92 (1939)
See George H. W. Bush 3

15 Our researchers into Public Opinion are
content
That he held the proper opinions for the time of
year;
When there was peace, he was for peace; when
there was war, he went.
"The Unknown Citizen" l. 22 (1939)

16 Was he free? Was he happy? The question is
absurd:
Had anything been wrong, we should certainly
have heard.
"The Unknown Citizen" l. 28 (1939)

17 When he laughed, respectable senators burst
with laughter,
And when he cried the little children died in
the streets.
"Epitaph on a Tyrant" l. 5 (1940)
See John Motley 1

18 The mercury sank in the mouth of the dying
day.
What instruments we have agree
The day of his death was a dark cold day.
"In Memory of W. B. Yeats" l. 4 (1940)

19 By mourning tongues
The death of the poet was kept from his poems.
"In Memory of W. B. Yeats" l. 10 (1940)

20 When the brokers are roaring like beasts on the
floor of the Bourse.
"In Memory of W. B. Yeats" l. 25 (1940)

21 You were silly like us; your gift survived it all:
The parish of rich women, physical decay,
Yourself. Mad Ireland hurt you into poetry.
"In Memory of W. B. Yeats" l. 32 (1940)

22 For poetry makes nothing happen: it survives
In the valley of its making where executives
Would never want to tamper.

"In Memory of W. B. Yeats" l. 36 (1940)
*See Auden 39; Andrew Fletcher 1; Samuel Johnson 22;
Percy Shelley 15; Twain 104*

23 Earth, receive an honored guest:
William Yeats is laid to rest.
Let the Irish vessel lie
Emptied of its poetry.
"In Memory of W. B. Yeats" l. 42 (1940)

24 In the nightmare of the dark
All the dogs of Europe bark,
And the living nations wait,
Each sequestered in its hate.

Intellectual disgrace
Stares from every human face,
And the seas of pity lie
Locked and frozen in each eye.
"In Memory of W. B. Yeats" l. 46 (1940)

25 In the prison of his days
Teach the free man how to praise.
"In Memory of W. B. Yeats" l. 64 (1940)

26 Time that with this strange excuse
Pardoned Kipling and his views,
And will pardon Paul Claudel,
Pardons him for writing well.
"In Memory of W. B. Yeats" pt. 3 (1940). Deleted in
later edition of Auden's poems.

27 Lay your sleeping head, my love,
Human on my faithless arm.
"Lullaby" l. 1 (1940)

28 About suffering they were never wrong,
The Old Masters: how well they understood
Its human position; how it takes place
While someone else is eating or opening a
window or just walking dully along.
"Musée des Beaux Arts" l. 1 (1940)

29   Even the dreadful martyrdom must run its
course
Anyhow in a corner, some untidy spot
Where the dogs go on with their doggy life and
the torturer's horse
Scratches its innocent behind on a tree.
"Musée des Beaux Arts" l. 10 (1940)

30   The expensive delicate ship that must have
seen
Something amazing, a boy falling out of
the sky,
Had somewhere to get to and sailed calmly on.
"Musée des Beaux Arts" l. 19 (1940)

31 And children swarmed to him like settlers. He
  became a land.
  "Edward Lear" l. 14 (1945)

32 She looked over his shoulder
  For vines and olive trees,
  Marble, well-governed cities
  And ships upon untamed seas,
  But there on the shining metal
  His hands had put instead
  An artificial wilderness
  And a sky like lead.
  "The Shield of Achilles" l. 1 (1952)

33 Out of the air a voice without a face
  Proved by statistics that some cause was just.
  "The Shield of Achilles" l. 16 (1952)

34 The mass and majesty of this world, all
  That carries weight and always weighs the
    same,
  Lay in the hands of others.
  "The Shield of Achilles" l. 38 (1952)

35   They lost their pride
  And died as men before their bodies died.
  "The Shield of Achilles" l. 43 (1952)

36 That girls are raped, that two boys knife a third,
  Were axioms to him, who'd never heard
  Of any world where promises were kept,
  Or one could weep because another wept.
  "The Shield of Achilles" l. 56 (1952)

37   The strong
  Iron-hearted man-slaying Achilles
  Who would not live long.
  "The Shield of Achilles" l. 65 (1952)

38 Some books are undeservedly forgotten; none
  are undeservedly remembered.
  The Dyer's Hand, and Other Essays pt. 1 (1962)

39 "The unacknowledged legislators of the world"
  describes the secret police, not the poets.
  The Dyer's Hand, and Other Essays pt. 1 (1962)
  *See Auden 22; Andrew Fletcher 1; Samuel Johnson 22;
  Percy Shelley 15; Twain 104*

40 Speaking for myself, the questions which
  interest me most when reading a poem are
  two. The first is technical: "Here is a verbal
  contraption. How does it work?" The second
  is, in the broadest sense, moral: "What kind of
  a guy inhabits this poem? What is his notion

of the good life or the good place? His notion
of the Evil One? What does he conceal from
the reader? What does he conceal even from
himself?"
  The Dyer's Hand, and Other Essays pt. 2 (1962)

41 Some thirty inches from my nose
  The frontier of my Person goes,
  And all the untilled air between
  Is private *pagus* or demesne.
  Stranger, unless with bedroom eyes
  I beckon you to fraternize,
  Beware of rudely crossing it:
  I have no gun, but I can spit.
  "Prologue: The Birth of Architecture" postscript
  (1966)

42 Of course, Behaviorism "works." So does
  torture. Give me a no-nonsense, down-to-earth
  behaviorist, a few drugs, and simple electrical
  appliances, and in six months I will have him
  reciting the Athanasian Creed in public.
  A Certain World "Behaviorism" (1970)

43 A professor is one who talks in someone else's
  sleep.
  Quoted in *The Pleasures of Publishing*, 15 Apr. 1940.
  The *Boston Globe*, 24 Sept. 1925, had "Do you talk
  in your sleep? . . . I talk in other people's sleep. . . .
  I'm a college professor!" A similar anecdote in the
  Amsterdam (N.Y.) *Evening Recorder*, 10 Oct. 1906, had
  the punch line, "he talks in other people's sleep. He
  is a preacher."

44   My face looks like a wedding-cake left out in
  the rain.
  Quoted in *Sunday Times Magazine* (London), 21 Nov.
  1965

Émile Augier
French poet and playwright, 1820–1889

1 *La nostalgie de la boue.*
  Yearning to be back in the mud.
  Le Mariage d'Olympe act 1, sc. 1 (1855)

St. Augustine
Christian church father, 354–430

1 To Carthage then I came, where all about me
  resounded a cauldron of dissolute loves.
  Confessions bk. 3, ch. 1 (397–398)

2 *Nondum amabam, et amare amabam . . .
  quaerebam quid amarem, amans amare.*

I loved not yet, yet I loved to love . . . I sought
what I might love, loving to love.
Confessions bk. 3, ch. 1 (397–398)

3 *Da mihi castitatem et continentiam, sed noli
modo.*
Give me chastity and continency—but not yet!
Confessions bk. 8, ch. 7 (397–398)

4 *Tolle lege, tolle lege.*
Take up and read, take up and read.
Confessions bk. 8, ch. 12 (397–398)

5 *Cum dilectione hominum et odio vitiorum.*
With love for mankind and hatred of sins.
Letter 211 (ca. 424). Famous in the form "Love the
sinner but hate the sin."
See Mohandas Gandhi 5

6 *Audi partem alteram.*
Hear the other side.
De Duabus Animabus Contra Manicheos ch. 14

7 *Inde etiam rescripta venerunt. Causa finita est.*
A report has come back. The proceeding is
ended.
Sermons no. 131. Traditionally summarized as *Roma
locuta est; causa finita est* (Rome has spoken; the case
is closed).

Augustus
Roman emperor, 63 B.C.–A.D. 14

1 [*Remark after Varus lost three legions fighting
Germanic tribes, A.D. 9:*] Quintilius Varus, give
me back my legions.
Quoted in Suetonius, *Lives of the Caesars*

2 Make haste deliberately.
Quoted in Suetonius, *Lives of the Caesars*

3 [*Of Rome:*] He [Augustus] could boast that he
inherited it brick and left it marble.
Reported in Suetonius, *Lives of the Caesars*

Aung San Suu Kyi
Burmese political leader, 1945–

1 It is not power that corrupts but fear. Fear of
losing power corrupts those who wield it and
fear of the scourge of power corrupts those who
are subject to it.
Acceptance message for Sakharov Prize for Freedom
of Thought, July 1991

Jane Austen
English novelist, 1775–1817

1 I do not want people to be very agreeable, as it
saves me the trouble of liking them a great deal.
Letter to Cassandra Austen, 24 Dec. 1798

2 We met . . . Dr. Hall in such very deep
mourning that either his mother, his wife, or
himself must be dead.
Letter to Cassandra Austen, 17 May 1799

3 An annuity is a very serious business.
Sense and Sensibility vol. 1, ch. 2 (1811)

4 Seven years would be insufficient to make
some people acquainted with each other, and
seven days are more than enough for others.
Sense and Sensibility vol. 2, ch. 12 (1811)

5 She was not a woman of many words; for,
unlike people in general, she proportioned
them to the number of her ideas.
Sense and Sensibility vol. 2, ch. 12 (1811)

6 It is a truth universally acknowledged, that a
single man in possession of a good fortune,
must be in want of a wife.
Pride and Prejudice ch. 1 (1813)

7 In nine cases out of ten, a woman had better
show *more* affection than she feels.
Pride and Prejudice ch. 6 (1813)

8 Everything nourishes what is strong already.
Pride and Prejudice ch. 9 (1813)

9 You have delighted us long enough.
   Pride and Prejudice ch. 18 (1813)

10 Your sister is crossed in love, I find. I
   congratulate her. Next to being married, a girl
   likes to be crossed in love a little now and then.
   Pride and Prejudice ch. 24 (1813)

11 One cannot be always laughing at a man
   without now and then stumbling on something
   witty.
   Pride and Prejudice ch. 40 (1813)

12 We all love to instruct, though we can teach
   only what is not worth knowing.
   Pride and Prejudice ch. 54 (1813)

13 For what do we live, but to make sport for our
   neighbors, and laugh at them in our turn?
   Pride and Prejudice ch. 57 (1813)

14 Be honest and poor, by all means—but I shall
   not envy you; I do not much think I shall even
   respect you. I have a much greater respect for
   those that are honest and rich.
   Mansfield Park ch. 22 (1814)

15 One half of the world cannot understand the
   pleasures of the other.
   Emma ch. 9 (1816)

16 Why not seize the pleasure at once?—How
   often is happiness destroyed by preparation,
   foolish preparation!
   Emma ch. 30 (1816)

17 How could I possibly join them on to the little
   bit (two inches wide) of ivory on which I work
   with so fine a brush, as produces little effect
   after much labor?
   Letter to J. Edward Austen, 16 Dec. 1816

18 "Oh! It is only a novel! . . ." in short, only some
   work in which the greatest powers of the mind
   are displayed, in which the most thorough
   knowledge of human nature, the happiest
   delineation of its varieties, the liveliest effusions
   of wit and humor, are conveyed to the world in
   the best-chosen language.
   Northanger Abbey ch. 5 (1818)

19 [*On history:*] The quarrels of popes and kings,
   with wars or pestilences in every page; the men
   all so good for nothing, and hardly any women
   at all, it is very tiresome; and yet I often think it

odd that it should be so dull, for a great deal of
it must be invention.
Northanger Abbey ch. 14 (1818)

20 One man's ways may be as good as another's,
   but we all like our own best.
   Persuasion ch. 13 (1818)

21 "My idea of good company, Mr. Elliot, is the
   company of clever, well-informed people, who
   have a great deal of conversation; that is what I
   call good company." "You are mistaken," said
   he gently, "that is not good company, that is the
   best."
   Persuasion ch. 16 (1818)

22 She gloried in being a sailor's wife, but she
   must pay the tax of quick alarm for belonging
   to that profession which is, if possible, more
   distinguished in its domestic virtues than in its
   national importance.
   Persuasion ch. 24 (1818)

Paul Auster
U.S. writer, 1947–

1 It was a wrong number that started it, the
  telephone ringing three times in the dead of
  night, and the voice on the other end asking for
  someone he was not.
  City of Glass ch. 1 (1985)

Gene Autry
U.S. singer and actor, 1907–1998

1 Back in the Saddle Again.
  Title of song (1940)

Averroës
Spanish-born Islamic philosopher, 1126–1198

1 Knowledge is the conformity of the object and
  the intellect.
  Tahāfut at-tahāfut (ca. 1180)

Tex Avery
U.S. cartoon animator, 1907–1980

1 What's up, Doc?
  A Wild Hare (animated cartoon) (1940). According to
  Jeff Lenburg, *The Encyclopedia of Animated Cartoons*
  (1991), Avery originated this phrase for the first Bugs
  Bunny cartoon, based on the line "What's up, Duke"
  from the film *My Man Godfrey* together with the

common use of the address "Doc" in Avery's native Texas.

Wilbert Awdry

English children's book writer, 1911–1997

1 You've a lot to learn about trucks, little Thomas. They are silly things and must be kept in their place. After pushing them about here for a few weeks, you'll know almost as much about them as Edward. Then you'll be a Really Useful Engine.

Thomas the Tank Engine (1946)

Hoyt Axton

U.S. singer and songwriter, 1938–1999

1 Jeremiah was a bullfrog
Was a good friend of mine.

"Joy to the World" (song) (1971)

2 Joy to the world . . .
Joy to the fishes in the deep blue sea
Joy to you and me.

"Joy to the World" (song) (1971)

Mae Boren Axton

U.S. songwriter, 1914–1997

1 Well since my baby left me
Well I found a new place to dwell
Well it's down at the end of lonely street
At Heartbreak Hotel.

"Heartbreak Hotel" (song) (1956). Cowritten with Tommy Durden and Elvis Presley.

Meher Baba
Indian guru, 1894–1969

1 Don't worry, be happy.

Quoted in Art Spiegelman and Bob Schneider, *Whole Grains: A Book of Quotations* (1973)

Charles Babbage
English mathematician and inventor, 1792–1871

1 On two occasions I have been asked—"Pray, Mr. Babbage, if you put into the machine wrong figures, will the right answers come out?" In one case a member of the Upper, and in the other a member of the Lower, House put this question. I am not able rightly to apprehend the kind of confusion of ideas that could provoke such a question.

Passages from the Life of a Philosopher ch. 5 (1864)
See Countess of Lovelace 1; Modern Proverbs 33

2 As soon as an Analytical Engine exists, it will necessarily guide the future course of science.

Passages from the Life of a Philosopher ch. 8 (1864)

Isaac Babel
Russian short-story writer, 1894–1941

1 No steel can pierce the human heart so chillingly as a period at the right moment.

"Guy de Maupassant" (1924) (translation by Max Hayward)

2 A phrase is born into the world both good and bad at the same time. The secret lies in a slight, an almost invisible twist. The lever should rest in your hand, getting warm, and you can only turn it once, not twice.

"Guy de Maupassant" (1924) (translation by Walter Morison)

3 You're trying to live without enemies. That's all you think about, not having enemies.

Red Cavalry "Argamak" (1926)

Lauren Bacall (Betty Joan Perske)
U.S. actress, 1924–2014

1 I think your whole life shows in your face and you should be proud of that.

Quoted in *Daily Telegraph* (London), 2 Mar. 1988

Johann Sebastian Bach
German composer, 1685–1750

1 There is nothing wonderful in that [playing the organ]; you have only to hit the right notes in the right time, and the instrument plays itself.

Attributed in *The Musical Visitor*, Aug. 1897

Francis Bacon
English jurist, philosopher, and man of letters, 1561–1626

1 I have taken all knowledge to be my province.

Letter to Lord Burghley, 1592

2 *Nam et ipsa scientia potestas est.*
For also knowledge itself is power.

Mediationes Sacrae "Of Heresies" (1597). Source of the proverb "knowledge is power."

3 If a man will begin with certainties, he shall
end in doubts; but if he will be content to begin
with doubts, he shall end in certainties.
The Advancement of Learning bk. 1, ch. 5, sec. 8 (1605)

4 We are much beholden to Machiavel and
others, that write what men do, and not what
they ought to do.
The Advancement of Learning bk. 2, ch. 2, sec. 9 (1605)

5 There are four classes of Idols which beset
men's minds. To these for distinction's sake I
have assigned names—calling the first class,
Idols of the Tribe; the second, Idols of the Cave;
the third, Idols of the Market-Place; the fourth,
Idols of the Theater.
Novum Organum bk. 1, aphorism 39 (1620)

6 Printing, gunpowder, and the mariner's needle
[compass] . . . these three have changed the
whole face and state of things throughout the
world.
Novum Organum bk. 1, aphorism 129 (1620)

7 Nothing is terrible except fear itself.
De Dignitate et Augmentis Scientiarum bk. 2 (1623)
*See Montaigne 4; Franklin Roosevelt 6; Thoreau 16;
Wellington 3*

8 There was a young man in Rome that was
very like Augustus Caesar; Augustus took
knowledge of it and sent for the man, and
asked him "Was your mother never at Rome?"
He answered "No Sir; but my father was."
Apophtegms New and Old no. 87 (1625). This anecdote
had appeared earlier in the first-century A.D. Latin
writings of Valerius Maximus and in Erasmus's
Apophthegmata (1531).

9 I had rather believe all the fables in the legend,
and the Talmud, and the Alcoran, than that this
universal frame is without a mind. . . . A little
philosophy inclineth man's mind to atheism,
but depth in philosophy bringeth men's minds
about to religion.
Essays "Of Atheism" (1625)

10 Men fear death as children fear to go in the
dark; and as that natural fear in children is
increased with tales, so is the other.
Essays "Of Death" (1625)

11 Cure the disease and kill the patient.
Essays "Of Friendship" (1625)

12 God Almighty first planted a garden; and,
indeed, it is the purest of human pleasures.
Essays "Of Gardens" (1625)

13 If a man be gracious and courteous to
strangers, it shows he is a citizen of the world.
Essays "Of Goodness, and Goodness of Nature" (1625)

14 Patience and gravity of hearing is an essential
part of justice; and an overspeaking judge is no
well-tuned cymbal.
Essays "Of Judicature" (1625)

15 He that hath wife and children hath given
hostages to fortune; for they are impediments
to great enterprises, either of virtue or
mischief. Certainly the best works and of
greatest merit for the public have proceeded
from the unmarried or childless men, which
both in affection and means have married and
endowed the public.
Essays "Of Marriage and the Single Life" (1625)
See Lucan 3

16 He was reputed one of the wise men that made
answer to the question when a man should
marry? "A young man not yet, an elder man
not at all."
Essays "Of Marriage and the Single Life" (1625)
See Punch 1

17 Revenge is a kind of wild justice, which the
more man's nature runs to, the more ought law
to weed it out.
Essays "Of Revenge" (1625)

18 Above all things, good policy is to be used
that the treasure and moneys in a state be
not gathered into few hands. For otherwise a
state may have a great stock, and yet starve.
And money is like muck, not good except it be
spread.
Essays "Of Seditions and Troubles" (1625)

19 The remedy is worse than the disease.
Essays "Of Seditions and Troubles" (1625)

20 The French are wiser than they seem, and the
Spaniards seem wiser than they are.
Essays "Of Seeming Wise" (1625)

21 Some books are to be tasted, others to be
swallowed, and some few to be chewed and
digested.
Essays "Of Studies" (1625)

22 Reading maketh a full man; conference a ready man; and writing an exact man.
Essays "Of Studies" (1625)

23 What is truth? said jesting Pilate; and would not stay for an answer.
Essays "Of Truth" (1625). The Biblical reference is to John 18:38.

24 It is the wisdom of the crocodiles, that shed tears when they would devour.
Essays "Of Wisdom for a Man's Self" (1625)

25 The end of our foundation is the knowledge of causes, and secret motions of things; and the enlarging of the bounds of human Empire, to the effecting of all things possible.
New Atlantis (1627)

26 [*Confession to Parliament of his being guilty of corruption as Lord Chancellor:*] I beseech your Lordships, be merciful unto a broken reed.
Quoted in *Journals of the House of Lords,* 30 Apr. 1621

Roger Bacon
English philosopher and scientist, ca. 1220–ca. 1292

1 If in other sciences we should arrive at certainty without doubt and truth without error, it behooves us to place the foundations of knowledge in mathematics.
Opus Majus bk. 1, ch. 4 (ca. 1267) (translation by Robert Burke)

Robert Stephenson Smyth Baden-Powell
English soldier and founder of the Boy Scouts, 1857–1941

1 The scouts' motto is founded on my initials, it is: BE PREPARED.
Scouting for Boys pt. 1 (1908)
See Lehrer 1

2 A Scout's Honor is to be Trusted.
Scouting for Boys pt. 1 (1908)

Joan Baez
U.S. folk singer, 1941–

1 The only thing that's been a worse flop than the organization of non-violence has been the organization of violence.
Daybreak (1968)

2 We both know what memories can bring
They bring diamonds and rust.
"Diamonds and Rust" (song) (1975)

Walter Bagehot
English economist and essayist, 1826–1877

1 You may talk of the tyranny of Nero and Tiberius; but the real tyranny is the tyranny of your next-door neighbor. . . . Public opinion is a permeating influence, and it exacts obedience to itself; it requires us to think other men's thoughts, to speak other men's words, to follow other men's habits.
"The Character of Sir Robert Peel" (1856)

2 Nations touch at their summits.
The English Constitution "The House of Lords" (1867)

3 The best reason why Monarchy is a strong government is, that it is an intelligible government. The mass of mankind understand it, and they hardly anywhere in the world understand any other.
The English Constitution "The Monarchy" (1867)

4 Our royalty is to be reverenced, and if you begin to poke about it you cannot reverence it. . . . Its mystery is its life. We must not let in daylight upon magic.
The English Constitution "The Monarchy (continued)" (1867)

5 The Sovereign has, under a constitutional monarchy such as ours, three rights—the right to be consulted, the right to encourage, the right to warn.
The English Constitution "The Monarchy (continued)" (1867)

P. J. Bailey
English poet, 1816–1902

1 Ye are all nations, I a single soul.
Yet shall this new world order outlast all.
Festus, 3rd ed. (1848)
See George H. W. Bush 7; George H. W. Bush 10; George H. W. Bush 12; Martin Luther King 1; Tennyson 45

Beryl Bainbridge
English novelist, 1932–2010

1 It never ceases to puzzle me, that, while men's and women's bodies fit jigsaw-tight in an

altogether miraculous way their minds remain wretchedly unaligned.

The Birthday Boys (1991)

Kenneth T. Bainbridge

U.S. physicist, 1904–1996

1 [*Comment after first atomic bomb test, Alamogordo, N.M., 1945:*] Now we're all sons-of-bitches.

Quoted in Lansing Lamont, *Day of Trinity* (1966)

Bruce Bairnsfather

Indian-born English cartoonist, 1888–1959

1 Well, if you knows of a better 'ole, go to it.

Fragments from France cartoon caption (1915)

Dorothy Baker

U.S. novelist, 1907–1968

1 He watched, stunned, and while he was watching, Rick died. He could tell when it happened. There was a difference.

Young Man with a Horn bk. 4, ch. 8 (1938)

George Baker

U.S. cartoonist, 1915–1975

1 The Sad Sack.

Title of comic strip (1942)

Howard H. Baker, Jr.

U.S. politician, 1925–2014

1 I'll tell you what my daddy told me after my first trial. I thought I was just great. I asked him, "How did I do?" He paused and said, "You've got to guard against speaking more clearly than you think."

Quoted in *Wash. Post*, 24 June 1973

2 What did the President know about Watergate and when did he know it?

Quoted in *Wash. Post*, 1 July 1973. This was Baker's recurrent question as a member of the U.S. Senate committee investigating the Nixon administration's Watergate scandal in 1973.

Michael Bakunin

Russian revolutionary and anarchist, 1814–1876

1 The urge for destruction is also a creative urge!

"Die Reaktion in Deutschland," Jahrbuch für Wissenschaft und Kunst (1842)

2 I shall continue to be an impossible person so long as those who are now possible remain possible.

Letter to Nikolai Ogarev, 14 June 1868

3 I am truly free only when all human beings, men and women, are equally free. The freedom of other men, far from negating or limiting my freedom, is, on the contrary, its necessary premise and confirmation.

"God and the State" (1871)

4 But it will scarcely be any easier on the people if the cudgel with which they are beaten is called the people's cudgel.

Statism and Anarchy ch. 1 (1873) (translation by Marshall Shatz)

James Baldwin

U.S. novelist and essayist, 1924–1987

1 Money, it turned out, was exactly like sex, you thought of nothing else if you didn't have it and thought of other things if you did.

"The Black Boy Looks at the White Boy" (1961)

2 If we do not now dare everything, the fulfillment of that prophecy, re-created from the Bible in song by a slave, is upon us: *God gave Noah the rainbow sign, No more water, the fire next time!*

The Fire Next Time (1963)
See Folk and Anonymous Songs 36

3 Do I really *want* to be integrated into a burning house?

The Fire Next Time (1963)

4 Consider the history of labor in a country in which, spiritually speaking, there are no workers, only candidates for the hand of the boss's daughter.

The Fire Next Time (1963)

5 Around the age of 5, 6, or 7. . . . It comes as a great shock to see Gary Cooper killing off the Indians and, although you are rooting for Gary Cooper, that the Indians are you.

Speech at Cambridge Union, Cambridge, England, 17 Feb. 1965

6 If they take you in the morning, they will be coming for us that night.

"Open Letter to My Sister Angela Y. Davis" (1971)

7 The White man, someone told me, *discovered the Cross by way of the Bible, but the Black man discovered the Bible by way of the Cross.*
Evidence of Things Not Seen (1985)

Stanley Baldwin
British prime minister, 1867–1947

1 I think it is well for the man in the street to realize that there is no power on earth that can protect him from being bombed. Whatever people may tell him, the bomber will always get through. The only defence is in offence, which means that you have to kill more women and children more quickly than the enemy if you want to save yourselves.
Speech in House of Commons, 10 Nov. 1932

2 I shall be but a short time tonight. I have seldom spoken with greater regret, for my lips are not yet unsealed.
Speech in House of Commons, 10 Dec. 1935. Popularly quoted as "my lips are sealed."

Arthur James Balfour
British prime minister, 1848–1930

1 His Majesty's Government view with favor the establishment in Palestine of a national home for the Jewish people, and will use their best endeavors to facilitate the achievement of this object, it being clearly understood that nothing shall be done which may prejudice the civil and religious rights of existing non-Jewish communities in Palestine, or the rights and political status enjoyed by Jews in any other country.
Letter to Lionel Walter, Lord Rothschild, 2 Nov. 1917. Known as the "Balfour Declaration."

2 In Palestine we do not propose even to go through the form of consulting the wishes of the present inhabitants of the country. . . . The Four Great Powers are committed to Zionism. And Zionism, be it right or wrong, good or bad, is rooted in age-long traditions, in present needs, in future hopes, of far profounder import than the desires and prejudices of the 700,000 Arabs who now inhabit that ancient land.
Memorandum respecting Syria, Palestine, and Mesopotamia, 11 Aug. 1919

3 [*To Frank Harris, who had said that "all the faults of the age come from Christianity and journalism":*] Christianity, of course . . . but why journalism?
Quoted in Margot Asquith, *Autobiography* (1920)

John Ball
U.S. writer, 1911–1988

1 They call me Mr. Tibbs.
In the Heat of the Night ch. 4 (1965)

Ballads
See also Folk and Anonymous Songs.

1 In Scarlet town, where I was born,
There was a fair maid dwellin',
Made every youth cry Well-a-day!
Her name was Barbara Allen.
"Barbara Allen's Cruelty"

2 Ye Highlands and ye Lawlands,
O where hae ye been?
They hae slain the Earl of Murray,
And hae laid him on the green.
"The Bonny Earl of Murray." Sylvia Wright in 1954 (*Harper's Magazine,* Nov.) coined the term *mondegreen* to refer to a misunderstood word derived from mishearing of song lyrics, inspired by the fact that "when I was a child, my mother used to read aloud to me from Percy's *Reliques,* and one of my favorite poems began, as I remember: Ye Highlands and ye Lowlands, Oh, where hae ye been? They hae slain the Earl Amurray, And Lady Mondegreen."

3 Turn again, Whittington . . .
Lord Mayor of London.
"Dick Whittington"

4 Och, Johnny, I hardly knew ye!
"Johnny, I Hardly Knew Ye"

5 "O where ha you been, Lord Randal, my son,
And where ha you been, my handsome
    young man?"
"I ha been at the greenwood; mother, mak my
    bed soon,
For I'm wearied wi hunting, and fain wad lie
    down."
"An wha met ye there, Lord Randal, my son?
An wha met you there, my handsome
    young man?"
"O I met wi my true-love; mother, mak my bed
    soon,

For I'm wearied wi huntin, an fain wad lie
    down."
"Lord Randal"

6 When captains courageous whom death could
    not daunt,
    Did march to the siege of the city of Gaunt,
    They mustered their soldiers by two and by
        three,
    And the foremost in battle was Mary Ambree.
"Mary Ambree"

7 The king sits in Dumferling toune,
    Drinking the blude-reid wine:
    "O whar will I get guid sailor,
    To sail this schip of mine?"
"Sir Patrick Spens"

8 Late late yestreen I saw the new moone,
    Wi the auld moone in hir arme,
    And I feir, I feir, my deir mastr,
    That we will cum to harme.
"Sir Patrick Spens"

Hank Ballard (John Henry Kendricks)
U.S. rhythm and blues singer, 1936–2003

1 Come on baby
    Let's do the twist.
"The Twist" (song) (1960)

J. G. (James Graham) Ballard
Chinese-born English writer, 1930–2009

1 Everything is becoming science fiction. From
    the margins of an almost invisible literature
    has sprung the intact reality of the 20th
    century.
"Fictions of Every Kind" (1971)

Honoré de Balzac
French novelist, 1799–1850

1 "I've been tormented by evil thoughts."
    "Of what sort? Ideas can cure you, you
        know."
    "They can?"
    "If you give in to them."
Le Père Goriot ch. 2 (1835) (translation by Burton
Raffel)
*See Clementina Graham 1; Mae West 19; Wilde 25;
Wilde 53*

2 *Le secret des grandes fortunes sans cause apparente
    est un crime oublié.*
    The secret of great fortunes without apparent
        source is a forgotten crime.
Le Père Goriot ch. 2 (1835). Source of the proverb
"Behind every great fortune there lies a crime," the
earliest occurrence of which was found in C. Wright
Mills, *The Power Elite* (1956).

3 *Je ne suis pas profond, mais très épais, et il faut du
    temps pour faire le tour de ma personne.*
    I am not deep, but I am very wide, and it takes
        time to walk round me.
Letter to Clara Carrara-Spinelli Maffei, Oct. 1837

4 *Le titre général* [of Balzac's novels] *est la
    Comédie humaine.*
    The general title [of Balzac's novels] is *The
    Human Comedy.*
Letter to an editor, Jan. 1840

George Bancroft
U.S. historian, 1800–1891

1 It is sometimes said, that the abundance of
    vacant land operates as the safety valve of our
    system.
"Reform," *New-England Magazine,* Jan. 1832
See Frederick Jackson Turner 1; Frederick Jackson Turner 2

Tallulah Bankhead
U.S. actress, 1903–1968

1 Cocaine habit-forming? Of course not. I ought
    to know. I've been using it for years.
Tallulah ch. 4 (1952)

2 Never practice two vices at once.
Tallulah ch. 4 (1952)

3 [*Remark to Alexander Woollcott after attending
    an unsuccessful revival of Maeterlinck's play
    Aglavaine and Selysette:*] There is less in this
    than meets the eye.
Quoted in *N.Y. Times,* 4 Jan. 1922

4 I'm as pure as the driven slush.
Quoted in *Tucson Daily Citizen,* 3 Sept. 1941

5 I don't know what I am, darling. I've tried
    several varieties of sex. The conventional
    position makes me claustrophobic. And the
    others give me either stiff neck or lockjaw.
Quoted in Lee Israel, *Miss Tallulah Bankhead* (1972)

6 They used to photograph Shirley Temple through gauze. They should photograph me through linoleum.

Quoted in Leslie Halliwell, *The Filmgoer's Book of Quotes* (1973)

7 There have been only two authentic geniuses in the world, Willie Mays and Willie Shakespeare.

Quoted in *The Baseball Card Engagement Book* (1987). Bankhead was quoted, saying something very similar to this, in *Chicago Daily Defender,* 23 Oct. 1962.

Ernie Banks
U.S. baseball player, 1931–2015

1 Isn't it a beautiful day? . . . The Cubs of Chicago versus the Phillies of Philadelphia, in beautiful, historic Wrigley Field. Let's go, let's go. It's Sunday in America.

Quoted in *Sport,* Dec. 1971

2 It's a great day for baseball. Let's play two.

Quoted in *Lowell* (Mass.) *Sun,* 12 Oct. 1972. Earlier version by Banks quoted in the *Valley Independent* (Monessen, Pa.), 23 June 1969: "It's a wonderful day, a great day to play two."

Iain Banks
Scottish writer, 1954–2013

1 It was the day my grandmother exploded.
The Crow Road ch. 1 (1992)

Russell Banks
U.S. writer, 1940–

1 Go, my book, and help destroy the world as it is.
Continental Drift envoi (1985)

Steve Bannon
U.S. political activist and media executive, 1953–

1 Darkness is good. Dick Cheney. Darth Vader. Satan. That's power.
Interview by *Hollywood Reporter,* 18 Nov. 2016

2 The media's the opposition party.
Interview by *N.Y. Times,* 26 Jan. 2017

Amiri Baraka (LeRoi Jones)
U.S. poet, 1934–2014

1 Who has ever stopped to think of the divinity of Lamont Cranston?
"In Memory of Radio" l. 1 (1961)

2 Saturday mornings we listened to *Red Lantern* & his undersea folk.
At 11, *Let's Pretend*
& we did
& I, the poet, still do, Thank God!
"In Memory of Radio" l. 18 (1961)

3 Lately, I've become accustomed to the way The ground opens up and envelops me Each time I go out to walk the dog.
"Preface to a Twenty Volume Suicide Note" l. 1 (1961)

4 We want "poems that kill."
Black Art (1966)

Walter "Red" Barber
U.S. sports broadcaster, 1908–1992

1 [*Expression for "sitting pretty":*] Sitting in the catbird seat.
Quoted in James Thurber, "The Catbird Seat" (1942). The use of the phrase *catbird seat* as a poker term dates back at least as early as 1916.

Maurice Baring
English writer, 1874–1945

1 [*Contrasting the two composers in Aleksandr Pushkin's play* Mozart and Salieri:] We see the contrast between the genius which does what it must and the talent which does what it can.
An Outline of Russian Literature ch. 3 (1914)
See Owen Meredith 2

Sabine Baring-Gould
English clergyman, 1834–1924

1 Onward, Christian soldiers,
Marching as to war,
With the Cross of Jesus
Going on before!
"Onward, Christian Soldiers" (hymn) (1866)

David Barker
U.S. poet, 1816–1874

1 But for *me*—and I care not a single fig If they say I am wrong or am right— I shall always go for the *weaker* dog: For the under dog in the fight.
"The Under Dog in the Fight" l.5 (1859). Appears to be the origin of the term *underdog,* previously thought to date from 1887.

Alben W. Barkley

U.S. politician, 1877–1956

1 I would rather be a servant in the House of the Lord than to sit in the seats of the mighty.

Speech at Washington and Lee University, Lexington, Va., 30 Apr. 1956. Immediately after delivering this line, the seventy-eight-year-old Barkley died. Jane R. Barkley writes in *I Married the Veep* (1958): "I am not sure, even now, how these words came into being, where they came from. I believe they were original with him but were based on the Old Testament, 84th Psalm: 10, 'I had rather be a doorkeeper in the house of my God, than to dwell in the tents of wickedness.'"
See Bible 115

Joel Barlow

U.S. poet and diplomat, 1754–1812

1 The Government of the United States of America is not, in any sense, founded on the Christian religion.

Treaty of peace and friendship with Tripoli art. 11 (1797)

Julian Barnes

English novelist, 1946–

1 Why does the writing make us chase the writer? Why can't we leave well enough alone? Why aren't the books enough?

Flaubert's Parrot ch. 1 (1984)

2 Books say: she did this because. Life says: she did this. Books are where things are explained to you; life is where things aren't.

Flaubert's Parrot ch. 13 (1984)

Peter Barnes

English playwright, 1931–2004

1 [*The Earl of Gurney, responding to the question, "How do you know you're . . . God?":*] Simple. When I pray to Him I find I'm talking to myself.

The Ruling Class act 1, sc. 4 (1969)

Natalie Clifford Barney

U.S.-born French writer, 1876–1972

1 The most beautiful life is one spent creating oneself, not procreating.

Éparpillements (1910)

P. T. Barnum

U.S. showman, 1810–1891

1 There is a sucker born every minute.

Attributed in *Daily Colonist* (Victoria, Canada), 21 July 1892. Although Barnum is closely associated with this quotation, the earliest known appearance of "There's a sucker born every minute" occurred in the *Inter-Ocean* (Chicago), 2 Jan. 1879, where no individual was credited for the saying. Garson O'Toole has tracked down many older variants, beginning with "There vash von fool born every minute" (*European Magazine and London Review*, Jan. 1806).

Roseanne Barr

U.S. comedian, 1953–

1 The only option for girls when I was growing up was mother, secretary, or teacher. Now I must say how lucky we are as women to live in an age where "dental hygienist" has been added to the list.

Quoted in *Chicago Tribune*, 16 Apr. 1989

2 I don't like the terms housewife and homemaker. I prefer to be called Domestic Goddess.

Quoted in *People*, 28 Apr. 1986

James M. Barrie

Scottish writer, 1860–1937

1 The tragedy of a man who has found himself out.

What Every Woman Knows act 4 (1908)

2 All children, except one, grow up.

Peter and Wendy ch. 1 (1911)

3 Every child is affected thus the first time he is treated unfairly. All he thinks he has a right to when he comes to you to be yours is fairness. After you have been unfair to him he will love you again, but he will never afterwards be quite the same boy.

Peter and Wendy ch. 8 (1911)

4 [*Response to being asked, "Where do you live?":*] Second to the right and then straight on till morning.

Peter Pan act 1 (1928)

5 You see, Wendy, when the first baby laughed for the first time, the laugh broke into a thousand

pieces and they all went skipping about, and that was the beginning of fairies.
Peter Pan act 1 (1928)

6 Every time a child says "I don't believe in fairies" there is a fairy somewhere that falls down dead.
Peter Pan act 1 (1928)

7 Do you know why swallows build in the eaves of houses? It is to listen to the stories.
Peter Pan act 1 (1928)

8 [*Explaining how to fly:*] You just think lovely wonderful thoughts and they lift you up in the air.
Peter Pan act 1 (1928)

9 To die will be an awfully big adventure.
Peter Pan act 3 (1928)
See Frohman 1

10 She [Tinker Bell] says she thinks she could get well again if children believed in fairies!
Peter Pan act 4 (1928)

11 Do you believe in fairies? Say quick that you believe! If you believe, clap your hands!
Peter Pan act 4 (1928)

12 Proud and insolent youth, prepare to meet thy doom.
Peter Pan act 5 (1928)

13 I'm youth, I'm joy, I'm a little bird that has broken out of the egg.
Peter Pan act 5 (1928)

George Barrington
Irish-born Australian criminal and author, 1755–1804

1 From distant climes, o'er wide-spread seas we come,
Though not with much éclat, or beat of drum,
True patriots all, for be it understood,
We left our country, for our country's good.
The History of New South Wales ch. 4 (1802). This poem may not have been written by Barrington.

Marion Barry
U.S. politician, 1936–2014

1 Outside of the killings, [Washington, D.C.] has one of the lowest crime rates in the country.
Quoted in *Chicago Tribune*, 28 Mar. 1989

2 Bitch set me up!
Quoted in *Wash. Post*, 29 June 1990. Barry was mayor of Washington, D.C., when he uttered this line while being arrested for smoking crack cocaine with a woman in a Washington hotel, 18 Jan. 1990.

Ethel Barrymore (Ethel Mae Blythe)
U.S. actress, 1879–1959

1 That's all there is, there isn't any more.
Curtain line, added to *Sunday* (play by Thomas Raceward) (1904)

John Barrymore (John Sidney Blyth)
U.S. actor, 1882–1942

1 The trouble with life is that there are so many beautiful women—and so little time.
Quoted in Evan Esar, *The Dictionary of Humorous Quotations* (1949)

John Barth
U.S. novelist, 1930–

1 [This book is] a floating opera, friend, chock-full of curiosities, melodrama, spectacle, instruction, and entertainment, but it floats willy-nilly on the tide of my vagrant prose: you'll catch sight of it, then lose it, then spy it again.
The Floating Opera ch. 1 (1956)

Karl Barth
Swiss theologian, 1886–1968

1 It may be that when the angels go about their task praising God, they play only Bach. I am sure, however, that when they are together *en famille*, they play Mozart.
Wolfgang Amadeus Mozart (1956) (translation by Clarence K. Pott)

Guillaume de Salluste, Seigneur du Bartas
French diplomat and poet, 1544–1590

1 In the jaws of death.
Divine Weeks and Works week 2, day 1, pt. 4 (1578)

Donald Barthelme
U.S. writer, 1931–1989

1 "You may not be interested in absurdity," she said firmly, "but absurdity is interested in you."
"A Shower of Gold" (1963)

2 The death of God left the angels in a strange position.
"On Angels" (1969)

Roland Barthes
French writer and critic, 1915–1980

1 I think that cars today are almost the exact equivalent of the great Gothic cathedrals: I mean the supreme creation of an era, conceived with passion by unknown artists, and consumed in image if not in usage by a whole population which appropriates them as a purely magical object.
Mythologies "La Nouvelle Citroën" (1957) (translation by Annette Lavers)

2 The birth of the reader must be at the cost of the death of the Author.
"The Death of the Author" (1968)

3 Opposite the writerly text, then, is its countervalue, its negative, reactive value: what can be read, but not written: the *readerly*. We call any readerly text a classic text.
S/Z (1970)

4 The goal of literary work (of literature as work) is to make the reader no longer a consumer, but a producer of the text. Our literature is characterized by the pitiless divorce which the literary institution maintains between the producer of the text and its user, between its owner and its consumer, between its author and its reader. This reader is thereby plunged into a kind of idleness—he is intransitive; he is, in short, *serious:* instead of functioning himself, instead of gaining access to the magic of the signifier, to the pleasure of writing, he is left with no more than the poor freedom either to accept or reject the text: reading is nothing more than a *referendum.*
S/Z (1970)

Bernard M. Baruch
U.S. financier and presidential adviser, 1870–1965

1 My fellow citizens of the world, we are here to make a choice between the quick and the dead. . . . Behind the black portent of the new atomic age lies a hope which, seized upon with faith, can work our salvation. . . . We must elect World Peace or World Destruction.
Speech to United Nations meeting, 14 June 1946
See Book of Common Prayer 9

2 Let us not be deceived—we are today in the midst of a cold war. Our enemies are to be found abroad and at home. Let us never forget this: Our unrest is the heart of their success. The peace of the world is the hope and the goal of our political system; it is the despair and defeat of those who stand against us.
Address at the unveiling of his portrait in the South Carolina Legislature, Columbia, S.C., 16 Apr. 1947. The term *cold war* was popularized by Baruch's speech and by Walter Lippmann's 1947 book with that title. An earlier use was by George Orwell writing in the *Tribune,* 19 Oct. 1945 (see Orwell for this and still older antecedents). Baruch credited speechwriter Herbert Bayard Swope with supplying him with this phrase in 1946 (in a draft speech about United States–Soviet relations).
See Orwell 27

3 Every man has the right to an opinion, but no man has a right to be wrong in his facts.
Quoted in *L.A. Times,* 9 Oct. 1946. This saying is now frequently stated as "Everyone is entitled to his own opinions, not his own facts," and is usually credited to Daniel Patrick Moynihan.

4 To me, old age is always fifteen years older than I am.
Quoted in Evan Esar, *The Dictionary of Humorous Quotations* (1949)

Jacques Barzun
French-born U.S. historian, 1907–2012

1 Whoever wants to know the heart and mind of America had better learn baseball, the rules and realities of the game—and do it by watching first some high school or small-town teams.
God's Country and Mine ch. 8 (1954)

2 If it were possible to talk to the unborn, one could never explain to them how it feels to be alive, for life is washed in the speechless real.
The House of Intellect ch. 6 (1959)

Matsuo Basho
Japanese poet, 1644–1694

1 Days and months are travellers of eternity. So are the years that pass by.
The Narrow Road to the Deep North (translation by Nobuyuki Yuasa)

2 An old pond—
A frog tumbles in—
The sound of water.
Poem (translation by Bernard Lionel Einbond)

3 Refinement's origin:
The remote north country's
Rice-planting song.
Poem (translation by Bernard Lionel Einbond)

4 Clouds now and again
Give a soul some respite from
Moon-gazing—behold.
Poem (translation by Bernard Lionel Einbond)

5 The summer grasses:
Of mighty warlords' visions
All that they have left.
Poem (translation by Bernard Lionel Einbond)

6 Cooling, so cooling,
With a wall against my feet,
Midday sleep—behold.
Poem (translation by Bernard Lionel Einbond)

7 On a withered branch
A crow has settled—
Autumn nightfall.
Poem (translation by Harold G. Henderson)

8 On a journey, ill,
And over fields all withered, dreams
Go wandering still.
Poem (translation by Harold G. Henderson)

Anselme Batbie
French jurist and government official, 1828–1887

1 *Celui qui n'est pas républicain à vingt ans fait
douter de la générosité de son âme; mais celui
qui, après trente ans, persévère, fait douter de la
rectitude de son esprit.*
He who is not a republican at twenty compels
one to doubt the generosity of his heart; but he
who, after thirty, persists, compels one to doubt
the soundness of his mind.

Quoted in Jules Claretie, *Portraits Contemporains*
vol. 1 (1875). Claretie indicates that Batbie wrote this
in a well-known letter and that Batbie was himself
quoting or paraphrasing a "paradox" of Edmund
Burke's. The Burke passage has not been traced.
*See John Adams 19; Clemenceau 5; George Bernard
Shaw 48*

Katherine Lee Bates
U.S. poet and educator, 1859–1929

1 O beautiful for spacious skies,
For amber waves of grain,
For purple mountain majesties
Above the fruited plain!
America! America!
God shed his grace on thee
And crown thy good with brotherhood
From sea to shining sea!
"America the Beautiful" (song) (1893)

Gregory Bateson
English social scientist, 1904–1980

1 What we mean by information—the elementary
unit of information—is a difference which
makes a difference, and it is able to make a
difference because the neural pathways along
which it travels and is continually transformed
are themselves provided with energy. The
pathways are ready to be triggered. We may
even say that the question is already implicit in
them.
General Semantics Bulletin no. 37 (1970)

William Bateson
English geneticist, 1861–1926

1 The best title would, I think, be "The Quick
Professorship of the study of Heredity." No
single word in common use quite gives this
meaning. Such a word is badly wanted, and
if it were desirable to coin one, "Genetics"
might do.
Letter to Adam Sedgewick, 18 Apr. 1905

John Batman
Australian explorer, 1801–1839

1 [*Of the future site of the city of Melbourne:*] This
will be the place for a Village.
Journal, June 1835

Charles Baudelaire
French poet and critic, 1821–1867

1 *Hypocrite lecteur,—mon semblable,—mon frère.*
Hypocrite reader—my likeness—my brother.
Les Fleurs du Mal "Au Lecteur" (1857)

2 *Les parfums, les couleurs, et les sons se répondent.*
  The sounds, the scents, the colors correspond.
  Les Fleurs du Mal "Correspondances" (1857)
  (translation by Richard Howard)

3 *Je suis la plaie et le couteau!*
  Je suis le soufflet et la joue!
  Je suis les membres et la roue,
  Et la victime et le bourreau!
  I am the knife and the wound it deals, I am the
     slap and the cheek, I am the wheel and the
     broken limbs, hangman and victim both!
  Les Fleurs du Mal "L'Héautontimorouménos" (1857)
  (translation by Richard Howard)

4 *Là, tout n'est qu'ordre et beauté,*
  Luxe, calme et volupté.
  All is order there, and elegance, pleasure,
     peace, and opulence.
  Les Fleurs du Mal "L'Invitation au Voyage" (1857)
  (translation by Richard Howard)

5 *Ô Mort, vieux capitaine, il est temps! levons*
     l'ancre.
  Death, old admiral, up anchor now.
  Les Fleurs du Mal "Le Voyage" (1857) (translation by
  Richard Howard)

6 *Nous voulons, tant ce feu nous brûle le cerveau,*
  Plonger au fond du gouffre, Enfer ou Ciel,
     qu'importe?
  Au fond de l'Inconnu pour trouver du nouveau!
  Once we have burned our brains out, we can
     plunge to Hell or Heaven—any abyss will
     do—deep in the Unknown to find the *new!*
  Les Fleurs du Mal "Le Voyage" (1857) (translation by
  Richard Howard)

7 *J'ai plus de souvenirs que si j'avais mille ans.*
  Souvenirs? More than if I had lived a thousand
     years!
  Les Fleurs du Mal "Spleen (II)" (1857) (translation by
  Richard Howard)

8 *La plus belle des ruses du Diable est de vous*
  persuader qu'il n'existe pas!
  The finest trick of the devil is to persuade you
     that he does not exist.
  "Le Joueur Généreux" (1864)

9 Belief in progress is a doctrine of idlers and
  Belgians. It is the individual relying upon his
  neighbors to do his work.
  Journaux Intimes "Mon Coeur Mis à Nu" no. 9 (1887)

10 Theory of the true civilization. It is not to
  be found in gas or steam or table turning.
  It consists in the diminution of the traces of
  original sin.
  Journaux Intimes "Mon Coeur Mis à Nu" no. 59
  (1887)

Baudouin
Belgian king, 1930–1993

1 America has been called a melting pot, but
  it seems better to call it a mosaic, for in it
  each nation, people, or race which has come
  to its shores has been privileged to keep its
  individuality, contributing at the same time its
  share to the unified pattern of a new nation.
  Quoted in *Reader's Digest*, Oct. 1959
  See Jimmy Carter 3; Crèvecoeur 1; Ralph Ellison 2;
  Victoria Hayward 1; Jesse Jackson 1; Zangwill 2

Jean Baudrillard
French philosopher, 1929–2007

1 It is the real, and not the map, whose vestiges
  subsist here and there, in the deserts which are
  no longer those of the Empire, but our own.
  The desert of the real itself.
  "The Precession of the Simulacra" (1981)
  See Korzybski 1

2 Everywhere one seeks to produce meaning, to
  make the world signify, to render it visible. We
  are not, however, in danger of lacking meaning;
  quite the contrary, we are gorged with meaning
  and it is killing us.
  The Ecstasy of Communication "Seduction, or the
  Superficial Abyss" (1987)

L. Frank Baum
U.S. writer, 1856–1919

1 The road to the City of Emeralds is paved with
  yellow brick.
  The Wonderful Wizard of Oz ch. 2 (1900). The phrase
  "yellow brick road" does not appear in this book.
  See Harburg 6

2 My name is Dorothy . . . and I am going to the
  Emerald City, to ask the great Oz to send me
  back to Kansas.
  The Wonderful Wizard of Oz ch. 3 (1900)

3 There is no place like home.
  The Wonderful Wizard of Oz ch. 4 (1900)
  See Hesiod 3; Payne 2

4 "I am Oz, the Great and Terrible. Who are you,
and why do you seek me?" . . . "I am Dorothy,
the Small and Meek. I have come to you for
help."
The Wonderful Wizard of Oz ch. 11 (1900)

5 I never thought a little girl like you would ever
be able to melt me and end my wicked deeds.
The Wonderful Wizard of Oz ch. 12 (1900)
See Film Lines 193

6 I'm really a very good man; but I'm a very bad
Wizard.
The Wonderful Wizard of Oz ch. 15 (1900)

7 True courage is in facing danger when you are
afraid.
The Wonderful Wizard of Oz ch. 15 (1900)

8 I think you are wrong to want a heart. It makes
most people unhappy.
The Wonderful Wizard of Oz ch. 15 (1900)

9 All you have to do is to knock the heels together
three times and command the shoes to carry
you wherever you wish to go.
The Wonderful Wizard of Oz ch. 23 (1900)

Vicki Baum
Austrian-born U.S. novelist, 1888–1960

1 In the Lounge, Doctor Otternschlag sat and
talked to himself. "It's dismal," he said. "Always
the same. Nothing happens. . . . "
Grand Hotel (1930)

2 Marriage always demands the finest arts of
insincerity possible between two human
beings.
Results of an Accident (1931) (translation by Margaret
Goldsmith)

Hans Baumann
German writer and songwriter, 1914–1988

1 *Denn heute da hört uns Deutschland
Und morgen die ganze Welt.*
For today Germany hears us,
But tomorrow the whole world shall.
"Es Zittern die Morschen Knochen" (song) (1932).
With the word *hört* changed to *gehört* ("belongs to"),
this took on the meaning "today Germany, tomorrow
the world!"

Arnold Bax
English composer, 1883–1953

1 [*Quoting a "sympathetic Scotsman":*] You should
make a point of trying every experience once,
excepting incest and folk-dancing.
Farewell, My Youth (1943)

Anne Baxter
U.S. actress, 1923–1985

1 Best to have failure happen early. [It] wakes up
the phoenix bird in you.
Quoted in *N.Y. Times*, 9 Jan. 1972

Thomas Haynes Bayly
English poet and playwright, 1797–1839

1 Tell me the tales that to me were so dear,
Long, long ago, long, long ago.
"Long, Long Ago" (song) (ca. 1835)

Todd M. Beamer
U.S. businessman, 1968–2001

1 [*Comment to fellow passengers preparing to
challenge hijackers on United Airlines Flight 93, 11
Sept. 2001:*] Let's roll!
Quoted in *Pittsburgh Post-Gazette*, 16 Sept. 2001

Charles A. Beard
U.S. historian, 1874–1948

1 It is for us . . . to inquire constantly and
persistently, when theories of national power or
states' rights are propounded: "What interests
are behind them and to whose advantage will
changes or the maintenance of old forms
accrue?" By refusing to do this we become
victims of history—clay in the hands of its
makers.
*An Economic Interpretation of the Constitution of the
United States* introduction (1935)
See Cicero 12

2 At no time, at no place, in solemn convention
assembled, through no chosen agents, had
the American people officially proclaimed
the United States to be a democracy. The
Constitution did not contain the word or
any word lending countenance to it, except
possibly the mention of "we, the people," in
the preamble. . . . When the Constitution was

framed no respectable person called himself or herself a democrat.

America in Midpassage vol. 2 (1939). Coauthored with Mary R. Beard.

Pierre-Augustin Caron de Beaumarchais

French playwright, 1732–1799

1 I hasten to laugh at everything for fear of being obliged to weep at it.

Le Barbier de Séville act 1, sc. 2 (1775)

2 If you assure me that your intentions are honorable.

Le Barbier de Séville act 4, sc. 6 (1775)

3 Drinking when we are not thirsty and making love all year round, madam; that is all there is to distinguish us from other animals.

Le Mariage de Figaro act 2, sc. 21 (1785)

4 *Vous vous êtes donné la peine de naître, et rien de plus.*

You went to some trouble to be born, and that's all.

Le Mariage de Figaro act 5, sc. 3 (1785)

Francis Beaumont

English poet and playwright, 1584–1616

1 Those have most power to hurt us that we love.

The Maid's Tragedy act 5 (written 1610–1611). Coauthored with John Fletcher.

Max Aitken, First Baron Beaverbrook

Canadian-born British newspaper owner and politician, 1879–1964

1 Let me say that the credit belongs to the boys in the back-rooms. It isn't the man who sits in the limelight like me who should have the praise. It is not the men who sit in prominent places. It is the men in the back-rooms.

Broadcast, 19 Mar. 1941

Cesare Bonesana, Marchese di Beccaria

Italian economist and criminologist, 1738–1794

1 If we glance at the pages of history, we will find that laws, which surely are, or ought to be, compacts of free men, have been, for the most part, a mere tool of the passions of some, or have arisen from an accidental and temporary need. Never have they been dictated by a dispassionate student of human nature who might, by bringing the actions of a multitude of men into focus, consider them from this single point of view: the greatest happiness shared by the greatest number.

Dei Delitti e Delle Pene (On Crimes and Punishments) introduction (1764)
See Bentham 1; Hutcheson 1

2 No man can be judged a criminal until he be found guilty; nor can society take from him the public protection, until it have been proved that he has violated the conditions on which it was granted. What right, then, but that of power, can authorize the punishment of a citizen, so long as there remains any doubt of his guilt? The dilemma is frequent. Either he is guilty, or not guilty. If guilty, he should only suffer the punishment ordained by the laws, and torture becomes useless, as his confession is unnecessary. If he be not guilty, you torture the innocent; for, in the eye of the law, every man is innocent, whose crime has not been proved.

Dei Delitti e Delle Pene (On Crimes and Punishments) ch. 16 (1764)

3 [*On the death penalty:*] It seems so absurd to me that the laws, that are the expression of the public will, that hate and punish the murder, make one themselves, and, to dissuade citizens from the murder, order a public murder.

Dei Delitti e Delle Pene (On Crimes and Punishments) ch. 28 (1764)

Dave Beck

U.S. labor leader, 1894–1993

1 I define a recession as when your neighbor loses his job, but a depression is when you lose your own.

Quoted in *Time*, 22 Feb. 1954. Frequently attributed to Harry Truman, but the earliest evidence of Truman's using it is later than 1954.

Carl Becker

U.S. historian, 1873–1945

1 The significance of man is that he is that part of the universe that asks the question, What is the significance of man? He alone can stand apart imaginatively and, regarding himself and the universe in their eternal aspects, pronounce

a judgment: The significance of man is that he is insignificant and is aware of it.
Progress and Power Lecture 3 (1935)

Samuel Beckett
Irish writer, 1906–1989

1 The sun shone, having no alternative, on the nothing new.
Murphy pt. 1 (1938)

2 Nothing to be done.
Waiting for Godot act 1 (1952)

3 [*Estragon:*] Let's go.
  [*Vladimir:*] We can't.
  [*Estragon:*] Why not?
  [*Vladimir:*] We're waiting for Godot.
Waiting for Godot act 1 (1952)

4 Nothing happens, nobody comes, nobody goes, it's awful!
Waiting for Godot act 1 (1952)

5 We always find something, eh Didi, to give us the impression we exist?
Waiting for Godot act 2 (1952)

6 We are all born mad. Some remain so.
Waiting for Godot act 2 (1952)

7 They give birth astride of a grave, the light gleams an instant, then it's night once more.
Waiting for Godot act 2 (1952)

8 Nothing is more real than nothing.
Malone Dies (1956)

9 There is no use indicting words, they are no shoddier than what they peddle.
Malone Dies (1956)

10 Where I am, I don't know, I'll never know, in the silence you don't know, you must go on, I can't go on, I'll go on.
The Unnamable (1959)

11 I could not have gone through the awful wretched mess of life without having left a stain upon the silence.
Quoted in Deirdre Bair, *Samuel Beckett* (1978)

Grace Bedell
U.S. schoolchild, 1848–1936

1 I am a little girl only eleven years old, but want you should be President of the United States.

. . . I have got 4 brother's and part of them will vote for you any way and if you let your whiskers grow I will try and get the rest of them to vote for you you would look a great deal better for your face is so thin. All the ladies like whiskers and they would tease their husband's to vote for you.
Letter to Abraham Lincoln, 15 Oct. 1860

Barnard Elliott Bee, Jr.
U.S. Confederate general, 1823–1861

1 [*Of Confederate general Thomas J. Jackson (thereafter known as "Stonewall" Jackson) at the Battle of Bull Run, 21 July 1861:*] There is Jackson standing like a stone wall.
Quoted in *Augusta Chronicle*, 26 July 1861

Henry Ward Beecher
U.S. clergyman, 1813–1887

1 It usually takes a hundred years to make a law; and then, after it has done its work, it usually takes a hundred years to get rid of it.
Life Thoughts (1858)

2 All words are pegs to hang ideas on.
Proverbs from Plymouth Pulpit (1887)

Max Beerbohm
English critic and caricaturist, 1872–1956

1 To give an accurate and exhaustive account of the period would need a far less brilliant pen than mine.
The Yellow Book, Jan. 1895

2 [*Of British music-hall comedian Dan Leno:*] Only mediocrity can be trusted to be always at its best. Genius must always have lapses proportionate to its triumphs.
Saturday Review, 5 Nov. 1904
See Maugham 11

3 Death cancels all engagements.
Zuleika Dobson ch. 7 (1911)

4 Anything that is worth doing has been done frequently. Things hitherto undone should be given, I suspect, a wide berth.
Mainly on the Air "From Bloomsbury to Baywater" (1946)

Ethel Lynn Beers

U.S. poet, 1827–1879

1 All quiet along the Potomac to-night
No sound save the rush of the river;
While soft falls the dew on the face of the
dead—
The picket's off duty forever!
"The Picket-Guard" l. 41 (1861)
See Remarque 1

Ludwig van Beethoven

German composer, 1770–1827

1 Prince, what you are, you are by accident of
birth; what I am, I am of myself. There are and
there will be thousands of princes. There is
only one Beethoven.
Letter to Prince Karl Lichnowsky, 1806

2 Beethoven can write music, thank God—but he
can do nothing else on earth.
Letter to Ferdinand Ries, 20 Dec. 1822

3 *Muss es sein? Es muss sein.*
Must it be? It must be.
String Quartet in F Major, Opus 135, epigraph to
fourth movement (1826)

4 [*"Last words," referring to his deafness:*] I shall
hear in heaven.
Quoted in *N.Y. Evening Post*, 8 Aug. 1845. This
quotation is undoubtedly apocryphal, and there
are alternative traditions with different "last words."

5 [*Reply to Goethe when the latter complained about
constant greetings from passers-by when the two
of them were walking together:*] Do not let that
trouble your Excellency, perhaps the greetings
are intended for me.
Attributed in Elliot Forbes, *Thayer's Life of Beethoven*
(1964)

Isabella Beeton

English writer, 1836–1865

1 The housekeeper must consider herself as the
immediate representative of her mistress, and
bring, to the management of the household,
all those qualities of honesty, industry, and
vigilance, in the same degree as if she were at
the head of her own family. . . . Cleanliness,
punctuality, order, and method, are essentials
in the character of a housekeeper.
Book of Cookery and Household Management ch. 2
(1861)

Menachem Begin

Israeli prime minister, 1913–1992

1 We fight, therefore we are!
The Revolt ch. 4 (1950)

Brendan Behan

Irish playwright, 1923–1964

1 So many belonging to me lay buried in
Kilbarrack, the healthiest graveyard in Ireland,
they said, because it was so near the sea.
Borstal Boy pt. 3 (1958)

2 I was courtmartialled in my absence and
sentenced to death in my absence, so I said
they could shoot me in my absence.
The Hostage act 1 (1958)

3 We're all the kids our mothers warned us
against.
Borstal Boy pt. 3 (1958). In the more famous form,
"We are the people our parents warned us about,"
this appears in Robert Reisner, *Graffiti* (1967).

4 All publicity is good, except an obituary notice.
Quoted in *Sunday Express* (London), 5 Jan. 1964
See Modern Proverbs 70; Wilde 22

5 I am married to a very dear girl who is an artist.
We have no children except me.
Quoted in Ulick O'Connor, *Brendan Behan* (1970)

Aphra Behn

English writer, 1640–1689

1 Variety is the soul of pleasure.
The Rover pt. 2, act 1 (1681)
See Cowper 7

2 Beauty unadorned.
The Rover pt. 2, act 4, sc. 2 (1681)

3 Love ceases to be a pleasure, when it ceases to
be a secret.
The Lover's Watch (1686)

4 Oh, what a dear ravishing thing is the
beginning of an Amour!
The Emperor of the Moon act 1, sc. 1 (1687)

5 The soft, unhappy sex.
The Wandering Beauty (1698)

Harry Belafonte

U.S. singer and actor, 1927–

1 Come, Mr. Tally Mon, tally me banana
Daylight come and he wan' go home
Day-o, day-ay-ay-o.

"Day-O (Banana Boat Song)" (song) (1957). Cowritten with Lord Burgess and Bill Attaway, but based on a Jamaican folk song.

2 You can cage the singer but not the song.

Quoted in *International Herald Tribune*, 3 Oct. 1988

Alexander Graham Bell

Scottish-born U.S. inventor, 1847–1922

1 [*The first intelligible words spoken on the telephone, to his assistant, Thomas Watson, 10 Mar. 1876:*]
Mr. Watson—come here—I want to see you.

Notebook, 10 Mar. 1876

Henry Bellamann

U.S. novelist, 1882–1945

1 [*The character Drake McHugh speaking, after discovering that his legs have been amputated:*]
Where's the rest of me?

Kings Row bk. 5, ch. 1 (1940)

Edward Bellamy

U.S. author, 1850–1898

1 There is no such thing as moral responsibility for past acts, no such thing as real justice in punishing them, for the reason that human beings are not stationary existences, but changing, growing, incessantly progressive organisms, which in no two moments are the same. Therefore justice, whose only possible mode of proceeding is to punish in present time for what is done in past time, must always punish a person more or less similar to, but never identical with, the one who committed the offense, and therein must be no justice.

Dr. Heidenhoff's Process (1880)

2 The nation guarantees the nurture, education, and comfortable maintenance of every citizen from the cradle to the grave.

Looking Backward, 2000–1887 ch. 9 (1888)

Francis Bellamy

U.S. clergyman and editor, 1856–1931

1 I pledge allegiance to my Flag and the Republic for which it stands: one Nation indivisible, with Liberty and Justice for all.

The Pledge of Allegiance to the Flag (1892). Introduced at the dedication of the World's Fair Grounds in Chicago, Ill., 21 Oct. 1892, and published in *The Youth's Companion*, 8 Sept. 1892, with the wording above. A number of changes were made over the years, most notably the addition of "under God" in 1954. The present version reads: "I pledge allegiance to the Flag of the United States of America, and to the Republic for which it stands, one Nation under God, indivisible, with liberty and justice for all."

Joachim du Bellay

French poet, 1522–1560

1 France, mother of arts, of warfare, and of laws.

Les Regrets Sonnet 9 (1558)

2 Happy he who like Ulysses has made a great journey.

Les Regrets Sonnet 31 (1558)

Melvin Belli

U.S. lawyer, 1907–1996

1 I'm no ambulance chaser. I always get there before the ambulance arrives.

Quoted in *Wash. Post*, 21 Apr. 1985

Hilaire Belloc

French-born English author and politician, 1870–1953

1 Child! do not throw this book about;
Refrain from the unholy pleasure
Of cutting all the pictures out!
Preserve it as your chiefest treasure.

A Bad Child's Book of Beasts dedication (1896)

2 The waterbeetle here shall teach
A sermon far beyond your reach;
He flabbergasts the Human race
By gliding on the water's face
With ease, celerity, and grace;
But if he ever stopped to think
Of how he did it, he would sink.

A Moral Alphabet (1899)

3 When I am dead, I hope it may be said:
   "His sins were scarlet, but his books were
      read."
   "On His Books" l. 1 (1923)

Saul Bellow
Canadian-born U.S. novelist, 1915–2005

1 I am an American, Chicago born—Chicago,
   that somber city—and go at things as I have
   taught myself, free-style, and will make the
   record in my own way: first to knock, first
   admitted; sometimes an innocent knock,
   sometimes a not so innocent.
   The Adventures of Augie March ch. 1 (1953)

2 Man's life is not a business.
   Herzog sec. 2 (1964)

3 New York makes one think of the collapse of
   civilization, about Sodom and Gomorrah, the
   end of the world. The end wouldn't come as a
   surprise here. Many people already bank on it.
   Mr. Sammler's Planet pt. 6 (1970)

4 The body, she says, is subject to the forces of
   gravity. But the soul is ruled by levity, pure.
   "Him with His Foot in His Mouth" (1984)

Ludwig Bemelmans
Italian-born children's book writer, 1898–1962

1 In an old house in Paris
   that was covered with vines
   lived twelve little girls in two straight lines.
   Madeline (1939)

Robert Benchley
U.S. humorist, 1889–1945

1 There may be said to be two classes of people
   in the world; those who constantly divide the
   people of the world into two classes, and those
   who do not.
   Vanity Fair, Feb. 1920

2 In America there are two classes of travel—first
   class, and with children.
   "Kiddie-Kar Travel" (1923)

3 Tell us your phobias and we will tell you what
   you are afraid of.
   My Ten Years in a Quandary and How They Grew
   "Phobias" (1936)

4 The surest way to make a monkey of a man is
   to quote him.
   My Ten Years in a Quandary and How They Grew
   "Quick Quotations" (1936)

5 It is rather to be chosen than great riches, unless
   I have omitted something from the quotation.
   Benchley—Or Else! (1947)

6 It'll be nice to get out of this wet suit and into a
   dry Martini!
   Quoted in *Daily News* (Frederick, Md.), 10 Sept. 1937.
   This occurrence, discovered by Barry Popik, was
   earlier than the quotation's appearance in the 1937
   film *Every Day's a Holiday*.

7 I do most of my work sitting down; that's where
   I shine.
   Quoted in *L.A. Times*, 4 Oct. 1942.

8 [*Suggested epitaph for a movie star:*] She sleeps
   alone at last.
   Quoted in Edmund Fuller, *2500 Anecdotes for All
   Occasions* (1943)

9 [*On his sharing a tiny office in the Metropolitan
   Opera House studios with Dorothy Parker:*] One
   cubic foot less and it would be adulterous.
   Quoted in *New Yorker*, 5 Jan. 1946

10 It took me 15 years to discover I had no talent
   for writing, but I couldn't give it up because by
   that time I was too famous.
   Quoted in *Reader's Digest*, Sept. 1949. Similar jokes
   have been traced by Garson O'Toole as far back as
   Puck, Feb. 1912 (the punch line there was "By that
   time I had a reputation").

11 [*Upon withdrawing his savings from a bank that
   had granted him a loan:*] I don't trust a bank that
   would lend money to such a poor risk.
   Quoted in *The Algonquin Wits,* ed. Robert E. Drennan
   (1968)
   *See Galsworthy 2; Joe E. Lewis 1; Lincoln 2; Groucho
   Marx 41; Twain 4*

12 [*Telegram to a friend upon arriving in Venice for a
   vacation:*] STREETS FLOODED. PLEASE ADVISE.
   Quoted in *The Algonquin Wits,* ed. Robert E.
   Drennan (1968). In an earlier version, Benchley was
   said to have telegraphed, "STREETS FULL OF WATER.
   ADVISE." (*Reader's Digest*, Oct. 1958).

13 Any one can do any amount of work, provided
   it isn't the work he is supposed to be doing at
   that moment.
   Chicago Tribune, 2 Feb. 1930

Julien Benda
French philosopher and novelist, 1867–1956

1 *La Trahison des Clercs.*
The Treason of the Intellectuals.
Title of book (1927)

Benedict XVI (Joseph Ratzinger)
German pope, 1927–

1 Dear brothers and sisters, after the great Pope
John Paul II, the cardinals have elected me—a
simple, humble worker in the vineyard of the
Lord.
Remarks from balcony at St. Peter's Basilica, Vatican
City, 19 Apr. 2005

Ruth Benedict
U.S. anthropologist, 1887–1948

1 The life-history of the individual is first and
foremost an accommodation to the patterns
and standards traditionally handed down in
his community. From the moment of his birth
the customs into which he is born shape his
experience and behavior. By the time he can
talk, he is the little creature of his culture,
and by the time he is grown and able to take
part in its activities, its habits are his habits,
its beliefs his beliefs, its impossibilities his
impossibilities.
Patterns of Culture ch. 1 (1934)

Stephen Vincent Benét
U.S. poet and writer, 1898–1943

1 I have fallen in love with American names.
"American Names" l. 1 (1927)

2 I shall not rest quiet in Montparnasse.
I shall not lie easy at Winchelsea.
You may bury my body in Sussex grass,
You may bury my tongue at Champmédy.
I shall not be there, I shall rise and pass.
Bury my heart at Wounded Knee.
"American Names" l. 30 (1927)

3 If two New Hampshiremen aren't a match for
the Devil, we might as well give the country
back to the Indians.
"The Devil and Daniel Webster" (1927)

David Ben-Gurion
Israeli prime minister, 1886–1973

1 In Israel, in order to be a realist, you must
believe in miracles.
Television broadcast, CBS, 5 Oct. 1956

Walter Benjamin
German literary and social critic, 1892–1940

1 A highly embroiled quarter, a network of
streets that I had avoided for years, was
disentangled at a single stroke when one day
a person dear to me moved there. It was as if
a searchlight set up at this person's window
dissected the area with pencils of light.
One-Way Street (1928) (translation by Edmund
Jephcott and Kingsley Shorter)

2 To articulate the past historically does not mean
to recognize it "the way it really was" (Ranke).
It means to seize hold of a memory as it flashes
up at a moment of danger.
"On the Concept of History" (1940)
See Ranke 1

Ernest Benn
English publisher and author, 1875–1954

1 Politics is the art of looking for trouble, finding
it whether it exists or not, diagnosing it
incorrectly and applying the wrong remedy.
Quoted in *Springfield* (Mass.) *Republican,* 27 July 1930

Jack Benny (Benjamin Kubelsky)
U.S. comedian, 1894–1974

1 [*Remark upon accepting an award:*] I don't
deserve all these kind words, but as a friend of
mine said, I've got arthritis and I don't deserve
that either.
Quoted in *Pittsburgh Post-Gazette,* 18 June 1959

A. C. Benson
English writer, 1862–1925

1 Land of Hope and Glory, Mother of the Free,
How shall we extol thee who are born of thee?
Wider still and wider shall thy bounds be set;
God who made thee mighty, make thee
    mightier yet.
"Land of Hope and Glory" (finale to Edward Elgar's
Coronation Ode) (1902)

Stella Benson

English novelist and poet, 1892–1933

1 Call no man foe, but never love a stranger.

This Is the End (1917)

Jeremy Bentham

English philosopher and jurist, 1748–1832

1 It is the greatest happiness of the greatest number that is the measure of right and wrong.

A Fragment on Government preface (1776). Bentham said that he derived this formula from either Joseph Priestley or Cesare Beccaria; Beccaria is the more likely. If Priestley was the source, then Bentham was paraphrasing him because the phrase is not found in Priestley's writings.
See Beccaria 1; Hutcheson 1

2 I dreamt t'other night that I was a founder of a sect; of course a personage of great sanctity and importance. It was called the sect of *utilitarians.*

Manuscript (ca. 1780). This passage, quoted in David Baumgardt, *Bentham and the Ethics of Today* (1952), represents the earliest known usage of the word *utilitarian.*

3 Nature has placed mankind under the governance of two sovereign masters, *pain* and *pleasure.* It is for them alone to point out what we ought to do, as well as to determine what we shall do.

An Introduction to the Principles of Morals and Legislation ch. 1 (1789)

4 The day *may* come, when the rest of the animal creation may acquire those rights which never could have been withholden from them but by the hand of tyranny. . . . The question is not, Can they *reason?* nor, Can they *talk?* but, Can they *suffer?*

An Introduction to the Principles of Morals and Legislation ch. 17 (1789)

5 The word *international,* it must be acknowledged, is a new one; though, it is hoped, sufficiently analogous and intelligible. It is calculated to express . . . the branch of law which goes commonly under the name of the *law of nations.*

An Introduction to the Principles of Morals and Legislation ch. 17 (1789)

6 All inequality that has no special utility to justify it is injustice.

Supply Without Burthen; or Escheat Vice Taxation (1795)

7 *Natural rights* is simple nonsense: natural and imprescriptible rights, rhetorical nonsense,— nonsense upon stilts.

Anarchical Fallacies art. 2 (1816)

8 The utility of all these arts and sciences,—I speak both of those of amusement and curiosity,—the value which they possess, is exactly in proportion to the pleasure they yield. . . . Prejudice apart, the game of push-pin is of equal value with the arts and sciences of music and poetry.

The Rationale of Reward bk. 3, ch. 1 (1825)

9 *"Whatever is, is right"* . . . This is called *following precedents.* . . . Thus it is—that, by the comparative blindness of man in each preceding period, the like blindness in each succeeding period is secured: without the trouble or need of reflection,—men, by opulence rendered indolent, and by indolence and self-indulgence doomed to ignorance, follow their leaders—as sheep follow sheep, and geese geese.

The Constitutional Code (1830)

E. Clerihew Bentley

English writer, 1875–1956

1 Sir Christopher Wren
Said, "I am going to dine with some men.
If anybody calls
Say I am designing St. Paul's."

Biography for Beginners (1905)

Richard Bentley

English classical scholar, 1662–1742

1 [*On Alexander Pope's translation of Homer's* Iliad:] It is a pretty poem, Mr. Pope, but you must not call it Homer.

Quoted in Samuel Johnson, "The Life of Pope" (1787)

Lloyd Bentsen

U.S. politician, 1921–2006

1 [*Responding to Dan Quayle's claim to have "as much experience in the Congress as Jack Kennedy did when he sought the presidency":*] Senator, I served with Jack Kennedy, I knew Jack Kennedy, Jack Kennedy was a friend of mine. Senator, you are no Jack Kennedy.

Remark in vice-presidential debate, 5 Oct. 1988

Charles William de la Poer, First Baron Beresford

British naval officer and author, 1846–1919

1 [*Telegram to Edward, Prince of Wales, responding to dinner invitation:*] Very sorry can't come. Lie follows by post.

Quoted in Ralph Nevill, *The World of Fashion 1837–1922* (1923)

Edgar Bergen

U.S. ventriloquist, 1903–1978

1 [*Catchphrase of dummy "Charlie McCarthy":*] Hard work never killed anybody, but why take a chance?

Quoted in Robert Byrne, *The Other 637 Best Things Anybody Ever Said* (1984)
See *Modern Proverbs* 39

Thomas Berger

U.S. novelist, 1924–2014

1 Whatever else you can say about the white man, it must be admitted that *you cannot get rid of him*. He is in never-ending supply. There has always been only a limited supply of Human Beings.

Little Big Man ch. 13 (1964)

Henri Bergson

French philosopher, 1859–1941

1 *L'élan vital.*
The vital spirit.

L'Évolution Créatrice ch. 2 (section title) (1907)

2 Religion is to mysticism what popularization is to science.

Two Sources of Morality and Religion ch. 3 (1932) (translation by R. Ashley Audra and Cloudesley Brereton)

3 The universe . . . is a machine for the making of gods.

Two Sources of Morality and Religion ch. 4 (1932) (translation by R. Ashley Audra and Cloudesley Brereton)

George Berkeley

Irish philosopher and bishop, 1685–1753

1 Upon the whole, I am inclined to think that the far greater part, if not all, of those difficulties which have hitherto amused philosophers, and

blocked up the way to knowledge, are entirely owing to our selves. That we have first raised a dust and then complain we cannot see.

A Treatise Concerning the Principles of Human Knowledge introduction, sec. 3 (1710)

2 All the choir of heaven and furniture of earth— in a word, all those bodies which compose the mighty frame of the world—have not any subsistence without a mind . . . their *being* is *to be perceived or known.*

A Treatise Concerning the Principles of Human Knowledge pt. 1, sec. 6 (1710)

3 Westward the course of empire takes its way;
The first four acts already past,
A fifth shall close the drama with the day:
Time's noblest offspring is the last.

"On the Prospect of Planting Arts and Learning in America" st. 6 (1752)

David Berkowitz (Richard David Falco)

U.S. criminal, 1953–

1 I am the "Son of Sam."

Letter to Joseph Borrelli, Apr. 1977

Adolf A. Berle, Jr.

U.S. diplomat, 1895–1971

1 The issue may well simmer down to whether the judgment of the courts of the United States, the executive arm of the United States, and, in fact though not in form, the apparent opinion of the great majority of the United States, considers essential this economic readjustment; or whether the nine old men of the Supreme Court are entitled to form their own opinion about it and to upset a movement of national scope solely on that opinion.

"The Law and the Social Revolution," *Survey Graphic*, Dec. 1933
See *Drew Pearson* 1

Irving Berlin (Israel Baline)

Russian-born U.S. songwriter, 1888–1989

1 Come on and hear, come on and hear,
Alexander's Ragtime Band.

"Alexander's Ragtime Band" (song) (1911)

2 Everybody's Doin' It Now.

Title of song (1911)

3 Oh! How I hate to get up in the morning,
   Oh! How I'd love to remain in bed.
   For the hardest blow of all
   Is to hear the bugler call:
   "You've got to get up,
   You've got to get up,
   You've got to get up this morning!"
   Some day I'm going to murder the bugler,
   Some day they're going to find him dead.
   I'll amputate his reveille,
   And step upon it heavily,
   And spend the rest of my life in bed.
   "Oh! How I Hate to Get Up in the Morning" (song)
   (1918)

4 A pretty girl is like a melody
   That haunts you night and day.
   "A Pretty Girl Is like a Melody" (song) (1919)

5 The Song Is Ended (But the Melody Lingers
   On).
   Title of song (1927)

6 Puttin' on the Ritz.
   Title of song (1928)

7 Heaven,
   I'm in heaven,
   And my heart beats so that I can hardly speak;
   And I seem to find the happiness I seek
   When we're out together dancing
   Cheek to cheek.
   "Cheek to Cheek" (song) (1935)

8 God bless America,
   Land that I love,
   Stand beside her and guide her
   Thru the night with a light from above.
   From the mountains to the prairies,
   To the oceans white with foam,
   God bless America,
   My home sweet home.
   "God Bless America" (song) (1939)
   See Peeke 1

9 This is the army, Mr. Jones,
   No private rooms or telephones,
   You had your breakfast in bed before,
   But you won't have it there anymore.
   "This Is the Army, Mr. Jones" (song) (1942)

10 I'm dreaming of a white Christmas
   Just like the ones I used to know.
   "White Christmas" (song) (1942)

11 I'm dreaming of a white Christmas
   With ev'ry Christmas card I write.
   "May your days be merry and bright,
   And may all your Christmases be white."
   "White Christmas" (song) (1942)

12 Anything you can do, I can do better,
   I can do anything better than you.
   "Anything You Can Do" (song) (1946)

13 Got no diamond, got no pearl,
   Still I think I'm a lucky girl,
   I got the sun in the morning
   And the moon at night.
   "I Got the Sun in the Morning" (song) (1946)

14 There's no bus'ness like show bus'ness,
   Like no bus'ness I know.
   Ev'rything about it is appealing,
   Ev'rything the traffic will allow.
   Nowhere could you get that happy feeling
   When you are stealing that extra bow.
   "There's No Business like Show Business" (song)
   (1946)

15 Even with a turkey that you know will fold,
   You may be stranded out in the cold,
   Still you wouldn't change it for a sack of gold.
   Let's go on with the show.
   "There's No Business like Show Business" (song)
   (1946)

16 They say that falling in love is wonderful.
   It's wonderful, so they say.
   And with a moon up above,
   It's wonderful,
   It's wonderful,
   So they tell me.
   "They Say It's Wonderful" (song) (1946)

Isaiah Berlin
Latvian-born English philosopher, 1909–1997

1 There exists a great chasm between those,
   on one side, who relate everything to a single
   central vision . . . and, on the other side, those
   who pursue many ends, often unrelated
   and even contradictory. . . . The first kind of
   intellectual and artistic personality belongs to
   the hedgehogs, the second to the foxes.
   The Hedgehog and the Fox sec. 1 (1953)
   See Archilochus 1

Hector Berlioz

French composer, 1803–1869

1 Time is a great teacher, they say; unfortunately it is an inhuman teacher that kills its pupils.
Letter to Jules-Henri Vernoy de Saint-Georges, 27 Nov. 1856

Georges Bernanos

French writer, 1888–1948

1 Hell, madam, is to love no more.
Journal d'un Curé de Campagne ch. 2 (1936)

Bernard of Chartres

French philosopher, fl. 1100

1 We are like dwarfs on the shoulders of giants, so that we can see more than they, and things at a greater distance, not by virtue of any sharpness of sight on our part, or any physical distinction, but because we are carried high and raised up by their giant size.
Quoted in John of Salisbury, *The Metalogicon* (1159)
See Robert Burton 1; Coleridge 30; Isaac Newton 1

St. Bernard of Clairvaux

French ecclesiastic, 1090–1153

1 You will find something more in woods than in books. Trees and stones will teach you that which you can never learn from masters.
Epistles no. 106

2 Hell is full of good intentions or desires.
Attributed in St. Francis de Sales, Letter 74
See Proverbs 255

Edward Bernays

Austrian public relations pioneer, 1891–1995

1 The engineering of consent is the very essence of the democratic process, the freedom to persuade and suggest.
Annals of the American Academy of Political and Social Science, Mar. 1947

Eric Berne

U.S. psychiatrist, 1910–1970

1 Games People Play: The Psychology of Human Relationships.
Title of book (1964)

Tim Berners-Lee

English computer scientist, 1955–

1 WorldWideWeb: Proposal for a HyperText Project.
Title of electronic document (1990). Coauthored with Robert A. Cailliau.

Bert Berns

U.S. songwriter and record producer, 1929–1967

1 Take another little piece of my heart now baby You know you got it if it makes you feel good.
"Piece of My Heart" (song) (1967). Cowritten with Jerry Ragovoy.

Yogi Berra

U.S. baseball player and sage, 1925–2015

1 [*Referring to rain that had just begun:*] Where is that coming from?
Yogi: It Ain't Over (1989)

2 [*While driving:*] We're lost, but we're making good time!
The Yogi Book (1998). This anecdote, worded slightly differently, appeared in *South Illinoisan* (Carbondale, Ill.), 28 Oct. 1963. Similar jokes, not attributed to Berra, can be found as early as *Collier's Weekly*, Oct. 1947.

3 You've got to be careful if you don't know where you're going 'cause you might not get there!
The Yogi Book (1998)

4 How can a guy hit and think at the same time?
Quoted in *N.Y. Times*, 12 June 1947

5 I wanna thank everyone for making this night necessary.

Quoted in *N.Y. Times*, 12 June 1947

6 It don't matter if you're ugly in this racket. All you have to do is hit the ball and I never saw anybody hit one with his face.

Quoted in Milton Gross, *Yankee Doodles* (1948)

7 If they don't want to come out [to the ballpark], nobody's gonna stop 'em.

Quoted in *New Orleans Times-Picayune*, 13 Sept. 1962. Sol Hurok was quoted as stating the same thing about filmgoers, in *Portland Oregonian*, 16 Aug. 1952.

8 It gets late early.

Quoted in *Lexington* (Ky.) *Leader*, 4 Oct. 1963. Berra says in *The Yogi Book* (1998) that he was referring here to the difficulty of playing left field in Yankee Stadium in late autumn when "the shadows would creep up on you and you had a tough time seeing the ball off the bat."

9 You can observe a lot by watchin'.

Quoted in *N.Y. Times*, 25 Oct. 1963

10 [*When asked for the time:*] You mean right now?

Quoted in *Fresno Bee*, 24 Nov. 1970

11 [*When asked if he wanted his pizza pie sliced into four or eight slices:*] Cut mine in four. I don't think I can eat eight.

Quoted in *Fresno Bee*, 24 Nov. 1970. A very similar comment by Milwaukee Braves pitcher Dan Osinski (with six slices instead of four) was quoted in the *High Point* (N.C.) *Enterprise*, 8 Aug. 1965.

12 [*Explaining why it is not necessary to have expensive luggage:*] You only use it for traveling.

Quoted in Phil Pepe, *The Wit and Wisdom of Yogi Berra* (1974)

13 Slump? I ain't in no slump. I just ain't hitting.

Quoted in Pete Rose, *Charlie Hustle* (1975)

14 It ain't over 'til it's over.

Quoted in *Wash. Post*, 26 Sept. 1977. Berra notes in *The Yogi Book* (1998): "That was my answer to a reporter when I was managing the New York Mets in July 1973. We were about nine games out of first place. We went on to win the division." Berra was quoted using the similar expression "You're not out of it until you're out of it" in *N.Y. Times*, 30 June 1974. "A ball game's never over until it's over" appeared in *The Delta of Sigma Nu Fraternity* (1921), quoting the *Indianapolis News*.
See Ralph Carpenter 1

15 It's déjà vu all over again.

Quoted in *Forbes*, 15 July 1985. Berra describes this as "My comment after Mickey Mantle and Roger Maris hit back-to-back home runs for the umpteenth time" (*The Yogi Book* [1998]). Jim Prior wrote "It's Déjà vu again" in a humorous poem in the *St. Petersburg* (Fla.) *Evening Independent*, 22 Sept. 1962, without mentioning Berra but in a context relating to home runs.

16 I really didn't say everything I said.

Quoted in *Sports Illustrated*, 17 Mar. 1986

17 [*Giving driving directions to Joe Garagiola:*] If you come to a fork in the road, take it.

Quoted in *Wall Street Journal*, 11 May 1987

18 [*Watching a Steve McQueen movie on television:*] He made that picture before he died.

Quoted in Phil Pepe, *The Wit and Wisdom of Yogi Berra*, 2nd ed. (1988)

Daniel Berrigan
U.S. priest and political activist, 1921–2016

1 Our apologies, good friends, for the fracture of good order, the burning of paper instead of children.

Night Flight to Hanoi preface (1968)

Chuck Berry
U.S. rock singer, 1926–2017

1 Roll over Beethoven
And tell Tchaikovsky the news.
"Roll Over, Beethoven" (song) (1956)

2 Just let me hear some of that
Rock and Roll Music,
Any old way you choose it . . .
It's got to be Rock and Roll Music,
If you want to dance with me.
"Rock and Roll Music" (song) (1957)

3 Hail, hail, rock 'n' roll,
Deliver me from the days of old.
"School Days" (song) (1957)

4 Go Johnny go!
"Johnny B. Goode" (song) (1958)

5 He never learned to read or write so well
But he could play a guitar just like ringing a bell.
"Johnny B. Goode" (song) (1958)

Richard Berry

U.S. singer and songwriter, 1935–1997

1 Louie, Louie,
Me gotta go. . . .
Three nights and days we sailed the sea;
Me think of girl constantly.
On the ship, I dream she there;
I smell the rose in her hair.

"Louie, Louie" (song) (1955). These are the true lyrics for the song. A raunchy version ("Each night at ten, I lay her again; I fuck my girl all kinds of ways") became world-famous after the Kingsmen's poorly enunciated 1963 cover of the song lent itself to creative interpretation.

John Berryman

U.S. poet, 1914–1972

1 We must travel in the direction of our fear.
"A Point of Age" l. 42 (1948)

2 Life, friends, is boring. We must not say so.
77 *Dream Songs* no. 14, l. 1 (1964)

Pierre Berton

Canadian writer and journalist, 1920–2004

1 A Canadian is somebody who knows how to make love in a canoe.
Quoted in *The Canadian,* 22 Dec. 1973

Bruce Bethke

U.S. science fiction writer, 1955–

1 Cyberpunk.
Title of story, *Amazing Stories,* Nov. 1983. Coinage of the term *cyberpunk.*

Theobald von Bethmann-Hollweg

German chancellor, 1856–1921

1 [*Remark to Edward Goschen, Berlin, 4 Aug. 1914:*] Just for a word "neutrality"—a word which in war time has so often been disregarded—just for a scrap of paper, Great Britain was going to make war on a kindred nation who desired nothing better than to be friends with her.
Attributed in Edward Goschen, Report, 18 Aug. 1914. The date of Goschen's report, which apparently originally read "August 18th," was altered to read "August 6th." It is not clear what Bethmann-Hollweg's true exact words were, nor even in what language they were spoken (English, German, or French?). Goschen's recollections may have been influenced by Victorien Sardou's 1860 play, *Les Pattes de Mouche,* translated into English as *A Scrap of Paper;* Goschen had appeared in an amateur production of the Sardou play.

Mary McLeod Bethune

U.S. educator and administrator, 1875–1955

1 [*Motto of National Council of Negro Women:*] Leave No One Behind.
Quoted in *N.Y. Times,* 17 Nov. 1985

John Betjeman

English poet, 1906–1984

1 He rose, and he put down *The Yellow Book.*
He staggered—and, terrible-eyed,
He brushed past the palms on the staircase
And was helped to a hansom outside.
"The Arrest of Oscar Wilde at the Cadogan Hotel" l. 33 (1937)

2 The sort of girl I like to see
Smiles down from her great height at me.
"The Olympic Girl" l. 1 (1954)

3 Oh! Would I were her racket pressed
With hard excitement to her breast.
"The Olympic Girl" l. 13 (1954)

Aneurin Bevan

British politician, 1897–1960

1 How can wealth persuade poverty to use its political freedom to keep wealth in power? Here lies the whole art of Conservative politics in the twentieth century.
In Place of Fear ch. 1 (1952)

2 We know what happens to people who stay in the middle of the road. They get run over.
Quoted in *Observer,* 9 Dec. 1953
See Hightower 2

Hugh M. Beville, Jr.

U.S. broadcasting executive, 1908–1988

1 In advertising there is a saying that if you can keep your head while all those around you are losing theirs—then you just don't understand the problem.
National Broadcasting Corporation brochure, 18 Nov. 1954. A similar statement appeared in the *Rhinebeck* (N.Y.) *Gazette,* 20 Sept. 1935.
See Kipling 31

Beyoncé (Beyoncé Giselle Knowles)

U.S. singer and songwriter, 1981–

1 If you liked it, then you should have put a ring on it.

"Single Ladies (Put a Ring on It)" (song) (2008). Cowritten with Terius Nash, Thaddis Harrell, and Christopher Stewart.

Bhagavadgita

Hindu poem, ca. 250 B.C.–ca. A.D. 250

1 If any man thinks he slays, and if another thinks he is slain, neither knows the ways of truth. The Eternal in man cannot kill: the Eternal in man cannot die. He is never born, and he never dies. He is in Eternity, he is for evermore. Never-born and eternal, beyond times gone or to come, he does not die when the body dies.

Bhagavadgita ch. 2, v. 19

2 If the radiance of a thousand suns were to burst forth at once in the sky, that would be like the splendor of the Mighty One.

Bhagavadgita ch. 11, v. 12
See Oppenheimer 3

3 I [Krishna] am mighty, world-destroying Time.

Bhagavadgita ch. 11, v. 32
See Oppenheimer 3

4 Only by love can men see me, and know me, and come unto me.

Bhagavadgita ch. 11, v. 54

Bible

Wording and chapter and verse numbers are from the Authorized (King James) Version (1611). Much of the language of the King James Bible, particularly the New Testament, derives from the translation by William Tyndale, printed between 1525 and 1535.

Genesis

1 In the beginning God created the heaven and the earth.
And the earth was without form, and void; and darkness was upon the face of the deep. And the Spirit of God moved upon the face of the waters.
And God said, Let there be light: and there was light.

Genesis 1:1–3

2 And the evening and the morning were the first day.

Genesis 1:5

3 And God saw that it was good.

Genesis 1:10

4 And God said, Let us make man in our image, after our likeness.

Genesis 1:26

5 Male and female created he them.

Genesis 1:27

6 Be fruitful, and multiply, and replenish the earth, and subdue it: and have dominion over the fish of the sea, and over the fowl of the air, and over every living thing that moveth upon the earth.

Genesis 1:28
See Woody Allen 1

7 And the Lord God planted a garden eastward in Eden.

Genesis 2:8

8 And out of the ground made the Lord God to grow every tree that is pleasant to the sight, and good for food; the tree of life also in the midst of the garden, and the tree of knowledge of good and evil.

Genesis 2:9

9 But of the tree of the knowledge of good and evil, thou shalt not eat of it: for in the day that thou eatest thereof thou shalt surely die.

Genesis 2:17

10 It is not good that the man should be alone; I will make him an help meet for him.

Genesis 2:18

11 And the rib, which the Lord God had taken from man, made he a woman.

Genesis 2:22

12 This is now bone of my bones, and flesh of my flesh: she shall be called Woman, because she was taken out of Man.

Genesis 2:23

13 Therefore shall a man leave his father and his mother, and shall cleave unto his wife: and they shall be one flesh.

Genesis 2:24

14 And they were both naked, the man and his
wife, and were not ashamed.
Genesis 2:25

15 Now the serpent was more subtil than any beast
of the field.
Genesis 3:1

16 Your eyes shall be opened, and ye shall be as
gods, knowing good and evil.
Genesis 3:5

17 And they sewed fig leaves together, and made
themselves aprons.
And they heard the voice of the Lord God
walking in the garden in the cool of the day.
Genesis 3:7–8

18 The woman whom thou gavest to be with me,
she gave me of the tree, and I did eat.
Genesis 3:12

19 The serpent beguiled me, and I did eat.
Genesis 3:13

20 In sorrow thou shalt bring forth children.
Genesis 3:16

21 In the sweat of thy face shalt thou eat bread.
Genesis 3:19

22 For dust thou art, and unto dust shalt thou
return.
Genesis 3:19
See Longfellow 1

23 Am I my brother's keeper?
Genesis 4:9

24 And the Lord set a mark upon Cain.
Genesis 4:15

25 And Cain went out from the presence of the
Lord, and dwelt in the land of Nod, on the east
of Eden.
Genesis 4:16

26 There were giants in the earth in those days.
Genesis 6:4

27 And of every living thing of all flesh, two of
every sort shalt thou bring into the ark.
Genesis 6:19

28 And the rain was upon the earth forty days and
forty nights.
Genesis 7:12

29 Therefore is the name of it called Babel;
because the Lord did there confound the
language of all the earth.
Genesis 11:9

30 His [Ishmael's] hand will be against every man,
and every man's hand against him.
Genesis 16:12

31 But his [Lot's] wife looked back from behind
him, and she became a pillar of salt.
Genesis 19:26

32 And he [Jacob] dreamed, and behold a ladder
set up on the earth, and the top of it reached
to heaven: and behold the angels of God
ascending and descending on it.
Genesis 28:12

33 Now Israel loved Joseph more than all his
children, because he was the son of his old age;
and he made him a coat of many colors.
Genesis 37:3

34 Jacob saw that there was corn in Egypt.
Genesis 42:1

35 But Benjamin's mess was five times so much as
any of theirs.
Genesis 43:34

36 God forbid.
Genesis 44:7

37 And ye shall eat the fat of the land.
Genesis 45:18

Exodus

38 I have been a stranger in a strange land.
Exodus 2:22

39 Behold, the bush burned with fire, and the
bush was not consumed.
Exodus 3:2

40 Put off thy shoes from off thy feet, for the place
whereon thou standest is holy ground.
Exodus 3:5

41 A land flowing with milk and honey.
Exodus 3:8

42 And God said unto Moses, I AM THAT I AM.
Exodus 3:14

43 Let my people go.
Exodus 5:1

44 And I will harden Pharaoh's heart, and multiply my signs and my wonders in the land of Egypt.
Exodus 7:3

45 Ye shall eat it in haste; it is the Lord's passover.
Exodus 12:11

46 For I will pass through the land of Egypt this night, and will smite all the firstborn in the land of Egypt, both man and beast.
Exodus 12:12

47 Seven days shall ye eat unleavened bread.
Exodus 12:15

48 Remember this day, in which ye came out from Egypt, out of the house of bondage.
Exodus 13:3

49 Would to God we had died by the hand of the Lord in the land of Egypt, when we sat by the flesh pots, and when we did eat bread to the full.
Exodus 16:3

50 I am the Lord thy God. . . .
Thou shalt have no other gods before me.
Exodus 20:2–3

51 Thou shalt not make unto thee any graven image.
Exodus 20:4

52 For I the Lord thy God am a jealous God, visiting the iniquity of the fathers upon the children unto the third and fourth generation of them that hate me.
Exodus 20:5

53 Thou shalt not take the name of the Lord thy God in vain.
Exodus 20:7

54 Remember the sabbath day, to keep it holy. Six days shalt thou labor, and do all thy work: But the seventh day . . . thou shalt not do any work.
Exodus 20:8–10

55 Honor thy father and thy mother: that thy days may be long upon the land which the Lord thy God giveth thee.
Exodus 20:12

56 Thou shalt not kill.
Exodus 20:13

57 Thou shalt not commit adultery.
Exodus 20:14

58 Thou shalt not steal.
Exodus 20:15

59 Thou shalt not bear false witness against thy neighbor.
Exodus 20:16

60 Thou shalt not covet thy neighbor's house, thou shalt not covet thy neighbor's wife, nor his manservant, nor his maidservant, nor his ox, nor his ass, nor any thing that is thy neighbor's.
Exodus 20:17

61 Eye for eye, tooth for tooth.
Exodus 21:24
See Fischer 1

62 A stiffnecked people.
Exodus 32:9

63 And he [Moses] was there with the Lord forty days and forty nights; he did neither eat bread, nor drink water. And he wrote upon the tables the words of the covenant, the ten commandments.
Exodus 34:28

Leviticus

64 Let him go for a scapegoat into the wilderness.
Leviticus 16:10

65 Thou shalt love thy neighbor as thyself.
Leviticus 19:18
See Bible 256

66 Ye shall hallow the fiftieth year, and proclaim liberty throughout all the land unto all the inhabitants thereof: it shall be a jubilee unto you.
Leviticus 25:10

Numbers

67 And your children shall wander in the wilderness forty years.
Numbers 14:33

68 What hath God wrought!
Numbers 23:23. Quoted by Samuel F. B. Morse in the first formal intercity message sent by electric telegraph (from Washington, D.C., to Baltimore, Md.), 24 May 1844.

Deuteronomy

69 Hear, O Israel: The Lord our God is one Lord.
Deuteronomy 6:4

70 Thou shalt love the Lord thy God with all thine
heart, and with all thy soul, and with all thy
might.
And these words, which I command thee this
day, shall be in thine heart:
And thou shalt teach them diligently unto thy
children.
Deuteronomy 6:5–7

71 The Lord thy God hath chosen thee to be a
special people unto himself.
Deuteronomy 7:6

72 Man doth not live by bread only, but by every
word that proceedeth out of the mouth of the
Lord doth man live.
Deuteronomy 8:3
See Bible 202

73 He found him in a desert land, and in the
waste howling wilderness; he led him about, he
instructed him, he kept him as the apple of his
eye.
Deuteronomy 32:10

Joshua

74 And it came to pass, when the people heard the
sound of the trumpet, and the people shouted
with a great shout, that the wall fell down
flat, so that the people went up into the city
[Jericho].
Joshua 6:20

75 Hewers of wood and drawers of water.
Joshua 9:21

Judges

76 Then said they unto him, Say now Shibboleth:
and he said Sibboleth: for he could not frame
to pronounce it right. Then they took him, and
slew him.
Judges 12:6

77 He smote them hip and thigh.
Judges 15:8

78 And Samson said, with the jawbone of an ass
. . . have I slain a thousand men.
Judges 15:16

79 All the people arose as one man.
Judges 20:8

80 In those days there was no king in Israel: every
man did that which was right in his own eyes.
Judges 21:25

Ruth

81 Whither thou goest, I will go; and where thou
lodgest, I will lodge: thy people shall be my
people, and thy God my God.
Ruth 1:16

I Samuel

82 God save the king.
I Samuel 10:24
See Henry Carey 2

83 A man after his own heart.
I Samuel 13:14

84 Go, and the Lord be with thee.
I Samuel 17:37

85 He fell likewise upon his sword.
I Samuel 31:5

II Samuel

86 The beauty of Israel is slain upon thy high
places: how are the mighty fallen!
II Samuel 1:19

87 Saul and Jonathan were lovely and pleasant
in their lives, and in their death they were not
divided: they were swifter than eagles, they
were stronger than lions.
II Samuel 1:23

88 Thy love to me was wonderful, passing the love
of women.
II Samuel 1:26

89 Would God I had died for thee, O Absalom, my
son, my son!
II Samuel 18:33

I Kings

90 Then will I cut off Israel out of the land which
I have given them; and this house, which I
have hallowed for my name, will I cast out of
my sight; and Israel shall be a proverb and a
byword among all people.
I Kings 9:7

91 The half was not told me: thy wisdom and
    prosperity exceedeth the fame which I heard.
    I Kings 10:7

92 How long halt ye between two opinions?
    I Kings 18:21

93 He girded up his loins.
    I Kings 18:46

94 But the Lord was not in the wind: and after
    the wind an earthquake; but the Lord was
    not in the earthquake:
    And after the earthquake a fire: but the Lord
    was not in the fire: and after the fire a still
    small voice.
    I Kings 19:11–12

95 Elijah passed by him, and cast his mantle
    upon him.
    I Kings 19:19

Job

96 And I only am escaped alone to tell thee.
    Job 1:15

97 Naked came I out of my mother's womb, and
    naked shall I return thither: the Lord gave,
    and the Lord hath taken away; blessed be the
    name of the Lord.
    Job 1:21

98 Let the day perish wherein I was born.
    Job 3:3

99 Miserable comforters are ye all.
    Job 16:2

100 I am escaped with the skin of my teeth.
    Job 19:20. Usually quoted as "by the skin of my
    teeth."

101 The root of the matter is found in me.
    Job 19:28

102 The price of wisdom is above rubies.
    Job 28:18

103 I am a brother to dragons, and a companion
    to owls.
    Job 30:29

104 Behold now behemoth, which I made with
    thee; he eateth grass as an ox.
    Job 40:15

105 Canst thou draw out leviathan with an hook?
    Job 41:1

Psalms

106 Thou shalt break them with a rod of iron; thou
    shalt dash them in pieces like a potter's vessel.
    Psalms 2:9

107 Out of the mouth of babes and sucklings hast
    thou ordained strength, because of thine
    enemies, that thou mightest still the enemy
    and the avenger.
    When I consider thy heavens, the work of thy
    fingers, the moon and the stars, which thou
    hast ordained;
    What is man, that thou art mindful of him?
    and the son of man, that thou visitest him?
    For thou hast made him a little lower than the
    angels.
    Psalms 8:2–5

108 The Lord is my shepherd; I shall not want.
    He maketh me to lie down in green pastures:
    he leadeth me beside the still waters.
    He restoreth my soul: he leadeth me in the
    paths of righteousness for his name's sake.
    Psalms 23:1–3

109 Yea, though I walk through the valley of the
    shadow of death, I will fear no evil: for
    thou art with me; thy rod and thy staff they
    comfort me.
    Thou preparest a table before me in the
    presence of mine enemies: thou anointest
    my head with oil; my cup runneth over.
    Surely goodness and mercy shall follow me all
    the days of my life: and I will dwell in the
    house of the Lord for ever.
    Psalms 23:4–6
    See Coolio 1

110 The earth is the Lord's, and the fullness
    thereof; the world, and they that dwell
    therein.
    For he hath founded it upon the seas, and
    established it upon the floods.
    Who shall ascend into the hill of the Lord? or
    who shall stand in his holy place?
    He that hath clean hands, and a pure heart;
    who hath not lifted up his soul unto vanity,
    nor sworn deceitfully.
    Psalms 24:1–4

111 Into thine hand I commend my spirit.
    Psalms 31:5
    See Bible 307

112 The meek shall inherit the earth.

Psalms 37:11
See Bible 205; Getty 1; Heinlein 16; John M. Henry 1

113 God is our refuge and strength, a very present
help in trouble.

Psalms 46:1

114 They are like the deaf adder that stoppeth
her ear;
Which will not hearken to the voice of
charmers, charming never so wisely.

Psalms 58:4–5
See John Adams 3

115 A day in thy courts is better than a thousand. I
had rather be a doorkeeper in the house of my
God, than to dwell in the tents of wickedness.

Psalms 84:10
See Barkley 1

116 For a thousand years in thy sight are but as
yesterday when it is past, and as a watch in
the night.

Psalms 90:4

117 The days of our years are threescore years
and ten; and if by reason of strength they be
fourscore years, yet is their strength labor and
sorrow; for it is soon cut off, and we fly away.

Psalms 90:10

118 They that go down to the sea in ships, that do
business in great waters.

Psalms 107:23

119 The fear of the Lord is the beginning of
wisdom.

Psalms 111:10

120 Except the Lord build the house, they labor
in vain that build it: except the Lord keep the
city, the watchman waketh but in vain.

Psalms 127:1

121 Out of the depths have I cried unto thee, O
Lord.

Psalms 130:1. Vulgate translation: *De profundis
clamavi ad te, Domine.*

122 By the rivers of Babylon, there we sat down,
yea, we wept, when we remembered Zion.

Psalms 137:1
See Smart 1

123 If I forget thee, O Jerusalem, let my right
hand forget her cunning.

If I do not remember thee, let my tongue
cleave to the roof of my mouth.

Psalms 137:5–6

Proverbs

124 Go to the ant, thou sluggard; consider her
ways, and be wise.

Proverbs 6:6

125 Wisdom hath builded her house, she hath
hewn out her seven pillars.

Proverbs 9:1

126 Stolen waters are sweet.

Proverbs 9:17

127 He that troubleth his own house shall inherit
the wind.

Proverbs 11:29

128 A righteous man regardeth the life of his
beast: but the tender mercies of the wicked
are cruel.

Proverbs 12:10

129 Lying lips are abomination to the Lord.

Proverbs 12:22

130 Hope deferred maketh the heart sick.

Proverbs 13:12
See Langston Hughes 8

131 He that spareth his rod hateth his son.

Proverbs 13:24

132 A soft answer turneth away wrath.

Proverbs 15:1

133 Pride goeth before destruction, and an
haughty spirit before a fall.

Proverbs 16:18. Frequently misquoted as "Pride
goeth before a fall."

134 Train up a child in the way he should go: and
when he is old, he will not depart from it.

Proverbs 22:6

135 If thine enemy be hungry, give him bread to
eat; and if he be thirsty, give him water to
drink.

For thou shalt heap coals of fire upon his
head, and the Lord shall reward thee.

Proverbs 25:21–22

136 As a dog returneth to his vomit, so a fool
returneth to his folly.

Proverbs 26:11
See Bible 386

137 Where there is no vision, the people perish.
Proverbs 29:18

138 Who can find a virtuous woman? for her price
is far above rubies.
Proverbs 31:10

Ecclesiastes

139 Vanity of vanities; all is vanity.
Ecclesiastes 1:2

140 One generation passeth away, and another
generation cometh: but the earth abideth
for ever.
The sun also ariseth.
Ecclesiastes 1:4–5

141 The thing that hath been, it is that which shall
be; and that which is done is that which shall
be done: and there is no new thing under the
sun.
Ecclesiastes 1:9. Often quoted as "There's nothing
new under the sun."

142 He that increaseth knowledge increaseth
sorrow.
Ecclesiastes 1:18

143 To every thing there is a season, and a time to
every purpose under the heaven:
A time to be born, and a time to die; a time to
plant, and a time to pluck up that which is
planted.
Ecclesiastes 3:1–2
See Pete Seeger 3

144 A time to kill, and a time to heal; a time to
break down, and a time to build up;
A time to weep, and a time to laugh; a time to
mourn, and a time to dance.
Ecclesiastes 3:3–4

145 A time to cast away stones, and a time to
gather stones together; a time to embrace,
and a time to refrain from embracing;
A time to get, and a time to lose; a time to
keep, and a time to cast away;
A time to rend, and a time to sew; a time to
keep silence, and a time to speak;
A time to love, and a time to hate; a time of
war, and a time of peace.
Ecclesiastes 3:5–8

146 A threefold cord is not quickly broken.
Ecclesiastes 4:12

147 A man hath no better thing under the sun,
than to eat, and to drink, and to be merry.
Ecclesiastes 8:15
See Bible 170

148 Whatsoever thy hand findeth to do, do it with
thy might; for there is no work, nor device,
nor knowledge, nor wisdom, in the grave,
whither thou goest.
Ecclesiastes 9:10

149 I returned, and saw under the sun, that the
race is not to the swift, nor the battle to the
strong, neither yet bread to the wise, nor
yet riches to men of understanding, nor yet
favor to men of skill; but time and chance
happeneth to them all.
Ecclesiastes 9:11
See Keough 1

150 Wine maketh merry: but money answereth all
things.
Ecclesiastes 10:19

151 Cast thy bread upon the waters: for thou shalt
find it after many days.
Ecclesiastes 11:1

152 And desire shall fail: because man goeth to
his long home, and the mourners go about
the streets:
Or ever the silver cord be loosed, or the
golden bowl be broken, or the pitcher be
broken at the fountain, or the wheel broken
at the cistern.
Then shall the dust return to the earth as it
was: and the spirit shall return unto God
who gave it.
Ecclesiastes 12:5–7

153 Of making many books there is no end; and
much study is a weariness of the flesh.
Ecclesiastes 12:12

154 Fear God, and keep his commandments: for
this is the whole duty of man.
Ecclesiastes 12:13

Song of Solomon

155 The song of songs, which is Solomon's.
Song of Solomon 1:1

156 I am black, but comely.
Song of Solomon 1:5
See Langston Hughes 5; Political Slogans 8

157 I am the rose of Sharon, and the lily of the
valleys.
Song of Solomon 2:1

158 The time of the singing of birds is come, and
the voice of the turtle is heard in our land.
Song of Solomon 2:12

159 Love is strong as death; jealousy is cruel as the
grave.
Song of Solomon 8:6

Isaiah

160 Come now, and let us reason together, saith
the Lord: though your sins be as scarlet, they
shall be as white as snow.
Isaiah 1:18

161 They shall beat their swords into plowshares,
and their spears into pruninghooks: nation
shall not lift up sword against nation, neither
shall they learn war any more.
Isaiah 2:4

162 What mean ye that ye beat my people to
pieces, and grind the faces of the poor?
Isaiah 3:15

163 I saw also the Lord sitting upon a throne, high
and lifted up, and his train filled the temple.
Above it stood the seraphims: each one had
six wings; with twain he covered his face,
and with twain he covered his feet, and
with twain he did fly.
And one cried unto another, and said, Holy,
holy, holy, is the Lord of hosts: the whole
earth is full of his glory.
Isaiah 6:1–3

164 Then said I, Lord, how long?
Isaiah 6:11

165 Behold, a virgin shall conceive, and bear a
son, and shall call his name Immanuel.
Butter and honey shall he eat, that he may
know to refuse the evil, and choose the good.
Isaiah 7:14–15

166 For unto us a child is born, unto us a son is
given: and the government shall be upon
his shoulder: and his name shall be called
Wonderful, Counsellor, The mighty God,
The everlasting Father, The Prince of Peace.
Of the increase of his government and peace
there shall be no end.
Isaiah 9:6–7

167 The wolf also shall dwell with the lamb, and
the leopard shall lie down with the kid; and
the calf and the young lion and the fatling
together; and a little child shall lead them.
Isaiah 11:6. Popularly quoted as "The lion shall lie
down with the lamb."
See Woody Allen 25

168 How art thou fallen from heaven, O Lucifer,
son of the morning!
Isaiah 14:12

169 Watchman, what of the night?
Isaiah 21:11

170 Let us eat and drink; for to morrow we shall
die.
Isaiah 22:13
See Bible 147

171 Lo, thou trusteth in the staff of this broken
reed.
Isaiah 36:6

172 The voice of him that crieth in the wilderness,
Prepare ye the way of the Lord, make straight
in the desert a highway for our God.
Isaiah 40:3
See Bible 199

173 Every valley shall be exalted, and every
mountain and hill shall be made low: and the
crooked shall be made straight, and the rough
places plain.
Isaiah 40:4

174 There is no peace, saith the Lord, unto the
wicked.
Isaiah 48:22

175 How beautiful upon the mountains are the
feet of him that bringeth good tidings, that
publisheth peace; that bringeth good tidings
of good, that publisheth salvation.
Isaiah 52:7

176 They shall see eye to eye.
Isaiah 52:8

177 He is despised and rejected of men; a man of
sorrows, and acquainted with grief.
Isaiah 53:3

178 He is brought as a lamb to the slaughter.
Isaiah 53:7

179 Arise, shine; for thy light is come, and the
glory of the Lord is risen upon thee.
Isaiah 60:1

180 I am holier than thou.
Isaiah 65:5

Jeremiah

181 The harvest is past, the summer is ended, and
we are not saved.
Jeremiah 8:20

182 Is there no balm in Gilead?
Jeremiah 8:22

183 Can the Ethiopian change his skin, or the
leopard his spots?
Jeremiah 13:23

184 The fathers have eaten a sour grape, and the
children's teeth are set on edge.
Jeremiah 31:29

Ezekiel

185 As it were a wheel in the middle of a wheel.
Ezekiel 1:16

186 As is the mother, so is her daughter.
Ezekiel 16:44
See Proverbs 201

187 The king of Babylon stood at the parting of
the way.
Ezekiel 21:21

188 O ye dry bones, hear the word of the Lord.
Ezekiel 37:4
See Folk and Anonymous Songs 20

Daniel

189 His legs of iron, his feet part of iron and part
of clay.
Daniel 2:33

190 And this is the writing that was written,
MENE, MENE, TEKEL, UPHARSIN.
This is the interpretation of the thing: MENE;
God hath numbered thy kingdom, and
finished it.

TEKEL; Thou art weighed in the balances, and
art found wanting.
PERES; Thy kingdom is divided, and given to
the Medes and Persians.
Daniel 5:25–28

191 Now, O king, establish the decree, and sign
the writing, that it be not changed, according
to the law of the Medes and Persians, which
altereth not.
Daniel 6:8

Hosea

192 They have sown the wind, and they shall reap
the whirlwind.
Hosea 8:7

Joel

193 Your old men shall dream dreams, your
young men shall see visions.
Joel 2:28

Micah

194 What doth the Lord require of thee, but to do
justly, and to love mercy, and to walk humbly
with thy God?
Micah 6:8

Apocrypha

195 Let us now praise famous men, and our
fathers that begat us.
Apocrypha: Ecclesiasticus 44:1

Matthew

196 Now when Jesus was born in Bethlehem
of Judaea in the days of Herod the king,
behold, there came wise men from the east
to Jerusalem,
Saying, Where is he that is born King of the
Jews? for we have seen his star in the east,
and are come to worship him.
Matthew 2:1–2

197 They saw the young child with Mary his
mother, and fell down, and worshipped him:
and . . . they presented unto him gifts; gold,
and frankincense, and myrrh.
Matthew 2:11

198 Repent ye: for the kingdom of heaven is at
hand.
Matthew 3:2

199 The voice of one crying in the wilderness,
Prepare ye the way of the Lord, make his
paths straight.
Matthew 3:3
See Bible 172

200 O generation of vipers, who hath warned you
to flee from the wrath to come?
Matthew 3:7

201 This is my beloved Son, in whom I am well
pleased.
Matthew 3:17

202 It is written, man shall not live by bread
alone, but by every word that proceedeth out
of the mouth of God.
Matthew 4:4. Echoes Deuteronomy 8:3.
See Bible 72

203 Follow me, and I will make you fishers of men.
Matthew 4:19

204 Blessed are the poor in spirit: for theirs is the
kingdom of heaven.
Blessed are they that mourn: for they shall be
comforted.
Matthew 5:3–4

205 Blessed are the meek: for they shall inherit
the earth.
Matthew 5:5
See Bible 112; Getty 1; Heinlein 16; John M. Henry 1

206 Blessed are they which do hunger and thirst
after righteousness: for they shall be filled.
Blessed are the merciful: for they shall obtain
mercy.
Blessed are the pure in heart: for they shall
see God.
Blessed are the peacemakers: for they shall be
called the children of God.
Matthew 5:6–9

207 Ye are the salt of the earth: but if the salt have
lost his savor, wherewith shall it be salted?
Matthew 5:13

208 Ye are the light of the world. A city that is set
on an hill cannot be hid.
Neither do men light a candle, and put it
under a bushel, but on a candlestick; and it
giveth light unto all that are in the house.

Let your light so shine before men, that they
may see your good works, and glorify your
Father which is in heaven.
Think not that I am come to destroy the law,
or the prophets: I am not come to destroy,
but to fulfill.
Matthew 5:14–17
See Winthrop 1

209 Whosoever looketh on a woman to lust after
her hath committed adultery with her already
in his heart.
Matthew 5:28
See Jimmy Carter 4

210 And if thy right eye offend thee, pluck it out,
and cast it from thee: for it is profitable
for thee that one of thy members should
perish, and not that thy whole body should
be cast into hell.
And if thy right hand offend thee, cut it off.
Matthew 5:29–30

211 Resist not evil: but whosoever shall smite thee
on thy right cheek, turn to him the other also.
Matthew 5:39

212 Whosoever shall compel thee to go a mile, go
with him twain.
Matthew 5:41

213 He maketh his sun to rise on the evil and on
the good, and sendeth rain on the just and on
the unjust.
Matthew 5:45
See Lord Bowen 2

214 When thou doest alms, let not thy left hand
know what thy right hand doeth.
Matthew 6:3

215 After this manner therefore pray ye: Our
Father which art in heaven, Hallowed be
thy name.
Thy kingdom come. Thy will be done in earth,
as it is in heaven.
Give us this day our daily bread.
And forgive us our debts, as we forgive our
debtors.
And lead us not into temptation, but deliver
us from evil: For thine is the kingdom, and
the power, and the glory, for ever. Amen.
Matthew 6:9–13
See Book of Common Prayer 12; Missal 5

216 Lay not up for yourselves treasures upon
earth, where moth and rust doth corrupt,
and where thieves break through and steal:
But lay up for yourselves treasures in heaven.
Matthew 6:19–20

217 Where your treasure is, there will your heart
be also.
Matthew 6:21

218 No man can serve two masters. . . . Ye cannot
serve God and mammon.
Matthew 6:24

219 Consider the lilies of the field, how they grow;
they toil not, neither do they spin:
And yet I say unto you, That even Solomon in
all his glory was not arrayed like one of these.
Matthew 6:28–29

220 Take therefore no thought for the morrow: for
the morrow shall take thought for the things
of itself. Sufficient unto the day is the evil
thereof.
Matthew 6:34

221 Judge not, that ye be not judged.
Matthew 7:1
See Lincoln 49

222 Why beholdest thou the mote that is in thy
brother's eye, but considerest not the beam
that is in thine own eye?
Matthew 7:3

223 Neither cast ye your pearls before swine.
Matthew 7:6

224 Ask, and it shall be given you; seek, and ye shall
find; knock, and it shall be opened unto you.
Matthew 7:7

225 Therefore all things whatsoever ye would that
men should do to you, do ye even so to them:
for this is the law and the prophets.
Matthew 7:12
See Aristotle 12; Chesterfield 4; Confucius 9; Hillel 2

226 Wide is the gate, and broad is the way, that
leadeth to destruction, and many there be that
go in thereat.
Matthew 7:13

227 Strait is the gate, and narrow is the way,
which leadeth unto life, and few there be that
find it.
Matthew 7:14

228 Beware of false prophets, which come to you
in sheep's clothing, but inwardly they are
ravening wolves.
Matthew 7:15

229 By their fruits ye shall know them.
Matthew 7:20

230 A foolish man, which built his house upon
the sand.
Matthew 7:26

231 But the children of the kingdom shall be
cast out into outer darkness: there shall be
weeping and gnashing of teeth.
Matthew 8:12

232 The foxes have holes, and the birds of the
air have nests; but the Son of man hath not
where to lay his head.
Matthew 8:20

233 Let the dead bury their dead.
Matthew 8:22
See Longfellow 3

234 Neither do men put new wine into old bottles.
Matthew 9:17

235 Whosoever shall not receive you, nor hear
your words, when ye depart out of that house
or city, shake off the dust of your feet.
Matthew 10:14

236 Be ye therefore wise as serpents, and
harmless as doves.
Matthew 10:16

237 I came not to send peace, but a sword.
Matthew 10:34

238 He that is not with me is against me.
Matthew 12:30

239 Some seeds fell by the wayside.
Matthew 13:4

240 The kingdom of heaven is like unto a
merchant man, seeking goodly pearls:
Who, when he had found one pearl of great
price, went and sold all that he had, and
bought it.
Matthew 13:45–46

241 A prophet is not without honor, save in his
own country, and in his own house.
Matthew 13:57

242 Be of good cheer; it is I; be not afraid.
Matthew 14:27

243 O thou of little faith, wherefore didst thou
doubt?
Matthew 14:31

244 If the blind lead the blind, both shall fall into
the ditch.
Matthew 15:14

245 Can ye not discern the signs of the times?
Matthew 16:3

246 Thou art Peter, and upon this rock I will build
my church; and the gates of hell shall not
prevail against it.
And I will give unto thee the keys of the
kingdom of heaven.
Matthew 16:18–19

247 Get thee behind me, Satan.
Matthew 16:23

248 Except ye be converted, and become as little
children, ye shall not enter into the kingdom
of heaven.
Matthew 18:3

249 What therefore God hath joined together, let
not man put asunder.
Matthew 19:6
See Book of Common Prayer 19

250 It is easier for a camel to go through the eye
of a needle, than for a rich man to enter into
the kingdom of God.
Matthew 19:24

251 With God all things are possible.
Matthew 19:26

252 But many that are first shall be last; and the
last shall be first.
Matthew 19:30

253 They made light of it.
Matthew 22:5

254 Many are called, but few are chosen.
Matthew 22:14

255 Render therefore unto Caesar the things
which are Caesar's; and unto God the things
that are God's.
Matthew 22:21

256 Thou shalt love the Lord thy God with all thy
heart, and with all thy soul, and with all thy
mind.
This is the first and great commandment.
And the second is like unto it, Thou shalt love
thy neighbor as thyself.
Matthew 22:37–39
See Bible 65

257 Ye blind guides, which strain at a gnat, and
swallow a camel.
Matthew 23:24

258 Whited sepulchres, which indeed appear
beautiful outward, but are within full of dead
men's bones.
Matthew 23:27

259 Ye shall hear of wars and rumors of wars.
Matthew 24:6

260 For nation shall rise against nation, and
kingdom against kingdom.
Matthew 24:7

261 Heaven and earth shall pass away, but my
words shall not pass away.
Matthew 24:35

262 Well done, thou good and faithful servant . . .
enter thou into the joy of the lord.
Matthew 25:21

263 Lord, I knew thee that thou art an hard man,
reaping where thou hast not sown, and
gathering where thou hast not strawed:
And I was afraid, and went and hid thy talent
in the earth: lo, there thou hast that is thine.
Matthew 25:24–25

264 Unto every one that hath shall be given, and
he shall have abundance: but from him that
hath not shall be taken away even that which
he hath.
Matthew 25:29
See Kahn 1; Merton 4; Modern Proverbs 75

265 And before him shall be gathered all nations:
and he shall separate them one from another,
as a shepherd divideth his sheep from the
goats.
Matthew 25:32

266 I was a stranger, and ye took me in.
Matthew 25:35

267 And they covenanted with him [Judas Iscariot] for thirty pieces of silver.
Matthew 26:15

268 Jesus took bread, and blessed it, and brake it, and gave it to the disciples, and said, Take, eat; this is my body.
Matthew 26:26

269 This night, before the cock crow, thou [Peter] shalt deny me thrice.
Matthew 26:34

270 Watch and pray, that ye enter not into temptation: the spirit indeed is willing but the flesh is weak.
Matthew 26:41

271 All they that take the sword shall perish with the sword.
Matthew 26:52

272 He [Pontius Pilate] took water, and washed his hands before the multitude, saying, I am innocent of the blood of this just person: see ye to it.
Matthew 27:24

273 His blood be on us, and on our children.
Matthew 27:25

274 Jesus cried out with a loud voice, saying, Eli, Eli, lama sabachthani? that is to say, My God, my God, why hast thou forsaken me?
Matthew 27:46

Mark

275 The sabbath was made for man, and not man for the sabbath.
Mark 2:27

276 If a house be divided against itself, that house cannot stand.
Mark 3:25
See Lincoln 11

277 My name is Legion: for we are many.
Mark 5:9

278 For what shall it profit a man, if he shall gain the whole world, and lose his own soul?
Mark 8:36
See Bolt 3

279 Lord, I believe; help thou mine unbelief.
Mark 9:24

280 Suffer the little children to come unto me, and forbid them not: for of such is the kingdom of God.
Mark 10:14

281 Go ye into all the world, and preach the gospel to every creature.
Mark 16:15

Luke

282 Hail, thou that art highly favored, the Lord is with thee: blessed art thou among women.
Luke 1:28
See Anonymous (Latin) 3

283 My soul doth magnify the Lord.
Luke 1:46

284 For he hath regarded the low estate of his handmaiden: for, behold, from henceforth all generations shall call me blessed.
Luke 1:48

285 He hath scattered the proud in the imagination of their hearts.
He hath put down the mighty from their seats, and exalted them of low degree.
Luke 1:51–52

286 He hath filled the hungry with good things; and the rich he hath sent empty away.
Luke 1:53

287 She brought forth her firstborn son, and wrapped him in swaddling clothes, and laid him in a manger; because there was no room for them in the inn.
Luke 2:7

288 And there were in the same country shepherds abiding in the field, keeping watch over their flock by night.
And, lo, the angel of the Lord came upon them, and the glory of the Lord shone round about them: and they were sore afraid.
Luke 2:8–9

289 And the angel said unto them, Fear not: for, behold, I bring you good tidings of great joy, which shall be to all people.
For unto you is born this day in the city of David a Savior, which is Christ the Lord.
Luke 2:10–11

290 Glory to God in the highest, and on earth peace, good will toward men.
Luke 2:14

291 Wist ye not that I must be about my Father's business?
Luke 2:49

292 Physician, heal thyself.
Luke 4:23

293 No man, having put his hand to the plough, and looking back, is fit for the kingdom of God.
Luke 9:62

294 The laborer is worthy of his hire.
Luke 10:7

295 A certain man went down from Jerusalem to Jericho, and fell among thieves.
Luke 10:30

296 That which ye have spoken in the ear in closets shall be proclaimed upon the housetops.
Luke 12:3

297 For unto whomsoever much is given, of him shall be much required: and to whom men have committed much, of him they will ask the more.
Luke 12:48
See John Kennedy 6

298 Bring in hither the poor, and the maimed, and the halt, and the blind.
Luke 14:21

299 Bring hither the fatted calf, and kill it.
Luke 15:23

300 Make to yourselves friends of the mammon of unrighteousness; that, when ye fail, they may receive you into everlasting habitations.
Luke 16:9

301 The crumbs which fell from the rich man's table.
Luke 16:21

302 The beggar died, and was carried by the angels into Abraham's bosom.
Luke 16:22

303 The kingdom of God is within you.
Luke 17:21

304 Out of thine own mouth will I judge thee.
Luke 19:22

305 Not my will, but thine, be done.
Luke 22:42

306 Father, forgive them: for they know not what they do.
Luke 23:34

307 And when Jesus had cried with a loud voice, he said, Father, into thy hands I commend my spirit: and having said thus, he gave up the ghost.
Luke 23:46
See Bible 111

John

308 In the beginning was the Word, and the Word was with God, and the Word was God.
John 1:1

309 And the light shineth in darkness; and the darkness comprehended it not.
John 1:5

310 He was not that Light, but was sent to bear witness of that Light.
That was the true Light, which lighteth every man that cometh into the world.
John 1:8–9

311 And the Word was made flesh, and dwelt among us, (and we beheld his glory, the glory as of the only begotten of the Father), full of grace and truth.
John 1:14

312 Behold the Lamb of God, which taketh away the sin of the world.
John 1:29
See Missal 6

313 Woman, what have I to do with thee? mine hour is not yet come.
John 2:4

314 Except a man be born again, he cannot see the kingdom of God.
John 3:3
See Jimmy Carter 2

315 God so loved the world, that he gave his only begotten Son, that whosoever believeth in him should not perish, but have everlasting life.
John 3:16

316 I am the bread of life: he that cometh to me
shall never hunger; and he that believeth on
me shall never thirst.
John 6:35

317 Verily, verily, I say unto you, He that believeth
on me hath everlasting life.
John 6:47

318 He that is without sin among you, let him
first cast a stone at her.
John 8:7

319 And ye shall know the truth, and the truth
shall make you free.
John 8:32

320 I am the good shepherd: the good shepherd
giveth his life for the sheep.
John 10:11

321 I am the resurrection, and the life.
John 11:25

322 Jesus wept.
John 11:35

323 The poor always ye have with you.
John 12:8

324 In my Father's house are many mansions. . . .
I go to prepare a place for you.
John 14:2

325 I am the way, the truth, and the life: no man
cometh unto the Father, but by me.
John 14:6

326 Greater love hath no man than this, that a
man lay down his life for his friends.
John 15:13
See James Joyce 21

327 Whither goest thou?
John 16:5. Vulgate translation: Quo vadis?

328 Now Barabbas was a robber.
John 18:40
See Byron 34

329 Behold the man!
John 19:5. Vulgate translation: Ecce homo.

330 Touch me not.
John 20:17

Acts of the Apostles

331 Saul, Saul, why persecutest thou me?
Acts of the Apostles 9:4

332 It is hard for thee to kick against the pricks.
Acts of the Apostles 9:5

333 God is no respecter of persons.
Acts of the Apostles 10:34
See John Brown 2

334 Certain lewd fellows of the baser sort.
Acts of the Apostles 17:5

335 I found an altar with this inscription, TO THE
UNKNOWN GOD.
Acts of the Apostles 17:23

336 It is more blessed to give than to receive.
Acts of the Apostles 20:35

337 But Paul said, I am a man which am a Jew of
Tarsus, a city in Cilicia, a citizen of no mean
city.
Acts of the Apostles 21:39

338 I appeal unto Caesar.
Acts of the Apostles 25:11

339 Paul, thou art beside thyself; much learning
doth make thee mad.
Acts of the Apostles 26:24

340 Almost thou persuadest me to be a Christian.
Acts of the Apostles 26:28

Romans

341 A law unto themselves.
Romans 2:14

342 Who against hope believed in hope, that he
might become the father of many nations.
Romans 4:18

343 Christ being raised from the dead dieth no
more; death hath no more dominion over
him.
Romans 6:9
See Dylan Thomas 3

344 The wages of sin is death.
Romans 6:23

345 For the good that I would I do not: but the evil
which I would not, that I do.
Romans 7:19

346 Vengeance is mine; I will repay, saith the
Lord.
Romans 12:19

347 The powers that be are ordained of God.
Romans 13:1

I Corinthians

348 Absent in body, but present in spirit.
I Corinthians 5:3

349 It is better to marry than to burn.
I Corinthians 7:9

350 I am made all things to all men.
I Corinthians 9:22

351 For the earth is the Lord's and the fulness
thereof.
I Corinthians 10:26

352 If a woman have long hair, it is a glory to her.
I Corinthians 11:15

353 Though I have all faith; so that I could remove
mountains, and have not charity, I am
nothing.
And though I bestow all my goods to feed
the poor, and though I give my body to be
burned, and have not charity, it profiteth
me nothing.
Charity suffereth long, and is kind; charity
envieth not; charity vaunteth not itself, is
not puffed up.
I Corinthians 13:2–4

354 Beareth all things, believeth all things, hopeth
all things, endureth all things.
Charity never faileth.
I Corinthians 13:7–8

355 When I was a child, I spake as a child, I
understood as a child, I thought as a child:
but when I became a man, I put away
childish things.
For now we see through a glass, darkly; but
then face to face: now I know in part; but
then shall I know even as also I am known.
And now abideth faith, hope, charity, these
three; but the greatest of these is charity.
I Corinthians 13:11–13

356 And last of all he was seen of me also, as of
one born out of due time.
For I am the least of the apostles, that am
not meet to be called an apostle, because I
persecuted the church of God.
But by the grace of God I am what I am.
I Corinthians 15:8–10

357 The last enemy that shall be destroyed is death.
I Corinthians 15:26

358 In a moment, in the twinkling of an eye, at
the last trump: for the trumpet shall sound,
and the dead shall be raised incorruptible,
and we shall be changed.
I Corinthians 15:52

359 O death, where is thy sting? O grave, where is
thy victory?
I Corinthians 15:55
See W. C. Fields 17

II Corinthians

360 The letter killeth, but the spirit giveth life.
II Corinthians 3:6

361 God loveth a cheerful giver.
II Corinthians 9:7

362 For ye suffer fools gladly, seeing ye yourselves
are wise.
II Corinthians 11:19

363 There was given to me a thorn in the flesh,
the messenger of Satan to buffet me.
II Corinthians 12:7

Galatians

364 Ye are fallen from grace.
Galatians 5:4

365 Be not deceived; God is not mocked: for
whatsoever a man soweth, that shall he also
reap.
Galatians 6:7

Ephesians

366 Be ye angry and sin not: let not the sun go
down upon your wrath.
Ephesians 4:26

367 See then that ye walk circumspectly, not as
fools, but as wise,
Redeeming the time, because the days are evil.
Ephesians 5:15–16

368 For we wrestle not against flesh and blood,
but against principalities, against powers,
against the rulers of the darkness of this
world, against spiritual wickedness in high
places.
Wherefore take unto you the whole armor of
God, that ye may be able to withstand in the
evil day, and having done all, to stand.
Ephesians 6:12–13

Philippians

369 At the name of Jesus every knee should bow,
of things in heaven, and things in earth, and
things under the earth.
Philippians 2:10

370 Work out your own salvation with fear and
trembling.
Philippians 2:12

371 The peace of God, which passeth all
understanding, shall keep your hearts and
minds through Christ Jesus.
Philippians 4:7

Colossians

372 Let your speech be alway with grace, seasoned
with salt.
Colossians 4:6

I Thessalonians

373 Remembering without ceasing your work of
faith and labor of love.
I Thessalonians 1:3

I Timothy

374 Refuse profane and old wives' fables, and
exercise thyself rather unto godliness.
I Timothy 4:7

375 Use a little wine for thy stomach's sake.
I Timothy 5:23

376 For we brought nothing into this world, and it
is certain we can carry nothing out.
I Timothy 6:7
See Proverbs 288

377 The love of money is the root of all evil.
I Timothy 6:10. Often quoted as simply, "Money is
the root of all evil."

378 Fight the good fight of faith, lay hold on
eternal life.
I Timothy 6:12

II Timothy

379 I have fought a good fight, I have finished my
course, I have kept the faith.
II Timothy 4:7
See Adam Clayton Powell 3

Titus

380 Unto the pure all things are pure.
Titus 1:15

Hebrews

381 Faith is the substance of things hoped for, the
evidence of things not seen.
Hebrews 11:1

382 Be not forgetful to entertain strangers:
for thereby some have entertained angels
unawares.
Hebrews 13:2

I Peter

383 Giving honor unto the wife, as unto the
weaker vessel.
I Peter 3:7

384 Charity shall cover the multitude of sins.
I Peter 4:8

385 Be sober, be vigilant; because your adversary
the devil, as a roaring lion, walketh about,
seeking whom he may devour.
I Peter 5:8

II Peter

386 The dog is turned to his own vomit again.
II Peter 2:22
See Bible 136

I John

387 He is antichrist, that denieth the Father and
the Son.
I John 2:22

388 He that loveth not knoweth not God; for God
is love.
I John 4:8
See Samuel Butler (1835–1902) 10; Gypsy Rose Lee 1

389 There is no fear in love; but perfect love
casteth out fear.
I John 4:18

Revelation

390 I am Alpha and Omega, the beginning and
the ending, saith the Lord.
Revelation 1:8

391 Be thou faithful unto death, and I will give
thee a crown of life.
Revelation 2:10

392 Behold a pale horse: and his name that sat on
him was Death, and Hell followed with him.
Revelation 6:8

393 These are they which came out of great
tribulation, and have washed their robes, and
made them white in the blood of the Lamb.
Revelation 7:14

394 God shall wipe away all tears from their eyes.
Revelation 7:17

395 And when he had opened the seventh seal,
there was silence in heaven about the space of
half an hour.
Revelation 8:1

396 And that no man might buy or sell, save he
that had the mark, or the name of the beast,
or the number of his name.
Revelation 13:17

397 Let him that hath understanding count the
number of the beast: for it is the number
of a man; and his number is Six hundred
threescore and six.
Revelation 13:18

398 And he gathered them together into a place
called in the Hebrew tongue Armageddon.
Revelation 16:16

399 And God shall wipe away all tears from their
eyes; and there shall be no more death,
neither sorrow, nor crying, neither shall
there be any more pain: for the former
things are passed away.
And he that sat upon the throne said, Behold,
I make all things new.
Revelation 21:4–5

Geneva Bible

400 Esau selleth his birthright for a mess of
pottage.
Geneva Bible heading of Genesis chapter 25 (1560)

Marie François Bichat
French anatomist, 1771–1802

1 *La vie est l'ensemble des fonctions qui résistent à
la mort.*

Life is the ensemble of functions that resist
death.
Recherches Physiologiques sur la Vie et la Mort article 1
(1800)

Alexander M. Bickel
Romanian-born U.S. legal scholar, 1924–1974

1 No society, certainly not a large and
heterogeneous one, can fail in time to explode
if it is deprived of the arts of compromise, if
it knows no ways of muddling through. No
good society can be unprincipled; and no viable
society can be principle-ridden.
The Least Dangerous Branch ch. 2 (1962)

Isaac Bickerstaffe
Irish playwright, 1733–ca. 1808

1 I care for nobody, not I,
If no one cares for me.
Love in a Village act 1, sc. 2 (1762)

Joseph Biden
U.S. politician, 1942–

1 [*Of Barack Obama:*] I mean, you got the first
mainstream African-American who is articulate
and bright and clean and a nice-looking guy. I
mean, that's a storybook, man.
Quoted in *New York Observer,* 4 Feb. 2007

Ambrose Bierce
U.S. journalist and author, 1842–ca. 1914

1 Peyton Farquhar was dead; his body, with a
broken neck, swung gently from side to side
beneath the timbers of the Owl Creek bridge.
"An Occurrence at Owl Creek Bridge" (1891)

2 Aborigines, *n.* Persons of little worth found
cumbering the soil of a newly discovered
country. They soon cease to cumber; they
fertilize.
The Cynic's Word Book (1906)

3 Accomplice, *n.* One associated with another
in a crime, having guilty knowledge and
complicity, as an attorney who defends a
criminal, knowing him guilty. This view of
the attorney's position in the matter has not
hitherto commanded the assent of attorneys,
no one having offered them a fee for assenting.
The Cynic's Word Book (1906)

4 Acquaintance, *n.* A person whom we know well enough to borrow from, but not well enough to lend to. A degree of friendship called slight when its object is poor or obscure, and "intimate" when he is rich or famous.
The Cynic's Word Book (1906)

5 Adherent, *n.* A follower who has not yet obtained all that he expects to get.
The Cynic's Word Book (1906)

6 Admiration, *n.* Our polite recognition of another's resemblance to ourselves.
The Cynic's Word Book (1906)

7 Advice, *n.* The smallest current coin.
The Cynic's Word Book (1906)

8 Age, *n.* That period of life in which we compound for the vices that remain by reviling those that we have no longer the vigor to commit.
The Cynic's Word Book (1906)

9 Alliance, *n.* In international politics, the union of two thieves who have their hands so deeply inserted in each other's pocket that they cannot separately plunder a third.
The Cynic's Word Book (1906)

10 Alone, *adj.* In bad company.
The Cynic's Word Book (1906)

11 Ambition, *n.* An overmastering desire to be vilified by enemies while living and made ridiculous by friends when dead.
The Cynic's Word Book (1906)

12 Applause, *n.* The echo of a platitude.
The Cynic's Word Book (1906)

13 Architect, *n.* One who drafts a plan of your house, and plans a draft of your money.
The Cynic's Word Book (1906)

14 Asperse, *v.t.* Maliciously to ascribe to another vicious actions which one has not had the temptation and opportunity to commit.
The Cynic's Word Book (1906)

15 Auctioneer, *n.* The man who proclaims with a hammer that he has picked a pocket with his tongue.
The Cynic's Word Book (1906)

16 Back, *n.* That part of your friend which it is your privilege to contemplate in your adversity.
The Cynic's Word Book (1906)

17 Befriend, *v.t.* To make an ingrate.
The Cynic's Word Book (1906)

18 Belladonna, *n.* In Italian a beautiful lady; in English a deadly poison. A striking example of the essential identity of the two tongues.
The Cynic's Word Book (1906)

19 Bore, *n.* A person who talks when you wish him to listen.
The Cynic's Word Book (1906)

20 Bride, *n.* A woman with a fine prospect of happiness behind her.
The Cynic's Word Book (1906)

21 Buddhism, *n.* A preposterous form of religious error perversely preferred by about three-fourths of the human race.
Wasp (San Francisco), 21 May 1881

22 Cartesian, *adj.* Relating to Descartes, a famous philosopher, author of the celebrated dictum, *Cogito, ergo sum*—whereby he was pleased to suppose he demonstrated the reality of human existence. The dictum might be improved, however, thus: *Cogito cogito, ergo cogito sum*—"I think that I think, therefore I think that I am"; as close an approach to certainty as any philosopher has yet made.
The Cynic's Word Book (1906)
See Descartes 4

23 Common-law, *n.* The will and pleasure of the judge.
Wasp (San Francisco), 5 Aug. 1881

24 Confidant, Confidante, *n.* One entrusted by A with the secrets of B confided to himself by C.
The Cynic's Word Book (1906)

25 Conservative, *n.* A statesman who is enamored of existing evils, as distinguished from the Liberal, who wishes to replace them with others.
The Cynic's Word Book (1906)

26 Consolation, *n.* The knowledge that a better man is more unfortunate than yourself.
The Cynic's Word Book (1906)

27 Consul, *v.t.* In American politics, a person who having failed to secure an office from the people is given one by the Administration on condition that he leave the country.
The Cynic's Word Book (1906)

28 Consult, *v.* To seek another's approval of a course already decided on.
The Cynic's Word Book (1906)

29 Corrupt, *adj.* In politics, holding an office of trust or profit.
Wasp (San Francisco), 7 Oct. 1881

30 Cynic, *n.* A blackguard whose faulty vision sees things as they are, not as they ought to be. Hence the custom among the Scythians of plucking out a cynic's eyes to improve his vision.
The Cynic's Word Book (1906)

31 Dawn, *n.* The time when men of reason go to bed. Certain old men prefer to rise at about that time, taking a cold bath and a long walk, with an empty stomach, and otherwise mortifying the flesh. They then point with pride to these practices as the cause of their sturdy health and ripe years; the truth being that they are hearty and old, not because of their habits, but in spite of them. The reason we find only robust persons doing this thing is that it has killed all the others who have tried it.
The Cynic's Word Book (1906)

32 Deliberation, *n.* The act of examining one's bread to determine which side it is buttered on.
The Cynic's Word Book (1906)

33 Demagogue, *n.* A political opponent.
Wasp (San Francisco), 20 Jan. 1882

34 Dictionary, *n.* A malevolent literary device for cramping the growth of language and making it hard and inelastic. This dictionary, however, is a most useful work.
The Cynic's Word Book (1906)

35 Diplomacy, *n.* The patriotic art of lying for one's country.
The Cynic's Word Book (1906)

36 Distress, *n.* A disease incurred by exposure to the prosperity of a friend.
The Cynic's Word Book (1906)

37 Effect, *n.* The second of two phenomena which always occur together in the same order. The first, called a Cause, is said to generate the other—which is no more sensible than it would be for one who has never seen a dog except in the pursuit of a rabbit to declare the rabbit the cause of the dog.
The Cynic's Word Book (1906)

38 Egotist, *n.* A person of low taste, more interested in himself than in me.
The Cynic's Word Book (1906)

39 Elysium, *n.* An imaginary delightful country which the ancients foolishly believed to be inhabited by the spirits of the good. This ridiculous and mischievous fable was swept off the face of the earth by the early Christians— may their souls be happy in Heaven!
The Cynic's Word Book (1906)

40 Equal, *adj.* As bad as something else.
Wasp (San Francisco), 24 May 1884

41 Err, *v.i.* To believe or act in a way contrary to my beliefs and actions.
Wasp (San Francisco), 24 May 1884

42 Eucharist, *n.* A sacred feast of the religious sect of Theophagi. A dispute once unhappily arose among the members of this sect as to what it was that they ate. In this controversy some five hundred thousand have already been slain, and the question is still unsettled.
The Cynic's Word Book (1906)

43 Expediency, *n.* The father of all the virtues.
Wasp (San Francisco), 7 June 1884

44 Faith, *n.* Belief without evidence in what is told by one who speaks without knowledge, of things without parallel.
The Cynic's Word Book (1906)

45 Fidelity, *n.* A virtue peculiar to those who are about to be betrayed.
The Cynic's Word Book (1906)

46 Forbidden, *pp.* Invested with a new and irresistible charm.
Wasp (San Francisco), 13 Dec. 1884

47 Forefinger, *n.* The finger commonly used in pointing out two malefactors.
The Cynic's Word Book (1906)

48 Friendless, *n.* Having no favors to bestow. Destitute of fortune. Addicted to utterance of truth and common sense.
The Cynic's Word Book (1906)

49 Future, *n.* That period of time in which our affairs prosper, our friends are true, and our happiness is assured.
The Cynic's Word Book (1906)

50 Generous, *adj.* Originally this word meant noble by birth and was rightly applied to a great multitude of persons. It now means noble by nature, and is taking a bit of a rest.
The Cynic's Word Book (1906)

51 Genuine, *adj.* Real, veritable, as, A genuine counterfeit, Genuine hypocrisy, etc.
Wasp (San Francisco), 28 Feb. 1885

52 Gold, *n.* A yellow metal greatly prized for its convenience in the various kinds of robbery known as trade. The word was formerly spelled "God"—the *l* was inserted to distinguish it from the name of another and inferior deity.
Wasp (San Francisco), 7 May 1885

53 Gratitude, *n.* A sentiment lying midway between a benefit received and a benefit expected.
Wasp (San Francisco), 28 May 1885

54 Gum, *n.* A substance greatly used by young women in place of a contented spirit and religious consolation.
Wasp (San Francisco), 4 Apr. 1885

55 Habit, *n.* A shackle for the free.
The Cynic's Word Book (1906)

56 Happiness, *n.* An agreeable sensation arising from contemplating the misery of another.
The Cynic's Word Book (1906)

57 Harmonists, *n.* A sect of Protestants, now extinct, who came from Europe in the beginning of the last century and were distinguished for the bitterness of their internal controversies and dissensions.
The Cynic's Word Book (1906)

58 Hatred, *n.* A sentiment appropriate to the occasion of another's success or superiority.
The Cynic's Word Book (1906)

59 Haughty, *adj.* Proud and disdainful, like a waiter.
Wasp (San Francisco), 25 Apr. 1885

60 Heaven, *n.* A place where the wicked cease from troubling you with talk of their personal affairs, and the good listen with attention while you expound your own.
The Cynic's Word Book (1906)

61 Historian, *n.* A broad-gauge gossip.
The Cynic's Word Book (1906)

62 Homesick, *adj.* Dead broke abroad.
Wasp (San Francisco), 18 July 1885

63 Idolator, *n.* One who professes a religion which we do not believe, with a symbolism different from our own. A person who thinks more of an image on a pedestal than of an image on a coin.
Wasp (San Francisco), 29 Aug. 1885

64 Immigrant, *n.* An unenlightened person who thinks one country better than another.
The Cynic's Word Book (1906)

65 Impunity, *n.* Wealth.
The Cynic's Word Book (1906)

66 Inhumanity, *n.* One of the signal and characteristic qualities of humanity.
Wasp (San Francisco), 17 Oct. 1885

67 Interpreter, *n.* One who enables two persons of different languages to understand each other by repeating to each what it would have been to the interpreter's advantage for the other to have said.
The Cynic's Word Book (1906)

68 Joy, *n.* An emotion variously excited, but in its highest degree arising from the contemplation of grief in another.
Wasp (San Francisco), 9 Jan. 1886

69 Labor, *n.* One of the processes by which A acquires property for B.
The Cynic's Word Book (1906)

70 Lawful, *adj.* Compatible with the will of a judge having jurisdiction.
The Cynic's Word Book (1906)

71 Legislator, *n.* A person who goes to the capital of his country to increase his own; one who makes laws and money.
Wasp (San Francisco), 19 June 1886

72 Lexicographer, *n.* A pestilent fellow who, under the pretense of recording some particular stage in the development of a language, does what he can to arrest its growth, stiffen its flexibility, and mechanize its methods. For your lexicographer, having written his dictionary, comes to be considered "as one having authority," whereas his function is only to make a record, not to give a law. The natural servility of the human understanding having invested him with judicial power, surrenders its right of reason and submits itself to a chronicle as if it were a statute.
The Cynic's Word Book (1906)

73 Liar, *n.* A lawyer with a roving commission.
The Cynic's Word Book (1906)

74 Literally, *adv.* Figuratively, as: "The pond was literally full of fish"; "The ground was literally alive with snakes," etc.
San Francisco Examiner, 4 Sept. 1887

75 Litigant, *n.* A person about to give up his skin for the hope of retaining his bones.
The Cynic's Word Book (1906)

76 Loquacity, *n.* A disorder which renders the sufferer unable to curb his tongue when you wish to talk.
The Devil's Dictionary (1911)

77 Mad, *adj.* Affected with a high degree of intellectual independence; not conforming to standards of thought, speech, and action derived by the conformants from study of themselves; at odds with the majority; in short, unusual.
The Devil's Dictionary (1911)

78 Mammon, *n.* The god of the world's leading religion. His chief temple is in the holy city of New York.
The Devil's Dictionary (1911)

79 Manna, *n.* A food miraculously given to the Israelites in the wilderness. When it was no longer supplied to them they settled down and tilled the soil, fertilizing it, as a rule, with the bodies of the original occupants.
The Devil's Dictionary (1911)

80 Marriage, *n.* The state or condition of a community consisting of a master, a mistress, and two slaves, making in all, two.
The Devil's Dictionary (1911)

81 Mythology, *n.* The body of a primitive people's beliefs concerning its origin, early history, heroes, deities, and so forth, as distinguished from the true accounts which it invents later.
The Devil's Dictionary (1911)

82 Oath, *n.* In law, a solemn appeal to the Deity, made binding upon the conscience by a penalty for perjury.
The Cynic's Word Book (1906)

83 Occident, *n.* The part of the world lying west (or east) of the Orient. It is largely inhabited by Christians, a powerful subtribe of the Hypocrites, whose principal industries are murder and cheating, which they are pleased to call "war" and "commerce."
The Devil's Dictionary (1911)

84 Ocean, *n.* A body of water occupying about two-thirds of a world made for man—who has no gills.
The Devil's Dictionary (1911)

85 Opera, *n.* A play representing life in another world, whose inhabitants have no speech but song, no motions but gestures, and no postures but attitudes. All acting is simulation, and the word *simulation* is from *simia,* an ape; but in opera the actor takes for his model *Simia audibilis* (or *Pithecanthropos stentor*)—the ape that howls.

The actor apes a man—at least in shape;
The opera performer apes an ape.
The Devil's Dictionary (1911)

86 Orphan, *n.* A living person whom death has deprived of the power of filial ingratitude.
The Devil's Dictionary (1911)

87 Outdo, *v.t.* To make an enemy.
The Devil's Dictionary (1911)

88 Pain, *n.* An uncomfortable frame of mind that may have a physical basis in something that is being done to the body, or may be purely mental, caused by the good fortune of another.
The Devil's Dictionary (1911)

89 Palace, *n.* A fine and costly residence, particularly that of a great official. The residence of a high dignitary of the Christian Church is called a palace; that of the Founder of his religion was known as a field, or wayside. There is progress.
The Devil's Dictionary (1911)

90 Palmistry, *n.* The 947th method (according to Mimbleshaw's classification) of obtaining money by false pretences. It consists in "reading character" in the wrinkles made by closing the hand. The pretence is not altogether false; character can really be read very accurately in this way, for the wrinkles in every hand submitted plainly spell the word "dupe." The imposture consists in not reading it aloud.
The Devil's Dictionary (1911)

91 Past, *n.* That part of Eternity with some small fraction of which we have a slight and regrettable acquaintance. A moving line called the Present parts it from an imaginary period known as the Future. These two grand divisions of Eternity, of which the one is continually effacing the other, are entirely unlike. The one is dark with sorrow and disappointment, the other bright with prosperity and joy. . . . Yet the Past is the Future of yesterday, the Future is the Past of to-morrow. They are one—the knowledge and the dream.
The Devil's Dictionary (1911)

92 Patience, *n.* A minor form of despair, disguised as a virtue.
The Devil's Dictionary (1911)

93 Patriot, *n.* One to whom the interests of a part seem superior to those of the whole. The dupe of statesmen and the tool of conquerors.
The Devil's Dictionary (1911)

94 Patriotism, *n.* . . . . In Dr. Johnson's famous dictionary patriotism is defined as the last resort of a scoundrel. With all due respect to an enlightened but inferior lexicographer I beg to submit that it is the first.
The Devil's Dictionary (1911)
See Samuel Johnson 80

95 Peace, *n.* In international affairs, a period of cheating between two periods of fighting.
The Devil's Dictionary (1911)

96 Penitent, *adj.* Undergoing or awaiting punishment.
The Devil's Dictionary (1911)

97 Piety, *n.* Reverence for the Supreme Being, based on His supposed resemblance to man.
The pig is taught by sermons and epistles
To think the God of Swine has snouts and bristles.
The Devil's Dictionary (1911)

98 Pillage, *v.* To carry on business candidly.
New York American, 22 Feb. 1906

99 Plagiarize, *v.* To take the thought or style of another writer whom one has never, never read.
The Devil's Dictionary (1911)

100 Plan, *v.t.* To bother about the best method of accomplishing an accidental result.
The Devil's Dictionary (1911)

101 Platonic, *adj.* . . . . Platonic Love is a fool's name for the affection between a disability and a frost.
The Devil's Dictionary (1911)

102 Please, *v.* To lay the foundation for a superstructure of imposition.
The Devil's Dictionary (1911)

103 Plebiscite, *n.* A popular vote to ascertain the will of the sovereign.
The Devil's Dictionary (1911)

104 Plutocracy, *n.* A republican form of government deriving its powers from the conceit of the governed—in thinking they govern.
New York American, 27 Jan. 1905

105 Polite, *adj.* Skilled in the art and practice of dissimulation.
New York American, 16 Mar. 1906

106 Politician, *n.* An eel in the fundamental mud upon which the superstructure of organized society is reared. When he wriggles he mistakes the agitation of his tail for the trembling of the edifice. As compared with the statesman, he suffers the disadvantage of being alive.
The Devil's Dictionary (1911)
See Thomas B. Reed 1; Truman 10

107 Politics, *n.* A strife of interests masquerading as a contest of principles. The conduct of public affairs for private advantage.
The Devil's Dictionary (1911)

108 Positive, *adj.* Mistaken at the top of one's voice.
The Devil's Dictionary (1911)

109 Pray, *v.* To ask that the laws of the universe be annulled in behalf of a single petitioner confessedly unworthy.
The Devil's Dictionary (1911)

110 Predict, *v.t.* To relate an event that has not occurred, is not occurring, and will not occur.
New York American, 30 May 1906

111 Preference, *n.* A sentiment, or frame of mind, induced by the erroneous belief that one thing is better than another.
The Devil's Dictionary (1911)

112 Present, *n.* Something given in expectation of something better. To-day's payment for to-morrow's service.
New York American, 30 May 1906

113 Present, *n.* That part of eternity dividing the domain of disappointment from the realm of hope.
The Devil's Dictionary (1911)

114 President, *n.* The leading figure in a small group of men of whom—and of whom only—it is positively known that immense numbers of their countrymen did not want any of them for President.
The Devil's Dictionary (1911). Bierce had earlier written in the *San Francisco Examiner*, 3 Nov. 1889 (addressing the wife of Benjamin Harrison): "With a single exception, your husband is the only man in the United States of whom it is certainly known that several millions of his fellow citizens did not wish him to be President this time."

115 Pretty, *adj.* Vain, conceited, as "a pretty girl." Tiresome, as "a pretty picture."
New York American, 14 June 1906

116 Prevaricator, *n.* A liar in the caterpillar state.
The Devil's Dictionary (1911)

117 Projectile, *n.* The final arbiter in international disputes. Formerly these disputes were settled by physical contact of the disputants, with such simple arguments as the rudimentary logic of the times could supply—the sword, the spear, and so forth. With the growth of prudence in military affairs the projectile came more and more into favor, and is now held in high esteem by the most courageous. Its capital defect is that it requires personal attendance at the point of propulsion.
The Devil's Dictionary (1911)

118 Prophecy, *n.* The art and practice of selling one's credibility for future delivery.
The Devil's Dictionary (1911)

119 Public, *n.* The negligible factor in problems of legislation.
New York American, 28 June 1906

120 Quotation, *n.* The act of repeating erroneously the words of another. The words erroneously repeated.
The Devil's Dictionary (1911)

121 Rash, *adj.* Insensible to the value of our advice.
The Devil's Dictionary (1911)

122 Really, *adv.* Apparently.
The Devil's Dictionary (1911)

123 Rebel, *n.* A proponent of a new misrule who has failed to establish it.
The Devil's Dictionary (1911)

124 Recount, *n.* In American politics, another throw of the dice, accorded to the player against whom they are loaded.
The Devil's Dictionary (1911)

125 Religion, *n*. A daughter of Hope and Fear, explaining to Ignorance the nature of the Unknowable.
The Devil's Dictionary (1911)

126 Resident, *adj*. Unable to leave.
The Devil's Dictionary (1911)

127 Resolute, *adj*. Obstinate in a course that we approve.
The Devil's Dictionary (1911)

128 Responsibility, *n*. A detachable burden easily shifted to the shoulders of God, Fate, Fortune, Luck, or one's neighbor. In the days of astrology it was customary to unload it upon a star.
The Devil's Dictionary (1911)

129 Revolution, *n*. In politics, an abrupt change in the form of misgovernment. Specifically, in American history, the substitution of the rule of an Administration for that of a Ministry, whereby the welfare and happiness of the people were advanced a full half-inch.
The Devil's Dictionary (1911)

130 Robber, *n*. A candid man of affairs.
   It is related of Voltaire that one night he and some traveling companions lodged at a wayside inn. The surroundings were suggestive, and after supper they agreed to tell robber stories in turn. When Voltaire's turn came he said: "Once there was a Farmer-General of the Revenues." Saying nothing more, he was encouraged to continue. "That," he said, "is the story."
The Devil's Dictionary (1911)

131 Saint, *n*. A dead sinner revised and edited.
The Devil's Dictionary (1911)

132 Scriptures, *n*. The sacred books of our holy religion, as distinguished from the false and profane writings on which all other faiths are based.
The Devil's Dictionary (1911)

133 Self-esteem, *n*. An erroneous appraisement.
The Devil's Dictionary (1911)

134 Self-evident, *adj*. Evident to one's self and to nobody else.
The Devil's Dictionary (1911)

135 Selfish, *adj*. Devoid of consideration for the selfishness of others.
The Devil's Dictionary (1911)

136 Telephone, *n*. An invention of the devil which abrogates some of the advantages of making a disagreeable person keep his distance.
The Devil's Dictionary (1911)

137 Telescope, *n*. A device having a relation to the eye similar to that of the telephone to the ear, enabling distant objects to plague us with a multitude of needless details. Luckily it is unprovided with a bell summoning us to the sacrifice.
The Devil's Dictionary (1911)

138 Truthful, *adj*. Dumb and illiterate.
The Devil's Dictionary (1911)

139 Ultimatum, *n*. In diplomacy, a last demand before resorting to concessions.
The Devil's Dictionary (1911)

140 Year, *n*. A period of three hundred and sixty-five disappointments.
The Devil's Dictionary (1911)

141 All men are created equal. Some, it appears, are created a little more equal than others.
Wasp (San Francisco), 16 Sept. 1882
See Orwell 25

142 The bold and discerning writer who, recognizing the truth that language must grow by innovation if it grow at all, makes new words and uses the old in an unfamiliar sense has no following and is tartly reminded that "it isn't in the dictionary"—although down to the time of the first lexicographer (Heaven forgive him!) no author ever had used a word that *was* in the dictionary.
The Cynic's Word Book (1906)

143 You are not permitted to kill a woman that has injured you, but nothing forbids you to reflect that she is growing older every minute. You are avenged 1440 times a day.
The Cynic's Word Book (1906)

144 [*One-sentence book review:*] The covers of this book are too far apart.
Quoted in Robert H. Davis, Introduction to *Work of Stephen Crane* vol. 2 (1925). "I think the covers are too far apart" as a comment about a book appeared as early as 1899 (*Logansport* [Ind.] *Pharos*, 28 Sept.).

Stephen Biko
South African political activist, 1946–1977

1 The most potent weapon in the hands of the oppressor is the mind of the oppressed.

"White Racism and Black Consciousness" (paper presented at workshop sponsored by Abe Bailey Institute of Interracial Studies), Cape Town, South Africa, Jan. 1971

Josh Billings (Henry Wheeler Shaw)
U.S. humorist, 1818–1885

1 We hate those who will not take our advise, an despise them who do.

Josh Billings, Hiz Sayings (1866)

2 I hate to be a kicker, I always long for peace,
But the wheel that does the squeaking is the
    one that gets the grease.

"The Kicker" (ca. 1870). This citation is traditional among quotation dictionaries, but it must be noted that no Billings poem called "The Kicker" or with words like these has ever been verified. The earliest documented version appears in Cal Stewart, Uncle Josh Weathersby's "Punkin Centre" Stories (1903): "I don't believe in kickin', / It ain't apt to bring one peace; / But the wheel what squeaks the loudest / Is the one what gets the grease." The saying is now proverbial, often with a form like "the squeaky wheel gets the grease."

3 It is better tew know nothing than tew know what ain't so.

Harrisburg Telegraph, 7 May 1869

4 As scarce as truth is, the supply has always been in excess of the demand.

Quoted in Evan Esar, The Dictionary of Humorous Quotations (1949)

Osama bin Laden
Saudi Arabian jihadist, 1957–2011

1 To kill Americans and their allies, both civilian and military, is an individual duty of every Muslim who can, in any country where this is possible, until the Aqsa mosque and the Haram mosque are freed from their grip, and until their armies, shattered and broken-winged, depart from all the lands of Islam, incapable of threatening any Muslim.

Declaration of jihad, Feb. 1998

2 We calculated in advance the number of casualties from the enemy, who would be killed based on the position of the tower. We calculated that the floors that would be hit would be three or four floors. I was the most optimistic of them all. . . . Due to my experience in this field, I was thinking that the fire from the gas in the plane would melt the iron structure of the building and collapse the area where the plane hit and all the floors above it only. That is all that we had hoped for.

Videotape released by U.S. government, Dec. 2001

Arthur Binstead
British journalist, 1861–1914

1 The great secret in life [is] not to open your letters for a fortnight. At the expiration of that period you will find that nearly all of them have answered themselves.

Pitcher's Proverbs (1909)

Laurence Binyon
English poet, 1869–1943

1 They shall grow not old, as we that are left grow old.
Age shall not weary them, nor the years condemn.
At the going down of the sun and in the morning
We will remember them.

"For the Fallen" l. 13 (1914)

Bion
Greek poet, ca. 325 B.C.–ca. 255 B.C.

1 Boys throw stones at frogs for fun, but the frogs don't die for "fun," but in sober earnest.

Quoted in Plutarch, Moralia

John Bird
English actor and satirist, 1936–

1 That Was the Week That Was.

Title of BBC television series (1962–1963)

Augustine Birrell
English politician and writer, 1850–1933

1 That great dust-heap called "history."

Obiter Dicta "Carlyle" (1884)
See Trotsky 2

Elizabeth Bishop

U.S. poet, 1911–1979

1   Until everything
was rainbow, rainbow, rainbow!
And I let the fish go.
"The Fish" l. 74 (1946)

2 I knew that nothing stranger
had ever happened.
"In the Waiting Room" l. 72 (1976)

3 How had I come to be here
like them, and overhear
a cry of pain that could have
got loud and worse but hadn't?
"In the Waiting Room" l. 86 (1976)

4 The art of losing isn't hard to master;
so many things seem filled with the intent
to be lost that their loss is no disaster.
"One Art" l. 1 (1976)

Otto von Bismarck

German statesman, 1815–1898

1 The great questions of the day will not be
settled by means of speeches and majority
decisions . . . but by iron and blood.
Speech to Prussian Diet, 30 Sept. 1862. Bismarck
later used the variant "blood and iron" (*Blut und
Eisen*) frequently. The expression "blood and iron"
had also been used much earlier in Quintilian,
Declamationes.

2 Politics is not an exact science.
Speech to Prussian legislature, 18 Dec. 1863

3 Let us put Germany in the saddle, so to
speak—it already knows how to ride.
Speech to North German Reichstag, 11 Mar. 1867

4 [*Of his dispute with Pope Pius IX over papal
authority in Germany, alluding to Emperor Henry
IV's obeisance to Pope Gregory VII at Canossa in
1077:*] We will not go to Canossa.
Speech to Reichstag, 14 May 1872

5 Whoever speaks of Europe is wrong, [it is] a
geographical concept.
Marginal note on letter from A. M. Gorchakov, Nov.
1876
See Klemens von Metternich 1

6 [*Of possible German military intervention in
the Balkans:*] Not worth the healthy bones of a
single Pomeranian grenadier.
Speech to Reichstag, 5 Dec. 1876

7 I do not regard the procuring of peace as a
matter in which we should play the role of
arbiter between different opinions . . . more
that of an honest broker who really wants to
press the business forward.
Speech to Reichstag, 19 Feb. 1878

8 We Germans fear God, but nothing else in the
world.
Speech to Reichstag, 6 Feb. 1888

9 [*Remark to Meyer von Waldeck, 11 Aug. 1867:*]
Die Politik ist die Lehre von Möglichen.
Politics is the art of the possible.
Quoted in Heinz Amelung, *Bismarck-Worte* (1918)

10 One day the great European War [will] come out
of some damned foolish thing in the Balkans.
Attributed in Winston Churchill, *The World Crisis*
(1923)

Hugo L. Black

U.S. judge, 1886–1971

1 It is my belief that there *are* "absolutes" in our
Bill of Rights, and that they were put there on
purpose by men who knew what words meant,
and meant their prohibitions to be "absolutes."
"The Bill of Rights," *New York University Law Review,*
Apr. 1960

2 An unconditional right to say what one pleases
about public affairs is what I consider to be the
minimum guarantee of the First Amendment.
New York Times Co. v. Sullivan (concurring opinion)
(1964)

3 When I was 40, my doctor advised me that
a man in his forties shouldn't play tennis. I
heeded his advice carefully and could hardly
wait until I reached 50 to start again.
Quoted in *Think*, Feb. 1963

Black Hawk

Native American leader, 1767–1838

1 The pathway to glory is rough, and many
gloomy hours obscure it. May the Great Spirit
shed light on yours, and that you may never
experience the humiliation that the power of
the American government has reduced me to,
is the wish of him who, in his native forests,
was once as proud as you.
The Autobiography of Black Hawk "Dedication to
General Atkinson" (1833)

2 [*Surrender speech, 1832:*] The white men despise the Indians, and drive them from their homes. But the Indians are not deceitful. The white men speak bad of the Indian, and look at him spitefully. But the Indian does not tell lies; Indians do not steal. An Indian, who is as bad as the white men, could not live in our nation; he would be put to death, and eat up by the wolves.

Quoted in Samuel G. Drake, *Biography and History of the Indians of North America,* 11th ed. (1841)

Harry A. Blackmun
U.S. judge, 1908–1999

1 This right of privacy, whether it be founded in the Fourteenth Amendment's concept of personal liberty and restrictions upon state action, as we feel it is, or . . . in the Ninth Amendment's reservation of rights to the people, is broad enough to encompass a woman's decision whether or not to terminate her pregnancy.

Roe v. Wade (1973)

2 In order to get beyond racism, we must first take account of race. There is no other way. And in order to treat some persons equally, we must treat them differently.

University of California Regents v. Bakke (opinion concurring in part and dissenting in part) (1978)

3 For today, at least, the law of abortion stands undisturbed. For today, the women of this Nation still retain the liberty to control their destinies. But the signs are evident and very ominous, and a chill wind blows. I dissent.

Webster v. Reproductive Health Services (opinion concurring in part and dissenting in part) (1989)

4 From this day forward, I no longer shall tinker with the machinery of death.

Callins v. Collins (dissenting opinion) (1994)

William Blackstone
English jurist, 1723–1780

1 Man was formed for society.

Commentaries on the Laws of England introduction, sec. 2 (1765)

2 Whence it is that in our law the goodness of a custom depends upon its having been used time out of mind; or, in the solemnity of our legal phrase, time whereof the memory of man runneth not to the contrary.

Commentaries on the Laws of England introduction, sec. 3 (1765)

3 In all tyrannical governments the supreme magistracy, or the right both of *making* and of *enforcing* the laws, is vested in one and the same man, or one and the same body of men; and wherever these two powers are united together, there can be no public liberty.

Commentaries on the Laws of England bk. 1, ch. 2 (1765)

4 The king, moreover, is not only incapable of *doing* wrong, but even of *thinking* wrong: he can never mean to do an improper thing: in him is no folly or weakness.

Commentaries on the Laws of England bk. 1, ch. 7 (1765)

5 The royal navy of England hath ever been its greatest defence and ornament: it is its ancient and natural strength; the floating bulwark of the island.

Commentaries on the Laws of England bk. 1, ch. 13 (1765)

6 That the king can do no wrong, is a necessary and fundamental principle of the English Constitution.

Commentaries on the Laws of England bk. 3, ch. 17 (1768)
See Proverbs 160

7 All presumptive evidence of felony should be admitted cautiously; for the law holds, that it is better that ten guilty persons escape, than that one innocent suffer.

Commentaries on the Laws of England bk. 4, ch. 27 (1769)
See Fortescue 1; Benjamin Franklin 37; Maimonides 1; Voltaire 3

Antoinette Brown Blackwell
U.S. reformer, 1825–1921

1 Mr. Darwin . . . has failed to hold definitely before his mind the principle that the difference of sex, whatever it may consist in, must itself be subject to *natural selection* and to evolution.

The Sexes Throughout Nature "Sex and Evolution" (1875)

Otis Blackwell

U.S. songwriter, 1931–2002

1 You shake my nerves and you rattle my brain.
Too much love drives a man insane.
You broke my will,
But what a thrill.
Goodness gracious, great balls of fire!
"Great Balls of Fire" (song) (1957)

Tony Blair

British prime minister, 1953–

1 We should be tough on crime and tough on the
causes of crime.
Speech at Labor Party conference, Bournemouth,
England, 5 Feb. 1993

2 We need to build a relationship of trust not just
within a firm but within a society. By trust, I
mean the recognition of a mutual purpose for
which we work together and in which we all
benefit. It is a Stakeholder Economy in which
opportunity is available to all, advancement is
through merit, and from which no group or
class is set apart or excluded.
Speech, Singapore, 8 Jan. 1996

3 Ask me my three main priorities for
Government, and I'll tell you: education,
education and education.
Speech at Labor Party Conference, Blackpool,
England, 1 Oct. 1996

4 I think most people who have dealt with me,
think I'm a pretty straight sort of guy, and I
am.
Interview on BBC TV "On the Record" show, 16 Nov.
1997

5 I feel the hand of history upon our shoulders.
Statement to press on arriving at Hillsborough
Castle for talks on Northern Ireland, Belfast, 7 Apr.
1998

6 This is not a battle between the United States
of America and terrorism, but between the
free and democratic world and terrorism. We,
therefore, here in Britain stand shoulder to
shoulder with our American friends in this
hour of tragedy, and we, like them, will not rest
until this evil is driven from our world.
Statement, 11 Sept. 2001

7 [Remark on hearing of Princess Diana's death:]
She was the People's Princess, and that is
how she will stay . . . in our hearts and in our
memories forever.
Quoted in Times (London), 1 Sept. 1997. Earliest usage
of the term People's Princess was found in a locally
published souvenir booklet from Prince Charles and
Lady Diana's tour of Australia in 1983; a section of the
booklet was titled "Diana: The People's Princess."

Eubie Blake

U.S. ragtime musician, 1883–1983

1 [When asked, at the age of ninety-seven, at
what age the sex drive ends:] You'll have to ask
somebody older than me.
Quoted in Ned Sherrin, In His Anecdotage (1993)
See Pauline Metternich 1

James W. Blake

U.S. songwriter, 1862–1935

1 East Side, West Side, all around the town
The kids sang "ring around rosie," "London
Bridge is falling down"
Boys and girls together, me and Mamie
O'Rourke
We tripped the light fantastic on the sidewalks
of New York.
"The Sidewalks of New York" (song) (1894)

William Blake

English poet and painter, 1757–1827

1 Love to faults is always blind,
Always is to joy inclin'd,
Lawless, wing'd, and unconfin'd,

And breaks all chains from every mind.
Note-Book "Love to Faults" (ca. 1791–1792)

2 If the doors of perception were cleansed
everything would appear to man as it is,
infinite.
The Marriage of Heaven and Hell "A Memorable Fancy"
plate 14 (1790–1793). Inspired the title of Aldous
Huxley's 1954 book about drug experimentation, *The
Doors of Perception,* which in turn inspired the name of
the 1960s rock group The Doors.

3 One Law for the Lion & Ox is Oppression.
The Marriage of Heaven and Hell "A Memorable
Fancy" plate 24 (1790–1793)

4 The road of excess leads to the palace of
wisdom.
The Marriage of Heaven and Hell "Proverbs of Hell"
(1790–1793)

5 Prisons are built with stones of Law, brothels
with bricks of Religion.
The Marriage of Heaven and Hell "Proverbs of Hell"
(1790–1793)

6 The pride of the peacock is the glory of God.
The lust of the goat is the bounty of God.
The wrath of the lion is the wisdom of God.
The nakedness of woman is the work of God.
The Marriage of Heaven and Hell "Proverbs of Hell"
(1790–1793)

7 The tygers of wrath are wiser than the horses of
instruction.
The Marriage of Heaven and Hell "Proverbs of Hell"
(1790–1793)

8 The reason Milton wrote in fetters when he
wrote of Angels and God, and at liberty when of
Devils and Hell, is because he was a true Poet,
and of the Devil's party without knowing it.
The Marriage of Heaven and Hell "The Voice of the
Devil" (note) (1790–1793)

9 O Rose, thou art sick!
Songs of Experience "The Sick Rose" (1794)

10 Tyger Tyger, burning bright,
In the forests of the night;
What immortal hand or eye,
Could frame thy fearful symmetry?
Songs of Experience "The Tiger" (1794)

11 What the hammer? What the chain?
In what furnace was thy brain?
What the anvil? What dread grasp
Dare its deadly terrors clasp?
Songs of Experience "The Tiger" (1794)

12 Did he smile his work to see?
Did he who made the Lamb make thee?
Songs of Experience "The Tiger" (1794)

13 May God us keep
From Single vision and Newton's sleep!
"Letter to Thomas Butts, 22 November 1802" (1802)

14 To see a world in a grain of sand
And a heaven in a wild flower,
Hold infinity in the palm of your hand
And eternity in an hour.
"Auguries of Innocence" l. 1 (ca. 1803)

15 A robin red breast in a cage
Puts all Heaven in a rage.
"Auguries of Innocence" l. 5 (ca. 1803)

16 A dog starv'd at his master's gate
Predicts the ruin of the State.
"Auguries of Innocence" l. 9 (ca. 1803)

17 To generalize is to be an idiot. To particularize
is the alone distinction of merit—general
knowledges are those knowledges that idiots
possess.
"Annotations to The Works of Sir Joshua Reynolds"
(ca. 1798–1809)

18 Great things are done when men and
mountains meet;
This is not done by jostling in the street.
Note-Book (1807–1809)

19 And did those feet in ancient time
Walk upon England's mountains green?
And was the Holy Lamb of God
On England's pleasant pastures seen?
And did the Countenance Divine
Shine forth upon our clouded hills?
And was Jerusalem builded here
Among these dark Satanic mills?
Milton preface (1804–1810)

20 Bring me my bow of burning gold:
Bring me my arrows of desire:
Bring me my spear: O clouds, unfold!
Bring me my chariot of fire.
Milton preface (1804–1810)

21 I will not cease from mental fight,
Nor shall my sword sleep in my hand,
Till we have built Jerusalem,
In England's green and pleasant land.
Milton preface (1804–1810)

22 I give you the end of a golden string;
   Only wind it into a ball:
   It will lead you in at Heaven's gate,
   Built in Jerusalem's wall.
   Jerusalem "I give you the end of a golden string" (1815)

23 Poetry fettered fetters the human race. Nations
   are destroyed, or flourish, in proportion as their
   poetry, painting, and music are destroyed or
   flourish!
   Jerusalem "To the Public" plate 1 (1815)

24 He who would do good to another must do it in
      minute particulars;
   General good is the plea of the scoundrel,
      hypocrite, and flatterer:
   For art and science cannot exist but in minutely
      organized particulars.
   Jerusalem ch. 3, plate 55, l. 60 (1815)

Jean Joseph Louis Blanc
Spanish-born French socialist, 1811–1882

1 *Dans la doctrine saint-simonienne, le problème de
   la répartition des bénéfices est résolu par cette
   fameuse formule:* à chacun suivant sa capacité;
   à chaque capacité suivant ses oeuvres.
   In the Saint-Simonian doctrine, the problem of
   the distribution of benefits is resolved by this
   famous saying: *To each according to his ability;
   to each ability according to its fruits.*
   Organisation du Travail (1841)
   See Karl Marx 12

Lesley Blanch
English writer, 1904–2007

1 She was an Amazon. Her whole life was spent
   riding at breakneck speed towards the wilder
   shores of love.
   The Wilder Shores of Love pt. 2, ch. 1 (1954)

James A. Bland
U.S. songwriter, 1854–1911

1 Carry me back to old Virginny,
   That's where the cotton and the corn and taters
      grow.
   "Carry Me Back to Old Virginny" (song) (1875)

2 Oh! Dem Golden Slippers.
   Title of song (1879)

Lloyd Blankfein
U.S. business executive, 1954–

1 [*Of his role as CEO of the investment firm
   Goldman Sachs at the time of the worldwide
   financial crisis:*] We have a social purpose . . .
   [I'm] doing God's work.
   Quoted in *Sunday Times* (London), 8 Nov. 2009

Vicente Blasco-Ibáñez
Spanish writer and politician, 1867–1928

1 *Los Cuatro Jinetes del Apocalipsis.*
   The Four Horsemen of the Apocalypse.
   Title of book (1916). A reference to the four
   allegorical horses in Revelation 6:1–8.
   See Grantland Rice 2; Margaret Chase Smith 1

Helena Petrovna Blavatsky
Russian traveler and theosophist, 1831–1891

1 [Theosophy] is the essence of all religion and of
   absolute truth, a drop of which only underlies
   every creed.
   The Key to Theosophy sec. 4 (1889)

Philip Paul Bliss
U.S. evangelist, 1838–1876

1 Hold the fort, for I am coming.
   Gospel Hymns and Sacred Songs no. 14 (1875). Inspired
   by General William Tecumseh Sherman's flag
   message.
   See William Tecumseh Sherman 2

Hans Blix
Swedish diplomat, 1928–

1 [*Of inspections for weapons of mass destruction in
   Iraq:*] We haven't found any smoking guns.
   News conference, New York, N.Y., 9 Jan. 2003

Arthur Bloch
U.S. writer, 1948–

1 The sum of the intelligence on the planet is a
   constant; the population is growing.
   *Murphy's Law and Other Reasons Why Things Go
   Wrong!* (1977)

Ernst Bloch
German philosopher, 1885–1977

1 It is important to learn hoping. Its work does
   not despair, it fell in love with succeeding

rather than with failure. Hoping, located above fearing, is neither passive like the latter nor imprisoned into nothingness. The emotion of hoping expands out of itself, makes people wider instead of narrower; insatiable, it wants to know what makes people purposeful on the inside and what might be allied with them on the outside.

The Principle of Hope vol. 1 (1959)

Robert Bloch

U.S. novelist and screenwriter, 1917–1994

1 She didn't swat it, and she hoped they were watching, because that *proved* what sort of a person she really was. Why, she wouldn't even harm a fly. . . .

Psycho ch. 17 (1959). Ellipsis in original text.

2 I have the heart of a small boy—I keep it on my desk, in a jar.

Quoted in *S.F. Chronicle,* 4 Nov. 1945

Alexander Blok

Russian poet, 1880–1921

1 The wind plays up; snow flutters down.
Twelve men are marching through the town.

"The Twelve" (1918) (translation by Jon Stallworthy and Peter France)

Harold Bloom

U.S. literary critic, 1930–2019

1 The Anxiety of Influence.

Title of book (1973)

Amelia Jenks Bloomer

U.S. feminist and reformer, 1818–1894

1 The costume of woman . . . should conduce at once to her health, comfort, and usefulness . . . while it should not fail also to conduce to her personal adornment, it should make that end of secondary importance.

Letter to Charlotte Joy, 3 June 1857

Henry Blossom

U.S. composer and writer, 1867–1919

1 I Want What I Want When I Want It.

Title of song (1905)

Gebhard Lebrecht Blücher

German military leader, 1742–1819

1 [*Of London, 1814:*] *Was für Plunder!*
What rubbish!

Quoted in *New Englander,* Jan. 1861

Ed Bluestone

U.S. comedian, 1948–

1 [*Caption of cover photograph of gun being pointed at dog:*] If You Don't Buy This Magazine, We'll Kill This Dog.

National Lampoon, Jan. 1973

Judy Blume (Judith Sussman)

U.S. children's book writer, 1938–

1 *Are you there God? It's me, Margaret. I just told my mother I want a bra. Please help me grow God. You know where.*

Are You There God? It's Me, Margaret. ch. 6 (1970)

Robert Bly

U.S. poet, 1926–

1 There is a privacy I love in this snowy night. Driving around, I will waste more time.

"Driving to Town Late to Mail a Letter" l. 4 (1962)

2 Every modern man has, lying at the bottom of his psyche, a large, primitive being covered with hair down to his feet. Making contact with this Wild Man is the step the Eighties male or the Nineties male has yet to take.

Iron John ch. 1 (1990)

Franz Boas

German-born U.S. anthropologist, 1858–1942

1 There is no fundamental difference in the ways of thinking of primitive and civilized man. A close connection between race and personality has never been established.

The Mind of Primitive Man preface (1938)

2 The behavior of an individual is therefore determined not by his racial affiliation, but by the character of his ancestry and his cultural environment.

Race and Democratic Society ch. 4 (1945)

3 No one has ever proved that a human being, through his descent from a certain group of

people must of necessity have certain mental characteristics.

Race and Democratic Society ch. 7 (1945)

Giovanni Boccaccio

Italian writer and humanist, 1313–1375

1 [*Of the Black Death:*] How many valiant men, how many fair ladies, breakfast with their kinfolk and the same night supped with their ancestors in the next world!

Decameron introduction (1348–1353)

2 [*Of the Black Death:*] The condition of the people was pitiable to behold. They sickened by the thousands daily, and died unattended and without help. Many died in the open street, others dying in their houses, made it known by the stench of their rotting bodies. Consecrated churchyards did not suffice for the burial of the vast multitude of bodies, which were heaped by the hundreds in vast trenches, like goods in a ship's hold and covered with a little earth.

Decameron introduction (1348–1353)

Ivan Boesky

U.S. financier, 1937–

1 Greed is all right. . . . Greed is healthy. You can be greedy and still feel good about yourself.

Commencement address at University of California School of Business Administration, Berkeley, Calif., 18 May 1986
See Film Lines 184

William J. H. Boetcker

U.S. clergyman, 1873–1962

1 1. You cannot bring about prosperity by discouraging thrift.

2. You cannot strengthen the weak by weakening the strong.

3. You cannot help small men up by tearing down big men.

4. You cannot help the poor by destroying the rich.

5. You cannot lift the wage earner up by pulling the wage payer down.

6. You cannot keep out of trouble by spending more than your income.

7. You cannot further the brotherhood of man by inciting class hatred.

8. You cannot establish sound social security on borrowed money.

9. You cannot build character and courage by taking away a man's initiative and independence.

10. You cannot help men permanently by doing for them what they could and should do for themselves.

"The Industrial Decalogue" (1916). These "ten cannots" are frequently, but falsely, attributed to Abraham Lincoln.

Boethius

Roman statesman and philosopher, ca. 476–524

1 For in every ill-turn of fortune the most unhappy sort of unfortunate man is the one who has been happy.

De Consolatione Philosophiae bk. 2, prose 4
See Dante Alighieri 7

Louise Bogan

U.S. poet, 1897–1970

1 What she has gathered, and what lost,
She will not find to lose again.
She is possessed by time, who once
Was loved by men.

"Portrait" l. 9 (1923)

2 Now that I have your heart by heart, I see.

"Song for the Last Act" l. 27 (1968)

Niels Bohr

Danish physicist, 1885–1962

1 The old saying of the two kinds of truth. To the one kind belongs statements so simple and clear that the opposite assertion obviously could not be defended. The other kind, the so-called "deep truths," are statements in which the opposite also contains deep truth.

Quoted in *Albert Einstein: Philosopher-Scientist*, ed. P. A. Schilpp (1949)
See Wilde 20

2 It is very difficult to predict, especially the future.

Attributed in *Bulletin of the Atomic Scientists*, Dec. 1971. This is often said to be "an old Danish proverb." K. K. Steincke, *Goodbye and Thanks* (1948), quotes it as a pun used in the Danish parliament in the late 1930s.

3 Anyone who is not shocked by quantum theory has not understood it.

Attributed in Kit Pedler, *Mind over Matter* (1981)

Nicolas Boileau

French critic and poet, 1636–1711

1 Nothing but truth is lovely, nothing fair.

Epistles no. 9 (1673)

2 At last came Malherbe, and he was the first in France to give poetry a proper flow.

L'Art Poétique canto 1 (1674)

3 A fool can always find a greater fool to admire him.

L'Art Poétique canto 1 (1674)

4 *Ce que l'on conçoit bien s'énonce clairement.* What is well conceived is clearly said.

L'Art Poétique canto 1 (1674)

Pierre le Pesant, Sieur de Boisguilbert

French economist, 1646–1714

1 *Il n'y avait qu'à laisser faire la nature et la liberté.* It was only necessary to let nature and liberty alone.

Factum de la France (1707). *Journal Oeconomique,* Apr. 1751, records the following: "Monsieur Colbert assembled several deputies of commerce at his house to ask what could be done for commerce; the most rational and the least flattering among them answered him in one word: *'Laissez-nous-faire'* [Leave us to do it]."
See Quesnay 1

Derek C. Bok

U.S. university president, 1930–

1 There is far too much law for those who can afford it and far too little for those who cannot.

"A Flawed System," *Harvard Magazine,* May-June 1983

2 If you think education is expensive—try ignorance.

Attributed in Paul Dickson, *The Official Rules* (1978). An earlier occurrence, without attribution to any individual, was in the *Washington Post,* 6 Oct. 1975.

Anne Boleyn

English queen, ca. 1501–1536

1 I heard say the executor [executioner] was very good, and I have a little neck.

Quoted in William Kingston, Letter to Thomas Cromwell, 19 May 1536

Simón Bolívar

Venezuelan statesman and military leader, 1783–1830

1 The hate that the Iberian peninsula has inspired in us is broader than the sea which separates us from it; it is less difficult to join both continents than to join both countries' souls.

"The Jamaican Letter" (1815)

2 All who have served the Revolution have plowed the sea.

Letter to Juan José Flores, 9 Nov. 1830

Robert Bolt

English playwright, 1924–1995

1 Yes, I'd give the Devil benefit of law, for my own safety's sake.

A Man for All Seasons act 1 (1960)

2 When the last law was down, and the Devil turned round on you—where would you hide, Roper, the laws all being flat? This country's planted thick with laws from coast to coast— Man's laws, not God's—and if you cut them down—and you're just the man to do it—d'you really think you could stand upright in the winds that would blow then?

A Man for All Seasons act 1 (1960)

3 It profits a man nothing to give his soul for the whole world . . . But for Wales—!

A Man for All Seasons act 2 (1960). Ellipsis in original text.
See Bible 278

Erma Bombeck

U.S. humorist, 1927–1996

1 The Grass Is Always Greener over the Septic Tank.

Title of book (1976)

2 If Life Is a Bowl of Cherries, What Am I Doing in the Pits?

Title of book (1978)
See Lew Brown 2

3 When You Look like Your Passport Photo, It's Time to Go Home.

Title of book (1991)

Carrie Jacobs Bond

U.S. songwriter, 1862–1946

1 Well, this is the end of a perfect day,
Near the end of a journey, too.
"A Perfect Day" (song) (1909)

Julian Bond

U.S. activist and politician, 1940–2015

1 Affirmative action really isn't about preferential
treatment for blacks, but about removing
preferential treatment whites have received
through history.
Speech at 89th NAACP Annual Convention, Atlanta,
Ga., 12 July 1998

Hermann Bondi

British mathematician and cosmologist, 1919–
2005

1 The Steady-State Theory of the Expanding
Universe.
Title of article, *Monthly Notices of the Royal
Astronomical Society* (1948). Coauthored with Thomas
A. Gold.

Mars Bonfire (Dennis McCrohan)

Canadian rock musician, 1943–

1 I like smoke and lightning
Heavy metal thunder
"Born to Be Wild" (song) (1968)
See William S. Burroughs 3

2 Like a true nature's child
We were born, born to be wild
We can climb so high
I never wanna die.
"Born to Be Wild" (song) (1968)

Dietrich Bonhoeffer

German clergyman and theologian, 1906–1945

1 The third possibility [for the church] is not just
to bandage the victims under the wheel, but to
put a spoke in the wheel itself.
"The Church and the Jewish Question" (1933)

2 Cheap grace is the deadly enemy of our
Church.
The Cost of Discipleship ch. 1 (1937)

3 When Christ calls a man, he bids him come
and die.
The Cost of Discipleship ch. 4 (1937)

4 We have learnt a bit too late in the day that
action springs not from thought, but from a
readiness for responsibility.
"Thoughts on the Baptism of D.W.R." (1944)

Bono (Paul Hewson)

Irish rock singer and songwriter, 1960–

1 I can't believe the news today
I can't close my eyes and make it go away.
How long, how long must we sing this song.
"Sunday Bloody Sunday" (song) (1983)

2 Early morning, April 4
Shots rang out in the Memphis sky
Free at last!
They took your life
But they could not take your pride.
"Pride (In the Name of Love)" (song) (1984)

3 One life, with each other
Sisters, brothers
One life, but we're not the same
We get to carry each other, carry each other.
"One" (song) (1991)

Salvatore Phillip "Sonny" Bono

U.S. singer and politician, 1935–1998

1 The Beat Goes On.
Title of song (1967)

The Book of Common Prayer

1 Whosoever shall be saved: before all things it is
necessary that he hold the Catholic Faith.
At Morning Prayer "Athanasian Creed" (1662)

2 Man that is born of a woman hath but a short
time to live, and is full of misery.
The Burial of the Dead "First Anthem" (1662)

3 In the midst of life we are in death.
The Burial of the Dead "First Anthem" (1662)

4 Forasmuch as it hath pleased Almighty God of
his great mercy to take unto himself the soul
of our dear brother here departed, we therefore
commit his body to the ground; earth to earth,
ashes to ashes, dust to dust; in sure and certain
hope of the Resurrection to eternal life.
The Burial of the Dead "Interment" (1662)

5 I believe in one God the Father Almighty,
Maker of heaven and earth, And of all things
visible and invisible:

And in one Lord Jesus Christ, the only-begotten Son of God, Begotten of his Father before all worlds, God of God, Light of Light, Very God of very God, Begotten, not made, Being of one substance with the Father, By whom all things were made.
Holy Communion "Nicene Creed" (1662)

6 And I believe one Catholick and Apostolick Church.
Holy Communion "Nicene Creed" (1662)

7 Have mercy upon us miserable sinners.
The Litany (1662)

8 From all the deceits of the world, the flesh, and the devil,
     Good Lord, deliver us.
The Litany (1662)

9 I believe in God the Father Almighty, Maker of heaven and earth:
     And in Jesus Christ his only Son our Lord, Who was conceived by the Holy Ghost, Born of the Virgin Mary, Suffered under Pontius Pilate, Was crucified, dead, and buried, He descended into hell; The third day he rose again from the dead, He ascended into heaven, And sitteth on the right hand of God, the Father Almighty; From thence he shall come to judge the quick and the dead. I believe in the Holy Ghost; The holy Catholick Church; The Communion of Saints; The Forgiveness of sins; The Resurrection of the body, And the life everlasting. Amen.
Morning Prayer "The Apostles' Creed" (1662)
See Baruch 1

10 We have left undone those things which we ought to have done; And we have done those things which we ought not to have done; And there is no health in us.
Morning Prayer "General Confession" (1662)

11 Glory be to the Father, and to the Son: and to the Holy Ghost; As it was in the beginning, is now, and ever shall be: world without end. Amen.
Morning Prayer "Gloria" (1662)

12 And forgive us our trespasses, As we forgive them that trespass against us.
Morning Prayer "The Lord's Prayer" (1662)
See Bible 215

13 If any of you know cause, or just impediment, why these two persons should not be joined together in holy Matrimony, ye are to declare it.
Solemnization of Matrimony "The Banns" (1662)

14 Wilt thou love her, comfort her, honor, and keep her in sickness and in health; and, forsaking all other, keep thee only unto her, so long as ye both shall live?
Solemnization of Matrimony "Betrothal" (1662)

15 To have and to hold from this day forward, for better for worse, for richer for poorer, in sickness and in health, to love, cherish, and to obey, till death us do part, according to God's holy ordinance; and thereto I give thee my troth.
Solemnization of Matrimony "Betrothal" (1662)

16 Dearly beloved, we are gathered together here in the sight of God, and in the face of this congregation, to join together this Man and this Woman in holy Matrimony.
Solemnization of Matrimony "Exhortation" (1662)

17 If any man can shew any just cause, why they may not lawfully be joined together, let him now speak, or else hereafter for ever hold his peace.
Solemnization of Matrimony "Exhortation" (1662)

18 With this Ring I thee wed, with my body I thee worship, and with all my worldly goods I thee endow.
Solemnization of Matrimony "Wedding" (1662)

19 Those whom God hath joined together let no man put asunder.
Solemnization of Matrimony "Wedding" (1662)
See Bible 249

Daniel Boone
U.S. pioneer, 1734–1820

1 [*Remark, June 1819:*] I can't say as ever I was lost, but I was *bewildered* once for three days.
Quoted in Chester Harding, *My Egotistigraphy* (1866)

Daniel J. Boorstin
U.S. historian, 1914–2004

1 A pseudo-event . . . comes about because someone has planned, planted, or incited it. Typically, it is not a train wreck or an earthquake, but an interview.
The Image ch. 1 (1962)

2 The celebrity is a person who is known for his well-knownness.

The Image ch. 1 (1962)

John Wilkes Booth
U.S. actor and assassin, 1838–1865

1 [*After shooting Abraham Lincoln, 14 Apr. 1865:*] Sic semper tyrannis!

Quoted in *N.Y. Times,* 15 Apr. 1865. *Sic semper tyrannis,* "Thus always to tyrants," is the state motto of Virginia. Booth is often said to have followed this with "the South is avenged," but these latter words do not appear in any contemporary source and may be apocryphal.
See Anonymous (Latin) 12

William Booth
English founder of the Salvation Army, 1829–1912

1 [*Of the poor:*] The submerged tenth.
In Darkest England pt. 1, title of ch. 2 (1890)

Émile Borel
French mathematician and government official, 1871–1956

1 *Concevons qu'on ait dressé un million de singes à frapper au hasard sur les touches d'une machine à écrire et que . . . ces singes dactylographes travaillent avec ardeur dix heures par jour avec un million de machines à écrire de types variés. . . . Et au bout d'un an, ces volumes se trouveraient renfermer la copie exacte des livres de toute nature et de toutes langues conservés dans les plus riches bibliothèques du monde.*

Let us imagine that a million monkeys have been trained to strike the keys of a typewriter at random, and that . . . these typist monkeys work eagerly ten hours a day on a million typewriters of various kinds. . . . And at the end of a year, these volumes turn out to contain the exact texts of the books of every sort and every language found in the world's richest libraries.

"Mécanique Statistique et Irréversibilité" (1913). Borel in his book *Le Hasard* (1914) specifically wrote of the monkeys typing all the books in the Bibliothèque Nationale. The venue of this quotation is changed to a different library by Gilbert N. Lewis, *The Anatomy of Science* (1926): "Borel makes the amusing supposition of a million monkeys allowed to play upon the keys of a million typewriters. What is

the chance that this wanton activity should reproduce exactly all of the volumes which are contained in the library of the British Museum?"
See Eddington 2; Wilensky 1

Jorge Luis Borges
Argentinian writer, 1899–1986

1 The universe (which others call the Library) is composed of an indefinite and perhaps infinite number of hexagonal galleries.

"The Library of Babel" (1941) (translation by James E. Irby)

2 It does not seem unlikely to me that there is a total book on some shelf of the universe; I pray to the unknown gods that a man—just one, even though it were thousands of years ago!—may have examined and read it. If honor and wisdom and happiness are not for me, let them be for others. Let heaven exist, though my place be in hell. Let me be outraged and annihilated, but for one instant, in one being, let Your enormous Library be justified.

"The Library of Babel" (1941) (translation by James E. Irby)

3 On those remote pages [of "a certain Chinese encyclopedia"] it is written that animals are divided into (a) those that belong to the Emperor, (b) embalmed ones, (c) those that are trained, (d) suckling pigs, (e) mermaids, (f) fabulous ones, (g) stray dogs, (h) those that are included in this classification, (i) those that tremble as if they were mad, (j) innumerable ones, (k) those drawn with a very fine camel's hair brush, (l) others, (m) those that have just broken a flower vase, (n) those that resemble flies from a distance.

"The Analytical Language of John Wilkins" (1942) (translation by Ruth L. C. Simms)

4 To die for a religion is easier than to live it absolutely.

"Deutsches Requiem" (1946) (translation by Julian Palley)

5 Time is a river which sweeps me along, but I am the river; it is a tiger which destroys me, but I am the tiger; it is a fire which consumes me, but I am the fire. The world, unfortunately, is real; I, unfortunately, am Borges.

"A New Refutation of Time" (1946) (translation by James E. Irby)

6 In the critics' vocabulary, the word "precursor"
is indispensable, but it should be cleansed of all
connotations of polemics or rivalry. The fact is
that every writer *creates* his own precursors. His
work modifies our conception of the past, as it
will modify the future.

"Kafka and His Precursors" (1951) (translation by
James E. Irby)

7 I . . . had always thought of Paradise
In form and image as a library.

"Poem of the Gifts" (1959) (translation by Alastair
Reid)

8 There are no moral or intellectual merits.
Homer composed the *Odyssey;* if we postulate
an infinite period of time, with infinite
circumstances and changes, the impossible
thing is not to compose the *Odyssey,* at least
once.

"The Immortal" (1968) (translation by James E. Irby)

Frank Borman

U.S. astronaut and business executive, 1928–

1 Capitalism without bankruptcy is like
Christianity without hell.

Quoted in *Forbes,* 8 June 1981

Pierre Bosquet

French general, 1810–1861

1 [*On the charge of the Light Brigade at Balaclava,
25 Oct. 1854:*] *C'est magnifique, mais ce n'est pas
la guerre.*
It is magnificent, but it is not war.

Quoted in Cecil Woodham-Smith, *The Reason Why*
(1953)

John Collins Bossidy

U.S. physician and poet, 1860–1928

1 I'm from good old Boston,
The home of the bean and the cod,
Where the Cabots speak only to the Lowells,
And the Lowells speak only with God.

Quoted in *Wash. Post,* 14 Feb. 1915. Recited at the
midwinter dinner of the alumni of Holy Cross
College in Boston in 1910. Bossidy was inspired
by a toast given at the twenty-fifth anniversary
dinner of the Harvard Class of 1880: "Here's to
old Massachusetts, / The home of the sacred cod,
/ Where the Adamses vote for Douglas / And the
Cabots walk with God."

James Boswell

Scottish biographer and lawyer, 1740–1795

1 That favourite subject, Myself.

Letter to William Temple, 26 July 1763

2 He who praises everybody, praises nobody.

Life of Samuel Johnson (1791) (footnote for 30 Mar.
1778 entry)

Horatio Bottomley

British journalist and financier, 1860–1933

1 [*When in prison and asked by a visitor whether he
were sewing:*] No, reaping.

Quoted in S. T. Felstead, *Horatio Bottomley* (1936)

Anthony Boucher (William Anthony
Parker White)

U.S. writer and critic, 1911–1968

1 Eliminate the impossible. Then if nothing
remains, some part of the "impossible" must
be possible.

Rocket to the Morgue epigraph (1942)
See Arthur Conan Doyle 10

F. W. Bourdillon

English poet, 1852–1921

1 The night has a thousand eyes,
And the day but one;
Yet the light of the bright world dies
With the dying sun.

Among the Flowers "Light" l. 1 (1878)
See Lyly 2

2 The light of a whole life dies
When love is gone.

Among the Flowers "Light" l. 7 (1878)

Margaret Bourke-White

U.S. photojournalist, 1906–1971

1 [*Of modern photojournalism:*] The beauty of the
past belongs to the past.

Diary, 11 May 1928

Randolph Bourne

U.S. writer, 1886–1918

1 War is the health of the State.

"Unfinished Fragment on the State" (1918)

Jim Bouton

U.S. baseball player, 1939–2019

1 You spend a good piece of your life gripping a baseball and in the end it turns out that it was the other way around all the time.
Ball Four (1970)

Elizabeth Bowen

Irish-born English writer, 1899–1973

1 There is no end to the violations committed by children on children, quietly talking alone.
The House in Paris pt. 1, ch. 2 (1935)

2 Fate is not an eagle, it creeps like a rat.
The House in Paris pt. 2, ch. 2 (1935)

3 Experience isn't interesting till it begins to repeat itself—in fact, till it does that, it hardly *is* experience.
The Death of the Heart pt. 1, ch. 1 (1938)

4 When you love someone all your saved-up wishes start coming out.
The Death of the Heart pt. 1, ch. 9 (1938)

Charles Synge Christopher, Lord Bowen

English judge, 1835–1894

1 The state of a man's mind is as much a fact as the state of his digestion.
Edginton v. Fitzmaurice (1885)

2 The rain, it raineth on the just
And also on the unjust fella:
But chiefly on the just, because
The unjust steals the just's umbrella.
Quoted in Walter Sichel, *Sands of Time* (1923)
See Bible 213

David Bowie (David Robert Jones)

English rock musician, 1947–2016

1 Ground control to Major Tom.
"Space Oddity" (song) (1969)

2 For here am I sitting in a tin can,
Far above the world.
Planet Earth is blue, and there's nothing I can do.
"Space Oddity" (song) (1969)

3 It's the terror of knowing
What this world is about

Watching some good friends
Screaming "Let me out."
"Under Pressure" (song) (1981). Cowritten with Queen (Rogers Meddows Taylor, Freddie Mercury, Brian Harold May, and John Richard Deacon).

4 'Cause love's such an old fashioned word
And love dares you to care
For the people on the edge of the night
And love dares you to change our way of
Caring about ourselves
This is our last dance
This is our last dance
This is ourselves
Under pressure.
"Under Pressure" (song) (1981). Cowritten with Queen (Rogers Meddows Taylor, Freddie Mercury, Brian Harold May, and John Richard Deacon).

Edward Boyd-Jones

English songwriter, fl. 1900

1 Tell Me, Pretty Maiden, Are There Any More at Home Like You?
Title of song (1899). Cowritten with Paul Rubens.

Charles Boyer

French actor, 1899–1978

1 Come with me to the Casbah.
Attributed in *Cleveland Plain Dealer*, 31 May 1944. Nigel Rees, *Cassell's Movie Quotations*, states that Boyer does not say this line in the 1938 film *Algiers*: "He is supposed to have said it to Hedy Lamarr. Boyer impersonators used it and the film was laughed at because of it, but it was simply a Hollywood legend that grew up. Boyer himself denied he had ever said it, and thought it had been invented by a press agent."

François Boyer

French writer, 1920–2003

1 *Jeux Interdits.*
Forbidden Games.
Title of book (1947)

Ray Bradbury

U.S. science fiction writer, 1920–2012

1 It was a pleasure to burn.
Fahrenheit 451 pt. 1 (1954)

John Bradford

English martyr, ca. 1510–1555

1 [*On seeing criminals being led to execution:*] But
for the grace of God there goes John Bradford.

Quoted in *The Writings of John Bradford* (1853). "Take
away the grace of God, and there goes John Bradford"
appears in *Free-will and Merit Fairly Examined* (1775).
Usually quoted as "There but for the grace of God
go I."
See Mankiewicz 1

William Bradford

English-born colonial American political leader,
1590–1657

1 Being brought safe to land, they fell upon their
knees and blessed the God of Heaven, who had
brought them over the vast and furious Ocean,
and delivered them from many perils and
miseries.

Quoted in Nathaniel Morton, *New Englands Memoriall*
(1669). Morton was quoting from Bradford's
manuscript, *Of Plymouth Plantation.*
See Evarts 1

2 They knew that they were *Pilgrims and Strangers*
here below.

Quoted in Nathaniel Morton, *New Englands Memoriall*
(1669). Morton was quoting from Bradford's
manuscript, *Of Plymouth Plantation.*

Joseph P. Bradley

U.S. judge, 1813–1892

1 Man is, or should be, woman's protector and
defender. The natural and proper timidity
and delicacy which belongs to the female sex
evidently unfits it for many of the occupations
of civil life. The constitution of the family
organization, which is founded in the divine
ordinance, as well as in the nature of things,
indicates the domestic sphere as that which
properly belongs to the domain and functions
of womanhood. The harmony, not to say
identity, of interests and views which belong,
or should belong, to the family institution is
repugnant to the idea of a woman adopting a
distinct and independent career from that of
her husband. . . . The paramount destiny and
mission of woman are to fulfil the noble and
benign offices of wife and mother. This is the
law of the Creator.

Bradwell v. State (concurring opinion) (1873)

Omar Bradley

U.S. general, 1893–1981

1 We have grasped the mystery of the atom and
rejected the Sermon on the Mount. . . . Ours is
a world of nuclear giants and ethical infants.

Speech on Armistice Day, Boston, Mass., 11 Nov.
1948

2 [*Of possible United States–Chinese conflict in the
Korean War:*] Red China is not the powerful
nation seeking to dominate the world. Frankly,
in the opinion of the Joint Chiefs of Staff, this
strategy would involve us in the wrong war, at
the wrong place, at the wrong time, and with
the wrong enemy.

Testimony before Senate Armed Services and Foreign
Affairs Committees, 15 May 1951

Anne Bradstreet

English-born colonial American poet, ca. 1612–
1672

1 I am obnoxious to each carping tongue,
Who says my hand a needle better fits.

"The Prologue" l. 25 (1650)

2 If ever two were one, then surely we.
If ever man were loved by wife, then thee;
If ever wife was happy in a man,
Compare with me ye women if you can.

"To My Dear and Loving Husband" l. 1 (1678)

Edward S. Bragg

U.S. politician and soldier, 1827–1912

1 [*Of Grover Cleveland:*] They love him for the
enemies he has made.

Nominating speech at Democratic National
Convention, Cleveland, Ohio, 9 July 1884

Tycho Brahe

Danish astronomer, 1546–1601

1 I noticed that a new and unusual star,
surpassing all the others in brilliancy, was
shining almost directly above my head. . . . A
miracle indeed, either the greatest of all that
have occurred in the whole range of nature
since the beginning of the world, or one
certainly that is to be classed with those attested
by the Holy Oracles.

De Stella Nova (On the New Star) (1573)

Harry Braisted

U.S. songwriter, fl. 1896

1 If you want to win her hand,
Let the maiden understand
That she's not the only pebble on the beach.
"You're Not the Only Pebble on the Beach" (song)
(1896)

George William Wilshere, Baron Bramwell

English judge, 1808–1892

1 The matter does not appear to me now as it
appears to have appeared to me then.
Andrews v. Styrap (1872)

Stewart Brand

U.S. author and futurist, 1938–

1 Why Haven't We Seen a Photograph of the
Whole Earth Yet?
Button (1966)

2 Once a new technology rolls over you, if you're
not part of the steamroller, you're part of the
road.
The Media Lab: Inventing the Future at MIT ch. 1
(1987)

3 A library doesn't need windows. A library is a
window.
How Buildings Learn ch. 3 (1994)

4 Information wants to be free.
Quoted in *Wash. Post*, 18 Nov. 1984

Louis D. Brandeis

U.S. lawyer and judge, 1856–1941

1 Political, social, and economic changes entail
the recognition of new rights, and the common
law, in its eternal youth, grows to meet the
demands of society. . . . Now the right to life
has come to mean the right to enjoy life,—the
right to be let alone; the right to liberty secures
the exercise of extensive civil privileges; and the
term "property" has grown to comprise every
form of possession—intangible, as well as
tangible.
"The Right to Privacy," *Harvard Law Review*, Dec.
1890. Coauthored with Samuel D. Warren.
See Brandeis 8

2 Instead of holding a position of independence,
between the wealthy and the people, prepared

to curb the expenses of either, able lawyers
have, to a large extent, allowed themselves to
become adjuncts of great corporations and have
neglected their obligation to use their powers
for the protection of the people. We hear much
of the "corporation lawyer," and far too little of
the "people's lawyer."
"The Opportunity in the Law," *American Law Review*,
July-Aug. 1905

3 Is there not a causal connection between
the development of these huge, indomitable
trusts and the horrible crimes now under
investigation? . . . Is it not irony to speak of the
equality of opportunity in a country cursed
with bigness?
Letter to the editor, *Survey*, 30 Dec. 1911

4 Publicity is justly commended as a remedy for
social and industrial diseases. Sunlight is said
to be the best of disinfectants; electric light the
most efficient policeman.
"What Publicity Can Do," *Harper's Weekly*, 20 Dec. 1913
See Ralph Waldo Emerson 42

5 [Those who won our independence knew] that
fear breeds repression; that repression breeds
hate; that hate menaces stable government;
that the path of safety lies in the opportunity
to discuss freely supposed grievances and
proposed remedies; and that the fitting remedy
for evil counsels is good ones.
Whitney v. California (concurring opinion) (1927)

6 Those who won our independence by revolution
were not cowards. They did not fear political
change. They did not exalt order at the cost of
liberty. To courageous, self-reliant men, with
confidence in the power of free and fearless
reasoning applied through the processes of
popular government, no danger flowing from
speech can be deemed clear and present,
unless the incidence of the evil apprehended is
so imminent that it may befall before there is
opportunity for full discussion. If there be time
to expose through discussion the falsehood
and fallacies, to avert the evil by the processes
of education, the remedy to be applied is more
speech, not enforced silence.
Whitney v. California (concurring opinion) (1927)
See Oliver Wendell Holmes, Jr. 29

7 As a means of espionage, writs of assistance and general warrants are but puny instruments of tyranny and oppression when compared with wire-tapping.
Olmstead v. United States (dissenting opinion) (1928)

8 The makers of our Constitution undertook to secure conditions favorable to the pursuit of happiness. They recognized the significance of man's spiritual nature, of his feelings, and of his intellect. They knew that only a part of the pain, pleasure, and satisfactions of life are to be found in material things. They sought to protect Americans in their beliefs, their thoughts, their emotions, and their sensations. They conferred, as against the Government, the right to be let alone—the most comprehensive of rights and the right most valued by civilized men.
Olmstead v. United States (dissenting opinion) (1928)
See Brandeis 1

9 Experience should teach us to be most on our guard to protect liberty when the Government's purposes are beneficent. Men born to freedom are naturally alert to repel invasion of their liberty by evil-minded rulers. The greatest dangers to liberty lurk in insidious encroachment by men of zeal, well-meaning but without understanding.
Olmstead v. United States (dissenting opinion) (1928)

10 Our Government is the potent, the omnipresent teacher. For good or for ill, it teaches the whole people by its example. Crime is contagious. If the Government becomes a lawbreaker, it breeds contempt for law; it invites every man to become a law unto himself; it invites anarchy. To declare that in the administration of the criminal law the end justifies the means—to declare that the Government may commit crimes in order to secure the conviction of a private criminal— would bring terrible retribution. Against that pernicious doctrine this Court should resolutely set its face.
Olmstead v. United States (dissenting opinion) (1928)

11 It is one of the happy incidents of the federal system that a single courageous State may, if its citizens choose, serve as a laboratory; and try novel social and economic experiments without risk to the rest of the country.
New State Ice Co. v. Liebmann (dissenting opinion) (1932)

12 We may have democracy, or we may have wealth concentrated in the hands of a few, but we can't have both.
Attributed in *Labor,* 14 Oct. 1941

Roger D. Branigin
U.S. politician, 1902–1975

1 [*Of newspaper publishers:*] I never argue with a man who buys ink by the barrel.
Quoted in *Indianapolis News,* 15 Jan. 1962. This is often attributed to publicist William I. Greener, Jr., and labeled as "Greener's Law," but the earliest known Greener attribution is not until 1978.

Sebastian Brant
German writer and jurist, 1458–1521

1 *Das Narrenschiff.*
The Ship of Fools.
Title of poem (1494)

Georges Braque
French painter, 1882–1963

1 Art is meant to disturb, science reassures.
Le Jour et la Nuit: Cahiers 1917–52 (1952)

Wernher von Braun
German-born U.S. rocket scientist, 1912–1977

1 Basic research is what I am doing when I don't know what I am doing.
Quoted in *Salt Lake City Tribune,* 19 Feb. 1959

2 There is just one thing I can promise you about the outer-space program: Your tax dollar will go farther.
Attributed in *Reader's Digest,* May 1961

Bertolt Brecht
German playwright, 1898–1956

1 Oh, the shark has pretty teeth, dear,
And he shows them pearly white.
Just a jackknife has Macheath, dear
And he keeps it out of sight.
The Threepenny Opera prologue (1928)

2 *Erst kommt das Fressen, dann die Moral.*
Food comes first, then morals.
The Threepenny Opera act 2, sc. 3 (1928)

3 What is robbing a bank compared with
founding a bank?
The Threepenny Opera act 3, sc. 3 (1928)

4 Unhappy the land that needs heroes.
The Life of Galileo sc. 13 (1939)

5 Don't tell me peace has broken out, when I've
just bought some new supplies.
Mother Courage sc. 8 (1939)

6 The Resistible Rise of Arturo Ui.
Title of play (1941)

7 [*On the East German uprising against Soviet
occupation:*]
Would it not be easier
In that case for the government
To dissolve the people
And elect another?
"The Solution" (1953)

L. Paul Bremer III
U.S. government official, 1941–

1 [*Announcing the capture of former Iraqi leader
Saddam Hussein:*] Ladies and gentlemen, we got
him.
News conference, Baghdad, 14 Dec. 2003

William J. Brennan, Jr.
U.S. judge, 1906–1997

1 All ideas having even the slightest redeeming
social importance—unorthodox ideas,
controversial ideas, even ideas hateful to the
prevailing climate of opinion—have the full
protection of the guaranties. . . . But implicit
in the history of the First Amendment is
the rejection of obscenity as utterly without
redeeming social importance. . . . We hold
that obscenity is not within the area of
constitutionally protected speech or press.
Roth v. United States (1957)

2 [*Standard for obscenity:*] Whether to the average
person, applying contemporary community
standards, the dominant theme of the material
taken as a whole appeals to prurient interest.
Roth v. United States (1957)

3 We consider this case against the background
of a profound national commitment to the
principle that debate on public issues should
be uninhibited, robust, and wide-open, and
that it may well include vehement, caustic,
and sometimes unpleasantly sharp attacks on
government and public officials.
New York Times Co. v. Sullivan (1964)

4 The constitutional guarantees require, we
think, a federal rule that prohibits a public
official from recovering damages for a
defamatory falsehood relating to his official
conduct unless he proves that the statement
was made with "actual malice"—that is, with
knowledge that it was false or with reckless
disregard of whether it was false or not.
New York Times Co. v. Sullivan (1964). The phrase
"actual malice" is first found in a 1908 libel case in
Kansas, *Coleman v. MacLennan;* the opinion there was
written by Rousseau A. Burch.

5 The chilling effect upon the exercise of First
Amendment rights may derive from the fact of
the prosecution, unaffected by the prospects of
its success or failure.
Dombrowski v. Pfister (1965). Popularized the use of
the term "chilling effect" to describe inhibition of
freedom of expression.

6 If the right of privacy means anything, it is the
right of the *individual,* married or single, to be
free from unwarranted governmental intrusion
into matters so fundamentally affecting a
person as the decision whether to bear or beget
a child.
Eisenstadt v. Baird (1972)

7 We current Justices read the Constitution in
the only way that we can: as Twentieth Century
Americans. We look to the history of the time
of framing and to the intervening history of
interpretation. But the ultimate question must
be, what do the words of the text mean in our
time. For the genius of the Constitution rests
not in any static meaning it might have had
in a world that is dead and gone, but in the
adaptability of its great principles to cope with
current problems and current needs.
"The Constitution of the United States:
Contemporary Ratification" (speech), Washington,
D.C., 12 Oct. 1985

Jimmy Breslin
U.S. journalist and writer, 1928–2017

1 The Gang That Couldn't Shoot Straight.
Title of book (1969)

2 All political power is primarily an illusion. . . .
Illusion. Mirrors and blue smoke, beautiful
blue smoke rolling over the surface of highly
polished mirrors, first a thin veil of blue smoke,
then a thick cloud that suddenly dissolves into
wisps of blue smoke, the mirrors catching it all,
bouncing it back and forth.
*How the Good Guys Finally Won: Notes from an
Impeachment Summer* (1975). Usually quoted as
"smoke and mirrors."

André Breton
French poet, 1896–1966

1 Beauty will be convulsive or will not be at all.
Nadja (1926)

2 It is impossible for me to envisage a picture
as being other than a window, and . . . my first
concern is then to know what it *looks out* on.
Surrealism and Painting (1928)

3 The imaginary is what tends to become real.
The White-Haired Revolver (1932)

4 It is at the movies that the only absolutely
modern mystery is celebrated.
Quoted in J. H. Matthews, *Surrealism and Film* (1971)

David J. Brewer
Turkish-born U.S. judge, 1837–1910

1 That woman's physical structure and the
performance of maternal functions place her at
a disadvantage in the struggle for subsistence
is obvious. This is especially true when the
burdens of motherhood are upon her. . . .
As healthy mothers are essential to vigorous
offspring, the physical well-being of woman
becomes an object of public interest and care in
order to preserve the strength and vigor of the
race.
Muller v. Oregon (1908)

Kingman Brewster, Jr.
U.S. university president, 1919–1988

1 I am appalled and ashamed that things should
have come to pass that I am skeptical of the
ability of Black revolutionaries to achieve a fair
trial anywhere in the United States.
Statement at Yale University faculty meeting, New
Haven, Conn., 23 Apr. 1970

Leonid Brezhnev
Soviet president, 1906–1982

1 When internal and external forces which are
hostile to Socialism try to turn the development
of any Socialist country towards the restoration
of a capitalist regime . . . it becomes not only
a problem of the people concerned, but a
common problem and concern of all Socialist
countries.
Speech to Congress of Polish Communist Party, 12
Nov. 1968

Aristide Briand
French statesman, 1862–1932

1 The high contracting powers solemnly declare
. . . that they condemn recourse to war and
renounce it . . . as an instrument of their
national policy towards each other. . . . The
settlement or the solution of all disputes or
conflicts of whatever nature or of whatever
origin they may be which may arise . . . shall
never be sought by either side except by pacific
means.
Treaty draft, 20 June 1927. Briand's language was
later incorporated into the Kellogg Pact (1928).

2 This war is too important to be left to military
men.
Quoted in Frances Stevenson, Diary, 23 Oct. 1916.
Also attributed to Clemenceau and Talleyrand, often
ending "entrusted to generals."
See Clemenceau 4; de Gaulle 10

Leslie Bricusse 1931– and Anthony Newley
1931–1999
English songwriters

1 What kind of fool am I
Who never fell in love?
It seems that I'm the only one
That I have been thinking of.
"What Kind of Fool Am I?" (song) (1961)

2 Stop the World, I Want to Get Off.
Title of musical comedy (1961). Current as graffiti
before 1961.

3 Maybe tomorrow
  I'll find what I'm after.
  I'll throw off my sorrow,
  Beg, steal, or borrow
  My share of laughter.
  "Who Can I Turn To (When Nobody Needs Me)"
  (song) (1964)

Robert Bridges
English poet, 1844–1930

1 When men were all asleep the snow came
    flying,
  In large white flakes falling on the city brown,
  Stealthily and perpetually settling and loosely
    lying,
  Hushing the latest traffic of the drowsy town.
  "London Snow" l. 1 (1890)

Robert Briffault
French-born British anthropologist and
novelist, 1876–1948

1 Democracy is the worst form of government.
  It is the most inefficient, the most clumsy, the
  most unpractical. . . . It reduces wisdom to
  impotence and secures the triumph of folly,
  ignorance, clap-trap, and demagogy. . . . Yet
  democracy is the only form of social order
  that is admissible, because it is the only one
  consistent with justice.
  Rational Evolution (The Making of Humanity) ch. 15
  (1930)
  See Winston Churchill 34

Le Baron Russell Briggs
U.S. educator, 1855–1934

1 As has often been said, the youth who loves his
  Alma Mater will always ask, not "What can she
  do for me?" but "What can I do for her?"
  Routine and Ideals "The Mistakes of College Life"
  (1904)
  *See Gibran 5; Oliver Wendell Holmes, Jr. 6; John
  Kennedy 4; John Kennedy 5; John Kennedy 16*

John Bright
English politician, 1811–1889

1 England is the mother of parliaments.
  Speech, Birmingham, England, 18 Jan. 1865

2 [*Of the American Civil War:*] My opinion is that
  the Northern States will manage somehow to
  muddle through.
  Quoted in Justin McCarthy, *Reminiscences* (1899)

Anthelme Brillat-Savarin
French jurist and gourmet, 1755–1826

1 *Dis-moi ce que tu manges, je te dirai ce que tu es.*
  Tell me what you eat and I will tell you what
    you are.
  Physiologie du Goût aphorism no. 4 (1825) (translation
  by Anne Drayton). Proverbial in the form "you are
  what you eat," the earliest known example of which is
  in *Longman's Magazine*, Dec. 1885.
  See Feuerbach 1

2 The discovery of a new dish does more for the
  happiness of mankind than the discovery of a
  star.
  Physiologie du Goût aphorism no. 9 (1825) (translation
  by Anne Drayton)

Mary Dow Brine
U.S. writer, ca. 1836–1925

1 She's somebody's mother, boys, you know,
  For all she's aged and poor and slow,
  And I hope some fellow will lend a hand
  To help my mother, you understand,
  If ever she's poor and old and gray,
  When her own dear boy is far away.
  "Somebody's Mother" l. 29 (1878)

André Brink
South African writer, 1935–2015

1 Perhaps all one can really hope for, all I am
  entitled to, is no more than this: to write it
  down. To report what I know. So that it will
  not be possible for any man ever to say again: *I
  knew nothing about it.*
  A Dry White Season epilogue (1980)

Terry Britten
Australian rock musician, fl. 1980

1 What's love got to do, got to do with it?
  What's love but a second hand emotion?
  What's love got to do, got to do with it?
  Who needs a heart when a heart can be broken?
  "What's Love Got to Do With It?" (song) (1984).
  Cowritten with Graham Lyle.

James Brockman

U.S. songwriter, 1886–1967

1 I'm forever blowing bubbles,
Pretty bubbles in the air.
"I'm Forever Blowing Bubbles" (song) (1919).
Cowritten with James Kendis and Nathaniel Vincent.

Tom Brokaw

U.S. broadcaster and author, 1940–

1 This is the greatest generation any society has
ever produced.
Remark on NBC "Meet the Press" television
broadcast, June 1994

Samuel Bronfman

Russian-born Canadian business executive and
philanthropist, 1889–1971

1 To turn $100 into $110 is work. But to turn
$100 million into $110 million is inevitable.
Quoted in Peter C. Newman, *Bronfman Dynasty: The
Rothschilds of the New World* (1978)

Anne Brontë

English poet and novelist, 1820–1849

1 All true histories contain instruction; though
in some, the treasure may be hard to find, and
when found, so trivial in quantity that the dry,
shrivelled kernel scarcely compensates for the
trouble of cracking the nut.
Agnes Grey ch. 1 (1847)

Charlotte Brontë

English novelist, 1816–1855

1 There was no possibility of taking a walk that
day.
Jane Eyre ch. 1 (1847)

2 "My bride is here," he said, again drawing me
to him, "because my equal is here, and my
likeness. Jane, will you marry me?"
Jane Eyre ch. 23 (1847)

3 You—poor and obscure, and small and plain
as you are—I entreat you to accept me as a
husband.
Jane Eyre ch. 23 (1847)

4 My future husband was becoming to me my
whole world; and more than the world: almost

my hope of heaven. He stood between me
and every thought of religion, as an eclipse
intervenes between man and the broad sun.
I could not, in those days, see God for His
creature: of whom I had made an idol.
Jane Eyre ch. 24 (1847)

5 Reader, I married him.
Jane Eyre ch. 38 (1847)

6 When his first-born was put into his arms, he
could see that the boy had inherited his own
eyes, as they once were—large, brilliant, and
black.
Jane Eyre ch. 38 (1847)

7 Of late years an abundant shower of curates has
fallen upon the North of England.
Shirley ch. 1 (1849)

8 Life is so constructed that the event does not,
cannot, will not, match the expectation.
Villette ch. 36 (1853)

Emily Brontë

English novelist and poet, 1818–1848

1 No coward soul is mine,
No trembler in the world's storm-troubled
sphere:
I see Heaven's glories shine,
And faith shines equal, arming me from fear.
"Last Lines" l. 1 (1846)

2 Cold in the earth—and fifteen wild Decembers,
From those brown hills, have melted into
spring.
"Remembrance" l. 9 (1846)

3 Nelly, I *am* Heathcliff.
Wuthering Heights ch. 9 (1847)

4 He's [Heathcliff's] more myself than I am.
Whatever our souls are made of, his and mine
are the same; and Linton's is as different as a
moonbeam from lightning, or frost from fire.
Wuthering Heights ch. 9 (1847)

5 And I pray one prayer—I repeat it till my
tongue stiffens—Catherine Earnshaw, may you
not rest as long as I am living; you said I killed
you—haunt me, then! The murdered *do* haunt
their murderers, I believe. I know that ghosts
have wandered on earth. Be with me always—

take any form—drive me mad! only *do* not leave me in this abyss, where I cannot find you! Oh, God! it is unutterable! I *cannot* live without my life! I *cannot* live without my soul!
Wuthering Heights ch. 16 (1847)

6 I lingered round them, under that benign sky: watched the moths fluttering among the heath and harebells, listened to the soft wind breathing through the grass, and wondered how any one could ever imagine unquiet slumbers for the sleepers in that quiet earth.
Wuthering Heights ch. 34 (1847)

Esther Eberstadt Brooke
U.S. author, 1894–1987

1 Luck, if you will, is something you work for, and the harder you work the more luck you have.
Career Clinic pt. 3, ch. 2 (1940)

Rupert Brooke
English poet, 1887–1915

1 If I should die, think only this of me:
That there's some corner of a foreign field
That is for ever England.
"The Soldier" l. 1 (1914)

2 Well this side of Paradise! . . .
There's little comfort in the wise.
"Tiare Tahiti" l. 76 (1914). Ellipsis in original.

Anita Brookner
English novelist, 1928–2016

1 Dr. Weiss, at forty, knew that her life had been ruined by literature.
A Start in Life ch. 1 (1981)

Frederick P. Brooks, Jr.
U.S. computer scientist, 1931–

1 ["*Brooks' Law*":] Adding manpower to a late software project makes it later.
"The Mythical Man-Month," *Datamation*, Dec. 1974

2 The bearing of a child takes nine months, no matter how many women are assigned.
"The Mythical Man-Month," *Datamation*, Dec. 1974

Gwendolyn Brooks
U.S. poet, 1917–2000

1 Abortions will not let you forget.
You remember the children you got that you did not get.
"the mother" l. 1 (1945)

2 We

Sing sin. We
Thin gin. We

Jazz June. We
Die soon.
"We Real Cool" l. 4 (1960)

Jack Brooks
English-born U.S. songwriter, 1912–1971

1 When the moon hits your eye
Like a big pizza pie,
That's amoré.
"That's Amoré (That's Love)" (song) (1953)

Mel Brooks (Melvin Kaminsky)
U.S. filmmaker and comedian, 1926–

1 [*Leo Bloom, played by Gene Wilder, speaking:*] It's simply a matter of creative accounting. Let's assume for a moment that you are a dishonest man. . . . It's very easy. You simply raise more money than you really need.
The Producers (motion picture) (1968)

2 [*Max Bialystock, played by Zero Mostel, speaking:*] That's it, baby! When you got it, flaunt it!
The Producers (motion picture) (1968)

3 [*Max Bialystock, played by Zero Mostel, speaking:*] A week? Are you kidding? This play has got to close on page four.
The Producers (motion picture) (1968)

4 [*Franz Liebkind, played by Kenneth Mars, speaking:*] Hitler was better looking than Churchill, he was a better dresser than Churchill, he had more hair, he told funnier jokes, and he could dance the pants off of Churchill.
The Producers (motion picture) (1968)

5 [*Max Bialystock, played by Zero Mostel, speaking:*] That's exactly why we want to produce this play. To show the world the true Hitler, the Hitler

you loved, the Hitler you knew, the Hitler with a song in his heart.

The Producers (motion picture) (1968)

6 Springtime for Hitler and Germany,
Deutschland is happy and gay.
We're marching to a faster pace,
Look out, here comes the Master Race!

The Producers (motion picture) (1968)

7 [*Roger De Bris, played by Christopher Hewett, speaking:*] Will the dancing Hitlers please wait in the wings, we are only seeing singing Hitlers.

The Producers (motion picture) (1968)

8 [*Max Bialystock, played by Zero Mostel, speaking:*] How could this happen? I was so careful. I picked the wrong play, the wrong director, the wrong cast. Where did I go right?

The Producers (motion picture) (1968)

9 [*Jury foreman, played by Bill Macy, returning verdict on Max Bialystock and Leo Bloom, played by Zero Mostel and Gene Wilder:*] We find the defendants incredibly guilty.

The Producers (motion picture) (1968). *The New Yorker Twenty-Fifth Anniversary Album, 1925–1950* (1951) includes a cartoon from the late 1940s in which a stern jury forewoman reads a verdict: "We find the defendant very, very guilty."

10 [*Governor William J. Le Petomane, played by Mel Brooks, addressing his secretary's breasts:*] Hello, boys . . . Have a good night's rest? . . . I missed you.

Blazing Saddles (motion picture) (1974)

11 [*The Waco Kid, played by Gene Wilder, speaking:*] You've got to remember that these are just simple farmers. These are people of the land. The common clay of the New West. You know—morons.

Blazing Saddles (motion picture) (1974)

12 [*Lili von Shtupp, played by Madeline Kahn, speaking to black cowboy Bart, played by Cleavon Little:*] Is it true how zey say zat you people are . . . gifted? Oh! It's twue! It's twue!

Blazing Saddles (motion picture) (1974)

13 [*King Louis XVI, played by Mel Brooks, speaking:*] It's good to be the king.

History of the World: Part I (motion picture) (1981)

14 Tragedy is when I cut my finger; comedy is when you walk into an open sewer and die.

Quoted in *Portland Oregonian*, 15 July 1973

15 Bad taste is simply saying the truth before it should be said.

Quoted in John Robert Columbo, *Popcorn in Paradise* (1980)

Van Wyck Brooks
U.S. essayist and critic, 1886–1963

1 [*Of Mark Twain:*] His wife not only edited his works but edited him.

The Ordeal of Mark Twain ch. 5 (1920)

Henry Peter Brougham
Scottish lawyer and politician, 1778–1868

1 An advocate, by the sacred duty which he owes his client, knows, in the discharge of that office, but one person in the world, that client and none other. To save that client . . . is the highest and most unquestioned of his duties; and he must not regard the alarm, the suffering, the torment, the destruction which he may bring upon any other. Nay . . . he must go on reckless of the consequences, if his fate it should unhappily be, to involve his country in confusion for his client's protection.

Argument at trial of Queen Caroline for adultery (1820). This speech was a veiled threat to King George IV that, if the king's bill of divorcement against the queen were pressed, Brougham would prove that George had forfeited his crown by secretly marrying a Roman Catholic.

Heywood Broun
U.S. journalist, 1888–1939

1 The tragedy of life is not that man loses but that he almost wins.

Pieces of Hate and Other Enthusiasms ch. 11 (1922)

2 "Trees" maddens me, because it contains the most insincere line ever written by mortal man. Surely the Kilmer tongue must have been not far from the Kilmer cheek when he wrote, "Poems are made by fools like me."

It Seems to Me "'Trees,' 'If,' and 'Invictus'" (1935)
See Kilmer 2

3 Obscenity is such a tiny kingdom that a single tour covers it completely.

Quoted in Bennett Cerf, *Shake Well Before Using* (1948)

4 The censor believes that he can hold back the mighty traffic of life with a tin whistle and a raised right hand. For, after all, it is life with which he quarrels.

Quoted in Ezra Goodman, *The Fifty-Year Decline and Fall of Hollywood* (1961)

Heywood Hale Broun
U.S. sports broadcaster, 1918–2001

1 Sports doesn't build character. . . . Sports reveals character.

Quoted in *Ames* (Iowa) *Daily Tribune*, 16 Jan. 1974

A. Seymour Brown
U.S. songwriter, 1885–1947

1 Oh You Beautiful Doll.

Title of song (1911)

Claude Brown
U.S. writer, 1937–2002

1 For where does one run to when he's already in the promised land?

Manchild in the Promised Land foreword (1965)

Fredric Brown
U.S. science fiction writer, 1906–1972

1 He turned to face the machine. "Is there a God?"

The mighty voice answered without hesitation, without the clicking of a single relay. "Yes, *now* there is a God."

"Answer" (1954)

Helen Gurley Brown
U.S. journalist and writer, 1922–2001

1 Sex and the Single Girl.

Title of book (1962)

2 Good girls go to heaven—bad girls go everywhere.

Quoted in *N.Y. Times*, 19 Sept. 1982. The *Cleveland Plain Dealer*, 3 Jan. 1980, printed: "Spotted on a Terminal Tower T-shirt: Good girls go to heaven, but bad girls go everywhere."

Henry B. Brown
U.S. judge, 1836–1913

1 Legislation is powerless to eradicate racial instincts or to abolish distinctions based upon physical differences, and the attempt to do so can only result in accentuating the difficulties of the present situation. If the civil and political rights of both races be equal one cannot be inferior to the other civilly or politically. If one race be inferior to the other socially, the Constitution of the United States cannot put them upon the same plane.

Plessy v. Ferguson (1896)

H. Rap Brown
U.S. civil rights leader, 1943–

1 Violence . . . is as American as cherry pie.

Press conference at Student Nonviolent Coordinating Committee headquarters, Washington, D.C., 27 July 1967

James Brown
U.S. singer, 1933–2006

1 Papa's Got a Brand New Bag.

Title of song (1965)

2 Say It Loud—I'm Black and I'm Proud.

Title of song (1968)
See Roddy Doyle 1

3 What we want—soul power! What we need— soul power!

"Soul Power" (song) (1971)

John Brown
U.S. abolitionist, 1800–1859

1 Had I interfered in the manner, which I admit, and which I admit has been fairly proved . . . had I so interfered in behalf of any of the rich, the powerful, the intelligent, the so-called great . . . and suffered and sacrificed what I have in this interference, it would have been all right, and every man in this court would have deemed it an act worthy of reward rather than punishment.

Speech at trial for treason and insurrection, Charlestown, Va., 2 Nov. 1859

2 I say I am yet too young to understand that God is any respecter of persons. I believe that to have interfered as I have done . . . in behalf

of His despised poor, is no wrong, but right. Now, if it is deemed necessary that I should forfeit my life for the furtherance of the ends of justice, and mingle my blood further with the blood of my children and with the blood of millions in this slave country whose rights are disregarded by wicked, cruel, and unjust enactments, I say let it be done.

Speech at trial for treason and insurrection, Charlestown, Va., 2 Nov. 1859
See Bible 333

3 I am fully persuaded that I am worth inconceivably more to hang for than for any other purpose.

Speech at trial for treason and insurrection, Charlestown, Va., 2 Nov. 1859

4 I, John Brown, am now quite certain that the crimes of this guilty land will never be purged away but with Blood.

Statement written on day of his execution, 2 Dec. 1859

5 This *is* a beautiful country.

Remark as Brown rode to the gallows seated on his coffin, Charlestown, Va., 2 Dec. 1859

John Mason Brown
U.S. critic, 1900–1969

1 TV seems to be chewing gum for the eyes.

Syracuse Herald-Journal, 21 Jan. 1955. Earlier, "chewing gum for the eyes" was used to refer to motion pictures by Henri Peyre in his book *Writers and Their Critics: A Study of Misunderstanding* (1944).

Lew Brown
U.S. songwriter, 1893–1958

1 Keep Your Sunny Side Up.

"Sunny Side Up" (song) (1929)

2 Life Is Just a Bowl of Cherries.

Title of song (1931)
See Bombeck 2

3 Don't Sit Under the Apple Tree with Anyone Else But Me.

Title of song (1942). Cowritten with Charles Tobias and Sam H. Stept.

Margaret Wise Brown
U.S. children's book writer, 1910–1952

1 In the great green room
There was a telephone

And a red balloon
And a picture of—
The cow jumping over the moon.

Goodnight Moon (1947)

2 And a quiet old lady who was whispering "hush."

Goodnight Moon (1947)

3 Goodnight stars
Goodnight air
Goodnight noises everywhere.

Goodnight Moon (1947)

Peter Brown
U.S. songwriter, 1953–

1 You know that we are living in a material world
And I am a material girl.

"I Am a Material Girl" (song) (1984). Cowritten with Robert Rans.

Rita Mae Brown
U.S. writer, 1944–

1 The only queer people are those who don't love anybody.

Speech at opening of Gay Olympics, San Francisco, Calif., 28 Aug. 1982

2 Insanity is doing the same thing over and over again, but expecting different results.

Sudden Death ch. 4 (1983). Earlier, "Insanity is repeating the same mistakes and expecting different results" appeared in a 1981 Narcotics Anonymous pamphlet (cited on the quoteinvestigator.com website).

3 Normal is the average of deviance.

Venus Envy ch. 21 (1993)

Sarah Frances Brown
U.S. [occupation unknown], 1913–2001

1 Twenty years from now you will be more disappointed by the things you didn't do than by the ones you did do. So throw off the bowlines. Sail away from the safe harbor. Catch the trade winds in your sails. Explore. Dream. Discover.

Quoted in H. Jackson Brown, Jr., *P.S. I Love You* (1990). Sarah Frances Brown was H. Jackson Brown, Jr.'s mother. The quotation is frequently misattributed to Mark Twain.

T. E. Brown

English poet and educator, 1830–1897

1 A garden is a lovesome thing, God wot!
"My Garden" l. 1 (1893)

Thomas Brown

English satirist, 1663–1704

1 I do not love you, Dr. *Fell,*
But why I cannot tell;
But this I know full well,
I do not love you, Dr. *Fell.*
Works vol. 4 (1744). Adaptation of an epigram by
Martial.
See Martial 1

Thomas Browne

English author and physician, 1605–1682

1 All things are artificial, for nature is the art of
God.
Religio Medici pt. 1, sec. 16 (1643)

2 For the world, I count it not an inn, but a
hospital; and a place not to live, but to die in.
Religio Medici pt. 2, sec. 11 (1643)

3 When the living might exceed the dead, and to
depart this world could not be properly said to
go unto the greater number.
Hydriotaphia Epistle Dedicatory (1658)

4 What song the Syrens sang, or what name
Achilles assumed when he hid himself among
women, though puzzling questions, are not
beyond all conjecture.
Hydriotaphia ch. 5 (1658)

Elizabeth Barrett Browning

English poet, 1806–1861

1 And lips say, "God be pitiful,"
Who ne'er said, "God be praised."
"The Cry of the Human" l. 7 (1844)

2 How do I love thee? Let me count the ways.
Sonnets from the Portuguese no. 43 (1850)

3 I love thee with the breath,
Smiles, tears, of all my life!—and if God
choose,
I shall but love thee better after death.
Sonnets from the Portuguese no. 43 (1850)

4 I should not dare to call my soul my own.
Aurora Leigh bk. 2, l. 786 (1857)

5 What was he doing, the great god Pan,
Down in the reeds by the river?
"A Musical Instrument" l. 1 (1862)

Frederick "Boy" Browning

British soldier, 1896–1965

1 [*Speaking to Field Marshal Bernard Montgomery,
10 Sept. 1944, about the planned Arnhem "Market
Garden" operation:*] I think we might be going a
bridge too far.
Attributed in R. E. Urquhart, *Arnhem* (1958).
According to Nigel Rees, *Cassell's Movie Quotations,*
"there is now a strong reason to doubt that Browning
ever said any such thing."

Robert Browning

English poet, 1812–1889

1 The year's at the spring
And day's at the morn;
Morning's at seven;
The hill-side's dew-pearled;
The lark's on the wing;
The snail's on the thorn:
God's in his heaven—
All's right with the world!
Pippa Passes pt. 1 (1841)

2 Then owls and bats
Cowls and twats
Monks and nuns in a cloister's moods,
Adjourn to the oak-stump pantry.
Pippa Passes pt. 4 (1841). Browning was misled into
thinking the word *twat* referred to a piece of nun's
clothing by an anonymous 1660 poem, "Vanity of
Vanities," which included the lines: "They talk't of his
having a Cardinalls Hat, / They'd send him as soon
an Old Nuns Twat."

3 That's my last Duchess painted on the wall,
Looking as if she were alive.
"My Last Duchess" l. 1 (1842)

4   She had
A heart—how shall I say?—too soon made
glad,
Too easily impressed; she liked whate'er
She looked on, and her looks went everywhere.
"My Last Duchess" l. 21 (1842)

5 She thanked men,—good! but thanked
  Somehow—I know not how—as if she ranked
  My gift of a nine-hundred-year-old name
  With anybody's gift.
  "My Last Duchess" l. 31 (1842)

6   Oh sir, she smiled, no doubt,
  Whene'er I passed her; but who passed without
  Much the same smile? This grew; I gave
      commands;
  Then all smiles stopped together. There she
      stands
  As if alive.
  "My Last Duchess" l. 42 (1842)

7   Notice Neptune, though,
  Taming a sea-horse, thought a rarity,
  Which Claus of Innsbruck cast in bronze
      for me!
  "My Last Duchess" l. 54 (1842)

8 Oh, to be in England
  Now that April's there.
  "Home-Thoughts, from Abroad" l. 1 (1845)

9 That's the wise thrush; he sings each song twice
      over,
  Lest you should think he never could recapture
  The first fine careless rapture!
  "Home-Thoughts, from Abroad" l. 14 (1845)

10 I sprang to the stirrup, and Joris, and he;
   I galloped, Dirck galloped, we galloped all
      three.
   "How They Brought the Good News from Ghent to
   Aix" l. 1 (1845)

11 Just for a handful of silver he left us,
   Just for a riband to stick in his coat.
   "The Lost Leader" l. 1 (1845). Refers to William
   Wordsworth.

12 Well, less is more, Lucrezia.
   "Andrea del Sarto" l. 78 (1855). Nigel Rees (*Quote . . .
   Unquote Newsletter*, Oct. 1997) points out a precursor
   to this saying: "In January 1774 . . . Wieland in his
   Teutsche Merkur . . . wrote: '*Und minder ist oft mehr*'
   [Less is often more]."
   See Mies van der Rohe 1; Venturi 1

13 Ah, but a man's reach should exceed his grasp,
   Or what's a heaven for?
   "Andrea del Sarto" l. 97 (1855)

14 Who knows but the world may end tonight?
   "The Last Ride Together" l. 22 (1855)

15 Ah, did you once see Shelley plain,
   And did he stop and speak to you
   And did you speak to him again?
   How strange it seems, and new!
   "Memorabilia" l. 1 (1855)

16 It was roses, roses, all the way.
   "The Patriot" l. 1 (1855)

17 What of soul was left, I wonder, when the
   kissing had to stop?
   "A Toccata of Galuppi's" l. 42 (1855)

18 The best way to escape His ire
   Is, not to seem too happy.
   "Caliban upon Setebos" l. 256 (1864)

19 Grow old along with me!
   The best is yet to be,
   The last of life, for which the first was made.
   "Rabbi Ben Ezra" l. 1 (1864)

Susan Brownmiller
U.S. writer, 1935–

1 Man's discovery that his genitalia could serve as
  a weapon to generate fear must rank as one of
  the most important discoveries of prehistoric
  times, along with the use of fire and the first
  crude stone axe. From prehistoric times to the
  present, I believe, rape has played a critical
  function. It is nothing more or less than a
  conscious process of intimidation by which *all
  men* keep *all women* in a state of fear.
  Against Our Will ch. 1 (1975)

2 My purpose in this book has been to give rape
  its history. Now we must deny it a future.
  Against Our Will ch. 12 (1975)

Ed Bruce
U.S. songwriter and singer, 1939–2021

1 Mammas, Don't Let Your Babies Grow Up to
  Be Cowboys.
  Title of song (1978). Cowritten with Patsy Bruce.

Lenny Bruce (Leonard Alfred Schneider)
U.S. comedian, 1925–1966

1 People should be taught what is, not what
  should be. All my humor is based on
  destruction and despair. If the whole world
  were tranquil, without disease and violence, I'd

be standing in the breadline—right back of J. Edgar Hoover.

The Essential Lenny Bruce, ed. John Cohen, epigram (1967)

2 The halls of justice. That's the only place you see the justice, is in the halls.

The Essential Lenny Bruce, ed. John Cohen (1967)

3 Every day people are straying away from the church and going back to God.

The Essential Lenny Bruce, ed. John Cohen (1967)

4 [*On his drug addiction:*] I'll die young but it's like kissing God.

Quoted in Richard Neville, *Playpower* (1970)

Giordano Bruno (Filippo Bruno)
Italian philosopher, 1548–1600

1 He is glorified not in one, but in countless suns, not in a single earth, a single world, but in a thousand thousand, I say in an infinity of worlds.

On the Infinite Universe and Worlds introduction (1584)

Alfred Bryan
U.S. songwriter, ca. 1870–1958

1 I Didn't Raise My Boy to Be a Soldier.

Title of song (1915)

William Jennings Bryan
U.S. politician, 1860–1925

1 I am in favor of an income tax. When I find a man who is not willing to bear his share of the burdens of the government which protects him, I find a man who is unworthy to enjoy the blessings of a government like ours.

Speech at Democratic National Convention, Chicago, Ill., 8 July 1896

2 There are those who believe that, if you will only legislate to make the well-to-do prosperous, their prosperity will leak through on those below. The Democratic idea, however, has been that if you make the masses prosperous, their prosperity will find its way up through every class, which rests upon them.

Speech at Democratic National Convention, Chicago, Ill., 8 July 1896

3 We will answer their demand for a gold standard by saying to them: You shall not press

down upon the brow of labor this crown of thorns, you shall not crucify mankind upon a cross of gold.

Speech at Democratic National Convention, Chicago, Ill., 8 July 1896. In an earlier speech in the House of Representatives, 22 Dec. 1894, Bryan had said: "I shall not help crucify mankind upon a cross of gold. I shall not aid in pressing down upon the bleeding brow of labor this crown of thorns."

William Cullen Bryant
U.S. poet and editor, 1794–1878

1 He who, from zone to zone,
Guides through the boundless sky thy certain flight,
In the long way that I must tread alone,
Will lead my steps aright.

"To a Waterfowl" l. 29 (1818)

2 To him who in the love of Nature holds
Communion with her visible forms, she speaks
A various language.

Thanatopsis l. 1 (1817–1821)

James Bryce
British statesman and historian, 1838–1922

1 To most people nothing is more troublesome than the effort of thinking.

Studies in History and Jurisprudence "Obedience" (1901)

Martin Buber
Austrian-born Israeli philosopher, 1878–1965

1 Through the Thou a person becomes I.

I and Thou (1923)

John Buchan, Baron Tweedsmuir
Scottish novelist and statesman, 1875–1940

1 It's a great life if you don't weaken.

Mr. Standfast ch. 5 (1919). Although this line is associated with Buchan, it appeared as a show-business saying as early as *Variety,* 27 Mar. 1914. The *Chicago Tribune,* 5 July 1914, credited singer Elizabeth Murray with supplying the same line to the libretto of the 1913 operatic farce *High Jinks* by Otto Hauerbach and Leo Dietrichstein.

2 I have heard an atheist defined as a man who has no invisible means of support.

Quoted in *Law Journal,* 2 Mar. 1935

Patrick J. Buchanan
U.S. politician, 1938–

1 [*On AIDS:*] The poor homosexuals . . . they
have declared war upon nature, and now nature
is exacting an awful retribution.
N.Y. Post, 24 May 1983

Georg Büchner
German playwright, 1813–1837

1 The Revolution is like Saturn, it devours its own
children.
Danton's Death act 1, sc. 5 (1835)
See Vergniaud 1

Gene Buck
U.S. songwriter, 1885–1957

1 That Shakespearian rag,—
Most intelligent, very elegant.
"That Shakespearian Rag" (song) (1912). Cowritten
with Herman Ruby.
See T. S. Eliot 48

Pearl S. Buck
U.S. writer, 1892–1973

1 It is better to be first with an ugly woman than
the hundredth with a beauty.
The Good Earth ch. 1 (1931)

2 "Rest assured, our father, rest assured. The land
is not to be sold." But over the old man's head
they looked at each other and smiled.
The Good Earth ch. 34 (1931)

3 Yet somehow our society must make it right
and possible for old people not to fear the
young or be deserted by them, for the test of
a civilization is in the way that it cares for its
helpless members.
My Several Worlds pt. 4 (1954)
*See Ramsey Clark 1; Dostoyevski 1; Humphrey 3; Samuel
Johnson 69; Helen Keller 4*

Richard M. Bucke
Canadian psychiatrist, 1837–1902

1 Cosmic consciousness.
Title of paper before American Medico-Psychological
Association, Philadelphia, Pa., 18 May 1894

William F. Buckley, Jr.
U.S. editor and writer, 1925–2008

1 [*The magazine* National Review] stands athwart
history yelling Stop.
National Review, 19 Nov. 1955

2 I would rather be governed by the first 2,000
people in the telephone directory than by the
Harvard University faculty.
Quoted in *Esquire*, Jan. 1961

3 [*Response when asked what he would do if he won
his third-party bid to be elected mayor of New
York:*] I'd demand a recount.
Quoted in *N.Y. Times*, 5 Sept. 1965

Michael Buffer
U.S. sports announcer, 1944–

1 [*Catchphrase in announcing professional wrestling
matches:*] Let's get ready to rumble!
Quoted in *Newsday*, 4 Feb. 1989

Warren Buffett
U.S. investor and businessman, 1930–

1 My friends and I have been coddled long
enough by a billionaire-friendly Congress.
N.Y. Times op-ed article, 15 Aug. 2011

2 It's only when the tide goes out that you learn
who's been swimming naked.
Quoted in *U.S. News & World Report*, 21 June 1993.
Although this quotation is strongly associated with
Buffett, it has been ascribed to others before 1993.
The Economist, 27 Feb. 1988, attributed "You don't
know if someone is swimming naked until the tide
goes out" to George Salem.

3 I'd be a bum on the street with a tin cup if the
markets were always efficient.
Quoted in *Fortune*, 3 Apr. 1995

George-Louis Leclerc, Comte de Buffon
French naturalist, 1707–1788

1 Style is the man himself.
Discours sur le Style (1753)

2 Genius is only a greater aptitude for patience.
Quoted in Hérault de Séchelles, *Voyage à Montbar*
(1803)
See Thomas Carlyle 19; Edison 2; Jane Ellice Hopkins 1

Mikhail A. Bulgakov

Russian novelist and playwright, 1891–1940

1 Manuscripts don't burn.

The Master and Margarita ch. 24 (1940) (translation by Mirra Ginsburg)

Arthur Buller

Canadian botanist, 1874–1944

1 There was a young lady named Bright,
Whose speed was far faster than light;
She set out one day
In a relative way
And returned on the previous night.

"Relativity" l. 1 (1923)

Bernhard von Bülow

German chancellor, 1849–1929

1 We desire to throw no one into the shade [in East Asia], but we also demand our own place in the sun.

Speech in Reichstag, 6 Dec. 1897
See Pascal 4; Wilhelm II 1

Edward George Bulwer-Lytton

British novelist and politician, 1803–1873

1 [*Opening line of book:*] It was a dark and stormy night.

Paul Clifford ch. 1 (1830). Charles M. Schulz used this line, typed by the character Snoopy, recurrently in his comic strip *Peanuts*. The earliest appearance there was 12 July 1965.

2 In other countries poverty is a misfortune— with us it is a crime.

England and the English (1833)

3 Beneath the rule of men entirely great,
The pen is mightier than the sword.

Richelieu act 2, sc. 2 (1839). The *Oxford Dictionary of Proverbs* documents similar formulations going back to 1582 ("The dashe of a Pen, is more greeuous then the counter use of a Launce" [George Whetstone, *Heptameron of Civil Discourses*]).
See Robert Burton 3

4 In the lexicon of youth, which fate reserves
For a bright manhood, there is no such word
As—*fail.*

Richelieu act 2, sc. 2 (1839)

Ralph J. Bunche

U.S. diplomat and political scientist, ca. 1903–1971

1 There are no warlike peoples—just warlike leaders.

Address to student conference, Madison, Wis., 1 May 1950

Luis Buñuel

Spanish film director, 1900–1983

1 *Le Charme Discret de la Bourgeoisie.*
The Discreet Charm of the Bourgeoisie.

Title of motion picture (1972)

2 *Cet Obscur Objet du Désir.*
That Obscure Object of Desire.

Title of motion picture (1977)

3 Thanks be to God, I am still an atheist.

Quoted in *Le Monde,* 16 Dec. 1959

John Bunyan

English writer and preacher, 1628–1688

1 As I walked through the wilderness of this world.

The Pilgrim's Progress pt. 1 (1678)

2 The name of the slough was Despond.

The Pilgrim's Progress pt. 1 (1678)

3 It beareth the name of Vanity-Fair, because the town where 'tis kept, is lighter than vanity.

The Pilgrim's Progress pt. 1 (1678)

4 Hanging is too good for him, said Mr. Cruelty.

The Pilgrim's Progress pt. 1 (1678)

5 So I awoke, and behold it was a dream.

The Pilgrim's Progress pt. 1 (1678)

6 A man that could look no way but downwards, with a muckrake in his hand.

The Pilgrim's Progress pt. 2 (1684)
See Theodore Roosevelt 15

7 So he [Mr. Valiant-for-Truth] passed over, and the trumpets sounded for him on the other side.

The Pilgrim's Progress pt. 2 (1684)

Samuel Dickinson Burchard

U.S. clergyman, 1812–1891

1 We are Republicans and don't propose to leave our party and identify ourselves with the party

whose antecedents are rum, Romanism, and rebellion.

Speech at Fifth Avenue Hotel, New York, N.Y., 29 Oct. 1884. Robert G. Caldwell, *James A. Garfield* (1931), quotes an 1876 letter by Garfield in which he attributed the apparent election victory of Samuel Tilden to "the combined power of rebellion, Catholicism, and whiskey."

Julie Burchill
English journalist and writer, 1960–

1 The freedom women were supposed to have found in the Sixties largely boiled down to easy contraception and abortion: things to make life easier for men, in fact.
   Damaged Goods "Born Again Cows" (1986)

2 Now, at last, this sad, glittering century has an image worthy of it: a wandering, wondering girl, a silly Sloane turned secular saint, coming home in her coffin to RAF Northolt like the good soldier she was.
   Guardian, 2 Sept. 1997

Robert Jones Burdette
U.S. clergyman and humorist, 1844–1914

1 Don't believe the world owes you a living. The world owes you nothing. It was here first.
   Quoted in *Evening Observer* (Dunkirk, N.Y.), 1 Feb. 1883

Eugene Burdick
U.S. writer, 1918–1965

1 The Ugly American.
   Title of book (1958). Coauthored with William Lederer.

Hannibal Buress
U.S. comedian, 1983–

1 [*Of Bill Cosby:*] He gets on TV, "Pull your pants up black people, I was on TV in the 80s! I can talk down to you because I had a successful sitcom!" Yeah, but you rape women, Bill Cosby, so turn the crazy down a couple notches.
   Comedy performance, Philadelphia, Pa., 17 Oct. 2014. Buress's remarks were influential in publicizing accusations of sexual assault against Cosby.

Anthony Burgess (John Wilson)
English novelist and critic, 1917–1993

1 Then I looked at its top sheet, and there was the name—A CLOCKWORK ORANGE . . . "—The attempt to impose upon man, a creature of growth and capable of sweetness, to ooze juicily at the last round the bearded lips of God, to attempt to impose, I say, laws and conditions appropriate to a mechanical creation, against this I raise my sword-pen—."
   A Clockwork Orange pt. 1, ch. 2 (1962)

2 But, gentlemen, enough of words. Actions speak louder than. Action now.
   A Clockwork Orange pt. 2, ch. 7 (1962)

3 I was cured all right.
   A Clockwork Orange pt. 3, ch. 6 (1962)

4 It was the afternoon of my eighty-first birthday, and I was in bed with my catamite when Ali announced that the archbishop had come to see me.
   Earthly Powers ch. 1 (1980)

Gelett Burgess
U.S. humorist and illustrator, 1866–1951

1 I never saw a Purple Cow,
   I never hope to see one;
   But I can tell you, anyhow,
   I'd rather see than be one!
   "The Purple Cow" l. 1 (1895)
   See Gelett Burgess 8

2 *Are you a Goop, or are you Not?*
   For, although it's Fun to See them,
   It is TERRIBLE to Be them.
   Goops and How to Be Them (1900)

3 The Goops they lick their fingers,
   And the Goops they lick their knives,
   They spill their broth on the tablecloth—
   Oh, they lead disgusting lives!
   Goops and How to Be Them (1900)

4 Are You a Bromide?
   Title of book (1906). Gave rise to the term *bromide* meaning "commonplace statement."

5 It isn't so much the heat . . . as the humidity.
   Are You a Bromide? (1906). Presumably not original with Burgess.

6 [*Included in list of familiar "bromides":*] I don't
know much about Art, but I know what I like.

Are You a Bromide? (1906). Burgess listed this as
number 1 in his collection of "bromides" (clichés),
so it clearly was not originated by him. *Scribner's
Monthly*, Feb. 1877, has: "When a person prefaces his
opinion of a picture or of a piece of music, with this
formula,—'I don't profess to know anything about art
(or music), but I know what I like,'—then look out for
dogmatism of the most flagrant sort."
See Thurber 12

7 YES, this is a "BLURB"! All the other
publishers commit them. Why shouldn't we?

Dust jacket for *Are You a Bromide?* (1907). Earliest
usage of the word *blurb*. This dust jacket, with a
portrait of "Miss Belinda Blurb," was apparently
specially added to copies of the 1906 book distributed
at the 1907 annual dinner of the American
Booksellers' Association.

8 Ah, yes! I wrote the "Purple Cow"—
I'm sorry, now, I wrote it!
But I can tell you anyhow,
I'll kill you if you quote it!

"Confession: and a Portrait Too, Upon a Background
that I Rue" l. 1 (1914)
See Gelett Burgess 1

Billie Burke

U.S. actress, 1884–1970

1 Age [doesn't matter] unless you're a cheese.
Quoted in *Baltimore Sun*, 8 Nov. 1959

Edmund Burke

British philosopher and statesman, 1729–1797

1 When bad men combine, the good must
associate; else they will fall, one by one, an
unpitied sacrifice in a contemptible struggle.
Thoughts on the Cause of the Present Discontents (1770)
See Edmund Burke 28; Mill 18

2 We set ourselves to bite the hand that feeds us.
Thoughts on the Cause of the Present Discontents (1770)

3 Here this extraordinary man [Charles
Townsend], then Chancellor of the Exchequer,
found himself in great straits. To please
universally was the object of his life; but to
tax and to please, no more than to love and
to be wise, is not given to men. However he
attempted it.
Speech on American Taxation, 19 Apr. 1774

4 He was bred to the law, which is, in my
opinion, one of the first and noblest of human
sciences; a science which does more to quicken
and invigorate the understanding, than all the
other kinds of learning put together; but it is
not apt, except in persons very happily born,
to open and liberalize the mind exactly in the
same proportion.
Speech on American Taxation, 19 Apr. 1774

5 Your representative owes you, not his industry
only, but his judgement; and he betrays,
instead of serving you, if he sacrifices it to your
opinion.
Speech to electors of Bristol, 3 Nov. 1774

6 [*Of the American colonies:*] In no country,
perhaps, in the world is the law so general a
study.
"On Moving His Resolutions for Conciliation with
the Colonies," 22 Mar. 1775

7 This study [of law] renders men acute,
inquisitive, dexterous, prompt in attack,
ready in defense, full of resources. In other
countries, the people, more simple, and of a
less mercurial cast, judge of an ill principle
in government only by an actual grievance;
here they anticipate the evil, and judge of the
pressure of the grievance by the badness of

the principle. They augur misgovernment at a distance, and snuff the approach of tyranny in every tainted breeze.

"On Moving His Resolutions for Conciliation with the Colonies," 22 Mar. 1775

8 I do not know the method of drawing up an indictment against an whole people.

"On Moving His Resolutions for Conciliation with the Colonies," 22 Mar. 1775

9 It is not, what a lawyer tells me I *may* do; but what humanity, reason, and justice, tells me I ought to do.

"On Moving His Resolutions for Conciliation with the Colonies," 22 Mar. 1775

10 All government, indeed every human benefit and enjoyment, every virtue and every prudent act, is founded on compromise and barter. We balance inconveniences; we give and take; we remit some rights, that we may enjoy others; and we choose rather to be happy citizens than subtle disputants.

"On Moving His Resolutions for Conciliation with the Colonies," 22 Mar. 1775

11 The people are the masters.

Speech in House of Commons, 11 Feb. 1780

12 Bad laws are the worst sort of tyranny.

Speech at the Guildhall, Bristol, England, 6 Sept. 1780

13 A state without the means of some change is without the means of its conservation.

Reflections on the Revolution in France (1790)

14 People will not look forward to posterity, who never look backward to their ancestors.

Reflections on the Revolution in France (1790)

15 To be attached to the subdivision, to love the little platoon we belong to in society, is the first principle (the germ, as it were) of public affections. It is the first link in the series by which we proceed towards a love to our country and to mankind.

Reflections on the Revolution in France (1790)

16 It is said that twenty-four millions ought to prevail over two hundred thousand. True, if the constitution of a kingdom be a problem of arithmetic.

Reflections on the Revolution in France (1790)

17 I thought ten thousand swords must have leapt from their scabbards to avenge even a look that threatened her [Queen Marie Antoinette] with insult.

Reflections on the Revolution in France (1790)

18 The age of chivalry is gone.—That of sophisters, economists, and calculators, has succeeded; and the glory of Europe is extinguished for ever.

Reflections on the Revolution in France (1790)

19 Because half a dozen grasshoppers under a fern make the field ring with their importunate chink, whilst thousands of great cattle, reposed beneath the shadow of the British oak, chew the cud and are silent, pray do not imagine that those who make the noise are the only inhabitants of the field.

Reflections on the Revolution in France (1790)

20 Society is indeed a contract. . . . As the ends of such a partnership cannot be obtained in many generations, it becomes a partnership not only between those who are living, but between those who are living, those who are dead, and those who are to be born.

Reflections on the Revolution in France (1790)

21 Superstition is the religion of feeble minds.

Reflections on the Revolution in France (1790)

22 He that wrestles with us strengthens our nerves, and sharpens our skill. Our antagonist is our helper.

Reflections on the Revolution in France (1790)

23 Old religious factions are volcanoes burnt out.

Speech on Petition of the Unitarians, 11 May 1792

24 *To innovate is not to reform.* The French revolutionists complained of everything; they refused to reform anything, and they left nothing, no, nothing at all, *unchanged.*

A Letter to a Noble Lord (1796)

25 Falsehood and delusion are allowed in no case whatsoever: But, as in the exercise of all the virtues, there is an economy of truth.

Two Letters on the Proposals for Peace with the Regicide Directory pt. 1 (1796)
See Robert Armstrong 1; Twain 86

26 Manners are of more importance than laws.
. . . Manners are what vex or soothe, corrupt

or purify, exalt or debase, barbarize or refine us, by a constant, steady, uniform, insensible operation, like that of the air we breathe in. They give their whole form and color to our lives.

"Three Letters to a Member of Parliament on the Proposals for Peace with the Regicide Directory of France" (1796–1797)

27 [*On the younger William Pitt's maiden speech in Parliament, Feb. 1781:*] Not merely a chip of the old "block," but the old block itself.

Quoted in Nathaniel W. Wraxall, *Historical Memoirs of My Own Time* (1904)

28 The only thing necessary for the triumph of evil is that good men should do nothing.

Attributed in *Volume of Proceedings of the Fourth International Congregational Council* (1921). Frequently attributed to Burke but never traced in his writings. The closest Burke passage appears to be the one cross-referenced below. Garson O'Toole has found that the *San Jose Mercury Herald*, 31 Oct. 1916, quoted a speech by Charles F. Aked stating: "It has been said that for evil men to accomplish their purpose it is only necessary that good men should do nothing."

See Edmund Burke 1; Mill 18

Johnny Burke
U.S. songwriter, 1908–1964

1 Ev'ry time it rains, it rains
Pennies from heaven.
Don't you know each cloud contains
Pennies from heaven?

"Pennies from Heaven" (song) (1936)

Tarana Burke
U.S. social activist, 1973–

1 [*Slogan of campaign against sexual abuse:*] Me Too.

Myspace (social network) page (2006)

Frances Hodgson Burnett
English-born U.S. writer, 1849–1924

1 Little Lord Fauntleroy.
Title of book (1886)

2 When Mary Lennox was sent to Misselthwaite Manor to live with her uncle, everybody said she was the most disagreeable-looking child ever seen.

The Secret Garden ch. 1 (1911)

Thomas E. Burnett, Jr.
U.S. businessman, 1963–2001

1 [*Telephone call to his wife from hijacked airplane, 11 Sept. 2001:*] I know we're all going to die—there's three of us who are going to do something about it.

Quoted in *S.F. Chronicle*, 12 Sept. 2001

W. R. Burnett
U.S. author, 1899–1982

1 "Mother of God," he said, "is this the end of Rico?"

Little Caesar pt. 7 (1929). In the 1930 film the line is "Mother of Mercy, is this the end of Rico?"

2 The Asphalt Jungle.

Title of book (1949). The *Oxford English Dictionary* records an earlier usage of this phrase in George Ade, *Hand-Made Fables* (1920): "After the newly arrived Delegate from the Asphalt Jungles had read a Telegram . . . he . . . sauntered back to the Bureau of Information."

See Evan Hunter 1

Fanny Burney
English novelist and diarist, 1752–1840

1 [*Of a wedding:*] O! how short a time does it take to put an end to a woman's liberty!

Diary, 20 July 1768

2 Travelling is the ruin of all happiness! There's no looking at a building here after seeing Italy.

Cecilia bk. 4, ch. 2 (1782)

3 "The whole of this unfortunate business," said Dr. Lyster, "has been the result of PRIDE AND PREJUDICE."

Cecilia bk. 10, ch. 10 (1782)

4 A little alarm now and then keeps life from stagnation.

Camilla bk. 3, ch. 11 (1796)

Daniel Burnham
U.S. architect, 1846–1912

1 Make no little plans; they have no magic to stir men's blood.

Quoted in *Louisville Courier-Journal*, 20 Oct. 1910. This is said by the *Courier-Journal* to be "From an address by Architect Daniel H. Burnham, of Chicago, at the town-planning conference in London, published in the *Chicago Record-Herald*."

George Burns (Nathan Birnbaum)
U.S. comedian, 1896–1996

1 Too bad that all the people who know how to run the country are busy driving taxicabs and cutting hair.

Quoted in *Life*, Dec. 1979

2 The main thing about acting is honesty. If you can fake that, you've got it made.

Quoted in *Playboy*, Mar. 1984. Often ascribed to Burns, but the *Morning Advocate* (Baton Rouge, La.), 6 Apr. 1962, quoted an anonymous actor: "Honesty . . . just as soon as I can learn to fake that, I'll have it made."

Robert Burns
Scottish poet, 1759–1796

1 Man's inhumanity to man
Makes countless thousands mourn!

"Man Was Made to Mourn" st. 7 (1786)

2 O wad some Pow'r the giftie gie us
To see oursels as others see us!
It wad frae mony a blunder free us,
And foolish notion.

"To a Louse" st. 8 (1786)

3 The best laid schemes o' mice an' men
Gang aft a-gley.

"To a Mouse" l. 39 (1786). Often misquoted as "best laid plans."
See Dickens 67; Disraeli 7; Modern Proverbs 100; Orwell 17; Plautus 3; Proverbs 2; Sayings 25

4 His locked, lettered, braw brass collar,
Shew'd him the gentleman and scholar.

"The Twa Dogs" l. 13 (1786)

5 A man's a man for a' that.

"For a' That and a' That" l. 12 (1790)

6 My heart's in the Highlands, my heart is not here;
My heart's in the Highlands a-chasing the deer;
Chasing the wild deer, and following the roe,
My heart's in the Highlands, wherever I go.

"My Heart's in the Highlands" l. 1 (1790)

7 The mirth and fun grew fast and furious.

"Tam o' Shanter" l. 143 (1791)

8 Should auld acquaintance be forgot
And never brought to mind?

"Auld Lang Syne" l. 1 (1796). James Watson, *Choice Collection of Comic and Serious Scots Poems*

(1711), contains a ballad beginning: "Should old acquaintance be forgot, / And never thought upon, / The flames of love extinguished, / And freely past and gone? / Is thy kind heart now grown so cold / In that loving breast of thine, / That thou canst never once reflect / On old-long-syne?"

9 We'll tak a cup o' kindness yet,
For auld lang syne.

"Auld Lang Syne" l. 7 (1796). The phrase "auld lang syne" appears in *Scotch Presbyterian Eloquence Display'd* (1694): "The good God said, Jonah, now billy Jonah, wilt thou go to Nineveh, for *Auld lang syne* (old kindness)."

10 Gin a body meet a body
Comin thro' the rye,
Gin a body kiss a body
Need a body cry?

"Comin Thro' the Rye" (song) (1796). The extent to which this song was original with Burns, as opposed to being a folk song collected by him, is uncertain.
See Salinger 4

11 O, my Luve's like a red, red rose
That's newly sprung in June;
O my Luve's like the melodie
That's sweetly play'd in tune.

"A Red Red Rose" l. 1 (1796). Based on various folk songs.

Aaron Burr
U.S. politician, 1756–1836

1 Law is whatever is boldly asserted and plausibly maintained.

Quoted in James Parton, *Life and Times of Aaron Burr*, 7th ed. (1858)

Edgar Rice Burroughs
U.S. writer, 1875–1950

1 That night a little son was born in the tiny cabin beside the primeval forest, while a leopard screamed before the door, and the deep notes of a lion's roar sounded from beyond the ridge.

Tarzan of the Apes ch. 3 (1914)

2 The Land That Time Forgot.

Title of short story (1924)

3 We wish to escape not alone the narrow confines of city streets for the freedom of the wilderness, but the restrictions of man made laws, and the inhibitions that society has placed

upon us. We would like to picture ourselves as roaming free, the lords of ourselves and of our world; in other words, we would each like to be Tarzan. At least I would; I admit it.

"The Tarzan Theme," *Writer's Digest*, June 1932

William S. Burroughs

U.S. novelist, 1914–1997

1 The title means exactly what the words say: NAKED Lunch—a frozen moment when everyone sees what is on the end of every fork.

Naked Lunch introduction (1959)

2 Junk is the ideal product . . . the ultimate merchandise. No sales talk necessary. The client will crawl through a sewer and beg to buy.

Naked Lunch (1959)

3 Just look there (another Heavy Metal Boy sank through the earth's crust and we got some good pictures . . .).

The Soft Machine (1961). Earliest usage of the modern term *heavy metal*.
See Bonfire 1

4 Kerouac opened a million coffee bars and sold a million pairs of Levis to both sexes. Woodstock rises from his pages.

The Adding Machine "Remembering Jack Kerouac" (1985)

5 A paranoid is someone who has all the facts.

Quoted in *Toronto Star*, 22 Apr. 1989

Nat Burton (Nat Schwartz)

U.S. songwriter, 1901–1945

1 There'll be bluebirds over the white cliffs of Dover,
Tomorrow, just you wait and see.

"The White Cliffs of Dover" (song) (1941)

Richard Francis Burton

English explorer, folklorist, and writer, 1821–1890

1 I have struggled for forty-seven years, distinguishing myself honorably in every way that I possibly could. I never had a compliment, nor a "thank you," nor a single farthing. I translate a doubtful book [the *Arabian Nights*]

in my old age, and I immediately make sixteen thousand guineas. Now that I know the tastes of England, we need never be without money.

Quoted in Isabel Burton, *The Life of Captain Sir Richard F. Burton* (1893)

Robert Burton

English clergyman and scholar, 1577–1640

1 A dwarf standing on the shoulders of a giant may see farther than a giant himself.

The Anatomy of Melancholy "Democritus Junior to the Reader" (1621–1651)
See Bernard of Chartres 1; Coleridge 30; Isaac Newton 1

2 Why doth one man's yawning make another yawn?

The Anatomy of Melancholy pt. 1, sec. 2 (1621–1651)

3 *Hinc quam sit calamus saevior ense patet.*
Hence you may see, the written word can be more cruel than the sword.

The Anatomy of Melancholy pt. 1, sec. 2 (1621–1651)
See Bulwer-Lytton 3

4 See one promontory (said Socrates of old), one mountain, one sea, one river, and see all.

The Anatomy of Melancholy pt. 1, sec. 2 (1621–1651)
See Agnew 1

5 One was never married, and that's his hell: another is, and that's his plague.

The Anatomy of Melancholy pt. 1, sec. 2 (1621–1651)

6 What is a ship but a prison?

The Anatomy of Melancholy pt. 2, sec. 3 (1621–1651)
See Samuel Johnson 50

7 To enlarge or illustrate this power and effect of love is to set a candle in the sun.

The Anatomy of Melancholy pt. 3, sec. 2 (1621–1651)

8 Be not solitary, be not idle.

The Anatomy of Melancholy pt. 3, sec. 4 (1621–1651)
See Samuel Johnson 97

Barbara Bush

U.S. First Lady, 1925–2018

1 [*Of Democratic vice-presidential candidate Geraldine Ferraro:*] That $4 million—I can't say it, but it rhymes with rich.

Quoted in *Wash. Post*, 9 Oct. 1984

George Herbert Walker Bush

U.S. president, 1924–2018

1 [*Of Ronald Reagan's proposals to increase government revenues by reducing taxes:*] Voodoo economics.

Campaign remarks, New Haven, Conn., Mar. 1980. Bush, after becoming Reagan's running mate, denied having used this term, but had to acknowledge having done so after the media produced evidence including footage of his referring to "voodoo economic policy" during an address on 10 Apr. 1980 at Carnegie Mellon University, Pittsburgh, Pa.

2 [*On the Iran-Contra scandal:*] Clearly, mistakes were made.

Speech to American Enterprise Institute, Washington, D.C., 3 Dec. 1986

3 We are a nation of communities, of tens and tens of thousands of ethnic, religious, social, business, labor union, neighborhood, regional, and other organizations, all of them varied, voluntary, and unique . . . a brilliant diversity spread like stars, like a thousand points of light in a broad and peaceful sky.

Acceptance speech at Republican National Convention, New Orleans, La., 18 Aug. 1988. Bush's speechwriter, Peggy Noonan, may have drawn the phrase "thousand points of light" from the writings of Thomas Wolfe, with which she was familiar. Wolfe's novels include at least three similar expressions: "a thousand tiny points of bluish light" (*Look Homeward, Angel* [1929]), "a thousand points of friendly light" (*The Web and the Rock* [1939]), and "ten thousand points of light" (*You Can't Go Home Again* [1940]). Ralph Keyes, *The Quote Verifier*, presents citations to several usages of "a thousand points of light" going back to 1866.
See Auden 14

4 Read my lips: no new taxes.

Acceptance speech at Republican National Convention, New Orleans, La., 18 Aug. 1988
See Curry 1; Film Lines 100; Joe Greene 1

5 I want a kinder, gentler nation.

Acceptance speech at Republican National Convention, New Orleans, La., 18 Aug. 1988. New York Governor Mario Cuomo, in a commencement address at Barnard College quoted in *Christian Science Monitor*, June 21, 1983, expressed hope to the graduates "that you will be wiser than we are, kinder, gentler, more caring."
See George H. W. Bush 6; Film Lines 91

6 America is never wholly herself unless she is engaged in high moral purpose. We as a people have such a purpose today. It is to make kinder the face of the nation and gentler the face of the world.

Inaugural Address, 20 Jan. 1989
See George H. W. Bush 5; Film Lines 91

7 Time and again in this century, the political map of the world was transformed. And in each instance, a new world order came about through the advent of a new tyrant, or the outbreak of a bloody global war, or its end. Now the world has undergone another upheaval, but this time, there's no war.

Speech at fund-raising dinner for Pete Wilson, San Francisco, Calif., 28 Feb. 1990
See Bailey 1; George H. W. Bush 10; George H. W. Bush 12; Martin Luther King 1; Tennyson 45

8 [*Of Iraq's invasion of Kuwait:*] This will not stand.

News conference, 5 Aug. 1990

9 [*Referring to United States actions against Iraq:*] A line has been drawn in the sand.

News conference, 8 Aug. 1990. Not a new expression, as shown by, "Brzezinski is more eager to draw a line in the sand and dare the Russians to cross it" (*Newsweek*, 24 July 1978).

10 We have before us the opportunity to forge for ourselves and for future generations a new world order—a world where the rule of law, not the law of the jungle, governs the conduct of nations.

Address to the nation announcing allied military action in the Persian Gulf, 16 Jan. 1991
See Bailey 1; George H. W. Bush 7; George H. W. Bush 12; Martin Luther King 1; Tennyson 45

11 The liberation of Kuwait has begun. In conjunction with the forces of our coalition partners, the United States has moved under the code name Operation Desert Storm to enforce the mandates of the United Nations Security Council.

Statement on allied military action in the Persian Gulf, 16 Jan. 1991

12 What is at stake is more than one small country; it is a big idea: a new world order, where diverse nations are drawn together in common cause to achieve the universal aspirations of mankind—peace and security, freedom and the rule of law.

State of the Union Address, 29 Jan. 1991
See Bailey 1; George H. W. Bush 7; George H. W. Bush 10; Martin Luther King 1; Tennyson 45

13 The biggest thing that has happened in the world in my life, in our lives, is this: By the grace of God, America won the Cold War.
State of the Union Address, 28 Jan. 1992

14 The big mo [momentum].
Quoted in *Economist*, 26 Jan. 1980

15 [*Remark after vice-presidential debate with Geraldine Ferraro:*] We tried to kick a little ass last night.
Quoted in *Wash. Post*, 13 Oct. 1984

16 [*On turning his attention to long-term objectives:*] Oh, the vision thing.
Quoted in *Time*, 26 Jan. 1987

17 [*Maintaining that he was not involved in discussions of trading arms for hostages in 1985:*] We were not in the loop.
Quoted in *Wash. Post*, 6 Aug. 1987. Frequently quoted as "I was out of the loop."

18 [*Of Ronald Reagan:*] For seven and a half years I have worked alongside him and I am proud to be his partner. We have had triumphs, we have made mistakes, we have had sex.
Quoted in *Financial Times*, 9 May 1988. This gaffe occurred at a campaign rally in Twin Falls, Idaho, 6 May 1988. Bush quickly corrected himself: "setbacks . . . we have had setbacks."

19 I do not like broccoli. And I haven't liked it since I was a little kid and my mother made me eat it. And I'm president of the United States, and I'm not going to eat any more broccoli!
Quoted in *N.Y. Times*, 23 Mar. 1990

20 We've kicked the Vietnam syndrome once and for all!
Quoted in *Newsweek*, 11 Mar. 1991

George W. Bush
U.S. president, 1946–

1 Now, some say it is unfair to hold disadvantaged children to rigorous standards. I say it is discrimination to require anything less—the soft bigotry of low expectations.
Remarks to Latin American Business Association, Los Angeles, Calif., 2 Sept. 1999

2 Rarely is the question asked: Is our children learning?
Speech, Florence, S.C., 11 Jan. 2000

3 To those of you who received honors, awards and distinctions, I say well done. And to the C students, I say you, too, can be president of the United States.
Commencement address at Yale University, New Haven, Conn., 21 May 2001

4 We will make no distinction between terrorists who committed these acts and those who harbor them.
Televised address, 12 Sept. 2001

5 [*After a person in the crowd yelled "I can't hear you":*] I can hear you. The rest of the world hears you. And the people who knocked these buildings down will hear all of us soon.
Remarks at World Trade Center site, New York, N.Y., 14 Sept. 2001

6 It is time for us to win the first war of the 21st century.
Press conference, 16 Sept. 2001

7 I want justice. And there's an old poster out West, that I recall, that said, "Wanted, Dead or Alive."
Remarks at Pentagon, Arlington, Va., 17 Sept. 2001

8 We will not tire, we will not falter, and we will not fail.
Address to joint session of Congress, 20 Sept. 2001
See Winston Churchill 19

9 Whether we bring our enemies to justice or bring justice to our enemies, justice will be done.

Address to joint session of Congress, 20 Sept. 2001

10 We have seen their kind before. They're the heirs of all the murderous ideologies of the 20th century. By sacrificing human life to serve their radical visions, by abandoning every value except the will to power, they follow in the path of fascism, Nazism, and totalitarianism. And they will follow that path all the way to where it ends in history's unmarked grave of discarded lies.

Address to joint session of Congress, 20 Sept. 2001

11 The course of this conflict is not known, yet its outcome is certain. Freedom and fear, justice and cruelty, have always been at war, and we know that God is not neutral between them.

Address to joint session of Congress, 20 Sept. 2001

12 States like these [Iraq, Iran, and North Korea] and their terrorist allies constitute an axis of evil, arming to threaten the peace of the world.

State of the Union Address, 29 Jan. 2002

13 All the world now faces a test, and the United Nations a difficult and defining moment. Are Security Council resolutions to be honored and enforced, or cast aside without consequence? Will the United Nations serve the purpose of its founding or will it be irrelevant?

Speech to United Nations General Assembly, New York, N.Y., 12 Sept. 2002

14 The British government has learned that Saddam Hussein recently sought significant quantities of uranium from Africa.

State of the Union message, 28 Jan. 2003

15 Saddam Hussein and his sons must leave Iraq within 48 hours. Their refusal to do so will result in military conflict, commenced at a time of our choosing.

Broadcast address, 17 Mar. 2003

16 My fellow Americans: Major combat operations in Iraq have ended. In the battle of Iraq, the United States and our allies have prevailed.

Address to the nation from USS *Abraham Lincoln*, 1 May 2003

17 I'm the master of low expectations.

Press interview, 4 June 2003

18 [*On Iraqi militants attacking U.S. forces:*] My answer is bring them on.

Remarks to press corps, Washington, D.C., 2 July 2003

19 Our enemies are innovative and resourceful, and so are we. They never stop thinking about new ways to harm our country and our people, and neither do we.

Remarks at signing of Department of Defense appropriations bill, 5 Aug. 2004

20 I earned capital in the campaign, political capital, and now I intend to spend it.

News conference, 4 Nov. 2004

21 Brownie, you're doing a heck of a job.

Remark to Federal Emergency Management Agency head Michael D. Brown after Hurricane Katrina, Mobile, Ala., 2 Sept. 2005

22 I'm the decider.

Remarks to press, Apr. 18, 2006

23 [*Of his youthful indiscretions:*] When I was young and irresponsible I was young and irresponsible.

Quoted in *Newsweek*, 2 Nov. 1998

24 I know how hard it is for you to put food on your family.

Quoted in *N.Y. Daily News*, 19 Feb. 2000

25 When I take action, I'm not going to fire a two-million-dollar missile at a ten-dollar empty tent and hit a camel in the butt. It's going to be decisive.

Quoted in *Newsweek*, 24 Sept. 2001

26 [*Of requests to give Iraq more time to disarm:*] This looks like a rerun of a bad movie and I'm not interested in watching it.

Quoted in *Wash. Post*, 22 Jan. 2003

27 [*Explaining why he did not consult his father, former President George H. W. Bush, on the decision to go to war with Iraq in 2003:*] There is a higher father that I appeal to.

Quoted in Bob Woodward, *Plan of Attack* (2004)

John Ellis "Jeb" Bush

U.S. politician, 1953–

1 [*Of Donald Trump:*] He's a chaos candidate. And he'd be a chaos president.

Republican presidential candidates debate, Las Vegas, Nev., 15 Dec. 2015

Comte de Bussy-Rabutin

French soldier and poet, 1618–1693

1 God is usually on the side of the big squadrons against the small.
Letter to Comte de Limoges, 18 Oct. 1677
See Frederick the Great 1; Tacitus 3; Turenne 1

Judith Butler

U.S. philosopher, 1956–

1 Gender is an identity tenuously constituted in time, instituted in an exterior space through a *stylized repetition of acts.*
Gender Trouble: Feminism and the Subversion of Identity pt. 3, ch. 4 (1990)

Octavia E. Butler

U.S. science fiction writer, 1947–2006

1 [*Advice to writers:*] First forget inspiration. Habit is more dependable. Habit will sustain you whether you're inspired or not. . . . Habit is persistence in practice.
"Furor Scribendi" (1993)

Robert N. Butler

U.S. physician, 1927–2010

1 We shall soon have to consider . . . a form of bigotry we now tend to overlook: age discrimination or age-ism, prejudice by one age group toward other age groups.
Gerontologist, Winter 1969. Coinage of the word *ageism.*

Samuel Butler

English poet, 1612–1680

1 For Justice, though she's painted blind, Is to the weaker side inclined.
Hudibras pt. 3, canto 3, l. 709 (1680)

Samuel Butler

English novelist, 1835–1902

1 A hen is only an egg's way of making another egg.
Life and Habit ch. 8 (1877)

2 Stowed away in a Montreal lumber room
The Discobolus standeth and turneth his face to the wall;

Dusty, cobweb-covered, maimed, and set at naught,
Beauty crieth in the attic and no man regardeth:
O God! O Montreal!
"A Psalm of Montreal" l. 1 (1878)

3 It was very good of God to let Carlyle and Mrs. Carlyle marry one another and so make only two people miserable instead of four.
Letter to E. M. A. Savage, 21 Nov. 1884

4 Some boys are born stupid; some achieve stupidity; and some have stupidity thrust upon them.
The Way of All Flesh ch. 1 (1903)
See Heller 4; Shakespeare 244

5 The family is a survival of the principle which is more logically embodied in the compound animal. . . . I would do with the family among mankind what nature has done with the compound animal, and confine it to the lower and less progressive races.
The Way of All Flesh ch. 24 (1903)

6 Sensible people get the greater part of their own dying done during their own lifetime. A man at five and thirty should no more regret not having had a happier childhood than he should regret not having been born a prince of the blood.
The Way of All Flesh ch. 24 (1903)

7 There are two classes of people in this world, those who sin, and those who are sinned against; if a man must belong to either, he had better belong to the first than to the second.
The Way of All Flesh ch. 26 (1903)

8 If there are one or two good ones in a very large family, it is as much as can be expected.
The Way of All Flesh ch. 66 (1903)

9 A man first quarrels with his father about three-quarters of a year before he is born.
The Way of All Flesh ch. 79 (1903)

10 God is Love—I dare say! But what a mischievous devil Love is!
Notebooks "God is Love" (1912)
See Bible 388; Gypsy Rose Lee 1

11 Life is the art of drawing sufficient conclusions from insufficient premises.
Notebooks "Life" (1912)

12 An apology for the Devil: It must be remembered that we have only heard one side of the case. God has written all the books.
Notebooks ch. 14 (1912)

David Byrne
Scottish-born U.S. rock musician, 1952–

1 And you may find yourself behind the wheel of
    a large automobile
And you may find yourself in a beautiful house
With a beautiful wife
And you may ask yourself
Well, how did I get here?
"Once in a Lifetime" (song) (1980). Cowritten with Brian Eno.

2 And you may ask yourself
What is that beautiful house?
And you may ask yourself
Where does that highway go?
And you may ask yourself
Am I right? . . . Am I wrong?
And you may tell yourself
MY GOD! . . . WHAT HAVE I DONE?
"Once in a Lifetime" (song) (1980). Cowritten with Brian Eno.

John Byrom
English poet, 1692–1763

1 Some say, that Signor Bononcini,
Compared to Handel's a mere ninny;
Others aver, that to him Handel
Is scarcely fit to hold a candle.
Strange! that such high dispute should be
'Twixt Tweedledum and Tweedledee.
"On the Feuds Between Handel and Bononcini" l. 1 (1727)

George Gordon, Lord Byron
English poet, 1788–1824

1 With just enough of learning to misquote.
English Bards and Scotch Reviewers l. 66 (1809)

2 [*Of Annabella Milbanke, Byron's future wife and an amateur mathematician:*] My Princess of Parallelograms.
Letter to Caroline Lamb, 18 Oct. 1812

3 When one subtracts from life infancy (which is vegetation),—sleep, eating, and swilling—

buttoning and unbuttoning—how much remains of downright existence? The summer of a dormouse.
Journal, 7 Dec. 1813

4 I wonder how the deuce any body could make such a world; for what purpose dandies, for instance, were ordained—and kings—and fellows of colleges—and women of "a certain age"—and many men of any age—and myself, most of all!
Journal, 14 Feb. 1814

5 The Assyrian came down like the wolf on the fold,
And his cohorts were gleaming in purple and gold;
And the sheen of their spears was like stars on the sea,
When the blue wave rolls nightly on deep Galilee.
"The Destruction of Sennacherib" l. 1 (1815)

6 For years fleet away with the wings of the dove.
"The First Kiss of Love" st. 7 (1815)

7 She walks in Beauty, like the night
Of cloudless climes and starry skies;
And all that's best of dark and bright
Meet in her aspect and her eyes:

Thus mellowed to that tender light
Which Heaven to gaudy day denies.
"She Walks in Beauty" l. 1 (1815)

8 There was a sound of revelry by night.
Childe Harold's Pilgrimage canto 3, st. 21 (1816)

9 On with the dance! let joy be unconfined.
Childe Harold's Pilgrimage canto 3, st. 22 (1816)

10 Here, where the sword united nations drew,
Our countrymen were warring on that day!
Childe Harold's Pilgrimage canto 3, st. 35 (1816).
Bartlett's Familiar Quotations notes: "This was the
passage Sir Winston Churchill quoted to Franklin D.
Roosevelt when both agreed to substitute the term
United Nations for Associated Powers in the pact that
the two leaders wished all the free nations to sign. [In
a conference at the White House, January 1942]."
See Minor 1

11 If I should meet thee
After long years,
How should I greet thee?—
With silence and tears.
"When We Two Parted" l. 29 (1816)

12 So we'll go no more a-roving
So late into the night,
Though the heart be still as loving,
And the moon be still as bright.
"So We'll Go No More A-Roving" l. 1 (1817)

13 I stood in Venice, on the Bridge of Sighs,
A palace and a prison on each hand.
Childe Harold's Pilgrimage canto 4, st. 1 (1818)

14 *There* were his young barbarians all at play,
There was their Dacian mother—he, their sire,
Butchered to make a Roman holiday.
Childe Harold's Pilgrimage canto 4, st. 141 (1818)

15 Roll on, thou deep and dark blue Ocean—roll!
Ten thousand fleets sweep over thee in vain;
Man marks the earth with ruin—his control
Stops with the shore.
Childe Harold's Pilgrimage canto 4, st. 179 (1818)

16 And Coleridge, too, has lately taken wing,
But, like a hawk encumbered with his hood,
Explaining metaphysics to the nation—
I wish he would explain his explanation.
Don Juan canto 1, dedication st. 2 (written 1818)

17 What men call gallantry, and gods adultery,
Is much more common where the climate's
sultry.
Don Juan canto 1, st. 63 (written 1818)

18 Christians have burnt each other, quite
persuaded
That all the Apostles would have done as
they did.
Don Juan canto 1, st. 83 (written 1818)

19 But who, alas! can love, and then be wise?
Not that remorse did not oppose temptation;
A little still she strove, and much repented,
And whispering "I will ne'er consent"—
consented.
Don Juan canto 1, st. 117 (written 1818)

20 Man's love is of man's life a thing apart,
'Tis woman's whole existence.
Don Juan canto 1, st. 194 (written 1818)
See Staël 1

21 I have been more ravished myself than any
body since the Trojan war.
Letter to Richard B. Hoppner, 29 Oct. 1819

22 Such writing [John Keats's] is a sort of mental
masturbation—he is always f—gg—g his
imagination.—I don't mean that he is indecent
but viciously soliciting his own ideas into a
state which is neither poetry nor any thing else
but a Bedlam vision produced by raw pork and
opium.
Letter to John Murray, 9 Nov. 1820

23 In her first passion woman loves her lover,
In all the others all she loves is love.
Don Juan canto 3, st. 3 (1821)

24 Think you, if Laura had been Petrarch's wife,
He would have written sonnets all his life?
Don Juan canto 3, st. 8 (1821)

25 And if I laugh at any mortal thing,
'Tis that I may not weep.
Don Juan canto 4, st. 4 (1821)

26 "Who killed John Keats?"
"I," said the Quarterly,
So savage and Tartarly;
"'Twas one of my feats."
"John Keats" l. 1 (1821)
See Byron 31

27 The "good old times"—all times when old are
good.

"The Age of Bronze" st. 1 (1823)

28 Year after year they voted cent per cent
Blood, sweat, and tear-wrung millions—why?
for rent!

"The Age of Bronze" st. 14 (1823)
*See Winston Churchill 9; Winston Churchill 12; Donne
4; Theodore Roosevelt 3*

29 A lady of a "certain age," which means
Certainly aged.

Don Juan canto 6, st. 69 (1823)

30 And after all, what is a lie? 'Tis but
The truth in masquerade.

Don Juan canto 11, st. 37 (1823)

31 John Keats, who was kill'd off by one critique,
Just as he really promis'd something great . . .
'Tis strange the mind, that very fiery particle,
Should let itself be snuffed out by an article.

Don Juan canto 11, st. 60 (1823)
See Byron 26

32 The English winter—ending in July,
To recommence in August.

Don Juan canto 13, st. 42 (1823)

33 'Tis strange—but true; for truth is always
strange;
Stranger than fiction.

Don Juan canto 14, st. 101 (1823)
See Chesterton 6; Twain 93

34 The tribe of Barabbas was unquestionably a
bookseller.

Quoted in Leigh Hunt, *Lord Byron and Some of His
Contemporaries* (1828). The later, commonly reported
story was that Byron, upon receiving a Bible from
his publisher, John Murray, returned it to Murray
with the words "Now Barabbas was a robber" altered
to "Now Barabbas was a publisher." This anecdote is
improbable on a number of accounts.
See Bible 328

35 I awoke one morning and found myself
famous.

Quoted in Thomas Moore, *Letters and Journals of Lord
Byron* (1830). Byron wrote this in his Memoranda
after the first two cantos of his poem *Childe Harold's
Pilgrimage* were published in 1812 and became
sensationally popular.

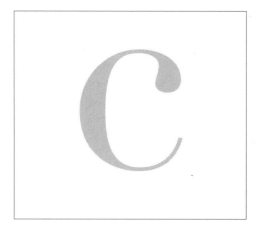

James Branch Cabell
U.S. novelist and essayist, 1879–1958

1 The optimist proclaims that we live in the best of all possible worlds; and the pessimist fears this is true.

The Silver Stallion bk. 4, ch. 26 (1926)
See Leibniz 3; Voltaire 7; Voltaire 8

Herb Caen
U.S. journalist, 1916–1997

1 *Look* magazine, preparing a picture spread on S.F.'s Beat Generation (oh, no, not AGAIN!) hosted a party in a No. Beach house for 50 Beatniks.

S.F. Chronicle, 2 Apr. 1958. Coinage of the word *beatnik*.

Irving Caesar
U.S. songwriter, 1895–1996

1 Picture you upon my knee,
Just tea for two and two for tea.

"Tea for Two" (song) (1924)

Julius Caesar
Roman statesman and general, 100 B.C.–44 B.C.

1 *Gallia est omnis divisa in partes tres.*
All Gaul is divided into three parts.

De Bello Gallico bk. 1, sec. 1

2 Men are nearly always willing to believe what they wish.

De Bello Gallico bk. 3, sec. 18. Demosthenes, *Third Olynthiac* sec. 19, had earlier said: "Nothing is easier than self-deceit. For what each man wishes, that he also believes to be true."

3 I wished my wife to be not so much as suspected.

Quoted in Plutarch, *Parallel Lives*. Refers to Caesar's wife Pompeia after he divorced her on the basis of unfounded aspersions; famous in the form "Caesar's wife must be above suspicion."

4 I had rather be the first man among those fellows than the second man in Rome.

Quoted in Plutarch, *Parallel Lives*

5 [*Proverb quoted by Caesar as he crossed the Rubicon River in defiance of restrictions on his army:*] The die is cast.

Quoted in Plutarch, *Parallel Lives*. According to Plutarch, Caesar spoke this in Greek.

6 *Veni, vidi, vici.*
I came, I saw, I conquered.

Quoted in Suetonius, *Lives of the Caesars*. Suetonius has this as an inscription displayed in Caesar's Pontic triumph, while Plutarch describes it in his *Parallel Lives* as appearing in a letter by Caesar announcing his victory at Zela.

7 You too, my son?

Quoted in Suetonius, *Lives of the Caesars*. Suetonius reports Caesar saying this in Greek. A famous Latin rendering is *Et tu, Brute?* (You too, Brutus?).
See Shakespeare 104

John Cage
U.S. composer, 1912–1992

1 I have nothing to say
and I am saying it and that is poetry.

"Lecture on Nothing" (1961)

2 Which is more musical, a truck passing by a factory or a truck passing by a music school?

Silence (1961)

James Cagney
U.S. actor, 1899–1986

1 You dirty, double-crossing rat.

Blonde Crazy (motion picture) (1931). Closest documented version of Cagney's alleged quotation, "You dirty rat," which the actor denied ever saying. Cagney says the line "Come out and take it, you dirty yellow-bellied rat" in *Taxi!* (1931), and "Listen, you dirty rats in there!" in *Each Dawn I Die* (1939).

Sammy Cahn
U.S. songwriter, 1913–1993

1 Love and marriage, love and marriage,
Go together like a horse and carriage.

"Love and Marriage" (song) (1955)

2 Love is lovelier
  The second time around.
  "The Second Time Around" (song) (1960)

3 Call me irresponsible,
  Call me unreliable,
  Throw in undependable, too.
  "Call Me Irresponsible" (song) (1962)

Herman Cain
U.S. business executive and politician, 1945–2020

1 When they ask me who is the president of Ubeki-beki-beki-beki-stan-stan I'm going to say, "You know, I don't know. Do you know?"
  Interview, Christian Broadcasting Network, 7 Oct. 2011

James M. Cain
U.S. novelist, 1892–1977

1 They threw me off the hay truck about noon.
  The Postman Always Rings Twice ch. 1 (1934)

2 I kissed her. . . . It was like being in church.
  The Postman Always Rings Twice ch. 3 (1934)

3 Hell could have opened for me then, and it wouldn't have made any difference. I had to have her, if I hung for it.
  The Postman Always Rings Twice ch. 8 (1934)

4 I knew I couldn't have her and never could have had her. I couldn't kiss the girl whose father I killed.
  Double Indemnity ch. 13 (1943)

Michael Caine (Maurice Micklewhite)
English actor, 1933–

1 Not Many People Know That.
  Title of book (1984). Catchphrase Caine used when relating obscure trivia. Caine has stated that this was actually originated by Peter Sellers.

Pedro Calderón de la Barca
Spanish playwright and poet, 1600–1681

1 All life is a dream, and dreams are dreams.
  La Vida es Sueño "Segunda Jornada" l. 2183 (1636)
  See Carroll 44; Folk and Anonymous Songs 67; Li Po 1; Proverbs 169

2 When love is not madness, it is not love.
  El Mayor Monstruo, Los Celos act 1 (1637)

Charles Calhoun (Jesse Stone)
U.S. songwriter, 1897–1972

1 Shake, Rattle and Roll.
  Title of song (1954)

Caligula (Gaius Julius Caesar Germanicus)
Roman emperor, A.D. 12–A.D. 41

1 *Utinam populus Romanus unam cervicem haberet!*
  Would that the Roman people had but one neck!
  Quoted in Suetonius, *Lives of the Caesars*

Callimachus
Greek scholar, ca. 305 B.C.–ca. 240 B.C.

1 Big book, big bore.
  Fragment 465. Often translated as "A great book is like great evil."

Cab Calloway
U.S. jazz musician, 1907–1994

1 Ho de ho de ho.
  "Minnie the Moocher" (song) (1931)

Charles Alexandre de Calonne
French statesman, 1734–1802

1 If it is possible, madam, the affair is done; if it is impossible, it shall be done!
  Quoted in Isaac Disraeli, *Domestic Anecdotes of the French Nation During the Last Thirty Years* (1794)
  See Nansen 1; Santayana 14; Trollope 3

John Calvin
French-born Swiss religious leader, 1509–1564

1 All the sum of our wisdom that deserves to be called true and certain wisdom is comprised of two parts, to know God and to know ourselves.
  Institutes of the Christian Religion pt. 1 (1541)

Italo Calvino
Italian writer, 1923–1985

1 The unconscious is the ocean of the unsayable, of what has been expelled from the land of language, removed as a result of ancient prohibitions.
  "Cybernetics and Ghosts" (1969)

2 I speak and speak, but the listener retains only the words he is expecting. . . . It is not the voice that commands the story: it is the ear.
Invisible Cities ch. 9 (1972)

3 You are about to begin reading Italo Calvino's new novel, *If on a winter's night a traveler.*
If on a Winter's Night a Traveler ch. 1 (1979)

4 And you say, "Just a moment, I've almost finished *If on a winter's night a traveler* by Italo Calvino."
If on a Winter's Night a Traveler ch. 12 (1979)

Hélder Câmara
Brazilian clergyman, 1909–1999

1 When I give food to the poor, they call me a Saint. When I ask why the poor have no food, they call me a Communist.
Quoted in *The Guardian*, 21 Jan. 1985

Pierre Jacques Étienne, Comte de Cambronne
French general, 1770–1842

1 *La Garde meurt, mais ne se rend pas.*
The Guards die but do not surrender.
Attributed in Henry Houssaye, *La Garde Meurt et ne se Rend pas* (1907). This sentence is attributed to Cambronne at the Battle of Waterloo, 18 June 1815, when he was asked to surrender, but he denied having said it. Another popular story has him saying *Merde!* (Shit!), which is consequently known in France as *le mot de Cambronne. Benham's Book of Quotations* (new and rev. ed.) states: "Also said to have been invented by the journalist Balison de Rougemont, in his account of Waterloo, 'Journal General,' June 24, 1815, wherein de Rougemont attributes the words to Cambronne."
See McAuliffe 1

William Bruce Cameron
U.S. sociologist, fl. 1960

1 Not everything that can be counted counts, and not everything that counts can be counted.
Informal Sociology (1963)

Luís Vaz de Camões
Portuguese poet, ca. 1524–1580

1 Love is a fire that burns unseen,
It is an injury that hurts unfelt,
It is unsatisfied satisfaction,

It is pain that causes despair without hurting.
"*Amor é um fogo que arde sem se ver*" (1598)

Frank B. Camp
U.S. writer, 1882–ca. 1967

1 When the final taps is sounded and we lay aside life's cares,
And we do the last and gloried parade on heaven's shining stairs,
And the angels bid us welcome and the harps begin to play
We can draw a million canteen checks and spend them in a day.
It is then we'll hear St. Peter tell us loudly with a yell,
"Take a front seat, you soldier men, you've done your hitch in Hell."
"Our Hitch in Hell" l. 29 (1917). A better known later variant is: "When he gets to Heaven, / To St. Peter he will tell, / One more Marine reporting, Sir, / I've served my time in Hell."

Roy Campanella
U.S. baseball player, 1921–1993

1 You have to be a man to be a big leaguer, but you have to have a lot of little boy in you, too.
Quoted in *Mt. Vernon* (Ill.) *Register-News*, 12 Apr. 1955

Beatrice Stella Tanner (Mrs. Patrick) Campbell
English actress, 1865–1940

1 [*On marriage:*] The deep, deep peace of the double-bed after the hurly-burly of the chaise-longue.
Quoted in Alexander Woollcott, *While Rome Burns* (1934)

2 What does it matter so long as they don't do it in the street and frighten the horses.
Quoted in Peter Daubeny, *Stage by Stage* (1952). Said to have been a rebuke to a young actress's complaint that an old actor in the company was overly fond of the young leading man. Noted in the *Oakland Tribune*, 13 Feb. 1910: "There is a saying in Leicestershire, 'We do not care what you do as long as you don't frighten the horses.'"

John W. Campbell, Jr.

U.S. science fiction editor and writer, 1910–1971

1 [*Remark to Isaac Asimov, 23 Dec. 1940:*] Look, Asimov, in working this out, you have to realize that there are three rules that robots have to follow. In the first place, they can't do any harm to human beings; in the second place, they have to obey orders without doing harm; in the third, they have to protect themselves, without doing harm or proving disobedient.

Quoted in Isaac Asimov, *In Memory Yet Green: The Autobiography of Isaac Asimov 1920–1954* (1979)
See Asimov 1; Asimov 2; Asimov 3

Joseph Campbell

U.S. scholar of mythology, 1904–1987

1 Follow your bliss.

Quoted in *Time,* 14 Sept. 1987. Campbell used the phrase "follow your own bliss" in an interview in *Psychology Today,* July 1971.

Luther Campbell

U.S. rap musician, 1960–

1 I'm like a dog in heat, a freak without warning
I have an appetite for sex, 'cause me so horny.

"Me So Horny" (song) (1989). The words "me so horny" are taken from dialogue in the 1987 film *Full Metal Jacket,* with screenplay by Stanley Kubrick and Michael Herr; the film dialogue is actually "sampled" in the song.

Roy Campbell

South African poet, 1901–1957

1 You praise the firm restraint with which they write—
I'm with you there, of course:
They use the snaffle and the curb all right,
But where's the bloody horse?

"On Some South African Novelists" l. 1 (1930)

Thomas Campbell

Scottish poet, 1777–1844

1 'Tis distance lends enchantment to the view,
And robes the mountain in its azure hue.

Pleasures of Hope pt. 1, l. 7 (1799). "The mountains too, at a distance, appear airy masses and smooth, but seen near at hand they are rough" appears in Diogenes Laertius, *Pyrrho* sec. 9.

2 O leave this barren spot to me!
Spare, woodman, spare the beechen tree.

"The Beech-Tree's Petition" l. 1 (1800)
See George Pope Morris 1

3 'Tis the sunset of life gives me mystical lore,
And coming events cast their shadows before.

"Lochiel's Warning" l. 55 (1801)

Timothy J. Campbell

U.S. politician, 1840–1904

1 What's the constitution between friends?

Attributed in *Chicago Daily Tribune,* 28 Oct. 1894. Grover Cleveland wrote in *Presidential Problems,* ch. 1 (1904): "An amusing story is told of a legislator who, endeavoring to persuade a friend and colleague to aid him in the passage of a certain measure in which he was personally interested, met the remark that his bill was unconstitutional with the exclamation, 'What does the Constitution amount to between friends?'"

Albert Camus

Algerian-born French writer, 1913–1960

1 *Aujourd'hui, maman est morte. Ou peut-être hier.*
Mother died today, or maybe it was yesterday.

L'Étranger (The Stranger) pt. 1, ch. 1 (1942)

2 I laid my heart open to the benign indifference of the universe. To feel it so like myself, indeed, so brotherly, made me realize that I'd been happy, and that I was happy still. For all to be accomplished, for me to feel less lonely, all that remained to hope was that on the day of my execution there should be a huge crowd of spectators and that they should greet me with howls of execration.

L'Étranger (The Stranger) pt. 2, ch. 5 (1942)

3 There is but one truly serious philosophical problem, and that is suicide. Judging whether life is or is not worth living amounts to answering the fundamental question of philosophy. All the rest—whether or not the world has three dimensions, whether the mind has nine or twelve categories—comes afterwards. These are games.

Le Mythe de Sisyphe (The Myth of Sisyphus)
"Absurdity and Suicide" (1942)

4 *La lutte elle-même vers les sommets suffit à remplir un coeur d'homme. Il faut imaginer Sisyphe heureux.*

The struggle itself toward the heights is enough to fill a man's heart. One must imagine Sisyphus happy.

Le Mythe de Sisyphe (The Myth of Sisyphus) "The Myth of Sisyphus" (1942)

5 Can one be a saint without God? That's the problem, in fact the only problem, I'm up against today.

La Peste (The Plague) pt. 4 (1947)

6 What is a rebel? A man who says no.

L'Homme Révolté (The Rebel) pt. 1 (1951)

7 In the midst of winter, I finally learned that there was in me an invincible summer.

L'Été (Summer) "Return to Tipasa" (1954)

8 *Je vais vous dire un grand secret, mon cher. N'attendez pas le jugement dernier. Il a lieu tous les jours.*

I'll tell you a big secret, my friend. Don't wait for the Last Judgment. It takes place every day.

La Chute (The Fall) (1956)

9 [*Remarks at debate, University of Stockholm, 1957:*] I have always denounced terrorism. I must also denounce a terrorism which is exercised blindly, in the streets of Algiers for example, and which some day could strike my mother or my family. I believe in justice, but I shall defend my mother above justice.

Quoted in Herbert R. Lottman, *Albert Camus: A Biography* (1979)

10 What I know most surely about morality and the duty of man I owe to sport.

Quoted in Herbert R. Lottman, *Albert Camus: A Biography* (1979)

Elias Canetti

Bulgarian-born British writer, 1905–1994

1 The great writers of aphorisms read as if they had all known each other very well.

The Human Province "1943" (1978) (translation by Joachim Neugroschel)

George Canning

British prime minister, 1770–1827

1 [*On his policy of recognizing the independence of former Spanish colonies in the Western Hemisphere:*] I called the New World into existence, to redress the balance of the Old.

Speech in House of Commons, 12 Dec. 1826

Eddie Cantor

U.S. entertainer, 1892–1964

1 Matrimony is not a word, it's a sentence.

Quoted in *Reader's Digest*, Mar. 1934

Karel Čapek

Czech writer, 1890–1938

1 Rossum's Universal Robots.

R.U.R. act 1 (1920). This Czech play introduced the word *robot*, which was coined by Čapek's brother Josef.

Al Capone

U.S. gangster, 1899–1944

1 [*Interview, 1930:*] Don't get the idea I'm one of these goddam radicals. Don't get the idea I'm knocking the American system.

Quoted in Claud Cockburn, *In Time of Trouble* (1956)

2 [*Of suburban Chicago:*] This is virgin territory out here for whorehouses.

Quoted in Kenneth Allsop, *The Bootleggers and Their Era* (1961)

3 You can get much further with a kind word and a gun than you can with a kind word alone.

Attributed in *Forbes*, 6 Oct. 1986. Usually associated with Capone, but Paul Dickson, *The Official Explanations* (1980), attributes to Irwin Corey, "You can get more with a kind word and a gun than you can with a kind word."

Truman Capote (Truman Streckfus Persons)

U.S. writer, 1924–1984

1 It was a terrible, strange-looking hotel. But Little Sunshine stayed on: it was his rightful home, he said, for if he went away, as he had once upon a time, other voices, other rooms, voices lost and clouded, strummed his dreams.

Other Voices, Other Rooms ch. 5 (1948)

2 I didn't want to harm the man. I thought he
  was a very nice gentleman. Soft-spoken. I
  thought so right up to the moment I cut his
  throat.
  In Cold Blood pt. 3 (1966)

3 [*Comment in television discussion about writers of
  the "Beat Generation":*] That isn't writing at all,
  it's typing.
  Quoted in *New Republic*, 9 Feb. 1959. In an interview
  in *Paris Review*, Spring–Summer 1957, Capote
  described "nonstylists": "They're not writers. They're
  typists."

Giovanni Capurro
Italian songwriter, 1859–1920

1 O Sole Mio.
  Title of song (1899)

Francesco Caracciolo
Italian naval commander and diplomat, 1752–
1799

1 There are in England sixty different religions
  and only one sauce.
  Attributed in Hugh Percy Jones, *Dictionary of Foreign
  Phrases* (1922). Charles-Augustin Sainte-Beuve,
  Nouveaux Lundis (1869), attributes a comment to
  Talleyrand that the United States had "thirty-two
  religions and only one dish."

Benjamin N. Cardozo
U.S. judge, 1870–1938

1 If the nature of a thing is such that it is
  reasonably certain to place life and limb in
  peril when negligently made, it is then a thing
  of danger. Its nature gives warning of the
  consequences to be expected. If to the element
  of danger there is added knowledge that the
  thing will be used by persons other than the
  purchaser, and used without new tests, then,
  irrespective of contract, the manufacturer of
  this thing of danger is under a duty to make it
  carefully.
  MacPherson v. Buick Motor Co. (1916)

2 The criminal is to go free because the constable
  has blundered.
  People v. Defore (1926)

3 Immunities that are valid as against the federal
  government by force of the specific pledges of
  particular amendments have been found to be
  implicit in the concept of ordered liberty, and
  thus, through the Fourteenth Amendment,
  become valid as against the states.
  Palko v. Connecticut (1937)

4 Of that freedom [freedom of thought and
  speech] one may say that it is the matrix, the
  indispensable condition, of nearly every other
  form of freedom.
  Palko v. Connecticut (1937)

Thomas Carew
English poet, ca. 1595–1640

1 Ask me no more where Jove bestows,
  When June is past, the fading rose;
  For in your beauty's orient deep
  These flowers, as in their causes, sleep.
  "A Song" l. 1 (1640)

Archibald Carey, Jr.
U.S. clergyman, 1908–1981

1 From every mountain side, let freedom ring.
  Not only from the Green Mountains and
  the White Mountains of Vermont and New
  Hampshire, not only from the Catskills of New
  York; but from the Ozarks in Arkansas, from
  the Stone Mountain in Georgia, from the Great
  Smokies of Tennessee and from the Blue Ridge
  Mountains of Virginia—let it ring . . . may
  the Republican party, under God, from every
  mountain side, LET FREEDOM RING!
  Address to Republican National Convention, Chicago,
  Ill., 8 July 1952
  See Martin Luther King 14; Samuel Francis Smith 1

Henry Carey
English playwright and songwriter,
ca. 1687–1743

1 Namby-Pamby.
  Title of poem (1725)

2 God save our gracious king!
  Long live our noble king!
  God save the king!
  Send him victorious,
  Happy, and glorious,

Long to reign over us:
God save the king!

"God Save the King" (song) (ca. 1740). The attribution to Carey is not certain. The words "God save the king" appear many times in the Old Testament, such as in I Samuel 4:24.
See Bible 82

Jane Welsh Carlyle
Scottish wife of Thomas Carlyle, 1801–1866

1 I am not at all the sort of person you and I took me for.
Letter to Thomas Carlyle, 7 May 1822

2 Medical men all over the world . . . merely entered into a tacit agreement to call all sorts of maladies people are liable to, in cold weather, by one name; so that one sort of treatment may serve for all, and their practice be thereby greatly simplified.
Letter to John Welsh, 4 Mar. 1837

Thomas Carlyle
Scottish historian and essayist, 1795–1881

1 A well-written Life is almost as rare as a well-spent one.
"Jean Paul Friedrich Richter" (1827)

2 The great law of culture is: Let each become all that he was created capable of being.
"Jean Paul Friedrich Richter" (1827)

3 A whiff of grapeshot.
History of the French Revolution vol. 1, bk. 5, ch. 3 (1837)

4 France was long a despotism tempered by epigrams.
History of the French Revolution vol. 3, bk. 7, ch. 7 (1837)

5 History is the essence of innumerable biographies.
Critical and Miscellaneous Essays "On History" (1838)
See Thomas Carlyle 12

6 There is no heroic poem in the world but is at bottom a biography, the life of a man; also, it may be said, there is no life of a man, faithfully recorded, but is a heroic poem of its sort, rhymed or unrhymed.
Critical and Miscellaneous Essays "Sir Walter Scott" (1838)

7 The three great elements of modern civilization, Gunpowder, Printing, and the Protestant Religion.
Critical and Miscellaneous Essays "The State of German Literature" (1838)

8 It were a real increase of human happiness, could all young men from the age of nineteen be covered under barrels, or rendered otherwise invisible; and there left to follow their lawful studies and callings, till they emerged, sadder and wiser, at the age of twenty-five.
Sartor Resartus ch. 4 (1838)

9 A witty statesman said, you might prove anything by figures.
Chartism ch. 2 (1839)
See Anonymous 15

10 It is not what a man outwardly has or wants that constitutes the happiness or misery of him. Nakedness, hunger, distress of all kinds, death itself have been cheerfully suffered, when the heart was right. It is the feeling of *injustice* that is insupportable to all men.
Chartism ch. 5 (1839)

11 Cash payment has become the sole nexus of man to man.
Chartism ch. 6 (1839)
See Marx and Engels 4

12 The history of the world is but the biography of great men.

On Heroes, Hero-Worship, and the Heroic "The Hero as Divinity" (1841)
See Thomas Carlyle 5

13 No sadder proof can be given by a man of his own littleness than disbelief in great men.

On Heroes, Hero-Worship, and the Heroic "The Hero as Divinity" (1841)

14 Burke said there were Three Estates in Parliament; but, in the Reporters' Gallery yonder, there sat a *Fourth Estate*, more important far than they all.

On Heroes, Hero-Worship, and the Heroic "The Hero as Man of Letters" (1841). Carlyle's attribution to Burke has never been verified.
See Hazlitt 4; Thomas Macaulay 4; Thackeray 10

15 The true University of these days is a collection of books.

On Heroes, Hero-Worship, and the Heroic "The Hero as Man of Letters" (1841)

16 All that mankind has done, thought, gained or been: it is lying as in magic preservation in the pages of books.

On Heroes, Hero-Worship, and the Heroic "The Hero as Man of Letters" (1841)

17 Captains of Industry.

Past and Present title of bk. 4, ch. 4 (1843)

18 [Economics is] not a "gay science," I should say, like some we have heard of; no, a dreary, desolate, and, indeed, quite abject and distressing one: what we might call, by way of eminence, the *dismal science*.

"Occasional Discourse on the Negro Question" (1849). Viewed in context, this remark should actually be a point of pride for economists, since Carlyle was criticizing them for being opposed to slavery.

19 "Genius" (which means transcendent capacity of taking trouble, first of all).

History of Friedrich II. of Prussia vol. 1, bk. 4, ch. 3 (1858). Often quoted as "Genius is an infinite capacity for taking pains."
See Buffon 2; Edison 2; Jane Ellice Hopkins 1

20 [*Commenting on Margaret Fuller's remark, "I accept the universe," ca. 1843:*] Gad! she'd better.

Quoted in William James, *The Varieties of Religious Experience* (1902). The earliest account of this remark was in Evert Duyckinck, Letter to George Duyckinck, 28 Jan. 1848. Duyckinck reported that Henry James, Sr., had said to Thomas Carlyle, "When I last saw Margaret Fuller she told me that she had got to this conclusion—to accept the Universe." Carlyle replied, "God, [deleted] Accept the Universe. Margaret Fooler accept the universe! [with a loud guffaw] Why perhaps upon the whole it is the best thing she could do—it is very kind of Margaret Fooler!"
See Margaret Fuller 3

Stokely Carmichael
Trinidadian-born U.S. political activist, 1941–1998

1 [*Response when asked what the position of women in the Student Nonviolent Coordinating Committee was:*] Prone.

Student Nonviolent Coordinating Committee conference, Waveland, Miss., Nov. 1964

2 Black power!

Remarks at rally following shooting of James Meredith, Greenwood, Miss., 16 June 1966
See Adam Clayton Powell 1; Richard Wright 3

Andrew Carnegie
Scottish-born U.S. industrialist and philanthropist, 1835–1919

1 "Don't put all your eggs in one basket" is all wrong. We tell you "put all your eggs in one basket, and then watch that basket."

Address to students at Curry Commercial College, Pittsburgh, Pa., 23 June 1885. This address was quoted in the *Yonkers Statesman*, 19 Aug. 1885. The quotation is almost universally attributed to Mark Twain, but Twain's usage was later, and in his notebook he credited Carnegie for it.
See Proverbs 84

2 Surplus wealth is a sacred trust which its possessor is bound to administer in his lifetime for the good of the community.

"Wealth," *North American Review*, June 1889

3 A man who dies rich dies disgraced.

Quoted in *Nonconformist and Independent* (London), 14 July 1887

Dale Carnegie
U.S. writer and lecturer, 1888–1955

1 How to Win Friends and Influence People.

Title of book (1936)

Julia Fletcher Carney
U.S. poet, 1823–1908

1 Little drops of water,
  Little grains of sand,

Make the mighty ocean
And the pleasant land.
"Little Things" l. 1 (1845)

Betty Carpenter
U.S. politician, fl. 1985

1 Politicians, like diapers, should be changed
regularly.
Quoted in *Cincinnati Enquirer*, 25 Oct. 1987

Ralph Carpenter
U.S. sports publicist, ca. 1932–1995

1 The opera ain't over until the fat lady sings.
Quoted in *Dallas Morning News*, 10 Mar. 1976.
Carpenter was sports information director at Texas
Tech University when he uttered this line during a
basketball game with Texas A&M. The expression
was popularized in 1978 by San Antonio sportscaster
Dan Cook and Washington Bullets basketball coach
Dick Motta. However, a 1976 booklet, *Southern Words
and Sayings* by Fabia Rue Smith and Charles Rayford
Smith, includes the saying "Church ain't out 'till
the fat lady sings," suggesting an ultimate origin in
Southern proverbial lore. "Church is never out till
the people get through singing" appeared in the *Fort
Worth Daily Gazette*, 17 Aug. 1894.
See Berra 14

Scott Carpenter
U.S. astronaut, 1925–2013

1 [*Comment upon the launching of Friendship
7 space flight, 20 Feb. 1962:*] Godspeed, John
Glenn.
Quoted in *People*, 30 Oct. 1983

Lewis Carroll (Charles L. Dodgson)
English writer and mathematician, 1832–1898

1 Down the Rabbit-Hole.
Alice's Adventures in Wonderland title of ch. 1 (1865)

2 "And what is the use of a book," thought Alice,
"without pictures or conversations?"
Alice's Adventures in Wonderland ch. 1 (1865)

3 [*The White Rabbit speaking:*] Oh dear! Oh dear! I
shall be too late!
Alice's Adventures in Wonderland ch. 1 (1865)

4 "Curiouser and curiouser!" cried Alice.
Alice's Adventures in Wonderland ch. 2 (1865)

5 How doth the little crocodile
Improve his shining tail,

And pour the waters of the Nile
On every golden scale!
Alice's Adventures in Wonderland ch. 2 (1865)
See Watts 1

6 How cheerfully he seems to grin,
How neatly spreads his claws,
And welcomes little fishes in
With gently smiling jaws!
Alice's Adventures in Wonderland ch. 2 (1865)

7 You're enough to try the patience of an oyster!
Alice's Adventures in Wonderland ch. 3 (1865)

8 Oh my fur and whiskers!
Alice's Adventures in Wonderland ch. 4 (1865)

9 "You are old, Father William," the young man
said,
"And your hair has become very white;
And yet you incessantly stand on your head—
Do you think, at your age, it is right?"
Alice's Adventures in Wonderland ch. 5 (1865)
See Southey 2

10 "In my youth," said his father, "I took to the
law,
And argued each case with my wife;
And the muscular strength, which it gave to
my jaw
Has lasted the rest of my life."
Alice's Adventures in Wonderland ch. 5 (1865)

11 One side will make you grow taller, and the other side will make you grow shorter.
Alice's Adventures in Wonderland ch. 5 (1865)
See Slick 1

12 Speak roughly to your little boy,
And beat him when he sneezes:
He only does it to annoy,
Because he knows it teases.
Alice's Adventures in Wonderland ch. 6 (1865)

13 [*Of the Cheshire Cat:*] "Well! I've often seen a cat without a grin," thought Alice; "but a grin without a cat! It's the most curious thing I ever saw in all my life!"
Alice's Adventures in Wonderland ch. 6 (1865)

14 Why is a raven like a writing-desk?
Alice's Adventures in Wonderland ch. 7 (1865). Carroll wrote in the preface to the 1896 edition: "Enquiries have been so often addressed to me, as to whether any answer to the Hatter's Riddle can be imagined, that I may as well put on record here what seems to me to be a fairly appropriate answer, viz: 'Because it can produce a few notes, tho they are very flat; and it is never put with the wrong end in front!' This, however, is merely an afterthought; the Riddle, as originally invented, had no answer at all." Others have subsequently suggested more satisfying answers, such as "Because Poe wrote on both" (Sam Loyd).

15 "Then you should say what you mean," the March Hare went on. "I do," Alice hastily replied; "at least—at least I mean what I say— that's the same thing, you know." "Not the same thing a bit!" said the Hatter. "Why, you might just as well say that 'I see what I eat' is the same thing as 'I eat what I see!'"
Alice's Adventures in Wonderland ch. 7 (1865)

16 Twinkle, twinkle, little bat!
How I wonder what you're at! . . .
Up above the world you fly,
Like a tea-tray in the sky.
Alice's Adventures in Wonderland ch. 7 (1865)
See Ann Taylor 2

17 "Take some more tea," the March Hare said to Alice, very earnestly. "I've had nothing yet," Alice replied in an offended tone, "so I can't take more." "You mean you can't take *less*," said the Hatter: "it's very easy to take *more* than nothing."
Alice's Adventures in Wonderland ch. 7 (1865)

18 [*The Queen of Hearts speaking:*] Off with her head!
Alice's Adventures in Wonderland ch. 8 (1865)

19 "I only took the regular course." "What was that?" inquired Alice. "Reeling and Writhing, of course, to begin with," the Mock Turtle replied; "and then the different branches of Arithmetic—Ambition, Distraction, Uglification, and Derision."
Alice's Adventures in Wonderland ch. 9 (1865)

20 "Will you walk a little faster?" said a whiting to a snail,
"There's a porpoise close behind us, and he's treading on my tail."
Alice's Adventures in Wonderland ch. 10 (1865)

21 Will you, won't you, will you, won't you, will you join the dance?
Alice's Adventures in Wonderland ch. 10 (1865)

22 I could tell you my adventures—beginning from this morning . . . but it's no use going back to yesterday, because I was a different person then.
Alice's Adventures in Wonderland ch. 10 (1865)

23 "Where shall I begin, please your Majesty?" he asked. "Begin at the beginning," the King said, very gravely, "and go on till you come to the end: then stop."
Alice's Adventures in Wonderland ch. 12 (1865)

24 Sentence first—verdict afterwards.
Alice's Adventures in Wonderland ch. 12 (1865)
See Molière 5; Walter Scott 11

25 You're nothing but a pack of cards!
Alice's Adventures in Wonderland ch. 12 (1865)

26 Who can tell whether the parallelogram, which in our ignorance we have defined and drawn, and the whole of whose properties we profess to know, may not be all the while panting for exterior angles, sympathetic with the interior, or sullenly repining at the fact that it cannot be inscribed in a circle?
The Dynamics of a Parti-cle (1865)

27 "The horror of that moment," the King went on, "I shall never, *never* forget!" "You will, though," the Queen said, "if you don't make a memorandum of it."
Through the Looking-Glass ch. 1 (1872)

28 'Twas brillig, and the slithy toves
   Did gyre and gimble in the wabe;
   All mimsy were the borogoves,
   And the mome raths outgrabe.

   Beware the Jabberwock, my son!
   The jaws that bite, the claws that catch!
   Beware the Jubjub bird, and shun
   The frumious Bandersnatch!
   Through the Looking-Glass ch. 1 (1872)

29 "And hast thou slain the Jabberwock?
   Come to my arms, my beamish boy!
   O frabjous day! Callooh! Callay!"
   He chortled in his joy.
   Through the Looking-Glass ch. 1 (1872). Coinage of the
   word *chortle*.

30 Now, *here* you see, it takes all the running *you*
   can do, to keep in the same place. If you want
   to get somewhere else, you must run at least
   twice as fast as that!
   Through the Looking-Glass ch. 2 (1872)

31 If it was so, it might be; and if it were so, it
   would be; but as it isn't, it ain't. That's logic.
   Through the Looking-Glass ch. 4 (1872)

32 The sun was shining on the sea,
   Shining with all his might:
   He did his very best to make
   The billows smooth and bright—
   And this was odd, because it was
   The middle of the night.
   Through the Looking-Glass ch. 4 (1872)

33 But four young oysters hurried up,
   All eager for the treat:
   Their coats were brushed, their faces washed,
   Their shoes were clean and neat—
   And this was odd, because, you know,
   They hadn't any feet.
   Through the Looking-Glass ch. 4 (1872)

34 "The time has come," the Walrus said,
   "To talk of many things:
   Of shoes—and ships—and sealing-wax—
   Of cabbages—and kings—
   And why the sea is boiling hot—
   And whether pigs have wings."
   Through the Looking-Glass ch. 4 (1872)

35 "O oysters," said the Carpenter.
   "You've had a pleasant run!

Shall we be trotting home again?"
But answer came there none—
And this was scarcely odd, because
They'd eaten every one.
Through the Looking-Glass ch. 4 (1872). "But answer
came there none" appeared in Walter Scott, *The
Bridal of Triermain* canto 3, st. 10 (1813).

36 The rule is, jam to-morrow and jam yesterday—
   but never jam to-day.
   Though the Looking-Glass ch. 5 (1872)

37 It's a poor sort of memory that only works
   backwards.
   Through the Looking-Glass ch. 5 (1872)

38 Why, sometimes I've believed as many as six
   impossible things before breakfast.
   Through the Looking-Glass ch. 5 (1872)

39 They gave it me,—for an un-birthday present.
   Through the Looking-Glass ch. 6 (1872)

40 "When *I* use a word," Humpty Dumpty said,
   in rather a scornful tone, "it means just what
   I choose it to mean—neither more nor less."
   "The question is," said Alice, "whether you *can*
   make words mean so many different things."
   "The question is," said Humpty Dumpty,
   "which is to be master—that's all."
   Through the Looking-Glass ch. 6 (1872)

41 *"Slithy"* means "lithe and slimy." . . . You see it's
   like a portmanteau—there are two meanings
   packed up into one word.
   Through the Looking-Glass ch. 6 (1872)

42 It's as large as life, and twice as natural!
   Through the Looking-Glass ch. 7 (1872). A play on the
   expression "as large as life and quite as natural."
   See Haliburton 1

43 I don't like belonging to another person's
   dream.
   Through the Looking-Glass ch. 8 (1872)

44 Life, what is it but a dream?
   Through the Looking-Glass ch. 12 (1872)
   *See Calderón de la Barca 1; Folk and Anonymous Songs
   67; Li Po 1; Proverbs 169*

45 For the Snark *was* a Boojum, you see.
   The Hunting of the Snark "Fit the Eighth: The
   Vanishing" (1876)

46 I am fond of children (except boys).
   Letter to Kathleen Eschwege, 24 Oct. 1879

Benjamin Carson

U.S. politician and physician, 1951–

1 [*On whether homosexuality is a choice:*] A lot of people who go into prison go into prison straight, and when they come out, they're gay. So, did something happen while they were in there?
CNN *New Day* television show, 4 Mar. 2015

Rachel Carson

U.S. naturalist and writer, 1907–1964

1 Over increasingly large areas of the United States, spring now comes unheralded by the return of the birds, and the early mornings are strangely silent where once they were filled with the beauty of bird song.
Silent Spring ch. 8 (1962)

2 As crude a weapon as the cave man's club, the chemical barrage has been hurled against the fabric of life.
Silent Spring ch. 17 (1962)

Sonny Carson

U.S. civil rights activist, 1936–2002

1 No justice, no peace.
Quoted in *N.Y. Times*, 6 July 1987

A. P. Carter

U.S. country singer, 1891–1960

1 Can the circle be unbroken
Bye and bye, Lord, bye and bye
There's a better home a-waiting
In the sky, Lord, in the sky.
"Can the Circle Be Unbroken" (song) (1935). Later versions of this song usually had the title "Will the Circle Be Unbroken."

Angela Carter (Angela Olive Carter-Pearce)

English writer, 1940–1992

1 I'm interested in the division that Judeo-Christianity has made between human nature and animal nature. None of the other great faiths in the world have got quite that division between us and them. . . . I think it's one of the scars in our culture that we have too high an opinion of ourselves. We align ourselves with the angels instead of the higher primates.
Quoted in *Marxism Today*, Jan. 1985

Graydon Carter

Canadian journalist, 1949–

1 [*Description of Donald Trump:*] Short-fingered vulgarian.
Spy, Jan.–Feb. 1988

Howard Carter

English archaeologist, 1873–1939

1 As my eyes grew accustomed to the light, details of the room within emerged slowly from the mist, strange animals, statues, and gold—everywhere the glint of gold. . . . When Lord Carnarvon, unable to stand the suspense any longer, inquired anxiously, "Can you see anything?" it was all I could do to get out the words, "Yes, wonderful things."
The Tomb of Tut-ankh-Amen vol. 1, ch. 5 (1923)

James Earl "Jimmy" Carter

U.S. president, 1924–

1 It is now time to stop and to ask ourselves the question which my last commanding officer, Admiral Hyman Rickover, asked me and every other young naval officer in the atomic submarine program.
  Why not the best?
Why Not the Best? ch. 1 (1975). Carter explained that Admiral Rickover responded to Carter's telling him that Carter had not always done his best at the Naval Academy by asking, "Why not?"

2 We believe that the first time we're born, as children, it's human life given to us; and when we accept Jesus as our Savior, it's a new life. That's what "born again" means.
Interview, 16 Mar. 1976
See Bible 314

3 We become not a melting pot but a beautiful mosaic. Different people, different beliefs, different yearnings, different hopes, different dreams.
Speech, Pittsburgh, Pa., 27 Oct. 1976
See Baudouin 1; Crèvecoeur 1; Ralph Ellison 2; Victoria Hayward 1; Jesse Jackson 1; Zangwill 2

4 I've looked on a lot of women with lust. I've committed adultery in my heart many times. This is something that God recognizes I will

do—and I have done it—and God forgives me for it.

Interview, *Playboy*, Nov. 1976
See Bible 209

5 [*In response to the question, "How fair do you believe it is then, that women who can afford to get an abortion can go ahead and have one, and women who cannot afford to are precluded?":*] There are many things in life that are not fair, that wealthy people can afford and poor people can't.

News conference, 12 July 1977. Usually misquoted as "Life is unfair."
See John Kennedy 24; Wilde 73

6 We have the heaviest concentration of lawyers on Earth—1 for every 500 Americans, three times as many as are in England, four times as many as are in West Germany, twenty-one times as many as there are in Japan. We have more litigation, but I am not sure that we have more justice. No resources of talent and training in our own society, even including the medical care, is more wastefully or unfairly distributed than legal skills. Ninety percent of our lawyers serve 10 percent of our people. We are over-lawyered and under-represented.

Remarks at 100th Anniversary Banquet of the Los Angeles County Bar Association, Los Angeles, Calif., 4 May 1978

7 I thought a lot about our Nation and what I should do as President. And Sunday night before last, I made a speech about two problems of our country—energy and malaise.

Remarks at town meeting, Bardstown, Ky., 31 July 1979, referring to a speech on energy and national goals broadcast 15 July 1979. The word *malaise* does not appear in the 15 July speech.

June Carter
U.S. country singer and songwriter, 1929–2003

1 I fell into a burning ring of fire
I went down, down, down
And the flames went higher.

"Ring of Fire" (song) (1963). Cowritten with Merle Kilgore.

Stephen Carter
U.S. legal scholar and writer, 1954–

1 The new grammar of race is constructed in a way that George Orwell would have appreciated, because its rules make some ideas impossible to express—unless, of course, one wants to be called a racist.

Reflections of an Affirmative Action Baby ch. 8 (1992)

Jacques Cartier
French explorer, 1491–1557

1 [*Account dated 26 July 1535:*] The sayd men did moreover certifie unto us, that there was the way and beginning of the great river of Hochelaga and ready way to Canada, which river the further it went the narrower it came, even unto Canada.

Quoted in Richard Hakluyt, *The Principal Navigations, Voyages, Traffiques and Discoveries of the English Nation* (1599). Earliest documentation of the word *Canada*, an Algonkian word for "huts."

Barbara Cartland
English novelist, 1901–2000

1 After forty a woman has to choose between losing her figure or her face. My advice is to keep your face, and stay sitting down.

Quoted in *Times* (London), 6 Oct. 1993. According to the *Oxford Dictionary of Quotations*, "similar remarks have been attributed since *c.* 1980."

John Cartwright
English political radical, 1740–1824

1 One man, one vote.

The People's Barrier Against Undue Influence and Corruption ch. 6 (1780).
See Chesterton 16; William O. Douglas 4

Carl Gustav Carus
German physician and philosopher, 1789–1869

1 *Der Schlüssel zur Erkenntnis vom Wesen des bewussten Seelenlebens liegt in der Region des Unbewusstseins.*
The key to an understanding of the nature of the conscious life of the soul lies in the sphere of the unconscious.

Psyche pt. 1, introduction (1846) (translation by Renata Welch)

Enrico Caruso
Italian opera singer, 1873–1921

1 You know whatta you do when you shit?
Singing, it's the same thing, only up!
Quoted in Heywood Hale Broun, *Whose Little Boy Are You?* (1983)

James Carville
U.S. political consultant, 1944–

1 [*Stating the priority of the Clinton presidential campaign:*] [It's] the economy, stupid.
Quoted in *Wash. Post,* 3 Aug. 1992

Joyce Cary
Irish novelist, 1888–1957

1 Sara could commit adultery at one end and weep for her sins at the other, and enjoy both operations at once.
The Horse's Mouth ch. 8 (1944)

Phoebe Cary
U.S. poet, 1824–1871

1 One sweetly solemn thought
Comes to me o'er and o'er:
I am nearer home to-day
Than I have ever been before.
"Nearer Home" l. 1 (1854)

Pablo Casals (Pau Casals i Defilló)
Spanish cellist and conductor, 1876–1973

1 The love of one's country is a splendid thing. But why should love stop at the border?
Quoted in Albert E. Kahn, *Joys and Sorrows: Reflections by Pablo Casals* (1974)

Giacomo Girolamo Casanova
Italian adventurer and author, 1725–1798

1 [Marriage] is the tomb of love.
History of My Life vol. 9, ch. 8 (1960)

Frank Case
U.S. hotel manager, 1872–1946

1 Time wounds all heels.
"Rudy Vallee Royal Gelatin Hour" radio broadcast, 17 June 1937. Although this line is associated with Case, it was attributed to a person named Marshall Reid in the *Lowell Sun,* 21 Dec. 1934.

Johnny Cash
U.S. country singer and songwriter, 1932–2003

1 I shot a man in Reno just to watch him die.
"Folsom Prison Blues" (song) (1956)

2 Because you're mine, I walk the line.
"I Walk the Line" (song) (1956)

3 San Quentin, I hate every inch of you.
You've cut me and have scarred me thru an' thru.
And I'll walk out a wiser weaker man;
Mister Congressman why can't you understand.
"San Quentin" (song) (1969)

Vera Caspary
U.S. screenwriter and novelist, 1899–1987

1 If the dreams of any so-called normal man were exposed . . . there would be no more gravity and dignity left for mankind.
Laura ch. 2 (1943)

Alfredo Cassello
Italian playwright, fl. 1925

1 Death Takes a Holiday.
Title of play (1925)

Jules-Antoine Castagnary
French art critic and politician, 1830–1888

1 If one wants to characterize them with a single word that explains their efforts [artists exhibiting at an 1874 show], one would have to create the new term impressionists.
"Exposition du Boulevard des Capucines—les Impressionnistes," *Le Siècle,* 29 Apr. 1874

Fidel Castro
Cuban president, 1926–2016

1 *La historia me absolverá.*
History will absolve me.
Speech at trial for raid on Moncada barracks, 16 Oct. 1953

2 I began revolution with 82 men. If I had [to] do it again, I do it with 10 or 15 and absolute faith. It does not matter how small you are if you have faith and plan of action.
Quoted in *N.Y. Times,* 22 Apr. 1959

3 How can the rope and the hanged man understand each other or the chain and the slave?

Quoted in Arthur M. Schlesinger, Jr., *A Thousand Days* (1965)

4 You Americans keep saying that Cuba is ninety miles from the United States. I say that the United States is ninety miles from Cuba and for us, that is worse.

Quoted in Herbert L. Matthews, *Castro: A Political Biography* (1969)

Willa Cather

U.S. novelist, 1873–1947

1 The history of every country begins in the heart of a man or a woman.

O Pioneers! pt. 1, ch. 5 (1913)

2 There are only two or three human stories, and they go on repeating themselves as fiercely as if they had never happened before.

O Pioneers! pt. 2, ch. 4 (1913)

3 I like trees because they seem more resigned to the way they have to live than other things do. I feel as if this tree knows everything I ever think of when I sit here. When I come back to it, I never have to remind it of anything; I begin just where I left off.

O Pioneers! pt. 2, ch. 8 (1913)

4 I tell you there is such a thing as creative hate!

The Song of the Lark pt. 1 (1915)

5 Her secret? It is every artist's secret . . . passion. That is all. It is an open secret, and perfectly safe. Like heroism, it is inimitable in cheap materials.

The Song of the Lark pt. 6, ch. 11 (1915)

6 Whatever we had missed, we possessed together the precious, the incommunicable past.

My Ántonia bk. 5, ch. 3 (1918)

7 When kindness has left people, even for a few moments, we become afraid of them, as if their reason had left them.

My Mortal Enemy pt. 1, ch. 6 (1926)

8 I shall not die of a cold. I shall die of having lived.

Death Comes for the Archbishop bk. 9 (1927)

9 Give the people a new word and they think they have a new fact.

"Four Letters: Escapism" (1936)

10 Religion and art spring from the same root and are close kin. Economics and art are strangers.

Commonweal, 17 Apr. 1936

Cato the Elder

Roman statesman and writer, 234 B.C.–149 B.C.

1 *Rem tene; verba sequentur.*
Grasp the subject, the words will follow.

Quoted in Caius Julius Victor, *Ars Rhetorica*

2 [*Habitual ending of his speeches in the Senate:*] *Delenda est Carthago.*
Carthage must be destroyed.

Quoted in Pliny the Elder, *Naturalis Historia*

3 I would much rather have men ask why I have no statue, than why I have one.

Quoted in Plutarch, *Parallel Lives*

Catullus

Roman poet, ca. 84 B.C.–ca. 54 B.C.

1 *Lugete, O Veneres Cupidinesque,*
Et quantum est hominum venustiorum.
Passer mortuus est meae puellae,
Passer, deliciae meae puellae.
Mourn, you powers of Charm and Desire, and all you who are endowed with charm. My lady's sparrow is dead, the sparrow which was my lady's darling.

Carmina no. 3

2 *Vivamus, mea Lesbia, atque amemus . . .*
Soles occidere et redire possunt:
Nobis cum semel occidit brevis lux
Nox est perpetua una dormienda.
Da mi basia mille.
Let us live and love, my Lesbia . . . Suns may set and rise again: for us, when our brief light has set, there's the sleep of perpetual night. Give me a thousand kisses.

Carmina no. 5

3 *Per caputque pedesque.*
Over head and heels.

Carmina no. 20

4 *Odi et amo: quare id faciam, fortasse requiris.*
Nescio, sed fieri sentio et excrucior.

I hate and I love: why I do so you may well ask.
   I do not know, but I feel it happen and am in
   agony.

Carmina no. 85

5 *Atque in perpetuum, frater, ave atque vale.*

And forever, O my brother, hail and farewell!

Carmina no. 101

Constantine Cavafy

Egyptian-born Greek poet, 1863–1933

1 What are we waiting for, gathered in the
   market-place?

The barbarians are to arrive today.

"Waiting for the Barbarians" (1904) (translation by
Edmund Keeley and Philip Sherrard)

2 And now, what will come of us without any
   barbarians?

Those people were a kind of solution.

"Waiting for the Barbarians" (1904) (translation by
Edmund Keeley and Philip Sherrard)

3 When you set out for Ithaka
ask that your way be long.

"Ithaka" (1911) (translation by Edmund Keeley and
Philip Sherrard)

Edith Cavell

English nurse, 1865–1915

1 [*On the eve of her execution by Germany for
helping British soldiers escape from Belgium:*] I
realize that patriotism is not enough. I must
have no hatred or bitterness towards anyone.

Quoted in *Times* (London), 23 Oct. 1915

Paul Celan

German poet, 1920–1970

1 *Der Tod ist ein Meister aus Deutschland.*
Death is a master from Germany.

"Death Fugue" (1952)

Louis-Ferdinand Céline (Louis Ferdinand
Auguste Destouches)

French novelist, 1894–1961

1 Those who talk about the future are scoundrels.
It is the present that matters. To evoke one's
posterity is to make a speech to maggots.

Voyage au Bout de la Nuit (Journey to the End of the
Night) (1932)

2 Almost every desire a poor man has is a
punishable offense.

Voyage au Bout de la Nuit (Journey to the End of the
Night) (1932)

Benvenuto Cellini

Italian artist, 1500–1571

1 Painting, in fact, is nothing else much than a
tree, a man, or any other object, reflected in the
water. The distinction between sculpture and
painting, is as great as between the shadow and
the substance.

Letter to Benedetto Varchi, 28 Jan. 1546 (translation
by Thomas Nugent)

Susannah Centlivre

English actress and playwright, ca. 1667–1723

1 There is a very pretty Collection of Prints in the
next Room, Madam, will you give me leave to
explain them to you?

The Man's Bewitched act 3 (1710)
See Dorothy Parker 22

2 The real Simon Pure.

A Bold Stroke for a Wife act 5, sc. 1 (1718)

3 He is as melancholy as an unbraced drum.

The Wonder! act 2, sc. 1 (1761)

Vinton G. Cerf

U.S. computer scientist, 1943–

1 Specification of Internet Transmission Control
Program.

"Request for Comments No. 675" (Network Working
Group, electronic text) (1974). Earliest use of the term
Internet.

Miguel de Cervantes Saavedra

Spanish novelist, 1547–1616

1 In a village of La Mancha, the name of which I
won't try to recall, there lived, not long ago, one
of those gentlemen, who usually keep a lance
upon a rack, an old shield, a lean horse, and a
greyhound for coursing.

Don Quixote pt. 1, ch. 1 (1605)

2 To tilt against windmills.

Don Quixote pt. 1, ch. 8 (1605)

3 *El Caballero de la Triste Figura.*
The Knight of the Doleful Countenance.
Don Quixote pt. 1, ch. 19 (1605)

4 We cannot all be friars, and many are the ways
by which God leads his own to eternal life.
Knight-errantry *is* religion.
Don Quixote pt. 2, ch. 8 (1615)

5 He's a muddle-headed fool, with frequent lucid
intervals.
Don Quixote pt. 2, ch. 18 (1615)

6 *Dos linajes solos hay en el mundo . . . que son el
tener y el no tener.*
There are only two families in the world . . . the
haves and the have-nots.
Don Quixote pt. 2, ch. 20 (1615)

7 *Digo, paciencia y barajar.*
What I say is, patience, and shuffle the cards.
Don Quixote pt. 2, ch. 23 (1615)

8 [*Don Quixote's epitaph:*] To die in wisdom,
having lived in folly.
Don Quixote pt. 2, ch. 74 (1615)

9 [*Of impending death:*] One foot already in the
stirrup.
Los Trabajos de Persiles y Sigismunda preface (1617)

Aimé Fernand Césaire
Martinican poet and political leader, 1913–2008

1 My mouth shall be the mouth of misfortunes
which have no mouth, my voice the freedoms
of those freedoms which break down in the
prison-cell of despair.
Cahier d'un Retour au Pays Natal (1939)

2 I see several Africas and one
vertical in the tumultuous event
with its screens and nodules,
a little separated, but within
the century, like a heart in reserve.
Ferrements "Pour Saluer le Tiers-Monde" (1960)

Paul Cézanne
French painter, 1839–1906

1 Treat nature in terms of the cylinder, the
sphere, the cone, all in perspective.
Letter to Émile Bernard, 15 Apr. 1904

2 The day was not far off when one solitary,
original carrot [depicted in a painting] might be
pregnant with revolution!
Quoted in Émile Zola, *L'Oeuvre* (1886) (translation
by Thomas Walton). In Zola's novel, uttered by a
character based on Cézanne.

3 [*Remark to Ambroise Vollard:*] Monet is only an
eye, but my God what an eye!
Quoted in Douglas Cooper, *Claude Monet: An
Exhibition of Paintings* (1957)

Zechariah Chafee, Jr.
U.S. legal scholar, 1885–1957

1 Each side takes the position of the man who
was arrested for swinging his arms and hitting
another in the nose, and asked the judge if he
did not have a right to swing his arms in a free
country. "Your right to swing your arms ends
just where the other man's nose begins."
Harvard Law Review, June 1919. "Your right to swing
your arm leaves off where my right not to have my
nose struck begins" appeared in a speech by John B.
Finch, Iowa City, Iowa, 7 May 1882.

Sri Chaitanya Mahaprabhu
Indian religious leader, 1486–1534

1 Hare Krishna Hare Krishna Krishna Krishna
Hare Hare
Hare Rama Hare Rama Rama Rama Hare
Hare.
Chant (ca. 1515)

Neville Chamberlain
British prime minister, 1869–1940

1 [*On Germany's annexing the Sudetenland:*] How
horrible, fantastic, incredible it is that we
should be digging trenches and trying on gas-
masks here because of a quarrel in a far away
country between people of whom we know
nothing.
Radio broadcast, 27 Sept. 1938

2 [*After returning from the Munich Conference:*]
This is the second time in our history that there
has come back from Germany to Downing
Street peace with honor. I believe it is peace for
our time.
Speech at 10 Downing Street, London, 30 Sept. 1938
See Disraeli 27; John Russell 1

3 This morning, the British Ambassador in Berlin handed the German government a final Note stating that, unless we heard from them by eleven o'clock that they were prepared at once to withdraw their troops from Poland, a state of war would exist between us. I have to tell you now that no such undertaking has been received, and that consequently this country is at war with Germany.
Radio broadcast, 3 Sept. 1939

4 Whatever may be the reason—whether it was that Hitler thought he might get away with what he had got without fighting for it, or whether it was that after all the preparations were not sufficiently complete—however, one thing is certain—he missed the bus.
Speech at Central Hall, Westminster, England, 4 Apr. 1940

Lindsay Chamberlain-Creighton
New Zealand–born Australian exonerated murder suspect, 1948–

1 The dingo's got my baby.
Quoted in *Canberra Times*, 16 Dec. 1980

Haddon Chambers
English playwright, 1860–1921

1 The long arm of coincidence.
Captain Swift act 2 (1888)

Nicolas-Sébastien Chamfort
French writer, 1741–1794

1 [*Revolutionary slogan, 1789:*] *Guerre aux châteaux! Paix aux chaumières!*
War on the palaces! Peace to the shacks!
Quoted in P. R. Anguis, *Oeuvres Complètes de Chamfort* "Notice sur la Vie de Chamfort" (1824)

2 [*Chamfort's interpretation of the revolutionary motto "Fraternity or death":*] Be my brother, or I kill you.
Quoted in P. R. Anguis, *Oeuvres Complètes de Chamfort* (1824)

Raymond Chandler
U.S. detective fiction writer, 1888–1959

1 I don't mind if you don't like my manners. They're pretty bad. I grieve over them on the long winter evenings.
The Big Sleep ch. 3 (1939)

2 What did it matter where you lay once you were dead? . . . You were dead, you were sleeping the big sleep, you were not bothered by things like that.
The Big Sleep ch. 32 (1939)

3 You just slept the big sleep, not caring about the nastiness of how you died or where you fell.
The Big Sleep ch. 32 (1939)

4 [*Credo of fictional detective Philip Marlowe:*] Trouble Is My Business.
Title of article, *Dime Detective Magazine*, Aug. 1939. Mary Roberts Rinehart used the expression "Trouble is my business too" in her 1934 detective story "The Inside Story."

5 It was a blonde. A blonde to make a bishop kick a hole in a stained glass window.
Farewell, My Lovely ch. 13 (1940)

6 She gave me a smile I could feel in my hip pocket.
Farewell, My Lovely ch. 18 (1940)

7 Law is where you buy it in this town.
Farewell, My Lovely ch. 19 (1940)

8 Down these mean streets a man must go who is not himself mean, who is neither tarnished nor afraid.
"The Simple Art of Murder," *Atlantic Monthly*, Dec. 1944
See Arthur Morrison 1

9 If my books had been any worse, I should not have been invited to Hollywood, and if they had been any better, I should not have come.
Atlantic Monthly, 12 Dec. 1945

10 Would you convey your compliments to the purist who reads your proofs and tell him or her that I write in a sort of broken-down patois which is something like the way a Swiss waiter talks, and that when I split an infinitive, God damn it, I split it so it will stay split.
Letter to Edward Weeks, 18 Jan. 1947

11 When in doubt have a man come through a door with a gun in his hand.
"The Simple Art of Murder," *Saturday Review of Literature,* 15 Apr. 1950

12 Alcohol is like love: the first kiss is magic, the second is intimate, the third is routine. After that you just take the girl's clothes off.
The Long Goodbye ch. 4 (1953)

Coco Chanel (Gabrielle Bonheur)
French fashion designer and perfumer, 1883–1971

1 Mode passes; style remains.

Interview, *McCall's*, Nov. 1965. Usually quoted as "Fashion fades, only style remains the same."

2 A woman should use perfume wherever she wants to be kissed.

Quoted in *Boston Globe*, 27 Dec. 1962

3 [*Of Christian Dior's "New Look":*] Clothes by a man who doesn't know women, never had one, and dreams of being one!

Quoted in *Vanity Fair*, June 1994

William Ellery Channing
U.S. clergyman, 1780–1842

1 No power in society, no hardship in your condition can depress you, keep you down, in knowledge, power, virtue, influence, but by your own consent.

"Self-Culture" (address), Boston, Mass., Sept. 1838
See Eleanor Roosevelt 6

Charles Spencer "Charlie" Chaplin
English comic actor and film director, 1889–1977

1 All I need to make a comedy is a park, a policeman, and a pretty girl.

My Autobiography ch. 10 (1964)

2 I am known in parts of the world by people who have never heard of Jesus Christ.

Quoted in Lita Grey Chaplin, *My Life with Chaplin: An Intimate Memoir* (1966)
See Zelda Fitzgerald 2; Lennon 13

Ralph Chaplin
U.S. political activist and songwriter, 1887–1961

1 Solidarity forever!
For the union makes us strong.

"Solidarity Forever" (song) (1915)

Arthur Chapman
U.S. poet, 1873–1935

1 Out where the hand-clasp's a little stronger,
Out where the smile dwells a little longer,
That's where the West begins.

"Out Where the West Begins" l. 1 (1916)

George Chapman
English playwright, ca. 1559–1634

1 Young men think old men are fools; but old men know young men are fools.

All Fools act 5, sc. 1 (1605)

2 I will neither yield to the song of the siren nor the voice of the hyena, the tears of the crocodile nor the howling of the wolf.

Eastward Ho act 5, sc. 1 (1605). The *Oxford English Dictionary* documents the term *crocodile tears* as early as 1563.

3 And let a scholar all Earth's volumes carry,
He will be but a walking dictionary.

The Tears of Peace l. 530 (1609)

4 Danger, the spur of all great minds.

The Revenge of Bussy D'Ambois act 5, sc. 1 (1613)

John Jay Chapman
U.S. writer, 1862–1933

1 The New Testament, and to a very large extent the Old, *is* the soul of man. You cannot criticize it. It criticizes you.

Letter to Elizabeth Chanler, 26 Mar. 1898

Tracy Chapman
U.S. singer and songwriter, 1964–

1 You got a fast car
I want a ticket to anywhere
Maybe we can make a deal
Maybe together we can get somewhere
Anyplace is better
Starting from zero, got nothing to lose.

"Fast Car" (song) (1988)

Charles I
British king, 1600–1649

1 [*Of five members of Parliament he had tried to arrest:*] I see all the birds are flown.

House of Commons, 4 Jan. 1642

Charles II
British king, 1630–1685

1 [*On his deathbed, referring to his former mistress, Nell Gwyn:*] Let not poor Nelly starve.

Quoted in Gilbert Burnet, *Bishop Burnet's History of His Own Time* (1724)

2 [*Report of "last words":*] He had been, he said, an unconscionable time dying; but he hoped they would excuse it.

Reported in Thomas Babington Macaulay, *History of England* (1849)

Charles V
Spanish king and Holy Roman Emperor, 1500–1558

1 *Le Grand Empereur, Charle-quint, disoit que s'il vouloit parler à Dieu, il luy parleroit en Espagnole; s'il vouloit parler à son Cheval, ce seroit en Allemand; s'il vouloit parler à sa Maitresse ce seroit en Italien; mais que s'il vouloit parler aux hommes ce seroit en François.*

The Great Emperor Charles V said that to God he would speak Spanish, to his horse he would speak German, to his mistress he would speak Italian, but to men he would speak French.

Reported in Lord Chesterfield, Letter to Philip Stanhope, 19 July 1762

Larry Charles
U.S. screenwriter, 1956–

1 [*Of homosexuality:*] Not that there's anything wrong with that.

Seinfeld (television show), 11 Feb. 1993

Charles, Prince of Wales
British prince, 1948–

1 [*Responding to being asked, after his engagement to Diana Spencer was announced, if he was "in love":*] Yes . . . whatever that may mean.

Interview, 24 Feb. 1981

2 [*On the proposed design for a new wing of the National Gallery:*] What is proposed is like a monstrous carbuncle on the face of a much-loved and elegant friend.

Speech to Royal Institute of British Architects, 30 May 1984. Charles's stepmother-in-law, Countess Spencer, had written in her 1983 book *The Spencers on Spas* (with Earl Spencer): "Alas, for our towns and cities. Monstrous carbuncles of concrete have erupted in gentle Georgian squares."

3 I just come and talk to the plants, really—very important to talk to them, they respond I find.

Television interview, 21 Sept. 1986

4 You have to give this much to the Luftwaffe: when it knocked down our buildings it did not replace them with anything more offensive than rubble. We did that.

Speech at Mansion House, London, 1 Dec. 1987

5 [*Replying to Camilla Parker-Bowles's remark, "Oh, you're going to come back as a pair of knickers" (so that he could live inside her trousers):*] Or, God forbid, a Tampax.

Intercepted telephone conversation, 18 Dec. 1989

Martin Charnin
U.S. songwriter, 1934–2019

1 It's the hard-knock life for us!
It's the hard-knock life for us!
'Steada treated,
We get tricked!
'Steada kisses,
We get kicked!

"It's the Hard Knock Life" (song) (1977)

2 Tomorrow, tomorrow, I love ya tomorrow,
You're always a day away!

"Tomorrow" (song) (1977)

Pierre Charron
French philosopher and theologian, 1541–1603

1 *La vraie science et la vraie étude de l'homme, c'est l'homme.*

The true science and the true study of man is man.

Traité de la Sagesse bk. 1, preface (1601)
See Pope 21

Mary Chase
U.S. playwright, 1907–1981

1 Doctor, I wrestled with reality for forty years, and I am happy to state that I finally won out over it.

Harvey act 2, sc. 2 (1944)

2 Dr. Chumley, my mother used to say to me, "In this world, Elwood"—she always called me Elwood—she'd say, "In this world, Elwood, you must be oh, so smart or oh, so pleasant." For years I was smart. I recommend pleasant.

Harvey act 3 (1944)

Salmon P. Chase

U.S. political leader and judge, 1808–1873

1 In God we trust.

Letter to James Pollock, 9 Dec. 1863. In the 1863 letter
to Director of the Mint Pollock, Chase, then secretary
of the treasury, proposed this as a motto on U.S. coins,
a proposal implemented on the two-cent coin in 1864.
Chase may have taken the words from a Civil War
(1862) battle cry of the Fifth Pennsylvania Volunteers.
In 1956 a Joint Resolution of Congress declared "In
God we trust" the national motto of the United States.
"In God we trust" was mentioned in the *Pennsylvania
Gazette*, 12 Jan. 1748, as one of a list of "Devices and
Mottoes painted on some of the Silk Colours of the
Regiments of Associators, in and near Philadelphia."
See Francis Scott Key 3

2 The Constitution, in all its provisions, looks
to an indestructible Union, composed of
indestructible States.

Texas v. White (1869)

François René de Chateaubriand

French author, 1768–1848

1 The original writer is not he who refrains from
imitating others, but he who can be imitated by
none.

Le Génie de Christianisme pt. 2, bk. 1, ch. 3 (1802)

2 Achilles exists only through Homer. Take away
the art of writing from this world, and you will
probably take away its glory.

Les Natchez preface (1826)

Geoffrey Chaucer

English poet, ca. 1343–1400

1 Oon ere it herde, at tother out it wente.

Troilus and Criseyde bk. 4, l. 434 (ca. 1385). Usually
quoted as "in one ear and out the other."

2 But manly sette the world on six and sevene;
And if thow deye a martyr, go to hevene!

Troilus and Criseyde bk. 4, l. 622 (ca. 1385)

3 Go, litel bok, go, litel myn tragedye.

Troilus and Criseyde bk. 5, l. 1786 (ca. 1385)

4 That lyf so short, the craft so long to lerne.

The Parliament of Fowls l. 1 (1380–1386)
See Hippocrates 1; Longfellow 2

5 For out of olde feldes, as men seyth,
Cometh al this newe corn fro yer to yere;
And out of olde bokes, in good feyth,
Cometh al this newe science that men lere.

The Parliament of Fowls l. 22 (1380–1386)

6 Whan that Aprill with his shoures soote
The droghte of March hath perced to the
roote.

The Canterbury Tales "The General Prologue" l. 1
(ca. 1387)

7 And smale foweles maken melodye,
That slepen al the nyght with open ye
(So priketh hem nature in hir corages),
Thanne longen folk to goon on pilgrimages.

The Canterbury Tales "The General Prologue" l. 9
(ca. 1387)

8 He was a verray, parfit gentil knyght.

The Canterbury Tales "The General Prologue" l. 72
(ca. 1387)

9 And gladly wolde he lerne and gladly teche.

The Canterbury Tales "The General Prologue" l. 308
(ca. 1387)

10 Ye been oure lord, dooth with youre owene
thyng
Right as yow list.

The Canterbury Tales "Clerk's Tale" l. 652 (ca. 1387).
Resembles the late-twentieth-century expression "do
your own thing."

11 Love wol nat been constreyned by maistrye.
When maistrie comth, the God of Love anon
Beteth his wynges, and farewel, he is gon!

The Canterbury Tales "The Franklin's Tale" l. 764
(ca. 1387)

12 And therefore, at the kynges court, my brother,
Ech man for hymself, ther is noon oother.

The Canterbury Tales "The Knight's Tale" l. 1181
(ca. 1387)

13 The bisy larke, messager of day.
The Canterbury Tales "The Knight's Tale" l. 1491 (ca. 1387)

14 The smylere with the knyf under the cloke.
The Canterbury Tales "The Knight's Tale" l. 1999 (ca. 1387)

15 Mordre wol out; that se we day by day.
The Canterbury Tales "The Nun's Priest's Tale" l. 3052 (ca. 1387)

16 Thurgh thikke and thurgh thenne.
The Canterbury Tales "The Reeve's Tale" l. 4066 (ca. 1387)

17 Yblessed be god that I have wedded fyve!
Welcome the sixte, whan that evere he shal.
The Canterbury Tales "The Wife of Bath's Prologue" l. 44 (ca. 1387)

18 Wommen desiren to have sovereynetee
As wel over hir housbond as hir love.
The Canterbury Tales "The Wife of Bath's Tale" l. 1038 (ca. 1387)

Cesar Chavez
U.S. labor leader, 1927–1993

1 [*Slogan of United Farm Workers:*] Viva la huelga. Long live the strike.
Quoted in *N.Y. Times*, 25 Mar. 1966

John Cheever
U.S. writer, 1912–1982

1 Wear dark clothes after 6 p.m. Eat fresh fish for breakfast when available. Avoid kneeling in unheated stone churches. Ecclesiastical dampness causes prematurely gray hair. Fear tastes like a rusty knife and do not let her into your house. Courage tastes of blood. Stand up straight. Admire the world. Relish the love of a gentle woman. Trust in the Lord.
The Wapshot Chronicle ch. 36 (1957)

2 It was at the highest point in the arc of a bridge that I became aware suddenly of the depth and bitterness of my feelings about modern life, and of the profoundness of my yearning for a more vivid, simple, and peaceable world.
Stories "The Angel of the Bridge" (1978)

Susan Cheever
U.S. writer, 1943–

1 When Tolstoy wrote that all happy families are alike, what he meant was that there are no happy families.
Treetops pt. 2, ch. 11 (1991)
See Tolstoy 8

Anton Chekhov
Russian playwright and short story writer, 1860–1904

1 I feel more confident and more satisfied when I reflect that I have two professions and not one. Medicine is my lawful wife and literature is my mistress. When I get tired of one I spend the night with the other. Though it's disorderly, it's not so dull, and besides, neither really loses anything through my infidelity.
Letter to A. S. Suvorin, 11 Sept. 1888

2 Brevity is the sister of talent.
Letter to Alexander Chekhov, 11 Apr. 1889

3 One must not put a loaded rifle on the stage if no one is thinking of firing it.
Letter to A. S. Lazarev, 1 Nov. 1889. Ilia Gurliand, in "Reminiscences of A. P. Chekhov," *Teatr i Iskusstvo*, 11 July 1904, states that Chekhov had told him the following in conversation at Yalta in the summer of 1889: "If in the first act you have hung a pistol on the wall, then in the following one it should be fired. Otherwise don't put it there."

4 I'm in mourning for my life, I'm unhappy.
The Seagull act 1 (1896)

5 I'm a seagull. No, that's wrong. Remember you shot a seagull? A man happened to come along, saw it and killed it, just to pass the time.
The Seagull act 4 (1896)

6 When a woman isn't beautiful, people always say, "You have lovely eyes, you have lovely hair."
Uncle Vanya act 3 (1897)

Richard B. Cheney
U.S. government official, 1941–

1 [*Of the Iraq War:*] My belief is we will, in fact, be greeted as liberators.
Interview by NBC *Meet the Press* television program, 16 Mar. 2003

2 The insurgency [in Iraq] is in its last throes.
Television interview, "Larry King Live," 30 May 2005

3 [*Of his five draft deferments during the Vietnam War:*] I had other priorities in the '60s than military service.
Quoted in interview in *Wash. Post*, 5 Apr. 1989

Cher (Cherilyn Sarkisian LaPierre)
U.S. singer and actress, 1946–

1 Mother told me a couple of years ago, "Sweetheart, settle down and marry a rich man." I said, "Mom, I am a rich man."
Quoted in *Observer* (London), 26 Nov. 1995

N. G. Chernyshevsky
Russian journalist and politician, 1828–1889

1 What Is to Be Done?
Title of book (1863)

Apsley Cherry-Garrard
English explorer, 1886–1959

1 [*Of Antarctic explorers:*] For a joint scientific and geographical piece of organization, give me Scott; for a Winter Journey, Wilson; for a dash to the Pole and nothing else, Amundsen: and if I am in the devil of a hole and want to get out of it, give me Shackleton every time.
The Worst Journey in the World vol. 1, preface (1922)

Philip Dormer Stanhope, Earl of Chesterfield
English writer and politician, 1694–1773

1 I have opposed measures not men.
Letter to Richard Chevenix, 6 Mar. 1742

2 Whatever is worth doing at all, is worth doing well.
Letters to His Son, 10 Mar. 1746

3 An injury is much sooner forgotten than an insult.
Letters to His Son, 9 Oct. 1746

4 Do as you would be done by is the surest method that I know of pleasing.
Letters to His Son, 16 Oct. 1747
See Aristotle 12; Bible 225; Confucius 9; Hillel 2

5 I knew, once, a very covetous, sordid fellow [William Lowndes], who used frequently to say, "Take care of the pence; for the pounds will take care of themselves."
Letters to His Son, 6 Nov. 1747

6 The chapter of knowledge is a very short, but the chapter of accidents is a very long one.
Letter to Solomon Dayrolles, 16 Feb. 1753

7 [*Of sex:*] The pleasure is momentary, the position is ridiculous, and the expense is damnable.
Attributed in W. Somerset Maugham, *Christmas Holiday* (1939). George Bernard Shaw, in a letter to St. John Ervine, 12 Mar. 1928, attributed "the position is ridiculous, the pleasure but momentary, and the expense damnable" to an unnamed "Aberdonian." "The pleasure is momentary, the attitudes ridiculous, and the expense _____" appeared, attributed to "a certain American," in the *Western Daily Press* (Bristol, England), 20 Nov. 1902.

G. K. Chesterton
English writer, 1874–1936

1 The person who is really in revolt is the optimist, who generally lives and dies in a desperate and suicidal effort to persuade all the other people how good they are.
The Defendant introduction (1901)

2 The act of defending any of the cardinal virtues has to-day all the exhilaration of a vice.
The Defendant "A Defence of Humility" (1901)

3 "My country, right or wrong," is a thing that no patriot would think of saying except in a desperate case. It is like saying "My mother, drunk or sober."
The Defendant "A Defence of Patriotism" (1901)
See Decatur 1; Schurz 1; Twain 114

4 They have invented a phrase, a phrase that is a black and white contradiction in two words— "free-love"—as if a lover ever had been, or ever could be, free. It is the nature of love to bind itself, and the institution of marriage merely paid the average man the compliment of taking him at his word.
The Defendant "A Defence of Rash Vows" (1902)

5 When you break the big laws, you do not get liberty; you do not even get anarchy. You get the small laws.
Daily News (London), 29 July 1905

6 Truth must of necessity be stranger than fiction . . . For fiction is the creation of the human mind, and therefore is congenial to it.
The Club of Queer Trades "The Singular Speculation of the House-Agent" (1905)
See Byron 33; Twain 93

7 It has often been said, very truly, that religion is the thing that makes the ordinary man feel extraordinary; it is an equally important truth that religion is the thing that makes the extraordinary man feel ordinary.
Charles Dickens: The Last of the Great Men ch. 1 (1906)

8 Creeds must disagree: it is the whole fun of the thing. If I think the universe is triangular, and you think it is square, there cannot be room for two universes. We may argue politely, we may argue humanely, we may argue with great mutual benefit: but, obviously, we must argue. Modern toleration is really a tyranny. It is a tyranny because it is a silence. To say that I must not deny my opponent's faith is to say I must not discuss it.
Illustrated London News, 10 Oct. 1908

9 Thieves respect property. They merely wish the property to become their property that they may more perfectly respect it.
The Man Who Was Thursday ch. 4 (1908)

10 Poets do not go mad; but chess-players do. Mathematicians go mad, and cashiers; but creative artists very seldom. I am not, as will be seen, in any sense attacking logic: I only say that this danger does lie in logic, not in imagination.
Orthodoxy ch. 2 (1908)

11 Tradition means giving votes to the most obscure of all classes, our ancestors. It is the democracy of the dead. Tradition refuses to submit to the small and arrogant oligarchy of those who merely happen to be walking about. All democrats object to men being disqualified by the accident of birth; tradition objects to their being disqualified by the accident of death.
Orthodoxy ch. 4 (1908)

12 Angels can fly because they can take themselves lightly.
Orthodoxy ch. 7 (1908)

13 You will hear everlastingly, in all discussions about newspapers, companies, aristocracies, or party politics, this argument that the rich man cannot be bribed. The fact is, of course, that the rich man is bribed; he has been bribed already. That is why he is a rich man.
Orthodoxy ch. 7 (1908)

14 Fairy-tales do not give a child his first idea of bogy. What fairy-tales give the child is his first clear idea of the possible defeat of bogy. The baby has known the dragon intimately ever since he had an imagination. What the fairy-tale provides for him is a St. George to kill the dragon.
Tremendous Trifles "The Red Angel" (1909)

15 Our civilization has decided, and very justly decided, that determining the guilt or innocence of men is a thing too important to be trusted to trained men. . . . When it wants a library catalogued, or the solar system discovered, or any trifle of that kind, it uses up its specialists. But when it wishes anything done which is really serious, it collects twelve of the ordinary men standing round. The same thing was done, if I remember right, by the Founder of Christianity.
Tremendous Trifles "The Twelve Men" (1909)

16 This diseased pride [of artistic individualists] was not even conscious of a public interest, and would have found all political terms utterly tasteless and insignificant. It was no longer a question of one man one vote, but of one man one universe.
George Bernard Shaw "The Progressive" (1910)
See Cartwright 1; William O. Douglas 4

17 The Christian ideal has not been tried and found wanting. It has been found difficult; and left untried.
What's Wrong with the World pt. 1, ch. 5 (1910)

18 If a thing is worth doing, it is worth doing badly.
What's Wrong with the World pt. 4, ch. 14 (1910)

19 The mystic does not bring doubts or riddles: the doubts and riddles exist already. We all feel the riddle of the earth without anyone to point it out. The mystery of life is the plainest part of it. The clouds and curtains of darkness, the confounding vapors, these are the daily weather of this world.
William Blake (1910)

20 The criminal is the creative artist; the detective only the critic.
The Innocence of Father Brown "The Blue Cross" (1911)

21 To be smart enough to get all that money you must be dull enough to want it.

A Miscellany of Men "The Miser and His Friends" (1912)

See Eugene McCarthy 1

22 Journalism largely consists in saying "Lord Jones Dead" to people who never knew that Lord Jones was alive.

The Wisdom of Father Brown "The Purple Wig" (1914)

23 I think I will not hang myself today.

"A Ballade of Suicide" l. 8 (1915)

24 All but the hard-hearted must be torn with pity for this pathetic dilemma of the rich man, who has to keep the poor man just stout enough to do the work and just thin enough to have to do it.

Utopia of Usurers, and Other Essays "The Utopia of Usurers" (1917)

25 The first effect of not believing in God is to believe in anything.

Attributed in Emile Cammaerts, *The Laughing Prophet* (1937). This quotation has not been traced in Chesterton's own writings. It may be a blend of two of his statements in the Father Brown stories: "It's the first effect of not believing in God that you lose your common sense" ("The Oracle of the Dog" [1923]) and "You hard-shelled materialists were all balanced on the very edge of belief—of belief in almost anything" ("The Miracle of Moon Crescent" [1924]).

Maurice Chevalier

French singer and actor, 1888–1972

1 Old age isn't so bad when you consider the alternative.

Quoted in *L.A. Times*, 15 May 1960. "Growing old isn't so bad when you consider the alternative" was printed as a "famous quotation" without attribution to any individual in the *Long Beach* (Calif.) *Press-Telegram*, 2 Aug. 1952.

2 Many a man has fallen in love with a girl in a light so dim he would not have chosen a suit by it.

Quoted in Helen Handley, *The Lover's Quotation Book* (1986)

Julia Child

U.S. chef, author, and television personality, 1912–2004

1 This is a book for the servantless American cook who can be unconcerned on occasion with budgets, waistlines, time schedules, children's meals, the parent-chauffeur-den mother syndrome, or anything else which might interfere with the enjoyment of producing something wonderful to eat.

Mastering the Art of French Cooking foreword (1961). Coauthored with Simone Beck and Louisette Bertholle.

Lydia Maria Child

U.S. abolitionist and women's right activist, 1802–1880

1 We first crush people to the earth, and then claim the right of trampling on them forever, because they are prostrate.

An Appeal in Favor of That Class of Americans Called Africans ch. 7 (1833)

2 Over the river and through the wood,
To grandfather's house we go;
The horse knows the way
To carry the sleigh,
Through the white and drifted snow.

Flowers for Children "Thanksgiving Day" l. 1 (1844–1846)

Shirley Chisholm

U.S. politician, 1924–2005

1 Unbought and Unbossed.

Title of book (1970)

2 Of my two "handicaps," being female put many more obstacles in my path than being black.

Unbought and Unbossed introduction (1970)

Hong-Yee Chiu

Chinese-born U.S. astrophysicist, 1932–

1 So far, the clumsily long name "quasi-stellar radio sources" is used to describe these objects. . . . For convenience, the abbreviated form *"quasar"* will be used throughout this paper.

Physics Today, May 1964

Joseph H. Choate

U.S. lawyer and diplomat, 1832–1917

1 You cannot live without the lawyers, and certainly you cannot die without them.

"The Bench and the Bar" (speech), New York, N.Y., 13 May 1879

2 America, the paradise of lawyers.
Lecture at Philosophical Institution of Edinburgh,
Edinburgh, Scotland, 13 Nov. 1900

3 At a certain drawing room in London . . . a
guest approached Mr. Choate, who was in the
conventional dress of the English waiter, and
said, "Call me a cab." "All right," said Mr.
Choate, "if you wish it. You're a cab."
Reported in *N.Y. Times*, 17 Nov. 1901

Rufus Choate
U.S. lawyer and politician, 1799–1859

1 Its constitution the glittering and sounding
generalities of natural right which make up the
Declaration of Independence.
Letter to Maine Whig State Central Committee, 9
Aug. 1856
See Ralph Waldo Emerson 43

Noam Chomsky
U.S. linguist and political activist, 1928–

1 The notion "grammatical" cannot be identified
with "meaningful" or "significant" in any
semantic sense. Sentences (1) and (2) are
equally nonsensical, but . . . only the former is
grammatical.
    (1) Colorless green ideas sleep furiously.
    (2) Furiously sleep ideas green colorless.
Syntactic Structures ch. 2 (1957)

2 We thus make a fundamental distinction
between *competence* (the speaker-hearer's
knowledge of his language) and *performance*
(the actual use of language in concrete
situations).
Aspects of the Theory of Syntax ch. 1 (1965)

3 The Internet is an élite organization; most of
the population of the world has never even
made a phone call.
Quoted in *Observer*, 18 Feb. 1996

Kate Chopin
U.S. writer, 1850–1904

1 Mrs. Pontellier was beginning to realize her
position in the universe as a human being, and
to recognize her relations as an individual to
the world within and about her.
The Awakening ch. 6 (1899)

2 The years that are gone seem like dreams—if
one might go on sleeping and dreaming—but
to wake up and find—oh! well! Perhaps it is
better to wake up after all, even to suffer, rather
than to remain a dupe to illusions all one's life.
The Awakening ch. 38 (1899)

3 For the first time in her life she stood naked
in the open air, at the mercy of the sun, the
breeze that beat upon her, and the waves that
invited her.
The Awakening ch. 39 (1899)

Agatha Christie
English detective fiction writer, 1890–1976

1 [Fictional detective Hercule] Poirot was an
extraordinary-looking little man. He was hardly
more than five feet four inches, but carried
himself with great dignity. His head was exactly
the shape of an egg, and he always perched it
a little on one side. His moustache was very
stiff and military. The neatness of his attire
was almost incredible; I believe a speck of dust
would have caused him more pain than a bullet
wound.
The Mysterious Affair at Styles ch. 2 (1920)

2 He [Hercule Poirot] tapped his forehead.
"These little grey cells. It is 'up to them.'"
The Mysterious Affair at Styles ch. 10 (1920)

3 With method and logic one can accomplish
anything.
Poirot Investigates "The Kidnapped Prime Minister"
(1924)

4 "My dear Mr. Mayherne," said Romaine, "you
do not see at all. I knew—he was guilty!"
"The Witness for the Prosecution" (1924)

5 It is completely unimportant. . . . That is why it
is so interesting.
The Murder of Roger Ackroyd ch. 7 (1926)

6 [*On being married to Max Mallowan:*] An
archeologist is the best husband any woman
can get. Just consider: The older she gets, the
more he is interested in her.
Attributed in *Milwaukee Journal*, 10 Jan. 1952

David Christy

U.S. abolitionist and geologist, 1802–ca. 1868

1 KING COTTON cares not whether he employs slaves or freemen.

Cotton Is King; or, the Economical Relations of Slavery conclusion (1855)

Chuang Tzu

Chinese philosopher, ca. 369 B.C.–286 B.C.

1 Once upon a time, Chuang Chou dreamed that he was a butterfly, a butterfly flitting about happily enjoying himself. He didn't know that he was Chou. Suddenly he awoke and was palpably Chou. He didn't know whether he were Chou who had dreamed of being a butterfly, or a butterfly who was dreaming that he was Chou.

Chuang Tzu ch. 2

Mary Lee, Lady Chudleigh

English poet, 1656–1710

1 'Tis hard we should be by the men despised,
   Yet kept from knowing what would make us
      prized;
   Debarred from knowledge, banished from the
      schools,
   And with the utmost industry bred fools.

The Ladies Defence (1701)

2 Wife and Servant are the same,
   But only differ in the Name.

"To the Ladies" l. 1 (1703)

Francis P. Church

U.S. journalist, 1839–1906

1 No Santa Claus! Thank God! he lives, and he lives forever. A thousand years from now, Virginia, nay, ten times ten thousand years from now, he will continue to make glad the heart of childhood.

"Is There a Santa Claus" (editorial), *Sun* (N.Y.), 21 Sept. 1897. Church was responding to a letter from eight-year-old Virginia O'Hanlon, asking "Some of my little friends say there is no Santa Claus. Papa says 'If you see it in *The Sun* it's so.' Please tell me the truth; is there a Santa Claus?"

2 Yes, Virginia, there is a Santa Claus. He exists as certainly as love and generosity and devotion exist.

"Is There a Santa Claus" (editorial), *Sun* (N.Y.), 21 Sept. 1897

3 You may tear apart the baby's rattle and see what makes the noise inside, but there is a veil covering the unseen world which not the strongest man, nor even the united strength of all the strongest men that ever lived, could tear apart. Only faith, fancy, poetry, love, romance, can push aside that curtain and view and picture the supernal beauty and glory beyond. Is it all real? Ah, Virginia, in all this world there is nothing else real and abiding.

"Is There a Santa Claus" (editorial), *Sun* (N.Y.), 21 Sept. 1897

Charles Churchill

English poet, 1731–1764

1   Be England what she will,
   With all her faults, she is my country still.

The Farewell l. 27 (1764)
See Cowper (1731–1800) 6

Frank E. Churchill

U.S. songwriter, 1901–1942

1 Who's Afraid of the Big Bad Wolf?

Title of song (1933)
See Albee 2

Randolph Henry Spencer, Lord Randolph Churchill

British political leader, 1849–1894

1 I decided some time ago that if the G.O.M. [William Ewart Gladstone, the "Grand Old Man"] went for Home Rule, the Orange card would be the one to play. Please God it may turn out the ace of trumps and not the two.

Letter to Lord Justice FitzGibbon, 16 Feb. 1886
See Robert Shapiro 1

2 Ulster will fight; Ulster will be right.

Public Letter, 7 May 1886

Winston Churchill

British statesman, 1874–1965

1 I pass with relief from the tossing sea of Cause and Theory to the firm ground of Result and Fact.

The Malakand Field Force ch. 3 (1898)

2 Nothing in life is so exhilarating as to be shot at without result.

The Malakand Field Force ch. 10 (1898)

3 It cannot in the opinion of His Majesty's government be classified as slavery in the extreme acceptation of the word without some risk of terminological inexactitude.

Speech in House of Commons, 22 Feb. 1906

4 Business carried on as usual during alterations on the map of Europe.

Speech at Guildhall, London, 9 Nov. 1914

5 [*Responding to criticism that he edited the* British Gazette *in a biased manner during the General Strike:*] I decline utterly to be impartial as between the fire brigade and the fire.

Speech in House of Commons, 7 July 1926

6 By being so long in the lowest form [at Harrow] I gained an immense advantage over the cleverer boys. . . . I got into my bones the essential structure of the ordinary British sentence—which is a noble thing.

My Early Life ch. 2 (1930)

7 It is a good thing for an uneducated man to read books of quotations. Bartlett's *Familiar Quotations* is an admirable work, and I studied it intently. The quotations when engraved upon the memory give you good thoughts. They also make you anxious to read the authors and look for more.

My Early Life ch. 9 (1930)

8 [*Of Ramsey MacDonald:*] I remember, when I was a child, being taken to the celebrated Barnum's circus, which contained an exhibition of freaks and monstrosities, but the exhibit on the program which I most desired to see was the one described as "The Boneless Wonder." My parents judged that the spectacle would be too revolting and demoralizing for my youthful eyes, and I have waited 50 years to see the boneless wonder sitting on the Treasury Bench.

Speech in House of Commons, 28 Jan. 1931

9 Their sweat, their tears, their blood bedewed the endless plain.

The Unknown War ch. 1 (1931)
See Byron 28; Winston Churchill 12; Donne 4; Theodore Roosevelt 3

10 [*Of Stanley Baldwin's Government:*] Decided only to be undecided, resolved to be irresolute, adamant for drift, solid for fluidity, all-powerful to be impotent.

Speech in House of Commons, 12 Nov. 1936

11 I cannot forecast to you the action of Russia. It is a riddle wrapped in a mystery inside an enigma.

Radio broadcast, 1 Oct. 1939

12 I would say to the House, as I said to those who have joined this Government: "I have nothing to offer but blood, toil, tears, and sweat."

Speech in House of Commons, 13 May 1940
See Byron 28; Winston Churchill 9; Donne 4; Theodore Roosevelt 3

13 You ask, what is our aim? I can answer in one word: It is victory, victory at all costs, victory in spite of all terror, victory, however long and hard the road may be; for without victory, there is no survival.

Speech in House of Commons, 13 May 1940

14 We shall fight on the beaches, we shall fight on the landing grounds, we shall fight in the fields and in the streets, we shall fight in the hills; we shall never surrender, and even if, which I do not for a moment believe, this island or a large part of it were subjugated and starving, then our Empire beyond the seas, armed and guarded by the British Fleet, would carry on the struggle, until, in God's good time, the New

World, with all its power and might, steps forth to the rescue and the liberation of the old.

Speech in House of Commons, 4 June 1940
See Clemenceau 3

15 Let us therefore brace ourselves to our duty, and so bear ourselves that, if the British Commonwealth and its Empire lasts for a thousand years, men will still say, "This was their finest hour."

Speech in House of Commons, 18 June 1940

16 What General Weygand called the Battle of France is over. I expect that the Battle of Britain is about to begin.

Speech in House of Commons, 18 June 1940

17 The gratitude of every home in our Island, in our Empire, and indeed throughout the world, except in the abodes of the guilty, goes out to the British airmen who, undaunted by odds, unwearied in their constant challenge and mortal danger, are turning the tide of the World War by their prowess and their devotion. Never in the field of human conflict was so much owed by so many to so few.

Speech in House of Commons, 20 Aug. 1940

18 We are waiting for the long-promised invasion. So are the fishes.

Radio broadcast to French people, 21 Oct. 1940

19 [*Addressing U.S. President Franklin Roosevelt:*] We shall not fail or falter; we shall not weaken or tire. Neither the sudden shock of battle, nor the long-drawn trials of vigilance and exertion will wear us down. Give us the tools, and we will finish the job.

Radio broadcast, 9 Feb. 1941
See George W. Bush 8

20 The people of London with one voice would say to Hitler: "You have committed every crime under the sun. . . . We will have no truce or parley with you, or the grisly gang who work your wicked will. You do your worst—and we will do our best."

Speech at County Hall, London, 14 July 1941

21 The V sign is the symbol of the unconquerable will of the occupied territories, and a portent of the fate awaiting the Nazi tyranny.

Message to people of Europe launching V for Victory propaganda campaign, 20 July 1941

22 Never give in, never give in, *never, never, never, never*—in nothing, great or small, large or petty—never give in except to convictions of honor and good sense.

Speech at Harrow School, Harrow, England, 29 Oct. 1941

23 Do not let us speak of darker days; let us rather speak of sterner days. These are not dark days: these are great days—the greatest days our country has ever lived; and we must all thank God that we have been allowed, each of us according to our stations, to play a part in making these days memorable in the history of our race.

Speech at Harrow School, Harrow, England, 29 Oct. 1941

24 When I warned them [the French] that Britain would fight on alone whatever they did, their generals told their Prime Minister and his divided Cabinet, "In three weeks England will have her neck wrung like a chicken." Some chicken! Some neck!

Speech to joint session of Canadian Parliament, Ottawa, 30 Dec. 1941

25 We have not journeyed all this way across the centuries, across the oceans, across the mountains, across the prairies, because we are made of sugar candy.

Speech to joint session of Canadian Parliament, Ottawa, 30 Dec. 1941

26 I have not become the King's First Minister in order to preside over the liquidation of the British Empire.

Speech at Lord Mayor's luncheon, London, 10 Nov. 1942

27 [*Of the Battle of Egypt:*] This is not the end. It is not even the beginning of the end. But it is, perhaps, the end of the beginning.

Speech at Mansion House, London, 10 Nov. 1942. An unsigned article in the *Economist*, 13 June 1942, stated, "Although this is not the end, it can be the beginning of the end."

28 We make this wide encircling movement in the Mediterranean, having for its primary object the recovery of the command of that vital sea, but also having for its object the exposure of the underbelly of the Axis, especially Italy, to heavy attack.

Speech in House of Commons, 11 Nov. 1942. Frequently misquoted as "soft underbelly."

29 The proud German army by its sudden collapse, sudden crumbling and breaking up, has once again proved the truth of the saying "The Hun is always either at your throat or at your feet."
Speech to U.S. Congress, 19 May 1943

30 The empires of the future are the empires of the mind.
Speech at Harvard University, Cambridge, Mass., 6 Sept. 1943

31 On the night of May 10, 1941, with one of the last bombs of the last serious raid our House of Commons was destroyed by the violence of the enemy, and we have now to consider whether we should build it up again, and how, and when. We shape our buildings, and afterwards our buildings shape us.
Speech in House of Commons, 28 Oct. 1943

32 We should not abandon our special relationship with the United States and Canada about the atomic bomb.
Speech in House of Commons, 7 Nov. 1945

33 A shadow has fallen upon the scenes so lately lighted by the Allied victory. . . . From Stettin in the Baltic to Trieste in the Adriatic, an iron curtain has descended across the Continent.
Address at Westminster College, Fulton, Mo., 5 Mar. 1946. Churchill's speech popularized the term *iron curtain* in reference to the political divide between the Soviet Union, and the nations dominated by that country, and the rest of the world. *Iron curtain* had been used in this sense as early as 1920 in Ethel Snowden, *Through Bolshevik Russia*. Churchill himself used the term in a telegram to President Harry S. Truman, 12 May 1945.
See Goebbels 3; Ethel Snowden 1; Troubridge 1

34 Many forms of Government have been tried, and will be tried in this world of sin and woe. No one pretends that democracy is perfect or all-wise. Indeed, it has been said that democracy is the worst form of Government except all those other forms that have been tried from time to time.
Speech in House of Commons, 11 Nov. 1947
See Briffault 1

35 In war: resolution. In defeat: defiance. In victory: magnanimity. In peace: goodwill.
The Second World War vol. 1, epigraph (1948). Churchill had earlier used these words in *My Early*

Life (1930), reporting that he had suggested them as an inscription for a monument in France.

36 On the night of the tenth of May [1940], at the outset of this mighty battle, I acquired the chief power in the State, which henceforth I wielded in ever-growing measure for five years and three months of world war, at the end of which time, all our enemies having surrendered unconditionally or being about to do so, I was immediately dismissed by the British electorate from all further conduct of their affairs.
The Second World War vol. 1 (1948)

37 I felt as if I were walking with destiny, and that all my past life had been but a preparation for this hour and this trial.
The Second World War vol. 1 (1948)

38 For my part, I consider that it will be found much better by all Parties to leave the past to history, especially as I propose to write that history myself.
Speech in House of Commons, 23 Jan. 1948

39 If Hitler invaded hell I would make at least a favorable reference to the devil in the House of Commons.
The Second World War vol. 3 (1950)

40 It may almost be said, "Before Alamein we never had a victory. After Alamein we never had a defeat."
The Second World War vol. 4 (1951)

41 The government of the world must be entrusted to satisfied nations, who wished nothing more for themselves than what they had. . . . Our power placed us above the rest. We were like rich men dwelling at peace within their habitations.
The Second World War vol. 5 (1951)

42 Meeting jaw to jaw is better than war.
Remarks at White House luncheon, Washington, D.C., 26 June 1954. This is frequently misquoted as "Jaw, jaw is better than war, war." The latter formulation seems to have been uttered by Harold Macmillan during a visit to Australia in 1958.

43 It was the nation and the race dwelling all round the globe that had the lion's heart. I had the luck to be called upon to give the roar.
Speech at Westminster Hall, London, 30 Nov. 1954

44 It is not easy to see how things could be worsened by a parley at the summit, if such a thing were possible.

Quoted in *Times* (London), 15 Feb. 1950

45 Naval tradition? Monstrous. Nothing but rum, sodomy, prayers, and the lash.

Quoted in Harold Nicolson, *Diary*, 17 Aug. 1950. Usually quoted as "rum, sodomy, and the lash."

46 [*Of Clement Attlee:*] A modest man who has a good deal to be modest about.

Quoted in *Chicago Tribune*, 27 June 1954. A nearly identical quip about Attlee, not attributed to Churchill, appears in the *New York Times*, 9 Dec. 1945.

47 I am ready to meet my Maker; whether my Maker is prepared for the great ordeal of meeting me is another matter.

Quoted in *L.A. Times*, 28 Nov. 1954

48 [*Describing Clement Attlee:*] A sheep in sheep's clothing.

Quoted in Geoffrey Willans and Charles Roetter, *The Wit of Winston Churchill* (1954)
See Gosse 1

49 [*Of Bernard Montgomery:*] In defeat unbeatable: in victory unbearable.

Quoted in Edward Marsh, *Ambrosia and Small Beer* (1964)

50 We are all worms. But I do believe that I am a glow-worm.

Quoted in Violet Bonham-Carter, *Winston Churchill as I Knew Him* (1965)

51 [*On the Chiefs of Staff system:*] You may take the most gallant sailor, the most intrepid airman, or the most audacious soldier, put them at a table together—what do you get? *The sum of their fears.*

Quoted in Harold Macmillan, *The Blast of War: 1939–45* (1968) (entry for 16 Nov. 1943)

52 [*On his portrait, painted by Graham Sutherland:*] I look as if I was having a difficult stool.

Quoted in *The Lyttelton Hart-Davis Letters*, ed. Rupert Hart-Davis (1978) (letter of 20 Nov. 1955)

53 [*To Anthony Eden about a long report from the latter:*] As far as I can see you have used every cliché except "God is Love" and "Please adjust your dress before leaving."

Attributed in *Life*, 9 Dec. 1940. The *Oxford Dictionary of 20th Century Quotations* notes that "when this story was repeated in the *Daily Mirror*, Churchill denied that it was true."

54 This is the kind of pedantic nonsense up with which I will not put!

Attributed in *Washington Post*, 30 Sept. 1946. Supposedly Churchill's marginal note in response to a civil servant's objection to his having ended a sentence with a preposition. However, the following appeared in *Strand Magazine*, May 1942: "When a memorandum passed round a certain Government department, one young pedant scribbled a postscript drawing attention to the fact that the sentence ended with a preposition, which caused the original writer to circulate another memorandum complaining that the anonymous postscript was 'offensive impertinence, up with which I will not put.'"

55 [*Replying to Nancy Astor's saying "If I were your wife I would put poison in your coffee!":*] And if I were your husband I would drink it.

Attributed in Consuelo Vanderbilt Balsan, *Glitter and Gold* (1952). George Thayer, who had worked as research assistant to Randolph Churchill on the latter's biography of Winston Churchill, wrote in 1971 that this anecdote was false. In fact, the joke appears to be an old one. The *Gazette-Telegraph* (Colorado Springs, Colo.), 19 Nov. 1899, printed the following: "'If you were my husband, sir, I'd give you a dose of poison!' The man looked at her. 'If I were your husband,' said he, 'I'd take it.'"

56 If you're going through hell, keep going.

Attributed in *Herald & Review* (Decatur, Ill.), 20 Oct. 1995. This attribution is undoubtedly apocryphal.

Count Galeazzo Ciano
Italian politician, 1903–1944

1 *La vittoria trova cento padri, e nessuno vuole riconoscere l'insuccesso.*

Victory has a hundred fathers, but no one wants to recognize defeat as his own.

Diary, 9 Sept. 1942. Often quoted with the words "but defeat is an orphan."
See John Kennedy 18

Colley Cibber
English playwright, 1671–1757

1 Off with his head—so much for Buckingham.

Richard III act 4, sc. 3 (1700) (adaptation of Shakespeare)

2 Perish the thought!

Richard III act 5, sc. 5 (1700) (adaptation of Shakespeare)

Marcus Tullius Cicero

Roman orator and statesman, 106 B.C.–43 B.C.

1 *Una navis est iam bonorum omnium.*
All loyalists are now in the same boat.
Ad Familiares bk. 12, ch. 25

2 *Sed nescio quo modo nihil tam absurde dici potest*
quod non dicatur ab aliquo philosophorum.
There is nothing so absurd but some
philosopher has said it.
De Divinatione bk. 2, ch. 119

3 *Salus populi suprema est lex.*
The good of the people is the supreme law.
De Legibus bk. 3, ch. 8

4 He used to raise a storm in a teapot.
De Legibus bk. 3, ch. 16

5 *Noxiae poena par esto.*
Let the punishment match the offense.
De Legibus bk. 3, ch. 20
See W. S. Gilbert 39

6 *Ipse dixit.*
He himself said.
De Natura Deorum bk. 1, ch. 10

7 *Summum bonum.*
The highest good.
De Officiis bk. 1, ch. 5

8 The sinews of war, unlimited money.
Fifth Philippic ch. 5

9 *O tempora, O mores!*
Oh, the times! Oh, the customs!
In Catilinam Speech 1, ch. 1

10 *Civis Romanus sum.*
I am a Roman citizen.
In Verrem Speech 5, ch. 147

11 *Silent enim leges inter arma.*
Laws are silent in time of war.
Pro Milone ch. 11

12 *Cui bono?*
Who stood to gain?
Pro Milone ch. 12. Quoting L. Cassius Longinus
Ravilla.
See Beard 1

13 *Cum dignitate otium.*
Leisure with dignity.
Pro Sestio ch. 98

14 *Errare mehercule malo cum Platone . . . quam*
cum istis vera sentire.
I would rather be wrong, by God, with Plato
. . . than be correct with those men [the
Pythagoreans].
Tusculanae Disputationes bk. 1, ch. 39

E. M. Cioran

Romanian-born French philosopher, 1911–1995

1 Without the possibility of suicide, I would have
killed myself long ago.
Quoted in *Independent* (London), 2 Dec. 1989

Sandra Cisneros

U.S. writer, 1954–

1 You can never have too much sky. You can fall
asleep and wake up drunk on sky and sky can
keep you safe when you are sad. Here there
is too much sadness and not enough sky.
Butterflies too are few and so are flowers and
most things that are beautiful. Still, we take
what we can get and make the best of it.
The House on Mango Street (1984)

2 No, this isn't my house I say and shake my head
as if shaking could undo the year I've lived
here. I don't belong. I don't ever want to come
from here.
The House on Mango Street (1984)

Henry Clapp, Jr.

U.S. journalist, 1814–1875

1 Horace Greeley is a self made man, and
worships his creator.
Quoted in *Springfield* (Mass.) *Republican,* 12 Mar.
1868

Eric Clapton (Eric Clapp)

English rock musician, 1945–

1 Would you know my name
If I saw you in heaven?
Would it be the same
If I saw you in heaven?
"Tears in Heaven" (song) (1992). Cowritten with Will
Jennings.

Sidney Clare

U.S. songwriter, 1892–1972

1 On the good ship
Lollipop
It's a sweet trip
To a candy shop
Where bon-bons play
On the sunny beach of Peppermint Bay.
"On the Good Ship Lollipop" (song) (1934)

Kenneth B. Clark

U.S. psychologist, 1917–1983

1 Negroes will not break out of the barriers of the ghetto unless whites transcend the barriers of their own minds, for the ghetto is to the Negro a reflection of the ghetto in which the white lives imprisoned. The poetic irony of American race relations is that the rejected Negro must somehow also find the strength to free the privileged white.
Dark Ghetto ch. 9 (1965)

Ramsey Clark

U.S. government official and political activist, 1927–

1 There are few better measures of the concern a society has for its individual members and its own well being than the way it handles criminals.
Keynote address to American Correctional Association conference, Miami Beach, Fla., Aug. 1967
See Pearl S. Buck 3; Dostoyevski 1; Humphrey 3; Samuel Johnson 69; Helen Keller 4

Susanna Clark

U.S. songwriter and painter, 1939–2012

1 You've got to sing like you don't need the
money
Love like you'll never get hurt
You've got to dance like nobody's watchin'
It's gotta come from the heart if you want it to
work.
"Come from the Heart" (song) (1987). Cowritten with Richard Leigh.

Arthur C. Clarke

English science fiction writer, 1917–2008

1 Overhead, without any fuss, the stars were going out.
"The Nine Billion Names of God" (1953)

2 When a distinguished but elderly scientist states that something is possible, he is almost certainly right. When he states that something is impossible, he is very probably wrong. . . . the only way to discover the limits of the possible is to go beyond them to the impossible.
Profiles of the Future ch. 2 (1962). These are "Clarke's First Law" and "Clarke's Second Law."

3 David Bowman had time for just one broken sentence which the waiting men in Mission Control, nine hundred million miles away and eighty minutes in the future, were never to forget: "The thing's hollow—it goes on forever—and—oh my God!—*it's full of stars!*"
2001: A Space Odyssey ch. 39 (1968)

4 Then he [the Star Child] waited, marshaling his thoughts and brooding over his still untested powers. For though he was master of the world, he was not quite sure what to do next.
    But he would think of something.
2001: A Space Odyssey ch. 47 (1968)

5 Any sufficiently advanced technology is indistinguishable from magic.
Letter to the editor, *Science*, 19 Jan. 1968. This is "Clarke's Third Law."

6 How inappropriate to call this planet Earth, when clearly it is Ocean.
Quoted in James E. Lovelock, *Gaia* (1979)

7 Two possibilities exist: Either we are alone in the Universe or we are not. Both are equally terrifying.
Quoted in Michio Kaku, *Visions: How Science Will Revolutionize the Twenty-First Century* (1999)

Grant Clarke

U.S. songwriter, 1891–1931

1 Ev'ryone knows
That I'm just second hand Rose
From Second Avenue.
"Second Hand Rose" (song) (1921)

Richard Clarke

U.S. government official, 1950–

1 [*Apology to families of victims of 11 Sept. 2001 terrorist attacks:*] Your government failed you, those entrusted with protecting you failed you, and I failed you.

Testimony Before National Commission on Terrorist Attacks upon the United States, Washington, D.C., 24 Mar. 2004

Karl von Clausewitz

German soldier and military theorist, 1780–1831

1 War is the realm of uncertainty; three-quarters of the factors on which action is based are wrapped in a fog of greater or lesser uncertainty.

On War bk. 1, ch. 3 (1833). Perhaps the closest Clausewitz comes to using the expression "the fog of war," which is often attributed to him. Jay M. Shafritz, *Words on War,* quotes Chevalier Floard, *Nouvelles Découvertes sur la Guerre* (1724): "The *coup d'oeuil* is a gift of God and cannot be acquired; but if professional knowledge does not perfect it, one only sees things imperfectly and in a fog."

2 War is regarded as *nothing but the continuation of state policy with other means.*

On War author's note (1833) (translation by O. J. Matthijs Jolles). The most common English-language version is "War is the continuation of politics by other means."

Rudolf Clausius

German physicist and mathematician, 1822–1888

1 In all cases where work is produced by heat, a quantity of heat proportional to the work done is expended; and inversely, by the expenditure of a like quantity of work, the same amount of heat may be produced.

"On the Moving Force of Heat, and the Laws Regarding the Nature of Heat Itself Which Are Deducible Therefrom" (1851)

2 Heat can never pass from a colder to a warmer body without some other change, connected therewith, occurring at the same time.

"On a Modified Form of the Second Fundamental Theorem in the Mechanical Theory of Heat" (1856)

3 1. The energy of the universe is constant.

2. The entropy of the universe tends toward a maximum.

"Ueber Verschiedene für die Anwendung Bequeme Formen der Hauptgleichungen der Mechanischen Warmetheorie" (1865). These are formulations of the "First Law of Thermodynamics" and "Second Law of Thermodynamics."

Henry Clay

U.S. politician, 1777–1852

1 I had rather be right than be President.

Quoted in *Niles' Register,* 23 Mar. 1839

Eldridge Cleaver

U.S. political activist, 1935–1998

1 Rape was an insurrectionary act. . . . I wanted to send waves of consternation throughout the white race.

Soul on Ice pt. 1 (1968)

2 You're either part of the solution or you're part of the problem.

Speech to San Francisco Barristers' Club, San Francisco, Calif., Sept. 1968. An earlier example of a similar formulation in the *Guthrian* (Guthrie Center, Iowa), 24 Jan. 1961: "Every person is either part of the problem, or part of the solution." An even earlier precursor was U.S. Senate Chaplain Peter Marshall's prayer printed in the *Congressional Record* for 10 Jan. 1947: "May we resolve, God helping us, to be part of the answer, and not part of the problem."

Sarah N. Cleghorn

U.S. poet and reformer, 1876–1959

1 The golf links lie so near the mill
That almost every day
The laboring children can look out
And watch the men at play.

"The Golf Links Lie So Near the Mill" l. 1 (1915)

Georges Clemenceau

French prime minister, 1841–1929

1 My home policy: I wage war; my foreign policy: I wage war. All the time I wage war.

Speech to French Chamber of Deputies, 8 Mar. 1918

2 It is easier to make war than to make peace.

Speech, Verdun, France, 20 July 1919

3 The Germans may take Paris, but that will not prevent me from going on with the war.

We will fight on the Loire, we will fight on the Garonne, we will fight even on the Pyrenees. And if at last we are driven off the Pyrenees, we will continue the war at sea.

Quoted in J. Hampden Jackson, *Clemenceau and the Third Republic* (1946)
See Winston Churchill 14

4 War is too serious a matter to entrust to military men.

Attributed in Georges Suarez, *Soixante Années d'Histoire Française* (1932)
See Briand 2; de Gaulle 10

5 [*Upon being told that his son had joined the Communist Party:*] My son is 22 years old. If he had not become a Communist at 22, I would have disowned him. If he is *still* a Communist at 30, I will do it then.

Attributed in Bennett Cerf, *Try and Stop Me* (1944)
See John Adams 19; Batbie 1; George Bernard Shaw 48

6 America is the only nation in history which miraculously has gone directly from barbarism to degeneration without the usual interval of civilization.

Attributed in *Saturday Review of Literature*, 1 Dec. 1945. "Americans are the only race which passed directly from barbarism to decadence without knowing civilization" appeared in the *Washington Post*, 16 July 1932, translating the French newspaper *La Liberté*.

7 [*Remark during Paris Peace Conference, 1919, about Woodrow Wilson's "Fourteen Points":*] The Good Lord had only ten.

Attributed in J. Hampden Jackson, *Clemenceau and the Third Republic* (1946)

8 Military justice is to justice as military music is to music.

Attributed in Herve Lauwick, *Les Français Sont Droles* (1966). This quotation, usually credited to Clemenceau, was ascribed as "the bon mot of a French minister after listening to bitter criticism of certain recent trials . . . *Journal du Dimanche*, Paris," in the *Hays* (Kan.) *Daily News*, 22 Jan. 1961.

Grover Cleveland
U.S. president, 1837–1908

1 A man had never yet been hung for breaking the spirit of a law.

Attributed in James Ford Rhodes, *History of the United States* (1919). Although this quotation is associated with Cleveland, Rhodes asserts: "It is impossible, I think, that Cleveland should have made the defence attributed by Ostrogorski to a certain high official that 'a man had never yet been hung for breaking of the spirit of a law.'" The reference is probably to Moisei Ostrogorski, *Democracy and the Organization of Political Parties* (1902).

Harlan Cleveland
U.S. government official, 1918–2008

1 The Revolution of Rising Expectations.

Title of speech at Colgate University, Hamilton, N.Y., 1949

2 Coalitions of the willing.

Quoted in Lincoln Bloomfield, Testimony Before House Subcommittee on International Organizations and Movements, Oct. 1971. Bloomfield had written in 1960 of "a protocol among the like-minded" and in July 1971 of a "coalition of the law-abiding."

Jimmy Cliff (James Chambers)
Jamaican reggae singer and songwriter, 1948–

1 Many rivers to cross
But I can't seem to find my way over.

"Many Rivers to Cross" (song) (1970)

2 As sure as the sun will shine
I'm going to get my share now, what's mine
And then the harder they come, the harder
   they fall
One and all.

"The Harder They Come" (song) (1971)
See Fitzsimmons 1

George Clinton
U.S. rhythm and blues musician, 1941–

1 Free Your Mind and Your Ass Will Follow.

Title of song (1971)

Hillary Rodham Clinton
U.S. politician, 1947–

1 [*Of her support of her husband Bill Clinton:*] You know, I'm not sitting here some little woman standing by my man like Tammy Wynette, I'm sitting here because I love him and I respect him and I honor what he's been through and what we've been through together.

Interview, *Sixty Minutes*, 26 Jan. 1992
See Wynette 4

2 I could have stayed home and baked cookies and had teas. But what I decided was to fulfill

my profession, which I entered before my husband was in public life.

Campaign remarks, Chicago, Ill., 16 Mar. 1992

3 We lack meaning in our individual lives and meaning collectively. We lack a sense that our lives are part of some greater effort, that we are connected to one another. We need a new politics of meaning. We need a new ethos of individual responsibility and caring. We need a new definition of civil society . . . that makes us feel that we are part of something bigger than ourselves.

Speech at University of Texas, Austin, Tex., 6 Apr. 1993

4 Human rights are women's rights and women's rights are human rights.

Speech at United Nations Fourth World Conference on Women, Beijing, 5 Sept. 1995

5 You know, we've been married for 22 years . . . and I have learned a long time ago that the only people who count in any marriage are the two that are in it.

Interview, NBC *Today Show*, 27 Jan. 1998

6 The great story here . . . is this vast right-wing conspiracy that has been conspiring against my husband since the day he announced for president.

Interview, NBC *Today Show*, 27 Jan. 1998

7 Although we weren't able to shatter that highest, hardest glass ceiling this time, thanks to you, it's got about 18 million cracks in it, and the light is shining through like never before.

Concession speech ending candidacy for 2008 Democratic presidential nomination, Washington, D.C., 7 June 2008

8 [*Of President Bill Clinton and herself:*] We came out of the White House not only dead broke, but in debt.

ABC News interview, 9 June 2014

9 A man you can bait with a tweet is not a man we can trust with nuclear weapons.

Presidential nomination acceptance speech, Democratic National Convention, Philadelphia, Pa., 28 July 2016

10 You could put half of Trump's supporters into what I call the "basket of deplorables."

Remarks at fundraiser, New York, N.Y., 9 Sept. 2016

11 [In politics] you need both a public and a private position.

Speech to National Multi-Housing Council, Dallas, Tex., 24 Apr. 2013. This private speech was released in a WikiLeaks email dump, 7 Oct. 2016.

William Jefferson "Bill" Clinton (William Jefferson Blythe III)
U.S. president, 1946–

1 [*Description of himself:*] The comeback kid.

Statement to supporters on night of New Hampshire primary, Concord, N.H., 18 Feb. 1992

2 [*Addressed to an AIDS activist accusing him of avoiding that issue:*] I feel your pain.

Remark at campaign reception, New York, N.Y., 26 Mar. 1992

3 There is nothing wrong with America that cannot be cured by what is right with America.

Inaugural Address, 20 Jan. 1993

4 This ceremony is held in the depth of winter. But, by the words we speak and the faces we show the world, we force the spring.

Inaugural Address, 20 Jan. 1993

5 [*Of veterans of the D-Day invasion in World War II:*] They may walk with a little less spring in their step, and their ranks are growing thinner, but let us never forget, when they were young, these men saved the world.

Remarks on the 50th anniversary of D-Day at the United States Cemetery, Colleville-sur-Mer, France, 6 June 1994

6 The era of big government is over.

State of the Union Address, 23 Jan. 1996

7 We do not need to build a bridge to the past, we need to build a bridge to the future, and that is what I commit to you to do! So tonight, let us resolve to build that bridge to the 21st century.

Nomination acceptance speech at Democratic National Convention, Chicago, Ill., 29 Aug. 1996. Clinton had earlier said, "We have to build a bridge to the 21st century," at a ceremony honoring teachers, 23 Apr. 1996.

8 I did not have sexual relations with that woman, Miss Lewinsky.

Comment during remarks on after-school child-care initiative, 26 Jan. 1998

9 [*Characterizing the truthfulness of his lawyer's statement, "There is absolutely no sex of any kind*

in any manner, shape, or form":] It depends on what the meaning of the word "is" is.

Grand jury testimony, Washington, D.C., 17 Aug. 1998. Clinton went on to say, "If the—if he—if 'is' means is and never has been, that is not—that is one thing. If it means there is none, that was a completely true statement."

10 I did have a relationship with Ms. Lewinsky that was not appropriate. In fact, it was wrong.

Address to the nation on testimony before the independent counsel's grand jury, 17 Aug. 1998

11 [*Explaining his affair with Monica Lewinsky:*] I did something for the worst possible reason—just because I could.

Interview on CBS News, 16 June 2004

12 Strength and wisdom are not opposing values.

Address to Democratic National Convention, Boston, Mass., 26 July 2004

13 The American people . . . [are] tired of the politics of personal destruction.

Quoted in *St. Louis Post-Dispatch,* 13 Mar. 1992

14 I experimented with marijuana a time or two. And I didn't like it, and I didn't inhale.

Quoted in *Wash. Post,* 30 Mar. 1992
See Richler 2

Robert Clive, Baron Clive of Plassey
British general and government official, 1725–1774

1 [*Remark during Parliamentary cross-examination, 1773:*] By God, Mr. Chairman, at this moment I stand astonished at my own moderation!

Quoted in G. R. Gleig, *The Life of Robert, First Lord Clive* (1848)

Arthur Hugh Clough
English poet, 1819–1861

1 Say not the struggle nought availeth,
  The labor and the wounds are vain,
  The enemy faints not, nor faileth,
  And as things have been, they remain.
  "Say Not the Struggle Nought Availeth" l. 1 (1855)

2 In front the sun climbs slow, how slowly,
  But westward, look, the land is bright.
  "Say Not the Struggle Nought Availeth" l. 15 (1855)

3 No graven images may be
  Worshipped, except the currency.
  "The Latest Decalogue" l. 3 (1862)

4 Thou shalt not kill; but need'st not strive
  Officiously to keep alive.
  "The Latest Decalogue" l. 11 (1862)

5 Thou shalt not steal; an empty feat,
  When it's so lucrative to cheat.
  "The Latest Decalogue" l. 15 (1862)

6 Thou shalt not covet; but tradition
  Approves all forms of competition.
  "The Latest Decalogue" l. 19 (1862)

Manfred Clynes
Austrian-born Australian neuroscientist, 1925–2020

1 For the exogenously extended organizational complex functioning as an integrated homeostatic system unconsciously, we propose the term "Cyborg." The Cyborg deliberately incorporates exogenous components extending the self-regulatory control function of the organism in order to adapt it to new environments.

Astronautics, Sept. 1960

Ronald Coase
English economist, 1910–2013

1 If you torture the data long enough, it will confess.

Quoted in *American Statistician,* June 1972

Kurt Cobain
U.S. rock musician and songwriter, 1967–1994

1 Here we are now, entertain us.
  "Smells like Teen Spirit" (song) (1991)

2 I found it hard, it was hard to find,
  Oh well, whatever, never mind.
  "Smells like Teen Spirit" (song) (1991)

3 I'd rather be dead than cool.
  "Stay Away" (song) (1991)

Irvin S. Cobb
U.S. novelist and playwright, 1876–1944

1 It is the private opinion of this court that not only is the late defendant sane but that he is the sanest man in this entire jurisdiction.

"Boys Will Be Boys" (1917)
See Film Lines 121

Will D. Cobb
U.S. songwriter, 1876–1930

1 School-days, school-days, dear old golden rule
   days,
   Readin' and 'ritin' and 'rithmetic,
   Taught to the tune of a hick'ry stick.
   "School-Days" (song) (1907)

Johnnie Cochran, Jr.
U.S. lawyer, 1937–2005

1 If it does not fit, then you must acquit.
   Closing argument for defense in trial of O. J.
   Simpson, Los Angeles, Calif., 27 Sept. 1995.
   Referring to a leather glove that was alleged to have
   belonged to Simpson, and more broadly to the entire
   prosecution case against Simpson.

Claud Cockburn
British author and journalist, 1904–1981

1 [*Suggested dull headline for* Times *(London), ca.*
   1929:] Small earthquake in Chile. Not many
   dead.
   Claud Cockburn, *A Discord of Trumpets* (1956)

Jean Cocteau
French writer, artist, and film director, 1889–
1963

1 *Je suis un mensonge qui dit toujours la vérité.*
   I am a lie who always speaks the truth.
   "Le Paquet Rouge" (1925)
   See Cocteau 3

2 Victor Hugo was a madman who thought he
   was Victor Hugo.
   Opium: The Diary of a Cure (1930)

3 *Les choses que je conte*
   Sont des mensonges vrais.
   The matters I relate
   Are true lies.
   Quoted in *Journals of Jean Cocteau,* ed. Wallace Fowlie
   (1956)
   See Cocteau 1

David Allan Coe
U.S. singer and songwriter, 1939–

1 Take This Job and Shove It.
   Title of song (1977)

Paulo Coelho
Brazilian writer, 1947–

1 When you want something, all the universe
   conspires in helping you to achieve it.
   The Alchemist pt. 1 (1988)

J. M. Coetzee
South African novelist, 1940–

1 The barbarians come out at night. Before
   darkness falls the last goat must be brought
   in, the gates barred, a watch set in every
   lookout to call the hours. All night, it is said,
   the barbarians prowl about bent on murder
   and rapine. Children in their dreams see
   the shutters part and fierce barbarian faces
   leer through. "The barbarians are here!" the
   children scream, and cannot be comforted.
   Waiting for the Barbarians ch. 5 (1980)

2 This is not the scene I dreamed of. Like much
   else nowadays I leave it feeling stupid, like a
   man who lost his way long ago but presses on
   along a road that may lead nowhere.
   Waiting for the Barbarians ch. 6 (1980)

William Sloane Coffin
U.S. clergyman and activist, 1924–2006

1 Even if you win a rat race, you're still a rat.
   Life, 30 Apr. 1965. In this *Life* magazine article,
   Coffin appears to have been quoting an anonymous
   student, but the line may have been something he
   himself had used earlier in the 1950s or 1960s. The
   Boston Herald, 11 Aug. 1956, quoted an unnamed
   person as saying "You can win the rat race, but you're
   still a rat."

George M. Cohan
U.S. actor and playwright, 1878–1942

1 I'm a Yankee Doodle dandy,
   A Yankee Doodle, do or die;
   A real live nephew of my Uncle Sam's,
   Born on the Fourth of July.
   "The Yankee Doodle Boy" (song) (1901)

2 Always Leave Them Laughing When You Say
   Good-Bye.
   Title of song (1903)

3 Give my regards to Broadway,
Remember me to Herald Square.
Tell all the gang at Forty-second Street
That I will soon be there.
"Give My Regards to Broadway" (song) (1904)

4 You're a grand old flag,
You're a high-flying flag,
And forever in peace may you wave.
You're the emblem of
The land I love,
The home of the free and the brave.
Ev'ry heart beats true
Under Red, White, and Blue,
Where there's never a boast or brag.
"You're a Grand Old Flag" (song) (1906)

5 Over there, over there,
Send the word, send the word over there,
That the Yanks are coming, the Yanks are
coming,
The drums rum-tumming ev'rywhere.
"Over There" (song) (1917)

6 We'll be over, we're coming over,
And we won't come back till it's over over there.
"Over There" (song) (1917)

7 My father thanks you, my mother thanks you,
my sister thanks you, I thank you.
Quoted in *N.Y. Times*, 2 Oct. 1921

8 Never let that ——— in this office again, unless
we need him.
Quoted in Alva Johnston, *The Great Goldwyn* (1937)

9 [*To a reporter in 1912:*] I don't care what you say
about me, as long as you say *something* about
me, and as long as you spell my name right.
Quoted in John McCabe, *George M. Cohan* (1973)

Leonard Cohen
Canadian singer and writer, 1934–2016

1 And when He knew for certain only drowning
men could see Him
He said "All men shall be sailors, then, until
the sea shall free them,"
But He Himself was broken long before the sky
would open.
Forsaken, almost human, He sank beneath
your wisdom like a stone.

"Suzanne" (song) (1966). The lyrics for this song first
appeared as the poem "Suzanne Takes You Down" in
Cohen's book *Parasites of Heaven* (1966).

2 And you want to travel with her,
And you want to travel blind;
And you know that you can trust her,
For she's touched your perfect body with her
mind.
"Suzanne" (song) (1966)

3 Now I've heard there was a secret chord
That David played, and it pleased the Lord
But you don't really care for music, do you?
It goes like this the fourth, the fifth
The minor fall, the major lift
The baffled king composing Hallelujah.
"Hallelujah" (song) (1984)

4 Everybody knows that the dice are loaded
Everybody rolls with their fingers crossed
Everybody knows that the war is over
Everybody knows the good guys lost
Everybody knows the fight was fixed
The poor stay poor, the rich get rich
That's how it goes
Everybody knows.
"Everybody Knows" (song) (1988). Cowritten with
Sharon Robinson.

5 Ring the bells that still can ring.
Forget your perfect offering.
There is a crack in everything.
That's how the light gets in.
"Anthem" (song) (1992)

Michael Cohen
U.S. lawyer, 1966–

1 In coordination with, and at the direction of, a
candidate for federal office [Donald Trump], I
and the CEO of a media company at the request
of the candidate worked together to keep an
individual with information that would be
harmful to the candidate and to the campaign
from publicly disclosing this information. . . .
I participated in this conduct, which on my
part took place in Manhattan, for the principal
purpose of influencing the election.
Statement to United States District Court pleading
guilty to felonies including illegal "payoff" campaign
contributions, New York, N.Y., 21 Aug. 2018

2 I know what Mr. Trump is. He is a racist. He is a conman. He is a cheat.

Testimony before House of Representatives Oversight Committee, 27 Feb. 2019

Edward Coke

English judge and lawyer, 1552–1634

1 The house of every one is to him as his castle and fortress, as well for his defence against injury and violence, as for his repose.

Semayne's Case (1603)
See Coke 8; Otis 2; William Pitt, Earl of Chatham 2

2 In many cases, the common law will control Acts of Parliament, and sometimes adjudge them to be utterly void: for when an Act of Parliament is against common right and reason, or repugnant, or impossible to be performed, the common law will control it, and adjudge such Act to be void.

Bonham's Case (1610)

3 How long soever it hath continued, if it be against reason, it is of no force in law.

The First Part of the Institutes of the Laws of England bk. 1, ch. 10 (1628). Derives from a gloss to Justinian's Digest (to Dig. 35, 1, 72, sec. 6) in *Corpus Iuris Civilis*, vol. 2 (1559), that reads: *"cessante cesset legatum, secus autem est in ratione legis."*

4 Reason is the life of the law, nay the common law itself is nothing else but reason.

The First Part of the Institutes of the Laws of England bk. 2, ch. 6 (1628)
See Oliver Wendell Holmes, Jr. 2

5 The law, which is the perfection of reason.

The First Part of the Institutes of the Laws of England bk. 2, ch. 6 (1628)

6 The gladsome light of Jurisprudence.

The First Part of the Institutes of the Laws of England epilogue (1628)

7 Magna Charta is such a fellow, that he will have no sovereign.

Speech in House of Commons, 17 May 1628

8 For a man's house is his castle, *et domus sua cuique est tutissimum refugium* [and each man's home is his safest refuge].

The Third Part of the Institutes of the Laws of England ch. 73 (1644)
See Coke 1; Otis 2; William Pitt, Earl of Chatham 2

9 They [corporations] cannot commit treason, nor be outlawed, nor excommunicate, for they have no souls.

Case of Sutton's Hospital (1658)

Stephen Colbert

U.S. comedian, 1964–

1 Truthiness. Now I'm sure some of the word police—the wordinistas—over at Webster's are gonna say, "hey, that's not a word." Well, anybody who knows me knows I'm no fan of dictionaries or reference books. . . . I don't trust books. They're all fact, no heart.

Colbert Report (television show), 17 Oct. 2005

Nat King Cole (Nathaniel Adams Coles)

U.S. singer and musician, 1919–1965

1 Straighten Up and Fly Right.

Title of song (1943). Cowritten with Irving Mills.

Paula Cole

U.S. singer and songwriter, 1968–

1 Where is my John Wayne?
Where is my prairie song?
Where is my happy ending?
Where have all the cowboys gone?

"Where Have All the Cowboys Gone?" (song) (1996)

Samuel Taylor Coleridge

English poet, critic, and philosopher, 1772–1834

1 It is an ancient Mariner,
And he stoppeth one of three.
"By thy long grey beard and glittering eye,
Now wherefore stopp'st thou me?"

"The Rime of the Ancient Mariner" l. 1 (1798)

2 The ice was here, the ice was there,
The ice was all around:
It crack'd and growl'd, and roar'd and howl'd,
Like noises in a swound!

"The Rime of the Ancient Mariner" l. 59 (1798)

3 "God save thee, ancient Mariner!
From the fiends that plague thee thus!—
Why look's thou so?"—With my cross-bow
I shot the Albatross.

"The Rime of the Ancient Mariner" l. 79 (1798)

4 We were the first that ever burst
  Into that silent sea.
  "The Rime of the Ancient Mariner" l. 105 (1798)

5 As idle as a painted ship
  Upon a painted ocean.
  "The Rime of the Ancient Mariner" l. 117 (1798)

6 Water, water, everywhere,
  And all the boards did shrink;
  Water, water, everywhere,
  Nor any drop to drink.
  "The Rime of the Ancient Mariner" l. 119 (1798).
  Popularly quoted as "Water, water, everywhere, and
  not a drop to drink."

7 The very deep did rot: O Christ!
  That ever this should be!
  Yea, slimy things did crawl with legs
  Upon the slimy sea.
  "The Rime of the Ancient Mariner" l. 123 (1798)

8 Her lips were red, her looks were free,
  Her locks were yellow as gold:
  Her skin was white as leprosy,
  The nightmare Life-in-Death was she,
  Who thicks man's blood with cold.
  "The Rime of the Ancient Mariner" l. 190 (1798)

9 I fear thee, ancient Mariner!
  I fear thy skinny hand!
  And thou art long, and lank, and brown,

As is the ribbed sea-sand.
  "The Rime of the Ancient Mariner" l. 225 (1798)

10 Alone, alone, all, all alone,
   Alone on a wide wide sea!
   "The Rime of the Ancient Mariner" l. 233 (1798)

11 Oh sleep! it is a gentle thing,
   Beloved from pole to pole.
   "The Rime of the Ancient Mariner" l. 293 (1798)

12 I pass, like night, from land to land;
   I have strange power of speech;
   That moment that his face I see,
   I know the man that must hear me;
   To him my tale I teach.
   "The Rime of the Ancient Mariner" l. 587 (1798)

13 He prayeth well, who loveth well
   Both man and bird and beast.
   "The Rime of the Ancient Mariner" l. 613 (1798)

14 He prayeth best, who loveth best
   All things both great and small;
   For the dear God who loveth us,
   He made and loveth all.
   "The Rime of the Ancient Mariner" l. 615 (1798)

15 A sadder and a wiser man,
   He rose the morrow morn.
   "The Rime of the Ancient Mariner" l. 625 (1798)

16 Poetry is not the proper antithesis to
   prose, but to science. Poetry is opposed to
   science, and prose to metre. The proper
   and immediate object of science is the
   acquirement, or communication, of truth; the
   proper and immediate object of poetry is the
   communication of immediate pleasure.
   "Definitions of Poetry" (1811)

17 Reviewers are usually people who would have
   been poets, historians, biographers, &c., if they
   could; they have tried their talents at one or
   the other, and have failed; therefore they turn
   critics.
   Seven Lectures on Shakespeare and Milton Lecture 1
   (1811–1812)
   See Disraeli 24

18 On awaking he . . . instantly and eagerly wrote
   down the lines that are here preserved. At this
   moment he was unfortunately called out by a
   person on business from Porlock.
   "Kubla Khan" preliminary note (1816)

19 In Xanadu did Kubla Khan
   A stately pleasure dome decree:
   Where Alph, the sacred river, ran
   Through caverns measureless to man
   Down to a sunless sea.
   "Kubla Khan" l. 1 (1816)

20 But oh! that deep romantic chasm which
     slanted
   Down the green hill athwart a cedarn cover!
   A savage place! as holy and enchanted
   As e'er beneath a waning moon was haunted
   By woman wailing for her demon-lover!
   "Kubla Khan" l. 12 (1816)

21 And 'mid this tumult Kubla heard from afar
   Ancestral voices prophesying war!
   "Kubla Khan" l. 29 (1816)

22 It was a miracle of rare device,
   A sunny pleasure-dome with caves of ice.
   "Kubla Khan" l. 35 (1816)

23 And all who heard should see them there,
   And all should cry, Beware! Beware!
   His flashing eyes, his floating hair!
   Weave a circle round him thrice,
   And close your eyes with holy dread,
   For he on honey-dew hath fed,
   And drunk the milk of Paradise.
   "Kubla Khan" l. 51 (1816)

24 Every reform, however necessary, will by weak
   minds be carried to an excess, that itself will
   need reforming.
   Biographia Literaria ch. 1 (1817)

25 The primary imagination I hold to be the
   living Power and prime Agent of all human
   Perception, and as a repetition in the finite
   mind of the eternal act of creation in the
   infinite I AM.
   Biographia Literaria ch. 13 (1817)

26 That willing suspension of disbelief for the
   moment, which constitutes poetic faith.
   Biographia Literaria ch. 14 (1817)

27 No man was ever yet a great poet, without being
   at the same time a profound philosopher.
   Biographia Literaria ch. 15 (1817)

28 Our *myriad-minded* Shakespeare.
   Biographia Literaria ch. 15 (1817)

29 In poetry, in which every line, every phrase,
   may pass the ordeal of deliberation and
   deliberate choice, it is possible, and barely
   possible, to attain that *ultimatum* which I have
   ventured to propose as the infallible test of a
   blameless style; namely: its *untranslatableness* in
   words of the same language without injury to
   the meaning.
   Biographia Literaria ch. 22 (1817)

30 The dwarf sees farther than the giant, when he
   has the giant's shoulder to mount on.
   The Friend vol. 2 "On the Principles of Political
   Knowledge" (1818)
   *See Bernard of Chartres 1; Robert Burton 1; Isaac
   Newton 1*

31 Evidences of Christianity! I am weary of the
   word. Make a man feel the want of it; rouse
   him, if you can, to the self-knowledge of his
   need of it; and you may safely trust it to his own
   Evidence.
   Aids to Reflection "Conclusion" (1825)

32 Exclusively of the abstract sciences, the largest
   and worthiest portion of our knowledge
   consists of aphorisms; and the greatest and best
   of men is but an aphorism.
   Aids to Reflection "Introductory Aphorisms" (1825)

33 He who begins by loving Christianity better
   than Truth will proceed by loving his own sect
   or church better than Christianity, and end by
   loving himself better than all.
   Aids to Reflection "Moral and Religious Aphorisms"
   (1825)

34 The happiness of life, on the contrary, is
   made up of minute fractions—the little, soon-
   forgotten charities of a kiss, a smile, a kind
   look, a heartfelt compliment in the disguise
   of playful raillery, and the countless other
   infinitesimals of pleasurable thought and genial
   feeling.
   "The Improvisatore" (1828)

35 Beneath this sod
   A poet lies, or that which once seem'd he—
   Oh, lift a thought for S.T.C.!
   That he, who many a year, with toil of breath,
   Found death in life, may here find life in death.
   "Stop, Christian Passer-by!—Stop, Child of God" l. 2
   (1833)

36 You abuse snuff! Perhaps it is the final cause of the human nose.
Table Talk 4 Jan. 1823 (1835)

37 [*Of Edmund Kean:*] To see him act, is like reading Shakespeare by flashes of lightning.
Table Talk 17 Apr. 1823 (1835)

38 Prose = words in their best order;—poetry = the *best* words in the best order.
Table Talk 12 July 1827 (1835)

39 The man's desire is for the woman; but the woman's desire is rarely other than for the desire of the man.
Table Talk 23 July 1827 (1835)

40 Shakespeare . . . is of no age—nor of any religion, or party or profession. The body and substance of his works came out of the unfathomable depths of his own oceanic mind.
Table Talk 15 Mar. 1834 (1835)

41 Iago's soliloquy—the motive-hunting of motiveless malignity.
The Literary Remains of Samuel Taylor Coleridge bk. 2 "Notes on the Tragedies of Shakespeare: Othello" (1836)

42 If a man could pass through Paradise in a dream, and have a flower presented to him as a pledge that his soul had really been there, and if he found the flower in his hand when he awoke—Aye! and what then?
Anima Poetae, ed. E. H. Coleridge (1895)

Sidonie-Gabrielle Colette
French novelist, 1873–1954

1 *Les femmes libres ne sont pas des femmes.*
Free women are not women at all.
Claudine à Paris (1901)

Michael Collins
Irish nationalist leader, 1890–1922

1 Think—what I have got for Ireland? Something which she has wanted these past 700 years. Will anyone be satisfied at the bargain? Will anyone? I tell you this—early this morning I signed my death warrant.
Letter, 6 Dec. 1921. Collins had just signed the treaty establishing the Irish Free State. He was in fact assassinated the next year.

2 [*Upon arriving at Dublin Castle and being told that he was seven minutes late for the transfer of power by British troops, 16 Jan. 1922:*] We've been waiting seven hundred years, you can have the seven minutes.
Attributed in Tim Pat Coogan, *Michael Collins* (1990)

Suzanne Collins
U.S. writer, 1962–

1 May the odds be *ever* in your favor!
The Hunger Games ch. 1 (2008)

2 "I volunteer!" I gasp. "I volunteer as tribute!"
The Hunger Games ch. 2 (2008)

Carlo Collodi (Carlo Lorenzini)
Italian children's book writer and journalist, 1826–1890

1 He had scarcely told the lie when his nose, which was already long, grew at once two fingers longer.
The Story of a Puppet or The Adventures of Pinocchio (1892) (translation by M. A. Murray)
See Film Lines 134

2 Upon awakening he discovered that he was no longer a wooden puppet, but that he had become instead a boy, like all other boys.
The Story of a Puppet or The Adventures of Pinocchio (1892) (translation by M. A. Murray)
See Film Lines 133

George Colman the Elder
English playwright, 1732–1794

1 Love and a cottage! Eh, Fanny! Ah, give me indifference and a coach and six!
The Clandestine Marriage act 1 (1766). Coauthored with David Garrick.

George Colman the Younger
English playwright, 1762–1836

1 Says he, "I am a handsome man, but I'm a gay deceiver."
Love Laughs at Locksmiths act 2 (1808)

John Robert Colombo
Canadian writer, 1936–

1 Canada could have enjoyed:
English government,

French culture,
and American know-how.

Instead it ended up with:
English know-how,
French government,
and American culture.
"Oh Canada" l. 1 (1965)

Charles W. Colson

U.S. government official and religious leader,
1931–2012

1 I would walk over my grandmother if necessary
[to get Richard Nixon reelected as president].

Quoted in *Wash. Post*, 30 Aug. 1972. In the *Wall
Street Journal*, 15 Oct. 1971, someone else is quoted
as saying that Colson "would walk over his own
grandmother if he had to."

Christopher Columbus

Italian explorer, 1451–1506

1 I should be judged as a captain who went
from Spain to the Indies to conquer a people
numerous and warlike, whose manners and
religion are very different from ours, who
live in sierras and mountains, without fixed
settlements, and where by divine will I have
placed under the sovereignty of the King and
Queen our Lords, an Other World, whereby
Spain, which was reckoned poor, is become the
richest of countries.

Letter to Doña Juana de Torres, Oct. 1500

2 Here the people could stand it no longer and
complained of the long voyage; but the Admiral
cheered them as best he could, holding out
good hope of the advantages they would have.
He added that it was useless to complain, he
had come [to go] to the Indies, and so had to
continue it until he found them, with the help
of Our Lord.

Reported in Bartolomé de las Casas, *Journal of the
First Voyage*, 10 Oct. 1492 (translation by Samuel Eliot
Morison)

3 At two hours after midnight appeared the
land, at a distance of 2 leagues. They handed
all sails and set the *treo*, which is the mainsail
without bonnets, and lay-to waiting for daylight
Friday, when they arrived at an island of the

Bahamas that was called in the Indians' tongue
Guanahaní.

Reported in Bartolomé de Las Casas, *Journal of the
First Voyage*, 12 Oct. 1492 (translation by Samuel Eliot
Morison)

Sean "Puffy" Combs

U.S. rap musician and producer, 1969–

1 It's All About the Benjamins.

Title of song (1997). "Benjamins" is a slang term for
hundred-dollar bills.

Betty Comden (Elizabeth Cohen) 1917–2006 and Adolph Green ca. 1915–2002

U.S. songwriters

1 New York,
A helluva town.
The Bronx is up and the Battery's down,
And people ride in a hole in the ground.
"New York, New York" (song) (1944)

2 Moses supposes his toeses are roses
But Moses supposes erroneously.
"Elocution" (song) (1952)

3 Why, O why, O why-o
Why did I ever leave Ohio,
Why did I wander
To find what lies yonder
When life was so cozy at home?
"Ohio" (song) (1953)

4 The party's over,
It's time to call it a day.
"The Party's Over" (song) (1956)
See Coward 11

5 Make
Someone happy,
Make just one
Someone happy,
And you
Will be happy too.
"Make Someone Happy" (song) (1960)

James Comey

U.S. government official, 1960–

1 In connection with an unrelated case, the F.B.I.
has learned of the existence of emails that
appear to be pertinent to the investigation [of

Hillary Clinton's use of a private email server while Secretary of State].

Letter to congressional committee chairs, 28 Oct. 2016

2 Our country is led by those who will lie about anything, backed by those who will believe anything, based on information from media sources that will say anything.

Tweet, 23 May 2018

Barry Commoner
U.S. biologist, 1917–2012

1 The First Law of Ecology: Everything Is
  Connected to Everything Else. . . .
  The Second Law of Ecology: Everything Must
  Go Somewhere. . . .
  The Third Law of Ecology: Nature Knows
  Best. . . .
  The Fourth Law of Ecology: There Is No Such
  Thing as a Free Lunch.

The Closing Circle ch. 2 (1971)
See Heinlein 3; Walter Morrow 1

Arthur H. Compton
U.S. physicist, 1892–1962

1 [*Coded telephone message to James B. Conant
  after first controlled nuclear chain reaction, 2 Dec.
  1942:*] The Italian navigator [Enrico Fermi] has
  landed in the New World.

Quoted in Corbin Allardice and Edward R. Trapnell, *The First Pile* (1946)

Ivy Compton-Burnett
English novelist, 1884–1969

1 There is more difference within the sexes than between them.

Mother and Son ch. 10 (1955)

Auguste Comte
French philosopher, 1798–1857

1 I think I should risk introducing this new term [*sociology*]. . . . The necessity for this coinage to correspond to the special objectives of this volume will, I hope, excuse this last exercise of a legitimate right which I believe I have always used with proper caution and without ceasing

to experience a deep feeling of repugnance for the systematic use of neologisms.

Cours de Philosophie Positive vol. 4 (1839) (translation by Yole G. Sills)

2 Conspiracy of silence.

Quoted in John Stuart Mill, *Auguste Comte and Positivism* (1865)

James Bryant Conant
U.S. chemist and university president, 1893–1978

1 Education is what is left after all that has been learnt is forgotten.

Diary as freshman at Harvard College (1910–1911). A very similar formulation appeared, attributed to Ralph Waldo Emerson, in *Education Times*, 2 Dec. 1907 ("Education is that which remains behind when all we have learned at school is forgotten").

2 There is only one proved method of assisting the advancement of pure science—that of picking men of genius, backing them heavily, and leaving them to direct themselves.

Letter to the Editor, *N.Y. Times*, 13 Aug. 1945

3 He who enters a university walks on hallowed ground.

Quoted in *Notes on the Harvard Tercentenary*, ed. David McCord (1936)

4 Behold the turtle. He only makes progress when he sticks his neck out.

Quoted in *The American Treasury: 1455–1955*, ed. Clifton Fadiman (1955)

Confucius
Chinese philosopher, 551 B.C.–479 B.C.

1 Is it not a pleasure to learn and to repeat or practice from time to time what has been learned? Is it not delightful to have friends coming from afar? Is one not a superior man if he does not feel hurt even though he does not feel recognized?

Analects ch. 1, v. 1 (translation by Wing-Tsit Chan)

2 A ruler who governs his state by virtue is like the north polar star, which remains in its place while all the other stars revolve around it.

Analects ch. 2, v. 1 (translation by Wing-Tsit Chan)

3 A man who reviews the old so as to find out the new is qualified to teach others.

Analects ch. 2, v. 11 (translation by Wing-Tsit Chan)

4 A superior man in dealing with the world is not for anything or against anything. He follows, righteousness as the standard.
Analects ch. 4, v. 10 (translation by Wing-Tsit Chan)

5 The Way of our Master is none other than conscientiousness of altruism.
Analects ch. 4, v. 15 (translation by Wing-Tsit Chan)

6 Man is born with uprightness. If one loses it he will be lucky if he escapes with his life.
Analects ch. 6, v. 17 (translation by Wing-Tsit Chan)

7 If we are not yet able to serve man, how can we serve spiritual beings? . . . If we do not yet know about life how can we know about death?
Analects ch. 11, v. 11 (translation by Wing-Tsit Chan)

8 To go too far is the same as not to go far enough.
Analects ch. 11, v. 15 (translation by Wing-Tsit Chan)

9 Do not do to others what you do not want them to do to you.
Analects ch. 15, v. 23 (translation by Wing-Tsit Chan). The negative version of "The Golden Rule." Similar formulations appear in many religious traditions, such as in the Buddhist *Udanavarga*, the Hindu *Mahabharata*, and the Zoroastrian *Dadistan-I Dinik*. *See Aristotle 12; Bible 225; Chesterfield 4; Hillel 2*

10 By nature men are alike. Through practice they have become far apart.
Analects ch. 17, v. 2 (translation by Wing-Tsit Chan)

William Congreve
English playwright, 1670–1729

1 Married in haste, we may repent at leisure.
The Old Bachelor act 5, sc. 1 (1693)

2 No mask like open truth to cover lies,
As to go naked is the best disguise.
The Double Dealer act 5, sc. 6 (1694)

3 O fie Miss, you must not kiss and tell.
Love for Love act 2, sc. 10 (1695)

4 I confess freely to you, I could never look long upon a monkey, without very mortifying reflections.
Letter to John Dennis, 10 July 1695

5 Music has charms to sooth a savage breast.
The Mourning Bride act 1, sc. 1 (1697)

6 Heaven has no rage, like love to hatred turned, Nor Hell a fury, like a woman scorned.
The Mourning Bride act 3, sc. 8 (1697). Often misquoted as "Hell hath no fury like a woman scorned."

7 Say what you will, 'tis better to be left than never to have been loved.
The Way of the World act 2, sc. 1 (1700)
See Tennyson 29

Roscoe Conkling
U.S. politician, 1829–1888

1 I have noticed there are three classes of people who always say "we" instead of "I." They are emperors, editors, and men with a tape worm.
Atlanta Daily Constitution, 23 Oct. 1877

Nellie Connally
U.S. wife of governor of Texas, 1919–2006

1 [*Remark to President John Kennedy immediately before his shooting in Dallas, 22 Nov. 1963:*] You can't say Dallas doesn't love you, Mr. President.
Quoted in *Chicago Tribune,* 25 Nov. 1963

Cyril Connolly
English writer, 1903–1974

1 I shall christen this style the Mandarin, since it is beloved by literary pundits, by those who would make the written word as unlike as possible to the spoken one. It is the style of all those writers whose tendency is to make their language convey more than they mean or more than they feel, it is the style of most artists and all humbugs.
Enemies of Promise ch. 2 (1938)

2 Whom the gods wish to destroy they first call promising.
Enemies of Promise ch. 13 (1938)
See Proverbs 123

3 Imprisoned in every fat man a thin one is wildly signalling to be let out.
The Unquiet Grave pt. 2 (1944)
See Orwell 10

4 It is closing time in the gardens of the West and from now on an artist will be judged only by the resonance of his solitude or the quality of his despair.
Horizon, Dec. 1949–Jan. 1950

5 [*Of George Orwell:*] He could not blow his nose without moralising on conditions in the handkerchief industry.
The Evening Colonnade pt. 3 (1973)

James Connolly
Irish nationalist and labor leader, 1868–1916

1 The worker is the slave of capitalist society, the female worker is the slave of that slave.
The Re-conquest of Ireland (1915)

James Scott "Jimmy" Connors
U.S. tennis player, 1952–

1 New Yorkers love it when you spill your guts out there. You spill your guts at Wimbledon, they make you stop and clean it up.
Quoted in *Sports Illustrated*, 17 Sept. 1984

Joseph Conrad (Teodor Josef Konrad Korzeniowski)
Polish-born English novelist, 1857–1924

1 It's only those who do nothing that make no mistakes, I suppose.
Outcast of the Islands pt. 3, ch. 2 (1896)

2 A work that aspires, however humbly, to the condition of art should carry its justification in every line.
The Nigger of the Narcissus preface (1897)

3 But the artist appeals to that part of our being which is not dependent on wisdom; to that in

us which is a gift and not an acquisition—and, therefore, more permanently enduring. He speaks to our capacity for delight and wonder, to the sense of mystery surrounding our lives: to our sense of pity, and beauty, and pain.
The Nigger of the Narcissus preface (1897)

4 My task which I am trying to achieve is by the power of the written word, to make you hear, to make you feel—it is, before all, to make you *see*. That—and no more, and it is everything.
The Nigger of the Narcissus preface (1897)

5 The problem of life seemed too voluminous for the narrow limits of human speech, and by common consent it was abandoned to the great sea that had from the beginning enfolded it in its immense grip; to the sea that knew all, and would in time infallibly unveil to each the wisdom hidden in all the errors, the certitude that lurks in doubts, the realm of safety and peace beyond the frontiers of sorrow and fear.
The Nigger of the Narcissus ch. 5 (1897)

6 One writes only half the book; the other half is with the reader.
Letter to Cunninghame Graham (1897)

7 There is a weird power in a spoken word. . . . And a word carries far—very far— deals destruction through time as the bullets go flying through space.
Lord Jim ch. 15 (1900)

8 That faculty of beholding at a hint the face of his desire and the shape of his dream, without which the earth would know no lover and no adventurer.
Lord Jim ch. 16 (1900)

9 A man that is born falls into a dream like a man who falls into the sea. If he tries to climb out into the air as inexperienced people endeavor to do, he drowns . . . and with the exertions of your hands and feet in the water make the deep, deep sea keep you up.
Lord Jim ch. 20 (1900)

10 To the destructive element submit yourself.
Lord Jim ch. 20 (1900)

11 The conquest of the earth, which mostly means the taking it away from those who have a different complexion or slightly flatter noses

than ourselves, is not a pretty thing when you look into it.
Heart of Darkness ch. 1 (1902)

12 We live, as we dream—alone.
Heart of Darkness ch. 1 (1902)

13 I don't like work—no man does—but I like what is in work—the chance to find yourself. Your own reality—for yourself, not for others— what no other man can ever know.
Heart of Darkness ch. 1 (1902)

14 No fear can stand up to hunger, no patience can wear it out, disgust simply does not exist where hunger is; and as to superstition, beliefs, and what you may call principles, they are less than chaff in a breeze.
Heart of Darkness ch. 2 (1902)

15 Exterminate all the brutes!
Heart of Darkness ch. 2 (1902)

16 The horror! The horror!
Heart of Darkness ch. 3 (1902)

17 Mistah Kurtz—he dead.
Heart of Darkness ch. 3 (1902)

18 The offing was barred by a black bank of clouds, and the tranquil waterway leading to the uttermost ends of the earth flowed sombre under an overcast sky—seemed to lead into the heart of an immense darkness.
Heart of Darkness ch. 3 (1902)

19 Only a moment; a moment of strength, of romance, of glamour—of youth! . . . A flick of sunshine upon a strange shore, the time to remember, the time for a sigh, and—good-bye!—Night—Good-bye . . . !"
"Youth" (1902). Ellipses in the original.

20 I remember my youth and the feeling that will never come back any more—the feeling that I could last for ever, outlast the sea, the earth, and all men; the deceitful feeling that lures us on to joys, to perils, to love, to vain effort—to death; the triumphant conviction of strength, the heat of life in the handful of dust, the glow in the heart that with every year grows dim, grows cold, grows small, and expires—and expires, too soon, too soon—before life itself.
"Youth" (1902)
See T. S. Eliot 43

21 The terrorist and the policeman both come from the same basket. Revolution, legality— counter-moves in the same game; forms of idleness at bottom identical.
The Secret Agent ch. 4 (1907)

22 A man's real life is that accorded to him in the thoughts of other men by reason of respect or natural love.
Under Western Eyes pt. 1, ch. 1 (1911)

23 The scrupulous and the just, the noble, humane, and devoted natures; the unselfish and the intelligent may begin a movement— but it passes away from them. They are not the leaders of a revolution. They are its victims.
Under Western Eyes pt. 2, ch. 3 (1911)

24 A belief in a supernatural source of evil is not necessary; men alone are quite capable of every wickedness.
Under Western Eyes pt. 2, ch. 4 (1911)

25 The perfect delight of writing tales where so many lives come and go at the cost of one which slips imperceptibly away.
A Personal Record ch. 5 (1912)

26 Only in men's imagination does every truth find an effective and undeniable existence. Imagination, not invention, is the supreme master of art, as of life.
Some Reminiscences ch. 1 (1912)

27 [*On wartime:*] Reality, as usual, beats fiction out of sight.
Letter, 11 Aug. 1915

Shirley Conran
English designer and journalist, 1932–

1 Life is too short to stuff a mushroom.
Superwoman epigraph (1975)

Pat Conroy
U.S. novelist, 1945–2016

1 It is the secret life that sustains me now, and as I reach the top of that bridge I say it in a whisper, I say it as a prayer, as regret, and as praise. I can't tell you why I do it or what it means, but each night when I drive toward my southern home and my southern life, I whisper these words: "Lowenstein, Lowenstein."
The Prince of Tides epilogue (1986)

John Constable

English painter, 1776–1837

1 There is nothing ugly; *I never saw an ugly thing in my life:* for let the form of an object be what it may,—light, shade, and perspective will always make it beautiful.

Quoted in Charles Robert Leslie, *Memoirs of the Life of John Constable* (1843)

Benjamin Constant de Rebecque

French writer and politician, 1767–1834

1 *L'art pour l'art.*
Art for art's sake.

Journal Intime, 11 Feb. 1804
See Cousin 1; Dietz 2

Constantine the Great

Roman emperor, ca. 288–337

1 By this, conquer.

Quoted in Eusebius, *Life of Constantine.* Supposedly the words of Constantine's vision before the battle of Saxa Rubra, 312.

Constitution of the United States

1 We the People of the United States, in Order to form a more perfect Union, establish Justice, ensure domestic Tranquility, provide for the common defence, promote the general Welfare, and secure the Blessings of Liberty to ourselves and our Posterity, do ordain and establish this Constitution for the United States of America.

Preamble (1787)
See Barbara Jordan 1

2 Representatives and direct Taxes shall be apportioned among the several States which may be included within this Union, according to their respective Numbers, which shall be determined by adding to the whole Number of free Persons, including those bound to Service for a Term of Years, and excluding Indians not taxed, three fifths of all other Persons.

Article 1, Section 2 (1787)

3 The Congress shall have Power . . . To make all Laws which shall be necessary and proper for carrying into Execution the foregoing Powers, and all other Powers vested by this Constitution in the Government of the United States, or in any Department or Officer thereof.

Article 1, Section 8 (1787)

4 Before he [the President] enter on the Execution of his Office, he shall take the following Oath of Affirmation:—"I do solemnly swear (or affirm) that I will faithfully execute the Office of President of the United States, and will to the best of my Ability, preserve, protect, and defend the Constitution of the United States."

Article 2, Section 1 (1787)

5 He [the President] shall have Power, by and with the Advice and Consent of the Senate, to make Treaties, provided two thirds of the Senators present concur; and he shall nominate, and by and with the Advice and Consent of the Senate, shall appoint Ambassadors, other public Ministers and Consuls, Judges of the supreme Court, and all other Officers of the United States.

Article 2, Section 2 (1787)

6 He [the President] shall from time to time give to the Congress Information of the State of the Union.

Article 2, Section 3 (1787)

7 The President, Vice President, and all civil Officers of the United States, shall be removed from Office on Impeachment for, and Conviction of, Treason, Bribery, or other high Crimes and Misdemeanors.

Article 2, Section 4 (1787)

8 Treason against the United States, shall consist only in levying War against them, or in adhering to their Enemies, giving them Aid and Comfort. No Person shall be convicted of Treason unless on the Testimony of two Witnesses to the same overt Act, or on Confession in open Court.

Article 3, Section 3 (1787)

9 Full Faith and Credit shall be given in each State to the public Acts, Records, and judicial Proceedings of every other State.

Article 4, Section 1 (1787)

10 This Constitution, and the Laws of the United States which shall be made in Pursuance thereof, and all Treaties made, or which shall be made, under the Authority of the United States, shall be the supreme Law of the Land; and the Judges in every State shall be bound

thereby, any Thing in the Constitution or Laws of any State to the Contrary notwithstanding.
Article 6 (1787)

11 Congress shall make no law respecting an establishment of religion, or prohibiting the free exercise thereof; or abridging the freedom of speech, or of the press; or of the right of the people peaceably to assemble, and to petition the Government for a redress of grievances.
First Amendment (1791)

12 A well regulated Militia, being necessary to the security of a free State, the right of the people to keep and bear Arms, shall not be infringed.
Second Amendment (1791)

13 The right of the people to be secure in their persons, houses, papers, and effects, against unreasonable searches and seizures, shall not be violated, and no Warrants shall issue, but upon probable cause, supported by Oath or affirmation, and particularly describing the place to be searched, and the persons or things to be seized.
Fourth Amendment (1791)

14 Nor shall any person be subject for the same offence to be twice put in jeopardy of life or limb; nor shall be compelled in any criminal case to be a witness against himself, nor be deprived of life, liberty, or property, without due process of law; nor shall private property be taken for public use, without just compensation.
Fifth Amendment (1791)

15 In all criminal prosecutions, the accused shall enjoy the right to a speedy and public trial, by an impartial jury of the State and district wherein the crime shall have been committed, which district shall have been previously ascertained by law, and to be informed of the nature and cause of the accusation; to be confronted with the witnesses against him; to have compulsory process for obtaining Witnesses in his favor, and to have the Assistance of Counsel for his defence.
Sixth Amendment (1791)

16 In Suits at common law, where the value in controversy shall exceed twenty dollars, the right of trial by jury shall be preserved, and no fact tried by a jury, shall be otherwise re-examined in any Court of the United States, than according to the rules of the common law.
Seventh Amendment (1791)

17 Excessive bail shall not be required, nor excessive fines imposed, nor cruel and unusual punishments inflicted.
Eighth Amendment (1791)

18 The enumeration in the Constitution, of certain rights, shall not be construed to deny or disparage others retained by the people.
Ninth Amendment (1791)

19 The powers not delegated to the United States by the Constitution, nor prohibited by it to the States, are reserved to the States respectively, or to the people.
Tenth Amendment (1791)

20 Neither slavery nor involuntary servitude, except as a punishment for crime whereof the party shall have been duly convicted, shall exist within the United States, or any place subject to their jurisdiction.
Thirteenth Amendment, Section 1 (1865)

21 No State shall make or enforce any law which shall abridge the privileges or immunities of citizens of the United States; nor shall any State deprive any person of life, liberty, or property, without due process of law; nor deny to any person within its jurisdiction the equal protection of the laws.
Fourteenth Amendment, Section 1 (1868)

22 The right of citizens of the United States to vote shall not be denied or abridged by the United States or by any State on account of race, color, or previous condition of servitude.
Fifteenth Amendment, Section 1 (1870)

23 The right of citizens of the United States to vote shall not be denied or abridged by the United States or by any State on account of sex.
Nineteenth Amendment (1920)

Kellyanne Conway
U.S. political operative, 1967–

1 Sean Spicer, our press secretary, gave alternative facts.
Interview on NBC "Meet the Press" television program, 22 Jan. 2017
See Todd 1

Rick Cook

U.S. science fiction writer, 1960–

1 Applications programming is a race between software engineers, who strive to produce idiot-proof programs, and the Universe which strives to produce bigger idiots.—Software engineers' saying

  So far the Universe is winning.—Applications programmers' saying
The Wizardry Compiled ch. 6 (1990)

Robin Cook

British politician, 1946–2005

1 Why is it now so urgent that we should take military action [against Iraq] to disarm a military capacity that has been there for twenty years, and which we helped to create?
Speech in House of Commons, 17 Mar. 2003

Sam Cooke

U.S. soul singer, 1931–1964

1 Don't know much about history
Don't know much biology.
"Wonderful World" (song) (1960)

2 It's been a long, long time coming
But I know a change is gonna come.
"A Change Is Gonna Come" (song) (1964)

Calvin Coolidge

U.S. president, 1872–1933

1 There is no right to strike against the public safety by anybody, anywhere, any time.
Telegram to Samuel Gompers, 14 Sept. 1919

2 One with the law is a majority.
Speech accepting Republican vice-presidential nomination, Northampton, Mass., 27 July 1920
See Douglass 7; Andrew Jackson 7; John Knox 1; Wendell Phillips 3; Thoreau 9

3 After all, the chief business of the American people is business.
Address before the American Society of Newspaper Editors, Washington, D.C., 17 Jan. 1925. Usually misquoted as "The business of America is business" or "The chief business of America is business."

4 I do not choose to run.
Statement to press regarding 1928 presidential election, Rapid City, S.D., 2 Aug. 1927

5 I won't pass the buck.
Quoted in Michael Hennessy, *From a Green Mountain Farm to the White House* (1924). Coolidge said these words (1920) after jitney operators threatened to "crucify" him politically in reaction to his intervention in a dispute between jitney and streetcar operators. He was governor of Massachusetts at the time.
See Truman 11

6 [*When asked by his wife what the minister had said in a sermon about sin:*] He was against it.
Quoted in *N.Y. Times*, 7 Dec. 1925.

7 [*On war debts owed by foreign nations to the United States, 1925:*] They hired the money, didn't they?
Attributed in *Wash. Post*, 31 May 1925. Coolidge's biographer, Claud M. Fuess, was unable to discover any evidence that Coolidge said this. Coolidge's wife stated, "I don't know whether he said it, but it is just what he might have said." This attribution appeared in a column by Will Rogers and strengthens the case for Coolidge having said this remark.

8 You lose.
Attributed in Gamaliel Bradford, *The Quick and the Dead* (1931). Supposedly Coolidge's response to a Washington matron's telling him, "I made a bet with someone that I could get more than two words out of you." The *New York Times*, 23 Apr. 1924, has the "you lose" response but without the "two words" part of the buildup.

9 When a great many people are unable to find work, unemployment results.
Attributed in Stanley Walker, *City Editor* (1934)

Coolio (Artis Ivey)

U.S. singer and songwriter, 1963–

1 As I walk through the valley of the shadow of death
I take a look at my life and realize there's not much left.
"Gangsta's Paradise" (song) (1995)
See Bible 109

2 Been spending most their lives, living in the gangsta's paradise.
"Gangsta's Paradise" (song) (1995)

Anna Julia Cooper

U.S. educator and writer, 1858–1964

1 Only the BLACK WOMAN can say "when and where I enter, in the quiet, undisputed dignity

of my womanhood, without violence and without suing or special patronage, then and there the whole *Negro race enters with me.*"
A Voice from the South pt. 1 (1892)

2 The cause of freedom is not the cause of a race or a sect, a party or a class,—it is the cause of human kind, the very birthright of humanity.
A Voice from the South pt. 1 (1892)

James Fenimore Cooper
U.S. novelist, 1789–1851

1 I am on the hilltop, and must go down into the valley; and when Uncas follows in my footsteps, there will no longer be any of the blood of the Sagamores, for my boy is the last of the Mohicans.
The Last of the Mohicans ch. 3 (1826)

2 It is a besetting vice of democracies to substitute publick opinion for law. This is the usual form in which masses of men exhibit their tyranny.
The American Democrat (1838)

3 The press, like fire, is an excellent servant, but a terrible master.
The American Democrat (1838)

Wendy Cope
English poet, 1945–

1 Making Cocoa for Kingsley Amis.
Title of poem (1986)

2 Bloody men are like bloody buses—

You wait for about a year
And as soon as one approaches your stop
Two or three others appear.
"Bloody Men" l. 1 (1992)

Nicolaus Copernicus
Polish astronomer, 1473–1543

1 The center of the earth is not the center of the universe, but only of gravity and of the lunar sphere. All the spheres revolve about the sun as their mid-point, and therefore the sun is the center of the universe.
"The Commentariolus" (ca. 1510) (translation by Edward Rosen)

Aaron Copland
U.S. composer, 1900–1990

1 This whole problem can be stated quite simply by asking, "Is there a meaning to music?" My answer to that would be "Yes." And "Can you state in so many words what the meaning is?" My answer to that would be "No."
What to Listen for in Music ch. 2 (1939)

Irwin Corey
U.S. comedian, 1914–2017

1 You can get more with a kind word and a gun than with just a kind word.
Quoted in *Variety*, 29 July 1953. Corey later comically attributed the wisecrack to Al Capone, who is now usually credited with it.

Bob Corker
U.S. politician, 1952–

1 [*Of the Trump administration:*] It's a shame the White House has become an adult day care center.
Tweet, 8 Oct. 2017

Avery Corman
U.S. novelist, 1935–

1 I don't do miracles. . . . The last miracle I did was the 1969 Mets . . . and before that I think you have to go back to the Red Sea.
Oh, God! ch. 2 (1977)

Pierre Corneille
French playwright, 1606–1684

1 *Va, cours, vole et nous venge.*
Go, run, fly and avenge us.
Le Cid act 1, sc. 5 (1637)

2 *Va, je ne te hais point.*
Go, I hate you not.
Le Cid act 3, sc. 4 (1637)

3 [Reply upon being asked "What could he have done when it was one against three?":] *Qu'il mourût.*
He should have died!
Horace act 3, sc. 6 (1641)

Frances Cornford

English poet, 1886–1960

1 O fat white woman whom nobody loves,
   Why do you walk through the fields in gloves
   When the grass is as soft as the breast of doves
   And shivering sweet to the touch?
   "To a Fat Lady Seen from the Train" l. 3 (1910)

Francis M. Cornford

English classical scholar, 1874–1943

1 Every public action, which is not customary,
   either is wrong, or, if it is right, is a dangerous
   precedent. It follows that nothing should ever
   be done for the first time.
   Microcosmographia Academica ch. 7 (1908)

Anne-Marie Bigot de Cornuel

French society hostess, 1605–1694

1 No man is a hero to his valet.
   Quoted in *Lettres de Mlle. Aïssé à Madame C.* Letter 13
   "De Paris, 1728" (1787)

Antonio Allegri Correggio

Italian painter, ca. 1489–1534

1 I, too, am a painter!
   Attributed in Luigi Pungileoni, *Memorie Istoriche di
   Antonio Allegri Detto il Correggio* (1817). Said to be
   Correggio's exclamation upon first seeing Raphael's
   painting *St. Cecilia* at Bologna, Italy, ca. 1525.

Gregory Corso

U.S. poet, 1930–2001

1 O God, and the wedding! All her family and her
   friends
   and only a handful of mine all scroungy and
   bearded
   just wait to get at the drinks and food—.
   "Marriage" l. 24 (1960)

2 It's just that I see love as odd as wearing
   shoes—
   I never wanted to marry a girl who was like my
   mother
   And Ingrid Bergman was always impossible.
   "Marriage" l. 100 (1960)

2 What if I'm 60 years old and not married,
   all alone in a furnished room with pee stains
   on my underwear
   and everybody else is married!
   "Marriage" l. 106 (1960)

3 Ah, yet well I know that were a woman possible
   as I am possible
   then marriage would be possible—
   Like SHE in her lonely alien gaud waiting her
   Egyptian lover
   so I wait—bereft of 2,000 years and the bath of
   life.
   "Marriage" l. 109 (1960)

Bob Costas

U.S. sportscaster, 1952–

1 It brings to mind a story Mickey liked to tell
   on himself. He pictured himself at the pearly
   gates, met by St. Peter, who shook his head and
   said, "Mick, we checked the record. We know
   some of what went on. Sorry, we can't let you
   in, but before you go, God wants to know if
   you'd sign these six dozen baseballs."
   Eulogy for Mickey Mantle, Dallas, Tex., 15 Aug. 1995

Elvis Costello (Declan MacManus)

English singer and songwriter, 1954–

1 Oh I used to be disgusted
   And now I try to be amused.
   "(The Angels Wanna Wear My) Red Shoes" (song)
   (1977)

2 Less Than Zero.
   Title of song (1977). This inspired the title of Bret
   Easton Ellis's 1985 novel.

Pierre de Coubertin

French sportsman and educator, 1863–1937

1 *L'important dans ces olympiades, c'est moins d'y
   gagner que d'y prendre part. . . . L'important
   dans la vie ce n'est point le triomphe mais le
   combat; l'essentiel ce n'est pas d'avoir vaincu
   mais de s'être bien battu.*
   The important thing in these Olympics is less
   to win than to take part. . . . The important
   thing in life is not the victory but the contest;
   the essential thing is not to have won but to
   have fought well.
   Speech to Olympic officials, London, 24 July 1908

Émile Coué

French psychologist, 1857–1926

1 [*Therapeutic formula to be said repeatedly each morning and evening:*] Every day, in every way, I am getting better and better.

De la Suggestion et de Ses Applications (1915)

Douglas Coupland

Canadian author, 1961–

1 Generation X: Tales for an Accelerated Culture.

Title of book (1991). The *Oxford English Dictionary* documents earlier uses of the term *Generation X* back to 1952, but Coupland popularized it.

2 Dag . . . was bored and cranky after eight hours of working his McJob ("Low pay, low prestige, low benefits, low future").

Generation X ch. 1 (1991). Earliest documented usage of *McJob* appeared in the *Washington Post*, 24 Aug. 1986: "The Fast-Food Factories: McJobs Are Bad for Kids."

Victor Cousin

French philosopher, 1792–1867

1 *Il faut de la religion pour la religion, de la morale pour la morale, de l'art pour l'art.*
We must have religion for religion's sake, morality for morality's sake, as with art for art's sake.

"Du Vrai, du Beau, et du Bien" (1818)
See Constant de Rebecque 1; Dietz 2

Jacques-Yves Cousteau

French marine explorer, 1910–1997

1 [*Description of nitrogen narcosis:*] *L'ivresse des grandes profoundeurs.*
The rapture of the deep.

Silent World ch. 2 (1953)

2 *Il faut aller voir.*
We must go and see for ourselves.

Quoted in *N.Y. Times*, 26 June 1997

Robert M. Cover

U.S. legal scholar, 1943–1986

1 No set of legal institutions or prescriptions exists apart from the narratives that locate it and give it meaning. For every constitution there is an epic, for each decalogue a scripture.

Once understood in the context of the narratives that give it meaning, law becomes not merely a system of rules to be observed, but a world in which we live.

"The Supreme Court, 1982 Term—Foreword: *Nomos and Narrative*," *Harvard Law Review*, Nov. 1983

Noël Coward

English playwright, actor, and composer, 1899–1973

1 I have never been able to take anything seriously after eleven o'clock in the morning.

The Young Idea act 1 (1921)

2 Poor little rich girl,
You're a bewitched girl,
Better beware!

"Poor Little Rich Girl" (song) (1925)
See Eleanor Gates 1

3 But I believe that since my life began
The most I've had is just
A talent to amuse.

"If Love Were All" (song) (1929)

4 I'll see you again,
Whenever Spring breaks through again.

"I'll See You Again" (song) (1929)

5 Very flat, Norfolk.

Private Lives act 1 (1930)

6 Certain women should be struck regularly, like gongs.

Private Lives act 3 (1930)

7 [*To T. E. Lawrence when the latter was a corporal in the Royal Air Force:*] Dear 338171 (May I call you 338?).

Letter to T. E. Lawrence, 25 Aug. 1930

8 Englishmen detest a siesta.

"Mad Dogs and Englishmen" (song) (1931)

9 In Bengal, to move at all
Is seldom, if ever, done,
But mad dogs and Englishmen
Go out in the midday sun.

"Mad Dogs and Englishmen" (song) (1931). Cole Lesley, in *The Life of Noël Coward*, notes earlier versions of this quotation. In 1835 Lovell Badcock wrote in *Rough Leaves from a Journal*: "The heat of the day, when dogs and English alone are seen to move." In 1874 G. N. Goodwin wrote, "Only newly arrived Englishmen and mad dogs expose themselves to it" (*Guide to Malta*). An earlier version found for this book is, "It is a common saying at *Rome,* 'None but dogs, ideots, and *Frenchmen* walk the streets in day-time'" (John George Keysler, *Travels Through Germany, Bohemia, Hungary, Switzerland, Italy and Lorrain* [1757]).

10 People are wrong when they say that the opera isn't what it used to be. It is what it used to be—that's what's wrong with it!

    Design for Living act 3, sc. 1 (1932)

11 The Party's Over Now.

    Title of song (1932)
    See Comden and Green 4

12 Don't put your daughter on the stage, Mrs.
      Worthington,
   Don't put your daughter on the stage.

    "Don't Put Your Daughter on the Stage, Mrs. Worthington" (song) (1935)

13 I have noticed . . . a certain tendency . . . to class me with the generation that was "ineradicably scarred by the war." . . . I was not in the least scarred by the war. . . . The reasons for my warped disenchantment with life must be sought elsewhere.

    Present Indicative pt. 3 (1937)

14 [*Advice on acting:*] Just say the lines and don't trip over the furniture.

    Quoted in Dick Richards, *The Wit of Noël Coward* (1968). According to Richards, Coward said this during the run of his play *Nude with Violin* (1956–1957).
    See Fontanne 1

15 I have never written for the intelligentsia. Sixteen curtain-calls and close on Saturday.

    Quoted in Dick Richards, *Wit of Noël Coward* (1968)
    See George Kaufman 4

Abraham Cowley

English poet, 1618–1667

1 Life is an incurable disease.

    "To Dr. Scarborough" l. 111 (1656)

2 God the first Garden made, and the first city *Cain.*

    "The Garden" l. 44 (1668)
    See Cowper (1731–1800) 5

Hannah Cowley

English playwright, 1743–1809

1 But what is woman?—only one of Nature's agreeable blunders.

    Who's the Dupe? act 2 (1779)
    See Nietzsche 22

William Cowper

English poet, 1731–1800

1 God moves in a mysterious way
   His wonders to perform;
   He plants his footsteps in the sea,
   And rides upon the storm.

    Olney Hymns "Light Shining Out of Darkness" l. 1 (1779)

2 A fool must now and then be right, by chance.

    "Conversation" l. 96 (1782)

3   Philologists, who chase
   A panting syllable through time and space,
   Start it at home, and hunt it in the dark
   To Gaul, to Greece, and into Noah's ark.

    "Retirement" l. 691 (1782)

4 I am monarch of all I survey,
   My right there is none to dispute.

    "Verses Supposed to Be Written by Alexander Selkirk" l. 1 (1782)

5 God made the country, and man made the town.

    The Task bk. 1 "The Sofa" l. 749 (1785)
    See Abraham Cowley 2

6 England, with all thy faults, I love thee still— My country!

    The Task bk. 2 "The Timepiece" l. 206 (1785)
    See Charles Churchill 1

7 Variety's the very spice of life,
   That gives it all its flavor.

    The Task bk. 2 "The Timepiece" l. 606 (1785). Often misquoted as "Variety is the spice of life."
    See Behn 1

William Cowper, First Earl Cowper

English lord chancellor, ca. 1660–1723

1 He who will have equity, or comes hither for equity, must do equity.

    Demandray v. Metcalf (1715)

Archibald Cox

U.S. legal scholar and government official,
1912–2004

1 Whether ours shall continue to be a
Government of laws and not of men is now for
Congress and ultimately the American people
[to decide].

Statement, 20 Oct. 1973. Cox had just been dismissed
by President Richard M. Nixon because he refused
to drop his lawsuit to obtain Watergate-related White
House tapes.
See John Adams 4; Gerald Ford 3; James Harrington 1

Coleman Cox

U.S. author, fl. 1925

1 I am a great believer in luck. The harder I work,
the more of it I seem to have.

Listen to This (1922)

Jimmy Cox

U.S. songwriter, 1882–1925

1 Nobody Knows You When You're Down and
Out.

Title of song (1923)

Dinah Mulock Craik

British novelist and poet, 1826–1887

1 Oh, the comfort—the inexpressible comfort
of feeling safe with a person—having neither
to weigh thoughts nor measure words, but
pouring them all right out, just as they are,
chaff and grain together; certain that a faithful
hand will take and sift them, keep what is worth
keeping, and then with the breath of kindness
blow the rest away.

A Life for a Life ch. 16 (1859)

2 O, my son's my son till he gets him a wife,
But my daughter's my daughter all her life.

"Magnus and Morna" sc. 2, l. 61 (1881)

Hart Crane

U.S. poet, 1899–1932

1 And yet this great wink of eternity,
Of rimless floods, unfettered leewardings,
Samite sheeted and processioned where
Her undinal vast belly moonward bends,
Laughing the wrapt inflections of love.

"Voyages II" l. 1 (1926)

2 How many dawns, chill from his rippling rest
The seagull's wings shall dip and pivot him,
Shedding white rings of tumult, building high
Over the chained bay waters Liberty.

The Bridge "Proem: To Brooklyn Bridge" l. 1 (1930)

3 O Sleepless as the river under thee,
Vaulting the sea, the prairies' dreaming sod,
Unto us lowliest sometimes sweep, descend
And of the curveship lend a myth to God.

The Bridge "Proem: To Brooklyn Bridge" l. 41 (1930)

Stephen Crane

U.S. writer, 1871–1900

1 In the desert
I saw a creature, naked, bestial,
Who, squatting upon the ground,
Held his heart in his hands,
And ate of it.
I said, "Is it good, friend?"
"It is bitter—bitter," he answered;
"But I like it
"Because it is bitter,
"And because it is my heart."

The Black Riders and Other Lines "In the Desert" l. 1
(1895)

2 At times he regarded the wounded soldiers in
an envious way. He conceived persons with
torn bodies to be peculiarly happy. He wished
that he, too, had a wound, a red badge of
courage.

The Red Badge of Courage ch. 9 (1895)

3 The red sun was pasted in the sky like a wafer.

The Red Badge of Courage ch. 9 (1895)

4 A man said to the universe:
"Sir, I exist!"
"However," replied the universe,
"The fact has not created in me
"A sense of obligation."

"A man said to the universe" l. 1 (1899)

Thomas Cranmer

English religious leader, 1489–1556

1 [Remark as he was being burned at the stake,
Oxford, England, 21 Mar. 1556:] This was the
hand that wrote it [his recantations of his faith],
therefore it shall suffer first punishment.

Quoted in John Richard Green, A Short History of the
English People (1874)

Adelaide Crapsey
U.S. poet, 1878–1914

1 These be
Three silent things:
The Falling snow . . . the hour
Before the dawn . . . the mouth of one
Just dead.
"Cinquain: Triad" l. 1 (1915)

Richard Crashaw
English poet, ca. 1612–1649

1 Love, thou art absolute sole Lord
Of life and death.
"Hymn to the Name and Honor of the Admirable
Saint Teresa" l. 1 (1652)

Cristina Crawford
U.S. writer, 1939–

1 She was my "Mommie dearest."
Mommie Dearest ch. 2 (1978)

Joan Crawford (Lucille Fay LeSueur)
U.S. actress, 1904–1977

1 [*On raiding her adoptive daughter's bedroom
closet:*] No wire hangers! No wire hangers!
Quoted in Christina Crawford, *Mommie Dearest*
(1978)

Julia Crawford
Irish poet and composer, ca. 1795–ca. 1855

1 Kathleen Mavourneen! the grey dawn is
breaking,
The horn of the hunter is heard on the hill.
"Kathleen Mavourneen" l. 1 (1835)

Robert Crawford
U.S. composer and pilot, 1899–1961

1 Off we go into the wild blue yonder,
Climbing high into the sun.
"The Air Force Song" (song) (1938)

2 We live in fame or go down in flame.
Nothing'll stop the Army Air Corps!
"The Air Force Song" (song) (1938)

Crazy Horse (Ta-Sunko-Witko)
Native American leader, ca. 1849–1877

1 One does not sell the earth upon which the
people walk.
Quoted in Dee Brown, *Bury My Heart at Wounded
Knee* (1970)

Robert Creeley
U.S. poet, 1926–2005

1 It is hard going to the door
cut so small in the wall where
the vision which echoes loneliness
brings a scent of wild flowers in the wood.
"The Door" l. 1 (1959)

2 I will go to the garden.
I will be a romantic. I will sell
myself in hell,
in heaven also I will be.
"The Door" l. 77 (1959)

3 shall we &
why not, buy a goddamn big car,

drive, he sd, for
christ's sake, look
out where yr going.
"I Know a Man" l. 8 (1962)

J. Hector St. John Crèvecoeur (Michel Guillaume Jean de Crèvecoeur)
French-born U.S. essayist, 1735–1813

1 Here individuals of all nations are melted into
a new race of men, whose labors and posterity
will one day cause great changes in the world.
Letters from an American Farmer Letter 3 (1782)
*See Baudouin 1; Jimmy Carter 3; Ralph Ellison 2;
Victoria Hayward 1; Jesse Jackson 1; Zangwill 2*

2 What then is the American, this new man? He
is either an European, or the descendant of an
European, hence that strange mixture of blood,
which you will find in no other country.
Letters from an American Farmer Letter 3 (1782)

3 [Lawyers] are plants that will grow in any
soil that is cultivated by the hands of others;
and when once they have taken root they will
extinguish every other vegetable that grows
around them. . . . The most ignorant, the most
bungling member of that profession, will, if

placed in the most obscure part of the country, promote litigiousness, and amass more wealth without labor, than the most opulent farmer, with all his toils.

Letters from an American Farmer Letter 7 (1782)

Michael Crichton
U.S. writer, 1942–2008

1 The history of evolution is that life escapes all barriers. Life breaks free. Life expands to new territories. Painfully, perhaps even dangerously. But life finds a way.

Jurassic Park "Third Iteration" (1990)

Francis Crick
English biophysicist, 1916–2004

1 We have built a model for the structure of [DNA] . . . we think we have found the basic copying mechanism by which life comes from life.

Letter to Michael Crick, 15 Mar. 1953

2 This [double helix] structure [of DNA] has novel features which are of considerable biological interest. . . . It has not escaped our notice that the specific pairing we have postulated immediately suggests a possible copying mechanism for the genetic material.

"Molecular Structure of Nucleic Acids," *Nature,* 25 Apr. 1953. Coauthored with James D. Watson.

3 *The Central Dogma* This states that once "information" has passed into protein *it cannot get out again.*

"On Protein Synthesis," *Symposia of the Society for Experimental Biology* (1958)

Quentin Crisp
English writer, 1908–1999

1 The young always have the same problem— how to rebel and conform at the same time. They have now solved this by defying their parents and copying one another.

The Naked Civil Servant ch. 19 (1968)

2 I became one of the stately homos of England.

The Naked Civil Servant ch. 24 (1968)
See Hemans 3; Woolf 4

3 [*Response to being asked by a U.S. immigration officer whether he was a "practising homosexual":*] Practising? Certainly not. I'm perfect.

Quoted in *Sunday Times* (London), 20 Jan. 1982

Jim Croce
U.S. singer and songwriter, 1943–1973

1 You don't tug on Superman's cape.

"You Don't Mess Around with Jim" (song) (1972)

Davy Crockett
U.S. frontiersman and politician, 1786–1836

1 I leave this rule for others when I'm dead,
Be always sure you're right—THEN GO AHEAD!

A Narrative of the Life of David Crockett epigraph (1834)

Oliver Cromwell
English statesman and soldier, 1599–1658

1 I beseech you, in the bowels of Christ, think it possible you may be mistaken.

Letter to General Assembly of the Kirk of Scotland, 3 Aug. 1650
See Hand 10

2 You have sat too long here for any good you have been doing. Depart, I say, and let us have done with you. In the name of God, go!

Remarks to Rump Parliament, 20 Apr. 1653. The *Oxford Dictionary of Quotations* describes this as "oral tradition." Bulstrode Whitlocke, *Memorials of the English Affairs* (1682), describes Cromwell as telling the House that "they has sate long enough, unles they had done more good."

3 [*Instructions to the court painter:*] Mr. Lely, I desire you would use all your skill to paint my picture truly like me, and not flatter me at all; but remark all these roughnesses, pimples, warts, and everything as you see me; otherwise I will never pay a farthing for it.

Quoted in Horace Walpole, *Anecdotes of Painting in England* (1763). Usually misquoted as "warts and all."

4 My boys trust in the Lord, and keep your powder dry.

Quoted in *House of Lords Hansard Sessional Papers,* 28 Feb. 1832

Walter Cronkite

U.S. broadcaster, 1916–2009

1 To say that we are closer to victory today is
to believe, in the face of the evidence, the
optimists who have been wrong in the past.
To suggest that we are on the edge of defeat
is to yield to unreasonable pessimism. To say
that we are mired in stalemate seems the only
realistic, yet unsatisfactory, conclusion.
Televised report on Vietnam War, 27 Feb. 1968

Harry "Bing" Crosby

U.S. singer and actor, 1903–1977

1 [*Proposed epitaph for himself:*] He was an average
guy who could carry a tune.
Quoted in *Newsweek*, 24 Oct. 1977

Norm Crosby

U.S. comedian, 1927–2020

1 There's so much lunacy in the world . . . look
at courtrooms. Where else would you place
yourself in the hands of 12 people who weren't
smart enough to get out of jury duty?
Quoted in *Sun-Star* (Merced, Calif.), 4 Aug. 1978

Douglas Cross

U.S. songwriter, 1920–1975

1 I left my heart in San Francisco
High on a hill it calls to me.
To be where little cable cars climb half-way to
   the stars.
"I Left My Heart in San Francisco" (song) (1954)

Aleister Crowley

English occultist, 1875–1947

1 Do what thou wilt shall be the whole of the Law.
Book of the Law (1909)

Tom Cruise (Thomas Cruise Mapother IV)

U.S. actor, 1962–

1 Psychiatry is a pseudoscience. . . . You don't
know the history of psychiatry. I do. . . . Matt,
Matt, Matt, Matt, Matt, Matt, you don't even—
you're glib. You don't even know what Ritalin is.
Remarks to Matt Lauer on NBC-TV "Today" show, 24
June 2005

Countee Cullen

U.S. poet, 1903–1946

1 One three centuries removed
From the scenes his fathers loved,
Spicy grove, cinnamon tree,
What is Africa to me?
"Heritage" l. 60 (1925)

2 Now I was eight and very small,
And he was no whit bigger,
And so I smiled, but he poked out
His tongue, and called me, "Nigger."
"Incident" l. 5 (1925)

3 I saw the whole of Baltimore
From May until December;
Of all the things that happened there
That's all that I remember.
"Incident" l. 9 (1925)

4 Yet do I marvel at this curious thing:
To make a poet black, and bid him sing!
"Yet Do I Marvel" l. 13 (1925)

R. V. Culter

U.S. cartoonist, 1883–1929

1 The Gay Nineties.
Title of cartoon series, *Life*, 9 Apr. 1925–22 Mar. 1928

Henry Frederick, Duke of Cumberland

English nobleman, 1745–1790

1 [*Addressing Edward Gibbon, who had presented to
him the second volume of* The Decline and Fall of
the Roman Empire, *1781:*] I suppose you are at
the old trade again—scribble, scribble, scribble.
Quoted in Miss Sayer, Letter to Madame Huber,
27 Jan. 1789. This letter is printed in *Journal and
Correspondence of William, Lord Auckland* vol. 2 (1861).
The quotation is usually attributed to Cumberland's
brother, William Henry, Duke of Gloucester, in
the form "Another damned, thick, square book!
Always scribble, scribble, scribble! Eh! Mr. Gibbon?"
However, the Gloucester version is not attested until
1829.

Richard Cumberland

English clergyman, 1631–1718

1 A man had better wear out, than rust out.
Quoted in Joseph Cornish, *The Life of Mr. Thomas
Firmin, Citizen of London* (1780)
See Neil Young 3

e.e. cummings (Edward Estlin Cummings)
U.S. poet, 1894–1962

1 All in green went my love riding
on a great horse of gold
into the silver dawn.
"All in green went my love riding" l. 1 (1923)

2 Buffalo Bill's
defunct.
"Buffalo Bill's" l. 1 (1923)

3 how do you like your blueeyed boy
Mister Death.
"Buffalo Bill's" l. 10 (1923)

4 in Just-
spring when the world is mud-
luscious the little
lame balloonman
whistles far and wee.
"Chansons Innocentes: I" l. 1 (1923)

5 when the world is puddle-wonderful.
"Chansons Innocentes: I" l. 9 (1923)

6 the Cambridge ladies who live in furnished
souls
are unbeautiful and have comfortable minds.
"Sonnets—Realities" no. 1, l. 1 (1923)

7 they believe in Christ and Longfellow, both
dead.
"Sonnets—Realities" no. 1, l. 5 (1923)

8 . . . the Cambridge ladies do not care, above
Cambridge if sometimes in its box of
sky lavender and cornerless, the
moon rattles like a fragment of angry candy.
"Sonnets—Realities" no. 1, l. 11 (1923). Ellipsis in the
original.

9 "next to of course god america i
love you land of the pilgrims" and so forth.
"next to of course god america i" l. 1 (1926)

10 these heroic happy dead
who rushed like lions to the roaring slaughter
they did not stop to think they died instead
then shall the voice of liberty be mute?
He spoke. And drank rapidly a glass of water.
"next to of course god america i" l. 10 (1926)

11 (dreaming,
et
cetera, of

Your smile
eyes knees and of your Etcetera).
"Two: 10" l. 21 (1926)

12 i sing of Olaf glad and big
whose warmest heart recoiled at war:
a conscientious object-or.
"i sing of Olaf glad and big" l. 1 (1931)

13 "I will not kiss your f.ing flag."
"i sing of Olaf glad and big" l. 19 (1931)

14 "there is some s. I will not eat."
"i sing of Olaf glad and big" l. 33 (1931)

15 unless statistics lie he was
more brave than me: more blond than you.
"i sing of Olaf glad and big" l. 41 (1931)

16 I'd rather learn from one bird how to sing
than teach ten thousand stars how not to dance.
"you shall above all things be glad and young" l. 13
(1938)

17 my father moved through dooms of love
through sames of am through haves of give,
singing each morning out of each night
my father moved through depths of height.
"my father moved through dooms of love" l. 1 (1940)

18 a politician is an arse upon
which everyone has sat except a man.
1 x 1 no. 10, l. 1 (1944)

19 pity this busy monster, manunkind,
not. Progress is a comfortable disease.
1 x 1 no. 14, l. 1 (1944)

20 tomorrow is our permanent address.
1 x 1 no. 39, l. 12 (1944)

Ray Cummings
U.S. science fiction writer, 1887–1957

1 Time is what keeps everything from happening
at once.
"The Time Professor" (1921)

Mario Cuomo
U.S. politician, 1932–2015

1 We campaign in poetry, but when we're elected
we're forced to govern in prose.
Speech at Yale University, New Haven, Conn., 15 Feb.
1985

Marie Curie (Manya Sklodowska)
Polish-born French chemist, 1867–1934

1 The various reasons which we have enumerated lead us to believe that the new radio-active substance contains a new element to which we propose to give the name of radium.
"Sur une Nouvelle Substance Fortement Radio-Active, Contenue dans la Pechblende" (1898). Coauthored with Pierre Curie and Gustave Bémont.

2 [*Remark, ca. 1904:*] In science we must be interested in things, not in persons.
Quoted in Eve Curie, *Madame Curie* (1938)

John Philpot Curran
Irish judge, 1750–1817

1 The condition upon which God hath given liberty to man is eternal vigilance; which condition if he break, servitude is at once the consequence of his crime, and the punishment of his guilt.
Speech on the right of election of the Lord Mayor of Dublin, 10 July 1790. Usually quoted as "Eternal vigilance is the price of liberty," which has been attributed to Thomas Jefferson, but no one has ever found this in his writings. *The Cabinet* (Schenectady, N.Y.), 30 Oct. 1816, has "Eternal vigilance is justly said to be the price of liberty."
See Andrew Jackson 5

Tim Curry
English actor and singer, 1946–

1 Read My Lips.
Title of record album (1978)
See George H. W. Bush 4; Film Lines 100; Joe Greene 1

Sonny Curtis
U.S. musician and songwriter, 1937–

1 I fought the law, and the law won.
"I Fought the Law" (song) (1961)

Tony Curtis (Bernard Schwartz)
U.S. actor, 1925–2010

1 Kissing Marilyn [Monroe] was like kissing Hitler.
Quoted in *Cumberland* (Md.) *Times,* 22 May 1960

George Curzon
English politician, 1859–1925

1 [*Instructing his wife on lovemaking:*] Ladies don't move.
Attributed in *The Lyttelton Hart-Davis Letters,* ed. Rupert Hart-Davis (1978–1984) (letter of 19 Aug. 1956)

Caleb Cushing
U.S. politician, 1800–1879

1 [*Of the impending civil war:*] Cruel war, war at home; and in the perspective distance, a man on horseback with a drawn sword in his hand, some Atlantic Caesar, or Cromwell, or Napoleon.
Speech, Bangor, Me., 11 Jan. 1860

Astolphe de Custine
French aristocrat and writer, 1790–1857

1 *Le gouvernement russe est une monarchie absolue tempérée par l'assassinat.*
The Russian government is an absolute monarchy tempered by assassination.
La Russie en 1839 vol. 1 (1843)

Savinien Cyrano de Bergerac
French writer, 1619–1655

1 A large nose is the mark of a witty, courteous, affable, generous, and liberal man.
The Other World: States and Empires of the Moon ch. 8 (1656)

Harry Dacre

English songwriter, 1860–1922

1 Daisy, Daisy, give me your answer do!
I'm half crazy, all for the love of you;
It won't be a stylish marriage,
I can't afford a carriage
But you'll look sweet upon the seat,
Of a bicycle built for two!
"Daisy Bell" (song) (1892)

Roald Dahl

Welsh-born English writer, 1916–1990

1 It's a funny thing about mothers and fathers.
Even when their own child is the most
disgusting little blister you could ever imagine,
they still think that he or she is wonderful.
Matilda (1988)

Edouard Daladier

French prime minister, 1884–1970

1 A phrase has spread from civilians to soldiers
and back again: "This is a phony war."
Speech to French Chamber of Deputies, 22 Dec. 1939

Dalai Lama (Tenzin Gyatso)

Tibetan religious and political leader, 1935–

1 We know our cause is just. Because violence
can only breed more violence and suffering,
our struggle must remain nonviolent and free
of hatred. We are trying to end the suffering of
our people, not to inflict suffering on others.
Speech accepting Nobel Peace Prize, Stockholm, 10
Dec. 1989

Richard J. Daley

U.S. politician, 1902–1976

1 [*Remark to press about riots during the Democratic
National Convention in Chicago, Ill., 1968:*] The
policeman isn't there to create disorder, the
policeman is there to preserve disorder.
Press conference, Chicago, Ill., 9 Sept. 1968

Salvador Dalí

Spanish painter, 1904–1989

1 The only difference between myself and a
madman is that I am not mad.
Lecture at Wadsworth Atheneum, Hartford, Conn.,
18 Dec. 1934

2 The first man to compare the cheeks of a young
woman to a rose was obviously a poet; the first
to repeat it was possibly an idiot.
Preface to Pierre Cabanne, *Dialogues with Marcel
Duchamp* (1968)

Mary Daly

U.S. feminist and theologian, 1928–2010

1 If God is male, then the male is God.
Beyond God the Father ch. 1 (1973)

Gerard Damiano

U.S. film director, 1928–2008

1 Deep Throat.
Title of motion picture (1972)

Charles A. Dana

U.S. newspaper editor, 1819–1897

1 You may see a dog bite a man. That would not
be news . . . but should you see a man biting a
dog . . . it would be "news."
Quoted in *Atchison* (Kan.) *Daily Champion*, 4 Mar.
1899. Often ascribed to John B. Bogart.

Rodney Dangerfield (Jacob Cohen)

U.S. comedian, 1921–2004

1 [*Catchphrase:*] I don't get no respect.
Quoted in *N.Y. Times*, 14 June 1970

2 I went to a fight last night and a hockey game
broke out.
Quoted in *Toronto Star*, 27 Sept. 1978.

3 If it weren't for pickpockets I'd have no sex life
at all.
Quoted in Robert Byrne, *The 637 Best Things Anybody
Ever Said* (1982)

Samuel Daniel

English poet and playwright, 1563–1619

1 This is the thing that I was born to do.

Musophilus, or Defence of All Learning st. 100 (1602–1603)

Dante Alighieri

Italian poet, 1265–1321

1 In that part of the book of my memory before which is little that can be read, there is a rubric, saying, "Incipit Vita Nova [The New Life Begins]."

La Vita Nuova (1293) (translation by Dante Gabriel Rossetti)

2 *Nel mezzo del cammin di nostra vita.*
In the middle of the journey of our life.

Divina Commedia "Inferno" canto 1, l. 1 (ca. 1310–1321)

3 [*Inscription at entrance to Hell:*] LASCIATE OGNI SPERANZA VOI CH' ENTRATE.

ABANDON EVERY HOPE, YE THAT ENTER.

Divina Commedia "Inferno" canto 3, l. 9 (ca. 1310–1321) (translation by John D. Sinclair)

4 *Non ragioniam di lor, ma guarda e passa.*
Let us not talk of them, but look thou and pass.

Divina Commedia "Inferno" canto 3, l. 51 (ca. 1310–1321) (translation by John D. Sinclair)

5 *Onorate l'altissimo poeta.*
Honor the lofty poet!

Divina Commedia "Inferno" canto 4, l. 80 (ca. 1310–1321) (translation by John D. Sinclair)

6 [*Of Aristotle:*] *Il maestro di color che sanno.*
The master of them that know.

Divina Commedia "Inferno" canto 4, l. 131 (ca. 1310–1321) (translation by John D. Sinclair)

7 *Nessun maggior dolore,*
Che ricordarsi del tempo felice
Nella miseria.
There is no greater pain than to recall the happy time in misery.

Divina Commedia "Inferno" canto 5, l. 121 (ca. 1310–1321) (translation by John D. Sinclair)
See Boethius 1

8 If thou follow thy star thou canst not fail of a glorious haven.

Divina Commedia "Inferno" canto 15, l. 55 (ca. 1310–1321) (translation by John D. Sinclair)

9 *Considerate la vostra semenza:*
Fatti non foste a viver come bruti,
Ma per seguir virtute e canoscenza.
Take thought of the seed from which you spring. You were not born to live as brutes, but to follow virtue and knowledge.

Divina Commedia "Inferno" canto 26, l. 118 (ca. 1310–1321) (translation by John D. Sinclair)

10 If I thought my answer were to one who would ever return to the world, this flame should stay without another movement; but since none ever returned alive from this depth, if what I hear is true, I answer thee without fear of infamy.

Divina Commedia "Inferno" canto 27, l. 60 (ca. 1310–1321) (translation by John D. Sinclair)

11 *E quindi uscimmo a riveder le stelle.*
And thence we came forth to see again the stars.

Divina Commedia "Inferno" canto 34, l. 139 (ca. 1310–1321) (translation by John D. Sinclair)

12 *E'n la sua volontade è nostra pace.*
And in His will is our peace.

Divina Commedia "Paradiso" canto 3, l. 85 (ca. 1310–1321) (translation by John D. Sinclair)

13 *Tu proverai sì come sa di sale*
Lo pane altrui, e comeè duro calle
Lo scendere e 'l salir per l'altrui scale.
Thou shalt prove how salt is the taste of another man's bread and how hard is the way up and down another man's stairs.

Divina Commedia "Paradiso" canto 17, l. 58 (ca. 1310–1321) (translation by John D. Sinclair)

14 *L' amor che move il sole e l'altre stelle.*
The Love that moves the sun and the other stars.

Divina Commedia "Paradiso" canto 33, l. 145 (ca. 1310–1321) (translation by John D. Sinclair)

Georges Jacques Danton

French revolutionary leader, 1759–1794

1 *De l'audace, et encore de l'audace, et toujours de l'audace!*
Boldness, and again boldness, and always boldness!

Speech to Legislative Committee of General Defence, 2 Sept. 1792

2 [*To his executioner, 5 Apr. 1794:*] Thou wilt show my head to the people: it is worth showing.

Quoted in Thomas Carlyle, *History of the French Revolution* (1837)

Lorenzo Da Ponte (Emmanuele Conegliano)

Italian librettist, 1749–1838

1 *Così fan tutte le belle.*

That's what all beautiful women do.

Le Nozze di Figaro (opera with music by Wolfgang Amadeus Mozart), act 1 (1778). *Così Fan Tutte* (That's What All Women Do) was the title of a Mozart/Da Ponte opera in 1790.

2 *Madamina, il catalogo è questo delle belle che ama il padron mio. In Italia sei cento e quaranta, in Almagna due cento e trent' una. Cento in Francia, in Turchia novant' una, ma in Ispagne, ma in Ispagna son già mille e tre!*

Dear my lady, this is the list of the beauties that my master has loved. Of Italians six hundred and forty, and in Germany two hundred thirty. Hundred in France and in Turkey 'twas ninety, Ah! but in Spain, ah! but in Spain were a thousand and three!

Don Giovanni (opera with music by Wolfgang Amadeus Mozart), act 1 (1787)

Hugh Antoine d'Arcy

French-born U.S. writer, 1843–1925

1 "Say, boys! if you give me just another whiskey I'll be glad,
And I'll draw right here a picture of the face that drove me mad.
Give me that piece of chalk with which you mark the baseball score,
You shall see the lovely Madeleine upon the bar-room floor."

"The Face upon the Floor" l. 61 (1887)

2 The vagabond began
To sketch a face that well might buy the soul of any man.
Then, as he placed another lock upon the shapely head,
With a fearful shriek, he leaped and fell across the picture—dead.

"The Face upon the Floor" l. 65 (1887)

Joe Darion

U.S. songwriter, 1917–2001

1 To dream the impossible dream,
To fight the unbeatable foe,
To bear with unbearable sorrow,
To run where the brave dare not go.

"The Impossible Dream (The Quest)" (song) (1965). This song was featured in the musical *Man of La Mancha*, book by Dale Wasserman. Wasserman had earlier included "To dream the impossible dream. To fight the unbeatable foe" in dialogue in his nonmusical teleplay *I, Don Quixote* (1959). It seems likely that Wasserman derived these key lines, perhaps unconsciously, from publicity matter appearing in a 1930 printing of Paul Kesler's play *Don Quixote: A Dramatization of Cervantes' Novel*. The publicity matter included: "To dream the impossible dream; to fight the unbeatable foe . . . these things are only for the quixotic few."

Byron Darnton

U.S. journalist, 1897–1942

1 No man who hates dogs and children can be all bad.

Quoted in *Harper's Magazine*, Nov. 1937. Usually attributed to Leo Rosten or W. C. Fields, but the Darnton remark predates these. In the *Harper's* article by Cedric Worth, "Dog Food for Thought," Worth recounts: "One afternoon a dog monopolized a small cocktail party on a penthouse roof. A dozen adults, instead of shifting pleasantly from business to evening gear, heard the symptoms of and remedies for mange recited and watched a small animal chase a ball round the floor. Several of us left at the same time. There was silence in the elevator for a few floors and then Mr. Byron Darnton relieved himself of a deathless truth. 'No man who hates dogs and children,' he said, 'can be all bad.'"

Charles B. Darrow

U.S. inventor, 1889–1967

1 Go to jail. Go directly to jail. Do not pass go. Do not collect $200.

Instruction in *Monopoly* board game (1933)

Clarence S. Darrow

U.S. lawyer, 1857–1938

1 I do not believe there is any sort of distinction between the real moral conditions of the people in and out of jail. One is just as good as the other. . . . I do not believe that people are in jail because they deserve to be. They are in jail

simply because they cannot avoid it on account of circumstances which are entirely beyond their control and for which they are in no way responsible.

Address to prisoners in Cook County Jail, Chicago, Ill. (1902)

2 You might as well hang a man because he is ill as because he is a criminal.

Crime: Its Cause and Treatment (1922)

3 Your Honor stands between the past and the future. You may hang these boys; you may hang them by the neck until they are dead. But in doing it you will turn your face toward the past. In doing it you are making it harder for every other boy who, in ignorance and darkness, must grope his way through the mazes which only childhood knows.

Closing argument in Leopold-Loeb trial, Chicago, Ill., 22 Aug. 1924

4 I am pleading for the future. I am pleading for a time when hatred and cruelty will not control the hearts of men, when we can learn by reason and judgment and understanding and faith that all life is worth saving, and that mercy is the highest attribute of man.

Closing argument in Leopold-Loeb trial, Chicago, Ill., 22 Aug. 1924

5 I do not consider it an insult, but rather a compliment to be called an agnostic. I do not pretend to know where many ignorant men are sure; that is all that agnosticism means.

Speech at Scopes trial, Dayton, Tenn., 15 July 1925

6 We are all murderers at heart. . . . I never killed anybody, but I often read an obituary notice with great satisfaction.

Testimony before House of Representatives Subcommittee on Judiciary, 1 Feb. 1926. Darrow had made a similar statement in a 13 Nov. 1922 speech printed in *The Institution Quarterly*, Sept.–Dec. 1922.

7 I don't believe in God because I don't believe in Mother Goose.

Speech, Toronto, Canada, 1930

8 Whenever I hear people discussing birth-control I always remember that I was the fifth.

The Story of My Life ch. 2 (1932)

9 There is no such thing as justice—in or out of court.

Quoted in *N.Y. Times*, 19 Apr. 1936

10 When I was a boy I was told that anybody could become President. I'm beginning to believe it.

Quoted in Irving Stone, *Clarence Darrow for the Defense* (1941)

Charles Darwin
English naturalist, 1809–1882

1 Origin of man now proved.—Metaphysics must flourish.—He who understands baboon would do more towards metaphysics than Locke.

Notebook, 16 Aug. 1838

2 I never saw a more striking coincidence. If [Alfred Russel] Wallace had my M.S. sketch written out in 1842 he could not have made a better short abstract! Even his terms now stand as Heads of my Chapters.

Letter to Charles Lyell, 18 June 1858

3 Owing to this struggle for life, any variation, however slight and from whatever cause proceeding, if it be in any degree profitable to an individual of any species, in its infinitely complex relations to other organic beings and to external nature, will tend to the preservation of that individual, and will generally be inherited by its offspring. The offspring, also, will thus have a better chance of surviving.

On the Origin of Species ch. 3 (1859)

4 I have called this principle, by which each slight variation, if useful, is preserved, by the term of Natural Selection, in order to mark its relation to man's power of selection.

On the Origin of Species ch. 3 (1859)

5 We will now discuss in a little more detail the Struggle for Existence.

On the Origin of Species ch. 3 (1859)
See Malthus 2

6 Thus, from the war of nature, from famine and death, the most exalted object which we are capable of conceiving, namely, the production of the higher animals, directly follows. There is grandeur in this view of life, with its several powers, having been originally breathed into a few forms or into one; and that, whilst this planet has gone cycling on according to the

fixed law of gravity, from so simple a beginning endless forms most beautiful and most wonderful have been, and are being, evolved.
On the Origin of Species ch. 14 (1859)

7 But the expression often used by Mr. Herbert Spencer of the Survival of the Fittest is more accurate, and is sometimes equally convenient.
On the Origin of Species, 5th ed., ch. 3 (1869)
See Philander Johnson 1; Herbert Spencer 5; Herbert Spencer 6

8 I cannot look at the universe as the result of blind chance, yet I can see no evidence of beneficent design or indeed of design of any kind, in the details.
Letter to J. D. Hooker, 12 July 1870

9 The Simiadae then branched off into two great stems, the New World and Old World monkeys; and from the latter at a remote period, Man, the wonder and the glory of the universe, proceeded.
The Descent of Man ch. 6 (1871)

10 False facts are highly injurious to the progress of science, for they often long endure; but false views, if supported by some evidence, do little harm, as everyone takes a salutary pleasure in proving their falseness; and when this is done, one path towards error is closed and the road to truth is often at the same time opened.
The Descent of Man ch. 21 (1871)

11 We thus learn that man is descended from a hairy quadruped, furnished with a tail and pointed ears, probably arboreal in its habits, and an inhabitant of the Old World.
The Descent of Man ch. 21 (1871)

12 For my own part I would as soon be descended from that heroic little monkey, who braved his dreaded enemy in order to save the life of his keeper; or from that old baboon, who, descending from the mountains, carried away in triumph his young comrade from a crowd of astonished dogs—as from a savage who delights to torture his enemies, offers up bloody sacrifices, practices infanticide without remorse, treats his wives like slaves, knows no decency, and is haunted by the grossest superstitions.
The Descent of Man ch. 21 (1871)

13 Man with all his noble qualities . . . with his god-like intellect which has penetrated into the movements and constitution of the solar system . . . still bears in his bodily frame the indelible stamp of his lowly origin.
The Descent of Man ch. 21 (1871)

Erasmus Darwin
English scientist and poet, 1731–1802

1 Would it be too bold to imagine, that all warm-blooded animals have arisen from one living filament, which THE GREAT FIRST CAUSE endued with animality, with the power of acquiring new parts . . . and of delivering down those improvements by generation to its posterity, world without end!
Zoonomia vol. 1 (1794)

Francis Darwin
English botanist, 1848–1925

1 In science the credit goes to the man who convinces the world, not to the man to whom the idea first occurs.
Eugenics Review, Apr. 1914

Jules Dassin
U.S.-born French film director, 1911–2008

1 *Pote tin Kyriaki.*
Never on Sunday.
Title of motion picture (1960)

Harry M. Daugherty
U.S. politician, 1860–1941

1 [*Remarks by General Leonard Wood in a speech, Toledo, Ohio, 1 Apr. 1920:*] What a distinguished political leader [Daugherty] recently said in Washington would be done in the 1920 Presidential nomination, namely, that about 2:11 A.M. the nomination would be settled by fifteen or twenty tired men sitting around a table in a smoke-filled room behind locked doors.
Reported in *N.Y. Times,* 2 Apr. 1920. *Safire's New Political Dictionary* gives a detailed account of Associated Press reporter Kirke Simpson suggesting the phrase *smoke-filled room* to Warren G. Harding's supporter, Daugherty, during the Republican National Convention in June 1920. However, the

Apr. 1920 speech above proves that *smoke-filled room* was used earlier in the year. It appears that Wood meant Daugherty as the "distinguished political leader," since an article of 21 Feb. 1920 in the same newspaper quoted Daugherty as predicting that "about eleven minutes after 2 o'clock on Friday morning at the convention, when fifteen or twenty men, somewhat weary, are sitting around a table some one of them will say: 'Who will we nominate?' At that decisive time the friends of Senator Harding can suggest him." (Harding was in fact nominated as Daugherty had predicted, including the time, which was approximately 2:00 in the morning.). It is possible, since the 21 Feb. article quoting Daugherty did not include the words "smoke-filled room," that the phrase was introduced by Wood.

Hugh "Duffy" Daugherty
U.S. football coach, 1915–1987

1 Football is not a contact sport; it's a collision sport. Dancing is a good example of a contact sport.
Quoted in *L.A. Times*, 5 Oct. 1963

Hal David
U.S. songwriter, 1921–2012

1 Why do stars fall down from the sky
Every time you walk by?
Just like me they long to be
Close to you.
"(They Long to Be) Close to You" (song) (1963)

2 What the world needs now is love, sweet love,
It's the only thing that there's just too little of.
"What the World Needs Now Is Love" (song) (1965)

3 What's it all about Alfie?
Is it just for the moment we live?
"Alfie" (song) (1966)

4 The moment I wake up
Before I put on my make-up
I say a little prayer for you.
"I Say a Little Prayer" (song) (1966)

5 Raindrops keep fallin' on my head,
But that doesn't mean my eyes will soon be turnin' red.
Cryin's not for me
'Cause I'm never gonna stop the rain by complainin'.
"Raindrops Keep Fallin' on My Head" (song) (1969)

Larry David
U.S. television producer, 1947–

1 It's about nothing, everything else is about something; this, it's about nothing.
Seinfeld (television show), 16 Sept. 1992

Ray Davies
English rock singer and songwriter, 1944–

1 Well I'm not dumb but I can't understand
Why she walked like a woman and talked like a man.
"Lola" (song) (1970)

2 Girls will be boys and boys will be girls
It's a mixed up muddled up shook up world.
"Lola" (song) (1970)

3 Everybody's a dreamer and everybody's a star,
And everybody's in movies, it doesn't matter who you are.
There are stars in every city,
In every house and every street,
And if you walk down Hollywood Boulevard
Their names are written in concrete!
"Celluloid Heroes" (song) (1972)

4 If you covered him with garbage,
George Sanders would still have style,
And if you stamped on Mickey Rooney
He would still turn round and smile,
But please don't tread on dearest Marilyn
'Cos she's not very tough,
She should have been made of iron or steel,
But she was only made of flesh and blood.
"Celluloid Heroes" (song) (1972)

Robertson Davies
Canadian novelist, 1913–1995

1 Canada is not really a place where you are encouraged to have large spiritual adventures.
The Enthusiasms of Robertson Davies (1990)

2 About 60 years ago, I said to my father, "Old Mr. Senex is showing his age; he sometimes talks quite stupidly." My father replied, "That isn't age. He's always been stupid. He is just losing his ability to conceal it."
N.Y. Times Book Review, 12 May 1991

W. H. (William Henry) Davies
Welsh poet, 1871–1940

1 What is this life if, full of care,
We have no time to stand and stare?
"Leisure" l. 1 (1911)

Angela Y. Davis
U.S. political activist, 1944–

1 Jails and prisons are designed to break
human beings, to convert the population into
specimens in a zoo—obedient to our keepers,
but dangerous to each other.
Angela Davis: An Autobiography ch. 1 (1974)

2 It is both humiliating and humbling to discover
that a single generation after the events that
constructed me as a public personality, I am
remembered as a hairdo.
"Afro Images: Politics, Fashion, and Nostalgia"
(1994)

Bette Davis
U.S. actress, 1908–1989

1 [*"Situation wanted" advertisement placed in
Hollywood trade papers after Davis's career had
declined:*] MOTHER OF THREE . . . DIVORCÉE.
AMERICAN. THIRTY YEARS EXPERIENCE AS AN
ACTRESS IN MOTION PICTURES. MOBILE STILL
AND MORE AFFABLE THAN RUMOR WOULD HAVE
IT. WANTS STEADY EMPLOYMENT IN HOLLYWOOD.
(HAS HAD BROADWAY.) . . . REFERENCES UPON
REQUEST.
Hollywood Reporter, 21 Sept. 1962

2 [*Of a starlet:*] There, standing at the piano, was
the original good time who had been had by all.
Attributed in Leslie Halliwell, *The Filmgoer's Book
of Quotes* (1973). Although Davis is now associated
with this remark, "There goes the original good time
that's been had by all" was credited to actress Leonora
Corbett in Earl Wilson, *Pikes Peak or Bust* (1946).
See Stevie Smith 3

David Davis
U.S. judge and political leader, 1815–1886

1 The Constitution of the United States is a
law for rulers and people, equally in war and
in peace, and covers with the shield of its
protection all classes of men, at all times, and
under all circumstances. No doctrine, involving
more pernicious consequences, was ever
invented by the wit of man than that any of its
provisions can be suspended during any of the
great exigencies of government.
Ex parte Milligan (1867)

Gussie L. Davis
U.S. songwriter, 1863–1899

1 Irene, goodnight,
Irene, goodnight,
Goodnight, Irene,
Goodnight, Irene,
I'll see you in my dreams.
"Irene, Good Night" (song) (1886)

Jefferson Davis
U.S. Confederate president, 1808–1889

1 If the Confederacy falls, there should be written
on its tombstone, "Died of a theory."
The Rise and Fall of the Confederate Government ch. 14
(1881). Davis was quoting a remark he had made in
1864.

Jimmie Davis
U.S. politician and songwriter, 1899–2000

1 You are my sunshine, my only sunshine,
You make me happy when skies are gray.
You'll never know, dear, how much I love you.
Please don't take my sunshine away.
"You Are My Sunshine" (song) (1930). Cowritten
with Charles Mitchell.

John W. Davis
U.S. lawyer and political leader, 1873–1955

1 True, we [lawyers] build no bridges. We raise
no towers. We construct no engines. We paint
no pictures—unless as amateurs for our own
principal amusement. There is little of all
that we do which the eye of man can see. But
we smooth out difficulties; we relieve stress;
we correct mistakes; we take up other men's
burdens and by our efforts we make possible
the peaceful life of men in a peaceful state.
Address, New York, N.Y., 16 Mar. 1946

2 Somewhere, sometime to every principle comes a moment of repose when it has been so often announced, so confidently relied upon, so long continued, that it passes the limits of judicial discretion and disturbance.

Argument before the U.S. Supreme Court, *Brown v. Board of Education*, Dec. 1953

Miles Davis

U.S. jazz musician, 1926–1991

1 A legend is an old man with a cane known for what he used to do. I'm still doing it.

Quoted in *International Herald Tribune*, 17 July 1991

2 If you understood everything I said, you'd be me.

Quoted in *Independent* (London), 6 Oct. 1991

Ossie Davis

U.S. actor and writer, 1917–2005

1 We shall know him . . . for what he was and is—a Prince, our own black shining Prince, who didn't hesitate to die, because he loved us so.

Eulogy at funeral of Malcolm X, New York, N.Y., 27 Feb. 1965

Sammy Davis, Jr.

U.S. entertainer, 1925–1990

1 Being a star has made it possible for me to get insulted in places where the average Negro could never *hope* to go and get insulted.

Yes I Can pt. 3, ch. 23 (1965)

Richard Dawkins

English biologist, 1941–

1 Let us understand what our own selfish genes are up to, because we may then at least have the chance to upset their designs.

The Selfish Gene ch. 1 (1976)

2 Much as we might wish to believe otherwise, universal love and the welfare of the species as a whole are concepts which simply do not make evolutionary sense.

The Selfish Gene ch. 1 (1976)

3 They are in you and in me; they created us, body and mind; and their preservation is the ultimate rationale for our existence . . . they go by the name of genes, and we are their survival machines.

The Selfish Gene ch. 2 (1976)

4 Natural selection, the blind, unconscious, automatic process which Darwin discovered, and which we now know is the explanation for the existence and apparently purposeful form of all life, has no purpose in mind. It has no mind and no mind's eye. It does not plan for the future. It has no vision, no foresight, no sight at all. If it can be said to play the role of watchmaker in nature, it is the *blind* watchmaker.

The Blind Watchmaker ch. 1 (1986)
See William Paley 3

5 The universe we obey has precisely the properties we should expect if there is, at bottom, no design, no purpose, no evil, and no good, nothing but blind, pitiless indifference. . . . DNA neither cares nor knows. DNA just is. And we dance to its music.

River Out of Eden ch. 4 (1995)

6 We are going to die, and that makes us the lucky ones. Most people are never going to die because they are never going to be born.

Unweaving the Rainbow ch. 1 (1998)

7 We are all atheists about most of the gods that humanity has ever believed in. Some of us just go one god further.

Forbes ASAP, 4 Oct. 1999

Clarence S. Day

U.S. writer, 1874–1935

1 If you don't go to other men's funerals . . . they won't go to yours.

Life with Father "Father Plans to Get Out" (1920). Although this quip is strongly associated with Day, Barry Popik has found "If I don't attend other people's funerals they won't come to mine" in James Frederick Shaw Kennedy, *The Youth of the Period* (1876).

2 The world of books is the most remarkable creation of man. Nothing else that he builds ever lasts. Monuments fall; nations perish; civilizations grow old and die out; and, after an era of darkness, new races build others. But in the world of books are volumes that have seen this happen again and again, and yet live on,

still young, still as fresh as the day they were written, still telling men's hearts of the hearts of men centuries dead.

And even the books that do not last long, penetrate their own times at last, sailing farther than Ulysses even dreamed of, like ships on the seas. It is the author's part to call into being their cargoes and passengers,—living thoughts and rich bales of study and jeweled ideas. And as for the publishers, it is they who build the fleet, plan the voyage, and sail on, facing wreck, till they find every possible harbor that will value their burden.

The Story of the Yale University Press Told by a Friend (1920)

3 What fairy story, what tale from the Arabian Nights of the jinns, is a hundredth part as wonderful as this true fairy story of simians! It is so much more heartening, too, than the tales we invent. A universe capable of giving birth to many such accidents is—blind or not—a good world to live in, a promising universe. . . . We once thought we lived on God's footstool; it may be a throne.

This Simian World ch. 19 (1920)

Moshe Dayan
Israeli military leader and politician, 1915–1981

1 If you want to make peace, you don't talk to your friends. You talk to your enemies.
Quoted in Barbara Rowes, *The Book of Quotes* (1979)

Howard Dean
U.S. politician, 1948–

1 Not only are we going to New Hampshire, Tom Harkin, we're going to South Carolina and Oklahoma and Arizona and North Dakota and New Mexico, and we're going to California and Texas and New York. And we're going to South Dakota and Oregon and Washington and Michigan. And then we're going to Washington, D.C. To take back the White House. Yeah.
Remarks after Iowa caucuses, Des Moines, Iowa, 19 Jan. 2004. The "Yeah" at the end of these

comments was perceived as a scream and contributed substantially to the decline of his presidential candidacy.

Jay Hanna "Dizzy" Dean
U.S. baseball player, 1910–1974

1 You can stick a fork in him folks—he's done.
Quoted in *Berkshire Evening Eagle* (Pittsfield, Mass.), 25 July 1944

2 It ain't braggin' if you can do it.
Quoted in *Wash. Post*, 3 Feb. 1983

John W. Dean
U.S. government official, 1938–

1 We have a cancer within, close to the Presidency, that is growing.
Nixon Presidential Transcripts, 21 Mar. 1973

Simone de Beauvoir
French novelist and feminist, 1908–1986

1 She appears essentially to the male as a sexual being. . . . She is defined and differentiated with reference to man and not he with reference to her; she is the incidental, the inessential as opposed to the essential. He is the Subject, he is the Absolute—she is the Other.
The Second Sex vol. 1, introduction (1949) (translation by H. M. Parshley)

2 *On ne naît pas femme, on le devient.*
One is not born, but rather becomes, a woman.
The Second Sex vol. 2, pt. 1, ch. 1 (1949) (translation by H. M. Parshley)

3 Few tasks are more like the torture of Sisyphus than housework, with its endless repetition. . . . The housewife wears herself out marking time: she makes nothing, simply perpetuates the present.
The Second Sex vol. 2, pt. 2, ch 1 (1949) (translation by H. M. Parshley)

Edward De Bono
Maltese-born English psychologist, 1933–

1 Some people are aware of another sort of thinking which . . . leads to those simple ideas that are obvious only after they have been thought of. . . . The term "lateral thinking"

has been coined to describe this other sort of thinking; "vertical thinking" is used to denote the conventional logical process.
The Use of Lateral Thinking foreword (1967)

Guy Debord
French philosopher, 1931–1994

1 Quotations are useful in periods of ignorance or obscurantist beliefs.
Panegyric pt. 1 (1989)

Régis Debray
French philosopher and journalist, 1940–

1 International life is right-wing, like nature. The social contract is left-wing, like humanity.
Charles de Gaulle ch. 7 (1994)

Eugene V. Debs
U.S. socialist, 1855–1926

1 When great changes occur in history, when great principles are involved, as a rule the majority are wrong. The minority are right.
Speech at trial, Cleveland, Ohio, 12 Sept. 1918
See Ibsen 16; Sydney Smith 6

2 While there is a lower class, I am in it; while there is a criminal element, I am of it; while there is a soul in prison, I am not free.
Speech at trial, Cleveland, Ohio, 14 Sept. 1918

Stephen Decatur
U.S. naval officer, 1779–1820

1 Our country! In her intercourse with foreign nations, may she always be in the right; but our country, right or wrong.
Toast at dinner, Norfolk, Va., Apr. 1816. This wording is quoted in Alexander Slidell Mackenzie, *Life of Stephen Decatur* (1848). According to *Respectfully Quoted*, ed. Suzy Platt, "*Niles' Weekly Register,* published in Baltimore, Maryland, gave a slightly different version in its April 20, 1816, issue (p. 136). A number of the toasts at the dinner for Decatur were included, probably reprinted from a Virginia newspaper, and Decatur's appeared as '*Our country—* In her intercourse with foreign nations may she always be in the *right*, and always *successful, right* or *wrong.*'"
See Chesterton 3; Schurz 1; Twain 114

Midge Decter
U.S. author, 1927–

1 Women's Liberation calls it enslavement but the real truth about the sexual revolution is that it has made of sex an almost chaotically limitless and therefore unmanageable realm in the life of women.
The New Chastity and Other Arguments Against Women's Liberation ch. 2 (1972)

Daniel Defoe
English novelist and journalist, 1660–1731

1 Why then should women be denied the benefits of instruction? If knowledge and understanding had been useless additions to the sex, God almighty would never have given them capacities.
An Essay upon Projects "Of Academies: An Academy for Women" (1697)

2 Nature has left this tincture in the blood,
That all men wou'd be tyrants if they cou'd.
The History of the Kentish Petition addenda (1701)
See Abigail Adams 1

3 It happened one day, about noon, going towards my boat, I was exceedingly surprised with the print of a man's naked foot on the shore, which was very plain to be seen in the sand. I stood like one thunderstruck, or as if I had seen an apparition.
Robinson Crusoe (1719)

4 My man Friday.
Robinson Crusoe (1719)

John William De Forest
U.S. writer, 1826–1906

1 The Great American Novel.
Title of article, *Nation,* 9 Jan. 1868

Edgar Degas
French artist, 1834–1917

1 Art is vice. You don't marry it legitimately, you rape it.
Quoted in Paul Lafond, *Degas* (1918)

2 Everybody has talent at twenty-five. The difficult thing is to have it at fifty.
Quoted in R. H. Ives Gammell, *The Shop-Talk of Edgar Degas* (1961)

Charles de Gaulle
French general and president, 1890–1970

1 France has lost a battle. But France has not lost the war!
Proclamation, 18 June 1940

2 Faced by the bewilderment of my countrymen, by the disintegration of a government in thrall to the enemy, by the fact that the institutions of my country are incapable, at the moment, of functioning, I General de Gaulle, a French soldier and military leader, realize that I now speak for France.
Speech, London, 19 June 1940

3 Since they whose duty it was to wield the sword of France have let it fall shattered to the ground, I have taken up the broken blade.
Radio address, 13 July 1940

4 All my life, I have had a certain idea of France.
Les Mémoires de Guerre vol. 1 (1954)

5 France cannot be France without greatness.
Les Mémoires de Guerre vol. 1 (1954)

6 *Je vous ai compris.*
I have understood you.
Speech to French colonists, Algiers, 4 June 1958

7 Treaties, you see, are like girls and roses: they last while they last.
Speech at Elysée Palace, 2 July 1963

8 *Vive le Québec! Vive le Québec libre! Vive le Canada français! Vive la France!*
Long live Quebec! Long live Free Quebec! Long live French Canada! Long live France!
Address to crowd before City Hall, Montreal, Canada, 24 July 1967

9 [*Responding to being compared to Robespierre:*] I always thought I was Jeanne d'Arc and Bonaparte—how little one knows oneself.
Quoted in *Figaro Littéraire* (1958)

10 Politics are too serious a matter to be left to the politicians.
Quoted in Clement Attlee, *A Prime Minister Remembers* (1961). "Politics has become too serious a matter to be left to politicians" appeared in an article by T. S. Eliot in the *Monthly Criterion*, Nov. 1927.
See Briand 2; Clemenceau 4

11 *Comment voulez-vous gouverner un pays qui a deux cent quarante-six variétés de fromage?*

How can anyone govern a nation that has two hundred and forty-six different kinds of cheese?
Quoted in Ernest Mignon, *Les Mots du Général* (1962). De Gaulle had earlier been quoted in the *N.Y. Times Magazine,* 29 June 1958, as saying, "How can one conceive of a one-party system in a country that has over two hundred varieties of cheeses?"

12 [*Remark at funeral of his disabled daughter, 1948:*] *Maintenant elle est comme les autres.*
Now she is like everybody else.
Quoted in Jean Lacouture, *De Gaulle* (1965)

13 [*Of Jean-Paul Sartre's political agitation:*] One does not arrest Voltaire.
Quoted in *Encounter,* June 1975

F. W. (Frederik Willem) de Klerk
South African statesman, 1936–

1 [*Of the results of a South African constitutional referendum:*] Today we have closed the book on apartheid.
Speech, Cape Town, South Africa, 18 Mar. 1992

Willem de Kooning
Dutch-born U.S. painter, 1904–1997

1 Flesh was the reason why oil painting was invented.
Quoted in *N.Y. Times,* 14 Oct. 1974

Walter de la Mare
English poet and novelist, 1873–1956

1 "Is there anybody there?" said the Traveller, Knocking on the moonlit door.
"The Listeners" l. 1 (1912)

2 "Tell them I came, and no one answered, That I kept my word," he said.
"The Listeners" l. 27 (1912)

Raphael De Leon
Trinidadian calypso singer and songwriter, 1908–1999

1 If you want to be happy living a king's life Never make a pretty woman your wife.
"Ugly Woman" (song) (1934)

2 That's from a logical point of view To always love a woman uglier than you.
"Ugly Woman" (song) (1934)

Jacques Delille

French poet, 1738–1813

1 *Le sort fait les parents, le choix fait les amis.*
Fate chooses our relatives, we choose our
friends.
Malheur et Pitié canto 1 (1803)

Don DeLillo

U.S. novelist, 1936–

1 This was worse than a retched nightmare. It
was the nightmare of real things, the fallen
wonder of the world.
The Names ch. 14 (1982)

2 Everything we need that is not food or love
is here in the tabloid racks. The tales of the
supernatural and the extraterrestrial. The
miracle vitamins, the cures for cancer, the
remedies for obesity. The cults of the famous
and the dead.
White Noise ch. 40 (1985)

3 A conspiracy is everything that ordinary
life is not. It's the inside game, cold, sure,
undistracted, forever closed off to us. We
are the flawed ones, the innocents, trying to
make some rough sense of the daily jostle.
Conspirators have a logic and a daring beyond
our reach.
Libra pt. 2 (1988)

Paul De Man

Belgian-born U.S. literary critic, 1919–1983

1 Death is a displaced name for a linguistic
predicament.
Quoted in David Lehman, *Signs of the Times* (1991)

W. Edwards Deming

U.S. management theorist, 1900–1993

1 There is no substitute for knowledge.
Quoted in *Wash. Post*, 29 May 1988

Democritus

Greek philosopher, ca. 460 B.C.–ca. 370 B.C.

1 By convention there is color, by convention
sweetness, by convention bitterness, but in
reality there are atoms and space.
Fragment 125

2 The first principles of the universe are atoms
and empty space. . . . The atoms are unlimited
in size and number, and they are borne along
in the whole universe in a vortex, and thereby
generate all composite things—fire, water, air,
earth. For even these are conglomerations of
given atoms.
Quoted in Diogenes Laertius, *Lives of Eminent
Philosophers*

Jack Dempsey

U.S. boxer, 1895–1983

1 I forgot to duck.
Quoted in *N.Y. Times*, 20 Feb. 1927. Said to his
wife after losing the world heavyweight boxing
championship to Gene Tunney, 23 Sept. 1926.
President Ronald W. Reagan joked to his wife,
"Honey, I forgot to duck!" after John Hinckley tried
to assassinate him 30 Mar. 1981.

Deng Xiaoping

Chinese political leader, 1904–1997

1 There are no fundamental contradictions
between a socialist system and a market
economy.
Interview, *Time*, 4 Nov. 1985

2 It doesn't matter whether a cat is black or white
as long as it catches mice.
Quoted in *Wash. Post*, 12 Aug. 1973. According to
Gucheng Li, *A Glossary of Political Terms of the People's
Republic of China*, at a June 1962 meeting of the
Secretariat of the Central Committee Deng quoted
a farmer about the boundary between communism
and capitalism: "We don't care if it is a black cat or
yellow cat; as long as it catches mice, it's a good cat."
During the Cultural Revolution the *People's Daily*,
3 Dec. 1967, ran an article subtitled "Repudiate the
Reactionary Fallacy of 'Black Cat, White Cat, as Long
as It Catches Mice, It's a Good Cat'" (translation of
Chinese original). The yellow/black saying appears to
be a Chinese proverb dating back to the seventeenth
century or earlier.

3 To get rich is glorious.
Attributed in *Adweek*, 16 Sept. 1985. Widely attributed
to Deng, but there is no evidence that he ever used
it. It was popularized by Orville Schell's 1984 book,
To Get Rich Is Glorious: China in the '80s. Schell has
stated that he probably encountered the phrase in
Chinese media reports.

Thomas Denman, First Baron Denman

English judge, 1779–1854

1 Trial by jury, instead of being a security to persons who are accused, will be a delusion, a mockery, and a snare.

O'Connell v. The Queen (1844)

Daniel Dennett

U.S. philosopher, 1942–

1 The juvenile sea squirt wanders through the sea searching for a suitable rock or hunk of coral to cling to and make its home for life. For this task, it has a rudimentary nervous system. When it finds its spot and takes root, it doesn't need its brain anymore so it eats it! (It's rather like getting tenure.)

Consciousness Explained ch. 7 (1991)

John Dennis

English writer, 1657–1734

1 The man that will make such an execrable pun as that . . . will pick my pocket.

Quoted in Benjamin Victor, *An Epistle to Sir Richard Steele* 2nd ed. (1722)

2 [*Upon hearing thunder sound effects invented by him used in a performance of* Macbeth, *after his own play featuring the effects had closed following a short run at the same theater, 1709:*] They will not let my Play run, but steal my Thunder.

Quoted in Thomas Whincop, *Scanderbeg* (1747). Alexander Pope, *The Dunciad* (note to book 2) (1729), quotes Dennis: "S'death! that is *my* thunder!"

John Denver (Henry John Deutschendorf, Jr.)

U.S. singer, 1943–1997

1 All my bags are packed, I'm ready to go
I'm standing here outside your door . . .
I'm leavin' on a jet plane
Don't know when I'll be back again.

"Leaving on a Jet Plane" (song) (1967)

Chauncey M. Depew

U.S. lawyer and politician, 1834–1928

1 I get my exercise serving as a pallbearer to my friends who take exercise.

Quoted in *L.A. Times*, 4 May 1954. Depew lived to be ninety-four years old.

Thomas De Quincey

English essayist and critic, 1785–1859

1 If once a man indulges himself in murder, very soon he comes to think little of robbing; and from robbing he comes next to drinking and sabbath-breaking, and from that to incivility and procrastination.

"On Murder, Considered as One of the Fine Arts" (1839)

Jacques Derrida

Algerian-born French philosopher and critic, 1930–2004

1 *Il n'y a pas de hors-texte.*
There is nothing outside of the text.

Of Grammatology pt. 2, sec. 2 (1967)

Anita Desai

Indian novelist, 1937–

1 Do you know anyone who would—secretly, sincerely, in his innermost self—*really* prefer to return to childhood?

The Clear Light of Day ch. 1 (1980)

René Descartes

French philosopher and mathematician, 1596–1650

1 Good sense is the best distributed thing in the world: for everyone thinks himself so well endowed with it that even those who are the hardest to please in everything else do not usually desire more of it than they possess.

Le Discours de la Méthode pt. 1 (1637)

2 While I was returning to the army from the coronation of the Emperor, the onset of winter detained me in quarters where, finding no conversation to divert me and fortunately having no cares or passions to trouble me, I stayed all day shut up alone in a stove-heated room, where I was completely free to converse with myself about my own thoughts.

Le Discours de la Méthode pt. 1 (1637)

3 The first [rule] was never to accept anything as true if I did not have evident knowledge of its truth: that is, carefully to avoid precipitate conclusions and preconceptions, and to include

nothing more in my judgements than what presented itself to my mind so clearly and so distinctly that I had no occasion to call it into doubt.

Le Discours de la Méthode pt. 1 (1637)

4 *Je pense, donc je suis.*
I think, therefore I am.

Le Discours de la Méthode pt. 4 (1637). Also famous in the form *"Cogito, ergo sum,"* from the Latin edition (1641) of this book.
See Bierce 22

5 Some years ago I was struck by the large number of falsehoods that I had accepted as true in my childhood, and by the highly doubtful nature of the whole edifice that I had subsequently based on them. I realized that it was necessary, once in the course of my life, to demolish everything completely and start again right from the foundations if I wanted to establish anything at all in the sciences that was stable and likely to last.

Meditationes "Meditation I" (1641)

6 But there is a deceiver of supreme power and cunning who is deliberately and constantly deceiving me. In that case I too undoubtedly exist, if he is deceiving me; and let him deceive me as much as he can, he will never bring it about that I am nothing so long as I think that I am something.

Meditationes "Meditation II" (1641)

7 It is quite evident that existence can no more be separated from the essence of God than the fact that its three angles equal two right angles can be separated from the idea of a triangle, or than the idea of a mountain can be separated from the idea of a valley. Hence it is just as much of a contradiction to think of God (that is, a supremely perfect being) lacking existence (that is, lacking a perfection), as it is to think of a mountain without a valley.

Meditationes "Meditation V" (1641)

8 It is contrary to reason to say that there is a vacuum or space in which there is absolutely nothing.

Principia Philosophiae pt. 2, sec. 16 (1644)

Philippe Néricault Destouches
French playwright, 1680–1754

1 Those not present are always wrong.

L'Obstacle Imprévu act 1, sc. 6 (1717)

Buddy DeSylva
U.S. songwriter, 1895–1950

1 So always look for the silver lining
And try to find the sunny side of life.

"Look for the Silver Lining" (song) (1920)
See Lena Ford 1; Proverbs 49

2 Though April showers may come your way,
They bring the flowers that bloom in May.

"April Showers" (song) (1921)

3 The moon belongs to ev'ryone,
The best things in life are free.

"The Best Things in Life Are Free" (song) (1927). Coauthored with Lew Brown and Ray Henderson.
See Howard E. Johnson 2

4 You're the Cream in My Coffee.

Title of song (1928). Coauthored with Lew Brown.

Eamonn de Valera
U.S.-born Irish president, 1882–1975

1 I was reared in a laborer's cottage here in Ireland. I have not lived solely among the intellectuals. The first fifteen years of my life that formed my character were lived among the Irish people down in Limerick; therefore I know what I am talking about, and whenever I wanted to know what the Irish people wanted, I had only to examine my own heart and it told me straight off what the Irish people wanted.

Speech in Dáil Éireann, 6 Jan. 1922

2 Soldiers of the Republic, Legion of the Rearguard: The Republic can no longer be defended successfully by your arms. Further sacrifice of life would now be in vain, and continuance of the struggle in arms unwise in the national interest and prejudicial to the future of our cause. Military victory must be allowed to rest for the moment with those who have destroyed the Republic. Other means must be sought to safeguard the Nation's right.

Message to Republican armed forces, 24 May 1923

3 That Ireland which we dreamed of would be the home of a people who valued material wealth only as a basis of right living, of a people who were satisfied with frugal comfort and devoted their leisure to the things of the spirit; a land whose countryside would be bright with cosy homesteads, whose fields and villages would be joyous with sounds of industry, the romping of sturdy children, the contests of athletic youths, the laughter of comely maidens; whose firesides would be the forums of the wisdom of serene old age.
Broadcast, 17 Mar. 1943

Peter De Vries
U.S. novelist, 1910–1993

1 It is the final proof of God's omnipotence that he need not exist in order to save us.
Mackerel Plaza ch. 1 (1958)

2 Nostalgia . . . ain't what it used to be.
Tents of Wickedness ch. 1 (1959)

Thomas Robert Dewar
Scottish distiller, 1864–1930

1 Minds are like parachutes—they function only when they are open.
Quoted in *Deseret News* (Salt Lake City, Utah), 7 Apr. 1928. Usually attributed to Dewar, but it should be noted that exactly the same words appeared, credited only to the *Louisville Times*, in the *Standard Examiner* (Ogden City, Utah), 20 Oct. 1927.

George Dewey
U.S. naval officer, 1837–1917

1 [*Order to the captain of his flagship* (Charles Vernon Gridley) *at the Battle of Manila Bay, 1 May 1898:*] You may fire when you are ready, Gridley.
Quoted in *Wash. Post,* 3 Oct. 1899

John Dewey
U.S. philosopher and educator, 1859–1952

1 The Great Society created by steam and electricity may be a society, but it is no community.
The Public and Its Problems ch. 3 (1927)
See Hamer 1; Lyndon Johnson 5; Lyndon Johnson 6; Lyndon Johnson 8; Wallas 1; William Wordsworth 30

Thomas E. Dewey
U.S. politician, 1902–1971

1 That's why it's time for a change!
Campaign speech, San Francisco, Calif., 21 Sept. 1944

John DeWitt
U.S. army officer, 1880–1962

1 There are indications that these [Japanese-Americans] are organized and ready for concerted action at a favorable opportunity. The very fact that no sabotage has taken place to date is a disturbing and confirming indication that such action will be taken.
Final Recommendation of the Commanding General, Western Defense Command and Fourth Army, Submitted to the Secretary of War, 14 Feb. 1942

Sergei Diaghilev
Russian ballet impresario, 1872–1929

1 [*To Jean Cocteau:*] *Étonne-moi.*
Astound me.
Quoted in *Journals of Jean Cocteau,* ed. Wallace Fowlie, ch. 1 (1956)

Diana, Princess of Wales
British princess, 1961–1997

1 I'd like to be a queen in people's hearts but I don't see myself being Queen of this country.
Interview on *Panorama* (television program), 20 Nov. 1995

2 [*Of her husband, Prince Charles, herself, and Charles's lover Camilla Parker Bowles:*] There were three of us in this marriage, so it was a bit crowded.
Interview on *Panorama* (television program), 20 Nov. 1995

3 You are going to get a big surprise with the next thing I do.
Quoted in *Guardian,* 16 July 1997

Porfirio Díaz
Mexican president, 1830–1915

1 Poor Mexico! So far from God, so close to the United States.
Attributed in Hudson Strode, *Timeless Mexico* (1944)

Philip K. Dick

U.S. science fiction writer, 1928–1982

1 Reality is that which when you stop believing in it, it doesn't go away.

Valis ch. 5 (1981). Originally appeared in a 1978 lecture by Dick entitled "How to Build a Universe That Doesn't Fall Apart in Two Days."
See Paktor 1

Charles Dickens

English novelist, 1812–1870

1 He had used the word [*humbug*] in its Pickwickian sense.

Pickwick Papers ch. 1 (1837)

2 I wants to make your flesh creep.

Pickwick Papers ch. 8 (1837)

3 "It's always best on these occasions to do what the mob do." "But suppose there are two mobs?" suggested Mr. Snodgrass. "Shout with the largest," replied Mr. Pickwick.

Pickwick Papers ch. 13 (1837)

4 Battledore and shuttlecock's a wery good game, vhen you an't the shuttlecock and two lawyers the battledores, in which case it gets too excitin' to be pleasant.

Pickwick Papers ch. 20 (1837)

5 Be wery careful o' vidders all your life.

Pickwick Papers ch. 20 (1837)

6 Dumb as a drum with a hole in it, sir.

Pickwick Papers ch. 25 (1837)

7 "Eccentricities of genius, Sam," said Mr. Pickwick.

Pickwick Papers ch. 30 (1837)

8 Keep yourself *to* yourself.

Pickwick Papers ch. 32 (1837)

9 Poetry's unnat'ral; no man ever talked poetry 'cept a beadle on boxin' day.

Pickwick Papers ch. 33 (1837)

10 A good, contented, well-breakfasted juryman, is a capital thing to get hold of. Discontented or hungry jurymen, my dear Sir, always find for the plaintiff.

Pickwick Papers ch. 34 (1837)

11 Oh Sammy, Sammy, vy worn't there a alleybi!

Pickwick Papers ch. 34 (1837)

12 She knows wot's wot, she does.

Pickwick Papers ch. 37 (1837)

13 *They* don't mind it; it's a regular holiday to them—all porter and skittles.

Pickwick Papers ch. 41 (1837)

14 Anythin' for a quiet life, as the man said wen he took the sitivation at the lighthouse.

Pickwick Papers ch. 43 (1837)

15 Please, sir, I want some more.

Oliver Twist ch. 2 (1838)

16 He avowed that among his intimate friends he was better known by the *sobriquet* of "The artful Dodger."

Oliver Twist ch. 8 (1838)

17 "Hard," replied the Dodger. "As Nails," added Charley Bates.

Oliver Twist ch. 9 (1838)

18 There is a passion *for hunting something* deeply implanted in the human breast.

Oliver Twist ch. 10 (1838)

19 I only know two sorts of boys. Mealy boys, and beef-faced boys.

Oliver Twist ch. 14 (1838)

20 [*Responding to being told that the law supposes a wife acts under a husband's direction:*] "If the law supposes that," said Mr. Bumble, . . . "the law is a ass—a idiot. If that's the eye of the law, the law's a bachelor; and the worst I wish the law is, that his eye may be opened by experience—by experience."

Oliver Twist ch. 51 (1838).
See Glapthorne 1

21 He had but one eye, and the popular prejudice runs in favor of two.
Nicholas Nickleby ch. 4 (1839)

22 Here's richness!
Nicholas Nickleby ch. 5 (1839)

23 Subdue your appetites my dears, and you've conquered human natur.
Nicholas Nickleby ch. 5 (1839)

24 "C-l-e-a-n, clean, verb active, to make bright, to scour. W-i-n, win, d-e-r, winder, a casement." When the boy knows this out of the book, he goes and does it.
Nicholas Nickleby ch. 8 (1839)

25 As she frequently remarked when she made any such mistake, it would all be the same a hundred years hence.
Nicholas Nickleby ch. 9 (1839). "It will be all one a hundred years hence" is a proverb dating at least as far back as the seventeenth century.
See Samuel Johnson 51

26 There are only two styles of portrait painting; the serious and the smirk.
Nicholas Nickleby ch. 10 (1839)

27 Language was not powerful enough to describe the infant phenomenon.
Nicholas Nickleby ch. 23 (1839)

28 The unities, sir . . . are a completeness—a kind of universal dovetailedness with regard to place and time.
Nicholas Nickleby ch. 24 (1839)

29 A demd, damp, moist, unpleasant body!
Nicholas Nickleby ch. 34 (1839)

30 All is gas and gaiters.
Nicholas Nickleby ch. 49 (1839)

31 He has gone to the demnition bow-wows.
Nicholas Nickleby ch. 64 (1839)

32 A smattering of everything, and a knowledge of nothing.
Sketches by Boz "Tales," ch. 3 (1839)

33 "There are strings," said Mr. Tappertit, ". . . in the human heart that had better not be wibrated."
Barnaby Rudge ch. 22 (1841)

34 She's the ornament of her sex.
The Old Curiosity Shop ch. 5 (1841). "The ornament of her sex" was used in print as early as the seventeenth century.

35 Codlin's the friend, not Short.
The Old Curiosity Shop ch. 19 (1841)

36 "Did you ever taste beer?" "I had a sip of it once," said the small servant. "Here's a state of things!" cried Mr. Swiveller. . . . "She *never* tasted it—it can't be tasted in a sip!"
The Old Curiosity Shop ch. 57 (1841)

37 It was a maxim with Foxey—our revered father, gentlemen—"Always suspect everybody."
The Old Curiosity Shop ch. 66 (1841)

38 Oh! but he was a tight-fisted hand at the grindstone, Scrooge! a squeezing, wrenching, grasping, scraping, clutching, covetous old sinner! Hard and sharp as flint, from which no steel had ever struck out generous fire, secret, and self-contained, and solitary as an oyster.
A Christmas Carol stave 1 (1843)

39 "Bah," said Scrooge. "Humbug!"
A Christmas Carol stave 1 (1843)

40 You may be an undigested bit of beef, a blot of mustard, a crumb of cheese, a fragment of an underdone potato. There's more of gravy than of grave about you, whatever you are!
A Christmas Carol stave 1 (1843)

41 [*Jacob Marley's ghost speaking:*] I wear the chain I forged in life.
A Christmas Carol stave 1 (1843)

42 "I am the Ghost of Christmas Past." "Long Past?" inquired Scrooge. . . . "No. Your past."
A Christmas Carol stave 2 (1843)

43 "I am the Ghost of Christmas Present," said the Spirit. "Look upon me!"
A Christmas Carol stave 3 (1843)

44 [*Of Tiny Tim:*] As good as gold.
A Christmas Carol stave 3 (1843)

45 "God bless us every one!" said Tiny Tim, the last of all.
A Christmas Carol stave 3 (1843)

46 "I am in the presence of the Ghost of Christmas Yet to Come?" said Scrooge.
A Christmas Carol stave 4 (1843)

47 I will honor Christmas in my heart, and try to keep it all the year.
A Christmas Carol stave 4 (1843)

48 It *was* a turkey! He could never have stood upon his legs, that bird! He would have snapped 'em off short in a minute, like sticks of sealing-wax.

A Christmas Carol stave 5 (1843)

49 With affection beaming in one eye, and calculation shining out of the other.

Martin Chuzzlewit ch. 8 (1844)

50 Keep up appearances whatever you do.

Martin Chuzzlewit ch. 11 (1844)

51 Here's the rule for bargains: "Do other men, for they would do you." That's the true business precept.

Martin Chuzzlewit ch. 11 (1844)

52 He'd make a lovely corpse.

Martin Chuzzlewit ch. 25 (1844)

53 "Bother Mrs. Harris!" said Betsey Prig. . . . "I don't believe there's no sich a person!"

Martin Chuzzlewit ch. 49 (1844)

54 "Wal'r, my boy," replied the Captain, "in the Proverbs of Solomon you will find the following words, 'May we never want a friend in need, nor a bottle to give him!' When found, make a note of."

Dombey and Son ch. 15 (1848)

55 Whether I shall turn out to be the hero of my own life, or whether that station will be held by anybody else, these pages must show.

David Copperfield ch. 1 (1850)

56 I am a lone lorn creetur . . . and everythink goes contrairy with me.

David Copperfield ch. 3 (1850)

57 Barkis is willin'.

David Copperfield ch. 5 (1850)

58 I have known him [Mr. Micawber] to come home to supper with a flood of tears, and a declaration that nothing was now left but a jail; and go to bed making a calculation of the expense of putting bow-windows to the house, "in case anything turned up," which was his favorite expression.

David Copperfield ch. 11 (1850)

59 "My other piece of advice, Copperfield," said Mr. Micawber, "you know. Annual income twenty pounds, annual expenditure nineteen nineteen six, result happiness. Annual income twenty pounds, annual expenditure twenty pounds nought and six, result misery."

David Copperfield ch. 12 (1850)

60 I never will desert Mr. Micawber.

David Copperfield ch. 12 (1850)

61 It's a mad world. Mad as Bedlam.

David Copperfield ch. 14 (1850)

62 [*Uriah Heep speaking:*] I'm a very umble person.

David Copperfield ch. 16 (1850)

63 The mistake was made of putting some of the trouble out of King Charles's head into my head.

David Copperfield ch. 17 (1850)

64 I only ask for information.

David Copperfield ch. 20 (1850)

65 What a world of gammon and spinnage it is, though, ain't it!

David Copperfield ch. 22 (1850)

66 Nobody's enemy but his own.

David Copperfield ch. 25 (1850)

67 Accidents will occur in the best-regulated families.

David Copperfield ch. 28 (1850). The *Oxford Dictionary of Proverbs* cites Peter Atall, *Hermit in America* (1819): "Accidents will happen in the best regulated families."
See Robert Burns 3; Disraeli 7; Modern Proverbs 100; Orwell 17; Plautus 3; Proverbs 2; Sayings 25

68 Ride on! Rough-shod if need be, smooth-shod if that will do, but ride on! Ride on over all obstacles, and win the race!

David Copperfield ch. 28 (1850)

69 A long pull, and a strong pull, and a pull altogether.

David Copperfield ch. 30 (1850)

70 "People can't die, along the coast," said Mr. Peggotty, "except when the tide's pretty nigh out. They can't be born, unless it's pretty nigh in—not properly born, till flood. He's a going out with the tide."

David Copperfield ch. 30 (1850)

71 It's only my child-wife.

David Copperfield ch. 44 (1850)

72 Circumstances beyond my individual control.

David Copperfield ch. 49 (1850)

73 A man must take the fat with the lean.
David Copperfield ch. 51 (1850)

74 Trifles make the sum of life.
David Copperfield ch. 53 (1850)

75 There is another well-known suit in Chancery, not yet decided, which was commenced before the close of the last century, and in which more than double the amount of seventy thousand pounds has been swallowed up in costs.
Bleak House preface (1853)

76 Fog everywhere. . . . The raw afternoon is rawest, and the dense fog is densest, and the muddy streets are muddiest, near that leaden-headed old obstruction, appropriate ornament for the threshold of a leaden-headed old corporation: Temple Bar. And hard by Temple Bar, in Lincoln's Inn Hall, at the very heart of the fog, sits the Lord High Chancellor in his High Court of Chancery.
Bleak House ch. 1 (1853)

77 Never can there come fog too thick, never can there come mud and mire too deep, to assort with the groping and floundering condition which this High Court of Chancery, most pestilent of hoary sinners, holds, this day, in the sight of heaven and earth.
Bleak House ch. 1 (1853)

78 Suffer any wrong that can be done you, rather than come here [to the Court of Chancery]!
Bleak House ch. 1 (1853)

79 Jarndyce and Jarndyce drones on. This scarecrow of a suit has, in course of time, become so complicated that no man alive knows what it means. The parties to it understand it least, but it has been observed that no two Chancery lawyers can talk about it for five minutes, without coming to a total disagreement as to all the premises.
Bleak House ch. 1 (1853)

80 Innumerable children have been born into the cause; innumerable young people have married into it; innumerable old people have died out of it. . . . The little plaintiff or defendant, who was promised a new rocking-horse when Jarndyce and Jarndyce should be settled, has grown up,

possessed himself of a real horse, and trotted away into the other world.
Bleak House ch. 1 (1853)

81 Jarndyce and Jarndyce still drags its dreary length before the Court, perennially hopeless.
Bleak House ch. 1 (1853)

82 This is a London particular. . . . A fog, miss.
Bleak House ch. 3 (1853)

83 "She is the child of the universe." "The universe makes rather an indifferent parent, I am afraid."
Bleak House ch. 6 (1853)

84 I only ask to be free. The butterflies are free. Mankind will surely not deny to Harold Skimpole what it concedes to the butterflies!
Bleak House ch. 6 (1853)

85 "Not to put too fine a point upon it"—a favorite apology for plain-speaking with Mr Snagsby.
Bleak House ch. 11 (1853)

86 I expect a Judgment. On the day of Judgment.
Bleak House ch. 14 (1853)

87 It is a melancholy truth that even great men have their poor relations.
Bleak House ch. 28 (1853)

88 The one great principle of the English law is, to make business for itself.
Bleak House ch. 39 (1853)

89 I call them [Miss Flite's birds] the Wards in Jarndyce. They are caged up with all the others. With Hope, Joy, Youth, Peace, Rest, Life, Dust, Ashes, Waste, Want, Ruin, Despair, Madness, Death, Cunning, Folly, Words, Wigs, Rags, Sheepskin, Plunder, Precedent, Jargon, Gammon, and Spinach!
Bleak House ch. 60 (1853)

90 Now, what I want is, Facts. . . . Facts alone are wanted in life.
Hard Times bk. 1, ch. 1 (1854)

91 There is a wisdom of the Head, and . . . a wisdom of the Heart.
Hard Times bk. 3, ch. 1 (1854)

92 I am the only child of parents who weighed, measured, and priced everything; for whom what could not be weighed, measured, and priced had no existence.
Little Dorrit bk. 1, ch. 2 (1857)

93 Whatever was required to be done, the Circumlocution Office was beforehand with all the public departments in the art of perceiving—HOW NOT TO DO IT.
Little Dorrit bk. 1, ch. 10 (1857)

94 There's milestones on the Dover Road!
Little Dorrit bk. 1, ch. 23 (1857)

95 You know, in a general way, what being a reference means. A person who can't pay, gets another person who can't pay, to guarantee that he can pay. Like a person with two wooden legs getting another person with two wooden legs, to guarantee that he has got two natural legs.
Little Dorrit bk. 1, ch. 23 (1857)

96 Papa, potatoes, poultry, prunes, and prism, are all very good words for the lips: especially prunes and prism.
Little Dorrit bk. 2, ch. 5 (1857)

97 It was the best of times, it was the worst of times, it was the age of wisdom, it was the age of foolishness, it was the epoch of belief, it was the epoch of incredulity, it was the season of Light, it was the season of Darkness, it was the spring of hope, it was the winter of despair, we had everything before us, we had nothing before us, we were all going direct to Heaven, we were all going direct the other way—in short, the period was so far like the present period, that some of its noblest authorities insisted on its being received, for good or for evil, in the superlative degree of comparison only.
A Tale of Two Cities bk. 1, ch. 1 (1859)

98 A wonderful fact to reflect upon, that every human creature is constituted to be that profound secret and mystery to every other.
A Tale of Two Cities bk. 1, ch. 3 (1859)

99 [*Sydney Carton's thoughts on the scaffold:*] It is a far, far better thing that I do, than I have ever done; it is a far, far better rest that I go to, than I have ever known.
A Tale of Two Cities bk. 3, ch. 15 (1859)

100 In the little world in which children have their existence, whosoever brings them up, there is nothing so finely perceived and so finely felt, as injustice.
Great Expectations ch. 8 (1861)

101 Now, I return to this young fellow. And the communication I have got to make is, that he has great expectations.
Great Expectations ch. 18 (1861)

102 What larks.
Great Expectations ch. 27 (1861)

103 Take nothing on its looks; take everything on evidence. There's no better rule.
Great Expectations ch. 40 (1861)

104 You have been in every prospect I have ever seen since—on the river, on the sails of the ships, on the marshes, in the clouds, in the light, in the darkness, in the wind, in the woods, in the sea, in the streets. You have been the embodiment of every graceful fancy that my mind has ever become acquainted with.
Great Expectations ch. 44 (1861)

105 I took her hand in mine, and we went out of the ruined place; and as the morning mists had risen long ago when I first left the forge, so the evening mists were rising now, and in all the broad expanse of tranquil light they showed to me, I saw no shadow of another parting from her.
Great Expectations ch. 59 (1862 ed.)

106 I want to be something so much worthier than the doll in the doll's house.
Our Mutual Friend bk. 1, ch. 5 (1865)

James Dickey
U.S. poet and novelist, 1923–1997

1 Drunk on the wind in my mouth,
Wringing the handlebar for speed,
Wild to be wreckage forever.
"Cherrylog Road" l. 106 (1963)

2 The air split into nine levels,
Some gift of tongues of the whistler.
"Buckdancer's Choice" l. 2 (1965)

3 For years, they have all been dying
Out, the classic buck-and-wing men.
"Buckdancer's Choice" l. 8 (1965)

Emily Dickinson

U.S. poet, 1830–1886

Poem texts are taken from The Poems of Emily Dickinson, *ed. R. W. Franklin (1998). The datings are dates of composition rather than of publication.*

1 Success is counted sweetest
　By those who ne'er succeed.
　To comprehend a nectar
　Requires sorest need—.
　"Success is counted sweetest" l. 1 (ca. 1859)

2 These are the days when Birds come back—
　A very few—a Bird or two—
　To take a backward look.
　"These are the days when birds" l. 1 (ca. 1859)

3 Surgeons must be very careful
　When they take the knife!
　Underneath their fine incisions
　Stirs the Culprit—*Life!*
　"Surgeons must be very careful" l. 1 (ca. 1860)

4 Inebriate of air am I,
　And debauchee of dew;—
　Reeling through endless summer days,
　From inns of molten blue.
　"I taste a liquor never brewed" l. 5 (ca. 1861)

5 I'm Nobody! Who are you?
　Are you—Nobody—too?
　Then there's a pair of us!
　Don't tell! they'd banish us—you know!
　"I'm nobody! Who are you?" l. 1 (ca. 1861)

6 There's a certain Slant of light,
　Winter Afternoons—
　That oppresses like the Heft
　Of Cathedral Tunes.
　"There's a certain slant of light" l. 1 (ca. 1861)

7 After great pain, a formal feeling comes—.
　"After great pain a formal feeling comes" l. 1 (ca. 1862)

8 Because I could not stop for Death—
　He kindly stopped for me—.
　"Because I could not stop for death" l. 1 (ca. 1862)

9 "Heaven"—is what I cannot reach!
　The Apple on the Tree—.
　"'Heaven' is what I cannot reach!" l. 1 (ca. 1862)

10 "Hope" is the thing with feathers—
　That perches in the soul—.
　"'Hope' is the thing with feathers" l. 1 (ca. 1862)
　See Woody Allen 20

11 I died for beauty—but was scarce
　Adjusted in the Tomb
　When One who died for Truth, was lain
　In an adjoining Room—.
　"I died for beauty but was scarce" l. 1 (ca. 1862)

12 I dwell in Possibility—
　A fairer House than Prose—
　More numerous of Windows—
　Superior—for Doors—.
　"I dwell in possibility" l. 1 (ca. 1862)

13 I like to see it lap the Miles—
　And lick the Valleys up.
　"I like to see it lap the miles" l. 1 (ca. 1862)

14 The Soul selects her own Society—
　Then—shuts the Door—
　To her divine Majority—
　Present no more—.
　"The Soul selects her own society" l. 1 (ca. 1862)

15 They shut me up in Prose—
　As when a little Girl
　They put me in the Closet—
　Because they liked me "still"—.
　"They shut me up in prose" l. 1 (ca. 1862)

16 Are you too deeply occupied to say if my Verse
　is alive?
　Letter to Thomas Wentworth Higginson, 15 Apr. 1862

17 Alter! When the hills do—
   Falter! When the Sun
   Question if His Glory
   Be the Perfect One—.
   "Alter! When the hills do" l. 1 (ca. 1863)

18 Much Madness is divinest Sense—
   To a discerning Eye—
   Much sense—the starkest Madness—
   'Tis the Majority
   In this, as all, prevail—.
   Assent—and you are sane—
   Demur—you're straightway dangerous—
   And handled with a Chain—.
   "Much madness is divinest sense" l. 1 (ca. 1863)

19 This is my letter to the World
   That never wrote to Me—.
   "This is my letter to the world" l. 1 (ca. 1863)

20 I never saw a Moor.
   I never saw the Sea—
   Yet know I how the Heather looks
   And what a Billow be—.
   "I never saw a moor" l. 1 (ca. 1864)

21 I never spoke with God
   Nor visited in heaven—
   Yet certain am I of the spot
   As if the Checks were given—.
   "I never saw a moor" l. 5 (ca. 1864). The word *Checks* is given as *chart* in many editions of Dickinson's poems.

22 The Bustle in a House
   The Morning after Death
   Is solemnest of industries
   Enacted upon Earth—.
   "The bustle in a house" l. 1 (ca. 1865)

23 If I can stop one Heart from breaking
   I shall not live in vain
   If I can ease one Life the Aching
   Or cool one Pain.
   "If I can stop one heart from breaking" l. 1 (ca. 1865)

24 Yet never met this fellow,
   Attended or alone,
   Without a tighter breathing,
   And zero at the bone.
   "A narrow fellow in the grass" l. 21 (ca. 1865)

25 There is no Frigate like a Book
   To take us Lands away
   Nor any Coursers like a Page
   Of prancing Poetry—.
   "There is no frigate like a book" l. 1 (ca. 1873)

26 The Pedigree of Honey
   Does not concern the Bee—
   A Clover, any time, to him,
   Is Aristocracy—.
   "The pedigree of honey" l.1 (ca. 1884)

27 My life closed twice before its close.
   "My life closed twice before its close" l. 1 (unknown date)

28 Parting is all we know of heaven,
   And all we need of hell.
   "My life closed twice before its close" l. 7 (unknown date)

29 If I read a book [and] it makes my whole body so cold no fire ever can warm me I know *that* is poetry. If I feel physically as if the top of my head were taken off, I know *that* is poetry. These are the only way I know it. Is there any other way.
   Quoted in Thomas Wentworth Higginson, Letter to Mary Channing Higginson, 16 Aug. 1870

John Dickinson
U.S. statesman, 1732–1808

1 Then join Hand in Hand brave Americans all,
  By uniting we stand, by dividing we fall.
  "The Liberty Song" (song) (1768). "United we stand, divided we fall!" became a slogan of the American Revolution.

Paul Dickson
U.S. writer, 1939–

1 Rowe's Rule: the odds are five to six that the light at the end of the tunnel is the headlight of an oncoming train.
  Washingtonian, Nov. 1978. Robert Lowell wrote in his 1977 poem "Since 1939": "If we see a light at the end of the tunnel, / it's the light of an oncoming train." "If you see the light at the end of the tunnel, don't forget that it may just be a train coming in the other direction" appeared in *ICC Practitioners' Journal*, Sept.–Oct. 1974.
  See Alsop 1; John Kennedy 29; Navarre 1

Denis Diderot

French philosopher and man of letters, 1713–1784

1 *On peut tromper quelques hommes, ou les tromper tous dans certains lieux & en certain tems [sic], mais non pas tous les hommes dans tous les lieux & dans tous les siècles.*

One can fool some men, or fool all men in some places and times, but one cannot fool all men in all places and ages.

Encyclopédie ou Dictionnaire raisonné des Sciences, des Arts et des Métiers vol. 4 (1754)
See Lincoln 66

2 If your little savage were left to himself and to his native blindness, he would in time join the infant's reasoning to the grown man's passion—he would strangle his father and sleep with his mother.

Rameau's Nephew (1762) (translation by Jacques Barzun and Ralph H. Bowen)

3 *L'esprit de l'escalier.*
Staircase wit.

Paradoxe sur le Comédien (written 1773–1778). Diderot meant by this the witty rejoinder that one thinks of only after leaving the drawing room and being already on one's way down the staircase.

4 *Et des boyaux du dernier prêtre
Serrons le cou du dernier roi.*
And with the guts of the last priest
Let us strangle the last king.

Dithrambe sur Fête des Rois (ca. 1780)
See Meslier 1

Joan Didion

U.S. writer, 1934–

1 Was there ever in anyone's life span a point free in time, devoid of memory, a point when choice was any more than sum of all the choices gone before?

Run River ch. 4 (1963)

2 Writers are always selling someone out.

Slouching Towards Bethlehem preface (1968)

3 It was the United States of America in the cold late spring of 1967, and the market was steady and the G.N.P. high and a great many articulate people seemed to have a sense of high social purpose and it might have been a spring of brave hopes and national promise, but it was not, and more and more people had the uneasy apprehension that it was not.

Slouching Towards Bethlehem (1968)

4 I think we are well advised to keep on nodding terms with the people we used to be, whether we find them attractive company or not. Otherwise they turn up unannounced and surprise us, come hammering on the mind's door at 4 a.m. of a bad night and demand to know who deserted them, who betrayed them, who is going to make amends.

Slouching Towards Bethlehem (1968)

5 We tell ourselves stories in order to live.

The White Album (1979)

Ngo Dinh Diem

South Vietnamese president, 1901–1963

1 Follow me if I advance! Kill me if I retreat! Revenge me if I die!

Quoted in *Time*, 8 Nov. 1963. Diem uttered these words after becoming president in 1954. Much earlier, the *Gentleman's Magazine*, June 1815, quoted Henri de la Roche Jacquelin: "If I advance, follow me; if I retreat, kill me; if I die, avenge me."

Marlene Dietrich

German actress, 1901–1992

1 How do you know that love is gone? If you said that you would be there at seven, you get there by nine and he or she has not called the police yet—it's gone.

Marlene Dietrich's ABC (1962)

2 Once a woman has forgiven her man, she must not reheat his sins for breakfast.

Marlene Dietrich's ABC (1962)

3 Sex. In America an obsession. In other parts of the world a fact.

Marlene Dietrich's ABC (1962)

Howard Dietz

U.S. motion picture executive and lyricist, 1896–1983

1 That's Entertainment.

Title of song (1953)

2 *Ars gratia artis.*

Quoted in *Zanesville* (Ohio) *Signal*, 3 Oct. 1928. Created about 1916 as a motto for the Metro-Goldwyn-Mayer motion picture studio. It translates as "art for art's sake," but was apparently intended to mean "Art is beholden to the artists."
See Constant de Rebecque 1; Cousin 1

3 A day away from Tallulah [Bankhead] is like a month in the country.

Quoted in Tallulah Bankhead, *Tallulah: My Autobiography* (1952)

Robert Diggs
U.S. rap musician and producer, 1969–

1 C.R.E.A.M. (Cash Rules Everything Around Me).
Title of song (1993)

Edsger Dijkstra
Dutch computer scientist, 1930–2002

1 The question of whether Machines Can Think . . . is about as relevant as the question of whether Submarines Can Swim.
Address at Association for Computing Machinery South Central Regional Conference, Austin, Tex., Nov. 1984

Annie Dillard
U.S. writer, 1945–

1 I read about an Eskimo hunter who asked the local missionary priest, "If I did not know about God and sin, would I go to hell?" "No," said the priest, "not if you did not know." "Then why," asked the Eskimo earnestly, "did you tell me?"
Pilgrim at Tinker Creek ch. 7 (1974)

2 This was the universe about which we have read so much and never before felt: the universe as a clockwork of loose spheres flung at stupefying, unauthorized speeds. How could anything moving so fast not crash.
"Total Eclipse" (1982)

Phyllis Diller
U.S. comedian, 1917–2012

1 Never go to bed mad. Stay up and fight.
Phyllis Diller's Housekeeping Hints (1966)

2 Cleaning your house while your kids are still growing

Is like shoveling the walk before it stops snowing.
Phyllis Diller's Housekeeping Hints (1966)

William Dillon
U.S. songwriter, 1877–1966

1 I want a girl just like the girl
That married dear old dad.
"I Want a Girl" (song) (1911)

Joe DiMaggio
U.S. baseball player, 1914–1999

1 [*Responding to his wife Marilyn Monroe's statement after returning from entertaining troops in Korea, "You never heard such cheering":*] Yes, I have.
Quoted in *Esquire,* July 1966

William Dimond
English playwright, 1780–1837

1 Captain, this is the twenty-seventh time I have heard you relate this story, and you invariably said, a chestnut, till now.
The Broken Sword act 1 (1816). Origin of the expression *chestnut* meaning an often-repeated story.

Isak Dinesen (Karen Blixen)
Danish author, 1885–1962

1 What is man, when you come to think upon him, but a minutely set, ingenious machine for turning, with infinite artfulness, the red wine of Shiraz into urine?
Seven Gothic Tales "The Dreamers" (1934)

2 I had a farm in Africa, at the foot of the Ngong Hills.
Out of Africa pt. 1, "The Ngong Farm" (1937)

3 A herd of elephant . . . pacing along as if they had an appointment at the end of the world.
Out of Africa pt. 1, ch. 1 (1937)

Diogenes
Greek philosopher, ca. 400 B.C.–ca. 325 B.C.

1 I am looking for an honest man.
Quoted in Diogenes Laertius, *Lives of Eminent Philosophers*

2 Alexander . . . asked him if he lacked anything. "Yes," said he, "that I do: that you stand out of my sun a little."
Reported in Plutarch, *Parallel Lives*

Everett M. Dirksen
U.S. politician, 1896–1969

1 A billion here, a billion there, pretty soon it begins to add up to real money.
Attributed in *N.Y. Times*, 28 Aug. 1975. The Dirksen Congressional Center has conducted an extensive search of audiotapes, newspaper clippings, Dirksen's own speech notes, transcripts of his speeches and media appearances, and other sources and found no concrete evidence of the senator's having uttered these words. The principal evidence for the quotation's authenticity consists of claims by various people that they heard Dirksen say it, but these claims remain uncorroborated. An earlier version appeared in the *N.Y. Times*, 10 Jan. 1938: "Well, now, about this new budget. It's a billion here and a billion there, and by and by it begins to mount up into money."

Walt Disney
U.S. animator and businessman, 1901–1966

1 I only hope that we never lose sight of one thing—that it was all started by a mouse.
"What Is Disneyland?" (television program), 27 Oct. 1954

2 Girls bored me—they still do. I love Mickey Mouse more than any woman I've ever known.
Quoted in Walter Wagner, *You Must Remember This* (1975)

Benjamin Disraeli, First Earl of Beaconsfield
British prime minister and novelist, 1804–1881

1 The microcosm of a public school.
Vivian Grey bk. 1, ch. 2 (1826)

2 To be a great lawyer, I must give up my chance of being a great man.
Vivian Grey bk. 1, ch. 9 (1826)

3 Experience is the child of Thought, and Thought is the child of Action. We cannot learn men from books.
Vivian Grey bk. 5, ch. 1 (1826)

4 A good eater must be a good man; for a good eater must have a good digestion, and a good digestion depends upon a good conscience.
The Young Duke bk. 1, ch. 14 (1831)

5 A *dark* horse, which had never been thought of, and which the careless St James had never even observed in the list, rushed past the grand stand in sweeping triumph.
The Young Duke bk. 2, ch. 5 (1831). The *Oxford English Dictionary* has this as its earliest citation for the term *dark horse*, and Disraeli is frequently considered to be the coiner. However, an earlier usage is in the *Edinburgh Advertiser*, 24 Sept. 1822: "What is termed an *outside* or a dark horse always tells well for heavy betters."

6 Read no history: nothing but biography, for that is life without theory.
Contarini Fleming pt. 1, ch. 23 (1832)
See Ralph Waldo Emerson 11

7 What we anticipate seldom occurs; what we least expected generally happens.
Henrietta Temple bk. 2, ch. 4 (1837)
See Robert Burns 3; Dickens 67; Modern Proverbs 100; Orwell 17; Plautus 3; Proverbs 2; Sayings 25

8 Though I sit down now, the time will come when you will hear me.
Maiden speech in House of Commons, 7 Dec. 1837

9 "A sound Conservative government," said Taper, musingly. "I understand: Tory men and Whig measures."
Coningsby bk. 2, ch. 6 (1844)

10 In England when a new character appears in our circles, the first question always is, "Who is he?" In France it is, "What is he?" In England,

"How much a year?" In France, "What has he done?"
Coningsby bk. 5, ch. 7 (1844)
See Twain 80

11 Let me see property acknowledging as in the old days of faith, that labor is his twin brother.
Coningsby bk. 8, ch. 3 (1844)

12 If you wish to be great, you must give men new ideas, you must teach them new words, you must modify their manners, you must change their laws, you must root out prejudices, subvert convictions. Greatness no longer depends on rentals: the world is too rich; nor on pedigrees: the world is too knowing.
Coningsby bk. 9, ch. 4 (1844)

13 To be conscious that you are ignorant is a great step to knowledge.
Sybil bk. 1, ch. 5 (1845)

14 "Two nations; between whom there is no intercourse and no sympathy; who are as ignorant of each other's habits, thoughts, and feelings, as if they were dwellers in different zones, or inhabitants of different planets; who are formed by a different breeding, are fed by a different food, are ordered by different manners, and are not governed by the same laws." "You speak of—" said Egremont, hesitatingly, "THE RICH AND THE POOR."
Sybil bk. 2, ch. 5 (1845)
See Kerner 1

15 Christianity is completed Judaism, or it is nothing. Christianity is incomprehensible without Judaism, as Judaism is incomplete without Christianity.
Sybil bk. 2, ch. 12 (1845)

16 Tobacco is the tomb of love.
Sybil bk. 2, ch. 16 (1845)

17 Mr Kremlin himself was distinguished for ignorance, for he had only one idea,—and that was wrong.
Sybil bk. 4, ch. 5 (1845)
See Samuel Johnson 66

18 A Conservative Government is an organized hypocrisy.
Speech in House of Commons, 17 Mar. 1845

19 All the great things have been done by little nations. It is the Jordan and the Ilyssus which have civilized the modern races.
Tancred bk. 3, ch. 7 (1847)

20 Finality is not the language of politics.
Speech in House of Commons, 28 Feb. 1859

21 Is man an ape or an angel? My Lord, I am on the side of the angels.
Speech at Diocesan Conference, Oxford, England, 25 Nov. 1864

22 Assassination has never changed the history of the world.
Speech in House of Commons, 1 May 1865

23 When a man fell into his anecdotage it was a sign for him to retire.
Lothair ch. 28 (1870). The *Oxford English Dictionary* documents the use of *anecdotage* as far back as 1835 and notes that it is attributed to John Wilkes.

24 You know who the critics are? The men who have failed in literature and art.
Lothair ch. 35 (1870)
See Coleridge 17

25 "My idea of an agreeable person," said Hugo Bohun, "is a person who agrees with me."
Lothair ch. 41 (1870)

26 [*Of the Treasury Bench:*] You behold a range of exhausted volcanoes.
Speech, Manchester, England, 3 Apr. 1872

27 Lord Salisbury and myself have brought you back peace—but a peace I hope with honor.
Speech on return from Congress of Berlin, 16 July 1878. Burton E. Stevenson, *Home Book of Quotations*, notes earlier examples of the phrase "peace with honor" going back to a letter from Theobald, Count of Champagne, to Louis the Great (ca. 1125).
See Chamberlain 2; John Russell 1

28 [*Of William E. Gladstone:*] A sophistical rhetorician, inebriated with the exuberance of his own verbosity, and gifted with an egotistical imagination that can at all times command an interminable and inconsistent series of arguments to malign an opponent and to glorify himself.
Speech, Knightsbridge, England, 27 July 1878

29 His Christianity was muscular.
Endymion ch. 14 (1880). The term *muscular Christianity* can be traced as far back as 1853 (*National Magazine*, June).

30 [*On becoming prime minister in 1868:*] I have climbed to the top of the greasy pole.

Quoted in William Fraser, *Disraeli and His Day* (1891)

31 [*Remark to Matthew Arnold, ca. 1880:*] Every one likes flattery; and when you come to Royalty you should lay it on with a trowel.

Quoted in G. W. E. Russell, *Collections and Recollections* (1898)

32 [*Of attacks in Parliament:*] Never complain and never explain.

Quoted in John Morley, *Life of William Ewart Gladstone* (1903). In *Cornhill Magazine*, Dec. 1893, Benjamin Jowett was quoted as having said, "Never retract, never explain, never apologise."
See John Arbuthnot Fisher 1; Elbert Hubbard 2

33 When I want to read a novel, I write one.

Quoted in Wilfred Meynell, *Benjamin Disraeli: An Unconventional Biography* (1903). "When I want to read a book, I write one" was ascribed to Disraeli by *Fraser's Magazine*, May 1868.

34 [*To an author who had sent him an unsolicited manuscript:*] Many thanks; I shall lose no time in reading it.

Quoted in Wilfrid Meynell, *Benjamin Disraeli: An Unconventional Biography* (1903). Although this line is associated with Disraeli, it appeared without attribution to him as early as 1871 ("I have received your book, and shall lose no time in reading it," *British Quarterly Review*, October).

35 [*On his deathbed, declining a visit from Queen Victoria:*] No it is better not. She would only ask me to take a message to Albert.

Quoted in Robert Blake, *Disraeli* (1966)

36 [*Correcting proofs of his last parliamentary speech, 31 Mar. 1881:*] I will not go down to posterity talking bad grammar.

Quoted in Robert Blake, *Disraeli* (1966)

37 [*Replying to anti-Semitic taunting in the House of Commons:*] Yes, I am a Jew! When the ancestors of the honorable gentleman were brutal savages in an unknown island, mine were priests in the temple!

Attributed in *Atlanta Constitution*, 14 Feb. 1892. Often said to have been addressed to Irish Member of Parliament Daniel O'Connell. An earlier Disraeli attribution appeared in *Phrenological Journal and Life Illustrated*, Mar. 1868: "My ancestors were lords of the tabernacle and princes of Israel when his were naked savages in the woods of Northern Germany." A very similar response to anti-Semitism is sometimes attributed to U.S. Senator Judah P. Benjamin; the earliest record of the Benjamin attribution that has been found occurs in Benjamin P. Poore, *Perley's Reminiscences of Sixty Years in the National Metropolis* (1886).

38 [*To Edward Bulwer-Lytton:*] Damn your principles! Stick to your party.

Attributed in Edward Latham, *Famous Sayings and Their Authors* (1904)

Dorothy Dix (Elizabeth Meriwether Gilmer)

U.S. journalist, 1870–1951

1 So many persons think divorce a panacea for every ill, who find out, when they try it, that the remedy is worse than the disease.

Dorothy Dix—Her Book (1926)

Tahar Djaout

Algerian writer, 1954–1993

1 Silence is death
And if you say nothing you die,
And if you speak you die.
So speak and die.

Quoted in *New Statesman & Society*, 19 Aug. 1994

Milovan Djilas

Yugoslavian political leader and writer, 1911–1995

1 The capitalist and other classes of ancient origin had in fact been destroyed, but a new class, previously unknown to history, had been formed. . . . This new class [is] the bureaucracy, or more accurately the political bureaucracy.

The New Class: An Analysis of the Communist System "The New Class" (1957)

J. Frank Dobie

U.S. educator and author, 1888–1964

1 The average Ph.D. thesis is nothing but a transference of bones from one graveyard to another.

A Texan in England ch. 1 (1945)

E. L. Doctorow

U.S. novelist, 1931–2015

1 By that time the era of Ragtime had run out, with the heavy breath of the machine, as if history were no more than a tune on a player piano.

Ragtime ch. 40 (1975)

Robert "Bob" Dole
U.S. political leader, 1923–

1 [*Of Gerald Ford, Jimmy Carter, and Richard Nixon at a reunion of former presidents:*] There they were, See No Evil, Hear No Evil, and Evil.
Remarks at Gridiron Club dinner, Washington, D.C., 26 Mar. 1983
See Modern Proverbs 80

2 [*Of the Clinton administration:*] A corps of the elite who never grew up, never did anything real, never sacrificed, never suffered, and never learned.
Acceptance speech for Republican presidential nomination, San Diego, Calif., 15 Aug. 1996

J. P. Donleavy
U.S.-born Irish writer, 1926–2017

1 But Jesus, when you don't have any money, the problem is food. When you have money, it's sex. When you have both, it's health, you worry about getting ruptured or something. If everything is simply jake then you're frightened of death.
The Ginger Man ch. 5 (1955)

2 Writing is turning one's worst moments into money.
Quoted in *Punch,* 22 Mar. 1978

John Donne
English poet and clergyman, 1572–1631

1 License my roving hands, and let them go, Behind, before, above, between, below. O my America, my new found land, My kingdom, safeliest when with one man manned.
Elegies "To His Mistress Going to Bed" (ca. 1595)

2 Death be not proud, though some have called thee
Mighty and dreadful, for thou art not so.
Holy Sonnets no. 6 (1609)

3 One short sleep past, we wake eternally, And death shall be no more; Death thou shalt die.
Holy Sonnets no. 6 (1609)

4 Mollify it with thy tears, or sweat, or blood.
An Anatomy of the World l. 430 (1611)
See Byron 28; Winston Churchill 9; Winston Churchill 12; Theodore Roosevelt 3

5 No man is an Island, entire of it self; every man is a piece of the Continent, a part of the main; if a clod be washed away by the sea, Europe is the less, as well as if a promontory were, as well as if a manor of thy friends or of thine own were; any man's death diminishes me, because I am involved in Mankind; And therefore never send to know for whom the bell tolls; it tolls for thee.
Devotions upon Emergent Occasions no. 17 (1624)

6 If poisonous minerals, and if that tree, Whose fruit threw death on else immortal us, If lecherous goats, if serpents envious Cannot be damn'd; alas; why should I be?
Holy Sonnets no. 5 (published 1633)

7 Thou art slave to fate, chance, kings, and desperate men.
Holy Sonnets no. 6 (published 1633)

8 What if this present were the world's last night?
Holy Sonnets no. 9 (published 1633)

9 Batter my heart, three-personed God; for, you As yet but knock, breathe, shine, and seek to mend.
Holy Sonnets no. 10 (published 1633)

10 I wonder by my troth, what thou, and I Did, till we loved, were we not weaned till then? But sucked on country pleasures, childishly? Or snorted we in the seven sleepers den?
Songs and Sonnets "The Good-Morrow" (published 1633)

11 Go, and catch a falling star, Get with child a mandrake root, Tell me, where all past years are, Or who cleft the Devil's foot, Teach me to hear mermaids singing.
Songs and Sonnets "Song: Go and catch a falling star" (published 1633)

12 Busy old fool, unruly sun, Why dost thou thus, Through windows, and through curtains call on us? Must to thy motions lovers' seasons run?
Songs and Sonnets "The Sun Rising" (published 1633)

13 I have done one braver thing
   Than all the Worthies did,
   And yet a braver thence doth spring,
   Which is, to keep that hid.
   Songs and Sonnets "The Undertaking" (published
   1633)

14 [*Letter to his wife, after being dismissed from the
   service of his father-in-law:*] John Donne, Anne
   Donne, Un-done.
   Quoted in Izaak Walton, *The Life of Dr. Donne* (1640)

T. A. Dorgan

U.S. cartoonist and sportswriter, 1877–1929

1 Quick, Watson, the needle.
   New Orleans Item, 24 Apr. 1911. This citation was
   discovered by Ben Zimmer. The phrase is often said
   to have originated in Henry Blossom's libretto for the
   operetta *The Red Mill* (1906), but the sole existing
   copy of that libretto, at the New York Public Library,
   does not include "Quick, Watson, the needle."

2 See what the boys in the back room will have.
   New York Evening Journal, 2 May 1914

3 Yes . . . we have no bananas.
   Wisconsin News, 18 July 1922. Became famous as the
   title of a 1923 song by Frank Silver and Irving Cohn.

Michael Dorris

U.S. writer, 1945–1997

1 My son will forever travel through a moonless
   night with only the roar of wind for company.
   . . . A drowning man is not separated from the
   lust for air by a bridge of thought—he is one
   with it—and my son, conceived and grown in
   an ethanol bath, lives each day in the act of
   drowning. For him there is no shore.
   The Broken Cord ch. 14 (1989)

Thomas A. Dorsey

U.S. gospel musician, 1901–1960

1 Precious Lord, take my hand,
   Lead me on, let me stand,
   I am tired, I am weak, I am worn;
   Thru the storm, thru the night,
   Lead me on to the light,
   Take my hand, precious Lord, lead me home.
   "Take My Hand, Precious Lord" (song) (1938)

John Dos Passos

U.S. writer, 1896–1970

1 all right we are two nations.
   The Big Money "The Camera Eye (50)" (1936)

Fyodor Dostoyevski

Russian novelist, 1821–1881

1 The degree of civilization in a society can be
   judged by entering its prisons.
   The House of the Dead (1862) (translation by
   Constance Garnett)
   See Pearl S. Buck 3; Ramsey Clark 1; Humphrey 3;
   Samuel Johnson 69; Helen Keller 4

2 I agree that two times two is four is an excellent
   thing; but if we're going to start praising
   everything, then two times two is five is
   sometimes also a most charming little thing.
   Notes from Underground pt. 1, ch. 9 (1864) (translation
   by Richard Pevear and Larissa Volokhonsky)

3 The world will be saved by beauty.
   The Idiot pt. 3, ch. 5 (1868) (translation by Alan
   Myers)

4 If you were to destroy in mankind the belief in
   immortality, not only love but every living force
   maintaining the life of the world would at once
   be dried up. Moreover, nothing then would be
   immoral, everything would be lawful.
   The Brothers Karamazov bk. 2, ch. 6 (1879–1880)
   (translation by Constance Garnett). This is one
   of several passages in the book that are famously
   paraphrased as "If God does not exist, then
   everything is permitted."

5 Imagine that you are creating a fabric of human
   destiny with the object of making men happy in
   the end, giving them peace and rest at least, but
   that it was essential and inevitable to torture to
   death only one tiny creature . . . and to found
   that edifice on its unavenged tears, would you
   consent to be the architect on those conditions?
   The Brothers Karamazov bk. 5, ch. 4 (1879–1880)
   (translation by Constance Garnett)

6 We have corrected Thy work and have founded
   it upon *miracle, mystery,* and *authority*. And men
   rejoiced that they were again led like sheep, and
   that the terrible gift that brought them such
   suffering, was, at last, lifted from their hearts.
   The Brothers Karamazov bk. 5, ch. 5 (1879–1880)
   (translation by Constance Garnett)

7 Who doesn't desire his father's death?

The Brothers Karamazov bk. 12, ch. 5 (1879–1880)
(translation by Constance Garnett)

8 They have their Hamlets, but we still have our
Karamazovs!

The Brothers Karamazov bk. 12, ch. 9 (1879–1880)
(translation by Constance Garnett)

9 We have all come out of Gogol's *Overcoat*.

Attributed in Eugène Melchior, *Le Roman Russe*
(1886). This statement about Gogol's influence on
Russian writers is reported by Melchior without
an attribution, but it is generally assigned to
Dostoyevski.

Mark Doty

U.S. poet, 1953–

1 And I swear sometimes
when I put my head to his chest
I can hear the virus humming
like a refrigerator.

"Faith" l. 40 (1995)

Lord Alfred Douglas

English poet, 1870–1945

1 I am the Love that dare not speak its name.

"Two Loves" (1894). Refers to homosexual love.
See Wilde 82; Wilde 83

Anselm Douglas

Trinidadian musician, 1964–

1 Who Let the Dogs Out?

Title of song (1997)

Norman Douglas

Scottish novelist and essayist, 1868–1952

1 You can tell the ideals of a nation by its
advertisements.

South Wind ch. 7 (1917)

William O. Douglas

U.S. judge, 1898–1980

1 A people who climb the ridges and sleep
under the stars in high mountain meadows,
who enter the forest and scale the peaks, who
explore glaciers and walk ridges buried deep in
snow—these people will give the country some
of the indomitable spirit of the mountains.

Of Men and Mountains ch. 22 (1950)

2 We are a religious people whose institutions
presuppose a Supreme Being. . . . We sponsor
an attitude on the part of government that
shows no partiality to any one group and that
lets each flourish according to the zeal of its
adherents and the appeal of its dogma.

Zorach v. Clauson (1952)

3 The Fifth Amendment is an old friend and a
good friend. It is one of the great landmarks
in man's struggle to be free of tyranny, to be
decent and civilized. It is our way of escape
from the use of torture.

An Almanac of Liberty (1954)

4 The conception of political equality from the
Declaration of Independence, to Lincoln's
Gettysburg Address, to the Fifteenth,
Seventeenth, and Nineteenth Amendments can
mean only one thing—one person, one vote.

Gray v. Sanders (1963)
See Cartwright 1; Chesterton 16

5 In other words, the First Amendment has a
penumbra where privacy is protected from
government intrusion.

Griswold v. Connecticut (1965)
See Oliver Wendell Holmes, Jr. 1

6 The foregoing cases suggest that specific
guarantees in the Bill of Rights have
penumbras, formed by emanations from
those guarantees that help give them life and
substance. . . . Various guarantees create zones
of privacy.

Griswold v. Connecticut (1965)

7 We deal with a right of privacy older than the
Bill of Rights—older than our political parties,
older than our school system. Marriage is
a coming together for better or for worse,
hopefully enduring, and intimate to the
degree of being sacred. It is an association that
promotes a way of life, not causes; a harmony
in living, not political faiths; a bilateral loyalty,
not commercial or social projects. Yet it is
an association for as noble a purpose as any
involved in our prior decisions.

Griswold v. Connecticut (1965)

Frederick Douglass

U.S. civil rights leader, ca. 1818–1895

1 [*Of slave songs:*] Every tone was a testimony against slavery, and a prayer to God for deliverance from chains.
Narrative of the Life of Frederick Douglass ch. 2 (1845)

2 You have seen how a man was made a slave; you shall see how a slave was made a man.
Narrative of the Life of Frederick Douglass ch. 10 (1845)

3 No, I make no pretension to patriotism. So long as my voice can be heard on this or the other side of the Atlantic, I will hold up America to the lightning scorn of moral indignation. In doing this, I shall feel myself discharging the duty of a true patriot; for he is a lover of his country who rebukes and does not excuse its sins.
Speech at Market Hall, New York, N.Y., 22 Oct. 1847

4 [*On the proposal to send American blacks to colonize Liberia:*] Our minds are made up to live here if we can, or die here if we must; so every attempt to remove us will be, as it ought to be, labor lost. Here we are, and here we shall remain.
The North Star, 26 Jan. 1849

5 It is not light that is needed, but fire; it is not the gentle shower, but thunder. We need the storm, the whirlwind, and the earthquake. The feeling of the nation must be quickened; the conscience of the nation must be roused; the propriety of the nation must be startled; the hypocrisy of the nation must be exposed;

and its crimes against God and man must be proclaimed and denounced.
Speech, Rochester, N.Y., 5 July 1852

6 What, to the American slave, is your 4th of July? I answer; a day that reveals to him, more than all other days in the year, the gross injustice and cruelty to which he is the constant victim. To him, your celebration is a sham.
Speech, Rochester, N.Y., 5 July 1852

7 The man who is right is a majority. He who has God and conscience on his side, has a majority against the universe. Though he does not represent the present state, he represents the future state. If he does not represent what we are, he represents what we ought to be.
Speech to National Free Soil Convention, Pittsburgh, Pa., 11 Aug. 1852
See Coolidge 2; Andrew Jackson 7; John Knox 1; Wendell Phillips 3; Thoreau 9

8 Power concedes nothing without a demand. It never did and it never will.
Speech, Canandaigua, N.Y., 4 Aug. 1857

9 If there is no struggle, there is no progress. Those who profess to favor freedom and yet deprecate agitation, are men who want crops without plowing up the ground, they want rain without thunder and lightning. They want the ocean without the awful roar of its many waters.
Speech, Canandaigua, N.Y., 4 Aug. 1857

10 The destiny of the colored American . . . is the destiny of America.
Speech at Emancipation League, Boston, Mass., 12 Feb. 1862

11 The relation subsisting between the white and colored people of this country is the great, paramount, imperative, and all-commanding question for this age and nation to solve.
Speech at the Church of the Puritans, New York, N.Y., May 1863

12 The story of our inferiority is an old dodge, as I have said; for wherever men oppress their fellows, wherever they enslave them, they will endeavor to find the needed apology for such enslavement and oppression in the character of the people oppressed and enslaved.
Speech at annual meeting of Massachusetts Anti-Slavery Society, Boston, Mass., Apr. 1865

13 In all the relations of life and death, we are met
by the color line.
Speech at the Convention of Colored Men, Louisville,
Ky., 24 Sept. 1883

14 No man can put a chain about the ankle of his
fellow man without at last finding the other end
fastened about his own neck.
Speech at Civil Rights Mass Meeting, Washington,
D.C., 22 Oct. 1883

15 The life of the nation is secure only while the
nation is honest, truthful, and virtuous.
Speech on the twenty-third anniversary of
emancipation in the District of Columbia,
Washington, D.C., Apr. 1885

16 Where justice is denied, where poverty is
enforced, where ignorance prevails, and where
any one class is made to feel that society is
an organized conspiracy to oppress, rob, and
degrade them, neither persons nor property
will be safe.
Speech on the twenty-fourth anniversary of
emancipation in the District of Columbia,
Washington, D.C., Apr. 1886

Rita Dove
U.S. poet, 1952–

1 Billie Holiday's burned voice
had as many shadows as lights,
a mournful candelabra against a sleek piano,
the gardenia her signature under that ruined
face. . . .

If you can't be free, be a mystery.
"Canary" l. 1, 11 (1989)

2 Poetry seems to exist in a parallel universe
outside daily life in America. . . . We tend to
be so bombarded with information, and we
move so quickly, that there's a tendency to treat
everything on the surface level and process
things quickly. This is antithetical to the kind of
openness and perception you have to have to be
receptive to poetry.
Quoted in N.Y. Times, 20 June 1993

Lorenzo Dow
U.S. evangelist, 1777–1834

1 [Of Calvinism:] You will be damned if you do—
And you will be damned if you don't.
Reflections on the Love of God ch. 6 (1836)

Maureen Dowd
U.S. journalist, 1952–

1 The Princess of Wales [Diana] was the queen
of surfaces, ruling over a kingdom where fame
was the highest value and glamour the most
cherished attribute.
N.Y. Times, 3 Sept. 1997

2 [Of the war in Iraq:] Why is all this a surprise
again? I know our hawks avoided serving in
Vietnam, but didn't they, like, read about it?
N.Y. Times, 30 Mar. 2003

Ernest Dowson
English poet, 1867–1900

1 I have been faithful to thee, Cynara! in my
fashion.
"Non Sum Qualis Eram" l. 6 (1896)
See Cole Porter 20

2 I have forgot much, Cynara! gone with the
wind.
"Non Sum Qualis Eram" l. 12 (1896)
See Mangan 1; Margaret Mitchell 4

3 They are not long, the days of wine and roses.
"Vitae Summa Brevis" l. 5 (1896)

Arthur Conan Doyle
British writer and physician, 1859–1930

1 [The first encounter between Sherlock Holmes and
Dr. Watson:] "You have been in Afghanistan, I
perceive."
"How on earth did you know that?"
A Study in Scarlet ch. 1 (1888)

2 London, that great cesspool into which all
the loungers and idlers of the Empire are
irresistibly drained.
A Study in Scarlet ch. 1 (1888)

3 Depend upon it there comes a time when
for every addition of knowledge you forget
something that you knew before. It is of the
highest importance, therefore, not to have
useless facts elbowing out the useful ones.
A Study in Scarlet ch. 2 (1888)

4 You say that we go round the sun. If we
went round the moon it would not make a
pennyworth of difference to me or to my work.
A Study in Scarlet ch. 2 (1888)

5 "Wonderful!" I ejaculated.
"Commonplace," said Holmes.
A Study in Scarlet ch. 3 (1888)

6 There's the scarlet thread of murder running
through the colorless skein of life, and our duty
is to unravel it, and isolate it, and expose every
inch of it.
A Study in Scarlet ch. 4 (1888)

7 It is cocaine . . . a seven per cent solution.
Would you care to try it?
The Sign of the Four ch. 1 (1890)

8 The only unofficial consulting detective. I am
the last and highest court of appeal in detection.
The Sign of the Four ch. 1 (1890)

9 Detection is, or ought to be, an exact science,
and should be treated in the same cold and
unemotional manner. You have attempted to
tinge it with romanticism, which produces
much the same effect as if you worked a love-
story or an elopement into the fifth proposition
of Euclid.
The Sign of the Four ch. 1 (1890)

10 How often have I said to you that when you
have eliminated the impossible, whatever
remains, *however improbable*, must be the truth?
The Sign of the Four ch. 6 (1890)
See Boucher 1

11 The unofficial force—the Baker Street
irregulars.
The Sign of the Four ch. 8 (1890)

12 Singularity is almost invariably a clue. The
more featureless and commonplace a crime is,
the more difficult it is to bring it home.
"The Boscombe Valley Mystery" (1891)

13 Beyond the obvious facts that he has at some
time done manual labor, that he takes snuff,
that he is a Freemason, that he has been to
China, and that he has done a considerable
amount of writing lately, I can deduce
nothing else.
"The Red-Headed League" (1891)

14 It is quite a three-pipe problem.
"The Red-Headed League" (1891)

15 To Sherlock Holmes she [Irene Adler] is always
the woman. I have seldom heard him mention
her under any other name. In his eyes she
eclipses and predominates the whole of her sex.
"A Scandal in Bohemia" (1891)

16 You see, but you do not observe.
"A Scandal in Bohemia" (1891)

17 I have no data yet. It is a capital mistake to
theorize before one has data. Insensibly one
begins to twist facts to suit theories, instead of
theories to suit facts.
"A Scandal in Bohemia" (1891)

18 My name is Sherlock Holmes. It is my business
to know what other people don't know.
"The Adventure of the Blue Carbuncle" (1892)

19 It is my belief, Watson, founded upon my
experience, that the lowest and vilest alleys in
London do not present a more dreadful record
of sin than does the smiling and beautiful
countryside.
"The Adventure of the Copper Beeches" (1892)

20 Your conversation is most entertaining. When
you go out close the door, for there is a decided
draught.
"The Adventure of the Speckled Band" (1892)

21 "Is there any other point to which you would
wish to draw my attention?"
"To the curious incident of the dog in the
night-time."

"The dog did nothing in the night-time."

"That was the curious incident," remarked Sherlock Holmes.

"Silver Blaze" (1892)

22 I should prefer that you do not mention my name at all in connection with the case, as I choose to be only associated with those crimes which present some difficulty in their solution.

"The Adventure of the Cardboard Box" (1893)

23 "Excellent," I cried. "Elementary," said he.

"The Adventure of the Crooked Man" (1893)
See Arthur Conan Doyle 39

24 You know my methods, Watson.

"The Adventure of the Crooked Man" (1893)

25 He [Professor Moriarty] is the Napoleon of crime, Watson. He is the organizer of half that is evil and of nearly all that is undetected in this great city. He is a genius, a philosopher, an abstract thinker. He has a brain of the first order.

"The Final Problem" (1893)

26 Then we rushed on into the captain's cabin . . . and there he lay . . . while the chaplain stood, with a smoking pistol in his hand.

"The Adventure of the *Gloria Scott*" (1893). Earliest known usage of *smoking gun* or *smoking pistol*.

27 There is nothing in which deduction is so necessary as in religion. It can be built up as an exact science by the reasoner. Our highest assurance of the goodness of Providence seems to me to rest in the flowers. All other things, our powers, our desires, our food, are all really necessary for our existence in the first instance. But this rose is an extra. Its smell and its color are an embellishment of life, not a condition of it. It is only goodness which gives extras, and so I say again that we have much to hope from the flowers.

"The Adventure of the Naval Treaty" (1893)

28 Like all Holmes's reasoning the thing seemed simplicity itself when it was once explained.

"The Adventure of the Stockbroker's Clerk" (1893)

29 Mr. Holmes, they were the footprints of a gigantic hound!

The Hound of the Baskervilles ch. 2 (1902)

30 Come, Watson, come! The game is afoot.

"The Adventure of the Abbey Grange" (1904)

31 [*Sherlock Holmes to Dr. Watson:*] The fair sex is your department.

"The Adventure of the Second Stain" (1904)

32 You will remember, Watson, how the dreadful business of the Abernetty family was first brought to my notice by the depth to which the parsley had sunk into the butter upon a hot day.

"The Adventure of the Six Napoleons" (1904)

33 It is fortunate for this community that I am not a criminal.

"The Adventure of the Bruce-Partington Plans" (1908)

34 I play the game for the game's own sake.

"The Adventure of the Bruce-Partington Plans" (1908)

35 Besides, on general principles it is best that I should not leave the country. Scotland Yard feels lonely without me, and it causes an unhealthy excitement among the criminal classes.

"The Disappearance of Lady Frances Carfax" (1911)

36 Mediocrity knows nothing higher than itself, but talent instantly recognizes genius.

The Valley of Fear ch. 1 (1915)

37 Good old Watson! You are the one fixed point in a changing age.

"His Last Bow" (1917)

38 The giant rat of Sumatra, a story for which the world is not yet prepared.

"The Adventure of the Sussex Vampire" (1924)

39 Elementary, my dear Watson.

Attributed in *Richmond Times-Dispatch*, 24 Aug. 1909. This phrase is popularly attributed to Sherlock Holmes but does not appear in any of the Holmes stories by Arthur Conan Doyle. The *Northhampton* (England) *Mercury*, 15 Nov. 1901, ran a humorous article in which "Dr. Potson" was told by "Shylock Combs": "Elementary, my dear Potson." Although the narrator's name was parodically altered to "Potson," clearly an existing phrase of "Elementary, my dear Watson" was being played upon. Even earlier, in the 22 Sept. 1893 issue of *English Mechanic and World of Science*, a letter to the editor included the words "All this is quite elementary, my dear 'Fellow of the Chemical Society.'" That may have been a coincidental expression unrelated to Sherlock Holmes, but it seems that it may have been an allusion to an early form, "Elementary, my dear fellow."

See Arthur Conan Doyle 23

Roddy Doyle

Irish novelist, 1958–

1 The Irish are the niggers of Europe, lads. . . .
  An' Dubliners are the niggers of Ireland. . . .
  An' the northside Dubliners are the niggers o'
  Dublin.—Say it loud, I'm black an' I'm proud.
  The Commitments (1987)
  See James Brown 2

Margaret Drabble

English novelist, 1939–

1 Sometimes it seems the only accomplishment
  my education ever bestowed on me was the
  ability to think in quotations.
  A Summer Birdcage ch. 1 (1963)

2 Lord knows what incommunicable small
  terrors infants go through, unknown to all. We
  disregard them, we say they forget, because
  they have not the words to make us remember.
  . . . By the time they learn to speak they have
  forgotten the details of their complaints, and so
  we never know. They forget so quickly, we say,
  because we cannot contemplate the fact that
  they never forget.
  The Millstone (1965)

3 Human contact seemed to her so frail a thing
  that the hope that two people might want each
  other in the same way, at the same time and
  with the possibility of doing something about
  it, seemed infinitely remote.
  The Waterfall (1969)

Drake (Aubrey Drake Graham)

Canadian rap singer and songwriter, 1986–

1 You only live once, that's the motto nigga YOLO
  We 'bout it every day, every day, every day.
  "The Motto" (song) (2011)
  See Modern Proverbs 54

Francis Drake

English admiral and explorer, ca. 1540–1596

1 [*On the expedition to Cadiz, 1587:*] The singeing
  of the King of Spain's Beard.
  Quoted in Francis Bacon, *Considerations Touching a
  War with Spain* (1629)

Michael Drayton

English poet, 1563–1631

1 Since there's no help, come let us kiss and part,
  Nay, I have done: you get no more of me,
  And I am glad, yea glad with all my heart,
  That thus so cleanly, I myself can free,
  Shake hands for ever, cancel all our vows.
  Idea Sonnet 61, l. 1 (1619)

2 Next these, learn'd Jonson, in this list I bring,
  Who had drunk deep of the Pierian spring.
  "To Henry Reynolds, of Poets and Poesy" l. 129
  (1627)
  See Pope 1

Theodore Dreiser

U.S. novelist and editor, 1871–1945

1 Oh, the moonlight's fair tonight along the
    Wabash,
  From the fields there comes the breath of new-
    mown hay;
  Through the sycamores the candle lights are
    gleaming
  On the banks of the Wabash, far away.
  "On the Banks of the Wabash" (song) (1898).
  Credited to Dreiser's brother, Paul Dresser, but
  Dreiser is believed to have written the lyrics to this
  chorus.

2 Our civilization is still in a middle stage,
  scarcely beast, in that it is no longer wholly
  guided by instinct; scarcely human, in that it is
  not yet wholly guided by reason.
  Sister Carrie ch. 8 (1900)

3 In your rocking-chair, by your window
  dreaming, shall you long, alone. In your
  rocking-chair, by your window, shall you dream
  such happiness as you may never feel.
  Sister Carrie ch. 47 (1900)

William Drennan

Irish poet, 1754–1820

1 Nor one feeling of vengeance presume to defile
  The cause, or the men, of the Emerald Isle.
  "Erin" l. 39 (1795). Appears to be the origin of the
  name *Emerald Isle* for Ireland.

William Driver

U.S. sailor, 1803–1886

1 [*Saluting a new flag hoisted on his ship, 10 Aug. 1831:*] I name thee Old Glory.

Attributed in *L.A. Times,* 31 July 1951. According to *Bartlett's Familiar Quotations:* "On August 10, 1831, a large American flag was presented to Captain William Driver of the brig *Charles Doggett* by a band of women, in recognition of his humane service in bringing back the British mutineers of the ship *Bounty* from Tahiti to their former home, Pitcairn Island. As the flag was hoisted to the masthead, Captain Driver proclaimed, 'I name thee Old Glory.' The flag is now in the Smithsonian Institution, Washington, D.C."

Peter Drucker

Austrian-born U.S. management theorist, 1909–2005

1 There is surely nothing quite so useless as doing with great efficiency what should not be done at all.

"Managing for Business Effectiveness," *Harvard Business Review,* May–June 1963

Charles Dryden

U.S. sportswriter, 1869–1931

1 Washington—First in war, first in peace, last in the American League.

Quoted in *Wash. Post,* 27 June 1904
See Henry Lee 1

John Dryden

English poet and playwright, 1631–1700

1 The famous rules, which the French call *Des Trois Unitez,* or, the Three Unities, which ought to be observed in every regular play; namely, of Time, Place, and Action.

An Essay of Dramatic Poesy (1668)

2 I am as free as nature first made man,
Ere the base laws of servitude began,
When wild in woods the noble savage ran.

The Conquest of Granada pt. 1, act 1, sc. 1 (1670)

3 Men are but children of a larger growth;
Our appetites as apt to change as theirs,
And full as craving too, and full as vain.

All for Love act 4, sc. 1 (1678)

4 Great wits are sure to madness near allied.

Absalom and Achitophel pt. 1, l. 163 (1681)

5 In friendship false, implacable in hate:
Resolved to ruin or to rule the state.

Absalom and Achitophel pt. 1, l. 173 (1681)

6 The rest to some faint meaning make pretence,
But Shadwell never deviates into sense.

MacFlecknoe l. 19 (1682)

7   Wit will shine
Through the harsh cadence of a rugged line.

"To the Memory of Mr. Oldham" l. 15 (1684)

8 Happy the man, and happy he alone,
He, who can call to-day his own:
He who, secure within, can say,
Tomorrow do thy worst, for I have lived today.

Imitation of Horace bk. 3, ode 29, l. 65 (1685)
See Horace 21

9 What passion cannot Music raise and quell?

A Song for St. Cecilia's Day st. 2 (1687)

10 None but the brave deserves the fair.

Alexander's Feast l. 7 (1697)

11 Arms, and the man I sing, who, forced by fate,
And haughty Juno's unrelenting hate,
Expelled and exiled, left the Trojan shore.

Translation of Virgil, *Aeneid,* bk. 1, l. 1 (1697)
See Virgil 1

12 [*Of Chaucer:*] 'Tis sufficient to say, according to the proverb, that here is God's plenty.

Fables Ancient and Modern preface (1700)

Alexander Dubček

Czechoslovak statesman, 1921–1992

1 In the service of the people we followed such a policy that socialism would not lose its human face.

Rudé Právo, 19 July 1968. Robert Stewart, in *Penguin Dictionary of Political Quotations,* states that Radovan Richta suggested "human face" to Dubček in conversation.

Al Dubin

Swiss-born U.S. songwriter, 1891–1945

1 Come and meet those dancing feet
On the avenue I'm taking you to
Forty Second Street.

"Forty-Second Street" (song) (1932)

2 Shuffle Off to Buffalo.

Title of song (1932)

3 We're in the money.
"The Gold Digger's Song (We're in the Money)"
(song) (1933)

W. E. B. Du Bois
U.S. reformer, educator, and writer, 1868–1963

1 The Negro is a sort of seventh son, born with
a veil, and gifted with second-sight in this
American world,—a world which yields him
no self-consciousness, but only lets him see
himself through the revelation of the other
world. It is a peculiar sensation, this double-
consciousness, this sense of always looking
at one's self through the eyes of others, of
measuring one's soul by the tape of a world that
looks on in amused contempt and pity.
"Strivings of the Negro People" (1897)

2 One ever feels his two-ness,—an American,
a Negro; two souls, two thoughts, two
unreconciled strivings; two warring ideals in
one dark body, whose dogged strength alone
keeps it from being torn asunder. The history
of the American Negro is the history of this
strife,—this longing to attain self-conscious
manhood, to merge his double self into a
better and truer self. In this merging he wishes
neither of the older selves to be lost.
"Strivings of the Negro People" (1897)

3 The Negro race, like all races, is going to be
saved by its exceptional men. The problem of
education, then, among Negroes must first of
all deal with the Talented Tenth.
"The Talented Tenth" (1903)

4 To be a poor man is hard, but to be a poor
race in a land of dollars is the very bottom of
hardships.
The Souls of Black Folk ch. 1 (1903)

5 The problem of the twentieth century is the
problem of the color-line,—the relation of the
darker to the lighter races of men in Asia and
Africa, in America and the islands of the sea.
The Souls of Black Folk ch. 2 (1903)

6 Herein lies the tragedy of the age: not that men
are poor,—all men know something of poverty;
not that men are wicked—who is good? not that
men are ignorant—what is Truth? Nay, but that
men know so little of men.
The Souls of Black Folk ch. 12 (1903)

7 The cost of liberty is less than the price of
repression, even though that cost be blood.
John Brown ch. 13 (1909)

8 Is a civilization naturally backward because it
is different? Outside of cannibalism, which
can be matched in this country, at least, by
lynching, there is no vice and no degradation
in native African customs which can begin to
touch the horrors thrust upon them by white
masters. Drunkenness, terrible diseases,
immorality, all these things have been gifts of
European civilization.
"Reconstruction and Africa" (1919)

9 What, then, is this dark world thinking? It
is thinking that as wild and awful as this
shameful war was, *it is nothing to compare with
that fight for freedom which black and brown
and yellow men must and will make unless their
oppression and humiliation and insult at the hands
of the White World cease.*
Darkwater ch. 2 (1920)

10 The Dark World is going to submit to its
present treatment just as long as it must and
not one moment longer.
Darkwater ch. 2 (1920)

11 Not even a Harvard School of Business can
make greed into a science.
In Battle for Peace ch. 14 (1952)

René Dubos
French-born U.S. biologist and
environmentalist, 1901–1982

1 In most human affairs, the idea is to think
globally and act locally.
"The Despairing Optimist," *American Scholar*, Spring
1977. The motto "Think Globally, Act Locally" was the
title of an interview with Dubos in *EPA Journal*, Apr.
1978. "We must think globally, but first act locally"
appeared in *Safety Education*, May 1942, where it was
said to be quoted from Edgar Dale in the Feb. 1942
issue of the newsletter of the Bureau of Educational
Research, Ohio State University. In addition, the
Vidette Messenger (Valparaiso, Ind.), 27 Mar. 1947,
quoted a letter from Jane Sense referring to "the
objective and slogan of the right worthy grand matron
and the general grand chapter [of the Indiana Order
of the Eastern Star]: 'World Friendship' and 'think
globally, act locally.'"

Madame Du Deffand (Marie de Vichy-Chamrond)

French literary hostess, 1697–1780

1 [*On the legend that St. Denis, carrying his own head, walked two leagues:*] *La distance n'y fait rien; il n'y a que le premier pas qui coûte.*
The distance is nothing; it is only the first step that is difficult.
Letter to Jean Le Rond d'Alembert, 7 July 1763

James S. Duesenberry

U.S. economist, 1918–2009

1 Economics is all about how people make choices. Sociology is all about why they don't have any choices to make.
Quoted in National Bureau of Economic Research, *Demographic and Economic Change in Developed Countries* (1960)

Du Fu

Chinese poet, 712–770

1 The nation is ruined, but mountains and rivers remain.
"Spring View" (755) (translation by Gary Snyder)

2 I am about to scream madly in the office,
Especially when they bring more papers to pile high on my desk.
Poem 109, quoted in William Hung, *Tu Fu: China's Greatest Poet* (1952)

3 Sundered by peaks unscalable,
Tomorrow shall we strangers be.
"Visiting an Old Friend," quoted in John A. Turner, *A Golden Treasury of Chinese Poetry* (1976)

Allen W. Dulles

U.S. government official, 1893–1969

1 When the fate of a nation and the lives of its soldiers are at stake, gentlemen do read each other's mail—if they can get their hands on it.
The Craft of Intelligence ch. 6 (1963)
See Stimson 1

John Foster Dulles

U.S. diplomat and lawyer, 1888–1959

1 If . . . the European Defense Community should not become effective; if France and Germany remain apart . . . That would compel an agonizing reappraisal of basic United States policy.
Speech to NATO Council, Paris, 14 Dec. 1953

2 Local defense must be reinforced by the further deterrent of massive retaliatory power.
Speech to Council on Foreign Relations, New York, N.Y., 12 Jan. 1954

3 The ability to get to the verge without getting into the war is the necessary art. . . . We walked to the brink and we looked it in the face.
Quoted in *Life*, 16 Jan. 1956
See Adlai Stevenson 9

4 [*In response to being asked whether he had ever been wrong:*] Yes, once . . . many, many years ago. I thought I had made a wrong decision. Of course, it turned out that I had been right all along. But I was wrong to have *thought* I was wrong.
Quoted in Henri Temianka, *Facing the Music* (1973)

Alexandre Dumas the Elder

French novelist and playwright, 1802–1870

1 She resisted me, so I killed her.
Antony act 5, sc. 4 (1831)

2 *Les Trois Mousquetaires.*
The Three Musketeers.
Title of book (1844)

3 *Tous pour un, un pour tous.*
All for one, one for all.
Les Trois Mousquetaires (The Three Musketeers) ch. 9 (1844)

4 Until the day when God will deign to reveal the future to man, all human wisdom is contained in these two words, Wait and hope.
The Count of Monte Cristo ch. 117 (1845)

5 *Cherchons la femme.*
Let us look for the woman.
Les Mohicans de Paris vol. 3, ch. 10 (1854–1855). Also attributed to Joseph Fouché in the form *Cherchez la femme.*

Alexandre Dumas the Younger

French writer, 1824–1895

1 *Le Demi-Monde.*
Title of play (1855). *Trésor de la Langue Française* records a somewhat different sense of the word *demi-monde* ("world of equivocal morals") as far back as 1789, but the modern usage derives from Dumas.

Daphne du Maurier
English novelist, 1907–1989

1 Last night I dreamt I went to Manderley again.
Rebecca ch. 1 (1938)

2 You thought I loved Rebecca? . . . I hated her.
Rebecca ch. 20 (1938)

3 And the ashes blew towards us with the salt wind from the sea.
Rebecca ch. 27 (1938)

Charles François Dumouriez
French general, 1739–1823

1 [*Of Louis XVIII:*] The courtiers who surround him have forgotten nothing and learnt nothing.
Examen Impartial d'un écrit Intitulé Déclaration de Louis XVIII (1795). Frequently attributed to Talleyrand, speaking of the Bourbon exiles and in the form "Ils n'ont rien appris, ni rien oublié" (They have learnt nothing, and forgotten nothing).

Paul Laurence Dunbar
U.S. poet, 1872–1906

1 We wear the mask that grins and lies,
It hides our cheeks and shades our eyes,—
This debt we pay to human guile . . .

But let the world dream otherwise,
We wear the mask!
"We Wear the Mask" l. 1, 14 (1895)

2 I know why the caged bird sings!
"Sympathy" l. 21 (1899)
See John Webster 2

Isadora Duncan
U.S. dancer, 1878–1927

1 Any intelligent woman who reads the marriage contract and then goes into it, deserves all the consequences.
My Life ch. 19 (1927)

2 [*"Last words," before breaking her neck when her scarf became entangled in a car wheel:*]
Adieu, mes amis. Je vais à la gloire.
Farewell, my friends. I go to glory.
Quoted in Mary Desti, *Isadora Duncan's End* (1929)

Irina Dunn
Australian educator, journalist, and politician, 1948–

1 A woman without a man is like a fish without a bicycle.
Quoted in *Sydney* (Australia) *Morning Herald*, 25 Jan. 1975. The newspaper stated: "We found this anonymous contribution . . . on a wall at Forest Lodge." This is the earliest printed documentation that has been found for the saying. Gloria Steinem, who is often said to be the originator, has credited Dunn as coiner. Dunn says she wrote "A woman needs a man like a fish needs a bicycle" on two toilet doors in Sydney, Australia, in 1970, paraphrasing "A man needs God like a fish needs a bicycle."
See Charles S. Harris 1

Finley Peter Dunne
U.S. humorist, 1867–1936

1 "Politics," he says, "ain't bean bag."
Mr. Dooley in Peace and in War preface (1898)

2 I knowed a society wanst to vote a monyment to a man an' refuse to help his fam'ly, all in wan night.
Mr. Dooley in Peace and in War "On Charity" (1898)

3 A fanatic is a man that does what he thinks th' Lord wud do if He knew th' facts iv th' case.
Mr. Dooley's Philosophy "Casual Observations" (1900)

4 I care not who makes th' laws iv a nation if I can get out an injunction.
Mr. Dooley's Philosophy "Casual Observations" (1900)

5 Thrust ivrybody—but cut th' ca-ards.
Mr. Dooley's Philosophy "Casual Observations" (1900)

6 A man that'd expict to thrain lobsters to fly in a year is called a loonytic; but a man that thinks men can be tur-rned into angels be an iliction is called a rayformer an' remains at large.
Mr. Dooley's Philosophy "Casual Observations" (1900)

7 Most vegetarians I ever see looked enough like their food to be classed as cannibals.
Mr. Dooley's Philosophy "Casual Observations" (1900)

8 No wan cares to hear what Hogan calls "Th' short and simple scandals iv th' poor."
"On Cross-Examinations" (1900)
See Thomas Gray 5

9 I tell ye Hogan's r-right when he says: "Justice is blind." Blind she is, an' deef an' dumb an' has a wooden leg!
"On Cross-Examinations" (1900)

10 No, sir, th' dimmcratic party ain't on speakin' terms with itsilf. Whin ye see two men with white neckties go into a sthreet car an' set in opposite corners while wan mutthers "Thraiter," an' th' other hisses, "Miscreent," ye can bet they're two dimmycratic leaders thryin' to reunite th' gran' ol' party.
"Mr. Dooley Discusses Party Prospects" (1901)

11 No matter whether th' constitution follows th' flag or not, th' Supreme Coort follows th' election returns.
"Mr. Dooley Reviews Supreme Court Decision" (1901)

12 "D'ye think th' colledges has much to do with th' progress iv th' wurruld?" asked Mr. Hennessy. "D'ye think," said Mr. Dooley, "'tis th' mill that makes th' wather run?"
"On the Celebration at Yale" (1901)

13 I don't believe in capital punishmint, Hinnissy, but 'twill niver be abolished while th' people injye it so much.
"On the Law's Delays" (1901)

14 Th' newspaper does ivrything fr us. It runs th' polis foorce an' th' banks, commands th' milishy, conthrols th' ligislachure, baptizes th' young, marries th' foolish, comforts th' afflicted, afflicts th' comfortable, buries th' dead an' roasts thim aftherward. They ain't annything it don't turn its hand to.
"On Newspaper Publicity" (1902)

15 "Ye know a lot about it [bringing up children]," said Mr. Hennessy. "I do," said Mr. Dooley. "Not bein' an author I'm a gr-reat critic."
"On the Bringing Up of Children" (1904)

16 Th' prisidincy is th' highest office in th' gift iv th' people. Th' vice-prisidincy is th' nex' highest an' th' lowest. It isn't a crime exactly. Ye can't be sint to jail fr it, but it's a kind iv a disgrace.
"On the Duties of Vice-President" (1904)

17 In me heart I think if people marry it ought to be fr life. Th' laws ar-re altogether too lenient with thim.
"On Short Marriage Contracts" (1904)

18 This home iv opporchunity where ivry man is th' equal iv ivry other man befure th' law if he isn't careful.
Dissertations by Mr. Dooley "The Food We Eat" (1906)

19 A law, Hinnissy, that might look like a wall to you or me wud look like a thriumphal arch to th' expeeryenced eye iv a lawyer.
"On the Power of the Press" (1906)

20 Th' lawyers make th' law; th' judges make th' errors, but th' iditors make th' juries.
"On the Power of the Press" (1906)

21 An appeal, Hinnissy, is where ye ask wan coort to show its contempt fr another coort.
"On the Big Fine" (1907)

22 [*Of John D. Rockefeller:*] He's kind iv a society fr the previntion of croolty to money. If he finds a man misusing his money he takes it away fr'm him an' adopts it.
"On the Big Fine" (1907)

23 Don't I think a poor man has a chanst in coort? Iv coorse he has. He has th' same chanst there that he has outside. He has a splendid, poor man's chanst.
"On the Recall of Judges" (1912)

Roberto Duran
Panamanian boxer, 1951–

1 [*Signaling his desire to end his welterweight championship fight against Sugar Ray Leonard, New Orleans, La., 25 Nov. 1980:*] No mas, no mas.
No more, no more.
Quoted in *N.Y. Times*, 26 Nov. 1980

Henry S. Durand
U.S. physician and songwriter, 1861–1929

1 For God, for Country, and for Yale!
"Bright College Years" (song) (1881). Cowritten with Carl Wilhelm.

Jimmy Durante
U.S. comedian, 1893–1980

1 [*Catchphrase:*] I've got a million of 'em!
Quoted in *Winnipeg Free Press*, 5 Oct. 1929

Marguerite Duras
French writer, 1914–1996

1 *Tu n'as rien vu à Hiroshima. Rien.*
You saw nothing in Hiroshima, nothing.
Hiroshima, Mon Amour (1960)

Adam Duritz
U.S. rock musician, 1964–

1 We all want something beautiful
Man, I wish I was beautiful.
"Mr. Jones" (song) (1993)

Émile Durkheim
French sociologist, 1858–1917

1 Our excessive tolerance with regard to suicide
is due to the fact that, since the state of mind
from which it springs is a general one, we
cannot condemn it without condemning
ourselves; we are too saturated with it not partly
to excuse it.
Suicide: A Study in Sociology bk. 3, ch. 3 (1897)
(translation by John A. Spaulding and George
Simpson)

Leo Durocher
U.S. baseball manager, 1906–1991

1 I never questioned the integrity of an umpire.
Their eyesight, yes.
Nice Guys Finish Last bk. 1 (1975)

2 [*Remark about New York Giants baseball team, 6
July 1946:*] The nice guys are all over there, in
seventh place.
Quoted in *N.Y. Journal-American*, 7 July 1946.
Ralph Keyes reports in "*Nice Guys Finish Seventh*"
that, when this newspaper column "was reprinted
in *Baseball Digest* that fall, Durocher's reference
to nice guys finishing in 'seventh place' had been
changed to 'last place.' . . . Before long Leo's credo
was bumper-stickered into 'Nice guys finish last.'"
The shift may have taken place even earlier, given
an article in *Sporting News*, 17 July 1946, headlined,
"'Nice Guys' Wind Up in Last Place, Scoffs Lippy."
The earliest occurrence of the exact famous quotation
may have been Durocher's article, titled "Nice Guys
Finish Last," in the Apr. 1948 issue of *Cosmopolitan*
magazine.

Lawrence Durrell
Indian-born English writer, 1912–1990

1 There are only three things to be done with a
woman. You can love her, suffer for her, or turn
her into literature.
Justine pt. 1 (1957)

Friedrich Dürrenmatt
Swiss playwright and novelist, 1921–1990

1 What was once thought can never be
unthought.
The Physicists act 2 (1962) (translation by James
Kirkup)

Ian Dury
English rock singer and songwriter, 1942–
2000

1 Sex and Drugs and Rock 'n' Roll.
Title of song (1976). Cowritten with Chaz Jankel.

Andrea Dworkin
U.S. feminist and writer, 1946–2005

1 Seduction is often difficult to distinguish from
rape. In seduction, the rapist bothers to buy a
bottle of wine.
"Sexual Economics: The Terrible Truth" (1976)

2 No woman needs intercourse; few women
escape it.
Right-Wing Women ch. 3 (1978)

3 The power of money is a distinctly male power.
Money speaks, but it speaks with a male voice.
In the hands of women, money stays literal;
count it out, it buys what it is worth or less. In
the hands of men, money buys women, sex,
status, dignity, esteem, recognition, loyalty, all
manner of possibility.
Pornography: Men Possessing Women ch. 1 (1981)

4 Women, for centuries not having access to
pornography and now unable to bear looking
at the muck on the supermarket shelves, are
astonished. Women do not believe that men
believe what pornography says about women.
But they do. From the worst to the best of them,
they do.
Pornography: Men Possessing Women ch. 5 (1981)

5 One of the differences between marriage and prostitution is that in marriage you only have to make a deal with one man.

Letters from a War Zone: Writings 1976–1989 "Feminism: An Agenda" (1988). This essay was originally a speech at Hamilton College, Clinton, N.Y., 8 Apr. 1983, then published in the college literary magazine, *The ABC's of Reading*, in 1984.

Bob Dylan (Robert Zimmerman)
U.S. singer and songwriter, 1941–

1 How many roads must a man walk down
Before you call him a man?
"Blowin' in the Wind" (song) (1962)

2 The answer, my friend, is blowin' in the wind,
The answer is blowin' in the wind.
"Blowin' in the Wind" (song) (1962)

3 How many deaths will it take till he knows
That too many people have died?
"Blowin' in the Wind" (song) (1962)

4 How many times can a man turn his head,
Pretending he just doesn't see?
"Blowin' in the Wind" (song) (1962)

5 I saw ten thousand talkers whose tongues were
all broken,
I saw guns and sharp swords in the hands of
young children,
And . . . it's a hard rain's a-gonna fall.
"A Hard Rain's A-Gonna Fall" (song) (1963)

6 Come senators, congressmen
Please heed the call
Don't stand in the doorway
Don't block up the hall.
"The Times They Are A-Changin'" (1963)

7 The order is
Rapidly fadin'.
And the first one now
Will later be last
For the times they are a-changin'.
"The Times They Are A-Changin'" (song) (1963)

8 Hey! Mr. Tambourine Man, play a song for me,
I'm not sleepy and there is no place I'm going
to.
Hey! Mr. Tambourine Man, play a song for me,
In the jingle jangle morning I'll come followin'
you.
"Mr. Tambourine Man" (song) (1964)

9 Yes, to dance beneath the diamond sky with
one hand waving free,
Silhouetted by the sea, circled by the circus
sands,
With all memory and fate driven deep beneath
the waves,
Let me forget about today until tomorrow.
"Mr. Tambourine Man" (song) (1964)

10 Ah, but I was so much older then,
I'm younger than that now.
"My Back Pages" (song) (1964)

11 Something is happening here
But you don't know what it is
Do you, Mister Jones?
"Ballad of a Thin Man" (song) (1965)

12 Yonder stands your orphan with his gun,
Crying like a fire in the sun.
Look out the saints are comin' through
And it's all over now, Baby Blue.
"It's All Over Now, Baby Blue" (song) (1965)

13 He not busy being born
Is busy dying.
"It's Alright, Ma (I'm Only Bleeding)" (song) (1965)

14 Even the president of the United States
Sometimes must have
To stand naked.
"It's Alright, Ma (I'm Only Bleeding)" (song) (1965)

15 Money doesn't talk, it swears.
"It's Alright, Ma (I'm Only Bleeding)" (song) (1965)

16 Once upon a time you dressed so fine
You threw the bums a dime in your prime,
didn't you?
"Like a Rolling Stone" (song) (1965)

17 How does it feel
    To be on your own
    With no direction home
    Like a complete unknown
    Like a rolling stone?
    "Like a Rolling Stone" (song) (1965)
    See Proverbs 257; Muddy Waters 1

18 You don't need a weather man
    To know which way the wind blows.
    "Subterranean Homesick Blues" (song) (1965). The revolutionary group the Weathermen, formed in 1969, took their name from this passage.

19 Don't follow leaders
    Watch the parkin' meters.
    "Subterranean Homesick Blues" (song) (1965)

20 But to live outside the law, you must be honest.
    "Absolutely Sweet Marie" (song) (1966). According to Robert Andrews, *New Penguin Dictionary of Modern Quotations,* "a similar line appears in Don Siegel's film *The Line-Up* (1958)."

21 "There must be some way out of here," said the joker to the thief,
    "There's too much confusion, I can't get no relief.
    Businessmen, they drink my wine, plowmen dig my earth,
    None of them along the line know what any of it is worth."
    "All Along the Watchtower" (song) (1968)

22 Lay, lady, lay, lay across my big brass bed.
    "Lay, Lady, Lay" (song) (1969)

23 Mama, take this badge off of me
    I can't use it anymore.
    It's getting dark, too dark for me to see
    I feel like I'm knockin' on heaven's door.
    "Knockin' on Heaven's Door" (song) (1973)

24 In a little hilltop village, they gambled for my clothes
    I bargained for salvation an' they gave me a lethal dose.
    "Shelter from the Storm" (song) (1974)

25 If I could only turn back the clock to when God and her were born.
    "Come in," she said,
    "I'll give you shelter from the storm."
    "Shelter from the Storm" (song) (1974)

26 Here comes the story of the Hurricane,
    The man the authorities came to blame
    For somethin' that he never done.
    Put in a prison cell, but one time he could-a been
    The champion of the world.
    "Hurricane" (song) (1975)

27 Now all the criminals in their coats and their ties
    Are free to drink martinis and watch the sun rise
    While Rubin sits like Buddha in a ten-foot cell
    An innocent man in a living hell.
    "Hurricane" (song) (1975)

Freeman Dyson
English-born U.S. physicist and mathematician, 1923–2020

1 Most of the papers which are submitted to the *Physical Review* are rejected, not because it is impossible to understand them, but because it is possible. Those which are impossible to understand are usually published.
   Scientific American, Sept. 1958

Will Dyson
Australian-born English cartoonist, 1880–1938

1 Curious! I seem to hear a child weeping!
   Cartoon caption, *Daily Herald* (London), 13 May 1919. The cartoon depicted Georges Clemenceau leaving the Palais de Versailles with Woodrow Wilson, David Lloyd George, and Vittorio Orlando after they had signed the peace treaty with Germany. The child represented the generation of 1940.

Amelia Earhart

U.S. aviator, 1897–1937

1 [*Letter left with her husband as she began her final flying journey:*] Please know I am quite aware of the hazards. I want to do it because I want to do it. Women must try to do things as men have tried. When they fail their failure must be but a challenge to others.

Letter to George Putnam, 1937

Max Eastman

U.S. editor and writer, 1883–1969

1 I don't know why it is we are in such a hurry to get up when we fall down. You might think we would lie there and rest a while.

The Enjoyment of Laughter pt. 3, ch. 4 (1935)

Abba Eban

South African–born Israeli statesman, 1915–2002

1 Nations do behave wisely once they have exhausted all other alternatives.

Quoted in *Evening Times* (Trenton, N.J.), 7 June 1967

2 [John Foster] Dulles often wrestled with his conscience and always won.

Personal Witness: Israel Through My Eyes ch. 14 (1992)

3 The P.L.O. [Palestine Liberation Organization] has never missed an opportunity to miss an opportunity.

Quoted in *N.Y. Times,* 18 Dec. 1988
See George Bernard Shaw 56

Fred Ebb

U.S. songwriter, 1935–2004

1 What good is sitting alone in your room?
Come hear the music play;
Life is a cabaret, old chum,
Come to the cabaret.
"Cabaret" (song) (1966)

2 Money makes the world go around.

"Money, Money" (song) (1966). As a proverb, "money makes the world go round" is found as early as *Beecher's Magazine,* Dec. 1870.

3 Meine Damen und Herren, Mesdames et
   Messieurs,
Ladies und Gentlemen—comment ça va?
Do you feel good? . . . I am your host . . .
Wilkommen! Bienvenue! Welcome!
Im Cabaret! Au Cabaret! To Cabaret!
"Wilkommen" (song) (1966)

4 We have no troubles here! Here life is beautiful.
The girls are beautiful.
Even the orchestra is beautiful!
"Wilkommen" (song) (1966)

5 These vagabond shoes
Are longing to stray
And make a brand new start of it
New York, New York
I want to wake up in the city that never sleeps.
"New York, New York" (song) (1977)

6 If I can make it there
I'll make it anywhere
It's up to you, New York, New York.

"New York, New York" (song) (1977). The *New York Times,* 8 Feb. 1959, quoted actress Julie Newmar: "That's why I came to New York. Because if you make it here, you make it anywhere."

Hermann Ebbinghaus

German psychologist, 1850–1909

1 What is true [in psychology] is alas not new, the new not true.

Über die Hartmannsche Philosophie des Unbewussten (1873). Earlier, "What is new is not good; and what is good is not new" appeared in Martin Sherlock, *Letters on Several Subjects* (1781).

Marie von Ebner-Eschenbach
Austrian novelist, 1830–1916

1 Be the first to say something obvious and achieve immortality.
Aphorisms (1905)

Umberto Eco
Italian historian and novelist, 1932–2016

1 I have never doubted the truth of signs, Adso; they are the only things man has with which to orient himself in the world. What I did not understand was the relation among signs. . . . I behaved stubbornly, pursuing a semblance of order, when I should have known well that there is no order in the universe.
The Name of the Rose "Seventh Day, Night" (1980)

Arthur S. Eddington
English physicist, 1882–1944

1 I shall use the phrase "time's arrow" to express this one-way property of time which has no analogue in space.
The Nature of the Physical World ch. 4 (1928)

2 If I let my fingers wander idly over the keys of a typewriter it *might* happen that my screed made an intelligible sentence. If an army of monkeys were strumming on typewriters they *might* write all the books in the British Museum.
The Nature of the Physical World ch. 4 (1928)
See Borel 1; Wilensky 1

3 Science is an edged tool, with which men play like children, and cut their own fingers.
Attributed in Robert L. Weber, *More Random Walks in Science* (1982)

Mary Baker Eddy
U.S. religious leader, 1821–1910

1 Our Father-Mother God, all-harmonious.
Science and Health with Key to the Scriptures 16:24 (1875)

2 Health is not a condition of matter, but of Mind; nor can the material senses bear reliable testimony on the subject of health.
Science and Health with Key to the Scriptures 120:15 (1875)

3 Jesus of Nazareth was the most scientific man that ever trod the globe. He plunged beneath the material surface of things, and found the spiritual cause.
Science and Health with Key to the Scriptures 313:23 (1875)

4 Spirit is the real and eternal; matter is the unreal and temporal.
Science and Health with Key to the Scriptures 468:9 (1875)

5 Then comes the question, how do drugs, hygiene, and animal magnetism heal? It may be affirmed that they do not heal, but only relieve suffering temporarily, exchanging one disease for another.
Science and Health with Key to the Scriptures 483:1 (1875)

6 Disease is an experience of so-called mortal mind. It is fear made manifest on the body.
Science and Health with Key to the Scriptures 493:17 (1875)

Marian Wright Edelman
U.S. lawyer and activist, 1939–

1 The question is not whether we can afford to invest in every child; it is whether we can afford not to.
The Measure of Our Success pt. 5 (1992)

Clarissa Eden
English spouse of prime minister, 1920–

1 [*Of the Suez crisis in October–November 1956:*] For the past few weeks I have really felt as if the Suez Canal was flowing through my drawing-room.
Speech, Gateshead, England, 20 Nov. 1956

Maria Edgeworth
English-born Irish novelist, 1768–1849

1 Well! Some people talk of morality, and some of religion, but give me a little snug property.
The Absentee ch. 2 (1812)

Thomas Alva Edison
U.S. inventor and businessman, 1847–1931

1 [*Suggesting "hello" as a standard telephone greeting:*] I do not think we shall need a call bell as Hello! can be heard 10 to 20 feet away.
Letter to T. B. A. David, 15 Aug. 1877

2 Genius is 1 per cent inspiration and 99 per cent perspiration.

Quoted in *Idaho Daily Statesman*, 6 May 1901. The *Ladies' Home Journal*, Apr. 1898, printed: "Once, when asked to give his definition of genius, Mr. Edison replied: 'Two per cent. is genius and ninety-eight per cent. is hard work.' At another time, when the argument that genius was inspiration was brought before him, he said: 'Bah! Genius is not inspired. Inspiration is perspiration.'"
See *Buffon 2; Thomas Carlyle 19; Jane Ellice Hopkins 1*

3 Opportunity is missed by most people because it comes dressed in overalls looking like hard work.

Attributed in *News Journal* (Mansfield, Ohio), 20 Feb. 1971. The popular attribution to Edison is undoubtedly apocryphal, as Barry Popik has found the following: "The reason most people do not recognize an opportunity when they meet it is because it usually goes around wearing overalls and looking like Hard Work," which was printed in the *Logansport* (Ind.) *Pharos-Tribune*, 18 May 1921, fifty years before the earliest known crediting to the famous inventor.

Jerry Edmonton (Gerald McCrohan)
Canadian rock musician, 1946–1993

1 Born to Be Wild.
Title of song (1968)

Edward VIII
British king, 1894–1972

1 I have found it impossible to carry the heavy burden of responsibility and to discharge my duties as King as I would wish to do without the help and support of the woman I love.
Radio broadcast after his abdication, 11 Dec. 1936

Herman Edwards
U.S. football player and coach, 1954–

1 You play to win the game.
News conference, Hempstead, N.Y., 30 Oct. 2002. Edwards was responding to a question as to whether his New York Jets team might give up during a difficult season.

John Edwards
U.S. politician, 1953–

1 There are two Americas—one for the powerful and the privileged and one for everybody else.
Quoted in *Baltimore Sun*, 9 Jan. 2004

Jonathan Edwards
Colonial American theologian and philosopher, 1703–1758

1 The God that holds you over the pit of hell, much as one holds a spider . . . abhors you, and is dreadfully provoked: his wrath towards you burns like fire; he looks upon you as worthy of nothing else, but to be cast into the fire.
"Sinners in the Hands of an Angry God" (sermon), Enfield, Conn., 8 July 1741

Oliver Edwards
English lawyer, 1711–1791

1 I have tried too in my time to be a philosopher; but, I don't know how, cheerfulness was always breaking in.
Quoted in James Boswell, *The Life of Samuel Johnson* (1791) (entry for 17 Apr. 1778)

Dave Eggers
U.S. writer, 1970–

1 A Heartbreaking Work of Staggering Genius.
Title of book (2000)

Barbara Ehrenreich
U.S. author and columnist, 1941–

1 Exercise is the yuppie version of bulimia.
N.Y. Times, 17 Jan. 1985

2 Take motherhood: nobody ever thought of putting it on a moral pedestal until some brash feminists pointed out, about a century ago, that the pay is lousy and the career ladder nonexistent.
Ms., Oct. 1986

3 Consider the standard two-person married couple. . . . They will *share* a VCR, a microwave, etc. This is not a matter of ideology or even personal inclination. It is practically the definition of marriage. Marriage is socialism among two people.
"Socialism in the Household" (1987)

Paul Ehrlich
U.S. ecologist, 1932–

1 The mother of the year should be a sterilized woman with two adopted children.
Quoted in Art Spiegelman and Bob Schneider, *Whole Grains: A Book of Quotations* (1973)

John Ehrlichman

U.S. government official, 1925–1999

1 [*Of Attorney General John Mitchell:*] He's the Big Enchilada.

Taped conversation, 27 Mar. 1973

2 [*Explaining a political move criticized in Washington, D.C.:*] It'll play in Peoria.

Quoted in *N.Y. Times*, 3 Aug. 1969

3 [*Of Patrick Gray, nominee for director of the Federal Bureau of Investigation, in telephone conversation with John Dean, Mar. 1973:*] I think we ought to let him hang there. Let him twist slowly, slowly in the wind.

Quoted in *Wash. Post*, 27 July 1973

Max Ehrmann

U.S. poet, 1872–1945

1 Go placidly amid the noise and the haste, and remember what peace there may be in silence. As far as possible, without surrender, be on good terms with all persons.

"Desiderata" (1927). The origins of this poem have become confused in the popular mind. Because it was distributed in 1956 by the rector of St. Paul's Church in Baltimore, Maryland, the poem was widely believed to have been written in 1692 and found later in that church. The 1692 date represents the founding of St. Paul's Church and is irrelevant to "Desiderata."

2 You are a child of the universe no less than the trees and the stars; you have a right to be here. And whether or not it is clear to you, no doubt the universe is unfolding as it should.

"Desiderata" (1927)

Albert Einstein

German-born U.S. physicist, 1879–1955

1 According to the assumption considered here, in the propagation of a light ray emitted from a point source, the energy is not distributed continuously over ever-increasing volumes of space, but consists of a finite number of energy quanta localized at points of space that move without dividing and can be absorbed or generated only as complete units.

"On a Heuristic Point of View Concerning the Production and Transformation of Light" (1905)

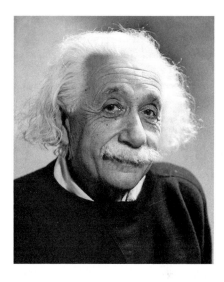

2 $E = mc^2$

"Manuscript on the Special Theory of Relativity" (1912). Einstein's original formulation of the equivalence of mass and energy, in his 1905 paper on relativity in *Annalen der Physik*, was "If a body emits the energy L in the form of radiation, its mass decreases by L/V^2" (translation). The familiar equation (energy equals mass times the square of the speed of light) came into being when Einstein substituted E for L in his 1912 manuscript.

3 I am by heritage a Jew, by citizenship a Swiss, and by makeup a human being, and *only* a human being, without any special attachment to any state or national entity whatsoever.

Letter to Alfred Kneser, 7 June 1918

4 To-day in Germany I am called a German man of science, and in England I am represented as a Swiss Jew. If I come to be regarded as a *bête noire*, the descriptions will be reversed, and I shall become a Swiss Jew for the Germans and a German man of science for the English!

Times (London), 28 Nov. 1919
See Einstein 6

5 As far as the laws of mathematics refer to reality, they are not certain; and as far as they are certain, they do not refer to reality.

Address to Prussian Academy of Sciences, Berlin, 27 Jan. 1921

6 If my theory of relativity is proven successful, Germany will claim me as a German and

France will declare that I am a citizen of the world. Should my theory prove untrue, France will say that I am a German and Germany will declare that I am a Jew.

Address to French Philosophical Society, Paris, 6 Apr. 1922
See Einstein 4

7 I find the idea quite intolerable that an electron exposed to radiation should choose *of its own free will*, not only its moment to jump off, but also its direction. In that case I would rather be a cobbler, or even an employee in a gaming-house, than a physicist.

Letter to Max Born, 29 Apr. 1924

8 Quantum mechanics is very worthy of regard. But an inner voice tells me that this is not yet the right track. The theory yields much, but it hardly brings us closer to the Old One's secrets. I, in any case, am convinced that *He* does not play dice.

Letter to Max Born, 4 Dec. 1926. Usually quoted as "God does not play dice with the universe."
See Einstein 16

9 Should we be unable to find a way to honest co-operation and honest pacts with the Arabs, then we shall have learned nothing from our 2,000 years of suffering and will deserve our fate.

Letter to Chaim Weizmann, 25 Nov. 1929

10 Nature conceals her secrets because she is sublime, not because she is a trickster.

Letter to Oscar Veblen, 30 Apr. 1930

11 We know nothing about it [God and the world] at all. All our knowledge is but the knowledge of schoolchildren. Possibly we shall know a little more than we do now. But the real nature of things, that we shall never know, never.

Interview, *The Jewish Sentinel*, Sept. 1931

12 As a human being, one has been endowed with just enough intelligence to be able to see clearly how utterly inadequate that intelligence is when confronted with what exists.

Letter to Queen Elisabeth of Belgium, 19 Sept. 1932

13 The eternal mystery of the world is its comprehensibility. . . . The fact that it is comprehensible is a miracle.

"Physics and Reality," *Journal of the Franklin Institute*, Mar. 1936. Often quoted as "The most

incomprehensible thing about the universe is that it is comprehensible."

14 Some recent work by E. Fermi and L. Szilard, which has been communicated to me in manuscript, leads me to expect that the element uranium may be turned into a new and important source of energy in the immediate future. Certain aspects of the situation which has arisen seem to call for watchfulness and, if necessary, quick action on the part of the Administration. . . .

This new phenomenon would also lead to the construction of bombs, and it is conceivable—though much less certain—that extremely powerful bombs of a new type may thus be constructed. A single bomb of this type, carried by boat or exploded in a port, might very well destroy the whole port together with some of the surrounding territory. However, such bombs might very well prove to be too heavy for transportation by air.

Letter to Franklin D. Roosevelt, 2 Aug. 1939 [delivered 11 Oct. 1939]. Drafted by Leo Szilard.

15 Science without religion is lame, religion without science is blind.

"Science, Philosophy, and Religion" (1940). According to *The Expanded Quotable Einstein*, ed. Alice Calaprice, "This may be a play on Kant's 'Notion without intuition is empty, intuition without notion is blind.'"

16 [*On quantum theory:*] It is hard to sneak a look at God's cards. But that he would choose to play dice with the world . . . is something I cannot believe for a single moment.

Letter to Cornel Lanczos, 21 Mar. 1942
See Einstein 8

17 The unleashed power of the atom has changed everything except our modes of thinking and we thus drift toward unparalleled catastrophe.

Telegram to prominent Americans, 24 May 1946

18 I do not know [how the Third World War will be fought]. But I can tell you what they'll use in the fourth—rocks!

Interview, *Liberal Judaism*, Apr.–May 1949. Usually credited to Einstein, but an army lieutenant was quoted as saying "in the war after the next war, sure as Hell, they'll be using spears!" in a Walter Winchell column in the *Wisconsin State Journal*, 23 Sept. 1946.

19 Every intellectual who is called before one of the committees ought to refuse to testify. . . . This kind of inquisition violates the spirit of the Constitution. If enough people are ready to take this grave step they will be successful. If not, then the intellectuals of this country deserve nothing better than the slavery which is intended for them.

Letter to William Frauenglass, 16 May 1953

20 It is true that my parents were worried because I began to speak fairly late, so that they even consulted a doctor. I can't say how old I was— but surely not less than three.

Letter to Sybille Blinoff, 21 May 1954

21 The most important aspect of our [Israel's] policy must be our ever-present, manifest desire to institute complete equality for the Arab citizens living in our midst. . . . The attitude we adopt toward the Arab minority will provide the real test of our moral standards as a people.

Letter to Zvi Lurie, 5 Jan. 1955

22 Why do people speak of great men in terms of nationality? Great Germans, great Englishmen? Goethe always protested against being called a German poet. Great men are simply men and are not to be considered from the point of view of nationality, nor should the environment in which they were brought up be taken into account.

Quoted in *N.Y. Times*, 18 Apr. 1926

23 I believe in Spinoza's God who reveals Himself in the orderly harmony of what exists, not in a God who concerns himself with fates and actions of human beings.

Quoted in *N.Y. Times*, 25 Apr. 1929

24 The Lord God is subtle, but malicious he is not.

Quoted in Philipp Frank, *Einstein: His Life and Times* (1947). *The Expanded Quotable Einstein*, ed. Alice Calaprice, notes: "Originally said to Princeton University mathematics professor Oscar Veblen, May 1921, while Einstein was in Princeton for a series of lectures, upon hearing that an experimental result by Dayton C. Miller of Cleveland, if true, would contradict his theory of gravitation. But the result turned out to be false. Some say by this remark Einstein meant that Nature hides her secrets by being subtle, while others say he meant that Nature is mischievous but not bent on trickery. Permanently inscribed in stone above the fireplace in the faculty lounge, 202 Jones Hall [at Princeton], in the original German: 'Raffiniert ist der Herr Gott, aber boshaft ist Er nicht.'"
See Einstein 34

25 If *A* is a success in life, then *A* equals *x* plus *y* plus *z*. Work is *x*; *y* is play; and *z* is keeping your mouth shut.

Quoted in *Observer*, 15 Jan. 1950

26 Common sense is nothing more than a deposit of prejudices laid down in the mind before you reach eighteen.

Quoted in Lincoln Barnett, *The Universe and Dr. Einstein* (1950)

27 If I would be a young man again and had to decide how to make my living, I would not try to become a scientist or scholar or teacher. I would rather choose to be a plumber or a peddler in the hope to find that modest degree of independence still available under present circumstances.

Quoted in *Reporter*, 18 Nov. 1954

28 [*Response to being asked why people could discover atoms but not the means to control them:*] That is simple, my friend: because politics is more difficult than physics.

Quoted in *N.Y. Times*, 22 Apr. 1955

29 When you sit with a nice girl for two hours you think it's only a minute, but when you sit on a hot stove for a minute you think it's two hours. That's relativity.

Quoted in *New York Times*, 15 Mar. 1929.

30 [*From an autobiographical handwritten note:*] Something deeply hidden had to be behind things.

Quoted in *N.Y. Times Magazine*, 2 Aug. 1964

31 Then I would feel sorry for the good Lord. The theory is correct anyway.

Quoted in Ilse Rosenthal-Schneider, *Reality and Scientific Truth* (1974). This was Einstein's response (1919) to doctoral student Ilse Rosenthal-Schneider's question about how he would have reacted had his general theory of relativity not been experimentally confirmed.

32 [*Remark to Philippe Halsman:*] When I was young, I found out that the big toe always ends up making a hole in a sock. So I stopped wearing socks.

Quoted in A. P. French, *Einstein: A Centenary Volume* (1979)

33 Nationalism is an infantile sickness. It is the measles of the human race.

Quoted in Helen Dukas and Banesh Hoffman, *Albert Einstein, the Human Side* (1979)

34 I have second thoughts. Maybe God *is* malicious.

Quoted in Jamie Sayen, *Einstein in America* (1985). Said to Vladimir Bargmann, with the meaning that God leads people to believe they understand things that they actually are far from understanding. *See Einstein 24*

35 The hardest thing in the world to understand is income taxes.

Attributed in *Time*, 22 Feb. 1963. Although this sounds like a classic apocryphal Einsteinism, it was said to be authentic by the scientist's tax preparer.

36 Everything should be made as simple as possible, but not simpler.

Attributed in *Zanesville* (Ohio) *Times Recorder*, 22 June 1972. A very similar attribution to Einstein appeared in the *New York Times*, 8 Jan. 1950. The actual source for the remark may be a statement in Einstein's 1933 lecture "On the Method of Theoretical Physics": "The supreme goal of all theory is to make the irreducible basic elements as simple and as few as possible without having to surrender the adequate representation of a single datum of experience."

37 The greatest invention of mankind is compound interest.

Attributed in *USA Today*, 2 Aug. 1991. An earlier version of this attribution appeared in the *Wall Street Journal*, 25 Aug. 1976.

38 Only two things are infinite, the universe and human stupidity, and I'm not sure about the former.

Attributed in Robert Byrne, *The Fourth . . . 637 Best Things Anybody Ever Said* (1990). Frederick S. Pearls, *In and Out the Garbage Pail* (1969), quoted Einstein as saying, "Two things are infinite, the universe and human stupidity, and I am not yet completely sure about the universe."

Loren Eiseley
U.S. writer and educator, 1907–1977

1 If there is magic in this planet, it is contained in water.

The Immense Journey "The Flow of the River" (1957)

Dwight D. Eisenhower
U.S. president and military leader, 1890–1969

1 I doubt whether any of these people [pacifists], with their academic or dogmatic hatred of war, detest it as much as I do. They probably have not seen bodies rotting on the ground and smelled the stench of decaying human flesh. . . . What separates me from the pacifists is that I hate the Nazis more than I hate war.

Letter to Arthur Eisenhower, 18 June 1943

2 Soldiers, Sailors, and Airmen of the Allied Expeditionary Force: You are about to embark upon the Great Crusade, toward which we have striven these many months. The eyes of the world are upon you.

Order of the Day, 2 June 1944

3 In war there is no substitute for victory.

Letter to Mamie Eisenhower, 2 Aug. 1944. A note in *Letters to Mamie* states, "The same aphorism was made famous by General Douglas MacArthur in 1951. It was probably a standard saying in the Army."

4 I shall go to Korea.

Campaign speech, Detroit, Mich., 24 Oct. 1952

5 Every gun that is made, every warship launched, every rocket fired, signifies, in the final sense, a theft from those who hunger and are not fed, those who are cold and are not clothed. The world in arms is not spending money alone. It is spending the sweat of its laborers, the genius of its scientists, the hopes of its children.

Speech to American Society of Newspaper Editors, Washington, D.C., 16 Apr. 1953

6 Don't join the book burners. Don't think you're going to conceal faults by concealing evidence that they ever existed. Don't be afraid to go in your library and read every book.

Remarks at Dartmouth College Commencement, Hanover, N.H., 14 June 1953

7 [*On the strategic importance of Indochina:*] You have the broader considerations that might

follow what you would call the "falling domino"
principle. You have a row of dominoes set up,
you knock over the first one, and what will
happen to the last one is the certainty that it
will go over very quickly. So you could have a
beginning of a disintegration that would have
the most profound influences.

News conference, 7 Apr. 1954

8 I think that people want peace so much that
one of these days governments had better get
out of the way and let them have it.

Broadcast discussion, 31 Aug. 1959

9 [*Response to a question asking him to name a
"major idea" that Vice-President Nixon had
initiated in the Eisenhower administration:*] If you
give me a week, I might think of one.

News conference, 25 Aug. 1960

10 This conjunction of an immense military
establishment and a large arms industry is
new in the American experience. The total
influence—economic, political, even spiritual—
is felt in every city, every statehouse, every
office of the federal government.

Farewell radio and television address to the American
people, 17 Jan. 1961

11 In the councils of government, we must
guard against the acquisition of unwarranted
influence, whether sought or unsought, by the
military-industrial complex. The potential for
the disastrous rise of misplaced power exists
and will persist.

Farewell radio and television address to the American
people, 17 Jan. 1961

12 I am convinced that the French could not
win the war because the internal political
situation in Vietnam, weak and confused,
badly weakened their military position. I have
never talked or corresponded with a person
knowledgeable in Indochinese affairs who did
not agree that had elections been held as of
the time of the fighting, possibly 80 per cent
of the population would have voted for the
Communist Ho Chi Minh as their leader rather
than Chief of State Bao Dai.

The White House Years vol. 1, ch. 14 (1963)

13 Plans are worthless, but planning is everything.

Speech to National Defense Executive Reserve
Conference, Washington, D.C., 14 Nov. 1957.
Eisenhower had written in a letter to Hamilton Fish
Armstrong, 31 Dec. 1950: "I always remember the
observation of a very successful soldier who said,
'Peace-time plans are of no particular value, but
peace-time planning is indispensable.'"

14 [*Of Douglas MacArthur:*] Oh yes, I studied
dramatics under him for 12 years.

Quoted in Quentin Reynolds, *By Quentin Reynolds*
(1963)

15 [*When asked if he had made any mistakes while he
had been president:*] Yes, two, and they are both
sitting on the Supreme Court.

Attributed in Henry J. Abraham, *Justices and
Presidents* (1974). Probably apocryphal. Elmo
Richardson, in his book *The Presidency of Dwight
D. Eisenhower* (1979), states that a similar remark
has been "ascribed to several other presidents."
The generic joke may have combined with actual
statements by Eisenhower about his disappointment
with appointee Earl Warren to inspire an apocryphal
story about Eisenhower's disappointment with *two*
justices (usually said to be Warren and William J.
Brennan, Jr.).

Edward Elgar

English composer, 1857–1934

1 My idea is that there is music in the air, music
all around us, the world is full of it and you
simply take as much as you require.

Quoted in Robert J. Buckley, *Sir Edward Elgar* (1905)

Charles W. Eliot

U.S. university president, 1834–1926

1 Enter to grow in wisdom.
Depart to serve better thy country and thy kind.

Inscriptions on Dexter Gate to Harvard Yard,
Cambridge, Mass. (1880)

2 To the Fifty-fourth Regiment of Massachusetts
Infantry:

The white officers . . . cast in their lot with
men of a despised race unproved in war, and
risked death as inciters of servile insurrection
if taken prisoners, besides encountering all
the common perils of camp march and battle.

The black rank and file volunteered when
disaster clouded the Union cause, served

without pay for eighteen months till given that of white troops, faced threatened enslavement if captured, were brave in action, patient under heavy and dangerous labors, and cheerful amid hardships and privations.

Together they gave to the nation and the world undying proof that Americans of African descent possess the pride, courage, and devotion of the patriot soldier. One hundred and eighty thousand such Americans enlisted under the Union flag in 1863–65.

Inscription on Robert Gould Shaw Monument, Boston, Mass. (1897)

George Eliot (Mary Ann Evans)
English novelist, 1819–1880

1 The first condition of human goodness is something to love; the second, something to reverence.
Scenes of Clerical Life "Jane's Repentance" ch. 10 (1858)

2 Anger and jealousy can no more bear to lose sight of their objects than love.
The Mill on the Floss bk. 1, ch. 10 (1860)

3 The dead level of provincial existence.
The Mill on the Floss bk. 5, ch. 3 (1860)

4 The happiest women, like the happiest nations, have no history.
The Mill on the Floss bk. 6, ch. 3 (1860)
See Montesquieu 6; Proverbs 54

5 I should like to know what is the proper function of women, if it is not to make reasons for husbands to stay at home, and still stronger reasons for bachelors to go out.
The Mill on the Floss bk. 6, ch. 6 (1860)

6 "Character," says Novalis, in one of his questionable aphorisms—"character is destiny."
The Mill on the Floss bk. 6, ch. 6 (1860)
See Heraclitus 2; Novalis 2

7 There's allays two 'pinions; there's the 'pinion a man has of himself, and there's the 'pinion other folks have on him. There'd be two 'pinions about a cracked bell, if the bell could hear itself.
Silas Marner ch. 6 (1861)

8 An election is coming. Universal peace is declared, and the foxes have a sincere interest in prolonging the lives of the poultry.
Felix Holt ch. 5 (1866)

9 A woman can hardly ever choose . . . she is dependent on what happens to her. She must take meaner things, because only meaner things are within her reach.
Felix Holt ch. 27 (1866)

10 Oh may I join the choir invisible
Of those immortal dead who live again
In minds made better by their presence.
"Oh May I Join the Choir Invisible" l. 1 (1867)

11 He said he should prefer not to know the sources of the Nile, and that there should be some unknown regions preserved as hunting-grounds for the poetic imagination.
Middlemarch bk. 1, ch. 9 (1871–1872)

12 Correct English is the slang of prigs.
Middlemarch bk. 1, ch. 11 (1871–1872)

13 Fred's studies are not very deep . . . he is only reading a novel.
Middlemarch bk. 1, ch. 11 (1871–1872)

14 Might, could, would—they are contemptible auxiliaries.
Middlemarch bk. 2, ch. 14 (1871–1872)

15 If we had a keen vision and feeling of all ordinary human life, it would be like hearing the grass grow and the squirrel's heart beat, and we should die of that roar which lies on the other side of silence.
Middlemarch bk. 2, ch. 20 (1871–1872)

16 The growing good of the world is partly
dependent on unhistoric acts; and that things
are not so ill with you and me as they might
have been, is half owing to the number who
have lived faithfully a hidden life, and rest in
unvisited tombs.
Middlemarch Finale (1871–1872)

17 A difference of taste in jokes is a great strain on
the affections.
Daniel Deronda bk. 2, ch. 15 (1876)

18 The Jews are among the aristocracy of every
land—if a literature is called rich in the
possession of a few classic tragedies, what shall
we say to a National Tragedy lasting for fifteen
hundred years, in which the poets and the
actors were also the heroes?
Daniel Deronda bk. 6, ch. 42 (1876)

19 Blessed is the man who, having nothing to say,
abstains from giving us wordy evidence of the
fact.
The Impressions of Theophrastus Such "A Man
Surprised at His Own Originality" (1879)

20 Debasing the Moral Currency.
The Impressions of Theophrastus Such title of essay
(1879)

T. S. (Thomas Stearns) Eliot
U.S.-born English poet and man of letters,
1888–1965

1 The readers of the *Boston Evening Transcript*
Sway in the wind like a field of ripe corn.
"The *Boston Evening Transcript*" l. 1 (1917)

2 Weave, weave the sunlight in your hair.
"La Figlia Che Piange" l. 3 (1917)

3 Let us go then, you and I,
When the evening is spread out against the sky
Like a patient etherized upon a table.
"The Love Song of J. Alfred Prufrock" l. 1 (1917)

4 In the room the women come and go
Talking of Michelangelo.
"The Love Song of J. Alfred Prufrock" l. 13 (1917)

5 Do I dare
Disturb the universe?
"The Love Song of J. Alfred Prufrock" l. 45 (1917)

6 I have measured out my life with coffee spoons.
"The Love Song of J. Alfred Prufrock" l. 51 (1917)

7 I should have been a pair of ragged claws
Scuttling across the floors of silent seas.
"The Love Song of J. Alfred Prufrock" l. 73 (1917)

8 I have seen the moment of my greatness flicker,
And I have seen the eternal Footman hold my
coat, and snicker,
And in short, I was afraid.
"The Love Song of J. Alfred Prufrock" l. 84 (1917)

9 No! I am not Prince Hamlet, nor was meant
to be.
"The Love Song of J. Alfred Prufrock" l. 111 (1917)

10 I grow old . . . I grow old . . .
I shall wear the bottoms of my trousers rolled.
"The Love Song of J. Alfred Prufrock" l. 120 (1917).
Ellipses in the original.

11 Shall I part my hair behind? Do I dare to eat a
peach?
I shall wear white flannel trousers, and walk
upon the beach.
I have heard the mermaids singing, each to
each.

I do not think that they will sing to me.
"The Love Song of J. Alfred Prufrock" l. 122 (1917)

12 We have lingered in the chambers of the sea
By sea-girls wreathed with seaweed red and
brown
Till human voices wake us, and we drown.
"The Love Song of J. Alfred Prufrock" l. 129 (1917)

13 He laughed like an irresponsible fetus.
"Mr. Apollinax" l. 7 (1917)

14 The winter evening settles down
With smell of steak in passageways.
Six o'clock.
The burnt-out ends of smoky days.
"Preludes" l. 1 (1917)

15 I am moved by fancies that are curled
Around these images, and cling:
The notion of some infinitely gentle
Infinitely suffering thing.
"Preludes" l. 48 (1917)

16 The worlds revolve like ancient women
Gathering fuel in vacant lots.
"Preludes" l. 53 (1917)

17 The nightingales are singing near
The Convent of the Sacred Heart,

And sang within the bloody wood
When Agamemnon cried aloud
And let their liquid siftings fall
To stain the stiff dishonored shroud.
"Sweeney Among the Nightingales" l. 35 (1919)

18 Webster was much possessed by death
And saw the skull beneath the skin;
And breastless creatures under ground
Leaned backward with a lipless grin.
"Whispers of Immortality" l. 1 (1919)

19 Grishkin is nice: her Russian eye
Is underlined for emphasis;
Uncorseted, her friendly bust
Gives promise of pneumatic bliss.
"Whispers of Immortality" l. 17 (1919)

20 And even the Abstract Entities
Circumambulate her charm;
But our lot crawls between dry ribs
To keep our metaphysics warm.
"Whispers of Immortality" l. 29 (1919)

21 Here I am, an old man in a dry month,
Being read to by a boy, waiting for rain.
"Gerontion" l. 1 (1920)

22 Signs are taken for wonders. "We would see a
sign!"
The word within a word, unable to speak a
word,
Swaddled with darkness. In the juvescence of
the year

Came Christ the tiger.
"Gerontion" l. 17 (1920)

23 After such knowledge, what forgiveness? Think
now
History has many cunning passages, contrived
corridors
And issues.
"Gerontion" l. 33 (1920)

24   Tenants of the house,
Thoughts of a dry brain in a dry season.
"Gerontion" l. 74 (1920)

25 The broad-backed hippopotamus
Rests on his belly in the mud;
Although he seems so firm to us
He is merely flesh and blood.
"The Hippopotamus" l. 1 (1920)

26 He shall be washed as white as snow,
By all the martyr'd virgins kist,
While the True Church remains below
Wrapt in the old miasmal mist.
"The Hippopotamus" l. 33 (1920)

27 The only way of expressing emotion in the form
of art is by finding an "objective correlative";
in other words, a set of objects, a situation,
a chain of events which shall be the formula
of that *particular* emotion; such that when
the external facts, which must terminate in
sensory experience, are given, the emotion is
immediately evoked.
The Sacred Wood "Hamlet and His Problems" (1920).
The *Oxford English Dictionary* traces the term *objective
correlative* as far back as Washington Allston, *Lectures
on Art, and Poems* (1850).
See Hemingway 14

28 Immature poets imitate; mature poets steal.
The Sacred Wood "Philip Massinger" (1920)

29 It [tradition] cannot be inherited, and if you
want it you must obtain it by great labor.
The Sacred Wood "Tradition and the Individual
Talent" (1920)

30 Some one said: "The dead writers are remote
from us because we *know* so much more than
they did." Precisely, and they are that which we
know.
The Sacred Wood "Tradition and the Individual
Talent" (1920)

31 The progress of an artist is a continual self-sacrifice, a continual extinction of personality.
The Sacred Wood "Tradition and the Individual Talent" (1920)

32 The more perfect the artist, the more completely separate in him will be the man who suffers and the mind which creates; the more perfectly will the mind digest and translate the passions which are its material.
The Sacred Wood "Tradition and the Individual Talent" (1920)

33 Poetry is not a turning loose of emotion, but an escape from emotion; it is not the expression of personality, but an escape from personality. But, of course, only those who have personality and emotions know what it means to want to escape from these things.
The Sacred Wood "Tradition and the Individual Talent" (1920)

34 In the seventeenth century a dissociation of sensibility set in, from which we have never recovered; and this dissociation, as is natural, was due to the influence of the two most powerful poets of the century, Milton and Dryden.
"The Metaphysical Poets" (1921)

35 Poets in our civilization, as it exists at present, must be *difficult*. . . . The poet must become more and more comprehensive, more allusive, more indirect, in order to force, to dislocate if necessary, language into its meaning.
"The Metaphysical Poets" (1921)

36 In using the myth, in manipulating a continuous parallel between contemporaneity and antiquity, Mr. Joyce is pursuing a method which others must pursue after him. . . . It is simply a way of controlling, of ordering, of giving a shape and a significance to the immense panorama of futility and anarchy which is contemporary history. . . . It is, I seriously believe, a step toward making the modern world possible in art.
"*Ulysses*, Order and Myth" (1922)

37 Leaving the bubbling beverage to cool, Fresca slips softly to the needful stool.
The Waste Land (deleted lines) (1922).

38 Odors, confected by the cunning French, Disguise the good old hearty female stench.
The Waste Land (deleted lines) (1922)

39 April is the cruellest month, breeding Lilacs out of the dead land, mixing Memory and desire, stirring Dull roots with spring rain.
The Waste Land l. 1 (1922)

40 Winter kept us warm, covering Earth in forgetful snow, feeding A little life with dried tubers.
The Waste Land l. 5 (1922)

41 In the mountains, there you feel free. I read, much of the night, and go south in the winter.
The Waste Land l. 17 (1922)

42 You know only A heap of broken images, where the sun beats, And the dead tree gives no shelter, the cricket no relief, And the dry stone no sound of water.
The Waste Land l. 21 (1922)

43 There is shadow under this red rock, (Come in under the shadow of this red rock), And I will show you something different from either Your shadow at morning striding behind you Or your shadow at evening rising to meet you; I will show you fear in a handful of dust.
The Waste Land l. 25 (1922)
See Conrad 20

44 Unreal City, Under the brown fog of a winter dawn, A crowd flowed over London Bridge, so many, I had not thought death had undone so many.
The Waste Land l. 60 (1922). The last line quotes Dante, *Inferno*, canto 3, l. 55: "so long a train of people, that I would have never believed death had undone so many."

45 The Chair she sat in, like a burnished throne, Glowed on the marble.
The Waste Land l. 77 (1922)
See Shakespeare 400

46 And still she cried, and still the world pursues, "Jug Jug" to dirty ears.
The Waste Land l. 102 (1922)
See Lyly 1

47 "My nerves are bad to-night. Yes, bad. Stay
      with me.
    "Speak to me. Why do you never speak. Speak.
      "What are you thinking of? What thinking?
        What?
    "I never know what you are thinking. Think."

    I think we are in rats' alley
    Where the dead men lost their bones.
    The Waste Land l. III (1922)

48 O O O O that Shakespeherian Rag—
    It's so elegant
    So intelligent.
    The Waste Land l. 128 (1922)
    See Gene Buck 1

49 HURRY UP PLEASE ITS TIME
    Goonight Bill. Goonight Lou. Goonight May.
      Goonight.
    Ta ta. Goonight. Goonight.
    Good night, ladies, good night, sweet ladies,
      good night, good night.
    The Waste Land l. 169 (1922)
    See Shakespeare 221

50 But at my back from time to time I hear
    The sound of horns and motors, which shall
      bring
    Sweeney to Mrs. Porter in the spring.
    O the moon shone bright on Mrs. Porter
    And on her daughter
    They wash their feet in soda water.
    The Waste Land l. 196 (1922)
    See Andrew Marvell 12

51 I Tiresias, old man with wrinkled dugs
    Perceived the scene, and foretold the rest—
    I too awaited the expected guest.
    The Waste Land l. 228 (1922)

52 One of the low on whom assurance sits
    As a silk hat on a Bradford millionaire.
    The Waste Land l. 233 (1922)

53 I Tiresias have foresuffered all
    Enacted on this same divan or bed;
    I who have sat by Thebes below the wall
    And walked among the lowest of the dead.
    The Waste Land l. 243 (1922)

54 When lovely woman stoops to folly and
    Paces about her room again, alone,
    She smoothes her hair with automatic hand,

And puts a record on the gramophone.
    The Waste Land l. 253 (1922)
    See Oliver Goldsmith 6

55 Phlebas the Phoenician, a fortnight dead,
    Forgot the cry of gulls, and the deep sea swell
    And the profit and loss.
    The Waste Land l. 312 (1922)

56 Here is no water but only rock.
    The Waste Land l. 331 (1922)

57 The awful daring of a moment's surrender
    Which an age of prudence can never retract
    By this, and this only, we have existed.
    The Waste Land l. 404 (1922)

58 *Dayadhvam:* I have heard the key
    Turn in the door once and turn once only
    We think of the key, each in his prison
    Thinking of the key, each confirms a prison.
    The Waste Land l. 412 (1922)

59   I sat upon the shore
    Fishing, with the arid plain behind me
    Shall I at least set my lands in order?
    The Waste Land l. 424 (1922)

60 These fragments I have shored against my
    ruins.
    The Waste Land l. 431 (1922)

61 Shantih shantih shantih.
    The Waste Land l. 434 (1922)
    See Upanishads 6

62 [The critic must] compose his differences
    with as many of his fellows as possible in the
    common pursuit of true judgement.
    "The Function of Criticism" (1923)

63 We are the hollow men
    We are the stuffed men
    Leaning together
    Headpiece filled with straw. Alas!
    "The Hollow Men" l. 1 (1925)

64 Shape without form, shade without color,
    Paralyzed force, gesture without motion.
    "The Hollow Men" l. 11 (1925)

65   Those who have crossed
    With direct eyes, to death's other Kingdom
    Remember us—if at all—not as lost
    Violent souls, but only
    As the hollow men
    The stuffed men.
    "The Hollow Men" l. 13 (1925)

66 Between the idea
  And the reality
  Between the motion
  And the act
  Falls the Shadow.
  "The Hollow Men" l. 72 (1925)

67 This is the way the world ends
  This is the way the world ends
  This is the way the world ends
  Not with a bang but a whimper.
  "The Hollow Men" l. 95 (1925)

68 A cold coming we had of it,
  Just the worst time of the year
  For a journey, and such a long journey:
  The ways deep and the weather sharp,
  The very dead of winter.
  "Journey of the Magi" l. 1 (1927)
  See Andrewes 1

69   Were we led all that way for
  Birth or Death? There was a Birth, certainly,
  We had evidence and no doubt. I had seen birth
    and death,
  But had thought they were different.
  "Journey of the Magi" l. 35 (1927)

70 We returned to our places, these Kingdoms,
  But no longer at ease here, in the old
    dispensation,
  With an alien people clutching their gods.
  I should be glad of another death.
  "Journey of the Magi" l. 40 (1927)

71 The great poet, in writing himself, writes his
    time.
  "Shakespeare and the Stoicism of Seneca" (1927)

72 Humility is the most difficult of all virtues to
    achieve; nothing dies harder than the desire to
    think well of oneself.
  "Shakespeare and the Stoicism of Seneca" (1927)

73 We know too much and are convinced of too
    little. Our literature is a substitute for religion,
    and so is our religion.
  "A Dialogue on Dramatic Poetry" (1928)

74 The general point of view may be described as
    classicist in literature, royalist in politics, and
    Anglo-Catholic in religion.
  For Lancelot Andrewes preface (1928)

75 Because I do not hope to turn again
  Because I do not hope
  Because I do not hope to turn.
  "Ash-Wednesday" l. 1 (1930). These lines echo Guido
  Cavalcanti's thirteenth-century ballad, *Perch'io non
  spero di tornar giamai* (Because I hope not ever to
  return).

76 Why should the aged eagle stretch its wings?
  "Ash-Wednesday" l. 6 (1930)

77 And pray to God to have mercy upon us
  And I pray that I may forget
  These matters that with myself I too much
    discuss
  Too much explain.
  "Ash-Wednesday" l. 26 (1930)

78 Because these wings are no longer wings to fly
  But merely vans to beat the air
  The air which is now thoroughly small and dry
  Smaller and dryer than the will
  Teach us to care and not to care
  Teach us to sit still.
  "Ash-Wednesday" l. 34 (1930)

79 Lady, three white leopards sat under a juniper-
    tree
  In the cool of the day, having fed to satiety
  On my legs my heart my liver and that which
    had been contained
  In the hollow round of my skull.
  "Ash-Wednesday" l. 42 (1930)

80 Terminate torment
  Of love unsatisfied
  The greater torment
  Of love satisfied.
  "Ash-Wednesday" l. 76 (1930)

81 Blown hair is sweet, brown hair over the mouth
    blown,
  Lilac and brown hair.
  "Ash-Wednesday" l. 112 (1930)

82 Redeem
  The time. Redeem
  The unread vision in the higher dream.
  "Ash-Wednesday" l. 137 (1930)

83 Against the Word the unstilled world still
    whirled
  About the center of the silent Word.
  "Ash-Wednesday" l. 156 (1930)

84 Wavering between the profit and the loss
   In this brief transit where the dreams cross
   The dreamcrossed twilight between birth and
      dying.
   "Ash-Wednesday" l. 188 (1930)

85 The white sails still fly seaward, seaward flying
   Unbroken wings.
   "Ash-Wednesday" l. 193 (1930)

86 And the lost heart stiffens and rejoices
   In the lost lilac and the lost sea voices
   And the weak spirit quickens to rebel
   For the bent golden-rod and the lost sea smell.
   "Ash-Wednesday" l. 195 (1930)

87 Even among these rocks,
   Our peace in His will.
   "Ash-Wednesday" l. 210 (1930)

88 Birth, and copulation, and death.
   That's all the facts when you come to brass
      tacks.
   Sweeney Agonistes (1932)

89 How unpleasant to meet Mr. Eliot!
   With his features of clerical cut,
   And his brow so grim
   And his mouth so prim.
   "Five-Finger Exercises" pt. 5 (1933)
   See Lear 3

90 Where is the wisdom we have lost in
      knowledge?
   Where is the knowledge we have lost in
      information?
   "Choruses from the Rock" pt. 1 (1934)

91 And the wind shall say "Here were decent
      godless people;
   Their only monument the asphalt road
   And a thousand lost golf balls."
   "Choruses from the Rock" pt. 3 (1934)

92 Yet we have gone on living,
   Living and partly living.
   Murder in the Cathedral pt. 1 (1935)

93 The last temptation is the greatest treason:
   To do the right deed for the wrong reason.
   Murder in the Cathedral pt. 1 (1935)

94 Time present and time past
   Are both perhaps present in time future,
   And time future contained in time past.

If all time is eternally present
All time is unredeemable.
Four Quartets "Burnt Norton" pt. 1 (1936)

95 Footfalls echo in the memory
   Down the passage which we did not take
   Towards the door we never opened
   Into the rose-garden.
   Four Quartets "Burnt Norton" pt. 1 (1936)

96   Human kind
   Cannot bear very much reality.
   Four Quartets "Burnt Norton" pt. 1 (1936)

97 At the still point of the turning world. Neither
   flesh nor fleshless.
   Four Quartets "Burnt Norton" pt. 2 (1936)

98   Words strain,
   Crack and sometimes break, under the
      burden,
   Under the tension, slip, slide, perish,
   Decay with imprecision, will not stay in place,
   Will not stay still.
   Four Quartets "Burnt Norton" pt. 5 (1936)

99 The Naming of Cats is a difficult matter,
   It isn't just one of your holiday games;
   You may think at first I'm as mad as a hatter
   When I tell you, a cat must have THREE
      DIFFERENT NAMES.
   Old Possum's Book of Practical Cats "The Naming of
   Cats" l. 1 (1939)

100 When you notice a cat in profound
      meditation,
   The reason, I tell you, is always the same:
   His mind is engaged in a rapt contemplation
   Of the thought, of the thought, of the thought
      of his name:
   His ineffable effable
   Effanineffable
   Deep and inscrutable singular Name.
   Old Possum's Book of Practical Cats "The Naming of
   Cats" l. 25 (1939)

101 In my beginning is my end. In succession
   Houses rise and fall, crumble, are extended,
   Are removed, destroyed, restored, or in their
      place
   Is an open field, or a factory, or a by-pass.
   Four Quartets "East Coker" pt. 1 (1940)
   See Mary, Queen of Scots 1

102 That was a way of putting it—not very
    satisfactory:
    A periphrastic study in a worn-out poetical
      fashion,
    Leaving one still with the intolerable wrestle
    With words and meanings.
    Four Quartets "East Coker" pt. 2 (1940)

103 The houses are all gone under the sea.
    The dancers are all gone under the hill.
    Four Quartets "East Coker" pt. 2 (1940)

104 O dark dark dark. They all go into the dark,
    The vacant interstellar spaces, the vacant into
      the vacant.
    Four Quartets "East Coker" pt. 3 (1940)
    See Milton 47

105 To arrive where you are, to get from where
      you are not,
    You must go by a way wherein there is no
      ecstasy.
    In order to arrive at what you do not know
    You must go by a way which is the way of
      ignorance.
    Four Quartets "East Coker" pt. 3 (1940)

106 The whole earth is our hospital
    Endowed by the ruined millionaire.
    Four Quartets "East Coker" pt. 4 (1940)

107 In spite of that, we call this Friday good.
    Four Quartets "East Coker" pt. 4 (1940)

108   And so each venture
    Is a new beginning, a raid on the inarticulate
    With shabby equipment always deteriorating
    In the general mess of imprecision of
      feeling,
    Undisciplined squads of emotion.
    Four Quartets "East Coker" pt. 5 (1940)

109 For us, there is only the trying. The rest is not
    our business.
    Four Quartets "East Coker" pt. 5 (1940)

110 Home is where one starts from. As we grow
      older
    The world becomes stranger, the pattern more
      complicated
    Of dead and living. Not the intense moment
    Isolated, with no before and after,
    But a lifetime burning in every moment
    And not the lifetime of one man only

But of old stones that cannot be deciphered.
    Four Quartets "East Coker" pt. 5 (1940)

111 Old men ought to be explorers.
    Four Quartets "East Coker" pt. 5 (1940)

112 We must be still and still moving
    Into another intensity
    For a further union, a deeper communion
    Through the dark cold and the empty
      desolation,
    The wave cry, the wind cry, the vast waters
    Of the petrel and the porpoise. In my end is
      my beginning.
    Four Quartets "East Coker" pt. 5 (1940)

113 I do not know much about gods; but I think
      that the river
    Is a strong brown god—sullen, untamed, and
      intractable.
    Four Quartets "The Dry Salvages" pt. 1 (1941)

114   Not fare well,
    But fare forward, voyagers.
    Four Quartets "The Dry Salvages" pt. 3 (1941)

115   Music heard so deeply
    That it is not heard at all, but you are the
      music
    While the music lasts.
    Four Quartets "The Dry Salvages" pt. 5 (1941)

116 Who are only undefeated
    Because we have gone on trying;
    We, content at the last
    If our temporal reversion nourish
    (Not too far from the yew-tree)
    The life of significant soil.
    Four Quartets "The Dry Salvages" pt. 5 (1941)

117   The communication
    Of the dead is tongued with fire beyond the
      language of the living.
    Four Quartets "Little Gidding" pt. 1 (1942)

118 In the uncertain hour before the morning
    Near the ending of interminable night
    At the recurrent end of the unending.
    Four Quartets "Little Gidding" pt. 2 (1942)

119   Our concern was speech, and speech
      impelled us
    To purify the dialect of the tribe.
    Four Quartets "Little Gidding" pt. 2 (1942)
    See Mallarmé 3

120 First, the cold friction of expiring sense
    Without enchantment, offering no promise
    But bitter tastelessness of shadow fruit
    As body and soul begin to fall asunder.
    Second, the conscious impotence of rage
    At human folly.
    Four Quartets "Little Gidding" pt. 2 (1942)

121 Who then devised the torment? Love.
    Love is the unfamiliar Name
    Behind the hands that wove
    The intolerable shirt of flame
    Which human power cannot remove.
        We only live, only suspire
        Consumed by either fire or fire.
    Four Quartets "Little Gidding" pt. 4 (1942)

122 What we call the beginning is often the end
    And to make an end is to make a beginning.
    The end is where we start from.
    Four Quartets "Little Gidding" pt. 5 (1942)

123   So, while the light fails
    On a winter's afternoon, in a secluded chapel
    History is now and England.
    Four Quartets "Little Gidding" pt. 5 (1942)

124 We shall not cease from exploration
    And the end of all our exploring
    Will be to arrive where we started
    And know the place for the first time.
    Four Quartets "Little Gidding" pt. 5 (1942)

125 A condition of complete simplicity
    (Costing not less than everything)
    And all shall be well and
    All manner of thing shall be well
    When the tongues of flame are in-folded
    Into the crowned knot of fire
    And the fire and the rose are one.
    Four Quartets "Little Gidding" pt. 5 (1942)
    See Julian of Norwich 1

126 What is hell?
    Hell is oneself,
    Hell is alone, the other figures in it
    Merely projections. There is nothing to escape
        from
    And nothing to escape to. One is always
        alone.
    The Cocktail Party act 1, sc. 3 (1950)
    See Sartre 5

127 [*On* The Waste Land:] Various critics have
    done me the honor to interpret the poem in
    terms of criticism of the contemporary world,
    have considered it, indeed, as an important
    bit of social criticism. To me it was only the
    relief of a personal and wholly insignificant
    grouse against life; it is just a piece of
    rhythmical grumbling.
    Quoted in *The Waste Land*, ed. Valerie Eliot (1971)

Elizabeth I
English queen, 1533–1603

1 I am your anointed Queen. I will never be by
    violence constrained to do anything. I thank
    God that I am endued with such qualities
    that if I were turned out of the Realm in my
    petticoat, I were able to live in any place in
    Christendom.
    Speech to Members of Parliament, 5 Nov. 1566

2 [*Upon the approach of the Spanish Armada:*]
    I know I have the body of a weak and feeble
    woman, but I have the heart and stomach of a
    king, and of a king of England too; and think
    foul scorn that Parma or Spain, or any prince
    of Europe, should dare to invade the borders
    of my realm.
    Speech to troops at Tilbury, England (1588).
    The authenticity of these words is open to
    question, since they are not included in the only
    contemporary account of the speech.

3 [*Remark to Edward de Vere, Earl of Oxford, after
    he had returned from a seven-year voluntary
    exile because of embarrassing flatulence he had
    experienced in the queen's presence:*] My Lord, I
    had forgot the fart.
    Quoted in John Aubrey, *Brief Lives* (1690)

4 [*Remark to Robert Cecil shortly before her death,
    when he told her she must go to bed:*] Must!—is
    "must" a word to be addressed to princes?
    Little man, little man, thy father, if he had
    been alive, durst not have used that word.
    Quoted in *Christian Review*, Oct. 1846

5 [*"Last words":*] All my possessions for a
    moment of time.
    Attributed in *Littell's Living Age*, 8 Nov. 1856.
    Undoubtedly an apocryphal remark.

Elizabeth II

British queen, 1926–

1 My husband and I . . .

Christmas Message (1953). The standard opening of the queen's speeches.

2 In the words of one of my more sympathetic correspondents, it has turned out to be an "annus horribilis."

Speech at Guildhall, London, 24 Nov. 1992

3 Nothing that can be said can begin to take away the anguish and pain of these moments. Grief is the price we pay for love.

Message to prayer service for the families of British victims of 9/11 terror attacks in New York, 21 Sept. 2001

4 Think what we would have missed if we had never . . . used a mobile phone or surfed the Net—or, to be honest, listened to other people talking about surfing the Net.

Quoted in *Daily Telegraph* (London), 21 Nov. 1997

Elizabeth the Queen Mother

British queen consort, 1900–2002

1 [*After being asked whether the princesses would leave England after the bombing of Buckingham Palace, 1940:*] The princesses could never leave without me—and I could not leave without the king—and, of course, the king will never leave.

Quoted in *N.Y. Times,* 28 May 1948

2 [*Remark to a London policeman, 13 Sept. 1940:*] I'm glad we've been bombed too. It makes me feel I can look those East End mothers in the face.

Quoted in Jennifer Ellis, *Elizabeth the Queen Mother* (1953)

Edward Kennedy "Duke" Ellington

U.S. jazz bandleader and composer, 1899–1974

1 Music is my mistress, and she plays second fiddle to no one.

Music Is My Mistress act 8 "Pedestrian Minstrel" (1973)

2 Playing "Bop" is like Scrabble with all the vowels missing.

Quoted in *Look,* 10 Aug. 1954

3 [*Responding to being turned down for a special Pulitzer Prize citation:*] Fate is being kind to me. Fate doesn't want me to be famous too young.

Quoted in *N.Y. Times Magazine,* 12 Sept. 1965

4 Jazz was like the kind of man you wouldn't want your daughter to associate with.

Quoted in *N.Y. Times Magazine,* 12 Sept. 1965

Jane Elliot

Scottish poet, 1727–1805

1 The flowers of the forest are a' wede away.

"Lament for Flodden" l. 4 (1776)

Ebenezer Elliott

English poet, 1781–1849

1 What is a communist? One who has yearnings For equal division of unequal earnings.

"Epigram" (1850)

Bret Easton Ellis

U.S. writer, 1964–

1 I've gotta return some videotapes.

American Psycho (1991)

2 There is an idea of a Patrick Bateman, some kind of abstraction, but there is no real me, only an entity, something illusory, and though I can hide my cold gaze and you can shake my hand and feel flesh gripping yours and maybe you can even sense our lifestyles are probably comparable: *I simply am not there.*

American Psycho (1991)

Havelock Ellis

English sexologist, 1859–1939

1 The sanitary and mechanical age we are now entering makes up for the mercy it grants to our sense of smell by the ferocity with which it assails our sense of hearing.

Impressions and Comments (1914)

2 The greatest task before civilization at present is to make machines what they ought to be, the slaves, instead of the masters of men; and if civilization fails at the task, then without doubt it and its makers will go down to a common destination.

Little Essays of Love and Virtue "The Individual and the Race" (1922)

3 Dancing is the loftiest, the most moving, the most beautiful of the arts, because it is no mere translation or abstraction from life; it is life itself.

The Dance of Life ch. 2 (1923)

Harlan Ellison

U.S. science fiction writer, 1934–2018

1 I Have No Mouth, and I Must Scream.

Title of book (1967)

2 Apart from hydrogen, the most common thing in the universe is stupidity.

An Edge in My Voice (1985). Usually quoted as "The two most common elements in the universe are hydrogen and stupidity."

Ralph Ellison

U.S. novelist, 1914–1994

1 I am an invisible man. . . . I am a man of substance, of flesh and bone, fiber and liquids—and I might even be said to possess a mind. I am invisible, understand, simply because people refuse to see me.

Invisible Man prologue (1952)

2 America is woven of many strands; I would recognize them and let it so remain. . . . Our fate is to become one, and yet many—This is not prophecy, but description.

Invisible Man epilogue (1952)
See Baudouin 1; Jimmy Carter 3; Crèvecoeur 1; Victoria Hayward 1; Jesse Jackson 1; Zangwill 2

3 Who knows but that, on the lower frequencies, I speak for you?

Invisible Man epilogue (1952)

4 While one can do nothing about choosing one's relatives, one can, as artist, choose one's "ancestors."

Shadow and Act "The World and the Jug" (1964)

Henry L. Ellsworth

U.S. government official, 1791–1858

1 The advancement of the arts from year to year taxes our credulity, and seems to presage the arrival of that period when human improvement must end.

Annual Report of the Commissioner of Patents (1843). Ellsworth was U.S. commissioner of patents.

This statement is the closest that has been found to an official source of the popular story that a commissioner of patents in the late nineteenth century resigned or advocated closing the Patent Office because there was nothing left to be invented. According to the folklorist David P. Mikkelson in the *New York Times*, 15 Oct. 1995: "The origins of this quotation were researched by Dr. Eber Jeffery more than 50 years ago as part of a project conducted under the aegis of the District of Columbia Historical Records Survey. He found no evidence that any official of the United States Patent Office (including Charles H. Duell, to whom the quotation is most often attributed) had ever resigned his post or recommended that the office be closed because he thought there was nothing left to invent." There was a joke in the English magazine *Punch*, 27 Dec. 1899, that may have given rise to the anecdote. A "genius" seeking a "clerk who can examine patents" is told at a publisher's office, "Everything that *can* be invented has been invented."

Paul Éluard (Eugène Grindel)

French poet, 1895–1952

1 *La Terre est Bleue Comme une Orange.*
The Earth Is Blue like an Orange.

Title of poem (1929)

2 *Adieu tristesse*
Bonjour tristesse.
Farewell sadness
Good-day sadness.

"À peine défigurée" (1932)

Ralph Waldo Emerson

U.S. writer, 1803–1882

1 When a whole nation is roaring Patriotism at the top of its voice, I am fain to explore the cleanness of its hands and purity of its heart.

Journal, 10 Dec. 1824

2 'Tis a queer life, and the only humor proper to it seems quiet astonishment. Others laugh, weep, sell, or proselyte. I admire.

Letter to Mary Moody Emerson, 1 Aug. 1826

3 A man is a god in ruins. When men are innocent, life shall be longer, and shall pass into the immortal, as gently as we awake from dreams.

Nature ch. 8 (1836). *Hitch Your Wagon to a Star*, ed. Keith W. Frome, notes: "Emerson says that a 'certain poet' sang this to him. Gay Wilson Allen and others

have speculated that this poet could have been Bronson Alcott, Plotinus, or Emerson himself."

4 Meek young men grow up in libraries,
believing it their duty to accept the views,
which Cicero, which Locke, which Bacon, have
given, forgetful that Cicero, Locke, and Bacon
were only young men in libraries, when they
wrote these books.
The American Scholar sec. 2 (1837)

5 Wherever Macdonald sits, there is the head of
the table.
The American Scholar sec. 3 (1837). This saying has
become proverbial, often with "Macgregor" instead of
"Macdonald."

6 By the rude bridge that arched the flood,
Their flag to April's breeze unfurled,
Here once the embattled farmers stood,
And fired the shot heard round the world.
"Concord Hymn" l. 1 (1837)

7 Nothing great was ever achieved without
enthusiasm.
Essays "Circles" (1841)

8 Commit a crime and the earth is made of glass.
Commit a crime, and it seems as if a coat of
snow fell on the ground, such as reveals in the
woods the track of every partridge and fox and
squirrel and mole.
Essays "Compensation" (1841)

9 Almost all people descend to meet.
Essays "Friendship" (1841)

10 The only reward of virtue is virtue; the only way
to have a friend is to be one.
Essays "Friendship" (1841)

11 All history becomes subjective; in other words
there is properly no history; only biography.
Essays "History" (1841)
See Disraeli 6

12 What is the hardest task in the world? To think.
Essays "Intellect" (1841)

13 All mankind love a lover.
Essays "Love" (1841)

14 In skating over thin ice, our safety is in our
speed.
Essays "Prudence" (1841)

15 But do your thing, and I shall know you.
Essays "Self-Reliance" (1841)

16 A foolish consistency is the hobgoblin of
little minds, adored by little statesmen and
philosophers and divines. With consistency a
great soul has simply nothing to do.
Essays "Self-Reliance" (1841)

17 To be great is to be misunderstood.
Essays "Self-Reliance" (1841)

18 A man Caesar is born, and for ages after we
have a Roman Empire. Christ is born, and
millions of minds so grow and cleave to his
genius that he is confounded with virtue and
the possible of man. An institution is the
lengthened shadow of one man.
Essays "Self-Reliance" (1841)

19 The lesson which these observations convey
is, Be, and not seem. Let us acquiesce. Let us
take our bloated nothingness out of the path of
the divine circuits. Let us unlearn our wisdom
of the world. Let us lie low in the Lord's power,
and learn that truth alone makes rich and great.
Essays "Spiritual Laws" (1841)

20 A man may love a paradox without either losing
his wit or his honesty.
"Walter Savage Landor" (1841)

21 Never strike a king unless you are sure you
shall kill him.
Journal, Aug.–Sept. 1843

22 Men are conservatives when they are least
vigorous, or when they are most luxurious.
They are conservatives after dinner, or before
taking their rest; when they are sick, or aged;
in the morning, or when their intellect or

their conscience has been aroused, when they hear music, or when they read poetry, they are radicals.

Essays, Second Series "New England Reformers" (1844)

23 The reward of a thing well done, is to have done it.

Essays, Second Series "New England Reformers" (1844)

24 Money, which represents the prose of life, and which is hardly spoken of in parlors without an apology, is, in its effects and laws, as beautiful as roses.

Essays, Second Series "Nominalist and Realist" (1844)

25 For, though the origin of most of our words is forgotten, each word was at first a stroke of genius, and obtained currency, because for the moment it symbolized the world to the first speaker and to the hearer. The etymologist finds the deadest word to have been once a brilliant picture.

Essays, Second Series "The Poet" (1844)

26 The wise know that foolish legislation is a rope of sand which perishes in the twisting; that the State must follow and not lead the character and progress of the citizen; . . . that the form of government which prevails is the expression of what cultivation exists in the population which permits it. The law is only a memorandum.

Essays, Second Series "Politics" (1844)

27 Good men must not obey the laws too well.

Essays, Second Series "Politics" (1844)

28 On the other side, the conservative party, composed of the most moderate, able, and cultivated part of the population, is timid, and merely defensive of property. It vindicates no right, it aspires to no real good, it brands no rime, it proposes no generous policy, it does not build, nor write, nor cherish the arts, nor foster religion, nor establish schools, nor encourage science, nor emancipate the slave, nor befriend the poor, or the Indian, or the immigrant.

Essays, Second Series "Politics" (1844)

29 The less government we have the better,—the fewer laws, and the less confided power.

Essays, Second Series "Politics" (1844)
See O'Sullivan 1; Shipley 1; Thoreau 3

30 Government exists to defend the weak and the poor and the injured party; the rich and the strong can better take care of themselves.

Address delivered on the anniversary of the emancipation of the negroes in the British West Indies, Concord, Mass., 1 Aug. 1844

31 Things are in the saddle,
And ride mankind.

"Ode Inscribed to W. H. Channing" l. 50 (1847)

32 The hand that rounded Peter's dome,
And groined the aisles of Christian Rome,
Wrought in a sad sincerity;
Himself from God he could not free;
He builded better than he knew;—
The conscious stone to beauty grew.

"The Problem" l. 19 (1847)

33 Standing on the bare ground, my head bathed by the blithe air, and uplifted into infinite space, all mean egotism vanishes. I become a transparent eye-ball; I am nothing; I see all; the currents of the Universal Being circulate through me; I am part and particle of God.

Nature, rev. ed., ch. 1 (1849)

34 I hate quotation. Tell me what you know.

Journal, May 1849

35 Keep cool: it will be all one a hundred years hence.

Representative Men "Montaigne; or the Skeptic" (1850)

36 The word *liberty* in the mouth of Mr. [Daniel] Webster sounds like the word *love* in the mouth of a courtesan.

Journal, Feb. 1851

37 I trust a good deal to common fame, as we all must. If a man has good corn, or wood, or boards, or pigs, to sell, or can make better chairs or knives, crucibles or church organs, than anybody else, you will find a broad hard-beaten road to his house, though it be in the woods.

Journal, Feb. 1855
See Ralph Waldo Emerson 51

38 Universities are, of course, hostile to geniuses, which seeing and using ways of their own, discredit the routine: as churches and monasteries persecute youthful saints.

English Traits "Universities" (1856)

39 Men are what their mothers made them.
The Conduct of Life "Fate" (1860)

40 In the Greek cities, it was reckoned profane, that any person should pretend a property in a work of art, which belonged to all who could behold it.
The Conduct of Life "Wealth" (1860)

41 The louder he talked of his honor, the faster we counted our spoons.
The Conduct of Life "Worship" (1860)
See Samuel Johnson 54

42 As gas-light is found to be the best nocturnal police, so the universe protects itself by pitiless publicity.
The Conduct of Life "Worship" (1860)
See Brandeis 4

43 [*Responding to Rufus Choate's characterization of the Declaration of Independence as "glittering and sounding generalities":*] "Glittering generalities!" They are blazing ubiquities.
"Books" (lecture), Boston, Mass., 25 Dec. 1864
See Rufus Choate 1

44 There are always two parties, the party of the Past and the party of the Future; the Establishment and the Movement.
"Historic Notes of Life and Letters in New England" (1867)
See Fairlie 1

45 Next to the originator of a good sentence is the first quoter of it. Many will read the book before one thinks of quoting a passage. As soon as he has done this, that line will be quoted east and west.
Journal (1867)

46 When Duty whispers low, *Thou must,* The youth replies, *I can.*
"Voluntaries" no. 3 (1867)

47 [*Of Abraham Lincoln:*] His heart was as great as the world, but there was no room in it to hold the memory of a wrong.
Letters and Social Aims "Greatness" (1876)

48 By necessity, by proclivity, and by delight, we all quote.
Letters and Social Aims "Quotation and Originality" (1876)

49 People go out to look at sunrises and sunsets who do not recognize their own, quietly and happily, but know that it is foreign to them. As they do by books, so they quote the sunset and the star, and do not make them theirs. Worse yet, they live as foreigners in the world of truth, and quote thoughts, and thus disown them. Quotation confesses inferiority.
Letters and Social Aims "Quotation and Originality" (1876)

50 Hitch your wagon to a star.
Quoted in Moncare D. Conway, *The Golden Hour* (1862)

51 If a man can write a better book, preach a better sermon or make a better mouse trap than his neighbors, though he builds his house in the woods, the world will make a beaten path to his door.
Quoted in *Detroit Free Press,* 7 May 1882. Robert Andrews notes in *Famous Lines:* "Ascribed to Emerson by Sarah Yule in the anthology *Borrowings* (1889), later said by her to originate in a lecture given by Emerson in 1871 [in San Francisco or Oakland]. A similar passage appears in Emerson's *Journals* (1909–1914), which provided material for many of his lectures and writings. The remark's authorship was also claimed by Elbert Hubbard in *A Thousand and One Epigrams* (1911)." The 1882 citation above is the earliest "mouse-trap" version found to date. Hubbard's claim is unlikely in view of the fact that he was born in 1859.
See Ralph Waldo Emerson 37

Eminem (Marshall Mathers)
U.S. rap musician, 1972–

1 My name is . . . Slim Shady!
Ahem . . . excuse me!
Can I have the attention of the class for one
   second?
Hi kids! Do you like violence?
Wanna see me stick Nine Inch Nails through
   each one of my eyelids?
Wanna copy me and do exactly like I did?
Try 'cid and get fucked up worse than my
   life is?
"My Name Is" (song) (1999)

2 I'm Slim Shady, yes I'm the real Shady
All you other Slim Shadys are just imitating
So won't the real Slim Shady please stand up,
   please stand up, please stand up?
"The Real Slim Shady" (song) (2000)

3 When a dude's gettin' bullied and shoots up his
    school
  And they blame it on Marilyn [Manson], and
    the heroin
  Where were the parents at? and look where
    it's at
  Middle America, now it's a tragedy
  Now it's so sad to see, an upper class city
  Havin' this happenin'
  Then attack Eminem 'cause I rap this way
  But I'm glad cause they feed me the fuel that I
    need for the fire
  To burn and it's burnin' and I have returned.
  "The Way I Am" (song) (2000)

Robert Emmet
Irish nationalist, 1778–1803

1 Let no man write my epitaph. . . . When my
  country takes her place among the nations of
  the earth, *then*, and *not till then*, let my epitaph
  be written.
  Speech at trial after being sentenced to death, 19
  Sept. 1803

Daniel Decatur Emmett
U.S. entertainer, 1815–1904

1 I wish I was in de land ob cotton,
  Old times dar am not forgotten,
  Look away! Look away! Look away! Dixie Land.
  "Dixie's Land" (song) st. 1 (1859). According to
  The Book of World-Famous Music, "the first line is
  traditional."

2 In Dixie's land, we'll took our stand,
  To lib and die in Dixie!
  Away, away, away down South in Dixie!
  "Dixie's Land" (song) st. 1 (1859)

William Empson
English poet and critic, 1906–1984

1 Seven Types of Ambiguity.
  Title of book (1930)

Friedrich Engels
German socialist, 1820–1895

1 The State is not "abolished," *it withers away.*
  Anti-Dühring pt. 3, ch. 2 (1878)

2 [The stock exchange is the] highest vocation
  for a capitalist, where property merges directly
  with theft.
  Letter to Eduard Bernstein, 10 Feb. 1883

3 The modern individual family is based on the
  open or disguised domestic enslavement of
  the woman. . . . Today, in the great majority
  of cases, the man has to be the earner, the
  breadwinner of the family, at least among
  the propertied classes, and this gives him
  a dominating position which requires no
  special legal privileges. In the family, he is the
  bourgeois; the wife represents the proletariat.
  The Origin of the Family, Private Property and the State
  ch. 2, pt. 4 (1884)

4 Naturally, the workers are perfectly free; the
  manufacturer does not force them to take his
  materials and his cards, but he says to them . . .
  "If you don't like to be frizzled in my frying-
  pan, you can take a walk into the fire."
  The Condition of the Working Class in England in 1844
  ch. 7 (1892)

H. C. Englebrecht
U.S. author, 1895–1939

1 Merchants of Death.
  Title of book (1934). Coauthored with F. C. Hanighen.

Eve Ensler
U.S. playwright, 1953–

1 The Vagina Monologues.
  Title of play (1996)

Nora Ephron
U.S. writer and director, 1941–2012

1 If pregnancy were a book, they would cut the
  last two chapters.
  Heartburn ch. 4 (1983)

2 [A successful parent is someone] who raises a
  child who grows up and is able to pay for his or
  her own psychoanalysis.
  Quoted in *People,* 10 Nov. 1986

Epimenides
Cretan poet and priest, Sixth cent. B.C.

1 All Cretans are liars.
  Attributed in Callimachus, *Hymn to Zeus*

Olaudah Equiano (Gustavus Vassa)

Nigerian abolitionist, ca. 1745–1797

1 When I recovered a little I found some black people about me . . . I asked them if we were not to be eaten by those white men with horrible looks, red faces, and loose hair.

Narrative of the Life of Olaudah Equiano ch. 3 (1789)

Desiderius Erasmus

Dutch scholar, ca. 1466–1536

1 *In regione caecorum rex est luscus.*
In the country of the blind the one-eyed man is king.

Adagia bk. 3, century 4, no. 96 (1500)

2 The first thing I shall do, as soon as the money arrives, is to buy some Greek authors; after that, I shall buy clothes.

Letter to Jacob Batt, 12 Apr. 1500. This is often paraphrased as "When I get a little money, I buy books; and, if any is left, I buy food and clothes."

3 [*Of Thomas More:*] *Omnium horarum hominem.*
A man of all hours.

In Praise of Folly prefatory letter (1509)
See Whittington 1

4 He calls figs figs and a spade a spade.

Adagia bk. 2, century 3, no. 5 (1515). Erasmus mistranslated "trough" in ancient Greek sources as "spade," thus creating the modern expression "to call a spade a spade." "Call a trough a trough" appears in Demosthenes' oration "Olynthus," quoting Philip of Macedon, and in a fragment by Menander.

Paul Erdös

Hungarian mathematician, 1913–1996

1 A mathematician is a machine for turning coffee into theorems.

Quoted in *Atlantic*, Nov. 1987. Sometimes credited to other mathematicians before Erdös, such as Paul Turan or Alfred Renyi.

Louise Erdrich

U.S. writer, 1954–

1 I was in love with the whole world and all that lived in its rainy arms.

Love Medicine ch. 15 (1984)

2 We started dying before the snow, and like the snow, we continued to fall.

Tracks ch. 1 (1988)

3 Life will break you. Nobody can protect you from that, and living alone won't either, for solitude will also break you with its yearning. You have to love. You have to feel. It is the reason you are here on earth. You are here to risk your heart. You are here to be swallowed up. And when it happens that you are broken, or betrayed, or left, or hurt, or death brushes near, let yourself sit by an apple tree and listen to the apples falling all around you in heaps, wasting their sweetness. Tell yourself you tasted as many as you could.

The Painted Drum pt. 4 (2005)

Erik Erikson

German-born U.S. psychologist, 1902–1994

1 The identity crisis . . . occurs in that period of the life cycle when each youth must forge for himself some central perspective and direction, some working unity, out of the effective remnants of his childhood and the hopes of his anticipated adulthood.

Young Man Luther ch. 1 (1958)

Thomas Erskine

Scottish lawyer and government official, 1750–1823

1 There should be a solemn pause before we rush to judgment.

Speech for the defense in treason trial of James Hadfield (1800)

Susan Ertz

U.S. writer, 1894–1985

1 Millions long for immortality who don't know what to do with themselves on a rainy Sunday afternoon.

Anger in the Sky ch. 5 (1943)
See France 4

Henri Estienne

French printer and publisher, 1531–1598

1 *Si jeunesse savait; si vieillesse pouvait.*
If youth knew; if age could.

Les Prémices bk. 4, epigram 4 (1594)

Euclid

Greek mathematician, fl. 300 B.C.

1 *Quod erat demonstrandum.*
Which was to be proved.

Elementa bk. 1, proposition 5. Latin translation from the original Greek, often abbreviated *QED*.

2 In right-angled triangles the square on the side opposite the right angle equals the sum of the squares on the sides containing the right angle.
Elementa bk. 1, proposition 47

3 [*Addressing Ptolemy I:*] There is no "royal road" to geometry.
Quoted in Proclus, *Commentary on the First Book of Euclid's Elementa*

Jeffrey Eugenides
U.S. writer, 1960–

1 It didn't matter in the end how old they had been, or that they were girls, but only that we had loved them, and that they hadn't heard us calling, still do not hear us, up here in the tree house, with our thinning hair and soft bellies, calling them out of those rooms where they went to be alone for all time, alone in suicide, which is deeper than death, and where we will never find the pieces to put them back together.
The Virgin Suicides ch. 5 (1993)

2 I was born twice: first, as a baby girl, on a remarkably smogless Detroit day in January of 1960; and then again, as a teenage boy, in an emergency room near Petoskey, Michigan, in August of 1974.
Middlesex bk. 1 (2002)

Leonhard Euler
Swiss mathematician and physicist, 1707–1783

1 [*Of his loss of the sight of one eye, 1735:*] Now I will have less distraction.
Quoted in Howard Eves, *Mathematical Circles* (1969)

Euripides
Greek playwright, ca. 485 B.C.–ca. 406 B.C.

1 Should I have left any stone unturned.
Heraclidae (translation by David Kovacs)

2 My tongue swore, but my mind is not on oath.
Hippolytus l. 612 (translation by David Kovacs)

3 Every man is like the company he is wont to keep.
Phoenix fragment 812 (translation by Morris Hickey Morgan). The modern proverb is "A man is known by the company he keeps."
See Proverbs 50

Linda Evangelista
Canadian fashion model, 1965–

1 [*Of supermodels:*] We don't wake up for less than $10,000 a day.
Quoted in *Vogue*, Oct. 1990

Dale Evans
U.S. actress and country singer, 1912–2001

1 Happy trails to you, until we meet again
Happy trails to you, keep smilin' until then.
"Happy Trails" (song) (1950)

Edith Evans
English actress, 1888–1976

1 When you leave the theater, if you don't walk several blocks in the wrong direction, the performance has been a failure.
Quoted in Garson Kanin, *Tracy and Hepburn* (1970)

William M. Evarts
U.S. politician, 1818–1901

1 The pious ones of Plymouth who, reaching the Rock, first fell upon their knees and then upon the aborigines.
Quoted in *Louisville Courier-Journal*, 4 July 1913. According to Robert Andrews, *Famous Lines*, this has also been attributed to Oliver Wendell Holmes, Sr., and Bill Nye.
See William Bradford 1

Gavin Ewart
English poet, 1916–1995

1 My life may be much happier to-morrow,
Hunger and love that press against the body,
The two eternal needs we recognize,—
Desires that so relentlessly pursue one,—
May get me down or raise me to the skies
And make me a Don Bradman or Don Juan.
"Days of Contempt" l. 3 (1939)

2 Miss Twye was soaping her breasts in her bath
When she heard behind her a meaning laugh
And to her amazement she discovered
A wicked man in the bathroom cupboard.
"Miss Twye" l. 1 (1939)

3 Everything was twice repeated,
Sometimes more than twice repeated,
As they worked through the agenda

(It seemed elastic, that agenda,
Becoming longer, never shorter),
Their utterances grew long, not shorter,
It was just like spreading butter.
"The Meeting" l. 11 (1982)

William Norman Ewer
British writer, 1885–1976

1 How odd
Of God
To choose
The Jews.

Quoted in *The Week-End Book* (1924). Cecil Browne
is said to have responded as follows: "But not so
odd / As those who choose / A Jewish God / Yet
spurn the Jews."

Winifred Ewing
Scottish politician, 1929–

1 The Scottish Parliament adjourned on the
25th day of March 1707 is hereby reconvened.
Speech at opening of new Scottish Parliament,
Edinburgh, Scotland, 12 May 1999

James Eyre
English judge, 1734–1799

1 A man must come into a court of equity with
clean hands.
Deering v. Earl of Winchelsea (1787)

Anne Fadiman
U.S. writer and editor, 1953–

1 [*On the travails of combining personal libraries with a spouse:*] Sharing a bed and a future was child's play compared to sharing my copy of *The Complete Poems of W. B. Yeats.*
Ex Libris: Confessions of a Common Reader "Marrying Libraries" (1998)

Clifton Fadiman
U.S. author and broadcast host, 1904–1999

1 Cheese, milk's leap toward immortality.
Introduction to Bob Brown, *The Complete Book of Cheese* (1955)

2 [*Of Gertrude Stein:*] I encountered the mama of dada again . . . and as usual withdrew worsted.
Party of One "Gertrude Stein" (1955)

3 When you reread a classic you do not see more in the book than you did before; you see more in *you* than there was before.
Any Number Can Play "War and Peace, Fifteen Years After" (1957)

Richard Fairbrass
English singer, 1953–

1 I'm too sexy for my love too sexy for my love
Love's going to leave me
I'm too sexy for my shirt too sexy for my shirt
So sexy it hurts.
"I'm Too Sexy" (song) (1991). Cowritten with Fred Fairbrass.

Henry Fairlie
English journalist, 1924–1990

1 I have several times suggested that what I call the "Establishment" in this country is today more powerful than ever before. By the "Establishment" I do not mean only the center of official power—though they are certainly part of it—but rather the whole matrix of official and social relations within which power is exercised.
The Spectator, 23 Sept. 1955. The *Oxford English Dictionary* traces as far back as 1923 the use of *the Establishment* in the sense of "a social group exercising power generally, or within a given field or institution, by virtue of its traditional superiority, and by the use esp. of tacit understandings and often a common mode of speech, and having as a general interest the maintenance of the *status quo.*" Even earlier evidence is found, however, in the quotation of Ralph Waldo Emerson cross-referenced here.
See Ralph Waldo Emerson 44

Jerry Falwell
U.S. religious leader and broadcaster, 1933–2007

1 [*Of homosexuality:*] God didn't create Adam and Steve, but Adam and Eve.
Quoted in *Wash. Post,* 15 Oct. 1979. Although this line was popularized by Falwell, it appeared as early as 1977, when the *New York Times* (19 Nov.) quoted a protest sign reading "God Made Adam and Eve, Not Adam and Steve."

Frantz Fanon
French West Indian writer, 1925–1961

1 National liberation, national renaissance, the restoration of nationhood to the people, commonwealth: whatever may be the headings used or the new formulas introduced, decolonization is always a violent phenomenon.
The Wretched of the Earth "Concerning Violence" (1961) (translation by Constance Farrington)

2 Leave this Europe where they are never done talking of Man, yet murder men everywhere they find them.
The Wretched of the Earth conclusion (1961) (translation by Constance Farrington)

3 When I search for Man in the technique and the style of Europe, I see only a succession of negations of man, and an avalanche of murders.
The Wretched of the Earth conclusion (1961) (translation by Constance Farrington)

Michael Faraday
English physicist and chemist, 1791–1867

1 I propose to distinguish these bodies by calling those *anions* which go to the *anode* of the decomposing body; and those passing to the *cathode, cations;* and when I have occasion to speak of these together, I shall call them *ions.*
Philosophical Transactions of the Royal Society of London (1834)

2 [*To William E. Gladstone, who asked what the usefulness of electricity was:*] Why, sir, there is every probability that you will soon be able to tax it!
Attributed in R. A. Gregory, *Discovery, Or the Spirit and Service of Science* (1916). This anecdote was not mentioned until well after Faraday's death and is most likely apocryphal. In the earliest known version, in William E. H. Lecky, *Democracy and Liberty* (1899), the reference is to "an important new discovery in science" rather than specifically to electricity.

Wallace Fard
U.S. founder of Nation of Islam, ca. 1891–1934

1 The blue-eyed devil white man.
Quoted in Malcolm X, *The Autobiography of Malcolm X* (1965)

Richard Fariña
U.S. writer and folk singer, 1937–1966

1 Been Down So Long It Looks Like Up to Me.
Title of book (1966)

Eleanor Farjeon
English writer, 1881–1965

1 Morning has broken, like the first morning, Blackbird has spoken, like the first bird.
"Morning Has Broken" (hymn) (1931)

Herbert Farjeon
English writer, 1887–1945

1 I'm the luckiest of females!
For I've danced with a man
Who's danced with a girl
Who's danced with the Prince of Wales!
"I've Danced With a Man Who's Danced With a Girl" (song) (1927)

James Farley
U.S. politician, 1888–1976

1 [*Of Franklin Roosevelt's 1936 reelection, carrying all states but two:*] As Maine goes, so goes Vermont.
Statement to press, 4 Nov. 1936
See Political Slogans 4

Philip José Farmer
U.S. science fiction writer, 1918–2009

1 THERE ARE UNIVERSES BEGGING FOR GODS yet He hangs around this one looking for work.
"Riders of the Purple Wage" (1967)

2 Confucius once said that a bear could not fart at the North Pole without causing a big wind in Chicago.
"Riders of the Purple Wage" (1967)
See Gleick 1; Edward Lorenz 1

Farouk I
Egyptian king, 1920–1965

1 [*Remark to Lord Boyd-Orr, Cairo, 1948:*] The whole world is in revolt. Soon there will be only five Kings left—the King of England, the King of Spades, the King of Clubs, the King of Hearts, and the King of Diamonds.
Quoted in *Life*, 10 Apr. 1950

George Farquhar
Irish playwright, 1678–1707

1 My Lady Bountiful.
The Beaux' Stratagem act 1, sc. 1 (1707)

David G. Farragut
U.S. admiral, 1801–1870

1 [*Remark at the Battle of Mobile Bay, 5 Aug. 1864:*] Damn the torpedoes!
Attributed in Foxhall A. Parker, *The Battle of Mobile Bay* (1878). Parker's full quotation is "Damn the torpedoes! Jouett, full speed!" Later sources usually quote Farragut as saying "Damn the torpedoes! Full speed ahead!" In fact, reports of the battle filed by the participants do not mention any version of "Damn the torpedoes!"; these words were probably never uttered.

Mia Farrow

U.S. actress, 1945–

1 [*Of Woody Allen:*] He had polyester sheets and I wanted to get cotton sheets. He discussed it with his shrink many times before he made the switch.

Quoted in *Independent*, 8 Feb. 1997

Ronan Farrow (Satchel Ronan O'Sullivan Farrow)

U.S. activist and journalist, 1987–

1 [*Of suspicions that his biological father was Frank Sinatra rather than Woody Allen:*] We're all *possibly* Frank Sinatra's son.

Tweet, 2 Oct. 2013

Howard Fast

U.S. novelist, 1914–2003

1 I will return and I will be millions.

Spartacus pt. 1 (1952). In Fast's novel these words are spoken by a crucified slave. Eva Perón's tomb in Buenos Aires, Argentina, bears the words, *"Volvere y sere milliones!"* ("I will come again and I will be millions"). Nigel Rees notes in *The Quote . . . Unquote Newsletter*, Jan. 2003: "According to Nicholas Fraser, co-author of *Eva Perón* (1980), 'She never said this last, but that doesn't keep it from being true,' though some sources give it as from a speech she made towards the end of her life." Perón died in 1952, but the tomb inscription is dated 1982.

William Faulkner

U.S. novelist, 1897–1962

1 Because no battle is ever won he said. They are not even fought. The field only reveals to man his own folly and despair, and victory is an illusion of philosophers and fools.

The Sound and the Fury pt. 2 (1929)

2 They [the Negroes] will endure. They are better than we are. Stronger than we are. Their vices are vices aped from white men or that white men and bondage have taught them: improvidence and intemperance and evasion— not laziness: evasion: of what white men had set them to, not for their aggrandizement or even comfort but his own.

The Bear pt. 4 (1932)

3 Too much happens. . . . Man performs, engenders, so much more than he can or should have to bear. That's how he finds that he can bear anything. . . . That's what's so terrible.

Light in August ch. 13 (1932)

4 Why do you hate the South?

I dont hate it. . . . I dont hate it. . . . *I dont hate it* he thought, panting in the cold air, the iron New England dark; *I dont. I dont! I dont hate it! I dont hate it!*

Absalom, Absalom! ch. 9 (1936). Ellipses in the original.

5 You cant understand it [the South]. You would have to be born there.

Absalom, Absalom! ch. 9 (1936)

6 JEFFERSON, YOKNAPATAWPHA CO., Mississippi. Area, 2400 Square Miles. Population, Whites, 6298; Negroes, 9313. WILLIAM FAULKNER, Sole Owner & Proprietor.

Absalom, Absalom! inscription on endpaper map (1936)

7 Between grief and nothing I will take grief.

If I Forget Thee, Jerusalem "The Wild Palms" (1939)

8 There are no longer problems of the spirit. There is only one question: When will I be blown up? Because of this, the young man or woman writing today has forgotten the problems of the human heart in conflict with itself which alone can make good writing because only that is worth writing about, worth the agony and the sweat.

Nobel Prize acceptance speech, Stockholm, 10 Dec. 1950

9 He [the writer] must teach himself that the basest of all things is to be afraid; and, teaching himself that, forget it forever, leaving no room in his workshop for anything but the old verities and truths of the heart, the old universal truths lacking which any story is ephemeral and doomed—love and honor and pity and pride and compassion and sacrifice.

Nobel Prize acceptance speech, Stockholm, 10 Dec. 1950

10 I decline to accept the end of man.

Nobel Prize acceptance speech, Stockholm, 10 Dec. 1950

11 I believe that man will not merely endure: he will prevail. He is immortal, not because he alone among creatures has an inexhaustible voice, but because he has a soul, a spirit capable of compassion and sacrifice and endurance.

Nobel Prize acceptance speech, Stockholm, 10 Dec. 1950

12 The poet's, the writer's duty is to write about these things. It is his privilege to help man endure by lifting his heart, by reminding him of the courage and honor and hope and pride and compassion and pity and sacrifice which have been the glory of his past. The poet's voice need not merely be the record of man, it can be one of the props, the pillars to help him endure and prevail.

Nobel Prize acceptance speech, Stockholm, 10 Dec. 1950

13 The past is never dead. It's not even past.

Requiem for a Nun act 1 (1951)

14 Oh yes, he will survive it because he has that in him which will endure even beyond the ultimate worthless tideless rock freezing slowly in the last red and heatless sunset, because already the next star in the blue immensity of space will be already clamorous with the uproar of his debarkation, his puny and inexhaustible voice still talking, still planning.

A Fable (1954)

15 The Long Hot Summer.

Title of motion picture (1958). Although listed here under Faulkner as the author, this film was actually written by Irving Ravetch and Harriet Frank, Jr., based on Faulkner's novel *The Hamlet* (1940). Book 3 of *The Hamlet* is titled "The Long Summer."

16 The writer's only responsibility is to his art. He will be completely ruthless if he is a good one. He has a dream. It anguishes him so much he must get rid of it. He has no peace until then. Everything goes by the board. . . . If a writer has to rob his mother, he will not hesitate; the *Ode on a Grecian Urn* is worth any number of old ladies.

Quoted in *Paris Review,* Spring 1956

17 Really the writer doesn't want success. . . . He knows he has a short span of life, that the day will come when he must pass through the wall of oblivion, and he wants to leave a scratch on

that wall—Kilroy was here—that somebody a hundred, or a thousand years later will see.

Quoted in *Faulkner in the University,* ed. Frederick L. Gwynn and Joseph L. Blotner (1959)

18 The ideal woman which is in every man's mind is evoked by a word or phrase or the shape of her wrist, her hand. The most beautiful description of a woman is by understatement. Remember, all Tolstoy ever said to describe Anna Karenina was that she was beautiful and could see in the dark like a cat. Every man has a different idea of what's beautiful, and it's best to take the gesture, the shadow of the branch, and let the mind create the tree.

Quoted in *Reader's Digest,* Mar. 1973

Kenneth Fearing
U.S. poet and novelist, 1902–1961

1 The big clock was running as usual. . . . Sometimes the hands of the clock actually raced, and at other times they hardly moved at all. But that made no difference to the big clock. The hands could move backward, and the time it told would be right just the same. It would still be running as usual, because all other watches have to be set by the big one.

The Big Clock ch. 1 (1946)

Lucien Febvre
French historian, 1878–1956

1 It is never a waste of time to study the history of a word.

"Civilisation: Evolution of a Word and a Group of Ideas" (1930)

James K. Feibleman
U.S. philosopher and writer, 1904–1987

1 A myth is a religion in which no-one any longer believes.

Understanding Philosophy ch. 3 (1973)
See Tom Wolfe 4

Jules Feiffer
U.S. cartoonist, 1929–

1 I used to think I was poor. Then they told me I wasn't poor, I was needy. Then they told me it was self-defeating to think of myself

as needy, I was culturally deprived. Then they told me deprived was a bad image, that I was underprivileged. Then they told me underprivileged was overused, that I was disadvantaged. I still don't have a dime, but I do have a *great* vocabulary.

Cartoon caption, quoted in Leonard L. Levinson, *Bartlett's Unfamiliar Quotations* (1971). Originally appeared in 1965.

Bruce Feirstein
U.S. writer, 1953–

1 Real Men Don't Eat Quiche.
Title of book (1982)

Federico Fellini
Italian director and screenwriter, 1920–1993

1 *La Dolce Vita.*
The Sweet Life.
Title of motion picture (1960)

Edna Ferber
U.S. writer, 1887–1968

1 Miss Ferber, never known for honeyed talk, clashed slightly with Noel Coward one day when they both turned up at the [Algonquin] Round Table sporting new double-breasted suits. "You look almost like a man," Mr. Coward told Miss Ferber. "So," Miss Ferber replied lightly, "do you."
Reported in Margaret Case Harriman, *The Vicious Circle: The Story of the Algonquin Round Table* (1951)

Ferdinand I
Holy Roman Emperor, 1503–1564

1 [*Motto:*] *Fiat justitia et pereat mundus.*
Let justice be done, though the world perish.
Quoted in Johannes Manlius, *Locorum Communium Collectanea* (1563)
See Lord Mansfield 1; William Watson 1

Lawrence Ferlinghetti
U.S. writer, 1919–2021

1 Constantly risking absurdity
and death
whenever he performs
above the heads
of his audience

the poet like an acrobat
climbs on rime.
"Constantly risking absurdity" l. 1 (1958)

2 Beauty stands and waits
with gravity
to start her death-defying leap.
"Constantly risking absurdity" l. 26 (1958)

3 In Goya's greatest scenes we seem to see
the people of the world
exactly at the moment when
they first attained the title of
"suffering humanity."
"In Goya's greatest scenes we seem to see" l. 1 (1958)

Pierre de Fermat
French mathematician, 1601–1665

1 *Cuius rei demonstrationem mirabilem sane detexi hanc marginis exiguitas non caperet.*
I have a truly marvelous demonstration of this proposition which this margin is too narrow to contain.
Quoted in *Diophanti Alexandrini Arithmeticorum*, ed. Clement-Samuel de Fermat (1670). Fermat wrote this comment about what has become known as "Fermat's last theorem." That theorem was written in the margin of Fermat's copy of *Diophantus' Arithmetica* and was later published in a 1670 edition of Diophantus that included Fermat's annotations. *See Gauss 1*

Enrico Fermi
Italian-born U.S. physicist, 1901–1954

1 [*Announcement during first controlled nuclear chain reaction, Chicago, Ill., 2 Dec. 1942:*] The reaction is self-sustaining.
Quoted in Corbin Allardice and Edward R. Trapnell, *The First Pile* (1949)

2 [*Commenting on the possibility of intelligent life on other planets:*] Where is everybody?
Quoted in Ralph E. Lapp, *Man and Space* (1961)

3 If I could remember the names of these particles, I would have been a botanist.
Quoted in Leon Lederman, Lecture at Brookhaven National Laboratory, Brookhaven, N.Y., 9 Jan. 1963

Macedonio Fernández
Argentinian philosopher and writer, 1874–1952

1 Everything has been written, everything has been said, everything has been made: that's

what God heard before creating the world, when there was nothing yet. I have also heard that one, he may have answered from the old, split Nothingness. And then he began.

Museo de la Novela de la Eterna (The Museum of Eternity's Novel) prologue (1967)

Will Ferrell
U.S. comedian, 1967–

1 [*Word coined to mock George W. Bush's communication skills:*] Strategery.

Saturday Night Live (television show), 7 Oct. 2000

Kathleen Ferrier
English opera singer, 1912–1953

1 [*"Last words," 1953:*] Now I'll have *eine kleine* Pause.

Quoted in Gerald Moore, *Am I Too Loud?* (1962)

Ludwig Feuerbach
German philosopher, 1804–1872

1 *Der Mensch ist, was er isst.*
Man is what he eats.

Quoted in Jacob Moleschott, *Lehre der Nahrungsmittel: Für das Volk* (1850)
See Brillat-Savarin 1

Richard P. Feynman
U.S. physicist, 1918–1988

1 To those who do not know mathematics it is difficult to get across a real feeling as to the beauty, the deepest beauty, of nature. . . . If you want to learn about nature, to appreciate nature, it is necessary to understand the language that she speaks in.

The Character of Physical Law ch. 2 (1965)

2 I think I can safely say that nobody understands quantum mechanics.

The Character of Physical Law ch. 6 (1965)

3 For a successful technology, reality must take precedence over public relations, for nature cannot be fooled.

Rogers Commission Report on the Space Shuttle Challenger Accident appendix (1986)

4 What I cannot create I do not understand.

Quoted in James Gleick, *Genius: The Life and Science of Richard Feynman* (1992)

Eugene Field
U.S. poet and journalist, 1850–1895

1 Wynken, Blynken, and Nod one night
Sailed off in a wooden shoe—
Sailed on a river of crystal light,
Into a sea of dew.

"Wynken, Blynken, and Nod" l. 1 (1889)

2 Wynken and Blynken are two little eyes,
And Nod is a little head,
And the wooden ship that sailed the skies
Is a wee one's trundle-bed.

"Wynken, Blynken, and Nod" l. 37 (1889)

Marshall Field
U.S. merchant, 1834–1906

1 [*Instruction to manager of his department store, Chicago, Ill.:*] Give the lady what she wants!

Quoted in Lloyd Wendt, *Give the Lady What She Wants!* (1952)

Sally Field
U.S. actress, 1946–

1 You like me. Right now! You like me!

Speech accepting Academy Award for Best Actress, Hollywood, Calif., 25 Mar. 1985. Field's words are usually misquoted as "You like me! You really like me!"

Helen Fielding
English writer, 1958–

1 Exes should never, never go out with or marry other people but should remain celibate to the end of their days in order to provide you with a mental fallback position.

Bridget Jones's Diary "August" (1996)

2 It's *amazing how much time and money* can be saved in the world of dating by close attention to detail. A white sock here, a pair of red braces there, a gray slip-on shoe, a swastika, are as often as not all one needs to tell you there's no point in writing down phone numbers and forking out for expensive lunches because it's never going to be a runner.

Bridget Jones's Diary "January" (1996)

3 I will not
Drink more than fourteen alcohol units a week.

Bridget Jones's Diary "New Year's Resolutions" (1996)

4 [I will not] sulk about having no boyfriend, but develop inner poise and authority and sense of self as woman of substance, complete *without* boyfriend, as best way to obtain boyfriend.

Bridget Jones's Diary "New Year's Resolutions" (1996)

Henry Fielding

English novelist and playwright, 1707–1754

1 The dusky night rides down the sky,
And ushers in the morn;
The hounds all join in glorious cry,
The huntsman winds his horn:
And a-hunting we will go.

Don Quixote in England act 2, sc. 5 (1733). "A-hunting they did go" was a line in an old ballad, "The Three Jovial Huntsmen."

2 I am as sober as a judge.

Don Quixote in England act 3, sc. 14 (1733)

3 To whom nothing is given, of him can nothing be required.

Joseph Andrews bk. 2, ch. 8 (1742)

4 He in a few minutes ravished this fair creature, or at least would have ravished her, if she had not, by a timely compliance, prevented him.

Jonathan Wild bk. 3, ch. 7 (1743)

5 Distinction without a difference.

Tom Jones bk. 6, ch. 13 (1749)

6 There are a set of religious, or rather moral writers, who teach that virtue is the certain road to happiness, and vice to misery, in this world. A very wholesome and comfortable doctrine, and to which we have but one objection, namely, that it is not true.

Tom Jones bk. 15, ch. 1 (1749)

7 It hath been often said, that it is not death, but dying, which is terrible.

Amelia bk. 3, ch. 4 (1751)

8 If we regard this world only, it is the interest of every man to be either perfectly good or completely bad. He had better destroy his conscience than gently wound it.

Amelia bk. 4, ch. 2 (1751)

9 A true Christian can never be disappointed if he doth not receive his reward in this world; the laborer might as well complain that he is not paid his hire in the middle of the day.

Amelia bk. 9, ch. 8 (1751)

Dorothy Fields

U.S. songwriter, 1905–1974

1 Grab your coat, and get your hat,
Leave your worry on the doorstep.
Just direct your feet
To the sunny side of the street.

"On the Sunny Side of the Street" (song) (1930)

2 I'm in the mood for love
Simply because you're near me.
Funny, but when you're near me,
I'm in the mood for love.

"I'm in the Mood for Love" (song) (1935)

3 The minute you walked in the joint,
I could see you were a man of distinction,
A real big spender.

"Big Spender" (song) (1966)

4 So, let me get right to the point,
I don't pop my cork for ev'ry guy I see.
Hey, big spender, spend
A little time with me.

"Big Spender" (song) (1966)

5 If My Friends Could See Me Now!

Title of song (1966)

James T. Fields

U.S. publisher, 1817–1881

1 Rally round the flag, boys—
Give it to the breeze!
That's the banner that we bore
On the land and seas.

"The Stars and Stripes" (song) (1862)
See George Frederick Root 2

W. C. Fields (William Claude Dukenfield)

U.S. comedian, 1880–1946

Lines uttered by Fields in his motion pictures have been listed under his name regardless of whether he was credited as a screenwriter for the film in question.

1 [*J. Effingham Bellweather, played by W. C. Fields, speaking:*] Godfrey Daniel!

The Golf Specialist (motion picture) (1930). Fields derived this euphemism for "goddamn" from the name of his uncle, Godfrey Dukenfield.

2 [*Rollo La Rue, played by W. C. Fields, speaking:*] My little chickadee.

If I Had a Million (motion picture) (1932)

3 [*Professor Quail, played by W. C. Fields, speaking:*] Now that I'm here, I shall dally in the valley— and believe me, I can dally.

International House (motion picture) (1932). The writers credited for this film were Walter DeLeon and Francis Martin.

4 [*Mr. Snavely, played by W. C. Fields, speaking:*] It ain't a fit night out for man or beast.

The Fatal Glass of Beer (motion picture) (1933). Fields stated in a letter of 8 Feb. 1944, printed in *W. C. Fields by Himself* (1974), that he first used this in a sketch in Earl Carroll's *Vanities*. However, Fields wrote, "I do not claim to be the originator of this line as it was probably used long before I was born in some old melodrama."

5 [*Harold Bissonette, played by W. C. Fields, replying to a real estate agent who said "You're drunk":*] Yeah, and you're crazy. I'll be sober tomorrow, but you'll be crazy the rest of your life.

It's a Gift (motion picture) (1934). The writers credited for this film were Jack Cunningham and Fields. In Augustus J. C. Hare's diary entry of 16 July 1882, a similar exchange is recorded, with the punch line "I shall be sober to-morrow morning; but you're a damned fool tonight, and you'll be a damned fool to-morrow morning."

6 [*Sam Bisbee, played by W. C. Fields, speaking:*] It's a funny old world—a man's lucky if he gets out of it alive.

You're Telling Me (motion picture) (1934). The writers credited for this film were Walter DeLeon and Paul M. Jones.

7 Now don't say you can't swear off drinking; it's easy. I've done it a thousand times.

"The Temperance Lecture" (radio broadcast) (1938)

8 You Can't Cheat an Honest Man.

Title of motion picture (1939). Fields is supposed to have said this also in the stage musical *Poppy* (1923).

9 [*Larsen E. Whipsnade, played by W. C. Fields, speaking:*] You kids are disgusting, skulking around here all day, reeking of popcorn and lollipops.

You Can't Cheat an Honest Man (motion picture) (1939). The writers credited for this film were Fields, Everett Freeman, Richard Mack, and George Marion, Jr.

10 [*Larsen E. Whipsnade, played by W. C. Fields, speaking:*] Some weasel took the cork out of my lunch.

You Can't Cheat an Honest Man (motion picture) (1939). The writers credited for this film were Fields, Everett Freeman, Richard Mack, and George Marion, Jr.

11 I'd rather have two girls at 21 each, than one girl at 42.

You Can't Cheat an Honest Man (motion picture) (1939). The writers credited for this film were Fields, Everett Freeman, Richard Mack, and George Marion, Jr. Garson O'Toole has found an analogous joke, with the ages "17" and "34," in the *Seattle Daily Times*, 23 Feb. 1915.

12 [*When asked whether he liked children:*] I do if they're properly cooked!

Fields for President ch. 7 (1940)

13 [*Cuthbert J. Twillie, played by W. C. Fields, responding to the question, "Is this a game of chance?":*] Not the way I play it.

My Little Chickadee (motion picture) (1940). The writers credited for this film were Fields and Mae West.

14 [*Cuthbert J. Twillie, played by W. C. Fields, speaking:*] A thing worth having is worth cheating for.

My Little Chickadee (motion picture) (1940). The writers credited for this film were Fields and Mae West.

15 [*Cuthbert J. Twillie, played by W. C. Fields, speaking:*] During one of our trips through Afghanistan, we lost our corkscrew. We had to live on food and water for several days.

My Little Chickadee (motion picture) (1940). The writers credited for this film were Fields and Mae West.

16 [*The Great Man, played by W. C. Fields, speaking:*] I was in love with a beautiful blonde

once. She drove me to drink. 'Tis the one thing I'm indebted to her for.

Never Give a Sucker an Even Break (motion picture) (1941). The writers credited for this film were Prescott Chaplin, Fields, and John T. Neville.

17 [*The Great Man, played by W. C. Fields, speaking:*] Drown in a vat of liquor? Death, where is thy sting?

Never Give a Sucker an Even Break (motion picture) (1941). The writers credited for this film were Prescott Chaplin, Fields, and John T. Neville. *See Bible 359*

18 [*Suggested epitaph for himself:*] Here lies W. C. Fields. I would rather be living in Philadelphia.

Quoted in *Vanity Fair*, June 1925. Frequently quoted as "On the whole, I'd rather be in Philadelphia." It did not ultimately appear on the vault holding his ashes, which reads "W. C. Fields, 1880–1946."

19 Never give a sucker an even break.

Quoted in *Variety*, 12 Apr. 1923. Fields had ad-libbed this saying in the stage musical *Poppy* (1923).

20 If at first you don't succeed, try, try again. Then quit. There's no use being a damn fool about it.

Quoted in *Reader's Digest*, Oct. 1949 *See Hickson 1*

21 Hell, I never vote *for* anybody. I always vote *against*.

Quoted in R. L. Taylor, *W. C. Fields* (1949). "It is said that the American people never vote for but just love to vote against" appeared in the *New York Times*, 26 Dec. 1932. *See Franklin P. Adams 3*

22 [*Of Charlie Chaplin:*] The son of a bitch is a ballet dancer. . . . He's the best ballet dancer that ever lived . . . and if I get a good chance I'll kill him with my bare hands.

Quoted in *Sight and Sound*, Feb. 1951

23 [*Deathbed remark while reading the Bible:*] I'm looking for loopholes.

Quoted in *Playboy*, Nov. 1960.

24 I am free of all prejudice. I hate everyone equally.

Quoted in *Saturday Review*, 28 Jan. 1967

25 I like to keep a bottle of stimulant handy in case I see a snake—which I also keep handy.

Quoted in Corey Ford, *The Time of Laughter* (1967)

26 I don't drink water because fish fuck in it.

Quoted in Robert Reisner, *Graffiti* (1971)

27 Last week, I went to Philadelphia, but it was closed.

Quoted in *"Godfrey Daniels!,"* ed. Richard J. Anobile (1975)

28 I've been drunk only once in my life. But that lasted for twenty-three years.

Quoted in *The Quotations of W. C. Fields*, ed. Martin Lewis (1976)

Edward A. Filene

U.S. business executive, 1860–1937

1 Why shouldn't the American people take half my money from me? I took all of it from them.

Attributed in Arthur M. Schlesinger, Jr., *The Coming of the New Deal* (1959)

Film Lines

See also Woody Allen, Mel Brooks, W. C. Fields, George Lucas, Groucho Marx, Monty Python's Flying Circus, Mario Puzo, and Mae West. *Film lines that merely repeat quotations that originated in the book or play upon which the motion picture was based are listed under the author of the book or play.*

1 [*Kip Laurie, played by David Wayne, speaking:*] Lawyers should never marry other lawyers. This is called inbreeding, from which comes idiot children and more lawyers.

Adam's Rib (1949). Screenplay by Ruth Gordon and Garson Kanin.

2 [*Buckaroo Banzai, played by Peter Weller, speaking:*] No matter where you go, there you are.

The Adventures of Buckaroo Banzai Across the 8th Dimension (1984). Screenplay by Earl Mac Rauch. Exactly the same words appeared in the *Hazelton Collegian*, 4 Mar. 1955.

3 [*Terry McKay, played by Deborah Kerr, speaking:*] Don't worry, darling. If . . . you can paint, I can walk. Anything can happen.

An Affair to Remember (1957). Screenplay by Leo McCarey.

4 [*Rose Sayer, played by Katharine Hepburn, speaking:*] I never dreamed that any mere physical experience could be so stimulating.

The African Queen (1951). Screenplay by James Agee and John Huston.

5 [*Rose Sayer, played by Katharine Hepburn, speaking:*] Nature, Mr. Allnut, is what we are put in this world to rise above.

The African Queen (1951). Screenplay by James Agee and John Huston.

6 [*Margo Channing, played by Bette Davis, speaking:*] Fasten your seat belts, it's going to be a bumpy night.

All About Eve (1950). Screenplay by Joseph L. Mankiewicz.

7 [*Margo Channing, played by Bette Davis, speaking:*] Funny business, a woman's career. The things you drop on your way up the ladder so you can move faster. You forget you'll need them again when you're back to being a woman.

All About Eve (1950). Screenplay by Joseph L. Mankiewicz.

8 [*Deep Throat, played by Hal Holbrook, advising Bob Woodward, played by Robert Redford, how to expose the Watergate story:*] Follow the money.

All the President's Men (1976). Screenplay by William Goldman. The *Omaha World Herald*, 11 June 1969, had an article headlined "To Find Fraud Villains, Just 'Follow the Money.'"

9 [*John "Bluto" Blutarsky, played by John Belushi, speaking:*] Over? Did you say "over"? Nothing is over until we decide it is! Was it over when the Germans bombed Pearl Harbor? Hell no!

Animal House (1978). Screenplay by Harold Ramis, Douglas Kenney, and Chris Miller.

10 [*John "Bluto" Blutarsky, played by John Belushi, speaking:*] Toga! Toga!

Animal House (1978). Screenplay by Harold Ramis, Douglas Kenney, and Chris Miller.

11 [*Anna Christie, played by Greta Garbo, speaking:*] Gimme a whiskey, ginger ale on the side. And don't be stingy, baby.

Anna Christie (1930). Screenplay by Frances Marion. Greta Garbo's first spoken motion picture lines.

12 [*Fran Kubelick, played by Shirley MacLaine, speaking:*] Shut up and deal.

The Apartment (1960). Screenplay by Billy Wilder and I. A. L. Diamond.

13 [*Bill Kilgore, played by Robert Duvall, speaking:*] Charlie don't surf!

Apocalypse Now (1979). Screenplay by John Milius and Francis Ford Coppola.

14 [*Lieutenant Colonel Bill Kilgore, played by Robert Duvall, speaking:*] I love the smell of napalm in the morning. You know, one time we had a hill bombed, for twelve hours. . . . The smell, you know that gasoline smell, the whole hill. Smelled like—victory.

Apocalypse Now (1979). Screenplay by John Milius and Francis Ford Coppola. Often misquoted as "I love the smell of napalm in the morning. It smells like victory."

15 [*Gene Kranz, played by Ed Harris, speaking:*] Failure is not an option.

Apollo 13 (1995). Screenplay by William Broyles, Jr., and Al Reinert.

16 [*Melvin Udall, played by Jack Nicholson, speaking:*] You make me want to be a better man.

As Good As It Gets (1997). Screenplay by Mark Andrus and James L. Brooks.

17 [*Austin Powers, played by Mike Myers, speaking:*] You're shagadelic, baby!

Austin Powers, International Man of Mystery (1997). Screenplay by Mike Myers.

18 [*Austin Powers, played by Mike Myers, speaking:*] Yeah, baby!

Austin Powers, International Man of Mystery (1997). Screenplay by Mike Myers.

19 [*Dr. Emmett Brown, played by Christopher Lloyd, speaking:*] Roads? Where we're going we don't need—roads.

Back to the Future (1985). Screenplay by Robert Zemeckis and Bob Gale.

20 [*Rosa Moline, played by Bette Davis, speaking:*] What a dump!

Beyond the Forest (1949). Screenplay by Lenore Coffee. This same line had appeared earlier in a number of motion pictures, including Coffee's *Night Court* (1932).

21 [*The Dude, played by Jeff Bridges, speaking:*] This rug . . . really tied the room together.

The Big Lebowski (1998). Screenplay by Ethan Coen and Joel Cohen.

22 [*The Dude, played by Jeff Bridges, speaking:*] The dude abides.

The Big Lebowski (1998). Screenplay by Ethan Coen and Joel Cohen.

23 [*Eldon Tyrell, played by Joe Turkel, speaking:*] The light that burns twice as bright burns half as long.

Blade Runner (1982). Screenplay by Hampton Fancher and David Webb Peoples.

24 [*Roy Batty, played by Rutger Hauer, speaking:*] I've seen things you people wouldn't believe.

Attack ships on fire off the shoulders of Orion. I watched C-beams glitter in the dark near the Tannhauser gate. All those moments will be lost in time, like tears in rain. Time to die.

Blade Runner (1982). Screenplay by Hampton Fancher and David Webb Peoples.

25 [*Gaff, played by Edward James Olmos, speaking:*] It's too bad she won't live! But then again, who does?

Blade Runner (1982). Screenplay by Hampton Fancher and David Webb Peoples.

26 [*Elwood Blues, played by Dan Aykroyd, speaking:*] We're on a mission from God.

The Blues Brothers (1980). Screenplay by Dan Aykroyd and John Landis.

27 [*Matty Walker, played by Kathleen Turner, speaking:*] You aren't too bright. I like that in a man.

Body Heat (1981). Screenplay by Lawrence Kasdan.

28 [*Clyde Barrow, played by Warren Beatty, speaking:*] We rob banks.

Bonnie and Clyde (1967). Screenplay by David Newman and Robert Benton.

29 [*William Wallace, played by Mel Gibson, speaking:*] Every man dies, not every man really lives.

Braveheart (1995). Screenplay by Randall Wallace.

30 [*Dr. Pretorius, played by Ernest Thesiger, speaking:*] To a new world of gods and monsters!

The Bride of Frankenstein (1935). Screenplay by William Hurlbut.

31 [*Closing line of film, spoken by Major Clipton, played by James Donald:*] Madness! Madness!

The Bridge on the River Kwai (1957). Screenplay by Carl Foreman.

32 [*David Huxley, played by Cary Grant, speaking:*] I've just gone gay . . . all of a sudden.

Bringing Up Baby (1938). Screenplay by Dudley Nichols and Hagar Wilde, but Grant actually ad-libbed this line. Grant's words are often said to be the first clear documented usage of the term *gay* to mean "homosexual." (The context in the film is that Grant, in a feather-trimmed dressing gown, is asked whether he always dresses like that.) Linguists, however, have discovered various earlier usages, for example, "a so-called gay party" (Robert McAlmon, *Distinguished Air* [1925]) and "I'm going gay" (Lew Levenson, *Butterfly Man* [1934]). Gertrude Stein also used *gay*, in "Miss Furr and Miss Skeene" (1922), in a way interpreted by some as a source of the modern usage.

See Stein 2

33 [*Annie Savoy, played by Susan Sarandon, speaking:*] I believe in the Church of Baseball. I tried all the major religions, and most of the minor ones. . . . I know things. For instance, there are 108 beads in a Catholic rosary and there are 108 stitches in a baseball. When I heard that, I gave Jesus a chance.

Bull Durham (1988). Screenplay by Ron Shelton.

34 [*Crash Davis, played by Kevin Costner, speaking:*] I believe in the soul, the cock, the pussy, the small of a woman's back, the hanging curve ball, high fiber, good Scotch, that the novels of Susan Sontag are self-indulgent, overrated crap. I believe Lee Harvey Oswald acted alone. I believe there ought to be a constitutional amendment outlawing Astroturf and the designated hitter. I believe in the sweet spot, soft-core pornography, opening your presents Christmas morning rather than Christmas Eve and I believe in long, slow, deep, soft, wet kisses that last three days.

Bull Durham (1988). Screenplay by Ron Shelton.

35 [*"Nuke" LaLoosh, played by Tim Robbins, speaking:*] Sometimes you win, sometimes you lose, sometimes it rains.

Bull Durham (1988). Screenplay by Ron Shelton. *See Modern Proverbs 97*

36 [*Butch Cassidy, played by Paul Newman, speaking:*] I have vision, and the rest of the world wears bifocals.

Butch Cassidy and the Sundance Kid (1969). Screenplay by William Goldman.

37 [*The Sundance Kid, played by Robert Redford, speaking to Butch Cassidy, played by Paul Newman:*] You just keep thinking, Butch. That's what you're good at.

Butch Cassidy and the Sundance Kid (1969). Screenplay by William Goldman.

38 [*Butch Cassidy, played by Paul Newman, speaking:*] Who are those guys?

Butch Cassidy and the Sundance Kid (1969). Screenplay by William Goldman.

39 [*Butch Cassidy, played by Paul Newman, speaking:*] If he'd just pay me what he's paying them to stop me robbing him, I'd stop robbing him!

Butch Cassidy and the Sundance Kid (1969). Screenplay by William Goldman.

40 [*Butch Cassidy, played by Paul Newman, speaking to the Sundance Kid, played by Robert Redford, after the latter balked at jumping off a cliff because he couldn't swim:*] Why you crazy, the fall will probably kill you.

Butch Cassidy and the Sundance Kid (1969). Screenplay by William Goldman.

41 [*Madge Norwood, played by Bette Davis, speaking:*] I'd love to kiss you, but I just washed my hair.

The Cabin in the Cotton (1932). Screenplay by Paul Green.

42 [*Ilsa Lund, played by Ingrid Bergman, speaking:*] Play it, Sam. Play "As Time Goes By."

Casablanca (1942). Screenplay by Julius J. Epstein, Philip G. Epstein, and Howard Koch. These lines are the closest in the film to the famous paraphrase "Play it again, Sam." Bill Mullins has discovered the following sentence in the *San Francisco Chronicle*, 12 Aug. 1943: "Dooley 'Play It Again, Sam' Wilson of 'Casablanca' fame has a stellar role in 'Stormy Weather,' the musical cavalcade at the Paramount." Woody Allen cemented the fame of the paraphrase by using *Play It Again, Sam* as the title of a 1969 play and 1972 motion picture.
See Woody Allen 4

43 [*Rick Blaine, played by Humphrey Bogart, speaking:*] Of all the gin joints in all the towns in all the world, she walks into mine.

Casablanca (1942). Screenplay by Julius J. Epstein, Philip G. Epstein, and Howard Koch.

44 [*Rick Blaine, played by Humphrey Bogart, speaking:*] Here's looking at you, kid.

Casablanca (1942). Screenplay by Julius J. Epstein, Philip G. Epstein, and Howard Koch. The toast "Here's looking at you" appears as early as 1881, in a glossary of saloon language in the *Washington Post*, 30 Nov.

45 [*Captain Louis Renault, played by Claude Rains, speaking:*] I'm shocked, *shocked* to find that gambling is going on in here!

Casablanca (1942). Screenplay by Julius J. Epstein, Philip G. Epstein, and Howard Koch.

46 [*Rick Blaine, played by Humphrey Bogart, speaking:*] If that plane leaves the ground and you're not with him, you'll regret it. Maybe not today, maybe not tomorrow, but soon and for the rest of your life.

Casablanca (1942). Screenplay by Julius J. Epstein, Philip G. Epstein, and Howard Koch.

47 [*Rick Blaine, played by Humphrey Bogart, speaking:*] We'll always have Paris.

Casablanca (1942). Screenplay by Julius J. Epstein, Philip G. Epstein, and Howard Koch.

48 [*Rick Blaine, played by Humphrey Bogart, speaking:*] Ilsa, I'm no good at being noble, but it doesn't take much to see that the problems of three little people don't amount to a hill of beans in this crazy world.

Casablanca (1942). Screenplay by Julius J. Epstein, Philip G. Epstein, and Howard Koch.

49 [*Captain Louis Renault, played by Claude Rains, speaking:*] Major Strasser has been shot. Round up the usual suspects.

Casablanca (1942). Screenplay by Julius J. Epstein, Philip G. Epstein, and Howard Koch.

50 [*Rick Blaine, played by Humphrey Bogart, speaking:*] Louis, I think this is the beginning of a beautiful friendship.

Casablanca (1942). Screenplay by Julius J. Epstein, Philip G. Epstein, and Howard Koch.

51 [*Evelyn Mulwray, played by Faye Dunaway, speaking:*] She's my sister *and* my daughter.

Chinatown (1974). Screenplay by Robert Towne.

52 [*Lawrence Walsh, played by Joe Mantell, speaking:*] Forget it, Jake. It's Chinatown.

Chinatown (1974). Screenplay by Robert Towne.

53 [*Charles Foster Kane, played by Orson Welles, uttering his dying words:*] Rosebud.

Citizen Kane (1941). Screenplay by Herman J. Mankiewicz and Orson Welles.

54 [*Mr. Bernstein, played by Everett Sloane, speaking:*] It's no trick to make a lot of money if what you want to do is make a lot of money.

Citizen Kane (1941). Screenplay by Herman J. Mankiewicz and Orson Welles.

55 [*Jerry Thompson, played by William Alland, speaking:*] Mr. Kane was a man who got everything he wanted, and then lost it. Maybe Rosebud was something he couldn't get or something he lost. Anyway, it wouldn't have explained anything. I don't think any word can explain a man's life. No, I guess Rosebud is just a piece in a jigsaw puzzle, a missing piece.

Citizen Kane (1941). Screenplay by Herman J. Mankiewicz and Orson Welles.

56 [*Captain, played by Strother Martin, speaking:*] What we've got here is failure to communicate.

Cool Hand Luke (1967). Screenplay by Donn Pearce and Frank R. Pierson.

57 [*Caption:*] Marriage isn't a word—it's a *sentence!*

The Crowd (1928). Screenplay by King Vidor.

58 [*The Joker, played by Heath Ledger, speaking:*]
Why so serious?

The Dark Knight (2008). Screenplay by Jonathan
Nolan and Christopher Nolan.

59 [*Alfred, played by Michael Caine, speaking:*] Some
men aren't looking for anything logical, like
money. They can't be bought, bullied, reasoned,
or negotiated with. Some men just want to
watch the world burn.

The Dark Knight (2008). Screenplay by Jonathan
Nolan and Christopher Nolan.

60 [*Robert Gold, played by Dirk Bogarde, speaking to
Diana Scott, played by Julie Christie:*] Your idea
of fidelity is not having more than one man in
bed at the same time.

Darling (1965). Screenplay by Frederic Raphael.

61 [*Frank Costello, played by Jack Nicholson,
speaking:*] I don't want to be a product of my
environment. I want my environment to be a
product of me.

The Departed (2006). Screenplay by William
Monahan.

62 [*Carlotta Vance, played by Marie Dressler,
responding to Jean Harlow's question, "Do you
know that the guy said that machinery is going to
take the place of every profession?":*] Oh my dear,
that's something you need never worry about.

Dinner at Eight (1933). Screenplay by Frances Marion
and Herman J. Mankiewicz.

63 [*Harry Callahan, played by Clint Eastwood,
speaking while holding a gun to a bank robber's
head:*] I know what you're thinking. Did he fire
six shots or only five? Well, to tell the truth,
in all this excitement, I've kind of lost track
myself. But being as this is a .44 Magnum,
the most powerful handgun in the world, and
would blow your head clean off, you've got to
ask yourself one question: "Do I feel lucky?"
Well, do ya, punk?

Dirty Harry (1971). Screenplay by Harry Julian Fink.

64 [*Sonny, played by Al Pacino, rallying crowd:*]
Attica! Attica!

Dog Day Afternoon (1975). Screenplay by Frank
Pierson.

65 [*Da Mayor, played by Ossie Davis, speaking:*]
Always do the right thing.

Do the Right Thing (1989). Screenplay by Spike Lee.

66 [*Count Dracula, played by Bela Lugosi, speaking:*]
I never drink . . . wine.

Dracula (1931). Screenplay by Garrett Fort.

67 [*General Jack D. Ripper, played by Sterling
Hayden, speaking:*] I can no longer sit back and
allow Communist infiltration, Communist
indoctrination, Communist subversion, and the
international Communist conspiracy to sap and
impurify all of our precious bodily fluids.

Dr. Strangelove (1964). Screenplay by Stanley Kubrick,
Terry Southern, and Peter George.

68 [*General Buck Turgidson, played by George C.
Scott, speaking:*] Mr. President, I'm not saying
we wouldn't get our hair mussed. But I do say
no more than ten to twenty million people
killed, tops, depending on the breaks.

Dr. Strangelove (1964). Screenplay by Stanley Kubrick,
Terry Southern, and Peter George.

69 [*Colonel Bat Guano, played by Keenan Wynn,
speaking:*] But if you don't get the President
of the United States on that phone, you know
what's gonna happen to you? . . . You're gonna
have to answer to the Coca-Cola company.

Dr. Strangelove (1964). Screenplay by Stanley Kubrick,
Terry Southern, and Peter George.

70 [*President Merkin Muffley, played by Peter Sellers,
speaking:*] Gentlemen, you can't fight in here.
This is the War Room!

Dr. Strangelove (1964). Screenplay by Stanley Kubrick,
Terry Southern, and Peter George.

71 [*Dr. Strangelove, played by Peter Sellers, rising
from his wheelchair as the world is about to be
destroyed:*] Mein Führer! I can walk!

Dr. Strangelove (1964). Screenplay by Stanley Kubrick,
Terry Southern, and Peter George.

72 [*John Merrick, played by John Hurt, speaking:*] I
am not an animal! I am a human being. I am a
man.

The Elephant Man (1980). Screenplay by Christopher
De Vore, Eric Bergren, and David Lynch.

73 [*Elliott, played by Henry Thomas, speaking:*] How
do you explain school to a higher intelligence?

E.T. the Extra-Terrestrial (1982). Screenplay by Melissa
Mathison.

74 [*E.T. speaking:*] E.T. phone home.

E.T. the Extra-Terrestrial (1982). Screenplay by Melissa
Mathison.

75 [*E.T. speaking, pointing to the forehead of Elliott, played by Henry Thomas:*] I'll be right here.

  E.T. the Extra-Terrestrial (1982). Screenplay by Melissa Mathison.

76 [*Irena, played by Rita Hayworth, speaking:*] Armies have marched over me.

  Fire Down Below (1957). Screenplay by Irwin Shaw.

77 [*Andre Delambre, played by David Hedison, speaking:*] Help me! Help me!

  The Fly (1958). Screenplay by James Clavell.

78 [*Veronica Quaife, played by Geena Davis, speaking:*] Be afraid. Be very afraid.

  The Fly (1986). Screenplay by Charles Edward Pogue and David Cronenberg.

79 [*Johnny Jones, played by Joel McCrea, speaking:*] I can't read the rest of the speech I had because the lights have gone out. It is as if the lights were out everywhere, except America. Keep those lights burning there! Cover them with steel! Ring them with guns! Build a canopy of battleships and bombing planes around them! Hello, America! Hang on to your lights, they're the only lights left in the world.

  Foreign Correspondent (1940). Screenplay by Charles Bennett.

80 [*Mrs. Gump, played by Sally Field, speaking:*] Life is a box of chocolates, Forrest. You never know what you're goin' to get.

  Forrest Gump (1994). Screenplay by Eric Roth.

81 [*Forrest Gump, played by Tom Hanks, speaking:*] Stupid is as stupid does.

  Forrest Gump (1994). Screenplay by Eric Roth. This same line appeared much earlier in Anthony Trollope, *Orley Farm* (1862).

82 [*Julian Marsh, played by Warner Baxter, speaking:*] You're going to go out a youngster—but you've *got* to come back a star!

  Forty-Second Street (1933). Screenplay by James Seymour and Rian James.

83 [*Dr. Henry Frankenstein, played by Colin Clive, speaking:*] It's alive! It's alive!

  Frankenstein (1931). Screenplay by Garrett Fort and Francis Edward Faragoh. Richard Brinsley Peake's 1823 play, *Presumption; or, The Fate of Frankenstein,* included the line "It lives! It lives!"

84 [*Fanny Brice, played by Barbra Streisand, speaking:*] Hello, gorgeous.

  Funny Girl (1968). Screenplay by Isobel Lennart.

85 [*Peter Venkman, played by Bill Murray, speaking:*] This chick is *toast!*

  Ghost Busters (1984). Screenplay by Dan Aykroyd and Harold Ramis.

86 [*Peter Venkman, played by Bill Murray, speaking:*] Human sacrifice, dogs and cats living together—mass hysteria!

  Ghost Busters (1984). Screenplay by Dan Aykroyd and Harold Ramis.

87 [*Maximus, played by Russell Crowe, speaking:*] Are you not entertained?

  Gladiator (2000). Screenplay by David Fanzoni, John Logan, and William Nicholson.

88 [*Blake, played by Alec Baldwin, speaking:*] First prize is a Cadillac Eldorado. . . . Second prize is a set of steak knives. Third prize is you're fired.

  Glengarry Glen Ross (1992). Screenplay by David Mamet.

89 [*Tommy De Vito, played by Joe Pesci, speaking:*] [I'm] funny how? I mean, funny like I'm a clown? I amuse you? I make you laugh? I'm here to fuckin' amuse you? How da fuck am I funny? What da fuck is so funny about me? Tell me, tell me what's funny.

  Goodfellas (1990). Screenplay by Nicholas Pileggi and Martin Scorsese.

90 [*Mr. Maguire, played by Walter Brooke, speaking:*] Just one more word. . . . Are you listening? . . . Plastics.

  The Graduate (1967). Screenplay by Calder Willingham and Buck Henry.

91 [*Jewish barber, played by Charlie Chaplin, speaking:*] More than cleverness, we need kindness and gentleness.

  The Great Dictator (1940). Screenplay by Charles Spencer "Charlie" Chaplin.
  See George H. W. Bush 5; George H. W. Bush 6

92 [*Colonel Mike Kirby, played by John Wayne, speaking:*] Out here, due process is a bullet.

  The Green Berets (1968). Screenplay by James Lee Barrett and Kenneth B. Facey.

93 [*Introductory narration, spoken by Laurence Olivier:*] This is the tragedy of a man who could not make up his mind.

  Hamlet (1948). Text by Alan Dent.

94 [*Helen, played by Jean Harlow, speaking:*] Would you be shocked if I put on something more comfortable?

Hell's Angels (1930). Screenplay by Howard Estabrook and Harry Behn. Often misquoted as "Do you mind if I put on something more comfortable?" or "Excuse me while I slip into something more comfortable."

95 [*Scott Carey, played by Grant Williams, speaking:*] So close, the Infinitesimal and the Infinite. But suddenly I knew they were really the two ends of the same concept. The unbelievably small and the unbelievably vast eventually meet, like the closing of a gigantic circle.

The Incredible Shrinking Man (1957). Screenplay by Richard Matheson.

96 [*Scott Carey, played by Grant Williams, speaking:*] That Existence begins and ends, is Man's conception, not Nature's. And I felt my body dwindling, melting, becoming nothing. My fears melted away, and in their place came acceptance. All this vast majesty of creation, it had to mean something, and then I meant something, too. Yes, smaller than the smallest, I meant something, too. To God there is no zero. I still exist.

The Incredible Shrinking Man (1957). Screenplay by Richard Matheson.

97 [*Dr. Moreau, played by Charles Laughton, speaking:*] They [the natives] are restless tonight.

Island of Lost Souls (1933). Screenplay by Waldemar Young and Philip Wylie.

98 [*Zuzu Bailey, played by Karolyn Grimes, speaking:*] Every time a bell rings, an angel gets his wings.

It's a Wonderful Life (1946). Screenplay by Frank Capra, Frances Goodrich, and Albert Hackett.

99 [*Professor Frankenstein, played by Whit Bissell, speaking:*] I know you have a civil tongue in your head—I sewed it there myself.

I Was a Teenage Frankenstein (1957). Screenplay by Kenneth Langtry.

100 [*Professor Frankenstein, played by Whit Bissell, speaking to the monster:*] Watch my lips. Good. Mor. Ning.

I Was a Teenage Frankenstein (1957). Screenplay by Kenneth Langtry.

See George H. W. Bush 4; Curry 1; Joe Greene 1

101 [*Martin Brody, played by Roy Scheider, speaking:*] You're gonna need a bigger boat.

Jaws (1975). Screenplay by Peter Benchley and Carl Gottlieb, although this line was not in the original script and was ad-libbed by Scheider.

102 [*Rod Tidwell, played by Cuba Gooding, Jr., speaking:*] You're gonna show me the money.

Jerry Maguire (1996). Screenplay by Cameron Crowe.

103 [*Dorothy Boyd, played by Renee Zellweger, speaking:*] You had me at "hello."

Jerry Maguire (1996). Screenplay by Cameron Crowe.

104 [*Ian Malcolm, played by Jeff Goldblum, responding to John Hammond's (played by Richard Attenborough) statement: "All major theme parks have delays. When they opened Disneyland in 1956, nothing worked":*] Yeah, but John, if the Pirates of the Caribbean breaks down, the pirates don't eat the tourists.

Jurassic Park (1993). Screenplay by Michael Crichton and David Koepp.

105 [*Sheik Mulhulla, played by Paul Harvey, speaking about alimony:*] Like buying oats for a dead horse.

Kid Millions (1934). Screenplay by Arthur Sheekman, Nunnally Johnson, and Nat Perrin.

106 [*Bill, played by David Carradine, speaking:*] What [Clark] Kent wears, the glasses, the business suit . . . that's the costume that Superman wears to blend in with us. Clark Kent is how Superman views us. And what are the characteristics of Clark Kent? He's weak, he's unsure of himself, he's a coward. Clark Kent is Superman's critique on the whole human race.

Kill Bill: Vol. 2 (2004). Screenplay by Quentin Tarantino.

107 [*Carl Denham, played by Robert Armstrong, speaking:*] Oh, no. It wasn't the airplanes. It was Beauty killed the Beast.

King Kong (1933). Screenplay by James Creelman and Ruth Rose.

108 [*Rupert Pupkin, played by Robert De Niro, speaking:*] Better to be a king for a night than a schmuck for a lifetime.

The King of Comedy (1983). Screenplay by Paul Zimmermann.

109 [*Jimmy Dugan, played by Tom Hanks, speaking:*] There's no crying in baseball!

A League of Their Own (1992). Screenplay by Lowell Ganz and Babaloo Mandel.

110 [*Mohammed Khan, played by Douglas Dumbrille, speaking:*] We have ways of making men talk.

Lives of a Bengal Lancer (1935). Screenplay by Waldemar Young.

111 [*Aragorn, played by Viggo Mortensen, speaking:*] A day may come when the courage of men fails, when we forsake our friends and break all bonds of fellowship, but it is not this day. An hour of wolves and shattered shields, when the age of men comes crashing down! But it is not this day! This day we fight! By all that you hold dear on this good Earth, I bid you stand, Men of the West!

The Lord of the Rings: The Return of the King (2003). Screenplay by Fran Walsh, Philippa Boyens, and Peter Jackson.

112 [*Sam Spade, played by Humphrey Bogart, responding to Detective Tom Polhaus's (played by Ward Bond) question about the falcon, "What is it?":*] The stuff that dreams are made of.

The Maltese Falcon (1941). Screenplay by John Huston.
See Shakespeare 443

113 [*Maxwell Scott, played by Carleton Young, speaking:*] This is the West, sir. When the legend becomes fact, print the legend.

The Man Who Shot Liberty Valance (1962). Screenplay by James Warner Bellah and Willis Goldbeck.

114 [*Morpheus, played by Laurence Fishburne, speaking:*] You take the red pill, you stay in Wonderland, and I show you how deep the rabbit hole goes.

The Matrix (1999). Screenplay by Andy Wachowski and Larry Wachowski.

115 [*"Ratso" Rizzo, played by Dustin Hoffman, speaking:*] I'm walking here! I'm walking here!

Midnight Cowboy (1969). Screenplay by Waldo Salt.

116 [*Fred Gailey, played by John Payne, speaking:*] Your Honor—every one of these letters is addressed to Santa Claus. The Post Office has delivered them. The Post Office is a branch of the Federal Government. Therefore, the United States Government recognizes this man, Kris Kringle, as the one and only Santa Claus.

Miracle on 34th Street (1947). Screenplay by George Seaton.

117 [*Gay Langland, played by Clark Gable, responding to the question, "How do you find your way back in the dark?":*] Just head for that big star straight on. The highway's under it. It'll take us right home.

The Misfits (1961). Screenplay by Arthur Miller.

118 [*Henri Verdoux, played by Charlie Chaplin, speaking:*] Wars, conflict, it's all business. One murder makes a villain. Millions a hero. Numbers sanctify.

Monsieur Verdoux (1947). Screenplay by Charles Spencer "Charlie" Chaplin.
See Stalin 5

119 [*Longfellow Deeds, played by Gary Cooper, speaking at Deeds's sanity hearing:*] Other people are doodlers. . . . That's a name we made up back home for people who make foolish designs on paper when they're thinking. It's called doodling.

Mr. Deeds Goes to Town (1936). Screenplay by Robert Riskin. Coinage of the term *doodle*.

120 [*Jane Faulkner, played by Margaret Seddon, speaking:*] Why, everybody in Mandrake Falls is pixilated—except us.

Mr. Deeds Goes to Town (1936). Screenplay by Robert Riskin.

121 [*Judge Walker, played by H. B. Warner, speaking at Longfellow Deeds's sanity hearing:*] Mr. Deeds, there's been a great deal of damaging testimony against you. Your behavior, to say the least, has been most strange. But, in the opinion of the court, you are not only sane but you're the sanest man that ever walked into this courtroom.

Mr. Deeds Goes to Town (1936). Screenplay by Robert Riskin.
See Irvin S. Cobb 1

122 [*Jefferson Smith, played by James Stewart, speaking:*] Dad always used to say the only causes worth fighting for were the lost causes.

Mr. Smith Goes to Washington (1939). Screenplay by Sidney Buchman. The line "Lost causes are the only causes worth fighting for" appeared earlier in *Blackwood's Magazine*, Dec. 1903.

123 [*Narrator Mark Hellinger speaking:*] There are eight million stories in the naked city. This has been one of them.
The Naked City (1948). Screenplay by Malvin Wald and Albert Maltz.

124 [*Howard Beale, played by Peter Finch, speaking:*] I want you to get up now. I want all of you to get up out of your chairs. I want you to get up right now and go to the window. Open it, and stick your head out, and yell "I'm mad as hell, and I'm not going to take this anymore!"
Network (1976). Screenplay by Paddy Chayevsky.

125 [*Ninotchka, played by Greta Garbo, speaking:*] Don't make an issue of my womanhood.
Ninotchka (1939). Screenplay by Billy Wilder, Charles Brackett, and Walter Reisch.

126 [*Ninotchka, played by Greta Garbo, speaking:*] The last mass trials were a great success. There are going to be fewer but better Russians.
Ninotchka (1939). Screenplay by Billy Wilder, Charles Brackett, and Walter Reisch.

127 [*Leon d'Algout, played by Melvyn Douglas, speaking:*] Ninotchka, it's midnight. One half of Paris is making love to the other half.
Ninotchka (1939). Screenplay by Billy Wilder, Charles Brackett, and Walter Reisch.

128 [*Terry Malloy, played by Marlon Brando, speaking:*] I could've had class. I could've been a contender. I could've been somebody, instead of a bum, which is what I am.
On the Waterfront (1954). Screenplay by Budd Schulberg.

129 [*Professor Charles W. Kingsfield, Jr., played by John Houseman, speaking:*] You come in here with a head full of mush and you leave thinking like a lawyer.
The Paper Chase (1973). Screenplay by James Bridges.

130 [*Mike Conovan, played by Spencer Tracy, speaking about Pat Pemberton, played by Katharine Hepburn:*] Not much meat on her, but what's there is cherce.
Pat and Mike (1952). Screenplay by Ruth Gordon and Garson Kanin.

131 [*Narrator Tim Conway speaking:*] All this has happened before, and it will all happen again, but this time, it happened in London.
Peter Pan (1953). Screenplay by Ted Sears.

132 [*The Blue Fairy speaking:*] Always let your conscience be your guide.
Pinocchio (1940). Screenplay by Ted Sears.

133 [*The Blue Fairy speaking to Pinocchio:*] Prove yourself brave, truthful, and unselfish, and someday, you will be a real boy.
Pinocchio (1940). Screenplay by Ted Sears. *See Collodi 2*

134 [*The Blue Fairy speaking:*] A lie keeps growing and growing, until it's as plain as the nose on your face.
Pinocchio (1940). Screenplay by Ted Sears. *See Collodi 1*

135 [*George Taylor, played by Charlton Heston, speaking:*] Take your stinking paws off me, you damned dirty ape.
Planet of the Apes (1968). Screenplay by Rod Serling and Michael Wilson.

136 [*George Taylor, played by Charlton Heston, speaking:*] You finally really did it. You maniacs! You blew it up! God damn you! God damn you all to hell!
Planet of the Apes (1968). Screenplay by Rod Serling and Michael Wilson.

137 [*Carol Anne Freeling, played by Heather O'Rourke, speaking:*] They're here.
Poltergeist (1982). Screenplay by Steven Spielberg, Michael Grais, and Mark Victor.

138 [*Blain, played by Jesse Ventura, speaking:*] I ain't got time to bleed.
Predator (1987). Screenplay by Jim Thomas and John Thomas.

139 [*Norman Bates, played by Anthony Perkins, speaking:*] Mother—what's the phrase?—isn't quite herself today.
Psycho (1960). Screenplay by Joseph Stefano.

140 [*Norman Bates, played by Anthony Perkins, speaking:*] A boy's best friend is his mother.
Psycho (1960). Screenplay by Joseph Stefano. This was proverbial long before its usage in *Psycho*, with the earliest appearance found in research for this book in an 1883 song. *See Henry Miller (U.S. songwriter) 1*

141 [*Voice of Norman Bates's mother, recorded by Virginia Gregg, speaking through Bates, played by Anthony Perkins:*] They'll see and they'll know and they'll say why, she wouldn't even harm a fly.
Psycho (1960). Screenplay by Joseph Stefano.

142 [*Mia Wallace, played by Uma Thurman, speaking:*] That was a little bit more information than I needed to know.
Pulp Fiction (1994). Screenplay by Quentin Tarantino.

143 [*Marsellus Wallace, played by Ving Rhames, speaking:*] I'm gonna get medieval on your ass.
Pulp Fiction (1994). Screenplay by Quentin Tarantino.

144 [*John Rambo, played by Sylvester Stallone, speaking:*] Sir, do we get to win this time?
Rambo: First Blood Part II (1985). Screenplay by Sylvester Stallone and James Cameron.

145 [*John Rambo, played by Sylvester Stallone, speaking:*] [I'm] your worst nightmare.
Rambo III (1988). Screenplay by Sylvester Stallone and Sheldon Lettich.

146 [*Joe Cabot, played by Lawrence Tierney, speaking:*] Let's go to work.
Reservoir Dogs (1992). Screenplay by Quentin Tarantino.

147 [*Mr. Blonde, played by Michael Madsen, speaking:*] Are you gonna bark all day, little doggy, or are you gonna bite?
Reservoir Dogs (1992). Screenplay by Quentin Tarantino.

148 [*Rocky Balboa, played by Sylvester Stallone, speaking:*] Yo, Adrian!
Rocky (1976). Screenplay by Sylvester Stallone.

149 [*Captain John Miller, played by Tom Hanks, speaking:*] Earn this.
Saving Private Ryan (1998). Screenplay by Robert Rodat.

150 [*Tony Montana, played by Al Pacino, speaking while holding an assault rifle:*] Say hello to my little friend!
Scarface (1983). Screenplay by Oliver Stone.

151 [*Ethan Edwards, played by John Wayne, speaking:*] That'll be the day.
The Searchers (1956). Screenplay by Frank S. Nugent.
See Holly 1

152 [*Kambei Shimada, played by Takashi Shimura, speaking:*] The farmers have won. We have lost.
The Seven Samurai (1954). Screenplay by Akira Kurosawa, Shinobu Hashimoto, and Hideo Oguni.

153 [*Joey Starrett, played by Brandon De Wilde, speaking:*] Shane! Come back!
Shane (1953). Screenplay by A. B. Guthrie, Jr.

154 [*Shanghai Lily, played by Marlene Dietrich, speaking:*] It took more than one man to change my name to Shanghai Lily.
Shanghai Express (1932). Screenplay by Jules Furthman.

155 [*Hannibal Lecter, played by Anthony Hopkins, speaking:*] I do wish we could chat longer but I'm having an old friend for dinner.
The Silence of the Lambs (1991). Screenplay by Ted Tally.

156 [*Cole Sear, played by Haley Joel Osment, speaking:*] I see dead people.
The Sixth Sense (1999). Screenplay by M. Night Shyamalan.

157 [*Sugar Kane, played by Marilyn Monroe, speaking:*] I always get the fuzzy end of the lollipop.
Some Like It Hot (1959). Screenplay by Billy Wilder and I. A. L. Diamond.

158 [*Osgood Fielding III, played by Joe E. Brown, speaking in response to his prospective fiancée's admission of being a man rather than a woman:*] Well, nobody's perfect.
Some Like It Hot (1959). Screenplay by Billy Wilder and I. A. L. Diamond.

159 [*Prologue:*] For those who believe in God no explanation is necessary. For those who do not believe in God no explanation is possible.
The Song of Bernadette (1943). Screenplay by George Seaton.

160 [*Detective Robert Thorn, played by Charlton Heston, speaking:*] Soylent Green is people!
Soylent Green (1973). Screenplay by Stanley R. Greenberg.

161 [*Antoninus, played by Tony Curtis, and others, speaking:*] I'm Spartacus!
Spartacus (1960). Screenplay by Dalton Trumbo.

162 [*Vicki Lester, played by Janet Gaynor, commemorating her late husband in the film's last line:*] Hello, everybody. This is Mrs. Norman Maine.
A Star Is Born (1937). Screenplay by Dorothy Parker, Alan Campbell, and Robert Carson.

163 [*Grant Matthews, played by Spencer Tracy, speaking:*] Don't you shut me off, I'm paying for this broadcast.

State of the Union (1948). Screenplay by Myles Connolly and Anthony Veiller. Ronald Reagan echoed this line at a Republican campaign debate in Nashua, N.H., 23 Feb. 1980; when the moderator tried to have Reagan's microphone turned off, Reagan responded, "I'm paying for this microphone."

164 [*Harry Callahan, played by Clint Eastwood, speaking:*] Go ahead, make my day.

Sudden Impact (1983). Screenplay by Joseph Stinson. Although *Sudden Impact* made this line world-famous, it was used earlier ("Go ahead, scumbag, make my day") in the 1982 film *Vice Squad* (spoken by the character Tom Walsh, played by Gary Swanson, screenplay by Sandy Howard, Kenneth Peters, and Robert Vincent O'Neil). *See Ronald Reagan 9*

165 [*Norma Desmond, played by Gloria Swanson, speaking in response to being told that she "used to be big":*] I am big. It's the pictures that got small.

Sunset Boulevard (1950). Screenplay by Billy Wilder, Charles Brackett, and D. M. Marshman, Jr.

166 [*Norma Desmond, played by Gloria Swanson, speaking about silent films:*] We didn't need dialogue. We had faces.

Sunset Boulevard (1950). Screenplay by Billy Wilder, Charles Brackett, and D. M. Marshman, Jr.

167 [*Norma Desmond, played by Gloria Swanson, speaking:*] This is my life. It always will be. There's nothing else. Just us and the cameras and those wonderful people out there in the dark. All right, Mr. De Mille, I'm ready for my close-up.

Sunset Boulevard (1950). Screenplay by Billy Wilder, Charles Brackett, and D. M. Marshman, Jr.

168 [*Bryan Mills, played by Liam Neeson, speaking:*] I will look for you, I will find you, and I will kill you.

Taken (2008). Screenplay by Luc Besson and Robert Mark Kamen.

169 [*Travis Bickle, played by Robert De Niro, speaking:*] You talkin' to me?

Taxi Driver (1976). Screenplay by Paul Schrader.

170 [*The Terminator, played by Arnold Schwarzenegger, speaking:*] I'll be back.

The Terminator (1984). Screenplay by James Cameron and Gale Ann Hurd.

171 [*The Terminator, played by Arnold Schwarzenegger, speaking:*] Hasta la vista, baby.

Terminator 2: Judgment Day (1991). Screenplay by James Cameron and William Wisher, Jr.

172 [*Daniel Plainview, played by Daniel Day-Lewis, speaking:*] I drink your milkshake!

There Will Be Blood (2007). Screenplay by Paul Thomas Anderson.

173 [*Ned Scott, played by Douglas Spencer, speaking:*] Watch the skies, everywhere! Keep looking. Keep watching the skies.

The Thing from Another World (1951). Screenplay by Charles Lederer.

174 [*Harry Lime, played by Orson Welles, speaking:*] In Italy for thirty years under the Borgias they had warfare, terror, murder, bloodshed— they produced Michelangelo, Leonardo da Vinci, and the Renaissance. In Switzerland they had brotherly love, five hundred years of democracy, and peace and what did that produce? The cuckoo clock.

The Third Man (1949). Orson Welles added these words to the screenplay by Graham Greene. In *Cassell's Movie Quotations*, Nigel Rees quotes Welles: "When the picture came out, the Swiss very nicely pointed out to me that they've never made any cuckoo clocks—they all come from the Schwarzwald in Bavaria!" *See Whistler 3*

175 [*King Leonidas, played by Gerard Butler, speaking:*] This is Sparta!

300 (2006). Screenplay by Zack Snyder, Kurt Johnstad, and Michael B. Gordon.

176 [*Jack Dawson, played by Leonardo Di Caprio, speaking:*] I'm the king of the world!

Titanic (1997). Screenplay by James Cameron.

177 [*Marie Browning, played by Lauren Bacall, speaking:*] You know how to whistle, don't you, Steve? You just put your lips together and blow.

To Have and Have Not (1944). Screenplay by Jules Furthman and William Faulkner.

178 [*Admiral Isoroku Yamamoto, played by Sô Yamamura, speaking:*] I fear all we have done is awaken a sleeping giant and fill him with a terrible resolve.

Tora! Tora! Tora! (1970). Screenplay by Larry Forrester, Hideo Oguni, and Ryuzo Kikushima. There is no reason to believe that Admiral Yamamoto said anything like this in reality.

179 [*Tanya, played by Marlene Dietrich, speaking:*]
He was some kind of a man. What does it
matter what you say about people?
Touch of Evil (1958). Screenplay by Orson Welles.

180 [*Buzz Lightyear, played by Tim Allen, speaking:*]
To infinity and beyond!
Toy Story (1995). Screenplay by Joss Whedon,
Andrew Stanton, Joel Cohen, and Alec Sokolow.

181 [*David Bowman, played by Keir Dullea,
speaking:*] Open the pod bay doors, HAL.
2001: A Space Odyssey (1968). Screenplay by Stanley
Kubrick and Arthur C. Clarke.

182 [*HAL speaking:*] Stop, Dave. I'm afraid. I'm
afraid, Dave. Dave, my mind is going. I can
feel it.
2001: A Space Odyssey (1968). Screenplay by Stanley
Kubrick and Arthur C. Clarke.

183 [*William Munny, played by Clint Eastwood,
speaking:*] Hell of a thing, killin' a man. You take
away all he's got and all he's ever gonna have.
Unforgiven (1992). Screenplay by David Webb
Peoples.

184 [*Gordon Gekko, played by Michael Douglas,
speaking:*] Greed, for lack of a better word, is
good. Greed is right. Greed works.
Wall Street (1987). Screenplay by Oliver Stone and
Stanley Weiser. Often quoted as simply "Greed is
good."
See Boesky 1

185 [*Harry Burns, played by Billy Crystal, speaking:*]
Men and women can't be friends because the
sex part always gets in the way.
When Harry Met Sally (1989). Screenplay by Nora
Ephron.

186 [*Older woman customer, played by Estelle Reiner,
speaking to waiter after seeing Sally Albright,
played by Meg Ryan, simulating an orgasm in a
restaurant:*] I'll have what she's having.
When Harry Met Sally (1989). Screenplay by Nora
Ephron.

187 [*Cody Jarrett, played by James Cagney, speaking:*]
Made it, Ma, top of the world!
White Heat (1949). Screenplay by Ivan Goff and
Ben Roberts.

188 [*Johnny Strabler, played by Marlon Brando,
after being asked what he is rebelling against:*]
What've you got?
The Wild One (1953). Screenplay by John Paxton.

189 [*Dorothy Gale, played by Judy Garland, speaking
to her dog:*] Toto, I've a feeling we're not in
Kansas any more.
The Wizard of Oz (1939). Screenplay by Noel
Langley, Florence Ryerson, and Edgar Allan Woolf.

190 [*Wicked Witch of the West, played by Margaret
Hamilton, speaking:*] I'll get you, my pretty,
and your little dog, too.
The Wizard of Oz (1939). Screenplay by Noel
Langley, Florence Ryerson, and Edgar Allan Woolf.

191 [*Dorothy Gale, played by Judy Garland,
speaking:*] Lions, and tigers, and bears! Oh,
my!
The Wizard of Oz (1939). Screenplay by Noel
Langley, Florence Ryerson, and Edgar Allan Woolf.

192 [*Cowardly Lion, played by Bert Lahr, speaking:*]
What makes the elephant charge his tusk
in the misty mist, or the dusky dusk? What
makes the muskrat guard his musk? Courage!
The Wizard of Oz (1939). Screenplay by Noel
Langley, Florence Ryerson, and Edgar Allan Woolf.

193 [*Wicked Witch of the West, played by Margaret
Hamilton, speaking:*] Who ever thought a
little girl like you could destroy my beautiful
wickedness?
The Wizard of Oz (1939). Screenplay by Noel
Langley, Florence Ryerson, and Edgar Allan Woolf.
See L. Frank Baum 5

194 [*Wicked Witch of the West, played by Margaret
Hamilton, speaking:*] I'm melting! I'm melting!
Oh, what a world! What a world!
The Wizard of Oz (1939). Screenplay by Noel
Langley, Florence Ryerson, and Edgar Allan Woolf.

195 [*The Wizard, played by Frank Morgan,
speaking:*] Pay no attention to that man behind
the curtain!
The Wizard of Oz (1939). Screenplay by Noel
Langley, Florence Ryerson, and Edgar Allan Woolf.

196 [*The Wizard, played by Frank Morgan, speaking
to the Tin Woodman, played by Jack Haley:*]
As for you, my galvanized friend, you want a
heart. You don't know how lucky you are not
to have one. Hearts will never be practical
until they can be made unbreakable.
The Wizard of Oz (1939). Screenplay by Noel
Langley, Florence Ryerson, and Edgar Allan Woolf.

197 [*The Wizard, played by Frank Morgan,
speaking:*] A heart is not judged by how much

you love; but by how much you are loved by others.

The Wizard of Oz (1939). Screenplay by Noel Langley, Florence Ryerson, and Edgar Allan Woolf.

198 [*Dorothy Gale, played by Judy Garland, speaking:*] If I ever go looking for my heart's desire again, I won't look any further than my own backyard, because if it isn't there, I never really lost it to begin with.

The Wizard of Oz (1939). Screenplay by Noel Langley, Florence Ryerson, and Edgar Allan Woolf.

199 [*John Talbot, played by Claude Rains, speaking:*] Even a man who is pure in heart and says his prayers by night, may become a wolf when the wolfbane blooms. And the autumn moon is bright.

The Wolf Man (1941). Screenplay by Curt Siodmak.

200 [*Cathy Linton, played by Merle Oberon, speaking:*] Go on, Heathcliff, run away. Bring me back the world!

Wuthering Heights (1939). Screenplay by Ben Hecht.

William "Bill" Finger
U.S. comic book creator, 1917–1974

1 [*Bruce Wayne's thoughts:*] I must have a disguise. Criminals are a superstitious cowardly lot. So my disguise must be able to strike terror into their hearts. I must be a creature of the night, black, terrible . . . a . . . a— [*A huge bat flies in the open window.*] A bat! That's it. It's an omen. . . . I shall become a BAT!

Detective Comics (comic book), Nov. 1939

James Finlayson
Scottish actor, 1887–1953

1 [*Professor Finlayson, played by James Finlayson, speaking:*] D-ohhhh!

Pardon Us (motion picture) (1931). Became well-known through the cartoon character Homer Simpson of the television show *The Simpsons*. Finlayson's usage of the exclamation is slightly different from Homer's in that Finlayson used it to imply that another person has said or done something stupid, whereas Homer uses it to imply that he himself has said or done something stupid.
See Groening 5

Louis Fischer
U.S. author and journalist, 1896–1970

1 "An eye for an eye" . . . in the end, would make everybody blind.

Gandhi and Stalin ch. 6 (1947). "An eye for an eye leaves the whole world blind" is frequently attributed to M. K. Gandhi. The Gandhi Institute for Nonviolence states that the Gandhi family believes it is an authentic Gandhi quotation, but no example of its use by the Indian leader has ever been discovered. A similar metaphor about "an eye for an eye and a tooth for a tooth" resulting in everyone being blind and toothless appeared in *Official Report of the Debates of the House of Commons of the Dominion of Canada*, 5 Feb. 1914.
See Bible 61

Williston Fish
U.S. lawyer and author, 1858–1939

1 To lovers I devise their imaginary world, with whatever they may need, as the stars of the sky, the red, red roses by the wall, the snow of the hawthorn, the sweet strains of music, or aught else they may desire to figure to each other the lastingness and beauty of their love.

"A Last Will," *Harper's Weekly*, 3 Sept. 1898

Carrie Fisher
U.S. actress and writer, 1956–2016

1 Here's how men think. . . . Sex, work—and those are reversible, depending on age—sex, work, food, sports, and lastly, begrudgingly, relationships. And here's how women think. Relationships, relationships, relationships, work, sex, shopping, weight, food.

Surrender the Pink ch. 9 (1990)

Dorothy Canfield Fisher
U.S. author, 1879–1958

1 A mother is not a person to lean on but a person to make leaning unnecessary.
Her Son's Wife ch. 37 (1926)

H. A. L. Fisher
English historian, 1856–1940

1 Men wiser and more learned than I have discerned in history a plot, a rhythm, a predetermined pattern. These harmonies are concealed from me. I can see only one

emergency following upon another as wave follows upon wave.

A History of Europe preface (1935)

2 Purity of race does not exist. Europe is a continent of energetic mongrels.

A History of Europe ch. 1 (1935)

Harry C. "Bud" Fisher

U.S. cartoonist, 1885–1954

1 Mutt and Jeff.

Title of comic strip (1907)

Irving Fisher

U.S. economist, 1867–1947

1 [*Statement to Purchasing Agents Association, New York, 15 Oct. 1929, shortly before stock market crash:*] [Stock prices have reached] what looks like a permanently high plateau.

Quoted in *N.Y. Times*, 16 Oct. 1929

John Arbuthnot Fisher

British admiral, 1841–1920

1 Never contradict. Never explain. Never apologize.

Letter to the Editor, *Times* (London), 5 Sept. 1919. *Littell's Living Age*, 30 Dec. 1893, quoted Benjamin Jowett: "Never retreat, never explain, never apologize."
See *Disraeli 32; Elbert Hubbard 2*

M. F. K. Fisher

U.S. writer, 1908–1992

1 When I write of hunger, I am really writing about love and the hunger for it, and warmth and the love of it and the hunger for it . . . and then the warmth and richness and fine reality of hunger satisfied . . . and it is all one.

The Gastronomical Me foreword (1943). Ellipses in the original.

George H. Fitch

U.S. author and journalist, 1877–1915

1 A reporter is a young man who blocks out the first draft of history each day on a rheumatic typewriter.

Lincoln (Nebr.) *Daily Star*, 3 July 1914. "The newspapers are making morning after morning the rough draft of history" appeared in *The State* (Columbia, S.C.), 5 Dec. 1905.

Edward FitzGerald

English poet and translator, 1809–1883

1 The Sultan asked for a Signet motto, that should hold good for Adversity or Prosperity. Solomon gave him, "This also shall pass away."

Polonius: A Collection of Wise Saws and Modern Instances (1852)
See *Lincoln 20; Walter Scott 8*

2 Come, fill the Cup, and in the fire of Spring
The Winter garment of Repentance fling:
The Bird of Time has but a little way
To fly—and Lo! the Bird is on the Wing.

The Rubáiyát of Omar Khayyám st. 7 (1859)

3 The moving finger writes; and, having writ,
Moves on: nor all your piety nor wit
Shall lure it back to cancel half a line,
Nor all thy tears wash out a word of it.

The Rubáiyát of Omar Khayyám st. 51 (1859)

4 Who *is* the potter, pray, and who the pot?

The Rubáiyát of Omar Khayyám st. 60 (1859)

5 Mrs. Browning's death is rather a relief to me, I must say: no more Aurora Leighs, thank God! A woman of real genius, I know; but what is the upshot of it all? She and her sex had better mind the kitchen and their children; and perhaps the poor: except in such things as little novels, they only devote themselves to what men do much better, leaving that which men do worse or not at all.

Letter to W. H. Thompson, 15 July 1861

6 Indeed the Idols I have loved so long
Have done my credit much wrong in Men's eye
Have drown'd my Glory in a shallow Cup
And sold my Reputation for a Song.

The Rubáiyát of Omar Khayyám, 2nd ed., st. 101 (1868)

7 Taste is the feminine of genius.

Letter to James Russell Lowell, Oct. 1877

8 A Book of Verses underneath the Bough,
A Jug of Wine, a Loaf of Bread—and Thou
Beside me singing in the Wilderness—
Oh, Wilderness were Paradise enow!

The Rubáiyát of Omar Khayyám, 4th ed., st. 11 (1879). In the first edition (1859) these words read: "Here with a Loaf of Bread beneath the Bough, / A Flask of Wine, a Book of Verse—and Thou / Beside me singing in the Wilderness— / And Wilderness is Paradise enow."

F. Scott Fitzgerald
U.S. writer, 1896–1940

1 "I know myself," he cried, "but that is all."
This Side of Paradise ch. 5 (1920)

2 An author ought to write for the youth of his own generation, the critics of the next, and the schoolmasters of ever after.
Letter to Booksellers' Convention, Apr. 1920

3 The victor belongs to the spoils.
The Beautiful and Damned epigraph (1922)

4 Tales of the Jazz Age.
Title of book (1922)

5 This is to tell you about a young man named Ernest Hemingway, who lives in Paris (an American), writes for the *Transatlantic Review* and has a brilliant future. . . . I'd look him up right away. He's the real thing.
Letter to Maxwell Perkins, Oct. 1924

6 Then wear the gold hat, if that will move her;
If you can bounce high, bounce for her too,
Till she cry, "Lover, gold-hatted, high-bouncing lover,
I must have you!"
The Great Gatsby epigraph (1925)

7 The intimate revelations of young men, or at least the terms in which they express them, are usually plagiaristic and marred by obvious suppressions.
The Great Gatsby ch. 1 (1925)

8 Reserving judgments is a matter of infinite hope.
The Great Gatsby ch. 1 (1925)

9 A sense of the fundamental decencies is parcelled out unequally at birth.
The Great Gatsby ch. 1 (1925)

10 I wanted no more riotous excursions with privileged glimpses into the human heart.
The Great Gatsby ch. 1 (1925)

11 If personality is an unbroken series of successful gestures, then there was something gorgeous about him, some heightened sensitivity to the promises of life, as if he were related to one of those intricate machines that register earthquakes ten thousand miles away.
The Great Gatsby ch. 1 (1925)

12 It is what preyed on Gatsby, what foul dust floated in the wake of his dreams that temporarily closed out my interest in the abortive sorrows and short-winded elations of men.
The Great Gatsby ch. 1 (1925)

13 Now I was going to bring back all such things into my life and become again that most limited of all specialists, the "well-rounded man." This isn't just an epigram—life is much more successfully looked at from a single window, after all.
The Great Gatsby ch. 1 (1925)

14 They had spent a year in France for no particular reason, and then drifted here and there unrestfully wherever people played polo and were rich together.
The Great Gatsby ch. 1 (1925)

15 That's the best thing a girl can be in this world, a beautiful little fool.
The Great Gatsby ch. 1 (1925)

16 I like large parties. They're so intimate. At small parties there isn't any privacy.
The Great Gatsby ch. 3 (1925)

17 Every one suspects himself of at least one of the cardinal virtues, and this is mine: I am one of the few honest people that I have ever known.
The Great Gatsby ch. 3 (1925)

18 I remembered, of course, that the World's Series had been fixed in 1919, but if I had

thought of it at all I would have thought of it as something that merely *happened,* the end of an inevitable chain. It never occurred to me that one man could start to play with the faith of fifty million people.

The Great Gatsby ch. 4 (1925)

19 His imagination had never really accepted them as his parents at all. The truth was that Jay Gatsby . . . sprang from his Platonic conception of himself. He was a son of God—a phrase which, if it means anything, means just that— and he must be about His Father's business, the service of a vast, vulgar, and meretricious beauty.

The Great Gatsby ch. 6 (1925)

20 Gatsby saw that the blocks of the sidewalks really formed a ladder and mounted to a secret place above the trees—he could climb to it, if he climbed alone, and once there he could suck on the pap of life, gulp down the incomparable milk of wonder.

The Great Gatsby ch. 6 (1925)

21 He knew that when he kissed this girl, and forever wed his unutterable vision to her perishable breath, his mind would never romp again like the mind of God.

The Great Gatsby ch. 6 (1925)

22 Then he kissed her. At his lips' touch she blossomed for him like a flower and the incarnation was complete.

The Great Gatsby ch. 6 (1925)

23 What'll we do with ourselves this afternoon . . . and the day after that, and the next thirty years?

The Great Gatsby ch. 7 (1925)

24 Her voice is full of money.

The Great Gatsby ch. 7 (1925)

25 There was no difference between men, in intelligence or race, so profound as the difference between the sick and the well.

The Great Gatsby ch. 7 (1925)

26 Thirty—the promise of a decade of loneliness, a thinning list of single men to know, a thinning brief-case of enthusiasm, thinning hair.

The Great Gatsby ch. 7 (1925)

27 [*Remark by attendee at Gatsby's funeral:*] The poor son-of-a-bitch.

The Great Gatsby ch. 9 (1925). Dorothy Parker made the same comment after Fitzgerald died in 1940.

28 That's my Middle West—not the wheat or the prairies or the lost Swede towns, but the thrilling returning trains of my youth, and the street lamps and sleigh bells in the frosty dark and the shadows of holly wreaths thrown by lighted windows on the snow. I am part of that, a little solemn with the feel of those long winters, a little complacent from growing up in the Carraway house in a city where dwellings are still called through decades by a family's name.

The Great Gatsby ch. 9 (1925)

29 I see now that this has been a story of the West, after all—Tom and Gatsby, Daisy and Jordan and I, were all Westerners, and perhaps we possessed some deficiency in common which made us subtly unadaptable to Eastern life.

The Great Gatsby ch. 9 (1925)

30 "I'm thirty," I said. "I'm five years too old to lie to myself and call it honor."

The Great Gatsby ch. 9 (1925)

31 They were careless people, Tom and Daisy— they smashed up things and creatures and then retreated back into their money or their vast carelessness, or whatever it was that kept them together, and let other people clean up the mess they had made.

The Great Gatsby ch. 9 (1925)

32 And as the moon rose higher the inessential houses began to melt away until gradually I became aware of the old island here that flowered once for Dutch sailors' eyes—a fresh, green breast of the new world.

The Great Gatsby ch. 9 (1925)

33 For a transitory enchanted moment man must have held his breath in the presence of this continent, compelled into an aesthetic contemplation he neither understood nor desired, face to face for the last time in history with something commensurate to his capacity for wonder.

The Great Gatsby ch. 9 (1925)

34 And as I sat there brooding on the old, unknown world, I thought of Gatsby's wonder when he first picked out the green light at the end of Daisy's dock. He had come a long way to this blue lawn, and his dream must have seemed so close that he could hardly fail to grasp it. He did not know that it was already behind him, somewhere back in that vast obscurity beyond the city, where the dark fields of the republic rolled on under the night.
The Great Gatsby ch. 9 (1925)

35 Gatsby believed in the green light, the orgastic future that year by year recedes before us. It eluded us then, but that's no matter—tomorrow we will run faster, stretch out our arms farther.
   . . . And one fine morning—
   So we beat on, boats against the current, borne back ceaselessly into the past.
The Great Gatsby ch. 9 (1925). Ellipsis in the original. In later editions, the word *orgastic* was changed to *orgiastic*, but the former was Fitzgerald's original choice.

36 Let me tell you about the very rich. They are different from you and me. They possess and enjoy early, and it does something to them, makes them soft where we are hard, and cynical where we are trustful.
"The Rich Boy" (1926)
See Hemingway 21

37 In the spring of '27, something bright and alien flashed across the sky. A young Minnesotan [Charles Lindbergh] who seemed to have had nothing to do with his generation did a heroic thing, and for a moment people set down their glasses in country clubs and speakeasies and thought of their old best dreams.
"Echoes of the Jazz Age" (1931)

38 The hangover became a part of the day as well allowed-for as the Spanish siesta.
"My Lost City" (1932)

39 One writes of scars healed, a loose parallel to the pathology of the skin, but there is no such thing in the life of an individual. There are open wounds, shrunk sometimes to the size of a pin-prick but wounds still. The marks of suffering are more comparable to the loss of a finger, or of the sight of an eye. We may not miss them, either, for one minute in a year, but if we should there is nothing to be done about it.
Tender Is the Night bk. 2, ch. 11 (1934)

40 The test of a first-rate intelligence is the ability to hold two opposed ideas in the mind at the same time, and still retain the ability to function.
"The Crack-Up" (1936)

41 In a real dark night of the soul it is always three o'clock in the morning, day after day.
"Handle with Care" (1936)
See St. John of the Cross 1

42 It was about then [1920] that I wrote a line which certain people will not let me forget: "She was a faded but still lovely woman of twenty-seven."
"Early Success" (1937)

43 When I was your age I lived with a great dream. The dream grew and I learned how to speak of it and make people listen. Then the dream divided one day when I decided to marry your mother after all. . . . I was a man divided—she wanted me to work too much for *her* and not enough for my dream. She realized too late that work was dignity, and the only dignity, and tried to atone for it by working herself, but it was too late and she broke and is broken forever.
Letter to Frances Scott Fitzgerald, 7 July 1938

44 I am not a great man, but sometimes I think the impersonal and objective quality of my talent and the sacrifices of it, in pieces, to preserve its essential value has some sort of epic grandeur.
Letter to Frances Scott Fitzgerald, Spring 1940

45 The wise and tragic sense of life. By this I mean . . . the sense that life is essentially a cheat and its conditions are those of defeat, and that the redeeming things are not "happiness and pleasure" but the deeper satisfactions that come out of struggle.
Letter to Frances Scott Fitzgerald, 5 Oct. 1940

46 There are no second acts in American lives.
The Last Tycoon "Hollywood, etc." (1941). In his essay "My Lost City" (1932), Fitzgerald had written: "I once thought that there were no second acts in American lives."

47 Show me a hero and I will write you a tragedy.
The Crack-Up "Note-Books" (1945)

48 No grand idea was ever born in a conference, but a lot of foolish ideas have died there.
The Crack-Up "Note-Books" (1945)

49 Egyptian Proverb: The worst things:
To be in bed and sleep not,
To want for one who comes not,
To try to please and please not.
The Crack-Up "Note-Books" (1945)

50 Listen, little Elia: draw your chair up close to the edge of the precipice and I'll tell you a story.
The Crack-Up "Note-Books" (1945)

51 It is in the thirties that we want friends. In the forties we know they won't save us any more than love did.
The Crack-Up "Note-Books" (1945)

52 All good writing is *swimming under water* and holding your breath.
Letter to Frances Scott Fitzgerald (undated)

Zelda Fitzgerald
U.S. writer, 1900–1948

1 [*On her husband F. Scott Fitzgerald's use of her diary and letters:*] Mr. Fitzgerald—I believe that is how he spells his name—seems to believe that plagiarism begins at home.
Quoted in *N.Y. Tribune,* 12 Apr. 1922

2 Ernest, don't you think Al Jolson is greater than Jesus?
Quoted in Ernest Hemingway, *A Moveable Feast* (1964)
See Charlie Chaplin 2; Lennon 13

Robert Fitzsimmons
English-born New Zealand boxer, 1862–1917

1 The bigger they are, the further they have to fall.
Quoted in *Brooklyn Daily Eagle,* 11 Aug. 1900. Garson O'Toole has discovered that "The bigger he is the harder he'll fall" appeared in a boxing article in the *Brooklyn Daily Eagle,* 12 Aug. 1884. "The larger they are, the harder they fall" was printed in the *Denver Post,* 28 Aug. 1899.
See Cliff 2

Jeff Flake
U.S. politician, 1962–

1 [*Of the Republican Party:*] Never has a party abandoned and fled its principles and deeply held beliefs so quickly as my party did in the face of the nativist juggernaut. We have become strangers to ourselves. . . . if we're going to cloister ourselves in the alternative truth of an erratic leader . . . then my party might not deserve to lead.
Speech to National Press Club, Washington, D.C., 15 Mar. 2018

Edward J. Flanagan
U.S. priest, 1886–1948

1 There are no bad boys.
Quoted in Fulton and Will Ousler, *Father Flanagan of Boys Town* (1949). In the 1938 film *Boys Town,* Spencer Tracy, playing Father Flanagan, says "There's no such thing in the world as a bad boy."

Gustave Flaubert
French novelist, 1821–1880

1 Human speech is like a cracked kettle on which we tap crude rhythms for bears to dance to, while we long to make music that will melt the stars.
Madame Bovary pt. 1, ch. 12 (1857) (translation by Francis Steegmuller)

2 *Madame Bovary, c'est moi!*
I am Madame Bovary.
Quoted in René Descharnes, *Flaubert* (1909)

3 *Le bon Dieu est dans le détail.*
God is in the details.
Attributed in Erwin Panofsky, *Meaning in the Visual Arts* (1955)
See Modern Proverbs 24; Mies van der Rohe 2; Warburg 1

Frederick Gard Fleay
English literary scholar, 1831–1909

1 In criticism, as in other matters, the test that decides between science and empiricism is this: "Can you say, not only of what kind, but how much? If you cannot weigh, measure, number your results, however you may be convinced yourself, you must not hope to convince others, or claim the position of

an investigator; you are merely a guesser, a propounder of hypotheses."

"On Metrical Tests as Applied to Dramatic Poetry," *Transactions of the New Shakespeare Society* (1874)
See Lord Kelvin 1

James Elroy Flecker
English poet, 1884–1915

1 For lust of knowing what should not be known,
We take the Golden Road to Samarkand.

The Golden Journey to Samarkand pt. 1, "Epilogue" (1913)

Charles Fleischer
U.S. entertainer, 1950–

1 If you remember the '60s, you really weren't there.

Quoted in *L.A. Times*, 13 June 1982

Alexander Fleming
English bacteriologist, 1881–1955

1 It has been demonstrated that a species of penicillium produces in culture a very powerful antibacterial substance which affects different bacteria in different degrees. . . . In addition to its possible use in the treatment of bacterial infections penicillin is certainly useful . . . for its power of inhibiting unwanted microbes in bacterial cultures so that penicillin insensitive bacteria can readily be isolated.

"On the Bacterial Action of Cultures of a Penicillium, with Special Reference to Their Use in the Isolation of B. Influenzae" (1929)

Ian Fleming
English novelist, 1908–1964

1 [*Said by James Bond in introducing himself:*]
Bond—James Bond.

Casino Royale ch. 7 (1953)

2 Live and Let Die.

Title of book (1954)

3 You have a double-o number, I believe—007, if I remember right. The significance of that double-o number, they tell me, is that you have had to kill a man in the course of some assignment.

Live and Let Die ch. 7 (1954)

4 From Russia with Love.

Title of book (1957)

5 The licence to kill for the Secret Service, the double-o prefix, was a great honor.

Dr. No ch. 2 (1958)

6 A medium Vodka dry Martini—with a slice of lemon peel. Shaken and not stirred.

Dr. No ch. 14 (1958). The sentence "The waiter brought the Martinis, shaken and not stirred, as Bond had stipulated" appeared in Fleming's *Diamonds Are Forever* (1956).

7 They have a saying in Chicago: "Once is happenstance. Twice is coincidence. The third time it's enemy action."

Goldfinger ch. 14 (1959)

8 You Only Live Twice.

Title of book (1964). The book's epigraph: "You only live twice: / Once when you are born / And once when you look death in the face," with the note "after Matsuo Basho, the Japanese poet (1644–1694)."

9 [*Notebook entry:*] Older women are best because they always think they may be doing it for the last time.

Quoted in John Pearson, *The Life of Ian Fleming* (1966)
See Benjamin Franklin 23

Peter Fleming
English travel writer, 1907–1971

1 Long Island represents the American's idea of what God would have done with Nature if he'd had the money.

Letter to Rupert Fleming, 29 Sept. 1929

Andrew Fletcher of Saltoun
Scottish patriot, 1655–1716

1 If a man were permitted to make all the ballads, he need not care who should make the laws of a nation.

"An Account of a Conversation Concerning a Right Regulation of Government for the Good of Mankind" (1704)
See Auden 22; Auden 39; Samuel Johnson 22; Percy Shelley 15; Twain 104

Ed Fletcher
U.S. musician, fl. 1982

1 Don't push me 'cause I'm close to the edge
I'm trying not to lose my head

It's like a jungle sometimes, it makes me
wonder
How I keep from going under.
"The Message" (song) (1982)

Curt Flood

U.S. baseball player, 1938–1997

1 After twelve years in the major leagues, I do
not feel I am a piece of property to be bought
and sold irrespective of my wishes.
Letter to Bowie Kuhn, 24 Dec. 1969

Jean-Pierre Claris de Florian

French writer, 1755–1794

1 Love's pleasure lasts but a moment;
Love's sorrow lasts all through life.
Célestine (1784)

Errol Flynn

Australian actor, 1909–1959

1 My main problem is reconciling my gross
habits with my net income.
Quoted in N.Y. Times, 6 Mar. 1955

Dario Fo

Italian playwright, 1926–2016

1 The worker knows 300 words while the boss
knows 1000. That is why he is the boss.
Grande Pantomima (1968)

Ferdinand Foch

French military leader, 1851–1929

1 [Of the Treaty of Versailles, 1919:] Ce n'est pas un
traité de paix, c'est un armistice de vingt ans.
This is not a peace treaty, it is an armistice for
twenty years.
Quoted in Paul Reynaud, Mémoires (1963)

2 [Dispatch during first Battle of the Marne, 8 Sept.
1914:] Mon centre cède, ma droite recule,
situation excellente. J'attaque!
My center is giving way, my right is retreating,
situation excellent, I am attacking.
Attributed in Raymond Recouly, Foch: Le Vainqueur
de la Guerre (1919). Othon Guerlac, Les Citations
Françaises, labels this as obviously being a legend,
citing the Marquis de Vogué's speech to the
Académie Française, 5 Feb. 1920. An early English-
language version appeared in the Washington Post, 25
July 1915: "My left has been forced back, my right is
routed; I shall attack with the center."

Jonathan Safran Foer

U.S. writer, 1977–

1 I've thought myself out of happiness one
million times, but never once into it.
Extremely Loud and Incredibly Close (2005)

2 Sometimes I can hear my bones straining
under the weight of all of the lives I'm not
living.
Extremely Loud and Incredibly Close (2005)

John Fogerty

U.S. singer and songwriter, 1945–

1 Some folks are born made to wave the flag,
Ooh, they're red, white, and blue.
And when the band plays "Hail to the Chief,"
Oh, they point the cannon at you, Lord,
It ain't me, it ain't me,
I ain't no senator's son,
It ain't me, it ain't me,
I ain't no fortunate one.
"Fortunate Son" (song) (1969)

J. Foley

British songwriter, 1906–1970

1 Old soldiers never die,
They simply fade away.
"Old Soldiers Never Die" (song) (1916). This song
was copyrighted by Foley, but he may well not have
been the author. The 1916 publication of the song
lyrics was in a book by Bruce Bairnsfather, Bullets &
Billets.
See MacArthur 2

Folk and Anonymous Songs

See also Ballads.

1 I got-a wings, you got-a wings
All o' God's chillun got-a wings . . .
I got shoes, you got shoes
All o' God's chillun got shoes.
"All God's Chillun Got Wings"

2 Alouette, gentille Alouette,
Alouette, je te plumerai.
Lark, nice lark, lark, I will pluck you.
"Alouette"

3   A tisket, a tasket
    A green and yellow basket
    I wrote a letter to my love
    And on the way I dropped it.
    "A Tisket, a Tasket"

4   *Au clair de la lune,*
    Mon ami Pierrot,
    Prête-moi ta plume
    Pour écrire un mot.
    By the light of the moon,
    My friend Pierrot,
    Lend me your pen
    To write a word.
    "Au Clair de la Lune"

5   Be kind to your web-footed friends
    For a duck may be somebody's mother,
    Be kind to your friends in the swamp
    Where the weather is always damp.
    "Be Kind to Your Webfooted Friends"

6   You may think that this is the end . . .
    Well you're right!
    "Be Kind to Your Webfooted Friends"

7   Blow the man down, to me aye, aye, blow the
        man down!
    Whether he's white man or black man or
        brown,
    Give me some time to blow the man down.
    "Blow the Man Down"

8   The pony jump, he run, he pitch,
    He threw my master in the ditch,
    He died and the jury wondered why,
    The verdict was the blue-tail fly.
    "The Blue-Tail Fly"

9   Jimmy, crack corn, and I don't care,
    Old massa's gone away.
    "The Blue-Tail Fly"

10 O ye'll tak' the high road, and I'll tak' the low
        road,
    And I'll be in Scotland afore ye,
    But me and my true love will never meet again,
    On the bonnie, bonnie banks o' Loch Lomon.
    "The Bonnie Banks of Loch Lomon"

11 My Bonnie lies over the ocean,
    My Bonnie lies over the sea,
    My Bonnie lies over the ocean,
    Oh, bring back my Bonnie to me.
    "Bring Back My Bonnie to Me"

12 Buffalo gals, woncha come out tonight,
    Woncha come out tonight, woncha come out
        tonight?
    Buffalo gals, woncha come out tonight,
    And dance by the light of the moon?
    "Buffalo Gals"

13 As I walked out in the streets of Laredo,
    As I walked out in Laredo one day,
    I spied a poor cowboy wrapped up in white
        linen,
    Wrapped up in white linen as cold as the clay.
    "The Cowboy's Lament"

14 Oh, bang the drum slowly and play the fife
        lowly,
    Play the Dead March as you carry me along;
    Take me to the green valley, there lay the sod
        o'er me,
    For I'm a young cowboy and I know I've done
        wrong.
    "The Cowboy's Lament"

15 For meeting is a pleasure and parting is a grief
    And a false-hearted lover's far worse than a
        thief
    A thief will but rob you and take all you've
        saved
    But an inconstant lover will turn you to the
        grave.
    "The Cuckoo"

16 Sumer is icumen in,
    Lhude sing cuccu!
    Groweth sed, and bloweth med,
    And springth the wude nu.
    "Cuckoo Song"

17 Deck the hall with boughs of holly,
    Fa la la la la, la la la la,
    'Tis the season to be jolly,
    Fa la la la la, la la la la.
    "Deck the Hall"

18 Down in the valley,
    The valley so low,
    Hang your head over
    And hear the wind blow.
    "Down in the Valley"

19 What shall we do with the drunken sailor,
    Early in the morning?
    "The Drunken Sailor"

20 They gonna walk around, dry bones,
　Why don't you rise and hear the word of the
　　Lord?
　"Dry Bones"
　See Bible 188

21 Ah, well, the toe bone connected with the foot
　　bone,
　The foot bone connected with the ankle bone,
　The ankle bone connected with the leg bone,
　The leg bone connected with the knee bone,
　The knee bone connected with the thigh bone,
　Rise and hear the word of the Lord!
　"Dry Bones"

22 For he's a jolly good fellow,
　Which nobody can deny.
　"For He's a Jolly Good Fellow"

23 Frankie and Johnny were lovers, O lordy how
　　they could love.
　Swore to be true to each other, true as the stars
　　above;
　He was her man but he done her wrong.
　"Frankie and Johnny"

24 Free at last, free at last,
　Thank God almighty, I'm free at last.
　"Free at Last"
　See Martin Luther King 14

25 Frère Jacques, Frère Jacques,
　Dormez-vous? Dormez-vous?
　Brother John, Brother John,
　Are you sleeping? Are you sleeping?
　"Frère Jacques"

26 Fuzzy Wuzzy was a bear;
　Fuzzy Wuzzy had no hair;
　Fuzzy Wuzzy wasn't very fuzzy,
　Was 'e?
　Wisconsin Rapids Daily Tribune, 31 July 1942

27 The Girl I Left Behind Me.
　Title of song

28 Give me that old time religion
　Tis the old time religion . . .
　And it's good enough for me.
　"Give Me That Old Time Religion"

29 Go down, Moses,
　Way down in Egypt land,
　Tell ole Pharaoh:
　Let my people go.
　"Go Down, Moses"

30 God rest you merry, gentlemen,
　Let nothing you dismay;
　Remember Christ our Savior
　Was born on Christmas Day.
　"God Rest You Merry, Gentlemen" (hymn)

31 Peas! Peas! Peas! Peas!
　Eating goober peas!
　Goodness, how delicious,
　Eating goober peas!
　"Goober Peas"

32 Go tell it on the mountain,
　Over the hills and everywhere,
　Go tell it on the mountain
　That Jesus Christ is Lord.
　"Go Tell It on the Mountain"

33 Happy Birthday to You.
　Title of song

34 He's got you and me, brother, in His hands . . .
　He's got the whole world in His hands.
　"He's Got the Whole World in His Hands"

35 Hush, little baby, don't say a word,
　Mama's going to buy you a mockingbird.
　And if that mockingbird don't sing,
　Mama's going to buy you a diamond ring.
　"Hush Little Baby"

36 God gave Noah the rainbow sign
　No more water but the fire next time.
　"I Got a Home in That Rock"
　See James Baldwin 2

37 I've been working on the railroad
　All the livelong day
　I've been working on the railroad
　Just to pass the time away.
　"I've Been Working on the Railroad"

38 Can't you hear the whistle blowing
　Rise up so early in the morn
　Can't you hear the captain shouting
　Dinah, blow your horn.
　"I've Been Working on the Railroad"

39 Someone's in the kitchen with Dinah
　Someone's in the kitchen I know
　Someone's in the kitchen with Dinah
　Strumming on the old banjo, and singing
　Fie, fi, fiddly i o.
　"I've Been Working on the Railroad"

40 John Brown's body lies a-mold'ring in the grave
   His soul goes marching on.
   "John Brown's Body"

41 Glory, Glory! Hallelujah! . . .
   His soul is marching on.
   "John Brown's Body"
   See Julia Ward Howe 2

42 John Henry was just a li'l baby,
   Settin' on his daddy's knee,
   He pint his finger at a little piece of steel, Lawd,
   "Steel gon' be the death of me."
   "John Henry"

43 John Henry told his captain,
   Says, "A man ain't nothin' but a man,
   And before I'd let your steam drill beat me
      down, Lawd,
   I'd die with this hammer in my hand."
   "John Henry"

44 Joshua fit the battle of Jericho,
   And the walls came tumbling down.
   "Joshua Fit the Battle of Jericho"

45 And where are the reeds?
   The girls have gathered them.
   And where are the girls?
   The girls have married and gone away.
   And where are the Cossacks?
   They've gone to war.
   "Koloda Duda." This Russian folksong, quoted in
   Mikhail Sholokhov's novel *And Quiet Flows the Don*,
   inspired Pete Seeger to write his song "Where Have
   All the Flowers Gone?"
   See Pete Seeger 4

46 *La cucaracha, la cucaracha*
   Ya no puede caminar
   Porque no tiene, porque le falta
   Marijuana que fumar.
   The cockroach, the cockroach
   Now he can't go traveling
   Because he doesn't have, because he lacks
   Marijuana to smoke.
   "La Cucaracha"

47 The Farmer's Dog leapt o'er the Stile,
   His name it was little Bingo;
   B with an I—I with an N
   N with a G—G with an O
   His name was little Bingo,
   B-I-N-G-O

And his name was little Bingo.
   "Little Bingo"

48 Mademoiselle from Armentières,
   Parlez-vous,
   Mademoiselle from Armentières,
   She hasn't been kissed for forty year,
   Hinky-dinky parlez-vous.
   "Mademoiselle from Armentières"

49 From the Halls of Montezuma
   To the shores of Tripoli;
   We fight our country's battles
   In air, on land, and sea;
   First to fight for right and freedom
   And to keep our honor clean;
   We are proud to claim the title
   Of United States Marine.
   "The Marine's Hymn." The first two lines transposed
   the words inscribed on the Colors of the Marine
   Corps: "From the Shores of Tripoli to the Halls of
   Montezuma."

50 If the Army and the Navy
   Ever look on Heaven's scenes,
   They will find the streets are guarded
   By United States Marines.
   "The Marine's Hymn"

51 Michael, row the boat ashore,
   Hallelujah!
   "Michael, Row the Boat Ashore"

52 One flew East, one flew West,
   One flew over the cuckoo's nest.
   "Miss Mary Mack"

53 Do you know the muffin man
   Who lives in Drury Lane?
   "The Muffin Man"

54 Here we go round the mulberry bush,
   On a cold and frosty morning.
   "The Mulberry Bush"

55 Greensleeves was all my joy,
   Greensleeves was my delight,
   Greensleeves was my heart of gold,
   And who but Lady Greensleeves?
   "A New Courtly Sonnet of the Lady Greensleeves, to
   the New Tune of 'Greensleeves'"

56 Nobody knows the trouble I see, Lord,
   Nobody knows like Jesus.
   "Nobody Knows the Trouble I See, Lord!"

57 O dear, what can the matter be?
   Johnny's so long at the fair.
   "O Dear, What Can the Matter Be?"

58 The old gray mare she ain't what she used to be,
   Many long years ago.
   "Old Gray Mare"

59 Old MacDonald had a farm, E-I-E-I-O.
   "Old MacDonald"

60 On top of Old Smokey,
   All covered with snow,
   I lost my true lover,
   For courting too slow.
   "On Top of Old Smokey"

61 Oh, I went down South for to see my Sal,
   Singing Polly Wolly Doodle all the day.
   "Polly-Wolly-Doodle"

62 Pop Goes the Weasel.
   Title of song (1853)

63 Come and sit by my side if you love me,
   Do not hasten to bid me adieu,
   But remember the Red River Valley
   And the girl that has loved you so true.
   "Red River Valley." In later versions the last line
   quoted became "the cowboy who loved you so true" or
   "the cowboy who's waiting for you."

64 Rise and shine,
   And give God the glory,
   For the year of jubilee.
   "Rise and Shine"

65 There is a house in New Orleans,
   They call the Rising Sun,
   It's been the ruin of many poor girls,
   And me, O Lord, for one.
   "The Rising Sun Blues"

66 Go tell my baby sister,
   Never do like I have done,
   Tell her shun that house in New Orleans,
   They call the Rising Sun.
   "The Rising Sun Blues"

67 Row, row, row your boat
   Gently down the stream.
   Merrily, merrily, merrily, merrily,
   Life is but a dream.
   "Row, Row, Row Your Boat"
   See Calderón de la Barca 1; Carroll 44; Li Po 1;
   Proverbs 169

68 Where are you going? To Scarborough Fair?
   Parsley, sage, rosemary and thyme,
   Remember me to a bonny lass there,
   For once she was a true lover of mine.
   "Scarborough Fair"

69 She'll be comin' round the mountain,
   When she comes. . . .
   She'll be drivin' six white horses,
   When she comes.
   "She'll Be Comin' Round the Mountain"

70 Around her neck she wore a yellow ribbon.
   "She Wore a Yellow Ribbon"
   See Levine 1

71 Mamma's little baby loves shortnin' bread.
   "Shortnin' Bread"

72 Skip to my Lou, my darling.
   "Skip to My Lou"

73 Sur le pont d'Avignon l'on y danse, l'on y danse.
   On the bridge of Avignon they dance, they
       dance.
   "Sur le Pont d'Avignon"

74 Swing low, sweet chariot,
   Coming for to carry me home.
   "Swing Low, Sweet Chariot"

75 There is a tavern in the town,
   And there my true love sits him down,
   And drinks his wine 'mid laughter free,
   And never, never thinks of me.
   "There Is a Tavern in the Town"

76 This train is bound for glory, this train!
   "This Train"

77 Hang down your head, Tom Dooley,
   Hang down your head and cry,
   Hang down your head, Tom Dooley,
   Poor boy, you're bound to die.
   "Tom Dooley"

78 O Paddy dear, an' did ye hear the news that's
       goin' round?
   The shamrock is by law forbid to grow on Irish
       ground!
   No more St. Patrick's Day we'll keep, his color
       can't be seen,
   For there's a cruel law agin the wearin' o' the
       Green!
   "The Wearing o' the Green"

79 For they're hangin' men and women there for
wearin' o' the Green.
"The Wearing o' the Green"

80 We're here
Because
We're here.
"We're Here"

81 Just like a tree that's standing by the water,
We shall not be moved.
"We Shall Not Be Moved"

82 Lord, I want to be in that number
When the saints come marchin' in.
"When the Saints Come Marchin' In"

83 Whoopee ti yi yo, git along, little dogies,
It's your misfortune and none of my own,
Whoopee ti yi yo, git along, little dogies,
For you know Wyoming will be your new
home.
"Whoopee Ti Yi Yo, Git Along, Little Dogies"

84 Yankee Doodle came to town
Riding on a pony
He stuck a feather in his hat
And called it macaroni.
"Yankee Doodle"

85 Yankee Doodle, keep it up,
Yankee Doodle dandy,
Mind the music and the step,
And with the girls be handy.
"Yankee Doodle"

86 There's a yellow rose in Texas, that I am going
to see,
No other darky knows her, no darky only me.
She cried so when I left her it like to broke my
heart,
And if I ever find her, we nevermore will part.
"Yellow Rose of Texas." Later versions replaced the
word "darky" with "soldier."

Jane Fonda
U.S. actress and businesswoman, 1937–

1 A man has every season while a woman only
has the right to spring.
Quoted in *Daily Mail* (London), 13 Sept. 1989

Lynn Fontanne
English actress, 1887–1983

1 [*Definition of acting, 1954:*] We move about the
stage without bumping into the furniture or
each other.
Quoted in *Morning Advocate* (Baton Rouge, La.), 24
Jan. 1955
See Coward 14

Bernard de Fontenelle
French philosopher, 1657–1757

1 We have already begun to fly; several persons,
here and there, have found the secret to fitting
wings to themselves, of setting them in motion,
so that they are held up in the air and are
carried across streams. . . . The art of flying is
only just being born; it will be perfected, and
some day we will go as far as the moon.
Entretiens sur la Pluralité des Mondes Habités (1686)

2 *Il n'y a point d'autres histoires anciennes que les
fables.*
There are no ancient histories other than
fables.
De l'Origine des Fables (1724)
See Voltaire 13

3 Not long ago he [Fontenelle, as a nonagenarian]
said to a young woman, to show her how
impressed he was by her beauty, "Ah, would
that I were only 80 years old!"
Reported in Friedrich Melchior von Grimm,
Correspondance Littéraire, Philosophique et Critique
(1813). This occurs, in French, in a letter dated 1 Feb.
1757.

4 *Du sublime au ridicule il n'y a qu'un pas.*
From the sublime to the ridiculous it is only
one step.
Attributed in *Pensées Nouvelles et Philosophiques* (1777)

Samuel Foote
English actor and playwright, 1720–1777

1 He is not only dull himself, but the cause of
dullness in others.
Quoted in James Boswell, *Life of Samuel Johnson*
(1791) (entry for 1783)
See Shakespeare 61

2 "Foote," (said lord Sandwich) "I have often
wondered what catastrophe would bring *you* to
your end; but I think, that you must either die

of the p-x, or the halter."—"My lord," (replied Foote instantaneously) *"that* will depend upon one of two contingencies;—whether I embrace your lordship's mistress, or your lordship's principles."

Quoted in Percival Stockdale, *The Memoirs of the Life and Writings of Percival Stockdale* (1809). An earlier, somewhat less punchy version of the same anecdote appeared in *Wits Museum, or the New London Jester* (ca. 1780). A still earlier version, involving Foote and an unnamed nobleman, was printed in the *Derby Mercury*, 3 Aug. 1764. The exchange is frequently attributed to Sandwich and John Wilkes, but the earliest evidence linking it to them is in a 1935 book.

3 So she went into the garden to cut a cabbage-leaf to make an apple-pie; and at the same time a great she-bear coming up the street, pops its head into the shop. "What! no soap?" So he died, and she very imprudently married the barber; and there were present the Picninnies, and the Joblillies, and the Garyulies, and the grand Panjandrum himself, with the little round button at top; and they all fell to playing the game of catch as catch can, till the gun powder ran out at the heels of their boots.

Quoted in Maria Edgeworth, *Harry and Lucy* (1825). Foote composed this nonsense to test the memory of actor Charles Macklin, who had claimed he could repeat any speech. The passage introduced into the English language the phrases *grand Panjandrum* (pretentious person) and (perhaps) *no soap* (no good).

Christine Blasey Ford
U.S. psychologist, 1966–

1 [*Describing her memory of an alleged sexual assault by Supreme Court nominee Brett Kavanaugh:*] Indelible in the hippocampus is the laughter.

U.S. Senate Judiciary Committee testimony, 27 Sept. 2018

Ford Madox Ford (Ford Madox Hueffer)
English writer, 1873–1939

1 This is the saddest story I have ever heard.
The Good Soldier pt. 1, sec. 1 (1915)

2 Only two classes of books are of universal appeal: the very best and the very worst.
Joseph Conrad pt. 3, sec. 1 (1924)

3 A fervent young admirer exclaimed: "By Jove, the Good Soldier is the finest novel in the English language!" whereupon my friend John Rodker, who has always had a properly tempered admiration for my work, remarked in his clear, slow drawl: "Ah, yes. It is, but you have left out a word. It is the finest French novel in the English language!"
The Good Soldier dedicatory letter (1927 edition)

Gerald R. Ford (Leslie L. King, Jr.)
U.S. president, 1913–2006

1 An impeachable offense is whatever a majority of the House of Representatives considers [it] to be at a given moment in history.
Remarks in House of Representatives, 15 Apr. 1970

2 I am a Ford, not a Lincoln.
Remarks on taking the vice-presidential oath, 6 Dec. 1973

3 My fellow Americans, our long national nightmare [the Watergate scandal] is over. Our Constitution works; our great Republic is a government of laws and not of men. Here the people rule.
Remarks upon taking oath of office, 9 Aug. 1974
See John Adams 4; Archibald Cox 1; James Harrington 1

4 Now, THEREFORE, I, Gerald R. Ford, President of the United States, pursuant to the pardon power conferred upon me by Article II, Section 2, of the Constitution, have granted and by these presents do grant a full, free, and absolute pardon unto Richard Nixon for all offenses against the United States which he, Richard Nixon, has committed or may have committed or taken part in during the period from January 20, 1969 through August 9, 1974.
Proclamation 4311, 8 Sept. 1974

5 There is no Soviet domination of Eastern Europe.
Televised presidential debate, 6 Oct. 1976

6 If the Government is big enough to give you everything you want, it is big enough to take away everything you have.
Quoted in John F. Parker, *If Elected, I Promise* (1960). Although this is associated with Ford, it appeared as early as 1952: "If your government is big enough to give you everything you want, it is big enough to take away from you everything you have" (Paul Harvey, *Remember These Things*).

Harrison Ford

U.S. actor, 1942–

1 [*Remark to George Lucas about Ford's lines in the 1977 motion picture* Star Wars:] George, you can type this shit, but you sure as hell can't say it.

Quoted in *The Guardian*, 24 Apr. 1999

Henry Ford

U.S. industrialist, 1863–1947

1 [*On the Model T Ford, 1909:*] Any customer can have a car painted any color that he wants so long as it is black.

My Life and Work ch. 2 (1922). Coauthored with Samuel Crowther.

2 History is more or less bunk.

Quoted in *Chicago Tribune*, 25 May 1916

3 Nothing is particularly hard if you divide it into small jobs.

Quoted in *Reader's Digest*, Mar. 1934

4 Whether you believe you can do a thing or not, you are right.

Attributed in *Reader's Digest*, Sept. 1947

John Ford

English playwright, 1586–1639

1 Of one so young, so rich in nature's store,
Who could not say, 'tis pity she's a whore?
'Tis Pity She's a Whore act 5, sc. 6 (1633)

Lena Guilbert Ford

English songwriter, 1870–1916

1 Keep the Home-fires burning,
While your hearts are yearning,
Though your lads are far away
They dream of Home.
There's a silver lining
Through the dark cloud shining;
Turn the dark cloud inside out,
Till the boys come Home.
"'Till the Boys Come Home!" (1914)
See DeSylva 1; Proverbs 49

Richard Ford

U.S. writer, 1944–

1 Married life requires shared mystery even when all the facts are known.
The Sportswriter ch. 5 (1986)

Rob Ford

Canadian politician, 1969–2016

1 Yes, I have smoked crack cocaine . . . Have I tried it? Um, probably in one of my drunken stupors.

Remarks to reporters, Toronto, Canada, 5 Nov. 2013

Howell Forgy

U.S. naval chaplain, 1908–1983

1 [*Remark while moving along a line of sailors passing ammunition by hand to the deck, Pearl Harbor, Hawaii, 7 Dec. 1941:*] Praise the Lord and pass the ammunition.

Quoted in *N.Y. Times*, 1 Nov. 1942. Often incorrectly attributed to William A. Maguire. The earliest known occurrence in print is in the *Tucson Daily Citizen*, 3 Feb. 1942; the attribution given there is only to an "unnamed Navy chaplain at Pearl Harbor."

Nathan Bedford Forrest

U.S. Confederate general, 1821–1877

1 Well, I got there first with the most men.

Quoted in Richard Taylor, *Destruction and Reconstruction* (1879). Forrest's prescription for success in warfare is frequently quoted as "git thar fustest with the mostest men," but there is no reliable evidence of his using the more colorful formulation.

E. M. Forster

English novelist, 1879–1970

1 Railway termini . . . are our gates to the glorious and the unknown. Through them we pass out into adventure and sunshine, to them, alas! we return.
Howards End ch. 2 (1910)

2 Mature as he was, she might yet be able to help him to the building of the rainbow bridge that should connect the prose in us with the passion. Without it we are meaningless fragments, half monks, half beasts, unconnected arches that have never joined into a man. With it love is born, and alights on the highest curve, glowing against the gray, sober against the fire.
Howards End ch. 22 (1910)

3 Only connect! That was the whole of her sermon. Only connect the prose and the passion, and both will be exalted, and human love will be seen at its height.
Howards End ch. 22 (1910)

4 The so-called white races are really pinko-gray.
A Passage to India ch. 7 (1924)

5 It is not that the Englishman can't feel—it is that he is afraid to feel. He has been taught at his public school that feeling is bad form. He must not express great joy or sorrow, or even open his mouth too wide when he talks—his pipe might fall out if he did.
Abinger Harvest "Notes on English Character" (1936)

6 A poem is true if it hangs together. Information points to something else. A poem points to nothing but itself.
Two Cheers for Democracy "Anonymity: An Enquiry" (1951)

7 Two cheers for Democracy: one because it admits variety and two because it permits criticism. Two cheers are quite enough: there is no occasion to give three.
Two Cheers for Democracy "What I Believe" (1951)

8 If I had to choose between betraying my country and betraying my friend, I hope I should have the guts to betray my country.
Two Cheers for Democracy "What I Believe" (1951)

Abe Fortas
U.S. lawyer and judge, 1910–1982

1 It can hardly be argued that either students or teachers shed their constitutional rights to freedom of speech or expression at the schoolhouse gate.
Tinker v. Des Moines Indep. Community School Dist. (1969)

John Fortescue
English judge, ca. 1394–ca. 1476

1 I should, indeed, prefer twenty guilty men to escape death through mercy, than one innocent to be condemned unjustly.
De Laudibus Legum Angliae ch. 27 (ca. 1470)
See Blackstone 7; Benjamin Franklin 37; Maimonides 1; Voltaire 3

Sam Walter Foss
U.S. poet, 1858–1911

1 But let me live by the side of the road
And be a friend to man.
"The House by the Side of the Road" l. 7 (1898)

Stephen Collins Foster
U.S. songwriter, 1826–1864

1 O, Susanna! O, don't you cry for me,
I've come from Alabama, with my banjo on my knee.
"O, Susanna" (song) (1848)

2 Gwine to run all night!
Gwine to run all day!
I'll bet my money on de bobtail nag—
Somebody bet on de bay.
"Camptown Races" (song) (1850)

3 Way down upon the Swanee River,
Far, far away,
There's where my heart is turning ever;
There's where the old folks stay.
"The Old Folks at Home" (song) (1851)

4 All the world is sad and dreary
Ev'rywhere I roam,
Oh! darkies, how my heart grows weary,
Far from the old folks at home.
"The Old Folks at Home" (song) (1851)

5 The sun shines bright in the old Kentucky home.
"My Old Kentucky Home" (song) (1853)

6 I dream of Jeanie with the light brown hair.
"Jeanie with the Light Brown Hair" (song) (1854)

7 Beautiful dreamer, wake unto me,
Starlight and dewdrop are waiting for thee.
"Beautiful Dreamer" (song) (1864)

Vince Foster
U.S. government official, 1945–1993

1 [*Suicide note:*] I was not meant for the spotlight of public life in Washington. Here, ruining people is considered a sport.
Quoted in *N.Y. Times*, 13 Aug. 1993

Michel Foucault
French philosopher, 1926–1984

1 As the archaeology of our thought easily shows, man is an invention of recent date. And one perhaps nearing its end.
The Order of Things: An Archaeology of the Human Sciences ch. 10 (1966)

2 If those arrangements [the fundamental arrangements of knowledge] were to disappear as they appeared . . . then one can certainly wager that man would be erased, like a face drawn in sand at the edge of the sea.
The Order of Things: An Archaeology of the Human Sciences ch. 10 (1966)

3 Homosexuality appeared as one of the forms of sexuality when it was transposed from the practice of sodomy into a kind of interior androgyny, a hermaphroditism of the soul. The sodomite had been a temporary aberration; the homosexual was now a species.
The History of Sexuality vol. 1, pt. 2, ch. 2 (1976) (translation by Robert Hurley)

Joseph Fouché
French statesman, 1759–1820

1 [*Of the execution of the Duc d'Enghien by Napoleon's troops, 1804:*] *C'est plus qu'un crime, c'est une faute!*
It is more than a crime, it is a blunder.
Quoted in Joseph Fouché, *Mémoires* (1824)

Charles Fourier
French social scientist, 1772–1837

1 The extension of women's rights is the basic principle of all social progress.
Theory of Four Movements vol. 2, ch. 4 (1808)

H. W. Fowler
English lexicographer and grammarian, 1858–1933

1 The English speaking world may be divided into (1) those who neither know nor care what a split infinitive is; (2) those who do not know, but care very much; (3) those who know and condemn; (4) those who know and approve; and (5) those who know and distinguish. Those who neither know nor care are the vast majority and are a happy folk, to be envied by most of the minority classes.
A Dictionary of Modern English Usage (1926)

John Fowles
English novelist, 1926–2005

1 I was born in 1927, the only child of middle-class parents, both English, and themselves born in the grotesquely elongated shadow . . . of that monstrous dwarf Queen Victoria.
The Magus ch. 1 (1966)

2 We all write poems; it is simply that poets are the ones who write in words.
The French Lieutenant's Woman ch. 19 (1969)

Charles James Fox
English statesman, 1749–1806

1 [*Of the fall of the Bastille:*] How much the greatest event it is that ever happened in the world! and how much the best!
Letter to Richard Fitzpatrick, 30 July 1789

Anatole France (Jacques-Anatole-François Thibault)
French novelist and man of letters, 1844–1924

1 Man is so made that he can only find relaxation from one kind of labor by taking up another.
The Crime of Sylvestre Bonnard pt. 2, ch. 4 (1881)

2 *Ils naquirent, ils souffrirent, ils moururent.*
They were born, they suffered, they died.
Opinions of Jérôme Coignard ch. 16 (1893)

3 The majestic equality of the law, which forbids the rich as well as the poor to sleep under bridges, to beg in the streets, and to steal bread.
Le Lys Rouge ch. 7 (1894)

4 The average man, who does not know what to do with his life, wants another one which will last forever.
The Revolt of the Angels ch. 21 (1914)
See Ertz 1

Francis I
French king, 1494–1547

1 [*Letter to his mother after his defeat at Pavia, 1525:*] *De toutes choses ne m'est demouré que l'honneur et la vie qui est sauve.*
Of all I had, only honor and life have been spared.
Quoted in *Registres Manuscrits de Parlement*, 10 Nov. 1525. Commonly quoted as "*Tout est perdu fors l'honneur* [All is lost save honor]."

St. Francis of Assisi
Italian friar, ca. 1181–1226

1 Praised be You, my Lord, with all your
    creatures,
  Especially Sir Brother Sun,
  Who is the day and through whom You give us
    light.
  "The Canticle of Brother Sun" (1225)

2 Lord, make me an instrument of Your peace!
  Where there is hatred, let me sow love.
  Where there is injury, pardon.
  Where there is doubt, faith.
  Where there is despair, hope.
  Where there is darkness, light.
  Where there is sadness, joy.
  Attributed in *Helena Independent*, 9 Nov. 1935. The
  attribution to St. Francis is undoubtedly apocryphal.
  This prayer appears to have first seen light, published
  anonymously, in a French religious magazine titled
  La Clochette, Dec. 1912.

3 Preach the gospel all the time—if necessary,
  use words.
  Attributed in *World Vision*, Aug.–Sept. 1989

Francis (Jorge Mario Bergoglio)
Argentinian pope, 1936–

1 If someone is gay and is searching for the Lord
  and has good will, then who am I to judge him?
  Press conference during airplane flight, 28 July 2013

2 The Earth, our home, is beginning to look more
  and more like an immense pile of filth.
  Laudato Si' (2015)

3 We cannot insist only on issues related
  to abortion, gay marriage, and the use of
  contraceptive methods . . . it is not necessary to
  talk about these issues all the time.
  Quoted in *America*, 30 Sept. 2013

Anne Frank
German diarist, 1929–1945

1 I want to go on living even after my death! And
  therefore I am grateful to God for giving me
  this gift, this possibility of developing myself
  and of writing, of expressing all that is in me. I
  can shake off everything if I write; my sorrows
  disappear, my courage is reborn.
  Diary, 4 Apr. 1944

2 Is discord going to show itself while we are
  still fighting, is the Jew once again worth less
  than another? Oh, it is sad, very sad, that once
  more, for the umpteenth time, the old truth
  is confirmed: "What one Christian does is his
  own responsibility, what *one* Jew does is thrown
  back at all Jews."
  Diary, 22 May 1944

3 In spite of everything I still believe that people
  are really good at heart.
  Diary, 15 July 1944

Barney Frank
U.S. politician, 1940–

1 [*Characterizing attitudes of some conservative
  legislators:*] Life begins at conception and ends at
  birth.
  Quoted in *N.Y. Times*, 16 Aug. 1981

Al Franken
U.S. humorist, 1951–

1 Rush Limbaugh Is a Big Fat Idiot.
  Title of book (1996)

Felix Frankfurter
Austrian-born U.S. judge and legal scholar,
1882–1965

1 The history of liberty has largely been the
  history of observance of procedural safeguards.
  McNabb v. United States (1943)

2 One who belongs to the most vilified and
  persecuted minority in history is not likely to
  be insensible to the freedom guaranteed by our
  Constitution. . . . But as judges we are neither
  Jew nor Gentile, neither Catholic nor agnostic.
  West Virginia State Bd. of Educ. v. Barnette (dissenting
  opinion) (1943)

3 It is a fair summary of history to say that the
  safeguards of liberty have frequently been
  forged in controversies involving not very nice
  people.
  United States v. Rabinowitz (dissenting opinion)
  (1950)

4 This is conduct that shocks the conscience.
  Illegally breaking into the privacy of the
  petitioner, the struggle to open his mouth and

remove what was there, the forcible extraction of his stomach's contents—this course of proceeding by agents of government to obtain evidence is bound to offend even hardened sensibilities. They are methods too close to the rack and the screw to permit of constitutional differentiation.

Rochin v. California (1952)

Aretha Franklin

U.S. rhythm and blues singer, 1942–2018

1 R-E-S-P-E-C-T
Find out what it means to me
R-E-S-P-E-C-T
Take care TCB.

"Respect" (song) (1967). Franklin added this refrain to Otis Redding's 1965 song "Respect."

Benjamin Franklin

U.S. statesman, scientist, and author, 1706–1790

1 The Body of B. Franklin, Printer; like the Cover of an old Book, its Contents torn out, and stript of its Lettering and Gilding, lies here, Food for Worms. But the Work shall not be wholly lost: for it will, as he believ'd, appear once more, in a new & more perfect Edition, corrected and amended by the Author.

"Epitaph" (1728). This did not ultimately appear on Franklin's tomb.

2 I am about Courting a Girl I have had but little Acquaintance with; how shall I come to a Knowledge of her Fawlts? and whether she has the Virtues I imagine she has?
    Answ. Commend her among her Female Acquaintances.

Pennsylvania Gazette, 12 Mar. 1732

3 After three days men grow weary of a wench, a guest, and weather rainy.

Poor Richard's Almanack, June 1733

4 God works wonders now and then;
Behold! a Lawyer, an honest Man!

Poor Richard's Almanack, Dec. 1733. Very similar passages occur in books as far back as *Alcilia Philoparthens Loving Folly* (1613).

5 Without justice courage is weak.

Poor Richard's Almanack, Jan. 1734

6 Blame-all and praise-all are two blockheads.

Poor Richard's Almanack, Feb. 1734

7 Lawyers, Preachers, and Tomtits Eggs, there are more of them hatch'd than come to perfection.

Poor Richard's Almanack, May 1734

8 He does not possess wealth; it possesses him.

Poor Richard's Almanack, Oct. 1734

9 Avarice and happiness never saw each other.

Poor Richard's Almanack, Nov. 1734

10 A little house well filled, a little field well tilled, and a little wife well willed are great riches.

Poor Richard's Almanack, Feb. 1735

11 Necessity never made a good bargain.

Poor Richard's Almanack, Apr. 1735

12 Opportunity is the great bawd.

Poor Richard's Almanack, Sept. 1735

13 Here comes the orator with his flood of words and his drop of reason.

Poor Richard's Almanack, Oct. 1735

14 Certainlie these things agree,
The Priest, the Lawyer, and Death all three:
Death takes both the weak and the strong,
The Lawyer takes from both right and wrong,

And the Priest from living and dead has his
 Fee.
Poor Richard's Almanack, July 1737

15 He that falls in love with Himself, will have no
 Rivals.
Poor Richard's Almanack, May 1738

16 If you would not be forgotten, as soon as you
 are dead and rotten, either write things worth
 reading, or do things worth the writing.
Poor Richard's Almanack, May 1738

17 There are three faithful friends: an old wife, an
 old dog, and ready money.
Poor Richard's Almanack, June 1738

18 Keep your eyes wide open before marriage, half
 shut afterwards.
Poor Richard's Almanack, June 1738

19 None but the well-bred man knows how to
 confess a fault or acknowledge himself in error.
Poor Richard's Almanack, Nov. 1738

20 At 20 years of age the will reigns; at 30 the wit;
 at 40 the judgment.
Poor Richard's Almanack, June 1741

21 Many a long dispute among Divines may be
  thus abridg'd:
 It is so, It is not so, It is so, It is not so.
Poor Richard's Almanack, Nov. 1743

22 Experience keeps a dear school, yet fools will
 learn in no other.
Poor Richard's Almanack, Dec. 1743

23 8th and lastly. They are so grateful!!
 "Reasons for Preferring an Elderly Mistress" (1745)
 See Ian Fleming 9

24 Dost thou love life? Then do not squander time,
 for that's the stuff life is made of.
Poor Richard's Almanack, June 1746

25 Remember that time is money.
 Advice to a Young Tradesman (1748). Although this
 proverb is associated with Franklin, "Time is Money"
 appeared earlier in *The Free-Thinker,* 18 May 1719.
 See Hugo 6

26 All would live long, but none would be old.
Poor Richard's Almanack, Sept. 1749

27 Old Boys have their Playthings as well as Young
 Ones; the Difference is only in the Price.
Poor Richard's Almanack, Aug. 1752

28 Those who would give up essential Liberty,
 to purchase a little temporary Safety, deserve
 neither Liberty nor Safety.
 "Pennsylvania Assembly: Reply to the Governor," 11
 Nov. 1755

29 Laws *too gentle* are seldom *obeyed; too severe,*
 seldom *executed.*
Poor Richard's Almanack, May 1756

30 Work as if you were to live 100 years; pray as if
 you were to die tomorrow.
Poor Richard's Almanack, May 1757

31 Three removes is as bad as a fire.
Poor Richard's Almanack preface, May 1758

32 The grand Leap of the Whale in that Chace
 up the Fall of Niagara is esteemed by all who
 have seen it, as one of the finest Spectacles in
 Nature!
 Letter, *The Public Advertiser,* 22 May 1765. This letter
 was intended to poke fun at British ignorance of
 America.

33 Rebellion to tyrants is obedience to God.
 Pennsylvania Evening Post, 14 Dec. 1775

34 We must all hang together, or most assuredly
 we shall all *hang separately.*
 Attributed remark at signing of Declaration of
 Independence, Philadelphia, 4 July 1776. The earliest
 known explicit attribution to Franklin was in the
 Jamestown (N.Y.) *Journal,* 30 Nov. 1836 (quoting the
 Rochester Daily Advertiser). Carter Braxton, a delegate
 to the Continental Congress, wrote in a letter to
 Landon Carter, 14 Apr. 1776: "It is a true saying of a
 Wit—We must hang together or separately." "A Wit"
 may have been a reference to Franklin.

35 There never was a good War, or a bad Peace.
 Letter to Joseph Banks, 27 July 1783

36 I wish the bald eagle had not been chosen
 as the representative of our country. . . . The
 turkey . . . is a much more respectable bird.
 Letter to Sarah Bache, 26 Jan. 1784

37 That it is better 100 guilty Persons should
 escape than that one innocent Person should
 suffer, is a Maxim that has been long and
 generally approved.
 Letter to Benjamin Vaughan, 14 Mar. 1785
 See Blackstone 7; Fortescue 1; Maimonides 1; Voltaire 3

38 Painters had found it difficult to distinguish
 in their art a rising from a setting sun. I have
 often and often in the course of the Session

[of the Constitutional Convention], and the vicissitudes of my hopes and fears as to its issue, looked at that [sun painted] behind the [chair of the] President without being able to tell whether it was rising or setting: but now at length I have the happiness to know that it is a rising and not a setting Sun.

Remarks upon the signing of the Constitution, Philadelphia, Pa., 17 Sept. 1787

39 Human Felicity is produc'd not so much by great Pieces of good Fortune that seldom happen, as by little Advantages that occur every Day.

Autobiography pt. 3 (written 1788)

40 The King of France's Picture set with Four hundred and Eight Diamonds, I give to my Daughter Sarah Bache requesting however that she would not form any of those Diamonds into Ornaments either for herself or Daughters and thereby introduce or countenance the expensive vain and useless Fashion of wearing Jewels in this Country.

Last Will and Testament, 17 July 1788

41 Our new Constitution is now established, and has an appearance that promises permanency; but in this world nothing can be said to be certain, except death and taxes.

Letter to Jean Baptiste Le Roy, 13 Nov. 1789
See Margaret Mitchell 6; Proverbs 63

42 [*Responding to skepticism about the usefulness of the first balloon flights:*] What good is a new-born baby?

Quoted in Frédéric-Melchior von Grimm, *Correspondance Littéraire* (1783)

43 Man is a tool-making animal.

Quoted in James Boswell, *Life of Samuel Johnson* (1791) (entry for 7 Apr. 1778)

44 [*After the conclusion of the Constitutional Convention, when asked by a woman, "Well, Doctor, what have we got, a republic or a monarchy?":*] A republic, if you can keep it.

Quoted in *American Historical Review*, Apr. 1906. The 1906 occurrence is taken from an anecdote about Franklin in the undated notes Constitutional Convention delegate James McHenry. Barry Popik has found an article from the *Republican, or Anti-Democrat* (Baltimore, Md.), 15 July 1803, quoting Franklin as saying "A republic, Madam, if you can keep it."

Rosalind E. Franklin
English biophysicist, 1920–1958

1 The results suggest a helical structure [of DNA] (which must be very closely packed) containing probably 2, 3, or 4 coaxial nucleic acid chains per helical unit and having the phosphate groups near the outside.

"Official Report," Feb. 1952

2 Conclusion: Big helix in several chains, phosphates on outside, phosphate-phosphate inter-helical bonds disrupted by water. Phosphate links available to proteins.

Lecture notes, 7 Feb. 1952

Stella Maria Miles Franklin
Australian novelist, 1879–1954

1 MY DEAR FELLOW AUSTRALIANS,
Just a few lines to tell you that this story is all about myself—for no other purpose do I write it.
   I make no apologies for being egotistical.

My Brilliant Career preface (1901)

2 Weariness! Weariness! This was life—my life— my career, my brilliant career! I was fifteen— fifteen! A few fleeting hours and I would be as old as those around me.

My Brilliant Career ch. 5 (1901)

3 I am proud that I am an Australian, a daughter of the Southern Cross, a child of the mighty bush. I am thankful I am a peasant, a part of the bone and muscle of my nation, and earn my bread by the sweat of my brow, as man was meant to do. I rejoice I was not born a parasite, one of the blood-suckers who loll on velvet and satin, crushed from the proceeds of human sweat and blood and souls.

My Brilliant Career ch. 38 (1901)

4 Judging by the few descendants from convicts in Australia to-day, most of the eighty-two thousand who came here must have been barren.

Pioneers on Parade (1939). Coauthored with Dymphna Cusack.

Jonathan Franzen
U.S. writer, 1959–

1 The madness of an autumn prairie cold front coming through. You could feel it: something terrible was going to happen. The sun low in the sky, a minor light, a cooling star. Gust after gust of disorder. Trees restless, temperatures falling, the whole northern religion of things coming to an end.
The Corrections (2001)

2 The human species was given dominion over the earth and took the opportunity to exterminate other species and warm the atmosphere and generally ruin things in its own image, but it paid this price for its privileges: that the finite and specific animal body of this species contained a brain capable of conceiving the infinite and wishing to be infinite itself.
The Corrections (2001)

3 She was seventy-five and she was going to make some changes in her life.
The Corrections (2001)

Malcolm Fraser
Australian prime minister, 1930–2015

1 Life is not meant to be easy.
Alfred Deakin Lecture, Melbourne, Australia, 20 July 1971. Although now associated with Fraser, this was also used earlier as a proverb going back at least to the nineteenth century.

James George Frazer
Scottish anthropologist, 1854–1941

1 The awe and dread with which the untutored savage contemplates his mother-in-law are amongst the most familiar facts of anthropology.
The Golden Bough ch. 18 (1922)

Charles Frazier
U.S. novelist, 1950–

1 Marrying a woman for her beauty makes no more sense than eating a bird for its singing. But it's a common mistake nonetheless.
Cold Mountain (1997)

Frederick the Great
Prussian king, 1712–1786

1 God is always with the strongest battalions.
Letter to Duchess Louise Dorothea von Gotha, 8 May 1760
See Bussy-Rabutin 1; Tacitus 3; Turenne 1

2 An army marches on its stomach.
Quoted in Thomas Carlyle, *History of Friedrich II. of Prussia* vol. 1, bk. 2, ch. 6 (1858). Carlyle's exact wording was actually "Leaders did not know then, as our little Friend at Berlin came to know, that 'an Army, like a serpent, goes upon its *belly*.'" Contemporary readers took the last nine words as belonging to Frederick. The proverb is now frequently attributed to Napoleon, but the earliest references to him using it began in 1862, and unambiguous internal evidence in Carlyle's book pointed to Frederick.

3 [*Exhortation to wavering troops, Kolin, 18 June 1757:*] *Hunde, wollt ihr ewig leben?*
Dogs, would you live forever?
Attributed in Bon Louis Henri Martin, *Histoire de France* (1865). According to Burton E. Stevenson, *Home Book of Quotations,* "Carlyle in his *Frederick the Great* (Bk. xviii, ch. 4) says this 'is to be counted pure myth,' but in his *French Revolution* (Pt. ii, bk. i, ch. 4) he writes, 'There were certain runaways whom Frederick the Great bullied back into the battle with a: "R——, wollt ihr ewig leben, Unprintable Offscouring of Scoundrels, would ye live forever!"' (The 'R——' perhaps for *Rindviehe* [cattle]) The phrase has been common to all wars."

Arthur Freed
U.S. songwriter and producer, 1894–1973

1 Singin' in the rain,
Just singin' in the rain.
What a glorious feeling,
I'm happy again.
I'm laughing at clouds
So dark up above,
The sun's in my heart
And I'm ready for love.
"Singin' in the Rain" (song) (1928)

Max C. Freedman
U.S. songwriter, ca. 1889–1962

1 One, two, three o'clock, four o'clock rock
Five, six, seven o'clock, eight o'clock rock
Nine, ten, eleven o'clock, twelve o'clock rock
We're gonna rock around the clock tonight.
"Rock Around the Clock" (song) (1953). Cowritten with Jimmy De Knight.

Marilyn French

U.S. author, 1929–2009

1 "I hate discussions of feminism that end up with who does the dishes," she said. So do I. But at the end, there are always the damned dishes.

The Women's Room ch. 1 (1977)

2 Whatever they may be in public life, whatever their relations with men, in their relations with women, all men are rapists, and that's all they are. They rape us with their eyes, their laws, and their codes.

The Women's Room ch. 5 (1977)

Clement Freud

German-born English broadcaster and politician, 1924–2009

1 If you resolve to give up smoking, drinking, and loving, you don't actually live longer; it just seems longer.

Quoted in *Observer* (London), 27 Dec. 1964. In the motion picture *Mr. Moto's Last Warning* (1939), Fabian, a ventriloquist played by Ricardo Cortez, says to his dummy, Alf: "Alf, you shouldn't belittle matrimony. Married men live longer than single ones." Alf responds: "Ha ha. It only seems longer."

Sigmund Freud

Austrian psychiatrist, 1856–1939

1 We have seen that hysterical symptoms immediately and permanently disappeared when we had succeeded in bringing clearly to light the memory of the event by which they were provoked and in arousing their accompanying affect, and when the patient had

described that event in the greatest possible detail and had put the affect into words. . . . Hysterics suffer mainly from reminiscences.

Studies on Hysteria ch. 3, sec. 4 (1893–1895). Coauthored with Josef Breuer.

2 I am inclined to suppose that children cannot find their way to acts of sexual aggression unless they have been seduced previously. The foundation for a neurosis would accordingly always be laid in childhood by adults.

"Heredity and the Aetiology of the Neuroses" (1896)

3 I owe my results to a new method of psycho-analysis, Josef Breuer's exploratory procedure; it is a little intricate, but irreplaceable, so fertile has it shown itself to be in throwing light upon the obscure unconscious mental processes.

"Heredity and the Aetiology of the Neuroses" (1896). First published appearance of the term *psycho-analysis.*

4 Being in love with the one parent and hating the other are among the essential constituents of the stock of psychical impulses which is formed at that time and which is of such importance in determining the symptoms of the later neurosis. . . . This discovery is confirmed by a legend that has come down to us from classical antiquity. . . . What I have in mind is the legend of King Oedipus.

The Interpretation of Dreams ch. 5 (1900)

5 I am actually not at all a man of science, not an observer, nor an experimenter, not a thinker. I am by temperament nothing but a conquistador—an adventurer . . . with all the curiosity, daring, and tenacity characteristic of a man of this sort.

Letter to Wilhelm Fliess, 1 Feb. 1900

6 The interpretation of dreams is the royal road to a knowledge of the unconscious activities of the mind.

The Interpretation of Dreams 2nd ed., ch. 7 (1909)

7 The individual's mental development repeats the course of human development in an abbreviated form.

Leonardo da Vinci pt. 3 (1910)
See Haeckel 1

8 The excremental is all too intimately and inseparably bound up with the sexual; the

position of the genitals—*inter urinas et faeces*—remains the decisive and unchangeable factor. One might say here, varying a well-known saying of the great Napoleon: "Anatomy is destiny."

"On the Universal Tendency to Debasement in the Sphere of Love" (1912). According to *Social Science Quotations*, ed. David L. Sills and Robert K. Merton, Freud's reference is "from a 1808 conversation with Goethe, whose report, written in German, was that Napoleon had said '*Die Politik ist das Schicksal*' (Politics is fate)."
See Napoleon 13

9 At bottom God is nothing other than an exalted father.
Totem and Taboo ch. 4 (1913)

10 If a man has been his mother's undisputed darling he retains throughout life the triumphant feeling, the confidence in success, which not seldom brings actual success along with it.
"A Childhood Recollection from *Dichtung und Wahrheit*" (1917)

11 The ego is not master in its own house.
"A Difficulty in the Path of Psycho-Analysis" (1917)

12 We know less about the sexual life of little girls than of boys. But we need not feel ashamed of this distinction: after all, the sexual life of adult women is a "dark continent" for psychology.
The Question of Lay Analysis pt. 4 (1926)

13 Before the problem of the artist, analysis must, alas, lay down its arms.
"Dostoyevsky and Parricide" (1928)

14 The ego's relation to the id might be compared with that of a rider to his horse. The horse supplies the locomotive energy, while the rider has the privilege of deciding on the goal and of guiding the powerful animal's movement. But only too often there arises between the ego and the id the not precisely ideal situation of the rider being obliged to guide the horse along the path by which it itself wants to go.
New Introductory Lectures on Psycho-analysis Lecture 31 (1933)

15 The poor ego . . . serves three severe masters and does what it can to bring their claims and demands into harmony with one another. . . .

Its three tyrannical masters are the external world, the super-ego, and the id.
New Introductory Lectures on Psycho-analysis Lecture 31 (1933)

16 Where id was, there ego shall be.
New Introductory Lectures on Psycho-analysis Lecture 31 (1933)

17 Homosexuality is assuredly no advantage, but it is nothing to be ashamed of, no vice, no degradation; it cannot be classified as an illness; we consider it to be a variation of the sexual function, produced by a certain arrest of sexual development. . . . It is a great injustice to persecute homosexuality as a crime—and a cruelty, too.
Letter to an American mother, 9 Apr. 1935

18 Intolerance of groups is often, strangely enough, exhibited more strongly against small differences than against fundamental ones.
Moses and Monotheism ch. 3, pt. 1 (1938)

19 Judaism had been a religion of the father; Christianity became a religion of the son. The old God the Father fell back behind Christ; Christ, the Son, took his place, just as every son had hoped to do in primeval times.
Moses and Monotheism ch. 3, pt. 1 (1938)

20 [*Remark on the occasion of his seventieth birthday:*] The poets and philosophers before me discovered the unconscious. . . . What I discovered was the scientific method by which the unconscious can be studied.
Quoted in Philip R. Lehrman, "Freud's Contributions to Science," *Harofe Haivri* (1940)

21 [*Remark to Marie Bonaparte, 8 Dec. 1925:*] The great question that has never been answered and which I have not yet been able to answer, despite my thirty years of research into the feminine soul, is "What does a woman want?"
Quoted in Ernest Jones, *The Life and Work of Sigmund Freud* (1955). In a footnote Jones gives the original German, "*Was will das Weib?*"

22 Yes, America is gigantic, but a gigantic mistake.
Quoted in Ernest Jones, *Memories of a Psycho-analyst* (1959)

23 Freud was once asked what he thought a normal person should be able to do well. The questioner probably expected a complicated

answer. But Freud, in the curt way of his old days, is reported to have said: "Lieben und arbeiten" (to love and to work).

Reported in Erik Erikson, *Childhood and Society* (1950). In *Civilization and Its Discontents* (1930), Freud wrote: "The communal life of human beings had, therefore, a two-fold foundation: the compulsion to work, which was created by external necessity, and the power of love."

24 Sometimes a cigar is just a cigar.

Attributed in *Law and Contemporary Problems,* Autumn 1954. In the slightly different form "A cigar is sometimes just a cigar," this was attributed to Freud in the journal *Psychiatry,* May 1950.

Marvin V. Frey

U.S. clergyman, 1918–1992

1 Come by here, my Lord,
Come by here.

"Come By Here" (song) (ca. 1935). Became well-known under the Angolan name "Kum Ba Yah."

Betty Friedan

U.S. feminist and author, 1921–2006

1 It was a strange stirring, a sense of dissatisfaction, a yearning that women suffered in the middle of the twentieth century in the United States. Each suburban wife struggled with it alone. As she made the beds, shopped for groceries, matched slipcover material, ate peanut butter sandwiches with her children, chauffeured Cub Scouts and Brownies, lay beside her husband at night—she was afraid to ask even of herself the silent question—"Is this all?"

The Feminine Mystique ch. 1 (1963)

2 The problem that has no name—which is simply the fact that American women are kept from growing to their full human capacities—is taking a far greater toll on the physical and mental health of our country than any known disease.

The Feminine Mystique ch. 14 (1963)

3 I think the energy locked up in . . . obsolete masculine and feminine roles is the social equivalent of the physical energy locked up in the realm of $e = mc^2$—the force that unleashed the holocaust of Hiroshima. I believe the locked-up sexual energies have helped to fuel,

more than anyone realizes, the terrible violence erupting in the nation and the world during these past ten years. If I am right, the sex-role revolution will liberate these energies from the service of death and will make it really possible for men and women to "make love, not war."

The Feminine Mystique epilogue (1983 edition)

Milton Friedman

U.S. economist, 1912–2006

1 History suggests only that capitalism is a necessary condition for political freedom. Clearly it is not a sufficient condition.

Capitalism and Freedom ch. 1 (1962)

2 Freedom in economic arrangements is itself a component of freedom broadly understood, so economic freedom is an end in itself. . . . Economic freedom is also an indispensable means toward the achievement of political freedom.

Capitalism and Freedom ch. 1 (1962)

3 A minimum-wage law is, in reality, a law that makes it illegal for an employer to hire a person with limited skills.

Interview, *Playboy,* Feb. 1973

4 Even the most ardent environmentalist doesn't really want to stop pollution. If he thinks about it, and doesn't just talk about it, he wants to have the *right amount* of pollution. We can't really *afford* to eliminate it—not without abandoning all the benefits of technology that we not only enjoy but on which we depend.

There's No Such Thing as a Free Lunch introduction (1975)

5 A society that puts equality—in the sense of equality of outcome—ahead of freedom will end up with neither equality nor freedom.

Free to Choose ch. 5 (1980). Coauthored with Rose Friedman.

6 We are all Keynesians now.

Quoted in *Time,* 31 Dec. 1965. Friedman popularized this saying, but it can be found earlier in the economics literature, for example in *American Economic Review,* May 1957.
See Harcourt 1

7 Inflation is the one form of taxation which can be imposed without any legislative action.

Quoted in *Challenge,* Nov.–Dec. 1973

8 Nothing is so permanent as a temporary
government program.

Quoted in *Cleveland Plain Dealer,* 27 Oct. 1993.
Although this line is now associated with Friedman,
Utah senator Wallace F. Bennett is recorded in
January 1964 hearings titled "Periodic Congressional
Review of Federal Grants-in-Aid" as stating: "It is an
age-old Washington axiom that there is nothing so
permanent as a temporary Government program."

Thomas L. Friedman

U.S. journalist and author, 1953–

1 No two countries that both have a McDonald's
have ever fought a war against each other.

N.Y. Times, 8 Dec. 1996

Max Frisch

Swiss novelist and playwright, 1911–1991

1 Technology . . . the knack of so arranging the
world that we need not experience it.

Homo Faber pt. 2 (1957)

William Harrison "Bill" Frist

U.S. politician and surgeon, 1952–

1 I can play hardball as well as anybody. That's
what I did, cut people's hearts out.

Quoted in *N.Y. Times,* 2 Feb. 2005

Lefty Frizzell

U.S. country singer, 1928–1975

1 If You've Got the Money, I've Got the Time.

Title of song (1950)

Charles Frohman

U.S. theatrical producer, 1860–1915

1 [*"Last words" before the sinking of the* Lusitania,
7 May 1915:] Why fear death? It is the most
beautiful adventure in life.

Quoted in Isaac F. Marcosson and Daniel Frohman,
Charles Frohman: Manager and Man (1916)
See Barrie 9

Robert Frost

U.S. poet, 1874–1963

1 "Home is the place where, when you have to go
there,
They have to take you in."

"I should have called it
Something you somehow haven't to deserve."
"The Death of the Hired Man" l. 121 (1914)

2 Something there is that doesn't love a wall.
"Mending Wall" l. 1 (1914)

3 My apple trees will never get across
And eat the cones under his pines, I tell him.
He only says, "Good fences make good
neighbors."
"Mending Wall" l. 25 (1914)
See Proverbs 125

4 Before I built a wall I'd ask to know
What I was walling in or walling out,
And to whom I was like to give offense.
Something there is that doesn't love a wall, that
wants it down.
"Mending Wall" l. 32 (1914)

5   I see him there
Bringing a stone grasped firmly by the top
In each hand, like an old-stone savage armed.
"Mending Wall" l. 38 (1914)

6 I'd like to get away from earth awhile
And then come back to it and begin over.
May no fate willfully misunderstand me
And half grant what I wish and snatch me away
Not to return.
"Birches" l. 48 (1916)

7 One could do worse than be a swinger of birches.
"Birches" l. 59 (1916)

8 Two roads diverged in a yellow wood.
"The Road Not Taken" l. 1 (1916)

9 I shall be telling this with a sigh
Somewhere ages and ages hence:
Two roads diverged in a wood, and I—
I took the one less traveled by,
And that has made all the difference.
"The Road Not Taken" l. 16 (1916)

10 Some say the world will end in fire,
Some say in ice.
"Fire and Ice" l. 1 (1923)

11 From what I've tasted of desire
I hold with those who favor fire.
"Fire and Ice" l. 3 (1923)

12 But if it had to perish twice,
I think I know enough of hate
To say that for destruction ice
Is also great
And would suffice.
"Fire and Ice" l. 5 (1923)

13 I met a Californian who would
Talk California—a state so blessed,
He said, in climate, none had ever died there
A natural death.
"New Hampshire" l. 16 (1923)

14 Whose woods these are I think I know.
His house is in the village, though;
He will not see me stopping here
To watch his woods fill up with snow.
"Stopping by Woods on a Snowy Evening" l. 1 (1923)

15 My little horse must think it queer
To stop without a farmhouse near.
"Stopping by Woods on a Snowy Evening" l. 5 (1923)

16 The woods are lovely, dark, and deep.
But I have promises to keep,
And miles to go before I sleep,
And miles to go before I sleep.
"Stopping by Woods on a Snowy Evening" l. 13 (1923)

17 I have been one acquainted with the night.
I have walked out in rain—and back in rain.
I have outwalked the furthest city light.
"Acquainted with the Night" l. 1 (1928)

18 Writing free verse is like playing tennis with
the net down.
Address to Milton Academy, Milton, Mass., 17 May
1935

19 I never dared be radical when young
For fear it would make me conservative when
old.
"Precaution" l. 1 (1936)

20 The figure a poem makes. It begins in delight
and ends in wisdom . . . in a clarification of
life—not necessarily a great clarification, such
as sects and cults are founded on, but in a
momentary stay against confusion.
Collected Poems preface (1939)

21 The land was ours before we were the land's.
She was our land more than a hundred years
Before we were her people.
"The Gift Outright" l. 1 (1942). Frost recited
this poem from memory at John F. Kennedy's
inauguration, 20 Jan. 1961, after wind prevented him
from reading his prepared text.

22 Such as we were we gave ourselves outright
(The deed of gift was many deeds of war)
To the land vaguely realizing westward,
But still unstoried, artless, unenhanced,
Such as she was, such as she would become.
"The Gift Outright" l. 12 (1942)

23 And were an epitaph to be my story
I'd have a short one ready for my own.
I would have written of me on my stone:
I had a lover's quarrel with the world.
"The Lesson for Today" l. 158 (1942)

24 Happiness Makes Up in Height for What It
Lacks in Length.
Title of poem (1942)

25 Poetry is what is lost in translation. It is also
what is lost in interpretation.
Quoted in Louis Untermeyer, *Robert Frost: A
Backward Look* (1964)

Christopher Fry
English playwright, 1907–2005

1 The Lady's Not for Burning.
Title of play (1949)
See Thatcher 4

Roger Fry
English critic, 1866–1934

1 Art is significant deformity.
Quoted in Virginia Woolf, *Roger Fry* (1940)

Mary Elizabeth Frye
U.S. poet, 1904–2004

1 Do not stand at my grave and weep,
  I am not there, I do not sleep.
  "Do Not Stand at My Grave and Weep" l. 1 (1932)

2 Do not stand at my grave and cry,
  I am not there—I do not die.
  "Do Not Stand at My Grave and Weep" l. 15 (1932).
  Later versions of the poem usually read "I did not
  die."

Mitsuo Fuchida
Japanese pilot, 1902–1976

1 [*Code words signaling the success of the Japanese
  attack on Pearl Harbor, 7 Dec. 1941:*] *Tora-tora-
  tora.*
  Quoted in *United States Naval Institute Proceedings,*
  Sept. 1952. *Tora* is Japanese for "tiger."

Carlos Fuentes
Mexican writer, 1928–2012

1 What America does best is to understand itself.
  What it does worst is to understand others.
  Quoted in *Time,* 16 June 1986

Francis Fukuyama
U.S. political theorist, 1953–

1 What we may be witnessing is not the end of
  the Cold War but the end of history as such;
  that is, the end point of man's ideological
  evolution and the universalization of Western
  liberal democracy.
  "The End of History?" *National Interest,* Summer
  1989
  See Sellar 3; Sellar 4

J. William Fulbright
U.S. politician, 1905–1995

1 The attitude above all others which I feel sure
  is no longer valid is the arrogance of power,
  the tendency of great nations to equate power
  with virtue and major responsibilities with a
  universal mission.
  The Arrogance of Power introduction (1967)

Robert Fulghum
U.S. author, 1937–

1 Share everything. Play fair. Don't hit people.
  Put things back where you found them. Clean
  up your own mess. Don't take things that
  aren't yours. Say you're sorry when you hurt
  somebody. Wash your hands before you eat.
  Flush. Warm cookies and cold milk are good
  for you. Live a balanced life—learn some and
  think some and draw and paint and sing and
  dance and play and work every day some.
  All I Really Need to Know I Learned in Kindergarten
  (1988)

"Blind Boy" Fuller (Fulton Allen)
U.S. blues musician, 1907–1941

1 Keep on truckin'.
  "Truckin' My Blues Away" (song) (1936)

Margaret Fuller
U.S. critic and reformer, 1810–1850

1 I myself am more divine than any I see.
  Letter to Ralph Waldo Emerson, 1 Mar. 1838

2 I now know all the people worth knowing in
  America, and I find no intellect comparable to
  my own.
  Quoted in *Memoirs of Margaret Fuller Ossoli,* ed. Ralph
  Waldo Emerson, William Henry Channing, and
  James Freeman Clarke (1852)

3 [*Remark to Henry James, Sr., Sept. 1843:*] I accept
  the universe.
  Quoted in *Daily Inter Ocean* (Chicago), 11 Mar. 1893
  See Thomas Carlyle 20

R. Buckminster Fuller
U.S. designer and architect, 1895–1983

1 Here is God's purpose—
  for God, to me, it seems,
  is a verb
  not a noun.
  No More Secondhand God (1963, written 1940).
  See Ulysses S. Grant 6; Hugo 5

2 For at least 2,000,000 years men have been
  reproducing and multiplying on a little
  automated spaceship called earth.
  "The Prospect for Humanity," *Saturday Review,* 29
  Aug. 1964

3 Synergy means
  Behavior of whole systems
  Unpredicted by
  The behavior of their parts.
  What I Have Learned "How Little I Know" (1968)

4 Now there is one outstandingly important fact
  regarding Spaceship Earth, and that is that no
  instruction book came with it.
  Operating Manual for Spaceship Earth ch. 4 (1969)

5 Either war is obsolete or men are.
  Quoted in *New Yorker*, 8 Jan. 1966

Ralph Fuller

U.S. cartoonist, 1890–1963

1 [*Caption of cartoon showing signalmen watching
  two trains about to collide:*] Tch, tch! What a way
  to run a railroad!
  Ballyhoo, June 1932

Thomas Fuller

English writer and physician, 1654–1734

1 Be you never so high the law is above you.
  Gnomologia (1752)

Rose Fyleman

English children's writer, 1877–1957

1 There are fairies at the bottom of our garden!
  "Fairies" l. 1 (1918)

Zsa Zsa Gabor
Hungarian-born U.S. actress, 1917–2016

1 I never hated a man enough to give him
diamonds back.
Quoted in *Observer* (London), 28 Aug. 1957

2 A man in love is incomplete until he has
married—and then he's finished.
Quoted in *Newsweek,* 28 Mar. 1960

3 Husbands are like fires. They go out when
unattended.
Quoted in *Newsweek,* 28 Mar. 1960

4 [*When asked how many husbands she had had:*]
You mean apart from my own?
Quoted in Kenneth Edwards, *I Wish I'd Said That!*
(1976)

William Gaddis
U.S. novelist, 1922–1998

1 What is it they want from a man that they didn't
get from his work? What do they expect? What
is there left of him when he's done his work?
What's any artist, but the dregs of his work? the
human shambles that follows it around.
The Recognitions pt. 1, ch. 3 (1955)

2 Money . . . ? in a voice that rustled.
JR (1975)

3 You get justice in the next world, in this world
you have the law.
A Frolic of His Own (1994)

Yuri Gagarin
Russian cosmonaut, 1934–1968

1 Let's go!
Radio communication at moment of launch of
the first space flight, Baikonur Cosmodrome,
Kazakhstan, 12 Apr. 1961

Neil Gaiman
English writer, 1960–

1 Google can bring you back, you know, a
hundred thousand answers. A librarian can
bring you back the right one.
McFadden Memorial Lecture, Indianapolis, Ind., 16
Apr. 2010

Ernest J. Gaines
U.S. writer, 1933–2019

1 What justice would there be to take this life?
Justice, gentlemen? Why, I would just as soon
put a hog in the electric chair as this.
A Lesson Before Dying ch. 1 (1994)

2 Good by mr wigin tell them im strong tell them
im a man.
A Lesson Before Dying ch. 29 (1994)

John Kenneth Galbraith
Canadian-born U.S. economist, 1908–2006

1 The Affluent Society.
Title of book (1958)

2 It will be convenient to have a name for the
ideas which are esteemed at any time for their
acceptability, and it should be a term that
emphasizes this predictability. I shall refer
to these ideas henceforth as the conventional
wisdom.
The Affluent Society ch. 2 (1958)

3 The leisure class has been replaced by another
and much larger class to which work has none
of the older connotation of pain, fatigue, or
other mental or physical discomfort. We have
failed to observe the emergence of this New
Class, as it may be simply called.
The Affluent Society ch. 24 (1958)

4 Much of the world's work, it has been said, is
done by men who do not feel quite well. Marx
is a case in point.
The Age of Uncertainty ch. 3 (1977)

5 The salary of the chief executive of the large corporation is not a market reward for achievement. It is frequently in the nature of a warm personal gesture by the individual to himself.

Annals of an Abiding Liberal ch. 6 (1979)

6 Trickle-down theory—the less than elegant metaphor that if one feeds the horse enough oats, some will pass through to the road for the sparrows.

The Culture of Contentment ch. 8 (1992)

Galen

Greek physician and writer, 129–199

1 That which *is* grows, while that which *is not* becomes.

On the Natural Faculties bk. 2, sec. 3

Tony "Two-Ton" Galento

U.S. boxer, 1910–1979

1 [*Remark to his manager Joe Jacobs before his losing heavyweight championship fight against Joe Louis, 1939:*] I'll moider that bum!

Quoted in Joe Louis, *My Life Story* (1947)

Galileo Galilei

Italian astronomer and physicist, 1564–1642

1 I do not feel obliged to believe that that same God who has endowed us with senses, reason, and intellect has intended to forgo their use and by some other means to give us knowledge which we can attain by them.

Letter to Madame Christina of Lorraine, Grand Duchess of Tuscany, 1615

2 Philosophy is written in this grand book, the universe, which stands continually open to our gaze. . . . It is written in the language of mathematics, and its characters are triangles, circles, and other geometric figures without which . . . one wanders about in a dark labyrinth.

The Assayer (1623) (translation by Stillman Drake)

3 Desiring to remove from the minds of Your Eminences, and of all faithful Christians, this vehement suspicion rightly conceived against me, with sincere heart and unpretended faith I abjure, curse, and detest the aforesaid errors and heresies . . . and I swear that in the future I will never again say or assert verbally or in writing, anything that might cause a similar suspicion toward me.

Abjuration after being sentenced for his advocacy of the Copernican system, Rome, 22 June 1633

4 [*Alleged remark after recanting his position that the earth moves around the sun, 1632:*] Eppur si muove.

And yet it does move.

Attributed in Giuseppe Baretti, *The Italian Library* (1757). Stillman Drake writes in *The Discoveries and Opinions of Galileo* (1957): "It is curious that this famous story should have first appeared so late and in an English book. . . . [Most serious writers rejected] the whole story as a myth created to fit Galileo's personality rather than the truth. But in 1911 the same Italian words . . . were discovered on a painting attributed to Murillo and dating no more than a decade after Galileo's death."

George H. Gallup

U.S. pollster, 1901–1984

1 I could prove God statistically. Take the human body—the chance that all functions of the individual would just happen is a statistical monstrosity.

Quoted in *Reader's Digest,* Oct. 1943

John Galsworthy

English novelist, 1867–1933

1 Nobody tells me anything.

The Man of Property pt. 1, ch. 1 (1906)

2 He [old Jolyon] had always had a contempt for the place [his Club], having joined it many years ago when they refused to have him at the "Hotch Potch" owing to his being "in trade." As if he were not as good as any of them! He naturally despised the Club that *did* take him.

The Man of Property pt. 1, ch. 2 (1906)
See Benchley 11; Joe E. Lewis 1; Lincoln 2; Groucho Marx 41; Twain 4

Francis Galton

English statistician and psychologist, 1822–1911

1 The phrase "nature and nurture" is a convenient jingle of words, for it separates under two distinct heads the innumerable elements of which personality is composed.

English Men of Science: Their Nature and Nurture ch. 1 (1874)

2 We greatly want a brief word to express the science of improving stock, which is by no means confined to questions of judicious mating, but which, especially in the case of man, takes cognizance of all influences that tend in however remote a degree to give to the more suitable races or strains of blood a better chance of prevailing speedily over the less suitable than they otherwise would have had. The word *eugenics* would sufficiently express the idea.

Inquiries into Human Faculty and Its Development (1883)

Indira Gandhi

Indian prime minister, 1917–1984

1 I am proud that I spent the whole of my life in the service of my people. . . . I shall continue to serve until my last breath and when I die, I can say, that every drop of my blood will invigorate India and strengthen it.

Speech, Bhubaneshwar, India, 30 Oct. 1984. Gandhi was assassinated the day after this speech.

Mohandas Karamchand (Mahatma) Gandhi

Indian nationalist and spiritual leader, 1869–1948

1 Satyagraha largely appears to the public as Civil Disobedience or Civil Resistance. It is civil in the sense that it is not criminal. . . . [The civil resister] considers certain laws to be so unjust as to render obedience to them a dishonor. He then openly and civilly breaks them and quietly suffers the penalty for their breach.

Young India, 14 Jan. 1920

2 Non-violence is the first article of my faith. It is also the last article of my creed.

Defense against charge of sedition, Shahi Bag, India, 18 Mar. 1922

3 Noncooperation with evil is as much a duty as is cooperation with good. But in the past, noncooperation has been deliberately expressed in violence to the evildoer. I am endeavoring to show to my countrymen that violent noncooperation only multiplies evil and that evil can only be sustained by violence,

withdrawal of support of evil requires complete abstention from violence.

Courtroom statement, Ahmadabad, India, 23 Mar. 1922

4 I am an uncompromising opponent of violent methods even to serve the noblest of causes.

Young India, 11 Dec. 1924

5 "Hate the sin and not the sinner" is a precept which, though easy enough to understand, is rarely practised, and that is why the poison of hatred spreads in the world.

An Autobiography: The Story of My Experiments with Truth pt. 4, ch. 9 (1929)
See Augustine 5

6 [*Upon being asked what he thought of Western civilization:*] It would be a good idea.

Quoted in CBS News television special, 17 Jan. 1967

7 You must be the change you want to see in the world.

Quoted in *Santa Fe New Mexican,* 22 Mar. 1987. According to the Gandhi Institute for Nonviolence, this has not been traced in Gandhi's writings but "the Gandhi family states that M. K. Gandhi was known to say this verse many times in his lifetime and believes it to be original with him." Garson O'Toole has found that Gandhi expressed a similar idea as early as 1913 in an article titled "Snake-Bite": "If we could change ourselves, the tendencies in the world would also change."

8 Whenever I despair, I remember that the way of truth and love has always won. There may be tyrants and murderers, and for a time, they may seem invincible, but in the end, they always fail. Think of it: always.

Attributed in *Gandhi* (motion picture) (1982). The Gandhi Institute for Nonviolence has been unable to find this in Gandhi's writings.

Greta Garbo (Greta Lovisa Gustafsson)

Swedish-born U.S. actress, 1905–1990

1 I want to be alone.

The Single Standard (motion picture) (1929). Listed here under Garbo's name rather than under Film Lines because it is so clearly identified with her as an actress and off-screen personality rather than with any individual movie line. Nigel Rees, *Cassell's Movie Quotations,* notes that in her 1927 silent film *Love* the words "I like to be alone" appeared as a screen title. In *The Single Standard* there was a title card reading "I am walking alone because I want to be alone." In *Grand Hotel* (1932) Garbo spoke "I want to be alone"

(the line had also appeared in Vicki Baum's 1930 play upon which that movie was based). By the early 1930s the phrase was indelibly linked with Garbo's persona, although there is no evidence of her actually saying it in "real life."
See Garbo 2

2 I never said, "I want to be alone." . . . I only said, "I want to be *let* alone." There is all the difference.
Quoted in John Bainbridge, *Garbo* (1955)
See Garbo 1

3 [*Response when Louis B. Mayer failed to meet her salary demands:*] I tank I go home.
Quoted in Norman Zierold, *Moguls* (1969)

Federico García Lorca
Spanish poet and playwright, 1899–1936

1 Green, how much I want you green.
Green wind. Green branches.
The ship upon the sea
and the horse in the mountain.
"Somnambule Ballad" (1928) (translation by Stephen Spender and Joan Gill)

2 At five in the afternoon.
Ah, that fatal five in the afternoon!
It was five by all the clocks!
It was five in the shade of the afternoon!
"The Goring and the Death" (1935) (translation by Stephen Spender and Joan Gill)

Gabriel García Márquez
Colombian novelist, 1927–2014

1 Many years later, as he faced the firing squad, Colonel Aureliano Buendia was to remember that distant afternoon when his father took him to discover ice.
One Hundred Years of Solitude (1967)

2 At that time Macondo was a village of twenty adobe houses, built on the bank of a river of clear water that ran along a bed of polished stones, which were white and enormous, like prehistoric eggs. The world was so recent that many things lacked names, and in order to indicate them it was necessary to point.
One Hundred Years of Solitude (1967)

3 Before reaching the final line, however, he had already understood that he would never leave that room, for it was foreseen that the city of

mirrors (or mirages) would be wiped out by the wind and exiled from the memory of men at the precise moment when Aureliano Babilonia would finish deciphering the parchments, and that everything written on them was unrepeatable since time immemorial and forever more, because races condemned to one hundred years of solitude did not have a second opportunity on the earth.
One Hundred Years of Solitude (1967)

4 Over the weekend the vultures got into the presidential palace by pecking through the screens on the balcony windows and the flapping of their wings stirred up the stagnant time inside, and at dawn on Monday the city awoke out of its lethargy of centuries with the warm, soft breeze of a great man dead and rotting grandeur.
The Autumn of the Patriarch (1975) (translation by Gregory Rabassa)

5 It was inevitable: the scent of bitter almonds always reminded him of the fate of unrequited love.
Love in the Time of Cholera (1985)

6 The problem with marriage is that it ends every night after making love, and it must be rebuilt every morning before breakfast.
Love in the Time of Cholera (1985)

Ava Gardner
U.S. actress, 1922–1990

1 Deep down, I'm pretty superficial.
Quoted in Roland Flamini, *Ava* (1983)

Ed Gardner
U.S. comedian, 1905–1963

1 In opera is when a guy gets stabbed in the back, instead of bleeding, he sings.
Duffy's Tavern (radio show), quoted in *Canton* (Ohio) *Repository*, 28 Nov. 1947

John Gardner
U.S. writer, 1933–1982

1 "Poor Grendel's had an accident," I whisper. "*So may you all.*"
Grendel ch. 12 (1971)

John W. Gardner

U.S. government official and activist, 1912–2002

1 We are all faced with a series of great opportunities—brilliantly disguised as insoluble problems.

Quoted in *Reader's Digest,* Mar. 1966

James A. Garfield

U.S. president, 1831–1881

1 [*Address to Williams College Alumni, New York, N.Y., 28 Dec. 1871:*] Take a log cabin in the West, put a wooden bench in it, with Mark Hopkins on one end and a student on the other, and you have a college.

Quoted in *New York Evangelist,* 17 July 1879. The earliest record, printed in the *Williams Vidette,* 27 Jan. 1872, read: "Offer him [Garfield] the finest college buildings, the largest library and the most complete physical appliances, and he would rather have Dr. Hopkins in a brick shanty than them all." A more familiar version is in a speech by John James Ingalls, ca. 1885–1890: "A pine log, with the student at one end and Doctor Hopkins at the other, would be a liberal education" (*A Collection of the Writings of John James Ingalls* [1902]).

2 [*Alleged speech calming a crowd, New York, N.Y., 17 Apr. 1865, after assassination of Lincoln:*] God reigns, and the Government at Washington still lives!

Attributed in *Bangor Daily Whig & Courier,* 29 June 1880. *Respectfully Quoted,* ed. Suzy Platt, cites Garfield biographer Theodore Clarke Smith: "Smith notes that while the tradition of this speech was so well established during Garfield's own lifetime as to become a 'familiar commonplace,' no clipping of it exists among Garfield's papers, nor did Garfield himself, so far as known, refer to it in later times." Paul F. Boller, Jr., and John George, *They Never Said It,* goes further: "It's a splendid story, but unfortunately it's not true. Garfield, an Ohio Congressman at the time, wasn't even in New York in April 1865."

Giuseppe Garibaldi

Italian patriot and military leader, 1807–1882

1 Men, I'm getting out of Rome. Anyone who wants to carry on the war against the outsiders, come with me. I can offer you neither honors nor wages; I offer you hunger, thirst, forced marches, battles, and death. Anyone who loves his country, follow me.

Attributed in Giuseppe Guerzoni, *Garibaldi* (1882)

Judy Garland (Frances Ethel Gumm)

U.S. singer and actress, 1922–1969

1 I was born at the age of twelve on a Metro-Goldwyn-Mayer lot.

Quoted in *Observer* (London), 18 Feb. 1951

Eric Garner

U.S. horticulturist, 1970–2014

1 [*Exclamation while being held by policemen, New York:*] I can't breathe!

Quoted in *N.Y. Daily News,* 18 July 2014

John Nance Garner

U.S. vice-president, 1868–1967

1 The Vice Presidency isn't worth a pitcher of warm spit.

Attributed in *L.A. Times,* 1 Apr. 1962. Garner's actual words were probably "pitcher of warm piss."

David Garrick

English actor and manager, 1717–1779

1 Heart of oak are our ships,
Heart of oak are our men:
We always are ready;
Steady, boys, steady;
We'll fight and we'll conquer again and again.

"Heart of Oak" (song) (1759)

William Lloyd Garrison

U.S. abolitionist, 1805–1879

1 I am in earnest—I will not equivocate—I will not excuse—I will not retreat a single inch—AND I WILL BE HEARD!

The Liberator, 1 Jan. 1831 (first issue)

2 Tell a man whose house is on fire to give a moderate alarm; tell him to moderately rescue his wife from the hands of the ravisher; tell the mother to gradually extricate her babe from the fire into which it has fallen; but urge me not to use moderation in a case like the present.

The Liberator, 1 Jan. 1831 (first issue)

3 I will be as harsh as truth and as uncompromising as justice. On this subject I do not wish to think, or speak, or write, with moderation.

The Liberator, 1 Jan. 1831 (first issue)

4 The compact which exists between the North and the South is "a covenant with death and an agreement with hell."

Resolution adopted by Massachusetts Anti-Slavery Society, 27 Jan. 1843. "A covenant with death and an agreement with hell" paraphrases Isaiah 28:15.

Marcus Garvey

Jamaican-born U.S. black nationalist leader, 1887–1940

1 We should say to the millions who are in Africa to hold the fort, for we are coming, four hundred million strong.

Speech at Liberty Hall, New York, N.Y., 25 Nov. 1922

2 Look Up, You Mighty Race!

Title of article, *Black Man*, Sept.–Oct. 1936

3 Day by day we hear the cry of AFRICA FOR THE AFRICANS. This cry has become a positive, determined one. It is a cry that is raised simultaneously the world over because of the universal oppression that affects the Negro.

Quoted in *The Philosophy and Opinions of Marcus Garvey* (1923)

Alicia Garza

U.S. political activist and writer, 1981–

1 Black people. I love you. I love us. Our lives matter. Black Lives Matter.

Facebook posting, July 2013. This appears to be the introduction of the slogan "Black lives matter."

Elizabeth Gaskell

English novelist, 1810–1865

1 A man . . . is *so* in the way in the house!

Cranford ch. 1 (1853)

2 I'll not listen to reason. . . . Reason always means what someone else has got to say.

Cranford ch. 14 (1853)

3 [*Of Mary Ann Evans's identity as "George Eliot," the author of* Adam Bede:] It is a noble grand book, whoever wrote it—but Miss Evans' life taken at the best construction, does so jar against the beautiful book that one cannot help hoping against hope.

Letter to George Smith, 4 Aug. 1859

4 That kind of patriotism which consists in hating all other nations.

Sylvia's Lovers ch. 1 (1863)

William H. Gass

U.S. writer, 1924–2016

1 YOU HAVE FALLEN INTO ART—RETURN TO LIFE.

Willie Masters' Lonesome Wife (1968)

Bill Gates

U.S. businessman and software engineer, 1955–

1 People often overestimate what will happen in the next two years and underestimate what will happen in ten.

The Road Ahead "Afterword" (1996). Joseph Licklider had earlier written in *Libraries of the Future* (1965), "A modern maxim says: People tend to overestimate what can be done in one year and to underestimate what can be done in five or ten years."

2 640K ought to be enough for anyone.

Attributed in *InfoWorld,* 1 Jan. 1990. This assertion about computer memory was supposedly uttered in 1981, but Gates has denied ever making such a statement. Two earlier precursor attributions to Gates appeared in *InfoWorld,* 29 Aug. 1985 ("When we set the upper limit of PC-DOS at 640K, we thought nobody would ever need that much memory.—William Gates") and *InfoWorld,* 14 Nov. 1988 ("Bill Gates once said 640K of memory was more than anyone needed").

Eleanor Gates

U.S. playwright, 1875–1951

1 You're the Poor Little Rich Girl.

The Poor Little Rich Girl act 2, sc. 1 (1912)
See Coward 2

Carl Friedrich Gauss

German mathematician, 1777–1855

1 I confess indeed that the Fermat theorem as an isolated proposition has little interest for me, since a multitude of such propositions, which one can neither prove nor refute, can be easily promulgated.

Letter to Wilhelm Olbers, 21 Mar. 1816
See Fermat 1

2 [Mathematics is] the queen of sciences.

Quoted in Sartorius von Waltershausen, *Gauss zum Gedächtniss* (1856)

Théophile Gautier
French poet and novelist, 1811–1872

1 Chance is perhaps the pseudonym of God
when he did not want to sign.
La Croix de Berny (1855)

2 *Toute passe.—L'art robuste*
Seul a l'éternité,
Le Buste
Survit à la cité.
Everything passes. Robust art
Alone is eternal,
The bust
Survives the city.
"L'Art" (1857)

Gavarni (Guillaume Sulpice Chevalier)
French caricaturist and illustrator, 1804–1866

1 *Les Enfants Terribles.*
The Terrible Children.
Title of series of prints (1842)

John Gay
English poet and playwright, 1685–1732

1 A miss for pleasure, and a wife for breed.
"The Toilette" l. 86 (1716)

2 Life is a jest; and all things show it.
I thought so once; but now I know it.
"My Own Epitaph" l. 1 (1720)

3 They'll tell thee, sailors, when away,
In ev'ry port a mistress find.
"Sweet William's Farewell to Black-Eyed Susan" l. 27
(1720)

4 I know you lawyers can, with ease,
Twist words and meanings as you please;
That language, by your skill made pliant,
Will bend to favor ev'ry client.
Fables "The Dog and the Fox" l. 1 (1738)

Marvin Gaye
U.S. singer and songwriter, 1939–1984

1 Mother, mother
There's too many of you crying
Brother, brother, brother
There's far too many of you dying.
"What's Going On" (song) (1971). Cowritten with
Renaldo Benson and Alfred Cleveland.

2 When I get that feeling,
I want some sexual healing.
"Sexual Healing" (song) (1982)

François Gayot de Pitaval
French author, 1673–1743

1 *Causes Célèbres.*
Title of series of books (1734–1743)

Eric Geddes
British politician, 1875–1937

1 The Germans, if this Government is returned,
are going to pay every penny; they are going to
be squeezed as a lemon is squeezed—until the
pips squeak.
Speech, Cambridge, England, 10 Dec. 1918

Henry Louis "Lou" Gehrig
U.S. baseball player, 1903–1941

1 Today I consider myself the luckiest man on
the face of the earth.
Farewell speech at Yankee Stadium, New York,
N.Y., 4 July 1939. Gehrig had been diagnosed with
amyotrophic lateral sclerosis, now known as "Lou
Gehrig's disease," and died two years later.

Bob Geldof
Irish rock singer, 1954–

1 Feed the world
Let them know it's Christmas time again.
"Do They Know It's Christmas?" (song) (1984).
Coauthored with Midge Ure.

Martha Gellhorn
U.S. journalist and author, 1908–1998

1 People often say, with pride, "I'm not interested
in politics." They might as well say, "I'm not
interested in my standard of living, my health,
my job, my rights, my freedoms, my future, or
any future."
"White into Black," *Granta* 10 (1984)

Genghis Khan
Mongol emperor, 1162–1227

1 [The greatest happiness is] to crush your
enemies, to see them fall at your feet—to

take their horses and goods and hear the
lamentation of their women.

Attributed in Harold Lamb, *Genghis Khan* (1927). A
version in French appears in volume 4 of *Revue des
Deux Mondes* (1843).

Arnold van Gennep
German-born French anthropologist, 1873–
1957

1 I have tried to assemble here all the ceremonial
patterns which accompany a passage from
one situation to another or from one cosmic
or social world to another. Because of the
importance of these transitions, I think it
legitimate to single out *rites of passage* as a
special category.

Rites de Passage ch. 1 (1908) (translation by Monika B.
Vizedom and Gabrielle L. Caffee)

George II
British king, 1683–1760

1 [*Response to the Duke of Newcastle, who had called
General James Wolfe a madman:*] If he is mad, I
hope to God he'll bite some of my generals.

Quoted in *New-York Magazine*, Nov. 1791. An earlier
version of this anecdote, without specific mention
of Wolfe, appeared in John Henderson, *Letters and
Poems* (1786).
See Lincoln 65

George IV
British king, 1762–1830

1 [*Replying to Sir Edmund Nagle's attempt to inform
him of the death of Napoleon:*] "Sir, your bitterest
enemy is dead."
"Is she, by God!" said the tender husband.

Reported in *Journal of Hon. Henry Edward Fox* (entry
for 25 Aug. 1821)

George V
British king, 1865–1936

1 [*Of his son, the future King Edward VIII:*] After
I am dead, the boy will ruin himself within
twelve months.

Quoted in Keith Middlemas and John Barnes,
Baldwin: A Biography (1969)

Rosemonde Gérard
French writer, 1871–1953

1 *Car, vois-tu, chaque jour je t'aime davantage,
Aujourd'hui plus qu'hier et bien moins que
demain.*

For, you see, each day I love you more,
Today more than yesterday and less than
tomorrow.

Les Pipeaux "L'Éternelle Chanson" (1889)

Hugo Gernsback
Luxembourg-born U.S. editor and inventor,
1884–1967

1 The editor of this publication [Gernsback]
addressed a number of letters to science fiction
lovers. The editor promised to pay $50.00 for
the best letter each month on the subject of
"What Science Fiction Means to Me."

Science Wonder Stories, June 1929. Gernsback here
popularized the term *science fiction*. William Wilson
had introduced it in an isolated usage in 1851, and T.
O'Conor Sloane had used the words in the magazine
Amazing Stories in 1927.
See William Wilson 1

Geronimo (Goyathlay)
Native American leader, ca. 1829–1909

1 [*Statement upon surrendering to General George
Crook, 25 Mar. 1886:*] Once I moved about like
the wind. Now I surrender to you and that is all.

Quoted in Dee Brown, *Bury My Heart at Wounded
Knee* (1970)

David Gerrold
U.S. science fiction writer, 1944–

1 You know what a virus is, don't you? . . . The
VIRUS program does the same thing.

When Harlie Was One (1972). First use of the term
virus for a maliciously designed computer program.

Ira Gershwin (Israel Gershowitz)
U.S. songwriter, 1896–1983

1 Oh lady, be good to me!
"Oh, Lady, Be Good!" (song) (1924)

2 Sweet and Low-Down.

Title of song (1925). Used earlier in Gershwin's song
"Singin' Pete," dropped from the 1924 show *Lady, Be
Good*.

3 'S wonderful! 'S marvelous—
You should care for me!
"'S Wonderful" (song) (1927)

4 Embrace me,
My sweet embraceable you.
"Embraceable You" (song) (1930)

5 I got rhythm,
I got music,
I got my man—
Who could ask for anything more?
"I Got Rhythm" (song) (1930)

6 I got plenty of nothin',
And nothin's plenty for me.
"I Got Plenty of Nothin'" (song) (1935)

7 It ain't necessarily so,
The things that you're liable
To read in the Bible,
It ain't necessarily so.
"It Ain't Necessarily So" (song) (1935)

8 You like potato and I like po-tah-to;
You like tomato and I like to-mah-to;
Potato, po-tah-to, tomato, to-mah-to—
Let's call the whole thing off!
"Let's Call the Whole Thing Off" (song) (1936)

9 Nice work if you can get it,
And you can get it if you try.
"Nice Work If You Can Get It" (song) (1937)

J. Paul Getty
U.S. business executive, 1892–1976

1 The meek shall inherit the earth—but NOT the
mineral rights.
Quoted in *Middlesboro* (Ky.) *Daily News*, 24 Apr. 1972.
Barry Popik has found a precursor in the *Titusville*
(Pa.) *Herald*, 24 Apr. 1924: "When the meek inherit
the earth they'll probably find that somebody else has
arranged for the oil leases and mineral rights."
See Bible 112; Bible 205; Heinlein 16; John M. Henry 1

2 [*Remark to reporters after his grandson had been
kidnapped and a ransom payment was demanded,
Guildford, England, 26 July 1973:*] I have 14 other
grandchildren and if I pay one penny now, I'll
have 14 other kidnapped grandchildren.
Quoted in *Minneapolis Star*, 27 July 1973

3 If you can count your money you don't have a
billion dollars.
Attributed in *Chicago Daily Tribune*, 28 Oct. 1957

Giuseppe Giacosa
Italian librettist, 1847–1906

1 *Che gelida manina, se la lasci riscaldar.*
Your tiny hand is frozen, let me warm it in my
own.
La Bohème (opera with music by Giacomo Puccini)
act 1 (1896). Cowritten with Luigi Illica.

2 *Mi chiamano Mimi ma'il mio nome è Lucia.*
They call me Mimi, but my real name is Lucia.
La Bohème (opera with music by Giacomo Puccini)
act 1 (1896). Cowritten with Luigi Illica.

3 *Vissi d'arte, vissi d'amore, non feci mai male ad
anima viva.*
I lived for art, I lived for love; never did I harm
a living soul.
Tosca (opera with music by Giacomo Puccini) act 2
(1900). Cowritten with Luigi Illica.

4 *Un bel dì, vedremo levarsi un fil di fumo sull'
estremo confin del mare, E poi la nave appare.*
He'll return one fine day, I'll see the telltale
smoke rise far above the far horizon before
his ship appears.
Madama Butterfly (opera with music by Giacomo
Puccini) act 2 (1904). Cowritten with Luigi Illica.

A. Bartlett Giamatti
U.S. university president and baseball
commissioner, 1938–1989

1 It [baseball] breaks your heart. It is designed
to break your heart. The game begins in the
spring, when everything else begins again,
and it blossoms in the summer, filling the
afternoons and evenings, and then as soon as
the chill rains come, it stops and leaves you to
face the fall alone.
"The Green Fields of the Mind," *Yale Alumni
Magazine*, Nov. 1977

2 [*Upon his appointment as president of Yale
University:*] All I ever wanted to be president of
was the American League.
Quoted in Bert Sugar, *Book of Sports Quotes* (1979)

3 Baseball has the largest library of law and lore
and custom and ritual, and therefore, in a
nation that fundamentally believes it is a nation
under law, well, baseball is America's most
privileged version of the level field.
Quoted in *Sports Illustrated*, 17 Apr. 1989

Edward Gibbon
English historian, 1737–1794

1 The Decline and Fall of the Roman Empire.
Title of book (1776)

2 The various modes of worship, which prevailed
in the Roman world, were all considered by the
people as equally true; by the philosopher, as
equally false; and by the magistrate, as equally
useful.
The Decline and Fall of the Roman Empire ch. 2
(1776–1788)

3 This long peace, and the uniform government
of the Romans, introduced a slow and secret
poison into the vitals of the empire. The minds
of men were gradually reduced to the same
level, the fire of genius was extinguished, and
even the military spirit evaporated.
The Decline and Fall of the Roman Empire ch. 2
(1776–1788)

4 His [Titus Antoninus Pius's] reign is marked
by the rare advantage of furnishing very few
materials for history, . . . the register of the
crimes, follies, and misfortunes of mankind.
The Decline and Fall of the Roman Empire ch. 3 (1776–
1788)
See Voltaire 15

5 [*Of Emperor Gordian II:*] Twenty-two
acknowledged concubines, and a library of sixty-
two thousand volumes, attested the variety of his
inclinations, and from the productions [children
and writings] which he left behind him, it
appears that the former as well as the latter were
designed for use rather than ostentation.
The Decline and Fall of the Roman Empire ch. 7
(1776–1788)

6 The pure and genuine influence of Christianity
may be traced in its beneficial, though
imperfect, effects on the Barbarian proselytes
of the North. If the decline of the Roman
empire was hastened by the conversion of
Constantine, his victorious religion broke the
violence of the fall, and mollified the ferocious
temper of the conquerors.
The Decline and Fall of the Roman Empire ch. 38
(1776–1788)

7 Experience had shewn him [Pope Gregory
the Great] the efficacy of these solemn and
pompous rites, to soothe the distress, confirm
the faith, to mitigate the fierceness, and to
dispel the dark enthusiasm of the vulgate, and
he readily forgave their tendency to promote
the reign of priesthood and superstition.
The Decline and Fall of the Roman Empire ch. 45
(1776–1788)

8 If we contrast the rapid progress of this
mischievous discovery [gunpowder] with the
slow and laborious advances of reason, science,
and the arts of peace, a philosopher, according
to his temper, will laugh or weep at the folly of
mankind.
The Decline and Fall of the Roman Empire ch. 65
(1776–1788)

9 I sighed as a lover, I obeyed as a son.
Memoirs of My Life ch. 4 (1796)

10 It was at Rome, on the 15th of October, 1764,
as I sat musing amidst the ruins of the Capitol,
while the barefoot friars were singing vespers
in the Temple of Jupiter, that the idea of writing
the decline and fall of the city first started to my
mind.
Memoirs of My Life ch. 6 (1796)

11 My English text is chaste, and all licentious
passages are left in the obscurity of a learned
language.
Memoirs of My Life ch. 8 (1796)

Stella Gibbons
English novelist, 1902–1989

1 Something nasty in the woodshed.
Cold Comfort Farm ch. 10 (1932)

Wolcott Gibbs
U.S. critic, 1902–1958

1 [*Parodying the style of the magazine* Time:]
Backward ran sentences until reeled the mind.
New Yorker, 28 Nov. 1936

2 [*Parodying the style of the magazine* Time:]
Where it will all end, knows God.
New Yorker, 28 Nov. 1936

Kahlil Gibran
Lebanese writer and painter, 1883–1931

1 If you could hear the whispering of the dream
you would hear no other sound.
The Prophet "Farewell" (1923)

2 Your children are not your children.
They are the sons and daughters of Life's
   longing for itself.
They came through you but not from you
And though they are with you yet they belong
   not to you.
You may give them your love but not your
   thoughts,
For they have their own thoughts.
You may house their bodies but not their souls.
The Prophet "On Children" (1923)

3 Let there be spaces in your togetherness.
The Prophet "On Marriage" (1923)

4 Work is love made visible.
The Prophet "On Work" (1923)

5 Are you a politician asking *what your country
can do for you* or a zealous one *asking what you
can do for your country?*
"The New Frontier" (1925). This is a loose translation
made in the 1970s and was undoubtedly influenced
by John F. Kennedy's words from 1960.
*See Briggs 1; Oliver Wendell Holmes, Jr. 6; John Kennedy
4; John Kennedy 5; John Kennedy 16*

William Gibson
U.S.-born Canadian science fiction writer,
1948–

1 I knew every chip in Bobby's simulator by
heart; it looked like your workaday Ono-Sendai
VII, the "Cyberspace Seven."
Omni, July 1982. Coinage of *cyberspace.*

2 The sky above the port was the color of
television, tuned to a dead channel.
Neuromancer ch. 1 (1984)

3 At twenty-two, had been a cowboy, a rustler,
one of the best in the Sprawl. . . . Had operated
on an almost permanent adrenaline high, a
byproduct of youth and proficiency, jacked into
a custom cyberspace deck that projected his
disembodied consciousness into the consensual
hallucination that was the Matrix.
Neuromancer ch. 1 (1984)

4 The future has arrived—it's just not evenly
distributed yet.
Quoted in *S.F. Examiner,* 19 Apr. 1992

André Gide
French novelist and critic, 1869–1951

1 Everything has been said before; but since
nobody listens, we have to keep going back and
beginning all over again.
Traite du Narcisse (1891)

2 Families, I hate you! Shut-in homes, closed
doors, jealous possessions of happiness.
Fruits of the Earth bk. 4 (1897)

3 *Croyez ceux qui cherchent la vérité, doutez de ceux
qui la trouvent.*
Believe those who are seeking the truth; doubt
those who find it.
Ainsi Soit-Il (1952) (translation by Justin O'Brien)

4 [*In response to being asked who was the greatest
nineteenth-century poet:*] Hugo,—*hélas!*
Hugo—alas!
Quoted in *L'Ermitage,* Feb. 1902

Gabrielle Giffords
U.S. politician, 1970–

1 [*Advocating gun control legislation after surviving
an assassination attempt:*] Speaking is difficult,
but I need to say something important.
Testimony at Senate Judiciary Committee hearing, 30
Jan. 2013

Fred Gilbert
English songwriter, 1850–1903

1 The Man Who Broke the Bank at Monte Carlo.
Title of song (1892)

Humphrey Gilbert
English explorer, ca. 1537–1583

1 We are as near to Heaven by sea as by land.
Quoted in Richard Hakluyt, *Third and Last Volume
of the Voyages* (1600). *Bartlett's Familiar Quotations*
quotes Thomas More, *Utopia* (1516): "The way to
heaven out of all places is of like length and distance."
Bartlett's also notes that "Gilbert, on the last day of his
life, was seen in his tiny pinnace *Squirrel* with a book
in hand, probably More's *Utopia,* which inspired
his last utterance. He was homeward bound from
Newfoundland, which he had just taken possession of
in the name of the queen [August 1583]."

Ray Gilbert

U.S. songwriter, 1912–1976

1 Zip-a-dee-doo-dah! Zip-a-dee-ay!
My, oh, my! What a wonderful day!
Plenty of sunshine headin' my way,
Zip-a-dee-doo-dah! Zip-a-dee-ay!
"Zip-a-dee-do-dah" (song) (1945)

W. S. (William Schwenck) Gilbert

English comic writer, 1836–1911
*Quotations are based on the libretti prepared by Ian
Bradley for* The Annotated Gilbert and Sullivan *(1982).*

1 I'm called Little Buttercup—dear Little
    Buttercup,
Though I could never tell why,
But still I'm called Buttercup—poor Little
    Buttercup,
Sweet Little Buttercup, I.
H.M.S. Pinafore act 1 (1878)

2 [*Captain:*] I am the Captain of the *Pinafore;*
[*All:*] And a right good captain, too!
H.M.S. Pinafore act 1 (1878)

3 [*Captain:*] And I'm never, never sick at sea!
[*All:*] What, never?
[*Captain:*] No, never!
[*All:*] What, *never?*
[*Captain:*] Well, hardly ever!
H.M.S. Pinafore act 1 (1878)

4 Then give three cheers, and one cheer more,
For the hardy Captain of the *Pinafore!*
H.M.S. Pinafore act 1 (1878)

5 [*Captain:*] I do my best to satisfy you all—
[*All:*] And with you we're quite content.
[*Captain:*] You're exceedingly polite,
    And I think it only right
    To return the compliment.
H.M.S. Pinafore act 1 (1878)

6 Bad language or abuse,
I never, never use,
Whatever the emergency;
Though, "Bother it," I may
Occasionally say,
I never use a big, big D—.
H.M.S. Pinafore act 1 (1878)

7 And so do his sisters, and his cousins, and his
    aunts!
His sisters and his cousins,
Whom he reckons up by dozens,
And his aunts!
H.M.S. Pinafore act 1 (1878)

8 When I was a lad I served a term
As office boy to an Attorney's firm.
I cleaned the windows and I swept the floor,
And I polished up the handle of the big front
    door. . . .
I polished up that handle so carefullee
That now I am the Ruler of the Queen's Navee!
H.M.S. Pinafore act 1 (1878)

9 I always voted at my party's call,
And I never thought of thinking for myself at
    all.
H.M.S. Pinafore act 1 (1878)

10 Stick close to your desks and never go to sea,
And you all may be Rulers of the Queen's
    Navee!
H.M.S. Pinafore act 1 (1878)

11 Things are seldom what they seem,
Skim milk masquerades as cream.
H.M.S. Pinafore act 2 (1878)

12 He is an Englishman!
For he himself has said it,
And it's greatly to his credit,
That he is an Englishman!
H.M.S. Pinafore act 2 (1878)

13 For he might have been a Roosian,
A French, or Turk, or Proosian,
Or perhaps Itali-an! . . .
But in spite of all temptations
To belong to other nations,
He remains an Englishman!
H.M.S. Pinafore act 2 (1878)

14 It is a glorious thing
   To be a Pirate King.
   The Pirates of Penzance act 1 (1879)

15 Poor wandering one!
   Though thou hast surely strayed,
   Take heart of grace,
   Thy steps retrace,
   Poor wandering one!
   The Pirates of Penzance act 1 (1879)

16 Poor wandering one!
   If such poor love as mine
   Can help thee find
   True peace of mind—
   Why, take it, it is thine!
   The Pirates of Penzance act 1 (1879)

17 Here's a first-rate opportunity
   To get married with impunity,
   And indulge in the felicity
   Of unbounded domesticity.
   The Pirates of Penzance act 1 (1879)

18 You shall quickly be parsonified,
   Conjugally matrimonified,
   By a doctor of divinity,
   Who is located in this vicinity.
   The Pirates of Penzance act 1 (1879)

19 I am the very model of a modern Major-General,
   I've information vegetable, animal, and
       mineral,
   I know the kings of England, and I quote the
       fights historical,
   From Marathon to Waterloo, in order
       categorical.
   The Pirates of Penzance act 1 (1879)

20 I'm very well acquainted too with matters
       mathematical,
   I understand equations, both the simple and
       quadratical,
   About binomial theorem I'm teeming with a lot
       o' news—
   With many cheerful facts about the square of
       the hypotenuse.
   The Pirates of Penzance act 1 (1879)

21 When the foeman bares his steel
       Tarantara! tarantara!
   We uncomfortable feel,
       Tarantara!
   The Pirates of Penzance act 2 (1879)

22 When a felon's not engaged in his employment
   Or maturing his felonious little plans,
   His capacity for innocent enjoyment
   Is just as great as any honest man's.
   The Pirates of Penzance act 2 (1879)

23 Our feelings we with difficulty smother
   When constabulary duty's to be done.
   Ah, take one consideration with another,
   A policeman's lot is not a happy one.
   The Pirates of Penzance act 2 (1879)

24 When the enterprising burglar isn't burgling,
   When the cut-throat isn't occupied in crime.
   The Pirates of Penzance act 2 (1879)

25 Twenty love-sick maidens we,
   Love-sick all against our will.
   Patience act 1 (1881)

26 The Law is the true embodiment
   Of everything that's excellent.
   It has no kind of fault or flaw,
   And I, my Lords, embody the Law.
   Iolanthe act 1 (1882)

27 I often think it's comical
   How Nature always does contrive
   That every boy and every gal,
   That's born into the world alive
   Is either a little Liberal
   Or else a little Conservative!
   Iolanthe act 2 (1882)

28 A wandering minstrel I—
   A thing of shreds and patches,
   Of ballads, songs, and snatches,
   And dreamy lullaby!
   The Mikado act 1 (1885)
   See Shakespeare 215

29 My family pride is something inconceivable. I
   can't help it. I was born sneering.
   The Mikado act 1 (1885)

30 Behold the Lord High Executioner!
   The Mikado act 1 (1885)

31 As some day it may happen that a victim must
       be found,
   I've got a little list—I've got a little list
   Of society offenders who might well be
       underground
   And who never would be missed—who never
       would be missed!
   The Mikado act 1 (1885)

32 Then the idiot who praises, with enthusiastic
tone,
All centuries but this, and every country but
his own.
The Mikado act 1 (1885)

33 And that singular anomaly, the lady novelist—
I don't think she'd be missed—I'm *sure* she'd
not be missed!
The Mikado act 1 (1885)

34 Three little maids from school are we,
Pert as a school-girl well can be,
Filled to the brim with girlish glee.
The Mikado act 1 (1885)

35 [*Yum-Yum:*] Everything is a source of fun.
[*Peep-Bo:*] Nobody's safe, for we care for none!
[*Pitti-Sing:*] Life is a joke that's just begun!
The Mikado act 1 (1885)

36 Three little maids who, all unwary,
Come from a ladies' seminary.
The Mikado act 1 (1885)

37 To sit in solemn silence in a dull, dark dock,
In a pestilential prison, with a life-long lock,
Awaiting the sensation of a short, sharp shock,
From a cheap and chippy chopper on a big
black block!
The Mikado act 1 (1885)

38 Here's a how-de-do!
The Mikado act 2 (1885)

39 My object all sublime
I shall achieve in time—
To let the punishment fit the crime.
The Mikado act 2 (1885)
See Cicero 5

40 And make each prisoner pent
Unwittingly represent
A source of innocent merriment!
The Mikado act 2 (1885)

41 [*The punishment of a billiard sharp:*]
And there he plays extravagant matches
In fitless finger-stalls
On a cloth untrue,
With a twisted cue
And elliptical billiard balls!
The Mikado act 2 (1885)

42 I have a left shoulder-blade that is a miracle of
loveliness. People come miles to see it. My right

elbow has a fascination that few can resist. It is
on view Tuesdays and Fridays, on presentation
of visiting card.
The Mikado act 2 (1885)

43 Merely corroborative detail, intended to give
artistic verisimilitude to an otherwise bald and
unconvincing narrative.
The Mikado act 2 (1885)

44 The flowers that bloom in the spring,
Tra la,
Have nothing to do with the case.
The Mikado act 2 (1885)

45 On a tree by a river a little tom-tit
Sang "Willow, titwillow, titwillow!"
And I said to him, "Dicky-bird, why do you sit
Singing 'Willow, titwillow, titwillow'?"
The Mikado act 2 (1885)

46 "Is it weakness of intellect, birdie?" I cried,
"Or a rather tough worm in your little inside?"
The Mikado act 2 (1885)

47 When every one is somebodee,
Then no one's anybody!
The Gondoliers act 2 (1889)

48 The world has joked incessantly for over fifty
centuries,
And every joke that's possible has long ago
been made.
His Excellency act 2 (1894)

Julia Gillard
Australian prime minister, 1961–

1 [*Responding to a speech by Opposition Leader Tony
Abbott:*] I will not be lectured about sexism and
misogyny by this man. I will not. . . . Not now,
not ever.
Speech to Australian House of Representatives, 9
Oct. 2012

Haven Gillespie
U.S. songwriter, 1888–1975

1 You better watch out,
You better not cry,
Better not pout,
I'm telling you why:
Santa Claus is comin' to town.
"Santa Claus Is Comin' to Town" (song) (1934)

2 He's making a list
And checking it twice,
Gonna find out
Who's naughty and nice.
"Santa Claus Is Comin' to Town" (song) (1934)

Penelope Gilliatt
U.S. critic and writer, 1932–1993

1 Sunday Bloody Sunday.

Title of motion picture (1971). According to Nigel Rees, *Cassell's Movie Quotations,* "Since the 19th century there has been the exclamation 'Sunday, *bloody* Sunday' to reflect frustration at the inactivity and boredom traditionally associated with the Sabbath. This was presumably the cue for the title of Penelope Gilliatt's screenplay." In 1983, the song title "Sunday Bloody Sunday" by the Irish band U2 referred to the "Bloody Sunday" massacre of thirteen Irish Catholics by British troops on 30 Jan. 1972.

Carol Gilligan
U.S. psychologist, 1936–

1 While an ethic of justice proceeds from the premise of equality—that everyone should be treated the same—an ethic of care rests on the premise of nonviolence—that no one should be hurt.

In a Different Voice ch. 6 (1982)

Strickland Gillilan
U.S. poet, 1869–1954

1 Bilin' down's reeport, wuz Finnigin.
An' he writed this here; "Musther Flannigan—
Off agin, on agin,
Gone agin.—Finnigin."

"Finnigin to Flannigan" l. 45 (1897). The source of the expression "off again on again."

2 Adam
Had 'em.

"The Antiquity of Microbes" l. 1 (1904). Said to be the shortest poem in the English language.

James Gillray
English cartoonist, ca. 1757–1815

1 [*Referring to the Bank of England:*] The Old Lady of Threadneedle Street.

Title of cartoon (1797)

Charlotte Perkins Gilman
U.S. feminist and writer, 1860–1935

1 There are things in that paper that nobody knows but me, or ever will.
Behind that outside pattern the dim shapes get clearer every day.
It is always the same shape, only very numerous.
And it is like a woman stooping down and creeping about behind that pattern.

"The Yellow Wallpaper" (1892)

2 There's a whining at the threshold—
There's a scratching at the floor—
To work! To work! In Heaven's name!
The wolf is at the door!

"The Wolf at the Door" l. 5 (1893)

3 The labor of women in the house, certainly enables men to produce more wealth than they otherwise could; and in this way women are economic factors in society. But so are horses.

Women and Economics ch. 1 (1898)

4 There is no female mind. The brain is not an organ of sex. As well speak of a female liver.

Women and Economics ch. 8 (1898)

5 The fact that women in the home have shut themselves away from the thought and life of the world has done much to retard progress. We fill the world with the children of 20th century A.D. fathers and 20th century B.C. mothers.

Speech at National American Convention, 1905

Samuel Gilman
U.S. clergyman, 1791–1858

1 Fair Harvard! Thy sons to thy Jubilee throng.

"Ode, Bicentennial, Harvard University" l. 1 (1836)

Gary Gilmore
U.S. murderer, 1941–1977

1 [*Remark before his execution for murder, 17 Jan. 1977:*] Let's do it!

Quoted in *Wash. Post,* 18 Jan. 1977

Grant Gilmore
U.S. legal scholar, 1910–1982

1 Law reflects but in no sense determines the moral worth of a society. The values of a

reasonably just society will reflect themselves in a reasonably just law. The better the society, the less law there will be. In Heaven there will be no law, and the lion will lie down with the lamb. The values of an unjust society will reflect themselves in an unjust law. The worse the society, the more law there will be. In Hell there will be nothing but law, and due process will be meticulously observed.

The Ages of American Law ch. 5 (1977)

John Gilmore

U.S. computer scientist, 1955–

1 The Net interprets censorship as damage and routes around it.

Quoted in *Information Week,* 29 Nov. 1993

Patrick S. Gilmore

Irish-born U.S. bandleader, 1829–1892

1 When Johnny comes marching home again, hurrah! hurrah!
We'll give him a hearty welcome then, hurrah, hurrah!
The men will cheer, the boys will shout,
The ladies they will all turn out,
And we'll all feel gay when Johnny comes marching home.

"When Johnny Comes Marching Home" (song) (1863)

Allen Ginsberg

U.S. poet, 1926–1997

1 America I've given you all and now I'm nothing.

"America" l. 1 (1956)

2 America when will you be angelic?
When will you take off your clothes?
When will you look at yourself through the grave?
When will you be worthy of your million Trotskyites?

"America" l. 8 (1956)

3 Are you being sinister or is this some form of practical joke?
I'm trying to come to the point.
I refuse to give up my obsession.

"America" l. 21 (1956)

4 Asia is rising against me
I haven't got a chinaman's chance.

"America" l. 48 (1956)

5 America how can I write a holy litany in your silly mood?

"America" l. 55 (1956)

6 I'd better get right down to the job.
It's true I don't want to join the Army or turn lathes in precision parts factories. I'm nearsighted and psychopathic anyway.
America I'm putting my queer shoulder to the wheel.

"America" l. 72 (1956)

7 I saw the best minds of my generation destroyed by madness, starving hysterical naked,
dragging themselves through the negro streets at dawn looking for an angry fix,
angelheaded hipsters burning for the ancient heavenly connection to the starry dynamo in the machinery of night.

"Howl" l. 1 (1956)
See Louis Simpson 1

8 who lost their loveboys to the three old shrews of fate the one eyed shrew of the heterosexual dollar the one eyed shrew that winks out of the womb and the one eyed shrew that does nothing but sit on her ass and snip the intellectual golden threads of the craftsman's loom.

"Howl" l. 40 (1956)

9 With the absolute heart of the poem of life butchered out of their own bodies good to eat a thousand years.

"Howl" l. 78 (1956)

10 There is nothing to be learned from history any more. We're in science fiction now.

Quoted in Christopher Butler, *After the Wake: An Essay on the Contemporary Avant-Garde* (1980)

Nikki Giovanni (Yolande Cornelia Giovanni)

U.S. poet, 1943–

1 It's a sex object if you're pretty
and no love
or love and no sex if you're fat.

"Woman Poem" l. 17 (1968)

2 And I really hope no white person ever has
    cause to write about me
  because they never understand Black love is
    Black wealth and they'll
  probably talk about my hard childhood and
    never understand that
  all the while I was quite happy.
  "Nikki-Rosa" l. 24 (1970)

3 So she replied: show me someone not full of
    herself
    and i'll show you a hungry person.
  "Poem for a Lady Whose Voice I Like" l. 20 (1970)

4 There're two people in the world that are not
  likeable: a master and a slave.
  Quoted in James Baldwin and Nikki Giovanni, *A
  Dialogue* (1973)

George Gipp
U.S. football player, 1895–1920

1 [*Alleged deathbed request to coach Knute Rockne:*]
  Tell them to go in there with all they've got and
  win just one for the Gipper.
  Attributed in *Collier's*, 22 Nov. 1930. Murray Sperber,
  in *Shake Down the Thunder: The Creation of Notre
  Dame Football* (1993), concludes that this version of
  a 1928 Rockne pep talk with the coach recounting
  these words was, in all probability, written by
  Rockne's ghostwriter at *Collier's*, John B. Kennedy.
  Rockne did apparently quote Gipp in 1928 (the *N.Y.
  Daily News*, 12 Nov. 1928, had the words as "On his
  deathbed George Gipp told me that some day, when
  the time came, he wanted me to ask a Notre Dame
  team to beat the Army for him"), but there is much
  evidence against Gipp having actually made such a
  request.

Delphine de Girardin
French writer, 1804–1855

1 *Les affaires, c'est l'argent des autres!*

  Business, it's other people's money.
  Marguerite ou Deux Amours ch. 17 (1852)

Jean Giraudoux
French writer, 1882–1944

1 There's no better way of exercising the
  imagination than the study of law. No poet
  ever interpreted nature as freely as a lawyer
  interprets the truth.
  La Guerre de Troie N'Aura pas Lieu act 2, sc. 4 (1935)

Lillian Gish
U.S. actress, 1893–1993

1 When I was making films, Lionel Barrymore
  first played my grandfather, later he played my
  father, and finally he played my husband. If he
  had lived, I am sure I would have played his
  mother. That's the way it is in Hollywood. The
  men get younger and the women get older.
  Quoted in *N.Y. Times*, 31 Dec. 1982

Rudolph W. Giuliani
U.S. politician, 1944–

1 [*In response to a question about estimated
  casualties at the World Trade Center after the 9/11
  terrorist attacks:*] More than any of us can bear.
  News conference, New York, N.Y., 11 Sept. 2001

2 Our hearts are broken, but they are beating,
  and they are beating stronger than ever. We
  choose to live our lives in freedom.
  Remarks on *Saturday Night Live* (television show), 29
  Sept. 2001

3 Truth isn't truth.
  NBC *Meet the Press* (television show), 19 Aug. 2018

William E. Gladstone
British statesman, 1809–1898

1 You cannot fight against the future. Time is on
  our side.
  Speech in House of Commons, 27 Apr. 1866

2 Justice delayed is justice denied.
  Speech in House of Commons, 16 Mar. 1868.
  Although Gladstone popularized this saying, it
  appeared earlier in the *Weekly Mississippian* (Jackson,
  Miss.), 23 Nov. 1838. Edward K. Conklin has found
  precursors dating back to "Another Word to the Wise,
  Shewing That the Delay of Justice, Is Great Injustice"
  (John Musgrave, Title of pamphlet [1646]) and
  "Justice delayed is little better than justice denied"
  (George Dillwyn, *Occasional Reflections* [1815]).

3 But, as the British Constitution is the most
  subtile organism which has proceeded from
  the womb and the long gestation of progressive
  history, so the American Constitution is, so
  far as I can see, the most wonderful work ever
  struck off at a given time by the brain and
  purpose of man.
  North American Review, Sept./Oct. 1878

4 All the world over, I will back the masses
against the classes.
Speech, Liverpool, England, 28 June 1886

Joseph Glanvill

English clergyman and philosopher, 1636–
1680

1 They that have never peep't beyond the
common belief in which their easie
understandings were at first indoctrinated,
are indubitately assur'd of the Truth, and
comparative excellency of their receptions,
while the larger Souls, that have travail'd the
divers *Climates* of *Opinions,* are more cautious
in their *resolves,* and more sparing to determine.
The Vanity of Dogmatizing (1661)
See Auden 7

Henry Glapthorne

English playwright, ca. 1610–ca. 1643

1 The law is such an Ass.
Revenge for Honor act 3, sc. 2 (1654)
See Dickens 20

Susan Glaspell

U.S. writer, 1876–1948

1 Nothing here but kitchen things.
Trifles (1916)

April Glaspie

U.S. diplomat, 1942–

1 [*Statement to Iraqi leader Saddam Hussein
four days before Hussein ordered the invasion of
Kuwait:*] We have no opinion on the Arab-Arab
conflicts like your border disagreement with
Kuwait. [Secretary of State James Baker] has
directed our official spokesman to emphasize
the instruction that the issue is not associated
with America.
Quoted in *Guardian,* 12 Sept. 1990

James Gleick

U.S. writer, 1954–

1 Tiny differences in input could quickly become
overwhelming differences in output. . . . In
weather, for example, this translates into what
is only half-jokingly known as the Butterfly
Effect—the notion that a butterfly stirring
the air today in Peking can transform storm
systems next month in New York.
Chaos prologue (1987)
See Farmer 2; Edward Lorenz 1

Denis Glover

New Zealand poet, 1912–1980

1 Quardle oodle ardle wardle doodle
The magpies said.
"The Magpies" l. 3 (1941)

Donald Glover

U.S. entertainer, 1983–

1 This is America
Don't catch you slippin' up.
"This Is America" (song) (2018)

Louise Glück

U.S. poet, 1943–

1 Soon the birds and ancients
Will be starting to arrive, bereaving points
South.
"The Racer's Widow" l. 3 (1968)

2 Even he did not get to keep that lovely body.
"The Racer's Widow" l. 12 (1968)

Elinor Glyn

English writer, 1864–1943

1 No matter what he does, one always forgives
him. It does not depend upon looks, either—
although this actual person is abominably good-
looking—it does not depend upon intelligence
or character or—anything—as you say, it is just
"it."
The Man and the Moment ch. 7 (1914)
See Kipling 30

2 He had that nameless charm, with a strong
magnetism which can only be called "It."
"It" ch. 1 (1927)
See Kipling 30

Martin H. Glynn

U.S. politician, 1871–1925

1 [*Of Woodrow Wilson:*] He kept us out of war!
Keynote speech at Democratic National Convention,
St. Louis, Mo., 15 June 1916

Jean-Luc Godard

French-Swiss director, 1930–

1 Photography is truth. The cinema is truth 24 times per second.

Le Petit Soldat (motion picture) (1960)

Kurt Gödel

Austrian-born U.S. logician and mathematician, 1906–1978

1 The development of mathematics toward greater precision has led, as is well known, to the formalization of large tracts of it, so that one can prove any theorem using nothing but a few mechanical rules. . . . One might therefore conjecture that these axioms and rules of inference are sufficient to decide *any* mathematical question that can at all be formally expressed in these systems. It will be shown below that this is not the case, that on the contrary there are in the two systems mentioned relatively simple problems in the theory of integers that cannot be decided on the basis of the axioms.

"On Formally Undecidable Propositions of *Principia Mathematica* and Related Systems I" (1931)

Arthur Godfrey

U.S. entertainer, 1903–1983

1 I'm proud to be paying taxes in the United States. The only thing is—I could be just as proud for half the money.

Quoted in *Reader's Digest,* Oct. 1951

Joseph Goebbels

German Nazi leader, 1897–1945

1 We can manage without butter but not, for example, without guns. If we are attacked we can only defend ourselves with guns not with butter.

Speech, Berlin, 17 Jan. 1936
See Goering 1

2 *Wollt Ihr den totalen Krieg?*
Do you want total war?

Speech at Sportpalast, Berlin, 18 Feb. 1943

3 Should the German people lay down their arms, the Soviets . . . would occupy all eastern and south-eastern Europe together with the greater part of the Reich. Over all this territory, which with the Soviet Union included, would be of enormous extent, an iron curtain would at once descend.

Das Reich, 25 Feb. 1945
See Winston Churchill 33; Ethel Snowden 1; Troubridge 1

Hermann Goering

German Nazi leader, 1893–1946

1 Would you rather have butter or guns? . . . Preparedness makes us powerful. Butter merely makes us fat.

Speech, Hamburg, Germany, 1936
See Goebbels 1

2 I herewith commission you to carry out all preparations with regard to . . . a *final solution* of the Jewish question in those territories of Europe which are under German influence.

Instructions to Reinhard Heydrich, 31 July 1941.
Drafted by Adolf Eichmann.
See Heydrich 1

3 The people can always be brought to the bidding of the leaders. That is easy. All you have to do is tell them they are being attacked and denounce the pacifists for lack of patriotism and exposing the country to danger. It works the same way in any country.

Quoted in Gustave M. Gilbert, *Nuremberg Diary* (1947). Gilbert recorded these words from a jail-cell interview with Goering during the Nuremberg war crimes trials, 18 Apr. 1946.

Johann Wolfgang von Goethe

German writer, 1749–1832

1 *Er kann mich im Arsch lecken.*
He can lick my ass.

Götz von Berlichingen act 3 (1773)

2 *Der Zauberlehrling.*
The Sorcerer's Apprentice.

Title of poem (1779)

3 Noble be man,
Helpful and good!
For that alone
Sets him apart
From every other creature
On earth.

"Das Göttliche" (1783)

4 *Du musst herrschen und gewinnen,*
  Oder dienen und verlieren,
  Leiden oder triumphieren
  Amboss oder Hammer sein.
  You must be master and win, or serve and
    lose, grieve or triumph, be the anvil or the
    hammer.
  Der Gross-Cophta act 2 (1791)

5 *Kennst du das Land, wo die Zitronen blühn?*
  Im dunkeln Laub die Gold-Orangen glühn,
  Ein sanfter Wind vom blauen Himmel weht,
  Die Myrte still und hoch der Lorbeer steht.
  Know you the land where the lemon-trees
    bloom? In the dark foliage the gold oranges
    glow; a gentle breeze wafts from an azure
    sky; the myrtle is still and the laurel
    stands tall.
  Wilhelm Meisters Lehrjahre bk. 3, ch. 1 (1795–1796)

6 *Nur, wer die Sehnsucht kennt,*
  Weiss, was ich leide!
  None but the lonely heart
  Knows what I suffer!
  Wilhelm Meisters Lehrjahre bk. 4, ch. 11 (1795–1796)

7 One ought, every day at least, to hear a little
  song, read a good poem, see a fine picture, and,
  if it were possible, to speak a few reasonable
  words.
  Wilhelm Meisters Lehrjahre bk. 5, ch. 1 (1795–1796)

8 We can't form our children on our own
  concepts; we must take them and love them as
  God gives them to us. Raise them the best we
  can, and leave them free to develop.
  Hermann and Dorothea pt. 3 (1797)

9 The fate of the architect is the strangest of
  all. How often he expends his whole soul, his
  whole heart and passion, to produce buildings
  into which he himself may never enter.
  Elective Affinities bk. 2, ch. 3 (1808)

10 *Es irrt der Mensch, so lang er strebt.*
   Man errs as long as he strives.
   Faust pt. 1 "Prolog im Himmel" (1808)

11 *Das also war des Pudels Kern.*
   So this, then, was the kernel of the brute!
   Faust pt. 1 "Studierzimmer" (1808)

12 *Ich bin der Geist der stets verneint.*
   I am the spirit that always denies.
   Faust pt. 1 "Studierzimmer" (1808)

13 *Zwei Seelen wohnen, ach! in meiner Brust.*
   Two souls dwell, alas! in my breast.
   Faust pt. 1 "Vor dem Thor" (1808)

14 *Die Wahlverwandtschaften.*
   Elective Affinities.
   Title of book (1809)

15 *Was man in der Jugend wünscht, hat man im*
     Alter die Fülle.
   What one has wished for in youth, in old age
     one has in abundance.
   Wahrheit und Dichtung (Poetry and Truth) pt. 2, ch. 6
   (1811–1833)
   See T. H. Huxley 4; Modern Proverbs 14; George
   Bernard Shaw 16; Teresa of Ávila 2; Wilde 56; Wilde 74

16 Against criticism a man can neither protest nor
   defend himself; he must act in spite of it, and
   then it will gradually yield to him.
   Maxims and Reflections (1819)

17 The first and last thing required of genius is the
   love of truth.
   Maxims and Reflections (1819)

18 Nothing hurts a new truth more than an old
   error.
   Maxims and Reflections (1819)

19 *Amerika, du hast es besser—als unser Kontinent,*
     das alte.
   America, you have it better than our continent,
     the old one.
   Almanac for the Muses (1831)

20 *Das Ewig-Weibliche zieht uns hinan.*
The Eternal Feminine draws us on.
Faust pt. 2 "Hochgebirg" (1832)

21 [*"Last words":*] *Mehr Licht!*
More light!
Quoted in K. W. Müller, *Goethes Letze Literarische Thätigkeit* (1832). The *Oxford Dictionary of Quotations* notes that this is an abbreviated version of *"Macht doch den zweiten Fensterladen auch auf, damit mehr Licht hereinkomme"* (Open the second shutter, so that more light can come in).

22 His high rank, as an English peer, was very injurious to Byron, for all genius is oppressed by the outer world;—how much more by high rank and great possessions! The middle station is most favorable to genius; you find the great artists and poets there.
Quoted in Johann Peter Eckermann, *Conversations with Goethe in the Last Years of His Life* (1836–1848) (entry for 24 Feb. 1825)

23 I compare the earth and her atmosphere to a great living being perpetually inhaling and exhaling.
Quoted in Johann Peter Eckermann, *Conversations with Goethe in the Last Years of His Life* (1836–1848) (entry for 11 Apr. 1827)
See Lovelock 1

24 Classicism is health, romanticism is disease.
Quoted in Johann Peter Eckermann, *Conversations with Goethe in the Last Years of His Life* (1836–1848) (entry for 2 Apr. 1829)

25 I don't know myself, and God forbid that I should.
Quoted in Johann Peter Eckermann, *Conversations with Goethe in the Last Years of His Life* (1836–1848) (entry for 10 Apr. 1829)

26 If any one asks me for good advice, I say I will give it, but only on condition that you promise me not to take it.
Quoted in Johann Peter Eckermann, *Conversations with Goethe in the Last Years of His Life* (1836–1848) (entry for 13 Feb. 1831)

Nikolai Gogol
Russian writer, 1809–1852

1 [Are not] you too, Russia, speeding along like a spirited *troika* that nothing can overtake? . . . Everything on earth is flying past, and looking askance, other nations and states draw aside and make way.
Dead Souls pt. 1, ch. 11 (1842) (translation by David Magarshak)

Isaac Goldberg
U.S. writer, 1887–1938

1 Diplomacy is to do and say
The nastiest thing in the nicest way.
The Reflex, Oct. 1927

Ludwig Max Goldberger
German banker, 1848–1913

1 [*Referring to the United States:*] Land of Unlimited Possibilities.
Title of book (1903)

William Golding
English novelist, 1911–1993

1 Fancy thinking the Beast was something you could hunt and kill! . . . You knew, didn't you? I'm part of you? Close, close, close! I'm the reason why it's no go? Why things are the way they are?
Lord of the Flies ch. 8 (1954). Ellipsis in the original.

2 Ralph wept for the end of innocence, the darkness of man's heart, and the fall through the air of the true, wise friend called Piggy.
Lord of the Flies ch. 12 (1954)

Emma Goldman
Lithuanian-born U.S. anarchist, 1869–1940

1 I did not believe that a Cause which stood for a beautiful ideal, for anarchism, for release and freedom from conventions and prejudice, should demand the denial of life and joy. I insisted that our Cause could not expect me to become a nun and that the movement should not be turned into a cloister. If it meant that, I did not want it.
Living My Life ch. 5 (1931). Rosalie Maggio, *The New Beacon Book of Quotations by Women*, posits this as a possible source for the abridgment "If I can't dance I don't want to be in your revolution." The abridgment apparently first appeared on T-shirts at a 1973 festival in New York City.

William Goldman

U.S. screenwriter and novelist, 1931–2018

1 Hello, my name is Inigo Montoya, you killed my father, prepare to die.
The Princess Bride ch. 5 (1973)

2 Life is pain. . . . Anybody that says different is selling something.
The Princess Bride ch. 5 (1973)

3 Is it safe?
Marathon Man ch. 21 (1974)

4 The single most important fact, perhaps, of the entire movie industry: NOBODY KNOWS ANYTHING.
Adventures in the Screen Trade ch. 1 (1983)

James Goldsmith

French-born English financier and politician, 1933–1997

1 [*Remark upon marrying Annabel Birley, 1978:*] If you marry your mistress, you create a job vacancy.
Quoted in Geoffrey Wansell, *Tycoon* (1987)

Oliver Goldsmith

British writer, 1728–1774

1 Such is the patriot's boast, where'er we roam, His first, best country ever is, at home.
The Traveller l. 73 (1764)

2 History of Little Goody Two-Shoes.
Title of book (1765). The authorship of this children's story has also been ascribed to people other than Goldsmith, such as John Newbery and Giles Jones.

3 Man wants but little here below, Nor wants that little long.
"Edwin and Angelina, or the Hermit" l. 31 (1766). Edward Young had written, in *Night Thoughts*, "Night 8" (1742–1745): "She gives but little, nor that little, long."

4 But soon a wonder came to light That show'd the rogues they lied: The man recovered of the bite, The dog it was that died.
"An Elegy on the Death of a Mad Dog" l. 29 (1766)

5 I find you want me to furnish you with argument and intellects too.
The Vicar of Wakefield ch. 7 (1766)
See Samuel Johnson 106

6 When lovely woman stoops to folly And finds too late that men betray, What charm can soothe her melancholy, What art can wash her guilt away?
The Vicar of Wakefield ch. 29 (1766)
See T. S. Eliot 54

7 Ill fares the land, to hast'ning ills a prey, Where wealth accumulates, and men decay; Princes and lords may flourish, or may fade; A breath can make them, as a breath has made; But a bold peasantry, their country's pride, When once destroyed, can never be supplied.
The Deserted Village l. 51 (1770)

8 At church, with meek and unaffected grace, His looks adorn'd the venerable place; Truth from his lips prevail'd with double sway, And fools, who came to scoff, remain'd to pray.
The Deserted Village l. 179 (1770)

9 The very pink of perfection.
She Stoops to Conquer act 1 (1773)

Barry M. Goldwater

U.S. politician, 1909–1998

1 Sometimes I think this country would be better off if we could just saw off the Eastern Seaboard and let it float out to sea.
Quoted in *Wash. Star*, 3 Dec. 1961

2 I will offer a choice, not an echo.
News conference, Paradise City, Ariz., 3 Jan. 1964

3 Extremism in the defense of liberty is no vice. Moderation in the pursuit of justice is no virtue.
Speech accepting nomination for president at Republican National Convention, San Francisco, Calif., 16 July 1964
See Thomas Paine 24

Samuel Goldwyn (Samuel Goldfish)

Polish-born U.S. motion picture producer, 1882–1974

1 Gentlemen, include me out.
Quoted in Alva Johnston, *The Great Goldwyn* (1937). Apparently uttered before storming out of a heated discussion of a Motion Pictures Producers and Distributors of America labor controversy in 1933.

2 I'll give you a definite maybe.
Quoted in *Dallas Morning News*, 29 Mar. 1940. "Definite maybe" was earlier credited to an unnamed producer in *Brooklyn Daily Eagle*, 14 Nov. 1933.

3 [*Of films with "messages":*] Messages are for Western Union.

Quoted in *Dallas Morning News*, 17 Apr. 1943

4 Why should people go out and pay to see bad movies when they can stay at home and see bad television for nothing?

Quoted in *Observer*, 9 Sept. 1956

5 The reason so many people showed up at [Louis B. Mayer's] funeral was because they wanted to make sure he was dead.

Quoted in Bosley Crowther, *Hollywood Rajah* (1960)
See Jessel 2

6 [*When urged to write his autobiography:*] Oh no. I can't do that—not until long after I'm dead.

Quoted in Norman Zierold, *The Moguls* (1969)

7 [*Of his film* The Best Years of Our Lives *before its opening, 1946:*] I don't care if it doesn't make a nickel, I just want every man, woman, and child in America to see it.

Quoted in Norman Zierold, *The Moguls* (1969)

8 A verbal contract isn't worth the paper it's written on.

Attributed in Alva Johnston, *The Great Goldwyn* (1937). According to Norman Zierold, *The Moguls* (1969), Goldwyn actually said, in praise of the trustworthiness of motion picture executive Joseph M. Schenck: "His verbal contract is worth more than the paper it's written on." The sentence was then "improved," like many other Goldwynisms, and became famous in the form above. There is evidence, however, of an older provenance. "A verbal agreement is not worth the paper it's written on" appeared, for example, in the *Irish Times and Solicitors' Journal*, 14 June 1890.

9 Our comedies are not to be laughed at.

Attributed in Alva Johnston, *The Great Goldwyn* (1937). The *Trenton Sunday Times-Advertiser*, 8 May 1921, attributed "My comedies are not to be laughed at" to an unnamed producer. The joke is an old one, traced by Garson O'Toole as far back as the *New-York Mirror*, 29 Aug. 1829 ("His efforts, like Cumberland's comedies, are not to be laughed at").

10 I read part of it all the way through.

Attributed in Alva Johnston, *The Great Goldwyn* (1937). According to Johnston, this was said by another producer but then "pinned" on Goldwyn.

11 I can answer you in two words, "Im possible."

Attributed in Alva Johnston, *The Great Goldwyn* (1937). According to Johnston: "Sam did not say it. It was printed late in 1925 in a humorous magazine and credited to an anonymous Potash or Perlmutter.

An executive in the Chaplin studio pointed it out to Charlie Chaplin, saying, 'It sounds like Sam Goldwyn.' Chaplin said, 'We'll pin it on Sam,' and he repeated it until it became a world-famous Goldwynism." An earlier version was in the *Daily Illini*, 26 Jan. 1928: "In two words I can tell you what's the matter with it: It's im-possible."

12 It rolls off my back like a duck.

Attributed in Alva Johnston, *The Great Goldwyn* (1937)

13 Anybody who goes to a psychiatrist should have his head examined.

Attributed in *N.Y. Herald Tribune*, 26 Dec. 1948. Probably an apocryphal Goldwynism.

14 Let's have some new clichés.

Attributed in *N.Y. Times*, 6 Sept. 1983. Labeled "perhaps apocryphal" in *The Oxford Dictionary of Twentieth Century Quotations*.

15 I want a film that begins with an earthquake and works up to a climax.

Attributed in *Wash. Post*, 23 Jan. 1944. Virtually identical language was attributed to "a film magnate" in *Spectator*, 4 Mar. 1938.

Daniel Goleman
U.S. psychologist, 1946–

1 What factors are at play, for example, when people of high IQ flounder and those of modest IQ do surprisingly well? I would argue that the difference quite often lies in the abilities called here *emotional intelligence,* which include self-control, zeal and persistence, and the ability to motivate oneself.

Emotional Intelligence "Aristotle's Challenge" (1995). Goleman popularized this term, although it is documented in a general sense by the *Oxford English Dictionary* as early as 1938.

Vernon Louis "Lefty" Gomez
U.S. baseball player, 1908–1989

1 [*Response after being asked to have his salary cut from $20,000 to $7,500 because he had had a poor season:*] Tell you what, you keep the salary and pay me the cut.

Quoted in Colin Jarman, *The Guinness Dictionary of Sports Quotations* (1990)

Ivan Goncharov

Russian novelist, 1812–1891

1 "And he was as intelligent as other people, his soul was pure and clear as crystal; he was noble and affectionate—and yet he did nothing!"

"But why? What was the reason?"

"The reason . . . what reason was there? Oblomovism!"

Oblomov pt. 4, ch. 12 (1859)

Maud Gonne

Irish nationalist and actress, 1867–1953

1 [*Remark to William Butler Yeats:*] Poets should never marry. The world should thank me for not marrying you.

Quoted in Margaret Ward, *Maud Gonne: A Life* (1990)

Alberto R. Gonzales

U.S. government official, 1955–

1 In my judgment, this new paradigm [the war on terrorism] renders obsolete Geneva's strict limitations on questioning of enemy prisoners and renders quaint some of its provisions.

Memorandum (written as White House legal counsel) to George W. Bush, 25 Jan. 2002

Miguel "Mike" Gonzales

Cuban baseball player and manager, 1890–1977

1 Good field. No hit.

Quoted in *N.Y. Times*, 2 Sept. 1927. In this 1924 telegram, Gonzalez gave his scouting assessment of the abilities of Moe Berg, a baseball catcher of limited (athletic) talents who later became a leading U.S. spy during World War II. The line is sometimes attributed to a Cuban scout named Adolpho Luque.

Amy Goodman

U.S. journalist, 1957–

1 [*Accepting an award for coverage of the 1991 massacre of Timorese by Indonesian troops:*] Go to where the silence is and say something.

Quoted in *Columbia Journalism Review,* Mar./Apr. 1994

Paul Goodman

U.S. author and activist, 1911–1972

1 Where there is official censorship it is a sign that speech is serious. Where there is none, it is pretty certain that the official spokesmen have all the loud-speakers.

Growing Up Absurd ch. 2 (1960)

Steve Goodman

U.S. singer and songwriter, 1948–1984

1 Good morning America how are you?
Don't you know me, I'm your native son,
I'm the train they call The City of New Orleans,
I'll be gone five hundred miles when the day is done.

"The City of New Orleans" (song) (1972)

2 The conductor sings his song again,
The passengers will please refrain
This train's got the disappearing railroad blues.

"The City of New Orleans" (song) (1972)

Joe Goodwin

U.S. songwriter, 1889–1943

1 When you're smiling, when you're smiling, the whole world smiles with you,
When you're laughing, when you're laughing, the sun comes shining through.
But when you're crying you bring on the rain, so stop your sighing, be happy again.
Keep on smiling, 'cause when you're smiling, the whole world smiles with you.

"When You're Smiling (The Whole World Smiles with You)" (song) (1928). Cowritten with Mark Fisher and Larry Shay.

Mikhail Sergeevich Gorbachev

Soviet statesman, 1931–

1 Democracy is the wholesome and pure air without which a socialist public organization cannot live a full-blooded life.

Speech to 27th Congress of Communist Party of the Soviet Union, Moscow, 25 Feb. 1986

2 The guilt of Stalin and his immediate entourage before the Party and the people for the mass repressions and lawlessness they committed is enormous and unforgivable.

Speech on seventieth anniversary of Russian Revolution, Moscow, 2 Nov. 1987

3 The idea of restructuring [*perestroika*] . . . combines continuity and innovation, the

historical experience of Bolshevism and the contemporaneity of socialism.

Speech on seventieth anniversary of Russian Revolution, Moscow, 2 Nov. 1987

Nadine Gordimer

South African writer, 1923–2014

1 It was a miracle; it was all a miracle: and one ought to have known, from the sufferings of saints, that miracles are horror.

July's People (1981)

Mack Gordon

Polish-born U.S. songwriter, 1904–1959

1 Pardon me, boy,
Is that the Chattanooga choo-choo?
Track twenty-nine.
Boy, you can give me a shine.

"Chattanooga Choo-Choo" (song) (1941)

Albert F. Gore, Jr.

U.S. politician, 1948–

1 High-capacity fiber optic networks will be the information superhighways of tomorrow.

Statement on Senate bill, 3 Jan. 1989. Apparent coinage of *information superhighway* to refer to the Internet.

2 My counsel advises me that there is no controlling legal authority or case that says that there was any violation of law whatsoever in the manner in which I asked people to contribute to our reelection campaign.

Press briefing, 3 Mar. 1997

3 During my service in the United States Congress, I took the initiative in creating the Internet.

CNN television interview, 9 Mar. 1999. This statement was controversial because the Internet was created in the early 1970s, but it was true that Gore had been a pioneer in advocating the construction of a national high-speed data network.

4 [*Remark to George W. Bush during their telephone call in which Gore retracted his election night concession:*] You don't have to get snippy.

Quoted in *Chicago Tribune*, 8 Nov. 2000

Maxim Gorky (Aleksei Maksimovich Peshkov)

Russian writer and political activist, 1868–1936

1 How marvelous is Man! How proud the word rings—Man!

The Lower Depths act 4 (1903)

Stuart Gorrell

U.S. songwriter, 1902–1963

1 Georgia, Georgia,
The whole day through;
Just an old sweet song
Keeps Georgia on my mind.

"Georgia on My Mind" (song) (1930)

Edmund Gosse

English writer, 1849–1928

1 [*Of Sturge Moore:*] A sheep in sheep's clothing.

Quoted in Ferris Greenslet, *Under the Bridge* (1943)
See Winston Churchill 48

Glenn Gould

Canadian pianist and composer, 1932–1982

1 The purpose of art is the lifelong construction of a state of wonder.

Commencement address at York University, Toronto, Canada, 6 Nov. 1982

Stephen Jay Gould

U.S. paleontologist and author, 1941–2002

1 But a man does not attain the status of Galileo merely because he is persecuted; he must also be right.

Natural History, Mar. 1975

2 In science "fact" can only mean "confirmed to such a degree that it would be perverse to withhold provisional assent."

Hen's Teeth and Horse's Toes "Evolution as Fact and Theory" (1983)

3 People in the past, in religious civilizations, had a real, profound terror of apocalyptic catastrophe. What frightens us in our secular age is the computer breakdown that'll occur if computers interpret the 00 of the year 2000 as a return to 1900.

Conversations About the End of Time introduction, ed. Catherine David et al. (1999)

Remy de Gourmont
French writer, 1858–1915

1 *De toutes les aberrations sexuelles, la plus singulière est peut-être la chasteté.*
Of all sexual aberrations perhaps the most curious is chastity.
La Physique de l'Amour: Essai sur l'Instincte Sexuel ch. 18 (1903) (translation by Ezra Pound)

Francisco José de Goya y Lucientes
Spanish painter, 1746–1828

1 The dream of reason produces monsters.
Los Caprichos caption of plate 43 (1799)

Baltasar Gracián
Spanish philosopher, 1601–1658

1 Never open the door to a lesser evil, for other and greater ones invariably slink in after it.
The Art of Worldly Wisdom (1647)

Alex Graham
Scottish cartoonist, 1917–1991

1 [*Addressed by two extraterrestrials to a horse, with a flying saucer parked in the field behind them:*] Kindly take us to your President!
New Yorker, 21 Mar. 1953 (cartoon caption). Apparently the source of the science fiction catchphrase, "Take me to your leader." The exact words "Take us to your leader!" appeared in Walter Winchell's newspaper column, 1 July 1955. In a non-science-fiction context, "take me to your leader" appeared in Burnett Hillman Streeter, *The Sadhu: A Study in Mysticism and Practical Religion* (1921).

Clementina Stirling Graham
Scottish writer, 1782–1877

1 The best way to get the better of temptation is just to yield to it.
Mystifications (1859)
See Balzac 1; Mae West 19; Wilde 25; Wilde 53

David Graham
U.S. lawyer, 1808–1852

1 A lawyer should never ask a witness on cross-examination a question unless in the first place he knew what the answer would be, or in the second place he didn't care.
Quoted in Francis L. Wellman, *The Art of Cross-Examination* (1903)

Martha Graham
U.S. dancer and choreographer, 1894–1991

1 We look at the dance to impart the sensation of living in an affirmation of life, to energize the spectator into keener awareness of the vigor, the mystery, the humor, the variety, and the wonder of life. This is the function of the American dance.
"The American Dance" (1935)

Kenneth Grahame
British children's book writer, 1859–1932

1 Believe me, my young friend, there is *nothing*— absolutely nothing—half so much worth doing as simply messing about in boats.
The Wind in the Willows ch. 1 (1908)

Cary Grant (Archibald Leach)
English actor, 1904–1986

1 Everybody wants to be Cary Grant. Even *I* want to be Cary Grant.
Quoted in *Newsweek*, 12 Mar. 1990

2 [*Responding to telegram to his movie studio,* HOW OLD CARY GRANT?:] OLD CARY GRANT FINE. HOW YOU?
Attributed in *St. Petersburg Times*, 8 Nov. 1959. Ralph Keyes, in his book *"Nice Guys Finish Seventh"* (1992), quotes Grant as denying the authenticity of this anecdote.

3 Judy Judy Judy.
Attributed in *Dallas Morning News*, 1 Dec. 1967. According to Ralph Keyes, *"Nice Guys Finish Seventh"* (1992), "Grant once had some sound men listen through all of his movies for the line. They couldn't find it. Where did he think it originated? 'I vaguely recall,' said Grant, 'that at a party someone introduced Judy Garland by saying "Judy, Judy, Judy," and it caught on, attributed to me.'" A claim of earlier usage is made by Marc Eliot, *Cary Grant* (2004): "Grant recorded a promo for the Lux Radio Theater version of *Only Angels Have Wings* in which he did actually say, 'Jee-u-dee, JEE-U-DEE, *JEE-U-DEE*.'" (*Only Angels Have Wings* was a 1939 film.)

Ulysses S. Grant
U.S. president and military leader, 1822–1885

1 No terms except an unconditional and immediate surrender can be accepted. I propose to move immediately upon your works.
Dispatch to General Simon Bolivar Buckner, Fort Donelson, Tenn., 16 Feb. 1862

2 [I] propose to fight it out on this line if it takes all Summer.

Dispatch from Spotsylvania (Va.) Court House, 11 May 1864. The *Oxford Dictionary of Quotations* quotes this as "I purpose to fight it out . . . ," but the wording appears as above in *The Papers of Ulysses S. Grant*, vol. 10, ed. John Y. Simon (1982).

3 I know no method to secure the repeal of bad or obnoxious laws so effective as their stringent execution.

First Inaugural Address, 4 Mar. 1869

4 Wars of extermination, engaged in by people pursuing commerce and all industrial pursuits, are expensive even against the weakest people, and are demoralizing and wicked.

Second Inaugural Address, 4 Mar. 1873

5 *Let no guilty man escape if it can be avoided.* Be specially vigilant—or instruct those engaged in the prosecution of fraud to be—against all who insinuate that they have high influence to protect—or to protect them. No personal consideration should stand in the way of performing a public duty.

Endorsement added to letter, received 29 July 1875. According to *Respectfully Quoted*, ed. Suzy Platt: "The exposure of the Whisky Ring, a secret association of distillers and federal officials defrauding the government, was a major scandal in 1875. W. D. W. Barnard, a St. Louis banker, wrote to [President] Grant that officials in St. Louis claimed Grant would sustain them to protect Orville Babcock, his private secretary. Grant added the above endorsement and referred the letter to Benjamin H. Bristow, secretary of the treasury, who led the efforts to expose the ring."

6 I am a verb.

Note to John H. Douglas, July 1885
See Buckminster Fuller 1; Hugo 5

7 I only know two tunes. One is Yankee Doodle, and the other isn't.

Quoted in George W. Childs, *Recollections of General Grant* (1890). Garson O'Toole has traced similar jokes, with different tunes named, as far back as 1839.

Günter Grass
German novelist, 1927–2015

1 Granted: I am an inmate of a mental hospital; my keeper is watching me, he never lets me out of his sight; there's a peephole in the door, and my keeper's eye is the shade of brown that can never see through a blue-eyed type like me.

The Tin Drum bk. 1, ch. 1 (1959)

2 You can declare at the very start that it's impossible to write a novel nowadays, but then, behind your back, so to speak, give birth to a whopper, a novel to end all novels.

The Tin Drum bk. 1, ch. 1 (1959)

3 Even bad books are books and therefore sacred.

The Tin Drum bk. 1, ch. 7 (1959)

4 Melancholy has ceased to be an individual phenomenon, an exception. It has become the class privilege of the wage earner, a mass state of mind that finds its cause wherever life is governed by production quotas.

From the Diary of a Snail (1972)

5 Memory likes to play hide-and-seek, to crawl away. It tends to hold forth, to dress up, often needlessly. Memory contradicts itself; pedant that it is, it will have its way.

Peeling the Onion "Skins Beneath the Skin" (2006)

Robert Graves
English writer, 1895–1985

1 As you are woman, so be lovely:
As you are lovely, so be various,
Merciful as constant, constant as various,
So be mine, as I yours for ever.

"Pygmalion to Galatea" l. 26 (1927)

2 Goodbye to All That.

Title of book (1929)

3 Down, wanton, down! Have you no shame
That at the whisper of Love's name,
Or Beauty's, presto! up you raise
Your angry head and stand at gaze!

"Down, Wanton, Down!" l. 1 (1933)

4 Tell me, my witless, whose one boast
Could be your staunchness at the post,
When were you made a man of parts
To think fine and profess the arts?

"Down, Wanton, Down!" l. 13 (1933)

5 Truth loving Persians do not dwell upon
The trivial skirmish fought near Marathon.

"The Persian Version" l. 1 (1945)

6 The reason why the hairs stand on end, the eyes water, the throat is constricted, the skin

crawls and a shiver runs down the spine when one writes or reads a true poem is that a true poem is necessarily an invocation of the White Goddess, or Muse, the Mother of All Living, the ancient power of fright and lust—the female spider or the queen bee whose embrace is death.
The White Goddess ch. 1 (1948)

7 For me, the naked and the nude
(By lexicographers construed
As synonyms that should express
The same deficiency of dress
Or shelter) stand as wide apart
As love from lies, or truth from art.
"The Naked and the Nude" l. 1 (1957)

Harold Gray
U.S. cartoonist, 1894–1968

1 Leapin lizards!
Little Orphan Annie (comic strip), 13 Oct. 1924

Thomas Gray
English poet, 1716–1771

1 Where ignorance is bliss,
'Tis folly to be wise.
"Ode on a Distant Prospect of Eton College" l. 99 (1747)

2 Not all that tempts your wand'ring eyes
And heedless hearts, is lawful prize;
Nor all, that glisters, gold.
"Ode on the Death of a Favorite Cat" l. 40 (1748)
See Proverbs 121

3 The curfew tolls the knell of parting day,
The lowing herd wind slowly o'er the lea,
The ploughman homeward plods his weary way,
And leaves the world to darkness and to me.
"Elegy Written in a Country Churchyard" l. 1 (1751)

4 Beneath those rugged elms, that yew-tree's shade,
Where heaves the turf in many a mouldering heap,
Each in his narrow cell for ever laid,
The rude forefathers of the hamlet sleep.
"Elegy Written in a Country Churchyard" l. 13 (1751)

5 Let not ambition mock their useful toil,
Their homely joys, and destiny obscure;
Nor grandeur hear with a disdainful smile,

The short and simple annals of the poor.
"Elegy Written in a Country Churchyard" l. 29 (1751)
See Dunne 8

6 The paths of glory lead but to the grave.
"Elegy Written in a Country Churchyard" l. 36 (1751)

7 Full many a gem of purest ray serene,
The dark unfathomed caves of ocean bear;
Full many a flower is born to blush unseen,
And waste its sweetness on the desert air.
"Elegy Written in a Country Churchyard" l. 53 (1751)

8 Some village-Hampden, that with dauntless breast
The little tyrant of his fields withstood;
Some mute inglorious Milton here may rest,
Some Cromwell guiltless of his country's blood.
"Elegy Written in a Country Churchyard" l. 57 (1751)
See Mencken 30

9 Far from the madding crowd's ignoble strife,
Their sober wishes never learned to stray;
Along the cool sequestered vale of life
They kept the noiseless tenor of their way.
"Elegy Written in a Country Churchyard" l. 73 (1751)

10 Here rests his head upon the lap of Earth
A youth to fortune and to fame unknown.
Fair Science frown'd not on his humble birth,
And Melancholy mark'd him for her own.
"Elegy Written in a Country Churchyard" l. 117 (1751)

11 Sweet is the breath of vernal shower,
The bee's collected treasures sweet,
Sweet music's melting fall, but sweeter yet
The still small voice of gratitude.
"Ode for Music" l. 61 (1769)

Rocky Graziano (Rocco Barbella)
U.S. boxer, 1921–1990

1 Somebody Up There Likes Me.
Title of book (1955)

Horace Greeley
U.S. journalist and politician, 1811–1872

1 The illusion that the times that were are better than those that are, has probably pervaded all ages.
The American Conflict ch. 1 (1864–1866)

2 Go West, young man.
Quoted in *Punchinello*, 20 Aug. 1870. This is one of the great examples of the prevalence of

misinformation about famous quotations. The *Oxford Dictionary of Quotations* says that Greeley used it in his book *Hints Toward Reform* (1850), then John Babson Lane Soule used it in an 1851 editorial in the *Terre Haute* (Indiana) *Express*. *Bartlett's Familiar Quotations* says that the Soule article inspired Greeley to use the quotation in an editorial in the *New York Tribune*. The *Oxford English Dictionary* gives a vague citation to Soule; many other reference works take pride in attributing the phrase to Soule rather than Greeley, who is closely associated with it in popular history. However, inspection of *Hints Toward Reform* shows that the quotation does not appear there. Thomas Fuller, writing in *Indiana Magazine of History*, Sept. 2004, found that these words also do not appear in the *Terre Haute Express* in 1851. There is no trace of the attribution to Soule before 1890, when the *Chicago Mail* made this assertion (30 June). Fuller concludes that "John Soule had nothing whatsoever to do with the phrase" and was also unable to find "go West, young man" in Greeley's writings, including the *New York Tribune* and other sources where various people have claimed it occurred. The *Punchinello* citation given is the earliest attribution to Greeley found to date, although Josiah Grinnell asserts plausibly in his autobiography *Men and Events of Forty Years* (1891) that Greeley gave Grinnell the famous advice in 1833. In his magazine *The New-Yorker*, 25 Aug. 1838, Greeley had written: "If any young man is about to commence the world . . . we say to him, publicly and privately, Go to the West."

Abel Green
U.S. editor, 1900–1973

1 [*Headline about rural filmgoers' rejection of motion pictures about rural life:*] Sticks Nix Hick Pix.
Variety, 17 July 1935

Eddie Green
U.S. entertainer, 1891–1950

1 A Good Man Is Hard to Find.
Title of song (1918)

Hannah Green (Joanne Greenberg)
U.S. novelist, 1927–1996

1 I Never Promised You a Rose Garden.
Title of book (1964)

John Green
U.S. novelist, 1977–

1 I believe the universe wants to be noticed. I think the universe is improbably biased toward

consciousness, that it rewards intelligence in part because the universe enjoys its elegance being observed. And who am I, living in the middle of history, to tell the universe that it—or my observation of it—is temporary?
The Fault in Our Stars ch. 14 (2012)

Graham Greene
English novelist, 1904–1991

1 There is always one moment in childhood when the door opens and lets the future in.
The Power and the Glory pt. 1, ch. 1 (1940)

2 No human being can really understand another, and no one can arrange another's happiness.
The Heart of the Matter pt. 3, ch. 1 (1948)

3 If we had not been taught how to interpret the story of the Passion, would we have been able to say from their actions alone whether it was the jealous Judas or the cowardly Peter who loved Christ?
The End of the Affair ch. 3 (1951)

4 He's a good chap in his way. Serious. Not one of those noisy bastards at the Continental. A quiet American.
The Quiet American ch. 1 (1955)

5 Fame is a potent aphrodisiac.
A Burnt-Out Case (1961)
See Kissinger 3; Napoleon 14

6 Catholics and Communists have committed great crimes, but at least they have not stood aside, like an established society, and been indifferent. I would rather have blood on my hands than water like Pilate.
The Comedians pt. 3, ch. 4 (1966)

7 The world is not black and white. More like black and grey.
Quoted in *Observer* (London), 19 Sept. 1982

Joe Greene
U.S. singer and songwriter, 1915–1986

1 Read My Lips.
Title of song (1957)
See George H. W. Bush 4; Curry 1; Film Lines 100

Robert Greene

English poet and playwright, ca. 1560–1592

1 [*Of Shakespeare:*] For there is an upstart Crow,
beautified with our feathers, that with his *Tygers
hart wrapt in a Players hyde,* supposes he is as
well able to bombast out a blanke verse as the
best of you: and being an absolute *Johannes fac
totum,* is in his owne conceit the only Shake-
scene in a countrey.
Groatsworth of Wit Bought with a Million of Repentance
(1592)

Alan Greenspan

U.S. government official, 1926–

1 How do we know when irrational exuberance
has unduly escalated asset values?
Remarks at American Enterprise Institute dinner,
Washington, D.C., 5 Dec. 1996

2 An infectious greed seemed to grip much of
our business community.
Testimony before Senate Committee on Banking,
Housing, and Urban Affairs, 16 July 2002

3 [*Of his reaction to the financial crisis of 2008:*] I
found a flaw in the model that I perceived is a
critical functioning structure that defines how
the world works.
Testimony before House of Representatives Oversight
Committee, 23 Oct. 2008

4 If I seem unduly clear to you, you must have
misunderstood what I said.
Quoted in *L.A. Times,* 27 Sept. 1987

Walter Greenwood

English writer, 1903–1974

1 Love on the Dole.
Title of book (1933)

Germaine Greer

Australian feminist, 1939–

1 It is exactly the element of quest in her
sexuality that the female is taught to deny.
She is not only taught to deny it in her sexual
contacts, but . . . in all her contacts, from
infancy onward, so that when she becomes
aware of her sex the pattern has sufficient
inertia to prevail over new forms of desire and

curiosity. This is the condition which is meant
by the term *female eunuch.*
The Female Eunuch (1970)

2 Freud is the father of psychoanalysis. It had no
mother.
The Female Eunuch (1970)

3 Woman . . . cannot be content with health
and agility: she must make exorbitant efforts
to appear something that never could exist
without a diligent perversion of nature. Is it too
much to ask that women be spared the daily
struggle for superhuman beauty in order to
offer it to the caresses of a subhumanly ugly
mate?
The Female Eunuch (1970)

4 Libraries are reservoirs of strength, grace, and
wit, reminders of order, calm, and continuity,
lakes of mental energy, neither warm nor cold,
light nor dark. The pleasure they give is steady,
unorgastic, reliable, deep, and long-lasting.
In any library in the world, I am at home,
unselfconscious, still, and absorbed.
Daddy, We Hardly Knew You (1989)

Gregory the Great

Italian pope, ca. 540–604

1 *Non Angli sed Angeli.*
Not Angles but Angels.
Quoted in Bede, *Historia Ecclesiastica.* The *Oxford
Dictionary of Quotations* states that Gregory uttered
this, according to oral tradition, "on seeing English
slaves in Rome . . . based on *Responsum est, quod Angli
vocarentur. At ille: 'Bene,' inquit; 'nam et angelicam
habent faciem, et tales angelorum in caelis decet esse
coheredes*" (It is well, for they have the faces of angels,
and such should be the co-heirs of the angels of
heaven).

Dick Gregory

U.S. comedian, 1932–2017

1 I happen to know quite a bit about the South.
Spent twenty years there one night.
From the Back of the Bus introduction (1962)

2 You gotta say this for the white race—its
self-confidence knows no bounds. Who
else could go to a small island in the South
Pacific where there's no poverty, no crime, no

unemployment, no war, and no worry—and call it a "primitive society"?

From the Back of the Bus (1962)

3 New York is the greatest city in the world—especially for my people. Where else, in this great and glorious land of ours, can I get on a subway, sit in any part of the train I please, get off at any station above 110th Street, and know I'll be welcome?

From the Back of the Bus (1962)

4 When the white Christian missionaries went to Africa, the white folks had the bibles and the natives had the land. When the missionaries pulled out, they had the land and the natives had the bibles.

Quoted in *Black Manifesto: Religion, Racism, and Reparations*, ed. Robert S. Lecky and H. Elliott Wright (1969)

Stephen Grellet
French missionary, 1773–1855

1 I expect to pass through this world but once. Any good thing therefore that I can do, or any kindness that I can show to any fellow creature, let me do it now. Let me not defer or neglect it, for I shall not pass this way again.

Attributed in W. Gurney Benham, *Benham's Book of Quotations, Proverbs, and Household Words* (1907). After noting that this has also been attributed to Emerson and others, Benham states, "There seems to be some authority in favor of Stephen Grellet being the author, but the passage does not occur in any of his printed works." The earliest appearance of "I will not pass this way again" found for this book is in the *Coshocton* (Ohio) *Age*, 15 Jan. 1868, where it is quoted anonymously.

Thomas Gresham
English financier, ca. 1519–1579

1 Ytt may pleasse your majesty to understande, thatt the firste occasion of the fall of exchainge did growe by the Kinges majesty, your latte ffather, in abasinge his quoyne ffrome vi ounces fine too iii ounces fine. Whereuppon the exchainge fell ffrome xxvis. viiid. to xiiis. ivd. which was the occasion thatt all your ffine goold was convayd ought of this your realme.

Letter to Queen Elizabeth I (1558). Printed in J. W. Burgon, *The Life and Times of Sir Thomas Gresham* (1839). This passage inspired Henry Dunning

Macleod in 1858 to use the term *Gresham's Law* to refer to the economic principle that "bad money drives out good."

See Aristophanes 8; Henry Macleod 1; Henry Macleod 2

Walter Gretzky
Canadian telephone technician, 1938–2021

1 [*Advice to his son, hockey player Wayne Gretzky:*] Skate to where the puck's going to be, not to where it has been.

Quoted in *Elgin* (Iowa) *Echo*, 27 Jan. 1982

Wayne Gretzky
Canadian hockey player, 1961–

1 100 percent of the shots you don't take don't go in the net.

Quoted in *Philadelphia Inquirer*, 9 Feb. 1983. Usually quoted as "You miss 100% of the shots you don't take."

Clifford Grey
English songwriter, 1887–1941

1 If you were the only girl in the world,
And I were the only boy,
Nothing else would matter in the world today,
We could go on loving in the same old way.

"If You Were the Only Girl in the World" (song) (1916)

Edward Grey, Viscount Grey of Fallodon
British politician, 1862–1933

1 [*Remark on the eve of World War I, 3 Aug. 1914:*] The lamps are going out all over Europe; we shall not see them lit again in our lifetime.

25 Years vol. 2, ch. 18 (1925)

Bill Griffith
U.S. cartoonist, 1944–

1 Are we having fun yet?

Zippy the Pinhead (comic strip) (1979)

Priscilla Grim
U.S. activist, fl. 2010

1 We Are the 99 Percent.

Flyer for assembly in New York City, Aug. 2011. Grim launched this slogan about opposition to Wall Street economic interests together with an activist named "Chris."

Angelina Grimké
U.S. reformer, 1805–1879

1 I know you do not make the laws but I also
know that *you are the wives and mothers, the
sisters and daughters of those who do.*
"Appeal to the Christian Women of the South," *The
Anti-Slavery Examiner*, Sept. 1836

Jacob Ludwig Carl Grimm 1785–1863 and Wilhelm Grimm 1786–1859
German philologists and folklorists

1 Rapunzel, Rapunzel,
Let your hair down.
Kinder- und Hausmärchen "Rapunzel" (1812)

2 "Oh, Grandmother, what big ears you have!"
"The better to hear you with."
"Oh, Grandmother, what big eyes you have!"
"The better to see you with."
"Oh, Grandmother, what big hands you have!"
"The better to grab you with!"
"Oh, Grandmother, what a big, scary mouth
    you have!"
"The better to eat you with!"
Kinder- und Hausmärchen "Rotkäppchen" (Little Red
Riding Hood) (1812)
See Perrault 1

3 Mirror, mirror, on the wall,
Who's the fairest of them all?
Kinder- und Hausmärchen "Sneewittchen" (Snow
White) (1812)

Matt Groening
U.S. cartoonist, 1954–

*For convenience, all quotations and catchphrases from the
television series* The Simpsons *are grouped together here
under Matt Groening, the show's creator.*

1 [*Catchphrase of character Bart Simpson:*] Don't
have a cow, man.
The Simpsons (television series) (1989–)

2 [*Catchphrase of character Bart Simpson:*] Aye,
Caramba!
The Simpsons (television series) (1989–)

3 [*Catchphrase of character C. Montgomery Burns:*]
Ex . . . cellent!
The Simpsons (television series) (1989–)

4 [*Catchphrase of character Bart Simpson:*] I'm Bart
Simpson. Who the hell are you?
The Simpsons (television series), 17 Dec. 1989

5 [*Catchphrase of character Homer Simpson:*]
D'oh . . .
The Simpsons (television series), 17 Dec. 1989
See Finlayson 1

6 [*Catchphrase of character Bart Simpson:*] Eat my
shorts!
The Simpsons (television series), 14 Jan. 1990.
Although this is famous as a *Simpsons* catchphrase,
the expression predated the show. The *Historical
Dictionary of American Slang* documents "eat my
shorts" to 1979, when it appeared in the *National
Lampoon.*

7 [*Groundskeeper Willie's characterization of the
French:*] Cheese-eating surrender monkeys.
The Simpsons (television series), 30 Apr. 1995. This
episode was written by Joshua Sternin, Jeffrey
Ventimilia, Al Jean, and Mike Reiss.

8 Trying is the first step towards failure.
The Simpsons (television series), 7 Dec. 1997. This
episode was written by Dan Greaney.

9 Love is a snowmobile racing across the tundra
and then suddenly it flips over, pinning you
underneath. At night, the ice weasels come.
Quoted in *L.A. Times*, 14 Feb. 1991

Andrei A. Gromyko
Soviet president, 1909–1989

1 [*Of Mikhail Gorbachev:*] Comrades, this man
has a nice smile, but he's got iron teeth.
Speech to Soviet Communist Party Central
Committee, 11 Mar. 1985

Walter Gropius
German-born U.S. architect, 1883–1969

1 Architects, painters, and sculptors must
recognize anew and learn to grasp the
composite character of a building both as an
entity and in its separate parts. Only then will
their work be imbued with the architectonic
spirit which it has lost as "salon art."
"The Bauhaus Proclamation April 1919" (1919)

2 Together let us desire, conceive, and create the
new structure of the future, which will embrace
architecture and sculpture and painting in
one unity and which will one day rise toward
heaven from the hands of a million workers like
the crystal symbol of a new faith.
"The Bauhaus Proclamation April 1919" (1919)

Hugo Grotius (Huig de Groot)
Dutch jurist and philosopher, 1583–1645

1 The following most specific and unimpeachable axiom of the Law of Nations, called a primary rule or first principle, the spirit of which is self-evident and immutable, to wit: Every nation is free to travel to every other nation, and to trade with it.
Mare Liberum (1609)

Andrew Grove (Gróf András)
Hungarian-born U.S. business executive, 1936–

1 Only the paranoid survive.
Quoted in *Electronic News,* 1 Apr. 1985

Edmund L. Gruber
U.S. soldier, 1879–1941

1 Over hill, over dale, we have hit the dusty trail
And those caissons go rolling along.
"The Caisson Song" (song) (1907)

2 Oh, it's hi-hi-yee! for the field artilleree,
Shout out your numbers loud and strong,
And where'er we go, you will always know
That those caissons are rolling along.
"The Caisson Song" (song) (1907)

John Guare
U.S. playwright, 1938–

1 Everybody on this planet is separated by only six other people. Six degrees of separation. Between us and everybody else on this planet.
Six Degrees of Separation (1989)

Philip Guedalla
English historian and biographer, 1889–1944

1 The work of Henry James has always seemed divisible by a simple dynastic arrangement into three reigns: James I, James II, and the Old Pretender.
Supers and Supermen "Some Critics" (1920)

2 The detective-story is the normal recreation of noble minds.
Quoted in Dorothy L. Sayers, *The Omnibus of Crime* (1929)

Edgar A. Guest
U.S. writer and journalist, 1881–1959

1 It takes a heap o' livin' in a house t' make it home,
A heap o' sun an' shadder, an' ye sometimes have t' roam
Afore ye really 'preciate the things ye lef' behind,
An' hunger fer 'em somehow, with 'em allus on yer mind.
"Home" l. 1 (1916)

Ernesto "Che" Guevara
Argentinian-born Cuban revolutionary, 1928–1967

1 Revolution that does not constantly become more profound is a regressive revolution.
"Guerilla Warfare—A Method," *Cuba Socialista* (1961)

2 In a revolution, one either triumphs or dies.
"Farewell Letter" (1965)

3 *Dos, tres . . . muchos Vietnam.*
Two, three . . . many Vietnams.
"Message to *Tricontinental* Magazine," *Bohemia,* 21 Apr. 1967

4 Let me say, with the risk of appearing ridiculous, that the true revolutionary is guided by strong feelings of love. It is impossible to think of an authentic revolutionary without this quality.
Quoted in Jon Lee Anderson, *Che Guevara: A Revolutionary Life* (1997)

Robert Guidry
U.S. songwriter, 1938–2010

1 See you later alligator,
After 'while, crocodile.
"See You Later Alligator" (song) (1956). According to the *Oxford Dictionary of Catchphrases,* these farewell words originated in U.S. "jive" of the 1930s.

Mary Louise Cecil Texas "Tex" Guinan
U.S. nightclub hostess, 1884–1933

1 [*Greeting to customers:*] Hello sucker!
Quoted in *Chicago Daily Tribune,* 8 Dec. 1926
See Mizner 2

Lani Guinier

U.S. legal scholar, 1950–

1 In a racially divided society majority rule is not a reliable instrument of democracy.

Boston Review, Sept.–Oct. 1992

Thom Gunn

English-born U.S. poet, 1929–2004

1 Small, black, as flies hanging in heat, the Boys,
Until the distance throws them forth, their
hum
Bulges to thunder held by calf and thigh.

"On the Move" l. 10 (1957)

2 At worst, one is in motion; and at best,
Reaching no absolute, in which to rest,
One is always nearer by not keeping still.

"On the Move" l. 38 (1957)

3 O wily painter, limiting the scene
From a cacophony of dusty forms
To the one convulsion.

"In Santa Maria del Popolo" l. 13 (1961)

4 The painter saw what was, an alternate
Candor and secrecy inside the skin.

"In Santa Maria del Popolo" l. 19 (1961)

Dorothy Frances Gurney

English poet, 1858–1932

1 The kiss of the sun for pardon,
The song of the birds for mirth,
One is nearer God's Heart in a garden
Than anywhere else on earth.

"God's Garden" l. 13 (1913)

Arlo Guthrie

U.S. folksinger and songwriter, 1947–

1 You can get anything you want at Alice's
Restaurant.

"Alice's Restaurant" (song) (1966)

Francis Guthrie

English mathematician, 1831–1899

1 If a figure be anyhow divided, and the
compartments differently colored, so that
figures with any portion of common boundary
line are differently colored—four colors may be
wanted, but no more.

Quoted in Augustus De Morgan, Letter to William
Rowan Hamilton, 23 Oct. 1852

Woodrow Wilson "Woody" Guthrie

U.S. folksinger and songwriter, 1912–1967

1 So long, it's been good to know you.

"Dusty Old Dust" (song) (1935)

2 Some will rob you with a six gun,
And some with a fountain pen.

"Pretty Boy Floyd" (song) (1939)

3 Green pastures of plenty from dry desert
ground
From the Grand Coulee Dam where the waters
run down
Every state in the Union us migrants have been
We'll work in this fight and we'll fight till we
win.

"Pastures of Plenty" (song) (1941)

4 Roll on, Columbia, roll on
Your power is turning our darkness to dawn
So roll on, Columbia, roll on.

"Roll On Columbia" (song) (1941)

5 Oh, you can't scare me, I'm sticking to the
union,
I'm sticking to the union 'til the day I die.

"The Union Maid" (song) (1941)

6 This land is your land, this land is my land,
From California to the New York Island,
From the redwood forest to the Gulf Stream
waters,
This land was made for you and me.

"This Land Is Your Land" (song) (1956)

7 [*Slogan posted on his guitar:*] This machine kills
fascists.

Quoted in *N.Y. Times,* 22 Mar. 1943

8 [*Message on mimeographed songbook mailed
to fans in 1930s:*] This song is copyrighted
. . . anybody caught singin' it without our
permission will be mighty good friends of ours,
'cause we don't give a dern. Publish it. Write it.
Sing it. Swing to it. Yodel it. We wrote it, that's
all we wanted to do.

Quoted in *Indiana* (Pa.) *Gazette,* 12 Oct. 1983

Edmund Gwenn

English actor, 1875–1959

1 [*Replying on his deathbed to George Seaton's remark, "I guess dying can be very hard":*] Yes, but *not as hard as playing comedy!*

Quoted in Don Widener, *Lemmon: A Biography* (1975). Usually quoted as "Dying is easy, comedy is hard."

Nell Gwyn

English actress and mistress to the king, 1650–1687

1 [*Remark to crowd, Oxford, England, during Popish Terror, 1681:*] Pray, good people, be civil. I am the Protestant whore.

Quoted in James Granger, *A Supplement, Consisting of Corrections and Large Additions, to a Biographical History of England* (1774)

Mark Haddon

English novelist, 1962–

1 Prime numbers are what is left when you have taken all the patterns away. I think prime numbers are like life.

The Curious Incident of the Dog in the Night-Time ch. 19 (2003)

Arthur Twining Hadley

U.S. economist and university president, 1856–1930

1 You always can tell a Harvard man when you see him, but you can't tell him much.

Quoted in *Chicago Daily Tribune*, 27 May 1906

Hadrian

Roman emperor, 76–138

1 *Animula vagula blandula,*
Hospes comesque corporis.
Ah! gentle, fleeting, wav'ring sprite,
Friend and associate of this clay!

"Ad Animam Suam"

Ernst Haeckel

German biologist and philosopher, 1834–1919

1 Ontogenesis, or the development of the individual, is a short and quick recapitulation of phylogenesis, or the development of the tribe to which it belongs, determined by the laws of inheritance and adaptation.

The History of Creation (1868). Haeckel's theory, now disproved, is frequently quoted as "Ontogeny recapitulates phylogeny."
See Sigmund Freud 7

2 There is no doubt that the course and character of the feared "European war" . . . will become the first world war in the full sense of the word.

Indianapolis Star, 20 Sept. 1914. Previously, the earliest known use of *First World War* has been dated to 1931.
See Repington 1

Walter Hagen

U.S. golfer, 1892–1969

1 Don't hurry, don't worry; you're here only a few hours, don't forget to smell the flowers.

Quoted in *Oakland Tribune*, 9 Jan. 1941

H. Rider Haggard

English writer, 1856–1925

1 She who must be obeyed.

She ch. 6 (1887)

Merle Haggard

U.S. country singer and songwriter, 1937–2016

1 I'm proud to be an Okie from Muskogee.

"Okie from Muskogee" (song) (1969). Cowritten with Roy Edward Burris.

Frank Hague

U.S. politician, 1876–1956

1 I am the law!

Quoted in *N.Y. Times*, 11 Nov. 1937. William Safire explains in *Safire's Political Dictionary* (1978): "Mayor Frank Hague of Jersey City . . . received a bum rap from history on this quotation. The episode involved two youths who wanted to change from day school to night school so that they could go to work, but who were denied working papers by the Board of Education's Special Services Director because the law required them to stay in day school. Mayor Hague cut through the red tape and ordered the official to give the boys working papers. As he proudly recounted the matter before the Men's Club of Emory Church in Jersey City on November 10, 1937, when the school official told him, 'That's the law,' he replied, 'Listen, here is the law. I am the law! Those boys go to work!' Today such an action would be lauded . . . but Hague had a well-deserved reputation for high-handedness, and the phrase soon lost its context and was used against him."

Alexander Haig

U.S. government official and general, 1924–2010

1 [*Articulating an erroneous interpretation of the succession of power, after the attempted assassination of President Ronald Reagan, 30 Mar.*

1981:] As of now, I am in control here in the White House.

Quoted in *Wash. Post*, 4 Apr. 1981

Douglas Haig, First Earl Haig
British military leader, 1861–1928

1 Every position must be held to the last man: there must be no retirement. With our backs to the wall and believing in the justice of our cause each one of us must fight on to the end.

Order to British troops, 11 Apr. 1918

Haile Selassie I (Ras Tafari Makonnen)
Ethiopian emperor, 1891–1975

1 Soldiers! When it is announced that a respected and beloved leader has died for our freedom in the course of a battle, do not grieve, do not lose hope! Observe that anyone who dies for his country is a fortunate man, but death takes what it wants, indiscriminately, in peacetime as well as in war. It is better to die with freedom than without it.

Address to Ethiopian Parliament, 18 July 1935

2 Outside the Kingdom of the Lord there is no nation which is greater than another. God and history will remember your judgment!

Speech to League of Nations, Geneva, Switzerland, 30 June 1936

3 Until the philosophy which holds one race superior and another inferior is finally and permanently discredited and abandoned: . . . until there are no longer first-class and second-class citizens of any nation; . . . until the color of a man's skin is of no more significance than the color of his eyes; . . . until the basic human rights are equally guaranteed to all without regard to race; . . . until that day, the dream of lasting peace and world citizenship and the rule of international morality will remain but a fleeting illusion, to be pursued but never attained.

Address to United Nations General Assembly, 4 Oct. 1963

Hakuin
Japanese monk and writer, 1686–1769

1 What is the Sound of the Single Hand? When you clap together both hands a sharp sound

is heard; when you raise the one hand there is neither sound nor smell.

"Yabuko-ji" (written 1753)

David Halberstam
U.S. journalist and author, 1934–2017

1 The Best and the Brightest.

Title of book (1972)
See Heber 1; Percy Shelley 16

J. B. S. Haldane
Scottish biologist, 1892–1964

1 Now, my own suspicion is that the universe is not only queerer than we suppose, but queerer than we *can* suppose.

Possible Worlds and Other Essays "Possible Worlds" (1927)

2 [*Reflecting on the fact that there are 400,000 species of beetles, as opposed to 8,000 species of mammals:*] The Creator, if He exists, has a special preference for beetles.

"A Report of Professor Haldane's Lecture to the Society on April 7, 1951," *Journal of the British Interplanetary Society*, July 1951. The title of the lecture was "Biological Problems of Space Flight." The frequently quoted form of the quotation, "an inordinate fondness for beetles," appeared in an article by G. E. Hutchinson in *American Naturalist*, May-June 1959.

H. R. Haldeman
U.S. government official, 1926–1993

1 [*Comment to John Dean about the Watergate scandal, 8 Apr. 1973:*] Once the toothpaste is out of the tube, it is awfully hard to get it back in.

Quoted in *Hearings Before the Select Committee on Presidential Campaign Activities of the United States Senate: Watergate and Related Activities* (1973). Although this saying is associated with Haldeman, it appears earlier in the *Sheboygan Press*, 5 Mar. 1940, as, "Have you ever tried squeezing the toothpaste back in the tube again?"

Edward Everett Hale
U.S. author and clergyman, 1822–1909

1 Nolan was proved guilty enough, as I say; yet you and I would never have heard of him, reader, but that, when the president of the court asked him at the close whether he wished to say anything to show that he had always been

faithful to the United States, he cried out, in a fit of frenzy,—

"Damn the United States! I wish I may never hear of the United States again!"

. . . "Prisoner, hear the sentence of the Court! The Court decides, subject to the approval of the President, that you never hear the name of the United States again."

"The Man Without a Country" (1863)

2 He loved his country as no other man has loved her, but no man deserved less at her hands.

"The Man Without a Country" (1863)

3 To look up and not down,
To look forward and not back,
To look out and not in,—
and
To lend a hand.

Ten Times One Is Ten ch. 9 (1871)

Nathan Hale

U.S. Revolutionary hero, 1755–1776

1 [*"Last words" before being hanged by British as a spy, New York, N.Y., 22 Sept. 1776:*] I only lament, that I have but one life to lose for my country.

Attributed in Abiel Holmes, *American Annals* (1805). These words, among the most famous in the chronicles of American history, are not supported by eyewitness accounts. The second earliest newspaper article about Hale's execution by the British as a Revolutionary spy did include a similar attributed quotation by Hale: "I am so satisfied with the cause in which I have engaged, that my only regret is, that I have not more lives than one to offer in its service" (*Boston Independent Chronicle*, 17 May 1781). The earliest article, in the *Essex Journal* (Newburyport, Mass.), 13 Feb. 1777, asserted that Hale had cried at the scaffold that "if he had ten thousand lives, he would lay them all down, if called to it, in defence of his injured, bleeding country." Hale's friend William Hull over a period of decades shaped such alleged words into the "but one life to lose" line. A possible inspiration to Hale or Hull was the remark by the English agitator John Lilburne: "I am sorry I have but one life to lose, in maintaining the truth, justice, and righteousness, of so gallant a piece" (*Englands New Chains Discovered* [1649]). Another possible source was the 1713 Joseph Addison quotation cross-referenced below.

See Addison 3

Sara Josepha Hale

U.S. writer, 1788–1879

1 Mary had a little lamb,
Its fleece was white as snow,
And everywhere that Mary went
The lamb was sure to go.
He followed her to school one day—
That was against the rule,
It made the children laugh and play,
To see a lamb at school.

"Mary's Lamb" l. 1 (1830). According to Iona and Peter Opie, *Oxford Dictionary of Nursery Rhymes*, 2nd ed., "E. V. Lucas came to the conclusion that these were the best-known four-line verses in the English language. . . . 'Mary had a little lamb' was the first utterance recorded on Edison's talking machine or phonograph (1877)."

Alex Haley

U.S. novelist and biographer, 1921–1992

1 Early in the spring of 1750, in the village of Juffure, four days upriver from the coast of The Gambia, West Africa, a manchild was born to Omoro and Binta Kinte.

Roots ch. 1 (1976)

Ed Haley

U.S. songwriter, 1862–1932

1 While strolling through the park one day,
All in the merry month of May,
A roguish pair of eyes they took me by surprise,
In a moment my poor heart they stole away!
Oh a sunny smile was all she gave to me.

"The Fountain in the Park" (song) (1884)

T. C. Haliburton

Canadian author and judge, 1796–1865

1 He marched up and down afore the street door like a peacock, as large as life and twice as natural.

The Clockmaker no. 17 (1837)
See Carroll 42

George Savile, Lord Halifax

English politician and essayist, 1633–1695

1 Men are not hanged for stealing horses, but that horses may not be stolen.

Political, Moral, and Miscellaneous Thoughts and Reflections "Of Punishment" (1750)

Jerry Hall

U.S. model, 1956–

1 Mama told me, be a maid in the living room, a cook in the kitchen and a mistress in the bedroom. But I hire someone to be a maid and someone to cook so I can take care of the rest.

Quoted in *St. Louis Post-Dispatch,* 13 June 1985. Similar advice to the first sentence is found as far back as 1959 (*Tucson Daily Citizen,* 8 Sept.).

Owen Hall (James Davis)

Irish librettist, 1853–1907

1 O tell me, pretty maiden, are there any more at home like you?

Florodora act 2 (1900)

Radclyffe Hall

English novelist, 1883–1943

1 The Well of Loneliness.

Title of book (1928)

2 [*Of lesbianism:*] You're neither unnatural, nor abominable, nor mad; you're as much a part of what people call nature as anyone else; only you're unexplained as yet—you've not got your niche in creation.

The Well of Loneliness ch. 20 (1928)

3 I am one of those whom God marked on the forehead. Like Cain, I am marked and blemished. If you come to me . . . the world will abhor you, will persecute you, will call you unclean. Our love may be faithful even unto death and beyond—yet the world will call it unclean.

The Well of Loneliness ch. 37 (1928)

James O. Halliwell

English literary scholar, 1820–1889

1 Presently came along a wolf, and knocked at the door, and said,—"Little pig, little pig, let me come in." To which the pig answered,—"No, no, by the hair of my chiny chin chin." The wolf then answered to that,—"Then I'll huff, and I'll puff, and I'll blow your house in."

Nursery Rhymes and Nursery Tales of England (1855)

Friedrich Halm

German poet and playwright, 1806–1871

1 *Zwei Seelen und ein Gedanke,*
Zwei Herzen und ein Schlag!
Two souls with but a single thought,
Two hearts that beat as one.

Der Sohn der Wildnis act 2 (1842) (translation by Maria Lovell)

Margaret Halsey

U.S. author, 1910–1997

1 Englishwomen's shoes look as if they had been made by someone who had often heard shoes described, but had never seen any.

With Malice Toward Some pt. 2 (1938)

2 The English never smash in a face. They merely refrain from asking it to dinner.

With Malice Toward Some pt. 3 (1938)

3 In a business society, the role of sex can be summed up in five pitiful little words. There is money in it.

The Folks at Home ch. 8 (1952)

William F. "Bull" Halsey

U.S. admiral, 1882–1959

1 [*Dispatch before Battle of Santa Cruz Islands, 26 Oct. 1942:*] ATTACK REPEAT ATTACK.

Quoted in William F. Halsey and J. Bryan III, *Admiral Halsey's Story* (1947)

2 [*Report in response to Japanese claims that most of the U.S. Third Fleet had been sunk or retired, 14 Oct. 1944:*] The Third Fleet's sunken and damaged ships have been salvaged and are retiring at high speed toward the enemy.

Quoted in Elmer B. Potter, *Bull Halsey* (1985)

Fannie Lou Hamer

U.S. civil rights leader, 1917–1977

1 If this is a Great Society, I'd hate to see a bad one.

The Worker, 13 July 1975
See *John Dewey 1; Lyndon Johnson 5; Lyndon Johnson 6; Lyndon Johnson 8; Wallas 1; William Wordsworth 30*

Alexander Hamilton

West Indian–born U.S. statesman, 1757–1804

1 The sacred rights of mankind are not to be rummaged for among old parchments or

musty records. They are written, as with a sunbeam, in the whole volume of human nature, by the hand of the divinity itself; and can never be erased or obscured by mortal power.

"The Farmer Refuted" (1775)

2 I hate Congress—I hate the army—I hate the world—I hate myself. The whole is a mass of fools and knaves.

Letter to John Laurens, 12 Sept. 1780

3 A national debt if it is not excessive will be to us a national blessing.

Letter to Robert Morris, 30 Apr. 1781
See Madison 11

4 Let Americans disdain to be the instruments of European greatness. Let the thirteen States, bound together in a strict and indissoluble Union, concur in erecting one great American system, superior to the control of all transatlantic force or influence, and able to dictate the terms of the connection between the old and the new world!

The Federalist no. 11 (1788)

5 Government implies the power of making laws. It is essential to the idea of a law, that it be attended with a sanction; or, in other words, a penalty or punishment for disobedience.

The Federalist no. 15 (1788)

6 Why has government been instituted at all? Because the passions of men will not conform to the dictates of reason and justice, without constraint.

The Federalist no. 15 (1788)

7 Laws are a dead letter without courts to expound and define their true meaning and operation.

The Federalist no. 22 (1788)

8 The judiciary, from the nature of its functions, will always be the least dangerous to the political rights of the constitution; because it will be least in a capacity to annoy or injure them. . . . The judiciary . . . has no influence over either the sword or the purse, no direction either of the strength or of the wealth of the society, and can take no active resolution whatever. It may truly be said to have neither

FORCE nor WILL, but merely judgment; and must ultimately depend upon the aid of the executive arm even for the efficacy of its judgments.

The Federalist no. 78 (1788)

9 Here [in the House of Representatives], sir, the people govern; here they act by their immediate representatives.

Remarks at New York convention on adoption of federal Constitution, Poughkeepsie, N.Y., 27 June 1788.

10 Every power vested in a government is in its nature *sovereign,* and includes, by *force* of the *term,* a right to employ all the *means* requisite . . . to the *ends* of such power.

Opinion on the Constitutionality of the Bank, 23 Feb. 1791

11 If the end be clearly comprehended within any of the specified powers, and if the measure have an obvious relation to that end, and is not forbidden by any particular provision of the Constitution, it may safely be deemed to come within the compass of the national authority.

Opinion on the Constitutionality of the Bank, 23 Feb. 1791

12 Your people, sir,—your people is a great beast!

Attributed in Theophilus Parsons, *The Memoir of Theophilus Parsons* (1859). Plato described the multitude as a "great strong beast" in *The Republic* bk. 6, 493-B.
See Horace 11

Andrew Hamilton

Scottish-born U.S. lawyer and politician, ca. 1676–1741

1 Power may justly be compar'd to a great River, while kept within it's [sic] due Bounds, is both Beautiful and Useful; but when it overflows, it's [sic] Banks, it is then too impetuous to be stemm'd, it bears down all before it, and brings Destruction and Desolation whenever it comes. If then this is the Nature of Power, let us at least do our Duty, and like wise Men (who value Freedom) use our utmost Care to support Liberty, the only Bulwark against lawless Power, which in all Ages has sacrificed to it's [sic] wild Lust and boundless Ambition, the Blood of the best Men that ever liv'd.

Argument in John Peter Zenger Trial, New York, N.Y. (1735)

2 The Question before the Court and you
Gentlemen of the Jury, is not of small nor
private Concern, it is not the Cause of the poor
Printer, nor of *New-York* alone, which you are
now trying: . . . It is the Cause of Liberty; . . .
every Man who prefers Freedom to a Life of
slavery will bless and honor You, as Men who
have baffled the Attempt of Tyranny; and by
an impartial and uncorrupt Verdict, have laid a
noble Foundation for securing to ourselves, our
Posterity, and our Neighbours, That, to which
Nature and the Laws of our Country have given
us a Right,—the Liberty—both of exposing and
opposing arbitrary Power (in these Parts of the
World, at least) by speaking and writing Truth.
Argument in John Peter Zenger Trial, New York, N.Y.
(1735)

Edith Hamilton

German-born U.S. classical scholar, 1867–1963

1 The fundamental fact about the Greek was that
he had to use his mind. The ancient priests had
said, "Thus far and no farther. We set the limits
to thought." The Greeks said, "All things are
to be examined and called into question. There
are no limits set to thought."
The Greek Way ch. 2 (1930)

Dag Hammarskjöld

Swedish statesman and U.N. Secretary-General,
1905–1961

1 We are not permitted to choose the frame of
our destiny. But what we put into it is ours.
Markings (1964)

2 I don't know Who—or what—put the question,
I don't know when it was put. I don't even
remember answering. But at some moment I
did answer Yes to Someone—or Something—
and from that hour I was certain that existence
is meaningful and that, therefore, my life, in
self-surrender, had a goal.
Markings (1964)

M. C. Hammer (Stanley Kirk Burrell)

U.S. rap musician, 1962–

1 U Can't Touch This.
Title of song (1990). Cowritten with Rick James and
Alonzo Miller.

Oscar Hammerstein II

U.S. songwriter, 1895–1960

1 Fish got to swim, birds got to fly,
I got to love one man till I die—
Can't help lovin' dat man of mine.
"Can't Help Lovin' Dat Man" (song) (1927)

2 Only make believe I love you,
Only make believe that you love me.
Others find peace of mind in pretending—
Couldn't you? Couldn't I? Couldn't we?
"Make Believe" (song) (1927)

3 But Ol' Man River,
He jes' keeps rollin' along.
"Ol' Man River" (song) (1927)

4 The last time I saw Paris her heart was warm
and gay.
"The Last Time I Saw Paris" (song) (1940)

5 Everythin's up to date in Kansas City.
They've gone about as fur as they c'n go!
"Kansas City" (song) (1943)

6 The corn is as high as a elephant's eye,
An' it looks like it's climbin' clear up to the sky.
"Oh, What a Beautiful Mornin'!" (song) (1943)

7 Oh what a beautiful mornin'!
Oh what a beautiful day!
I got a beautiful feelin'
Everythin's goin' my way.
"Oh, What a Beautiful Mornin'!" (song) (1943)

8 Oklahoma,
Where the wind comes sweepin' down the
plain,
And the wavin' wheat

Can sure smell sweet
When the wind comes right behind the rain.
"Oklahoma!" (song) (1943)

9 Don't sigh and gaze at me
(Your sighs are so like mine),
Your eyes mustn't glow like mine—
People will say we're in love!
"People Will Say We're in Love" (song) (1943)

10 Chicks and ducks and geese better scurry
When I take you out in the surrey,
When I take you out in the surrey with the
fringe on top.
"The Surrey with the Fringe on Top" (song) (1943)

11 June is bustin' out all over
All over the meadow and the hill!
"June Is Bustin' Out All Over" (song) (1945)

12 Walk on, walk on with hope in your heart,
And you'll never walk alone!
"You'll Never Walk Alone" (song) (1945)

13 I'm Gonna Wash That Man Right Outa My
Hair.
Title of song (1949)

14 Some enchanted evening,
You may see a stranger . . .
Across a crowded room.
"Some Enchanted Evening" (song) (1949)

15 There is nothin' like a dame! . . .
There is nothin' you can name
That is anythin' like a dame!
"There Is Nothin' like a Dame" (song) (1949)

16 I'm as corny as Kansas in August,
High as a flag on the Fourth of July!
"A Wonderful Guy" (song) (1949)

17 Younger than springtime are you.
"Younger Than Springtime" (song) (1949)

18 You've got to be taught to be afraid
Of people whose eyes are oddly made,
Of people whose skin is a different shade.
You've got to be carefully taught.
"You've Got to Be Carefully Taught" (song) (1949)

19 Hello, young lovers, whoever you are,
I hope your troubles are few.
All my good wishes go with you tonight—
I've been in love like you.
"Hello, Young Lovers" (song) (1951)

20 I know how it feels to have wings on your heels,
And to fly down the street in a trance.
You fly down a street on the chance that you'll
meet,
And you meet—not really by chance.
"Hello, Young Lovers" (song) (1951)

21 Whenever I feel afraid
I hold my head erect
And whistle a happy tune,
So no one will suspect
I'm afraid.
"I Whistle a Happy Tune" (song) (1951)

22 Shall we dance?
On a bright cloud of music shall we fly?
"Shall We Dance" (song) (1951)

23 Climb ev'ry mountain,
Ford every stream,
Follow every rainbow
Till you find your dream.
"Climb Ev'ry Mountain" (song) (1959)

24 Doe—a deer, a female deer,
Ray—a drop of golden sun.
"Do Re Mi" (song) (1959)

25 Raindrops on roses and whiskers on kittens,
Bright copper kettles and warm woolen mittens,
Brown paper packages tied up with strings—
These are a few of my favorite things.
"My Favorite Things" (song) (1959)

26 When the dog bites,
When the bee stings,
When I'm feeling sad,
I simply remember my favorite things
And then I don't feel so bad!
"My Favorite Things" (song) (1959)

27 The hills are alive
With the sound of music,
With songs they have sung
For a thousand years.
"The Sound of Music" (song) (1959)

Dashiell Hammett

U.S. detective fiction writer, 1894–1961

1 I won't play the sap for you.
The Maltese Falcon ch. 20 (1930)

2 When a man's partner is killed he's supposed
to do something about it. It doesn't make
any difference what you thought of him. He

was your partner and you're supposed to do something about it.

The Maltese Falcon ch. 20 (1930)

3 Don't be too sure I'm as crooked as I'm supposed to be. That kind of reputation might be good business—bringing in high-priced jobs and making it easier to deal with the enemy.

The Maltese Falcon ch. 20 (1930)

Jupiter Hammon

U.S. writer, 1711–ca. 1805

1 If we should ever get to Heaven, we shall find nobody to reproach us for being black, or being slaves.

An Address to the Negroes in the State of New-York (1787)

Amadou Hampâté Bâ

Malian author and anthropologist, 1901–1991

1 In Africa, when an old man dies, it is a library burning.

Speech at UNESCO conference, Paris, Dec. 1960

Knut Hamsun

Norwegian writer, 1859–1952

1 It was during the time I wandered about and starved in Christiana: Christiana, this singular city, from which no man departs without carrying away the traces of his sojourn there.

Hunger pt. 1 (1890) (translation by George Egerton)

2 Nought availed; I was dying helplessly, with my eyes wide open—staring straight up at the roof. At length, I stuck my forefinger in my mouth, and took to sucking it. Something stirred in my brain, a thought that bored its way in there—a stark-mad notion. Supposing I were to take a bite? And without a moment's reflection, I shut my eyes, and clenched my teeth on it. I sprang up. At last I was thoroughly awake.

Hunger pt. 3 (1890) (translation by George Egerton)

John Hancock

U.S. statesman, 1737–1793

1 [*Remark upon signing his name boldly on the engrossed copy of the Declaration of Independence, 2 Aug. 1776:*] There John Bull can read my name without spectacles.

Attributed in *Public Ledger* (Philadelphia), 10 July 1841. This quotation is undoubtedly apocryphal.

Learned Hand

U.S. judge, 1872–1961

1 I must say that as a litigant I should dread a lawsuit beyond almost anything else short of sickness and death.

"The Deficiencies of Trials to Reach the Heart of the Matter" (lecture at Association of the Bar of the City of New York) (1921)

2 A transaction, otherwise within an exception of the tax law, does not lose its immunity, because it is actuated by a desire to avoid, or, if one choose, to evade, taxation. Any one may so arrange his affairs that his taxes shall be as low as possible; he is not bound to choose the pattern which will best pay the Treasury; there is not even a patriotic duty to increase one's taxes.

Helvering v. Gregory (1934)

3 This much I think I do know—that a society so riven that the spirit of moderation is gone, no court *can* save; that a society where that spirit flourishes, no court *need* save; that in a society which evades its responsibility by thrusting upon the courts the nurture of that spirit, that spirit in the end will perish.

"The Contribution of an Independent Judiciary to Civilization" (speech), Boston, Mass., 21 Nov. 1942
See Hand 5

4 Right conclusions are more likely to be gathered out of a multitude of tongues, than through any kind of authoritative selection. To many this is, and always will be, folly; but we have staked upon it our all.

United States v. Associated Press (1943)

5 I often wonder whether we do not rest our hopes too much upon constitutions, upon laws and upon courts. These are false hopes, believe me, these are false hopes. Liberty lies in the hearts of men and women; when it dies there, no constitution, no law, no court can save it; no constitution, no law, no court can even do much to help it. While it lies there it needs no constitution, no law, no court to save it.

"The Spirit of Liberty" (speech), New York, N.Y., 21 May 1944
See Hand 3

6 What then is the spirit of liberty? I cannot define it; I can only tell you my own faith. The spirit of liberty is the spirit which is not too sure that it is right; the spirit of liberty is the spirit which seeks to understand the minds of other men and women; the spirit of liberty is the spirit which weighs their interests alongside its own without bias.

"The Spirit of Liberty" (speech), New York, N.Y., 21 May 1944

7 In each case [the courts] must ask whether the gravity of the "evil," discounted by its improbability, justifies such invasion of free speech as is necessary to avoid the danger.

United States v. Dennis (1950)

8 Law has always been unintelligible, and I might say that perhaps it ought to be. And I will tell you why, because I don't want to deal in paradoxes. It ought to be unintelligible because it ought to be in words—and words are utterly inadequate to deal with the fantastically multiform occasions which come up in human life.

"Thou Shalt Not Ration Justice" (1951)

9 If we are to keep our democracy, there must be one commandment: Thou shalt not ration justice.

"Thou Shalt Not Ration Justice" (1951)

10 One utterance of [Oliver Cromwell] . . . has always hung in my mind. It was just before the Battle of Dunbar; he beat the Scots in the end . . . but he wrote them before the battle, trying to get them to accept a reasonable composition. These were his words: "I beseech ye in the bowels of Christ, think ye may be mistaken." I should like to have that written over the portals of every church, every school, and every court house, and, may I say, of every legislative body in the United States. I should like to have every court begin, "I beseech ye in the bowels of Christ, think that we may be mistaken."

Testimony before Senate committee, 28 June 1951
See *Cromwell 1*

11 For myself I had rather take my chance that some traitors will escape detection than spread abroad a spirit of general suspicion and distrust. . . . I believe that that community is already in process of dissolution where each

man begins to eye his neighbor as a possible enemy, where nonconformity with the accepted creed, political as well as religious, is a mark of disaffection; where denunciation, without specification or backing, takes the place of evidence; where orthodoxy chokes freedom of dissent; where faith in the eventual supremacy of reason has become so timid that we dare not enter our convictions in the open lists, to win or lose.

"A Plea for the Open Mind and Free Discussion" (speech), Albany, N.Y., 24 Oct. 1952

George Frederick Handel
German-born English composer, 1685–1759

1 Whether I was in my body or out of my body [as he wrote the "Hallelujah Chorus" in *Messiah*] I know not. God knows it!

Attributed in *Harvard Magazine*, Dec. 1862. Handel here echoed II Corinthians 12:2: "I knew a man in Christ above fourteen years ago (whether in the body, I cannot tell; or whether out of the body, I cannot tell: God knoweth)."

J. B. (John Bernard) Handelsman
U.S. cartoonist, 1922–2007

1 [*Lawyer to potential client:*] You have a pretty good case, Mr. Pitkin. How much justice can you afford?

New Yorker, 24 Dec. 1973 (cartoon caption)

Jack Handey
U.S. humorist, 1949–

1 If trees could scream, would we be so cavalier about cutting them down? We might, if they screamed all the time, for no good reason.

Saturday Night Live (television program), 12 Oct. 1991

2 I can picture in my mind a world without war, a world without hate. And I can picture us attacking that world, because they'd never expect it.

Quoted in *L.A. Times,* 18 Jan. 1999

W. C. Handy
U.S. blues musician, 1873–1958

1 Memphis Blues.

Title of song (1912). Earliest documented occurrence of the term *blues.*

2 I hate to see de ev'nin' sun go down,
   Hate to see de ev'nin' sun go down,
   'Cause ma baby he done lef dis town.
   "St. Louis Blues" (song) (1914)

3 St. Louis woman, wid her diamon' rings,
   Pulls dat man 'roun' by her apron strings.
   "St. Louis Blues" (song) (1914)

4 Got de St. Louis Blues jes as blue as ah can be,
   Dat man got a heart lak a rock cast in the sea,
   Or else he wouldn't have gone so far from me.
   "St. Louis Blues" (song) (1914)

5 If Beale Street could talk, if Beale Street could
      talk,
   Married men would have to take their beds and
      walk,
   Except one or two, who never drink booze,
   And the blind man on the corner who sings the
      Beale Street Blues.
   "Beale Street Blues" (song) (1916)

Carol Hanisch

U.S. feminist, fl. 1969

1 The Personal Is Political.
   Title of article, *Notes from the Second Year* (1969).
   Hanisch later stated that her article's title was
   supplied by editors Shulamith Firestone and
   Anne Koedt.

Lorraine Hansberry

U.S. playwright, 1930–1965

1 In my mother's house there is still God.
   A Raisin in the Sun act 1, sc. 1 (1959)

2 [*To winners of a creative writing contest sponsored
   by* Reader's Digest *and the United Negro College
   Fund:*] Though it be a thrilling and marvellous
   thing to be merely young and gifted in such
   times, it is doubly so—doubly dynamic—to be
   young, gifted *and black.*
   Negro Digest, Aug. 1964

Beck Hansen

U.S. musician, 1970–

1 In the time of chimpanzees I was a monkey.
   "Loser" (song) (1993)

2 I'm a loser baby, why don't you kill me.
   "Loser" (song) (1993)

Edmond Haraucourt

French poet, 1856–1941

1 *Partir c'est mourir un peu,
   C'est mourir à ce qu'on aime.*
   To go away is to die a little,
   It is to die to that which one loves.
   "Rondel de l'Adieu" (1891)

Donna Haraway

U.S. cultural theorist, 1944–

1 Though both are bound in the spiral dance, I
   would rather be a cyborg than a goddess.
   "A Manifesto for Cyborgs: Science, Technology, and
   Socialist Feminism in the 1980s" (1985)

Otto Harbach

U.S. songwriter, 1873–1963

1 When a lovely flame dies,
   Smoke gets in your eyes.
   "Smoke Gets in Your Eyes" (song) (1933)

E. Y. Harburg

U.S. songwriter, 1896–1981

1 Brother, Can You Spare a Dime?
   Title of song (1932)

2 Ding Dong! The Wicked Witch is dead.
   "Ding Dong! The Witch Is Dead!" (song) (1939)

3 I could while away the hours
   Conversin' with the flowers,
   Consultin' with the rain;
   With the thoughts I'd be thinkin'
   I could be another Lincoln,
   If I only had a brain.
   "If I Only Had a Brain" (song) (1939)

4 Somewhere over the rainbow
   Skies are blue,
   And the dreams that you dare to dream
   Really do come true.
   "Over the Rainbow" (song) (1939)

5 Somewhere over the rainbow
   Bluebirds fly,
   Birds fly over the rainbow
   Why then oh why can't I?
   "Over the Rainbow" (song) (1939)

6 Follow the yellow brick road.

"We're Off to See the Wizard (The Wonderful Wizard of Oz)" (song) (1939)
See L. Frank Baum 1

7 We're off to see the wizard.
The wonderful wizard of Oz.
We hear he is
A whiz of a Wiz
If ever a Wiz there was.

"We're Off to See the Wizard (The Wonderful Wizard of Oz)" (song) (1939)

William Harcourt

British politician, 1827–1904

1 We are all Socialists now.

Speech in House of Commons, 11 Aug. 1887
See Milton Friedman 6

Garrett Hardin

U.S. biologist, 1915–2003

1 We can never do merely one thing.

Perspectives in Biology and Medicine, Autumn 1963

2 The Tragedy of the Commons.

Title of article, *Science,* 13 Dec. 1968

3 Ruin is the destination toward which all men rush, each pursuing his own best interest in a society that believes in the freedom of the commons. Freedom in a commons brings ruin to all.

"The Tragedy of the Commons," *Science,* 13 Dec. 1968

4 Picture a pasture open to all. . . . The rational herdsman concludes that the only sensible course for him to pursue is to add another animal to his herd. And another; and another. . . . But this is the conclusion reached by each and every rational herdsman sharing a commons. Therein is the tragedy. Each man is locked into a system that compels him to increase his herd without limit—in a world that is limited.

"The Tragedy of the Commons," *Science,* 13 Dec. 1968. The second ellipsis is in the original.

Warren G. Harding

U.S. president, 1865–1923

1 America's present need is not heroics but healing; not nostrums but normalcy; not

revolution but restoration; . . . not surgery but serenity.

Speech, Boston, Mass., 14 May 1920. Harding was widely derided for coining the word *normalcy,* but in fact this word was already current and the *Oxford English Dictionary* documents it as early as 1857. Apparently Harding's manuscript had the word as *normality,* but he misspoke it as *normalcy.*

Elizabeth Hardwick

U.S. critic and author, 1916–2007

1 This is the unspoken contract of a wife and her works. In the long run wives are to be paid in a peculiar coin—consideration for their feelings. And it usually turns out this is an enormous, unthinkable inflation few men will remit, or if they will, only with a sense of being overcharged.

Seduction and Betrayal: Women and Literature
"Amateurs" (1974)

G. H. Hardy

English mathematician, 1877–1947

1 Archimedes will be remembered when Aeschylus is forgotten, because languages die and mathematical ideas do not. "Immortality" may be a silly word, but probably a mathematician has the best chance of whatever it may mean.

A Mathematician's Apology ch. 8 (1940)

2 The mathematician's patterns, like the painter's or the poet's, must be *beautiful;* the ideas, like the colors or the words, must fit together in a harmonious way. Beauty is the first test: there is no permanent place in the world for ugly mathematics.

A Mathematician's Apology ch. 10 (1940)

3 A science is said to be useful if its development tends to accentuate the existing inequalities in the distribution of wealth, or more directly promotes the destruction of human life.

A Mathematician's Apology ch. 21 (1940)

Thomas Hardy

English novelist and poet, 1840–1928

1 The difference between a common man and a recognized poet is, that one has been deluded,

and cured of his delusion, and the other continues deluded all his days.
Desperate Remedies ch. 3 (1871)

2 Though a good deal is too strange to be believed, nothing is too strange to have happened.
Notebook, Feb. 1871

3 Good, but not religious-good.
Under the Greenwood Tree ch. 2 (1872)

4 Uniform pleasantness is rather a defect than a faculty. It shows that a man hasn't sense enough to know whom to despise.
A Pair of Blue Eyes ch. 9 (1873)

5 Anybody's life may be just as romantic and strange and interesting if he or she fails as if he or she succeed. All the difference is, that the last chapter is wanting in the story.
A Pair of Blue Eyes ch. 19 (1873)

6 There is no regular path for getting out of love as there is for getting in. Some people look upon marriage as a short cut that way, but it has been known to fail.
Far from the Madding Crowd ch. 5 (1874)

7 If a woman did not invariably form an opinion of her choice before she has half seen him, and love him before she has half formed an opinion, there would be no tears and pining in the whole feminine world, and poets would starve for want of a topic.
The Hand of Ethelberta ch. 19 (1876)

8 Women the most delicate get used to strange moral situations. Eve probably regained her normal sweet composure about a week after the Fall.
Two on a Tower ch. 35 (1882)

9 MICHAEL HENCHARD'S WILL
"That Elizabeth-Jane Farfrae be not told of my death, or made to grieve on account of me.
"& that I be not bury'd in consecrated ground.
"& that no sexton be asked to toll the bell.
"& that nobody is wished to see my dead body.
"& that no murners walk behind me at my funeral.
"& that no flours be planted on my grave.
"& that no man remember me.
"To this I put my name.
The Mayor of Casterbridge ch. 45 (1886)

10 A woeful fact—that the human race is too extremely developed for its corporeal conditions, the nerves being evolved to an activity abnormal in such an environment. Even the higher animals are in excess in this respect. It may be questioned if Nature, or what we call nature, so far back as when she crossed the line from invertebrates to vertebrates, did not exceed her mission. This planet does not supply the materials for happiness to higher existences.
Notebook, 7 Apr. 1889

11 Did it never strike your mind that what every woman says some women may feel?
Tess of the D'Urbervilles ch. 12 (1891)

12 Considering his position he became wonderfully free from the chronic melancholy which is taking hold of the civilized races with the decline of belief in a beneficent Power.
Tess of the D'Urbervilles ch. 18 (1891)

13 "Justice" was done, and the President of the Immortals (in Aeschylean phrase) had ended his sport with Tess.
Tess of the D'Urbervilles ch. 59 (1891)

14 And so, standing before the aforesaid officiator, the two swore that at every other time of their lives till death took them, they would assuredly believe, feel, and desire precisely as they had believed, felt, and desired during the few preceding weeks. What was as remarkable as the undertaking itself was the fact that nobody seemed at all surprised at what they swore.
Jude the Obscure pt. 1, ch. 9 (1896)

15 The social moulds civilization fits us into have no more relation to our actual shapes than the conventional shapes of the constellations have to the real star-patterns.
Jude the Obscure pt. 4, ch. 1 (1896)

16 If the marriage ceremony consisted in an oath and signed contract between the parties to cease loving from that day forward . . . and to avoid each other's society as much as possible in public, there would be more loving couples than there are now. Fancy the secret meetings between the perjuring husband and wife, the denials of having seen each other, the clambering in at bedroom windows, and the hiding in closets! There'd be little cooling then.
Jude the Obscure pt. 5, ch. 1 (1896)

17 People go on marrying because they can't resist natural forces, although many of them may know perfectly well that they are possibly buying a month's pleasure with a life's discomfort.
Jude the Obscure pt. 5, ch. 1 (1896)

18 That excessive regard of parents for their own children, and their dislike of other people's, is, like class-feeling, patriotism, save-your-own-soul-ism, and other virtues, a mean exclusiveness at bottom.
Jude the Obscure pt. 5, ch. 3 (1896)

19 [*Suicide note by a child who killed himself and two siblings:*] Done because we are too menny.
Jude the Obscure pt. 6, ch. 2 (1896)

20 An aged thrush, frail, gaunt, and small, In blast-beruffled plume.
"The Darkling Thrush" l. 21 (1902)

21 Pessimism (or rather what is called such) is, in brief, playing the sure game. You cannot lose at it; you may gain. It is the only view of life in which you can never be disappointed. Having reckoned what to do in the worst possible circumstances, when better arise, as they may, life becomes child's play.
Notebook, 1 Jan. 1902

22 A local thing called Christianity.
The Dynasts pt. 1, act 1, sc. 6 (1904)

23 War makes rattling good history; but Peace is poor reading.
The Dynasts pt. 1, act 2, sc. 5 (1904)

24 Yes; quaint and curious war is!
You shoot a fellow down
You'd treat if met where any bar is,
Or help to half-a-crown.
"The Man He Killed" l. 17 (1909)

25 And as the smart ship grew
In stature, grace, and hue,
In shadowy silent distance grew the
Iceberg too.
"The Convergence of the Twain (Lines on the Loss of the *Titanic*)" l. 22 (1912)

26 Till the Spinner of the Years
Said "Now!" And each one hears,
And consummation comes, and jars two
hemispheres.
"The Convergence of the Twain (Lines on the Loss of the *Titanic*)" l. 31 (1912)

27 Yonder a maid and her wight
Come whispering by:
War's annals will cloud into night
Ere their story die.
"In Time of 'The Breaking of Nations'" l. 9 (1915)

28 I am the family face;
Flesh perishes, I live on,
Projecting trait and trace
Through time to times anon,
And leaping from place to place
Over oblivion.
"Heredity" l. 1 (1917)

29 The years-heired feature that can
In curve and voice and eye
Despise the human span
Of durance—that is I;
The eternal thing in man,
That heeds no call to die.
"Heredity" l. 7 (1917)

30 [*Remark, 1918:*] My opinion is that a poet should express the emotion of all the ages and the thought of his own.

Quoted in Florence Emily Hardy, *The Later Years of Thomas Hardy* (1930)

John Harington

English writer and translator, 1561–1612

1 Treason doth never prosper, what's the reason?
For if it prosper, none dare call it treason.

Epigrams "Of Treason" (1618)

John M. Harlan

U.S. judge, 1833–1911

1 By the Louisiana statute, the validity of which is here involved, all railway companies (other than street railroad companies) carrying passengers in that State are required to have separate but equal accommodations for white and colored persons.

Plessy v. Ferguson (dissenting opinion) (1896). The statute used the phrase "equal but separate," but Harlan's opinion popularized "separate but equal." An earlier usage of the latter formulation appears in the argument of counsel in an 1889 Mississippi case, *Louisville, N.O. & T.R. Co. v. State.* The Declaration of Independence referred to "the separate and equal station to which the laws of Nature and of Nature's God entitle" a people.
See Kerner 1; Earl Warren 1

2 But in view of the Constitution, in the eye of the law, there is in this country no superior, dominant, ruling class of citizens. There is no caste here. Our Constitution is color-blind, and neither knows nor tolerates classes among citizens. In respect of civil rights, all citizens are equal before the law. The humblest is the peer of the most powerful.

Plessy v. Ferguson (dissenting opinion) (1896)

3 The arbitrary separation of citizens, on the basis of race, while they are on a public highway, is a badge of servitude wholly inconsistent with the civil freedom and the equality before the law established by the Constitution. . . . We boast of the freedom enjoyed by our people above all other peoples. But it is difficult to reconcile that boast with a state of the law which, practically, puts the brand of servitude and degradation upon a large class of our fellow-citizens, our equals

before the law. The thin disguise of "equal" accommodations for passengers in railroad coaches will not mislead any one, nor atone for the wrong this day done.

Plessy v. Ferguson (dissenting opinion) (1896)

John M. Harlan

U.S. judge, 1899–1971

1 One man's vulgarity is another man's lyric.

Cohen v. California (1971)

Sheldon Harnick

U.S. songwriter, 1924–

1 Matchmaker, matchmaker, make me a match,
Find me a find,
Catch me a catch.

"Matchmaker" (song) (1964)

Robert Goodloe Harper

U.S. politician, 1765–1825

1 Millions for defense but not a cent for tribute.

Toast at dinner for John Marshall, Philadelphia, Pa., 18 June 1798. According to Burton E. Stevenson, *The Home Book of Quotations,* this was "published in the *American Daily Advertiser,* 20 June, 1798. . . . Harper afterwards explained that what he had in mind was . . . that, instead of permitting France to plunder American merchant vessels of millions in tribute, he would spend them in defense." This quotation is often ascribed to Charles Cotesworth Pinckney as a response to a demand for a $250,000 bribe made by a French secret agent in 1797, but Pinckney said that his response was "Not a penny; not a penny."

James Harrington

English philosopher, 1611–1677

1 These I conceive to be the principles upon which Aristotle and Livy . . . have grounded their assertion that a commonwealth is an empire of laws and not of men.

The Commonwealth of Oceana pt. 1 (1656)
See John Adams 4; Archibald Cox 1; Gerald Ford 3

Michael Harrington

U.S. political scientist and socialist, 1928–1989

1 The other America, the America of poverty, is hidden today in a way that it never was before. Its millions are socially invisible to the rest of us.

The Other America: Poverty in the United States ch. 1 (1962)

2 For the middle class, the police protect property, give directions, and help old ladies. For the urban poor, the police are those who arrest you. In almost any slum there is a vast conspiracy against the forces of law and order.
The Other America: Poverty in the United States ch. 1 (1962)

3 To be a Negro is to participate in a culture of poverty and fear that goes far deeper than any law for or against discrimination. . . . After the racist statutes are all struck down, after legal equality has been achieved in the schools and in the courts, there remains the profound institutionalized and abiding wrong that white America has worked on the Negro for so long.
The Other America: Poverty in the United States ch. 4 (1962)

Charles K. Harris
U.S. songwriter, 1867–1930

1 Many a heart is aching, if you could read them all,
Many the hopes that have vanished, after the ball.
"After the Ball" (song) (1892)

Charles S. Harris
U.S. psychologist, 1937–

1 A man without faith is like a fish without a bicycle.
Swarthmore Phoenix, 7 Apr. 1958. Often repeated as "a man without God . . ." It inspired the feminist slogan "A woman without a man is like a fish without a bicycle." A very early precursor appeared in the *Hartford Courant,* 31 Dec. 1898, which referred to a town in Spain: "The place didn't need an American consul any more than a cow needs a bicycle."
See Dunn 1

Joanne Harris
English novelist, 1964–

1 She closes her eyes again, and I begin to sing softly: . . . Hoping that this time it will remain a lullaby. That this time the wind will not hear. That this time—*please, just this once*—it will leave without us.
Chocolat ch. 39 (1999)

Joel Chandler Harris
U.S. writer, 1848–1908

1 Tar-baby ain't sayin' nuthin', en Brer Fox, he lay low.
Uncle Remus and His Legends of the Old Plantation "The Wonderful Tar-Baby Story" (1881)

Mark Harris (Mark Finkelstein)
U.S. writer, 1922–2007

1 From here on in I rag nobody.
Bang the Drum Slowly ch. 17 (1956)

Robert Harris
English journalist and author, 1957–

1 There can now be no doubt that it is Stalin rather than Hitler who is the most alarming figure of the twentieth century. I say this—I say this not merely because Stalin killed more people than Hitler—though clearly he did—and not even because Stalin was more of a psychopath than Hitler—although clearly he was. I say it because Stalin was not a one-off like Hitler, an eruption from nowhere. Stalin stands in a historical tradition of rule by terror which existed before him, which he refined, and which could exist again. His, not Hitler's, is the spectre that should worry us.
Archangel ch. 11 (1998)

2 The great western myth. . . . That just because a place has a McDonald's and MTV and takes American Express it's exactly the same as everywhere else—it doesn't have a past any more, it's Year Zero.
Archangel ch. 16 (1998)

Rolf Harris
Australian television host, 1930–

1 Tie Me Kangaroo Down, Sport.
Title of song (1960)

Thomas Harris
U.S. novelist, 1940–

1 A census taker tried to quantify me once. I ate his liver with some fava beans and a big Amarone.
The Silence of the Lambs ch. 3 (1991)

Thomas A. Harris
U.S. psychiatrist and author, 1910–1995

1 I'm OK—You're OK.
Title of book (1969)

George Harrison
English rock musician, 1943–2001

1 I look at you all see the love there that's sleeping
While my guitar gently weeps.
"While My Guitar Gently Weeps" (song) (1968)

Deborah Harry (Angela Trimble)
U.S. singer and songwriter, 1945–

1 Cover me with kisses, baby
Cover me with love
Roll me in designer sheets
I'll never get enough.
"Call Me" (song) (1980)

Frances Noyes Hart
U.S. writer, 1890–1943

1 It's the greatest murder trial of the century—
about every two years another one of 'em comes
along.
The Bellamy Trial (1928)

Gary Hart (Gary Warren Hartpence)
U.S. politician, 1936–

1 [*On allegations of his womanizing before his
scandal with Donna Rice:*] Follow me around. I
don't care. I'm serious. If anybody wants to put
a tail on me, go ahead. They'd be very bored.
Quoted in *N.Y. Times Magazine,* 3 May 1987

Josephine Hart
Irish writer, 1942–2011

1 Damaged people are dangerous. They know
they can survive.
Damage ch. 12 (1991)

Lorenz Hart
U.S. songwriter, 1895–1943

1 We'll have Manhattan,
The Bronx and Staten
Island too.
"Manhattan" (song) (1925)

2 With a Song in My Heart.
Title of song (1930)

3 When love congeals
It soon reveals
The faint aroma of performing seals,
The double crossing of a pair of heels.
I wish I were in love again!
"I Wish I Were in Love Again" (song) (1937)

4 Johnny One Note.
Title of song (1937)

5 That's why the lady is a tramp.
"The Lady Is a Tramp" (song) (1937)

6 Falling in love with love
Is falling for make-believe.
Falling in love with love
Is playing the fool.
"Falling in Love with Love" (song) (1938)

7 I fell in love,
With love everlasting,
But love fell out with me.
"Falling in Love with Love" (song) (1938)

8 Bewitched, Bothered, and Bewildered.
Title of song (1941)

Moss Hart
U.S. playwright, 1904–1961

1 [*Referring to the Broadway theater:*] The Fabulous
Invalid.
Title of play (1938). Coauthored with George S.
Kaufman.

2 George Washington slept here.
George Washington Slept Here act 1, sc. 1 (1941).
Coauthored with George S. Kaufman.

Bret Harte
U.S. writer, 1836–1902

1 Beneath this tree lies the body of John
Oakhurst, who struck a streak of bad luck on
the 23rd of November, 1850, and handed in his
checks on the 7th December, 1850.
"The Outcasts of Poker Flat" (1869)

L. P. Hartley
English novelist, 1895–1972

1 The past is a foreign country: they do things
differently there.
The Go-Between prologue (1953)

William Harvey
English physician and anatomist, 1578–1657

1 I profess both to learn and to teach anatomy, not from books but from dissections; not from the positions of philosophers but from the fabric of nature.
On the Motion of the Heart and Blood in Animals (1628) (translation by Robert Willis)

Henry S. Haskins
U.S. stockbroker and author, 1875–1957

1 What lies behind us and what lies before us are tiny matters compared to what lies within us.
Meditations in Wall Street (1940)

Robert Hass
U.S. poet, 1941–

1 All the new thinking is about loss.
In this it resembles the old thinking.
"Meditation at Lagunitas" l. 1 (1979)

2 A word is elegy to what it signifies.
"Meditation at Lagunitas" l. 11 (1979)

3 Longing, we say, because desire is full of endless distances.
"Meditation at Lagunitas" l. 24 (1979)

4 There are moments when the body is as numinous
as words, days that are the good flesh continuing.
Such tenderness, those afternoons and evenings,
saying blackberry, blackberry, blackberry.
"Meditation at Lagunitas" l. 28 (1979)

Václav Havel
Czech president and playwright, 1936–2011

1 A specter is haunting Eastern Europe: the specter of what in the West is called "dissent."
"The Power of the Powerless" (1978) (translation by Paul Wilson)

2 There's always something suspect about an intellectual on the winning side.
Disturbing the Peace ch. 5 (1986) (translation by Paul Wilson)

Stephen W. Hawking
English physicist, 1942–2018

1 Someone told me that each equation I included in the book would halve the sales.
A Brief History of Time acknowledgments (1988)

2 A well-known scientist (some say it was Bertrand Russell) once gave a public lecture on astronomy. He described how the earth orbits around the sun and how the sun, in turn, orbits around the center of a vast collection of stars called our galaxy. At the end of the lecture, a little old lady at the back of the room got up and said: "What you have told us is rubbish. The world is really a flat plate supported on the back of a giant tortoise." The scientist gave a superior smile before replying, "What is the tortoise standing on?" "You're very clever, young man, very clever," said the old lady. "But it's turtles all the way down!"
A Brief History of Time ch. 1 (1988). A very similar anecdote, in which an old woman speaks of "rocks all the way down," is found as early as 1838 (*The New-Yorker*, 18 Aug.).

3 If we do discover a complete theory [of the universe], it should in time be understandable in broad principle by everyone, not just a few scientists. Then we shall all, philosophers, scientists, and just ordinary people, be able to take part in the discussion of the question of why it is that we and the universe exist. If we find the answer to that, it would be the ultimate triumph of human reason—for then we would know the mind of God.
A Brief History of Time ch. 11 (1988)

4 What is it that breathes fire into the equations and makes a universe for them to describe. . . . Why does the universe go to all the bother of existing?
A Brief History of Time ch. 11 (1988)

5 The best evidence we have that time travel is not possible, and never will be, is that we have not been invaded by hordes of tourists from the future.
Darwin Lecture at Cambridge University, Cambridge, England, Jan. 1991

Edwin Hawkins

U.S. gospel musician, 1943–2018

1 Oh happy day
  When Jesus . . . washed my sins away.
  "Oh Happy Day" (song) (1969)

Nathaniel Hawthorne

U.S. novelist and short story writer, 1804–1864

1 By the sympathy of your human hearts for sin
  ye shall scent out all the places—whether in
  church, bedchamber, street, field, or forest—
  where crime has been committed, and shall
  exult to behold the whole earth one stain of
  guilt, one mighty blood spot.
  "Young Goodman Brown" (1835)

2 We sometimes congratulate ourselves at the
  moment of waking from a troubled dream; it
  may be so the moment after death.
  Journal, 25 Oct. 1836

3 The Scarlet Letter.
  Title of book (1850)

4 If a man, sitting all alone, cannot dream
  strange things, and make them look like truth,
  he need never try to write romances.
  The Scarlet Letter "The Custom-House" (1850)

5 On the breast of her gown, in fine red cloth,
  surrounded with an elaborate embroidery and
  fantastic flourishes of gold thread, appeared the
  letter A.
  The Scarlet Letter ch. 2 (1850)

6 My heart was a habitation large enough for
  many guests, but lonely and chill, and without
  a household fire. I longed to kindle one! It
  seemed not so wild a dream.
  The Scarlet Letter ch. 4 (1850)

7 But there is a fatality, a feeling so irresistible
  and inevitable that it has the force of doom,
  which almost invariably compels human
  beings to linger around and haunt, ghost-like,
  the spot where some great and marked event
  has given the color to their lifetime; and still
  the more irresistibly, the darker the tinge that
  saddens it.
  The Scarlet Letter ch. 5 (1850)

8 Let the black flower blossom as it may!
  The Scarlet Letter ch. 14 (1850)

9 Let men tremble to win the hand of woman,
  unless they win along with it the utmost
  passion of her heart!
  The Scarlet Letter ch. 15 (1850)

10 What we did had a consecration of its own.
  The Scarlet Letter ch. 17 (1850)

11 The scarlet letter was her passport into
  regions where other women dared not tread.
  Shame, Despair, Solitude! These had been her
  teachers,—stern and wild ones,—and they had
  made her strong, but taught her much amiss.
  The Scarlet Letter ch. 18 (1850)

12 We must not always talk in the market-place of
  what happens to us in the forest.
  The Scarlet Letter ch. 22 (1850)

13 She assured them, too, of her firm belief, that,
  at some brighter period, when the world should
  have grown ripe for it, in Heaven's own time,
  a new truth would be revealed, in order to
  establish the whole relation between man and
  woman on a surer ground of mutual happiness.
  The Scarlet Letter ch. 24 (1850)

14 Not to be deficient in this particular, the author
  has provided himself with a moral;—the truth,
  namely, that the wrong-doing of one generation
  lives into the successive ones.
  The House of the Seven Gables preface (1851)

15 God will give him blood to drink!
  The House of the Seven Gables ch. 1 (1851)

16 For, what other dungeon is so dark as one's
  own heart! What jailer so inexorable as one's
  self!
  The House of the Seven Gables ch. 11 (1851)

17 What we call real estate . . . is the broad
  foundation on which nearly all the guilt of this
  world rests.
  The House of the Seven Gables ch. 17 (1851)

18 The world owes all its onward impulses to men
  ill at ease. The happy man inevitably confines
  himself within ancient limits.
  The House of the Seven Gables ch. 20 (1851)
  See George Bernard Shaw 22

19 The greatest obstacle to being heroic is the doubt whether one may not be going to prove one's self a fool; the truest heroism is to resist the doubt; and the profoundest wisdom to know when it ought to be resisted, and when to be obeyed.
The Blithedale Romance ch. 2 (1852)

20 It is my belief—yes, and my prophecy, should I die before it happens—that, when my sex shall achieve its rights, there will be ten eloquent women where there is now one eloquent man. Thus far, no woman in the world has ever once spoken out her whole heart and her whole mind. The mistrust and disapproval of the vast bulk of society throttles us, as with two gigantic hands at our throats! We mumble a few weak words, and leave a thousand better ones unsaid.
The Blithedale Romance ch. 14 (1852)

21 America is now wholly given over to a d——d mob of scribbling women.
Letter to William D. Ticknor, 19 Jan. 1855

22 "It is very lonesome at the summit!" "Like a man's life, when he has climbed to eminence."
The Marble Faun ch. 28 (1860)
See Modern Proverbs 55

John Milton Hay

U.S. statesman, 1838–1905

1 True luck consists not in holding the best of the cards at the table:
Luckiest he who knows just when to rise and go home.
Distichs no. 15 (1890)
See Schlitz 1

2 [*Of the Spanish-American War:*] It has been a splendid little war, begun with the highest motives, carried on with magnificent intelligence and spirit, favored by that Fortune which loves the brave.
Letter to Theodore Roosevelt, 27 July 1898

S. I. Hayakawa

U.S. semanticist and politician, 1906–1992

1 We should hang on to it [the Panama Canal]. We stole it fair and square.
Quoted in *L.A. Times*, 7 Oct. 1976

Joseph Hayden

U.S. songwriter, fl. 1896

1 There'll be a hot time in the old town tonight.
"A Hot Time in the Old Town" (song) (1896)

Robert Hayden

U.S. poet, 1913–1980

1 What did I know
of love's austere and lonely offices?
"Those Winter Sundays" l. 10 (1962)

Tom Hayden

U.S. political activist, 1939–2016

1 We are people of this generation, bred in at least modest comfort, housed now in universities, looking uncomfortably to the world we inherit.
"The Port Huron Statement of the Students for a Democratic Society" (1962)

Franz Joseph Haydn

Austrian composer, 1732–1809

1 Before God and as an honest man I tell you that your son is the greatest composer known to me either in person or by name: He has taste, and, furthermore, the most profound knowledge of composition.
Quoted in Leopold Mozart, Letter to Maria Anna Mozart, 16 Feb. 1785

2 [*To Mozart, who had advised him not to visit England because Haydn lacked knowledge of foreign languages, 1790:*] My language is understood all over the world.
Quoted in Albert Christoph Die, *Biographical Accounts of Joseph Haydn* (1810) (translation by Vernon Gotwals)

Friedrich A. von Hayek

Austrian-born British economist, 1899–1992

1 The system of private property is the most important guaranty of freedom, not only for those who own property, but scarcely less for those who do not.
The Road to Serfdom ch. 8 (1944)

2 I am certain that nothing has done so much to destroy the juridical safeguards of individual

freedom as the striving after this mirage of social justice.
Economic Freedom and Representative Government (1973)

Alfred Hayes

U.S. songwriter, 1911–1985

1 I dreamed I saw Joe Hill last night
Alive as you and me.
Says I, "But Joe, you're ten years dead."
"I never died," says he.
"I Dreamed I Saw Joe Hill Last Night" (song) (1936)

Isaac Hayes

U.S. singer and songwriter, 1942–2008

1 Who's the black private dick
That's a sex machine to all the chicks
Shaft, you're damn right.
"Theme from *Shaft*" (song) (1971)

Wayne Woodrow "Woody" Hayes

U.S. football coach, 1913–1987

1 When you throw a pass three things can happen to it, and two of them are bad.
Quoted in *Dallas Morning News*, 23 Nov. 1962. This 1962 source attributed the quotation to Darrell Royal, but Royal in 2005 gave credit to Hayes as the originator.

Tony Hayward

English business executive, 1957–

1 [*Comment to reporters about his company BP's catastrophic oil leak in the Gulf of Mexico, 30 May 2010:*] I'd like my life back.
Quoted in *Guardian*, 2 June 2010

Victoria Hayward

U.S. travel writer, fl. 1922

1 [*Of Canadian cultural diversity:*] It is indeed a mosaic of vast dimensions and great breadth.
Romantic Canada ch. 24 (1922)
See Baudouin 1; Jimmy Carter 3; Crèvecoeur 1; Ralph Ellison 2; Jesse Jackson 1; Zangwill 2

Rita Hayworth (Margarita Carmen Cansino)

U.S. actress, 1918–1987

1 [*Of one of her film characters:*] Men fall in love with Gilda, but they wake up with me.
Quoted in John Kobal, *Rita Hayworth: Portrait of a Love Goddess* (1977)

Robert Hazard (Robert Rimato)

U.S. rock musician, 1948–2008

1 When the working day is done
Girls—they want to have fun
Oh girls just want to have fun.
"Girls Just Want to Have Fun" (song) (1979)

Lee Hazlewood

U.S. singer and songwriter, 1929–2007

1 These boots are made for walkin'
And that's just what they'll do
One of these days these boots are gonna walk all over you.
"These Boots Are Made for Walkin'" (song) (1966)

William Hazlitt

English essayist, 1778–1830

1 Hamlet is a name: his speeches and sayings but the idle coinage of the poet's brain. What then, are they not real? They are as real as our own thoughts. Their reality is in the reader's mind. It is *we* who are Hamlet.
Characters of Shakespeare's Plays "Hamlet" (1817)

2 This play [*Hamlet*] has a prophetic truth, which is above that of history.
Characters of Shakespeare's Plays "Hamlet" (1817)

3 Man is the only animal that laughs and weeps; for he is the only animal that is struck with the difference between what things are, and what they ought to be.
Lectures on the English Comic Writers "On Wit and Humor" (1818)

4 One has no notion of him [William Cobbett] as making use of a fine pen, but a great mutton-fist; his style stuns his readers. . . . He is too much for any single newspaper antagonist; "lays waste" a city orator or Member of Parliament, and bears hard upon the government itself. He is a kind of *fourth estate* in the politics of the country.
Table Talk "Character of Cobbett" (1821)
See Thomas Carlyle 14; Thomas Macaulay 4; Thackeray 10

5 A great chess-player is not a great man, for he leaves the world as he found it. No act terminating in itself constitutes greatness.
Table Talk "The Indian Jugglers" (1822)

6 Perhaps the best cure for the fear of death is to reflect that life has a beginning as well as an end. There was a time when we were not: this gives us no concern—why then should it trouble us that a time will come when we shall cease to be?

Table Talk "On the Fear of Death" (1822)

Bessie Head

South African–born Botswanan writer, 1937–1986

1 I am building a stairway to the stars. I have the authority to take the whole of mankind up there with me. That is why I write.

"Why Do I Write?" (1985)

John Healy

U.S. journalist, fl. 1877

1 The Mounties fetch their man every time.

Fort Benton (Montana) *Record,* 13 Apr. 1877. Healy's line inspired the Royal Canadian Mounted Police's unofficial motto, "The Mounties always get their man."

Timothy Michael Healy

Irish politician, 1855–1931

1 [*Responding to John Redmond's statement, at Irish Parliamentary Party meeting, 6 Dec. 1890, that "He [William Ewart Gladstone] is the master of the [Irish] party":*] Who is to be the mistress of the party?

Quoted in St. John Ervine, *Parnell* (1925). Healy was alluding to Katherine O'Shea, whose involvement with Charles Stewart Parnell was devastating to Parnell's political leadership.

Seamus Heaney

Irish poet, 1939–2013

1 I rhyme
To see myself, to set the darkness echoing.
"Personal Helicon" l. 19 (1965)

2 The cold smell of potato mould, the squelch and slap
Of soggy peat, the curt cuts of an edge
Through living roots awaken in my head.
But I've no spade to follow men like them.
Between my finger and my thumb

The squat pen rests.
I'll dig with it.
"Digging" l. 25 (1966)

3 God is a foreman with certain definite views
Who orders life in shifts of work and leisure.
"Docker" l. 10 (1966)

4   The famous
Northern reticence, the tight gag of place
And times: yes, yes. Of the "wee six" I sing
Where to be saved you only must save face
And whatever you say, you say nothing.
"Whatever You Say Say Nothing" l. 32 (1975)

5 Is there a life before death? That's chalked up
In Ballymurphy. Competence with pain,
Coherent miseries, a bite and sup,
We hug our little destiny again.
"Whatever You Say Say Nothing" l. 85 (1975)

6 But don't be surprised
If I demur, for, be advised
My passport's green.
No glass of ours was ever raised
To toast *The Queen.*
"An Open Letter" l. 80 (1983). Heaney was objecting to his being included in *The Penguin Book of Contemporary British Poetry.*

7 You lose more of yourself than you redeem
Doing the decent thing.
Station Island pt. 12 (1984)

8 History says don't hope
On this side of the grave.
But then, once in a lifetime
The longed for tidal wave
Of justice can rise up
And hope and history rhyme.
"Doubletake" l. 13 (1990)

William Randolph Hearst

U.S. newspaper publisher, 1863–1951

1 [*Telegram to Frederic Remington, whom Hearst had sent to Cuba to cover a rebellion there:*] You furnish the pictures, and I'll furnish the war.

Attributed in James Creelman, *On the Great Highway* (1901). Howard Langer, *America in Quotations,* notes: "Some scholars now question Creelman's reliability, pointing out that neither Remington nor Davis [a correspondent accompanying Remington to Cuba] ever confirmed it and that Hearst flatly denied it."

2 News is something which somebody wants suppressed: all the rest is advertising.

Attributed in *Time & Tide*, 29 Oct. 1955. "News is what somebody does not want you to print. All the rest is advertising" appeared, attributed to an unnamed newspaper editor, in *The Motor*, Dec. 1937.

Edward Heath

British prime minister, 1916–2005

1 [*Of the Lonrho affair:*] The unpleasant and unacceptable face of capitalism.

Speech in House of Commons, 15 May 1973

Reginald Heber

English clergyman, 1783–1826

1 Brightest and Best of the Sons of the Morning.

Title of hymn (1819)
See Halberstam 1; Percy Shelley 16

Ben Hecht

U.S. author, 1894–1964

1 The son of a bitch stole my watch!

The Front Page act 2 (1928). Coauthored with Charles MacArthur.

Georg Wilhelm Friedrich Hegel

German philosopher, 1770–1831

1 What is rational is actual and what is actual is rational.

Philosophy of Right (1821)

2 The owl of Minerva spreads its wings only with the falling of dusk.

Philosophy of Right (1821)

3 What experience and history teach is this—that people and governments never have learned anything from history, or acted upon any lessons they might have drawn from it.

Lectures on the Philosophy of History: Introduction introduction (1830)

4 The History of the World is nothing but the development of the Idea of Freedom.

Lectures on the Philosophy of History introduction (1837)

5 Napoleon was twice defeated, and the Bourbons twice expelled. By repetition that which at first appeared merely a matter of chance

and contingency, becomes a real and ratified existence.

Lectures on the Philosophy of History pt. 3, sec. 3 (1837)
See Karl Marx 4

Martin Heidegger

German philosopher, 1889–1976

1 Language is the house of Being. In its home man dwells.

"Letter on Humanism" (1947)

2 *Die Sprache spricht.*
Language speaks.

"Language" (1950)

Robert L. Heilbroner

U.S. economist, 1919–2005

1 [The great economists] can be called the worldly philosophers, for they sought to embrace in a scheme of philosophy the most worldly of all of man's activities—his drive for wealth.

The Worldly Philosophers introduction (1953)

Carolyn Heilbrun

U.S. literary scholar and mystery novelist, 1926–2003

1 In former days, everyone found the assumption of innocence so easy; today we find fatally easy the assumption of guilt.

Poetic Justice ch. 2 (1970). Written under the pseudonym Amanda Cross.

2 One hires lawyers as one hires plumbers, because one wants to keep one's hands off the beastly drains.

The Question of Max ch. 5 (1976). Written under the pseudonym Amanda Cross.

Cynthia Heimel

U.S. writer and humorist, 1947–2018

1 If You Can't Live Without Me, Why Aren't You Dead Yet?

Title of book (1991)

Heinrich Heine

German poet, 1797–1856

1 *Dort, wo man Bücher*
Verbrennt, verbrennt man auch am Ende
Menschen.

Wherever they burn books they will also, in the end, burn human beings.

Almansor: A Tragedy l. 245 (1823)

2 *Auf Flügeln des Gesanges.*
On Wings of Song.

Title of song (1823)

3 Mark this well, you proud men of action:
You are nothing but the unwitting agents of
the men of thought who often, in quiet self-
effacement, mark out most exactly all your
doings in advance.

History of Religion and Philosophy in Germany vol. 3
(1834)
See Keynes 12

4 People in those old times had convictions; we
moderns only have opinions. And it needs
more than a mere opinion to erect a Gothic
cathedral.

The French Stage ch. 9 (1837)

5 [*Deathbed remark:*] *Dieu me pardonnera, c'est son
métier.*
God will pardon me, it is His trade.

Quoted in Alfred Meissner, *Heinrich Heine* (1856)

Robert A. Heinlein

U.S. science fiction writer, 1907–1988

1 You have attributed conditions to villainy that
simply result from stupidity.

"Logic of Empire" (1941). Thomas F. Woodcock
wrote in the *Wall Street Journal,* 22 Dec. 1937: "In
this world much of what the victims believe to be
malice is explicable on the ground of ignorance or
incompetence, or a mixture of both."

2 Women should be obscene but not heard.

Stranger in a Strange Land ch. 35 (1961). Richard F.
Carroll was quoted in *Billboard,* 19 Dec. 1908, as
saying "little girls should be obscene and not heard."

3 Oh, "tanstaafl." Means "There ain't no such
thing as a free lunch."

The Moon Is a Harsh Mistress ch. 11 (1966). There is
also a 1949 book by Pierre Dos Utt titled *Tanstaafl: A
Plan for a New Economic World Order.*
See Commoner 1; Walter Morrow 1

4 Always listen to experts. They'll tell you what
can't be done, and why. Then do it.

Time Enough for Love "Intermission" (1973)

5 There are hidden contradictions in the minds
of people who "love Nature" while deploring

the "artificialities" with which "Man has
spoiled 'Nature.'" The obvious contradiction
lies in their choice of words, which imply that
Man and his artifacts are *not* part of "Nature"—
but beavers and their dams *are.*

Time Enough for Love "Intermission" (1973)

6 Democracy is based on the assumption that a
million men are wiser than one man. How's
that again? I missed something.

Time Enough for Love "Intermission" (1973)

7 God is omnipotent, omniscient, and
omnibenevolent—it says so right here on the
label. If you have a mind capable of believing all
three of these divine attributes simultaneously,
I have a wonderful bargain for you. No checks,
please. Cash and in small bills.

Time Enough for Love "Intermission" (1973)

8 The two highest achievements of the human
mind are the twin concepts of "loyalty" and
"duty." Whenever these twin concepts fall
into disrepute—get out of there fast! You may
possibly save yourself, but it is too late to save
that society. It is doomed.

Time Enough for Love "Intermission" (1973)

9 Anyone who cannot cope with mathematics
is not fully human. At best he is a tolerable
subhuman who has learned to wear shoes,
bathe, and not make messes in the house.

Time Enough for Love "Intermission" (1973)

10 A human being should be able to change a
diaper, plan an invasion, butcher a hog, conn a
ship, design a building, write a sonnet, balance
accounts, build a wall, set a bone, comfort the
dying, take orders, give orders, cooperate, act
alone, solve equations, analyze a new problem,
pitch manure, program a computer, cook
a tasty meal, fight efficiently, die gallantly.
Specialization is for insects.

Time Enough for Love "Intermission" (1973)

11 The most preposterous notion that H. sapiens
has ever dreamed up is that the Lord God of
Creation, Shaper and Ruler of all the Universes,
wants the saccharine adoration of His
creatures, can be swayed by their prayers, and
becomes petulant if He does not receive this
flattery. Yet this absurd fantasy, without a shred

of evidence to bolster it, pays all the expenses of the oldest, largest, and least productive industry in all history.

Time Enough for Love "Intermission" (1973)

12 Everybody lies about sex.

Time Enough for Love "Intermission" (1973)

13 Never attempt to teach a pig to sing; it wastes your time and annoys the pig.

Time Enough for Love "Prelude II" (1973)

14 Does history record *any* case in which the majority was right?

Time Enough for Love "Second Intermission" (1973)
See Ibsen 14; Roscommon 1; Twain 119

15 Never try to outstubborn a cat.

Time Enough for Love "Second Intermission" (1973)

16 Maybe Jesus was right when he said that the meek shall inherit the earth—but they inherit very small plots, about six feet by three.

Time Enough for Love "Variations on a Theme VI" (1973)
See Bible 112; Bible 205; Getty 1; John M. Henry 1

17 Premenstrual Syndrome: Just before their periods women behave the way men do all the time.

The Cat Who Walks Through Walls: A Comedy of Manners ch. 15 (1985)

18 Women and Cats do what they do; there is nothing a man can do about it.

The Cat Who Walks Through Walls: A Comedy of Manners ch. 29 (1985)

Werner Heisenberg

German physicist, 1901–1976

1 The more precisely we determine the position [of an electron], the more imprecise is the determination of velocity at this instant, and vice versa.

"On the Perceptual Content of Quantum Theoretical Kinematics and Mechanics" (1927). Known as "Heisenberg's uncertainty principle."

2 Since the measuring device has been constructed by the observer . . . we have to remember that what we observe is not nature in itself but nature exposed to our method of questioning.

Physics and Philosophy (1958)

Joseph Heller

U.S. novelist, 1923–1999

1 It was love at first sight. The first time Yossarian saw the Chaplain he fell madly in love with him.

"Catch-18" (1955)

2 He had decided to live forever or die in the attempt, and his only mission each time he went up was to come down alive.

Catch-22 ch. 3 (1961)

3 There was only one catch and that was Catch-22, which specified that a concern for one's own safety in the face of dangers that were real and immediate was the process of a rational mind. Orr was crazy and could be grounded. All he had to do was ask; and as soon as he did, he would no longer be crazy and would have to fly more missions. Orr would be crazy to fly more missions and sane if he didn't, but if he was sane he had to fly them. If he flew them he was crazy and didn't have to; but if he didn't want to he was sane and had to. Yossarian was moved very deeply by the absolute simplicity of this clause of Catch-22 and let out a respectful whistle.

Catch-22 ch. 5 (1961). Heller originally wrote "Catch-18," and the first chapter of *Catch-22* was published under that title in the collection *New World Writing: Seventh Mentor Selection* in 1955, but the phrase was changed because Leon Uris had a book out at the same time titled *Mila 18*.

4 Some men are born mediocre, some men achieve mediocrity, and some men have mediocrity thrust upon them. With Major Major it had been all three.

Catch-22 ch. 9 (1961)
See Samuel Butler (1835–1902) 4; Shakespeare 244

5 How much reverence can you have for a Supreme Being who finds it necessary to include such phenomena as phlegm and tooth decay in His divine system of creation?

Catch-22 ch. 18 (1961)

6 Dear Mrs., Mr., Miss, or Mr. And Mrs. Daneeka: Words cannot express the deep personal grief I experienced when your husband, son, father, or brother was killed, wounded, or reported missing in action.

Catch-22 ch. 31 (1961)

7 Kissinger brought peace to Vietnam the same way Napoleon brought peace to Europe: by losing.

Good as Gold (1979)

Lillian Hellman
U.S. playwright, 1905–1984

1 I cannot and will not cut my conscience to fit this year's fashions, even though I long ago came to the conclusion that I was not a political person and could have no comfortable place in any political group.

Letter to John S. Wood, 19 May 1952. Hellman declared in this letter to the chairman of the House Un-American Activities Committee that she would testify about her own leftist political associations but not about those of others.

2 It is a mark of many famous people that they cannot part with their brightest hour.

Pentimento "Theatre" (1973)

3 Truth made you a traitor as it often does in a time of scoundrels.

Scoundrel Time (1976)

Hermann Ludwig Ferdinand von Helmholtz
German physicist and anatomist, 1821–1894

1 Nature as a whole possesses a store of force which cannot in any way be either increased or diminished . . . therefore, the quantity of force in Nature is just as eternal and unalterable as the quantity of matter. . . . I have named [this] general law "The Principle of the Conservation of Force."

Über die Erhaltung der Kraft (1847) (translation by E. Atkinson). Modern physicists use *energy* for Helmholtz's word *force*.

Leona Helmsley
U.S. hotel executive, 1920–2007

1 We don't pay taxes. Only the little people pay taxes.

Quoted in *N.Y. Times*, 12 July 1989. A comment Helmsley made to her housekeeper in 1983, reported at Helmsley's tax evasion trial.

Héloise
French nun and writer, ca. 1095–1164

1 God knows I never sought anything in you except yourself; I wanted simply you, nothing of yours.

Letter to Peter Abelard, ca. 1132

2 My heart was not in me but with you, and now, even more, if it is not with you it is nowhere.

Letter to Peter Abelard, ca. 1132

Robert Murray Helpmann
Australian dancer and actor, 1909–1986

1 [*Comment after opening night of play* Oh, Calcutta!, *1969:*] The trouble with nude dancing is that not everything stops when the music stops.

Quoted in Frank Muir, *The Frank Muir Book* (1976)

Mark Helprin
U.S. writer and journalist, 1947–

1 There was a white horse, on a quiet winter morning when snow covered the streets gently and was not deep, and the sky was swept with vibrant stars, except in the east, where dawn was beginning in a light blue flood. The air was motionless, but would soon start to move as the sun came up and winds from Canada came charging down the Hudson.

Winter's Tale pt. 1 (1983)

Felicia Hemans
English poet, 1793–1835

1 The breaking waves dash'd high
On a stern and rock-bound coast,
And the woods against a stormy sky
Their giant branches toss'd.

"The Landing of the Pilgrim Fathers in New England" l. 1 (1826)

2 The boy stood on the burning deck
Whence all but he had fled;
The flame that lit the battle's wreck
Shone round him o'er the dead.

"Casabianca" l. 1 (1826)

3 The stately Homes of England,
How beautiful they stand!
Amidst their tall ancestral trees,

O'er all the pleasant land.
"The Homes of England" l. 1 (1827)
See Crisp 2; Woolf 4

Ernest Hemingway

U.S. writer, 1899–1961

1 You and me, we've made a separate peace.
In Our Time ch. 6 (1924)

2 It was all a nothing and a man was nothing too.
It was only that and light was all it needed and
a certain cleanness and order. Some lived in it
and never felt it but he knew it all was nada y
pues nada y nada y pues nada. Our nada who
art in nada, nada be thy name thy kingdom
nada thy will be nada in nada as it is in nada.
Give us this nada our daily nada and nada us
our nada as we nada our nadas and nada us not
into nada but deliver us from nada; pues nada.
Hail nothing full of nothing, nothing is with
thee.
"A Clean, Well-Lighted Place" (1926)

3 Nobody ever lives their life all the way up except
bull-fighters.
The Sun Also Rises ch. 2 (1926)

4 I did not care what it [the world] was all about.
All I wanted to know was how to live in it.
Maybe if you found out how to live in it you
learned from that what it was all about.
The Sun Also Rises ch. 14 (1926)

5 It makes one feel rather good deciding not to be
a bitch. . . . It's sort of what we have instead of
God.
The Sun Also Rises ch. 19 (1926)

6 "Oh, Jake," Brett said, "we could have had such
a damned good time together." . . .
"Yes," I said. "Isn't it pretty to think so?"
The Sun Also Rises ch. 19 (1926)

7 In the fall the war was always there but we did
not go to it any more.
Men Without Women "In Another Country" (1927)

8 In the late summer of that year we lived in a
house in a village that looked across the river
and the plain to the mountains. In the bed of
the river there were pebbles and boulders, dry
and white in the sun, and the water was clear
and swiftly moving and blue in the channels.
A Farewell to Arms ch. 1 (1929)

9 I had seen nothing sacred, and the things that
were glorious had no glory and the sacrifices
were like the stockyards at Chicago if nothing
was done with the meat except to bury it. . . .
Abstract words such as glory, honor, courage,
or hallow were obscene.
A Farewell to Arms ch. 27 (1929)

10 The world breaks everyone and afterward many
are strong at the broken places. But those that
will not break it kills. It kills the very good and
the very gentle and the very brave impartially.
If you are none of these you can be sure that
it will kill you too but there will be no special
hurry.
A Farewell to Arms ch. 34 (1929)

11 You never had time to learn. They threw you
in and told you the rules and the first time they
caught you off base they killed you.
A Farewell to Arms ch. 41 (1929)

12 It was like saying good-bye to a statue. After
a while I went out and left the hospital and
walked back to the hotel in the rain.
A Farewell to Arms ch. 41 (1929)

13 I know only that what is moral is what you feel
good after and what is immoral is what you feel
bad after.
Death in the Afternoon ch. 1 (1932)
See Lincoln 57

14 I was trying to write then and I found the greatest difficulty, aside from knowing truly what you really felt, rather than what you were supposed to feel, had been taught to feel, was to put down what really happened in action; what the actual things were which produced the emotion that you experienced . . . the real thing, the sequence of motion and fact which made the emotion and which would be as valid in a year or in ten years or, with luck and if you stated it purely enough, always.
Death in the Afternoon ch. 1 (1932)
See T. S. Eliot 27

15 If a writer of prose knows enough about what he is writing about he may omit things that he knows and the reader, if the writer is writing truly enough, will have a feeling of those things as strongly as though the writer had stated them. The dignity of movement of an ice-berg is due to only one-eighth of it being above water. A writer who omits things because he does not know them only makes hollow places in his writing.
Death in the Afternoon ch. 16 (1932)

16 If he wrote it he could get rid of it. He had gotten rid of many things by writing them.
Winner Take Nothing "Fathers and Sons" (1933)

17 All good books are alike in that they are truer than if they had really happened and after you are finished reading one you will feel that all that happened to you and afterwards it all belongs to you; the good and the bad, the ecstasy, the remorse and sorrow, the people and the places and how the weather was. If you can get so that you can give that to people, then you are a writer.
Esquire, Dec. 1934

18 All modern American literature comes from one book by Mark Twain called *Huckleberry Finn*. All American writing comes from that. There was nothing before. There has been nothing as good since.
Green Hills of Africa ch. 1 (1935)

19 No matter how a man alone ain't got no bloody fucking chance.
To Have and Have Not ch. 23 (1937)

20 Kilimanjaro is a snow-covered mountain 19,710 feet high, and is said to be the highest mountain in Africa. Its western summit is called the Masai "Ngàje Ngài," the House of God. Close to the western summit there is the dried and frozen carcass of a leopard. No one has explained what the leopard was seeking at that altitude.
"The Snows of Kilimanjaro" (1938)

21 The rich were dull and they drank too much. . . . He remembered poor Julian and his romantic awe of them and how he had started a story once that began, "The very rich are different from you and me." And how someone had said to Julian, Yes, they have more money.
"The Snows of Kilimanjaro" (1938). In the story's original magazine publication in 1936, Hemingway wrote, "poor Scott Fitzgerald." He later changed the name to "Julian" at Fitzgerald's request. According to Matthew J. Bruccoli, *Scott and Ernest* (1978), Hemingway remarked at a lunch in 1936 that "I am getting to know the rich." Critic Mary Colum replied, "The only difference between the rich and other people is that the rich have more money."
See F. Scott Fitzgerald 36

22 [*Referring to kissing:*] Where do the noses go? I always wondered where the noses would go.
For Whom the Bell Tolls ch. 7 (1940)

23 [*After sex:*] But did thee feel the earth move?
For Whom the Bell Tolls ch. 13 (1940)

24 If we win here we will win everywhere. The world is a fine place and worth the fighting for and I hate very much to leave it.
For Whom the Bell Tolls ch. 43 (1940)

25 Cowardice, as distinguished from panic, is almost always simply a lack of ability to suspend the functioning of the imagination.
Men at War introduction (1942)

26 A writer should be of as great probity and honesty as a priest of God. He is either honest or not, as a woman is either chaste or not, and after one piece of dishonest writing he is never the same again.
Men at War introduction (1942)

27 "I would like to take the great DiMaggio fishing," the old man said. "They say his father was a fisherman. Maybe he was as poor as we are and would understand."
The Old Man and the Sea (1952)

28 But man is not made for defeat. A man can be destroyed but not defeated.

The Old Man and the Sea (1952)

29 The old man was dreaming about the lions.

The Old Man and the Sea (1952)

30 If you are lucky enough to have lived in Paris as a young man, then wherever you go for the rest of your life, it stays with you, for Paris is a moveable feast.

A Moveable Feast epigraph (1964). A. E. Hotchner writes in *Papa Hemingway: A Personal Memoir* (1966) that Hemingway made this remark to him in 1950. Also in 1950, Hemingway wrote, "Happiness, as you know, is a moveable feast," in *Across the River and into the Trees.*

31 His [F. Scott Fitzgerald's] talent was as natural as the pattern that was made by the dust on a butterfly's wings. At one time he understood it no more than the butterfly did and he did not know when it was brushed or marred. Later he became conscious of his damaged wings and of their construction and he learned to think and could not fly any more because the love of flight was gone and he could only remember when it had been effortless.

A Moveable Feast "Scott Fitzgerald" (1964)

32 [*Definition of* guts:] Grace under pressure.

Quoted in *New Yorker*, 30 Nov. 1929 (profile by Dorothy Parker). Earlier, Hemingway had used "grace under pressure" in a letter to F. Scott Fitzgerald, 20 Apr. 1926. In the 1926 letter Hemingway stated that he was *not* referring to guts.

33 Time is the least thing we have of.

Quoted in *New Yorker*, 13 May 1950

34 I started out very quiet and I beat Mr. Turgenev. Then I trained hard and I beat Mr. de Maupassant. I've fought two draws with Mr. Stendhal and I think I had an edge in the last one. But nobody's going to get me in any ring with Mr. Tolstoy unless I'm crazy or I keep getting better.

Quoted in *New Yorker*, 13 May 1950

35 The most essential gift for a good writer is a built-in, shock-proof shit detector. This is the writer's radar and all great writers have had it.

Quoted in *Paris Review*, Spring 1958

36 Poor Faulkner. Does he really think big emotions come from big words? He thinks I don't know the ten-dollar words. I know them all right. But there are older and simpler and better words, and those are the ones I use.

Quoted in A. E. Hotchner, *Papa Hemingway* (1966)

37 [*Example of a short story consisting of only six words:*] For sale. Baby shoes. Never worn.

Attributed in John de Groot, *Papa: A Play Based on the Legendary Lives of Ernest Hemingway* act 1 (1989). This is now often ascribed to Hemingway, but Garson O'Toole has found that there is no evidence that he authored it. Similar pre-Hemingway items have been uncovered by O'Toole, such as "The great American dramatist will be the man or woman who can write a one-act play as poignant as a seven-word want ad which the *Houston Post* discovers: For Sale, a baby carriage; never used" (*Life Magazine*, 16 June 1921).

Thomas "Hollywood" Henderson

U.S. football player, 1953–

1 Terry Bradshaw is so dumb he couldn't spell "cat" if you spotted him a "c" and an "a."

Quoted in *Ottawa Journal*, 22 Jan. 1978

Jimi Hendrix

U.S. rock musician, 1942–1970

1 Are You Experienced?

Title of song (1967)

2 Hey Joe, I said where you goin' with that gun in your hand?
I'm goin' down to shoot my old lady,
Caught her messin' around with another man.

"Hey Joe" (song) (1967)

3 'Scuse me while I kiss the sky.

"Purple Haze" (song) (1967)

4 You've got me blowing, blowing my mind
Is it tomorrow or just the end of time?

"Purple Haze" (song) (1967)

5 Third Stone from the Sun.

Title of song (1967)

Don Henley

U.S. rock musician, 1947–

1 You can check out anytime you like,
But you can never leave.

"Hotel California" (song) (1976). Cowritten with Glenn Frey.

W. E. Henley
English poet and playwright, 1849–1903

1 Under the bludgeonings of chance
My head is bloody, but unbowed.
"Invictus" l. 5 (1888)

2 It matters not how strait the gate,
How charged with punishments the scroll,
I am the master of my fate:
I am the captain of my soul.
"Invictus" l. 13 (1888)

3 What have I done for you,
England, my England?
"Pro Rege Nostro" l. 1 (1900)

Henri IV
French king, 1553–1610

1 I want there to be no peasant in my kingdom
so poor that he is unable to have a chicken in
his pot every Sunday.
Quoted in Hardouin de Péréfixe, *Histoire de Henry le
Grand* (1681)
See Herbert Hoover 3; Political Slogans 12

2 *Paris vaut bien une messe.*
Paris is well worth a mass.
Attributed in Henry Wikoff, *The Four Civilizations
of the World* (1874). *Caquets de l'Accouchée* (1622)
attributes "*la couronne vaut bien une messe*" (the Crown
is worth a mass) to Henri's minister Sully. *Mémoires
du Comte de Brienne* (1719) attributes to Henri the
remark "*la couronne de France vaut bien une messe!*"
The reference is to Henri's conversion to Roman
Catholicism in order to gain the French crown.

Henry II
English king, 1133–1189

1 [*Of Thomas à Becket, 1170:*] Who will deliver me
from this turbulent Priest?
Attributed in Robert Dodsley, *The Chronicle of the
Kings of England* (1740). W. L. Warren, noting that
there is no way of knowing whether Henry actually
spoke these words, writes in *Henry II* (1973): "The
chroniclers and the biographers of Becket tell
differing tales. That he uttered some such words is,
however, beyond doubt." Accounts of language by the
king to the same effect are found in *Materials for the
History of Thomas Becket, Archbishop of Canterbury*
(1875–1885).

John M. Henry
Nationality/Occupation unknown, fl. 1962

1 Probably the meek really will inherit the earth;
they won't have the nerve to refuse.
Quoted in *Reader's Digest*, May 1962
See Bible 112; Bible 205; Getty 1; Heinlein 16

Matthew Henry
English clergyman, 1662–1714

1 Those that die by famine die by inches.
An Exposition on the Old and New Testament Psalm 59
(1710)

O. Henry (William Sydney Porter)
U.S. short story writer, 1862–1910

1 In the constitution of this small, maritime
banana republic was a forgotten section that
provided for the maintenance of a navy.
Cabbages and Kings ch. 8 (1904). Appears to be the
coinage of *banana republic,* previously thought to trace
back to 1935.

2 Three times Della counted it. One dollar and
eighty-seven cents. And the next day would be
Christmas.
The Four Million "The Gift of the Magi" (1906)

3 If men knew how women pass the time when
they are alone, they'd never marry.
The Four Million "Memoirs of a Yellow Dog" (1906)

4 [*Of New York City:*] Little old Bagdad-on-the-
Subway.
The Trimmed Lamp "A Madison Square Arabian
Night" (1907)

5 Busy as a one-armed man with the nettle-rash
pasting on wallpaper.
The Gentle Grafter "The Ethics of Pig" (1908)

6 It was beautiful and simple as all truly great
swindles are.
The Gentle Grafter "The Octopus Marooned" (1908)

7 She plucked from my lapel the invisible strand
of lint (the universal act of woman to proclaim
ownership).
Strictly Business "A Rumble in Aphasia" (1910)

8 [*"Last words":*] Turn up the lights; I don't want
to go home in the dark.
Quoted in Charles Alphonso Smith, *O. Henry* (1916)
See Harry Williams 2

Patrick Henry

U.S. Revolutionary leader, 1736–1799

1 Caesar had his Brutus—Charles the first, his Cromwell, and George the third—("Treason!" cried the speaker) . . . *may profit by their example.* If *this* be treason, make the most of it.

Speech in Virginia House of Burgesses, Williamsburg, Va., May 1765. These words are attributed to Henry in William Wirt's biography, *Sketches of the Life and Character of Patrick Henry* (1817), on the authority of Thomas Jefferson and two other eyewitnesses. Very similar wording appears in John Burk, *History of Virginia* vol. 3 (1805). However, the *American Heritage Dictionary of American Quotations* states: "Notes made by a French visitor to Williamsburg at the time, but not discovered until 1921, suggest that Henry actually backed down when interrupted by the Speaker." The anonymous Frenchman's notes are published in "Journal of a French Traveller in the Colonies, 1765," *American Historical Review,* July 1921.

2 Is life so dear, or peace so sweet, as to be purchased at the price of chains and slavery? Forbid it, Almighty God!—I know not what course others may take; but as for me, give me liberty, or give me death!

Speech in Virginia Convention, Richmond, Va., 23 Mar. 1775. The words of Henry's speech are known through their being reported in William Wirt, *Sketches of the Life and Character of Patrick Henry* (1817). Wirt reconstructed the speech from people who had heard it, but the passage of time renders his precise text questionable.

3 That religion, or the duty which we owe to our Creator, and the manner of discharging it, can be directed only by reason and conviction, not by force or violence; and therefore all men are equally entitled to the free exercise of religion, according to the dictates of conscience; and that it is the mutual duty of all to practice Christian forbearance, love, and charity towards each other.

Virginia Bill of Rights article 16 (1776)

Philip Henry

English clergyman, 1631–1696

1 All this, and Heaven too!

Quoted in Matthew Henry, *An Account of the Life and Death of Mr. Philip Henry* (1698)

Katharine Hepburn

U.S. actress, 1907–2003

1 Sometimes I wonder if men and women really suit each other. Perhaps they should live next door and just visit now and then.

Quoted in Barbara Rowes, *The Book of Quotes* (1979)

2 Acting isn't really a very high-class way to make a living, is it? Nobody ever won a Nobel Prize for acting. You have to remember that Shirley Temple could do it at the age of four.

Quoted in *Detroit Free Press,* 23 Jan. 1979

Heraclitus

Greek philosopher, ca. 540 B.C.–ca. 480 B.C.

1 The road up and the road down are one and the same.

On the Universe fragment 69

2 A man's character is his fate.

On the Universe fragment 121
See George Eliot 6; Novalis 2

3 You can't step twice into the same river.

Quoted in Plato, *Cratylus*

4 All is flux, nothing stays still.

Quoted in Plato, *Cratylus*

5 Nothing endures but change.

Quoted in Plato, *Cratylus*

Anne Herbert

U.S. writer, 1950–2015

1 Anything we do randomly and frequently starts to make its own sense and changes the world into itself. Senseless violence makes more and more sense when vengeance and fear take us closer and closer to a world where everyone is dead for no reason. But violence isn't the only thing that is senseless until it makes its own sense. Anything you want there to be more of, do it randomly. It will make itself be more, senselessly. Scrawl it on the wall: RANDOM KINDNESS AND SENSELESS ACTS OF BEAUTY.

Whole Earth Review, July 1985

2 Libraries will get you through times of no money better than money will get you through times of no libraries.

Quoted in *The Next Whole Earth Catalog: Access to Tools*, ed. Stewart Brand (1980). Herbert derived this quotation from Gilbert Shelton's statement about drugs and money.
See Gilbert Shelton 1

Frank Herbert
U.S. science fiction writer, 1920–1986

1 I must not fear. Fear is the mind-killer. Fear is the little-death that brings total obliteration. I will face my fear. I will permit it to pass over me and through me. And when it has gone past I will turn the inner eye to see its path. Where the fear has gone there will be nothing. Only I will remain.

Dune bk. 1 (1965)

George Herbert
English poet and clergyman, 1593–1633

1 I struck the board, and cry'd, No more.
   I will abroad.

"The Collar" l. 1 (1633)

2 But as I rav'd and grew more fierce and wilde
   At every word,
   Me thoughts I heard one calling, *Child!*
   And I reply'd, *My Lord.*

"The Collar" l. 33 (1633)

3 Who sayes that fictions onely and false hair
   Become a verse? Is there in truth no beautie?

"Jordan (1)" l. 1 (1633)
See Keats 5; Keats 16

4 Love bade me welcome: yet my soul drew back,
   Guilty of dust and sinne
   But quick-ey'd Love, observing me grow slack
   From my first entrance in,
   Drew nearer to me, sweetly questioning,
   If I lack'd any thing.

"Love" l. 1 (1633)

5 You must sit down, sayes Love, and taste my
      meat:
   So I did sit and eat.

"Love" l. 17 (1633)

6 Sweet spring, full of sweet dayes and roses,
   A box where sweets compacted lie.

"Virtue" l. 9 (1633)

Jerry Herman
U.S. songwriter, 1931–2019

1 Hello, Dolly,
   Well, hello, Dolly,
   It's so nice to have you back where you belong.

"Hello, Dolly!" (song) (1964)

Gerald V. Hern
U.S. sports editor, 1911–1992

1 Pitch Spahn and Sain, Then Pray for Rain.

Boston Post, 14 Sept. 1948. Warren Spahn and Johnny Sain were the star pitchers of the Boston Braves baseball team.

Herodotus
Greek historian, ca. 485 B.C.–ca. 425 B.C.

1 In peace, children inter their parents; war violates the order of nature and causes parents to inter their children.

Histories bk. 1, sec. 87

2 The most hateful torment for men is to have knowledge of everything but power over nothing.

Histories bk. 9, sec. 16

Don Herold
U.S. humorist, 1889–1966

1 "If I Had My Life to Live Over—" I'd Pick More Daisies.

Title of article, *Reader's Digest*, Oct. 1953

Michael Herr
U.S. writer, 1940–2016

1 There was a famous story, some reporters asked a door gunner, "How can you shoot women and children?" and he'd answered, "It's easy, you just don't lead 'em so much."

Dispatches ch. 3 (1977)

2 I think that Vietnam was what we had instead of happy childhoods.

Dispatches ch. 3 (1977)

3 We were walking across 57th Street one afternoon and passed a blind man carrying a sign that read, MY DAYS ARE DARKER THAN YOUR NIGHTS. "Don't bet on it, man," the ex-medic said.

Dispatches ch. 3 (1977)

Robert Herrick
English poet, 1591–1674

1 A sweet disorder in the dress
 Kindles in clothes a wantonness.
 "Delight in Disorder" l. 1 (1648)

2 Fair daffodils, we weep to see
 You haste away so soon.
 "To Daffodils" l. 1 (1648)

3 Gather ye rosebuds while ye may,
 Old Time is still a-flying:
 And this same flower that smiles to-day,
 To-morrow will be dying.
 "To the Virgins, to Make Much of Time" l. 1 (1648)

4 Whenas in silks my Julia goes,
 Then, then (methinks) how sweetly flows
 That liquefaction of her clothes.
 Next, when I cast mine eyes and see
 That brave vibration each way free;
 O how that glittering taketh me!
 "Upon Julia's Clothes" l. 1 (1648)

James Herriot (James Alfred Wight)
British veterinarian and author, 1916–1995

1 I have long held the notion that if a vet can't
 catch his patient there's nothing much to worry
 about.
 Vet in Harness ch. 20 (1974)

John Hersey
Chinese-born U.S. writer, 1914–1993

1 There, in the tin factory, in the first moment of
 the atomic age, a human being was crushed by
 books.
 Hiroshima ch. 1 (1946)

June Hershey
U.S. songwriter, fl. 1941

1 Deep in the Heart of Texas.
 Title of song (1941)

Markus Herz
German physician and philosopher, 1747–1803

1 [*Of patients who read medical books:*] My dear
 friend, you will some day die of a misprint.
 Quoted in Ernst von Feuchtersleben, *Dietetics of the
 Soul* (1841)

Theodor Herzl
Hungarian-born Austrian Zionist, 1860–1904

1 If you will it, it is no dream.
 Altneuland epigraph (1902)

Hesiod
Greek poet, fl. 700 B.C.

1 The half is greater than the whole.
 Works and Days l. 40

2 The man who does evil to another does evil to
  himself,
 and the evil counsel is most evil
 for him who counsels it.
 Works and Days l. 265

3 There's no place like home.
 Works and Days l. 365
 See L. Frank Baum 3; Payne 2

Hermann Hesse
German novelist and poet, 1877–1962

1 If you hate a person, you hate something in
 him that is part of yourself. What isn't part of
 ourselves doesn't disturb us.
 Demian ch. 6 (1919)

2 I looked at my life, and it was also a river.
 Siddhartha ch. 9 (1922)

3 Wisdom cannot be passed on. Wisdom which
 a wise man tries to pass on to someone always
 sounds like foolishness.
 Siddhartha ch. 12 (1922)

4 He went on two legs, wore clothes, and was
 a human being, but nevertheless he was in
 reality a wolf of the Steppes. He had learned
 a good deal . . . and was a fairly clever fellow.
 What he had not learned, however, was this: to
 find contentment in himself and his own life.
 The cause of this apparently was that at the
 bottom of his heart he knew all the time (or
 thought he knew) that he was in reality not a
 man, but a wolf of the Steppes.
 Steppenwolf pt. 1 (1927)

5 I understood it all. I understood Pablo. I
 understood Mozart, and somewhere behind me
 I heard his ghastly laughter. I knew that all the
 hundred thousand pieces of life's game were in

my pocket. . . . I would traverse not once more, but often, the hell of my inner being. One day I would be a better hand at the game. One day I would learn how to laugh. Pablo was waiting for me, and Mozart too.

Steppenwolf pt. 6 (1927)

Gordon Hewart, Viscount Hewart

British judge, 1870–1943

1 Justice should not only be done, but should manifestly and undoubtedly be seen to be done.

Rex v. Sussex Justices (1924). J. B. Atlay, *The Victorian Chancellors* vol. 2 (1908), states that when Lord Herschell "was at the Bar, Sir George Jessel once attempted to cut him short in an argument. Herschell . . . retorted on the Master of the Rolls that, important as it was that people should get justice, it was even more important that they should be made to feel and see that they were getting it."

Foster Hewitt

Canadian sports broadcaster, 1904–1985

1 He shoots! He scores!

Radio broadcast of hockey game, 4 Apr. 1933

Reinhard Heydrich

German Nazi leader, 1904–1942

1 [*On plans to exterminate millions of European Jews:*] Now the rough work has been done we begin the period of finer work. We need to work in harmony with the civil administration. We count on you gentlemen as far as the final solution is concerned.

Speech, Wannsee, Germany, 20 Jan. 1942
See Goering 2

Edward Heyman

U.S. songwriter, 1907–1981

1 You oughta be in pictures,
You're wonderful to see.

"You Oughta Be in Pictures" (song) (1934)

2 When I fall in love
It will be forever.

"When I Fall in Love" (song) (1952)

DuBose Heyward

U.S. writer, 1885–1940

1 Summertime
And the livin' is easy,

Fish are jumpin',
And the cotton is high.

"Summertime" (song) (1935)

Thomas Heywood

English playwright, ca. 1574–1641

1 A Woman Killed with Kindness.

Title of play (1607)

2 Seven cities warred for Homer, being dead,
Who, living, had no roof to shroud his head.

The Hierarchy of the Blessed Angels (1635)

W. E. (William Edward) Hickson

English educational writer, 1803–1870

1 'Tis a lesson you should heed,
Try, try, try again;
If at first you don't succeed,
Try, try, try again.

The Singing Master (1836). This song, titled "Perseverance; or, Try Again," may not have been authored by Hickson.
See W. C. Fields 20

Jim Hightower

U.S. politician, 1943–

1 [*Of George H. W. Bush's inherited wealth:*] He is a man who was born on third base and thinks he hit a triple.

Speech at Democratic National Convention, Atlanta, Ga., 19 July 1988. "Born on third base and thinks he hit a triple" was used earlier (about another wealthy heir) in *Fortune*, 30 May 1983.

2 Ain't nothing in the middle of the road but yellow stripes and dead armadillos.

Quoted in *N.Y. Times*, 22 July 1984. Although this line is associated with Hightower, *The Dictionary of Modern Proverbs* documents versions as far back as 1967 ("The middle of the road is where there's a yellow line and dead cats") and 1970 ("The middle of the road is where you find the yellow stripe and dead skunks").
See Bevan 2

Brewster M. Higley

U.S. physician, 1823–1911

1 Oh, give me a home
Where the buffalo roam
Where the deer and the antelope play
Where seldom is heard

A discouraging word,
And the sky is not cloudy all day.

"Oh, Give Me a Home Where the Buffalo Roam"
(1873). These words became famous as the lyrics of
the song "Home on the Range."

David Hilbert

German mathematician, 1862–1943

1 We must know, we will know.

Address to the Society of German Scientists and
Physicians, Königsberg, Germany, 8 Sept. 1930

2 One can measure the importance of a scientific
work by the number of earlier publications
rendered superfluous by it.

Quoted in Howard Eves, *Mathematical Circles
Revisited* (1971)

Hildegard of Bingen

German abbess and polymath, 1098–1179

1 A feather does not fly of its own accord, it is
borne up by the air. So too I am not imbued
with human doctrine or strong powers. . . .
Rather, I depend entirely on God's help.

Letter to Odo of Soissons (1148) (translation by Mark
Atherton)

Geoffrey Hill

English poet, 1932–2016

1 Beware
The soft-voiced owl, the ferret's smile,
The hawk's deliberate stoop in air,
Cold eyes, and bodies hooped in steel,
Forever bent upon the kill.

"Genesis" l. 16 (1959)

2 By blood we live, the hot, the cold,
To ravage and redeem the world:
There is no bloodless myth will hold.

"Genesis" l. 40 (1959)

3 As estimated, you died. Things marched,
sufficient, to that end.
Just so much Zyklon and leather, patented
terror, so many routine cries.

"September Song" l. 4 (1968)

4 Platonic England, house of solitudes,
rests in its laurels and its injured stone.

"An Apology for the Revival of Christian Architecture
in England" st. 34 (1978)

Joe Hill (Joel Hägglund)

Swedish-born U.S. labor leader and songwriter,
1879–1915

1 You will eat, bye and bye,
In that glorious land in the sky;
Work and pray, live on hay,
You'll get pie in the sky when you die.

"Preacher and the Slave" (song) (1911)

2 Don't waste any time mourning—organize!

Telegram to William D. Haywood, 18 Nov. 1915. Hill
was a member of the Industrial Workers of the World
(the "Wobblies") and was their leading songwriter.
He was executed on 19 November 1915, on the basis
of highly suspect evidence, for murdering a Utah
grocer.

Rowland Hill

English clergyman, 1744–1833

1 He did not see any reason why the devil should
have all the good tunes.

Reported in Edward W. Broome, *The Rev. Rowland
Hill* (1881). This is usually attributed to Hill, but the
Monthly Review vol. 6 (1791) credits "Why should the
devil have all the good times?" to George Whitefield
(1714–1770), one of the founders of Methodism, and a
very similar formulation is attributed to Whitefield in
the *New-York Journal*, 24 Nov. 1787.

Edmund Hillary

New Zealand explorer, 1919–2008

1 [*After completing the first ascent of Mount Everest,
29 May 1953:*] Well, we knocked the bastard off!

Quoted in Edmund Hillary, *Nothing Venture, Nothing
Win* (1975)

Hillel

Jewish teacher, ca. 60 B.C.–ca. A.D. 9

1 If I am not for myself, who is for me? And
when I am for myself, what am I? And if not
now, when?

Talmud Mishnah "Pirqei Avot" 1:14

2 What is hateful to you do not do to your
neighbor. That is the whole Torah. The rest is
commentary.

Talmud "Shabbat" 31a
See Aristotle 12; Bible 225; Chesterfield 4; Confucius 9

Alice Hillingdon

English noblewoman, fl. 1912

1 I am happy now that Charles calls on my bedchamber less frequently than of old. As it is, I now endure but two calls a week and when I hear his steps outside my door I lie down on my bed, close my eyes, open my legs, and think of England.

Attributed in Jonathan Gathorne-Hardy, *The Rise and Fall of the British Nanny* (1972). Gathorne-Hardy ascribes this passage to Lady Hillingdon's "journal," but no such journal appears to exist and it is likely that the quotation is apocryphal. An earlier version is in the *Washington Post*, 18 May 1943: "Stanley Baldwin's son tells this story of the day his sister went out with a young man who wanted to marry her. She asked her mother for advice, in case the young man should want to kiss her . . . 'Do what I did,' said her mother, reminiscing of the beginning of her romance with the man who was to become Prime Minister. 'Just close your eyes and think of England.'" (Ellipsis in the original.)

James Hilton

English novelist, 1900–1954

1 The austere serenity of Shangri-La.
Lost Horizon ch. 5 (1933)

2 Nothing really wrong with him—only anno domini, but that's the most fatal complaint of all, in the end.
Goodbye, Mr. Chips ch. 1 (1934)

Chester Himes

U.S. writer, 1909–1984

1 My feelings are too intense. I hate too bitterly, I love too exaltingly, I pity too extravagantly, I hurt too painfully. We American blacks call that "soul."
The Quality of Hurt vol. 1, bk. 3, ch. 5 (1972)

Paul von Hindenburg

German military leader and president, 1847–1934

1 As an English general has very truly said, "The German army was 'stabbed in the back.'"
Statement to Reichstag committee of inquiry, 18 Nov. 1919. Hindenburg apparently was referring to a conversation between British general Neill Malcolm and German military leader Erich von Ludendorff in Berlin in late 1918. Malcolm's words are said to have been: "You mean, General Ludendorff, that you were—were stabbed in the back?"

S. E. (Susan Eloise) Hinton

U.S. novelist, 1948–

1 When I stepped out into the bright sunlight from the darkness of the movie house, I had only two things on my mind: Paul Newman and a ride home.
The Outsiders ch. 1 (1967)

2 Stay gold, Ponyboy. Stay gold.
The Outsiders ch. 9 (1967)

Hippocrates

Greek physician, ca. 460 B.C.–357 B.C.

1 Life is short, the art long.
Aphorisms sec. 1, para. 1. Often quoted in the Latin form, *Ars longa, vita brevis*, from Seneca's *De Brevitate Vitae* sec. 1.
See Chaucer 4; Longfellow 2

2 As to diseases make a habit of two things—to help, or at least, to do no harm.
Epidemics bk. 1, ch. 11

3 I swear by Apollo Physician, by Asclepius, by Health, by Panacea, and by all the gods and goddesses, making them my witnesses, that I will carry out, according to my ability and judgment, this oath and this indenture.
The Physician's Oath (translation by W. H. S. Jones)

4 I will use treatment to help the sick according to my ability and judgment, but never with a view to injury and wrongdoing. Neither will I administer a poison to anybody when asked to do so, nor will I suggest such a course. Similarly, I will not give to a woman a pessary to cause abortion. I will keep pure and holy both my life and my art.
The Physician's Oath (translation by W. H. S. Jones)

5 In whatsoever houses I enter, I will enter to help the sick, and I will abstain from all intentional wrongdoing and harm, especially from abusing the bodies of man or woman, bond or free. And whatsoever I shall see or hear in the course of my profession in my intercourse with men, if it be what should not be published abroad, I will never divulge, holding such things to be holy secrets. Now if I carry out this oath, and break it not, may I gain forever the reputation among all men for my life and for my art.
The Physician's Oath (translation by W. H. S. Jones)

Hirohito

Japanese emperor, 1901–1989

1 The war situation has developed not necessarily to Japan's advantage.
Broadcast announcing Japan's surrender, 15 Aug. 1945

2 The enemy has begun to employ a new and most cruel bomb, the power of which to do damage is indeed incalculable, taking the toll of many innocent lives. Should we continue to fight, it would not only result in an ultimate collapse and obliteration of the Japanese nation, but it would also lead to the total extinction of human civilization.
Broadcast announcing Japan's surrender, 15 Aug. 1945

3 The ties between us and our people . . . do not depend upon mere legends and myths . . . predicated on the false conception that the Emperor is divine and that the Japanese people are superior to other races and fated to rule the world.
Address denying his divinity, 1 Jan. 1946

Alfred Hitchcock

English film director, 1899–1980

1 In regard to the tune, we have a name in the studio, and we call it the "MacGuffin." It is the mechanical element that usually crops up in any story. In crook stories it is always the necklace and in spy stories it is always the papers. We just try to be a little more original.
Lecture at Columbia University, New York, N.Y., 30 Mar. 1939. According to Donald Spoto, *The Dark Side of Genius: The Life of Alfred Hitchcock* (1983), Hitchcock picked up the term *MacGuffin* from film editor Angus MacPhail.

2 Actors are cattle.
Quoted in *Wash. Post*, 26 July 1940

Christopher Hitchens

English author and journalist, 1949–2011

1 The secular state is the guarantee of religious pluralism. This apparent paradox, again, is the simplest and most elegant of political truths.
"Ireland" (1998)

Adolf Hitler

German dictator, 1889–1945

1 The broad mass of a nation . . . will more easily fall victim to a big lie than to a small one.
Mein Kampf vol. 1, ch. 10 (1925)

2 [*Referring to his massacre of Ernst Roehm and associates in June 1934:*] The night of the long knives.
Speech to Reichstag, 13 July 1934

3 I go the way that Providence dictates with the assurance of a sleepwalker.
Speech, Munich, Germany, 15 Mar. 1936

4 [*On the Sudetenland:*] It is the last territorial claim which I have to make in Europe.
Speech, Berlin, 26 Sept. 1938

5 After fifteen years of work I have achieved, as a common German soldier and merely with my fanatical will-power, the unity of the German nation, and have freed it from the death sentence of Versailles.
Proclamation, 21 Dec. 1941

6 This war . . . is one of those elemental conflicts which usher in a new millennium and which shake the world once in a thousand years.
Speech to Reichstag, 26 Apr. 1942

7 [*Question by telephone to General Alfred Jodl after Hitler had ordered Paris to be set on fire by retreating German troops, 25 Aug. 1944:*] *Brennt Paris?*

Is Paris burning?
Quoted in Larry Collins and Dominique Lapierre, *Is Paris Burning?* (1965). Lapierre relates in *A Thousand Suns: Witness to History* (1999) that he was told of this quotation by General Walter Warlimont, former deputy chief of staff of the Wehrmacht, who recorded it in his diary for 25 Aug. 1944.

8 [*Explaining why he was willing to invade Poland, 1939:*] Who, after all, speaks to-day of the annihilation of the Armenians?
Attributed in Louis Lochner, *What About Germany?* (1942). This alleged remark has not been verified in official records of Hitler's 1939 speeches.

9 The streets of our country are in turmoil. The universities are filled with students rebelling and rioting. Communists are seeking to destroy our country. Russia is threatening us with her might and the Republic is in danger. Yes,

danger from within and from without. We need law and order. Yes, without law and order our nation cannot survive. Elect us and we shall restore law and order.

Attributed in *Saturday Review,* 17 May 1969. According to Ralph Keyes, *"Nice Guys Finish Seventh":* "This statement was used by defenders of student rebels to imply that their critics were crypto-fascists. It was put in play by a liberal newsletter which said the sentences came from a 1932 speech Hitler made in Hamburg." Researchers have been unable to trace an authentic Hitler source.

Benjamin Hoadly

English clergyman, 1676–1761

1 Whoever hath an *absolute authority* to *interpret* any written or spoken laws, it is *He* who is truly the Law Giver to all intents and purposes, and not the Person who first wrote or spoke them.

Sermon before the King of England, 31 Mar. 1717

Thomas Hobbes

English philosopher, 1588–1679

1 For by art is created that great Leviathan, called a commonwealth or state, (in Latin *civitas*) which is but an artificial man . . . and in which, the sovereignty is an artificial soul.

Leviathan introduction (1651)

2 True and False are attributes of speech, not of things. And where speech is not, there is neither Truth nor Falsehood.

Leviathan pt. 1, ch. 4 (1651)

3 For words are wise men's counters, they do but reckon by them: but they are the money of fools, that value them by the authority of an Aristotle, a Cicero, or a Thomas, or any other doctor whatsoever, if but a man.

Leviathan pt. 1, ch. 4 (1651)

4 The power of a man, to take it universally, is his present means, to obtain some future apparent good; and is either original or instrumental. . . . Reputation of power, is power.

Leviathan pt. 1, ch. 10 (1651)

5 In the first place, I put for a general inclination of all mankind, a perpetual and restless desire of power after power, that ceaseth only in death.

Leviathan pt. 1, ch. 11 (1651)

6 *Religion;* which by reason of the different fancies, judgments, and passions of several men, hath grown up into ceremonies so different, that those which are used by one man, are for the most part ridiculous to another.

Leviathan pt. 1, ch. 12 (1651)

7 During the time men live without a common power to keep them all in awe, they are in that condition which is called war; and such a war as is of every man against every man.

Leviathan pt. 1, ch. 13 (1651)

8 [*Describing a state of nature:*] No arts; no letters; no society; and which is worst of all, continual fear, and danger of violent death; and the life of man, solitary, poor, nasty, brutish, and short.

Leviathan pt. 1, ch. 13 (1651)

9 Force, and fraud, are in war the two cardinal virtues.

Leviathan pt. 1, ch. 13 (1651)

10 Such truth as opposeth no man's profit nor pleasure is to all men welcome.

Leviathan "A Review and Conclusion" (1651)

11 [*"Last words":*] Death, is a leap into the dark.

Quoted in *The Last Sayings, or, Dying Legacy of Mr. Thomas Hobbs of Malmesbury* (1680). Usually rendered as "I am about to take my last voyage, a great leap in the dark."

Edward W. Hoch

U.S. politician, 1848–1925

1 There is so much good in the worst of us,
And so much bad in the best of us,
That it hardly becomes any of us
To talk about the rest of us.

Attributed in *The Reader,* 7 Sept. 1907. *Home Book of Quotations* notes the following: "Attributed to Edward Wallis Hoch, ex-Governor of Kansas, because first printed in the *Record,* of Marion, Kansas, of which he was editor." The claims that Hoch was the author and that the quotation first appeared in the *Record* are extremely dubious. The earliest version found by the editor of this book ("There is so much good in the worst of us / And so much bad in the best of us / That it little behooves any of us / To say much of the rest of us") was printed in the *Brown County World* (Hiawatha, Kan.), 14 Aug. 1896, without attribution to any individual.

Ho Chi Minh

North Vietnamese president, 1890–1969

1 All men are created equal; they are endowed
by their creator with certain inalienable rights;
among these are Life, Liberty and the pursuit
of happiness. This immortal statement was
made in the Declaration of Independence of the
United States of America in 1776. In a broader
sense, this means: All the peoples on the earth
are equal from birth, all the peoples have a
right to live, to be happy and free.

Proclamation of independence, 2 Sept. 1945
See Jefferson 2

2 Men and women, old and young, regardless of
creeds, political parties, or nationalities, all the
Vietnamese must stand up to fight the French
colonialists to save the fatherland. Those who
have rifles will use their rifles; those who have
swords will use their swords; those who have no
swords will use spades, hoes, or sticks.

Proclamation, 19 Dec. 1946 (translation by Peter
Wiles)

3 [*Remark, ca. 1946:*] It is better to sniff the
French dung for a while than eat China's all our
lives.

Quoted in Jean Lacouture, *Ho Chi Minh: A Political
Biography* (1968) (translation by Peter Wiles)

4 Nothing is more precious than independence
and liberty.

Quoted in *N.Y. Times*, 25 Jan. 1973

Russ Hodges

U.S. sportscaster, ca. 1909–1971

1 The Giants win the pennant! The Giants win
the pennant!

Television broadcast of Giant-Dodger baseball playoff
game, 3 Oct. 1951

William H. "Red" Hodgson

U.S. songwriter, fl. 1930

1 The Music Goes 'Round and Around.

Title of song (1931). Burton E. Stevenson, *Home Book
of Quotations*, states: "The authorship . . . has also
been credited to Eddy Farley and Mike Riley, but
Hodgson seems to have the prior claim. The song is
said to have been suggested by some lines in a joke
book for the Ford automobile, published in 1915: You
push the first pedal down, The wheels go 'round and
around."

Don C. Hoefler

U.S. journalist, ca. 1922–1986

1 Silicon Valley USA.

Title of article, *Electronic News*, 11 Jan. 1971. First
appearance in print of *Silicon Valley*, referring to an
area in California where many electronics firms were
located. Hoefler later recalled that the term "was used
occasionally mostly by Easterners" before his series
of articles, but Hoefler's usage popularized it.

Abbie Hoffman

U.S. political activist, 1936–1989

1 Today is the first day of the rest of your life.

Revolution for the Hell of It (1968). There is also 1968
evidence for this saying's being used by the antidrug
movement Synanon, and it may have been originated
by Synanon's founder, Charles Dederich.

2 Steal This Book.

Title of book (1971)

3 Sacred cows make the tastiest hamburger.

Quoted in *N.Y. Times*, 20 Apr. 1989. Although this is
associated with Hoffman, *The Daily Collegian* (Penn
State University), 19 Oct. 1965, printed "Sacred cows
make the best hamburger," crediting it to *Aardvark*
magazine.

4 I believe in compulsory cannibalism. If people
were forced to eat what they killed there would
be no war.

Quoted in James Charlton, *The Military Quotation
Book* (1990)

Al Hoffman

U.S. songwriter, 1902–1960

1 Takes Two to Tango.

Title of song (1952). Cowritten with Dick Manning.

August Heinrich Hoffmann, von Fallersleben

German poet, 1798–1874

1 *Deutschland Über Alles.*
Germany Above All.

Title of poem (1841)

Douglas R. Hofstadter

U.S. computer scientist and author, 1945–

1 *Hofstadter's Law:* It always takes longer than
you expect, even when you take into account
Hofstadter's Law.

Gödel, Escher, Bach ch. 5 (1979)

William Hogarth
English painter and engraver, 1697–1764

1 The Rake's Progress.
Title of series of paintings and engravings (1735)

Friedrich Hölderlin
German poet, 1770–1843

1 Near and
Hard to grasp, the god.
Yet where danger lies,
Grows that which saves.
"Patmos" (1802) (translation by Richard Sieburth)

Billie Holiday (Eleanora Fagan)
U.S. singer, 1915–1959

1 Mama may have
Papa may have
But God bless the child that's got his own.
"God Bless the Child" (song) (1941). Coauthored with
Arthur Herzog, Jr.

2 I can't stand to sing the same song the same
way two nights in succession, let alone two
years or ten years. If you can, then it ain't
music, it's close-order drill or exercise or
yodeling or something, not music.
Lady Sings the Blues ch. 4 (1956). Coauthored with
William Duffy.

3 You can be up to your boobies in white satin,
with gardenias in your hair and no sugar cane
for miles, but you can still be working on a
plantation.
Lady Sings the Blues ch. 11 (1956). Coauthored with
William Duffy.

Eddie Holland
U.S. songwriter, 1939–

1 Set me free, why don't cha, baby
Get out my life, why don't cha, baby
'Cause you don't really love me
You just keep me hangin' on.
"You Keep Me Hangin' On" (song) (1966)

Henry Scott Holland
English clergyman, 1847–1918

1 Death is nothing at all; it does not count. I have
only slipped away into the next room.
Sermon in St. Paul's Cathedral, London, 15 May 1910

John Hollander
U.S. poet, 1929–2013

1 The periodic table folded up. Now again
The elements are four: I myself, whose hand
and heart
And inner eye are one and indivisible; ink,
Discursive, drying into characters; the hard,
white
Ground of this very page; and for the fourth,
yourself: air
In which I burn? Or the fire by which I am
consumed.
Powers of Thirteen no. 7, l. 8 (1983)

2 The odd, evening hour, neither yours nor mine,
but ours,
When our hands reach out to touch like object
and image
Moving toward the mirror's surface each
through the magic
Space that the other's world must needs
transform in order
To comprehend.
Powers of Thirteen no. 169, l. 7 (1983)

Buddy Holly (Charles Hardin Holley)
U.S. rock singer and musician, 1937–1959

1 That'll be the day when I die.
"That'll Be the Day" (song) (1957). Cowritten with
Jerry Allison and Norman Petty.
See Film Lines 151

Fanny Dixwell Holmes
U.S. socialite and wife of Oliver Wendell
Holmes, Jr., 1840–1929

1 [*Remark to President Theodore Roosevelt at White
House dinner honoring Justice Oliver Wendell
Holmes, Jr., 8 Jan. 1903:*] Washington is full
of famous men and the women they married
when they were young.
Quoted in Catherine Drinker Bowen, *Yankee from
Olympus* (1944)

John H. Holmes
U.S. clergyman, 1879–1964

1 This universe is not hostile, nor yet is it
friendly. It is simply indifferent.
The Sensible Man's View of Religion ch. 4 (1932)

Oliver Wendell Holmes

U.S. writer and physician, 1809–1894

1 And if I should live to be
The last leaf upon the tree
In the spring,
Let them smile, as I do now,
At the old forsaken bough
Where I cling.
"The Last Leaf" l. 43 (1831)

2 The state should, I think, be called
"Anaesthesia." This signifies insensibility.
. . . The adjective will be "Anaesthetic." Thus
we might say the state of Anaesthesia, or the
anaesthetic state.
Letter to W. T. G. Morton, 21 Nov. 1846

3 What a satire, by the way, is that machine
[Charles Babbage's calculating machine] on the
mere mathematician! A Frankenstein-monster,
a thing without brains and without heart, too
stupid to make a blunder; that turns out results
like a corn-sheller, and never grows any wiser
or better, though it grind a thousand bushels of
them!
The Autocrat of the Breakfast-Table ch. 1 (1858)

4 Good Americans, when they die, go to Paris.
The Autocrat of the Breakfast-Table ch. 6 (1858).
Holmes attributed this comment to "one of the
wittiest of men," probably referring to his friend
Thomas Gold Appleton.
See Wilde 30

5 Boston State-House is the hub of the solar
system.
The Autocrat of the Breakfast-Table ch. 6 (1858)

6 Every now and then a man's mind is stretched
by a new idea or sensation, and never shrinks
back to its former dimensions.
The Autocrat of the Breakfast-Table ch. 11 (1858)

7 Have you heard of the wonderful one-hoss shay,
That was built in such a logical way
It ran a hundred years to a day.
The Autocrat of the Breakfast-Table ch. 11, "The
Deacon's Masterpiece" l. 1 (1858)

8 End of the wonderful one-hoss shay.
Logic is logic. That's all I say.
The Autocrat of the Breakfast-Table ch. 11, "The
Deacon's Masterpiece" l. 119 (1858)

9 Build thee more stately mansions, O my soul.
"The Chambered Nautilus" l. 29 (1858)

10 He comes of the Brahmin caste of New
England. This is the harmless, inoffensive,
untitled aristocracy referred to, and which
many readers will at once acknowledge.
Elsie Venner ch. 1 (1861)

11 Life is a fatal complaint, and an eminently
contagious one.
The Poet at the Breakfast Table ch. 12 (1872)

Oliver Wendell Holmes, Jr.

U.S. judge, 1841–1935

1 It is better to have a line drawn somewhere in
the penumbra between darkness and light, than
to remain in uncertainty.
"The Theory of Torts" (1873). Appears to be the first
use of the "penumbra" metaphor in American law.
See William O. Douglas 5

2 The life of the law has not been logic: it has been
experience. The felt necessities of the time, the
prevalent moral and political theories, intuitions
of public policy, avowed or unconscious, even
the prejudices which judges share with their
fellow-men, have had a good deal more to do
than the syllogism in determining the rules by
which men should be governed.
The Common Law Lecture 1 (1881). The first sentence
appeared verbatim in Holmes's review of Christopher
C. Langdell's A Selection of Cases on the Law of
Contracts, published in the American Law Review,
Mar. 1880.
See Coke 4

3 The law embodies the story of a nation's development through many centuries, and it cannot be dealt with as if it contained only the axioms and corollaries of a book of mathematics.

The Common Law Lecture 1 (1881)

4 Vengeance imports a feeling of blame, and an opinion, however distorted by passion, that a wrong has been done. It can hardly go very far beyond the case of a harm intentionally inflicted: even a dog distinguishes between being stumbled over and being kicked.

The Common Law Lecture 1 (1881)

5 The truth is, that the law is always approaching, and never reaching, consistency. It is forever adopting new principles from life at one end, and it always retains old ones from history at the other, which have not yet been absorbed or sloughed off. It will become entirely consistent only when it ceases to grow.

The Common Law Lecture 1 (1881)

6 We pause to become conscious of our national life and to rejoice in it, to recall what our country has done for each of us, and to ask ourselves what we can do for our country in return.

Memorial Day Address, Keene, N.H., 30 May 1884
See Briggs 1; Gibran 5; John Kennedy 4; John Kennedy 5; John Kennedy 16

7 I think that, as life is action and passion, it is required of a man that he should share the passion and action of his time at peril of being judged not to have lived.

Memorial Day Address, Keene, N.H., 30 May 1884

8 The law, wherein, as in a magic mirror, we see reflected, not only our own lives, but the lives of all men that have been!

"The Law" (address to Suffolk Bar Association dinner), Boston, Mass., 5 Feb. 1885. The "magic mirror" is probably an allusion to Alfred Tennyson's poem, "The Lady of Shalott," in which the Lady's only view of the world is through reflections in a mirror.

9 The external and immediate result of an advocate's work is but to win or lose a case. But remotely what the lawyer does is to establish, develop, or illuminate rules which are to govern the conduct of men for centuries; to set in motion principles and influences which shape

the thought and action of generations which know not by whose command they move.

"Sidney Bartlett" (eulogy), Boston, Mass., 23 Mar. 1889

10 If you want to know the law and nothing else, you must look at it as a bad man, who cares only for the material consequences which such knowledge enables him to predict, not as a good one, who finds his reasons for conduct, whether inside the law or outside of it, in the vaguer sanctions of conscience.

"The Path of the Law" (1897)

11 The prophecies of what the courts will do in fact, and nothing more pretentious, are what I mean by the law.

"The Path of the Law" (1897)

12 Certainty generally is illusion, and repose is not the destiny of man.

"The Path of the Law" (1897)

13 For the rational study of the law the black-letter man may be the man of the present, but the man of the future is the man of statistics and the master of economics.

"The Path of the Law" (1897)

14 It is revolting to have no better reason for a rule of law than that so it was laid down in the time of Henry IV. It is still more revolting if the grounds upon which it was laid down have vanished long since, and the rule simply persists from blind imitation of the past.

"The Path of the Law" (1897)

15 The remoter and more general aspects of the law are those which give it universal interest. It is through them that you not only become a great master in your calling, but connect your subject with the universe and catch an echo of the infinite, a glimpse of its unfathomable process, a hint of the universal law.

"The Path of the Law" (1897)

16 Life is an end in itself, and the only question as to whether it is worth living is whether you have enough of it.

Speech to Bar Association of Boston, Boston, Mass., 7 Mar. 1900

17 Great cases like hard cases make bad law. For cases are called great, not by reason of their real

importance in shaping the law of the future, but because of some accident of immediate overwhelming interest which appeals to the feelings and distorts the judgment. These immediate interests exercise a kind of hydraulic pressure which makes what previously was clear seem doubtful, and before which even well settled principles of law will bend.

Northern Securities Co. v. United States (dissenting opinion) (1904)
See Proverbs 136

18 This case is decided upon an economic theory which a large part of the country does not entertain. If it were a question whether I agreed with that theory, I should desire to study it further and long before making up my mind. But I do not conceive that to be my duty, because I strongly believe that my agreement or disagreement has nothing to do with the right of a majority to embody their opinions in law.

Lochner v. New York (dissenting opinion) (1905)

19 The Fourteenth Amendment does not enact [the economic theories of] Mr. Herbert Spencer's Social Statics.

Lochner v. New York (dissenting opinion) (1905)

20 A constitution is not intended to embody a particular economic theory. . . . It is made for people of fundamentally differing views, and the accident of our finding certain opinions natural and familiar or novel and even shocking ought not to conclude our judgment upon the question whether statutes embodying them conflict with the Constitution of the United States.

Lochner v. New York (dissenting opinion) (1905)

21 Life is painting a picture, not doing a sum.
"The Class of '61" (speech), Cambridge, Mass., 28 June 1911

22 We are very quiet there [at the Supreme Court], but it is the quiet of a storm centre, as we all know.
"Law and the Court" (speech to Harvard Law School Association of New York), 15 Feb. 1913

23 I do not think we need trouble ourselves with the thought that my view depends upon differences of degree. The whole law does so as soon as it is civilized. . . . Negligence is all

degree—that of the defendant here degree of the nicest sort; and between the variations according to distance that I suppose to exist and the simple universality of the rules in the Twelve Tables of the Leges Barbarorum, there lies the culture of two thousand years.

LeRoy Fibre Co. v. Chicago, Milwaukee & St. Paul Ry. (concurring opinion) (1914)

24 The common law is not a brooding omnipresence in the sky but the articulate voice of some sovereign or quasi-sovereign that can be identified.

Southern Pacific Co. v. Jensen (dissenting opinion) (1917)

25 I abhor, loathe, and despise these long discourses, and agree with Carducci the Italian poet who died some years ago that a man who takes half a page to say what can be said in a sentence will be damned.

Letter to Frederick Pollock, 1 June 1917

26 A word is not a crystal, transparent and unchanged, it is the skin of a living thought and may vary greatly in color and content according to the circumstances and the time in which it is used.

Towne v. Eisner (1918)

27 Persecution for the expression of opinions seems to be perfectly logical. If you have no doubt of your premises or your power and want a certain result with all your heart you naturally express your wishes in law and sweep away all opposition.

Abrams v. United States (dissenting opinion) (1919)

28 But when men have realized that time has upset many fighting faiths, they may come to believe even more than they believe the very foundations of their own conduct that the ultimate good desired is better reached by free trade in ideas—that the best test of truth is the power of the thought to get itself accepted in the competition of the market, and that truth is the only ground upon which their wishes safely can be carried out. That at any rate is the theory of our Constitution. It is an experiment, as all life is an experiment.

Abrams v. United States (dissenting opinion) (1919)
See Milton 8

29 The most stringent protection of free speech would not protect a man in falsely shouting fire in a theatre and causing a panic.... The question in every case is whether the words used are used in such circumstances and are of such a nature as to create a clear and present danger that they will bring about the substantive evils that Congress has a right to prevent.

Schenck v. United States (1919). The sentence about "falsely shouting fire in a theatre" is often misquoted by omitting the word "falsely" or by adding the word "crowded" before "theatre." Holmes appears to have taken the theater example from the closing argument of prosecutor Edwin S. Wertz in the sedition trial of Eugene V. Debs in 1918. Wertz stated: "A man in a crowded auditorium, or any theatre, who yells 'fire' and there is no fire, and a panic ensues and someone is trampled to death, may be rightfully indicted and charged with murder."
See Brandeis 6

30 I ... probably take the extremest view in favor of free speech, (in which, in the abstract, I have no very enthusiastic belief, though I hope I would die for it).

Letter to Frederick Pollock, 26 Oct. 1919

31 Upon this point a page of history is worth a volume of logic.

New York Trust Co. v. Eisner (1921)

32 It will need more than the Nineteenth Amendment to convince me that there are no differences between men and women, or that legislation cannot take those differences into account.

Adkins v. Children's Hospital (dissenting opinion) (1922)

33 But I have long thought that if you knew a column of advertisements by heart, you could achieve unexpected felicities with them. You can get a happy quotation anywhere if you have the eye.

Letter to Harold Laski, 31 May 1923

34 It is said that this manifesto is more than a theory, that it was an incitement. Every idea is an incitement.

Gitlow v. New York (dissenting opinion) (1925)

35 It is better for all the world, if instead of waiting to execute degenerate offspring for crime, or to let them starve for their imbecility, society can prevent those who are manifestly unfit from continuing their kind. The principle that sustains compulsory vaccination is broad enough to cover cutting the Fallopian tubes.... Three generations of imbeciles are enough.

Buck v. Bell (1927)

36 Taxes are what we pay for civilized society.

Compañía General de Tabacos de Filipinas v. Collector of Internal Revenue (dissenting opinion) (1927). "Taxation is the price which we pay for civilization" has been found by Garson O'Toole to have appeared in Journal of the House of Representatives of the State of Vermont (1852).

37 The government ought not to use evidence obtained and only obtainable, by a criminal act.... For my part I think it a less evil that some criminals should escape than that the Government should play an ignoble part.

Olmstead v. United States (dissenting opinion) (1928)

38 The power to tax is not the power to destroy while this Court sits.

Panhandle Oil Co. v. Mississippi ex rel. Knox (dissenting opinion) (1928)
See John Marshall 7; Daniel Webster 2

39 If there is any principle of the Constitution that more imperatively calls for attachment than any other it is the principle of free thought—not free thought for those who agree with us but freedom for the thought that we hate.

United States v. Schwimmer (dissenting opinion) (1929)

40 The riders in a race do not stop short when they reach the goal. There is a little finishing canter before coming to a standstill. There is time to hear the kind voice of friends and to say to one's self: "The work is done." But just as one says that, the answer comes: "The race is over, but the work never is done while the power to work remains." The canter that brings you to a standstill need not be only coming to rest. It cannot be, while you still live. For to live is to function. That is all there is in living.

Radio address on his 90th birthday, 8 Mar. 1931

41 Life seems to me like a Japanese picture which our imagination does not allow to end with the margin. We aim at the infinite and when our arrow falls to earth it is in flames.

Letter to Federal Bar Association, 29 Feb. 1932

42 No generalization is wholly true—not even this one.

Quoted in Owen Wister, *Roosevelt: The Story of a Friendship* (1930)

43 [*In response to a well-wisher who called out "Now justice will be administered in Washington" as Holmes embarked to take his seat on the U.S. Supreme Court, 1902:*] Don't be too sure. I am going there to administer *the law.*

Quoted in Charles Henry Butler, *A Century at the Bar of the Supreme Court of the United States* (1942)

44 [*Of Franklin D. Roosevelt, after meeting him when Holmes was in his nineties and Roosevelt had just become president, 1933:*] A second-class intellect, but a first-class temperament.

Quoted in James MacGregor Burns, *Roosevelt: The Lion and the Fox* (1956)
See Theodore Roosevelt 29

Homer

Greek poet, Eighth cent. B.C.

1 Sing, goddess, the wrath of Peleus' son Achilles, a destroying wrath which brought upon the Achaeans myriad woes, and sent forth to Hades most valiant souls of heroes.
Iliad bk. 1, l. 1

2 Speaking, he addressed her winged words.
Iliad bk. 1, l. 201

3 From his tongue flowed speech sweeter than honey.
Iliad bk. 1, l. 249

4 Smiling through her tears.
Iliad bk. 6, l. 484

5 The most preferable of evils.
Iliad bk. 17, l. 105
See Mae West 13

6 It lies in the lap of the gods.
Iliad bk. 17, l. 514

7 [*Of Odysseus:*] Tell me, muse, of the man of many resources who wandered far and wide after he had sacked the holy citadel of Troy, and he saw the cities and learned the thoughts of many men.
Odyssey bk. 1, l. 1
See Pope 8

8 Rosy-fingered dawn.
Odyssey bk. 2, l. 1

9 The wine-dark sea.
Odyssey bk. 2, l. 420

Thomas Hood

English poet, 1799–1845

1 There is a silence where hath been no sound,
There is a silence where no sound may be,
In the cold grave—under the deep, deep sea.
"Silence" l. 1 (1827)

Richard Hooker

English theologian, ca. 1554–1600

1 Of Law there can be no less acknowledged, than that her seat is the bosom of God, her voice the harmony of the world: all things in heaven and earth do her homage, the very least as feeling her care, and the greatest as not exempted from her power.
Of the Laws of Ecclesiastical Polity bk. 1, ch. 16 (1593)

Richard Hooker (H. Richard Hornberger)

U.S. physician, 1924–1997

1 We're the pros from Dover.
M*A*S*H ch. 8 (1968). Developed by the character Hawkeye as a way of claiming to be a pro from an ambiguous golf club in order to wangle invitations to play free rounds.

bell hooks (Gloria Jean Watkins)

U.S. author and feminist, 1952–

1 The academy is not paradise. But learning is a place where paradise can be created.
Teaching to Transgress ch. 14 (1994)

Ellen Sturgis Hooper

U.S. poet, 1816–1841

1 I slept, and dreamed that life was Beauty;
I woke, and found that life was Duty.
"I Slept, and Dreamed That Life Was Beauty" l. 1 (1840)

Herbert C. Hoover

U.S. president, 1874–1964

1 Our country has deliberately undertaken a great social and economic experiment, noble in motive and far-reaching in purpose.
Letter to William E. Borah, 23 Feb. 1928. Referring to the prohibition of liquor, thereafter known as "the noble experiment."

2 We were challenged with a peace-time choice between the American system of rugged individualism and a European philosophy of diametrically opposed doctrines—doctrines of paternalism and static socialism.

Campaign speech, New York, N.Y., 22 Oct. 1928. The term *rugged individualism* is found earlier in *Godey's Magazine,* May 1898.

3 The slogan of progress is changing from the full dinner pail to the full garage.

Campaign speech, New York, N.Y., 22 Oct. 1928. Often quoted as "a car in every garage and a chicken in every pot."
See Henri IV 1; Political Slogans 12

4 [*Of members of Congress introducing bill for unemployment relief:*] They are playing politics at the expense of human misery.

Statement to press, 9 Dec. 1930

5 Older men declare war. But it is youth that must fight and die. And it is youth who must inherit the tribulation, the sorrow, and the triumphs that are the aftermath of war.

Address to Republican National Convention, Chicago, Ill., 27 June 1944
See Grantland Rice 3

J. Edgar Hoover
U.S. government official, 1895–1972

1 I regret to say that we of the FBI are powerless to act in cases of oral-genital intimacy, unless it has in some way obstructed interstate commerce.

Attributed in Irving Wallace, *Intimate Sex Lives of Famous People* (1981)

Anthony Hope (Anthony Hope Hopkins)
English novelist, 1863–1933

1 His foe was folly & his weapon wit.

Inscription on W. S. Gilbert Memorial, London (1915)

Laurence Hope (Adela Florence Nicolson)
English poet, 1865–1904

1 Pale hands I loved beside the Shalimar,
Where are you now? Who lies beneath your spell?
Whom do you lead on Rapture's roadway, far,
Before you agonize them in farewell?

"Kashmiri Song" l. 1 (1901)

2 Less than the dust, beneath thy Chariot wheel,
Less than the rust, that never stained thy Sword,
Less than the trust thou hast in me, O Lord,
Even less than these!

"Less Than the Dust" l. 1 (1901)

Gerard Manley Hopkins
English poet, 1844–1889

1 Elected Silence, sing to me
And beat upon my whorlèd ear.

"The Habit of Perfection" l. 1 (written 1866)

2 The world is charged with the grandeur of God.

"God's Grandeur" l. 1 (written 1877)

3 Glory be to God for dappled things.

"Pied Beauty" l. 1 (written 1877)

4 All things counter, original, spare, strange;
Whatever is fickle, freckled (who knows how?)
With swift, slow; sweet, sour; adazzle, dim;
He fathers-forth whose beauty is past change:
Praise him.

"Pied Beauty" l. 7 (written 1877)

5 I caught this morning morning's minion,
kingdom of daylight's dauphin, dapple-dawn-drawn Falcon, in his riding
Of the rolling level underneath him steady air,
and striding
High there, how he rung upon the rein of a
wimpling wing
In his ecstasy!

"The Windhover" l. 1 (written 1877)

6 Márgarét, áre you grieving
Over Goldengrove unleaving?

"Spring and Fall: to a young child" l. 1 (written 1880)

7 It is the blight man was born for,
It is Margaret you mourn for.

"Spring and Fall: to a young child" l. 12 (written 1880)

8 O the mind, mind has mountains; cliffs of fall
Frightful, sheer, no-man-fathomed. Hold them cheap
May who ne'er hung there.

"No worst, there is none" l. 9 (written 1885)

Harry Hopkins

U.S. government official, 1890–1946

1 We are going to spend and spend and spend,
tax and tax and tax and elect and elect and elect.

Quoted in *Daily Times* (Beaver and Rochester, Pa.),
26 Oct. 1938. This appears to be the origin of the
political phrase "tax and spend."

Jane Ellice Hopkins

English reformer, 1836–1904

1 Genius . . . an infinite capacity for taking pains.

Work Amongst Working Men ch. 4 (1870)
See Buffon 2; Thomas Carlyle 19; Edison 2

Joseph Hopkinson

U.S. politician, 1770–1842

1 Hail, Columbia! happy land!
Hail, ye heroes! heaven-born band!

"Hail, Columbia" l. 1 (1798)

Edward Hopper

U.S. painter, 1882–1967

1 If you could say it in words there'd be no reason
to paint.

Quoted in *Time*, 24 Dec. 1956

Grace Murray Hopper

U.S. computer scientist, 1906–1992

1 [*Notation next to moth taped into log:*] First actual
case of bug being found.

Logbook entry, 9 Sept. 1947. The moth taped into
Hopper's log after being found inside the early Mark
II computer supposedly gave rise to the term *bug*
meaning a defect in computer hardware or software.
This insect is real—it is preserved at the Smithsonian
Institution; however, much earlier usages of *bug* by
Thomas Edison and others disprove the notion that
the moth's discovery inspired the term.

2 Always remember that it's much easier to
apologize than to get permission.

Quoted in *Chicago Tribune*, 9 Dec. 1982. "It's easier
to get forgiveness than permission," not attributed to
Hopper, appeared in *Southern Education Report*, Aug.
1966.

Horace (Quintus Horatius Flaccus)

Roman poet, 65 B.C.–8 B.C.

1 *Inceptis gravibus plerumque et magna professis*
Purpureus, late qui splendeat, unus et alter
Adsuitur pannus.

Works of serious purpose and grand promises
often have a purple patch or two stitched on,
to shine far and wide.

Ars Poetica l. 14

2 *Multa renascentur quae iam cecidere, cadentque*
Quae nunc sunt in honore vocabula, si volet usus,
Quem penes arbitrium est et ius et norma
loquendi.

Many terms which have now dropped out of
favor will be revived, and those that are at
present respectable will drop out, if usage
so choose, with whom lies the decision, the
judgment, and the rule of speech.

Ars Poetica l. 70

3 *Grammatici certant et adhuc sub iudice lis est.*
Scholars dispute, and the case is still before the
courts.

Ars Poetica l. 78

4 *Proicit ampullas et sesquipedalia verba.*
He throws aside his paint-pots and his words a
foot and a half long.

Ars Poetica l. 97

5 *Parturient montes, nascetur ridiculus mus.*
Mountains will go into labor, and a silly little
mouse will be born.

Ars Poetica l. 139

6 *Semper ad eventum festinat et in medias res*
Non secus ac notas auditorem rapit.
He always hurries to the main event and
whisks his audience into the middle of
things as though they knew already.

Ars Poetica l. 148

7 *Laudator temporis acti.*
A praiser of past times.

Ars Poetica l. 173

8 *Quandoque bonus dormitat Homerus.*
Sometimes even excellent Homer nods.

Ars Poetica l. 359

9 *Ut pictura poesis.*
A poem is like a painting.

Ars Poetica l. 361

10 *Si possis recte, si non, quocumque modo rem.*
If possible honestly, if not, somehow, make
money.

Epistles bk. 1, no. 1, l. 66

11 *Belua multorum es capitum.*
The people are a many-headed beast.
Epistles bk. 1, no. 1, l. 76
See Alexander Hamilton 12

12 *Concordia discors.*
Discordant harmony.
Epistles bk. 1, no. 12, l. 19

13 *Et semel emissum volat irrevocabile verbum.*
And once sent out a word takes wing beyond recall.
Epistles bk. 1, no. 18, l. 71

14 *Atque inter silvas Academi quaerere verum.*
And seek for truth in the groves of Academe.
Epistles bk. 2, no. 2, l. 45

15 *Multa fero, ut placem genus irritabile vatum.*
I have to put up with a lot, to please the touchy breed of poets.
Epistles bk. 2, no. 2, l. 102

16 *Nil desperandum.*
Never despair.
Odes bk. 1, no. 7, l. 27

17 *Carpe diem, quam minimum credula postero.*
Seize the day, put no trust in the future.
Odes bk. 1, no. 11, l. 7
See Seale 1

18 *Nunc est bibendum, nunc pede libero*
Pulsanda tellus.
Now for drinking, now the Earth must shake beneath a lively foot.
Odes bk. 1, no. 37, l. 1

19 *Auream quisquis mediocritatem diligit.*
Someone who loves the golden mean.
Odes bk. 2, no. 10, l. 5
See Anonymous 21; Horace 26; Proverbs 195

20 *Dulce et decorum est pro patria mori.*
Lovely and honorable it is to die for one's country.
Odes bk. 3, no. 2, l. 13
See Wilfred Owen 3

21 *Ille potens sui*
Laetusque deget, cui licet in diem
Dixisse Vixi: cras vel atra
Nube polum pater occupato
Vel sole puro.
That man shall live as his own master and in happiness who can say each day "I have

lived": tomorrow let the Father fill the sky with a black cloud or clear sunshine.
Odes bk. 3, no. 29, l. 41
See John Dryden 8

22 *Exegi monumentum aere perennius.*
I have erected a monument more lasting than bronze.
Odes bk. 3, no. 30, l. 1

23 *Non omnis moriar.*
I shall not altogether die.
Odes bk. 3, no. 30, l. 6

24 *Non sum qualis eram bonae*
Sub regno Cinarae.
I was not as I was when good Cinara was my queen.
Odes bk. 4, no. 1, l. 3

25 *Vixere fortes ante Agamemnona*
Multi; sed omnes illacrimabiles
Urgentur ingotique longa
Nocte, carent quia vate sacro.
Many brave men lived before Agamemnon's time; but they are all, unmourned and unknown, covered by the long night, because they lack their sacred poet.
Odes bk. 4, no. 9, l. 25

26 *Est modus in rebus.*
There is moderation in everything.
Satires bk. 1, no. 1, l. 106
See Anonymous 21; Horace 19; Proverbs 195

27 *[Of Ennius:] Disiecti membra poetae.*
The limbs of a dismembered poet.
Satires bk. 1, no. 4, l. 62

28 *Hoc erat in votis: modus agri non ita magnus,*
Hortus ubi et tecto vicinus iugis aquae fons
Et paulum silvae super his foret.
This was among my prayers: a piece of land not so very large, where a garden should be and a spring of ever-flowing water near the house, and a bit of woodland as well as these.
Satires bk. 2, no. 6, l. 1

Donald Horne
Australian writer, 1921–2005

1 Australia is a lucky country.
The Lucky Country ch. 10 (1964). Horne meant this comment as a criticism, but it is often repeated with a positive sense.

Karen Horney

German-born U.S. psychoanalyst and author, 1885–1952

1 Fortunately analysis [psychoanalysis] is not the only way to resolve inner conflicts. Life itself still remains a very effective therapist.
Our Inner Conflicts: A Constructive Theory of Neuroses conclusion (1945)

Khaled Hosseini

Afghan-born U.S. novelist, 1965–

1 I became what I am today at the age of twelve, on a frigid overcast day in the winter of 1975.
The Kite Runner ch. 1 (2003)

2 He was already turning the street corner, his rubber boots kicking up snow. He stopped, turned. He cupped his hands around his mouth. "For you a thousand times over!" he said.
The Kite Runner ch. 7 (2003)

A. E. Housman

English poet, 1859–1936

1 Loveliest of trees, the cherry now
Is hung with bloom along the bough,
And stands about the woodland ride
Wearing white for Eastertide.
A Shropshire Lad no. 2, l. 1 (1896)

2 Into my heart an air that kills
From yon far country blows:
What are those blue remembered hills,
What spires, what farms are those?
A Shropshire Lad no. 40, l. 1 (1896)

3 That is the land of lost content,
I see it shining plain,
The happy highways where I went
And cannot come again.
A Shropshire Lad no. 40, l. 5 (1896)

4 Terence, this is stupid stuff:
You eat your victuals fast enough:
There can't be much amiss, 'tis clear,
To see the rate you drink your beer.
A Shropshire Lad no. 62, l. 1 (1896)

5 And malt does more than Milton can
To justify God's ways to man.
A Shropshire Lad no. 62, l. 21 (1896)
See Milton 18; Milton 49

6 I tell the tale that I heard told.
Mithridates, he died old.
A Shropshire Lad no. 62, l. 75 (1896)

7 I, a stranger and afraid
In a world I never made.
Last Poems no. 12, l. 17 (1922)

8 If a line of poetry strays into my memory, my skin bristles so that the razor ceases to act.
The Name and Nature of Poetry (1933)

Charles Hamilton Houston

U.S. lawyer, 1895–1950

1 [*Of United States civil rights and foreign policy:*] The failure of the Government to enforce democratic practices and to protect minorities in its own capital makes its expressed concern for national minorities abroad somewhat specious, and its interference in the domestic affairs of other countries very premature.
Letter to Harry S. Truman, 3 Dec. 1945

Sam Houston

U.S. general and president of Republic of Texas, 1793–1863

1 He has every characteristic of a dog except loyalty.
Quoted in Leon A. Harris, *The Fine Art of Political Wit* (1964)

Richard Hovey

U.S. poet, 1864–1900

1 For it's always fair weather
When good fellows get together,
With a stein on the table and a good song ringing clear.
"A Stein Song" l. 5 (1896)

Barbara Howar

U.S. writer and socialite, 1934–

1 [*Of Henry Kissinger:*] Henry's idea of sex is to slow the car down to thirty miles an hour when he drops you off at the door.
Quoted in Barbara Rowes, *The Book of Quotes* (1979)

Bart Howard (Howard Gustafsson)

U.S. songwriter and musician, 1915–2004

1 Fly me to the moon, and let me play among the stars.

"Fly Me to the Moon (In Other Words)" (song) (1954)

Edgar W. Howe

U.S. editor and humorist, 1853–1937

1 What people say behind your back is your standing in the community.

Quoted in *The American Treasury: 1455–1955*, ed. Clifton Fadiman (1955)

Julia Ward Howe

U.S. suffragist and reformer, 1819–1910

1 Mine eyes have seen the glory of the coming of the Lord:

He is trampling out the vintage where the grapes of wrath are stored;

He hath loosed the fateful lightning of his terrible swift sword:

His truth is marching on.

"Battle Hymn of the Republic" l. 1 (1862)

2 Glory! Glory! Hallelujah! Glory! Glory! Hallelujah!

Glory! Glory! Hallelujah! His truth is marching on.

"The Battle Hymn of the Republic" l. 5 (1862). The music and words of this chorus appeared earlier in a hymn titled "Brothers, Will You Meet Us?," copyright G. S. Scofield, 1858.

See Folk and Anonymous Songs 41

3 In the beauty of the lilies Christ was born across the sea,

With a glory in His bosom that transfigures you and me:

As He died to make men holy, let us die to make men free;

While God is marching on.

"The Battle Hymn of the Republic" l. 25 (1862)

William Dean Howells

U.S. author, 1837–1920

1 I don't see why, when it comes to falling in love, a man shouldn't fall in love with a rich girl as easily as a poor one.

The Rise of Silas Lapham ch. 5 (1885)

See Thackeray 9

Mary Howitt

English children's writer, 1799–1888

1 "Will you walk into my parlor?" said a spider to a fly:

"'Tis the prettiest little parlor that ever you did spy."

"The Spider and the Fly" l. 1 (1834). Often misquoted as "said the spider to the fly."

Edmond Hoyle

English writer on games, 1672–1769

1 When in doubt, win the trick.

Hoyle's Games Improved, ed. Charles Jones (1790). Although this is associated with Hoyle, it appears slightly earlier in *The Aberdeen Magazine, Literary Chronicle, and Review* vol. 1 (1788): "When in doubt win the trick."

Fred Hoyle

English astrophysicist, 1915–2001

1 One [idea] was that the Universe started its life a finite time ago in a single huge explosion. . . . This big bang idea seemed to me to be unsatisfactory.

The Nature of the Universe ch. 5 (1950)

Roman L. Hruska

U.S. politician, 1904–1999

1 There are a lot of mediocre judges and people and lawyers, and they are entitled to a little representation [on the Supreme Court], aren't they? We can't have all Brandeises, Frankfurters, and Cardozos.

Quoted in *N.Y. Times*, 17 Mar. 1970

Elbert Hubbard

U.S. writer, 1856–1915

1 [President William] McKinley gave Rowan a letter to be delivered to Garcia; Rowan took the letter & did not ask, "Where is he at?" By the Eternal! there is a man whose form should be cast in deathless bronze & the statue placed in every college of the land. It is not book-learning young men need, nor instruction about this and that, but a stiffening of the vertebrae which will cause them to be loyal to a trust, to act promptly, concentrate their energies: do the thing—"Carry a message to Garcia!"

"A Message to Garcia" (1899)

2 Never explain—your friends do not need it and
your enemies will not believe you anyhow.
The Motto Book (1907)
See Disraeli 32; John Arbuthnot Fisher 1

3 One machine can do the work of fifty ordinary
men. No machine can do the work of one
extraordinary man.
A Thousand and One Epigrams (1911)

4 Editor: a person employed by a newspaper,
whose business it is to separate the wheat from
the chaff, and to see that the chaff is printed.
The Roycroft Dictionary of Epigrams (1914)

5 If you want work well done, select a busy man.
The Philosophy of Elbert Hubbard (1916).
See Modern Proverbs 11

6 A genius is a man who takes the lemons that
Fate hands him and starts a lemonade-stand
with them.
Quoted in *Literary Digest,* 23 Jan. 1909
See Modern Proverbs 48

Frank McKinney "Kin" Hubbard
U.S. humorist, 1868–1930

1 It's no disgrace t' be poor, but it might as
well be.
"Short Furrows" (1911)

2 It's what we learn after we think we know it all
that counts.
Fairmount (Ind.) *News,* 17 Feb. 1913

3 Now an' then a innocent man is sent t' th'
legislature.
Wash. Herald, 15 Mar. 1913

4 When a feller says, "It hain't th' money, but th'
principle o' the thing," it's th' money.
Rockford (Ill.) *Morning Star,* 23 Nov. 1916
See Sayings 30

5 Nobody ever forgets where he buried a hatchet.
Quoted in Evan Esar, *The Dictionary of Humorous
Quotations* (1949)

Charles Evans Hughes
U.S. judge and politician, 1862–1948

1 We are under a Constitution, but the
Constitution is what the judges say it is.
Speech, Elmira, N.Y., 3 May 1907

Howard Hughes, Jr.
U.S. industrialist, aviator, and motion picture
producer, 1905–1976

1 [*Of Clark Gable:*] That man's ears make him
look like a taxi-cab with both doors open.
Quoted in Charles Higham and Joel Greenberg,
Celluloid Muse (1969)

Langston Hughes
U.S. writer, 1902–1967

1 I've known rivers ancient as the world and
older than the flow of human blood in human
veins.
"The Negro Speaks of Rivers" l. 1 (1921)

2 I too, sing America.
I am the darker brother.
They send me to eat in the kitchen
When company comes,
But I laugh,
And eat well,
And grow strong.
"I, Too" l. 1 (1925)

3 They'll see how beautiful I am
And be ashamed—
I, too, am America.
"I, Too" l. 16 (1925)

4 Got the Weary Blues
And can't be satisfied—
I ain't happy no mo'
And I wish that I had died.
"The Weary Blues" l. 27 (1926)

5 It is the duty of the younger Negro artist . . .
to change through the force of his art that
old whispering "I want to be white," hidden
in the aspirations of his people, to "Why
should I want to be white? I am a Negro—and
beautiful!"
Nation, 23 June 1926
See Bible 156; Political Slogans 8

6 Hold fast to dreams
For if dreams die
Life is a broken-winged bird
That cannot fly.
"Dreams" l. 1 (1929)

7 I swear to the Lord
  I still can't see
  Why Democracy means
  Everybody but me.
  "The Black Man Speaks" l. 1 (1943)

8 What happens to a dream deferred?
  Does it dry up
  like a raisin in the sun?
  Or fester like a sore—
  And then run?
  Does it stink like rotten meat?
  Or crust and sugar over—
  like a syrupy sweet?
  Maybe it just sags
  Like a heavy load.
  Or does it explode?
  "Harlem" l. 1 (1951)
  See Bible 130

9 As I learn from you,
  I guess you learn from me—
  although you're older—and white—
  and somewhat more free.
  This is my page for English B.
  "Theme for English B" l. 37 (1951)

10 "It's powerful," he said.
   "What?"
   "That one drop of Negro blood—because
      just *one* drop of black blood makes a man
      colored. *One* drop—you are a Negro!"
   Simple Takes a Wife ch. 20 (1953)

Ted Hughes

English poet, 1930–1998

1 Grey silent fragments
  Of a grey silent world.
  "The Horses" l. 14 (1957)

2 Cold, delicately as the dark snow,
  A fox's nose touches twig, leaf;
  Two eyes serve a movement, that now
  And again now, and now, and now
  Sets neat prints into the snow.
  "The Thought-Fox" l. 9 (1957)

3 With a sudden sharp hot stink of fox,
  It enters the dark hole of the head.
  The window is starless still; the clock ticks,
  The page is printed.
  "The Thought-Fox" l. 21 (1957)

4 I sit in the top of the wood, my eyes closed.
  Inaction, no falsifying dream
  Between my hooked head and hooked feet:
  Or in sleep rehearse perfect kills and eat.
  "Hawk Roosting" l. 1 (1960)

5 It took the whole of Creation
  To produce my foot, my each feather:
  Now I hold Creation in my foot
  Or fly up, and revolve it all slowly—
  I kill where I please because it is all mine.
  There is no sophistry in my body:
  My manners are tearing off heads—
  The allotment of death.
  "Hawk Roosting" l. 10 (1960)

6 Pike, three inches long, perfect
  Pike in all parts, green tigering the gold.
  Killers from the egg; the malevolent aged grin.
  "Pike" l. 1 (1960)

7 The jaws' hooked clamp and fangs
  Not to be changed at this date;
  A life subdued to its instrument.
  "Pike" l. 13 (1960)

8 Stilled legendary depth:
  It was as deep as England. It held
  Pike too immense to stir, so immense and old
  That past nightfall I dared not cast.
  "Pike" l. 33 (1960)

Thomas Hughes

English jurist, reformer, and writer, 1822–1896

1 Life isn't all beer and skittles; but beer and
  skittles, or something better of the same sort,
  must form a good part of every Englishman's
  education.
  Tom Brown's Schooldays pt. 1, ch. 2 (1857)
  See Proverbs 170

Victor Hugo

French writer, 1802–1885

1 *Asile!*
  Sanctuary!
  The Hunchback of Notre Dame bk. 8, ch. 6 (1831)

2 *Oh! que ne suis-je de pierre comme toi!*
  Oh, why am I not of stone, like you?
  The Hunchback of Notre Dame bk. 9, ch. 4 (1831)

3 *Les États Unis d'Europe.*
  The United States of Europe.
  Speech, Anvers, France, 1 Aug. 1852

4 Waterloo! Waterloo! Waterloo! Dismal plain!
  "L'Expiation" (1853)

5 *Le mot, c'est le Verbe, et le Verbe, c'est Dieu.*
  The word is the Verb, and the Verb is God.
  Contemplations bk. 1, no. 8 (1856)
  See Buckminster Fuller 1; Ulysses S. Grant 6

6 Take away *time is money,* and what is left of
  England? take away *cotton is king,* and what is
  left of America?
  Les Misérables vol. 3, bk. 4, ch. 4 (1862)
  See Benjamin Franklin 25

7 The first symptom of true love in a young man
  is timidity; in a young woman, it is boldness.
  Les Misérables vol. 4, bk. 3, ch. 6 (1862)

8 *On résiste à l'invasion des armées; on ne résiste pas
  à l'invasion des idées.*
  One can resist the invasion of armies; one
     cannot resist the invasion of ideas.
  Histoire d'un Crime (1877). Frequently paraphrased
  as "nothing is so powerful as an idea whose time has
  come." In the *Atlanta Constitution,* 8 June 1919, Hugo
  is quoted: "There is one thing stronger than armies,
  and that is an idea whose time has come."

9 Jesus wept; Voltaire smiled. From that divine
  tear and from that human smile is derived the
  grace of present civilization.
  "Centenaire de Voltaire" (1878)

David Hume
Scottish philosopher, 1711–1776

1 Generally speaking, the errors in religion are
  dangerous; those in philosophy only ridiculous.
  A Treatise upon Human Nature bk. 1 (1739)

2 We speak not strictly and philosophically when
  we talk of the combat of passion and of reason.
  Reason is, and ought only to be the slave of the
  passions, and can never pretend to any other
  office than to serve and obey them.
  A Treatise upon Human Nature bk. 2 (1739)

3 It is not contrary to reason to prefer the
  destruction of the whole world to the scratching
  of my finger.
  A Treatise upon Human Nature bk. 2 (1739)

4 Of all the animals with which this globe is
  peopled, there is none towards whom nature
  seems, at first sight, to have exercis'd more
  cruelty than towards man, in the numberless
  wants and necessities, with which she has
  loaded him, and in the slender means, which
  she affords to the relieving these necessities.
  A Treatise upon Human Nature bk. 3 (1739)

5 In contriving any system of government, and
  fixing the several checks and controuls of the
  constitution, every man ought to be supposed
  a *knave,* and to have no other end, in all his
  actions, than private interest.
  "Of the Independency of Parliament" (1741)

6 Money . . . is none of the wheels of trade: it is
  the oil which renders the motion of the wheels
  more smooth and easy.
  Essays: Moral and Political "Of Money" (1741–1742)

7 No testimony is sufficient to establish a miracle,
  unless the testimony be of such a kind that its
  falsehood would be more miraculous than the
  fact which it endeavors to establish.
  An Enquiry Concerning Human Understanding "Of
  Miracles" (1748)

8 The Christian religion not only was at first
  attended with miracles, but even at this day
  cannot be believed by any reasonable person
  without one. Mere reason is insufficient to
  convince us of its veracity: and whoever is
  moved by faith to assent to it, is conscious
  of a continued miracle in his own person,
  which subverts all the principles of his
  understanding, and gives him a determination
  to believe what is most contrary to custom and
  experience.
  An Enquiry Concerning Human Understanding "Of
  Miracles" (1748)

9 Custom, then, is the great guide of human life.
  An Enquiry Concerning Human Understanding sec. 5,
  pt. 1 (1748)

10 If we take in our hand any volume; of divinity
  or school metaphysics, for instance; let us ask,
  *Does it contain any abstract reasoning concerning
  quantity or number?* No. *Does it contain any
  experimental reasoning, concerning matter of fact
  and existence?* No. Commit it then to the flames:

for it can contain nothing but sophistry and illusion.

An Enquiry Concerning Human Understanding sec. 12, pt. 3 (1748)

11 Bear-baiting was esteemed heathenish and unchristian: the sport of it, not the inhumanity, gave offence.

The History of England vol. 7, ch. 62 (1763)
See Thomas Macaulay 12

Hubert H. Humphrey
U.S. politician, 1911–1978

1 There are not enough jails, not enough policemen, not enough courts to enforce a law not supported by the people.

Speech, Williamsburg, Va., 1 May 1965

2 Here we are the way politics ought to be in America, the politics of happiness, the politics of purpose, and the politics of joy.

Speech, Washington, D.C., 27 Apr. 1968

3 It was once said that the moral test of government is how that government treats those who are in the dawn of life, the children; those who are in the twilight of life, the elderly; and those who are in the shadows of life, the sick, the needy, and the handicapped.

Speech at dedication of Hubert H. Humphrey Building, Washington, D.C., 1 Nov. 1977
See Pearl S. Buck 3; Ramsey Clark 1; Dostoyevski 1; Samuel Johnson 69; Helen Keller 4

G. W. Hunt
English songwriter, ca. 1829–1904

1 We don't want to fight, but, by jingo if we do,
We've got the ships, we've got the men, we've got the money too.

"We Don't Want to Fight" (song) (1878). Inspired the political usage of *jingo* and *jingoism* to refer to bellicose nationalism. The *Oxford English Dictionary* traces the expression *by jingo* as far back as Motteux' translation of Rabelais (1694).

Leigh Hunt
English poet and essayist, 1784–1859

1 [*Of Prince George:*] This Adonis in loveliness was a corpulent man of fifty.

The Examiner, 22 Mar. 1812

2 Abou Ben Adhem (may his tribe increase!)
"Abou Ben Adhem" l. 1 (1838)

3 Write me as one that loves his fellow-men.
"Abou Ben Adhem" l. 14 (1838)

4 And showed the names whom love of God had blessed,
And lo! Ben Adhem's name led all the rest!
"Abou Ben Adhem" l. 17 (1838)

5 Jenny kissed me when we met,
Jumping from the chair she sat in;
Time, you thief, who love to get
Sweets into your list, put that in:
Say I'm weary, say I'm sad,
Say that health and wealth have missed me,
Say I'm growing old, but add,
Jenny kissed me.
"Rondeau" l. 1 (1838)

Evan Hunter (Salvatore Lombino)
U.S. novelist, 1926–2005

1 The Blackboard Jungle.
Title of book (1954)
See W. R. Burnett 2

Robert Hunter (Robert Burns)
U.S. rock musician and songwriter, 1941–2019

1 Sometimes the light's all shining on me
Other times I can barely see
Lately it occurs to me
What a long, strange trip it's been.
"Truckin'" (song) (1970)

2 Driving that train, high on cocaine
Casey Jones you'd better watch your speed.
Trouble ahead
Trouble behind
And you know that notion
Just crossed my mind.
"Casey Jones" (song) (1971)

Collis P. Huntington
U.S. businessman, 1821–1900

1 Whatever is not nailed down is mine. Whatever I can pry loose is not nailed down.

Attributed in H. L. Mencken, *A New Dictionary of Quotations* (1942). The attribution to Huntington has been shown by Garson O'Toole to be a confused interpretation of a statement that seems to have originated with David Starr Jordan, *The Call of the Nation* (1910): "Whatever is not nailed down is mine. . . . Whatever can be pried loose is not nailed down."

Herman Hupfeld

U.S. songwriter, 1894–1951

1 You must remember this,
A kiss is still a kiss,
A sigh is just a sigh;
The fundamental things apply,
As time goes by.
"As Time Goes By" (song) (1931)

2 And when two lovers woo
They still say, "I love you,"
On that you can rely.
"As Time Goes By" (song) (1931)

Fannie Hurst

U.S. novelist, 1885–1968

1 A woman has to be twice as good as a man to
go half as far.
Quoted in *Reader's Digest*, Oct. 1958. A later satirical
version of this saying added to the end "Luckily, this
is not difficult" (Paul Dickson, *The Official Rules*
[1978]).
See Eleanor Roosevelt 2

Zora Neale Hurston

U.S. novelist and folklorist, 1891–1960

1 I do not weep at the world—I am too busy
sharpening my oyster knife.
World Tomorrow "How It Feels to Be Colored Me"
(1928)

2 Ships at a distance have every man's wish on
board. For some they come in with the tide. For
others they sail forever on the same horizon,
never out of sight, never landing until the
Watcher turns his eyes away in resignation, his
dreams mocked to death by Time. That is the
life of men.
Their Eyes Were Watching God ch. 1 (1937)

3 Now, women forget all those things they don't
want to remember, and remember everything
they don't want to forget. The dream is the
truth. Then they act and do things accordingly.
Their Eyes Were Watching God ch. 1 (1937)

4 De nigger woman is de mule uh de world so
fur as Ah can see.
Their Eyes Were Watching God ch. 2 (1937)

5 The wind came back with triple fury, and
put out the light for the last time. They sat in
company with the others in other shanties,
their eyes straining against crude walls and
their souls asking if He meant to measure
their puny might against His. They seemed
to be staring at the dark, but their eyes were
watching God.
Their Eyes Were Watching God ch. 18 (1937)

6 I have been in Sorrow's kitchen and licked out
all the pots. Then I have stood on the peaky
mountain wrapped in rainbows, with a harp
and a sword in my hands.
Dust Tracks on a Road ch. 16 (1942)

Jan Hus

Bohemian religious reformer, ca. 1372–1415

1 *O sancta simplicitas!*
O holy simplicity!
Quoted in Julius W. Zincgreff, *Apophthegmata* (1653).
Hus's "last words," uttered upon seeing an elderly
peasant adding twigs to the pile at Hus's burning at
the stake.
See St. Jerome 1

Saddam Hussein

Iraqi president, 1937–2006

1 What midgets they are! May they, most of all
Bush and his servants Fahd and Husni, be
accursed. . . . Everybody must realize that this
battle will be the mother of all battles.
Broadcast statement, 20 Sept. 1990

2 I am Saddam Hussein, the president of Iraq.
Statement at arraignment, Baghdad, 1 July 2004.
Hussein said almost the identical words when he
was captured by U.S. troops near Tikrit, Iraq, 13 Dec.
2003. At the arraignment the judge instructed the
clerk to write "former" in brackets before "president"
in transcribing Hussein's statement.

3 [*Remark to U.S. Ambassador April Glaspie,
Baghdad, 25 July 1990:*] Yours is a society that
cannot accept 10,000 dead in one battle.
Quoted in *Wash. Post*, 13 Sept. 1990

Francis Hutcheson

Scottish philosopher, 1694–1746

1 *That Action* is *best*, which accomplishes the
greatest Happiness for the *greatest Numbers.*
*An Inquiry into the Original of Our Ideas of Beauty and
Virtue* treatise 2, sec. 3 (1725)
See Beccaria 1; Bentham 1

Robert M. Hutchins

U.S. educator, 1899–1977

1 The law may . . . depend on what the judge has had for breakfast.

"The Autobiography of an Ex-Law Student," *American Law School Review*, Apr. 1934

2 The death of democracy is not likely to be an assassination from ambush. It will be a slow extinction from apathy, indifference, and undernourishment.

Great Books of the Western World vol. 1, ch. 10 (1952)

Gennifer Hutchison

U.S. screenwriter, 1977–

1 I am not in danger, Skyler. I am the danger! A guy opens his door and gets shot and you think that of me? No. I am the one who knocks!

Breaking Bad (television show), 21 Aug. 2011

Aldous Huxley

English novelist, 1894–1963

1 Facts do not cease to exist because they are ignored.

Proper Studies "A Note on Dogma" (1927)

2 "If you look up 'Intelligence' in the new volumes of the *Encyclopaedia Britannica*," he had said, "you'll find it classified under the following three heads: Intelligence, Human; Intelligence, Animal; Intelligence, Military. My stepfather's a present specimen of Intelligence, Military."

Point Counter Point ch. 7 (1928)

3 How do you know that the earth isn't some other planet's hell?

Point Counter Point ch. 17 (1928)

4 The end cannot justify the means, for the simple and obvious reason that the means employed determine the nature of the ends produced.

Ends and Means ch. 1 (1937)
See Proverbs 85

5 [*Describing a mescaline-induced experience:*] I looked down by chance, and went on passionately staring by choice, at my own crossed legs. Those folds in the trousers—what a labyrinth of endlessly significant complexity!

And the texture of the gray flannel—how rich, how deeply, mysteriously sumptuous!

The Doors of Perception (1954)

6 If we evolved a race of Isaac Newtons, that would not be progress. For the price Newton had to pay for being a supreme intellect was that he was incapable of friendship, love, fatherhood, and many other desirable things. As a man he was a failure; as a monster he was superb.

Quoted in J. W. N. Sullivan, *Contemporary Mind* (1934)

Thomas Henry Huxley

English biologist, 1825–1895

1 Science is, I believe, nothing but *trained and organised common sense*, differing from the latter only as a veteran may differ from a raw recruit: and its methods differ from those of common sense only so far as the guardsman's cut and thrust differ from the manner in which a savage wields his club.

"On the Educational Value of the Natural History Sciences" (1854)

2 Truly it has been said, that to a clear eye the smallest fact is a window through which the Infinite may be seen.

"The Study of Zoology" (1861)

3 The great tragedy of Science—the slaying of a beautiful hypothesis by an ugly fact.

"Biogenesis and Abiogenesis" (1870)

4 A man's worst difficulties begin when he is able to do as he likes.

"Address on University Education" (1876)
See Goethe 15; Modern Proverbs 14; George Bernard Shaw 16; Teresa of Ávila 2; Wilde 56; Wilde 74

5 The great end of life is not knowledge but action.

"Technical Education" (1877)

6 History warns us, however, that it is the customary fate of new truths to begin as heresies and to end as superstitions.

"The Coming of Age of 'The Origin of Species'" (1880)

7 My reflection, when I first made myself master of the central idea of the "Origin" [Charles Darwin's *Origin of Species*], was,

"How extremely stupid not to have thought of that!"

"On the Reception of the 'Origin of Species'" (1888)

8 [*Replying to Bishop Samuel Wilberforce in their debate on Charles Darwin's theory of evolution, Oxford, England, 30 June 1860:*] A man has no reason to be ashamed of having an ape for his grandfather. If there were an ancestor whom I should feel shame in recalling it would rather be a *man*—a man of restless and versatile intellect—who, not content with an equivocal success in his own sphere of activity, plunges into scientific questions with which he has no real acquaintance, only to obscure them with an aimless rhetoric, and distract the attention of his hearers from the real point at issue by eloquent digressions and skilled appeals to religious prejudice.

Quoted in Leonard Huxley, *Life and Letters of Thomas Henry Huxley* (1900)

9 I have always been Darwin's bulldog.

Quoted in Henry Fairfield Osborn, *Impressions of Great Naturalists* (1924)

Joris-Karl Huysmans (Georges-Charles Huysmans)
French writer, 1848–1907

1 *À Rebours.*
Against the Grain.
Title of book (1884)

Lee Iacocca
U.S. business executive, 1924–2019

1 People want economy, and they will pay any
price to get it.
Quoted in *N.Y. Times*, 13 Oct. 1974

Janis Ian
U.S. singer and songwriter, 1951–

1 One of these days I'm gonna stop my listening
Gonna raise my head up high.
One of these days I'm gonna raise up my
glistening wings and fly.
But that day will have to wait for a while.
Baby I'm only society's child.
When we're older things may change,
But for now this is the way they must remain.
"Society's Child" (song) (1967)

2 To those of us who knew the pain
Of valentines that never came
And those whose names were never called
When choosing sides for basketball
It was long ago and far away
The world was younger than today
When dreams were all they gave for free
To ugly duckling girls like me.
"At Seventeen" (song) (1975)

Dolores Ibarruri (La Pasionaria)
Spanish Communist leader, 1895–1989

1 It is better to die on your feet than to live on
your knees!
Radio broadcast, 18 July 1936. It is often claimed
that Emiliano Zapata used this expression earlier in
the century, but documentation for Zapata's usage

is lacking. "Better to die on your feet than live on
your knees" is mentioned as a Mexican aphorism
in the *Appleton* (Wis.) *Post Crescent*, 4 June 1925. An
article by Roberto Habermann in *Survey*, 1 May 1924,
stated: "The day he [Zapata, assassinated in 1919] was
murdered, and the news of it reached Cuernavaca, a
barefooted peon scratched with his penknife in crude
letters on one of the posts of the Boarda Garden, the
old Maximilian palace, the following: 'Rebels of the
South, it is more honorable to die on your feet than to
live on your knees.'"

2 *No pasarán!*
They [the fascists] shall not pass!
Radio broadcast, Paris, 18 July 1936
See Pétain 1

Ibn Battutah
Arab explorer and geographer, 1304–1368

1 Never to travel any road a second time.
Travels in Asia and Africa (translation by H. A. R.
Gibb)

Ibn-Khaldūn
Arab historian, 1332–1406

1 Geometry enlightens the intellect and sets
one's mind right.
Muqaddimah vol. 3 (ca. 1380)

Henrik Ibsen
Norwegian playwright, 1828–1906
Quotations are based on The Oxford Ibsen, *translated
and edited by James Walter McFarlane.*

1 She knew well she was to give me All or
Nothing!
Brand act 3 (1866)

2 Being a prophet is a horrible business!
Peer Gynt act 4 (1867)

3 Turn to the Jewish nation, the nobility of the
human race. How has it preserved itself—
isolated, poetical—despite all the barbarity
from without? Because it had no state to
burden it. Had the Jewish nation remained in
Palestine, it would long since have been ruined
in the process of construction, like all the other
nations.
Letter to George Brandes, 17 Feb. 1871

4 And you call yourselves pillars of society!
Pillars of Society act 3 (1877)

5 Our house has never been anything but a
play-room. I have been your doll wife, just
as at home I was Daddy's doll child. And the

children in turn have been my dolls. I thought it was fun when you came and played with me, just as they thought it was fun when I went and played with them. That's been our marriage, Torvald.

A Doll's House act 3 (1879)

6 If I'm ever to reach any understanding of myself and the things around me, I must learn to stand alone. That's why I can't stay here with you any longer.

A Doll's House act 3 (1879)

7 I have another duty equally sacred. . . . My duty to myself.

A Doll's House act 3 (1879)

8 [*Helmer:*] First and foremost, you are a wife and mother.
[*Nora:*] That I don't believe any more. I believe that first and foremost I am an individual.

A Doll's House act 3 (1879)

9 I'm inclined to think that we are all ghosts, Pastor Manders, every one of us. It's not just what we inherit from our mothers and fathers that haunts us. It's all kinds of old defunct theories, all sorts of old defunct beliefs, and things like that.

Ghosts act 2 (1881)

10 I've only to pick up a newspaper and I seem to see ghosts gliding between the lines. Over

the whole country there must be ghosts, as numerous as the sands of the sea. And here we are, all of us, abysmally afraid of the light.

Ghosts act 2 (1881)

11 Mother, give me the sun.

Ghosts act 3 (1881)

12 This meeting declares that it considers Dr. Thomas Stockmann, Medical Officer to the Baths, to be an enemy of the people.

An Enemy of the People act 4 (1882)

13 The worst enemy of truth and freedom in our society is the compact majority.

An Enemy of the People act 4 (1882)

14 The majority is never right.

An Enemy of the People act 4 (1882)
See Heinlein 14; Roscommon 1; Twain 119

15 Who are the people that make up the biggest proportion of the population—the intelligent ones or the fools? I think we can agree it's the fools, no matter where you go in this world, it's the fools that form the overwhelming majority. But I'll be damned if that means it's right that the fools should dominate the intelligent.

An Enemy of the People act 4 (1882)

16 The minority is always right.

An Enemy of the People act 4 (1882)
See Debs 1; Sydney Smith 6

17 The life of a normally constituted truth is generally, say, about seventeen or eighteen years, at most twenty; rarely longer. But truths as elderly as that have always worn terribly thin. But it's only *then* that the majority will have anything to do with them; then it will recommend them as wholesome food for thought. But there's no great food-value in that sort of diet.

An Enemy of the People act 4 (1882)

18 I love this town so much that I'd rather destroy it than see it prosper on a lie.

An Enemy of the People act 4 (1882)

19 You should never have your best trousers on when you turn out to fight for freedom and truth.

An Enemy of the People act 5 (1882)

20 The party programs grab hold of every young and promising idea and wring its neck.
An Enemy of the People act 5 (1882)

21 The strongest man in the world is the man who stands alone.
An Enemy of the People act 5 (1882)

22 Always do that, wild ducks do. Go plunging right to the bottom . . . as deep as they can get . . . hold on with their beaks to the weeds and stuff—and all the other mess you find down there. Then they never come up again.
The Wild Duck act 2 (1884)

23 Our common lust for life.
Hedda Gabler act 2 (1890)

24 With vine leaves in his hair.
Hedda Gabler act 2 (1890)

25 But, good God Almighty . . . People don't do such things.
Hedda Gabler act 4 (1890)

26 Castles in the air—they're so easy to take refuge in. So easy to build, too.
The Master Builder act 3 (1892)

27 [*"Last words," responding to a nurse's remark that he "seemed to be a little better":*] On the contrary.
Quoted in Michael Meyer, *Ibsen* (1967)

I Ching (The Book of Changes), ca. 2000 B.C.

1 It is unlucky to sound off about happiness.
No. 16 (translation by Thomas Cleary)

2 Change proves true on the day it is finished.
No. 49 (translation by Thomas Cleary)

3 Cultured people practice self-examination with trepidation and fear.
No. 51 (translation by Thomas Cleary)

Harold L. Ickes
U.S. politician, 1874–1952

1 [Thomas E. Dewey] threw his diaper in the ring.
Quoted in *N.Y. Times*, 12 Dec. 1939

St. Ignatius of Loyola (Iñigo de Oñez y Loyola)
Spanish theologian, 1491–1556

1 To arrive at the truth in all things, we ought always to be ready to believe that what seems to us white is black if the hierarchical Church so defines it.
Spiritual Exercises (1548)

Ivan Illich
Austrian-born U.S. social critic, 1926–2002

1 In a consumer society there are inevitably two kinds of slaves: the prisoners of addiction and the prisoners of envy.
Tools for Conviviality ch. 3 (1973)

William Ralph Inge
English prelate and author, 1860–1954

1 It takes in reality only one to make a quarrel. It is useless for the sheep to pass resolutions in favor of vegetarianism, while the wolf remains of a different opinion.
Outspoken Essays: First Series "Patriotism" (1919)

2 We have enslaved the rest of the animal creation, and have treated our distant cousins in fur and feathers so badly that beyond doubt, if they were able to formulate a religion, they would depict the Devil in human form.
Outspoken Essays: Second Series "The Idea of Progress" (1922)

3 A man may build himself a throne of bayonets, but he cannot sit on it.
Philosophy of Plotinus Lecture 22 (1923)
See Talleyrand-Périgord 1

4 Originality, I fear, is too often only undetected and frequently unconscious plagiarism.
Quoted in *Wit and Wisdom of Dean Inge*, ed. James Marchant (1927)

Robert G. Ingersoll
U.S. orator, 1833–1899

1 Like an armed warrior, like a plumed knight, James G. Blaine marched down the halls of the American Congress and threw his shining lances full and fair against the brazen foreheads of every defamer to his country and maligner of its honor.
Speech nominating James G. Blaine for president, Republican National Convention, Cincinnati, Ohio, 15 June 1876

Jean Auguste Dominique Ingres
French painter, 1780–1867

1 What do these so-called artists mean when they preach the discovery of the "new"? Is there anything new? Everything has been done, everything has been discovered.
Quoted in Henri Delaborde, Ingres, Sa Vie, Ses Travaux, Sa Doctrine (1870)

Eugène Ionesco
Romanian-born French playwright, 1912–1994

1 A civil servant doesn't make jokes.
Tuer sans Gages (The Killer) act 1 (1958)

2 Living is abnormal.
Rhinocéros act 1 (1959)

John Irving (John Wallace Blunt, Jr.)
U.S. novelist, 1942–

1 Jenny Garp . . . liked to describe herself as her father had described a novelist.

"A doctor who sees only terminal cases."

. . . Her famous grandmother, Jenny Fields, once thought of us as Externals, Vital Organs, Absentees, and Goners. But in the world according to Garp, we are all terminal cases.
The World According to Garp ch. 19 (1978)

2 Good night, you Princes of Maine—you Kings of New England!
The Cider House Rules ch. 3 (1985)

3 I am doomed to remember a boy with a wrecked voice—not because of his voice, or because he was the smallest person I ever knew, or even because he was the instrument of my mother's death, but because he is the reason I believe in God; I am a Christian because of Owen Meany.
A Prayer for Owen Meany ch. 1 (1989)

Washington Irving
U.S. writer, 1783–1859

1 The renowned and antient city of Gotham.
Salmagundi ch. 17 (1807). Coinage of the nickname Gotham for New York City (before this, Gotham was a proverbial name for a village famed for the folly of its inhabitants).

2 This sequestered glen has long been known by the name of Sleepy Hollow.
The Sketch Book of Geoffrey Crayon "The Legend of Sleepy Hollow" (1819–1820)

3 A sharp tongue is the only edged tool that grows keener with constant use.
The Sketch Book of Geoffrey Crayon "Rip Van Winkle" (1819–1820)

4 His father had once seen them [strange beings] in their old Dutch dresses playing at nine-pins in a hollow of the mountain; and . . . he himself had heard, one summer afternoon, the sound of their balls, like distant peals of thunder.
The Sketch Book of Geoffrey Crayon "Rip Van Winkle" (1819–1820)

5 The almighty dollar.
New-York Mirror, 4 Nov. 1836. Slightly earlier than the previous oldest known usage of the term almighty dollar.

Christopher Isherwood
English-born U.S. novelist, 1904–1986

1 I am a camera with its shutter open, quite passive, recording, not thinking. Recording the man shaving at the window opposite and the woman in the kimono washing her hair. Some day, all this will have to be developed, carefully printed, fixed.
Goodbye to Berlin "Berlin Diary" (1939)

2 [Of T. E. Lawrence:] There are those who have tried to dismiss his story with a flourish of the Union Jack, a psycho-analytical catchword or a sneer; it should move our deepest admiration and pity. Like Shelley and like Baudelaire, it may be said of him that he suffered, in his own person, the neurotic ills of an entire generation.
Exhumations (1966)

Kazuo Ishiguro
Japanese-born English novelist, 1954–

1 An Artist of the Floating World.
Title of book (1986)

2 A "great" butler can only be, surely, one who can point to his years of service and say that he has applied his talents to serving a great gentleman—and through the latter, to serving humanity.
The Remains of the Day (1989)

3 I can't even say I made my own mistakes.
Really—one has to ask oneself—what dignity is
there in that?
The Remains of the Day (1989)

4 Perhaps it is indeed time I began to look
at this whole matter of bantering more
enthusiastically. After all, when one thinks
about it, it is not such a foolish thing to
indulge in—particularly if it is the case that in
bantering lies the key to human warmth.
The Remains of the Day (1989)

Kobayashi Issa

Japanese poet, 1763–1827

1 Look, don't kill that fly!
It is making a prayer to you
By rubbing its hands and feet.
Poem

Molly Ivins

U.S. journalist, 1944–2007

1 Many people did not care for Pat Buchanan's
speech; it probably sounded better in the
original German.
Nation, 14 Sept. 1992

2 There are two kinds of humor. One kind that
makes us chuckle about our foibles and our
shared humanity—like what Garrison Keillor
does. The other kind holds people up to public
contempt and ridicule—that's what I do.
Quoted in *People,* 9 Dec. 1991

Andrew Jackson
U.S. president and general, 1767–1845

1 Our Union: It must be preserved.

Toast at Jefferson Day dinner, 13 Apr. 1830. Jackson altered the wording to "Our Federal Union" before it was given to the newspapers, and it is often reported thus.

2 Every man is equally entitled to protection by law. But when the laws undertake to add . . . artificial distinctions, to grant titles, gratuities, and exclusive privileges—to make the rich richer and the potent more powerful—the humble members of society—the farmers, mechanics, and laborers, who have neither the time nor the means of securing like favors to themselves, have a right to complain of the injustice of their government.

Veto Message on Bank Bill, 10 July 1832

3 There are no necessary evils in government. Its evils exist only in its abuses. If it would confine itself to equal protection, and, as Heaven does its rains, shower its favors alike on the high and the low, the rich and the poor, it would be an unqualified blessing.

Veto Message on Bank Bill, 10 July 1832

4 The wisdom of man never yet contrived a system of taxation that would operate with perfect equality.

Proclamation, 10 Dec. 1832

5 Eternal vigilance by the people is the price of liberty.

Farewell Address, 4 Mar. 1837
See Curran 1

6 John Marshall has made his decision: *now let him enforce it!*

Attributed in Horace Greeley, *The American Conflict* (1864). This response to the U.S. Supreme Court decision in *Worcester v. Georgia* (1832) was first attributed to Jackson in the 1864 Greeley book. While the remark does represent Jackson's views, he probably never spoke these actual words.

7 One man with courage makes a majority.

Attributed in *Wash. Post,* 7 Feb. 1964. Although this saying is strongly associated with Jackson, the earliest discoverable occurrence, in the form "Desperate courage makes one a majority," is in the *Atlantic Monthly,* Nov. 1858, without attribution to any individual.
See Coolidge 2; Douglass 7; John Knox 1; Wendell Phillips 3; Thoreau 9

Charles Jackson
U.S. novelist, 1903–1968

1 The Lost Weekend.
Title of book (1944)

George Jackson
U.S. activist and author, 1941–1971

1 Being born a slave in a captive society and never experiencing any objective basis for expectation had the effect of preparing me for the progressively traumatic misfortunes that led to so many blackmen to the prison gate. I was prepared for prison. It required only minor psychic adjustments.
Soledad Brother (1970)

2 Patience has its limits. Take it too far, and it's cowardice.
Soledad Brother (1970)

Glenda Jackson
English actress and politician, 1936–

1 The important thing in acting is to be able to laugh and cry. If I have to cry, I think of my sex life. If I have to laugh, I think of my sex life.
Quoted in Robert Byrne, *The 637 Best Things Anybody Ever Said* (1982)

Jesse Jackson
U.S. politician, 1941–

1 Our flag is red, white, and blue, but our nation is a rainbow—red, yellow, brown, black, and white—and all are precious in God's sight. America is not like a blanket—one piece of

unbroken cloth, the same color, the same texture, the same size. It is more like a quilt—many patches, many pieces, many colors, and many sizes, all woven and held together by a common thread.

Address to Democratic National Convention, San Francisco, Calif., 17 July 1984
See Baudouin 1; Jimmy Carter 3; Crèvecoeur 1; Ralph Ellison 2; Victoria Hayward 1; Zangwill 2

2 I hear that melting-pot stuff a lot, and all I can say is that we haven't melted.

Quoted in *Playboy,* Nov. 1969

3 When we're unemployed we're called lazy; when the whites are unemployed, it's called a depression.

Quoted in David Frost, *The Americans* (1970)

Mahalia Jackson

U.S. gospel singer, 1911–1972

1 [*Exhortation to Martin Luther King, Jr., inspiring King to deliver his "I Have a Dream" speech at the March on Washington, 28 Aug. 1963:*] Tell them about your dream, Martin. Tell them about the dream.

Quoted in *Boston Globe,* 27 Aug. 1983

Michael Jackson

U.S. singer and songwriter, 1958–2009

1 We are the world,
We are the children.

"We Are the World" (song) (1985). Cowritten with Lionel Richie.

2 Before you judge me, try hard to love me, look within your heart
Then ask,—have you seen my childhood?

"Childhood" (song) (1995)

3 [*Defending his practice of sharing his bed with young boys:*] Why can't you share your bed? The most loving thing to do is to share your bed with someone.

Broadcast interview on ITV network, 3 Feb. 2003

4 [*Upon being asked in court testimony whether he had memory lapses:*] Not that I recall.

Quoted in *The Sun,* 5 Dec. 2002

Reggie Jackson

U.S. baseball player, 1946–

1 If I played in New York, they'd name a candy bar after me.

Quoted in *Wash. Post,* 15 Apr. 1976

2 [*Of Tom Seaver:*] He's so good that blind people come to the park just to hear him pitch.

Quoted in *N.Y. Times,* 1 Jan. 1978

3 You know, this team . . . it all flows from me. . . . I'm the straw that stirs the drink.

Attributed in *Sport,* June 1977. Jackson denied having said this.

Robert H. Jackson

U.S. judge and government official, 1892–1954

1 The very purpose of a Bill of Rights was to withdraw certain subjects from the vicissitudes of political controversy, to place them beyond the reach of majorities and officials and to establish them as legal principles to be applied by the courts. One's right to life, liberty, and property, to free speech, a free press, freedom of worship and assembly, and other fundamental rights may be submitted to no vote; they depend on the outcome of no elections.

West Virginia State Bd. of Educ. v. Barnette (1943)

2 Those who begin coercive elimination of dissent soon find themselves exterminating dissenters. Compulsory unification of opinion achieves only the unanimity of the graveyard.

West Virginia State Bd. of Educ. v. Barnette (1943)

3 The case is made difficult, not because the principles of its decision are obscure, but because the flag involved is our own. . . . To believe that patriotism will not flourish if patriotic ceremonies are voluntary and spontaneous instead of a compulsory routine is to make an unflattering estimate of the appeal of our institutions to free minds.

West Virginia State Bd. of Educ. v. Barnette (1943)

4 But freedom to differ is not limited to things that do not matter much. That would be a mere shadow of freedom. The test of its substance is the right to differ as to things that touch the heart of the existing order. If there is any

fixed star in our constitutional constellation, it is that no official, high or petty, can prescribe what shall be orthodox in politics, nationalism, religion, or other matters of opinion or force citizens to confess by word or act their faith therein.
West Virginia State Bd. of Educ. v. Barnette (1943)

5 The privilege of opening the first trial in history for crimes against the peace of the world imposes a grave responsibility. The wrongs which we seek to condemn and punish have been so calculated, so malignant and so devastating, that civilization cannot tolerate their being ignored, because it cannot survive their being repeated. That four great nations, flushed with victory and stung with injury, stay the hands of vengeance and voluntarily submit their captive enemies to the judgment of the law is one of the most significant tributes that Power ever has paid to Reason.
Opening statement for the prosecution before International Military Tribunal, Nuremberg, Germany, 21 Nov. 1945

6 We must never forget that the record on which we judge these defendants today is the record on which history will judge us tomorrow. To pass these defendants a poisoned chalice is to put it to our own lips as well. We must summon such detachment and intellectual integrity to our task that this trial will commend itself to posterity as fulfilling humanity's aspirations to do justice.
Opening statement for the prosecution before International Military Tribunal, Nuremberg, Germany, 21 Nov. 1945

7 If you were to say of these men that they are not guilty, it would be as true to say there has been no war, there are no slain, there has been no crime.
Concluding speech for the prosecution before International Military Tribunal, Nuremberg, Germany, 26 July 1946

8 The choice is not between order and liberty. It is between liberty with order and anarchy without either. There is danger that, if the Court does not temper its doctrinaire logic with a little practical wisdom, it will convert the constitutional Bill of Rights into a suicide pact.
Terminiello v. Chicago (dissenting opinion) (1949)

9 The priceless heritage of our society is the unrestricted constitutional right of each member to think as he will. Thought control is a copyright of totalitarianism, and we have no claim to it. It is not the function of our Government to keep the citizen from falling into error; it is the function of the citizen to keep the Government from falling into error.
American Communications Ass'n v. Douds (1950) (concurring in part and dissenting in part)

10 I used to say that, as Solicitor General, I made three arguments of every case. First came the one that I planned—as I thought, logical, coherent, complete. Second was the one actually presented—interrupted, incoherent, disjointed, disappointing. The third was the utterly devastating argument that I thought of after going to bed that night.
Lecture before State Bar of California, San Francisco, Calif., 23 Aug. 1951

11 The day that this country ceases to be free for irreligion it will cease to be free for religion— except for the sect that can win political power.
Zorach v. Clauson (dissenting opinion) (1952)

12 There is no doubt that if there were a super-Supreme Court, a substantial proportion of our reversals of state courts would also be reversed. We are not final because we are infallible, but we are infallible only because we are final.
Brown v. Allen (concurring opinion) (1953)

13 Procedural fairness and regularity are of the indispensable essence of liberty. Severe substantive laws can be endured if they are fairly and impartially applied. Indeed, if put to the choice, one might well prefer to live under Soviet substantive law applied in good faith by our common-law procedures than under our substantive law enforced by Soviet procedural practices.
Shaughnessy v. United States (dissenting opinion) (1953)

Shirley Jackson
U.S. writer, 1916–1965

1 "It isn't fair, it isn't right," Mrs. Hutchinson screamed, and then they were upon her.
"The Lottery" (1948)

2 No live organism can continue for long to exist sanely under conditions of absolute reality; even larks and katydids are supposed, by some, to dream. Hill House, not sane, stood by itself against its hills, holding darkness within; it had stood so for eighty years and might stand for eighty more. Within, walls continued upright, bricks met neatly, floors were firm, and doors were sensibly shut; silence lay steadily against the wood and stone of Hill House, and whatever walked there, walked alone.
The Haunting of Hill House ch. 1 (1959)

Thomas J. "Stonewall" Jackson
U.S. Confederate general, 1824–1863

1 [*"Last words":*] Let us cross the river and rest under the shade of the trees.
Quoted in *Macon* (Ga.) *Telegraph*, 25 May 1863

Harriet Jacobs
U.S. writer and abolitionist, 1813–1897

1 Reader, be assured this narrative is no fiction.
Incidents in the Life of a Slave Girl preface (1860)

Jane Jacobs
U.S.-born Canadian social and architectural critic, 1916–2006

1 But look what we have built. . . . This is not the rebuilding of cities. This is the sacking of cities.
The Death and Life of Great American Cities introduction (1961)

2 There must be eyes upon the street, eyes belonging to those we might call the natural proprietors of the street. The buildings on a street equipped to handle strangers and to insure the safety of both residents and strangers, must be oriented to the street. They cannot turn their backs or blank sides on it and leave it blind.
The Death and Life of Great American Cities ch. 2 (1961)

Joe Jacobs
U.S. boxing manager, 1896–1940

1 We wuz robbed!
Quoted in *Wash. Post*, 19 Sept. 1934. Spoken after heavyweight champion Max Schmeling, whom Jacobs managed, was defeated by Jack Sharkey, 21 June 1932.

2 I should have stood in bed.
Quoted in *Reno Evening Gazette*, 30 Dec. 1935. Referring to a game he attended during the 1935 World Series.

Mick Jagger
English rock musician and songwriter, 1943–

1 [*Response, at press conference in New York, 26 Nov. 1969, to being asked whether the Rolling Stones were more "satisfied" now:*] Financially dissatisfied, sexually satisfied, philosophically trying.
Quoted in *N.Y. Times*, 28 Nov. 1969

2 I'd rather be dead than sing "Satisfaction" when I'm 45.
Quoted in *People*, 9 June 1975

Mick Jagger 1943– and Keith Richards 1943–
English rock musicians and songwriters

1 Time is on my side, yes it is.
"Time Is on My Side" (song) (1964)

2 I can't get no satisfaction.
"(I Can't Get No) Satisfaction" (song) (1965)

3 When I'm watchin' my TV
And that man comes on to tell me
How white my shirts can be
But he can't be a man 'cause he doesn't smoke
The same cigarettes as me.
"(I Can't Get No) Satisfaction" (song) (1965)

4 And though she's not really ill
There's a little yellow pill
She goes running for the shelter of a mother's little helper
And it helps her on her way, gets her through her busy day.
"Mother's Little Helper" (song) (1966)

5 Doctor please, some more of these
Outside the door, she took four more
What a drag it is getting old.
"Mother's Little Helper" (song) (1966)

6 Goodbye, Ruby Tuesday
Who could hang a name on you
When you change with every new day?
Still I'm gonna miss you.
"Ruby Tuesday" (song) (1967)

7 When I search a faceless crowd
  A swirling mass of gray and black and white
  They don't look real to me
  In fact, they look so strange.
  "Salt of the Earth" (song) (1968)

8 But what can a poor boy do
  Except to sing for a rock & roll band?
  Cause in sleepy London town there's just no
    place for
  Street fighting man.
  "Street Fighting Man" (song) (1968)

9 Please allow me to introduce myself
  I'm a man of wealth and taste
  I've been around for a long, long year
  Stole many a man's soul and faith.
  "Sympathy for the Devil" (song) (1968)

10 Pleased to meet you, hope you guess my name
   But what's puzzling you is the nature of my
     game.
   "Sympathy for the Devil" (song) (1968)

11 I shouted out, "Who killed the Kennedys?"
   When after all it was you and me.
   "Sympathy for the Devil" (song) (1968)

12 Just as every cop is a criminal and all the
   sinners saints.
   "Sympathy for the Devil" (song) (1968)

13 Oh, a storm is threatening my very life today
   If I don't get some shelter, oh yeah, I'm going
     to fade away
   War, children, it's just a shot away.
   "Gimme Shelter" (song) (1969)

14 I met a gin-soaked, bar-room queen in
     Memphis,
   She tried to take me upstairs for a ride.
   She had to heave me right across her shoulder
   'Cause I just can't seem to drink you off my
     mind.
   "Honky Tonk Woman" (song) (1969)

15 You can't always get what you want
   But if you try sometime you just might find
   You get what you need.
   "You Can't Always Get What You Want" (song) (1969)

16 No sweeping exits or offstage lines
   Could make me feel bitter or treat you
     unkind . . .
   Wild horses couldn't drag me away.
   "Wild Horses" (song) (1971)

17 It's Only Rock and Roll.
   Title of song (1974)

Evan James
Welsh songwriter, 1809–1878

1 O land of my fathers, O land of my love.
  "Land of My Fathers" (song) (1856)

Henry James
U.S. novelist, 1843–1916

1 To write well and worthily of American things
  one need even more than elsewhere to be a
  master.
  Letter to Charles Eliot Norton, 16 Jan. 1871

2 The curious thing is that the more the mind
  takes in, the more it has space for, and that all
  one's ideas are like the Irish people at home
  who live in the different corners of a room, and
  take boarders.
  Roderick Hudson ch. 3 (1876)

3 We stand like a race with shrunken muscles,
  staring helplessly at the weights our forefathers
  easily lifted.
  Roderick Hudson ch. 3 (1876)

4 It takes a great deal of history to produce a little
  literature.
  Hawthorne ch. 1 (1879)

5 [*Of Henry David Thoreau:*] He was worse than
  provincial—he was parochial.
  Hawthorne ch. 4 (1879)

6 Cats and monkeys—monkeys and cats—all
  human life is there!
  The Madonna of the Future vol. 1 (1879)

7 The only reason for the existence of a novel is
  that it does compete with life.
  "The Art of Fiction" (1884)

8 The only obligation to which in advance we may
  hold a novel without incurring the accusation of
  being arbitrary, is that it be interesting.
  "The Art of Fiction" (1884)

9 Experience is never limited and it is never
  complete; it is an immense sensibility, a kind
  of huge spider-web, of the finest silken threads,
  suspended in the chamber of consciousness and
  catching every air-borne particle in its tissue.
  "The Art of Fiction" (1884)

10 If I should certainly say to a novice, "Write from experience, and experience only," I should feel that this was a rather tantalising monition if I were not careful immediately to add, "Try to be one of the people on whom nothing is lost!"
"The Art of Fiction" (1884)

11 What is character but the determination of incident? What is incident but the illustration of character?
"The Art of Fiction" (1884)

12 We work in the dark—we do what we can—we give what we have. Our doubt is our passion and our passion is our task. The rest is the madness of art.
"The Middle Years" (1893)

13 The time-honored bread-sauce of the happy ending.
Theatricals: 2nd Series "Note" (1895)

14 Vereker's secret, my dear man—the general intention of his books: the string the pearls were strung on, the buried treasure, the figure in the carpet.
The Figure in the Carpet ch. 11 (1896)

15 We were alone with the quiet day, and his little heart, dispossessed, had stopped.
The Turn of the Screw ch. 24 (1898)

16 She couldn't dress it away, nor walk it away, nor read it away, nor think it away; she could neither smile it away in any dreamy absence nor blow it away in any softened sigh. She couldn't have lost it if she had tried—that was what it was to be really rich. It had to be *the* thing you were.
The Wings of the Dove ch. 5 (1902)

17 Live all you can; it's a mistake not to. It doesn't so much matter what you do in particular, so long as you have your life. If you haven't had that, what *have* you had?
The Ambassadors bk. 5, ch. 11 (1903)

18 The house of fiction has in short not one window, but a million . . . They are, singly or together, as nothing without the posted presence of the watcher.
The Portrait of a Lady preface (1908)

19 In art economy is always beauty.
The Altar of the Dead preface (1909)

20 The terrible *fluidity of self-revelation.*
The Ambassadors preface (1909)

21 The historian, essentially, wants more documents than he can really use; the dramatist only wants more liberties than he can really take.
The Aspern Papers preface (1909)

22 Life being all inclusion and confusion, and art being all discrimination and selection, the latter, in search of the hard latent *value* with which it alone is concerned, sniffs round the mass as instinctively and unerringly as a dog suspicious of some buried bone.
The Spoils of Poynton preface (1909)

23 The fatal futility of Fact.
The Spoils of Poynton preface (1909)

24 We must know, as much as possible, in our beautiful art . . . what we are talking about—& the only way to know it is to have lived & loved & cursed & floundered & enjoyed & suffered—I think I don't regret a single "excess" of my responsive youth—I only regret, in my chilled age, certain occasions & possibilities I didn't *embrace.*
Letter to Hugh Walpole, 21 Aug. 1913

25 The black and merciless things that are behind the great possessions.
The Ivory Tower notes (1917)

26 The war has used up words.
Quoted in *N.Y. Times,* 21 Mar. 1915

27 [*On experiencing his initial stroke:*] So here it is at last, the distinguished thing!
Quoted in Edith Wharton, *A Backward Glance* (1934)

28 Summer afternoon—summer afternoon; to me those have always been the two most beautiful words in the English language.
Quoted in Edith Wharton, *A Backward Glance* (1934)

LeBron James
U.S. basketball player, 1984–

1 [*Announcing his decision to leave the Cleveland Cavaliers team for the Miami Heat:*] I'm taking my talents to South Beach.
ESPN TV broadcast, 8 July 2010

P. D. James

English detective fiction writer, 1920–2014

1 Early this morning, 1 January 2021, three minutes after midnight, the last human being to be born on earth was killed in a pub brawl in a suburb of Buenos Aires, aged twenty-five years two months and twelve days.
The Children of Men bk. 1, ch. 1 (1992)

2 What the detective story is about is not murder but the restoration of order.
Quoted in *Face*, Dec. 1986

3 I had an interest in death from an early age. It fascinated me. When I heard, "Humpty Dumpty sat on a wall," I thought, "Did he fall or was he pushed?"
Quoted in *Paris Review* no. 135 (1995)

William James

U.S. philosopher and psychologist, 1842–1910

1 My first act of free will shall be to believe in free will.
Diary, 30 Apr. 1870

2 The best way to define a man's character would be to seek out the particular mental or moral attitude in which, when it came upon him, he felt himself most deeply and intensely active and alive. At such moments there is a voice inside which speaks and says: "*This* is the real me!"
Letter to Alice Gibbons James, 1878

3 All our scientific and philosophic ideals are altars to unknown gods.
"The Dilemma of Determinism" (1884)

4 Habit is thus the enormous fly-wheel of society, its most precious conservative agent. It alone is what keeps us all within the bounds of ordinance.
The Principles of Psychology vol. 1, ch. 4 (1890)

5 Consciousness, then, does not appear to itself chopped up in bits. Such words as "chain" or "train" do not describe it fitly as it presents itself in the first instance. It is nothing jointed; it flows. A "river" or a "stream" are the metaphors by which it is most naturally described. *In talking of it hereafter, let us call*

it the stream of thought, of consciousness, or of subjective life.
The Principles of Psychology vol. 1, ch. 9 (1890). James had earlier written about the "stream of our consciousness" in "On Some Omissions of Introspective Psychology," *Mind*, Jan. 1884. The term *stream of consciousness* is documented by the *Oxford English Dictionary* still earlier, in Alexander Bain, *The Senses and the Intellect* (1855).

6 *In its widest possible sense . . . a man's Self is the sum total of all that he* can *call his*, not only his body and his psychic powers, but his clothes and his house, his wife and children, his ancestors and friends, his reputation and works, his lands and horses, and yacht and bank-account. All these things give him the same emotions. If they wax and prosper, he feels triumphant; if they dwindle and die away, he feels cast down.
The Principles of Psychology vol. 1, ch. 10 (1890)

7 *Some people are far more sensitive to resemblances, and far more ready to point out wherein they consist, than others are.* They are the wits, the poets, the inventors, the scientific men, the practical geniuses.
The Principles of Psychology vol. 1, ch. 13 (1890)

8 Objective evidence and certitude are doubtless very fine ideals to play with, but where on this moonlit and dream-visited planet are they found?
"The Will to Believe" (1896)

9 Although all the special manifestations of religion may have been absurd (I mean its creeds and theories), yet the life of it as a whole is mankind's most important function.
Letter to Frances Morse, 13 Apr. 1900

10 Religion . . . is a man's total reaction upon life.
The Varieties of Religious Experience Lecture 2 (1902)

11 We can act *as if* there were a God; feel *as if* we were free; consider Nature *as if* she were full of special designs; lay plans *as if* we were to be immortal; and we find then that these words do make a genuine difference in our moral life.
The Varieties of Religious Experience Lecture 3 (1902)

12 A genuine first-hand religious experience . . . is bound to be a heterodoxy to its witnesses, the prophet appearing as a mere lonely

madman. If his doctrine prove contagious enough to spread to any others, it becomes a definite and labeled heresy. But if it then still prove contagious enough to triumph over persecution, it becomes itself an orthodoxy, its day of inwardness is over: the spring is dry; the faithful live at second hand exclusively and stone the prophets in their turn.

The Varieties of Religious Experience Lectures 14–15 (1902)

13 One hears of the mechanical equivalent of heat. What we now need to discover in the social realm is the moral equivalent of war: something heroic that will speak to men as universally as war does, and yet will be as compatible with their spiritual selves as war has proved itself to be incompatible.

The Varieties of Religious Experience Lectures 14–15 (1902)

14 The God whom science recognizes must be a God of universal laws exclusively, a God who does a wholesale, not a retail business. He cannot accommodate his processes to the convenience of individuals.

The Varieties of Religious Experience Lecture 20 (1902)

15 Most people live, whether physically, intellectually, or morally, in a very restricted circle of their potential being. They *make use* of a very small portion of their possible consciousness, and of their soul's resources in general, much like a man who, out of his whole bodily organism, should get into a habit of using and moving only his little finger. Great emergencies and crises show us how much greater our vital resources are than we had supposed.

Letter to Wincenty Lutoslawski, 6 May 1906

16 The moral flabbiness born of the exclusive worship of the bitch-goddess SUCCESS. That— with the squalid cash interpretation put on the word success—is our national disease.

Letter to H. G. Wells, 11 Sept. 1906

17 The philosophy which is so important in each of us is not a technical matter; it is our more or less dumb sense of what life honestly and deeply means. It is only partly got from books; it is our individual way of just seeing and feeling the total push and pressure of the cosmos.

Pragmatism: A New Name for Some Old Ways of Thinking Lecture 1 (1907)

18 I myself believe that the evidence for God lies primarily in inner personal experiences.

Pragmatism: A New Name for Some Old Ways of Thinking Lecture 3 (1907)

19 First, you know, a new theory is attacked as absurd; then it is admitted to be true, but obvious and insignificant; finally it is seen to be so important that its adversaries claim that they themselves discovered it.

Pragmatism: A New Name for Some Old Ways of Thinking Lecture 6 (1907)

20 True ideas are those that we can assimilate, validate, corroborate, and verify. False ideas are those that we cannot.

Pragmatism: A New Name for Some Old Ways of Thinking Lecture 6 (1907)

21 The truth of an idea is not a stagnant property inherent in it. Truth *happens* to an idea. It *becomes* true, is *made* true by events. Its verity *is* in fact an event, a process: the process namely of its verifying itself, its veri-*fication*. Its validity is the process of its valid-*ation*.

Pragmatism: A New Name for Some Old Ways of Thinking Lecture 6 (1907)

22 I firmly disbelieve, myself, that our human experience is the highest form of experience extant in the universe. I believe rather that we stand in much the same relation to the whole of the universe as our canine and feline pets do to the whole of human life. They inhabit our drawing-rooms and libraries. They take part in scenes of whose significance they have no inkling. They are merely tangent to curves of history the beginnings and ends and forms of which pass wholly beyond their ken. So we are tangent to the wider life of things.

Pragmatism: A New Name for Some Old Ways of Thinking Lecture 8 (1907)

23 My thesis . . . is that *the bodily changes follow directly the perception of the exciting fact, and that our feeling of the same changes as they occur is the emotion.*

Psychology ch. 24 (1909)

Tama Janowitz

U.S. novelist and short story writer, 1957–

1 Long after the bomb falls and you and your good deeds are gone, cockroaches will still be here, prowling the streets like armored cars.
Slaves of New York "Modern Saint 271" (1986)

Elliott Jaques

Canadian psychologist, 1917–2003

1 The crises which occur around the age of 35—which I shall term the mid-life crisis.
International Journal of Psycho-analysis vol. 46 (1965). Coinage of the term *mid-life crisis*.

Randall Jarrell

U.S. poet, 1914–1965

1 From my mother's sleep I fell into the State,
And I hunched in its belly till my wet fur froze.
Six miles from earth, loosed from its dream of life,
I woke to black flak and the nightmare fighters.
When I died they washed me out of the turret with a hose.
"The Death of the Ball Turret Gunner" l. 1 (1945)

Alfred Jarry

French writer, 1873–1907

1 *Merdre!*
Shit!
Ubu Roi act 1 (1896). This vulgarity, unprecedented in the modern stage, caused a near-riot when it was uttered as the first line of Jarry's play. Jarry intentionally misspelled *merde* for humorous effect.

Robert Jastrow

U.S. astrophysicist, 1925–2008

1 For the scientist who has lived by his faith in the power of reason, the story ends like a bad dream. He has scaled the mountains of ignorance; he is about to conquer the highest peak; as he pulls himself over the final rock, he is greeted by a band of theologians who have been sitting there for centuries.
God and the Astronomers ch. 9 (1978)

Jay Z (Shawn Carter)

U.S. rapper and businessman, 1969–

1 I'm not afraid of dying
I'm afraid of not trying.
"Beach Chair" (song) (2006)

James Jeans

English physicist and astronomer, 1877–1946

1 From the intrinsic evidence of his creation, the Great Architect of the Universe now begins to appear as a pure mathematician.
The Mysterious Universe ch. 5 (1930)

2 If we assume that the last breath of, say, Julius Caesar has by now become thoroughly scattered through the atmosphere, then the chances are that each of us inhales one molecule of it with every breath we take.
An Introduction to the Kinetic Theory of Gases ch. 2 (1940)

Robinson Jeffers

U.S. poet, 1887–1962

1 I'd sooner, except the penalties, kill a man than a hawk.
"Hurt Hawks" l. 18 (1928)

Thomas Jefferson

U.S. president, 1743–1826

1 When in the Course of human events, it becomes necessary for one people to dissolve the political bands which have connected them with another, and to assume among the powers of the earth, the separate and equal station to which the Laws of Nature and of Nature's God entitle them, a decent respect to the opinions of mankind requires that they should declare the causes which impel them to the separation.
Declaration of Independence (1776)

2 We hold these truths to be self-evident, that all men are created equal, that they are endowed by their Creator with certain unalienable Rights, that among these are Life, Liberty, and the pursuit of Happiness. That to secure these rights, Governments are instituted among Men, deriving their just powers from the consent of the governed, That whenever

any Form of Government becomes destructive of these ends, it is the Right of the People to alter or to abolish it, and to institute new Government, laying its foundation on such principles and organizing its powers in such form, as to them shall seem most likely to effect their Safety and Happiness.
Declaration of Independence (1776). Jefferson had used the word *inalienable* in a handwritten rough draft, but it was changed to *unalienable* for the final draft.
See Ho Chi Minh 1; George Mason 1

3 Prudence, indeed, will dictate that Governments long established should not be changed for light and transient causes; and accordingly all experience hath shewn, that mankind are more disposed to suffer, while evils are sufferable, than to right themselves by abolishing the forms to which they are accustomed.
Declaration of Independence (1776)

4 The history of the present King of Great Britain is a history of repeated injuries and usurpations, all having in direct object the establishment of an absolute Tyranny over these States. To prove this, let Facts be submitted to a candid world.
Declaration of Independence (1776)

5 He has erected a multitude of New Offices, and sent hither swarms of Officers to harrass our people, and eat out their substance.
Declaration of Independence (1776)

6 We must, therefore, acquiesce in the necessity, which denounces our Separation, and hold them [the British], as we hold the rest of mankind, Enemies in War, in Peace Friends.
Declaration of Independence (1776)

7 That these United Colonies are, and of Right ought to be Free and Independent States; that they are Absolved from all Allegiance to the British Crown, and that all political connection between them and the State of Great Britain, is and ought to be totally dissolved.
Declaration of Independence (1776)

8 And for the support of this Declaration, with a firm reliance on the protection of Divine Providence, we mutually pledge to each other our Lives, our Fortunes and our sacred Honor.
Declaration of Independence (1776)

9 Truth is great and will prevail if left to herself; that she is the proper and sufficient antagonist to error, and has nothing to fear from the conflict unless by human interposition disarmed of her natural weapons, free argument and debate; errors ceasing to be dangerous when it is permitted freely to contradict them.
"A Bill for Establishing Religious Freedom" (1779)

10 It is error alone which needs the support of government. Truth can stand by itself.
Notes on the State of Virginia, query 17 (1781–1785)

11 It does me no injury for my neighbor to say there are twenty gods, or no God. It neither picks my pocket nor breaks my leg.
Notes on the State of Virginia, query 17 (1781–1785)

12 Is uniformity [of opinion] attainable? Millions of innocent men, women, and children, since the introduction of Christianity, have been burnt, tortured, fined, imprisoned; yet we have not advanced one inch towards uniformity. What has been the effect of coercion? To make one half the world fools, and the other half hypocrites.
Notes on the State of Virginia, query 17 (1781–1785)

13 [*On slavery:*] Can the liberties of a nation be thought secure when we have removed their only firm basis, a conviction in the minds of the people that these liberties are of the gift of god? That they are not to be violated but with his wrath? Indeed I tremble for my country when I reflect that god is just; that his justice cannot sleep forever.
Notes on the State of Virginia, query 18 (1781–1785)

14 What a stupendous, what an incomprehensible machine is man! Who can endure toil, famine, stripes, imprisonment, & death itself in vindication of his own liberty, and the next moment . . . inflict on his fellow men a bondage, one hour of which is fraught with more misery than ages of that which he rose in rebellion to oppose.
Letter to Jean Nicholas Demeunier, 24 Jan. 1786

15 Were it left to me to decide whether we should have a government without newspapers or newspapers without a government, I should not hesitate a moment to prefer the latter.
Letter to Edward Carrington, 16 Jan. 1787

16 I hold it that a little rebellion now and then is a good thing, & as necessary in the political world as storms in the physical. Unsuccessful rebellions indeed generally establish the incroachments on the rights of the people which have produced them. An observation of this truth should render honest republican governors so mild in their punishment of rebellions, as not to discourage them too much. It is a medicine necessary for the sound health of government.
Letter to James Madison, 30 Jan. 1787

17 The tree of liberty must be refreshed from time to time with the blood of patriots & tyrants. It is its natural manure.
Letter to William Stephens Smith, 13 Nov. 1787

18 God forbid we should ever be 20 years without such a rebellion. . . . What country can preserve its liberties, if their rulers are not warned from time to time that their people preserve the spirit of resistance? Let them take arms. . . . What signify a few lives lost in a century or two?
Letter to William Stephens Smith, 13 Nov. 1787

19 A bill of rights is what the people are entitled to against every government on earth, general or particular, and what no just government should refuse, or rest on inference.
Letter to James Madison, 20 Dec. 1787

20 If we cannot secure all our rights, let us secure what we can.
Letter to James Madison, 15 Mar. 1789

21 The earth belongs to the living and not to the dead.
Letter to James Madison, 6 Sept. 1789

22 We are not to expect to be translated from despotism to liberty in a feather bed.
Letter to Marquis de Lafayette, 2 Apr. 1790

23 I would rather be exposed to the inconveniencies attending too much liberty than those attending too small a degree of it.
Letter to Archibald Stewart, 23 Dec. 1791

24 The second office of this government is honorable & easy, the first is but a splendid misery.
Letter to Elbridge Gerry, 13 May 1797

25 In questions of power, then, let no more be said of confidence in man, but bind him down from mischief by the chains of the Constitution.
Kentucky Resolutions of 1798, resolution 9 (1798)

26 The war hawks talk of septembrizing, deportation, and the examples for quelling sedition set by the French Executive.
Letter to James Madison, 26 Apr. 1798. Jefferson's usage of *hawk* here is earlier than any political usage of that word previously recorded.

27 I have sworn upon the altar of god, eternal hostility against every form of tyranny over the mind of man.
Letter to Benjamin Rush, 23 Sept. 1800

28 If there be any among us who would wish to dissolve this Union or to change its republican form, let them stand undisturbed as monuments of the safety with which error of opinion may be tolerated where reason is left free to combat it.
First Inaugural Address, 4 Mar. 1801

29 All, too, will bear in mind this sacred principle, that though the will of the majority is in all

cases to prevail, that will to be rightful must be reasonable; that the minority possess their equal rights, which equal law must protect, and to violate would be oppression.
First Inaugural Address, 4 Mar. 1801

30 Equal and exact justice to all men, of whatever state or persuasion, religious or political; peace, commerce, and honest friendship, with all nations; entangling alliances with none . . . freedom of religion; freedom of the press, and freedom of person under the protection of the habeas corpus, and trial by juries impartially selected. These principles form the bright constellation which has gone before us and guided our steps through an age of revolution and reformation. The wisdom of our sages and blood of our heroes have been devoted to their attainment. They should be the creed of our political faith, the text of civic instruction, the touchstone by which to try the services of those we trust; and should we wander from them in moments of error or of alarm, let us hasten to retrace our steps and to regain the road which alone leads to peace, liberty, and safety.
First Inaugural Address, 4 Mar. 1801

31 We are all Republicans, we are all Federalists.
First Inaugural Address, 4 Mar. 1801

32 If a due participation of office is a matter of right, how are vacancies to be obtained? Those by death are few; by resignation none.
Letter to Elias Shipman and others, 12 July 1801. Often paraphrased as "Few die and none resign."

33 Believing with you that religion is a matter which lies solely between man and his god, that he owes account to none other for his faith or his worship, that the legitimate powers of government reach actions only, and not opinions, I contemplate with sovereign reverence that act of the whole American people which declared that *their* legislature should make no law respecting an establishment of religion, or prohibiting the free exercise thereof, thus building a wall of separation between church and state.
Reply to Nehemiah Dodge, Ephraim Robbins, and Stephen S. Nelson (committee of the Danbury, Conn., Baptist Association), 1 Jan. 1802. Roger Williams had written in *Mr. Cotton's Letter Lately Printed, Examined and Answered* (1644) of "the hedge or wall of separation between the garden of the church and the wilderness of the world."

34 It behoves every man who values liberty of conscience for himself, to resist invasions of it in the case of others; or their case may, by change of circumstances, become his own.
Letter to Benjamin Rush, 21 Apr. 1803

35 He who knows most, knows how little he knows.
"Batture at New Orleans" (1812)

36 He who receives an idea from me, receives instruction himself without lessening mine; as he who lights his taper at mine, receives light without darkening me.
Letter to Isaac McPherson, 13 Aug. 1813

37 The new circumstances under which we are placed call for new words, new phrases, and for the transfer of old words to new objects. An American dialect will therefore be formed.
Letter to John Waldo, 16 Aug. 1813

38 I agree with you that there is a natural aristocracy among men. The grounds of this are virtue & talents.
Letter to John Adams, 28 Oct. 1813

39 I am . . . mortified to be told that, *in the United States of America*, a question about the sale of a book can be carried before the civil magistrate. . . . Are we to have a censor whose imprimatur shall say what books may be sold, and what we may buy? . . . Whose foot is to be the measure to which ours are all to be cut and stretched?
Letter to N. G. Dufief, 19 Apr. 1814

40 I cannot live without books.
Letter to John Adams, 10 June 1815

41 If a nation expects to be ignorant & free, in a state of civilization, it expects what never was & never will be. The functionaries of every government have propensities to command at will the liberty & property of their constituents. There is no safe deposit for these but with the people themselves; nor can they be safe with them without information. Where the press is free and every man able to read, all is safe.
Letter to Charles Yancey, 6 Jan. 1816

42 There are indeed (who might say Nay) gloomy & hypochondriac minds, inhabitants of diseased bodies, disgusted with the present, & despairing of the future; always counting that the worst will happen, because it may happen. To these I say How much pain have cost us the evils which have never happened!

Letter to John Adams, 8 Apr. 1816
See Twain 148

43 Some men look at constitutions with sanctimonious reverence, and deem them like the ark of the covenant, too sacred to be touched. . . . Laws and institutions must go hand in hand with the progress of the human mind. . . . We might as well require a man to wear still the coat which fitted him when a boy, as civilized society to remain ever under the regimen of their barbarous ancestors.

Letter to Samuel Kercheval, 12 July 1816

44 When angry count 10. before you speak. If very angry 100.

Letter to Charles Clay, 12 July 1817. Jefferson is quoting advice he had given to Paul Clay.

45 But this momentous question, like a fire bell in the night, awakened and filled me with terror. I considered it at once as the knell of the Union.

Letter to John Holmes, 22 Apr. 1820. Jefferson was referring to the issue of whether to admit Missouri as a slave state but prohibit slavery in the remainder of the Louisiana Purchase.

46 Dictionaries are but the depositories of words already legitimated by usage. Society is the work-shop in which new ones are elaborated. When an individual uses a new word, if illformed it is rejected in society, if wellformed, adopted, and, after due time, laid up in the depository of dictionaries.

Letter to John Adams, 15 Aug. 1820

47 I know no safe depository of the ultimate powers of the society, but the people themselves: and if we think them not enlightened enough to exercise their control with a wholesome discretion, the remedy is not to take it from them, but to inform their discretion by education.

Letter to William Charles Jarvis, 28 Sept. 1820

48 The boisterous sea of liberty indeed is never without a wave.

Letter to Marquis de Lafayette, 26 Dec. 1820. Jefferson had earlier used *boisterous sea of liberty* in a letter to Philip Mazzei, 24 Apr. 1796.

49 We are not afraid to follow truth wherever it may lead, nor to tolerate any error so long as reason is left free to combat it.

Letter to William Roscoe, 27 Dec. 1820

50 If the present Congress errs in too much talking, how can it be otherwise in a body to which the people send 150. lawyers, whose trade it is to question everything, yield nothing, and talk by the hour? That 150. lawyers should do business together ought not to be expected.

Autobiography (1821)

51 The only security of all is in a free press. The force of public opinion cannot be resisted, when permitted freely to be expressed. The agitation it produces must be submitted to. It is necessary to keep the waters pure.

Letter to Marquis de Lafayette, 4 Nov. 1823

52 Speeches measured by the hour, die with the hour.

Letter to David Harding, 20 Apr. 1824

53 Here was buried Thomas Jefferson author of the Declaration of American Independence of the Statute of Virginia for Religious Freedom and father of the University of Virginia.

Epitaph (1826) on Jefferson's gravestone at his home, Monticello, at Charlottesville, Va.

54 The general spread of the light of science has already laid open to every view the palpable truth that the mass of mankind has not been born, with saddles on their backs, nor a favored few booted and spurred, ready to ride them legitimately, by the grace of god.

Letter to Roger C. Weightman, 24 June 1826. From Jefferson's last letter before his death.

55 [*Last words, 4 July 1826:*] This is the Fourth?

Quoted in Henry S. Randall, *The Life of Thomas Jefferson* (1858). Jefferson was asking whether the date was July 4th, the anniversary of the Declaration of Independence.
See John Adams 21

56 Dissent is the highest form of patriotism.

Attributed in *Boston Globe*, 2 June 1991. The widespread attribution to Jefferson is clearly apocryphal. The earliest known occurrence of these exact words or near-identical ones was in Friends Peace Committee, *The Use of Force in International Affairs* (1961) ("is dissent the highest form of patriotism?"); Barry Popik has traced similar formulations as far back as 1925.

Francis, Lord Jeffrey
Scottish critic, 1773–1850

1 [*Of William Wordsworth's poem* The Excursion:] This will never do.

Edinburgh Review, Nov. 1814

Charles Jennens
English librettist, 1700–1773

1 And He shall reign for ever and ever.

"Hallelujah Chorus" (libretto to music by G. F. Handel) (1741). Taken from Revelation 11:15: "The kingdoms of this world are become the kingdoms of our Lord and of his Christ; and he shall reign for ever and ever."

Jerome K. Jerome
English writer, 1859–1927

1 I like work; it fascinates me. I can sit and look at it for hours.

Three Men in a Boat ch. 15 (1889)

St. Jerome
Christian church father, ca. 342–420

1 *Venerationi mihi semper fuit non verbosa rusticitas, sed sancta simplicitas.*
I have always revered not crude verbosity but holy simplicity.

Letter 57 (translation by W. H. Fremantle)
See Hus 1

George Jessel
U.S. entertainer, 1898–1981

1 Well, sue me.

Quoted in *Boston Globe*, 17 Feb. 1929

2 [*On the large crowd attending a celebrity's funeral:*] You see, you give the people what they want and they'll come.

Quoted in *Saturday Review*, 13 Aug. 1955. Jessel was credited with a similar remark earlier, in the *Washington Post*, 8 Mar. 1942.
See Goldwyn 5

Juan Ramón Jiménez
Spanish poet, 1881–1958

1 *Si te dan papel rayado, escribe de través.*
If they give you ruled paper, write the other way.

España, 20 Nov. 1920

Piyush "Bobby" Jindal
U.S. politician, 1971–

1 We've got to stop being the stupid party. . . . It's time for a new Republican Party that talks like adults.

Speech at Republican National Committee Winter Meeting, Charlotte, N.C., 24 Jan. 2013

Muhammad Ali Jinnah
Pakistani statesman, 1876–1948

1 [*Of Muslims and Hindus:*] If we cannot agree, let us at any rate agree to differ, but let us part as friends.

Speech at All Parties National Convention, Calcutta, India, 22 Dec. 1928

2 You are free; you are free to go to your temples, you are free to go to your mosques or to any other place of worship in this State of Pakistan. You may belong to any religion or caste or creed—that has nothing to do with the fundamental principle that we are all citizens and equal citizens of one state.

Presidential Address to the Constituent Assembly, Karachi, Pakistan, 11 Aug. 1947

Joan of Arc
French military leader and saint, 1412–1431

1 Of the love or hatred God has for the English, I know nothing, but I do know that they will all be thrown out of France, except those who die there.

Response to interrogation by English, 15 Mar. 1431

Steven Jobs
U.S. business executive and computer inventor, 1955–2011

1 [*Description of the Macintosh computer:*] Insanely great.

Quoted in *Time*, 30 Jan. 1984

2 [*Inviting John Sculley, then president of PepsiCo, to join Apple Computer:*] Do you want to spend the rest of your life selling sugared water or do you want a chance to change the world?
Quoted in John Sculley, *Odyssey* (1987)

3 [*Remark to Apple employees, 1982:*] It's more fun to be a pirate than to join the Navy.
Quoted in John Sculley, *Odyssey* (1987)

4 It's really hard to design products by focus groups. A lot of times, people don't know what they want until you show it to them.
Quoted in *Business Week*, 12 May 1998

5 Oh wow. Oh wow. Oh wow.
"Last words," 5 Oct. 2011, quoted in Mona Simpson's eulogy for Jobs, Stanford, Calif., 16 Oct. 2011

Billy Joel
U.S. singer and songwriter, 1949–

1 Sing us a song you're the piano man
Sing us a song tonight
Well we're all in the mood for a melody
And you've got us feeling alright.
"The Piano Man" (song) (1973)

2 I'm in a New York state of mind.
"New York State of Mind" (song) (1976)

3 Come out, Virginia, don't let me wait.
You Catholic girls start much too late,
Ah, but sooner or later it comes down to fate.
I might as well be the one.
"Only the Good Die Young" (song) (1977)

4 I'd rather laugh with the sinners than cry with
  the saints
Sinners are much more fun.
"Only the Good Die Young" (song) (1977)

5 We didn't start the fire
It was always burning
Since the world's been turning.
"We Didn't Start the Fire" (song) (1989)

Wilhelm Ludvig Johannsen
Danish botanist, 1857–1927

1 It appears as most simple to use the last syllable "gen" taken from Darwin's well-known word pangene. . . . Thus, we will say for "das pangene" and "die pangene" simply "Das Gen" and "Die Gene."
Elemente der Exakten Erblichkeitslehre (1909) (translation by G. E. Allen). Coinage of the term *gene*.

John XXIII (Angelo Giuseppe Roncalli)
Italian pope, 1881–1963

1 If civil authorities legislate for or allow anything that is contrary to that order and therefore contrary to the will of God, neither the laws made nor the authorizations granted can be binding on the consciences of the citizens, since *we must obey God rather than men.*
Pacem in Terris pt. 2 (1963)

2 The social progress, order, security, and peace of each country are necessarily linked with the social progress, order, security, and peace of every other country.
Pacem in Terris pt. 4 (1963)

3 It often happens that I wake at night and begin to think about a serious problem and decide I must tell the Pope about it. Then I wake up completely and remember that I am the Pope.
Quoted in *Forbes*, 14 May 1990

Elton John (Reginald Dwight) 1947– and Bernie Taupin 1950–
English singer and songwriter; songwriter

1 It seems to me you lived your life
Like a candle in the wind.
Never knowing who to cling to
When the rain set in. . . .
The candle burned out long before
Your legend ever did.
"Candle in the Wind" (song) (1973). This original version of the song was addressed to Marilyn Monroe.

2 Goodbye England's rose;
May you ever grow in our hearts. . . .
And your footsteps will always fall here
On England's greenest hills;
Your candle's burned out long before
Your legend ever will.
"Candle in the Wind" (revised version of song) (1997). The revised version of this song was sung by John at the funeral of Diana, Princess of Wales, 7 Sept. 1997.

St. John of the Cross
Spanish mystic and poet, 1542–1591

1 *Noche oscura.*

Dark night.

Title of poem (1578–1580). Frequently quoted as "dark night of the soul"; that phrase appears in translator David Lewis's chapter heading for the poem in the saint's *Complete Works* vol. 1, bk. 1, ch. 3 (1864).
See F. Scott Fitzgerald 41

John Paul II (Karol Wojtyla)
Polish pope, 1920–2005

1 This right [to join a free trade union] is not given to us by the State. . . . This right is given by the Creator.

Speech, Katowice, Poland, 20 June 1983

2 The culture of life means respect for nature and protection of God's work of creation. In a special way, it means respect for human life from the first moment of conception until its natural end.

Speech, Denver, Colo., 15 Aug. 1993

3 [*Response to suggestion that it was inappropriate for him as a cardinal to ski, ca. 1968:*] It is unbecoming for a cardinal to ski badly.

Quoted in *St. Petersburg Times,* 7 Sept. 1987

Charles R. Johnson
U.S. writer, 1948–

1 Of all the things that drive men to sea, the most common disaster, I've come to learn, is women.

Middle Passage (1990)

Claudia Alta "Lady Bird" Johnson
U.S. First Lady, 1912–2007

1 Mrs. Kennedy is going to marry Aristotle Socrates Onassis! . . . I feel strangely freer. No shadow walks beside me down the halls of the White House.

A White House Diary (1970) (entry for 19 Oct. 1968)

Diane Johnson
U.S. author, 1934–

1 Men are generally more law-abiding than women. . . . Women have a feeling that since they didn't make the rules, the rules have nothing to do with them.

Lying Low ch. 9 (1978)

Howard E. Johnson
U.S. songwriter, 1887–1941

1 "M" is for the million things she gave me,
"O" means only that she's growing old,
"T" is for the tears were shed to save me,
"H" is for her heart of purest gold;
"E" is for her eyes, with love-light shining,
"R" means right, and right she'll always be,
Put them all together, they spell "MOTHER,"
A word that means the world to me.

"M-O-T-H-E-R (A Word That Means the World to Me)" (song) (1915)

2 The Best Things in Life Are Free.

Title of song (1917). Many reference works erroneously attribute this proverb to Buddy DeSylva, who wrote a song of the same name in 1927.
See DeSylva 3

James Weldon Johnson
U.S. author, 1871–1938

1 Lift Ev'ry Voice and Sing.

Title of poem (1900)

2 Young man, yo' arm's too short to box wid God!

The Autobiography of an Ex-Colored Man ch. 10 (1912). Johnson was quoting an African-American preacher named John Brown.

3 O black and unknown bards of long ago,
How came your lips to touch the sacred fire?

"O Black and Unknown Bards" l. 1 (1917)

4 And God stepped out on space,
And he looked around and said:
I'm lonely—
I'll make me a world.

"The Creation" l. 1 (1927)

Lyndon B. Johnson
U.S. president, 1908–1973

1 I am a free man, an American, a United States Senator, and a Democrat, in that order. I am also a liberal, a conservative, a Texan, a taxpayer, a rancher, a businessman, a consumer, a parent, a voter, and not as young

as I used to be nor as old as I expect to be—and I am all of these things in no fixed order.

Texas Quarterly, Winter 1958

2 [*After the assassination of John F. Kennedy:*] All I have I would have given gladly not to be standing here today.

Address before Joint Session of Congress, 27 Nov. 1963

3 We have talked long enough in this country about equal rights. We have talked for one hundred years or more. It is time now to write the next chapter, and to write it in the books of law.

Address before Joint Session of Congress, 27 Nov. 1963

4 This administration today, here and now, declares unconditional war on poverty in America. I urge this Congress and all Americans to join with me in that effort.

State of the Union Address, 8 Jan. 1964

5 We are trying to build a great society that will make your children and your grandchildren and the people three or four generations from today proud of what we are doing.

Remarks to a group in connection with the Montana Territorial Centennial, Washington, D.C., 17 Apr. 1964. Johnson's first usage of the phrase *great society*. *See John Dewey 1; Hamer 1; Lyndon Johnson 6; Lyndon Johnson 8; Wallas 1; William Wordsworth 30*

6 In your time we have the opportunity to move not only toward the rich society and the powerful society, but upward to the Great Society.

Speech at University of Michigan, Ann Arbor, Mich., 22 May 1964 *See John Dewey 1; Hamer 1; Lyndon Johnson 5; Lyndon Johnson 8; Wallas 1; William Wordsworth 30*

7 We Americans know, although others appear to forget, the risks of spreading conflict. We still seek no wider war.

Broadcast speech, 4 Aug. 1964

8 This Nation—this generation—in this hour, has man's first chance to build the Great Society—a place where the meaning of man's life matches the marvels of man's labor.

Address accepting Democratic presidential nomination, Atlantic City, N.J., 27 Aug. 1964 *See John Dewey 1; Hamer 1; Lyndon Johnson 5; Lyndon Johnson 6; Wallas 1; William Wordsworth 30*

9 We are not about to send American boys 9 or 10,000 miles away from home to do what Asian boys ought to be doing for themselves.

Speech at Akron University, Akron, Ohio, 21 Oct. 1964 *See Franklin Roosevelt 21*

10 I shall not seek, and I will not accept, the nomination of my party for another term as your President.

Broadcast address to the nation, 31 Mar. 1968

11 [*Of Gerald R. Ford:*] That's what happens when you play football too long without a helmet.

Quoted in *N.Y. Times,* 30 Apr. 1967

12 [*Of J. Edgar Hoover:*] Better to have him inside the tent pissing out, than outside pissing in.

Quoted in *N.Y. Times,* 31 Oct. 1971

13 [*Of a prospective assistant:*] I don't want loyalty. I want *loyalty.* I want him to kiss my ass in Macy's window at high noon and tell me it smells like roses. I want his pecker in my pocket.

Quoted in David Halberstam, *The Best and the Brightest* (1972)

14 [*Of Gerald Ford:*] So dumb he can't fart and chew gum at the same time.

Quoted in Richard Reeves, *A Ford, Not a Lincoln* (1975). Barry Popik has traced "he can't walk and chew gum at the same time" as far back as 1954 (*Paris* [Tex.] *News,* 16 Mar. 1954).

Philander C. Johnson
U.S. humorist, 1866–1939

1 Every man who has attained to high position is a sincere believer of the survival of the fittest.

Senator Sorghum's Primer of Politics (1906) *See Charles Darwin 7; Herbert Spencer 5; Herbert Spencer 6*

Philip C. Johnson
U.S. architect, 1906–2005

1 The automobile is the greatest catastrophe in the entire history of City architecture.

"The Town and the Automobile or the Pride of Elm Street" (1955)

2 Architecture is the art of how to waste space.

Quoted in *N.Y. Times,* 27 Dec. 1964

Robert Johnson

U.S. blues musician, 1911–1938

1 I went down to the crossroad,
Fell down on my knees.
Asked the Lord above,
"Have mercy, now, save poor Bob, if you
please."
"Cross Road Blues" (song) (1936)

2 When the train, it left the station
With two lights on behind—
Well, the blue light was my blues
And the red light was my mind.
"Love in Vain" (song) (1936)

3 Blues fallin' down like hail
And the day keeps on worryin' me
There's a hell hound on my trail.
"Hell Hound on My Trail" (song) (1937)

4 You can squeeze my lemon
'Til the juice run down my leg.
"Travelling Riverside Blues" (song) (1937)

Samuel Johnson

English man of letters, 1709–1784

1 More knowledge may be gained of a man's real
character, by a short conversation with one of
his servants, than from a formal and studied
narrative, begun with his pedigree and ended
with his funeral.
The Rambler no. 60 (13 Oct. 1750)

2 To neglect at any time preparation for death, is
to sleep on our post at a siege, but to omit it in
old age, is to sleep at an attack.
The Rambler no. 78 (15 Dec. 1750)

3 Such is the delight of mental superiority, that
none on whom nature or study *have* conferred
it, would purchase the gifts of fortune by its
loss.
The Rambler no. 150 (24 Aug. 1751)

4 Every other author may aspire to praise; the
lexicographer can only hope to escape reproach.
A Dictionary of the English Language preface (1755)

5 I am not yet so lost in lexicography, as to forget
that *words are the daughters of earth, and that
things are the sons of heaven.*
A Dictionary of the English Language preface (1755)
See Madden 1

6 I have studiously endeavored to collect
examples and authorities from the writers
before the restoration, whose works I regard as
the wells of English undefiled, as the pure sources
of genuine diction.
A Dictionary of the English Language preface (1755)
See Spenser 6

7 But these were the dreams of a poet doomed at
last to wake a lexicographer.
A Dictionary of the English Language preface (1755)

8 The *English Dictionary* was written with
little assistance of the learned, and without
any patronage of the great; not in the soft
obscurities of retirement, or under the shelter
of academick bowers, but amidst inconvenience
and distraction, in sickness and in sorrow.
A Dictionary of the English Language preface (1755)

9 DULL. . . . Not exhilarating; not delightful; as, *to
make dictionaries is* dull *work.*
A Dictionary of the English Language (1755)

10 EXCISE. . . . A hateful tax levied upon
commodities, and adjudged not by the common
judges of property, but wretches hired by those
to whom excise is paid.
A Dictionary of the English Language (1755)

11 FAVORITE. . . . One chosen as a companion
by his superior; a mean wretch whose whole
business is by any means to please.
A Dictionary of the English Language (1755)

12 GRUBSTREET. . . . Originally the name of a street in Moorfields in London, much inhabited by writers of small histories, dictionaries, and temporary poems; whence any mean production is called *grubstreet*.
A Dictionary of the English Language (1755)

13 LEXICOGRAPHER. . . . A writer of dictionaries; a harmless drudge.
A Dictionary of the English Language (1755)

14 NETWORK. . . . Anything reticulated or decussated, at equal distances, with interstices between the intersections.
A Dictionary of the English Language (1755)

15 OATS. . . . A grain, which in England is generally given to horses, but in Scotland supports the people.
A Dictionary of the English Language (1755)

16 PATRON. . . . Commonly a wretch who supports with insolence, and is paid with flattery.
A Dictionary of the English Language (1755)

17 PENSION. . . . In England it is generally understood to mean pay given to a state hireling for treason to his country.
A Dictionary of the English Language (1755)

18 STAMMEL. . . . Of this word I know not the meaning.
A Dictionary of the English Language (1755)

19 No people can be great who have ceased to be virtuous.
"An Introduction to the Political State of Great Britain" (1756)

20 No sooner are we supplied with every thing that nature can demand, than we sit down to contrive artificial appetites.
The Idler no. 30 (11 Nov. 1758)

21 Among the calamities of war may be justly numbered the diminution of the love of truth, by the falsehoods which interest dictates and credulity encourages.
The Idler no. 30 (11 Nov. 1758)
See Modern Proverbs 96

22 He [the poet] must write as the interpreter of nature, and the legislator of mankind, and consider himself as presiding over the thoughts and manners of future generations; as a being superior to time and place.
Rasselas ch. 10 (1759)
See Auden 22; Auden 39; Andrew Fletcher 1; Percy Shelley 15; Twain 104

23 Human life is every where a state in which much is to be endured, and little to be enjoyed.
Rasselas ch. 11 (1759)

24 Marriage has many pains, but celibacy has no pleasures.
Rasselas ch. 26 (1759)

25 Nature has given women so much power that the law has very wisely given them little.
Letter to John Taylor, 18 Aug. 1763

26 How small, of all that human hearts endure,
That part which laws or kings can cause or cure.
Lines added to Oliver Goldsmith's *The Traveller* (1764)

27 [*Of Shakespeare:*] He that tries to recommend him by select quotations, will succeed like the pedant in Hierocles, who, when he offered his house to sale, carried a brick in his pocket as a specimen.
The Plays of William Shakespeare preface (1765)

28 While, an author is yet living we estimate his powers by his worst performance, and when he is dead we rate them by his best.
The Plays of William Shakespeare preface (1765)

29 Shakespeare is above all writers, at least above all modern writers, the poet of nature; the poet that holds up to his readers a faithful mirror of manners and of life.
The Plays of William Shakespeare preface (1765)

30 [*On the American colonies:*] How is it that we hear the loudest yelps for liberty among the drivers of negroes?
Taxation No Tyranny (1775)

31 [*On a work by Congreve:*] It is praised by the biographers. . . . I would rather praise it than read it.
Lives of the English Poets "Congreve" (1779–1781)

32 About the beginning of the seventeenth century appeared a race of writers that may be termed the *metaphysical poets*.
Lives of the English Poets "Cowley" (1779–1781)

33 Words being arbitrary must owe their power to association, and have the influence, and that only, which custom has given them. Language is the dress of thought.

Lives of the English Poets "Cowley" (1779–1781)
See Samuel Wesley 1

34 [*Of the death of David Garrick:*] I am disappointed by that stroke of death, which has eclipsed the gaiety of nations and impoverished the public stock of harmless pleasure.

Lives of the English Poets "Edmund Smith" (1779–1781)

35 In the character of his [Thomas Gray's] *Elegy* I rejoice to concur with the common reader; for by the common sense of readers uncorrupted with literary prejudices . . . must be finally decided all claim to poetical honors.

Lives of the English Poets "Gray" (1779–1781)

36 [*Of Italian opera:*] An exotic and irrational entertainment, which has always been combated, and always has prevailed.

Lives of the English Poets "Hughes" (1779–1781)

37 The want of human interest is always felt. *Paradise Lost* is one of the books which the reader admires and lays down, and forgets to take up again. None ever wished it longer than it is.

Lives of the English Poets "Milton" (1779–1781)

38 [*Of Alexander Pope's* The Rape of the Lock:] New things are made familiar, and familiar things are made new.

Lives of the English Poets "Pope" (1779–1781)

39 [*Referring to his fits of melancholia:*] The black dog I hope always to resist, and in time to drive. . . . When I rise my breakfast is solitary, the black dog waits to share it, from breakfast to dinner he continues barking. . . . Night comes at last, and some hours of restlessness and confusion bring me again to a day of solitude. What shall exclude the black dog from a habitation like this?

Letter to Mrs. Thrale, 28 June 1783

40 Dictionaries are like watches; the worst is better than none, and the best cannot be expected to go quite true.

Letter to Francesco Sastres, 21 Aug. 1784

41 A lawyer has no business with the justice or injustice of the cause which he undertakes, unless his client asks his opinion, and then he is bound to give it honestly. The justice or injustice of the cause is to be decided by the judge.

Quoted in James Boswell, *The Journal of a Tour to the Hebrides* (1785) (entry for 15 Aug. 1773)

42 The law is the last result of human wisdom acting upon human experience for the benefit of the public.

Quoted in Heather Lynch Piozzi, *Anecdotes of . . . Johnson* (1786)

43 [*After being absent from a tutorial at Oxford because he had been "sliding in Christ Church meadow":*] JOHNSON: I had no notion that I was wrong or irreverent to my tutor.

BOSWELL: That, Sir, was great fortitude of mind.

JOHNSON: No, Sir; stark insensibility.

Quoted in James Boswell, *Life of Samuel Johnson* (1791) (entry for 31 Oct. 1728)

44 A man may write at any time, if he will set himself doggedly to it.

Quoted in James Boswell, *The Life of Samuel Johnson* (1791) (entry for Mar. 1750)

45 [*Of Lord Chesterfield's* Letters:] They teach the morals of a whore, and the manners of a dancing master.

Quoted in James Boswell, *The Life of Samuel Johnson* (1791) (entry for 1754)

46 [*Of Lord Chesterfield:*] This man I thought had been a Lord among wits; but, I find, he is only a wit among Lords.

Quoted in James Boswell, *The Life of Samuel Johnson* (1791) (entry for 1754)

47 [*To a woman who asked him why he had defined* pastern *in his* Dictionary of the English Language *as a horse's knee:*] Ignorance, Madam, pure ignorance.

Quoted in James Boswell, *The Life of Samuel Johnson* (1791) (entry for 1755)

48 If a man does not make new acquaintance as he advances through life, he will soon find himself left alone. A man, Sir, should keep his friendship *in constant repair.*

Quoted in James Boswell, *The Life of Samuel Johnson* (1791) (entry for 1755)

49 Is not a Patron, my Lord, one who looks with unconcern on a man struggling for life in the water, and, when he has reached ground, encumbers him with help? The notice which you have been pleased to take of my labors, had it been early, had been kind; but it has been delayed till I am indifferent, and cannot enjoy it; till I am solitary, and cannot impart it; till I am known, and do not want it.

Quoted in James Boswell, *The Life of Samuel Johnson* (1791) (letter to Lord Chesterfield, 7 Feb. 1755)

50 No man will be a sailor who has contrivance enough to get himself into a jail; for being in a ship is being in a jail, with the chance of being drowned. . . . A man in a jail has more room, better food, and commonly better company.

Quoted in James Boswell, *The Life of Samuel Johnson* (1791) (entry for 16 Mar. 1759)
See Robert Burton 6

51 Consider, Sir, how insignificant this will appear a twelvemonth hence.

Quoted in James Boswell, *The Life of Samuel Johnson* (1791) (entry for 6 July 1763)
See Dickens 25

52 The noblest prospect which a Scotchman ever sees, is the high road that leads him to England!

Quoted in James Boswell, *The Life of Samuel Johnson* (1791) (entry for 6 July 1763)

53 A man ought to read just as inclination leads him: for what he reads as a task will do him little good.

Quoted in James Boswell, *The Life of Samuel Johnson* (entry for 14 July 1763)

54 If he does really think that there is no distinction between virtue and vice, why, Sir, when he leaves our houses, let us count our spoons.

Quoted in James Boswell, *The Life of Samuel Johnson* (1791) (entry for 14 July 1763)
See Ralph Waldo Emerson 41

55 Your levellers wish to level *down* as far as themselves; but they cannot bear levelling *up* to themselves.

Quoted in James Boswell, *The Life of Samuel Johnson* (1791) (entry for 21 July 1763)

56 [*Of a female Quaker:*] Sir, a woman's preaching is like a dog's walking on his hinder legs. It is

not done well; but you are surprised to find it done at all.

Quoted in James Boswell, *The Life of Samuel Johnson* (1791) (entry for 31 July 1763)

57 This was a good dinner enough, to be sure; but it was not a dinner to *ask* a man to.

Quoted in James Boswell, *The Life of Samuel Johnson* (1791) (entry for 31 July 1763)

58 [*In response to Boswell's observation that George Berkeley's theory of the nonexistence of matter could not be refuted, Johnson kicked a large stone and said:*] I refute it *thus.*

Quoted in James Boswell, *The Life of Samuel Johnson* (1791) (entry for 6 Aug. 1763)

59 [*Of John Hawkins:*] Sir John, Sir, is a very unclubable man.

Quoted in James Boswell, *The Life of Samuel Johnson* (1791) (entry for Spring 1764)

60 So far is it from being true that men are naturally equal, that no two people can be half an hour together, but one shall acquire an evident superiority over the other.

Quoted in James Boswell, *The Life of Samuel Johnson* (1791) (entry for 15 Feb. 1766)

61 Sir, we *know* our will is free, and *there's* an end on 't.

Quoted in James Boswell, *The Life of Samuel Johnson* (1791) (entry for 16 Oct. 1769)

62 BOSWELL: But is not the fear of death natural to man?

JOHNSON: So much so, Sir, that the whole of life is but keeping away the thoughts of it.

Quoted in James Boswell, *The Life of Samuel Johnson* (1791) (entry for 19 Oct. 1769)

63 Most schemes of political improvement are very laughable things.

Quoted in James Boswell, *The Life of Samuel Johnson* (1791) (entry for 26 Oct. 1769)

64 It matters not how a man dies, but how he lives. The act of dying is not of importance, it lasts so short a time.

Quoted in James Boswell, *The Life of Samuel Johnson* (1791) (entry for 26 Oct. 1769)

65 Being told she was remarkable for her humility and condescension to inferiors, he observed, that those were very laudable qualities, but it

might not be so easy to discover who the lady's inferiors were.

Quoted in James Boswell, *The Life of Samuel Johnson* (1791) (entry for 1770)
See Dorothy Parker 32

66 That fellow seems to me to possess but one idea, and that is a wrong one.

Quoted in James Boswell, *The Life of Samuel Johnson* (1791) (entry for 1770)
See Disraeli 17

67 Johnson observed, that "he did not care to speak ill of any man behind his back, but he believed the gentleman was an *attorney.*"

Quoted in James Boswell, *The Life of Samuel Johnson* (1791) (entry for 1770)

68 [*Of a man who remarried after the death of his first wife, with whom he had been unhappy:*] The triumph of hope over experience.

Quoted in James Boswell, *The Life of Samuel Johnson* (1791) (entry for 1770)

69 A decent provision for the poor, is the true test of civilisation.

Quoted in James Boswell, *The Life of Samuel Johnson* (1791) (entry for 1770)
See Pearl S. Buck 3; Ramsey Clark 1; Dostoyevski 1; Humphrey 3; Helen Keller 4

70 [*Of Lord Mansfield, born in Scotland but educated in England:*] Much may be made of a Scotchman, if he be *caught* young.

Quoted in James Boswell, *The Life of Samuel Johnson* (1791) (entry for Spring 1772)

71 Sir, it is so far from natural for a man and woman to live in a state of marriage, that we find all the motives which they have for remaining in that connection, and the restraints which civilized society imposes to prevent separation, are hardly sufficient to keep them together.

Quoted in James Boswell, *The Life of Samuel Johnson* (1791) (entry for 31 Mar. 1772)

72 I would not give half a guinea to live under one form of government rather than another. It is of no moment to the happiness of an individual.

Quoted in James Boswell, *The Life of Samuel Johnson* (1791) (entry for 31 Mar. 1772)

73 [*Of Oliver Goldsmith's apology in the* London Chronicle *for assaulting Thomas Evans:*] He

has, indeed, done it very well; but it is a foolish thing well done.

Quoted in James Boswell, *The Life of Samuel Johnson* (1791) (entry for 3 Apr. 1773)

74 [*Replying to the question, "What, have you not read it through?":*] No, Sir, do *you* read books *through?*

Quoted in James Boswell, *The Life of Samuel Johnson* (1791) (entry for 19 Apr. 1773)

75 [*Quoting an old college tutor:*] Read over your compositions and where ever you meet with a passage which you think is particularly fine, strike it out.

Quoted in James Boswell, *The Life of Samuel Johnson* (1791) (entry for 30 Apr. 1773)

76 [*Of Lady Diana Beauclerk:*] The woman's a whore, and there's an end on 't.

Quoted in James Boswell, *The Life of Samuel Johnson* (1791) (entry for 7 May 1773)

77 Why, sir, a man grows better humored as he grows older. He improves by experience. When young, he thinks himself of great consequence, and every thing of importance. As he advances in life, he learns to think himself of no consequence, and little things of little importance; and so he becomes more patient, and better pleased.

Quoted in James Boswell, *The Life of Samuel Johnson* (1791) (entry for 14 Sept. 1773)

78 [*Of Thomas Gray:*] He was dull in a new way, and that made many people think him *great.*

Quoted in James Boswell, *The Life of Samuel Johnson* (1791) (entry for 28 Mar. 1775)

79 The greatest part of a writer's time is spent in reading, in order to write: a man will turn over half a library to make one book.

Quoted in James Boswell, *The Life of Samuel Johnson* (1791) (entry for 6 Apr. 1775)

80 Patriotism is the last refuge of a scoundrel.

Quoted in James Boswell, *The Life of Samuel Johnson* (1791) (entry for 7 Apr. 1775)
See Bierce 94

81 Knowledge is of two kinds. We know a subject ourselves, or we know where we can find information upon it.

Quoted in James Boswell, *The Life of Samuel Johnson* (1791) (entry for 18 Apr. 1775)

82 We would all be idle if we could.

Quoted in James Boswell, *The Life of Samuel Johnson* (1791) (entry for 1776)

83 A man should be careful never to tell tales of himself to his own disadvantage. People may be amused and laugh at the time, but they will be remembered, and brought out against him upon some subsequent occasion.

Quoted in James Boswell, *The Life of Samuel Johnson* (1791) (entry for 25 Mar. 1776)

84 No, Sir; to act from pure benevolence is not possible for finite beings. Human benevolence is mingled with vanity, interest, or some other motive.

Quoted in James Boswell, *The Life of Samuel Johnson* (1791) (entry for Apr. 1776)

85 No man but a blockhead ever wrote, except for money.

Quoted in James Boswell, *The Life of Samuel Johnson* (1791) (entry for 5 Apr. 1776)

86 It is better that some should be unhappy, than that none should be happy, which would be the case in a general state of equality.

Quoted in James Boswell, *The Life of Samuel Johnson* (1791) (entry for 7 Apr. 1776)

87 Sir, you have but two topics, yourself and me. I am sick of both.

Quoted in James Boswell, *The Life of Samuel Johnson* (1791) (entry for May 1776)

88 *Olivarii Goldsmith,*
Poetae, Physici, Historici,
Qui nullum fere scribendi genus
Non tetigit,
Nullum quod tetigit non ornavit.
To Oliver Goldsmith, Poet, Naturalist, Historian, who left scarcely any style of writing untouched, and touched nothing that he did not adorn.

Quoted in James Boswell, *The Life of Samuel Johnson* (1791) (entry for 22 June 1776)

89 Depend upon it, Sir, when a man knows he is to be hanged in a fortnight, it concentrates his mind wonderfully.

Quoted in James Boswell, *The Life of Samuel Johnson* (1791) (entry for 19 Sept. 1777)

90 When a man is tired of London, he is tired of life; for there is in London all that life can afford.

Quoted in James Boswell, *The Life of Samuel Johnson* (1791) (entry for 20 Sept. 1777)

91 [*Of the existence of ghosts:*] All argument is against it; but all belief is for it.

Quoted in James Boswell, *The Life of Samuel Johnson* (1791) (entry for 31 Mar. 1778)

92 Johnson had said that he could repeat a complete chapter of "The Natural History of Iceland," from the Danish of *Horrebow,* the whole of which was exactly thus:—"CHAP. LXXII. *Concerning snakes.* There are no snakes to be met with throughout the whole island."

Quoted in James Boswell, *The Life of Samuel Johnson* (1791) (entry for 13 Apr. 1778). *Bartlett's Familiar Quotations* points out that ch. 42 is even shorter: "There are no owls of any kind in the whole island."

93 I am willing to love all mankind, *except an American.*

Quoted in James Boswell, *The Life of Samuel Johnson* (1791) (entry for 15 Apr. 1778)

94 All censure of a man's self is oblique praise. It is in order to show how much he can spare.

Quoted in James Boswell, *The Life of Samuel Johnson* (1791) (entry for 25 Apr. 1778)

95 I am always for getting a boy forward in his learning; for that is a sure good. I would let him at first read *any* English book which happens to engage his attention; because you have done a great deal when you have brought him to have entertainment from a book. He'll get better books afterwards.

Quoted in James Boswell, *The Life of Samuel Johnson* (1791) (entry for 16 Apr. 1779)

96 [*On the Giant's Causeway in Ireland:*] Worth seeing, yes; but not worth going to see.

Quoted in James Boswell, *The Life of Samuel Johnson* (1791) (entry for 12 Oct. 1779)

97 If you are idle, be not solitary; if you are solitary, be not idle.

Quoted in James Boswell, *The Life of Samuel Johnson* (1791) (letter to Boswell, 27 Oct. 1779)
See Robert Burton 8

98 [*To a follower of George Berkeley's philosophy, which held that things exist only insofar as they are perceived by a mind:*] Pray, Sir, don't leave us; for we may perhaps forget to think of you, and then you will cease to exist.

Quoted in James Boswell, *The Life of Samuel Johnson* (1791) (entry for 1780)

99 [*When asked what he considered to be the real value of the Thrale Brewery, which, as executor, he was attempting to sell:*] We are not here to sell a parcel of boilers and vats, but the potentiality of growing rich beyond the dreams of avarice.

Quoted in James Boswell, *The Life of Samuel Johnson* (1791) (entry for 6 Apr. 1781)
See Edward Moore 2

100 [Quotation] is a good thing; there is a community of mind in it. Classical quotation is the *parole* of literary men all over the world.

Quoted in James Boswell, *The Life of Samuel Johnson* (1791) (entry for 8 May 1781)

101 Resolve not to be poor: whatever you have, spend less. Poverty is a great enemy to human happiness; it certainly destroys liberty, and it makes some virtues impracticable, and others extremely difficult.

Quoted in James Boswell, *The Life of Samuel Johnson* (1791) (letter to Boswell, 7 Dec. 1782)

102 It is strange that there should be so little reading in the world, and so much writing. People in general do not willingly read, if they can have any thing else to amuse them.

Quoted in James Boswell, *The Life of Samuel Johnson* (1791) (entry for 1 May 1783)

103 Clear your *mind* of cant.

Quoted in James Boswell, *The Life of Samuel Johnson* (1791) (entry for 15 May 1783)

104 As I know more of mankind I expect less of them, and am ready now to call a man *a good man,* upon easier terms than I was formerly.

Quoted in James Boswell, *The Life of Samuel Johnson* (1791) (entry for Sept. 1783)

105 If a man were to go by chance at the same time with [Edmund] Burke under a shed, to shun a shower, he would say—"this is an extraordinary man."

Quoted in James Boswell, *The Life of Samuel Johnson* (1791) (entry for 15 May 1784)

106 Sir, I have found you an argument; but I am not obliged to find you an understanding.

Quoted in James Boswell, *The Life of Samuel Johnson* (1791) (entry for June 1784)
See Oliver Goldsmith 5

107 [*On hearing a violin solo:*] Difficult do you call it, Sir? I wish it were impossible.

Quoted in William Seward, *Supplement to the Anecdotes of Distinguished Persons* (1797)

108 What is written without effort is in general read without pleasure.

Quoted in William Seward, *Biographia* (1799)

109 [*On overindulgence in drink, to the extent of becoming a beast:*] He who makes a *beast* of himself gets rid of the pain of being a man.

Quoted in Percival Stockdale, *The Memoirs of the Life, and Writings of Percival Stockdale* (1809)

110 [*To two women who commended him on his omission of vulgar words from his* Dictionary of the English Language:] What! my dears! then you have been looking for them?

Quoted in Henry G. Beste, *Personal and Literary Memorials* (1829). A very similar anecdote about Johnson, with the punch line "I find, however, that you have been looking for them," appeared in *Gentleman's Magazine,* Apr. 1785.

Hanns Johst
German playwright, 1890–1978

1 *Wenn ich Kultur höre . . . entsichere ich meinen Browning.*
When I hear the word "culture" . . . I reach for my gun.

Schlageter act 1, sc. 1 (1933). Frequently attributed to Hermann Goering.

Al Jolson (Asa Yoelson)
Russian-born U.S. singer and actor, 1886–1950

1 California, here I come right back where I started from.

"California Here I Come" (song) (1924). Cowritten with Buddy DeSylva and Joseph Meyer.

2 Wait a minute, wait a minute. You ain't heard nothin' yet!

The Jazz Singer (motion picture) (1927). This ad-libbed line is celebrated because it constituted the first spoken words in the first prominent talking motion picture. Jolson had earlier recorded a song titled "You Ain't Heard Nothing Yet" (1919, written by Gus Kahn and Buddy DeSylva). Nigel Rees notes in *Cassell Companion to Quotations:* "Martin Abramson in *The Real Story of Al Jolson* (1950) suggests that Jolson had also uttered the slogan in San Francisco as long before as 1906. Interrupted by noise from a building site across the road from a café in which he was performing, Jolson had shouted, 'You think that's noise—you ain't heard nuttin' yet!' Listening to the film soundtrack makes it clear that Jolson did not add 'folks' at the end of his mighty line, as Bartlett . . . and the [*Oxford Dictionary of Quotations*] say he did."

3 Sonny Boy.

Title of song (1928). Cowritten with Buddy DeSylva, Lew Brown, and Ray Henderson.

Booker T. Jones
U.S. rhythm and blues musician, 1944–

1 If it wasn't for bad luck, I wouldn't have no luck at all.

"Born Under a Bad Sign" (song) (1967). Cowritten with William Bell.

James Jones
U.S. novelist, 1921–1977

1 They shouldnt teach their immigrants' kids all about democracy unless they mean to let them have a little of it, it ony makes for trouble. Me and the United States is disassociating our alliance as of right now, until the United States can find time to read its own textbooks a little.

From Here to Eternity ch. 39 (1951)

John Paul Jones (John Paul)
U.S. admiral, 1747–1792

1 I wish to have no Connection with any Ship that does not sail *fast,* for I intend to go *in harm's way.*

Letter to Le Ray de Chaumont, 16 Nov. 1778

2 [*Remark during Battle off Flamborough Head, 23 Sept. 1779:*] I have not yet begun to fight.

Quoted in John Henry Sherburne, *Life and Character of the Chevalier John Paul Jones* (1825). According to *Respectfully Quoted,* ed. Suzy Platt: "The exact wording of his reply is uncertain, and several accounts exist. The standard version . . . is from an account of the engagement by one of Jones's officers, First Lieutenant Richard Dale."

Mother Jones (Mary Harris Jones)
Irish-born U.S. labor organizer, 1830–1930

1 Pray for the dead and fight like hell for the living!

The Autobiography of Mother Jones ch. 6 (1925)

T. A. D. Jones
U.S. football coach, 1887–1957

1 [*To Yale football players preparing for game against Harvard, 24 Nov. 1923:*] Gentlemen, you are now going out to play football against Harvard. Never again in your whole life will you do anything so important.

Quoted in Tim Cohane, *The Yale Football Story* (1951)

Tom Jones
U.S. songwriter, 1928–

1 Try to remember the kind of September When life was slow and oh so mellow.

"Try to Remember" (song) (1960)

2 Deep in December it's nice to remember The fire of September that made us mellow Deep in December our hearts should remember And follow . . .

"Try to Remember" (song) (1960)

William Jones
British philologist and jurist, 1746–1794

1 The law is a jealous science.

Letter to Mr. Howard, 4 Oct. 1774
See Story 1

2 The Sanskrit language, whatever be its antiquity, is of a wonderful structure; more perfect than the Greek, more copious than the Latin, and more exquisitely refined than either, yet bearing to both of them a stronger affinity, both in the roots of verbs, and in the forms of grammar, than could possibly have been produced by accident; so strong, indeed, that no philologer could examine them all three, without believing them to have sprung from some common source, which, perhaps, no longer exists.

"The Third Anniversary Discourse, on the Hindus" (1786)

William Jones
U.S. politician, 1753–1822

1 The Continental ship Providence, now lying at Boston, is bound on a short cruise, immediately; a few good men are wanted to make up her complement.

Providence Gazette, 20 Mar. 1779

Erica Jong
U.S. writer, 1942–

1 Everyone has talent. What is rare is the courage to follow the talent to the dark place where it leads.

"The Artist as Housewife" (1972)

2 Fear of Flying.

Title of book (1973)

3 Bigamy is having one husband too many. Monogamy is the same.

Fear of Flying epigraph (1973). Jong was quoting an anonymous source here. "They say bigamy means one wife too many; but so does monogamy sometimes" appeared in Robert Webster Jones, *Light Interviews with Shades* (1922).

4 There were 117 psychoanalysts on the Pan Am flight to Vienna and I'd been treated by at least six of them.

Fear of Flying ch. 1 (1973)

5 The zipless fuck is absolutely pure. It is free of ulterior motives. There is no power game. The man is not "taking" and the woman is not "giving." No one is attempting to cuckold a husband or humiliate a wife. No one is out to prove anything or get anything out of anyone. The zipless fuck is the purest thing there is. And it is rarer than the unicorn.

Fear of Flying ch. 1 (1973). Jong explains: "Zipless because when you come together zippers fell away like petals."

6 Gossip is the opiate of the oppressed.

Fear of Flying ch. 6 (1973)

7 Coupling doesn't always have to do with sex. . . . Two people holding each other up like flying buttresses. Two people depending on each other and babying each other and defending each other against the world outside. Sometimes it was worth all the disadvantages of marriage just to have that: one friend in an indifferent world.

Fear of Flying ch. 10 (1973)

8 Men and women, women and men. It will never work.

Fear of Flying ch. 16 (1973)

Ben Jonson
English playwright and poet, ca. 1573–1637

1 Queen and huntress, chaste and fair,
Now the sun is laid to sleep,
Seated in thy silver chair,
State in wonted manner keep:
Hesperus entreats thy light,
Goddess, excellently bright.

Cynthia's Revels act 5, sc. 3 (1600)

2 Still to be neat, still to be drest,
As you were going to a feast.

Epicene act 1, sc. 1 (1609)

3 Such sweet neglect more taketh me,
Than all the adulteries of art;
They strike mine eyes, but not my heart.

Epicene act 1, sc. 1 (1609)

4 Fortune, that favors fools.

The Alchemist prologue (1610)

5 Rest in soft peace, and, asked, say here doth lie
Ben Jonson his best piece of poetry.

"On My First Son" l. 9 (1616)

6 Drink to me only with thine eyes,
And I will pledge with mine;
Or leave a kiss but in the cup,
And I'll not look for wine.

"To Celia" l. 1 (1616). The following appears in Philostratus (ca. 181–250), *Letter 24:* "Drink to me with your eyes alone. . . . And if you will, take the cup to your lips and fill it with kisses, and give it to me."

7 [*On Shakespeare's portrait:*]
This figure that thou here seest put,
It was for gentle Shakespeare cut,
Wherein the graver had a strife
With Nature, to out-do the life.

First Folio Shakespeare "To the Reader" l. 1 (1623)

8 [*On William Shakespeare:*]
Reader, look
Not on his picture, but his book.

First Folio Shakespeare "To the Reader" l. 9 (1623)

9 Thou hadst small Latin, and less Greek.

"To the Memory of My Beloved, the Author, Mr. William Shakespeare" l. 31 (1623)

10 He was not of an age, but for all time!

"To the Memory of My Beloved, the Author, Mr. William Shakespeare" l. 38 (1623)

11 Sweet Swan of Avon!

"To the Memory of My Beloved, the Author, Mr. William Shakespeare" l. 66 (1623)

Janis Joplin

U.S. rock singer, 1943–1970

1 Down on me, down on me
Looks like everyone in this whole round world
Is down on me.

"Down on Me" (song) (1967)

2 Lord, won't you buy me a Mercedes-Benz?
My friends all drive Porsches
I must make amends.

"Mercedes-Benz" (song) (1970)

3 Get It While You Can.

Title of song (1971)

4 [*Of Dwight Eisenhower, whose death pushed Joplin off the cover of* Newsweek:] Fourteen heart attacks and he had to die in my week.

Quoted in *New Music Express,* 12 Apr. 1969

5 On stage I make love to twenty-five thousand people; then I go home alone.

Quoted in Barbara Rowes, *The Book of Quotes* (1979)

Barbara C. Jordan

U.S. politician, 1936–1996

1 Earlier today we heard the beginning of the Preamble to the Constitution of the United States. "We the people." It is a very eloquent beginning. But, when that document was completed on the 17th of September in 1787, I was not included in that "We, the people." I felt somehow for many years that George Washington and Alexander Hamilton just left me out by mistake. But, through the process of amendment, interpretation, and court decision, I have finally been included in "We, the people."

Statement before House Judiciary Committee considering impeachment of Richard Nixon, 25 July 1974

See Constitution of the United States 1

2 My faith in the Constitution is whole, it is complete, it is total. I am not going to sit here and be an idle spectator to the diminution, the subversion, the destruction of the Constitution.

Statement before House Judiciary Committee considering impeachment of Richard Nixon, 25 July 1974

Henry Jordan

U.S. football player, 1935–1977

1 [*Of coach Vince Lombardi:*] The coach is very fair. He treats us all like dogs.

Quoted in *Boston Globe,* 23 Dec. 1965

Louis Jordan

U.S. rhythm and blues musician, 1908–1975

1 Is You or Is You Ain't My Baby?

Title of song (1943). Cowritten with Billy Austin.

2 Let the Good Times Roll.

Title of song (1946). Jordan popularized this expression, but Barry Popik has unearthed uses of it or variants such as "Let the good times roll in upon us" as early as the *Atlanta Constitution,* 4 Sept. 1898.

Joseph II

Holy Roman emperor, 1741–1790

1 [*Of Mozart's opera,* The Escape from the Seraglio, *1782:*] Too beautiful for our ears and an extraordinary number of notes, dear Mozart.

Quoted in Franz Xavier Niemetschek, *Life of Mozart* (1798). According to Niemetschek, Mozart replied, "Just as many, Your Majesty, as are necessary."

Chief Joseph

Native American chief, ca. 1840–1904

1 If you tie up a horse to a stake, do you expect he will grow fat? If you pen an Indian up on a small spot of earth, and compel him to stay there, he will not be contented, nor will he grow and prosper. I have asked some of the great white chiefs where they get their authority to say to the Indian that he shall stay in one place, while he sees white men going where they please. They can not tell me.

North American Review, Apr. 1879

2 [*Speech of surrender at end of Nez Percé War, 5 Oct. 1877:*] I am tired of fighting. . . . I want to have time to look for my children and see how

many of them I can find. Maybe I shall find them among the dead.

Quoted in Herbert J. Spinden, *The Nez Percé Indians* (1908)

3 [*Statement to General Miles at end of Nez Percé War, 5 Oct. 1877:*] From where the sun now stands I will fight no more.

Quoted in Herbert J. Spinden, *The Nez Percé Indians* (1908)

Jenny Joseph
English poet, 1932–2018

1 When I am an old woman I shall wear purple
  With a red hat which doesn't go, and doesn't
    suit me.
  And I shall spend my pension on brandy and
    summer gloves
  And satin sandals, and say we've no money for
    butter.

"Warning" l. 1 (1965)

Francis de Jouvenot
French playwright, fl. 1888

1 *Fin de Siècle.*
  End of Century.

Title of play (1888). Coauthored with H. Micard.

William N. "Bill" Joy
U.S. computer scientist, 1954–

1 The experiences of the atomic scientists clearly show the need to take personal responsibility, the danger that things will move too fast, and the way in which a process can take on a life of its own. We can, as they did, create insurmountable problems in almost no time flat. We must do more thinking up front if we are not to be similarly surprised and shocked by the consequences of our inventions.

"Why the Future Doesn't Need Us: Our Most Powerful 21st-Century Technologies—Robotics, Genetic Engineering, and Nanotech—Are Threatening to Make Humans an Endangered Species," *Wired,* Apr. 2000

James Joyce
Irish writer, 1882–1941

1 Yes, the newspapers were right: snow was general all over Ireland. It was falling on every part of the dark central plain, on the treeless

hills, falling softly upon the Bog of Allen and, further westward, softly falling into the dark mutinous Shannon waves.

Dubliners "The Dead" (1914)

2 His soul swooned slowly as he heard the snow falling faintly through the universe and faintly falling, like the descent of their last end, upon all the living and the dead.

Dubliners "The Dead" (1914)

3 He looked down the slope and, at the base, in the shadow of the wall of the Park, he saw some human figures lying. Those venal and furtive loves filled him with despair. He gnawed the rectitude of his life; he felt that he had been outcast from life's feast.

Dubliners "A Painful Case" (1914)

4 Once upon a time and a very good time it was there was a moocow coming down along the road and this moocow that was down along the road met a nicens little boy named baby tuckoo.

A Portrait of the Artist as a Young Man ch. 1 (1916)

5 Ireland is the old sow that eats her farrow.

A Portrait of the Artist as a Young Man ch. 5 (1916)

6 Pity is the feeling which arrests the mind in the presence of whatsoever is grave and constant in human sufferings and unites it with the human sufferer. Terror is the feeling which arrests the mind in the presence of whatsoever is grave and constant in human sufferings and unites it with the secret cause.

A Portrait of the Artist as a Young Man ch. 5 (1916)

7 The artist, like the God of the creation, remains within or behind or beyond or above his

handiwork, invisible, refined out of existence, indifferent, paring his fingernails.

A Portrait of the Artist as a Young Man ch. 5 (1916). The character Lynch responds to this statement of Stephen Dedalus with the comment, "Trying to refine them also out of existence."

8 [*Upon being asked whether he intended to become a Protestant:*] I said that I had lost the faith, Stephen answered, but not that I had lost self-respect. What kind of liberation would that be to forsake an absurdity which is logical and coherent and to embrace one which is illogical and incoherent?

A Portrait of the Artist as a Young Man ch. 5 (1916)

9 I will try to express myself in some mode of life or art as freely as I can and as wholly as I can, using for my defense the only arms I allow myself to use, silence, exile, and cunning.

A Portrait of the Artist as a Young Man ch. 5 (1916)

10 Mother is putting my new secondhand clothes in order. She prays now, she says, that I may learn in my own life and away from home and friends what the heart is and what it feels. Amen. So be it.

A Portrait of the Artist as a Young Man ch. 5 (1916)

11 Welcome, O life! I go to encounter for the millionth time the reality of experience and to forge in the smithy of my soul the uncreated conscience of my race.

A Portrait of the Artist as a Young Man ch. 5 (1916)

12 Old father, old artificer, stand me now and ever in good stead.

A Portrait of the Artist as a Young Man ch. 5 (1916)

13 Stately, plump Buck Mulligan came from the stairhead, bearing a bowl of lather on which a mirror and a razor lay crossed.

Ulysses (1922)

14 The snotgreen sea. The scrotumtightening sea.

Ulysses (1922)

15 It is a symbol of Irish art. The cracked lookingglass of a servant.

Ulysses (1922)

16 Agenbite of inwit. Conscience.

Ulysses (1922). *Ayenbite of Inwyt* was the title of a fourteenth-century treatise by Dan Michel of Northgate.

17 History, Stephen said, is a nightmare from which I am trying to awake.

Ulysses (1922)

18 Lawn Tennyson, gentleman poet.

Ulysses (1922)

19 A man of genius makes no mistakes. His errors are volitional and are the portals of discovery.

Ulysses (1922)

20 Love loves to love love.

Ulysses (1922)

21 Greater love than this, he said, no man hath that a man lay down his wife for his friend.

Ulysses (1922)
See Bible 326

22 He kissed me under the Moorish wall and I thought well as well him as another and then I asked him with my eyes to ask again yes and then he asked me would I yes to say yes my mountain flower and first I put my arms around him yes and drew him down to me so he could feel my breasts all perfume yes and his heart was going like mad and yes I said yes I will Yes.

Ulysses (1922)

23 riverrun, past Eve and Adam's, from swerve of shore to bend of bay, brings us by a commodious vicus of recirculation back to Howth Castle and Environs.

Finnegans Wake pt. 1 (1939)

24 Three quarks for Muster Mark!
Sure he hasn't got much of a bark
And sure any he has it's all beside the mark.

Finnegans Wake pt. 2 (1939). Physicist Murray Gell-Mann was influenced by this line when in 1963 he chose the name *quark* to denote a group of subatomic particles.

25 By an epiphany he meant a sudden spiritual manifestation, whether in vulgarity of speech or of gesture or in a memorable phase of the mind itself.

Stephen Hero ch. 25 (1944)

26 The demand that I make of my reader is that he should devote his whole life to reading my works.

Quoted in *Harper's Magazine*, Oct. 1931

27 When a young man came up to him in Zurich and said, "May I kiss the hand that wrote *Ulysses?*" Joyce replied, somewhat like King Lear, "No, it did lots of other things too."
Quoted in Richard Ellmann, *James Joyce* (1959)

28 I want to give a picture [in *Ulysses*] of Dublin so complete that if the city one day suddenly disappeared from the earth it could be reconstructed out of my book.
Quoted in Frank Budgen, *James Joyce and the Making of* Ulysses, *and Other Writings* (1960)

29 Why all this fuss and bother about the mystery of the unconscious? What about the mystery of the conscious? What do they know about that?
Quoted in Frank Budgen, *James Joyce and the Making of* Ulysses, *and Other Writings* (1960)

Benito Juárez
Mexican president, 1806–1872

1 *Entre los individuos, como entre las Naciones, el respeto al derecho ajeno es la paz.*
Among individuals, as among nations, respect for the rights of others is peace.
Manifesto, 15 July 1867

Jack Judge
English entertainer, 1878–1938

1 It's a long way to Tipperary,
It's a long way to go;
It's a long way to Tipperary,
To the sweetest girl I know!
"It's a Long Way to Tipperary" (song) (1912)

Julian the Apostate (Flavius Claudius Julianus)
Roman emperor, 331–363

1 [*Traditional version of his dying words:*] Vicisti, Galilaee.
You have won, Galilean.
Attributed in Theodoret, *Ecclesiastical History* (ca. 450). According to the *Oxford Dictionary of Quotations,* this is actually "a late embellishment of Theodoret."

Julian of Norwich
English anchoress, ca. 1342–ca. 1413

1 Sin is behovely, but all shall be well and all shall be well and all manner of thing shall be well.
Revelations of Divine Love ch. 27 (ca. 1380)
See T. S. Eliot 125

Carl Gustav Jung
Swiss psychologist, 1875–1961

1 The great problems of life, including of course sex, are always related to the primordial images of the collective unconscious. These images are balancing and compensating factors that correspond to the problems which life confronts us with in reality. This is not matter for astonishment, since these images are deposits of thousands of years of experience of the struggle for existence and for adaptation.
Psychological Types ch. 5 (1921)

2 Among all my patients in the second half of life—that is to say, over thirty-five—there has not been one whose problem in the last resort was not that of finding a religious outlook on life.
"Psychotherapists or the Clergy" (1932)

3 The dream is a little hidden door in the innermost and most secret recesses of the soul, opening into that cosmic night which was psyche long before there was any ego-consciousness, and which will remain psyche no matter how far our ego-consciousness extends.
"The Meaning of Psychology for Modern Man" (1933)

4 The contents of the collective unconscious . . . are known as *archetypes.*
Eranos Jahrbuch (1934)

5 As far as we can discern, the sole purpose of human existence is to kindle a light of meaning in the darkness of mere being.
Memories, Dreams, Reflections ch. 11 (1962)

6 Every form of addiction is bad, no matter whether the narcotic be alcohol or morphine or idealism.
Memories, Dreams, Reflections ch. 12 (1962)

Junius

English pseudonymous author, fl. 1770

1 The liberty of the press is the *Palladium* of all the civil, political, and religious rights of an Englishman.

The Letters of Junius "Dedication to the English Nation" (1772)

Donald Justice

U.S. poet, 1925–2004

1 Men at forty
Learn to close softly
The doors to rooms they will not be
Coming back to.

"Men at Forty" l. 1 (1967)

Justinian

Byzantine emperor, 483–565

1 Justice is the constant and perpetual wish to render to every one his due.

Institutes bk. 1, ch. 1, para. 1

Juvenal

Roman satirist, ca. 60–ca. 130

1 *Omnia Romae cum pretio.*
Everything in Rome has its price.

Satires no. 3, l. 183

2 *Rara avis in terris nigroque simillima cycno.*
A rare bird on earth, comparable to a black swan.

Satires no. 6, l. 165

3 *Sed quis custodiet ipsos custodes?*
But who is to guard the guards themselves?

Satires no. 6, l. 347

4 *Tenet insanabile multos*
Scribendi cacoethes et aegro in corde senescit.
Many suffer from the incurable disease of writing, and it becomes chronic in their sick minds.

Satires no. 7, l. 51

5 *Duas tantum res anxius optat,*
Panem et circenses.
Only two things does he [the modern citizen] anxiously wish for—bread and circuses.

Satires no. 10, l. 80

6 *Mens sana in corpore sano.*
A sound mind in a sound body.

Satires no. 10, l. 356

7 *Maxima debetur puero reverentia.*
The greatest respect is due the child.

Satires no. 14, l. 47

Pauline Kael

U.S. film critic, 1919–2001

1 The words "Kiss Kiss Bang Bang," which I
saw on an Italian movie poster, are perhaps
the briefest statement imaginable of the basic
appeal of movies.
Kiss Kiss Bang Bang "A Note on the Title" (1968)
See Powdermaker 1

2 [*Remark in address to Modern Language
Association, Dec. 1972, after Richard Nixon's
landslide election win:*] I live in a rather special
world. I only know one person who voted for
Nixon. Where they are I don't know. They're
outside my ken. But sometimes when I'm in a
theater I can feel them.
Quoted in *N.Y. Times*, 28 Dec. 1972

Colin Kaepernick

U.S. football player, 1987–

1 I am not going to stand up to show pride in a
flag for a country that oppresses black people
and people of color.
Interview by NFL Media, 26 Aug. 2016

Franz Kafka

Czech novelist, 1883–1924

1 A book must be the ax for the frozen sea
within us.
Letter to Oskar Pollak, 27 Jan. 1904

2 Everyone strives to reach the Law.
"Before the Law" (1914) (translation by Willa and
Edwin Muir)

3 No one else could ever be admitted here, since
this gate was made only for you. I am now
going to shut it.
"Before the Law" (1914) (translation by Willa and
Edwin Muir)

4 As Gregor Samsa awoke one morning from
uneasy dreams he found himself transformed
in his bed into a gigantic insect.
The Metamorphosis ch. 1 (1915) (translation by Willa
and Edwin Muir)

5 The Messiah will come only when he is no
longer necessary, he will come only one day
after his arrival, he will not come on the last
day, but on the last day of all.
"The Third Notebook," 4 Dec. 1917 (translation by
Ernst Kaiser and Eithne Wilkins)

6 In the struggle between yourself and the world
second the world.
"The Third Notebook," 8 Dec. 1917 (translation by
Ernst Kaiser and Eithne Wilkins)

7 Only our concept of Time makes it possible
for us to speak of the Day of Judgment by
that name; in reality it is a summary court in
perpetual session.
"Reflections on Sin, Pain, Hope, and the True Way"
(1917–1920)

8 Someone must have traduced Joseph K., for
without having done anything wrong he was
arrested one fine morning.
The Trial ch. 1 (1925) (translation by Willa and Edwin
Muir)

9 You may object that it is not a trial at all; you
are quite right, for it is only a trial if I recognize
it as such.
The Trial ch. 2 (1925) (translation by Willa and Edwin
Muir)

10 It's often better to be in chains than to be free.
The Trial ch. 8 (1925) (translation by Willa and Edwin
Muir)

11 "Like a dog!" he said: it was as if the shame of it
must outlive him.
The Trial ch. 10 (1925) (translation by Willa and
Edwin Muir)

12 This village belongs to the Castle, and whoever
lives here or passes the night here does so in a
manner of speaking in the Castle itself. Nobody
may do that without the Count's permission.
The Castle ch. 1 (1926) (translation by Willa and
Edwin Muir)

Gus Kahn
U.S. songwriter, 1886–1941

1 There's nothing surer,
  The rich get rich and the poor get children,
  In the meantime,
  In between time,
  Ain't we got fun?
  "Ain't We Got Fun" (song) (1920). Cowritten with
  Raymond B. Egan.
  See Bible 264; Merton 4; Modern Proverbs 75

2 Nothing could be finer
  Than to be in Carolina
  In the morning.
  "Carolina in the Morning" (song) (1922)

3 I'll See You in My Dreams.
  Title of song (1924)

4 It Had to Be You.
  Title of song (1924)

5 Yes, Sir, that's my baby,
  No, Sir, don't mean "maybe,"
  Yes, Sir, that's my baby now.
  "Yes, Sir! That's My Baby" (song) (1925)

6 Love Me or Leave Me.
  Title of song (1928)
  See Dorothy Parker 16; Political Slogans 3

7 Makin' Whoopee.
  Title of song (1928)

Daniel Kahneman
Israeli-born U.S. psychologist and economist,
1934–

1 Nothing in life is as important as you think it is
  when you are thinking about it.
  Thinking, Fast and Slow ch. 38 (2011)

Kālidāsa
Indian playwright and poet, fl. ca. 400

1 We have watered the trees that blossom in the
  summer-time. Now let's sprinkle those whose
  flowering-time is past. That will be a better
  deed because we shall not be working for a
  reward.
  Shakuntala act 1 (translation by Arthur W. Ryder)

Wendy Kaminer
U.S. lawyer and writer, 1949–

1 Only people who die very young learn all they
  really need to know in kindergarten.
  I'm Dysfunctional, You're Dysfunctional introduction
  (1992). Kaminer is referring to Robert Fulghum's
  1988 book, *All I Really Need to Know I Learned in
  Kindergarten.*

Wassily Kandinsky
Russian painter, 1866–1944

1 Every work of art is the child of its age and, in
  many cases, the mother of our emotions.
  Concerning the Spiritual in Art pt. 1 (1911)

Helen Kane
U.S. singer, 1903–1966

1 Boop-boop-a-doop.
  "That's My Weakness Now" (song) (1928). Kane
  interpolated these syllables while singing "That's My
  Weakness Now" in 1928. Beginning in 1930 they
  were used as the catchphrase of cartoon character
  Betty Boop, who was modeled on Kane.

Immanuel Kant
German philosopher, 1724–1804

1 Out of the crooked timber of humanity no
  straight thing can ever be made.
  The Idea of a Universal History proposition 6 (1784)

2 There is nothing it is possible to think of
  anywhere in the world, or indeed anything at all
  outside it, that can be held to be good without
  limitation, excepting only a *good will.*
  Groundwork for the Metaphysics of Morals sec. 1 (1785)
  (translation by Allen W. Wood)

3 I ought never to conduct myself except so *that I
  could also will that my maxim become a universal
  law.*
  Groundwork for the Metaphysics of Morals sec. 1 (1785)
  (translation by Allen W. Wood)

4 Finally, there is one imperative that, without
  being grounded on any other aim to be
  achieved through a certain course of conduct
  as its condition, commands this conduct
  immediately. This imperative is *categorical.* . . .
  This imperative may be called that *of morality.*
  Groundwork for the Metaphysics of Morals sec. 2 (1785)
  (translation by Allen W. Wood)

5 Act so that you use humanity, as much in your own person as in the person of every other, always at the same time as end and never merely as means.

Groundwork for the Metaphysics of Morals sec. 2 (1785) (translation by Allen W. Wood)

6 Two things fill the mind with ever new and increasing admiration and awe, the oftener and more steadily we reflect on them: the starry heavens above me and the moral law within me.

Critique of Practical Reason conclusion (1788) (translation by Lewis White Beck)

Alphonse Karr

French novelist and journalist, 1808–1890

1 *Si l'on veut abolir la peine de mort en ce cas, que MM. les assassins commencent.*

If the death penalty is to be abolished, let those gentlemen, the murderers, do it first.

Les Guêpes, Jan. 1849

2 *Plus ça change, plus c'est la même chose.*

The more things change, the more they remain the same.

Les Guêpes, July 1848

Beatrice Kaufman

U.S. writer, 1895–1945

1 I've been poor and I've been rich. Rich is better!

Quoted in *Wash. Post,* 12 May 1937. This quotation is invariably attributed to Sophie Tucker, but the usage by Kaufman occurs years before any evidence linking it to Tucker.

Bel Kaufman

German-born U.S. writer and teacher, 1911–2014

1 Up the Down Staircase.

Title of book (1965)

George S. Kaufman

U.S. playwright, 1889–1961

1 We're in the widget business.

Beggar on Horseback pt. 1 (1924). Coauthored with Marc Connelly. Appears to be the origin of the nonsense-word *widget.*

2 Merrily We Roll Along.

Title of song (1931)

3 The Man Who Came to Dinner.

Title of play (1939). Coauthored with Moss Hart.

4 Satire is something that closes on Saturday night.

Quoted in *Wash. Post,* 26 July 1937
See Coward 15

5 Everything I've ever said will be credited to Dorothy Parker.

Quoted in Scott Meredith, *George S. Kaufman and His Friends* (1974)

Irving R. Kaufman

U.S. judge, 1910–1992

1 Your crime is worse than murder. . . . Who knows but that millions more of innocent people may pay the price of your treason. Indeed, by your betrayal you undoubtedly have altered the course of history to the disadvantage of our country.

Remarks sentencing Julius and Ethel Rosenberg to death for espionage of atomic bomb secrets, New York, N.Y., 5 Apr. 1951

Kenneth D. Kaunda

Zambian president, 1924–

1 Let the West have its Technology and Asia its Mysticism! Africa's gift to world culture must be in the realm of Human Relationships.

A Humanist in Africa ch. 1 (1966)

Brett Kavanaugh

U.S. judge, 1965–

1 This whole two-week effort has been a calculated and orchestrated political hit, fueled with . . . revenge on behalf of the Clintons.

U.S. Senate Judiciary Committee testimony on his nomination to the Supreme Court, 27 Sept. 2018

2 I liked beer. I still like beer. But I did not drink beer to the point of blacking out and I never sexually assaulted anyone.

U.S. Senate Judiciary Committee testimony on his nomination to the Supreme Court, 27 Sept. 2018

Yasunari Kawabata

Japanese writer, 1899–1972

1 The train came out of the long tunnel into the snow country. The earth lay white under the night sky.

Snow Country pt. 1 (1947) (translation by Edward G. Seidensticker)

Alan Kay

U.S. computer scientist, 1940–

1 [*Remark at meeting between Palo Alto Research Center scientists and Xerox planners, 1971:*] The best way to predict the future is to invent it.

Quoted in *InfoWorld,* 26 Apr. 1982

Susanna Kaysen

U.S. writer, 1948–

1 This time I read the title of the painting: *Girl Interrupted at Her Music.* Interrupted at her music: as my life had been, interrupted in the music of being seventeen, as her life had been, snatched and fixed on canvas: one moment made to stand still and to stand for all the other moments, whatever they would be or might have been. What life can recover from that?

Girl, Interrupted (1993)

Nikos Kazantzakis

Greek writer, 1883–1957

1 How simple and frugal a thing is happiness: a glass of wine, a roast chestnut, a wretched little brazier, the sound of the sea. . . . All that is required to feel that here and now is happiness is a simple, frugal heart.

Zorba the Greek ch. 7 (1946) (translation by Carl Wildman)

2 "Life is trouble," Zorba continued. "Death, no. To live—do you know what that means? To undo your belt and look for trouble!"

Zorba the Greek ch. 8 (1946) (translation by Carl Wildman)

Bil Keane

U.S. cartoonist, 1922–2011

1 Yesterday's the past, tomorrow's the future, but today is a GIFT. That's why it's called the present.

The Family Circus (comic strip), 31 Aug. 1994

John Keats

English poet, 1795–1821

1 Much have I travelled in the realms of gold.

"On First Looking into Chapman's Homer" l. 1 (1817)

2 Oft of one wide expanse had I been told
That deep-brow'd Homer ruled as his demesne;
Yet did I never breathe its pure serene
Till I heard Chapman speak out loud and bold.

"On First Looking into Chapman's Homer" l. 5 (1817)

3 Then felt I like some watcher of the skies
When a new planet swims into his ken;
Or like stout Cortez when with eagle eyes
He stared at the Pacific—and all his men
Looked at each other with a wild surmise—
Silent, upon a peak in Darien.

"On First Looking into Chapman's Homer" l. 9 (1817)

4 To one who has been long in city pent,
'Tis very sweet to look into the fair
And open face of heaven.

"To One Who Has Been Long in City Pent" l. 1 (1817)
See Milton 40

5 I am certain of nothing but the holiness of the heart's affections and the truth of imagination—what the imagination seizes as beauty must be truth—whether it existed before or not.

Letter to Benjamin Bailey, 22 Nov. 1817
See George Herbert 3; Keats 16

6 At once it struck me, what quality went to form a Man of Achievement especially in Literature & which Shakespeare possessed so enormously—I mean *Negative Capability,* that is, when man is capable of being in uncertainties, Mysteries, doubts, without any irritable reaching after fact & reason.

Letter to George and Thomas Keats, 21 Dec. 1817

7 When I have fears that I may cease to be
Before my pen has gleaned my teeming brain.

"When I Have Fears" l. 1 (written 1818)

8 There is not a fiercer hell than the failure in a great object.

Endymion preface (1818)

9 A thing of beauty is a joy for ever:
Its loveliness increases; it will never
Pass into nothingness; but still will keep
A bower quiet for us, and a sleep

Full of sweet dreams, and health, and quiet
    breathing.
Endymion bk. 1, l. 1 (1818)

10 If poetry comes not as naturally as the leaves to
a tree it had better not come at all.
Letter to John Taylor, 27 Feb. 1818

11 I think I shall be among the English Poets after
my death.
Letter to George and Georgiana Keats, 14 Oct. 1818

12 Call the world if you please "The vale of soul-
making."
Letter to George and Georgiana Keats, 21 Apr. 1819

13 Oh, what can ail thee knight-at-arms,
Alone and palely loitering?
"La Belle Dame Sans Merci" l. 1 (1820)

14 I saw pale kings and princes too,
Pale warriors, death-pale were they all;
They cried—"La Belle Dame sans Merci
Hath thee in thrall!"
"La Belle Dame Sans Merci" l. 37 (1820)

15 Heard melodies are sweet, but those unheard
Are sweeter; therefore, ye soft pipes, play on;
Not to the sensual ear, but, more endeared,
Pipe to the spirit ditties of no tone.
"Ode on a Grecian Urn" l. 11 (1820)

16 When old age shall this generation waste,
Thou shalt remain, in midst of other woe
Than ours, a friend to man, to whom thou
    say'st,
"Beauty is truth, truth beauty,"—that is all
Ye know on earth, and all ye need to know.
"Ode on a Grecian Urn" l. 46 (1820)
See George Herbert 3; Keats 5

17 She dwells with Beauty—Beauty that must die;
And Joy, whose hand is ever at his lips
Bidding adieu.
"Ode on Melancholy" l. 21 (1820)

18 Not charioted by Bacchus and his pards,
But on the viewless wings of Poesy,
Though the dull brain perplexes and retards:
Already with thee! tender is the night,
And haply the Queen-Moon is on her throne.
"Ode to a Nightingale" l. 32 (1820)

19 Thou wast not born for death, immortal bird!
No hungry generations tread thee down;
The voice I hear this passing night was heard

In ancient days by emperor and clown:
Perhaps the self-same song that found a path
Through the sad heart of Ruth, when, sick for
    home,
She stood in tears amid the alien corn;
The same that oft-times hath
Charmed magic casements, opening on the
    foam
Of perilous seas, in faery lands forlorn.
"Ode to a Nightingale" l. 61 (1820)

20 Season of mists and mellow fruitfulness,
Close bosom-friend of the maturing sun;
Conspiring with him how to load and bless
With fruit the vines that round the thatch-eaves
    run.
"To Autumn" l. 1 (1820)

21 Where are the songs of Spring? Ay, where are
    they?
Think not of them, thou hast thy music too.
"To Autumn" l. 23 (1820)

22 "If I should die," said I to myself, "I have left no
immortal work behind me—nothing to make
my friends proud of my memory—but I have
loved the principle of beauty in all things, and
if I had had time I would have made myself
remembered."
Letter to Fanny Brawne, ca. Feb. 1820

23 I always made an awkward bow.
Letter to Charles Armitage Brown, 30 Nov. 1820

24 Among the many things he [Keats] has
requested of me to-night, this is the principal
one,—that on his grave-stone shall be this,—
HERE LIES ONE WHOSE NAME WAS WRIT IN WATER.
John Keats, reported in Joseph Severn, Letter to
Charles Armitage Brown, 14 Feb. 1821. Keats is
thought to have been inspired by a line in Francis
Beaumont and John Fletcher's 1620 play *Philaster*:
"All your better deeds / Shall be in water writ."
See Shakespeare 453

John Keble
English clergyman, 1792–1866

1 The trivial round, the common task,
Would furnish all we ought to ask.
The Christian Year "Morning" (1827)

"Wee Willie" Keeler (William Henry O'Kelleher)

U.S. baseball player, 1872–1923

1 Hit 'em where they ain't.

Quoted in *Brooklyn Eagle*, 29 July 1901

Garrison Keillor

U.S. humorous writer and broadcaster, 1942–

1 [*Catchphrase describing fictional Minnesota town of Lake Wobegon:*] Where all the women are strong, all the men are good-looking, and all the children are above average.

A Prairie Home Companion (radio series) (1974–1987)

2 Ronald Reagan, the President who never told bad news to the American people.

We Are Still Married introduction (1989)

3 My ancestors were Puritans from England. They arrived here in 1648 in the hope of finding greater restrictions than were permissible under English law at that time.

Quoted in *N.Y. Times*, 30 Mar. 1990

Helen Keller

U.S. writer and reformer, 1880–1968

1 One can never consent to creep when one feels an impulse to soar.

Address to American Association to Promote the Teaching of Speech to the Deaf, Philadelphia, Pa., 8 July 1896

2 The mystery of language was revealed to me. I knew then that "w-a-t-e-r" meant the wonderful cool something that was flowing over my hand. That living word awakened my soul, gave it light, joy, set it free!

The Story of My Life ch. 4 (1902)

3 Although the world is full of suffering, it is full also of the overcoming of it.

Optimism pt. 1 (1903)

4 The test of a democracy is not the magnificence of buildings or the speed of automobiles or the efficiency of air transportation, but rather the care given to the welfare of all the people.

The Home Magazine, Apr. 1935
See Pearl S. Buck 3; Ramsey Clark 1; Dostoyevski 1; Humphrey 3; Samuel Johnson 69

5 Life is either a daring adventure or nothing. To keep our faces toward change and behave like free spirits in the presence of fate is strength undefeatable.

Let Us Have Faith (1940)

6 Avoiding danger is no safer in the long run than outright exposure. The fearful are caught as often as the bold.

Let Us Have Faith (1940)

James Keller

U.S. priest and broadcaster, 1900–1977

1 A Christopher spends his time improving, not disapproving, because he knows that *"it is better to light one candle than to curse the darkness."*

You Can Change the World! "Explaining the Christophers" (1948). Keller chose this "ancient Chinese proverb" as the motto of the Christophers, a religious society he founded in 1945. This may indeed have been a Chinese saying, given the *Frederick* (Md.) *Post* printing the following on 8 July 1940: "One of the leaders of new China said to a friend of mine recently, 'I had rather light a candle in the darkness than to curse the darkness.'" On the other hand, "It is far better to light the candle than to curse the darkness" appeared in a 1907 American book, *The Supreme Conquest and Other Sermons* by W. L. Watkinson.
See Adlai Stevenson 14

Bridget Anne Kelly

U.S. state government official, 1972–

1 [*Instigating closure of bridge entrances as retribution against an opponent of New Jersey governor Chris Christie:*] Time for some traffic problems in Fort Lee.

Email to David Wildstein, 13 Aug. 2013

Ned Kelly

Australian outlaw, 1855–1880

1 [*"Last words" on the scaffold:*] Such is life.

Attributed in *Melbourne Herald*, 12 Nov. 1880

Walt Kelly

U.S. cartoonist, 1913–1973

1 Deck us all with Boston Charlie, Walla Walla, Wash, and Kalamazoo!

Nora's freezin' on the trolley, Swaller dollar cauliflower Alleygaroo!

Pogo (comic strip), 22 Dec. 1948

2 Don't take life so serious, son, it ain't nohow permanent.

Pogo (comic strip), 24 June 1950

3 Resolve, then, that on this very ground, with small flags waving and tinny blasts on tiny trumpets, we shall meet the enemy, and not only may he be ours, he may be us.

The Pogo Papers foreword (1953)
See Walt Kelly 4; Oliver Hazard Perry 2

4 We have met the enemy and he is us.

Poster for Earth Day (1970). Also appeared in the *Pogo* comic strip for 8 Aug. 1970.
See Walt Kelly 3; Oliver Hazard Perry 2

William Thomson, Lord Kelvin
Irish-born Scottish physicist and mathematician, 1824–1907

1 I often say that when you can measure what you are speaking about, and express it in numbers, you know something about it; but when you cannot measure it, when you cannot express it in numbers, your knowledge is of a meagre and unsatisfactory kind: it may be the beginning of knowledge, but you have scarcely, in your thoughts, advanced to the stage of *science,* whatever the matter may be.

Popular Lectures and Addresses "Electrical Units of Measurement" (1889). The lecture from which this passage is taken was delivered 3 May 1883.
See Fleay 1

Thomas Ken
English clergyman, 1637–1711

1 Praise God, from whom all blessings flow! Praise Him, all creatures here below! Praise Him above, ye heavenly host! Praise Father, Son, and Holy Ghost!

"Awake my soul, and with the sun" (hymn) (1695)

William Kendall
U.S. architect, 1856–1941

1 Neither snow nor rain nor heat nor gloom of night stays these couriers from the swift completion of their appointed rounds.

Inscription on U.S. Post Office Building, New York, N.Y. (1912). Kendall, who was the designer of the Post Office Building, wrote these words as a free translation of Herodotus, *Histories,* vol. 4, book 8, verse 98. A more exact translation, by A. D. Godley,

reads: "It is said that as many days as there are in the whole journey, so many are the men and horses that stand along the road, each horse and man at the interval of a day's journey, and these are stayed neither by snow nor rain nor heat nor darkness from accomplishing their appointed course with due speed."

Thomas Keneally
Australian writer, 1935–

1 The list is an absolute good. The list is life. All around its cramped margins lies the gulf.

Schindler's Ark ch. 31 (1982)

George Kennan
U.S. explorer and author, 1845–1924

1 [*Proverb of Caucasian mountaineers:*] Heroism is endurance for one moment more.

Journal of the American Geographical Society vol. 15 (1883)

George F. Kennan
U.S. diplomat, 1904–2005

1 It is clear that the main element of any United States policy toward the Soviet Union must be that of a long-term, patient but firm and vigilant containment of Russian expansive tendencies.

"The Sources of Soviet Conduct," *Foreign Affairs,* July 1947

Anthony Kennedy
U.S. judge, 1936–

1 [On same-sex couples seeking the right to marry:] These men and women . . . ask for equal dignity in the eyes of the law. The Constitution grants them that right.

Obergefell v. Hodges (2015)

Edward M. Kennedy
U.S. politician, 1932–2009

1 For me, a few hours ago, this campaign came to an end. For all those whose cares have been our concern, the work goes on, the cause endures, the hope still lives, and the dream shall never die.

Speech at Democratic National Convention, New York, N.Y., 13 Aug. 1980

Florynce Kennedy
U.S. lawyer, 1916–2000

1 Oppressed people are frequently very oppressive when first liberated. And why wouldn't they be? They know best two positions. Somebody's foot on their neck or their foot on somebody's neck.

"Institutionalized Oppression *vs.* the Female" (1970)

2 If men could get pregnant, abortion would be a sacrament.

Quoted in *Off Our Backs,* 24 June 1971. This citation was referring to a speech Kennedy gave at a Washington, D.C., rally on 15 May 1971. Gloria Steinem later stated that the witticism was originated with an elderly female Irish cabdriver who was transporting Kennedy and Steinem around Boston or Cambridge.

3 There are very few jobs that actually require a penis or vagina. All other jobs should be open to everybody.

Quoted in *Ms.,* Mar. 1973

Jimmy Kennedy
Irish songwriter, 1902–1984

1 Today's the day the teddy bears have their picnic.

"The Teddy Bears' Picnic" (song) (1932)

2 In out in out shake it all about,
  You do the Hokey Cokey
  And you turn around.
  That's what it's all about.

"Hokey Cokey" (song) (1942). William Wells Newell, *Games and Songs of American Children* (1883), records the following: "Put your right elbow in, Put your right elbow out, Shake yourselves a little, And turn yourselves about."

3 Even old New York was once New Amsterdam
  Why they changed it I can't say
  People just liked it better that way.

"Istanbul (Not Constantinople)" (song) (1953)

4 Why did Constantinople get the works
  That's nobody's business but the Turks'.

"Istanbul (Not Constantinople)" (song) (1953)

John F. Kennedy
U.S. president, 1917–1963

1 I have just received the following telegram from my generous Daddy. It says, "Dear Jack:

Don't buy a single vote more than necessary. I'll be damned if I'm going to pay for a landslide."

Remarks at Gridiron Dinner, Washington, D.C., 15 Mar. 1958. The telegram was undoubtedly an invention of the younger Kennedy's.

2 When written in Chinese, the word *crisis* is composed of two characters. One represents danger and the other represents opportunity.

Speech to United Negro College Fund, Indianapolis, Ind., 12 Apr. 1959. The assertion about the Chinese characters, which is a questionable one, appeared as early as the Jan. 1938 issue of the journal *Chinese Recorder.*

3 This is not a time to keep the facts from the people—to keep them complacent. To sound the alarm is not to panic but to seek action from an aroused public. For, as the poet Dante once said: "The hottest places in hell are reserved for those who, in a time of great moral crisis, maintain their neutrality."

Speech, Tulsa, Okla., 16 Sept. 1959 (printed in John F. Kennedy, *The Strategy of Peace,* ed. Allan Nevins [1960]). No passage in Dante matches Kennedy's words, so the quotation seems to belong to Kennedy rather than the poet. Arthur M. Schlesinger, Jr., states in *A Thousand Days* (1965) that Kennedy wrote "The hottest places in Hell are reserved for those who, in a period of moral crisis, maintain their neutrality" in a loose-leaf notebook of quotations Kennedy kept in 1945–1946 and attributed these words to Dante. Kennedy may have gotten the sentence from Henry Powell Spring, *What Is Truth* (1944), where it appeared identically and was attributed to Dante.

4 We stand today on the edge of a new frontier— the frontier of the Nineteen Sixties— the frontier of unknown opportunities and perils—the frontier of unfulfilled hopes and unfilled threats. . . . The New Frontier of which

I speak is not a set of promises—it is a set of challenges. It sums up not what I intend to offer to the American people, but what I intend to ask of them.

Speech accepting Democratic presidential nomination, Los Angeles, Calif., 15 July 1960. According to *American Heritage Dictionary of American Quotations*, ed. Margaret Miner and Hugh Rawson, "The 'new frontier' phrase had been used before. In 1934, Henry Wallace published a book entitled *New Frontiers*, and in 1936 Alf Landon, the Republican candidate for president also spoke of 'a new frontier . . . a frontier of invention and new wants.'" Walt W. Rostow is credited with suggesting the phrase "new frontier" to Kennedy at a Boston cocktail party, 16 June 1960.
See Briggs 1; Gibran 5; Oliver Wendell Holmes, Jr. 6; John Kennedy 5; John Kennedy 16

5 We do not campaign stressing what our country is going to do for us as a people. We stress what we can do for the country.

Speech at Sheraton Park Hotel, Washington, D.C., 20 Sept. 1960
See Briggs 1; Gibran 5; Oliver Wendell Holmes, Jr. 6; John Kennedy 4; John Kennedy 16

6 For those to whom much is given, much is required. And when at some future date the high court of history sits in judgment on each of us—recording whether in our brief span of service we fulfilled our responsibilities to the state—our success or failure, in whatever office we hold, will be measured by the answers to four questions: First, were we truly men of courage. . . . Secondly, were we truly men of judgment. . . . Third, were we truly men of integrity. . . . Finally, were we truly men of dedication.

Address to Massachusetts legislature, 9 Jan. 1961
See Bible 297

7 Let the word go forth from this time and place, to friend and foe alike, that the torch has been passed to a new generation of Americans— born in this century, tempered by war, disciplined by a hard and bitter peace, proud of our ancient heritage.

Inaugural Address, 20 Jan. 1961

8 Let every nation know, whether it wishes us well or ill, that we shall pay any price, bear any burden, meet any hardship, support any friend, oppose any foe to assure the survival and the success of liberty.

Inaugural Address, 20 Jan. 1961

9 If a free society cannot help the many who are poor, it cannot save the few who are rich.

Inaugural Address, 20 Jan. 1961

10 To our sister republics south of our border, we offer a special pledge—to convert our good words into good deeds—in a new alliance for progress—to assist free men and free governments in casting off the chains of poverty.

Inaugural Address, 20 Jan. 1961

11 Let us never negotiate out of fear. But let us never fear to negotiate.

Inaugural Address, 20 Jan. 1961

12 If a beach-head of cooperation may push back the jungle of suspicion, let both sides join in creating a new endeavor, not a new balance of power, but a new world of law, where the strong are just and the weak secure and the peace preserved. All this will not be finished in the first one hundred days. Nor will it be finished in the first one thousand days, nor in the life of this Administration, nor even perhaps in our lifetime on this planet. But let us begin.

Inaugural Address, 20 Jan. 1961

13 Now the trumpet summons us again—not as a call to bear arms, though arms we need—not as a call to battle, though embattled we are— but a call to bear the burden of a long twilight struggle, year in and year out, "rejoicing in hope, patient in tribulation"—a struggle against the common enemies of man: tyranny, poverty, disease, and war itself.

Inaugural Address, 20 Jan. 1961. The words in quotation marks are from the Bible, Romans 12:12.

14 In the long history of the world, only a few generations have been granted the role of defending freedom in its hour of maximum danger. I do not shrink from this responsibility—I welcome it.

Inaugural Address, 20 Jan. 1961

15 The energy, the faith, the devotion which we bring to this endeavor will light our country and all who serve it—and the glow from that fire can truly light the world.

Inaugural Address, 20 Jan. 1961

16 And so, my fellow Americans: ask not what your country can do for you—ask what you can do for your country. My fellow citizens of the world: ask not what America will do for you, but what together we can do for the freedom of man.

Inaugural Address, 20 Jan. 1961
See Briggs 1; Gibran 5; Oliver Wendell Holmes, Jr. 6; John Kennedy 4; John Kennedy 5

17 With a good conscience our only sure reward, with history the final judge of our deeds, let us go forth to lead the land we love, asking His blessing and His help, but knowing that here on earth God's work must truly be our own.

Inaugural Address, 20 Jan. 1961

18 [*Referring to the Bay of Pigs disaster:*] There's an old saying that victory has 100 fathers and defeat is an orphan.

Press conference, 21 Apr. 1961
See Ciano 1

19 First, I believe that this nation should commit itself to achieving the goal, before this decade is out, of landing a man on the moon and returning him safely to the earth. No single space project in this period will be more impressive to mankind, or more important for the long-range exploration of space; and none will be so difficult or expensive to accomplish.

Special message to joint session of Congress on urgent national needs, 25 May 1961

20 I do not think it altogether inappropriate to introduce myself to this audience. I am the man who accompanied Jacqueline Kennedy to Paris, and I have enjoyed it.

Speech at SHAPE headquarters, Paris, 2 June 1961

21 Mankind must put an end to war or war will put an end to mankind.

Address to United Nations General Assembly, New York, N.Y., 25 Sept. 1961

22 Somebody once said that Washington was a city of Northern charm and Southern efficiency.

Remarks to trustees and advisory committee of national cultural center, 14 Nov. 1961. Although this bon mot is associated with Kennedy, Warren Magnuson (senator from Washington) was quoted in the *New Orleans Times-Picayune*, 2 Oct. 1945: "Washington—with its Northern charm and Southern efficiency."

23 Those who make peaceful revolution impossible will make violent revolution inevitable.

Address on first anniversary of Alliance for Progress, 13 Mar. 1962

24 Some men are killed in a war and some men are wounded, and some men never leave the country, and some men are stationed in the Antarctic and some are stationed in San Francisco. It's very hard in military or in personal life to assure complete equality. Life is unfair.

News conference, 21 Mar. 1962
See Jimmy Carter 5; Wilde 73

25 I think this is the most extraordinary collection of talent, of human knowledge, that has ever been gathered together at the White House, with the possible exception of when Thomas Jefferson dined alone.

Remarks at dinner honoring Nobel Prize winners of the Western Hemisphere, Washington, D.C., 29 Apr. 1962

26 A rising tide lifts all the boats.

Remarks, Pueblo, Colo., 17 Aug. 1962. In a later address Kennedy referred to this as a saying from Cape Cod, Massachusetts. Earlier occurrences date as far back as *The Missionary Voice*, May 1911: "The rising tide lifts all boats."

27 We choose to go to the moon in this decade and do the other things, not because they are easy, but because they are hard, because that goal will serve to organize and measure the best of our energies and skills.

Address at Rice University on nation's space effort, Houston, Tex., 12 Sept. 1962

28 We are prepared to discuss a détente affecting NATO and the Warsaw pact.

Message to Nikita Khrushchev, Oct. 1962

29 We don't see the end of the tunnel, but I must say I don't think it is darker than it was a year ago, and in some ways lighter.

News conference, 12 Dec. 1962
See Alsop 1; Dickson 1; Navarre 1

30 We can help make the world safe for diversity. For, in the final analysis, our most basic common link is that we all inhabit this small planet. We all breathe the same air. We all

cherish our children's future. And we are all mortal.

Commencement Address at American University, Washington, D.C., 10 June 1963

31 Every American ought to have the right to be treated as he would wish to be treated, as one would wish his children to be treated. But this is not the case.

Broadcast address on civil rights, 11 June 1963

32 No one has been barred on account of his race from fighting or dying for America—there are no "white" or "colored" signs on the foxholes or graveyards of battle.

Special Message to Congress on Civil Rights, 19 June 1963

33 All free men, wherever they may live, are citizens of Berlin, and, therefore, as a free man, I take pride in the words "Ich bin ein Berliner" [I am a Berliner].

Remarks in Rudolf Wilde Platz, West Berlin, Germany, 26 June 1963. Kennedy's statement is frequently cited as an example of an unintentional gaffe because *Berliner* in German can have the meaning "jelly-filled doughnut." Reinhold Aman has debunked this legend, arguing that Kennedy's listeners would have clearly understood him to be referring to a "male inhabitant of Berlin" (*Maledicta* vol. II).

34 Yesterday a shaft of light cut into the darkness. . . . For the first time, an agreement has been reached on bringing the forces of nuclear destruction under international control.

Broadcast address on Nuclear Test Ban Treaty, 26 July 1963

35 When power leads man towards arrogance, poetry reminds him of his limitations. When power narrows the areas of man's concern, poetry reminds him of the richness and diversity of his existence. When power corrupts, poetry cleanses. For art establishes the basic human truth which must serve as the touchstone of our judgment.

Remarks upon receiving an honorary degree from Amherst College, Amherst, Mass., 26 Oct. 1963

36 The definition of happiness of the Greeks . . . is full use of your powers along lines of excellence. I find, therefore, the Presidency provides some happiness.

News conference, 31 Oct. 1963

37 [*Remark to advisers after United States Steel raised prices on the heels of a labor settlement negotiated by Kennedy, 12 Apr. 1962:*] My father always told me that all business men were sons-of-bitches but I never believed it till now!

Quoted in *N.Y. Times*, 23 Apr. 1962

38 [*On the appointment of his brother Robert F. Kennedy as attorney general:*] I can't see that it's wrong to give him a little legal experience before he goes out to practice law.

Quoted in Victor Lasky, *J.F.K.: The Man and the Myth* (1963)

39 [*Of the Bay of Pigs invasion:*] All my life I've known better than to depend on the experts. How could I have been so stupid, to let them go ahead?

Quoted in Theodore C. Sorensen, *Kennedy* (1965)

40 [*Responding to the question, "How did you become a war hero?":*] It was involuntary. They sank my boat.

Quoted in Arthur M. Schlesinger, Jr., *A Thousand Days* (1965)

41 [*Remark, 13 Oct. 1960:*] Do you realize the responsibility I carry? I'm the only person standing between Nixon and the White House.

Quoted in Arthur M. Schlesinger, Jr., *A Thousand Days* (1965)

Joseph P. Kennedy
U.S. businessman and politician, 1888–1969

1 Don't get mad, get even.

Quoted in Ben Bradlee, *Conversations with Kennedy* (1975). An earlier occurrence appeared in the *Chicago Tribune*, 21 Feb. 1967: "The motto of the Irish Mafia which Bobby [Kennedy] inherited has always been, 'Don't get mad—get even,' a slogan which predates the Kennedys in Massachusetts politics." Still earlier, "Don't get mad—get even" appeared in a list of teenagers' expressions in the *Newport* (R.I.) *Daily News*, 14 June 1956.

Robert F. Kennedy
U.S. politician, 1925–1968

1 Always forgive your enemies—but never forget their names.

Quoted in Nancy McPhee, *The Second Book of Insults* (1981)

William Kennedy
U.S. novelist, 1928–

1 I don't hold no grudges more'n five years.
Ironweed ch. 3 (1983)

X. J. Kennedy (Joseph Charles Kennedy)
U.S. writer, 1929–

1 In a car like the Roxy I'd roll to the track,
  A steel-guitar trio, a bar in the back,
  And the wheels made no noise, they turned
    over so fast,
  Still it took you ten minutes to see me go past.
  "In a Prominent Bar in Secaucus One Day" l. 21
  (1961)

2 Let you hold in mind, girls, that your beauty
    must pass
  Like a lovely white clover that rusts with its
    grass.
  Keep your bottoms off barstools and marry you
    young
  Or be left—an old barrel with many a bung.
  "In a Prominent Bar in Secaucus One Day" l. 29
  (1961)

Jomo Kenyatta
Kenyan president, 1891–1978

1 The African is conditioned, by the cultural and
  social institutions of centuries, to a freedom
  of which Europe has little conception, and it
  is not in his nature to accept serfdom forever.
  He realizes that he must fight unceasingly
  for his own emancipation; for without this
  he is doomed to remain the prey of rival
  imperialisms.
  Facing Mount Kenya conclusion (1938)

Hugh Keough
U.S. journalist, 1864–1912

1 The race is not always to the swift, nor the
  battle to the strong; but that is the way to bet.
  Quoted in *Collier's*, Feb. 1919. Garson O'Toole has
  found that Hugh S. Fullerton, in a 1912 booklet titled
  By HEK, quoted Keough as follows: "The race is not
  always to the swift, but that is where to look." O'Toole
  also found "The race is—if not always—ninety-nine
  times in a hundred—to the swift, and the battle to the
  strong" (*Blackwood's Edinburgh Magazine*, Oct. 1833).
  See Bible 149

Johannes Kepler
German astronomer, 1571–1630

1 The most true path of the planet [Mars] is
  an ellipse, which Dürer also calls an oval,
  or certainly so close to an ellipse that the
  difference is insensible.
  Letter to David Fabricius, 11 Oct. 1605

2 I write the book, to be read, either now or by
  posterity. Which, I care not. It may well wait a
  century for a reader, as long as God waited six
  thousand years for a discoverer.
  Harmonices Mundi (Harmony of the World) bk. 5,
  preface (1619)

Otto Kerner, Jr.
U.S. politician, 1908–1976

1 This is our basic conclusion: Our Nation is
  moving toward two societies, one black, one
  white—separate and unequal.
  *Report of the National Advisory Commission on Civil
  Disorders* introduction (1968)
  *See Disraeli 14; John M. Harlan (1833–1911) 1; Earl
  Warren 1*

Jack Kerouac
U.S. novelist, 1922–1969

1 The only people for me are the mad ones,
  the ones who are mad to live, mad to talk,
  mad to be saved, desirous of everything at the
  same time, the ones who never yawn or say a
  commonplace thing, but burn, burn, burn like
  fabulous yellow roman candles exploding like
  spiders across the stars and in the middle you
  see the blue centerlight pop and everybody goes
  "Awww!"
  On the Road pt. 1, ch. 1 (1957)

2 I think of Dean Moriarty, I even think of Old
  Dean Moriarty the father we never found, I
  think of Dean Moriarty.
  On the Road pt. 5 (1957)

3 Jack speaks to Alan (in a letter written and
  mailed here) about the "beat generation," the
  "generation of furtives."
  Reported in John Clellon Holmes, Journal, 10 Dec.
  1948. This reference in Holmes's journal, preserved
  at the Boston University Library, is the earliest known
  use of the term *beat generation*.

Jean Kerr

U.S. writer, 1923–2003

1 I'm tired of all this nonsense about beauty
being only skin-deep. That's deep enough.
What do you want—an adorable pancreas?
The Snake Has All the Lines (1958)
See Proverbs 18

Nancy Kerrigan

U.S. figure skater, 1969–

1 Why? Why? It hurts so much. Why me?
Quoted in *Time*, 17 Jan. 1994. Kerrigan said this after
being hit on the leg by an assailant with a metal rod
at Cobo Arena, Detroit, Mich., 6 Jan. 1994.

John Kerry

U.S. politician, 1943–

1 [*Of the Vietnam War:*] How do you ask a man to
be the last man to die for a mistake?
Testimony before Senate Foreign Relations
Committee, 22 Apr. 1971

2 [*Of a 2003 Senate vote against funds for the
war in Iraq, criticized in Republican campaign
advertisements:*] I actually did vote for the $87
billion, before I voted against it.
Remarks at Marshall University, Huntington, W.V.,
16 Mar. 2004

Ken Kesey

U.S. novelist, 1935–2001

1 When I get out of here the first woman that
takes on ol' Red McMurphy the ten-thousand-
watt psychopath, she's gonna light up like a
pinball machine and pay off in silver dollars!
One Flew Over the Cuckoo's Nest pt. 4 (1962)

2 Mostly, I'd just like to look over the country
around the gorge again, just to bring some of
it clear in my mind again. I been away a long
time.
One Flew Over the Cuckoo's Nest pt. 4 (1962)

3 There are going to be times when we can't wait
for somebody. Now, you're either on the bus or
off the bus. If you're on the bus, and you get left
behind, then you'll find it again. If you're off
the bus in the first place—then it won't make a
damn.
Quoted in Tom Wolfe, *The Electric Kool-Aid Acid Test*
(1968)

Joseph Kesselring

U.S. playwright, 1902–1967

1 Insanity runs in my family. It practically *gallops!*
Arsenic and Old Lace act 2 (1941)

Charles F. Kettering

U.S. electrical engineer and inventor, 1876–1958

1 I am interested in the future because I expect to
spend the rest of my life in the future.
Quoted in *L.A. Times*, 19 July 1939

Thomas Kettle

Irish economist and poet, 1880–1916

1 Dublin Castle, if it did not know what the
Irish people want, could not so infallibly have
maintained its tradition of giving them the
opposite.
Quoted in Ulick O'Connor, *The Troubles: Ireland,
1912–1922* (1975)

Ellen Karolina Sofia Key

Swedish writer and feminist, 1849–1926

1 The emancipation of women is practically the
greatest egoistic movement of the nineteenth
century, and the most intense affirmation of the
right of the self that history has yet seen.
The Century of the Child ch. 2 (1900)

2 The worst barbarity of war is that it forces
men collectively to commit acts against which
individually they would revolt with their whole
being.
War, Peace, and the Future ch. 6 (1916) (translation by
Hildegard Norberg)

Francis Scott Key

U.S. lawyer, 1779–1843

1 Oh, say, can you see by the dawn's early light,
What so proudly we hailed at the twilight's last
gleaming?
Whose broad stripes and bright stars, through
the perilous fight,
O'er the ramparts we watched were so gallantly
streaming?
"The Star-Spangled Banner" (song) st. 1 (1814).
These lyrics and the ones below first appeared in
Key's 1814 poem "Defence of Fort McHenry." "The
Star-Spangled Banner" was designated the national
anthem of the United States in 1916.

2 And the rockets' red glare, the bombs bursting
 in air,
Gave proof through the night that our flag was
 still there.
Oh, say, does that star-spangled banner yet wave
O'er the land of the free and the home of the
 brave?
"The Star-Spangled Banner" (song) st. 1 (1814). The
words *Star Spangled flag* had been used in a poem by
Key published in 1805.

3 Then conquer we must, when our cause it
 is just,
And this be our motto, "In God is our trust."
"The Star-Spangled Banner" (song) st. 4 (1814)
See Salmon P. Chase 1

Daniel Keyes
U.S. writer, 1927–2014

1 Dr. Strauss says I shud rite down what I think
and evrey thing that happins to me from now
on. I dont know why but he says its important
so they will see if they will use me. I hope
they use me. Miss Kinnian says maybe they
can make me smart. I want to be smart. My
name is Charlie Gordon. I am 37 years old and
2 weeks ago was my birthday. I have nuthing
more to rite now so I will close for today.
"Flowers for Algernon" (1959)

John Maynard Keynes
English economist, 1883–1946

1 I work for a Government I despise for ends I
think criminal.
Letter to Duncan Grant, 15 Dec. 1917

2 He [Clemenceau] had one illusion—France;
and one disillusion—mankind, including
Frenchmen.
The Economic Consequences of the Peace ch. 3 (1919)

3 Lenin was certainly right. There is no subtler,
no surer means of overturning the existing
basis of society than to debauch the currency.
The process engages all the hidden forces of
economic law on the side of destruction, and
does it in a manner which not one man in a
million is able to diagnose.
The Economic Consequences of the Peace ch. 6 (1919).
The attributed Lenin discussion here has never been
found in Lenin's writings, and Keynes may have
invented it.

4 But this *long run* is a misleading guide to
current affairs. *In the long run* we are all dead.
A Tract on Monetary Reform ch. 3 (1923)

5 Professor [Max] Planck of Berlin, the famous
originator of the Quantum Theory, once
remarked to me that in early life he had
thought of studying economics, but had found
it too difficult!
Essays in Biography "Alfred Marshall: 1842–1924"
(1924)

6 Marxian Socialism must always remain a
portent to the historians of Opinion—how
a doctrine so illogical and so dull can have
exercised so powerful and enduring an
influence over the minds of men, and, through
them, the events of history.
The End of Laissez-Faire pt. 3 (1926)

7 I believe that in many cases the ideal size
for the unit of control and organization lies
somewhere between the individual and the
modern State. I suggest, therefore, that
progress lies in the growth and the recognition
of semi-autonomous bodies within the State.
The End of Laissez-Faire pt. 4 (1926)

8 The important thing for Government is not to
do things which individuals are doing already,
and to do them a little better or a little worse;
but to do those things which at present are not
done at all.
The End of Laissez-Faire pt. 4 (1926)

9 A "sound" banker, alas! is not one who foresees
danger and avoids it, but one who, when he
is ruined, is ruined in a conventional and
orthodox way along with his fellows, so that no
one can really blame him.
"The Consequences to the Banks of the Collapse of
Money Values" (1931)

10 The love of money as a possession—as
distinguished from the love of money as
a means to the enjoyment and realities of
life—will be recognized for what it is, a
somewhat disgusting morbidity, one of those
semicriminal, semi-pathological propensities
which one hands over with a shudder to the
specialists in mental disease.
Essays in Persuasion pt. 5 (1931)

11 If the Treasury were to fill old bottles with
banknotes, bury them at suitable depths in

disused coalmines which are then filled up to the surface with town rubbish, and leave it to private enterprise on well-tried principles of *laissez-faire* to dig the notes up again . . . there need be no more unemployment.

The General Theory of Employment, Interest and Money bk. 3, ch. 10 (1936)

12 Practical men, who believe themselves to be quite exempt from any intellectual influences, are usually the slaves of some defunct economist. Madmen in authority, who hear voices in the air, are distilling their frenzy from some academic scribbler of a few years back.

The General Theory of Employment, Interest and Money bk. 6, ch. 24 (1936)
See Heine 3

13 Owe your banker £1,000 and you are at his mercy; owe him £1 million and the position is reversed.

"Overseas Financial Policy in Stage III" (1945)

14 When my information changes, I change my mind. What do you do?

Attributed in *Wall Street Journal*, 13 Oct. 1978. The 1978 attribution was made by economist Paul Samuelson. Eight years earlier, Samuelson himself had said the following without attribution to Keynes: "When events change, I change my mind. What do you do?" (*Daily Labor Report*, 21 Dec. 1970). (These citations were found by Garson O'Toole.) The most common wording now is "When the facts change, I change my mind. What do you do, sir?"

Khizr Khan
Pakistani-born U.S. lawyer, 1950–

1 [*Addressing Donald Trump:*] Have you even read the United States Constitution? . . . You have sacrificed nothing and no one.

Speech at Democratic National Convention, Philadelphia, Pa., 28 July 2016

Ruhollah Khomeini
Iranian religious and political leader, 1900–1989

1 Music is no different from opium. Music affects the human mind in a way that makes people think of nothing but music and sensual matters. . . . Music is a treason to the country, a treason to our youth, and we should cut out all this music and replace it with something instructive.

Ramadan speech, 23 July 1979

2 The author of the book entitled *The Satanic Verses*, which has been compiled, printed, and published in opposition to Islam, the Prophet and the Qur'an, as well as those publishers who were aware of its contents, have been sentenced to death. I call on all zealous Muslims to execute them quickly, wherever they find them.

Fatwa against Salman Rushdie, 14 Feb. 1989

Nikita S. Khrushchev
Russian statesman, 1894–1971

1 If anyone believes that our smiles involve abandonment of the teaching of Marx, Engels, and Lenin he deceives himself poorly. Those who wait for that must wait until a shrimp learns to whistle.

Speech at dinner for visiting East German dignitaries, Moscow, 17 Sept. 1955

2 Comrades! We must abolish the cult of the individual decisively, once and for all.

Speech to secret session of Twentieth Congress of Communist Party, 25 Feb. 1956. Frequently translated as "cult of personality."

3 Whether you like it or not, history is on our side. We will bury you.

Speech to Western diplomats, Moscow, 18 Nov. 1956. Khrushchev later explained that he meant "bury" in the sense of "outlive."

4 The Soviet Government . . . has given a new order to dismantle the arms which you describe as offensive [Soviet arms in Cuba], and to crate and return them to the Soviet Union.

Letter to John F. Kennedy, 28 Oct. 1962

5 [*Remark, Belgrade, 21 Aug. 1963:*] [Politicians] are the same all over. They promise to build a bridge even where there is no river.

Quoted in *N.Y. Herald Tribune*, 22 Aug. 1963

6 [*Remark during visit to New York, N.Y., Oct. 1960:*] There is no greenery. It is enough to make a stone sad.

Quoted in Barbara Rowes, *The Book of Quotes* (1979)

7 [*Of nuclear war:*] The living will envy the dead.

Attributed in *Harper's*, Aug. 1979. According to *Respectfully Quoted*, ed. Suzy Platt, "no form of this quotation has been verified in the speeches or writings of Khrushchev." A similar line appears in an article by Oliver Loud in *Phylon* vol. 9, no. 1 (1948).

Søren Kierkegaard

Danish philosopher, 1813–1855

1 It is quite true what Philosophy says: that Life must be understood backwards. But that makes one forget the other saying: that it must be lived—forwards.

Diary (1843)

2 "The absurd . . . the fact that with God all things are possible." The absurd is not one of the factors which can be discriminated within the proper compass of the understanding: it is not identical with the improbable, the unexpected, the unforeseen.

Fear and Trembling "Problemata: Preliminary Expectoration" (1843)

3 Truth Is Subjectivity.

Concluding Unscientific Postscript ch. 2 (1846)

James R. Killian

U.S. university president and government official, 1904–1988

1 It is useful to distinguish among four factors which give importance, urgency, and inevitability to the advancement of space technology. The first of these factors is the compelling urge of man to explore and to discover, the thrust of curiosity that leads men to try to go where no one has gone before.

Statement of President's Science Advisory Committee, 26 Mar. 1958
See Roddenberry 1; Roddenberry 2; Roddenberry 3

Joyce Kilmer

U.S. poet and journalist, 1886–1918

1 I think that I shall never see
A poem lovely as a tree.

"Trees" l. 1 (1913)
See Nash 7

2 Poems are made by fools like me,
But only God can make a tree.

"Trees" l. 11 (1913)
See Heywood Broun 2

B. B. King (Riley B. King)

U.S. blues musician, 1925–2015

1 I woke up this morning,
My baby was gone.

"Woke Up This Morning (My Baby's Gone)" (song) (1952)

2 Nobody loves me but my mother—
And she could be jivin', too.

"Nobody Loves Me But My Mother" (song) (1970)

3 Being a blues singer is like being black two times.

Quoted in *Guitar Player*, Sept. 1980

Carole King (Carole Klein)

U.S. singer and songwriter, 1942–

1 You make me feel like
A natural woman.

"(You Make Me Feel Like) A Natural Woman" (song) (1967)

2 Winter, spring, summer, or fall,
All you have to do is call
And I'll be there.
You've got a friend.

"You've Got a Friend" (song) (1971)

Larry L. King

U.S. writer, 1929–2012

1 The only way you can lose this election, Joe, is to get caught in bed with a live man or a dead woman.

Harper's, Nov. 1966

Martin Luther King, Jr. (Michael King, Jr.)

U.S. civil rights leader, 1929–1968

1 It is historically and biologically true that there can be no birth and growth without birth and growing pains. Whenever there is the emergence of the new we confront the recalcitrance of the old. So the tensions which we witness in the world today are indicative of the fact that a new world order is being born and an old order is passing away.

Address at First Annual Institute on Nonviolence and Social Change, Montgomery, Ala., 3 Dec. 1956
See Bailey 1; George H. W. Bush 7; George H. W. Bush 10; George H. W. Bush 12; Tennyson 45

2 Government action is not the whole answer to the present crisis, but it is an important partial answer. Morals cannot be legislated, but behavior can be regulated. The law cannot make an employer love me, but it can keep him from refusing to hire me because of the color of my skin.

Stride Toward Freedom: The Montgomery Story ch. 11 (1958)

3 Injustice anywhere is a threat to justice everywhere.

Stride Toward Freedom: The Montgomery Story ch. 11 (1958)

4 The law may not change the heart, but it can restrain the heartless.

Speech at National Press Club, Washington, D.C., 19 July 1962

5 I have a dream tonight. One day my little daughter and my two sons will grow up in a world not conscious of the color of their skin but only conscious of the fact that they are members of the human race.

Speech, Rocky Mount, N.C., 27 Nov. 1962. King apparently first used "I have a dream" during a mass meeting in Albany, Ga., 16 Nov. 1962.
See Martin Luther King 10; Martin Luther King 12; Martin Luther King 13

6 Freedom is never voluntarily given by the oppressor; it must be demanded by the oppressed.

"Letter from Birmingham Jail," 16 Apr. 1963

7 One who breaks an unjust law must do so *openly, lovingly,* . . . and with a willingness to accept the penalty.

"Letter from Birmingham Jail," 16 Apr. 1963

8 I submit that an individual who breaks a law that conscience tells him is unjust, and who willingly accepts the penalty of imprisonment in order to arouse the conscience of the community over its injustice, is in reality expressing the highest respect for law.

"Letter from Birmingham Jail," 16 Apr. 1963

9 We can never forget that everything Adolf Hitler did in Germany was "legal" and everything the Hungarian freedom fighters did in Hungary was "illegal."

"Letter from Birmingham Jail," 16 Apr. 1963

10 I have a dream this afternoon that my four little children, that my four little children will not come up in the same young days that I came up within, but they will be judged on the basis of the content of their character, and not the color of their skin.

Speech at civil rights rally, Detroit, Mich., June 1963
See Martin Luther King 5; Martin Luther King 12; Martin Luther King 13

11 When the architects of our republic wrote the magnificent words of the Constitution and the Declaration of Independence, they were signing a promissory note to which every American was to fall heir . . . America has defaulted on this promissory note in so far as her citizens of color are concerned.

Speech at Civil Rights March, Washington, D.C., 28 Aug. 1963

12 I have a dream that one day on the red hills of Georgia the sons of former slaves and the sons of former slave owners will be able to sit down together at the table of brotherhood.

Speech at Civil Rights March, Washington, D.C., 28 Aug. 1963
See Martin Luther King 5; Martin Luther King 10

13 I have a dream that my four little children will one day live in a nation where they will not be judged by the color of their skin but by the content of their character.

Speech at Civil Rights March, Washington, D.C., 28 Aug. 1963
See Martin Luther King 5; Martin Luther King 10

14 From every mountainside, let freedom ring. And when this happens, and when we allow freedom to ring, and when we let it ring from every village and every hamlet, from every state and every city, we will be able to speed up that day when all of God's children, black men and white men, Jews and Gentiles, Protestants and Catholics, will be able to join hands and sing in the words of that old Negro spiritual, "Free at last! Free at last! Thank God Almighty, we are free at last!"

Speech at Civil Rights March, Washington, D.C., 28 Aug. 1963
See Archibald Carey 1; Folk and Anonymous Songs 24; Samuel Francis Smith 1

15 The means by which we live have outdistanced the ends for which we live. Our scientific power has outrun our spiritual power. We have guided missiles and misguided men.

Strength to Love ch. 7 (1963)

16 I believe that unarmed truth and unconditional love will have the final word in reality. This is why right temporarily defeated is stronger than evil triumphant.

Nobel Prize acceptance speech, Oslo, Norway, 10 Dec. 1964

17 A riot is at bottom the language of the unheard.

Where Do We Go from Here? ch. 4 (1967)

18 Even if it falls your lot to be a street sweeper, go on out and sweep streets like Michelangelo painted pictures; sweep streets like Handel and Beethoven composed music; sweep streets like Shakespeare wrote poetry; sweep streets so well that all the host of heaven and earth will have to pause and say, "Here lived a great street sweeper who swept his job well."

Sermon at New Covenant Baptist Church, Chicago, Ill., 9 Apr. 1967

19 [*Suggesting his own eulogy:*] Yes, if you want to say that I was a drum major, say that I was a drum major for justice; say that I was a drum major for peace; I was a drum major for righteousness.

Sermon delivered at Ebenezer Baptist Church, Atlanta, Ga., 4 Feb. 1968

20 Like anybody, I would like to live a long life. Longevity has its place. But I'm not concerned about that now. I just want to do God's will. And He's allowed me to go up to the mountain. And I've looked over, and I've seen the promised land. I may not get there with you, but I want you to know tonight that we as a people will get to the promised land.

Address to sanitation workers, Memphis, Tenn., 3 Apr. 1968. King was assassinated the day after making this address. In a sermon in Montgomery, Ala., 27 Jan. 1957, King had stated: "If I had to die tomorrow morning I would die happy because I've been to the mountaintop and I've seen the promised land and it's going to be here in Montgomery."

21 I want to be the white man's brother, not his brother-in-law.

Quoted in *New York Journal-American,* 10 Sept. 1962

Rodney King
U.S. construction worker, 1965–2012

1 [*Calling for an end to rioting provoked by the acquittal of four Los Angeles police officers accused of beating King:*] People, I just want to say . . . can we all get along? Can we get along?

Public statement, Los Angeles, Calif., 1 May 1992

Stephen King
U.S. writer, 1947–

1 The man in black fled across the desert, and the gunslinger followed.

"The Gunslinger" (1978)

2 Remember that hope is a good thing, Red, maybe the best of things, and no good thing ever dies.

Different Seasons "Rita Hayworth and Shawshank Redemption" (1982)

3 Either get busy living or get busy dying.

Different Seasons "Rita Hayworth and Shawshank Redemption" (1982)

4 I hope the Pacific is as blue as it has been in my dreams. I *hope.*

Different Seasons "Rita Hayworth and Shawshank Redemption" (1982)

William Lyon Mackenzie King
Canadian prime minister, 1874–1950

1 If some countries have too much history, we have too much geography.

Speech in Canadian House of Commons, 18 June 1936

Charles Kingsley
English writer and clergyman, 1819–1875

1 Be good, sweet maid, and let who will be clever.

"A Farewell" l. 5 (1858)

2 When all the world is young, lad,
And all the trees are green;
And every goose a swan, lad,
And every lass a queen;
Then hey for boot and horse, lad,
And round the world away:
Young blood must have its course, lad,
And every dog his day.

The Water Babies "Young and Old" l. 1 (1863)

Hugh Kingsmill (Hugh Kingsmill Lunn)
English writer, 1889–1949

1 [*Of friends:*] God's apology for relations.
Quoted in Michael Holroyd, *The Best of Hugh Kingsmill* (1970)

Barbara Kingsolver
U.S. writer, 1955–

1 God doesn't need to punish us. He just grants us a long enough life to punish ourselves.
The Poisonwood Bible bk. 4 (1998)

2 Her body moved with the frankness that comes from solitary habits. But solitude is only a human presumption. Every quiet step is thunder to beetle life underfoot; every choice is a world made new for the chosen. All secrets are witnessed.
Prodigal Summer ch. 1 (2000)

Galway Kinnell
U.S. poet, 1927–2014

1 after making love, quiet, touching along the
    length of our bodies,
familiar touch of the long-married.
"After Making Love We Hear Footsteps" l. 10 (1980)

2 this one whom habit of memory propels to the
    ground of his making,
sleeper only the mortal sounds can sing awake,
this blessing love gives again into our arms.
"After Making Love We Hear Footsteps" l. 21 (1980)

Neil Kinnock
British politician, 1942–

1 [*Replying to a heckler saying that Margaret Thatcher "showed guts" in the Falklands War:*] It's a pity others had to leave theirs on the ground at Goose Green [battlefield] to prove it.
Television interview, 6 June 1983

2 If Margaret Thatcher wins on Thursday—I warn you not to be ordinary, I warn you not to be young, I warn you not to fall ill, I warn you not to get old.
Speech, Bridgend, England, 7 June 1983

3 Why am I the first Kinnock in a thousand generations to be able to get to a university?
Broadcast, 21 May 1987. Later plagiarized by U.S. Senator Joseph Biden.

W. P. Kinsella
Canadian writer, 1935–2016

1 Two years ago at dusk on a spring evening, when the sky was a robin's-egg blue and the wind as soft as a day-old chick, as I was sitting on the verandah of my farm home in eastern Iowa, a voice very clearly said to me, "If you build it, he will come."
"Shoeless Joe Jackson Comes to Iowa" (1979)

2 "This must be heaven," he says. "No. It's Iowa," I reply automatically.
"Shoeless Joe Jackson Comes to Iowa" (1979)

3 They'll pass over the money without even looking at it—for it is money they have, and peace they lack.
Shoeless Joe pt. 4 (1982)

4 The memories will be so thick that the outfielders will have to brush them away from their faces.
Shoeless Joe pt. 4 (1982)

5 The one constant through all the years has been baseball. America has been erased like a blackboard, only to be rebuilt and then erased again. But baseball has marked time while America has rolled by like a procession of steamrollers.
Shoeless Joe pt. 4 (1982)

Alfred C. Kinsey
U.S. biologist, 1894–1956

1 Caricatures of the English-American [sexual] position are performed around the communal campfires, to the great amusement of the [South Pacific] natives, who refer to the position as the "missionary position."
Sexual Behavior in the Human Male ch. 10 (1948)

2 Males do not represent two discrete populations, heterosexual and homosexual. The world is not to be divided into sheep and goats. Not all things are black nor all things white. It is a fundamental of taxonomy that nature rarely deals with discrete categories. Only the human mind invents categories and tries to force facts into separated pigeon-holes. The living world is a continuum in each and every one of its aspects. The sooner we learn this concerning human sexual behavior the sooner we shall

reach a sound understanding of the realities of sex.

Sexual Behavior in the Human Male ch. 21 (1948)

3 The vaginal walls are quite insensitive in the great majority of females. . . . There is no . . . evidence that the vagina is ever the sole source of arousal, or even the primary source of erotic arousal in any female.

Sexual Behavior in the Human Female ch. 14 (1953)

4 The only unnatural sex act is that which one cannot perform.

Attributed in *Mattachine Review*, Aug. 1963

Michael Kinsley

U.S. journalist, 1951–

1 A "gaffe" is . . . when a politician tells the truth.

L.A. Times, 15 May 1984

Rudyard Kipling

Indian-born English writer, 1865–1936

1 A woman is only a woman, but a good Cigar is a Smoke.

"The Betrothed" st. 25 (1886)

2 Lalun is a member of the most ancient profession in the world.

In Black and White "On the City Wall" (1888)

3 There will never be any more great men in India. They will all, when they are boys, go whoring after strange gods.

In Black and White "On the City Wall" (1888)

4 The silliest woman can manage a clever man; but it needs a very clever woman to manage a fool.

Plain Tales from the Hills "Three and—An Extra" (1888)

5 Yes, makin' mock o' uniforms that guard you while you sleep
Is cheaper than them uniforms, an' they're starvation cheap.

"Tommy" st. 3 (1890)

6 Oh, East is East, and West is West, and never the twain shall meet,
Till Earth and Sky stand presently at God's great Judgement Seat;
But there is neither East nor West, Border, nor Breed, nor Birth,

When two strong men stand face to face, tho' they come from the ends of earth!

"The Ballad of East and West" st. 1 (1892)

7 We know that the tail must wag the dog, for the horse is drawn by the cart;
But the Devil whoops, as he whooped of old:
"It's clever, but is it Art?"

"The Conundrum of the Workshops" st. 6 (1892)

8 What should they know of England who only England know?

"The English Flag" st. 1 (1892)

9 We're poor little lambs who've lost our way,
Baa! Baa! Baa!
We're little black sheep who've gone astray,
Baa-aa-aa!
Gentlemen rankers out on the spree,
Damned from here to Eternity.
God ha' mercy on such as we,
Baa! Yah! Bah!

"Gentlemen-Rankers" st. 1 (1892)

10 An' for all 'is dirty 'ide
'E was white, clear white, inside
When 'e went to tend the wounded under fire!

"Gunga Din" st. 3 (1892)

11 Though I've belted you and flayed you,
By the livin' Gawd that made you,
You're a better man than I am, Gunga Din!

"Gunga Din" st. 5 (1892)

12 On the road to Mandalay,
   Where the flyin'-fishes play,
   An' the dawn comes up like thunder outer
     China 'crost the Bay!
   "Mandalay" st. 1 (1892)

13 Ship me somewheres east of Suez, where the
     best is like the worst,
   Where there aren't no Ten Commandments an'
     a man can raise a thirst.
   "Mandalay" st. 6 (1892)

14 When Earth's last picture is painted, and the
     tubes are twisted and dried,
   When the oldest colors have faded, and the
     youngest critic has died,
   We shall rest, and, faith, we shall need it—lie
     down for an eon or two,
   Till the Master of All Good Workmen shall put
     us to work anew.
   "When Earth's Last Picture Is Painted" l. 1 (1892)

15 And only the Master shall praise us, and only
     the Master shall blame;
   And no one will work for money, and no one
     shall work for fame,
   But each for the joy of the working, and each, in
     his separate star,
   Shall draw the Thing as he sees It for the God
     of Things as They are!
   "When Earth's Last Picture Is Painted" l. 9 (1892)

16 He wrapped himself in quotations—as a
   beggar would enfold himself in the purple of
   emperors.
   Many Inventions "The Finest Story in the World"
   (1893)

17 The Law of the Jungle.
   The Jungle Book "Mowgli's Brothers" (1894)

18 Now this is the Law of the Jungle—as old and
     as true as the sky;
   And the Wolf that shall keep it may prosper, but
     the Wolf that shall break it must die.
   The Second Jungle Book "The Law of the Jungle" st. 1
   (1895)

19 Now these are the Laws of the Jungle, and
     many and mighty are they;
   But the head and the hoof of the Law and the
     haunch and the hump is—Obey!
   The Second Jungle Book "The Law of the Jungle" st. 19
   (1895)

20 When you get to a man in the case,
   They're like as a row of pins—
   For the Colonel's Lady an' Judy O'Grady
   Are sisters under their skins!
   "The Ladies" st. 8 (1896)

21 Lord God of Hosts, be with us yet,
   Lest we forget—lest we forget!
   "Recessional" st. 1 (1897)

22 The tumult and the shouting dies—
   The captains and the kings depart—
   Still stands Thine ancient sacrifice,
   An humble and a contrite heart.
   "Recessional" st. 2 (1897)

23 Such boasting as the Gentiles use,
   Or lesser breeds without the Law.
   "Recessional" st. 4 (1897)

24 A fool there was and he made his prayer
   (Even as you and I!)
   To a rag and a bone and hank of hair
   (We called her the woman who did not care)
   But the fool he called her his lady fair—
   (Even as you and I!)
   "The Vampire" st. 1 (1897)

25 Take up the White Man's burden—
   Send forth the best ye breed—
   Go, bind your sons to exile
   To serve your captives' need.
   "The White Man's Burden" st. 1 (1899)

26 The Cat That Walked by Himself.
   Just So Stories title of story (1902)

27 I keep six honest serving-men
   (They taught me all I knew);
   Their names are What and Why and When
   And How and Where and Who.
   Just So Stories "The Elephant's Child" (1902)

28 One Elephant—a new Elephant—an Elephant's
   Child—who was full of 'satiable curiosity.
   Just So Stories "The Elephant's Child" (1902)

29 The flannelled fools at the wicket or the
     muddied oafs at the goals.
   "The Islanders" l. 31 (1903)

30 That's the secret. 'Tisn't beauty, so to speak, nor
   good talk necessarily. It's just It. Some women'll
   stay in a man's memory if they once walked
   down a street.
   Traffics and Discoveries "Mrs. Bathurst" (1904)
   See Elinor Glyn 1; Elinor Glyn 2

31 If you can keep your head when all about you
   Are losing theirs and blaming it on you,
   If you can trust yourself when all men doubt
      you,
   But make allowance for their doubting too.
   "If—" st. 1 (1910)
   See Beville 1

32 If you can meet with Triumph and Disaster
   And treat those two impostors just the same.
   "If—" st. 2 (1910)

33 If you can talk with crowds and keep your
      virtue,
   Or walk with Kings—nor lose the common
      touch,
   If neither foes nor loving friends can hurt you,
   If all men count with you, but none too much,
   If you can fill the unforgiving minute
   With sixty seconds' worth of distance run,
   Yours is the Earth and everything that's in it,
   And—which is more—you'll be a Man, my son!
   "If—" st. 4 (1910)

34 The female of the species is more deadly than
      the male.
   "The Female of the Species" st. 1 (1911)

35 It is always a temptation to a rich and lazy
      nation,
   To puff and look important and to say:—
   "Though we know we should defeat you,
      we have not the time to meet you.
   We will therefore pay you cash to go away."
   And that is called paying the Dane-geld;
   But we've proved it again and again,
   That if once you have paid him the Dane-geld
   You never get rid of the Dane.
   School History "Dane-Geld (A.D. 980–1016)" (1911).
   Coauthored with C. R. L. Fletcher.

36 If any question why we died,
   Tell them, because our fathers lied.
   "Common Form" l. 1 (1919)

37 Fiction is Truth's elder sister. Obviously. No one
   in the world knew what truth was till somebody
   had told a story.
   A Book of Words "Fiction" (1928)

38 Every nation, like every individual, walks in a
   vain show—else it could not live with itself—
   but I never got over the wonder of a people
   who, having extirpated the aboriginals of their

continent more completely than any modern
race had ever done, honestly believed that they
were a godly little New England community,
setting examples to brutal mankind.
Something of Myself ch. 5 (1937)

39 [*Remark to Lord Beaverbrook, ca. 1917:*] Power
   without responsibility: the prerogative of the
   harlot throughout the ages.
   Quoted in *Kipling Journal*, Dec. 1971

Henry Kissinger
German-born U.S. statesman, 1923–

1 A conventional army loses if it does not win.
  The guerilla army wins if he does not lose.
  Foreign Affairs, Jan. 1969

2 There cannot be a crisis next week. My
  schedule is already full.
  Quoted in *N.Y. Times Magazine*, 1 June 1969

3 Power is the great aphrodisiac.
  Quoted in *N.Y. Times*, 19 Jan. 1971
  See Graham Greene 5; Napoleon 14

4 The illegal we do immediately; the
  unconstitutional takes a little longer.
  Quoted in *Wash. Post*, 23 Dec. 1973

5 [*Remark after the invasion of Cambodia, 1970:*]
  We are all the President's men.
  Quoted in *Sunday Times* (London), 4 May 1975

6 [Richard Nixon] would have been a great, great
  man had somebody loved him.
  Quoted in Stephen Ambrose, *Nixon: Ruin and
  Recovery 1973–1990* (1991)

Horatio Herbert Kitchener, First Earl Kitchener
British general and statesman, 1850–1916

1 [*To the Prince of Wales during World War I:*] I
  don't mind your being killed, but I object to
  your being taken prisoner.
  Quoted in *Journals and Letters of Reginald Viscount
  Esher* (1938) (entry for 18 Dec. 1914)

Walter Kittredge
U.S. songwriter, 1834–1905

1 Many are the hearts that are weary to-night,
  Wishing for the war to cease,
  Many are the hearts looking for the right,

To see the dawn of peace.
Tenting to-night, tenting to-night,
Tenting on the old campground.

"Tenting on the Old Campground" (song) (1864)

Paul Klee

Swiss artist, 1879–1940

1 Art does not reproduce the visible; rather, it
makes visible.

"Creative Credo" sec. 1 (1920)

2 [*Of drawing:*] An active line on a walk, moving
freely without a goal. A walk for a walk's sake.

Pedagogical Sketchbook ch. 1 (1925)

Heinrich von Kleist

German playwright, 1777–1811

1 We've had some very caustic writings
Unwilling to concede that God exists.
However, the devil, so far as I'm aware,
No atheist has yet quite proved away.

The Broken Jug sc. 11 (1808) (translation by David
Constantine)

William "Bill" Klem

U.S. baseball umpire, 1874–1951

1 It ain't nothin' till I call it.

Quoted in Mel Allen and Ed Fitzgerald, *You Can't
Beat the Hours* (1964). Although this is commonly
attributed to Klem, it is worth noting that the *L.A.
Times*, 20 Mar. 1948, attributed "It ain't nothin' until
I call it" to a different umpire, Charlie Moran.

B. Kliban

U.S. cartoonist, 1935–1990

1 Cat: One Hell of a nice animal, frequently
mistaken for a meatloaf.

Cat (1975)

Friedrich Maximilian von Klinger

German playwright, 1752–1831

1 *Sturm und Drang.*
Storm and Stress.

Title of play (1775). This title was suggested by
Christoph Kaufmann.

Friedrich Klopstock

German poet, 1724–1803

1 God and I both knew what it meant once; now
God alone knows.

Quoted in Cesare Lombroso, *The Man of Genius*
(1891)

Damon Knight

U.S. science fiction writer, 1922–2002

1 [*Punch line of story about aliens taking human
beings to their planet:*] It's a cookbook!

"To Serve Man" (1950)

Mark Knopfler

Scottish rock musician, 1949–

1 Now look at them yo-yo's that's the way you
do it
You play the guitar on the M.T.V.
That ain't workin' that's the way you do it
Money for nothin' and chicks for free.

"Money for Nothing" (song) (1985). Cowritten with
Sting.

John Knowles

U.S. writer, 1926–2001

1 My war ended before I even put on a uniform; I
was on active duty all my time at school; I killed
my enemy there.

A Separate Peace ch. 13 (1959)

2 All of them, all except Phineas, constructed at
infinite cost to themselves these Maginot Lines
against this enemy they thought they saw across
the frontier, this enemy who never attacked that
way—if he ever attacked at all; if he was indeed
the enemy.

A Separate Peace ch. 13 (1959)

John Knox

Scottish religious leader, ca. 1505–1572

1 *Un homme avec Dieu est toujours dans la
majorité.*
A man with God is always in the majority.

Quoted in Inscription on Reformation Monument,
Geneva, Switzerland
*See Coolidge 2; Douglass 7; Andrew Jackson 7; Wendell
Phillips 3; Thoreau 9*

Philander C. Knox

U.S. politician, 1853–1921

1 Oh, Mr. President, do not let so great an achievement suffer from any taint of legality.

Quoted in Tyler Dennett, *John Hay: From Poetry to Politics* (1933). Knox's reply, as attorney general, to President Theodore Roosevelt's 1903 request for a legal justification of his acquisition of the Panama Canal Zone.

Ronald Knox

English writer and priest, 1888–1957

1 It is stupid of modern civilization to have given up believing in the devil, when he is the only explanation of it.

Let Dons Delight ch. 8 (1939)

2 It is alleged by a friend of my family that I used to suffer from insomnia at the age of four; and that when she asked me how I managed to occupy my time at night I answered, "I lie awake and think about the past."

Literary Distractions (1958)

3 There once was a man who said, "God
Must think it exceedingly odd
If he finds that this tree
Continues to be
When there's no one about in the Quad."

Quoted in Langford Reed, *Complete Limerick Book* (1924). Quotation dictionaries typically add an anonymous response to this:

Dear Sir,

Your astonishment's odd:

I am always about in the Quad.

And that's why the tree

Will continue to be,

Since observed by

Yours faithfully,

God.

Donald Knuth

U.S. computer scientist, 1938–

1 Beware of bugs in the above code; I have only proved it correct, not tried it.

Memorandum to Peter van Emde Boas, 29 Mar. 1977

Edward I. Koch

U.S. politician, 1924–2013

1 [*Catchphrase:*] How'm I doing?

Quoted in *N.Y. Times,* 26 Feb. 1978. In the slightly different form, "How am I doing?," this was quoted in the *N.Y. Times,* 26 June 1977.

Kenneth Koch

U.S. writer, 1925–2002

1 I chopped down the house that you had been saving to live in next summer.
I am sorry, but it was morning, and I had nothing to do and its wooden beams were so inviting.

"Variations on a Theme by William Carlos Williams" l. 1 (1962)

2 In the yard across the street we saw a snowman holding a garbage can lid smashed into a likeness of the mad English king, George the Third.

"You Were Wearing" l. 13 (1962)

Anne Koedt

U.S. feminist, 1941–

1 Whenever female orgasm and frigidity are discussed, a false distinction is made between the vaginal and the clitoral orgasm. Frigidity has generally been defined by men as the failure of women to have vaginal orgasms. Actually the vagina is not a highly sensitive area and is not constructed to achieve orgasm. It is the clitoris which is the center of sexual sensitivity and which is the female equivalent of the penis.

"The Myth of the Vaginal Orgasm," *Notes from the First Year* (1968)

Ted Koehler

U.S. songwriter, 1894–1973

1 Between the Devil and the Deep Blue Sea.

Title of song (1931)

2 Don't know why there's no sun up in the sky.
Stormy weather,
Since my man and I ain't together.

"Stormy Weather" (song) (1933)

Arthur Koestler

Hungarian-born English writer, 1905–1983

1 The definition of the individual was: a multitude of one million divided by one million.

Darkness at Noon (1941) (translation by Daphne Hardy)

2 The God That Failed.

Title of book (1949). Koestler collaborated on the book, whose title referred to Communism, with five other writers.

3 Behaviorism is indeed a kind of flat-earth view of the mind . . . it has substituted for the erstwhile anthropomorphic view of the rat, a ratomorphic view of man.

The Ghost in the Machine pt. 1, ch. 1 (1967)

The Koran

Quotations are taken from the translation by Arthur J. Arberry, The Koran Interpreted *(1955).*

1 In the Name of God, the Merciful, the Compassionate.

Sura 1

2 We believe in God, and
in that which has been sent down on us
and sent down on Abraham, Ishmael,
Isaac, and Jacob, and the Tribes,
and that which was given to Moses and Jesus
and the Prophets, of their Lord; we
make no division between any of them, and to
Him we surrender.

Sura 2

3 The month of Ramadan, wherein the Koran
was sent down to be a guidance
to the people, and as clear signs
of the Guidance and the Salvation.
So let those of you, who are present
at the month, fast it.

Sura 2

4 God
there is no god but He, the
Living, the Everlasting.
Slumber seizes Him not, neither sleep;
to Him belongs
all that is in the heavens and the earth.
Who is there that shall intercede with Him
save by His leave?

He knows what lies before them
and what is after them,
and they comprehend not anything of His
knowledge
save such as He wills.
His Throne comprises the heavens and earth;
the preserving of them oppresses Him not;
He is the All-high, the All-glorious.

Sura 2

5 No compulsion is there in religion.

Sura 2

6 God charges no soul save to its capacity . . .
Our Lord,
do Thou not burden us
beyond what we have the strength to bear.
And pardon us,
and forgive us,
and have mercy on us;
Thou art our Protector.
And help us against the people
of the unbelievers.

Sura 2

7 There is no god but God.

Sura 3. "There is no god but God, and Muhammad is his messenger" is the creed known as the *Shahada*.

8 Men are the managers of the affairs of women.

Sura 4

9 Righteous women are therefore obedient,
guarding the secret for God's guarding. And
those you fear may be rebellious admonish;
banish them to their couches, and beat them.

Sura 4

10 Whosoever fights in the way of God and is
slain, or conquers, We shall bring him a
mighty wage.

Sura 4

11 Glory be to Him, who carried His servant by
night
from the Holy Mosque to the Further Mosque
the precincts of which We have blessed,
that We might show him some of Our signs.

Sura 17

12 God is the Light of the heavens and the earth;
the likeness of His Light is as a niche
wherein is a lamp . . .
kindled from a Blessed Tree,

an olive that is neither of the East nor of
  the West
whose oil wellnigh would shine, even if no fire
  touched it;
Light upon Light.
  Sura 24

13 We indeed created man; and We know
what his soul whispers within him,
and We are nearer to him than the jugular vein.
  Sura 50

14 He [God] is the First and the Last, the Outward
  and the Inward.
  Sura 57

15 Recite: In the Name of thy Lord who created,
created Man of a blood-clot.
Recite: And thy Lord is the Most Generous,
who taught by the Pen,
taught man that he knew not.
  Sura 96

Alexander Korda (Sáncor Lászlo Kellner)
Hungarian-born English film director and
producer, 1893–1956

1 It's not enough to be Hungarian, you must
have talent too.
  Quoted in Karol Kulik, *Alexander Korda: The Man
  Who Could Work Miracles* (1975)

Alfred Korzybski
Polish-born U.S. philosopher of language,
1879–1950

1 A map *is not* the territory.
  Science and Sanity (1933). This phrase was used in "A
  Non-Aristotelian System and Its Necessity for Rigour
  in Mathematics and Physics," a paper presented
  before the American Mathematical Society, New
  Orleans, La., 28 Dec. 1931.
  See Baudrillard 1

Jerzy Kosinski (Jerzy Lewinkopf)
Polish-born U.S. novelist, 1933–1991

1 I like to watch.
  Being There pt. 5 (1971)

Larry Kramer
U.S. playwright and novelist, 1935–2020

1 We're all going to go crazy, living this epidemic
[AIDS] every minute, while the rest of the world
goes on out there, all around us, as if nothing
is happening, going on with their own lives and
not knowing what it's like, what we're going
through. We're living through war, but where
they're living it's peacetime, and we're all in the
same country.
  The Normal Heart act 2, sc. 11 (1985)

Stanley Kramer
U.S. film director, 1913–2001

1 Guess Who's Coming to Dinner.
  Title of motion picture (1967)

Karl Kraus
Austrian satirist, 1874–1936

1 Intercourse with a woman is sometimes a
satisfactory substitute for masturbation. But it
takes a lot of imagination to make it work.
  Die Fackel, 2 July 1907

2 There is no more unfortunate creature under
the sun than a fetishist who yearns for a
woman's shoe and has to settle for the whole
woman.
  Beim Wort Genommen (1909) (translation by Harry
  Zohn)

Herbert Kretzmer
South African–born English journalist and
songwriter, 1925–2020

1 To love another person
Is to see the face of God!
  "Wedding Chorale" (song) (1985). Appeared in the
  English version of the musical play *Les Misérables.*
  There is a similar quotation in Victor Hugo's novel
  Les Misérables, vol. 4, bk. 5, ch. 4: "Dieu est derrière
  tout, mais tout cache Dieu. Les choses sont noires,
  les créatures sont opaques. Aimer un être, c'est le
  rendre transparent" (God is behind everything, but
  everything hides God. Things are dark, creatures
  are opaque. To love a being is to render that being
  transparent).

Seymour Krim
U.S. writer and journalist, 1922–1989

1 [*The New Yorker* magazine stretches] its now
rubber conscience to include tokens of radical

chic and impressiveness on top but not at the bottom where it counts.

Shake It for the World, Smartass (1970). This book was published in January 1970, and the essay in question was written in 1962 (although not published at that time). Therefore it was Krim, and not Tom Wolfe, who coined the term *radical chic,* since Wolfe's usage was in June 1970.
See Tom Wolfe 1

Jiddu Krishnamurti
Indian theosophist, 1895–1986

1 Meditation is not a means to an end. It is both the means and the end.
Quoted in *The Penguin Krishnamurti Reader,* ed. Mary Lutyens (1970)

Julia Kristeva
Bulgarian-born French philosopher and literary critic, 1941–

1 Any text is constructed as a mosaic of quotations; any text is the absorption and transformation of another. The notion of *intertextuality* replaces that of intersubjectivity.
"Word, Dialogue and Novel" (1969)

Kris Kristofferson
U.S. singer and actor, 1936–

1 Freedom's just another word for nothin' left to lose,
Nothin' ain't worth nothin', but it's free.
"Me and Bobby McGee" (song) (1969). Cowritten with Fred L. Foster.

Irving Kristol
U.S. journalist and author, 1920–2009

1 History does not provide us with any instance of a society that repressed the economic liberties of the individual while being solicitous of his other liberties.
Two Cheers for Capitalism preface (1978)

2 If you believe that no one was ever corrupted by a book, you have also to believe that no one was ever improved by a book (or a play or a movie).
Reflections of a Neoconservative ch. 4 (1983)

3 [A neoconservative is] a liberal who has been mugged by reality.
Quoted in *N.Y. Times,* 6 Dec. 1981

Ray Kroc
U.S. business executive, 1902–1984

1 What do you do when your competitor is drowning? Get a live hose and stick it in his mouth.
Quoted in *Fortune,* 28 Oct. 1996

Arthur Krock
U.S. journalist, 1886–1974

1 New Dealers and conservatives . . . are together in their opposition to what a press gallery wit has called "government by crony."
N.Y. Times, 10 Feb. 1946. Krock later stated that "the press gallery wit" was himself.

Leopold Kronecker
German mathematician, 1823–1891

1 God made integers, all else is the work of man.
Quoted in Jahresbericht der Deutschen Mathematiker-Vereinigung (1893). Kronecker made this statement in a speech before the Society of German Scientists and Doctors in Berlin in 1886.

Pyotr Alexeevich Kropotkin
Russian revolutionary, geographer, and philosopher, 1842–1921

1 Sociability is as much a law of nature as mutual struggle . . . mutual aid is as much a law of animal life as mutual struggle.
Mutual Aid (1902)

Joseph Wood Krutch
U.S. critic and naturalist, 1893–1970

1 The most serious charge which can be brought against New England is not Puritanism but February.
The Twelve Seasons: A Perpetual Calendar for the Country "February: The One We Could Do Without" (1949)

2 Cats seem to go on the principle that it never does any harm to ask for what you want.
The Twelve Seasons: A Perpetual Calendar for the Country "February: The One We Could Do Without" (1949)

Stanley Kubrick
U.S. film director, 1928–1999

1 Dr. Strangelove; or, How I Learned to Stop Worrying and Love the Bomb.
Title of motion picture (1964). Cowritten with Terry Southern and Peter George.

Maggie Kuhn
U.S. activist, 1905–1995

1 Stand before the people you fear and speak your mind—even if your voice shakes.
No Stone Unturned ch. 7 (1991)

Thomas S. Kuhn
U.S. historian of science, 1922–1996

1 "Normal science" means research firmly based upon one or more past scientific achievements, achievements that some particular scientific community acknowledges for a time as supplying the foundation for its further practice.
The Structure of Scientific Revolutions ch. 2 (1962)

2 As in political revolutions, so in paradigm choice—there is no standard higher than the assent of the relevant community. To discover how scientific revolutions are effected, we shall therefore have to examine not only the impact of nature and of logic, but also the techniques of persuasive argumentation effective within the quite special groups that constitute the community of scientists.
The Structure of Scientific Revolutions ch. 9 (1962)

3 In a sense that I am unable to explicate further, the proponents of competing paradigms practice their trades in different worlds.
The Structure of Scientific Revolutions ch. 12 (1962)

Maxine Kumin
U.S. poet, 1925–2014

1 I took the lake between my legs.
"Morning Swim" l. 10 (1965)

Milan Kundera
Czech novelist, 1929–

1 The struggle of man against power is the struggle of memory against forgetting.
The Book of Laughter and Forgetting pt. 1, sec. 2 (1980) (translation by Michael Henry Heim)

2 The only reason people want to be masters of the future is to change the past.
The Book of Laughter and Forgetting pt. 1, sec. 17 (1980) (translation by Michael Henry Heim)

3 Her drama was a drama not of heaviness but of lightness. What fell to her lot was not the burden but the unbearable lightness of being.
The Unbearable Lightness of Being pt. 3, ch. 10 (1984) (translation by Michael Henry Heim)

4 Up out of the lampshade, startled by the overhead light, flew a large nocturnal butterfly that began circling the room. The strains of the piano and violin rose up weakly from below.
The Unbearable Lightness of Being pt. 7, ch. 7 (1984) (translation by Michael Henry Heim)

Andrei, Prince Kurbsky
Russian military leader, 1528–1583

1 Oh, Satan! . . . Why have you planted such a godless seed in the heart of a Christian tsar [Ivan the Terrible], from which such a fire swept over all the Holy Russian land.
History of the Grand Prince of Moscow (ca. 1580)

Harvey Kurtzman
U.S. cartoonist and magazine editor, 1924–1993

1 What—me worry?
Mad, July 1955. Catchphrase of the *Mad* magazine mascot Alfred E. Neuman. It may have had a prehistory as an advertising slogan in the early 1900s.

Raymond Kurzweil
U.S. inventor, 1948–

1 The fate of the universe is a decision yet to be made, one which we will intelligently consider when the time is right.
The Age of Spiritual Machines epilogue (1999)

Harold S. Kushner
U.S. author and rabbi, 1935–

1 There is only one question which really matters: why do bad things happen to good people?
When Bad Things Happen to Good People ch. 1 (1981)

Tony Kushner

U.S. playwright, 1956–

1 There are no gods here, no ghosts and spirits in America, there are no angels in America, no spiritual past, no racial past, there's only the political, and the decoys and the ploys to maneuver around the inescapable battle of politics.

Angels in America: Millennium Approaches act 3, sc. 2 (1992)

Mikhail I. Kutuzov

Russian military leader, 1745–1813

1 [*Remark, 13 Sept. 1812:*] Napoleon is like a stormy torrent which we are as yet unable to stop. Moscow will be the sponge that will suck him in.

Quoted in Eugene Tarle, *Napoleon's Invasion of Russia, 1812* (1942)

Jean de la Bruyère
French moralist, 1645–1696

1 Most men employ the first years of their life in making the last miserable.
The Characters "Of Mankind" (1688) (translation by Henri Van Laun)

2 There are but three events which concern man: birth, life, and death. They are unconscious of their birth, they suffer when they die, and they neglect to live.
The Characters "Of Mankind" (1688) (translation by Henri Van Laun)

3 The common people have scarcely any culture, the great have no soul. . . . Were I to choose between the two, I should select, without hesitation, being a plebeian.
The Characters "Of the Great" (1688) (translation by Henri Van Laun)

Jacques Lacan
French psychologist, 1901–1981

1 The unconscious is structured like a language.
"The Agency of the Letter in the Unconscious, or Reason Since Freud" (1957)

Pierre Choderlos de Laclos
French novelist and general, 1741–1803

1 A man enjoys the happiness he feels, a woman the happiness she gives.
Les Liaisons Dangereuses letter 130 (1782)

Lady Gaga (Stefani Joanne Angelina Germanotta)
U.S. singer and songwriter, 1986–

1 I was born this way.
"Born This Way" (song) (2011). Cowritten with Jeppe Laursen.

Robert M. La Follette, Sr.
U.S. politician, 1855–1925

1 Every nation has its war party. It is not the party of democracy. It is the party of autocracy. It seeks to dominate absolutely. It is commercial, imperialistic, ruthless. . . . If there is not sufficient reason for war, the war party will make war on one pretext, then invent another.
Quoted in *The Progressive,* June 1917

Suzanne LaFollette
U.S. editor and author, 1893–1983

1 Most people, no doubt, when they espouse human rights, make their own mental reservations about the proper application of the word "human."
Concerning Women "The Beginnings of Emancipation" (1926)

2 There is nothing more innately human than the tendency to transmute what has become customary into what has been divinely ordained.
Concerning Women "The Beginnings of Emancipation" (1926)

3 What its children become, that will the community become.
Concerning Women "Woman and Marriage" (1926)

Jean de la Fontaine
French poet, 1621–1695

1 You were singing? I'm very glad, very well, start dancing now.
Fables bk. 1, Fable 1 (1668)

2 The opinion of the strongest is always the best.
Fables bk. 1, Fable 10 (1668)

3 I bend but do not break.
Fables bk. 1, Fable 22 (1668)

Selma Lagerlöf

Swedish novelist, 1858–1940

1 If you have learned anything at all from us [wild geese], Tummetott, you no longer think that the humans should have the whole earth to themselves.

The Further Adventures of Nils (1907) (translation by Velma Swanston Howard)

Joseph Louis Lagrange

French mathematician and astronomer, 1736–1813

1 [*Remark the day after the guillotining of the great chemist Antoine Lavoisier on 8 May 1794:*] *Il ne leur a fallu qu'un moment pour faire tomber cette tête, et cent années, peut-être, ne suffiront pas pour en reproduire une semblable.*

It took them only an instant to cut off that head, but it is unlikely that a hundred years will suffice to reproduce a similar one.

Quoted in J. B. Delambre, "Éloge de Lagrange," *Mémoires de l'Institut* (1812)

Fiorello H. La Guardia

U.S. politician, 1882–1947

1 [*Looking back on his appointment of Herbert O'Brien as a judge:*] When I make a mistake, it's a beaut.

Quoted in *N.Y. Times*, 12 Feb. 1941

Nilanjana Sudeshna "Jhumpa" Lahiri

English-born U.S. writer, 1967–

1 In a few minutes he will go downstairs, join the party, his family. But for now his mother is distracted, laughing at a story a friend is telling her, unaware of her son's absence. For now, he starts to read.

The Namesake ch. 12 (2003)

R. D. Laing

Scottish psychiatrist, 1927–1989

1 Madness need not be all breakdown. It may also be break-through.

The Politics of Experience ch. 6 (1967)

Jess Lair

U.S. author, 1926–2000

1 If you want something very, very badly, let it go free. If it comes back to you, it's yours forever. If it doesn't, it was never yours to begin with.

I Ain't Much Baby—But I'm All I've Got ch. 19 (1969). Lair had his students at Montana State University write comments, questions, or feelings on index cards. This passage appeared on one of the students' cards, although it might have been copied by the student from another source. When these words became famous, a harsh parody arose: "If you want something very very badly, let it go free. If it doesn't come back to you, hunt it down and kill it."

Jean-Baptiste Lamarck

French naturalist, 1744–1829

1 It is interesting to observe the result of habit in the peculiar shape and size of the giraffe (*Camelo-pardalis*): this animal, the largest of the mammals, is known to live in the interior of Africa in places where the soil is nearly always arid and barren, so that it is obliged to browse on the leaves of trees and to make constant efforts to reach them. From this habit long maintained in all its race, it has resulted that the animal's fore-legs have become longer than its hind legs, and that its neck is lengthened to such a degree that the giraffe, without standing up on its hind legs, attains a height of six metres.

Philosophie Zoologique pt. 1, ch. 7 (1809)

2 FIRST LAW. In every animal . . . a more frequent and continuous use of any organ gradually strengthens, develops, and enlarges that organ . . . while the permanent disuse of any organ imperceptibly weakens and deteriorates it, and progressively diminishes its functional capacity, until it finally disappears.

Philosophie Zoologique pt. 2, ch. 7 (1809)

3 SECOND LAW. All the acquisitions or losses wrought by nature in individuals . . . are preserved by reproduction to the new individuals which arise.

Philosophie Zoologique pt. 2, ch. 7 (1809)

4 Habits form a second nature.

Philosophie Zoologique pt. 2, ch. 7 (1809)

Hedy Lamarr (Hedwig Eva Maria Kiesler)
Austrian-born U.S. actress, 1913–2000

1 Any girl can be glamorous. All you have to do is stand still and look stupid.
Quoted in *Hartford Daily Courant*, 1 Aug. 1941

Alphonse de Lamartine
French poet, 1790–1869

1 Only one being is wanting, and your whole world is bereft of people.
"L'Isolement" (1820)

2 O Time! arrest your flight, and you, propitious hours, stay your course.
"Le Lac" (1820)

Arthur J. Lamb
U.S. songwriter, 1870–1928

1 Her beauty was sold for an old man's gold, She's a bird in a gilded cage.
"A Bird in a Gilded Cage" (song) (1900)

Caroline Lamb
English writer, 1785–1828

1 [*Of Lord Byron after their first meeting:*] Mad, bad, and dangerous to know.
Diary, Mar. 1812

Charles Lamb
English writer, 1775–1834

1 I have had playmates, I have had companions, In my days of childhood, in my joyful schooldays,—
All, all are gone, the old familiar faces.
"The Old Familiar Faces" l. 1 (1798)

2 [*Of Samuel Taylor Coleridge:*] An Archangel a little damaged.
Letter to William Wordsworth, 26 Apr. 1816

3 Lawyers, I suppose, were children once.
Essays of Elia "The Old Benchers of the Inner Temple" (1823)

Anne Lamott
U.S. writer, 1954–

1 You can safely assume you've created God in your own image when it turns out that God hates all the same people you do.
Bird by Bird pt. 1 (1994). Lamott attributed this quotation to "my priest friend Tom."

2 Lighthouses don't go running all over an island looking for boats to save; they just stand there shining.
Bird by Bird pt. 5 (1994)

Giuseppe di Lampedusa
Italian writer, 1896–1957

1 If we want things to stay as they are, things will have to change.
The Leopard ch. 1 (1957) (translation by Archibald Colquhoun)

Bert Lance
U.S. politician, 1931–2013

1 If it ain't broke, don't fix it.
Quoted in *Wash. Post,* 23 Dec. 1976. Lance popularized this expression, but *Approach: The Naval Aviation Safety Review,* Apr. 1964, printed the following: "As someone recently said, 'if it ain't broke don't fix it.'"

Elsa Lanchester
English-born U.S. actress, 1902–1986

1 [*Of Maureen O'Hara:*] She looked as if butter wouldn't melt in her mouth—or anywhere else.
Quoted in Gary Herman, *The Book of Hollywood Quotes* (1979)

Edwin H. Land
U.S. inventor and businessman, 1909–1991

1 The bottom line is in heaven.
Speech at shareholders' meeting of Polaroid Corporation, 26 Apr. 1977

Jon Landau
U.S. music critic and record producer, 1947–

1 Last Thursday, at the Harvard Square theatre, I saw my rock'n'roll past flash before my eyes. And I saw something else: I saw rock and roll future and its name is Bruce Springsteen. And on a night when I needed to feel young, he made me feel like I was hearing music for the very first time.
The Real Paper, 22 May 1974

Ann Landers (Esther Pauline "Eppie" Lederer)

U.S. newspaper columnist, 1918–2002

1 Wake up and smell the coffee.

Chicago Tribune, 21 Dec. 1955. Landers popularized this expression, but an earlier anonymous usage is found in the *Chicago Daily Tribune,* 18 Jan. 1943.

2 [*Announcing her divorce in her newspaper advice column:*] One of the world's best marriages that didn't make it to the finish line.

Quoted in *Newsweek,* 14 July 1975

3 Television has proved that people will look at anything rather than each other.

Quoted in Barbara Rowes, *The Book of Quotes* (1979)

Walter Savage Landor

English poet, 1775–1864

1 I strove with none; for none was worth my strife;

Nature I loved, and, next to Nature, Art.

"Dying Speech of an Old Philosopher" l. 1 (1853)

Wanda Landowska

Polish musician, 1877–1959

1 [*To another musician:*] Oh, well, you play Bach *your* way. I'll play him *his.*

Quoted in Harold C. Schonberg, *The Great Pianists* (1963)

Andrew Lang

Scottish author, 1844–1912

1 He uses statistics as a drunken man uses lampposts—for support rather than for illumination.

Attributed in *Reader's Digest,* Apr. 1937

Christopher C. Langdell

U.S. legal scholar, 1826–1906

1 Law is a science, and . . . all the available materials of that science are contained in printed books. . . . The library is the proper workshop of professors and students alike; . . . it is to us all that the laboratories of the university are to the chemists and physicists, the museum of natural history to the zoologists, the botanical garden to the botanists.

Speech at Harvard University, Cambridge, Mass., 1887

Susanne K. Langer

U.S. philosopher, 1895–1985

1 Art is the objectification of feeling, and the subjectification of nature.

Mind: An Essay in Human Feeling vol. 1, pt. 2, ch. 4 (1967)

William Langland

English poet, ca. 1330–ca. 1400

1 In a somer seson, whan softe was the sonne.

The Vision of Piers Plowman B text, prologue, l. 1 (1362–1390)

2 Grammer, the ground of al.

The Vision of Piers Plowman B text, Passus 15, l. 370 (1362–1390)

Meyer Lansky

Russian-born U.S. mobster, 1902–1983

1 [*Of organized crime:*] We're bigger than U.S. Steel.

Attributed in *N.Y. Times,* 5 Sept. 1967. In *"Nice Guys Finish Seventh"* (1992), Ralph Keyes describes this as a paraphrase of a somewhat inaudible comment recorded by FBI surveillance.

Lao Tzu

Chinese philosopher, ca. 604 B.C.–ca. 531 B.C.

1 The Tao [Way] that can be told of is not the eternal Tao.

Tao-te Ching ch. 1 (translation by Wing-Tsit Chan)

2 Heaven and earth are not humane
They regard all things as straw dogs.
The sage is not humane,
He regards all people as straw dogs.

Tao-te Ching ch. 5 (translation by Wing-Tsit Chan)

3 The best [rulers] are those whose existence is [merely] known by the people.
The next best are those who are loved and praised.
The next are those who are feared.
And the next are those who are reviled . . .
[The great rulers] accomplish their task; they complete their work.
Nevertheless their people say that they simply follow Nature.

Tao-te Ching ch. 17 (translation by Wing-Tsit Chan)

4 Let people hold on to these:
Manifest plainness,

Embrace simplicity,
Reduce selfishness,
Have few desires.
Tao-te Ching ch. 19 (translation by Wing-Tsit Chan)

5 Reversion is the action of the Tao.
Weakness is the function of the Tao.
All things in the world come from being.
And being comes from non-being.
Tao-te Ching ch. 40 (translation by Wing-Tsit Chan)

6 One may know the world without going out of
doors.
One may see the Way of Heaven without
looking through windows.
The further one goes, the less one knows.
Tao-te Ching ch. 47 (translation by Wing-Tsit Chan)

7 He who knows does not speak.
He who speaks does not know.
Tao-te Ching ch. 56 (translation by Wing-Tsit Chan)

8 The more laws and orders are made prominent,
The more thieves and bandits there will be.
Tao-te Ching ch. 57 (translation by Wing-Tsit Chan)

9 The journey of a thousand *li* starts from where
one stands.
Tao-te Ching ch. 64 (translation by Wing-Tsit Chan).
Commonly rendered as "A journey of a thousand
miles must begin with a single step."

10 Heaven's net is indeed vast.
Though its meshes are wide, it misses nothing.
Tao-te Ching ch. 73 (translation by Wing-Tsit Chan)

11 There is nothing softer and weaker than water.
And yet there is nothing better for attacking
hard and strong things.
For this reason there is no substitute for it.
All the world knows that the weak overcomes
the strong and the soft overcomes the hard.
But none can practice it.
Tao-te Ching ch. 78 (translation by Wing-Tsit Chan)

12 The sage does not accumulate for himself.
The more he uses for others, the more he has
himself.
The more he gives to others, the more he
possesses of his own.
The Way of Heaven is to benefit others and not
to injure.
The Way of the sage is to act but not to
compete.
Tao-te Ching ch. 81 (translation by Wing-Tsit Chan)

Wayne LaPierre
U.S. gun rights advocate, 1949–

1 The only thing that's stopping these bad guys
with a gun is a good guy with a gun.
Quoted in *USA Today,* 21 Dec. 2007

Pierre Simon de Laplace
French astronomer and mathematician, 1749–
1827

1 Given for one instant an intelligence which
could comprehend all the forces by which
nature is animated and the respective positions
of the beings which compose it, if moreover this
intelligence were vast enough to submit these
data to analysis, it would embrace in the same
formula both the movements of the largest
bodies in the universe and those of the lightest
atom; to it nothing would be uncertain, and the
future as the past would be present to its eyes.
Oeuvres vol. 7, introduction (1812–1820)

2 [*Replying to Napoleon Bonaparte's comment upon
receiving a copy of Laplace's* Système du monde,
"*M. Laplace, they tell me you have written this
large book on the system of the universe, and have
never even mentioned its Creator":*] Je n'avais pas
besoin de cette hypothèse-là.
I have no need for that hypothesis.
Quoted in Augustus De Morgan, *A Budget of
Paradoxes* (1872). An earlier version of the anecdote
appeared in *Mémoires du Docteur F. Antommarchi*
(1825). Laplace may have been denying that God
occasionally intervenes to maintain the workings of
the universe, rather than denying that God exists.
Napoleon is said to have repeated Laplace's reply
to the mathematician Joseph Louis Lagrange, who
responded, *"Ah! c'est une belle hypothèse; ça explique
beaucoup de choses."* (Ah! It is a beautiful hypothesis; it
explains many things.)

Ring Lardner
U.S. writer, 1885–1933

1 Are you lost daddy I arsked tenderly.
Shut up he explained.
The Young Immigrunts ch. 10 (1920)

2 A good many young writers make the mistake
of enclosing a stamped, self-addressed
envelope, big enough for the manuscript to
come back in. This is too much of a temptation
to the editor.
How to Write Short Stories preface (1924)

3 [*After reading a poem written by someone twenty years dead:*] Did he write it before or after he died?

Quoted in *The Algonquin Wits*, ed. Robert E. Drennan (1968)

Philip Larkin

English poet, 1922–1985

1 What will survive of us is love.

"An Arundel Tomb" l. 42 (1964)

2 Sexual intercourse began
In nineteen sixty-three
(Which was rather late for me)—
Between the end of the *Chatterley* ban
And the Beatles' first LP.

"Annus Mirabilis" l. 1 (1974)

3 They fuck you up, your mum and dad,
They may not mean to, but they do.
They fill you with the faults they had
And add some extra, just for you.

"This Be the Verse" l. 1 (1974)

François, Sixth Duc de la Rochefoucauld

French writer, 1613–1680

1 In the misfortune of our best friends, we always find something which is not displeasing to us.

Réflections ou Maximes Morales maxim 99 (1665)

2 Self-love is the greatest of all flatterers.

Maximes no. 2 (1678)

3 We are all strong enough to bear the misfortunes of others.

Maximes no. 19 (1678)

4 There are good marriages, but no delightful ones.

Maximes no. 113 (1678)

5 *L'hypocrisie est un hommage que le vice rend à la vertu.*
Hypocrisy is a tribute which vice pays to virtue.

Maximes no. 218 (1678)

6 Absence diminishes commonplace passions and increases great ones, as the wind extinguishes candles and kindles fire.

Maximes no. 276 (1678)

7 In most of mankind gratitude is merely a secret hope for greater favors.

Maximes no. 298 (1678)

8 *L'enfer des femmes, c'est la vieillesse.*
The hell of women is old age.

Maximes Posthumes no. 562 (1696)

François Alexandre Frédéric, Duc de la Rochefoucauld-Liancourt

French reformer, 1747–1827

1 [*Responding to Louis XVI's July 1789 statement upon hearing of the fall of the Bastille, "C'est une grande révolte" (It is a big revolt):*] Non, Sire, c'est une grande révolution.
No, Sire, it is a big revolution.

Attributed in Ferdinand-Dreyfus, *Un Philanthrope d'Autrefois: La Rochefoucauld-Liancourt* (1903). Although Louis XVI was indeed awakened in the middle of the night of 14–15 July 1789 to be told of the uprising, Rochefoucauld-Liancourt's statement is probably an embellishment.

Harold J. Laski

English politician and political scientist, 1893–1950

1 [*Of sitting next to Virginia Woolf at lunch:*] It was like watching someone organize her own immortality. Every phrase and gesture was studied. Now and again, when she said something a little out of the ordinary, she wrote it down herself in a notebook.

Letter to Oliver Wendell Holmes, Jr., 30 Nov. 1930

Ferdinand Lassalle

German socialist and labor leader, 1825–1864

1 Wages . . . cannot fall with anything like permanence below the ordinary rate of living. . . . This is the cruel, rigorous law that governs wages under the present system.

"Open Letter to the National Labor Association of Germany" (1862)

Harold D. Lasswell

U.S. political scientist, 1902–1978

1 Politics is the study of *who gets what, when, and how.*

World Politics and Personal Insecurity ch. 1 (1935)

Hugh Latimer
English bishop, 1485–1555

1 [*To fellow martyr Nicholas Ridley, as they were about to be burned at the stake for heresy, Oxford, England, 16 Oct. 1555:*] Be of good comfort Master Ridley, and play the man. We shall this day light such a candle by God's grace in England, as (I trust) shall never be put out.
Quoted in John Foxe, *Actes and Monuments* (1570)

Harry Lauder
Scottish entertainer, 1870–1950

1 I love a lassie, a bonnie, bonnie lassie.
"I Love a Lassie" (song) (1905)

2 Roamin' in the Gloamin'.
Title of song (1911)

John Keith Laumer
U.S. science fiction writer, 1925–1993

1 Only a free society . . . can produce the technology that makes tyranny possible.
"Test to Destruction" (1967)

Stan Laurel
English-born U.S. comedian, 1890–1965

1 [*Ollie, played by Oliver Hardy, speaking to Stan Laurel:*] Here's another nice mess you've gotten us into.
The Laurel-Hardy Murder Case (motion picture) (1930). First appearance of Laurel and Hardy's catchphrase, usually quoted as "another fine mess."

Ralph Lauren (Ralph Lifshitz)
U.S. fashion designer, 1939–

1 I don't design clothes, I design dreams.
Quoted in *N.Y. Times*, 19 Apr. 1986

William L. Laurence
U.S. journalist, 1888–1977

1 [*Reporting on the first atomic bomb explosion, 16 July 1945:*] A great ball of fire about a mile in diameter, changing colors as it kept shooting upward, from deep purple to orange, expanding, growing bigger, rising as it was expanding, an elemental force freed from its bonds after being chained for billions of years.
N.Y. Times, 26 Sept. 1945

2 At first it was a giant column that soon took the shape of a supramundane mushroom.
N.Y. Times, 26 Sept. 1945

Wilfrid Laurier
Canadian prime minister, 1841–1919

1 The nineteenth century was the century of the United States. I think we can claim that it is Canada that shall fill the twentieth century.
Address to Canadian Club, Ottawa, 18 Jan. 1904. Commonly quoted as "The twentieth century belongs to Canada."

Johann Kaspar Lavater
Swiss theologian and poet, 1741–1801

1 Say not you know another entirely, till you have divided an inheritance with him.
Aphorisms on Man no. 157 (ca. 1788)

Frank Lawler
U.S. politician, 1842–1896

1 Gentlemen you should not get impatient with nature. All things equalize themselves—the rich man gets his ice in summer and the poor man gets his in winter.
Quoted in *Kansas City Times*, 18 Dec. 1886

D. H. Lawrence
English novelist and poet, 1885–1930

1 Not I, not I, but the wind that blows through me!
A fine wind is blowing the new direction of Time.
"Song of a Man Who Has Come Through" l. 1 (1920)

2 It is the three strange angels.
Admit them, admit them.
"Song of a Man Who Has Come Through" l. 17 (1920)

3 Sin is a queer thing. It isn't the breaking of divine commandments. It is the breaking of one's own integrity.
Studies in Classic American Literature ch. 8 (1923)

4 Why were we crucified into sex?
Why were we not left rounded off, and finished in ourselves,
As we began,
As he certainly began, so perfectly alone?
"Tortoise Shout" l. 9 (1923)

5 There are only two great diseases in the world today—Bolshevism and Americanism; and Americanism is the worse of the two, because Bolshevism only smashes your house or your business or your skull, but Americanism smashes your soul.

The Plumed Serpent ch. 2 (1926)

6 John Thomas says good-night to Lady Jane, a little droopingly, but with a hopeful heart.

Lady Chatterley's Lover ch. 19 (1928). "John Thomas" and "Lady Jane" are euphemisms for the male and female genitalia.

7 How beastly the bourgeois is
Especially the male of the species.

"How Beastly the Bourgeois Is" l. 1 (1929)

8 And if tonight my soul may find her peace
In sleep, and sink in good oblivion,
And in the morning wake like a new-opened flower
Then I have been dipped again in God, and new-created.

"Shadows" l. 1 (1932)

9 Now it is autumn and the falling fruit
And the long journey towards oblivion.

"The Ship of Death" l. 1 (1932)

10 Have you built your ship of death, O have you?
O build your ship of death, for you will need it.

"The Ship of Death" l. 8 (1932)

11 We are dying, we are dying, we are all of us dying.

"The Ship of Death" l. 43 (1932)

12 Pornography is the attempt to insult sex, to do dirt on it.

Phoenix "Pornography and Obscenity" ch. 3 (1936)

Jerome Lawrence (Jerome Lawrence Schwartz)
U.S. playwright, 1915–2004

1 Life is a banquet, and most poor sons-of-bitches are *starving* to death! Live!

Auntie Mame act 2, sc. 6 (1957). Coauthored with Robert E. Lee.

T. E. Lawrence
British military leader and writer, 1888–1935

1 I loved you, so I drew these tides of men into my hands and wrote my will across the sky in stars

To earn you freedom, the seven pillared worthy house, that your eyes might be shining for me
When we came.

The Seven Pillars of Wisdom dedication, l. 1 (1926)

2 Men prayed me that I set our work, the inviolate house,
As a memory of you.
But for fit monument I shattered it, unfinished: and now
The little things creep out to patch themselves hovels
In the marred shadow
Of your gift.

The Seven Pillars of Wisdom dedication, l. 16 (1926)

3 All men dream, but not equally. Those who dream by night in the dusty recesses of their minds wake in the day to find that it was vanity; but the dreamers of the day are dangerous men, for they may act their dream with open eyes, to make it possible. This I did.

The Seven Pillars of Wisdom suppressed introductory chapter (1926).

4 There could be no honor in a sure success, but much might be wrested from a sure defeat.

Revolt in the Desert ch. 19 (1927)

Henry Lawson
Australian writer, 1867–1922

1 And the sun sank again on the grand Australian bush—the nurse and tutor of eccentric minds, the home of the weird, and of much that is different from things in other lands.

"The Bush Undertaker" (1896)

Irving Layton
Romanian-born Canadian poet, 1912–2006

1 Only the tiniest fraction of mankind want freedom.
All the rest want someone to tell them they are free.

The Whole Bloody Bird "Aphs" (1969)

2 In Pierre Elliott Trudeau, Canada has at last produced a political leader worthy of assassination.

The Whole Bloody Bird "Obs II" (1969)

Emma Lazarus
U.S. poet, 1849–1887

1 Not like the brazen giant of Greek fame,
With conquering limbs astride from land to
     land,
Here at our sea-washed, sunset gates shall
     stand
A mighty woman with a torch, whose flame
Is the imprisoned lightning, and her name
Mother of Exiles.

"The New Colossus" l. 1 (1883). Inscribed on a plaque
in the pedestal of the Statue of Liberty in New York
Harbor.

2   Give me your tired, your poor,
Your huddled masses yearning to breathe free,
The wretched refuse of your teeming shore.
Send these, the homeless, tempest-tost to me,
I lift my lamp beside the golden door!

"The New Colossus" l. 10 (1883). Inscribed on a
plaque in the pedestal of the Statue of Liberty in New
York Harbor.

Stephen Leacock
English-born Canadian humorist, 1869–1944

1 Lord Ronald said nothing; he flung himself
from the room, flung himself upon his horse,
and rode madly off in all directions.

Nonsense Novels "Gertrude the Governess; or, Simple
Seventeen" (1911)

2 Advertising may be described as the science of
arresting human intelligence long enough to
get money from it.

Garden of Folly "The Perfect Salesman" (1924)

3 I am what is called a *professor emeritus*—from
the Latin *e,* "out," and *meritus,* "so he ought to
be."

Here Are My Lectures ch. 14 (1938)

Frank Leahy
U.S. football coach, 1908–1973

1 When the going gets tough, the tough get
going.

Quoted in *Charleston* (W.V.) *Daily Mail,* 4 May 1954.
Frequently attributed to Joseph P. Kennedy, but
Leahy's usage is eight years earlier than the earliest
known Kennedy reference. This 1954 article refers to
the quotation as "his own personal football motto."
There was a still earlier occurrence, in the *Boston
Herald,* 10 Oct. 1949, in an advertisement with no
attribution to any individual.

William D. Leahy
U.S. military leader, 1875–1959

1 The lethal possibilities of atomic warfare in the
future are frightening. My own feeling was that
in being the first to use it, we had adopted an
ethical standard common to the barbarians of
the Dark Ages. I was not taught to make war
in that fashion, and wars cannot be won by
destroying women and children.

I Was There ch. 23 (1950)

Edward Lear
English artist and humorous writer, 1812–1888

1 There was an Old Man with a beard,
Who said, "It is just as I feared!—
Two Owls and a Hen,
Four Larks and a Wren,
Have all built their nests in my beard!"

A Book of Nonsense (1846)

2 Far and few, far and few,
Are the lands where the Jumblies live;
Their heads are green, and their hands are
     blue,
And they went to sea in a Sieve.

"The Jumblies" l. 11 (1871)

3 "How pleasant to know Mr. Lear!"
Who has written such volumes of stuff!
Some think him ill-tempered and queer,
But a few think him pleasant enough.

Nonsense Songs preface (1871)
See T. S. Eliot 89

4 The Owl and the Pussy-Cat went to sea
In a beautiful pea-green boat.
They took some honey, and plenty of money,
Wrapped up in a five-pound note.

"The Owl and the Pussy-Cat" l. 1 (1871)

5 The Owl looked up to the Stars above
And sang to a small guitar,
"Oh lovely Pussy! O Pussy, my love,
What a beautiful Pussy you are."

"The Owl and the Pussy-Cat" l. 5 (1871)

6 Pussy said to the Owl, "You elegant fowl!
How charmingly sweet you sing!
O let us be married! too long we have tarried:
But what shall we do for a ring?"
They sailed away for a year and a day,
To the land where the Bong-tree grows,

And there in a wood a Piggy-wig stood
With a ring at the end of his nose.
"The Owl and the Pussy-Cat" l. 9 (1871)

7 They dined on mince, and slices of quince,
Which they ate with a runcible spoon;
And hand in hand, on the edge of the sand,
They danced by the light of the moon.
"The Owl and the Pussy-Cat" l. 21 (1871)

Timothy Leary
U.S. psychologist and countercultural activist,
1920–1996

1 Turn on, tune in, and drop out.
Quoted in *East Village Other*, 15 Apr.–1 May 1966.
Leary stated that this slogan was given to him by
Marshall McLuhan in conversation.

Mary Lease
U.S. reformer, 1850–1933

1 [*Addressed to Kansas farmers:*] Raise less corn
and more hell.
Quoted in *L.A. Times*, 30 Oct. 1903. The attribution to
Lease may be apocryphal.

William Least Heat-Moon (William Trogdon)
U.S. writer, 1939–

1 Whoever the last true cowboy in America turns
out to be, he's likely to be an Indian.
Blue Highways: A Journey into America ch. 5 (1983)

Fran Lebowitz
U.S. humorist, 1950–

1 Stand firm in your refusal to remain conscious
during algebra. In real life, I assure you, there
is no such thing as algebra.
Social Studies "Tips for Teens" (1981)

2 Being a woman is of special interest only to
aspiring male transsexuals. To actual women, it
is simply a good excuse not to play football.
Metropolitan Life "Letters" (1978)

3 All God's children are not beautiful. Most of
God's children are, in fact, barely presentable.
Metropolitan Life "Manners" (1978)

4 There is no such thing as inner peace. There is
only nervousness or death.
Metropolitan Life "Manners" (1978)

5 Sleep is death without the responsibility.
Metropolitan Life "Why I Love Sleep" (1978)

6 Your responsibility as a parent is not as great
as you might imagine. You need not supply
the world with the next conqueror of disease
or a major movie star. If your child simply
grows up to be someone who does not use the
word "collectible" as a noun, you can consider
yourself an unqualified success.
Social Studies "Parental Guidance" (1981)

7 Original thought is like original sin: both
happened before you were born to people you
could not have possibly met.
Social Studies "People" (1981)

8 Remember that as a teenager you are at the last
stage in your life when you will be happy to
hear that the phone is for you.
Social Studies "Tips for Teens" (1981)

9 If you removed all of the homosexuals and
homosexual influence from what is generally
regarded as American culture you would be
pretty much left with "Let's Make a Deal."
N.Y. Times, 13 Sept. 1987

Stanislaw Jerzy Lec
Polish writer, 1909–1966

1 Is it progress if a cannibal uses knife and fork?
Unkempt Thoughts (1962)

2 Proverbs contradict each other. That is the
wisdom of a nation.
Unkempt Thoughts (1962)

3 No snowflake in an avalanche ever feels
responsible.
More Unkempt Thoughts (1968)

John le Carré (David John Moore Cornwell)
English novelist, 1931–2020

1 The Spy Who Came in from the Cold.
Title of book (1963)

2 We have to live without sympathy, don't we?
That's impossible of course. We act it to one
another, this hardness; but we aren't like that
really. I mean . . . one can't be out in the cold all
the time; one has to come in from the cold . . .
do you see what I mean?
The Spy Who Came in from the Cold ch. 2 (1963)

3 We do disagreeable things so that ordinary
people here and elsewhere can sleep safely in
their beds at night.
The Spy Who Came in from the Cold ch. 2 (1963)
See Orwell 20

4 Do you know what love is? . . . It is whatever
you can still betray.
The Looking-Glass War ch. 18 (1965)

William E. H. Lecky
Irish historian, 1838–1903

1 The Augustinian doctrine of the damnation of
unbaptized infants and the Calvinistic doctrine
of reprobation . . . surpass in atrocity any tenets
that have ever been admitted into any pagan
creed.
History of European Morals vol. 1, ch. 1 (1869)

2 It had been boldly predicted by some of the
early Christians that the conversion of the world
would lead to the establishment of perpetual
peace. In looking back, with our present
experience, we are driven to the melancholy
conclusion that, instead of diminishing the
number of wars, ecclesiastical influence has
actually and very seriously increased it.
History of European Morals vol. 2, ch. 4 (1869)

Le Corbusier (Charles-Édouard Jeanneret)
French architect, 1887–1965

1 *Une maison est une machine-à-habiter.*
A house is a machine for living in.
Vers une Architecture ch. 1 (1923)

William Lederer
U.S. author, 1912–2009

1 The Ugly American.
Title of book (1958). Coauthored with Eugene
Burdick.

Alexandre Auguste Ledru-Rollin
French politician, 1807–1874

1 Ah well! I am their leader, I really had to follow
them!
Attributed in Eugène de Mirecourt, *Les Contemporains*
(1857). May be apocryphal.

Bruce Lee (Lee Jun-fan)
U.S. martial artist and actor, 1940–1973

1 I fear not the man who has practiced 10,000
kicks once, but I fear the man who has
practiced one kick 10,000 times.
Quoted in *Baltimore Sun,* 6 Nov. 2011

Gypsy Rose Lee (Rose Louise Hovick)
U.S. striptease artist, 1914–1970

1 God is love, but get it in writing.
Quoted in *N.Y. Times,* 1 Dec. 1988
See Bible 388; Samuel Butler (1835–1902) 10

Harper Lee
U.S. novelist, 1926–2016

1 Mockingbirds don't do one thing but make
music for us to enjoy . . . but sing their
heart out for us. That's why it's a sin to kill a
mockingbird.
To Kill a Mockingbird ch. 10 (1960)

2 The one thing that doesn't abide by majority
rule is a person's conscience.
To Kill a Mockingbird ch. 11 (1960)

3 But there is one way in this country in which
all men are created equal—there is one human
institution that makes a pauper the equal of
a Rockefeller, the stupid man the equal of an
Einstein, and the ignorant man the equal of any
college president. That institution, gentlemen,
is a court.
To Kill a Mockingbird ch. 20 (1960)

4 I'm no idealist to believe firmly in the integrity
of our courts and in the jury system—that is
no ideal to me, it is a living, working reality.
Gentlemen, a court is no better than each man
of you sitting before me on this jury. A court is
only as sound as its jury, and a jury is only as
sound as the men who make it up.
To Kill a Mockingbird ch. 20 (1960)

5 As you grow older, you'll see white men cheat
black men every day of your life, but let me
tell you something and don't you forget it—
whenever a white man does that to a black
man, no matter who he is, how rich he is, or
how fine a family he comes from, that white
man is trash.
To Kill a Mockingbird ch. 23 (1960)

Henry "Light-Horse Harry" Lee
U.S. soldier and politician, 1756–1818

1 First in war—first in peace—and first in the hearts of his countrymen.
   Funeral oration on the death of George Washington, Philadelphia, Pa., 1800
   See Charles Dryden 1

Nathaniel Lee
English playwright, ca. 1653–1692

1 When Greeks joined Greeks, then was the tug of war!
   The Rival Queens act 4, sc. 2 (1677)

Richard Henry Lee
U.S. political leader, 1732–1794

1 That these colonies are, and of right ought to be, free and independent states; that they are absolved from all allegiance to the British crown; and that all political connection between them and the State of Great Britain is, and ought to be, totally dissolved.
   Resolution presented to Continental Congress, 7 June 1776

Robert E. Lee
U.S. Confederate military leader, 1807–1870

1 [*Remark to General James Longstreet at Battle of Fredericksburg, Va., 13 Dec. 1862:*] It is well this [war] is so terrible—we would grow too fond of it!
   Quoted in John Esten Cooke, *Surry of Eagle's-Nest* (1866)

2 [*"Last words," 12 Oct. 1870:*] Strike the tent.
   Quoted in J. W. Jones, *Personal Reminiscences of General Robert E. Lee* (1874)

Stan Lee (Stanley Lieber)
U.S. comic book creator, 1922–2018

1 With great power there must also come—great responsibility!
   Amazing Fantasy no. 15 (comic book), Aug. 1962. Used in the original Spider-Man story. "The possession of great power necessarily implies great responsibility" appeared much earlier in Thomas C. Hansard, *Parliamentary Debates*, 27 June 1817.

2 [*First words of character Mary Jane Watson to Peter Parker:*] Face it, tiger . . . you just hit the jackpot!
   The Amazing Spider-Man (comic book) #42, Nov. 1966. Ellipses are in original.

Antoni van Leeuwenhoek
Dutch naturalist, 1632–1723

1 [*First observation of protozoa:*] Examining this water . . . I found floating therein divers earthy particles, and some green streaks, spirally wound serpent-wise. . . . I judge that some of these little creatures were above a thousand times smaller than the smallest ones I have ever yet seen, upon the rind of cheese, in wheaten flour, mould, and the like.
   Letter to Henry Oldenburg, 7 Sept. 1674

Gershon Legman
U.S. folklorist, 1917–1999

1 Murder is a crime. Describing murder is not. Sex is not a crime. Describing sex *is*.
   Love & Death: A Study in Censorship (1949)

2 Make love not war.
   Speech at Ohio University, Athens, Ohio, Nov. 1963. This speech was attested, in correspondence with the editor of this book, by Legman's widow Judith Legman; however, no actual documentation has ever been unearthed. The earliest verified citation is *Oakland Tribune*, 12 Mar. 1965.

Ursula Le Guin
U.S. science fiction writer, 1929–2018

1 You must not change one thing, one pebble, one grain of sand, until you know what good and evil will follow on that act.
   A Wizard of Earthsea ch. 3 (1968)

2 When action grows unprofitable, gather information; when information grows unprofitable, sleep.
   The Left Hand of Darkness ch. 3 (1969)

3 The only thing that makes life possible is permanent, intolerable uncertainty: not knowing what comes next.
   The Left Hand of Darkness ch. 5 (1969)

4 The king was pregnant.
   The Left Hand of Darkness ch. 8 (1969)

5 He had grown up in a country run by
politicians who sent the pilots to man the
bombers to kill the babies to make the world
safe for children to grow up in.
The Lathe of Heaven ch. 6 (1971)

6 Love doesn't just sit there, like a stone, it has to
be made, like bread; re-made all the time, made
new.
The Lathe of Heaven ch. 10 (1971)

7 A man can endure the entire weight of the
universe for eighty years. It is unreality that he
cannot bear.
The Lathe of Heaven ch. 11 (1971)

8 If you want your writing to be taken seriously,
don't marry and have kids, and above all, don't
die. But if you have to die, commit suicide.
They approve of that.
"Prospects for Women in Writing" (speech), Portland,
Me., Sept. 1986

Ernest Lehman
U.S. screenwriter, 1915–2005

1 I allowed the soothing music and the muted
sounds of the city and the rich, sweet smell
of success that permeated the room to lull my
senses.
"Tell Me About It Tomorrow" (1950)

Tom Lehrer
U.S. satirist, 1928–

1 Be prepared! That's the Boy Scouts' solemn
creed,
Be prepared! And be clean in word and deed.
Don't solicit for your sister, that's not nice,
Unless you get a good percentage of her price.
"Be Prepared" (song) (1953)
See Baden-Powell 1

2 Plagiarize! Let no one else's work evade your
eyes,
Remember why the good Lord made your eyes.
"Lobachevski" (song) (1953)

3 Oh, the poor folks hate the rich folks,
And the rich folks hate the poor folks.
All of my folks hate all of your folks,
It's American as apple pie.
"National Brotherhood Week" (song) (1965)

4 If you visit American city,
You will find it very pretty.
Just two things of which you must beware:
Don't drink the water and don't breathe the air!
"Pollution" (song) (1965)

5 So long, mom,
I'm off to drop the bomb,
So don't wait up for me.
"So Long, Mom (A Song for World War III)" (song)
(1965)

6 I'll look for you when the war is over,
An hour and a half from now!
"So Long, Mom (A Song for World War III)" (song)
(1965)

7 It is a sobering thought . . . that when Mozart
was my age he had been dead for two years.
That Was the Year That Was (record album) (1965)

8 First you get down on your knees,
Fiddle with your rosaries,
Bow your heads with great respect,
And genuflect, genuflect, genuflect!
"The Vatican Rag" (song) (1965)

9 "Once the rockets are up, who cares where they
come down?
That's not my department," says Wernher von
Braun.
"Wernher von Braun" (song) (1965)

Jerry Leiber
U.S. songwriter, 1933–2011

1 You ain't nothin' but a hound dog cryin' all the
time.
Well, you ain't never caught a rabbit and you
ain't no friend of mine.
"Hound Dog" (song) (1956). Coauthored with Mike
Stoller.

Gottfried Wilhelm Leibniz
German philosopher and mathematician,
1646–1716

1 *Nihil est sine ratione.*
There is nothing without a reason.
Studies in Physics and the Nature of Body (1671)

2 *Eadem sunt quorum unum potest substitui alteri
salva veritate.*

Two things are identical if one can be substituted for the other without affecting the truth.

"Table de définitions" (1704)

3 It may be said likewise in respect of perfect wisdom, which is no less orderly than mathematics, that if there were not the best among all possible worlds, God would not have produced any.

Theodicy: Essays on the Goodness of God and Freedom of Man and the Origin of Evil (1710)
See Cabell 1; Voltaire 7; Voltaire 8

Carolyn Leigh
U.S. songwriter, 1926–1983

1 Fairy tales can come true,
It can happen to you
If you're young at heart.

"Young at Heart" (song) (1954)

2 Hey, look me over,
Lend me an ear,
Fresh out of clover,
Mortgaged up to here.

"Hey, Look Me Over" (song) (1960)

Fred W. Leigh
British songwriter, 1871–1924

1 Why am I always the bridesmaid,
Never the blushing bride?

"Why Am I Always the Bridesmaid?" (song) (1917). Cowritten with Charles Collins and Lily Morris.
See Proverbs 36

Richard Leigh
U.S. songwriter, 1951–

1 Don't It Make My Brown Eyes Blue.

Title of song (1976)

Erwin Leiser
German film director, 1923–1996

1 [*Of the Holocaust:*] It must never happen again—never again.

Den Blodiga Tiden (motion picture) (1960)

Curtis E. LeMay
U.S. Air Force officer, 1906–1990

1 My solution to the problem [of North Vietnam] would be to tell them frankly that they've got to draw in their horns and stop their aggression, or we're going to bomb them back into the Stone Age.

Mission with LeMay: My Story bk. 8 (1965)

Raphael Lemkin
Polish legal scholar, 1900–1959

1 By genocide we mean the destruction of a nation or of an ethnic group.

Axis Rule in Occupied Europe preface (1944). This represents the coinage of the word *genocide*.

Madeleine L'Engle
U.S. writer, 1918–2007

1 A Wrinkle in Time.

Title of book (1963)

Nikolai Lenin (Vladimir Ilyich Ulyanov)
Russian revolutionary and political leader, 1870–1924

1 One Step Forward, Two Steps Back.

Title of pamphlet (1904). The *Oxford English Dictionary* records an earlier usage: "When a man has fully made up his mind to retreat, he bluster the most; and one step forward often promises two backward" (James Fenimore Cooper, *Homeward Bound* [1838]).

2 "The revolution's decisive victory over tsarism" means the establishment of the *revolutionary-democratic dictatorship of the proletariat and the peasantry.*

Two Tactics of Social-Democracy ch. 6 (1905)

3 Imperialism is the monopoly stage of capitalism.

Imperialism, the Highest Stage of Capitalism ch. 7 (1916)

4 We shall now proceed to construct the socialist order.

Speech at Congress of Soviets, 26 Oct. 1917

5 Communism is Soviet power plus the electrification of the whole country.

Report on the Work of the Council of People's Commissars, 22 Dec. 1920

6 [*Of George Bernard Shaw:*] A good man fallen among Fabians.

Quoted in Arthur Ransome, *Six Weeks in Russia in 1919* (1919)

7 They [capitalists] will furnish credits which will serve us for the support of the Communist Party in their countries and, by supplying us materials and technical equipment which we lack, will restore our military industry necessary for our future attacks against our suppliers. To put it in other words, they will work on the preparation of their own suicide.

Quoted in *Novyi Zhurnal/New Review,* Sept. 1961. According to *Respectfully Quoted,* ed. Suzy Platt, this was copied by I. U. Annenkov from Lenin manuscripts he examined shortly after Lenin's death. Platt notes, "The popular and widely-quoted paraphrase, 'The capitalists are so hungry for profits that they will sell us the rope to hang them with,' has often been considered spurious because it had not been found in Lenin's published works."

8 [*Definition of* political science:] Who masters whom?

Quoted in *Polnoe Sobranie Sochinenii* (1970) (entry for 17 Oct. 1921)

9 It is true that liberty is precious—so precious that it must be rationed.

Attributed in Sidney and Beatrice Webb, *Soviet Communism: A New Civilization* (1936)

10 [The United States will fall] like an over-ripe fruit into our hands.

Attributed in *Wash. Post,* 5 Sept. 1951. Long a popular quotation in anti-Communist circles, but diligent efforts by the Library of Congress and other researchers have failed to unearth anything by Lenin resembling it. The saying is undoubtedly fallacious.

11 [*Of left-liberals in the West:*] Useful idiots.

Attributed in *Italy Today* (1951). The phrase appeared in the *New York Times,* 21 June 1948, without reference to Lenin. Anti-Communists have often used this to attack those thought to be Soviet sympathizers, but the Library of Congress has never been able to trace the phrase in Lenin's writings. Like many other putative Leninisms, it seems to be a myth.

12 In dictatorships the masses vote with their feet.

Attributed in *N.Y. Times,* 4 Nov. 1954. Appeared in the *Times* without quotation marks and may have been a paraphrase.

John Lennon
English rock singer and songwriter, 1940–1980

1 Will the people in the cheaper seats clap your hands? All the rest of you, if you'll just rattle your jewelry.

Royal Variety Performance, 4 Nov. 1963

2 There was no reason for Michael to be sad that morning, (the little wretch); everyone liked him, (the scab). He'd had a hard day's night that day, for Michael was a Cocky Watchtower.

In His Own Write "Sad Michael" (1964)
See Lennon and McCartney 4

3 God is a concept
By which we measure
Our pain.
"God" (song) (1970)

4 I don't believe in Elvis
I don't believe in Zimmerman
I don't believe in Beatles
I just believe in me
Yoko and me
And that's reality.
"God" (song) (1970). "Zimmerman" refers to singer Bob Dylan, whose original name is Robert Zimmerman.

5 The dream is over . . .
I was the Dreamweaver
But now I'm reborn
I was the Walrus
But now I'm John.
"God" (song) (1970)

6 They hurt you at home and they hit you at school
They hate you if you're clever and they despise a fool
Till you're so fucking crazy you can't follow their rules
A working class hero is something to be.
"Working Class Hero" (song) (1970)

7 There's room at the top they are telling you still
But first you must learn how to smile as you kill.
"Working Class Hero" (song) (1970)

8 Imagine there's no heaven
It's easy if you try
No hell below us
Above us only sky
Imagine all the people
Living for today.
"Imagine" (song) (1971)

9 Imagine there's no countries
It isn't hard to do
Nothing to kill or die for.
"Imagine" (song) (1971)

10 You may say that I'm a dreamer
But I'm not the only one
I hope someday you'll join us
And the world will be as one.
"Imagine" (song) (1971)

11 Mind Games.
Title of song (1973)

12 Whatever Gets You Thru the Night.
Title of song (1974)

13 [*Of the Beatles:*] We're more popular than
Jesus now.
Quoted in *Evening Standard,* 4 Mar. 1966
See Charlie Chaplin 2; Zelda Fitzgerald 2

John Lennon 1940–1980 and **Paul
McCartney** 1942–
English rock singers and songwriters

1 I Want to Hold Your Hand.
Title of song (1963)

2 She loves you yeah, yeah, yeah.
"She Loves You" (song) (1963)

3 For I don't care too much for money,
For money can't buy me love.
"Can't Buy Me Love" (song) (1964)

4 It's been a hard day's night,
And I've been working like a dog,
It's been a hard day's night,
I should be sleeping like a log.
"A Hard Day's Night" (song) (1964)
See Lennon 2

5 Michelle ma belle
These are words that go together well, my
Michelle,

Michelle ma belle,
Sont des mots qui vont très bien ensemble.
"Michelle" (song) (1965)

6 He's a real Nowhere Man,
Sitting in his Nowhere Land,
Making all his Nowhere plans for nobody.
"Nowhere Man" (song) (1965)

7 Yesterday,
All my troubles seemed so far away,
Now it looks as though they're here to stay,
Oh, I believe in yesterday.
"Yesterday" (song) (1965)

8 All the lonely people, where do they all come
from?
All the lonely people, where do they all belong?
"Eleanor Rigby" (song) (1966)

9 Eleanor Rigby died in the church and was
buried along with her name.
Nobody came.
Father McKenzie, wiping the dirt from his
hands as he walks from the grave.
No one was saved.
"Eleanor Rigby" (song) (1966)

10 We all live in a yellow submarine.
"Yellow Submarine" (song) (1966)

11 All You Need Is Love.
Title of song (1967)

12 I heard the news today oh boy
Four thousand holes in Blackburn, Lancashire
And though the holes were rather small
They had to count them all
Now they know how many holes it takes
To fill the Albert Hall.
"A Day in the Life" (song) (1967). According to
Nigel Rees, *Cassell Companion to Quotations,* John
Lennon was inspired by an item in the *Daily Mail,*
17 Jan. 1967: "There are 4,000 holes in the road in
Blackburn, Lancashire."

13 I'd love to turn you on.
"A Day in the Life" (song) (1967)

14 I Am the Walrus.
Title of song (1967)

15 Lucy in the Sky with Diamonds.
Title of song (1967)

16 Sgt. Pepper's Lonely Hearts Club Band.
Title of song (1967)

17 Will you still need me, will you still feed me,
When I'm sixty-four?
"When I'm Sixty-Four" (song) (1967)

18 I get by with a little help from my friends.
"With a Little Help from My Friends" (song) (1967)

19 Helter Skelter.
Title of song (1968)

20 You say you want a revolution
Well, you know
We all want to change the world.
"Revolution" (song) (1968)

21 But when you talk about destruction,
Don't you know that you can count me out.
"Revolution" (song) (1968)

22 You say you got a real solution
Well, you know
We'd all love to see the plan.
"Revolution" (song) (1968)

23 Christ, you know it ain't easy,
You know how hard it can be,
The way things are going
They're going to crucify me.
"The Ballad of John and Yoko" (song) (1969)

24 And in the end the love you take is equal to the
love you make.
"The End" (song) (1969)

25 All we are saying is give peace a chance.
"Give Peace a Chance" (song) (1969)

26 Let It Be.
Title of song (1970)

Annie Lennox
Scottish rock musician, 1954–

1 Some of them want to use you
Some of them want to get used by you
Some of them want to abuse you
Some of them want to be abused
Sweet dreams are made of this
Who am I to disagree?
"Sweet Dreams (Are Made of This)" (song) (1983).
Cowritten with David A. Stewart.

2 Sisters Are Doin' It for Themselves.
Title of song (1985). Cowritten with Dave Stewart.

Leo XIII
Italian pope, 1810–1903

1 It is one thing to have a right to the possession
of money and another to have a right to use
money as one wills.
Rerum Novarum (1891)

2 Every man has by nature the right to possess
property as his own.
"Rights and Duties of Capital and Labor" art. 6 (1891)

Elmore Leonard
U.S. novelist, 1925–2013

1 If work was a good thing the rich would have it
all and not let you do it.
Split Images ch. 1 (1981)

2 I asked him one time what type of writing
brought the most money and the agent says,
"Ransom notes."
Get Shorty ch. 9 (1990)

3 [*Of his writing:*] I try to leave out the parts that
people skip.
Quoted in *Publishers Weekly*, 8 Mar. 1985

Leonardo da Vinci
Italian artist and engineer, 1452–1519

1 The span of a man's outstretched arms is equal
to his height.
The Notebooks of Leonardo da Vinci (translation by
Edward MacCurdy)

2 A bird is an instrument working according
to mathematical law, which instrument it is
within the capacity of man to reproduce with all
its movements.
The Notebooks of Leonardo da Vinci (translation by
Edward MacCurdy)

3 [*Text accompanying sketch of man with
parachute:*] If a man have a tent made of linen
of which the apertures have all been stopped
up, and it be twelve braccia across and twelve
in depth, he will be able to throw himself down
from any height without sustaining any injury.
The Notebooks of Leonardo da Vinci (translation by
Edward MacCurdy)

4 Whoever in discussion adduces authority uses
not intellect but rather memory.
The Notebooks of Leonardo da Vinci (translation by
Edward MacCurdy)

5 In her [Nature's] inventions nothing is lacking, and nothing is superfluous.

The Notebooks of Leonardo da Vinci (translation by Edward MacCurdy)

Ruggiero Leoncavallo

Italian composer, 1858–1919

1 *Vesti la giubba e la faccia infarina. Le gente paga e rider vuole qua. Ridi, Pagliacci, sul tuo amore in franto!*

Put on your make-up and then smear on the powder! The people pay you and they must have their laugh. Laugh now, Pagliacci, for the love that is gone now.

I Pagliacci (opera) act 1, sc. 4 (1892)

2 *La commedia è finita.*

The comedy is finished.

I Pagliacci (opera) act 2, sc. 2 (1892)

Sergio Leone

Italian film director, 1929–1989

1 *Il Buono, il Brutto, il Cattivo.*

The Good, the Bad, and the Ugly.

Title of motion picture (1966)

Aldo Leopold

U.S. ecologist, 1886–1948

1 When we see land as a community to which we belong, we may begin to use it with love and respect.

A Sand County Almanac foreword (1949)

2 A thing is right when it tends to preserve the integrity, stability, and beauty of the biotic community. It is wrong when it tends otherwise.

A Sand County Almanac pt. 3 (1949)

3 If the land mechanism as a whole is good, then every part is good, whether we understand it or not. If the biota, in the course of aeons, has built something we like but do not understand, then who but a fool would discard seemingly useless parts? To keep every cog and wheel is the first precaution of intelligent tinkering.

Round River: From the Journals of Aldo Leopold "Conservation" (1953). Usually quoted as "The first rule of intelligent tinkering is to save all the parts."

Mikhail Lermontov

Russian novelist and poet, 1814–1841

1 I was traveling post from Tiflis. My cart's entire load consisted of one small valise, which was half filled with travel notes about Georgia. Of these, the greater part, fortunately for you, have been lost.

A Hero of Our Time pt. 1, ch. 1 (1840) (translation by Marian Schwartz)

2 Of two friends, one is always the other's slave.

A Hero of Our Time pt. 2, ch. 2 (1840) (translation by Marian Schwartz)

Alan Jay Lerner

U.S. songwriter, 1918–1986

1 What a day this has been!
What a rare mood I'm in!
Why, it's . . . almost like being in love!

"Almost Like Being in Love" (song) (1947). Ellipsis in the original.

2 I'm getting married in the morning!
Ding dong! the bells are gonna chime.
Pull out the stopper!
Let's have a whopper!
But get me to the church on time!

"Get Me to the Church on Time" (song) (1956)

3 Why can't a woman be more like a man?

"A Hymn to Him" (song) (1956)

4 I could have danced all night!
And still have begged for more.
I could have spread my wings
And done a thousand things
I've never done before.

"I Could Have Danced All Night" (song) (1956)

5 I'd be equally as willing
For a dentist to be drilling
Than to ever let a woman in my life!

"I'm an Ordinary Man" (song) (1956)

6 I've grown accustomed to her face!
She almost makes the day begin.
I've grown accustomed to the tune
She whistles night and noon.

"I've Grown Accustomed to Her Face" (song) (1956)

7 "Thanks a lot, King," says I, in a manner well-bred;
"But all I want is 'enry 'iggins' 'ead!"

"Just You Wait" (song) (1956)

8 I have often walked down this street before,
But the pavement always stayed beneath my
    feet before.
All at once am I
Several storeys high,
Knowing I'm on the street where you live.
"On the Street Where You Live" (song) (1956)

9 Why can't the English teach their children how
    to speak?
This verbal class distinction by now should be
    antique.
If you spoke as she does, sir,
Instead of the way you do,
Why, you might be selling flowers, too.
"Why Can't the English?" (song) (1956)

10 There even are places where English completely
    disappears.
In America, they haven't used it for years!
"Why Can't the English?" (song) (1956)

11 The Lord above made man to help his neighbor,
No matter where, on land, or sea, or foam.
The Lord above made man to help his
    neighbor—but
With a little bit of luck . . .
When he comes around you won't be home!
"With a Little Bit of Luck" (song) (1956)

12 There'll be spring ev'ry year without you.
England still will be here without you.
"Without You" (song) (1956)

13 All I want is a room somewhere,
Far away from the cold night air;
With one enormous chair
Oh, wouldn't it be luverly?
"Wouldn't It be Luverly?" (song) (1956)

14 Oh, Gigi, have I been standing up too close
Or back too far?
When did your sparkle turn to fire?
And your warmth become desire?
Oh, what miracle has made you the way you
    are?
"Gigi" (song) (1958)

15 Thank heaven for little girls!
For little girls get bigger every day.
Thank heaven for little girls!
They grow up in the most delightful way.
"Thank Heaven for Little Girls" (song) (1958)

16 The winter is forbidden till December,
And exits March the second on the dot.
By order summer lingers through September
In Camelot.
"Camelot" (song) (1960)

17 Don't let it be forgot
That once there was a spot
For one brief shining moment that was known
As Camelot.
"Camelot" (song) (1960)

Sammy Lerner
Romanian-born U.S. songwriter, 1903–1989

1 I'm Popeye the sailor man.
I'm strong to the "fin-ich"
'Cause I eats me spinach;
I'm Popeye the sailor man.
"I'm Popeye the Sailor Man" (song) (1934)

Edgar Leslie
U.S. songwriter, 1885–1976

1 The bells are ringing
For me and my gal.
The birds are singing
For me and my gal.
"For Me and My Gal" (song) (1917). Cowritten with
E. Ray Goetz.

Doris Lessing
Iranian-born British novelist, 1919–2013

1 There's only one real sin, and that is to
persuade oneself that the second-best is
anything but the second-best.
The Golden Notebook "Free Women: 5" (1962)

2 None of you [men] ask for anything—except
everything, but just for so long as you need it.
The Golden Notebook "Free Women: 5" (1962)

Gotthold Ephraim Lessing
German playwright and critic, 1729–1781

1 *Ein einziger dankbarer Gedanke gen Himmel ist
    das vollkommenste Gebet.*
One single grateful thought raised to heaven is
    the most perfect prayer.
Minna von Barnhelm act 2, sc. 7 (1767)

2 No person must have to.
Nathan der Weise act 1, sc. 3 (1779)

3 The true beggar is . . . the true king!
Nathan der Weise act 2 (1779)

Julius Lester

U.S. author, 1939–2018

1 To be a slave was to be a human being under conditions in which humanity was denied. They were not slaves. They were people. Their condition was slavery.
To Be a Slave ch. 1 (1968)

Kathy Lette

Australian-born English novelist, 1958–

1 I didn't "fall" pregnant! I was bloody well pushed.
Foetal Attraction pt. 1 (1993)

Oscar Levant

U.S. pianist and actor, 1906–1972

1 An epigram is a gag that's played Carnegie Hall.
Quoted in Edmund Fuller, *Thesaurus of Quotations* (1941). In later occurrences, the word *wisecrack* was used rather than *gag*.

2 Strip away the phony tinsel of Hollywood and you find the real tinsel underneath.
Quoted in *L.A. Times*, 17 Sept. 1961. A very similar remark about Hollywood was attributed to Ed Gardner in the *L.A. Times*, 27 Nov. 1947: "Scratch beneath the phony tinsel and you will find the real tinsel."

Sam Levenson

U.S. humorist, 1911–1980

1 Insanity is hereditary. You can get it from your children.
Quoted in *Ada* (Okla.) *Weekly News*, 6 Apr. 1961

Denise Levertov

English-born U.S. poet, 1923–1997

1 Two by two in the ark of
the ache of it.
"The Ache of Marriage" l. 10 (1963)

Carlo Levi

Italian writer and painter, 1902–1975

1 To this shadowy land, that knows neither sin nor redemption from sin, where evil is not moral but is only the pain residing forever in earthly things, Christ did not come. Christ stopped at Eboli.
Christ Stopped at Eboli ch. 1 (1945)

2 Christ never came this far, nor did time, nor the individual soul, nor hope, nor the relation of cause to effect, nor reason nor history.
Christ Stopped at Eboli ch. 1 (1945)

Primo Levi

Italian novelist and poet, 1919–1987

1 [*Of the Auschwitz concentration camp:*] Our language lacks words to express this offence, the demolition of a man.
If This Is a Man (1958). Newsman Edward R. Murrow, in his CBS radio broadcast from the Buchenwald concentration camp, 15 Apr. 1945, said, "For most of it I have not words."

2 Today I think that if for no other reason than that an Auschwitz existed, no one in our age should speak of Providence.
Survival in Auschwitz ch. 17 (1960) (translation by Stuart Woolf)

Irwin Levine

U.S. songwriter, 1938–1997

1 Whoa tie a yellow ribbon
'Round the old oak tree
It's been three long years
Do ya still want me?
"Tie a Yellow Ribbon 'Round the Old Oak Tree" (song) (1972). Cowritten with L. Russell Brown. *See Folk and Anonymous Songs* 70

Duc de Lévis

French soldier and writer, 1764–1830

1 *Noblesse oblige.*
Nobility has its obligations.
Maximes et Réflexions (1808)

Claude Lévi-Strauss

French anthropologist, 1908–2009

1 The world began without man, and it will end without him.
Tristes Tropiques pt. 9, ch. 40 (1955)

2 I therefore claim to show, not how men think in myths, but how myths operate in men's minds without their being aware of the fact.
The Raw and the Cooked (1964)

Monica Lewinsky

U.S. White House intern, 1973–

1 I would just like to say that no one ever asked me to lie and I was never promised a job for my silence. And that I'm sorry. I'm really sorry for everything that's happened. And I hate Linda Tripp.
Grand jury testimony, 6 Aug. 1998

C. S. Lewis

English novelist and essayist, 1898–1963

1 The safest road to Hell is the gradual one— the gentle slope, soft underfoot, without sudden turnings, without milestones, without signposts.
The Screwtape Letters ch. 12 (1941)

2 The Future . . . something which everyone reaches at the rate of sixty minutes an hour, whatever he does, whoever he is.
The Screwtape Letters ch. 25 (1941)

3 Either this man [Jesus] was, and is, the Son of God: or else a madman or something worse. You can shut Him up for a fool, you can spit at Him and kill Him as a demon; or you can fall at His feet and call Him Lord and God. But let us not come with any patronizing nonsense about His being a great human teacher. He has not left that open to us. He did not intend to.
Broadcast Talks "The Shocking Alternative" (1942). This argument, now known as "Lewis's trilemma," was anticipated by nineteenth-century preachers such as Mark Hopkins and John Duncan.

4 Though the Witch knew the Deep Magic, there is a magic deeper still which she did not know. Her knowledge goes back only to the dawn of Time.
The Lion, the Witch and the Wardrobe ch. 15 (1950)

5 There was a boy called Eustace Clarence Scrubb, and he almost deserved it.
The Voyage of the Dawn Treader ch. 1 (1952)

Joe E. Lewis

U.S. comedian, 1902–1971

1 [A banker is] a man who will lend you money if you can prove to him that you don't need it.
Quoted in *Wash. Post*, 16 Oct. 1944. The same thought was expressed by Ogden Nash in his 1938 poem "Bankers Are Just like Anybody Else, Except Richer."
See Benchley 11; Galsworthy 2; Lincoln 2; Groucho Marx 41; Twain 4

2 Rooting for the Yankees is like rooting for U.S. Steel.
Quoted in *N.Y. Times*, 29 June 1958. The 1958 usage does not attribute these words to Lewis, but Paul Dickson states in *Baseball's Greatest Quotations* (1991) that "the wide-mouthed comic appears to have said it first." The variation "Rooting against the Yankees is like rooting against U.S. Steel" appears in *Sporting News*, 21 Oct. 1953.

Paul Lewis

U.S. literary scholar, 1949–

1 Ever since Mary Shelley's baron rolled his improved human out of the lab, scientists have been bringing just such good things to life. If they want to sell us Frankenfood, perhaps it's time to gather the villagers, light some torches, and head to the castle.
Letter to the editor, *N.Y. Times*, 16 June 1992

Richard Lewis

U.S. comedian, 1947–

1 [*Self-description:*] Comedian from hell.
Quoted in *Chicago Tribune*, 20 Apr. 1986. Lewis popularized the expression "the ——— from hell."

Sam M. Lewis

U.S. songwriter, 1885–1959

1 How 'Ya Gonna Keep 'Em Down on the Farm (After They've Seen Paree)?
Title of song (1919). Cowritten with Joe Young.

2 Five foot two, eyes of blue,
But oh! what those five feet could do,
Has anybody seen my girl?
"Five Foot Two, Eyes of Blue" (song) (1925). Cowritten with Joe Young.

Sinclair Lewis
U.S. novelist, 1885–1951

1 Main Street.
Title of book (1920)

2 His name was George F. Babbitt. He was 46 years old now, in April 1920, and he made nothing in particular, neither butter nor shoes nor poetry, but he was nimble in the calling of selling houses for more than people could afford to pay.
Babbitt ch. 1 (1922)

3 Every compulsion is put upon writers to become safe, polite, obedient, and sterile. In protest I declined election to the National Institute of Arts and Letters some years ago, and now I must decline the Pulitzer Prize.
Letter declining Pulitzer Prize in fiction (1926)

4 Our American professors like their literature clear and cold and pure and very dead.
Nobel Prize address, Stockholm, 12 Dec. 1930

5 It Can't Happen Here.
Title of book (1935)

Wyndham Lewis
English writer and painter, 1882–1957

1 The earth has become one big village, with telephones laid on from one end to the other, and air transport, both speedy and safe.
America and Cosmic Man ch. 2 (1948)
See McLuhan 3; McLuhan 4; McLuhan 6

Robert Ley
German Nazi leader, 1890–1945

1 *Kraft durch Freude.*
Strength through joy.
Instruction for German Labor Front, 2 Dec. 1933

George Leybourne (Joe Saunders)
English entertainer, 1842–1884

1 He'd fly through the air with the greatest of ease,
A daring young man on the flying trapeze.
"The Flying Trapeze" (song) (1868)

Liberace (Wladziu Valentino Liberace)
U.S. entertainer, 1919–1987

1 After reading [a] bitter attack on the Liberace show, the famous Milwaukee piano player wrote the critic, "My manager and I laughed all the way to the bank."
Reported in *San Mateo* (Calif.) *Times*, 7 Nov. 1953. The sentence "Some of them heard Mason laugh all the way to the bank" appeared in F. Hopkinson Smith, *Peter* (1908).

2 He [Liberace] repeated his crack that when his brother read Crosby's insults, he "cried all the way to the bank."
Reported in *Detroit Free Press*, 7 May 1954. An earlier version appeared in Walter Winchell's column in the *Cincinnati Enquirer*, 2 Sept. 1946: "Eddie Walker perhaps is the wealthiest fight manager in the fight game . . . The other night when his man Belloise lost, Eddie had the miseries . . . He felt so terrible that he cried all the way to the bank" [ellipses in original].

Georg Christoph Lichtenberg
German scientist and satirist, 1742–1799

1 To do just the opposite is also a form of imitation.
Aphorisms (1775–1779) (translation by Franz H. Mautner and Henry Hatfield)

2 A book is a mirror: when a monkey looks in, no apostle can look out.
Aphorisms (1775–1779) (translation by Franz H. Mautner and Henry Hatfield)

3 Everyone is a genius at least once a year. The real geniuses simply have their bright ideas closer together.
Aphorisms (1779–1788) (translation by Franz H. Mautner and Henry Hatfield)

4 A donkey appears to me like a horse translated into Dutch.
Aphorisms (1779–1788) (translation by Franz H. Mautner and Henry Hatfield)

J. C. R. Licklider
U.S. computer scientist, 1915–1990

1 It seems reasonable to envision, for a time 10 or 15 years hence, a "thinking center" that will incorporate the functions of present-day libraries together with anticipated advances in information storage and retrieval. . . . The picture readily enlarges itself into a network of such centers, connected to one another

by wide-band communication lines and to individual users by leased-wire services.
"Man-Computer Symbiosis" (1960)

A. J. Liebling
U.S. journalist, 1904–1963

1 Freedom of the press is guaranteed only to those who own one.
New Yorker, 14 May 1960

2 I can write faster than anyone who can write better, and I can write better than anyone who can write faster.
Quoted in *Wash. Post,* 19 Jan. 1964

Gordon Lightfoot
Canadian folk singer and songwriter, 1938–

1 The legend lives on from the Chippewa on
down
Of the big lake they call "Gitche Gumee."
Superior, they said, never gives up her dead
When the gales of November come early!
"The Wreck of the Edmund Fitzgerald" (song) (1976)

2 Does anyone know where the love of God goes
When the waves turn the minutes to hours?
"The Wreck of the Edmund Fitzgerald" (song) (1976)

Lydia Kamekeha Liliuokalani
Hawaiian queen and songwriter, 1838–1917

1 Farewell to thee, farewell to thee . . .
Until we meet again.
"Aloha Oe" (song) (1878)

Beatrice Lillie
Canadian comedian, 1898–1989

1 Every Other Inch a Lady.
Title of book (1927)
See Woollcott 5

2 [*To a waiter who had spilled soup on her dress:*]
Never darken my Dior again.
Quoted in Lore and Maurice Cowan, *The Wit of Women* (1969)

Maya Lin
U.S. architect and sculptor, 1959–

1 I saw the Vietnam Veterans Memorial not as an object placed into the earth but as a cut in the earth that has then been polished, like a geode.
Quoted in *Smithsonian Magazine,* Aug. 1996

Abraham Lincoln
U.S. president, 1809–1865

1 There is no grievance that is a fit object of redress by mob law.
Address before the Young Men's Lyceum, Springfield, Ill., 27 Jan. 1838

2 I have now come to the conclusion never again to think of marrying; and for this reason; I can never be satisfied with any one who would be blockhead enough to have me.
Letter to Mrs. Orville H. Browning, 1 Apr. 1838
See Benchley 11; Galsworthy 2; Joe E. Lewis 1; Groucho Marx 41; Twain 4

3 Any people anywhere, being inclined and having the power, have the *right* to rise up, and shake off the existing government, and form a new one that suits them better.
Speech in House of Representatives, 12 Jan. 1848

4 Discourage litigation. Persuade your neighbors to compromise whenever you can. Point out to them how the nominal winner is often a real loser—in fees, expenses, and waste of time. As a peacemaker the lawyer has a superior opportunity of being a good man. There will still be business enough.
"Notes for a Law Lecture," ca. 1 July 1850

5 The ant, who has toiled and dragged a crumb to his nest, will furiously defend the fruit of his labor, against whatever robber assails him. So plain, that the most dumb and stupid slave that ever toiled for a master, does constantly *know* that he is wronged. So plain that no one, high or low, ever does mistake it, except in a plainly

selfish way; for although volume upon volume is written to prove slavery a very good thing, we never hear of the man who wishes to take the good of it, *by being a slave himself.*

"Fragment on Slavery" ca. 1 July 1854

6 We were proclaiming ourselves political hypocrites before the world, by thus fostering Human Slavery and proclaiming ourselves, at the same time, the sole friends of Human Freedom.

Speech, Springfield, Ill., 4 Oct. 1854

7 This *declared* indifference, but as I must think, covert *real* zeal for the spread of slavery, I can not but hate. I hate it because of the monstrous injustice of slavery itself. I hate it because it deprives our Republican example of its just influence in the world—enables the enemies of free institutions, with plausibility, to taunt us as hypocrites—causes the real friends of freedom to doubt our sincerity, and especially because it forces so many really good men amongst ourselves into an open war with the very fundamental principles of civil liberty—criticizing the Declaration of Independence, and insisting that there is no right principle of action but *self-interest.*

Speech, Peoria, Ill., 16 Oct. 1854

8 No man is good enough to govern another man, *without that other's consent.* I say this is the leading principle—the sheet anchor of American republicanism.

Speech, Peoria, Ill., 16 Oct. 1854

9 Our progress in degeneracy appears to me to be pretty rapid. As a nation, we began by declaring that "all men are created equal." We now practically read it "all men are created equal, except Negroes." When the Know-Nothings get control, it will read "all men are created equal, except Negroes and foreigners and Catholics." When it comes to this, I shall prefer emigrating to some country where they make no pretense of loving liberty—to Russia, for instance, where despotism can be taken pure and without the base alloy of hypocrisy.

Letter to Joshua F. Speed, 24 Aug. 1855

10 To give the victory to the right, not *bloody bullets,* but *peaceful ballots* only, are necessary.

"Fragment of a Speech" ca. 18 May 1858. This is the closest documented Lincoln passage to the frequently quoted "The ballot is stronger than the bullet."

11 "A house divided against itself cannot stand." I believe this government cannot endure, permanently half *slave* and half *free.* I do not expect the Union to be *dissolved*—I do not expect the house to *fall*—but I *do* expect it will cease to be divided. It will become *all* one thing, or *all* the other.

Speech at Republican state convention nominating him to run for U.S. senator, Springfield, Ill., 16 June 1858
See Bible 276

12 They have seen in his [Senator Stephen A. Douglas's] round, jolly, fruitful face, post offices, land offices, marshalships, and cabinet appointments, chargeships and foreign missions, bursting and sprouting out in wonderful exuberance ready to be laid hold of by their greedy hands. . . . Nobody has ever expected me to be President. In my poor, lean, lank face nobody has ever seen that any cabbages were sprouting out.

Speech, Springfield, Ill., 17 July 1858

13 As I would not be a *slave,* so I would not be a *master.* This expresses my idea of democracy. Whatever differs from this, to the extent of the difference, is no democracy.

"Definition of Democracy," ca. 1 Aug. 1858

14 I am not, nor ever have been in favor of bringing about in any way the social and political equality of the white and black races. . . . I am not nor ever have been in favor of making voters or jurors of negroes, nor of qualifying them to hold office, nor to intermarry with white people; and I will say in addition to this that there is a physical difference between the white and black races which I believe will for ever forbid the two races living together on terms of social and political equality. And inasmuch as they cannot so live, while they do remain together there must be the position of superior and inferior, and I as much as any other man am in favor of having the superior assigned to the white race.

Fourth Debate with Stephen A. Douglas, Charleston, Ill., 18 Sept. 1858

15 I have never seen to my knowledge a man, woman, or child who was in favor of producing a perfect equality, social and political, between negroes and white men.
Fourth Debate with Stephen A. Douglas, Charleston, Ill., 18 Sept. 1858

16 [*Referring to Senator Stephen A. Douglas's argument about popular sovereignty:*] Has it not got down as thin as the homeopathic soup that was made by boiling the shadow of a pigeon that had starved to death?
Sixth Debate with Stephen A. Douglas, Quincy, Ill., 13 Oct. 1858

17 This is a world of compensations; and he who would *be* no slave, must consent to *have* no slave. Those who deny freedom to others deserve it not for themselves and under a just God, can not long retain it.
Letter to Henry L. Pierce and Others, 6 Apr. 1859

18 Negro equality! Fudge!! How long, in the government of a God great enough to make and maintain this Universe, shall there continue knaves to vend, and fools to gulp, so low a piece of demagogueism as this.
Notes for Speech, ca. Sept. 1859

19 I hold that if the Almighty had ever made a set of men that should do all the eating and none of the work, he would have made them with mouths only and no hands, and if he had ever made another class that he intended should do all the work and none of the eating, he would have made them without mouths and with all hands.
Speech (omitted portion), Cincinnati, Ohio, 17 Sept. 1859

20 It is said an Eastern monarch once charged his wise men to invent him a sentence, to be ever in view, and which should be true and appropriate in all times and situations. They presented him the words: *"And this, too, shall pass away."*
Address before Wisconsin State Agricultural Society, Milwaukee, Wis., 30 Sept. 1859
See Edward FitzGerald 1; Walter Scott 8

21 If a house was on fire there could be but two parties. One in favor of putting out the fire. Another in favor of the house burning.
Second Speech at Leavenworth, Kansas, 5 Dec. 1859

22 Let us have faith that right makes might, and in that faith, let us, to the end, dare to do our duty as we understand it.
Address at Cooper Institute, New York, N.Y., 27 Feb. 1860

23 I am glad to know that there is a system of labor where the laborer can strike if he wants to! I would to God that such a system prevailed all over the world.
Speech, Hartford, Conn., 5 0-Mar. 1860

24 Whether the owners of this species of property [slavery] do really see it as it is, it is not for me to say, but if they do, they see it as it is through 2,000,000,000 of dollars, and that is a pretty thick coating.
Speech, New Haven, Conn., 5 Mar. 1860

25 Why should there not be a patient confidence in the ultimate justice of the people? Is there any better or equal hope, in the world?
First Inaugural Address, 4 Mar. 1861

26 It is safe to assert that no government proper ever had a provision in its organic law for its own termination. Continue to execute all the express provisions of our national Constitution, and the Union will endure forever—it being impossible to destroy it, except by some action not provided for in the instrument itself.
First Inaugural Address, 4 Mar. 1861

27 If, by the mere force of numbers, a majority should deprive a minority of any clearly written constitutional right, it might, in a moral point of view, justify revolution—certainly would, if such right were a vital one.
First Inaugural Address, 4 Mar. 1861

28 Physically speaking, we cannot separate. We cannot remove our respective sections from each other, nor build an impassable wall between them. A husband and wife may be divorced, and go out of the presence, and beyond the reach of each other; but the different parts of our country cannot do this. They cannot but remain face to face; and intercourse, either amicable or hostile, must continue between them.
First Inaugural Address, 4 Mar. 1861

29 This country, with its institutions, belongs to the people who inhabit it. Whenever they shall grow weary of the existing government, they can exercise their *constitutional* right of amending it, or their *revolutionary* right to dismember, or overthrow it.
First Inaugural Address, 4 Mar. 1861

30 We are not enemies, but friends. We must not be enemies. Though passion may have strained, it must not break our bonds of affection. The mystic chords of memory, stretching from every battle-field, and patriot grave, to every living heart and hearthstone, all over this broad land, will yet swell the chorus of the Union, when again touched, as surely they will be, by the better angels of our nature.
First Inaugural Address, 4 Mar. 1861

31 Labor is prior to, and independent of, capital. Capital is only the fruit of labor, and could never have existed if labor had not first existed. Labor is the superior of capital, and deserves much the higher consideration.
Annual Message to Congress, 3 Dec. 1861

32 If there be those who would not save the Union, unless they could at the same time *save* slavery, I do not agree with them. If there be those who would not save the Union unless they could at the same time *destroy* slavery, I do not agree with them. My paramount object in this struggle is to save the Union, and is *not* either to save or to destroy slavery. If I could save the Union without freeing *any* slave I would do it, and if I could save it by freeing *all* the slaves I would do it; and if I could save it by freeing some and leaving others alone I would also do that. What I do about slavery, and the colored race, I do because I believe it helps to save the Union; and what I forbear, I forbear because I do *not* believe it would help to save the Union.
Letter to Horace Greeley, 22 Aug. 1862

33 In great contests each party claims to act in accordance with the will of God. Both *may* be, and one *must* be, wrong. God can not be *for* and *against* the same thing at the same time.
"Meditation on the Divine Will," ca. 2 Sept. 1862

34 On the first day of January in the year of our Lord, one thousand eight hundred and sixty-three, all persons held as slaves within any state, or designated part of a state, the people whereof shall then be in rebellion against the United States shall be then, thenceforward, and forever free.
Preliminary Emancipation Proclamation, 22 Sept. 1862

35 I have just read your dispatch about sore tongued and fatigued horses. Will you pardon me for asking what the horses of your army have done since the battle of Antietam that fatigue anything?
Letter to George B. McClellan, 24 Oct. 1862

36 The dogmas of the quiet past are inadequate to the stormy present. The occasion is piled high with difficulty, and we must rise with the occasion. As our case is new, so we must think anew, and act anew. We must disenthrall ourselves, and then we shall save our country.
Annual Message to Congress, 1 Dec. 1862

37 Fellow-citizens, *we* cannot escape history. We of this Congress and this administration, will be remembered in spite of ourselves. No personal significance, or insignificance, can spare one or another of us. The fiery trial through which we pass, will light us down, in honor or dishonor, to the latest generation. We *say* we are for the Union. The world will not forget that we say this. We know how to save the Union. The world knows we do know how to save it. We— even we *here*—hold the power, and bear the responsibility. In *giving* freedom to the *slave,* we *assure* freedom to the *free*—honorable alike in what we give, and what we preserve. We shall nobly save, or meanly lose, the last best, hope of earth.
Annual Message to Congress, 1 Dec. 1862

38 I do order and declare that all persons held as slaves within said designated States, and part of States, are, and henceforward shall be free; . . . And upon this act, sincerely believed to be an act of justice, warranted by the Constitution, upon military necessity, I invoke the considerate judgment of mankind, and the gracious favor of Almighty God.
Emancipation Proclamation, 1 Jan. 1863

39 The signs look better. The Father of Waters [the Mississippi River] again goes unvexed to the sea.
Letter to James C. Conkling, 26 Aug. 1863

40 I do, therefore, invite my fellow citizens . . . to set apart and observe the last Thursday of November next, as a day of Thanksgiving and Praise to our beneficent Father who dwelleth in the Heavens.
Proclamation, 3 Oct. 1863

41 Four score and seven years ago our fathers brought forth on this continent, a new nation, conceived in Liberty, and dedicated to the proposition that all men are created equal.
Now we are engaged in a great civil war, testing whether that nation, or any nation so conceived and so dedicated, can long endure. We are met on a great battlefield of that war. We have come to dedicate a portion of that field, as a final resting place for those who here gave their lives that that nation might live. It is altogether fitting and proper that we should do this.
Gettysburg Address, Gettysburg, Pa., 19 Nov. 1863

42 But, in a larger sense, we cannot dedicate—we cannot consecrate—we cannot hallow—this ground. The brave men, living and dead, who struggled here, have consecrated it far above our poor power to add or detract. The world will little note, nor long remember what we say here, but it can never forget what they did here. It is for us the living, rather, to be dedicated here to the unfinished work which they who fought here have thus far so nobly advanced. It is rather for us to be here dedicated to the great task remaining before us—that from these honored dead we take increased devotion to that cause for which they gave the last full measure of devotion—that we here highly resolve that these dead shall not have died in vain—that this nation, under God, shall have a new birth of freedom—and that government of the people, by the people, for the people, shall not perish from the earth.
Gettysburg Address, Gettysburg, Pa., 19 Nov. 1863. Burton E. Stevenson notes in *The Home Book of Quotations* that "Herndon, in his *Life of Lincoln,* asserts that he gave a copy of this pamphlet [Theodore Parker's *On the Effect of Slavery on the*

American People, printing Parker's 1858 sermon] to Lincoln, who marked" the passage there with the words "over all the people, for all the people, by all the people." Henry Wilson, in a letter to James Redpath et al., 27 Nov. 1860 (printed in the *Evening Transcript* [Boston], 4 Dec. 1860), wrote, "Ours is a government of constitutions and laws, . . . a government of the people, by the people, for the people."
See Theodore Parker 1; Theodore Parker 3; Daniel Webster 5

43 I am naturally anti-slavery. If slavery is not wrong, nothing is wrong. I can not remember when I did not so think, and feel.
Letter to Albert G. Hodges, 4 Apr. 1864

44 By general law life *and* limb must be protected; yet often a limb must be amputated to save a life; but a life is never wisely given to save a limb.
Letter to Albert G. Hodges, 4 Apr. 1864

45 I claim not to have controlled events, but confess plainly that events have controlled me.
Letter to Albert G. Hodges, 4 Apr. 1864

46 The world has never had a good definition of the word liberty, and the American people, just now, are much in want of one. We all declare for liberty; but in using the same *word* we do not all mean the same *thing.* . . . The shepherd drives the wolf from the sheep's throat, for which the sheep thanks the shepherd as a *liberator,* while the wolf denounces him for the same act as the destroyer of liberty, especially as the sheep was a black one. Plainly the sheep and the wolf are not agreed upon a definition of the word liberty; and precisely the same difference prevails today among us human creatures.
Address at Sanitary Fair, Baltimore, Md., 18 Apr. 1864

47 [*On the possibility of his reelection:*] I have not permitted myself, gentlemen, to conclude that I am the best man in the country; but I am reminded, in this connection, of a story of an old Dutch farmer, who remarked to a companion once that "it was not best to swap horses when crossing streams."
Reply to Delegation from National Union League, 9 June 1864. A precursor of this expression appeared in the *New-Hampshire Sentinel,* 19 Feb. 1840 (citing the *Albany Advertiser*): "An Irishman, (said Mr. Hamer) in crossing a river in a boat, with his

mare and colt, was thrown into the river, and clung to the colt's tail. The colt showed signs of exhaustion, and a man on shore told him to leave the colt and cling to the mare's tail. 'Och! faith honey! this is no time to swap horses,' was his reply."

48 Dear Madam,—I have been shown in the files of the War Department a statement of the Adjutant General of Massachusetts, that you are the mother of five sons who have died gloriously on the field of battle. I feel how weak and fruitless must be any words of mine which should attempt to beguile you from the grief of a loss so overwhelming. But I cannot refrain from tendering to you the consolation that may be found in the thanks of the Republic they died to save. I pray that our Heavenly Father may assuage the anguish of your bereavement, and leave you only the cherished memory of the loved and lost, and the solemn pride that must be yours, to have laid so costly a sacrifice upon the altar of Freedom.

Letter to Lydia Bixby, 21 Nov. 1864. Later information corrected the records of Mrs. Bixby's loss from five sons to two sons.

49 It may seem strange that any men should dare to ask a just God's assistance in wringing their bread from the sweat of other men's faces; but let us judge not that we be not judged.

Second Inaugural Address, 4 Mar. 1865
See Bible 221

50 Fondly do we hope—fervently do we pray—that this mighty scourge of war may speedily pass away. Yet, if God wills that it continue, until all the wealth piled by the bond-man's two hundred and fifty years of unrequited toil shall be sunk, and until every drop of blood drawn with the lash, shall be paid by another drawn with the sword, as was said three thousand years ago, so still it must be said "the judgments of the Lord, are true and righteous altogether."

Second Inaugural Address, 4 Mar. 1865

51 With malice toward none; with charity for all; with firmness in the right, as God gives us to see the right, let us strive on to finish the work we are in; to bind up the nation's wounds; to care for him who shall have borne the battle, and for his widow, and his orphan—to do all which may achieve and cherish a just, and a lasting peace, among ourselves, and with all nations.

Second Inaugural Address, 4 Mar. 1865
See John Quincy Adams 2

52 Whenever [I] hear any one, arguing for slavery I feel a strong impulse to see it tried on him personally.

Speech to 140th Indiana regiment, 17 Mar. 1865

53 [*Commenting on his loss to Stephen A. Douglas for senator from Illinois in 1858:*] I feel just like the boy who stubbed his toe—*too d——d badly hurt to laugh and too d——d proud to cry!*

Quoted in *Cincinnati Enquirer*, 16 Sept. 1859

54 Common looking people are the best in the world: that is the reason the Lord makes so many of them.

Quoted in John Hay, Diary, 24 Dec. 1863. Hay's diary relates that Lincoln said these words in a dream, in response to someone in the dream saying of him, "He is a very common-looking man." The more familiar version of the quotation, "God must love the common people, He's made so many of 'em," appeared in the *New York Tribune*, 20 Dec. 1903.

55 If I were to try to read, much less answer, all the attacks made on me, this shop might as well be closed for other business.

Quoted in Francis B. Carpenter, *The Inner Life of Abraham Lincoln: Six Months at the White House* (1869)

56 If the end brings me out all right, what's said against me won't amount to anything. If the end brings me out wrong, ten angels swearing I was right would make no difference.

Quoted in Francis B. Carpenter, *The Inner Life of Abraham Lincoln: Six Months at the White House* (1869)

57 [*Recollection of comment by an old man at an Indiana church meeting, ca. 1810:*] When I do good, I feel good, when I do bad, I feel bad, and that's my religion.

Quoted in William H. Herndon and Jesse W. Weik, *Herndon's Lincoln: The True Story of a Great Life* (1889)
See Hemingway 13

58 That [man] can compress the most words in the fewest ideas of any man I ever knew.

Quoted in Henry Clay Whitney, *Life on the Circuit with Lincoln* (1892)

59 [*Critique of book:*] People who like this sort of thing will find this the sort of thing they like.

Quoted in G. W. E. Russell, *Collections and Recollections* (1898). David Mearns suggests in the *Lincoln Herald* (1965) that the source for this remark was a mock testimonial by Artemus Ward: "For people who like the kind of lectures you deliver, they are just the kind of lectures such people like" (these exact words by Ward appeared in the *Daily Eastern Argus* [Portland, Me.], 23 Oct. 1863).

60 [*Upon meeting Harriet Beecher Stowe, Nov. 1862:*] So you're the little woman who wrote the book that made this great war!

Quoted in *McClure's Magazine*, Apr. 1911. *McClure's* adds: "Mr. Charles Edward Stowe, one of the authors of this article, accompanied his mother on this visit to Lincoln, and remembers this occasion distinctly."

61 Folks are usually about as happy as they make up their minds to be.

Quoted in *Syracuse Herald*, 1 Jan. 1914

62 [*Remark at conference of cabinet members and generals, 10 Jan. 1862:*] If General McClellan did not want to use the army, he would like to borrow it.

Reported in Henry J. Raymond, *The Life and Public Services of Abraham Lincoln* (1865)

63 He [Lincoln] used to liken the case to that of the boy who, when asked how many legs his calf would have if he called its tail a leg, replied, "Five," to which the prompt response was made that *calling* the tail a leg would not make it a leg.

Reported in *Reminiscences of Abraham Lincoln*, ed. A. T. Rice (1886). Garson O'Toole has found an earlier version of this Lincoln anecdote told in the *Daily Milwaukee News*, 23 Sept. 1862, and he has found a very similar, non-Lincoln precursor of the "five legs" riddle in the *Berkshire* (Mass.) *Star*, 28 Apr. 1825.

64 Mr. Lincoln [told] the story of the young man who had an aged father and mother owning considerable property. The young man being an only son and believing that the old people had lived out their usefullness assassinated them both. He was accused, tried, and convicted of the murder. When the judge came to pass sentence upon him and called upon him to give any reason he might have why the sentence of death should not be passed upon him, he with great promptness replied he hoped the court would be lenient upon him because he was a poor orphan.

Reported in Ward Hill Lamon, *Administration of Lincoln* (1886)
See Artemus Ward 1

65 [*After being requested to remove Ulysses S. Grant from command because he drank too much:*] Can you tell me where he gets his whiskey? . . . Because, if I can only find out, I will send a barrel of this wonderful whiskey to every general in the army.

Attributed in *N.Y. Herald*, 18 Sept. 1863. P. M. Zall notes in *Abe Lincoln Laughing* (1982): "This is a switch on an old jestbook favorite, appearing, for instance, in *Joe Miller's Complete Jest Book* (1845), p. 494, where the King of England makes the comment about General James Wolfe." Zall also cites evidence that Lincoln on one occasion denied having invented it, specifically referring to a King George–General Wolfe original in which the King, told that Wolfe was mad, replied, "I wish he would bite some of my other generals then."
See George II 1

66 You can fool part of the people some of the time, you can fool some of the people all of the time, but you cannot fool all the people all of the time.

Attributed in *Albany Times*, 8 Mar. 1886. According to *The Collected Works of Abraham Lincoln*, ed. Roy P. Basler, "Tradition has come to attribute to the Clinton [Illinois] speeches [2 September 1858]" this "most famous" of Lincoln's utterances. Basler indicates, however, that there is no evidence of this saying in Lincoln documents. P. T. Barnum has also been a putative source for the quotation. Garson O'Toole has found "You can fool all the people part of the time, or you can fool some people all the time, but you cannot fool all people all the time," without attribution to any individual, in the *Syracuse Daily Standard*, 9 Sept. 1885.
See Abbadie 1; Diderot 1

67 It is better to remain silent at the risk of being thought a fool, than to talk and remove all doubt of it.

Attributed in Maurice Switzer, *Mrs. Goose, Her Book* (1907)

68 "The sun," said Mr. Bull, "never sets on English dominion. Do you understand how that is?" "Oh, yes," said the Indian, "that is because God is afraid to trust them in the dark."

Attributed in Emanuel Hertz, *Lincoln Talks* (1939)
See North 1

69 A lawyer's time and advice are his stock in trade.

Attributed in *Bulletin, Lincoln National Life Foundation,* 11 July 1949. Michael J. Musmanno notes in his dissenting opinion in *Sterling v. Philadelphia* (1954): "A study of Lincoln's accredited writings fails to produce this aphorism. . . . The Lincoln National Life Foundation, which makes an effort to trace the origin of supposed Lincoln sayings, reports that this one . . . apparently came to life in a plaque produced by the Allen Smith Company in Indianapolis . . . (Bulletin, Lincoln National Life Foundation No. 1057, July 11, 1949.)"

Anne Morrow Lindbergh
U.S. author, 1906–2001

1 The Wave of the Future.
   Title of book (1940)

2 I . . . understand why the saints were rarely married women. I am convinced it has nothing inherently to do, as I once supposed, with chastity or children. It has to do primarily with distractions. . . . Women's normal occupations in general run counter to creative life, or contemplative life or saintly life.
   Gift from the Sea ch. 2 (1955)

3 The most exhausting thing in life, I have discovered, is being insincere.
   Gift from the Sea ch. 2 (1955)

4 By and large, mothers and housewives are the only workers who do not have regular time off. They are the great vacationless class.
   Gift from the Sea ch. 3 (1955)

5 Him that I love, I wish to be
   Free—
   Even from me.
   "Even—" (1956)

6 [*Diary entry, 5 Aug. 1939:*] Life itself is always pulling you away from the understanding of life.
   War Within and War Without (1980)

Charles Lindbergh
U.S. aviator, 1902–1974

1 We (that's my ship and I) took off rather suddenly. We had a report somewhere around 4 o'clock in the afternoon before that the weather would be fine, so we thought we would try it.
   N.Y. Times, 23 May 1927

2 I saw a fleet of fishing boats. . . . I flew down almost touching the craft and yelled at them, asking if I was on the right road to Ireland. They just stared. Maybe they didn't hear me. Maybe I didn't hear them. Or maybe they thought I was just a crazy fool. An hour later I saw land.
   N.Y. Times, 23 May 1927

R. M. Lindner
U.S. psychologist, 1914–1956

1 Rebel Without a Cause.
   Title of book (1944)

Vachel Lindsay
U.S. poet, 1879–1931

1 A bronzed, lank man! His suit of ancient black,
   A famous high top-hat and plain worn shawl
   Make him the quaint figure that men love,
   The prairie-lawyer, master of us all.
   "Abraham Lincoln Walks at Midnight" l. 9 (1914)

2 It breaks his heart that men must murder still,
   That all his hours of travail here for men
   Seem yet in vain. And who will bring white
      peace
   That he may sleep upon his hill again?
   "Abraham Lincoln Walks at Midnight" l. 29 (1914)

Carolus Linnaeus
Swedish botanist and taxonomist, 1707–1778

1 I ask you and the whole world for a generic differentia between man and ape which conforms to the principles of natural history. I certainly know of none.
   Letter to J. G. Gmelin, 14 Jan. 1747 (translation by Gunnar Broberg)

2 Nature does not make jumps.
   Philosophia Botanica aphorism 77 (1751)

Lin Yutang
Chinese author and linguist, 1895–1976

1 The Chinese do not draw any distinction between food and medicine.
   The Importance of Living ch. 9 (1938)

Li Po
Chinese poet, 701–762

1 Since Life is but a Dream,
   Why toil to no avail?
   "A Homily on Ideals in Life, Uttered in Springtime on Rising from a Drunken Slumber" (ca. 750)
   See Calderón de la Barca 1; Carroll 44; Folk and Anonymous Songs 67; Proverbs 169

2 Beneath the blossoms with a pot of wine,
   No friends at hand, so I poured alone;

I raised my cup to invite the moon,
Turned to my shadow, and we became three.
"Drinking Alone in the Midnight" (eighth cent.)
(translation by Elling Eide)

Walter Lippmann
U.S. journalist, 1889–1974

1 The newspaper is in all literalness the bible
of democracy, the book out of which a people
determines its conduct. It is the only serious
book most people read. It is the only book they
read every day.
Liberty and the News ch. 2 (1920)

2 The subtlest and most pervasive of all
influences are those which create and maintain
the repertory of stereotypes. We are told about
the world before we see it. We imagine most
things before we experience them.
Public Opinion ch. 6 (1922)

3 Franklin D. Roosevelt is no crusader. He is
no tribune of the people. He is no enemy of
entrenched privilege. He is a pleasant man
who, without any important qualifications
for the office, would very much like to be
President.
N.Y. Herald Tribune, 8 Jan. 1932

Franz Liszt
Hungarian composer and pianist, 1811–1886

1 [*In response to the suggestion that his music was
being neglected:*] I can wait.
Quoted in Frederic Lamond, *Memoirs* (1949)

Little Richard (Richard Penniman)
U.S. rock musician, 1932–2020

1 A-wop-bop-a-loo-bop a-lop-bam-boo.
Tutti Frutti, aw-rootie.
"Tutti-Frutti" (song) (1955). Cowritten with J. Lubin
and Dorothy La Bostrie.

Maxim Litvinov
Soviet diplomat, 1876–1951

1 Peace is indivisible.
Note to Allies, 25 Feb. 1920

Jay Livingston
U.S. songwriter, 1915–2001

1 Que sera, sera,
Whatever will be will be;
The future's not ours to see.
"Whatever Will Be, Will Be (Que Sera, Sera)" (song)
(1955). Cowritten with Ray Evans.
See Proverbs 203

LL Cool J (James Todd Smith)
U.S. musician and actor, 1968–

1 Don't call it a comeback
I've been here for years.
"Mama Said Knock You Out" (song) (1991)

Richard Llewellyn
Welsh novelist and playwright, 1907–1983

1 How green was my Valley . . . and the Valley of
them that have gone.
How Green Was My Valley ch. 42 (1939)

Alain Locke
U.S. writer and philosopher, 1885–1954

1 Of all the voluminous literature on the
Negro, so much is mere external view and
commentary that we may warrantably say that
nine-tenths of it is *about* the Negro rather than
of him, so that it is the Negro problem rather
than the Negro that is known.
The New Negro foreword (1925)

John Locke
English philosopher, 1632–1704

1 New opinions are always suspected, and usually
opposed, without any other reason but because
they are not already common.
An Essay Concerning Human Understanding
"Dedicatory Epistle" (1690)

2 Let us suppose the mind to be, as we say, white
paper, void of all characters, without any ideas;
how comes it to be furnished? Whence comes it
by that vast store which the busy and boundless
fancy of man has painted on it with an almost
endless variety? Whence has it all the materials
of reason and knowledge? To this I answer, in
one word, from *experience*.
An Essay Concerning Human Understanding bk. 2,
ch. 1, sec. 2 (1690)

3 It is one thing to show a man that he is in error, and another to put him in possession of truth.

An Essay Concerning Human Understanding bk. 4, ch. 7, sec. 11 (1690)

4 All men are liable to error; and most men are, in many points, by passion or interest, under temptation to it.

An Essay Concerning Human Understanding bk. 4, ch. 20, sec. 17 (1690)

5 In the beginning all the World was *America*.

Second Treatise of Civil Government ch. 5, sec. 49 (1690)

6 The end of law is, not to abolish or restrain, but to preserve and enlarge freedom.

Second Treatise of Civil Government ch. 6, sec. 57 (1690)

7 Man being . . . by nature all free, equal, and independent, no one can be put out of this estate, and subjected to the political power of another, without his own consent.

Second Treatise of Civil Government ch. 8, sec. 95 (1690)

8 The great and chief end, therefore, of men's uniting into commonwealths, and putting themselves under government, is the preservation of their property.

Second Treatise of Civil Government ch. 9, sec. 124 (1690)

9 Wherever Law ends, Tyranny begins.

Second Treatise of Civil Government ch. 18, sec. 202 (1690)

10 Good and evil, reward and punishment, are the only motives to a rational creature: these are the spur and reins whereby all mankind are set on work, and guided.

Some Thoughts Concerning Education sec. 54 (1693)

11 Virtue is harder to be got than a knowledge of the world; and, if lost in a young man, is seldom recovered.

Some Thoughts Concerning Education sec. 70 (1693)

12 The only fence against the world is a thorough knowledge of it.

Some Thoughts Concerning Education sec. 88 (1693)

Belva Lockwood
U.S. lawyer and feminist, 1830–1917

1 [*Arguing for the admittance of women to practice law before the U.S. Supreme Court:*] The glory of each generation is to make its own precedents.

Speech to National Convention of Woman Suffrage Association, Washington, D.C., 16–17 Jan. 1877

David Lodge
English novelist, 1935–

1 Literature is mostly about having sex and not much about having children. Life is the other way around.

The British Museum Is Falling Down ch. 4 (1965)

Frank Loesser
U.S. songwriter, 1910–1969

1 See what the boys in the backroom will have
And tell them I'm having the same.

"The Boys in the Backroom" (song) (1939)

2 I'd love to get you
On a slow boat to China.
All to myself alone.

"On a Slow Boat to China" (song) (1948). The expression "slow boat to China" predated Loesser. The *Washington Post*, 23 Dec. 1947, for example, states, "As the old proverb says, I'd like to get him on a slow boat to China."

3 Once in love with Amy,
Always in love with Amy.

"Once in Love with Amy" (song) (1948)

4 I got the horse right here,
The name is Paul Revere.

"Fugue for Tinhorns" (song) (1950)

5 When you meet a gent
Paying all kinds of rent
For a flat
That could flatten the Taj Mahal.
Call it sad, call it funny,
But it's better than even money
That the guy's only doing it for some doll.

"Guys and Dolls" (song) (1950)

6 Luck Be a Lady Tonight.

Title of song (1950)

7 Sit Down, You're Rockin' the Boat.

Title of song (1950)

Frederick Loewe

German-born U.S. composer, 1904–1988

1 I don't like my music, but what is my opinion against that of millions of others.

Quoted in Nat Shapiro, *An Encyclopedia of Quotations About Music* (1978)

Logan

Native American leader, 1725–1780

1 I appeal to any white man to say, if ever he entered Logan's cabin hungry, and he gave him not meat; if ever he came cold and naked, and he clothed him not.

Address to council with Governor of Virginia, 11 Nov. 1774

Horace Logan

U.S. radio producer, ca. 1916–2002

1 Elvis has left the building.

Announcement at end of Elvis Presley concert, Shreveport, La., 15 Dec. 1956. This became a habitual close to Presley's concerts and more generally a phrase connoting finality.

Friedrich von Logau

German poet, 1604–1655

1 Though the mills of God grind slowly, yet they grind exceeding small.

Sinnegedichte no. 3224 (1654) (translation by Henry Wadsworth Longfellow). The *Oxford Dictionary of Quotations* notes that this is a "translation of an anonymous verse in Sextus Empiricus *Adversus Mathematicos* bk. 1, sect. 287."
See Proverbs 192

Christopher Logue

English poet, 1926–2011

1 Come to the edge.
We might fall.
Come to the edge.
It's too high!
COME TO THE EDGE!
And they came
and he pushed
and they flew . . .

"Come to the Edge" l. 1 (1969)

Vince Lombardi

U.S. football coach, 1913–1970

1 Winning isn't everything, but wanting to win is!

Quoted in *Esquire*, Nov. 1962
See Modern Proverbs 99; "Red"Sanders 1

Jack London (John Griffith Chaney)

U.S. novelist, 1876–1916

1 The Call of the Wild.

Title of book (1903)

2 I would rather be ashes than dust! I would rather that my spark should burn out in a brilliant blaze than it should be stifled by dry-rot. I would rather be a superb meteor, every atom of me in magnificent glow, than a sleepy and permanent planet. The proper function of man is to live, not to exist. I shall not waste my days in trying to prolong them. I shall use my time.

Quoted in *Bulletin* (San Francisco), 2 Dec. 1916. Known as London's Credo.

Huey Long

U.S. politician, 1893–1935

1 Every Man a King.

Title of book (1933). Long was quoting William Jennings Bryan, who had said, "every man a king, but no one wears a crown."

2 For the present you can just call me the Kingfish.

Every Man a King ch. 27 (1933)

3 Huey Long once remarked that America probably would have Fascism some day, but, he added, "when we get it we won't call it Fascism, we'll call it anti-Fascism."

Reported in *Owosso* (Mich.) *Argus-Press*, 11 Oct. 1938. Norman Thomas, in a speech in Cincinnati, attributed a similar remark to Long, according to the *Cincinnati Enquirer*, 22 Feb. 1936.

Russell B. Long

U.S. politician, 1918–2003

1 [*Describing tax reform:*] Don't tax you, don't tax me, tax that fellow behind the tree.

Quoted in *Forbes*, 15 Dec. 1976

Henry Wadsworth Longfellow
U.S. poet, 1807–1882

1 Tell me not, in mournful numbers,
   Life is but an empty dream!
   For the soul is dead that slumbers,
   And things are not what they seem.
   Life is real! Life is earnest!
   And the grave is not its goal;
   Dust thou art, to dust returnest,
   Was not spoken of the soul.
   "A Psalm of Life" st. 1–2 (1838)
   See Bible 22

2 Art is long, and Time is fleeting,
   And our hearts, though stout and brave,
   Still, like muffled drums, are beating
   Funeral marches to the grave.
   "A Psalm of Life" st. 4 (1838)
   See Chaucer 4; Hippocrates 1

3 Trust no Future, howe'er pleasant!
   Let the dead Past bury its dead!
   Act,—act in the living Present!
   Heart within, and God o'erhead!
   "A Psalm of Life" st. 6 (1838)
   See Bible 233

4 Lives of great men all remind us
   We can make our lives sublime,
   And, departing, leave behind us
   Footprints on the sands of time.
   "A Psalm of Life" st. 7 (1838)

5 Let us, then, be up and doing,
   With a heart for any fate;
   Still achieving, still pursuing,
   Learn to labor and to wait.
   "A Psalm of Life" st. 9 (1838)

6 There is a Reaper whose name is Death,
   And, with his sickle keen,
   He reaps the bearded grain at a breath,
   And the flowers that grow between.
   "The Reaper and the Flowers" st. 1 (1839)

7 Under a spreading chestnut tree
   The village smithy stands;
   The smith, a mighty man is he,
   With large and sinewy hands;
   And the muscles of his brawny arms
   Are strong as iron bands.
   "The Village Blacksmith" st. 1 (1839)

8 His brow is wet with honest sweat,
   He earns whate'er he can,
   And looks the whole world in the face,
   For he owes not any man.
   "The Village Blacksmith" st. 2 (1839)

9 Each morning sees some task begin,
   Each evening sees it close;
   Something attempted, something done,
   Has earned a night's repose.
   "The Village Blacksmith" st. 7 (1839)

10 The shades of night were falling fast,
    As through an Alpine village passed
    A youth, who bore, 'mid snow and ice,
    A banner with the strange device,
    Excelsior!
    "Excelsior" st. 1 (1841)

11 Into each life some rain must fall,
    Some days must be dark and dreary.
    "The Rainy Day" st. 3 (1842)

12   The bards sublime,
    Whose distant footsteps echo
    Through the corridors of Time.
    "The Day Is Done" st. 5 (1844)

13 And the night shall be filled with music,
    And the cares, that infest the day,
    Shall fold their tents, like the Arabs,
    And as silently steal away.
    "The Day Is Done" st. 11 (1844)

14 I shot an arrow into the air,
     It fell to earth, I know not where.
       "The Arrow and the Song" st. 1 (1845)

15 This is the forest primeval. The murmuring
         pines and the hemlocks,
     Bearded with moss, and in garments green,
         indistinct in the twilight,
     Stand like Druids of old, with voices sad and
         prophetic.
       Evangeline introduction (1847)

16 Thou too, sail on, O Ship of State!
     Sail on, O Union, strong and great!
     Humanity with all its fears,
     With all the hopes of future years,
     Is hanging breathless on thy fate!
       "The Building of the Ship" l. 378 (1849)

17 By the shores of Gitche Gumee,
     By the shining Big-Sea-Water,
     Stood the wigwam of Nokomis,
     Daughter of the Moon, Nokomis.
       The Song of Hiawatha pt. 3 (1855)

18 From the waterfall he named her,
     Minnehaha, Laughing Water.
       The Song of Hiawatha pt. 4 (1855)

19 As unto the bow the cord is,
     So unto the man is woman,
     Though she bends him, she obeys him,
     Though she draws him, yet she follows,
     Useless each without the other!
       The Song of Hiawatha pt. 10 (1855)

20 A Lady with a Lamp shall stand
     In the great history of the land,
     A noble type of good,
     Heroic womanhood.
       "Santa Filomena" st. 10 (1858). Longfellow was
       writing here of Florence Nightingale.

21 Between the dark and the daylight,
     When the night is beginning to lower,
     Comes a pause in the day's occupations,
     That is known as the Children's Hour.
       "The Children's Hour" st. 1 (1859)

22 I hear in the chamber above me
     The patter of little feet.
       "The Children's Hour" st. 2 (1859)

23 Listen, my children, and you shall hear
     Of the midnight ride of Paul Revere,

On the eighteenth of April in Seventy-five;
     Hardly a man is now alive
     Who remembers that famous day and year.
       Tales of a Wayside Inn pt. 1 "The Landlord's Tale: Paul
       Revere's Ride" st. 1 (1863)

24 One if by land and two if by sea;
     And I on the opposite shore will be,
     Ready to ride and sound the alarm
     Through every Middlesex village and farm.
       Tales of a Wayside Inn pt. 1 "The Landlord's Tale: Paul
       Revere's Ride" st. 2 (1863)
       See Revere 1

25 The fate of a nation was riding that night.
       Tales of a Wayside Inn pt. 1 "The Landlord's Tale: Paul
       Revere's Ride" st. 8 (1863)

26 Ships that pass in the night, and speak each
         other in passing;
     Only a signal shown and a distant voice in the
         darkness;
     So on the ocean of life we pass and speak one
         another,
     Only a look and a voice; then darkness again
         and a silence.
       Tales of a Wayside Inn pt. 3 "The Theologian's Tale:
       Elizabeth" pt. 4 (1874)

27 The love of learning, the sequestered nooks,
     And all the sweet serenity of books.
       "Morituri Salutamus" st. 21 (1875)

28 There was a little girl
     Who had a little curl
     Right in the middle of her forehead,
     When she was good
     She was very, very good,
     But when she was bad she was horrid.
       Attributed in Blanche Roosevelt Tucker Macchetta,
       The Home Life of Henry W. Longfellow (1882).
       Longfellow is said to have composed a version of this
       and sung it to his young daughter in the 1850s. In the
       Macchetta book the exact wording is as follows:
       There was a little durl,
       And she had a little curl
       That hung in the middle of her forehead,
       When she was dood,
       She was very dood indeed,
       But when she was bad she was horrid.
       The *Oxford Dictionary of Nursery Rhymes,* however,
       casts doubt on Longfellow's authorship, suggesting a
       possible British origin. The earliest known printing
       was in a pre-1870 broadside titled "Wrong Side Up.
       A Poem."
       See Mae West 6

Alice Roosevelt Longworth

U.S. socialite, 1884–1980

1 [Calvin Coolidge looks as if he was] weaned on a pickle.

Quoted in *Wash. Post*, 12 Oct. 1924

2 [*Of Thomas E. Dewey:*] How can you vote for a man who looks like the bridegroom on a wedding cake?

Quoted in *Time*, 10 July 1944. This was later usually phrased as "the little man on the wedding cake." Longworth herself said she had taken this witticism from Ethel Barrymore or someone else, and Walter Winchell claimed coinage.

3 [*Of Thomas E. Dewey's second nomination for president, 1948:*] You can't make a soufflé rise twice.

Quoted in *Philadelphia Inquirer*, 8 Nov. 1948

4 [*Motto embroidered on sofa pillow:*] If you can't say something good about someone, sit right here by me.

Quoted in *Saturday Evening Post*, 4 Dec. 1965
See Modern Proverbs 78

5 I have a simple philosophy. Fill what's empty, empty what's full, and scratch where it itches.

Quoted in Peter Passell and Leonard Ross, *The Best* (1974)

Nicholas Longworth

U.S. politician, 1869–1931

1 Perhaps his most crushing riposte was directed at a presumptuous Congressman who passed his hand over Longworth's bald head and remarked, "Feels just like my wife's bottom." Longworth passed his own hand over his own head, and then said thoughtfully: "By golly, it does, doesn't it?"

Reported in Stewart Alsop, *The Center: People and Power in Political Washington* (1968). Although this anecdote is now associated with Longworth, Garson O'Toole has traced precursors as far back as 1924, when the *Roswell* (N.M.) *Daily Record*, 12 July, printed a version referring to "my wife's cheek."

Anita Loos

U.S. writer, 1893–1981

1 Gentlemen Prefer Blondes.

Title of book (1925)

2 So I really think that American gentlemen are the best after all, because kissing your hand may make you feel very very good but a diamond and safire bracelet lasts forever.

Gentlemen Prefer Blondes ch. 4 (1925)
See Advertising Slogans 38; Robin 2

Lisa "Left Eye" Lopes

U.S. rhythm and blues musician, 1971–2002

1 Don't go chasing waterfalls
Please stick to the rivers and the lakes that you're used to
I know that you're gonna have it your way or nothing at all
But I think you're moving too fast.

"Waterfalls" (song) (1994)

Lorde (Ella Marija Lani Yelich-O'Connor)

New Zealand singer and songwriter, 1996–

1 I've never seen a diamond in the flesh
I cut my teeth on wedding rings in the movies.

"Royals" (song) (2013)

Audre Lorde

West Indian–born U.S. writer and educator, 1934–1992

1 The Master's Tools Will Never Dismantle the Master's House.

Title of essay (1979)

2 Pain is an event, an experience that must be recognized, named, and then used in some way in order for the experience to change, to be transformed into something else, strength or knowledge or action.

Sister Outsider "Eye to Eye: Black Women, Hatred, and Anger" (1984)

Sophia Loren

Italian actress, 1934–

1 Sex appeal is 50 per cent what you've got and 50 per cent what people think you've got.

Quoted in *Anniston* (Ala.) *Star*, 13 Dec. 1957

2 Everything you see I owe to spaghetti.

Quoted in *Mansfield* (Ohio) *News Journal*, 10 Nov. 1963

Edward N. Lorenz

U.S. meteorologist, 1917–2008

1 Predictability: Does the Flap of a Butterfly's Wings in Brazil Set Off a Tornado in Texas?

Title of paper delivered to the American Association for the Advancement of Science, Washington, D.C., 29 Dec. 1972
See Farmer 2; Gleick 1

Konrad Lorenz

Austrian zoologist, 1903–1989

1 It is a good morning exercise for a research scientist to discard a pet hypothesis every day before breakfast.

On Aggression ch. 2 (1966)

2 Man appears to be the missing link between anthropoid apes and human beings.

Quoted in *N.Y. Times Magazine*, 11 Apr. 1965

Trent Lott

U.S. politician, 1941–

1 I want to say this about my state: When Strom Thurmond ran for president, we voted for him. We're proud of it. And if the rest of the country had followed our lead, we wouldn't have had all these problems over all these years, either.

Remarks at Strom Thurmond's one-hundredth birthday party, Washington, D.C., 5 Dec. 2002. These comments, apparently endorsing Thurmond's legacy of racism, caused a furor culminating in Lott's resignation as Senate majority leader (Republican).

Louis XIV

French king, 1638–1715

1 Every time I fill an office I make a hundred malcontents and one ingrate.

Quoted in Voltaire, *Siècle de Louis XIV* (1753)

2 [*Probably apocryphal remark before the Parlement de Paris, 13 Apr. 1655:*] L'État c'est moi.
I am the State.

Attributed in Charles Pinot Duclos, *Mémoires Secrets sur les Règnes de Louis XIV et de Louis XV* (1791)

3 [*Remark after a coach he had ordered arrived barely in time for him:*] I almost had to wait.

Attributed in Edouard Fournier, *L'Esprit dans l'Histoire* (1857)

Louis XVI

French king, 1754–1793

1 [*Diary entry on the day of the storming of the Bastille, 14 July 1789:*] Rien.
Nothing.

Quoted in Simon Schama, *Citizens* (1989)

Louis XVIII

French king, 1755–1824

1 *Rappelez-vous bien qu'il n'est aucun de vous qui n'ait dans sa giberne le bâton de maréchal du duc de Reggio.*
Remember that there is not one of you who does not carry in his cartridge-pouch the marshal's baton of the duke of Reggio.

Speech to cadets of St. Cyr, 9 Aug. 1819

2 *L'exactitude est la politesse des rois.*
Punctuality is the politeness of kings.

Attributed in *Souvenirs de J. Lafitte* (1844)

Joe Louis (Joseph Louis Barrow)

U.S. boxer, 1914–1981

1 [*Of World War II:*] We're goin' to do our part, and we'll win 'cause we're on God's side.

Quoted in *N.Y. Times*, 16 Mar. 1942. Popularly quoted as "God's on our side."

2 [*Remark to reporter before his June 1946 heavyweight championship fight against Billy Conn:*] He can run but he can't hide.

Quoted in *N.Y. Times*, 20 June 1946. The *Times* story stated, "That bit of homespun philosophy was offered in his training camp by Joe Louis less than a fortnight ago." Earlier, the *Los Angeles Times*, 3 July 1939, had quoted Louis: "Remember one thing—when you're in the ring you can run—but you can't hide."

Louis Philippe

French king, 1773–1850

1 [*Of friendly relations between France and England:*] L'entente cordiale.

Speech from the throne, 27 Dec. 1843

Richard Louv

U.S. author and journalist, 1949–

1 When I talk about nature-deficit disorder with groups of parents and educators, the meaning of the phrase is clear. Nature-deficit disorder

describes the human costs of alienation from nature, among them: diminished use of the senses, attention difficulties, and higher rates of physical and emotional illnesses.

Last Child in the Woods ch. 3 (2005)

H. P. Lovecraft

U.S. writer, 1890–1937

1 The most merciful thing in the world, I think, is the inability of the human mind to correlate all its contents.

The Call of Cthulhu ch. 1 (1928)

2 [*On Ambrose Bierce's* Devil's Dictionary:] That sort of thing wears thin—for when one's cynicism becomes perfect and absolute, there is no longer anything amusing in the stupidity and hypocrisy of the herd. It is all to be expected—what else *could* human nature produce?—so irony annuls itself by means of its own victories!

Letter to August W. Derleth, Jan. 1928

Augusta Ada King, Countess of Lovelace

English mathematician, 1815–1852

1 The Analytical Engine [Charles Babbage's visionary computer] has no pretensions whatever to *originate* anything. It can do whatever we *know how to order* it to perform. It can *follow* analysis; but it has no power of *anticipating* any analytical relations or truths.

Taylor's Scientific Memoirs, Sept. 1843
See Babbage 1; Modern Proverbs 33

2 We may say most aptly that the Analytical Engine [Charles Babbage's visionary computer] *weaves algebraical patterns* just as the Jacquard loom weaves flowers and leaves.

Taylor's Scientific Memoirs, Sept. 1843

Richard Lovelace

English poet, 1618–1658

1 Stone walls do not a prison make,
  Nor iron bars a cage.

"To Althea, from Prison" l. 25 (1649)

2 I could not love thee, Dear, so much,
  Loved I not honor more.

"To Lucasta, Going to the Wars" l. 11 (1649)

James Lovell

U.S. astronaut, 1928–

1 Houston, we've had a problem.

Transmission on Apollo 13 mission to the moon, 13 Apr. 1970. This sentence was made famous by the 1995 motion picture *Apollo 13*, where it was spoken as "Houston, we have a problem." Lovell's command module pilot, Jack Swigert, actually preceded Lovell's line by saying, "Hey, we've got a problem here. . . . Okay, Houston, we've had a problem here."

James Lovelock

English environmentalist, 1919–

1 We have . . . defined Gaia as a complex entity involving the Earth's biosphere, atmosphere, oceans, and soil: the totality constituting a feedback or cybernetic system which seeks an optimal physical and chemical environment for life on this planet.

Gaia: A New Look at Life on Earth ch. 1 (1979). Lovelock credited writer William Golding with suggesting the goddess *Gaia* as the name of the hypothetical entity.
See Goethe 23

David Low

New Zealand–born British political cartoonist, 1891–1963

1 Very well, alone.

Caption of cartoon, *Evening Standard* (London), 18 June 1940. Low's cartoon showed a British soldier gesturing defiantly to a sky full of bombers after the fall of France to Germany.

2 I have never met anyone who wasn't against war. Even Hitler and Mussolini were, according to themselves.

Quoted in *N.Y. Times Magazine,* 10 Feb. 1946

A. Lawrence Lowell

U.S. university president, 1856–1943

1 [*On why universities have so much learning:*] The freshmen bring a little in and the seniors take none out, so it accumulates through the years.

Quoted in *Reader's Digest,* May 1949. Although this line is associated with Lowell, James Pycroft, *A Course of English Reading* (1844), included the following attribution: "[Jonathan] Swift said that the reason a certain university was a learned place was, that most persons took some learning there, and few brought any away with them, so it accumulated."

Amy Lowell

U.S. poet, 1874–1925

1 All books are either dreams or swords,
You can cut, or you can drug, with words.
"Sword Blades and Poppy Seeds" l. 291 (1914)

2 For the man who should loose me is dead,
Fighting with the Duke in Flanders,
In a pattern called a war.
Christ! What are patterns for?
"Patterns" l. 104 (1916)

James Russell Lowell

U.S. writer and diplomat, 1819–1891

1 Blessed are the horny hands of toil!
"A Glance Behind the Curtain" l. 205 (1843)
See Salisbury 2

2 Truth forever on the scaffold, Wrong forever on
the throne.
"The Present Crisis" st. 8 (1845)

3 And what is so rare as a day in June?
Then, if ever, come perfect days.
"The Vision of Sir Launfal" prelude to pt. 1, st. 5
(1848)

4 Democ'acy gives every man
The right to be his own oppressor.
The Biglow Papers, Second Series, "Ef I a song or two
could make" l. 97 (1867)

5 Though old the thought and oft expressed,
'Tis his at last who says it best.
"For an Autograph" st. 5 (1868)

Robert Lowell

U.S. poet, 1917–1977

1 These are the tranquillized Fifties,
and I am forty. Ought I to regret my seedtime?
I was a fire-breathing Catholic C.O.,
and made my manic statement,
telling off the state and president, and then
sat waiting sentence in the bull pen
beside a negro boy with curlicues
of marijuana in his hair.
"Memories of West Street and Lepke" l. 12 (1959)

2 Their monument sticks like a fishbone
in the city's throat.
"For the Union Dead" l. 29 (1964)

3 Everywhere,
giant finned cars nose forward like fish;
a savage servility
slides by on grease.
"For the Union Dead" l. 65 (1964)

Janette Sebring Lowrey

U.S. children's book writer, 1892–1986

1 Five little puppies dug a hole under the fence
and went for a walk in the wide, wide world.
The Poky Little Puppy (1942)

2 "Now where in the world is that poky little
puppy?," they wondered.
The Poky Little Puppy (1942)

Malcolm Lowry

English novelist, 1909–1957

1 How alike are the groans of love to those of the
dying.
Under the Volcano ch. 12 (1947)

Robert Lowry

U.S. songwriter and theologian, 1826–1899

1 Yes, we'll gather at the river,
The beautiful, the beautiful river—
Gather with the saints at the river
That flows by the throne of God.
"Beautiful River" (song) (1864)

Lucan (Marcus Annaeus Lucanus)

Roman poet, 39–65

1 It is not granted to know which man took up
arms with more right on his side. Each pleads
his cause before a great judge: the winning
cause pleased the gods, but the losing cause
pleased Cato.
Pharsalia bk. 1, l. 128
See Pollard 1

2 [Of Julius Caesar:] Thinking nothing done while
anything remained to be done.
Pharsalia bk. 2, l. 657

3 I have a wife, I have sons: we have given so
many hostages to the fates.
Pharsalia bk. 6, l. 661
See Francis Bacon 15

George Lucas
U.S. film director, 1944–

1 Star Wars.
Title of motion picture (1977)

2 [*Opening title:*] A long time ago in a galaxy far, far away . . .
Star Wars (motion picture) (1977)

3 [*Obi-Wan Kenobi, played by Alec Guinness, speaking:*] Vader was seduced by the dark side of the Force. . . . The Force is what gives the Jedi his power. It's an energy field created by all living things. It surrounds us, it permeates us, it binds the galaxy together.
Star Wars (motion picture) (1977)

4 [*Obi-Wan Kenobi, played by Alec Guinness, speaking:*] Mos Eisley Spaceport. You will never find a more wretched hive of scum and villainy.
Star Wars (motion picture) (1977)

5 [*Obi-Wan Kenobi, played by Alec Guinness, speaking:*] There is a great disturbance in the Force.
Star Wars (motion picture) (1977)

6 [*Obi-Wan Kenobi, played by Alec Guinness, speaking:*] May the Force be with you!
Star Wars (motion picture) (1977)

7 [*Obi-Wan Kenobi, played by Alec Guinness, speaking:*] Use the Force, Luke.
Star Wars (motion picture) (1977)

8 [*Darth Vader, voiced by James Earl Jones, speaking about Luke Skywalker:*] The Force is strong with this one!
Star Wars (motion picture) (1977)

9 [*Obi-Wan Kenobi, played by Alec Guinness, speaking:*] The Force will be with you—always.
Star Wars (motion picture) (1977)

10 The Empire Strikes Back.
Title of motion picture (1980). Coauthored with Leigh Brackett and Lawrence Kasdan.

11 [*Opening title:*] It is a period of civil war. Rebel spaceships, striking from a hidden base, have won their first victory against the evil Galactic Empire.
The Empire Strikes Back (motion picture) (1980)
See Ronald Reagan 6

12 [*Yoda, voiced by Frank Oz, speaking:*] My ally is the Force, and a powerful ally it is. . . . Its energy surrounds us and binds us. Luminous beings are we, not this crude matter. You must feel the Force around you, between you, me, the tree, the rock, everywhere. Yes, even between the land and the ship.
The Empire Strikes Back (motion picture) (1980). Coauthored with Leigh Brackett and Lawrence Kasdan.

13 [*Han Solo, played by Harrison Ford, speaking:*] Never tell me the odds!
The Empire Strikes Back (motion picture) (1980). Coauthored with Leigh Brackett and Lawrence Kasdan.

14 [*Yoda, voiced by Frank Oz, speaking:*] Do. Or do not. There is no try.
The Empire Strikes Back (motion picture) (1980). Coauthored with Leigh Brackett and Lawrence Kasdan.

15 [*Darth Vader, voiced by James Earl Jones, speaking to Luke Skywalker, played by Mark Hamill:*] I am your father.
The Empire Strikes Back (motion picture) (1980). Coauthored with Leigh Brackett and Lawrence Kasdan.

16 [*Darth Vader, voiced by James Earl Jones, speaking to Luke Skywalker, played by Mark Hamill:*] Join me, and together we can rule the galaxy as father and son.
The Empire Strikes Back (motion picture) (1980). Coauthored with Leigh Brackett and Lawrence Kasdan.

17 [*Yoda, voiced by Frank Oz, speaking:*] When nine hundred years old you reach, look as good you will not.
Return of the Jedi (motion picture) (1983)

18 [*Padmé, played by Natalie Portman, speaking:*] This is how liberty dies—with thunderous applause.
Revenge of the Sith (motion picture) (2005)

Clare Boothe Luce
U.S. politician and writer, 1903–1987

1 Nature abhors . . . a virgin—a frozen asset.
The Women act 1, sc. 1 (1937)

2 You know, that's the only good thing about divorce; you get to sleep with your mother.
The Women act 2, sc. 4 (1937)

3 But much of what Mr. [Vice-President Henry] Wallace calls his global thinking is, no matter how you slice it, still "globaloney." Mr. Wallace's warp of sense and his woof of nonsense is very tricky cloth out of which to cut the pattern of a post-war world.

Remarks in House of Representatives, 9 Feb. 1943

4 But if God had wanted us to think just with our wombs, why did He give us a brain?

Slam the Door Softly (1970)

5 All history shows that the hand that cradles the *rock* has ruled the world, *not* the hand that rocks the cradle!

Slam the Door Softly (1970)
See Proverbs 133

6 Whenever a Republican leaves one side of the aisle and goes to the other [Democratic side], it raises the intelligence quotient of both parties.

Quoted in James C. Humes, *Speaker's Treasury of Anecdotes About the Famous* (1978)

7 No good deed goes unpunished.

Attributed in *Miami Daily News*, 27 July 1949. Usually associated with Luce, but there is an earlier occurrence in Walter Winchell's column, *Cincinnati Enquirer*, 2 Oct. 1942: "Reminds me of the line diplomats use: 'No good deed goes unpunished in Washington.'" The saying may in fact be proverbial; the *Oxford Dictionary of Proverbs* cites "1938 J. AGATE *Ego 3* 25 Jan. 275 Pavia was in great form to-day: 'Every good deed brings its own punishment.'"

Henry R. Luce
U.S. editor and publisher, 1898–1967

1 The world of the 20th century, if it is to come to life in any viability of health and vigor, must be to a significant degree an American century.

Life, 17 Feb. 1941

Lucretius (Titus Lucretius Carus)
Roman poet, ca. 94 B.C.–55 B.C.

1 *Tantum religio potuit suadere malorum.*
So much wrong could religion induce.

De Rerum Natura bk. 1, l. 101

2 *Nil posse creari de nilo.*
Nothing can be created out of nothing.

De Rerum Natura bk. 1, l. 155

3 *Augescunt aliae gentes, aliae minuuntur,*
Inque brevi spatio mutantur saecla animantum

Et quasi cursores vitai lampada tradunt.
Some races increase, others are reduced, and in a short while the generations of living creatures are changed and like runners relay the torch of life.

De Rerum Natura bk. 2, l. 8

4 *Ut quod ali cibus est aliis fuat acre venenum.*
What is food to one, is to others bitter poison.

De Rerum Natura bk. 4, l. 637
See Proverbs 190

Fray Luis de León
Spanish poet and religious writer, ca. 1527–1591

1 [*Words upon resuming a lecture after being imprisoned for five years, Salamanca University, 1577:*] We were saying yesterday . . .

Attributed in Aubrey F. G. Bell, *Luis de León* (1925). Bell states, "The story was first recorded by Nicolas Cruesen, a Flemish Augustinian, acquainted with Spain personally and by report; it was written by him not later than 1612 and published in 1623."

Luiz Inácio Lula da Silva
Brazilian president, 1945–

1 A war can perhaps be won single-handedly. But peace—lasting peace—cannot be secured without the support of all.

Speech to United Nations General Assembly, New York, N.Y., 23 Sept. 2003

Saville Lumley
English artist, 1876–1960

1 What did you do in the Great War, Daddy?

British World War I recruiting poster (1917)

Patrice Lumumba
Congolese independence leader, 1925–1961

1 History will one day have its say, but it will not be the history that Brussels, Paris, Washington, or the United Nations will teach, but that which they will teach in the countries emancipated from colonialism and its puppets. Africa will write its own history, and it will be, to the north and to the south of the Sahara, a history of glory and dignity.

Letter to Pauline Lumumba, 8 Jan. 1961

2 A minimum of comfort is necessary for the practice of virtue.

Congo, My Country ch. 16 (1962)

Martin Luther
German religious leader, 1483–1546

1 *Hier stehe ich. Ich kann nicht anders. Gott helfe
   mir. Amen.*
   Here I stand. I can do no other. God help me.
   Amen.

   Speech at Diet of Worms, 18 Apr. 1521. This is the
   commonly attributed wording, but Richard Marius
   states in *Luther* (1974): "Later on the words 'Here I
   stand; I can do no other' were inserted before 'God
   help me' in printed editions of this speech. They do
   not appear in the extensive stenographic accounts
   taken down as Luther spoke."

2 For, where God built a church, there the devil
   would also build a chapel. . . . In such sort is
   the devil always God's ape.

   Colloquia Mensalia ch. 2 (1566) (translation by
   Henry Bell)

3 So our Lord God commonly gives riches to
   those gross asses to whom He vouchsafes
   nothing else.

   Quoted in *Tischreden oder Colloquia*, ed. Johann
   Aurifaber (1566)
   See Steele 2; Jonathan Swift 8

4 *Wer nicht liebt Wein, Weib, und Gesang,*
   Der bleibt ein Narr sein Lebenlang.
   Who loves not wine, woman, and song,
   Remains a fool his whole life long.

   Attributed in Matthias Claudius, *Der Wandsbecker
   Bothe* (1775). According to Wolfgang Mieder, the triad
   "Wein, Weib, und Gesang" first appeared in print in a
   German folk song recorded in 1602.

Rosa Luxemburg
German revolutionary, 1871–1919

1 Bourgeois society stands at the crossroads,
   either transition to Socialism or regression into
   Barbarism.

   "The Junius Pamphlet" (1916)

2 *Freiheit ist immer nur Freiheit des anders Denkenden.*
   Freedom is always and exclusively freedom for
   the one who thinks differently.

   Die Russische Revolution sec. 4 (1918)

Lu Xun (Chou Shu Jen)
Chinese writer, 1881–1936

1 Hope is like a road in the country; there was
   never a road, but when many people walk on it,
   the road comes into existence.

   Quoted in Lin Yutang, *The Wisdom of China* (1944)

John Lyly
English poet and playwright, ca. 1554–1606

1 What bird so sings, yet so does wail?
   O 'tis the ravished nightingale.
   Jug, jug, jug, jug, tereu, she cries,
   And still her woes at midnight rise.

   Campaspe act 5, sc. 1 (1584)
   See T. S. Eliot 46

2 Night hath a thousand eyes.
   The Maydes Metamorphosis act 3, sc. 1 (1600)
   See Bourdillon 1

Peter Lynch
U.S. businessman and investor, 1944–

1 [*Investment advice:*] Go for a business that any
   idiot can run—because sooner or later any idiot
   probably is going to be running it.
   Quoted in *USA Today*, 7 Mar. 1989

Robert S. Lynd
U.S. sociologist, 1892–1970

1 It is characteristic of mankind to make as little
   adjustment as possible in customary ways
   in the face of new conditions; the process
   of social change is epitomized in the fact
   that the first Packard car body delivered to
   the manufacturers had a whipstock on the
   dashboard.

   Middletown ch. 29 (1929). Coauthored with Helen
   M. Lynd.

Loretta Lynn
U.S. country singer, 1932–

1 Well, I was born a coal miner's daughter
   In a cabin on a hill in Butcher Holler
   We were poor but we had love
   That's the one thing my Daddy made sure of.
   "Coal Miner's Daughter" (song) (1970)

Henry Francis Lyte
English hymnwriter, 1793–1847

1 Abide with me: fast falls the eventide;
   The darkness deepens; Lord, with me abide:
   When other helpers fail, and comforts flee,
   Help of the helpless, O abide with me.
   "Abide with Me" l. 1 (1847)

Jackie "Moms" Mabley (Loretta
Mary Aiken)
U.S. comedian, 1899–1975

1 An old man can't do nothin' for me except to
bring me a message from a young man.
*Quoted in Joe Franklin, Joe Franklin's Encyclopedia of
Comedians* (1979)

Douglas MacArthur
U.S. military leader, 1880–1964

1 I have returned. By the grace of Almighty God
our forces stand again on Philippine soil.
Broadcast to Filipino people, 21 Oct. 1944

2 I still remember the refrain of one of the most
popular barracks ballads of that day, which
proclaimed most proudly that old soldiers never
die; they just fade away. I now close my military
career and just fade away.
Address to joint meeting of Congress, 19 Apr. 1951
See Foley 1

3 It is fatal to enter any war without the will to
win it.
*Speech at Republican National Convention, Chicago,
Ill., 7 July 1952*

4 But in the evening of my memory always I
come back to West Point. Always there echoes
and re-echoes: Duty, honor, country.
*Farewell address to cadets of U.S. Military Academy,
West Point, N.Y., 12 May 1962*

5 Today marks my final roll call with you. But I
want you to know that when I cross the river,
my last conscious thoughts will be of the corps,
and the corps, and the corps.
*Farewell address to cadets of U.S. Military Academy,
West Point, N.Y., 12 May 1962*

6 [*Statement, Adelaide, Australia, 20 Mar. 1942:*]
The President of the United States ordered
me to break through the Japanese lines and
proceed from Corregidor to Australia for the
purpose, as I understand it, of organizing the
American offensive against Japan, a primary
object of which is the relief of the Philippines. I
came through and I shall return.
Quoted in N.Y. Times, 21 Mar. 1942

7 Eisenhower was the best clerk I ever had.
Quoted in N.Y. Times Magazine, 6 July 1952

Harry Macarthy
English-born U.S. entertainer, 1834–1888

1 Hurrah! Hurrah!
For Southern rights hurrah!
Hurrah for the Bonnie Blue Flag
That bears a single star.
"The Bonnie Blue Flag" (song) (ca. 1861)

Rose Macaulay
English writer, 1881–1958

1 "Take my camel, dear," said my aunt Dot, as
she climbed down from this animal on her
return from High Mass.
The Towers of Trebizond ch. 1 (1956)

Thomas Babington Macaulay
British author and statesman, 1800–1859

1 As civilization advances, poetry almost
necessarily declines. . . . In proportion as men
know more and think more, they look less at
individuals and more at classes. They therefore
make better theories and worse poems.
"Milton" (1825)

2 There is only one cure for the evils which newly
acquired freedom produces; and that cure is
freedom.
"Milton" (1825)

3 Many politicians of our time are in the habit of
laying it down as a self-evident proposition, that
no people ought to be free till they are fit to use
their freedom. The maxim is worthy of the fool
in the old story, who resolved not to go into the
water till he had learnt to swim. If men are to
wait for liberty till they become wise and good
in slavery, they may indeed wait forever.
"Milton" (1825)

4 The gallery in which the reporters sit has become a fourth estate of the realm.
"Hallam's Constitutional History" (1828)
See Thomas Carlyle 14; Hazlitt 4; Thackeray 10

5 Facts are the mere dross of history. It is from the abstract truth which interpenetrates them, and lies latent among them, like gold in the ore, that the mass derives its whole value: and the precious particles are generally combined with the baser in such a manner that the separation is a task of the utmost difficulty.
"History" (1828)

6 We know no spectacle so ridiculous as the British public in one of its periodical fits of morality.
"Moore's *Life of Lord Byron*" (1830)

7 No particular man is necessary to the State. We may depend on it that, if we provide the country with popular institutions, those institutions will provide it with great men.
Speech in House of Commons, 2 Mar. 1831

8 Every schoolboy knows who imprisoned Montezuma, and who strangled Atahualpa.
"Lord Clive" (1840)
See Jonathan Swift 23; Jeremy Taylor 1

9 She [the Catholic Church] may still exist in undiminished vigor when some traveller from New Zealand shall, in the midst of a vast solitude, take his stand on a broken arch of London Bridge to sketch the ruins of St. Paul's.
"Ranke's History of the Popes" (1840)
See Walpole 2

10 The Church of Rome . . . thoroughly understands, what no other church has ever understood, how to deal with enthusiasts. In some sects, particularly in infant sects— enthusiasm is suffered to be rampant. In other sects, particularly in sects long established and richly endowed, it is regarded with aversion. The Catholic Church neither submits to enthusiasm nor proscribes it, but uses it.
"Ranke's History of the Popes" (1840)

11 [*Of Richard Rumbold:*] He never would believe that Providence had sent a few men into the world ready booted and spurred to ride, and millions ready saddled and bridled to be ridden.
The History of England vol. 1, ch. 1 (1849)

12 The Puritan hated bear-baiting, not because it gave pain to the bear, but because it gave pleasure to the spectators.
The History of England vol. 1, ch. 2 (1849)
See Hume 11

13 Your constitution [the Constitution of the United States] is all sail and no anchor.
Letter to Henry S. Randall, 23 May 1857

Ewan MacColl (Jimmie Miller)
English folksinger and songwriter, 1915–1989

1 The first time ever I saw your face
I thought the sun rose in your eyes,
And the moon and the stars were the gifts you gave
To the dark and empty skies.
"The First Time Ever I Saw Your Face" (song) (1962)

Pat MacDonald
U.S. songwriter, 1952–

1 The Future's So Bright I Gotta Wear Shades.
Title of song (1986)

Joaquim Machado de Assis
Brazilian writer, 1839–1908

1 Marcela loved me during fifteen months and three thousand dollars; nothing more.
Posthumous Memoirs of Brás Cubas ch. 17 (1881)

2 It is better to fall from above the clouds than from the third floor.
Posthumous Memoirs of Brás Cubas ch. 119 (1881)

Niccolò Machiavelli
Italian statesman and political philosopher, 1469–1527

1 It is necessary for him who lays out a state and arranges laws for it to presuppose that all men are evil and that they are always going to act according to the wickedness of their spirits whenever they have free scope.
Discourse upon the First Ten Books of Livy bk. 1, ch. 3 (written 1513–1517) (translation by Allan Gilbert)

2 Men must either be caressed or extinguished; because they avenge themselves of light offenses, but of the grave ones they cannot. So

the offense one does to a man must be such that one not fear vengeance for it.

The Prince ch. 3 (1532) (translation by Angelo M. Codevilla)

3 Nothing is more difficult to transact, nor more dubious to succeed, nor more dangerous to manage, than to make oneself chief to introduce new orders. Because the introducer has for enemies all those whom the old orders benefit, and has for lukewarm defenders all those who might benefit by the new orders.

The Prince ch. 6 (1532) (translation by Angelo M. Codevilla)

4 A prince must not have any objective nor any thought, nor take up any art, other than the art of war and its ordering and discipline; because it is the only art that pertains to him who commands. And it is of such virtue that not only does it maintain those who were born princes, but many times makes men rise to that rank from private station.

The Prince ch. 14 (1532) (translation by Angelo M. Codevilla)

5 Many have imagined for themselves republics and principalities that no one has ever seen or known to be in reality. Because how one ought to live is so far removed from how one lives that he who lets go of what is done for that which one ought to do sooner learns ruin than his own preservation.

The Prince ch. 15 (1532) (translation by Angelo M. Codevilla)

6 From this springs a dispute: whether it is better to be loved than feared or the reverse. It is answered that one would want to be both; but, because it is difficult to force them together whenever one has to do without either of the two, it is much more secure to be feared than to be loved.

The Prince ch. 17 (1532) (translation by Angelo M. Codevilla)

7 Since a prince is constrained by necessity to know well how to use the beast, among [the beasts] he must choose the fox and the lion; because the lion does not defend itself from traps, the fox does not defend itself from the wolves. One therefore needs to be a fox

to recognize traps, and a lion to dismay the wolves.

The Prince ch. 18 (1532) (translation by Angelo M. Codevilla)
See Plutarch 3

Charles Mackay
Scottish author, 1814–1889

1 Men, it has been well said, think in herds; it will be seen that they go mad in herds, while they only recover their sense slowly, and one by one.

Memoirs of Extraordinary Popular Delusions vol. 1 (1841)

Dorothea Mackellar
Australian writer, 1885–1968

1 I love a sunburnt country,
A land of sweeping plains,
Of ragged mountain ranges,
Of droughts and flooding rains.

"My Country" l. 9 (1908)

Halford Mackinder
English geographer and educator, 1861–1947

1 Who rules East Europe commands the
    Heartland:
Who rules the Heartland commands the World-
    Island:
Who rules the World-Island commands the
    World.

Democratic Ideals and Reality ch. 6 (1919)

Catharine MacKinnon
U.S. legal scholar, 1946–

1 The law sees and treats women the way men see and treat women.

"Feminism, Marxism, Method, and the State: Toward Feminist Jurisprudence," *Signs*, Spring 1982

2 This has been at the heart of every women's initiative for civil equality from suffrage to the Equal Rights Amendment: the simple notion that law—only words, words that set conditions as well as express them, words that are their own kind of art, words in power, words in authority, words in life—respond to women as well as men.

Feminism Unmodified afterword (1987)

3 In conceiving a cognizable injury from the viewpoint of the reasonable rapist, the rape law affirmatively rewards men with acquittals for not comprehending women's point of view on sexual encounters.
Toward a Feminist Theory of the State ch. 9 (1989)

James Mackintosh
Scottish philosopher and historian, 1765–1832

1 The Commons, faithful to their system, remained in a wise and masterly inactivity.
Vindiciae Gallicae sec. 1 (1791)

Charles Macklin
Irish actor and playwright, ca. 1697–1797

1 The law is a sort of hocus-pocus science.
Love à la Mode act 2, sc. 1 (1759)

Shirley MacLaine (Shirley MacLean Beaty)
U.S. actress, 1934–

1 I've played so many hookers they don't pay me the regular way anymore. They leave it on the dresser.
Quoted in *Guardian,* 23 May 1977

Ian Maclaren (John Watson)
Scottish author and theologian, 1850–1907

1 Be pitiful, for every man is fighting a hard battle.
Quoted in *Congregationalist,* 6 Jan. 1898. "Pitiful" here is used to mean "feeling pity." This quotation is now frequently worded with "be kind" instead of "be pitiful."

Norman Maclean
U.S. writer, 1902–1990

1 In our family, there was no clear line between religion and fly fishing.
"A River Runs Through It" (1976)

2 Eventually, all things merge into one, and a river runs through it. The river was cut by the world's great flood and runs over rocks from the basement of time. On some of the rocks are timeless raindrops. Under the rocks are the words, and some of the words are theirs. I am haunted by waters.
"A River Runs Through It" (1976)

Archibald MacLeish
U.S. writer and government official, 1892–1982

1 The Oklahoma Ligno and Lithograph Co Weeps at a nude by Michael Angelo.
"Corporate Entity" l. 13 (1924)

2 A poem should not mean
But be.
"Ars Poetica" l. 23 (1926)

3 To see the earth as we now see it, small and blue and beautiful in that eternal silence where it floats, is to see ourselves as riders on the earth together, brothers on that bright loveliness in the unending night—brothers who *see* now they are truly brothers.
Riders on the Earth "Bubble of Blue Air" (1978)

Henry Dunning Macleod
Scottish economist, 1821–1902

1 The illustrious Gresham, who has the great merit of being, as far as we can discover, the first who discerned the great fundamental law of the currency, that good and bad money cannot circulate together . . . Now, as he was the first to perceive that a bad and debased currency is the *cause* of the disappearance of the good money, we are only doing what is just in calling this great fundamental law of the currency by his name. We may call it Gresham's law of the currency.
The Elements of Political Economy (1858)
See Aristophanes 8; Gresham 1; Henry Macleod 2

2 Bad money drives out good.
A Dictionary of Political Economy vol. 1 (1863). This is the most famous formulation of "Gresham's Law." "The bad money drives out the good money" appeared in Thomas Macaulay, *The History of England from the Accession of James the Second* (1855). Macleod wrote, "That bad coin will drive out good coin from circulation, is an unerring law of nature," in the first edition of *The Theory and Practice of Banking* (1856).
See Aristophanes 8; Gresham 1; Henry Macleod 1

Iain Macleod
British politician, 1913–1970

1 This new victory for the Nanny State represents the wrong approach. . . . [T]he decision to

smoke or not is for the individual, and it should be left to him.

Spectator, 12 Feb. 1965. This is the earliest known use of the term "Nanny State."

2 We now have the worst of both worlds—not just inflation on the one side or stagnation on the other side, but both of them together. We have a sort of "stagflation" situation.

Speech in House of Commons, 17 Nov. 1965

Maurice de MacMahon
French president and soldier, 1808–1893

1 [*Remark upon the taking of the Malakoff fortress during the Crimean War, 8 Sept. 1855:*] *J'y suis et j'y reste!*

Here I am, and here I stay.

Attributed in Antoine de Castellane, Speech to Tribune de la Chambre, 18 Nov. 1873. According to the *Oxford Dictionary of Quotations*, "MacMahon later denied that he had expressed himself in such 'lapidary form.'"

Harold Macmillan
British prime minister, 1894–1986

1 Let us be frank about it: most of our people have never had it so good.

Speech, Bedford, England, 20 July 1957

2 The wind of change is blowing through the continent [Africa].

Address to South African Parliament, 4 Feb. 1960

3 [*When asked what worried him most:*] Events, dear boy, events.

Quoted in *Sunday Times* (London), 15 Nov. 1992

Emmanuel Macron
French president, 1977–

1 Make our planet great again.

Statement on withdrawal of United States from Paris climate agreement, 1 June 2017
See Political Slogans 26

Samuel Madden
Irish writer and philanthropist, 1686–1765

1 Words are men's daughters, but God's sons are things.

Boulter's Monument l. 377 (1745)
See Samuel Johnson 5

James Madison
U.S. president, 1751–1836

1 It is proper to take alarm at the first experiment on our liberties. . . . Who does not see that the same authority which can establish Christianity, in exclusion of all other Religions, may establish with the same ease any particular sect of Christians, in exclusion of all other Sects?

"Memorial and Remonstrance Against Religious Assessments" (1785)

2 By a faction I understand a number of citizens, whether amounting to a majority or minority of the whole, who are united and actuated by some common impulse of passion, or of interest, adverse to the rights of other citizens, or to the permanent and aggregate interests of the community.

The Federalist no. 10 (1788)

3 Liberty is to faction what air is to fire, an aliment without which it instantly expires. But it could not be a less folly to abolish liberty, which is essential to political life, because it nourishes faction than it would be to wish the annihilation of air, which is essential to animal life, because it imparts to fire its destructive agency.

The Federalist no. 10 (1788)

4 The diversity in the faculties of men, from which the rights of property originate, is not less an insuperable obstacle to a uniformity of interests. The protection of these faculties is the first object of government. From the protection of different and unequal faculties of acquiring property, the possession of different degrees and kinds of property immediately results.

The Federalist no. 10 (1788)

5 The most common and durable source of factions, has been the various and unequal distribution of property. Those who hold, and those who are without property, have ever formed distinct interests in society.

The Federalist no. 10 (1788)

6 To secure the public good and private rights against the danger of . . . faction, and at the same time to preserve the spirit and the form of

popular government, is then the great object to which our inquiries are directed.

The Federalist no. 10 (1788)

7 The accumulation of all powers, legislative, executive, and judiciary, in the same hands, whether of one, a few, or many, and whether hereditary, self-appointed, or elective, may justly be pronounced the very definition of tyranny.

The Federalist no. 47 (1788)

8 But the great security against a gradual concentration of the several powers in the same department, consists in giving to those who administer each department, the necessary constitutional means, and personal motives, to resist encroachments of the others. . . . Ambition must be made to counteract ambition. . . . If men were angels, no government would be necessary. . . . In framing a government which is to be administered by men over men, the great difficulty lies in this: you must first enable the government to control the governed; and in the next place, oblige it to control itself.

The Federalist no. 51 (1788)

9 It will be of little avail to the people that the laws are made by men of their own choice, if the laws be so voluminous that they cannot be read, or so incoherent that they cannot be understood.

The Federalist no. 62 (1788). This number of *The Federalist* may have been authored by Alexander Hamilton rather than by Madison.

10 Since the general civilization of mankind, I believe there are more instances of the abridgment of the freedom of the people, by gradual and silent encroachments of those in power, than by violent and sudden usurpations.

Speech at Virginia Convention, 5 June 1788

11 I go on the principle that a public debt is a public curse, and in a Republican Government a greater curse than in any other.

Letter to Henry Lee, 13 Apr. 1790
See Alexander Hamilton 3

12 In every political society, parties are unavoidable. A difference of interests, real or supposed, is the most natural and fruitful

source of them. . . . The great art of politicians lies in making them checks and balances to each other.

"Parties" (1792)

13 Some degree of abuse is inseparable from the proper use of every thing; and in no instance is this more true, than in that of the press. It has accordingly been decided by the practice of the states, that it is better to leave a few of its noxious branches, to their luxuriant growth, than by pruning them away, to injure the vigor of those yielding the proper fruits.

"Report on the Virginia Resolutions" (1799–1800)

14 A popular Government, without popular information, or the means of acquiring it, is but a Prologue to a Farce or a Tragedy; or perhaps both. Knowledge will forever govern ignorance.

Letter to W. T. Barry, 4 Aug. 1822

Madonna (Madonna Louise Ciccione)
U.S. singer, 1958–

1 Papa don't preach, I'm in trouble deep
Papa don't preach, I've been losing sleep
But I made up my mind, I'm keeping my baby.

"Papa Don't Preach" (song) (1986). Cowritten with Brian Elliot.

2 They had style, they had grace
Rita Hayworth gave good face
Lauren, Katherine, Lana too
Bette Davis, we love you.

"Vogue" (song) (1990). Cowritten with Shep Pettibone.

3 I always thought of losing my virginity as a career move.

Quoted in Christopher Andersen, *Madonna Unauthorized* (1991)

Maurice Maeterlinck
Belgian writer, 1862–1949

1 And nowhere, surely, should we discover more painful and absolute sacrifice. . . . The queen bids farewell to freedom, the light of day. . . . The workers give five or six years of their life, and shall never know love, or the joys of maternity.

"The Life of the Bee" (1901)

2 *Il n'y a pas de morts.*
There are no dead.
L'Oiseau Bleu act 4 (1909)

John G. Magee, Jr.
Chinese-born U.S. aviator, 1922–1941

1 Oh! I have slipped the surly bonds of Earth
And danced the skies on laughter-silvered
wings.
"High Flight" l. 1 (1941). Magee flew with the Royal
Canadian Air Force during World War II. Three
months before his death during a training mission,
he wrote the poem "High Flight." President Ronald
Reagan quoted this passage and the one below in a
televised address to the nation after the explosion of
the space shuttle *Challenger* on 28 January 1986.

2 And, while with silent lifting mind I've trod
The high untrespassed sanctity of space,
Put out my hand, and touched the face of God.
"High Flight" l. 12 (1941)

Magna Carta

1 No free man shall be taken or imprisoned or
dispossessed, or outlawed or exiled, or in any
way destroyed, nor will we go upon him, nor
will we send against him except by the lawful
judgement of his peers or by the law of the land.
Clause 39 (1215)

2 To no man will we sell, or deny, or delay, right
or justice.
Clause 40 (1215)

René Magritte
Belgian painter, 1898–1967

1 *Ceci n'est pas une pipe.*
This is not a pipe.
Writing on painting of pipe (*"La Trahison des Images"*)
(1929)

Naguib Mahfouz
Egyptian novelist, 1911–2006

1 What I want is to draw inspiration only
from the truth. . . . My qualifications for
this important role include a large head, an
enormous nose, disappointment in love, and
expectations of ill health.
Palace of Desire ch. 40 (1957) (translation by William
Maynard Hutchins, Lorne M. Kenny, and Olive E.
Kenny)

2 Hating England is a form of self-defense. That
kind of nationalism is nothing more than a
local manifestation of a concern for human
rights.
Palace of Desire ch. 40 (1957) (translation by William
Maynard Hutchins, Lorne M. Kenny, and Olive E.
Kenny)

Gustav Mahler
Austrian composer, 1860–1911

1 [*On visiting Niagara Falls:*] Fortissimo at last!
Quoted in Kurt Blaukopf, *Gustav Mahler* (1973)

2 [*Remark to Jean Sibelius, Helsinki, 1907:*] The
symphony must be like the world. It must
embrace everything.
Quoted in Kurt Blaukopf, *Mahler: His Life, His Work
and His World* (1976)

Norman Mailer
U.S. novelist and essayist, 1923–2007

1 The hipster has absorbed the existentialist
synapses of the Negro, and for practical
purposes could be considered a White Negro.
"The White Negro" (1954)

2 There is probably no sensitive heterosexual
alive who is not preoccupied at one time or
another with his latent homosexuality.
"The Homosexual Villain" (1957)

3 Once a newspaper touches a story, the facts are
lost forever, even to the protagonists.
Esquire, June 1960

4 Factoids . . . that is, facts which have no
existence before appearing in a magazine or
newspaper, creations which are not so much
lies as a product to manipulate emotion in the
Silent Majority.
Marilyn ch. 1 (1973)

5 [*Of Marilyn Monroe:*] So we think of Marilyn
who was every man's love affair with America.
Marilyn Monroe who was blonde and beautiful
and had a sweet little rinky-dink of a voice and
all the cleanliness of all the clean American
backyards. She was our angel, the sweet angel
of sex, and the sugar of sex came up from her
like a resonance of sound in the clearest grain
of a violin.
Marilyn ch. 1 (1973)

6 All the security around the American president is just to make sure the man who shoots him gets caught.

Quoted in *Sunday Telegraph*, 4 Mar. 1990

Maimonides (Moses ben Maimon)
Spanish Jewish philosopher and scholar, 1135–1204

1 It is better and more satisfactory to acquit a thousand guilty persons than to put a single innocent man to death once in a way.

Sefer Hamitzvot Negative Commandment 290 (translation by Charles B. Chavel) (ca. 1170)
See Blackstone 7; Fortescue 1; Benjamin Franklin 37; Voltaire 3

2 Astrology is a disease, not a science.

Laws of Repentance (ca. 1175)

3 When I find the road narrow, and can see no other way of teaching a well established truth except by pleasing one intelligent man and displeasing ten thousand fools—I prefer to address myself to the man.

The Guide for the Perplexed introduction (ca. 1190)

Henry Maine
English jurist, 1822–1888

1 The movement of the progressive societies has hitherto been a movement *from Status to Contract.*

Ancient Law ch. 5 (1861)

2 So great is the ascendancy of the Law of Actions in the infancy of Courts of Justice, that substantive law has at first the look of being gradually secreted in the interstices of procedure.

Dissertations on Early Law and Custom ch. 11 (1883)

Natalie Maines
U.S. singer, 1974–

1 [*Remark to concert audience, London, 10 Mar. 2003:*] Just so you know, we're ashamed the president of the United States is from Texas.

Quoted in *Houston Chronicle*, 14 Mar. 2003

Joseph de Maistre
French diplomat and writer, 1753–1821

1 *Toute nation a le gouvernement qu'elle mérite.*
Every country has the government it deserves.

Lettres et Opuscules Inédits vol. 1, no. 53 (1851) (letter of 15 Aug. 1811)

Frederick W. Maitland
British legal historian and jurist, 1850–1906

1 Such is the unity of all history that any one who endeavors to tell a piece of it must feel that his first sentence tears a seamless web.

"Prologue to a History of English Law," *Law Quarterly Review*, Jan. 1898. Frequently quoted as "the law is a seamless web."

2 The forms of action we have buried, but they still rule us from their graves.

Forms of Action at Common Law Lecture 1 (1909)

John Major
British prime minister, 1943–

1 [*On inflation:*] If the policy isn't hurting, it isn't working.

Speech, Northampton, England, 27 Oct. 1989

2 Society needs to condemn a little more and understand a little less.

Interview, *Mail on Sunday* (London), 21 Feb. 1993

Bernard Malamud
U.S. novelist, 1914–1986

1 When I walk down the street I bet people will say there goes Roy Hobbs, the best there ever was in the game.

The Natural pt. 1 (1952)
See Theodore "Ted" Williams 2

2 We have two lives . . . the life we learn with and the life we live with after that.

The Natural pt. 6 (1952)

Janet Malcolm
U.S. writer, 1934–

1 Every journalist who is not too stupid or too full of himself to notice what is going on knows that what he does is morally indefensible. He is a kind of confidence man, preying on people's vanity, ignorance, or loneliness, gaining their trust and betraying them without remorse.

The Journalist and the Murderer pt. 1 (1990)

Malcolm X (Malcolm Little)
U.S. civil rights leader, 1925–1965

1 There is nothing in our book the Koran, that teaches us to suffer peacefully. Our religion teaches us to be intelligent. Be peaceful, be courteous, obey the law, respect everyone; but if someone puts his hand on you, send him to the cemetery. That's a good religion.
"Message to the Grass Roots" (speech), Detroit, Mich., 10 Nov. 1963

2 We didn't land on Plymouth Rock, my brothers and sisters—Plymouth Rock landed on *us*.
The Autobiography of Malcolm X (as told to Alex Haley) ch. 12 (1964)
See Cole Porter 4

3 It [the assassination of John F. Kennedy] was, as I saw it, a case of "the chickens coming home to roost." I said that the hate in white men had not stopped with the killing of defenseless black people, but that hate, allowed to spread unchecked, had finally struck down this nation's Chief Magistrate.
The Autobiography of Malcolm X (as told to Alex Haley) ch. 16 (1964)

4 That's our motto. We want freedom by any means necessary. We want justice by any means necessary. We want equality by any means necessary.
Speech at rally of Organization of Afro-American Unity, New York, N.Y., 28 June 1964

François de Malherbe
French poet, 1555–1628

1 And a rose, she lived as roses do, the space of a morn.
"Consolation à M. du Périer" (1599)

Bronislaw Malinowski
Polish-born U.S. anthropologist, 1884–1942

1 There can be no doubt that we have here a new type of linguistic use—*phatic communion* I am tempted to call it . . .—a type of speech in which ties of union are created by a mere exchange of words.
"The Problem of Meaning in Primitive Languages" (1923)

2 There are no peoples however primitive without religion and magic. Nor are there, it must be added at once, any savage races lacking either in the scientific attitude or in science, though this lack has been frequently attributed to them.
"Magic, Science and Religion" (1925)

3 The anthropologist must relinquish his comfortable position in the long chair on the veranda of the missionary compound, Government station, or planter's bungalow, where, armed with pencil and notebook and at times with a whisky and soda, he has been accustomed to collect statements from informants. . . . He must go out into the villages, and see the natives at work in gardens, on the beach, in the jungle; he must sail with them to distant sandbanks and to foreign tribes.
Myth in Primitive Psychology ch. 5 (1926)

Stéphane Mallarmé
French poet, 1842–1898

1 *Prélude à l'Après-Midi d'un Faune.*
Prelude to the Afternoon of a Faun.
Title of poem (ca. 1865)

2 *Tel qu'en Lui-Même enfin l'éternité le change.*
Such as into Himself at last Eternity has changed him.
"Le Tombeau d'Edgar Poe" (1877)

3 *Donner un sens plus pur aux mots de la tribu.*
To give a purer sense to the words of the tribe.
"Le Tombeau d'Edgar Poe" (1877)
See T. S. Eliot 119

4 *La chair est triste, hélas! et j'ai lu tous les livres.*
Alas, the flesh is weary, and I've read all the books.
"Brise Marin" st. 1 (1887)

5 *Un Coup de Dés Jamais N'Abolira le Hasard.*
A Throw of the Dice Will Never Abolish Chance.
Title of poem (1897)

George Leigh Mallory
English mountain climber, 1886–1924

1 [*When asked why he wanted to climb Mount Everest:*] Because it's there.
Quoted in *N.Y. Times*, 18 Mar. 1923

Thomas Malory

English writer, fl. 1470

1 Whoso pulleth out this sword of this stone and
anvil is rightwise King born of all England.
Le Morte d'Arthur bk. 1, ch. 4 (1485)

2 I shall curse you with book and bell and candle.
Le Morte d'Arthur bk. 21, ch. 1 (1485)
See Shakespeare 69

3 And many men say that there is written upon
his tomb this verse: *Hic iacet Arthurus, rex
quondam rexque futurus* [Here lies Arthur, the
once and future king].
Le Morte D'Arthur bk. 31, ch. 7 (1485)

André Malraux

French writer and art historian, 1901–1976

1 *La Condition Humaine.*
The Human Condition.
Title of book (1933)

2 *L'art est un anti-destin.*
Art is a revolt against man's fate.
Les Voix du Silence pt. 4, ch. 7 (1951)

3 The extermination camps, in endeavoring to
turn man into a beast, intimated that it is not
life alone which makes him man.
Anti-Memoirs "La Condition Humaine" sec. 2 (1967)

Thomas Robert Malthus

English economist, 1766–1834

1 Population, when unchecked, increases in a
geometrical ratio. Subsistence increases only
in an arithmetical ratio. A slight acquaintance
with numbers will shew the immensity of the
first power in comparison of the second.
An Essay on the Principle of Population ch. 1 (1798)

2 The perpetual struggle for room and food.
An Essay on the Principle of Population ch. 3 (1798)
See Charles Darwin 5

3 A foresight of the difficulties attending the
rearing of a family acts as a preventive check,
and the actual distresses of some of the lower
classes, by which they are disabled from giving
the proper food and attention to their children,
act as a positive check to the natural increase of
population.
An Essay on the Principle of Population ch. 4 (1798)

4 Moral restraint . . . may be defined to be,
abstinence from marriage, either for a time or
permanently, from prudential considerations,
with a strictly moral conduct towards the sex
in the interval. And this is the only mode of
keeping population on a level with the means of
subsistence which is perfectly consistent with
virtue and happiness.
A Summary View of the Principle of Population (1830)

David Mamet

U.S. writer, 1947–

1 Always be closing.
Glengarry Glen Ross act 2 (1984). Although now
associated with the Mamet play, this appeared
in writings about salesmanship as early as 1950
(*Successful Investment Salesmanship: A Series of Lectures*).

Nelson Mandela

South African president, 1918–2013

1 I have fought against white domination, and I
have fought against black domination. I have
cherished the ideal of a democratic and free
society in which all persons live together in
harmony with equal opportunities. It is an ideal
which I hope to live for, and to see realized. But
my lord, if needs be, it is an ideal for which I
am prepared to die.
Statement at trial, Johannesburg, South Africa, 20
Apr. 1964

2 Only free men can negotiate. Prisoners cannot
enter into contracts.
Statement from prison, 10 Feb. 1985

3 Out of the experience of an extraordinary
human disaster that lasted too long, must be
born a society of which all humanity will be
proud. . . . Never, never, and never again shall it
be that this beautiful land will again experience
the oppression of one by another.
Presidential Inaugural Address, 10 May 1994

Winnie Mandela

South African political activist, 1934–

1 Together, hand-in-hand with our sticks of
matches, with our necklaces, we shall liberate
this country.
Speech in black townships, 13 Apr. 1986. The
"necklace" was a tire doused with gasoline, placed
around the neck of a suspected government
collaborator and set afire.

Benoit Mandelbrot

Polish-born French-U.S. mathematician, 1924–2010

1 How Long Is the Coast of Britain?
Title of article, *Science*, 5 May 1967

Nadezhda Mandelstam

Russian writer, 1899–1980

1 If nothing else is left, one must scream. Silence is the real crime against humanity.
Hope Against Hope ch. 11 (1970) (translation by Max Hayward)

Osip Mandelstam

Russian poet, 1891–1938

1 Our lives no longer feel ground under them.
At ten paces you can't hear our words.
But whenever there's a snatch of talk
It turns to the Kremlin mountaineer.
"The Stalin Epigram" st. 1–2 (1934) (translation by W. S. Merwin)

2 He forges decrees in a line like horseshoes,
One for the groin, one the forehead, temple, eye,
He rolls the executions on his tongue like berries.
He wishes he could hug them like big friends from home.
"The Stalin Epigram" st. 7–8 (1934) (translation by W. S. Merwin)

Bernard de Mandeville

Dutch-born English satirist and philosopher, 1670–1733

1 The Fable of the Bees: or, Private Vices, Publick Benefits.
Title of book (1714)

James Clarence Mangan

Irish poet, 1803–1849

1 Solomon! where is thy throne? It is gone in the wind.
Babylon! where is thy might? It is gone in the wind.
Happy in death are they only whose hearts have consigned

All Earth's affections and longings and cares to the wind.
"Gone in the Wind" l. 25 (1842)
See Dowson 2; Margaret Mitchell 4

Marcus Manilius

Latin poet, First cent.

1 [*Of human intelligence:*] Eripuitque Jovi fulmen viresque tonandi, et sonitum ventis concessit, nubibus ignem.
And snatched from Jove the lightning shaft and power to thunder, and attributed the noise to the winds, the flame to the clouds.
Astronomica bk. 1, l. 104

Herman J. Mankiewicz

U.S. screenwriter, 1897–1953

1 [*Of Orson Welles:*] There, but for the grace of God, goes God.
Quoted in *N.Y. Times*, 29 Nov. 1941. The 1941 newspaper article refers to this only as "someone's comment on Orson Welles," but later writers name Mankiewicz as the source. The quotation is also frequently credited to Winston Churchill, speaking about Stafford Cripps, but the earliest documentation of a Churchill version is dated 1943.
See John Bradford 1

2 [*Telegram to screenwriter Ben Hecht, 1925, urging Hecht to come to Hollywood:*] Millions are to be grabbed out here and your only competition is idiots. Don't let this get around.
Quoted in Ben Hecht, *A Child of the Century* (1954)

Robert Mankoff

U.S. cartoonist, 1944–

1 [*Businessman talking into the telephone:*] No, Thursday's out. How about never—is never good for you?
Cartoon caption, *New Yorker*, 3 May 1993

Mary de la Rivière Manley

English novelist and playwright, 1663–1724

1 No time like the present.
The Lost Lover act 4, sc. 1 (1696)

Horace Mann

U.S. educator and politician, 1796–1859

1 Be ashamed to die until you have won some
victory for humanity.

Address at Antioch College, Yellow Springs, Ohio, 29
June 1859

Thomas Mann

German novelist, 1875–1955

1 Beauty can pierce one like a pain.

Buddenbrooks pt. 11, ch. 2 (1903)

2 Time has no divisions to mark its passage,
there is never a thunderstorm or blare of
trumpets to announce the beginning of a
new month or year. Even when a new century
begins it is only we mortals who ring bells and
fire off pistols.

The Magic Mountain ch. 4 (1924) (translation by H. T.
Lowe-Porter)

3 Speech is civilization itself. The word, even the
most contradictory word, preserves contact—it
is silence which isolates.

The Magic Mountain ch. 6 (1924) (translation by H. T.
Lowe-Porter)

4 A man's dying is more the survivors' affair than
his own.

The Magic Mountain ch. 6 (1924) (translation by H. T.
Lowe-Porter)

5 What we call mourning for our dead is not so
much grief at not being able to call them back
as it is grief at not being able to want to do so.

The Magic Mountain ch. 7 (1924) (translation by H. T.
Lowe-Porter)

6 [*Remark after arriving in New York, N.Y., 21 Feb.
1938:*] Where I am, there is Germany.

Quoted in *N.Y. Times,* 22 Feb. 1938

Katherine Mansfield (Kathleen Mansfield Beauchamp)

New Zealand–born British short story writer,
1888–1923

1 I want, by understanding myself, to understand
others. I want to be all that I am capable of
becoming. . . . This all sounds very strenuous
and serious. But now that I have wrestled with
it, it's no longer so. I feel happy—deep down.
All is well.

Journal, 1922

2 Whenever I prepare for a journey I prepare as
though for death. Should I never return, all is
in order. This is what life has taught me.

Journal, 29 Jan. 1922

3 Looking back, I imagine I was always writing.
Twaddle it was, too. But better far write twaddle
or anything, anything, than nothing at all.

Journal, July 1922

4 Risk! Risk anything! Care no more for the
opinions of others, for those voices. Do the
hardest thing on earth for you. Act for yourself.
Face the truth.

Journal, 10 Oct. 1922

5 But then there comes that moment rare
When, for no cause that I can find,
The little voices of the air
Sound above all the sea and wind.

"Voices of the Air" l. 1 (1923)

William Murray, Lord Mansfield

Scottish lawyer and politician, 1705–1793

1 The constitution does not allow reasons
of state to influence our judgments: God
forbid it should! We must not regard political
consequences; however formidable soever
they might be: if rebellion was the certain
consequence, we are bound to say *"fiat justitia,
ruat caelum."*

Rex v. Wilkes (1768). The Latin maxim here, "Let
justice be done though the heavens fall," was
popularized by Mansfield's usage.
See Ferdinand I 1; William Watson 1

2 The state of slavery is of such a nature, that it is
incapable of being introduced on any reasons,
moral or political, but only by positive law,
which preserves its force long after the reasons,
occasion, and time itself from whence it was
created, is erased from memory. It is so odious,
that nothing can be suffered to support it, but
positive law.

Sommersett's Case (1771)

3 Most of the disputes of the world arise from
words.

Morgan v. Jones (1773)

4 Dost not know that old Mansfield, who writes
    like the Bible,

Says the more 'tis a truth, sir, the more 'tis a
    libel?

Reported in Robert Burns, "The Libeller's Self-
Reproof" (ca. 1787). This legal maxim, usually
attributed to Mansfield, is most often formulated
as "the greater the truth the greater the libel." The
earliest occurrence of this formulation found is in an
1825 Massachusetts case, *Commonwealth v. Blanding*
(in which the precise wording is "the greater the truth
is, the greater is the libel").

Mao Tse-tung
Chinese political leader, 1893–1976

1 A revolution is not a dinner party.
   "Report on an Investigation into the Peasant
   Movement in Hunan" (1927)

2 The enemy advances, we retreat; the enemy
   camps, we harass; the enemy tires, we attack;
   the enemy retreats, we pursue.
   Letter, 5 Jan. 1930. *Respectfully Quoted,* ed. Suzy Platt,
   notes that "Mao was quoting from a letter from the
   Front Committee to the Central Committee, on
   guerrilla tactics."

3 Many people think it is impossible for the
   guerrilla to exist long in the enemy's realm.
   Such a belief reveals a lack of understanding
   of the relationship that should exist between
   the people and the troops. The former may be
   likened to water and the latter to the fish that
   swim in it.
   On Guerrilla Warfare (1937)

4 Political power grows out of the barrel of a gun.
   Speech at Communist Party Meeting, Hankou,
   China, 7 Aug. 1927

5 The atom bomb is a paper tiger which the
   United States reactionaries use to scare people.
   It looks terrible, but in fact it isn't. . . . All
   reactionaries are paper tigers.
   Interview by Anne Louise Strong, Aug. 1946

6 Letting a hundred flowers blossom and a
   hundred schools of thought contend is the
   policy for promoting progress in the arts and
   the sciences and a flourishing socialist culture
   in our land.
   Speech, Beijing, China, 27 Feb. 1957. Maurice
   Cranston, *Glossary of Political Terms,* traces Mao's use
   of these words back as far as 1951.

7 All erroneous ideas, all poisonous weeds, all
   ghosts and monsters, must be subjected to
   criticism; in no circumstance should they be
   allowed to spread unchecked.
   Speech at Chinese Communist Party's National
   Conference on Propaganda Work, Beijing, China,
   12 Mar. 1957

Diego Maradona
Argentinian soccer player, 1960–2020

1 [*Of a controversial goal in Argentina's World Cup
   game against England:*] That goal was scored a
   little bit by the hand of God and another bit by
   Maradona's head.
   Quoted in *L.A. Times,* 24 June 1986

William March
U.S. writer, 1893–1954

1 The Bad Seed.
   Title of book (1954)

Guglielmo Marconi
Italian physicist and inventor, 1874–1937

1 Let it be so.
   Wireless telegraph message, 13 May 1897. This was
   the first wireless transmission across water (across
   the Bristol Channel between England and Wales).

Marcus Aurelius Antoninus
Roman emperor and philosopher, 121–180

1 Nothing happens to anybody which he is not
   fitted by nature to bear.
   Meditations bk. 5, sec. 18

Herbert Marcuse
German-born U.S. philosopher, 1898–1979

1 Free election of masters does not abolish the
   masters or the slaves.
   One-Dimensional Man ch. 1 (1964)

William L. Marcy
U.S. politician, 1786–1857

1 If they [politicians] are successful, they claim,
   as a matter of right, the advantages of success.
   They see nothing wrong in the rule, that to the
   victor belong the spoils of the enemy.
   Remarks in Senate, 25 Jan. 1832

Emilio Filippo Tomasso Marinetti

Italian writer, 1876–1944

1 We affirm that the world's magnificence has been enriched by a new beauty: the beauty of speed. A racing car whose hood is adorned with great pipes, like serpents of explosive breath—a roaring car that seems to ride on grapeshot is more beautiful than the *Victory of Samothrace.*
"Manifesto of Futurism" (1909)

2 It is from Italy that we launch through the world this violently upsetting incendiary manifesto of ours. With it, today, we establish *Futurism,* because we want to free this land from its smelly gangrene of professors, archaeologists, *ciceroni,* and antiquarians. For too long Italy has been a dealer in second-hand clothes. We mean to free her from the numberless museums that cover her like so many graveyards.
"Manifesto of Futurism" (1909)

Beryl Markham

English aviator and author, 1902–1986

1 I have learned that if you must leave a place that you have lived in and loved and where all your yesterdays are buried deep—leave it any way except a slow way; leave it the fastest way you can. Never turn back and never believe that an hour you remember is a better hour because it is dead. Passed years seem safe ones, vanquished ones, while the future lives in a cloud, formidable from a distance.
West with the Night ch. 11 (1942)

2 One day the stars will be as familiar to each man as the landmarks, the curves, and the hills on the road that leads to his door, and one day this will be an airborne life. But by then men will have forgotten how to fly; they will be passengers on machines whose conductors are carefully promoted to a familiarity with labelled buttons, and in whose minds knowledge of the sky and the wind and the way of weather will be extraneous as passing fiction. And the days of the clipper ships will be recalled again—and people will wonder if clipper means ancients of the sea or ancients of the air.
West with the Night ch. 15 (1942)

Edwin Markham

U.S. poet, 1852–1940

1 Bowed by the weight of centuries he leans
Upon his hoe and gazes on the ground,
The emptiness of ages in his face,
And on his back the burden of the world.
Who made him dead to rapture and despair,
A thing that grieves not and that never hopes,
Stolid and stunned, a brother to the ox?
"The Man with the Hoe" l. 1 (1899)

Johnny Marks

U.S. songwriter, 1909–1985

1 Rudolph, the Red-Nosed Reindeer
Had a very shiny nose,
And if you ever saw it,
You would even say it glows.
"Rudolph, the Red-Nosed Reindeer" (song) (1949)

Walter Marks

U.S. songwriter, 1934–

1 I want to live, not merely survive
And I won't give up this dream of life that
   keeps me alive
I've gotta be me.
"I've Gotta Be Me" (song) (1968)

2 I'll go it alone, that's how it must be
I can't be right for somebody else if I'm not
   right for me
I gotta be free, I've gotta be free
Daring to try, to do it or die
I've gotta be me.
"I've Gotta Be Me" (song) (1968)

Sarah Jennings Churchill, Duchess of Marlborough

English noblewoman, 1660–1744

1 His Grace returned from the wars this morning and pleasured me twice in his top-boots.
Attributed in James Agate, *Ego 4* (1940)

Bob Marley

Jamaican reggae musician and songwriter, 1945–1981

1 Get up, stand up,
Stand up for your rights.

Get up, stand up,
Never give up the fight.

"Get Up, Stand Up" (song) (1973). Cowritten with Peter Tosh.

2 I shot the sheriff
But I swear it was in self-defence.

"I Shot the Sheriff" (song) (1974)

3 Emancipate yourselves from mental slavery.
None but ourselves can free our minds.

"Redemption Song" (song) (1980)

4 [*"Last words":*] Money can't buy life.

Quoted in *Reggae & African Beat*, June 1987

Christopher Marlowe

English playwright and poet, 1564–1593

1 Come live with me, and be my love,
And we will all the pleasures prove,
That valleys, groves, hills, and fields,
Woods or steepy mountain yields.

"The Passionate Shepherd to His Love" l. 1
(ca. 1589)

2 I count religion but a childish toy,
And hold there is no sin but ignorance.

The Jew of Malta prologue (ca. 1592)

3 [*Friar Barnardine:*] Thou hast committed—
[*Barabas:*] Fornication? But that was in
another country: and besides, the wench is
dead.

The Jew of Malta act 4, sc. 1 (ca. 1592)

4 My men, like satyrs grazing on the lawns,
Shall with their goat feet dance an antic hay.

Edward II act 1, sc. 1 (1593)

5 Where both deliberate, the love is slight;
Who ever loved that loved not at first sight?

Hero and Leander First Sestiad, l. 175 (1598). "None
ever loved but at first sight they loved" appeared in
George Chapman, *The Blind Beggar of Alexandria*
(1596).

6 Why, this is hell, nor am I out of it.

Doctor Faustus act 1, sc. 3 (1604)

7 Hell hath no limits nor is circumscribed
In one self place, where we are is Hell,
And to be short, when all the world dissolves,
And every creature shall be purified,
All places shall be hell that are not heaven.

Doctor Faustus act 2, sc. 1 (1604)

8 Was this the face that launched a thousand
ships,
And burnt the topless towers of Ilium?

Doctor Faustus act 5, sc. 1 (1604). Nigel Rees notes
in *Cassell Companion to Quotations* that Marlowe had
anticipated this line in *Tamburlaine the Great*, pt. 2,
act 2, sc. 4 (1587): "Helen, whose beauty . . . / Drew a
thousand ships to Tenedos."

9 Sweet Helen, make me immortal with a kiss.
Her lips suck forth my soul; see where it flies!
Come, Helen, come, give me my soul again.
Here will I dwell, for heaven be in these lips,
And all is dross that is not Helena.

Doctor Faustus act 5, sc. 1 (1604). Nigel Rees notes in
Cassell Companion to Quotations that Marlowe wrote
earlier in *Dido, Queen of Carthage*, act 4, sc. 4 (1594):
"He'll make me immortal with a kiss."

10 Now hast thou but one bare hour to live,
And then thou must be damned perpetually.
Stand still, you ever-moving spheres of heaven,
That time may cease, and midnight never
come.

Doctor Faustus act 5, sc. 2 (1604)

11 *O lente lente currite noctis equi.*
The stars move still, time runs, the clock will
strike,
The devil will come, and Faustus must be
damned.
O I'll leap up to my God: who pulls me down?
See, see, where Christ's blood streams in the
firmament.
One drop would save my soul, half a drop, ah
my Christ.

Doctor Faustus act 5, sc. 2 (1604)
See Ovid 1

12 Cut is the branch that might have grown full
straight,
And burned is Apollo's laurel bough,
That sometime grew within this learned man.

Doctor Faustus act 5, sc. 3 (1604)

Don Marquis

U.S. humorist, 1878–1937

1 an optimist is a guy
that has never had
much experience.

archy and mehitabel "certain maxims of archy" (1927)

2 When a man tells you that he got rich through hard work, ask him: "Whose?"

Quoted in Edward Anthony, *O Rare Don Marquis* (1962)

3 Poetry is what Milton saw when he went blind.

Quoted in Edward Anthony, *O Rare Don Marquis* (1962)

Anthony Marriott

English playwright, 1931–2014

1 No sex, please—we're British!!!!!!

No Sex Please, We're British act 2 (1971). Coauthored with Alistair Foot.

Frederick Marryat

English naval officer and novelist, 1792–1848

1 [*Excuse made for an illegitimate baby:*] If you please, ma'am, it was a very little one.

Mr. Midshipman Easy ch. 3 (1836)

Dave Marsh

U.S. rock music critic, 1950–

1 Needless to say, it was impossible, even after two nights running of Tina Turner, to miss such a landmark exposition of punk-rock.

Creem, May 1971. Earliest known use of the term *punk rock*. A somewhat different usage of the words appeared in the *Chicago Tribune*, 22 Mar. 1970, where Ed Sanders was quoted describing an album of his as "punk rock—redneck sentimentality."

Alfred Marshall

English economist, 1842–1924

1 Political Economy or Economics is a study of mankind in the ordinary business of life.

Principles of Economics bk. 1, ch. 1 (1890)

George C. Marshall, Jr.

U.S. military leader and statesman, 1880–1959

1 [*Proposing the "Marshall Plan" to reconstruct Europe after World War II:*] Our policy is directed not against any country or doctrine, but against hunger, poverty, desperation, and chaos. Its purpose should be the revival of a working economy in the world so as to permit the emergence of political and social conditions in which free institutions can exist.

Speech at Harvard University, Cambridge, Mass., 5 June 1947

John Marshall

U.S. judge, 1755–1835

1 It is a proposition too plain to be contested, that the constitution controls any legislative act repugnant to it; or, that the legislature may alter the constitution by an ordinary act.

Marbury v. Madison (1803)

2 Certainly all those who have framed written constitutions contemplate them as forming the fundamental and paramount law of the nation, and consequently the theory of every such government must be, that an act of the legislature, repugnant to the constitution, is void.

Marbury v. Madison (1803)

3 It is emphatically the province and duty of the judicial department to say what the law is.

Marbury v. Madison (1803)

4 We must never forget, that it is *a constitution* we are expounding.

McCulloch v. Maryland (1819)

5 This provision is made in a constitution intended to endure for ages to come, and, consequently, to be adapted to the various *crises* of human affairs.

McCulloch v. Maryland (1819)

6 Let the end be legitimate, let it be within the scope of the constitution, and all means which are appropriate, which are plainly adapted to that end, which are not prohibited, but consist with the letter and spirit of the constitution, are constitutional.

McCulloch v. Maryland (1819)

7 That the power to tax involves the power to destroy; that the power to destroy may defeat and render useless the power to create; that there is a plain repugnance, in conferring on one government a power to control the constitutional measures of another, which other, with respect to those very measures, is declared to be supreme over that which exerts the control, are propositions not to be denied.

McCulloch v. Maryland (1819)
See Oliver Wendell Holmes, Jr. 38; Daniel Webster 2

8 The acme of judicial distinction means the ability to look a lawyer straight in the eyes for two hours and not hear a damned word he says.
Quoted in Albert J. Beveridge, *Life of John Marshall* (1919)

Thomas R. Marshall

U.S. politician, 1854–1925

1 The chief need of the country . . . is a really good 5-cent cigar.
Quoted in *Daily Northwestern* (Oshkosh, Wis.), 6 Feb. 1914. Marshall is usually said to have uttered this in 1920. In both the 1914 newspaper article and the standard 1920 account, Marshall is responding to a senator's speech about "what this country needs." However, there is a much earlier occurrence in the *Hartford Courant*, 22 Sept. 1875: "What this country really needs is a good five cent cigar.—*New York Mail.*"

Thurgood Marshall

U.S. judge and lawyer, 1908–1993

1 If the First Amendment means anything, it means that a State has no business telling a man, sitting alone in his own house, what books he may read or what films he may watch.
Stanley v. Georgia (1969)

2 We will see that the true miracle was not the birth of the Constitution, but its life, a life nurtured through two turbulent centuries of our own making, and a life embodying much good fortune that was not. Thus, in this bicentennial year, we may not all participate in the festivities with flag-waving fervor. Some may more quietly commemorate the suffering, struggle, and sacrifice that has triumphed over much of what was wrong with the original document, and observe the anniversary with hopes not realized and promises not fulfilled.
Speech, Maui, Hawaii, 6 May 1987

Yann Martel

Spanish-born Canadian novelist, 1963–

1 I know zoos are no longer in people's good graces. Religion faces the same problem. Certain illusions about freedom plague them both.
Life of Pi ch. 4 (2001)

2 To choose doubt as a philosophy of life is akin to choosing immobility as a means of transportation.
Life of Pi ch. 7 (2001)

3 I can well imagine an atheist's last words: "White, white! L-L-Love! My God!"—and the deathbed leap of faith. Whereas the agnostic, if he stays true to his reasonable self, if he stays beholden to dry, yeastless factuality, might try to explain the warm light bathing him by saying, "Possibly a f-f-failing oxygenation of the b-b-brain," and, to the very end, lack imagination and miss the better story.
Life of Pi ch. 22 (2001)

José Martí

Cuban patriot and poet, 1853–1895

1 [Our objective is to prevent] the annexation of the nations of our America by the unruly and brutal North which despises them. I have lived in the bowels of the beast and I know it from the inside.
Letter to Manuel Mercado, 18 Mar. 1895

Martial

Roman epigrammatist, ca. 40–ca. 104

1 *Non amo te, Sabidi, nec possum dicere quare:*
Hoc tantum possum dicere, non amo te.
I don't love you, Sabidius, and I can't tell you why; all I can tell you is this, that I don't love you.
Epigrammata bk. 1, no. 32
See Thomas Brown 1

2 *Difficilis facilis, iucundus acerbus es idem:*
Nec tecum possum vivere nec sine te.
Difficult or easy, pleasant or bitter, you are the same you: I cannot live with you—or without you.
Epigrammata bk. 12, no. 46 (47)
See Aristophanes 5

3 *Rus in urbe.*
Country in the town.
Epigrammata bk. 12, no. 57

Alfred Manuel "Billy" Martin

U.S. baseball manager and player, 1928–1989

1 [*Of player Reggie Jackson and New York Yankees owner George Steinbrenner:*] The two of them deserve each other. One's a born liar, the other's convicted.

Quoted in *N.Y. Times,* 24 July 1978. Steinbrenner had been convicted of making illegal campaign contributions.

George R. R. Martin

U.S. novelist, 1948–

1 Winter is coming.

A Game of Thrones (1996)

2 When you play the game of thrones, you win or you die. There is no middle ground.

A Game of Thrones (1996)

3 You know nothing, Jon Snow.

A Storm of Swords (2000)

Harriet Martineau

English novelist and economist, 1802–1876

1 Wealth and opinion were practically worshipped before Washington opened his eyes on the sun which was to light him to his deeds, and the worship of Opinion is, to this day, the established religion of the United States.

Society in America vol. 2 (1837)

Andrew Marvell

English poet and satirist, 1621–1678

1 The forward Youth that would appear
Must now forsake his Muses dear,
Nor in the Shadows sing
His Numbers languishing.

"An Horatian Ode upon Cromwell's Return from Ireland" l. 1 (written 1650)

2 The inglorious Arts of Peace.

"An Horatian Ode upon Cromwell's Return from Ireland" l. 10 (written 1650)

3 Though Justice against Fate complain,
And plead the antient Rights in vain:
But those do hold or break
As Men are strong or weak.

"An Horatian Ode upon Cromwell's Return from Ireland" l. 37 (written 1650)

4 [*On the execution of King Charles I:*]
He nothing common did, or mean,
Upon that memorable Scene:
But with his keener Eye
The Axe's edge did try.

"An Horatian Ode upon Cromwell's Return from Ireland" l. 57 (written 1650)

5 But bow'd his comely Head
Down, as upon a Bed.

"An Horatian Ode upon Cromwell's Return from Ireland" l. 63 (written 1650)

6 So much one Man can do,
That does both act and know.

"An Horatian Ode upon Cromwell's Return from Ireland" l. 75 (written 1650)

7 March indefatigably on,
And for the last effect
Still keep thy Sword erect:
Besides the force it has to fright
The Spirits of the shady Night;
The same Arts that did gain
A Pow'r must it maintain.

"An Horatian Ode upon Cromwell's Return from Ireland" l. 114 (written 1650)

8 Oh! let our voice His praise exalt,
Till it arrive at Heaven's vault,
Which, thence (perhaps) rebounding, may
Echo beyond the Mexique Bay.

"Bermudas" l. 33 (ca. 1653)

9 Annihilating all that's made
To a green thought in a green shade.

"The Garden" l. 47 (1681)

10 Had we but world enough and time,
This coyness, Lady, were no crime.

"To His Coy Mistress" l. 1 (1681)

11   I would
Love you ten years before the Flood,
And you should, if you please, refuse
Till the Conversion of the Jews.
My vegetable love should grow
Vaster than empires, and more slow.

"To His Coy Mistress" l. 7 (1681)

12 But at my back I always hear
Time's winged chariot hurrying near,
And yonder all before us lie
Deserts of vast eternity.

"To His Coy Mistress" l. 21 (1681)
See T. S. Eliot 50

13 Then worms shall try
   That long preserved virginity,
   And your quaint honor turn to dust,
   And into ashes all my lust.
   "To His Coy Mistress" l. 27 (1681)

14 The grave's a fine and private place,
   But none, I think, do there embrace.
   "To His Coy Mistress" l. 31 (1681)

15 Let us roll all our strength and all
   Our sweetness up into one ball
   And tear our pleasures with rough strife
   Thorough the iron gates of life.
   Thus, though we cannot make our sun
   Stand still, yet we will make him run.
   "To His Coy Mistress" l. 41 (1681)

Holt Marvell (Eric Maschwitz)

English songwriter, 1901–1969

1 A cigarette that bears a lipstick's traces,
   An airline ticket to romantic places,
   And still my heart has wings:
   These foolish things
   Remind me of you.
   "These Foolish Things Remind Me of You" (song)
   (1935)

Julius Henry "Groucho" Marx

U.S. comedian, 1890–1977

Lines from Marx Brothers films are listed here, regardless of screenwriter or whether Groucho Marx spoke them.

1 [*Hammer, played by Groucho Marx, speaking:*]
   Three years ago I came to Florida without a
   nickel in my pocket. And now I've got a nickel
   in my pocket.
   The Cocoanuts (motion picture) (1929). Screenplay by
   George S. Kaufman.

2 [*Hammer, played by Groucho Marx, speaking:*]
   I'll meet you tonight under the moon. Oh, I

can see you now, you and the moon. You wear a
necktie so I'll know you.
The Cocoanuts (motion picture) (1929). Screenplay by
George S. Kaufman.

3 [*Line repeatedly spoken by Chico Marx when
   Groucho Marx refers to a* viaduct:] Why a duck?
   The Cocoanuts (motion picture) (1929). Screenplay by
   George S. Kaufman.

4 From the moment I picked up your book until
   I put it down, I was convulsed with laughter.
   Some day I intend reading it.
   Dust jacket for S. J. Perelman, *Dawn Ginsbergh's
   Revenge* (1929).

5 [*Captain Jeffrey T. Spaulding, played by Groucho
   Marx, singing:*] Hello, I must be going.
   Animal Crackers (motion picture) (1930). Screenplay
   by George S. Kaufman and Morrie Ryskind; however,
   these words actually appeared in a song titled
   "Hooray for Captain Spaulding," written by Harry
   Ruby and Bert Kalmar.

6 [*Mrs. Whitehead, played by Margaret Irving,
   speaking:*] Why, that's bigamy.
   [*Captain Jeffrey T. Spaulding, played by Groucho
   Marx, speaking:*] Yes, and it's big of me too.
   Animal Crackers (motion picture) (1930). Screenplay
   by George S. Kaufman and Morrie Ryskind. The
   same exchange occurred earlier in "the Napoleon
   sketch," written by Will B. Johnstone and Groucho
   Marx for the Marx Brothers' 1924 stage play *I'll Say
   She Is!*

7 [*Captain Jeffrey T. Spaulding, played by Groucho
   Marx, speaking:*] One morning I shot an
   elephant in my pajamas. How he got in my
   pajamas, I don't know.
   Animal Crackers (motion picture) (1930). Screenplay
   by George S. Kaufman and Morrie Ryskind.

8 [*Groucho Marx speaking:*] Do you suppose I
   could buy back my introduction to you?
   Monkey Business (motion picture) (1931). Screenplay
   by Will B. Johnstone and S. J. Perelman.

9 [*Groucho Marx, replying to the comment, "You're
   awfully shy for a lawyer":*] You bet I'm shy. I'm a
   shyster lawyer.
   Monkey Business (motion picture) (1931). Screenplay
   by Will B. Johnstone and S. J. Perelman.

10 [*Groucho Marx speaking:*] I worked myself up
   from nothing to a state of extreme poverty.
   Monkey Business (motion picture) (1931). Screenplay
   by Will B. Johnstone and S. J. Perelman.

11 [*Groucho Marx speaking after a woman says, "I don't like this innuendo":*] That's what I always say. Love flies out the door when money comes innuendo.

Monkey Business (motion picture) (1931). Screenplay by Will B. Johnstone and S. J. Perelman.

12 [*Groucho Marx speaking:*] Come, Kapellmeister, let the violas throb! My regiment leaves at dawn.

Monkey Business (motion picture) (1931). Screenplay by Will B. Johnstone and S. J. Perelman.

13 [*Professor Wagstaff, played by Groucho Marx, speaking:*]

I don't know what they have to say,
It makes no difference anyway,
Whatever it is, I'm against it.

Horse Feathers (motion picture) (1932). Screenplay by Will B. Johnstone, Bert Kalmar, S. J. Perelman, and Harry Ruby.

14 [*Professor Wagstaff, played by Groucho Marx, speaking:*] You're a disgrace to our family name of Wagstaff, if such a thing is possible.

Horse Feathers (motion picture) (1932). Screenplay by Will B. Johnstone, Bert Kalmar, S. J. Perelman, and Harry Ruby.

15 [*Professor Wagstaff, played by Groucho Marx, speaking:*] I'd horsewhip you if I had a horse.

Horse Feathers (motion picture) (1932). Screenplay by Will B. Johnstone, Bert Kalmar, S. J. Perelman, and Harry Ruby.

16 [*Professor Wagstaff, played by Groucho Marx, speaking:*] Baravelli, you've got the brain of a four-year-old boy, and I bet he was glad to get rid of it.

Horse Feathers (motion picture) (1932). Screenplay by Will B. Johnstone, Bert Kalmar, S. J. Perelman, and Harry Ruby.

17 [*Rufus T. Firefly, played by Groucho Marx, speaking:*] If you can't get a taxi you can leave in a huff. If that's too soon, you can leave in a minute and a huff.

Duck Soup (motion picture) (1933). Screenplay by Bert Kalmar and Harry Ruby.

18 [*Rufus T. Firefly, played by Groucho Marx, speaking:*] You know you haven't stopped talking since I came here? You must have been vaccinated with a phonograph needle.

Duck Soup (motion picture) (1933). Screenplay by Bert Kalmar and Harry Ruby.

19 [*Rufus T. Firefly, played by Groucho Marx, speaking:*] Will you marry me? Did he leave you any money? Answer the second question first.

Duck Soup (motion picture) (1933). Screenplay by Bert Kalmar and Harry Ruby.

20 [*Rufus T. Firefly, played by Groucho Marx, speaking:*] I could dance with you till the cows come home. On second thought, I'd rather dance with the cows till you come home.

Duck Soup (motion picture) (1933). Screenplay by Bert Kalmar and Harry Ruby.

21 [*Rufus T. Firefly, played by Groucho Marx, speaking:*] Clear? Huh! Why, a four-year-old child could understand this report. Run out and find me a four-year-old child. I can't make head or tail out of it.

Duck Soup (motion picture) (1933). Screenplay by Bert Kalmar and Harry Ruby.

22 [*Ambassador Tarentino, played by Louis Calhern, speaking:*] This means war!

Duck Soup (motion picture) (1933). Screenplay by Bert Kalmar and Harry Ruby.

23 [*Rufus T. Firefly, played by Groucho Marx, speaking:*] Go, and never darken my towels again!

Duck Soup (motion picture) (1933). Screenplay by Bert Kalmar and Harry Ruby.

24 [*Chicolini, played by Chico Marx, speaking:*] Who you gonna believe, me or your own eyes?

Duck Soup (motion picture) (1933). Screenplay by Bert Kalmar and Harry Ruby.

25 [*Rufus T. Firefly, played by Groucho Marx, speaking:*] Chicolini here may talk like an idiot, and look like an idiot, but don't let that fool you. He really is an idiot.

Duck Soup (motion picture) (1933). Screenplay by Bert Kalmar and Harry Ruby.

26 [*Rufus T. Firefly, played by Groucho Marx, speaking:*] Remember you're fighting for this woman's honor, which is probably more than she ever did.

Duck Soup (motion picture) (1933). Screenplay by Bert Kalmar and Harry Ruby.

27 [*Otis B. Driftwood, played by Groucho Marx, speaking:*] That's—that's in every contract. That's—that's what they call a sanity clause.
[*Fiorello, played by Chico Marx, speaking:*] You can't fool me. There ain't no Sanity Claus.

A Night at the Opera (motion picture) (1935). Screenplay by George S. Kaufman and Morrie Ryskind.

28 [*"Doctor" Hugo Z. Hackenbush, played by Groucho Marx, attempting to take Harpo's pulse:*] Either he's dead, or my watch has stopped.

A Day at the Races (motion picture) (1937). Screenplay by Robert Pirosh, George Seaton, and George Oppenheimer.

29 [*"Doctor" Hugo Z. Hackenbush, played by Groucho Marx, speaking:*] If I hold you any closer, I'll be in back of you.

A Day at the Races (motion picture) (1937). Screenplay by Robert Pirosh, George Seaton, and George Oppenheimer.

30 [*"Doctor" Hugo Z. Hackenbush, played by Groucho Marx, answering the question, "Are you a man or a mouse?":*] You put a piece of cheese down there and you'll find out.

A Day at the Races (motion picture) (1937). Screenplay by Robert Pirosh, George Seaton, and George Oppenheimer.

31 [*"Doctor" Hugo Z. Hackenbush, played by Groucho Marx, speaking:*] Don't point that beard at me. It might go off.

A Day at the Races (motion picture) (1937). Screenplay by Robert Pirosh, George Seaton, and George Oppenheimer.

32 [*"Doctor" Hugo Z. Hackenbush, played by Groucho Marx, speaking:*] Emily, I have a little confession to make. I really am a horse doctor. But marry me and I'll never look at any other horse.

A Day at the Races (motion picture) (1937). Screenplay by Robert Pirosh, George Seaton, and George Oppenheimer.

33 [*Gordon Miller, played by Groucho Marx, speaking:*] Room service? Send up a larger room.

Room Service (motion picture) (1938). Screenplay by Morrie Ryskind.

34 [*J. Cheever Loophole, played by Groucho Marx, after being told that "the bottom of your shoe creates a suction that holds you up in the ceiling":*] No, no, I'd rather not. I have an agreement with the houseflies. The flies don't practice law and I don't walk on the ceiling.

At the Circus (motion picture) (1939). Screenplay by Irving Brecher.

35 [*J. Cheever Loophole, played by Groucho Marx, speaking:*] I bet your father spent the first year of your life throwing rocks at the stork.

At the Circus (motion picture) (1939). Screenplay by Irving Brecher.

36 What a revoltin' development this is!

Catchphrase (1940s). Groucho Marx originated this phrase during a telephone conversation with Irving Brecher in the 1940s. Brecher later used it as the catchphrase of Chester A. Riley, played by Jackie Gleason followed by William Bendix, on the television series *The Life of Riley* (1949–1958). Daffy Duck also uttered this expression in the animated feature *Mexican Joyride* (1947).

37 [*Responding to a woman contestant who, explaining why she had twenty-two children, said "because I love children, and I think that's our purpose here on earth, and I love my husband":*] I love my cigar too, but I take it out of my mouth once in a while.

Censored line, *You Bet Your Life* (radio and television program) (1947–1961). Groucho experts are divided about whether this line is real or apocryphal, and Groucho himself at different times remembered it both ways. The strongest evidence for its authenticity is that *You Bet Your Life* head writer Bernie Smith affirmed it. There was a similar line that is documented to have actually aired on the show: "Well, I like pancakes, but I haven't got closetsful of them" (said in 1955 to a woman with seventeen children).

38 [*Question asked of losers on quiz show so that they would go away with some money:*] Who is buried in Grant's Tomb?

You Bet Your Life (radio and television series) (1947–1961). This question predates Groucho's usage; for example, "What famous general was buried in Grant's tomb" appears in the *Pittsburgh Press*, 8 June 1925.

39 Say the secret word and win a hundred dollars.

Catchphrase, *You Bet Your Life* (radio and television series) (1947–1961)

40 I never forget a face—but I'm going to make an exception in your case.

Quoted in *L.A. Times*, 16 Feb. 1937

41 [*Explaining his resignation from the Hollywood chapter of the Friars Club:*] I don't want to belong to any club that would accept me as one of its members.

Quoted in *Dunkirk* (N.Y.) *Evening Observer*, 20 Oct. 1949.
See Benchley 11; Galsworthy 2; Joe E. Lewis 1; Lincoln 2; Twain 4

42 I find television very educating. Every time somebody turns on the set I go into the other room and read a book.

Quoted in *Reader's Digest*, Aug. 1950.

43 I've been around so long, I knew Doris Day before she was a virgin.

Quoted in Max Wilk, *The Wit and Wisdom of Hollywood* (1972). Oscar Levant had earlier referred to "Doris Day's first picture; that was before she became a virgin" in *The Memoirs of an Amnesiac* (1965).

44 [*Responding to a beach club telling him he couldn't join because he was Jewish:*] My son's only half Jewish. Would it be all right if he went in the water up to his knees?

Quoted in Arthur Marx, *Son of Groucho* (1973). The earliest version found by the editor of this book is from Leo Rosten, *The Many Worlds of Leo Rosten* (1964): "He once expressed interest in joining a certain beach club in Santa Monica. A friend told him uneasily, 'You don't want to apply for membership in that beach club, Groucho.' 'Why not?' asked Marx. 'Well, frankly, they're anti-Semitic.' Marx, a Jew whose wife wasn't, said, 'Will they let my son go into the water up to his knees?'"

45 A man is only as old as the woman he feels.

Quoted in Laurence J. Peter, *Peter's Quotations* (1977)
See Proverbs 185

46 These are my principles. If you don't like them I have others.

Quoted in *Legal Times*, 7 Feb. 1983. Earlier versions go back at least as far as 1873: "Them's my principles; but if you don't like them—I kin change them!" (*New Zealand Tablet, Weekly Epitome*, 18 Oct.).

47 I've had a wonderful evening, but this wasn't it!

Attributed in *Reader's Digest*, Mar. 1941. Although this is associated with Groucho, an earlier attribution of "I had a lovely evening, but this wasn't it" was made to Hugh Herbert in the *Augusta Chronicle*, 14 Oct. 1936.

48 Military intelligence is a contradiction in terms.

Attributed in *N.Y. Times*, 21 Feb. 1971. Garson O'Toole has found the following statement in John Charteris, *At G.H.Q.* (1931): "Curzon did not give much time to intelligence work. I fancy Military Intelligence to him is a contradiction in terms."

49 Outside of a dog, a book is a man's best friend. That's because inside of a dog, it's too dark to read.

Attributed in *Philadelphia Daily News*, 5 Apr. 1973. "Clever comic Jimmy Husson's observation: 'Book is man's best friend, outside of a dog. Inside, it's too dark to read anyhow'" appeared in the *Tennessean* (Nashville), 23 Nov. 1952.

Karl Marx

German political philosopher, 1818–1883

1 The criticism of religion is the basis of all criticism.

A Contribution to the Critique of Hegel's Philosophy of Right introduction (1843–1844)

2 Religion is the sigh of the oppressed creature, the heart of a heartless world, just as it is the spirit of spiritless conditions. It is the opium of the people.

A Contribution to the Critique of Hegel's Philosophy of Right introduction (1843–1844)
See Joan Robinson 3

3 The philosophers have only interpreted the world in various ways; the point is to change it.

Theses on Feuerbach no. 11 (written 1845). This is the epitaph on Marx's tombstone in Highgate Cemetery, London. Although written in 1845, *Theses on Feuerbach* was not published until 1888.

4 Hegel remarks somewhere that all great world-historic facts and personages appear, so to speak, twice. He forgot to add: the first time as tragedy, the second time as farce.

The Eighteenth Brumaire of Louis Napoleon pt. 1 (1852)
See Hegel 5

5 Men make their own history, but they do not make it just as they please; they do not make it under circumstances chosen by themselves, but under circumstances directly encountered,

given, and transmitted from the past. The tradition of all the dead generations weighs like a nightmare on the brain of the living.

The Eighteenth Brumaire of Louis Napoleon pt. 1 (1852)

6 My own contribution was: 1. to show that the *existence of classes* is merely bound up with *certain historical phases in the development of production;* 2. that the class struggle necessarily leads to the *dictatorship of the proletariat;* 3. that this dictatorship itself constitutes no more than a transition to the *abolition of all classes* and to a *classless society.*

Letter to Joseph Weydemeyer, 5 Mar. 1852. The *Oxford Dictionary of Quotations* states: "The phrase 'dictatorship of the proletariat' had been used earlier in the Constitution of the World Society of Revolutionary Communists (1850), signed by Marx and others. . . . Marx claimed that the phrase had been coined by Auguste Blanqui (1805–81), but it has not been found in this form in Blanqui's work."

7 Society does not consist of individuals; it expresses the sum of connections and relationships in which individuals find themselves.

Grundrisse (1857–1858)

8 Nothing can be a value without being an object of utility. If the thing is useless, so is the labor contained in it; the labor does not count as labor, and therefore creates no value.

Das Kapital vol. 1, ch. 1 (1867) (translation by Ben Fowkes)

9 [*Of John Stuart Mill:*] On a level plain, simple mounds look like hills; and the insipid flatness of our present bourgeoisie is to be measured by the altitude of its "great intellects."

Das Kapital vol. 1, ch. 16 (1867) (translation by Ben Fowkes)

10 [The effect of capitalist development is to] distort the worker into a fragment of a man, . . . degrade him to the level of an appendage of a machine, they destroy the actual content of his labor by turning it into a torment.

Das Kapital vol. 1, ch. 25 (1867) (translation by Ben Fowkes)

11 The centralization of the means of production and the socialization of labor reach a point at which they become incompatible with their capitalist integument. This integument is burst

asunder. The knell of capitalist private property sounds. The expropriators are expropriated.

Das Kapital vol. 1, ch. 32 (1867) (translation by Ben Fowkes)

12 From each according to his abilities, to each according to his needs.

Critique of the Gotha Program pt. 1 (1875). The *North British Review,* vol. 10 (1849), included this passage: "The formula of Communism, as propounded by Cabet, may be expressed thus:—'the duty of each is according to his faculties; his right according to his wants.'"
See Blanc 1

13 *Ce qu'il y a de certain, c'est que moi je ne suis pas Marxiste.*

What is certain is that I am no Marxist.

Quoted in Friedrich Engels, Letter to Eduard Bernstein, 2–3 Nov. 1882

Karl Marx 1818–1883 and **Friedrich Engels** 1820–1895

German political philosopher; German socialist

1 A specter is haunting Europe, the specter of Communism.

The Communist Manifesto introduction (1848)

2 The history of all hitherto existing society is the history of class struggles.

The Communist Manifesto sec. 1 (1848)

3 The executive of the modern State is but a committee for managing the common affairs of the whole bourgeoisie.

The Communist Manifesto sec. 1 (1848)

4 The bourgeoisie, wherever it has got the upper hand, has put an end to all feudal, patriarchal, idyllic relations. It has pitilessly torn asunder the motley feudal ties that bound man to his "natural superiors," and has left remaining no other bond between man and man than naked self-interest, than callous "cash payment."

The Communist Manifesto sec. 1 (1848)
See Thomas Carlyle 11

5 The bourgeoisie has subjected the country to the rule of the towns. It has created enormous cities, has greatly increased the urban population as compared with the rural, and has thus rescued a considerable part of the population from the idiocy of rural life.

The Communist Manifesto sec. 1 (1848)

6 In this sense, the theory of the Communists may be summed up in the single sentence: Abolition of private property.

The Communist Manifesto sec. 2 (1848)

7 What else does the history of ideas prove, than that intellectual production changes in character in proportion as material production is changed? The ruling ideas of each age have ever been the ideas of its ruling class.

The Communist Manifesto sec. 2 (1848)

8 The Communists disdain to conceal their views and aims. They openly declare that their ends can be attained only by the forcible overthrow of all existing social conditions. Let the ruling classes tremble at a Communist revolution. The proletarians have nothing to lose but their chains. They have a world to win. Working men of all countries, unite!

The Communist Manifesto sec. 4 (1848). Usually quoted as "Workers of the world, unite!" The party congress of the League of the Just headed its draft articles, dated 9 June 1847: "Proletarier aller Länder, Vereinigt Euch!" ("Proletarians of all countries, unite!").

Mary I

English queen, 1516–1558

1 When I am dead and opened, you shall find Calis lieng in my hart ["Calais" lying in my heart].

Quoted in Raphael Holinshed, *Holinshed's Chronicles* (1587)

Queen Mary

British queen consort, 1867–1953

1 [*On the abdication of the Duke of Windsor, formerly Edward VIII, as king:*] I do not think you have ever realized the shock, which the attitude you took up caused your family and the whole nation. It seemed inconceivable to those who had made such sacrifices during the war that you, as their King, refused a lesser sacrifice.

Letter to Duke of Windsor, July 1938

Mary, Queen of Scots

Scottish queen, 1542–1587

1 *En ma fin git mon commencement.*
In my end is my beginning.

Motto. The *Oxford Dictionary of Quotations* states that this motto was "embroidered with an emblem of her mother, Mary of Guise, and quoted in a letter from William Drummond of Hawthornden to Ben Jonson in 1619."
See T. S. Eliot 101

John Masefield

English poet, 1878–1967

1 I must go down to the seas again, to the lonely sea and the sky,
   And all I ask is a tall ship and a star to steer her by.

"Sea Fever" l. 1 (1902). The word *go* was mistakenly omitted from the original publication.

2 I must go down to the seas again, for the call of the running tide
   Is a wild call and a clear call that may not be denied.

"Sea Fever" l. 5 (1902)

Abraham Maslow

U.S. psychologist, 1908–1970

1 It is tempting, if the only tool you have is a hammer, to treat everything as if it were a nail.

The Psychology of Science: A Reconnaissance ch. 2 (1966). Maslow's formulation was preceded by a similar saying by Abraham Kaplan, who called it "the law of the instrument": "Give a boy a hammer and everything he meets has to be pounded" (quoted in *Journal of Medical Education*, June 1962). Silvan S. Tomkins, in *Computer Simulation of Personality* (1963), wrote "If one has a hammer one tends to look for nails."

Donald F. Mason

U.S. naval officer, 1913–1990

1 Sighted sub. Sank same.

Radio message to U.S. Navy Department, 28 Jan. 1942. It has subsequently been questioned whether Mason actually sank a submarine on this date.

George Mason

U.S. politician, 1725–1792

1 That all men are by nature equally free and independent, and have certain inherent rights,

of which, when they enter into a state of society, they cannot by any compact deprive or divest their posterity; namely, the enjoyment of life and liberty, with the means of acquiring and possessing property, and pursuing and obtaining happiness and safety.
Virginia Bill of Rights article 1 (1776)
See Jefferson 2

2 Government is, or ought to be instituted for the common benefit, protection, and security of the people, nation, or community; of all the various modes and forms of government, that is best which is capable of producing the greatest degree of happiness and safety, and is most effectually secured against the danger of maladministration.
Virginia Bill of Rights article 3 (1776)

3 The freedom of the press is one of the greatest bulwarks of liberty, and can never be restrained but by despotic governments.
Virginia Bill of Rights article 12 (1776)

Philip Massinger
English playwright, 1583–1640

1 A New Way to Pay Old Debts.
Title of play (1632)

Cotton Mather
U.S. clergyman, 1662–1728

1 That there is a *Devil,* is a thing doubted by none but such as are under the influence of the *Devil.* For any to deny the being of a *Devil* must be from an ignorance or profaneness, worse than *diabolical.*
The Wonders of the Invisible World (1692)

Richard Matheson
U.S. writer, 1926–2013

1 Robert Neville looked out over the new people of the earth. He knew he did not belong to them; he knew that, like the vampires, he was anathema and black terror to be destroyed. And abruptly, the concept came, amusing to him even in his pain. . . . I am legend.
I Am Legend ch. 21 (1954)

Henri Matisse
French painter, 1869–1954

1 I want to reach that state of condensation of sensations which constitutes a picture.
Notes d'un Peintre (1908)

2 What I dream of is an art of balance, of purity and serenity devoid of troubling or depressing subject matter . . . a soothing, calming influence on the mind, rather like a good armchair which provides relaxation from physical fatigue.
Notes d'un Peintre (1908)

Leonard Matlovich
U.S. soldier, 1943–1988

1 [*Inscription on tombstone:*] A gay Vietnam veteran . . . they gave me a medal for killing two men—and a discharge for loving one.
Quoted in *Wash. Post,* 22 Apr. 1988

W. Somerset Maugham
French-born English novelist, 1874–1965

1 Like all weak men he laid an exaggerated stress on not changing one's mind.
Of Human Bondage ch. 39 (1915)

2 There's always one who loves and one who lets himself be loved.
Of Human Bondage ch. 71 (1915)

3 I forget who it was that recommended men for their soul's good to do each day two things they disliked . . . it is a precept that I have followed scrupulously; for every day I have got up and I have gone to bed.
The Moon and Sixpence ch. 2 (1919)

4 It is not difficult to be unconventional in the eyes of the world when your unconventionality is but the convention of your set.
The Moon and Sixpence ch. 14 (1919)

5 The tragedy of love is indifference.
The Trembling of a Leaf ch. 4 (1921)

6 Poor Henry [James], he's spending eternity wandering round and round a stately park and the fence is just too high for him to peep over and they're having tea just too far away for him to hear what the countess is saying.
Cakes and Ale ch. 11 (1930)

7 From the earliest times the old have rubbed it into the young that they are wiser than they, and before the young had discovered what nonsense this was they were old too, and it profited them to carry on the imposture.
Cakes and Ale ch. 11 (1930)

8 You cannot imagine the kindness I've received at the hands of perfect strangers.
The Narrow Corner ch. 15 (1932)
See Tennessee Williams 5

9 I [Death] was astounded to see him in Baghdad, for I had an appointment with him tonight in Samarra.
Sheppey act 3 (1933). Nigel Rees reports in *"Quote . . . Unquote" Newsletter*, Apr. 2004, that Maugham's Samarra anecdote traces to a Persian tradition including a version of this legend in Rumi's thirteenth-century epic *Masnavi-ye Ma'navi*, and to even earlier Jewish and Islamic sources.

10 It is a funny thing about life, if you refuse to accept anything but the best, you very often get it: if you utterly decline to make do with what you get, then somehow or other you are very likely to get what you want.
The Mixture as Before "The Treasure" (1940)

11 Only a mediocre writer is always at his best.
The Portable Dorothy Parker introduction (1944)
See Beerbohm 2

Bill Mauldin
U.S. cartoonist, 1921–2003

1 I feel like a fugitive from th' law of averages.
Up Front cartoon caption (1945)

2 Look at an infantryman's eyes, and you can tell how much war he has seen.
Up Front cartoon caption (1945)

3 [*Infantryman speaking to another:*] Why th' hell couldn't you have been born a beautiful woman?
Up Front cartoon caption (1945)

4 [*Advice from one soldier to another aiming a pistol at a rat:*] Aim between th' eyes, Joe. Sometimes they charge when they're wounded.
Up Front cartoon caption (1945)

5 [*Officer looking at a magnificent mountain vista:*] Beautiful view. Is there one for the enlisted men?
Up Front cartoon caption (1945)

6 [*American soldier looking around a European village in which all the men and women look exactly like himself:*] This is th' town my pappy told me about.
Up Front cartoon caption (1945)

Guy de Maupassant
French writer, 1850–1893

1 What would have happened if she hadn't lost the necklace? Who knows? Who knows? How strange life is, how full of changes! How little it takes to doom you or save you!
"The Necklace" (1884)

François Mauriac
French author, 1885–1970

1 I love Germany so dearly that I hope there will always be two of them.
Quoted in *Newsweek*, 20 Nov. 1989

Maury Maverick
U.S. politician, 1895–1954

1 Stay off gobbledygook language. It only fouls people up. For the Lord's sake, be short and say what you're talking about.
Memorandum to staff of Smaller War Plants Corporation, 24 Mar. 1944. Earliest known usage of the word *gobbledygook*.

James Clerk Maxwell
Scottish physicist, 1813–1879

1 We can scarcely avoid the inference that light consists in the transverse undulations of the same medium which is the cause of electric and magnetic phenomena.
"On Physical Lines of Force" (1862)

2 The opinion seems to have got abroad, that in a few years all the great physical constants will have been approximately estimated, and that the only occupation which will be left to men of science will be to carry on these measurements to another place of decimals.
Inaugural Address as Cavendish Professor at Cambridge University, Cambridge, England, Oct. 1871

Vladimir Mayakovski

Russian poet, 1893–1930

1 If you wish,
  I shall grow irreproachably tender:
  Not a man, but a cloud in trousers!
  "The Cloud in Trousers" (1915) (translation by George
  Reavey)

Percy Mayfield

U.S. songwriter, 1920–1984

1 Hit the road Jack and don't you come back no
  more.
  "Hit the Road Jack" (song) (1961)

William J. Mayo

U.S. physician, 1861–1939

1 A specialist is one who knows more and more
  about less and less.
  Quoted in *Philadelphia Inquirer*, 26 July 1927. This
  is usually credited to Mayo, but an earlier occurrence
  without attribution to any individual was in the
  Canton (Ohio) *Repository*, 11 June 1926: "The expert
  . . . becomes a man who knows more and more about
  less and less."

Willie Mays

U.S. baseball player, 1931–

1 Say, hey.
  Quoted in *Newport* (R.I.) *Daily News,* 26 Jan. 1953

Emil Mazey

U.S. labor leader, 1913–1983

1 I can't prove you are a Communist. But when
  I see a bird that quacks like a duck, walks
  like a duck, has feathers and webbed feet and
  associates with ducks—I'm certainly going to
  assume that he is a duck.
  Quoted in *Milwaukee Sentinel,* 29 Sept. 1946

Giuseppe Mazzini

Italian revolutionary leader, 1805–1872

1 [Thomas Carlyle] loves silence somewhat
  platonically.
  Quoted in Jane Welsh Carlyle, Letter to Mrs. Stirling,
  Oct. 1843
  See Proverbs 271

William G. McAdoo

U.S. politician, 1863–1941

1 [*Of Warren G. Harding:*] His speeches leave the
  impression of an army of pompous phrases
  moving over the landscape in search of an idea.
  Sometimes these meandering words would
  actually capture a straggling thought and bear
  it triumphantly a prisoner in their midst until it
  died of servitude and overwork.
  Quoted in Leon A. Harris, *The Fine Art of Political
  Wit* (1964)

Ward McAllister

U.S. socialite, 1827–1895

1 There are only about 400 people in fashionable
  New-York society.
  Quoted in *N.Y. Tribune,* 25 Mar. 1888

Anthony McAuliffe

U.S. general, 1898–1975

1 [*Replying to the German demand that the 101st
  Airborne Division, besieged at Bastogne, Belgium,
  surrender, 22 Dec. 1944:*] Nuts!
  Quoted in *N.Y. Times,* 28 Dec. 1944. McAuliffe may
  have said something stronger, with "Nuts" being
  an expurgated version. However, some accounts
  maintain that he did actually say "Nuts."
  See Cambronne 1

John McCain

U.S. politician and naval officer, 1936–2018

1 The fundamentals of America's economy are
  strong.
  Interview on Bloomberg TV, 17 Apr. 2008

2 To fear the world we have organized and led
  for three-quarters of a century, to abandon
  the ideals we have advanced around the globe,
  to refuse the obligations of international
  leadership and our duty to remain "the last
  best hope of earth" for the sake of some
  half-baked, spurious nationalism cooked up
  by people who would rather find scapegoats
  than solve problems is as unpatriotic as an
  attachment to any other tired dogma of the past
  that Americans consigned to the ash heap of
  history.
  Speech accepting Liberty Medal, Philadelphia, Pa.,
  16 Oct. 2017

Meghan McCain

U.S. broadcaster, 1984–

1 We gather to mourn the passing of American greatness, the real thing, not cheap rhetoric from men who will never come near the sacrifice he gave so willingly, nor the opportunistic appropriation of those that live lives of comfort and privilege while he suffered and served.
Eulogy for John McCain, Washington, D.C., 1 Sept. 2018

2 The America of John McCain has no need to be made great again because America was always great.
Eulogy for John McCain, Washington, D.C., 1 Sept. 2018

William McCall

U.S. psychologist, 1891–1982

1 Anything that exists in amount can be measured.
How to Measure in Education ch. 1 (1922)
See Thorndike 1

Cormac McCarthy

U.S. novelist, 1933–

1 He never sleeps, the judge. He is dancing, dancing. He says that he will never die.
Blood Meridian ch. 23 (1985)

2 Scars have the strange power to remind us that our past is real.
All the Pretty Horses ch. 2 (2000)

3 What's the most you ever saw lost on a coin toss?
No Country for Old Men ch. 2 (2005)

4 It takes very little to govern good people. Very little. And bad people cant be governed at all. Or if they could I never heard of it.
No Country for Old Men ch. 3 (2005)

5 It's a mess, aint it Sheriff?
If it aint it'll do till a mess gets here.
No Country for Old Men ch. 3 (2005)

6 You never know what worse luck your bad luck has saved you from.
No Country for Old Men ch. 9 (2005)

7 He knew only that the child was his warrant. He said: If he is not the word of God God never spoke.
The Road (2006)

8 You forget what you want to remember and you remember what you want to forget.
The Road (2006)

Eugene McCarthy

U.S. politician, 1916–2005

1 Being in politics is like being a football coach. You have to be smart enough to understand the game and dumb enough to think it's important.
Quoted in *Wash. Post*, 12 Nov. 1967
See Chesterton 21

John McCarthy

U.S. computer scientist, 1927–2011

1 A Proposal for the Dartmouth Summer Research Project on Artificial Intelligence.
Title of proposal (1955). Coinage of *artificial intelligence*.

Joseph McCarthy

U.S. politician, 1908–1957

1 I have here in my hand a list of two hundred and five that were known to the Secretary of State as being members of the Communist Party and who nevertheless are still working and shaping the policy of the State Department.
Speech, Wheeling, W.V., 9 Feb. 1950

Mary McCarthy

U.S. novelist, 1912–1989

1 The Man in the Brooks Brothers Shirt.
The Company She Keeps title of story (1942)

2 The happy ending is our national belief.
"America the Beautiful: The Humanist in the Bathtub" (1947)

3 The immense popularity of American movies abroad demonstrates that Europe is the unfinished negative of which America is the proof.
"America the Beautiful: The Humanist in the Bathtub" (1947)

4 You mustn't force sex to do the work of love or love to do the work of sex.
The Group ch. 2 (1954)

5 If someone tells you he is going to make "a realistic decision," you immediately understand that he has resolved to do something bad.
On the Contrary "The American Realist Playwrights" (1961)

6 [*Of Lillian Hellman:*] Every word she writes is a lie, including "and" and "the."
Dick Cavett Show (television program), 26 Jan. 1980. McCarthy here was referring to an interview with her published in *Paris Metro,* 15 Feb. 1978, in which she had actually said of Hellman: "every word she writes is false, including 'and' and 'but.'" The 1980 remark occasioned a $2 million lawsuit by Hellman.

Harry McClintock
U.S. singer and songwriter, 1882–1957

1 O—the buzzing of the bees in the cigarette trees
Round the soda-water fountain,
Where the lemonade springs and the bluebird sings
In the Big Rock Candy Mountains.
"The Big Rock Candy Mountains" (song) (1928)

Robert McCloskey
U.S. State Department spokesman, 1922–1996

1 [*Remark at press briefing during Vietnam War:*] I know that you believe that you understood what you think I said, but I am not sure you realize that what you heard is not what I meant.
Quoted in *TV Guide,* 31 Mar. 1984

Mitch McConnell
U.S. politician, 1942–

1 [*Silencing Sen. Elizabeth Warren's reading of a letter by Coretta Scott King, criticizing Jeff Sessions, in Senate debate:*] Senator Warren was giving a lengthy speech. She had appeared to violate the rule. She was warned. She was given an explanation. Nevertheless, she persisted.
Remarks in United States Senator chamber, 7 Feb. 2017

David McCord
U.S. poet, 1897–1997

1 [*Epitaph for a waiter:*]
By and by
God caught his eye.
"Remainders" (1935)

Peter Dodds McCormick
Scottish-born Australian songwriter, 1834–1916

1 In joyful strains then let us sing
Advance Australia fair.
"Advance Australia Fair" (song) (1878). This song is the Australian national anthem.

Frank McCourt
U.S. writer, 1930–2009

1 Worse than the ordinary miserable childhood is the miserable Irish childhood, and worse yet is the miserable Irish Catholic childhood.
Angela's Ashes: A Memoir ch. 1 (1996)

2 Above all—we were wet.
Angela's Ashes: A Memoir ch. 1 (1996)

Horace McCoy
U.S. novelist, 1897–1955

1 "Why did you kill her?" the policeman in the rear seat asked.

"She asked me to," I said. . . .

"Is that the only reason you got?" the policeman in the rear seat asked.

"They shoot horses, don't they?" I said.
They Shoot Horses, Don't They? ch. 13 (1935)

John McCrae
Canadian poet, 1872–1918

1 In Flanders fields the poppies blow
Between the crosses, row on row.
"In Flanders Fields" l. 1 (1915)

2 To you from failing hands we throw
The torch; be yours to hold it high.
"In Flanders Fields" l. 11 (1915)

3 If ye break faith with us who die
We shall not sleep, though poppies grow
In Flanders fields.
"In Flanders Fields" l. 13 (1915)

Carson McCullers

U.S. writer, 1917–1967

1 The Heart Is a Lonely Hunter.

Title of book (1940)
See Sharp 1

2 Love is a joint experience between two
persons—but the fact that it is a joint
experience does not mean that it is a similar
experience to the two people involved. There
are the lover and the beloved, but these two
come from different countries. Often the
beloved is only a stimulus for all the stored-up
love which has lain quiet within the lover for a
long time hitherto.

"The Ballad of the Sad Cafe" (1943)

3 The curt truth is that, in a deep secret way,
the state of being beloved is intolerable to
many. The beloved fears and hates the lover,
and with the best of reasons. For the lover is
forever trying to strip bare his beloved. The
lover craves any possible relation with the
beloved, even if this experience can cause him
only pain.

"The Ballad of the Sad Cafe" (1943)

Colleen McCullough

Australian novelist, 1937–2015

1 There is a legend about a bird which sings
just once in its life, more sweetly than any
other creature on the face of the earth. From
the moment it leaves the nest it searches for a
thorn tree, and does not rest until it has found
one. Then, singing among the savage branches,
it impales itself upon the longest, sharpest
spine. And, dying, it rises above its own agony
to out-carol the lark and the nightingale. One
superlative song, existence the price. But the
whole world stills to listen, and God in His
heaven smiles. For the best is only bought at
the cost of great pain.

The Thorn Birds epigraph (1977)

2 The bird with the thorn in its breast, it follows
an immutable law; it is driven by it knows
not what to impale itself, and die singing. At
the very instant the thorn enters there is no
awareness in it of the dying to come; . . . But
we, when we put the thorns in our breasts, we

know. We understand. And still we do it. Still
we do it.

The Thorn Birds ch. 7 (1977)

Hattie McDaniel

U.S. actress, 1893–1952

1 It has made me feel very, very humble and I
shall always hold it as a beacon for anything
that I may be able to do in the future. I
sincerely hope I shall always be a credit to my
race and to the motion picture industry.

Acceptance speech for Academy Award for Best
Supporting Actress, 29 Feb. 1940

2 Why should I complain about making seven
thousand dollars a week playing a maid? If
I didn't, I'd be making seven dollars a week
actually being one!

Quoted in Donald Bogle, *Toms, Coons, Mulattoes,
Mammies, and Bucks* (1973)

"Country" Joe McDonald

U.S. rock musician and songwriter, 1942–

1 And it's one, two, three
What are we fighting for
Don't ask me, I don't give a damn
Next stop is Viet Nam.

"Feel Like I'm Fixin' to Die Rag" (song) (1969)

W. J. "Bill" McDonald

U.S. policeman, 1852–1918

1 One riot, one Ranger.

Texas Rangers motto. This motto is a synthesis of
two statements by McDonald quoted in biographies
by Albert B. Paine. In *Captain Bill McDonald: Texas
Ranger* Paine quotes McDonald, sent to Dallas to
prevent a boxing match, as responding to the mayor's
question, "Where are the others?," by saying "Hell!
ain't I enough? There's only one prize-fight!" In
Paine's 1909 book McDonald's creed is given as "No
man in the wrong can stand up against a fellow that's
in the right and keeps on a-comin."

John McEnroe

German-born U.S. tennis player, 1959–

1 [*Comment to umpire at Wimbledon tennis
tournament:*] You can't be serious.

Quoted in *N.Y. Post*, 22 June 1981. According to the
Oxford Dictionary of Catchphrases, this line was first
said "during the 1981 Wimbledon tournament, when
McEnroe was playing Tom Gullikson in the first

round, and had just seen chalk fly up from a serve of his which was called long." Audiotapes of the incident indicate that McEnroe followed "you can't be serious" with the words "you *cannot be serious!*," and it is the latter form that has become famous.

Ian McEwan
English novelist, 1948–

1 It wasn't only wickedness and scheming that made people unhappy, it was confusion and misunderstanding; above all, it was the failure to grasp the simple truth that other people are as real as you.
Atonement (2001)

2 But now I must sleep.
Atonement (2001)

3 [*Of the last messages sent by people trapped by 9/11 terror attacks:*] I love you. . . . that is what they were all saying down their phones, from the hijacked planes and the burning towers. There is only love, and then oblivion. Love was all they had to set against the hatred of their murderers.
Guardian, 15 Sept. 2001

Donald McGill
English cartoonist, 1875–1962

1 [*Caption of postcard:*]
He: "Do you like Kipling?"
She: "I don't know, you naughty boy, I've never kippled."
Quoted in Elfreda Buckland, *The World of Donald McGill* (1984). This postcard is said to be the bestselling one of all time. The joke seems to have predated McGill; Garson O'Toole has unearthed it dating as early as 1907 (Paul Pierce, *Suppers: Novel Suggestions for Social Occasions*).

George S. McGovern
U.S. politician, 1922–2012

1 [I'm] 1000% for Tom Eagleton . . . [and have] no intention of dropping him from the ticket.
Quoted in *N.Y. Times*, 27 July 1972. Democratic presidential nominee McGovern was affirming his support for his running mate Senator Thomas Eagleton after it was revealed that the latter had undergone electroshock therapy for depression. A few days later, McGovern dropped Eagleton from the ticket.

Frank Edwin "Tug" McGraw
U.S. baseball player, 1944–2004

1 You gotta believe.
Quoted in *N.Y. Daily News*, 2 Oct. 1973. According to Paul Dickson, *Baseball's Greatest Quotations*, McGraw uttered this phrase after a clubhouse speech by New York Mets chairman M. Donald Grant in July 1973, and it became the slogan of the Mets' miraculous drive to the National League pennant that year. The *New York Daily News*, 24 Sept. 1973, reported that two nuns at a Mets game held up a sign saying "You Got to Believe." If the McGraw story is true, then the nuns were probably echoing his prior usage of the slogan.

Mark McGwire
U.S. baseball player, 1963–

1 [*Responding to questions about his steroid use:*] I'm not here to talk about the past.
Testimony at House of Representatives Government Reform Committee hearing, 17 Mar. 2005

Jay McInerney
U.S. novelist, 1955–

1 You are not the kind of guy who would be at a place like this at this time of the morning. But here you are, and you cannot say that the terrain is entirely unfamiliar, although the details are fuzzy.
Bright Lights, Big City (1984)

2 You get down on your knees and tear open the bag. The smell of warm dough envelops you. The first bite sticks in your throat and you almost gag. You will have to go slowly. You will have to learn everything all over again.
Bright Lights, Big City (1984)

Claude McKay
Jamaican-born U.S. poet and novelist, 1890–1948

1 If we must die, let it not be like hogs
Hunted and penned in some inglorious spot.
"If We Must Die" l. 1 (1917)

2 What though before us lies the open grave?
Like men we'll face the murderous, cowardly pack,
Pressed to the wall, dying, but fighting back!
"If We Must Die" l. 12 (1917)

Sarah McLachlan

Canadian singer and songwriter, 1968–

1 You strut your rasta wear
  And your suicide poem
  And a cross from a faith that died
  Before Jesus came
  You're building a mystery.
  "Building a Mystery" (song) (1997)

Mignon McLaughlin

U.S. author and editor, 1913–1983

1 Hope is the feeling we have that the feeling we
  have is not permanent.
  The Neurotic's Notebook ch. 5 (1963)

2 Every society honors its live conformists, and
  its dead troublemakers.
  The Neurotic's Notebook ch. 7 (1963)

Don McLean

U.S. singer and songwriter, 1945–

1 Something touched me deep inside
  The day the music died.
  "American Pie" (song) (1971)

2 So bye bye Miss American Pie,
  Drove my Chevy to the levee
  But the levee was dry.
  Them good old boys were drinkin' whisky and
    rye
  Singin', This'll be the day that I die.
  "American Pie" (song) (1971)

Marshall McLuhan

Canadian communications theorist, 1911–1980

1 But the fury for change is in the form and not
  the message of the new media.
  "Culture Without Literacy," *Explorations*, Dec. 1953
  See McLuhan 5; McLuhan 8

2 The media are not toys; they should not be
  in the hands of Mother Goose and Peter Pan
  executives. They can be entrusted only to new
  artists, because they are art forms.
  Counterblast (1954). Earliest known usage of *the media*
  to refer to all forms of communication.

3 The tribe is a unit, which, extending the
  bounds of the family to include the whole
  society, becomes the only way of organizing

society when it exists in a kind of Global
Village pattern. It is important to understand
that the Global Village pattern is caused by the
instantaneous movement of information from
every quarter to every point at the same time.
Letter to Edward S. Morgan, 16 May 1959
See Wyndham Lewis 1; McLuhan 4; McLuhan 6

4 Postliterate man's electronic media contract
  the world to a village or tribe where everything
  happens to everyone at the same time: everyone
  knows about, and therefore participates in,
  everything that is happening the minute
  it happens. Television gives this quality of
  simultaneity to events in the global village.
  Explorations in Communication introduction (1960).
  Coauthored with Edmund Carpenter.
  See Wyndham Lewis 1; McLuhan 3; McLuhan 6

5 Another way of getting at this aspect of
  languages as macromyths is to say that the
  medium is the message.
  "Myth and Mass Media," *Daedalus, Spring 1959*
  See McLuhan 1; McLuhan 8

6 The new electronic interdependence recreates
  the world in the image of a global village.
  *The Gutenberg Galaxy: The Making of Typographic
  Man* (1962)
  See Wyndham Lewis 1; McLuhan 3; McLuhan 4

7 Dewey in reacting against passive print culture
  was surf-boarding along on the new electronic
  wave.
  *The Gutenberg Galaxy: The Making of Typographic
  Man* (1962)

8 The Medium Is the Message.
  Understanding Media title of ch. 1 (1964). According
  to John Robert Colombo, *Colombo's All-Time Great
  Canadian Quotations,* "McLuhan first uttered the
  now-famous formulation on the evening of July
  30, 1959, at a reception in the Vancouver home of
  educator Alan Thomas, following a symposium at
  the University of British Columbia on the subject
  of music and the mass media. . . . According
  to anthropologist Edmund Carpenter, writing
  in *Canadian Notes & Queries,* Spring 1992, the
  talismanic sentence came from a lecture delivered by
  Ashley Montagu titled 'The Method Is the Message.'"
  See McLuhan 1; McLuhan 5

9 There is a basic principle that distinguishes
  a hot medium like radio from a cool one like
  the telephone, or a hot medium like the movie
  from a cool one like TV. . . . Hot media . . . are

low in participation, and cool media are high in participation or completion by the audience.

Understanding Media ch. 2 (1964)

10 Television brought the brutality of war into the comfort of the living room. Vietnam was lost in the living rooms of America—not on the battlefields of Vietnam.

Quoted in *Montreal Gazette,* 16 May 1975

11 Gutenberg made everybody a reader. Xerox makes everybody a publisher.

Quoted in *Wash. Post,* 15 May 1977

Terry McMillan

U.S. novelist, 1951–

1 I worry about if and when I'll ever find the *right* man, if I'll ever be able to exhale. The more I try not to think about it, the more I think about it.

Waiting to Exhale (1992)

Scott McNealy

U.S. businessman, 1954–

1 You have zero privacy anyway. Get over it.

Quoted in *Wired,* 26 Jan. 1999

John McNulty

U.S. writer, 1895–1956

1 They were talking about a certain hangout and Johnny said, "Nobody goes there anymore. It's too crowded."

New Yorker, 10 Feb. 1943. Often erroneously attributed to Yogi Berra. An earlier version, attributed to a "flutterbrained cutie named Suzanne Ridgeway," appeared in the *Helena Independent,* 10 Sept. 1941 ("Now I know why nobody ever comes here; it's too crowded"). Barry Popik has found an even earlier precursor in the *Philadelphia Inquirer,* 19 Dec. 1907: "She—'Oh, don't go there on Saturday; it's so frightfully crowded. Nobody goes there then!'"

William H. McRaven

U.S. admiral, 1955–

1 Geronimo EKIA.

Message to Leon Panetta, 2 May 2011. This was a code for "Enemy Killed in Action," referring to the mission to apprehend Osama bin Laden.

Norris McWhirter

English writer and political activist, 1925–2004

1 Ladies and gentlemen, here is the result of event nine, the one mile: first, number forty one, R. G. Bannister, Amateur Athletic Association and formerly of Exeter and Merton Colleges, Oxford, with a time which is a new meeting and track record, and which—subject to ratification—will be a new English Native, British National, All-Comers, European, British Empire and World Record. The time was three . . .

Announcement of winner of one-mile race at track meet, Oxford, England, 6 May 1954. In this race Roger Bannister became the first sub-four-minute miler; his time was drowned out after the word "three" by the roar of the crowd.

Margaret Mead

U.S. anthropologist, 1901–1978

1 As the traveller who has been once from home is wiser than he who has never left his own door step, so a knowledge of one other culture should sharpen our ability to scrutinise more steadily, to appreciate more lovingly, our own.

Coming of Age in Samoa introduction (1928)

2 Historically our own culture has relied for the creation of rich and contrasting values upon many artificial distinctions, the most striking of which is sex. . . . If we are to achieve a richer culture, rich in contrasting values, we must recognize the whole gamut of human potentialities, and so weave a less arbitrary social fabric, one in which each diverse human gift will find a fitting place.

Sex and Temperament in Three Primitive Societies conclusion (1935)

3 Warfare . . . is just an invention, older and more widespread than the jury system, but none the less an invention.

"Warfare Is Only an Invention—Not a Biological Necessity" (1940)

4 Female animals defending their young are notoriously ferocious and lack the playful delight in combat which characterizes the mock combats of males of the same species. There seems very little ground for claiming that the mother of young children is more peaceful,

more responsible, and more thoughtful for the welfare of the human race than is her husband or brother.

Male and Female introduction (1955 edition)

5 We know of no culture that has said, articulately, that there is no difference between men and women except in the way they contribute to the creation of the next generation.

Male and Female ch. 1 (1949)

6 Between the layman's "*Naturally* no human society" and the anthropologist's "No *known* human society" lie thousands of detailed and painstaking studies, made by hurricane-lamp and firelight, by explorer and missionary and modern scientists, in many parts of the world.

Male and Female ch. 2 (1949)

7 The mind is not sex-typed.

Blackberry Winter ch. 5 (1972)

8 Because of their age-long training in human relations—for that is what feminine intuition really is—women have a special contribution to make to any group enterprise, and I feel it is up to them to contribute the kinds of awareness that relatively few men . . . have incorporated through their education.

Blackberry Winter ch. 14 (1972)

9 I was brought up to believe that the only thing worth doing was to add to the sum of accurate information in this world.

Quoted in *N.Y. Times*, 9 Aug. 1964

10 Never doubt that a small group of thoughtful, committed citizens can change the world: indeed, it's the only thing that ever has.

Attributed in Donald Keys, *Earth at Omega: Passage to Planetization* (1982)

Shepherd Mead

U.S. advertising executive and author, 1914–1994

1 How to Succeed in Business Without Really Trying.

Title of book (1952)

Hughes Mearns

U.S. writer, 1875–1965

1 As I was going up the stair
I met a man who wasn't there.
He wasn't there again today.
I wish, I wish he'd stay away.

The Psycho-ed (1910)

Robert Megarry

English judge, 1910–2006

1 Whereas in England all is permitted that is not expressly prohibited, it has been said that in Germany all is prohibited unless expressly permitted and in France all is permitted that is expressly prohibited. In the European Common Market no-one knows what is permitted and it all costs more.

"Law and Lawyers in a Permissive Society" (lecture), 22 Mar. 1972

Henri Meilhac

French playwright, 1830–1897

1 *L'amour est un oiseau rebelle que nul ne peut apprivoiser.*

Love's a rebellious bird that flies so free it cannot be tamed.

Carmen (opera with music by Georges Bizet) act 1 (1875). Cowritten with Ludovic Halévy.

2 *Toréador en garde! Toréador, Toréador, et songe bien, ou, songe en combatant qu'un oeil noir te regarde.*

Toreador, be ready, Toreador, Toreador, and consider well while fighting that a dark eye is watching you.

Carmen (opera with music by Georges Bizet) act 2 (1875). Cowritten with Ludovic Halévy.

Golda Meir

Russian-born Israeli prime minister, 1898–1978

1 Let me tell you something that we Israelis have against Moses. He took us 40 years through the desert in order to bring us to the one spot in the Middle East that has no oil.

Speech at state dinner for Willy Brandt, Jerusalem, 10 June 1973

2 Don't be so humble—you're not that great.

Quoted in *N.Y. Times*, 18 Mar. 1969

3 There were no such things as Palestinians. When was there an independent Palestinian people with a Palestinian state? . . . It was not as though there was a Palestinian people in Palestine considering itself as a Palestinian people and we came and threw them out and took their country away from them. They did not exist.

Quoted in *Sunday Times* (London), 15 June 1969

4 Our secret weapon is no alternative.

Quoted in *N.Y. Times*, 26 Oct. 1969

5 A leader who doesn't hesitate before he sends his nation into battle is not fit to be a leader.

Quoted in Israel and Mary Shenker, *As Good as Golda: The Warmth and Wisdom of Israel's Prime Minister* (1970)

Nellie Melba

Australian opera singer, 1861–1931

1 [*Advice to Dame Clara Butt before the latter's concert tour of Australia, ca. 1901:*] Sing 'em muck!

Quoted in John Hetherington, *Melba: A Biography* (1967)

William Lamb, Second Viscount Melbourne

British prime minister, 1779–1848

1 I wish that I knew any thing as well as Tom Macaulay knows every thing.

Quoted in *Graham's Magazine,* Aug. 1851. Often quoted later as "I wish I was as cocksure of anything as Tom Macaulay is of everything."

John Mellencamp

U.S. singer and songwriter, 1951–

1 Oh yeah, life goes on long after the thrill of livin' is gone.

"Jack and Diane" (song) (1982)

Herman Melville

U.S. novelist, 1819–1891

1 Genius all over the world stands hand in hand, and one shock of recognition runs the whole circle round.

"Hawthorne and His Mosses" (1850)

2 Call me Ishmael.

Moby-Dick ch. 1 (1851)

3 Better sleep with a sober cannibal than a drunken Christian.

Moby-Dick ch. 3 (1851)

4 A whaleship was my Yale College and my Harvard.

Moby-Dick ch. 24 (1851)

5 And this is what ye have shipped for, men! to chase that white whale on both sides of land, and over all sides of earth, till he spouts black blood and rolls fin out.

Moby-Dick ch. 36 (1851)

6 All visible objects, man, are but as pasteboard masks . . . strike, strike through the mask!

Moby-Dick ch. 36 (1851)

7 All that most maddens and torments; all that stirs up the lees of things; all truth with malice in it; all that cracks the sinews and cakes the brain; all the subtle demonisms of life and thought; all evil, to crazy Ahab, were visibly personified, and made practically assailable in Moby Dick. He piled upon the whale's white hump the sum of all the general rage and hate felt by his whole race from Adam down; and then, as if his chest had been a mortar, he burst his hot heart's shell upon it.

Moby-Dick ch. 41 (1851)

8 Though in many of its aspects this visible world seems formed in love, the invisible spheres were formed in fright.

Moby-Dick ch. 42 (1851)

9 To produce a mighty book, you must choose a mighty theme. No great and enduring volume can ever be written on the flea, though many there be who have tried it.
Moby-Dick ch. 104 (1851)

10 By heaven, man, we are turned round and round in this world, like yonder windlass, and Fate is the handspike.
Moby-Dick ch. 132 (1851)

11 Aye, toil as we may, we all sleep at last on the field. Sleep? Aye, and rust amid greenness; as last year's scythes flung down, and left in the half-cut swaths.
Moby-Dick ch. 132 (1851)

12 Towards thee I roll thou all-destroying but unconquering whale; to the last I grapple with thee; from hell's heart I stab at thee; for hate's sake I spit my last breath at thee.
Moby-Dick ch. 135 (1851)

13 The great shroud of the sea rolled on as it rolled five thousand years ago.
Moby-Dick ch. 135 (1851)

14 It was the devious-cruising Rachel, that in her retracing search after her missing children, only found another orphan.
Moby-Dick epilogue (1851)

15 One trembles to think of that mysterious thing in the soul, which seems to acknowledge no human jurisdiction, but in spite of the individual's own innocent self, will still dream horrid dreams, and mutter unmentionable thoughts.
Pierre bk. 4 (1852)

16 A smile is the chosen vehicle for all ambiguities.
Pierre bk. 4 (1852)

17 I would prefer not to.
"Bartleby the Scrivener" (1856)

18 Ah, Bartleby! Ah, humanity!
"Bartleby the Scrivener" (1856)

19 Games in which all may win remain as yet in this world uninvented.
The Confidence Man ch. 10 (1857)

20 God bless Captain Vere!
Billy Budd, Sailor ch. 25 (1924)

21 But me they'll lash in hammock, drop me deep.
    Fathoms down, fathoms down, how I'll dream
        fast asleep.
    I feel it stealing now. Sentry, are you there?
    Just ease these darbies at the wrist,
    And roll me over fair!
    I am sleepy, and the oozy weeds about me twist.
Billy Budd, Sailor ch. 25 (1924)

Menander
Greek playwright, 342 B.C.–ca. 292 B.C.

1 Whom the gods love dies young.
Dis Exapaton fragment 4

2 The man who runs may fight again.
Sententiae

3 A god from the machine.
The Woman Possessed with a Divinity fragment 227. The Latin form of this expression is *deus ex machina*.

Mencius (Meng-tzu)
Chinese philosopher, 371 B.C.–289 B.C.

1 The great man is the one who does not lose his child's heart.
The Book of Mencius bk. 4, pt. 2, v. 12

2 If you let people follow their feelings, they will be able to do good. This is what is meant by saying that human nature is good.
The Book of Mencius bk. 6, pt. 1, v. 6

H. L. Mencken
U.S. journalist, 1880–1956

1 Love is the delusion that one woman differs from another.
A Little Book in C Major ch. 1 (1916)

2 Democracy is the theory that the common people know what they want, and deserve to get it good and hard.
A Little Book in C Major ch. 2 (1916)

3 An idealist is one who, on noticing that a rose smells better than a cabbage, concludes that it is also more nourishing.
A Little Book in C Major ch. 2 (1916)

4 A man is called a good fellow for doing things which, if done by a woman, would land her in a lunatic asylum.
A Little Book in C Major ch. 3 (1916)

5 A lawyer is one who protects you against robbers by taking away the temptation.
A Little Book in C Major ch. 4 (1916)

6 Archbishop: a Christian ecclesiastic of a rank superior to that attained by Christ.
A Little Book in C Major ch. 4 (1916)

7 Conscience: the inner voice which warns us that someone may be looking.
A Little Book in C Major ch. 4 (1916)

8 The penalty for laughing in a courtroom is six months in jail. If it were not for this penalty, the jury would never hear the evidence.
A Little Book in C Major ch. 4 (1916)

9 Courtroom: a place where Jesus Christ and Judas Iscariot would be equals, with the odds in favor of Judas.
A Little Book in C Major ch. 4 (1916)

10 It is a sin to believe evil of others, but it is seldom a mistake.
A Little Book in C Major ch. 5 (1916)

11 Suicide: a belated acquiescence in the opinion of one's wife's relatives.
A Little Book in C Major ch. 5 (1916)

12 When women kiss it always reminds one of prize-fighters shaking hands.
A Little Book in C Major ch. 6 (1916)

13 Alimony is the ransom that the happy pay to the devil.
A Little Book in C Major ch. 6 (1916)

14 The virulence of the national appetite for bogus revelation.
A Book of Prefaces ch. 1 (1917)

15 Time is a great legalizer, even in the field of morals.
A Book of Prefaces ch. 4 (1917)

16 The public . . . demands certainties. . . . But there *are* no certainties.
Prejudices, First Series ch. 3 (1919)

17 The great artists of the world are never Puritans, and seldom even ordinarily respectable.
Prejudices, First Series ch. 16 (1919)

18 ADULTERY. Democracy applied to love.
A Book of Burlesques ch. 11 (1920)

19 IMMORALITY. The morality of those who are having a better time.
A Book of Burlesques ch. 11 (1920)

20 LOVER. An apprentice second husband; victim no. 2 in the larval stage.
A Book of Burlesques ch. 11 (1920)

21 PLATITUDE. An idea *(a)* that is admitted to be true by everyone, and *(b)* that is not true.
A Book of Burlesques ch. 11 (1920)

22 There is always a well-known solution to every human problem—neat, plausible, and wrong.
Prejudices, Second Series ch. 4 (1920). Now usually quoted with "easy solution" instead of "well-known solution." Some sources trace the quotation to the earliest version of the essay "The Divine Afflatus" by Mencken, published in the *New York Evening Mail*, 16 Nov. 1917, but it does not appear in the 1917 version.

23 To sum up: 1. The cosmos is a gigantic flywheel making 10,000 revolutions a minute. 2. Man is a sick fly taking a dizzy ride on it. 3. Religion is the theory that the wheel was designed and set spinning to give him the ride.
Smart Set, Dec. 1920

24 How long will the human race sweat under the superstition that, in order to be happy and useful and intelligent, it is necessary to believe in things? What nonsense indeed! Human progress consists, not in acquiring beliefs, but in getting rid of them.
Smart Set, Mar. 1921

25 If, after I depart this vale, you ever remember me and have thought to please my ghost, forgive some sinner and wink your eye at some homely girl.
Smart Set, Dec. 1921

26 Democracy is grounded upon so childish a complex of fallacies that they must be protected by a rigid system of taboos, else even half-wits would argue it to pieces.
In Defense of Women, rev. ed., introduction (1922)

27 Women decide the larger questions of life correctly and quickly, not because they are lucky guessers, not because they are divinely inspired, not because they practise a magic inherited from savagery, but simply and solely because they have sense. They see at a glance what most men could not see with searchlights and telescopes. . . . They are the supreme realists of the race.
In Defense of Women, rev. ed., pt. 1, ch. 5 (1922)

28 No sane man, employing an American plumber to repair a leaky drain, would expect him to do it at the first trial, and in precisely the same way no sane man, observing an American Secretary of State in negotiation with Englishmen and Japs, would expect him to come off better than second best. Third-rate men, of course, exist in all countries, but it is only here that they are in full control of the state, and with it of all the national standards.
Prejudices, Third Series ch. 1 (1922)

29 Injustice is relatively easy to bear; what stings is justice.
Prejudices, Third Series ch. 3 (1922)

30 There are no mute, inglorious Miltons, save in the hallucinations of poets. The one sound test of a Milton is that he functions as a Milton.
Prejudices, Third Series ch. 3 (1922)
See Thomas Gray 8

31 Faith may be defined briefly as an illogical belief in the occurrence of the improbable.
Prejudices, Third Series ch. 14 (1922)

32 The old game, I suspect, is beginning to play out, even in the Bible Belt.
American Mercury, Nov. 1924. Earliest known usage of *Bible belt*, antedating the previous date of 1926 found in historical dictionaries.

33 The difference between a moral man and a man of honor is that the latter regrets a discreditable act, even when it has worked and he has not been caught.
Prejudices, Fourth Series ch. 11 (1924)

34 The Klan is actually as thoroughly American as Rotary or the Moose. Its childish mummery is American, its highfalutin bombast is American, and its fundamental philosophy is American. The very essence of Americanism is the doctrine that the other fellow, if he happens to be in a minority, has absolutely no rights— that enough is done for him when he is allowed to live at all.
American Mercury, Mar. 1925

35 No one in this world, so far as I know—and I have searched the records for years, and employed agents to help me—has ever lost money by underestimating the intelligence of the great masses of the plain people.
Chicago Tribune, 19 Sept. 1926. Often misquoted as "Nobody ever went broke underestimating the intelligence of the American public."

36 The average man doesn't want to be free. He wants to be safe.
Notes on Democracy pt. 3 (1926)

37 Life may not exactly be pleasant, but at least it is not dull. Heave yourself into Hell today, and you may miss, tomorrow or next day, another Scopes trial, or another War to End War, or perchance a rich and buxom widow with all her first husband's clothes. There are always more Hardings hatching. I advocate hanging on as long as possible.
American Mercury, Apr. 1928

38 Capitalism undoubtedly has certain boils and blotches upon it, but has it as many as government? Has it as many as marriage? Has it as many as religion? I doubt it. It is the only basic institution of modern man that shows any genuine health and vigor.
American Mercury, Aug. 1928

39 It might be a good idea to relate strip-teasing in some way . . . to the associated zoölogical phenomenon of molting. . . . A resort to the scientific name for molting, which is ecdysis, produces both ecdysist and ecdysiast.
Letter to Georgia Sothern, 5 Apr. 1940

40 When *A* annoys or injures *B* on the pretense of saving or improving *X*, *A* is a scoundrel.
Newspaper Days: 1899–1906 ch. 2 (1941)

41 Love is the most fun you can have without
laughing.

A New Dictionary of Quotations (1942). This quotation
is attributed as "Author unidentified." In Walter
Winchell's column in the *Wilkes-Barre* (Pa.) *Times
Leader*, 25 Jan. 1938, the following appeared: "The
latest definition of necking: How you can have the
most fun without laughing."
See Woody Allen 28

42 Puritanism—The haunting fear that someone,
somewhere, may be happy.

A Mencken Chrestomathy ch. 30 (1949). Mencken
used this definition earlier, in *American Mercury*,
Jan. 1925.

43 It is now quite lawful for a Catholic woman to
avoid pregnancy by a resort to mathematics,
though she is still forbidden to resort to physics
and chemistry.

Minority Report: H. L. Mencken's Notebooks (1956)

44 There are people who read too much: the
bibliobibuli. I know some who are constantly
drunk on books, as other men are drunk on
whiskey or religion. They wander through this
most diverting and stimulating of worlds in a
haze, seeing nothing and hearing nothing.

Minority Report: H. L. Mencken's Notebooks (1956)

45 We must respect the other fellow's religion,
but only in the sense and to the extent that we
respect his theory that his wife is beautiful and
his children smart.

Minority Report: H. L. Mencken's Notebooks (1956)

Johann Gregor Mendel
Czech geneticist and monk, 1822–1884

1 In this generation, *along with the dominating*
traits, the *recessive* ones also reappear, their
individuality fully revealed, and they do so in
the decisively expressed average proportion
of 3:1, so that among each four plants of this
generation three receive the dominating and
one the recessive characteristic.

"Experiments on Plant Hybrids" (1865)

2 Those traits that pass into hybrid association
entirely or almost entirely unchanged, thus
themselves representing the traits of the
hybrid, are termed *dominating* and those that
become latent in the association, *recessive*.

"Experiments on Plant Hybrids" (1865)

Dmitri Ivanovich Mendeleev
Russian chemist, 1834–1907

1 If all the elements are arranged in the order of
their atomic weights, a periodic repetition of
properties is obtained. This is expressed by the
law of periodicity.

Principles of Chemistry vol. 2 (1905)

Robert Menzies
Australian prime minister, 1894–1978

1 [*Response to a heckler who had yelled, "I wouldn't
vote for you if you were the Archangel Gabriel":*]
If I were the Archangel Gabriel, madam, I'm
afraid you would not be in my constituency.

Quoted in Ray Robinson, *The Wit of Robert Menzies*
(1966)

Johnny Mercer
U.S. songwriter, 1909–1976

1 Jeepers creepers!
Where'd ya get those peepers?
"Jeepers Creepers" (song) (1937)

2 You must have been a beautiful baby,
You must have been a beautiful child.
"You Must Have Been a Beautiful Baby" (song) (1938)

3 That Old Black Magic.
Title of song (1942)

4 You've got to
Accent-tchu-ate the positive,
E-lim-my-nate the negative,
Latch on to the affirmative,
Don't mess with Mister In-between.
"Accentuate the Positive" (song) (1944)

5 Moon River,
Wider than a mile:
I'm crossin' you in style
Some day.
"Moon River" (song) (1961)

6 Two drifters
Off to see the world,
There's such a lot of world
To see.
"Moon River" (song) (1961)

Leigh Mercer

English puzzle composer, 1893–1977

1 A man, a plan, a canal—Panama!

Notes and Queries, 13 Nov. 1948. One of the best-known palindromes (a word or words that spell the same thing forward and backward).

Freddie Mercury (Farrokh Bulsara)

Zanzibar-born English rock singer and songwriter, 1946–1991

1 Nothing really matters,
Anyone can see,
Nothing really matters, nothing really matters
   to me.

"Bohemian Rhapsody" (song) (1975)

George Meredith

English novelist and poet, 1828–1909

1 Ah, what a dusty answer gets the soul
When hot for certainties in this our life!

Modern Love st. 50 (1862)

2 Enter these enchanted woods,
You who dare.

"The Woods of Westermain" l. 1 (1883)

Owen Meredith (Edward Robert Bulwer Lytton, Lord Lytton)

English poet, 1831–1891

1 We may live without friends; we may live
   without books;
But civilized man can not live without cooks.

Lucile pt. 1, canto 2 (1860)

2 Genius does what it must, and Talent does
what it can.

"Last Words of a Sensitive Second-Rate Poet" (1868)
See Baring 1

Peter Merholz

U.S. computer scientist, 1972–

1 I've decided to pronounce the word "weblog" as
wee-blog. Or "blog" for short.

Peterme.com website, 23 May 1999. Coinage of the word *blog*.

Ethel Merman (Ethel Agnes Zimmermann)

U.S. singer and actress, 1908–1984

1 [*Of Mary Martin:*] Oh, she's all right, if you like
talent.

Quoted in *Theater Arts*, Sept. 1958

Bob Merrill

U.S. songwriter and composer, 1920–1998

1 How much is that doggie in the window?
The one with the waggily tail.

"How Much Is That Doggie in the Window?" (song)
(1953)

2 People who need people
Are the luckiest people
In the world.

"People" (song) (1963)

James Merrill

U.S. poet, 1926–1995

1 Always that same old story—
Father Time and Mother Earth,
A marriage on the rocks.

"The Broken Home" l. 40 (1966)

2 What we dream up must be lived down, I think.

"The Book of Ephraim" sec. 1 (1976)

Dixon Lanier Merritt

U.S. humorist, 1879–1972

1 Oh, a wondrous bird is the pelican!
His beak holds more than his belican.
He takes in his beak
Food enough for a week.
But I'll be darned if I know how the helican.

Nashville Banner, 22 Apr. 1913

Robert K. Merton (Meyer R. Schkolnick)

U.S. sociologist, 1910–2003

1 Four sets of institutional imperatives—
universalism [truth-claims are to be subjected
to preestablished impersonal criteria],
communism [scientific property is a heritage
held in common], disinterestedness, organized
skepticism—are taken to comprise the ethos of
modern science.

"Science and Technology in a Democratic Order"
(1942). Square brackets are in the original text.

2 The self-fulfilling prophecy is, in the beginning, a *false* definition of the situation evoking a new behavior which makes the originally false conception come *true*. The specious validity of the self-fulfilling prophecy perpetuates a reign of error. For the prophet will cite the actual course of events as proof that he was right from the very beginning.
"The Self-Fulfilling Prophecy" (1948)

3 The *distinctive* intellectual contributions of the sociologist are found primarily in the study of unintended consequences . . . of social practices as well as in the study of anticipated consequences.
Social Theory and Social Structure: Toward the Codification of Theory and Research "Manifest and Latent Functions" (1949)

4 [The] complex pattern of the misallocation of credit for scientific work must quite evidently be described as "the Matthew effect," for . . . the Gospel According to St. Matthew puts it this way: For unto every one that hath shall be given, and he shall have abundance: but from him that hath not shall be taken away even that which he hath. Put in less stately language, the Matthew effect consists of the accruing of greater increments of recognition for particular scientific contributions to scientists of considerable repute and the withholding of such recognition from scientists who have not yet made their mark.
"The Matthew Effect in Science: The Reward and Communication Systems of Science Are Considered," *Science*, 5 Jan. 1968. Merton based this principle on analysis of Harriet Zuckerman's interviews with Nobel laureates.
See Bible 264; Kahn 1; Modern Proverbs 75

W. S. (William Stanley) Merwin
U.S. poet, 1927–2019

1 who should moor at his edge
And fare on afoot would find gates of no gardens,
But the hill of dark underfoot diving,
Closing overhead, the cold deep, and drowning.
He is called Leviathan, and named for rolling.
"Leviathan" l. 18 (1956)

2 Then I will no longer
Find myself in life as in a strange garment.
"For the Anniversary of My Death" l. 6 (1967)

3 The ghosts of the villages trail in the sky
Making a new twilight.
"The Asians Dying" l. 8 (1967)

4 Rain falls into the open eyes of the dead
Again again with its pointless sound
When the moon finds them they are the color
of everything.
"The Asians Dying" l. 10 (1967)

Jean Meslier
French priest, 1664–1729

1 I remember, on this matter, the wish made once by an ignorant, uneducated man . . . that all the great men in the world and all the nobility could be hanged, and strangled with the guts of priests.
Testament vol. 1, ch. 2 (1864)
See Diderot 4

Grace Metalious
U.S. novelist, 1924–1964

1 Peyton Place.
Title of book (1956)

Klemens Wenzel Nepomuk Lothar von Metternich
Austrian statesman, 1773–1859

1 Italy is a geographical expression.
Dispatch to Count Apponyi, 6 Aug. 1847
See Bismarck 5

2 [*Remark, 1848:*] Error has never approached my spirit.
Quoted in François Pierre G. Guizot, *Mémoires* (1858–1867)

3 [*Remark, 1830:*] When Paris sneezes, the rest of Europe catches a cold.
Quoted in *Journal of Politics*, Aug. 1949

Pauline Metternich
Austrian princess, 1836–1921

1 [*In response to being asked at what age a woman's sexual urges cease:*] I do not know, I am only sixty-five.
Quoted in Simone de Beauvoir, *The Second Sex* (1949)
See Eubie Blake 1

Jean de Meun
French poet, fl. 1277

1 Thou shalt make castels thanne in Spayne,
And dreme of joye, all but in vayne.
The Romaunt of the Rose fragment B, l. 2573 (ca. 1277)
(translation by Geoffrey Chaucer)

Andrew Meyer
U.S. activist, 1986–

1 [*Plea to University of Florida police who were
using a Taser stun gun to drag him away from
questioning Senator John Kerry, Gainesville, Fla.,
17 Sept. 2007:*] Don't Tase me, bro!
Quoted in *St. Petersburg Times*, 20 Sept. 2007

Al Michaels
U.S. sportscaster, 1944–

1 [*At conclusion of victory by U.S. Olympic ice
hockey team over the heavily favored Soviet Union:*]
Do you believe in miracles? Yes!
Television broadcast of Olympic hockey game, 24
Feb. 1980

Anne Michaels
Canadian poet and novelist, 1958–

1 Do you realize Beethoven composed all his
music without ever having looked upon
the sea?
Fugitive Pieces "The Gradual Instant" (1997)

Michelangelo
Italian artist and poet, 1475–1564

1 [*On the completion of the Sistine chapel ceiling:*]
I've finished that chapel I was painting. The
Pope is quite satisfied.
Letter to his father, Oct. 1512

2 The marble not yet carved can hold the form
Of every thought the greatest artist has.
Sonnet 15 (translation by Elizabeth Jennings)

Jules Michelet
French historian, 1798–1874

1 Man is his own Prometheus.
Histoire de France preface (1869)

Albert A. Michelson
German-born U.S. physicist, 1852–1931

1 The more important fundamental laws
and facts of physical science have all been
discovered, and these are now so firmly
established that the possibility of their ever
being supplanted in consequence of new
discoveries is exceedingly remote.
Light Waves and Their Uses lecture 2 (1903)

Thomas Middleton
English playwright, 1580–1627

1 Anything for a Quiet Life.
Anything for a Quiet Life prologue (ca. 1620)

Ludwig Mies van der Rohe
German-born U.S. architect and designer,
1886–1969

1 Less is more.
Quoted in Philip Johnson, *Mies van der Rohe* (1947)
See Robert Browning 12; Venturi 1

2 God is in the Details.
Quoted in *Architectural Forum*, May 1958
See Flaubert 3; Modern Proverbs 24; Warburg 1

Bette Midler
U.S. singer and actress, 1945–

1 When it's three o'clock in New York, it's still
1938 in London.
Quoted in *Jerusalem Post*, 24 Feb. 1989

George Mikes
Hungarian-born English writer, 1912–1987

1 On the Continent people have good food; in
England people have good table manners.
How to Be an Alien ch. 1 (1946)

2 Continental people have sex life; the English
have hot-water bottles.
How to Be an Alien ch. 1 (1946)

Alfred Hart Miles
U.S. naval officer, 1883–1956

1 Anchors aweigh, my boys,
Anchors aweigh!
Farewell to college joys,
We sail at break of day.
"Anchors Aweigh" (song) (1906). Cowritten with R.
Lovell.

John Stuart Mill

English philosopher and economist, 1806–1873

1 No man made the land. It is the original inheritance of the whole species. Its appropriation is wholly a question of general expediency. When private property in land is not expedient, it is unjust.
Principles of Political Economy bk. 2, ch. 2 (1848)

2 The sole end for which mankind are warranted, individually or collectively, in interfering with the liberty of action of any of their number is self-protection.
On Liberty ch. 1 (1859)

3 The only purpose for which power can be rightfully exercised over any member of a civilized community, against his will, is to prevent harm to others. His own good, either physical or moral, is not a sufficient warrant.
On Liberty ch. 1 (1859)

4 The only part of the conduct of any one, for which he is amenable to society, is that which concerns others. In the part which merely concerns himself, his independence is, of right, absolute. Over himself, over his own body and mind, the individual is sovereign.
On Liberty ch. 1 (1859)

5 If all mankind minus one were of one opinion, and only one person were of the contrary opinion, mankind would be no more justified in silencing that one person, than he, if he had the power, would be justified in silencing mankind.
On Liberty ch. 2 (1859)

6 He who knows only his own side of the case, knows little of that.
On Liberty ch. 2 (1859)

7 The fatal tendency of mankind to leave off thinking about a thing when it is no longer doubtful is the cause of half their errors.
On Liberty ch. 2 (1859)

8 We can never be sure that the opinion we are endeavoring to stifle is a false opinion; and if we were sure, stifling it would be an evil still.
On Liberty ch. 2 (1859)

9 The liberty of the individual must be thus far limited; he must not make himself a nuisance to other people.
On Liberty ch. 3 (1859)

10 Whatever crushes individuality is despotism, by whatever name it may be called.
On Liberty ch. 3 (1859)

11 Everyone who receives the protection of society owes a return for the benefit.
On Liberty ch. 4 (1859)

12 The individual is not accountable to society for his actions, insofar as these concern the interests of no person but himself.
On Liberty ch. 5 (1859)

13 Liberty consists in doing what one desires.
On Liberty ch. 5 (1859)

14 Instead of the function of governing, for which it is radically unfit, the proper office of a representative assembly is to watch and control the government.
Considerations on Representative Government ch. 5 (1861)

15 The Conservatives . . . being by the law of their existence the stupidest party.
Considerations on Representative Government ch. 7 (1861)

16 It is better to be a human being dissatisfied than a pig satisfied; better to be Socrates dissatisfied than a fool satisfied.
Utilitarianism ch. 2 (1861)

17 I will call no being good, who is not what I mean when I apply that epithet to my fellow-creatures; and if such a being can sentence me to hell for not so calling him, to hell I will go.
Examination of Sir William Hamilton's Philosophy ch. 7 (1865)

18 Bad men need nothing more to compass their ends than that good men should look on and do nothing.
"On Education" (1867)
See Edmund Burke 1; Edmund Burke 28

19 The principle which regulates the existing social relations between the two sexes—the legal subordination of one sex to the other— is wrong in itself, and now one of the chief hindrances to human improvement; and . . . it

ought to be replaced by a principle of perfect equality, admitting no power or privilege on the one side, nor disability on the other.
The Subjection of Women ch. 1 (1869)

20 So true is it that unnatural generally means only uncustomary, and that everything that is usual appears natural. The subjection of women to men being a universal custom, any departure from it quite naturally appears unnatural.
The Subjection of Women ch. 1 (1869)

21 What is now called the nature of women is an eminently artificial thing—the result of forced repression in some directions, unnatural stimulation in others.
The Subjection of Women ch. 1 (1869)

22 No slave is a slave to the same lengths, and in so full a sense of the word, as a wife is.
The Subjection of Women ch. 2 (1869)

23 Marriage is the only actual bondage known to our law. There remain no legal slaves, except the mistress of every house.
The Subjection of Women ch. 4 (1869)

24 Ask yourself whether you are happy, and you cease to be so.
Autobiography ch. 5 (1873)

25 Human existence is girt round with mystery: the narrow region of our experience is a small island in the midst of a boundless sea.
Nature, the Utility of Religion, and Theism "The Utility of Religion" (1874)

26 Unearned increment of value.
Quoted in *Scotsman*, 10 Aug. 1871

Margaret Millar
Canadian-born U.S. novelist, 1915–1994

1 Most conversations are simply monologues delivered in the presence of a witness.
The Weak-Eyed Bat ch. 8 (1942)

Edna St. Vincent Millay
U.S. poet, 1892–1950

1 All I could see from where I stood
Was three long mountains and a wood.
"Renascence" l. 1 (1917)

2 The heart can push the sea and land
Farther away on either hand;
The soul can split the sky in two,
And let the face of God shine through.
"Renascence" l. 207 (1917)

3   I forgot in Camelot
The man I loved in Rome.
"Fugitive" l. 3 (1919)

4 My candle burns at both ends;
It will not last the night;
But, ah, my foes, and, oh, my friends—
It gives a lovely light.
A Few Figs from Thistles "First Fig" l. 1 (1920)

5 I would indeed that love were longer-lived,
And vows were not so brittle as they are,
But so it is, and nature has contrived
To struggle on without a break thus far,—
Whether or not we find what we are seeking
Is idle, biologically speaking.
"Four Sonnets—IV" l. 9 (1922)

6   Euclid alone
Has looked on Beauty bare. Fortunate they
Who, though once only and then but
       far away,
Have heard her massive sandal set on stone.
"Euclid Alone Has Looked on Beauty Bare" l. 11 (1923)

7 It's not true that life is one damn thing after another—it's one damn thing over and over.
Letter to Arthur Davison Ficke, 24 Oct. 1930
See Modern Proverbs 51

8 Love is not all: it is not meat nor drink
Nor slumber nor a roof against the rain;
Nor yet a floating spar to men that sink.
"Love Is Not All" l. 1 (1931)

9 Childhood Is the Kingdom Where Nobody Dies.
Title of poem (1934)

Arthur Miller
U.S. playwright, 1915–2005

1 For a salesman, there is no rock bottom to the life. He don't put a bolt to a nut, he don't tell you the law or give you medicine. He's a man way out there in the blue, riding on a smile and

a shoeshine. And when they start not smiling back—that's an earthquake.

Death of a Salesman "Requiem" (1949)

2 A salesman is got to dream, boy. It comes with the territory.

Death of a Salesman "Requiem" (1949)

3 Willy Loman never made a lot of money. His name was never in the paper. . . . But he's a human being, and a terrible thing is happening to him. So attention must be paid. He's not to be allowed to fall into his grave like an old dog. Attention, attention must be finally paid to such a person.

Death of a Salesman act 1 (1949)

4 The structure of a play is always the story of how the birds came home to roost.

Harper's, Aug. 1958

5 A suicide kills two people, Maggie, that's what it's for!

After the Fall act 2 (1964)

Bill Miller
U.S. political consultant, 1951–

1 Politics is show business for ugly people.

Quoted in *Dallas Morning News*, 13 Oct. 1991

Edgar E. "Rip" Miller
U.S. football player and coach, 1901–1991

1 [A tie in a football game is] just like kissing your sister.

Quoted in *Pittsburgh Post-Gazette*, 5 Dec. 1946. Although this quotation is often attributed to Duffy Daugherty, the 1946 citation predates any Daugherty evidence. Other metaphors involving sister-kissing go back as far as the nineteenth century.

Henry Miller
U.S. songwriter, fl. 1883

1 A Boy's Best Friend Is His Mother.

Title of song (1883)
See Film Lines 140

Henry Miller
U.S. writer, 1891–1980

1 This then? This is not a book. This is libel, slander, defamation of character. This is not a book, in the ordinary sense of the word. No,

this is a prolonged insult, a gob of spit in the face of Art, a kick in the pants to God, Man, Destiny, Time, Love, Beauty . . . what you will. I am going to sing for you, a little off key, perhaps, but I will sing. I will sing while you croak, I will dance over your dirty corpse.

Tropic of Cancer ch. 1 (1934)

2 Sex is one of the nine reasons for reincarnation. The other eight are unimportant.

Sexus ch. 21 (1949)

Joaquin Miller (Cincinnatus Heine Miller)
U.S. poet and frontiersman, 1837–1913

1 The mail must go through.

"Greeley's Ride with Hank Monk" l. 30 (1885)

Jonathan Miller
English writer and director, 1934–2019

1 I'm not really a *Jew*. Just Jew-*ish*. Not the whole hog, you know.

Beyond the Fringe (1960). Coauthored with Alan Bennett, Peter Cook, and Dudley Moore.

2 [*Of reading from a computer screen:*] A sort of cognitive equivalent of a condom—it's a layer of contraceptive rubber between the direct experience and the cognitive system.

Quoted in *Independent on Sunday* (London), 14 Jan. 1996

Max Miller
U.S. journalist, 1899–1967

1 I Cover the Waterfront.

Title of book (1932)

Roger Miller
U.S. country singer and songwriter, 1936–1992

1 Trailer for sale or rent;
Rooms to let, fifty cents;
No phone, no pool, no pets;
I ain't got no cigarettes.

"King of the Road" (song) (1964)

2 Ah, but two hours of pushing broom
Buys a eight by twelve four-bit room.
I'm a man of means by no means,
King of the road.

"King of the Road" (song) (1964)

Kate Millett

U.S. feminist and writer, 1934–2017

1 Sexual Politics.

Title of book (1970)

2 Perhaps patriarchy's greatest psychological weapon is simply its universality and longevity. . . . Patriarchy has a still more tenacious or powerful hold through its successful habit of passing itself off as nature.

Sexual Politics ch. 2 (1970)

Terence Alan "Spike" Milligan

Irish comedian, 1918–2002

1 Money couldn't buy friends, but you got a better class of enemy.

Puckoon ch. 6 (1963). This quotation is associated with Milligan, but it appeared before him. The earliest citation found is "Money can't get you friends, but it can get you a better class of enemies" (*Charleroi* [Pa.] *Mail*, 19 Aug. 1953).

C. Wright Mills

U.S. sociologist, 1916–1962

1 By the power elite, we refer to those political, economic, and military circles which as an intricate set of overlapping cliques share decisions having at least national consequences. In so far as national events are decided, the power elite are those who decide them.

The Power Elite ch. 1 (1956)

2 The sociological imagination enables us to grasp history and biography and the relations between the two within society.

The Sociological Imagination ch. 1 (1959)

Irving Mills

U.S. songwriter, 1894–1985

1 It don't mean a thing
If it ain't got that swing.

"It Don't Mean a Thing" (song) (1932). Duke Ellington noted in *Jazz Journal*, Dec. 1965, that trumpeter Bubber Miley was the first man he had heard use this expression.

A. A. Milne

English children's book writer, 1882–1956

1 They're changing guard at Buckingham
   Palace—

Christopher Robin went down with Alice.
Alice is marrying one of the guard.
"A soldier's life is terrible hard,"
Says Alice.

When We Were Very Young "Buckingham Palace" l. 1 (1924)

2 James James
Morrison Morrison
Weatherby George Dupree
Took great
Care of his Mother,
Though he was only three.
James James
Said to his Mother,
"Mother," he said, said he;
"You must never go down to the end of the town, if you don't go down with me."

When We Were Very Young "Disobedience" l. 1 (1924)

3 If you were a cloud, and sailed up there,
You'd sail on water as blue as air,
And you'd see me here in the fields and say:
"Doesn't the sky look green today?"

When We Were Very Young "Spring Morning" l. 9 (1924)

4 If you were a bird, and lived on high,
You'd lean on the wind when the wind came by,
You'd say to the wind when it took you away:
"*That's* where I wanted to go today!"

When We Were Very Young "Spring Morning" l. 17 (1924)

5 I am a Bear of Very Little Brain, and long words Bother me.

Winnie-the-Pooh ch. 4 (1926)

Czeslaw Milosz

Lithuanian-born Polish writer, 1911–2004

1 Grow your tree of falsehood from a small grain of truth.

Do not follow those who lie in contempt of reality.

Let your lie be even more logical than the truth itself,

So the weary travelers may find repose in the lie.

"Child of Europe" sec. 4 (1946) (translation by Jan Darowski)

John Milton

English poet, 1608–1674

1 Come, knit hands, and beat the ground,
In a light fantastic round.

Comus l. 143 (1637)

2 Fame is the spur that the clear spirit doth raise
(That last infirmity of noble mind).

"Lycidas" l. 70 (1638). A 1619 play thought to be
written by John Fletcher, *Sir John van Olden Barnavelt*
act 1, sc. 1, refers to "the desire of glory (That last
infirmity of noble minds)." That play was lost and
not rediscovered until 1883, so Milton's parallel words
were coincidental.

3 Look homeward angel now, and melt with ruth.

"Lycidas" l. 163 (1638)

4 At last he rose, and twitched his mantle blue:
Tomorrow to fresh woods, and pastures new.

"Lycidas" l. 192 (1638)

5 Truth . . . never comes into the world but like
a bastard, to the ignominy of him that brought
her forth.

The Doctrine and Discipline of Divorce introduction
(1643)

6 As good almost kill a man as kill a good book:
who kills a man kills a reasonable creature,
God's image; but he who destroys a good book,
kills reason itself, kills the image of God, as it
were in the eye.

Areopagitica (1644)

7 I cannot praise a fugitive and cloistered virtue,
unexercised and unbreathed, that never sallies
out and sees her adversary, but slinks out of
the race, where that immortal garland is to
be run for, not without dust and heat . . . that
which purifies us is trial, and trial is by what is
contrary.

Areopagitica (1644)

8 And though all the winds of doctrine were to
be let loose to play upon the earth, so Truth be
in the field, we do injuriously by licensing and
prohibiting to misdoubt her strength. Let her
and Falsehood grapple; who ever knew Truth
put to the worse, in a free and open encounter?

Areopagitica (1644)
See Oliver Wendell Holmes, Jr. 28

9 Time the subtle thief of youth.

"How soon hath time" l. 1 (1645)

10 Where glowing embers through the room
Teach light to counterfeit a gloom,
Far from all resort of mirth,
Save the cricket on the hearth.

"Il Penseroso" l. 79 (1645)

11 Nods, and becks, and wreathed smiles.

"L'Allegro" l. 28 (1645)

12 Come, and trip it as ye go
On the light fantastic toe.

"L'Allegro" l. 33 (1645)

13 New *Presbyter* is but old *Priest* writ large.

"On the New Forcers of Conscience Under the Long
Parliament" (1646)

14 None can love freedom heartily, but good men;
the rest love not freedom, but licence.

The Tenure of Kings and Magistrates (1649)

15   Peace hath her victories
No less renowned than war.

"To the Lord General Cromwell" l. 10 (written 1652)

16 What I have spoken, is the language of that
which is not called amiss *The good old Cause.*

*The Ready and Easy Way to Establish a Free
Commonwealth,* 2nd ed. (1660)

17 Of man's first disobedience, and the fruit
Of that forbidden tree, whose mortal taste
Brought death into the world, and all our woe,
With loss of Eden.

Paradise Lost bk. 1, l. 1 (1667)

18   What in me is dark
Illumine, what is low raise and support;
That to the height of this great argument
I may assert eternal providence,
And justify the ways of God to men.
Paradise Lost bk. 1, l. 22 (1667)
See Housman 5; Milton 49

19 No light, but rather darkness visible
Served only to discover sights of woe.
Paradise Lost bk. 1, l. 63 (1667)

20   What though the field be lost?
All is not lost; the unconquerable will,
And study of revenge, immortal hate,
And courage never to submit or yield.
Paradise Lost bk. 1, l. 105 (1667)

21 The mind is its own place, and in itself
Can make a heaven of hell, a hell of heaven.
Paradise Lost bk. 1, l. 254 (1667)

22 Better to reign in hell, than serve in heaven.
Paradise Lost bk. 1, l. 263 (1667)

23 The imperial ensign, which full high advanced
Shone like a meteor streaming to the wind.
Paradise Lost bk. 1, l. 536 (1667)

24   Let none admire
That riches grow in hell; that soil may best
Deserve the precious bane.
Paradise Lost bk. 1, l. 690 (1667)

25   From morn
To noon he fell, from noon to dewy eve,
A summer's day; and with the setting sun
Dropped from the zenith like a falling star.
Paradise Lost bk. 1, l. 742 (1667)

26   Pandemonium, the high capital
Of Satan and his peers.
Paradise Lost bk. 1, l. 756 (1667)

27 Belial, in act more graceful and humane;
A fairer person lost not heaven; he seemed
For dignity composed and high exploit:
But all was false and hollow; though his tongue
Dropped manna, and could make the worse
      appear
The better reason.
Paradise Lost bk. 2, l. 109 (1667)
See Aristophanes 1

28   With grave
Aspect he rose, and in his rising seemed
A pillar of state; deep on his front engraven

Deliberation sat and public care;
And princely counsel in his face yet shone,
Majestic though in ruin.
Paradise Lost bk. 2, l. 300 (1667)

29   Long is the way
And hard, that out of hell leads up to light.
Paradise Lost bk. 2, l. 432 (1667)

30   Chaos umpire sits,
And by decision more embroils the fray.
Paradise Lost bk. 2, l. 907 (1667)

31 Me miserable! which way shall I fly
Infinite wrath, and infinite despair?
Which way I fly is hell; myself am hell.
Paradise Lost bk. 4, l. 73 (1667)

32 Evil, be thou my good.
Paradise Lost bk. 4, l. 110 (1667)

33 Adam, the goodliest man of men since born
His sons, the fairest of her daughters Eve.
Paradise Lost bk. 4, l. 323 (1667)

34 With thee conversing I forget all time,
All seasons, and their change; all please alike.
Sweet is the breath of morn, her rising sweet,
With charm of earliest birds.
Paradise Lost bk. 4, l. 639 (1667)

35 Millions of spiritual creatures walk the earth
Unseen, both when we wake, and when we
      sleep.
Paradise Lost bk. 4, l. 677 (1667)

36 But wherefore thou alone? Wherefore with thee
Came not all hell broke loose?
Paradise Lost bk. 4, l. 917 (1667). "Hell were broken
loose" appears in Ben Jonson, *Every Man in His
Humor* act 3, sc. 4 (1601).

37 Best image of myself and dearer half.
Paradise Lost bk. 5, l. 95 (1667)

38   Oft-times nothing profits more
Than self-esteem, grounded on just and right
Well managed.
Paradise Lost bk. 8, l. 571 (1667)

39 The serpent subtlest beast of all the field.
Paradise Lost bk. 9, l. 86 (1667)

40 As one who long in populous city pent,
Where houses thick and sewers annoy the air,
Forth issuing on a summer's morn to breathe
Among the pleasant villages and farms

Adjoined, from each thing met conceives
  delight.
Paradise Lost bk. 9, l. 445 (1667)
See Keats 4

41   I shall temper so
Justice with mercy.
Paradise Lost bk. 10, l. 77 (1667)

42 The world was all before them, where to choose
Their place of rest, and Providence their guide:
They hand in hand, with wandering steps and
  slow,
Through Eden took their solitary way.
Paradise Lost bk. 12, l. 646 (1667)

43   The childhood shows the man,
As morning shows the day.
Paradise Regained bk. 4, l. 220 (1671)
See William Wordsworth 12

44 Athens, the eye of Greece, mother of arts
And eloquence . . .
See there the olive grove of Academe,
Plato's retirement, where the Attic bird
Trills her thick-warbled notes the summer long.
Paradise Regained bk. 4, l. 240 (1671)

45 The first and wisest of them all professed
To know this only, that he nothing knew.
Paradise Regained bk. 4, l. 293 (1671)
See Socrates 2

46 Ask for this great deliverer now, and find him
Eyeless in Gaza at the mill with slaves.
Samson Agonistes l. 40 (1671)

47 O dark, dark, dark, amid the blaze of noon,
Irrecoverably dark, total eclipse
Without all hope of day!
Samson Agonistes l. 80 (1671)
See T. S. Eliot 104

48 To live a life half dead, a living death.
Samson Agonistes l. 100 (1671)

49 Just are the ways of God,
And justifiable to men;
Unless there be men who think not God at all.
Samson Agonistes l. 293 (1671)
See Housman 5; Milton 18

50 His servants he, with new acquist
Of true experience from this great event,
With peace and consolation hath dismissed,
And calm of mind, all passion spent.
Samson Agonistes l. 1755 (1671)

51 Licence they mean when they cry liberty;
For who loves that, must first be wise and good.
"I did but prompt the age" l. 11 (1673)

52 When I consider how my light is spent,
E're half my days, in this dark world and wide,
And that one talent which is death to hide
Lodged with me useless.
"When I consider how my light is spent" l. 1 (1673)

53 They also serve who only stand and wait.
"When I consider how my light is spent" l. 14 (1673)

Charles Miner
U.S. businessman and politician, 1780–1865

1 When I see a man, holding a fat office,
sounding "the horn on the borders," to call
the people to support the man, on whom he
depends for his office, well thinks I, no wonder
the man is zealous in the cause, he evidently
has an axe to grind.
Luzerne County Federalist, 7 Sept. 1810. This is the
conclusion of an anecdote recalling a childhood
incident in which a stranger tricked Miner into
grinding an axe for him.

Raleigh C. Minor
U.S. legal scholar, 1869–1923

1 For the sake of convenience of discussion,
arbitrary terms have been used in designating
the union [a federal league of nations proposed
by Minor], the compact, and the officials
supposed to act under it. Thus the union
is spoken of as "The United Nations"; the
compact of government, as the "Constitution"
of the United Nations.
*A Republic of Nations: A Study of the Organization of
a Federal League of Nations* ch. 3 (1918). Here Minor
used the term *United Nations* for a federal league of
nations proposed by him, twenty-four years earlier
than the generally accepted coinage of the term.
See Byron 10

Newton N. Minow
U.S. government official, 1926–

1 I invite you to sit down in front of your
television set when your station goes on the air
. . . and keep your eyes glued to that set until
the station signs off. I can assure you that you
will observe a vast wasteland.
Speech before National Association of Broadcasters,
Washington, D.C., 9 May 1961

Lin-Manuel Miranda

U.S. playwright, songwriter, and actor 1980–

1 How does a bastard, orphan, son of a whore
And a Scotsman, dropped in the middle of a
    forgotten spot
In the Caribbean by Providence, impoverished,
    in squalor
Grow up to be a hero and a scholar?
Hamilton act 1 (2015)

2 Alexander Hamilton
My name is Alexander Hamilton
And there's a million things I haven't done
But just you wait, just you wait.
Hamilton act 1 (2015)

3 I'm just like my country
I'm young, scrappy and hungry
And I am not throwing away my shot.
Hamilton act 1 (2015)

4 Look around, look around at how
Lucky we are to be alive right now.
Hamilton act 1 (2015)

5 Immigrants: we get the job done.
Hamilton act 1 (2015)

6 I want to be in the room where it happens.
Hamilton act 2 (2015)

7 And love is love is love is love is love is love is
love is love cannot be killed or swept aside.
Poem about Orlando massacre read at Tony Awards
ceremony, New York, N.Y., 12 June 2016

Helen Mirren (Helen Lydia Mironoff)

English actress, 1945–

1 [*Of nudity:*] The part never calls for it. And I've
never ever used that excuse. The box office calls
for it.
Quoted in *Independent* (London), 22 Mar. 1994

Ludwig von Mises

Austrian-born U.S. economist, 1881–1973

1 The market economy as such does not respect
political frontiers. Its field is the world.
Human Action: A Treatise on Economics ch. 15 (1949)

2 Laissez faire does not mean: Let soulless
mechanical forces operate. It means: Let each
individual choose how he wants to cooperate in
the social division of labor; let the consumers
determine what the entrepreneurs should
produce. Planning means: Let the government
alone choose and enforce its rulings by the
apparatus of coercion and compulsion.
Human Action: A Treatise on Economics ch. 27 (1949)

3 Everybody thinks of economics whether he is
aware of it or not. In joining a political party
and in casting his ballot, the citizen implicitly
takes a stand upon essential economic theories.
Human Action: A Treatise on Economics ch. 38 (1949)

Yukio Mishima (Hiraoka Kimitake)

Japanese writer, 1925–1970

1 As he saw it, there was only one choice—to be
strong and upright, or to commit suicide.
"Ken" (1963) (translation by John Bester)

2 Human beings . . . they go on being born
and dying, dying and being born. It's kind of
boring, isn't it?
"Ken" (1963) (translation by John Bester)

The Missal

1 *Requiescant in pace.*
May they rest in peace.
Order of Mass for the Dead

2 *In Nomine Patris, et Filii, et Spiritus Sancti.*
In the Name of the Father, and of the Son, and
of the Holy Ghost.
The Ordinary of the Mass

3 *Peccavi nimis cogitatione, verbo, et opere, mea
culpa, mea culpa, mea maxima culpa.*
I have sinned exceedingly in thought, word, and
deed, through my fault, through my fault,
through my most grievous fault.
The Ordinary of the Mass

4 *Sanctus, sanctus, sanctus, Dominus Deus Sabaoth.
Pleni sunt coeli et terra gloria tua. Hosanna in
excelsis. Benedictus qui venit in nomine Domini.*
Holy, holy, holy, Lord God of Hosts. Heaven
and earth are full of thy glory. Hosanna in
the highest. Blessed is he that cometh in the
name of the Lord.
The Ordinary of the Mass

5 *Pater noster, qui es in coelis, sanctificetur nomen
  tuum; adveniat regnum tuum; fiat voluntas tua
  sicut in coelo, et in terra . . . sed libera nos a
  malo.*

  Our Father, who art in heaven, hallowed be thy
  name; thy kingdom come; thy will be done
  on earth, as it is in heaven . . . but deliver us
  from evil.

  The Ordinary of the Mass
  See Bible 215

6 *Agnus Dei, qui tollis peccata mundi, miserere
  nobis.*

  Lamb of God, who takest away the sins of the
  world, have mercy on us.

  The Ordinary of the Mass
  See Bible 312

7 *Credo in unum Deum.*
  I believe in one God.
  The Ordinary of the Mass "The Nicene Creed"

George Mitchell
U.S. politician, 1933–

1 Although he is regularly asked to do so, God
  does not take sides in American politics, and
  in America disagreement with the policies
  of the government is not evidence of lack of
  patriotism.
  Statement at Senate Hearings on Iran-Contra
  scandal, 13 July 1987

John N. Mitchell
U.S. attorney general, 1913–1988

1 [*Addressing black civil rights workers protesting
  Nixon administration actions regarding the Voting
  Rights Act:*] You'd be better informed if instead
  of listening to what we say, you watch what we
  do.
  Quoted in *Wash. Post,* 7 July 1969. Usually
  misquoted as "Watch what we do, not what we say."

2 [*Remark during telephone interview, 29 Sept.
  1972:*] Katie Graham's [*Washington Post*
  publisher Katharine Graham] gonna get her
  tit caught in a big fat wringer if that's ever
  published.
  Quoted in Carl Bernstein and Bob Woodward, *All
  the President's Men* (1974). Mitchell was referring
  to an article about his involvement in a secret fund
  financing illegal campaign activities.

Joni Mitchell (Roberta Joan Anderson)
Canadian-born U.S. singer and songwriter,
1943–

1 I've looked at life from both sides now,
  From win and lose and still somehow
  It's life's illusions I recall;
  I really don't know life at all.
  "Both Sides Now" (song) (1967)

2 They paved paradise
  And put up a parking lot.
  "Big Yellow Taxi" (song) (1969)

3 We are stardust,
  We are golden,
  And we've got to get ourselves
  Back to the garden.
  "Woodstock" (song) (1969)

4 By the time we got to Woodstock we were half a
  million strong
  And everywhere was song and celebration
  And I dreamed I saw the bombers riding
  shotgun in the sky
  Turning into butterflies above our nation.
  "Woodstock" (song) (1969)

5 All the people at this party, they've got a lot of
  style,
  They've got stamps of many countries, they've
  got passport smiles.
  Some are friendly, some are cutting, some are
  watchin' it from the wings,
  Some are standin' in the center givin' to get
  something.
  "People's Parties" (song) (1974)

Margaret Mitchell
U.S. novelist, 1900–1949

1 Land is the only thing in the world that
  amounts to anything, for 'tis the only thing
  in this world that lasts. . . . 'Tis the only thing
  worth working for, worth fighting for—worth
  dying for.
  Gone with the Wind pt. 1, ch. 2 (1936)

2 What most people don't seem to realize is that
  there is just as much money to be made out
  of the wreckage of a civilization as from the
  upbuilding of one.
  Gone with the Wind pt. 2, ch. 9 (1936)

3 Ah doan know nuthin' 'bout bringin' babies.

Gone with the Wind pt. 3, ch. 21 (1936). In the 1939 motion picture, this line by the character Prissy is changed to "birthin' babies."

4 Was Tara still standing? Or was Tara also gone with the wind that had swept through Georgia?

Gone with the Wind pt. 3, ch. 24 (1936)
See Dowson 2; Mangan 1

5 As God is my witness, as God is my witness, the Yankees aren't going to lick me. I'm going to live through this, and when it's over, I'm never going to be hungry again. No, nor any of my folks. If I have to steal or kill—as God is my witness, I'm never going to be hungry again.

Gone with the Wind pt. 3, ch. 25 (1936)

6 Death and taxes and childbirth! There's never any convenient time for any of them!

Gone with the Wind pt. 4, ch. 38 (1936)
See Benjamin Franklin 41; Proverbs 63

7 I wish I could care what you do or where you go but I can't. . . . My dear, I don't give a damn.

Gone with the Wind pt. 5, ch. 63 (1936). In the 1939 motion picture these words of Rhett Butler are changed to "Frankly, my dear, I don't give a damn." Inclusion of the last word in the film was accomplished only over great opposition from the Hollywood censors.

8 I'll think of some way to get him back. After all, tomorrow is another day.

Gone with the Wind pt. 5, ch. 63 (1936)
See Proverbs 302

Maria Mitchell
U.S. astronomer, 1818–1889

1 Endow the already established institution with money. Endow the woman who shows genius with *time*.

Journal, 10 Feb. 1887

Nancy Mitford
English author, 1904–1973

1 The great advantage of living in a large family is that early lesson of life's essential unfairness.

The Pursuit of Love ch. 1 (1945)

2 Love in a Cold Climate.

Title of book (1949)
See Southey 1

3 I love children, especially when they cry, because then someone takes them away.

The Water Beetle pt. 2, ch. 8 (1962)

Wilson Mizner
U.S. playwright, 1876–1933

1 Be kind to everyone on the way up; you'll meet the same people on the way down.

Quoted in *S.F. Chronicle*, 5 July 1932. Colonel Tom Parker, Elvis Presley's manager, is said to have remarked, "You don't have to be nice to people you meet on the way up if you're not coming back down again."

2 Hello, sucker!

Quoted in Edward Dean Sullivan, *The Fabulous Wilson Mizner* (1935). According to Ralph Keyes, *"Nice Guys Finish Seventh"* (1992), Mizner's "trademark greeting was a hearty 'Hello, Sucker!' This was adopted by flamboyant speakeasy hostess Texas Guinan . . . as her own signature line."
See Guinan 1

3 I respect faith, but doubt is what gets you an education.

Quoted in Edward Dean Sullivan, *The Fabulous Wilson Mizner* (1935)

4 A fellow who is always declaring he's no fool, usually has his suspicions.

Quoted in Edward Dean Sullivan, *The Fabulous Wilson Mizner* (1935)

5 [*On his deathbed, telling a priest he had no need to speak with him:*] I've been talking to your boss, Father.

Quoted in Edward Dean Sullivan, *The Fabulous Wilson Mizner* (1935)

6 When you take stuff from one writer it's plagiarism, but when you take from many writers it's called research.

Quoted in Frank Case, *Tales of a Wayward Inn* (1938). Wallace Notestein was earlier quoted very similarly: "If you copy from one book, that's plagiarism; if you copy from many books, that's research" (*California District News Letter* [U.S. Forest Service], 1 Nov. 1929).

7 The only sure thing about luck is that it will change.

Quoted in Evan Esar, *The Dictionary of Humorous Quotations* (1949)

8 A good listener is not only popular everywhere, but after a while he knows something.

Quoted in Evan Esar, *The Dictionary of Humorous Quotations* (1949)

9 You're a mouse studying to be a rat.

Quoted in Alva Johnston, *The Legendary Mizners* (1953)

10 You sparkle with larceny.

Quoted in Alva Johnston, *The Legendary Mizners* (1953)

11 Treat a whore like a lady and a lady like a whore.

Quoted in Alva Johnston, *The Legendary Mizners* (1953)

12 [*Of Hollywood:*] It's a trip through a sewer in a glass-bottomed boat.

Quoted in Alva Johnston, *The Legendary Mizners* (1953)

13 I never saw a mob rush across town to do a good deed.

Quoted in John Burke, *Rogue's Progress: The Fabulous Adventures of Wilson Mizner* (1975)

14 Wilson Mizner . . . recalls his embarrassment when he first came into the world, and found a woman in bed with him.

Reported in Groucho Marx, *Beds* (1930)

Modern Proverbs

Refers to proverbs whose earliest known documented usage is 1900 or later. Proverbs are listed alphabetically by first significant word of the proverb text. Citations are those of the earliest known English-language usage, based on extensive research in online texts. The wording given is exactly that of the earliest known usage, with older variant wordings explained in annotations. See also Proverbs, Sayings, *and* Anonymous. *Quotations with a known originator that have become proverbial are listed elsewhere in this book under the originator's name.*

1 An apple a day keeps the doctor away.

Anaconda (Mont.) *Standard*, 23 Dec. 1900. This newspaper states that the item was reprinted from the *Pall Mall Gazette*. In 1866 *Notes and Queries* recorded "A Pembrokeshire Proverb—'Eat an apple on going to bed. And you'll keep the doctor from earning his bread.'"

2 You can't argue against success.

Florida Magazine, June 1902

3 There are no atheists in fox-holes.

Springfield (Mass.) *Republican*, 11 Apr. 1942. This is often said to have been originated by chaplain William Thomas Cummings or other participants in the American defense of the Philippines in World War II. However, Bonnie Taylor-Blake and Garson O'Toole have traced very similar sayings to World War I, with the earliest they have uncovered being:

"We have no atheists in the trenches" (*Western Times* [Devon, England], 6 Nov. 1914, attributed there to an anonymous chaplain).

4 You have to take the bad with the good.

Proceedings of the 29th Convention of . . . the Middle States (1916)

5 That's the way the ball bounces.

George Mandel, *Flee the Angry Strangers* (1952)

6 If you can't beat 'em, join 'em.

Puck, 10 July 1901

7 It is better to be a big fish in a small pond than a small fish in a mighty ocean.

N.Y. Times, 25 Dec. 1927

8 You can't have it both ways.

McClure's Magazine, Mar. 1914

9 Never send a boy to do a man's work.

L.A. Times, 10 Aug. 1911. The wording in this 1911 occurrence was "duty" instead of "work." "It is not well to get a boy to do a man's work" appeared in Josephine Pollard, *The History of the United States* (1884).

10 Do not burn your bridges behind you.

Dental Digest, Sept. 1907

11 When you want a thing done, you must ask a busy person to do it.

Margaret Sangster, *Eastover Parish* (1912)
See Elbert Hubbard 5

12 [*Arab proverb:*] If the camel once gets his nose in the tent his body will soon follow.

Robert Christy, *Proverbs, Maxims, and Phrases of All Ages* (1907)

13 The camera does not lie.

Chicago Tribune, 27 May 1900. "The camera cannot lie" appeared in *Field and Fireside*, 17 Feb. 1866.

14 Be careful what you wish for, you'll probably get it.

Wash. Post, 19 Nov. 1954. "Be careful what you wish for in this world, for if you wish hard enough you are sure to get it" appeared in the *Atlantic Monthly*, May 1891.
See Goethe 15; T. H. Huxley 4; George Bernard Shaw 16; Teresa of Ávila 2; Wilde 56; Wilde 74

15 Too many chiefs, not enough Indians.

Nevada State Journal, 16 Feb. 1947

16 That's the way the cookie crumbles.

Helena (Mont.) *Independent Record*, 27 Nov. 1955

17 Don't do the crime if you can't do the time.

Lowell (Mass.) *Sun*, 23 May 1957

18 A criminal always returns to the scene of the crime.

Wash. Post, 24 Apr. 1905

19 Never criticize anybody until you have walked a mile in his moccasins.

Lincoln (Neb.) *Star*, 10 Oct. 1930. This 1930 usage is actually worded "never criticize the other boy or girl unless," etc., described as an "Indian maxim." Later versions sometimes refer to "shoes" rather than "moccasins."

20 Curiosity killed the cat.

L.A. Times, 22 Aug. 1901. "Curiosity killed a cat" appeared in *Papers of the Manchester Literary Club* (1880).

21 The customer is always right.

Boston Herald, 3 Sept. 1905
See Ritz 1

22 Any day above ground is a good day.

Transcript (North Adams, Mass.), 29 Sept. 1973. The exact wording in the 1973 source given starts with "Each day . . ."

23 The best defense is a good offense.

Chicago Daily Tribune, 27 Nov. 1903. The *Oxford Dictionary of Proverbs* gives earlier versions beginning with "offensive operations, often times, is the surest, if not the only . . . means of defence" (George Washington, 1799).

24 The devil is in the details.

Richard Mayne, *The Community of Europe* (1963)
See Flaubert 3; Mies van der Rohe 2; Warburg 1

25 Different strokes for different folks.

Philadelphia Tribune, 19 May 1945

26 Elephants never forget.

Saki, *Reginald* (1904)

27 It's not the end of the world.

Margaret A. Barnes, *Years of Grace* (1930)

28 Fair's fair.

Charles Barry, *Corpse on the Bridge* (1928)

29 You can't fight City Hall.

Brooklyn Daily Eagle, 12 June 1940. *The Dictionary of Modern Proverbs* documents similar sayings as far back as 1933.

30 The first hundred years are the hardest.

Bridgeport Telegram, 29 July 1918

31 Give a man a fish, and he will eat for a day. Teach him how to fish, and he will eat the rest of his life.

Boston Globe, 27 June 1963. In this 1963 occurrence, the saying is said to be "a Chinese proverb"; however, in 1911 M. Loane, *The Common Growth*, included the sentence "It is an oft-quoted saying . . . 'Give a man a fish, and he will be hungry again to-morrow; teach him to catch a fish, and he will be richer all his life.'"

32 Flattery will get you nowhere.

Redbook, Mar. 1946

33 Garbage in, garbage out.

Traffic Quarterly, July 1957

34 Go with the flow.

Military Cold War Education and Speech Review Policies (1962)

35 What goes around, comes around.

Proceedings of the Fourteenth Biennial Convention of the International Longshoremen's and Warehousemen's Union (1961)

36 Grab them by the balls, and their hearts and minds will follow.

William C. Anderson, *The Gooney Bird* (1968)

37 Your guess is as good as mine.

Henry Strong, *Miscellanies* (1902)

38 No guts, no glory.

N.Y. Times, 30 Aug. 1945

39 Hard work never hurt anybody.

Boston Daily Globe, 11 June 1901. "Hard work never killed anybody" appeared in *Bristol* (England) *Mercury*, 11 May 1844.
See Bergen 1

40 There is no harm in asking.

N.Y. Times, 11 Sept. 1921

41 History is written by the survivors.

Social Forces, Oct. 1931. Often worded with "winners" or "victors" instead of "survivors." George Graham Vest, senator from Missouri, used "History is written by the victors" in a speech in Kansas City, Mo., 20 Aug. 1891, printed the next day in the *Kansas City Gazette*.

42 When you are in a hole, stop digging.

Wall Street Journal, 16 Sept. 1977. The wording of the 1977 occurrence was "you don't keep digging."

43 When you're hot, you're hot.

Jerry Reed, Title of song (1969). Often used in an expanded form of "When you're hot, you're hot, and when you're not, you're not"; the unexpanded and expanded forms are both in the lyrics of the Reed song.

44 There's no "I" in team.

L.A. Times, 14 Aug. 1960

45 It's what's on the inside that counts.

Hamilton Drane, *Madison Hood* (1913)

46 Choose a job you love, and you will never have to work a day in your life.

Computerworld, 3 June 1985

47 It's not what you know that counts so much, as who you know.

Electrical Worker vol. 13 (1914)

48 If life hands you a lemon, make lemonade.

Dallas Morning News, 4 Oct. 1972. "If anyone 'hands you a lemon' take it home and make lemonade of it" appeared in William G. Haupt, *The Art of Business College Soliciting* (1910); and "If life hands you a lemon adjust your rose colored glasses and start to selling pink lemonade" appeared in the *New Oxford* (Pa.) *Item*, 19 Apr. 1917.
See Elbert Hubbard 6

49 Life is a journey and not a destination.

Christian Advocate, 19 Feb. 1920

50 Life is not the amount of breaths you take, it's the moments that take your breath away.

Vicki Corona, *Tahitian Choreographies* (1989)

51 Life is one damn thing after another.

Wilkes-Barre (Pa.) *Times*, 5 Mar. 1909. The exact wording in the Wilkes-Barre newspaper was "Life: (A new definition) One damn thing after another." Elbert Hubbard wrote "Life is just one damned thing after another" in the *Philistine*, Dec. 1909, but the citation above indicates that the expression predated Hubbard. Frank Ward O'Malley also sometimes is assigned the origination.
See Millay 7

52 Life's a bitch, and then you die.

Wash. Post, 10 Oct. 1982

53 Live every day as though it were your last.

Scranton Republican, 27 June 1903

54 You only live once.

Chicago Daily Tribune, 17 Feb. 1902. "We only live once" was printed in *The Lady's Magazine and Museum*, Feb. 1837.
See Aubrey Drake 1

55 It is lonely at the top.

Outlook and Independent, 12 Nov. 1930. The precise wording in this 1930 source was "It is always lonely at the top."
See Hawthorne 22

56 Don't make waves.

Palm Beach (Fla.) *Daily News*, 2 Feb. 1939. This may have derived from the punch line of a scatological joke, attested as early as 1925. The joke involved a new arrival in Hell being implored, while joining others standing in a pool up to their necks in excrement, not to make waves.

57 Those who mind don't matter, and those who matter don't mind.

Journal of the Institution of Municipal & County Engineers, 1 Feb. 1938

58 Never mix business with pleasure.

Lippincott's Monthly Magazine, Oct. 1905

59 There are some things money can't buy.

Indianapolis Journal, 7 Dec. 1902

60 Money doesn't grow on trees.

The Commoner (Lincoln, Neb.), 12 July 1901. In the form "Money does not grow on trees," this appeared in the *Connecticut Courant*, 6 July 1819.

61 Put your money where your mouth is.

N.Y. Tribune, 24 Aug. 1913

62 Monkey see, monkey do.

Sailors' Magazine and Seamen's Friend, Jan. 1901

63 Never say never.

Scotsman, 29 Aug. 1901

64 "No" means no.

State v. Lederer (1980)

65 If it isn't one thing it's another.

L.A. Times, 9 June 1903

66 Opposites attract.

L.A. Times, 30 May 1901. "Opposites attract each other" appeared in Andrew Jackson Davis, *The Great Harmonia* (1850).

67 A picture is worth a thousand words.

Arthur Brisbane, quoted in *New Orleans Item*, 26 July 1915. Brisbane, a well-known newspaper editor, earlier was quoted in the *Syracuse Post Standard*, 28 Mar. 1911: "Use a picture. It's worth a thousand words." Kathleen Caffyn, in her book *He for God Only* (1903), wrote "One look is worth a thousand words." The proverb has long been credited to Frederick Barnard, who used a "One look is worth" version in *Printers' Ink*, 8 Dec. 1921, and a "one picture is worth" version in the same periodical, 10 Mar. 1927. The citations above, however, disprove the Barnard coinage.
See Turgenev 3

68 Never wrestle with a pig; you will both get dirty, and the pig likes it.

Daily Mail (Charleston, W.V.), 31 May 1948. The exact wording in this 1948 occurrence is "My father told me never to roll in the mud with a pig. Because you both get covered with mud—and the pig likes it."

69 Before you meet the handsome prince, you have to kiss a lot of toads.

Better Homes and Gardens, Dec. 1975

70 All publicity is good publicity.

San Francisco Call, 25 June 1910
See Behan 4; Wilde 22

71 Publish or perish.

Clarence Marsh Case, "Scholarship in Sociology," *Sociology and Social Research*, Mar.–Apr. 1928

72 [A] quitter never wins. A winner never quits.

Salt Lake Telegram, 12 May 1921. "A winner never quits; a quitter never wins" appeared in *The Fraternal Builder of the Fraternal Monitor*, Nov. 1918.

73 The man who doesn't read hasn't any advantage over the man who can't read.

The Dodge Idea, Oct. 1914

74 Records are made to be broken.

Munsey's Magazine, Jan. 1900. "Road records seem to resemble promises and piecrust, inasmuch as they are only made to be broken" appeared in the magazine *Outing*, July 1889.

75 The rich get richer and the poor get poorer.

Huntington (Ind.) *Weekly Herald*, 22 May 1903. William Sargant, *Taxation: Past, Present, and Future* (1874), wrote, "as the rich get richer the poor get poorer."
See Bible 264; Kahn 1; Merton 4

76 Safety first.

Transactions of the Connecticut Academy of Arts and Sciences, May 1907

77 Don't make the same mistake twice.

American Gardening, 1 Feb. 1902

78 If you cannot say something good about anybody, don't say anything at all.

Smart Set, Dec. 1903
See Alice Longworth 4

79 It's not what you say, it's how you say it.

Arthur Miller, *Death of a Salesman* (1949)

80 See no evil, hear no evil, speak no evil.

Forum, Feb. 1913. The *Dallas Morning News*, 9 July 1905, has "speak no evil, see no evil, hear no evil." "Don't see any wrong . . . don't hear any wrong . . . don't talk any wrong" appears in Robert C. Hope, *The Temples and Shrines of Nikko* (1896). Hope is describing carvings at the Sacred Stable, Nikko, Japan, which are the original depiction of the "three monkeys" (one covering its mouth with its paws, one covering its eyes, and one covering its ears) that gave rise to the proverb.
See Dole 1

81 Shit happens.

Connie Eble, "UNC-CH Slang," Spring 1983

82 Shit or get off the pot.

Djuna Barnes, *Nightwood: Original Version and Related Drafts* (1934)

83 Shoot first and ask questions afterward.

N.Y. Times, 11 Aug. 1907

84 Size doesn't matter.

Boston Globe, 25 May 1989

85 Don't stick your neck out.

Wash. Post, 13 May 1939

86 Stupid is forever.

Wash. Post, 19 Dec. 1969

87 It is the thought that counts.

Racine (Wis.) *Journal Times*, 6 May 1904

88 Three strikes, you're out.

Proceedings of the New York State Stenographers' Association . . . Twenty-sixth Annual Meeting (1901)
See Norworth 3

89 Time flies when you're having fun.

George S. Kaufman and Moss Hart, *The Man Who Came to Dinner* (1939)

90 Time you enjoy wasting is not wasted time.

Marthe Troly-Curtin, *Phrynette Married* (1912)

91 Timing is everything.

C. W. Saleeby, *The Whole Armour of Man* (1919)

92 Trust but verify.

Problems in Communism, Jan.–Feb. 1966
See Reagan 12

93 The truth hurts.

N.Y. Times, 24 Nov. 1909

94 Use it or lose it.

Living Age, 25 July 1908

95 It takes a village to raise a child.

Toni Morrison, quoted in *Essence*, Apr. 1984. Earlier, an interview with Morrison in *Essence*, July 1981, quoted her: "I don't think one parent can raise a child. I don't think two parents can raise a child. You really need the whole village." According to *The Dictionary of Modern Proverbs*, "The saying is often referred to as an 'African' or a 'West African' proverb; however, no prototype from Africa has been discovered—though several sayings from that continent do urge cooperation in child rearing and other enterprises ('One hand cannot nurse a child,' 'One finger cannot crush a louse,' etc.)." S. S. Farsi, *Swahili Sayings from Zanzibar* (1962) includes "Mkono mmoja haulei mwana (One hand cannot nurse a child)."

96 Truth is the first casualty in war.

Ethel Snowden, "Women and War," *Journal of Proceedings and Addresses of the National Education Association* (1915). "The first casualty when war comes is truth" is often attributed to remarks in the U.S. Senate by Hiram Johnson in 1918, but according to the *Oxford Dictionary of Proverbs*, "it does not occur in the record of the relevant speech."
See Samuel Johnson 21

97 You win a few, you lose a few.

N.Y. Times, 11 Mar. 1958. In the form "You're going to lose some, win some and some are going to be rained out," this appeared in the *Greensboro* (N.C.) *Record,* 13 Dec. 1939.
See Film Lines 35

98 We can't win them all.

Norfolk Virginian-Pilot, 24 May 1900. The headline "Can't Win 'Em All" appeared in the *Cleveland Plain Dealer,* 1 Aug. 1894.

99 Winning isn't everything.

Atlanta Constitution, 11 Feb. 1912
See Lombardi 1; "Red" Sanders 1

100 If anything can go wrong it will.

Genetic Psychology Monographs, May 1951. Earliest documented occurrence of the celebrated "Murphy's Law" (also often phrased as "Anything that can go wrong, will go wrong"). In popular legend, Murphy's Law originated in 1949 at Edwards Air Force Base in California, coined by project manager George E. Nichols after hearing Edward A. Murphy, Jr., complain about a wrongly wired rocket sled experiment. When the editor of this book spoke to Nichols in Sept. 2003, Nichols stated that the original formulation was "If it can happen, it will happen." According to Nichols, this law was used by Air Force colonel John Paul Stapp at a 5 Jan. 1950 news conference. However, there is no trace of documentation of the aviation Murphy's Law until 1955. Barry Popik has read through most issues of the Edwards AFB base periodical *Desert Wings* from the 1950s, as well as other relevant publications, and found no mentions of the law.

In *Genetic Psychology Monographs,* May 1951, Anne Roe published an interview with an unidentified physicist in which she stated, "As for himself he realized that this was the inexorable working of the second law of the thermodynamics which stated Murphy's law 'If anything can go wrong it will.'" Stephen Goranson has tracked down, in Roe's papers, identification of the physicist as Howard Percy Robertson and, in Robertson's papers, evidence that the interview occurred in the first three months of 1949. Since the Edwards AFB incident is supposed to have happened in June or later of 1949, it appears that such an incident cannot be the explanation of the christening of Murphy's Law.

Murphy's Law is actually an old proverb in many fields. Bill Mullins has discovered Murphyesque statements in magicians' magazines going back to 1908, when British conjuror Nevil Maskelyne wrote in *The Magic Circular* (June): "It is an experience common to all men to find that, on any special occasion, such as the production of a magical effect for the first time in public, everything that can go wrong will go wrong." An earlier specialized version of the law has been unearthed by Stephen Goranson. The 1877 *Minutes of Proceedings of the Institution of Civil Engineers* contained this statement by Alfred Holt: "It is found that anything that can go wrong at sea generally does go wrong sooner or later." Still earlier, an article in the *Economist,* 22 Mar. 1862, included the following: "The lawyer does not see the whole of mercantile life. He sees only the failures. . . . His instinct, therefore, is that business as a rule fails,— that what can go wrong will go wrong."
See Robert Burns 3; Dickens 67; Disraeli 7; Orwell 17; Plautus 3; Proverbs 2; Sayings 25

101 You're only young once.

Dallas Morning News, 25 May 1913. An older version was "One is only young once" (Mrs. Herman Philip, *Above Her Station* [1863]).

Joseph Mohr
Austrian clergyman, 1792–1848

1 Silent night! Holy night!
All is calm, all is bright.
"Holy Night" (hymn) (1818)

Emilio Mola
Spanish general, 1887–1937

1 [*Describing supporters within Madrid as he was besieging the city with four columns of Nationalist troops:*] Fifth column.
Quoted in *N.Y. Times,* 17 Oct. 1936

Molière (Jean-Baptiste Poquelin)
French playwright, 1622–1673

1 I prefer an accommodating vice to an obstinate virtue.
Amphitryon act 1, sc. 4 (1666)

2 *Nous avons changé tout cela.*
We have changed all that.
Le Médecin Malgré Lui act 2, sc. 4 (1667)

3 You've asked for it, Georges Dandin, you've asked for it.
Georges Dandin act 1, sc. 9 (1668)

4 *Il faut manger pour vivre et non pas vivre pour manger.*

One should eat to live, and not live to eat.

L'Avare act 3, sc. 1 (1669)

5 Here [in Paris] they hang a man first, and try him afterwards.

Monsieur de Pourceaugnac act 1, sc. 5 (1670)
See Carroll 24; Walter Scott 11

6 All that is not prose is verse; and all that is not verse is prose.

Le Bourgeois Gentilhomme act 2, sc. 4 (1671)

7 *Par ma foi! il y a plus de quarante ans que je dis de la prose sans que j'en susse rien.*

Good heavens! For more than forty years I have been speaking prose without knowing it.

Le Bourgeois Gentilhomme act 2, sc. 4 (1671)

8 My fair one, let us swear an eternal friendship.

Le Bourgeois Gentilhomme act 4, sc. 1 (1671)

9 I will maintain it before the whole world.

Le Bourgeois Gentilhomme act 4, sc. 5 (1671)

10 What the devil was he doing in that galley?

Les Fourberies de Scapin act 2, sc. 11 (1671)

11 Grammar, which knows how to control even kings.

Les Femmes Savantes act 2, sc. 6 (1672)

12 *Le Malade Imaginaire.*

The Imaginary Invalid.

Title of play (1673)

13 Nearly all men die of their remedies, and not of their illnesses.

Le Malade Imaginaire act 3, sc. 3 (1673)

Billy Moll

U.S. songwriter, 1905–1968

1 I Scream, You Scream, We All Scream for Ice Cream.

Title of song (1927)

Helmuth von Moltke

Prussian military leader, 1800–1891

1 No plan of operations reaches with any certainty beyond the first encounter with the enemy's main force.

Kriegsgeschichtliche Einzelschriften (1880)

2 Everlasting peace is a dream, and not even a pleasant one; and war is a necessary part of God's arrangement of the world. . . . Without war the world would deteriorate into materialism.

Letter to J. K. Bluntschli, 11 Dec. 1880 (translation by Mary Herms)

Arthur R. "Pop" Momand

U.S. cartoonist, fl. 1913

1 Keeping Up with the Joneses.

Title of comic strip (1913)

Walter Mondale

U.S. politician, 1928–

1 When I hear your new ideas I'm reminded of that ad, "Where's the beef?"

Televised debate with Gary Hart, 11 Mar. 1984
See Advertising Slogans 132

Piet Mondrian (Pieter Cornelis Mondriaan)

Dutch painter, 1872–1944

1 I construct lines and color combinations on a flat surface, in order to express general beauty with the utmost awareness. Nature (or, that which I see) inspires me, puts me, as with any painter, in an emotional state so that an urge comes about to make something, but I want to come as close as possible to the truth and abstract everything from that, until I reach the foundation (still just an external foundation!) of things.

Letter to H. P. Bremmer, 29 Jan. 1914

2 I believe it is possible that, through horizontal and vertical lines constructed with awareness, but not with calculation, led by high intuition, and brought to harmony and rhythm, these basic forms of beauty, supplemented if necessary by other direct lines or curves, can become a work of art, as strong as it is true.
Letter to H. P. Bremmer, 29 Jan. 1914

3 Why should art continue to follow nature when every other field has left nature behind?
Quoted in Frank Elgar, *Mondrian* (1968)

Cosmo Monkhouse
English poet and critic, 1840–1901

1 There once was an old man of Lyme
Who married three wives at a time;
When asked "Why a third?"
He replied, "One's absurd!"
"And bigamy, sir, is a crime."
"There Once Was an Old Man of Lyme" l. 1 (date unknown)

2 There was a young lady of Niger
Who smiled as she rode on a Tiger;
They came back from the ride
With the lady inside,
And the smile on the face of the Tiger.
"There Was a Young Lady of Niger" l. 1 (date unknown). Usually attributed to Monkhouse, but it appears without credit in the *Los Angeles Times,* 5 Nov. 1891, with the following wording: "There was a young lady from Niger, / Who rode with a smile on a tiger; / When they returned from the ride, / The young lady was inside, / And the smile on the face of the tiger."

James Monroe
U.S. president, 1758–1831

1 In the wars of the European powers in matters relating to themselves we have never taken any part, nor does it comport with our policy so to do.
Seventh Annual Message to Congress (The Monroe Doctrine), 2 Dec. 1823

2 The American continents, by the free and independent condition which they have assumed and maintain, are henceforth not to be considered as subjects for future colonization by any European powers.
Seventh Annual Message to Congress (The Monroe Doctrine), 2 Dec. 1823

3 We owe it, therefore, to candor, and to the amicable relations existing between the United States and those powers to declare that we should consider any attempt on their part to extend their system to any portion of this hemisphere as dangerous to our peace and safety.
Seventh Annual Message to Congress (The Monroe Doctrine), 2 Dec. 1823

4 With the existing colonies or dependencies of any European power we have not interfered and shall not interfere. But with the Governments who have declared their independence and maintained it, and whose independence we have, on great consideration and on just principles, acknowledged, we could not view any interposition for the purpose of oppressing them, or controlling in any other manner their destiny, by any European power in any other light than as the manifestation of an unfriendly disposition toward the United States.
Seventh Annual Message to Congress (The Monroe Doctrine), 2 Dec. 1823

Marilyn Monroe
U.S. actress, 1926–1962

1 [*Declining an invitation to a party:*]
Unfortunately, I am involved in a freedom ride protesting the loss of the minority rights belonging to the few remaining earthbound stars. All we demanded was our right to twinkle.
Telegram to Robert and Ethel Kennedy, 13 June 1962

2 That's the trouble, a sex symbol becomes a thing. I just hate to be a thing.
Quoted in *Life,* 3 Aug. 1962

3 [*Responding to a question about whether she had posed for a calendar in 1947 with nothing on:*] I had the radio on.
Quoted in *Time,* 11 Aug. 1952

4 [*Responding to being asked what she wore in bed:*] Chanel Number 5.
Quoted in *Saturday Evening Post,* 12 May 1956

5 I just want to be wonderful.
Quoted in Cleveland Amory, *International Celebrity Register* (1959).

6 A career is born in public—talent in privacy.
  Quoted in *Ms.*, Aug. 1972

7 People feel fame gives them some kind of
  privilege to walk up to you and say anything
  to you, of any kind of nature—and it won't
  hurt your feelings—like it's happening to your
  clothing.
  Quoted in *Ms.*, Aug. 1972

8 Hollywood's a place where they'll pay you a
  thousand dollars for a kiss, and fifty cents for
  your soul. I know, because I turned down the
  first offer often enough and held out for the
  fifty cents.
  Attributed in *My Story* (1974)

Ashley Montagu (Israel Ehrenberg)
English-born U.S. anthropologist, 1905–1999

1 "Race" is the witchcraft of our time. The
  means by which we exorcise demons. It is the
  contemporary myth. Man's most dangerous
  myth.
  Man's Most Dangerous Myth: The Fallacy of Race ch. 1
  (1942)

Mary Wortley Montagu
English writer, 1689–1762

1 And we meet with champagne and a chicken
    at last.
  Six Town Eclogues "The Lover" l. 25 (1747)

2 Oh! was there a man (but where shall I find
  Good sense and good nature so equally join'd?)
  Would value his pleasure, contribute to mine.
  "The Lover: A Ballad" l. 11 (1748)

3 No entertainment is so cheap as reading, nor
  any pleasure so lasting.
  Letter to Mary, Countess of Bute, 28 Jan. 1753

4 Civility costs nothing, and buys everything.
  Letter to Mary, Countess of Bute, 30 May 1756

Charles Edward Montague
English novelist and essayist, 1867–1928

1 There is no limit, someone has said, to what
  a man can do who does not care who gets the
  credit for it.
  "Memoir: Middle Life," in William T. Arnold, *Studies
  of Roman Imperialism* (1906). Garson O'Toole has

found that, in *Notes from a Diary 1851–1872* (1897)
(diary entry dated 21 Sept. 1863), Mountstuart E.
Grant Duff wrote: "Father Strickland, an English
Jesuit . . . said to me—'I have observed, throughout
life, that a man may do an immense deal of good, if
he does not care who gets the credit for it.'"

Michel Eyquem de Montaigne
French essayist, 1533–1592

1 I want to be seen here in my simple, natural,
  and ordinary fashion, without straining or
  artifice; for it is myself that I portray.
  Essais "Au Lecteur" (1580)

2 I am myself the matter of my book.
  Essais "Au Lecteur" (1580)

3 Truly man is a marvelously vain, diverse, and
  undulating object. It is hard to found any
  constant and uniform judgment on him.
  Essais bk. 1, ch. 1 (1580)

4 *C'est ce dequoy j'ay le plus de peur que la peur.*
  The thing I fear the most is fear.
  Essais bk. 1, ch. 18 (1580)
  *See Francis Bacon 7; Franklin Roosevelt 6; Thoreau 16;
  Wellington 3*

5 I want . . . death to find me planting my
  cabbages.
  Essais bk. 1, ch. 20 (1580)

6 The ceaseless labor of your life is to build the
  house of death.
  Essais bk. 1, ch. 20 (1580)

7 He who would teach men to die would teach
  them to live.
  Essais bk. 1, ch. 20 (1580)
  See Porteus 2

8 It should be noted that children at play are not
  playing about; their games should be seen as
  their most serious-minded activity.
  Essais bk. 1, ch. 23 (1580)

9 There is scarcely any less bother in the running
  of a family than in that of an entire state. And
  domestic business is no less importunate for
  being less important.
  Essais bk. 1, ch. 39 (1580)

10 The greatest thing in the world is to know how
   to be oneself.
   Essais bk. 1, ch. 39 (1580)

11 *Quand je me jouë à ma chatte, qui sçait si elle
   passe son temps de moy plus que je ne fay d'elle.*
   When I play with my cat, who knows whether
   she isn't amusing herself with me more than
   I am with her?
   Essais bk. 2, ch. 12 (1580)

12 *Que sçay-je?*
   What do I know?
   Essais bk. 2, ch. 12 (1580)

13 Man is quite insane. He would not how to
   create a mite, and he creates gods by the
   dozens.
   Essais bk. 2, ch. 12 (1580)

14 *Chaque homme porte la forme entière de
   l'humaîne condition.*
   Every man bears the whole stamp of the
   human condition.
   Essais bk. 3, ch. 2 (1580)

15 [*Of marriage:*] It happens as with cages: the
   birds who are outside despair to get in, and
   those inside despair of getting out.
   Essais bk. 3, ch. 5 (1580)

16 There is no man so good that if he submitted
   all his actions and thoughts to the scrutiny of
   the laws, he would not deserve hanging ten
   times in his life.
   Essais bk. 3, ch. 9 (1580)

17 It could be said of me that I have here only
   made a nosegay of other men's flowers,
   providing of my own only the string that ties
   them together.
   Essais bk. 3, ch. 12 (1580)

18 Nature is a gentle guide, yet not more gentle
   than prudent and just.
   Essais bk. 3, ch. 13 (1580)

19 No matter that we may mount on stilts, we still
   must walk on our own legs. And on the highest
   throne in the world, we still sit only on our own
   bottom.
   Essais bk. 3, ch. 13 (1580)

Charles-Louis de Secondat, Baron de La Brède et de Montesquieu

French political philosopher, 1689–1755

1 How can anyone be Persian?
  Lettres Persanes no. 30 (1721)

2 Men should be bewailed at their birth, and not
  at their death.
  Lettres Persanes no. 40 (1721)

3 *Si les triangles faisoient un Dieu, ils lui
   donneroient trois côtés.*
   If the triangles were to make a God they would
   give him three sides.
   Lettres Persanes no. 59 (1721)

4 Liberty is the right of doing whatever the laws
  permit.
  De l'Esprit des Loix (The Spirit of the Laws) bk. 11
  (1748)

5 When the legislative and executive powers
  are united in the same person, or in the same
  body of magistrats, there can be no liberty.
  . . . Again, there is no liberty, if the judiciary
  power be not separated from the legislative and
  executive.
  De l'Esprit des Loix (The Spirit of the Laws) bk. 11
  (1748)

6 Happy the people whose annals are blank in
  history-books!
  Attributed in Thomas Carlyle, *History of Frederick the
  Great* (1858–1865)
  See George Eliot 4; Proverbs 54

Maria Montessori

Italian educator, 1870–1952

1 If education is always to be conceived along the
  same antiquated lines of a mere transmission
  of knowledge, there is little to be hoped from
  it in the bettering of man's future. For what
  is the use of transmitting knowledge if the
  individual's total development lags behind?
  The Absorbent Mind ch. 1 (1949)

2 The greatest sign of success for a teacher . . .
  is to be able to say, "The children are now
  working as if I did not exist."
  The Absorbent Mind ch. 27 (1949)

Bernard Law Montgomery

British military leader, 1887–1976

1 Rule 1, on page 1 of the book of war, is: "Do not
  march on Moscow" . . . [Rule 2] is: "Do not go
  fighting with your land armies in China."
  Speech in House of Lords, 30 May 1962

2 [*In debate on Sexual Offences Bill:*] I have heard
  some say . . . that such [homosexual] practices

are allowed in France and in other NATO countries. We are not French, and we are not other nationals. We are British, thank God!

Speech in House of Lords, 24 May 1965

Lucy Maud Montgomery
Canadian writer, 1874–1942

1 When twilight drops her curtain down
And pins it with a star
Remember that you have a friend
Though she may wander far.

Anne of Green Gables ch. 17 (1908)

2 "Marilla, isn't it nice to think that tomorrow is a new day with no mistakes in it yet?"

Anne of Green Gables ch. 21 (1908)

Percy Montrose
U.S. songwriter, fl. 1884

1 In a cavern, in a canyon,
Excavating for a mine,
Dwelt a miner, 'Forty-Niner,
And his daughter Clementine.

"Oh, My Darling Clementine" (song) (1884)

2 Oh my darling Clementine!
Thou art lost and gone for ever, dreadful sorry,
Clementine.

"Oh, My Darling Clementine" (song) (1884). An earlier song, "Down by the River Lived a Maiden," by H. S. Thompson (1863), contained this chorus: "Oh! my darling Clementine, / Now you are gone and lost forever, / I'm dreadful sorry Clementine."

3 Light she was and like a fairy,
And her shoes were number nine.

"Oh, My Darling Clementine" (song) (1884)

Monty Python's Flying Circus
British comedy group

"Monty Python's Flying Circus" was a comedy group consisting of Graham Chapman, John Cleese, Terry Gilliam, Eric Idle, Terry Jones, and Michael Palin.

1 And now for something completely different.

Monty Python's Flying Circus (television series) episode 2 (1969). This catchphrase also appeared in the earlier Python series *At Last the 1948 Show* (1967).

2 Your wife interested in er . . . photographs, eh? Know what I mean? . . . Nudge nudge. Snap snap. Grin, grin, wink, wink, say no more.

Monty Python's Flying Circus (television series) episode 3 (1969)

3 It's not pining, it's passed on. This parrot is no more. It has ceased to be. It's expired and gone to meet its maker. This is a late parrot. It's a stiff. Bereft of life, it rests in peace. If you hadn't nailed it to the perch, it would be pushing up the daisies. It's rung down the curtain and joined the choir invisible. This is an ex-parrot.

Monty Python's Flying Circus (television series) episode 8 (1969)

4 I'm a lumberjack and I'm OK,
I sleep all night and I work all day.

Monty Python's Flying Circus (television series) episode 9 (1969)

5 I cut down trees, I skip and jump,
I like to press wild flowers.
I put on women's clothing
And hang around in bars.

Monty Python's Flying Circus (television series) episode 9 (1969)

6 Nobody expects the Spanish Inquisition.

Monty Python's Flying Circus (television series) episode 15 (1970)

7 Spam, spam, spam, spam, spam . . . spam, spam, spam, spam . . . lovely spam, wonderful spam.

Monty Python's Flying Circus (television series) episode 25 (1970). Spam is a trademark of Hormel Foods for a brand of canned spiced ham. In this skit, the words are chanted by Vikings sitting in a restaurant. The skit is often said to be the source for the term *spam* referring to unsolicited bulk e-mail. This theory is probably erroneous, however, because the earliest documented uses of *spam* in this sense seem to derive from the tendency of spam to splatter messily when hurled, but Python probably influenced the development of this meaning.

8 [*Dead Body That Claims It Isn't, played by John Young, speaking:*] I'm not dead.

Monty Python and the Holy Grail (motion picture) (1975)

9 [*Large Man:*] Who's that then?
[*Dead Collector:*] I dunno, must be a king.
[*Large Man:*] Why?
[*Dead Collector:*] He hasn't got shit all over him.

Monty Python and the Holy Grail (motion picture) (1975)

10 [*Dennis, played by Michael Palin, speaking:*] Listen, strange women lyin' in ponds distributin' swords is no basis for a system of

government! Supreme executive power derives from a mandate from the masses, not from some farcical aquatic ceremony!

Monty Python and the Holy Grail (motion picture) (1975)

11 [*Dennis, played by Michael Palin, speaking:*] You can't expect to wield supreme executive power just because some watery tart threw a sword at you.

Monty Python and the Holy Grail (motion picture) (1975)

12 [*Knight 1 speaking:*] We are the Knights who say . . . NI!

Monty Python and the Holy Grail (motion picture) (1975)

13 [*Reg, played by John Cleese, speaking:*] All right, but apart from the sanitation, medicine, education, wine, public order, irrigation, roads, the fresh water system, and public health, what have the Romans ever done for us?

Life of Brian (motion picture) (1979)

Clement C. Moore
U.S. writer, 1779–1863

1 'Twas the night before Christmas, when all through the house
   Not a creature was stirring, not even a mouse.
   "A Visit from St. Nicholas" l. 1 (1823)

2 The children were nestled all snug in their beds,
   While visions of sugar-plums danced in their heads.
   "A Visit from St. Nicholas" l. 5 (1823)

3 Now, Dasher! now, Dancer! now, Prancer and Vixen!
   On, Comet! on, Cupid! on, Donder and Blitzen!
   "A Visit from St. Nicholas" l. 21 (1823)

4 He had a broad face and a little round belly,
   That shook when he laughed, like a bowl full of jelly.
   "A Visit from St. Nicholas" l. 43 (1823)

5 "Happy Christmas to all, and to all a goodnight!"
   "A Visit from St. Nicholas" l. 56 (1823)

Edward Moore
English playwright, 1712–1757

1 This is adding insult to injuries.
   The Foundling act 5, sc. 5 (1748)

2 I am rich beyond the dreams of avarice.
   The Gamester act 2, sc. 2 (1753)
   See Samuel Johnson 99

Gordon E. Moore
U.S. businessman and computer scientist, 1929–

1 The complexity for minimum component costs has increased at a rate of roughly a factor of two per year. . . . Certainly over the short term this rate can be expected to continue, if not to increase.
   Electronics, 19 Apr. 1965. This statement became known as "Moore's Law" of integrated circuits and computers, predicting that the number of transistors the computer industry would be able to place on a chip would double every couple of years.

Hoyt A. Moore
U.S. lawyer, 1870–1958

1 The story, doubtless apocryphal, has long been told that when some of his partners [at the firm of Cravath, Swaine and Moore] urged that the office was under such pressure as to make additions to the staff imperative, Moore replied: "That's silly. No one is under pressure. There wasn't a light on when I left at two o'clock this morning."
   Reported in Robert T. Swaine, *The Cravath Firm and Its Predecessors, 1819–1948* (1948)

Jo Moore
British government official, 1963–

1 [*E-mail thirty minutes after terrorist attack, 11 Sept. 2001:*] It's now a very good day to get out anything we want to bury.
   Quoted in *Times* (London), 9 Oct. 2001

Marianne Moore
U.S. poet, 1887–1972

1 I, too, dislike it: there are things that are important
      beyond all this fiddle.
   "Poetry" l. 1 (1920)

2 Imaginary gardens with real toads in them.
"Poetry" l. 32 (1935)

3 My father used to say,
"Superior people never make long visits,
have to be shown Longfellow's grave
or the glass flowers at Harvard."
"Silence" l. 1 (1935)

4   Beauty is everlasting
        And dust is for a time.
"In Distrust of Merit" st. 8 (1944)

Michael Moore
U.S. film director and author, 1954–

1 The bad guys are just a bunch of silly, stupid
white men. And there's a helluva lot more of us
than there are of them. Use your power.
Stupid White Men ch. 12 (2002)

2 We live in fictitious times. We live in the time
where we have fictitious election results that
elect a fictitious president. We live in a time
where we have a man sending us to war for
fictitious reasons.
Remarks after receiving Academy Award, Los
Angeles, Calif., 23 Mar. 2003

Thomas Moore
Irish musician and songwriter, 1779–1852

1 Believe me, if all those endearing young
    charms,
Which I gaze on so fondly today,
Were to change by tomorrow, and fleet in my
    arms,
Like fairy gifts fading away!
Irish Melodies "Believe Me, If All Those Endearing
Young Charms" (1807)

2 The harp that once through Tara's halls
The soul of music shed,
Now hangs as mute on Tara's walls
As if that soul were fled.
Irish Melodies "The Harp That Once Through Tara's
Halls" (1807)

3 No, there's nothing half so sweet in life
As love's young dream.
Irish Melodies "Love's Young Dream" (1807)

4 Oh! ever thus, from childhood's hour,
I've seen my fondest hope decay;

I never loved a tree or flower,
But 'twas the first to fade away.
I never nurs'd a dear gazelle
To glad me with its soft black eye,
But when it came to know me well,
And love me, it was sure to die.
Lalla Rookh pt. 5 (1817)

Harry "Breaker" Morant
English-born Australian poet and soldier,
ca. 1864–1902

1 [*To the firing squad at his execution, 27 Feb. 1902:*]
Shoot straight you bastards. Don't make a mess
of it.
Quoted in Bill Hornadge, *The Australian Slanguage*
(1980)

Alberto Moravia
Italian novelist, 1907–1990

1 The ratio of literacy to illiteracy is constant, but
nowadays the illiterates can read and write.
Quoted in *Observer* (London), 14 Oct. 1979

Thomas Osbert Mordaunt
English soldier, 1730–1809

1 One crowded hour of glorious life
Is worth an age without a name.
"A Poem, Said to Be Written by Major Mordaunt
During the Last German War" l. 3 (1791)

Hannah More
English writer and philanthropist, 1745–1835

1 Going to the opera, like getting drunk, is a sin
that carries its own punishment with it, and
that a very severe one.
Letter to her sister, 1775

2 Since trifles make the sum of human things,
And half our mis'ry from our foibles springs.
"Sensibility: An Epistle to the Honorable Mrs.
Boscawen" l. 293 (1782)

3 He liked those literary cooks
Who skim the cream of others' books;
And ruin half an author's graces
By plucking bon-mots from their places.
Florio pt. 1, l. 123 (1786)

Thomas More

English scholar, saint, and Lord Chancellor, 1478–1535

1 Utopia.
   Title of book (1516)

2 They have no lawyers among them, for they consider them as a sort of people whose profession it is to disguise matters.
   Utopia bk. 1 (1516)

3 [*Before ascending the steps of the scaffold:*] I pray you, master Lieutenant, see me safe up, and my coming down let me shift for my self.
   Quoted in William Roper, *Life of Sir Thomas More* (1626)

4 [*Drawing his beard aside before placing his head on the block:*] This hath not offended the king.
   Attributed in Francis Bacon, *Apothegms* (1624)

Mantan Moreland

U.S. actor, 1902–1973

1 Feets, don't fail me now!
   Attributed in *Wash. Post*, 30 Sept. 1973. Often said to be a catchphrase uttered by Moreland in the Charlie Chan detective films, but no one has actually found the expression in any of those motion pictures. Moreland may have used it in his nightclub act.

Thomas Morell

English librettist, 1703–1784

1 See, the conquering hero comes!
   Sound the trumpets, beat the drums!
   Judas Maccabeus (1747) (music by G. F. Handel)

Larry Morey

U.S. songwriter, 1905–1971

1 Oh! The World Owes Me a Living.
   Title of song (1934)

2 Heigh-ho, heigh-ho,
   It's off to work we go.
   "Heigh-Ho" (song) (1937)

3 Someday My Prince Will Come.
   Title of song (1937)

4 Whistle While You Work.
   Title of song (1937)

J. P. Morgan

U.S. financier, 1837–1913

1 I don't know as I want a lawyer to tell me what I cannot do. I hire him to tell me how to do what I want to do.
   Quoted in Ida M. Tarbell, *The Life of Elbert H. Gary* (1925)

2 Don't sell America short.
   Quoted in *N.Y. Times*, 27 Aug. 1925. Burton E. Stevenson, *Home Book of Quotations*, states the following: "J. PIERPONT MORGAN. Quoted by his son in talk at the Chicago Club, 10 Dec. 1908. J. P. Morgan was paraphrasing his father, Junius Spencer Morgan, who is credited with the injunction, 'Never sell a bear on the United States.'" James J. Hill was quoted, "Don't Sell America Short," in a headline in the *Fort Worth Star-Telegram*, 13 Sept. 1914, and anonymous advice "never to sell the United States short" was mentioned in Montgomery Rollins, *Money and Investments* (1907).

3 [*Of owning a yacht:*] If it makes the slightest difference to you what it costs, don't try it.
   Quoted in W. P. Bonbright, Letter to Herbert L. Satterlee, 20 May 1927. Jean Strouse, *Morgan: American Financier* (1999), cites this letter found among papers in the Pierpont Morgan Library. Slightly earlier evidence has been found in the *Wall Street Journal*, 14 Sept. 1926, where Morgan answers the query, "Do you think I could afford a yacht?" by saying, "If there is any doubt in your mind, you can't." The quotation is famous in the form "If you have to ask, you can't afford it."

4 A man always has two reasons for what he does—a good one, and the real one.
   Quoted in Owen Wister, *Roosevelt: The Story of a Friendship* (1930). Garson O'Toole has found various precursors for this quotation, with the earliest very similar one being "Some wise person says, 'There is always two reasons for doing a thing: one is a good reason and the other is the real reason'" (*Rockford* [Ill.] *Daily Register-Gazette*, 11 Feb. 1905).

5 [*To President Theodore Roosevelt on the antitrust prosecution of the Northern Securities Corporation:*] If we have done anything wrong, send your man [the Attorney-General] to my man [naming one of his lawyers] and they can fix it up.
   Quoted in Matthew Josephson, *The Robber Barons* (1934)

Robin Morgan

U.S. feminist and author, 1941–

1 Don't accept rides from strange men,
and remember that all men are strange as hell.
Sisterhood Is Powerful "Letter to a Sister
Underground" (1970)

2 Pornography is the theory, and rape the
practice.
Going Too Far "Theory and Practice: Pornography and
Rape" (1977)

Sidney Morgenbesser

U.S. philosopher, 1921–2004

1 A philosopher of language once presented a
formal lecture in which he announced that a
double negative is known to mean a negative
in some languages and a positive in others
but that no natural language had yet been
discovered in which a double positive means
a negative. Whereupon professor Sidney
Morgenbesser is said to have piped up from
the back of the room with an instant, sarcastic,
"Yeah, yeah."
Reported in *N.Y. Times Magazine,* 14 Aug. 1977

Samuel Eliot Morison

U.S. historian, 1887–1976

1 America was discovered accidentally by a
great seaman who was looking for something
else; when discovered it was not wanted; and
most of the exploration for the next fifty years
was done in the hope of getting through or
around it. America was named after a man who
discovered no part of the New World. History is
like that, very chancy.
The Oxford History of the American People ch. 2 (1965)

Akio Morita

Japanese industrialist, 1921–1999

1 [*On the approach of Japanese business toward
jobs:*] We believe if you have a family you can't
just eliminate certain members of that family
because profits are down.
Quoted in *International Management,* Sept. 1988

Christopher Morley

U.S. writer, 1890–1957

1 When Abraham Lincoln was murdered
The thing that interested Matthew Arnold
Was that the assassin
Shouted in Latin
As he leapt on the stage.
This convinced Matthew
There was still hope for America.
"Point of View" l. 1 (1923)

2 Thunder on the Left.
Title of book (1925)

3 Life is a foreign language: all men
mispronounce it.
Thunder on the Left ch. 14 (1925)

4 Dancing is wonderful training for girls, it's
the first way you learn to guess what a man is
going to do before he does it.
Kitty Foyle ch. 11 (1939)

John Morley, Viscount Morley of Blackburn

English writer and politician, 1838–1923

1 Where it is a duty to worship the sun, it is
pretty sure to be a crime to examine the laws of
heat.
A Biographical Critique of Voltaire ch. 1 (1872)

2 You have not converted a man, because you
have silenced him.
On Compromise ch. 5 (1874)

3 It is too often the case to be a mere accident
that men who become eminent for wide
compass of understanding and penetrating
comprehension, are in their adolescence
unsettled and desultory.
Encyclopaedia Britannica "Edmund Burke" (1876)

Desmond Morris

English anthropologist, 1928–

1 There are one hundred and ninety-three living
species of monkeys and apes. One hundred
and ninety-two of them are covered with hair.
The exception is a naked ape self-named *Homo
sapiens.*
The Naked Ape introduction (1967)

George Pope Morris

U.S. poet, 1802–1864

1 Woodman, spare that tree!
Touch not a single bough!
In youth it sheltered me,
And I'll protect it now.
"Woodman, Spare That Tree" l. 1 (1830)
See Thomas Campbell 2

William Morris

English writer and artist, 1834–1896

1 If you want a golden rule that will fit
everything, this is it: Have nothing in your
houses that you do not know to be useful or
believe to be beautiful.
Hopes and Fears for Art "The Beauty of Life" (1882)

2 Art is man's expression of his joy in labor.
"Art Under Plutocracy" (1883)

3 Men fight and lose the battle, and the thing that
they fought for comes about in spite of their
defeat, and when it comes turns out not to be
what they meant, and other men have to fight,
for what they meant under another name.
A Dream of John Ball ch. 4 (1888)

4 The question of who are the best people to take
charge of children is a very difficult one; but
it is quite certain that the parents are the very
worst.
Quoted in George Bernard Shaw, *Everybody's Political
What's What?* (1944)

Arthur Morrison

English novelist and short story writer, 1863–
1945

1 Tales of Mean Streets.
Title of book (1894). The *Oxford English Dictionary*
records an earlier use of the term *mean streets:*
"Deal is not very seductive to the sojourner, with its
labyrinths of mean streets" (*Chambers' Journal,* 5 Oct.
1861).
See Chandler 8

Herbert Morrison

U.S. broadcaster, 1905–1989

1 [*Describing the crash of the German airship*
Hindenburg *and the death of passengers,
Lakehurst, N.J., 6 May 1937:*] Oh, the humanity!
Radio broadcast, 6 May 1937

Jim Morrison

U.S. rock singer and songwriter, 1943–1971

1 This is the end, beautiful friend
This is the end, my only friend, the end.
"The End" (song) (1967)

2 You know that it would be untrue
You know that I would be a liar
If I was to say to you
Girl we couldn't get much higher.
"Light My Fire" (song) (1967). Cowritten with Robbie
Krieger and Ray Manzarek.

3 Come on, baby, light my fire
Try to set the night on fire.
"Light My Fire" (song) (1967). Cowritten with Robbie
Krieger and Ray Manzarek.

4 Five to one, baby, one in five,
No one here gets out alive.
"Five to One" (song) (1968)

5 Riders on the storm
Into this house we're born
Into this world we're thrown
Like a dog without a bone
An actor out on loan
Riders on the storm.
"Riders on the Storm" (song) (1971). Cowritten
with John Densmore, Robbie Krieger, and Ray
Manzarek.

Toni Morrison (Chloe Anthony Wofford)

U.S. novelist, 1931–2019

1 Like any artist with no art form, she became
dangerous.
Sula pt. 2 (1973)

2 I know what every colored woman in this
country is doing. . . . Dying. Just like me. But
the difference is they dying like a stump. Me,
I'm going down like one of those redwoods. I
sure did live in this world.
Sula pt. 2 (1973)

3 It was a fine cry—loud and long—but it had
no bottom and it had no top, just circles and
circles of sorrow.
Sula pt. 2 (1973)

4 124 was spiteful. Full of a baby's venom.
Beloved pt. 1 (1987)

5 This is not a story to pass on.
Beloved pt. 3 (1987)

6 [*Of Bill Clinton:*] This is our first black President.
New Yorker, 5 Oct. 1998

7 They shoot the white girl first.
Paradise (1998)

Alanis Morrissette

Canadian singer and songwriter, 1974–

1 What it all comes down to
Is that I haven't got it all figured out just yet
I've got one hand in my pocket
And the other one is giving the peace sign.
"Hand in My Pocket" (song) (1995)

2 An old man turned ninety-eight
He won the lottery and died the next day
It's a black fly in your Chardonnay
It's a death row pardon two minutes too late
Isn't it ironic . . . don't you think.
"Ironic" (song) (1995)

3 I recommend getting your heart trampled on to anyone
I recommend walking around naked in your living room
Swallow it down (what a jagged little pill).
"You Learn" (song) (1995)

4 Is she perverted like me
Would she go down on you in a theater?
"You Oughta Know" (song) (1995)

Dwight Morrow

U.S. lawyer, banker, and diplomat, 1873–1931

1 Any party which takes credit for the rain must not be surprised if its opponents blame it for the drought.
Campaign speech, Newark, N.J., 13 Oct. 1930

Walter Morrow

U.S. journalist, ca. 1895–1949

1 There ain't no such thing as free lunch.
El Paso Herald-Post, 27 June 1938. The 1938 anonymous editorial containing the quotation was titled "Economics in Eight Words." In this fable, a king asks his advisers to summarize economics in a "short and simple text." After they initially respond with eighty-seven volumes of six hundred pages each,

the king's wrath and resulting executions force the economists to restate their science in ever-briefer summations. Finally, the last economist produces an eight-word distillation: "There ain't no such thing as free lunch." A later reprint of the editorial identified the author as Morrow. Although the Morrow editorial seems to have popularized the "free lunch" proverb, a very close precursor appeared in an item in the *Washington Herald,* 2 Nov. 1909: "Mr. Tillman's idea that free lunch is good enough for anybody—or even Presidents—may appear sound to some people, but, as a matter of fact, there is no such thing as free lunch. Somebody has to pay for it."
See Commoner 1, Heinlein 3

Theodora Morse (Alfreda Strandberg)

U.S. songwriter, 1883–1953

1 Hail! Hail! the gang's all here,—
What the hell do we care?
"Hail, Hail, the Gang's All Here" (song) (1917)

John Mortimer

English novelist and lawyer, 1923–2009

1 No brilliance is needed in the law. Nothing but common sense, and relatively clean fingernails.
A Voyage Round My Father act 1 (1971)

Rogers Morton

U.S. politician, 1914–1979

1 [*After having lost five primaries as Gerald Ford's campaign manager:*] I'm not going to rearrange the furniture on the deck of the Titanic.
Quoted in *Wash. Post,* 16 May 1976. A similar expression appeared earlier in the *Charleston* (W.V.) *Gazette,* 29 Dec. 1969: "One clergyman has been quoted as saying the numerous reforms taking place today are only 'shuffling deck chairs on the Titanic.'"

Thomas Morton

English playwright, ca. 1764–1838

1 What will Mrs. Grundy zay? What will Mrs. Grundy think?
Speed the Plough act 1, sc. 1 (1798)

Edwin Moses

U.S. track and field athlete, 1955–

1 I don't really see the hurdles. I sense them, like a memory.
Quoted in Bruce Jenner, *Finding the Champion Within* (1996)

Stanley Mosk
U.S. judge, 1912–2001

1 [*Of John Birch Society members:*] Little old ladies in tennis shoes.

Quoted in *Wash. Post*, 4 Aug. 1961

Charles Moskos
U.S. sociologist, 1934–2008

1 [*Suggested policy toward homosexuals in the military:*] Don't ask, don't tell.

Quoted in *Chicago Tribune*, 31 Jan. 1993. When the editor of this book queried Moskos, the latter replied that he coined this phrase in a letter to Senator Sam Nunn, ca. Jan. 1993.

John Lothrop Motley
U.S. historian, 1814–1877

1 [*Of William of Orange:*] As long as he lived, he was the guiding-star of a whole brave nation, and when he died the little children cried in the streets.

The Rise of the Dutch Republic pt. 6, ch. 7 (1856). According to Burton E. Stevenson, *Home Book of Quotations*, this was: "A literal translation of the official report made by Greffier Corneille Aertsens to the magistracy of Brussels, 11 July, 1584: 'Dont par toute la ville l'on est en si grand dull tellement que les petits enfants en pleurent par les rues.'" *See Auden 17*

2 Give us the luxuries of life, and we will dispense with its necessities.

Quoted in Oliver Wendell Holmes, *Autocrat of the Breakfast-Table* (1857–1858)

Willard Motley
U.S. novelist, 1912–1965

1 Live fast, die young, and have a good-looking corpse!

Knock on Any Door ch. 35 (1947). Earlier, "I intend to live a fast life, die young and be a beautiful corpse" appeared in the *Riverside* (Calif.) *Daily Press*, 25 Aug. 1920. Courtenay Terrett, *Only Saps Work* (1930), referred to a very similar formulation as "an old cowboy proverb."

Lucretia Mott
U.S. reformer, 1798–1880

1 The legal theory is, that marriage makes the husband and wife one person, and that person is the husband.

"Discourse on Woman" (1849)

2 In the true marriage relation, the independence of the husband and wife is equal, the dependence mutual and their obligations reciprocal.

Letter to Elizabeth Cady Stanton, Nov. 1880. A similar statement, about the relations between men and women in general, was made by Mott in a speech in Boston, Mass., 23 Sept. 1841.

Stephen Moylan
U.S. Army officer, 1737–1811

1 I should like vastly to go with full and ample powers from the United States of America to Spain.

Letter to Joseph Reed, 2 Jan. 1776. Earliest known use of the term *United States of America*.

Daniel Patrick Moynihan
U.S. politician and social scientist, 1927–2003

1 The time may have come when the issue of race could benefit from a period of "benign neglect."

Memorandum to Richard Nixon on the status of blacks, 16 Jan. 1970. This memo was quoted in an article in the *New York Times*, 1 Mar. 1970, which reported: "The phrase 'benign neglect,' Mr. Moynihan said in a telephone interview, came from an 1839 report on Canada by the British Earl of Durham. The Durham report, he said, described Canada as having grown more competent and capable of governing herself 'through many years of benign neglect' by Britain, and recommended full self-government."

Wolfgang Amadeus Mozart
Austrian composer, 1756–1791

1 I cannot write in verse, for I am no poet. I cannot arrange the parts of speech with such art as to produce effects of light and shade, for I am no painter. Even by signs and gestures I cannot express my thoughts and feelings, for I am no dancer. But I can do so by means of sounds, for I am a musician.

Letter to Leopold Mozart, 8 Nov. 1777

2 I like to enjoy myself, but rest assured that I can be as serious as anyone else can.

Letter to Leopold Mozart, 20 Dec. 1777

3 The two valets sit at the top of the table, but at least I have the honor of being placed above the cooks.

Letter to Leopold Mozart, 17 Mar. 1781

4 Passion, whether violent or not, must never be
expressed to the point of exciting disgust, and
. . . music, even in the most terrible situations,
must never offend the ear.
Letter to Leopold Mozart, 26 Sept. 1781

Hosni Said Mubarak
Egyptian president, ca. 1928–

1 [*Of the invasion of Iraq by the United States and
other Western nations:*] Instead of having one bin
Laden, we will have 100 bin Ladens.
Speech to soldiers, Suez, Egypt, 31 Mar. 2003

Robert Mueller
U.S. musician, fl. 1957

1 I asked a Burmese why women, after centuries
of following their men, now walk ahead. He
said there were many unexploded land mines
since the war.
Quoted in *Look,* 5 Mar. 1957

Malcolm Muggeridge
English journalist and writer, 1903–1990

1 The greatest artists, saints, philosophers, and,
until quite recent times, scientists . . . have
all assumed that the New Testament promise
of eternal life is valid. . . . I'd rather be wrong
with Dante and Shakespeare and Milton, with
Augustine of Hippo and Francis of Assisi, with
Dr. Johnson, Blake, and Dostoevsky than right
with Voltaire, Rousseau, the Huxleys, Herbert
Spencer, H. G. Wells, and Bernard Shaw.
Quoted in *Vintage Muggeridge,* ed. Geoffrey Barlow
(1985)

John Muir
Scottish-born U.S. naturalist, 1838–1914

1 When we try to pick out anything by itself we
find that it is bound fast by a thousand invisible
cords that cannot be broken, to everything in
the universe.
Journal, 27 July 1869

2 In God's wildness lies the hope of the world—
the great fresh unblighted, unredeemed
wilderness.
"Alaska Fragment" (1890)

3 Climb the mountains and get their good
tidings, Nature's peace will flow into you as
sunshine flows into trees. The winds will blow
their own freshness into you and the storms
their energy, while cares will drop off like
autumn leaves.
Atlantic Monthly, Apr. 1898

Martin Mull
U.S. actor and comedian, 1943–

1 Writing about music is like dancing about
architecture.
Quoted in *Detroit Free Press,* 18 Feb. 1979. Garson
O'Toole has discovered a similar formulation,
"Writing about music is as illogical as singing about
economics," in the *New Republic,* 9 Feb. 1918.

Friedrich Max Müller
German-born English philologist, 1823–1900

1 Mythology . . . is in truth a disease of language.
Lectures on the Science of Language Lecture 1 (1862)

2 To me an ethnologist who speaks of Aryan
race, Aryan blood, Aryan eyes and hair, is as
great a sinner as a linguist who speaks of a
dolichocephalic dictionary or a brachycephalic
grammar.
Biographies of Words and the House of the Aryas ch. 6
(1888)

Herbert J. Muller
U.S. historian, 1905–1980

1 Few have heard of Fra Luca Pacioli, the inventor
of double-entry bookkeeping; but he has
probably had much more influence on human
life than has Dante or Michelangelo.
Uses of the Past ch. 8 (1957)

Lewis Mumford
U.S. architectural and cultural critic, 1895–
1990

1 Every generation revolts against its fathers and
makes friends with its grandfathers.
The Brown Decades ch. 1 (1931)

Edvard Munch
Norwegian painter, 1863–1944

1 I was walking along the road with two friends.
The sun was setting.

I felt a breath of melancholy—
Suddenly the sky turned blood-red.
I stopped, and leaned against the railing,
    deathly tired—
looking out across the flaming clouds that hung
    like blood and a sword over the blue-black
    fjord and town.
My friends walked on—I stood there, trembling
    with fear.
And I sensed a great, infinite scream pass
    through nature.

Diary, 22 Jan. 1892. This experience inspired Munch to create his painting *The Scream*.

Theodore T. Munger
U.S. clergyman, 1830–1910

1 A purpose is the eternal condition of success. Nothing will take its place. Talent will not; nothing is more common than unsuccessful men of talent. Genius will not; unrewarded genius is a proverb. . . . Education will not; the country is full of unsuccessful educated men. . . . There is no road to success but through a clear, strong purpose.
On the Threshold ch. 1 (1881). Garson O'Toole has demonstrated that this passage was later transmuted by other authors into a paean to "persistence" rather than "purpose." Calvin Coolidge is now usually credited for the "persistence" version, but it seems to have originated with Edward H. Hart in a 1902 speech.

Alice Munro
Canadian short story writer, 1931–

1 When a man goes out of the room, he leaves everything in it behind. . . . When a woman goes out she carries everything that happened in the room along with her.
"Too Much Happiness" (2009)

Haruki Murakami
Japanese writer, 1949–

1 In a place far away from anyone or anywhere, I drifted off for a moment.
The Wind-Up Bird Chronicle ch. 39 (1995)

Murasaki Shikibu
Japanese writer, ca. 978–ca. 1031

1 Thus anything whatsoever may become the subject of a novel, provided only that it happens in this mundane life and not in some fairyland beyond our human ken.
The Tale of Genji pt. 3, ch. 7 (translation by Arthur Waley)

Iris Murdoch
English novelist and philosopher, 1919–1999

1 All our failures are ultimately failures in love.
The Bell ch. 19 (1958)

2 Love is the extremely difficult realization that something other than oneself is real.
"The Sublime and the Good" (1959)

3 One doesn't have to get anywhere in a marriage. It's not a public conveyance.
A Severed Head ch. 3 (1961)

4 I think being a woman is like being Irish. . . . Everyone says you're important and nice, but you take second place all the same.
The Red and the Green ch. 2 (1965)

5 He led a double life. Did that make him a liar? He did not feel a liar. He was a man of two truths.
The Sacred and Profane Love Machine (1974)

Rupert Murdoch
Australian-born U.S. media executive, 1931–

1 This is the most humble day of my life.
Testimony before U.K. Parliamentary committee hearing on phone hacking scandal, 19 July 2011

Anna Pauline "Pauli" Murray
U.S. activist, 1910–1985

1 I spent many hours digging up weeds, cutting grass and tending the family plot. It was only a few feet from the main highway between Durham and Chapel Hill. I wanted the white people who drove by to be sure to see this banner and me standing by it. Whatever else they denied me, they could not take from me this right and the undiminished stature it gave me. For there at least at Grandfather's grave with the American flag in my hands, I could stand very tall and in proud shoes.
Proud Shoes ch. 20 (1956)

2 Hope is a song in a weary throat.
"Dark Testament" pt. 8, l. 11 (1970)

Clara Murray (Etta Austin McDonald)

U.S. author, 1872–1963

1 Run, Spot, run! . . . See Spot run.

The Wide Awake Primer (1904). These lines became famous through their later use in the "Dick and Jane" readers.

James A. H. Murray

Scottish lexicographer, 1837–1915

1 The circle of the English language has a well-defined center but no discernible circumference.

A New English Dictionary on Historical Principles "General Explanations" (1888)

K. M. Elisabeth Murray

English educator and author, 1909–1998

1 Caught in the Web of Words.

Title of book (1977)

Edward R. Murrow

U.S. journalist, 1908–1965

1 [*Signoff line:*] Good night, and good luck.

Radio and television broadcasts (1940–1958)

2 I pray to you to believe what I have said about Buchenwald. I have reported what I saw and heard, but only part of it. For most of it I have no words.

Radio broadcast from Buchenwald concentration camp, 15 Apr. 1945

3 We must not confuse dissent with disloyalty.

"Report on Senator Joseph R. McCarthy" (television documentary), 7 Mar. 1954

4 No one can terrorize a whole nation, unless we are all his accomplices.

"Report on Senator Joseph R. McCarthy" (television documentary), 7 Mar. 1954

5 [*Of Winston Churchill:*] He mobilized the English language and sent it into battle.

Broadcast, 30 Nov. 1954

6 Anyone who isn't confused doesn't really understand the situation.

Quoted in Walter Bryan, *The Improbable Irish* (1969)

Robert Musil

Austrian writer, 1880–1942

1 There is nothing in this world as invisible as a monument.

"Monuments" (1927)

2 *Der Mann ohne Eigenschaften.*
The Man Without Qualities.

Title of book (1930)

3 The number of portraits one saw of [Emperor Franz Joseph] was almost as great as the number of inhabitants of his realms. . . . Believing in his existence was rather like seeing certain stars although they ceased to exist thousands of years ago.

The Man Without Qualities bk. 1, ch. 20 (1930) (translation by Eithne Wilkins and Ernst Kaiser)

Alfred de Musset

French poet and playwright, 1810–1857

1 Never mind the bottle, as long as it gets you drunk.

La Coupe et les Lèvres (1832)

2 *On ne Badine pas avec l'Amour.*
Do Not Trifle with Love.

Title of play (1834)

Benito Mussolini

Italian dictator, 1883–1945

1 War alone brings up to their highest tension all human energies and imposes the stamp of nobility upon the peoples who have the courage to make it.

Encyclopedia Italiana "The Political and Social Doctrine of Fascism" (1932)

2 Rome-Berlin axis.

Speech, Milan, Italy, 2 Nov. 1936

3 [*To a railway stationmaster:*] We must leave exactly on time. . . . From now on everything must function to perfection.

Quoted in Giorgio Pini, *Mussolini* (1939). Infanta Eulalia of Spain wrote in *Courts and Countries After the War* (1925): "The first benefit of Benito Mussolini's direction in Italy begins to be felt when one crosses the Italian Frontier and hears '*Il treno arriva all'orario* [The train is arriving on time].'" "Italian trains now run on time" appears in the *Decatur* (Ill.) *Daily Review*, 13 July 1923.

A. J. Muste
U.S. author and pacifist, 1885–1967

1 There is no way to peace. Peace is the way.
Quoted in *N.Y. Times,* 16 Nov. 1967

Meiji Mutsohito
Japanese emperor, 1852–1912

1 Knowledge shall be sought for all over the
world and thus shall be strengthened the
foundation of the imperial polity.
"The Charter Oath" (statement ending Japan's
isolation from the West) (1868)

Gunnar Myrdal
Swedish economist and sociologist, 1898–1987

1 The treatment of the Negro is America's
greatest and most conspicuous scandal.
An American Dilemma vol. 2 (1944)

2 The facts about unemployment and its
immediate causes are well known in America.
. . . Less often observed and commented upon
is the tendency of the changes under way
to trap an "underclass" of unemployed and,
gradually, unemployable persons and families
at the bottom of a society.
Challenge to Affluence ch. 3 (1962)

Vladimir Nabokov

Russian-born U.S. novelist, 1899–1977

1 Our existence is but a brief crack of light between two eternities of darkness.
Speak, Memory ch. 1 (1951)

2 Lolita, light of my life, fire of my loins. My sin, my soul. Lo-lee-ta: the tip of the tongue taking a trip of three steps down the palate to tap, at three, on the teeth. Lo. Lee. Ta.
Lolita pt. 1, ch. 1 (1955)

3 You can always count on a murderer for a fancy prose style.
Lolita pt. 1, ch. 1 (1955)

4 Between the age limits of nine and fourteen there occur maidens who, to certain bewitched travellers, twice or many times older than they, reveal their true nature which is not human, but nymphic (that is, demoniac); and these chosen creatures I propose to designate as "nymphets."
Lolita pt. 1, ch. 5 (1955)

5 I am thinking of aurochs and angels, the secret of durable pigments, prophetic sonnets, the refuge of art. And this is the only immortality you and I may share, my Lolita.
Lolita pt. 2, ch. 36 (1955)

6 Like so many aging college people, Pnin had long since ceased to notice the existence of students on the campus.
Pnin ch. 3 (1957)

7 Human life is but a series of footnotes to a vast obscure unfinished masterpiece.
Pale Fire "Commentary" (1962)

8 Treading the soil of the moon, palpating its pebbles, tasting the panic and splendor of the event, feeling in the pit of one's stomach the separation from terra . . . these form the most romantic sensation an explorer has ever known . . . this is the only thing I can say about the matter. The utilitarian results do not interest me.
N.Y. Times, 21 July 1969

9 One of those "Two Cultures" is really nothing but utilitarian technology; the other is B-grade novels, ideological fiction, popular art. Who cares if there exists a gap between such "physics" and such "humanities"?
Strong Opinions ch. 6 (1973)
See Snow 2

10 Literature was born not the day when a boy crying wolf, wolf came running out of the Neanderthal valley with a big gray wolf at his heels: literature was born on the day when a boy came crying wolf, wolf and there was no wolf behind him.
Lectures on Literature "Good Readers and Good Writers" (1980)

11 Her exotic daydreams do not prevent her from being small-town bourgeois at heart, clinging to conventional ideas or committing this or that conventional violation of the conventional, adultery being a most conventional way to rise above the conventional.
Lectures on Literature "Madame Bovary" (1980)

Ralph Nader

U.S. reformer, 1934–

1 Unsafe at Any Speed.
Title of book (1965). U.S. journalist John Keats (1920–) had earlier written in *The Insolent Chariots* ch. 4 (1958), "Our automobiles are so poorly designed as to be unsafe at *any* speed, and more speed simply increases the danger."

V. S. Naipaul

Trinidadian novelist, 1932–2018

1 Worse, to have lived without even attempting to lay claim to one's portion of the earth; to have lived and died as one has been born, unnecessary and unaccommodated.
A House for Mr. Biswas prologue (1961)

2 It isn't that there's no right and wrong here.
There's no right.
A Bend in the River ch. 2 (1979)

Carolina Oliphant, Baroness Nairne
Scottish poet, 1766–1845

1 Charlie he's my darling, the young Chevalier.
"Charlie Is My Darling" (song) (date unknown). Also
attributed to James Hogg.

Joe Namath
U.S. football player, 1943–

1 [*Predicting the upset victory by the New York Jets
in the Super Bowl:*] We'll win. I guarantee it.
Quoted in *N.Y. Times,* 13 Jan. 1969. According to the
Times article, Namath made his guarantee on 9 Jan.
1969.

Lewis B. Namier
Polish-born English historian, 1888–1960

1 One would expect people to remember the
past and to imagine the future. But in fact,
when discoursing or writing about history, they
imagine it in terms of their own experience,
and when trying to gauge the future they cite
supposed analogies from the past: till, by a
double process of repetition, they imagine the
past and remember the future.
"Symmetry and Repetition" (1941)

Fridtjof Nansen
Norwegian explorer, 1861–1930

1 The difficult is that which can be done at once:
the impossible is that which takes a little longer.
*Verbatim Record of the Sixth Assembly of the League of
Nations, Eighteenth Plenary Meeting,* 26 Sept. 1925
See Calonne 1; Santayana 14; Trollope 3

Napoleon I
French emperor and general, 1769–1821

1 [*Of the English Channel:*] It is a mere ditch, and
will be crossed as soon as someone has the
courage to attempt it.
Letter to Consul Cambacérès, 16 Nov. 1803

2 I want the whole of Europe to have one
currency; it will make trading much easier.
Letter to Louis Bonaparte, 6 May 1807

3 *Ce n'est pas possible . . . cela n'est pas français.*

It is not possible . . . that is not French.
Letter to Lemarois (commandant of Magdebourg), 9
July 1813. Usually quoted as "Impossible? The word
is not French."

4 [*Remark to the Polish ambassador, De Pradt, after
the retreat from Moscow, 1812:*] *Du sublime au
ridicule il n'y a qu'un pas.*
There is only one step from the sublime to the
ridiculous.
Quoted in D. G. De Pradt, *Histoire de l'Ambassade
dans le Grand-Duché de Varsovie en 1812* (1815)
See Thomas Paine 30

5 *L'Angleterre est une nation de boutiquiers.*
England is a nation of shopkeepers.
Quoted in Barry E. O'Meara, *Napoleon in Exile* (1822).
The *Pennsylvania Gazette,* 20 Aug. 1794, prints
"Barrere's Report of the Naval Action of the 1st of
June" to the National Convention of France, 16 June.
Included in this report is the sentence: "Let Pitt then
boast of this victory of his nation of shop-keepers
(national boutiquiere.)" The author was revolutionary
and legislator Bertrand Barrère.
See Samuel Adams 1; Adam Smith 7; Josiah Tucker 1

6 *La carrière ouverte aux talents.*
The career open to the talents.
Quoted in Barry E. O'Meara, *Napoleon in Exile* (1822)

7 I love a brave soldier who has undergone, *le
baptême du fer* [baptism of fire], whatever nation
he may belong to.
Quoted in Barry E. O'Meara, *Napoleon in Exile* (1822)

8 [*Speech to army before Battle of the Pyramids, 21 July 1798:*] *Soldats, songez que, du haut de ces pyramides, quarante siècles vous contemplent.*
Soldiers, think of it, from the summit of these pyramids, forty centuries look down upon you.
Quoted in Gaspard Gourgaud, *Mémoires* (1823)

9 I have very rarely met with two o'clock in the morning courage: I mean instantaneous courage.
Quoted in E. A. de Las Cases, *Mémorial de Ste-Hélène* (1823) (entry for 4–5 Dec. 1815)

10 [*Remark at Battle of Montereau, 18 Feb. 1814:*] The bullet which is to kill me is not yet cast.
Quoted in J. T. Headley, *The Imperial Guard of Napoleon* (1851)

11 War is hell.
Quoted in John Livingston, *Portraits of Eminent Americans Now Living* (1854). Livingston cited an unspecified 1835 publication by Charles Brooks that stated, "Bonaparte said,—'War is hell.'" This preceded by many years the use of the expression by William Tecumseh Sherman, who has long been accepted as the originator.
See William Tecumseh Sherman 1; William Tecumseh Sherman 4

12 Society cannot exist without inequality of fortunes, and inequality of fortunes cannot exist without religion. When a man is dying of hunger beside another who has engorged himself, it is impossible for him to accept that difference unless there is an authority that tells him to.
Quoted in Pierre Louis Roederer, *Autour de Bonaparte* (1909)

13 Politics is fate.
Quoted in J. Christopher Herold, *The Mind of Napoleon* (1955). Napoleon said this in conversation with Goethe in 1808; the latter wrote that Napoleon had said *"Die Politik ist das Schicksal."*
See Sigmund Freud 8

14 [Women] belong to the highest bidder. Power is what they like—it is the greatest of all aphrodisiacs.
Attributed in Constant Louis Wairy, *Mémoires de Constant, Premier Valet de l'Empereur* (1830–1831)
See Graham Greene 5; Kissinger 3

15 Able was I ere I saw Elba.
Attributed in *Gazette of the Union*, 8 July 1848. This most famous of palindromes (words or phrases spelling the same forwards or backwards) was

obviously not really created by the French-speaking Napoleon. The *Gazette of the Union* credited a person in Baltimore identified only with the initials "J. T. R." with constructing it.

16 ["Last words":] *Tête . . . Armée.*
Chief of the Army.
Attributed in Louis Cohen, *Napoleonic Anecdotes* (1925)

Janet Napolitano
U.S. politician, 1957–

1 You show me a 50-foot wall and I'll show you a 51-foot ladder at the border. That's the way the border works.
News conference, Phoenix, Ariz., 21 Dec. 2005

Nas (Nasir Bin Olu Dara Jones)
U.S. rap musician, 1973–

1 I never sleep, 'cause sleep is the cousin of death.
"N.Y. State of Mind" (song) (1994). "Sleep is the brother of death" is an ancient Greek saying.

Petroleum V. Nasby (David Ross Locke)
U.S. humorist, 1833–1888

1 [*Referring to the Civil War:*] The late onpleasantniss.
"Mr. Nasby Projects a College" (1866). This piece by Nasby was reprinted in *The Struggles (Social, Financial and Political) of Petroleum V. Nasby* (1872) and antedates the first citation for the term *late unpleasantness* (1868) given in historical dictionaries.

Ogden Nash
U.S. humorist, 1902–1971

1 The Bronx?
No, thonx!
"Geographical Reflection" l. 1 (1931)

2 Gird up your l—ns,
Smite h-p and th-gh,
We'll all be Kansas
By and by.
"Invocation" l. 7 (1931)

3 Senator Smoot is an institute
Not to be bribed with pelf;
He guards our homes from erotic tomes
By reading them all himself.
"Invocation" l. 23 (1931)

4 Candy
Is dandy
But liquor
Is quicker.
"Reflection on Ice-breaking" l. 1 (1931)

5 The turtle lives twixt plated decks
Which practically conceal its sex.
I think it clever of the turtle
In such a fix to be so fertile.
"The Turtle" l. 1 (1931)

6 Sure, deck your lower limbs in pants;
Yours are the limbs, my sweeting.
You look divine as you advance—
Have you seen yourself retreating?
"What's the Use?" l. 1 (1931)

7 I think that I shall never see
A billboard lovely as a tree.
Perhaps, unless the billboards fall,
I'll never see a tree at all.
"Song of the Open Road" l. 1 (1933)
See Kilmer 1

8 Bankers Are Just Like Anybody Else, Except
Richer.
Title of poem (1938)

9 Every Englishman is convinced of one thing,
viz.:
That to be an Englishman is to belong to the
most exclusive club there is.
"England Expects" l. 3 (1938)

10 I'm a Stranger Here Myself.
Title of book (1938)

11 There was a young belle of old Natchez
Whose garments were always in patchez.
When comment arose
On the state of her clothes,
She drawled, When Ah itchez, Ah scratchez!
"Requiem" l. 1 (1938)

12 The trouble with a kitten is
THAT
Eventually it becomes a
CAT.
"The Kitten" l. 1 (1940)

13 I believe a little incompatibility is the spice of
life, particularly if he has income and she is
pattable.
"I Do, I Will, I Have" l. 12 (1949)

14 A door is what a dog is perpetually on the
wrong side of.
The Private Dining Room "A Dog's Best Friend Is His
Illiteracy" (1953)

15 The only compliment he ever paid her was
You sweat less than any fat girl I know.
"But I Could Not Love Thee, Ann, So Much, Loved I
Not Honoré More" l. 14 (1972)

Thomas Nashe
English satirist and playwright, 1567–1601

1 O, tis a precious apothegmatical Pedant, who
will find matter enough to dilate a whole day
of the first invention of Fy, fa, fum, I smell the
blood of an English-man.
Have with You to Saffron-walden (1596)
See Shakespeare 301

2 Brightness falls from the air;
Queens have died young and fair;
Dust hath closed Helen's eye.
I am sick, I must die.
Lord have mercy on us.
Summer's Last Will and Testament l. 1590 (1600)

Thomas Nast
German-born U.S. cartoonist, 1840–1902

1 Boss Tweed, "As long as I count the Votes, what
are you going to do about it?"
Caption of cartoon, Harper's Weekly, 7 Oct. 1871. This
cartoon put these words in the mouth of New York
politician William Marcy "Boss" Tweed, and they are
usually attributed to Tweed, but Nast almost certainly
originated them.
See Somoza 1; Stoppard 4

George Jean Nathan
U.S. drama critic, 1882–1958

1 The test of a real comedian is whether you
laugh at him before he opens his mouth.
American Mercury, Sept. 1929

2 Patriotism, as I see it, is often an arbitrary
veneration of real estate above principles.
Testament of a Critic bk. 1 (1931)

Carry Nation
U.S. temperance activist, 1846–1911

1 [Remark, ca. 1901:] You have put me in here
[jail], but I will come out roaring like a lion, and
I will make all hell howl!
Quoted in Carleton Beals, Cyclone Carry (1962)

Henri-Eugène Navarre

French general, 1898–1983

1 [*On the French war in Indochina, which ended in defeat in 1954:*] A year ago none of us could see victory. There wasn't a prayer. Now we can see it clearly—like light at the end of a tunnel.

Quoted in *Time,* 28 Sept. 1953. Although this quotation is associated with Navarre, the *Time* article attributes it to an unnamed acquaintance of Navarre's.

See Alsop 1; Dickson 1; John Kennedy 29

Martina Navratilova

Czechoslovakian-born U.S. tennis player, 1956–

1 In Czechoslovakia there is no such thing as freedom of the press. In the United States there is no such thing as freedom from the press.

Quoted in Lee Green, *Sportswit* (1984)

Holly Near

U.S. singer and songwriter, 1949–

1 Why do we kill people who are killing people
To show that killing people is wrong.

"Foolish Notion" (song) (1981). Although this quotation is associated with Near, the *Los Angeles Times,* 10 Mar. 1969, quoted a junior high school student who wrote, "Why do we kill people to show people killing people is wrong?"

Jawaharlal Nehru

Indian statesman, 1889–1964

1 [*On India's achieving independence from Great Britain:*] Long years ago we made a tryst with destiny . . . At the stroke of the midnight hour, while the world sleeps, India will awake to life and freedom.

Speech to Indian Constituent Assembly, 14 Aug. 1947

2 The light has gone out of our lives and there is darkness everywhere.

Broadcast after the assassination of Gandhi, 30 Jan. 1948

3 I am the last Englishman to rule in India.

Quoted in John Kenneth Galbraith, *A Life in Our Times* (1981)

Gaylord Nelson

U.S. politician and environmentalist, 1916–2005

1 The economy is a wholly owned subsidiary of the environment. All economic activity is dependent upon that environment and its underlying resource base of forests, water, air, soil, and minerals. When the environment is finally forced to file for bankruptcy because its resource base has been polluted, degraded, dissipated, and irretrievably compromised, the economy goes into bankruptcy with it.

Beyond Earth Day ch. 2 (2002)

Horatio, Viscount Nelson

English admiral, 1758–1805

1 When I came to explain to them the *"Nelson touch,"* it was like an electric shock.

Letter to Emma Hamilton, 1 Oct. 1805

2 I leave Emma Lady Hamilton [Nelson's mistress], therefore, a Legacy to my King and Country, that they will give her an ample provision to maintain her rank in life.

Codicil to Nelson's will, 21 Oct. 1805. The British government did not comply with Nelson's request, made immediately before the Battle of Trafalgar.

3 [*Remark before the Battle of the Nile, 1798:*] Before this time to-morrow I shall have gained a peerage, or Westminster Abbey.

Quoted in Robert Southey, *Life of Nelson* (1813). Nigel Rees, *Cassell Companion to Quotations,* notes: "Earlier, at the Battle of Cape St Vincent (1797), he is reported to have said: 'Westminster Abbey or victory!' Both of these echo Shakespeare, *Henry VI, Part 3* (II.ii.174): 'And either victory, or else a grave.'"

4 [*Remark at the Battle of Copenhagen, 2 Apr. 1801:*] I have only one eye,—I have a right to be blind sometimes. . . . I really do not see the signal!

Quoted in Robert Southey, *Life of Nelson* (1813). These words, uttered while placing his long glass to his blind eye, were attributed to Nelson by then-Colonel William Stewart. They are often said to be the source of the expression "turn a blind eye," but the *Oxford English Dictionary* documents that phrase as far back as 1698.

5 [*Of his mistress Lady Emma Hamilton:*] Brave Emma! Good Emma! If there were more Emmas there would be more Nelsons.

Quoted in Robert Southey, *Life of Nelson* (1813). According to Captain Henry Blackwood, Nelson uttered these words in Sept. 1805, when Nelson was on leave shortly before the Battle of Trafalgar.

6 [*Memorandum to captains before Battle of Trafalgar, Oct. 1805:*] In case signals cannot be seen or clearly understood, no captain can do wrong if he places his ship alongside that of an enemy.

Quoted in Robert Southey, *Life of Nelson* (1813)

7 [*Signal to the fleet at the Battle of Trafalgar, 21 Oct. 1805:*] England expects that every man will do his duty.

Quoted in Robert Southey, *Life of Nelson* (1813). Burton E. Stevenson, in *Home Dictionary of Quotations,* states: "In the London *Times,* 26 Dec., 1805, it was given: 'England expects every officer and man to do his duty this day.' . . . Captain Pasco, Nelson's flag-lieutenant, stated that Nelson's order was: 'Say to the fleet, England confides that every man will do his duty,' and that he suggested the substitution of 'expects' for 'confides.'"

8 [*Dying remark at Battle of Trafalgar, 21 Oct. 1805:*] Kiss me, Hardy.

Quoted in Robert Southey, *Life of Nelson* (1813)

9 [*At the Battle of Trafalgar, 21 Oct. 1805:*] Thank God, I have done my duty.

Quoted in Robert Southey, *Life of Nelson* (1813). These words, attributed by Dr. William Beatty, the surgeon aboard H.M.S. *Victory,* were Nelson's last.

10 To that quarter of an hour [of being habitually early to appointments] I owe every thing in life.

Quoted in *Chester* [England] *Chronicle,* 1 Jan. 1819

Ted Nelson

U.S. computer scientist, 1937–

1 Let me introduce the word "hypertext" to mean a body of written or pictorial material interconnected in such a complex way that it could not conveniently be presented or represented on paper.

Proceedings of the 20th National Conference of the Association of Computing Machinery (1965)

Nero (Lucius Domitius Ahenobarbus)

Roman emperor, 37–68

1 *Qualis artifex pereo!*
What an artist dies with me!

Quoted in Suetonius, *Lives of the Caesars*

Pablo Neruda (Neftalí Ricardo Reyes y Basualto)

Chilean poet, 1904–1973

1 I have gone marking the atlas of your body with crosses of fire.
My mouth went across: a spider, trying to hide. In you, behind you, timid, driven by thirst.

Twenty Love Poems and a Song of Despair "Poem 13" l. 1 (1924) (translation by W. S. Merwin)

2 You are like nobody else since I love you.

Twenty Love Poems and a Song of Despair "Poem 14" l. 5 (1924) (translation by W. S. Merwin)

3 I want
to do with you what spring does with the cherry trees.

Twenty Love Poems and a Song of Despair "Poem 14" l. 35 (1924) (translation by W. S. Merwin)

4 I like for you to be still, and you seem far away.

Twenty Love Poems and a Song of Despair "Poem 15" l. 9 (1924) (translation by W. S. Merwin)

5 Tonight I can write the saddest lines.

Write, for example, "The night is starry and the stars are blue and shiver in the distance."

The night wind revolves in the sky and sings.

Tonight I can write the saddest lines. I love her, and sometimes she loved me too.

Twenty Love Poems and a Song of Despair "Poem 20" l. 1 (1924) (translation by W. S. Merwin)

6 Love is so short, forgetting is so long.

Twenty Love Poems and a Song of Despair "Poem 20" l. 28 (1924) (translation by W. S. Merwin)

7 Peace goes into the making of a poet as flour goes into the making of bread.

Memoirs (1974) (translation by Hardie St. Martin)

Gérard de Nerval (Gérard Labrunie)

French poet, 1808–1855

1 *Je suis le ténébreux,—le veuf,—l'inconsolé, Le prince d'Aquitaine à la tour abolie.*
I am the darkly shaded, the bereaved, the inconsolate, the prince of Aquitaine, with the blasted tower.

Les Chimères "El Desdichado" (1854)

2 *Dieu est mort!*
God is dead!

Les Chimères "Le Christ aux Oliviers" (1854). The
Oxford Dictionary of Quotations notes that this
epigraph is "summarizing a passage in Jean Paul's
Blumen-Frucht-und Dornstücke (1796–1797) in which
God's children are referred to as 'orphans.'"
See Nietzsche 7; Nietzsche 12

3 [*Explaining why he walked a lobster on a leash
in the gardens of the Palais Royal:*] I have a
liking for lobsters. They are peaceful, serious
creatures. They know the secrets of the sea,
they don't bark, and they don't gnaw upon one's
monadic privacy like dogs do.

Quoted in Théophile Gautier, *Portraits et Souvenirs
Littéraires* (1875) (translation by Richard Holmes)

Allan Nevins

U.S. historian, 1890–1971

1 The former allies have blundered in the past by
offering Germany too little, and offering even
that too late, until finally Nazi Germany had
become a menace to all mankind.

Current History, May 1935

Simon Newcomb

Canadian-born U.S. astronomer, 1835–1909

1 May not our mechanicians . . . be ultimately
forced to admit that aerial flight is one of that
great class of problems with which man can
never cope, and give up all attempts to grapple
with it?

The Independent: A Weekly Magazine, Oct. 22, 1903

New England Primer

1 In *Adam's* Fall
we sinned all.

The New-England Primer, Enlarged (1727)

2 Now I lay me down to sleep,
I pray the Lord my Soul to keep.
If I should die before I 'wake,
I pray the Lord my Soul to take.

The New-England Primer (1735). The *Oxford Dictionary
of Nursery Rhymes* states that the wording was "Now I
lay me down to take my sleep" in the 1737 edition of
the *Primer.* The *Oxford Dictionary of Quotations* says
that this rhyme did not appear until the 1781 edition,
and *Bartlett's Familiar Quotations* has the wording
above as first being printed in the 1784 edition.
Inspection of the actual books, however, shows
that the words above appeared in all early editions

beginning in 1735, and there is no trace in the early
editions of "lay me down to take my sleep."

John Henry Newman

English religious leader, 1801–1890

1 Lead, kindly Light, amid the encircling gloom,
Lead thou me on.

"Lead, Kindly Light" l. 1 (1834)

2 *We can believe what we choose.* We are
answerable for what we choose to believe.

Letter to Mrs. William Froude, 27 June 1848

Paul Newman

U.S. actor, 1925–2008

1 [*Of his marriage to Joanne Woodward:*] I have
steak at home. Why should I go out for
hamburger?

Quoted in *Good Housekeeping,* Feb. 1971

Isaac Newton

English mathematician and physicist, 1642–
1727

1 If I have seen further it is by standing on the
shoulders of giants.

Letter to Robert Hooke, 5 Feb. 1676
See Bernard of Chartres 1; Robert Burton 1; Coleridge 30

2 I frame no hypotheses; for whatever is not
deduced from the phenomena is to be called
an hypothesis; and hypotheses, whether
metaphysical or physical, whether of occult
qualities or mechanical, have no place in
experimental philosophy.

Letter to Robert Hooke, 5 Feb. 1676

3 Errors are not in the art but in the artificers.

Principia Mathematica preface (1687) (translation by
Andrew Motte)

4 Every body continues in its state of rest, or
of uniform motion in a right line, unless it
is compelled to change that state by forces
impressed upon it.

Principia Mathematica "Laws of Motion" 1 (1687)
(translation by Andrew Motte)

5 The alteration of motion is ever proportional to
the motive force impressed; and is made in the
direction of the right line in which that force is
impressed.

Principia Mathematica "Laws of Motion" 2 (1687)
(translation by Andrew Motte)

6 To every action there is always opposed an
   equal reaction: or, the mutual actions of two
   bodies upon each other are always equal, and
   directed to contrary parts.
   Principia Mathematica "Laws of Motion" 3 (1687)
   (translation by Andrew Motte)

7 I do not know what I may appear to the world;
   but to myself I seem to have been only a boy
   playing on the shore, diverting myself in
   now and then finding a smoother pebble or a
   prettier shell than ordinary, whilst the great
   ocean of truth lay all undiscovered before me.
   Quoted in *Christian Monitor, and Religious
   Intelligencer,* 4 July 1812. An almost identical
   quotation by Newton, said to have been uttered "a
   little before he died," appears in Joseph Spence,
   *Anecdotes, Observations, and Characters of Books and
   Men,* published in 1820 but extant in manuscript
   form from around 1730. A paraphrase of Newton's
   words was printed in a note in a 1797 edition of *The
   Works of Alexander Pope.*

8 O *Diamond! Diamond!* thou little knowest the
   mischief done!
   Attributed in Thomas Maude, *Wensleydale: or Rural
   Contemplations* (1771). This remark, allegedly said to
   a pet dog who knocked over a candle and set fire to
   papers representing several years of Newton's work, is
   probably apocryphal.

John Newton
English clergyman, 1725–1807

1 Amazing grace! how sweet the sound
   That saved a wretch like me!
   I once was lost, but now am found,
   Was blind, but now I see.
   Olney Hymns "Amazing Grace" (1779)

St. Niceta
Serbian saint, fl. 400

1 *Te Deum laudamus: Te Dominum confitemur.*
   We praise thee, God: we own thee Lord.
   "Te Deum" (hymn) (ca. 390)

Nicholas I
Russian tsar, 1796–1855

1 [*Referring to Turkey:*] I am not so eager about
   what shall be done when the sick man dies, as
   I am to determine with England what shall not
   be done upon that event taking place.
   Quoted in *Annual Register* (1853). Gave rise to the
   expression "sick man of Europe" in reference to
   Turkey. The *Oxford English Dictionary* states that this
   is from "a conversation between the Tsar Nicholas I
   and Sir G. Seymour at St. Petersburg on the 21 Feb.
   1853."

2 Russia has two generals in whom she can
   confide—Generals Janvier [January] and Février
   [February].
   Attributed in *Punch,* 10 Mar. 1855

Nicholas II
Russian tsar, 1868–1918

1 There are senseless dreams of the participation
   of local government representatives in the
   affairs of internal administration. I shall
   maintain the principle of autocracy just as
   firmly and unflinchingly as it was upheld by my
   own, ever to be remembered dead father.
   Declaration, 17 Jan. 1896

Stevie Nicks (Stephanie Lynn Nicks)
U.S. singer and songwriter, 1948–

1 Well, I've been afraid of changing
   'Cause I've built my life around you
   But time makes you bolder
   Even children get older
   And I'm getting older too.
   "Landslide" (song) (1975)

Harold Nicolson
English politician and writer, 1886–1968

1 We are too prone to judge ourselves by our
   ideals and other people by their acts.
   Quoted in *N.Y. Times,* 17 May 1930. Garson O'Toole
   has traced similar statements as far back as Edward
   Wigglesworth, *Reflections* (1885), said to be reprinting
   something first published in 1850 or 1851: "We
   judge others by their doings, but ourselves by our
   intentions."

Reinhold Niebuhr
U.S. theologian, 1892–1971

1 Man's capacity for justice makes democracy
   possible; but man's inclination to injustice
   makes democracy necessary.
   The Children of Light and the Children of Darkness
   foreword (1944)

Martin Niemöller

German theologian, 1892–1984

1 When Hitler attacked the Jews I was not a Jew, therefore, I was not concerned. And when Hitler attacked the Catholics, I was not a Catholic, and therefore, I was not concerned. And when Hitler attacked the unions and the industrialists, I was not a member of the unions and I was not concerned. Then, Hitler attacked me and the Protestant church—there was nobody left to be concerned.

Attributed in *Congressional Record,* 14 Oct. 1968. This is usually quoted in a form such as "In Germany, they came first for the Communists and I didn't speak up because I was not a Communist," etc. Different versions have different lists of groups who were attacked. The quotation has never actually been found in Niemöller's speeches or sermons, although the general idea is found in remarks of his from 1946, in which he referred to Communists, disabled people, Jews, and Jehovah's Witnesses; he does not appear to have mentioned Catholics. Harold Marcuse, who has studied the quotation intensively, concludes, "Yes, I think MN did say something to this effect, or he would certainly have denied it during his lifetime."

Friedrich Nietzsche

German philosopher, 1844–1900

1 In dreams we all resemble this savage.

Human, All Too Human vol. 1, sec. 12 (1878) (translation by R. J. Hollingdale)

2 Every tradition now continually grows more venerable the farther away its origin lies and the more this origin is forgotten; the respect paid to it increases from generation to generation, the tradition at last becomes holy and evokes awe and reverence; and thus the morality of piety is in any event a much older morality than that which demands unegoistic actions.

Human, All Too Human vol. 1, sec. 96 (1878) (translation by R. J. Hollingdale)

3 Convictions are more dangerous enemies of truth than lies.

Human, All Too Human vol. 1, sec. 483 (1878) (translation by R. J. Hollingdale)

4 When his work opens its mouth, the author has to shut his.

Human, All Too Human vol. 2, pt. 1, sec. 140 (1878) (translation by R. J. Hollingdale)

5 A witticism is an epigram on the death of a feeling.

Human, All Too Human vol. 2, pt. 1, sec. 202 (1878) (translation by R. J. Hollingdale)

6 An excellent quotation can annihilate entire pages, indeed an entire book, in that it warns the reader and seems to cry out to him: "Beware, I am the jewel and around me there is lead, pallid, ignominious lead!"

Human, All Too Human vol. 2, pt. 2, sec. 111 (1878) (translation by R. J. Hollingdale)

7 *Gott ist tot: aber so wie die Art der Menschen ist, wird es vielleicht noch Jahrtausende lang Höhlen geben, in denen man seinen Schatten zeigt.—Und wir—wir müssen auch noch seinen Schatten besiegen!*

God is dead, but given the way of men, there may still be caves for thousands of years in which his shadow will be shown.—And we— we still have to vanquish his shadow, too.

The Gay Science bk. 3, sec. 108 (1882) (translation by Walter Kaufmann)
See Nerval 2; Nietzsche 12

8 Morality is herd-instinct in the individual.

The Gay Science bk. 3, sec. 116 (1882) (translation by Josefine Nauckhoff)

9 No victor believes in chance.

The Gay Science bk. 3, no. 258 (1882) (translation by Walter Kaufmann)

10 What is originality? *To see* something that has no name as yet and hence cannot be mentioned although it stares us all in the face. The way men usually are, it takes a name to make something visible for them.

The Gay Science bk. 3, sec. 261 (1882) (translation by Walter Kaufmann)

11 The secret for harvesting from existence the greatest fruitfullness and the greatest enjoyment is—to *live dangerously!*

The Gay Science bk. 4, sec. 283 (1882) (translation by Walter Kaufmann)

12 When Zarathustra was alone he spoke thus to his heart: "Could it be possible? This old saint in the forest has not yet heard anything of this, that *God is dead!*"

Thus Spake Zarathustra prologue, sec. 2 (1883) (translation by Walter Kaufmann)
See Nerval 2; Nietzsche 7

13 *Ich lehre euch den Übermenschen. Der Mensch ist Etwas, das überwunden werden soll.*

I teach you the overman. Man is something that shall be overcome.

Thus Spake Zarathustra prologue, sec. 3 (1883) (translation by Walter Kaufmann). This is often translated as "I teach you the superman." *See Radio Catchphrases 21; Radio Catchphrases 22; George Bernard Shaw 11; Siegel 1; Television Catchphrases 6*

14 One must still have chaos in oneself to be able to give birth to a dancing star.

Thus Spake Zarathustra prologue, sec. 5 (1883) (translation by Walter Kaufmann)

15 I would believe only in a God who could dance.

Thus Spake Zarathustra pt. 1, ch. 7 (1883) (translation by Walter Kaufmann)

16 You are going to women? Do not forget the whip!

Thus Spake Zarathustra pt. 1, ch. 18 (1883) (translation by Walter Kaufmann)

17 Whoever fights with monsters should see to it that he does not become one himself. And when you stare for a long time into an abyss, the abyss stares back into you.

Beyond Good and Evil pt. 4, sec. 146 (1886) (translation by Judith Norman)

18 There is a *master morality* and a *slave morality*.

Beyond Good and Evil pt. 9, sec. 260 (1886) (translation by Judith Norman)

19 At the center of all these noble races we cannot fail to see the blond beast of prey, the magnificent *blond beast* avidly prowling round for spoil and victory.

Genealogy of Morals essay 1, aphorism 11 (1887) (translation by Carol Diethe)

20 What can largely be achieved by punishment, in man or beast, is the increase of fear, the intensification of intelligence, the mastering of desires: punishment *tames* man in this way but does not make him "better"—we would be more justified in asserting the opposite.

Genealogy of Morals essay 2, aphorism 15 (1887) (translation by Carol Diethe)

21 There was only *one* Christian, and he died on the cross.

The Antichrist aphorism 39 (1888) (translation by Walter Kaufmann)

22 God created woman. And indeed, that was the end of boredom—but of other things too! Woman was God's *second* mistake.

The Antichrist aphorism 48 (1888) (translation by Walter Kaufmann)
See Hannah Cowley 1

23 As far as Germany extends, she *corrupts* culture.

Ecce Homo "Why I Am So Clever" (1888) (translation by Walter Kaufmann)

24 I believe only in French culture and consider everything else in Europe today that calls itself "culture" a misunderstanding—not to speak of German culture.

Ecce Homo "Why I Am So Clever" (1888) (translation by Walter Kaufmann)

25 What does not destroy me, makes me stronger.

The Twilight of the Idols "Maxims and Arrows" sec. 8 (1888) (translation by Walter Kaufmann). Popularly rendered as "Whatever does not kill me makes me stronger."

26 I mistrust all systematizers and I avoid them. The will to a system is a lack of integrity.

The Twilight of the Idols "Maxims and Arrows" sec. 26 (1888) (translation by Walter Kaufmann)

27 Liberal institutions straightway cease to be liberal, as soon as they are attained: later on, there are no worse and no more thorough injurers of freedom than liberal institutions.

The Twilight of the Idols "Skirmishes of an Untimely Man" sec. 38 (1888) (translation by Walter Kaufmann)

28 *Der Wille zur Macht.*
The Will to Power.
Title of book (1901)

29 It is precisely facts that do not exist, only *interpretations.*

The Will to Power notes (1901) (translation by Walter Kaufmann)

Florence Nightingale
English nurse, 1820–1910

1 No *man*, not even a doctor, ever gives any other definition of what a nurse should be than this—"devoted and obedient." This definition would do just as well for a porter. It might even do for a horse. It would not do for a policeman.

Notes on Nursing (1860)

Chester W. Nimitz
U.S. admiral, 1885–1966

1 [*Of the battle of Iwo Jima:*] Uncommon valor was a common virtue.
CINCPOA Communiqué No. 300, 16 Mar. 1945

Anaïs Nin
French-born U.S. writer, 1903–1977

1 Woman does not forget she needs the fecundator, she does not forget that every thing that is born of her is planted in her.
Diary, Aug. 1937

2 Electric flesh-arrows . . . traversing the body. A rainbow of color strikes the eye-lids. A foam of music falls over the ears. It is the gong of the orgasm.
Diary, Oct. 1937

3 Anxiety is love's greatest killer. It creates the failures. It makes others feel as you might when a drowning man holds on to you. You want to save him, but you know he will strangle you with his panic.
Diary, Feb. 1947

David Niven
English actor, 1910–1983

1 [*Remark, as host of the Academy Awards ceremony, 2 Apr. 1974, about a "streaker" who had run naked across the stage:*] The only laugh that man will ever get in his life is by stripping off his clothes and showing his shortcomings.
Quoted in *Philadelphia Inquirer*, 3 Apr. 1974

Richard M. Nixon
U.S. president, 1913–1994

1 The kids, like all kids, loved the dog [Checkers], and I just want to say this, right now, that regardless of what they say about it, we are going to keep it.
Broadcast speech responding to allegations of a political "slush fund," 23 Sept. 1952

2 Pat [his wife] doesn't have a mink coat. But she does have a respectable Republican cloth coat.
Broadcast speech responding to allegations of a political "slush fund," 23 Sept. 1952

3 [*After being defeated for governor of California:*] You don't have Nixon to kick around anymore because, gentlemen, this is my last press conference.
Press conference, Los Angeles, Calif., 7 Nov. 1962

4 What America needs most today is what it once had, but has lost: the lift of a driving dream.
Campaign speech, Concord, N.H., 3 Feb. 1968

5 [*Quoting a sign held up by a young girl on the campaign trail:*] Bring us together again.
Speech, New York, N.Y., 31 Oct. 1968

6 The greatest honor history can bestow is the title of peacemaker.
First Inaugural Address, 20 Jan. 1969

7 [*Welcoming back the crew of Apollo 11 from the first moon landing:*] This is the greatest week in the history of the world since the Creation.
Remarks aboard U.S.S. *Hornet*, 24 July 1969

8 After a third of a century of power flowing from the people and the States to Washington it is time for a New Federalism in which power, funds, and responsibility will flow from Washington to the States and to the people.
Address to the Nation on Domestic Programs, 8 Aug. 1969

9 North Vietnam cannot defeat or humiliate the United States. Only Americans can do that.
Address to the Nation on the War in Vietnam, 3 Nov. 1969

10 Let historians not record that when America was the most powerful nation in the world we passed on the other side of the road and allowed the last hopes for peace and freedom of

millions of people to be suffocated by the forces of totalitarianism. And so tonight—to you, the great silent majority of my fellow Americans—I ask for your support.

Address to the Nation on Vietnam War, 3 Nov. 1969. The term *silent majority* is found as early as 1870, when the *Economist* (19 Nov.) referred to "the silent majority which so seldom appears at the polls." *See Petronius 2; Edward Young 1*

11 If when the chips are down, the world's most powerful nation . . . acts like a pitiful, helpless giant, the forces of totalitarianism and anarchy will threaten free nations and free institutions throughout the world.

Televised speech announcing offensive into Cambodia, 30 Apr. 1970

12 [*Requesting aides to resist exposure of Watergate scandal:*] I want you all to stonewall it, let them plead the Fifth Amendment, cover-up or anything else, if it'll save it—save the plan.

Presidential transcript, 22 Mar. 1973

13 [*On the Watergate scandal:*] There can be no whitewash at the White House.

Televised speech, 30 Apr. 1973

14 People have got to know whether or not their President is a crook. Well, I am not a crook.

Speech, Orlando, Fla., 17 Nov. 1973

15 In the past few days . . . it has become evident to me that I no longer have a strong enough political base in the Congress to justify continuing that effort [to remain in office as president despite the Watergate scandal]. . . . But with the disappearance of that base, I now believe that the constitutional purpose has been served, and there is no longer a need for the process to be prolonged.

Address to the Nation Announcing Decision to Resign the Office of President, 8 Aug. 1974

16 I have never been a quitter. To leave office before my term is completed is abhorrent to every instinct in my body. But as President I must put the interests of America first. . . . Therefore, I shall resign the presidency, effective at noon tomorrow.

Address to the Nation Announcing Decision to Resign the Office of President, 8 Aug. 1974

17 Always give your best, never get discouraged, never be petty; always remember, others may hate you. Those who hate you don't win unless you hate them. And then you destroy yourself.

Address to members of administration on leaving office as president, 9 Aug. 1974

18 When the President does it, that means that it is not illegal.

Television interview by David Frost, 19 May 1977

19 I brought myself down. I gave them a sword. And they stuck it in and they twisted it with relish.

Television interview by David Frost, 19 May 1977

20 I hope that . . . television, radio, and the press first recognize the great responsibility they have to report all the news and, second, recognize that they have a right and a responsibility, if they are against a candidate—give him the shaft. But also recognize, if they give him the shaft—put one lonely reporter on the campaign who will report what the candidate says, now and then.

Quoted in *L. A. Times*, 8 Nov. 1962

21 [*Of John Dean:*] A loose cannon.

Quoted in *Wash. Post*, 3 May 1974

22 [*Remark to General Alexander Haig, 7 Aug. 1974:*] You fellows, in your business, have a way of handling problems like this. Somebody leaves a pistol in the drawer. I don't have a pistol.

Quoted in Bob Woodward and Carl Bernstein, *The Final Days* (1976)

Thelma Catherine "Pat" Nixon
U.S. First Lady, 1912–1993

1 [*Remark, 1960:*] I have sacrificed everything in my life that I consider precious in order to advance the political career of my husband.

Quoted in Betty Medsger, *Women at Work* (1975)

Louis Nizer
English-born U.S. lawyer, 1902–1994

1 When a man points a finger at someone else, he should remember that four of his fingers are pointing to himself.

My Life in Court ch. 1 (1961)

2 Yes, there's such a thing as luck in trial law but it only comes at 3 o'clock in the morning. . . . You'll still find me in the library looking for luck at 3 o'clock in the morning.
Quoted in *Reader's Digest,* Oct. 1984

Kwame Nkrumah
Ghanaian statesman, 1909–1972

1 We prefer self government with danger to servitude in tranquillity.
Motto of *Accra Evening News* (1948)

2 The best way of learning to be an independent sovereign state is to be an independent sovereign state.
Speech to legislative assembly, Accra, Ghana, 18 May 1956

3 Revolutions are brought about by men, by men who think as men of action and act as men of thought.
Consciencism ch. 2 (1964)

Alfred Bernhard Nobel
Swedish chemist and industrialist, 1833–1896

1 The whole of my remaining realizable estate shall be dealt with the following way: the capital, invested in safe securities by my executors, shall constitute a fund, the interest on which shall be annually distributed in the form of prizes to those who, during the preceding year, shall have conferred the greatest benefit on mankind.
Will (1895)

2 [The Nobel Peace Prize shall be awarded to] the person who shall have done the most or the best work for fraternity between nations, for the abolition or reduction of standing armies and for the holding and promotion of peace congresses.
Will (1895)

Albert Jay Nock
U.S. author and editor, 1870–1945

1 As sheer casual reading matter, I still find the English dictionary the most interesting book in our language.
Memoirs of a Superfluous Man ch. 1 (1943)

Peggy Noonan
U.S. speechwriter, 1950–

1 The battle for the mind of Ronald Reagan was like the trench warfare of World War I: never have so many fought so hard for such barren terrain.
What I Saw at the Revolution ch. 14 (1990)

2 Beware the politically obsessed. They are often bright and interesting, but they have something missing in their natures; there is a hole, an empty place, and they use politics to fill it up. It leaves them somehow misshapen.
What I Saw at the Revolution "Another Epilogue" (1990)

Grover Norquist
U.S. political activist, 1956–

1 I don't want to abolish government. I simply want to reduce it to the size where I can drag it into the bathroom and drown it in the bathtub.
Quoted in *Indiana* (Pa.) *Gazette,* 7 Oct. 1985

2 Bipartisanship is another name for date rape.
Quoted in *Denver Post,* 26 May 2003

Frank Norris (Benjamin Franklin Norris, Jr.)
U.S. novelist and journalist, 1870–1902

1 [I] don't like to *write,* but like *having written.*
Quoted in *The Bellman,* 4 Dec. 1915

Christopher North (John Wilson)
Scottish literary critic, 1785–1854

1 His Majesty's dominions, on which the sun never sets.
Blackwood's Magazine, Apr. 1829. North was preceded by George Macartney, who wrote about "this vast [British] empire on which the sun never sets" (*An Account of Ireland in 1773 by a Late Chief Secretary of that Kingdom* [1773]). A similar older saying related to the Spanish empire, the earliest known example being, "as one saith in a brave kind of expression, the sun never sets in the Spanish dominions" (Francis Bacon, "An Advertisement Touching an Holy War" [1629]).
See Lincoln 68

2 Laws were made to be broken.
Blackwood's Magazine, May 1830

Caroline Sheridan Norton
English poet and songwriter, 1808–1877

1 A soldier of the Legion lay dying in Algiers,
  There was a lack of woman's nursing, there was
    dearth of woman's tears;
  But a comrade stood beside him, while his
    lifeblood ebbed away.
  "Bingen on the Rhine" l. 1 (1850)

2 For death and life, in ceaseless strife,
  Beat wild on this world's shore,
  And all our calm is in that balm—
  Not lost but gone before.
  "Not Lost but Gone Before" (ca. 1850). Burton E.
  Stevenson, *Home Book of Quotations,* and the
  Oxford Dictionary of Quotations trace "Not lost, but
  gone before" and similar expressions to Seneca,
  St. Cyprian, and Matthew Henry.

Jack Norworth
U.S. songwriter, 1879–1959

1 Oh! shine on, shine on, harvest moon
  Up in the sky.
  "Shine On, Harvest Moon" (song) (1908)

2 Take me out to the ball game,
  Take me out with the crowd.
  Buy me some peanuts and cracker-jack—
  I don't care if I never get back.
  "Take Me Out to the Ball Game" (song) (1908)

3 Let me root, root, root for the home team,
  If they don't win it's a shame.
  For it's one, two, three strikes, "You're out!"
  At the old ball game.
  "Take Me Out to the Ball Game" (song) (1908)
  See Modern Proverbs 88

Notorious B.I.G. (Christopher Wallace)
U.S. rap musician, 1972–1997

1 Birthdays was the worst days
  Now we sip champagne when we thirsty.
  "Juicy" (song) (1994)

Novalis (Friedrich von Hardenberg)
German poet and novelist, 1772–1801

1 *Spinotza ist ein gotttrunkener Mensch.*
  Spinoza is a God-intoxicated man.
  Fragment 562 (1800)

2 I often feel, and ever more deeply I realize, that
  Fate and character are the same conception.
  Heinrich von Ofterdingen bk. 2 (1802). Often quoted
  as "character is destiny" or "character is fate."
  See George Eliot 6; Heraclitus 2

Alfred Noyes
English poet, 1880–1958

1 The moon was a ghostly galleon tossed upon
    cloudy seas,
  The road was a ribbon of moonlight over the
    purple moor,
  And the highwayman came riding—
  Riding—riding—
  The highwayman came riding, up to the old
    inn-door.
  "The Highwayman" l. 3 (1907)

2 Then look for me by moonlight,
  Watch for me by moonlight,
  I'll come to thee by moonlight, though hell
    should bar the way!
  "The Highwayman" l. 29 (1907)

Robert Nozick
U.S. philosopher, 1938–2002

1 Individuals have rights, and there are things
  no person or group may do to them (without
  violating their rights).
  Anarchy, State, and Utopia preface (1974)

2 A minimal state, limited to the narrow
  functions of protection against force, theft,
  fraud, enforcement of contracts, and so on,
  is justified; that any more extensive state will
  violate persons' rights not to be forced to do
  certain things, and is unjustified; and that the
  minimal state is inspiring as well as right.
  Anarchy, State, and Utopia preface (1974)

3 Is there really someone who, searching for a
  group of wise and sensitive persons to regulate
  him for his own good, would choose that group
  of people who constitute the membership of
  both houses of Congress?
  Anarchy, State, and Utopia ch. 2 (1974)

4 The socialist society would have to forbid
  capitalist acts between consenting adults.
  Anarchy, State, and Utopia ch. 7 (1974)

5 No state more extensive than the minimal state
   can be justified.
   Anarchy, State, and Utopia ch. 10 (1974)

Nursery Rhymes

*Arranged alphabetically on the basis of the most
prominent word in the quotation. Wording and citation,
the latter representing the earliest known documented
usage, are taken in the great majority of instances from
the* Oxford Dictionary of Nursery Rhymes, *2nd ed., ed.
Iona and Peter Opie.*

1 Hush-a-bye, baby, on the tree top,
   When the wind blows the cradle will rock;
   When the bough breaks the cradle will fall,
   Down will come baby, cradle, and all.
   Mother Goose's Melody (ca. 1765)

2 Ride a cock-horse to Banbury Cross,
   To see a fine lady upon a white horse;
   Rings on her fingers and bells on her toes,
   And she shall have music wherever she goes.
   Gammer Gurton's Garland (1784)

3 Where have you been all the day,
   My boy Billy?
   I have been all the day
   Courting of a lady gay;
   Although she is a young thing,
   And just come from her mammy.
   David Herd, *Scots Songs and Ballads* (manuscript)
   (1776)

4 Once I saw a little bird
   Come hop, hop, hop,
   And I cried, Little bird,
   Will you stop, stop, stop?
   Little Rhymes for Little Folks (1823)

5 Baa, baa, black sheep,
   Have you any wool?
   Yes, sir, yes, sir,
   Three bags full;
   One for the master,
   And one for the dame,
   And one for the little boy
   Who lives down the lane.
   Tommy Thumb's Pretty Song Book (ca. 1744)

6 Little Bo-peep has lost her sheep,
   And can't tell where to find them;
   Leave them alone, and they'll come home,
   And bring their tails behind them.
   Francis Douce Manuscript (ca. 1805)

7 Little Boy Blue,
   Come blow your horn,
   The sheep's in the meadow,
   The cow's in the corn;
   But where is the boy
   Who looks after the sheep?
   He's under a haycock,
   Fast asleep.
   The Famous Tommy Thumb's Little Story Book
   (ca. 1760)

8 Hot cross buns!
   Hot cross buns!
   One a penny, two a penny,
   Hot cross buns!
   Christmas Box (1797)

9 Can you make me a cambric shirt,
   Parsley, sage, rosemary, and thyme,
   Without any seam or needlework?
   And you shall be a true lover of mine.
   Gammer Gurton's Garland (1784)

10 The first day of Christmas,
   My true love sent to me
   A partridge in a pear tree.
   Mirth Without Mischief (ca. 1780). Verses about
   subsequent days of Christmas include as gifts "two
   turtle doves," "three French hens," etc.

11 Here is the church, and here is the steeple;
   Open the door and here are the people.
   William Wells Newell, *Games and Songs of American
   Children* (1883)

12 Who killed Cock Robin?
   I, said the Sparrow,
   With my bow and arrow,
   I killed Cock Robin.
   Tommy Thumb's Pretty Song Book (ca. 1744)

13 Old King Cole
   Was a merry old soul,
   And a merry old soul was he;
   He called for his bottle and he called for his
     pipe,
   And he called for his music masters three.
   Vocal Harmony (ca. 1806). The most common variant
   has "called for his fiddlers three."

14 Ding, dong, bell,
   Pussy's in the well.
   Mother Goose's Melody (ca. 1765)

15 Bow, wow, wow,
   Whose dog art thou?
   Little Tom Tinker's dog,
   Bow, wow, wow.
   Mother Goose's Melody (ca. 1765)
   See Pope 36

16 Eena, meena, mina, mo,
   Catch a nigger by his toe;
   If he squeals, let him go,
   Eena, meena, mina, mo.
   William W. Newell, *Games and Songs of American Children* (1883). Henry C. Bolton, *The Counting-Out Rhymes of Children* (1888), has the following variant: "Eeny, meeny, miny, mo, / Catch a nigger by the toe! / If he hollers let him go! / Eeny, meeny, miny, mo."

17 The farmer in the dell,
   The farmer in the dell,
   Heigh ho! for Rowley O!
   The farmer in the dell.
   William W. Newell, *Games and Songs of American Children* (1883)

18 Georgie Porgie, pudding and pie,
   Kissed the girls and made them cry;
   When the boys came out to play,
   Georgie Porgie ran away.
   J. O. Halliwell, *Nursery Rhymes* (1844)

19 Goosey, goosey gander,
   Whither shall I wander?
   Upstairs and downstairs
   And in my lady's chamber.
   Gammer Gurton's Garland (1784)

20 Hark, hark,
   The dogs do bark,
   The beggars are coming to town;
   Some in rags,
   And some in jags,
   And some in velvet gowns.
   Gammer Gurton's Garland (1784)

21 Hickety, pickety, my black hen,
   She lays eggs for gentlemen.
   James O. Halliwell, *The Nursery Rhymes of England* (1853)
   See Dorothy Parker 37

22 Hey diddle diddle,
   The cat and the fiddle,
   The cow jumped over the moon;
   The little dog laughed

To see such sport,
And the dish ran away with the spoon.
Mother Goose's Melody (ca. 1765)

23 Hickory, dickory, dock,
   The mouse ran up the clock.
   The clock struck one,
   The mouse ran down,
   Hickory, dickory, dock.
   Tommy Thumb's Pretty Song Book (ca. 1744)

24 Humpty Dumpty sat on a wall,
   Humpty Dumpty had a great fall;
   All the king's horses,
   And all the king's men,
   Couldn't put Humpty together again.
   Mother Goose's Melody (manuscript addition to Bussell copy) (ca. 1803). The ca. 1803 manuscript has the last line as "Could not set Humpty Dumpty up again."

25 Is gote eate yvy.
   Mare eate ootys.
   William Wyrcestre, Medical manuscript (ca. 1450). According to the *Oxford Dictionary of Nursery Rhymes*, this was "a catch which, when said quickly, appears to be in Latin." In 1943 Milton Drake, Al Hoffman, and Jerry Livingston's song "Mairzy Doats" employed similar words.

26 Jack and Jill went up the hill
   To fetch a pail of water;
   Jack fell down and broke his crown,
   And Jill came tumbling after.
   Mother Goose's Melody (ca. 1765)

27 Jack be nimble,
   Jack be quick,
   Jack jump over
   The candle stick.
   Douce Manuscript (ca. 1815)

28 This is the house that Jack built.
   Nurse Truelove's New-Year's-Gift (ca. 1750)

29 Little Jack Horner
   Sat in the corner,
   Eating a Christmas pie;
   He put in his thumb,
   And pulled out a plum,
   And said, what a good boy am I!
   Henry Carey, *Namby Pamby* (1725)

30 Jack Sprat could eat no fat,
   His wife could eat no lean,
   And so between them both, you see,
   They licked the platter clean.
   John Clarke, *Paroemiologia Anglo-Latina* (1639)

31 Diddle, diddle, dumpling, my son John,
   Went to bed with his trousers on;
   One shoe off, and one shoe on,
   Diddle, diddle, dumpling, my son John.
   Newest Christmas Box (ca. 1797)

32 Three little kittens they lost their mittens,
   And they began to cry.
   Eliza Follen, *New Nursery Songs* (1853)

33 Ladybird, ladybird,
   Fly away home,
   Your house is on fire
   And your children are gone.
   Nancy Cock's Pretty Song Book (ca. 1780)

34 London Bridge is broken down,
   Broken down, broken down,
   London Bridge is broken down,
   My fair lady.
   Henry Carey, *Namby Pamby* (1725). "London Bridge is
   falling down" is a popular variant.

35 See-saw, sacradown,
   Which is the way to London town?
   One foot up and the other foot down,
   That is the way to London town.
   Henry Carey, *Namby Pamby* (1725)

36 Where are you going,
   My pretty maiden fair,
   With your red rosy cheeks,
   And your coal-black hair?
   I'm going a-milking,
   Kind sir, says she.
   James Orchard Halliwell, *The Nursery Rhymes of
   England* (1846). Modern versions of this also include
   the well-known lines: "What is your fortune, my
   pretty maid? My face is my fortune, sir, she said."

37 There was a crooked man, and he walked a
      crooked mile,
   He found a crooked sixpence against a crooked
      stile;
   He bought a crooked cat, which caught a
      crooked mouse,
   And they all lived together in a little crooked
      house.
   James O. Halliwell, *The Nursery Rhymes of England*
   (1842)

38 This old man he played one,
   He played nick nack on my drum,

Nick, nack, paddy whack, give a dog a bone,
This old man came rolling home.
Living Age, 23 Nov. 1918

39 See-saw, Margery Daw,
   Jacky shall have a new master;
   Jacky shall have but a penny a day,
   Because he can't work any faster.
   Mother Goose's Melody (ca. 1765)

40 To market, to market,
   To buy a plum bun:
   Home again, home again,
   Market is done.
   John Florio, *World of Wordes* (1611)

41 Mary, Mary, quite contrary,
   How does your garden grow?
   With silver bells and cockle shells,
   And pretty maids all in a row.
   Tommy Thumb's Pretty Song Book (ca. 1744). The exact
   wording in the ca. 1744 source is as follows: "Mistress
   Mary, Quite contrary, / How does your Garden
   grow? / With Silver Bells, And Cockle Shells, / And
   so my Garden grows."

42 Three blind mice, see how they run!
   They all ran after the farmer's wife,
   Who cut off their tails with a carving knife,
   Did you ever see such a thing in your life,
   As three blind mice?
   Thomas Ravenscroft, *Deuteromelia* (1609).
   Ravenscroft's original wording was actually, "Three
   blinde Mice, three blinde Mice, Dame Iulian, Dame
   Iulian, the Miller and his merry olde Wife, shee
   scrapte her tripe licke thou the knife."

43 Monday's child is fair in face,
   Tuesday's child is full of grace,
   Wednesday's child is full of woe,
   Thursday's child has far to go,
   Friday's child is loving and giving,
   Saturday's child works hard for its living;
   And a child that's born on a Christmas day,
   Is fair and wise, good and gay.
   A. E. Bray, *A Description of . . . Part of Devonshire* (1836)

44 I see the moon,
   And the moon sees me;
   God bless the moon,
   And God bless me.
   Gammer Gurton's Garland (1784)

45 Old Mother Hubbard
   Went to the cupboard,
   To fetch her poor dog a bone;

But when she came there
The cupboard was bare
And so the poor dog had none.
Sarah Catherine Martin, *The Comic Adventures of Old Mother Hubbard and Her Dog* (1805)

46 Mother may I go out to swim?
Yes, my darling daughter,
But hang your clothes on a hickory limb
And don't go near the water.
Ray Wood, *The American Mother Goose* (1940)

47 Little Miss Muffet
Sat on a tuffet,
Eating her curds and whey;
There came a big spider,
Who sat down beside her
And frightened Miss Muffet away.
Songs for the Nursery (1805)

48 One to make ready,
And two to prepare;
Good luck to the rider,
And away goes the mare.
James O. Halliwell, *The Nursery Rhymes of England* (1853)

49 One, two,
Buckle my shoe;
Three, four,
Knock at the door;
Five, six,
Pick up sticks;
Seven, eight,
Lay them straight;
Nine, ten,
A big, fat hen.
Songs for the Nursery (1805)

50 Oranges and lemons,
Say the bells of St. Clement's.
You owe me five farthings,
Say the bells of St. Martin's.
When will you pay me?
Say the bells of Old Bailey.
When I grow rich,
Say the bells of Shoreditch.
Tommy Thumb's Pretty Song Book (ca. 1744)

51 Here comes a candle to light you to bed,
Here comes a chopper to chop off your head.
James Orchard Halliwell, *The Nursery Rhymes of England* (1844)

52 Pat-a-cake, pat-a-cake, baker's man,
Bake me a cake as fast as you can;
Pat it and prick it, and mark it with B,
Put it in the oven for baby and me.
Tom D'Urfey, *The Campaigners* (1698)

53 Pease porridge hot,
Pease porridge cold,
Pease porridge in the pot
Nine days old.
Some like it hot,
Some like it cold,
Some like it in the pot
Nine days old.
Newest Christmas Box (ca. 1797)

54 Peter, Peter, pumpkin eater,
Had a wife and couldn't keep her;
He put her in a pumpkin shell
And there he kept her very well.
Infant Institutes (1797)

55 Peter Piper picked a peck of pickled pepper.
Peter Piper's Practical Principles of Plain and Perfect Pronunciation (1813)

56 This little pig went to market,
This little pig stayed at home,
This little pig had roast beef,
This little pig had none,
And this little pig cried, Wee-wee-wee-wee-wee,
I can't find my way home.
The Famous Tommy Thumb's Little Story Book (ca. 1760)

57 Polly put the kettle on,
We'll all have tea.
Charles Dickens, *Barnaby Rudge* (1841)

58 I love little pussy,
Her coat is so warm,
And if I don't hurt her
She'll do me no harm.
So I'll not pull her tail,
Nor drive her away,
But pussy and I
Very gently will play.
Hints for the Formation of Infant Schools (1829)

59 Pussy cat, pussy cat, where have you been?
I've been to London to look at the queen.
Pussy cat, pussy cat, what did you there?
I frightened a little mouse under her chair.
Songs for the Nursery (1805)

60 The Queen of Hearts
   She made some tarts,
   All on a summer's day;
   The Knave of Hearts
   He stole the tarts,
   And took them clean away.
   European Magazine, Apr. 1782

61 Rain, rain, go away,
   Come again another day.
   James Howell, *Proverbs* (1659)

62 Ring-a-ring o' roses,
   A pocket full of posies,
   A-tishoo! A-tishoo!
   We all fall down.
   Kate Greenaway, *Mother Goose* (1881)

63 The rose is red, the violet's blue,
   The honey's sweet, and so are you.
   Gammer Gurton's Garland (1784)

64 Rub-a-dub-dub,
   Three men in a tub,
   And how do you think they got there?
   The butcher, the baker,
   The candlestick-maker.
   Mother Goose's Quarto (ca. 1825)

65 As I was going to St. Ives,
   I met a man with seven wives,
   Each wife had seven sacks,
   Each sack had seven cats,
   Each cat had seven kits:
   Kits, cats, sacks, and wives,
   How many were there going to St. Ives?
   Harley Manuscript (ca. 1730). The original wording in
   the manuscript begins "As I went to St. Ives / I met
   Nine Wives / And every Wife had nine Sacs / And
   every Sac had nine Cats / And every Cat had Nine
   Kittens."

66 A diller, a dollar,
   A ten o'clock scholar,
   What makes you come so soon?
   You used to come at ten o'clock,
   But now you come at noon.
   Gammer Gurton's Garland (1784)

67 Thirty days hath September,
   April, June, and November;
   All the rest have thirty-one,
   Excepting February alone,
   And that has twenty-eight days clear

And twenty-nine in each leap year.
   Stevins Manuscript (ca. 1555)

68 Simple Simon met a pieman,
   Going to the fair;
   Says Simple Simon to the pieman,
   Let me taste your ware.
   Simple Simon (chapbook advertisement) (1764)

69 Sing a song of sixpence,
   A pocket full of rye;
   Four and twenty blackbirds,
   Baked in a pie.
   When the pie was opened,
   The birds began to sing;
   Was not that a dainty dish,
   To set before the king?
   Nancy Cock's Pretty Song Book (ca. 1780)

70 Star light, star bright,
   First star I've seen tonight,
   I wish you may, I wish you might,
   Give me the wish, I wish tonight.
   Folk-Lore from Maryland, ed. Annie Weston Whitney
   and Caroline Canfield Bullock (1925)

71 Tinker,
   Tailor,
   Soldier,
   Sailor,
   Rich man,
   Poor man,
   Beggarman,
   Thief.
   Edward Moor, *Suffolk Words* (1823). In *Suffolk Words*,
   the exact sequence is "tinker, tailor, sowja, sailor,
   richman, poorman, plow-boy, poticarry, thief."

72 There was a sick man of Tobago
   Liv'd long on rice-gruel and sago;
   But at last, to his bliss,
   The physician said this—
   "To a roast leg of mutton you may go."
   Anecdotes and Adventures of Fifteen Gentlemen
   (ca. 1822). This may be said to be the original
   limerick, in that it directly inspired Edward Lear to
   use this verse form in his *Book of Nonsense*.

73 Tom, Tom, the piper's son,
   Stole a pig and away he run;
   The pig was eat
   And Tom was beat,
   And Tom went howling down the street.
   Tom, the Piper's Son (ca. 1795)

74 Little Tommy Tucker,
   Sings for his supper:
   What shall we give him?
   White bread and butter.
   Tommy Thumb's Pretty Song Book (ca. 1744)

75 Wee Willie Winkie runs through the town,
   Upstairs and downstairs in his night-gown,
   Rapping at the window, crying through
      the lock,
   Are the children all in bed, for now it's eight
      o'clock?
   J. G. Rusher, *Cries of Banbury and London* (ca. 1840)

76 There was an old woman tossed up in a basket,
   Seventeen times as high as the moon;
   Where she was going I couldn't but ask it,
   For in her hand she carried a broom.
   Old woman, old woman, old woman, quoth I,
   Where are you going to up so high?
   To brush the cobwebs off the sky!
   May I go with you?
   Aye, by-and-by.
   Mother Goose's Melody (ca. 1765)

77 There was an old woman who lived in a shoe,
   She had so many children she didn't know
      what to do;

She gave them some broth without any bread;
She whipped them all soundly and put them
   to bed.
Gammer Gurton's Garland (1784)

Bill Nye
U.S. humorist, 1850–1896

1 Wagner's music, I have been informed, is really
  much better than it sounds.
  Quoted in *Indianapolis News*, 22 Nov. 1889. Nye
  was quoted saying virtually the same thing about
  "classical music" in the *Wichita Daily Beacon*, 4 Aug.
  1887.

Laura Nyro
U.S. singer and songwriter, 1948–1997

1 And when I die, and when I'm gone,
  There'll be one child born in this world to
     carry on.
  "And When I Die" (song) (1966). Cowritten with
  Jerry Sears.

Michael Oakeshott
English philosopher, 1901–1990

1 To be conservative, then, is to prefer the familiar to the unknown, to prefer the tried to the untried, fact to mystery, the actual to the possible, the limited to the unbounded, the near to the distant, the sufficient to the superabundant, the convenient to the perfect, present laughter to utopian bliss.
"On Being Conservative" (1956)

Joyce Carol Oates
U.S. writer, 1938–

1 The worst cynicism: a belief in luck.
Do with Me What You Will ch. 15 (1973)

2 For what links us are elemental experiences—emotions—forces that have no intrinsic language and must be imagined as art if they are to be contemplated at all.
Where Are You Going, Where Have You Been? afterword (1993)

Lawrence Oates
English explorer, 1880–1912

1 [*Last words, before walking to his death in extreme weather conditions during the ill-fated 1912 Scott Antarctic expedition:*] I am just going outside and may be some time.
Quoted in Robert Falcon Scott, Diary, 16–17 Mar. 1912

Johnson Oatman, Jr.
U.S. songwriter, 1856–1922

1 Count your blessings.
"When upon Life's Billows" (hymn) (1897)

Barack Obama
U.S. president, 1961–

1 The pundits like to slice and dice our country into red states and blue states. Red states for Republicans, blue states for Democrats. But I've got news for them, too. We worship an awesome God in the blue states, and we don't like federal agents poking around in our libraries in the red states. We coach Little League in the blue states and, yes, we've got some gay friends in the red states.
Keynote address at Democratic National Convention, Boston, Mass., 27 July 2004

2 The hope of a skinny kid with a funny name who believes that America has a place for him, too. Hope in the face of difficulty, hope in the face of uncertainty, the audacity of hope.
Keynote address at Democratic National Convention, Boston, Mass., 27 July 2004. "The Audacity to Hope" was the title of a sermon by Jeremiah Wright, Jr., in 1990.

3 You go into some of these small towns in Pennsylvania, a lot like a lot of small towns in the Midwest, the jobs have been gone now for 25 years and nothing's replaced them. And they fell through the Clinton administration, and the Bush administration, and each successive administration has said that somehow these communities are gonna regenerate and they have not. So it's

not surprising then that they get bitter, they cling to guns or religion or antipathy towards people who aren't like them or anti-immigrant sentiment or anti-trade sentiment as a way to explain their frustrations.

Speech at fundraiser, San Francisco, Calif., 6 Apr. 2008

4 If there is anyone out there who still doubts that America is a place where all things are possible, who still wonders if the dream of our founders is alive in our time, who still questions the power of our democracy, tonight is your answer.

Victory speech in presidential election, Chicago, Ill., 4 Nov. 2008

5 As for our common defense, we reject as false the choice between our safety and our ideals.

First Inaugural Address, 20 Jan. 2009

6 We are a nation of Christians and Muslims, Jews and Hindus, and non-believers.

First Inaugural Address, 20 Jan. 2009

7 To those who cling to power through corruption and deceit and the silencing of dissent, know that you are on the wrong side of history, but that we will extend a hand if you are willing to unclench your fist.

First Inaugural Address, 20 Jan. 2009

8 A man whose father less than sixty years ago might not have been served at a local restaurant can now stand before you to take a most sacred oath.

First Inaugural Address, 20 Jan. 2009

9 If you were successful, somebody along the line gave you some help. There was a great teacher somewhere in your life. Somebody helped to create this unbelievable American system that we have that allowed you to thrive. Somebody invested in roads and bridges. If you've got a business—you didn't build that.

Remarks at campaign appearance, Roanoke, Va., 13 July 2012

10 You mentioned the Navy, for example, and that we have fewer ships than we did in 1916. Well, Governor, we also have fewer horses and bayonets because the nature of our military has changed. We have these things called aircraft carriers where planes land on them. We have these ships that go underwater, nuclear submarines.

Remarks at presidential debate, Boca Raton, Fla., 22 Oct. 2012

11 When they go low we go high.

Quoted in Michelle Obama, Commencement speech at Jackson State University, Jackson, Miss., 23 Apr. 2016. A tweet from the *Steve Harvey Show* after an interview with Michelle Obama, 11 Dec. 2012, quoted Barack Obama: "When someone hits low . . . You Go high" (ellipsis in original).

Michelle Obama

U.S. First Lady and lawyer, 1964–

1 For the first time in my adult lifetime, I'm really proud of my country, and not just because Barack has done well but because I think people are hungry for change.

Remarks at campaign rally, Madison, Wis., 18 Feb. 2008

Edna O'Brien

Irish writer, 1930–

1 The vote, I thought, means nothing to women, we should be armed.

Girls in Their Married Bliss ch. 7 (1964)

Tim O'Brien

U.S. novelist, 1946–

1 They carried the soldier's greatest fear, which was the fear of blushing. Men killed, and died, because they were embarrassed not to.

The Things They Carried (1990)

2 A true war story is never moral. It does not instruct, nor encourage virtue, nor suggest models of proper human behavior, nor restrain men from doing the things men have always done. If a story seems moral, do not believe it. If at the end of a war story you feel uplifted, or if you feel that some small bit of rectitude has been salvaged from the larger waste, then you have been made the victim of a very old and terrible lie.

The Things They Carried (1990)

3 In many ways he was like America itself, big and strong, full of good intentions, a roll of fat jiggling at his belly, slow of foot but always plodding along, always there when you needed

him, a believer in the virtues of simplicity and directness and hard labor.

The Things They Carried (1990)

Sean O'Casey

Irish playwright, 1884–1964

1 The whole worl's in a state o' chassis!

Juno and the Paycock act 1 (1925)

2 [*Of P. G. Wodehouse:*] English literature's performing flea.

Quoted in P. G. Wodehouse, *Performing Flea* (1953)

William of Occam

English philosopher, ca. 1285–1349

1 Plurality should not be assumed unnecessarily.

Quodlibeta no. 5, question 1, art. 2 (ca. 1324). This is the closest Occam came to the paraphrase now known as "Occam's Razor": "No more things should be presumed to exist than are absolutely necessary." The *Oxford Dictionary of Quotations* describes "Occam's Razor" as "an ancient philosophical principle often attributed to Occam but earlier in origin" and states that it is "not found in this form in his writings, although he frequently used similar expressions" such as the one set forth above. The *Oxford Dictionary of Scientific Quotations* cites "It is vain to do with more what can be done with less" from "*Summa logicae* (The Sum of All Logic) [before 1324], Part I, chapter 12. William of Ockham borrowing from Petrus Aureolus, *The Eloquent Doctor*, 2 Sent. distinction 12, question 1."

Adolph Ochs

U.S. newspaper owner, 1858–1935

1 All the news that's fit to print.

N.Y. Times, 25 Oct. 1896. Nigel Rees notes in *Brewer's Quotations:* "This slogan was devised by Ochs when he bought the *New York Times*, it has been used in every edition since—at first on the editorial page, on 25 October 1896, and from the following February on the front page near the masthead." Actually, the motto appeared on the masthead directly below the title on 25 Oct. The words had appeared slightly earlier in the newspaper: "The New-York Times has obtained possession of the wall for this season and has displayed in colored lights the following announcement: NEW-YORK TIMES. ALL THE NEWS THAT'S FIT TO PRINT." (4 Oct. 1896).

Phil Ochs

U.S. folksinger, 1940–1976

1 Oh I marched to the battle of New Orleans
At the end of the early British war
The young land started growing

The young blood started flowing
But I ain't marchin' anymore.

"I Ain't Marchin' Anymore" (song) (1965)

2 It's always the old to lead us to the war
It's always the young to fall
Now look at all we've won with the sabre and
the gun
Tell me is it worth it all.

"I Ain't Marchin' Anymore" (song) (1965)

Daniel O'Connell

Irish politician, 1775–1847

1 England's difficulty is Ireland's opportunity.

Quoted in *Tribune,* 19 Jan. 1856

Edwin O'Connor

U.S. novelist, 1918–1968

1 The Last Hurrah.

Title of book (1956)

Flannery O'Connor

U.S. writer, 1925–1964

1 In case of an accident, anyone seeing her dead on the highway would know at once she was a lady.

"A Good Man Is Hard to Find" (1955)

2 I have found that anything that comes out of the South is going to be called grotesque by the Northern reader, unless it is grotesque, in which case it is going to be called realistic.

"Some Aspects of the Grotesque in Southern Fiction" (1960)

3 While the South is hardly Christ-centered, it is most certainly Christ-haunted.

"Some Aspects of the Grotesque in Southern Fiction" (1960)

4 Everywhere I go I'm asked if I think the universities stifle writers. My opinion is that they don't stifle enough of them. There's many a best-seller that could have been prevented by a good teacher. The idea of being a writer attracts a good many shiftless people, those who are merely burdened with poetic feelings or afflicted with sensibility.

Mystery and Manners: Occasional Prose "The Nature and Aims of Fiction" (1969). The first two sentences appeared, with slightly different wording, in an interview with O'Connor in the *Atlanta Constitution*, 20 May 1960.

Sandra Day O'Connor

U.S. judge, 1930–

1 Liberty finds no refuge in a jurisprudence of doubt.

Planned Parenthood v. Casey (joint opinion) (1992). Coauthored with Anthony M. Kennedy and David H. Souter.

2 We expect that 25 years from now, the use of racial preferences will no longer be necessary to further the interest approved today.

Grutter v. Bollinger (2003)

3 A state of war is not a blank check for the President when it comes to the rights of the Nation's citizens.

Hamdi v. Rumsfeld (2004)

William D. O'Connor

U.S. author, 1832–1889

1 [*Referring to Walt Whitman:*] The Good Gray Poet.

Title of pamphlet (1866)

Clifford Odets

U.S. playwright, 1906–1963

1 He walks down the street respected—the golden boy!

The Golden Boy act 1, sc. 3 (1937)

Christine O'Donnell

U.S. politician, 1969–

1 I'm not a witch.

Television advertisement as Republican candidate for senator from Delaware, Oct. 2010

Kirk O'Donnell

U.S. lawyer and political adviser, 1946–1998

1 [Social security is the] third rail of American politics.

Quoted in *Newsweek*, 24 May 1982. The *Newsweek* article credits this line "in the words of one Democrat," but it is generally agreed that O'Donnell was the originator, in 1981.

Charlton Ogburn, Jr.

U.S. author, 1911–1998

1 We trained hard, but it seemed that every time we were beginning to form up into teams we would be reorganized. Presumably the plans for our employment were being changed. I was to learn later in life that, perhaps because we are so good at organizing, we tend as a nation to meet any new situation by reorganizing; and a wonderful method it can be for creating the illusion of progress while producing confusion, inefficiency and demoralization.

Harper's Magazine, Jan. 1957. This is often misattributed to the ancient Roman writer Petronius.

David Ogilvy

English-born U.S. advertising executive, 1911–1999

1 It is the professional duty of the advertising agent to conceal his artifice. When Aeschines spoke, they said, "How well he speaks." But when Demosthenes spoke, they said, "Let us march against Philip."

Confessions of an Advertising Man ch. 5 (1963)

2 The consumer isn't a moron; she is your wife. You insult her intelligence if you assume that a mere slogan and a few vapid adjectives will persuade her to buy anything.

Confessions of an Advertising Man ch. 5 (1963)

Frank O'Hara

U.S. poet, 1926–1966

1 I get a little Verlaine
for Patsy with drawings by Bonnard although I do
   think of Hesiod, trans. Richmond Lattimore or
Brendan Behan's new play or Le Balcon or Les
   Negres
of Genet, but I don't, I stick with Verlaine
after practically going to sleep with
   quandariness.

"The Day Lady Died" l. 14 (1964)

2 thinking of
leaning on the john door in the 5 SPOT
while she whispered a song along the keyboard
to Mal Waldron and everyone and I stopped
   breathing.

"The Day Lady Died" l. 26 (1964)

John O'Hara

U.S. writer, 1905–1970

1 George [Gershwin] died on July 11, 1937, but I don't have to believe that if I don't want to.

Quoted in *Newsweek*, 15 July 1940

Georgia O'Keeffe
U.S. artist, 1887–1986

1 When you take a flower in your hand and really look at it, it's your world for the moment. I want to give that world to someone else. Most people in the city rush around so, they have no time to look at a flower. I want them to see it whether they want to or not.
Quoted in *N.Y. Post,* 16 May 1946

2 I hate flowers—I paint them because they're cheaper than models and they don't move.
Quoted in *N.Y. Herald Tribune,* 18 Apr. 1954

Daniel Okrent
U.S. writer and editor, 1948–

1 [*"Okrent's Law":*] The pursuit of balance can create imbalance, because sometimes something is true.
Quoted in *New Yorker,* 3 May 2004

Chauncey Olcott
U.S. singer and songwriter, 1858–1932

1 When Irish eyes are smiling,
Sure, 'tis like the morn in spring
In the lilt of Irish laughter
You can hear the angels sing.
"When Irish Eyes Are Smiling" (song) (1912). Cowritten with George Graff, Jr.

Claes Oldenburg
Swedish-born U.S. sculptor, 1929–

1 I am for an art that tells you the time of day, or where such and such a street is. I am for an art that helps old ladies across the street.
Store Days: Documents from the Store (1961)

William Fitzjames Oldham
Indian-born U.S. clergyman, 1854–1937

1 [Some people] think they are thinking when they are merely rearranging their prejudices.
Quoted in *Zion's Herald,* 7 Nov. 1906

John Oliver
English comedian, 1977–

1 One failed attempt at a shoe bomb and we all take off our shoes at the airport. Thirty-one

school shootings since Columbine and no change in our regulation of guns.
Quoted in *Michigan Journal,* 11 Mar. 2014

Mary Oliver
U.S. poet, 1935–2019

1 When it's over I don't want to wonder
if I have made of my life something particular,
and real.
I don't want to find myself sighing and
frightened,
or full of argument.
I don't want to end up simply having visited
this world.
"When Death Comes" l. 24 (1992)

Laurence Olivier
English actor, 1907–1989

1 [*To Dustin Hoffman, who had stayed up for three nights to portray a sleepless character in the motion picture* Marathon Man:] Dear boy, why not try acting?
Quoted in *Times* (London), 17 May 1982

Kenneth H. Olsen
U.S. businessman, 1926–2011

1 There is no reason for any individual to have a computer in their home.
Attributed in Christopher Cerf and Victor Navasky, *The Experts Speak* (1984). Cerf and Navasky specify "Convention of the World Future Society in Boston, 1977" as the venue for Olson's quotation, stating in a footnote that David H. Ahl cited this in a 1982 "interview with the authors."

Tillie Olsen
U.S. writer, 1912–2007

1 Better mankind born without mouths and stomachs than always to worry for money to buy, to shop, to fix, to cook, to wash, to clean.
Tell Me a Riddle title story (1961)

Omar
Muslim caliph, ca. 581–644

1 [*Remark on burning the library of Alexandria, Egypt, 641:*] If these writings of the Greeks agree with the book of God, they are useless

and need not be preserved; if they disagree, they are pernicious and ought to be destroyed.

Quoted in Edward Gibbon, *The Decline and Fall of the Roman Empire* (1776–1788)

Aristotle Onassis

Greek shipowner, 1906–1975

1 If women didn't exist, all the money in the world would have no meaning.

Quoted in Barbara Rowes, *The Book of Quotes* (1979)

2 The secret of business is to know something that nobody else knows.

Attributed in *Indianapolis News*, 23 June 1977

Jacqueline Kennedy Onassis

U.S. First Lady, 1929–1994

1 If you bungle raising your children I don't think whatever else you do well matters very much.

Interview, NBC News, 1 Oct. 1960

2 [*Of John F. Kennedy:*] Now he is a legend when he would have preferred to be a man.

Look magazine, 27 Nov. 1967

3 The one thing I do not want to be called is First Lady. It sounds like a saddle horse.

Quoted in Peter Collier and David Horowitz, *The Kennedys* (1984)

Michael Ondaatje

Sri Lankan–born Canadian writer, 1943–

1 The heart is an organ of fire.

The English Patient ch. 3 (1992)

2 We die containing a richness of lovers and tribes, tastes we have swallowed, bodies we have plunged into and swum up as if rivers of wisdom, characters we have climbed into as if trees, fears we have hidden as if in caves.

The English Patient ch. 9 (1992)

Eugene O'Neill

U.S. playwright, 1888–1953

1 For de little stealin' dey gits you in jail soon or late. For de big stealin' dey makes you Emperor and puts you in de Hall o' Fame when you croaks.

The Emperor Jones sc. 1 (1921)

2 Dat ole davil, sea.

Anna Christie act 1 (1922)

3 Gimme a whiskey—ginger ale on the side. And don't be stingy, baby.

Anna Christie act 1 (1922). In the motion picture version of the play, these were Greta Garbo's first spoken words on screen.

4 Strange interlude! Yes, our lives are merely strange dark interludes in the electrical display of God the Father!

Strange Interlude pt. 2, act 9 (1928)

5 [*"Last words," Nov. 1953:*] Born in a hotel room— and God damn it—died in a hotel room!

Quoted in Arthur and Barbara Gelb, *O'Neill* (1962)

James H. O'Neill

U.S. military chaplain, 1892–1972

1 Almighty and most merciful Father, we humbly beseech Thee, of Thy great goodness, to restrain these immoderate rains with which we have had to contend. Grant us fair weather for the battle. Graciously hearken to us as soldiers who call upon Thee that, armed with Thy power, we may advance from victory to victory, and crush the oppression and wickedness of our enemies, and establish Thy justice among men and nations.

Quoted in *N.Y. Times*, 18 Jan. 1945. This "Weather Prayer" was composed by O'Neill for the use of General George S. Patton.

Paul H. O'Neill

U.S. government official and businessman, 1935–2020

1 [*Of George W. Bush leading Cabinet meetings:*] Like a blind man in a roomful of deaf people.

Quoted in Ron Suskind, *The Price of Loyalty: George W. Bush, the White House, and the Education of Paul O'Neill* (2004)

Thomas P. "Tip" O'Neill, Jr.

U.S. politician, 1912–1994

1 All politics is local.

Quoted in *Wall Street Journal*, 6 Dec. 1976. Although this line is associated with O'Neill, it appeared much earlier, such as in the *Frederick* (Md.) *News*, 1 July 1932.

Yoko Ono
Japanese-born U.S. artist and writer, 1933–

1 Woman is the nigger of the world.
Quoted in *Nova* (London), Mar. 1969

J. Robert Oppenheimer
U.S. physicist, 1904–1967

1 In some sort of crude sense which no vulgarity, no humor, no over-statement can quite extinguish, the physicists have known sin, and this is a knowledge which they cannot lose.
Physics in the Contemporary World (1947)

2 When you see something that is technically sweet, you go ahead and do it and you argue about what to do about it only after you have had your technical success. That is the way it was with the atomic bomb.
Quoted in *In the Matter of J. Robert Oppenheimer:* USAEC *Transcript of Hearing Before Personnel Security Board* (1954)

3 [*On the first atomic bomb explosion, Alamogordo, N.M., 16 July 1945:*] I remembered the line from the Hindu scripture, the *Bhagavad Gita.* . . . "I am become death, the destroyer of worlds."
Quoted in Len Giovannitti and Fred Freed, *The Decision to Drop the Bomb* (1965). An article in *Time,* 8 Nov. 1948, referred to Oppenheimer as recalling "I am become death, the shatterer of worlds." According to Robert Jungk, *Brighter Than a Thousand Suns: A Personal History of the Atomic Scientists* (1958), Oppenheimer also remembered another line from the same scripture: "If the radiance of a thousand suns . . ."
See Bhagavadgita 2; Bhagavadgita 3

Frederick B. Opper
U.S. cartoonist, 1857–1937

1 "After you, my dear Alphonse!"
"You first, my dear Gaston!"
Alphonse & Gaston (comic strip) (1902)

Susie Orbach
U.S. psychologist, 1946–

1 Fat Is a Feminist Issue.
Title of book (1978)

Roy Orbison
U.S. singer and songwriter, 1936–1988

1 Only the Lonely (Know the Way I Feel).
Title of song (1960). Cowritten with Joe Melson.

Baroness Emmuska Orczy
Hungarian-born English playwright and novelist, 1865–1947

1 We seek him here, we seek him there,
Those Frenchies seek him everywhere.
Is he in heaven?—Is he in hell?
That demmed, elusive Pimpernel?
The Scarlet Pimpernel ch. 12 (1905)

Dolores Mary O'Riordan
Irish singer and songwriter, 1971–2018

1 It's the same old theme since 1916
In your head, in your head they're still fightin'
With their tanks and their bombs
And their bombs, and their guns
In your head, in your head they are dyin'
In your head, in your head, Zombie, Zombie
In your head, what's in your head Zombie.
"Zombie" (song) (1994)

P. J. O'Rourke
U.S. humorist, 1947–

1 Marijuana is . . . self-punishing. It makes you acutely sensitive and in this world, what worse punishment could there be?
Rolling Stone, Nov. 1989

2 Every government is a parliament of whores. The trouble is, in a democracy the whores are us.
Parliament of Whores (1991)

3 Liberals have invented whole college majors—psychology, sociology, women's studies—to prove that nothing is anybody's fault.
Give War a Chance introduction (1992)

José Ortega y Gasset
Spanish writer and philosopher, 1883–1955

1 I am I plus my surroundings, and if I do not preserve the latter I do not preserve myself.
Meditaciones del Quijote "Lector" (1914)

2 The characteristic of the hour is that the commonplace mind, knowing itself to be commonplace, has the assurance to proclaim the rights of the commonplace and to impose them wherever it will.
La Rebelión de las Masas ch. 1 (1930)

3 Civilization is nothing else than the attempt to reduce force to being the last resort.
La Rebelión de las Masas ch. 8 (1930)

Joe Orton
English playwright, 1933–1967

1 I'd the upbringing a nun would envy and that's the truth. Until I was fifteen I was more familiar with Africa than my own body.
Entertaining Mr. Sloane act 1 (1964)

George Orwell (Eric Blair)
English novelist and journalist, 1903–1950

1 He was an embittered atheist (the sort of atheist who does not so much disbelieve in God as personally dislike Him).
Down and Out in Paris and London ch. 30 (1933)

2 I shall never again think that all tramps are drunken scoundrels, nor expect a beggar to be grateful when I give him a penny, nor be surprised if men out of work lack energy, nor subscribe to the Salvation Army, nor pawn my clothes, nor refuse a handbill, nor enjoy a meal at a smart restaurant.
Down and Out in Paris and London ch. 37 (1933)

3 However delicately it is disguised, charity is still horrible; there is a malaise, almost a secret hatred, between the giver and the receiver.
Keep the Aspidistra Flying ch. 9 (1936)

4 For my own part I don't object to old jokes—indeed, I reverence them. When sea-sickness and adultery have ceased to be funny, western civilization will have ceased to exist.
New English Weekly, 23 Jan. 1936

5 In Moulmein, in Lower Burma, I was hated by large numbers of people—the only time in my life that I have been important enough for this to happen to me.
"Shooting an Elephant" (1936)

6 Afterwards I was very glad that the coolie had been killed; it put me legally in the right and it gave me a sufficient pretext for shooting the elephant. I often wondered whether any of the others grasped that I had done it solely to avoid looking a fool.
"Shooting an Elephant" (1936)

7 As with the Christian religion, the worst advertisement for Socialism is its adherents.
The Road to Wigan Pier ch. 11 (1937)

8 The Communist and the Catholic are not saying the same thing, in a sense they are even saying opposite things, and each would gladly boil the other in oil if circumstances permitted; but from the point of view of an outsider they are very much alike.
The Road to Wigan Pier ch. 11 (1937)

9 The high-water mark, so to speak, of Socialist literature is W. H. Auden, a sort of gutless Kipling.
The Road to Wigan Pier ch. 11 (1937)

10 Has it ever struck you that there's a thin man inside every fat man, just as they say there's a statue inside every block of stone?
Coming Up for Air pt. 1, ch. 3 (1939)
See Cyril Connolly 3

11 [T. S. Eliot achieves] the difficult feat of making modern life out to be worse than it is.
"Inside the Whale" (1940)

12 The only "ism" that has justified itself is pessimism.
"The Limit to Pessimism" (1940)

13 Whatever is funny is subversive, every joke is ultimately a custard pie. . . . A dirty joke is not, of course, a serious attack upon morality, but it is a sort of mental rebellion, a momentary wish that things were otherwise.
"The Art of Donald McGill" (1941)

14 The clatter of clogs in the Lancashire mill towns, the to-and-fro of the lorries on the Great North Road, the queues outside the

Labour Exchanges, the rattle of pin-tables in the Soho pubs, the old maids biking to Holy Communion through the mists of the autumn mornings—all these are not only fragments, but *characteristic* fragments, of the English scene.

The Lion and the Unicorn pt. 1, sec. 1 (1941)

15 Probably the battle of Waterloo *was* won on the playing-fields of Eton, but the opening battles of all subsequent wars have been lost there.

The Lion and the Unicorn pt. 1, sec. 4 (1941)
See Wellington 8

16 War is the greatest of all agents of change. It speeds up all processes, wipes out minor distinctions, brings realities to the surface. Above all, war brings it home to the individual that he is *not* altogether an individual. It is only because they are aware of this that men will die on the field of battle.

The Lion and the Unicorn pt. 3, sec. 2 (1941)

17 If there is a wrong thing to do, it will be done, infallibly. One has come to believe in that as if it were a law of nature.

War-time Diary, 18 May 1941. Essentially states what would later be called "Murphy's Law."
See Robert Burns 3; Dickens 67; Disraeli 7; Modern Proverbs 100; Plautus 3; Proverbs 2; Sayings 25

18 I know it is the fashion to say that most of recorded history is lies anyway. I am willing to believe that history is for the most part inaccurate and biased, but what is peculiar to our own age is the abandonment of the idea that history *could* be truthfully written.

"Looking Back on the Spanish War" sec. 4 (1942)

19 Nazi theory indeed specifically denies that such a thing as "the truth" exists. . . . The implied objective of this line of thought is a nightmare world in which the Leader, or some ruling clique, controls not only the future but *the past*. If the Leader says of such and such an event, "It never happened"—well, it never happened. If he says that two and two are five—well, two and two are five. This prospect frightens me much more than bombs.

"Looking Back on the Spanish War" sec. 4 (1942)
See Orwell 37; Orwell 41

20 He [Kipling] sees clearly that men can only be highly civilized while other men, inevitably less civilized, are there to guard and feed them.

"Rudyard Kipling" (1942). This is the closest passage in Orwell's writings that has been found to the following quotation popularly attributed to him: "People sleep peaceably in their beds at night only because rough men stand ready to do violence on their behalf" (or sometimes, "We sleep safely at night because rough men stand ready to visit violence on those who would harm us").
See le Carré 3

21 If liberty means anything at all it means the right to tell people what they do not want to hear.

"The Freedom of the Press" (1945)

22 One has to belong to the intelligentsia to believe things like that: no ordinary man could be such a fool.

"Notes on Nationalism" (1945)

23 Serious sport has nothing to do with fair play. It is bound up with hatred, jealousy, boastfulness, disregard of all rules, and sadistic pleasure in witnessing violence: in other words it is war minus the shooting.

"The Sporting Spirit" (1945)

24 FOUR LEGS GOOD, TWO LEGS BAD.

Animal Farm ch. 3 (1945)

25 ALL ANIMALS ARE EQUAL

BUT SOME ANIMALS ARE MORE EQUAL THAN OTHERS.

Animal Farm ch. 10 (1945)
See Bierce 141

26 The creatures outside looked from pig to man, and from man to pig, and from pig to man again; but already it was impossible to say which was which.

Animal Farm ch. 10 (1945)

27 A State which was . . . in a permanent state of "cold war" with its neighbors.

Tribune (London), 19 Oct. 1945. Orwell's usage of *cold war* here is the first known that refers to tension between a state like the Soviet Union and other nations. In 1938 the *Nation* had a headline, "Hitler's Cold War" (26 Mar.). According to Luis Garcia Arias, *El Concepto de Guerra y la Denominada "Guerra Fria"* (1956), a thirteenth-century Spanish writer, Don Juan Manuel, used "guerra fria" to refer to the coexistence of Islam and Christendom in medieval Spain.
See Baruch 2

28 In our time, political speech and writing are largely the defence of the indefensible.
"Politics and the English Language" (1946)

29 The great enemy of clear language is insincerity. When there is a gap between one's real and one's declared aims, one turns as it were instinctively to long words and exhausted idioms, like a cuttlefish squirting out ink. . . . But if thought corrupts language, language can also corrupt thought.
"Politics and the English Language" (1946)

30 One can cure oneself of the *not un-* formation by memorizing this sentence: A not unblack dog was chasing a not unsmall rabbit across a not ungreen field.
"Politics and the English Language" (1946)

31 Political language . . . is designed to make lies sound truthful and murder respectable, and to give an appearance of solidity to pure wind.
"Politics and the English Language" (1946)

32 The Catholic and the Communist are alike in assuming that an opponent cannot be both honest and intelligent.
"The Prevention of Literature" (1946)

33 It was a bright cold day in April, and the clocks were striking thirteen.
Nineteen Eighty-Four pt. 1, ch. 1 (1949)

34 BIG BROTHER IS WATCHING YOU.
Nineteen Eighty-Four pt. 1, ch. 1 (1949)

35 WAR IS PEACE
FREEDOM IS SLAVERY
IGNORANCE IS STRENGTH.
Nineteen Eighty-Four pt. 1, ch. 1 (1949)

36 If the Party could thrust its hand into the past and say of this or that event, *it never happened—*that, surely was more terrifying than mere torture and death?
Nineteen Eighty-Four pt. 1, ch. 3 (1949)

37 "Who controls the past," ran the Party slogan, "controls the future: who controls the present controls the past."
Nineteen Eighty-Four pt. 1, ch. 3 (1949)
See Orwell 19

38 Don't you see that the whole aim of Newspeak is to narrow the range of thought? In the

end we shall make thoughtcrime literally impossible, because there will be no words in which to express it.
Nineteen Eighty-Four pt. 1, ch. 5 (1949)

39 Every year fewer and fewer words, and the range of consciousness always a little smaller.
Nineteen Eighty-Four pt. 1, ch. 5 (1949)

40 Under the spreading chestnut tree
I sold you and you sold me:
There lie they, and here lie we
Under the spreading chestnut tree.
Nineteen Eighty-Four pt. 1, ch. 7 (1949)

41 Freedom is the freedom to say that two plus two make four. If that is granted, all else follows.
Nineteen Eighty-Four pt. 1, ch. 7 (1949)
See Orwell 19

42 And when memory failed and written records were falsified—when that happened, the claim of the Party to have improved the conditions of human life had got to be accepted, because there did not exist, and never again could exist, any standard against which it could be tested.
Nineteen Eighty-Four pt. 1, ch. 8 (1949)

43 To do anything that suggested a taste for solitude, even to go for a walk by yourself, was always slightly dangerous. There was a word for it in Newspeak: *ownlife,* it was called, meaning individualism and eccentricity.
Nineteen Eighty-Four pt. 1, ch. 8 (1949)

44 *Doublethink* means the power of holding two contradictory beliefs in one's mind simultaneously, and accepting both of them.
Nineteen Eighty-Four pt. 2, ch. 9 (1949)

45 Power is not a means, it is an end. One does not establish a dictatorship in order to safeguard a revolution; one makes the revolution in order to establish the dictatorship. The object of persecution is persecution. The object of torture is torture. The object of power is power.
Nineteen Eighty-Four pt. 3, ch. 3 (1949)

46 If you want a picture of the future, imagine a boot stamping on a human face—for ever.
Nineteen Eighty-Four pt. 3, ch. 3 (1949)

47 If you want to keep a secret you must also hide it from yourself.

Nineteen Eighty-Four pt. 3, ch. 4 (1949)

48 The thing that is in Room 101 is the worst thing in the world.

Nineteen Eighty-Four pt. 3, ch. 5 (1949)

49 HE LOVED BIG BROTHER.

Nineteen Eighty-Four pt. 3, ch. 6 (1949)

50 One cannot really be Catholic & grown-up.

Notebook (1949)

51 At 50, everyone has the face he deserves.

Notebook, 17 Apr. 1949. These were Orwell's last words in his notebook. He died on 21 Jan. 1950, at the age of forty-six.

52 In a time of deceit, telling the truth is a revolutionary act.

Attributed in Venturino Venturini, *Partners in Ecocide* (1982). The attribution to Orwell is undoubtedly apocryphal. Usually quoted as "In a time of universal deceit . . . "

John Jay Osborn, Jr.
U.S. writer, 1945–

1 The Paper Chase.

Title of book (1971)

John Osborne
English playwright, 1929–1994

1 Look Back in Anger.

Title of play (1956)
See Leslie Paul 1

2 Asking a working writer what he thinks about critics is like asking a lamppost what it feels about dogs.

Quoted in *Time*, 31 Oct. 1977

Arthur O'Shaughnessy
English poet, 1844–1881

1 Yet we are the movers and shakers
Of the world for ever, it seems.

"Ode" l. 7 (1874)

William Osler
Canadian physician, 1849–1919

1 A desire to take medicine is, perhaps, the great feature which distinguishes man from other animals.

"Recent Advances in Medicine," *Science*, Mar. 1891

2 Take the sum of human achievement in action, in science, in art, in literature—subtract the work of the men above forty, and while we should miss great treasures, even priceless treasures, we would practically be where we are today. . . . The effective, moving, vitalizing work of the world is done between the ages of twenty-five and forty.

Address at Johns Hopkins University, Baltimore, Md., 22 Feb. 1905

3 My second fixed idea is the uselessness of men above sixty years of age, and the incalculable benefit it would be in commercial, political, and in professional life if as a matter of course, men stopped work at this age.

Address at Johns Hopkins University, Baltimore, Md., 22 Feb. 1905

4 Listen to the patient's story—he is telling you the diagnosis.

Attributed in *Central African Journal of Medicine* vol. 1 (1955). This may have been an adage that was current in medicine before it was attributed to Osler.

John L. O'Sullivan
U.S. journalist and diplomat, 1813–1895

1 Understood as a central consolidated power, managing and directing the various general interests of the society, all government is evil, and the parent of evil. . . . The best government is that which governs least.

United States Magazine and Democratic Review, 1 Oct. 1837. "That is the best Government, that governs the least" appeared in *Southern Review*, Nov. 1831.
See Ralph Waldo Emerson 29; Shipley 1; Thoreau 3

2 A spirit of hostile interference against us . . . checking the fulfillment of our manifest destiny to overspread the continent allotted by Providence for the free development of our yearly multiplying millions.

United States Magazine and Democratic Review, July–Aug. 1845

Lee Harvey Oswald
U.S. former Marine, 1939–1963

1 I'm just a patsy!

Remark while in police custody after allegedly assassinating President John F. Kennedy, Dallas, Tex., 22 Nov. 1963

James Otis
U.S. patriot, 1725–1783

1 Your Honors will find in the old book, concerning the office of a justice of peace, precedents of general warrants to search suspected houses. But in more modern books you will find only special warrants to search such and such houses specially named, in which the complainant has before sworn he suspects his goods are concealed; and you will find it adjudged *that special warrants only are legal.* In the same manner I rely on it, that the writ prayed for in this petition being general is illegal. It is a power that places the liberty of every man in the hands of every petty officer.

Argument against the writs of assistance, Boston, Mass., Feb. 1761

2 Now one of the most essential branches of English liberty, is the freedom of one's house. A man's house is his castle; and while he is quiet, he is as well guarded as a prince in his castle. This writ [of assistance], if it should be declared legal, would totally annihilate this privilege.

Argument against the writs of assistance, Boston, Mass., Feb. 1761. Burton Stevenson, *Home Book of Proverbs, Maxims and Familiar Phrases* (1948), traces the proverb "A man's house is his castle" back to 1567 and notes legal usages of it by Sir Edward Coke in the seventeenth century.
See Coke 1; Coke 8; William Pitt, Earl of Chatham 2

3 An act against the Constitution is void.

Argument against the writs of assistance, Boston, Mass., Feb. 1761

4 [*Motto:*] *Ubi libertas, ibi patria.*
Where liberty is, there is my country.

Quoted in Mercy Otis Warren, *The Rise, Progress and Termination of the American Revolution* (1805). Although this motto is often associated with Otis, the earliest evidence for it found in research for this book is in Charles Jones, *Great Britain's Nosegay* (1768), where it is attributed to the Earl of Essex.

5 [*Of Faneuil Hall in Boston, Mass.:*] Cradle of American liberty.

Quoted in Justin Winsor, *Memorial History of Boston* (1880–1881)

6 Taxation without representation is tyranny.

Attributed in John Adams, Letter to William Tudor, 29 Mar. 1818. This maxim, which is often quoted as the rallying cry for the American Revolution, has been attributed to Otis's argument against the writs of assistance before the Superior Court of Massachusetts in February 1761. However, there is no contemporary record of Otis using these words. John Adams, in describing the event fifty-seven years later, referred in his letter to Tudor to "Mr Otis's maxim, that 'taxation without representation was tyranny.'"

Ouida (Maria Louise Ramé)
English novelist, 1839–1908

1 In a few generations more, there will probably be no room at all allowed for animals on the earth: no need of them, no toleration of them. An immense agony will have then ceased, but with it there will also have passed away the last smile of the world's youth.

Critical Studies "The Quality of Mercy" (1900)

Ovid (Publius Ovidius Naso)
Roman poet, 43 B.C.–ca. A.D. 17

1 *Lente currite noctis equi.*
Run slowly, horses of the night.

Amores bk. 1, no. 13, l. 40
See Marlowe 11

2 *Expedit esse deos, et, ut expedit, esse putemus.*
It is convenient that there be gods, and, as it is convenient, let us believe that there are.

Ars Amatoria bk. 1, l. 637
See Voltaire 18

3 *Medio tutissimus ibis.*
You will go most safely by the middle way.

Metamorphoses bk. 2, l. 137

4 *Video meliora, proboque;*
Deteriora sequor.
I see the better things, and approve; I follow the worse.

Metamorphoses bk. 7, l. 20

5 *Tempus edax rerum.*
Time the devourer of everything.

Metamorphoses bk. 15, l. 234

Richard Owen
English anatomist and paleontologist, 1804–1892

1 The combination of such characters, some, as the sacral ones, altogether peculiar among Reptiles, others borrowed, as it were, from groups now distinct from each other, and all manifested by creatures far surpassing in size the largest of existing reptiles, will, it is

presumed, be deemed sufficient ground for establishing a distinct tribe or sub-order of Saurian Reptiles, for which I would propose the name of *Dinosauria*.

Report of the Eleventh Meeting of the British Association for the Advancement of Science "Report on British Fossil Reptiles" (1842)

Wilfred Owen
English poet, 1893–1918

1 What passing-bells for these who die as cattle? Only the monstrous anger of the guns.
  "Anthem for Doomed Youth" l. 1 (written 1917)

2 The pallor of girls' brows shall be their pall; Their flowers the tenderness of patient minds, And each slow dusk a drawing-down of blinds.
  "Anthem for Doomed Youth" l. 12 (written 1917)

3 If you could hear, at every jolt, the blood Come gargling from the froth-corrupted lungs, Obscene as cancer, bitter as the cud Of vile, incurable sores on innocent tongues,— My friend, you would not tell with such high zest To children ardent for some desperate glory, The old Lie: Dulce et decorum est Pro patria mori.
  "Dulce et Decorum Est" l. 21 (written 1918)
  See Horace 20

4 Above all, this book is not concerned with Poetry,
  The subject of it is War, and the pity of War.
  The Poetry is in the pity.
  All a poet can do is warn.
  Poems preface (1920)

Jesse Owens
U.S. track and field athlete, 1913–1980

1 [*Of Franklin Roosevelt:*] Hitler didn't snub me— it was our president who snubbed me. The president didn't even send me a telegram.
  Quoted in *Austin Statesman,* 16 Oct. 1936

Count Axel Gustafsson Oxenstierna
Swedish statesman, 1583–1654

1 Dost thou not know, my son, with how little wisdom the world is governed?
  Letter to his son (1648)

Edward de Vere, Earl of Oxford
English poet, 1550–1604

1 My mind to me a kingdom is.
  "In Praise of a Contented Mind" l. 1 (1588). Also attributed to Edward Dyer.

Herbert L. Packer
U.S. legal scholar, 1925–1972

1 Crime is a sociopolitical artifact, not a natural phenomenon. We can have as much or as little crime as we please, depending on what we choose to count as criminal.
The Limits of the Criminal Sanction conclusion (1968)

Ignacy Jan Paderewski
Polish pianist, composer, and statesman, 1860–1941

1 If I don't practice for one day, I know it; if I don't practice for two days, the critics know it; if I don't practice for three days, the audience knows it.
Quoted in Nat Shapiro, *An Encyclopedia of Quotations About Music* (1978)

William Tyler Page
U.S. congressional clerk, 1868–1942

1 I believe in the United States of America as a government of the people, by the people, for the people, whose just powers are derived from the consent of the governed; a democracy in a republic; a sovereign Nation of many sovereign States; a perfect Union, one and inseparable, established upon those principles of freedom, equality, justice, and humanity for which American patriots sacrificed their lives and fortunes. I therefore believe it is my duty to my country to love it, to support its Constitution, to obey its laws, to respect its flag, and to defend it against all enemies.
"American's Creed" (1918)

Camille Paglia
U.S. author and critic, 1947–

1 If civilization had been left in female hands, we would still be living in grass huts.
Sexual Personae ch. 1 (1990)

2 There is no female Mozart because there is no female Jack the Ripper.
Sexual Personae ch. 8 (1990)

Marcel Pagnol
French playwright and film director, 1895–1974

1 One has to look out for engineers—they begin with sewing machines and end up with the atomic bomb.
Critique des Critiques ch. 3 (1949)

Leroy Robert "Satchel" Paige
U.S. baseball player, 1906–1982

1 Avoid fried meats which angry up the blood.
"How to Keep Young," *Collier's*, 13 June 1953

2 If your stomach disputes you, lie down and pacify it with cool thoughts.
"How to Keep Young," *Collier's*, 13 June 1953

3 Keep the juices flowing by jangling around gently as you move.
"How to Keep Young," *Collier's*, 13 June 1953

4 Go very lightly on the vices, such as carrying on in society. The social ramble ain't restful.

"How to Keep Young," *Collier's,* 13 June 1953

5 Avoid running at all times.

"How to Keep Young," *Collier's,* 13 June 1953

6 Don't look back. Something might be gaining on you.

"How to Keep Young," *Collier's,* 13 June 1953

7 There ain't no man can avoid being born average. But there ain't no man got to be common.

Quoted in *Reader's Digest,* Oct. 1958

8 [*Response when asked his age:*] How old would you be if you didn't know how old you are?

Quoted in Garson Kanin, *It Takes a Long Time to Become Young* (1978)

9 Age is a question of mind over matter. If you don't mind, it doesn't matter.

Quoted in Bert Sugar, *Book of Sports Quotes* (1979)

10 I never threw an illegal pitch. The trouble is, once in a while I toss one that ain't never been seen by this generation.

Quoted in *Wash. Post,* 10 June 1982

11 [*On his induction into the Hall of Fame, 9 Aug. 1971:*] The one change is that baseball has turned Paige from a second-class citizen into a second-class immortal.

Quoted in Paul Dickson, *Baseball's Greatest Quotations* (1991)

12 Don't pray when it rains if you don't pray when the sun shines.

Quoted in Deirdre Mullane, *Words to Make My Dream Children Live: A Book of African American Quotations* (1995)

Robert Treat Paine

U.S. politician, 1731–1814

1 If therefore in the examination of this Cause the Evidence is not sufficient to Convince you beyond reasonable doubt of the Guilt of all or of any of the Prisoners by the Benignity and Reason of the Law you will acquit them.

Closing argument in Boston Massacre Trial, Boston, Mass. (1770). Paine, counsel for the British Crown in this trial, here makes the earliest known reference to the "reasonable doubt" standard of guilt in criminal cases.

Thomas Paine

English-born U.S. political philosopher, 1737–1809

1 I scarcely ever quote; the reason is, I always think.

"The Forester's Letters," 22 Apr. 1776

2 The cause of America is in a great measure the cause of all mankind.

Common Sense introduction (1776)

3 Government, even in its best state, is but a necessary evil; in its worst state, an intolerable one. . . . Government, like dress, is the badge of lost innocence; the palaces of kings are built upon the ruins of the bowers of paradise.

Common Sense (1776)

4 But where, say some, is the king of America? . . . in America the law is king.

Common Sense (1776)

5 [*Addressing America:*] Freedom hath been hunted round the globe. Asia and Africa have long expelled her. Europe regards her like a stranger, and England hath given her warning to depart. O! receive the fugitive, and prepare in time an asylum for mankind.

Common Sense (1776)

6 As to religion, I hold it to be the indispensable duty of government to protect all conscientious

professors thereof, and I know of no other business which government hath to do therewith.

Common Sense (1776)

7 We have it in our power to begin the world over again.

Common Sense appendix (1776)

8 These are the times that try men's souls: The summer soldier and the sunshine patriot will, in this crisis, shrink from the service of his country; but he that stands it NOW, deserves the love and thanks of man and woman.

The American Crisis, 19 Dec. 1776

9 What we obtain too cheap, we esteem too lightly:—'Tis dearness only that gives every thing its value. Heaven knows how to set a proper price upon its goods; and it would be strange indeed, if so celestial an article as FREEDOM should not be highly rated.

The American Crisis, 19 Dec. 1776

10 A bad cause will ever be supported by bad means and bad men.

The American Crisis, 13 Jan. 1777

11 Those who expect to reap the blessings of Freedom, must, like men, undergo the fatigue of supporting it.

The American Crisis, 12 Sept. 1777

12 We fight, not to enslave, but to set a country free, and to make room upon the earth for honest men to live in.

The American Crisis, 12 Sept. 1777

13 It is the object only of war that makes it honorable. And if there was ever *a just* war since the world began, it is this which America is now engaged in.

The American Crisis, 21 Mar. 1778

14 War involves in its progress such a train of unforeseen and unsupposed circumstances . . . that no human wisdom can calculate the end. It has but one thing certain, and that is to increase taxes.

Prospects on the Rubicon (1787)

15 A share in two revolutions is living to some purpose.

Letter to George Washington, 16 Oct. 1789

16 [Edmund Burke] is not affected by the reality of distress touching his heart, but by the showy resemblance of it striking his imagination. He pities the plumage, but forgets the dying bird.

The Rights of Man pt. 1 (1791)

17 The idea of hereditary legislators is as inconsistent as that of hereditary judges, or hereditary juries; and as absurd as an hereditary mathematician, or an hereditary wise man; and as ridiculous as an hereditary poet laureate.

The Rights of Man pt. 1 (1791)

18 Persecution is not an original feature in *any* religion; but it is always the strongly marked feature of all law-religions, or religions established by law.

The Rights of Man pt. 1 (1791)

19 The American constitutions were to liberty, what a grammar is to language: they define its parts of speech, and practically construct them into syntax.

The Rights of Man pt. 1 (1791)

20 [*Of Edmund Burke's House of Commons debate with Charles James Fox concerning the French Revolution:*] As he rose like a rocket, he fell like the stick.

Letter to the Addressers on the Late Proclamation (1792)

21 [*Of monarchy:*] I compare it to something behind a curtain, about which there is a great deal of bustle and fuss, and a wonderful air of seeming solemnity; but when, by any accident, the curtain happens to be open, and the company see what it is, they burst into laughter.

The Rights of Man pt. 2, ch. 3 (1792)

22 When, in countries that are called civilized, we see age going to the workhouse and youth to the gallows, something must be wrong in the system of government.

The Rights of Man pt. 2, ch. 5 (1792)

23 My country is the world, and my religion is to do good.

The Rights of Man pt. 2, ch. 5 (1792)

24 A thing moderately good is not so good as it ought to be. Moderation in temper is always a virtue; but moderation in principle is always a vice.

The Rights of Man pt. 2, ch. 5 (1792)
See Goldwater 3

25 The Age of Reason.
Title of book (1794)

26 I believe in one God and no more, and I hope
for happiness beyond this life. I believe in the
equality of man; and I believe that religious
duties consist in doing justice, loving mercy,
and endeavoring to make our fellow creatures
happy.
The Age of Reason pt. 1 (1794)

27 It is necessary to the happiness of man that he
be mentally faithful to himself. Infidelity does
not consist in believing, or in disbelieving, it
consists in professing to believe what one does
not believe.
The Age of Reason pt. 1 (1794)

28 The church has set up a system of religion very
contradictory to the character of the person
whose name it bears. It has set up a religion of
pomp and of revenue in pretended imitation of
a person whose life was humility and poverty.
The Age of Reason pt. 1 (1794)

29 Any system of religion that has any thing in it
that shocks the mind of a child cannot be a true
system.
The Age of Reason pt. 1 (1794)

30 The sublime and the ridiculous are often
so nearly related, that it is difficult to class
them separately. One step above the sublime,
makes the ridiculous; and one step above the
ridiculous, makes the sublime again.
The Age of Reason pt. 2 (1795)
See Napoleon 4

David Paktor
U.S. computer scientist, fl. 1973

1 Reality is that stuff which, no matter what you
believe, just won't go away.
Quoted in *Thursday* (MIT student newspaper), 8 Mar.
1973
See Dick 1

Chuck Palahniuk
U.S. novelist, 1962–

1 The first rule about fight club is you don't talk
about fight club. . . . The second rule about fight
club is you don't talk about fight club.
Fight Club ch. 6 (1996)

2 You are not a beautiful and unique snowflake.
You are the same decaying organic matter as
everyone else, and we are all part of the same
compost pile.
Fight Club ch. 17 (1996)

Grace Paley
U.S. writer and political activist, 1922–2007

1 Enormous Changes at the Last Minute.
Title of book (1974)

William Paley
English theologian and philosopher, 1743–1805

1 Who can refute a sneer?
Principles of Moral and Political Philosophy bk. 5, ch.
9 (1785)

2 The infidelity of the gentile world, and that
more especially of men of rank and learning
in it, is resolved into a principle, which, in my
judgment, will account for the inefficacy of
any argument, or any evidence whatever, viz.
contempt prior to examination.
A View of the Evidences of Christianity pt. 3, ch. 2
(1794)

3 Suppose I had found a *watch* upon the ground,
and it should be enquired how the watch
happened to be in that place . . . the inference,
we think, is inevitable; that the watch must
have had a maker, that there must have existed,
at some time and at some place or other, an
artificer or artificers, who formed it for the
purpose which we find it actually to answer;
who comprehended its construction, and
designed its use.
Natural Theology ch. 1 (1802)
See Dawkins 4

Pali Tripitaka
Buddhist collection of sacred texts, ca. Second
cent. B.C.

1 For hate is not conquered by hate: hate is
conquered by love. This is a law eternal.
Dhammapada v. 5

2 [*First Sermon of the Buddha:*] Avoiding both
these extremes [sensual pleasure and self-
mortification] the Tathagata has realized
the Middle Path: it gives vision, it gives

knowledge, and it leads to calm, to insight, to enlightenment, to Nirvana.

Samyutta-nikāya pt. 56

3 [*First Sermon of the Buddha:*] The Noble Truth of Suffering is this: Birth is suffering, ageing is suffering; sickness is suffering; death is suffering; sorrow and lamentation, pain, grief, and despair are suffering; association with the unpleasant is suffering; dissociation from the pleasant is suffering; not to get what one wants is suffering.

Samyutta-nikāya pt. 56

4 [*First Sermon of the Buddha:*] The Noble Truth of the Path leading to the Cessation of suffering is this: It is simply the Noble Eightfold Path, namely right view; right thought; right speech; right action; right livelihood; right effort; right mindfulness; right concentration.

Samyutta-nikāya pt. 56

5 [*"The Five Precepts":*] 1) Refraining from taking life. 2) Refraining from taking what is not given. 3) Refraining from incontinence. 4) Refraining from falsehood. 5) Refraining from strong drink, intoxicants, and liquor, which are occasions of carelessness.

Vinaya, Mahāv 1, 56

Sarah Palin
U.S. politician, 1964–

1 What's the difference between a hockey mom and a pitbull? Lipstick.

Speech to Republican National Convention, St. Paul, Minn., 3 Sept. 2008

2 They're [the Russians] our next-door neighbors and you can actually see Russia from land here in Alaska, from an island in Alaska.

Interview on ABC *Nightline (*television program), 11 Sept. 2008. This statement, which Palin presented as a kind of foreign-policy credential, was parodied by comedian Tina Fey on the *Saturday Night Live* television broadcast, 13 Sept. 2008. Fey's satirical version was "I can see Russia from my house!"

3 [*Response to Katie Couric's asking her to specifically name newspapers or magazines she read:*] All of them, any of them that have been in front of me over all these years.

Interview on CBS News television broadcast, 1 Oct. 2008

4 The America I know and love is not one in which my parents or my baby with Down Syndrome will have to stand in front of Obama's "death panel" so his bureaucrats can decide, based on a subjective judgment of their "level of productivity in society," whether they are worthy of health care. Such a system is downright evil.

Facebook page, 7 Aug. 2009

5 Don't retreat, reload.

Tweet, Mar. 23, 2010

John F. Palmer
U.S. songwriter, fl. 1895

1 His brain was so loaded, it nearly exploded,
The poor girl would shake with alarm.
He'd ne'er leave the girl with the strawberry curls,
And the band played on.

"The Band Played On" (song) (1895)

Henry John Temple, Viscount Palmerston
British prime minister, 1784–1865

1 We have no eternal allies and we have no perpetual enemies. Our interests are eternal and perpetual, and those interests it is our duty to follow.

Speech in House of Commons, 1 Mar. 1848

2 Lord Palmerston, with characteristic levity had once said that only three men in Europe had ever understood [the Schleswig-Holstein question], and of these the Prince Consort was dead, a Danish statesman (unnamed) was in an asylum, and he himself had forgotten it.

Reported in Robert W. Seton-Watson, *Britain in Europe 1789–1914* (1937). Garson O'Toole has found a very similar anecdote in an Italian book, namely Alfonso La Marmora, *Un Po' Piudi Luce Sugli Eventi Politici e Militari dell' Anno 1866*, 2nd ed. (1873).

Orhan Pamuk
Turkish novelist, 1952–

1 Mankind's greatest error, the biggest deception of the past thousand years is this: to confuse poverty with stupidity.

Snow ch. 31 (2002) (translation by Maureen Freely)

Christabel Pankhurst

English women's rights activist, 1880–1958

1 [*Childhood remark, ca. 1890:*] How long you
women have been trying for the vote. For my
part, I mean to get it.
Quoted in Emmeline Pankhurst, *My Own Story*
(1914)

Emmeline Pankhurst

English feminist, 1858–1928

1 There is something that Governments care
for far more than human life, and that is the
security of property. So it is through property
that we shall strike the enemy. . . . Be militant
each in your own way. . . . I incite this meeting
to rebellion.
Speech at Royal Albert Hall, London, 17 Oct. 1912

2 Women had always fought for men, and for
their children. Now they were ready to fight for
their own human rights.
My Own Story ch. 3 (1914)

3 The argument of the broken window pane is
the most valuable argument in modern politics.
Quoted in George Dangerfield, *The Strange Death of
Liberal England* (1936)

Charlie "Bird" Parker

U.S. saxophonist, bandleader, and composer,
1920–1955

1 If you don't live it, it won't come out of your
horn.
Quoted in Nat Shapiro and Nat Hentoff, *Hear Me
Talkin' to Ya* (1955)

2 They teach you there's a boundary line to
music. But, man, there's no boundary line
to art.
Quoted in Nat Shapiro and Nat Hentoff, *Hear Me
Talkin' to Ya* (1955)

Dorothy Parker

U.S. critic and humorist, 1893–1967

1 [*Caption accompanying drawings of models:*]
Brevity is the soul of lingerie.
Vogue, 1 Oct. 1916
See Shakespeare 174

2 Scratch a lover, and find a foe.
"Ballade of a Great Weariness" l. 8 (1926)

3 Oh, life is a glorious cycle of song,
A medley of extemporanea;
And love is a thing that can never go wrong;
And I am Marie of Roumania.
"Comment" l. 1 (1926)

4 Woman wants monogamy;
Man delights in novelty. . . .
Woman lives but in her lord;
Count to ten, and man is bored.
With this the gist and sum of it,
What earthly good can come of it?
"General Review of the Sex Situation" l. 1 (1926)

5 Four be the things I am wiser to know:
Idleness, sorrow, a friend, and a foe.
"Inventory" l. 1 (1926)

6 Four be the things I'd been better without:
Love, curiosity, freckles, and doubt.
"Inventory" l. 3 (1926)

7 Men seldom make passes
At girls who wear glasses.
"News Item" l. 1 (1926)

8 Why is it no one ever sent me yet
One perfect limousine, do you suppose?
Ah no, it's always just my luck to get
One perfect rose.
"One Perfect Rose" l. 9 (1926)

9 Guns aren't lawful;
   Nooses give;
   Gas smells awful;
   You might as well live.
   "Résumé" l. 5 (1926)

10 Lady, lady, should you meet
   One whose ways are all discreet,
   One who murmurs that his wife
   Is the lodestar of his life,
   One who keeps assuring you
   That he never was untrue,
   Never loved another one . . .
   Lady, lady, better run!
   "Social Note" l. 1 (1926). Ellipsis in the original.

11 By the time you swear you're his,
   Shivering and sighing,
   And he vows his passion is
   Infinite, undying—
   Lady, make a note of this:
   One of you is lying.
   "Unfortunate Coincidence" l. 1 (1926)

12 The affair between Margot Asquith and Margot
   Asquith will live as one of the prettiest love
   stories in all literature.
   New Yorker, 22 Oct. 1927

13 If, with the literate, I am
   Impelled to try an epigram,
   I never seek to take the credit;
   We all assume that Oscar said it.
   "A Pig's-Eye View of Literature" l. 10 (1928)

14 It costs me never a stab nor squirm
   To tread by chance upon a worm.
   "Aha, my little dear," I say,
   "Your clan will pay me back one day."
   "Thought for a Sunshiny Morning" l. 1 (1928)

15 Salary is no object; I want only enough to keep
   body and soul apart.
   New Yorker, 4 Feb. 1928

16 Take me or leave me; or, as is the usual order of
   things, both.
   New Yorker, 4 Feb. 1928
   See Kahn 6; Political Slogans 3

17 It may be that this autobiography [Aimee
   Semple McPherson's] is set down in sincerity,
   frankness, and simple effort. It may be, too, that
   the Statue of Liberty is situated in Lake Ontario.
   New Yorker, 25 Feb. 1928

18 [Reviewing A. A. Milne's The House at Pooh
   Corner in her "Constant Reader" column:]
   Tonstant Weader Fwowed up.
   New Yorker, 20 Oct. 1928

19 [Of Ernest Hemingway:] He has a capacity for
   enjoyment so vast that he gives away great
   chunks to those about him, and never even
   misses them. . . . He can take you to a bicycle
   race and make it raise your hair.
   New Yorker, 30 Nov. 1929

20 Drink and dance and laugh and lie,
   Love, the reeling midnight through,
   For tomorrow we shall die!
   (But, alas, we never do.)
   "The Flaw in Paganism" l. 1 (1931)

21 [Reviewing Channing Pollock's The House
   Beautiful:] "The House Beautiful" is, for me,
   the play lousy.
   New Yorker, 21 Mar. 1931

22 Come on down to my apartment—I want to
   show you some remarkably fine etchings I just
   bought.
   New Yorker, 25 July 1931
   See Centlivre 1

23 How do people go to sleep? I'm afraid I've lost
   the knack. . . . I might repeat to myself, slowly
   and soothingly, a list of quotations beautiful
   from minds profound; if I can remember any
   of the damn things.
   Here Lies "The Little Hours" (1939)

24 Sorrow is tranquility remembered in emotion.
   Here Lies "Sentiment" (1939)
   See William Wordsworth 6

25 [Her suggested epitaph for herself:] Excuse My
   Dust.
   Quoted in Vanity Fair, June 1925

26 [When asked about the most beautiful words in
   the English language:] The ones I like . . . are
   "cheque" and "inclosed."
   Quoted in N.Y. Herald Tribune, 12 Dec. 1932

27 That woman speaks eighteen languages, and
   can't say No in any of them.
   Quoted in Hearst's International Cosmopolitan,
   Aug. 1933

28 [Telegram to Mary Sherwood, who finally had her
   baby after a much-ballyhooed pregnancy, 1915:]

Good work, Mary. We all knew you had it in you.

Quoted in *Hearst's International Cosmopolitan*, Aug. 1933

29 [*Of a performance by Katharine Hepburn:*] Let's all go to see Miss Hepburn and hear her run the gamut of emotions from A to B!

Quoted in *N.Y. Sun*, 6 Jan. 1934

30 [*When told of the death of Calvin Coolidge:*] How can they tell?

Quoted in Max Eastman, *The Enjoyment of Laughter* (1936)

31 [*Of a cocktail party she had attended:*] One more drink and I'd have been under the host!

Quoted in Bennett Cerf, *Try and Stop Me* (1944)

32 [*Of an actress who was said to be kind to her inferiors:*] Where does she find them?

Quoted in *Milwaukee Sentinel*, 23 June 1937. A similar joke appeared as early as James Boswell, *Life of Samuel Johnson* (1791).
See Samuel Johnson 65

33 [*Responding to a hostess being described as "outspoken":*] Outspoken by whom?

Quoted in Bennett Cerf, *Try and Stop Me* (1944). This quip is associated with Parker, but Garson O'Toole has traced the "outspoken . . . by whom?" formulation back as far as the *New York Times*, 7 Oct. 1901.

34 There's a hell of a distance between wise-cracking and wit. Wit has truth in it; wise-cracking is simply calisthenics with words.

Quoted in *Paris Review*, Summer 1956

35 [*On women writers:*] As artists they're rot, but as providers they're oil wells; they gush. Norris said she never wrote a story unless it was fun to do. I understand Ferber whistles at her typewriter. And there was that poor sucker Flaubert rolling around on his floor for three days looking for the right word.

Quoted in *Paris Review*, Summer 1956

36 [*Advice to a friend whose ailing cat had to be "put away":*] Have you tried curiosity?

Quoted in *New Orleans Times-Picayune*, 6 Aug. 1966

37 [*Completing the nursery rhyme "Higgledy piggledy, my white hen; / She lays eggs for gentlemen":*] You cannot persuade her with gun or lariat To come across for the proletariat.

Quoted in *N.Y. Times*, 8 June 1967
See Nursery Rhymes 21

38 [*On being informed that editor Harold Ross had called her on her honeymoon demanding a belated article:*] Tell Ross I'm too fucking busy and vice versa.

Quoted in *Ramparts*, Sept. 1967

39 [*Upon being challenged to use the word* horticulture *in a sentence:*] You can lead a whore to culture, but you can't make her think.

Quoted in *The Algonquin Wits*, ed. Robert E. Drennan (1968). In *Horizon* magazine, July 1962, Parker was quoted as saying, "You may lead a whore to culture but you can't make her think." Walter Winchell, in the *Richmond Times-Dispatch*, 1 Mar. 1935, referred to Parker's having made up a sentence containing the word horticulture but did not provide any details.
See Proverbs 148

40 [*In book review:*] This is not a novel to be tossed aside lightly. It should be thrown with great force.

Quoted in *The Algonquin Wits*, ed. Robert E. Drennan (1968). A very similar line appeared, attributed to Sid Ziff, in *Reader's Digest*, Feb. 1960.

41 [*On being told at a party that people were ducking for apples:*] There, but for a typographical error, is the story of my life.

Quoted in *The Algonquin Wits*, ed. Robert E. Drennan (1968). A very similar anecdote about Parker was told in Ben Hecht, *Charlie* (1957).

42 I was the toast of two continents: Greenland and Australia.

Quoted in John Keats, *You Might As Well Live: The Life and Times of Dorothy Parker* (1970)

43 [*On her abortion:*] It serves me right for putting all my eggs in one bastard.

Quoted in John Keats, *You Might as Well Live: The Life and Times of Dorothy Parker* (1970)
See Proverbs 84

44 [*Habitual response upon hearing the doorbell or telephone ring:*] What fresh hell is this?

Quoted in John D. Tumpane, *Scotch and Holy Water* (1981). In the form "What fresh hell can this be?," this was quoted in John Keats, *You Might as Well Live: The Life and Times of Dorothy Parker* (1970).

45 [*On being warned by her doctor that if she didn't stop drinking she would be dead within a month:*] Promises, promises!

Quoted in *The Sayings of Dorothy Parker*, ed. S. T. Brownlow (1992)

46 People ought to be one of two things, young or old. No; what's the use of fooling? People ought to be one of two things, young or dead.

Quoted in *The Sayings of Dorothy Parker,* ed. S. T. Brownlow (1992)

47 And there was that wholesale libel on a Yale prom. If all the girls attending it were laid end to end, Mrs. Parker said, she wouldn't be at all surprised.

Reported in Alexander Woollcott, *While Rome Burns* (1934)

48 Then I remember her comment on one friend who had lamed herself while in London. It was Mrs. Parker who voiced the suspicion that this poor lady had injured herself while sliding down a barrister.

Reported in Alexander Woollcott, *While Rome Burns* (1934)

49 The two ladies [Dorothy Parker and Clare Boothe Luce] were trying to get out of a doorway at the same time. Clare drew back and cracked, "Age before beauty, Miss Parker." As Dotty swept out, she turned to the other guests and said, "Pearls before swine."

Reported in *Hartford Courant,* 14 Oct. 1938. Luce denied that this exchange ever happened, and Dorothy Parker's biographer John Keats treated it as inauthentic.

John Parker
U.S. army officer, 1729–1775

1 Don't fire unless fired upon. But if they want to have a war, let it begin here.

Quoted in *The Historical Magazine, and Notes and Queries Concerning the Antiquities, History, and Biography of America,* July 1860. Captain Parker, a commander of the Minutemen, is said to have uttered these words to his troops at Lexington, Mass., before the beginning of the 19 Apr. 1775 battle with the British.

Ray Parker, Jr.
U.S. musician, 1954–

1 If there's something strange in your neighborhood,
Who you gonna call? Ghostbusters.

"Ghostbusters" (song) (1984)

Ross Parker
English songwriter, 1914–1974

1 There'll always be an England
While there's a country lane,
Wherever there's a cottage small
Beside a field of grain.

"There'll Always Be an England" (song) (1939). Cowritten with Hughie Charles.

2 We'll meet again, don't know where,
Don't know when,
But I know we'll meet again some sunny day.

"We'll Meet Again" (song) (1939). Cowritten with Hughie Charles.

Theodore Parker
U.S. clergyman and abolitionist, 1810–1860

1 A democracy,—that is, a government of all the people, by all the people, for all the people.

Speech at Anti-Slavery Convention, Boston, Mass., 29 May 1850
See Lincoln 42; Theodore Parker 3; Daniel Webster 5

2 I do not pretend to understand the moral universe; the arc is a long one, my eye reaches but little ways; I cannot calculate the curve and complete the figure by the experience of sight; I can divine it by conscience. And from what I see I am sure it bends toward justice.

Ten Sermons on Religion "Justice and the Conscience" (1853). This was later paraphrased by Martin Luther King, Jr., in a sermon on 31 March 1968, and by Barack Obama in a speech on 2 Feb. 2007.

3 Democracy is direct self-government, over all the people, for all the people, by all the people.

Sermon at Music Hall, Boston, Mass., 4 July 1858
See Lincoln 42; Theodore Parker 1; Daniel Webster 5

Camilla Parker Bowles
British duchess, 1947–

1 [*Reputed remark to Prince Charles upon their first meeting:*] My great-grandmother was your great-great-grandfather's mistress. How about it?

Attributed in *Mail on Sunday,* 15 Nov. 1992

C. Northcote Parkinson
English writer, 1909–1993

1 Work expands so as to fill the time available for its completion.

"Parkinson's Law," *Economist,* 19 Nov. 1955

2 Time spent on any item of the agenda will be in inverse proportion to the sum involved.
Parkinson's Law ch. 3 (1957)

3 Perfection of planned layout is achieved only by institutions on the point of collapse.
Parkinson's Law ch. 6 (1957)

4 The man who is denied the opportunity of taking decisions of importance begins to regard as important the decisions he is allowed to take.
Parkinson's Law ch. 10 (1957)

5 Men enter local politics solely as a result of being unhappily married.
Parkinson's Law ch. 10 (1957)

6 Expenditure rises to meet income.
The Law and the Profits ch. 1 (1960)

7 Expansion means complexity and complexity, decay; or to put it even more plainly—the more complex, the sooner dead.
In-Laws and Outlaws (1962)

8 Successful research attracts the bigger grant which makes further research impossible.
"Parkinson's Laws in Medical Research," *Bulletin of the Atomic Scientists,* Nov. 1962

9 It is the essence of grantsmanship to persuade the Foundation executives that it was *they* who suggested the research project and that you were a belated convert, agreeing reluctantly to all they had proposed.
"Parkinson's Laws in Medical Research," *Bulletin of the Atomic Scientists,* Nov. 1962

10 The printed word expands to fill the space available for it.
"Parkinson's New Law," *Reader's Digest,* Feb. 1963

11 The effectiveness of a telephone conversation is in inverse proportion to the time spent on it.
"Now Parkinson's Telephone Law," *N.Y. Times Magazine,* 12 Apr. 1964

12 Heat produced by pressure expands to fill the mind available from which it can pass only to a cooler mind.
Mrs. Parkinson's Law ch. 7 (1968)

13 Delay is the deadliest form of denial.
The Law of Delay ch. 13 (1971)

14 An enterprise employing more than 1000 people becomes a self-perpetuating empire, creating so much internal work that it no

longer needs any contact with the outside world.
Quoted in *Management Science Journal,* Oct. 1960

Gordon Parks
U.S. photographer and film director, 1912–2006

1 The Learning Tree.
Title of book (1964)

Rosa Parks
U.S. civil rights activist, 1913–2005

1 [*On her refusal to relinquish her seat to a white man, triggering the Montgomery, Ala., bus boycott, 1955:*] All I was doing was trying to get home from work.
Quoted in *Time,* 15 Dec. 1975

2 I had felt for a long time, that if I was ever told to get up so a white person could sit, that I would refuse to do so.
Quoted in David J. Garrow, *Bearing the Cross* (1986)

Charles Stewart Parnell
Irish politician, 1846–1891

1 No man has a right to fix the boundary of the march of a nation; no man has a right to say to his country—thus far shalt thou go and no further.
Speech, Cork, Ireland, 21 Jan. 1885

Elsie Clews Parsons
U.S. anthropologist and feminist critic, 1874–1941

1 Some day there may be a "masculism" movement to allow men to act "like women."
The Journal of a Feminist, Apr. 1914

Talcott Parsons
U.S. sociologist, 1902–1979

1 If, however, the culture of the deviant group, like that of the delinquent gang, remains a "counter-culture" it is difficult to find the bridges by which it can acquire influence over wider circles.
The Social System ch. 11 (1951). Earliest known occurrence of the word *counterculture,* preceding by nineteen years the earliest use given by historical dictionaries. Parson's usage was unearthed through a search on the JSTOR electronic journal archive.

Eric Partridge
New Zealand–born English lexicographer,
1894–1979

1 That old lady who, on borrowing a dictionary
from her municipal library, returned it with the
comment, "A very unusual book indeed—but
the stories are extremely short, aren't they?"
The Gentle Art of Lexicography ch. 1 (1963)

Blaise Pascal
French mathematician and philosopher,
1623–1662

1 *Je n'ai fait celle-ci plus longue que parce que je n'ai
pas eu le loisir de la faire plus courte.*
I have made this [letter] longer than usual, only
because I have not had the time to make it
shorter.
Lettres Provinciales no. 16 (1657)
See Thoreau 34; Woodrow Wilson 25

2 *Le nez de Cléopâtre s'il eût été plus court toute la
face de la terre aurait changé.*
Cleopatra's nose, had it been shorter, the whole
face of the world would have been changed.
Pensées no. 32 (1658)

3 How vain painting is, exciting admiration by
its resemblance to things of which we do not
admire the originals.
Pensées no. 74 (1658)

4 *C'est là ma place au soleil.*
That's my place in the sun.
Pensées no. 98 (1658)
See Bülow 1; Wilhelm II 1

5 What is it, then, that this desire and this
inability proclaim to us, but that there was
once in man a true happiness of which there
now remain to him only the mark and empty
trace, which he in vain tries to fill from all his
surroundings, seeking from things absent the
help he does not obtain in things present? But
these are all inadequate, because the infinite
abyss can only be filled by an infinite and
immutable object, that is to say, only by God
Himself.
Pensées no. 181 (1658). Popularly paraphrased as
"There is a God-shaped vacuum in every heart."

6 We shall die alone.
Pensées no. 184 (1658)

7 What is man in nature? A nothing in relation
to the infinite, an all in relation to nothing, a
middle between nothing and all.
Pensées no. 230 (1658)

8 *L'homme n'est qu'un roseau, le plus faible de la
nature, mais c'est un roseau pensant.*
Man is only a reed, the weakest in nature, but
he is a thinking reed.
Pensées no. 231 (1658)

9 [*On the heavens:*] The eternal silence of these
infinite spaces terrifies me.
Pensées no. 233 (1658)

10 When we see a natural style, we are quite
surprised and delighted, for we expected to see
an author and we find a man.
Pensées no. 554 (1658)

11 I lay it down as a fact that if all men knew what
others say of them, there would not be four
friends in the world.
Pensées no. 646 (1658)

12 *Dieu est, ou il n'est pas. Mais de quel côté
pencherons-nous? La raison n'y peut rien
déterminer. Il y'a un chaos infini qui nous
sépare. Il se joue un jeu, à l'extrémité de cette
distance infinie, où il arrivera croix ou pile: que
gagerez-vous?*
God is, or He is not. But to which side shall
we incline? Reason can decide nothing here.

There is an infinite chaos which separates us. A game is being played at the extremity of this infinite distance, where heads or tails will turn up: what will you wager?

Pensées no. 680 (1658). Popularly known as "Pascal's wager."

13 *Pesons le gain et la perte, en prenant croix que Dieu est. Estimons ces deux cas: Si vous gagnez, vous gagnez tout; si vous perdez, vous ne perdez rien. Gagez donc qu'il est, sans hésiter!*

Let us weigh the gain and the loss in wagering that God is. Let us estimate the two chances. If you win, you win everything; if you lose, you lose nothing. Wager then without hesitation that He is!

Pensées no. 680 (1658). Popularly known as "Pascal's wager."

14 *Le coeur a ses raisons, que la raison ne connaît point.*

The heart has its reasons which reason knows nothing of.

Pensées no. 680 (1658)

15 Men never do evil so completely and cheerfully as when they do it from religious conviction.

Pensées no. 894 (1670 ed.)

Boris Pasternak

Russian novelist and poet, 1890–1960

1 Man is born to live, not to prepare for life.

Doctor Zhivago ch. 9 (1958) (translation by Max Hayward and Manya Harari)

2 I don't like people who have never fallen or stumbled. Their virtue is lifeless and it isn't of much value. Life hasn't revealed its beauty to them.

Doctor Zhivago ch. 13 (1958) (translation by Max Hayward and Manya Harari)

3 All customs and traditions, all our way of life, everything to do with home and order, has crumbled into dust in the general upheaval and reorganization of society. The whole human way of life has been destroyed and ruined. All that's left is the naked human soul stripped to the last shred, for which nothing has changed because it was always cold and shivering and reaching out to its nearest neighbor, as cold and lonely as itself.

Doctor Zhivago ch. 13 (1958) (translation by Max Hayward and Manya Harari)

4 One day Lara went out and did not come back. . . . She died or vanished somewhere, forgotten as a nameless number on a list which was afterwards mislaid.

Doctor Zhivago ch. 15 (1958) (translation by Max Hayward and Manya Harari)

5 Yet the order of the acts is planned
And the end of the way inescapable.
I am alone; all drowns in the Pharisees' hypocrisy.
To live your life is not as simple as to cross a field.

Doctor Zhivago "Zhivago's Poems: Hamlet" (1958) (translation by Max Hayward and Manya Harari)

Louis Pasteur

French chemist and bacteriologist, 1822–1895

1 Where observation is concerned, chance favors only the prepared mind.

Address at inauguration of Faculty of Science, University of Lille, Lille, France, 7 Dec. 1854

Walter Pater

English critic and essayist, 1839–1894

1 [Of the *Mona Lisa:*] She is older than the rocks among which she sits; like the vampire, she has been dead many times, and learned the secrets of the grave; and has been a diver in deep seas, and keeps their fallen day about her; and trafficked for strange webs with Eastern merchants; and as Leda, was the mother of Helen of Troy, and as Saint Anne, the mother of Mary; and all this has been to her but as the sound of lyres and flutes, and lives only in the delicacy with which it has moulded the changing lineaments, and tinged the eyelids and the hands.

Studies in the History of the Renaissance "Leonardo da Vinci" (1873)

2 All art constantly aspires towards the condition of music.

Studies in the History of the Renaissance "The School of Giorgione" (1873)

3 To burn always with this hard, gemlike flame, to maintain this ecstasy, is success in life.

Studies in the History of the Renaissance "Conclusion" (1873)

Andrew Barton "Banjo" Paterson
Australian poet, 1864–1941

1 There was movement at the station, for the
    word had passed around
That the colt from old Regret had got away,
And had joined the wild bush horses—he was
    worth a thousand pound,
So all the cracks had gathered to the fray.
"The Man from Snowy River" l. 1 (1895)

2 Once a jolly swagman camped by a billabong,
Under the shade of a coolibah tree;
And he sang as he watched and waited till his
    "Billy" boiled:
"You'll come a-waltzing, Matilda, with me."
"Waltzing Matilda" (song) (1903)

Alan Paton
South African writer, 1903–1988

1 I see only one hope for our country, and that is
    when white men and black men . . . desiring
    only the good of their country, come together
    to work for it. . . . I have one great fear in my
    heart, that one day when they are turned to
    loving, they will find we are turned to hating.
Cry, the Beloved Country ch. 7 (1948)

2 Cry, the beloved country, for the unborn child
    that is the inheritor of our fear.
Cry, the Beloved Country ch. 12 (1948)

3 No second Johannesburg is needed upon the
    earth. One is enough.
Cry, the Beloved Country ch. 23 (1948)

George S. Patton, Jr.
U.S. military leader, 1885–1945

1 War will be won by Blood and Guts alone.
Address to officers, Fort Benning, Ga., 1940

2 [Remark at press conference, Bad-Toelz, Germany:]
The Nazi thing is just like a Democrat and
Republican election fight.
Quoted in N.Y. Times, 30 Sept. 1945

3 No dumb bastard ever won a war by going out
    and dying for his country. He won it by making
    some other dumb bastard die for his country.
Attributed in James M. Gavin, War and Peace in the
Space Age (1958). This is said to have been uttered
in various speeches by Patton in 1943 and 1944, but

definitive documentation is lacking. "Don't die for
your dear country's sake, / But let the other chap die
for his" appeared in War Poems by Thomas W. H.
Crosland (1917).

Elliot Paul
U.S. writer and editor, 1891–1958

1 The last time I see Paris will be on the day I
    die. The city was inexhaustible, and so is its
    memory.
The Last Time I Saw Paris pt. 2 (1942)

Herbert Paul
English author and politician, 1853–1935

1 After all, what is originality? It is merely
    undetected plagiarism.
The Nineteenth Century, Apr. 1896

Jean Paul (Johann Paul Friedrich Richter)
German writer, 1763–1825

1 Weltschmerz.

World-pain.
Selina (1827)

Leslie Paul
Irish writer, 1905–1985

1 Angry Young Man.
Title of book (1951)
See John Osborne 1

Wolfgang Pauli
Austrian-born Swiss physicist, 1900–1958

1 [Comment about an inadequate paper by a young
    physicist:] It is not even wrong.
Quoted in Rudolf Peierls, "Wolfgang Ernst Pauli,
1900–1958," Biographical Memoirs of Fellows of the
Royal Society (1960)

Luciano Pavarotti
Italian opera singer, 1935–2007

1 The wife of one famous tenor says her husband
    does not make love for two days before a
    performance and for two days after it. And he
    gives a performance every four days.
Quoted in People Weekly, 17 Nov. 1980

Ivan Petrovich Pavlov

Russian physiologist and psychologist,
1849–1936

1 Mankind will possess incalculable advantages
and extraordinary control over human
behavior when the scientific investigator will
be able to subject his fellow men to the same
external analysis he would employ for any
natural object, and when the human mind will
contemplate itself not from within but from
without.

"Scientific Study of the So-Called Psychical Processes
in the Higher Animals" (1906)

J. H. Payne

U.S. actor, playwright, and songwriter,
1791–1852

1 Home, Sweet Home.

Title of song (1823). Appeared in the opera, *Clari,
or, The Maid of Milan*. The phrase "Home, sweet
Home" appeared in a poem titled "Home" by Joseph
Beaumont (1615–1699).

2 Mid pleasures and palaces though we may
   roam,
   Be it ever so humble, there's no place like
   home.

"Home, Sweet Home" (song) (1823). "No place like
home" appeared even earlier in Piomingo, *The Savage*
(1810).
See L. Frank Baum 3; Hesiod 3

Octavio Paz

Mexican writer and diplomat, 1914–1998

1 The North American wants to use reality rather
than to know it.

The Labyrinth of Solitude ch. 1 (1950) (translation by
Lysander Kemp)

2 No doubt the nearness of death and the
brotherhood of men-at-arms, at whatever time
and in whatever country, always produces an
atmosphere favorable to the extraordinary, to
all that rises above the human condition and
breaks the circle of solitude that surrounds
each one of us.

The Labyrinth of Solitude ch. 1 (1950) (translation by
Lysander Kemp)

3 Solitude is the profoundest fact of the human
condition. Man is the only being who knows

he is alone, and the only one who seeks out
another.

The Labyrinth of Solitude ch. 9 (1950) (translation by
Lysander Kemp)

4 We are condemned
to kill time:
Thus we die
bit by bit.

"Cuento de los Jardines" (1968)

5 Wit *invents;* inspiration *reveals.*

Sor Juana ch. 4 (1982)

Thomas Love Peacock

English novelist and poet, 1785–1866

1 A book that furnishes no quotations is, *me
judice,* no book—it is a plaything.

Crochet Castle ch. 9 (1831)

Norman Vincent Peale

U.S. religious broadcaster and writer, 1898–
1993

1 The Power of Positive Thinking.

Title of book (1952)

Patrick Pearse

Irish nationalist, 1879–1916

1 Ireland unfree shall never be at peace.

Speech at grave of Jeremiah O'Donovan Rossa, 1 Aug.
1915

Drew Pearson

U.S. journalist, 1897–1969

1 [*Referring to U.S. Supreme Court:*] The Nine Old
Men.

Title of book (1936). Coauthored with Robert S.
Allen.
See Berle 1

Hesketh Pearson

English actor and biographer, 1887–1964

1 Misquotation is, in fact, the pride and privilege
of the learned. A widely-read man never quotes
accurately, for the rather obvious reason that he
has read too widely.

Common Misquotations introduction (1934)

Lester Pearson
Canadian prime minister, 1897–1972

1 The grim fact is that we prepare for war like precocious giants and for peace like retarded pygmies.
Speech, Toronto, Canada, 14 Mar. 1955

Margaret B. Peeke
U.S. novelist and traveler, 1838–1908

1 And God bless America,
When other lands are falling,
Because to Him, in every tongue
Her children will be calling.
"Totus in Uno" l. 21 (1882)
See Irving Berlin 8

George Peele
English playwright and poet, 1556–1596

1 A Farewell to Arms.
Title of poem (1590)

Westbrook Pegler
U.S. journalist, 1894–1969

1 [*Of the post–World War I decade:*] The Era of Wonderful Nonsense.
'*T Aint Right* (1936)

Benjamin Peirce
U.S. mathematician, 1809–1880

1 Mathematics is the science which draws necessary conclusions.
"Linear Associative Algebra" (1870)

Charles Sanders Peirce
U.S. philosopher and physicist, 1839–1914

1 Consider what effects, that might conceivably have practical bearings, we conceive the object of our conception to have. Then, our conception of these effects is the whole of our conception of the object.
"How to Make Our Ideas Clear" (1878). This has become known as "the pragmatic maxim."

2 My word "pragmatism" has gained general recognition. . . . The writer, finding his bantling "pragmatism" so promoted, feels that it is time to kiss his child good-by and relinquish it to its higher destiny; while to serve the precise purpose of expressing the original definition, he begs to announce the birth of the word "pragmaticism," which is ugly enough to be safe from kidnappers.
"What Pragmatism Is" (1905)

3 I define a Sign as anything which is so determined by something else, called its Object, and so determines an effect upon a person, which effect I call its Interpretant, that the latter is thereby mediately determined by the former.
Letter to Victoria Welby, 23 Dec. 1908

Pelé (Edson Arantes do Nascimento)
Brazilian soccer player, 1940–

1 I dedicate this book to all the people who have made this great game the Beautiful Game.
My Life and the Beautiful Game dedication (1977)

Nancy Pelosi
U.S. politician, 1940–

1 [*Of the Affordable Care Act:*] We have to pass the bill so that you can find out what is in it.
Speech to National Association of Counties, Washington, D.C., 9 Mar. 2010. "I admit this new bill is too complicated to understand . . . we'll just have to pass it to find out how it works!" (ellipsis in original) was the caption of George Lichty's newspaper cartoon "Grin and Bear It," 12 Mar. 1947.

2 [*Comment on Donald Trump's desire to build a border wall, 11 Dec. 2018:*] It's like a manhood thing with him—as if manhood can be associated with him.
Quoted in *N.Y. Times,* 12 Dec. 2018

Sean Penn
U.S. actor, 1960–

1 The difference between being a director and being an actor is the difference between being the carpenter banging the nails into the wood, and being the piece of wood the nails are being banged into.
Quoted in *Guardian,* 28 Nov. 1991

William Penn

English colonizer and reformer, 1644–1718

1 No pain, no palm; no thorns, no throne; no gall, no glory; no cross, no crown.
No Cross, No Crown (1669)
See Proverbs 212

Samuel Pepys

English diarist, 1633–1703

1 And so to bed.
Diary, 4 Jan. 1660

2 A strange slavery that I stand in to beauty, that I value nothing near it.
Diary, 6 Sept. 1664

3 Up, and all day at the office, but a little at dinner, and there late till past 12. So home to bed, pleased as I always am after I have rid a great deal of work, it being very satisfactory to me.
Diary, 6 May 1665

4 God forgive me! I do still see that my nature is not to be quite conquered, but will esteem pleasure above all things, though yet in the middle of it, it has reluctances after my business, which is neglected by my following my pleasure. However music and women I cannot but give way to, whatever my business is.
Diary, 9 Mar. 1666

5 [*Final entry of* Diary:] And so I betake myself to that course, which is almost as much as to see myself go into my grave—for which, and all the discomforts that will accompany my being blind, the good God prepare me!
Diary, 31 May 1669

Walker Percy

U.S. writer, 1916–1990

1 The fact is I am quite happy in a movie, even a bad movie. Other people, so I have read, treasure memorable moments in their lives.
The Moviegoer ch. 1 (1961)

S. J. Perelman

U.S. humorist, 1904–1979

1 I've got Bright's Disease. And he's got mine.
Caption of cartoon, *Judge*, 16 Nov. 1929

Dom Perignon

French monk and winemaker, 1640–1715

1 [*Alleged remark upon inventing champagne:*]
Come quickly, I am tasting stars!
Attributed in Robert Byrne, *The Other 637 Best Things Anybody Ever Said* (1984). This remark, as well as Perignon's invention of champagne, appear to be apocryphal.

Carl Perkins

U.S. singer and songwriter, 1932–1998

1 Well it's one for the money,
Two for the show,
Three to get ready,
Now go, cat, go.
But don't you
Step on my blue suede shoes.
"Blue Suede Shoes" (song) (1956)

Thomas Perkins

U.S. businessman, 1932–2016

1 I would call attention to the parallels of fascist Nazi [Germany's] war on its "one percent," namely its Jews, to the progressive war on the American one percent, namely the "rich." . . . I perceive a rising tide of hatred of the successful one percent.
Letter to the editor, *Wall Street Journal*, 24 Jan. 2014

Frederick S. Perls

German-born U.S. psychiatrist, 1893–1970

1 I do my thing, and you do your thing.
I am not in this world to live up to your
    expectations
And you are not in this world to live up to
    mine.
You are you and I am I,
And if by chance we find each other, it's
    beautiful;
If not, it can't be helped.
"Gestalt Therapy Verbatim" (1969)

H. Ross Perot

U.S. businessman and politician, 1930–2019

1 [*Of U.S. trade agreements with other nations:*] If you're paying $12, $13, $14 an hour for a factory worker, and you can move your factory south of the border, pay $1 an hour for labor . . .

Have no environmental controls, no pollution controls, and no retirement. And you don't care about anything but making money. There will be a giant sucking sound going south.
Presidential debate, 15 Oct. 1992

2 [*Contrasting the corporate cultures of his former company, EDS, and General Motors, which had acquired EDS:*] The first EDSer to see a snake kills it. At GM, first thing you do is organize a committee on snakes. Then you bring in a consultant who knows a lot about snakes. Third thing you do is talk about it for a year.
Quoted in *Business Week,* 6 Oct. 1986

3 [*Responding to George H. W. Bush's emphasis on the value of experience to presidential candidates:*] I don't have any experience in running up a $4 trillion debt.
Quoted in *Newsweek,* 19 Oct. 1992

Charles Perrault
French poet and critic, 1628–1703

1 "Oh Grandmother! What big ears you have!" "All the better to hear you with."
Stories and Tales of Past Times "Little Red Riding Hood" (1697)
See Grimm and Grimm 2

2 It belongs to my lord the Marquis of Carabas.
Stories and Tales of Past Times "Puss in Boots" (1697)

Freddie Perren
U.S. songwriter and record producer, 1943–2004

1 As long as I know how to love, I know I'll stay alive
I've got all my life to live
And I've got all my love to give
I'll survive
I will survive.
"I Will Survive" (song) (1979). Cowritten with Dino Fekaris.

James Richard "Rick" Perry
U.S. politician, 1950–

1 [*Remark after unsuccessfully attempting to remember the third federal agency he would eliminate:*] Oops.
Republican presidential campaign debate, 9 Nov. 2011

Oliver Hazard Perry
U.S. naval officer, 1785–1819

1 Don't give up the ship.
Inscription on battle flag, 10 Sept. 1813. According to *Respectfully Quoted,* ed. Suzy Platt: "Although this quotation has been attributed to several historical figures, the only documented source is the blue battle-flag inscribed with these words ordered and used by Oliver Hazard Perry as a signal during the battle of Lake Erie, September 10, 1813. Although popularly attributed to Captain James Lawrence as his dying words during a battle with a British frigate off the coast of Boston on June 1, 1813, there remains the possibility these words were not his, but those of someone reporting the battle."

2 We have met the enemy and they are ours—two ships, two brigs, one schooner, and a sloop.
Message to William Henry Harrison, 10 Sept. 1813. The source is Perry's dispatch from the U.S. brig *Niagara* to General Harrison, announcing that victory at the Battle of Lake Erie was secure. The dispatch was written in pencil on the back of an old letter; it is quoted in Robert B. McAfee, *History of the Late War in the Western Country* (1816).
See Walt Kelly 3; Walt Kelly 4

Ted Perry
U.S. screenwriter, 1937–

1 How can you buy or sell the sky, the warmth of the land?
Home (television movie) (1972). Part of a speech Perry wrote for a film on ecology produced by the Southern Baptist Radio and Television Commission. Perry put the speech in the mouth of nineteenth-century Suquamish Indian Chief Seattle; as a result, the televised speech has been widely but incorrectly credited to Seattle.

2 We are part of the earth, and it is part of us.
Home (television movie) (1972). See the comment above for Perry 1.

3 I have seen a thousand rotting buffalos on the prairie, left by the white man who shot them from a passing train. I am a savage and I do not understand how the smoking iron horse can be more important than the buffalo that we kill only to stay alive.
Home (television movie) (1972). See the comment above for Perry 1.

4 The earth does not belong to man; man belongs to the earth.
Home (television movie) (1972). See the comment above for Perry 1.

5 All things are connected. Whatever befalls the earth befalls the sons of the earth. Man did not weave the web of life; he is merely a strand in it. Whatever he does to the web, he does to himself.

Home (television movie) (1972). See the comment above for Perry 1.

Fernando Pessoa
Portuguese writer, 1888–1935

1 The poet is a pretender.
He pretends so completely
That he even pretends that it is pain
The pain he really feels.

"Autopsicografia" (1932)

2 Was it worthy? Everything is worthy.
If the soul is not small.

"Mar Português" (1934)

Henri Philippe Pétain
French soldier and statesman, 1856–1951

1 They shall not pass.

Quoted in *N.Y. Times,* 28 Apr. 1916. This exhortation at the Battle of Verdun is often said to first be recorded in General Nivelle's Order of the Day, 23 June 1916, but the citation above predates that order. *See Ibarruri 2*

Laurence J. Peter
Canadian author, 1919–1990

1 In a hierarchy, each employee tends to rise to his level of incompetence.

Phi Delta Kappan, Mar. 1967. Peter later called this "the Peter principle."
See Scott Adams 1

2 Every post tends to be occupied by an employee incompetent to execute its duties.

Phi Delta Kappan, Mar. 1967

3 The work is done by people who have not yet attained final placement at their level of incompetence.

Quoted in *Wall Street Journal,* 8 June 1967

Thomas Peters
U.S. business author, 1942–

1 When's the last time you washed a rental car?

Speech at Second National Labor-Management Conference, Washington, D.C., June 1984. Peters was quoting an anonymous Air Force officer.

Petrarch (Francesco Petrarca)
Italian poet and scholar, 1304–1374

1 We are continually dying; I while I am writing these words, you while you are reading them. I shall be dying when you read this, you die while I write, we both are dying, we all are dying, we are dying forever.

Letter to Philippe de Cabassoles, ca. 1360 (translation by Morris Bishop)

Petronius Arbiter
Roman satirist, First cent.

1 *Cave canem.*
Beware of the dog.

Satyricon ch. 29

2 *Abiit ad plures.*
He's gone to join the majority [the dead].

Satyricon ch. 42
See Richard Nixon 10; Edward Young 1

3 Not worth his salt.

Satyricon ch. 57

Pheidippides
Greek messenger, ca. 530 B.C.–ca. 490 B.C.

1 [*Dying words, announcing victory over the Persians in the Battle of Marathon after running from Marathon to Athens:*] Joy, we win!

Quoted in Lucian, "Pro Lapsu Inter Salutandum" (translation by F. G. Fowler and H. W. Fowler)

Kim Philby (Harold Adrian Russell Philby)
Indian-born English spy, 1912–1988

1 To betray, you must first belong. I never belonged.

Quoted in *Sunday Times* (London), 17 Dec. 1967

John Woodward Philip
U.S. naval officer, 1840–1900

1 [*At the Battle of Santiago, 4 July 1898:*] Don't cheer boys. Those poor devils are dying.

Quoted in *Wash. Post,* 6 July 1898

Prince Philip, Duke of Edinburgh
Greek-born British prince consort, 1921–2021

1 I have very little experience of self-government. In fact, I am one of the most governed people in the world.

Quoted in *N.Y. Times,* 30 Dec. 1959

A. A. Phillips
Australian literary critic, 1900–1985

1 We cannot shelter from invidious comparisons behind the barrier of a separate language; we have no long-established or interestingly different cultural tradition to give security and distinction to its interpreters; and the centrifugal pull of the great cultural metropolises works against us. Above our writers—and other artists—looms the intimidating mass of Anglo-Saxon achievement. Such a situation almost inevitably produces the characteristic Australian Cultural Cringe.
Meanjin vol. 9, no. 4 (1950)

Wendell Phillips
U.S. reformer, 1811–1884

1 There stands the bloody [fugitive slave] clause—you cannot fret the seal off the bond. The fault is in allowing such a constitution to live an hour. When I look upon these crowded thousands and see them trample on their consciences and the rights of their fellow-men, at the bidding of a piece of parchment, I say, my CURSE be on the Constitution of these United States.
Speech at Faneuil Hall, Boston, Mass., 30 Oct. 1842

2 The greatest praise government can win is, that its citizens know their rights, and dare to maintain them. The best use of good laws is to teach men to trample bad laws under their feet.
Speech, Boston, Mass., 12 Apr. 1852

3 One on God's side is a majority.
Speech on John Brown, Brooklyn, N.Y., 1 Nov. 1859
See Coolidge 2; Douglass 7; Andrew Jackson 7; John Knox 1; Thoreau 9

4 How prudently most men creep into nameless graves while now and then one or two forget themselves into immortality.
National Anti-Slavery Standard, 27 Apr. 1867

Jean Piaget
Swiss psychologist, 1896–1980

1 The child's first year of life is unfortunately still an abyss of mysteries for the psychologist. If only we could know what was going on in a baby's mind while observing him in action, we could certainly understand everything there is to psychology.
"La Première Année de l'Enfant" (1927)

Francesco Maria Piave
Italian librettist, 1810–1876

1 *La donna è mobile.*
Woman is fickle.
Rigoletto (opera with music by Giuseppe Verdi) act 3 (1851)
See Virgil 6

Pablo Picasso
Spanish painter, 1881–1973

1 We all know that Art is not truth. Art is a lie that makes us realize truth.
The Arts, May 1923

2 [*Comment to Herbert Read while viewing an exhibition of children's drawings:*] When I was the age of these children I could draw like Raphael: it took me many years to learn how to draw like these children.
Quoted in *Times* (London), 27 Oct. 1956

3 God is really only another artist. He invented the giraffe, the elephant, and the cat. He has no real style. He just goes on trying other things.
Quoted in Françoise Gilot and Carlton Lake, *Life with Picasso* (1964)

4 [*Of computers:*] They are useless. They can only give you answers.
Quoted in *Paris Review,* Summer–Fall 1964

5 When I was a child my mother said to me, "If you are a soldier, you will become a general. If you are a monk, you will become the Pope." Instead, I was a painter, and became Picasso.
Quoted in Françoise Gilot and Carlton Lake, *Life with Picasso* (1964)

6 [I am] only a public entertainer, who has understood his time.
Attributed in *Wash. Post,* 30 Nov. 1952. The *Post* article is quoting an article in *Quick Magazine* from the summer of 1951. According to a letter by William S. Rubin in the *New York Times,* 5 Jan. 1969, this is "a trumpery originated in *Il Libro Nero* published by Giovanni Papini in 1951."

7 Every child is an artist. The problem is how to remain an artist once he grows up.
Attributed in *Time,* 4 Oct. 1976

Marge Piercy

U.S. writer, 1936–

1 The pitcher cries for water to carry
and a person for work that is real.
"To Be of Use" l. 26 (1973)

2 You called me bad and I posed like a gutter
queen in a dress sewn of knives.
All I feared was being stuck in a box
with a lid. A good woman appeared to me
indistinguishable from a dead one
except that she worked all the time.
"My Mother's Body" l. 119 (1985)

James L. Pierpont

U.S. composer, 1822–1893

1 Dashing through the snow
On a one-horse open sleigh,
Over the fields we go,
Laughing all the way;
Bells on bob-tail ring,
Making spirits bright,
What fun it is to ride and sing
A sleighing song tonight.
"Jingle Bells" (song) (1857)

2 Jingle Bells, Jingle Bells,
Jingle all the way!
Oh what fun it is to ride
In a one-horse open sleigh.
"Jingle Bells" (song) (1857)

Steven Pinker

Canadian-born U.S. psychologist and linguist,
1954–

1 Believe it or not—and I know that most
people do not—violence has declined over
long stretches of time, and today we may be
living in the most peaceable era in our species'
existence.
The Better Angels of Our Nature preface (2011)

Harold Pinter

English playwright, 1930–2008

1 [*Response when asked what his plays were about:*]
The weasel under the cocktail cabinet.
Quoted in J. Russell Taylor, *Anger and After* (1962)

Watty Piper (Arnold Munk)

Hungarian-born U.S. publisher, ca. 1888–1957

1 The Little Engine That Could.
Title of book (1930). A similar story with the same
title had appeared in Olive B. Miller, *My Book House*
(1920).

2 I think I can. I think I can. I think I can.
The Little Engine That Could (1930). Very similar
phraseology occurs in many pre-1930 versions of the
same story, beginning with a 1902 article by Gustaf
Cederschiöld in a Swedish academic journal, *Nordisk
Tidskrift För Vetenskap Konst Och Industri*, using these
English words: "I think I can. I think—I can."

Luigi Pirandello

Italian playwright and novelist, 1867–1936

1 Six Characters in Search of an Author.
Title of play (1921)

2 Yes, but haven't you perceived that it isn't
possible to live in front of a mirror which not
only freezes us with the image of ourselves, but
throws our likeness back at us with a horrible
grimace?
Six Characters in Search of an Author act 3 (1921)

Robert M. Pirsig

U.S. writer and philosopher, 1928–2017

1 Zen and the Art of Motorcycle Maintenance.
Title of book (1974)

2 The Buddha, the Godhead, resides quite as
comfortably in the circuits of a digital computer
or the gears of a cycle transmission as he does
at the top of a mountain or in the petals of a
flower.
Zen and the Art of Motorcycle Maintenance pt. 1, ch. 1
(1974)

3 You are never dedicated to something you have
complete confidence in. (No one is fanatically
shouting that the sun is going to rise tomorrow.
They *know* it's going to rise tomorrow.) When
people are fanatically devoted to political or
religious faiths or any other kinds of dogmas or
goals, it's always because these dogmas or goals
are in doubt.
Zen and the Art of Motorcycle Maintenance pt. 2, ch. 13
(1974)

4 Other people can talk about how to expand the destiny of mankind. I just want to talk about how to fix a motorcycle. I think that what I have to say has more lasting value.

Zen and the Art of Motorcycle Maintenance pt. 3, ch. 25 (1974)

Walter B. Pitkin
U.S. writer and teacher, 1878–1953

1 Life Begins at Forty.

Title of book (1932)

William Pitt
British prime minister, 1759–1806

1 [*Remark after Napoleon's victory at the Battle of Austerlitz, Dec. 1805:*] Roll up that map [of Europe]; it will not be wanted these ten years.

Quoted in Earl Stanhope, *Life of the Rt. Hon. William Pitt* (1862)

William Pitt, Earl of Chatham
British prime minister, 1708–1778

1 The atrocious crime of being a young man . . . I shall neither attempt to palliate or deny.

Speech in House of Commons, 2 Mar. 1741

2 The poorest man may in his cottage bid defiance to all the forces of the Crown. It may be frail—its roof may shake—the wind may blow through it—the storm may enter—the rain may enter—but the King of England cannot enter!—all his force dares not cross the threshold of the ruined tenement!

Speech in House of Commons, ca. March 1763
See Coke 1; Coke 8; Otis 2

3 Unlimited power is apt to corrupt the minds of those who possess it.

Speech in House of Lords, 9 Jan. 1770
See Acton 3

4 There is something behind the throne greater than the King himself.

Speech in House of Lords, 2 Mar. 1770. Source of the phrase "power behind the throne."

Pius IX (Giovanni Maria Mastai-Ferretti)
Italian pope, 1792–1878

1 We declare, pronounce, and define that the doctrine which holds that the most Blessed Virgin Mary, in the first instance of her conception, by a singular grace and privilege granted by Almighty God, in view of the merits of Jesus Christ, the Savior of the human race, was preserved free from all stain of original sin, is a doctrine revealed by God and therefore to be believed firmly and constantly by all the faithful.

"Dogma of the Immaculate Conception" (papal bull), 8 Dec. 1854

Francisco Pizarro
Spanish conquistador, ca. 1475–1541

1 Friends and comrades! On that side [the south] are toil, hunger, nakedness, the drenching storm, desertion, and death; on this side ease and pleasure. There lies Peru with its riches; here, Panama and its poverty. Choose, each man, what best becomes a brave Castilian. For my part, I go to the south.

Quoted in William H. Prescott, *History of the Conquest of Peru* (1848)

Max Planck
German physicist, 1858–1947

1 Anybody who has been seriously engaged in scientific work of any kind realizes that over the entrance to the gates of the temple of science are written the words: *Ye must have faith.* It is a quality which the scientist cannot dispense with.

Where Is Science Going? epilogue (1932)

2 A new scientific truth does not triumph by convincing its opponents and making them see the light, but rather because its opponents eventually die, and a new generation grows up that is familiar with it.

Scientific Autobiography, and Other Papers "Scientific Autobiography" (1948) (translation by Frank Gaynor)

Jacques Plante
Canadian hockey player, 1929–1986

1 How would you like a job where, every time you make a mistake, a big red light goes on and 18,000 people boo?

Quoted in J. R. Colombo, *Colombo's All Time Great Canadian Quotations* (1994)

Sylvia Plath

U.S. poet, 1932–1963

1 My boy, it's your last resort.
Will you marry it, marry it, marry it.
"The Applicant" l. 39 (1962)

2 It was a queer, sultry summer, the summer
they executed the Rosenbergs, and I didn't
know what I was doing in New York.
The Bell Jar ch. 1 (1963)

3 If neurotic is wanting two mutually exclusive
things at one and the same time, then I'm
neurotic as hell. I'll be flying back and forth
between one mutually exclusive thing and
another for the rest of my days.
The Bell Jar ch. 8 (1963)

4 To the person in the bell jar, blank and stopped
as a dead baby, the world itself is the bad
dream.
The Bell Jar ch. 20 (1963)

5 Every woman adores a Fascist,
The boot in the face, the brute
Brute heart of a brute like you.
"Daddy" l. 48 (1963)

6 Dying
Is an art, like everything else.
I do it exceptionally well.

I do it so it feels like hell
I do it so it feels real.
I guess you could say I've a call.
"Lady Lazarus" l. 43 (1963)

7 Out of the ash
I rise with my red hair
And I eat men like air.
"Lady Lazarus" l. 82 (1963)

8 The woman is perfected.
Her dead
Body wears the smile of accomplishment.
"Edge" l. 1 (1965)

Plato

Greek philosopher, 429 B.C.–347 B.C.
Translations and citation information are from The
Collected Dialogues of Plato, *ed. Edith Hamilton and
Huntington Cairns (1961).*

1 [*Socrates speaking, describing the charge against
him:*] Socrates is guilty of corrupting the minds
of the young, and of believing in deities of his
own invention instead of the gods recognized
by the state.
Apology 24b

2 [*Socrates speaking:*] Life without this sort of
examination is not worth living.
Apology 38a. Frequently quoted as "The life which is
unexamined is not worth living."

3 [*Socrates speaking:*] Is what is holy holy because
the gods approve it, or do they approve it
because it is holy?
Euthyphro 10a

4 [*Of Socrates:*] Such, Echecrates, was the end of
our comrade, who was, we may fairly say, of all
those whom we knew in our time, the bravest
and also the wisest and most upright man.
Phaedo 118a

5 [*Socrates speaking:*] If men learn this [writing],
it will implant forgetfulness in their souls;
they will cease to exercise memory because
they rely on that which is written, calling
things to remembrance no longer from within
themselves, but by means of external marks.
. . . And it is no true wisdom that you offer
your disciples, but only its semblance, for by
telling them of many things without teaching
them you will make them seem to know much,
while for the most part they know nothing,
and as men filled, not with wisdom, but with
the conceit of wisdom, they will be a burden to
their fellows.
Phaedrus 275a

6 [*Thrasymachus speaking:*] I affirm that the just is
nothing else than the advantage of the stronger.
The Republic bk. 1, 338c

7 [*Socrates speaking:*] Unless either philosophers
become kings in our states or those whom
we now call our kings and rulers take to the
pursuit of philosophy seriously and adequately,
and there is a conjunction of these two things,
political power and philosophical intelligence,
while the motley horde of the natures who at
present pursue either apart from the other
are compulsorily excluded, there can be no
cessation of troubles, dear Glaucon, for our
states, nor, I fancy, for the human race either.

Nor, until this happens, will this constitution which we have been expounding in theory ever be put into practice within the limits of possibility and see the light of the sun.

The Republic bk. 5, 473c

8 [*Socrates speaking:*] Picture men dwelling in a sort of subterranean cavern with a long entrance open to the light on its entire width. . . . Like to us. . . . Tell me do you think that these men would have seen anything of themselves or of one another except the shadows cast from the fire on the wall of the cave that fronted them?

The Republic bk. 7, 514a

9 [*Socrates speaking:*] Democracy . . . would, it seems, be a delightful form of government, anarchic and motley, assigning a kind of equality indiscriminately to equals and unequals alike!

The Republic bk. 8, 558c

10 [*Socrates speaking:*] Let us suppose that every mind contains a kind of aviary stocked with birds of every sort, some in flocks apart from the rest, some in small groups, and some solitary, flying in any direction among them all. . . . When we are babies we must suppose this receptacle empty, and take the birds to stand for pieces of knowledge. Whenever a person acquires any piece of knowledge and shuts it up in his enclosure, we must say he has learned or discovered the thing of which this is the knowledge, and that is what "knowing" means.

Theaetetus 197e

11 God ever geometrizes.

Attributed in Plutarch, *Moralia*

Plautus
Roman playwright, ca. 250 B.C.–184 B.C.

1 *Lupus est homo homini, non homo.*
A man is a wolf rather than a man to another man.

Asinaria l. 495
See Vanzetti 1

2 No host can be hospitable enough to prevent a friend who has descended on him from becoming tiresome after three days.

Miles Gloriosus l. 741

3 Things which you do not hope happen more frequently than things which you do hope.

Mostellaria act 1, sc. 3, l. 40
See Robert Burns 3; Dickens 67; Disraeli 7; Modern Proverbs 100; Orwell 17; Proverbs 2; Sayings 25

4 *Dictum sapienti sat est.*
A sentence is enough for a sensible man.

Persa l. 729. Source of the proverb *Verbum sapienti sat est* (A word is enough for the wise).

Willis Player
U.S. business executive, 1915–1995

1 A liberal is a person whose interests aren't at stake at the moment.

Quoted in *Reader's Digest,* Nov. 1966

Georgi Valentinovich Plekhanov
Russian political philosopher and revolutionary, 1857–1918

1 He [Hegel] proved that we are free only insofar as we know the laws of nature and sociohistorical development and insofar as we, submitting to them, rely upon them. This was a tremendous gain in the field of philosophy and also in that of social science again which, however, only modern, dialectical materialism has exploited to the full.

"For the Sixtieth Anniversary of Hegel's Death" (1891). Earliest known usage of *dialectical materialism.*

Pliny the Elder
Roman scholar, 23–79

1 *Semper aliquid novi Africam adferre.*
Africa always brings something new.

Historia Naturalis bk. 8, sec. 42. Frequently quoted as *"Ex Africa semper aliquid novi"* (always something new out of Africa). Pliny refers to it as a Greek proverb.

2 *Addito salis grano.*
With the addition of a grain of salt.

Historia Naturalis bk. 23, sec. 149. Usually quoted as *"Cum grano salis"* (with a grain of salt). The reference is to salt being added to Pompey's antidote to poison.

William Plomer
South African–born English writer, 1903–1973

1 On a sofa upholstered in human skin
Mona did researches in original sin.

"Mews Flat Mona: A Memory of the 'Twenties" l. 22 (1940)

George Washington Plunkitt

U.S. politician, 1842–1924

1 There's an honest graft, and I'm an example of how it works. I might sum up the whole thing by sayin': "I seen my opportunities and I took 'em."

Plunkitt of Tammany Hall "Honest Graft and Dishonest Graft" (1905)

Plutarch

Greek biographer, ca. 46–ca. 120

1 As geographers, Sosius, crowd into the edges of their maps parts of the world which they do not know about, adding notes in the margin to the effect that beyond this lies nothing but sandy deserts full of wild beasts, and unapproachable bogs.

Parallel Lives "Theseus" sec. 1

2 For we are told that when a certain man was accusing both of them to him, he [Julius Caesar] said that he had no fear of those fat and long-haired fellows, but rather of those pale and thin ones [Brutus and Cassius].

Parallel Lives "Anthony" sec. 11
See Shakespeare 99

3 Where the lion's skin will not reach, you must patch it out with the fox's.

Parallel Lives "Lysander" sec. 7
See Machiavelli 7

Edgar Allan Poe

U.S. writer, 1809–1849

1 Thy Naiad airs have brought me home,
To the glory that was Greece
And the grandeur that was Rome.

"To Helen" l. 8 (1831)

2 They who dream by day are cognizant of many things which escape those who dream only by night.

"Eleonora" (1841)

3 It appears to me that this mystery is considered insoluble, for the very reason which should cause it to be regarded as easy of solution—I mean for the outré character of its features.

"The Murders in the Rue Morgue" (1841)

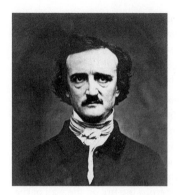

4 True!—nervous—very, very dreadfully nervous I had been and am; but why will you say that I am mad? The disease had sharpened my senses—not destroyed—not dulled them.

"The Tell-Tale Heart" (1843)

5 I admit the deed!—tear up the planks! here, here!—It is the beating of his hideous heart!

"The Tell-Tale Heart" (1843)

6 Once upon a midnight dreary, while I
   pondered, weak and weary,
Over many a quaint and curious volume of
   forgotten lore,
While I nodded, nearly napping, suddenly
   there came a tapping,
As of someone gently rapping, rapping at my
   chamber door.

"The Raven" l. 1 (1845)

7 Ah, distinctly I remember it was in the bleak
   December;
And each separate dying ember wrought its
   ghost upon the floor.
Eagerly I wished the morrow,—vainly had I
   sought to borrow
From my books surcease of sorrow—sorrow for
   the lost Lenore—
For the rare and radiant maiden whom the
   angels name Lenore—
Nameless *here* for evermore.
And the silken, sad, uncertain rustling of each
   purple curtain
Thrilled me—filled me with fantastic terrors
   never felt before.

"The Raven" l. 7 (1845)

8 Deep into that darkness peering, long I stood
    there wondering, fearing,
  Doubting, dreaming dreams no mortal ever
    dared to dream before.
  "The Raven" l. 25 (1845)

9 "Ghastly grim and ancient Raven wandering
    from the Nightly shore—
  Tell me what the lordly name is on the Night's
    Plutonian shore!"
  Quoth the Raven, "Nevermore."
  "The Raven" l. 46 (1845)

10 "Prophet!" said I, "thing of evil!—prophet still,
    if bird or devil!"
  "The Raven" l. 85 (1845)

11 Take thy beak from out my heart, and take thy
    form from off my door!
  Quoth the Raven, "Nevermore."
  "The Raven" l. 101 (1845)

12 And the Raven, never flitting, still is sitting, *still*
    is sitting,
  On the pallid bust of Pallas just above my
    chamber door.
  "The Raven" l. 103 (1845)

13 And his eyes have all the seeming of a demon's
    that is dreaming.
  "The Raven" l. 105 (1845)

14 And my soul from out that shadow that lies
    floating on the floor
  Shall be lifted—nevermore!
  "The Raven" l. 107 (1845)

15 And this maiden she lived with no other
    thought
  Than to love and be loved by me.
  "Annabel Lee" l. 5 (1849)

16 *I* was a child and *she* was a child,
  In this kingdom by the sea;
  But we loved with a love that was more than
    love—
  I and my Annabel Lee—
  With a love that the winged seraphs of Heaven
  Coveted her and me.
  "Annabel Lee" l. 7 (1849)

17 In her sepulchre there by the sea,
  In her tomb by the sounding sea.
  "Annabel Lee" l. 40 (1849)

18 While the stars that oversprinkle
  All the heavens, seem to twinkle
  With a crystalline delight;
  Keeping time, time, time,
  In a sort of Runic rhyme,
  To the tintinnabulation that so musically wells
  From the bells, bells, bells, bells,
  Bells, bells, bells.
  "The Bells" l. 6 (1849)

19 All that we see or seem
  Is but a dream within a dream.
  "A Dream Within a Dream" l. 10 (1849)

Henri Poincaré
French mathematician, 1854–1912

1 Thought is only a gleam in the midst of a long
  night. But it is this gleam which is everything.
  The Value of Science (1904) (translation by George B.
  Halsted)

2 Sociology is the science with the greatest
  number of methods and the least results.
  Science et Méthode ch. 1 (1908)

3 To doubt everything or to believe everything are
  two equally convenient solutions; both dispense
  with the necessity of reflection.
  Quoted in Bertrand Russell, preface to *Science and
  Method* (1913) (the English translation of Poincaré's
  book).

John M. Poindexter
U.S. naval officer and government official,
1936–

1 [*Of the Iran-Contra arms-for-hostages scheme:*] I
  made a very deliberate decision not to ask the
  President, so that I could insulate him from the
  decision and provide some future deniability
  for him if it ever leaked out.
  Testimony at Iran-Contra congressional hearings,
  15 July 1987

Political Slogans

1 All power to the Soviets.
  Slogan of workers in Petrograd (1917)

2 All the Way with LBJ [Lyndon B. Johnson].
  Democratic campaign slogan (1964)

3 America: Love It or Leave It.
  Pro–Vietnam War slogan
  See Kahn 6; Dorothy Parker 16

4 As Maine goes, so goes the nation.

U.S. political saying (ca. 1840)
See Farley 1

5 Ban the bomb.

Campaign for Nuclear Disarmament slogan (1953)

6 Better dead than Red.

Anti-Communist slogan. May have originated with
Josef Goebbels's propaganda phrase during World
War II, *"Lieber tot als rot."*
See Political Slogans 7

7 Better Red than dead.

Nuclear disarmament slogan of late 1950s
See Political Slogans 6

8 Black is beautiful.

Civil rights slogan of mid-1960s
See Bible 156; Langston Hughes 5

9 Blaine, Blaine, Blaine,
The continental liar from the State of Maine.

Democratic campaign jingle (1884)

10 Burn, baby, burn!

African-American militant slogan (1965)

11 Change we can believe in.

Democratic campaign slogan (2008)

12 A Chicken in Every Pot, A Car in Every Garage.

Republican campaign slogan (1928)
See Henri IV 1; Herbert Hoover 3

13 *Ein Reich, ein Volk, ein Führer.*
One realm, one people, one leader.

Nazi Party slogan of early 1930s

14 Fifty-four Forty or Fight.

Slogan of proponents of expansionism (1846).
Frequently said to be a slogan of the war party in
the 1844 presidential campaign and to have been
originated by Senator William Allen of Ohio.
However, Hans Sperber and Travis Trittschuh, in
American Political Terms: An Historical Dictionary,
state that this "is nothing but an unfounded, though
amazingly stubborn legend. We have failed to find
it in sources of that year [1844], and we can state
confidently that it was not used in Allen's senatorial
speeches." The earliest known occurrence of the
slogan was in the *Dollar Newspaper* (Philadelphia,
Pa.), 8 Apr. 1846, where it is humorously spelled
"Phifty-Phour Phorty or Phight." (54°40' is the
latitude of the disputed Oregon territory.)

15 Get the Government Off Our Backs.

Republican campaign slogan (1980)

16 Give 'em hell, Harry.

Democratic campaign slogan (1948)
See Truman 7

17 Guns don't die, people die.

Slogan of supporters of gun control

18 Guns don't kill people, people kill people.

Slogan of opponents of gun control

19 Hell no, we won't go!

Anti–Vietnam War slogan

20 Hey, hey, LBJ, how many kids did you kill
today?

Anti–Vietnam War slogan

21 I Like Ike.

Republican campaign slogan (1952). These words,
referring to Dwight D. Eisenhower, appeared on
buttons as early as 1947.

22 I'll give up my gun when they pry it from my
cold dead hands.

National Rifle Association slogan

23 [*Referring to Barry Goldwater:*] In Your Heart
You Know He's Right.

Republican campaign slogan (1964)

24 Keep Cool with Coolidge.

Republican campaign slogan (1924)

25 Ma! Ma! Where's my pa? Gone to the White
House, ha, ha, ha!

Democratic campaign jingle (1884). The first part of
this was a jibe by hecklers at Democratic candidate
Grover Cleveland, referring to his alleged fathering
of a child out of wedlock; the second part was the
Democrats' rejoinder.

26 Make America great again.

Donald Trump campaign slogan (2016)
See Macron 1

27 Nixon's the One.

Republican campaign slogan (1968)

28 Power to the people.

Black Panther Party slogan (ca. 1968)

29 Prosperity Is Just Around the Corner.

Republican campaign slogan (1932)

30 Save the Whales.

Animal Welfare Institute slogan (1971)

31 Soak the Rich.

Slogan associated with progressive taxation

32 Tippecanoe and Tyler too.

Whig campaign slogan (1840)

33 Turn the rascals out!

Liberal Republican campaign slogan (1872)

34 We'll stand pat!
   Republican campaign slogan (1900)

35 What Britain needs is an iron lady.
   Conservative campaign slogan (1979)

36 When guns are outlawed, only outlaws will have guns.
   Slogan of opponents of gun control

37 The whole world is watching.
   Chant of demonstrators at Democratic National Convention, Chicago, Ill. (1968)

38 Would you buy a used car from this man?
   Anti–Richard Nixon slogan (1960)

39 Yes, we can!
   Democratic Barack Obama campaign slogan for Illinois senator (2004) and U.S. president (2008). The United Farm Workers earlier used the slogan "*Sí se puede* (Yes, it can be done)."
   See Toussaint 1

E. A. Pollard
U.S. journalist and author, 1831–1872

1 The Lost Cause.
   Title of book (1866)
   See Lucan 1

Katha Pollitt
U.S. author, 1949–

1 When you consider that God could have commanded anything he wanted—anything!—the Ten have got to rank as one of the great missed moral opportunities of all time. How different history would have been had he clearly and unmistakably forbidden war, tyranny, taking over other people's countries, slavery, exploitation of workers, cruelty to children, wife-beating, stoning, treating women—or anyone—as chattel or inferior beings.
   Nation, 4 Sept. 2003

Jackson Pollock
U.S. painter, 1912–1956

1 There was a reviewer a while back who wrote that my pictures didn't have any beginning or any end. He didn't mean it as a compliment, but it was. It was a fine compliment.
   Interview, *New Yorker*, 5 Aug. 1950

Marco Polo
Italian traveler, 1254–1324

1 [*"Last words":*] I have not told half of what I saw.
   Attributed in Jacopo d'Acqui, *Imago Mundi seu Chronica* (ca. 1330)

John Pomfret
English clergyman, 1667–1702

1 We live and learn, but not the wiser grow.
   "Reason" l. 112 (1700)

Madame de Pompadour (Jeanne-Antoinette Poisson)
French royal favorite, 1721–1764

1 *Après nous le déluge.*
   After us the deluge.
   Quoted in Madame du Hausset, *Mémoires* (1824). Said to be Pompadour's response to Louis XV after the French defeat in the Battle of Rossbach, 5 Nov. 1757. Some sources attribute the comment to the king himself. In reality, it predated 1757 in French proverbial usage. "Après nous le Déluge" appeared in *Les Principales Aventures de l'Admirable Don Quichotte* (1746).

Alexander Pope
English poet, 1688–1744

1 A little learning is a dangerous thing;
   Drink deep, or taste not the Pierian spring:

There shallow draughts intoxicate the brain,
And drinking largely sobers us again.

An Essay on Criticism l. 215 (1711). Often misquoted as
"A little knowledge is a dangerous thing."
See Drayton 2

2 True wit is Nature to advantage dressed,
   What oft was thought, but ne'er so well
      expressed.

An Essay on Criticism l. 297 (1711)

3 True ease in writing comes from art, not
      chance,
   As those move easiest who learn'd to dance.
   'Tis not enough no harshness gives offence,
   The sound must seem an echo to the sense.

An Essay on Criticism l. 362 (1711)

4 To err is human; to forgive, divine.

An Essay on Criticism l. 525 (1711). The *Oxford
Dictionary of Proverbs* notes, "Although known in
Latin (*humanum est errare*, it is human to err) and
in earlier English versions, this saying is generally
quoted in Pope's words." The *ODP* cites "To offend
is humaine, to repent diuine" (Henry Wotton, 1578)
and "To erre is humane, to repent is divine" (James
Howell, 1659).

5 Fools rush in where angels fear to tread.

An Essay on Criticism l. 625 (1711)

6 The hungry judges soon the sentence sign,
   And wretches hang that jury-men may dine.

The Rape of the Lock canto 3, l. 21 (1714)

7 How happy is the blameless vestal's lot!
   The world forgetting, by the world forgot.
   Eternal sunshine of the spotless mind!

"Eloisa to Abelard" l. 207 (1717)

8 Tell me, Muse, of the man of many wiles.

Translation of the Odyssey, bk. 1, l. 1 (1725–1756)
See Homer 7

9 True friendship's laws are by this rule
      express'd,
   Welcome the coming, speed the parting guest.

Translation of the Odyssey, bk. 15, l. 83 (1725–1756)

10 I never knew any man in my life who could
    not bear another's misfortunes perfectly like a
    Christian.

"Thoughts on Various Subjects" (1727)

11 Nature, and Nature's laws lay hid in night.
    God said, *Let Newton be!* and all was light.

"Epitaph: Intended for Sir Isaac Newton" l. 1 (1730)
See Squire 1

12 Sir, I admit your gen'ral rule
    That every poet is a fool:
    But you yourself may serve to show it,
    That every fool is not a poet.

"Epigram from the French" l. 1 (1732)

13 You beat your pate, and fancy wit will come:
    Knock as you please, there's nobody at home.

"Epigram: You beat your pate" l. 1 (1732)

14 Who shall decide, when doctors disagree?

Epistles to Several Persons "To Lord Bathurst" l. 1 (1733)

15 Die, and endow a college, or a cat.

Epistles to Several Persons "To Lord Bathurst" l. 98
(1733)

16 The ruling passion, be it what it will,
    The ruling passion conquers reason still.

Epistles to Several Persons "To Lord Bathurst" l. 155
(1733)

17 In wit, a man, simplicity, a child.

"Epitaph: On Mr. Gay in Westminster Abbey" l. 2
(1733)

18 Hope springs eternal in the human breast:
    Man never Is, but always To be blest.

An Essay on Man Epistle 1, l. 95 (1733)

19 Vast chain of Being, which from God began,
    Natures aethereal, human, angel, man,
    Beast, bird, fish, insect! what no eye can see,
    No glass can reach; from Infinite to thee,
    From thee to Nothing!

An Essay on Man Epistle 1, l. 237 (1733)

20 And, spite of Pride, in erring Reason's spite,
    One truth is clear, "Whatever IS, is RIGHT."

An Essay on Man Epistle 1, l. 293 (1733)

21 Know then thyself, presume not God to scan;
    The proper study of mankind is man.

An Essay on Man Epistle 2, l. 1 (1733)
See Charron 1

22 Created half to rise, and half to fall;
    Great lord of all things, yet a prey to all;
    Sole judge of truth, in endless error hurled;
    The glory, jest, and riddle of the world!

An Essay on Man Epistle 2, l. 15 (1733)

23 For forms of government let fools contest;
    Whate'er is best administered is best.

An Essay on Man Epistle 3, l. 303 (1733)

24 'Tis education forms the common mind,
   Just as the twig is bent, the tree's inclined.
   Epistles to Several Persons "To Lord Cobham" l. 101
   (1734)

25 Worth makes the man, and want of it the
     fellow;
   The rest is all but leather or prunella.
   An Essay on Man Epistle 4, l. 203 (1734)

26 An honest man's the noblest work of God.
   An Essay on Man Epistle 4, l. 248 (1734)

27 If parts allure thee, think how Bacon shined,
   The wisest, brightest, meanest of mankind.
   An Essay on Man Epistle 4, l. 281 (1734)

28 Thou wert my guide, philosopher, and friend.
   An Essay on Man Epistle 4, l. 390 (1734)

29 All our knowledge is, ourselves to know.
   An Essay on Man Epistle 4, l. 398 (1734)

30 There St. John mingles with my friendly bowl
   The feast of reason and the flow of soul.
   Imitations of Horace bk. 2, Satire 1, l. 127 (1734)

31 The Muse but served to ease some friend, not
     wife,
   To help me through this long disease, my life.
   "An Epistle to Dr. Arbuthnot" l. 131 (1735)

32 Damn with faint praise, assent with civil leer,
   And without sneering, teach the rest to sneer;
   Willing to wound, and yet afraid to strike,
   Just hint a fault, and hesitate dislike.
   "An Epistle to Dr. Arbuthnot" l. 201 (1735)
   See Wycherley 1

33 Satire or sense, alas! can Sporus feel?
   Who breaks a butterfly upon a wheel?
   "An Epistle to Dr. Arbuthnot" l. 307 (1735)

34 Unlearn'd, he knew no schoolman's subtle art,
   No language, but the language of the heart.
   "An Epistle to Dr. Arbuthnot" l. 398 (1735)

35 Chaste to her husband, frank to all beside,
   A teeming mistress, but a barren bride.
   Epistles to Several Persons "To a Lady" l. 71 (1735)

36 I am his Highness' dog at Kew;
   Pray, tell me sir, whose dog are you?
   "Epigram Engraved on the Collar of a Dog Which I
   Gave to His Royal Highness" (1738)
   See Nursery Rhymes 15

37 Poetic Justice, with her lifted scale.
   The Dunciad bk. 1, l. 52 (1742)

Karl Popper
Austrian-born English philosopher, 1902–1994

1 I shall certainly admit a system as empirical
   or scientific only if it is capable of being *tested*
   by experience. These considerations suggest
   that not the *verifiability* but the *falsifiability*
   of a system is to be taken as a criterion of
   demarcation. . . . *It must be possible for an
   empirical scientific system to be refuted by
   experience.*
   The Logic of Scientific Discovery ch. 1 (1934)

Cole Porter
U.S. songwriter, 1891–1964

1 Night and day you are the one,
   Only you beneath the moon and under the sun.
   "Night and Day" (song) (1932)

2 In olden days, a glimpse of stocking
   Was looked on as something shocking,
   But now, God knows,
   Anything goes.
   "Anything Goes" (song) (1934)

3 Good authors too who once knew better words
   Now only use four-letter words,
   Writing prose,
   Anything goes.
   "Anything Goes" (song) (1934)

4 Times have changed,
   And we've often rewound the clock,
   Since the Puritans got a shock,

When they landed on Plymouth Rock.
If today,
Any shock they should try to stem,
'Stead of landing on Plymouth Rock,
Plymouth Rock would land on them.
"Anything Goes" (song) (1934)
See Malcolm X 2

5 I get no kick from champagne.
Mere alcohol doesn't thrill me at all,
So tell me why should it be true
That I get a kick out of you?
"I Get a Kick Out of You" (song) (1934)

6 You're the top!
You're the Colosseum.
You're the top!
You're the Louvre Museum.
"You're the Top" (song) (1934)

7 You're a melody from a symphony by Strauss,
You're a Bendel bonnet,
A Shakespeare sonnet,
You're Mickey Mouse.
"You're the Top" (song) (1934)

8 You're the Nile,
You're the Tow'r of Pisa,
You're the smile
On the Mona Lisa.
"You're the Top" (song) (1934)

9 You're the top!
You're Mahatma Gandhi.
You're the top!
You're Napoleon brandy.
"You're the Top" (song) (1934)

10 I'm a toy balloon that is fated soon to pop,
But if, baby, I'm the bottom
You're the top!
"You're the Top" (song) (1934)

11 When they begin the beguine
It brings back the sound of music so tender,
It brings back a night of tropical splendor,
It brings back a memory ever green.
"Begin the Beguine" (song) (1935)

12 It was just one of those things,
Just one of those crazy flings,
One of those bells that now and then rings,
Just one of those things.
"Just One of Those Things" (song) (1935)

13 It was just one of those nights,
Just one of those fabulous flights,
A trip to the moon on gossamer wings,
Just one of those things.
"Just One of Those Things" (song) (1935)

14 It's delightful, it's delicious, it's de-lovely.
"It's De-Lovely" (song) (1936)

15 I've got you under my skin,
I've got you deep in the heart of me,
So deep in my heart, you're really a part of me,
I've got you under my skin.
"I've Got You Under My Skin" (song) (1936)

16 My Heart Belongs to Daddy.
Title of song (1938)

17 Oh, give me land, lots of land under starry skies
above,
Don't fence me in.
"Don't Fence Me In" (song) (1944). The lyrics for this
song closely follow a song written by Bob Fletcher, for
which Porter purchased the rights.

18 I want to ride to the ridge where the West
commences,
Gaze at the moon till I lose my senses,
Can't look at hobbles and I can't stand fences,
Don't fence me in.
"Don't Fence Me In" (song) (1944)

19 Ev'ry time we say goodbye
I die a little,
Ev'ry time we say goodbye
I wonder why a little.
"Ev'ry Time We Say Goodbye" (song) (1944)

20 But I'm always true to you, darlin', in my
fashion,
Yes, I'm always true to you, darlin', in my way.
"Always True to You in My Fashion" (song) (1948)
See Dowson 1

21 All the world loves a clown.
"Be a Clown" (song) (1948)

22 Brush up your Shakespeare,
Start quoting him now.
"Brush Up Your Shakespeare" (song) (1948)

23 I love Paris in the springtime.
"I Love Paris" (song) (1953)

24 I love the look of you, the lure of you
The sweet of you, and the pure of you

The eyes, the arms, and the mouth of you
The east, west, north, and the south of you.
"All of You" (song) (1954)

25 Birds do it, bees do it,
Even educated fleas do it.
Let's do it, let's fall in love.
"Let's Do It" (song) (1954). These words were added
to the original 1928 song, replacing lines including
"Chinks do it, Japs do it" because Porter realized that
those lyrics were offensive.

26 Who Wants to Be a Millionaire?
Title of song (1956)

Eleanor Porter
U.S. novelist, 1868–1920

1 Pollyanna.
Title of book (1913)

Katherine Anne Porter
U.S. writer, 1890–1980

1 Miracles are instantaneous, they cannot be
summoned, but come of themselves, usually at
unlikely moments and to those who least expect
them.
Ship of Fools pt. 3 (1962)

Robert P. Porter
U.S. government official, 1852–1917

1 Up to and including 1880 the country had
a frontier of settlement, but at present the
unsettled area has been so broken into by
isolated bodies of settlement that there can
hardly be said to be a frontier line. In the
discussion of its extent and its westward
movement it can not, therefore, any longer have
a place in the census reports.
Report on Population of the United States at the Eleventh
Census: 1890 "Progress of the Nation: 1790 to 1890"
(1895)
See Frederick Jackson Turner 2

Beilby Porteus
English poet and bishop, 1731–1808

1 One murder made a villain,
Millions a hero.
Death l. 154 (1759)
See Jean Rostand 1; Edward Young 3

2 Teach him how to live,
And, oh! still harder lesson! how to die.
Death l. 319 (1759)
See Montaigne 7

Beatrix Potter
English children's book writer, 1866–1943

1 Once upon a time there were four little Rabbits,
and their names were Flopsy, Mopsy, Cotton-
tail, and Peter.
The Tale of Peter Rabbit (1902)

2 Don't go into Mr. McGregor's garden: your
father had an accident there, he was put into a
pie by Mrs. McGregor.
The Tale of Peter Rabbit (1902)

3 NO MORE TWIST.
The Tailor of Gloucester (1903)

4 But Tom Kitten has always been afraid of a
rat; he never durst face anything that is bigger
than—A Mouse.
The Tale of Samuel Whiskers (1908)

Stephen Potter
English writer and radio producer, 1900–1969

1 What is gamesmanship? . . . "The Art of
Winning Games Without Actually Cheating"—
that is my personal "working definition."
The Theory and Practice of Gamesmanship ch. 1 (1947)

2 One-Upmanship.
Title of book (1952)

Eugène Pottier
French politician, 1816–1887

1 Debout! les damnés de la terre!
Debout! les forçats de la faim!
La raison tonne en son cratère,
C'est l'éruption de la fin . . .
Nous ne sommes rien, soyons tout!
C'est la lutte finale
Groupons-nous, et, demain,
L'Internationale
Sera le genre humain.
On your feet, you damned souls of the earth!
On your feet, inmates of hunger's prison!
Reason is rumbling in its crater, and its final
eruption is on its way. . . . We are nothing, let

us be everything! This is the final conflict: let us form up and, tomorrow, the International will encompass the human race.
"L'Internationale" (song) (1871)

Ezra Pound

U.S. poet, 1885–1972

1 Poetry is about as much a "criticism of life" as red-hot iron is a criticism of fire.
The Spirit of Romance ch. 9 (1910)

2 Poetry must be *as well written as prose*.
Letter to Harriet Monroe, Jan. 1915

3 Objectivity and again objectivity, and expression: no hindside-before-ness, no straddled adjectives ("as addled mosses dank"), no Tennysonianness of speech; nothing—nothing that you couldn't, in some circumstance, in the stress of some emotion, actually say.
Letter to Harriet Monroe, Jan. 1915

4 The apparition of these faces in the crowd; Petals on a wet, black bough.
"In a Station of the Metro" l. 1 (1916)

5 I make a pact with you, Walt Whitman— I have detested you long enough.
"A Pact" l. 1 (1916)

6 We have one sap and one root— Let there be commerce between us.
"A Pact" l. 8 (1916)

7 Your mind and you are our Sargasso Sea.
"Portrait d'une Femme" l. 1 (1916)

8 Winter is icummen in,
Lhude sing Goddamm,
Raineth drop and staineth slop,
And how the wind doth ramm!
"Ancient Music" l. 1 (1917)

9 For three years, out of key with his time,
He strove to resuscitate the dead art
Of poetry; to maintain "the sublime"
In the old sense. Wrong from the start—
No, hardly, but seeing he had been born
In a half savage country, out of date.
Hugh Selwyn Mauberley "E. P. *Ode Pour l'Élection de Son Sépulchre*" l. 1 (1920)

10 His true Penelope was Flaubert,
He fished by obstinate isles;
Observed the elegance of Circe's hair
Rather than the mottoes on sun-dials.
Hugh Selwyn Mauberley "E. P. *Ode Pour l'Élection de Son Sépulchre*" l. 13 (1920)

11 Unaffected by "the march of events,"
He passed from men's memory in *l'an trentuniesme*
De son eage; the case presents
No adjunct to the Muses' diadem.
Hugh Selwyn Mauberley "E. P. *Ode Pour l'Élection de Son Sépulchre*" l. 17 (1920)

12 The age demanded an image
Of its accelerated grimace,
Something for the modern stage,
Not, at any rate, an Attic grace.
Hugh Selwyn Mauberley "E. P. *Ode Pour l'Élection de Son Sépulchre*" l. 21 (1920)

13 Better mendacities
Than the classics in paraphrase!
Hugh Selwyn Mauberley "E. P. *Ode Pour l'Élection de Son Sépulchre*" l. 27 (1920)

14 There died a myriad,
And of the best among them,
For an old bitch gone in the teeth,
For a botched civilization.
Hugh Selwyn Mauberley "E. P. *Ode Pour l'Élection de Son Sépulchre*" l. 88 (1920)

15 Lie quiet Divus.
Cantos no. 1, l. 68 (1925)

16 Hang it all, Robert Browning,
there can be but the one "Sordello."
Cantos no. 2, l. 1 (1925)

17 And even I can remember
   A day when the historians left blanks in their
      writings,
   I mean for things they didn't know.
   Cantos no. 13, l. 69 (1925)

18 Great literature is simply language charged
   with meaning to the utmost possible degree.
   How to Read pt. 2 (1931)

19 Literature is news that STAYS news.
   The ABC of Reading ch. 2 (1934)

20 Genius is the capacity to see ten things where
   the ordinary man sees one, and the man of
   talent sees two or three, PLUS the ability to
   register that multiple perception in the material
   of his art.
   Jefferson and/or Mussolini ch. 23 (1935)

21 With usura hath no man a house of good stone
   each block cut smooth and well fitting.
   Cantos no. 45, l. 1 (1937)

22 No picture is made to endure nor to live with
   but it is made to sell and sell quickly
   with usura, sin against nature,
   is thy bread ever more of stale rags
   is thy bread dry as paper.
   Cantos no. 45, l. 11 (1937)

23 Usura slayeth the child in the womb
   It stayeth the young man's courting
   It hath brought palsey to bed, lyeth
   between the young bride and her bridegroom
   CONTRA NATURAM
   They have brought whores for Eleusis
   Corpses are set to banquet
   at behest of usura.
   Cantos no. 45, l. 42 (1937)

24 What thou lovest well remains, the rest is dross
   What thou lov'st well shall not be reft from thee
   What thou lov'st well is thy true heritage
   Whose world, or mine or theirs or is it of none?
   First came the seen, then thus the palpable
      Elysium, though it were in the halls of hell.
   Cantos no. 81, l. 134 (1948)

25 The ant's a centaur in his dragon world.
   Pull down thy vanity, it is not man
   Made courage, or made order, or made grace,
      Pull down thy vanity, I say pull down.
   Cantos no. 81, l. 144 (1948)

26 Learn of the green world what can be thy place
   In scaled invention or true artistry,
   Pull down thy vanity,
      Paquin pull down!
   The green casque has outdone your elegance.
   Cantos no. 81, l. 148 (1948)

27 Thou art a beaten dog beneath the hail,
   A swollen magpie in a fitful sun,
   Half black half white
   Nor knowst'ou wing from tail.
   Cantos no. 81, l. 155 (1948)

28 To have gathered from the air a live tradition
      or from a fine old eye the unconquered
      flame
   This is not vanity.
   Here error is all in the not done,
      all in the diffidence that faltered.
   Cantos no. 81, l. 170 (1948)

29 America, my country, is almost a continent and
   hardly yet a nation.
   Patria Mia pt. 1, sec. 1 (1950)

30 But the beauty is not the madness
   Tho' my errors and wrecks lie about me.
   And I am not a demigod,
   I cannot make it cohere.
   Cantos no. 116, l. 26 (1972)

Roscoe Pound
U.S. legal scholar, 1870–1964

1 Law must be stable and yet it cannot stand still.
   Interpretations of Legal History Lecture 1 (1923)

Nicolas Poussin
French painter, 1594–1665

1 The grand manner consists of four elements:
   subject or theme, concept, structure, and style.
   The first requirement, fundamental to all the
   others, is that the subject and the narrative be
   grandiose, such as battles, heroic actions, and
   religious themes.
   Quoted in Giovanni Pietro Bellori, *Lives of the Modern
   Painters, Sculptors and Architects* (1672)

Hortense Powdermaker

U.S. anthropologist, 1896–1970

1 South Sea natives who have been exposed to American movies classify them into two types, "kiss-kiss" and "bang-bang."

Hollywood, the Dream Factory: An Anthropologist Looks at the Movie-Makers introduction (1950)
See Kael 1

Adam Clayton Powell, Jr.

U.S. politician, 1908–1972

1 To demand these God-given rights is to seek black power.

Baccalaureate address at Howard University, Washington, D.C., 29 May 1966
See Carmichael 2; Richard Wright 3

2 A man's respect for law and order exists in precise relationship to the size of his paycheck.
Keep the Faith, Baby! "Black Power: A Form of Godly Power" (1967)

3 Keep the faith, Baby.
Quoted in *Wash. Post*, 10 Oct. 1966
See Bible 379

Anthony Powell

English novelist, 1905–2000

1 All women are stimulated by the news that any wife has left any husband.
The Acceptance World ch. 4 (1955)

Colin Powell

U.S. government official and military leader, 1937–

1 Our strategy to go after this [Iraq's] army is very, very simple. First, we are going to cut it off, and then we are going to kill it.
News conference, 23 Jan. 1991

2 We have gone forth from our shores repeatedly over the last hundred years and we've done this as recently as the last year in Afghanistan and put wonderful young men and women at risk, many of whom have lost their lives, and we have asked for nothing except enough ground to bury them in.
Remarks at World Economic Forum, Davos, Switzerland, 26 Jan. 2003

3 There can be no doubt that Saddam Hussein has biological weapons and the capability to rapidly produce more, many more.
Speech to United Nations Security Council, New York, N.Y., 5 Feb. 2003

4 [*Comment during lead-up to Iraq War, upon being reminded that George W. Bush claimed to sleep like a baby:*] I sleep like a baby, too—every two hours I wake up screaming.
Quoted in *New Yorker*, 10 Feb. 2003

Lewis F. Powell, Jr.

U.S. judge, 1907–1998

1 Under the First Amendment there is no such thing as a false idea. However pernicious an opinion may seem, we depend for its correction not on the conscience of judges and juries but on the competition of other ideas.
Gertz v. Robert Welch, Inc. (1974)

Thomas Reed Powell

U.S. legal scholar, 1880–1955

1 If you think that you can think about a thing inextricably attached to something else without thinking of the thing which it is attached to, then you have a legal mind.
Quoted in Thurman W. Arnold, *The Symbols of Government* (1935)

Helen Prejean

U.S. nun and activist, 1939–

1 [*On her opposition to the death penalty:*] People are more than the worst thing they have ever done in their lives.
Quoted in *N.Y. Times Magazine*, 9 May 1993

Elvis Presley

U.S. singer, 1935–1977

1 Love me tender, love me sweet,
Never let me go.
"Love Me Tender" (song) (1956). Cowritten with Vera Matson.

2 I don't know anything about music. In my line you don't have to.
Quoted in Robert Byrne, *The Other 637 Best Things Anybody Ever Said* (1984)

Jacques Prévert

French poet and screenwriter, 1900–1977

1 *Je suis comme je suis*
Je suis faite comme ça.
I am what I am
I am made like that.
Paroles "Je Suis Comme Je Suis" (1945)
See Segar 2

Marcel Prévost

French novelist and playwright, 1862–1941

1 *Les Demi-Vierges.*
The Demi-Virgins.
Title of book (1894)

Prince (Prince Rogers Nelson)

U.S. rock musician, 1958–2016

1 Tonight I'm gonna party like it's nineteen
ninety nine.
"1999" (song) (1982)

2 I never meant to cause you any sorrow
I never meant to cause you any pain
I only wanted to one time see you laughing
I only wanted to see you laughing in the purple
rain.
"Purple Rain" (song) (1984)

3 Dream if you will a courtyard
An ocean of violets in bloom
Animals strike curious poses
They feel the heat
Between me and you.
"When Doves Cry" (song) (1984)

Matthew Prior

English poet, 1664–1721

1 No, no; for my virginity,
When I lose that, says Rose, I'll die:
Behind the elms last night, cried Dick,
Rose, were you not extremely sick?
"A True Maid" (1718)

V. S. (Victor Sawdon) Pritchett

English writer and critic, 1900–1997

1 The principle of procrastinated rape is said to
be the ruling one in all the great best-sellers.
The Living Novel "Clarissa" (1946)

Adelaide Ann Procter

English poet, 1825–1864

1 A Lost Chord.
Title of poem (1858)

2 Seated one day at the organ,
I was weary and ill at ease,
And my fingers wandered idly
Over the noisy keys.
"A Lost Chord" l. 1 (1858)

3 But I struck one chord of music,
Like the sound of a great Amen.
"A Lost Chord" l. 7 (1858)

4 No star is ever lost we once have seen,
We always may be what we might have been.
"A Legend of Provence" l. 284 (1861)

Propertius

Roman poet, ca. 54 B.C.–A.D. 2

1 *Semper in absentes felicior aestus amantes.*
Absence makes the heart grow fonder.
Elegies bk. 2, elegy 33, l. 43
See Proverbs 1

Protagoras

Greek philosopher, ca. 485 B.C.–ca. 410 B.C.

1 There are two sides to every question.
Quoted in Diogenes Laertius, *Lives of Eminent Philosophers*

2 Man is the measure of all things.
Quoted in Plato, *Theaetetus*

Pierre-Joseph Proudhon

French reformer, 1809–1865

1 *La propriété c'est le vol.*
Property is theft.
Qu'est-ce que la Propriété? (What Is Property?) ch. 1
(1840)

2 *La Guerre et la Paix.*
War and Peace.
Title of book (1862). *Cassell Companion to Quotations*,
ed. Nigel Rees, notes that, according to Henry
Troyat's biography of Tolstoy, the latter borrowed the
title of his novel from Proudhon.

Annie Proulx

U.S. writer, 1935–

1 You know, one of the tragedies of real life is that there is no background music.
The Shipping News ch. 10 (1993)

2 For if Jack Buggit could escape from the pickle jar, if a bird with a broken neck could fly away, what else might be possible? Water may be older than light, diamonds crack in hot goat's blood, mountaintops give off cold fire, forests appear in mid-ocean, it may happen that a crab is caught with the shadow of a hand on its back, that the wind be imprisoned in a bit of knotted string. And it may be that love sometimes occurs without pain or misery.
The Shipping News ch. 39 (1993)

3 I wish I knew how to quit you.
"Brokeback Mountain" (1997)

Marcel Proust

French novelist, 1871–1922

1 *À la Recherche du Temps Perdu.*
In Search of Lost Time.
Title of multivolume book (1913–1927). Translated into English by C. K. Scott Moncrieff (1922–1931) with the title *Remembrance of Things Past*.
See Shakespeare 417

2 For a long time I used to go to bed early.
Du Côté de Chez Swann (Swann's Way) (1913) (translation by C. K. Scott Moncrieff and Terence Kilmartin)

3 And suddenly the memory revealed itself. The taste was that of the little piece of madeleine which . . . my aunt Léonie used to give me, dipping it first in her own cup of tea or tisane.
Du Côté de Chez Swann (Swann's Way) (1913) (translation by C. K. Scott Moncrieff and Terence Kilmartin)

4 Everything we think of as great has come to us from neurotics. It is they and they alone who found religions and create great works of art. The world will never realize how much it owes to them and what they have suffered in order to bestow their gifts on it.
Le Côté de Guermantes (The Guermantes Way) pt. 1 (1921). George Seldes, *The Great Thoughts*, quotes Ramon Guthrie: "This passage was meant to show what fools people who are capable of uttering such idiocies are. . . . It is slap-stick irony that Proust puts into the mouth of a fool (Boulbon) in order to show what a fool he was."

5 It is in sickness that we are compelled to recognize that we do not live alone but are chained to a being from a different realm, from whom we are worlds apart, who has no knowledge of us and by whom it is impossible to make ourselves understood: our body. . . . To ask pity of our body is like discoursing in front of an octopus, for which our words can have no more meaning than the sound of the tides, and with which we should be appalled to find ourselves condemned to live.
Le Côté de Guermantes (The Guermantes Way) pt. 1 (1921) (translation by C. K. Scott Moncrieff and Terence Kilmartin)

6 An artist has no need to express his thought directly in his work for the latter to reflect its quality; it has even been said that the highest praise of God consists in the denial of Him by the atheist who finds creation so perfect that it can dispense with a creator.
Le Côté de Guermantes (The Guermantes Way) pt. 2 (1921) (translation by C. K. Scott Moncrieff and Terence Kilmartin)

7 The idea of Time was of value to me for yet another reason: it was a spur. . . . This life that we live in half-darkness can be illumined, this life that at every moment we distort can be restored to its true pristine shape, that a life, in short, can be realized within the confines of a book! How happy would be, I thought, the man who had the power to write such a book! What a task awaited him!
Le Temps Retrouvé (Time Regained) (1926) (translation by C. K. Scott Moncrieff and Terence Kilmartin)

8 The truth is that every morning war is declared afresh. And the men who wish to continue it are as guilty as the men who began it, more guilty perhaps, for the latter perhaps did not foresee all its horrors.
Le Temps Retrouvé (Time Regained) (1926) (translation by C. K. Scott Moncrieff and Terence Kilmartin)

9 In reality every reader is, while he is reading, the reader of his own self. The writer's work is merely a kind of optical instrument which he

offers to the reader to enable him to discern what, without this book, he would perhaps never have perceived in himself.

Le Temps Retrouvé (Time Regained) (1926) (translation by C. K. Scott Moncrieff and Terence Kilmartin)

Olive Higgins Prouty

U.S. novelist, 1882–1974

1 O Jerry . . . Don't let's ask for the moon! We have the stars!

Now, Voyager ch. 29 (1941). Ellipsis in the original.

Proverbs

Listed alphabetically by first significant word of the proverb. Citations are those of the earliest known documented English-language usage. Most of the first uses are taken from the Oxford Dictionary of Proverbs, *but many of the usages in the ODP have been improved upon. The wording given for the proverb is that of the earliest known usage unless otherwise indicated, with older variant wordings or analogues in other languages explained in annotations. This Proverbs category includes only those proverbs attested before 1900; those whose evidence begins after 1900 are listed under Modern Proverbs. See also Sayings and Anonymous. Quotations with a known originator that have become proverbial are listed under the originator's name.*

1 Absence makes the heart grow fonder.

Godey's Magazine and Lady's Book, Nov. 1844. The *Oxford Dictionary of Proverbs* notes that Propertius much earlier wrote "Passion [is] always warmer towards absent lovers" in his *Elegies.*
See Propertius 1

2 Accidents will happen.

Robert Shiells, *The Lives of the Poets of Great Britain and Ireland* (1753)
See Robert Burns 3; Dickens 67; Disraeli 7; Modern Proverbs 100; Orwell 17; Plautus 3; Sayings 25

3 There is no accounting for tastes.

Ann Radcliffe, *The Mysteries of Udolpho* (1794). Also current in the form "There is no accounting for taste." The *Oxford Dictionary of Proverbs* states: "The saying is a version of the Latin tag *de gustibus non est disputandum,* there is no disputing about tastes. Cf. 1599 J. MINSHEU *Dialogues in Spanish* 6 Against ones liking there is no disputing."

4 Actions speak louder than words.

Melancholy State of Province (1736)

5 After a storm comes a calm.

Claudius Hollyband, *French Littleton* (1576)

6 Age before beauty.

Western Horticultural Review, Nov. 1851

7 All good things must come to an end.

Henry M. Field, *Summer Pictures* (1859)

8 It takes all sorts to make a world.

Douglas Jerrold, *Story of a Feather* (1844). The *Oxford Dictionary of Proverbs* records "In the world there must bee of all sorts" (1620) and "The World . . . has people of all sorts" (1767).

9 All things come to those who wait.

Violet Fane, *From Dawn to Noon* (1872). The *Oxford Dictionary of Proverbs* documents earlier variants back to 1530, including "everything comes if a man will only wait" (Disraeli, 1847) and "all things come to him who will but wait" (Longfellow, 1863).

10 Any port in a storm.

John Cleland, *Memoirs of a Woman of Pleasure* (1749)

11 Appearances are deceptive.

Toby Meanwell, *A Voyage Through Hell* (1770). Giovanni Torriano, in *Italian Proverbs* (1666), has "Appearance oft deceives." The *Oxford Dictionary of Proverbs* cites "appearances are very deceitful" (1748). Today the form "appearances are deceiving" is the usual one.

12 An apple does not fall far from the tree.

Jewish South (Richmond, Va.), 13 Oct. 1893. Wolfgang Mieder, in *Strategies of Wisdom: Anglo-American and German Proverb Studies* (2000), notes that "The apple does not fall far from the stem" appears in Ralph Waldo Emerson's notebook covering the years 1824 to 1836. Mieder also traces the proverb back to 1554 in German.

13 April showers bring forth May flowers.

John Ray, *English Proverbs* (1670). The *Oxford Dictionary of Proverbs* records similar formulations dating back to ca. 1560.

14 Ask me no questions and I'll tell you no lies.

Oliver Goldsmith, *She Stoops to Conquer* (1773). Goldsmith's wording was "fibs" instead of "lies."

15 Bad news travels fast.

Lady's Book, 1 Oct. 1830. The earliest variant in the *Oxford Dictionary of Proverbs* is in Thomas Kyd, *The Spanish Tragedy* (1592), "euill newes flie faster still than good."

16 A bad penny is sure to return.

Rose H. Thorpe, *The Fenton Family* (1884). The *Oxford Dictionary of Proverbs* records similar expressions beginning with "like a bad penny it returnd. to me again" (Abigail Adams, 1766) and "the bad shilling is sure enough to come back again" (Walter Scott, 1824).

17 Beauty is in the eye of the beholder.

> Richard Cumberland, *The Observer* (1788). Cumberland's wording is "Beauty, gentlemen, is in the eye, I aver it to be in the eye of the beholder and not in the object itself." The *Oxford Dictionary of Proverbs* states: "The idea is a very old one: THEOCRITUS *Idyll* . . . for in the eyes of love that which is not beautiful often seems beautiful. Cf. 1742 HUME *Essays Moral & Political* II. 151 Beauty, properly speaking, lyes . . . in the Sentiment or Taste of the Reader."

18 Beauty is only skin-deep.

> Thomas Adams, *The Blacke Devil or the Apostate* (1615). Adams's actual wording was "the beauty of the fairest woman is but skin-deep."
> *See Jean Kerr 1*

19 Beggars can't be choosers.

> *Vermont Watchman and State Journal* (Montpelier, Vt.), 5 Mar. 1846. The *Oxford Dictionary of Proverbs* notes: "Cf. mid 15th-cent. Fr. *qui empruncte ne peult choisir*, he who borrows cannot choose. 1546 J. HEYWOOD *Dialogue of Proverbs* I. x. D1 Folke say alwaie, beggers shulde be no choosers."

20 The best things come in small packages.

> *Atlanta Constitution*, 19 Nov. 1899. According to the *Oxford Dictionary of Proverbs*, "*Parcels* sometimes replaces *packages*. Cf. 13th-cent. Fr. *menue[s] parceles ensemble sunt beles*, small packages considered together are beautiful; 1659 J. HOWELL *Proverbs* (French) 10 The best ointments are put in little boxes." The *ODP* cites an 1877 letter: "the best things are (said to be) wrapped in small parcels (proverb)."

21 It's best to be on the safe side.

> *Lady's Book*, Oct. 1832. The *Oxford Dictionary of Proverbs* records expressions involving "safe side" or "sure side" back to 1668.

22 Better be safe than sorry.

> *N.Y. Times*, 3 Mar. 1882. The *Oxford Dictionary of Proverbs* records "it's betther be sure than sorry" from Samuel Lover, *Rory O'More* (1837).

23 Better late than never.

> John Lydgate, *The Assembly of Gods* (ca. 1450). A note in the *Oxford Dictionary of Proverbs* reads: "Cf. DIONYSIUS OF HALICARNASSUS *Roman Antiquities* ix. 9 . . . it is better to start doing what one has to late than not at all."

24 Better the devil you know than the devil you don't know.

> Anthony Trollope, *Barchester Towers* (1857)

25 The bigger the better.

> *N.Y. Times*, 21 June 1891

26 A bird in the hand is worth two in the bush.

> John Bunyan, *Pilgrim's Progress* (1678). The *Oxford Dictionary of Proverbs* notes: "Cf. 13th-cent. L. *plus valet in manibus avis unica quam dupla silvis*, one bird in the hands is worth more than two in the woods. . . . *c* 1470 *Harley MS 3362* f.4 Betyr ys a byrd in the hond than tweye in the wode."

27 Birds of a feather flock together.

> John Minsheu, *A Spanish Grammar* (1599). The *Oxford Dictionary of Proverbs* cites Ecclesiasticus 27:9 ("The birds will resort unto their like") and a 1545 source ("Byrdes of on kynde and color flok and flye allwayes together").

28 Don't bite off more than you can chew.

> *Sacramento Daily Record-Union*, 3 Aug. 1881

29 Blessed is the man who expects nothing, for he shall never be disappointed.

> John Gay and Alexander Pope, Letter to Fortescue, 23 Sept. 1725

30 There's no getting blood out of a turnip.

> Frederick Marryat, *Japhet* (1836). The *Oxford Dictionary of Proverbs* documents similar expressions going back to ca. 1435, when John Lydgate wrote, "Harde to likke hony out of a marbil stoon."

31 Blood's thicker than water.

> Allan Ramsay, *A Collection of Scots Proverbs* (1750). The *Oxford Dictionary of Proverbs* compares this proverb with the twelfth-century German one, "*ouch hoer ich sagen, daz sippebluot von wassere niht verdirbet*, also I hear it said that kin-blood is not spoiled by water."

32 Don't judge a book by its cover.

> *L.A. Times*, 14 Mar. 1897. "Never judge a book by the cover" appeared in Horace Smith, *The Tin Trumpet* (1859).

33 Boys will be boys.

> *Lady's Book*, Apr. 1832. The *Oxford Dictionary of Proverbs* records "youth will be youthfull" from 1601, and "girls will be girls" from 1826.

34 What is bred in the bone will appear in the flesh.

> *New-York Weekly Museum*, 6 Apr. 1816. The *Oxford Dictionary of Proverbs* documents variants back to ca. 1470: "Harde hit ys to take oute off the fleysshe that ys bredde in the bone" (Thomas Malory, *Morte d'Arthur*). That dictionary also notes "medieval L. *osse radicatum raro de carne recedit*, that which is rooted in the bone rarely comes out from the flesh."

35 You can't make bricks without straw.

> T. Hyde, Letter (1658). Hyde's wording is "It is an hard task to make bricks without straw." According to the *Oxford Dictionary of Proverbs*, this expression is "frequently used as a metaphorical phrase, *to make bricks without straw*. A (misapplied) allusion to EXODUS v. 7 (AV) Ye shall no more give the people straw to make brick, as heretofore: let them go and gather straw for themselves."

36 Always a bridesmaid, never a bride.

Godey's Lady's Book and Magazine, Feb. 1871. The actual wording in this source is "Three times a bridesmaid, never a bride."
See Fred W. Leigh 1

37 A burnt child dreads the fire.

Proverbs of Hending (ca. 1250). The wording in this source is "Brend child fuir fordredeth."

38 Business before pleasure.

L. E. Landon, *Francesca Carrara* (1834)

39 Let the buyer beware.

John Fitzherbert, *A Book of Husbandry* (1523). Fitzherbert's actual words are "And [if] he [a horse] be tame and haue ben rydden vpon than caveat emptor be ware thou byer." The *Oxford Dictionary of Proverbs* notes, "The Latin tag *caveat emptor* is also frequently found: *caveat emptor, quia ignorare non debuit quod jus alienum emit,* let the purchaser beware, for he ought not to be ignorant of the nature of the property which he is buying from another party."

40 Let bygones be bygones.

Francis Nethersole, *Parables* (1648). The *Oxford Dictionary of English Proverbs* records earlier variants going back to 1577.

41 When the cat's away, the mice will play.

Thomas Heywood, *A Woman Killed with Kindness* (1607). The wording in Heywood is "when the cats away, the mouse may play." The *Oxford Dictionary of Proverbs* states: "Cf. early 14th-cent. Fr. *ou chat na rat regne,* where there is no cat the rat is king; *c* 1470 *Harley MS 3362* . . . The mows lordchypythe [rules] ther a cat ys nawt."

42 All cats are gray in the dark.

Thomas Lodge, *A Margarite of America* (1596). The *Oxford Dictionary of Proverbs* also records "when all candels be out, all cats be grey" (ca. 1549).

43 A chain cannot be stronger than its weakest link.

John Walker, *Euclid's Elements of Plane Geometry* (1827)

44 Some things never change.

Saturday Evening Post, 7 Feb. 1885

45 Charity begins at home.

John Wycliffe, *English Works* (ca. 1383). Wycliffe's wording is "Charite schuld bigyne at hem-self."

46 Children should be seen and not heard.

John Quincy Adams, *Memoirs* (1820). Adams's words are "children in company should be seen and not heard." The *Oxford Dictionary of Proverbs* records earlier versions, referring to women rather than children, going back to ca. 1400 ("a mayde schuld be seen, but not herd").

47 Circumstances alter cases.

W. Heath, *Memoirs* (1776)

48 Clothes make the man.

Cincinnati Literary Gazette, 9 Apr. 1825. The *Oxford Dictionary of Proverbs* gives much older versions, beginning with the Greek "the man is his clothing."

49 Every cloud has a silver lining.

American Publishers' Circular and Literary Gazette, 15 Dec. 1855. The *Oxford Dictionary of Proverbs* notes the following older quotation: "1634 MILTON *Comus* I. 93 Was I deceiv'd, or did a sable cloud Turn forth her silver lining on the night?"
See DeSylva 1; Lena Ford 1

50 A man is known by the company he keeps.

Hopkinsian Magazine, Feb. 1826. The *Oxford Dictionary of Proverbs* cites similar statements back to 1541.
See Euripides 3

51 Comparisons are odious.

Gilbert of Hay's Prose MS (1456). The *Oxford Dictionary of Proverbs* notes: "Cf. early 14th-cent. Fr. *comparisons sont haÿneuses,* comparisons are hateful."

52 Confession is good for the soul.

David Fergusson, *Scottish Proverbs* (ca. 1641)

53 Don't count your chickens before they are hatched.

Thomas Howell, *New Sonnets* (ca. 1570). Howell's wording is "Counte not thy Chickens that vnhatched be."

54 Happy is the country which has no history.

Thomas Jefferson, Letter, 29 Mar. 1807. Jefferson's wording is "Blest is that nation whose silent course of happiness furnishes nothing for history to say." The *Oxford Dictionary of Proverbs* refers to Benjamin Franklin's *Poor Richard's Almanack* (1740): "Happy that Nation,—fortunate that age, whose history is not diverting."
See George Eliot 4; Montesquieu 6

55 Give credit where credit is due.

City Gazette and Daily Advertiser (Charleston, S.C.), 14 Aug. 1812. The *Oxford Dictionary of Proverbs* records the earlier "may Honor be given to whom Honor may be due" (John Adams, 1777). It also notes Romans 13:7: "Render therefore to all men their due: . . . to whom honor, honor."

56 Crime does not pay.

Law Magazine and Law Review vol. 8 (1860)

57 Do not cross the bridge till you come to it.

Henry Wadsworth Longfellow, Journal, 29 Apr. 1850

58 There's no use crying over spilt milk.

James Howell, *Proverbs* (1659). Howell's wording is "No weeping for shed milk."

59 Don't cut off your nose to spite your face.

Marshall County Republican (Plymouth, Ind.), 10 Jan. 1878. The *Oxford Dictionary of Proverbs* notes a mid-fourteenth-century French proverb, *qui cope son nès, sa face est despechie* (the man who cuts off his nose spites his face), as well as a ca. 1560 English citation, "He that byteth hys nose of, shameth hys face."

60 If you want to dance, you must pay the fiddler.

Abraham Lincoln, Speech, 11 Jan. 1837. Lincoln's words are "he that dances should always pay the fiddler." The *Oxford Dictionary of Proverbs* has "those that dance must pay the Musicke" documented from 1638.

61 The darkest hour is just before the dawn.

Thomas Fuller, *A Pisgah Sight of Palestine* (1650). Fuller's words are "It is always darkest just before the Day dawneth."

62 Dead men tell no tales.

John Dryden, *The Spanish Friar* (1681). The *Oxford Dictionary of Proverbs* has variants dating back to 1560.

63 'Tis impossible to be sure of any thing but Death and Taxes.

Christopher Bullock, *The Cobler of Preston* (1716). Edward Ward, in *The Dancing Devils* (1724), has "Death and Taxes, they are certain." These citations predate the famous 1789 quotation by Benjamin Franklin.
See Benjamin Franklin 41; Margaret Mitchell 6

64 Death is the great leveller.

Thomas Hall and George Swinnock, *The Beauty of Magistracy in an Exposition of the 82 Psalm* (1660). The *Oxford Dictionary of Proverbs* also cites Claudian, *De Raptu Proserpinae:* "omnia mors aequat, death levels all things."

65 Desperate diseases must have desperate remedies.

Robert Sanderson, *Episcopacy . . . Not Prejudicial to Regal Power* (1661). The *Oxford Dictionary of Proverbs* records various similar sayings, including the Latin "*extremis malis extrema remedia*, extreme remedies for extreme ills"; "Diseases desperate grown By desperate appliance are reliev'd, Or not at all" (Shakespeare, *Hamlet* [1600–1601]); and "A desperate disease must have a desperate remedy" (John Rushworth, *Historical Collections* [1659]).
See Shakespeare 219

66 The devil is not so black as he is painted.

Thomas More, *Dialogue of Comfort* (1534)

67 Devil take the hindmost.

Francis Beaumont and John Fletcher, *Philaster* (1620)

68 You can only die once.

Torrent of Portugal (ca. 1435). The *Oxford Dictionary of Proverbs* lists many variants, beginning with "a man schall but onnys Dyee" (the ca. 1435 citation above) and "a man can die but once" (William Shakespeare, *Henry IV, Pt. 2* [1597–1598]).

69 Throw dirt enough, and some will stick.

B. R., *Letter to Popish Friends* (1678). The exact wording is "'Tis a blessed line in Matchiavel—If durt enough be thrown, some will stick." The *Oxford Dictionary of Proverbs* notes a Latin equivalent, *calumniare fortiter, et aliquid adhaerebit* (slander strongly and some will stick).

70 Divide and rule.

Joseph Hall, *Meditations and Vowes* (1605). The *Oxford Dictionary of Proverbs* refers to the Latin *divide et impera* and the German *entzwei und gebiete.*

71 Do as I say, not as I do.

John Selden, *Table-Talk* (1689). The *Oxford Dictionary of Proverbs* cites a similar Anglo-Saxon quotation, dating from before 1100.

72 Do or die.

Pittscottie's Chronicles (1577)

73 Do right and fear no man.

Book of Precedence (ca. 1450). The wording of this source is actually "doe well, and drede no man."

74 Every dog has his day.

Randle Cotgrave, *Dictionary of French and English* (1611). The *Oxford Dictionary of Proverbs* has earlier citations for "a dogge hath a day" (Richard Taverner, translation of *Erasmus' Adages* [1545]) and "dog will have his day" (Shakespeare, *Hamlet* [1600–1601]).

75 The dog is man's best friend.

Thomas Hood, *Whimsicalities* (1843)

76 Whatever is worth doing at all is worth doing well.

Lord Chesterfield, Letter, 9 Oct. 1746

77 What's done is done.

Humphrey Mill and John Droeshout, *Poems Occasioned by a Melancholy Vision* (1639). The *Oxford Dictionary of Proverbs* gives variants back to ca. 1450 in English and the early fourteenth century in French.

78 A drowning man will clutch at a straw.

Samuel Richardson, *Clarissa* (1748). Richardson says "catch" instead of "clutch." The *Oxford Dictionary of Proverbs* cites an earlier version: "We do not as men redie to be drowned, catch at euery straw" (John Prime, *Fruitful and Brief Discourse* [1583]).

79 To each his own.

John Wise, *Churches Quarrel Espoused* (1713)

80 The early bird catches the worm.

William Camden, *Remains Concerning Britain*, 5th ed. (1636)

81 Early to bed and early to rise makes a man healthy, wealthy, and wise.

John Clarke, *Paroemiologia Anglo-Latina* (1639). The *Oxford Dictionary of Proverbs* gives similar expressions back to 1496.
See Thurber 8

82 Easy come, easy go.

Samuel Warren, *Diary of a Late Physician* (1832). The *Oxford Dictionary of Proverbs* cites Anne Bradstreet, in *Tenth Muse* (1650): "That which easily comes, as freely goes."

83 Easy does it.

Eclectic Magazine of Foreign Literature, June 1848

84 Don't put all your eggs in one basket.

Samuel Palmer, *Proverbs* (1710). Palmer's wording is "don't venture all your eggs in one basket." The *Oxford Dictionary of Proverbs* cites a 1662 reference to an Italian proverb translation, "to put all ones Eggs in a Paniard."
See Andrew Carnegie 1; Dorothy Parker 43

85 The end justifies the means.

Éléazar de Mauvillon, *The Life of Frederick-William I* (1750). The *Oxford Dictionary of Proverbs* refers to Ovid, *Heroides*: "*exitus acta probat*, the outcome justifies the deeds."
See Aldous Huxley 4

86 The enemy of my enemy is my friend.

Gabriel Manigault, *A Political Creed* (1884). Often attributed to the *Arthasastra*, a pre–fourth century B.C. Sanskrit text by Kautilya, but it appears to be a summary of strategic advice given there.

87 Enough is enough.

John Heywood, *Dialogue of Proverbs* (1546)

88 Every little helps.

Richard Johnson, *A Defence of the Grammatical Categories* (1707). The *Oxford Dictionary of Proverbs* cites "1590 G. MEURIER *Deviz Familiers* A6 *peu ayde, disçoit le formy, pissant en mer en plein midy*, every little helps, said the ant, pissing into the sea at midday."

89 Every man has his price.

William Wyndham, *Bee* (1734)

90 Every man to his own taste.

Laurence Sterne, *Tristram Shandy* (1760). The *Oxford Dictionary of Proverbs* notes: "Cf. STATIUS *Silvae* II. ii. 73 *sua cuique voluptas*, everyone has his own pleasures; Fr. *chacun à son goût*, each to his taste."

91 The exception proves the rule.

John Wilson, *Cheats* (1664). This is perhaps the most misunderstood of proverbs. It is widely believed to mean, illogically, that a rule is proved by examples contradicting it. Others believe that the word "prove" is used here in an archaic sense of "test." In reality, the meaning is that the very fact of there being an exception proves the existence of a rule. The *Oxford Dictionary of Proverbs* cites G. Watts, *Bacon's Advancement of Learning* (1640) ("exception strengthens the force of a law in cases not excepted") and refers to a Latin maxim, *exceptio probat regulam in casibus non exceptis* (the exception confirms the rule in cases not excepted).

92 There is an exception to every rule.

T. F., *News from North* (1579). The actual wording is "there is no rule so generall, that it admitteth not exception."

93 Experience is the best teacher.

Thomas Taylor, *David's Learning* (1617). The *Oxford Dictionary of Proverbs* refers to the Latin tag *experientia docet* (experience teaches) as the source of this expression.

94 Eyes are the windows of the soul.

H.V., *Counsel for Youth* (1650). The *Oxford Dictionary of Proverbs* records older variants, including the Latin "*vultus est index animi* (also *oculus animi index*), the face (also, eye) is the index of the mind," and "The eyes . . . are the wyndowes of the mynde" (1545).

95 Faint heart never won fair lady.

William Camden, *Remains Concerning Britain* (1614). The *Oxford Dictionary of Proverbs* has an earlier variant: "1580 LYLY *Euphues & His England* II. 131 Faint hart Philautus neither winneth Castell nor Lady."

96 All's fair in love and war.

The Universal Songster (1826). "All Advantages are fair in Love and War" appears earlier in William Taverner, *The Artful Husband* (1717).

97 Faith can move mountains.

Frederick Henniker, *Notes, During a Visit to Egypt* (1823). The *Oxford Dictionary of Proverbs* states: "With allusion to MATTHEW xvii. 20 (AV) If ye have faith as a grain of mustard seed, ye shall say unto this mountain; Remove hence to yonder place; and it shall remove. Cf. I CORINTHIANS xiii. 2 (AV) though I have all faith; so that I could remove mountains; and have not charity, I am nothing."

98 Familiarity breeds contempt.

Thomas Fuller, *Comment on Ruth* (1654). The *Oxford Dictionary of Proverbs* notes earlier forms, including "*Nimia familiaritas parit contemptum*, too much familiarity breeds contempt" (Augustine, *Scala Paradisi*), and "Ouermuche familiaritie myght breade him contempte" (Richard Taverner, *Garden of Wisdom* [1539]).

99 Father knows best.

Youth's Companion, 18 Dec. 1835

100 Like father like son.

Thomas Draxe, *Adages* (1616). The *Oxford Dictionary of Proverbs* notes: "Cf. L. *qualis pater talis filius*, as is the father, so is the son."

101 Fight fire with fire.

P. T. Barnum, *Struggles and Triumphs* (1869). The *Oxford Dictionary of Proverbs* cites earlier versions back to the early-fourteenth-century French "*lung feu doit estaindre lautre*, one fire must put out another."

102 He who fights and runs away, may live to fight another day.

N.Y. Daily Tribune, 12 Sept. 1842. Earlier versions in the *Oxford Dictionary of Proverbs* include "A man who flees will fight again" (Menander) and "That same manne, that renneth awaye, Maye again fight, an other daye" (*Erasmus' Apophthegms* [1542]).

103 Finders keepers, losers weepers.

St. Paul Globe, 13 May 1902. The *Oxford Dictionary of Proverbs* records variants back to 1825.

104 First come first served.

Henry Brinkelow, *Complaint of Roderick Mars* (1548). The *Oxford Dictionary of Proverbs* notes French versions of "he who comes first to the mill may grind first" dating back to the late thirteenth century.

105 First impressions are the most lasting.

Jonas Hanway, *A Journal of Eight Days Journey* (1756)

106 First things first.

The Christian Observer vol. 30 (1831)

107 There is a first time for everything.

Ballou's Dollar Monthly Magazine vol. 15 (1862). The *Oxford Dictionary of Proverbs* cites an earlier version from the *Papers of Alexander Hamilton* (1792): "But there is always a *first time*."

108 Fish always stinks from the head downwards.

Stefano Guazzo, *Civil Conversation*, trans. George Pettie (1581). Pettie's wording is "fishe beginneth first to smell at the head." The *Oxford Dictionary of Proverbs* refers to "a fish begins to stink from the head" as a Greek proverb.

109 There are plenty of other fish in the sea.

J. W. De Forest, *Seacliff* (1859). The *Oxford Dictionary of Proverbs* gives other "fish in sea" expressions going back to ca. 1573.

110 Fish or cut bait.

Joliet (Ill.) Signal, 1 Aug. 1848

111 A fool and his money are soon parted.

John Bridges, *Defence of the Government* (1587)

112 A man who is his own lawyer has a fool for a client.

Port Folio (Philadelphia), Aug. 1809. This source has the wording "he who is always his own counseller will often have a fool for his client." An earlier version appears in William De Britaine, *Humane Prudence*, 9th ed. (1702): "He who will be his own Counsellor, shall be sure to have a Fool for his Client."

113 There's no fool like an old fool.

John Heywood, *Dialogue of Proverbs* (1546)

114 Forewarned is forearmed.

The Knickerbocker, Feb. 1847. The *Oxford Dictionary of Proverbs* notes a Latin proverb, "*praemonitus, praemunitus*, forewarned, forearmed."

115 Forgive and forget.

William Langland, *The Vision of Piers Plowman* (1377)

116 This is a free country.

James Flint, *Letters from America* (1822). The letter containing this sentence is dated 28 June 1819.

117 A friend in need is a friend indeed.

John Smith, *The Mysterie of Rhetorique* (1665). The *Oxford Dictionary of Proverbs* notes similar expressions going back to Euripides, *Hecuba*: "In adversity good friends are most clearly seen."

118 Never look a gift horse in the mouth.

Samuel Palmer, *Proverbs* (1710). The *Oxford Dictionary of Proverbs* refers to Jerome, *Commentary on Epistle to Ephesians* (ca. 400), "Do not, as the common proverb says, look at the teeth of a gift horse," as well as pre-1710 English-language variants.

119 Give the devil his due.

Thomas Nashe, *Saffron Walden* (1596). The *Oxford Dictionary of Proverbs* has "Giue them their due though they were diuels" cited from John Lyly, *Pap with Hatchet* (1589).

120 People who live in glass houses shouldn't throw stones.

George Herbert, *Outlandish Proverbs* (1640). The precise wording is "Whose house is of glasse, must not throw stones at another."

121 All that glitters is not gold.

Hali Meidenhad (ca. 1220). The wording in this source is "Nis hit nower neh gold al that ter schineth." Other early versions recorded by the *Oxford Dictionary of Proverbs* include "All that glisters is not gold" (William Shakespeare, *Merchant*

of *Venice* [1596]) and a Latin proverb, "*non omne quod nitet aurum est*, not all that shines is gold."
See Thomas Gray 2

122 **God helps them that help themselves.**

Benjamin Franklin, *Poor Richard's Almanack* (1736). The *Oxford Dictionary of Proverbs* records various similar expressions going back to Aeschylus, *Fragments*: "God likes to assist the man who toils."

123 **Whom the gods would destroy they first make mad.**

North American Review, Jan. 1836. The *Oxford Dictionary of Proverbs* has "Cf. *Trag. Graec. Fragm. Adesp.* 296 (Nauck) . . . when divine anger ruins a man, it first takes away his good sense; L. *quos Deus vult perdere, prius dementat.*" Another citation there is "1640 G. HERBERT *Outlandish Proverbs* no. 688 When God will punish, hee will first take away the understanding."
See Cyril Connolly 2

124 **The good die young.**

J. A. Heraud, *The Descent into Hell* (1830). The *Oxford Dictionary of Proverbs* notes an earlier version in Daniel Defoe, *Character of Dr. Annesley* (1697): "The Good die early."

125 **Good fences make good neighbors.**

Genesee Farmer and Gardener's Journal, 24 May 1834. Predates the famous 1914 usage by Robert Frost.
See Frost 3

126 **The only good Indian is a dead Indian.**

Daily Miners' Register (Central City, Colo.), 30 May 1866. The wording of this 1866 occurrence, which is a reprint of an item from the *Salt Lake City Vidette*, is "The only good Indians on the plains are the dead ones." The earliest instance that has been found of the precise form "The only good Indian is a dead one" is the *Sacramento Daily Union,* 9 Oct. 1867, and the earliest instance of "The only good Indian is a dead Indian" is the *Atchison* (Kan.) *Daily Patriot,* 30 July 1870. The usual attribution of the saying's origin to General Philip Sheridan is clearly erroneous, since the putative Sheridan usage is dated 1869.

127 **One good turn deserves another.**

Thomas Randolph, *Amyntas* (1638). The *Oxford Dictionary of Proverbs* has earlier versions dating back to "early 14th-cent. Fr. *lune bonté requiert lautre,* one good deed deserves another."

128 **The grass is always greener in the next pasture.**

Asheville (N.C.) *Gazette-News,* 21 Feb. 1912. The *Oxford Dictionary of Proverbs* refers to a much older antecedent: "OVID *Ars Amatoria* I. 349 *fertilior seges est alienis semper in agris,* the harvest is always more fruitful in another man's fields."

129 **Behind every great man is a great woman.**

Philip Slaughter, *Christianity the Key to the Character and Career of Washington* (1886)
See Schreiner 3

130 **Great minds think alike.**

Godey's Lady's Book and Magazine, Apr. 1856. The *Oxford Dictionary of Proverbs* documents an earlier version (1618), "good wits jump," with *jump* used in an obsolete meaning of "agree completely."

131 **Beware of the Greeks bearing gifts.**

Bristol (Tenn.) *News,* 6 Apr. 1880. The *Oxford Dictionary of Proverbs* notes: "The original Latin version is also quoted: VIRGIL *Aeneid* II. 49 *timeo Danaos, et dona ferentes,* I fear the Greeks, even when bringing gifts (said by Laocoön as a warning to the Trojans not to admit the wooden horse)."
See Virgil 4

132 **One half of the world knows not how the other half lives.**

Joseph Hall, *Holy Observations* (1607). The *Oxford Dictionary of Proverbs* presents an earlier French citation: "1532 RABELAIS *Pantagruel* II. xxxii. *la moytié du monde ne sçait comment l'autre vit,* one half of the world knows not how the other lives."

133 **The hand that rocks the cradle rules the world.**

Zion's Herald, 25 May 1836. This has usually been attributed to an 1865 poem by William Ross Wallace.
See Clare Boothe Luce 5

134 **One hand washes the other.**

James Sanforde, *The Garden of Pleasure* (1573). The *Oxford Dictionary of Proverbs* quotes "one hand washes the other" in a much earlier Greek usage, from Epicharmus, *Apophthegm.*

135 **Handsome is as handsome does.**

Oliver Goldsmith, *The Vicar of Wakefield* (1766). The *Oxford Dictionary of Proverbs* also has an earlier version: "He is handsome that handsome doth" (N. R., *Proverbs* [1659]).

136 **Hard cases make bad law.**

Hodgens v. Hodgens (1837)
See Oliver Wendell Holmes, Jr. 17

137 **Haste makes waste.**

John Heywood, *Dialogue of Proverbs* (1546)

138 **You can't have everything.**

Godey's Magazine and Lady's Book, June 1852

139 **You can't have your cake and eat it too.**

John Davies, *Scourge of Folly* (1611). Davies's wording is "a man cannot eat his cake and haue it stil." The *Oxford Dictionary of Proverbs* quotes an earlier version: "Wolde ye bothe eate your cake, and haue your cake?" (John Heywood, *Dialogue of Proverbs* [1546]).

140 Here today and gone tomorrow.

John Calvin, *Life and Conversion of a Christian Man* (1549)

141 He who hesitates is lost.

W. Bullock, *Practical Lectures upon the Story of Joseph and His Brethren* (1826). Precursors recorded in the *Oxford Dictionary of Proverbs* include "The woman that deliberates is lost" (Joseph Addison, *Cato* [1713]) and "She who doubts is lost" (1865).

142 History repeats itself.

George Eliot, *Scenes of Clerical Life* (1858). The precise wording is "history, we know, is apt to repeat itself."

143 Home is where the heart is.

Graham's Magazine, Mar. 1847

144 Honesty is the best policy.

Edwin Sandys, *Europae Speculum* (1605)

145 Honey catches more flies than vinegar.

Giovanni Torriano, *Italian Proverbs* (1666). Torriano's wording is "honey gets more flyes to it, than doth viniger."

146 There is honor among thieves.

The Involuntary Inconstant (1772)

147 Hope for the best and prepare for the worst.

Roger l'Estrange, *Seneca's Morals* (1702). The *Oxford Dictionary of Proverbs* documents similar expressions dating back to 1565.

148 You can lead a horse to water, but you can't make him drink.

John Heywood, *Dialogue of Proverbs* (1546). Heywood's wording is "a man may well bryng a horse to the water, but he can not make hym drynke without he will."
See Dorothy Parker 39

149 Horses for courses.

A. E. T. Watson, *Turf* (1891)

150 [The] husband is always the last to know.

Works of Honore de Balzac (1896). Similar expressions about cuckolds are recorded in the *Oxford Dictionary of Proverbs* back to 1604. "[The] wife is always the last one to find out" appeared in the *San Francisco Chronicle*, 15 Oct. 1911.

151 An idle brain is the Devil's workshop.

William Perkins, *Works* (ca. 1600). Perkins's words are "the idle bodie and the idle braine is the shoppe of the deuill."

152 Idleness is the root of all evil.

George Farquhar, *The Beaux' Stratagem* (1707). The *Oxford Dictionary of Proverbs* notes earlier expressions relating to idleness and vice back to the fourteenth century.

153 Ignorance of the law is no excuse.

Christopher St. German, *Dialogues in English* (1530). St. German's words are "ignorance of the law though it be inuincible doth not excuse." According to the *Oxford Dictionary of Proverbs*, "there is a hoary L. legal maxim: *ignorantia iuris neminem excusat*, ignorance of the law excuses nobody."
See Selden 1

154 It's an ill wind that blows no good.

John Heywood, *Dialogue of Proverbs* (1546). Heywood's wording is "an yll wynde that blowth no man to good."

155 Imitation is the sincerest form of flattery.

Charles Caleb Colton, *Lacon* (1820). Colton's words are "imitation is the sincerest of flattery."

156 Every man is to be held innocent until proved guilty.

Monthly Magazine, Mar. 1803. Kenneth Pennington, in his article "Innocent Until Proven Guilty: The Origins of a Legal Maxim," *A Ennio Cortese* (2001), traces this saying to the French canonist Johannes Monachus (d. 1313). According to Pennington, Monachus wrote, *"item quilbet presumitur innocens nisi probetur nocens"* (a person is presumed innocent until proven guilty).

157 No man should be judge in his own cause.

Reginald Pecock, *Repressor of Blaming of Clergy* (ca. 1449). Pecock's words are "Noman oughte be iuge in his owne cause." The *Oxford Dictionary of Proverbs* notes the Latin legal maxim *nemo debet esse iudex in propria causa* (no one should be judge in his own cause).

158 Keep your eye on the ball.

Century Illustrated Magazine, Aug. 1892

159 Keep your shop and your shop will keep you.

George Chapman, *Eastward Ho* (1605)
See Mae West 15

160 The King can do no wrong.

John Selden, *Table-Talk* (1689)
See Blackstone 6

161 What you don't know can't hurt you.

George Pettie, *Petit Palace* (1576). Pettie's wording is "so long as I know it not, it hurteth mee not."

162 You never know what you can do until you try.

Henry Morford, *Shoulder-Straps* (1863). The *Oxford Dictionary of Proverbs* has an earlier variant: "A man knows not what he can do 'till he tries" (William Cobbett, *A Year's Residence in the United States of America* [1818]).

163 The last straw breaks the camel's back.

Charles Dickens, *Dombey and Son* (1848). Dickens's wording is "the last straw breaks the laden camel's back." The *Oxford Dictionary of Proverbs* records earlier similar expressions, dealing with feathers and horses, back to 1655.

164 He laughs best who laughs last.

Christmas Prince (ca. 1607). The wording in this source is "hee laugheth best that laugheth to the end."

165 One law for the rich and another for the poor.

Hugh Sempill, *A Short Address to the Public* (1793)

166 Leave well enough alone.

George Cheyne, *Essay on Regimen* (1740). Cheyne's words are "let well alone."

167 A liar ought to have a good memory.

Robert South, *Twelve Sermons* (ca. 1690). The *Oxford Dictionary of Proverbs* refers to a Latin version: "*mendacem memorem esse oportet*, a liar ought to have a good memory" (Quintilian, *Institutio Oratoria*). It also cites an English variant from ca. 1540.

168 A lie will go round the world while truth is pulling its boots on.

C. H. Spurgeon, *Gems from Spurgeon* (1859). An earlier version appears in the *Portland* (Me.) *Gazette*, 5 Sept. 1820: "Falsehood will fly from Maine to Georgia, while truth is pulling her boots on." Still earlier, Jonathan Swift wrote in *The Examiner*, 9 Nov. 1710: "Falsehood flies, and the truth comes limping after it."

169 Life is but a dream.

Charles Cotton, "The Sleeper" (1689)
See Calderón de la Barca 1; Carroll 44; Folk and Anonymous Songs 67; Li Po 1

170 Life isn't all beer and skittles.

Thomas C. Haliburton, *Nature and Human Nature* (1855)
See Thomas Hughes 1

171 While there's life, there's hope.

John Ray, *English Proverbs* (1670). Earlier versions recorded by the *Oxford Dictionary of Proverbs* include "THEOCRITUS *Idyll* iv. 42 . . . there's hope among the living; CICERO *Ad Atticum* IX. x. *dum anima est, spes esse dicitur*, as the saying is, while there's life there's hope; also ECCLESIASTES ix. 4 ["To him that is joined to all the living, there is hope"] . . . 1539 R. TAVERNER tr. *Erasmus' Adages* . . . The sycke person whyle he hath lyfe, hath hope."

172 Lightning never strikes twice in the same place.

Baltimore Republican, 25 July 1832

173 Live and learn.

Roxburghe Ballads (ca. 1620)

174 Live and let live.

David Fergusson, *Scottish Proverbs* (1641). An earlier example from 1622 cited in the *Oxford Dictionary of Proverbs* refers to "the Dutche prouerbe . . . To liue and to let others liue."

175 Look before you leap.

Robert Greene, *Greenes Never Too Late* (1590). Earlier versions in the *Oxford Dictionary of Proverbs* go back to "First loke and aftirward lepe" (*Douce MS 52* [ca. 1350]).

176 No man can lose what he never had.

Izaak Walton, *The Compleat Angler,* 5th ed. (1676)

177 One man's loss becomes another man's gain.

"*Well-wisher to Trade*," *A General Treatise of Monies and Exchanges* (1707)

178 Love is blind.

Geoffrey Chaucer, *The Canterbury Tales* (ca. 1387). The *Oxford Dictionary of Proverbs* notes a Greek version: "THEOCRITUS Idyll x. 19 . . . love is blind."

179 Love makes the world go round.

Universal Songster (1826). The words in this songbook are "'tis love that makes the world go round."

180 Love me, love my dog.

John Heywood, *Dialogue of Proverbs* (1546). The *Oxford Dictionary of Proverbs* notes: "Cf. ST. BERNARD Sermon: In Festo Sancti Michaelis iii. *qui me amat, amat et canem meum*, who loves me, also loves my dog; early 14th-cent. Fr. *et ce dit le sage qui mayme il ayme mon chien*, and so says the sage, who loves me loves my dog."

181 Love will find a way.

Thomas Deloney, *The Pleasant and Princely History of the Gentle-Craft* (ca. 1600). The wording in Deloney is "love you see can finde a way."

182 Lucky at cards, unlucky in love.

New Monthly Belle Assemblée, June 1851

183 Make hay while the sun shines.

John Heywood, *Dialogue of Proverbs* (1546). Heywood's wording is "whan the sunne shynth make hey."

184 As you must make your bed, so you must lie on it.

Gabriel Harvey, *Marginalia* (ca. 1590). Harvey's wording is "lett them . . . go to there bed, as themselues shall make it." The *Oxford Dictionary of Proverbs* notes the late fifteenth-century French *comme on faict son lict, on le treuve* (as one makes one's bed, so one finds it).

185 A man is as old as he feels, and a woman as old as she looks.

Belgravia, Oct. 1867
See Groucho Marx 45

186 Man proposes and God disposes.

Thomas à Kempis, *De Imitatione Christi* (ca. 1450). This dating is for the English translation, which included the words "man purposith and god disposith." The original (ca. 1420) has the Latin *homo proponit, sed Deus disponit.*
See Thomas à Kempis 1

187 There's many a slip 'twixt cup and lip.

The Attic Nights of Aulus Gellius (1795). Earlier versions in the *Oxford Dictionary of Proverbs* include "CATO THE ELDER in Aulus Gellius *Noctes Atticae* XIII. xviii. 1 . . . many things can come between mouth and morsel; PALLADAS (attrib.) in *Anthologia Palatina* x. 32 . . . there are many things between the cup and the edge of the lip."

188 March comes in like a lion, and goes out like a lamb.

John Fletcher, *A Wife for a Month* (1624). Fletcher's words are "I would chuse March, for I would come in like a Lion. . . . But you'd go out like a Lamb when you went to hanging."

189 Marriages are made in heaven.

John Lyly, *Euphues and His England* (1580). The *Oxford Dictionary of Proverbs* has a slightly earlier version, "marriages be don in Heaven" (William Painter, *The Palace of Pleasure* [1567]).

190 One man's meat is another man's poison.

Plato's Cap (1604). The *Oxford Dictionary of Proverbs* refers to Lucretius, *De Rerum Natura* ("*quod ali cibus est aliis fuat acre venenum*, what is food to one person may be bitter poison to others"), and Thomas Whythorne, *Autobiography* (1576) ("On bodies meat iz an otherz poizon").
See Lucretius 4

191 Might is right.

Political song (ca. 1325). The *Oxford Dictionary of Proverbs* cites this from Thomas Wright, *Political Songs of England;* also refers to "*mensuraque iuris vis erat,* might was the measure of right" (Lucan, *Pharsalia*).

192 The mills of God grind slowly, yet they grind exceeding small.

George Herbert, *Outlandish Proverbs* (1640). Herbert's wording is "Gods Mill grinds slow, but sure." The *Oxford Dictionary of Proverbs* has

the following earlier version: "Quoted in SEXTUS EMPIRICUS *Against Professors* I. 287 . . . the mills of the gods are late to grind, but they grind small."
See Logau 1

193 Misery loves company.

A Collection of Papers, Lately Printed in the Daily Advertiser (1740). The *Oxford Dictionary of Proverbs* documents earlier similar sayings in both Latin and English going back to the fourteenth century.

194 A miss is as good as a mile.

The Bee Reviv'd (1750)

195 Moderation in all things.

The Polyanthos, Apr. 1813. The *Oxford Dictionary of Proverbs* cites "HESIOD *Works & Days* I. 694 . . . moderation is best in all things; PLAUTUS *Poenulus* l. 238 *modus omnibus rebus . . . optimus est habitu,* moderation in all things is the best policy."
See Anonymous 21; Horace 19; Horace 26

196 There are some things that money cannot buy.

N.Y. Times, 31 May 1864

197 Money isn't everything.

Harriet Beecher Stowe, *Uncle Tom's Cabin* (1852). Stowe's wording was "money an't everything."

198 Money talks.

Aphra Behn, *The Rover* (1681). Behn's wording is "money speaks." "Money talks" appears in the *National Police Gazette,* 8 Dec. 1883.

199 The more the merrier.

Pearl (ca. 1380)

200 Mother knows best.

Robert Merry's Museum, Jan. 1844

201 Like mother, like daughter.

Roger Williams, *Bloody Tenet of Persecution* (1644). The *Oxford Dictionary of Proverbs* refers to Ezekiel 16:44: "Every one . . . shall use this proverb against thee, saying, As is the mother, so is her daughter."
See Bible 186

202 If the mountain will not come to Mahomet, Mahomet must go to the mountain.

Thomas Fuller, *Gnomologia* (1732). The *Oxford Dictionary of Proverbs* also cites Francis Bacon, *Essays,* "Of Boldness": "If the Hill will not come to Mahomet, Mahomet wil go to the hil."

203 What must be, must be.

Francis Beaumont and John Fletcher, *The Scornful Lady* (1616). The *Oxford Dictionary of Proverbs* also notes "That the whiche muste be wyll be" (William Horman, *Vulgaria* [1519]) and the Italian "*che sarà, sarà,* what will be, will be."
See Livingston 1

204 Nature abhors a vacuum.

Robert Boyle, *A Defence of the Doctrine Touching the Spring and Weight of the Air* (1662). The *Oxford Dictionary of Proverbs* also refers to the Latin *"natura abhorret vacuum*, Nature abhors a vacuum" and "Naturall reason abhorreth vacuum" (Thomas Cranmer, *Answer to Gardiner* [1551]).

205 Necessity is the mother of invention.

Richard Franck, *Northern Memoirs* (1658)

206 Never is a long time.

The Mirror of Literature, Amusement and Instruction (1823). The *Oxford Dictionary of Proverbs* cites an earlier variant: "Never is a long Term" (James Kelly, *Scottish Proverbs* [1721]).

207 Never say die.

Diary of Benjamin F. Palmer, Privateersman (1814)

208 It is never too late to learn.

Roger l'Estrange, *Seneca's Morals* (1678)

209 Never too old to learn.

John Ray, *English Proverbs* (1670)

210 The new broom sweeps clean.

John Heywood, *Dialogue of Proverbs* (1546)

211 No news is good news.

James Howell, *Familiar Letters*, 3 June 1640

212 No pains, no gains.

Robert Herrick, *Hesperides* (1648). The *Oxford Dictionary of Proverbs* records an earlier variant: "They must take pain that look for any gayn" (N. Breton, *Works of Young Wit* [1577]). The popular modern version is "No pain, no gain." *See William Penn 1*

213 No rest for the weary.

Wash. Post, 18 May 1880

214 Nobody is perfect.

John Barker, *Sermons on the Following Subjects* (1763)

215 A nod is as good as a wink to a blind horse.

William Goodall, *The True Englishman's Miscellany* (1740)

216 Nothing comes of nothing.

William Shakespeare, *King Lear* (1605–1606). Shakespeare's formulation is "nothing will come of nothing." The *Oxford Dictionary of Proverbs* refers to "ALCAEUS *Fragment* CCCXX. . . . nothing comes of nothing."

217 Nothing lasts forever.

Southern Literary Journal and Magazine of Arts, Oct. 1836

218 There's nothing so good for the inside of a man as the outside of a horse.

Boston Daily Traveller, 12 Apr. 1859. The wording in the 1859 source is "The outside of a horse is good for the inside of a man."

219 Nothing succeeds like success.

A Biographical Sketch . . . of M. De Lamartine (1849)

220 Nothing ventured, nothing gained.

Thomas Heywood, *The Captives* (1624). Heywood's wording is "hee that nought venters, nothinge gaynes." The *Oxford Dictionary of Proverbs* documents similar sayings back to the late fourteenth century, such as "Noght venter noght haue" (John Heywood, *Dialogue of Proverbs* [1546]).

221 Now or never.

Geoffrey Chaucer, *Troilus and Criseyde* (ca. 1380)

222 Oil and water don't mix.

Alice Cary, *Married, Not Mated* (1856). Cary's words are "Ile and water . . . won't mix."

223 Old habits die hard.

Arthur Reade, *Tea and Tea Drinking* (1884). An earlier similar expression in the *Oxford Dictionary of Proverbs* is "Old habits are not easily broken" (Jeremy Belknap, *The Foresters* [1792]).

224 Omelets are not made without breaking eggs.

Walker's Hibernian Magazine, May 1796. The French "on ne fait pas d'omelette sans casser des oeufs" is older.

225 Once bit twice shy.

Rachel Hunter, *Lady Maclairn: The Victim of Villainy* (1806). In the United States, the proverb is commonly "once burned, twice shy."

226 When one door shuts, another opens.

Lazarillo, trans. D. Rowland (1586)

227 Opportunity never knocks twice.

Chicago Daily Tribune, 30 Aug. 1896

228 Other times, other manners.

Jean de la Bruyère, *Characters* (1709). The *Oxford Dictionary of Proverbs* records "Other times, other wayes" from 1576 (George Pettie, *Petit Palace*).

229 Out of sight, out of mind.

Erasmus' Adages, 2nd ed., trans. Richard Taverner (1545). An earlier variant in the *Oxford Dictionary of Proverbs* is "Whan Man is oute of sight, son be he passith oute of mynde" (trans. *Thomas à Kempis' De Imitatione Christi* [ca. 1450]).

230 Those who pay the piper call the tune.

Guardian (London), 26 Dec. 1868

231 A penny saved is a penny earned.

Thomas Fuller, *The Worthies of England* (1662). Fuller's wording is "a penny saved is a penny gained."

232 Penny wise and pound foolish.

Edward Topsell, *History of Four-footed Beasts* (1607)

233 The pitcher will go to the well once too often.

N. Shaw, *Collections of New London County Historical Society* (1777). The *Oxford Dictionary of Proverbs* refers to the early-fourteenth-century French "*tant va pot a eve qu'il brise*, the pot goes so often to the water that it breaks."

234 A place for everything, and everything in its place.

Ohio Repository, Dec. 1827. The wording in the 1827 source is "Have a place for every thing, and keep every thing in its proper place."

235 If you play with fire you get burnt.

John Wesley, Letter to Miss Loxdale, 12 July 1782. Wesley's words were "If you play with fire, will you not be burnt sooner or later?"

236 You can't please everyone.

E. Paston, Letter, 16 May 1472. Paston's language is "he can not plese all partys."

237 Politics makes strange bedfellows.

William Gifford, *The Baviad, and Maeviad*, new ed. revised (1797). Gifford's wording is "I can only say that politics, like misery, 'bring a man acquainted with strange bedfellows!'" "Politics *do* make strange bedfellows" appears in *Workingman's Advocate*, 10 Mar. 1832.
See Charles Dudley Warner 2

238 A poor workman blames his tools.

Scribner Monthly, May 1873. The *Oxford Dictionary of Proverbs* records variants as far back as 1611 in English and notes: "Cf. late 13th-cent. Fr. *mauvés ovriers ne trovera ja bon hostill*, a bad workman will never find a good tool."

239 Possession is nine points of the law.

Thomas Draxe, *Adages* (1616). The modern version is usually "Possession is nine-tenths of the law."

240 When poverty comes in at the door, love flies out of the window.

John Clarke, *Paroemiologia Anglo-Latina* (1639). Clarke's words are "when povertie comes in at doores, love leapes out at windowes."

241 Practice makes perfect.

The Present State of the Republick of Letters for August 1730 (1730)

242 Practise what you preach.

Roger l'Estrange, *Seneca's Morals* (1678). L'Estrange's words are "we must practise what we preach."

243 An ounce of prevention is worth a pound of cure.

Benjamin Franklin, *Pennsylvania Gazette*, 11 Feb. 1735

244 A promise is a promise.

The Juvenile Miscellany, Mar. 1827

245 Promises, like pie-crust, are made to be broken.

Heraclitus Ridens (1681). This source has the wording "he makes no more of breaking Acts of Parliaments, than if they were like Promises and Pie-crust made to be broken."

246 The proof of the pudding is in the eating.

William Camden, *Remains Concerning Britain*, 3rd ed. (1623)

247 It is easier to pull down than to build up.

James Howell, *Dodona's Grave* (1644). The *Oxford Dictionary of Proverbs* also cites "It is easie to raze, but hard to buylde" (Holinshed, *Chronicles* [1577]).

248 Never put off till tomorrow what you can do today.

Thomas Draxe, *Adages* (1616). Draxe's wording is "deferre not vntill to morrow, if thou canst do it to day." The *Oxford Dictionary of Proverbs* notes some similar expressions dating from the fourteenth century.
See Wilde 113

249 Put up or shut up.

Montana Post (Virginia City, Mont.), 5 Nov. 1864

250 It never rains but it pours.

John Arbuthnot, title of book (1726). Arbuthnot's words are "it cannot rain but it pours."

251 Red sky at night is the sailor's delight; red in the morning the sailors take warning.

Henry McCook, *The Teacher's Commentary on the Gospel Narrative* (1871). The *Oxford Dictionary of Proverbs* records earlier versions back to ca. 1454 and notes: "With allusion to MATTHEW xvi. 2–3 (AV) When it is evening, ye say, It will be fair weather: for the sky is red. And in the morning, It will be foul weather to day: for the sky is red and louring."

252 Revenge can be eaten cold.

Eugène Sue, *Matilda* (1843)

253 Revenge is sweet.

Jean Bodin, *Six Books of a Commonweale* (1606) (translation by Richard Knolles)

254 He who rides a tiger is afraid to dismount.

William Scarborough, *A Collection of Chinese Proverbs* (1875)

255 The road to hell is paved with good intentions.

H. G. Bohn, *Hand-Book of Proverbs* (1855). The *Oxford Dictionary of Proverbs* states: "Earlier forms of the proverb omit the first three words. Cf. st. francis de sales, *Letter* lxxiv. *le proverbe tiré de notre saint Bernard, 'L'enfer est plein de bonnes volontés ou désirs,'* the proverb taken from our St. Bernard, 'Hell is full of good intentions or desires.'" *See Bernard of Clairvaux 2*

256 All roads lead to Rome.

The Correspondence of Baron Armfelt (1795). The *Oxford Dictionary of Proverbs* notes: "Cf. medieval L. *mille vie ducunt hominem per secula Romam,* a thousand roads lead man for ever towards Rome. . . . 1806 r. thomson tr. *La Fontaine's Fables* iv. xii. xxiv. All roads alike conduct to Rome."

257 A rolling stone gathers no moss.

Stephen Gosson, *Ephemerides of Phialo* (1579). The *Oxford Dictionary of Proverbs* refers to "erasmus *Adages* III. iv. . . . *musco lapis volutus haud obducitur,* a rolling stone is not covered with moss." *See Dylan 17; Muddy Waters 1*

258 When in Rome, do as the Romans do.

Erasmus' Adages, 3rd ed., trans. Richard Taverner (1552). Taverner's translation is worded "whan you art at Rome, do as they do at Rome." Earlier versions in the *Oxford Dictionary of Proverbs* date back to St. Ambrose; see the cross-reference. *See Ambrose 1*

259 Rome was not built in a day.

Erasmus' Adages, 2nd ed., trans. Richard Taverner (1545). The *Oxford Dictionary of Proverbs* notes: "Cf. medieval Fr. *Rome ne fut pas faite toute en un jour,* Rome was not made in one day."

260 Root, hog, or die.

Davy Crockett, *A Narrative of the Life of David Crockett* (1834)

261 Give a man rope enough and he will hang himself.

John Ray, *English Proverbs* (1670). Ray's wording was "Give a thief rope enough, and he'll hang himself."

262 No rose without a thorn.

John Ray, *English Proverbs* (1670). Earlier versions in the *Oxford Dictionary of Proverbs* date back to the fifteenth century, beginning with "There is no rose . . . in garden, but there be sum thorne" (John Lydgate, *Bochas* [1430–1440]).

263 Rules are made to be broken.

N.Y. Sun, 28 Feb. 1893

264 There is safety in numbers.

Peterson's Magazine, July 1869

265 What's sauce for the goose is sauce for the gander.

John Ray, *English Proverbs* (1670). Ray's wording is "that that's good sawce for a goose, is good for a gander."

266 Scratch my back and I'll scratch yours.

Dublin University Magazine, Aug. 1833. The *Oxford Dictionary of Proverbs* has an earlier version: "Scratch me, says one, and I'll scratch thee" (E. Ward, *All Men Mad* [1704]).

267 Seeing is believing.

S. Harward MS (Trinity College, Cambridge) (1609)

268 Self-preservation is the first law of nature.

John Donne, *Biathanatos* (ca. 1608). Donne writes, "selfe-preservation is of Naturall Law." The *Oxford Dictionary of Proverbs* also refers to Cicero, *De Finibus:* "*primamque ex natura hanc habere appetitionem, ut conservemus nosmet ipsos,* by nature our first impulse is to preserve ourselves."

269 If the shoe fits, wear it.

New-York Gazette and Weekly Mercury, 17 May 1773. The actual wording there is "let those whom the shoe fits wear it."

270 The show must go on.

Wash. Post, 3 July 1879

271 Silence is golden.

Thomas Carlyle, *Fraser's Magazine,* June 1834. Carlyle's usage reads "As the Swiss Inscription says: *Sprechen ist silbern, Schweigen ist golden* (Speech is silvern, Silence is golden)." *See Mazzini 1*

272 You can't make a silk purse out of a sow's ear.

Stephen Gosson *Ephemerides of Phialo* (1579). Gosson's words are "seekinge . . . too make a silke purse of a Sowes eare."

273 Let sleeping dogs lie.

Geoffrey Chaucer, *Troilus and Criseyde* (ca. 1385). Chaucer's wording is "it is nought good a slepyng hound to wake." The *Oxford Dictionary of Proverbs* notes: "Cf. early 14th-cent. Fr. *n'esveillez pas lou chien qui dort,* wake not the sleeping dog."

274 Slow and steady wins the race.

Robert Lloyd, *Poems* (1762)

275 It's a small world.

The Theatre, 1 May 1882

276 No smoke without fire.

G. Delamothe, *The French Alphabet* (1592). The *Oxford Dictionary of Proverbs* also notes: "Cf. PLAUTUS *Curculio* 53 *flamma fumo est proxima*, the flame is right next to the smoke; late 13th-cent. Fr. *nul feu est sens fumee ne fumee sans feu*, no fire is without smoke, nor smoke without fire."

277 You don't get something for nothing.

The Cultivator, Feb. 1835. The actual wording here is "It is idle to expect something for nothing."

278 Something is better than nothing.

John Heywood, *Dialogue of Proverbs* (1546). Heywood's wording is "somwhat is better than nothyng." The *Oxford Dictionary of Proverbs* notes: "Cf. early 15th-cent. Fr. *mieulx vault aucun bien que neant*, something is better than nothing."

279 My son is my son till he gets him a wife, but my daughter's my daughter all the days of her life.

John Ray, *English Proverbs* (1670)

280 Spare the rod and spoil the child.

John Clarke, *Paroemiologia Anglo-Latina* (1639). The *Oxford Dictionary of Proverbs* notes: "With allusion to PROVERBS xiii. 24 (AV) He that spareth his rod, hateth his son. . . . 1377 LANGLAND *Piers Plowman* B. v. 41 Salamon seide. . . . *Qui parcit virge, odit filium*. The Englich of this latyn is . . . Who-so spareth the sprynge [switch], spilleth [ruins] his children."

281 Never speak ill of the dead.

S. Harward MS (Trinity College, Cambridge) (1609). The exact wording is "Speake not evill of the dead." The *Oxford Dictionary of Proverbs* also notes: "Cf. Gr. . . . speak no evil of the dead (attributed to the Spartan ephor [civil magistrate] Chilon, 6th cent. BC); L. *de mortuis nil nisi bonum*, say nothing of the dead but what is good."

282 One step at a time.

Charlotte M. Yonge, *Heir of Redclyffe* (1853)

283 Sticks and stones will break my bones, but words will never harm me.

Christian Recorder, 22 Mar. 1862

284 Still waters run deep.

John Lydgate, *Minor Poems* (ca. 1410). Lydgate's words are "smothe waters ben ofte sithes depe." The *Oxford Dictionary of Proverbs* notes: "Cf. Q. CURTIUS *De Rebus Gestis Alexandri Magni* VII. iv. 13 *altissima quaeque flumina minimo sono labi*, the deepest rivers flow with least sound [said there to be a Bactrian saying]."

285 A stitch in time saves nine.

Thomas Tusser, *Tusser Redivivus* (1710)

286 Stuff a cold and starve a fever.

Emerald and Baltimore Literary Gazette, 28 Feb. 1829. An earlier form is "nurse a cold, and starve a fever" (James M. Adair, *Medical Cautions, for the Consideration of Invalids* [1786]). "Feed a cold and starve a fever" is a common modern variant.

287 Strike while the iron is hot.

Geoffrey Chaucer, *The Canterbury Tales* (ca. 1387). Chaucer's words are "whil that iren is hoot, men sholden smyte." The *Oxford Dictionary of Proverbs* notes: "Cf. late 13th-cent. Fr. *len doit batre le fer tandis cum il est chauz*, one must strike the iron while it is hot."

288 You can't take it with you.

Southern Literary Journal and Monthly Magazine, June 1836
See Bible 376

289 Never tell tales out of school.

Varley Banks, *The Manchester Man* (1876). The *Oxford Dictionary of Proverbs* records similar phrases back to 1530.

290 Talk is cheap.

All Pleas'd at Last (1783). "Seying goes good cheap" is cited in the *Oxford Dictionary of Proverbs* from 1668 (R. B., *Adagia Scotica*).

291 Tall oaks from little acorns grow.

David Everett, *The Columbian Orator* (1777). Earlier variants given by the *Oxford Dictionary of Proverbs* go back to ca. 1385.

292 You can't teach an old dog new tricks.

William Camden, *Remains Concerning Britain*, 5th ed. (1636). Camden's wording is "it is hard to teach an old dog trickes."

293 Things are not always what they seem.

Edward Lewis, *The Italian Husband* (1754)

294 Three may keep a secret, if two of them are dead.

Benjamin Franklin, *Poor Richard's Almanack*, July 1735

295 Don't throw the baby out with the bathwater.

Thomas Carlyle, *The Nigger Question*, 2nd ed. (1853). The actual language in Carlyle is "the Germans say, 'you must empty out the bathing-tub, but not the baby along with it.'" Wolfgang Mieder, in *Proverbs Are Never Out of Season* (1993), gives references in German to this proverb going back as far as 1512.

296 There is a time and place for everything.

Alexander Barclay, *Ship of Fools* (1509)

297 Time and tide wait for no man.

Robert Greene, *Disputations between He Cony-catcher and She Cony-catcher* (1592). Greene's wording is "tyde nor time tarrieth no man."

298 Time flies.

> Thomas Lodge et al., *The Workes of Lucius Annaeus Seneca* (1614). The *Oxford Dictionary of Proverbs* refers to "L. *tempus fugit*, time flies."

299 There is a time for everything.

> Geoffrey Chaucer, *The Canterbury Tales* (ca. 1387). Chaucer writes "but Salomon seith 'every thyng hath tyme.'" According to the *Oxford Dictionary of Proverbs*, this is "with allusion to ECCLESIASTES iii. 1 (AV) To every thing there is a season."

300 Time is a great healer.

> *National Republican* (Washington, D.C.), 12 Apr. 1875. The *Oxford Dictionary of Proverbs* refers to Menander, *Fragments* ("time is the healer of all necessary evils").

301 Time will tell.

> *Appendix to the Considerations on the Measures Carrying On with Respect to the British Colonies in North America* (1775). The *Oxford Dictionary of Proverbs* traces similar expressions back to Menander, *Monosticha* ("time brings the truth to light").

302 Tomorrow is a new day.

> John Rastell, *Calisto and Melebea* (ca. 1527)
> *See Margaret Mitchell 8*

303 Too many cooks spoil the broth.

> Balthazar Gerbier, *Principles of Building* (1662). An earlier variant in the *Oxford Dictionary of Proverbs* is "the more cooks the worse potage" (1575).

304 There may be too much even of a good thing.

> *The History and Adventures of the Renowned Don Quixote* (1770). The *Oxford Dictionary of Proverbs* gives "A man may take too much of a good thing" (Cotgrave, *Dictionary of French and English* [1611]).

305 Trade follows the flag.

> *Grand County Herald* (Lancaster, Wis.), 18 June 1862

306 Many a true word has been spoken in jest.

> *Roxburghe Ballads* (ca. 1665)

307 Every tub must stand on its own bottom.

> John Clarke, *Paroemiologia Anglo-Latina* (1639). The *Oxford Dictionary of Proverbs* cites William Bullein, *Dialogue Against Fever* (1564), "Let euery Fatte [vat] stande vpon his owne bottome."

308 Turnabout is fair play.

> *The Life and Uncommon Adventures of Capt. Dudley Bradstreet* (1755)

309 Two can live as cheap as one.

> *London Saturday Journal*, Feb. 1840

310 Two heads are better than one.

> John Heywood, *Dialogue of Proverbs* (1546). Slightly earlier in the *Oxford Dictionary of Proverbs* is "Two wittes be farre better than one" (John Palsgrave, *L'Éclaircissement de la Langue Française* [1530]).

311 Two is company, three is a crowd.

> *North American Review*, Jan. 1856

312 There are two sides to every question.

> John Adams, *Autobiography* (1802). Adams's wording is "there were two sides to a question." The *Oxford Dictionary of Proverbs* also cites "PROTAGORAS Aphorism (in Diogenes Laertius *Protagoras* IX. li.) . . . there are two sides to every question."

313 Two wrongs will not make one right.

> Charles Howard, *Thoughts, Essays, and Maxims* (1768)

314 Union is strength.

> S. Robinson, Letter, 29 Dec. 1848. The *Oxford Dictionary of Proverbs* has earlier versions of this going back to Homer's *Iliad:* "Even weak men have strength in unity."

315 What goes up must come down.

> Theodore Sedgwick, *Hints to My Countrymen* (1826)

316 Virtue is its own reward.

> Thomas Browne, *Religio Medici* (1642). The *Oxford Dictionary of Proverbs* documents earlier usage in Latin: "*Virtutem pretium . . . esse sui*, virtue is its own reward" (Ovid, *Ex Ponto*).

317 We must walk before we run.

> Alban Butler, *A Letter on Prayer* (1755). Earlier versions in the *Oxford Dictionary of Proverbs* include "You must learn to creep before you go" (John Ray, *English Proverbs* [1670]).

318 Walls have ears.

> G. Delamothe, *The French Alphabet* (1592). Delamothe's wording is "the walles may have some eares."

319 If you want a thing to be well done, you must do it yourself.

> Henry Wadsworth Longfellow, "The Courtship of Miles Standish" (1858). The *Oxford Dictionary of Proverbs* also cites "If a man will haue his business well done, he must doe it himselfe" from Thomas Draxe, *Adages* (1616).

320 For want of a nail the shoe is lost, for want of a shoe the horse is lost, for want of a horse the rider is lost.

> George Herbert, *Outlandish Proverbs* (1640). The *Oxford Dictionary of Proverbs* refers to similar French sayings going back to the fifteenth century.

321 It will all come out in the wash.

Tony Hart, Title of song (1886)

322 Waste not, want not.

Monthly Review vol. 58 (1778)

323 A watched pot never boils.

Cobbett's Weekly Political Register, 16 July 1808. "Watched milk never boils" appears in Charles Dibdin, Jr., *The Wild Man* (1833).

324 The way to a man's heart is through his stomach.

Fraser's Magazine, Apr. 1837. The wording of the 1837 source is "the direct road to a man's heart is through his stomach." The *Oxford Dictionary of Proverbs* quotes John Adams, Letter, 15 Apr. 1814: "The shortest road to men's hearts is down their throats."

325 There's more than one way to skin a cat.

Logansport (Ind.) *Canal Telegraph*, 30 Jan. 1836

326 All's well that ends well.

R. Hill, *Commonplace Book* (ca. 1530). The *Oxford Dictionary of Proverbs* cites an earlier version: "If the ende be wele, than is alle wele" (1381, in J. R. Lumby, *Chronicon Henrici Knighton* [1895]).

327 Where there's a will, there's a way.

The Happiness of Having God for a Friend in Time of Trial (1797). The *Oxford Dictionary of Proverbs* cites an earlier version from George Herbert, *Outlandish Proverbs* (1640): "To him that will, wais are not wanting."

328 It is a wise child that knows its own father.

Robert Greene, *Menaphon* (1589). Greene's wording is "wise are the Children in these dayes that know their owne fathers."

329 If wishes were horses, beggars would ride.

James Carmichaell, *Proverbs in Scots* (ca. 1620). Carmichaell's version is "and wishes were horses pure [poor] men wald ryde."

330 A woman's place is in the home.

New Sporting Magazine, Aug. 1832. The actual words here are "a woman's place is her own home." *See Sayings 65*

331 A woman's work is never done.

Roxburghe Ballads (1629). The *Oxford Dictionary of Proverbs* documents an earlier version: "Huswiues affaires haue never none ende" (Thomas Tusser, *Husbandry*, rev. ed. [1570]).

332 Wonders will never cease.

H. Bates, Letter (1776)

333 A man's word is his bond.

Lancelot of Lake (ca. 1500). This source, with the wording "o kingis word shuld be o kingis bonde," is the earliest version given by the *Oxford Dictionary of Proverbs*.

334 All work and no play makes Jack a dull boy.

James Howell, *Proverbs* (1659)

335 Work before play.

Edward Bulwer Lytton, *The Last of the Barons* (1843)

336 Youth must be served.

Pierce Egan, *Boxiana*, 2nd Ser. (1829)

Richard Pryor

U.S. comedian, 1940–2005

1 Marriage is really tough because you have to deal with feelings and lawyers.

Quoted in Robert Byrne, *The Third and Possibly the Best 637 Things Anybody Ever Said* (1986)

Ptahhotep

Egyptian government official, Twenty-fourth cent. B.C.

1 To resist him that is set in authority is evil.

The Maxims of Ptahhotep no. 31

Pu Yi

Chinese emperor, 1906–1967

1 For the past forty years I had never folded my own quilt, made my own bed, or poured out my washing water. I had never even washed my own feet or tied my shoes.

From Emperor to Citizen ch. 8 (1964)

Publilius Syrus

Roman playwright, First cent. B.C.

1 *Necessitas dat legem non ipsa accipit.*
Necessity gives the law without itself acknowledging one.

Sententiae no. 444. Gave rise to the proverb *Necessitas non habet legem* (Necessity has no law).

Giacomo Puccini

Italian composer, 1858–1924

1 [*After hearing Enrico Caruso sing at an audition:*] Who sent you to me—God?

Quoted in Derek Watson, *Chambers Music Quotations* (1991)

Thomas Puccio

U.S. lawyer, 1944–2012

1 I [a prosecutor] could indict a ham sandwich.

Quoted in *Wash. Post*, 23 Feb. 1982. The *Democrat and Chronicle* (Rochester, N.Y.), 2 Sept. 1979, printed the following: "'The district attorney could get the grand jury to indict a ham sandwich if he wanted to,' one Rochester defense lawyer said."

Manuel Puig

Argentinian novelist, 1932–1990

1 Outside of this cell we may have our oppressors, yes, but not inside. Here no one oppresses the other. The only thing that seems to disturb me . . . because I'm exhausted, or conditioned, or perverted . . . is that someone wants to be nice to me, without asking anything back for it.

Kiss of the Spider Woman ch. 11 (1976)

Punch

English periodical

1 Advice to persons about to marry.—"Don't."

4 Jan. 1845
See Francis Bacon 16

2 It's worse than wicked, my dear, it's vulgar.

Almanac (1876)

Eugene I. "Buck" Purcell

U.S. government official, 1882–1936

1 If a man can't stand the heat, he ought to stay out of the kitchen.

Quoted in *Independence* (Mo.) *Examiner*, 1 Jan. 1931. Often quoted by Harry S. Truman, who referred to it in a speech of 17 Dec. 1952 as "a saying I used to hear from my old friend and colleague on the Jackson County Court."

Aleksander Sergeevich Pushkin

Russian poet, 1799–1837

1 "My uncle always was respected;
But his grave illness, I confess,
Is more than could have been expected:
A stroke of genius, nothing less.
He offers all a grand example;
But, God, such boredom who would sample?—
Daylong, nightlong, thus to be bid
To sit beside an invalid!
Low cunning must assist devotion

To one who is but half-alive:
You smooth his pillow and contrive
Amusement while you mix his potion;
You sigh, and think with furrowed brow—
'Why can't the devil take you now?'"

Eugene Onegin ch. 1, st. 1 (1833) (translation by Babette Deutsch)

2 Moscow: those syllables can start
A tumult in the Russian heart.

Eugene Onegin ch. 7, st. 36 (1833) (translation by Babette Deutsch)

3 Blessed is he who leaves the glory
Of life's gay feast ere time is up,
Who does not drain the brimming cup,
Nor read the ending of the story,
But drops it without more ado,
As, my Onegin, I drop you.

Eugene Onegin ch. 8, st. 51 (1833) (translation by Babette Deutsch)

Vladimir Putin

Russian political leader, 1952–

1 The collapse of the Soviet Union was the greatest geopolitical catastrophe of the century.

Address to the Russian Parliament, 25 Apr. 2005

Israel Putnam

U.S. general, 1718–1790

1 [*Remark at Battle of Bunker Hill, 17 June 1775:*] Men, you know you are all marksmen, you can take a squirrel from the tallest tree. Don't fire till you see the whites of their eyes.

Attributed in S. Swett, *Notes to His Sketch of Bunker Hill Battle* (1825). The authenticity of these words is often questioned because, according to most sources, they are not documented until 1873; however, this 1825 citation, based on a deposition of a participant in the battle, seems plausible as documentation. In addition, "Don't throw away a single shot, but take good aim; nor touch a trigger, till you can see the whites of their eyes" is attributed to Putnam in M. L. Weems, *The Life of George Washington*, 8th ed. (1809). *The Columbian Phoenix and Boston Review*, June 1800, reported: "He [Putnam] harangued his men as the British first advanced, charged them to reserve their fire, till they were near, 'till they could see the white of their eyes,' were his words." The *Oxford English Dictionary* states that "similar expressions in a number of other European languages are also anecdotally attributed to 18th-cent. military commanders; however, German parallels are attested from as early as the early 17th cent. (see J. Grimm & W. Grimm *Deutsches Wörterbuch* at *weisz* D. 1a)."

Mario Puzo

U.S. writer, 1920–1999

1 A lawyer with his briefcase can steal more than a hundred men with guns.

The Godfather ch. 1 (1969). This line does not appear in the movie version of *The Godfather*.

2 He's a businessman. I'll make him an offer he can't refuse.

The Godfather ch. 1 (1969). The line "I've made Denton an offer he can't refuse" appeared in the 1933 motion picture *Riders of Destiny*.

3 [*Tessio, played by Abe Vigoda, explaining the meaning of a package of fish:*] It's a Sicilian message. It means Luca Brasi sleeps with the fishes.

The Godfather (motion picture) (1972). Coauthored with Francis Ford Coppola. In Puzo's book *The Godfather*, ch. 8, the passage reads: "'The fish means that Luca Brasi is sleeping on the bottom of the ocean,' he [Hagen] said. 'It's an old Sicilian message.'"

4 [*Michael Corleone, played by Al Pacino, speaking:*] If anything in this life is certain, if history has taught us anything, it's that you can kill anyone.

The Godfather: Part II (motion picture) (1974). Coauthored with Francis Ford Coppola.

5 [*Michael Corleone, played by Al Pacino, speaking:*] My father taught me many things here. He taught me: Keep your friends close, but your enemies closer.

The Godfather: Part II (motion picture) (1974). Coauthored with Francis Ford Coppola.

6 [*Michael Corleone, played by Al Pacino, speaking:*] Just when I thought that I was out they pull me back in.

The Godfather: Part III (motion picture) (1990). Coauthored with Francis Ford Coppola.

Thomas Pynchon

U.S. novelist, 1937–

1 A screaming comes across the sky.

Gravity's Rainbow episode 1 (1973)

2 Paranoids are not paranoid because they're paranoid, but because they keep putting themselves, fucking idiots, deliberately into paranoid situations.

Gravity's Rainbow episode 28 (1973)

3 If they can get you asking the wrong questions, they don't have to worry about answers.

Gravity's Rainbow episode 28 (1973)

Pyrrhus

Epirian king, 319 B.C.–272 B.C.

1 [*Remark after defeating the Romans at the Battle of Asculum, 279 B.C.:*] One more such victory and we are lost.

Quoted in Plutarch, *Parallel Lives*

Francis Quarles

English poet, 1592–1644

1 We spend our midday sweat, our midnight oil;
We tire the night in thought, the day in toil.
Emblems bk. 2, no. 2, l. 33 (1635)
See Yeats 40

Dan Quayle

U.S. politician, 1947–

1 [The Holocaust was] an obscene period in our
nation's history. We all lived in this century. I
didn't live in this century, but in this century's
history.
Campaign remark, Moore, Okla., 15 Sept. 1988.
These remarks were quoted in the *L.A. Times*, 16
Sept. 1988.

2 What a waste it is to lose one's mind—or not to
have a mind. . . . How true that is.
Speech to United Negro College Fund, Washington,
D.C., 9 May 1989. This remark was quoted in *USA
Today*, 10 May 1989.
See Advertising Slogans 120

3 If we do not succeed, then we run the risk of
failure.
Speech to Phoenix Republican Forum, Phoenix,
Ariz., 23 Mar. 1990

4 It doesn't help matters when prime time TV has
Murphy Brown—a character who supposedly
epitomized today's intelligent, highly paid,
professional woman—mocking the importance
of fathers by bearing a child alone, and calling
it just another "lifestyle choice."
Remarks to Commonwealth Club of California, San
Francisco, Calif., 19 May 1992

5 Take a breath, Al. . . . Inhale.
Vice-Presidential Debate with Albert Gore, 13 Oct.
1992

6 Space is almost infinite. As a matter of fact, we
think it is infinite.
Quoted in *Daily Telegraph*, 8 Mar. 1989

7 I believe we are on an irreversible trend toward
more freedom and democracy—but that could
change.
Quoted in *Wall Street Journal*, 26 May 1989

8 [*Convincing twelve-year-old spelling bee contestant
William Figueroa to add an e to the word potato,
which Figueroa had spelled correctly:*] That's fine
phonetically, but you're missing just a little bit.
Quoted in *N.Y. Times*, 17 June 1992. This remark
occurred at a school in Trenton, N.J., 15 June 1992.

John Sholto Douglas, Marquess of Queensberry

Scottish nobleman and sports patron, 1844–
1900

1 For Oscar Wilde posing somdomite [*sic*].
Card left at Oscar Wilde's club, 18 Feb. 1895. This
card provoked Wilde's disastrous libel suit against
Queensberry.

Raymond Queneau

French author and critic, 1903–1976

1 You talk, you talk, that's all you know how to do.
Zazie dans le Métro (1959)

François Quesnay

French political economist, 1694–1774

1 *Laisser faire.*
Freedom of action [in commerce].
Quoted in M. Alpha, Letter to Quesnay (1767)
See Boisguilbert 1

Lambert-Adolphe-Jacques Quételet

Belgian statistician, 1796–1874

1 This determination of the average man is not
merely a matter of speculative curiosity; it
may be of the most important service to the
science of man and the social system. It ought
necessarily to precede every other inquiry
into social physics, since it is, as it were, the
basis. The average man, indeed, is in a nation
what the center of gravity is in a body; it is by
having that central point in view that we arrive

at the apprehension of all the phenomena of equilibrium and motion.

A Treatise on Man and the Development of His Faculties bk. 4, ch. 1 (1835) (translation by Robert Knox)

Arthur Quiller-Couch
English writer and critic, 1863–1944

1 Whenever you feel an impulse to perpetrate a piece of exceptionally fine writing, obey it— whole-heartedly—and delete it before sending your manuscript to press. *Murder your darlings.*
On the Art of Writing "On Style" (1916)

Willard Van Orman Quine
U.S. philosopher and mathematician, 1908– 2000

1 To be is to be the value of a variable.
Journal of Philosophy, 21 Dec. 1939

François Rabelais
French humanist and satirist, ca. 1494–ca. 1553

1 *Rire est le propre de l'homme.*
To laugh is proper to man.
Gargantua bk. 1, "Rabelais to the Reader" (1534)

2 The appetite grows by eating.
Gargantua bk. 1, ch. 5 (1534)

3 *Fais ce que voudras.*
Do what you like.
Gargantua bk. 1, ch. 57 (1534)

4 [*"Last words":*] I am going to seek a grand perhaps; draw the curtain, the farce is played.
Attributed in Peter Motteux, *Life of Rabelais* (1693–1694). These words are probably apocryphal.

Yitzhak Rabin
Israeli prime minister and military leader, 1922–1995

1 We say to you today in a loud and a clear voice: enough of blood and tears. Enough.
Remark to Palestinians upon signing of the Israel-Palestine Declaration, Washington, D.C., 13 Sept. 1993

2 One does not make peace with one's friends. One makes peace with one's enemy.
Jerusalem Post, 26 Nov. 1993

3 [*Comment on the "intifada" rebellion:*] I've learned something in the past two and a half months. Among other things is that you can't rule by force over 1.5 million Palestinians.
Quoted in *St. Petersburg Times*, 25 Feb. 1988

Jean Racine
French playwright, 1639–1699

1 *Je l'ai trop aimé pour ne le point haïr!*
I have loved him too much not to feel any hatred for him.
Andromaque act 2, sc. 1 (1667)

2 In a month, in a year, how will we bear that so many seas separate me from you?
Bérénice act 4, sc. 5 (1670)

3 *Je le vis, je rougis, je pâlis à sa vue.*
I saw him, I blushed, I paled at his view.
Phèdre act 1, sc. 3 (1677)

4 *Ce n'est plus une ardeur dans mes veines cachée:*
C'est Vénus tout entière à sa proie attachée.
It's no longer a burning within my veins: it's Venus entire latched onto her prey.
Phèdre act 1, sc. 3 (1677)

5 The day is not purer than the depths of my heart.
Phèdre act 4, sc. 2 (1677)

Ann Radcliffe
English novelist, 1764–1823

1 Fate sits on these dark battlements, and frowns,
And, as the portals open to receive me,
Her voice, in sullen echoes through the courts,
Tells of a nameless deed.
The Mysteries of Udolpho vol. 1, epigraph (1794)

Radio Catchphrases
See also Television Catchphrases.

1 Hey, Abbott!
Abbott and Costello Program

2 I'm a ba-a-a-d boy!
Abbott and Costello Program

3 This is Ray Goulding reminding you to write if you get work . . . and Bob Elliott reminding you to hang by your thumbs.
Bob and Ray

4 My name's Friday. I'm a cop.
Dragnet. On the later television series of *Dragnet*, this became "This is the city. Los Angeles, California. I work here. I carry a badge. My name's Friday."

5 All we want are the facts, ma'am.
Dragnet. Frequently misquoted as "Just the facts, ma'am."

6 The story you have just heard is true. Only
the names have been changed to protect the
innocent.
Dragnet

7 [*Opening of show:*] Hello, Duffy's Tavern, where
the elite meet to eat.
Duffy's Tavern

8 This is—London.
Edward R. Murrow radio broadcasts from London
during World War II

9 'Tain't funny, McGee.
Fibber McGee

10 Now, cut that out.
Jack Benny Show

11 Anaheim, Azusa, and Cu-ca-monga.
Jack Benny Show

12 Vas you dere, Sharlie?
Jack Pearl Show

13 Everybody wants to get into da act!
Jimmy Durante Show

14 What a revoltin' development this is!
Life of Riley

15 The Lone Ranger rides again!
The Lone Ranger

16 Hi-yo Silver!
The Lone Ranger

17 Kemo Sabe.
The Lone Ranger. This phrase may have been intended
to mean "Faithful Friend" or "Trusty Scout," and
may have been taken from the name of a boys' camp
("Kee-Mo-Sah-Bee") established at Mullet Lake,
Mich., in 1911.

18 Who was that masked man?
The Lone Ranger

19 The wheel of fortune goes 'round and 'round
and where she stops nobody knows.
Major Bowes and His Original Amateur Hour

20 Who knows what evil lurks in the hearts of
men? The Shadow knows.
The Shadow

21 Faster than an airplane, more powerful than a
locomotive, impervious to bullets. "Up in the
sky—look!" "It's a giant bird." "It's a plane."
"It's superman!" And now, Superman—A
being no larger than an ordinary man but
possessed of powers and abilities never before
realized on Earth: able to leap into the air
an eighth of a mile at a single bound, hurtle
a 20-story building with ease, race a high-
powered bullet to its target, lift tremendous
weights and rend solid steel in his bare hands
as though it were paper. Superman—a strange
visitor from a distant planet: champion of the
oppressed, physical marvel extraordinary who
has sworn to devote his existence on Earth to
helping those in need.
Superman. This original opening was written
by Robert Joffe Maxwell and Allen Ducovny and
broadcast on 12 Feb. 1940. The opening had many
later variations, including the following well-known
form:
"Faster than a speeding bullet! More powerful than
a locomotive! Able to leap tall buildings at a single
bound!"
"Look! Up in the sky!"
"It's a bird!"
"It's a plane!"
"It's Superman!"
See Nietzsche 13; Radio Catchphrases 22; George Bernard
Shaw 11; Siegel 1; Television Catchphrases 6

22 Up, up, and away!
Superman
See Nietzsche 13; Radio Catchphrases 21; George Bernard
Shaw 11; Siegel 1; Television Catchphrases 6

23 The sixty-four dollar question.
Take It or Leave It. In the television version of this
show in the 1950s, the show title and catchphrase was
"the sixty-four thousand dollar question."

24 [*Opening of broadcasts:*] Good evening, Mr. and
Mrs. North and South America and all the
ships at sea. . . . Let's go to press!
Walter Winchell newscasts

James Rado (James Alexander Radomski)
U.S. songwriter, 1932–

1 When the moon is in the seventh house,
And Jupiter aligns with Mars,
Then peace will guide the planets,
And love will steer the stars;
This is the dawning of the age of Aquarius.
"Aquarius" (song) (1967). Cowritten with Gerome
Ragni.

John Rae

Scottish-born Canadian-U.S. economist, 1796–1872

1 The things to which vanity seems most readily to apply itself are those to which the use or consumption is most apparent, and of which the effects are most difficult to discriminate. Articles of which the consumption is not conspicuous, are incapable of gratifying this passion.

Statement of Some New Principles on the Subject of Political Economy ch. 11 (1834). This anticipated Thorstein Veblen's use of the term *conspicuous consumption.*
See Veblen 2

Craig Raine

English poet, 1944–

1 Caxtons are mechanical birds with many wings
And some are treasured for their markings—
They cause the eyes to melt
Or the body to shriek without pain.
"A Martian Sends a Postcard Home" l. 1 (1979)

2 In homes, a haunted apparatus sleeps,
That snores when you pick it up.
If the ghost cries, they carry it
To their lips and soothe it to sleep
With sounds. And yet, they wake it up
Deliberately, by tickling with a finger.
"A Martian Sends a Postcard Home" l. 19 (1979)

Rakim (William Michael Griffin, Jr.)

U.S. rap musician, 1968–

1 I start to think, and then I sink
Into the paper like I was ink
When I'm writing, I'm trapped in between the lines
I escape when I finish the rhyme.
"I Know You Got Soul" (song) (1987)

Walter Ralegh

English courtier and explorer, ca. 1552–1618

1 Say to the court, it glows
And shines like rotten wood;
Say to the church, it shows
What's good, and doth no good:
If church and court reply,
Then give them both the lie.
"The Lie" l. 7 (1608)

2 Fain would I climb, yet fear I to fall.

Quoted in Thomas Fuller, *History of the Worthies of England* (1662). Written on a window-pane; Queen Elizabeth I wrote under it, "If thy heart fails thee, climb not at all."

Walter Raleigh

English lecturer and critic, 1861–1922

1 I wish I loved the Human Race;
I wish I loved its silly face;
I wish I liked the way it walks;
I wish I liked the way it talks;
And when I'm introduced to one
I wish I thought *What Jolly Fun!*
"Wishes of an Elderly Man" l. 1 (1923)

Srinavasa Ramanujan

Indian mathematician, 1887–1920

1 [*Replying to G. H. Hardy's statement that the number on the back of a taxicab (1729) was a dull number:*] No, it is a very interesting number, it is the smallest number expressible as a sum of two cubes in two different ways.

Quoted in *Proceedings of the London Mathematical Society,* 26 May 1921

2 Sir, an equation has no meaning for me unless it expresses a thought of God.

Quoted in Shiyali Ramamrita Ranganathan, *Ramanujan, the Man and the Mathematician* (1967)

Joey Ramone (Jeffrey Ross Hyman)

U.S. musician, 1951–2001

1 Twenty-twenty-twenty four hours to go
I wanna be sedated
Nothing to do, nowhere to go
I wanna be sedated.
"I Wanna Be Sedated" (song) (1978)

Tommy Ramone (Tamás Erdélyi)

Hungarian-born U.S. musician, 1949–2014

1 Hey ho, let's go.
"Blitzkrieg Bop" (song) (1976)

Ayn Rand (Alissa Rosenbaum)

Russian-born U.S. writer, 1905–1982

1 Howard Roark laughed.
The Fountainhead pt. 1, ch. 1 (1943)

2 Kill reverence and you've killed the hero
in man.
The Fountainhead pt. 4, ch. 14 (1943)

3 Civilization is the progress toward a society of
privacy. The savage's whole existence is public,
ruled by the laws of his tribe. Civilization is the
process of setting men free from men.
The Fountainhead pt. 4, ch. 18 (1943)

4 It had to be said. The world is perishing from
an orgy of self-sacrificing.
The Fountainhead pt. 4, ch. 18 (1943)

5 Who is John Galt?
Atlas Shrugged pt. 1, ch. 1 (1957)

6 I swear by my life and my love of it that I will
never live for the sake of another man, nor ask
another man to live for mine.
Atlas Shrugged pt. 3, ch. 1 (1957)

James Ryder Randall
U.S. journalist and poet, 1839–1908

1 Avenge the patriotic gore
That flecked the streets of Baltimore,
And be the battle queen of yore,
Maryland! My Maryland!
"Maryland! My Maryland!" (song) (1861)

Leopold von Ranke
German historian, 1795–1886

1 To history has been assigned the office of
judging the past, of instructing the present for
the benefit of future generations. This work
does not have such a lofty ambition. It wants
only to show what actually happened.
*History of the Romance and Germanic Peoples, 1492–
1535* preface (1824)
See Benjamin 2

Jeannette Rankin
U.S. politician and activist, 1880–1973

1 [*Casting her vote against U.S. declaration entering
World War I, 1917:*] I want to stand by my
country, but I cannot vote for war. I vote no.
Quoted in Hannah Josephson, *Jeannette Rankin: First
Lady in Congress* (1974)

2 [*Explaining her vote in Congress against the
United States entering World War II, Dec. 1941:*]
As a woman I can't go to war, and I refuse to
send anyone else.
Quoted in Hannah Josephson, *Jeannette Rankin: First
Lady in Congress* (1974)

3 You can no more win a war than you can win
an earthquake.
Quoted in Hannah Josephson, *Jeannette Rankin: First
Lady in Congress* (1974)

François-Vincent Raspail
French natural philosopher, 1794–1878

1 *Omnis cellua e cellula.*
Every cell is derived from another cell.
Annales des Sciences Naturelles (1825)

Dan Rather
U.S. news broadcaster, 1931–

1 [*Response to President Richard Nixon's question
at a Houston, Tex., press conference, Mar. 1974,
"Are you running for something?":*] No, sir, Mr.
President. Are you?
Quoted in *Wash. Post,* 21 Apr. 1974

Terence Rattigan
English playwright, 1911–1977

1 Do you know what *"le vice Anglais"*—the
English vice—really is? Not flagellation, not
pederasty—whatever the French believe it to
be. It's our refusal to admit our emotions. We
think they demean us, I suppose.
In Praise of Love act 2 (1973)

Maurice Ravel
French composer, 1875–1937

1 [*"Last words":*] I've still so much music in my
head. I have said nothing. I have so much more
to say.
Quoted in Hélène Jourdan-Morhange, *Ravel et Nous*
(1945)

Marjorie Rawlings
U.S. novelist, 1896–1953

1 A woman has got to love a bad man once or
twice in her life, to be thankful for a good one.
The Yearling ch. 12 (1938)

John Rawls
U.S. philosopher, 1921–2002

1 Justice is the first virtue of social institutions, as truth is of systems of thought. A theory however elegant and economical must be rejected or revised if it is untrue; likewise laws and institutions no matter how efficient and well-arranged must be reformed or abolished if they are unjust.
A Theory of Justice ch. 1 (1971)

2 Each person possesses an inviolability founded on justice that even the welfare of society as a whole cannot override.
A Theory of Justice ch. 1 (1971)

3 The principles of justice are chosen behind a veil of ignorance.
A Theory of Justice ch. 1 (1971)

Elizabeth Ray
U.S. congressional clerk, 1943–

1 [*Remark upon revealing that she was the mistress, paid by the government, of Congressman Wayne Hays:*] I can't type. I can't file. I can't even answer the phone.
Quoted in *Wash. Post,* 23 May 1976

Sam Rayburn
U.S. politician, 1882–1961

1 If you want to get along, go along.
N.Y. Times, 19 Feb. 1955. This was Speaker of the House of Representatives Rayburn's advice to new members of Congress. The *Kerrville* (Tex.) *Times,* 14 Oct. 1952, referred to "Get-Along, Go-Along Sam Rayburn."

Don Raye (Donald Macrae Wilhoite, Jr.)
U.S. songwriter, 1909–1985

1 He's the Boogie Woogie Bugle Boy of Company B.
"Boogie Woogie Bugle Boy" (song) (1941). Cowritten with Hughie Prince.

Eric S. Raymond
U.S. computer programmer, 1957–

1 Given enough eyeballs, all bugs are shallow.
"The Cathedral and the Bazaar" (paper published on Internet) (1997). Raymond called this "Linus' Law" after Linus Torvalds.

Andy Razaf
U.S. songwriter, 1895–1973

1 Ain't misbehavin',
I'm savin' my love for you.
"Ain't Misbehavin'" (song) (1929)

2 The Joint Is Jumpin'.
Title of song (1938). Cowritten with J. C. Johnson.

Carveth Read
English philosopher, 1848–1931

1 It is better to be vaguely right than exactly wrong.
Logic: Deductive and Inductive ch. 22 (1898)

Nancy Reagan
U.S. First Lady, 1921–2016

1 A woman is like a tea bag. You never know her strength until she is in hot water.
Remarks to National Federation of Republican Women, 12 Mar. 1981. As far back as 14 Dec. 1876, the *New Orleans Republican* printed "a person's real strength of character is not drawn out until he gets in hot water." The "woman" variant showed up by 1963, in the *Dallas Morning News,* 29 Oct.

Ronald W. Reagan
U.S. president, 1911–2004

1 No government ever voluntarily reduces itself in size. Government programs, once launched, never disappear. Actually, a government bureau is the nearest thing to eternal life we'll ever see on this earth!
Television broadcast, 27 Oct. 1964. "The nearest approach to immortality on earth is a government bureau" appeared earlier in James F. Byrnes, *Speaking Frankly* (1947).

2 Politics is supposed to be the second oldest profession. I have come to realize that it bears a very close resemblance to the first.
Conference, Los Angeles, Calif., 2 Mar. 1977

3 I've noticed that everyone that is for abortion has already been born.
Presidential campaign debate, 21 Sept. 1980. Similar statements (not by Reagan) referring to "birth control" rather than "abortion" are recorded as early as 1965.

4 Next Tuesday all of you will go to the polls, will stand there in the polling place and make a decision. I think when you make that decision it might be well if you would ask yourself: Are you better off than you were four years ago?
Televised presidential debate, 28 Oct. 1980

5 [To his Democratic opponent Jimmy Carter:] There you go again!
Televised presidential debate, 28 Oct. 1980

6 In your discussions of the nuclear freeze proposals, I urge you to beware the temptation of pride—the temptation of blithely declaring yourselves above it all and label both sides equally at fault, to ignore the facts of history and the aggressive impulses of an evil empire.
Remarks at Annual Convention of National Association of Evangelicals, Orlando, Fla., 8 Mar. 1983
See George Lucas 11

7 My fellow Americans, I am pleased to tell you I just signed legislation which outlaws Russia forever. The bombing begins in five minutes.
Remarks during radio microphone test, 11 Aug. 1984

8 [Referring to his younger opponent, Walter Mondale:] I will not make age an issue of this campaign. I am not going to exploit, for political purposes, my opponent's youth and inexperience.
Televised presidential debate, 22 Oct. 1984

9 I have my veto pen drawn and ready for any tax increase that Congress might even think of sending up. And I have only one thing to say to the tax increasers: Go ahead, make my day.
Remarks to American Business Conference, Washington, D.C., 13 Mar. 1985
See Film Lines 164

10 We're especially not going to tolerate these attacks from outlaw states run by the strangest collection of misfits, looney tunes, and squalid criminals since the advent of the Third Reich.
Remarks at American Bar Association Annual Convention, Washington, D.C., 8 July 1985

11 Back then [before 1981], government's view of the economy could be summed up in a few short phrases: If it moves, tax it. If it keeps moving, regulate it. And if it stops moving, subsidize it.
Remarks to state chairs of National White House Conference on Small Business, 15 Aug. 1986. "If it moves, control it; if you cannot control it, tax it; if you cannot tax it, subsidize it" appeared in the Chicago Daily Tribune, 20 July 1952.

12 I did say something in our negotiations in Iceland in Russian: Dovorey no provorey. That means trust, but verify.
Remarks at campaign rally, Springfield, Mo., 23 Oct. 1986
See Modern Proverbs 92

13 A few months ago I told the American people I did not trade arms for hostages. My heart and my best intentions still tell me that is true, but the facts and the evidence tell me it is not.
Televised address to nation, 4 Mar. 1987

14 Mr. Gorbachev, open this gate! Mr. Gorbachev, tear down this wall!
Remarks at Brandenburg Gate, West Berlin, Germany, 12 June 1987

15 I have recently been told that I am one of the millions of Americans who will be afflicted with Alzheimer's Disease. . . . I now begin the journey that will lead me into the sunset of my life. I know that for America there will always be a bright dawn ahead.
Letter to the American people, 5 Nov. 1994

16 We should declare war on North Vietnam.
. . . We could pave the whole country and put parking stripes on it, and still be home for Christmas.
Quoted in Fresno Bee, 10 Oct. 1965

17 The Government is like a baby's alimentary canal, with a healthy appetite at one end and no responsibility at the other.
Quoted in N.Y. Times Magazine, 14 Nov. 1965. Although this line is associated with Reagan, Reader's Digest, July 1937, attributed "BABY: An alimentary canal with a loud voice at one end and no responsibility at the other" to Elizabeth I. Adamson.

18 A tree's a tree. How many more do you need to look at?

> Quoted in *Sacramento Bee*, 12 Mar. 1966. Speech to Western Wood Products Association, 12 Sept. 1965.

19 Approximately 80% of our air pollution stems from hydrocarbons released by vegetation, so let's not go overboard in setting and enforcing tough emission standards from man-made sources.

> Quoted in *Sierra*, 10 Sept. 1980

20 [*To the surgeons about to operate on him after he was shot by John Hinckley:*] Please tell me you're Republicans.

> Quoted in *Wash. Post*, 31 Mar. 1981

Red Cloud
Native American leader, 1822–1909

1 You have the sound of the white soldier's axe upon the Little Piney. His presence here is . . . an insult to the spirits of our ancestors. Are we then to give up their sacred graves to be ploughed for corn? Dakotas, I am for war!

> Speech at council, Fort Laramie, Wyo., 1866

2 When the white men came we gave them lands, and did not wish to hurt them. But the white man drove us back and took our lands. Then the Great Father [president of the United States] made us many promises, but they are not kept. He promised to give us large presents, and when they came to us they were small; they seemed to be lost on the way.

> Speech at Council of Peace, New York, N.Y., 15 June 1870

Red Jacket
Native American leader, ca. 1751–1830

1 Brother, our seats were once large, and yours were small. You have now become a great people, and we have scarcely a place left to spread our blankets. You have got our country, but are not satisfied; you want to force your religion upon us.

> Quoted in Norman B. Wood, *Lives of Famous Indian Chiefs* (1906). The original source is a speech to a Christian missionary in 1805.

Otis Redding
U.S. musician and songwriter, 1941–1967

1 What you want baby I got it
What you need you know I got it
All I'm askin' for is a little respect.
> "Respect" (song) (1965)

2 I'm sittin' on the dock of the bay,
Watchin' the tide roll away,
I'm just sittin' on the dock of the bay,
Wasting time.
> "Sittin' on the Dock of the Bay" (song) (1968). Cowritten with Steve Cropper.

Helen Reddy
Australian singer, ca. 1941–2020

1 I am woman hear me roar
In numbers too big to ignore
And I know too much to go back and pretend.
> "I Am Woman" (song) (1971)

2 If I have to, I can do anything.
I am strong, I am invincible, I am woman.
> "I Am Woman" (song) (1971)

Florence Reece
U.S. labor activist, 1900–1986

1 Come all of you good workers,
Good news to you I'll tell
Of how the good old union
Has come in here to dwell.
Which side are you on,
Tell me, which side are you on?
> "Which Side Are You On?" (song) (1931)

Henry Reed
English poet and playwright, 1914–1986

1 Today we have naming of parts. Yesterday,
We had daily cleaning. And tomorrow morning,
We shall have what to do after firing. But today,
Today we have naming of parts. Japonica
Glistens like coral in all of the neighbor gardens,
And today we have naming of parts.
> "Lessons of the War: 1, Naming of Parts" l. 1 (1946)

2 We can slide it
Rapidly backwards and forwards: we call this

Easing the spring. And rapidly backwards and
   forwards
The early bees are assaulting and fumbling the
   flowers:
They call it easing the Spring.
"Lessons of the War: 1, Naming of Parts" l. 20 (1946)

3 They call it easing the Spring; it is
   perfectly easy
If you have any strength in your thumb: like the
   bolt,
And the breech, and the cocking-piece, and the
   point of balance,
Which in our case we have not got; and the
   almond blossom
Silent in all of the gardens and the bees going
   backwards and forwards,
For today we have naming of parts.
"Lessons of the War: 1, Naming of Parts" l. 25 (1946)

4   And as for war, my wars
Were global from the start.
"Lessons of the War: 3, Unarmed Combat" l. 35
(1946)

John Reed
U.S. journalist and revolutionary, 1887–1920

1 Ten Days That Shook the World.
Title of book (1919)

Lou Reed
U.S. rock musician, 1942–2013

1 I don't know just where I'm going
But I'm gonna try for the kingdom, if I can
'Cause it makes me feel like I'm a man
When I put a spike into my vein
And I tell you things aren't quite the same
When I'm rushing on my run
And I feel just like Jesus's son
And I guess that I just don't know
And I guess that I just don't know.
"Heroin" (song) (1967)

2 It's such a perfect day
I'm glad I spent it with you
Oh, such a perfect day
You just keep me hanging on.
"Perfect Day" (song) (1972)

3 Holly came from Miami F-L-A
Hitchhiked her way across the U.S.A.
Plucked her eyebrows on the way

Shaved her legs and then he was a she
She says, Hey babe, take a walk on the wild
   side.
"Walk on the Wild Side" (song) (1972)
See Algren 1

Thomas B. Reed
U.S. politician, 1839–1902

1 [Remark, ca. 1880:] A statesman is a successful
politician—who is dead.
Quoted in State (Columbia, S.C.), 27 Feb. 1892
See Bierce 106; Truman 10

2 They [two fellow Congressmen] never open
their mouths without subtracting from the sum
of human knowledge.
Quoted in Samuel W. McCall, The Life of Thomas
Brackett Reed (1914)

Martin Rees
English astronomer, 1942–

1 Absence of evidence is not evidence of absence.
Quoted in Project Cyclops: A Design Study of a System
for Detecting Extraterrestrial Intelligent Life, rev. ed., ed.
B. M. Oliver and J. Billingham (1973). Although this
is associated with Rees, a much earlier occurrence
was by Dugald Bell, quoted in The Glacialists'
Magazine, Dec. 1895. "The distinction between
absence of evidence and evidence of absence" was
mentioned in Live Stock Journal, 16 Oct. 1891.

Billy Reeves
U.S. songwriter, fl. 1866

1 Shoo fly, don't bother me, shoo fly, don't
   bother me,
Shoo fly, don't bother me, I belong to
   Company G.
"Shoo Fly, Don't Bother Me" (song) (1866)

Max Reger
German composer, 1873–1916

1 [Response to negative review by Rudolf Louis of
   Reger's Sinfonietta, 1906:] Ich sitze in dem
   kleinsten Zimmer in meinem Hause. Ich habe
   Ihre Kritik vor mir. Im nächsten Augenblick
   wird sie hinter mir sein.
I am sitting in the smallest room of my house.
   I have your review before me. In a moment it
   will be behind me.
Quoted in Nicholas Slonimsky, Lexicon of Musical
Invective: Critical Assaults on Composers Since

Beethoven's Time (1953). Nigel Rees points out in *Cassell's Humorous Quotations* that an earlier version of this jab appeared in a 1785 letter reported as follows: "When Mr. Eden, afterwards Lord Auckland, deserted the standard of Fox for that of Pitt, he sent, in justification of his apostacy, a circular letter to his former political colleagues. The reply of Lord Sandwich [John George Montagu] was sufficiently laconic: 'Sir,' he said, 'your letter is before me, and will presently be behind'" (John Heneage Jesse, *George Selwyn and His Contemporaries* vol. 1 [1843]).

Charles A. Reich
U.S. legal scholar and author, 1928–2019

1 The institution called property guards the troubled boundary between individual man and the state. . . . In a society that chiefly values material well-being, the power to control a particular portion of that well-being is the very foundation of individuality.
"The New Property," *Yale Law Journal*, Apr. 1964

2 If an individual is to survive in a collective society, he must have protection against its ruthless pressures. There must be sanctuaries or enclaves where no majority can reach. . . . Just as the Homestead Act was a deliberate effort to foster individual values at an earlier time, so we must try to build an economic basis for liberty today—a Homestead Act for rootless twentieth century man. We must create a new property.
"The New Property," *Yale Law Journal*, Apr. 1964

3 The good society must have its hiding places— its protected crannies for the soul. Under the pitiless eye of safety the soul will wither. If I choose to get in my car and drive somewhere, it seems to me that where I am coming from, and where I am going, are nobody's business; I know of no law that requires me to have either a purpose or a destination. If I choose to take an evening walk to see if Andromeda has come up on schedule, I think I am entitled to look for the distant light of Almach and Mirach without finding myself staring into the blinding beam of a police flashlight.
"Police Questioning of Law Abiding Citizens," *Yale Law Journal*, June 1966

4 There is a revolution coming. It will not be like revolutions of the past. It will originate with the individual and with culture, and it will change the political structure only as its final act. It will not require violence to succeed, and it cannot be successfully resisted by violence.
The Greening of America ch. 1 (1970)

5 The extraordinary thing about this new consciousness is that it has emerged out of the wasteland of the Corporate State. For one who thought the world was irretrievably encased in metal and plastic and sterile stone, it seems a remarkable greening of America.
The Greening of America ch. 12 (1970)

Erich Maria Remarque
German novelist, 1898–1970

1 He fell in October 1918, on a day that was so quiet and still on the whole front, that the army report confined itself to the single sentence: All quiet on the Western Front.
　　He had fallen forward and lay on the earth as though sleeping. Turning him over one saw that he could not have suffered long; his face had an expression of calm, as though almost glad the end had come.
All Quiet on the Western Front ch. 12 (1929) (translation by A. W. Wheen)
See Beers 1

Ernest Renan
French philologist and historian, 1823–1892

1 War is a condition of progress; the whip-cut that prevents a country from going to sleep and forces satisfied mediocrity to shake off its apathy.
La Réforme Intellectuelle et Morale (1871)

2 The simplest schoolboy is now familiar with facts for which Archimedes would have sacrificed his life.
Souvenirs d'Enfance et de Jeunesse preface (1883)

Jean Renoir
French film director, 1894–1979

1 A director makes only one film in his life. Then he breaks it into pieces and makes it again.
Quoted in Leslie Halliwell, *Halliwell's Filmgoer's Companion* (1993)

Pierre-Auguste Renoir
French painter, 1841–1919

1 It's with my brush that I make love.

Quoted in Albert André, *Renoir* (1919). Another commonly quoted version is "I paint with my prick."

2 I have a predilection for painting that lends joyousness to a wall.

Quoted in Ambroise Vollard, *Auguste Renoir* (1920)

3 In a few generations you can breed a racehorse. The recipe for making a man like Delacroix is less well known.

Quoted in Jean Renoir, *Renoir My Father* (1958)

Charles à Repington
English journalist, 1858–1925

1 [*Diary entry, 10 Sept. 1918:*] We discussed the right name of the war. I said that we called it now *The War,* but that this could not last. The Napoleonic War was *The Great War.* To call it *The German War* was too much flattery for the Boche. I suggested *The World War* as a shade better title, and finally we mutually agreed to call it *The First World War* in order to prevent the millennium folk from forgetting that the history of the world was the history of war.

The First World War, 1914–18 (1920)
See Haeckel 2

Jean-François Paul de Gondi, Cardinal de Retz
French cardinal, 1613–1679

1 *Il n'y a rien dans le monde qui n'ait son moment décisif.*
There is nothing in the world which does not have its decisive moment.

Mémoires bk. 2 (1717)

David Reuben
U.S. psychiatrist, 1933–

1 Everything You Always Wanted to Know About Sex, But Were Afraid to Ask.

Title of book (1969)

Paul Reubens
English composer, 1875–1917

1 Tonight's the Night.

Title of song and musical comedy (1915)

Paul Revere
Colonial American revolutionary leader and businessman, 1735–1818

1 If the British went out by Water, we would shew two Lanthorns in the North Church Steeple; and if by Land, one, as a Signal.

Letter to Jeremy Belknap, 1798
See Longfellow 24

2 [*Alleged cry while riding to warn American colonists of the approach of British troops:*] The British are coming!

Attributed in Nathaniel Shatswell Dodge, *Stories of a Grandfather About American History* (1874). This famous line is apocryphal; the colonists would have thought of themselves as British. Revere may instead have said "The Regulars are coming out!"

Charles H. Revson
U.S. business executive, 1906–1975

1 In the factory, we make cosmetics; in the store we sell hope.

Quoted in Andrew P. Tobias, *Fire and Ice* (1976)

H. A. Rey
German-born U.S. children's book writer, 1898–1977

1 This is George. He lived in Africa. He was a good little monkey and always very curious.

Curious George (1941)

Malvina Reynolds
U.S. songwriter, 1900–1978

1 Little boxes on the hillside,
Little boxes made of ticky-tacky,
Little boxes on the hillside,
Little boxes all the same.

"Little Boxes" (song) (1962)

Trent Reznor
U.S. rock musician, 1965–

1 I hurt myself today
To see if I still feel.

"Hurt" (song) (1994)

J. B. Rhine
U.S. psychologist, 1895–1980

1 Let us merely say . . . "perception by means that are outside of the recognized senses,"

and indicate this meaning by "Extra-Sensory Perception" or E.S.P.

Extra-Sensory Perception preface (1934)

Deborah L. Rhode

U.S. legal scholar, 1952–2021

1 Lawyers like to leave no stone unturned, provided they can charge by the stone.

Stanford Law Review, Jan. 1985

Cecil J. Rhodes

South African statesman, 1853–1902

1 I also desire to encourage and foster an appreciation of the advantages which I implicitly believe will result from the union of the English-speaking peoples throughout the world and to encourage in the students from the United States of North America who will benefit from the American Scholarships to be established for the reason above given at the University of Oxford under this my Will an attachment to the country from which they have sprung but without I hope withdrawing them or their sympathies from the land of their adoption or birth.

The Last Will and Testament of Cecil John Rhodes, ed. W. T. Stead (1902)

2 [*Remark on the day of his death:*] So little done, so much to do.

Quoted in Lewis Mitchell, *Life of Rhodes* (1910)
See Tennyson 31

3 Remember that you are an Englishman, and have consequently won first prize in the lottery of life.

Attributed in Peter Ustinov, *Dear Me* (1977)

Jean Rhys

Dominica-born English novelist, 1890–1979

1 They say when trouble comes close ranks, and so the white people did.

Wide Sargasso Sea pt. 1 (1966)

Abraham Ribicoff

U.S. politician, 1910–1998

1 And with George McGovern as President of the United States we wouldn't have to have Gestapo tactics in the streets of Chicago.

Speech nominating George McGovern, Democratic National Convention, Chicago, Ill., 28 Aug. 1968

Mirella Ricciardi

Kenyan-born English photographer, 1931–

1 Black people are natural, they possess the secret of joy.

African Saga ch. 14 (1981)
See Alice Walker 8; Alice Walker 9

Condoleezza Rice

U.S. government official and educator, 1954–

1 [*Response to questioning about whether the President's Daily Brief of 6 Aug. 2001 warned against Al Qaida attacks within the United States:*] I believe the title was, "Bin Laden Determined to Attack Inside the United States."

Testimony before National Commission on Terrorist Attacks upon the United States, 7 Apr. 2004

2 There was no silver bullet that could have prevented the 9/11 attacks.

Testimony before National Commission on Terrorist Attacks upon the United States, 8 Apr. 2004. Rice had made similar statements in broadcast interviews in Mar. 2004.

Grantland Rice

U.S. sportswriter, 1880–1954

1 For when the One Great Scorer comes to write
   against your name,
He marks—not that you won or lost—but how
   you played the Game.

"Alumnus Football" l. 63 (1908)

2 [*Reporting Notre Dame's football victory over Army:*] Outlined against a blue-gray October sky, the Four Horsemen rode again. In dramatic lore they were known as Famine, Pestilence, Destruction, and Death. These are only aliases. Their real names are Stuhldreher, Miller, Crowley, and Layden.

N.Y. Herald Tribune, 19 Oct. 1924. The "Four Horsemen" is a reference to the four allegorical horses in Revelation 6:1–8.
See Blasco-Ibáñez 1; Margaret Chase Smith 1

3 All wars are planned by old men
In council rooms apart.

"Two Sides of War" l. 1 (1930)
See Herbert Hoover 5

Tim Rice

English songwriter, 1944–

1 Jesus Christ
Who are you? What have you sacrificed?
"Superstar" (song) (1971)

2 Jesus Christ
Superstar
Do you think you're what they say you are?
"Superstar" (song) (1971)

3 Don't cry for me Argentina
The truth is I never left you
All through my wild days
My mad existence
I kept my promise
Don't keep your distance.
"Don't Cry for Me Argentina" (song) (1976)

Mandy Rice-Davies

English model and showgirl, 1944–2014

1 [*On Lord Astor's denying her allegations
implicating him in sex scandal:*] He would,
wouldn't he?
Testimony at trial of Stephen Ward, 29 June 1963

Adrienne Rich

U.S. poet, 1929–2012

1 Split at the root, neither Gentile nor Jew,
Yankee, nor Rebel, born
in the face of two ancient cults,
I'm a good reader of histories.
"Readings in History" pt. 5, l. 9 (1963)

2 A thinking woman sleeps with monsters.
The beak that grips her, she becomes.
"Snapshots of a Daughter-in-Law" l. 26 (1963)

3 I put on
the body-armor of black rubber
the absurd flippers
the grave and awkward mask.
"Diving into the Wreck" l. 5 (1973)

4 I came to explore the wreck.
The words are purposes.
The words are maps.
I came to see the damage that was done
and the treasures that prevail.
"Diving into the Wreck" l. 51 (1973)

5 I stroke the beam of my lamp
slowly along the flank
of something more permanent
than fish or weed.
"Diving into the Wreck" l. 57 (1973)

6 The thing I came for:
the wreck and not the story of the wreck
the thing itself and not the myth
the drowned face always staring
toward the sun.
"Diving into the Wreck" l. 61 (1973)

7 We are, I am, you are
by cowardice or courage
the one who find our way
back to this scene
carrying a knife, a camera
a book of myths
in which
our names do not appear.
"Diving into the Wreck" l. 87 (1973)

8 The true nature of poetry. The drive
to connect. The dream of a common language.
"Origins and History of Consciousness" pt. 1, l. 11
(1972–1974)

Janet Radcliffe Richards

English philosopher, 1944–

1 It seems most unlikely that so much effort
would have been put into making women
artificially dependent on men if they had been
naturally so.
The Sceptical Feminist: A Philosophical Enquiry ch. 5
(1980)

2 Men may have had their own very good reasons
for bringing women up in servitude, but the
soul of a servant is not an attractive thing,
and one of the most infuriating aspects of
women's constricted upbringing is that it has
made them less attractive, even in the eyes of
their constrictors, than they should have been.
Man has twisted and pruned women out of all
recognition and *then not liked the results.*
The Sceptical Feminist: A Philosophical Enquiry ch. 5
(1980)

Keith Richards

English rock musician and songwriter, 1943–

1 [*Responding to a fan's request that he autograph a school chemistry book:*] Sure thing, man. I used to be a laboratory myself once.
Quoted in *Independent on Sunday*, 7 Aug. 1994

Laura Elizabeth Richards

U.S. writer, 1850–1943

1 Once there was an elephant,
Who tried to use the telephant—
No! No! I mean an elephone
Who tried to use the telephone.
"Eletelephony" l. 1 (ca. 1880)

Samuel Richardson

English novelist, 1689–1761

1 Power and riches never want advocates.
Pamela Letter 24 (1740–1744)

Armand Jean du Plessis, Duc de Richelieu

French statesman and cardinal, 1585–1642

1 *Qu'on me donne six lignes écrites de la main du plus honnête homme, j'y trouverai de quoi le faire pendre.*
If you give me six lines written by the hand of the most honest of men, I will find something in them which will hang him.
Attributed in Édouard Fournier, *L'Esprit dans l'Histoire: Recherches et Curiosités sur les Mots Historiques* (1857). Fournier actually rejects the quotation's attribution to Richelieu. Othon Guerlac, *Les Citations Françaises* cites the eighteenth-century *Mémoires de Mme. de Motteville* as quoting Richelieu: "with two lines of writing by a man one can indict the most innocent." Guerlac states, however, that the saying is generally credited to the judge Laubardemont.

Mordecai Richler

Canadian writer, 1931–2001

1 I'm world-famous, Dr. Parks said, all over Canada.
The Incomparable Atuk pt. 1, ch. 4 (1963)

2 Even in Paris, I remained a Canadian. I puffed hashish, but I didn't inhale.
St. Urbain's Horseman ch. 2 (1971)
See Bill Clinton 14

3 The Canadian kid who wants to grow up to be Prime Minister isn't thinking big, he is setting a limit to his ambitions rather early.
Quoted in *Time* (Canadian ed.), 31 May 1971

Johann Paul Friedrich Richter

German novelist, 1763–1825

1 *Weltschmerz.*
World pain.
Selina; or, Above Immortality (1827)

Branch Rickey

U.S. baseball executive, 1881–1965

1 Luck is the residue of design.
Quoted in *Lexington* (Ky.) *Herald*, 1 Nov. 1915

Hyman G. Rickover

U.S. admiral, 1900–1986

1 When men in Communist Russia fail, in Government or in industry, they are summarily dismissed. We, on the other hand, protect those who fail and grasp them even more tightly to the Government's bosom. We let them privatize profits and socialize losses.
Testimony before Subcommittee on Priorities and Economy in Government of the Joint Economic Committee, U.S. Congress, 28 Apr. 1971

David Riesman

U.S. sociologist, 1909–2002

1 The Lonely Crowd.
Title of book (1951)

Rig Veda

Indian collection of hymns, Second millennium B.C.

1 When they divided the Man, into how many parts did they apportion him? What did they call his mouth, his two arms and thighs and feet?
His mouth became the Brahman; his arms were made into the Warrior, his thighs the People, and from his feet the Servants were born.
Hymn of Man bk. 10, hymn 190, v. 11

James Whitcomb Riley
U.S. poet, 1849–1916

1 An' all us other children, when the supper
   things is done,
We set around the kitchen fire an' has the
   mostest fun
A'list'nin' to the witch tales 'at Annie tells
   about,
An' the gobble-uns 'at gits you
Ef you
   Don't
      Watch
         Out!
"Little Orphant Annie" l. 5 (1885). This poem was
originally published under the title "The Elf-Child."

Rainer Maria Rilke
German poet, 1875–1926

1 But, once the realization is accepted that even
between the *closest* human beings infinite
distances continue to exist, a wonderful living
side by side can grow up, if they succeed in
loving the distance between them which makes
it possible for each to see the other whole and
against a wide sky!
Letter to Emanuel von Bodman, 17 Aug. 1901

2 Who, if I cried out, would hear me among the
   angels'
hierarchies?
Duino Elegies no. 1 (written 1912) (translation by
Stephen Mitchell)

3   Beauty is nothing
but the beginning of terror, which we still are
   just able to endure,
and we are so awed because it serenely disdains
to annihilate us. Every angel is terrifying.
Duino Elegies no. 1 (written 1912) (translation by
Stephen Mitchell)

4 If no one else, the dying
must notice how unreal, how full of pretense,
is all that we accomplish here, where nothing
is allowed to be itself.
Duino Elegies no. 4 (written 1912) (translation by
Stephen Mitchell)

Arthur Rimbaud
French poet, 1854–1891

1 *A noir, E blanc, I rouge, U vert, O bleu: voyelles,*
  Je dirai quelque jour vos naissances latentes.
Black A, white E, red I, green U, blue O:
   vowels,
Someday I shall recount your latent births.
"Voyelles" (1870)

2 *JE est un autre.*
"I" is someone else.
"Lettre du Voyant" (1871)

3 *Elle est retrouvée.*
  Quoi?—L'éternité.
  C'est la mer allée
  Avec le soleil.
It is found again.
What? Eternity.
It is the sea
Gone with the sun.
"L'Éternité" (1872)

4 One evening, I sat Beauty in my lap.—And I
found her bitter.—And I cursed her.
"Une Saison en Enfer" (1873)

5   *Je me suis baigné dans le Poème*
  De la Mer.
      I have bathed in the Poem
  Of the Sea.
"Le Bateau Ivre" (1883)

6 *Je regrette l'Europe aux anciens parapets!*
  I long for Europe of the ancient parapets!
"Le Bateau Ivre" (1883)

Mary Roberts Rinehart
U.S. detective fiction writer, 1876–1958

1 Conscription may form a great and admirable
machine, but it differs from the trained army of
volunteers as a body differs from a soul. But it
costs a country heavy in griefs, does a volunteer
army; for the flower of the country goes.
Kings, Queens and Pawns preface (1915)

Hal Riney
U.S. advertising executive, 1932–2008

1 [*Slogan for Ronald Reagan's 1984 presidential
campaign:*] It's morning again in America.
Quoted in *Fortune*, 6 Aug. 1984

Robert L. Ripley
U.S. cartoonist, 1893–1949

1 Believe It or Not.
Title of syndicated newspaper cartoon series (1919)

César Ritz
Swiss hotel owner, 1850–1918

1 *Le client n'a jamais tort.*
The customer is never wrong.
Quoted in Ralph Nevill and C. E. Jerningham,
Piccadilly to Pall Mall (1908)
See Modern Proverbs 21

Antoine de Rivarol
French writer, 1753–1801

1 *Ce qui n'est pas clair n'est pas français.*
What is not clear is not French.
Discours sur l'Universalité de la Langue Française (1784)

Diego Rivera
Mexican painter, 1886–1957

1 The subject is to the painter what the rails are
to the locomotive. He cannot do without it.
In fact, when he refuses to seek or accept a
subject, his own plastic methods and his own
esthetic theories become his subject instead.
And even if he escapes them, he himself
becomes the subject of his work. He becomes
nothing but an illustrator of his own state of
mind, and in trying to liberate himself he falls
into the worst sort of slavery.
Quoted in Walter Lippmann, *A Preface to Morals*
(1929)

Joan Rivers (Joan Molinsky)
U.S. comedian, 1933–2014

1 There is not one female comic who was
beautiful as a little girl.
Quoted in *L.A. Times*, 10 May 1974

2 [*Catchphrase:*] Can we talk?
Quoted in *Wash. Post*, 24 Aug. 1982

3 A man can sleep around, no questions asked. A
woman can make 19 or 20 mistakes and she's a
tramp.
Quoted in *L.A. Times*, 5 June 1983

4 I hate housework! You make the beds, you do
the dishes—and six months later you have to
start all over again.
Quoted in Michèle Brown and Ann O'Connor,
Woman Talk (1984)

5 It's been so long since I made love I can't even
remember who gets tied up.
Quoted in Robert Byrne, *The Other 637 Best Things
Anybody Ever Said* (1984)

Joan Riviere
U.S. psychologist, 1883–1962

1 Civilization and Its Discontents.
Title of book (1930). Riviere's translation of Sigmund
Freud, *Das Unbehagen in der Kultur.*

Tom Robbins
U.S. novelist, 1932–

1 Who knows how to make love stay? . . . Tell
love you are going to Junior's Deli on Flatbush
Avenue in Brooklyn to pick up a cheesecake,
and if love stays, it can have half. It will
stay. . . . Wake love up in the middle of the
night. Tell it the world is on fire. Dash to the
bedroom window and pee out of it. Casually
return to bed and assure love that everything
is going to be all right. Fall asleep. Love will be
there in the morning.
Still Life with Woodpecker ch. 45 (1980)

Allan Roberts
U.S. songwriter, 1905–1966

1 You Always Hurt the One You Love.
Title of song (1944)
See Wilde 92

John G. Roberts, Jr.
U.S. judge, 1955–

1 The way to stop discrimination on the basis of
race is to stop discriminating on the basis of
race.
*Parents Involved in Community Schools v. Seattle School
District No. 1* (2007)

Pat Robertson
U.S. religious broadcaster, 1930–

1 [*On rainbow flags put up by gay activists in
support of sexual diversity:*] I would warn
Orlando [Fla.] that you're right in the way of

some serious hurricanes, and I don't think I'd be waving those flags in God's face if I were you. This is not a message of hate; this is a message of redemption. But a condition like this will bring about the destruction of your nation. It'll bring about terrorist bombs; it'll bring earthquakes, tornadoes, and possibly a meteor.

Quoted in *Wash. Post*, 10 June 1998. Two months after Robertson's warning, Hurricane Bonnie detoured around Orlando but slammed into Robertson's own headquarters city, Virginia Beach, Va.

Robbie Robertson (Jaime Royal Robertson)
Canadian rock musician, 1943–

1 I pulled into Nazareth, was feelin' 'bout half-past dead
I just need some place where I can lay my head
Hey, mister, can you tell me where a man might find a bed?
He just grinned and shook my hand; "No" was all he said.
"The Weight" (song) (1968)

2 The Night They Drove Old Dixie Down.
Title of song (1969)

Paul Robeson
U.S. singer, actor, political activist, and athlete, 1898–1976

1 The artist must elect to fight for freedom or slavery. I have made my choice. I had no alternative.
Speech at antifascist rally, Royal Albert Hall, London, 24 June 1937

2 It is unthinkable [that American Negroes] would go to war on behalf of those who have oppressed us for generations against a country [the Soviet Union] which in one generation has raised our people to the full dignity of mankind.
Speech at World Peace Congress, Paris, 20 Apr. 1949

3 My father was a slave and my people died to build this country, and I'm going to stay right here and have a part of it, just like you. And no fascist-minded people like you will drive me from it. Is that clear?
Testimony before House Un-American Activities Committee, 12 June 1956

4 You are the un-Americans, and you ought to be ashamed of yourselves.
Testimony Before House Un-American Activities Committee, 12 June 1956

Maximilien-François-Marie-Isidore de Robespierre
French revolutionary, 1758–1794

1 *Liberté, Égalité, Fraternité.*
Liberty, Equality, Fraternity.
"Discours sur l'Organisation des Gardes Nationales," 5 Dec. 1790. Became the motto of the French Revolution.

2 Any law which violates the inalienable rights of man is essentially unjust and tyrannical; it is not a law at all.
Déclaration des Droits de l'Homme art. 6 (1793)

3 Any institution which does not suppose the people good, and the magistrate corruptible, is evil.
Déclaration des Droits de l'Homme art. 25 (1793)

Leo Robin
U.S. songwriter, 1895–1984

1 Thanks for the Memory.
Title of song (1937). Cowritten with Ralph Rainger.

2 A kiss on the hand may be quite Continental,
But diamonds are a girl's best friend.
"Diamonds Are a Girl's Best Friend" (song) (1949)
See Advertising Slogans 38; Loos 2

Edwin Arlington Robinson
U.S. poet, 1869–1935

1 But still he fluttered pulses when he said, "Good morning," and he glittered when he walked.
"Richard Cory" l. 7 (1897)

2 So on we worked, and waited for the light, And went without the meat, and cursed the bread,
And Richard Cory, one calm summer night, Went home and put a bullet through his head.
"Richard Cory" l. 13 (1897)

3 I shall have more to say when I am dead.
"John Brown" l. 199 (1920)

Frank Robinson

U.S. baseball player and executive, 1935–2019

1 Close don't count in baseball. Close only counts in horseshoes and grenades.

Quoted in *Time,* 31 July 1973. Usually attributed to Robinson, but earlier evidence appeared in the *Elwood* (Ind.) *Call-Leader,* 4 Dec. 1965: "Close counts only in horseshoes and hand grenades."

Jackie Robinson

U.S. baseball player, 1919–1972

1 Today as I look back on that opening game of my first world series, I must tell you that it was Mr. [Branch] Rickey's drama and that I was only a principal actor. As I write this twenty years later, I cannot stand and sing the anthem. I cannot salute the flag; I know that I am a black man in a white world. In 1972, in 1947, at my birth in 1919, I know that I never had it made.

I Never Had It Made introduction (1972)

Joan Robinson

English economist, 1903–1983

1 Any government which had both the power and the will to remedy the major defects of the capitalist system would have the will and the power to abolish it altogether, while governments which have the power to retain the system lack the will to remedy its defects.

Economic Journal, Dec. 1936

2 One of the main effects . . . of orthodox traditional economics was . . . a plan for explaining to the privileged class that their position was morally right and was necessary for the welfare of society.

Essays in the Theory of Employment "An Economist's Sermon" (1937)

3 Marxism is the opium of the Marxists.

On Re-Reading Marx title page (1953)
See Karl Marx 2

4 The purpose of studying economics is not to acquire a set of ready-made answers to economic questions, but to learn how to avoid being deceived by economists.

"Marx, Marshall and Keynes" (1955)

5 Economics limps along with one foot in untested hypotheses and the other in untestable slogans.

"Metaphysics, Morals and Science" (1962)

6 Marx did not have very much to say about the economics of socialism. As Kalecki once remarked, it was not his business to write science fiction.

"Economics Versus Political Economy" (1968)

7 In the natural sciences, controversies are settled in a few months, or at a time of crisis, in a year or two, but in the social so-called sciences, absurd misunderstanding can continue for sixty or a hundred years without being cleared up.

"Thinking About Thinking" (1979)

Marilynne Robinson

U.S. writer, 1943–

1 This is an interesting planet. It deserves all the attention you can give it.

Gilead (2004)

Mary Robinson

English poet, 1758–1800

1 Pavement slippery, people sneezing,
Lords in ermine, beggars freezing;
Titled gluttons dainties carving,
Genius in a garret starving.

"January, 1795" l. 1 (1795)

William "Smokey" Robinson

U.S. singer and songwriter, 1940–

1 I've got sunshine on a cloudy day.
When it's cold outside I've got the month
    of May.
I guess you'd say
What can make me feel this way?
My girl
Talkin' 'bout my girl.

"My Girl" (song) (1964). Cowritten with Ronald White.

2 Oh, but if you feel like lovin' me,
If you got the notion, I second that emotion.

"I Second That Emotion" (song) (1967). Cowritten with Alfred Cleveland.

3 So take a good look at my face.
You'll see my smile
Looks out of place.
If you look closer it's easy to trace
The tracks of my tears.
"The Tracks of My Tears" (song) (1965). Cowritten with Warren Moore and Marvin Tarplin.

Ludwig von Rochau

German journalist and politician, 1810–1873

1 *Grundsätze der Realpolitik.*
Fundamentals of Realpolitik.
Title of book (1853)

John Wilmot, Earl of Rochester

English poet, 1647–1680

1 Reason, which fifty times for one does err,
Reason, an ignis fatuus of the mind.
"A Satire Against Mankind" l. 11 (1675)

2 Then Old Age and Experience, hand in hand,
Lead him to death, and make him understand,
After a search so painful and so long,
That all his life he has been in the wrong.
"A Satire Against Mankind" l. 25 (1675)

3 A merry monarch, scandalous and poor.
"A Satire on Charles II" l. 15 (1697)

4 [*Of Charles II:*]
Here lives a Great and Mighty Monarch,
Whose Promise none relies on,
Who never said a foolish Thing,
Nor ever did a wise one.
Quoted in *The Miscellaneous Works of the Right Honorable the Late Earls of Rochester and Roscommon* (1707)

Chris Rock

U.S. comedian, 1965–

1 You know the world is going crazy when the best rapper is a white guy, the best golfer is a black guy, the tallest guy in the NBA is Chinese, the Swiss hold the America's Cup, France is accusing the U.S. of arrogance, and Germany doesn't want to go to war.
Quoted in *Calgary Sun*, 5 May 2003

John D. Rockefeller

U.S. businessman and philanthropist, 1839–1937

1 The growth of a large business is merely a survival of the fittest. . . . The American Beauty rose can be produced in the splendor and fragrance which bring cheer to its beholder only by sacrificing the early buds which grow up around it.
Quoted in W. J. Ghent, *Our Benevolent Feudalism* (1902). Ellipsis in the original.

2 [*Comment in 1905 interview:*] God gave me my money. I believe the power to make money is a gift from God—to be developed and used to the best of our ability for the good of mankind. Having been endowed with the gift I possess, I believe it is my duty to make money and still more money and to use the money I make for the good of my fellow man according to the dictates of my conscience.
Quoted in Peter Collier and David Horowitz, *The Rockefellers, an American Dynasty* (1976)

John D. Rockefeller, Jr.

U.S. philanthropist, 1874–1960

1 Brotherhood of man under the fatherhood of God.
Radio speech, 8 July 1941

Nelson A. Rockefeller

U.S. politician, 1908–1979

1 I never wanted to be vice-president of anything.
Quoted in James Desmond, *Nelson Rockefeller: A Political Biography* (1964)

Knute Rockne

Norwegian-born U.S. football coach, 1888–1931

1 Show me a good loser and I will show you a failure.
Quoted in *Wash. Post,* 15 Aug. 1943. This citation was found by Barry Popik, who also traced the more popular form "Show me a good loser and I'll show you a loser" as far back as *Life,* 21 June 1963 (quoting quarterback Frankie Albert).

Gene Roddenberry
U.S. television producer, 1921–1991
See also Star Trek.

1 Space, the final frontier. These are the voyages of the starship *Enterprise*. Its five-year mission: to explore strange new worlds, to seek out new life and new civilizations, to boldly go where no man has gone before.

Star Trek (television series). This opening narration was first used in the episode "The Corbomite Maneuver" (1966).
See Killian 1; Roddenberry 2; Roddenberry 3

2 Space, the final frontier. These are the continuing voyages of the starship *Enterprise*. Her ongoing mission: to explore strange new worlds, to seek out new life-forms and new civilizations, to boldly go where no man has gone before.

The Wrath of Khan (motion picture) (1982)
See Killian 1; Roddenberry 1; Roddenberry 3

3 Space. The final frontier. These are the voyages of the starship *Enterprise*. Its continuing mission, to explore strange new worlds, to seek out new life and new civilizations, to boldly go where no one has gone before.

Star Trek: The Next Generation (television series). This third mission statement was first used in the episode "Encounter at Farpoint" (1987).
See Killian 1; Roddenberry 1; Roddenberry 2

Fred Rodell
U.S. legal scholar, 1907–1980

1 There are two things wrong with almost all legal writing. One is its style. The other is its content.

"Goodbye to Law Reviews," *Virginia Law Review*, Nov. 1936

2 The Law is the killy-loo bird of the sciences. The killy-loo, of course, was the bird that insisted on flying backward because it didn't care where it was going but was mightily interested in where it had been. . . . Only The Law, inexorably devoted to all its most ancient principles and precedents, makes a vice of innovation and a virtue of hoariness.

Woe unto You, Lawyers! ch. 2 (1939)

Auguste Rodin
French sculptor, 1840–1917

1 I invent nothing. I rediscover.

Quoted in Camille Mauclair, *Auguste Rodin* (1905) (translation by Clementina Black)

Wilhelm Conrad Roentgen
German physicist, 1845–1923

1 All bodies are transparent to this agent. . . . For brevity's sake I shall use the expression "rays"; and to distinguish them from others of this name I shall call them "X-rays."

"On a New Kind of Rays" (1895)

Theodore Roethke
U.S. poet, 1908–1963

1 Over this damp grave I speak the words of my love:
I, with no rights in this matter,
Neither father nor lover.

"Elegy for Jane" l. 20 (1953)

Fred Rogers
U.S. children's television show host, 1928–2003

1 It's a beautiful day in this neighborhood,
A beautiful day for a neighbor.
Would you be mine?
Could you be mine?

"Won't You Be My Neighbor?" (song) (1967)

Robert Emmons Rogers
U.S. educator, 1888–1941

1 Be a snob. You will find it is just as easy to marry the boss's daughter as the stenographer.

Address at graduation banquet of Massachusetts Institute of Technology, Cambridge, Mass., 3 June 1929

Will Rogers (William Penn Adair)
U.S. humorist, 1879–1935

1 All I Know Is What I Read in the Papers.

Title of article, *Life*, 16 Nov. 1922. Rogers used this line earlier beginning with his appearances in Florenz Ziegfeld's Broadway shows in 1915.

2 I tell you Folks, all Politics is Apple Sauce.

The Illiterate Digest "Breaking into the Writing Game" (1924)

3 Everybody is ignorant, only on different subjects.

The Illiterate Digest "Defending My Soup Plate Position" (1924)

4 The Income Tax has made more Liars out of the American people than Golf has. Even when you make one out on the level, you don't know when it's through if you are a Crook or a Martyr.

The Illiterate Digest "Helping the Girls with Their Income Taxes" (1924)

5 More men have been elected between Sundown and Sunup, than ever were elected between Sunup and Sundown.

The Illiterate Digest "Mr. Ford and Other Political Self-Starters" (1924)

6 Everything is funny as long as it is happening to somebody Else.

The Illiterate Digest "Warning to Jokers: Lay Off the Prince" (1924)

7 I dont see why a man shouldn't pay an inheritance tax. If a Country is good enough to pay taxes to while you are living, it's good enough to pay in after you die. By the time you die you should be so used to paying taxes that it would just be almost second nature to you.

"They've Got a New Dictionary at Ellis Island" (1926)

8 I never yet met a man that I didn't like.

Saturday Evening Post, 6 Nov. 1926

9 The Nineteenth Amendment—I think that's the one that made Women humans by Act of Congress.

"Mr. Toastmaster and Democrats" (1929)

10 Everytime a lawyer writes something, he is not writing for posterity, he is writing so that endless others of his craft can make a living out of trying to figure out what he said, course perhaps he hadent really said anything, that's what makes it hard to explain.

"The Lawyers Talking" (1935)

11 The minute you read something and you can't understand it you can almost be sure that it was drawn up by a lawyer.

"The Lawyers Talking" (1935)

12 America has a unique record. We never lost a war and we never won a conference in our lives.

Will Rogers Wit and Wisdom (1936)

13 My people didn't come over on the Mayflower but we were there to meet the folks when they landed.

Quoted in *Dallas Morning News*, 5 Nov. 1926

14 You can't say civilization don't advance, however, for in every war they kill you in a new way.

Quoted in *N.Y. Times*, 23 Dec. 1929

15 I am not a member of any organized party—I am a Democrat.

Quoted in P. J. O'Brien, *Will Rogers, Ambassador of Good Will, Prince of Wit and Wisdom* (1935). Rogers was quoted in the *Dubuque* (Iowa) *Telegraph-Herald and Times-Journal*, 3 Oct. 1930: "I am a member of no political organization. I am a democrat."

Madame Roland (Marie-Jeanne Philipon)
French revolutionary, 1754–1793

1 [*Remark before being guillotined, 1793:*] *O liberté! que de crimes on commet en ton nom!*

O liberty! what crimes are committed in thy name!

Quoted in Honoré Riouffe, *Mémoires d'un Détenu* (1794)

2 The more I see of men, the more I like dogs.

Attributed in *Notes and Queries*, 5 Sept. 1908
See Toussenel 1

Romain Rolland
French writer, 1866–1944

1 This intimate alliance—which for me makes the true man—of pessimism of the intelligence, which penetrates every illusion, and optimism of the will.

L'Humanité, 19 Mar. 1920

Irma S. Rombauer (Irma von Starkloff)
U.S. cookbook author, 1877–1962

1 The Joy of Cooking.

Title of book (1931)

2 We are frequently asked what is the ideal number for a dinner party. Estimates vary. . . . We are reminded of the response made to this question by a . . . nineteenth-century gourmet: "Myself and the headwaiter."

The Joy of Cooking, 5th rev. ed. (1975)

Oscar Arnulfo Romero y Galdames
Salvadoran archbishop, 1917–1980

1 I would like to make a special appeal to the members of the Army. . . . In the name of God, in the name of your tormented people whose cries rise up . . . I beseech you, I beg you, I command you: STOP THE REPRESSION!
Sermon, San Salvador, 23 Mar. 1980. Delivered the day before Romero's murder by paramilitary death squads.

Erwin Johannes Eugen Rommel
German general, 1891–1944

1 [*Statement to his aide, Captain Hellmuth Lang, northern France, ca. Mar. 1944:*] Believe me, Lang, the first twenty-four hours of the invasion will be decisive . . . for the Allies, as well as Germany, it will be the longest day.
Quoted in Cornelius Ryan, The Longest Day: June 6, 1944 (1959)

George Romney
U.S. politician, 1907–1995

1 I just had the greatest brainwashing that anyone can get when you go over to Vietnam, not only by the generals, but also by the diplomatic corps over there, and they do a very thorough job.
Television interview, 31 Aug. 1967

Mitt Romney
U.S. politician, 1947–

1 There are 47 percent of the people who will vote for the president no matter what . . . who are dependent upon government, who believe that they are victims. . . . These are people who pay no income tax. . . . and so my job is not to worry about those people. I'll never convince them that they should take personal responsibility and care for their lives.
Remarks at private fundraiser, Boca Raton, Fla., 17 May 2012

2 We took a concerted effort to go out and find women who had backgrounds that could be qualified to become members of our cabinet [in Massachusetts]. I went to a number of women's groups and said, "Can you help us find folks?"

and they brought us whole binders full of women.
Remarks at presidential debate, Hempstead, N.Y., 16 Oct. 2012

Pierre de Ronsard
French poet, 1524–1585

1 *Le temps s'en va, le temps s'en va, ma Dame,*
Las! le temps non, mais nous nous en allons.
For time speeds onward, time speeds on, my lady,
Alas! it's we who must speed on, not time.
"Amours de Marie" (1555–1556)

2 *Cueillez dès aujourd'hui les roses de la vie.*
Gather the roses of life today.
Sonnets pour Hélène bk. 1, no. 43 (1578)

3 *Quand vous serez bien vieille, au soir, à la*
chandelle,
Assise auprès du feu, dévidant et filant,
Direz, chantant mes vers, en vous émerveillant,
Ronsard me célébrait du temps que j'étais belle.
When you are very old, and sit in the candle-light at evening spinning by the fire, you will say, as you murmur my verses, a wonder in your eyes, "Ronsard sang of me in the days when I was fair."
Sonnets pour Hélène bk. 2, no. 43 (1578)

Eleanor Roosevelt
U.S. humanitarian and diplomat, 1884–1962

1 All of us in this country give lip service to the ideals set forth in the Bill of Rights and emphasized by every additional amendment, and yet when war is stirring in the world, many of us are ready to curtail our civil liberties. We do not stop to think that curtailing these liberties may in the end bring us a greater danger than the danger we are trying to avert.
Cosmopolitan, Feb. 1940

2 A woman will always have to be better than a man in any job she undertakes.
"My Day" (newspaper column), 29 Nov. 1945
See Hurst 1

3 You will find that [as the First Lady] you are no longer clothing yourself, you are dressing a public monument.
N.Y. Herald Tribune, 27 Oct. 1960

4 You gain strength, courage, and confidence by every experience in which you really stop to look fear in the face. . . . *You must do the thing you think you cannot do.*

You Learn by Living ch. 2 (1960)

5 Life was meant to be lived, and curiosity must be kept alive. One must never, for whatever reason, turn his back on life.

The Autobiography of Eleanor Roosevelt preface (1961)

6 No one can make you feel inferior without your consent.

Quoted in *Reader's Digest*, Sept. 1940
See Channing 1

7 When you cease to make a contribution you begin to die.

Quoted in Joseph P. Lash, *Eleanor: The Years Alone* (1972)

8 The future belongs to those who believe in the beauty of their dreams.

Attributed in Gerson G. Eisenberg, *Learning Vacations* (1986). An earlier occurrence, not credited to Roosevelt, was published in the *Surrey* (British Columbia) *Leader*, 15 Mar. 1978.

Franklin D. Roosevelt
U.S. president, 1882–1945

1 [*Of Alfred E. Smith:*] He is the Happy Warrior of the political battlefield.

Nominating speech at Democratic National Convention, New York, N.Y., 26 June 1924
See William Wordsworth 7

2 These unhappy times call for the building of plans that rest upon the forgotten, the unorganized but the indispensable units of economic power, for plans like those of 1917 that build from the bottom up and not from the

top down, that put their faith once more in the forgotten man at the bottom of the economic pyramid.

Radio address, 7 Apr. 1932
See Sumner 3

3 The country needs and, unless I mistake its temper, the country demands bold, persistent experimentation. It is common sense to take a method and try it: If it fails, admit it frankly and try another. But above all, try something.

Address at Oglethorpe University, Atlanta, Ga., 22 May 1932

4 I pledge you, I pledge myself, to a new deal for the American people.

Speech to Democratic National Convention accepting presidential nomination, Chicago, Ill., 2 July 1932. The earliest figurative use of the term *new deal* that has been found is in a letter from John Rathbone to Nicholas Biddle, 18 Jan. 1834, referring to "a new bank and a New Deal." Roosevelt or his speechwriters may have picked up the phrase from earlier political usages by Mark Twain or Woodrow Wilson.
See Twain 40; Woodrow Wilson 4

5 The first theory is that if we make the rich richer, somehow they will let a part of their prosperity trickle down to the rest of us. The second theory . . . was the theory that if we make the average of mankind comfortable and secure, their prosperity will rise upward . . . through the ranks.

Campaign address, Detroit, Mich., 2 Oct. 1932

6 Let me assert my firm belief that the only thing we have to fear is fear itself—nameless, unreasoning, unjustified terror which paralyzes needed efforts to convert retreat into advance.

First Inaugural Address, 4 Mar. 1933
See Francis Bacon 7; Montaigne 4; Thoreau 16; Wellington 3

7 In the field of world policy I would dedicate this nation to the policy of the good neighbor— the neighbor who resolutely respects himself and, because he does so, respects the rights of others—the neighbor who respects his obligations and respects the sanctity of his agreements in and with a world of neighbors.

First Inaugural Address, 4 Mar. 1933. According to Hans Sperber and Travis Trittschuh, *American Political Terms: An Historical Dictionary,* Herbert Hoover prominently used the term "good neighbor" during his tour of South America after the 1928 presidential election.

8 I hope your committee will not permit doubts
   as to constitutionality, however reasonable, to
   block the suggested legislation [the Bituminous
   Coal Conservation Act of 1935].
   Letter to Samuel B. Hill (chairman of House Ways
   and Means Committee), 6 July 1935

9 There is a mysterious cycle in human events.
   To some generations much is given. Of other
   generations much is expected. This generation
   of Americans has a rendezvous with destiny.
   Speech accepting renomination as president,
   Philadelphia, Pa., 27 June 1936

10 Out of this modern civilization economic
   royalists carved new dynasties. . . . The royalists
   of the economic order have conceded that
   political freedom was the business of the
   Government, but they have maintained that
   economic slavery was nobody's business.
   Speech accepting renomination as president,
   Philadelphia, Pa., 27 June 1936

11 I have seen war. . . . I hate war.
   Speech, Chautauqua, N.Y., 14 Aug. 1936

12 The true conservative seeks to protect the
   system of private property and free enterprise
   by correcting such injustices and inequalities
   as arise from it. The most serious threat to our
   institutions comes from those who refuse to
   face the need for change. Liberalism becomes
   the protection for the far-sighted conservative.
   Campaign address, Syracuse, N.Y., 29 Sept. 1936

13 I see one-third of a nation ill-housed, ill-clad,
   ill-nourished. . . . The test of our progress is
   not whether we add more to the abundance of
   those who have much; it is whether we provide
   enough for those who have too little.
   Second Inaugural Address, 20 Jan. 1937

14 We have always known that heedless self-
   interest was bad morals; we now know that
   it is bad economics. Out of the collapse of
   a prosperity whose builders boasted their
   practicality has come the conviction that in the
   long run economic morality pays.
   Second Inaugural Address, 20 Jan. 1937

15 Modern complexities call also for a constant
   infusion of new blood in the courts, just as
   it is needed in executive functions of the
   Government and in private business. A lowered
   mental or physical vigor leads men to avoid

an examination of complicated and changed
conditions. Little by little, new facts become
blurred through old glasses fitted, as it were,
for the needs of another generation; older men,
assuming that the scene is the same as it was in
the past, cease to explore or to inquire into the
present or the future.
Message to Congress recommending reorganization
of judicial branch, 5 Feb. 1937

16 [*On the "court-packing plan" increasing the
   number of U.S. Supreme Court justices:*] This
   plan will save our national Constitution from
   hardening of the judicial arteries.
   Radio broadcast, 9 Mar. 1937

17 Remember, remember always that all of us,
   and you and I especially, are descended from
   immigrants and revolutionists.
   Remarks before Daughters of the American
   Revolution Convention, Washington, D.C., 21 Apr.
   1938. Often paraphrased as Roosevelt's addressing
   the DAR as "my fellow immigrants."

18 A radical is a man with both feet firmly
   planted—in the air. A conservative is a man
   with two perfectly good legs who, however, has
   never learned to walk forward. A reactionary is
   a somnambulist walking backwards. A liberal
   is a man who uses his legs and his hands at the
   behest . . . of his head.
   Radio address, 26 Oct. 1939

19 The Soviet Union, as everybody who has
   the courage to face the fact knows, is run
   by a dictatorship as absolute as any other
   dictatorship in the world.
   Address to American Youth Congress, 10 Feb. 1940

20 On this tenth day of June 1940 the hand that
   held the dagger has struck it into the back of its
   neighbor.
   Address at University of Virginia, Charlottesville, Va.,
   10 June 1940

21 I have said this before, but I shall say it again
   and again and again: Your boys are not going to
   be sent into any foreign wars.
   Speech, Boston, Mass., 30 Oct. 1940
   See Lyndon Johnson 9

22 We must be the great arsenal of democracy.
   Radio broadcast, 29 Dec. 1940. According to Walter
   Isaacson and Evan Thomas, *The Wise Men* (1986),
   this slogan was picked up for Roosevelt's address
   after it was used in conversation by John McCloy, who
   had gotten it from Jean Monnet.

23 In the future days, which we seek to make secure, we look forward to a world founded upon four essential human freedoms. The first is freedom of speech and expression—everywhere in the world. The second is freedom of every person to worship God in his own way—everywhere in the world. The third is freedom from want . . . everywhere in the world. The fourth is freedom from fear . . . anywhere in the world.

Annual Message to Congress, 6 Jan. 1941
See Roosevelt and Churchill 3

24 When you see a rattlesnake poised to strike, you do not wait until he has struck before you crush him.

Radio talk, 11 Sept. 1941

25 Yesterday, December 7, 1941—a date which will live in infamy—the United States of America was suddenly and deliberately attacked by naval and air forces of the Empire of Japan.

Address to joint session of Congress asking for declaration of war on Japan, 8 Dec. 1941

26 We all know that books burn—yet we have the greater knowledge that books can not be killed by fire. People die, but books never die. No man and no force can abolish memory. No man and no force can put thought in a concentration camp forever. No man and no force can take from the world the books that embody man's eternal fight against tyranny of every kind. In this war, we know, books are weapons. And it is a part of your dedication always to make them weapons for man's freedom.

"Message to the Booksellers of America" (1942)

27 Poverty anywhere constitutes a danger to prosperity everywhere.

Address to Conference of International Labor Organization, Washington, D.C., 17 May 1944. These words were part of a Declaration of the International Labor Organization, but Roosevelt repeated and illustrated them at the conference.

28 [Referring to his dog:] Fala's Scotch, and being a Scottie, as soon as he learned that the Republican fiction writers in Congress and out had concocted a story that I had left him behind on an Aleutian Island and had sent a destroyer back to find him—at a cost to the taxpayers of two or three, or eight or twenty million dollars—his Scotch soul was furious. He has not been the same dog since.

Speech at Hotel Statler, Washington, D.C., 23 Sept. 1944

29 More than an end to war, we want an end to the beginnings of all wars.

Address written for Jefferson Day Dinner, 13 Apr. 1945. This address was never delivered because of Roosevelt's death on 12 April.

30 [Of Nicaraguan dictator Anastasio Somoza:] He may be a son of a bitch, but he's our son of a bitch.

Quoted in Washington Quarterly, Summer 1982. An earlier version ("As a Nicaraguan might say, he's a sonofabitch but he's ours") was credited to Roosevelt in Time, 15 Nov. 1948. The basic pattern can be found as far back as 1868, when a "but he is our rascal" anecdote appeared in the Cincinnati Enquirer, 22 July.

31 When you get to the end of your rope, tie a knot and hang on.

Attributed in Evan Esar, The Dictionary of Humorous Quotations (1949). Although this is usually credited to Roosevelt, the Daily Ardmoreite (Ardmore, Okla.), 16 Jan. 1920, printed the following without any attribution: "You get to the end of your rope, tie a knot in it and hang on!"

Franklin D. Roosevelt 1882–1945 and Winston Churchill 1874–1965
U.S. president, British statesman

1 First, their countries seek no aggrandizement, territorial or other.

Atlantic Charter, 14 Aug. 1941

2 Second, they desire to seek no territorial changes that do not accord with the freely expressed wishes of the peoples concerned.

Atlantic Charter, 14 Aug. 1941

3 Sixth, after the final destruction of the Nazi tyranny, they hope to see established a peace which will afford to all nations the means of dwelling in safety within their own boundaries, and which will afford assurance that all the men in all the lands may live out their lives in freedom from fear and want.

Atlantic Charter, 14 Aug. 1941
See Franklin Roosevelt 23

4 Eighth, they believe that all of the nations of the world, for realistic as well as spiritual reasons, must come to the abandonment of the use of force. Since no future peace can be maintained if land, sea, or air armaments continue to be employed by nations which threaten, or may threaten, aggression outside of their frontiers, they believe, pending the establishment of a wider and permanent system of general security, that the disarmament of such nations is essential.

Atlantic Charter, 14 Aug. 1941

Theodore Roosevelt

U.S. president, 1858–1919

1 The man who really counts in the world is the doer, not the mere critic, the man who actually does the work, even if roughly and imperfectly, not the man who only talks or writes about how it ought to be done.

New York ch. 14 (1891)
See Theodore Roosevelt 2; Theodore Roosevelt 5; Theodore Roosevelt 18

2 Criticism is necessary and useful; it is often indispensable; but it can never take the place of action, or be even a poor substitute for it. The function of the mere critic is of very subordinate usefulness. It is the doer of deeds who actually counts in the battle for life, and not the man who looks on and says how the

fight ought to be fought, without himself sharing the stress and the danger.

"The College Graduate and Public Life" (1894)
See Theodore Roosevelt 1; Theodore Roosevelt 5; Theodore Roosevelt 18

3 Every man among us is more fit to meet the duties and responsibilities of citizenship because of the perils over which, in the past, the nation has triumphed; because of the blood and sweat and tears, the labor and the anguish, through which, in the days that have gone, our forefathers moved on to triumph.

Speech at Naval War College, Newport, R.I., June 1897
See Byron 28; Winston Churchill 9; Winston Churchill 12; Donne 4

4 To borrow a simile from the football field, we believe that men must play fair, but that there must be no shirking, and that the success can only come to the player who "hits the line hard."

Speech, Oyster Bay, N.Y., Oct. 1897

5 Far better it is to dare mighty things, to win glorious triumphs, even though checkered by failure, than to take rank with those poor spirits who neither enjoy much nor suffer much, because they live in the gray twilight that knows not victory nor defeat.

Speech to Hamilton Club, Chicago, Ill., 10 Apr. 1899
See Theodore Roosevelt 1; Theodore Roosevelt 2; Theodore Roosevelt 18

6 I wish to preach, not the doctrine of ignoble ease, but the doctrine of the strenuous life.

Speech to Hamilton Club, Chicago, Ill., 10 Apr. 1899

7 I have always been fond of the West African proverb: "Speak softly and carry a big stick; you will go far."

Letter to Henry L. Sprague, 26 Jan. 1900

8 Death is always and under all circumstances a tragedy, for if it is not, then it means that life itself has become one.

Letter to Cecil Spring-Rice, 12 Mar. 1900

9 [*Responding to the question of whether he was available to run for vice-president:*] I am as strong as a bull moose and you can use me to the limit.

Letter to Mark Hanna, 17 June 1900. Roosevelt had used the expression "I feel as strong as a bull-moose" in an earlier letter of 29 Oct. 1895.

10 The first requisite of a good citizen in this
Republic of ours is that he shall be able and
willing to pull his weight.

Speech, New York, N.Y., 11 Nov. 1902

11 A man who is good enough to shed his blood
for his country is good enough to be given a
square deal afterwards. More than that no man
is entitled, and less than that no man shall
have.

Speech, Springfield, Ill., 4 July 1903
See Theodore Roosevelt 12

12 We must treat each man on his worth and
merits as a man. We must see that each is given
a square deal, because he is entitled to no more
and should receive no less.

Speech at New York State Fair, Syracuse, N.Y., 7 Sept.
1903
See Theodore Roosevelt 11

13 No man is above the law and no man is below
it; nor do we ask any man's permission when
we require him to obey it. Obedience to the law
is demanded as a right; not asked as a favor.

Third Annual Message to Congress, 7 Dec. 1903.
"No one is above the law" appears as early as Henry
Fielding, *Don Quixote in England* (1734).

14 Chronic wrongdoing, or an impotence
which results in a general loosening of the
ties of civilized society, may in America, as
elsewhere, ultimately require intervention
by some civilized nation, and in the Western
Hemisphere the adherence of the United States
to the Monroe Doctrine may force the United
States, however reluctantly, in flagrant cases of
such wrongdoing or impotence, to the exercise
of an international police power.

Annual Message to Congress, 6 Dec. 1904. Known as
the "Roosevelt Corollary" to the Monroe Doctrine.

15 The men with the muck-rakes are often
indispensable to the well-being of society;
but only if they know when to stop raking the
muck.

Speech, Washington, D.C., 14 Apr. 1906
See Bunyan 6

16 Let individuals contribute as they desire; but let
us prohibit in effective fashion all corporations
from making contributions for any political
purpose, directly or indirectly.

Sixth Annual Message to Congress, 3 Dec. 1906

17 Malefactors of great wealth.

Speech, Provincetown, Mass., 20 Aug. 1907

18 It is not the critic who counts; not the man who
points out how the strong man stumbles, or
where the doer of deeds could have done them
better. The credit belongs to the man who is
actually in the arena, whose face is marred by
dust and sweat and blood; who strives valiantly;
who errs, and comes short again and again,
because there is no effort without error and
shortcoming; but who does actually strive to do
the deeds; who knows the great enthusiasms,
the great devotions; who spends himself in a
worthy cause; who at the best knows in the end
the triumph of high achievement, and who at
the worst, if he fails, at least fails while daring
greatly, so that his place shall never be with
those cold and timid souls who know neither
victory nor defeat.

Address at the Sorbonne, Paris, 23 Apr. 1910. Richard
M. Nixon quoted this passage in his address to
the nation announcing his decision to resign the
presidency, 8 Aug. 1974.
*See Theodore Roosevelt 1; Theodore Roosevelt 2; Theodore
Roosevelt 5*

19 My position as regards the monied interests
can be put in a few words. In every civilized
society property rights must be carefully
safeguarded; ordinarily and in the great
majority of cases, human rights and property
rights are fundamentally and in the long run,
identical; but when it clearly appears that there
is a real conflict between them, human rights
must have the upper hand; for property belongs
to man and not man to property.

Address at the Sorbonne, Paris, 23 Apr. 1910

20 It would be a master stroke if those great Powers
honestly bent on peace would form a league
of peace, not only to keep the peace among
themselves, but to prevent, by force if necessary,
its being broken by others. The man or statesman
who should bring about such a condition would
have earned his place in history for all time and
his title to the gratitude of all mankind.

Nobel Prize Lecture, Christiana, Norway, 5 May 1910

21 The New Nationalism puts the national need
before sectional or personal advantage.

"The New Nationalism" (speech), Osawatomie, Kan.,
31 Aug. 1910

22 The man who wrongly holds that every human right is secondary to his profit must now give way to the advocate of human welfare, who rightly maintains that every man holds his property subject to the general right of the community to regulate its use to whatever degree the public welfare may require it.

Speech, Osawatomie, Kan., 31 Aug. 1910

23 My hat's in the ring. The fight is on and I'm stripped to the buff.

Newspaper interview, 21 Feb. 1912

24 The various admirable movements in which I have been engaged have always developed among their members a large lunatic fringe.

Letter to Henry Cabot Lodge, 27 Feb. 1913. This, along with two other 1913 usages, represents the earliest known use of the phrase *lunatic fringe* referring to extremist individuals. However, Roosevelt appears to have been playing on an older sense of *lunatic fringe* referring to bangs of hair (documented as far back as Feb. 1874 in *Oliver Optic's Magazine*).

25 There is no room in this country for hyphenated Americanism.

Speech, New York, N.Y., 12 Oct. 1915

26 One of our defects as a nation is a tendency to use what have been called "weasel words." When a weasel sucks eggs the meat is sucked out of the egg. If you use a "weasel word" after another there is nothing left of the other.

Speech, St. Louis, Mo., 31 May 1916. The *Oxford English Dictionary* documents usage of the term *weasel word* as early as 1900.

27 [*On the presidency:*] I have got such a bully pulpit!

Quoted in *Outlook* (N.Y.), 27 Feb. 1909

28 I took the canal zone and let Congress debate, and while the debate goes on the canal does also.

Quoted in *N.Y. Times*, 24 Mar. 1911

29 I have only a second rate brain but I think I have a capacity for action.

Quoted in Owen Wister, *Roosevelt: The Story of a Friendship* (1930)
See Oliver Wendell Holmes, Jr. 44

30 I could carve out of a banana a Justice with more backbone than that.

Quoted in Silas Bent, *Justice Oliver Wendell Holmes* (1932)

Elihu Root

U.S. statesman and lawyer, 1845–1937

1 There is a useless lawsuit in every useless word of a statute and every loose, sloppy phrase plays the part of the typhoid carrier.

"The Layman's Criticism of the Lawyer," *American Bar Association Report* (1914)

2 About half the practice of a decent lawyer consists in telling would-be clients that they are damned fools and should stop.

Quoted in Philip C. Jessup, *Elihu Root* (1938)

George Frederick Root

U.S. songwriter, 1820–1895

1 Tramp! Tramp! Tramp! the boys are marching,
Cheer up, comrades, they will come,
And beneath the starry flag
We shall breathe the air again
Of the free land in our own beloved home.

"Tramp! Tramp! Tramp!" (song) (1862)

2 The Union forever,
Hurray! boys, Hurrah!
Down with the traitor, up with the star;
While we rally round the flag boys, rally once again,
Shouting the battle cry of freedom.

"The Battle Cry of Freedom" (song) (1863). According to the *American Heritage Dictionary of American Quotations*, "The phrase 'rally 'round the flag' has been ascribed to Gen. Andrew Jackson at the Battle of New Orleans and was used in political campaigns before Root picked it up for this popular war song."
See James T. Fields 1

Wentworth Dillon, Earl of Roscommon

Irish poet and critic, ca. 1633–1685

1 The multitude is always in the wrong.

Essay on Translated Verse l. 183 (1684)
See Heinlein 14; Ibsen 14; Twain 119

Billy Rose

U.S. songwriter and producer, 1899–1966

1 Barney Google, with the goo-goo-goo-ga-ly eyes.

"Barney Google" (song) (1923). Cowritten with Con Conrad.

2 Fifty Million Frenchmen Can't Be Wrong.

Title of song (1927). Cowritten with Willie Ruskin.

3 Never invest your money in anything that eats or needs repainting.
Quoted in *N.Y. Post*, 26 Oct. 1957

R. D. Rosen
U.S. journalist and critic, 1949–

1 We are living, practically no one has to be reminded, in a therapeutic age. The sign in every storefront reads: "Psychobabble spoken here." Personal liberation, relating, being in touch with one's feelings (an aspiration that sadly presumes we are so out of touch with our feelings that we must now make a project of reclaiming them)—the whole pop vocabulary and grammar of human growth appear more and more suspect.
Boston Phoenix, 27 May 1975. Coinage of the term *psychobabble.*

Ethel Rosenberg
U.S. alleged spy, 1915–1953

1 We are innocent, as we have proclaimed and maintained from the time of our arrest. This is the whole truth. To forsake this truth is to pay too high a price even for the priceless gift of life—for life thus purchased we could not live out in dignity and self-respect.
Petition for executive clemency, 9 Jan. 1953. Coauthored with her husband Julius Rosenberg.

2 Suffice it to say that my husband and I shall die innocent before we lower ourselves to live guilty! And nobody, not even you, whom we continue to love as our own true brother, can dictate terms to the Rosenbergs, who follow only the dictates of heart and soul, truth and conscience, and the God-blessed love we bear our fellows!
Letter to Emanuel H. Bloch, 30 Jan. 1953.

3 We are the first victims of American Fascism.
Quoted in Julius Rosenberg, Letter to Emanuel Bloch, 19 June 1953

Harold Rosenberg
U.S. art critic, 1906–1978

1 At a certain moment the canvas began to appear to one American painter after another as an arena in which to act—rather than as a space in which to reproduce, re-design, analyze, or express an object, actual or imagined. What was to go on the canvas was not a picture but an event.
"The American Action Painter," *Art News,* Dec. 1952

Harold Ross
U.S. journalist and editor, 1892–1951

1 The *New Yorker* will be the magazine which is not edited for the old lady from Dubuque.
Prospectus for *New Yorker* magazine (1925). Frequently quoted as "little old lady from Dubuque."

Jerry Ross
U.S. songwriter, 1926–1955

1 You've gotta have heart
All you really need is heart.
"Heart" (song) (1955)

Christina Rossetti
English poet, 1830–1894

1 My heart is like a singing bird
Whose nest is in a watered shoot.
"A Birthday" l. 1 (1862)

2 Better by far you should forget and smile
Than that you should remember and be sad.
"Remember" l. 13 (1862)

3 Silence more musical than any song.
"Rest" l. 10 (1862)

4 Does the road wind up-hill all the way?
Yes, to the very end.
Will the day's journey take the whole long day?
From morn to night, my friend.
"Up-Hill" l. 1 (1862)

5 When I am dead, my dearest,
Sing no sad songs for me;
Plant thou no roses at my head,
Nor shady cypress tree.
Be the green grass above me
With showers and dewdrops wet;
And if thou wilt, remember
And if thou wilt, forget.
"When I am dead, my dearest" l. 1 (1862)

Alice S. Rossi
U.S. sociologist and feminist, 1922–2009

1 Without the means to prevent, and to control the timing of, conception, economic

and political rights have limited meaning for women. If women cannot plan their pregnancies, they can plan little else in their lives.

The Feminist Papers pt. 3 (1973)

Gioacchino Rossini

Italian composer, 1792–1868

1 Wagner has lovely moments but awful quarters of an hour.

Letter to Emile Naumann, Apr. 1867

2 Give me a laundry list and I'll set it to music.

Attributed in *Cincinnati Enquirer*, 21 Sept. 1941. Garson O'Toole has found that a similar remark was attributed to Rossini in *Rivista d'Italia* vol. 2 (1913) and that there were eighteenth-century references to Jean-Philippe Rameau making a comparable assertion about the *Gazette of Holland.*

Edmond Rostand

French playwright, 1868–1918

1 The Cadets of Gascoyne.

Cyrano de Bergerac act 2 (1897) (translation by Brian Hooker)

2 There is one crown I bear away with me,
And to-night, when I enter before God,
My salute shall sweep all the stars away
From the blue threshold! One thing without stain,
Unspotted from the world, in spite of doom
Mine own!
. . . My white plume.

Cyrano de Bergerac act 5 (1897) (translation by Brian Hooker)

Jean Rostand

French biologist, 1894–1977

1 Kill a man, and you are an assassin. Kill millions of men, and you are a conqueror. Kill everyone, and you are a god.

Pensées d'un Biologiste ch. 5 (1939)
See Porteus 1; Edward Young 3

Theodore Roszak

U.S. author, 1933–2011

1 The technocratic imperative: "What can be done must be done."

The Making of the Counter Culture: Reflections on the Technocratic Society appendix (1969)

Philip Roth

U.S. novelist, 1933–2018

1 The first time I saw Brenda she asked me to hold her glasses.

"Goodbye, Columbus" (1959)

2 A Jewish man with parents alive is a fifteen-year-old boy, and will remain a fifteen-year-old boy until *they die!*

Portnoy's Complaint (1969)

3 Doctor, doctor, what do you say, LET'S PUT THE ID BACK IN YID!

Portnoy's Complaint (1969)

4 Now vee may perhaps to begin. Yes?

Portnoy's Complaint (1969)

5 In Israel it's enough to live—you don't have to do anything else and you go to bed exhausted. Have you ever noticed that Jews shout? Even one ear is more than you need.

The Counterlife ch. 2 (1987)

6 I write fiction and I'm told it's autobiography, I write autobiography and I'm told it's fiction, so since I'm so dim and they're so smart, let *them* decide what it is or it isn't.

Deception (1990)

7 All that we don't know is astonishing. Even more astonishing is what passes for knowing.

The Human Stain ch. 4 (2000)

8 Old age isn't a battle; old age is a massacre.

Everyman (2006)

9 [*Contrasting writers in the United States and in Eastern Europe:*] In my situation, everything goes and nothing matters; in their situation, nothing goes and everything matters.

Quoted in *N.Y. Times*, 11 May 1981

Mark Rothko (Markus Yakovlevich Rotkovich)

Latvian-born U.S. painter, 1903–1970

1 I'm *not* an abstractionist. . . . The people who weep before my pictures are having the same religious experience I had when I painted them. And if you, as you say, are moved only by their color relationships, then you miss the point!

Quoted in Selden Rodman, *Conversations with Artists* (1957)

2 Silence is so accurate.
Quoted in *Art News Annual* (1958)

Nathan Mayer Rothschild
German-born English financier, 1777–1836

1 [*Investment advice:*] Buy when the blood is
running in the streets.
Attributed in Harry D. Schultz, *Bear Markets* (1964).
In many attributions, it is not clear which member of
the Rothschild family this is being attributed to, and
any attribution may well be apocryphal.

Johnny Rotten (John Joseph Lydon)
English rock singer, 1956–

1 I am an antichrist
I am an anarchist
Don't know what I want
But I know how to get it
I wanna destroy passer by
Cause I
Wanna be
Anarchy.
"Anarchy in the UK" (song) (1976). Cowritten with
Paul Cook, Steve Jones, and Glen Matlock.

2 There's no future in England's dreaming
No future, no future, no future for you
No future, no future, no future for me.
"God Save the Queen" (song) (1977)

3 Ever get the feeling you've been cheated?
Remark to audience at concert, San Francisco, Calif.,
14 Jan. 1978

4 Love is three minutes of squelching noises.
Quoted in Nigel Rees, *Graffiti 3* (1981)

Julie Rottenberg
U.S. screenwriter, fl. 2010

1 He's just not that into you.
Sex and the City (television show), 13 July 2003.
Cowritten with Elisa Zuritsky.

Claude-Joseph Rouget de Lisle
French soldier, 1760–1836

1 *Allons, enfants de la patrie,*
Le jour de gloire est arrivé.
Come, children of our country,
The day of glory has arrived.
"La Marseillaise" (song) (1792)

2 *Aux armes, citoyens!*
Formez vos bataillons!
To arms, citizens!
Form your battalions!
"La Marseillaise" (song) (1792)

Jean-Jacques Rousseau
Swiss-born French philosopher and novelist,
1712–1778

1 The first person who, having fenced off a
plot of ground, took it into his head to say
this is mine and found people simple enough
to believe him, was the true founder of civil
society.
*Discourse on the Origins and Foundations of Inequality
Among Men* pt. 2 (1755)

2 *Du Contrat Social.*
The Social Contract.
Title of book (1762)

3 *L'homme est né libre, et partout il est dans les fers.*
Man was born free, and everywhere he is
chains.
Du Contrat Social bk. 1, ch. 1 (1762)

4 The strongest is never strong enough to be
always the master, unless he transforms
strength into right, and obedience into duty.
Hence the right of the strongest, which, though
to all seeming meant ironically, is really laid
down as a fundamental principle.
Du Contrat Social bk. 1, ch. 3 (1762)

5 If we take the term in the strict sense, there
never has been a real democracy, and there
never will be. It is against the natural order for
the many to govern and the few to be governed.
It is unimaginable that the people should
remain continually assembled to devote their
time to public affairs, and it is clear that they
cannot set up commissions for that purpose
without the form of administration being
changed.
Du Contrat Social bk. 3, ch. 4 (1762)

6 The body politic, like the human body, begins
to die from its birth, and bears in itself the
causes of its destruction.
Du Contrat Social bk. 3, ch. 11 (1762)

7 Good laws lead to the making of better ones; bad ones bring about worse. As soon as any man says of the affairs of the State *What does it matter to me?* the State may be given up for lost.
Du Contrat Social bk. 3, ch. 15 (1762)

8 Everything is good as it leaves the hands of the Author of things; everything degenerates in the hands of man. He forces one soil to nourish the products of another, one tree to bear the fruit of another. He mixes and confuses the climates, the elements, the seasons. He mutilates his dog, his horse, his slave. He turns everything upside down; he disfigures everything; he loves deformity, monsters. He wants nothing as nature made it, not even man; for him, man must be trained like a school horse; man must be fashioned in keeping with his fancy like a tree in his garden.
Émile bk. 1 (1762)

9 I am commencing an undertaking, hitherto without precedent, and which will never find an imitator. I desire to set before my fellows the likeness of a man in all the truth of nature, and that man myself.
Confessions bk. 1 (1782)

10 At length I recollected the thoughtless saying of a great princess, who, on being informed that the country people had no bread, replied, "Then let them eat cake."
Confessions bk. 6 (1782). The words "let them eat cake" are usually attributed to Marie-Antoinette, but the Rousseau usage, written in 1766–1767 before she had even arrived in France, makes it clear that the saying predated this famous queen.

Martin Joseph Routh
English classicist, 1755–1854

1 Let me recommend to you the practice of always verifying your references, sir.
Quoted in John W. Burgon, *The Last Twelve Verses of the Gospel According to S. Mark* (1871)

Adolphe-Basile Routhier
Canadian poet and judge, 1839–1920

1 *O Canada! Terre de nos aïeux,*
Ton front est ceint de fleurons glorieux!
Car ton bras sait porter l'épee,
Il sait porter la croix!

O Canada! Our home and native land!
True patriot love in all thy sons command.
With glowing hearts we see thee rise,
The True North strong and free!
"*O Canada*" (song) (1880) (translation by Robert Stanley Weir [1856–1926], a Canadian lawyer)

Karl Rove
U.S. political advisor, 1950–

1 The aide said that guys like me were "in what we call the reality-based community," which he defined as people who "believe that solutions emerge from your judicious study of discernible reality." . . . "That's not the way the world really works anymore," he continued. "We're an empire now, and when we act, we create our own reality. And while you're studying that reality—judiciously, as you will—we'll act again, creating other new realities, which you can study too, and that's how things will sort out. We're history's actors . . . and you, all of you, will be left to just study what we do."
Reported in *N.Y. Times Magazine*, 17 Oct. 2004. Ron Suskind, the journalist writing the *Times Magazine* story, did not identify the quoted aide, but the aide is widely believed to have been Rove.

Matthew Rowbottom
English rock musician, fl. 1996

1 I'll tell you what I want what I really really want
(So tell me what you want, what you really really want)
If you wanna be my lover
Gotta get with my friends
Make it last forever
Friendship never ends!
"Wannabe" (song) (1996). Cowritten with Richard Stannard.

Nicholas Rowe
English playwright, 1674–1718

1 Is this that haughty, gallant, gay Lothario?
The Fair Penitent act 5, sc. 1 (1703)

Helen Rowland
U.S. writer, 1875–1950

1 When you see what some girls marry, you realize how they must hate to work for a living.
Reflections of a Bachelor Girl (1909)

2 A husband is what is left of a lover, after the nerve has been extracted.
A Guide to Men prelude (1922)

3 It takes one woman twenty years to make a man of her son—and another woman twenty minutes to make a fool of him.
A Guide to Men prelude (1922)

4 Somehow, a bachelor never quite gets over the idea that he is a thing of beauty and a boy forever!
A Guide to Men "Bachelors" (1922)

5 Love, the quest; marriage, the conquest; divorce, the inquest.
A Guide to Men "Divorces" (1922)

6 Before marriage, a man will go home and lie awake all night thinking about something you said; after marriage, he'll go to sleep before you finish saying it.
A Guide to Men "First Interlude" (1922)

7 The follies which a man regrets the most, in his life, are those which he didn't commit when he had the opportunity.
A Guide to Men "Improvisations" (1922)

8 When a girl marries she exchanges the attentions of many men for the inattention of one.
Quoted in Evan Esar, *The Dictionary of Humorous Quotations* (1949)

Richard Rowland
U.S. motion picture producer, ca. 1881–1947

1 [*Of the 1919 takeover of the United Artists film company by Charlie Chaplin, Mary Pickford, Douglas Fairbanks, and D. W. Griffith:*] The lunatics are running the asylum!
Quoted in *Seattle Daily Times*, 16 Mar. 1924

J. K. Rowling
English-born Scottish novelist, 1965–

1 "A Muggle," said Hagrid, "it's what we call nonmagic folk like them. An' it's your bad luck you grew up in a family o' the biggest Muggles I ever laid eyes on."
Harry Potter and the Philosopher's Stone ch. 4 (1997)

2 It does not do to dwell on dreams and forget to live, remember that.
Harry Potter and the Philosopher's Stone ch. 12 (1997)

3 It takes a great deal of bravery to stand up to our enemies, but just as much to stand up to our friends.
Harry Potter and the Philosopher's Stone ch. 17 (1997)

4 It is our choices, Harry, that show what we truly are, far more than our abilities.
Harry Potter and the Chamber of Secrets ch. 18 (1999)

5 You can exist without your soul, you know, as long as your brain and heart are still working. But you'll have no sense of self any more, no memory, no . . . anything. There's no chance at all of recovery. You'll just—exist. As an empty shell.
Harry Potter and the Prisoner of Azkaban ch. 12 (1999). Ellipsis in the original.

6 Differences of habit and language are nothing at all if our aims are identical and our hearts are open.
Harry Potter and the Goblet of Fire ch. 37 (2000)

7 The one with the power to vanquish the Dark Lord approaches. . . . Born to those who have thrice defied him, born as the seventh month dies . . . and the Dark Lord will mark him as his equal, but he will have power the Dark Lord knows not . . . and either must die at the hand of the other for neither can live while the other survives.
Harry Potter and the Order of the Phoenix ch. 37 (2003). Ellipses in the original.

8 The scar had not pained Harry for nineteen years. All was well.
Harry Potter and the Deathly Hallows epilogue (2007)

Arundhati Roy
Indian author, 1961–

1 The secret of the Great Stories is that they *have* no secrets. The Great Stories are the ones you have heard and want to hear again. The ones you can enter anywhere and inhabit comfortably. They don't deceive you with thrills and trick endings. They don't surprise you with the unforeseen. They are as familiar as the house you live in. Or the smell of your lover's skin. You know how they end, yet you listen as though you don't. In the way that although you know that one day you will die, you live as though you won't. In the Great Stories you know who lives, who dies, who finds love, who

doesn't. And yet you want to know again. *That is their mystery and their magic.*
The God of Small Things ch. 12 (1997)

Maude Royden
English religious writer, 1876–1956

1 The Church should go forward along the path of progress and be no longer satisfied only to represent the Conservative Party at prayer.
Speech at Queen's Hall, London, 16 July 1917

Rick Rubin
U.S. music producer, 1963–

1 You gotta fight
For your right
To party.
"Fight for Your Right (to Party)" (song) (1986). Cowritten with Adam Yauch and The King.

Rita Rudner
U.S. comedian, 1953–

1 Men with pierced ears are better prepared for marriage—they've experienced pain and bought jewelry.
Quoted in *Time*, 1 Oct. 1990

Muriel Rukeyser
U.S. poet, 1913–1980

1   I am in the world
to change the world.
"Käthe Kollwitz" sec 1, l. 12 (1968)

2 What would happen if one woman told the truth about her life?
The world would split open.
"Käthe Kollwitz" sec. 3, l. 25 (1968)

Donald Rumsfeld
U.S. government official, 1932–

1 As we know, there are known knowns; there are things we know we know. We also know there are known unknowns; that is to say we know there are some things we do not know. But there are also unknown unknowns—the ones we don't know we don't know.
Defense Department news briefing, 12 Feb. 2002

2 Now, you're thinking of Europe as Germany and France. I don't. I think that's old Europe. If you look at the entire NATO Europe today, the center of gravity is shifting to the east.
Briefing at Foreign Press Center, Washington, D.C., 22 Jan. 2003

3 [*On looting after the fall of Baghdad:*] Stuff happens!
Defense Department press briefing, 11 Apr. 2003

4 I don't do quagmires.
Defense Department news briefing, 24 July 2003

5 You go to war with the Army you have. They're not the Army you might want or wish to have at a later time.
Remarks at town hall meeting, Kuwait, 8 Dec. 2004

6 Simply because a problem can be shown to exist, it doesn't necessarily follow that there is a solution.
Quoted in *Interavia Business & Technology*, 1 Jan. 2001. One of "Rumsfeld's Rules."

7 Learn to say, "I don't know." If used when appropriate, it will be often.
Quoted in *N.Y. Times*, 8 Jan. 2001. One of "Rumsfeld's Rules."

8 If you are not criticized, you may not be doing much.
Quoted in *N.Y. Times*, 8 Jan. 2001. One of "Rumsfeld's Rules."

9 [*Statement on lawlessness in Iraq after the entry of U.S. troops:*] Freedom's untidy. And free people are free to make mistakes and commit crimes and do bad things.
Quoted in *N.Y. Times*, 12 Apr. 2003

10 There aren't any good targets in Afghanistan and there are lots of good targets in Iraq.
Quoted in *N.Y. Daily News*, 20 Mar. 2004. Former U.S. counterterrorism chief Richard Clarke alleged that Rumsfeld said these words on 12 Sept. 2001. Rumsfeld was explaining why the United States should bomb Iraq despite the fact that Al Qaida terrorists were located in Afghanistan. Clarke says he responded, "Well, there are lots of good targets in lots of places, but Iraq had nothing to do with [the September 11 attacks]."

Damon Runyon
U.S. writer, 1884–1946

1 Always try to rub up against money, for if you rub up against money long enough, some of it may rub off on you.
"A Very Honorable Guy" (1929)

2 "Some day, somewhere," he says, "a guy is going to come to you and show you a nice brand-new deck of cards on which the seal is never broken, and this guy is going to offer to bet you that the jack of spades will jump out of this deck and squirt cider in your ear. But son," the old guy says, "do not bet him, for as sure as you do you are going to get an ear full of cider."
"The Idyll of Miss Sarah Brown," *Collier's*, 28 Jan. 1933

3 I long ago come to the conclusion that all life is 6 to 5 against.
Collier's, 8 Sept. 1934

Norman Rush
U.S. writer, 1933–

1 In Africa, you want more, I think.
Mating ch. 1 (1991)

Salman Rushdie
Indian-born English novelist, 1947–

1 I was born in the city of Bombay . . . once upon a time. No, that won't do, there's no getting away from the date: I was born in Doctor Narlikar's Nursing Home on August 15th, 1947. . . . On the stroke of midnight, as a matter of fact.
Midnight's Children bk. 1, "The Perforated Sheet" (1981). First ellipsis in the original.

2 To be born again . . . first you have to die.
The Satanic Verses pt. 1 (1988)

3 A poet's work. . . . To name the unnamable, to point at frauds, to take sides, start arguments, shape the world, and stop it from going to sleep.
The Satanic Verses pt. 2 (1988)

4 Your blasphemy, Salman, can't be forgiven. . . . To set your words against the Words of God.
The Satanic Verses pt. 6 (1988)

5 Literature is the one place in any society where, within the secrecy of our own heads, we can hear voices talking about everything in every possible way.
"Is Nothing Sacred?" (1990)

Dean Rusk
U.S. politician, 1909–1994

1 Physicists and astronomers see their own implications in the world being round, but to me it means that only one-third of the world is asleep at any given time and the other two-thirds is up to something.
Speech to American Bar Association, Atlanta, Ga., 22 Oct. 1964

2 [*On the Cuban missile crisis, 24 Oct. 1962:*] We're eyeball to eyeball, and I think the other fellow just blinked.
Quoted in *Saturday Evening Post*, 8 Dec. 1962

John Ruskin
English art and social critic, 1819–1900

1 He is the greatest artist who has embodied, in the sum of his works, the greatest number of the greatest ideas.
Modern Painters vol. 1, pt. 1, ch. 2 (1843)

2 I believe the right question to ask, respecting all ornament, is simply this: Was it done with enjoyment—was the carver happy while he was about it?
Seven Lamps of Architecture "The Lamp of Life" sec. 24 (1849)

3 When we build, let us think that we build for ever.
Seven Lamps of Architecture "The Lamp of Memory" sec. 10 (1849)

4 Remember that the most beautiful things in the world are the most useless; peacocks and lilies for instance.
Stones of Venice vol. 1, ch. 2, sec. 17 (1851)

5 All violent feelings . . . produce in us a falseness in all our impressions of external things, which I would generally characterize as the "Pathetic Fallacy."
Modern Painters vol. 3, pt. 4, ch. 12 (1856)

6 To see clearly is poetry, prophecy, and religion—all in one.
Modern Painters vol. 3, pt. 4 "Of Modern Landscape" (1856)

7 Mountains are the beginning and the end of all natural scenery.
Modern Painters vol. 4, pt. 5, ch. 20 (1856)

8 Value is the life-giving power of anything; cost, the quantity of labor required to produce it; price, the quantity of labor which its possessor will take in exchange for it.
Munera Pulveris ch. 1 (1862)

9 Let us reform our schools, and we shall find little reform needed in our prisons.
Unto This Last Essay 2 (1862)

10 Government and cooperation are in all things the laws of life; anarchy and competition the laws of death.
Unto This Last Essay 3 (1862)

11 Whereas it has long been known and declared that the poor have no right to the property of the rich, I wish it also to be known and declared that the rich have no right to the property of the poor.
Unto This Last Essay 3 (1862)

12 Life being very short, and the quiet hours of it few, we ought to waste none of them in reading valueless books.
Sesame and Lilies preface (1865)

13 Be sure that you go to the author to get at his meaning, not to find yours.
Sesame and Lilies "Of Kings' Treasuries" (1865)

14 All books are divisible into two classes, the books of the hour, and the books of all time.
Sesames and Lilies "Of Kings' Treasuries" (1865)

15 Give a little love to a child, and you get a great deal back.
The Crown of Wild Olive Lecture 1 (1866)

16 Taste . . . is the *only* morality. . . . Tell me what you like, and I'll tell you what you are.
The Crown of Wild Olive Lecture 2 (1866)

17 The first duty of a State is to see that every child born therein shall be well housed, clothed, fed, and educated, till it attains years of discretion.
Time and Tide Letter 13 (1867)

18 Life without industry is guilt, and industry without art is brutality.
Lectures on Art Lecture 3, sec. 95 (1870)

19 Every increased possession loads us with a new weariness.
The Eagle's Nest ch. 5 (1872)

20 [*Of James McNeill Whistler's painting* Nocturne in Black and Gold:] I have seen, and heard, much of Cockney impudence before now; but never expected to hear a coxcomb ask two hundred guineas for flinging a pot of paint in the public's face.
Fors Clavigera Letter 79, 18 June 1877. This comment was the basis for Whistler's 1878 libel suit against Ruskin.

21 Great nations write their autobiographies in three manuscripts—the book of their deeds, the book of their words, and the book of their art.
St. Mark's Rest preface (1877)

22 There was a rocky valley between Buxton and Bakewell. . . . You enterprised a railroad . . . you blasted its rocks away. . . . And now, every fool in Buxton can be at Bakewell in half-an-hour, and every fool in Bakewell at Buxton.
Praeterita vol. 3 (1889)

23 There is scarcely anything in this world that some man cannot make a little worse and sell a little cheaper, and the buyers, who consider price only, are this man's lawful prey.
Attributed in *Chicago Daily Tribune*, 3 Oct. 1927. This quotation, repeated in many commercial advertisements, has not been found anywhere in Ruskin's works. An earlier unattributed occurrence appeared in the *Winston-Salem Journal*, 11 Nov. 1905: "There is hardly anything that some man cannot make a little worse and sell a little cheaper, and . . . people who consider price only, are that man's lawful prey."

Benjamin Russell
U.S. editor, 1761–1845

1 [*Of James Monroe's administration:*] The Era of Good Feelings.

Title of article, *Columbian Centinel* (Boston), 12 July 1817

Bertrand Russell
English philosopher and mathematician, 1872–1970

1 Mathematics may be defined as the subject in which we never know what we are talking about, nor whether what we are saying is true.

"Mathematics and Metaphysicians" (1901)

2 Mathematics, rightly viewed, possesses not only truth, but supreme beauty—a beauty cold and austere, like that of sculpture, without appeal to any part of our weaker nature, without the gorgeous trappings of painting or music, yet sublimely pure, and capable of a stern perfection such as only the greatest art can show.

"The Study of Mathematics" (1902)

3 We are thus led to a somewhat vague distinction between what we may call "hard" data and "soft" data. . . . I mean by "hard" data those which resist the solvent influence of critical reflection, and by "soft" data those which, under the operation of this process, become to our minds more or less doubtful.

Our Knowledge of the External World Lecture 3 (1915)

4 One is often told that it is a very wrong thing to attack religion, because religion makes men virtuous. So I am told; I have not noticed it.

"Why I Am Not a Christian" (1927)

5 The infliction of cruelty with a good conscience is a delight to moralists. That is why they invented Hell.

Sceptical Essays "On the Value of Scepticism" (1928)

6 The fact that an opinion has been widely held is no evidence whatever that it is not utterly absurd; indeed in view of the silliness of the majority of mankind, a widespread belief is more likely to be foolish than sensible.

Marriage and Morals ch. 5 (1929)

7 It seems to be the fate of idealists to obtain what they have struggled for in a form which destroys their ideals.

Marriage and Morals ch. 7 (1929)

8 The psychology of adultery has been falsified by conventional morals, which assume, in monogamous countries, that attraction to one person cannot coexist with a serious affection for another. Everybody knows that this is untrue.

Marriage and Morals ch. 16 (1929)

9 A dog cannot relate his autobiography; however eloquently he may bark, he cannot tell you that his parents were honest but poor.

Human Knowledge: Its Scope and Limits pt. 2, ch. 1 (1948)

10 Aristotle maintained that women have fewer teeth than men; although he was twice married, it never occurred to him to verify this statement by examining his wives' mouths.

Impact of Science on Society ch. 1 (1952)

11 The opinions that are held with passion are always those for which no good ground exists; indeed the passion is the measure of the holder's lack of rational conviction. Opinions in politics and religion are almost always held passionately.

Sceptical Essays "Introduction: On the Value of Skepticism" (1961)

12 [*Of Aldous Huxley:*] You could always tell by his conversation which volume of the *Encyclopedia Britannica* he'd been reading. One day it would be Alps, Andes, and Apennines, and the next it would be the Himalayas and the Hippocratic Oath.

Letter to R. W. Clark, July 1965

13 Three passions, simple but overwhelmingly strong, have governed my life: the longing for love, the search for knowledge, and unbearable pity for the suffering of mankind.

Autobiography prologue (1967)

Dora Russell
English feminist, 1894–1986

1 We want better reasons for having children than not knowing how to prevent them.

Hypatia ch. 4 (1925)

John Russell

British statesman, 1792–1878

1 If peace cannot be maintained with honor, it is
no longer peace.

Speech, Greenock, Scotland, 19 Sept. 1853
See Chamberlain 2; Disraeli 27

2 Among the defects of the Bill . . . one provision
was conspicuous by its presence and another by
its absence.

Speech to electors of London, Apr. 1859

3 [*Definition of a proverb:*] One man's wit, and all
men's wisdom.

Quoted in *Memoirs of the Life of the Right Honourable
Sir James Mackintosh*, ed. Robert James Mackintosh
(1835) (entry for 6 Oct. 1823)

William Howard Russell

British journalist, 1820–1907

1 [*Of the British infantry at the Battle of Balaclava:*]
That thin red streak topped with a line of steel.

Times (London), 14 Nov. 1854. In Russell's book, *The
British Expedition to the Crimea* (1877), the words
read, "They dashed on towards that thin red line
tipped with steel."

George Herman "Babe" Ruth

U.S. baseball player, 1895–1948

1 [*Self-description at age fifteen:*] George H Ruth
World's worse singer, world's best pitcher.

Inscription in hymnbook (1910)

2 [*Replying to a reporter's criticism that Ruth was
demanding a higher salary than that of President
Herbert Hoover in 1930:*] I had a better year than
he did.

Quoted in Tom Meany, *Babe Ruth* (1947)

Ernest Rutherford

New Zealand–born English physicist, 1871–
1937

1 Radioactivity is shown to be accompanied
by chemical changes in which new types of
matter are being continually produced. . . .
The conclusion is drawn that these chemical
changes must be sub-atomic in character.

"The Cause and Nature of Radioactivity," *Philosophical
Magazine*, Sept. 1902

2 In order to explain these and other results,
it is necessary to assume that the electrified
particle passes through an intense electric
field within the atom. The scattering of the
electrified particles is considered for a type of
atom which consists of a central electric charge
concentrated at a point and surrounded by
a uniform spherical distribution of opposite
electricity equal in amount.

"The Scattering of the *3 and *4 Rays and the
Structure of the Atom," *Proceedings of the Manchester
Literary and Philosophical Society* (1911)

3 From the results so far obtained it is difficult
to avoid the conclusion that the long-range
atoms arising from collision of *3 particles with
nitrogen are not nitrogen atoms but probably
atoms of hydrogen, or atoms of mass 2. If this
be the case, we must conclude that the nitrogen
atom is disintegrated under the intense forces
developed in a close collision with a swift
*3 particle, and that the hydrogen atom which
is liberated formed a constituent part of the
nitrogen nucleus.

"Collisions of *3 Particles with Light Atoms. IV.
An Anomalous Effect in Nitrogen," *Philosophical
Magazine*, June 1919

4 We haven't any money so we've got to think.

Quoted in *Chemical and Process Engineering*, Aug.
1952

5 [*Responding to the statement, "Lucky fellow
Rutherford, always on the crest of the wave":*] Well,
I made the wave, didn't I?

Quoted in C. P. Snow, *The Two Cultures and the
Scientific Revolution* (1959)

6 [Science may be divided into either one of]
physics and stamp-collecting.

Attributed in *Scientific Monthly*, Sept. 1945

7 If you can't explain your physics to a barmaid, it
is probably not very good physics.

Attributed in *Journal of Advertising Research*, Mar./
Apr. 1998. Kurt Vonnegut wrote in *Cat's Cradle*
(1963), "Any scientist who couldn't explain to an
eight-year-old what he was doing was a charlatan."

Paul Ryan

U.S. politician, 1970–

1 [*Of Donald Trump's criticism of Judge Gonzalo
Curiel:*] Claiming a person can't do their
job because of their race is . . . the textbook
definition of a racist comment.

News conference, Washington, D.C., 7 June 2016
See Trump 11

Matthew Rycroft
British diplomat, 1968–

1 Bush wanted to remove Saddam, through
military action, justified by the conjunction
of terrorism and WMD [weapons of mass
destruction]. But the intelligence and facts were
being fixed around the policy.

Memo to David Manning summarizing British
government meeting of 23 July 2002, quoted in
Sunday Times, 1 May 2005

Richard D. Ryder
English psychologist, 1940–

1 I use the word "speciesism" to describe the
widespread discrimination that is practised by
man against the other species. . . . Speciesism
and racism (and indeed sexism) overlook or
underestimate the similarities between the
discriminator and those discriminated against.

Victims of Science: The Use of Animals in Research
ch. 1 (1975). Ryder is said to have coined the word
speciesism earlier in a leaflet privately printed in
Oxford, England, in 1970.

Gilbert Ryle
English philosopher, 1900–1976

1 [*On Descartes's philosophy of mind:*] Such in
outline is the official theory. I shall often speak
of it, with deliberate abusiveness, as the dogma
of the Ghost in the Machine.

The Concept of Mind ch. 1 (1949)

Rafael Sabatini
Italian-born English author, 1875–1950

1 He was born with a gift of laughter and a sense that the world was mad. And that was all his patrimony.
Scaramouche ch. 1 (1921)

Howard Sackler
U.S. playwright, 1929–1982

1 The White Hope! Every paper in the country is calling you that.
The Great White Hope act 1, sc. 1 (1968)

Oliver Sacks
U.S. author and neurologist, 1933–2015

1 The Man Who Mistook His Wife for a Hat.
Title of book (1985)

Victoria "Vita" Sackville-West
English writer, 1892–1962

1 The greater cats with golden eyes
Stare out between the bars.
Deserts are there, and different skies,
And night with different stars.
The King's Daughter vol. 2, no. 1 (1929)

Anwar al-Sadat
Egyptian president, 1918–1981

1 Peace is much more precious than a piece of land.
Speech, Cairo, 8 Mar. 1978

Donatien-Alphonse-François, Marquis de Sade
French writer and libertine, 1740–1814

1 Far from being a vice, cruelty is the primary feeling that nature imprints in us. The infant breaks its rattle, bites its nurse's nipple, and strangles a bird, well before reaching the age of reason.
La Philosophie dans le Boudoir "Third Dialogue" (1795)

Sadi (Muslih-ud-Din)
Persian poet, ca. 1184–1291

1 I never complained of the vicissitudes of fortune, nor suffered my face to be overcast at the revolution of the heavens, except once when my feet were bare, and I had not the means of obtaining shoes. I came to the chief of Kūfah in a state of much dejection, and saw there a man who had no feet. I returned thanks to God and acknowledged his mercies, and endured my want of shoes with patience.
The Gulistān, or Rose Garden ch. 3, story 19 (1258) (translation by Edward B. Eastwick). Modern versions of this are often cited as Arabian proverbs, with wordings such as "I thought I was abused because I had no shoes until I met a man who had no feet."

William Safire
U.S. journalist and author, 1929–2009

1 A man who lies, thinking it is the truth, is an honest man, and a man who tells the truth, believing it to be a lie, is a liar.
Before the Fall: An Inside View of the Pre-Watergate White House prologue (1975)

Carl Sagan
U.S. astronomer and author, 1934–1996

1 But the fact that some geniuses were laughed at does not imply that all who are laughed at are geniuses. They laughed at Columbus, they laughed at Fulton, they laughed at the Wright Brothers. But they also laughed at Bozo the Clown.
Broca's Brain ch. 5 (1979)

2 A galaxy is composed of gas and dust and stars—billions upon billions of stars.
Cosmos ch. 1 (1980). Sagan denied using the phrase "billions and billions," as caricatured by comedian Johnny Carson, but the above quote approaches that phrase, and Sagan was extremely fond in his writing of the word *billion* or *billions*.

3 If you wish to make an apple pie from scratch, you must first invent the universe.
Cosmos ch. 9 (1980)

4 In science it often happens that scientists say, "You know that's a really good argument; my position is mistaken," and then they actually change their minds and you never hear that old view from them again. They really do it. It doesn't happen as often as it should, because scientists are human and change is sometimes painful. But it happens every day. I cannot recall the last time something like that has happened in politics or religion.
"The Burden of Skepticism" (1987)

Françoise Sagan (Françoise Quoirez)
French writer, 1935–2004

1 To jealousy, nothing is more frightful than laughter.
La Chamade ch. 9 (1965)

2 I shall live bad if I do not write and I shall write bad if I do not live.
Quoted in *N.Y. Times,* 11 Nov. 1956

Mohammed al-Sahhaf
Iraqi minister of information, 1940–

1 The infidels are committing suicide by the hundreds on the gates of Baghdad.
Quoted in *S.F. Chronicle,* 7 Apr. 2003

2 I triple guarantee you, there are no American soldiers in Baghdad.
Quoted in *Daily Telegraph* (London), 10 Apr. 2003

Edward Said
Palestinian-born U.S. social and literary critic, 1935–2003

1 Orientalism can be discussed and analyzed as the corporate institution for dealing with the Orient—dealing with it by making statements about it, authorizing views of it, describing it, by teaching it, settling it, ruling over it: in short, Orientalism as a Western style for dominating, restructuring, and having authority over the Orient.
Orientalism introduction (1978)

Antoine de Saint-Exupéry
French novelist, 1900–1944

1 Although human life is priceless, we always act as if something had an even greater price than life. . . . But what is that something?
Night Flight ch. 14 (1931)

2 Experience shows us that love does not consist in gazing at each other but in looking together in the same direction.
Terre des Hommes ch. 8 (1939)

3 Grown-ups never understand anything for themselves, and it is tiresome for children to be always and forever explaining things to them.
Le Petit Prince ch. 1 (1943)

4 It is much more difficult to judge oneself than to judge others. If you succeed in judging yourself rightly, then you are indeed a man of true wisdom.
Le Petit Prince ch. 10 (1943)

5 It is only with the heart that one can see rightly; what is essential is invisible to the eye.
Le Petit Prince ch. 21 (1943)

Charles-Augustin Sainte-Beuve
French critic, 1804–1869

1 *Et Vigny plus secret,*
Comme en sa tour d'ivoire, avant midi rentrait.
And Vigny more discreet, as if in his ivory tower, returned before noon.
Les Pensées d'Août, à M. Villemain (1837). Origin of the term *ivory tower.*

Buffy Sainte-Marie
Canadian singer and songwriter, 1941–

1 He's five feet two and he's six feet four.
He fights with missiles and with spears.
He's all of thirty-one and he's only seventeen.
He's been a soldier for a thousand years.
"The Universal Soldier" (song) (1963)

2 He's a Cath'lic, a Hindu, an atheist, a Jain,
A Buddhist and a Baptist and a Jew.
And he knows he shouldn't kill
And he knows he always will.
"The Universal Soldier" (song) (1963)

Andrei Sakharov

Russian physicist and political activist, 1921–1989

1 Intellectual freedom is essential to human society—freedom to obtain and distribute information, freedom for open-minded and unfearing debate, and freedom from pressure by officialdom and prejudices.

"Reflections on Progress, Peaceful Coexistence, and Intellectual Freedom" (1968)

2 Freedom of thought is the only guarantee of the feasibility of a scientific democratic approach to politics, economy, and culture.

"Reflections on Progress, Peaceful Coexistence, and Intellectual Freedom" (1968)

Saki (Hector Hugh Munro)

Burmese-born Scottish writer, 1870–1916

1 Everyone heard that I'd written the book and got it in the press. After that, I might have been a gold-fish in a glass bowl for all the privacy I got.

Reginald "The Innocence of Reginald" (1904)

2 The cook was a good cook, as cooks go; and as cooks go, she went.

Reginald "Reginald on Besetting Sins" (1904)

3 I'm living so far beyond my means that we may almost be said to be living apart.

The Unbearable Bassington ch. 5 (1912)

4 Waldo is one of those people who would be enormously improved by death.

Beasts and Super-Beasts "The Feast of Nemesis" (1914)

J. D. Salinger

U.S. novelist and short story writer, 1919–2010

1 If you really want to hear about it, the first thing you'll probably want to know is where I was born, and what my lousy childhood was like . . . and all that David Copperfield kind of crap, but I don't feel like going into it, if you want to know the truth.

The Catcher in the Rye ch. 1 (1951)

2 What really knocks me out is a book that, when you're all done reading it, you wish the author that wrote it was a terrific friend of yours and you could call him up on the phone whenever you felt like it.

The Catcher in the Rye ch. 3 (1951)

3 Sex is something I really don't understand too hot. You never know *where* the hell you are. I keep making up these sex rules for myself, and then I break them right away.

The Catcher in the Rye ch. 9 (1951)

4 Anyway, I keep picturing all these little kids playing some game in this big field of rye and all. . . . What I have to do, I have to catch everybody if they start to go over the cliff—I mean if they're running and they don't look where they're going I have to come out from somewhere and catch them. That's all I'd do all day. I'd just be the catcher in the rye.

The Catcher in the Rye ch. 22 (1951)
See Robert Burns 10

5 Don't ever tell anybody anything. If you do, you start missing everybody.

The Catcher in the Rye ch. 26 (1951)

6 A confessional passage has probably never been written that didn't stink a little bit of the writer's pride in having given up his pride.

"Seymour: An Introduction" (1959)

7 There isn't anyone *any*where that isn't Seymour's Fat Lady. Don't you know that? Don't you know that goddam secret yet? And don't you know—*listen* to me, now—*don't you know who that Fat Lady really is?* . . . Ah, buddy. Ah, buddy. It's Christ Himself. Christ Himself, buddy.

Franny and Zooey (1961). Ellipsis in the original.

Robert Arthur Talbot Gascoyne-Cecil, Marquis of Salisbury

British prime minister, 1830–1903

1 [*Of Disraeli's amendment on Disestablishment:*] Too clever by half.

Speech in House of Commons, 30 Mar. 1868

2 Horny-handed sons of toil.

Quarterly Review, Oct. 1873. Popularized in the United States by Denis Kearney.
See James Russell Lowell 1

Jonas E. Salk

U.S. physician and virologist, 1914–1995

1 [*When asked by journalist Edward R. Murrow who held the patent to his vaccine against polio:*] Well the people, I would say. There is no patent. Could you patent the sun?

See It Now (television show), 12 Apr. 1955

Sallust (Gaius Sallustius Crispus)

Roman historian, 86 B.C.–35 B.C.

1 [*Of Rome:*] A venal city ripe to perish, if a buyer can be found.

Jugurtha sec. 35

2 *Punica fide.*
With Carthaginian trustworthiness [treachery].

Jugurtha sec. 108

Narcisse Achille, Comte de Salvandy

French government official and writer, 1795–1856

1 We are dancing on a volcano.

Quoted in *Paris ou le Livre des Cent-et-Un* (1832). This remark was made at a fête given by the Duc d'Orleans for the King of Naples at the Palais-Royal, 31 May 1830.

Paul A. Samuelson

U.S. economist, 1915–2009

1 Wall Street indexes predicted nine out of the last five recessions.

Newsweek, 19 Sept. 1966

George Sand (Amandine-Aurore Lucie Dupin, Baronne Dudevant)

French novelist, 1804–1876

1 We cannot tear out a single page of our life; but we can throw the book in the fire.

Mauprat ch. 11 (1837)

2 There is only one happiness in life, to love and be loved.

Letter to Lina Calamatta, 31 Mar. 1862

3 Faith is an excitement and an enthusiasm, a state of intellectual magnificence which we must safeguard like a treasure, not squander on our way through life in the small coin of empty words and inexact, pedantic arguments.

Letter to Marie-Théodore Desplanches, 25 May 1866

4 Happiness lies in the consciousness we have of it.

Handsome Lawrence ch. 3 (1872)

5 Art for art's sake is an empty phrase. Art for the sake of the true, art for the sake of the good and the beautiful, that is the faith I am searching for.

Letter to Alexandre Saint-Jean, 1872

Carl Sandburg

U.S. writer, 1878–1967

1 Hog Butcher for the World,
Tool Maker, Stacker of Wheat,
Player with Railroads and the Nation's Freight
 Handler;
Stormy, husky, brawling,
City of the big shoulders.

"Chicago" l. 1 (1916)

2 They tell me you are wicked and I believe them,
 for I have seen your painted women under
 the gas lamps luring the farm boys.

"Chicago" l. 6 (1916)

3 And they tell me you are brutal and my reply is:
 On the faces of women and children I have
 seen the marks of wanton hunger.
And having answered so I turn once more to
 those who sneer at this my city, and I give
 them back the sneer and say to them:
Come and show me another city with lifted
 head singing so proud to be alive and coarse
 and strong and cunning.

"Chicago" l. 10 (1916)

4 The fog comes
on little cat feet.
It sits looking
over the harbor and city
on silent haunches
and then moves on.

"Fog" l. 1 (1916)

5 I am the people—the mob—the crowd—the
 mass.
Do you know that all the great work of the
 world is done through me?

"I Am the People, the Mob" l. 1 (1916)

6 When Abraham Lincoln was shoveled into
the tombs, he forgot the copperheads and the
assassin . . . in the dust, in the cool tombs.
"Cool Tombs" l. 1 (1918). Ellipsis in the original.

7 Pile the bodies high at Austerlitz and Waterloo.
Shovel them under and let me work—
I am the grass; I cover all.
"Grass" l. 1 (1918)

8 Two years, ten years, and passengers ask the
conductor:
What place is this?
Where are we now?
"Grass" l. 7 (1918)

9 Why is there always a secret singing
When a lawyer cashes in?
Why does a hearse horse snicker
Hauling a lawyer away?
"The Lawyers Know Too Much" l. 16 (1920)

10 Sometime they'll give a war and nobody will
come.
The People, Yes pt. 23 (1936). The popular form of this
expression was crystallized when Charlotte Keyes
published an article titled "Suppose They Gave a War
and No One Came?" in *McCall's,* Oct. 1966.

11 The people will live on.
The learning and blundering people will
live on.
The People, Yes pt. 107 (1936)

12 A baby is God's opinion that life should go on.
Remembrance Rock ch. 2 (1948)

13 Slang is language that takes off its coat, spits on
its hands, and goes to work.
Quoted in Maurice H. Weseen, *The Dictionary of
American Slang* (1934).

Bernie Sanders
U.S. politician, 1941–

1 If [a company] is too big to fail, then it is too big
to exist.
News release, 18 Sept. 2008

2 [*To Hillary Clinton:*] The American people are
sick and tired of hearing about your damn
emails.
Democratic presidential debate, Las Vegas, Nev.,
13 Oct. 2015

George Sanders
Russian-born English actor, 1906–1972

1 Dear World, I am leaving you because I am
bored. I feel I have lived long enough. I am
leaving you with your worries in this sweet
cesspool. Good luck.
Suicide note, 25 Apr. 1972

Henry R. "Red" Sanders
U.S. football coach, 1905–1958

1 Winning isn't everything. . . . It's the only thing!
Quoted in *L.A. Times,* 18 Oct. 1950. Often attributed
to Vince Lombardi, but the Sanders citation predates
any reference to Lombardi's using it. A little earlier,
the *Tallahassee Democrat,* 7 Feb. 1950, printed the
following (citation discovered by Garson O'Toole):
"Tulane football coach Henry Frnka recently
asked UCLA mentor Red Sanders, 'Winning isn't
everything, is it, Red?' To which Sanders replied,
'No, it isn't everything; it's just the ONLY thing.'"
David Maraniss, *When Pride Still Mattered: A Life
of Vince Lombardi* (1999), quotes Sanders's friend
Fred Russell: "I remember hearing him saying it
back in the mid-1930s when he was coaching at the
Columbia Military Academy."
See Lombardi 1; Modern Proverbs 99

Margaret Sanger
U.S. reformer, 1883–1966

1 Women of the working class, especially wage
workers, should not have more than two
children at most. The average working man
can support no more and the average working
woman can take care of no more in decent
fashion.
Family Limitation introduction (1914)

2 A mutual and satisfied sexual act is of great
benefit to the average woman, the magnetism
of it is health giving, and acts as a beautifier
and tonic. When it is not desired on the part of
the woman and she has no response, it should
not take place. This is an act of prostitution and
is degrading to the woman's finer sensibility,
all the marriage certificates on earth to the
contrary notwithstanding.
Family Limitation (1914)

3 No woman can call herself free who cannot
choose the time to be a mother or not as she
sees fit.
"The Case for Birth Control," *Physical Culture,* Apr.
1917

4 No woman can call herself free who does not own and control her body. No woman can call herself free until she can choose consciously whether she will or will not be a mother.
Woman and the New Race ch. 8 (1920)

5 Woman was and is condemned to a system under which the lawful rapes exceed the unlawful ones a million to one.
Woman and the New Race ch. 14 (1920)

6 Woman's role has been that of an incubator and little more. She has given birth to an incubated race.
Woman and the New Race ch. 18 (1920)

George Santayana

Spanish-born U.S. philosopher and critic, 1863–1952

1 Fanaticism consists in redoubling your effort when you have forgotten your aim.
The Life of Reason vol. 1, introduction (1905)

2 That life is worth living is the most necessary of assumptions, and were it not assumed, the most impossible of conclusions.
The Life of Reason vol. 1, ch. 10 (1905)

3 Progress, far from consisting in change, depends on retentiveness. . . . When experience is not retained, as among savages, infancy is perpetual. Those who cannot remember the past are condemned to repeat it. . . . This is the condition of children and barbarians, in whom instinct has learned nothing from experience.
The Life of Reason vol. 1, ch. 12 (1905)

4 Each religion, so dear to those whose life it sanctifies, and fulfilling so necessary a function in the society that has adopted it, necessarily contradicts every other religion, and probably contradicts itself.
The Life of Reason vol. 3, ch. 1 (1905)

5 What religion a man shall have is a historical accident, quite as much as what language he shall speak.
The Life of Reason vol. 3, ch. 1 (1905)

6 Miracles are propitious accidents, the natural causes of which are too complicated to be readily understood.
The Ethics of Spinoza introduction (1910)

7 I like to walk about amidst the beautiful things that adorn the world; but private wealth I should decline, or any sort of personal possessions, because they would take away my liberty.
Soliloquies in England and Later Soliloquies "The Irony of Liberalism" (1922)

8 My atheism, like that of Spinoza, is true piety towards the universe and denies only gods fashioned by men in their own image, to be servants of their human interests.
Soliloquies in England and Later Soliloquies "On My Friendly Critics" (1922)

9 Only the dead have seen the end of war.
Soliloquies in England and Later Soliloquies "Tipperary" (1922). Frequently attributed to Plato, as on the wall of the Imperial War Museum in London, in General Douglas MacArthur's farewell address at West Point in 1962, and in the film *Black Hawk Down,* but it does not appear in Plato's works.

10 There is no cure for birth and death save to enjoy the interval.
Soliloquies in England and Later Soliloquies "War Shrines" (1922)

11 Scepticism is the chastity of the intellect, and it is shameful to surrender it too soon or to the first comer.
Scepticism and Animal Faith ch. 9 (1923)

12 It is a great advantage for a system of philosophy to be substantially true.
The Unknowable (1923)

13 There is nothing impossible, therefore, in the existence of the supernatural; its existence seems to me decidedly probable; there is infinite room for it on every side.
"The Genteel Tradition at Bay" (1931)

14 The Difficult is that which can be done immediately; the Impossible that which takes a little longer.
Quoted in *Reader's Digest,* Nov. 1939. "The difference between the difficult and the 'impossible' is that the impossible takes a little longer time" appeared in the *Oakland Tribune,* 31 Mar. 1924, quoting a sermon by John Snape.
See Calonne 1; Nansen 1; Trollope 3

15 There is no God and Mary is His Mother.
Attributed in Robert Lowell, *Life Studies* (1953). May be a paraphrase of Santayana's ideas or a Catholic joke that became attached to his name.

Edward Sapir

U.S. anthropologist and linguist, 1884–1939

1 Were a language ever completely "grammatical," it would be a perfect engine of conceptual expression. Unfortunately, or luckily, no language is tyrannically consistent. All grammars leak.
Language: An Introduction to the Study of Speech ch. 2 (1921)

2 Language and our thought-grooves are inextricably interwoven, are, in a sense, one and the same.
Language: An Introduction to the Study of Speech ch. 10 (1921)

Sappho

Greek poet, Seventh cent. B.C.

1 Equal to the gods seems to me that man who sits facing you and hears you nearby sweetly speaking and softly laughing. This sets my heart to fluttering in my breast, for when I look on you a moment, then can I speak no more, but my tongue falls silent, and at once a delicate flame courses beneath my skin, and with my eyes I see nothing, and my ears hum, and a cold sweat bathes me, and a trembling seizes me all over, and I am paler than grass, and I feel that I am near to death.
Fragment 2

2 The moon has set, and the Pleiades; it is midnight, and time passes, and I sleep alone.
Fragment 94

3 [*Of a girl before marriage:*] As an apple reddens on the high bough; high atop the highest bough the apple pickers passed it by—no, not passed it by, but they could not reach it.
Fragment 116

John Singer Sargent

U.S. painter, 1856–1925

1 Every time I paint a portrait I lose a friend.
Quoted in Evan Esar, *A Dictionary of Humorous Quotations* (1949)

David Sarnoff

U.S. business executive, 1891–1971

1 For some years I have had in mind a plan of development which would make radio a "household utility" in the same sense as a piano or phonograph.
Memorandum to Owen D. Young, 31 Jan. 1920

2 [*Announcing the inauguration of regular television programming by the National Broadcasting Company:*] And now we add radio sight to sound.
Broadcast speech, 20 Apr. 1939

William Saroyan

U.S. writer, 1908–1981

1 In the time of your life, live—so that in that good time there shall be no ugliness or death for yourself or for any life your life touches.
The Time of Your Life preface (1939)

2 If you give to a thief he cannot steal from you, and then he is no longer a thief.
The Human Comedy ch. 4 (1943)

George Sarton

Belgian-born U.S. historian of science, 1884–1956

1 The most ominous conflict of our time is the difference of opinion, of outlook, between men of letters, historians, philosophers, the so-called humanists, on the one side and scientists on the other. The gap cannot but increase because of the intolerance of both and the fact that science is growing by leaps and bounds.
"The History of Science and the History of Civilization" (1930)
See Snow 3

May Sarton

Belgian-born U.S. poet, 1912–1995

1 I come to you with only this straight gaze.
These are not hours of fire but years of praise,
The glass full to the brim, completely full,
But held in balance so no drop can spill.
"Because What I Want Most Is Permanence" l. 20 (1954)

2 And one cold starry night
Whatever your belief
The phoenix will take flight
Over the seas of grief
To sing her thrilling song
To stars and waves and sky

For neither old nor young
The phoenix does not die.
"The Phoenix Again" l. 17 (1988)

Jean-Paul Sartre
French philosopher and writer, 1905–1980

1 Everything is gratuitous, this garden, this city and myself. When you suddenly realize it, it makes you feel sick and everything begins to drift . . . that's nausea.
La Nausée (Nausea) (1938)

2 I am condemned to be free.
L'Être et le Néant (Being and Nothingness) pt. 4, ch. 1 (1943)

3 *L'homme est une passion inutile.*
Man is a useless passion.
L'Être et le Néant (Being and Nothingness) pt. 4, ch. 2 (1943)

4 Human life begins on the far side of despair.
Les Mouches (The Flies) act 3, sc. 2 (1943)

5 *L'Enfer, c'est les Autres.*
Hell is other people.
Huis Clos (No Exit) (1944)
See T. S. Eliot 126

6 Well, well, let's get on with it.
Huis Clos (No Exit) (1944)

7 Man cannot will unless he has first understood that he can count on nothing but himself: that he is alone, left alone on earth in the middle of his infinite responsibilities, with neither help nor succor, with no other goal but the one he will set for himself, with no other destiny but the one he will forge on this earth.
"A More Precise Characterization of Existentialism" (1944) (translation by Richard McCleary). The previous attribution of this quotation to Sartre's *L'Être et le Néant* (Being and Nothingness) is incorrect.

8 Existence precedes essence.
L'Existentialisme Est un Humanisme (1946)

9 When the rich wage war it's the poor who die.
Le Diable et le Bon Dieu act 1, tableau 1 (1951)

10 [*Declining to accept the Nobel Prize for Literature:*] A writer must refuse, therefore, to allow himself to be transformed into an institution.
Declaration read at Stockholm, Sweden, 22 Oct. 1964

Siegfried Sassoon
English writer, 1886–1967

1 You smug-faced crowds with kindling eye
Who cheer when soldier lads march by,
Sneak home and pray you'll never know
The hell where youth and laughter go.
"Suicide in the Trenches" l. 9 (1918)

Allen Saunders
U.S. cartoonist, 1899–1986

1 Life is what happens to us while we are making other plans.
Quoted in *Reader's Digest,* Jan. 1957. Often credited to John Lennon, but this citation considerably predates Lennon's usage.

John Monk Saunders
U.S. writer, 1895–1940

1 It seemed like a good idea . . . at the time.
Single Lady ch. 12 (1931). Ellipsis in the original.

Ferdinand de Saussure
Swiss linguist, 1857–1913

1 But what is language [*langue*]? It is not to be confused with human speech [*langage*], of which it is only a definite part, though certainly an essential one. It is both a social product of the faculty of speech and a collection of necessary conventions that have been adopted by a social body to permit individuals to exercise that faculty.
Course in General Linguistics introduction, ch. 3 (1916) (translation by Wade Baskin)

2 *A science that studies the life of signs within society* is conceivable; it would be a part of social psychology and consequently of general psychology; I shall call it *semiology* (from Greek *sēmeîon* "sign").
Course in General Linguistics introduction, ch. 3 (1916) (translation by Wade Baskin)

3 I call the combination of a concept and a sound-image a *sign.* . . . I propose to retain the word *sign* [*signe*] to designate the whole and to replace *concept* and *sound-image* respectively by *signified* [*signifié*] and *signifier* [*signifiant*]. . . . The bond between the signifier and the signified is arbitrary.
Course in General Linguistics pt. 1, ch. 1 (1916) (translation by Wade Baskin)

4 Language can . . . be compared with a sheet of paper: thought is the front and the sound the back; one cannot cut the front without cutting the back at the same time; likewise in language, one can neither divide sound from thought nor thought from sound; the division could be accomplished only abstractedly, and the result would be either pure psychology or pure phonology.
Course in General Linguistics pt. 2, ch. 4 (1916) (translation by Wade Baskin)

Alfred Sauvy

French demographer, 1898–1990

1 *Ce Tiers Monde ignoré, exploité, méprisé comme le*
   Tiers Etat, veut, lui aussi, être quelque chose.
This Third World, ignored, exploited, scorned
   like the Third Estate, wants also to be
   something.
L'Observateur, 14 Aug. 1952. Coinage of the term *Tiers Monde* or *Third World*.

Mario Savio

U.S. political activist, 1942–1996

1 There's a time when the operation of the machine becomes so odious, makes you so sick at heart, that you can't take part; you can't even passively take part. And you've got to put your bodies on the gears and on the levers, and on all the apparatus, and you've got to make it stop.
Speech, Berkeley, Calif., 3 Nov. 1964
See Thoreau 7

John G. Saxe

U.S. poet, 1816–1887

1 Laws, like sausages, cease to inspire respect in proportion as we know how they are made.
Quoted in *University Chronicle* (University of Michigan), 27 Mar. 1869. Today this is usually credited to Otto von Bismarck, but the earliest Bismarck attribution that has been found is in Claudius O. Johnson, *Government in the United States* (1933).

Jean Baptiste Say

French economist, 1767–1832

1 It is production which opens a demand for products. . . . A product is no sooner created, than it, from that instant, affords a market for other products to the full extent of its own value.
A Treatise on Political Economy (1803)

Dorothy L. Sayers

English detective fiction writer, 1893–1957

1 I always have a quotation for everything—it saves original thinking.
Have His Carcase ch. 4 (1932)

2 Many words have no legal meaning. Others have a legal meaning very unlike their ordinary meaning. For example, the word "daffy-down-dilly." It is a criminal libel to call a lawyer a "daffy-down-dilly." Ha! Yes, I advise you never to do such a thing. No, I certainly advise you *never* to do it.
Unnatural Death ch. 14 (1955)

3 As years come in and years go out
I totter toward the tomb,
Still caring less and less about
Who goes to bed with whom.
Letter to John Benjamin, 2 Feb. 1953

Henry J. Sayers

U.S. songwriter, 1854–1932

1 Ta-ra-ra-boom-de-ay!
Title of minstrel show number (1891)

Sayings

This category lists expressions that are not strictly proverbs, that is, not traditional sentences offering advice or a moral pithily, but that resemble most proverbs in the respect that their authorship is probably impossible to trace. The citation given for each is that of the earliest occurrence that has been found in research for this book. The sayings are arranged alphabetically by their first significant word. See also Proverbs, Modern Proverbs, *and* Anonymous.

1 Age and treachery will overcome youth and skill.
Reno Evening Gazette, 2 May 1977

2 All the world is queer . . . but thee and me, and thee knows thee is queer sometimes.
Good Literature, 16 June 1883. Frequently attributed to Robert Owen, but no evidence has ever been produced supporting that claim.

3 The butler did it.
Variety, 29 Oct. 1924. "His ex-butler did it!" appears in Gilbert Wolf Gabriel, *Jiminy* (1922).

4 The check is in the mail.
Berkshire Evening Eagle, 20 Feb. 1947

5 Chicken Little was right.
Max Steele, *Debby* (1950)

6 Close, but no cigar.

Annie Oakley (motion picture) (1935). The actual phrasing here is "Close, Colonel, but no cigar!"

7 A committee is a group of the unwilling, appointed by the unfit, to do the unnecessary.

Detroit Medical News, 8 Dec. 1952

8 Curses, foiled again.

Yale Forest School News, July 1923

9 Do not fold, spindle, or mutilate.

Kansas City Star, 16 July 1941. The basic directive on punched computer cards. A later development was "I am a human being—do not fold, spindle, or mutilate." The earliest example of the latter found in research for this book is in two 1967 books: Alan Robbins, *The Guide to College Graffiti;* and Robert Reisner, *Great Wall Writing & Button Graffiti.*

10 Don't call us, we'll call you.

Lowell (Mass.) *Sun*, 17 Mar. 1944

11 Don't sweat the small stuff.

Atlanta Constitution, 17 Aug. 1957. A popular extension of this is: "Don't sweat the small stuff. And try to remember it's all small stuff" (*N.Y. Times*, 23 Oct. 1979).

12 Feminism is the radical notion that women are people.

Orlando Sentinel, 20 Feb. 1993

13 [*Formula used at the beginning of an automobile race:*] Gentlemen—start your engines!

Iowa City Press-Citizen, 24 May 1952. "Gentlemen, start your motors" appeared in the 1950 edition of *Floyd Clymer's Indianapolis 500 Yearbook.*

14 Get a life.

Wash. Post, 23 Jan. 1983

15 [*Supposed Jesuit maxim:*] Give me a child until he is seven years old, and you may do what you like with him afterwards.

The Mother's Mission (1859). This has never been verified in any Jesuit source.
See Spark 2

16 Remember the golden rule. . . . Whoever has the gold makes the rules.

Wizard of Id (comic strip), 3 May 1965

17 Happy ever after.

William M. Thackeray, *The History of Pendennis* (1849). "And they lived happily ever after" or variants is a standard fairy tale ending. The Thackeray quotation antedates the earliest (1853) citation given by the *Oxford English Dictionary.*

18 [They snatched] defeat from the jaws of victory.

Daily Inter-Ocean (Chicago), 24 May 1874

19 I don't care what you call me, as long as you don't call me late to dinner.

Huron Reflector (Norwalk, Ohio), 16 July 1833. The exact words used by this source are "Call me what you please, but don't call me too late to dinner."

20 If a tree falls in a forest and there is no one to hear it, does it make a sound?

Wash. Post, 9 Apr. 1935. A similar question involving a tree falling on an island appeared in *The Chautauquan*, June 1883. The saying is a popularization of the philosophy of George Berkeley.

21 If English was good enough for Jesus, it's good enough for me.

New Yorker, 4 Dec. 1926. An earlier version appeared in the *New York Times*, 15 Jan. 1905: "If English was good enough for St. Paul to write the Bible in it's good enough for me."

22 [*Military saying:*] If it moves salute it. If it doesn't move pick it up. If you can't pick it up, paint it.

Chicago Defender, 16 Dec. 1944

23 If I'd have known I was going to live this long, I would have taken better care of myself.

Wash. Post, 24 Nov. 1966. Frequently attributed to Eubie Blake, Adolph Zukor, or others, but this occurrence significantly predates any evidence for these individuals using the saying.

24 If voting could change anything it would be made illegal.

Lowell (Mass.) *Sun*, 24 Sept. 1976

25 When did I ever drop my bread and butter—and it seldom got to my mouth without some such circuit—but it fell on the buttered side?

Blackwood's Edinburgh Magazine, Jan. 1822
See Robert Burns 3; Dickens 67; Disraeli 7; Modern Proverbs 100; Orwell 17; Plautus 3; Proverbs 2

26 In God we trust; all others pay cash.

Chester (Pa.) *Daily Times*, 21 Apr. 1877. The exact wording here is "In God we trust, all others cash."

27 It's a long time between drinks.

Henry Morford, *Red-Tape and Pigeon-Hole Generals* (1864). "A d—d long time between drinks" appears in the *Southern Literary Messenger*, Dec. 1862. A popular story ascribes the origin of the phrase to the governor of North Carolina speaking to the governor of South Carolina, or vice versa.

28 [New York is] a nice place to visit, but I wouldn't want to live there.

Brattleboro (Vt.) *Daily Reformer*, 1 Feb. 1919

29 [*Definition of death:*] It's nature's way of telling you to slow down.

Newsweek, 25 Apr. 1960

30 It's not the money, it's the principle.

Catherine G. F. Smith, *Quixote, the Weaver* (1892) See "Kin" Hubbard 4

31 Just because you're paranoid doesn't mean you're not being followed.

Fitchburg (Mass.) *Sentinel,* 9 Sept. 1971. This 1971 source referred to the saying as being a graffito. A similar quotation, "Even Paranoids Have Real Enemies" (printed on a button), was cited in *Christianity Today,* 21 July 1967. Nigel Rees, *Cassell's Humorous Quotations,* records two earlier versions: "Because a person has monomania she need not be wrong about her facts" (Dorothy L. Sayers, *Murder Must Advertise* ch. 16 [1933]); and "Has it ever struck you that when people get persecution mania, they usually have a good deal to feel persecuted about?" (C. P. Snow, *The Affair* ch. 11 [1960]).

32 Keep it simple, stupid.

Robesonian (Lumberton, N.C.), 23 July 1958. Usually given as the expansion of the abbreviation KISS.

33 Kilroy was here.

Sheppard Field Texacts, 14 July 1945. Graffito popularized by U.S. soldiers in the 1940s. An earlier version appeared in the *Kearns Air Force Post Review,* 26 June 1945 ("To the Unknown Soldier—Kilroy *Sleeps* Here"), and the *Texacts* newspaper of the Sheppard Field Army base in Texas had posed the question "Who is Kilroy?" in its 21 Apr. 1945 issue.

34 *Le roi est mort! Vive le roi!*
The king is dead! Long live the king!

Encyclopaedia Americana (1851). This official formula dates at least from the sixteenth century and was used by a French court dignitary to announce the death of the sovereign and the immediate advent of his successor.

35 Let's run it up the flagpole and see if anyone salutes.

Twelve Angry Men (motion picture) (1957)

36 [*Formula used to begin motion picture filming:*] Lights, camera, action.

L.A. Times, 10 Oct. 1926

37 [*Describing the three most important things about real estate:*] Location, location, location.

Omaha World Herald, 13 July 1920

38 The mail must go through.

Motto of Pony Express (1860–1861)

39 [*"Chinese curse":*] May you live in interesting times.

Yorkshire Post, 21 Mar. 1936. No authentic Chinese saying to this effect has ever been found.

40 Meanwhile back at the ranch.

Oakland Tribune, 21 July 1940. Zane Grey's *Riders of the Purple Sage* (1912) contains the phrase "Meantime, at the ranch."

41 No more Mr. Nice Guy.

Terre Haute Tribune, 8 Sept. 1960

42 [*Pseudo-Latin for "Don't let the bastards grind you down":*] Ne illigitimi carborundum.

Racine (Wis.) *Journal-Times,* 19 May 1945

43 Not tonight, Josephine.

Houston Post, 12 June 1910. Supposedly Napoleon's rejection of his wife's advances, but it appears to be a much later catchphrase.

44 One man's terrorist is another man's freedom fighter.

Christian E. Hauer, Jr., *Crisis and Conscience in the Middle East* (1970). The exact wording in the 1970 book was "heroic freedom fighter."

45 The operation was successful, but the patient died.

Hartford Daily Courant, 28 Aug. 1851

46 [*Response to request for directions, "How do you get to Carnegie Hall?":*] Practice, practice.

N.Y. Times, 26 Mar. 1961. With the single-word answer, "Practice!," this appeared in the *Washington Post,* 13 Mar. 1955.

47 Sex is like money—even when it's bad, it's good.

Robert Reisner, *Graffiti* (1971)

48 The South will rise again.

Baltimore Sun, 10 July 1865

49 Thank God It's Friday.

Lima (Ohio) *News,* 16 Dec. 1937. Often abbreviated TGIF.

50 [*Of computer defects:*] That's not a bug, that's a feature.

CoEvolution Quarterly, Spring 1981

51 There ain't nobody here but us chickens.

Times-Democrat (New Orleans), 22 Sept. 1912. A racially charged version appeared as early as 1908: "'Tain't nobody in heah 'ceptin' us chickens" (*Life,* 11 June). According to Eric Partridge, *Dictionary of Catch Phrases,* this saying "had existed prob. since late or latish C19 and was based on a story about a chicken-thief surprised by the owner, who calls 'Anybody there?' and is greeted by this resourceful reply."

52 [*British description of U.S. soldiers stationed in England during World War II:*] They're over-paid, they're over-sexed, and they're over here.
Wash. Post, 30 Apr. 1944

53 This hurts me more than you.
Harry Graham, *Ruthless Rhymes* (1899)

54 [*Native American pre-battle motto:*] This is a good day to die.
Leavenworth (Kan.) *Weekly Times*, 18 Aug. 1881

55 Hours spent fishing are not deducted from man's allotted span.
Angling Yarns (1936)

56 To err is human. To really foul up—it takes a computer.
Newark (Ohio) *Advocate*, 3 Oct. 1969

57 *Vive la différence.*
Long live the difference [between men and women].
N.Y. Times, 5 Sept. 1943

58 Wait till next year.
Sporting Life, 5 Nov. 1884. Phrase used by disappointed sports fans.

59 [*Alluding to perfunctory sexual intercourse:*] Wham bam thank you, ma'am!
Thomas Heggens, *Mister Roberts* (1948)

60 What's black and white and red all over?
Barbara Bee, *One Thousand Riddles* (1882). The answer is "A newspaper."

61 When all else fails, try reading the instructions.
The Aeroplane, 4 Apr. 1954

62 Which . . . is first, the chicken or the egg?
Stephen Pearl Andrews, *The Basic Outline of Universology* (1872)

63 Who's minding the store?
Wash. Post, 16 Apr. 1942

64 Will you still respect me in the morning?
N.Y. Times, 11 Oct. 1979

65 A woman's place is in the House, and the Senate, too.
Burlington (N.C.) *Daily Times News*, 7 May 1973. "A woman's place is in the House" appeared as a campaign slogan of Bella Abzug's in the *Mansfield* (Ohio) *News Journal*, 13 July 1970.
See Proverbs 330

66 Women and children first.
William D. O'Connor, *Harrington* (1860)

67 You can't win. . . . You can't even break even. . . . You can't get out of the game!
Astounding Science-Fiction, Dec. 1956

Wallace S. Sayre
U.S. political scientist, 1905–1972

1 Academic politics is the most vicious and bitter form of politics, because the stakes are so low.
Quoted in *Wall Street Journal*, 20 Dec. 1973. Political scientist Herbert Kaufman has attested to the editor of this dictionary that Sayre usually stated this as "The politics of the university are so intense because the stakes are so low" and that Sayre originated the quip by the early 1950s. Philosopher Charles Frankel said in a 1969 speech, "It used to be said of politics on the university campus that it was the worst of all kinds of politics because the stakes were so small" ("Education and the Barricades," in American Association of School Administrators, *Your AASA in Nineteen Sixty-Eight–Sixty-Nine*).

Al Scalpone
U.S. advertising writer, fl. 1947

1 The family that prays together stays together.
Family Theater of the Air (radio program), 6 Mar. 1947. According to the *Oxford Dictionary of Proverbs*, "The saying was invented by Al Scalpone, a professional commercial-writer, and was used as the slogan of the Roman Catholic Family Rosary Crusade by Father Patrick Peyton. . . . The crusade began in 1942 and the slogan was apparently first broadcast" as above.

Friedrich von Schelling
German philosopher, 1775–1854

1 *Architektur ist überhaupt die erstarrte Musik.*
Architecture in general is frozen music.
Philosophie der Kunst (1809). Nigel Rees notes in the *Cassell Companion to Quotations:* "[Schelling] had already used the 'frozen' phrase in a lecture in 1802–3. . . . Madame de Staël wrote in *Corinne* (1807) about St. Peter's in Rome: '*La vue d'un tel monument est comme une musique continuelle et fixée.*' As she was in touch with leading German intellectuals . . . she may well have known Schelling's phrase." Rees also explains that Schopenhauer in *Die Welt als Wille und Vorstellung* (written 1814–1818) refers to architecture as *gefrorene* music; *gefrorene* translates more clearly as "frozen" than *erstarrte*, whose meaning is more that of "fixed" or "petrified."

Claudia Schiffer
German fashion model, 1970–

1 [*On her retirement from the catwalk:*] I ate a whole chocolate bar.
Quoted in *Guardian* (London), 27 Sept. 1996

Johann Christoph Friedrich von Schiller
German poet and playwright, 1759–1805

1 *Freude, schöner Götterfunken,*
Tochter aus Elysium,
Wir betreten feuertrunken,
Himmlische, dein Heiligtum.
Deine Zauber binden wieder,
Was die Mode streng geteilt.
Alle Menschen werden Brüder,
Wo dein sanfter Flügel weilt.
Joy, beautiful radiance of the gods, daughter of Elysium, we set foot in your heavenly shrine dazzled by your brilliance. Your charms re-unite what common use has harshly divided. All men become brothers under your tender wings.
"An die Freude" (1785)

2 *Die Weltgeschichte ist das Weltgericht.*
The world's history is the world's judgment.
"Resignation" (1786)

3 Whatever is not forbidden is permitted.
Wallenstein's Camp sc. 6 (1798)

4 *Mit der Dummheit kämpfen Götter selbst vergebens.*
With stupidity the gods themselves struggle in vain.
The Maid of Orleans act 3, sc. 6 (1801)

Walter M. "Wally" Schirra
U.S. astronaut, 1923–2007

1 It's interesting because we couldn't see the borders of the different countries [from space]. I'm always amazed at how geopoliticians made those borders—rulers meaning dictators, kings, or politicians—and apparently we the humans have gone along with it.
Quoted in *Newark Star-Ledger*, 4 May 2007

Friedrich von Schlegel
German philosopher and writer, 1772–1829

1 A historian is a prophet in reverse.
Athenäum vol. 1 "Fragmente" (1798)

Friedrich Schleiermacher
German theologian and philosopher, 1768–1834

1 I lie on the bosom of the infinite world. At the moment I am its soul, for I feel all its powers and its infinite life as my own.
On Religion: Speeches to Its Cultured Despisers (1799)

Arthur M. Schlesinger, Jr.
U.S. historian, 1917–2007

1 [*Of John F. Kennedy:*] He read partly for information, partly for comparison, partly for insight, partly for the sheer joy of felicitous statement. He delighted particularly in quotations which distilled the essence of an argument.
A Thousand Days ch. 4 (1965)

2 The constitutional Presidency—as events so apparently disparate as the Indochina War and the Watergate affair showed—has become the imperial Presidency.
The Imperial Presidency foreword (1973)

Moritz Schlick
German philosopher, 1882–1936

1 The Meaning of a Proposition is the Method of its Verification.
"Form and Content" (1932)

Don Schlitz
U.S. songwriter, 1952–

1 You got to know when to hold 'em,
Know when to fold 'em,
Know when to walk away,
And when to run.
"The Gambler" (song) (1977)
See Hay 1

Mary Schmich
U.S. journalist, 1953–

1 Ladies and gentlemen of the class of '97: Wear sunscreen. If I could offer you only one tip for

the future, sunscreen would be it. The long-term benefits of sunscreen have been proved by scientists, whereas the rest of my advice has no basis more reliable than my own meandering experience. I will dispense this advice now. . . . But trust me on the sunscreen.

Chicago Tribune, 1 June 1997. This column became widely misattributed as a commencement address by Kurt Vonnegut to the MIT Class of 1997.

2 Do one thing every day that scares you.
Chicago Tribune, 1 June 1997

Eric Schmidt
U.S. business executive, 1955–

1 The Internet is the first thing that humanity has built that humanity doesn't understand, the largest experiment in anarchy that we have ever had.

Speech at Netscape Communications Developers' conference, New York, N.Y., 18 Oct. 1996

Carl Schmitt
German legal scholar and political philosopher, 1888–1985

1 Sovereign is he who decides on the exception.
Political Theology ch. 1 (1922) (translation by George Schwab)

Artur Schnabel
Austrian pianist and composer, 1882–1951

1 The notes I handle no better than many pianists. But the pauses between the notes—ah, that is where the art resides.
Quoted in *Chicago Daily News,* 11 June 1958

2 The sonatas of Mozart are unique; they are too easy for children, and too difficult for artists.
Quoted in Nat Shapiro, *An Encyclopedia of Quotations About Music* (1978)

Max Schneckenburger
German poet, 1819–1849

1 *Lieb Vaterland, magst ruhig sein,*
Fest steht und treu die Wacht am Rhein.
Dear Fatherland, no danger thine:
Firm stands thy watch along the Rhine.
"Die Wacht am Rhein" (The Watch on the Rhine) (1840)

Lorraine Schneider
U.S. artist, 1925–1972

1 War is not healthy for children and other living things.
Poster (1965)

Arnold Schoenberg
Austrian-born U.S. composer, 1874–1951

1 I have made a discovery [twelve-tone composition], which will ensure the supremacy of German music for the next hundred years.
Attributed in Josef Rufer, *Das Werk Arnold Schönbergs* (1959). This quotation, based on Rufer's long-after-the-fact recollection of a 1921 conversation, is suspect; its extreme nationalism would have been uncharacteristic of Schoenberg.

Hans Scholl
German resistance activist, 1918–1943

1 [*"Last words" before being executed for treason, Munich, 22 Feb. 1943:*] *Es lebe die Freiheit!*
Long live freedom!
Quoted in Joachim Remak, *The Nazi Years* (1969)

Arthur Schopenhauer
German philosopher, 1788–1860

1 Every man takes the limits of his own field of vision for the limits of the world.
Studies in Pessimism "Psychological Observations" (1851) (translation by T. Bailey Saunders)

Olive Schreiner
South African writer and feminist, 1855–1920

1 Men are like the earth and we are the moon; we turn always one side to them, and they think there is no other, because they don't see it but there is.
The Story of an African Farm pt. 2, ch. 4 (1883)

2 A little weeping, a little wheedling, a little self-degradation, a little careful use of our advantages, and then some man will say Come, be my wife! With good looks and youth marriage is easy to attain. There are men enough; but a woman who has sold herself, even for a ring and a new name, need hold her skirt aside for no creature in the street. They both earn their bread in one way. Marriage for love is the beautifullest external symbol of

the union of souls; marriage without it is the uncleanliest traffic that defiles the world.
The Story of an African Farm pt. 2, ch. 4 (1883)

3 There was never a great man who had not a great mother.
The Story of an African Farm pt. 2, ch. 4 (1883)
See Proverbs 129

4 Of all cursed places under the sun, where the hungriest soul can hardly pick up a few grains of knowledge, a girl's boarding-school is the worst. They are called finishing schools, and the name tells accurately what they are. They finish everything but imbecility and weakness, and that they cultivate. They are nicely adapted machines for experimenting on the question, Into how little space a human being can be crushed? I have seen some souls so compressed that they would have fitted into a small thimble, and found room to move there—wide room.
The Story of an African Farm pt. 2, ch. 4 (1883)

5 We were equals once when we lay new-born babes on our nurse's knees. We will be equal again when they tie up our jaws for the last sleep.
The Story of an African Farm pt. 2, ch. 4 (1883)

6 I have no conscience, none, but I would not like to bring a soul into this world. When it sinned and when it suffered something like a dead hand would fall on me, You did it, you, for your own pleasure you created this thing! See your work! If it lived to be eighty it would always hang like a millstone round my neck, have the right to demand good from me, and curse me for its sorrow. A parent is only like to God: if his work turns out bad so much the worse for him; he dare not wash his hands of it. Time and years can never bring the day when you can say to your child, Soul, what have I to do with you?
The Story of an African Farm pt. 2, ch. 6 (1883)

Erwin Schrödinger
Austrian physicist, 1887–1961

1 [*Describing the "Schrödinger's cat" thought experiment:*] If one has left this entire system to itself for an hour, one would say that the cat still lives if meanwhile no atom has decayed. The psi-function of the entire system would

express this by having in it the living and dead cat (pardon the expression) mixed or smeared out in equal parts.
"The Present Situation in Quantum Mechanics" (1935) (translation by John D. Trimmer)

Patricia Schroeder
U.S. politician, 1940–

1 Ronald Reagan . . . is attempting a great breakthrough in political technology—he has been perfecting the Teflon-coated Presidency. He sees to it that nothing sticks to him.
Speech in House of Representatives, 2 Aug. 1983

2 [*Responding to the question of how she could be both a member of Congress and a mother:*] I have a brain and a uterus, and I use both.
Quoted in *Current Biography 1978* (1978)

Budd Schulberg
U.S. writer, 1914–2009

1 What Makes Sammy Run?
Title of book (1941)

Robert H. Schuller
U.S. clergyman and author, 1926–2015

1 Tough Times Never Last, But Tough People Do.
Title of book (1983). In this book Schuller described his origination of the expression during a 1982 lecture.

Charles M. Schulz
U.S. cartoonist, 1922–2000

1 Good grief, Charlie Brown!
Peanuts (comic strip), 12 Nov. 1955

2 Happiness is a warm puppy.
Peanuts (comic strip), 25 Apr. 1960

3 I love mankind . . . it's *people* I can't stand!!
Peanuts (comic strip), 12 Nov. 1959. Ellipsis in the original.

4 Big sisters are the crab grass in the lawn of life.
Peanuts (comic strip), 17 June 1961

5 No problem is so big or so complicated that it can't be run away from.
Peanuts (comic strip), 27 Feb. 1963

6 There's no heavier burden than a great potential!
You're a Brave Man, Charlie Brown (1963)

7 [*Imprecation of the dog Snoopy, imagining himself to be a World War I flying ace, to Baron von Richthoven:*] Curse you, Red Baron!
Peanuts (comic strip), 6 Feb. 1966

E. F. Schumacher

German-born English economist, 1911–1977

1 When I first began to travel the world, visiting rich and poor countries alike, I was tempted to formulate the first law of economics as follows: "The amount of real leisure a society enjoys tends to be in inverse proportion to the amount of labor-saving machinery it employs."
Small Is Beautiful: Economics As If People Mattered pt. 2, ch. 5 (1973)

2 I have no doubt that it is possible to give a new direction to technological development, a direction that shall lead it back to the real needs of man, and that also means: *to the actual size of man*. Man is small, and, therefore, small is beautiful. To go for giantism is to go for self-destruction.
Small Is Beautiful: Economics As If People Mattered pt. 2, ch. 5 (1973)

3 It is of little use trying to suppress terrorism if the production of deadly devices continues to be deemed a legitimate employment of man's creative powers.
Small Is Beautiful: Economics As If People Mattered epilogue (1973)

Robert Schuman

Luxembourgian-born French prime minister, 1886–1963

1 World peace cannot be safeguarded without the making of creative efforts proportionate to the dangers which threaten it.
Declaration, 9 May 1950. This declaration on behalf of the French government, which laid the foundation for the European Union, was drafted by Jean Monnet.

Robert Schumann

German composer, 1810–1856

1 [*Of Frédéric Chopin:*] Hats off, gentlemen—a genius!
Allgemeine Musikalische Zeitung, Dec. 1831

Joseph A. Schumpeter

Austro-Hungarian–born U.S. economist, 1883–1950

1 The spirit of a people, its cultural level, its social structure, the deeds its policy may prepare—all this and more is written in its fiscal history, stripped of all phrases. He who knows how to listen to its message here discerns the thunder of world history more clearly than anywhere else.
"The Crisis of the Tax State" (1918)

2 Marxism *is* a religion. To the believer it presents, first, a system of ultimate ends that embody the meaning of life and are absolute standards by which to judge events and actions; and, secondly, a guide to those ends which implies a plan of salvation and the indication of the evil from which mankind, or a chosen section of mankind, is to be saved.
Capitalism, Socialism, and Democracy ch. 1 (1942)

3 The opening up of new markets, foreign or domestic, and the organizational development from the craft shop and factory to such concerns as U.S. Steel illustrate the same process of industrial mutation . . . that incessantly revolutionizes the economic structure *from within,* incessantly destroying the old one, incessantly creating a new one. This process of Creative Destruction is the essential fact about capitalism.
Capitalism, Socialism, and Democracy ch. 7 (1942)

Carl Schurz

German-born U.S. politician and general, 1829–1906

1 The Senator from Wisconsin cannot frighten me by exclaiming, "My country, right or wrong." In one sense I say so too. My country; and my country is the great American Republic. My country, right or wrong; if right, to be kept right; and if wrong, to be set right.
Remarks in Senate, 29 Feb. 1872
See Chesterton 3; Decatur 1; Twain 114

Delmore Schwartz

U.S. poet, 1913–1966

1 May memory restore again and again
The smallest color of the smallest day:

Time is the school in which we learn,
Time is the fire in which we burn.
"For Rhoda" l. 40 (1938)

Arnold Schwarzenegger
Austrian-born U.S. actor, bodybuilder, and
politician, 1947–

1 I think that gay marriage is something that
should be between a man and a woman.
Radio interview, 27 Aug. 2003

Albert Schweitzer
French missionary and theologian, 1875–1965

1 Late on the third day, at the very moment when,
at sunset, we were making our way through a
herd of hippopotamuses, there flashed upon
my mind, unforeseen and unsought, the
phrase, "Reverence for Life."
Out of My Life and Thought ch. 13 (1949)

2 Happiness is nothing more than good health
and a bad memory.
Attributed in L.A. Times, 3 May 1959

C. P. Scott
English newspaper editor, 1846–1932

1 Comment is free, but facts are sacred.
Manchester Guardian, 5 May 1921

John Scott, Earl of Eldon
English jurist, 1751–1838

1 Christianity is part of the law of England.
In re Bedford Charity (1819)

Robert Falcon Scott
Scottish explorer, 1868–1912

1 [Of the South Pole:] Great God! this is an awful
place.
Diary, 17 Jan. 1912

2 [Final entry before dying of starvation and
exposure:] For God's sake look after our people.
Diary, 29 Mar. 1912

3 Had we lived, I should have had a tale to tell of
the hardihood, endurance, and courage of my
companions which would have stirred the heart
of every Englishman. These rough notes and
our dead bodies must tell the tale.
"Message to the Public," Times (London), 11 Feb. 1913

Walter Scott
Scottish novelist and poet, 1771–1832

1 In peace, Love tunes the shepherd's reed;
In war, he mounts the warrior's steed;
In halls, in gay attire is seen;
In hamlets, dances on the green.
Love rules the court, the camp, the grove,
And men below, and saints above;
For love is heaven, and heaven is love.
The Lay of the Last Minstrel canto 3, st. 2 (1805)

2 Breathes there the man, with soul so dead,
Who never to himself hath said,
This is my own, my native land!
Whose heart hath ne'er within him burned,
As home his footsteps he hath turned
From wandering on a foreign strand!
The Lay of the Last Minstrel canto 6, st. 1 (1805)

3 For him no Minstrel raptures swell;
High though his titles, proud his name,
Boundless his wealth as wish can claim;
Despite those titles, power, and pelf,
The wretch, concentred all in self,
Living, shall forfeit fair renown,
And, doubly dying, shall go down
To the vile dust, from whence he sprung,
Unwept, unhonour'd, and unsung.
The Lay of the Last Minstrel canto 6, st. 1 (1805)

4   And dar'st thou, then,
To beard the lion in his den,
The Douglas in his hall?
Marmion canto 6, introduction, st. 14 (1808)

5 O what a tangled web we weave,
When first we practise to deceive!
Marmion canto 6, st. 17 (1808)

6 O Woman! in our hours of ease,
Uncertain, coy, and hard to please,
And variable as the shade
By the light quivering aspen made;
When pain and anguish wring the brow,
A ministering angel thou!
Marmion canto 6, st. 30 (1808)
See Shakespeare 228

7 Hail to the Chief who in triumph advances!
The Lady of the Lake canto 2, st. 19 (1810)

8 Your Lordship will probably recollect where
the Oriental tale occurs, of a Sultan who
consulted Solomon on the proper inscription

for a signet-ring, requiring that the maxim which it conveyed should be at once proper for moderating the presumption of prosperity and tempering the pressure of adversity. The apophthegm supplied by the Jewish sage was, I think, admirably adapted for both purposes, being comprehended in the words "And this also shall pass away."

Letter to Lord Byron, 6 Nov. 1813
See Edward FitzGerald 1; Lincoln 20

9 "That sounds like nonsense, my dear."
"May be so, my dear: but it may be very good law for all that."

Guy Mannering ch. 9 (1815)

10 A lawyer without history or literature is a mechanic, a mere working mason; if he possesses some knowledge of these, he may venture to call himself an architect.

Guy Mannering ch. 37 (1815)

11 The criminals came in so fast that they were fain to execute them first and afterwards try them at leisure.

Letter to Lady Compton, 16 Apr. 1816
See Carroll 24; Molière 5

12 Sea of upturned faces.

Rob Roy ch. 20 (1817)

13 Tell that to the marines—the sailors won't believe it.

Redgauntlet vol. 2, ch. 7 (1824). The *Oxford Dictionary of English Proverbs* traces the expression "Tell it to the marines" back to 1805.

14 Rouse the lion from his lair.

The Talisman ch. 6 (1825)

15 [*Of his need to raise money to pay huge debts by writing:*] My own right hand shall do it.

Journal, 22 Jan. 1826

Winfield Scott

U.S. general, 1786–1866

1 Say to the seceded States, "Wayward sisters, depart in peace."

Letter to William H. Seward, 3 Mar. 1861

Gil Scott-Heron

U.S. writer, 1949–2011

1 The Revolution Will Not Be Televised.

Title of song (1974)

Bobby Seale

U.S. activist, 1936–

1 Seize the Time.

Title of book (1970)
See Horace 17

John R. Searle

U.S. philosopher, 1932–

1 "Could a machine think?" My own view is that *only* a machine could think, and indeed only very special kinds of machines, namely brains and machines that had the same causal powers as brains. . . . Whatever else intentionality is, it is a biological phenomenon, and it is as likely to be as causally dependent on the specific biochemistry of its origins as lactation, photosynthesis, or any other biological phenomena.

"Minds, Brains, and Programs" (1980)

2 The reason that no computer program can ever be a mind is simply that a computer program is only syntactical, and minds are more than syntactical. Minds are semantical, in the sense that they have more than a formal structure, they have a content.

Minds, Brains, and Science ch. 2 (1984)

Alice Sebold

U.S. author, 1963–

1 My name was Salmon, like the fish; first name, Susie. I was fourteen when I was murdered on December 6, 1973.

The Lovely Bones ch. 1 (2002)

2 These were the lovely bones that had grown around my absence: the connections— sometimes tenuous, sometimes made at great cost, but often magnificent—that happened after I was gone. And I began to see things in a way that let me hold the world without me in it. The events that my death wrought were merely the bones of a body that would become whole at some unpredictable time in the future. The price of what I came to see as this miraculous body had been my life.

The Lovely Bones ch. 23 (2002)

John Sedgwick

U.S. general, 1813–1864

1 [*Words shortly before being fatally wounded by a bullet during the Civil War, Spotsylvania, Va., 8 May 1864:*] They could not hit an elephant at that distance.

Quoted in Theodore Lyman, Letter to Elizabeth Russell Lyman, 20 May 1864. These "last words" are popularly said to have been cut off in the middle of "distance" as the bullet hit.

Alan Seeger

U.S. poet, 1888–1916

1 I have a rendezvous with Death
At some disputed barricade,
When Spring comes back with rustling shade
And apple-blossoms fill the air.
"I Have a Rendezvous with Death" l. 1 (1916)

2 But I've a rendezvous with Death
At midnight in some flaming town,
When Spring trips north again this year,
And I to my pledged word am true,
I shall not fail that rendezvous.
"I Have a Rendezvous with Death" l. 20 (1916)

Pete Seeger

U.S. folksinger and songwriter, 1919–2014

1 If I had a hammer,
I'd hammer in the morning,
I'd hammer in the evening
All over this land.
"If I Had a Hammer (The Hammer Song)" (song) (1949). Cowritten with Lee Hays.

2 I'd hammer out danger
I'd hammer out a warning,
I'd hammer out love between
All of my brothers
All over this land.
"If I Had a Hammer (The Hammer Song)" (song) (1949). Cowritten with Lee Hays. The original lyrics above were changed to "my brothers and my sisters" by Libby Frank in 1952.

3 To everything, turn, turn, turn,
There is a season, turn, turn, turn,
And a time for every purpose under heaven . . .
A time of love, a time of hate
A time for peace, I swear, it's not too late.
"Turn! Turn! Turn! (To Everything There Is a Season)" (song) (1954)
See Bible 143

4 Where have all the flowers gone?
Long time passing
Where have all the flowers gone?
Long time ago
Where have all the flowers gone?
Young girls picked them every one
When will they ever learn?
"Where Have All the Flowers Gone?" (song) (1961)
See Folk and Anonymous Songs 45

5 O deep in my heart, I do believe
We shall overcome some day.
"We Shall Overcome" (song) (1963). This civil rights anthem traces to Charles A. Tindley's gospel song "I'll Overcome Some Day," although Tindley may have had an older spiritual as a source. In 1946 Lucille Simmons introduced a labor version using "we will overcome." Pete Seeger then altered the words to "we shall."
See Tindley 1

6 We're waist deep in the big muddy
And the big fool says to push on.
"Waist Deep in the Big Muddy" (song) (1967)

John Seeley

English historian, 1834–1895

1 We [the English] seem, as it were, to have conquered and peopled half the world in a fit of absence of mind.
The Expansion of England lecture 1 (1883)

Giorgos Seferis (Georgios Seferiades)

Greek poet and diplomat, 1900–1971

1 When on his way to Thebes Oedipus encountered the Sphinx, his answer to its riddle was: "Man." That simple word destroyed the monster. We have many monsters to destroy. Let us think of the answer of Oedipus.
Speech at Nobel Prize banquet, Stockholm, Sweden, 10 Dec. 1963

Erich Segal

U.S. novelist, 1937–2010

1 What can you say about a twenty-five-year-old girl who died? That she was beautiful. And brilliant. That she loved Mozart and Bach. And the Beatles. And me. Once, when she specifically lumped me with those musical types, I asked her what the order was, and she replied, smiling, "Alphabetical."
Love Story ch. 1 (1970)

2 Love means not ever having to say you're sorry.

Love Story ch. 13 (1970). In the motion picture this line was "Love means never having to say you're sorry" and become famous in this form. Segal actually wrote the screenplay before he wrote the novel.

E. C. Segar
U.S. cartoonist, 1894–1938

1 [*Popeye speaking*:] Blow me down!

Thimble Theatre (comic strip), 21 Jan. 1929

2 [*Popeye speaking*:] I yam what I yam and that's what I yam.

Thimble Theatre (comic strip), 6 Nov. 1929. Segar introduced the classic formulation, "I yam what I yam an' tha's all I yam" in the strip for 17 Apr. 1931.
See Prévert 1

3 [*Wimpy speaking*:] I would gladly pay you Tuesday for a hamburger to-day.

Thimble Theatre (comic strip), 20 Mar. 1932. An earlier version ("Cook me up a hamburger. I'll pay you Thursday.") appeared in the strip on 21 June 1931.

T. Lawrence Seibert
U.S. songwriter, 1877–1917

1 Come all you rounders if you want to hear
A story 'bout a brave engineer.
Casey Jones was the rounder's name;
On a six eight-wheeler, boys, he won his fame.

"Casey Jones" (song) (1909). Siebert's version was adapted from an original one sung by Wallace Saunders.

Jerry Seinfeld
U.S. comedian, 1954–

1 Everyone lies about sex. People lie during sex. If it weren't for lies, there'd be no sex.

Quoted in *N.Y. Times*, 7 Aug. 1998

John Selden
English jurist and antiquarian, 1584–1654

1 Ignorance of the law excuses no man; not that all men know the law, but because 'tis an excuse every man will plead, and no man can tell how to confute him.

Table-Talk "Law" (1689)
See Proverbs 153

2 Take a straw and throw it up into the air, you shall see by that which way the wind is.

Table-Talk "Libels" (1689)

H. Gordon Selfridge
U.S.-born English department store owner, 1858–1947

1 Complete satisfaction or money cheerfully refunded.

Quoted in A. H. Williams, *No Name on the Door* (1957)

W. C. Sellar
British writer, 1898–1951

1 The Roman Conquest was, however, a *Good Thing*, since the Britons were only natives at the time.

1066 and All That ch. 1 (1930). Coauthored with R. J. Yeatman.
See Martha Stewart 1

2 Gladstone . . . spent his declining years trying to guess the answer to the Irish Question; unfortunately whenever he was getting warm, the Irish secretly changed the Question.

1066 and All That ch. 57 (1930). Coauthored with R. J. Yeatman.

3 [*On World War I:*] This pacific and inevitable struggle was undertaken in the reign of His Good and memorable Majesty King George V and it was the cause of nowadays and the end of History.

1066 and All That ch. 61 (1930). Coauthored with R. J. Yeatman.
See Fukuyama 1; Sellar 4

4 AMERICA was thus clearly top nation, and History came to a .

1066 and All That ch. 62 (1930). Coauthored with R. J. Yeatman.
See Fukuyama 1; Sellar 3

David O. Selznick
U.S. motion picture executive, 1902–1965

1 I don't get ulcers. I give them!

Quoted in *The Democrat and Leader* (Davenport, Iowa), 31 Mar. 1947. Selznick was not named in the 1947 newspaper column, but the columnist later identified the person quoted as Selznick.

Amartya Sen
Indian economist, 1933–

1 No famine has ever taken place in the history of the world in a functioning democracy.

Development as Freedom ch. 1 (1999)

Maurice Sendak

U.S. children's book writer, 1928–2012

1 Sipping once
sipping twice
sipping chicken soup
with rice.
Chicken Soup with Rice: A Book of Months (1962)

2 Where the Wild Things Are.
Title of book (1963)

3 Let the wild rumpus start!
Where the Wild Things Are (1963)

4 Oh please don't go—we'll eat you up—we love
you so!
Where the Wild Things Are (1963)

5 Max stepped into his private boat and waved
goodbye and sailed back over a year and in and
out of weeks and through a day and into the
night of his very own room where he found his
supper waiting for him—and it was still warm.
Where the Wild Things Are (1963)

Seneca (the Younger)

Roman philosopher and poet, ca. 4 B.C.–
A.D. 65

1 *Tanta stultitia mortalium est!*
What fools these mortals be.
Epistulae ad Lucilium Epistle 1, sec. 3
See Shakespeare 55

Léopold Sédar Senghor

Senegalese poet, 1906–2001

1 I chose my black people struggling, my country
people, all country people, in the world.
Chants d'Ombre "Que M'Accompagnent Kára et
Balafong, 3" (1945)

2 Only rhythm brings about a poetic short-circuit
and transforms the copper into gold, the words
into life.
Éthiopiques postface (1956)

Rod Serling

U.S. screenwriter and television producer,
1924–1975

1 You're traveling through another dimension, a
dimension not only of sight and sound but of
mind; a journey into a wondrous land whose
boundaries are that of imagination. That's

the signpost up ahead—your next stop, the
Twilight Zone.
The Twilight Zone (television series), opening
narration (1959)

2 The tools of conquest do not necessarily come
with bombs and explosions and fallout. There
are weapons that are simply thoughts, attitudes,
prejudices—to be found only in the minds
of men. For the record, prejudices can kill
and suspicion can destroy, and a thoughtless,
frightened search for a scapegoat has a fallout
all its own—for the children, and the children
yet unborn. And the pity of it is that these
things cannot be confined to the Twilight Zone.
The Twilight Zone (television show), 4 Mar. 1960

3 You unlock this door with the key of
imagination. Beyond it is another dimension.
A dimension of sound. A dimension of sight.
A dimension of mind. You're moving into a
land of both style and substance, of things and
ideas. You've just crossed over into the Twilight
Zone.
The Twilight Zone (television series), opening
narration (1961)

4 There is a fifth dimension beyond that which
is known to man. It is a dimension as vast
as space and timeless as infinity. It is the
middle ground between light and shadow,
between science and superstition, and it lies
between the pit of man's fears and the summit
of his knowledge. This is the dimension of
imagination. It is an area which we call the
Twilight Zone.
The Twilight Zone (television series), opening
narration (1963)

Robert W. Service

Canadian poet, 1874–1958

1 The Northern Lights have seen queer sights,
But the queerest they ever did see
Was the night on the marge of Lake Lebarge
I cremated Sam McGee.
"The Cremation of Sam McGee" l. 5 (1907)

2 This is the law of the Yukon, that only the
Strong shall thrive;
That surely the Weak shall perish, and only the
Fit survive.
"The Law of the Yukon" l. 71 (1907)

3 A bunch of the boys were whooping it up in the
   Malamute saloon;
   The kid that handles the music-box was hitting
   a rag-time tune;
   Back of the bar, in a solo game, sat Dangerous
   Dan McGrew,
   And watching his luck was his light-o'-love, the
   lady that's known as Lou.
   "The Shooting of Dan McGrew" l. 1 (1907)

4 Ah, the clock is always slow;
   It is later than you think.
   "It Is Later Than You Think" l. 56 (1921)

Vikram Seth
Indian novelist and poet, 1952–

1 If we cannot eschew hatred, at least let us
   eschew group hatred.
   Two Lives pt. 5, ch. 23 (2005)

Dr. Seuss (Theodor Seuss Geisel)
U.S. children's book author, 1904–1991

1 I meant what I said
   And I said what I meant . . .
   An elephant's faithful
   One hundred per cent!
   Horton Hatches the Egg (1940). Ellipsis in the original.

2 I'll sail to Ka-Troo
   And bring back an it-kutch,

A preep, and a proo,
A nerkle, a NERD,
And a seersucker, too!
If I Ran the Zoo (1950). Earliest known appearance
in print of the word *nerd*. However, *Newsweek*, 8 Oct.
1951, noted that "In Detroit, someone who once
would be called a drip or a square is now, regrettably,
a nerd," raising the possibility that *nerd* existed before
If I Ran the Zoo.

3 The sun did not shine.
   It was too wet to play.
   So we sat in the house
   All that cold, cold, wet day.
   The Cat in the Hat (1957)

4 Oh, I do not like it!
   Not one little bit!
   The Cat in the Hat (1957)

5 You will see something new.
   Two things. And I call them
   Thing One and Thing Two.
   The Cat in the Hat (1957)

6 What would YOU do
   If your mother asked YOU?
   The Cat in the Hat (1957)

7 Every *Who*
   Down in *Who*-ville
   Liked Christmas a lot . . .
   But the Grinch,
   Who lived just north of *Who*-ville,
   Did *NOT!*
   How the Grinch Stole Christmas (1957). Ellipsis in the
   original.

8 The most likely reason of all
   May have been that his heart was two sizes too
   small.
   How the Grinch Stole Christmas (1957)

9 "Maybe Christmas," he thought,
   "*doesn't* come from a store.
   Maybe Christmas . . . perhaps . . . means
   a little bit more!"
   How the Grinch Stole Christmas (1957). Ellipses in the
   original.

10 I am Sam
   Sam I am.
   Green Eggs and Ham (1960)

11 I do not like
   green eggs
   and ham!

I do not like them,
Sam-I-am.
Green Eggs and Ham (1960)

12 I am the Lorax. I speak for the trees.
The Lorax (1971)

13 UNLESS someone like you
cares a whole awful lot,
nothing is going to get better.
It's not.
The Lorax (1971)

14 Plant a new Truffula. Treat it with care.
Give it clean water. And feed it fresh air.
Grow a forest. Protect it from axes that hack.
Then the Lorax
and all of his friends
may come back.
The Lorax (1971)

15 You're in pretty good shape
for the shape you are in!
You're Only Old Once! (1986)

16 Adults are obsolete children, and the hell with
them.
Quoted in Thomas Fensch, *Of Sneetches and Whos
and the Good Dr. Seuss* (1997)

17 Don't cry because it's over, smile because it
happened.
Attributed in *Rockland* (N.Y.) *Journal-News*, 6 June
1998. A very similar quotation was included in the
1899 poem "*Leuchtende Tage*" by German writer
Ludwig Jacobowski.

William H. Seward
U.S. politician, 1801–1872

1 There is a higher law than the Constitution.
Speech in Senate during debate on Compromise of
1850, 11 Mar. 1850

2 [*On the slavery controversy:*] It is an irrepressible
conflict between opposing and enduring forces.
Speech, Rochester, N.Y., 25 Oct. 1858

Anna Sewell
English novelist, 1820–1878

1 Though I am an old horse, and have seen and
heard a great deal, I never yet could make out
why men are so fond of this sport; they often
hurt themselves, often spoil good horses, and
tear up the fields, and all for a hare or a fox,

or a stag, that they could get more easily some
other way; but we are only horses, and don't
know.
Black Beauty ch. 2 (1877)

2 We have no right to distress any of God's
creatures without a very good reason; we call
them dumb animals, and so they are, for they
cannot tell us how they feel, but they do not
suffer less because they have no words.
Black Beauty ch. 46 (1877)

Anne Sexton
U.S. poet, 1928–1974

1 You, Doctor Martin, walk
from breakfast to madness.
"You, Doctor Martin" l. 1 (1960)

2 In a dream you are never eighty.
"Old" l. 18 (1962)

3 But suicides have a special language.
Like carpenters they want to know *which tools*.
They never ask *why build*.
"Wanting to Die" l. 7 (1966)

4 She has always been there, my darling.
She is, in fact, exquisite.
Fireworks in the dull middle of February
and as real as a cast-iron pot.
"For My Lover, Returning to His Wife" l. 5 (1969)

5 Set forth three children under the moon,
three cherubs drawn by Michelangelo,
done this with her legs spread out
in the terrible months in the chapel.
"For My Lover, Returning to His Wife" l. 19 (1969)

6 As for me, I am a watercolor.
I wash off.
"For My Lover, Returning to His Wife" l. 47 (1969)

7 It doesn't matter who my father was; it matters
who I *remember* he was.
Journal, 1 Jan. 1972

Scott Sforza
U.S. media producer, ca. 1963–

1 Mission Accomplished.
Banner on aircraft carrier U.S.S. *Abraham Lincoln*,
1 May 2003. This banner, used as a backdrop for
a speech by President George W. Bush, became
controversial when the lack of closure of the Iraq War
was apparent.

Ernest H. Shackleton

Irish explorer, 1874–1922

1 Difficulties are just things to overcome after all.
Diary, 11 Dec. 1908

2 [*Remark to Frank Worsley, 1916:*] Superhuman
effort isn't worth a damn unless it achieves
results.
Quoted in Frank Worsley, *Endurance* (1931)

3 Men wanted for hazardous journey to South
Pole. Small wages, bitter cold, long months
of complete darkness, constant danger. Safe
return doubtful. Honor and recognition in case
of success.
Attributed in Carl Hopkins Elmore, *Quit You Like
Men* (1944). This advertisement was allegedly printed
in London newspapers in 1900, but a search in the
Times Digital Archive fails to retrieve it, and no trace
of it has been found before the 1944 Elmore book.

Peter Shaffer

English playwright, 1926–2016

1 Mediocrities everywhere—now and to come—I
absolve you all.
Amadeus act 2, sc. 19 (1980)

William Shakespeare

English playwright and poet, 1564–1616

The text and line numbers follow the Arden
Shakespeare Complete Works, *rev. ed., ed. Richard
Proudfoot, Ann Thompson, and David Scott Kastan
(2001).*

King Richard III

1 Now is the winter of our discontent
Made glorious summer by this sun of York.
King Richard III act 1, sc. 1, l. 1 (1591)

2 This weak piping time of peace.
King Richard III act 1, sc. 1, l. 24 (1591)

3 Talk'st thou to me of ifs! Thou art a traitor:
Off with his head!
King Richard III act 3, sc. 4, l. 75 (1591)

4 I am not in the giving vein today.
King Richard III act 4, sc. 2, l. 116 (1591)

5 A horse! A horse! My kingdom for a horse!
King Richard III act 5, sc. 4, l. 7 (1591)

King Henry VI, Part 2

6 The first thing we do, let's kill all the lawyers.
King Henry VI, Part 2 act 4, sc. 2, l. 72 (1592). This
quotation, although beloved by lawyer-haters, is
in context complimentary to lawyers, spoken by a
would-be tyrant.

King Henry VI, Part 3

7 O tiger's heart wrapp'd in a woman's hide!
King Henry VI, Part 3 act 1, sc. 4, l. 137 (1592)

The Taming of the Shrew

8 Kiss me, Kate, we will be married o' Sunday.
The Taming of the Shrew act 2, sc. 1, l. 318 (1592)

9 This is a way to kill a wife with kindness.
The Taming of the Shrew act 4, sc. 1, l. 196 (1592)

10 A woman mov'd is like a fountain troubled,
Muddy, ill-seeming, thick, bereft of beauty.
The Taming of the Shrew act 5, sc. 2, l. 143 (1592)

King Richard II

11 The purest treasure mortal times afford
Is spotless reputation—that away,
Men are but gilded loam, or painted clay.
King Richard II act 1, sc. 1, l. 177 (1595)

12 We were not born to sue, but to command.
King Richard II act 1, sc. 1, l. 196 (1595)

13 How long a time lies in one little word!
Four lagging winters and four wanton springs
End in a word: such is the breath of kings.
King Richard II act 1, sc. 3, l. 213 (1595)

14 There is no virtue like necessity.
King Richard II act 1, sc. 3, l. 278 (1595)

15 As the last taste of sweets, is sweetest last,
Writ in remembrance more than things long
past.
King Richard II act 2, sc. 1, l. 13 (1595)

16 This royal throne of kings, this scept'red isle,
This earth of majesty, this seat of Mars,
This other Eden, demi-paradise,
This fortress built by Nature for herself
Against infection and the hand of war,
This happy breed of men, this little world,
This precious stone set in the silver sea.
King Richard II act 2, sc. 1, l. 40 (1595)

17 This blessed plot, this earth, this realm, this
England.
King Richard II act 2, sc. 1, l. 50 (1595)

18 Grace me no grace, nor uncle me no uncle.
King Richard II act 2, sc. 3, l. 86 (1595)

19 Not all the water in the rough rude sea
Can wash the balm off from an anointed king.
King Richard II act 3, sc. 2, l. 54 (1595)

20 Let's talk of graves, of worms, and epitaphs,
Make dust our paper, and with rainy eyes
Write sorrow on the bosom of the earth.
Let's choose executors and talk of wills.
King Richard II act 3, sc. 2, l. 145 (1595)

21 For God's sake let us sit upon the ground
And tell sad stories of the death of kings.
King Richard II act 3, sc. 2, l. 155 (1595)

22   Within the hollow crown
That rounds the mortal temples of a king
Keeps Death his court.
King Richard II act 3, sc. 2, l. 160 (1595)

23   How sour sweet music is
When time is broke and no proportion kept!
So is it in the music of men's lives.
King Richard II act 5, sc. 5, l. 42 (1595)

24 I wasted time, and now doth time waste me.
King Richard II act 5, sc. 5, l. 49 (1595)

Love's Labour's Lost

25 When daisies pied and violets blue
And lady-smocks all silver-white
And cuckoo-buds of yellow hue

Do paint the meadows with delight,
The cuckoo then on every tree
Mocks married men; for thus sings he:
"Cuckoo!"
Love's Labour's Lost act 5, sc. 2, l. 885 (1595)

26 When icicles hang by the wall
And Dick the shepherd blows his nail
And Tom bears logs into the hall
And milk comes frozen home in pail,
When blood is nipped and ways be foul,
Then nightly sings the staring owl:
"Tu-whit, Tu-whoo!"
A merry note,
While greasy Joan doth keel the pot.
Love's Labour's Lost act 5, sc. 2, l. 903 (1595)

Romeo and Juliet

27 A pair of star-cross'd lovers.
Romeo and Juliet prologue, l. 6 (1595)

28 O then I see Queen Mab hath been with you.
She is the fairies' midwife, and she comes
In shape no bigger than an agate stone.
Romeo and Juliet act 1, sc. 4, l. 53 (1595)

29 You and I are past our dancing days.
Romeo and Juliet act 1, sc. 5, l. 32 (1595)

30 It seems she hangs upon the cheek of night
As a rich jewel in an Ethiop's ear—
Beauty too rich for use, for earth too dear.
Romeo and Juliet act 1, sc. 5, l. 45 (1595)

31 My only love sprung from my only hate.
Too early seen unknown, and known too late.
Romeo and Juliet act 1, sc. 5, l. 138 (1595)

32 He jests at scars that never felt a wound.
But soft, what light through yonder window
breaks?
It is the east and Juliet is the sun!
Romeo and Juliet act 2, sc. 1, l. 1 (1595)

33 O Romeo, Romeo, wherefore art thou Romeo?
Deny thy father and refuse thy name.
Or if thou wilt not, be but sworn my love
And I'll no longer be a Capulet.
Romeo and Juliet act 2, sc. 1, l. 33 (1595)

34 What's in a name? That which we call a rose
By any other word would smell as sweet.
Romeo and Juliet act 2, sc. 2, l. 43 (1595)

35 O swear not by the moon, th'inconstant moon,
  That monthly changes in her circled orb,
  Lest that thy love prove likewise variable.
  Romeo and Juliet act 2, sc. 2, l. 109 (1595)

36 Do not swear at all.
  Or if thou wilt, swear by thy gracious self,
  Which is the god of my idolatry.
  Romeo and Juliet act 2, sc. 2, l. 111 (1595)

37 It is too rash, too unadvis'd, too sudden.
  Romeo and Juliet act 2, sc. 2, l. 118 (1595)

38   O for a falconer's voice
  To lure this tassel-gentle back again.
  Romeo and Juliet act 2, sc. 2, l. 158 (1595)

39 Good night, good night. Parting is such sweet
    sorrow
  That I shall say good night till it be morrow.
  Romeo and Juliet act 2, sc. 2, l. 184 (1595)

40 I am the very pink of courtesy.
  Romeo and Juliet act 2, sc. 4, l. 56 (1595)

41 No, 'tis not so deep as a well, nor so wide as a
  church door, but 'tis enough, 'twill serve.
  Romeo and Juliet act 3, sc. 1, l. 97 (1595)

42 A plague o'both your houses.
  Romeo and Juliet act 3, sc. 1, l. 107 (1595)

43 O, I am fortune's fool.
  Romeo and Juliet act 3, sc. 1, l. 137 (1595)

44 Gallop apace, you fiery-footed steeds,
  Toward Phoebus' lodging.
  Romeo and Juliet act 3, sc. 2, l. 1 (1595)

45 Give me my Romeo; and when I shall die
  Take him and cut him out in little stars,
  And he will make the face of heaven so fine
  That all the world will be in love with night,
  And pay no worship to the garish sun.
  Romeo and Juliet act 3, sc. 2, l. 21 (1595)

46 Adversity's sweet milk, philosophy.
  Romeo and Juliet act 3, sc. 3, l. 55 (1595)

47 Night's candles are burnt out, and jocund day
  Stands tiptoe on the misty mountain tops.
  Romeo and Juliet act 3, sc. 5, l. 9 (1595)

48 Thank me no thankings nor proud me no
    prouds.
  Romeo and Juliet act 3, sc. 5, l. 152 (1595)

49 Tempt not a desperate man.
  Romeo and Juliet act 5, sc. 3, l. 59 (1595)

50 How oft when men are at the point of death
  Have they been merry!
  Romeo and Juliet act 5, sc. 3, l. 88 (1595)

A Midsummer Night's Dream

51 The course of true love never did run smooth.
  A Midsummer Night's Dream act 1, sc. 1, l. 134 (1595–
  1596)

52 Love looks not with the eyes, but with the mind,
  And therefore is wing'd Cupid painted blind.
  A Midsummer Night's Dream act 1, sc. 1, l. 234 (1595–
  1596)

53 Over hill, over dale,
  Thorough bush, thorough briar,
  Over park, over pale,
  Thorough flood, thorough fire.
  A Midsummer Night's Dream act 2, sc. 1, l. 2 (1595–
  1596)

54 Ill met by moonlight, proud Titania.
  A Midsummer Night's Dream act 2, sc. 1, l. 60 (1595–
  1596)

55 Lord, what fools these mortals be!
  A Midsummer Night's Dream act 3, sc. 2, l. 115 (1595–
  1596)
  See Seneca 1

56 The lunatic, the lover, and the poet
  Are of imagination all compact.
  A Midsummer Night's Dream act 5, sc. 1, l. 7 (1595–
  1596)

57 The poet's eye, in a fine frenzy rolling,
  Doth glance from heaven to earth, from earth
    to heaven;
  And as imagination bodies forth
  The forms of things unknown, the poet's pen
  Turns them to shapes, and gives to airy nothing
  A local habitation and a name.
  A Midsummer Night's Dream act 5, sc. 1, l. 12 (1595–
  1596)

58 The best in this kind are but shadows.
  A Midsummer Night's Dream act 5, sc. 1, l. 209
  (1595–1596)

King Henry IV, Part 1

59 Let me tell the world.
  King Henry IV, Part 1 act 5, sc. 2, l. 65 (1597)

60 The better part of valor is discretion.
  King Henry IV, Part 1 act 5, sc. 4, l. 118 (1597)

King Henry IV, Part 2

61 I am not only witty in myself, but the cause that wit is in other men.

King Henry IV, Part 2 act 1, sc. 2, l. 9 (1597)
See Foote 1

62 He hath eaten me out of house and home.

King Henry IV, Part 2 act 2, sc. 1, l. 74 (1597)

63 Is it not strange that desire should so many years outlive performance?

King Henry IV, Part 2 act 2, sc. 4, l. 260 (1597)

64 Uneasy lies the head that wears a crown.

King Henry IV, Part 2 act 3, sc. 1, l. 31 (1597)

65 We have heard the chimes at midnight.

King Henry IV, Part 2 act 3, sc. 2, l. 214 (1597)

66 Thy wish was father, Harry, to that thought.

King Henry IV, Part 2 act 4, sc. 5, l. 92 (1597)

The Merry Wives of Windsor

67 Why then, the world's mine oyster,
Which I with sword will open.

The Merry Wives of Windsor act 2, sc. 2, l. 2 (1597)

68 As good luck would have it.

The Merry Wives of Windsor act 3, sc. 5, l. 77 (1597)

King John

69 Bell, book, and candle shall not drive me back.

King John act 3, sc. 2, l. 22 (1591–1598). Refers to a Roman Catholic formula of excommunication.
See Malory 2

70 To gild refined gold, to paint the lily,
To throw a perfume on the violet,
To smooth the ice, or add another hue
Unto the rainbow, or with taper-light
To seek the beauteous eye of heaven to garnish,
Is wasteful and ridiculous excess.

King John act 4, sc. 2, l. 11 (1591–1598). Source of the expression "to gild the lily."

The Merchant of Venice

71 I will buy with you, sell with you, talk with you, walk with you, and so following: but I will not eat with you, drink with you, nor pray with you. What news on the Rialto?

The Merchant of Venice act 1, sc. 3, l. 34 (1596–1598)

72 The devil can cite Scripture for his purpose.

The Merchant of Venice act 1, sc. 3, l. 96 (1596–1598)

73 (For suffrance is the badge of all our tribe)
You call me misbeliever, cut-throat dog,
And spet upon my Jewish gaberdine.

The Merchant of Venice act 1, sc. 3, l. 108 (1596–1598)

74 It is a wise father that knows his own child.

The Merchant of Venice act 2, sc. 2, l. 73 (1596–1598)

75 My daughter! O my ducats! O my daughter!

The Merchant of Venice act 2, sc. 8, l. 15 (1596–1598)

76 Hath not a Jew eyes? hath not a Jew hands, organs, dimensions, senses, affections, passions? fed with the same food, hurt with the same weapons, subject to the same diseases, healed by the same means, warmed and cooled by the same winter and summer as a Christian is?— if you prick us do we not bleed? if you tickle us do we not laugh? if you poison us do we not die? and if you wrong us shall we not revenge?

The Merchant of Venice act 3, sc. 1, l. 54 (1596–1598)

77 Tell me where is Fancy bred,
Or in the heart, or in the head?

The Merchant of Venice act 3, sc. 2, l. 63 (1596–1598)

78 I never knew so young a body with so old a head.

The Merchant of Venice act 4, sc. 1, l. 161 (1596–1598)

79 The quality of mercy is not strain'd,
It droppeth as the gentle rain from heaven
Upon the place beneath.

The Merchant of Venice act 4, sc. 1, l. 182 (1596–1598)

80 Wrest once the law to your authority,—
To do a great right, do a little wrong.

The Merchant of Venice act 4, sc. 1, l. 213 (1596–1598)

81 A Daniel come to judgment: yea a Daniel!

The Merchant of Venice act 4, sc. 1, l. 221 (1596–1598)

82 He is well paid that is well satisfied.

The Merchant of Venice act 4, sc. 1, l. 413 (1596–1598)

As You Like It

83 O how full of briers is this working-day world!

As You Like It act 1, sc. 3, l. 11 (1599)

84 Sweet are the uses of adversity,
Which like the toad, ugly and venomous,
Wears yet a precious jewel in his head;
And this our life, exempt from public haunt,

Finds tongues in trees, books in the running
brooks,
Sermons in stones, and good in everything.
As You Like It act 2, sc. 1, l. 12 (1599)

85 Under the greenwood tree,
Who loves to lie with me,
And turn his merry note
Unto the sweet bird's throat,
Come hither, come hither, come hither.
Here shall he see
No enemy,
But winter and rough weather.
As You Like It act 2, sc. 5, l. 1 (1599)

86 And so from hour to hour, we ripe, and ripe,
And then from hour to hour, we rot, and rot,
And thereby hangs a tale.
As You Like It act 2, sc. 7, l. 26 (1599)

87 True is it that we have seen better days.
As You Like It act 2, sc. 7, l. 120 (1599)

88   All the world's a stage,
And all the men and women merely players.
They have their exits and their entrances,
And one man in his time plays many parts,
His acts being seven ages.
As You Like It act 2, sc. 7, l. 139 (1599)

89   At first the infant,
Mewling and puking in the nurse's arms.
Then, the whining school-boy with his satchel
And shining morning face, creeping like snail
Unwillingly to school.
As You Like It act 2, sc. 7, l. 143 (1599)

90   Then, a soldier,
Full of strange oaths, and bearded like the pard,
Jealous in honour, sudden, and quick in
quarrel,
Seeking the bubble reputation
Even in the cannon's mouth.
As You Like It act 2, sc. 7, l. 149 (1599)

91   Second childishness and mere oblivion,
Sans teeth, sans eyes, sans taste, sans
everything.
As You Like It act 2, sc. 7, l. 165 (1599)

92 Blow, blow, thou winter wind,
Thou art not so unkind
As man's ingratitude.
As You Like It act 2, sc. 7, l. 174 (1599)

93 Thank heaven, fasting, for a good man's love.
As You Like It act 3, sc. 5, l. 58 (1599)

94 Men have died from time to time and worms
have eaten them, but not for love.
As You Like It act 4, sc. 1, l. 101 (1599)

95 Men are April when they woo, December
when they wed. Maids are May when they
are maids, but the sky changes when they are
wives.
As You Like It act 4, sc. 1, l. 140 (1599)

96 A poor virgin sir, an ill-favored thing sir, but
mine own.
As You Like It act 5, sc. 4, l. 56 (1599)

Julius Caesar

97 Beware the Ides of March.
Julius Caesar act 1, sc. 2, l. 18 (1599)

98 Why, man, he doth bestride the narrow world
Like a colossus, and we petty men
Walk under his huge legs and peep about
To find ourselves dishonorable graves.
Men at some time are masters of their fates.
The fault, dear Brutus, is not in our stars
But in ourselves, that we are underlings.
Julius Caesar act 1, sc. 2, l. 134 (1599)

99 Let me have men about me that are fat,
Sleek-headed men, and such as sleep
a-nights.
Yond Cassius has a lean and hungry look:
He thinks too much: such men are
dangerous.
Julius Caesar act 1, sc. 2, l. 191 (1599)
See Plutarch 2

100 Let's carve him as a dish fit for the gods,
Not hew him as a carcass fit for hounds.
Julius Caesar act 2, sc. 1, l. 172 (1599)

101 When beggars die there are no comets seen;
The heavens themselves blaze forth the death
of princes.
Julius Caesar act 2, sc. 2, l. 30 (1599)

102 Cowards die many times before their deaths;
The valiant never taste of death but once.
Julius Caesar act 2, sc. 2, l. 32 (1599)

103 But I am constant as the northern star,
Of whose true-fixed and resting quality
There is no fellow in the firmament.
Julius Caesar act 3, sc. 1, l. 60 (1599)

104 *Et tu, Brute?*—Then fall, Caesar.
Julius Caesar act 3, sc. 1, l. 77 (1599)
See Caesar 7

105 The choice and master spirits of this age.
Julius Caesar act 3, sc. 1, l. 163 (1599)

106 O pardon me, thou bleeding piece of earth,
That I am meek and gentle with these
butchers.
Thou art the ruins of the noblest man
That ever lived in the tide of times.
Julius Caesar act 3, sc. 1, l. 254 (1599)

107 Cry havoc and let slip the dogs of war.
Julius Caesar act 3, sc. 1, l. 273 (1599)

108 Not that I loved Caesar less, but that I loved
Rome more.
Julius Caesar act 3, sc. 2, l. 21 (1599)

109 As he was valiant, I honor him: but as he was
ambitious, I slew him.
Julius Caesar act 3, sc. 2, l. 25 (1599)

110 Who is here so base, that would be a
bondman? If any, speak, for him have I
offended. . . . I pause for a reply.
Julius Caesar act 3, sc. 2, l. 29 (1599)

111 Friends, Romans, countrymen, lend me your
ears:
I come to bury Caesar, not to praise him.
The evil that men do lives after them:
The good is oft interred with their bones.
So let it be with Caesar.
Julius Caesar act 3, sc. 2, l. 74 (1599)

112   The noble Brutus
Hath told you Caesar was ambitious:
If it were so, it was a grievous fault,
And grievously hath Caesar answered it.
Julius Caesar act 3, sc. 2, l. 78 (1599)

113 For Brutus is an honorable man;
So are they all, all honorable men.
Julius Caesar act 3, sc. 2, l. 83 (1599)

114 He was my friend, faithful and just to me.
Julius Caesar act 3, sc. 2, l. 86 (1599)

115 When that the poor have cried, Caesar hath
wept:
Ambition should be made of sterner stuff.
Julius Caesar act 3, sc. 2, l. 92 (1599)

116 You all did see, that on the Lupercal
I thrice presented him a kingly crown,
Which he did thrice refuse. Was this
ambition?
Julius Caesar act 3, sc. 2, l. 96 (1599)

117 O judgement, thou art fled to brutish beasts
And men have lost their reason.
Julius Caesar act 3, sc. 2, l. 105 (1599)

118 But yesterday the word of Caesar might
Have stood against the world. Now lies he
there,
And none so poor to do him reverence.
Julius Caesar act 3, sc. 2, l. 119 (1599)

119 If you have tears, prepare to shed them now.
Julius Caesar act 3, sc. 2, l. 167 (1599)

120 This was the most unkindest cut of all:
For when the noble Caesar saw him stab,
Ingratitude, more strong than traitor's arms,
Quite vanquished him: then burst his mighty
heart;
And in his mantle muffling up his face,
Even at the base of Pompey's statue,
Which all the while ran blood, great Caesar
fell.
Julius Caesar act 3, sc. 2, l. 181 (1599)

121 O what a fall was there, my countrymen!
Then I, and you, and all of us fell down,
Whilst bloody treason flourished over us.
Julius Caesar act 3, sc. 2, l. 188 (1599)

122 I am no orator, as Brutus is,
But, as you know me all, a plain blunt man.
Julius Caesar act 3, sc. 2, l. 210 (1599)

123 For I have neither wit, nor words, nor worth,
Action, nor utterance, nor the power of speech
To stir men's blood. I only speak right on.
Julius Caesar act 3, sc. 2, l. 214 (1599)

124 I tell you that which you yourselves do know,
Show you sweet Caesar's wounds, poor poor
dumb mouths,
And bid them speak for me. But were I
Brutus,
And Brutus Antony, there were an Antony
Would ruffle up your spirits and put a tongue
In every wound of Caesar that should move
The stones of Rome to rise and mutiny.
Julius Caesar act 3, sc. 2, l. 217 (1599)

125 Here was a Caesar! when comes such
another?
Julius Caesar act 3, sc. 2, l. 243 (1599)

126 Now let it work. Mischief, thou art afoot:
Take thou what course thou wilt.
Julius Caesar act 3, sc. 2, l. 251 (1599)

127 Let me tell you, Cassius, you yourself
Are much condemned to have an itching
palm.
Julius Caesar act 4, sc. 3, l. 9 (1599)

128 There is a tide in the affairs of men
Which, taken at the flood, leads on to fortune.
Julius Caesar act 4, sc. 3, l. 215 (1599)

129 O Julius Caesar, thou art mighty yet.
Thy spirit walks abroad and turns our swords
In our own proper entrails.
Julius Caesar act 5, sc. 3, l. 92 (1599)

130 This was the noblest Roman of them all:
All the conspirators save only he
Did that they did in envy of great Caesar.
He only, in a general honest thought
And common good to all, made one of them.
Julius Caesar act 5, sc. 5, l. 68 (1599)

131 His life was gentle, and the elements
So mixed in him that nature might stand up
And say to all the world, "This was a man!"
Julius Caesar act 5, sc. 5, l. 73 (1599)

King Henry V

132 O for a muse of fire, that would ascend
The brightest heaven of invention.
King Henry V prologue (1599)

133 Once more unto the breach, dear friends,
once more,
Or close the wall up with our English dead.
In peace there's nothing so becomes a man
As modest stillness and humility;
But when the blast of war blows in our ears,
Then imitate the action of the tiger:
Stiffen the sinews, conjure up the blood,
Disguise fair nature with hard-favored rage.
Then lend the eye a terrible aspect.
King Henry V act 3, sc. 1, l. 1 (1599)

134 I see you stand like greyhounds in the slips,
Straining upon the start. The game's afoot.
Follow your spirit, and upon this charge

Cry "God for Harry! England and St. George!"
King Henry V act 3, sc. 1, l. 31 (1599)

135 And what have kings that privates have
not too,
Save ceremony, save general ceremony?
King Henry V act 4, sc. 1, l. 234 (1599)

136 This day is called the feast of Crispian.
He that outlives this day and comes safe home
Will stand a-tiptoe when this day is named
And rouse him at the name of Crispian.
King Henry V act 4, sc. 3, l. 40 (1599)

137   Our names,
Familiar in his mouth as household words.
King Henry V act 4, sc. 3, l. 51 (1599)

138 We few, we happy few, we band of brothers.
For he today that sheds his blood with me
Shall be my brother; be he ne'er so vile,
This day shall gentle his condition.
And gentlemen in England now abed
Shall think themselves accursed they were not
here,
And hold their manhoods cheap whiles any
speaks
That fought with us upon Saint Crispin's day.
King Henry V act 4, sc. 3, l. 60 (1599)

Much Ado About Nothing

139 Sigh no more, ladies, sigh no more,
Men were deceivers ever.
Much Ado About Nothing act 2, sc. 3, l. 61 (1598–
1599)

Hamlet

140 For this relief much thanks. 'Tis bitter cold,
And I am sick at heart.
Hamlet act 1, sc. 1, l. 8 (1601)

141 Not a mouse stirring.
Hamlet act 1, sc. 1, l. 11 (1601)

142 In the most high and palmy state of Rome,
A little ere the mightiest Julius fell,
The graves stood tenantless and the sheeted
dead
Did squeak and gibber in the Roman streets.
Hamlet act 1, sc. 1, l. 116 (1601)

143 And then it started like a guilty thing
Upon a fearful summons.
Hamlet act 1, sc. 1, l. 152 (1601)

144 It faded on the crowing of the cock.
　　Some say that ever 'gainst that season comes
　　Wherein our Savior's birth is celebrated,
　　This bird of dawning singeth all night long;
　　And then, they say, no spirit dare stir abroad.
　　Hamlet act 1, sc. 1, l. 162 (1601)

145 But look, the morn in russet mantle clad
　　Walks o'er the dew of yon high eastward hill.
　　Hamlet act 1, sc. 1, l. 171 (1601)

146 Though yet of Hamlet our dear brother's
　　　　death
　　The memory be green.
　　Hamlet act 1, sc. 2, l. 1 (1601)

147 A little more than kin, and less than kind.
　　Hamlet act 1, sc. 2, l. 65 (1601)

148 Not so, my lord, I am too much in the sun.
　　Hamlet act 1, sc. 2, l. 67 (1601)

149 O that this too too sullied flesh would melt,
　　Thaw and resolve itself into a dew,
　　Or that the Everlasting had not fix'd
　　His canon 'gainst self-slaughter.
　　Hamlet act 1, sc. 2, l. 129 (1601). Another reading of
　　"sullied" here is "solid."

150 How weary, stale, flat, and unprofitable
　　Seem to me all the uses of this world!
　　Hamlet act 1, sc. 2, l. 133 (1601)

151 So excellent a king, that was to this
　　Hyperion to a satyr, so loving to my mother
　　That he might not beteem the winds of
　　　　heaven
　　Visit her face too roughly. Heaven and earth,
　　Must I remember? Why, she would hang on
　　　　him
　　As if increase of appetite had grown
　　By what it fed on.
　　Hamlet act 1, sc. 2, l. 139 (1601)

152 Frailty, thy name is woman.
　　Hamlet act 1, sc. 2, l. 146 (1601)

153 A little month, or ere those shoes were old
　　With which she follow'd my poor father's
　　　　body,
　　Like Niobe, all tears—why, she—
　　O God, a beast that wants discourse of reason
　　Would have mourn'd longer.
　　Hamlet act 1, sc. 2, l. 147 (1601)

154 It is not, nor it cannot come to good.
　　But break, my heart, for I must hold my
　　　　tongue.
　　Hamlet act 1, sc. 2, l. 158 (1601)

155 Thrift, thrift, Horatio. The funeral bak'd
　　　　meats
　　Did coldly furnish forth the marriage tables.
　　Hamlet act 1, sc. 2, l. 180 (1601)

156 'A was a man, take him for all in all:
　　I shall not look upon his like again.
　　Hamlet act 1, sc. 2, l. 187 (1601)

157 A countenance more in sorrow than in anger.
　　Hamlet act 1, sc. 2, l. 231 (1601)

158 Himself the primrose path of dalliance treads,
　　And recks not his own rede.
　　Hamlet act 1, sc. 3, l. 50 (1601)

159 　　Beware
　　Of entrance to a quarrel, but being in,
　　Bear't that th'opposed may beware of thee.
　　Give every man thy ear, but few thy voice;
　　Take each man's censure, but reserve thy
　　　　judgment.
　　Costly thy habit as thy purse can buy,
　　But not express'd in fancy; rich, not gaudy;
　　For the apparel oft proclaims the man.
　　Hamlet act 1, sc. 3, l. 65 (1601)

160 Neither a borrower nor a lender be,
　　For loan oft loses both itself and friend,
　　And borrowing dulls the edge of husbandry.
　　Hamlet act 1, sc. 3, l. 75 (1601)

161 This above all: to thine own self be true,
　　And it must follow as the night the day
　　Thou canst not then be false to any man.
　　Hamlet act 1, sc. 3, l. 78 (1601)

162 Ay, springes to catch woodcocks.
　　Hamlet act 1, sc. 3, l. 115 (1601)

163 But to my mind, though I am native here
　　And to the manner born, it is a custom
　　More honor'd in the breach than the
　　　　observance.
　　Hamlet act 1, sc. 4, l. 14 (1601)

164 Angels and ministers of grace defend us!
　　Hamlet act 1, sc. 4, l. 39 (1601)

165 Something is rotten in the state of Denmark.
　　Hamlet act 1, sc. 4, l. 90 (1601)

166 I could a tale unfold whose lightest word
    Would harrow up thy soul, freeze thy young
      blood,
    Make thy two eyes like stars start from their
      spheres,
    Thy knotted and combined locks to part,
    And each particular hair to stand an end
    Like quills upon the fretful porpentine.
    Hamlet act 1, sc. 5, l. 15 (1601)

167 Murder most foul, as in the best it is.
    Hamlet act 1, sc. 5, l. 27 (1601)

168 O my prophetic soul! My uncle!
    Hamlet act 1, sc. 5, l. 41 (1601)

169 O villain, villain, smiling damned villain!
    My tables. Meet it is I set it down
    That one may smile, and smile, and be a
      villain.
    Hamlet act 1, sc. 5, l. 106 (1601)

170 There are more things in heaven and earth,
    Horatio,
    Than are dreamt of in your philosophy.
    Hamlet act 1, sc. 5, l. 174 (1601)

171 To put an antic disposition on.
    Hamlet act 1, sc. 5, l. 180 (1601)

172 Rest, rest, perturbed spirit.
    Hamlet act 1, sc. 5, l. 190 (1601)

173 The time is out of joint. O cursed spite,
    That ever I was born to set it right.
    Hamlet act 1, sc. 5, l. 196 (1601)

174 Brevity is the soul of wit.
    Hamlet act 2, sc. 2, l. 90 (1601)
    See Dorothy Parker 1

175 More matter with less art.
    Hamlet act 2, sc. 2, l. 95 (1601)

176 [*Hamlet speaking, after being asked by Polonius,*
    "What do you read, my lord?":] Words, words,
    words.
    Hamlet act 2, sc. 2, l. 191 (1601)

177 Though this be madness, yet there is
    method in't.
    Hamlet act 2, sc. 2, l. 205 (1601). Commonly quoted
    as "There's method in his madness."

178 There is nothing either good or bad but
    thinking makes it so.
    Hamlet act 2, sc. 2, l. 250 (1601)

179 O God, I could be bounded in a nutshell and
    count myself a king of infinite space—were it
    not that I have bad dreams.
    Hamlet act 2, sc. 2, l. 255 (1601)

180 This goodly frame the earth seems to me a
    sterile promontory, this most excellent canopy
    the air, look you, this brave o'erhanging
    firmament, this majestical roof fretted with
    golden fire, why, it appeareth nothing to
    me but a foul and pestilent congregation of
    vapours.
    Hamlet act 2, sc. 2, l. 300 (1601)

181 What piece of work is a man, how noble in
    reason, how infinite in faculties, in form and
    moving how express and admirable, in action
    how like an angel, in apprehension how like
    a god: the beauty of the world, the paragon
    of animals—and yet, to me, what is this
    quintessence of dust? Man delights not me—
    nor woman neither, though by your smiling
    you seem to say so.
    Hamlet act 2, sc. 2, l. 305 (1601)

182 I am but mad north-north-west. When the
    wind is southerly, I know a hawk from a
    handsaw.
    Hamlet act 2, sc. 2, l. 379 (1601)

183 The play, I remember, pleased not the million,
    'twas caviare to the general.
    Hamlet act 2, sc. 2, l. 436 (1601)

184 Use every man after his desert, and who shall
    scape whipping?
    Hamlet act 2, sc. 2, l. 530 (1601)

185 O what a rogue and peasant slave am I!
    Hamlet act 2, sc. 2, l. 550 (1601)

186 What's Hecuba to him, or he to her,
    That he should weep for her?
    Hamlet act 2, sc. 2, l. 559 (1601)

187   The play's the thing
    Wherein I'll catch the conscience of the King.
    Hamlet act 2, sc. 2, l. 605 (1601)

188 To be, or not to be, that is the question:
    Whether 'tis nobler in the mind to suffer
    The slings and arrows of outrageous fortune,
    Or to take arms against a sea of troubles
    And by opposing end them.
    Hamlet act 3, sc. 1, l. 56 (1601)

189 To die—to sleep,
    No more; and by a sleep to say we end
    The heart-ache and the thousand natural
      shocks
    That flesh is heir to: 'tis a consummation
    Devoutly to be wish'd. To die, to sleep;
    To sleep, perchance to dream—ay, there's the
      rub:
    For in that sleep of death what dreams may
      come,
    When we have shuffled off this mortal coil,
    Must give us pause—there's the respect
    That makes calamity of so long life.
    Hamlet act 3, sc. 1, l. 60 (1601)

190 For who would bear the whips and scorns of
      time,
    Th'oppressor's wrong, the proud man's
      contumely,
    The pangs of dispriz'd love, the law's delay,
    The insolence of office, and the spurns
    That patient merit of th'unworthy takes,
    When he himself might his quietus make
    With a bare bodkin?
    Hamlet act 3, sc. 1, l. 70 (1601)

191   Who would fardels bear,
    To grunt and sweat under a weary life,
    But that the dread of something after death,
    The undiscover'd country, from whose bourn
    No traveller returns, puzzles the will,
    And makes us rather bear those ills we have
    Than fly to others that we know not of?
    Hamlet act 3, sc. 1, 76 (1601)

192 Thus conscience does make cowards of us all,
    And thus the native hue of resolution
    Is sicklied o'er with the pale cast of thought,
    And enterprises of great pitch and moment
    With this regard their currents turn awry
    And lose the name of action.
    Hamlet act 3, sc. 1, l. 83 (1601)

193   Nymph, in thy orisons
    Be all my sins remember'd.
    Hamlet act 3, sc. 1, l. 88 (1601)

194 Get thee to a nunnery.
    Hamlet act 3, sc. 1, l. 121 (1601)

195 Be thou as chaste as ice, as pure as snow, thou
    shalt not escape calumny.
    Hamlet act 3, sc. 1, l. 137 (1601)

196 I have heard of your paintings well enough.
    God hath given you one face and you make
    yourselves another.
    Hamlet act 3, sc. 1, l. 143 (1601)

197 O, what a noble mind is here o'erthrown!
    The courtier's, soldier's, scholar's, eye, tongue,
      sword.
    Hamlet act 3, sc. 1, l. 151 (1601)

198 The glass of fashion and the mould of form,
    Th'observ'd of all observers, quite, quite
      down!
    Hamlet act 3, sc. 1, l. 154 (1601)

199 Now see that noble and most sovereign reason
    Like sweet bells jangled out of tune and
      harsh.
    Hamlet act 3, sc. 1, l. 158 (1601)

200 Speak the speech, I pray you, as I pronounced
    it to you, trippingly on the tongue.
    Hamlet act 3, sc. 2, l. 1 (1601)

201 I would have such a fellow whipped for
    o'erdoing Termagant. It out-Herods Herod.
    Hamlet act 3, sc. 2, l. 13 (1601)

202 Suit the action to the word, the word to the
    action.
    Hamlet act 3, sc. 2, l. 18 (1601)

203 To hold as 'twere the mirror up to nature.
    Hamlet act 3, sc. 2, l. 22 (1601)

204 The lady doth protest too much, methinks.
    Hamlet act 3, sc. 2, l. 232 (1601)

205 Let the galled jade wince, our withers are
    unwrung.
    Hamlet act 3, sc. 2, l. 244 (1601)

206 Why, let the strucken deer go weep,
    The hart ungalled play;
    For some must watch while some must sleep,
    Thus runs the world away.
    Hamlet act 3, sc. 2, l. 273 (1601)

207 You would pluck out the heart of my mystery.
    Hamlet act 3, sc. 2, l. 368 (1601)

208 Very like a whale.
    Hamlet act 3, sc. 2, l. 384 (1601)

209 They fool me to the top of my bent.
    Hamlet act 3, sc. 2, l. 386 (1601)

210 'Tis now the very witching time of night,
When churchyards yawn and hell itself
      breathes out
Contagion to this world.
Hamlet act 3, sc. 2, l. 390 (1601)

211 O, my offence is rank, it smells to heaven;
It hath the primal eldest curse upon't—
A brother's murder.
Hamlet act 3, sc. 3, l. 36 (1601)

212 Now might I do it pat, now a is a-praying.
And now I'll do't. And so a goes to heaven;
And so am I reveng'd.
Hamlet act 3, sc. 3, l. 73 (1601)

213 My words fly up, my thoughts remain below.
Words without thoughts never to heaven go.
Hamlet act 3, sc. 3, l. 97 (1601)

214 How now? A rat! Dead for a ducat, dead.
Hamlet act 3, sc. 4, l. 22 (1601)

215 A king of shreds and patches.
Hamlet act 3, sc. 4, l. 103 (1601)
See W. S. Gilbert 28

216 Assume a virtue if you have it not.
Hamlet act 3, sc. 4, l. 162 (1601)

217 I must be cruel only to be kind.
Hamlet act 3, sc. 4, l. 180 (1601)

218   'Tis the sport to have the enginer
Hoist with his own petard.
Hamlet act 3, sc. 4, l. 208 (1601)

219   Diseases desperate grown
By desperate appliance are reliev'd,
Or not at all.
Hamlet act 4, sc. 3, l. 9 (1601)
See Proverbs 65

220 How all occasions do inform against me,
And spur my dull revenge.
Hamlet act 4, sc. 4, l. 32 (1601)

221 Come, my coach. Good night, ladies, good
night. Sweet ladies, good night, good night.
Hamlet act 4, sc. 5, l. 71 (1601)
See T. S. Eliot 49

222 When sorrows come, they come not single
      spies,
But in battalions.
Hamlet act 4, sc. 5, l. 78 (1601)

223 There's such divinity doth hedge a king
That treason can but peep to what it would.
Hamlet act 4, sc. 5, l. 123 (1601)

224 There's rosemary, that's for remembrance—
pray you, love, remember. And there is
pansies, that's for thoughts.
Hamlet act 4, sc. 5, l. 173 (1601)

225 You must wear your rue with a difference.
There's a daisy. I would give you some violets,
but they withered all when my father died.
Hamlet act 4, sc. 5, l. 180 (1601)

226 Alas, poor Yorick. I knew him, Horatio,
a fellow of infinite jest, of most excellent
fancy. He hath bore me on his back a
thousand times, and now—how abhorred
in my imagination it is. My gorge rises at
it. Here hung those lips that I have kissed I
know not how oft. Where be your gibes now,
your gambols, your songs, your flashes of
merriment, that were wont to set the table
on a roar? Not one now to mock your own
grinning? Quite chop-fallen? Now get you to
my lady's chamber and tell her, let her paint
an inch thick, to this favor she must come.
Make her laugh at that.
Hamlet act 5, sc. 1, l. 182 (1601). The first line
is frequently quoted "Alas, poor Yorick, I knew
him well."

227 Imperious Caesar, dead and turn'd to clay,
Might stop a hole to keep the wind away.
Hamlet act 5, sc. 1, l. 211 (1601)

228 A minist'ring angel shall my sister be
When thou liest howling.
Hamlet act 5, sc. 1, l. 238 (1601)
See Walter Scott 6

229 Sweets to the sweet. Farewell.
Hamlet act 5, sc. 1, l. 241 (1601)

230 There's a divinity that shapes our ends,
Rough-hew them how we will.
Hamlet act 5, sc. 2, l. 10 (1601)

231 Not a whit. We defy augury. There is special
providence in the fall of a sparrow. If it be
now, 'tis not to come; if it be not to come, it
will be now; if it be not now, yet it will come.
The readiness is all.
Hamlet act 5, sc. 2, l. 218 (1601)

232 A hit, a very palpable hit.
 Hamlet act 5, sc. 2, l. 285 (1601)

233 This fell sergeant, Death,
 Is strict in his arrest.
 Hamlet act 5, sc. 2, l. 343 (1601)

234 I am more an antique Roman than a Dane.
 Hamlet act 5, sc. 2, l. 348 (1601)

235 If thou didst ever hold me in thy heart,
 Absent thee from felicity awhile,
 And in this harsh world draw thy breath in
  pain
 To tell my story.
 Hamlet act 5, sc. 2, l. 353 (1601)

236 The rest is silence.
 Hamlet act 5, sc. 2, l. 364 (1601)

237 Now cracks a noble heart. Good night, sweet
  prince,
 And flights of angels sing thee to thy rest.
 Hamlet act 5, sc. 2, l. 365 (1601)

238 Rosencrantz and Guildenstern are dead.
 Hamlet act 5, sc. 2, l. 378 (1601)

Twelfth Night

239 If music be the food of love, play on,
 Give me excess of it, that, surfeiting,
 The appetite may sicken, and so die.
 That strain again, it had a dying fall:
 O, it came o'er my ear like the sweet sound
 That breathes upon a bank of violets,
 Stealing and giving odor.
 Twelfth Night act 1, sc. 1, l. 1 (1601)

240 What is love? 'Tis not hereafter,
 Present mirth hath present laughter:
 What's to come is still unsure.
 In delay there lies no plenty,
 Then come kiss me, sweet and twenty:
 Youth's a stuff will not endure.
 Twelfth Night act 2, sc. 3, l. 47 (1601)

241 Dost thou think because thou art virtuous,
 there shall be no more cakes and ale?
 Twelfth Night act 2, sc. 3, l. 113 (1601)

242 Let still the woman take
 An elder than herself; so wears she to him,
 So sways she level in her husband's heart.
 Twelfth Night act 2, sc. 4, l. 29 (1601)

243 Come away, come away death,
 And in sad cypress let me be laid.
 Twelfth Night act 2, sc. 4, l. 51 (1601)

244 But be not afraid of greatness. Some are born
 great, some achieve greatness, and some have
 greatness thrust upon 'em.
 Twelfth Night act 2, sc. 5, l. 139 (1601)
 See Samuel Butler (1835–1902) 4; Heller 4

245 Thus the whirligig of time brings in his
 revenges.
 Twelfth Night act 5, sc. 1, l. 369 (1601)

246 When that I was and a little tiny boy,
 With hey, ho, the wind and the rain,
 A foolish thing was but a toy,
 For the rain it raineth every day.
 Twelfth Night act 5, sc. 1, l. 381 (1601)

Troilus and Cressida

247 Take but degree away, untune that string,
 And hark what discord follows.
 Troilus and Cressida act 1, sc. 3, l. 109 (1602)

248 To be wise and love
 Exceeds man's might.
 Troilus and Cressida act 3, sc. 2, l. 152 (1602)

249 Time hath, my lord, a wallet at his back,
 Wherein he puts alms for oblivion.
 Troilus and Cressida act 3, sc. 3, l. 147 (1602)

250 One touch of nature makes the whole world
  kin.
 Troilus and Cressida act 3, sc. 3, l. 177 (1602)

251 The end crowns all,
 And that old common arbitrator, Time,
 Will one day end it.
 Troilus and Cressida act 4, sc. 5, l. 224 (1602)

All's Well That Ends Well

252 My friends were poor, but honest.
 All's Well That Ends Well act 1, sc. 3, l. 192 (1603–1604)

Measure for Measure

253 O, it is excellent
 To have a giant's strength, but it is tyrannous
 To use it like a giant.
 Measure for Measure act 2, sc. 2, l. 108 (1604)

254   Man, proud man,
Dress'd in a little brief authority,
Most ignorant of what he's most assur'd—
His glassy essence—like an angry ape
Plays such fantastic tricks before high heaven
As makes the angels weep.
Measure for Measure act 2, sc. 2, l. 118 (1604)

255   Thou hast nor youth, nor age,
But as it were an after-dinner's sleep
Dreaming on both; for all thy blessed youth
Becomes as aged, and doth beg the alms
Of palsied eld: and when thou art old and
rich,
Thou hast neither heat, affection, limb, nor
beauty
To make thy riches pleasant.
Measure for Measure act 3, sc. 1, l. 32 (1604)

256   If I must die,
I will encounter darkness as a bride
And hug it in mine arms.
Measure for Measure act 3, sc. 1, l. 82 (1604)

257   Ay, but to die, and go we know not where;
To lie in cold obstruction, and to rot.
Measure for Measure act 3, sc. 1, l. 117 (1604)

Othello

258   But I will wear my heart upon my sleeve
For daws to peck at.
Othello act 1, sc. 1, l. 63 (1602–1604)

259   Even now, now, very now, an old black ram
Is tupping your white ewe!
Othello act 1, sc. 1, l. 87 (1602–1604)

260   Your daughter and the Moor are now making
the beast with two backs.
Othello act 1, sc. 1, l. 114 (1602–1604)

261   Keep up your bright swords, for the dew will
rust them.
Othello act 1, sc. 2, l. 59 (1602–1604)

262   I will a round unvarnished tale deliver.
Othello act 1, sc. 3, l. 91 (1602–1604)

263   And of the cannibals that each other eat,
The Anthropophagi, and men whose heads
Do grow beneath their shoulders.
Othello act 1, sc. 3, l. 144 (1602–1604)

264   She loved me for the dangers I had passed
And I loved her that she did pity them.
Othello act 1, sc. 3, l. 168 (1602–1604)

265   I do perceive here a divided duty.
Othello act 1, sc. 3, l. 181 (1602–1604)

266   To suckle fools, and chronicle small beer.
Othello act 2, sc. 1, l. 160 (1602–1604)

267   O, I have lost my reputation, I have lost the
immortal part of myself—and what remains
is bestial.
Othello act 2, sc. 3, l. 254 (1602–1604)

268   Excellent wretch! perdition catch my soul
But I do love thee! and when I love thee not
Chaos is come again.
Othello act 3, sc. 1, l. 90 (1602–1604)

269   Who steals my purse steals trash—'tis
something-nothing,
'Twas mine, 'tis his, and has been slave to
thousands—
But he that filches from me my good name
Robs me of that which not enriches him
And makes me poor indeed.
Othello act 3, sc. 1, l. 160 (1602–1604)

270   O beware, my lord, of jealousy!
It is the green-eyed monster, which doth
mock
The meat it feeds on.
Othello act 3, sc. 1, l. 167 (1602–1604)

271   If I do prove her haggard,
Though that her jesses were my dear heart-
strings,
I'd whistle her off and let her down the wind
To prey at fortune.
Othello act 3, sc. 3, l. 264 (1602–1604)

272   I had rather be a toad
And live upon the vapor of a dungeon
Than keep a corner in the thing I love
For others' uses.
Othello act 3, sc. 3, l. 274 (1602–1604)

273   Trifles light as air
Are to the jealous confirmations strong
As proofs of holy writ.
Othello act 3, sc. 3, l. 325 (1602–1604)

274   Farewell the tranquil mind, farewell content!
Farewell the plumed troops and the big wars
That makes ambition virtue!
Othello act 3, sc. 3, l. 351 (1602–1604)

275   Pride, pomp, and circumstance of glorious war!
Othello act 3, sc. 3, l. 357 (1602–1604)

276 Othello's occupation's gone.
Othello act 3, sc. 3, l. 360 (1602–1604)

277 This denoted a foregone conclusion.
Othello act 3, sc. 3, l. 430 (1602–1604)

278 But yet the pity of it, Iago—O, Iago, the pity
of it, Iago!
Othello act 4, sc. 1, l. 192 (1602–1604)

279 The poor soul sat sighing by a sycamore tree,
Sing all a green willow:
Her hand on her bosom, her head on her
knee,
Sing willow, willow, willow.
Othello act 4, sc. 3, l. 39 (1602–1604)

280 Put out the light, and then put out the light!
Othello act 5, sc. 2, l. 7 (1602–1604)

281 Here is my journey's end, here is my butt
And very sea-mark of my utmost sail.
Othello act 5, sc. 2, l. 267 (1602–1604)

282 I have done the state some service, and they
know't:
No more of that. I pray you, in your letters,
When you shall these unlucky deeds relate,
Speak of me as I am. Nothing extenuate,
Nor set down aught in malice. Then must you
speak
Of one that loved not wisely, but too well;
Of one not easily jealous, but, being wrought,
Perplexed in the extreme; of one whose hand,
Like the base Indian, threw a pearl away
Richer than all his tribe.
Othello act 5, sc. 2, l. 339 (1602–1604)

King Lear

283 Nothing will come of nothing.
King Lear act 1, sc. 1, l. 90 (1605–1606)

284 [*Lear:*] So young and so untender?
[*Cordelia:*] So young, my lord, and true.
King Lear act 1, sc. 1, l. 107 (1605–1606)

285   I want that glib and oily art
To speak and purpose not.
King Lear act 1, sc. 1, l. 226 (1605–1606)

286   Why bastard? Wherefore base?
When my dimensions are as well compact,
My mind as generous and my shape as true
As honest madam's issue?
King Lear act 1, sc. 2, l. 6 (1605–1606)

287 Now gods, stand up for bastards!
King Lear act 1, sc. 2, l. 22 (1605–1606)

288 This is the excellent foppery of the world,
that when we are sick in fortune, often the
surfeits of our own behavior, we make guilty
of our disasters the sun, the moon, and the
stars, as if we were villains on necessity, fools
by heavenly compulsion, knaves, thieves,
and treachers by spherical predominance;
drunkards, liars, and adulterers by an
enforced obedience of planetary influence.
King Lear act 1, sc. 2, l. 119 (1605–1606)

289 How sharper than a serpent's tooth it is
To have a thankless child.
King Lear act 1, sc. 4, l. 280 (1605–1606)

290   O sir, you are old:
Nature in you stands on the very verge
Of her confine.
King Lear act 2, sc. 2, l. 338 (1605–1606)

291 O, reason not the need! Our basest beggars
Are in the poorest things superfluous;
Allow not nature more than nature needs,
Man's life is cheap as beast's.
King Lear act 2, sc. 2, l. 456 (1605–1606)

292 Blow winds and crack your cheeks! Rage, blow!
You cataracts and hurricanoes, spout
Till you have drenched our steeples, drowned
the cocks!
You sulphurous and thought-executing fires,
Vaunt-couriers of oak-cleaving thunderbolts,
Singe my white head!
King Lear act 3, sc. 2, l. 1 (1605–1606)

293 I tax not you, you elements, with unkindness.
King Lear act 3, sc. 2, l. 16 (1605–1606)

294   I am a man
More sinned against than sinning.
King Lear act 3, sc. 2, l. 59 (1605–1606)

295 O, that way madness lies, let me shun that.
King Lear act 3, sc. 4, l. 21 (1605–1606)

296   Take physic, pomp,
Expose thyself to feel what wretches feel.
King Lear act 3, sc. 4, l. 33 (1605–1606)

297 Thou art the thing itself. Unaccommodated
man is no more but such a poor, bare, forked
animal as thou art.
King Lear act 3, sc. 4, l. 105 (1605–1606)

298 The green mantle of the standing pool.
King Lear act 3, sc. 4, l. 130 (1605–1606)

299 The prince of darkness is a gentleman.
King Lear act 3, sc. 4, l. 139 (1605–1606)

300 Poor Tom's a-cold.
King Lear act 3, sc. 4, l. 143 (1605–1606)

301 Childe Rowland to the dark tower came,
His word was still "Fie, foh, and fum,
I smell the blood of a British man."
King Lear act 3, sc. 4, l. 178 (1605–1606)
See Nashe 1

302   Out, vile jelly,
Where is thy luster now?
King Lear act 3, sc. 7, l. 82 (1605–1606)

303   The worst is not
So long as we can say "This is the worst."
King Lear act 4, sc. 1, l. 29 (1605–1606)

304 As flies to wanton boys are we to the gods,
They kill us for their sport.
King Lear act 4, sc. 1, l. 38 (1605–1606)

305 Ay, every inch a king.
King Lear act 4, sc. 6, l. 106 (1605–1606)

306   Die—die for adultery? No!
The wren goes to't and the small gilded fly
Does lecher in my sight.
King Lear act 4, sc. 6, l. 110 (1605–1606)

307   Get thee glass eyes,
And like a scurvy politician seem
To see the things thou dost not.
King Lear act 4, sc. 6, l. 166 (1605–1606)

308 When we are born we cry that we are come
To this great stage of fools.
King Lear act 4, sc. 6, l. 178 (1605–1606)

309   Mine enemy's dog
Though he had bit me should have stood that
night
Against my fire.
King Lear act 4, sc. 7, l. 36 (1605–1606)

310 Thou art a soul in bliss, but I am bound
Upon a wheel of fire.
King Lear act 4, sc. 7, l. 46 (1605–1606)

311 I am a very foolish, fond old man,
Fourscore and upward, not an hour more or
less;

And to deal plainly,
I fear I am not in my perfect mind.
King Lear act 4, sc. 7, l. 60 (1605–1606)

312   Men must endure
Their going hence even as their coming
hither.
Ripeness is all.
King Lear act 5, sc. 2, l. 9 (1605–1606)

313   Come, let's away to prison;
We two alone will sing like birds i'the cage.
When thou dost ask me blessing I'll kneel
down
And ask of thee forgiveness.
King Lear act 5, sc. 3, l. 8 (1605–1606)

314 The gods are just and of our pleasant vices
Make instruments to plague us.
King Lear act 5, sc. 3, l. 168 (1605–1606)

315 The wheel is come full circle.
King Lear act 5, sc. 3, l. 172 (1605–1606)

316 Howl, howl, howl, howl! O, you are men of
stones!
Had I your tongues and eyes, I'd use them so
That heaven's vault should crack: she's gone
for ever.
King Lear act 5, sc. 3, l. 255 (1605–1606)

317   Her voice was ever soft,
Gentle and low, an excellent thing in woman.
King Lear act 5, sc. 3, l. 270 (1605–1606)

318 And my poor fool is hanged. No, no, no life!
Why should a dog, a horse, a rat have life
And thou no breath at all? O thou'lt come no
more
Never, never, never, never, never.
King Lear act 5, sc. 3, l. 304 (1605–1606)

319 Vex not his ghost; O, let him pass. He hates
him
That would upon the rack of this tough world
Stretch him out longer.
King Lear act 5, sc. 3, l. 312 (1605–1606)

320 The weight of this sad time we must obey,
Speak what we feel, not what we ought to say.
The oldest hath borne most; we that are
young
Shall never see so much, nor live so long.
King Lear act 5, sc. 3, l. 322 (1605–1606)

Macbeth

321 When shall we three meet again?
In thunder, lightning, or in rain?
Macbeth act 1, sc. 1, l. 1 (1606)

322 Fair is foul, and foul is fair:
Hover through the fog and filthy air.
Macbeth act 1, sc. 1, l. 11 (1606)

323 A sailor's wife had chestnuts in her lap,
And mounch'd, and mounch'd, and
mounch'd: "Give me," quoth I:—
"Aroynt thee, witch!" the rump-fed ronyon
cries.
Macbeth act 1, sc. 3, l. 4 (1606)

324 Sleep neither night nor day
Hang upon his penthouse lid;
He shall live a man forbid.
Weary sev'n-nights nine times nine,
Shall he dwindle, peak, and pine:
Though his bark cannot be lost,
Yet it shall be tempest-tost.
Macbeth act 1, sc. 3, l. 19 (1606)

325 The Weird Sisters, hand in hand,
Posters of the sea and land,
Thus do go about, about.
Macbeth act 1, sc. 3, l. 32 (1606)

326 So foul and fair a day I have not seen.
Macbeth act 1, sc. 3, l. 38 (1606)

327 If you can look into the seeds of time,
And say which grain will grow, and which
will not.
Macbeth act 1, sc. 3, l. 58 (1606)

328 Two truths are told,
As happy prologues to the swelling act
Of the imperial theme.
Macbeth act 1, sc. 3, l. 127 (1606)

329 Present fears
Are less than horrible imaginings.
Macbeth act 1, sc. 3, l. 137 (1606)

330 Come what come may,
Time and the hour runs through the roughest
day.
Macbeth act 1, sc. 3, l. 147 (1606)

331 Nothing in his life
Became him like the leaving it.
Macbeth act 1, sc. 4, l. 7 (1606)

332 There's no art
To find the mind's construction in the face.
Macbeth act 1, sc. 4, l. 11 (1606)

333 Glamis thou art, and Cawdor; and shalt be
What thou art promis'd.—Yet do I fear thy
nature:
It is too full o'th' milk of human kindness,
To catch the nearest way.
Macbeth act 1, sc. 5, l. 14 (1606)

334 The raven himself is hoarse,
That croaks the fatal entrance of Duncan
Under my battlements.
Macbeth act 1, sc. 5, l. 37 (1606)

335 Unsex me here,
And fill me, from the crown to the toe, top-
full
Of direst cruelty!
Macbeth act 1, sc. 5, l. 40 (1606)

336 Come to my woman's breasts,
And take my milk for gall, you murth'ring
ministers.
Macbeth act 1, sc. 5, l. 46 (1606)

337 Your face, my Thane, is as a book, where men
May read strange matters.
Macbeth act 1, sc. 5, l. 61 (1606)

338 Look like th'innocent flower,
But be the serpent under't.
Macbeth act 1, sc. 5, l. 64 (1606)

339 This guest of summer,
The temple-haunting martlet.
Macbeth act 1, sc. 6, l. 3 (1606)

340 If it were done, when 'tis done, then 'twere
well
It were done quickly: if th'assassination
Could trammel up the consequence, and
catch
With his surcease success; that but this blow
Might be the be-all and the end-all—here,
But here, upon this bank and shoal of time,
We'd jump the life to come.
Macbeth act 1, sc. 7, l. 1 (1606)

341 This even-handed Justice
Commends th'ingredience of our poison'd
chalice
To our own lips.
Macbeth act 1, sc. 7, l. 10 (1606)

342   Besides, this Duncan
Hath borne his faculties so meek, hath been
So clear in his great office, that his virtues
Will plead like angels, trumpet-tongu'd, against
The deep damnation of his taking-off.
Macbeth act 1, sc. 7, l. 16 (1606)

343   I have no spur
To prick the sides of my intent, but only
Vaulting ambition, which o'erleaps itself
And falls on th'other.
Macbeth act 1, sc. 7, l. 25 (1606)

344   He hath honor'd me of late; and I have bought
Golden opinions from all sorts of people.
Macbeth act 1, sc. 7, l. 32 (1606)

345   Letting "I dare not" wait upon "I would,"
Like the poor cat i'th'adage?
Macbeth act 1, sc. 7, l. 44 (1606)

346   I dare do all that may become a man;
Who dares do more, is none.
Macbeth act 1, sc. 7, l. 46 (1606)

347   I have given suck, and know
How tender 'tis to love the babe that
milks me:
I would, while it was smiling in my face,
Have pluck'd my nipple from his boneless
gums,
And dash'd the brains out, had I so sworn
As you have done to this.
Macbeth act 1, sc. 7, l. 54 (1606)

348   [*Macbeth:*] If we should fail?
[*Lady Macbeth:*] We fail?
But screw your courage to the sticking-place,
And we'll not fail.
Macbeth act 1, sc. 7, l. 59 (1606)

349   False face must hide what the false heart doth
know.
Macbeth act 1, sc. 7, l. 83 (1606)

350   Is this a dagger, which I see before me,
The handle toward my hand? Come, let me
clutch thee:—
I have thee not, and yet I see thee still.
Art thou not, fatal vision, sensible
To feeling, as to sight? or art thou but
A dagger of the mind, a false creation,
Proceeding from the heat-oppressed brain?
Macbeth act 2, sc. 1, l. 33 (1606)

351   The bell invites me.
Hear it not, Duncan; for it is a knell
That summons thee to Heaven, or to Hell.
Macbeth act 2, sc. 1, l. 62 (1606)

352   It was the owl that shriek'd, the fatal bellman,
Which gives the stern'st good-night.
Macbeth act 2, sc. 2, l. 3 (1606)

353   Had he not resembled
My father as he slept, I had done't.
Macbeth act 2, sc. 2, l. 12 (1606)

354   Methought, I heard a voice cry, "Sleep no
more!
Macbeth does murther Sleep,"—the innocent
Sleep;
Sleep, that knits up the ravell'd sleave of care.
Macbeth act 2, sc. 2, l. 34 (1606)

355   Glamis hath murther'd Sleep, and therefore
Cawdor
Shall sleep no more, Macbeth shall sleep no
more!
Macbeth act 2, sc. 2, l. 41 (1606)

356   Infirm of purpose!
Give me the daggers. The sleeping, and the
dead,
Are but as pictures; 'tis the eye of childhood
That fears a painted devil.
Macbeth act 2, sc. 2, l. 51 (1606)

357   Will all great Neptune's ocean wash this blood
Clean from my hand? No, this my hand will
rather
The multitudinous seas incarnadine,
Making the green one red.
Macbeth act 2, sc. 2, l. 59 (1606)

358   Drink, Sir, is a great provoker. . . . Lechery,
Sir, it provokes, and unprovokes: it provokes
the desire, but it takes away the performance.
Macbeth act 2, sc. 3, l. 24 (1606)

359   The labor we delight in physics pain.
Macbeth act 2, sc. 3, l. 50 (1606)

360   Confusion now hath made his masterpiece!
Macbeth act 2, sc. 3, l. 66 (1606)

361   Shake off this downy sleep, death's
counterfeit.
Macbeth act 2, sc. 3, l. 75 (1606)

362 Had I but died an hour before this chance,
  I had liv'd a blessed time; for, from this
      instant,
  There's nothing serious in mortality;
  All is but toys: renown, and grace, is dead;
  The wine of life is drawn, and the mere lees
  Is left this vault to brag of.
    Macbeth act 2, sc. 3, l. 89 (1606)

363 A falcon, towering in her pride of place,
  Was by a mousing owl hawk'd at, and kill'd.
    Macbeth act 2, sc. 4, l. 12 (1606)

364 I must become a borrower of the night,
  For a dark hour, or twain.
    Macbeth act 3, sc. 1, l. 26 (1606)

365   Things without all remedy
  Should be without regard; what's done is
      done.
    Macbeth act 3, sc. 2, l. 11 (1606)

366   Duncan is in his grave;
  After life's fitful fever he sleeps well;
  Treason has done his worst: nor steel, nor
      poison,
  Malice domestic, foreign levy, nothing
  Can touch him further!
    Macbeth act 3, sc. 2, l. 22 (1606)

367   Come, seeling Night,
  Scarf up the tender eye of pitiful Day,
  And, with thy bloody and invisible hand,
  Cancel, and tear to pieces, that great bond
  Which keeps me pale!
    Macbeth act 3, sc. 2, l. 46 (1606)

368 Now spurs the lated traveller apace,
  To gain the timely inn.
    Macbeth act 3, sc. 3, l. 6 (1606)

369 But now, I am cabin'd, cribb'd, confin'd,
      bound in
  To saucy doubts and fears.
    Macbeth act 3, sc. 4, l. 23 (1606)

370 Now, good digestion wait on appetite,
  And health on both!
    Macbeth act 3, sc. 4, l. 37 (1606)

371 Thou canst not say, I did it: never shake
  Thy gory locks at me.
    Macbeth act 3, sc. 4, l. 49 (1606)

372 Stand not upon the order of your going.
    Macbeth act 3, sc. 4, l. 118 (1606)

373 It will have blood, they say: blood will have
      blood.
    Macbeth act 3, sc. 4, l. 121 (1606)

374   I am in blood
  Stepp'd in so far, that, should I wade no more,
  Returning were as tedious as go o'er.
    Macbeth act 3, sc. 4, l. 135 (1606)

375 Double, double toil and trouble:
  Fire, burn; and, cauldron, bubble.
    Macbeth act 4, sc. 1, l. 10 (1606)

376 Eye of newt, and toe of frog,
  Wool of bat, and tongue of dog.
    Macbeth act 4, sc. 1, l. 14 (1606)

377 By the pricking of my thumbs,
  Something wicked this way comes.
    Macbeth act 4, sc. 1, l. 44 (1606)

378 How now, you secret, black, and midnight
      hags!
    Macbeth act 4, sc. 1, l. 48 (1606)

379 Be bloody, bold, and resolute: laugh to scorn
  The power of man, for none of woman born
  Shall harm Macbeth.
    Macbeth act 4, sc. 1, l. 79 (1606)

380 But yet I'll make assurance double sure,
  And take a bond of Fate.
    Macbeth act 4, sc. 1, l. 83 (1606)

381 Macbeth shall never vanquish'd be, until
  Great Birnam wood to high Dunsinane hill
  Shall come against him.
    Macbeth act 4, sc. 1, l. 92 (1606)

382 Give sorrow words; the grief, that does not
      speak,
  Whispers the o'er-fraught heart, and bids it
      break.
    Macbeth act 4, sc. 3, l. 209 (1606)

383 He has no children.—All my pretty ones?
  Did you say all?—O Hell-kite!—All?
  What, all my pretty chickens, and their dam,
  At one fell swoop?
    Macbeth act 4, sc. 3, l. 216 (1606)

384 Out, damned spot! out, I say!
    Macbeth act 5, sc. 1, l. 36 (1606)

385 Who would have thought the old man to have
  had so much blood in him?
    Macbeth act 5, sc. 1, l. 40 (1606)

386 The Thane of Fife had a wife: where is she
now?
Macbeth act 5, sc. 1, l. 43 (1606)

387 All the perfumes of Arabia will not sweeten
this little hand.
Macbeth act 5, sc. 1, l. 51 (1606)

388 The devil damn thee black, thou cream-fac'd
loon!
Where gott'st thou that goose look?
Macbeth act 5, sc. 3, l. 11 (1606)

389 I have liv'd long enough: my way of life
Is fall'n into the sere, the yellow leaf.
Macbeth act 5, sc. 3, l. 22 (1606)

390 Canst thou not minister to a mind diseas'd.
Macbeth act 5, sc. 3, l. 40 (1606)

391 Throw physic to the dogs: I'll none of it.
Macbeth act 5, sc. 3, l. 46 (1606)

392 I have supp'd full with horrors.
Macbeth act 5, sc. 5, l. 13 (1606)

393 She should have died hereafter:
There would have been a time for such a
word.—
To-morrow, and to-morrow, and to-morrow,
Creeps in this petty pace from day to day,
To the last syllable of recorded time;
And all our yesterdays have lighted fools
The way to dusty death. Out, out, brief candle!
Macbeth act 5, sc. 5, l. 17 (1606)

394 Life's but a walking shadow; a poor player,
That struts and frets his hour upon the stage,
And then is heard no more: it is a tale
Told by an idiot, full of sound and fury,
Signifying nothing.
Macbeth act 5, sc. 5, l. 24 (1606)

395 I bear a charmed life; which must not yield
To one of woman born.
Macbeth act 5, sc. 8, l. 12 (1606)

396   Macduff was from his mother's womb
Untimely ripp'd.
Macbeth act 5, sc. 8, l. 15 (1606)

397   Lay on, Macduff;
And damn'd be him that first cries, "Hold,
enough!"
Macbeth act 5, sc. 8, l. 33 (1606). Frequently
misquoted as "Lead on, Macduff."

Antony and Cleopatra

398 Let Rome in Tiber melt, and the wide arch
Of the ranged empire fall!
Antony and Cleopatra act 1, sc. 1, l. 34 (1606–1607)

399   My salad days,
When I was green in judgement.
Antony and Cleopatra act 1, sc. 5, l. 77 (1606–1607)

400 The barge she sat in, like a burnished throne,
Burned on the water.
Antony and Cleopatra act 2, sc. 2, l. 201 (1606–1607)
See T. S. Eliot 45

401   For her own person,
It beggared all description.
Antony and Cleopatra act 2, sc. 2, l. 207 (1606–
1607)

402 Age cannot wither her, nor custom stale
Her infinite variety. Other women cloy
The appetites they feed, but she makes
hungry
Where most she satisfies.
Antony and Cleopatra act 2, sc. 2, l. 245 (1606–1607)

403 I am dying, Egypt, dying.
Antony and Cleopatra act 4, sc. 15, l. 19 (1606–1607)

404   I shall see
Some squeaking Cleopatra boy my greatness
I'th' posture of a whore.
Antony and Cleopatra act 5, sc. 2, l. 217 (1606–1607)

405 Give me my robe. Put on my crown. I have
Immortal longings in me.
Antony and Cleopatra act 5, sc. 2, l. 278 (1606–1607)

Timon of Athens

406 Men shut their doors against a setting sun.
Timon of Athens act 1, sc. 2, l. 146 (ca. 1607)

407 We have seen better days.
Timon of Athens act 4, sc. 2, l. 27 (ca. 1607)

Pericles

408 [*First Fisherman:*] Master, I marvel how the
fishes live in the sea.
[*Third Fisherman:*] Why, as men do a-land: the
great ones eat up the little ones.
Pericles act 2, sc. 1, l. 26 (1606–1608)

Sonnets

409 To the only begetter of these ensuing sonnets
Mr. W. H.

Sonnets dedication (1609). This dedication may have
been written by the publisher, Thomas Thorpe.

410 From fairest creatures we desire increase,
That thereby beauty's rose might never die.

Sonnets 1, l. 1 (1609)

411 Shall I compare thee to a summer's day?
Thou art more lovely and more temperate:
Rough winds do shake the darling buds of
May,
And summer's lease hath all too short a date.

Sonnets 18, l. 1 (1609)

412 But thy eternal summer shall not fade.

Sonnets 18, l. 9 (1609)

413 When in disgrace with fortune and men's eyes
I all alone beweep my outcast state,
And trouble deaf heav'n with my bootless
cries.

Sonnets 29, l. 1 (1609)

414 Desiring this man's art and that man's scope,
With what I most enjoy contented least.

Sonnets 29, l. 7 (1609)

415 Haply I think on thee, and then my state,
Like to the lark at break of day arising,
From sullen earth sings hymns at heaven's
gate.

Sonnets 29, l. 10 (1609)

416 For thy sweet love remembered such wealth
brings
That then I scorn to change my state with
kings.

Sonnets 29, l. 13 (1609)

417 When to the sessions of sweet silent thought
I summon up remembrance of things past.

Sonnets 30, l. 1 (1609)
See Proust 1

418 Full many a glorious morning have I seen.

Sonnets 33, l. 1 (1609)

419 Not marble, nor the gilded monuments
Of princes, shall outlive this powerful rhyme.

Sonnets 55, l. 1 (1609)

420 Like as the waves make towards the pebbled
shore,
So do our minutes hasten to their end.

Sonnets 60, l. 1 (1609)

421 That time of year thou mayst in me behold,
When yellow leaves, or none, or few do hang
Upon those boughs which shake against the
cold,
Bare ruined choirs where late the sweet birds
sang.

Sonnets 73, l. 1 (1609)

422 Farewell, thou art too dear for my possessing.

Sonnets 87, l. 1 (1609)

423 In sleep a king, but waking no such matter.

Sonnets 87, l. 14 (1609)

424 They that have power to hurt, and will do
none,
That do not do the thing they most do show,
Who, moving others, are themselves as stone,
Unmoved, cold, and to temptation slow;
They rightly do inherit heaven's graces,
And husband nature's riches from expense.

Sonnets 94, l. 1 (1609)

425 Lilies that fester smell far worse than weeds.

Sonnets 94, l. 14 (1609). Pliny the Elder wrote in
Natural History bk. 16, ch. 15: "As in the nature of
things, those which most admirably flourish, most
swiftly fester or putrefy, as roses, lilies, violets,
while others last: so in the lives of men, those that
are most blooming, are soonest turned into the
opposite."

426 When in the chronicle of wasted time
I see descriptions of the fairest wights.

Sonnets 106, l. 1 (1609)

427 Alas, 'tis true, I have gone here and there,
And made myself a motley to the view.

Sonnets 110, l. 1 (1609)

428 My nature is subdued
To what it works in, like the dyer's hand.

Sonnets 111, l. 6 (1609)

429 Let me not to the marriage of true minds
Admit impediments; love is not love
Which alters when it alteration finds.

Sonnets 116, l. 1 (1609)

430 Love alters not with his brief hours and
weeks,
But bears it out even to the edge of doom.

If this be error, and upon me proved,
I never writ, nor no man ever loved.
Sonnets 116, l. 11 (1609)

431 Th'expense of spirit in a waste of shame
Is lust in action.
Sonnets 129, l. 1 (1609)

432 My mistress' eyes are nothing like the sun;
Coral is far more red than her lips' red;
If snow be white, why then her breasts are
dun;
If hairs be wires, black wires grow on her
head.
Sonnets 130, l. 1 (1609)

433 Two loves I have, of comfort and despair,
Which, like two spirits, do suggest me still:
The better angel is a man right fair,
The worser spirit a woman colored ill.
Sonnets 144, l. 1 (1609)

434 For I have sworn thee fair, and thought thee
bright,
Who art as black as hell, as dark as night.
Sonnets 147, l. 13 (1609)

Cymbeline

435 Hark, hark, the lark at heaven's gate sings.
Cymbeline act 2, sc. 3, l. 20 (1609–1610)

436 The game is up.
Cymbeline act 3, sc. 3, l. 106 (1609–1610)

437 Fear no more the heat o'th' sun,
Nor the furious winter's rages,
Thou thy worldly task has done,
Home art gone and ta'en thy wages.
Golden lads and girls all must,
As chimney-sweepers, come to dust.
Cymbeline act 4, sc. 2, l. 258 (1609–1610)

The Tempest

438   My library
Was dukedom large enough.
The Tempest act 1, sc. 2, l. 109 (1611)

439 Full fathom five thy father lies,
Of his bones are coral made;
Those are pearls that were his eyes,
Nothing of him that doth fade
But doth suffer a sea-change
Into something rich and strange.
The Tempest act 1, sc. 2, l. 397 (1611)

440 What's past is prologue.
The Tempest act 2, sc. 1, l. 254 (1611)

441 Misery acquaints a man with strange
bedfellows!
The Tempest act 2, sc. 2, l. 39 (1611)

442 Our revels now are ended. These our actors,
As I foretold you, were all spirits and
Are melted into air, into thin air;
And—like the baseless fabric of this vision—
The cloud-capped towers, the gorgeous
palaces,
The solemn temples, the great globe itself,
Yea, all which it inherit, shall dissolve,
And like this insubstantial pageant faded,
Leave not a rack behind.
The Tempest act 4, sc. 1, l. 148 (1611)

443   We are such stuff
As dreams are made on, and our little life
Is rounded with a sleep.
The Tempest act 4, sc. 1, l. 156 (1611)
See Film Lines 112

444   But this rough magic
I here abjure.
The Tempest act 5, sc. 1, l. 50 (1611)

445   I'll break my staff,
Bury it certain fathoms in the earth,
And deeper than did ever plummet sound
I'll drown my book.
The Tempest act 5, sc. 1, l. 54 (1611)

446 Where the bee sucks, there suck I,
In a cowslip's bell I lie;
There I couch when owls do cry.
On the bat's back I do fly
After summer merrily.
Merrily, merrily, shall I live now,
Under the blossom that hangs on the bough.
The Tempest act 5, sc. 1, l. 88 (1611)

447 How beauteous mankind is! O brave new
world
That has such people in't.
The Tempest act 5, sc. 1, l. 184 (1611)

The Winter's Tale

448 [*Stage direction:*] Exit, pursued by a bear.
The Winter's Tale act 3, sc. 3, l. 58 (1610–1611)

449 When daffodils begin to peer,
    With heigh! the doxy over the dale,
    Why then comes in the sweet o'the year.
    The Winter's Tale act 4, sc. 3, l. 1 (1610–1611)

450 Jog on, jog on, the foot-path way,
    And merrily hent the stile-a:
    A merry heart goes all the day,
    Your sad tires in a mile-a.
    The Winter's Tale act 4, sc. 3, l. 121 (1610–1611)

King Henry VIII

451 Orpheus, with his lute, made trees
    And the mountain tops that freeze
    Bow themselves, when he did sing.
    King Henry VIII act 3, sc. 1, l. 3 (1613)

452 Had I but served my God with half the zeal
    I served my King, he would not in mine age
    Have left me naked to mine enemies.
    King Henry VIII act 3, sc. 2, l. 455 (1613)
    See Wolsey 1

453 Men's evil manners live in brass, their virtues
    We write in water.
    King Henry VIII act 4, sc. 2, l. 45 (1613)
    See Keats 24

Miscellaneous

454 Item, I give unto my wife my second best bed
    with the furniture.
    Will (1616)

455 Good friend, for Jesu's sake forbear
    To dig the dust enclosed here.
    Blest be the man that spares these stones,
    And curst be he that moves my bones.
    Inscription on his grave, Stratford-upon-Avon,
    England

Tupac Shakur

U.S. rap musician, 1971–1996

1 California love!
    California—knows how to party . . .
    In the city of L.A.
    In the city of good ol' Watts
    In the city, the city of Compton
    We keep it rockin'!
    "California Love" (song) (1996)

Ntozake Shange (Paulette Williams)

U.S. writer, 1948–2018

1 For Colored Girls Who Have Considered
    Suicide When the Rainbow Is Enuf.
    Title of play (1975)

Bill Shankly

British soccer manager, 1914–1981

1 Some people think football is a matter of life
    and death. . . . I can assure them it is much
    more serious than that.
    Quoted in *Sunday Times*, 4 Oct. 1981. Barry Popik
    has found that UCLA football coach Henry Russell
    "Red" Sanders was quoted as using virtually the same
    words, in reference to his team's rivalry with the
    University of Southern California, in 1966, at which
    time it was already called "an old Red Sanders line."

John Patrick Shanley

U.S. playwright, 1950–

1 In the pursuit of wrongdoing, one steps away
    from God. Of course there's a price. . . . I have
    doubts! I have such doubts!
    Doubt: A Parable sc. 9 (2004)

Fred R. Shapiro

U.S. lexicographer and librarian, 1954–

1 Law is the intersection of language and power.
    Oxford Dictionary of American Legal Quotations
    preface (1993)

Karl Jay Shapiro

U.S. poet, 1913–2000

1 Our throats were tight as tourniquets.
    "Auto Wreck" l. 22 (1942)

2 But this invites the occult mind,
    Cancels our physics with a sneer,
    And spatters all we knew of denouement
    Across the expedient and wicked stones.
    "Auto Wreck" l. 35 (1942)

3 Backwardly tolerant, Faustus was expelled
    From the Third Reich in Nineteen Thirty-nine.
    His exit caused the breaching of the Rhine,
    Except for which the frontier might have held.
    Five years unknown to enemy and friend
    He hid, appearing on the sixth to pose
    In an American desert at war's end
    Where, at his back, a dome of atoms rose.
    "The Progress of Faust" l. 49 (1958)

4 To hurt the Negro and avoid the Jew
  Is the curriculum.
  "University" l. 1 (1958)

Robert Shapiro
U.S. lawyer, 1942–

1 [*On defense lawyers' strategy at the trial of O. J. Simpson:*] Not only did we play the race card, we played it from the bottom of the deck.
  Quoted in *Times* (London), 5 Oct. 1995. Before Shapiro's comment, the *Lakeland* (Fla.) *Ledger*, 28 Aug. 1995, headlined an article by Joseph Wambaugh, "Johnnie Cochran Plays the Race Card from Bottom of Deck." Still earlier in a non-O.J. context, historian Lawrence Powell was quoted, "two Republican administrations have been playing this race card from the bottom of the deck" (*Chicago Tribune*, 17 Nov. 1991).
  See Randolph Churchill 1

William Sharp
Scottish novelist and poet, 1855–1905

1 My heart is a lonely hunter that hunts on a lonely hill.
  "The Lonely Hunter" l. 24 (1896)
  See McCullers 1

Bernard Shaw
U.S. journalist, 1940–

1 [*Question asked by Shaw to presidential candidate Michael Dukakis regarding his wife:*] Governor, if Kitty Dukakis were raped and murdered, would you favor an irrevocable death penalty for the killer?
  Presidential debate, 13 Oct. 1988

David T. Shaw
U.S. singer, fl. 1843

1 O Columbia the gem of the ocean,
  The home of the brave and the free,
  The shrine of each patriot's devotion,
  A world offers homage to thee.
  "Columbia, the Gem of the Ocean" (song) (1843)

George Bernard Shaw
Irish author and socialist, 1856–1950

1 The Family is a petty despotism; . . . a school in which men learn to despise women and women to mistrust men (much more than is necessary); a slaughterhouse for children (the

firstborn succumbing to unskilled treatment, the lastborn to neglect). . . . Unfortunately, we cannot as yet do without it; and therefore we put a good face on the matter by conferring upon it the conventional attribute of sacredness, and impudently proclaiming it the source of all the virtues it has well-nigh killed in us.
  "Socialism and the Family" (1886)

2 The man of business . . . goes on Sunday to the church with the regularity of the village blacksmith, there to renounce and abjure before his God the line of conduct which he intends to pursue with all his might during the following week.
  Fabian Essays in Socialism pt. 1 "Economic" (1889)

3 We do not seek for truth in the abstract. . . . Every man sees what he looks for, and hears what he listens for, and nothing else.
  Letter to E. C. Chapman, 29 July 1891

4 The fickleness of the women I love is only equaled by the infernal constancy of the women who love me.
  The Philanderer act 2 (1893)

5 Patriotism is, fundamentally, a conviction that a particular country is the best in the world because you were born in it.
  The World, 15 Nov. 1893

6 I dread success. To have succeeded is to have finished one's business on earth, like the male spider, who is killed by the female the moment he has succeeded in his courtship. I like a state of continual becoming, with a goal in front and not behind.
  Letter to Ellen Terry, 28 Aug. 1896

7 With the single exception of Homer, there is no eminent writer, not even Sir Walter Scott, whom I can despise so entirely as I despise Shakespeare when I measure my mind against his.
Saturday Review, 26 Sept. 1896

8 I . . . once read the Old Testament and the four Gospels straight through, from a vainglorious desire to do what nobody else had done.
Saturday Review, 6 Feb. 1897

9 Oh, you are a very poor soldier—a chocolate cream soldier!
Arms and the Man act 1 (1898)

10 There is nothing so bad or so good that you will not find Englishmen doing it; but you will never find an Englishman in the wrong. He does everything on principle. He fights you on patriotic principles; he robs you on business principles; he enslaves you on imperial principles.
The Man of Destiny (1898)

11 Man and Superman.
Title of play (1903)
See Nietzsche 13; Radio Catchphrases 21; Radio Catchphrases 22; Siegel 1; Television Catchphrases 6

12 This is the true joy in life, the being used for a purpose recognized by yourself as a mighty one; the being thoroughly worn out before you are thrown on the scrap heap; the being a force of nature instead of a feverish selfish little clod of ailments and grievances complaining that the world will not devote itself to making you happy.
Man and Superman epistle dedicatory (1903)

13 A lifetime of happiness! No man alive could bear it: it would be hell on earth.
Man and Superman act 1 (1903)

14 Hell is full of musical amateurs: music is the brandy of the damned.
Man and Superman act 3 (1903)

15 An Englishman thinks he is moral when he is only uncomfortable.
Man and Superman act 3 (1903)

16 There are two tragedies in life. One is not to get your heart's desire. The other is to get it.
Man and Superman act 4 (1903)
See Goethe 15; T. H. Huxley 4; Modern Proverbs 14; Teresa of Ávila 2; Wilde 56; Wilde 74

17 He who can, does. He who cannot, teaches.
Man and Superman "Maxims for Revolutionists" (1903). A further extension appears in Jacob M. Braude, *Speaker's Encyclopedia of Stories, Quotations, and Anecdotes* (1955): "Those who can, do; those who can't teach; and those who can't do anything at all, teach the teachers."

18 The golden rule is that there are no golden rules.
Man and Superman "Maxims for Revolutionists" (1903)

19 Democracy substitutes election by the incompetent many for appointment by the corrupt few.
Man and Superman "Maxims for Revolutionists" (1903)

20 Marriage is popular because it combines the maximum of temptation with the maximum of opportunity.
Man and Superman "Maxims for Revolutionists" (1903)

21 If you strike a child take care that you strike it in anger, even at the risk of maiming it for life. A blow in cold blood neither can nor should be forgiven.
Man and Superman "Maxims for Revolutionists" (1903)

22 The reasonable man adapts himself to the world: the unreasonable one persists in trying to adapt the world to himself. Therefore all progress depends on the unreasonable man.
Man and Superman "Maxims for Revolutionists" (1903)
See Hawthorne 18

23 Every man over forty is a scoundrel.
Man and Superman "Maxims for Revolutionists" (1903)

24 On Christmas Day it is proclaimed that Christianity established peace on earth and good will towards men. Next day the Christian, with refreshed soul, goes back to the manufacture of submarines and torpedoes.
"The Solidarity of Social-Democracy" (1906)

25 It's usually pointed out that women are not fit for political power, and ought not to be trusted with a vote because they are politically ignorant, socially prejudiced, narrow-minded, and selfish. True enough, but precisely the same is true of men!
Tribune (London), 12 Mar. 1906

26 The greatest of our evils and the worst of crimes is poverty.

Major Barbara preface (1907)

27 I am a Millionaire. That is my religion.

Major Barbara act 2 (1907)

28 All professions are conspiracies against the laity.

The Doctor's Dilemma act 1 (1911)

29 When two people are under the influence of the most violent, most insane, most delusive, and most transient of passions, they are required to swear that they will remain in that excited, abnormal, and exhausting condition continuously until death do them part.

Getting Married preface (1911)

30 The early Christian rules of life were not made to last, because the early Christians did not believe that the world itself was going to last.

Getting Married (1911)

31 Assassination is the extreme form of censorship.

The Shewing-up of Blanco Posnet preface (1911)

32 If you demand my authorities for this and that, I must reply that only those who have never hunted up the authorities as I have believe that there is any authority who is not contradicted flatly by some other authority.

Androcles and the Lion preface (1913)

33 I have not wasted my life trifling with literary fools in taverns as [Samuel] Johnson did when he should have been shaking England with the thunder of his spirit.

Misalliance preface (1914)

34 A perpetual holiday is a good working definition of hell.

Misalliance preface (1914)

35 Anybody on for a game of tennis?

Misalliance (1914). "Tennis, anyone?" was later a catchphrase associated with drawing room comedies. Humphrey Bogart is often said to have originated that phrase, but no example of its use has ever been found in the plays in which he appeared. The earliest example found to date for "Tennis, anyone?" is in the *Oakland Tribune*, 14 Mar. 1935.

36 I've got a soul: don't tell me I haven't. Cut me up and you can't find it. Cut up a steam engine and you can't find the steam. But, by George, it makes the engine go.

Misalliance (1914)

37 [*Referring to World War I:*] When all the world goes mad, one must accept madness as sanity, since sanity is, in the last analysis, nothing but the madness on which the whole world happens to agree.

Letter to Maxim Gorky, 28 Dec. 1915

38 It is impossible for an Englishman to open his mouth without making some other Englishman despise him.

Pygmalion preface (1916)

39 Women upset everything. When you let them into your life, you find that the woman is driving at one thing and you're driving at another.

Pygmalion act 2 (1916)

40 Gin was mother's milk to her.

Pygmalion act 3 (1916)

41 Walk! Not bloody likely.

Pygmalion act 3 (1916). This line created a sensation because of the taboo status at the time of the word *bloody*.

42 We all profess the deepest regard for liberty; but no sooner does anyone claim to exercise it than we declare with horror that we are in favor of liberty but not of licence, and demand indignantly whether true freedom can ever mean freedom to do wrong, to preach sedition and immorality, to utter blasphemy. Yet this is exactly what liberty does mean.

W. E. A. Education Year Book preface to pt. 1 (1918)

43 All great truths begin as blasphemies.

Annajanska (1919)

44 I am the sort of man who devotes his life to the salvation of humanity in the abstract, and can't bear to give a penny to a starving widow.

Letter to Sister Ethna, 1 Oct. 1920

45 You see things; and you say "Why?" But I dream things that never were; and I say "Why not?"

Back to Methuselah pt. 1, act 1 (1921). This was a favorite quotation of Robert F. Kennedy's, and Edward M. Kennedy used it in his eulogy of Robert Kennedy.

46 I have defined the 100 per cent American as 99 per cent an idiot.

N.Y. Times, 19 Dec. 1930

47 Democracy, then, cannot be government by the people: it can only be government by consent of the governed. Unfortunately, when democratic statesmen propose to govern us by our own consent, they find that we don't want to be governed at all, and that we regard rates and taxes and rents and death duties as intolerable burdens. What we want to know is how little government we can get along with without being murdered in our beds.

The Apple Cart preface (1930)

48 If you don't begin to be a revolutionist at the age of twenty, then at fifty you will be a most impossible old fossil. If you are a red revolutionary at the age of twenty, you have some chance of being up-to-date when you are forty!

"Universities and Education" (speech at University of Hong Kong), 12 Feb. 1933
See John Adams 19; Batbie 1; Clemenceau 5

49 The rain in Spain stays mainly in the plains.

Pygmalion (motion picture) (1938). Nigel Rees notes in *Cassell's Movie Quotations:* "(Note that is *plains.*) An elocution exercise said to have been invented by the director, Anthony Asquith, and approved by Shaw (though this [does] not appear in Shaw's published scenes for the film script)."

50 In Hampshire, Hereford, and Hertford, Hurricanes hardly ever happen.

Pygmalion (motion picture) (1938). See note for quotation above.

51 [*Henry Higgins, played by Leslie Howard, speaking:*] Where the devil are my slippers, Eliza?

Pygmalion (motion picture) (1938). According to Nigel Rees, *Cassell's Movie Quotations,* these were "Last words of film, not in Shaw's original text nor in his screenplay. He disapproved of anything that even hinted at a romantic interest between Higgins and Eliza."

52 We speak of war gods, but not of mathematician gods, poet or painter gods, or inventor gods. Nobody has ever called me a god; I am at best a sage. We worship all the conquerors, but have only one Prince of Peace, who was horribly put to death, and if he lived

in these islands, would have some difficulty in getting exempted from military service as a conscientious objector.

Everybody's Political What's What? ch. 16 (1944)

53 A government which robs Peter to pay Paul can always depend on the support of Paul.

Everybody's Political What's What? ch. 30 (1944)

54 [*Referring to film producer Samuel Goldwyn:*] Well, Mr. Goldwyn, there is not much use in going on. There is this difference between you and me: You are only interested in art and I am only interested in money.

Quoted in *Baltimore American,* 1 May 1921

55 [*When Isadora Duncan regretted that they could not have a child together, saying, "Think what a child it would be, with my body and your brain":*] I know, but suppose the child was so unlucky as to have my body and your brain?

Quoted in Lewis and Faye Copeland, *10,000 Jokes, Toasts, & Stories* (1939). Garson O'Toole has discovered a similar anecdote from 1925, with Duncan allegedly writing to Shaw and Shaw allegedly replying: "It might happen that our child would have my body and your brain" (*Minutes of the Seventeenth Session of the Interfraternity Conference*). A still earlier discovery by O'Toole shows that the *Boston Globe,* 7 Dec. 1923, recounted an analogous putative exchange between Duncan and Anatole France.

56 [*Of Archibald Primrose, Fifth Earl of Rosebery:*] [A] man who never missed a chance of missing an opportunity.

Quoted in Robert Rhodes, *Rosebery* (1963)
See Eban 3

57 Youth . . . is wasted on the young.

Attributed in Frank H. Lee, *Tokyo Calendar* (1934). In the *Rockford* (Ill.) *Register-Republic,* 14 Feb. 1931, Shaw was quoted as saying about youth, "What a pity that it has to be wasted on children!"

58 England and America are two countries separated by the same language.

Attributed in *Christian Science Monitor,* 5 Sept. 1942
See Wilde 4

59 [Dancing is] a perpendicular expression of a horizontal desire.

Attributed in *New Statesman,* 23 Mar. 1962

Hartley Shawcross

German-born English politician and lawyer, 1902–2003

1 We are the masters at the moment, and not only at the moment, but for a very long time to come.

Speech in House of Commons, 2 Apr. 1946. Frequently misquoted as "We are the masters now."

John A. Shedd

U.S. author, 1859–1928

1 A ship in harbor is safe, but that is not what ships are built for.

Salt from My Attic (1928)

Wilfrid Sheed

English novelist, 1930–2011

1 Suicide . . . is about life, being in fact the sincerest form of criticism life gets.

N.Y. Times Book Review, 7 May 1972

Charlie Sheen (Carlos Irwin Estévez)

U.S. actor, 1965–

1 I'm so tired of pretending like my life isn't perfect and bitching and just winning every second.

Alex Jones radio show, 24 Feb. 2011

2 I am on a drug. It's called "Charlie Sheen." It's not available because if you try it once, you will die. Your face will melt off and your children will weep over your exploded body.

ABC *Good Morning America* (television program), 28 Feb. 2011

3 [That way of life] was written for normal people, people who aren't special, people who don't have tiger blood and Adonis DNA.

NBC *Today Show* (television program), 28 Feb. 2011

Charles Sheldon

U.S. clergyman, 1857–1946

1 What would Jesus do?

In His Steps ch. 1 (1896). This slogan was popularized by Sheldon, but the words can be found earlier, for example in Charles Bullock, *Home Words for Heart and Hearth* (1880).

Mary Wollstonecraft Shelley

English novelist, 1797–1851

1 Frankenstein.

Title of book (1818)

2 It was the secrets of heaven and earth that I desired to learn.

Frankenstein ch. 2 (1818)

3 I beheld the wretch—the miserable monster whom I had created.

Frankenstein ch. 5 (1818)

4 All men hate the wretched; how, then, must I be hated, who am miserable beyond all living things! Yet you, my creator, detest and spurn me, thy creature, to whom thou art bound by ties only dissoluble by the annihilation of one of us.

Frankenstein ch. 10 (1818)

5 Everywhere I see bliss, from which I alone am irrevocably excluded.

Frankenstein ch. 10 (1818)

6 Nothing contributes so much to tranquilize the mind as a steady purpose—a point on which the soul may fix its intellectual eye.

Frankenstein Letter 1 (1818)

7 You seek for knowledge and wisdom as I once did; and I ardently hope that the gratification of your wishes may not be a serpent to sting you, as mine has been.

Frankenstein Letter 4 (1818)

8 [*Replying to someone who advised her to send her son to a school "where they will teach him to think for himself!":*] Teach him to think for himself? Oh, my God, teach him rather to think like other people!

Quoted in Matthew Arnold, *Essays in Criticism, Second Series* (1888)

Percy Bysshe Shelley

English poet, 1792–1822

1 Thou Paradise of exiles, Italy!

"Julian and Maddalo" l. 57 (1818)

2 I met Murder on the way—
He had a mask like Castlereagh.

"The Mask of Anarchy" l. 5 (1819)

3 Oh, lift me as a wave, a leaf, a cloud!
  I fall upon the thorns of life! I bleed!
  "Ode to the West Wind" l. 53 (1819)

4 If Winter comes, can Spring be far behind?
  "Ode to the West Wind" l. 70 (1819)

5 I met a traveller from an antique land
  Who said: Two vast and trunkless legs of stone
  Stand in the desert.
  "Ozymandias" l. 1 (1819)

6 Near them, on the sand,
  Half sunk, a shattered visage lies, whose frown,
  And wrinkled lip, and sneer of cold command,
  Tell that its sculptor well those passions read.
  "Ozymandias" l. 3 (1819)

7 And on the pedestal these words appear:
  "My name is Ozymandias, king of kings:
  Look on my works, ye Mighty, and despair!"
  Nothing beside remains. Round the decay
  Of that colossal wreck, boundless and bare
  The lone and level sands stretch far away.
  "Ozymandias" l. 9 (1819)

8 An old, mad, blind, despised, and dying king.
  "Sonnet: England in 1819" l. 1 (written 1819)

9 Hail to thee, blithe Spirit!
  Bird thou never wert.
  "To a Skylark" l. 1 (1819)

10 And singing still dost soar, and soaring ever
   singest.
   "To a Skylark" l. 10 (1819)

11 Our sincerest laughter
   With some pain is fraught;
   Our sweetest songs are those that tell of saddest
   thought.
   "To a Skylark" l. 88 (1819)

12 The dust of creeds outworn.
   Prometheus Unbound act 1, l. 697 (1820)

13 I weep for Adonais—he is dead!
   Oh, weep for Adonais! though our tears
   Thaw not the frost which binds so dear a head!
   Adonais l. 1 (1821)

14 The One remains, the many change and pass;
   Heaven's light forever shines, Earth's shadows
   fly;
   Life, like a dome of many-colored glass,
   Stains the white radiance of Eternity.
   Adonais l. 460 (1821)

15 Poets are the hierophants of an unapprehended
   inspiration; the mirrors of the gigantic shadow
   which futurity casts upon the present; the
   words which express what they understand not;
   the trumpets which sing to battle, and feel not
   what they inspire; the influence which is moved
   not, but moves. Poets are the unacknowledged
   legislators of the world.
   A Defence of Poetry (written 1821)
   *See Auden 22; Auden 39; Andrew Fletcher 1; Samuel
   Johnson 22; Twain 104*

16 Best and brightest, come away!
   "To Jane: The Invitation" l. 1 (1822)
   See Halberstam 1; Heber 1

17 Swiftly walk o'er the western wave,
   Spirit of Night!
   "To Night" l. 1 (1824)

18 The desire of the moth for the star,
   Of the night for the morrow,
   The devotion to something afar
   From the sphere of our sorrow.
   "To—: One word is too often profaned" l. 13 (1824)

Gilbert Shelton
U.S. cartoonist, 1940–

1 Dope will get you through times of no money
  better than money will get you through times of
  no dope.
  Quoted in *The Rag* (Austin, Tex.), 24 Nov. 1969
  See Anne Herbert 2

Ron Shelton
U.S. screenwriter and film director, 1945–

1 White Men Can't Jump.
  Title of motion picture (1992)

Alan Shepard
U.S. astronaut, 1923–1998

1 [*Transmitted question to Mission Control when his
  space flight's liftoff was repeatedly delayed:*] Why
  don't you fix your little problem and light this
  candle?
  Quoted in *L.A. Times*, 5 May 1966

2 [*Alleged comment before entering his capsule for
  the first American space flight, 5 May 1961:*] Just
  think, the contract on this thing went to the
  lowest bidder.
  Attributed in *Bryant* (Tex.) *Daily Eagle*, 26 Apr. 1963

Philip Henry Sheridan

U.S. general, 1831–1888

1 If I owned Texas and Hell, I would rent out Texas and live in Hell.

Quoted in Independent, *19 Apr. 1866*

Richard Brinsley Sheridan

Irish playwright and orator, 1751–1816

1 You write with ease, to show your breeding, But easy writing's vile hard reading.

"Clio's Protest" (written 1771)

2 He is the very pineapple of politeness!

The Rivals *act 3, sc. 3 (1775)*

3 If I reprehend any thing in this world, it is the use of my oracular tongue, and a nice derangement of epitaphs!

The Rivals *act 3, sc. 3 (1775)*

4 She's as headstrong as an allegory on the banks of the Nile.

The Rivals *act 3, sc. 3 (1775)*

5 Here's to the maiden of bashful fifteen
Here's to the widow of fifty
Here's to the flaunting, extravagant quean;
And here's to the housewife that's thrifty.

The School for Scandal *act 3, sc. 3 (1777)*

6 An unforgiving eye, and a damned disinheriting countenance!

The School for Scandal *act 4, sc. 1 (1777)*

John Sherman

U.S. politician, 1823–1900

1 I [have] come home to look after my fences.

Quoted in N.Y. Times, *27 Mar. 1887. Sherman's remark is said to have inspired the political phrase "fence-mending." He explained to the* Times: *"While I was Secretary of the Treasury I came home to Mansfield [Ohio] for a few days at one time. As soon as I got there there was an influx of newspaper correspondents from all parts. . . . One of them came to me and boldly asked me what I was doing in Ohio. It just happened that on that day I had contracted with a man to repair some fences on my place that were in a tumble-down condition. So when that newspaper man asked me what I was doing in Ohio I told him that I had come home to look after my fences."*

Robert B. Sherman

U.S. songwriter, 1925–2012

1 Supercalifragilisticexpialidocious!

Title of song (1964). "The word" was popularized by this song in the movie Mary Poppins. *However, usage of very similar words has been documented as far back as 1931.*

Sidney Sherman

U.S. general, 1805–1873

1 Remember the Alamo!

Battle cry, San Jacinto, 21 Apr. 1836. These words, chanted by advancing troops in the battle of San Jacinto, are traditionally attributed to their commander, Sherman. Sam Houston's letter to David G. Burnet, 25 Apr. 1836, stated: "Col. Sherman with his regiment having commenced the action upon our left wing, the whole line at the centre and on the right, advancing in double quick time, rung the war cry 'Remember the Alamo.'"

William Tecumseh Sherman

U.S. military leader, 1820–1891

1 You cannot qualify war in harsher terms than I will. War is cruelty, and you cannot refine it; and those who brought war into our country deserve all the curses and maledictions a people can pour out.

Letter to Mayor Calhoun of Atlanta, Ga., and others, 12 Sept. 1864
See Napoleon 11; William Tecumseh Sherman 4

2 Hold on to Allatoona, to the last. I will help you.

Flag signal at Battle of Allatoona, Ga., to General John Murray Corse, 5 Oct. 1864. Usually quoted as "Hold the fort! I am coming!"
See Bliss 1

3 I hereby state, and mean all that I say, that I never have been and never will be a candidate for President; that if nominated by either party I should peremptorily decline, and even if unanimously elected I should decline to serve.

Letter to N.Y. Herald, *25 May 1871*
See William Tecumseh Sherman 5

4 There is many a boy here to-day who looks on war as all glory, but, boys, it is all hell.

Speech to reunion of veterans, Columbus, Ohio, 11 Aug. 1880. Sherman's words are famous in the paraphrase "War is hell," but, as shown in the above record of the speech as given in the Ohio State Journal, *12 Aug. 1880, Sherman did not utter this precise saying there.* Bartlett's Familiar Quotations

prints "war is hell" with the source "Attributed to a graduation address at Michigan Military Academy [June 19, 1879]." However, research by Buzz Brown, president of the Greater West Bloomfield [Ohio] Historical Society, shows that this attribution rests solely on the recollections of Charles Oliver Brown decades later. The real coiner of "war is hell" may be Napoleon Bonaparte.
See Napoleon 11; William Tecumseh Sherman 1

5 I will not accept if nominated, and will not serve if elected.

Telegram to General Henderson (1884). Sherman's telegram, sent to the Republican National Convention while he was being urged to run for president, was quoted by his son in an addendum to the elder Sherman's *Memoirs* (4th ed., 1891). The words are frequently quoted as "If nominated, I will not run. If elected, I will not serve."
See William Tecumseh Sherman 3

6 General Grant *is a great general*. I know him well. He stood by me when I was crazy, and I stood by him when he was drunk; and now, sir, we stand by each other always.

Quoted in L. P. Brockett, *Our Great Captains* (1865)

Robert E. Sherwood
U.S. playwright, 1896–1955

1 The trouble with me is, I belong to a vanishing race. I'm one of the intellectuals.
The Petrified Forest act 1 (1934)

2 Poor, dear God. Playing Idiot's Delight. The game that never means anything, and never ends.
Idiot's Delight act 2, sc. 2 (1936)

Brooke Shields
U.S. actress, 1965–

1 Smoking . . . kills you, and if you are killed, you have lost a very important part of your life.
Testimony at House of Representatives hearings on cigarette advertising, 25 June 1981

Shijing (Book of Songs)
Chinese poetry collection

1 Merrily the ospreys cry,
On the islet in the stream.
Gentle and graceful is the girl,
A fit wife for the gentleman.
"Crying Ospreys: Zhou and the South" (translation by Xianyi and Gladys Yang)

Gary Shilling
U.S. economist, 1937–

1 Markets can remain irrational a lot longer than you and I can remain solvent.
Forbes, 15 Feb. 1993

Jonathan Shipley
English clergyman, 1714–1788

1 The true art of government consists in *not governing too much*.
A Sermon Preached Before the Incorporated Society for the Propagation of the Gospel in Foreign Parts (1773)
See Ralph Waldo Emerson 29; O'Sullivan 1; Thoreau 3

Keith Shocklee
U.S. music producer, 1962–

1 Fight the Power.
Title of song (1989). Cowritten with Carlton Ridenhour and Eric Sadler.

2 Elvis was a hero to most but he never meant shit to me
You see straight-up racist that sucker was Simple and plain
Motherfuck him and John Wayne
Cos I'm black and I'm proud
I'm ready and hyped plus I'm amped
Most of my heroes don't appear on no stamps.
"Fight the Power" (song) (1989). Cowritten with Carlton Ridenhour and Eric Sadler.

Mikhail Sholokhov
Russian novelist, 1905–1984

1 And Quiet Flows the Don.
Title of book (1934)

Robert Shrum
U.S. political consultant, 1943–

1 [*On the Republican Party's idea of diversity in their ticket:*] Presidents of two different oil companies.
Quoted in *L.A. Times*, 27 July 2000. Also often attributed to film director Rob Reiner, but this citation predates documented Reiner usages.

Algernon Sidney
English conspirator, 1622–1683

1 The law is established, which no passion can disturb. 'Tis void of desire and fear, lust and anger . . . 'Tis deaf, inexorable, inflexible.
Discourses Concerning Government ch. 3, sec. 15 (1698)
See John Adams 3

Philip Sidney
English poet and soldier, 1554–1586

1 Thou blind man's mark, thou fool's self-chosen snare,
Fond fancy's scum, and dregs of scatt'red thought,
Band of all evils, cradle of causeless care,
Thou web of will, whose end is never wrought;

Desire, desire! I have too dearly bought,
With price of mangled mind, thy worthless ware;
Too long, too long, asleep thou hast me brought,
Who should my mind to higher things prepare.
Certain Sonnets no. 31, l. 1 (written 1577–1581)

2 Leave me, O Love which reachest but to dust,
And thou, my mind, aspire to higher things;
Grow rich in that which never taketh rust;
Whatever fades, but fading pleasure brings.
Certain Sonnets no. 32, l. 1 (written 1577–1581)

3 *Splendidis longum valedico nugis.*
A long farewell to shining trifles.
Certain Sonnets no. 32, l. 15 (written 1577–1581)

4 My dear, my better half.
Arcadia bk. 3, ch. 12 (1581)

5 With how sad steps, O Moon, thou climb'st the skies;
How silently, and with how wan a face.
Astrophel and Stella sonnet 31 (1591)

6 [*Remark while giving his water to a soldier more seriously wounded than himself, Battle of Zutphen, 1586:*] Thy necessity is yet greater than mine.
Quoted in Fulke Greville, *Life of Sir Philip Sidney* (1652). Usually quoted as "Thy need . . ."

Jerry Siegel
U.S. comic book writer, 1914–1996

1 When maturity was reached, he [Superman] discovered he could easily: leap 1/8th of a

mile; hurdle a twenty-story building . . . raise tremendous weights . . . run faster than an express train . . . and that nothing less than a bursting shell could penetrate his skin!
Action Comics no. 1, June 1938. Cowritten with Joe Shuster.
See Nietzsche 13; Radio Catchphrases 21; Radio Catchphrases 22; George Bernard Shaw 11; Television Catchphrases 6

Henryk Sienkiewicz
Polish writer, 1846–1916

1 The greater philosopher a man is, the more difficult it is for him to answer the foolish questions of common people.
Quo Vadis ch. 19 (1896) (translation by Jeremiah Curtin)

Emmanuel Joseph Sieyès
French clergyman and statesman, 1748–1836

1 Who will dare deny that the Third Estate contains within itself all that is needed to constitute a nation? . . . What would the Third Estate be without the privileged classes? It would be a whole in itself, and a prosperous one. Nothing can be done without it, and everything would be done far better without the others.
Qu'est-ce que le Tiers-État? (1789)

2 [*Response when asked what he had done during the French Revolution:*] *J'ai vécu.*
I survived.
Quoted in F. A. M. Mignet, *Notice Historique sur la Vie et les Travaux de M. le Comte de Sieyès* (1836)

Simone Signoret
French actress, 1921–1985

1 Chains do not hold a marriage together. It is thread, hundreds of tiny threads which sew people together through the years.
Quoted in *Daily Mail* (London), 4 July 1978

Norodom Sihanouk
Cambodian king and prime minister, 1922–2012

1 [*On the U.S. bombing of Cambodia:*] What is the difference between burning and gassing people

in ovens and doing it to a whole nation out in the open?

My War with the CIA: Cambodia's Fight for Survival ch. 18 (1973)

Leslie Marmon Silko

U.S. writer, 1948–

1 It is only a matter of time, Indian
you can't sleep with the river forever.

"Indian Song: Survival" l. 34 (1981)

Alan Sillitoe

English writer, 1928–2010

1 The Loneliness of the Long-Distance Runner.

Title of book (1959)

Sime Silverman

U.S. newspaper publisher, 1873–1933

1 [*Headline reporting stock market crash:*] Wall St. Lays an Egg.

Variety, 30 Oct. 1929

Shel Silverstein

U.S. cartoonist, children's book author, and songwriter, 1930–1999

1 A Boy Named Sue.

Title of song (1969)

Georges Simenon

Belgian-born French novelist, 1903–1989

1 I have made love to ten thousand women since I was thirteen and a half. It wasn't in any way a vice. I've no sexual vices. But I needed to communicate.

Quoted in *L'Express*, 21 Feb. 1977

Georg Simmel

German sociologist, 1858–1918

1 One need not be a Caesar truly to understand Caesar, nor a second Luther to understand Luther.

Die Probleme der Geschichtsphilosophie, 2nd ed., ch. 1 (1905)

Carly Simon

U.S. singer and songwriter, 1945–

1 You walked into the party like you were walking onto a yacht.

"You're So Vain" (song) (1972)

2 You're so vain, you probably think this song is about you.

"You're So Vain" (song) (1972)

Neil Simon

U.S. playwright, 1927–2018

1 The Odd Couple.

Title of play (1965)

Paul Simon

U.S. singer and songwriter, 1941–

1 Hello darkness my old friend
I've come to talk with you again.

"The Sounds of Silence" (song) (1964)

2 And the sign said, "The words of the prophets
Are written on subway walls
And tenement halls."
And whisper'd in the sounds of silence.

"The Sounds of Silence" (song) (1964)

3 Time, time, time, see what's become of me
While I looked around for my possibilities.
I was so hard to please,
Look around
Leaves are brown
And the sky is a hazy shade of winter.

"A Hazy Shade of Winter" (song) (1966)

4 Counting the cars
On the New Jersey Turnpike.
They've all come
To look for America.

"America" (song) (1968)

5 In the clearing stands a boxer,
And a fighter by his trade
And he carries the reminders
Of ev'ry glove that laid him down
Or cut him till he cried out
In his anger and his shame,
"I am leaving, I am leaving."
But the fighter still remains.

"The Boxer" (song) (1968)

6 Going to the candidates debate
Laugh about it, shout about it
When you've got to choose
Ev'ry way you look at it, you lose.
"Mrs. Robinson" (song) (1968)

7 Where have you gone, Joe DiMaggio?
A nation turns its lonely eyes to you
What's that you say, Mrs. Robinson
Joltin' Joe has left and gone away.
"Mrs. Robinson" (song) (1968)

8 Like a bridge over troubled water
I will lay me down.
"Bridge over Troubled Water" (song) (1969).
According to the *New Penguin Dictionary of Modern
Quotations,* "the words are said to have been inspired
by 'Mary Don't You Weep,' a song by the gospel group
the Swan Silvertones, which included the line 'I'll be
a bridge over deep water if you trust in my name.'"

9 We come on the ship they call the Mayflower
We come on the ship that sailed the moon
We come in the age's most uncertain hours
And sing an American tune.
"American Tune" (song) (1973)

10 There must be fifty ways to leave your lover . . .
You just slip out the back, Jack
Make a new plan, Stan
You don't need to be coy, Roy.
"50 Ways to Leave Your Lover" (song) (1975)

11 Slip slidin' away, slip slidin' away
You know the nearer your destination, the more
    you're slip slidin' away.
"Slip Slidin' Away" (song) (1977)

12 The Mississippi Delta was shining
Like a National guitar.
"Graceland" (song) (1986)

Simonides

Greek poet, ca. 556 B.C.–468 B.C.

1 [*Epitaph for the Spartans killed at the Battle of
Thermopylae, 480 B.C.:*]
Go, tell the Spartans, thou who passest by,
That here obedient to their laws we lie.
Quoted in Herodotus, *Histories*

George Gaylord Simpson

U.S. paleontologist, 1902–1984

1 Man is the result of a purposeless and
materialistic process that did not have him in
mind.
The Meaning of Evolution epilogue (1949)

Louis Simpson

Jamaican-born U.S. poet, 1923–2012

1 I saw the best minds of my generation
Reading their poems to Vassar girls,
Being interviewed by Mademoiselle.
Having their publicity handled by professionals.
When can I go into an editorial office
And have my stuff published because I'm
    weird?
I could go on writing like this forever.
"Squeal" l. 28 (1959)
See Ginsberg 7

O. J. Simpson

U.S. football player, entertainer, and alleged
murderer, 1947–

1 Absolutely, 100 percent not guilty.
Plea at murder trial, Los Angeles, Calif., 22 July 1994

2 If I Did It.
Title of book (2007)

Valerie Simpson

U.S. songwriter and singer, 1946–

1 'Cause baby there ain't no mountain high
    enough
Ain't no valley low enough
Ain't no river wide enough
To keep me from getting to you babe.
"Ain't No Mountain High Enough" (song) (1967).
Cowritten with Nickolas Ashford.

Frank Sinatra

U.S. singer and actor, 1915–1998

1 Do be do be do.
"Strangers in the Night" (song) (1966). Although the
lyrics for this song were written by Charles Singleton
and Eddie Snyder, this quotation is thoroughly
identified with Sinatra as the singer.

2 May you live a thousand years, and may the last
voice you hear be mine.
Quoted in *Lima* (Ohio) *News*, 13 June 1977

Upton Sinclair

U.S. author and socialist, 1878–1968

1 [*Of his book* The Jungle:] I aimed at the public's heart, and by accident I hit it in the stomach.
Cosmopolitan, Oct. 1906

2 They put him in a place where the snow could not beat in, where the cold could not eat through his bones; they brought him food and drink—why, in the name of heaven, if they must punish him, did they not put his family in jail and leave him outside—why could they find no better way to punish him than to leave three weak women and six helpless children to starve and freeze?
The Jungle ch. 16 (1906)

3 All art is propaganda.
Mammonart ch. 2 (1925)

4 I used to say to our audiences: "It is difficult to get a man to understand something, when his salary depends upon his not understanding it!"
I, Candidate for Governor ch. 20 (1935)

Isaac Bashevis Singer

Polish-born U.S. writer, 1904–1991

1 Buildings will collapse, power plants will stop generating electricity. Generals will drop atomic bombs on their own populations. Mad revolutionaries will run in the streets, crying fantastic slogans. I have often thought it would begin in New York. This metropolis has all the symptoms of a mind gone berserk.
Collected Stories "The Cafeteria" (1986)

2 We have to believe in free will. We have no choice.
Quoted in *N.Y. Times,* 15 June 1982

Peter Singer

Australian philosopher, 1946–

1 Killing them [infants], therefore, cannot be equated with killing normal human beings, or any other self-conscious beings. No infant—disabled or not—has as strong a claim to life as beings capable of seeing themselves as distinct entities, existing over time.
Practical Ethics ch. 7 (1979)

Sir Mix-a-Lot (Anthony Ray)

U.S. rap musician, 1963–

1 I like big butts and I cannot lie
You other brothers can't deny.
"Baby Got Back" (song) (1992)

Noble Sissle

U.S. songwriter, 1889–1975

1 I'm just wild about Harry,
And Harry's wild about me.
"I'm Just Wild About Harry" (song) (1921)

Sitting Bull

Native American leader, ca. 1830–1890

1 The life of white men is slavery. They are prisoners in towns or farms. The life my people want is a life of freedom. I have seen nothing that a white man has, houses or railways or clothing or food, that is as good as the right to move in the open country, and live in our own fashion.
Quoted in James Creelman, *On the Great Highway: The Wanderings and Adventures of a Special Correspondent* (1901)

Edith Sitwell

English poet and critic, 1887–1964

1 Jane, Jane,
Tall as a crane,
The morning light creaks down again.
"Aubade" l. 1 (1923)

2 [*Of Richard Porson:*] There were moments when his memory failed him; and he would forget to eat dinner, though he never forgot a quotation.
English Eccentrics ch. 8 (1933)

3 Still falls the Rain—
Dark as the world of man, black as our loss—
Blind as the nineteen hundred and forty nails
Upon the Cross.
"Still Falls the Rain" l. 1 (1942)

4 A lady asked me why, on most occasions, I wore black.
"Are you in mourning?"
"Yes."
"For whom are you in mourning?"
"For the world."
Taken Care Of ch. 1 (1965)

B. F. Skinner

U.S. psychologist, 1904–1990

1 The real question is not whether machines think but whether men do.
Contingencies of Reinforcement ch. 9 (1969)

Cornelia Otis Skinner

U.S. actress and author, 1901–1979

1 Woman's virtue is man's greatest invention.
Quoted in *Lima* (Ohio) *News*, 8 Nov. 1957

Grace Slick

U.S. rock singer, 1939–

1 One pill makes you larger
And one pill makes you small
And the ones that mother gives you
Don't do anything at all.
Go ask Alice
When she's ten feet tall.
"White Rabbit" (song) (1967)
See Carroll 11

2 Remember what the dormouse said:
"Feed your head."
"White Rabbit" (song) (1967)

Edwin E. Slosson

U.S. author and chemist, 1865–1929

1 Learning is that mysterious process by means of which the contents of the note-book of the professor are transferred through the instrument of the fountain pen to the note-book of the student without passing through the mind of either.
Quoted in Harry L. Miller, *Creative Learning and Teaching* (1927)

Elizabeth Smart

Canadian poet and novelist, 1913–1986

1 By Grand Central Station I Sat Down and Wept.
Title of book (1945)
See Bible 122

George Smathers

U.S. politician, 1913–2007

1 [*Of his opponent in a Florida election primary:*]
Are you aware that Claude Pepper is known all over Washington as a shameless extrovert? Not only that, but this man is reliably reported to practice nepotism with his sister-in-law, and he has a sister who was once a thespian in wicked New York. Worst of all, it is an established fact that Mr. Pepper before his marriage habitually practiced celibacy.
Attributed in *Time*, 17 Apr. 1950. These comments were undoubtedly fabricated by journalists and not actually uttered by Smathers.

Adam Smith

Scottish economist and philosopher, 1723–1790

1 The rich . . . divide with the poor the produce of all their improvements. They are led by an invisible hand to make nearly the same distribution of the necessaries of life, which would have been made, had the earth been divided into equal proportions among all its inhabitants.
Theory of Moral Sentiments pt. 4, sec. 1 (1759).
This usage of *invisible hand* is earlier than Smith's employment of it in *Wealth of Nations* (1776), which is the one cited by standard reference works.
See Adam Smith 6

2 It is not from the benevolence of the butcher, the brewer, or the baker, that we expect our dinner, but from their regard to their own interest. We address ourselves not to their humanity but their self-love.
An Inquiry into the Nature and Causes of the Wealth of Nations vol. 1, bk. 1, ch. 2 (1776)

3 People of the same trade seldom meet together, even for merriment and diversion, but the conversation ends in a conspiracy against the public, or in some contrivance to raise prices.
An Inquiry into the Nature and Causes of the Wealth of Nations vol. 1, bk. 1, ch. 10 (1776)

4 With the greater part of rich people, the chief enjoyment of riches consists in the parade of riches, which in their eyes is never so complete as when they appear to possess those decisive marks of opulence which nobody can possess but themselves.
An Inquiry into the Nature and Causes of the Wealth of Nations vol. 1, bk. 1, ch. 11 (1776)

5 It is the highest impertinence and presumption, therefore, in kings and ministers,

to pretend to watch over the economy of private people, and to restrain their expence either by sumptuary laws, or by prohibiting the importation of foreign luxuries. They are themselves always, and without any exception, the greatest spendthrifts in the society. Let them look well after their own expence, and they may safely trust private people with theirs. If their own extravagance does not ruin the state, that of their subjects never will.
An Inquiry into the Nature and Causes of the Wealth of Nations vol. 1, bk. 2, ch. 3 (1776)

6 Every individual necessarily labors to render the annual revenue of the society as great as he can. He generally, indeed, neither intends to promote the public interest, nor knows how much he is promoting it. . . . He intends only his own gain, and he is in this, as in many other cases, led by an invisible hand to promote an end which was no part of his intention.
An Inquiry into the Nature and Causes of the Wealth of Nations vol. 2, bk. 4, ch. 2 (1776)
See Adam Smith 1

7 To found a great empire for the sole purpose of raising up a people of customers, may at first sight appear a project fit only for a nation of shopkeepers. It is, however, a project altogether unfit for a nation of shopkeepers; but extremely fit for a nation that is governed by shopkeepers.
An Inquiry into the Nature and Causes of the Wealth of Nations vol. 2, bk. 4, ch. 7 (1776). Other quotation compilations have this ending with "whose government is influenced by shopkeepers," but the first edition reads as above.
See Samuel Adams 1; Napoleon 5; Josiah Tucker 1

Alfred E. Smith
U.S. politician, 1873–1944

1 Let's look at the record.
Speech at convention dinner of New York State League of Women Voters, Albany, N.Y., 2 Dec. 1927

2 [*On Ogden Mills after Hearst endorsed Mills for governor of New York:*] William Randolph Hearst gave him the kiss of death.
Quoted in *N.Y. Times*, 25 Oct. 1926. Earliest known usage of *kiss of death*, antedating the 1948 citation given by historical dictionaries.

3 No sane local official who has hung up an empty stocking over the municipal fireplace, is going to shoot Santa Claus just before a hard Christmas.
Quoted in *New Outlook*, Dec. 1933

Betty Smith (Elizabeth Wehmer)
U.S. writer, 1904–1972

1 There's a tree that grows in Brooklyn. Some people call it the Tree of Heaven. No matter where its seed falls, it makes a tree which struggles to reach the sky.
A Tree Grows in Brooklyn epigraph (1943)

2 "Dear God," she prayed, "let me be *something* every minute of every hour of my life."
A Tree Grows in Brooklyn ch. 48 (1943)

Dodie Smith
English novelist and playwright, 1896–1990

1 I write this sitting in the kitchen sink.
I Capture the Castle pt. 1, ch. 1 (1948)

Edgar Smith
English songwriter, 1857–1938

1 Heaven Will Protect the Working Girl.
Title of song (1910)

Elliott Dunlap Smith
U.S. author, 1891–1976

1 The law is the only profession which records its mistakes carefully, exactly as they occurred, and yet does not identify them as mistakes.
Quoted in *Journal of the American Judicature Society*, June 1955

Frederick Edwin Smith, First Earl of Birkenhead
British politician and lawyer, 1872–1930

1 The world continues to offer glittering prizes to those who have stout hearts and sharp swords.
Rectorial Address, Glasgow University, Glasgow, Scotland, 7 Nov. 1923

2 [*To a judge who complained that he was none the wiser after listening to Smith's argument:*] Possibly not, My Lord, but far better informed.
Quoted in Earl of Birkenhead, *Frederick Edwin, Earl of Birkenhead* (1933)

H. Allen Smith

U.S. journalist and author, 1906–1976

1 Low Man on a Totem Pole.

Title of book (1941)

Henry John Stephen Smith

English mathematician, 1826–1883

1 [*Toast:*] Pure mathematics; may it never be of any use to anyone.

Quoted in Alexander Macfarlane, *Ten British Mathematicians of the Nineteenth Century* (1916). "Pure mathematics; may it never be of use to any man!" is cited as the toast of the Mathematical Society of England in *Science*, 10 Dec. 1886.

Joseph Smith

U.S. founder of Church of Jesus Christ of Latter-day Saints (Mormon Church), 1805–1844

1 He called me by name, and said unto me that he was a messenger sent from the presence of God to me, and that . . . God had a work for me to do.

"History of Joseph Smith," *Times and Seasons*, 15 Apr. 1842

Logan Pearsall Smith

U.S.-born English essayist, 1865–1946

1 An improper mind is a perpetual feast.

Afterthoughts ch. 1 (1931)

2 There is one thing that matters—to set a chime of words tinkling in the minds of a few fastidious people.

Quoted in *New Statesman*, 9 Mar. 1946

Margaret Chase Smith

U.S. politician, 1897–1995

1 [*Of the tactics of Senator Joseph McCarthy:*] I don't want to see the Republican Party ride to political victory on the four horsemen of calumny—fear, ignorance, bigotry, and smear.

Speech in Senate, 1 June 1950
See Blasco-Ibáñez 1; Grantland Rice 2

Patti Smith

U.S. singer and songwriter, 1946–

1 Jesus died for somebody's sins but not mine.
"Oath" l. 1 (1970)

2 Take me now baby here as I am
Pull me close, try and understand
Desire is hunger is the fire I breathe
Love is a banquet on which we feed.
"Because the Night" (song) (1978). Coauthored with Bruce Springsteen.

Samuel Francis Smith

U.S. poet and clergyman, 1808–1895

1 My country, 'tis of thee,
Sweet land of liberty,
Of thee I sing:
Land where my fathers died,
Land of the pilgrims' pride,
From every mountain-side
Let freedom ring.
"America" (song) (1831)
See Archibald Carey 1; Martin Luther King 14

Stevie Smith (Florence Margaret Smith)

English poet and novelist, 1902–1971

1 If you cannot have your dear husband for a comfort and a delight, for a breadwinner and a crosspatch, for a sofa, chair, or a hot-water bottle, one can use him as a Cross to be Borne.
Novel on Yellow Paper (1936)

2 This Englishwoman is so refined
She has no bosom and no behind.
"This Englishwoman" l. 1 (1937)

3 A Good Time Was Had by All.
Title of book (1937). Smith took this phrase from parish magazines describing church picnics or other social occasions. Searches of historical electronic texts yield occurrences as far back as 1889: "During the evening the prizes were given the successful players and a good time was had by all" (*Wash. Post*, 22 Sept.).
See Bette Davis 2

4 I was much too far out all my life
And not waving but drowning.
"Not Waving but Drowning" l. 11 (1957)

Sydney Smith

English clergyman and essayist, 1771–1845

1 The moment the very name of Ireland is mentioned, the English seem to bid adieu to common feeling, common prudence, and

common sense, and to act with the barbarity of tyrants, and the fatuity of idiots.
Letters of Peter Plymley Letter 2 (1807)

2 I look upon Switzerland as an inferior sort of Scotland.
Letter to Lord Holland, 1815

3 In the four quarters of the globe, who reads an American book, or goes to an American play, or looks at an American picture or statue? . . . Under which of the old tyrannical governments of Europe is every sixth man a slave, whom his fellow-creatures may buy, and sell, and torture?
Edinburgh Review, Jan.–May 1820

4 I have no relish for the country; it is a kind of healthy grave.
Letter to G. Harcourt, 1838

5 If you choose to represent the various parts in life by holes upon a table, of different shapes— some circular, some triangular, some square, some oblong—and the persons acting these parts by bits of wood of similar shapes, we shall generally find that the triangular person has got into the square hole, the oblong into the triangular, and a square person has squeezed himself into the round hole.
Sketches of Moral Philosophy Lecture 9 (1849). Frequently paraphrased as "a square peg in a round hole."

6 *Minorities* . . . are almost always in the right.
Quoted in Hesketh Pearson, *The Smith of Smiths* (1934)
See Debs 1; Ibsen 16

7 No furniture so charming as books.
Quoted in Lady Holland, *Memoir* (1855)

8 Daniel Webster struck me much like a steam-engine in trousers.
Quoted in Lady Holland, *Memoir* (1855)

9 My definition of marriage . . . it resembles a pair of shears, so joined that they cannot be separated; often moving in opposite directions, yet always punishing anyone who comes between them.
Quoted in Lady Holland, *Memoir* (1855)

10 Serenely full, the epicure would say,
Fate cannot harm me, I have dined to-day.
Quoted in Lady Holland, *Memoir* (1855)

11 What you don't know would make a great book.
Quoted in Lady Holland, *Memoir* (1855)

12 [*Of Thomas Babington Macaulay:*] He has occasional flashes of silence, that make his conversation perfectly delightful.
Quoted in Lady Holland, *Memoirs* (1855)

13 I never read a book before reviewing it; *it prejudices a man so.*
Quoted in *Metropolitan Magazine*, Feb. 1848

Walter Wellesley "Red" Smith
U.S. sportswriter, 1905–1982

1 [*Explaining why writing is easy:*] You simply sit down at the typewriter, open your veins and bleed.
Quoted in *Philadelphia Inquirer*, 6 Apr. 1949

Zadie Smith
English novelist, 1975–

1 We are so convinced of the goodness of ourselves, and the goodness of our love, we cannot bear to believe that there might be something more worthy of love than us, more worthy of worship. Greeting cards routinely tell us everybody deserves love. No. Everybody deserves clean water. Not everybody deserves love all the time.
White Teeth ch. 17 (2000)

2 But surely to tell these tall tales and others like them would be to spread the myth, the wicked lie, that the past is always tense and the future, perfect.
White Teeth ch. 20 (2000)

James Smithson (James Louis Macie)
French-born English chemist and philanthropist, 1765–1829

1 I bequeath the whole of my property . . . to the United States of America to found at Washington under the name of the Smithsonian Institution, an establishment for the increase and diffusion of knowledge among men.
Bequest (1829)

Tobias Smollett
Scottish novelist, 1721–1771

1 He was formed for the ruin of our sex.
The Adventures of Roderick Random ch. 22 (1748)

2 That great Cham of literature, Samuel Johnson.
Letter to John Wilkes, 16 Mar. 1759

3 I am pent up in frowzy lodgings, where there is not room enough to swing a cat.
Humphry Clinker vol. 1 (1771)

Jan Christiaan Smuts
South African prime minister, 1870–1950

1 This community of nations, which I prefer to call the British Commonwealth of nations.
The British Commonwealth of Nations (1917). The Earl of Rosebery said "The British Empire is a commonwealth of nations" in a speech in Adelaide, Australia, 18 Jan. 1884.

2 The whole-making, holistic tendency, or Holism, operating in and through particular wholes, is seen at all stages of existence.
Holism and Evolution ch. 5 (1926)

W. D. (William De Witt) Snodgrass
U.S. poet, 1926–2009

1 Up the reputable walks of old established trees
They stalk, children of the nouveaux riches; chimes
Of the tall Clock Tower drench their heads in blessing:
"I don't wanna play at your house;
I don't like you any more."
"The Campus on the Hill" l. 1 (1959)

2 Before we drained out one another's force
With lies, self-denial, unspoken regret
And the sick eyes that blame; before the divorce
And the treachery.
"Mementos, 1" l. 19 (1968)

Snoop Doggy Dogg (Calvin Broadus)
U.S. rap musician and actor, 1971–

1 One, two, three and to the fo'
Snoop Doggy Dogg and Dr. Dre is at the do' . . .
Ain't nuthin' but a G thang, baby!
"Nuthin' But a 'G' Thang" (song) (1992). Cowritten with Leon Haywood and Frederick Knight.

2 Rollin' down the street, smokin' indo'
Sippin' on gin and juice
Laid back (with my mind on my money and my money on my mind).
"Gin and Juice" (song) (1993)

C. P. Snow
English novelist and physicist, 1905–1980

1 The official world, the corridors of power.
Homecomings ch. 22 (1956)

2 The separation between the two cultures has been getting deeper under our eyes; there is now precious little communication between them. . . . The traditional culture . . . is, of course, mainly literary . . . the scientific culture is expansive, not restrictive.
New Statesman, 6 Oct. 1956
See Nabokov 9

3 Literary intellectuals at one pole—at the other scientists, and as the most representative, the physical scientists. Between the two a gulf of mutual incomprehension—sometimes (particularly among the young) hostility and dislike, but most of all lack of understanding.
The Two Cultures (1959)
See George Sarton 1

4 A good many times I have been present at gatherings of people who, by the standards of the traditional culture, are thought highly educated and who have with considerable gusto been expressing their incredulity at the illiteracy of scientists. Once or twice I have been provoked and have asked the company how many of them could describe the Second Law of Thermodynamics. The response was cold: it was also negative. Yet I was asking something which is about the scientific equivalent of: *Have you read a work of Shakespeare's?*
The Two Cultures (1959)

Edward Snowden
U.S. activist, 1983–

1 I don't want to live in a world where everything that I say, everything I do, everyone I talk to, every expression of creativity or love or friendship is recorded.
Interview, Guardian, 9 July 2013

Ethel Snowden

English reformer, 1881–1951

1 We were behind the "iron curtain" at last!
Through Bolshevik Russia ch. 2 (1920)
See Winston Churchill 33; Goebbels 3; Troubridge 1

Gary Snyder

U.S. poet, 1930–

1 I cannot remember things I once read
A few friends, but they are in cities.
Drinking cold snow-water from a tin cup
Looking down for miles
Through high still air.
"Mid-August at Sourdough Mountain Lookout" l. 6 (1959)

2 each rock a word
a creek-washed stone
Granite: ingrained
with torment of fire and weight.
"Riprap" l. 19 (1959)

Socrates

Greek philosopher, 469 B.C.–399 B.C.
See Plato for other quotations attributed by him to Socrates.

1 [*On looking at an expensive shop:*] How many things I can do without!
Quoted in Diogenes Laertius, *Lives of the Philosophers*

2 I know nothing except the fact of my ignorance.
Quoted in Diogenes Laertius, *Lives of the Philosophers*
See Milton 45

3 The rest of the world lives to eat, while I eat to live.
Quoted in Diogenes Laertius, *Lives of the Philosophers*

4 [*"Last words":*] Crito, we ought to offer a cock to Asclepius. See to it, and don't forget.
Quoted in Plato, *Phaedo*

5 The children now love luxury, they have bad manners, contempt for authority, they show disrespect for elders and love chatter in place of exercise. Children are now tyrants, not the slaves of their households. They no longer rise when an elder enters the room, they contradict their parents, chatter before company, gobble up the dainties at the table, cross their legs and tyrannize over their pedagogues.
Attributed in *Olean* (N.Y.) *Evening Herald,* 16 June 1922. This spurious quotation, trying to make the point that adults have always complained about the behavior of youths, became very popular in the 1960s. Researchers have never found anything like it in the words of Socrates or Plato. Kenneth John Freeman, *Schools of Hellas* (1907), has a very similar passage, attributed there to Xenophon, that may well have inspired newspaper items such as the one above.

Alan Sokal

U.S. physicist and mathematician, 1955–

1 Anyone who believes that the laws of physics are mere social conventions is invited to try transgressing those conventions from the windows of my apartment. I live on the twenty-first floor.
"Transgressing the Boundaries: Toward a Transformative Hermeneutics of Quantum Gravity" (1996)

Valerie Solanas

U.S. feminist, 1936–1988

1 The male is a biological accident: the Y (male) gene is an incomplete X (female) gene, that is, has an incomplete set of chromosomes. In other words, the male is an incomplete female, a walking abortion, aborted at the gene stage. To be male is to be deficient, emotionally limited; maleness is a deficiency disease and males are emotional cripples.
The S.C.U.M. Manifesto (1967)

Ezra Solomon

U.S. economist, 1920–2002

1 The only function of economic forecasting is to make astrology look respectable.
Quoted in *Psychology Today,* Mar. 1984

Solon

Greek lawgiver, ca. 640 B.C.–ca. 550 B.C.

1 I grow old ever learning many things.
Fragment 22

2 Call no man happy before he dies, he is at best but fortunate.
Quoted in Herodotus, *Histories*

Alexander I. Solzhenitsyn

Russian writer, 1918–2008

1 You only have power over people as long as you don't take *everything* away from them. But

when you've robbed a man of *everything* he's no longer in your power—he's free again.
The First Circle ch. 17 (1968)

2 A great writer is, so to speak, a second government. That's why no regime anywhere has ever loved its great writers, only its minor ones.
The First Circle ch. 57 (1968)

3 The Gulag Archipelago had already begun its malignant life and would shortly metastasize throughout the whole body of the nation.
The Gulag Archipelago, 1918–1956 vol. 1, ch. 2 (1973)

4 I have spent all my life under a Communist regime and I will tell you that a society without any objective legal scale is a terrible one indeed. But a society with no other scale but the legal one is not quite worthy of man either.
Commencement address at Harvard University, Cambridge, Mass., 8 June 1978

5 A society based on the letter of the law and never reaching any higher fails to take advantage of the full range of human possibilities. The letter of the law is too cold and formal to have a beneficial influence on society. Whenever the tissue of life is woven of legalistic relationships, this creates an atmosphere of spiritual mediocrity that paralyzes man's noblest impulses.
Commencement address at Harvard University, Cambridge, Mass., 8 June 1978

William Somerville
English poet, 1675–1742

1   The chase, the sport of kings;
Image of war, without its guilt.
The Chase bk. 1, l. 14 (1735)

Anastasio Somoza
Nicaraguan president, 1925–1980

1 You won the elections, but I won the count.
Quoted in *Guardian*, 17 June 1977
See Nast 1; Stoppard 4

Stephen Sondheim
U.S. songwriter, 1930–

1 I like to be in America!
O.K. by me in America!

Everything free in America
For a small fee in America!
"America" (song) (1957)

2 Tonight, tonight, won't be just any night.
Tonight there will be no morning star.
"Tonight" (song) (1957)

3 Everything's Coming Up Roses.
Title of song (1959)

4 The Ladies Who Lunch.
Title of song (1970)

5 [It's the] concerts you enjoy together
Neighbors you annoy together
Children you destroy together
That make marriage a joy.
"The Little Things You Do Together" (song) (1970)

6 Isn't it rich?
Are we a pair?
Me here at last on the ground,
You in mid-air.
Send in the clowns.
"Send in the Clowns" (song) (1973)

7 Isn't it rich?
Isn't it queer?
Losing my timing this late
In my career?
"Send in the Clowns" (song) (1973)

8 The history of the world, my sweet,
Is who gets eaten and who gets to eat.
"A Little Priest" (song) (1979)

Susan Sontag
U.S. writer, 1933–2004

1 Interpretation is the revenge of the intellect upon art.
"Against Interpretation" (1964)

2 The truth is that Mozart, Pascal, Boolean algebra, Shakespeare, parliamentary government, baroque churches, Newton, the emancipation of women, Kant, Marx, and Balanchine ballets don't redeem what this particular civilization has wrought upon the world. The white race *is* the cancer of human history.
"What's Happening in America" (1966)

3 What pornography is really about, ultimately, isn't sex but death.
"The Pornographic Imagination" (1967)

4 What pornographic literature does is precisely to drive a wedge between one's existence as a full human being and one's existence as a sexual being.

"The Pornographic Imagination" (1967)

5 Much of modern art is devoted to lowering the threshold of what is terrible. By getting us used to what, formerly, we could not bear to see or hear, because it was too shocking, painful, or embarrassing, art changes morals.

On Photography "America, Seen Through Photographs, Darkly" (1977)

6 Though collecting quotations could be considered as merely an ironic mimetism—victimless collecting, as it were . . . in a world that is well on its way to becoming one vast quarry, the collector becomes someone engaged in a pious work of salvage. The course of modern history having already sapped the traditions and shattered the living wholes in which precious objects once found their place, the collector may now in good conscience go about excavating the choicer, more emblematic fragments.

On Photography "Melancholy Objects" (1977)

7 Illness is the night-side of life, a more onerous citizenship. Everyone who is born holds dual citizenship, in the kingdom of the well and in the kingdom of the sick.

Illness as Metaphor preface (1978)

8 [*Of the terrorist attacks of 11 Sept. 2001:*] Where is the acknowledgment that this was not a "cowardly" attack on "civilization" or "liberty" or "humanity" or "the free world" but an attack on the world's self-proclaimed superpower, undertaken as a consequence of specific American alliances and actions?

New Yorker, 24 Sept. 2001

Sophocles
Greek playwright, ca. 496 B.C.–406 B.C.

1 Nobody likes the man who brings bad news.

Antigone l. 277. Sophocles's words are the earliest version that has been traced for the modern saying "Don't shoot the messenger."

2 There are many wonderful things, and nothing is more wonderful than man.

Antigone l. 333

3 Not to be born is, past all prizing, best.

Oedipus Coloneus l. 1225

4 Someone asked Sophocles, "How is your sex-life now? Are you still able to have a woman?" He replied, "Hush, man; most gladly indeed am I rid of it all, as though I had escaped from a mad and savage master."

Reported in Plato, *Republic*

Aaron Sorkin
U.S. screenwriter, 1961–

1 You can't handle the truth.

A Few Good Men act 2 (1989)

2 We live in a world that has walls. And those walls have to be guarded by men with guns. Who's gonna do it? You? . . . You can't handle it. Because deep down, in places you don't talk about, you *want* me on that wall. You need me there. We use words like honor, code, loyalty. We use these words as a backbone to a life spent defending something. You use them as a punchline. I have neither the time nor the inclination to explain myself to a man who rises and sleeps under the blanket of the very freedom I provide, then questions the manner in which I provide it.

A Few Good Men act 2 (1989)

George Soros
Hungarian-born U.S. businessman and philanthropist, 1930–

1 The Bush doctrine . . . is built on two pillars: First, the United States will do everything in its power to maintain its unquestioned military supremacy and, second, the United States arrogates the right to preemptive action. Taken together, these two pillars support two classes of sovereignty: the sovereignty of the United States, which takes precedence over international treaties and obligations, and the sovereignty of all other states, which is subject to the Bush doctrine.

The Bubble of American Supremacy: The Costs of Bush's War in Iraq ch. 1 (2004)

Sonia Sotomayor
U.S. judge, 1954–

1 I would hope that a wise Latina woman with the richness of her experiences would more often than not reach a better conclusion than a white male who hasn't lived that life.

Address at University of California Law School, Berkeley, Calif., 26 Oct. 2001. Sotomayor had made similar statements in other speeches going back to 1994.

Terry Southern
U.S. writer, 1924–1995

1 While the hopeless ecstasy of his huge pent-up spasm began, and sweet Candy's melodious voice rang out through the temple in truly mixed feelings: *"GOOD GRIEF—IT'S DADDY!"*

Candy ch. 15 (1958). Coauthored with Mason Hoffenberg.

2 Listen, who do I have to fuck to get *off* this picture?!?

Blue Movie ch. 1 (1970). Nigel Rees, *Cassell's Movie Quotations*, presents evidence that versions of this quotation predated 1970.

Robert Southey
English author, 1774–1843

1 [*Of Mary Wollstonecraft's letters from Scandinavia:*] She has made me in love with a cold climate.

Letter to Thomas Southey, 28 Apr. 1797
See Mitford 2

2 You are old, Father William, the young man cried,
　The few locks which are left you are grey;
You are hale, Father William, a hearty old man,
　Now tell me the reason, I pray.

"The Old Man's Comforts and How He Gained Them" l. 1 (1799)
See Carroll 9

3 "I am cheerful, young man," Father William replied;
　"Let the cause thy attention engage;
In the days of my youth I remembered my God,
　And He hath not forgotten my age."

"The Old Man's Comforts and How He Gained Them" l. 21 (1799)

4 But what they fought each other for,
　I could not well make out.

"The Battle of Blenheim" l. 33 (1800)

5 "And everybody praised the Duke,
　Who this great fight did win."
"But what good came of it at last?"
　Quoth little Peterkin.
"Why that I cannot tell," said he;
　"But 'twas a famous victory."

"The Battle of Blenheim" l. 61 (1800)

6 Curses are like young chickens, they always come home to roost.

The Curse of Kehama motto (1810). Geoffrey Chaucer wrote something similar in "The Parson's Tale" (ca. 1387): "And ofte tyme swich cursynge wrongfully retorneth agayn to hym that curseth, as a bryd that retorneth agayn to his owene nest."

7 What are little boys made of?
　Snips and snails and puppy-dog tails,
And such are little boys made of.

"What All the World Is Made Of" (ca. 1820)

8 What are young women made of?
　Sugar and spice and all things nice,
And such are young women made of.

"What All the World Is Made Of" (ca. 1820)

9 "Somebody has been at my porridge!" said the Great, Huge Bear, in his great, rough, gruff voice.

"Story of the Three Bears" (1837)

10 "Somebody has been at my porridge, and has eaten it all up!" said the Little, Small, Wee Bear, in his little, small, wee voice.

"Story of the Three Bears" (1837)

11 "Somebody has been lying in my bed!" said the Great, Huge Bear, in his great, rough, gruff voice.

"Story of the Three Bears" (1837)

Robert Southwell
English poet and Jesuit martyr, ca. 1561–1595

1 As I in hoary winter night stood shivering in the snow,
　Surprised was I with sudden heat which made my heart to glow;
And lifting up a fearful eye to view what fire was near

A pretty Babe all burning bright did in the air
  appear.
"The Burning Babe" l. 1 (ca. 1590)

Thomas Sowell

U.S. economist and author, 1930–

1 Envy was once considered to be one of the
seven deadly sins before it became one of the
most admired virtues under its new name,
"social justice."
The Quest for Cosmic Justice ch. 2 (1999)

Wole Soyinka

Nigerian writer, 1934–

1 But the skin of progress
Masks, unknown, the spotted wolf of sameness.
The Lion and the Jewel "Night" (1962)

Muriel Spark

Scottish novelist and satirist, 1918–2006

1 I am putting old heads on your young
shoulders . . . all my pupils are the crème de la
crème.
The Prime of Miss Jean Brodie ch. 1 (1961)

2 Give me a girl at an impressionable age, and
she is mine for life.
The Prime of Miss Jean Brodie ch. 1 (1961)
See Sayings 15

3 One's prime is elusive. You little girls, when
you grow up, must be on the alert to recognize
your prime at whatever time of your life it may
occur. You must then live it to the full.
The Prime of Miss Jean Brodie ch. 1 (1961)

4 To me education is a leading out of what is
already there in the pupil's soul. To Miss
Mackay it is a putting in of something that is
not there, and that is not what I call education, I
call it intrusion.
The Prime of Miss Jean Brodie ch. 2 (1961)

Nicholas Sparks

U.S. novelist, 1965–

1 I am nothing special; of this I am sure. I am a
common man with common thoughts, and I've
led a common life. There are no monuments
dedicated to me and my name will soon be

forgotten, but I've loved another with all my
heart and soul, and to me, this has always been
enough.
The Notebook (1996)

Phil Spector (Harvey Philip Spector)

U.S. record producer, 1939–2021

1 To Know Him Is to Love Him.
Title of song (1958). Nigel Rees, in the *Cassell
Companion to Quotations*, notes that Spector took
this title from his father's gravestone, which read
"To Have Known Him Was To Have Loved Him."
Rees also quotes Samuel Rogers's poem "Jacqueline"
(1814) ("To know her was to love her") and a 1928
hymn ("To know Him is to love Him").

2 You've lost that lovin' feelin'
Now it's gone gone gone.
"You've Lost That Lovin' Feelin'" (song) (1964).
Cowritten with Barry Mann and Cynthia Weil.

John H. Speke

English explorer, 1827–1864

1 The expedition had now performed its
functions. I saw that old Father Nile without
any doubt rises in the Victoria N'yanza, and, as
I had foretold, that lake is the great source of
the holy river which cradled the first expounder
of our religious belief.
Journal of the Discovery of the Source of the Nile ch. 15
(1863)

Charles Edward Maurice Spencer, Ninth Earl Spencer

English nobleman, 1964–

1 It is a point to remember that, of all the ironies
about Diana, perhaps the greatest was this:
a girl given the name of the ancient goddess
of hunting was, in the end, the most hunted
person of the modern age.
Funeral tribute for his sister, Princess Diana, 7 Sept.
1997

2 [*Of Princess Diana and her sons, Princes William
and Harry:*] We, your blood family, will do all
we can to continue the imaginative way in
which you were steering these two exceptional
young men so that their souls are not simply
immersed by duty and tradition but can sing
openly as you planned.
Funeral tribute for his sister, Princess Diana, 7 Sept.
1997

3 [*On the death of his sister, Princess Diana, in an automobile crash while being pursued by photographers:*] I always believed the press would kill her in the end. But not even I could believe they would take such a direct hand in her death as seems to be the case. . . . Every proprietor and editor of every publication that has paid for intrusive and exploitative photographs of her . . . has blood on their hands today.
Quoted in *Daily Telegraph* (London), 1 Sept. 1997

Herbert Spencer
English sociologist and philosopher, 1820–1903

1 Progress . . . is not an accident, but a necessity. Instead of civilization being artificial, it is a part of nature.
Social Statics pt. 1, ch. 2 (1850)

2 Every active force produces more than one change—every cause produces more than one effect.
"Progress: Its Law and Cause" (1857)

3 Science is organized knowledge.
Education ch. 2 (1861)

4 Evolution . . . is—a change from an indefinite, incoherent homogeneity, to a definite coherent heterogeneity.
First Principles ch. 16 (1862)

5 This survival of the fittest, which I have here sought to express in mechanical terms, is that which Mr Darwin has called "natural selection, or the preservation of favored races in the struggle for life."
The Principles of Biology vol. 1, pt. 3, ch. 12 (1864). This is the coinage of the phrase *survival of the fittest. Bartlett's Familiar Quotations* erroneously indicates that Charles Darwin used that phrase in *On the Origin of Species* (1859); he did not actually use it until 1868.
See Darwin 7; Philander Johnson 1; Herbert Spencer 6

6 The law is the survival of the *fittest.* . . . The law is not the survival of the "better" or the "stronger," if we give to those words any thing like their ordinary meanings. It is the survival of those which are constitutionally fittest to thrive under the conditions in which they are placed; and very often that which, humanly speaking, is inferiority, causes the survival.
"Mr. Martineau on Evolution" (1872)
See Darwin 7; Philander Johnson 1; Herbert Spencer 5

Oswald Spengler
German historian and philosopher, 1880–1936

1 The decline of the West, which at first sight may appear, like the corresponding decline of the Classical Culture, a phenomenon limited in time and space, we now perceive to be a philosophical problem that, when comprehended in all its gravity, includes within itself every great question of Being.
The Decline of the West ch. 1 (1918) (translation by Charles Francis Atkinson)

Edmund Spenser
English poet, ca. 1552–1599

1 And he that strives to touch the stars,
Oft stumbles at a straw.
The Shepherd's Calendar "July" l. 99 (1579)

2 So now they have made our English tongue a gallimaufry or hodgepodge of all other speeches.
The Shepherd's Calendar "Letter to Gabriel Harvey" (1579)

3 Sleep after toil, port after stormy seas,
Ease after war, death after life does greatly please.
The Faerie Queen bk. 1, canto 9, st. 40 (1596)

4 And with rich metal loaded every rift.
The Faerie Queen bk. 2, canto 7, st. 28 (1596)

5 And all for love, and nothing for reward.
The Faerie Queen bk. 2, canto 8, st. 2 (1596)

6 Dan Chaucer, well of English undefiled.
The Faerie Queen bk. 4, canto 2, st. 32 (1596)
See Samuel Johnson 6

7 Sweet Thames, run softly, till I end my song.
Prothalamion l. 18 (1596)

Sean Spicer
U.S. government official, 1971–

1 [*Of Donald Trump's presidential inauguration:*] This was the largest audience to ever witness an inauguration.
Statement to media, 21 Jan. 2017. Spicer's claim was erroneous.

Steven Spielberg
U.S. film director, 1946–

1 Close Encounters of the Third Kind.
   Title of motion picture (1977). The title refers to a categorization of UFO sightings created by UFO researcher J. Allen Hynek. A "close encounter 3" was actual contact with aliens.

2 The most expensive habit in the world is celluloid not heroin and I need a fix every two years.
   Quoted in *Time*, 16 Apr. 1979

Baruch Spinoza
Dutch philosopher, 1632–1677

1 There is no Hope without Fear, and no Fear without Hope.
   Ethics pt. 3 (1677) (translation by Edwin Curley)

2 Of Human Bondage.
   Ethics title of pt. 4 (1677)

3 *Deus, sive Natura.*
   God, *or* Nature.
   Ethics pt. 4 (1677) (translation by Edwin Curley)

4 To bring aid to everyone in need far surpasses the powers and advantage of a private person. . . . So the case of the poor falls upon society as a whole.
   Ethics pt. 4, appendix (1677) (translation by Edwin Curley)

5 All things excellent are as difficult as they are rare.
   Ethics pt. 5 (1677) (translation by Edwin Curley)

6 I have taken great care not to deride, bewail, or execrate human actions, but to understand them.
   Tractatus Politicus ch. 1 (1677) (translation by Samuel Shirley)

Benjamin Spock
U.S. physician and author, 1903–1998

1 Trust yourself. You know more than you think you do.
   The Common Sense Book of Baby and Child Care ch. 1 (1946)

2 The more people have studied different methods of bringing up children the more they have come to the conclusion that what good mothers and fathers instinctively feel like doing for their babies is the best after all.
   The Common Sense Book of Baby and Child Care ch. 1 (1946)

3 I was proud of the youths who opposed the war in Vietnam because they were my babies.
   Quoted in *Times* (London), 2 May 1988

William Spooner
English clergyman and academic, 1844–1930

1 In a dark, glassly.
   Quoted in William Hayter, *Spooner: A Biography* (1977)

2 Poor soul, very sad; her late husband, you know, a very sad death—eaten by missionaries—poor soul!
   Quoted in William Hayter, *Spooner: A Biography* (1977)

3 Kinquering congs their titles take.
   Attributed in *Echo* (Oxford, England), 4 May 1892

4 [*Addressing an undergraduate:*] You have tasted your worm, you have hissed my mystery lectures, and you must leave by the first town drain.
   Attributed in *Oxford University What's What* (1948). This is undoubtedly an apocryphal "Spoonerism."

5 [*Toast:*] To our queer old dean.
   Attributed in *Oxford University What's What* (1948)

Cecil Spring-Rice
British diplomat, 1859–1918

1 The love that makes undaunted the final sacrifice.
   "I Vow to Thee, My Country" (hymn) (written 1918)

Bruce Springsteen
U.S. rock singer and songwriter, 1949–

1 In the day we sweat it out in the streets
   Of a runaway American dream
   At night we ride through mansions of
   Glory in suicide machines.
   "Born to Run" (song) (1974)

2 Baby this town rips the bones from your back
   It's a death trap, it's a suicide rap
   We gotta get out while we're young
   'Cause tramps like us, baby, we were born
      to run.
   "Born to Run" (song) (1974)

3 Is a dream a lie if it don't come true,
   Or is it something worse?
   "The River" (song) (1980)

4 Born down in a dead man's town
   First kick I took was when I hit the ground.
   "Born in the U.S.A." (song) (1984)

5 So they put a rifle in my hand
   Sent me off to a foreign land
   To go and kill the yellow man
   Born in the U.S.A.
   "Born in the U.S.A." (song) (1984)

6 We made a promise we swore we'd always
   remember
   No retreat, baby, no surrender.
   "No Surrender" (song) (1984)

7 57 Channels (and Nothin' On).
   Title of song (1992)

J. C. Squire
English man of letters, 1884–1958

1 It did not last: the Devil howling "Ho!
   Let Einstein be!" restored the status quo.
   "In Continuation of Pope on Newton" l. 1 (1926)
   See Pope 11

Madame de Staël (Anne-Louise-Germaine Necker)
French writer, 1766–1817

1 *L'amour est l'histoire de la vie des femmes; c'est un*
   épisode dans celle des hommes.
   Love is the whole history of a woman's life, it is
   only an episode in man's.
   De l'Influence des Passions preface (1796)
   See Byron 20

2 A man must know how to defy opinion; a
   woman how to submit to it.
   Delphine epigraph (1802)

3 *Tout comprendre rend très indulgent.*
   To understand everything makes one tolerant.
   Corinne bk. 18, ch. 5 (1807)

Josef Stalin (Iosif Vissarionovich Dzhugashvili)
Soviet political leader, 1879–1953

1 You are engineers of human souls.
   Speech to writers at Maxim Gorky's house, 26 Oct.
   1932

2 History shows that there are no invincible
   armies.
   Broadcast address, 3 July 1941

3 In case of a forced retreat of Red Army units,
   all rolling stock must be evacuated; to the
   enemy must not be left a single engine, a
   single railway car, not a single pound of grain
   or a gallon of fuel. . . . In occupied regions
   conditions must be made unbearable for the
   enemy and all his accomplices. They must be
   hounded and annihilated at every step and all
   their measures frustrated.
   Broadcast address, 3 July 1941. This became known
   as the "scorched earth" policy.

4 [*When asked by French Foreign Minister Pierre*
   Laval to encourage Catholicism in the Soviet
   Union in order to appease the Pope, 13 May 1935:]
   The Pope? How many divisions has he got?
   Quoted in Winston S. Churchill, *The Gathering Storm*
   (1948)

5 A single death is a tragedy, a million deaths is a
   statistic.
   Quoted in *N.Y. Times Book Review,* 28 Sept. 1958.
   An earlier version quoted Stalin as saying, "If only
   one man dies of hunger, that is a tragedy. If millions
   die, that's only statistics" (*Washington Post,* 30 Jan.
   1947). Stephen Goranson has discovered an article
   by German journalist Kurt Tucholsky, published
   in the newspaper *Vossische Zeitung,* 23 Aug. 1925,
   quoting an unnamed French diplomat as saying
   "Der Tod eines Menschen: das ist eine Katastrophe.
   Hunderttausend Tote: das ist eine Statistik!" ("The
   death of one man: that is a catastrophe. One hundred
   thousand deaths: that is a statistic!")
   See Film Lines 118

6 [*Remark upon being informed that the United*
   States had developed the atom bomb:] Well, that's
   fine. Let's use it. What's the next item on the
   agenda?
   Quoted in James B. Reston, *Deadline* (1991)

Josiah Stamp
English economist, 1880–1941

1 The individual source of the statistics may
   easily be the weakest link. Harold Cox tells
   a story of his life as a young man in India.
   He quoted some statistics to a Judge, an
   Englishman, and a very good fellow. His friend
   said, "Cox, when you are a bit older, you will
   not quote Indian statistics with that assurance.

The Government are very keen on amassing statistics—they collect them, add them, raise them to the *n*th power, take the cube root and prepare wonderful diagrams. But what you must never forget is that every one of those figures comes in the first instance from the *chowty dar* (village watchman), who just puts down what he damn pleases."

Some Economic Factors in Modern Life ch. 8 (1929)

2 A pessimist looks at his glass and says it is half empty; an optimist looks at it and says it is half full.

Attributed in *N.Y. Times,* 13 Nov. 1935

Konstantin Stanislavsky

Russian theatrical director and actor, 1863–1938

1 There are no small parts, there are only small actors.

My Life in Art ch. 28 (1924) (translation by J. J. Robbins)

2 In the creative process there is the father, the author of the play; the mother, the actor pregnant with the part; and the child, the role to be born.

An Actor Prepares ch. 16 (1936)

Bessie A. Stanley

U.S. writer, 1879–1952

1 He has achieved success who has lived well, laughed often, and loved much; who has enjoyed the trust of pure women, the respect of intelligent men and the love of little children; who has filled his niche and accomplished his task; who has left the world better than he found it, whether by an improved poppy, a perfect poem, or a rescued soul; who has never lacked appreciation of earth's beauty or failed to express it; who has always looked for the best in others and given them the best he had; whose life was an inspiration; whose memory is a benediction.

Quoted in John Bartlett, *Familiar Quotations,* 11th ed. (1937). Often said to be by Ralph Waldo Emerson and to be titled "Success." In fact, however, it was written in 1905 by Stanley and was the first-prize winner in a contest sponsored by the magazine *Modern Women.* Anthony W. Shipps wrote in *Notes and Queries* in 1976: "The versions printed in the two local newspapers in 1905 do not agree, and in the many later appearances in print which I have seen, the wording has varied somewhat. However, the essayist's son, Judge Arthur J. Stanley, Jr., of Leavenworth, writes me that the correct text is the one given in the eleventh edition (1937) of *Bartlett's Familiar Quotations.*"

Henry Morton Stanley (John Rowlands)

Welsh-born U.S. explorer and journalist, 1841–1904

1 [*Remark on meeting David Livingstone, Ujiji, Central Africa, 10 Nov. 1871:*] Dr. Livingstone, I presume?

Quoted in Henry Morton Stanley, *How I Found Livingstone* (1872). In Richard Brinsley Sheridan's play *School for Scandal,* act 5, sc. 1, the line "Mr. Stanley, I presume?" appears.

Vivian Stanshall

English musician and entertainer, 1943–1995

1 Cool Britannia
Britannia, you are cool
Take a trip
Britons ever ever ever shall be hip.

"Cool Britannia" (song) (1967)

Charles E. Stanton

U.S. soldier, 1859–1933

1 [*Statement after arrival of first U.S. troops joining Allied forces in World War I:*] *Lafayette, nous voilà!*
Lafayette, we are here!

Address at tomb of Marquis de Lafayette, Paris, 4 July 1917

Edwin M. Stanton

U.S. politician, 1814–1869

1 [*Of Abraham Lincoln after his assassination, 15 Apr. 1865:*] Now he belongs to the ages.

Quoted in *Century Illustrated Magazine,* Jan. 1890. This is sometimes quoted with "angels" as the last word instead of "ages," and one of the observers at Lincoln's deathbed, James Tanner, is said to have recorded the "angels" version.

Elizabeth Cady Stanton

U.S. feminist, 1815–1902

1 We hold these truths to be self-evident: that all men and women are created equal.

Declaration of Sentiments, First Woman's Rights Convention, Seneca Falls, N.Y., 19–20 July 1848

2 The history of mankind is a history of repeated injuries and usurpations on the part of man toward woman, having in direct object the establishment of an absolute tyranny over her. To prove this, let facts be submitted to a candid world.

Declaration of Sentiments, First Woman's Rights Convention, Seneca Falls, N.Y., 19–20 July 1848

3 Now, in view of this entire disfranchisement of one-half the people of this country, their social and religious degradation—in view of the unjust laws above mentioned, and because women do feel themselves aggrieved, oppressed, and fraudulently deprived of their most sacred rights, we insist that they have immediate admission to all the rights and privileges which belong to them as citizens of the United States.

Declaration of Sentiments, First Woman's Rights Convention, Seneca Falls, N.Y., 19–20 July 1848

4 *Resolved,* That all laws which prevent women from occupying such a station in society as her conscience shall dictate, or which place her in a position inferior to that of man, are contrary to the great precept of nature, and therefore of no force or authority.

Resolutions, First Woman's Rights Convention, Seneca Falls, N.Y., 19–20 July 1848

5 *Resolved,* That the same amount of virtue, delicacy, and refinement of behavior, that is required of woman in the social state, should also be required of man, and the same transgressions should be visited with equal severity on both man and woman.

Resolutions, First Woman's Rights Convention, Seneca Falls, N.Y., 19–20 July 1848

6 *Resolved,* That it is the duty of the women of this country to secure to themselves their sacred right to the elective franchise.

Resolutions, First Woman's Rights Convention, Seneca Falls, N.Y., 19–20 July 1848

7 Would to God you could know the burning indignation that fills woman's soul when she turns over the pages of your statute books, and sees there how like feudal barons you freemen hold your women.

Address to New York State Legislature, Albany, N.Y., Feb. 1854

8 Who of you appreciate the galling humiliation, the refinements of degradation, to which women . . . are subject, in this the last half of the nineteenth century? How many of you have ever read even the laws concerning them that now disgrace your statute-books? In cruelty and tyranny, they are not surpassed by any slaveholding code in the Southern States.

Address to New York State Legislature, Albany, N.Y., 18 Feb. 1860

9 The point I wish plainly to bring before you on this occasion is the individuality of each human soul; our Protestant idea, the right of individual conscience and judgment—our republican idea, individual citizenship. In discussing the rights of woman, we are to consider, first, what belongs to her as an individual, in a world of her own, the arbiter of her own destiny, an imaginary Robinson Crusoe with her woman Friday on a solitary island. Her rights under such circumstances are to use all her faculties for her own safety and happiness.

Speech before Senate Judiciary Committee, 18 Jan. 1892

10 The isolation of every human soul and the necessity of self-dependence must give each individual the right, to choose his own surroundings. The strongest reason for giving woman all the opportunities for higher education, for the full development of her faculties, her forces of mind and body; for giving her the most enlarged freedom of thought and action; a complete emancipation from all forms of bondage, of custom, dependence, superstition; from all the crippling influences of fear, is the solitude and personal responsibility of her own individual life.

Speech before Senate Judiciary Committee, 18 Jan. 1892

11 The strongest reason why we ask for woman a voice in the government under which she lives; in the religion she is asked to believe; equality in social life, where she is the chief factor; a place in the trades and professions, where she may earn her bread, is because of her birthright to self-sovereignty; because, as an individual, she must rely on herself.

Speech before Senate Judiciary Committee, 18 Jan. 1892

12 To throw obstacles in the way of a complete education is like putting out the eyes; to deny the rights of property, like cutting off the hands. To deny political equality is to rob the ostracized of all self-respect; of credit in the market place; of recompense in the world of work; of a voice among those who make and administer the law; a choice in the jury before whom they are tried, and in the judge who decides their punishment.

Speech before Senate Judiciary Committee, 18 Jan. 1892

13 Nothing strengthens the judgment and quickens the conscience like individual responsibility. Nothing adds such dignity to character as the recognition of one's self-sovereignty; the right to an equal place, every where conceded; a place earned by personal merit, not an artificial attainment, by inheritance, wealth, family, and position.

Speech before Senate Judiciary Committee, 18 Jan. 1892

14 The talk of sheltering woman from the fierce storms of life is the sheerest mockery, for they beat on her from every point of the compass, just as they do on man, and with more fatal results, for he has been trained to protect himself, to resist, to conquer.

Speech before Senate Judiciary Committee, 18 Jan. 1892

Barbara Stanwyck (Ruby Catherine Stevens)
U.S. actress, 1907–1990

1 My only problem is finding a way to play my fortieth fallen female in a different way from my thirty-ninth.

Quoted in *Indianapolis Star*, 29 June 1953

Star Trek
Television series

Catchphrases are cited to the first episode in which they were used, according to Quotable Star Trek, *ed. Jill Sherwin (1999) and other sources. See also* Gene Roddenberry *and* Film Lines.

1 Engage.

"The Cage" pilot episode, 1966

2 Energize.

"Where No Man Has Gone Before" episode, 22 Sept. 1966

3 He's dead, Jim.

"The Enemy Within" episode, 6 Oct. 1966

4 Hailing frequencies still open, sir.

"The Corbomite Maneuver" episode, 10 Nov. 1966

5 Fascinating.

"The Corbomite Maneuver" episode, 10 Nov. 1966

6 Live long and prosper.

"Amok Time" episode, 15 Sept. 1967

7 Beam us up, Mr. Scott.

"Gamesters of Triskelion" episode, 5 Jan. 1968. This is the closest approach in the television series to the apocryphal line "Beam me up, Scotty!" "Beam us up, Scotty" is said to occur in the animated *Star Trek* episode "The Lorelei Signal," 29 Sept. 1973. The earliest known occurrence of the actual words "beam me up, Scotty" was in *Aeronautical Journal*, Apr. 1975.

8 The Prime Directive. . . . No identification of self or mission. No interference with the social development of said planet. No reference to space or the fact that there *are* other worlds or more advanced civilizations.

"Bread and Circuses" episode, 15 Mar. 1968. The "Return of the Archons" episode, 9 Feb. 1967, referred to the "prime directive of non-interference."

9 Make it so.

"Encounter at Farpoint" episode of *Star Trek: The Next Generation* series, 28 Sept. 1987

10 [*Catchphrase of the Borg:*] Resistance is futile.

"The Best of Both Worlds" episode of Star Trek: The *Next Generation* series, 6 Apr. 1990. "Resistance is useless" had earlier been a catchphrase on the British television series *Doctor Who*.

John Stark
U.S. general, 1728–1822

1 Live free or die.

Letter "To My Friends and Fellow Soldiers," 31 July 1809. Adopted in 1945 as the official motto of New Hampshire. *The General Advertiser* (Philadelphia), 26 July 1791, printed "live Free, or Die" as a translation of a French revolutionary oath.

2 [*Exhortation before Battle of Bennington, 16 Aug. 1777:*] You see those *red coats* yonder! They must fall into our hands in fifteen minutes, or— Molly Stark is a widow.

Quoted in *New Hampshire Sentinel*, 20 July 1819

Christina Stead

Australian novelist, 1902–1983

1 A self-made man is one who believes in luck and sends his son to Oxford.
House of All Nations (1938)

Richard Steele

Irish essayist and playwright, 1672–1729

1 [*Of Elizabeth Hastings:*] Though her mien carries much more invitation than command, to behold her is an immediate check to loose behavior; and to love her is a liberal education.
The Tatler no. 49, 2 Aug. 1709

2 It was very prettily said, that we may learn the little value of fortune by the persons on whom heaven is pleased to bestow it.
The Tatler no. 203, 27 July 1710
See Luther 3; Jonathan Swift 8

Gwen Stefani

U.S. singer, 1969–

1 Don't speak, I know
Just what you're saying
So, please stop explaining
Don't tell me 'cause it hurts
Don't speak, I know
What you're thinking
I don't need your reasons
Don't tell me 'cause it hurts.
"Don't Speak" (song) (1997). Cowritten with Eric Stefani.

Vilhjalmur Steffanson

Canadian explorer and author, 1879–1962

1 A land may be said to be discovered the first time a white European, preferably an Englishman, sets foot on it.
Quoted in *N.Y. Times*, 21 May 1967

Lincoln Steffens

U.S. journalist, 1866–1936

1 The Shame of the Cities.
Title of book (1904)

2 [*Describing a visit to the Soviet Union:*] I have seen the future; and it works.

Letter to Marie Howe, 3 Apr. 1919. The *Oxford Dictionary of Quotations* notes: "Steffens had composed the expression before he had even arrived in Russia."

Edward Steichen

Luxembourg-born U.S. photographer, 1879–1973

1 The mission of photography is to explain man to man and each man to himself.
Quoted in Cornell Capa, *The Concerned Photographer* (1972)

Gertrude Stein

U.S. writer, 1874–1946

1 Rose is a rose is a rose is a rose, is a rose.
"Sacred Emily" (1913). Frequently misquoted as "a rose is a rose is a rose." The allusion may have been to English painter Francis Rose.

2 They were regular in being gay, they learned little things that are things in being gay, they learned many little things that are things in being gay, they were gay every day, they were regular, they were gay, they were gay the same length of time every day, they were gay, they were quite regularly gay.
Geography and Plays "Miss Furr and Miss Skeene" (1922). Some scholars regard this as the genesis or popularization of the term *gay* to mean "homosexual."
See Film Lines 32

3 Before the Flowers of Friendship Faded Friendship Faded.
Title of story (written 1930)

4 Remarks are not literature.
The Autobiography of Alice B. Toklas ch. 7 (1933)

5 [*Of Ezra Pound:*] A village explainer, excellent if you were a village, but if you were not, not.
The Autobiography of Alice B. Toklas ch. 7 (1933)

6 Pigeons on the grass alas.
Four Saints in Three Acts act 3, sc. 2 (1934)

7 America is my country and Paris is my hometown.
"An American and France" (1936)

8 In the United States there is more space where nobody is than where anybody is. That is what makes America what it is.
The Geographical History of America (1936)

9 More great Americans were failures than they were successes. They mostly spent their lives in not having a buyer for what they had for sale.
Everybody's Autobiography ch. 2 (1937)

10 It is funny the two things most men are proudest of is the thing that any man can do and doing does in the same way, that is being drunk and being the father of their son.
Everybody's Autobiography ch. 2 (1937)

11 I do want to get rich but I never want to do what there is to do to get rich.
Everybody's Autobiography ch. 3 (1937)

12 What was the use of my having come from Oakland it was not natural to have come from there yes write about it if I like or anything if I like but not there, there is no there there.
Everybody's Autobiography ch. 4 (1937)

13 You are all a lost generation.
Quoted in Ernest Hemingway, *The Sun Also Rises* (1926). In Stein's *Everybody's Autobiography* (1937), she wrote: "It was this hotel-keeper who said what it is said I said in this way. He said that every man becomes civilized between the ages of eighteen and twenty-five. If he does not go through a civilizing experience at that time in his life he will not be a civilized man. And the men who went to war at eighteen missed the period of civilizing, and they could never be civilized. They were a lost generation."

14 [*Of Ernest Hemingway:*] Anyone who marries three girls from St. Louis hasn't learned much.
Quoted in James R. Mellow, *Charmed Circle: Gertrude Stein & Company* (1974)

15 Just before she died she asked, "What *is* the answer?" No answer came. She laughed and said, "In that case, what is the question?" Then she died.
Reported in Donald Sutherland, *Gertrude Stein: A Biography of Her Work* (1951). Stein's companion Alice B. Toklas, who was with her at her death, reported Stein's words as, "What is the answer? . . . In that case . . . what is the question?" (Alice B. Toklas, *What Is Remembered* [1963]), and did not identify these specifically as the last words.

16 [*Remark, 1925:*] The Jews have produced only three originative geniuses; Christ, Spinoza, and myself.
Attributed in *Exile,* Autumn 1928

John Steinbeck
U.S. novelist, 1902–1968

1 I know this—a man got to do what he got to do.
The Grapes of Wrath ch. 18 (1939)

2 Okie use' ta mean you was from Oklahoma. Now it means you're a dirty son-of-a-bitch. Okie means you're scum. Don't mean nothing itself, it's the way they say it.
The Grapes of Wrath ch. 18 (1939)

3 Why, Tom, we're the people that live. They ain't gonna wipe us out. Why, we're the people— we go on.
The Grapes of Wrath ch. 20 (1939)

4 Maybe that makes us tough. Rich fellas come up an' they die, an' their kids ain't no good, an' they die out. But, Tom, we keep a-comin'.
The Grapes of Wrath ch. 20 (1939)

5 Wherever they's a fight so hungry people can eat, I'll be there. Wherever they's a cop beating up a guy, I'll be there. . . . I'll be in the way guys yell when they're mad an'—I'll be in the way kids laugh when they're hungry an' they know supper's ready. An' when our folks eat the stuff they raise an' live in the houses they build— why, I'll be there.
The Grapes of Wrath ch. 28 (1939)

6 Men really need sea-monsters in their personal oceans. . . . An ocean without its unnamed monsters would be like a completely dreamless sleep.
Sea of Cortez ch. 4 (1941)

Gloria Steinem

U.S. feminist and editor, 1934–

1 There are times when a woman reading *Playboy* feels a little like a Jew reading a Nazi manual.
McCall's, Oct. 1970

2 Any woman who chooses to behave like a full human being should be warned that the armies of the status quo will treat her as something of a dirty joke. That's their natural and first weapon. She will *need* her sisterhood.
Ms., Spring 1972

3 Some of us are becoming the men we wanted to marry.
Speech at Yale University, New Haven, Conn., 23 Sept. 1981

4 Pornography is about dominance. Erotica is about mutuality.
Outrageous Acts and Everyday Rebellions "Erotica vs. Pornography" (1983)

5 I have yet to hear a man ask for advice on how to combine marriage and a career.
Quoted in Robert Byrne, *The Fourth—and by Far the Most Recent—637 Best Things Anybody Ever Said* (1990)

George Steiner

French-born U.S. critic and novelist, 1929–2020

1 We know that a man can read Goethe or Rilke in the evening, that he can play Bach and Schubert, and go to his day's work at Auschwitz in the morning.
Language and Silence preface (1967)

2 We Jews walk closer to our children than other men . . . because to have children is possibly to condemn them.
Quoted in *Guardian*, 6 Jan. 1996

Peter Steiner

U.S. cartoonist, 1940–

1 On the Internet, nobody knows you're a dog.
Cartoon caption, *New Yorker*, 5 July 1993

Frances Steloff

U.S. bookstore owner, 1887–1989

1 [*Sign for Gotham Book Mart, New York, N.Y.*:] Wise men fish here.
Quoted in *Wash. Post*, 21 Sept. 1933

Stendhal (Henri Beyle)

French novelist, 1783–1842

1 One can acquire everything in solitude—except character.
"De l'Amour" fragment 1 (1822)

2 Every true passion thinks only of itself.
Le Rouge et le Noir bk. 2, ch. 1 (1830)

3 *Un roman est un miroir qui se promène sur une grande route.*
A novel is a mirror that strolls along a highway.
Le Rouge et le Noir bk. 2, ch. 19 (1830)

4 *La politique au milieu des intérêts d'imagination, c'est un coup de pistolet au milieu d'un concert.*
Politics in the middle of things concerning the imagination are like a pistol shot in the middle of a concert.
Le Rouge et le Noir bk. 2, ch. 22 (1830)

5 I know of only one rule: style cannot be too *clear*, too *simple*.
Letter to Honoré de Balzac, 30 Oct. 1840

Charles Dillon "Casey" Stengel

U.S. baseball manager, ca. 1890–1975

1 I had many years that I was not so successful as a ball player, as it is a game of skill.
Testimony before Senate Antitrust and Monopoly Subcommittee, 9 July 1958

2 [*Comment as manager of the last-place New York Mets in 1962:*] Can't anybody here play this game?
Quoted in *Wash. Post*, 29 Mar. 1963

3 [*Remark to a barber, after losing a doubleheader:*] Don't cut my throat. I may want to do that later myself.

Quoted in Joseph Durso, *Casey: The Life and Legend of Charles Dillon Stengel* (1967)

4 A lot of people my age are dead at the present time.

Quoted in Leo Rosten, *People I Have Loved, Known, or Admired* (1970). Paul Dickson, in *Baseball's Greatest Quotations*, credits this to Stengel "on being asked by a reporter what people 'your age' thought of modern-day ballplayers or, depending on the source, being asked about his future. It appears to date from the spring of 1965."

5 [*Of the new New York baseball franchise, on Thanksgiving Day, 1961*] The Mets are gonna be amazin'.

Quoted in *S.F. Examiner*, 30 Sept. 1975

6 Going to bed with a woman never hurt a ballplayer. It's staying up all night looking for them that does you in.

Quoted in Barbara Rowes, *The Book of Quotes* (1979)

7 Good pitching will always stop good hitting and vice versa.

Quoted in Paul Dickson, *The Official Explanations* (1980)

8 There comes a time in every man's life and I've had plenty of them.

Quoted in *Wash. Post*, 6 May 1981. This quotation marks Stengel's grave.

9 All you have to do is keep the five players who hate your guts away from the five who are undecided.

Quoted in *The Guardian Book of Sports Quotes*, ed. John Samuel (1985)

10 Most ball games are lost, not won.

Quoted in Paul Dickson, *Baseball's Greatest Quotations* (1991)

J. K. Stephen

English journalist and poet, 1859–1892

1 When the Rudyards cease from kipling
And the Haggards ride no more.

"To R. K." l. 15 (1891)

James Fitzjames Stephen

English jurist, 1829–1894

1 The criminal law stands to the passion of revenge in much the same relation as marriage to the sexual appetite.

A General View of the Criminal Law of England ch. 4 (1863)

2 Complete moral tolerance is possible only when men have become completely indifferent to each other—that is to say, when society is at an end.

Liberty, Equality, Fraternity ch. 4 (1873)

Andrew B. Sterling

U.S. songwriter, 1874–1955

1 Meet me in St. Louis, Louis,
Meet me at the fair.

"Meet Me in St. Louis, Louis" (song) (1904)

Bruce Sterling

U.S. science fiction writer, 1954–

1 Information is not power. If information were power, then librarians would be the most powerful people on the planet.

Speech at Social Work Futures Conference, Houston, Tex., 23 May 1994

John W. Sterling

U.S. lawyer, 1844–1918

1 [The ideal client is] the very wealthy man in very great trouble.

Quoted in *American Bar Association Journal*, Apr. 1960

Laurence Sterne

Irish novelist, 1713–1768

1 I wish either my father or my mother, or indeed both of them, as they were in duty both equally bound to it, had minded what they were about when they begot me.

Tristram Shandy bk. 1, ch. 1 (1759–1767)

2 "Pray, my dear," quoth my mother, "have you not forgot to wind up the clock?"—"Good G—!" cried my father, making an exclamation, but taking care to moderate his voice at the same time,—"Did ever woman, since the creation

of the world, interrupt a man with such a silly question?"

Tristram Shandy bk. 1, ch. 1 (1759–1767)

3 That's another story, replied my father.

Tristram Shandy bk. 2, ch. 17 (1759–1767)

4 L—d! said my mother, "what is all this story about?"—"A Cock and a Bull," said Yorick.

Tristram Shandy bk. 9, ch. 33 (1759–1767). The *Oxford English Dictionary* points out that the origins of the notion of the "cock and bull story" are obscure.

5 They order, said I, this matter better in France.

A Sentimental Journey (1768)

John Paul Stevens

U.S. judge, 1920–2019

1 Although we may never know with complete certainty the identity of the winner of this year's presidential election, the identity of the loser is perfectly clear. It is the nation's confidence in the judge as an impartial guardian of the rule of law.

Bush v. Gore (dissenting opinion) (2000)

2 While American democracy is imperfect, few outside the majority of this court would have thought its flaws included a dearth of corporate money in politics.

Citizens United v. Federal Election Commission (dissenting opinion) (2010)

Wallace Stevens

U.S. poet, 1879–1955

1 I placed a jar in Tennessee,
  And round it was, upon a hill,
  It made the slovenly wilderness
  Surround that hill.

"Anecdote of the Jar" l. 1 (1923)

2 It did not give of bird or bush,
  Like nothing else in Tennessee.

"Anecdote of the Jar" l. 11 (1923)

3 Call the roller of big cigars,
  The muscular one, and bid him whip
  In kitchen cups concupiscent curds.

"The Emperor of Ice-Cream" l. 1 (1923)

4 Let be be finale of seem.
  The only emperor is the emperor of ice-cream.

"The Emperor of Ice-Cream" l. 7 (1923)

5 If her horny feet protrude, they come
  To show how cold she is, and dumb.

"The Emperor of Ice-Cream" l. 13 (1923)

6 Poetry is the supreme fiction, madame.

"A High-Toned Old Christian Woman" l. 1 (1923)

7 Beauty is momentary in the mind—
  The fitful tracing of a portal;
  But in the flesh it is immortal.

"Peter Quince at the Clavier" l. 51 (1923)

8 Complacencies of the peignoir, and late
  Coffee and oranges in a sunny chair.

"Sunday Morning" l. 1 (1923)

9 She sang beyond the genius of the sea.

"The Idea of Order at Key West" l. 1 (1935)

10 The water never formed to mind or voice,
   Like a body wholly body, fluttering
   Its empty sleeves, and yet its mimic motion
     made constant cry.

"The Idea of Order at Key West" l. 2 (1935)

11 The ever-hooded, tragic-gestured sea
   Was merely a place by which she walked to
     sing.

"The Idea of Order at Key West" l. 16 (1935)

12   It was her voice that made
   The sky acutest at its vanishing.
   She measured to the hour its solitude.
   She was the single artificer of the world
   In which she sang.

"The Idea of Order at Key West" l. 33 (1935)

13 Oh, Blessed rage for order, pale Ramon,
   The maker's rage to order words of the sea,
   Words of the fragrant portals, dimly-starred,
   And of ourselves and of our origins,
   In ghostlier demarcations, keener sounds.

"The Idea of Order at Key West" l. 59 (1935)

14 A. A violent order is disorder; and
   B. A great disorder is an order. These
   Two things are one.

"Connoisseur of Chaos" l. 1 (1942)

15 The palm at the end of the mind,
   Beyond the last thought, rises
   In the bronze distance.

"Of Mere Being" l. 1 (1957)

Adlai E. Stevenson

U.S. politician, 1900–1965

1 The problem of cat versus bird is as old as time. If we attempt to resolve it by legislation who knows but what we may be called upon to take sides as well in the age old problems of dog versus cat, bird versus bird, or even bird versus worm. In my opinion, the State of Illinois and its local governing bodies already have enough to do without trying to control feline delinquency.

Veto message, 23 Apr. 1949

2 Let's talk sense to the American people. Let's tell them the truth, that there are no gains without pains, that we are now on the eve of great decisions, not easy decisions, like resistance when you're attacked, but a long, patient, costly struggle which alone can assure triumph over the great enemies of man—war, poverty, and tyranny—and the assaults upon human dignity which are the most grievous consequences of each.

Speech accepting presidential nomination, Democratic National Convention, Chicago, Ill., 26 July 1952

3 I yield to no man—if I may borrow that majestic parliamentary phrase—I yield to no man in my belief in the principle of free debate, inside or outside the halls of Congress. The sound of tireless voices is the price we pay for the right to hear the music of our own opinions. But there is also, it seems to me, a moment at which democracy must prove its capacity to act. Every man has a right to be heard; but no man has the right to strangle democracy with a single set of vocal cords.

Speech to the State Committee of the Liberal Party, New York, N.Y., 28 Aug. 1952

4 A hungry man is not a free man.

Speech, Kasson, Minn., 6 Sept. 1952

5 The time to stop a revolution is at the beginning, not the end.

Speech, San Francisco, Calif., 9 Sept. 1952

6 I have been thinking that I would make a proposition to my Republican friends. . . . That if they will stop telling lies about the Democrats, we will stop telling the truth about them.

Campaign remark, Fresno, Calif., 10 Sept. 1952. Garson O'Toole has traced the reverse statement to a speech by Asa W. Tenney quoted in the *Buffalo Evening News*, 27 Sept. 1888: "If the Democrats will stop lying about Harrison the Republicans will stop telling the truth about Cleveland."

7 [*Of Richard Nixon*] The young man who asks you to set him one heart-beat from the Presidency of the United States.

Speech, Cleveland, Ohio, 23 Oct. 1952

8 [*Remark after he was defeated in the presidential election:*] A funny thing happened to me on the way to the White House.

Speech, Washington, D.C., 13 Dec. 1952

9 We hear the Secretary of State [John Foster Dulles] boasting of his brinkmanship—the art of bringing us to the edge of the abyss.

Speech, Hartford, Conn., 25 Feb. 1956
See John Foster Dulles 3

10 Our nation stands at a fork in the political road. In one direction lies a land of slander and scare; the land of sly innuendo, the poison pen, the anonymous phone call and hustling, pushing, shoving; the land of smash and grab and anything to win. This is Nixonland. But I say to you that it is not America.

Speech, Los Angeles, Calif., 27 Oct. 1956

11 Do you, Ambassador Zorin, deny that the U.S.S.R. has placed and is placing medium- and intermediate-range missiles and sites in Cuba? Yes or no? Don't wait for the translation. . . . I am prepared to wait for my answer until Hell freezes over, if that's your decision. And I am also prepared to present the evidence in this room!

Statement to United Nations Security Council, 25 Oct. 1962

12 We travel together, passengers on a little space ship, dependent on its vulnerable reserves of air and soil; all committed for our safety to its security and peace; preserved from annihilation only by the care, the work, and, I will say, the love we give our fragile craft. We cannot maintain it half fortunate, half miserable, half confident, half despairing, half slave—to

the ancient enemies of man—half free in a liberation of resources undreamed of until this day. No craft, no crew can travel safely with such vast contradictions. On their resolution depends the survival of us all.

Speech to Economic and Social Council of United Nations, Geneva, Switzerland, 9 July 1965

13 [The Republican Party] had to be dragged kicking and screaming into the twentieth century.

Quoted in *N.Y. Times,* 19 Oct. 1952

14 [*Paying tribute to Eleanor Roosevelt after her death on 7 Nov. 1962:*] I have lost more than a beloved friend. I have lost an inspiration. She would rather light a candle than curse the darkness, and her glow has warmed the world.

Quoted in *N.Y. Times,* 8 Nov. 1962
See James Keller 1

Robert Louis Stevenson

Scottish novelist, 1850–1894

1 For my part, I travel not to go anywhere, but to go. I travel for travel's sake. The great affair is to move.

Travels with a Donkey "Cheylard and Luc" (1879)

2 Books are good enough in their own way, but they are a mighty bloodless substitute for life.

Virginibus Puerisque "An Apology for Idlers" (1881)

3 It is better to be a fool than to be dead.

Virginibus Puerisque "Crabbed Age and Youth" (1881)

4 Some people swallow the universe like a pill; they travel on through the world, like smiling images pushed from behind. For God's sake give me the young man who has brains enough to make a fool of himself!

Virginibus Puerisque "Crabbed Age and Youth" (1881)

5 To travel hopefully is a better thing than to arrive, and the true success is to labor.

Virginibus Puerisque "El Dorado" (1881)

6 Falling in love is the one illogical adventure, the one thing of which we are tempted to think as supernatural, in our trite and reasonable world.

Virginibus Puerisque title essay (1881)

7 Politics is perhaps the only profession for which no preparation is thought necessary.

Familiar Studies of Men and Books "Yoshida-Torajiro" (1882)

8 Fifteen men on the dead man's chest
Yo-ho-ho, and a bottle of rum!
Drink and the devil had done for the rest—
Yo-ho-ho, and a bottle of rum!

Treasure Island ch. 1 (1883). Stevenson took the phrase *dead man's chest* from a pirate name for an isle in Charles Kingsley, *At Last,* ch. 1 (1870).

9 Pieces of eight, pieces of eight, pieces of eight!

Treasure Island ch. 10 (1883)

10 Them that die'll be the lucky ones.

Treasure Island ch. 20 (1883)

11 There is but one art—to omit! O if I knew how to omit, I would ask no other knowledge.

Letter to R. A. M. Stevenson, Oct. 1883

12 In winter I get up at night
And dress by yellow candle-light.
In summer, quite the other way,—
I have to go to bed by day.

A Child's Garden of Verses "Bed in Summer" l. 1 (1885)

13 The world is so full of a number of things,
I'm sure we should all be as happy as kings.

A Child's Garden of Verses "Happy Thought" l. 1 (1885)

14 How do you like to go up in a swing,
Up in the air so blue?
Oh, I do think it the pleasantest thing
Ever a child can do!

A Child's Garden of Verses "The Swing" l. 1 (1885)

15 A birdie with a yellow bill
Hopped upon the window sill,
Cocked his shining eye and said:
"Ain't you 'shamed, you sleepy-head!"

A Child's Garden of Verses "Time to Rise" l. 1 (1885)

16 A child should always say what's true,
And speak when he is spoken to,
And behave mannerly at table;
At least as far as he is able.

A Child's Garden of Verses "Whole Duty of Children" l. 1 (1885)

17 Am I no a bonny fighter?

Kidnapped ch. 10 (1886)

18 Strange Case of Dr. Jekyll and Mr. Hyde.

Title of book (1886)

19 I have thus played the sedulous ape to Hazlitt, to Lamb, to Wordsworth, to Sir Thomas Browne, to Defoe, to Hawthorne, to Montaigne, to Baudelaire, and to Obermann.

Memories and Portraits ch. 4 (1887)

20 No human being ever spoke of scenery for
   above two minutes at a time, which makes me
   suspect we hear too much of it in literature.
   Memories and Portraits ch. 10 (1887)

21 Under the wide and starry sky
   Dig the grave and let me lie.
   Glad did I live and gladly die,
   And I laid me down with a will.

   This be the verse you grave for me:
   "Here he lies where he longed to be;
   Home is the sailor, home from sea,
   And the hunter home from the hill."
   Underwoods "Requiem" (1887). Engraved on
   Stevenson's tomb in Samoa, with the seventh line
   reading "home from the sea," which is a frequently
   quoted variant.

22 A Footnote to History.
   Title of book (1892)

23 I hate writing, but I love having written.
   Attributed in *Wash. Post,* 3 Oct. 1954

Jon Stewart (Jonathan Stuart Leibowitz)
U.S. comedian and political commentator, 1962–

1 We live in hard times, not end times.
  Speech at Rally to Restore Sanity and/or Fear,
  Washington, D.C., 30 Oct. 2010

2 The press can hold its magnifying glass up
  to our problems, bringing them into focus,
  illuminating issues heretofore unseen, or they
  can use that magnifying glass to light ants on
  fire. And then perhaps host a week of shows
  on the sudden, unexpected, dangerous flaming
  ant epidemic. If we amplify everything, we hear
  nothing.
  Speech at Rally to Restore Sanity and/or Fear,
  Washington, D.C., 30 Oct. 2010

Martha Stewart
U.S. businesswoman and media personality,
1941–

1 It's a good thing.
  Quoted in *Palm Beach* (Fla.) *Post,* 24 Dec. 1994
  See Sellar 1

Potter Stewart
U.S. judge, 1915–1985

1 I have reached the conclusion . . . that under the
  First and Fourteenth Amendments criminal

laws in this area [obscenity] are constitutionally
limited to hard-core pornography. I shall not
today attempt further to define the kinds of
materials I understand to be embraced within
that shorthand description; and perhaps I could
never succeed in intelligibly doing so. But I
know it when I see it; and the motion picture
involved in this case is not that.
Jacobellis v. Ohio (concurring opinion) (1964)

Henry L. Stimson
U.S. statesman, 1867–1950

1 Gentlemen do not read each other's mail.
  On Active Service in Peace and War ch. 7 (1948).
  Stimson was explaining his action, while secretary
  of state in 1929, in closing the State Department's
  code-breaking office. The 1948 book, coauthored with
  McGeorge Bundy, is the earliest known appearance
  of this quotation. Louis Kruh, in his article "Stimson,
  the Black Chamber, and the 'Gentleman's Mail'
  Quote," *Cryptologia,* Apr. 1988, concludes that these
  words accurately represented Stimson's feelings in
  1929 but that "whether he also said it then remains
  unknown."
  See Allen Dulles 1

Sting (Gordon Matthew Sumner)
English rock singer and songwriter, 1951–

1 Roxanne
  You don't have to
  Put on the red light
  Those days are over
  You don't have to sell
  Your body to the night.
  "Roxanne" (song) (1979)

2 Every breath you take
  Every move you make . . .
  I'll be watching you.
  "Every Breath You Take" (song) (1983)

3 Every vow you break
  Every smile you fake
  Every claim you stake
  I'll be watching you.
  "Every Breath You Take" (song) (1983)

John Michael Stipe
U.S. rock musician and songwriter, 1960–

1 It's the End of the World As We Know It (and I
  Feel Fine).
  Title of song (1988)

2 That's me in the corner
That's me in the spotlight
Losing my religion.

"Losing My Religion" (song) (1991). "Losing my religion" is a Southern expression for losing one's temper.

3 Everybody hurts sometimes
Everybody cries.

"Everybody Hurts" (song) (1992)

James B. Stockdale
U.S. admiral, 1923–2005

1 [*Remark during vice-presidential campaign debate, Atlanta, Ga., 13 Oct. 1992:*] Who am I? Why am I here?

Quoted in *Wash. Post*, 14 Oct. 1992. In fairness to Admiral Stockdale, who was Ross Perot's running mate on the Reform Party ticket, it should be noted that he had not had time to prepare for the debate, being notified that he would participate only two days beforehand.

David Stockman
U.S. government official, 1946–

1 None of us really understands what's going on with all these numbers.

Quoted in *Atlantic Monthly*, Dec. 1981. Stockman, director of the Office of Management and Budget during the Reagan administration, was referring to the U.S. budget.

Frank R. Stockton
U.S. editor, humorist, and short story writer, 1834–1902

1 And so I leave it with all of you:
Which came out of the opened door—the lady, or the tiger?

The Lady, or the Tiger? title story (1884)

Bram Stoker
Irish writer, 1847–1912

1 I am Dracula; and I bid you welcome.

Dracula ch. 2 (1897)

2 The mouth, so far as I could see it under the heavy moustache, was fixed and rather cruel-looking, with peculiarly sharp white teeth; these protruded over the lips, whose remarkable ruddiness showed astonishing vitality in a man of his years.

Dracula ch. 2 (1897)

3 [*Of howling wolves:*] Listen to them—the children of the night. What music they make!

Dracula ch. 2 (1897)

Leopold Stokowski
English conductor, 1882–1977

1 A painter paints his pictures on canvas. But musicians paint their pictures on silence.

Quoted in *N.Y. Times*, 11 May 1967

Clifford Stoll
U.S. astronomer and computer expert, 1950–

1 There's a relationship between data, information, knowledge, understanding, and wisdom. Our networks are awash in data. A little of it's information. A smidgen of this shows up as knowledge. Combined with ideas, some of that is actually useful. Mix in experience, context, compassion, discipline, humor, tolerance, and humility, and perhaps knowledge becomes wisdom.

Silicon Snake Oil ch. 11 (1995)

Harlan F. Stone
U.S. judge, 1872–1946

1 Nor need we enquire . . . whether prejudice against discrete and insular minorities may be a special condition, which tends seriously to curtail the operation of those political processes ordinarily to be relied upon to protect minorities, and which call for a correspondingly more searching judicial inquiry.

United States v. Carolene Products Co. (footnote 4) (1938)

Irving Stone
U.S. novelist, 1903–1989

1 The Agony and the Ecstasy.

Title of book (1961)

Lucy Stone
U.S. reformer, 1818–1893

1 While acknowledging our mutual affection by publicly assuming the relationship of husband and wife, . . . we deem it a duty to declare that this act on our part implies no sanction of, nor promise of voluntary obedience to such

of the present laws of marriage, as refuse to recognize the wife as an independent, rational being, while they confer upon the husband an injurious and unnatural superiority.

Statement read at marriage of Stone and Henry B. Blackwell (1855)

2 We believe that personal independence and equal human rights can never be forfeited, except for crime; that marriage should be an equal and permanent partnership, and so recognized by law; that until it is so recognized, married partners should provide against the radical injustice of present laws, by every means in their power.

Statement read at marriage of Stone and Henry B. Blackwell (1855)

Winifred Sackville Stoner, Jr.
U.S. child prodigy and poet, 1902–1983

1 In fourteen hundred ninety-two, Columbus sailed the ocean blue.

"The History of the United States" (1919)

Marie Stopes
Scottish reformer, 1880–1958

1 An impersonal and scientific knowledge of the structure of our bodies is the surest safeguard against prurient curiosity and lascivious gloating.

Married Love ch. 5 (1918)

Tom Stoppard (Thomas Straussler)
Czech-born English playwright, 1937–

1 Eternity is a terrible thought. I mean, where's it going to end?

Rosencrantz and Guildenstern Are Dead act 2 (1967)

2 Life is a gamble at terrible odds—if it was a bet, you wouldn't take it.

Rosencrantz and Guildenstern Are Dead act 3 (1967)

3 Skill without imagination is craftsmanship and gives us many useful objects such as wickerwork picnic baskets. Imagination without skill gives us modern art.

Artist Descending a Staircase (1972)

4 It's not the voting that's democracy, it's the counting.

Jumpers act 1 (1972)
See Nast 1; Somoza 1

5 [*On James Joyce:*] An essentially private man who wished his total indifference to public notice to be universally recognized.

Travesties act 1 (1975)

6 What is an artist? For every thousand people there's nine hundred doing the work, ninety doing well, nine doing good, and one lucky bastard who's the artist.

Travesties act 1 (1975)

7 I learned three things in Zurich during the war. I wrote them down. Firstly, you're either a revolutionary or you're not, and if you're not you might as well be an artist as anything else. Secondly, if you can't be an artist, you might as well be a revolutionary . . . I forget the third thing.

Travesties act 2 (1975). Ellipsis in the original.

Joseph Story
U.S. judge and legal scholar, 1779–1845

1 [*Of the law:*] It is a jealous mistress, and requires a long and constant courtship. It is not to be won by trifling favors, but by lavish homage.

"The Value and Importance of Legal Studies" (1829). Earlier, the following passage appeared in Roger North, *A Discourse on the Study of the Laws* (1824): "The law is not so jealous a mistress as to exclude every other object from the mind of her devotee." See William Jones (1746–1794) 1

Harriet Beecher Stowe
U.S. novelist, 1811–1896

1 Eliza made her desperate retreat across the river just in the dusk of twilight. The gray mist of evening, rising slowly from the river, enveloped her as she disappeared up the bank, and the swollen current and floundering masses of ice presented a hopeless barrier between her and her pursuer.

Uncle Tom's Cabin ch. 8 (1852)

2 [*The character Topsy speaking:*] I s'pect I growed. Don't think nobody never made me.

Uncle Tom's Cabin ch. 20 (1852)

3 Whipping and abuse are like laudanum; you have to double the dose as the sensibilities decline.

Uncle Tom's Cabin ch. 20 (1852)

4 My soul an't yours, Mas'r! You haven't bought
it,—ye can't buy it! It's been bought and paid
for, by one that is able to keep it.
Uncle Tom's Cabin ch. 33 (1852)

5 Every nation that carries in its bosom great and
unredressed injustice has in it the elements of
this last convulsion.
Uncle Tom's Cabin ch. 45 (1852)

6 I did not write it. God wrote it. I merely did His
dictation.
Uncle Tom's Cabin introduction (1879 edition)

Lytton Strachey
English biographer and critic, 1880–1932

1 The history of the Victorian Age will never
be written: we know too much about it.
For ignorance is the first requisite of the
historian—ignorance, which simplifies and
clarifies, which selects and omits, with a placid
perfection unattainable by the highest art.
Eminent Victorians preface (1918)

2 The art of biography seems to have fallen on
evil times in England. . . . With us, the most
delicate and humane of all the branches of
the art of writing has been relegated to the
journeymen of letters; we do not reflect that it
is perhaps as difficult to write a good life as to
live one.
Eminent Victorians preface (1918)

3 [*Responding to the chairman of the military
tribunal's question, "What would you do if you saw
a German soldier trying to violate your sister?":*] I
would try to get between them.
Quoted in Robert Graves, *Good-bye to All That* (1929).
Strachey's comment is sometimes quoted as "I
should interpose my body."

4 [*Deathbed remark:*] If this is dying, then I don't
think much of it.
Quoted in Michael Holroyd, *Lytton Strachey* (1968)

Mark Strand
Canadian-born U.S. poet, 1934–2014

1 We all have reasons
for moving.
I move
to keep things whole.
"Keeping Things Whole" l. 14 (1969)

2 Ink runs from the corners of my mouth.
There is no happiness like mine.
I have been eating poetry.
"Eating Poetry" l. 1 (1980)

Lewis L. Strauss
U.S. government official, 1896–1974

1 Our children will enjoy in their homes
electrical energy too cheap to meter.
Speech at twentieth anniversary of National
Association of Science Writers, New York, N.Y., 16
Sept. 1954. Strauss was chairman of the Atomic Energy
Commission and was referring to atomic energy.

Igor Stravinsky
Russian-born U.S. composer, 1882–1971

1 Now that Mr. [John] Cage's most successful
opus is undoubtedly the delectable silent
piece *4'33"*, we may expect his example to be
followed by more and more silent pieces by
younger composers who, in rapid escalation,
will produce their silences with more and more
varied and beguiling combinations. . . . I only
hope they turn out to be works of major length.
Themes and Episodes pt. 1 "Conspiracy of Silence"
(1966)

2 My music is best understood by children and
animals.
Quoted in *Observer*, 8 Oct. 1961

Cheryl Strayed
U.S. writer, 1968–

1 How wild it was, to let it be.
Wild ch. 19 (2012)

Barbra Streisand
U.S. singer and actress, 1942–

1 Success to me is having ten honeydew melons
and eating only the top half of each one.
Quoted in *Life,* 20 Sept. 1963

August Strindberg
Swedish playwright and novelist, 1849–1912

1 The Family! Home of all social evils, a
charitable institution for indolent women, a
prison workhouse for family breadwinners, and
a hell for children!
The Son of a Servant ch. 1 (1886) (translation by Evert
Spinchorn)

2 I detest dogs, those protectors of cowards who have not the courage to bite the assailant themselves.
The Madman's Manifesto pt. 3 (1895) (translation by Anthony Swerling)

Muriel Strode
U.S. writer, 1875–1964

1 I will not follow where the path may lead, but I will go where there is no path, and I will leave a trail.
Open Court, Aug. 1903

Joe Strummer (John Graham Mellor)
Turkish-born English rock musician, 1952–2002

1 The ice age is coming, the sun's zooming in Meltdown expected, the wheat is growing thin Engines stop running, but I have no fear 'Cause London is drowning and I live by the river.
"London Calling" (song) (1979)

William Strunk, Jr.
U.S. educator, 1869–1946

1   Omit needless words.
   Vigorous writing is concise. A sentence should contain no unnecessary words, a paragraph no unnecessary sentences, for the same reason that a drawing should have no unnecessary lines and a machine no unnecessary parts. This requires not that the writer make all his sentences short, or that he avoid all detail and treat his subjects only in outline, but that every word tell.
The Elements of Style ch. 2 (1918)

Simeon Strunsky
Russian-born U.S. journalist and essayist, 1879–1948

1 Famous remarks are very seldom quoted correctly.
No Mean City ch. 38 (1944)

Theodore Sturgeon
U.S. science fiction writer, 1918–1985

1 Ninety-percent of *everything* is crud.
Venture Science Fiction Magazine, Sept. 1957. This is known as "Sturgeon's Law," although the author originally described it as "Sturgeon's Revelation." According to James Gunn in *The New York Review of Science Fiction*, Sept. 1995, Sturgeon used it in a talk at the 1953 World Science Fiction Convention, Philadelphia, Pa., saying: "Ninety percent of science fiction is crud. But then ninety percent of everything is crud, and it's the ten percent that isn't crud that is important. And the ten percent of science fiction that isn't crud is as good as or better than anything being written anywhere." The *Oxford English Dictionary* adds that "the aphorism was apparently first formulated in 1951 or 1952 at a lecture at New York University."

John Suckling
English poet and playwright, 1609–1642

1 Why so pale and wan, fond lover? Prithee, why so pale?
Aglaura act 4, sc. 1 (1637)

Sukarno (Kusno Sosrodihardjo)
Indonesian president, 1901–1970

1 A Year of Living Dangerously.
Title of speech, Jakarta, 17 Aug. 1964

Brendan V. Sullivan, Jr.
U.S. lawyer, 1942–

1 [*Upon being told to allow his client, Lieutenant Colonel Oliver North, to object for himself if he wished, at the Senate hearings on the Iran-Contra scandal:*] I'm not a potted plant. . . . I'm here as the lawyer. That's my job.
Remarks at Senate hearing, 9 July 1987

Louis H. Sullivan
U.S. architect, 1856–1924

1 Form ever follows function.
"The Tall Office Building Artistically Considered," *Lippincott's Magazine*, Mar. 1896

William Graham Sumner
U.S. sociologist, 1840–1910

1 It would be hard to find a single instance of a direct assault by positive effort upon poverty,

vice, and misery which has not either failed or, if it has not failed directly and entirely, has not entailed other evils greater than the one which it removed.
"Sociology" (1881)

2 We are born into no right whatever but what has an equivalent and corresponding duty right alongside of it. There is no such thing on this earth as something for nothing.
"The Forgotten Man" (1883)

3 The Forgotten Man . . . works, he votes, generally he prays—but he always pays—yes, above all, he pays. He does not want an office; his name never gets into the newspaper except when he gets married or dies. He keeps production going on. . . . He does not frequent the grocery or talk politics at the tavern. Consequently, he is forgotten. . . . All the burdens fall on him, or on her, for it is time to remember that the Forgotten Man is not seldom a woman.
"The Forgotten Man" (1883)
See Franklin Roosevelt 2

4 The Absurd Attempt to Make the World Over.
Title of article, Forum, Mar. 1894

5 If we put together all that we have learned from anthropology and ethnography about primitive men and primitive society, we perceive that the first task of life is to live. Men begin with acts, not with thoughts.
Folkways ch. 1 (1906)

6 A differentiation arises between ourselves, the we-group, or in-group, and everybody else, or the others-groups, out-groups.
Folkways ch. 1 (1906)

7 [Ethnocentrism is] the view of things in which one's own group is the center of everything and all others are scaled and rated with reference to it. . . . Each group nourishes its own pride and vanity, boasts itself superior, exalts its own divinities, and looks with contempt on outsiders.
Folkways ch. 1 (1906)

8 The mores come down to us from the past. Each individual is born into them as he is born into the atmosphere, and he does not reflect on

them, or criticise them any more than a baby analyzes the atmosphere before he begins to breathe it.
Folkways ch. 2 (1906)

9 The men, women, and children who compose a society at any time are the unconscious depositaries and transmitters of the mores. They inherited them without knowing it; they are molding them unconsciously; they will transmit them involuntarily. The people cannot make the mores. They are made by them.
Folkways ch. 11 (1906)

Sun Tzu
Chinese collective name for authors of *The Art of War*, fl. ca. 400 B.C.

1 War is a vital matter of state.
The Art of War ch. 1 (translation by Roger T. Ames)

2 Warfare is the art of deceit.
The Art of War ch. 1 (translation by Roger T. Ames)

3 There has never been a state that has benefited from an extended war.
The Art of War ch. 2 (translation by Roger T. Ames)

4 To win a hundred victories in a hundred battles is not the highest excellence; the highest excellence is to subdue the enemy's army without fighting at all.
The Art of War ch. 3 (translation by Roger T. Ames)

5 He who knows the enemy and himself
Will never in a hundred battles be at risk.
The Art of War ch. 3 (translation by Roger T. Ames)

6 The victorious army only enters battle after having first won the victory, while the defeated army only seeks victory after having first entered the fray.
The Art of War ch. 4 (translation by Roger T. Ames)

7 So veiled and subtle,
To the point of having no form;
So mysterious and miraculous,
To the point of making no sound.
Therefore he can be arbiter of the enemy's fate.
The Art of War ch. 6 (translation by Roger T. Ames)

8 Hence a commander who advances without any thought of winning personal fame and withdraws in spite of certain punishment, whose only concern is to protect his people and

promote the interests of his ruler, is the nation's treasure.

The Art of War ch. 10 (translation by Roger T. Ames)

Sun Yat-sen

Chinese president, 1866–1925

1 The Chinese people have only family and clan solidarity; they do not have national spirit . . . they are just a heap of loose sand. . . . Other men are the carving knife and serving dish; we are the fish and the meat.

"China as a Heap of Loose Sand" (1924)

2 The National Government shall construct the Republic of China on the revolutionary basis of the Three Principles of the People. The primary requisite of reconstruction lies in the people's livelihood. . . . Second in importance is the people's sovereignty. . . . Third comes nationalism.

Fundamentals of National Reconstruction (1924)

Jacqueline Susann

U.S. novelist, 1921–1974

1 Valley of the Dolls.

Title of book (1966)

2 [*Of Philip Roth:*] He's a fine writer, but I wouldn't want to shake hands with him.

Quoted in Barbara Seaman, *Lovely Me* (1987)

Willie Sutton

U.S. criminal, 1901–1980

1 [*Explanation of why he robbed banks:*] That's where the money is.

Quoted in *Saturday Evening Post*, Jan. 1951

Han Suyin (Elisabeth Rosalie Matthilde Clare Chou)

Chinese novelist and physician, 1917–2012

1 Love Is a Many-Splendored Thing.

Title of book (1952)
See Francis Thompson 1

Claude A. Swanson

U.S. politician, 1862–1939

1 When in doubt, do right.

Quoted in *Current Opinion,* 1 July 1923

Gloria Swanson (Gloria Josephine Mae Swenson)

U.S. actress, 1899–1983

1 When I die, my epitaph should read: *She Paid the Bills.* That's the story of my life.

Quoted in *Saturday Evening Post,* 22 July 1950

Edwin Swayzee

U.S. jazz musician, 1906–1935

1 Jitter Bug.

Title of song (1934). Swayzee wrote this song for Cab Calloway. The actual coiner of the term *jitterbug* was trombonist-drummer Harry Alexander White; Swayzee picked up the word from White.

May Swenson

U.S. poet, 1919–1989

1 Body my house
my horse my hound
what will I do
when you are fallen.

"Question" l. 1 (1954)

Jonathan Swift

Irish-born English satirist and clergyman, 1667–1745

1 Instead of dirt and poison we have rather chosen to fill our hives with honey and wax; thus furnishing mankind with the two noblest of things, which are sweetness and light.

The Battle of the Books (1704)
See Matthew Arnold 27

2 Last week I saw a woman flayed, and you will hardly believe, how much it altered her person for the worse.

A Tale of a Tub ch. 9 (1704)

3 Laws are like Cobwebs, which may catch small Flies, but let Wasps and Hornets break through.

A Critical Essay upon the Faculties of the Mind (1709)
See Anacharsis 1

4 We have just Religion enough to make us *hate*, but not enough to make us *love* one another.

Thoughts on Various Subjects (1711)

5 When a true Genius appears in the World, you may know him by this Sign; that the Dunces are all in Confederacy against him.

Thoughts on Various Subjects (1711)

6 The stoical scheme of supplying our wants, by lopping off our desires, is like cutting off our feet when we want shoes.

Thoughts on Various Subjects (1711)

7 Proper words in proper places, make the true definition of a style.

Letter to a Young Gentleman Lately Entered into Holy Orders, 9 Jan. 1720

8 If Heaven had looked upon riches to be a valuable thing, it would not have given them to such a scoundrel.

Letter to Miss Vanhomrigh, 12–13 Aug. 1720
See Luther 3; Steele 2

9 All *Government* without the Consent of the *Governed*, is the *very Definition of Slavery*.

The Drapier's Letters no. 4 (1724)

10 I have ever hated all nations, professions, and communities, and all my love is towards individuals. . . . I hate and detest that animal called man, although I heartily love John, Peter, Thomas, and so forth.

Letter to Alexander Pope, 29 Sept. 1725

11 I cannot but conclude the Bulk of your Natives, to be the most pernicious Race of little odious Vermin that Nature ever suffered to crawl upon the Surface of the Earth.

Gulliver's Travels "A Voyage to Brobdingnag" ch. 6 (1726)

12 Whoever could make two Ears of Corn, or two Blades of Grass to grow upon a Spot of Ground where only one grew before; would deserve better of Mankind, and do more essential Service to his Country, than the whole Race of Politicians put together.

Gulliver's Travels "A Voyage to Brobdingnag" ch. 7 (1726)

13 He replied, That I must needs be mistaken, or that I *said the thing which was not*. (For they have no Word in their Language to express Lying or Falsehood.)

Gulliver's Travels "A Voyage to the Houyhnhnms" ch. 3 (1726)

14 [*On lawyers:*] I said there was a Society of Men among us, bred up from their Youth in the Art of proving by Words multiplied for the Purpose, that *White* is *Black,* and *Black* is *White,* according as they are paid. To this Society all the rest of the People are Slaves.

Gulliver's Travels "A Voyage to the Houyhnhnms" ch. 5 (1726)

15 It is a Maxim among these Lawyers, that whatever hath been done before, may legally be done again.

Gulliver's Travels "A Voyage to the Houyhnhnms" ch. 5 (1726)

16 I told him . . . that we eat when we were not hungry, and drank without the Provocation of Thirst.

Gulliver's Travels "A Voyage to the Houyhnhnms" ch. 6 (1726)

17 But when I behold a Lump of Deformity, and Diseases both in Body and Mind, smitten with *Pride*, it immediately breaks all the Measures of my Patience.

Gulliver's Travels "A Voyage to the Houyhnhnms" ch. 12 (1726)

18 He had been Eight Years upon a Project for extracting Sun-Beams out of Cucumbers, which were to be put into Vials hermetically sealed, and let out to warm the Air in raw inclement Summers.

Gulliver's Travels "A Voyage to Laputa, etc." ch. 5 (1726)

19 Men are never so serious, thoughtful, and intent, as when they are at Stool.

Gulliver's Travels "A Voyage to Laputa, etc." ch. 6 (1726)

20 It is computed, that eleven Thousand Persons have, at several Times, suffered Death, rather than submit to break their Eggs at the smaller End. Many large Volumes have been published upon this Controversy: But the Books of the *Big-Endians* have been long forbidden, and the whole Party rendered incapable by Law of holding Employments.

Gulliver's Travels "A Voyage to Lilliput" ch. 4 (1726)

21 Ingratitude is among them a capital Crime, . . . For they reason thus: that whoever makes ill Returns to his Benefactor, must needs be a common Enemy to the rest of Mankind, from whom he hath received no Obligation; and therefore such a Man is not fit to live.

Gulliver's Travels "A Voyage to Lilliput" ch. 6 (1726)

22 They will never allow, that a Child is under any Obligation to his Father for begetting him, or his Mother for bringing him into the World; which, considering the Miseries of human Life, was neither a Benefit in itself, nor intended so by his Parents, whose Thoughts in their Love-encounters were otherwise employed.

Gulliver's Travels "A Voyage to Lilliput" ch. 6 (1726)

23 How haughtily he lifts his nose,
To tell what every schoolboy knows.

"The Journal" l. 81 (1727)
See Thomas Macaulay 8; Jeremy Taylor 1

24 Every man desires to live long; but no man would be old.

Thoughts on Various Subjects (1727 edition)

25 Hail, fellow, well met,
All dirty and wet:
Find out, if you can,
Who's master, who's man.

"My Lady's Lamentation" l. 165 (written 1728)

26 A Modest Proposal for Preventing the Children of Poor People from Being a Burden to their Parents, or the Country, and for Making Them Beneficial to the Public.

Title of pamphlet (1729)

27 I have been assured by a very knowing *American* of my Acquaintance in *London,* that a young healthy Child, well nursed, is, at a Year old, a most delicious, nourishing, and wholesome Food; whether *Stewed, Roasted,*

Baked, or *Boiled;* and, I make no doubt, that it will equally serve in a *Fricasie,* or *Ragoust.*

A Modest Proposal for Preventing the Children of Poor People from Being a Burden to their Parents, or the Country, and for Making Them Beneficial to the Public (1729)

28 Hobbes clearly proves, that every creature Lives in a state of war by nature.

"On Poetry" l. 319 (1733)

29 So, Nat'ralists observe, a Flea
Hath smaller Fleas that on him prey,
And these have smaller Fleas to bite 'em,
And so proceed *ad infinitum:*
Thus ev'ry Poet in his Kind,
Is bit by him that comes behind.

"On Poetry" l. 337 (1733)

30 The Sight of you is good for sore Eyes.

Polite Conversation "First Conversation" (1738)

31 He was a bold man that first eat an oyster.

Polite Conversation "Second Conversation" (1738)

32 There was all the World, and his Wife.

Polite Conversation "Third Conversation" (1738)

33 I'm going to the Land of Nod.

Polite Conversation "Third Conversation" (1738)

34 *Ubi saeva indignatio ulterius cor lacerare nequit.*
  Abi Viator et imitare, si poteris, strenuum, pro virili, libertatis vindicatorem.
Where savage indignation can no longer
  tear his heart. Go, traveller, and imitate
  him if you can, a man who to his utmost
  championed liberty.

Epitaph (1745). These words, in St. Patrick's Cathedral in Dublin, have been described by William Butler Yeats as "the greatest epitaph in history."
See Yeats 58

35 Although reason were intended by Providence to govern our passions, yet it seems that, in two points of the greatest moment to the being and continuance of the world, God hath intended our passions to prevail over reason. The first is, the propagation of our species, since no wise man ever married from the dictates of reason. The other is, the love of life, which, from the dictates of reason, every man would despise, and wish it at an end, or that it never had a beginning.

Thoughts on Religion (1765)

36 I heard the little bird say so.
   Journal to Stella (1768) (entry for 23 May 1711)

37 The other day we had a long discourse with
   [Lady Orkney] about love; and she told us a
   saying . . . which I thought excellent, that *in
   men, desire begets love;* and *in women, love begets
   desire.*
   Journal to Stella (1768) (entry for 30 Oct. 1712)

38 Good God! what a genius I had when I wrote
   that book [*A Tale of a Tub*].
   Quoted in *Works of Swift*, ed. Walter Scott (1814)

39 [*Of angling:*] A stick and a string, with a worm
   at one end and a fool at the other.
   Attributed in *Monthly Review*, Apr. 1805. Francis
   Grose, *A Classical Dictionary of the Vulgar Tongue*, 2nd
   ed. (1788), had earlier written: "A fool at the end of
   a stick; a fool at one end, and a maggot at the other:
   gibes on an angler." A similar remark has also been
   attributed to Samuel Johnson.

Taylor Swift
U.S. singer and songwriter, 1989–

1 Nice to meet you, where you been?
   I could show you incredible things
   Magic, madness, heaven, sin
   Saw you there and I thought
   Oh my God, look at that face
   You look like my next mistake
   Love's a game, wanna play?
   "Blank Space" (song) (2014). This song was
   coauthored with Max Martin and Shellback.

Algernon Charles Swinburne
English poet, 1837–1909

1 When the hounds of spring are on winter's
         traces,
   The mother of months in meadow or plain
   Fills the shadows and windy places
   With lisp of leaves and ripple of rain.
   Atalanta in Calydon chorus (1865)

2 For winter's rains and ruins are over,
   And all the season of snows and sins;
   The days dividing lover and lover,
   The light that loses, the night that wins;
   And time remembered is grief forgotten,
   And frosts are slain and flowers begotten,
   And in green underwood and cover
   Blossom by blossom the spring begins.
   Atalanta in Calydon chorus (1865)

3 From too much love of living,
   From hope and fear set free,
   We thank with brief thanksgiving
   Whatever gods may be
   That no man lives forever,
   That dead men rise up never;
   That even the weariest river
   Winds somewhere safe to sea.
   "The Garden of Proserpine" l. 81 (1866)

4 If love were what the rose is,
   And I were like the leaf,
   Our lives would grow together
   In sad or singing weather.
   "A Match" l. 1 (1866)

5 As a god self-slain on his own strange altar,
   Death lies dead.
   "A Forsaken Garden" l. 79 (1878)

John Swinton
U.S. journalist, 1829–1901

1 There is no such thing in America as an
   independent press. . . . There is not one of you
   who dares to write your honest opinions, and
   if you did, you know beforehand that it would
   never appear in print. I am paid $150 a week
   for keeping my honest opinions out of the
   paper I am connected with.
   Quoted in *Chicago Labor Enquirer*, 12 May 1888

2 The business of the New York journalist is to
   destroy the truth; to lie outright; to pervert; to
   vilify; to fawn at the feet of mammon, and to
   sell his race and his country for his daily bread.
   Quoted in *Chicago Labor Enquirer*, 12 May 1888

3 We are the tools and vassals of rich men behind
   the scenes. We are the jumping jacks, they
   pull the strings and we dance. Our talents, our
   possibilities, and our lives are all the property
   of other men. We are intellectual prostitutes.
   Quoted in *Chicago Labor Enquirer*, 12 May 1888

Herbert Bayard Swope
U.S. editor and journalist, 1882–1958

1 I can not give you [the formula for success], but
   I can give you the formula for failure—which
   is: Try to please everybody.
   Quoted in *Miami News*, 27 Dec. 1950

Charles J. Sykes

U.S. writer, 1954–

1 Be nice to nerds. You may end up working for them.

San Diego Union-Tribune, 19 Sept. 1996

J. A. Symonds

English scholar, 1840–1893

1 The author [Richard Francis Burton] endeavoured to co-ordinate a large amount of miscellaneous matter, and to frame a general theory regarding the origin and prevalence of homosexual passions.

A Problem in Modern Ethics ch. 8 (1891). Appears to be the earliest printed occurrence in English of the word *homosexual*.

Arthur Symons

Welsh literary critic, 1865–1945

1 There is not a dream which may not come true, if we have the energy which makes or chooses our own fate. . . . It is only the dreams of those light sleepers who dream faintly that do not come true.

Poems of Ernest Dowson introduction (1900)

John Millington Synge

Irish playwright, 1871–1909

1 "A translation is no translation," he said, "unless it will give you the music of a poem along with the words of it."

The Aran Islands pt. 3 (1907)

2 Oh my grief, I've lost him surely. I've lost the only Playboy of the Western World.

The Playboy of the Western World act 3 (1907)

Thomas Szasz

Hungarian-born U.S. psychiatrist, 1920–2012

1 Happiness is an imaginary condition, formerly often attributed by the living to the dead, now usually attributed by adults to children, and by children to adults.

The Second Sin "Emotions" (1973)

2 If you talk to God, you are praying; if God talks to you, you have schizophrenia.

The Second Sin "Schizophrenia" (1973)

3 Formerly, when religion was strong and science weak, men mistook magic for medicine; now, when science is strong and religion weak, men mistake medicine for magic.

The Second Sin "Science and Scientism" (1973)

4 Traditionally, sex has been a very private, secretive activity. Herein perhaps lies its powerful force for uniting people in a strong bond. As we make sex less secretive, we may rob it of its power to hold men and women together.

The Second Sin "Sex" (1973)

Cornelius Tacitus
Roman historian, ca. 56–ca. 120

1 [*Referring to the Romans:*] They make a desert and call it peace.
Agricola ch. 30. These are allegedly Calgacus's words at the battle of the Grampians.

2 [*Of Petronius:*] *Elegantiae arbiter.*
The arbiter of taste.
Annals bk. 16, ch. 18

3 *Deos fortioribus adesse.*
The gods are on the side of the stronger.
Histories bk. 4, ch. 17
See Bussy-Rabutin 1; Frederick the Great 1; Turenne 1

4 *Experientia docuit.*
Experience has taught.
Histories bk. 5, ch. 6. Usually quoted as "*Experientia docet* [Experience teaches]."

William Howard Taft
U.S. president and judge, 1857–1930

1 [*Of the 350-pound Taft:*] Taft, stuck at a water-tank railroad station and learning that the train would only stop if a number of passengers wished to come aboard, telegraphed to the conductor: "Stop at Hicksville. Large party waiting to catch train."
Reported in Malcolm Ross, *Death of a Yale Man* (1939)

2 When I suggested to him [Taft, who weighed more than three hundred pounds] . . . that he occupy a Chair of Law at the University, he said that he was afraid that a Chair would not be adequate, but that if we would provide a Sofa of Law, it might be all right.
Reported in Anson Phelps Stokes, Letter to Frederick C. Hicks, 10 May 1940

William Tager
U.S. criminal, fl. 1986

1 What is the frequency, Kenneth?
Quoted in *Chicago Tribune*, 8 Oct. 1986. Television broadcaster Dan Rather was assaulted in New York City by two men, one of whom cryptically asked Rather, "What is the frequency, Kenneth?" The speaker was later identified as Tager.

Rabindranath Tagore
Indian poet and philosopher, 1861–1941

1 On the seashore of endless worlds children meet. Tempest roams in the pathless sky, ships are wrecked in the trackless water, death is abroad and children play. On the seashore of endless worlds is the great meeting of children.
"On the Seashore" l. 6 (1918)

2 Bigotry tries to keep truth safe in its hand
With a grip that kills it.
Fireflies (1928)

Hippolyte Adolphe Taine
French critic, historian, and philosopher, 1828–1893

1 *Le vice et la vertu sont des produits comme le vitriol et le sucre.*
Vice and virtue are products like vitriol and sugar.
Histoire de la Littérature Anglaise introduction (1863)

Nassim Nicholas Taleb
Lebanese-born U.S. author and statistician, 1960–

1 Our world is dominated by the extreme, the unknown, and the very improbable (improbable according to our current knowledge)—and all the while we spend our time engaged in small talk, focusing on the known, and the repeated.
The Black Swan: The Impact of the Highly Improbable prologue (2007)

2 Economic, financial, and political predictors . . . are quite ashamed to say anything outlandish to their clients—and yet *events, it turns out, are almost always outlandish.*
The Black Swan: The Impact of the Highly Improbable ch. 10 (2007)

S. G. Tallentyre (Evelyn Beatrice Hall)
English writer, 1868–1956

1 [*Paraphrase of Voltaire's attitude:*] I disapprove of what you say, but I will defend to the death your right to say it.

The Friends of Voltaire ch. 7 (1906). *Bartlett's Familiar Quotations* traces this to a letter by Voltaire to a M. le Riche, 6 Feb. 1770, but that is based on an error in Norbert Guterman, *A Dictionary of French Quotations.* The quotation does not appear in Voltaire's letter to François-Louis-Henri Leriche of that date nor anywhere else in Voltaire's writings.

Charles Maurice de Talleyrand-Périgord
French statesman, 1754–1838

1 You can do anything with bayonets except sit on them.

Quoted in *N.Y. Times,* 18 Dec. 1898. Although this is associated with Talleyrand, *Littell's Living Age,* 31 Jan. 1852, printed the following: "There may be some truth in that humorous Parisian bon mot, in which a queer sort of point has been given by attributing it to Prince Schwartzenberg, that 'a man may do anything with bayonets except sit upon them.'"

See Inge 3

2 [*Response to the tsar of Russia's criticism of those who "betrayed the cause of Europe":*] That, Sire, is a question of dates.

Quoted in Duff Cooper, *Talleyrand* (1932). Often quoted as "treason is a matter of dates."

3 [*Of Napoleon's costly victory at the Battle of Borodino, 1812:*] C'est le commencement de la fin. This is the beginning of the end.

Attributed in Édouard Fournier, *L'Esprit dans l'Historie* (1857)

Talmud
Jewish traditional compilation, ca. sixth cent.

1 If the soft [water] can wear away the hard [stone], how much more can the words of the Torah, which are hard like iron, carve a way into my heart which is of flesh and blood!

Babylonian Talmud "Avot de Rabbi Nathan" 20b

2 Even an iron partition cannot interpose between Israel and their Father in Heaven.

Babylonian Talmud "Pesahim" 85b

3 [*Of the laws of the Torah:*] *He shall live by them,* but he shall not die because of them.

Babylonian Talmud "Yoma" 85b

4 On Passover eve the son asks his father, and if the son is unintelligent, his father instructs him to ask: Why is this night different from all other nights?

Mishnah "Pesahim" 10:4

5 The day is short, the labor long, the workers are idle, and reward is great, and the Master is urgent.

Mishnah "Pirqei Avot" 2:15

6 The tradition is a fence around the Law.

Mishnah "Pirqei Avot" 3:14

7 [*Of the Torah:*] Turn it and turn it again, for everything is in it.

Mishnah "Pirqei Avot" 5:22

8 Whoever destroys a single life is as guilty as though he had destroyed the entire world; and whoever rescues a single life earns as much merit as though he had rescued the entire world.

Mishnah "Sanhedrin" 4:5

Amy Tan
U.S. novelist, 1952–

1 Fate is shaped half by expectation, half by inattention.

The Joy Luck Club (1989)

Roger B. Taney
U.S. judge and cabinet officer, 1777–1864

1 They [slaves and their descendants] are not included, and are not intended to be included, under the word "citizens" in the Constitution, and can therefore, claim none of the rights and privileges which that instrument provides for and secures to citizens of the United States.

Dred Scott v. Sandford (1857)

2 They had for more than a century before been regarded as beings of an inferior order, and altogether unfit to associate with the white race, either in social or political relations; and so far inferior, that they had no rights which the white man was bound to respect; . . . This opinion was at that time fixed and universal in the civilized portion of the white race.

Dred Scott v. Sandford (1857)

T'ao Ch'ien

Chinese poet, 365–427

1 They told him that their ancestors had fled the disorders of Ch'in times and, having taken refuge here with wives and children and neighbors, had never ventured out again; consequently they had lost all contact with the outside world.
"The Peach Blossom Spring" (ca. 500) (translation by James Robert Hightower)

Siegbert Tarrasch

German chess player, 1862–1934

1 Chess, like love, like music, has the power to make men happy.
The Game of Chess ch. 9 (1931)

Donna Tartt

U.S. novelist, 1963–

1 The snow in the mountains was melting and Bunny had been dead for several weeks before we came to understand the gravity of our situation.
The Secret History prologue (1992)

Torquato Tasso

Italian poet, 1544–1595

1 Much wished, hoped little, and demanded nought.
Jerusalem Delivered bk. 2, st. 16 (1580)

Ann Taylor

English children's book writer, 1782–1866

1 Who ran to help me when I fell,
And would some pretty story tell,
Or kiss the place to make it well?
My mother.
"My Mother" l. 21 (1804)

2 Twinkle, twinkle, little star,
How I wonder what you are!
Up above the world so high,
Like a diamond in the sky!
Rhymes for the Nursery "The Star" l. 1 (1806). Book authored with Jane Taylor, who wrote "The Star."
See Carroll 16

Bert L. Taylor

U.S. journalist, 1866–1921

1 A bore is a man who, when you ask him how he is, tells you.
The So-Called Human Race (1922)

James Taylor

U.S. singer and songwriter, 1948–

1 Just yesterday morning they let me know you were gone,
Suzanne the plans they made put an end to you.
I walked out this morning and I wrote down this song,
I just can't remember who to send it to.
"Fire and Rain" (song) (1969)

2 I've seen fire and I've seen rain
I've seen sunny days that I thought would never end
I've seen lonely times when I could not find a friend
But I always thought that I'd see you again.
"Fire and Rain" (song) (1969)

3 There's a song that they sing when they take to the highway
A song that they sing when they take to the sea
A song that they sing of their home in the sky
Maybe you can believe it if it helps you to sleep
But singing works just fine for me.
"Sweet Baby James" (song) (1970)

4 The first of December was covered with snow
So was the turnpike from Stockbridge to Boston
The Berkshires seemed dream-like on account of that frosting
With ten miles behind me and ten thousand more to go.
"Sweet Baby James" (song) (1970)

Jeremy Taylor

English clergyman and author, 1613–1667

1 This thing . . . that can be understood and not expressed, may make a neuter gender; and every School-boy knows it.
The Real Presence and Spiritual of Christ in the Blessed Sacrament sec. 5 (1653)
See Thomas Macaulay 8; Jonathan Swift 23

2 Marriage is . . . the union of hands and hearts.
XXV Sermons Preached at Golden Grove "The Marriage Ring" pt. 1 (1653)

Tell Taylor

U.S. entertainer, 1876–1937

1 Down by the old mill stream where I first
     met you,
  With your eyes of blue, dressed in
     gingham too,
  It was there I knew that you loved me true,
  You were sixteen, my village queen, by the old
     mill stream.
"Down by the Old Mill Stream" (song) (1910)

2 You're in the Army now,
  You're not behind a plow;
  You'll never get rich
  A-diggin' a ditch,
  You're in the Army now.
"You're in the Army Now" (song) (1917). Cowritten with Ole Olsen.

Sara Teasdale

U.S. poet, 1884–1933

1 Time is a kind friend, he will make us old.
"Let It Be Forgotten" l. 4 (1919)

Tecumseh

Native American leader, 1768–1813

1 Sell a country! Why not sell the air, the clouds, and the great sea, as well as the earth? Did not the Great Spirit make them all for the use of his children?
Speech to William Henry Harrison, Vincennes, Indiana Territory, 14 Aug. 1810

2 Sleep not longer, O Choctaws and Chickasaws, in false security and delusive hopes. Our broad domains are fast escaping from our grasp. Every year our white intruders become more greedy, exacting, oppressive, and overbearing.
Speech before joint council of Choctaws and Chickasaws, Sept. 1811

3 Where today are the Pequot? Where are the Narragansett, the Mohican, the Pokanoket, and many other once powerful tribes of our people? They have vanished before the avarice and oppression of the white man, as snow before the summer sun.
Quoted in Dee Brown, *Bury My Heart at Wounded Knee* (1970)

Pierre Teilhard de Chardin

French philosopher and paleontologist, 1881–1955

1 *Tout ce qui monte converge.*
  Everything that rises must converge.
"Faith in Man" (1947)

2 The day will come when, after harnessing space, the winds, the tides, gravitation, we shall harness for God the energies of love. And, on that day, for the second time in the history of the world, man will have discovered fire.
The Evolution of Chastity (1934)

Television Catchphrases

See also Radio Catchphrases, Star Trek, Gene Roddenberry, Matt Groening, Rod Serling, Tex Avery, Larry David, *and* Larry Charles.

1 Up close and personal.
ABC Sports broadcasts

2 [*Caution by daredevil Evel Knievel:*] Kids, do not try this at home.
ABC's Wide World of Sports

3 The thrill of victory, the agony of defeat.
ABC's Wide World of Sports

4 The envelope, please.
Academy Awards broadcasts

5 And the winner is . . .
Academy Awards broadcasts

6 Superman! . . . strange visitor from another planet who came to Earth with powers and abilities far beyond those of mortal men. Superman! who can change the course of mighty rivers, bend steel in his bare hands. And who, disguised as Clark Kent, mild-mannered reporter for a great metropolitan newspaper, fights a never-ending battle for Truth, Justice, and the American way!
Adventures of Superman
See Nietzsche 13; Radio Catchphrases 21; Radio Catchphrases 22; George Bernard Shaw 11; Siegel 1

7 [*Catchphrase of Flo Castleberry, played by Polly Holliday:*] Kiss my grits!
Alice

8 [*Catchphrase of Donald Trump:*] You're fired!
   The Apprentice

9 [*Catchphrase of Hannibal Smith, played by George Peppard:*] I love it when a plan comes together.
   The A-Team

10 Still wanted by the government, they survive as soldiers of fortune. If you have a problem, if no one else can help, and if you can find them, maybe you can hire the A-Team.
   The A-Team

11 [*Catchphrase of Sheldon Cooper, played by Jim Parsons:*] Bazinga!
   The Big Bang Theory

12 Smile! You're on Candid Camera!
   Candid Camera

13 [*Signoff of Walter Cronkite:*] And that's the way it is.
   CBS Evening News

14 This is CNN.
   CNN news network broadcasts

15 [*Catchphrase of Jon Stewart:*] Here it is, your moment of Zen.
   The Daily Show

16 What'chu talkin' 'bout, Willis?
   Different Strokes

17 Tonight, we have a re-e-eally big shew!
   The Ed Sullivan Show

18 Bam!
   Emeril Live

19 [*Catchphrase of Fred Flintstone:*] Yabba, Dabba Do!
   The Flintstones

20 Clear eyes, full hearts, can't lose.
   Friday Night Lights

21 [*Catchphrase of Joey Tribbiani, played by Matt LeBlanc:*] How *you* doin'?
   Friends

22 [*Catchphrase of Ross Geller, played by David Schwimmer:*] We were on a break!
   Friends

23 [*Catchphrase of George Burns, said to Gracie Allen:*] Say goodnight, Gracie.
   The George Burns and Gracie Allen Show. It is often said that Allen would respond, "Goodnight, Gracie."

Burns, however, in his book *Gracie: A Love Story* (1988) describes this response as a show business myth. That myth may have been reinforced by analogous banter between Dan Rowan and Dick Martin in the series *Rowan and Martin's Laugh-In,* in which Martin would actually respond to "Say goodnight, Dick" by saying "Goodnight, Dick."

24 [*Catchphrase of Maxwell Smart, played by Don Adams:*] Would you believe . . .
   Get Smart. Earlier used by Adams on the *Bill Dana Show.*

25 [*Catchphrase of Jimmy Walker:*] Dy-No-Mite!
   Good Times

26 [*Catchphrase of Fonzie, played by Henry Winkler:*] Aaay.
   Happy Days

27 [*Catchphrase of Steve McGarrett, played by Jack Lord:*] Book 'em, Danno!
   Hawaii Five-O

28 [*Catchphrase of Sergeant Phil Esterhaus, played by Michael Conrad:*] Let's be careful out there.
   Hill Street Blues

29 [*Catchphrase of Ralph Kramden, played by Jackie Gleason:*] One of these days, Alice . . . POW!, right in the kisser!
   The Honeymooners

30 [*Catchphrase of Ralph Kramden, played by Jackie Gleason:*] To the moon, Alice!
   The Honeymooners

31 Everybody lies.
   House

32 [*War cry of Chief Thunderthud:*] Kowabunga!
   The Howdy Doody Show

33 [*Catchphrase of Buffalo Bob Smith:*] Say kids, what time is it? It's Howdy Doody Time!
   The Howdy Doody Show

34 [*Catchphrase of Barney Stinson, played by Neil Patrick Harris:*] Legendary.
   How I Met Your Mother

35 [*Catchphrase of Barney Stinson, played by Neil Patrick Harris:*] Suit up!
   How I Met Your Mother

36 [*Catchphrase of Ricky Ricardo, played by Desi Arnaz:*] Lucy, I'm ho-o-ome.
   I Love Lucy

37 [*Catchphrase of David Banner, played by Bill Bixby:*] Don't make me angry. You wouldn't like me when I'm angry.
The Incredible Hulk

38 How sweet it is!
The Jackie Gleason Show

39 [*Catchphrase of Lt. Theo Kojak, played by Telly Savalas:*] Who loves ya, baby?
Kojak

40 Wunnerful, wunnerful.
The Lawrence Welk Show

41 [*Catchphrase of robot:*] Danger! Danger, Will Robinson!
Lost in Space

42 [*Catchphrase of Maynard G. Krebs, played by Bob Denver:*] You rang?
The Many Loves of Dobie Gillis. This was also a catchphrase of Lurch, played by Ted Cassidy, on the later television series *The Addams Family*.

43 [*Catchphrase of Maynard G. Krebs, played by Bob Denver:*] Work!
The Many Loves of Dobie Gillis

44 Now it's time to say goodbye to all our company. M-I-C (see you real soon). K-E-Y (why? because we like you). M-O-U-S-E.
The Mickey Mouse Club

45 Good morning, Mr. Phelps. . . . Your mission . . . should you decide to accept it, is to [mission of the week described]. As always, should you or any member of your IM Force be caught or killed, the secretary will disavow any knowledge of your actions. This tape will self-destruct in five seconds.
Mission Impossible. In the show's first season, the beginning was "Good morning, Mr. Briggs."

46 [*Catchphrase of Robot AF709, played by Julie Newmar:*] Does not compute.
My Living Doll

47 There is nothing wrong with your television set. Do not attempt to adjust the picture. We are controlling the transmission.
The Outer Limits

48 Thanks . . . I needed that.
The Perry Como Show

49 You really know how to hurt a guy.
The Perry Como Show

50 Come on down!
The Price Is Right

51 [*Catchphrase of "Number Six," played by Patrick McGoohan:*] I am not a number! I am a free man!
The Prisoner

52 [*Catchphrase of "Number Six," played by Patrick McGoohan:*] I will not be pushed, stamped, filed, indexed, briefed, debriefed, or numbered. My life is my own.
The Prisoner

53 [*Catchphrase of Tim Gunn:*] Make it work.
Project Runway

54 [*Catchphrase of Ashton Kutcher:*] You've been punk'd.
Punk'd

55 Sock it to me!
Rowan and Martin's Laugh-In. Was in use before this show, appearing in a song sung by Stepin Fetchit in the 1945 short film "Big Times."

56 [*Catchphrase of Arte Johnson:*] Very interesting . . . but stupid.
Rowan and Martin's Laugh-In

57 You bet your sweet bippy.
Rowan and Martin's Laugh-In

58 [*Catchphrase of Gary Owen:*] Beautiful downtown Burbank.
Rowan and Martin's Laugh-In

59 [*Catchphrase of Sammy Davis, Jr., and Flip Wilson:*] Here come de judge.
Rowan and Martin's Laugh-In. This phrase derived most immediately from a routine of Dewey "Pigmeat" Markham's, but the *Oxford Dictionary of Catchphrases* states, "The 'here comes the judge' vaudeville routine written and performed by blacks for black audiences dates to the early part of the century, and particularly the 1920s."

60 [*Catchphrase of Fred Sanford, played by Redd Foxx:*] This is the big one! Elizabeth, I'm coming to join you honey!
Sanford and Son

61 [*Catchphrase of Steve Martin:*] Exc-u-u-u-se me!
Saturday Night Live

62 [*Catchphrase of Mike Myers and Dana Carvey in "Wayne's World" skits:*] We're not worthy!
Saturday Night Live

63 [*Catchphrase of Mike Myers and Dana Carvey in "Wayne's World" skits, indicating that a female was attractive:*] Schwing!
Saturday Night Live

64 [*Catchphrase of Dan Aykroyd, speaking to Jane Curtin:*] Jane, you ignorant slut.
Saturday Night Live

65 [*Catchphrase of Steve Martin and Dan Aykroyd:*] We are two wild and crazy guys!
Saturday Night Live

66 [*Catchphrase of Mike Myers and Dana Carvey in "Wayne's World" skits, negating the entire statement preceding it:*] Not!
Saturday Night Live. This usage of the word *not* was not original with the "Wayne's World" skits; the *Historical Dictionary of American Slang* documents it as far back as 1893.

67 [*Catchphrase of Mike Myers and Dana Carvey in "Wayne's World" skits:*] No way?! Way!
Saturday Night Live

68 Live from New York, it's Saturday Night!
Saturday Night Live

69 Hello, Newman.
Seinfeld

70 [*Catchphrase of Paris Hilton:*] That's hot.
The Simple Life

71 [*Indicating approval of a motion picture:*] Two thumbs up!
Siskel & Ebert at the Movies

72 Oh my God! They killed Kenny!
South Park

73 The tribe has spoken.
Survivor

74 Voted off the island.
Survivor

75 [*Catchphrase of Ed McMahon, introducing host Johnny Carson:*] He-e-ere's . . . Johnny!
The Tonight Show

76 [*Catchphrase of Johnny Carson:*] I did not know that.
The Tonight Show

77 Will the real [name of person] please stand up?
To Tell the Truth

78 [*Catchphrase of Dale Cooper, played by Kyle MacLachlan:*] Damn good coffee.
Twin Peaks

79 [*Title of series:*] Upstairs, Downstairs.
Upstairs, Downstairs

80 [*Catchphrase of Road Runner:*] Beep! Beep!
Warner Brothers cartoons. First appeared in the animated short film *Fast and Furry-Ous* (1949), directed by Chuck Jones.

81 [*Catchphrase of Tweety Pie:*] I tawt I taw a puddy tat!
Warner Brothers cartoons. First appeared in the 1942 cartoon "A Tale of Two Kitties."

82 [*Catchphrase of Sylvester the Cat:*] Thufferin' Thuccotash!
Warner Brothers cartoons. Mel Blanc, who voiced Sylvester, had previously used this phrase for a traveling salesman character named Roscoe E. Wortle on the radio program *The Judy Canova Show*.

83 [*Signoff of Porky the Pig:*] Th-th-th-th-that's all, folks!
Warner Brothers cartoons. Before Porky, "That's all, folks!" was used by other characters ending Looney Tunes cartoons.

84 [*Catchphrase of Anne Robinson:*] You are the weakest link. Goodbye!
The Weakest Link

85 [*Steve Allen's regular question:*] Is it bigger than a breadbox?
What's My Line

86 Is that your final answer?
Who Wants to Be a Millionaire?

87 The truth is out there.
The X-Files

88 [*Catchphrase of Snagglepuss the lion:*] Exit, stage left [or "right"].
Yogi Bear

89 [*Catchphrase of Snagglepuss the lion:*] Heavens to Murgatroyd!
Yogi Bear. This was used earlier by Bert Lahr in the 1944 film *Meet the People*.

90 Smarter than the average bear.
Yogi Bear

Shirley Temple Black
U.S. actress and diplomat, 1928–2014

1 I stopped believing in Santa Claus when I was six. Mother took me to see him in a department store and he asked for my autograph.
Quoted in Leslie Halliwell, *Halliwell's Filmgoer's Companion* (1984)

George Tenet

U.S. government official, 1953–

1 It's a slam-dunk case.

Quoted in Bob Woodward, *Plan of Attack* (2004). Tenet's response to President George W. Bush when the latter asked him, during a White House meeting, 21 Dec. 2002, about the evidence that Iraq possessed weapons of mass destruction.

John Tenniel

English cartoonist and illustrator, 1820–1914

1 [*On Bismarck's leaving office:*] Dropping the pilot.

Cartoon caption and title of poem, *Punch,* 29 Mar. 1890

Alfred, Lord Tennyson

English poet, 1809–1892

1 Out flew the web and floated wide;
The mirror cracked from side to side;
"The curse is come upon me," cried
The Lady of Shalott.
"The Lady of Shalott" pt. 3, st. 5 (1832)

2 Break, break, break,
On thy cold gray stones, O Sea!
And I would that my tongue could utter
The thoughts that arise in me.
"Break, Break, Break" l. 1 (1842)

3 And the stately ships go on
To their haven under the hill;
But O for the touch of a vanish'd hand,
And the sound of a voice that is still!
"Break, Break, Break" l. 9 (1842)

4 Kind hearts are more than coronets,
And simple faith than Norman blood.
"Lady Clara Vere de Vere" l. 55 (1842)

5 In the spring a young man's fancy lightly turns
to thoughts of love.
"Locksley Hall" l. 20 (1842)

6 For I dipp'd into the future, far as human eye
could see,
Saw the vision of the world, and all the wonder
that would be.
"Locksley Hall" l. 119 (1842)

7 Heard the heavens fill with shouting, and there
rain'd a ghastly dew
From the nations' airy navies grappling in the
central blue.
"Locksley Hall" l. 123 (1842)

8 Till the war-drum throbbed no longer, and the
battle-flags were furl'd
In the Parliament of man, the Federation of the
world.
"Locksley Hall" l. 127 (1842)

9 I will take some savage woman, she shall rear
my dusky race.
"Locksley Hall" l. 168 (1842)

10 I the heir of all the ages, in the foremost files of
time.
"Locksley Hall" l. 178 (1842)

11 Forward, forward let us range,
Let the great world spin for ever down the
ringing grooves of change.
"Locksley Hall" l. 181 (1842)

12 Better fifty years of Europe than a cycle of
Cathay.
"Locksley Hall" l. 184 (1842)

13 My strength is as the strength of ten,
Because my heart is pure.
"Sir Galahad" l. 3 (1842)

14 It little profits that an idle king,
By this still hearth, among these barren crags,
Match'd with an aged wife, I mete and dole
Unequal laws unto a savage race
That hoard, and sleep, and feed, and know
not me.
"Ulysses" l. 1 (1842)

15 I cannot rest from travel; I will drink
Life to the lees: all times I have enjoy'd
Greatly, have suffer'd greatly.
"Ulysses" l. 6 (1842)

16 I am become a name.
  "Ulysses" l. 11 (1842)

17 Much have I seen and known; cities of men
  And manners, climates, councils, governments,
  Myself not least, but honor'd of them all;
  And drunk delight of battle with my peers,
  Far on the ringing plains of windy Troy.
  I am a part of all that I have met.
  "Ulysses" l. 13 (1842)

18 Yet all experience is an arch wherethro'
  Gleams that untravell'd world, whose margin
    fades
  For ever and for ever when I move.
  "Ulysses" l. 19 (1842)

19 How dull it is to pause, to make an end,
  To rust unburnish'd, not to shine in use!
  As tho' to breathe were life.
  "Ulysses" l. 22 (1842)

20 And this gray spirit yearning in desire
  To follow knowledge like a sinking star,
  Beyond the utmost bound of human thought.
  "Ulysses" l. 30 (1842)

21 This is my son, mine own Telemachus,
  To whom I leave the scepter and the isle.
  "Ulysses" l. 33 (1842)

22 He works his work, I mine.
  "Ulysses" l. 43 (1842)

23 Death closes all: but something ere the end,
  Some work of noble note, may yet be done,
  Not unbecoming men that strove with gods.
  "Ulysses" l. 51 (1842)

24   The deep
  Moans round with many voices. Come, my
    friends,
  'Tis not too late to seek a newer world.
  "Ulysses" l. 55 (1842)

25   For my purpose holds
  To sail beyond the sunset, and the baths
  Of all the western stars, until I die.
  It may be that the gulfs will wash us down:
  It may be we shall touch the Happy Isles,
  And see the great Achilles, whom we knew.
  "Ulysses" l. 59 (1842)

26 Tho' much is taken, much abides; and tho'
  We are not now that strength which in old days

Moved earth and heaven: That which we are,
    we are;
  One equal temper of heroic hearts,
  Made weak by time and fate, but strong in will
  To strive, to seek, to find, and not to yield.
  "Ulysses" l. 65 (1842)

27 In Memoriam.
  Title of poem (1850)

28 Let knowledge grow from more to more,
  But more of reverence in us dwell;
  That mind and soul, according well,
  May make one music as before.
  In Memoriam prologue, st. 7 (1850)

29 I hold it true, whate'er befall;
  I feel it, when I sorrow most;
  'Tis better to have loved and lost
  Than never to have loved at all.
  In Memoriam canto 27 (1850)
  See Congreve 7

30 Nature, red in tooth and claw.
  In Memoriam canto 56 (1850)

31 So many worlds, so much to do,
  So little done, such things to be.
  In Memoriam canto 73 (1850)
  See Rhodes 2

32 He seems so near and yet so far.
  In Memoriam canto 97 (1850)

33 Ring out the old, ring in the new,
  Ring, happy bells, across the snow:
  The year is going, let him go;
  Ring out the false, ring in the true.
  In Memoriam canto 106 (1850)

34   Wearing all that weight
  Of learning lightly like a flower.
  In Memoriam epilogue, st. 10 (1850)

35 One God, one law, one element,
  And one far-off divine event,
  To which the whole creation moves.
  In Memoriam epilogue, st. 36 (1850)

36 He clasps the crag with crooked hands;
  Close to the sun in lonely lands,
  Ringed with the azure world, he stands.

  The wrinkled sea beneath him crawls;
  He watches from his mountain walls,
  And like a thunderbolt he falls.
  "The Eagle" l. 1 (1851)

37 Half a league, half a league,
 Half a league onward,
 All in the valley of Death
 Rode the six hundred.
 "Forward the Light Brigade!"
 "The Charge of the Light Brigade" l. 1 (1854)

38 Was there a man dismay'd?
 Not tho' the soldier knew
 Some one had blunder'd.

 "The Charge of the Light Brigade" l. 6 (1854).
 Tennyson was inspired to write this poem by reading
 the account of the Battle of Balaclava in the *Times*
 (London), 13 Nov. 1854. In that account, written by
 William Russell, this passage appears: "The British
 soldier will do his duty, even to certain death, and is
 not paralyzed by feeling that he is the victim of some
 hideous blunder."

39 Theirs not to make reply,
 Theirs not to reason why,
 Theirs but to do and die:
 Into the valley of Death
 Rode the six hundred.
 "The Charge of the Light Brigade" l. 13 (1854)

40 Cannon to right of them,
 Cannon to left of them,
 Cannon in front of them
 Volley'd and thunder'd.
 "The Charge of the Light Brigade" l. 18 (1854)

41 Into the jaws of Death,
 Into the mouth of Hell.
 "The Charge of the Light Brigade" l. 24 (1854)

42 Mastering the lawless science of our law,
 That codeless myriad of precedent,
 That wilderness of single instances.
 "Aylmer's Field" st. 18 (1864)

43 The woods decay, the woods decay and fall,
 The vapors weep their burthen to the ground,
 Man comes and tills the field and lies beneath,
 And after many a summer dies the swan.
 "Tithonus" l. 1 (1860–1864)

44 For why is all around us here
 As if some lesser god had made the world,
 But had not force to shape it as he would?
 Idylls of the King "The Passing of Arthur" l. 13 (1869)

45 The old order changeth, yielding place to new,
 And God fulfils himself in many ways,
 Lest one good custom should corrupt the world.

Idylls of the King "The Passing of Arthur" l. 408
(1869)
*See Bailey 1; George H. W. Bush 7; George H. W. Bush
10; George H. W. Bush 12; Martin Luther King 1*

46 For tho' from out our bourne of time and place
 The flood may bear me far,
 I hope to see my pilot face to face
 When I have crossed the bar.
 "Crossing the Bar" l. 13 (1889)

Terence (Publius Terentius Afer)
Roman playwright, ca. 190 B.C.–159 B.C.

1 *Hinc illae lacrimae.*
 Hence those tears.
 Andria l. 126

2 *Nullumst iam dictum quod non dictum sit prius.*
 Nothing is said that has not been said before.
 Eunuchus prologue, l. 41

3 *Homo sum: humani nil a me alienum puto.*
 I am a man, and nothing human is foreign
  to me.
 Heauton Timorumenos l. 77

4 *Fortunis fortuna adiuvat.*
 Fortune helps the brave.
 Phormio l. 203
 See Virgil 12

5 *Quot homines tot sententiae.*
 There are as many opinions as there are people.
 Phormio l. 454

Mother Teresa (Agnes Gonxha Bojaxhiu)
Albanian-born Indian missionary, 1910–1997

1 God loves me, and I have an opportunity to love
 others as he loves me, not in big things, but in
 small things with great love.
 Nobel Peace Prize Lecture, Stockholm, Sweden,
 11 Dec. 1979

2 Let us do something beautiful for God.
 Quoted in Malcom Muggeridge, *Mother Teresa of
 Calcutta* (1971)

Teresa of Ávila (Teresa de Cepeda y Ahumada)
Spanish mystic and saint, 1512–1582

1 I die because I do not die.
 "Versos Nacidos del Fuego del Amor de Dios"
 (ca. 1571–1573)

2 More tears are shed over answered prayers than
unanswered ones.
Attributed in The Complete Stories of Truman Capote
(2004)
See Goethe 15; T. H. Huxley 4; Modern Proverbs 14;
George Bernard Shaw 16; Wilde 56; Wilde 74

Paul Terry
U.S. cartoonist and filmmaker, 1887–1971

1 When I feel like exercising, I just lie down until
the feeling goes away.
Quoted in Cleveland Plain Dealer, 13 June 1937

Tertullian (Quintus Septimius Florens Tertullianus)
Latin Church father, ca. 160–ca. 225

1 *Domina mater ecclesia.*
Mother Church.
Ad Martyras ch. 1

2 We grow up in greater number as often as
we are cut down by you. The blood of the
Christians is their harvest seed.
Apologeticus ch. 50, sec. 13. Often quoted as "The
blood of the martyrs is the seed of the Church."

3 *Certum est, quia impossibile est.*
It is certain because it is impossible.
De Carne Christi ch. 5. Often quoted as *Credo quia
impossibile* (I believe because it is impossible).

Nikola Tesla
Croatian-born U.S. electrical engineer and
inventor, 1856–1943

1 Ere many generations pass, our machinery will
be driven by a power obtainable at any point
of the universe. . . . Throughout space there is
energy . . . it is a mere question of time when
men will succeed in attaching their machinery
to the very wheelwork of nature.
"Experiments with Alternate Currents of High
Potential and High Frequency" (1892)

2 In the twenty-first century the robot will take
the place which slave labor occupied in ancient
civilization.
"A Machine to End War" (1935)

3 When wireless is perfectly applied the whole
earth will be converted into a huge brain,
which in fact it is, all things being particles of

a real and rhythmic whole. We shall be able
to communicate with one another instantly,
irrespective of distance. Not only this, but
through television and telephony we shall see
and hear one another as perfectly as though we
were face to face, despite intervening distances
of thousands of miles; and the instruments
through which we shall be able to do this
will be amazingly simple compared with our
present telephone. A man will be able to carry
one in his vest pocket.
Quoted in Collier's, 30 Jan. 1926

Tewodros II
Ethiopian emperor, ca. 1820–1868

1 I know their game. First, the traders and the
missionaries: then the ambassadors: then the
cannon. It's better to go straight to the cannon.
Quoted in Basil Davidson, Africa in Modern History:
The Search for a New Society (1978)

William Makepeace Thackeray
Indian-born English novelist, 1811–1863

1 There is a skeleton in every house.
"Punch in the East" (1845)

2 He who meanly admires mean things is a
Snob.
The Book of Snobs ch. 2 (1848)

3 A woman with fair opportunities and without a
positive hump, may marry whom she likes.
Vanity Fair ch. 4 (1847–1848)

4 Them's my sentiments!
Vanity Fair ch. 21 (1847–1848)

5 How to live well on nothing a year.
Vanity Fair ch. 36 (chapter title) (1847–1848)

6 I think I could be a good woman if I had five
thousand a year.
Vanity Fair ch. 36 (1847–1848)

7 Ah! *Vanitas Vanitatum!* Which of us is happy
in this world? Which of us has his desire? or,
having it, is satisfied?—Come, children, let us
shut up the box and the puppets, for our play is
played out.
Vanity Fair ch. 67 (1847–1848)

8 It is best to love wisely, no doubt: but to love foolishly is better than not to be able to love at all.

The History of Pendennis ch. 6 (1848–1850)

9 Remember, it is as easy to marry a rich woman as a poor woman.

The History of Pendennis ch. 28 (1848–1850)
See Howells 1

10 Of the Corporation of the Goosequill—of the Press . . . of the fourth estate.

The History of Pendennis ch. 30 (1848–1850)
See Thomas Carlyle 14; Hazlitt 4; Thomas Macaulay 4

11 'Tis not the dying for a faith that's so hard, Master Harry—every man of every nation has done that—'tis the living up to it that is difficult.

The History of Henry Esmond bk. 1, ch. 6 (1852)

12 'Tis strange what a man may do, and a woman yet think him an angel.

The History of Henry Esmond bk. 1, ch. 7 (1852)

13 [*Of Jonathan Swift:*] An immense genius: an awful downfall and ruin. So great a man he seems to me, that thinking of him is like thinking of an empire falling.

The English Humorists of the Eighteenth Century: A Series of Lectures "Swift" (1853)

14 The wicked are wicked, no doubt, and they go astray and they fall, and they come by their deserts; but who can tell the mischief which the very virtuous do?

The Newcomes ch. 20 (1853–1855)

15 Next to the very young, I suppose the very old are the most selfish.

The Virginians ch. 61 (1857–1859)

16 Whatever you are, try to be a good one.

Attributed in *St. Nicholas*, Mar. 1897. Thackeray was said by Laurence Hutton to have given this advice to Hutton in the 1850s.

Margaret Thatcher

British prime minister, 1925–2013

1 In politics, if you want anything said ask a man, if you want anything done ask a woman.

Speech to National Council of the Townswomen's Guilds, London, 20 May 1965

2 No woman in my time will be Prime Minister or Chancellor or Foreign Secretary—not the top jobs.

Interview, *Sunday Telegraph* (London), 26 Oct. 1969

3 They've [the Labor Government] got the usual Socialist disease—they've run out of other people's money.

Speech to Conservative Party Conference, Blackpool, England, 10 Oct. 1975. This is usually quoted as "The trouble with socialism is that you eventually run out of other people's money."

4 To those waiting with bated breath for that favorite media catchphrase, the U-turn, I have only this to say. "You turn if you want; the lady's not for turning."

Speech at Conservative Party Conference, Brighton, England, 10 Oct. 1980
See Christopher Fry 1

5 [*On the reconquest of South Georgia in the Falklands War:*] Just rejoice at that news and congratulate our forces and the Marines. Rejoice!

Statement to journalists at 10 Downing Street, London, 25 Apr. 1982. Usually quoted as "Rejoice, rejoice!"

6 We know we can do it—we haven't lost the ability. That is the Falklands Factor.

Speech at Conservative Party rally, Cheltenham, England, 3 July 1982

7 [*Of the Irish Republican Army bombing in Brighton intended to assassinate her:*] This was the day I was meant not to see.

Television interview on Channel 4, 15 Oct. 1984

8 [*Of Soviet leader Mikhail Gorbachev:*] We can do business together.

BBC television interview, 17 Dec. 1984

9 We must try to find ways to starve the terrorist and the hijacker of the oxygen of publicity on which they depend.

Speech to American Bar Association, London, 15 July 1985

10 The President of the Commission, Mr. Delors, said at a press conference the other day that he wanted the European Parliament to be the democratic body of the Community, he wanted the Commission to be the Executive and he wanted the Council of Ministers to be the Senate. No. No. No.

Statement in House of Commons, 30 Oct. 1990

11 In my lifetime all the problems have come from mainland Europe and all the solutions have come from the English-speaking nations across the world.

Speech at reception for Scottish delegates to Conservative Party conference, Blackpool, England, 5 Oct. 1999

12 There is no such thing as Society. There are individual men and women, and there are families.

Quoted in *Woman's Own*, 31 Oct. 1987

13 We have become a grandmother.

Quoted in *Times* (London), 4 Mar. 1989

Bob Thaves

U.S. cartoonist, 1924–2006

1 [*Of Fred Astaire:*] Sure he was great, but don't forget that Ginger Rogers did everything *he* did, . . . backwards and in high heels.

Frank and Ernest (comic strip), 3 May 1982. Often attributed to Ann Richards, Linda Ellerbee, or Faith Whittlesey, but no reference before Thaves's strip has been found, and Thaves confirmed to the editor of this book that he was the originator.

Ernest L. Thayer

U.S. journalist, 1863–1940

1 The outlook wasn't brilliant for the Mudville nine that day.

"Casey at the Bat" l. 1 (1888)

2 There was ease in Casey's manner as he stepped into his place.

"Casey at the Bat" l. 21 (1888)

3 The sneer is gone from Casey's lip, his teeth are clenched in hate,
He pounds with cruel violence his bat upon the plate.
And now the pitcher holds the ball, and now he lets it go,
And now the air is shattered by the force of Casey's blow.

"Casey at the Bat" l. 45 (1888)

4 Oh! somewhere in this favored land the sun is shining bright;
The band is playing somewhere, and somewhere hearts are light,
And somewhere men are laughing, and somewhere children shout;
But there is no joy in Mudville—mighty Casey has struck out.

"Casey at the Bat" l. 49 (1888)

William Roscoe Thayer

U.S. historian, 1859–1923

1 [*Biography of James A. Garfield:*] From Log-Cabin to the White House.

Title of book (1881)

Themistocles

Greek general and statesman, ca. 528 B.C.–ca. 462 B.C.

1 [*To Spartan admiral Eurybiades, when the latter raised his staff:*] Strike, but hear me.

Quoted in Plutarch, *Lives*

Clarence Thomas

U.S. judge, 1948–

1 [*Of the contentious hearings for his nomination as a Supreme Court justice:*] This is a circus. It's a national disgrace. From my standpoint as a black American, it is a high-tech lynching for

uppity blacks who in any way deign to think for
themselves, to do for themselves.
Quoted in *N.Y. Times,* 12 Oct. 1991

Dylan Thomas
Welsh poet, 1914–1953

1 The force that through the green fuse drives the
  flower
Drives my green age; that blasts the roots of
  trees
Is my destroyer.
"The Force That Through the Green Fuse Drives the
Flower" l. 1 (1934)

2 I see the boys of summer in their ruin
Lay the gold tithings barren,
Setting no store by harvest, freeze the soils.
"I See the Boys of Summer" l. 1 (1934)

3 And death shall have no dominion.
Dead men naked they shall be one
With the man in the wind and the west moon.
"And Death Shall Have No Dominion" l. 1 (1936)
See Bible 343

4 The hand that signed the paper felled a city;
Five sovereign fingers taxed the breath,
Doubled the globe of dead and halved a
  country;
These five kings did a king to death.
"The Hand That Signed the Paper Felled a City" l. 1
(1936)

5 When All My Five and Country Senses See.
Title of poem (1939)

6 Now as I was young and easy under the apple
  boughs
About the lilting house and happy as the grass
  was green.
"Fern Hill" l. 1 (1946)

7 Oh as I was young and easy in the mercy of his
  means,
Time held me green and dying
Though I sang in my chains like the sea.
"Fern Hill" l. 52 (1946)

8 In my craft or sullen art
Exercised in the still night
When only the moon rages
And the lovers lie abed
With all their griefs in their arms.
"In My Craft or Sullen Art" l. 1 (1946)

9 But for the lovers, their arms
Round the griefs of the ages,
Who pay no praise or wages
Nor heed my craft or art.
"In My Craft or Sullen Art" l. 17 (1946)

10 It was my thirtieth year to heaven
Woke to my hearing from harbor and neighbor
  wood
And the mussel pooled and the heron
Priested shore
The morning beckon.
"Poem in October" l. 1 (1946)

11 And I rose
In rainy autumn
And walked abroad in a shower of all my days.
"Poem in October" l. 14 (1946)

12 A child's
Forgotten mornings when he walked with his
  mother
Through the parables
Of sunlight
And the legends of the green chapels

And the twice-told fields of infancy.
"Poem in October" l. 46 (1946)

13 And there could I marvel my birthday
Away but the weather turned around. And the
  true

Joy of the long dead child sang burning
In the sun.
"Poem in October" l. 61 (1946)

14 O may my heart's truth
Still be sung
On this high hill in a year's turning.
"Poem in October" l. 68 (1946)

15 And I must enter again the round
Zion of the water bead
And the synagogue of the ear of corn.
"A Refusal to Mourn the Death, by Fire, of a Child in London" l. 7 (1946)

16 Deep with the first dead lies London's daughter,
Robed in the long friends,
The grains beyond age, the dark veins of her mother,
Secret by the unmourning water
Of the riding Thames.
After the first death, there is no other.
"A Refusal to Mourn the Death, by Fire, of a Child in London" l. 19 (1946)

17 Do not go gentle into that good night,
Old age should burn and rave at close of day;
Rage, rage against the dying of the light.
"Do Not Go Gentle into That Good Night" l. 1 (1952)

18 And you, my father, there on the sad height,
Curse, bless me now with your fierce tears, I pray.
Do not go gentle into that good night.
Rage, rage against the dying of the light.
"Do Not Go Gentle into That Good Night" l. 16 (1952)

19 I read somewhere of a shepherd who, when asked why he made, from within fairy rings, ritual observances to the moon to protect his flocks, replied: I'd be a damn fool if I didn't! These poems, with all their crudities, doubts, and confusions, are written for the love of Man and in praise of God, and I'd be a damn fool if they weren't.
Collected Poems introduction (1953)

20 It is spring, moonless night in the small town, starless and bible-black.
Under Milk Wood (1954)

21 [*Definition of an alcoholic:*] A man you don't like who drinks as much as you do.
Quoted in Constantine FitzGibbon, *The Life of Dylan Thomas* (1965)

22 [*"Last words":*] I've had eighteen straight whiskies. I think that is the record.
Quoted in Barnaby Conrad, *Famous Last Words* (1961)

J. Parnell Thomas
U.S. politician, 1895–1970

1 [*Standard question posed to witnesses testifying before the House Committee on Un-American Activities:*] Are you now or have you ever been a member of the Communist Party?
Quoted in *N.Y. Times*, 29 Oct. 1947

Lewis Thomas
U.S. physician and author, 1913–1993

1 Viewed from the distance of the moon, the astonishing thing about the earth . . . is that it is alive. . . . Aloft, floating free beneath the moist, gleaming membrane of bright blue sky, is the rising earth, the only exuberant thing in this part of the cosmos. . . . It has the organized, self-contained look of a live creature, full of information, marvelously skilled in handling the sun.
The Lives of a Cell "The World's Biggest Membrane" (1974)

M. Carey Thomas
U.S. feminist and educator, 1857–1935

1 [*Of Bryn Mawr–educated women:*] Our failures only marry.
Attributed in Vivian Gornick and Barbara K. Moran, *Woman in Sexist Society* (1971). According to the Bryn Mawr College Archives, Thomas denied having said this. The quotation is sometimes rendered as "Only our failures marry."

Marlo Thomas
U.S. actress and feminist, 1937–

1 Free to Be . . . You and Me.
Title of record album (1972)

W. I. Thomas
U.S. sociologist, 1863–1947

1 If men define situations as real, they are real in their consequences.
The Child in America ch. 13 (1928). Coauthored with Dorothy Swaine Thomas.

Thomas à Kempis

German clergyman and writer, ca. 1380–1471

1 *Nam homo proponit, sed Deus disponit.*
For man proposes, but God disposes.
De Imitatione Christi bk. 1, ch. 19, sec. 2 (ca. 1420)
See Proverbs 186

2 *Hodie homo est: et cras non comparet. Cum autem sublatus fuerit ab oculis: etiam cito transit a mente.*
Today man is, and tomorrow he will be seen no more. And being removed out of sight, quickly also he is out of mind.
De Imitatione Christi bk. 1, ch. 23, sec. 1 (ca. 1420)

E. P. (Edward Palmer) Thompson

English historian and activist, 1924–1993

1 I am seeking to rescue the poor stockinger, the Luddite cropper, the "obsolete" hand-loom weaver, the "utopian" artisan, and even the deluded follower of Joanna Southcott, from the enormous condescension of posterity. . . . they lived through these times of acute social disturbance, and we did not. Their aspirations were valid in terms of their own experience; and, if they were casualties of history, they remain, condemned in their own lives, as casualties.
The Making of the English Working Class preface (1964)

Francis Thompson

English poet, 1859–1907

1 The angels keep their ancient places;—
Turn but a stone, and start a wing!
'Tis ye, 'tis your estranged faces,
That miss the many-splendored thing.
"The Kingdom of God" l. 13 (1913)
See Suyin 1

Hunter S. Thompson

U.S. writer, 1939–2005

1 Fear and Loathing in Las Vegas.
Title of articles, *Rolling Stone*, 11 and 25 Nov. 1971. Thompson said that he took the phrase "fear and loathing" from Thomas Wolfe's book *The Web and the Rock.*

2 We were somewhere around Barstow on the edge of the desert when the drugs began to take hold.
Fear and Loathing in Las Vegas pt. 1 (1971)

3 No point mentioning those bats, I thought. The poor bastard will see them soon enough.
Fear and Loathing in Las Vegas pt. 1 (1971)

4 It is Nixon himself who represents that dark, venal, and incurably violent side of the American character almost every other country in the world has learned to fear and despise.
Fear and Loathing: On the Campaign Trail '72 (1973)

5 When the going gets weird, the weird turn pro.
"Fear and Loathing at the Super Bowl" (1974)

6 *Gonzo* journalism . . . is a style of "reporting" based on William Faulkner's idea that the best fiction is far more *true* than any kind of journalism—and the best journalists have always known this.
The Great Shark Hunt "Jacket Copy for Fear and Loathing in Las Vegas" (1979)

7 The TV business . . . is normally perceived as some kind of cruel and shallow money trench through the heart of the journalism industry, a long plastic hallway where thieves and pimps run free and good men die like dogs, for no good reason.
S.F. Examiner, 4 Nov. 1985

8 Going to trial with a lawyer who considers your whole life-style a Crime in Progress is not a happy prospect.
Letter, *The Champion,* July 1990

9 I hate to advocate drugs, alcohol, violence, or insanity to anyone . . . but they've always worked for me.
Quoted in *Life,* Jan. 1981. In the 1980 film *Where the Buffalo Roam,* based on stories by Thompson, Bill Murray, playing Thompson, says: "I hate to advocate drugs or liquor, violence, insanity to anyone. But in my case it's worked."

W. J. Thoms

English scholar, 1803–1900

1 What we in England designate as Popular Antiquities, or Popular Literature (though . . . it . . . would be most aptly described by a good Saxon compound, Folk-Lore, the Lore of the People).
Athenaeum, 22 Aug. 1846. Coinage of the term *folklore.*

James Thomson

Scottish poet, 1700–1748

1 When Britain first, at heaven's command,
  Arose from out the azure main,
  This was the charter of the land,
  And guardian angels sung this strain:
  "Rule, Britannia, rule the waves;
  Britons never will be slaves."

Alfred: A Masque act 2 (1740). The words to this song may have been written by David Mallet rather than Thomson.

2 Delightful task! to rear the tender thought,
  To teach the young idea how to shoot.

The Seasons "Spring" l. 1152 (1746)

Roy Thomson, First Baron Thomson of Fleet

Canadian-born Scottish media proprietor, 1894–1976

1 A licence to put commercial programs on the air in Britain is a licence to print your own money.

Quoted in *Times* (London), 16 Mar. 1961

Henry David Thoreau

U.S. writer, 1817–1862

1 I am a parcel of vain strivings tied
  By a chance bond together.

"Sic Vita" l. 1 (1841)

2 Perchance, coming generations will not abide the dissolution of the globe, but, availing themselves of future inventions in aerial locomotion, and the navigation of space, the entire race may migrate from the earth, to settle some vacant and more western planet. . . . It took but little art, a simple application of natural laws, a canoe, a paddle, and a sail of matting, to people the isles of the Pacific, and a little more will people the shining isles of space.

"Paradise (to Be) Regained" (1843)

3 I heartily accept the motto, "That government is best which governs least"; and I should like to see it acted up to more rapidly and systematically. Carried out, it finally amounts to this, which also I believe,—"That government is best which governs not at all"; and when men are prepared for it, that will be the kind of government which they will have.

Civil Disobedience (1849)
See Ralph Waldo Emerson 29; O'Sullivan 1; Shipley 1

4 The objections which have been brought against a standing army, and they are many and weighty, and deserve to prevail, may also at last be brought against a standing government.

Civil Disobedience (1849)

5 I think that we should be men first, and subjects afterwards. It is not desirable to cultivate a respect for the law, so much as for the right. The only obligation which I have a right to assume is to do at any time what I think right.

Civil Disobedience (1849)

6 The mass of men serve the state thus, not as men mainly, but as machines, with their bodies. They are the standing army, and the militia, jailers, constables, posse comitatus, etc. In most cases there is no free exercise whatever of the judgement or of the moral sense; but they put themselves on a level with wood and earth and stones; and wooden men can perhaps be manufactured that will serve the purpose as well.

Civil Disobedience (1849)

7 If the injustice is part of the necessary friction of the machine of government, let it go, let it go: perchance it will wear smooth,—certainly the machine will wear out. If the injustice has a spring, or a pulley, or a rope, or a crank, exclusively for itself, then perhaps you

may consider whether the remedy will not be worse than the evil; but if it is of such a nature that it requires you to be the agent of injustice to another, then, I say, break the law. Let your life be a counter-friction to stop the machine.

Civil Disobedience (1849)
See Savio 1

8 As for adopting the ways which the State has provided for remedying the evil, I know not of such ways. They take too much time, and a man's life will be gone. I have other affairs to attend to. I came into this world, not chiefly to make this a good place to live in, but to live in it, be it good or bad.

Civil Disobedience (1849)

9 I do not hesitate to say, that those who call themselves Abolitionists should at once effectually withdraw their support, both in person and property, from the government of Massachusetts, and not wait until they constitute a majority of one, before they suffer the right to prevail through them. I think that it is enough if they have God on their side, without waiting for that other one. Moreover, any man more right than his neighbors constitutes a majority of one already.

Civil Disobedience (1849)
See Coolidge 2; Douglass 7; Andrew Jackson 7; John Knox 1; Wendell Phillips 3

10 Under a government which imprisons any unjustly, the true place for a just man is also a prison.

Civil Disobedience (1849)

11 When I meet a government which says to me, "Your money or your life," why should I be in haste to give it my money?

Civil Disobedience (1849)

12 The lawyer's truth is not Truth, but consistency or a consistent expediency.

Civil Disobedience (1849)

13 It is remarkable that, notwithstanding the universal favor with which the New Testament is outwardly received, and even the bigotry with which it is defended, there is no hospitality shown to, there is no appreciation of, the order of truth with which it deals. I know of no book

that has so few readers. There is none so truly strange, and heretical, and unpopular.

A Week on the Concord and Merrimack Rivers (1849)

14 It takes two to speak the truth,—one to speak, and another to hear.

A Week on the Concord and Merrimack Rivers (1849)

15 Some circumstantial evidence is very strong, as when you find a trout in the milk.

Journal, 11 Nov. 1850

16 Nothing is so much to be feared as fear.

Journal, 7 Sept. 1851
See Francis Bacon 7; Montaigne 4; Franklin Roosevelt 6; Wellington 3

17 The fate of the country . . . does not depend on what kind of paper you drop into the ballot box once a year, but on what kind of man you drop from your chamber into the street every morning.

"Slavery in Massachusetts" (address), Framingham, Mass., 4 July 1854

18 The mass of men lead lives of quiet desperation. What is called resignation is confirmed desperation.

Walden ch. 1 (1854)

19 Beware of all enterprises that require new clothes.

Walden ch. 1 (1854)

20 Our inventions are wont to be pretty toys, which distract our attention from serious things. They are but improved means to an unimproved end. . . . We are in great haste to construct a magnetic telegraph from Maine to Texas, but Maine and Texas, it may be, have nothing important to communicate.

Walden ch. 1 (1854)

21 There are a thousand hacking at the branches of evil to one who is striking at the root.

Walden ch. 1 (1854)

22 A man is rich in proportion to the number of things which he can afford to let alone.

Walden ch. 2 (1854)

23 I went to the woods because I wished to live deliberately, to front only the essential facts of life, and see if I could not learn what it had to teach, and not, when I came to die, to discover that I had not lived.

Walden ch. 2 (1854)

24 Our life is frittered away by detail. . . . Simplify, simplify.
  Walden ch. 2 (1854)

25 We do not ride on the railroad; it rides upon us.
  Walden ch. 2 (1854)

26 I had three chairs in my house; one for solitude, two for friendship; three for society. When visitors came in larger and unexpected numbers there was but the third chair for them all, but they generally economized the room by standing up.
  Walden ch. 6 (1854)

27 [*Of wood stumps:*] They warmed me twice—once while I was splitting them, and again when they were on the fire.
  Walden ch. 13 (1854)

28 I learned this, at least, by my experiment: that if one advances confidently in the direction of his dreams, and endeavors to live the life which he has imagined, he will meet with a success unexpected in common hours.
  Walden ch. 18 (1854)

29 If you have built castles in the air, your work need not be lost; that is where they should be. Now put the foundations under them.
  Walden ch. 18 (1854)

30 If a man does not keep pace with his companions, perhaps it is because he hears a different drummer. Let him step to the music which he hears, however measured or far away.
  Walden ch. 18 (1854). Frequently quoted as "marches to the tune of a different drummer."

31 Only that day dawns to which we are awake. There is more day to dawn. The sun is but a morning star.
  Walden ch. 18 (1854)

32 Don't spend your time in drilling soldiers, who may turn out hirelings after all, but give to undrilled peasantry a *country* to fight for.
  Letter to Harrison Blake, 26 Sept. 1855

33 That man is the richest whose pleasures are the cheapest.
  Journal, 11 Mar. 1856

34 Not that the story need be long, but it will take a long while to make it short.
  Letter to Harrison Blake, 16 Nov. 1857
  See Pascal 1; Woodrow Wilson 25

35 I hear many condemn these men because they were so few. When were the good and the brave ever in a majority?
  "A Plea for Captain John Brown" (1859)

36 We preserve the so-called peace of a community by deeds of petty violence everyday. Look at the policeman's billy and handcuffs! Look at the jail! Look at the gallows!
  "A Plea for Captain John Brown" (1859)

37 The West of which I speak is but another name for the Wild; and what I have been preparing to say is, that in Wildness is the preservation of the World.
  "Walking" (1862)

38 If a man walk in the woods for love of them half of each day, he is in danger of being regarded as a loafer; but if he spends his whole day as a speculator, shearing off those woods and making earth bald before her time, he is esteemed an industrious and enterprising citizen. As if the town had no interest in its forests but to cut them down!
  "Life Without Principle" (1863)

39 [*Reply to Ralph Waldo Emerson's questioning why Thoreau had gone to jail in 1843 for not paying the Massachusetts poll tax as a protest against slavery:*] Why are you not here also?
  Attributed in *Christian Examiner,* July 1865. Henry Seidel Canby, in his book *Thoreau* (1939), argues that there is no evidence that Emerson visited Thoreau in jail, and also notes that Emerson is unlikely to have asked this question because he knew very well why Thoreau was in prison.

Edward L. Thorndike
U.S. psychologist, 1874–1949

1 Whatever exists at all exists in some amount. To know it thoroughly involves knowing its quantity as well as its quality.
  "The Nature, Purposes, and General Methods of Measurements of Educational Products," *17th Yearbook of the National Society for the Study of Education* (1918)
  See McCall 1

Rose Hartwick Thorpe
U.S. poet, 1850–1939

1 Curfew shall not ring to-night!
  "Curfew Must Not Ring Tonight" l. 30 (1887)

Thucydides

Greek historian, ca. 455 B.C.–ca. 400 B.C.

1 The absence of romance in my history will, I fear, detract somewhat from its interest; but if it be judged useful by those inquirers who desire an exact interpretation of the future, which in the course of human things must resemble if it does not reflect it, I shall be content. In fine, I have written my work, not as an essay which is to win the applause of the moment, but as a possession for all time.
History of the Peloponnesian War bk. 1, ch. 1

2 Happiness depends on being free, and freedom depends on being courageous.
History of the Peloponnesian War bk. 2, ch. 4

3 Revolution . . . ran its course from city to city, and the places which it arrived at last, from having heard what had been done before carried to a still greater excess the refinement of their inventions, as manifested to the cunning of their enterprises and the atrocity of their reprisals. Words had to change their ordinary meaning and to take that which was now given them.
History of the Peloponnesian War bk. 3, ch. 10

James Thurber

U.S. humorist, 1894–1961

1 All right, have it your way—you heard a seal bark!
Cartoon caption, *New Yorker*, 30 Jan. 1932

2 I suppose that the high-water mark of my youth in Columbus, Ohio was the night the bed fell on my father.
My Life and Hard Times ch. 1 (1933)

3 Her own mother lived the latter years of her life in the horrible suspicion that electricity was dripping invisibly all over the house.
My Life and Hard Times ch. 2 (1933)

4 The War Between Men and Women.
Title of cartoon series, *New Yorker*, 20 Jan.–28 Apr. 1934

5 It's a naïve domestic Burgundy without any breeding, but I think you'll be amused by its presumption.
Cartoon caption, *New Yorker*, 27 Mar. 1937

6 Well, if I called the wrong number, why did you answer the phone?
Cartoon caption, *New Yorker*, 5 June 1937

7 He doesn't know anything except facts.
Cartoon caption, *New Yorker*, 12 Dec. 1937

8 Early to rise and early to bed makes a male healthy and wealthy and dead.
"The Shrike and the Chipmunks," *New Yorker*, 18 Feb. 1939
See Proverbs 81

9 The Secret Life of Walter Mitty.
Title of story (1939)

10 Then, with that faint fleeting smile playing about his lips, he faced the firing squad; erect and motionless, proud and disdainful, Walter Mitty, the undefeated, inscrutable to the last.
"The Secret Life of Walter Mitty," *New Yorker*, 18 Mar. 1939

11 I love the idea of there being two sexes, don't you?
Cartoon caption, *New Yorker*, 22 Apr. 1939

12 He knows all about art, but he doesn't know what he likes.
Cartoon caption, *New Yorker*, 4 Nov. 1939
See Gelett Burgess 6

13 You Could Look It Up.
Title of story (1941). Later popularized by Casey Stengel.

14 How is it possible, woman, in the awful and magnificent times we live in, to be preoccupied exclusively with the piddling?
Cartoon caption, *New Yorker*, 16 Feb. 1946

Rex Tillerson

U.S. government official and business executive, 1952–

1 If our leaders seek to conceal the truth, or we as people become accepting of alternative realities that are no longer grounded in facts, then we as American citizens are on a pathway to relinquishing our freedom.
Commencement address at Virginia Military Institute, Lexington, Va., 16 May 2018

Paul Tillich

German-born U.S. theologian and philosopher, 1886–1965

1 Neurosis is the way of avoiding non-being by avoiding being.
The Courage to Be pt. 2, ch. 3 (1952)

2 I had the great honor and luck to be the first non-Jewish professor dismissed from a German university.
Quoted in *Minneapolis Star*, 23 Oct. 1965

Justin Timberlake

U.S. singer, 1981–

1 [*Of Janet Jackson's exposure of her breast:*] I am sorry if anyone was offended by the wardrobe malfunction during the halftime performance of the Super Bowl.
Quoted in *N.Y. Times*, 2 Feb. 2004

Nicholas Conyngham Tindal

English judge, 1776–1846

1 To establish a defence on the ground of insanity, it must be clearly proved that, at the time of the committing of the act, the party accused was laboring under such a defect of reason, from disease of the mind, as not to know the nature and quality of the act he was doing; or, if he did know it, that he did not know he was doing what was wrong.
M'Naghten's Case (1843)

Charles A. Tindley

U.S. songwriter and clergyman, 1851–1933

1 I'll overcome some day
If in my heart I do not yield,
I'll overcome some day.
"I'll Overcome Some Day" (song) (1900)
See Pete Seeger 5

Titus Flavius Sabinus Vespasianus

Roman emperor, 39–81

1 [*Remark upon the fact that he had done nothing to help anyone all day:*] Amici, diem perdidi.
Friends, I have lost a day.
Quoted in Suetonius, *Lives of the Caesars*

Alexis de Tocqueville

French historian and statesman, 1805–1859

1 I know of no country, indeed, where the love of money has taken stronger hold on the affections of men, and where a profounder contempt is expressed for the theory of the permanent equality of property.
Democracy in America vol. 1, ch. 3 (1835) (translation by Henry Reeve)

2 The power vested in the American courts of justice of pronouncing a statute to be unconstitutional, forms one of the most powerful barriers which has ever been devised against the tyranny of political assemblies.
Democracy in America vol. 1, ch. 6 (1835) (translation by Henry Reeve)

3 I have never been more struck by the good sense and the practical judgment of the Americans than in the ingenious devices by which they elude the numberless difficulties resulting from their Federal Constitution.
Democracy in America vol. 1, ch. 8 (1835) (translation by Henry Reeve)

4 There is no medium between servitude and extreme licence; in order to enjoy the inestimable benefits which the liberty of the

press ensures, it is necessary to submit to the inevitable evils which it engenders.
Democracy in America vol. 2, ch. 3 (1835) (translation by Henry Reeve)

5 In countries where associations are free, secret societies are unknown. In America there are numerous factions, but no conspiracies.
Democracy in America vol. 2, ch. 4 (1835) (translation by Henry Reeve)

6 [*Section title:*] Tyranny of the Majority.
Democracy in America vol. 2, ch. 7 (1835) (translation by Henry Reeve)

7 In America, the majority raises very formidable barriers to the liberty of opinion: within these barriers an author may write whatever he pleases, but he will repent it if he ever step beyond them.
Democracy in America vol. 2, ch. 7 (1835) (translation by Henry Reeve)

8 I cannot believe that a republic could subsist at the present time, if the influence of lawyers in public business did not increase in proportion to the power of the people.
Democracy in America vol. 2, ch. 8 (1835) (translation by Henry Reeve)

9 In America there are no nobles or literary men, and the people is apt to mistrust the wealthy; lawyers consequently form the highest political class, and the most cultivated circle of society. They have therefore nothing to gain by innovation, which adds a conservative interest to their natural taste for public order. If I were asked where I place the American aristocracy, I should reply without hesitation, that it is not composed of the rich, who are united together by no common tie, but that it occupies the judicial bench and the bar.
Democracy in America vol. 2, ch. 8 (1835) (translation by Henry Reeve)

10 The more we reflect upon all that occurs in the United States, the more shall we be persuaded that the lawyers as a body, form the most powerful, if not the only counterpoise to the democratic element. In that country we perceive how eminently the legal profession is qualified by its powers, and even by its defects, to neutralize the vices which are inherent in popular government.
Democracy in America vol. 2, ch. 8 (1835) (translation by Henry Reeve)

11 Scarcely any question arises in the United States which does not become, sooner or later, a subject of judicial debate; hence all parties are obliged to borrow the ideas, and even the language usual in judicial proceedings, in their daily controversies. . . . The language of the law thus becomes, in some measure, a vulgar tongue; the spirit of the law, which is produced in the schools and courts of justice, gradually penetrates beyond their walls into the bosom of society, where it descends to the lowest classes, so that the whole people contracts the habits and the tastes of the magistrate.
Democracy in America vol. 2, ch. 8 (1835) (translation by Henry Reeve)

12 The jury . . . may be regarded as a gratuitous public school, ever open, in which every juror learns to exercise his rights, enters into daily communication with the most learned and enlightened members of the upper classes, and becomes practically acquainted with the laws of his country.
Democracy in America vol. 2, ch. 8 (1835) (translation by Henry Reeve)

13 The time will therefore come when one hundred and fifty millions of men will be living in North America, equal in condition, the progeny of one race, owing their origin to the same cause, and preserving the same civilization, the same language, the same religion, the same habits, the same manners, and imbued with the same opinions, propagated under the same forms.
Democracy in America vol. 2, ch. 10 (1835) (translation by Henry Reeve)

14 There are, at the present time, two great nations in the world, which seem to tend towards the same end, although they started from different points: I allude to the Russians and the Americans. . . . Their starting-point is different, and their courses are not the same; yet each of them seems marked out by the will of Heaven to sway the destinies of half the globe.
Democracy in America vol. 2, ch. 10 (1835) (translation by Henry Reeve)

15 Democratic nations care but little for what has been, but they are haunted by visions of what will be; in this direction their unbounded

imagination grows and dilates beyond all measure. . . . Democracy, which shuts the past against the poet, opens the future before him.
Democracy in America vol. 2, sec. 1, ch. 17 (1840) (translation by Henry Reeve)

16 Not only does democracy make every man forget his ancestors, but it hides his descendants and separates his contemporaries from him; it throws him back forever upon himself alone and threatens to the end to confine him entirely within the solitude of his own heart.
Democracy in America vol. 2, sec. 2, ch. 2 (1840) (translation by Henry Reeve)

17 Wherever at the head of some new undertaking you see the government in France, or a man of rank in England, in the United States you will be sure to find an association.
Democracy in America vol. 2, sec. 2, ch. 5 (1840) (translation by Henry Reeve)

18 I believe that [in the United States] the social changes that bring nearer to the same level the father and son, the master and servant, and, in general, superiors and inferiors will raise woman and make her more and more the equal of man.
Democracy in America vol. 2, sec. 3, ch. 12 (1840) (translation by Henry Reeve)

19 If I were asked . . . to what the singular prosperity and growing strength of that people [the Americans] ought mainly to be attributed, I should reply: To the superiority of their women.
Democracy in America vol. 2, sec. 3, ch. 12 (1840) (translation by Henry Reeve)

20 The love of wealth is therefore to be traced, as either a principal or an accessory motive, at the bottom of all that the Americans do; this gives to all their passions a sort of family likeness.
Democracy in America vol. 2, sec. 3, ch. 17 (1840) (translation by Henry Reeve)

21 In no country in the world is the love of property more active and more anxious than in the United States; nowhere does the majority display less inclination for those principles which threaten to alter, in whatever manner, the laws of property.
Democracy in America vol. 2, sec. 3, ch. 21 (1840) (translation by Henry Reeve)

22 If ever America undergoes great revolutions, they will be brought about by the presence of the black race on the soil of the United States; that is to say, they will owe their origin, not to the equality, but to the inequality of condition.
Democracy in America vol. 2, sec. 3, ch. 21 (1840) (translation by Henry Reeve)

23 All those who seek to destroy the liberties of a democratic nation ought to know that war is the surest and the shortest means to accomplish it.
Democracy in America vol. 2, sec. 3, ch. 22 (1840) (translation by Henry Reeve)

24 Not until I went into the churches of America and heard her pulpits flame with righteousness did I understand the secret of her genius and power. America is great because America is good, and if America ever ceases to be good America will cease to be great.
Attributed in *Herald and Presbyter*, 6 Sept. 1922. Nothing like this passage actually appears anywhere in Tocqueville's writings.

Chuck Todd
U.S. newscaster, 1972–

1 Alternative facts are not facts, they're falsehoods.
Interview of Kellyanne Conway on NBC *Meet the Press* (television program), 22 Jan. 2017
See Conway 1

Alvin Toffler
U.S. writer, 1928–2016

1 Culture shock is relatively mild in comparison with a much more serious malady that might be called "future shock." Future shock is the dizzying disorientation brought on by the premature arrival of the future.
Horizon, Summer 1965

Hideki Tojo
Japanese prime minister and general, 1884–1948

1 [*Final testimony before International Tribunal for the Far East, Tokyo, Nov. 1945:*]
This is farewell.
I shall wait beneath the moss,
Until the flowers again are fragrant
In this island country of Japan.
Quoted in Robert J. C. Butow, *Tojo and the Coming of the War* (1961)

Tokugawa Iemitsu
Japanese shogun, 1604–1651

1 Japanese ships are strictly forbidden to leave for foreign countries.
Edict 1 (1635)

2 No Japanese is permitted to go abroad. If there is anyone who attempts to do so secretly, he must be executed. The ship so involved must be impounded and its owner arrested, and the matter must be reported to the higher authority.
Edict 2 (1635)

3 If any Japanese returns from overseas after residing there, he must be put to death.
Edict 3 (1635)

J. R. R. Tolkien
South African–born English novelist and philologist, 1892–1973

1 In a hole in the ground there lived a hobbit. Not a nasty, dirty, wet hole, filled with the ends of worms and an oozy smell, nor yet a dry, bare, sandy hole with nothing in it to sit down on or to eat: it was a hobbit-hole, and that means comfort.
The Hobbit ch. 1 (1937). In a letter to W. H. Auden, 7 June 1955, Tolkien stated that in the late 1920s he had written the first line of this passage impulsively on a blank leaf of an examination paper he was correcting.

2 Never laugh at live dragons.
The Hobbit ch. 12 (1937)

3 I desired dragons with a profound desire. Of course, I in my timid body did not wish to have them in the neighborhood, intruding into my relatively safe world, in which it was, for instance, possible to read stories in peace of mind, free from fear. But the world that contained even the imagination of Fáfnir was richer and more beautiful, at whatever cost of peril.
"On Fairy-Stories" (1947)

4 [*Gollum speaking of the Ring:*] Where iss it? Where iss it? . . . Losst it is, my precious, lost, lost! Curse us and crush us, my precious is lost!
The Hobbit, 2nd ed., ch. 5 (1951)

5 Do not laugh! But once upon a time (my crest has long since fallen) I had a mind to make a

body of more or less connected legend, ranging from the large and cosmogonic, to the level of romantic fairy-story—the larger founded on the lesser in contact with the earth, the lesser drawing splendor from the vast backcloths—which I could dedicate simply to: to England; to my country.
Letter to Milton Waldman, ca. Dec. 1951

6 One Ring to rule them all, One Ring to find them
One Ring to bring them all and in the darkness bind them.
The Fellowship of the Ring epigraph (1954)

7 The Road goes ever on and on
Down from the door where it began.
Now far ahead the Road has gone,
And I must follow, if I can,
Pursuing it with eager feet,
Until it joins some larger way
Where many paths and errands meet.
And whither then? I cannot say.
The Fellowship of the Ring bk. 1, ch. 1 (1954)

8 Do not meddle in the affairs of Wizards, for they are subtle and quick to anger.
The Fellowship of the Ring bk. 1, ch. 3 (1954)

9 Not all those who wander are lost.
The Fellowship of the Ring bk. 1, ch. 10 (1954)

10 "I will take the Ring," he said, "though I do not know the way."
The Fellowship of the Ring bk. 2, ch. 2 (1954)

11 "The realm of Sauron is ended!" said Gandalf. "The Ring-bearer has fulfilled his Quest."
The Return of the King bk. 6, ch. 4 (1955)

12 [*Sam Gamgee speaking*:] "Well, I'm back," he said.
The Return of the King bk. 6, ch. 9 (1955)

13 I speak no comfort to you, for there is no comfort for such pain within the circles of the world. The uttermost choice is before you: to repent and go to the Havens and bear away into the West the memory of our days together that shall there be evergreen but never more than memory; or else to abide the Doom of Men.
The Return of the King Appendix A, "A Part of the Tale of Aragon and Arwen" (1955)

14 I am in fact a Hobbit (in all but size). I like gardens, trees, and unmechanized farmlands; I smoke a pipe, and like good plain food (unrefrigerated), but detest French cooking; I like, and even dare to wear in these dull days, ornamental waistcoats. I am fond of mushrooms (out of a field); have a very simple sense of humor (which even my appreciative critics find tiresome); I go to bed late and get up late (when possible). I do not travel much.
Letter to Deborah Webster, 25 Oct. 1958

Leo Tolstoy
Russian novelist, 1828–1910

1 "What's this? Am I falling? My legs are giving way," thought he, and fell on his back. He opened his eyes, hoping to see how the struggle of the Frenchmen with the gunners ended, whether the red-haired gunner had been killed or not, and whether the cannon had been captured or saved. But he saw nothing. Above him there was nothing but the sky—the lofty sky, not clear yet still immeasurably lofty, with grey clouds gliding slowly across it.
War and Peace bk. 3, ch. 16 (1865–1869) (translation by Louise and Aylmer Maude)

2 If I were not myself, but the handsomest, cleverest, and best man in the world, and were free, I would this moment ask on my knees for your hand and your love!
War and Peace bk. 8, ch. 22 (1865–1869) (translation by Louise and Aylmer Maude)

3 In historic events the so-called great men are labels giving names to events, and like labels they have but the smallest connexion with the event itself. Every act of theirs, which appears to them an act of their own will, is in an historical sense involuntary, and is related to the whole course of history and predestined from eternity.
War and Peace bk. 9, ch. 1 (1865–1869) (translation by Louise and Aylmer Maude)

4 A king is history's slave.
War and Peace bk. 9, ch. 1 (1865–1869) (translation by Louise and Aylmer Maude)

5 Not only does a good army commander not need any special qualities, on the contrary he needs the absence of the highest and best human attributes—love, poetry, tenderness, and philosophic inquiring doubt. He should be limited, firmly convinced that what he is doing is very important (otherwise he will not have sufficient patience), and only then will he be a brave leader. God forbid that he should be humane, should love, or pity, or think of what is just and unjust.
War and Peace bk. 9, ch. 11 (1865–1869) (translation by Louise and Aylmer Maude)

6 Our body is a machine for living. It is organized for that, it is its nature. Let life go on in it unhindered and let it defend itself, it will do more than if you paralyze it by encumbering it with remedies.
War and Peace bk. 10, ch. 29 (1865–1869) (translation by Louise and Aylmer Maude)

7 All newspaper and journalistic activity is an intellectual brothel from which there is no retreat.
  Letter to Prince V. P. Meshchersky, 22 Aug. 1871

8 All happy families resemble one another, but each unhappy family is unhappy in its own way.
  Anna Karenina pt. 1, ch. 1 (1875–1877) (translation by Louise and Aylmer Maude)
  See Susan Cheever 1

9 The eternal error men make in imagining that happiness consists in the gratification of their wishes.
  Anna Karenina pt. 5, ch. 8 (1875–1877) (translation by Louise and Aylmer Maude)

10 A desire for desires—boredom.
  Anna Karenina pt. 5, ch. 8 (1875–1877) (translation by Louise and Aylmer Maude)

11 Six feet from his head to his heels was all that he needed.
  How Much Land Does a Man Need? ch. 9 (1886) (translation by Louise and Aylmer Maude)

12 I sit on a man's back, choking him and making him carry me, and yet assure myself and others that I am very sorry for him and wish to ease his load by all possible means—except by getting off his back.
  What Then Must We Do? ch. 16 (1886) (translation by Aylmer Maude)

13 Ivan Ilych's life had been most simple and most ordinary and therefore most terrible.
  The Death of Ivan Ilych ch. 2 (1886) (translation by Aylmer Maude and J. D. Duff)

14 It is generally supposed the Conservatives are usually old people, and that those in favor of change are the young. That is not quite correct. Usually Conservatives are young people: those who want to live but who do not think about how to live, and have not time to think, and therefore take as a model for themselves a way of life that they have seen.
  The Devil ch. 1 (1889) (translation by Louise and Alymer Maude)

15 Man survives earthquakes, epidemics, the horrors of disease, and all the agonies of the soul, but for all time his most tormenting tragedy has been, is, and will be the tragedy of the bedroom.
  Quoted in Maxim Gorky, *Lev Nikolayevich Tolstoy* (1920)

Lily Tomlin
U.S. comedian, 1939–

1 If truth is beauty, how come no one has their hair done in the library?
  Quoted in *Adweek*, 7 Sept. 1987

Henry M. Tomlinson
English novelist, 1873–1958

1 We do not see things as they are, but as we are ourselves.
  Out of Soundings ch. 10 (1931)

Theobald Wolfe Tone
Irish nationalist and lawyer, 1763–1798

1 To unite the whole people of Ireland, to abolish the memory of all past dissentions, and to substitute the common name of Irishman, in place of the denominations of Protestant, Catholic, and Dissenter—these were my means.
  "Life of Theobald Wolfe Tone" (1796)

John Kennedy Toole
U.S. novelist, 1937–1969

1 A green hunting cap squeezed the top of the fleshy balloon of a head.
  A Confederacy of Dunces ch. 1 (1980)

Jean Toomer
U.S. writer, 1894–1967

1 And there, a field rat, startled, squealing bleeds, His belly close to ground. I see the blade, Blood-stained, continue cutting weeds and shade.
  "Reapers" l. 6 (1923)

Augustus Montague Toplady
English clergyman, 1740–1778

1 Rock of Ages, cleft for me, Let me hide myself in Thee.
  "Rock of Ages, Cleft for Me" (hymn) (1776)

Allen Toussaint
U.S. musician and songwriter, 1938–2015

1 I know we can make it, I know that we can I know darn well we can work it out Yes we can, I know we can can

Yes we can can, why can't we
If we wanna it yes we can can.
"Yes We Can" (song) (1970)
See Political Slogans 39

Toussaint-Louverture (François-Dominique Toussaint)
Haitian general and liberator, 1743–1803

1 Brothers and Friends,
I am Toussaint Louverture; perhaps my name has made itself known to you. I have undertaken vengeance. I want Liberty and Equality to reign in Saint Domingue. I am working to make that happen. Unite yourselves to us, brothers, and fight with us for the same cause.
Proclamation from Camp Turel, 29 Aug. 1793

2 [*Remarks, 1802, while boarding the ship taking him to his death in France:*] In overthrowing me, you have cut down in San Domingo only the trunk of the tree of liberty. It will spring up again by the roots, for they are numerous and deep.
Quoted in *Negro Digest*, Aug. 1964

A. Toussenel
French writer, 1803–1885

1 *Plus on apprend à connaître l'homme, plus on apprend à estimer le chien.*
The more one gets to know of men, the more one values dogs.
L'Esprit des Bêtes ch. 3 (1847). Garson O'Toole has found an earlier, anonymously attributed citation: "Plus je connais les hommes, mieux j'aime les chiens" ("the more I know men, the better I like dogs"), published in *Tablettes Historiques et Littéraires*, 13 Nov. 1822, quoting prior usage in *Miroir de la Somme*.
See Roland 2

Sue Townsend
English writer, 1946–2014

1 The Secret Diary of Adrian Mole, Aged 13¾.
Title of book (1982)

Peter Townshend
English rock musician and songwriter, 1945–

1 Hope I die before I get old.
"My Generation" (song) (1965)

2 See me, feel me
Touch me, heal me.
"Go to the Mirror" (song) (1969)

3 I don't need to fight
To prove I'm right . . .
It's only teenage wasteland.
"Baba O'Riley" (song) (1971)

4 No one knows what it's like
To be the bad man
To be the sad man
Behind blue eyes.
"Behind Blue Eyes" (song) (1971)

5 But my dreams
They aren't as empty
As my conscience seems to be.
"Behind Blue Eyes" (song) (1971)

6 I'll tip my hat to the new constitution
Take a bow for the new revolution . . .
And I'll get on my knees and pray
We don't get fooled again.
"Won't Get Fooled Again" (song) (1971)

7 Meet the new boss
Same as the old boss.
"Won't Get Fooled Again" (song) (1971)

Arnold J. Toynbee
English historian, 1889–1975

1 The so-called racial explanation of differences in human performance and achievement is either an ineptitude or a fraud.
A Study of History vol. 1 (1934)

2 The nature of the breakdowns of civilizations can be summed up in three points: a failure of creative power in the minority, an answering withdrawal of mimesis on the part of the majority, and a consequent loss of social unity in the society as a whole.
A Study of History (D. C. Somervell abridgement), bk. 4, ch. 13 (1947)

3 Though sixteen civilizations may have perished already to our knowledge, and nine others may be now at the point of death, we—the twenty-sixth—are not compelled to submit the riddle of our fate to the blind arbitrament of statistics. The divine spark of creative power is still alive in us, and, if we have the grace to kindle it into

flame, then the stars in their courses cannot defeat our efforts to attain the goal of human endeavor.

A Study of History (D. C. Somervell abridgement), bk. 4, ch. 14 (1947)

B. Traven

U.S. writer, 1890–1969

1 Badges, to god-damned hell with badges! We have no badges. In fact, we don't need badges. I don't have to show you any stinking badges.

The Treasure of the Sierra Madre ch. 13 (1935). This quotation was immortalized by its use in the 1948 film. (In the film it is worded "Badges? We ain't got no badges. We don't need no badges. I don't have to show you any stinking badges!") Now it is frequently quoted as "Badges? We don't need no stinking badges!" The latter version was popularized by the motion picture *Blazing Saddles* (1974) but appeared earlier in a 1967 episode of the television series *The Monkees*.

Pamela Lyndon Travers (Helen Lyndon Goff)

Australian-born English writer, 1899–1996

1 Feed the Birds, Tuppence a Bag!

Mary Poppins ch. 7 (1934)

Merle Travis

U.S. country singer, 1917–1983

1 You load sixteen tons, what do you get?
Another day older and deeper in debt.
Saint Peter, don't you call me 'cause I can't go
I owe my soul to the company store.

"Sixteen Tons" (song) (1947)

William B. Travis

U.S. lawyer and soldier, 1809–1836

1 Victory or Death.

Letter from the Alamo to people of Texas and "all Americans," 24 Feb. 1836

Herbert Beerbohm Tree

English actor and theatrical manager, 1852–1917

1 [*Remark to a man in the street carrying a grandfather clock:*] My poor fellow, why not carry a watch?

Quoted in Hesketh Pearson, *Beerbohm Tree* (1956)

G. M. Trevelyan

English historian, 1876–1962

1 Our modern system of popular Education was indeed indispensable and has conferred great benefits on the country, but it has been a disappointment in some important respects. . . . It has produced a vast population able to read but unable to distinguish what is worth reading.

English Social History ch. 18 (1942)

Calvin Trillin

U.S. humorist, 1935–

1 [*Definition of insider trading:*] Stealing too fast.

"The Inside on Insider Trading" (1987)

Linda R. Tripp

U.S. government employee, 1949–2020

1 [*Explanation of why she covertly tape-recorded conversations of her friend, Monica Lewinsky:*] I'm you. I'm just like you. I'm an average American who found herself in a situation not of her own making.

Statement after testifying to grand jury, Washington, D.C., 29 July 1998

Anthony Trollope

English novelist, 1815–1882

1 It is not the prize that can make us happy; it is not even the winning of the prize. . . . [It is] the struggle, the long hot hour of the honest fight. . . . There is no human bliss equal to twelve hours of work with only six hours in which to do it.

Orley Farm ch. 49 (1862)

2 [*Concluding words of the Barsetshire novels:*] To me Barset has been a real county, and its city a real city, and the spires and towers have been before my eyes, and the voices of the people are known to my ears, and the pavement of the city ways are familiar to my footsteps. . . . I have been induced to wander among them too long by my love of old friendships, and by the sweetness of old faces.

The Last Chronicle of Barset ch. 84 (1867)

3 What was it the French Minister said. If it is simply difficult it is done. If it is impossible, it shall be done.

Phineas Redux ch. 29 (1873)
See Calonne 1; Nansen 1; Santayana 14

4 If men were equal to-morrow and all wore the same coats, they would wear different coats the next day.
The Way We Live Now ch. 42 (1875)

Leon Trotsky (Lev Davidovich Bronstein)
Russian revolutionary, 1879–1940

1 The Literary "Fellow Travelers" of the Revolution.
Literature and Revolution title of ch. 2 (1923)

2 [*Remark to Julius Martov, 7 Nov. 1917:*] You [the Mensheviks] are pitiful isolated individuals; you are bankrupts; your role is played out. Go where you belong from now on—into the dustbin of history!
History of the Russian Revolution ch. 47 (1930) (translation by Max Eastman)
See Birrell 1

3 It was the supreme expression of the mediocrity of the apparatus that Stalin himself rose to his position.
My Life ch. 40 (1930)

T. St. Vincent Troubridge
British army officer, 1895–1963

1 At present an iron curtain of silence has descended, cutting off the Russian zone from the Western Allies.
Sunday Empire News, 21 Oct. 1945
See Winston Churchill 33; Goebbels 3; Ethel Snowden 1

Pierre Elliott Trudeau
Canadian prime minister, 1919–2000

1 There's no place for the state in the bedrooms of the nation.
Interview, Ottawa, 21 Dec. 1967. Trudeau was paraphrasing Martin O'Malley's statement in the *Globe and Mail* (Toronto), 12 Dec. 1967, which read: "Obviously, the state's responsibility should be to legislate rules for a well-ordered society. It has no right or duty to creep into the bedrooms of the nation."

2 [*Response to question asking how far he would go in suspending civil liberties to restore order in Quebec province:*] Just watch me.
Interview by CBC reporter Tim Ralfe, Ottawa, Canada, 13 Oct. 1970

Harry S. Truman
U.S. president, 1884–1972

1 [*After the death of President Franklin D. Roosevelt:*] When they told me yesterday what had happened, I felt like the moon, the stars, and all the planets had fallen on me.
Remarks to reporters, 13 Apr. 1945

2 Sixteen hours ago an American airplane dropped one bomb on Hiroshima. . . . It is a harnessing of the basic powers of the universe. The force from which the sun draws its powers has been loosed against those who brought war to the Far East.
Statement on first use of atomic bomb in combat, 6 Aug. 1945

3 I believe that it must be the policy of the United States to support free peoples who are resisting attempted subjugation by armed minorities or by outside pressures.
Address to joint session of Congress, 12 Mar. 1947

4 The Government has been informed that a Jewish state has been proclaimed in Palestine, and recognition has been requested by the provisional government thereof. The United States recognizes the provisional government of the *de facto* authority of the new state of Israel.
Statement, 14 May 1948

5 Every segment of our population and every individual has a right to expect from our Government a fair deal.

State of the Union Address, 4 Jan. 1949

6 I've just read your lousy review [of a concert by Truman's daughter, Margaret]. I've come to the conclusion that you are an "eight ulcer man on four ulcer pay." It seems to me that you are a frustrated old man who wishes he could have been successful. When you write such poppy-cock as was in the back section of the paper you work for it shows conclusively that you're off the beam and at least four of your ulcers are at work. Some day I hope to meet you. When that happens you'll need a new nose, a lot of beefsteak for black eyes, and perhaps a supporter below!

Letter to Paul Hume, 6 Dec. 1950

7 Now they accuse me of going up and down the Nation on a whistlestop train, and the slogans that they hurl at me most of the time are "Give 'em hell, Harry." That reputation I did not earn. All I do is to tell them [the Republicans] the truth, and that hurts a lot worse than giving them hell.

Address at Palace Hotel, San Francisco, Calif., 4 Oct. 1952
See Political Slogans 16

8 Those who want the Government to regulate matters of the mind and spirit are like men who are so afraid of being murdered that they commit suicide to avoid assassination.

Address at National Archives, Washington, D.C., 15 Dec. 1952

9 I have found the best way to give advice to your children is to find out what they want, and then advise them to do it.

Television interview by Edward R. Murrow, CBS, 27 May 1955

10 A statesman is a politician who's been dead 10 or 15 years.

Speech to Reciprocity Club, Washington, D.C., 11 Apr. 1958
See Bierce 106; Thomas B. Reed 1

11 The buck stops here.

Quoted in *Wash. Post*, 15 Dec. 1946. Described by the *Post* as a "desk gadget . . . a little thing" on which these four words were printed. The *Oxford Dictionary of Catchphrases* states, "The sign was made in the Federal Reformatory at El Reno, Oklahoma, and mailed to President Truman on 2 October 1945, appearing at different times on his desk until late in his administration." The phrase is now firmly associated with Truman but appears to have an older history. Garson O'Toole has found that an article in the journal *Hospital Management*, Oct. 1939, stated: "[General] Warfield spoke on 'Co-operation,' emphasizing the value of doing his job without seeking to escape responsibility by referring to a motto he keeps on his desk—'The buck stops here.'" Still earlier, the *Lincoln* (Nebr.) *Evening Journal*, 2 Oct. 1929, noted: "Capt. Joe Lehman tells a story . . . about the second lieutenant in the war department whose desk was back in the corner among the boxes and barrels. . . . Above the desk the second looey had placed a card which read: 'The buck stops here'" (citation found by Barry Popik).
See Coolidge 5

12 There is nothing new in the world except the history you do not know.

Quoted in William Hillman, *Mr. President* (1952)

13 [*On General Douglas MacArthur:*] I fired him because he wouldn't respect the authority of the President. That's the answer to that. I didn't fire him because he was a dumb son of a bitch, although he was, but that's not against the law for generals. If it was, half to three-quarters of them would be in jail.

Quoted in Merle Miller, *Plain Speaking: An Oral Biography of Harry S. Truman* (1974)

Dalton Trumbo

U.S. screenwriter and novelist, 1905–1976

1 You plan the wars you masters of men plan the wars and point the way and we will point the gun.

Johnny Got His Gun ch. 20 (1939)

2 [*Of the Hollywood blacklist of suspected Communists:*] There was bad faith and good, honesty and dishonesty, courage and cowardice, selflessness and opportunism, wisdom and stupidity, good and bad on both sides; and almost every individual involved, no matter where he stood, combined some or all of these antithetical qualities in his own person, in his own acts. . . . It will do no good to search for villains or heroes or saints or devils because there were none; there were only victims.

Speech accepting an award from the Writers' Guild, 13 Mar. 1970

Donald Trump

U.S. president and businessman, 1946–

1 Deals are my art form. Other people paint beautifully on canvas or write wonderful poetry. I like making deals, preferably big deals. That's how I get my kicks.

Trump: The Art of the Deal ch. 1 (1987)

2 You know, I'm automatically attracted to beautiful—I just start kissing them. It's like a magnet. Just kiss. I don't even wait. And when you're a star, they let you do it. You can do anything. . . . Grab 'em by the pussy. You can do anything.

Recorded remarks to anchorman of *Access Hollywood* television program, Burbank, Calif., Sept. 2005

3 When Mexico sends its people, they're not sending their best. . . . They're bringing drugs. They're bringing crime. They're rapists. And some, I assume, are good people.

Announcement of presidential candidacy, New York, N.Y., 16 June 2015

4 I will build a great, great wall on our southern border. And I will have Mexico pay for that wall.

Announcement of presidential candidacy, New York, N.Y., 16 June 2015

5 [*Of illegal immigrants:*] Who's doing the raping?

CNN *The Situation Room* (television program), 1 July 2015

6 [*Of John McCain:*] He's not a war hero. . . . He's a war hero because he was captured. I like people that weren't captured.

Interview at Family Leadership Summit, Ames, Iowa, 18 July 2015

7 [*Of newscaster Megyn Kelly:*] She gets out and she starts asking me all sorts of ridiculous questions, and you know, you can see there was blood coming out of her eyes, blood coming out of her wherever.

Interview on CNN television, 7 Aug. 2015

8 My father gave me a small loan of a million dollars.

Today Show televised town hall, 26 Oct. 2015

9 I could stand in the middle of Fifth Avenue and shoot somebody, and I wouldn't lose any voters.

Speech at campaign rally, Sioux Center, Iowa, 23 Jan. 2016

10 [*Of Judge Gonzalo Curiel, who was presiding over a fraud case against Trump University:*] I've been treated very unfairly by this judge. Now, this judge is of Mexican heritage. I'm building a wall, okay? I'm building a wall.

CNN television interview, 3 June 2016
See Ryan 1

11 I alone can fix it.

Speech at Republican National Convention, Cleveland, Ohio, 21 July 2016

12 Russia, if you're listening, I hope you're able to find the thirty thousand emails [of Hillary Clinton] that are missing. I think you will probably be rewarded mightily by our press.

Press conference, Doral, Fla., 27 July 2016

13 [*Responding to Hillary Clinton's suggestion that he paid no federal income taxes:*] That makes me smart.

Presidential debate, 26 Sept. 2016

14 [*Of Hillary Clinton:*] Such a nasty woman.

Presidential debate, 19 Oct. 2016

15 Nobody knew that health care could be so complicated.

Remarks at National Governors Association meeting, Washington, D.C., 27 Feb. 2017

16 [*Explaining the firing of FBI director James Comey:*] I just fired the head of the FBI. He

was crazy, a real nut job. I faced great pressure because of Russia. That's taken off.
Remarks to visiting Russian officials, Washington, D.C., 10 May 2017

17 North Korea best not make any more threats to the United States. They will be met with fire and fury like the world has never seen.
Remarks to reporters, Bedminster, N.J., 8 Aug. 2017

18 [*Of the confrontation at a nationalist rally in Charlottesville, Va.:*] I think there's blame on both sides, you look at, you look at both sides.
News conference, New York, N.Y., 15 Aug. 2017

19 North Korean Leader Kim Jong Un just stated that the "Nuclear Button is on his desk at all times." Will someone from his depleted and food starved regime please inform him that I too have a Nuclear Button, but it is a much bigger & more powerful one than his, and my Button works!
Tweet, 2 Jan. 2018

20 [I am] not smart, but genius . . . and a very stable genius at that!
Tweet, 6 Jan. 2018

21 Trade wars are good, and easy to win.
Tweet, 2 Mar. 2018

22 [*Of interference with the 2016 U.S. presidential election:*] My people came to me . . . they said they think it's Russia. I have President Putin; he just said it's not Russia. I will say this: I don't see any reason why it would be.
News conference, Helsinki, Finland, 16 July 2018. Trump later asserted that he had meant to say "why it wouldn't be Russia."

23 I have a gut, and my gut tells me more sometimes than anybody else's brain can ever tell me.
Interview, *Wash. Post*, 28 Nov. 2018

24 I would like you to do us a favor, though.
Memorandum of telephone conversation with Ukrainian president Volodymyr Zelensky, 25 July 2019

25 One day, it's [the novel coronavirus is] like a miracle, it will disappear.
Remarks at African-American History Month reception at White House, 27 Feb. 2020

26 When somebody is the president of the United States the authority is total.
Remarks at White House Coronavirus Task Force press briefing, 14 Apr. 2020

27 I see the disinfectant, where it knocks it [the coronavirus that causes COVID-19] out in a minute. One minute. And is there a way we can do something like that, by injection inside or almost a cleaning.
Remarks at White House Coronavirus Task Force press briefing, 23 Apr. 2020

28 [*Of rival candidate Carly Fiorina's appearance:*] Look at that face! Would anyone vote for that?
Quoted in *Rolling Stone*, 24 Sept. 2015

29 [*Reported comment to senators at White House meeting on immigration, 11 Jan. 2018:*] Why are we having all these people from shithole countries come here?
Quoted in *Wash. Post*, 12 Jan. 2018

Donald Trump, Jr.
U.S. businessman, 1977–

1 [*Responding to Rob Goldstone's offer of incriminating information on Hillary Clinton:*] If it's what you say I love it.
Email, 3 June 2016

Sojourner Truth (Isabella Baumfree)
U.S. evangelist and reformer, ca. 1797–1883

1 Dat man ober dar say dat womin needs to be helped into carriages, and lifted ober ditches, and to hab de best place everywhar. Nobody eber helps me into carriages, or ober mud-puddles, or gibs me any best place! An a'n't I a woman? Look at me! Look at my arm! I have ploughed, and planted, and gathered into barns, and no man could head me! And a'n't I a woman? I could work as much and eat as much as a man—when I could get it—and bear de lash as well! And a'n't I a woman? I have borne thirteen chilern, and seen 'em mos' all sold off to slavery and when I cried out with my mother's grief, none but Jesus heard me! And a'n't I a woman?
Speech at Women's Rights Convention, Akron, Ohio, 29 May 1851. This is a version of Truth's speech not recorded until 1863 and appears to have been embellished by Frances Dana Gage.

2 Den dat little man in black dar, he say women can't have as much rights as men, 'cause Christ wan't a woman! Whar did your Christ come from? Whar did your Christ come from? From God and a woman! Man had nothin' to do wid Him.

Speech at Women's Rights Convention, Akron, Ohio, 29 May 1851. See comment above.

3 My name was Isabella; but when I left the house of bondage, I left everything behind. I wa'n't goin' to keep nothin' of Egypt on em, an' so I went to the Lord an' asked him to give me a new name. And the Lord gave me Sojourner, because I was to travel up an' down the land, showin' the people their sins, an' bein' a sign unto them. Afterward I told the Lord I wanted another name, 'cause everybody else had two names; and the Lord gave me Truth, because I was to declare Truth to the people.

Quoted in *Atlantic Monthly*, Apr. 1863

Marcello Truzzi

Danish-born U.S. sociologist, 1935–2003

1 Extraordinary claims require extraordinary proof.

Letter to the editor, *Parapsychology Review*, Nov.–Dec. 1975. This idea can be traced as far back as David Hume and Pierre-Simon Laplace, and in 1824 "Extraordinary claims can rest only on extraordinary proofs" appeared in Craig Brownlee, *A Careful and Free Inquiry into the True Nature and Tendency of the Religious Principles of the Society of Friends*.

Harriet Tubman (Araminta Green)

U.S. abolitionist, 1821–1913

1 There was one of two things I had a right to, liberty, or death; if I could not have one, I would take de oder; for no man should take me alive; I should fight for my liberty as long as my strength lasted, and when de time came for me to go, de Lord would let dem take me.

Quoted in Sarah Bradford, *Harriet, the Moses of Her People* (1969)

2 I had crossed de line of which I had so long been dreaming. I was free; but dere was no one to welcome me to de land of freedom. I was a stranger in a strange land, and my home after all was down in de old cabin quarter, wid de ole folks, and my brudders and sisters. But to dis solemn resolution I came; I was free, and dey should be free also; I would make a home for dem in de North, and de Lord helping me, I would bring dem all dere.

Quoted in Sarah Bradford, *Harriet, the Moses of Her People* (1969)

3 I was the conductor of the Underground Railroad for eight years, and I can say what most conductors can't say—I never ran my train off the track and I never lost a passenger.

Quoted in Lyde Cullen Sizer, *Divided Houses* (1992)

Barbara W. Tuchman

U.S. historian and writer, 1912–1989

1 Dead battles, like dead generals, hold the military mind in their dead grip and Germans, no less than other peoples, prepare for the last war.

The Guns of August ch. 2 (1962). J. L. Schley wrote in *The Military Engineer*, Jan.–Feb. 1929: "It has been said critically that there is a tendency in many armies to spend the peace time studying how to fight the last war."

2 For one August in its history Paris was French—and silent.

The Guns of August ch. 20 (1962)

3 No more distressing moment can ever face a British government than that which requires it to come to a hard and fast and specific decision.

The Guns of August ch. 9 (1962)

4 Every successful revolution puts on in time the robes of the tyrant it has deposed.

Stilwell and the American Experience in China 1911–45 ch. 8 (1971)

Dick Tuck

U.S. politician, 1924–2018

1 [*Conceding defeat in 1966 primary for California State Senate seat:*] The people have spoken, the bastards.

Quoted in *Independent Press Telegram* (Long Beach, Calif.), 24 Sept. 1972

Benjamin R. Tucker

U.S. anarchist, 1854–1939

1 We enact many laws that manufacture criminals, and then a few that punish them.

Address before Unitarian Ministers' Institute, Salem, Mass., 14 Oct. 1890

Gideon J. Tucker

U.S. judge, 1826–1899

1 The error arose from want of diligent watchfulness in respect to legislative changes. He did not remember that it might be necessary to look at the statutes of the year before. Perhaps he had forgotten the saying, that "no man's life, liberty, or property are safe while the Legislature is in session."
Final Accounting in the Estate of A.B. (1866)

Josiah Tucker

English clergyman, 1711–1799

1 A Shop-keeper will never get the more Custom by beating his Customers: And what is true of a Shop-keeper, is true of a Shop-keeping Nation.
A Letter from a Merchant in London to his Nephew in North America (1766)
See Samuel Adams 1; Napoleon 5; Adam Smith 7

Sophie Tucker

Russian-born U.S. entertainer, 1884–1966

1 From birth to age eighteen, a girl needs good parents. From eighteen to thirty-five, she needs good looks. From thirty-five to fifty-five, she needs a good personality. From fifty-five on, she needs good cash.
Quoted in John Bartlett, *Familiar Quotations*, 13th ed. (1955)

John W. Tukey

U.S. statistician, 1915–2000

1 Today the "software" comprising the carefully planned interpretive routines, compilers, and other aspects of automative programming are at least as important to the modern electronic calculator as its "hardware" of tubes, transistors, wires, tapes, and the like.
American Mathematical Monthly, Jan. 1958. Apparent coinage of the word *software*.

2 Far better an approximate answer to the *right* question, which is often vague, than an *exact* answer to the wrong question, which can always be made precise.
Annals of Mathematical Statistics, Mar. 1962

Peppino Turco

Italian journalist, 1846–1903

1 Funiculì—Funiculà.
Title of song (1880)

Henri de La Tour d'Auvergne, Vicomte de Turenne

French military leader, 1611–1675

1 *La fortune est toujours pour les gros bataillons.*
Fortune is always for the big battalions.
Quoted in Madame de Sévigné, Letter, 22 Dec. 1673
See Bussy-Rabutin 1; Frederick the Great 1; Tacitus 3

Ivan Turgenev

Russian novelist, 1818–1883

1 A nihilist is a man who does not bow down before any authority, who does not take any principle on faith, whatever reverence that principle may be enshrined in.
Fathers and Sons ch. 5 (1862) (translation by Constance Garnett)

2 I don't adopt any one's ideas; I have my own.
Fathers and Sons ch. 13 (1862) (translation by Constance Garnett)

3 The drawing shows me at a glance what would be spread over ten pages in a book.
Fathers and Sons ch. 16 (1862) (translation by Constance Garnett)
See Modern Proverbs 67

4 Whatever a man prays for, he prays for a miracle. Every prayer reduces itself to this: Great God, grant that twice two be not four.
Poems in Prose "Prayer" (1881)

Alan Turing

English mathematician, 1912–1954

1 I propose to consider the question, "Can machines think?"
"Computing Machinery and Intelligence" (1950)

2 The new form of the problem can be described in terms of a game which we call the "imitation game."
"Computing Machinery and Intelligence" (1950)

3 I believe that at the end of the century the use of words and general educated opinion will have altered so much that one will be able to

speak of machines thinking without expecting to be contradicted.

"Computing Machinery and Intelligence" (1950)

4 [*Loud comment about computer intelligence, made in an AT&T cafeteria:*] No, I'm not interested in developing a powerful brain. All I'm after is just a mediocre brain, something like the President of the American Telephone and Telegraph Company.

Quoted in Andrew Hodges, *Alan Turing: The Enigma of Intelligence* (1983)

Frederick Jackson Turner
U.S. historian, 1861–1932

1 Up to our own day American history has been in a large degree the history of the colonization of the Great West. The existence of an area of free land, its continuous recession, and the advance of American settlement westward, explain American development.

"The Significance of the Frontier in American History" (1893)
See Bancroft 1; Frederick Jackson Turner 2

2 What the Mediterranean Sea was to the Greeks, breaking the bond of custom, offering new experiences, calling out new institutions and activities, that, and more, the ever retreating frontier has been to the United States directly, and to the nations of Europe more remotely. And now, four centuries from the discovery of America, at the end of a hundred years of life under the Constitution, the frontier has gone, and with its going has closed the first period of American history.

"The Significance of the Frontier in American History" (1893)
See Bancroft 1; Robert P. Porter 1; Frederick Jackson Turner 1

J. M. W. (Joseph Mallord William) Turner
English painter, 1775–1851

1 [*On first seeing a daguerreotype photograph:*] This is the end of Art. I am glad I have had my day.

Quoted in J. G. Links, *Canaletto and His Patrons* (1977)

2 [*"Last words":*] The Sun is God.

Attributed in John Ruskin, *Fors Clavigera* Letter 45, 2 Aug. 1874

Nat Turner
U.S. rebel, 1800–1831

1 'Twas my object to carry terror and devastation wherever we went.

The Confessions of Nat Turner (1831)

Thomas Tusser
English poet, ca. 1524–1580

1 At Christmas play, and make good cheer,
For Christmas comes, but once a year.

Five Hundred Pointes of Good Husbandrie (1580)

Desmond Tutu
South African religious leader, 1931–

1 There is no peace in Southern Africa. There is no peace because there is no justice.

Nobel Lecture, Oslo, Norway, 11 Dec. 1984

2 Having looked the past in the eye, having asked for forgiveness and having made amends, let us shut the door on the past—not in order to forget it but in order not to allow it to imprison us.

Report of South Africa's Truth and Reconciliation Commission foreword (1998)

3 If you are neutral in situations of injustice, you have chosen the side of the oppressor. If an elephant has its foot on the tail of a mouse and you say that you are neutral, the mouse will not appreciate your neutrality.

Quoted in Robert McAfee Brown, *Unexpected News* (1984)

Mark Twain (Samuel Langhorne Clemens)
U.S. writer, 1835–1910

1 I have often noticed that you shun exertion. There comes the difference between us. I court exertion. I love work. Why, sir, when I have a piece of work to perform, I go away to myself, sit down in the shade, and muse over the coming enjoyment.

Letter to John T. Moore, 6 July 1859

2 The serene confidence which a Christian feels in four aces.

Territorial Enterprise, 1–15 May 1864

3 What a good thing Adam had—when he said a good thing he knew nobody had said it before.

Notebook, 2 July 1867

4 If I were settled I would quit all nonsense & swindle some girl into marrying me. But I wouldn't expect to be *"worthy"* of her. I wouldn't *have* a girl that *I* was worthy of. *She* wouldn't do. She wouldn't be respectable enough.
Letter to Mary Fairbanks, 12 Dec. 1867
See Benchley 11; Galsworthy 2; Joe E. Lewis 1; Lincoln 2; Groucho Marx 41

5 They spell it Vinci and pronounce it Vinchy; foreigners always spell better than they pronounce.
The Innocents Abroad ch. 19 (1869)

6 To do something, say something, see something, before *anybody* else—these are things that confer a pleasure compared with which other pleasures are tame and commonplace, other ecstasies cheap and trivial.
The Innocents Abroad ch. 26 (1869)

7 [*Deleted dedication of Twain's book* Roughing It:] To the Late Cain, This Book is Dedicated, Not on account of respect for his memory, for it merits little respect; not on account of sympathy with him, for his bloody deed placed him without the pale of sympathy, strictly speaking; but out of a mere human commiseration for him in that it was his misfortune to live in a dark age that knew not the beneficent Insanity Plea.
Letter to Elisha Bliss, 15 May 1871

8 Soap and education are not as sudden as a massacre, but they are more deadly in the long run.
A Curious Dream "Facts Concerning the Recent Resignation" (1872)

9 When the peremptory challenges were all exhausted, a jury of twelve men were impaneled—a jury who swore that they had neither heard, read, talked about, nor expressed an opinion concerning a murder which the very cattle in the corrals, the Indians in the sage-brush, and the stones in the street were cognizant of!
Roughing It ch. 48 (1872)

10 The jury system puts a ban upon intelligence and honesty, and a premium upon ignorance, stupidity, and perjury.
Roughing It ch. 48 (1872)

11 [*On women in the United States:*] They live in the midst of a country where there is no end to the laws and no beginning to the execution of them.
"The Temperance Crusade and Woman's Rights" (1873)

12 To my mind Judas Iscariot was nothing but a low, mean, premature Congressman.
Letter to the Editor, *N.Y. Daily Tribune*, 10 Mar. 1873

13 The Gilded Age.
Title of book (1873). Coauthored with Charles Dudley Warner.

14 The chances are that a man cannot get into congress now without resorting to arts and means that should render him unfit to go there.
The Gilded Age ch. 50 (1873). Coauthored with Charles Dudley Warner.
See Douglas Adams 7

15 Tom appeared on the sidewalk with a bucket of whitewash and a long-handled brush. He surveyed the fence, and all gladness left him and a deep melancholy settled down upon his spirit. Thirty yards of board fence nine feet high. Life to him seemed hollow, and existence but a burden.
The Adventures of Tom Sawyer ch. 2 (1876)

16 He [Tom Sawyer] had discovered a great law of human action, without knowing it—namely, that in order to make a man or a boy covet a thing, it is only necessary to make the thing difficult to attain. If he had been a great and wise philosopher, like the writer of this book, he would now have comprehended that Work

consists of whatever a body is *obliged* to do and that Play consists of whatever a body is not obliged to do.

The Adventures of Tom Sawyer ch. 2 (1876)

17 The widder eats by a bell; she goes to bed by a bell; she gits up by a bell—everything's so awful reg'lar a body can't stand it.

The Adventures of Tom Sawyer ch. 35 (1876)

18 There is a sumptuous variety about the New England weather that compels the stranger's admiration—and regret. . . . In the spring I have counted one hundred and thirty-six different kinds of weather inside of four-and-twenty hours.

Address at New England Society's Seventy-First Annual Dinner, New York, N.Y., 22 Dec. 1876

19 I am a great & sublime fool. But then I am God's fool, & all His works must be contemplated with respect.

Letter to William Dean Howells, 28 [?] Dec. 1877

20 Anywhere is better than Paris. Paris the cold, Paris the drizzly, Paris the rainy, Paris the Damnable. More than a hundred years ago, somebody asked Quin, "Did you ever *see* such a winter in all your life before?" "Yes," said he, "last summer." I judge he spent his summer in Paris.

Letter to Lucius Fairchild, 28 Apr. 1880. This letter is the closest source that has been found for the saying, frequently credited to Twain, that "The coldest winter I ever spent was a summer in San Francisco." The Quin referred to was an eighteenth-century actor and wit.

21 A pretty air in an opera is prettier there than it could be anywhere else, I suppose, just as an honest man in politics shines more than he would elsewhere.

A Tramp Abroad ch. 9 (1880)

22 In the matter of intellect the ant must be a strangely overrated bird. During many summers, now, I have watched him, when I ought to have been in better business, and I have not yet come across a living ant that seemed to have any more sense than a dead one. I refer to the ordinary ant, of course; I have had no experience of those wonderful Swiss and African ones which vote, keep drilled armies, hold slaves, and dispute about religion.

A Tramp Abroad ch. 22 (1880)

23 We have not the reverent feeling for the rainbow that a savage has, because we know how it is made. We have lost as much as we gained by prying into that matter.

A Tramp Abroad ch. 42 (1880)

24 What chance has the ignorant, uncultivated liar against the educated expert? What chance have I . . . against a lawyer?

"On the Decay of the Art of Lying" (1882)

25 I was gratified to be able to answer promptly, and I did. I said I didn't know.

Life on the Mississippi ch. 6 (1883)

26 There is something fascinating about science. One gets such wholesale returns of conjecture out of such a trifling investment of fact.

Life on the Mississippi ch. 17 (1883)

27 All the modern inconveniences.

Life on the Mississippi ch. 43 (1883)

28 Persons attempting to find a motive in this narrative will be prosecuted; persons attempting to find a moral in it will be banished; persons attempting to find a plot in it will be shot.

The Adventures of Huckleberry Finn "Notice" (1884)

29 You don't know about me, without you have read a book by the name of "The Adventures of Tom Sawyer," but that ain't no matter. That book was made by Mr. Mark Twain, and he told the truth, mainly.

The Adventures of Huckleberry Finn ch. 1 (1884)

30 I thought a minute, and says to myself, hold on,—s'pose you'd a done right and give Jim up; would you felt better than what you do now? No, says I, I'd feel bad—I'd feel just the same way I do now. Well, then, says I, what's the use you learning to do right, when it's troublesome to do right and ain't no trouble to do wrong, and the wages is just the same?

The Adventures of Huckleberry Finn ch. 16 (1884)

31 We said there warn't no home like a raft, after all. Other places do seem so cramped up and smothery, but a raft don't. You feel mighty free and easy and comfortable on a raft.

The Adventures of Huckleberry Finn ch. 18 (1884)

32 All kings is mostly rapscallions.
The Adventures of Huckleberry Finn ch. 23 (1884)

33 Hain't we got all the fools in town on our side? and ain't that a big enough majority in any town?
The Adventures of Huckleberry Finn ch. 26 (1884)

34 You can't pray a lie.
The Adventures of Huckleberry Finn ch. 31 (1884)

35 It was a close place. I took it up, and held it in my hand. I was trembling, because I'd got to decide, forever, betwixt two things, and I knowed it. I studied a minute, sort of holding my breath, and then says to myself: "All right, then, I'll go to hell"—and tore it up.
The Adventures of Huckleberry Finn ch. 31 (1884)

36 I reckon I got to light out for the Territory ahead of the rest, because Aunt Sally she's going to adopt me and sivilize me and I can't stand it. I been there before.
The Adventures of Huckleberry Finn ch. 43 (1884)

37 Loyalty to petrified opinions never yet broke a chain or freed a human soul in *this* world—and never *will*.
Speech, Hartford, Conn., 1884

38 The difference between the *almost*-right word & the *right* word is really a large matter—it's the difference between the lightning-bug & the lightning.
Letter to George Bainton, 15 Oct. 1888

39 My kind of loyalty was loyalty to one's country, not to its institutions or its office-holders.
A Connecticut Yankee in King Arthur's Court ch. 13 (1889)

40 Here I was, in a country where a right to say how the country should be governed was restricted to six persons in each thousand of its population. . . . I was become a stockholder in a corporation where nine hundred and ninety-four of the members furnished all the money and did all the work, and the other six elected themselves a permanent board of direction and took all the dividends. It seemed to me that what the nine hundred and ninety-four dupes needed was a new deal.
A Connecticut Yankee in King Arthur's Court ch. 13 (1889)
See Franklin Roosevelt 4; Woodrow Wilson 4

41 A man has no business to be depressed by a disappointment, anyway; he ought to make up his mind to get even.
A Connecticut Yankee in King Arthur's Court ch. 22 (1889)

42 Whenever the literary German dives into a sentence, that is the last you are going to see of him till he emerges on the other side of his Atlantic with his verb in his mouth.
A Connecticut Yankee in King Arthur's Court ch. 22 (1889)

43 The master minds of all nations, in all ages, have sprung in affluent multitude from the mass of the nation, and from the mass of the nation only—not from its privileged classes.
A Connecticut Yankee in King Arthur's Court ch. 25 (1889)

44 Don't you know, there are some things that can beat smartness and foresight? Awkwardness and stupidity can. The best swordsman in the world doesn't need to fear the second best swordsman in the world; no, the person for him to be afraid of is some ignorant antagonist who has never had a sword in his hand before; he doesn't do the thing he ought to.
A Connecticut Yankee in King Arthur's Court ch. 34 (1889)

45 Words are only painted fire; a look is the fire itself.
A Connecticut Yankee in King Arthur's Court ch. 35 (1889)

46 Dying man couldn't make up his mind which place to go to—both have their advantages, "heaven for climate, hell for company!"
Notebook, 1889–1890. Ben Wade was quoted as saying "heaven has the better climate, but hell has the better company" in the 1885 *Proceedings of the National Conference of Charities and Correction*.

47 Bill Styles . . . spoke of the low grade of legislative morals. "Kind of discouraging. You see, it's so hard to find men of a so high type of morals that they'll *stay bought*."
Notebook, 1890–1891. "An honest politician is one who, when he is bought, will stay bought" is often attributed to Simon Cameron. However, Erwin S. Bradley, in *Simon Cameron, Lincoln's Secretary of War* (1966), states that "apparently there is no basis for the definition of an honest politician commonly attributed to him." The *New York Times*, 8 Sept. 1866,

printed the following: "'I call a man honest,' said a New-Jersey politician, 'who when he is bought, stays bought.'"

48 In the first place God made idiots. This was for practice. Then he made proofreaders.

Notebook, 1893

49 Cheer up—the worst is yet to come.

Letter to Olivia Clemens, 19 Apr. 1894. After initially writing "worst is," Clemens crossed these words out and wrote "best is."

50 Of all God's creatures there is only one that cannot be made the slave of the lash. That one is the cat. If man could be crossed with a cat it would improve man, but it would deteriorate the cat.

Notebook, 1894

51 Familiarity breeds contempt—and children.

Notebook, 1894

52 There is no character, howsoever good and fine, but it can be destroyed by ridicule, howsoever poor and witless. Observe the ass, for instance: his character is about perfect, he is the choicest spirit among all the humbler animals, yet see what ridicule has brought him to. Instead of feeling complimented when we are called an ass, we are left in doubt.

Pudd'nhead Wilson "A Whisper to the Reader," "Pudd'nhead Wilson's Calendar" (1894)

53 Tell the truth or trump—but get the trick.

Pudd'nhead Wilson ch. 1, "Pudd'nhead Wilson's Calendar" (1894)

54 A home without a cat—and a well-fed, well-petted, and properly revered cat—may be a perfect home, perhaps, but how can it prove title?

Pudd'nhead Wilson ch. 1 (1894)

55 Adam was but human—this explains it all. He did not want the apple for the apple's sake, he wanted it only because it was forbidden. The mistake was in not forbidding the serpent: then he would have eaten the serpent.

Pudd'nhead Wilson ch. 2, "Pudd'nhead Wilson's Calendar" (1894)

56 Whoever has lived long enough to find out what life is, knows how deep a debt of gratitude we owe to Adam, the first great benefactor of our race. He brought death into the world.

Pudd'nhead Wilson ch. 3, "Pudd'nhead Wilson's Calendar" (1894)

57 Adam and Eve had many advantages, but the principal one was, that they escaped teething.

Pudd'nhead Wilson ch. 4, "Pudd'nhead Wilson's Calendar" (1894)

58 Training is everything. The peach was once a bitter almond; cauliflower is nothing but cabbage with a college education.

Pudd'nhead Wilson ch. 5, "Pudd'nhead Wilson's Calendar" (1894)

59 Let us endeavor so to live that when we come to die even the undertaker will be sorry.

Pudd'nhead Wilson ch. 6, "Pudd'nhead Wilson's Calendar" (1894)

60 One of the most striking differences between a cat and a lie is that a cat has only nine lives.

Pudd'nhead Wilson ch. 7, "Pudd'nhead Wilson's Calendar" (1894)

61 The holy passion of Friendship is of so sweet and steady and loyal and enduring a nature that it will last through a whole lifetime, if not asked to lend money.

Pudd'nhead Wilson ch. 8, "Pudd'nhead Wilson's Calendar" (1894)

62 Why is it that we rejoice at a birth and grieve at a funeral? It is because we are not the person involved.

Pudd'nhead Wilson ch. 9, "Pudd'nhead Wilson's Calendar" (1894)

63 It is easy to find fault, if one has that disposition. There was once a man who, not being able to find any other fault with his coal, complained that there were too many prehistoric toads in it.

Pudd'nhead Wilson ch. 9, "Pudd'nhead Wilson's Calendar" (1894)

64 When angry, count four; when very angry, swear.

Pudd'nhead Wilson ch. 10, "Pudd'nhead Wilson's Calendar" (1894)

65 Courage is resistance to fear, mastery of fear—not absence of fear. Except a creature be part coward it is not a compliment to say it is brave; it is merely a loose misapplication of the word. Consider the flea!—incomparably the bravest of all the creatures of God, if ignorance of fear were courage.

Pudd'nhead Wilson ch. 12, "Pudd'nhead Wilson's Calendar" (1894)

66 When I reflect upon the number of disagreeable people who I know have gone to a better world, I am moved to lead a different life.

Pudd'nhead Wilson ch. 13, "Pudd'nhead Wilson's Calendar" (1894)

67 October. This is one of the peculiarly dangerous months to speculate in stocks in. The others are July, January, September, April, November, May, March, June, December, August, and February.

Pudd'nhead Wilson ch. 13, "Pudd'nhead Wilson's Calendar" (1894)

68 Nothing so needs reforming as other people's habits.

Pudd'nhead Wilson ch. 15, "Pudd'nhead Wilson's Calendar" (1894)

69 If you pick up a starving dog and make him prosperous, he will not bite you. This is the principal difference between a dog and a man.

Pudd'nhead Wilson ch. 16, "Pudd'nhead Wilson's Calendar" (1894)

70 Even popularity can be overdone. In Rome, along at first, you are full of regrets that Michelangelo died; but by and by you only regret that you didn't see him do it.

Pudd'nhead Wilson ch. 17, "Pudd'nhead Wilson's Calendar" (1894)

71 *Thanksgiving Day.* Let us all give humble, hearty, and sincere thanks, now, but the turkeys. In the island of Fiji they do not use turkeys; they use plumbers. It does not become you and me to sneer at Fiji.

Pudd'nhead Wilson ch. 18, "Pudd'nhead Wilson's Calendar" (1894)

72 Few things are harder to put up with than the annoyance of a good example.

Pudd'nhead Wilson ch. 19, "Pudd'nhead Wilson's Calendar" (1894)

73 It were not best that we should all think alike; it is difference of opinion that makes horse-races.

Pudd'nhead Wilson ch. 19, "Pudd'nhead Wilson's Calendar" (1894)

74 Even the clearest and most perfect circumstantial evidence is likely to be at fault, after all, and therefore ought to be received with great caution. Take the case of any pencil, sharpened by any woman: if you have witnesses, you will find she did it with a knife;

but if you take simply the aspect of the pencil, you will say she did it with her teeth.

Pudd'nhead Wilson ch. 20, "Pudd'nhead Wilson's Calendar" (1894)

75 *April 1.* This is the day upon which we are reminded of what we are on the other three hundred and sixty-four.

Pudd'nhead Wilson ch. 21, "Pudd'nhead Wilson's Calendar" (1894)

76 It was wonderful to find America, but it would have been more wonderful to miss it.

Pudd'nhead Wilson conclusion, "Pudd'nhead Wilson's Calendar" (1894)

77 I've thought it all over . . . and there ain't no way to find out why a snorer can't hear himself snore.

Tom Sawyer Abroad ch. 10 (1894)

78 I asked Tom if countries always apologized when they had done wrong, and he says: "Yes; the little ones does."

Tom Sawyer Abroad ch. 12 (1894)

79 He saw nearly all things as through a glass eye, darkly.

"Fenimore Cooper's Literary Offenses" (1895)

80 [*Quoting an "American joke":*] In Boston they ask, How much does he know? in New York, How much is he worth? in Philadelphia, Who were his parents?

"What Paul Bourget Thinks of Us" (1895)
See Disraeli 10

81 He is the only animal that loves his neighbor as himself, and cuts his throat if his theology isn't straight.

"Man's Place in the Animal World" (ca. 1896)

82 Talking of patriotism what humbug it is; it is a word which always commemorates a robbery. There isn't a foot of land in the world which doesn't represent the ousting and re-ousting of a long line of successive "owners," who each in turn, as "patriots," with proud swelling hearts defended it against the next gang of "robbers" who came to steal it and *did*—and became swelling-hearted patriots in *their* turn.

Notebook, 26 May 1896

83 Be good & you will be lonesome.

Following the Equator flyleaf (1897)

84 When in doubt, tell the truth.

> *Following the Equator* ch. 2, "Pudd'nhead Wilson's New Calendar" (1897)

85 Noise proves nothing. Often a hen who has laid an egg cackles as if she had laid an asteroid.

> *Following the Equator* ch. 5, "Pudd'nhead Wilson's New Calendar" (1897)

86 Truth is the most valuable thing we have. Let us economize it.

> *Following the Equator* ch. 7, "Pudd'nhead Wilson's New Calendar" (1897)
> *See Robert Armstrong 1; Edmund Burke 25*

87 It could probably be shown by facts and figures that there is no distinctly native American criminal class except Congress.

> *Following the Equator* ch. 8, "Pudd'nhead Wilson's New Calendar" (1897)

88 Everything human is pathetic. The secret source of Humor itself is not joy but sorrow. There is no humor in heaven.

> *Following the Equator* ch. 10, "Pudd'nhead Wilson's New Calendar" (1897)

89 We should be careful to get out of an experience only the wisdom that is in it—and stop there; lest we be like the cat that sits down on a hot stove-lid. She will never sit down on a hot stove-lid again—and that is well; but also she will never sit down on a cold one any more.

> *Following the Equator* ch. 11, "Pudd'nhead Wilson's New Calendar" (1897)

90 Faith is believing what you know ain't so.

> *Following the Equator* ch. 12, "Pudd'nhead Wilson's New Calendar" (1897)

91 The timid man yearns for full value and demands a tenth. The bold man strikes for double value and compromises on par.

> *Following the Equator* ch. 13, "Pudd'nhead Wilson's New Calendar" (1897)

92 We can secure other people's approval, if we do right and try hard; but our own is worth a hundred of it, and no way has been found out of securing that.

> *Following the Equator* ch. 14, "Pudd'nhead Wilson's New Calendar" (1897)

93 Truth *is* stranger than fiction, but it is because Fiction is obliged to stick to possibilities; Truth isn't.

> *Following the Equator* ch. 15, "Pudd'nhead Wilson's New Calendar" (1897)
> *See Byron 33; Chesterton 6*

94 It is easier to stay out than to get out.

> *Following the Equator* ch. 18, "Pudd'nhead Wilson's New Calendar" (1897)

95 It is by the goodness of God that in our country we have those three unspeakably precious things: freedom of speech, freedom of conscience, and the prudence never to practise either of them.

> *Following the Equator* ch. 20, "Pudd'nhead Wilson's New Calendar" (1897)

96 There is no such thing as "the Queen's English." The property has gone into the hands of a joint stock company and we own the bulk of the shares!

> *Following the Equator* ch. 24, "Pudd'nhead Wilson's New Calendar" (1897)

97 *"Classic."* A book which people praise and don't read.

> *Following the Equator* ch. 25, "Pudd'nhead Wilson's New Calendar" (1897)

98 Man is the Only Animal that Blushes. Or needs to.

> *Following the Equator* ch. 27, "Pudd'nhead Wilson's New Calendar" (1897)

99 To succeed in the other trades, capacity must be shown; in the law, concealment of it will do.

> *Following the Equator* ch. 37, "Pudd'nhead Wilson's New Calendar" (1897)

100 By trying we can easily learn to endure adversity. Another man's, I mean.

> *Following the Equator* ch. 39, "Pudd'nhead Wilson's New Calendar" (1897)

101 Few of us can stand prosperity. Another man's, I mean.

> *Following the Equator* ch. 40, "Pudd'nhead Wilson's New Calendar" (1897)

102 Each person is born to one possession which outvalues all his others—his last breath.

> *Following the Equator* ch. 42, "Pudd'nhead Wilson's New Calendar" (1897)

103 It takes your enemy and your friend, working together, to hurt you to the heart; the one to slander you and the other to get the news to you.

Following the Equator ch. 45, "Pudd'nhead Wilson's New Calendar" (1897)

104 Let me make the superstitions of a nation and I care not who makes its laws or its songs either.

Following the Equator ch. 51, "Pudd'nhead Wilson's New Calendar" (1897)
See Auden 22; Auden 39; Andrew Fletcher 1; Samuel Johnson 22; Percy Shelley 15

105 There are two times in a man's life when he should not speculate: when he can't afford to, and when he can.

Following the Equator ch. 56, "Pudd'nhead Wilson's New Calendar" (1897)

106 Don't part with your illusions. When they are gone you may still exist but you have ceased to live.

Following the Equator ch. 59, "Pudd'nhead Wilson's New Calendar" (1897)

107 In the first place God made idiots. This was for practice. Then He made School Boards.

Following the Equator ch. 61, "Pudd'nhead Wilson's New Calendar" (1897)

108 Every one is a moon, and has a dark side which he never shows to anybody.

Following the Equator ch. 66, "Pudd'nhead Wilson's New Calendar" (1897)

109 What are the proper proportions of a maxim? A minimum of sound to a maximum of sense.

More Tramps Abroad ch. 23, "Pudd'nhead Wilson's New Calendar" (1897)

110 A successful book is not made of what is *in* it, but of what is left *out* of it.

Letter to H. H. Rogers, 26–28 Apr. 1897

111 I have no race prejudices, and I think I have no color prejudices nor caste prejudices nor creed prejudices. Indeed, I know it. I can stand any society. All that I care to know is that a man is a human being—that is enough for me; he can't be any worse.

"Concerning the Jews" (1899)

112 Good breeding consists in concealing how much we think of ourselves and how little we think of the other person.

Notebook, 1899

113 Always do right. This will gratify some people & astonish the rest.

Note to Young People's Society, Greenpoint Presbyterian Church, Brooklyn, N.Y., 16 Feb. 1901

114 I would throw out the old maxim, "My country, right or wrong," and instead I would say, "My country when she is right."

"Training That Pays" (speech), 16 Mar. 1901
See Chesterton 3; Decatur 1; Schurz 1

115 What is the difference between a taxidermist and a tax collector? The taxidermist takes only your skin.

Notebook, Dec. 1902

116 The man who is a pessimist before 48 knows too much; if he is an optimist after it, he knows too little.

Notebook, Dec. 1902

117 To create man was a fine and original idea; but to add the sheep was tautology.

Notebook, Dec. 1902

118 Man was made at the end of the week's work, when God was tired.

Notebook, 1903

119 Whenever you find that you are on the side of the majority, it is time to reform.

Notebook, 1905
See Heinlein 14; Ibsen 14; Roscommon 1

120 Laws are sand, customs are rock. Laws can be evaded and punishment escaped, but an openly transgressed custom brings sure punishment.

"The Gorky Incident" (1906)

121 The language [German] which enables a man to travel all day in one sentence without changing cars.

Christian Science bk. 1, ch. 1 (1907)

122 In all matters of opinion our adversaries are insane.

Christian Science bk. 1, ch. 5 (1907)

123 When I was younger I could remember anything, whether it happened or not; but my

faculties are decaying, now, and soon I shall be so I cannot remember any but the latter. It is sad to go to pieces like this, but we all have to do it.

"Mark Twain's Own Autobiography," *North American Review*, 1 Mar. 1907

124 Thunder is good, thunder is impressive; but it is lightning that does the work.

Letter to Henry W. Ruoff, 28 Aug. 1908

125 Power, Money, Persuasion, Supplication, Persecution—these can lift at a colossal humbug—push it a little—crowd it a little—weaken it a little, century by century: but only Laughter can blow it to rags and atoms at a blast. Against the assault of Laughter nothing can stand.

The Mysterious Stranger ch. 10 (1916)

126 There is no God, no universe, no human race, no earthly life, no heaven, no hell. It is all a dream, a grotesque and foolish dream. Nothing exists but you. And you are but a *thought*—a vagrant thought, a useless thought, a homeless thought, wandering forlorn among the empty eternities!

The Mysterious Stranger ch. 11 (1916)

127 You tell me whar a man gits his corn pone, en I'll tell you what his 'pinions is.

Europe and Elsewhere "Corn-Pone Opinions" (1923)

128 Biographies are but the clothes and buttons of the man—the biography of the man himself cannot be written.

Autobiography vol. 1 (1924)

129 Life does not consist mainly—or even largely—of facts and happenings. It consists mainly of the storm of thoughts that is forever blowing through one's head.

Autobiography vol. 1 (1924)

130 News is history in its first and best form, its vivid and fascinating form . . . history is the pale and tranquil reflection of it.

Autobiography vol. 1 (1924)

131 [Man] has imagined a heaven, and has left entirely out of it the supremest of all his delights, the one ecstasy that stands first and foremost in the heart of every individual of his race—and of ours—sexual intercourse!

It is as if a lost and perishing person in a roasting desert should be told by a rescuer he might choose and have all longed for things but one, and he should elect to leave out water!

"Letters from the Earth" (1940)

132 [*On the Bible:*] It is full of interest. It has noble poetry in it; and some clever fables; and some blood-drenched history; and some good morals; and a wealth of obscenity; and upwards of a thousand lies.

"Letters from the Earth" (1940)

133 Man is the Religious Animal. He is the only Religious Animal. He is the only animal that has the True Religion—several of them.

"The Lowest Animal" (1940)

134 I believe that our Heavenly Father invented man because he was disappointed in the monkey.

Mark Twain in Eruption (1940)

135 Annihilation has no terrors for me, because I have already tried it before I was born—a hundred million years—and I have suffered more in an hour, in this life, than I remember to have suffered in the whole hundred million years put together. There was a peace, a serenity, an absence of all sense of responsibility, an absence of worry, an absence of care, grief, perplexity; and the presence of a deep content and unbroken satisfaction in that hundred million years of holiday which I look back upon with a tender longing and with a grateful desire to resume, when the opportunity comes.

Autobiography ch. 49 (1959)

136 In religion and politics people's beliefs and convictions are in almost every case gotten at second-hand, and without examination.

Autobiography ch. 78 (1959)

137 God made man, without man's consent, and made his nature, too; made it vicious instead of angelic, and then said, Be angelic, or I will punish you and destroy you. But no matter, God is responsible for everything man does, all the same; He can't get around that fact. There is only one Criminal, and it is not man.

"Little Bessie" (1972)

138 The report of my death was an exaggeration.

Quoted in *N.Y. Journal,* 2 June 1897. These words were preceded by "James Ross Clemens, of St. Louis, a cousin of mine, was seriously ill two or three weeks ago in London, but is well now. The report of my illness grew out of his illness." The quotation is usually reported as "Reports of my death have been greatly exaggerated." Much earlier (5 July 1863), the following appeared in a letter by Twain to the *Territorial Enterprise:* "There was a report about town, last night, that Charles Strong, Esq., Superintendent of the Gould & Curry, had been shot and very effectually killed. I asked him about it at church this morning. He said there was no truth in the rumor."

139 In certain trying circumstances, urgent circumstances, desperate circumstances, profanity furnishes a relief denied even to prayer.

Quoted in Albert B. Paine, *Mark Twain: A Biography* (1912)

140 Suppose you were an idiot. And suppose you were a member of Congress. But I repeat myself.

Quoted in Albert B. Paine, *Mark Twain: A Biography* (1912)

141 [Christian nations are the most enlightened and progressive] in spite of their religion, not because of it. The Church has opposed every innovation and discovery from the day of Galileo down to our own time, when the use of anesthetics in child-birth was regarded as a sin because it avoided the biblical curse pronounced against Eve.

Quoted in Albert B. Paine, *Mark Twain: A Biography* (1912)

142 [*To his wife Olivia, who had repeated his swearing:*] You got the words right, Livy, but you don't know the tune.

Quoted in Albert B. Paine, *Mark Twain: A Biography* (1912)

143 Clothes make the man. Naked people have little or no influence in society.

Quoted in *More Maxims of Mark,* ed. Merle Johnson (1927)

144 A lawyer one day spoke to him [Mark Twain] with his hands in his pockets. "Is it not a curious sight to see a lawyer with his hands in his *own* pockets?" remarked the humorist in his quiet drawl.

Reported in Max O'Rell, *Jonathan and His Continent* (1889)

145 A well known American writer said once that, while everybody talked about the weather, nobody seemed to do anything about it.

Reported in *Hartford Courant,* 24 Aug. 1897. This witticism is famous in the form "Everybody talks about the weather, but nobody does anything about it." The "well-known American writer" is usually taken to be Twain, but the writer could also have been Charles Dudley Warner, who was the editor of the *Hartford Courant* in 1897. There is an 1884 reference to Warner saying about New England weather that "it is a matter about which a great deal is said, but very little done" (*Proceedings of the Chamber of Commerce of the State of New York, Twenty-seventh Annual Report*).

146 I made it [a] rule never to smoke more than one cigar at a time.

Attributed in *Wash. Post,* 11 Aug. 1929. Twain did apparently utter this in a speech at his seventieth birthday dinner, 5 Dec. 1905, but may have been recycling an already existing joke, as the *Burlington* (Iowa) *Weekly Hawk-Eye,* 12, Jan. 1882, published "I will only smoke one cigar at a time" as a New Year's resolution.

147 I have no respect for a man who can spell a word only one way.

Attributed in *Chicago Daily Tribune,* 22 May 1932. Without attribution to Twain, this appears as early as 1880, in Marshall Brown, *Wit and Humor:* "A man must be a great fool *who can't spell a word more than one way.*" Without attribution, this appeared as early as 1855, in *The Farmer's Cabinet,* 13 Sept.: "A man must be a great fool who can't spell a word more than one way."

148 I am an old man and have known a great many troubles, but most of them never happened.

Attributed in *Reader's Digest,* Apr. 1934. A similar remark, attributed to an anonymous old man, appeared in Andrew Carnegie, *An American Four-in-Hand in Britain* (1883).
See Jefferson 42

149 When I was a boy of fourteen, my father was so ignorant I could hardly stand to have the old man around. But when I got to be twenty-one, I was astonished at how much he had learned in seven years.

Attributed in *Reader's Digest,* Sept. 1937. A similar attribution to Twain occurred in *The Square Deal,* Dec. 1915.

150 If you don't like the weather in New England, just wait a few minutes.

Attributed in Bennett Cerf, *Try and Stop Me* (1944). An earlier version, not attributed to any individual, appeared in Thomas Morris Longstreth, *Reading the Weather* (1915), and referred to the St. Lawrence River valley: "If you don't like our weather, wait a minute."

151 I have never let my schooling interfere with my education.

Attributed in *Reader's Digest*, Oct. 1946. The writer Grant Allen complained that "we should . . . be compelled to let our boys' schooling interfere with their education!" in his 1894 book *Post-Prandial Philosophy*.

152 Golf is a good walk spoiled.

Attributed in *Reader's Digest*, Dec. 1948. Commonly attributed to Twain, but the *Stevens Point* (Wis.) *Daily Journal*, 19 Dec. 1913, printed the following without attribution to any named individual: "Golf, of course, has been defined as a good walk spoiled."

153 Twenty-four years ago I was strangely handsome; in San Francisco in the rainy season I was often mistaken for fair weather.

Attributed in Evan Esar, *The Dictionary of Humorous Quotations* (1949). This is an abridgment of a passage in an unmailed letter of Twain's dated 8 Sept. 1887.

154 History never repeats itself, but it rhymes.

Attributed in *N.Y. Times*, 25 Jan. 1970

Harrison Tweed

U.S. lawyer, 1885–1969

1 I have a high opinion of lawyers. With all their faults, they stack up well against those in every other occupation or profession. They are better to work with or play with or fight with or drink with than most other varieties of mankind.

Quoted in Bernard Botein, *Trial Judge* (1952). Inscribed on a plaque in the reading room of the Harvard Law Library.

Twiggy (Leslie Hornby)

English model, 1949–

1 [*Remarks in 1968 interview:*] Oh! God! When did you say it happened? Where? Hiroshima? But that's ghastly. A hundred thousand dead? It's frightful. Men are mad.

Quoted in R. Buckminster Fuller, *I Seem to Be a Verb* (1970)

Anne Tyler

U.S. novelist, 1941–

1 "While armchair travelers dream of going places," Julian said, "traveling armchairs dream of staying put."

The Accidental Tourist ch. 6 (1985)

2 Once upon a time, there was a woman who discovered she had turned into the wrong person.

Back When We Were Grownups ch. 1 (2001)

Kenneth Tynan

English theater critic, 1927–1980

1 What, when drunk, one sees in other women, one sees in Garbo sober.

Curtains pt. 2 (1961)

2 A critic is a man who knows the way but can't drive the car.

N.Y. Times, 1 Dec. 1963

Mike Tyson

U.S. boxer, 1966–

1 Everybody has a plan until they get punched in the mouth.

Quoted in *L.A. Times*, 6 July 2004

Alexander Fraser Tytler, Lord Woodhouselee

Scottish historian and lawyer, 1747–1813

1 A true democracy cannot exist as a permanent form of government. It can only exist until the electorate discovers it can vote itself largess out of the public treasury.

Attributed in *Brainerd* (Minn.) *Daily Dispatch*, 1 June 1946. Researchers have failed to find this in Tytler's writings, and the often-made attribution to him is probably apocryphal.

Tristan Tzara (Samy Rosenstock)

Romanian-born French writer and editor, 1896–1963

1 *Dada ne signifie rien.*
Dada means nothing.

"Manifeste Dada 1918" (1918)

Harlan K. Ullman
U.S. military theorist, 1941–

1 In Rapid Dominance, the aim of affecting the adversary's will, understanding, and perception through achieving Shock and Awe is multifaceted.

Shock and Awe: Achieving Rapid Dominance ch. 2 (1996). Coauthored with James P. Wade.

Ulpian (Domitius Ulpianus)
Roman jurist, ca. 170–228

1 *Nulla iniuria est, quae in volentem fiat.*
No injustice is done to someone who wants that thing done.

Corpus Iuris Civilis Digests, bk. 47, ch. 10, sec. 1. Commonly quoted as *"Volenti non fit iniuria"* (To a willing person it is not wrong).

Laurel Thatcher Ulrich
U.S. historian, 1938–

1 Well-behaved women seldom make history.
American Quarterly, Spring 1976

Miguel de Unamuno
Spanish philosopher and writer, 1864–1937

1 Life is doubt,
And faith without doubt is nothing but death.
"Salmo II" (1907)

Jesse M. Unruh
U.S. politician, 1922–1987

1 Money is the mother's milk of politics.
Quoted in *Time,* 14 Dec. 1962

2 [*Of lobbyists and California legislators:*] If you can't eat their food, drink their booze, screw their women and then vote against them, you have no business being up here.
Lou Cannon, *Ronnie and Jesse: A Political Odyssey* (1969)

Upanishads
Hindu sacred texts, ca. 800 B.C.–200 B.C.

1 As the bees make honey by gathering juices from many flowering plants and trees, and as these juices reduced to one honey do not know from what flowers they severally come, similarly, my son, all creatures, when they are merged in that one Existence, whether in dreamless sleep or in death, know nothing of their past or present state, because of the ignorance enveloping them—know not that they are merged in him and that from him they came. "Whatever these creatures are, whether a lion, or a tiger, or a boar, or a worm, or a gnat, or a mosquito, that they remain after they come back from dreamless sleep." All these have their self in him alone. He is the truth.
   He is the subtle essence of all. He is the Self. And that, Svetaketu, THAT ART THOU.
Chāndogya Upanishad ch. 6, pt. 14

2 Abiding in the midst of ignorance, thinking themselves wise and learned, fools go aimlessly hither and thither, like blind led by the blind.
Katha Upanishad ch. 2, v. 5

3 If any man thinks he slays, and if another thinks he is slain, neither knows the ways of truth. The Eternal in man cannot kill: the Eternal in man cannot die.
Katha Upanishad ch. 2, v. 19

4 Sages say the path is narrow and difficult to tread, narrow as the edge of a razor.
Katha Upanishad ch. 3, v. 15

5 The sound of Brahman is OM. At the end of OM is silence. It is a silence of joy.
Maitri Upanishad ch. 6, v. 23

6 *Shantih, shantih, shantih.*
Peace, peace, peace!
Taittirīya Upanishad ch. 1, pt. 1, mantra
See T. S. Eliot 61

John Updike

U.S. novelist, 1932–2009

1 [*On Ted Williams's last baseball game at Fenway Park, Boston, Mass.*:] Our noise for some seconds passed beyond excitement into a kind of immense open anguish, a cry to be saved. But immortality is nontransferable. The papers said that the other players, and even the umpires on the field, begged him to come out and acknowledge us in some way, but he never had and did not now. Gods do not answer letters.
New Yorker, 22 Oct. 1960

2 The first breath of adultery is the freest; after it, constraints aping marriage appear.
Couples ch. 5 (1968)

3 Writing criticism is to writing fiction and poetry as hugging the shore is to sailing in the open sea.
Hugging the Shore foreword (1984)

4 To say that war is madness is like saying that sex is madness: true enough, from the standpoint of a stateless eunuch, but merely a provocative epigram for those who must make their arrangements in the world as given.
Self-Consciousness ch. 4 (1989)

5 Rabbit realized the world was not solid and benign, it was a shabby set of temporary arrangements rigged up for the time being, all for the sake of the money. You just passed through, and they milked you for what you were worth, mostly when you were young and gullible.
Rabbit at Rest ch. 3 (1990)

Lauren Caitlin Upton

U.S. beauty contestant, 1989–

1 [*Response to a pageant question about why one-fifth of Americans are unable to locate the United States on a world map:*] I personally believe that U.S. Americans are unable to do so because some people out there in our nation don't have maps and I believe that our education like such as in South Africa and the Iraq and everywhere like such as and I believe that they should our education over here in the U.S. should help the U.S. or should help South Africa and should help Iraq and the Asian countries so we will be able to build up our future for our children.
Television broadcast of Miss Teen USA competition, 24 Aug. 2007

Urban II

French pope, ca. 1042–1099

1 [*Exhortation to faithful to embark on the First Crusade:*] Rid God's sanctuary of the wicked; expel the robbers; bring in the pious. . . . Let no attachment to your native soil be an impediment; because, in different points of view, all the world is exile to the Christian and all the world his country. Thus exile is his country, and his country exile.
Speech to Council of Clermont, 27 Nov. 1095. There were no immediate contemporary accounts of Urban's speech; the quotation here is taken from William of Malmesbury, *De Gestis Regum Anglorum*.

James Ussher

Irish prelate and scholar, 1581–1656

1 [*Calculating that the Creation occurred in the year 4004 B.C.:*] Which beginning of time according to our Chronology, fell upon the entrance of the night preceding the twenty third day of *Octob.* in the year of the Julian Calendar, 710.
The Annals of the World (1658)

Paul Valéry

French poet and man of letters, 1871–1945

1 *Nous autres, civilisations, nous savons maintenant que nous sommes mortelles.*
We others, civilizations, we know now that we are mortal.
"La Crise de l'Esprit" Letter 1 (1919)

2 *Un poème n'est jamais achevé—c'est toujours un accident qui le termine.*
A poem is never finished—it's always an accident that ends it.
Littérature (1929)

3 Liberty is the hardest test that one can inflict on a people. To know how to be free is not given equally to all men and all nations.
Regards sur le Monde Actuel (1931)

4 History justifies whatever we want it to. It teaches absolutely nothing, for it contains everything and gives examples of everything.
Regards sur le Monde Actuel (1931)

5 *L'avenir est comme le reste: il n'est plus ce qu'il était.*
The future, like everything else, is no longer quite what it used to be.
"Notre Destin et les Lettres" (1937)

6 *Dieu créa l'homme, et ne le trouvant pas assez seul, il lui donne une compagne pour lui faire mieux sentir sa solitude.*
God created man and, finding him not sufficiently alone, gave him a companion to make him feel his solitude more keenly.
Tel Quel 1 "Moralités" (1941)

7 Politics is the art of preventing people from taking part in affairs which properly concern them.
Tel Quel 2 "Rhumbs" (1943)

Martin Van Buren

U.S. president, 1782–1862

1 I believe . . . that constitutions are the work of time and not the invention of ingenuity; and that to frame a complete system of government, depending on the habits of reverence and experience, was an attempt as absurd as to build a tree or manufacture an opinion.
Remarks at New York State Constitutional Convention, 25 Sept. 1820

Paul J. Vance

U.S. songwriter, 1929–

1 It was an itsy bitsy teenie weenie yellow polkadot bikini
That she wore for the first time today.
"Itsy Bitsy Teenie Weenie Yellow Polkadot Bikini" (song) (1960). Cowritten with Lee Pockriss.

Arthur Moeller van den Bruck

German poet and political writer, 1876–1925

1 I offer the ideal of the Third Reich. It is an old German concept and a great one. It arose when our First Reich fell; it was accelerated by the thought of a Thousand-Year Reich, but its underlying concept is the dawn of a German age, in which the German people would for the first time fulfill their destiny on earth.
Das Dritte Reich (The Third Reich), preface (1923)

Cornelius Vanderbilt

U.S. financier, 1794–1877

1 What do I care about the law? Hain't I got the power?
Quoted in Matthew Josephson, *The Robber Barons* (1934)

2 [*Comment in letter:*] Gentlemen, you have undertaken to cheat me. I won't sue you, for law is too slow. I'll ruin you.
Attributed in *N.Y. Times*, 5 Jan. 1877

William H. Vanderbilt
U.S. businessman, 1821–1885

1 [*Comment to news reporters:*] The public be damned.

Quoted in *Chicago Herald*, 9 Oct. 1882. In a letter to the *New York Times* published on 13 Oct. 1882, Vanderbilt denied having said this. The reporters who had interviewed the railroad magnate, however, affirmed that "he certainly did say" the words in question. Earlier, the *New York Herald*, 25 July 1873, quoted a "guano speculator" as exclaiming "Public be damned!"

Laurens van der Post
South African soldier, explorer, and writer, 1906–1996

1 Human beings are perhaps never more frightening than when they are convinced beyond doubt that they are right.
The Lost World of the Kalahari ch. 3 (1958)

Charles Van Doren
U.S. quiz show contestant and editor, 1926–2019

1 [*Acknowledging that he had been involved in fraud as a contestant on the television quiz show* Twenty One:] I have deceived my friends, and I had millions of them.
Testimony before House of Representatives Subcommittee on Legislative Oversight, 2 Nov. 1959

Vincent van Gogh
Dutch painter, 1853–1890

1 I cannot help it that my paintings do not sell. The time will come when people will see that they are worth more than the price of the paint.
Letter to Theo van Gogh, 24 Oct. 1888

Ronnie Van Zant
U.S. songwriter, 1948–1977

1 Sweet home Alabama
Where skies are so blue
Sweet home Alabama
Lord, I'm coming home to you.
"Sweet Home Alabama" (song) (1974). Cowritten with Ed King and Gary Rossington.

Bartolomeo Vanzetti
Italian-born U.S. political radical, 1888–1927

1 I . . . found myself compelled to fight back from my eyes the tears, and quanch my heart trobling to my throat to not weep before him— this man called thief and assassin and doomed. But Sacco's name will live in the hearts of the people and in their gratitude when Katzmann's and yours bones will be disperse by time, when your name, his [Katzmann's] name, your laws, institutions, and your false god are but a *deem rememoring of a cursed past in which man was wolf to the man.*
Notes for speech to the court, 9 Apr. 1927
See Plautus 1

2 If it had not been for these thing, I might have live out my life talking at street corners to scorning men. I might have die, unmarked, unknown, a failure. Now we are not a failure. This is our career and our triumph. Never in our full life could we hope to do such work for tolerance, for joostice, for man's onderstanding of man as now we do by accident.

Our words—our lives—our pains—nothing! The taking of our lives—lives of a good shoemaker and a poor fish-peddler—all! That last moment belongs to us—that agony is our triumph.
Statement after being sentenced to death, Dedham, Mass., 9 Apr. 1927

Mario Vargas Llosa
Peruvian writer and politician, 1936–

1 At what precise moment had Peru fucked itself up?
Conversation in the Cathedral ch. 1 (1969)

Giorgio Vasari
Italian artist and art historian, 1511–1574

1 [*Of Michelangelo's* David:] Anyone who sees this statue need not be concerned with seeing any other piece of sculpture done in our times or in any other period by any other artist.
The Lives of the Most Excellent Painters, Sculptors, and Architects "The Life of Michelangelo Buonarroti" (1550) (translation by Julia Conaway Bondanella and Peter Bondanella)

Michel Vaucaire
French songwriter, 1904–1980

1 *Non, Je ne Regrette rien.*
No, I Regret Nothing.
Title of song (1960)

Henry Vaughan
English poet, 1622–1695

1 Happy those early days, when I
Shined in my angel-infancy.
Before I understood this place
Appointed for my second race,
Or taught my soul to fancy aught
But a white, celestial thought.
Silex Scintillans "The Retreat" l. 1 (1650–1655)

Louis Vauxcelles
French art critic, 1870–1943

1 The purity of this bust comes as a surprise
in the midst of the orgy of pure colors: it is
Donatello among the wild beasts.
Gil Blas, 17 Oct. 1905. The reference (*"Donatello
chez les fauves"* in the original French) is to a bust
by Albert Marquet, exhibited among the works of
Matisse and others at the Salon d'Automne, Paris, in
1905; it gave rise to the term *fauvism* to describe an
early-twentieth-century movement in painting.

Thorstein Veblen
U.S. economist and social critic, 1857–1929

1 In order to gain and to hold the esteem of men
it is not sufficient merely to possess wealth
or power. The wealth or power must be put
in evidence, for esteem is awarded only on
evidence.
The Theory of the Leisure Class ch. 3 (1899)

2 Conspicuous consumption of valuable goods
is a means of reputability to the gentleman of
leisure.
The Theory of the Leisure Class ch. 4 (1899)
See Rae 1

3 From the foregoing survey of the growth
of conspicuous leisure and consumption, it
appears that the utility of both alike for the
purposes of reputability lies in the element of
waste that is common to both. In the one case it
is a waste of time and effort, in the other it is a
waste of goods.
The Theory of the Leisure Class ch. 4 (1899)

4 With the exception of the instinct of self-
preservation, the propensity for emulation
is probably the strongest and most alert and
persistent of the economic motives proper.
The Theory of the Leisure Class ch. 5 (1899)

5 The outcome of any serious research can only
be to make two questions grow where one
question grew before.
"Evolution of the Scientific Point of View" (1908)

6 The law school belongs in the modern
university no more than a school of fencing or
dancing.
The Higher Learning in America ch. 7 (1918)

Bill Veeck
U.S. baseball team owner, 1914–1986

1 Sometimes the best trades are the ones you
don't make.
Quoted in *Daily Ardmoreite* (Ardmore, Okla.), 6
Oct. 1948. Paul Dickson notes in *Baseball's Greatest
Quotations* that Veeck said this "after the 1948 season,
when Veeck had refrained from trading manager-
shortstop Lou Boudreau and the Indians went on to
win the pennant and the World Series."

Lope de Vega
Spanish playwright and poet, 1562–1635

1 Harmony is pure love, for love is complete
agreement.
Fuenteovejuna act 1 (ca. 1613) (translation by Angel
Flores and Muriel Kittel)

2 Except for God, the King's our only lord and
master.
Fuenteovejuna act 3 (ca. 1613) (translation by Angel
Flores and Muriel Kittel)

Vegetius (Flavius Vegetius Renatus)
Roman military writer, fl. 375

1 *Qui desiderat pacem, praeparet bellum.*
Let him who desires peace, prepare for war.
Epitoma Rei Militaris bk. 3, prologue
See Aristotle 4

Robert Venturi
U.S. architect, 1925–

1 Less is a bore.
Complexity and Contradiction in Architecture ch. 2
(1966)
See Robert Browning 12; Mies van der Rohe 1

Pierre Vergniaud

French revolutionary, 1753–1793

1 *Il a été permis de craindre que la Révolution,*
   comme Saturne, dévorât successivement tous ses
   enfants.
   There is reason to fear that the Revolution may,
   like Saturn, devour each of her children one
   by one.
   Remark at his trial, Oct. 1793
   See Büchner 1

Paul Verlaine

French poet, 1844–1896

1 *Les sanglots longs*
   Des violons
   De l'automne
   Blessent mon coeur
   D'une langueur
   Monotone.
   The drawn-out sobs of autumn's violins wound
      my heart with a monotonous languor.
   "Chanson d'Automne" (1866)

2 *Il pleure dans mon coeur*
   Comme il pleut sur la ville.
   There are tears in my heart
   Like the rain falling on the city.
   Romances sans Paroles "Ariettes Oubliées" no. 3 (1874)

3 *Et tout le reste est littérature.*
   All the rest is literature.
   "Art Poétique" (1882)

4 *De la musique avant toute chose.*
   Music above all.
   "Art Poétique" (1882)

5 *Prends l'éloquence et tords-lui le cou.*
   Take eloquence and break its neck.
   Jadis et Naguère (1884)

6 *Et, Ô ces voix d'enfants chantants dans la coupole!*
   And O those children's voices, singing beneath
      the dome!
   "Parsifal" (1886)

Jules Verne

French science fiction writer, 1828–1905

1 Science, my lad, has been built upon many
   errors; but they are errors which it was good to
   fall into, for they led to the truth.
   Journey to the Center of the Earth ch. 31 (1864)

2 The sea is everything. It covers seven tenths
   of the terrestrial globe. Its breath is pure and
   healthy. It is an immense desert, where man
   is never lonely, for he feels life stirring on all
   sides. The sea is only the embodiment of a
   supernatural and wonderful existence. It is
   nothing but love and emotion.
   Twenty Thousand Leagues Under the Sea pt. 1, ch. 10
   (1870)

Vespasian

Roman emperor, 9–79

1 [*Remark during fatal illness:*] *Vae, puto deus fio.*
   Woe is me, I think I am becoming a god.
   Quoted in Suetonius, *Lives of the Caesars*

Amerigo Vespucci

Italian explorer, 1454–1512

1 Those new regions which we found and
   explored with the fleet . . . we may rightly call
   a New World . . . a continent more densely
   peopled and abounding in animals than our
   Europe or Asia or Africa; and, in addition, a
   climate milder than in any other region known
   to us.
   Mundus Novus (1503) (translation by G. T. Northup)

Giovanni Battista Vico

Italian jurist, philologist, and philosopher,
1668–1744

1 But in the night of thick darkness enveloping
   the earliest antiquity, so remote from ourselves,
   there shines the eternal and never failing light
   of a truth beyond all question: that the world of
   civil society has certainly been made by men.
   The New Science bk. 1, par. 331 (1725)

Victoria

British queen, 1819–1901

1 The Queen is most anxious to enlist everyone
   who can speak or write to join in checking this
   mad, wicked folly of Woman's Rights with all
   its attendant horrors on which her poor, feeble
   sex is bent, forgetting every sense of womanly
   feeling and propriety.
   Letter to Theodore Martin, 29 May 1870

2 [*Remark upon being shown the line of succession to the throne, 11 Mar. 1830:*] I will be good.

Quoted in Theodore Martin, *The Prince Consort* (1875). Victoria was crowned in 1837.

3 We are not amused.

Quoted in *Fitchburg* (Mass.) *Daily Sentinel*, 31 Jan. 1887. This article relates: "Sir Arthur Helps, who was her private secretary, used to tell an amusing anecdote of being snubbed by her for telling a rather funny story down the table, among the ladies-in-waiting to relieve the monotony of a dreary dinner, when the queen remarked: 'What is it? We are not amused.'" "We are not amused" was earlier attributed to an unnamed royal in James Payn, *The Talk of the Town* (1885).

4 [*Remark to Arthur J. Balfour regarding the Boer War, Dec. 1899:*] We are not interested in the possibilities of defeat—they do not exist.

Quoted in Gwendolen Cecil, *Life of Robert, Marquis of Salisbury* (1931)

5 [*Of William Gladstone:*] He talks to me as if I were a public meeting.

Attributed in *Saturday Review*, 27 Mar. 1897. Alexis de Tocqueville had written in *Democracy in America*, vol. 1, ch. 14 (1835): "An American . . . speaks to you as if he was addressing a meeting."

Gore Vidal

U.S. novelist and critic, 1925–2012

1 He will lie even when it is inconvenient, the sign of the true artist.

Two Sisters (1970)

2 [*Of Richard Nixon:*] He turned being a Big Loser into a perfect triumph by managing to lose the presidency in a way bigger and more original than anyone else had ever lost it before.

Esquire, Dec. 1983

3 As societies grow decadent, the language grows decadent too. Words are used to disguise, not to illuminate, action: You liberate a city by destroying it. Words are used to confuse, so that at election time people will solemnly vote against their own interests.

"The Day the American Empire Ran Out of Gas" (1986)

4 Whenever a friend succeeds, a little something in me dies.

Quoted in *Sunday Times Magazine*, 16 Sept. 1973

5 I'm all for bringing back the birch, but only between consenting adults.

Quoted in *Sunday Times Magazine*, 16 Sept. 1973

6 It is not enough to succeed; others must fail.

Quoted in *Newport* (R.I.) *Daily News*, 3 Nov. 1978. Although this line is associated with Vidal, Garson O'Toole has found that Iris Murdoch wrote in *The Black Prince* (1973): "Some clever writer (probably a Frenchman) has said: it is not enough to succeed; others must fail." O'Toole also found that Somerset Maugham was quoted in *The Daily Messenger* (Canandaigua, N.Y.), 8 July 1959: "Now that I've grown old, I realize that for most of us it is not enough to have achieved personal success. One's best friend must also have failed."

7 [*Of Ronald Reagan:*] A triumph of the embalmer's art.

Quoted in *Observer*, 26 Apr. 1981

Peter Viereck

U.S. poet and historian, 1916–2006

1 Catholic-baiting is the anti-Semitism of the liberals.

Shame and Glory of the Intellectuals ch. 3 (1953)

Alfred de Vigny

French poet, 1797–1863

1 *Dieu! que le son du cor est triste au fond des bois!*
God! how sad is the sound of the horn deep in the woods!

"Le Cor" (1826)

2 *J'aime la majesté des souffrances humaines.*
I love the majesty of human suffering.

La Maison du Berger (1844)

George Villiers, Second Duke of Buckingham

English courtier and writer, 1628–1687

1 Ay, now the plot thickens very much upon us.

The Rehearsal act 3, sc. 2 (1672)

Philippe-Auguste Villiers de L'Isle-Adam

French writer, 1838–1889

1 *Vivre? les serviteurs feront cela pour nous.*
Living? The servants will do that for us.

Axël pt. 4, sec. 2 (1890)

François Villon

French poet, 1431–ca. 1465

1 *Mais où sont les neiges d'antan?*
But where are the snows of yesteryear?
Le Grand Testament "Ballade des Dames du Temps Jadis" (1461) (translation by Dante Gabriel Rossetti)

2 *Frères humains, qui après nous vivez,*
N'ayez les coeurs contre nous endurcis.
Brothers in humanity who live after us,
Let not your hearts be hardened against us.
"Ballade des Pendus" (ca. 1463)

St. Vincent of Lérins

French ecclesiastical writer, fl. 434

1 *Quod ubique, quod semper, quod ab omnibus creditum est.*
[That faith is catholic] which is everywhere, which is always, which is by all people believed.
Commonitorium Primum sec. 2 (434)

Virgil (Publius Vergilius Maro)

Roman poet, 70 B.C.–19 B.C.

1 *Arma virumque cano.*
Of arms and the man I sing.
Aeneid bk. 1, l. 1
See John Dryden 11

2 *Forsan et haec olim meminisse iuvabit.*
Maybe one day it will be cheering to remember even these things.
Aeneid bk. 1, l. 203

3 *Sunt lacrimae rerum et mentem mortalia tangunt.*
There are tears shed for things even here and mortality touches the heart.
Aeneid bk. 1, l. 462

4 *Timeo Danaos et dona ferentes.*
I fear Greeks even when they bring gifts.
Aeneid bk. 2, l. 49
See Proverbs 131

5 *Dis aliter visum.*
The gods thought otherwise.
Aeneid bk. 2, l. 428

6 *Varium et mutabile semper femina.*
Fickle and changeable always is woman.
Aeneid bk. 4, l. 569
See Piave 1

7 *Bella, horrida bella,*
Et Thybrim multo spumantem sanguine cerno.
I see wars, horrible wars, and the Tiber foaming with much blood.
Aeneid bk. 6, l. 86

8 *Facilis descensus Averno:*
Noctes atque dies patet atri ianua Ditis;
Sed revocare gradum superasque evadere ad auras,
Hoc opus, hic labor est.
Easy is the way down to the Underworld: by night and by day dark Hades' door stands open; but to retrace one's steps and to make a way out to the upper air, that's the task, that is the labor.
Aeneid bk. 6, l. 126

9 *Manibus date lilia plenis.*
Give me lilies in armfuls.
Aeneid bk. 6, l. 883

10 *Geniumque loci primamque deorum*
Tellurem Nymphasque et adhuc ignota precatur
Flumina.
He prays to the genius of the place and to Earth, the first of the gods, and to the Nymphs and as yet unknown rivers.
Aeneid bk. 7, l. 136

11 *Macte nova virtute, puer, sic itur ad astra.*
Blessings on your young courage, boy; that's the way to the stars.
Aeneid bk. 9, l. 641

12 *Audentis Fortuna iuvat.*
Fortune favors the brave.
Aeneid bk. 10, l. 284
See Terence 4

13 *Experto credite.*
Believe an expert.
Aeneid bk. 11, l. 283

14 *Latet anguis in herba.*
There's a snake hidden in the grass.
Eclogues no. 3, l. 93

15 *Ultima Cumaei venit iam carminis aetas;*
Magnum ab integro saeclorum nascitur ordo.
Iam redit et virgo, redeunt Saturnia regna,
Iam nova progenies caelo demittitur alto.
Now has come the last age according to the oracle at Cumae; the great series of lifetimes starts anew. Now too the virgin goddess

returns, the golden days of Saturn's reign
return, now a new race is sent down from
high heaven.

Eclogues no. 4, l. 4

16 *Non omnia possumus omnes.*
We can't all do everything.

Eclogues no. 8, l. 63

17 *Omnia vincit Amor: et nos cedamus Amori.*
Love conquers all things: let us too give in to
Love.

Eclogues no. 10, l. 69

18 *Ultima Thule.*
Farthest Thule.

Georgics no. 1, l. 30

19 *Audacibus annue coeptis.*
Look with favor upon a bold beginning.

Georgics no. 1, l. 40. *Annuit coeptis* (He [God] has
favored our undertakings) appears on the reverse of
the Great Seal of the United States.

20 [*Of Lucretius:*] *Felix qui potuit rerum cognoscere
causas.*
Happy the man who could search out the
causes of things.

Georgics no. 2, l. 490

21 *Fugit inreparabile tempus.*
Time is flying never to return.

Georgics no. 3, l. 284. Usually quoted as *"tempus fugit"*
(time flies).

22 Death twitches my ear. "Live," he says; "I am
coming."

Minor Poems "Copa" l. 38

23 *E pluribus unus.*
One composed of many.

Minor Poems "Moretum" l. 104. *E pluribus unum* was
used on the title page of the *Gentleman's Magazine*
beginning in 1731 and as the motto on the face of the
Great Seal of the United States, adopted in 1782.

Voltaire (François-Marie-Arouet)
French writer and philosopher, 1694–1778

1 If there were only one religion in England,
there would be danger of tyranny; if there were
two, they would cut each other's throats; but
there are thirty, and they live happily together
in peace.

"On the Presbyterians" (1732)

2 *Il meglio, è l'inimico del bene.*
The best is the enemy of the good.

Letter to Duc de Richelieu, 18 June 1744. Although
this saying is now associated with Voltaire, he is
obviously quoting an Italian proverb here. The
French form, which he used later, is *Le mieux est
l'ennemi du bien.*

3 That generous maxim, that it is much more
prudence to acquit two persons, though actually
guilty, than to pass sentence of condemnation
on one that is virtuous and innocent.

Zadig ch. 6 (1749)
See Blackstone 7; Fortescue 1; Benjamin Franklin 37;
Maimonides 1

4 It is one of the superstitions of mankind to
have imagined that virginity could be a virtue.

"The Leningrad Notebooks" (ca. 1735–1750)

5 *Ce Corps qui s'appellait, & qui s'appelle encor,
le saint Empire Romain, n'était en aucune
maniére, ni saint, ni Romain, ni Empire.*
This agglomeration which was called and which
still calls itself the Holy Roman Empire was
neither Holy, nor Roman, nor an empire.

*Essay sur l'Histoire Générale et sur les Moeurs et l'Esprit
des Nations,* new ed., vol. 2, ch. 66 (1761)

6 In Westphalie, in Baron Thunder-ten-tronckh's castle, there was a young boy upon whom nature had bestowed the gentlest manners. His soul shined through his face. He had fairly sound judgment, with the simplest spirit; this is why, I believe, they called him Candide.
Candide ch. 1 (1759)

7 *Ce meilleur des mondes possibles . . . tout est au mieux.*
This best of possible worlds . . . all is for the best.
Candide ch. 1 (1759). Usually quoted as "best of all possible worlds."
See Cabell 1; Leibniz 3; Voltaire 8

8 If this is the best of all possible worlds, what are the others like?
Candide ch. 6 (1759)
See Cabell 1; Leibniz 3; Voltaire 7

9 *Dans ce pays-ci il est bon de tuer de temps en temps un amiral pour encourager les autres.*
In this country [England] it is useful to kill an admiral from time to time to encourage the others.
Candide ch. 23 (1759). Voltaire refers here to the execution of Admiral Byng for his failure to relieve Minorca, besieged by the French.

10 *Il faut cultiver notre jardin.*
We must cultivate our garden.
Candide ch. 30 (1759)

11 In this world we run the risk of having to choose between being either the anvil or the hammer.
Dictionnaire Philosophique "Tyranny" (1764)

12 Very learned women are to be found, in the same manner as female warriors; but they are seldom or never inventors.
Dictionnaire Philosophique "Women" (1764)

13 *Toutes les histoires anciennes, comme le disait un de nos beaux esprits, ne sont que des fables convenues.*
Ancient histories, as one of our wits has said, are but fables that have been agreed upon.
Jeannot et Colin (1764). Although this is usually associated with Voltaire, "L'histoire n'est qu'une fable convenue" was attributed to Bernard de Fontenelle in Claude Helvétius, *De l'esprit* (1758).
See Fontenelle 2

14 *Le sens commun est fort rare.*
Common sense is not so common.
Dictionnaire Philosophique "Common Sense" (1765)

15 History is nothing more than a tableau of crimes and misfortunes.
L'Ingénu ch. 10 (1767)
See Gibbon 4

16 I have never made but one prayer to God, a very short one: "O Lord, make my enemies ridiculous." And God granted it.
Letter to M. Damilaville, 16 May 1767

17 I want my attorney, my tailor, my valets, and even my wife to believe in God, and I fancy that then I'll be robbed and cuckolded less.
"Dialogues Between A, B, and C" (1768)

18 *Si Deux n'existait pas, il faudrait l'inventer.*
If God did not exist, it would be necessary to invent him.
Épîtres no. 96, "À l'Auteur du Livre des Trois Imposteurs" (1770)
See Ovid 2

Kurt Vonnegut, Jr.
U.S. novelist, 1922–2007

1 Every passing hour brings the Solar System forty-three thousand miles closer to Globular Cluster M13 in Hercules—and still there are some misfits who insist that there is no such thing as progress.
The Sirens of Titan epigraph (1959)

2 I was the victim of a series of accidents, as are we all.
The Sirens of Titan ch. 10 (1959)

3 We Bokonists believe that humanity is organized into teams, teams that do God's Will without ever discovering what they are doing. Such a team is called a *karass* by Bokonon.
Cat's Cradle ch. 1 (1960)

4 A seeming team that was meaningless in terms of the way God gets things done, a textbook example of what Bokonon calls a *granfalloon*. Other examples of *granfalloons* are the Communist party, the Daughters of the American Revolution, the General Electric Company, the International Order of Odd Fellows—and any nation, anytime, anywhere.
Cat's Cradle ch. 42 (1960)

5 So it goes.
Slaughterhouse-Five ch. 1 (1969)

6 Billy Pilgrim has come unstuck in time.
Slaughterhouse-Five ch. 2 (1969)

7 We had forgotten that wars were fought by
babies. When I saw those freshly shaved faces,
it was a shock. "My God, my God—" I said to
myself, "it's the Children's Crusade."
Slaughterhouse-Five ch. 5 (1969)

John von Neumann
Hungarian-born U.S. mathematician and
computer scientist, 1903–1957

1 Is the sum of all payments received by all
players (at the end of the game) always zero.
. . . All games which are actually played
for entertainment are of this type. But the
economically significant schemes are most
essentially not such. There the sum of all
payments, the total social product, will in
general not be zero. . . . We shall call games of
the first mentioned type *zero-sum* games, and
those of the latter type *non-zero-sum* games.
Theory of Games and Economic Behavior ch. 2 (1944).
Coauthored with Oskar Morgenstern.

2 In mathematics you don't understand things,
you just get used to them.
Quoted in Gary Zukav, *The Dancing Wu Li Masters*
(1979)

Don Von Tress
U.S. country songwriter, fl. 1990

1 Achy Breaky Heart.
Title of song (1990)

Johann Heinrich Voss
German poet, 1751–1826

1 *Dein redseliges Buch lehrt mancherlei Neues und
  Wahres: Wäre das Wahre nur neu, wäre das
  Neue nur wahr.*
Your garrulous book teaches many things new
  and true: If only the true were new, if only
  the new were true!
Vossicher Musenalmanach (1772)

Andrei Voznesensky
Russian poet, 1933–2010

1 I am Goya
of the bare field, by the enemy's beak gouged
till the craters of my eyes gape,
I am grief,
I am the tongue
of war, the embers of cities
on the snows of the year 1941
I am hunger.
"Goya" (1960) (translation by Stanley Kunitz)

Diana Vreeland
U.S. fashion journalist, 1903–1989

1 I love London. It is the most swinging city in
the world at the moment.
Quoted in *Weekly Telegraph Magazine*, 30 Apr. 1965

Bill W. (William Wilson)

U.S. founder of Alcoholics Anonymous, 1895–1971

1 We admitted we were powerless over alcohol—that our lives had become unmanageable.
We came to believe that a Power greater than ourselves would restore us to sanity.

Alcoholics Anonymous (1939). The first two of the "Twelve Steps" that form the program of Alcoholics Anonymous to combat alcoholism.

John Francis Wade

English hymnwriter, ca. 1710–1786

1 O come, all ye faithful, joyful and triumphant,
O come ye, O come ye, to Bethlehem.
Come and behold Him, born the King of angels.

"Adeste Fidelis" (hymn) (ca. 1743) (translation from the original Latin by Frederick Oakeley, 1852)

2 O come, let us adore Him,
Christ the Lord.

"Adeste Fidelis" (hymn) (ca. 1743) (translation from the original Latin by Frederick Oakeley, 1852)

Jane Wagner

U.S. writer, 1935–

1 Reality is a crutch for people who can't cope with drugs.

Appearing Nitely (1977). "Reality is a crutch" was quoted as graffiti in the *New York Times*, 12 Feb. 1967.

2 What is reality anyway? Nothin' but a collective hunch.

The Search for Signs of Intelligent Life in the Universe pt. 1 (1985)

3 I've always wanted to *be* somebody. But I see now I should have been more specific.

The Search for Signs of Intelligent Life in the Universe pt. 1 (1985)

4 I personally think we developed language because of our deep inner need to complain.

The Search for Signs of Intelligent Life in the Universe pt. 2 (1985)

Richard Wagner

German composer, 1813–1883

1 *O du mein holder Abendstern.*
O thou, my gracious evening star.

Tannhäuser (opera) act 3, sc. 1 (1845)

2 *Nacht und Nebel niemand gleich.*
Night and fog make you no one.

Das Rheingold (opera) (1869). *Nacht und Nebel* (Night and Fog) was the title of a 1941 decree by Adolf Hitler consigning opponents of German occupation to concentration camps.

3 *Götterdämmerung.*
Twilight of the Gods.

Title of opera (1876)

Tom Waits

U.S. singer and songwriter, 1949–

1 I'd rather have a bottle in front of me than a frontal lobotomy.

Fernwood2night (television show), 1 Aug. 1977. A similar bottle in front/frontal lobotomy saying appeared in Carlton W. Berenda, *World Visions and the Image of Man* (1965).

Derek Walcott

West Indian poet and playwright, 1930–2017

1 I who have cursed
The drunken officer of British rule, how choose
Between this Africa and the English tongue I love?

"A Far Cry from Africa" l. 28 (1962)

George Wald

U.S. biologist, 1906–1997

1 A physicist is an atom's way of knowing about atoms.

Foreword to L. J. Henderson, *The Fitness of the Environment* (1958)

2 [*Of evolution:*] We are the products of editing, rather than of authorship.

"The Origin of Optical Activity" (1975)

Martin Waldseemüller

German cartographer, 1470–1518

1 Now that these regions are truly and amply explored and another fourth part has been discovered by Amerigo Vespucci I do not see why anyone can prohibit its being given the name of its discoverer, Amerigo, wise man of genius.

Cosmographiae Introductio (1507). Introduction of the name *America* for the lands of the Western Hemisphere.

Lech Walesa

Polish president, 1943–

1 [*Comment during his first trip to Western Europe:*] You have riches and freedom here but I feel no sense of faith or direction. You have so many computers, why don't you use them in the search for love?

Quoted in *Daily Telegraph* (London), 14 Dec. 1988

Alice Walker

U.S. novelist and poet, 1944–

1 In search of my mother's garden, I found my own.

"In Search of Our Mother's Gardens" (1974)

2 The good news may be that Nature is phasing out the white man, but the bad news is that's who She thinks we all are.

Black Scholar, Spring 1982

3 The trouble with our people is as soon as they got out of slavery they didn't want to give the white man nothing else. But the fact is, you got to give 'em something. Either your money, your land, your woman, or your ass.

The Color Purple (1982)

4 She say, Celie, tell the truth, have you ever found God in church? I never did. I just found a bunch of folks hoping for him to show. Any God I ever felt in church I brought in with me.

The Color Purple (1982)

5 I think it pisses God off if you walk by the color purple in a field somewhere and don't notice it.

The Color Purple (1982)

6 I'm pore, I'm black, I may be ugly and can't cook, a voice say to everything listening. But I'm here.

The Color Purple (1982)

7 Womanist is to feminist as purple is to lavender.

In Search of Our Mothers' Gardens epigraph (1983)

8 There are those who believe Black people possess the secret of joy and that it is this that will sustain them through any spiritual or moral or physical devastation.

Possessing the Secret of Joy epigraph (1992)
See Ricciardi 1; Alice Walker 9

9 *Resistance* is the secret of joy!

Possessing the Secret of Joy (1992)
See Ricciardi 1; Alice Walker 8

James J. Walker

U.S. politician, 1881–1946

1 Will You Love Me in December as You Do in May?

Title of song (1905). *Bartlett's Familiar Quotations* quotes an undated poem by John Alexander Joyce (1842–1915): "I shall love you in December / With the love I gave in May!" These lines are said by *Bartlett's* to be from stanza 8 of "Question and Answer."

Katherine Kent Child Walker

U.S. author, 1840–1916

1 I believe in the total depravity of inanimate things.

"The Total Depravity of Inanimate Things," *Atlantic Monthly*, Sept. 1864

David Foster Wallace

U.S. writer, 1962–2008

1 Most really pretty girls have pretty ugly feet, and so does Mindy Metalman, Lenore notices, all of a sudden.

The Broom of the System (1987)

2 "You can trust me," R.V. said, watching her hand. "I'm a man of my

The Broom of the System (1987)

3 I do things like get in a taxi and say, "The library, and step on it."

Infinite Jest (1996)

4 Acceptance is mostly a matter of fatigue rather than anything else.
Infinite Jest (1996)

5 Everybody is identical in their secret unspoken belief that way deep down they are different from everyone else.
Infinite Jest (1996)

6 The truth will set you free. But not until it is finished with you.
Infinite Jest (1996)

7 If you are bored and disgusted by politics and don't bother to vote, you are in effect voting for the entrenched Establishments of the two major parties, who please rest assured are not dumb, and who are keenly aware that it is in their interests to keep you disgusted and bored and cynical and to give you every possible reason to stay at home doing one-hitters and watching MTV on primary day. By all means stay home if you want, but don't bullshit yourself that you're not voting. In reality, there is *no such thing as not voting*: you either vote by voting, or you vote by staying home and tacitly doubling the value of some Diehard's vote.
Up, Simba! (2000)

8 Because here's something else that's weird but true: in the day-to day trenches of adult life, there is actually no such thing as atheism.

There is no such thing as not worshipping. Everybody worships. The only choice we get is what to worship.
Commencement address at Kenyon College, Gambier, Ohio, 21 May 2005

9 The really important kind of freedom involves attention and awareness and discipline, and being able truly to care about other people and to sacrifice for them over and over in myriad petty, unsexy ways every day.
Commencement address at Kenyon College, Gambier, Ohio, 21 May 2005

10 The capital-T Truth is about life *before* death. It is about making it to 30, or maybe 50, without wanting to shoot yourself in the head. It is about simple awareness—awareness of what is so real and essential, so hidden in plain sight all around us, that we have to keep reminding ourselves, over and over: "This is water, this is water."
Commencement address at Kenyon College, Gambier, Ohio, 21 May 2005

George C. Wallace
U.S. politician, 1919–1998

1 Segregation now, segregation tomorrow, and segregation forever!
Inaugural Speech as governor of Alabama, Montgomery, Ala., 19 Jan. 1963

Henry A. Wallace
U.S. politician, 1888–1965

1 The century on which we are entering—the century which will come out of this war—can be and must be the century of the common man.
Speech to Free World Association, New York, N.Y., 8 May 1942

Lew Wallace
U.S. politician, general, and novelist, 1827–1905

1 A man is never so on trial as in the moment of excessive good fortune.
Ben Hur: A Tale of the Christ bk. 5, ch. 7 (1880)

2 Would you hurt a man keenest, strike at his self-love.
Ben Hur: A Tale of the Christ bk. 6, ch. 2 (1880)

Oliver Wallace
English-born U.S. composer, 1887–1963

1 When der Fuehrer says we is de master race
We heil heil right in der Fuehrer's face.
"Der Fuehrer's Face" (song) (1942)

Graham Wallas
English political scientist, 1858–1932

1 Economists have invented the term The Great
Industry for the special aspect of this change
[in scale] which is dealt with by their science,
and sociologists may conveniently call the
whole result The Great Society.
The Great Society ch. 1 (1914)
*See John Dewey 1; Hamer 1; Lyndon Johnson 5; Lyndon
Johnson 6; Lyndon Johnson 8; William Wordsworth 30*

2 The little girl had the making of a poet in her
who, being told to be sure of her meaning
before she spoke, said, "How can I know what I
think till I see what I say?"
The Art of Thought ch. 4 (1926)

Edmund Waller
English poet, 1606–1687

1 Go, lovely rose!
Tell her, that wastes her time and me,
That now she knows,
When I resemble her to thee,
How sweet and fair she seems to be.
"Go, Lovely Rose!" l. 1 (1645)

Robert James Waller
U.S. author, 1939–2017

1 In a universe of ambiguity, this kind of
certainty comes only once, and never again, no
matter how many lifetimes you live.
The Bridges of Madison County (1992)

Thomas "Fats" Waller
U.S. jazz musician and composer, 1904–1943

1 One never know, do one?
Stormy Weather (motion picture) (1943). Waller used
this phrase as an actor in this film, but it was earlier a
catchphrase in his singing performances.

2 [*When asked to explain jazz:*] Lady, if you got to
ask, you ain't got it.
Quoted in *Wash. Post,* 17 July 1947. Often attributed
to Louis Armstrong.

Horace Walpole
English writer, 1717–1797

1 *Serendipity* . . . You will understand it better
by the derivation than by the definition. I once
read a silly fairy tale, called "The Three Princes
of Serendip": as their Highnesses traveled, they
were always making discoveries, by accidents
and sagacity, of things which they were not in
quest of.
Letter to Horace Mann, 28 Jan. 1754. Coinage of the
word *serendipity.*

2 The next Augustan age will dawn on the other
side of the Atlantic. There will, perhaps, be
a Thucydides at Boston, a Xenophon at New
York, and, in time, a Virgil at Mexico, and a
Newton at Peru. At last, some curious traveler
from Lima will visit England and give a
description of the ruins of St. Paul's, like the
editions of Balbec and Palmyra.
Letter to Horace Mann, 24 Nov. 1774
See Thomas Macaulay 9

3 I have often said, and oftener think, that this
world is a comedy to those that think, a tragedy
to those that feel.
Letter to Horace Mann, 31 Dec. 1769

Izaak Walton
English writer, 1593–1683

1 No man can lose what he never had.
The Compleat Angler pt. 1, ch. 5 (1653)

2 We may say of angling as Dr. Boteler said of
strawberries: "Doubtless God could have made
a better berry, but doubtless God never did."
The Compleat Angler, 2nd ed., pt. 1, ch. 5 (1655). "Dr.
Boteler" refers to English physician William Butler.

Sam Walton
U.S. businessman, 1918–1992

1 There is only one boss—the customer. And he
can fire everybody in the company from the
chairman on down, simply by spending his
money somewhere else.
Quoted in *Telemarketing,* Oct. 1994

John Wanamaker
U.S. businessman, 1838–1922

1 I am convinced that about one-half the money I spend for advertising is wasted, but I have never been able to decide which half.

Quoted in Bible Conference, *Winona Echoes* (1919). David Ogilvy, in *Confessions of an Advertising Man* (1963), asserts that Lord Leverhulme voiced this complaint before Wanamaker.

Aby Warburg
German art historian, 1866–1929

1 *Der liebe Gott steckt im Detail.*
God is in the details.

Notice of seminar at Hamburg University, Hamburg, Germany, 11 Nov. 1925. This is documented in papers at the Warburg Institute at the University of London, described in Dieter Wuttke, *Ausgewählte Schriften und Würdigungen* (1980).
See Flaubert 3; Modern Proverbs 24; Mies van der Rohe 2

Artemus Ward (Charles Farrar Browne)
U.S. humorist, 1834–1867

1 The hardest case we ever heard of lived in Arkansas. He was only fourteen years old. One night he deliberately murdered his father and mother in cold blood, with a meat-axe. He was tried and found guilty. The judge drew on his black cap, and in a voice choked with emotion asked the young prisoner if he had anything to say before the sentence of the Court was passed on him. . . . "Why, no," replied the prisoner, "I think I haven't, though I hope yer Honor will show some consideration FOR THE FEELINGS OF A POOR ORPHAN!"

Artemus Ward in London "A Hard Case" (1867)
See Lincoln 64

2 [*Of Brigham Young:*] He is dreadfully married. He's the most married man I ever saw in my life.

Artemus Ward's Lecture "Brigham Young's Palace" (1869)

3 Why is this thus? What is the reason of this thusness?

Artemus Ward's Lecture "Mr. Heber C. Kimball's Harem" (1869)

Barbara Ward
English economist and writer, 1914–1981

1 We have forgotten how to be good guests, how to walk lightly on the earth as its other creatures do.

Only One Earth (1972)

Mary Jane Ward
U.S. writer, 1905–1981

1 The Snake Pit.
Title of book (1946)

Andy Warhol (Andrew Warhola)
U.S. artist, 1927–1987

1 Making money is art and working is art and good business is the best art.

The Philosophy of Andy Warhol ch. 6 (1975)

2 If you want to know all about Andy Warhol, just look at the surface of my paintings and films and me, and there I am. There's nothing behind it.

Quoted in *Free Press* (Los Angeles), 17 Mar. 1967

3 In the future everybody will be world famous for fifteen minutes.

Quoted in *Andy Warhol* (exhibition catalogue, Moderna Museet, Stockholm, Sweden) (1968). Usually quoted simply with "famous" rather than "world famous." *Time* magazine, 13 Oct. 1967, stated that Warhol had predicted "the day 'when everyone will be famous for 15 minutes.'"

Anna Bartlett Warner
U.S. writer, 1827–1915

1 Jesus loves me—this I know,
For the Bible tells me so.

"The Love of Jesus" l. 1 (1858)

Charles Dudley Warner
U.S. editor and essayist, 1829–1900

1 What small potatoes we all are, compared with what we might be!

My Summer in a Garden "Fifteenth Week" (1870)

2 Politics makes strange bed-fellows.

My Summer in a Garden "Fifteenth Week" (1870)
See Proverbs 237

3 The thing generally raised on city land is taxes.

My Summer in a Garden "Sixteenth Week" (1870)

4 It seems to superficial observers that all Americans are born busy. It is not so. They are born with a fear of not being busy.
A Little Journey in the World ch. 1 (1889)

Jack L. Warner

Polish-born U.S. motion picture producer, 1892–1978

1 [*On hearing that Ronald Reagan was running for governor of California:*] No, *no! Jimmy Stewart* for governor—Reagan for his best friend.
Quoted in Max Wilk, *The Wit and Wisdom of Hollywood* (1972)

Mary Warnock

English philosopher, 1924–2019

1 But without *some* element of objectivity, without *any* criterion for preferring one scheme of values to another, except the criterion of what looks most attractive to oneself, there cannot in fact be any morality at all, and moral theory must consist only in the assertion that there is no morality.
Existentialist Ethics ch. 5 (1967)

Earl Warren

U.S. judge and politician, 1891–1974

1 To separate them [black children] from others of similar age and qualifications solely because of their race generates a feeling of inferiority as to their status in the community that may affect their hearts and minds in a way unlikely ever to be undone. . . . We conclude that in the field of public education the doctrine of "separate but equal" has no place. Separate educational facilities are inherently unequal.
Brown v. Board of Education (1954)
See *John M. Harlan (1833–1911)* 1; *Kerner* 1

2 The judgments below . . . are accordingly reversed and the cases are remanded to the District Courts to take such proceedings and enter such orders and decrees consistent with this opinion as are necessary and proper to admit to public schools on a racially nondiscriminatory basis with all deliberate speed the parties to these cases.
Brown v. Board of Education (1955). It appears that Felix Frankfurter contributed the crucial phrase

"deliberate speed" to Chief Justice Warren's opinion in the implementation stage of *Brown v. Board of Education* and, earlier, to the government's oral argument in a connected case. Frankfurter's source was Oliver Wendell Holmes, Jr., who used it in a 1909 letter and a 1911 opinion. Although Holmes in the 1909 letter attributed the phrase to "the language of the English chancery," the earliest usage that has been found occurred in Thomas Beddoes's medical book *Hygëia* (1802).

3 Prior to any questioning, the person must be warned that he has a right to remain silent, that any statement he does make may be used as evidence against him, and that he has a right to the presence of an attorney, either retained or appointed.
Miranda v. Arizona (1966)

4 I always turn to the sports section first. The sports page records man's accomplishments; the front page has nothing but man's failures.
Quoted in *Sports Illustrated*, 22 July 1968. A similar statement appeared in an article by William Lyon Phelps in *Scribner's Magazine*, Nov. 1922.

Edward H. "Bull" Warren

U.S. legal scholar, 1873–1945

1 [*"Address of Welcome" to incoming students at Harvard Law School:*] Look well to the right of you, look well to the left of you, for one of you three won't be here next year.
Quoted in *Harvard Law Review*, Oct. 1945. A very similar Harvard Law School admonition appeared, without identification of the speaker, in *Life* magazine, 1 Nov. 1937.

2 On one occasion a student made a curiously inept response to a question from Professor Warren. "The Bull" roared at him, "You will never make a lawyer. You might just as well pack up your books now and leave the school." The student rose, gathered his notebooks, and started to leave, pausing only to say in full voice, "I accept your suggestion, Sir, but I do not propose to leave without giving myself the pleasure of telling you to go plumb straight to Hell." "Sit down, Sir, sit down," said "The Bull." "Your response makes it clear that my judgment was too hasty."
Reported in *Harvard Law Review*, Oct. 1945

Elizabeth Warren
U.S. politician and legal scholar, 1949–

1 There is nobody in this country who got rich on his own. Nobody. You built a factory out there—good for you! But I want to be clear. You moved your goods to market on the roads the rest of us paid for. You hired workers the rest of us paid to educate. You were safe in your factory because of police forces and fire forces that the rest of us paid for.
Remarks, Andover, Mass., Aug. 2011

Rick Warren
U.S. clergyman and author, 1954–

1 The Purpose Driven Life.
Title of book (2002)

2 It's not about you.
The Purpose Driven Life (2002)

Robert Penn Warren
U.S. poet and novelist, 1905–1989

1 The law is always too short and too tight for growing humankind. The best you can do is do something and then make up some law to fit and by the time that law gets on the books you would have done something different.
All the King's Men ch. 3 (1946)

Booker T. Washington
U.S. educator, 1856–1915

1 No race can prosper till it learns that there is as much dignity in tilling a field as in writing a poem.
Address at Atlanta International Exposition, Atlanta, Ga., 18 Sept. 1895

2 To those of my race who . . . underestimate the importance of cultivating friendly relations with the Southern white man, who is their next-door neighbor, I would say, "Cast down your bucket where you are"—cast it down in making friends in every manly way of the people of all races by whom we are surrounded.
Address at Atlanta International Exposition, Atlanta, Ga., 18 Sept. 1895

3 In all things that are purely social we can be as separate as the fingers, yet one as the hand in all things essential to mutual progress.
Address at Atlanta International Exposition, Atlanta, Ga., 18 Sept. 1895

4 Ignorance is more costly to the State than education.
The Future of the American Negro ch. 6 (1899)

George Washington
U.S. president and military leader, 1732–1799

1 When we assumed the Soldier, we did not lay aside the Citizen.
Letter to New York Legislature, 26 June 1775

2 Few men have virtue to withstand the highest bidder.
Letter to Robert Howe, 17 Aug. 1779

3 The preservation of the sacred fire of liberty and the destiny of the republican model of government are justly considered as *deeply,* perhaps as *finally,* staked on the experiment entrusted to the hands of the American people.
First Inaugural Address, New York, N.Y., 30 Apr. 1789

4 Happily the Government of the United States, which gives to bigotry no sanction, to persecution no assistance requires only that they who live under its protection should demean themselves as good citizens, in giving it on all occasions their effectual support.
Letter to Hebrew congregation of Newport, R.I., 17 Aug. 1790

5 The basis of our political Systems is the right of the people to make and to alter their Constitutions of Government. But the Constitution which at any time exists, 'till changed by an explicit and authentic act of the whole People, is sacredly obligatory upon all.
Farewell Address, Philadelphia, Pa., 19 Sept. 1796

6 Avoid the necessity of those overgrown Military establishments, which under any form of Government are inauspicious to liberty, and which are to be regarded as particularly hostile to Republican Liberty.
Farewell Address, Philadelphia, Pa., 19 Sept. 1796

7 Observe good faith and justice towards all nations. Cultivate peace and harmony with all.
Farewell Address, Philadelphia, Pa., 19 Sept. 1796

8 The Nation, which indulges towards another an habitual hatred, or an habitual fondness, is in some degree a slave. It is a slave to its animosity or to its affection, either of which is sufficient to lead it astray from its duty and its interest.
Farewell Address, Philadelphia, Pa., 19 Sept. 1796

9 'Tis our true policy to steer clear of permanent Alliances, with any portion of the foreign World.
Farewell Address, Philadelphia, Pa., 19 Sept. 1796

10 It is too probable that no plan we propose will be adopted. Perhaps another dreadful conflict is to be sustained. If to please the people, we offer what we ourselves disapprove, how can we afterwards defend our work? Let us raise a standard to which the wise and the honest can repair. The event is in the hand of God.
Attributed in Gouverneur Morris, oration on death of Washington, New York, N.Y., 31 Dec. 1799. This quotation, said to have been uttered at the Constitutional Convention in Philadelphia in 1787, does not appear in any contemporaneous documentation.

11 Government is not reason, it is not eloquence,—it is force! Like fire, it is a dangerous servant, and a fearful master; never for a moment should it be left to irresponsible action.
Attributed in *Christian Science Journal*, Nov. 1902. The attribution to Washington is undoubtedly apocryphal.

Ned Washington
U.S. songwriter, 1901–1976

1 Hi Diddle Dee Dee (An Actor's Life for Me).
Title of song (1940)

2 When you wish upon a star,
Makes no diff'rence who you are,
Any thing your heart desires will come to you.
"When You Wish upon a Star" (song) (1940)

3 Do not forsake me, oh my darlin'.
"The Ballad of High Noon" (song) (1952)

Wendy Wasserstein
U.S. playwright, 1950–2006

1 No matter how lonely you get or how many birth announcements you receive, the trick is not to get frightened. There's nothing wrong with being alone.
Isn't It Romantic act 1, sc. 6 (1983)

Keith Waterhouse
English writer, 1929–2009

1 Lying in bed, I abandoned the facts again and was back in Ambrosia.
Billy Liar ch. 1 (1959)

Maxine Waters
U.S. politician, 1938–

1 If you see anybody from that Cabinet in a restaurant, in a department store, at a gasoline station, you get out and you create a crowd! And you push back on them. And you tell them they're not welcome anymore, anywhere.
Remarks at rally, Los Angeles, Calif., 23 June 2018

2 I like to laugh, I like to have a great time. But I also have a right to my anger, and I don't want anybody telling me I shouldn't be, that it's not nice to be, and that something's wrong with me because I get angry.
Quoted in Brian Lanker, *I Dream a World* (1989)

Muddy Waters (McKinley Morganfield)
U.S. blues singer and songwriter, 1913–1983

1 Well, my mother told my father
Just before I was born,
"I got a boy child comin',
Gonna be a rollin' stone."
"Rollin' Stone" (song) (1950). This song inspired the Rolling Stones rock group and *Rolling Stone* magazine to choose their names.
See Dylan 17; Proverbs 257

2 Got My Mojo Workin'.
Title of song (1960)

Roger Waters

English rock musician, ca. 1944–

1 So, so you think you can tell
  Heaven from Hell,
  Blue skies from pain?
  "Wish You Were Here" (song) (1975)

2 We don't need no education.
  We don't need no thought control.
  No dark sarcasm in the classroom.
  Hey teacher, leave those kids alone.
  "Another Brick in the Wall (Part 2)" (song) (1979)

James D. Watson

U.S. biologist, 1928–

1 I was twenty-five and too old to be unusual.
  The Double Helix ch. 29 (1968)

John B. Watson

U.S. psychologist, 1878–1958

1 Psychology, as the behaviorist views it, is
  a purely objective, experimental branch of
  natural science which needs introspection
  as little as do the sciences of chemistry and
  physics. . . . The position is taken here that the
  behavior of man and the behavior of animals
  must be considered in the same plane.
  "Psychology as the Behaviorist Views It" (1913)

2 The rule, or measuring rod, which the
  behaviorist puts in front of him always is: Can
  I describe this bit of behavior I see in terms of
  "stimulus and response"?
  Behaviorism ch. 1 (1924)

3 Give me a dozen healthy infants, well-formed,
  and my own specified world in which to bring
  them up in and I'll guarantee to take any one
  at random and train him to become any type of
  specialist I might select—doctor, lawyer, artist,
  merchant chief, and, yes, even beggarman
  and thief, regardless of his talents, penchants,
  tendencies, abilities, vocations, and race of his
  ancestors.
  Behaviorism ch. 5 (1924)

4 The universe will change if you bring up your
  children, not in the freedom of the libertine,
  but in behavioristic freedom—a freedom which

we cannot even picture in words, so little do we
know of it.
  Behaviorism ch. 12 (1924)

5 There are . . . for us no instincts—we no longer
  need the term in psychology. Everything we
  have been in the habit of calling an "instinct"
  today is a result largely of training—belonging
  to man's *learned behavior*.
  "What the Nursery Has to Say About Instincts"
  (1926)

6 At three years of age the child's whole
  emotional life plan has been laid down, his
  emotional disposition set. At that age the
  parents have already determined for him
  whether he is to grow into a happy person,
  wholesome and good-natured, whether he is to
  be a whining, complaining neurotic, an anger-
  driven, vindictive, over-bearing slave driver,
  or one whose every move in life is definitely
  controlled by fear.
  "Are You Giving Your Child a Chance?" (1927)

7 The Behaviorist cannot find consciousness in
  the test-tube of his science.
  "Behaviorism—The Modern Note in Psychology"
  (1928)

8 Dedicated to the First Mother Who Brings Up a
  Happy Child.
  Psychological Care of Infant and Child dedication
  (1928)

Thomas J. Watson, Jr.

U.S. business executive and diplomat, 1914–
1993

1 I think there is a world market for about five
  computers.
  Attributed in Chris Morgan and David Langford,
  *Facts and Fallacies: A Book of Definitive Mistakes and
  Misguided Predictions* (1981). IBM (of which Watson
  served as chairman) states that it believes that this
  statement "is a misunderstanding of remarks made
  at IBM's annual stockholders meeting on April 28,
  1953. In referring specifically and only to the IBM
  701 Electronic Data Processing Machine—which had
  been introduced the year before as the company's
  first production computer designed for scientific
  calculations—Thomas Watson, Jr., told stockholders
  that 'IBM had developed a paper plan for such a
  machine and took this paper plan across the country
  to some 20 concerns that we thought could use such
  a machine. I would like to tell you that the machine

rents for between \$12,000 and \$18,000 a month, so it was not the type of thing that could be sold from place to place. But, as a result of our trip, on which we expected to get orders for five machines, we came home with orders for 18.'" Earlier, Sir Charles Darwin (grandson of the great biologist) had written in a 1946 proposal that "it is very possible that . . . one machine would suffice to solve all the problems that are demanded of it from the whole country" ("Automatic Computing Engine [ACE]," National Physical Laboratory, 17 Apr.). American computer pioneer Howard Aiken was cited even earlier as having exactly the same concern: "He could not conceive of there being enough work for more than one such giant" (*Popular Science*, Oct. 1944). According to Kevin Maney, *The Maverick and His Machine*, "Aiken revised his forecast while working on the Mark I with IBM, saying 5 or 10 might be built, according to Aiken contemporaries. That prediction by Aiken could have been mistakenly attributed to Watson, or perhaps Watson repeated Aiken's prediction."

Thomas J. Watson, Sr.

U.S. businessman, 1874–1956

1 THINK.

Corporate motto (1911). According to Kevin Maney, in *The Maverick and His Machine: Thomas Watson, Sr. and the Making of IBM* (2003), Thomas J. Watson, Sr., when he was managing the sales and advertising departments of the National Cash Register Company, is reported to have said at a sales meeting: "The trouble with every one of us is that we don't think enough!" Then Watson wrote "THINK" on an easel behind him. This motto proliferated on signs throughout NCR, then followed Watson to IBM's predecessor company (in 1914) and finally to IBM itself, where it became the main corporate slogan.

William Watson

English conspirator, ca. 1559–1603

1 *Fiat justitia et ruant coeli.*
Let justice be done though the heavens fall.
A Decacordon of Ten Quodlibeticall Questions Concerning Religion and State (1602)
See Ferdinand I 1; Lord Mansfield 1

James G. Watt

U.S. government official, 1938–

1 [*Of the composition of a commission studying coal-leasing policies of the Department of the Interior:*] I have a black, a woman, two Jews, and a cripple.
Speech to U.S. Chamber of Commerce, Washington, D.C., 21 Sept. 1983. Watt had to resign as secretary of the interior because of controversy engendered by this remark.

Bill Watterson

U.S. cartoonist, 1958–

1 Sometimes I think the surest sign that intelligent life exists elsewhere in the universe is that none of it has tried to contact us.
Calvin and Hobbes (comic strip), 8 Nov. 1989

Isaac Watts

English hymnwriter, 1674–1748

1 How doth the little busy Bee
Improve each shining Hour,
And gather Honey all the day
From every opening Flower!
Divine Songs for Children "Against Idleness and Mischief" l. 1 (1715)
See Carroll 5

2 For *Satan* finds some Mischief still
For idle Hands to do.
Divine Songs for Children "Against Idleness and Mischief" l. 11 (1715)

3 Joy to the world! the Lord is come;
Let earth receive her King.
Let ev'ry heart prepare Him room,
And heav'n and nature sing.
The Psalms of David Imitated Psalm 98 (1719)

Evelyn Waugh

English novelist, 1903–1966

1 I expect you'll be becoming a schoolmaster, sir. That's what most of the gentlemen does, sir, that gets sent down for indecent behavior.
Decline and Fall "Prelude" (1928)

2 Almost all crime is due to the repressed desire for aesthetic expression.
Decline and Fall pt. 3, ch. 1 (1928)

3 Any one who has been to an English public school will always feel comparatively at home in prison.
Decline and Fall part 3, ch. 4 (1928)

4 In the dying world I come from quotation is a national vice. No one would think of making an after-dinner speech without the help of poetry. It used to be the classics, now it's lyric verse.
The Loved One ch. 9 (1948)

5 [*After Randolph Churchill's lung was removed and found not to have malignancies:*] A typical triumph of modern science to find the only part of Randolph that was not malignant and remove it.
Diary, Mar. 1964

6 You have no idea how much nastier I would be if I was not a Catholic. Without supernatural aid I would hardly be a human being.
Quoted in Noel Annan, *Our Age* (1990)

John Wayne (Marion Morrison)
U.S. actor, 1907–1979

1 [*Of the treatment of Native Americans by white settlers:*] There were great numbers of people who needed new land, and the Indians were selfishly trying to keep it for themselves.
Interview, *Playboy,* May 1971

2 [*Explaining why he did not serve in the military during World War II:*] I would have had to go in as a private. I took a dim view of that.
Quoted in *Time,* 8 Aug. 1969
See Cheney 3

Frederic Weatherly
English songwriter and lawyer, 1848–1929

1 Oh, Danny boy, the pipes, the pipes are calling
From glen to glen, and down the mountain
   side.
"Danny Boy" (song) (1913)

Richard M. Weaver
U.S. philosopher, 1910–1963

1 Ideas Have Consequences.
Title of book (1948)

Beatrice Potter Webb
English reformer and social scientist, 1858–1943

1 Religion is love; in no case is it logic.
My Apprenticeship ch. 2 (1926)

Charles Webb
U.S. writer, 1939–2020

1 "Mrs. Robinson," he said, turning around, "you are trying to seduce me." . . . "Aren't you?"
The Graduate ch. 1 (1963)

Sidney Webb
English socialist, 1859–1947

1 The inevitability of gradualness.
Presidential address to annual conference of Labor Party, 26 June 1923

Joseph Weber
U.S. comedian, 1867–1942

1 Who was that lady I saw you with last night? She ain't no lady; she's my wife.
Vaudeville routine (1887). In collaboration with Lew Fields.

Max Weber
German sociologist, 1864–1920

1 The Protestant Ethic and the Spirit of Capitalism.
Title of article, *Archiv für Sozialwissenschaft Sozialpolitik* (1904–1905)

2 For when asceticism was carried out of monastic cells into everyday life, and began to dominate worldly morality, it did its part in building the tremendous cosmos of the modern economic order. This order is now bound to the technical and economic conditions of machine production which to-day determine the lives of all the individuals who are born into this mechanism, not only those directly concerned with economic acquisition, with irresistible force. Perhaps it will so determine them until the last ton of fossilized coal is burnt.
The Protestant Ethic and the Spirit of Capitalism ch. 5 (1920) (translation by Talcott Parsons)

3 The term "charisma" will be applied to a certain quality of an individual personality by virtue of which he is considered extraordinary and treated as endowed with supernatural, superhuman, or at least specifically exceptional powers or qualities. These are such as are not accessible to the ordinary person, but are regarded as of divine origin or as exemplary, and on the basis of them the individual concerned is treated as a "leader."
Economy and Society ch. 3 (1922)

Daniel Webster

U.S. statesman and lawyer, 1782–1852

1 It is, Sir, as I have said, a small college. And yet *there are those who love it!*

Argument before U.S. Supreme Court, *Trustees of Dartmouth College v. Woodward*, 10 Mar. 1818

2 An *unlimited* right to tax, implies a right to destroy.

Argument before U.S. Supreme Court, *McCulloch v. Maryland*, 22 Feb. 1819
See Oliver Wendell Holmes, Jr. 38; John Marshall 7

3 It is my living sentiment, and by the blessing of God it shall be my dying sentiment—Independence now and Independence forever.

Discourse in Commemoration of Adams and Jefferson, Faneuil Hall, Boston, Mass., 2 Aug. 1826

4 I shall enter on no encomium upon Massachusetts; she needs none. There she is. Behold her, and judge for yourselves. There is her history; the world knows it by heart. The past, at least, is secure. There is Boston, and Concord, and Lexington, and Bunker Hill; and there they will remain for ever.

Second Speech on Foote's Resolution, U.S. Senate, 26 Jan. 1830. Often misquoted as "Massachusetts, there she stands."

5 It is, Sir, the people's Constitution, the people's government, made for the people, made by the people, and answerable to the people.

Second Speech on Foote's Resolution, U.S. Senate, 26 Jan. 1830
See Lincoln 42; Theodore Parker 1; Theodore Parker 3

6 When my eyes shall be turned to behold for the last time the sun in heaven, may I not see him shining on the broken and dishonored

fragments of a once glorious Union; on States dissevered, discordant, belligerent; on a land rent with civil feuds, or drenched, it may be, in fraternal blood!

Second Speech on Foote's Resolution, U.S. Senate, 26 Jan. 1830

7 Liberty *and* Union, now and for ever, one and inseparable!

Second Speech on Foote's Resolution, U.S. Senate, 26 Jan. 1830

8 There is no refuge from confession but suicide, and suicide is confession.

Summation in murder trial of John Francis Knapp, Salem, Mass., 1830

9 He smote the rock of the national resources, and abundant streams of revenue gushed forth. He touched the dead corpse of the Public Credit, and it sprung upon his feet. The fabled birth of Minerva, from the brain of Jove, was hardly more sudden or more perfect than the financial system of the United States, as it burst forth from the conceptions of Alexander Hamilton.

Speech, New York, N.Y., 10 Mar. 1831

10 There is no happiness, there is no liberty, there is no enjoyment of life, unless a man can say when he rises in the morning, I shall be subject to the decision of no unjust judge to-day.

Speech, New York, N.Y., 24 Mar. 1831

11 Gentlemen, the citizens of this republic cannot sever their fortunes. . . . Let us then stand by the Constitution as it is, and by our country as it is, one, united, and entire: let it be a truth engraven on our hearts, let it be borne on the flag under which we rally, in every exigency, that we have ONE COUNTRY, ONE CONSTITUTION, ONE DESTINY.

Speech at Niblo's Saloon, New York, N.Y., 15 Mar. 1837

12 Justice, Sir, is the great interest of man on earth.

Oration on day of Justice Story's funeral, Boston, Mass., 12 Sept. 1845

13 I can give it as the condensed history of most, if not all, good lawyers, that they lived well and died poor.

Speech at Charleston Bar Dinner, Charleston, S.C., 10 May 1847

14 The Law: It has honored us, may we honor it.
> Speech at Charleston Bar Dinner, Charleston, S.C.,
> 10 May 1847

15 Liberty exists in proportion to wholesome
restraint.
> Speech at Charleston Bar Dinner, Charleston, S.C.,
> 10 May 1847

16 I was born an American; I will live an
American; I shall die an American.
> Speech in Senate on Compromise Bill, 17 July 1850

17 [*Response to advice not to enter the legal profession
because it was too crowded:*] There is room
enough at the top.
> Quoted in *Bangor Daily Whig & Courier*, 27 Feb. 1866.
> Often quoted later as "There is always room at the
> top." Webster was quoted with the wording "There is
> room higher up" in Edward Everett Hale, *Christian
> Duty to Emigrants* (1852).

John Webster
English playwright, ca. 1580–ca. 1625

1 But keep the wolf far hence that's foe to men,
For with his nails he'll dig them up again.
> *The White Devil* act 5, sc. 4 (1612)

2 We think caged birds sing, when indeed they cry.
> *The White Devil* act 5, sc. 4 (1612)
> See Dunbar 2

3 Cover her face; mine eyes dazzle: she died
    young.
> *The Duchess of Malfi* act 4, sc. 2 (1623)

Mason Locke "Parsons" Weems
U.S. clergyman and biographer, 1759–1825

1 [*Apocryphal remark of the young George
Washington, confessing to having chopped down a
cherry tree:*] I can't tell a lie, Pa, you know I can't
tell a lie, I did cut it with my little hatchet.
> *The Life of Washington the Great*, 5th ed., ch. 2 (1806)

Simone Weil
French philosopher, social activist, and mystic,
1909–1943

1 What a country calls its vital economic interests
are not the things which enable its citizens to
live, but the things which enable it to make war;
petrol is more likely than wheat to be a cause of
international conflict.
> "The Power of Words" (1937)

2 Who were the fools who spread the story that
brute force cannot kill ideas? Nothing is easier.
And once they are dead they are no more than
corpses.
> "Three Letters on History: Thophile de Viau" (written
> 1938–1939)

3 The needs of a human being are sacred. Their
satisfaction cannot be subordinated either to
reasons of state, or to any consideration of
money, nationality, race, or color, or to the
moral or other value attributed to the human
being in question, or to any consideration
whatsoever.
> "Draft for a Statement of Human Obligation" (1943)

4 All sins are attempts to fill voids.
> *La Pesanteur et la Grâce* "Désirer sans Objet" (1948)

5 Every time that I think of the crucifixion of
Christ, I commit the sin of envy.
> *Waiting on God* Letter 4 (1950)

Jack Weinberg
U.S. political activist, 1940–

1 We have a saying in the movement that you
can't trust anybody over 30.
> Quoted in *S.F. Chronicle*, 15 Nov. 1964

Steven Weinberg
U.S. physicist, 1933–

1 It is even harder to realize that this present
universe has evolved from an unspeakably
unfamiliar early condition, and faces a future
extinction of endless cold or intolerable heat.
The more the universe seems comprehensible,
the more it also seems pointless.
> *The First Three Minutes* ch. 8 (1977)

2 With or without [religion] you would have
good people doing good things and evil people
doing evil things. But for good people to do evil
things, that takes religion.
> Address at Conference on Cosmic Design,
> Washington, D.C., Apr. 1999

Max Weinreich
Lithuanian-born U.S. linguist, 1893–1969

1 *A shprakh iz a dialekt mit an armey un flot.*
A language is a dialect with an army and navy.
> *Yivo Bleter*, Jan.–Feb. 1945. Weinreich was quoting an
> unnamed student who spoke to him after a lecture at
> the Yidisher Visnshaftlekher Institut in 1944.

Johnny Weismuller

U.S. actor and swimmer, 1904–1984

1 Me Tarzan, you Jane.

Quoted in *Photoplay*, June 1932. Weissmuller's full quotation in this interview was "I didn't have to act in *Tarzan, the Ape Man*—just said, 'Me Tarzan, you Jane.'" This was a paraphrase of the real film dialogue, which had Tarzan alternately tapping himself and Jane Parker while repeating each of their names.

George David Weiss

U.S. songwriter, 1921–2010

1 I see skies of blue, and clouds of white,
The bright blessed day, the dark sacred night
And I think to myself what a wonderful world.

"What a Wonderful World" (song) (1968). Cowritten with Bob Thiele.

Hazel Weiss

U.S. sports executive's wife, fl. 1969

1 I married him for better or for worse—but not for lunch.

Quoted in *Wash. Post*, 27 Apr. 1969. Supposedly said after her husband, George Weiss, retired as general manager of the New York Yankees in 1960. The *Dallas Morning News* on 5 May 1962 has the following, credited to "the wife of the fired baseball manager": "I married the guy for better or worse. But not for lunch."

Peter Weiss

German novelist and playwright, 1916–1982

1 *Die Verfolgung und Ermordung Jean Paul Marats, Dargestellt Durch die Schauspielgruppe des Hospizes zu Charenton Unter Anleitung des Herrn de Sade.*

The Persecution and Assassination of Jean-Paul Marat: As Performed by the Inmates of the Asylum of Charenton Under the Direction of the Marquis de Sade.

Title of play (1964, translation 1965)

Victor Weisskopf

Austrian-born U.S. physicist, 1908–2002

1 It was absolutely marvelous working for [Wolfgang] Pauli. You could ask him anything. There was no worry that he would think a particular question was stupid, since he thought *all* questions were stupid.

American Journal of Physics, May 1977

Joseph N. Welch

U.S. lawyer, 1890–1960

1 Until this moment, Senator, I think I never really gauged your cruelty or your recklessness. . . . Let us not assassinate this lad further, Senator. You have done enough. Have you no sense of decency, sir, at long last? Have you left no sense of decency?

Remark to Senator Joseph McCarthy, 9 June 1954. Welch was counsel for the U.S. Army in a Senate hearing on alleged subversive activities in the army. McCarthy had charged that a lawyer in Welch's firm had once belonged to a Communist front group. Welch's statement was decisive in triggering McCarthy's political downfall.

Fay Weldon (Franklin Birkinshaw)

English writer, 1931–

1 The Life and Loves of a She-Devil.

Title of book (1983)

Orson Welles

U.S. director and actor, 1915–1985

1 Ladies and gentlemen, I have a grave announcement to make. Incredible as it may seem, strange beings who landed in New Jersey tonight are the vanguard of an invading army from Mars.

Radio broadcast of *The War of the Worlds*, 31 Oct. 1938

2 [*Punch line of joke about a scorpion stinging a frog that is carrying him across a river despite the fact that this would result in both their deaths:*] I can't help it. It's my nature.

Mr. Arkadin bk. 1 (1956)

3 [*Of a Hollywood movie studio:*] This is the biggest electric train [set] any boy ever had!

Quoted in Leo Rosten, *Hollywood* (1941)

4 I started at the top and worked my way down.

Quoted in Leslie Halliwell, *The Filmgoer's Book of Quotes* (1973)

5 [*Response when asked which film directors he most admired:*] I like the old masters, by which I mean John Ford, John Ford, and John Ford.

Quoted in Paul F. Boller, Jr., and Ronald L. Davis, *Hollywood Anecdotes* (1988)

Arthur Wellesley, Duke of Wellington

British military leader and prime minister, 1769–1852

1 Up Guards and at them!

> Quoted in John Booth, *The Battle of Waterloo* (1815). Wellington denied having said this. The attributed comment appears to be the source of the expression "Up and at 'em!"

2 [*Of Napoleon:*] I used to say of him that his presence on the field made the difference of forty thousand men.

> Quoted in Philip Henry Stanhope, *Notes of Conversations with the Duke of Wellington* (1888) (entry for 2 Nov. 1831)

3 The only thing I am afraid of is fear.

> Quoted in Philip Henry Stanhope, *Notes of Conversations with the Duke of Wellington* (1888) (entry for 3 Nov. 1831)
> See Francis Bacon 7; Montaigne 4; Franklin Roosevelt 6; Thoreau 16

4 [*Of the British Army:*] Ours is composed of the scum of the earth—the mere scum of the earth.

> Quoted in Philip Henry Stanhope, *Notes of Conversations with the Duke of Wellington* (1888) (entry for 4 Nov. 1831)

5 [*Of troops sent to fight the United States in the War of 1812:*] They wanted this iron fist to command them.

> Quoted in Philip Henry Stanhope, *Notes of Conversations with the Duke of Wellington* (1888) (entry for 8 Nov. 1840)

6 Write and be damned.

> Attributed in Julia Johnstone, *Confessions of Julia Johnstone* (1825). This exclamation, usually quoted as "Publish and be damned!," was Wellington's alleged response in 1824 to a blackmail threat from a publisher about to release the *Memoirs* of courtesan Harriette Wilson, who had been the duke's mistress and was ready to "name names." The words supposedly were written in bright red ink on the blackmailing letter, with the letter then returned to the publisher. However, the letter survives at Apsley House and has no trace of such a reply.

7 [*Of the disposition of Napoleon's ashes:*] How they settle the matter I care not one two-penny damn.

> Quoted in Thomas Babington Macaulay, Letter to Mr. Ellis, 6 Mar. 1849

8 The Battle of Waterloo was won in the playing fields of Eton.

> Attributed in *Daily News* (London), 2 Mar. 1860. The earliest known trace of this quotation was in Charles

de Montalembert, *De l'Avenir Politique de l'Angleterre* (1856). Montalembert quoted Wellington, supposedly visiting his old school, in French: *"C'est ici qu'a été gagnée la bataille de Waterloo."* In fact, Wellington was a notably unenthusiastic alumnus of Eton, and Elizabeth Longford, in *Wellington: The Years of the Sword* (1969), concludes that "probably he never said or thought anything of the kind."
> See Orwell 15

H. G. Wells

English novelist, 1866–1946

1 Would you like to see the Time Machine itself?

> *The Time Machine* ch. 1 (1895)

2 Are we not Men?

> *The Island of Dr. Moreau* ch. 12 (1896)

3 The War That Will End War.

> Title of book (1914)

4 Nothing could have been more obvious to the people of the earlier twentieth century than the rapidity with which war was becoming impossible. And as certainly they did not see it. They did not see it until the atomic bombs burst in their fumbling hands.

> *The World Set Free* ch. 2 (1914). Earliest use of the term *atomic bomb*.

5 The catastrophe of the atomic bombs which shook men out of cities and businesses and economic relations, shook them also out of their old-established habits of thought, and out of the lightly held beliefs and prejudices that came down to them from the past.

> *The World Set Free* ch. 4 (1914)

6 The professional military mind is by necessity an inferior and unimaginative mind; no man of high intellectual quality would willingly imprison his gifts in such a calling.

> *The Outline of History* ch. 40 (1920)

7 Human history becomes more and more a race between education and catastrophe.

> *The Outline of History* ch. 41 (1920)

8 The Shape of Things to Come.

> Title of book (1933)

9 The brain upon which my experiences have been written is not a particularly good one. If there were brain-shows, as there are cat and dog shows, I doubt if it would get even a third class prize.

> *Experiment in Autobiography* introduction (1934)

Rebecca Wells

U.S. novelist, 1952–

1 I have been missing the point. The point is not *knowing* another person, or learning to *love* another person. The point is simply this: how tender can we bear to be? What good manners can we show as we welcome ourselves and others into our hearts?

The Divine Secrets of the Ya-Ya Sisterhood ch. 31 (1996)

Robert Wells

U.S. songwriter, 1922–1998

1 Chestnuts roasting on an open fire,
Jack Frost nipping at your nose.

"The Christmas Song" (song) (1946)

Ida Wells-Barnett

U.S. journalist and activist, 1862–1931

1 I felt that one had better die fighting against injustice than to die like a dog or a rat in a trap. I had already determined to sell my life as dearly as possible if attacked. I felt if I could take one lyncher with me, this would even up the score a little bit.

A Red Record: Tabulated Statistics and Alleged Causes of Lynching in the United States (1895)

Irvine Welsh

Scottish novelist, 1957–

1 It's nae good blamin' it oan the English fir colonising us. Ah don't hate the English. They're just wankers. We can't even pick a decent vibrant, healthy culture to be colonised by.

Trainspotting (1993)

2 Choose us. Choose life. Choose mortgage payments; choose washing machines; choose cars; choose sitting oan a couch watching mind-numbing and spirit-crushing game shows, stuffing fuckin junk food intae yir mooth. Choose rotting away, pishing and shiteing yersel in a home, a total fuckin embarrassment tae the selfish, fucked-up brats ye've produced. Choose life.

Trainspotting (1993)

Eudora Welty

U.S. novelist and short story writer, 1909–2001

1 Never think you've seen the last of anything.

The Optimist's Daughter ch. 1 (1969)

2 It had been startling and disappointing to me to find out that story books had been written by *people,* that books were not natural wonders, coming up of themselves like grass.

One Writer's Beginnings ch. 1 (1983)

Charles Wesley

English clergyman and hymnwriter, 1707–1788

1 Hark how all the Welkin rings—
Glory to the Kings of Kings.
Peace on earth and mercy mild,
God and sinners reconciled.

Hymns and Sacred Poems "Hymn for Christmas-Day" (1739). George Whitefield, in *A Collection of Hymns for Social Worship* (1753), altered Wesley's first two lines to "Hark! The Herald Angels sing / Glory to the new-born King!"

John Wesley

English religious leader, 1703–1791

1 I look upon all the world as my parish.

Sermon, 11 May 1739

2 Slovenliness is no part of religion; that neither this, nor any text of Scripture, condemns neatness of apparel. Certainly this is a duty, not a sin. "Cleanliness is, indeed, next to godliness."

Sermons on Several Occasions Sermon 88 (1788). The *Oxford Dictionary of Proverbs* notes, "*Next* in this proverb means 'immediately following,' as in serial order." The *ODP* refers to a passage in Francis Bacon, *Advancement of Learning* (1605), reading, "Cleannesse of bodie was euer esteemed to proceed from a due reverence to God."

Samuel Wesley

English clergyman and poet, 1662–1735

1 Style is the dress of thought; a modest dress,
Neat, but not gaudy, will true critics please.

"An Epistle to a Friend Concerning Poetry" l. 138 (1700)
See Samuel Johnson 33

Dorothy West

U.S. writer, 1907–1998

1 Color was a false distinction; love was not.

The Wedding ch. 17 (1995)

Jessamyn West
U.S. author, 1903–1984

1 Writing is so difficult that I often feel that writers, having had their hell on earth, will escape all punishment hereafter.
To See the Dream ch. 1 (1957)

2 It is very easy to forgive others their mistakes; it takes more grit and gumption to forgive them for having witnessed our own.
To See the Dream ch. 5 (1957)

3 Sex and religion are bordering states. They use the same vocabulary, share like ecstasies, and often serve as a substitute for one another.
Hide and Seek ch. 21 (1973)

4 A rattlesnake that doesn't bite teaches you nothing.
The Life I Really Lived ch. 2 (1979)

Kanye West
U.S. musician, 1977–

1 George Bush doesn't care about black people.
NBC "A Concert for Hurricane Relief" telethon, 2 Sept. 2005

2 Imma let you finish, but Beyoncé had one of the best videos of all time!
Remarks interrupting Taylor Swift's acceptance speech at the MTV Video Music Awards, 13 Sept. 2009

3 You don't have to agree with Trump but the mob can't make me not love him. We are both dragon energy. He is my brother. I love everyone.
Tweet, 25 Apr. 2018

Mae West
U.S. actress, 1893–1980
Lines West spoke in her motion pictures have been listed under her name here regardless of whether she was credited as a screenwriter for the film in question.

1 I always like a man in uniform, and that one fits you grand. Say, why don't you drop in and see me some time? Home every evening you know. . . . Why don't you come up some time?
Diamond Lil act 1 (1928). These lines do not appear in the Library of Congress copy of the play but do appear in a copy at the Shubert Archive in New York. Jill Watts, in *Mae West: An Icon in Black and White*, notes that West's 1927 play *The Drag* has the line "Come up sometime and I'll bake you a pan of biscuits." Watts

also writes, "Perry Bradford, the African-American songwriter, boasted that the [1922] song 'He May Be Your Man but He Comes to See Me Sometimes,' which he provided to West years before, was the inspiration for Lil's line."
See Mae West 2; Mae West 10

2 You know, I always liked a man in uniform. . . . That one fits you perfect. Say, why don't you come up some time. I'm home every evening.
Diamond Lil (1932). The novel version of *Diamond Lil* (see the comment to the quotation above).
See Mae West 1; Mae West 10

3 [*Mandie Triplett, played by Mae West, responding to being told, "Goodness, what beautiful diamonds":*] Goodness had nothing to do with it, dearie.
Night After Night (motion picture) (1932)

4 [*Tira, played by Mae West, speaking:*] Peel me a grape.
I'm No Angel (motion picture) (1933). Usually quoted as "Beulah, peel me a grape."

5 [*Tira, played by Mae West, speaking:*] It's not the men in my life that counts—it's the life in my men.
I'm No Angel (motion picture) (1933)

6 [*Tira, played by Mae West, speaking:*] When I'm good, I'm very, very good. But when I'm bad, I'm better.
I'm No Angel (motion picture) (1933)
See Longfellow 28

7 [*Tira, played by Mae West, speaking:*] I've been things and seen places.
I'm No Angel (motion picture) (1933)

8 [*Tira, played by Mae West, speaking:*] She's the kind of girl who climbed the ladder of success, wrong by wrong.
I'm No Angel (motion picture) (1933)

9 [*Tira, played by Mae West, speaking:*] Marriage is a great institution—but I'm not ready for an institution.
I'm No Angel (motion picture) (1933). Nigel Rees, in his *Quote . . . Unquote Newsletter,* has found this joke appearing earlier in the cartoon "Pop" in 1921: "WOMAN: 'You say what you like, Pop! Marriage is a jolly good institution!' POP: 'Yes! But who wants to live in an institution?'"

10 [*Lady Lou, played by Mae West, speaking:*] Why don't you come up sometime and see me?
She Done Him Wrong (motion picture) (1933). Often misquoted as "Come up and see me sometime."
See Mae West 1; Mae West 2

11 [*Lady Lou, played by Mae West, speaking:*] When women go wrong, men go right after them.
She Done Him Wrong (motion picture) (1933)

12 [*Ruby Carter, played by Mae West, speaking:*] It's better to be looked over than overlooked.
Belle of the Nineties (motion picture) (1934)

13 [*The Frisco Doll, played by Mae West, speaking:*] Between two evils, I always pick the one I never tried before.
Klondike Annie (motion picture) (1936)
See Homer 5

14 [*The Frisco Doll, played by Mae West, speaking:*] Give a man a free hand and he'll try to put it all over you.
Klondike Annie (motion picture) (1936)

15 [*Peaches O'Day, played by Mae West, speaking:*] I always say, keep a diary and someday it'll keep you.
Every Day's a Holiday (motion picture) (1937). Margot Asquith was quoted in the *Schenectady Gazette,* 25 May 1922, as follows: "Keep a diary, my dear, and later on, perhaps, the diary will keep you."
See Proverbs 159

16 [*Peaches O'Day, played by Mae West, speaking:*] It ain't no sin if you crack a few laws now and then, just so long as you don't break any.
Every Day's a Holiday (motion picture) (1937)

17 [*Flower Belle Lee, played by Mae West, speaking:*] Oh, arithmetic. I was always pretty good at figures myself.
My Little Chickadee (motion picture) (1940)

18 [*Flower Belle Lee, played by Mae West, replying to judge's question, "Are you trying to show contempt for the court?":*] No, I'm doing my best to hide it.
My Little Chickadee (motion picture) (1940). Henry Hupfeld, in *Encyclopaedia of Wit and Wisdom* (1871), includes a joke in which Thaddeus Stevens responds to a similar question from a judge by saying, "Express my contempt for this court! No, sir, I am trying to conceal it, your honor."

19 [*Flower Belle Lee, played by Mae West, speaking:*] I generally avoid temptation unless I can't resist it.
My Little Chickadee (motion picture) (1940)
See Balzac 1; Clementina Graham 1; Wilde 25; Wilde 53

20 Catherine was a great empress. She also had three hundred lovers. I did the best I could in a couple of hours.
Curtain speech after performances of play *Catherine Was Great* (1945)

21 [*Letter to Royal Air Force, 1941, when the term "Mae West," referring to an inflatable life jacket used by airmen in World War II, was entered into a dictionary:*] I've been in *Who's Who,* and I know what's what, but it'll be the first time I ever made the dictionary.
Goodness Had Nothing to Do With It ch. 17 (1959)

22 Too much of a good thing can be wonderful.
Goodness Had Nothing to Do With It ch. 21 (1959)

23 I used to be Snow White, but I drifted.
Quoted in *Augusta Chronicle,* 4 May 1938. Earlier, *Phi Gamma Delta,* Nov. 1921 (quoting the *Yale Record*), printed "She was as pure and as white as snow." "Yes, but she drifted."

24 Is that a gun in your pocket, or are you just glad to see me?
Quoted in *The Wit and Wisdom of Mae West,* ed. Joseph Weintraub (1967). Often ascribed to West's film *She Done Him Wrong,* but the line does not appear in that or any of her other pre-1967 movies. According to Jill Watts, in *Mae West: An Icon in Black and White* (2001), "Upon [West's] arrival [in Los Angeles in 1936], she coined one of her most famous lines; she greeted an LAPD officer assigned to escort her home with 'Is that a gun in your pocket or are you happy to see me?'"

Nathanael West (Nathan von Wallenstein Weinstein)
U.S. novelist, 1903–1940

1 Dear Miss Lonelyhearts . . . I would like to have boy friends like the other girls and go out on Saturday nites, but no boy will take me because I was born without a nose—although I am a good dancer and have a nice shape and my father buys me pretty clothes.
Miss Lonelyhearts ch. 1 (1933)

Rebecca West (Cicily Isabel Fairfield)
English novelist and journalist, 1892–1983

1 I myself have never been able to find out precisely what Feminism is: I only know that people call me a Feminist whenever I express sentiments that differentiate me from a doormat or a prostitute.
The Clarion, 14 Nov. 1913

2 It was in dealing with the early feminist that the Government acquired the tact and skillfulness with which it is now handling Ireland.
Daily News (London), 7 Aug. 1916

3 [*Of the James brothers, Henry and William:*] One of whom grew up to write fiction as though it were philosophy and the other to write philosophy as though it were fiction.
Henry James ch. 1 (1916)

4 There is no such thing as conversation. It is an illusion. There are intersecting monologues, that is all.
"There Is No Conversation" (1928). In the earliest publication of West's story, "intersecting" was erroneously printed as "interesting."

5 Just how difficult it is to write biography can be reckoned by anybody who sits down and considers just how many people know the real truth about his or her love affairs.
"The Art of Scepticism" (1952)

6 Before a war, military science seems a real science, like astronomy. After a war it seems more like astrology.
Quoted in Jonathon Green, *Morrow's International Dictionary of Contemporary Quotations* (1982)

7 Journalism is the ability to meet the challenge of filling space.
Quoted in *N.Y. Times*, 10 Dec. 1989

Richard Bethell, First Baron Westbury
English lawyer, 1800–1873

1 [*Remark to a solicitor who had said that "he had turned the matter over in his mind":*] Turn it over once more in what you are *pleased to call* your mind.
Quoted in Thomas A. Nash, *The Life of Richard Lord Westbury* (1888)

William C. Westmoreland
U.S. military leader, 1914–2005

1 Vietnam was the first war ever fought without any censorship. Without censorship, things can get terribly confused in the public mind.
Quoted in *Wash. Post*, 19 Mar. 1982

Edith Wharton
U.S. writer, 1862–1937

1 There are two ways of spreading light; to be
The candle or the mirror that reflects it.
I let my wick burn out—there yet remains
To spread an answering surface to the flame
That others kindle.
"Vesalius in Zante (1564)" st. 12 (1902)

2 He seemed a part of the mute melancholy landscape, an incarnation of its frozen woe, with all that was warm and sentient in him fast bound below the surface.
Ethan Frome preface (1911)

3 Almost everybody in the neighborhood had "troubles," frankly localized and specified; but only the chosen had "complications." To have them was in itself a distinction, though it was also, in most cases, a death warrant. People struggled on for years with "troubles," but they almost always succumbed to "complications."
Ethan Frome ch. 7 (1911)

4 Mrs. Ballinger is one of the ladies who pursue Culture in bands, as though it were dangerous to meet it alone.
Xingu and Other Stories "Xingu" (1916)

5 An unalterable and unquestioned law of the musical world required that the German text of French operas sung by Swedish artists should be translated into Italian for the clearer understanding of English-speaking audiences.
The Age of Innocence ch. 1 (1920)

6 In the rotation of crops there was a recognized season for wild oats; but they were not sown more than once.
The Age of Innocence ch. 31 (1920)

7 It was the old New York way of taking life "without effusion of blood": the way of people who dreaded scandal more than disease, who placed decency above courage, and who considered that nothing was more ill-bred than "scenes," except the behavior of those who gave rise to them.
The Age of Innocence ch. 33 (1920)

8 The worst of doing one's duty was that it apparently unfitted one for doing anything else.
The Age of Innocence ch. 34 (1920)

9 In spite of illness, in spite even of the arch-enemy sorrow, one *can* remain alive long past the usual date of disintegration if one is unafraid of change, insatiable in intellectual curiosity, interested in big things, and happy in small ways.
A Backward Glance "A First Word" (1934)

Richard Whately
English philosopher and clergyman, 1787–1863

1 It is not that pearls fetch a high price *because* men have dived for them; but on the contrary, men dive for them because they fetch a high price.
Introductory Lectures on Political Economy, 2nd ed., lecture 9 (1832)

Phillis Wheatley
U.S. poet, ca. 1753–1784

1 'Twas mercy brought me from my *Pagan* land, Taught my benighted soul to understand That there's a God, that there's a *Savior* too: Once I redemption neither sought nor knew.
"On Being Brought from Africa to America" l. 1 (1773)

2 *Imagination!* who can sing thy force? Or who describe the swiftness of thy course? Soaring through air to find the bright abode, Th' empyreal palace of the thund'ring God, We on thy pinions can surpass the wind, And leave the rolling universe behind.
"On Imagination" l. 13 (1773)

3 Wisdom is higher than a fool can reach.
"On Virtue" l. 3 (1773)

4 In every human breast, God has implanted a principle, which we call love of freedom; it is impatient of oppression, and pants for deliverance; and by the leave of our modern Egyptians I will assert, that the same principle lives in us.
Letter to Samson Occom, Feb. 1774

Elmer Wheeler
U.S. marketing expert, 1903–1968

1 Don't Sell the Steak—*Sell the Sizzle!*
Tested Sentences That Sell ch. 1 title (1937)

John Hall Wheelock
U.S. poet, 1886–1978

1 "A planet doesn't explode of itself," said drily The Martian astronomer, gazing off into the air—
"That they were able to do it is proof that highly
Intelligent beings must have existed there."
"Earth" l. 1 (1970)

William Whewell
English philosopher and scientist, 1794–1866

1 Hence no force however great can stretch a cord however fine into an horizontal line which is accurately straight.
Elementary Treatise on Mechanics ch. 4 (1819). This is an instance of unintentional rhyme and meter. After the passage's poetical qualities were pointed out to him, Whewell altered it in subsequent editions of the book.

2 We need very much a name to describe a cultivator of science in general. I should incline to call him a Scientist.
The Philosophy of the Inductive Sciences vol. 1 (1840). Whewell coined *scientist* at a meeting of the British Association for the Advancement of Science in the early 1830s.

James McNeill Whistler
U.S. artist, 1834–1903

1 I maintain that two and two the mathematician would continue to make four, in spite of the whine of the amateur for three, or the cry of the critic for five. We are told that Mr. Ruskin has devoted his long life to art, and as a result— is "Slade Professor" at Oxford. In the same sentence, we have thus his position and its worth. It suffices not, Messieurs! a life passed among pictures makes not a painter—else the policeman in the National Gallery might assert himself.
"Whistler v. Ruskin: Art and Art Critics" (1878)

2 [*Response to the question, in cross-examination, "The labor of two days is that for which you ask two hundred guineas?":*] No, I ask it for the knowledge I have gained in the work of a lifetime.
Testimony in *Whistler v. Ruskin* libel trial, 1878

3 The Swiss in their mountains. What more worthy people! . . . yet, the perverse and scornful [goddess, Art] will none of it, and the sons of patriots are left with the clock that turns the mill, and the sudden cuckoo, with difficulty restrained in its box! For this was Tell a hero! For this did Gessler die!
"Mr. Whistler's Ten O'Clock" (1885)
See Film Lines 174

4 I am not arguing with you—I am telling you.
The Gentle Art of Making Enemies "A Proposal" (1890)

5 [*Response to Oscar Wilde's comment, "I wish I had said that":*] You will, Oscar! You will!
Quoted in *Daily Inter Ocean* (Chicago), 4 Apr. 1892. An earlier version was printed in the *Sunday Herald* (Boston), 24 Jan. 1886: "Wilde . . . approved Mr. Whistler's brightness, and wondered why he had not thought of the witticism himself. 'You will,' promptly replied Whistler, 'you will.'"

6 [*Comment on his having failed chemistry while a student at the U.S. Military Academy:*] Had silicon been a gas, I would have been a major general.
Quoted in Joseph Pennell, *The Life of James McNeill Whistler* (1908)

7 "There are, Mr. Whistler," said one of his numerous worshippers, "only two painters in the world, yourself and Velasquez." "Why drag in Velasquez?" said Whistler.
Reported in *Derby* (England) *Mercury*, 13 Aug. 1884

Andrew D. White
U.S. educator, 1832–1918

1 [*Explanation of why, as president of Cornell University, he was prohibiting Cornell from playing the University of Michigan in football, 1873:*] I will not permit thirty men to travel 400 miles merely to agitate a bag of wind.
Quoted in *N.Y. Times*, 7 Nov. 1944

E. B. White
U.S. writer, 1899–1985

1 [*Mother:*] It's broccoli, dear.
[*Child:*] I say it's spinach, and I say the hell with it.
Cartoon caption, *New Yorker*, 8 Dec. 1928

2 Democracy is the recurrent suspicion that more than half of the people are right more than half of the time.
New Yorker, 3 July 1943

3 When Mrs. Frederick C. Little's second son was born, everybody noticed that he was not much bigger than a mouse. The truth of the matter was, the baby looked very much like a mouse in every way. He was only two inches high; and he had a mouse's sharp nose, a mouse's tail, a mouse's whiskers, and the pleasant, shy manner of a mouse. Before he was many days old he was not only looking like a mouse but acting like one, too—wearing a gray hat and carrying a small cane.
Stuart Little ch. 1 (1945)

4 The city, for the first time in its long history, is destructible. A single flight of planes no bigger than a wedge of geese can quickly end this island fantasy, burn the towers, crumble the bridges, turn the underground passages into lethal chambers, cremate the millions. The intimation of mortality is part of New York now: in the sound of jets overhead, in the black headlines of the latest edition.
Here Is New York (1949)

5 All dwellers in cities must live with the stubborn fact of annihilation . . . of all targets, New York has a certain clear priority. In the mind of whatever perverted dreamer might loose the lightning, New York must hold a steady, irresistible charm.
Here Is New York (1949)

6 "Where's Papa going with that axe?" said Fern to her mother as they were setting the table for breakfast.

Charlotte's Web ch. 1 (1952)

7 It was the best place to be, thought Wilbur, this warm delicious cellar, with the garrulous geese, the changing seasons, the heat of the sun, the passage of swallows, the nearness of rats, the sameness of sheep, the love of spiders, the smell of manure, and the glory of everything.

Charlotte's Web ch. 22 (1952)

8 It is not often that someone comes along who is a true friend and a good writer. Charlotte was both.

Charlotte's Web ch. 22 (1952)

Edmund White
U.S. writer, 1940–

1 The AIDS epidemic has rolled back a big rotting log and revealed all the squirming life underneath it, since it involves, all at once, the main themes of our existence: sex, death, power, money, love, hate, disease, and panic. No American phenomenon has been so compelling since the Vietnam War.

States of Desire: Travels in Gay America "Afterword—AIDS: An American Epidemic" (1986)

Patrick White
English-born Australian novelist, 1912–1990

1 So that, in the end, there was no end.

The Tree of Man ch. 26 (1955)

T. H. White
Indian-born English writer, 1906–1964

1 Learn why the world wags and what wags it. That is the only thing which the poor mind can never exhaust, never alienate, never be tortured by, never fear or distrust, and never dream of regretting.

The Sword in the Stone ch. 21 (1939)

Alfred North Whitehead
English mathematician and philosopher, 1861–1947

1 It is a profoundly erroneous truism, repeated by all copy-books and by eminent people when they are making speeches, that we should cultivate the habit of thinking of what we are doing. The precise opposite is the case. Civilization advances by extending the number of important operations which we can perform without thinking about them. Operations of thought are like cavalry charges in a battle— they are strictly limited in number, they require fresh horses, and must only be made at decisive moments.

An Introduction to Mathematics ch. 5 (1911)

2 To come very near to a true theory, and to grasp its precise application, are two very different things, as the history of a science teaches us. Everything of importance has been said before by somebody who did not discover it.

"The Organization of Thought" (1917)

3 Seek simplicity and distrust it.

The Concept of Nature ch. 7 (1920)

4 The science of pure mathematics, in its modern developments, may claim to be the most original creation of the human spirit.

Science and the Modern World ch. 2 (1925)

5 The greatest invention of the nineteenth century was the invention of the method of invention.

Science and the Modern World ch. 6 (1925)

6 The religious vision, and its history of persistent expansion, is our one ground for optimism. Apart from it, human life is a flash of occasional enjoyments lighting up a mass of pain and misery, a bagatelle of transient experience.

Science and the Modern World ch. 12 (1925)

7 The safest general characterization of the European philosophical tradition is that it consists of a series of footnotes to Plato.

Process and Reality pt. 2, ch. 1 (1929)

8 It is more important that a proposition be interesting than that it be true. . . . But of course a true proposition is more apt to be interesting than a false one.

Adventures of Ideas pt. 4, ch. 16 (1933)

9 There are no whole truths; all truths are half-truths. It is trying to treat them as whole truths that plays the devil.

Dialogues prologue (1954)

10 What is morality in any given time or place? It is what the majority then and there happen to like, and immorality is what they dislike.
Dialogues (1954) (entry for 30 Aug. 1941)

11 The ideas of Freud were popularized by people who only imperfectly understood them, who were incapable of the great effort required to grasp them in their relationship to larger truths, and who therefore assigned to them a prominence out of all proportion to their true importance.
Dialogues (1954) (entry for 3 June 1943)

12 Art is the imposing of a pattern on experience, and our aesthetic enjoyment is recognition of the pattern.
Dialogues (1954) (entry for 10 June 1943)

Katharine Whitehorn
English journalist, 1928–2021

1 In our society mothers take the place elsewhere occupied by the Fates, the System, Negroes, Communism, or Reactionary Imperialist Plots; mothers go on getting blamed until they're eighty, but shouldn't take it personally.
Observations ch. 10 (1970)

Norman Whitfield
U.S. songwriter, 1940–2008

1 I heard it through the grapevine
Not much longer would you be mine.
Oh I heard it through the grapevine.
Oh and I'm just about to lose my mind.
"I Heard It Through the Grapevine" (song) (1968). Cowritten with Barrett Strong.

George Whiting
U.S. songwriter, 1884–1943

1 When You're All Dressed Up and Have No Place to Go.
Title of song (1912)

Gough Whitlam
Australian prime minister, 1916–2014

1 [*Of Governor-General Sir John Kerr, who had just dismissed Whitlam as prime minister:*] Well may we say, "God save the Queen," because nothing will save the Governor-General.
Speech, Canberra, Australia, 11 Nov. 1975

Walt Whitman
U.S. poet, 1819–1892

1 I Sing the Body Electric.
Title of poem (1855)

2 The United States themselves are essentially the greatest poem.
Leaves of Grass preface (1855)

3 I celebrate myself, and sing myself,
And what I assume you shall assume,
For every atom belonging to me as good belongs to you.
"Song of Myself" l. 1 (written 1855)

4 Stop this day and night with me and you shall possess the origin of all poems,
You shall possess the good of the earth and sun, (there are millions of suns left,)
You shall no longer take things at second or third hand, nor look through the eyes of the dead, nor feed on the spectres in books,
You shall not look through my eyes either, nor take things from me,
You shall listen to all sides and filter them from your self.
"Song of Myself" l. 33 (written 1855)

5 Walt Whitman, a kosmos, of Manhattan the son,
Turbulent, fleshy, sensual, eating, drinking and breeding,
No sentimentalist, no stander above men and women or apart from them,
No more modest than immodest.
"Song of Myself" l. 497 (written 1855)

6 I think I could turn and live with animals, they are so placid and self-contain'd,
I stand and look at them long and long.

They do not sweat and whine about their condition,
They do not lie awake in the dark and weep for their sins,
They do not make me sick discussing their duty to God,
Not one is dissatisfied, not one is demented with the mania of owning things,
Not one kneels to another, nor to his kind that lived thousands of years ago,
Not one is respectable or unhappy over the whole earth.
"Song of Myself" l. 684 (written 1855)

7 Behold, I do not give lectures or a little charity,
   When I give I give myself.
   "Song of Myself" l. 994 (written 1855)

8 Do I contradict myself?
   Very well then I contradict myself,
   (I am large, I contain multitudes.)
   "Song of Myself" l. 1324 (written 1855)

9 I too am not a bit tamed, I too am
   untranslatable,
   I sound my barbaric yawp over the roofs of the
   world.
   "Song of Myself" l. 1332 (written 1855)

10 I hear America singing, the varied carols I hear.
   "I Hear America Singing" l. 1 (1867)

11 O Captain! my Captain! our fearful trip is done,
   The ship has weather'd every rack, the prize we
   sought is won,
   The port is near, the bells I hear, the people all
   exulting.
   "O Captain! My Captain!" l. 1 (1871)

12 The ship is anchor'd safe and sound, its voyage
   closed and done,
   From fearful trip the victor ship comes in with
   object won;
   Exult O shores, and ring O bells!
   But I with mournful tread,
   Walk the deck my Captain lies,
   Fallen cold and dead.
   "O Captain! My Captain!" l. 19 (1871)

13 Passage to India.
   Title of poem (1871)

14 The untold want by life and land ne'er granted,
   Now voyager sail thou forth to seek and find.
   "The Untold Want" l. 1 (1871)

15 A noiseless patient spider,
   I mark'd where on a little promontory it stood
   isolated,
   Mark'd how to explore the vacant vast
   surrounding,
   It launch'd forth filament, filament, filament
   out of itself,
   Ever unreeling them, ever tirelessly speeding
   them.
   "A Noiseless Patient Spider" l. 1 (1881)

16 Out of the cradle endlessly rocking,
   Out of the mocking-bird's throat, the musical
   shuttle,

Out of the Ninth-month midnight,
Over the sterile sands and the fields beyond,
   where the child leaving his bed wander'd
   alone, bareheaded, barefoot.
"Out of the Cradle Endlessly Rocking" l. 1 (1881)

17 We must march my darlings, we must bear the
   brunt of danger,
   We the youthful sinewy races, all the rest on us
   depend,
   Pioneers! O pioneers!
   "Pioneers! O Pioneers!" l. 6 (1881)

18 When lilacs last in the dooryard bloom'd,
   And the great star early droop'd in the western
   sky in the night,
   I mourn'd, and yet shall mourn with ever-
   returning spring.
   "When Lilacs Last in the Dooryard Bloom'd" l. 1
   (1881)

19 *The Real War Will Never Get in the Books.* And
   so good-bye to the war.
   Specimen Days "The Real War Will Never Get in the
   Books" (1882)

Beth Slater Whitson
U.S. songwriter, 1879–1930

1 Let me call you Sweetheart
   I'm in love with you.
   Let me hear you whisper that you love me too.
   "Let Me Call You Sweetheart" (song) (1910)

John Greenleaf Whittier
U.S. poet, 1807–1892

1 For of all sad words of tongue or pen,
   The saddest are these: "It might have been!"
   "Maud Muller" l. 105 (1854)

2 Blessings on thee, little man,
   Barefoot boy, with cheek of tan!
   "The Barefoot Boy" l. 1 (1856)

3 "Shoot, if you must, this old gray head,
   But spare your country's flag," she said.
   "Barbara Frietchie" l. 35 (1863)

4 "Who touches a hair of yon gray head
   Dies like a dog! March on!" he said.
   "Barbara Frietchie" l. 41 (1863)

Robert Whittington

English grammarian, ca. 1480–ca. 1553

1 [*Of Thomas More:*] As time requireth, a man of marvellous mirth and pastimes, and sometime of as sad gravity, as who say: a man for all seasons.

Vulgaria pt. 2 (1521)
See Erasmus 3

Benjamin Lee Whorf

U.S. linguist, 1897–1941

1 We dissect nature along lines laid down by our native languages. The categories and types that we isolate from the world of phenomena we do not find there because they stare every observer in the face; on the contrary, the world is presented in a kaleidoscopic flux of impressions which has to be organized by our minds—and this means largely by the linguistic systems in our minds. We cut nature up, organize it into concepts, and ascribe significances as we do, largely because we are parties to an agreement to organize it in this way—an agreement that holds throughout our speech community and is codified in the patterns of our language.

"Science and Linguistics" (1946)

William H. Whyte, Jr.

U.S. writer and sociologist, 1917–1999

1 The great enemy of communication, we find, is the illusion of it.

Fortune, Sept. 1950. This is frequently paraphrased as "the biggest problem in communication is the illusion that it has taken place."

2 This book is about the organization man. . . . The people I am talking about . . . are not the workers, nor are they the white-collar people in the usual, clerk sense of the word. These people only work for the Organization. The ones I am talking about *belong* to it as well.

The Organization Man ch. 1 (1956)

Ann Widdecombe

British politician, 1947–

1 [*Of Michael Howard:*] [He has] something of the night in his personality.

Quoted in *Observer* (London), 11 May 1997

Norbert Wiener

U.S. mathematician, 1894–1964

1 We have decided to call the entire field of control and communication theory, whether in the machine or the animal, by the name *Cybernetics,* which we form from the Greek [for] *steersman.*

Cybernetics introduction (1948)

2 Scientific discovery consists in the interpretation for our own convenience of a system of existence which has been made with no eye to our convenience at all.

The Human Use of Human Beings ch. 7 (1949)

3 The automatic machine . . . is the precise economic equivalent of slave labor. . . . It is perfectly clear that this will produce an unemployment situation, in comparison with which . . . the depression of the thirties will seem a pleasant joke.

The Human Use of Human Beings ch. 10 (1950)

Elie Wiesel

Romanian-born U.S. writer, 1928–2016

1 Never shall I forget that night, the first night in [a concentration] camp, which has turned my life into one long night, seven times cursed and seven times sealed. . . . Never shall I forget those moments which murdered my God and my soul and turned my dreams to dust. Never shall I forget these things, even if I am condemned to live as long as God Himself. Never.

Night ch. 3 (1960)

2 Take sides. Neutrality helps the oppressor, never the victim. Silence encourages the tormentor, never the tormented.

Nobel Peace Prize acceptance speech, Oslo, Norway, 11 Dec. 1986

3 The opposite of love is not hate, it's indifference.

Quoted in *U.S. News and World Report,* 27 Oct. 1986. The same quotation, with "it is" instead of "it's," appeared in Jess Lair, *I Ain't Much Baby—But I'm All I've Got* (1969) (quoting an anonymous student).

4 God of forgiveness, do not forgive those murderers of Jewish children here [at Auschwitz].

Quoted in *Times* (London), 27 Jan. 1995

Kate Douglas Wiggin

U.S. children's book writer and educator, 1856–1923

1 When Joy and Duty clash
Let Duty go to smash.
Rebecca of Sunnybrook Farm ch. 11 (1903)

Richard Wilbur

U.S. poet, 1921–2017

1 We milk the cow of the world.
"Epistemology" l. 3 (1950)

2 The good grey guardians of art
Patrol the halls on spongy shoes,
Impartially protective, though
Perhaps suspicious of Toulouse.
"Museum Piece" l. 1 (1950)

3 Mind in its purest play is like some bat
That beats about in caverns all alone,
Contriving by a kind of senseless wit
Not to conclude against a wall of stone.
"Mind" l. 1 (1956)

Ella Wheeler Wilcox

U.S. poet, 1850–1919

1 Laugh and the world laughs with you;
Weep, and you weep alone.
"Solitude" l. 1 (1883)

2 No question is ever settled
Until it is settled right.
"Settle the Question Right" l. 7 (1888)

3 To sin by silence, when we should protest,
Makes cowards out of men.
"Protest" l. 1 (1914)

Oscar Wilde

Irish playwright and poet, 1854–1900

1 The things of nature do not really belong to
us; we should leave them to our children as we
have received them.
Speech, Ottawa, 12 May 1882

2 That he is indeed one of the very greatest
masters of painting is my opinion. And I may
add that in this opinion Mr. Whistler himself
entirely concurs.
"Mr. Whistler's Ten O'Clock," *Pall Mall Gazette,* Feb.
1885

3 Every great man nowadays has his disciples,
and it is usually Judas who writes the
biography.
"The Butterfly's Boswell" (1887)

4 We have really everything in common with
America nowadays, except, of course, language.
The Canterville Ghost pt. 1 (1887)
See George Bernard Shaw 58

5 Pathology is rapidly becoming the basis of
sensational literature, and in art, as in politics,
there is a great future for monsters.
Saturday Review, 7 May 1887

6 Day by day the old order of things changes,
and new modes of thought pass over our
world, and it may be that, before many years,
talking will have taken the place of literature,
and the personal screech silenced the music of
impersonal utterance. Something of the dignity
of the literary calling will probably be lost, and
it is perhaps a dangerous thing for a country to
be too eloquent.
"Should Geniuses Meet?" (1887)

7 The public is wonderfully tolerant. It forgives
everything except genius.
Intentions "The Critic as Artist" pt. 1 (1891)

8 [George] Meredith's a prose Browning, and so
is Browning. He used poetry as medium for
writing in prose.
Intentions "The Critic as Artist" pt. 1 (1891)

9 Nothing that is worth knowing can be taught.
Intentions "The Critic as Artist" pt. 1 (1891)

10 Anybody can write a three-volumed novel. It merely requires a complete ignorance of both life and literature.
Intentions "The Critic as Artist" pt. 1 (1891)

11 More difficult to do a thing than to talk about it? Not at all. That is a gross popular error. It is very much more difficult to talk about a thing than to do it. In the sphere of actual life that is of course obvious. Anybody can make history. Only a great man can write it.
Intentions "The Critic as Artist" pt. 1 (1891)

12 The criticism which I have quoted is criticism of the highest kind. It treats the work of art simply as a starting-point for a new creation. It does not confine itself . . . to discovering the real intention of the artist and accepting that as final.
Intentions "The Critic as Artist" pt. 1 (1891)

13 All art is immoral. . . . For emotion for the sake of emotion is the aim of art, and emotion for the sake of action is the aim of life, and of that practical organization of life that we call society.
Intentions "The Critic as Artist" pt. 2 (1891)

14 Man is least himself when he talks in his own person. Give him a mask, and he will tell you the truth.
Intentions "The Critic as Artist" pt. 2 (1891)

15 In matters of religion, it [truth] is simply the opinion that has survived.
Intentions "The Critic as Artist" pt. 2 (1891)

16 As long as war is regarded as wicked, it will always have its fascination. When it is looked upon as vulgar, it will cease to be popular.
Intentions "The Critic as Artist" pt. 2 (1891)

17 The English mind is always in a rage. The intellect of the race is wasted in the sordid and stupid quarrels of second-rate politicians or third-rate theologians.
Intentions "The Critic as Artist" pt. 2 (1891)

18 The proper school to learn art in is not Life but Art.
Intentions "The Decay of Lying" (1891)

19 Life imitates Art far more than Art imitates Life.
Intentions "The Decay of Lying" (1891)

20 The essay simply represents an artistic standpoint, and in aesthetic criticism attitude is everything. For in art there is no such thing as a universal truth. A Truth in art is that whose contradictory is also true.
Intentions "The Truth of Masks" (1891)
See Bohr 1

21 There is no such thing as a moral or an immoral book. Books are well written, or badly written. That is all.
The Picture of Dorian Gray preface (1891)

22 There is only one thing in the world worse than being talked about, and that is not being talked about.
The Picture of Dorian Gray ch. 1 (1891)
See Behan 4; Modern Proverbs 70

23 Conscience and cowardice are really the same things, Basil. Conscience is the trade-name of the firm. That is all.
The Picture of Dorian Gray ch. 1 (1891)

24 I choose my friends for their good looks, my acquaintances for their good characters, and my enemies for their good intellects. A man cannot be too careful in the choice of his enemies.
The Picture of Dorian Gray ch. 1 (1891)

25 The only way to get rid of a temptation is to yield to it.
The Picture of Dorian Gray ch. 2 (1891)
See Balzac 1; Clementina Graham 1; Mae West 19; Wilde 53

26 The only difference between a caprice and a life-long passion is that the caprice lasts a little longer.
The Picture of Dorian Gray ch. 2 (1891)

27 How sad it is! I shall grow old, and horrible, and dreadful. But this picture will remain always young. It will never be older than this particular day of June. . . . If it were only the other way! If it were I who was to be always young, and the picture that was to grow old! For that—for that—I would give everything! Yes, there is nothing in the whole world I would not give! I would give my soul for that!
The Picture of Dorian Gray ch. 2 (1891)

28 I adore simple pleasures. . . . They are the last refuge of the complex.
The Picture of Dorian Gray ch. 2 (1891)

29 I wonder who it was defined man as a rational animal. It was the most premature definition ever given. Man is many things, but he is not rational.

The Picture of Dorian Gray ch. 2 (1891)

30 [*Sir Thomas Burdon:*] They say that when good Americans die they go to Paris. . . .
[*Lady Agatha:*] Really! And where do bad Americans go to when they die? . . .
[*Lord Henry:*] They go to America.

The Picture of Dorian Gray ch. 3 (1891). Similar dialogue appears in Wilde's *A Woman of No Importance* (1893) as well.
See Oliver Wendell Holmes 4

31 Nowadays most people die of a sort of creeping common sense, and discover when it is too late that the only things one never regrets are one's mistakes.

The Picture of Dorian Gray ch. 3 (1891)

32 Nowadays people know the price of everything and the value of nothing.

The Picture of Dorian Gray ch. 4 (1891). In Wilde's play *Lady Windermere's Fan*, act 3 (1892), Lord Darlington replies to the question "What is a cynic?": "A man who knows the price of everything and the value of nothing."

33 Men marry because they are tired; women, because they are curious; both are disappointed.

The Picture of Dorian Gray ch. 4 (1891). Wilde used the same words in *A Woman of No Importance* (1893).

34 When one is in love one always begins by deceiving one's self, and one always ends by deceiving others.

The Picture of Dorian Gray ch. 4 (1891). A very similar statement is found in Wilde's play *A Woman of No Importance*, act 3 (1893).

35 Experience was of no ethical value. It was merely the name men gave to their mistakes.

The Picture of Dorian Gray ch. 4 (1891). A similar quotation occurs in Wilde's play *Lady Windermere's Fan*, act 3 (1892).

36 Children begin by loving their parents; as they grow older they judge them; sometimes they forgive them.

The Picture of Dorian Gray ch. 5 (1891). This passage is repeated in Wilde's play *A Woman of No Importance* (1893) with the words "rarely, if ever" instead of "sometimes."

37 Modern morality consists in accepting the standard of one's age. I consider that for any man of culture to accept the standard of his age is a form of the grossest immorality.

The Picture of Dorian Gray ch. 6 (1891)

38 There is a luxury in self-reproach. When we blame ourselves, we feel that no one else has a right to blame us. It is the confession, not the priest, that gives us absolution.

The Picture of Dorian Gray ch. 8 (1891)

39 Ernest Harrowden, one of those middle-aged mediocrities so common in London clubs who have no enemies, but are thoroughly disliked by their friends.

The Picture of Dorian Gray ch. 15 (1891)
See Wilde 104

40 Her capacity for family affection is extraordinary. When her third husband died, her hair turned quite gold from grief.

The Picture of Dorian Gray ch. 15 (1891). A similar quotation appears in Wilde's play *The Importance of Being Earnest*, act 1 (1895).

41 When a woman marries again it is because she detested her first husband. When a man marries again, it is because he adored his first wife. Women try their luck; men risk theirs.

The Picture of Dorian Gray ch. 15 (1891)

42 Crime belongs exclusively to the lower orders. I don't blame them in the smallest degree. I should fancy that crime was to them what art is to us, simply a method of procuring extraordinary sensations.

The Picture of Dorian Gray ch. 19 (1891)

43 To get back my youth I would do anything in the world, except take exercise, get up early, or be respectable.

The Picture of Dorian Gray ch. 19 (1891)

44 The books that the world calls immoral are books that show the world its own shame.

The Picture of Dorian Gray ch. 19 (1891)

45 The recognition of private property has really harmed Individualism, and obscured it, by confusing a man with what he possesses.

"The Soul of Man Under Socialism" (1891)

46 The true perfection of man lies, not in what man has, but in what man is.

"The Soul of Man Under Socialism" (1891)

47 To live is the rarest thing in the world. Most people exist, that is all.

"The Soul of Man Under Socialism" (1891)

48 All authority is quite degrading. It degrades those who exercise it, and degrades those over whom it is exercised.

"The Soul of Man Under Socialism" (1891)

49 The fact is, that civilization requires slaves. The Greeks were quite right there. Unless there are slaves to do the ugly, horrible, uninteresting work, culture and contemplation become almost impossible. Human slavery is wrong, insecure, and demoralizing. On mechanical slavery, on the slavery of the machine, the future of the world depends.

"The Soul of Man Under Socialism" (1891)

50 We are dominated by Journalism. In America the President reigns for four years, and Journalism governs for ever and ever.

"The Soul of Man Under Socialism" (1891)

51 The fact is, that the public have an insatiable curiosity to know everything, except what is worth knowing.

"The Soul of Man Under Socialism" (1891)

52 It is absurd to divide people into good and bad. People are either charming or tedious.

Lady Windermere's Fan act 1 (1892)

53 I can resist everything except temptation.

Lady Windermere's Fan act 1 (1892)
See Balzac 1; Clementina Graham 1; Mae West 19; Wilde 25

54 Whenever people agree with me, I always feel I must be wrong.

Lady Windermere's Fan act 3 (1892)

55 We are all in the gutter, but some of us are looking at the stars.

Lady Windermere's Fan act 3 (1892)

56 In this world there are only two tragedies. One is not getting what one wants, and the other is getting it.

Lady Windermere's Fan act 3 (1892)
See Goethe 15; T. H. Huxley 4; Modern Proverbs 14; George Bernard Shaw 16; Teresa of Ávila 2; Wilde 74

57 We [women] have a much better time than they [men] have. There are far more things forbidden to us than are forbidden to them.

A Woman of No Importance act 1 (1893)

58 It is perfectly monstrous the way people go about, nowadays, saying things against one behind one's back that are absolutely and entirely true.

A Woman of No Importance act 1 (1893)

59 You can't make people good by Act of Parliament.

A Woman of No Importance act 1 (1893)

60 One knows so well the popular idea of health. The English country gentleman galloping after a fox—the unspeakable in full pursuit of the uneatable.

A Woman of No Importance act 1 (1893)

61 Twenty years of romance make a woman look like a ruin; but twenty years of marriage make her something like a public building.

A Woman of No Importance act 1 (1893)

62 Men always want to be a woman's first love. That is their clumsy vanity. We women have a more subtle instinct about things. What we like is to be a man's last romance.

A Woman of No Importance act 2 (1893)

63 Study the Peerage. . . . It is the best thing in fiction the English have ever done.

A Woman of No Importance act 3 (1893)

64 Moderation is a fatal thing, Lady Hunstanton. Nothing succeeds like excess.

A Woman of No Importance act 3 (1893)

65 Wickedness is a myth invented by good people to account for the curious attractiveness of others.

"Phrases and Philosophies for the Use of the Young" (1894)

66 It is only by not paying one's bills that one can hope to live in the memory of the commercial classes.

"Phrases and Philosophies for the Use of the Young" (1894)

67 Any preoccupation with ideas of what is right or wrong in conduct shows an arrested intellectual development.

"Phrases and Philosophies for the Use of the Young" (1894)

68 Ambition is the last refuge of the failure.

"Phrases and Philosophies for the Use of the Young" (1894)

69 A truth ceases to be true when more than one person believes in it.

"Phrases and Philosophies for the Use of the Young" (1894)

70 The old believe everything: the middle-aged suspect everything: the young know everything.

"Phrases and Philosophies for the Use of the Young" (1894)

71 To love oneself is the beginning of a life-long romance.

"Phrases and Philosophies for the Use of the Young" (1894)

72 Science can never grapple with the irrational. That is why it has no future before it, in this world.

An Ideal Husband act 1 (1895)

73 Life is never fair.

An Ideal Husband act 2 (1895)
See Jimmy Carter 5; John Kennedy 24

74 In all things connected with money I have had a luck so extraordinary that sometimes it has made me almost afraid. I remember having read somewhere, in some strange book, that when the gods wish to punish us they answer our prayers.

An Ideal Husband act 2 (1895)
See Goethe 15; T. H. Huxley 4; Modern Proverbs 14; George Bernard Shaw 16; Teresa of Ávila 2; Wilde 56

75 Morality is simply the attitude we adopt towards people whom we personally dislike.

An Ideal Husband act 2 (1895)

76 The truth is rarely pure, and never simple.

The Importance of Being Earnest act 1 (1895)

77 I have invented an invaluable permanent invalid called Bunbury, in order that I may be able to go down into the country whenever I choose.

The Importance of Being Earnest act 1 (1895)

78 To lose one parent may be regarded as a misfortune; to lose both seems like carelessness.

The Importance of Being Earnest act 1 (1895)

79 Relations are simply a tedious pack of people, who haven't got the remotest knowledge of how to live, nor the smallest instinct about when to die.

The Importance of Being Earnest act 1 (1895)

80 All women become like their mothers. That is their tragedy. No man does. That's his.

The Importance of Being Earnest act 1 (1895). The same lines appear, as a dialogue between Lord Illingworth and Mrs. Allonby, in A Woman of No Importance, act 2 (1893).

81 The good ended happily, and the bad unhappily. That is what fiction means.

The Importance of Being Earnest act 2 (1895)

82 The "Love that dare not speak its name" in this century is such a great affection of an elder for a younger man as there was between David and Jonathan, such as Plato made the very basis of his philosophy, and such as you find in the sonnets of Michael Angelo and Shakespeare.

Testimony at his first trial, 30 Apr. 1895
See Alfred Douglas 1; Wilde 83

83 On account of it ["the Love that dare not speak its name"] I am placed where I am now. It is beautiful, it is fine, it is the noblest form of affection. There is nothing unnatural about it. It is intellectual, and it repeatedly exists between an elder and a younger man, when the elder man has intellect, and the younger man has all the joy, hope, and glamour of life before him.

Testimony at his first trial, 30 Apr. 1895
See Alfred Douglas 1; Wilde 82

84 And I? May I say nothing, my Lord?

Remark before being led from courtroom after his second trial, 25 May 1895

85 Where there is Sorrow there is holy ground.

Letter to Alfred Douglas, Jan.–Mar. 1897

86 I was a man who stood in symbolic relations to the art and culture of my age. . . . The gods had given me almost everything. I had genius, a distinguished name, high social position, brilliancy, intellectual daring: I made art a philosophy, and philosophy an art: I altered the minds of men and the colors of things: there was nothing I said or did that did not make people wonder.

Letter to Alfred Douglas, Jan.–Mar. 1897

87 I treated Art as the supreme reality, and life as a mere mode of fiction: I awoke the imagination of my century so that it created myth and legend around me: I summed up all systems in a phrase, and all existence in an epigram.

Letter to Alfred Douglas, Jan.–Mar. 1897

88 Most people are other people. Their thoughts are someone else's opinions, their lives a mimicry, their passions a quotation.
Letter to Alfred Douglas, Jan.–Mar. 1897

89 Just as there are false dawns before the dawn itself, and winter-days so full of sudden sunlight that they will cheat the wise crocus into squandering its gold before its time, and make some foolish bird call to its mate to build on barren boughs, so there were Christians before Christ. . . . The unfortunate thing is that there have been none since.
Letter to Alfred Douglas, Jan.–Mar. 1897

90 To recognize that the soul of a man is unknowable is the ultimate achievement of Wisdom. The final mystery is oneself. When one has weighed the sun in a balance, and measured the steps of the moon, and mapped out the seven heavens star by star, there still remains oneself. Who can calculate the orbit of his own soul?
Letter to Alfred Douglas, Jan.–Mar. 1897

91 I never saw a man who looked
With such a wistful eye
Upon that little tent of blue
Which prisoners call the sky.
The Ballad of Reading Gaol pt. 1, st. 3 (1898)

92 Yet each man kills the thing he loves,
By each let this be heard,
Some do it with a bitter look,
Some with a flattering word.
The coward does it with a kiss,
The brave man with a sword!
The Ballad of Reading Gaol pt. 1, st. 7 (1898)
See Roberts 1

93   He who lives more lives than one
More deaths than one must die.
The Ballad of Reading Gaol pt. 3, st. 37 (1898)

94 I know not whether Laws be right,
Or whether Laws be wrong;
All that we know who lie in gaol
Is that the wall is strong;
And that each day is like a year,
A year whose days are long.
The Ballad of Reading Gaol pt. 5, st. 1 (1898)

95 How else but through a broken heart
May Lord Christ enter in?
The Ballad of Reading Gaol pt. 5, st. 14 (1898)

96 Over the piano was printed a notice: Please do not shoot the pianist. He is doing his best.
Impressions of America (1906). The *Atchison* (Kan.) *Globe*, 19 Mar. 1883, describes an after-dinner speech made by Wilde in Paris about his experiences in the United States: "The brightest and best of the many stories he related was one to the effect that at a ball in Leadville he saw a notice over the piano which read: 'Please don't shoot the pianist. He is doing his best.'" Barry Popik has found a reference in *Harper's Bazaar*, 20 Dec. 1879, to a California church sign stating, "It is requested that you will not shoot at the organist. He does his best."

97 Every American bride is taken there [Niagara Falls], and the sight of the stupendous waterfall must be one of the earliest, if not the keenest, disappointments in American married life.
Impressions of America (1906). Wilde was earlier quoted by the *Daily Patriot* (Harrisburg, Pa.), 13 Aug. 1883: "Niagara . . . is the first disappointment in the married life of many Americans who spend their honeymoon there."

98 This is one of the compliments that mediocrity pays to those who are not mediocre.
Quoted in *N.Y. Daily Tribune*, 6 Jan. 1882. Sometimes quoted as "Caricature is the tribute which mediocrity pays to genius." Wilde was referring to Gilbert and Sullivan's satirization of him in their opera *Patience*.

99 Poets, you know, are always ahead of science; all the great discoveries of science have been stated before in poetry.
Quoted in *Philadelphia Press*, 17 Jan. 1882

100 California is an Italy without its art. There are subjects for the artist, but it is universally true that the only scenery which inspires utterance is that which man feels himself the master of. The mountains of California are so gigantic that they are not favorable to art or poetry. There are good poets in England but none in Switzerland. There the mountains are too high. Art cannot add to nature.
Quoted in *Denver Tribune*, Apr. 1882

101 As for borrowing Mr. Whistler's ideas about art, the only thoroughly original ideas I have

ever heard him express have had reference to his own superiority as a painter over painters greater than himself.

Quoted in *Truth,* Jan. 1890

102 It is indeed a burning shame that there should be one law for men and another law for women. . . . I think that there should be no law for anybody.

Quoted in *The Sketch,* 9 Jan. 1895

103 I have put my genius into my life; I have put only my talent into my works.

Quoted in André Gide, Letter to his mother, 30 Jan. 1895

104 [*Of George Bernard Shaw:*] An excellent man; he has no enemies; and none of his friends like him.

Quoted in George Bernard Shaw, Letter to Ellen Terry, 25 Sept. 1896
See Wilde 39

105 I have been correcting the proofs of my poems. In the morning, after hard work, I took a comma out of one sentence. . . . In the afternoon, I put it back again.

Quoted in Robert Sherard, *The Life of Oscar Wilde* (1906). Wilde was earlier quoted making a similar comma comment, in the *Daily Graphic* (New York, N.Y.), 8 May 1884.

106 [*Reply when asked, as an Oxford undergraduate, why he was staring raptly at a pair of vases on his mantelpiece:*] Oh, would that I could live up to my blue china!

Quoted in Robert Sherard, *The Life of Oscar Wilde* (1906). Wilde was earlier quoted in the *St. Louis Daily Globe-Democrat,* 10 Sept. 1881: "We must try to live up to our blue china."

107 There are works which wait, and which one does not understand for a long time; the reason is that they bring answers to questions which have not yet been raised; for the question often arrives a terribly long time after the answer.

Quoted in André Gide, *Oscar Wilde: In Memoriam* (1910)

108 [*To a customs official upon arriving in New York in 1882:*] I have nothing to declare but my genius.

Quoted in Archibald Henderson, *European Dramatists* (1913). Arthur Ransome, in *Oscar Wilde: A Critical Study* (1912), wrote that "Wilde sailed for

New York . . . to tell Customs Officials that he had nothing to declare except his genius." No earlier reference to Wilde's alleged statement has been found.

109 Work is the curse of the drinking classes of this country.

Quoted in Frank Harris, *Oscar Wilde: His Life and Confessions* (1916). "Work is the curse of the drinkin' classes" appeared earlier in the *Ottumwa* (Iowa) *Semi-Weekly Courier,* 8 Apr. 1902.

110 Prayer must never be answered: if it is, it ceases to be prayer, and becomes a correspondence.

Quoted in Laurence Housman, *Écho de Paris* (1923)

111 One must have a heart of stone to read the death of Little Nell [in Charles Dickens's *The Old Curiosity Shop*] without laughing.

Quoted in *Letters to the Sphinx from Oscar Wilde* (1930)

112 We Irish are too poetical to be poets; we are a nation of brilliant failures, but we are the greatest talkers since the Greeks.

Quoted in W. B. Yeats, *Autobiography* (1938)

113 I never put off till to-morrow what I can possibly do . . . the day after.

Quoted in Hesketh Pearson, *Oscar Wilde, His Life and Wit* (1946). Ellipsis in the original. Mark Twain had written, "Never put off till to-morrow what you can do day after to-morrow just as well" (*The Galaxy,* July 1870).
See Proverbs 248

114 It is sad. One half of the world does not believe in God, and the other half does not believe in me.

Quoted in Hesketh Pearson, *Oscar Wilde, His Life and Wit* (1946). Appeared in French in an article about Wilde in *Écho de Paris,* 6 Dec. 1891.

115 Each class preaches the importance of those virtues it need not exercise. The rich harp on the value of thrift, the idle grow eloquent over the dignity of labor.

Quoted in Hesketh Pearson, *Oscar Wilde, His Life and Wit* (1946)

116 Don't tell me that you have exhausted life. When a man says that one knows that Life has exhausted him.

Quoted in Hesketh Pearson, *Oscar Wilde, His Life and Wit* (1946)

117 Each time one loves is the only time that one has ever loved. Difference of object does not alter singleness of passion. It merely intensifies it.

Quoted in Hesketh Pearson, *Oscar Wilde, His Life and Wit* (1946)

118 [*Reply when asked to name the hundred best books of all time:*] I fear that would be impossible, because I have only written five.

Quoted in Hesketh Pearson, *Oscar Wilde, His Life and Wit* (1946)

119 To believe is very dull. To doubt is intensely engrossing. To be on the alert is to live, to be lulled into security is to die.

Quoted in Hesketh Pearson, *Oscar Wilde, His Life and Wit* (1946)

120 I am dying, as I have lived, beyond my means.

Quoted in Hesketh Pearson, *Oscar Wilde: His Life and Wit* (1946). Karl Beckson, in *I Can Resist Everything Except Temptation,* notes: "On December 14, 1900, Robert Ross wrote to More Adey that Wilde 'said he was "dying above his means,"' though Ross does not say what prompted the remark (*Letters,* 847); the earliest published version of Wilde's famous remark is apparently that in Robert Sherard's *Life of Oscar Wilde* (New York, 1906), 421, reporting Wilde's reaction to a 'huge fee' for an operation ('I suppose that I shall have to die beyond my means'); in Harris, ch. 26 (as in Pearson), Wilde responds to the cost of champagne (. . . 'when it was brought [he] declared that he was dying as he had lived, "beyond his means."'"

121 Consistency is the last refuge of the unimaginative.

Quoted in Hesketh Pearson, *Oscar Wilde: His Life and Wit* (1946)

122 Mr. Whistler always spelt art, and we believe still spells it, with a capital "I."

Quoted in Hesketh Pearson, *Oscar Wilde: His Life and Wit* (1946)

123 Decidedly one of us will have to go.

Quoted in H. Montgomery Hyde, *Oscar Wilde* (1975). Wilde allegedly made this remark on his deathbed in reference to the wallpaper in his Paris hotel room. A variant of this is quoted in a letter from William Butler Yeats to Lady Gregory, 17 Dec. 1908: "This friend of Oscar Wilde told me a strange heroic thing about Wilde. . . . He was in great poverty, often with not money for food & had declared that it was his wall paper that was killing him. 'One of us had to go' he said."

Billy Wilder
Polish-born U.S. film director and screenwriter, 1906–2002

1 [*Of Marilyn Monroe:*] Marilyn was mean. Terribly mean. The meanest woman I have ever met around this town. I have never met anybody as mean as Marilyn Monroe nor as utterly fabulous on the screen, and that includes Garbo.

Quoted in Earl Wilson, *The Show Business Nobody Knows* (1971)

2 Hindsight is always twenty-twenty.

Quoted in J. R. Colombo, *Wit and Wisdom of the Moviemakers* (1979). Earlier, the *Cleveland Plain Dealer,* 28 Nov. 1948, quoted Richard Armour in the *Saturday Evening Post:* "Most people's hindsight is 20-20."

3 You have Van Gogh's ear for music.

Quoted in *L.A. Times,* 26 Apr. 1964

Laura Ingalls Wilder
U.S. writer, 1867–1957

1 [*Comment by the author's mother upon serving blackbird pie after blackbirds destroyed the family's crops:*] There's no great loss without some small gain.

Little House on the Prairie (1935)

Matthew Wilder (Matthew Weiner)
U.S. musician, 1953–

1 Ain't nothin' gonna break my stride
Nobody's gonna slow me down, oh-no
I got to keep on movin'.

"Break My Stride" (song) (1984)

Thornton Wilder
U.S. writer, 1897–1975

1 There is a land of the living and a land of the dead and the bridge is love, the only survival, the only meaning.

The Bridge of San Luis Rey pt. 5 (1928)

2 The dead don't stay interested in us living people for very long. Gradually, gradually, they let go hold of the earth . . . and the ambitions they had . . . and the pleasures they had . . . and the things they suffered . . . and the people they loved. They get weaned away from earth—that's the way I put it—weaned away.

Our Town act 3 (1938). Ellipses in the original.

3 Oh, earth, you're too wonderful for anyone to realize you. . . . Do any human beings ever realize life while they live it?—every, every minute?

Our Town act 3 (1938)

4 The best part of married life is the fights. The rest is merely so-so.

The Matchmaker act 2 (1954)

Robert Wilensky

U.S. computer scientist, 1951–2013

1 We've all heard that a million monkeys banging on a million typewriters will eventually reproduce the entire works of Shakespeare. Now, thanks to the Internet, we know this is not true.

Quoted in *Daily Telegraph* (London), 11 Feb. 1997. Responding to a query from the editor of this book, Wilensky said: "I made this comment as part of some remarks I made to the attendees of [the University of California, Berkeley's] 'Industrial Liaison Program,' I believe in March 1996. . . . I believe I heard this from someone else, but that person said it wasn't original with him either, and I was never able to track down an authoritative source." Less elegant versions of this quip were around long before Wilensky. Bill Dietrich posted a message on the net.misc newsgroup, 29 Nov. 1984: "a million monkeys on a million typewriters will immediately produce Usenet." *See Borel 1; Eddington 2*

Andrew Wiles

English mathematician, 1953–

1 [*Concluding the lecture in which he claimed to have proved the Taniyama-Weil Conjecture for a class of examples, including those necessary to prove Fermat's Last Theorem, 23 June 1993:*] I'll stop here.

Quoted in Simon Singh, *Fermat's Enigma: The Quest to Solve the World's Greatest Mathematical Problem* (1997)

Wilhelm II

German emperor and Prussian king, 1859–1941

1 We have . . . fought for our place in the sun and have won it. It will be my business to see that we retain this place in the sun unchallenged, so that the rays of that sun may exert a fructifying influence upon our foreign trade and traffic.

Speech, Hamburg, Germany, 18 June 1901
See Bülow 1; Pascal 4

2 But should any one essay to detract from our just rights or to injure us, then up and at him with your mailed fist.

Quoted in *Times* (London), 17 Dec. 1897

3 It is my Royal and Imperial command that you concentrate your energies, for the immediate present, upon one single purpose, and that is that you address all your skill and all the valor of my soldiers to exterminate first the treacherous English and walk over General French's contemptible little army.

Attributed in British Expeditionary Force Routine Order, 24 Sept. 1914. This supposed order of 19 Aug. 1914 appears to have been a British forgery, probably written by General Frederick Maurice. General French was John French, the BEF commander.

Wilhelmina

Dutch queen, 1880–1962

1 [*Response to Kaiser Wilhelm II's boast that his guards stood seven feet high:*] Indeed, and when I order my dykes to be thrown open, the water is ten feet deep.

Quoted in *Current Opinion*, 1 Apr. 1923

John Wilkins

English clergyman and scientist, 1614–1672

1 Yet I doe seriously, and upon good grounds, affirme it possible to make a flying Chariot. In which a man may sit, and give such a motion unto it, as shall convey him through the aire. And this perhaps might bee made large enough to carry divers men at the same time, together with foode for their viaticum, and commodities for traffique. It is not the bignesse of any thing in this kind, that can hinder its motion, if the motive faculty be answerable thereunto. We see a great ship swimmes as well as a small corke, and an Eagle flies in the aire as well as a little gnat. . . . So that notwithstanding all these seeming impossibilities, tis likely enough, that there may be a meanes invented of journying to the Moone; And how happy shall they be, that are first successfull in this attempt?

A Discourse Concerning a New World and Another Planet book 1, proposition 14 (1640)

Paul Wilkinson

English political scientist, 1937–2011

1 Fighting terrorism is like being a goalkeeper. You can make a hundred brilliant saves but the only shot that people remember is the one that gets past you.

Quoted in *Daily Telegraph* (London), 1 Sept. 1992

George F. Will

U.S. journalist, 1941–

1 The American condition can be summed up in three sentences we're hearing these days:

"Your check is in the mail."

"I will respect you as much in the morning."

"I am from the government and I am here to help you."

Quoted in *Frederick* (Md.) *News*, 19 July 1976

2 Football combines the two worst features of American life. It is violence punctuated by committee meetings.

Quoted in *N.Y. Times Book Review*, 1 Apr. 1990. An earlier version appeared in *Newsweek*, 6 Sept. 1976: "Football . . . is committee meetings, called huddles, separated by outbursts of violence."

3 Americans are conservative. What they want to conserve is the New Deal.

Quoted in Lou Cannon, *President Reagan: The Role of a Lifetime* (1991)

Emma Willard

U.S. educator, 1787–1870

1 Rocked in the cradle of the deep.

"The Cradle of the Deep" l. 1 (1831)

Frances E. Willard

U.S. educator and reformer, 1839–1898

1 The capacity of the human mind to resist knowledge is nowhere more painfully illustrated than in the postulate laid down by average minds that home is always to be just what it is now—forgetting that in no two consecutive generations has it remained the same.

Quoted in Anna A. Gordon, *What Frances E. Willard Said* (1905)

William III

Dutch-born British king, 1650–1702

1 There was a sure way never to see [my country] lost, and that was to die in the last ditch.

Quoted in Gilbert Burnet, *Bishop Burnet's History of His Own Time* (1724)

Alexander S. Williams

Canadian-born U.S. law enforcement official, 1839–1917

1 [*Remark in 1870s:*] There is more law at the end of a nightstick than in all the statute books.

Quoted in *N.Y. Times*, 23 Mar. 1911

Hank Williams

U.S. country singer and songwriter, 1923–1953

1 Hear that lonesome whippoorwill?
He sounds too blue to fly.
The midnight train is whining low,
I'm so lonesome I could cry.

"I'm So Lonesome I Could Cry" (song) (1942)

2 Hey, good lookin',
What cha got cookin'?
How about cookin' somethin' up with me?

"Hey, Good Lookin'" (song) (1951)

Harry Williams

English songwriter, 1879–1922

1 In the Shade of the Old Apple Tree.

Title of song (1905)

2 I'm Afraid to Come Home in the Dark.

Title of song (1907)
See O. Henry 8

Margery Williams (Margery Bianco)

English-born U.S. children's book writer, 1881–1944

1 "Real isn't how you are made," said the Skin Horse. "It's a thing that happens to you. When a child loves you for a long, long time, not just to play with, but REALLY loves you, then you become Real."

The Velveteen Rabbit (1922)

Robert L. Williams

U.S. psychologist, 1930–2020

1 Ebonics may be defined as the linguistic and paralinguistic features which on a concentric continuum represents the communicative competence of the West African, Caribbean, and United States slave descendant of African origin.

Ebonics: The True Language of Black Folks (1975)

Robin Williams

U.S. comedian, 1951–2014

1 Cocaine is God's way of telling us we make too much money.

Quoted in *Winnipeg Free Press,* 8 Aug. 1981

2 If it's the Psychic Network why do they need a phone number?

Quoted in *Manly* (Australia) *Daily,* 30 Mar. 2004

Sarah Williams

English poet, 1837–1868

1 Though my soul may set in darkness, it will rise in perfect light;
I have loved the stars too truly to be fearful of the night.

"The Old Astronomer" l. 15 (1868)

Tennessee Williams (Thomas Lanier Williams III)

U.S. playwright, 1911–1983

1 They told me to take a streetcar named Desire, and transfer to one called Cemeteries, and ride six blocks and get off at—Elysian Fields!

A Streetcar Named Desire sc. 1 (1947)

2 Turn that off! I won't be looked at in this merciless glare!

A Streetcar Named Desire sc. 1 (1947)

3 STELL-LAHHHHH!

A Streetcar Named Desire sc. 3 (1947)

4 I don't want realism. I want magic!

A Streetcar Named Desire sc. 9 (1947)

5 I have always depended on the kindness of strangers.

A Streetcar Named Desire sc. 11 (1947)
See Maugham 8

6 Mrs. Stone found herself thinking that surely such beauty was a world of its own whose anarchy had a sort of godly license.

The Roman Spring of Mrs. Stone pt. 1 (1950). The 1961 film of this novel (screenplay by Gavin Lambert) has the line "People who are very beautiful make their own laws."

7 *Make voyages!—Attempt them!*—there's nothing else.

Camino Real block 8 (1953)

8 What is the victory of a cat on a hot tin roof?—I wish I knew. . . . Just staying on it, I guess, as long as she can . . .

Cat on a Hot Tin Roof act 1 (1955). Ellipses in the original.

9 I'm not living with you. We occupy the same cage.

Cat on a Hot Tin Roof act 1 (1955)

10 We're all of us sentenced to solitary confinement inside our own skins, for life!

Orpheus Descending act 2, sc. 1 (1958)

Theodore S. "Ted" Williams

U.S. baseball player, 1918–2002

1 I think without question the hardest single thing to do in sport is to hit a baseball. A .300 hitter, that rarest of breeds these days, goes through life with the certainty that he will fail at his job seven out of ten times.

My Turn at Bat pt. 4 (1969)

2 When I walk down the street I'd like for them to say, There goes Ted Williams, the best hitter in baseball.

Quoted in *Nevada State Journal,* 6 July 1941. Later, Williams's self-image became more grandiose: "A man has to have goals—for a day, for a lifetime—and that was mine, to have people say, 'There goes Ted Williams, the greatest hitter who ever lived'" (*My Turn at Bat,* pt. 1 [1969]).
See Malamud 1

William Carlos Williams

U.S. poet, 1883–1963

1 Who shall say I am not
the happy genius of my household?

"Danse Russe" l. 18 (1917)

2 So much depends
upon

a red wheel

barrow

glazed with rain
water

beside the white
chickens.

"The Red Wheelbarrow" l. 1 (1923)

3 Your thighs are appletrees
whose blossoms touch the sky.
Which sky? The sky
Where Watteau hung a lady's
slipper.

"Portrait of a Lady" l. 1 (1934)

4   Your knees
are a southern breeze—or
a gust of snow. Agh! what
sort of man was Fragonard?

"Portrait of a Lady" l. 5 (1934)

5 Say it, no ideas but in things.

Paterson bk. 1, sec. 1 (1946)

6 It is difficult
to get the news from poems
yet men die miserably every day
for lack
of what is found there.

"Asphodel, That Greeny Flower" bk. 1, l. 317 (1955)

Marianne Williamson

U.S. author, 1952–

1 Our deepest fear is not that we are inadequate.
Our deepest fear is that we are powerful beyond
measure. It is our light, not our darkness, that
most frightens us.

A Return to Love ch. 7 (1992). Frequently
misattributed to Nelson Mandela.

Roy Williamson

Scottish folk musician, 1937–1990

1 O Flower of Scotland,
When will we see
Your like again,
That fought and died for
Your wee bit hill and glen
And stood against him,
Proud Edward's Army,
And sent him homeward
Tae think again.

"Flower of Scotland" (song) (1968)

Wendell Willkie

U.S. politician and lawyer, 1892–1944

1 The Constitution does not provide for first and
second class citizens.

An American Program ch. 2 (1944)

Meredith Willson (Robert Meredith Reiniger)

U.S. composer and playwright, 1902–1984

1 Seventy-six trombones led the big parade,
With a hundred and ten cornets close at hand.
They were followed by rows and rows
Of the finest virtuosos,
The cream of ev'ry famous band.

"Seventy-six Trombones" (song) (1957)

2 Ya got trouble, folks, right here in River City.
Trouble, with a capital "T" and that rhymes with
"P" and that stands for pool!

"Ya Got Trouble" (song) (1957)

Alexander Wilson

Scottish-born U.S. naturalist and poet, 1766–1813

1 The woods are full of them!

American Ornithology preface (1808). Wilson tells
the story of a boy who brought flowers to his mother,
saying "Look, my dear ma! What beautiful flowers I
have found growing in our place! Why, all the woods
are full of them!"

August Wilson (Frederick August Kittel)

U.S. playwright, 1945–2005

1 White folks don't understand about the blues.
They hear it come out, but they don't know how
it got there. They don't understand that's life's
way of talking. You don't sing to feel better. You
sing 'cause that's a way of understanding life.

Ma Rainey's Black Bottom act 2 (1984)

2 You line up at the door with your hands out. I
give you the lint from my pockets. I give you
my sweat and my blood. I ain't got no tears. I
done spent them.

Fences act 1, sc. 3 (1985)

Brian Wilson

U.S. rock musician and songwriter, 1942–

1 And she'll have fun, fun, fun
Till her daddy takes the T-bird away.

"Fun, Fun, Fun" (song) (1964)

2 I wish they all could be California girls.
"California Girls" (song) (1965)

Charles E. Wilson

U.S. businessman and government official,
1890–1961

1 For years I thought what was good for our
country was good for General Motors, and vice
versa. The difference did not exist.

Testimony at confirmation hearing, 15 Jan. 1953.
Wilson, formerly president of General Motors, was
nominated to become secretary of defense. At his
confirmation hearing he was asked whether he could
make a decision furthering the interests of the U.S.
government but adverse to the interests of General
Motors or other companies in which he held stock.
Wilson's comment is often misquoted "What's good
for General Motors is good for the country." Ralph
Keyes points out in *Nice Guys Finish Seventh* (1992)
that a precursor of the quotation is "a line from a
corrupt banker in the 1939 movie *Stagecoach*: 'And
remember this: What's good for the bank is good for
the country.'"

Edmund Wilson

U.S. writer, 1895–1972

1 [*Statement in interview, 1962:*] I attribute such
success as I have had to the use of the periodic
sentence.

Quoted in John Bartlett, *Familiar Quotations*, 14th ed.
(1968)

Harold Wilson

British prime minister, 1916–1995

1 All these financiers, all the little gnomes in
Zurich.

Speech in House of Commons, 12 Nov. 1956. Earlier
in the same year, the *Manchester Guardian*, 7 Mar.
1956, had referred to "little gnomes sitting over ticker
tapes in Zurich."

2 The Britain that is going to be forged in the
white heat of this revolution will be no place for
restrictive practices or for outdated methods on
either side of industry.

Speech at Labor Party Conference, Scarborough,
England, 1 Oct. 1963. Often quoted as "white heat
of technology" or "white heat of the technological
revolution."

3 A week is a long time in politics.

Quoted in *N.Y. Times*, 24 July 1966. The wording in
this 1966 *Times* article was actually "One of Harold
Wilson's favorite sayings is that a week is a long time

in the life of a Prime Minister." *The Dictionary of
Modern Proverbs* has earlier citations not associated
with Wilson, from *New York Times Magazine*, 3 Dec.
1961 ("a week is a long time in African politics") and
George Wolfskill, *Revolt of the Conservatives* (1962)
("in politics a week is a long time").

Harriette Wilson

English courtesan, 1789–1846

1 I shall not say why and how I became, at
the age of fifteen, the mistress of the Earl of
Craven.
Memoirs (1825)

2 "*Vous me voyez là, madame, honnête homme, de
    cinq pieds et neuf pouces.*"
"*Madame est persuadée de vos cinq pieds, mais elle
    n'est pas si sûre de vos neuf pouces.*"
"You see me, madame, an honest man of five
    feet nine inches."
"Madame is persuaded of your five feet, but she
    is not so sure of your nine inches."
Memoirs (1825)

Harry L. Wilson

U.S. writer, 1867–1939

1 I'll be pushed just so far and no farther.
Ruggles of Red Gap ch. 3 (1915)

James Wilson

U.S. politician and judge, 1742–1798

1 "The United States," instead of the "People of
the United States," is the toast given. This is
not politically correct.
Chisholm v. Georgia (1793). Earliest known use of the
phrase *politically correct.*

Robert R. Wilson

U.S. physicist, 1914–2000

1 [*Of a proposed particle accelerator:*] It has nothing
to do directly with defending our country,
except to make it worth defending.
Testimony before U.S. Congress, Joint Committee on
Atomic Energy, 16 Apr. 1969

Sloan Wilson

U.S. novelist, 1920–2003

1 The Man in the Gray Flannel Suit.
Title of book (1955)

William Wilson
English author, fl. 1851

1 We hope it will not be long before we may have other works of Science-Fiction, as we believe such works likely to fulfil a good purpose, and create an interest, where, unhappily, science alone might fail. . . . Campbell says that "Fiction in Poetry is not the reverse of truth, but her soft and enchanting resemblance." Now this applies especially to Science-Fiction, in which the revealed truths of Science may be given, interwoven with a pleasing story which may itself be poetical and *true*—thus circulating a knowledge of the Poetry of Science, clothed in a garb of the Poetry of Life.

A Little Earnest Book upon a Great Old Subject ch. 10 (1851). Earliest known usage of the term *science fiction*. See Gernsback 1

Woodrow Wilson
U.S. president, 1856–1924

1 The most conservative persons I ever met are college undergraduates. The radicals are the men past middle life.

Speech to Inter-Church Conference on Federation, New York, N.Y., 19 Nov. 1905

2 The wisest thing to do with a fool is to encourage him to hire a hall and discourse to his fellow-citizens. Nothing chills nonsense like exposure to the air.

Constitutional Government in the United States ch. 2 (1908)

3 The President is at liberty, both in law and conscience, to be as big a man as he can.

Constitutional Government in the United States ch. 3 (1908)

4 If it is reorganization, a new deal, and a change you are seeking, it is Hobson's choice. I am sorry for you, but it is really vote for me or not vote at all.

Address, Camden, N.J., 24 Oct. 1910
See Franklin Roosevelt 4; Twain 40

5 A presidential campaign may easily degenerate into a mere personal contest and so lose its real dignity and significance. There is no indispensable man.

Speech accepting Democratic presidential nomination, Seagirt, N.J., 7 Aug. 1912

6 When I resist, therefore, when I as a Democrat resist the concentration of power, I am resisting the processes of death, because the concentration of power is what always precedes the destruction of human initiative, and, therefore of human energy.

Address, New York, N.Y., 4 Sept. 1912

7 And there will be no greater burden in our generation than to organize the forces of liberty in our time, in order to make conquest of a new freedom for America.

Campaign speech, Indianapolis, Ind., 3 Oct. 1912

8 We shall not, I believe, be obliged to alter our policy of watchful waiting. And then, when the end comes, we shall hope to see constitutional order restored in distressed Mexico by the concert and energy of such of her leaders as prefer the liberty of their people to their own ambitions.

State of the Union Address, 2 Dec. 1913

9 Our whole duty, for the present, at any rate, is summed up in the motto, "America first."

Speech, New York, N.Y., 20 Apr. 1915

10 There is such a thing as a man being too proud to fight.

Speech, Philadelphia, Pa., 10 May 1915

11 One cool judgment is worth a thousand hasty counsels. The thing to be supplied is light, not heat.

Address on preparedness, Pittsburgh, Pa., 29 Jan. 1916

12 Never . . . murder a man who is committing suicide.

Letter to Bernard Baruch, 19 Aug. 1916. According to the *American Heritage Dictionary of American*

13 It must be a peace without victory. . . . Only a peace between equals can last. Only a peace the very principle of which is equality and a common participation in a common benefit.

Address to Senate on essential terms of peace in Europe, 22 Jan. 1917

14 A little group of willful men [eleven senators conducting a filibuster against a bill authorizing the president to arm U.S. merchant ships], representing no opinion but their own, have rendered the great government of the United States helpless and contemptible.

Statement to the nation, 4 Mar. 1917

15 The world must be made safe for democracy.

Address to Joint Session of Congress asking for declaration of war, 2 Apr. 1917
See Thomas Wolfe 1

16 It is a fearful thing to lead this great peaceful people into war, into the most terrible and disastrous of all wars, civilization itself seeming to be in the balance. But the right is more precious than peace, and we shall fight for the things which we have always carried nearest our hearts. . . . To such a task we dedicate our lives and our fortunes, everything that we are and everything that we have, with the pride of those who know that the day has come when America is privileged to spend her blood and her might for the principles that gave her birth and happiness and the peace which she has treasured.

Address to Joint Session of Congress asking for declaration of war, 2 Apr. 1917

17 The program of the world's peace, therefore, is our program; and that program, the only possible program, as we see it, is this: I. Open covenants of peace, openly arrived at, after which there shall be no private understandings of any kind but diplomacy shall proceed always frankly and in the public view.

"Fourteen Points" Address to Joint Session of Congress, 8 Jan. 1918

18 II. Absolute freedom of navigation upon the seas, outside territorial waters, alike in peace and in war, except as the seas may be closed in whole or in part by international action for the enforcement of international covenants.

"Fourteen Points" Address to Joint Session of Congress, 8 Jan. 1918

19 III. The removal, so far as possible, of all economic barriers and the establishment of an equality of trade conditions among all the nations consenting to the peace and associating themselves for its maintenance.

"Fourteen Points" Address to Joint Session of Congress, 8 Jan. 1918

20 IV. Adequate guarantees given and taken that national armaments will be reduced to the lowest point consistent with domestic safety.

"Fourteen Points" Address to Joint Session of Congress, 8 Jan. 1918

21 V. A free, open-minded, and absolutely impartial adjustment of all colonial claims, based upon a strict observance of the principle that in determining all such questions of sovereignty the interests of the populations concerned must have equal weight with the equitable claims of the government whose title is to be determined.

"Fourteen Points" Address to Joint Session of Congress, 8 Jan. 1918

22 XIV. A general association of nations must be formed under specific covenants for the purpose of affording mutual guarantees of political independence and territorial integrity to great and small states alike.

"Fourteen Points" Address to Joint Session of Congress, 8 Jan. 1918

23 Sometimes people call me an idealist. Well, that is the way I know I am an American. America, my fellow citizens—I do not say it in disparagement of any other great people—America is the only idealistic nation in the world.

Address supporting League of Nations, Sioux Falls, S.D., 8 Sept. 1919

24 Once lead this people into war and they'll forget there ever was such a thing as tolerance.

Quoted in John Dos Passos, Mr. Wilson's War (1917)

25 If it is a ten-minute speech it takes me all of two weeks to prepare it; if it is a half-hour

speech it takes me a week; if I can talk as long as I want to it requires no preparation at all. I am ready now.

Quoted in *The Operative Miller,* Apr. 1918. This citation was discovered by Garson O'Toole, who also found a precursor: "Lincoln once made a most apt suggestion applicable to such cases. When asked to appear upon some important occasion and deliver a five-minute speech, he said that he had no time to prepare five-minute speeches, but that he could go and speak an hour at any time." (First Biennial Message of Governor H. H. Markham to the Legislature of the State of California, 3 Jan. 1893) *See Pascal 1; Thoreau 34*

26 [*Alleged comment upon viewing the film* Birth of a Nation, *18 Feb. 1915:*] It is like writing history with lightning. And my only regret is that it is all so terribly true.

Attributed in *Scribner's Magazine,* Nov. 1937. This is the earliest documented evidence for this quotation, and it appears unlikely to be authentic. Marjorie Brown King, the last survivor among the people at the 1915 screening, said that Wilson walked out of the room afterwards without comment. However, at least the first part of the quotation may have been associated with Wilson as early as February 1915. According to a 2004 article by Arthur Lennig, the *New York American,* 28 Feb. 1915, quoted *Birth of a Nation* director D. W. Griffith commenting that the film "received very high praise from high quarters in Washington. . . . I was gratified when a man we all revere, or ought to, said it teaches history by lightning."

Dale Wimbrow
U.S. writer, 1895–1954

1 When you get what you want in your struggle for pelf,
And the world makes you King for a day,
Then go to the mirror and look at yourself,
And see what that guy has to say.
"The Guy in the Glass," l. 1, *American Magazine,* May 1934

2 You can fool the whole world down the pathway of years,
And get pats on the back as you pass,
But your final reward will be heartaches and tears
If you've cheated the guy in the glass.
"The Guy in the Glass" l. 17, *American Magazine,* May 1934

Duchess of Windsor (Wallis Simpson)
U.S.-born British aristocrat, 1896–1986

1 You can't be too rich or too thin.

Quoted in *L.A. Times,* 17 June 1970. This line is associated with the Duchess of Windsor, but *Harper's Bazaar,* July 1963, referred to "You can never be too rich or too thin" as a "wise old adage." According to Alec Lewis, *The Quotable Quotations Book,* Truman Capote claimed to have said "No woman can be too rich or too thin" on the *David Susskind Show* in 1958.

Amy Winehouse
English singer and songwriter, 1983–2011

1 They tried to make me go to Rehab
I said no, no, no
Yes, I've been black, but when I come back
You'll know, know, know!
I ain't got the time
And if my daddy thinks I'm fine
Just try to make me go to rehab
I won't go, go, go.
"Rehab" (song) (2006)

Septimus Winner
U.S. songwriter, 1827–1902

1 Listen to the mockingbird, listen to the mockingbird,
Still singing where the weeping willows wave.
"Listen to the Mockingbird" (song) (1855)

2 Oh where, oh where ish mine little dog gone;
Oh where, oh where can he be . . .
His ears cut short and his tail cut long:
Oh where, oh where ish he.
"Der Deitcher's Dog" (song) (1864)

Ella Winter
Australian-born English writer, 1898–1980

1 [*Remark to Thomas Wolfe, who then asked to use the phrase as title for his 1937 book:*] Don't you know you can't go home again?
Quoted in Ella Winter, Letter to Elizabeth Nowell, 7 May 1943

Jeanette Winterson
English novelist and critic, 1959–

1 [Roger Fry] gave us the term "Post-Impressionist," without realizing that the

late twentieth century would soon be entirely fenced in with posts.

Art Objects pt. 1 (1995)

John Winthrop

English-born colonial American governor, 1588–1649

1 For we must consider that we shall be as a City upon a hill. The eyes of all people are upon us. Soe that if we shall deal falsely with our God in this work we have undertaken, and so cause him to withdraw his present help from us, we shall be made a story and a byword throughout the world.

"A Modell of Christian Charity" (1630). Winthrop, governor of the Massachusetts Bay Colony, wrote this in a discourse composed aboard the *Arbella* during its voyage to Massachusetts.
See Bible 208

Owen Wister

U.S. novelist, 1860–1938

1 Fetterman Events, 1885–1886. Card game going on. Big money. Several desperadoes playing. One John Lawrence among others. A player calls him a son-of-a-b——. John Lawrence does not look as if he had heard it. Merely passes his fingers strokingly up and down his pile of chips. When his hand is done, he looks across at the man and says, "You smile when you call me that."

"Frontier Notes, 1894" (1894). Wister's "Frontier Notes, 1894" are reprinted in *Owen Wister Out West: His Journals and Letters,* ed. Fanny Kemble Wister (1958).

2 When you call me that, *smile!*
The Virginian ch. 2 (1902)

Forest E. Witcraft

U.S. Scouting administrator, 1894–1967

1 A hundred years from now it will not matter what my bank account was, the sort of house I lived in, or the kind of car I drove. But the world may be different, because I was important in the life of a boy.

"Within My Power," *Scouting,* Oct. 1950

Ludwig Wittgenstein

Austrian-born English philosopher, 1889–1951

1 *Die Welt ist alles, was der Fall ist.*
The world is everything that is the case.
Tractatus Logico-Philosophicus Proposition 1 (1922)

2 *Die Grenzen meiner Sprache bedeuten die Grenzen meiner Welt.*
The limits of my language mean the limits of my world.
Tractatus Logico-Philosophicus Proposition 5.6 (1922)

3 *Wovon man nicht sprechen kann, darüber muss man schweigen.*
What we cannot speak about we must pass over in silence.
Tractatus Logico-Philosophicus Proposition 7 (1922)

4 What is your aim in philosophy?—To show the fly the way out of the fly-bottle.
Philosophical Investigations pt. 1, sec. 309 (1953)

P. G. Wodehouse

English writer, 1881–1975

1 To Herbert Westbrook, without whose never-failing advice, help, and encouragement this book would have been finished in half the time.
A Gentleman of Leisure dedication (1910)

2 He spoke with a certain what-is-it in his voice, and I could see that, if not actually disgruntled, he was far from being gruntled.
The Code of the Woosters ch. 1 (1938)

3 Slice him where you like, a hellhound is always a hellhound.
The Code of the Woosters ch. 1 (1938)

4 Ice formed on the butler's upper slopes.
Pigs Have Wings ch. 5 (1952)

5 "I hate you, I hate you!" cried Madeline, a thing I didn't know anyone ever said except in the second act of a musical comedy.
Stiff Upper Lip, Jeeves ch. 15 (1963)

6 It is never difficult to distinguish between a Scotsman with a grievance and a ray of sunshine.
Quoted in Richard Usborne, *Wodehouse at Work to the End* (1977)

Jim Wohlford

U.S. baseball player, 1951–

1 Ninety per cent of this game is half mental.
   Quoted in *Maryville* (Mo.) *Daily Forum*, 4 Apr. 1974.
   This or a similar formulation is often attributed to
   Yogi Berra, but the evidence for Wohlford's having
   said it predates that for Berra.

Christa Wolf

German writer, 1929–2011

1 It is this ability to bear what is unbearable and
   to go on living, to go on doing what one is used
   to doing—it is this uncanny ability that the
   existence of the human species is based on.
   Medea ch. 10 (1996) (translation by John Cullen)

Naomi Wolf

U.S. writer, 1962–

1 We are in the midst of a violent backlash
   against feminism that uses images of female
   beauty as a political weapon against women's
   advancement: the beauty myth.
   *The Beauty Myth: How Images of Beauty Are Used
   Against Women* ch. 1 (1990)

2 "Beauty" is a currency system like the gold
   standard. Like any economy it is determined
   by politics, and in the modern age in the West
   it is the last, best belief system that keeps male
   dominance intact.
   The Beauty Myth ch. 1 (1990)

3 When women breached the power structure in
   the 1980s, the two economies finally merged.
   Beauty was no longer just a symbolic form of
   currency; it literally *became* money.
   The Beauty Myth ch. 2 (1990)

4 What little girls learn is not the desire for the
   other, but the desire to be desired.
   The Beauty Myth ch. 5 (1990)

Humbert Wolfe

Italian-born English poet and government
official, 1886–1940

1 You cannot hope
   to bribe or twist,
   thank God! the
   British journalist.

   But, seeing what

the man will do
unbribed, there's
no occasion to.
The Uncelestial City (1930)

James Wolfe

British general, 1727–1759

1 The General . . . repeated nearly the whole of
   Gray's Elegy . . . adding, as he concluded, that
   he would prefer being the author of that poem
   to the glory of beating the French to-morrow.
   Reported in J. Playfair, "Biographical Account
   of J. Robison," *Transactions of the Royal Society of
   Edinburgh* (1815)

Thomas Wolfe

U.S. novelist, 1900–1938

1 "Where they got you stationed now, Luke?" . . .
   ["]In Norfolk at the Navy base," Luke answered,
   "m-m-making the world safe for hypocrisy."
   Look Homeward, Angel pt. 3, ch. 36 (1929)
   See Woodrow Wilson 15

2 Duh poor guy! . . . Maybe he's found out by now
   dat he'll neveh live long enough to know duh
   whole of Brooklyn. It'd take a guy a lifetime
   to know Brooklyn t'roo an' t'roo. An' even den,
   yuh wouldn't know it all.
   "Only the Dead Know Brooklyn" (1935)

3 If a man has talent and cannot use it, he has
   failed. If he has a talent and uses only half of
   it, he has partly failed. If he has a talent and
   learns somehow to use the whole of it, he has
   gloriously succeeded, and won a satisfaction
   and a triumph few men ever know.
   The Web and the Rock ch. 29 (1939)

Tom Wolfe

U.S. writer, 1930–2018

1 Radical Chic . . . is only radical in Style; in its
   heart it is part of Society and its tradition—
   Politics, like Rock, Pop, and Camp, has its uses.
   New York, 8 June 1970
   See Krim 1

2 All these years, in short, I had assumed that
   in art, if nowhere else, seeing is believing.
   Well—how very shortsighted! . . . I had gotten
   it backward all along. Not "seeing is believing,"

you ninny, but "believing is seeing," for *Modern Art has become completely literary: the paintings and other works exist only to illustrate the text.*
The Painted Word introduction (1975)

3 The "Me" Decade and the Third Great Awakening.
Title of article, *New York Magazine*, 23 Aug. 1976

4 A sect, incidentally, is a religion with no political power.
"The 'Me' Decade and the Third Great Awakening" (1976). In later repetitions of this thought, Wolfe used the word *cult* rather than *sect*.
See Feibleman 1

5 One of the phrases that kept running through their conversation was "pushing the outside of the envelope." The "envelope" was a flight-test term referring to the limits of a particular aircraft's performance, how tight a turn it could make at such-and-such a speed, and so on. "Pushing the outside," probing the outer limits, of the envelope seemed to be the great challenge and satisfaction of flight test.
The Right Stuff ch. 1 (1979)

6 The idea was to prove at every foot of the way up that you were one of the elected and anointed ones who had *the right stuff* and could move higher and higher and even—ultimately, God willing, one day—that you might be able to join that special few at the very top, that elite who had the capacity to bring tears to men's eyes, the very Brotherhood of the Right Stuff itself.
The Right Stuff ch. 2 (1979)

7 The Bonfire of the Vanities.
Title of book (1987). Wolfe derived his title from the 1497 public burning of objects considered sinful by the priest Girolamo Savonarola in Florence, Italy.

8 On Wall Street he and a few others—how many?—three hundred, four hundred, five hundred?—had become precisely that . . . Masters of the Universe.
The Bonfire of the Vanities ch. 1 (1987). Ellipsis in the original. Wolfe took the phrase "Masters of the Universe" from a name used in the early 1980s for action figures by the Mattel toy company and in a related television cartoon show.

9 A liberal is a conservative who has been arrested.
The Bonfire of the Vanities ch. 24 (1987). An earlier version ("A liberal is a conservative who just got arrested") was printed in Peter Kreeft, *The Unaborted Socrates* (1983).

Raymond Wolfinger
U.S. political scientist, 1931–2015

1 The plural of anecdote is data.
Quoted in *Issues in Health Care Regulation*, ed. Richard S. Gordon (1980). Far more popular is a later counter-proverb, "The plural of anecdote is not data," first attested in 1982.

Mary Wollstonecraft
English feminist, 1759–1797

1 Nothing, I am sure, calls forth the faculties so much as the being obliged to struggle with the world.
Thoughts on the Education of Daughters "Matrimony" (1787)

2 Virtue can only flourish amongst equals.
A Vindication of the Rights of Men (1790)

3 She [woman] was created to be the toy of man, his rattle, and it must jingle in his ears whenever, dismissing reason, he chooses to be amused.
A Vindication of the Rights of Woman ch. 2 (1792)

4 Till women are more rationally educated, the progress of human virtue and improvement in knowledge must receive continual checks.
A Vindication of the Rights of Woman ch. 3 (1792)

5 To give a sex to mind was not very consistent with the principles of a man [Jean-Jacques Rousseau] who argued so warmly, and so well, for the immortality of the soul.
A Vindication of the Rights of Woman ch. 3 (1792)

6 Taught from their infancy that beauty is woman's sceptre, the mind shapes itself to the body, and roaming round its gilt cage, only seeks to adorn its prison.
A Vindication of the Rights of Woman ch. 3 (1792)

7 If women be educated for dependence; that is, to act according to the will of another fallible being, and submit, right or wrong, to power, where are we to stop?
A Vindication of the Rights of Woman ch. 3 (1792)

8 How can a rational being be ennobled by any thing that is not obtained by its *own* exertions?
A Vindication of the Rights of Woman ch. 3 (1792)

9 A king is always a king—and a woman always a woman: his authority and her sex, ever stand between them and rational converse.
A Vindication of the Rights of Woman ch. 4 (1792)

10 Women are systematically degraded by receiving the trivial attentions, which men think it manly to pay to the sex, when, in fact, they are insultingly supporting their own superiority.
A Vindication of the Rights of Woman ch. 4 (1792)

11 It would be an endless task to trace the variety of meannesses, cares, and sorrows, into which women are plunged by the prevailing opinion, that they were created rather to feel than reason, and that all the power they obtain, must be obtained by their charms and weakness.
A Vindication of the Rights of Woman ch. 4 (1792)

12 I do not wish them [women] to have power over men; but over themselves.
A Vindication of the Rights of Woman ch. 4 (1792)

13 Women ought to have representatives, instead of being arbitrarily governed without having any direct share allowed them in the deliberations of government.
A Vindication of the Rights of Woman ch. 9 (1792)

14 Till society is very differently constituted, parents, I fear, will still insist on being obeyed, because they will be obeyed, and constantly endeavor to settle that power on a Divine right which will not bear the investigation of reason.
A Vindication of the Rights of Woman ch. 11 (1792)

15 The pure animal spirits, which make both mind and body shoot out, and unfold the tender blossoms of hope, are turned sour, and vented in vain wishes or pert repinings, that contract the faculties and spoil the temper; else they mount to the brain, and sharpening the understanding before it gains proportional strength, produce that pitiful cunning which disgracefully characterizes the female mind— and I fear will characterize it whilst women remain the slaves of power!
A Vindication of the Rights of Woman ch. 12 (1792)

16 Executions, far from being useful examples to the survivors, have, I am persuaded, a quite contrary effect, by hardening the heart they ought to terrify. Besides, the fear of an ignominious death, I believe, never deterred anyone from the commission of a crime, because in committing it the mind is roused to activity about present circumstances.
Letters Written During a Short Residence in Sweden, Norway, and Denmark Letter 19 (1796)

17 The same energy of character which renders a man a daring villain would have rendered him useful to society, had that society been well organized.
Letters Written During a Short Residence in Sweden, Norway, and Denmark Letter 19 (1796)

18 It is the preservation of the species, not of individuals, which appears to be the design of Deity throughout the whole of nature.
Letters Written During a Short Residence in Sweden, Norway, and Denmark Letter 22 (1796)

19 Was not the world a vast prison, and women born slaves?
The Wrongs of Woman; or, Maria ch. 1 (1798)

Thomas Wolsey
English cardinal and statesman, ca. 1475–1530

1 If I had served God as diligently as I have done the King, He would not have given me over in my gray hairs.

Quoted in George Cavendish, *The Life and Death of Cardinal Wolsey* (manuscript at British Museum, 1558)
See Shakespeare 452

Kenneth Wolstenholme
English sportscaster, 1920–2002

1 They think it's all over—it is now.

Television broadcast in final moments of World Cup soccer championship, 30 July 1966

Stevie Wonder (Steveland Judkins Hardaway)
U.S. singer and songwriter, 1950–

1 You are the sunshine of my life
That's why I'll always be around,
You are the apple of my eye,
Forever you'll stay in my heart.

"You Are the Sunshine of My Life" (song) (1972)

Natalie Wood
U.S. actress, 1938–1981

1 The only time a woman really succeeds in changing a man is when he's a baby.

Quoted in Barbara Rowes, *The Book of Quotes* (1979)

Victoria Claflin Woodhull
U.S. reformer, 1838–1927

1 I have an inalienable constitutional and natural right to love whom I may, to love as long or as short a period as I can, to change that love every day if I please!

Woodhull and Claflin's Weekly, 20 Nov. 1871

Bob Woodward
U.S. journalist, 1943–

1 Democracy dies in darkness.

Quoted in *Berkshire Eagle,* 10 Dec. 2008. This was adopted as the slogan of the *Washington Post* in 2017.

C. Vann Woodward
U.S. historian, 1908–1999

1 Southerners have repeated the American rhetoric of self admiration and sung the perfection of American institutions ever since the Declaration of Independence. But for half that time they lived intimately with a great social evil and the other half with its aftermath. . . . The South's preoccupation was with guilt, not with innocence, with the reality of evil, not with the dream of perfection. Its experience . . . was on the whole a thoroughly un-American one.

The Burden of Southern History ch. 1 (1960)

Stanley Woodward
U.S. sportswriter, 1894–1965

1 A proportion of our eastern ivy colleges are meeting little fellows another Saturday before plunging into the strife and the turmoil.

N.Y. Herald Tribune, 14 Oct. 1933. This football reference is the earliest known usage of the term *ivy colleges,* later Ivy League. Ivy League first appeared (as far as is known) in articles in the *Christian Science Monitor* and other newspapers, 7 Feb. 1935, antedating the first use of 1939 given by historical dictionaries.

William E. Woodward
U.S. author, 1874–1950

1 De-bunking means simply taking the bunk out of things.

Bunk ch. 1 (1923)

Virginia Woolf (Adeline Virginia Stephen)
English novelist, 1882–1941

1 Each had his past shut in him like the leaves of a book known to him by heart; and his friends could only read the title.

Jacob's Room ch. 5 (1922)

2 [*Of James Joyce's* Ulysses:] Never did I read such tosh. As for the first 2 chapters we will let them pass, but the 3rd 4th 5th 6th—merely the scratching of pimples on the body of the bootboy at Claridges.

Letter to Lytton Strachey, 24 Apr. 1922

3 On or about December 1910 human character changed. . . . All human relations have shifted—those between masters and servants, husbands and wives, parents and children. And when human relations change there is at the same time a change in religion, conduct, politics, and literature.
"Mr. Bennett and Mrs. Brown" (1924)

4 Those comfortably padded lunatic asylums which are known, euphemistically, as the stately homes of England.
The Common Reader "Lady Dorothy Nevill" (1925)
See Crisp 2; Hemans 3

5 [*Of Elizabethan drama:*] The word-coining genius, as if thought plunged into a sea of words and came up dripping.
The Common Reader "Notes on an Elizabethan Play" (1925)

6 Mrs. Dalloway said she would buy the flowers herself.
Mrs. Dalloway pt. 1, sec. 1 (1925)

7 I found myself thinking with intense curiosity about death. Yet if I'm persuaded of anything, it is of mortality—Then why this sense that death is going to be a great excitement?—something positive, active?
Letter to Vita Sackville-West, 19 Nov. 1926

8 It was done; it was finished. Yes, she thought, laying down her brush in extreme fatigue, I have had my vision.
To the Lighthouse pt. 3, ch. 14 (1927)

9 A woman must have money and a room of her own if she is to write fiction.
A Room of One's Own ch. 1 (1929)

10 Why are women . . . so much more interesting to men than men are to women?
A Room of One's Own ch. 2 (1929)

11 Women have served all these centuries as looking-glasses possessing the magic and delicious power of reflecting the figure of a man at twice its natural size.
A Room of One's Own ch. 2 (1929)

12 When, however, one reads of a witch being ducked, of a woman possessed by devils, of a wise woman selling herbs, or even of a very remarkable man who had a mother, then I think we are on the track of a lost novelist, a suppressed poet, of some mute and inglorious Jane Austen, some Emily Brontë who dashed her brains out on the moor or mopped and mowed about the highways crazed with the torture that her gift had put her to. Indeed, I would venture to guess that Anon, who wrote so many poems without signing them, was often a woman.
A Room of One's Own ch. 3 (1929)

13 This is an important book, the critic assumes, because it deals with war. This is an insignificant book because it deals with the feelings of women in a drawing-room.
A Room of One's Own ch. 4 (1929)

14 I have lost friends, some by death . . . others through sheer inability to cross the street.
The Waves (1931)

15 Death is the enemy. . . . Against you I will fling myself, unvanquished and unyielding, O Death!
The Waves (1931)

16 Therefore if you insist upon fighting to protect me, or "our" country, let it be understood, soberly and rationally between us, that you are fighting to gratify a sex instinct which I cannot share; to procure benefits which I have not shared and probably will not share; but not to gratify my instincts, or to protect myself or my country. For . . . in fact, as a woman, I have no country. As a woman I want no country. As a woman my country is the whole world.
Three Guineas pt. 3 (1938)

17 One has to secrete a jelly in which to slip
quotations down people's throats—and one
always secretes too much jelly.

Letter to Margaret Llewelyn Davies, 4 July 1938

18 [*Final diary entry*:] Occupation is essential. And
now with some pleasure I find that it's seven;
and must cook dinner. Haddock and sausage
meat. I think it is true that one gains a certain
hold on sausage and haddock by writing them
down.

Diary, 8 Mar. 1941. Woolf committed suicide on 28
Mar. 1941.

19 Dearest, I feel certain that I am going mad
again: I feel we cant go through another of
those terrible times. And I shant recover
this time. I begin to hear voices, and cant
concentrate. So I am doing what seems the best
thing to do.

Suicide note to her husband, 18 Mar. 1941

20 Everything has gone from me but the certainty
of your goodness. I cant go on spoiling your life
any longer. I dont think two people could have
been happier than we have been.

Suicide note to her husband, 18 Mar. 1941

21 Further, the war—our waiting while the knives
sharpen for the operation—has taken away the
outer wall of security. . . . We pour to the edge
of a precipice . . . and then? I can't conceive that
there will be a 27th June 1941.

A Writer's Diary (1953) (entry for 22 June 1940).
Woolf committed suicide on 28 Mar. 1941.

Alexander Woollcott
U.S. writer, 1887–1943

1 The ink-stained wretches who turn out books
and plays.

N.Y. Times, 18 Sept. 1921

2 The two oldest professions in the world—
ruined by amateurs.

Shouts and Murmurs "The Actor and the Streetwalker"
(1922)

3 Germany was the cause of Hitler just as much
as Chicago is responsible for the Chicago
Tribune.

Radio broadcast, 23 Jan. 1943. Woollcott's last words
before the microphone.

4 All the things I really like to do are either
immoral, illegal, or fattening.

Quoted in *Readers Digest*, Dec. 1933. Although this
quip is usually credited to Woollcott, Garson O'Toole
has discovered an article in the *Albany Evening News*,
16 Sept. 1933, indicating that Woollcott, in a radio
broadcast, told a story about a Mr. Frank Rand of St.
Louis, in which Rand stated: "It seems as if anything
I like is either illegal or immoral or fattening."

5 [Michael] Arlen, for all his reputation, is not a
bounder. He is every other inch a gentleman.

Quoted in Louis Untermeyer, *A Treasury of Laughter*
(1946). Sometimes attributed to Rebecca West, but
the earliest known reference to West's having said it
is not until 1980.
See Lillie 1

John M. Woolsey
U.S. judge, 1877–1945

1 The words which are criticized as dirty [in
James Joyce's *Ulysses*] are old Saxon words
known to almost all men and, I venture, to
many women, and are such words as would be
naturally and habitually used, I believe, by the
types of folk whose life, physical and mental,
Joyce is seeking to describe. In respect of the
recurrent emergence of the theme of sex in
the minds of his characters, it must always be
remembered that his locale was Celtic and his
season spring.

United States v. One Book Called "Ulysses" (1933)

2 I am quite aware that owing to some of its
scenes *Ulysses* is a rather strong draught to
ask some sensitive, though normal, persons
to take. But my considered opinion, after long
reflection, is that, whilst in many places the
effect of *Ulysses* on the reader undoubtedly
is somewhat emetic, nowhere does it tend to
be an aphrodisiac. *Ulysses* may, therefore, be
admitted into the United States.

United States v. One Book Called "Ulysses" (1933)

Dorothy Wordsworth
English writer, 1771–1855

1 I never saw daffodils so beautiful. They grew
among the mossy stones about and about them;
some rested their heads upon these stones as
on a pillow for weariness; and the rest tossed

and reeled and danced, and seemed as if they verily laughed with the wind that blew upon them over the lake.

"Grasmere Journal," 15 Apr. 1802
See William Wordsworth 25

William Wordsworth

English poet, 1770–1850

1 That best portion of a good man's life,
His little, nameless, unremembered, acts
Of kindness and of love.

"Lines Composed a Few Miles Above Tintern Abbey" l. 34 (1798)

2 We are laid asleep
In body, and become a living soul:
While with an eye made quiet by the power
Of harmony, and the deep power of joy,
We see into the life of things.

"Lines Composed a Few Miles Above Tintern Abbey" l. 46 (1798)

3 We murder to dissect.

"The Tables Turned" l. 28 (1798)

4 The wiser mind
Mourns less for what Age takes away
Than what it leaves behind.

"The Fountain" l. 34 (1799)

5 The harvest of a quiet eye.

"A Poet's Epitaph" l. 51 (1800)

6 Poetry is the spontaneous overflow of powerful feelings: it takes its origin from emotion recollected in tranquillity.

Lyrical Ballads 2nd ed., preface (1802)
See Dorothy Parker 24

7 Who is the happy Warrior? Who is he
Whom every man in arms should wish to be?

"Character of the Happy Warrior" l. 1 (1807)
See Franklin Roosevelt 1

8 Earth has not anything to show more fair:
Dull would he be of soul who could pass by
A sight so touching in its majesty.

"Composed upon Westminster Bridge" l. 1 (1807)

9 It is a beauteous evening, calm and free,
The holy time is quiet as a nun
Breathless with adoration.

"It Is a Beauteous Evening" l. 1 (1807)

10 Never forget what I believe was observed to you by Coleridge, that every great and original writer, in proportion as he is great and original, must himself create the taste by which he is to be relished.

Letter to Lady Beaumont, 21 May 1807

11 Milton! thou shouldst be living at this hour:
England hath need of thee: she is a fen
Of stagnant waters: altar, sword, and pen,
Fireside, the heroic wealth of hall and bower,
Have forfeited their ancient English dower
Of inward happiness.

"London, 1802" l. 1 (1807)

12 My heart leaps up when I behold
A rainbow in the sky:
So was it when my life began;
So is it now I am a man;
So be it when I shall grow old,
Or let me die!
The Child is father of the Man;
And I could wish my days to be
Bound each to each by natural piety.

"My Heart Leaps Up When I Behold" l. 1 (1807). Wordsworth also used the last three lines as the epigraph for his poem "Ode: Intimations of Immortality from Recollections of Early Childhood" (1807).
See Milton 43

13 There was a time when meadow, grove, and
        stream,
    The earth, and every common sight,
    To me did seem
    Apparelled in celestial light,
    The glory and the freshness of a dream.
    "Ode: Intimations of Immortality from Recollections
    of Early Childhood" l. 1 (1807)

14 Our birth is but a sleep and a forgetting:
    The Soul that rises with us, our life's Star,
    Hath had elsewhere its setting,
    And cometh from afar:
    Not in entire forgetfulness,
    And not in utter nakedness,
    But trailing clouds of glory do we come
    From God, who is our home:
    Heaven lies about us in our infancy!
    Shades of the prison-house begin to close
    Upon the growing boy.
    "Ode: Intimations of Immortality from Recollections
    of Early Childhood" l. 58 (1807)

15 And by the vision splendid
    Is on his way attended;
    At length the man perceives it die away,
    And fade into the light of common day.
    "Ode: Intimations of Immortality from Recollections
    of Early Childhood" l. 73 (1807)

16 High instincts before which our mortal nature
    Did tremble like a guilty thing surprised.
    "Ode: Intimations of Immortality from Recollections
    of Early Childhood" l. 146 (1807)

17 Though nothing can bring back the hour
    Of splendor in the grass, of glory in the flower.
    "Ode: Intimations of Immortality from Recollections
    of Early Childhood" l. 177 (1807)

18 To me the meanest flower that blows can give
    Thoughts that do often lie too deep for tears.
    "Ode: Intimations of Immortality from Recollections
    of Early Childhood" l. 202 (1807)

19 I thought of Chatterton, the marvellous boy,
    The sleepless soul that perished in its pride;
    Of him who walked in glory and in joy
    Behind his plough, upon the mountain side:
    By our own spirits are we deified;
    We poets in our youth begin in gladness;
    But thereof comes in the end despondency and
        madness.
    "Resolution and Independence" l. 43 (1807)

20   Thou hast left behind
    Powers that will work for thee; air, earth, and
        skies;
    There's not a breathing of the common wind
    That will forget thee; thou hast great allies;
    Thy friends are exultations, agonies,
    And love, and man's unconquerable mind.
    "To Toussaint L'Ouverture" l. 8 (1807)

21 The world is too much with us; late and soon,
    Getting and spending, we lay waste our powers:
    Little we see in Nature that is ours.
    . . . Great God! I'd rather be
    A Pagan suckled in a creed outworn;
    So might I, standing on this pleasant lea,
    Have glimpses that would make me less
        forlorn;
    Have sight of Proteus rising from the sea;
    Or hear old Triton blow his wreathèd horn.
    "The World Is Too Much with Us" l. 10 (1807)

22 Plain living and high thinking are no more:
    The homely beauty of the good old cause
    Is gone.
    "Written in London. September, 1802" l. 11 (1807)

23 Bliss was it in that dawn to be alive,
    But to be young was very heaven!
    "The French Revolution, as It Appeared to
    Enthusiasts" l. 4 (1809). The same lines appear in
    Wordsworth's *The Prelude*, bk. 9, l. 108 (1850).

24 Wisdom is oft-times nearer when we stoop
    Than when we soar.
    The Excursion bk. 3, l. 231 (1814)

25 I wandered lonely as a cloud
    That floats on high o'er vales and hills,
    When all at once I saw a crowd,
    A host, of golden daffodils.
    "I Wandered Lonely As a Cloud" l. 1 (1815 ed.)
    See Dorothy Wordsworth 1

26 For oft, when on my couch I lie
    In vacant or in pensive mood,
    They flash upon that inward eye
    Which is the bliss of solitude;
    And then my heart with pleasure fills,
    And dances with the daffodils.
    "I Wandered Lonely as a Cloud" l. 19 (1815 ed.)

27 Surprised by joy—impatient as the wind.
    "Surprised by Joy" l. 1 (1815)

28 Scorn not the Sonnet; Critic, you have frowned,
   Mindless of its just honors; with this key
   Shakespeare unlocked his heart.
   "Scorn not the Sonnet" l. 1 (1827)

29 The statue stood
   Of Newton, with his prism, and silent face:
   The marble index of a mind for ever
   Voyaging through strange seas of Thought,
     alone.
   The Prelude bk. 3, l. 60 (1850)

30 One great society alone on Earth,
   The noble Living, and the noble Dead.
   The Prelude bk. 11, l. 393 (1850)
   See John Dewey 1; Hamer 1; Lyndon Johnson 5; Lyndon Johnson 6; Lyndon Johnson 8; Wallas 1

Henry Clay Work

U.S. songwriter, 1832–1884

1 My grandfather's clock was too large for the
   shelf,
   So it stood ninety years on the floor.
   "Grandfather's Clock" (song) (1876)

Henry Wotton

English poet and diplomat, 1568–1639

1 An ambassador is an honest man sent to lie
   abroad for the good of his country.
   Quoted in Izaak Walton, *Reliquiae Wottonianae* (1651).
   Written in the album of Christopher Fleckmore in
   1604.

Herman Wouk

U.S. novelist, 1915–2019

1 The Navy is a master plan designed by geniuses
   for execution by idiots.
   The Caine Mutiny ch. 9 (1951)

2 I kid you not.
   The Caine Mutiny ch. 13 (1951)

Stephen Wozniak

U.S. computer inventor, 1950–

1 Never trust a computer you can't throw out of a
   window.
   Quoted in *Newsbytes*, 26 Sept. 1997

Christopher Wren

British government official and antiquarian,
1675–1747

1 *Si monumentum requiris, circumspice.*
   If you seek a monument, gaze around.
   Inscription in St. Paul's Cathedral, London. This
   reference to the cathedral as the monument of its
   architect, the elder Christopher Wren (1632–1723),
   is attributed to the latter's son, the antiquarian of the
   same name.

Frank Lloyd Wright

U.S. architect, 1867–1959

1 No house should ever be *on* any hill or *on*
   anything. It should be *of* the hill, belonging to
   it, so hill and house could live together each the
   happier for the other.
   An Autobiography bk. 2 (1932)

2 Go as far away as possible from home to build
   your first buildings. The physician can bury his
   mistakes—but the Architect can only advise his
   client to plant vines.
   Two Lectures on Architecture (1931)

3 Tip the world over on its side and everything
   loose will land in Los Angeles.
   Quoted in Art Spiegelman and Bob Schneider, *Whole
   Grains: A Book of Quotations* (1973). Although usually
   attributed to Wright, it was credited to Will Rogers
   ("Tilt this country on end and everything loose will
   slide into Los Angeles") in the *Washington Post*, 17
   May 1964.

James Wright

U.S. poet, 1927–1980

1 I lean back, as the evening darkens and
     comes on.
   A chicken hawk floats over, looking for home.
   I have wasted my life.
   "Lying on a Hammock at William Duffy's Farm in
   Pine Island, Minnesota" l. 11 (1963)

Michael Wright

U.S. musician, 1957–

1 I said a hip hop
   The hippie the hippie
   To the hip hip hop, a you don't stop the rock it

To the bang bang boogie, say up jumped the
   boogie
To the rhythm of the boogie, the beat.
"Rapper's Delight" (song) (1979). Popularized the
term *hip hop*.

Richard Wright

U.S. writer, 1908–1960

1 Goddamit, look! We live here and they live
there. We black and they white. They got things
and we ain't. They do things and we can't. It's
just like living in jail.
Native Son bk. 1 (1940)

2 Who knows when some slight shock,
disturbing the delicate balance between social
order and thirsty aspiration, shall send the
skyscrapers in our cities toppling?
Native Son bk. 1 (1940)

3 Black Power.
Title of book (1954)
See Carmichael 2; Adam Clayton Powell 1

Wilbur Wright 1867–1912 and Orville Wright 1871–1948

U.S. inventors

1 Success. Four flights Thursday morning. All
against twenty-one-mile wind. Started from
level with engine power alone. Average speed
through air thirty-one miles. Longest fifty-nine
seconds. Inform press. Home Christmas.
Telegram to Milton Wright from Kitty Hawk, N.C., 17
Dec. 1903

William Wrigley, Jr.

U.S. industrialist, 1861–1932

1 When two men [in a business] always agree,
one of them is unnecessary.
Quoted in *American Magazine*, Mar. 1931

Allie Wrubel

U.S. songwriter, 1905–1973

1 Zip a dee doo dah,
Zip a dee ay,
My, oh my, what a wonderful day.
"Zip A Dee Doo Dah" (song) (1946)

Thomas Wyatt

English poet, ca. 1503–1542

1 They flee from me, that sometime did me seek
With naked foot, stalking in my chamber.
"They Flee from Me That Sometime Did Me Seek" l.
1 (1557)

William Wycherley

English playwright, ca. 1640–1716

1 You who scribble, yet hate all who write . . .
And with faint praises one another damn.
The Plain Dealer prologue (1677)
See Pope 32

Winnifred Crane Wygal

U.S. social service organization official, 1884–
1972

1 Oh, God, give us courage to change what must
be altered, serenity to accept what cannot be
helped, and insight to know the one from the
other.
The Woman's Press, Mar. 1933. This is the "Serenity
Prayer," the most famous and beloved prayer of
modern times. It is most commonly quoted as,
"God grant me the serenity to accept the things I
cannot change, courage to change the things I can,
and wisdom to know the difference." There has
been considerable controversy and misinformation
about this prayer's origins, and it has usually been
attributed to the great theologian Reinhold Niebuhr.
The first edition of the *Yale Book of Quotations* listed
Niebuhr as the author, but a new interpretation by
William FitzGerald in a forthcoming book (based
on discoveries made by the *Yale Book of Quotations*
editor) argues for Wygal as author. It is not unusual
for important quotations by obscure women to be
ascribed to prominent men.

    The March 1933 sentence above, the beginning of
an article by Wygal, is the earliest known occurrence
of the Serenity Prayer. The other oldest versions
all appeared in contexts related to the Young
Women's Christian Association, of which Wygal
was a longtime staff member, and all followed
Wygal's wording very closely. No attributions of
the prayer to Niebuhr by others have been found
from before 1937, and no one has ever definitively
documented any pre-1950 uses by Niebuhr himself.
In a book devoted to the Serenity Prayer, Niebuhr's
daughter Elisabeth Sifton repeatedly told a story
about his composition of it, with a firmly asserted
dating of 1943. Niebuhr believed he was the author,
although his statements on the origination were
vague. Alcoholics Anonymous, which has made
extensive use of the prayer, has credited him for it.

Wygal was an associate of Niebuhr, and in her diary entry for 31 Oct. 1932 she quoted him as follows: "The victorious man in the day of crisis is the man who has the serenity to accept what he cannot help and the courage to change what must be altered." That sentence featured some of the elements of the Serenity Prayer yet lacked the key "insight" or "wisdom" element, and it was not a prayer. Three times in the 1937 to 1943 period, Wygal herself linked the Serenity Prayer to Niebuhr's name. However, Professor FitzGerald suggests that she may have been motivated by her high regard for Niebuhr and by the power of patriarchy. The textual evidence of Wygal's priority, presented by numerous citations, is overwhelming. Although the answer to the issue of provenance is not certain, the demonstrable facts point to Winnifred Wygal as the coiner who combined pieces apparently drawn from Niebuhr with important other pieces of her own devising to create a most memorable prayer.

Philip Wylie

U.S. author, 1902–1971

1 She ["Mom"] is the bride at every funeral and the corpse at every wedding.
Generation of Vipers ch. 11 (1942)

Tammy Wynette

U.S. country music singer, 1942–1998

1 Our D-I-V-O-R-C-E becomes final today
Me and Little Joe will be going away
I love you both and this will be pure
    H-E-double L for me.
Oh, I wish that we could stop this
    D-I-V-O-R-C-E.
"D-I-V-O-R-C-E" (song) (1968). Cowritten with Bobby Braddock and Curly Putnam.

2 Sometimes it's hard to be a woman
Giving all your love to just one man.
"Stand by Your Man" (song) (1968). Cowritten with Billy Sherrill.

3 Stand by your man.
Give him two arms to cling to
And something warm to come to.
"Stand by Your Man" (song) (1968). Cowritten with Billy Sherrill.

4 Stand by your man
And tell the world you love him
Keep giving all the love you can.
"Stand by Your Man" (song) (1968). Cowritten with Billy Sherrill.
See Hillary Clinton 1

Ed Wynn

U.S. comedian, 1886–1966

1 I have no ambition to be the wealthiest man in the cemetery.
Quoted in *Boston Globe,* 19 Jan. 1932

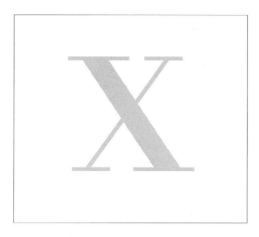

Augustin, Marquis de Ximénèz
French poet, 1726–1817

1 *Attaquons dans ses eaux*
   La perfide Albion!
   Let us attack in her own waters perfidious
       Albion!
   "L'Ère des Français" (1793)

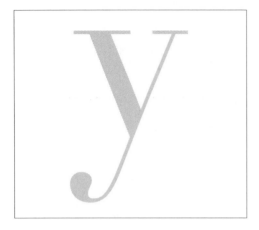

Isoroku Yamamoto
Japanese admiral, 1884–1943

1 Climb Mount Niitaka.

Signal to Japanese strike force to launch attack on Pearl Harbor, 7 Dec. 1941

2 [*Statement to Prime Minister Konoye, 1940:*] If I am told to fight regardless of consequence, I shall run wild considerably for the first six months or a year, but I have utterly no confidence for the second and third years.

Asahi Shimbun, 20–31 Dec. 1945

Leon R. Yankwich
Romanian-born U.S. judge, 1888–1975

1 There are no illegitimate children, only illegitimate parents.

Quoted in *L.A. Times,* 9 Aug. 1928

Victor J. Yannacone, Jr.
U.S. lawyer and environmentalist, 1936–

1 Sue the bastards!

Speech, East Lansing, Mich., 22 Apr. 1970

Peter Yarrow
U.S. folksinger, 1938–

1 Puff, the magic dragon lived by the sea
And frolicked in the autumn mist in a land called Honah Lee.

"Puff (The Magic Dragon)" (song) (1963). Cowritten with Leonard Lipton.

2 A dragon lives forever, but not so little boys,
Painted wings and giant rings make way for other toys.

"Puff (The Magic Dragon)" (song) (1963). Cowritten with Leonard Lipton. The lyrics are based on a 1959 poem by Lipton.

W. B. (William Butler) Yeats
Irish poet, 1865–1939

1 The Celtic Twilight.

Title of book (1893)

2 I will arise and go now, and go to Innisfree,
And a small cabin build there, of clay and wattles made:
Nine bean-rows will I have there, a hive for the honey-bee,
And live alone in the bee-loud glade.

"The Lake Isle of Innisfree" l. 1 (1893)

3 I hear lake water lapping with low sounds by the shore;
While I stand on the roadway, or on the pavements grey,
I hear it in the deep heart's core.

"The Lake Isle of Innisfree" l. 10 (1893)

4 When you are old and grey and full of sleep,
And nodding by the fire, take down this book,
And slowly read.

"When You Are Old" l. 1 (1893)

5 I have spread my dreams under your feet;
Tread softly because you tread on my dreams.

"He Wishes for the Cloths of Heaven" l. 7 (1899)

6 I will find out where she has gone,
And kiss her lips and take her hands;
And walk among long dappled grass,
And pluck till time and times are done
The silver apples of the moon,
The golden apples of the sun.

"The Song of Wandering Aengus" l. 19 (1899)

7 The friends that have it I do wrong
  When ever I remake a song
  Should know what issue is at stake,
  It is myself that I remake.

  *Collected Works in Verse and Prose of William Butler
  Yeats* vol. 2, preliminary poem, l. 1 (1908)

8 Though leaves are many, the root is one;
  Through all the lying days of my youth
  I swayed my leaves and flowers in the sun;
  Now I may wither into the truth.

  "The Coming of Wisdom with Time" l. 1 (1910)

9 The fascination of what's difficult
  Has dried the sap of my veins, and rent
  Spontaneous joy and natural content
  Out of my heart.

  "The Fascination of What's Difficult" l. 1 (1910)

10   A mind
  That nobleness made simple as a fire,
  With beauty like a tightened bow.

  "No Second Troy" l. 6 (1910)

11 Why, what could she have done, being what
      she is?
  Was there another Troy for her to burn?

  "No Second Troy" l. 11 (1910)

12 Where, where but here have Pride and Truth,
  That long to give themselves for wage,
  To shake their wicked sides at youth
  Restraining reckless middle-age?

  "On Hearing that the Students of Our New
  University Have Joined the Agitation Against
  Immoral Literature" l. 1 (1910)

13 I made my song a coat
  Covered with embroideries
  Out of old mythologies.

  "A Coat" l. 1 (1914)

14 Song, let them take it,
  For there's more enterprise
  In walking naked.

  "A Coat" l. 8 (1914)

15 Now as at all times I can see in my mind's eye,
  In their stiff, painted clothes, the pale
      unsatisfied ones . . .
      Hoping to find once more,
  Being by Calvary's turbulence unsatisfied,
  The uncontrollable mystery on the bestial floor.

  "The Magi" l. 1, 6 (1914)

16 In dreams begins responsibility.

  Responsibilities epigraph (1914). Said to be from an
  "Old Play."

17 Romantic Ireland's dead and gone,
  It's with O'Leary in the grave.

  "September, 1913" l. 7 (1914)

18 Be secret and exult,
  Because of all things known
  That is most difficult.

  "To a Friend Whose Work Has Come to Nothing"
  l. 14 (1914)

19 Bald heads, forgetful of their sins,
  Old, learned, respectable bald heads
  Edit and annotate the lines
  That young men tossing on their beds,
  Rhymed out in love's despair
  To flatter beauty's ignorant ear.

  "The Scholars" l. 1 (1915)

20 And cried, "Before I am old
  I shall have written him one
  Poem maybe as cold
  And passionate as the dawn."

  "The Fisherman" l. 37 (1917)

21 I know that I shall meet my fate
  Somewhere among the clouds above;
  Those that I fight I do not hate,
  Those that I guard I do not love;
  My country is Kiltartan Cross,
  My countrymen Kiltartan's poor.

  "An Irish Airman Foresees His Death" l. 1 (1919)

22 Nor law, nor duty bade me fight,
  Nor public men, nor cheering crowds,
  A lonely impulse of delight
  Drove to this tumult in the clouds;
  I balanced all, brought all to mind,
  The years to come seemed waste of breath,
  A waste of breath the years behind
  In balance with this life, this death.

  "An Irish Airman Foresees His Death" l. 9 (1919)

23 It's certain that fine women eat
  A crazy salad with their meat
  Whereby the Horn of Plenty is undone.

  "A Prayer for my Daughter" l. 30 (1919)

24 An intellectual hatred is the worst,
  So let her think opinions are accursed.

  "A Prayer for my Daughter" l. 57 (1919)

25 All think what other people think;
   All know the man their neighbor knows.
   Lord, what would they say
   Did their Catullus walk that way?
   "The Scholars" l. 9 (1919)

26 I have met them at close of day
   Coming with vivid faces
   From counter or desk among grey
   Eighteenth-century houses.
   I have passed with a nod of the head
   Or polite meaningless words.
   "Easter 1916" l. 1 (1921)

27 All changed, changed utterly:
   A terrible beauty is born.
   "Easter 1916" l. 15 (1921)

28 Too long a sacrifice
   Can make a stone of the heart.
   "Easter 1916" l. 57 (1921)

29 Turning and turning in the widening gyre
   The falcon cannot hear the falconer;
   Things fall apart; the center cannot hold;
   Mere anarchy is loosed upon the world,
   The blood-dimmed tide is loosed, and
      everywhere
   The ceremony of innocence is drowned;
   The best lack all conviction, while the worst
   Are full of passionate intensity.
   "The Second Coming" l. 1 (1921)

30 The darkness drops again; but now I know
   That twenty centuries of stony sleep
   Were vexed to nightmare by a rocking cradle,
   And what rough beast, its hour come round at
      last,
   Slouches towards Bethlehem to be born?
   "The Second Coming" l. 18 (1921)

31 We make out of the quarrel with others, rhetoric,
   but of the quarrel with ourselves, poetry.
   "Anima Hominis" (1924)

32 We are one of the great stocks of Europe. We
   are the people of Burke; we are the people of
   Grattan; we are the people of Swift, the people
   of Emmet, the people of Parnell. We have
   created most of the modern literature of this
   country. We have created the best of its political
   intelligence.
   Speech in Seanad on government measure outlawing
   divorce, 11 June 1925

33 I am still of opinion that only two topics can be
   of the least interest to a serious and studious
   mind—sex and the dead.
   Letter to Olivia Shakespear, Oct. 1927

34   The children's eyes
   In momentary wonder stare upon
   A sixty-year-old smiling public man.
   "Among School Children" l. 6 (1928)

35 I dream of a Ledaean body, bent
   Above a sinking fire.
   "Among School Children" l. 9 (1928)

36 For even daughters of the swan can share
   Something of every paddler's heritage.
   "Among School Children" l. 20 (1928)

37 And I though never of Ledaean kind
   Had pretty plumage once—enough of that,
   Better to smile on all that smile, and show
   There is a comfortable kind of old scarecrow.
   "Among School Children" l. 31 (1928)

38 What youthful mother . . .
   Would think her son, did she but see that shape
   With sixty or more winters on its head,
   A compensation for the pang of his birth,
   Or the uncertainty of his setting forth?
   "Among School Children" l. 33, 37 (1928)

39 Both nuns and mothers worship images,
   But those the candles light are not as those
   That animate a mother's reveries,
   But keep a marble or a bronze repose.
   "Among School Children" l. 49 (1928)

40 Labor is blossoming or dancing where
   The body is not bruised to pleasure soul,
   Nor beauty born out of its own despair,
   Nor blear-eyed wisdom out of midnight oil.
   "Among School Children" l. 57 (1928)
   See Quarles 1

41 O chestnut tree, great-rooted blossomer,
   Are you the leaf, the blossom, or the bole?
   O body swayed to music, O brightening glance,
   How can we know the dancer from the dance?
   "Among School Children" l. 61 (1928)

42 A sudden blow: the great wings beating still
   Above the staggering girl.
   "Leda and the Swan" l. 1 (1928)

43 How can those terrified vague fingers push
  The feathered glory from her loosening thighs?
  "Leda and the Swan" l. 5 (1928)

44 A shudder in the loins engenders there
  The broken wall, the burning roof and tower
  And Agamemnon dead.
  "Leda and the Swan" l. 9 (1928)

45 Being so caught up,
  So mastered by the brute blood of the air,
  Did she put on his knowledge with his power
  Before the indifferent beak could let her drop?
  "Leda and the Swan" l. 11 (1928)

46 That is no country for old men. The young
  In one another's arms, birds in the trees
  —Those dying generations—at their song.
  "Sailing to Byzantium" l. 1 (1928)

47 An aged man is but a paltry thing,
  A tattered coat upon a stick, unless
  Soul clap its hands and sing, and louder sing
  For every tatter in its mortal dress.
  "Sailing to Byzantium" l. 9 (1928)

48 Consume my heart away; sick with desire
  And fastened to a dying animal
  It knows not what it is; and gather me
  Into the artifice of eternity.
  "Sailing to Byzantium" l. 21 (1928)

49 Once out of nature I shall never take
  My bodily form from any natural thing,
  But such a form as Grecian goldsmiths make.
  "Sailing to Byzantium" l. 25 (1928)

50 Set upon a golden bough to sing
  To lords and ladies of Byzantium
  Of what is past, or passing, or to come.
  "Sailing to Byzantium" l. 30 (1928)

51 Locke sank into a swoon;
  The Garden died;
  God took the spinning-jenny
  Out of his side.
  "Fragments" l. 1 (1931)

52 A woman can be proud and stiff
  When on love intent;
  But Love has pitched his mansion in
  The place of excrement;
  For nothing can be sole or whole
  That has not been rent.
  "Crazy Jane Talks with the Bishop" l. 13 (1932)

53 The unpurged images of day recede;
  The Emperor's drunken soldiery are abed;
  Night resonance recedes, night-walkers' song
  After great cathedral gong.
  "Byzantium" l. 1 (1933)

54 A starlit or a moonlit dome disdains
  All that man is,
  All mere complexities,
  The fury and the mire of human veins.
  "Byzantium" l. 5 (1933)

55 I hail the superhuman;
  I call it death-in-life and life-in-death.
  "Byzantium" l. 15 (1933)

56 An agony of flame that cannot singe a sleeve.
  "Byzantium" l. 32 (1933)

57 Those images that yet
  Fresh images beget,
  That dolphin-torn, that gong-tormented sea.
  "Byzantium" l. 38 (1933)

58 Savage indignation there
  Cannot lacerate his breast.
  Imitate him if you dare,
  World-besotted traveller; he
  Served human liberty.
  "Swift's Epitaph" l. 1 (1933)
  See Jonathan Swift 34

59 We poets would die of loneliness but for
  women, & we choose our men friends that we
  may have somebody to talk about women with.
  Letter to Ethel Mannin, 15 Nov. 1936. Incorrectly cited
  in some other reference works as from a letter to
  Olivia Shakespear.

60 I must lie down where all the ladders start,
  In the foul rag-and-bone shop of the heart.
  "The Circus Animals' Desertion" l. 39 (1939)

61 Irish poets, learn your trade,
  Sing whatever is well made.
  "Under Ben Bulben" l. 68 (1939)

62 Cast your mind on other days
  That we in coming days may be
  Still the Indomitable Irishry.
  "Under Ben Bulben" l. 81 (1939)

63 Under bare Ben Bulben's head
  In Drumcliff churchyard Yeats is laid.
  "Under Ben Bulben" l. 84 (1939)

64 No marble, no conventional phrase;
   On limestone quarried near the spot
   By his command these words are cut:
   Cast a cold eye
   On life, on death.
   Horseman, pass by!
   "Under Ben Bulben" l. 89 (1939). The final three
   lines are in fact inscribed on Yeats's gravestone.

Jack Yellen
U.S. songwriter, 1892–1991

1 Ain't she sweet?
  See her coming down the street!
  Now I ask you very confidentially,
  Ain't she sweet?
  "Ain't She Sweet?" (song) (1927)

2 The Last of the Red-Hot Mamas.
  Title of song (1928)

3 Happy days are here again!
  The skies above are clear again.
  Let us sing a song of cheer again,
  Happy days are here again!
  "Happy Days Are Here Again" (song) (1929)

Yevgeny Yevtushenko
Russian poet, 1933–2017

1 No Jewish blood runs among my blood,
  But I am as bitterly and hardly hated
  By every anti-Semite
  As if I were a Jew. By this
  I am a Russian.
  "Babi Yar" (1961)

Rafael Yglesias
U.S. writer, 1954–

1 People don't so much believe in God as that
  they choose not to believe in nothing.
  Fearless ch. 17 (1993)

Andrew Young
U.S. politician and civil rights leader, 1932–

1 Nothing is illegal if one hundred businessmen
  decide to do it.
  Quoted in Paul Dickson, *The Official Explanations*
  (1980)

Brigham Young
U.S. religious leader, 1801–1877

1 [*Remark upon first seeing the Great Salt Lake
  valley, 24 July 1847:*] This is the right place.
  Quoted in Wilford Woodruff, *The Utah Pioneers*
  (1880)

Edward Young
English poet and playwright, 1683–1765

1 Life is the desert, life the solitude;
  Death joins us to the great majority.
  The Revenge act 4 (1721)
  See Richard Nixon 10; Petronius 2

2 Be wise with speed;
  A fool at forty is a fool indeed.
  The Love of Fame Satire 2, l. 282 (1725–1728)

3 One to destroy, is murder by the law;
  And gibbets keep the lifted hand in awe;
  To murder thousands, takes a specious name,
  "War's glorious art," and gives immortal fame.
  The Love of Fame Satire 7, l. 55 (1725–1728)
  See Porteus 1; Jean Rostand 1

4 Procrastination is the thief of time.
  Night Thoughts "Night 1" l. 393 (1742–1745)

5 Too low they build, who build beneath the stars.
  Night Thoughts "Night 8" l. 215 (1742–1745)

Michael Young
English sociologist, 1915–2002

1 Today we frankly recognize that democracy
  can be no more than aspiration, and have rule
  not so much by the people as by the cleverest
  people; not an aristocracy of birth, not a
  plutocracy of wealth, but a true meritocracy of
  talent.
  The Rise of the Meritocracy ch. 1 (1958). Apparent
  coinage of the word *meritocracy*.

Neil Young
Canadian singer and songwriter, 1945–

1 Look at Mother Nature on the run
  In the nineteen seventies.
  "After the Gold Rush" (song) (1970)

2 Tin soldiers and Nixon coming,
  We're finally on our own.
  This summer I hear the drumming,
  Four dead in Ohio.

  "Ohio" (song) (1970)

3 My my, hey hey
  Rock and roll is here to stay
  It's better to burn out
  Than to fade away.

  "My My Hey Hey (Out of the Blue)" (song) (1978).
  The last sentence was quoted by singer-songwriter
  Kurt Cobain in his suicide note, 8 Apr. 1994.
  See Richard Cumberland 1

4 Ain't singin' for Pepsi
  Ain't singin' for Coke
  I don't sing for nobody
  Makes me look like a joke
  This note's for you.

  "This Note's for You" (song) (1988)

5 There's a warnin' sign on the road ahead
  There's a lot of people sayin' we'd be better off
    dead
  Don't feel like Satan, but I am to them
  So I try to forget it, any way I can.
  Keep on rockin' in the free world.

  "Rockin' in the Free World" (song) (1989)

6 There's one more kid that will never go to
    school
  Never get to fall in love, never get to be cool.

  "Rockin' in the Free World" (song) (1989)

Rida Johnson Young
U.S. songwriter, 1869–1926

1 Ah, sweet mystery of life
  At last I found thee.

  "Ah! Sweet Mystery of Life" (song) (1910)

Thomas Young
English physicist, physician, and philologist,
1773–1829

1 Radiant light consists in Undulations of the
  Luminiferous Ether.

  "On the Theory of Light and Colors," *Philosophical
  Transactions* (1802)

2 Another ancient and extensive class of
  languages, united by a greater number of
  resemblances than can well be altogether
  accidental, may be denominated the Indo-
  european, comprehending the Indian, the West
  Asiatic, and almost all the European languages.

  "Adelung's Mithridates," *Quarterly Review* (1813).
  Coinage of the term *Indo-European* for the most
  extensive family of languages.

Henny Youngman
U.S. comedian, 1906–1998

1 Take my wife . . . please.

  Quoted in *Chicago Daily Tribune*, 14 June 1959.
  In an interview in *Eye*, 17 Sept. 1992, Youngman
  recalled the origins of this, his trademark line: "'My
  wife came in with several women at the last minute,'
  Youngman says from his New York apartment, as he
  talks about the night he accidentally discovered the
  joke during an airing of Kate Smith's radio show. 'I
  had got her tickets, and I said to the usher, "Take my
  wife, please." I meant get her in the audience, you
  know, and that stuck all these years.'"

2 When I read about the evils of drinking, I gave
  up reading.

  Quoted in *Rocky Mountain News*, 15 July 1994

Marguerite Yourcenar
Belgian-born French-U.S. writer, 1903–1987

1 The true birthplace is that wherein for the first
  time one looks intelligently upon oneself; my
  first homelands have been books.

  Memoirs of Hadrian (1951)

2 There is more than one kind of wisdom, and all
  are essential in the world; it is not bad that they
  should alternate.

  Memoirs of Hadrian (1951)

Malala Yousafzai
Pakistani education activist, 1997–

1 So let us wage a glorious struggle against
  illiteracy, poverty, and terrorism, let us pick
  up our books and our pens, they are the most
  powerful weapons.

  Speech to United Nations General Assembly, New
  York, N.Y., 12 July 2013

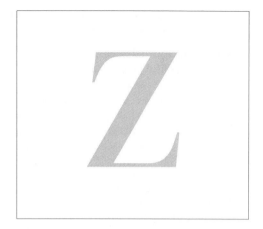

Arnold Zack

U.S. lawyer, 1931–

1 No one on his deathbed ever said, "I wish I had spent more time on my business."
Quoted in Paul Tsongas, *Heading Home* (1984)

Jan Zamojski

Polish general and statesman, 1542–1605

1 [*Advice to King Sigismund III:*] Reign, but do not govern!
Speech to Polish Diet, 1605. In 1830 French politician Adolphe Thiers introduced into French politics the phrase "The king neither administers nor governs, he reigns."

Israel Zangwill

English playwright and novelist, 1864–1926

1 Scratch the Christian and you find the pagan—spoiled.
Children of the Ghetto bk. 2, ch. 6 (1892)

2 America is God's Crucible, the great Melting-Pot where all the races of Europe are melting and reforming!
The Melting-Pot act 1 (1908). This passage popularized the term *melting pot* in the sense of an amalgamation of peoples (an earlier usage with this meaning occurs in the *New York Times*, 2 Sept. 1889). *See Baudouin 1; Jimmy Carter 3; Crèvecoeur 1; Ralph Ellison 2; Victoria Hayward 1; Jesse Jackson 1*

Frank Zappa

U.S. rock musician and songwriter, 1940–1993

1 Valley Girl.
Title of song (1982)

2 Rock journalism is people who can't write interviewing people who can't talk for people who can't read.
Quoted in *Toronto Star*, 24 Sept. 1977

3 Politics is the entertainment branch of industry.
Quoted in *Keyboard*, Feb. 1987

Robert Zemeckis

U.S. film director, 1952–

1 Back to the Future.
Title of motion picture (1985). Coauthored with Bob Gale.

Warren Zevon

U.S. singer and songwriter, 1947–2003

1 He's the hairy-handed gent who ran amuck in Kent
Lately he's been overheard in Mayfair
Better stay away from him
He'll rip your lungs out, Jim
I'd like to meet his tailor
Werewolves of London.
"Werewolves of London" (song) (1975). Cowritten with Leroy P. Marinell and Robert Wachtel.

2 I'll Sleep When I'm Dead.
Title of song (1976). This has become associated with Zevon but appeared much earlier in Charles Yale Harrison, *Clarence Darrow* (1931), quoting a ca. 1923 remark by Darrow himself.

3 Send lawyers, guns, and money, the shit has hit the fan.
"Lawyers, Guns, and Money" (song) (1978)

4 [*On his terminal illness:*] I might have made a tactical error in not going to a physician for twenty years.
The Late Show with David Letterman (television program), 30 Oct. 2002

5 [*On life after being diagnosed with a terminal illness:*] Enjoy every sandwich.
The Late Show with David Letterman (television program), 30 Oct. 2002

Ronald L. Ziegler

U.S. government official, 1939–2003

1 [*Of the Watergate break-in:*] A third-rate burglary attempt.
Press conference, Key Biscayne, Fla., 19 June 1972

2 [President Nixon's latest statement] is the Operative White House Position . . . and all previous statements are inoperative.

Quoted in *Boston Globe*, 18 Apr. 1973

Émile Zola

French novelist, 1840–1902

1 I am little concerned with beauty or perfection. I don't care for the great centuries. All I care about is life, struggle, intensity. I am at ease in my generation.

My Hates (1866)

2 A work of art is a corner of creation seen through a temperament.

My Hates (1866)

3 *La vérité est en marche; rien ne peut plus l'arrêter.*
Truth is on the march and nothing can stop it.

Le Figaro, 25 Nov. 1897

4 *J'accuse.*
I accuse.

Title of open letter to president of French Republic, *L'Aurore*, 13 Jan. 1898. Georges Clemenceau later asserted that he gave the title to Zola's letter. The letter concerned the "Dreyfus affair."

KEYWORD INDEX

A

appeared the letter A   Hawthorne 5
gamut of emotion from A to B
    Dorothy Parker 29

aaay
A.   Television Catchphrases 26

abandon
A. EVERY HOPE   Dante 3

Abbott
Hey, A.   Radio Catchphrases 1

abhors
Nature a. a vacuum   Proverbs 204

abide
A. with me   Lyte 1

abilities
each according to his a.   Karl Marx 12

ability
to each according to his a.   Blanc 1

abjure
I a., curse, and detest   Galileo 3

able
A. was I ere I saw Elba   Napoleon 15

abolish
a. the masters or the slaves   Marcuse 1

abolition
A. of private property
    Marx and Engels 6

abomination
Lying lips are a. to the Lord   Bible 129

aborigines
A., *n*. Persons of little   Bierce 2
then upon the a.   Evarts 1

abortion
a. would be a sacrament
    Florynce Kennedy 2
everyone that is for a.
    Ronald W. Reagan 3
law of a. remains undisturbed
    Blackmun 3

abortions
A. will not let you forget
    Gwendolyn Brooks 1

Abou
A. Ben Adhem   Leigh Hunt 2

about
A. suffering they were never wrong
    Auden 28
It's not a. you   Rick Warren 2

above
all the children are a. average   Keillor 1
Caesar's wife must be a. suspicion
    Julius Caesar 3

No man is a. the law
    Theodore Roosevelt 13

Abraham
A. Lincoln was shoveled   Sandburg 6
A.'s bosom   Bible 302

abroad
I will a.   George Herbert 1

Absalom
A., my son, my son   Bible 89

absence
A. diminishes commonplace passions
    la Rochefoucauld 6
A. makes the heart grow fonder
    Propertius 1
A. makes the heart grow fonder
    Proverbs 1
A. of evidence   Rees 1
another by its a.   John Russell 2
fit of a. of mind   Seeley 1
shoot me in my a.   Behan 2

absent
A. in body, but present in spirit
    Bible 348

absolute
a. power corrupts absolutely   Acton 3
a. power over Wives   Abigail Adams 2
list is an a. good   Keneally 1

absolutely
absolute power corrupts a.   Acton 3
When it a., positively
    Advertising Slogans 47

absolutes
"a." in our Bill of   Black 1

absolve
History will a. me   Castro 1

abstract
even the A. Entities   T. S. Eliot 20
humanity in the a.
    George Bernard Shaw 44

abstractionist
I'm *not* an a.   Rothko 1

absurd
A. Attempt to Make the World
    Sumner 4
a. is not one of the factors
    Kierkegaard 2
There is nothing so a.   Cicero 2

absurdity
a. is interested   Barthelme 1
Constantly risking a.   Ferlinghetti 1

abyss
a. stares back into you   Nietzsche 17

academe
in the groves of A.   Horace 14

olive grove of A.   Milton 44

academic
A. politics is the most vicious   Sayre 1

accent-tchu-ate
a. the positive   Johnny Mercer 4

accept
a. the standard of his age   Wilde 37
I a. the universe   Margaret Fuller 3
I decline to a. the end of man
    Faulkner 10
I will not a. the nomination
    Lyndon B. Johnson 10
society that cannot a.   Hussein 3
will not a. if nominated
    William Tecumseh Sherman 5

acceptance
A. is mostly a matter
    David Foster Wallace 4

accident
A. counts for as much in
    Henry Adams 2
historical a.   Santayana 5

accidents
A. will happen   Proverbs 2
A. will occur   Dickens 67
chapter of a.   Chesterfield 6
victim of a series of a.   Vonnegut 2

accommodating
prefer an a. vice   Molière 1

accompanied
man who a. Jacqueline Kennedy
    John F. Kennedy 20

accomplice
A., *n*. One associated   Bierce 3

accomplices
we are all his a.   Murrow 4

according
in the world a. to Garp   John Irving 1

accounting
matter of creative a.   Mel Brooks 1
no a. for tastes   Proverbs 3

accumulates
it a. through the years
    A. Lawrence Lowell 1

accurate
sum of a. information   Margaret Mead 9

accursed
think themselves a.   Shakespeare 138

accuse
J'a.   Zola 4

accustomed
grown a. to her face   Alan Jay Lerner 6

aces
Christian feels in four a   Twain 2

ache
ark of the a. of it   Levertov 1

achieve
some a. greatness   Shakespeare 244

achieved
Nothing great was ever a.
    Ralph Waldo Emerson 7

Achilles
A. exists only through Homer
    Chateaubriand 2
Iron-hearted man-slaying A.   Auden 37
see the great A.   Tennyson 25

achy
A. Breaky Heart   Von Tress 1

acme
a. of judicial distinction
    John Marshall 8

acorns
oaks from little a.   Proverbs 291

acquaintance
A., n. A person whom   Bierce 4
Should auld a. be forgot   Robert Burns 8

acquaintances
among her Female A.
    Benjamin Franklin 2

acquainted
one a. with the night   Frost 17

acquire
One can a. everything   Stendhal 1

acquit
a. two persons   Voltaire 3
you must a.   Cochran 1

act
a. against the Constitution   Otis 3
both a. and know   Andrew Marvell 6
good by A. of Parliament   Wilde 59
My first a. of free will   William James 1
think globally and a. locally   Dubos 1
wants to get into da a.
    Radio Catchphrases 13

acting
A. isn't really   Hepburn 2
why not try a.   Olivier 1

action
a. springs not from   Bonhoeffer 4
forms of a. we have buried   Maitland 2
life is a. and passion
    Oliver Wendell Holmes, Jr. 7
Lights, camera, a.   Sayings 36
lose the name of a.   Shakespeare 192
not knowledge but a.   T. H. Huxley 5
Suit the a. to the word   Shakespeare 202
Time, Place, and A.   John Dryden 1
To every a. there is always
    Isaac Newton 6

actions
A. speak louder than
    Anthony Burgess 2
A. speak louder than words   Proverbs 4

actor
A.'s Life for Me   Ned Washington 1
Five stages in the life of an a.
    Mary Astor 1

actors
A. are cattle   Hitchcock 2
These our a.   Shakespeare 442

acts
a. of kindness and of love
    William Wordsworth 1

no second a. in American
    F. Scott Fitzgerald 46
RANDOM KINDNESS AND SENSELESS A.
    Anne Herbert 1

actual
made with "a. malice"   Brennan 4
What is rational is a.   Hegel 1

actually
a. say   Ezra Pound 3

ad
a. majorem Dei gloriam
    Anonymous (Latin) 1

Adam
A., the goodliest man   Milton 33
A. had a chance   Nancy Astor 1
A. had 'em   Gillian 2
create A. and Steve   Falwell 1
gratitude we owe to A.   Twain 56
In A.'s Fall   New England Primer 1
What a good thing A. had   Twain 3

adamant
a. for drift   Winston Churchill 10

adapts
reasonable man a. himself
    George Bernard Shaw 22

add
a. to the sum of accurate
    Margaret Mead 9

adder
deaf a. that stoppeth   Bible 114

addiction
Every form of a. is bad   Jung 6
prisoners of a.   Illich 1

adding
a. insult to injuries   Edward Moore 1
A. manpower to a late software
    Frederick Brooks 1

adherent
A., n. A follower   Bierce 5

adherents
Socialism is its a.   Orwell 7

adjunct
no a. to the Muses' diadem
    Ezra Pound 11

adjust
a. the picture
    Television Catchphrases 47

administered
Whate'er is best a.   Pope 23

admiral
kill an a.   Voltaire 9

admiration
A., n. Our polite   Bierce 6

admit
A. them   D. H. Lawrence 2

adolescence
in their a. unsettled   John Morley 3

Adonais
I weep for A.   Percy Shelley 13

Adonis
This A. in loveliness   Leigh Hunt 1

adorable
a. pancreas   Jean Kerr 1

adore
come, let us a. Him   Wade 2

adorn
seeks to a. its prison   Wollstonecraft 6
touched nothing that he did not a.
    Samuel Johnson 88

Adrian
Yo, A.   Film Lines 148

adult
a. day care center   Corker 1

adulterous
it would be a.   Benchley 9

adultery
a. being a most conventional
    Nabokov 11
A. Democracy applied to love
    Mencken 18
and gods a.   Byron 17
commit a. at one end   Joyce Cary 1
committed a. with her already
    Bible 209
die for a.   Shakespeare 306
first breath of a.   Updike 2
I've committed a. in my heart
    "Jimmy" Carter 4
psychology of a.   Bertrand Russell 8
Thou shalt not commit a.   Bible 57

adults
A. are obsolete children   Seuss 16
only between consenting a.   Vidal 5

advanced
Any sufficiently a. technology
    Arthur C. Clarke 5

advances
if one a. confidently   Thoreau 28

advantage
great a. for a system   Santayana 12
Homosexuality is assuredly no a.
    Sigmund Freud 17
not necessarily to Japan's a.   Hirohito 1

adventure
most beautiful a.   Frohman 1
To die will be an awfully big a.   Barrie 9

adversaries
our a. are insane   Twain 122

adversity
A.'s sweet milk   Shakespeare 46
learn to endure a.   Twain 100
Sweet are the uses of a.   Shakespeare 84

advertisements
ideals of a nation by its a.
    Norman Douglas 1

advertising
A. may be described as the science
    Leacock 2
all the rest is a.   Hearst 2
money I spend for a.   Wanamaker 1

advice
A., n. The smallest   Bierce 7
A. and Consent of the Senate
    Constitution 5
A. to persons about to marry   Punch 1
asks me for good a.   Goethe 26
give a. to your children   Truman 9

advise
those who will not take our a.   Billings 1

advocates
never want a.   Richardson 1

aerial
a. flight is one of   Newcomb 1

aesthetic
desire for a. expression   Waugh 2

affair
a. between Margot Asquith
    Dorothy Parker 12

more the survivors' a.   Thomas Mann 4
affairs
tide in the a. of men   Shakespeare 128
affection
woman had better show more a.
Austen 7
affinities
Elective A.   Goethe 14
affirmative
A. action really   Julian Bond 1
afflicted
comforts th' a.   Dunne 14
afflicts
a. th' comfortable   Dunne 14
affluent
A. Society   Galbraith 1
afford
How much justice can you a.
Handelsman 1
when he can't a. to   Twain 105
you can't a. it   J. P. Morgan 3
Afghanistan
You have been in A., I perceive
Arthur Conan Doyle 1
afoot
game is a.   Arthur Conan Doyle 30
game's a.   Shakespeare 134
Mischief, thou art a.   Shakespeare 126
afraid
Be a. Be very a.   Film Lines 78
But Were A. to Ask   Reuben 1
in short, I was a.   T. S. Eliot 8
It's not that I'm a. to die
Woody Allen 19
only thing I am a. of   Wellington 3
stranger and a.   Housman 7
they were sore a.   Bible 288
Who's A. of the Big Bad Wolf
Frank E. Churchill 1
Who's a. of Virginia Woolf   Albee 2
Africa
A. FOR THE AFRICANS   Garvey 3
A. will write its own   Lumumba 1
A.'s gift to world culture   Kaunda 1
I had a farm in A.   Dinesen 2
In A., you want more   Rush 1
millions who are in A.   Garvey 1
something new out of A.   Pliny 1
What is A. to me   Cullen 1
African
A. is conditioned   Kenyatta 1
African American
first mainstream A.   Biden 1
Africas
I see several A.   Césaire 2
after
A. a storm comes a calm   Proverbs 5
A. great pain, a formal feeling
Emily Dickinson 7
A. I am dead, the boy   George V 1
a. many a summer   Tennyson 43
A. such knowledge   T. S. Eliot 23
a. the ball   Charles K. Harris 1
A. the first death   Dylan Thomas 16
Happy ever a.   Sayings 17
man a. his own heart   Bible 83
after-dinner
a.'s sleep   Shakespeare 255

afterlife
there is an a.   Woody Allen 24
afternoon
It was five in the a.   García Lorca 2
Prelude to the A. of a Faun   Mallarmé 1
summer a.; to me those have always
Henry James 28
afterward
ask questions a.   Modern Proverbs 83
afterwards
try him a.   Molière 5
again
Except a man be born a.   Bible 314
I shall not pass this way a.   Grellet 1
never a.   Leiser 1
South will rise a.   Sayings 48
against
He was a. it   Coolidge 6
I always vote a.   W. C. Fields 21
life is 6 to 5 a.   Runyon 3
most people vote a. somebody
Franklin P. Adams 3
not with me is a. me   Bible 238
whatever it is, I'm a. it
"Groucho" Marx 13
Who a. hope believed in hope   Bible 342
Agamemnon
A. dead   Yeats 44
Many brave men lived before A.'s
Horace 25
when A. cried aloud   T. S. Eliot 17
age
A., n. That period   Bierce 8
A. and treachery will overcome
Sayings 1
A. before beauty   Dorothy Parker 49
A. before beauty   Proverbs 6
A. cannot wither her   Shakespeare 402
a. demanded an image   Ezra Pound 12
A. doesn't matter   Billie Burke 1
A. is a question of mind   Paige 9
a. of Aquarius   Rado 1
a. of chivalry is gone   Edmund Burke 18
A. of Reason   Thomas Paine 25
drives my green a.   Dylan Thomas 1
Gilded A.   Twain 13
hast nor youth, nor a.   Shakespeare 255
He was not of an a.   Jonson 10
hell of women is old a.
la Rochefoucauld 8
I will not make a. an issue
Ronald W. Reagan 8
If youth knew; if a. could   Estienne 1
in the first moment of the atomic a.
Hersey 1
lady of a "certain a."   Byron 29
old a. is always fifteen years older
Baruch 4
Old a. isn't so bad   Chevalier 1
old a. should burn and rave
Dylan Thomas 17
people my a. are dead   Stengel 4
what A. takes away
William Wordsworth 4
worth an a. without a name
Mordaunt 1
aged
a. man is but a paltry   Yeats 47
Why should the a. eagle   T. S. Eliot 76

age-ism
age discrimination or a.
Robert N. Butler 1
agenbite
A. of inwit   Joyce 16
agenda
Time spent on any item of the a.
Parkinson 2
ages
heir of all the a.   Tennyson 10
Now he belongs to the a.
Edwin M. Stanton 1
Rock of A.   Toplady 1
aggrandizement
countries seek no a.
Roosevelt and Churchill 1
agitate
a. a bag of wind   Andrew D. White 1
agnostic
compliment to be called an a.
Clarence S. Darrow 5
agnus
A. Dei   Missal 6
ago
long time a. in a galaxy   George Lucas 2
agonizing
a. reappraisal   John Foster Dulles 1
agony
A. and the Ecstasy   Irving Stone 1
a. of defeat   Television Catchphrases 3
agree
always a.   Wrigley 1
people a. with me   Wilde 54
agreeable
My idea of an a. person   Disraeli 25
want people to be very a.   Austen 1
agreed
fables that have been a.   Voltaire 13
agrees
person who a. with me   Disraeli 25
ah
A., love, let us be true   Arnold 18
aid
giving them A. and Comfort
Constitution 8
AIDS
A. epidemic has rolled   Edmund White 1
ail
what can a. thee   Keats 13
aim
when you have forgotten your a.
Santayana 1
aimed
a. at the public's heart   Sinclair 1
ain't
A. misbehavin'   Razaf 1
A. she sweet   Yellen 1
a. we got fun   Gus Kahn 1
It a. necessarily so   Gershwin 7
You a. heard nothin' yet   Jolson 2
air
a. is shattered   Ernest L. Thayer 3
a. split into nine   Dickey 2
built castles in the a.   Thoreau 29
Castles in the a.   Ibsen 26
don't breathe the a.   Lehrer 4
England was too pure an A.
Anonymous 14
He'd fly through the a.   Leybourne 1

air (cont.):

I eat men like a.   Plath 7
I shot an arrow into the a.   Longfellow 14
I would like to be the a.   Atwood 2
melted into a.   Shakespeare 442

airplanes
It wasn't the a.   Film Lines 107

airport
as pretty as an a.   Douglas Adams 9

Alabama
I've come from A.   Stephen Foster 1
Sweet home A.   Van Zant 1

Alamein
After A. we never had a defeat
                          Winston Churchill 40

Alamo
Remember the A.   Sidney Sherman 1

alarm
little a. now and then   Burney 4

alarms
confused a. of struggle and flight
                            Matthew Arnold 19

alas
A., poor Yorick   Shakespeare 226

albatross
With my cross-bow I shot the A.
                                Coleridge 3

Albert
take a message to A.   Disraeli 35

Albion
perfidious A.   Ximénèz 1

alcohol
A. is like love   Raymond Chandler 12
Mere a. doesn't thrill   Cole Porter 5
powerless over a.   Bill W. 1

ale
no more cakes and a.   Shakespeare 241

Alexander
A. . . . asked him if he lacked
                                Diogenes 2
A. Hamilton   Miranda 2
A.'s Ragtime Band   Irving Berlin 1
If I were not A., I would be Diogenes
                        Alexander the Great 1

Alfie
What's it all about A.   Hal David 3

algebra
no such thing as a.   Lebowitz 1

algebraical
weaves a. patterns
                    Countess of Lovelace 2

Algiers
lay dying in A.   Caroline Norton 1

aliases
These are only a.   Grantland Rice 2

Alice
at A.'s Restaurant   Arlo Guthrie 1
Christopher Robin went down with A.
                                Milne 1
One of these days, A.
                Television Catchphrases 29
To the moon, A.
                Television Catchphrases 30

alien
a. people clutching   T. S. Eliot 70
amid the a. corn   Keats 19

alike
All good books are a.   Hemingway 17
By nature men are a.   Confucius 10

Great minds think a.   Proverbs 130
alimentary
like a baby's a. canal
                        Ronald W. Reagan 17
alimony
A. is the ransom   Mencken 13
alive
dawn to be a.   William Wordsworth 23
hardly a man is now a.   Longfellow 23
hills are a.   Hammerstein 27
It's a.   Film Lines 83
lucky if he gets out of it a.
                              W. C. Fields 6
No one here gets out a.   Jim Morrison 4
remain a. long past   Wharton 9
all
a. around the town   James W. Blake 1
A. art is immoral   Wilde 13
a. be the same a hundred   Dickens 25
A. children, except one, grow up
                                Barrie 2
A. Cretans are liars   Epimenides 1
A. Dressed Up   Whiting 1
a. for love   Spenser 5
A. for one, one for all Dumas the Elder 3
A. Gaul is divided into three parts
                            Julius Caesar 1
A. good books are alike   Hemingway 17
A. good things must come   Proverbs 7
A. good writing is swimming under
                        F. Scott Fitzgerald 52
a. hell broke loose   Milton 36
A. I Know Is What I Read   Will Rogers 1
a. I want is 'enry 'iggins' 'ead
                            Alan Jay Lerner 7
A. in green went my love riding
                            e.e. cummings 1
A. is flux   Heraclitus 4
A. is not lost   Milton 20
a. is vanity   Bible 139
A. mankind love a lover
                        Ralph Waldo Emerson 13
a. manner of thing   Julian of Norwich 1
A. men are created equal
                            Ho Chi Minh 1
a. men are created equal   Jefferson 2
a. men are rapists   French 2
a. men keep all women   Brownmiller 1
a. men would be tyrants   Defoe 2
A. music is folk music
                        Louis Armstrong 1
A. of them, any of them   Palin 3
a. o' God's chillun got-a wings
                    Folk and Anonymous Songs 1
a. others pay cash   Sayings 26
A. politics is local   "Tip" O'Neill 1
A. power to the Soviets
                        Political Slogans 1
A. quiet along the Potomac to-night
                                Beers 1
A. quiet on the Western Front
                              Remarque 1
A. roads lead to Rome   Proverbs 256
a. shall be well   T. S. Eliot 125
A. that glitters is not gold   Proverbs 121
a. that I am capable
                        Katherine Mansfield 1
A. that is necessary for the triumph
                            Edmund Burke 28

a. the king's horses Nursery Rhymes 24
A. the news that's fit to print
                            Adolph Ochs 1
a. the President's men   Kissinger 5
a. the ships at sea
                    Radio Catchphrases 24
a. the way home they walked   Agee 3
a. the way through   Goldwyn 10
A. the way with LBJ   Political Slogans 2
a. the World, and his Wife
                        Jonathan Swift 32
a. the world as my parish   John Wesley 1
A. the world is sad and dreary
                            Stephen Foster 4
A. the world loves a clown
                            Cole Porter 21
A. the world's a stage   Shakespeare 88
a. things are connected   Ted Perry 5
a. things are possible   Bible 251
a. things both great and small
                            Coleridge 14
A. things bright and beautiful
                        Cecil Alexander 1
A. things come to those   Proverbs 9
A. things counter
                    Gerard Manley Hopkins 4
A. this, and Heaven too   Philip Henry 1
A. You Need Is Love
                    Lennon and McCartney 11
a. your eggs in one basket   Proverbs 84
A.'s fair in love and war   Proverbs 96
a.'s right with the world
                        Robert Browning 1
best among a. possible worlds Leibniz 3
books of a. time   Ruskin 14
but for a. time   Jonson 10
but that is a.   F. Scott Fitzgerald 1
cried a. the way to the bank
                                Liberace 2
give me A. or Nothing   Ibsen 1
I am made a. things to a. men Bible 350
Is this a.   Friedan 1
it's a. over now, Baby Blue   Dylan 12
laughed a. the way to the bank
                                Liberace 1
Love conquers a. things   Virgil 17
Love is not a.   Millay 8
man for a. seasons   Whittington 1
Man is the measure of a. things
                            Protagoras 2
man of a. hours   Erasmus 3
nor a., that glisters, gold Thomas Gray 2
readiness is a.   Shakespeare 231
shower of a. my days   Dylan Thomas 11
take him for a. in a.   Shakespeare 156
Th-th-th-th-that's a., folks
                    Television Catchphrases 83
willing to love a. mankind
                        Samuel Johnson 93
allegiance
I pledge a. to my Flag Francis Bellamy 1
allegory
a. on the banks of the Nile
                    Richard Brinsley Sheridan 4
alles
Deutschland über a.   Hoffmann 1
alleybi
vy worn't there a a.   Dickens 11

alliance
 A., *n.* In international   Bierce 9
 new a. for progress   John F. Kennedy 10
alliances
 entangling a. with none   Jefferson 30
 steer clear of permanent A.
   George Washington 9
allied
 to madness near a.   John Dryden 4
allies
 We have no eternal a.   Palmerston 1
alligator
 See you later a.   Guidry 1
allons
 A., enfants de la patrie   Rouget de Lisle 1
Allstate
 good hands with A.
   Advertising Slogans 8
almighty
 a. dollar   Washington Irving 5
almost
 a. like being in love   Alan Jay Lerner 1
 A. thou persuadest me   Bible 340
 but that he a. wins   Heywood Broun 1
alone
 afford to let a.   Thoreau 22
 A., *adj.* In bad company   Bierce 10
 A. on a wide wide sea   Coleridge 10
 he is a.   Sartre 7
 I must learn to stand a.   Ibsen 6
 I want to be a.   Garbo 1
 I want to be let a.   Garbo 2
 Leave well enough a.   Proverbs 166
 man a. ain't got no bloody
   Hemingway 19
 man who stands a.   Ibsen 21
 nothing wrong with being a.
   Wasserstein 1
 right to be let a.   Brandeis 1
 right to be let a.   Brandeis 8
 She sleeps a. at last   Benchley 8
 that the man should be a.   Bible 10
 then I go home a.   Joplin 5
 Very well, a.   Low 1
 We live, as we dream—a.   Conrad 12
 We shall die a.   Pascal 6
 you'll never walk a.   Hammerstein 12
along
 can we all get a.   Rodney King 1
Alouette
 A., gentille A.
   Folk and Anonymous Songs 2
Alph
 where A., the sacred river, ran
   Coleridge 19
alpha
 I am A. and Omega   Bible 390
Alphonse
 After you, my dear A.   Opper 1
already
 a. been born   Ronald W. Reagan 3
altar
 a. with this inscription   Bible 335
 I have sworn upon the a. of god
   Jefferson 27
 upon the a. of Freedom   Lincoln 48
altars
 a. to unknown gods   William James 3

alter
 A.! When the hills do
   Emily Dickinson 17
 Circumstances a. cases   Proverbs 47
altered
 a. her person for the worse
   Jonathan Swift 2
alternative
 a. facts   Conway 1
 A. facts are not facts   Todd 1
 a. truth of an erratic   Flake 1
 accepting of a. realities   Tillerson 1
 secret weapon is no a.   Meir 4
 when you consider the a.   Chevalier 1
alternatives
 exhausted all other a.   Eban 1
altitude
 leopard was seeking at that a.
   Hemingway 20
altruism
 conscientiousness of a.   Confucius 5
always
 A. a bridesmaid   Proverbs 36
 a. at his best   Maugham 11
 A. be closing   Mamet 1
 A. do right   Twain 113
 A. suspect everybody   Dickens 37
 a. true to you   Cole Porter 20
 customer is a. right
   Modern Proverbs 21
 Force will be with you—a.
   George Lucas 9
 he knows he a. will   Sainte-Marie 2
 It's a. fair weather   Hovey 1
 poor a. ye have with you   Bible 323
 There'll a. be an England   Ross Parker 1
 We'll a. have Paris   Film Lines 47
 You A. Hurt the One You Love
   Allan Roberts 1
Alzheimer's
 afflicted with A. Disease
   Ronald W. Reagan 15
amateurs
 ruined by a.   Woollcott 2
amazin'
 Mets are gonna be a.   Stengel 5
amazing
 A. grace   John Newton 1
ambassador
 a. is an honest man   Wotton 1
amber
 For a. waves of grain   Bates 1
ambiguities
 vehicle for all a.   Melville 16
ambiguity
 Seven Types of A.   Empson 1
ambition
 A., *n.* An overmastering   Bierce 11
 A. is the last refuge   Wilde 68
 A. must be made to counteract
   Madison 8
 a. should be made of sterner
   Shakespeare 115
 vaulting a.   Shakespeare 343
ambitious
 as he was a.   Shakespeare 109
 told you Caesar was a.   Shakespeare 112
Ambrosia
 back in A.   Keith Waterhouse 1

ambulance
 I'm no a. chaser   Belli 1
amending
 constitutional right of a. it   Lincoln 29
amendment
 Fourteenth A. does not enact
   Oliver Wendell Holmes, Jr. 19
America
 all the World was A.   John Locke 5
 A.! A.!   Bates 1
 A., the paradise of lawyers
   Joseph H. Choate 2
 A., you have it better   Goethe 19
 A. first   Woodrow Wilson 9
 A. I'm putting my queer shoulder
   Ginsberg 6
 A. is a place where all   Barack Obama 4
 A. is gigantic   Sigmund Freud 22
 A. is great   Tocqueville 24
 A. is my country   Stein 7
 A. is never wholly herself
   George Herbert Walker Bush 6
 A. is the only nation   Clemenceau 6
 A. is woven of many strands
   Ralph Ellison 2
 A. I've given you all   Ginsberg 1
 A.: Love It or Leave It   Political Slogans 3
 A. was always great   Meghan McCain 2
 A. was discovered accidentally
   Morison 1
 A. won the Cold War
   George Herbert Walker Bush 13
 cause of A.   Thomas Paine 2
 come to look for A.   Paul Simon 4
 Don't sell A. short   J. P. Morgan 2
 England and A. are two
   George Bernard Shaw 58
 God bless A.   Irving Berlin 8
 God bless A.   Peeke 1
 Good morning A. how are you
   Steve Goodman 1
 greening of A.   Reich 5
 he was like A. itself   Tim O'Brien 3
 I, too, am A.   Langston Hughes 3
 I hear A. singing   Whitman 10
 I like to be in A.   Sondheim 1
 I too, sing A.   Langston Hughes 2
 In A., they haven't used it
   Alan Jay Lerner 10
 in common with A.   Wilde 4
 is the destiny of A.   Douglass 10
 It's morning again in A.   Riney 1
 Make A. great again   Political Slogans 26
 Merrill Lynch is bullish on A.
   Advertising Slogans 82
 my A., my new found land   Donne 1
 next to of course god a.
   e.e. cummings 9
 no angels in A.   Tony Kushner 1
 nothing wrong with A.
   William Jefferson "Bill" Clinton 3
 other A.   Michael Harrington 1
 still hope for A.   Christopher Morley 1
 This is A.   Donald Glover 1
 What A. does best is to understand
   Fuentes 1
 wonderful to find A.   Twain 76

annuity
a. is a very serious business   Austen 3
annus
"a. horribilis"   Elizabeth II 2
anointed
a. king   Shakespeare 19
Anon
venture to guess that A.
        Virginia Woolf 12
another
A. man's, I mean   Twain 100
a. man's gain   Proverbs 177
a. man's poison   Proverbs 190
a. nice mess   Laurel 1
a. Troy for her to burn   Yeats 11
live to fight a. day   Proverbs 102
One good turn deserves a.   Proverbs 127
one thing it's a.   Modern Proverbs 65
that was in a. country   Marlowe 3
That's a. story   Sterne 3
tomorrow is a. day   Margaret Mitchell 8
when comes such a.   Shakespeare 125
answer
a. came there none   Carroll 35
a. is blowin' in the wind   Dylan 2
A. the second question first
        "Groucho" Marx 19
a. to the Coca-Cola company
        Film Lines 69
Gods do not a. letters   Updike 1
Is that your final a.
        Television Catchphrases 86
soft a. turneth away wrath   Bible 132
they a. our prayers   Wilde 74
What is the a.   Stein 15
why did you a. the phone   Thurber 6
answered
a. prayers   Teresa of Ávila 1
Prayer must never be a.   Wilde 110
answers
they bring a. to questions   Wilde 107
They can only give you a.   Picasso 4
will the right a. come out   Babbage 1
ant
a. must be a strangely   Twain 22
a.'s a centaur   Ezra Pound 25
Go to the a., thou sluggard   Bible 124
Antarctica
inform you proceeding A.   Amundsen 1
anthropologist
a. must relinquish   Malinowski 3
antic
dance an a. hay   Marlowe 4
put an a. disposition   Shakespeare 171
antichrist
He is a., that denieth   Bible 387
anticipate
What we a. seldom occurs   Disraeli 7
anti-fascism
we'll call it a.   Huey Long 3
antique
more an a. Roman   Shakespeare 234
traveller from an a. land   Percy Shelley 5
anti-Semitism
Catholic-baiting is the a.   Viereck 1
antithesis
Poetry is not the proper a.   Coleridge 16
anvil
a. or the hammer   Goethe 4

a. or the hammer   Voltaire 11
anxiety
A. is love's greatest killer   Nin 3
A. of Influence   Bloom 1
any
A. port in a storm   Proverbs 10
by a. means necessary   Malcolm X 4
anybody
A. can win   Ade 2
a. here play this game   Stengel 2
anything
A. for a Quiet Life   Middleton 1
a. goes   Cole Porter 2
A. that is worth doing   Beerbohm 4
A. you can do, I can do better
        Irving Berlin 12
don't know a. about music   Presley 2
don't say a. at all   Modern Proverbs 78
If a. can go wrong
        Modern Proverbs 100
in case a. turned up   Dickens 58
You can get a. you want   Arlo Guthrie 1
apart
said to be living a.   Saki 3
You mean a. from my own   Gabor 4
apartheid
closed the book on a.   de Klerk 1
ape
between man and a.   Linnaeus 1
exception is a naked a.
        Desmond Morris 1
played the sedulous a.
        Robert Louis Stevenson 19
you damned dirty a.   Film Lines 135
aphorism
best of men is but an a.   Coleridge 32
aphorisms
great writers of a.   Canetti 1
aphrodisiac
Fame is a potent a.   Graham Greene 5
Power is the great a.   Kissinger 3
aphrodisiacs
greatest of all a.   Napoleon 14
apologize
it's much easier to a.
        Grace Murray Hopper 2
apology
God's a. for relations   Kingsmill 1
app
There's an a. for that
        Advertising Slogans 15
apparel
a. oft proclaims the man
        Shakespeare 159
apparition
a. of these faces in the crowd
        Ezra Pound 4
appeal
a., Hinnissy   Dunne 21
I a. unto Caesar   Bible 338
appear
matter does not a. to me now
        Bramwell 1
our names do not a.   Rich 7
worse a. the better reason   Milton 27
appearances
A. are deceptive   Proverbs 11
Keep up a. whatever you do   Dickens 50

appetite
a. grows by eating   Rabelais 2
as if increase of a.   Shakespeare 151
appetites
contrive artificial a.   Samuel Johnson 20
Subdue your a. my dears   Dickens 23
applause
A., n. The echo   Bierce 12
with thunderous a.   George Lucas 18
apple
all politics is A. Sauce   Will Rogers 2
a. a day keeps the doctor
        Modern Proverbs 1
a. does not fall far   Proverbs 12
As an a. reddens   Sappho 3
did not want the a.   Twain 55
Don't Sit Under the A. Tree
        Lew Brown 3
kept him as the a. of his eye   Bible 73
Shade of the Old A. Tree
        Harry Williams 1
under the a. boughs   Dylan Thomas 6
apples
golden a. of the sun   Yeats 6
appointed
completion of their a. rounds   Kendall 1
appointment
a. with him tonight in Samarra
        Maugham 9
apprehension
in a. how like a god   Shakespeare 181
apprentice
Sorcerer's A.   Goethe 2
appropriate
that was not a.
        William Jefferson "Bill" Clinton 10
approval
other people's a.   Twain 92
après
A. nous le déluge   Pompadour 1
April
A. 1   Twain 75
A. is the cruellest month   T. S. Eliot 39
A. showers bring forth   Proverbs 13
A. showers may come your way
        DeSylva 2
bright cold day in A.   Orwell 33
now that A.'s there   Robert Browning 8
Aprill
Whan that A.   Chaucer 6
aptitude
Genius is only a greater a.   Buffon 2
Aqua
something about an A. Velva
        Advertising Slogans 16
Aquarius
age of A.   Rado 1
aquatic
some farcical a. ceremony
        Monty Python 10
Aquitaine
prince of A.   Nerval 1
Arab
equality for the A. citizens   Einstein 21
Arabia
All the perfumes of A.   Shakespeare 387
Arabs
fold their tents, like the A.   Longfellow 13
honest pacts with the A.   Einstein 9

arbeit
A. *macht frei*   Anonymous 3
arbiter
a. of taste   Tacitus 2
arc
a. is a long one   Theodore Parker 2
Arcadia
Et in A. ego   Anonymous (Latin) 7
arch
all experience is an a.   Tennyson 18
look like a thriumphal a.   Dunne 19
archaeologist
a. is the best husband   Christie 6
archangel
A. a little damaged   Charles Lamb 2
If I were the A. Gabriel   Menzies 1
archbishop
A.: a Christian   Mencken 6
archetypes
known as a.   Jung 4
Archimedes
A. would have sacrificed   Renan 2
archipelago
Gulag A.   Solzhenitsyn 3
architect
A., *n.* One who drafts   Bierce 13
a. can only advise Frank Lloyd Wright 2
call himself an a.   Walter Scott 10
fate of the a.   Goethe 9
Great A. of the Universe   Jeans 1
architects
A., painters   Gropius 1
architecture
A. in general is frozen music
                  Schelling 1
A. is the art of how to waste
          Philip C. Johnson 2
dancing about a.   Mull 1
arena
man who is actually in the a.
        Theodore Roosevelt 18
Argentina
Don't cry for me A.   Tim Rice 3
argue
can't a. with success Modern Proverbs 2
arguing
not a. with you   Whistler 4
argument
a. and intellects Oliver Goldsmith 5
a. of the broken window
        Emmeline Pankhurst 3
I have found you an a.
        Samuel Johnson 106
arguments
three a. of every case
        Robert H. Jackson 10
arise
A., shine; for thy light   Bible 179
I will a. and go now   Yeats 2
ariseth
sun also a.   Bible 140
aristocracy
natural a. among men   Jefferson 38
place the American a. Tocqueville 9
Aristotle
A. maintained that women
        Bertrand Russell 10
arithmetic
different branches of A.   Carroll 19

problem of a.   Edmund Burke 16
ark
shalt thou bring into the a.   Bible 27
arm
a.'s too short to box
       James Weldon Johnson 4
long a. of coincidence   Chambers 1
armadillos
yellow stripes and dead a. Hightower 2
Armageddon
called in the Hebrew tongue A.
                 Bible 398
armaments
a. will be reduced Woodrow Wilson 20
armchairs
traveling a.   Tyler 1
armed
We should be a.   Edna O'Brien 1
Armenians
extermination of the A.   Hitler 8
Armentières
Mademoiselle from A.
      Folk and Anonymous Songs 48
armes
Aux a., citoyens Rouget de Lisle 2
armies
A. have marched over me Film Lines 76
ignorant a. clash by night
          Matthew Arnold 19
no invincible a.   Stalin 2
armistice
a. for twenty years   Foch 1
arms
A., and the man I sing John Dryden 11
Farewell to A.   Peele 1
keep and bear a.   Constitution 12
man's outstretched a.
        Leonardo da Vinci 1
Of a. and the man I sing   Virgil 1
take a. against a sea Shakespeare 188
trade a. for hostages
        Ronald W. Reagan 13
army
a. marches on its stomach
       Frederick the Great 2
a. of pompous phrases   McAdoo 1
Chief of the A.   Napoleon 16
contemptible little a.   Wilhelm II 3
conventional a. loses   Kissinger 1
did not want to use the a. Lincoln 62
go to war with the A. you have
           Rumsfeld 5
If an a. of monkeys   Eddington 2
language is a dialect with an a.
           Weinreich 1
This is the a., Mr. Jones Irving Berlin 9
You're in the A. now   Tell Taylor 2
Arnold
interested Matthew A.
        Christopher Morley 1
around
Money makes the world go a. Ebb 2
What goes a., comes a.
        Modern Proverbs 35
arrayed
not a. like one of these   Bible 219
arrest
One does not a. Voltaire de Gaulle 13
strict in his a.   Shakespeare 233

arrested
a. intellectual   Wilde 67
conservative who has been a.
        Tom Wolfe 9
he was a. one fine morning Kafka 8
arresting
a. human intelligence long enough
           Leacock 2
arrests
feeling which a. the mind   Joyce 6
arrive
To a. where you are T. S. Eliot 105
arrogance
a. of power   Fulbright 1
arrow
I shot an a. into the air Longfellow 14
our a. falls to earth
     Oliver Wendell Holmes, Jr. 41
time's a.   Eddington 1
arrows
a. of outrageous fortune
        Shakespeare 188
ars
A. gratia artis   Dietz 2
arse
politician is an a. upon
        e.e. cummings 18
arsenal
a. of democracy
     Franklin D. Roosevelt 22
art
All a. constantly aspires   Pater 2
All a. is immoral   Wilde 13
an a. of balance   Matisse 2
a. being all discrimination
        Henry James 22
A. does not reproduce the visible Klee 1
A. for art's sake Constant de Rebecque 1
a. for art's sake   Cousin 1
A. for the sake of the true Sand 5
A. is a lie   Picasso 1
A. is a revolt   Malraux 2
A. is long   Longfellow 2
A. is man's expression William Morris 2
A. is meant to disturb   Braque 1
a. is propaganda   Sinclair 3
A. is significant deformity Roger Fry 1
A. is the imposing   Whitehead 12
A. is the objectification   Langer 1
A. is vice   Degas 1
a. of losing   Bishop 4
a. that tells you the time Oldenburg 1
book of their a.   Ruskin 21
Desiring this man's a. Shakespeare 414
Dying is an a.   Plath 6
Economics and a. are strangers
        Cather 9
Every work of a.   Kandinsky 1
gives us modern a.   Stoppard 3
good grey guardians of a. Wilbur 2
He knows all about a. Thurber 12
I don't know much about A.
       Gelett Burgess 6
In a. economy   Henry James 19
In my craft or sullen a. Dylan Thomas 8
Life imitates A.   Wilde 19
Life is short, the a. long Hippocrates 1
Making money is a.   Warhol 1
Modern A. has become Tom Wolfe 2

More matter with less a.
　　　　　　Shakespeare 175
Much of modern a.　　　　Sontag 5
next to Nature, A.　　　　Landor 1
no boundary line to a.
　　　Charlie "Bird" Parker 2
only interested in a.
　　George Bernard Shaw 54
Politics is the a. of the possible
　　　　　　　　Bismarck 9
property in a work of a.
　　Ralph Waldo Emerson 40
purpose of a.　　　Glenn Gould 1
rest is the madness of a.
　　　　　　Henry James 12
There's no a.　　Shakespeare 332
This is the end of A.　J. M. W. Turner 1
Why should a. continue　Mondrian 3
work of a. is a corner　　　Zola 2
artful
a. Dodger　　　　　Dickens 16
arthritis
I've got a.　　　　　Benny 1
article
snuffed out by an a.　　Byron 31
artifice
a. of eternity　　　　Yeats 48
artificer
Old father, old a.　　　Joyce 12
artificers
not in the art but in the a.
　　　　　Isaac Newton 3
artificial
All things are a., for nature
　　　　Thomas Browne 1
a. distinctions　Andrew Jackson 2
A. Intelligence　John McCarthy 1
a. wilderness　　　　Auden 32
contrive a. appetites　Samuel Johnson 20
eminently a. thing　　　Mill 21
which is but an a. man　Hobbes 1
artist
a., like the God　　　Joyce 7
A. of the Floating　Ishiguro 1
a. with no art form　Toni Morrison 1
Before the problem of the a.
　　　　Sigmund Freud 13
Every child is an a.　Picasso 7
lucky bastard who's the a.　Stoppard 6
more perfect the a.　T. S. Eliot 32
really only another a.　Picasso 3
What an a. dies with me　Nero 1
artists
great a. of the world　Mencken 17
arts
inglorious A. of Peace　Andrew Marvell 2
same A. that did gain　Andrew Marvell 7
think fine and profess the a.　Graves 4
Aryan
A. race, A. blood　　Müller 2
as
act a. if there were　William James 11
asceticism
a. was carried out　Max Weber 2
ashes
a. to a., dust to dust
　　Book of Common Prayer 4
rather be a. than dust　London 2

Asia
A. is rising against me　Ginsberg 4
ask
A., and it shall be given you　Bible 224
a. a woman　　　Thatcher 1
a. for what you want　Krutch 2
A. me no more where Jove　Carew 1
A. me no questions　Proverbs 14
a. not what your country
　　John F. Kennedy 16
a. what you can do　John F. Kennedy 16
A. yourself whether you are happy
　　　　　　　Mill 24
But Were Afraid to A.　Reuben 1
Don't a., don't tell　Moskos 1
Don't let's a. for the moon　Prouty 1
have to a. somebody older　Eubie Blake 1
if you got to a.　　"Fats" Waller 2
If you have to a.　J. P. Morgan 3
not a dinner to a. a man to
　　　Samuel Johnson 57
passengers will a. the conductor
　　　　　　Sandburg 8
Shoot first and a. questions
　　　Modern Proverbs 83
who could a. for anything more
　　　　　　Gershwin 5
asked
You've a. for it　　Molière 3
asking
no harm in a.　Modern Proverbs 40
aspect
lend the eye a terrible a.　Shakespeare 133
asperse
A., v. Maliciously to ascribe　Bierce 14
asphalt
A. Jungle　　W. R. Burnett 2
aspires
All art constantly a.　Pater 2
Asquith
affair betweeen Margot A.
　　　Dorothy Parker 12
ass
get medieval on your a.　Film Lines 143
He can lick my a.　Goethe 1
I want him to kiss my a.
　　Lyndon B. Johnson 13
law is a a.　　　Dickens 20
law is such an A.　Glapthorne 1
we are called an a.　Twain 52
We tried to kick a little a.
　　George Herbert Walker Bush 15
Your A. Will Follow　George Clinton 1
assassination
A. has never changed the history
　　　　　Disraeli 22
A. is the extreme form
　　George Bernard Shaw 31
know about an a.　Ambler 1
leader worthy of a.　Layton 2
monarchy tempered by a.　Custine 1
Persecution and A.　Peter Weiss 1
assault
Against the a. of Laughter　Twain 125
asset
virgin—a frozen a.　Clare Boothe Luce 1
association
sure to find an a.　Tocqueville 17

assume
A. a virtue　　Shakespeare 216
what I a. you shall a.　Whitman 3
assurance
on whom a. sits　T. S. Eliot 52
asteroid
she had laid an a.　Twain 85
astonish
a. the rest　　　Twain 113
astound
A. me　　　Diaghilev 1
astrology
A. is a disease　Maimonides 2
asunder
let no man put a.
　　Book of Common Prayer 19
let not man put a.　Bible 249
asylum
land her in a lunatic a.　Mencken 4
lunatics are running the a.
　　　Richard Rowland 1
asylums
padded lunatic a.　Virginia Woolf 4
ate
a. his liver with some fava beans
　　　Thomas Harris 1
a. the whole thing　Advertising Slogans 5
A-Team
you can hire the A.
　　Television Catchphrases 10
atheism
My a.　　　Santayana 8
atheist
a. defined as a man　Buchan 2
a.'s last words　Martel 3
He was an embittered a.　Orwell 1
I am still an a.　Buñuel 3
atheists
no a. in fox-holes　Modern Proverbs 3
atom
a.'s way of knowing　Wald 1
grasped the mystery of the a.
　　　Omar Bradley 1
unleashed power of the a.　Einstein 17
atomic
a. bombs burst　H. G. Wells 4
a. warfare in the future　William Leahy 1
catastrophe of the a. bombs
　　　H. G. Wells 5
in the first moment of the a. age
　　　　　　Hersey 1
atoms
a. and empty space　Democritus 2
dome of a. rose　Karl Jay Shapiro 3
there are a. and space　Democritus 1
atone
a. for the wrong
　　John M. Harlan (1833–1911) 3
attack
A. REPEAT A.　William F. Halsey 1
attacking
I am a.　　　Foch 2
attacks
all the a. made on me　Lincoln 55
attempt
live forever or die in the a.　Heller 2
attended
he had a. business college　Ade 1

attention
a. must be paid   Arthur Miller 3
attentions
a. of many men   Helen Rowland 8
trivial a. which men   Wollstonecraft 10
Attica
A.! A.!   Film Lines 64
attorney
gentleman was an a.
                                Samuel Johnson 67
attract
Opposites a.   Modern Proverbs 66
attractiveness
curious a. of others   Wilde 65
auctioneer
A., *n.* The man who   Bierce 15
audace
De l'a., et encore de l'a.   Danton 1
audacity
a. of hope   Barack Obama 2
audience
largest a. to ever witness   Spicer 1
August
corny as Kansas in A.   Hammerstein 16
Augustus
very like A. Caesar   Francis Bacon 8
auld
Should a. acquaintance be forgot
                                Robert Burns 8
aunts
his cousins, and his a.   W. S. Gilbert 7
Aurora
no more A. Leighs, thank God
                           Edward FitzGerald 5
Auschwitz
day's work at A.   George Steiner 1
that an A. existed   Primo Levi 2
To write poetry after A.   Adorno 1
austere
love's a. and lonely offices
                            Robert Hayden 1
Austerlitz
A. and Waterloo   Sandburg 7
Australia
A. is a lucky country   Horne 1
Advance A. fair   McCormick 1
Australian
proud that I am an A.   Stella Franklin 3
author
a. has to shut his   Nietzsche 4
a. is yet living   Samuel Johnson 28
a. ought to write for the youth
                           F. Scott Fitzgerald 2
death of the A.   Barthes 2
Every other a. may aspire
                            Samuel Johnson 4
expected to see an a.   Pascal 10
in Search of an A.   Pirandello 1
influence of an a.   Henry Adams 9
Not bein' an a.   Dunne 15
prefer being the a.   James Wolfe 1
you wish the a.   Salinger 2
authority
a. is quite degrading   Wilde 48
a. who is not contradicted
                        George Bernard Shaw 32
discussion adduces a.
                         Leonardo da Vinci 4
him that is set in a.   Ptahhotep 1

miracle, mystery, and a.   Dostoyevski 6
no controlling legal a.   Gore 2
authors
buy some Greek a.   Erasmus 2
autocracy
principle of a.   Nicholas II 1
autograph
he asked for my a.   Temple Black 1
automobile
a. is the greatest catastrophe
                          Philip C. Johnson 1
avarice
A. and happiness never saw
                         Benjamin Franklin 9
beyond the dreams of a.
                          Samuel Johnson 99
beyond the dreams of a.
                           Edward Moore 2
ave
A. Maria, gratia plena
                         Anonymous (Latin) 3
avenge
fly and a. us   Corneille 1
avenue
on the a. I'm taking you to   Dubin 1
average
a. guy who could carry   "Bing" Crosby 1
determination of the a. man   Quételet 1
I'm an a. American   Tripp 1
Smarter than the a. bear
                      Television Catchphrases 90
averages
fugitive from th' law of a.   Mauldin 1
Avignon
Sur le pont d'A.
                   Folk and Anonymous Songs 73
avis
Rara a.   Juvenal 2
avoid
A. fried meats   Paige 1
a. looking a fool   Orwell 6
A. running at all times   Paige 5
Avon
Sweet Swan of A.   Jonson 11
awake
trying to a.   Joyce 17
awaken
a. a sleeping giant   Film Lines 178
away
been a. a long time   Kesey 2
they simply fade a.   Foley 1
This also shall pass a.
                          Edward FitzGerald 1
Up, up, and a.   Radio Catchphrases 22
When the cat's a.   Proverbs 41
awe
Shock and A.   Ullman 1
aweigh
Anchors a.   Alfred Hart Miles 1
awful
this is an a. place   Robert Falcon Scott 1
awfully
To die will be an a. big adventure
                                 Barrie 9
awkward
I always made an a. bow   Keats 23
awoke
I a., and behold   Bunyan 5
I a. one morning and found   Byron 35

aww
everybody goes "A."   Kerouac 1
ax
book must be the a.   Kafka 1
Lizzie Borden took an a.   Anonymous 18
axe
a. to grind   Miner 1
Papa going with that a.   E. B. White 6
axioms
decided on the basis of the a.   Gödel 1
Were a. to him   Auden 36
axis
a. of evil   George W. Bush 12
Rome-Berlin a.   Mussolini 2
aye
A., Caramba   Groening 2

B

baa
B., b., black sheep   Nursery Rhymes 5
ba-a-a-d
I'm a b. boy   Radio Catchphrases 2
Babbitt
His name was George F. B.
                            Sinclair Lewis 2
babe
pretty B. all burning bright   Southwell 1
Babel
name of it called B.   Bible 29
babes
Out of the mouth of b.   Bible 107
babies
B. are our business
                        Advertising Slogans 55
nuthin' 'bout bringin' b.
                         Margaret Mitchell 3
they were my b.   Spock 3
baboon
He who understands b.
                           Charles Darwin 1
baby
b. is God's opinion   Sandburg 12
b. out with the bathwater   Proverbs 295
B. shoes   Hemingway 37
Burn, b., burn   Political Slogans 10
Hush, little b.
                    Folk and Anonymous Songs 35
Hush-a-bye, b., on the tree top
                           Nursery Rhymes 1
Is You or Is You Ain't My B.
                             Louis Jordan 1
it's all over now, B. Blue   Dylan 12
Keep the faith, B.
                     Adam Clayton Powell, Jr. 3
like a b.'s alimentary canal
                           Ronald W. Reagan 17
Mamma's little b. loves shortnin'
                    Folk and Anonymous Songs 71
must have been a beautiful b.
                            Johnny Mercer 2
my b. he done lef   Handy 2
my b. was gone   B. B. King 1
Well since my b. left me
                          Mae Boren Axton 1
What good is a new-born b.
                        Benjamin Franklin 42
when he's a b.   Wood 1
when the first b. laughed   Barrie 5

Who loves ya, b.
Television Catchphrases 39
Yes, Sir, that's my b.   Gus Kahn 5
You've come a long way b.
Advertising Slogans 129

Babylon
By the rivers of B.   Bible 122
Hollywood B.   Anger 1

Bach
they play only B.   Karl Barth 1

bachelor
b. never quite gets over
Helen Rowland 4

bachelors
reasons for b. to go out
George Eliot 5

back
at my b. from time to time T. S. Eliot 50
at my b. I always hear
Andrew Marvell 12
B., *n.* That part of your   Bierce 16
B. in the Saddle Again   Autry 1
B. to the Future   Zemeckis 1
b. to the old drawing board   Arno 1
Don't look b.   Paige 6
Empire Strikes B.   George Lucas 10
If it comes b. to you   Lair 1
Look B. in Anger   John Osborne 1
May the wind be ever at your b.
Anonymous 19
rolls off my b. like a duck   Goldwyn 12
Scratch my b.   Proverbs 266
See what the boys in the b. room
Dorgan 2
sit on a man's b.   Tolstoy 12
stabbed in the b.   Hindenburg 1
straw breaks the camel's b. Proverbs 163
Well, I'm b.   Tolkien 12
What people say behind your b.
Edgar W. Howe 1

backbone
more b. than that
Theodore Roosevelt 30

background
there is no b. music   Proulx 1

backroom
what the boys in the b.   Loesser 1

back-rooms
boys in the b.   Beaverbrook 1

backs
beast with two b.   Shakespeare 260
Get the Government Off Our B.
Political Slogans 15
With our b. to the wall   Haig 1

backward
B. ran sentences until reeled   Gibbs 1
Is a civilization naturally b.   Du Bois 8

backwardly
B. tolerant, Faustus   Karl Jay Shapiro 3

backwards
b. and in high heels   Thaves 1
Life must be understood b.
Kierkegaard 1
memory that only works b.   Carroll 37

backyard
further than my own b.   Film Lines 198

Bacon
think how B. shined   Pope 27

bad
b. cause will ever be supported
Thomas Paine 10
b. girls go everywhere
Helen Gurley Brown 2
B. laws are the worst sort of tyranny
Edmund Burke 12
B. men need nothing more   Mill 18
B. money drives out good
Henry Dunning Macleod 2
B. news travels fast   Proverbs 15
b. penny is sure to return   Proverbs 16
B. Seed   March 1
B. taste is simply saying the truth
Mel Brooks 15
down to posterity talking b. grammar
Disraeli 36
even when it's b.   Sayings 47
Good, the B., and the Ugly   Leone 1
good health and a b. memory
Schweitzer 2
good War, or a b. Peace
Benjamin Franklin 35
Hard cases make b. law   Proverbs 136
If it wasn't for b. luck Booker T. Jones 1
I'm a very b. Wizard   L. Frank Baum 6
look at it as a b. man
Oliver Wendell Holmes, Jr. 10
Mad, b., and dangerous to know
Caroline Lamb 1
man who brings b. news   Sophocles 1
President who never told b. news
Keillor 2
regarded as a b. move Douglas Adams 4
take the b. with the good
Modern Proverbs 4
There are no b. boys   Flanagan 1
trample b. laws   Wendell Phillips 2
When b. men combine
Edmund Burke 1
when I do b., I feel b.   Lincoln 57
When I'm b., I'm better   Mae West 6
when she was b. she was horrid
Longfellow 28
Who's Afraid of the Big B. Wolf
Frank E. Churchill 1
why do b. things happen
Harold S. Kushner 1

bade
Love b. me welcome   George Herbert 4

badge
b. of all our tribe   Shakespeare 73
b. of lost innocence   Thomas Paine 3
b. of servitude
John M. Harlan (1833–1911) 3
red b. of courage   Stephen Crane 2

badges
show you any stinking b.   Traven 1

badly
it is worth doing b.   Chesterton 18

bag
agitate a b. of wind   Andrew D. White 1
Papa's Got a Brand New B.
James Brown 1

Bagdad
B.-on-the-Subway   O. Henry 4

Baghdad
no American soldiers in B.   Sahhaf 2
on the gates of B.   Sahhaf 1

bah
"B.," said Scrooge   Dickens 39

bait
Fish or cut b.   Proverbs 110

bake
b. me a cake   Nursery Rhymes 52

baked
b. in a pie   Nursery Rhymes 69
stayed home and b. cookies
Hillary Clinton 2

Baker
B. Street irregulars
Arthur Conan Doyle 11
butcher, the b.   Nursery Rhymes 64

balanced
Fair and b.   Advertising Slogans 51
I b. all   Yeats 22

balances
checks and b.   Madison 12
Thou art weighed in the b.   Bible 190

bald
I wish the b. eagle
Benjamin Franklin 36

Balkans
foolish thing in the B.   Bismarck 10

ball
after the b.   Charles K. Harris 1
Keep your eye on the b.   Proverbs 158
Take me out to the b. game Norworth 2
way the b. bounces Modern Proverbs 5

ballads
make all the b.   Andrew Fletcher 1

ballet
son of a bitch is a b. dancer
W. C. Fields 22

balloon
I'm a toy b.   Cole Porter 10

ballots
peaceful b. only   Lincoln 10

balls
Grab 'em by the b. Modern Proverbs 36
great b. of fire   Otis Blackwell 1

balm
b. in Gilead   Bible 182
wash the b. off   Shakespeare 19

Baltimore
I saw the whole of B.   Cullen 3

bam
B.   Television Catchphrases 18
Wham b. thank you   Sayings 59

ban
B. the bomb   Political Slogans 5

banality
b. of evil   Arendt 5

banana
b. republic   O. Henry 1
carve out of a b. Theodore Roosevelt 30

bananas
Yes . . . we have no b.   Dorgan 3

Banbury
cock-horse to B. Cross
Nursery Rhymes 2

band
Alexander's Ragtime B.   Irving Berlin 1
b. played on   John F. Palmer 1
we b. of brothers   Shakespeare 138

bane
deserve the precious b.   Milton 24

bang
    b. the drum slowly
        Folk and Anonymous Songs 14
    "kiss-kiss" and "b.-b."   Powdermaker 1
    Kiss Kiss B. B.   Kael 1
    not with a b. but a whimper
        T. S. Eliot 67
    This big b. idea   Fred Hoyle 1
banjo
    with my b. on my knee Stephen Foster 1
bank
    all the way to the b.   Liberace 2
    b. that would lend money   Benchley 11
    laughed all the way to the b.   Liberace 1
    Man Who Broke the B.   Fred Gilbert 1
    What is robbing a b.   Brecht 3
banker
    Owe your b.   Keynes 13
    "sound" b., alas!   Keynes 9
bankers
    B. Are Just Like Anybody Else   Nash 8
banknotes
    fill old bottles with b.   Keynes 11
bankruptcy
    Capitalism without b.   Borman 1
banks
    on the b. of the Wabash   Dreiser 1
    We rob b.   Film Lines 28
banner
    star-spangled b. yet wave
        Francis Scott Key 2
banquet
    Life is a b.   Jerome Lawrence 1
    love is a b.   Patti Smith 2
bantering
    in b. lies the key   Ishiguro 4
baptism
    b. of fire   Napoleon 7
bar
    upon the b.-room floor   D'Arcy 1
    when I have crossed the b.   Tennyson 46
Barabbas
    B. was a robber   Bible 328
    tribe of B.   Byron 34
Barbara
    Her name was B. Allen   Ballads 1
barbarians
    B., Philistines, and Populace
        Matthew Arnold 23
    b. are to arrive today   Cavafy 1
    b. come out at night   Coetzee 1
    in my own mind, the B.
        Matthew Arnold 28
    without any b.   Cavafy 2
barbaric
    I sound my b. yawp   Whitman 9
barbarism
    from b. to degeneration   Clemenceau 6
bards
    black and unknown b.
        James Weldon Johnson 3
bare
    b. ruined choirs   Shakespeare 421
    bend steel in his b. hands
        Television Catchphrases 6
    I am Goya of the b. field   Voznesensky 1
    looked on Beauty b.   Millay 6
barefoot
    b. boy, with cheek of tan   Whittier 2

bares
    When the foeman b. his steel
        W. S. Gilbert 21
bargain
    Necessity never made a good b.
        Benjamin Franklin 11
bargains
    Here's the rule for b.   Dickens 51
barge
    b. she sat in   Shakespeare 400
bark
    Are you gonna b. all day Film Lines 147
    hark, the dogs do b. Nursery Rhymes 20
    you heard a seal b.   Thurber 1
Barkis
    B. is willin'   Dickens 57
barmaid
    explain your physics to a b. Rutherford 7
Barney
    B. Google   Rose 1
barrel
    buys ink by the b.   Branigin 1
    power grows out of the b.
        Mao Tse-tung 4
barrels
    be covered under b.   Thomas Carlyle 8
barren
    for such b. terrain   Noonan 1
barrister
    sliding down a b.   Dorothy Parker 48
bars
    nor iron b. a cage   Richard Lovelace 1
Barset
    B. has been a real county   Trollope 2
Bartleby
    Ah, B.   Melville 18
base
    born on third b.   Hightower 1
    Wherefore b.   Shakespeare 286
baseball
    [b.] breaks your heart   Giamatti 1
    b. has marked time   Kinsella 5
    B. has the largest library   Giamatti 3
    had better learn b.   Barzun 1
    I believe in the Church of B.
        Film Lines 33
    life gripping a b.   Bouton 1
    no crying in b.   Film Lines 109
baseless
    b. fabric of this vision Shakespeare 442
baser
    lewd fellows of the b. sort   Bible 334
basic
    B. research is what   Braun 1
basket
    all your eggs in one b.   Proverbs 84
    b. of deplorables   Hillary Clinton 10
    both come from the same b.   Conrad 21
    eggs in one b.   Andrew Carnegie 1
    tossed up in a b.   Nursery Rhymes 76
bastard
    all my eggs in one b.   Dorothy Parker 43
    How does a b., orphan   Miranda 1
    like a b.   Milton 5
    No dumb b. ever won a war   Patton 3
    we knocked the b. off   Hillary 1
    Why b.   Shakespeare 286
bastards
    people have spoken, the b.   Tuck 1

    stand up for b.   Shakespeare 287
    Sue the b.   Yannacone 1
bat
    I shall become a B.   Finger 1
    Twinkle, twinkle, little b.   Carroll 16
bath
    b. of life   Corso 4
bathed
    b. in the Poem   Rimbaud 5
bathtub
    drown it in the b.   Norquist 1
bathwater
    baby out with the b.   Proverbs 295
baton
    marshal's b.   Louis XVIII 1
bats
    No point mentioning those b.
        Hunter S. Thompson 3
battalions
    for the big b.   Turenne 1
    with the strongest b.
        Frederick the Great 1
batter
    B. my heart   Donne 9
battle
    b. cry of freedom
        George Frederick Root 2
    b. for Truth, Justice
        Television Catchphrases 6
    B. of Britain is about to begin
        Winston Churchill 16
    B. of Waterloo was won   Wellington 8
    fighting a hard b.   Maclaren 1
    France has lost a b.   de Gaulle 1
    Joshua fit the b. of Jericho
        Folk and Anonymous Songs 44
    no b. is ever won   Faulkner 4
    nor the b. to the strong   Bible 149
    sent it into b.   Murrow 5
battles
    Dead b.   Tuchman 1
    mother of all b.   Hussein 1
    opening b. of all subsequent   Orwell 15
bay
    sittin' on the dock of the b.   Redding 2
bayonets
    do anything with b.   Talleyrand 1
    fewer horses and b.   Barack Obama 10
    throne of b.   Inge 3
bazinga
    B.   Television Catchphrases 11
be
    B. all that you can b.
        Advertising Slogans 122
    B. fruitful, and multiply   Bible 6
    B. not solitary, b. not idle
        Robert Burton 8
    B. of good cheer   Bible 242
    B. PREPARED   Baden-Powell 1
    To b., or not to b.   Shakespeare 188
beach
    only pebble on the b.   Braisted 1
beaches
    We shall fight on the b.
        Winston Churchill 14
Beale
    If B. Street could talk   Handy 5
beam
    B. me up   Star Trek 7

b. that is in thine own eye   Bible 222

bean

"Politics," he says, "ain't b. bag"
                    Dunne 1

home of the b. and the cod   Bossidy 1

beans

amount to a hill of b.   Film Lines 48

bear

b. another's misfortunes   Pope 10

b. any burden   John F. Kennedy 8

B.-baiting was esteemed heathenish
                    David Hume 11

b. could not fart   Farmer 2

b. false witness   Bible 59

B. of Very Little Brain   Milne 5

b. witness of that Light   Bible 310

Exit, pursued by a b.   Shakespeare 448

finds that he can b. anything   Faulkner 3

Human kind cannot b.   T. S. Eliot 96

keep and b. arms   Constitution 12

More than any of us can b.   Giuliani 1

Puritan hated b.-baiting
                    Thomas Macaulay 12

Smarter than the average b.
            Television Catchphrases 90

unreality that he cannot b.   Le Guin 7

what we have the strength to b.   Koran 6

beard

b. the lion in his den   Walter Scott 4

Don't point that b. at me
            "Groucho" Marx 31

Old Man with a b.   Lear 1

singeing of the King of Spain's B.
                    Francis Drake 1

bearing

b. of a child takes nine months
                Frederick Brooks 2

Greeks b. gifts   Proverbs 131

bears

Lions, and tigers, and b.   Film Lines 191

beast

b. with two backs   Shakespeare 260

Beauty killed the B.   Film Lines 107

blond b.   Nietzsche 19

both man and bird and b.   Coleridge 13

either a b. or a god   Aristotle 10

Fancy thinking the B.   Golding 1

fit night out for man or b.   W. C. Fields 4

in the bowels of the b.   Martí 1

life is cheap as b.'s   Shakespeare 291

makes a b. of himself
                Samuel Johnson 109

name of the b.   Bible 396

number of the b.   Bible 397

people are a many-headed b.   Horace 1

serpent subtlest b.   Milton 39

what rough b.   Yeats 30

your people is a great b.
            Alexander Hamilton 12

beastly

How b. the bourgeois is
                D. H. Lawrence 7

beasts

brokers are roaring like b.   Auden 20

fled to brutish b.   Shakespeare 117

beat

b. generation   Kerouac 3

B. Goes On   "Sonny" Bono 1

b. him when he sneezes   Carroll 12

b. them   Koran 9

I b. people up   Ali 8

If you can't b. 'em   Modern Proverbs 6

They shall b. their swords   Bible 161

two hearts that b. as one   Halm 1

we b. on, boats against
                F. Scott Fitzgerald 35

beaten

Thou art a b. dog   Ezra Pound 27

world will make a b. path
                Ralph Waldo Emerson 51

beating

b. of his hideous heart   Poe 5

beatniks

beach house for 50 B.   Caen 1

beaut

it's a b.   La Guardia 1

beautie

Is there in truth no b.   George Herbert 3

beautiful

All things bright and b.
                Cecil Alexander 1

b. and ineffectual angel
                Matthew Arnold 30

b. as a little girl   Rivers 1

b. day in this neighborhood
                Fred Rogers 1

b. downtown Burbank
            Television Catchphrases 58

B. dreamer, wake unto me
                Stephen Foster 7

B. Game   Pelé 1

b. little fool   F. Scott Fitzgerald 15

b. river   Robert Lowry 1

been born a b. woman   Mauldin 3

beginning of a b. friendship
                Film Lines 50

Black is b.   Political Slogans 8

find yourself in a b. house   Byrne 1

Here life is b.   Ebb 4

How b. upon the mountains   Bible 175

I am a Negro—and b.
                Langston Hughes 5

Isn't it a b. day   Ernie Banks 1

I wish I was b.   Duritz 1

most b. adventure   Frohman 1

most b. things   Ruskin 2

most b. words   Woody Allen 37

must have been a b. baby
                Johnny Mercer 2

O b. for spacious skies   Bates 1

Oh what a b. mornin'   Hammerstein 7

Oh You B. Doll   A. Seymour Brown 1

slaying of a b. hypothesis   T. H. Huxley 3

small is b.   Schumacher 2

something b. for God   Mother Teresa 2

"The House B." is, for me
                Dorothy Parker 21

They'll see how b. I am
                Langston Hughes 3

This is a b. country   John Brown 5

When a woman isn't b.   Chekhov 6

beauty

Age before b.   Dorothy Parker 49

Age before b.   Proverbs 6

B. and the Beast   Ashman 2

b. being only skin-deep   Jean Kerr 1

b. born out of its own despair   Yeats 40

B. can pierce one   Thomas Mann 1

b. cold and austere   Bertrand Russell 2

b. hardly   Matthew Arnold 21

"B." is a currency   Naomi Wolf 2

B. is everlasting   Marianne Moore 4

B. is in the eye of the beholder
                Proverbs 17

B. is momentary   Wallace Stevens 7

B. is nothing but   Rilke 3

B. is only skin-deep   Proverbs 18

B. is truth, truth b.   Keats 16

B. killed the Beast   Film Lines 107

b. like a tightened bow   Yeats 10

b. of their dreams   Eleanor Roosevelt 8

B. of the past   Bourke-White 1

B. stands and waits   Ferlinghetti 2

B. unadorned   Behn 2

B. was no longer just   Naomi Wolf 3

B. will be convulsive   Breton 1

daily struggle for superhuman b.
                Greer 3

dreamed that life was B.   Hooper 1

flatter b.'s ignorant ear   Yeats 19

I died for b.   Emily Dickinson 11

I have loved the principle of b.   Keats 22

I sat B. in my lap   Rimbaud 4

images of female b.   Naomi Wolf 1

looked on B. bare   Millay 6

seizes as b. must be truth   Keats 5

SENSELESS ACTS OF B.   Anne Herbert 1

She dwells with B.   Keats 11

She walks in b.   Byron 7

slavery that I stand in to b.   Pepys 2

such b. was a world
                Tennessee Williams 6

terrible b. is born   Yeats 27

thing of b. is a joy   Keats 9

world will be saved by b.   Dostoyevski 3

your b. must pass   X. J. Kennedy 2

beavers

b. and their dams are   Heinlein 5

became

b. him like the leaving it
                Shakespeare 331

because

B. I could not stop for Death
                Emily Dickinson 8

B. I do not hope to turn again
                T. S. Eliot 75

b. it is bitter   Stephen Crane 1

b. it is my heart   Stephen Crane 1

B. it's there   Mallory 1

just b. I could
            William Jefferson "Bill" Clinton 11

becks

Nods, and b.   Milton 11

become

I am b. a name   Tennyson 16

Let each b.   Thomas Carlyle 2

becomes

one b. one   de Beauvoir 2

that which is not b.   Galen 1

becoming

all that I am capable of b.
                Katherine Mansfield 1

b. the men we wanted   Steinem 3

I am b. a god   Vespasian 1

bed

And so to b.   Pepys 1

Early to b. and early to rise   Proverbs 81

billboard
b. lovely as a tree · Nash 7

Billie
B. Holiday's burned voice · Dove 1

billion
b. here, a b. there · Dirksen 1

billionaire
b.-friendly Congress · Buffett 1

billions
b. upon b. of stars · Carl Sagan 2

bills
not paying one's b. · Wilde 66
She Paid the B. · Gloria Swanson 1

Billy
my boy B. · Nursery Rhymes 3

binders
b. full of women · Mitt Romney 2

bin Ladens
100 b. · Mubarak 1

bingo
his name it was little B.
Folk and Anonymous Songs 47

biographies
essence of innumerable b.
Thomas Carlyle 5

biography
art of b. seems to have fallen · Strachey 2
b. of the man himself · Twain 128
history of the world is but the b.
Thomas Carlyle 12
Judas who writes the b. · Wilde 3
no history; only b.
Ralph Waldo Emerson 11
nothing but b. · Disraeli 6
write b. · Rebecca West 5

biological
b. weapons · Colin Powell 3

bipartisanship
B. is another name · Norquist 2

bippy
bet your sweet b.
Television Catchphrases 57

birch
bringing back the b. · Vidal 5

birches
swinger of b. · Frost 7

bird
b. does not sing · Anglund 1
b. in a gilded cage · Arthur J. Lamb 1
b. in the hand · Proverbs 26
b. is an instrument · Leonardo da Vinci 2
B. is on the Wing · Edward FitzGerald 2
B. thou never wert · Percy Shelley 9
b. with the thorn · McCullough 2
both man and b. and beast · Coleridge 13
did not give of b. or bush
Wallace Stevens 2
early b. catches the worm · Proverbs 80
forgets the dying b. · Thomas Paine 16
I heard the little b. say so
Jonathan Swift 36
I know why the caged b. sings · Dunbar 2
if b. or devil · Poe 10
I'm a little b. that has broken · Barrie 13
immortal b. · Keats 19
It's a b. · Radio Catchphrases 21
learn from one b. · e.e. cummings 16
legend about a b. · McCullough 1

life is a broken-winged b.
Langston Hughes 6
Once I saw a little b. · Nursery Rhymes 4
problem of cat versus b.
Adlai E. Stevenson 1
rare b. · Juvenal 2

birds
all the b. are flown · Charles I 1
b. came home to roost · Arthur Miller 4
B. do it, bees do it · Cole Porter 25
b. got to fly · Hammerstein 1
B. of a feather flock together
Proverbs 27
b. who are outside despair · Montaigne 15
caged b. sing · John Webster 2
charm of earliest b. · Milton 34
Feed the B. · Travers 1
Soon the b. and ancients · Glück 1
unheralded by the return of the b.
Rachel Carson 1

Birnam
Great B. wood · Shakespeare 381

birth
bewailed at their b. · Montesquieu 2
B., and copulation, and death
T. S. Eliot 88
b., life, and death · la Bruyère 2
give b. to a dancing star · Nietzsche 14
hear people discussing b.-control
Clarence S. Darrow 8
I had seen b. and death · T. S. Eliot 69
new b. of freedom · Lincoln 42
no cure for b. and death · Santayana 10
pang of his b. · Yeats 38
rejoice at a b. · Twain 62
They give b. astride of a grave · Beckett 7

birthday
Happy B. to You
Folk and Anonymous Songs 33

birthdays
B. was the worst days
Notorious B.I.G. 1

birthright
selleth his b. for a mess · Bible 400

bishop
blonde to make a b.
Raymond Chandler 5

bit
Not one little b. · Seuss 4
Once b. twice shy · Proverbs 225

bitch
B. set me up · Barry 2
b.-goddess SUCCESS · William James 16
deciding not to be a b. · Hemingway 5
Life's a b. · Modern Proverbs 52
old b. gone in the teeth · Ezra Pound 14
our son of a b. · Franklin D. Roosevelt 30

bite
b. off more than you can chew
Proverbs 28
b. some of my generals · George II 1
b. the hand that feeds us
Edmund Burke 2
courage to b. · Strindberg 2
he will not b. you · Twain 69
rattlesnake that doesn't b.
Jessamyn West 4
smaller Fleas to b. 'em
Jonathan Swift 29

Take a b. out of crime
Advertising Slogans 89

bites
When the dog b. · Hammerstein 26

bitter
because it is b. · Stephen Crane 1
scent of b. almonds · García Márquez 5
'Tis b. cold · Shakespeare 140

bitterest
Sir, your b. enemy is dead · George IV 1

black
Baa, baa, b. sheep · Nursery Rhymes 5
being b. two times · B. B. King 3
b. and merciless things · Henry James 25
b. and unknown bards
James Weldon Johnson 3
b. and white and red · Sayings 60
b. as hell · Shakespeare 434
b. dog I hope always to resist
Samuel Johnson 39
B. is beautiful · Political Slogans 8
B. Lives Matter · Garza 1
B. love is B. wealth · Giovanni 2
b. man discovered the Bible
James Baldwin 7
B. people are natural · Ricciardi 1
B. people possess · Alice Walker 8
B. power · Carmichael 2
b. power · Adam Clayton Powell, Jr. 1
B. Power · Richard Wright 3
chose my b. people struggling
Senghor 1
devil is not so b. · Proverbs 66
first b. President · Toni Morrison 6
I am b., but comely · Bible 156
I'm B. and I'm Proud · James Brown 2
Let the b. flower blossom · Hawthorne 8
my b. hen · Nursery Rhymes 21
not b. and white · Graham Greene 7
Only the B. WOMAN can say
Anna Julia Cooper 1
presence of the b. race · Tocqueville 22
reproach us for being b. · Hammon 1
so long as it is b. · Henry Ford 1
That Old B. Magic · Johnny Mercer 3
to make a poet b. · Cullen 4
whether a cat is b. or white
Deng Xiaoping 2
white is b. · Ignatius 1
white men cheat b. men · Harper Lee 5
Who's the b. private dick · Isaac Hayes 1
young, gifted, and b. · Hansberry 2

blackbird
b. has spoken · Eleanor Farjeon 1

blackbirds
four and twenty b. · Nursery Rhymes 69

blackboard
B. Jungle · Evan Hunter 1

blacks
B. should be used to play · Angelou 3

blade
taken up the broken b. · de Gaulle 3

Blaine
B., B. · Political Slogans 9

blame
b. it for the drought · Dwight Morrow 1
b. it on Marilyn · Eminem 3
B.-all and praise-all
Benjamin Franklin 6

blames
workman b. his tools   Proverbs 238
blank
b. white spaces   Atwood 3
not a b. check   Sandra Day O'Connor 3
people whose annals are b.
                              Montesquieu 6
blanket
b. of the very freedom   Sorkin 2
blanks
historians left b.   Ezra Pound 17
blasphemies
great truths begin as b.
                              George Bernard Shaw 43
blasphemy
Your b., Salman   Rushdie 4
blazing
b. ubiquities   Ralph Waldo Emerson 43
bleed
ain't got time to b.   Film Lines 138
do we not b.   Shakespeare 76
I b.   Percy Shelley 3
open your veins and b.   "Red" Smith 1
bleeding
instead of b., he sings   Ed Gardner 1
pardon me, thou b.   Shakespeare 106
bless
God b. America   Irving Berlin 8
God b. America   Peeke 1
God b. the child   Holiday 1
God b. us every one   Dickens 45
blessed
all generations shall call me b. Bible 284
B. are the meek   Bible 205
B. are the peacemakers   Bible 206
B. are the poor in spirit   Bible 204
B. are the pure in heart   Bible 206
b. art thou among women   Bible 282
B. is he who leaves   Pushkin 2
B. is the man who expects   Proverbs 29
more b. to give   Bible 336
blessing
will be to us a national b.
                              Alexander Hamilton 3
blessings
Count your b.   Oatman 1
from whom all b. flow   Ken 1
blest
B. be the man that spares
                              Shakespeare 455
blight
b. man was born for
                              Gerard Manley Hopkins 7
blind
accompany my being b.   Pepys 5
b. led by the b.   Upanishads 2
b. people come to the park
                              Reggie Jackson 2
B. she is, an' deef   Dunne 9
b. watchmaker   Dawkins 4
Cupid painted b.   Shakespeare 52
halt, and the b.   Bible 298
If the b. lead the b.   Bible 244
In the country of the b.   Erasmus 1
Like a b. man in a roomful
                              Paul H. O'Neill 1
Love is b.   Proverbs 178
Milton saw when he went b.   Marquis 3
old, mad, b., despised   Percy Shelley 8

religion without science is b.   Einstein 15
right to be b. sometimes
                              Horatio Nelson 4
Three b. mice   Nursery Rhymes 42
was b., but now I see   John Newton 1
wink to a b. horse   Proverbs 215
would make everybody b.   Fischer 1
blinked
other fellow just b.   Rusk 2
bliss
B. was it in that dawn
                              William Wordsworth 23
Everywhere I see b.   Mary Shelley 5
Follow your b.   Joseph Campbell 1
soul in b.   Shakespeare 310
where ignorance is b.   Thomas Gray 1
blithe
Hail to thee, b. Spirit   Percy Shelley 9
block
chip of the old "b."   Edmund Burke 27
each b. cut smooth   Ezra Pound 21
blockhead
b. enough to have me   Lincoln 2
No man but a b. ever wrote
                              Samuel Johnson 85
blog
"b." for short   Merholz 1
blond
b. beast   Nietzsche 19
blonde
b. to make a bishop
                              Raymond Chandler 5
let me live it as a b.
                              Advertising Slogans 32
blondes
b. have more fun
                              Advertising Slogans 30
Gentlemen Prefer B.   Loos 1
blood
all the while ran b.   Shakespeare 120
b., sweat, and tear-wrung millions
                              Byron 28
b., toil, tears, and sweat
                              Winston Churchill 12
b. and sweat and tears
                              Theodore Roosevelt 3
b. coming out of her   Trump 7
b. is running in the streets Rothschild 1
b. of patriots   Jefferson 17
b. of the martyrs   Tertullian 2
b. on their hands   Charles Spencer 3
b. will have b.   Shakespeare 373
B.'s thicker than water   Proverbs 31
By b. we live   Geoffrey Hill 2
by iron and b.   Bismarck 1
enough of b. and tears   Rabin 1
God will give him b.   Hawthorne 15
have had so much b.   Shakespeare 385
His b. be on us   Bible 273
I smell the b.   Shakespeare 301
in b. stepp'd in so far   Shakespeare 374
never be purged away but with B.
                              John Brown 4
no getting b. out of a turnip Proverbs 30
one drop of Negro b.
                              Langston Hughes 10
sweat, their tears, their b.
                              Winston Churchill 9
thy tears, or sweat, or b.   Donne 4

Tiber foaming with much b.   Virgil 7
War will be won by B. and Guts Patton 1
wash this b. clean   Shakespeare 357
white in the b. of the Lamb   Bible 393
blood-clot
created Man of a b.   Koran 15
bloodless
b. substitute for life
                              Robert Louis Stevenson 2
bloody
b., but unbowed   W. E. Henley 1
B. men are like b. buses   Cope 2
Not b. likely   George Bernard Shaw 41
sang within the b. wood   T. S. Eliot 17
Sunday B. Sunday   Gilliatt 1
where's the b. horse   Roy Campbell 1
bloom
flowers that b. in the spring
                              W. S. Gilbert 44
blossom
Let the black flower b.   Hawthorne 8
Letting a hundred flowers b.
                              Mao Tse-tung 6
blossoming
Labor is b.   Yeats 40
blow
B., b., thou winter wind Shakespeare 92
B. me down   Segar 1
B. the man down
                              Folk and Anonymous Songs 7
B. winds   Shakespeare 292
come b. your horn   Nursery Rhymes 7
Dinah, b. your horn
                              Folk and Anonymous Songs 38
He could not b. his nose
                              Cyril Connolly 5
I'll b. your house in   Halliwell 1
put your lips together and b.
                              Film Lines 177
Western wind, when will thou b.
                              Anonymous 33
blowin'
answer is b. in the wind   Dylan 2
blowing
I'm forever b. bubbles   Brockman 1
blown
B. hair is sweet   T. S. Eliot 81
blows
ill wind that b. no good   Proverbs 154
know which way the wind b.   Dylan 18
when the wind b.   Nursery Rhymes 1
wind that b. through me
                              D. H. Lawrence 1
bludgeonings
under the b. of chance   W. E. Henley 1
blue
awesome God in the b. states
                              Barack Obama 1
behind b. eyes   Townshend 4
b.-gray October sky   Grantland Rice 2
Columbus sailed the ocean b.   Stoner 1
Devil and the Deep B.   Koehler 1
Don't It Make My Brown Eyes B.
                              Richard Leigh 1
eyes of b.   Sam M. Lewis 2
Hurrah for the Bonnie B. Flag
                              Macarthy 1
I hope the Pacific is as b. Stephen King 4
it's all over now, Baby B.   Dylan 12

book (cont.):
do not throw this b. about   Belloc 1
Don't join the b. burners   Eisenhower 6
Go, my b.   Russell Banks 1
half a library to make one b.
                    Samuel Johnson 79
he who destroys a good b.   Milton 6
I picked up your b.   "Groucho" Marx 4
If I read a b.   Emily Dickinson 29
If pregnancy were a b.   Ephron 1
I'll drown my b.   Shakespeare 445
It is a noble grand b.   Gaskell 3
judge a b. by its cover   Proverbs 32
matter of my b.   Montaigne 2
moral or an immoral b.   Wilde 21
not on his picture, but his b.   Jonson 8
One writes only half the b.   Conrad 6
read a b. before reviewing
                    Sydney Smith 13
Steal This B.   Abbie Hoffman 2
There is no Frigate like a B.
                    Emily Dickinson 25
This is an insignificant b.
                    Virginia Woolf 13
This is not a b.
              Henry Miller (1891–1980) 1
total b. on some shelf   Borges 2
what is the use of a b.   Carroll 2
within the confines of a b.   Proust 7
would make a great b.   Sydney Smith 11
written in this grand b.   Galileo 2
bookkeeping
inventor of double-entry b.   Muller 1
books
All good b. are alike   Hemingway 17
b. are either dreams   Amy Lowell 1
B. are good enough
              Robert Louis Stevenson 2
b. are weapons
              Franklin D. Roosevelt 26
B. are where things   Julian Barnes 2
b. of the hour   Ruskin 14
b. that the world calls immoral Wilde 44
collection of b.   Thomas Carlyle 15
constantly drunk on b.   Mencken 44
do you read b. through
                    Samuel Johnson 74
Even bad b. are b.   Grass 3
first homelands have been b.
                    Yourcenar 1
God has written all the b.
                Samuel Butler (1835–1902) 12
his b. were read   Belloc 3
human being was crushed by b.
                      Hersey 1
I cannot live without b.   Jefferson 40
If my b. had been any worse
                Raymond Chandler 9
I've read all the b.   Mallarmé 4
more in woods than in b.   St. Bernard 1
Never Get in the B.   Whitman 19
No furniture so charming as b.
                    Sydney Smith 7
not from b. but from dissections
                      Harvey 1
Of making many b.   Bible 153
Only two classes of b.
                  Ford Madox Ford 2

preservation in the pages of b.
                  Thomas Carlyle 16
Some b. are to be tasted
                    Francis Bacon 21
Some b. are undeservedly forgotten
                      Auden 38
story b. had been written   Welty 2
We cannot learn men from b.   Disraeli 3
Wherever they burn b.   Heine 1
world of b. is the most   Day 2
bookseller
unquestionably a b.   Byron 34
boop
B.-b.-a-doop   Kane 1
boot
b. in the face   Plath 5
b. stamping on a human face Orwell 46
bootboy
b. at Claridges   Virginia Woolf 2
booted
b. and spurred to ride
                  Thomas Macaulay 11
favored few b. and spurred   Jefferson 54
bootless
my b. cries   Shakespeare 413
boots
b. are made for walkin'   Hazlewood 1
truth is pulling its b. on   Proverbs 168
bop
Playing "B." is like   Ellington 2
Borden
Lizzie B. took an ax   Anonymous 18
border
love stop at the b.   Casals 1
borders
we couldn't see the b.   Schirra 1
bore
B., n. A person who talks   Bierce 19
b. is a man   Bert L. Taylor 1
b. me on his back   Shakespeare 226
Less is a b.   Venturi 1
bored
b. by people who used to   Nancy Astor 3
They'd be very b.   Gary Hart 1
boredom
desire for desires—b.   Tolstoy 10
Borges
I, unfortunately, am B.   Borges 5
boring
kind of b., isn't it   Mishima 2
Life, friends, is b.   John Berryman 2
born
already been b.   Ronald W. Reagan 3
beauty b. out of its own   Yeats 40
because you were b. in it
              George Bernard Shaw 5
b. in the city of Bombay   Rushdie 1
b. in the U.S.A.   Springsteen 5
b. on Christmas Day
            Folk and Anonymous Songs 30
b. on earth   P. D. James 1
b. on the Fourth of July   Cohan 1
b. on third base   Hightower 1
b. sneering   W. S. Gilbert 29
b. this way   Lady Gaga 1
b. to be wild   Bonfire 2
B. to Be Wild   Edmonton 1
b. to set it right   Shakespeare 173
b. with a gift of laughter   Sabatini 1

day perish wherein I was b.   Bible 98
Except a man be b. again   Bible 314
He not busy being b.   Dylan 13
I was b. twice   Eugenides 2
man that is b. falls into a dream
                      Conrad 9
Man that is b. of a woman
              Book of Common Prayer 2
Man was b. free   Rousseau 3
never going to be b.   Dawkins 6
none of woman b.   Shakespeare 379
not b. to sue   Shakespeare 12
Not to be b.   Sophocles 3
One is not b. a woman   de Beauvoir 2
One's a b. liar   "Billy" Martin 1
other powerless to be b.
                  Matthew Arnold 2
Some are b. great   Shakespeare 244
Some men are b. mediocre   Heller 4
some trouble to be b.   Beaumarchais 4
terrible beauty is b.   Yeats 27
That's what "b. again" means
                  "Jimmy" Carter 2
There's a sucker b. every minute
                      Barnum 1
They were b., they suffered   France 2
thing that I was b. to do   Daniel 1
Thou wast not b. for death   Keats 19
time to be b.   Bible 143
To be b. again   Rushdie 1
to the manner b.   Shakespeare 163
towards Bethlehem to be b.   Yeats 30
We are all b. mad   Beckett 6
we were b. to run   Springsteen 2
When we are b.   Shakespeare 308
You would have to be b. there
                      Faulkner 5
borne
b. back ceaselessly F. Scott Fitzgerald 35
borrow
he would like to b. it   Lincoln 62
borrower
b. of the night   Shakespeare 364
Neither a b. nor a lender be
                  Shakespeare 160
borrowing
b. dulls the edge of husbandry
                  Shakespeare 160
bosom
Abraham's b.   Bible 302
her seat is the b. of God
                  Richard Hooker 1
no b. and no behind   Stevie Smith 2
boss
hand of the b.'s daughter
                  James Baldwin 4
I've been talking to your b.   Mizner 5
marry the b.'s daughter
              Robert Emmons Rogers 1
Meet the new b.   Townshend 7
That is why he is the b.   Fo 1
Boston
B. State-House is the hub
              Oliver Wendell Holmes 5
B. telephone directory   Buckley 3
I'm from good old B.   Bossidy 1
In B. they ask   Twain 80
just returned from B.   Fred Allen 4

botanist
I would have been a b.　　Fermi 3
botched
b. civilization　　Ezra Pound 14
both
blame on b. sides　　Trump 18
can't have it b. ways　Modern Proverbs 8
from b. sides now　　Joni Mitchell 1
I am sick of b.　　Samuel Johnson 87
My candle burns at b. ends　　Millay 4
plague o'b. your houses　Shakespeare 42
so long as ye b. shall live
　　Book of Common Prayer 14
usual order of things, b.
　　Dorothy Parker 16
bother
universe go to all the b.　　Hawking 4
bothered
Bewitched, B. and Bewildered
　　Lorenz Hart 8
bottle
b. in front of me　　Waits 1
Never mind the b.　　Musset 1
Yo-ho-ho, and a b. of rum
　　Robert Louis Stevenson 8
bottles
fill old b. with banknotes　　Keynes 11
new wine into old b.　　Bible 234
bottom
b. line is in heaven　　Land 1
b. of the deck　　Robert Shapiro 1
my wife's b.　　Nicholas Longworth 1
no rock b. to the life　　Arthur Miller 1
sit only on our own b.　　Montaigne 19
stand on its own b.　　Proverbs 307
bottoms
wear the b. of my trousers　T. S. Eliot 10
bough
petals on a wet, black b.　　Ezra Pound 4
when the b. breaks　　Nursery Rhymes 1
boughs
Deck the hall with b. of holly
　　Folk and Anonymous Songs 17
bought
b. and paid for　　Stowe 4
I b. the company
　　Advertising Slogans 105
stay b.　　Twain 47
bounces
way the ball b.　　Modern Proverbs 5
bound
b. upon a wheel of fire　Shakespeare 310
This train is b. for glory
　　Folk and Anonymous Songs 76
utmost b. of human thought
　　Tennyson 20
white man was b. to respect　　Taney 2
boundary
no b. line to art　Charlie "Bird" Parker 2
bountiful
My Lady B.　　Farquhar 1
bourgeois
B. society stands　　Luxemburg 1
How beastly the b. is　D. H. Lawrence 7
bourgeoisie
Discreet Charm of the B.　　Buñuel 1
Bourse
beasts on the floor of the B.　　Auden 20

Bovary
Madame B., c'est moi　　Flaubert 2
bow
beauty like a tightened b.　　Yeats 10
Bring me my b. of burning gold
　　William Blake 20
every knee should b.　　Bible 369
I always made an awkward b.　　Keats 23
bowed
B. by the weight　　Edwin Markham 1
bowels
I beseech ye in the b.　　Hand 10
in the b. of Christ　　Cromwell 1
bowl
golden b. be broken　　Bible 152
goldfish in a glass b.　　Saki 1
If Life Is a B. of Cherries　　Bombeck 2
Life Is Just a B. of Cherries　Lew Brown 2
bow-wows
He has gone to the demnition b.
　　Dickens 31
box
arm's too short to b. wid God
　　James Weldon Johnson 2
Life is a b. of chocolates　Film Lines 80
boxer
In the clearing stands a b.　Paul Simon 5
boxes
Little b. on the hillside
　　Malvina Reynolds 1
boy
After I am dead, the b.　　George V 1
barefoot b.　　Whittier 2
b. falling out of the sky　　Auden 30
B. Named Sue　　Silverstein 1
b. playing on the shore　Isaac Newton 7
b. stood on the burning deck　Hemans 2
b.'s best friend is his mother
　　Film Lines 140
B.'s Best Friend Is His Mother
　　Henry Miller (fl. 1883) 1
he had become instead a b.　　Collodi 2
I Didn't Raise My B. to Be a Soldier
　　Alfred Bryan 1
important in the life of a b.　　Witcraft 1
Little B. Blue　　Nursery Rhymes 7
makes Jack a dull b.　　Proverbs 334
marvellous b.　William Wordsworth 19
my b. Billy　　Nursery Rhymes 3
Never send a b.　　Modern Proverbs 9
respected—the golden b.　　Odets 1
When I was a b. of fourteen　Twain 149
When the b. knows this　　Dickens 24
when the b. shouted　　Aesop 1
you will be a real b.　　Film Lines 133
boyfriend
best way to obtain b.　Helen Fielding 4
boys
As flies to wanton b.　Shakespeare 304
b. are marching
　　George Frederick Root 1
b. are not going to be sent
　　Franklin D. Roosevelt 21
b. in the back room　　Dorgan 2
b. in the backroom　　Loesser 1
b. in the back-rooms　　Beaverbrook 1
B. throw stones at frogs　　Bion 1
B. will be b.　　Proverbs 33
Girls will be b.　　Ray Davies 2

hanging in heat, the B.　　Gunn 1
I am fond of children (except b.)
　　Carroll 46
I see the b. of summer　Dylan Thomas 2
Mealy b., and beef-faced b.　Dickens 19
Old B. have their Playthings
　　Benjamin Franklin 27
There are no bad b.　　Flanagan 1
What are little b. made of　　Southey 7
Bozo
laughed at B. the Clown　　Carl Sagan 1
braggin'
It ain't b. if you can do it
　　Jay Hanna "Dizzy" Dean 2
Brahmin
comes of the B. caste of New
　　Oliver Wendell Holmes 10
brain
Bear of Very Little B.　　Milne 5
b. and a uterus　　Schroeder 2
b. is not an organ of sex
　　Charlotte Gilman 4
b. of a four-year-old
　　"Groucho" Marx 16
idle b. is the Devil's workshop
　　Proverbs 151
If I only had a b.　　Harburg 3
If there were b.-shows　　H. G. Wells 9
mediocre b.　　Turing 4
my body and your b.
　　George Bernard Shaw 55
My b.? It's my second favorite
　　Woody Allen 13
second rate b.　Theodore Roosevelt 29
thoughts of a dry b.　　T. S. Eliot 24
why did He give us a b.
　　Clare Boothe Luce 4
your b. on drugs　Advertising Slogans 98
brains
b. enough to make a fool
　　Robert Louis Stevenson 4
brainwashing
greatest b. that anyone can get
　　George Romney 1
branch
Cut is the b.　　Marlowe 12
branches
hacking at the b. of evil　　Thoreau 21
brand
Papa's Got a B. New Bag　James Brown 1
brandy
music is the b. of the damned
　　George Bernard Shaw 14
brass
facts when you come to b. tacks
　　T. S. Eliot 88
brave
b. new world　　Shakespeare 447
Fortune favors the b.　　Virgil 12
Fortune helps the b.　　Terence 4
home of the b.　Francis Scott Key 2
home of the free and the b.　　Cohan 3
Many b. men lived before　　Horace 25
None but the b.　　John Dryden 10
braver
I have done one b. thing　　Donne 13
brazen
Not like the b. giant　　Lazarus 1

breach
  more honor'd in the b. Shakespeare 163
  Once more unto the b. Shakespeare 133
bread
  b. and circuses Juvenal 5
  b. of life Bible 316
  Cast thy b. upon the waters Bible 151
  drop my b. and butter Sayings 25
  Give us this day our daily b. Bible 215
  Jug of Wine, a Loaf of B.
      Edward FitzGerald 8
  Man doth not live by b. only Bible 72
  man shall not live by b. alone Bible 202
  shalt thou eat b. Bible 21
  taste of another man's b. Dante 13
breadbox
  bigger than a b.
      Television Catchphrases 85
breadline
  standing in the b. Lenny Bruce 1
bread-sauce
  time-honored b. Henry James 13
break
  bend but do not b. la Fontaine 3
  B., b., b. Tennyson 2
  b. my bones Proverbs 283
  b. of day arising Shakespeare 415
  b. the law Thoreau 7
  gonna b. my stride Matthew Wilder 1
  Never give a sucker an even b.
      W. C. Fields 19
  We were on a b.
      Television Catchphrases 22
  When you b. the big laws Chesterton 5
  You can't even b. even Sayings 67
  You deserve a b. today
      Advertising Slogans 80
breakdown
  Verge of a Nervous B. Almodóvar 1
breakfast
  B. of Champions
      Advertising Slogans 134
  judge has had for b. Hutchins 1
  six impossible things before b.
      Carroll 38
  your b. in bed before Irving Berlin 9
breaking
  hung for b. the spirit Grover Cleveland 1
  stop one Heart from b.
      Emily Dickinson 23
  without b. eggs Proverbs 224
breaks
  b. a butterfly upon a wheel Pope 33
  It b. your heart Giamatti 1
  One who b. an unjust law
      Martin Luther King, Jr. 7
  straw b. the camel's back Proverbs 163
  world b. everyone Hemingway 10
break-through
  It may also be b. Laing 1
breast
  alas! in my b. Goethe 13
  cannot lacerate his b. Yeats 58
  charms to sooth a savage b. Congreve 5
  eternal in the human b. Pope 18
  fresh, green b. F. Scott Fitzgerald 32
breath
  Every b. you take Sting 2
  his last b. Twain 102

  last b. of, say, Julius Caesar Jeans 2
  such is the b. of kings Shakespeare 13
  Sweet is the b. of morn Milton 34
breathe
  as tho' to b. were life Tennyson 19
  don't b. the air Lehrer 4
  I can't b. Eric Garner 1
  too pure an Air for Slaves to b.
      Anonymous 14
breathes
  b. fire into the equations Hawking 4
  B. there the man Walter Scott 2
breathing
  everyone and I stopped b.
      Frank O'Hara 2
breaths
  amount of b. you take
      Modern Proverbs 50
bred
  b. in at least modest comfort
      Tom Hayden 1
  What is b. in the bone Proverbs 34
  where is Fancy b. Shakespeare 77
breed
  wife for b. Gay 1
breeds
  Familiarity b. contempt Proverbs 98
  Familiarity b. contempt Twain 51
  lesser b. without the Law Kipling 23
brekekekex
  B., koax, koax Aristophanes 7
brevity
  B. is the sister of talent Chekhov 2
  B. is the soul of lingerie Dorothy Parker 1
  B. is the soul of wit Shakespeare 174
bribe
  b. or twist Humbert Wolfe 1
bribed
  rich man is b. Chesterton 13
brick
  carried a b. in his pocket
      Samuel Johnson 27
  Follow the yellow b. road Harburg 6
  inherited it b. and left it marble
      Augustus 3
  paved with yellow b. L. Frank Baum 1
bricks
  make b. without straw Proverbs 35
bride
  B., n. A woman with Bierce 20
  never a b. Proverbs 36
  never the blushing b. Fred W. Leigh 1
bridesmaid
  Always a b. Proverbs 36
  always the b. Fred W. Leigh 1
bridge
  B. of Sighs Byron 13
  b. over troubled water Paul Simon 8
  b. to the 21st century
      William Jefferson "Bill" Clinton 7
  By the rude b. Ralph Waldo Emerson 6
  Do not cross that b. Proverbs 57
  going a b. too far Frederick Browning 1
  highest point in the arc of a b.
      John Cheever 2
  London B. is broken down
      Nursery Rhymes 34
  promise to build a b. Khrushchev 5

bridges
  burn your b. behind you
      Modern Proverbs 10
  sleep under b. France 3
brief
  one b. shining moment
      Alan Jay Lerner 17
briefcase
  lawyer with his b. Puzo 1
brigade
  Forward the Light B. Tennyson 37
bright
  All things b. and beautiful
      Cecil Alexander 1
  b. cold day in April Orwell 33
  Future's So B. Pat MacDonald 1
  I've got B.'s Disease Perelman 1
  something b. and alien
      F. Scott Fitzgerald 37
  Star light, star b. Nursery Rhymes 70
  sun shines b. Stephen Foster 5
  You aren't too b. Film Lines 27
  young lady named B. Buller 1
brightest
  Best and b. Percy Shelley 16
  Best and the B. Halberstam 1
  B. and Best of the Sons Heber 1
  part with their b. hour Hellman 2
brightness
  B. falls from the air Nashe 2
brilliant
  far less b. pen than mine Beerbohm 1
  my b. career Stella Franklin 2
  outlook wasn't b. Ernest L. Thayer 1
brillig
  'Twas b. Carroll 28
bring
  b. a soul into this world Schreiner 6
  b. back my Bonnie to me
      Folk and Anonymous Songs 11
  b. good things to life
      Advertising Slogans 54
  B. me back the world Film Lines 200
  B. me my bow of burning gold
      William Blake 20
  B. me my chariot of fire
      William Blake 20
  B. us together again Richard Nixon 5
  even when they b. gifts Virgil 4
  I b. you tidings Bible 289
  My answer is b. them on
      George W. Bush 18
  thou shalt b. forth children Bible 20
  Whether we b. our enemies to justice
      George W. Bush 9
brings
  man who b. bad news Sophocles 1
brink
  We walked to the b. John Foster Dulles 3
brinkmanship
  boasting of his b. Adlai E. Stevenson 9
bristles
  my skin b. Housman 8
Britain
  Battle of B. is about to begin
      Winston Churchill 16
  How Long Is the Coast of B.
      Mandelbrot 1

Britannia
Cool B.   Stanshall 1
Rule, B.   James Thomson 1
Britannica
volume of the *Encyclopedia B.*
                              Bertrand Russell 12
British
all the books in the B. Museum
                                    Eddington 2
B. are coming   Revere 2
B. Commonwealth   Smuts 1
B. journalist   Humbert Wolfe 1
B. public in one of its
                         Thomas Macaulay 6
face a B. government   Tuchman 3
if the B. Commonwealth
                         Winston Churchill 15
liquidation of the B. Empire
                         Winston Churchill 26
No sex, please—we're B.   Marriott 1
We are B., thank God
                     Bernard Montgomery 2
Britons
B. never will be slaves James Thomson 1
broad
b. is the way   Bible 226
broadcast
I'm paying for this b.   Film Lines 163
Broadway
Give my regards to B.   Cohan 3
broccoli
not going to eat any more b.
                  George Herbert Walker Bush 19
broke
all hell b. loose   Milton 36
b. his crown   Nursery Rhymes 26
If it ain't b.   Lance 1
Man Who B. the Bank   Fred Gilbert 1
not only dead b.   Hillary Clinton 8
then b. the mold   Ariosto 1
broken
argument of the b. window
                     Emmeline Pankhurst 3
be merciful unto a b. reed
                         Francis Bacon 26
He Himself was b.   Leonard Cohen 1
heap of b. images   T. S. Eliot 42
I have taken up the b. blade   de Gaulle 3
Laws were made to be b.   North 2
life is a b.-winged bird
                     Langston Hughes 6
made to be b.   Proverbs 245
Our hearts are b.   Giuliani 2
Records are made to be b.
                     Modern Proverbs 74
Rules are made to be b.   Proverbs 263
staff of this b. reed   Bible 171
strong at the b. places   Hemingway 10
through a b. heart   Wilde 95
broker
honest b.   Bismarck 7
brokers
b. are roaring like beasts   Auden 20
bromide
Are You a B.   Gelett Burgess 4
Bronx
B. is up   Comden and Green 1
B.? No, thonx!   Nash 1

brooding
b. omnipresence in the sky
                 Oliver Wendell Holmes, Jr. 24
sat there b. on the old
                     F. Scott Fitzgerald 34
Brooklyn
lifetime to know B.   Thomas Wolfe 2
tree that grows in B.   Betty Smith 1
Brooks
Man in the B. Brothers
                         Mary McCarthy 1
broom
new b. sweeps clean   Proverbs 210
broth
Too many cooks spoil the b.
                             Proverbs 303
brothel
intellectual b.   Tolstoy 7
brothels
b. with bricks of Religion
                         William Blake 5
brother
Am I my b.'s keeper   Bible 23
Be my b.   Chamfort 2
BIG B. IS WATCHING YOU   Orwell 34
B., Can You Spare a Dime   Harburg 1
especially Sir B. Sun   St. Francis 1
He loved Big B.   Orwell 49
I am a b. to dragons   Bible 103
white man's b.
                     Martin Luther King, Jr. 21
brotherhood
B. of man   John D. Rockefeller, Jr. 1
brother-in-law
not his b.   Martin Luther King, Jr. 21
brothers
we band of b.   Shakespeare 138
brought
b. all to mind   Yeats 22
brow
b. is wet with honest sweat
                         Longfellow 8
brown
Don't It Make My B. Eyes Blue
                         Richard Leigh 1
John B.'s body lies a-mold'ring
                 Folk and Anonymous Songs 40
Brownie
B., you're doing a heck
                         George W. Bush 21
Browning
Hang it all, Robert B.   Ezra Pound 16
Mrs. B.'s death is rather a relief
                     Edward FitzGerald 5
prose B., and so is B.   Wilde 8
brush
B. up your Shakespeare   Cole Porter 22
with my b. that I make love
                 Pierre-Auguste Renoir 1
with so fine a b.   Austen 17
brutal
they tell me you are b.   Sandburg 3
brutality
without art is b.   Ruskin 18
Brute
Et tu, B.   Julius Caesar 7
Et tu, B.   Shakespeare 104
brutes
Exterminate all the b.   Conrad 15

not born to live as b.   Dante 9
brutish
fled to b. beasts   Shakespeare 117
nasty, b., and short   Hobbes 8
Brutus
B. is an honorable man
                         Shakespeare 113
fault, dear B.   Shakespeare 98
were I B.   Shakespeare 124
bubble
seeking the b. reputation
                         Shakespeare 90
bubbles
I'm forever blowing b.   Brockman 1
buck
B. Stops Here   Truman 11
I won't pass the b.   Coolidge 5
Stately, plump B. Mulligan   Joyce 13
buck-and-wing
classic b. men   Dickey 3
bucket
cast down your b.
                 Booker T. Washington 2
Buckingham
changing guard at B. Palace   Milne 1
so much for B.   Cibber 1
buckle
One, two, b. my shoe
                     Nursery Rhymes 49
Bud
This B.'s for you   Advertising Slogans 21
Buddha
while Rubin sits like B.   Dylan 27
Buddhism
B., *n.* A preposterous   Bierce 21
buff
I'm stripped to the b.
                     Theodore Roosevelt 23
Buffalo
B. Bill's defunct   e.e. cummings 2
B. gals, woncha come out
                 Folk and Anonymous Songs 12
Shuffle Off to B.   Dubin 2
where the b. roam   Higley 1
buffalos
thousand rotting b.   Ted Perry 3
bug
First actual case of b. being found
                 Grace Murray Hopper 1
not a b., that's a feature   Sayings 50
bugle
Boogie Woogie B. Boy   Raye 1
bugs
all b. are shallow   Raymond 1
Beware of b.   Knuth 1
build
b. that bridge to the 21st century
             William Jefferson "Bill" Clinton 7
I will b. my church   Bible 246
If you b. it, he will come   Kinsella 1
Too low they b.   Edward Young 5
we b. for ever   Ruskin 3
we b. no bridges   John W. Davis 1
you didn't b. that   Barack Obama 9
builded
He b. better than he knew
                 Ralph Waldo Emerson 32
was Jerusalem b. here   William Blake 19

building
b. a mystery   McLachlan 1
Elvis has left the b.   Horace Logan 1
hurdle a twenty-story b.   Siegel 1
like a public b.   Wilde 61
buildings
b. into which he himself   Goethe 9
B. will collapse   Isaac Bashevis Singer 1
We shape our b.   Winston Churchill 31
builds
B. Strong Bodies
       Advertising Slogans 137
built
b. castles in the air   Thoreau 29
b. his house upon the sand   Bible 230
b. your ship of death   D. H. Lawrence 10
house that Jack b.   Nursery Rhymes 28
Rome was not b. in a day   Proverbs 259
till we have b. Jerusalem
       William Blake 21
bulimia
yuppie version of b.   Ehrenreich 1
bull
Cock and a B.   Sterne 4
strong as a b. moose
       Theodore Roosevelt 9
bullet
b. which is to kill me   Napoleon 10
due process is a b.   Film Lines 92
Faster than a speeding b.
       Radio Catchphrases 21
no silver b.   Condoleezza Rice 2
put a b. through his head
       Edwin Arlington Robinson 2
bullets
not bloody b.   Lincoln 10
bull-fighters
all the way up except b.   Hemingway 3
bullish
Merrill Lynch is b. on America
       Advertising Slogans 82
bully
got such a b. pulpit
       Theodore Roosevelt 27
bulwark
floating b. of the island   Blackstone 5
bum
I'll moider that b.   Galento 1
somebody, instead of a b.   Film Lines 128
bump
things that go b. in the night
       Anonymous 11
bumping
b. into the furniture   Fontanne 1
bumpy
going to be a b. night   Film Lines 6
bums
you threw the b. a dime   Dylan 16
Bunbury
permanent invalid called B.   Wilde 77
bunk
History is more or less b.   Henry Ford 2
buns
hot cross b.   Nursery Rhymes 8
Burbank
beautiful downtown B.
       Television Catchphrases 58
burden
do Thou not b. us   Koran 6

no heavier b. than a great   Schulz 6
White Man's b.   Kipling 25
bureaucracy
b., the rule of nobody   Arendt 2
burglar
enterprising b. isn't burgling
       W. S. Gilbert 24
burglary
third-rate b.   Ziegler 1
burgling
enterprising burglar isn't b.
       W. S. Gilbert 24
Burgundy
naïve domestic B.   Thurber 5
buried
b. along with her name
       Lennon and McCartney 9
forgets where he b. a hatchet
       "Kin" Hubbard 5
Who is b. in Grant's Tomb
       "Groucho" Marx 38
Burke
B. is so great because
       Matthew Arnold 10
burn
another Troy for her to b.   Yeats 11
better to b. out   Neil Young 3
better to marry than to b.   Bible 349
B., baby, b.   Political Slogans 10
b., b., b.   Kerouac 1
b. always with this hard   Pater 3
b. the towers   E. B. White 4
b. your bridges behind you
       Modern Proverbs 10
fire in which we b.   Schwartz 1
in the end, b. human beings   Heine 1
It was a pleasure to b.   Bradbury 1
Manuscripts don't b.   Bulgakov 1
watch the world b.   Film Lines 59
Wherever they b. books   Heine 1
burned
bush b. with fire   Bible 39
candle's b. out   John and Taupin 2
burners
Don't join the book b.   Eisenhower 6
burning
boy stood on the b. deck   Hemans 2
b. and gassing people   Sihanouk 1
b. of paper   Berrigan 1
integrated into a b. house
       James Baldwin 3
Is Paris b.   Hitler 7
Keep the Home-fires b.   Lena Ford 1
Lady's Not for B.   Christopher Fry 1
Tyger tiger, b. bright   William Blake 10
burnished
like a b. throne   T. S. Eliot 45
like a b. throne   Shakespeare 400
burns
b. twice as bright   Film Lines 23
My candle b. at both ends   Millay 4
burnt
b. child dreads the fire   Proverbs 37
b. the topless towers   Marlowe 8
b.-out ends of smoky days   T. S. Eliot 14
volcanoes b. out   Edmund Burke 23
you get b.   Proverbs 235

burst
then b. his mighty heart
       Shakespeare 120
bury
B. my heart at Wounded Knee   Benét 2
get out anything we want to b.
       Jo Moore 1
I come to b. Caesar   Shakespeare 111
Let the dead b. their dead   Bible 233
Let the dead Past b. its dead
       Longfellow 3
We will b. you   Khrushchev 3
bus
either on the b. or off the b.   Kesey 3
he missed the b.   Chamberlain 4
buses
men are like bloody b.   Cope 2
bush
b. burned with fire   Bible 39
B. doctrine   Soros 1
did not give of bird or b.
       Wallace Stevens 2
grand Australian b.   Lawson 1
round the mulberry b.
       Folk and Anonymous Songs 54
worth two in the b.   Proverbs 26
bushel
put it under a b.   Bible 208
business
all b. men were sons-of-bitches
       John F. Kennedy 37
Babies are our b.   Advertising Slogans 55
B. before pleasure   Proverbs 38
B. carried on as usual
       Winston Churchill 4
b. of the American people   Coolidge 3
growth of a large b.
       John D. Rockefeller 1
How to Succeed in B.   Shepherd Mead 1
I must be about my Father's b.
       Bible 291
make b. for itself   Dickens 88
man of b. . . . goes on Sunday
       George Bernard Shaw 2
Man's life is not a b.   Bellow 2
mix b. with pleasure
       Modern Proverbs 58
more time on my b.   Zack 1
no other b. which government
       Thomas Paine 6
Not even a Harvard School of B.
       Du Bois 11
ordinary b. of life   Alfred Marshall 1
rest is not our b.   T. S. Eliot 109
robs you on b. principles
       George Bernard Shaw 10
secret of b. is to know
       Aristotle Onassis 2
We can do b. together   Thatcher 8
bus'ness
no b. like show b.   Irving Berlin 14
bust
b. survives the city   Gautier 2
bustle
B. in a House   Emily Dickinson 22
busy
ask a b. person   Modern Proverbs 11
B. as a one-armed man   O. Henry 5

fear of not being b.
                    Charles Dudley Warner 4
He not b. being born   Dylan 13
I'm too fucking b.   Dorothy Parker 38
pity this b. monster   e.e. cummings 19
select a b. man   Elbert Hubbard 5
too b. sharpening my oyster   Hurston 1
Butch
keep thinking, B.   Film Lines 37
butcher
benevolence of the b.   Adam Smith 2
b., the baker   Nursery Rhymes 64
Hog B. for the World   Sandburg 1
butchered
b. out of their own bodies   Ginsberg 9
butchers
gentle with these b.   Shakespeare 106
butler
A "great" b.   Ishiguro 2
b. did it   Sayings 3
butt
hit a camel in the b.   George W. Bush 25
butter
guns not with b.   Goebbels 1
parsley had sunk into the b.
                    Arthur Conan Doyle 32
rather have b. or guns   Goering 1
buttercup
I'm called Little B.   W. S. Gilbert 1
buttered
fell on the b. side   Sayings 25
butterflies
b. are free   Dickens 84
butterfly
breaks a b. upon a wheel   Pope 33
B. Effect   Gleick 1
dreamed of being a b.   Chuang Tzu 1
dust on a b.'s wings   Hemingway 31
Flap of a B.'s Wings Edward N. Lorenz 1
Float like a b.   Ali 3
large nocturnal b.   Kundera 4
button
my B. works   Trump 19
butts
I like big b.   Sir Mix-a-Lot 1
Buxton
every fool in B.   Ruskin 22
buy
as thy purse can b.   Shakespeare 159
b. back my introduction
                      "Groucho" Marx 8
b. me a Mercedes-Benz   Joplin 2
b. the flowers herself Virginia Woolf 6
Don't b. a single vote more
                      John F. Kennedy 1
How can you b. or sell the sky
                            Ted Perry 1
money cannot b.   Proverbs 196
money can't b. me love
                    Lennon and McCartney 3
Money couldn't b. friends   Milligan 1
some things money can't b.
                     Modern Proverbs 59
Would you b. a used car
                     Political Slogans 38
buyer
if a b. can be found   Sallust 1
Let the b. beware   Proverbs 39

buyers
b. who consider price only   Ruskin 23
by
B. and b. God caught his eye   McCord 1
B. their fruits ye shall know   Bible 229
bygones
Let b. be b.   Proverbs 40
byword
Israel shall be a proverb and a b.
                                Bible 90

C

to the C students   George W. Bush 3
cab
Call me a c.   Joseph H. Choate 3
cabaret
Life is a c., old chum   Ebb 1
cabbage
c. with a college   Twain 58
cabbages
c. were sprouting out   Lincoln 12
of c.—and kings   Carroll 34
planting my c.   Montaigne 5
cabin
entered Logan's c. hungry   Logan 1
cable
little c. cars climb half-way   Cross 1
Cabots
C. speak only to the Lowells   Bossidy 1
cackles
c. as if she had laid   Twain 85
Caesar
C. hath wept   Shakespeare 115
C.'s wife must be above suspicion
                         Julius Caesar 3
envy of great C.   Shakespeare 130
great C. fell   Shakespeare 120
Hail C.   Anonymous (Latin) 2
I appeal unto C.   Bible 338
I come to bury C.   Shakespeare 111
Not that I loved C. less   Shakespeare 108
One need not be a C.   Simmel 1
Render therefore unto C.   Bible 255
Then fall, C.   Shakespeare 104
cage
bird in a gilded c.   Arthur J. Lamb 1
c. the singer   Belafonte 2
nor iron bars a c.   Richard Lovelace 1
round its gilt c.   Wollstonecraft 6
We occupy the same c.
                     Tennessee Williams 9
caged
c. birds sing   John Webster 2
I know why the c. bird sings   Dunbar 2
Cain
Lord set a mark upon C.   Bible 24
caissons
those c. go rolling along   Gruber 1
cake
bake me a c.   Nursery Rhymes 52
have your c. and eat it   Proverbs 139
let them eat c.   Rousseau 10
cakes
no more c. and ale   Shakespeare 241
calamities
Among the c. of war   Samuel Johnson 21

calamity
makes c. of so long life   Shakespeare 189
calculated
We c. in advance   bin Laden 2
calculation
c. shining out of the other   Dickens 49
calf
Bring hither the fatted c.   Bible 299
c. won't get much sleep   Woody Allen 25
California
all could be C. girls   Brian Wilson 2
C., here I come   Jolson 1
C. is a fine place to live   Fred Allen 3
C. is an Italy   Wilde 100
C. love   Tupac Shakur 1
Californian
I met a C.   Frost 13
Calis
C. lieng in my hart   Mary I 1
calisthenics
wise-cracking is simply c.
                     Dorothy Parker 34
call
ain't nothin' till I c. it   Klem 1
C. me a cab   Joseph H. Choate 3
C. me irresponsible   Cahn 3
C. me Ishmael   Melville 2
C. of the Wild   London 1
c. that may not be denied   Masefield 2
c. the tune   Proverbs 230
Don't c. us, we'll c. you   Sayings 10
it's time to c. it a day
                    Comden and Green 4
Let me c. you Sweetheart   Whitson 1
make a desert and c. it peace   Tacitus 1
none dare c. it treason   Harington 1
smile when you c. me that   Wister 1
They c. me Mr. Tibbs   Ball 1
we c. this Friday good   T. S. Eliot 107
When you c. me that   Wister 2
called
Many are c.   Bible 254
calling
c. the tail a leg   Lincoln 63
calls
He c. figs figs   Erasmus 4
calm
After a storm comes a c.   Proverbs 5
reached the c. of water   Henry Adams 7
calumny
escape c.   Shakespeare 195
four horsemen of c.
                  Margaret Chase Smith 1
Calvins
between me and my C.
                  Advertising Slogans 24
Cambridge
C. ladies who live in furnished
                       e.e. cummings 6
came
c. to scoff, remain'd to pray
                     Oliver Goldsmith 8
I c., I saw, I conquered   Julius Caesar 6
I c. through   Douglas MacArthur 6
Spy Who C. in from the Cold   le Carré 1
camel
easier for a c.   Bible 250
hit a c. in the butt   George W. Bush 25
straw breaks the c.'s back   Proverbs 163

camel (cont.):
swallow a c.   Bible 257
Take my c., dear   Rose Macaulay 1
walk a mile for a C.
                       Advertising Slogans 25
Camelot
I forgot in C.   Millay 3
camera
c. does not lie   Modern Proverbs 13
I am a c.   Isherwood 1
Lights, c., action   Sayings 36
Smile! You're on Candid C.
                   Television Catchphrases 12
campaign
We c. in poetry   Cuomo 1
campground
tenting on the old c.   Kittredge 1
can
c. we all get along   Rodney King 1
C. we talk   Rivers 2
He who c., does
                   George Bernard Shaw 17
I think I c.   Watty Piper 2
What c. be done must be done   Roszak 1
Yes, we c.   Political Slogans 39
youth replies, I c.
                 Ralph Waldo Emerson 46
can't
c. always get what you want
                   Jagger and Richards 15
c. get no satisfaction
                    Jagger and Richards 2
c. help lovin' dat man of mine
                         Hammerstein 1
c. live with them, or without them
                       Aristophanes 5
Canada
all over C.   Richler 1
C. could have enjoyed   Colombo 1
C. is not really a place
                     Robertson Davies 1
C. that shall fill the twentieth   Laurier 1
even unto C.   Cartier 1
O C.   Routhier 1
Canadian
C. is somebody who knows   Berton 1
canal
I took the c. zone
                 Theodore Roosevelt 28
cancer
ideology of the c. cell   Abbey 1
We have a c. within   John W. Dean 1
white race is the c.   Sontag 2
candid
Smile! You're on C. Camera
                   Television Catchphrases 12
submitted to a c. world   Jefferson 4
candidates
Going to the c. debate   Paul Simon 6
Candide
they called him C.   Voltaire 6
candle
Bell, book, and c.   Shakespeare 69
better to light one c.   James Keller 1
book and bell and c.   Malory 2
c.'s burned out   John and Taupin 2
Jack jump over the c. stick
                   Nursery Rhymes 27
like a c. in the wind   John and Taupin 1

My c. burns at both ends   Millay 4
Out, out, brief c.   Shakespeare 393
rather light a c.   Adlai E. Stevenson 14
set a c. in the sun   Robert Burton 7
this day light such a c.   Latimer 1
candles
yellow roman c.   Kerouac 1
candlestick
baker, the c.-maker   Nursery Rhymes 64
candy
Big Rock C. Mountains   McClintock 1
C. is dandy   Nash 4
like a fragment of angry c.
                        e.e. cummings 8
name a c. bar after me   Reggie Jackson 1
we are made of sugar c.
                   Winston Churchill 25
cannibal
c. uses knife and fork   Lec 1
cannibalism
I believe in compulsory c.
                       Abbie Hoffman 4
cannibals
c. that each other eat   Shakespeare 263
cannon
C. to right of them   Tennyson 40
even in the c.'s mouth   Shakespeare 90
go straight to the c.   Tewodros 1
loose c.   Richard Nixon 21
cannot
He who c., teaches
                   George Bernard Shaw 17
You c. bring about prosperity   Boetcker 1
canoe
knows how to make love in a c.   Berton 1
canopy
most excellent c.   Shakespeare 180
Canossa
We will not go to C.   Bismarck 4
cant
Clear your mind of c.
                   Samuel Johnson 103
capability
Negative C.   Keats 6
capable
all that I am c. of becoming
                   Katherine Mansfield 1
capacity
c. for enjoyment so vast
                   Dorothy Parker 19
Genius is an infinite c.   Jane Hopkins 1
his c. for wonder   F. Scott Fitzgerald 33
our c. for delight and wonder   Conrad 3
capital
C. is only the fruit of labor   Lincoln 31
don't believe in c. punishmint   Dunne 13
I earned c.   George W. Bush 20
capitalism
c. is a necessary condition
                   Milton Friedman 1
C. undoubtedly has certain   Mencken 38
C. without bankruptcy   Borman 1
face of c.   Heath 1
Spirit of C.   Max Weber 1
capitalist
forbid c. acts   Nozick 4
caprice
c. lasts a little longer   Wilde 26

captain
c. of my soul   W. E. Henley 2
C. of the *Pinafore*   W. S. Gilbert 2
hardy C. of the *Pinafore*   W. S. Gilbert 4
no c. can do wrong   Horatio Nelson 6
O C.! my C.   Whitman 11
right good c., too   W. S. Gilbert 2
walk the deck my C. lies   Whitman 12
captains
c. and the kings depart   Kipling 22
c. courageous whom death   Ballads 6
C. of Industry   Thomas Carlyle 17
car
C. in Every Garage   Political Slogans 12
customer can have a c. painted
                        Henry Ford 1
In a c. like the Roxy   X. J. Kennedy 1
Would you buy a used c.
                   Political Slogans 38
Carabas
Marquis of C.   Perrault 2
caramba
Aye, C.   Groening 2
carborundum
Ni illigitimi c.   Sayings 42
carbuncle
monstrous c. on the face
           Charles, Prince of Wales 2
card
Orange c. would be the one
                   Randolph Churchill 1
play the race c.   Robert Shapiro 1
cardinal
one of the c. virtues
                   F. Scott Fitzgerald 17
cards
Lucky at c.   Proverbs 182
nothing but a pack of c.   Carroll 25
patience, and shuffle the c.   Cervantes 7
care
ethic of c. rests on the premise
                        Gilligan 1
I c. for nobody, not I   Bickerstaffe 1
taken better c. of myself   Sayings 23
teach us to c. and not to c.   T. S. Eliot 78
When you c. enough to send
                   Advertising Slogans 58
career
c. open to the talents   Napoleon 6
Funny business, a woman's c.
                        Film Lines 7
my brilliant c.   Stella Franklin 2
careful
Be c. what you wish for
                   Modern Proverbs 14
Be wery c. o' vidders   Dickens 5
c. if you don't know   Berra 3
Let's be c. out there
                   Television Catchphrases 28
carefully
got to be c. taught   Hammerstein 18
careless
They were c. people
                   F. Scott Fitzgerald 31
cares
if no one c. for me   Bickerstaffe 1
caressed
Men must either be c.   Machiavelli 2

Carlyle
let C. and Mrs. C. marry
    Samuel Butler (1835–1902) 3
Carnegie
gag that's played C. Hall   Levant 1
Carolina
than to be in C.   Gus Kahn 2
carpe
C. diem   Horace 17
carpet
figure in the c.   Henry James 14
carriage
like a horse and c.   Cahn 1
carried
They c. the soldier's   Tim O'Brien 1
carrot
original c.   Cézanne 2
carry
c. a big stick   Theodore Roosevelt 7
C. a message to Garcia
    Elbert Hubbard 1
c. its justification   Conrad 2
C. me back to old Virginny   Bland 1
could c. a tune   "Bing" Crosby 1
we can c. nothing out   Bible 376
cars
c. today are almost the exact   Barthes 1
Counting the c.   Paul Simon 4
giant finned c. nose forward
    Robert Lowell 3
Cartesian
C., *adj.* Relating to Descartes   Bierce 22
Carthage
C. must be destroyed   Cato 2
To C. then I came   Augustine 1
Carthaginian
C. trustworthiness   Sallust 2
carve
c. out of a banana   Theodore Roosevelt 30
carving
with a c. knife   Nursery Rhymes 42
Cary
Even *I* want to be C. Grant   Cary Grant 1
OLD C. GRANT FINE   Cary Grant 2
Casbah
Come with me to the C.   Charles Boyer 1
case
c. is still before the courts   Horace 3
everything that is the c.   Wittgenstein 1
only his own side of the c.   Mill 6
Rome has spoken; the c. is closed
    Augustine 7
cases
Circumstances alter c.   Proverbs 47
Great c. like hard c.
    Oliver Wendell Holmes, Jr. 17
Hard c. make bad law   Proverbs 136
we are all terminal c.   John Irving 1
Casey
C. Jones was the rounder's name
    Seibert 1
C. Jones you'd better watch
    Robert Hunter 2
ease in C.'s manner   Ernest L. Thayer 2
mighty C. has struck out
    Ernest L. Thayer 4
cash
all others pay c.   Sayings 26
c. payment   Marx and Engels 4

C. payment has become
    Thomas Carlyle 11
C. Rules Everything   Diggs 1
casque
green c. has outdone   Ezra Pound 26
Cassius
Yon C. has a lean   Shakespeare 99
cast
C. a cold eye   Yeats 64
c. down your bucket
    Booker T. Washington 2
c. out into outer darkness   Bible 231
C. thy bread upon the waters   Bible 151
c. ye your pearls before swine   Bible 223
coming events c. their shadows before
    Thomas Campbell 3
die is c.   Julius Caesar 5
kill me is not yet c.   Napoleon 2
let him first c. a stone   Bible 318
castels
c. thanne in Spayne   Meun 1
castle
man's house is his c.   Coke 8
man's house is his c.   Otis 2
This village belongs to the C.   Kafka 12
to him as his c. and fortress   Coke 1
Castlereagh
He had a mask like C.   Percy Shelley 2
castles
built c. in the air   Thoreau 29
C. in the air   Ibsen 26
casualty
first c. of war   Modern Proverbs 96
cat
c. and a lie   Twain 60
c. and the fiddle   Nursery Rhymes 22
c. on a hot tin roof
    Tennessee Williams 8
C.: One Hell of a nice animal   Kliban 1
c. that sits down   Twain 89
C. That Walked by Himself   Kipling 26
couldn't spell "c."   Henderson 1
Curiosity killed the c.
    Modern Proverbs 20
deteriorate the c.   Twain 50
endow a college, or a c.   Pope 15
eventually it becomes a C.   Nash 2
fog comes on little c. feet   Sandburg 4
grin without a c.   Carroll 13
home without a c.   Twain 54
like the poor c.   Shakespeare 345
living and dead c.   Schrödinger 1
Never try to outstubborn a c.
    Heinlein 15
problem of c. versus bird
    Adlai E. Stevenson 1
Pussy c., pussy c.   Nursery Rhymes 59
room enough to swing a c.   Smollett 3
way to skin a c.   Proverbs 325
When I play with my c.   Montaigne 11
When the c.'s away   Proverbs 41
whether a c. is black or white
    Deng Xiaoping 2
catamite
bed with my c.   Anthony Burgess 4
catastrophe
drift toward unparalleled c.   Einstein 17
catbird
Sitting in the c. seat   Barber 1

catch
c. a falling star   Donne 11
c. a nigger by his toe
    Nursery Rhymes 16
c. the conscience of the King
    Shakespeare 187
one c. and that was C.-22   Heller 3
catcher
c. in the rye   Salinger 4
catches
as long as it c. mice   Deng Xiaoping 2
early bird c. the worm   Proverbs 80
Honey c. more flies   Proverbs 145
categorical
This imperative is c.   Kant 4
catharsis
c. of such emotions   Aristotle 5
Cathay
cycle of C.   Tennyson 12
cathedra
when he speaks *ex c.*   Anonymous 25
cathedral
to erect a Gothic c.   Heine 4
cathedrals
equivalent of the great Gothic c.
    Barthes 1
Catherine
C. was a great empress   Mae West 20
Catholic
C. & grown-up   Orwell 50
C. and the Communist are alike
    Orwell 32
C. girls start much too late   Joel 3
C. woman to avoid pregnancy
    Mencken 43
C.-baiting is the anti-Semitism
    Viereck 1
Communist and the C.   Orwell 8
Catholick
I believe one C.
    Book of Common Prayer 6
Catholics
C. and Communists have committed
    Graham Greene 6
cats
All c. are gray in the dark   Proverbs 42
C. and monkeys   Henry James 6
C. seem to go on the principle   Krutch 2
greater c. with golden eyes
    Sackville-West 1
Naming of C.   T. S. Eliot 99
Women and C. do what they do
    Heinlein 18
catsup
Shake and shake the c. bottle   Armour 1
cattle
Actors are c.   Hitchcock 2
these who die as c.   Wilfred Owen 1
Catullus
did their C. walk that way   Yeats 25
caught
C. in the Web of Words
    K. M. Elisabeth Murray 1
get c. in bed   Larry L. King 1
God c. his eye   McCord 1
if he be c. young   Samuel Johnson 70
man who shoots him gets c.   Mailer 6
they c. you off base   Hemingway 11
worked and he has not been c.
    Mencken 33

cauldron
c. of dissolute loves   Augustine 1
cauliflower
c. is nothing but   Twain 58
cause
bad c. will ever be supported
        Thomas Paine 10
c. of America   Thomas Paine 2
c. of dullness in others   Foote 1
C. of Liberty   Andrew Hamilton 2
c. that wit is   Shakespeare 61
every c. produces more than one
        Herbert Spencer 2
good old C.   Milton 16
good old c.   William Wordsworth 22
judge in his own c.   Proverbs 157
Lost C.   Pollard 1
Rebel Without a C.   Lindner 1
upon probable c.   Constitution 13
We know our c. is just   Dalai Lama 1
causes
C. Célèbres   Gayot de Pitaval 1
c. of its destruction   Rousseau 6
fighting for were the lost c.
        Film Lines 122
Home of lost c.   Matthew Arnold 8
search out the c. of things   Virgil 20
cave
as the c. man's club   Rachel Carson 2
on the wall of the c.   Plato 8
cavern
In a c.   Montrose 1
caverns
through c. measureless to man
        Coleridge 19
caves
c. for thousands of years   Nietzsche 7
caviare
c. to the general   Shakespeare 183
cavities
Look Ma! No c.   Advertising Slogans 37
Caxtons
C. are mechanical   Raine 1
cease
I will not c. from mental fight
        William Blake 21
then you will c. to exist
        Samuel Johnson 98
We shall not c. from exploration
        T. S. Eliot 124
When I have fears that I may c.   Keats 7
Wonders will never c.   Proverbs 332
ceased
who have c. to be virtuous
        Samuel Johnson 19
you have c. to live   Twain 106
celebrate
I c. myself   Whitman 3
celebrity
c. is a person who is known   Boorstin 2
c. is a person who works   Fred Allen 7
celestial
c. thought   Henry Vaughan 1
celibacy
c. has no pleasures   Samuel Johnson 24
cell
Every c. is derived   Raspail 1
cells
These little grey c.   Christie 2

celluloid
c. not heroin   Spielberg 2
Celtic
C. Twilight   Yeats 1
his locale was C.   Woolsey 1
Celts
C. certainly have it   Matthew Arnold 20
cemetery
send him to the c.   Malcolm X 1
wealthiest man in the c.   Wynn 1
censor
Are we to have a c.   Jefferson 39
c. believes that he can hold back
        Heywood Broun 4
censorship
extreme form of c.
        George Bernard Shaw 31
Net interprets c.   John Gilmore 1
Where there is official c.
        Paul Goodman 1
Without c., things can get
        Westmoreland 1
censure
c. of a man's self   Samuel Johnson 94
census
c. taker tried to quantify me
        Thomas Harris 1
cent
Millions for defense but not a c.
        Robert Harper 1
centaur
ant's a c.   Ezra Pound 25
center
c. cannot hold   Yeats 29
c. of the silent Word   T. S. Eliot 83
My c. is giving way   Foch 2
sun is the c.   Copernicus 1
well-defined c.   James Murray 1
central
C. Dogma   Crick 3
centuries
all c. but this   W. S. Gilbert 32
forty c. look down   Napoleon 8
century
American c.   Henry R. Luce 1
c. of the common man
        Henry A. Wallace 1
fill the twentieth c.   Laurier 1
glittering c. has an image   Burchill 2
trial of the c.   Frances Noyes Hart 1
wait a c. for a reader   Kepler 2
We all lived in this c.   Quayle 1
ceremony
c. of innocence is drowned   Yeats 29
save c.   Shakespeare 135
some farcical aquatic c.
        Monty Python 10
certain
c. because it is impossible   Tertullian 3
lady of a "c. age"   Byron 29
nothing can be said to be c.
        Benjamin Franklin 41
they are not c.   Einstein 5
yet c. am I of the spot
        Emily Dickinson 21
certainties
hot for c.   George Meredith 1
If a man will begin with c.
        Francis Bacon 3

there are no c.   Mencken 16
certainty
c. comes only once   Robert Waller 1
C. generally is illusion
        Oliver Wendell Holmes, Jr. 12
cesspool
London, that great c.
        Arthur Conan Doyle 2
this sweet c.   George Sanders 1
chaff
see that the c. is printed
        Elbert Hubbard 4
chain
c. cannot be stronger   Proverbs 43
I wear the c. I forged   Dickens 41
No man can put a c.   Douglass 14
Vast c. of Being   Pope 19
chained
c. to a being   Proust 5
chains
better to be in c.   Kafka 10
c. of the Constitution   Jefferson 25
everywhere he is in c.   Rousseau 3
I sang in my c. like the sea
        Dylan Thomas 7
nothing to lose but their c.
        Marx and Engels 8
chair
C. she sat in   T. S. Eliot 45
chairs
I had three c.   Thoreau 26
chalice
poison'd c.   Shakespeare 341
poisoned c.   Robert H. Jackson 6
cham
great C. of literature   Smollett 2
chambers
lingered in the c.   T. S. Eliot 12
champagne
c. and a chicken   Mary Montagu 1
I get no kick from c.   Cole Porter 5
champions
Breakfast of C.   Advertising Slogans 134
chance
bludgeonings of c.   W. E. Henley 1
c. favors only the prepared   Pasteur 1
C. is perhaps   Gautier 1
give peace a c.
        Lennon and McCartney 25
no bloody fucking c.   Hemingway 19
No victor believes in c.   Nietzsche 9
Will Never Abolish C.   Mallarmé 5
chancery
another well-known suit in C.
        Dickens 75
this High Court of C.   Dickens 77
Chanel
C. Number 5   Marilyn Monroe 4
change
can c. the world   Margaret Mead 10
chance to c. the world   Jobs 2
c. is gonna come   Cooke 2
c. it for a sack of gold   Irving Berlin 15
c. my name to Shanghai Lily
        Film Lines 154
C. proves true on the day   I Ching 2
c. the world   Rukeyser 1
C. we can believe in   Political Slogans 11
c. you want to see   Mohandas Gandhi 7

If voting could c. anything   Sayings 24
more things c.   Karr 2
must not c. one thing   Le Guin 1
Nothing endures but c.   Heraclitus 5
point is to c. it   Karl Marx 3
ringing grooves of c.   Tennyson 11
scorn to c. my state   Shakespeare 416
Some things never c.   Proverbs 44
that could c.   Quayle 7
things will have to c.   Lampedusa 1
time for a c.   Thomas E. Dewey 1
wind of c. is blowing   Macmillan 2
changed
Assassination has never c.   Disraeli 22
c. everything except our modes
    Einstein 17
c. utterly   Yeats 27
human character c.   Virginia Woolf 3
names have been c.
    Radio Catchphrases 6
We have c. all that   Molière 2
changes
make some c. in her life   Franzen 3
changeth
old order c.   Tennyson 45
changing
c. guard at Buckingham Palace   Milne 1
I've been afraid of c.   Nicks 1
not c. one's mind   Maugham 1
channel
tuned to a dead c.   Gibson 2
channels
57 C. (and Nothin' On)   Springsteen 7
chaos
c. candidate   "Jeb" Bush 1
c. often breeds life   Henry Adams 8
C. umpire sits   Milton 30
have c. in oneself   Nietzsche 14
chaotically
made of sex an almost c. limitless
    Decter 1
chapel
I've finished that c.   Michelangelo 1
chapels
legends of the green c.
    Dylan Thomas 12
chapter
last c. is wanting   Thomas Hardy 5
chapters
cut the last two c.   Ephron 1
Heads of my C.   Charles Darwin 2
character
c. is destiny   George Eliot 6
content of their c.
    Martin Luther King, Jr. 10
content of their c.
    Martin Luther King, Jr. 13
Fate and c. are the same   Novalis 2
human c. changed   Virginia Woolf 3
man's c. is his fate   Heraclitus 2
Now c. is capable of being taught
    Matthew Arnold 21
Sports doesn't build c.
    Heywood Hale Broun 1
What is c. but the determination
    Henry James 11
characteristic
every c. of a dog except loyalty
    Sam Houston 1

characters
Six C. in Search   Pirandello 1
charge
c. when they're wounded   Mauldin 4
charged
language c. with meaning
    Ezra Pound 18
world is c. with the grandeur
    Gerard Manley Hopkins 2
chariot
Bring me my c. of fire
    William Blake 20
make a flying C.   Wilkins 1
Swing low, sweet c.
    Folk and Anonymous Songs 74
time's winged c.   Andrew Marvell 12
charisma
term "c." will be applied   Max Weber 3
charity
C. begins at home   Proverbs 45
c. is still horrible   Orwell 3
C. never faileth   Bible 354
C. shall cover the multitude   Bible 384
have not c., I am nothing   Bible 353
In c. to all mankind
    John Quincy Adams 2
now abideth faith, hope, c.   Bible 355
with c. for all   Lincoln 51
Charles
King C.'s head   Dickens 63
Charlie
C. don't surf   Film Lines 13
C. he's my darling   Nairne 1
Good grief, C. Brown   Schulz 1
My name is C. Gordon   Keyes 1
Charlotte
C. was both   E. B. White 8
charm
c. of earliest birds   Milton 34
city of Northern c.   John F. Kennedy 22
Discreet C. of the Bourgeoisie   Buñuel 1
charmed
I bear a c. life   Shakespeare 395
charming
c. or tedious   Wilde 52
No furniture so c. as books
    Sydney Smith 7
charms
all those endearing young c.
    Thomas Moore 1
Music has c. to sooth   Congreve 5
Chartres
like the Virgin, build C.
    Henry Adams 16
chase
Paper C.   Osborn 1
chassis
state o' c.   O'Casey 1
chaste
C. to her husband   Pope 35
My English text is c.   Gibbon 11
Queen and huntress, c. and fair
    Jonson 1
chastity
c. of the intellect   Santayana 11
Give me c. and continency   Augustine 3
most curious is c.   Gourmont 1
Chattanooga
C. choo-choo   Gordon 1

Chatterton
C., the marvellous boy
    William Wordsworth 19
Chaucer
Dan C., well of English   Spenser 6
che
C. gelida manina   Giacosa 1
cheap
C. grace is the deadly   Bonhoeffer 2
energy too c. to meter   Strauss 1
man's life is c.   Shakespeare 291
Talk is c.   Proverbs 290
Two can live as c.   Proverbs 309
cheaper
sell a little c.   Ruskin 23
cheapest
whose pleasures are the c.   Thoreau 33
cheat
Can't C. an Honest Man   W. C. Fields 8
cheated
feeling you've been c.   Rotten 3
cheating
worth c. for   W. C. Fields 14
check
c. is in the mail   Sayings 4
c. to the natural increase   Malthus 3
so it may be a c. upon both
    John Adams 5
You can c. out   Don Henley 1
checking
c. it twice   Gillespie 2
checks
c. and balances   Madison 12
cheek
c. of tan   Whittier 2
dancing c. to c.   Irving Berlin 7
smite thee on thy right c.   Bible 211
cheer
Be of good c.   Bible 242
Don't c. boys   Philip 1
cheerful
God loveth a c. giver   Bible 361
cheerfulness
c. was always breaking   Oliver Edwards 1
cheers
give three c.   W. S. Gilbert 4
Two c. for Democracy   Forster 7
cheese
C.-eating surrender monkeys
    Groening 7
C., milk's leap   Clifton Fadiman 1
different kinds of c.   de Gaulle 11
put a piece of c. down there
    "Groucho" Marx 30
chemical
c. barrage has been hurled
    Rachel Carson 2
chemistry
Better Living . . . Through C.
    Advertising Slogans 43
cheque
"c." and "inclosed"   Dorothy Parker 26
cherce
what's there is c.   Film Lines 130
cherchez
C. la femme   Dumas the Elder 5
cherries
If Life Is a Bowl of C.   Bombeck 2
Life Is Just a Bowl of C.   Lew Brown 2

cherry
  as American as c. pie   H. Rap Brown 1
  spring does with the c. trees   Neruda 3
chesnut
  you invariably said, a c.   Dimond 1
chess
  C., like love   Tarrasch 1
  great c.-player is not a great man
    Hazlitt 5
chest
  dead man's c. Robert Louis Stevenson 8
chestnut
  O c. tree   Yeats 41
  Under a spreading c. tree   Longfellow 7
  Under the spreading c. tree   Orwell 40
chestnuts
  C. roasting at an open fire
    Robert Wells 1
chevalier
  darling, the young C.   Nairne 1
Chevrolet
  See the USA in a C.
    Advertising Slogans 28
Chevy
  drove my C. to the levee   McLean 2
chew
  more than you can c.   Proverbs 28
  So dumb he can't fart and c. gum
    Lyndon B. Johnson 14
chewing
  c. gum for the eyes John Mason Brown 1
chic
  radical c.   Krim 1
  Radical C.   Tom Wolfe 1
Chicago
  American, C. born   Bellow 1
  streets of C.   Ribicoff 1
chick
  This c. is toast   Film Lines 85
chickadee
  My little c.   W. C. Fields 2
chicken
  champagne and a c.   Mary Montagu 1
  C. in Every Pot   Political Slogans 12
  c. in his pot every Sunday   Henri 1
  C. Little was right   Sayings 5
  c. or the egg   Sayings 62
  c. soup with rice   Sendak 1
  make a tender c.
    Advertising Slogans 101
  Some c.   Winston Churchill 24
chickens
  beside the white c.
    William Carlos Williams 2
  c. coming home to roost   Malcolm X 3
  Curses are like young c.   Southey 6
  Don't count your c.   Proverbs 53
  nobody here but us c.   Sayings 51
chief
  C. of the Army   Napoleon 16
  Hail to the C.   Walter Scott 7
chiefs
  too many c.   Modern Proverbs 15
child
  burnt c. dreads the fire   Proverbs 37
  C. is father of the Man
    William Wordsworth 12
  C. is under any Obligation
    Jonathan Swift 22

c. of the universe   Ehrmann 2
c.'s first year of life   Jean Piaget 1
c. should always say what's true
    Robert Louis Stevenson 16
c. was his warrant Cormac McCarthy 7
ever a c. can do
    Robert Louis Stevenson 14
Every c. is an artist   Picasso 7
Experience is the c. of Thought
    Disraeli 3
find me a four-year-old c.
    "Groucho" Marx 21
Give a little love to a c.   Ruskin 15
Give me a c. until he is seven Sayings 15
God bless the c.   Holiday 1
greatest respect is due the c.   Juvenal 7
I heard one calling, "C."
    George Herbert 2
I seem to hear a c. weeping
    Will Dyson 1
If you strike a c.
    George Bernard Shaw 21
invest in every c.   Edelman 1
It's only my c.-wife   Dickens 71
knows his own c.   Shakespeare 74
little c. shall lead them   Bible 167
Make me a c. again   Elizabeth Allen 1
Monday's c. is fair in face
    Nursery Rhymes 43
not lose his c.'s heart   Mencius 1
one c. born in this world   Nyro 1
shocks the mind of a c.
    Thomas Paine 29
simplicity, a c.   Pope 17
society's c.   Janis Ian 1
Spare the rod and spoil the c.
    Proverbs 280
Train up a c.   Bible 134
when their own c.   Dahl 1
wise c. that knows   Proverbs 328
young healthy C.   Jonathan Swift 27
childbirth
  Death and taxes and c.
    Margaret Mitchell 6
childhood
  C. Is the Kingdom   Millay 9
  c. shows the man   Milton 43
  have you seen my c. Michael Jackson 2
  make glad the heart of c.   Church 1
  miserable Irish c.   McCourt 1
  old are in a second c. Aristophanes 2
  prefer to return to c.   Desai 1
childhoods
  instead of happy c.   Herr 2
childish
  count religion but a c. toy   Marlowe 2
  put away c. things   Bible 355
children
  after her missing c.   Melville 14
  All c., except one, grow up   Barrie 2
  all the c. are above average   Keillor 1
  better reasons for having c.
    Dora Russell 1
  breeds contempt—and c.   Twain 51
  bringing up c.   Spock 2
  bungle raising your c.
    Jacqueline Kennedy Onassis 1
  c. and other living Lorraine Schneider 1
  c. at play   Montaigne 8

C. begin by loving   Wilde 36
c. now love luxury   Socrates 5
c. of the night   Stoker 3
C. should be seen and not heard
    Proverbs 46
c. swarmed to him   Auden 31
devour each of her c.   Vergniaud 1
draw like these c.   Picasso 2
first class, and with c.   Benchley 2
give advice to your c.   Truman 9
his c. smart   Mencken 45
I am fond of c. (except boys) Carroll 46
I love c.   Mitford 3
if c. believed in fairies   Barrie 10
Is our c. learning   George W. Bush 2
it devours its own c.   Büchner 1
it's the C.'s Crusade   Vonnegut 7
know where your c. are
    Advertising Slogans 104
known as the C.'s Hour   Longfellow 21
laboring c. can look out   Cleghorn 1
Lawyers, I suppose, were c. once
    Charles Lamb 3
leave them to our c.   Wilde 1
Listen, my c.   Longfellow 23
Men are but c. of a larger growth
    John Dryden 3
my four little c.
    Martin Luther King, Jr. 13
No man who hates dogs and c.
    Darnton 1
not more than two c.   Sanger 1
not much about having c.   Lodge 1
O those c.'s voices   Verlaine 6
on us, and on our c.   Bible 273
poor get c.   Gus Kahn 1
remember the c. you got
    Gwendolyn Brooks 1
Set forth three c.   Sexton 5
so many c. she didn't know
    Nursery Rhymes 77
Suffer the little c.   Bible 280
take charge of c.   William Morris 4
thou shalt bring forth c.   Bible 20
violations committed by c.
    Elizabeth Bowen 1
we are the c.   Michael Jackson 1
We can't form our c.   Goethe 8
We have no c. except me   Behan 5
What its c. become   LaFollette 3
when he died the little c. John Motley 1
Women and c. first   Sayings 66
Your c. are not your c.   Gibran 2
chill
  c. wind blows   Blackmun 3
chilling
  c. effect   Brennan 5
chills
  Nothing c. nonsense Woodrow Wilson 2
chillun
  all o' God's c. got-a wings
    Folk and Anonymous Songs 1
chime
  set a c. of words tinkling
    Logan Pearsall Smith 2
chimes
  c. at midnight   Shakespeare 65
chimpanzees
  In the time of c.   Hansen 1

chin
   hair of my chiny c.   Halliwell 1
China
   eat C.'s all our lives   Ho Chi Minh 3
   live up to my blue c.   Wilde 106
   slow boat to C.   Loesser 2
Chinatown
   It's C.   Film Lines 52
Chinese
   C. do not draw any distinction
        Lin Yutang 1
   C. people have only family Sun Yat-sen 1
chip
   c. of the old "block" Edmund Burke 27
chivalry
   age of c. is gone   Edmund Burke 18
chocolate
   c. cream soldier
      George Bernard Shaw 9
   I ate a whole c. bar   Schiffer 1
   makes the very best c.
      Advertising Slogans 91
chocolates
   Life is a box of c.   Film Lines 80
choice
   c., not an echo   Goldwater 2
   c. and master spirits Shakespeare 105
   c. of his enemies   Wilde 24
   just another "lifestyle c." Quayle 4
choices
   c. gone before   Didion 1
   It is our c., Harry   Rowling 4
choir
   join the c. invisible George Eliot 10
choirs
   bare ruined c.   Shakespeare 421
choo-choo
   Chattanooga c.   Gordon 1
choose
   C. life   Welsh 2
   c. the frame of our destiny
      Hammarskjöld 1
   I do not c. to run   Coolidge 4
   We c. to go to the moon
      John F. Kennedy 27
   woman can hardly ever c.
      George Eliot 9
choosers
   Beggars can't be c.   Proverbs 19
chooses
   Fate c. our relatives   Delille 1
chopped
   c. down the house Kenneth Koch 1
chopper
   Here comes a c. to chop off
      Nursery Rhymes 51
chord
   Lost C.   Procter 1
   struck one c. of music   Procter 3
chords
   mystic c. of memory   Lincoln 30
chortled
   he c. in his joy   Carroll 29
chosen
   few are c.   Bible 254
   Lord thy God hath c. thee Bible 71
Chou
   C. who had dreamed Chuang Tzu 1

Christ
   C. never came this far Carlo Levi 2
   C. stopped at Eboli   Carlo Levi 1
   C.! what are patterns for Amy Lowell 2
   C.-haunted   Flannery O'Connor 3
   It's C. Himself   Salinger 7
   may Lord C. enter in   Wilde 95
   remember C. our Savior
     Folk and Anonymous Songs 30
   that attained by C.   Mencken 6
   they believe in C. and Longfellow
      e.e. cummings 7
   When C. calls a man Bonhoeffer 3
   which is C. the Lord   Bible 289
Christian
   C. ideal has not been tried
      Chesterton 17
   C. religion not only was David Hume 8
   confidence which a C. feels Twain 2
   founded on the C. religion Barlow 1
   I am a C. because   John Irving 3
   Next day the C.
      George Bernard Shaw 24
   Onward, C. soldiers   Baring-Gould 1
   perfectly like a C.   Pope 10
   persuadest me to be a C. Bible 340
   Scratch the C.   Zangwill 1
   than a drunken C.   Melville 3
   There was only one C. Nietzsche 21
Christianity
   begins by loving C.   Coleridge 33
   C., of course   Balfour 3
   C. became a religion of the son
      Sigmund Freud 19
   C. is completed Judaism Disraeli 15
   C. is part of the law John Scott 1
   Evidences of C.   Coleridge 31
   His C. was muscular   Disraeli 29
   local thing called C. Thomas Hardy 22
   pure and genuine influence of C.
      Gibbon 6
Christians
   C. have burnt each other Byron 18
   early C. did not believe
     George Bernard Shaw 30
   there were C. before Christ Wilde 89
Christmas
   C. comes, but once a year Tusser 1
   C. won't be C. Louisa May Alcott 1
   first day of C.   Nursery Rhymes 10
   Ghost of C. Past   Dickens 42
   Ghost of C. Present   Dickens 43
   Ghost of C. Yet to Come Dickens 46
   Happy C. to all Clement C. Moore 5
   I will honor C. in my heart Dickens 47
   I'm dreaming of a white C.
      Irving Berlin 10
   Let them know it's C. time again
      Geldof 1
   Maybe C. . . . perhaps . . . means
      Seuss 9
   next day would be C. O. Henry 2
   On C. Day it is proclaimed
     George Bernard Shaw 24
   'Twas the night before C.
      Clement C. Moore 1
   was born on C. Day
     Folk and Anonymous Songs 30

Christmases
   may all your C. be white Irving Berlin 11
Christopher
   C. Robin went down with Alice Milne 1
   Sir C. Wren   E. Clerihew Bentley 1
church
   C. has opposed every innovation
      Twain 141
   get me to the c. on time
      Alan Jay Lerner 2
   God I ever felt in c.   Alice Walker 4
   Here is the c.   Nursery Rhymes 11
   I believe in the c. of Baseball
      Film Lines 33
   I will build my c.   Bible 246
   It was like being in c. James M. Cain 2
   Mother C.   Tertullian 1
   no other c. has ever understood
     Thomas Macaulay 10
   separation between c. and state
      Jefferson 33
   straying away from the c. Lenny Bruce 3
   True C. remains below T. S. Eliot 26
Churchill
   Hitler was better looking than C.
      Mel Brooks 4
cider
   ear full of c.   Runyon 2
cigar
   Close, but no c.   Sayings 6
   good C. is a Smoke   Kipling 1
   I love my c. too "Groucho" Marx 37
   really good 5-cent c.
     Thomas R. Marshall 1
   smoke more than one c. Twain 146
   Sometimes a c. is just a c.
     Sigmund Freud 24
cigarette
   C. Smoking Is Dangerous
     Anonymous 32
   tastes good like a c. should
     Advertising Slogans 135
cigarettes
   he doesn't smoke the same c.
     Jagger and Richards 3
cigars
   roller of big c.   Wallace Stevens 3
Cinara
   when good C. was my queen Horace 24
cinema
   c. is truth 24 times   Godard 1
circle
   Can the c. be unbroken A. P. Carter 1
   c. of the English language
      James Murray 1
   wheel is come full c. Shakespeare 315
circuits
   c. of a digital computer Pirsig 2
circumambulate
   c. her charm   T. S. Eliot 20
circumlocution
   C. Office was beforehand Dickens 93
circumstance
   Pride, pomp, and c. Shakespeare 275
circumstances
   C. alter cases   Proverbs 47
   C. beyond my individual control
      Dickens 72

circumstantial
c. evidence is very strong   Thoreau 15
circuses
bread and c.   Juvenal 5
cite
devil can c. Scripture   Shakespeare 72
cities
Seven c. warred for Homer   Heywood 2
Shame of the C.   Steffens 1
This is the sacking of c.   Jane Jacobs 1
citizen
he is a c. of the world   Francis Bacon 13
I am a c. of the world   Einstein 6
I am a Roman c.   Cicero 10
lay aside the C.   George Washington 1
citizens
first and second class c.   Willkie 1
under the word "c."   Taney 1
citoyens
Aux armes, c.   Rouget de Lisle 2
city
been long in c. pent   Keats 4
C. of New Orleans   Steve Goodman 1
c. of the big shoulders   Sandburg 1
c. that is set on a hill   Bible 208
c. that never sleeps   Ebb 5
C. upon a hill   Winthrop 1
long in populous c. pent   Milton 40
raised on c. land
    Charles Dudley Warner 3
stories in the naked c.   Film Lines 123
Unreal C.   T. S. Eliot 44
venal c. ripe to perish   Sallust 1
You can't fight C. Hall
    Modern Proverbs 29
civil
C. Disobedience or Civil Resistance
    Mohandas Gandhi 1
c. servant doesn't make   Ionesco 1
curtail our c. liberties
    Eleanor Roosevelt 1
founder of c. society   Rousseau 1
I know you have a c. tongue
    Film Lines 99
civilisation
true test of c.   Samuel Johnson 69
civility
C. costs nothing   Mary Montagu 4
civilization
botched c.   Ezra Pound 14
C. advances by extending   Whitehead 1
C. and Its Discontents   Riviere 1
c. had been left in female   Paglia 1
degree of c. in a society   Dostoyevski 1
Our c. is still   Dreiser 2
social moulds c. fits us into
    Thomas Hardy 15
test of a c.   Pearl S. Buck 3
Theory of the true c.   Baudelaire 10
usual interval of c.   Clemenceau 6
civilizations
breakdowns of c.   Toynbee 2
sixteen c. may have perished   Toynbee 3
civilized
countries that are called c.
    Thomas Paine 22
what we pay for c. society
    Oliver Wendell Holmes, Jr. 36

claim
last territorial c.   Hitler 4
clair
Au c. de la lune
    Folk and Anonymous Songs 4
clan
Your c. will pay me back
    Dorothy Parker 14
clap
If you believe, c. your hands   Barrie 11
Clark
C. Kent is Superman's   Film Lines 106
clasps
He c. the crag   Tennyson 36
class
better c. of enemy   Milligan 1
emergence of this New C.   Galbraith 3
history of c. struggles
    Marx and Engels 2
new c.   Djilas 1
classes
curse of the drinking c.   Wilde 109
masses against the c.   Gladstone 4
two c. of people   Benchley 1
classic
"C." A book which people   Twain 97
When you reread a c.   Clifton Fadiman 3
classical
C. quotation is the parole
    Samuel Johnson 100
classicism
C. is health   Goethe 24
classicist
c. in literature   T. S. Eliot 74
classics
c. in paraphrase   Ezra Pound 13
Claus
which C. of Innsbruck cast
    Robert Browning 7
claw
Nature, red in tooth and c.   Tennyson 30
claws
pair of ragged c.   T. S. Eliot 7
clay
friend and associate of this c.   Hadrian 1
his feet part of iron and part of c.
    Bible 189
clean
court of equity with c. hands   Eyre 1
new broom sweeps c.   Proverbs 210
cleaning
C. your house while your kids   Diller 2
cleanliness
C. is, indeed, next   John Wesley 2
clear
c. and present danger
    Oliver Wendell Holmes, Jr. 29
C. eyes, full hearts
    Television Catchphrases 20
C. your mind of cant
    Samuel Johnson 103
great enemy of c. language   Orwell 29
no c. line between religion
    Norman Maclean 1
not c. is not French   Rivarol 1
unduly c. to you   Greenspan 4
clearly
c. said   Boileau 4
To see c.   Ruskin 6

cleave
c. unto his wife   Bible 13
let my tongue c. to the roof   Bible 123
Clementine
his daughter C.   Montrose 1
Oh my darling C.   Montrose 2
Cleopatra
C.'s nose   Pascal 2
some squeaking C.   Shakespeare 404
clerk
best c. I ever had   Douglas MacArthur 7
clever
let who will be c.   Kingsley 1
Too c. by half   Salisbury 1
very c. woman   Kipling 4
cliché
you have used every c.
    Winston Churchill 53
clichés
Let's have some new c.   Goldwyn 14
client
fool for a c.   Proverbs 112
sacred duty which he owes his c.
    Brougham 1
clients
telling would-be c.   Elihu Root 2
cliffs
white c. of Dover   Nat Burton 1
climate
heaven for c.   Twain 46
in love with a cold c.   Southey 1
Love in a Cold C.   Mitford 2
where the c.'s sultry   Byron 17
whole c. of opinion   Auden 7
climates
diverse C. of Opinions   Glanvill 1
climax
works up to a c.   Goldwyn 15
climb
C. ev'ry mountain   Hammerstein 23
C. Mount Niitaka   Yamamoto 1
C. the mountains   Muir 3
Fain would I c.   Ralegh 2
climbed
c. the ladder   Mae West 8
c. to the top   Disraeli 30
cling
c. to guns or religion   Barack Obama 3
clock
big c. was running as usual   Fearing 1
mouse ran up the c.   Nursery Rhymes 23
My grandfather's c.   Work 1
rock around the c.   Freedman 1
The cuckoo c.   Film Lines 174
clocks
c. were striking thirteen   Orwell 33
Stop all the c.   Auden 1
clockwork
C. ORANGE   Anthony Burgess 1
cloistered
fugitive and c. virtue   Milton 7
close
C., but no cigar   Sayings 6
C. Encounters of the Third Kind
    Spielberg 1
c. my eyes   Hillingdon 1
C. only counts in horseshoes
    Frank Robinson 1
c. on Saturday   Coward 15

c. to the edge   Ed Fletcher 1
got to c. on page four   Mel Brooks 3
met them at c. of day   Yeats 26
so c. to the United States   Díaz 1
Stick c. to your desks   W. S. Gilbert 10
they long to be c. to you   Hal David 1
When you go out c. the door
                              Arthur Conan Doyle 20

closed
My life c. twice   Emily Dickinson 27
Rome has spoken; the case is c.
                              Augustine 7
went to Philadelphia, but it was c.
                              W. C. Fields 27

closer
If I hold you any c.   "Groucho" Marx 29
your enemies c.   Puzo 5

closes
c. on Saturday night
                              George S. Kaufman 4

close-up
I'm ready for my c.   Film Lines 167

closing
Always be c.   Mamet 1
It is c. time in the gardens
                              Cyril Connolly 4

cloth
Republican c. coat   Richard Nixon 2

clothes
C. make the man   Proverbs 48
Emperor's New C.   Andersen 2
I don't design c.   Lauren 1
require new c.   Thoreau 19
take the girl's c. off
                              Raymond Chandler 12
wrapped him in swaddling c.   Bible 287

clothing
come to you in sheep's c.   Bible 228
sheep in sheep's c.   Gosse 1
Wolf in Sheep's C.   Aesop 3

cloud
c. in trousers   Mayakovski 1
c.-capped towers   Shakespeare 442
Every c. has a silver lining Proverbs 49
wandered lonely as a c.
                              William Wordsworth 25

cloudcuckooland
C.   Aristophanes 3

clouds
C. now and again   Basho 4
fall from above the c.
                              Machado de Assis 2
trailing c. of glory
                              William Wordsworth 14

clover
C., any time, to him Emily Dickinson 26

clown
All the world loves a c.   Cole Porter 21

clowns
Send in the c.   Sondheim 6

club
belong to any c. that would accept
                              "Groucho" Marx 41
despised the C.   Galsworthy 2
first rule about fight c.   Palahniuk 1

clutch
drowning man will c. at a straw
                              Proverbs 78

clutching
alien people c. their gods   T. S. Eliot 70

CNN
This is C.   Television Catchphrases 14

coal
c. miner's daughter   Lynn 1

coalitions
C. of the willing   Harlan Cleveland 2

coast
How Long Is the C. of Britain
                              Mandelbrot 1

coat
c. of many colors   Bible 33
c. which fitted him   Jefferson 43
her c. is so warm   Nursery Rhymes 58
made my song a c.   Yeats 13
Republican cloth c.   Richard Nixon 2
takes off its c.   Sandburg 13

coats
wear different c.   Trollope 4

cobbler
would rather be a c.   Einstein 7

cobwebs
Laws are like C.   Jonathan Swift 3

Coca-Cola
answer to the C. company
                              Film Lines 69

cocaine
C. habit-forming   Bankhead 1
C. is God's way   Robin Williams 1
Driving that train, high on c.
                              Robert Hunter 2
smoked crack c.   Rob Ford 1

cock
before the c. crow   Bible 269
C. and a Bull   Sterne 4
faded on the crowing of the c.
                              Shakespeare 144
Ride a c.-horse   Nursery Rhymes 2
we ought to offer a c.   Socrates 4
Who killed C. Robin
                              Nursery Rhymes 12

Cockney
C. impudence   Ruskin 20

cockroaches
c. will still be here   Janowitz 1

cocoa
Making C. for Kingsley   Cope 1

cod
home of the bean and the c.   Bossidy 1

Codlin
C.'s the friend, not Short   Dickens 35

coffee
Damn good c.
                              Television Catchphrases 78
my life with c. spoons   T. S. Eliot 6
turning c. into theorems   Erdös 1
Wake up and smell the c.   Landers 1
You're the Cream in My C.   DeSylva 4

cohere
I cannot make it c.   Ezra Pound 30

coil
shuffled off this mortal c.
                              Shakespeare 189

coin
lost on a c. toss   Cormac McCarthy 3

coincidence
long arm of c.   Chambers 1

coins
c. for common use   Aristophanes 8

coitum
Post c. omne animal triste
                              Anonymous (Latin) 10

Coke
Ain't singin' for C.   Neil Young 4
Things go better with C.
                              Advertising Slogans 36

cokey
you do the Hokey C.   Jimmy Kennedy 2

cold
America won the C. War
                              George Herbert Walker Bush 13
bright c. day in April   Orwell 33
Cast a c. eye   Yeats 64
c. and passionate as the dawn Yeats 20
c. coming they had of it   Andrewes 1
c. coming we had of it   T. S. Eliot 68
c. friction of expiring sense
                              T. S. Eliot 120
c. never bothered me
                              Anderson-Lopez 1
"c. war" with its neighbors   Orwell 27
Europe catches a c.
                              Klemens von Metternich 3
fallen c. and dead   Whitman 12
in love with a c. climate   Southey 1
in the midst of a c. war   Baruch 2
Love in a C. Climate   Mitford 2
out in the c. all the time   le Carré 2
pry it from my c. dead hand
                              Political Slogans 22
Revenge can be eaten c.   Proverbs 252
shall not die of a c.   Cather 8
sneer of c. command   Percy Shelley 6
so c. no fire ever can warm me
                              Emily Dickinson 29
Spy Who Came in from the C.
                              le Carré 1
Stuff a c.   Proverbs 286
'Tis bitter c.   Shakespeare 140

colder
c. to a warmer body   Clausius 2

Cole
Old King C.   Nursery Rhymes 13

collar
Ring around the c.
                              Advertising Slogans 136

collect
Do not c. $200   Charles B. Darrow 1

collectible
use the word "c." as a noun   Lebowitz 6

collection
c. of books   Thomas Carlyle 15

collective
images of the c. unconscious Jung 1

colledges
c. has much to do   Dunne 12

college
cabbage with a c.   Twain 58
endow a c., or a cat   Pope 15
small c.   Daniel Webster 1

collision
it's a c. sport Hugh "Duffy" Daugherty 1

colonial
adjustment of all c. claims
                              Woodrow Wilson 21

colonies
these c. are   Richard Henry Lee 1
colonization
c. of the Great West
          Frederick Jackson Turner 1
subjects for future c.   James Monroe 2
color
any c. he wants   Henry Ford 1
c. of television, tuned to a dead
          Gibson 2
c. of their skin
          Martin Luther King, Jr. 10
c. of their skin   Martin Luther King, Jr. 5
c. was a false   Dorothy West 1
judged by the c. of their skin
          Martin Luther King, Jr. 13
Our Constitution is c.-blind
          John M. Harlan (1833–1911) 2
problem of the c.-line   Du Bois 5
walk by the c. purple   Alice Walker 5
we are met by the c. line   Douglass 13
colored
destiny of the c. American   Douglass 10
For C. Girls   Shange 1
white and c. people   Douglass 11
colorless
C. green ideas sleep   Chomsky 1
colors
coat of many c.   Bible 33
four c. may be wanted   Francis Guthrie 1
Colosseum
You're the C.   Cole Porter 6
colossus
like a c.   Shakespeare 98
Columbia
C. the gem of the ocean David T. Shaw 1
Hail, C.   Joseph Hopkinson 1
Roll on, C.   "Woody" Guthrie 4
Columbus
C. sailed the ocean blue   Stoner 1
column
Fifth c.   Mola 1
combat
Major c. operations in Iraq
          George W. Bush 16
reason is left free to c. it   Jefferson 49
combine
how to c. marriage   Steinem 5
come
all c. out in the wash   Proverbs 321
All things c. to those   Proverbs 9
c., all ye faithful   Wade 1
c., let us adore Him   Wade 2
c. across for the proletariat
          Dorothy Parker 37
c. again some other day
          Nursery Rhymes 61
C. and sit by my side
          Folk and Anonymous Songs 63
c. blow your horn   Nursery Rhymes 7
c. home to roost   Southey 6
c. in from the cold   le Carré 2
C. live with me   Marlowe 1
C. on and hear   Irving Berlin 1
C. on down   Television Catchphrases 50
c. out to the park   Berra 7
c. to the aid of the party   Anonymous 22
C. to the edge   Logue 1
c. up some time   Mae West 1

c. up some time   Mae West 2
c. up sometime and see me
          Mae West 10
C. what may   Shakespeare 330
C. with me to the Casbah
          Charles Boyer 1
Easy c., easy go   Proverbs 82
First c. first served   Proverbs 104
harder they c.   Cliff 2
I c. to bury Caesar   Shakespeare 111
If you build it, he will c.   Kinsella 1
I'm trying to c. to the point   Ginsberg 3
It's gotta c. from the heart
          Susanna Clark 1
its hour c. round   Yeats 30
I've c. from Alabama   Stephen Foster 1
mine hour is not yet c.   Bible 313
must c. down   Proverbs 315
must c. to an end   Proverbs 7
nobody will c.   Sandburg 10
Shape of Things to C.   H. G. Wells 8
Someday My Prince Will C.   Morey 3
thy kingdom c.   Missal 5
till the cows c. home "Groucho" Marx 20
wheel is c. full circle   Shakespeare 315
won't c. back till it's over   Cohan 6
worst is yet to c.   Twain 49
comeback
c. kid   William Jefferson "Bill" Clinton 1
Don't call it a c.   LL Cool J 1
comedian
test of a real c.   Nathan 1
comedie
C. humaine   Balzac 4
comedies
c. are not to be laughed at   Goldwyn 9
comedy
All I need to make a c.
          "Charlie" Chaplin 1
c. is when you walk   Mel Brooks 14
c. to those that think   Walpole 3
not as hard as playing c.   Gwenn 1
time equals c.   Steve Allen 1
comes
It c. with the territory   Arthur Miller 2
Nothing c. of nothing   Proverbs 216
What goes around, c. around
          Modern Proverbs 35
wicked this way c.   Shakespeare 377
comets
there are no c. seen   Shakespeare 101
comfort
c. of feeling safe   Craik 1
giving them Aid and C.   Constitution 8
minimum of c. is necessary
          Lumumba 2
comfortable
afflicts th' c.   Dunne 14
put on something more c.   Film Lines 94
comforters
Miserable c. are ye all   Bible 99
comforts
c. th' afflicted   Dunne 14
comin
C. thro' the rye   Robert Burns 10
coming
British are c.   Revere 2
chickens c. home to roost   Malcolm X 3
cold c. we had of it   T. S. Eliot 68

c. events cast their shadows before
          Thomas Campbell 3
c. for us that night   James Baldwin 6
Everything's C. Up Roses   Sondheim 3
glory of the c. of the Lord
          Julia Ward Howe 1
Guess Who's C. to Dinner
          Stanley Kramer 1
I'm c. to join you
          Television Catchphrases 60
Yanks are c.   Cohan 4
comma
took a c. out   Wilde 105
command
but to c.   Shakespeare 12
by whose c. they move
          Oliver Wendell Holmes, Jr. 9
sneer of cold c.   Percy Shelley 6
commander
c. who advances   Sun Tzu 8
good army c.   Tolstoy 5
commandments
words of the covenant, the ten c.
          Bible 63
commedia
La c. è finita   Leoncavallo 2
commences
where the West c.   Cole Porter 18
commend
C. her among her Female
          Benjamin Franklin 2
I c. my spirit   Bible 111
into thy hands I c. my spirit   Bible 307
commensurate
something c. to his capacity
          F. Scott Fitzgerald 33
comment
C. is free   C. P. Scott 1
commentary
rest is c.   Hillel 2
commerce
let there be c. between us   Ezra Pound 6
commercial
memory of the c. classes   Wilde 66
commit
C. a crime and the earth
          Ralph Waldo Emerson 8
C. it then to the flames   David Hume 10
Thou shalt not c. adultery   Bible 57
committed
what crimes are c.   Roland 1
committee
c. on snakes   Perot 2
c. is a group   Sayings 7
punctuated by c. meetings   Will 2
committing
infidels are c. suicide   Sahhaf 1
murder a man who is c.
          Woodrow Wilson 12
common
century of the c. man
          Henry A. Wallace 1
c. law is not a brooding
          Oliver Wendell Holmes, Jr. 24
C. looking people   Lincoln 54
C. sense is not so c.   Voltaire 14
C. sense is nothing more   Einstein 26
c. task   Keble 1
c.-law, n. The will   Bierce 23

concur with the c. reader
Samuel Johnson 35
creeping c. sense Wilde 31
dream of a c. language Rich 8
He nothing c. did or mean
Andrew Marvell 4
light of c. day William Wordsworth 15
no man got to be c. Paige 7
nor lose the c. touch Kipling 33
sprung from some c. source
William Jones (1746–1794) 2
trained and organised c. sense
T. H. Huxley 1
commonplace
"C.," said Holmes
Arthur Conan Doyle 5
c. mind, knowing itself
Ortega y Gasset 2
commons
every rational herdsman sharing a c.
Hardin 4
Freedom in a c. Hardin 3
Tragedy of the C. Hardin 2
commonwealth
British C. Smuts 1
communicate
failure to c. Film Lines 56
I needed to c. Simenon 1
communication
c. of the dead T. S. Eliot 117
great enemy of c. Whyte 1
communion
c. with her visible forms
William Cullen Bryant 2
phatic c. Malinowski 1
communism
C. is Soviet power Lenin 5
specter of C. Marx and Engels 1
communist
Catholic and the C. are alike Orwell 32
C. and the Catholic are not saying
Orwell 8
If he is still a C. at 30 Clemenceau 5
member of the C. Party
J. Parnell Thomas 1
members of the C. Party
Joseph McCarthy 1
they call me a C. Câmara 1
What is a c. Elliott 1
Communists
Catholics and C. have committed
Graham Greene 6
community
contemporary c. standards Brennan 2
godly little New England c. Kipling 38
compact
c. majority Ibsen 13
c. which exists between the Garrison 4
imagination all c. Shakespeare 56
company
c. he is wont to keep Euripides 3
hell for c. Twain 46
I bought the c. Advertising Slogans 105
known by the c. he keeps Proverbs 50
Misery loves c. Proverbs 193
that is not good c. Austen 21
Two is c. Proverbs 311
comparable
no intellect c. to my own
Margaret Fuller 2

compare
Shall I c. thee Shakespeare 411
comparisons
C. are odious Proverbs 51
compete
it does c. with life Henry James 7
competence
distinction between c. Chomsky 2
competition
c. of the market
Oliver Wendell Holmes, Jr. 28
competitor
c. is drowning Kroc 1
complacencies
C. of the peignoir Wallace Stevens 8
complain
against Fate c. Andrew Marvell 3
deep inner need to c. Jane Wagner 4
Never c. and never explain Disraeli 32
complained
c. of the long voyage Columbus 2
complaint
Life is a fatal c.
Oliver Wendell Holmes 11
that's the most fatal c. Hilton 2
complete
C. satisfaction Selfridge 1
completed
Christianity is c. Judaism Disraeli 15
complex
last refuge of the c. Wilde 28
military-industrial c. Eisenhower 11
more c., the sooner dead Parkinson 7
complexion
Keep that schoolgirl c.
Advertising Slogans 97
complexities
all mere c. Yeats 54
complexity
endlessly significant c. Aldous Huxley 5
compliance
by a timely c., prevented him
Henry Fielding 4
complicated
become still more c. Poul Anderson 1
complications
only the chosen had "c." Wharton 3
compliment
to return the c. W. S. Gilbert 5
compliments
c. that mediocrity pays Wilde 98
compose
not to c. the Odyssey Borges 8
composer
greatest c. known to me Haydn 1
compound
c. interest Einstein 37
comprehended
If the end be clearly c.
Alexander Hamilton 11
comprehensible
that it is c. is a miracle Einstein 13
universe seems c. Steven Weinberg 1
compress
c. the most words Lincoln 58
compromise
deprived of the arts of c. Bickel 1
founded on c. and barter
Edmund Burke 10

compulsion
Every c. is put upon writers
Sinclair Lewis 3
No c. is there in religion Koran 5
compulsory
I believe in c. cannibalism
Abbie Hoffman 4
computation
means of mechanical c. Howard Aiken 1
compute
Does not c. Television Catchphrases 46
computer
circuits of a digital c. Pirsig 2
individual to have a c.
Kenneth H. Olsen 1
it takes a c. Sayings 56
Never trust a c. Wozniak 1
no c. program can ever be a mind
Searle 2
computers
market for about five c.
Thomas J. Watson, Jr. 1
You have so many c. Walesa 1
conceal
losing his ability to c. it
Robertson Davies 2
concealing
c. how much we think Twain 112
concedes
Power c. nothing Douglass 8
conceive
virgin shall c. Bible 165
conceived
new nation, c. in Liberty Lincoln 41
concentrates
c. his mind wonderfully
Samuel Johnson 89
concentration
resist the c. of power
Woodrow Wilson 6
concept
God is a c. Lennon 3
conception
first instance of her c. Pius 1
concern
our c. was speech T. S. Eliot 119
concise
Vigorous writing is c. Strunk 1
conclusion
foregone c. Shakespeare 277
conclusions
drawing sufficient c.
Samuel Butler (1835–1902) 11
draws necessary c. Benjamin Peirce 1
condemn
c. a little more Major 2
condemned
c. to be free Sartre 2
c. to kill time Paz 4
c. to repeat it Santayana 3
condensation
c. of sensations Matisse 1
condition
aspires towards the c. of music Pater 2
Human C. Malraux 1
stamp of the human c. Montaigne 14
conditions
without moralising on c.
Cyril Connolly 5

condom
equivalent of a c.   Jonathan Miller 2
conduct
I consider your c.   Arno 1
conductor
passengers will ask the c.   Sandburg 8
confected
Odors, c. by the cunning French
T. S. Eliot 38
confederacy
Dunces are all in C.   Jonathan Swift 5
conference
c. is a gathering   Fred Allen 2
idea was ever born in a c.
F. Scott Fitzgerald 48
my last press c.   Richard Nixon 3
won a c.   Will Rogers 12
confess
how to c. a fault   Benjamin Franklin 19
confession
C. is good for the soul   Proverbs 52
suicide is c.   Daniel Webster 8
confessional
A c. passage has   Salinger 6
confidant
C., Confidante, n.   Bierce 24
confidence
nation's c. in the judge
John Paul Stevens 1
patient c. in the ultimate   Lincoln 25
serene c. which a Christian feels
Twain 2
confine
verge of her c.   Shakespeare 290
confinement
sentenced to solitary c.
Tennessee Williams 10
conflict
irrepressible c.   Seward 2
Never in the field of human c.
Winston Churchill 17
conform
how to rebel and c.   Crisp 1
conformists
honors its live c.   McLaughlin 2
confronted
c. with the witnesses   Constitution 15
confuse
c. dissent with disloyalty   Murrow 3
confused
Anyone who isn't c.   Murrow 6
c. alarms of struggle and flight
Matthew Arnold 19
confusing
c. a man with what he possesses
Wilde 45
confusion
C. now hath made his masterpiece
Shakespeare 360
congress
both houses of C.   Nozick 3
criminal class except C.   Twain 87
man cannot get into c.   Twain 14
suppose you were a member of C.
Twain 140
congressman
premature C.   Twain 12
congs
Kinquering c.   Spooner 3

conjecture
best c. possible   Agassiz 2
conjunction
c. of an immense military
Eisenhower 10
connect
c. the prose and the passion   Forster 3
c. the prose in us   Forster 2
connected
All things are c.   Ted Perry 5
toe bone c. with the foot bone
Folk and Anonymous Songs 21
connection
ancient heavenly c.   Ginsberg 7
conquer
By this, c.   Constantine the Great 1
conquered
hate is c. by love   Pali Tripitaka 1
I came, I saw, I c.   Julius Caesar 6
conquering
c. hero comes   Morell 1
conquers
Love c. all things   Virgil 17
conquest
c. of the earth   Conrad 11
conquistador
nothing but a c.   Sigmund Freud 5
conscience
catch the c. of the King   Shakespeare 187
conduct that shocks the c.   Frankfurter 5
C. and cowardice   Wilde 23
c. does make cowards   Shakespeare 192
C.: the inner voice   Mencken 7
cut my c. to fit   Hellman 1
let your c. be your guide   Film Lines 132
person's c.   Harper Lee 2
uncreated c. of my race   Joyce 11
values liberty of c.   Jefferson 34
wrestled with his c.   Eban 2
conscious
c. that you are ignorant   Disraeli 13
mystery of the c.   Joyce 29
consciousness
Behaviorist cannot find c.
John B. Watson 7
C. was upon him   Amis 1
Cosmic c.   Bucke 1
stream of thought, of c.   William James 5
consecration
c. of its own   Hawthorne 10
consensual
c. hallucination that was the Matrix
Gibson 3
consent
Advice and C. of the Senate
Constitution 5
but by your own c.   Channing 1
C. of the Governed   Jonathan Swift 9
feel inferior without your c.
Eleanor Roosevelt 6
I will ne'er c.   Byron 19
without his own c.   John Locke 7
without that other's c.   Lincoln 8
consented
"I will ne'er consent"—c.   Byron 19
consenting
only between c. adults   Vidal 5
consequences
c. of our inventions   Joy 1

Ideas Have C.   Weaver 1
study of unintended c.   Merton 3
conservation
Principle of the C. of Force
Helmholtz 1
conservative
Americans are c.   Will 3
C., n. A statesman who   Bierce 25
C. Government is an organized
Disraeli 18
C. Party at prayer   Royden 1
c. who has been arrested   Tom Wolfe 9
make me c. when old   Frost 19
most c. persons I ever met
Woodrow Wilson 1
or else a little C.   W. S. Gilbert 27
other side, the c. party
Ralph Waldo Emerson 28
To be c., then, is to prefer   Oakeshott 1
true c. seeks to protect
Franklin D. Roosevelt 12
whole art of c. politics   Bevan 1
conservatives
C. are young people   Tolstoy 14
C. . . . being by the law   Mill 15
Men are c. when they are
Ralph Waldo Emerson 22
conserve
What they want to c.   Will 3
consider
c. her ways, and be wise   Bible 124
C. the lilies of the field   Bible 219
c. your conduct   Arno 1
Today I c. myself the luckiest   Gehrig 1
when you c. the alternative   Chevalier 1
consistency
C. is the last refuge   Wilde 121
foolish c. is the hobgoblin
Ralph Waldo Emerson 16
consistent
It will become entirely c.
Oliver Wendell Holmes, Jr. 5
consolation
C., n. The knowledge   Bierce 26
conspicuous
c. by its presence   John Russell 2
C. consumption   Veblen 2
consumption is not c.   Rae 1
conspiracies
All professions are c.
George Bernard Shaw 28
no c.   Tocqueville 5
conspiracy
c. against the public   Adam Smith 3
c. is everything that ordinary   DeLillo 3
C. of silence   Comte 2
vast c. against the forces
Michael Harrington 2
vast right-wing c.   Hillary Clinton 6
conspirators
all the c. save only he   Shakespeare 130
constable
because the c. has blundered   Cardozo 2
constabulary
when c. duty's to be done
W. S. Gilbert 23
constancy
infernal c. of the women
George Bernard Shaw 4

constant
c. as the northern star   Shakespeare 103
energy of the universe is c.   Clausius 3
friendship in c. repair
    Samuel Johnson 48
one c. through all the years   Kinsella 5
constantly
c. risking absurdity   Ferlinghetti 1
Constantinople
Why did C. get the works
    Jimmy Kennedy 4
constitution
act against the C. is void   Otis 3
American C. is, so far   Gladstone 3
C., in all its provisions
    Salmon P. Chase 2
c. controls any legislative
    John Marshall 1
c. intended to endure   John Marshall 5
c. is not intended to embody
    Oliver Wendell Holmes, Jr. 20
C. is what the judges
    Charles Evans Hughes 1
C. of the United States is a law
    David Davis 1
c. we are expounding   John Marshall 4
C. which at any time exists
    George Washington 5
higher law than the C.   Seward 1
my CURSE be on the C.
    Wendell Phillips 1
My faith in the C. is whole
    Barbara C. Jordan 2
not the birth of the C.
    Thurgood Marshall 2
ordain and establish this C.
    Constitution 1
Our C. is color-blind
    John M. Harlan (1833–1911) 2
preserve, protect, and defend the C.
    Constitution 4
read the C. in the only way   Brennan 7
repugnant to the c.   John Marshall 2
resulting from their Federal C.
    Tocqueville 3
What's the c. between friends
    Timothy J. Campbell 1
Your c. is all sail   Thomas Macaulay 13
constitutionality
doubts as to c.   Franklin D. Roosevelt 8
constitutions
American c. were to liberty
    Thomas Paine 19
c. are the work of time   Van Buren 1
look at c.   Jefferson 43
constraints
c. aping marriage   Updike 2
construct
c. the socialist order   Lenin 4
I c. lines and color   Mondrian 1
consul
C., v.t. In American politics   Bierce 27
consult
C., v. To seek another's   Bierce 28
consulting
only unofficial c. detective
    Arthur Conan Doyle 8
consumed
c. by either fire or fire   T. S. Eliot 121

consumer
c. isn't a moron   Ogilvy 2
consummation
c. devoutly to be wish'd
    Shakespeare 189
consumption
Conspicuous c.   Veblen 2
c. is not conspicuous   Rae 1
contact
C. light   Neil A. Armstrong 1
Football is not a c. sport
    Hugh "Duffy" Daugherty 1
contain
I c. multitudes   Whitman 8
contained
c. nothing but itself   Henry Adams 7
containment
c. of Russian expansionist
    George F. Kennan 1
contempt
c. prior to examination   Paley 2
coort to show its c.   Dunne 21
Familiarity breeds c.   Proverbs 98
Familiarity breeds c.   Twain 51
contemptible
c. little army   Wilhelm II 3
contender
I could've been a c.   Film Lines 128
content
c. of their character
    Martin Luther King, Jr. 10
c. of their character
    Martin Luther King, Jr. 13
I am c.   John Quincy Adams 3
land of lost c.   Housman 3
other is its c.   Rodell 1
contented
c. least   Shakespeare 414
contents
mind to correlate all its c.   Lovecraft 1
contest
not the victory but the c.   Coubertin 1
continent
almost a c.   Ezra Pound 29
C. isolated   Anonymous 4
"dark c." for psychology
    Sigmund Freud 12
continental
c. liar   Political Slogans 9
Jehovah and the C. Congress
    Ethan Allen 1
may be quite C.   Robin 2
continents
toast of two c.   Dorothy Parker 42
continuation
nothing but the c. of state policy
    Clausewitz 2
continuing
c. voyages of the starship   Roddenberry 3
contra
C. NATURAM   Ezra Pound 23
contraception
fast word about oral c.   Woody Allen 2
contract
movement from Status to C.   Maine 1
reads the marriage c.   Duncan 1
Social C.   Rousseau 2
Society is indeed a c.   Edmund Burke 20
unspoken c. of a wife   Hardwick 1

verbal c. isn't worth   Goldwyn 8
contracts
Prisoners cannot enter into c.
    Nelson Mandela 2
contradict
Do I c. myself   Whitman 8
Never c.   John Arbuthnot Fisher 1
contradiction
intelligence is a c. in terms
    "Groucho" Marx 48
contradictory
c. is also true   Wilde 20
contradicts
c. every other religion   Santayana 4
contrary
Mary, Mary, quite c.   Nursery Rhymes 41
On the c.   Ibsen 27
contribution
When you cease to make a c.
    Eleanor Roosevelt 7
contrive
c. artificial appetites
    Samuel Johnson 20
contrived
Country has in its Wisdom c.
    John Adams 12
control
Circumstances beyond my individual c.
    Dickens 72
c. even kings   Molière 11
I am in c. here   Haig 1
controlled
not to have c. events   Lincoln 45
controlling
no c. legal authority   Gore 2
controls
c. not only the future   Orwell 19
Who c. the past   Orwell 37
convenient
as it is c., let us believe   Ovid 2
convention
c. of your set   Maugham 4
conventional
c. army loses   Kissinger 1
c. wisdom   Galbraith 2
converge
Everything that rises must c.
    Teilhard de Chardin 1
conversation
no such thing as c.   Rebecca West 4
conversations
Most c. are simply   Millar 1
converse
c. with myself   Descartes 2
conversion
till the C. of the Jews   Andrew Marvell 11
converted
You have not c. a man   John Morley 2
conveyance
not a public c.   Iris Murdoch 3
convicted
other's c.   "Billy" Martin 1
conviction
best lack all c.   Yeats 29
convictions
C. are more dangerous enemies
    Nietzsche 3
convicts
few descendants from c.
    Stella Franklin 4

convinced
c. beyond doubt   van der Post 1
convulsive
Beauty will be c.   Breton 1
cook
American c.   Julia Child 1
as c. go, she went   Saki 2
cookbook
It's a c.   Knight 1
cooked
I do if they're properly c. W. C. Fields 12
cookie
way the c. crumbles Modern Proverbs 16
cookies
stayed home and baked c.
                       Hillary Clinton 2
cooking
Joy of C.   Rombauer 1
cooks
being placed above the c.   Mozart 3
can not live without c. Owen Meredith 1
He liked those literary c.
                     Hannah More 3
Too many c. spoil the broth
                      Proverbs 303
cool
C. Britannia   Stanshall 1
c. media are high   McLuhan 9
I'd rather be dead than c.   Cobain 3
in the c. of the day   Bible 17
in the c. tombs   Sandburg 6
Keep c.   Ralph Waldo Emerson 35
Keep C. with Coolidge
                    Political Slogans 24
never get to be c.   Neil Young 6
Coolidge
Keep Cool with C.   Political Slogans 24
cop
every c. is a criminal
                   Jagger and Richards 12
I'm a c.   Radio Catchphrases 4
Copperfield
all that David C.   Salinger 1
copulation
Birth, and c., and death   T. S. Eliot 88
cord
threefold c. is not quickly   Bible 146
cordiale
L'entente c.   Louis Philippe 1
core
deep heart's c.   Yeats 3
cork
Some weasel took the c. out
                     W. C. Fields 10
corn
amid the alien c.   Keats 19
cometh al this newe c.   Chaucer 5
c. in Egypt   Bible 34
c. is as high   Hammerstein 6
Jimmy, crack c.
          Folk and Anonymous Songs 9
make two Ears of C.   Jonathan Swift 12
Raise less c. and more hell   Lease 1
whar a man gits his c. pone Twain 127
corner
c. of a foreign field   Rupert Brooke 1
Prosperity Is Just Around the C.
                    Political Slogans 29

corny
c. as Kansas in August Hammerstein 16
coronets
Kind hearts are more than c. Tennyson 4
corporate
c. money in politics John Paul Stevens 2
corporations
c. from making contributions
                   Theodore Roosevelt 16
corps
effete c. of impudent snobs   Agnew 2
thoughts will be of the c.
                  Douglas MacArthur 5
corpse
have a good-looking c.   Willard Motley 1
He'd make a lovely c.   Dickens 52
corpulent
c. man of fifty   Leigh Hunt 1
correct
politically c.   James Wilson 1
than be c. with those men   Cicero 14
theory is c. anyway   Einstein 31
correlate
mind to c. all its contents   Lovecraft 1
correlative
finding an "objective c."   T. S. Eliot 27
correspondence
becomes a c.   Wilde 110
corridors
c. of power   Snow 1
through the c. of Time   Longfellow 12
corrupt
C., adj. In politics   Bierce 29
Power tends to c.   Acton 3
Unlimited power is apt to c.
              William Pitt, Earl of Chatham 3
corrupting
c. the minds of the young   Plato 1
Cortez
like stout C.   Keats 3
Cosby
you rape women, Bill C.   Buress 1
cosi
C. fan tutte le belle   da Ponte 1
cosmic
C. consciousness   Bucke 1
cosmos
total push and pressure of the c.
                    William James 17
cost
c. of liberty is less than   Du Bois 7
costly
C. thy habit   Shakespeare 159
costume
c. of woman   Bloomer 1
cottage
Love and a c.   Colman the Elder 1
poorest man may in his c.
              William Pitt, Earl of Chatham 2
cotton
in de land ob c.   Emmett 1
KING C.   Christy 1
could
just because I c.
        William Jefferson "Bill" Clinton 11
Little Engine That C.   Watty Piper 1
counsel
Assistance of C. for his defence
                    Constitution 15

count
As long as I c. the Votes   Nast 1
c. on a murderer   Nabokov 3
C. your blessings   Oatman 1
Don't c. your chickens   Proverbs 53
I won the c.   Somoza 1
If you can c. your money   Getty 3
Let me c. the ways
            Elizabeth Barrett Browning 2
let us c. our spoons   Samuel Johnson 54
only people who c. in any marriage
                  Hillary Clinton 5
When angry c. 10.   Jefferson 44
you can c. me out
            Lennon and McCartney 21
counted
can be c. counts   Cameron 1
faster we c. our spoons
              Ralph Waldo Emerson 41
Success is c. sweetest
                  Emily Dickinson 1
countenance
Knight of the Doleful C.   Cervantes 3
counter-culture
remains a c.   Talcott Parsons 1
counterfeit
death's c.   Shakespeare 361
counters
words are wise men's c.   Hobbes 3
counting
C. the cars   Paul Simon 4
it's the c.   Stoppard 4
countries
c. always apologized   Twain 78
Imagine there's no c.   Lennon 9
join both c.' souls   Bolívar 1
No two c. that both have a McDonald's
                  Thomas L. Friedman 1
some c. have too much history
          William Lyon Mackenzie King 1
two c. separated
              George Bernard Shaw 58
country
America is my c.   Stein 7
Anyone who loves his c.   Garibaldi 1
ask not what your c. can do
                  John F. Kennedy 16
betraying my c.   Forster 8
chief need of the c.
                  Thomas R. Marshall 1
C. has in its Wisdom contrived
                    John Adams 12
c. to fight for   Thoreau 32
c.'s planted thick with laws   Bolt 2
Cry, the beloved c.   Paton 2
die but once to serve our c.   Addison 3
Duty, honor, c.   Douglas MacArthur 4
every c. but his own   W. S. Gilbert 32
Every c. has the government   Maistre 1
for C., and for Yale   Durand 1
for our c.'s good   Barrington 1
God made the c.   William Cowper 5
going out and dying for his c.   Patton 3
good for our c.   Charles E. Wilson 1
Happy is the c.   Proverbs 54
his first, best c.   Oliver Goldsmith 1
history of every c.   Cather 1
I love a sunburnt c.   Mackellar 1
I love thee still—my c.
                  William Cowper 6

I tremble for my c.   Jefferson 13
In the c. of the blind   Erasmus 1
like a month in the c.   Dietz 3
lose for my c.   Nathan Hale 1
loyalty to one's c.   Twain 39
My c., right or wrong   Schurz 1
My c., 'tis of thee
    Samuel Francis Smith 1
my c. is Kiltartan   Yeats 21
My c. is the world   Thomas Paine 23
no c. for old men   Yeats 46
no relish for the c.   Sydney Smith 4
ONE C., ONE CONSTITUTION
    Daniel Webster 11
our c., right or wrong   Decatur 1
our c. is going to do for us
    John F. Kennedy 5
past is a foreign c.   Hartley 1
peace of each c.   John XXIII 2
save in his own c.   Bible 241
she is my c. still   Charles Churchill 1
that was in another c.   Marlowe 3
there is my c.   Otis 4
This is a beautiful c.   John Brown 1
This is a free c.   Proverbs 116
undiscover'd c.   Shakespeare 191
what our c. has done
    Oliver Wendell Holmes, Jr. 6
what we can do for the c.
    John F. Kennedy 5
what your c. can do for you   Gibran 5
When my c. takes her place
    Robert Emmet 1
Your King and C. need you
    Advertising Slogans 138

countrymen
first in the hearts of his c.
    "Light-Horse Harry" Lee 1
Friends, Romans, c.   Shakespeare 111
countryside
smiling and beautiful c.
    Arthur Conan Doyle 19
counts
Close only c. in horseshoes
    Frank Robinson 1
It's the thought that c.
    Modern Proverbs 87
what's inside that c. Modern Proverbs 45
couple
Odd C.   Neil Simon 1
courage
C. is resistance to fear   Twain 65
c. of men fails   Film Lines 111
c. to change   Wygal 1
guard his musk? C.!   Film Lines 192
One man with c.   Andrew Jackson 7
red badge of c.   Stephen Crane 2
True c. is facing danger
    L. Frank Baum 7
two o'clock in the morning c.
    Napoleon 9
Without justice c. is weak
    Benjamin Franklin 5
courageous
When captains c. whom death Ballads 6
couriers
stays these c. from the swift   Kendall 1
course
c. of true love   Shakespeare 51
take thou what c.   Shakespeare 126

Westward the c. of empire takes
    Berkeley 3
courses
Horses for c.   Proverbs 149
court
institution, gentlemen, is a c.
    Harper Lee 3
courtesan
in the mouth of a c.
    Ralph Waldo Emerson 36
courtesy
very pink of c.   Shakespeare 40
courtroom
C.: a place where Jesus   Mencken 9
cousins
his sisters, and his c.   W. S. Gilbert 7
covenant
c. with death   Garrison 4
covenants
Open c. of peace   Woodrow Wilson 17
cover
C. me with kisses   Harry 1
c. the multitude of sins   Bible 384
I c. all   Sandburg 7
I C. the Waterfront   Max Miller 1
judge a book by its c.   Proverbs 32
covered
all c. with snow
    Folk and Anonymous Songs 60
If you c. him with garbage   Ray Davies 4
covers
c. of this book   Bierce 144
covet
Thou shalt not c.   Clough 6
Thou shalt not c. thy neighbor's
    Bible 60
coveted
c. her and me   Poe 16
cow
c. jumped over the moon
    Nursery Rhymes 22
Don't have a c.   Groening 1
never saw a Purple C.   Gelett Burgess 1
coward
No c. soul is mine   Emily Brontë 1
cowardice
Conscience and c.   Wilde 23
C., as distinguished   Hemingway 25
cowardly
not a "c." attack   Sontag 8
cowards
conscience does make c.
    Shakespeare 192
C. die many times   Shakespeare 102
cowboy
last true c.   Least Heat-Moon 1
cowboys
Grow Up to Be C.   Ed Bruce 1
Where have all the c. gone Paula Cole 1
cows
dance with you till the c.
    "Groucho" Marx 20
Sacred c. make the tastiest
    Abbie Hoffman 3
coxcomb
c. ask two hundred guineas   Ruskin 20
coyness
this c., Lady, were no crime
    Andrew Marvell 10

crab
Big sisters are the c. grass   Schulz 4
crack
c. a few laws   Mae West 16
c. in everything   Leonard Cohen 5
heaven's vault should c. Shakespeare 316
Jimmy, c. corn, and I don't care
    Folk and Anonymous Songs 9
cracked
c. lookingglass of a servant   Joyce 15
Human speech is like a c. kettle
    Flaubert 1
mirror c. from side to side   Tennyson 1
crackers
It's c. to slip   Allingham 2
cracks
Now c. a noble heart   Shakespeare 237
cradle
C. of American liberty   Otis 5
c. will rock   Nursery Rhymes 1
from the c. to the grave
    Edward Bellamy 2
hand that rocks the c.   Proverbs 133
Out of the c.   Whitman 16
Rocked in the c. of the deep
    Emma Willard 1
cradles
hand that c. the rock
    Clare Boothe Luce 5
craft
c. so long to lerne   Chaucer 4
In my c. or sullen art   Dylan Thomas 8
crag
He clasps the c.   Tennyson 36
crane
Jane, tall as a c.   Sitwell 1
crawl
client will c. through a sewer
    William S. Burroughs 2
crawls
our lot c. between dry ribs   T. S. Eliot 20
crazy
c. salad with their meat   Yeats 23
Here's to the c. ones
    Advertising Slogans 13
when I was c.
    William Tecumseh Sherman 6
wild and c. guys
    Television Catchphrases 65
you'll be c. the rest of your life
    W. C. Fields 5
cream
chocolate c. soldier
    George Bernard Shaw 9
skim milk masquerades as c.
    W. S. Gilbert 11
We All Scream for Ice C.   Moll 1
You're the C. in My Coffee   DeSylva 4
create
himself c. the taste
    William Wordsworth 10
What I cannot c.   Feynman 4
created
all men are c. equal   Jefferson 2
all men are c. equal   Lincoln 41
C. half to rise   Pope 22
In the beginning God c.   Bible 1
men and women are c. equal
    Elizabeth Cady Stanton 1
Universe was c.   Douglas Adams 4

creates
he c. gods by the dozens   Montaigne 13
creating
spent c. oneself   Barney 1
creation
got your niche in c.   Radclyffe Hall 2
present at the C.   Alfonso 1
since the C.   Richard Nixon 7
took the whole of C.   Ted Hughes 5
whole c. moves   Tennyson 35
creative
C. Destruction   Schumpeter 3
In the c. process   Stanislavsky 2
matter of c. accounting   Mel Brooks 1
such a thing as c. hate   Cather 4
creator
dispense with a c.   Proust 6
given to us by the C.   John Paul II 1
creature
not a c. was stirring
    Clement C. Moore 1
reasonable c., God's image   Milton 6
creatures
All c. great and small   Cecil Alexander 1
c. outside looked from pig to man
    Orwell 26
Millions of spiritual c.   Milton 35
these little c.   Leeuwenhoek 1
credit
Full Faith and C.   Constitution 9
Give c. where c. is due   Proverbs 55
In science the c.   Francis Darwin 1
takes c. for the rain   Dwight Morrow 1
who gets the c. for it   Montague 1
credo
C. in unum Deum   Missal 7
creed
Pagan suckled in a c.
    William Wordsworth 21
creeds
C. must disagree   Chesterton 8
dust of c. outworn   Percy Shelley 12
creep
make your flesh c.   Dickens 2
creepers
Jeepers c.   Johnny Mercer 1
creeping
c. common sense   Wilde 31
creeps
c. in this petty pace   Shakespeare 393
crème
pupils are the c.   Spark 1
Cretans
All C. are liars   Epimenides 1
cricket
c. on the hearth   Milton 10
cried
c. all the way to the bank   Liberace 2
little children c. in the streets
    John Motley 1
when he c. the little children   Auden 17
cries
my bootless c.   Shakespeare 413
crieth
voice of him that c.   Bible 172
crime
bigamy, sir, is a c.   Monkhouse 2
Commit a c. and the earth
    Ralph Waldo Emerson 8

C. does not pay   Proverbs 56
C. is a sociopolitical   Packer 1
c. is due   Waugh 2
c. of being a young man
    William Pitt, Earl of Chatham 1
c. to examine the laws   John Morley 1
c. was to them what art   Wilde 42
Don't do the c.   Modern Proverbs 17
He is the Napoleon of c.
    Arthur Conan Doyle 25
It isn't a c. exactly   Dunne 16
let the punishment fit the c.
    W. S. Gilbert 39
lowest c. rates   Barry 1
more than a c.   Fouché 1
Murder is a c.   Legman 1
returns to the scene of the c.
    Modern Proverbs 18
specific c. has appeared   Arendt 6
this coyness, Lady, were no c.
    Andrew Marvell 10
tough on c.   Blair 1
your whole life-style a C. in Progress
    Hunter S. Thompson 8
crimes
c. of this guilty land   John Brown 4
high C. and Misdemeanors
    Constitution 7
register of the c., follies   Gibbon 4
tableau of c. and misfortunes   Voltaire 15
what c. are committed   Roland 1
criminal
because he is a c.   Clarence S. Darrow 2
c. always returns to the scene
    Modern Proverbs 18
c. class except Congress   Twain 87
c. is the creative artist   Chesterton 20
c. is to go free   Cardozo 2
c. law stands to the passion
    James Fitzjames Stephen 1
every cop is a c.   Jagger and Richards 12
for ends I think c.   Keynes 1
I am not a c.   Arthur Conan Doyle 33
criminals
all the c. in their coats   Dylan 27
laws that manufacture c.
    Benjamin R. Tucker 1
some c. should escape
    Oliver Wendell Holmes, Jr. 37
the way it handles c.   Ramsey Clark 1
cringe
Australian Cultural C.   A. A. Phillips 1
cripple
two Jews, and a c.   Watt 1
crises
c. of human affairs   John Marshall 5
crisis
c. is composed of two characters
    John F. Kennedy 2
cannot be a c. next week   Kissinger 2
identity c.   Erikson 1
Crispian
at the name of C.   Shakespeare 136
critic
c. is a man who knows   Tynan 2
doer, not the mere c.
    Theodore Roosevelt 1
function of the mere c.
    Theodore Roosevelt 2

not the c. who counts
    Theodore Roosevelt 18
criticism
Against c. a man   Goethe 16
c. of life   Ezra Pound 1
c. of religion   Karl Marx 1
my own definition of c.
    Matthew Arnold 12
Poetry is at bottom a c. of life
    Matthew Arnold 34
sincerest form of c.   Sheed 1
criticize
You cannot c. it   John Jay Chapman 1
criticized
If you are not c.   Rumsfeld 8
criticizes
It c. you   John Jay Chapman 1
critics
You know who the c. are   Disraeli 24
Crito
C., we ought to offer a cock   Socrates 4
crocodile
After 'while, c.   Guidry 1
How doth the little c.   Carroll 5
tears of the c.   George Chapman 2
crocodiles
wisdom of the c.   Francis Bacon 24
crony
government by c.   Krock 1
crook
I am not a c.   Richard Nixon 14
crooked
c. shall be made straight   Bible 173
c. timber of humanity   Kant 1
I'm as c. as I'm supposed   Hammett 3
There was a c. man   Nursery Rhymes 37
cross
ask a witness on c.-examination
    David Graham 1
crucify mankind upon a c. of gold
    William Jennings Bryan 3
Do not c. that bridge   Proverbs 57
he died on the c.   Nietzsche 21
hot c. buns   Nursery Rhymes 8
inability to c. the street
    Virginia Woolf 14
Let us c. over the river
    "Stonewall" Jackson 1
Many rivers to c.   Cliff 1
With my c.-bow I shot   Coleridge 3
crossed
girl likes to be c. in love   Austen 10
when I have c. the bar   Tennyson 46
crossing
swap horses when c.   Lincoln 47
crossroad
I went down to the c.   Robert Johnson 1
crow
before the cock c.   Bible 269
c. has settled   Basho 7
For there is an upstart C.
    Robert Greene 1
crowd
Far from the madding c.'s
    Thomas Gray 9
Lonely C.   Riesman 1
these faces in the c.   Ezra Pound 4
three is a c.   Proverbs 311

crowded
 it was a bit c.
  Diana, Princess of Wales 2
 It's too c.   McNulty 1
 One c. hour of glorious life Mordaunt 1
crowing
 faded on the c. of the cock
  Shakespeare 144
crown
 c. thy good with brotherhood Bates 1
 head that wears a c.   Shakespeare 64
 presented him a kingly c.
  Shakespeare 116
 Within the hollow c. Shakespeare 22
crucified
 Why were we c. into sex
  D. H. Lawrence 4
crucifixion
 think of the c.   Weil 5
crucify
 c. mankind upon a cross
  William Jennings Bryan 3
 they're going to c. me
  Lennon and McCartney 23
crud
 Ninety percent of everything is c.
  Sturgeon 1
crude
 As c. a weapon   Rachel Carson 2
cruel
 c. and unusual punishments
  Constitution 17
 c. only to be kind Shakespeare 217
cruellest
 April is the c. month   T. S. Eliot 39
cruelty
 c. is the primary feeling   Sade 1
 In c. and tyranny
  Elizabeth Cady Stanton 8
crumbles
 way the cookie c.   Modern Proverbs 16
crumbs
 c. which fell from the rich man's
  Bible 301
crusade
 Children's C.   Vonnegut 7
crush
 c. them all under you   Alexandra 1
 We first c. people Lydia Maria Child 1
crushed
 c. by books   Hersey 1
crushes
 Whatever c. individuality   Mill 10
crutch
 Reality is a c. for people Jane Wagner 1
cry
 battle c. of freedom
  George Frederick Root 2
 C., the beloved country   Paton 1
 C. havoc and let slip Shakespeare 107
 Do not stand at my grave and c. Frye 2
 Don't c. because it   Seuss 17
 Don't c. for me Argentina   Tim Rice 3
 don't you c. for me   Stephen Foster 1
 It was a fine c.   Toni Morrison 3
 made them c.   Nursery Rhymes 18
 proud to c.   Lincoln 53
 so lonesome I could c. Hank Williams 1

crying
 c. in the wilderness   Bible 199
 c. like a fire in the sun   Dylan 12
 no c. in baseball   Film Lines 109
 no use c. over spilt milk Proverbs 58
crystal
 word is not a c.
  Oliver Wendell Holmes, Jr. 26
Cuba
 ninety miles from C.   Castro 4
cubic
 One c. foot less and it would be
  Benchley 9
Cu-ca-monga
 Anaheim, Azusa, and C.
  Radio Catchphrases 11
cucaracha
 La c., la c.
  Folk and Anonymous Songs 46
cuccu
 Lhude sing c.
  Folk and Anonymous Songs 16
cuckolded
 robbed and c. less often   Voltaire 17
cuckoo
 one flew over the c.'s nest
  Folk and Anonymous Songs 52
 sudden c.   Whistler 3
 The c. clock   Film Lines 174
 thus sings he: "C.!"   Shakespeare 25
cucumbers
 Sun-Beams out of C. Jonathan Swift 18
cui
 C. bono   Cicero 12
culpa
 mea c.   Missal 3
culprit
 stirs the C.—Life! Emily Dickinson 3
cult
 c. of the individual   Khrushchev 2
cultivate
 We must c. our garden   Voltaire 10
cultural
 Australian C. Cringe   A. A. Phillips 1
 only c. advantage   Woody Allen 27
culture
 believe only in French c.   Nietzsche 24
 c. being a pursuit of our total
  Matthew Arnold 22
 c. of life   John Paul 2
 knowledge of one other c.
  Margaret Mead 1
 lead a whore to c. Dorothy Parker 39
 little creature of his c. Ruth Benedict 1
 pursue C. in bands   Wharton 4
 vibrant, healthy c.   Welsh 1
 When I hear the word "c."   Johst 1
cultured
 C. people practice   I Ching 3
cultures
 One of those "Two C."   Nabokov 9
 separation between the two c.   Snow 2
cunning
 Odors, confected by the c. French
  T. S. Eliot 38
 right hand forget her c.   Bible 123
 silence, exile, and c.   Joyce 9
cup
 many a slip 'twixt c.   Proverbs 187

 my c. runneth over   Bible 109
 We'll tak a c. o' kindness yet
  Robert Burns 9
cupboard
 c. was bare   Nursery Rhymes 45
Cupid
 C. painted blind   Shakespeare 52
curates
 abundant shower of c.
  Charlotte Brontë 7
curds
 eating her c. and whey
  Nursery Rhymes 47
cure
 C. the disease and kill the patient
  Francis Bacon 11
 no c. for birth and death   Santayana 10
 worth a pound of c.   Proverbs 243
cured
 I was c. all right   Anthony Burgess 3
curfew
 C. shall not ring   Thorpe 1
 c. tolls the knell of parting
  Thomas Gray 3
curiosity
 C. killed the cat   Modern Proverbs 20
 full of 'satiable c.   Kipling 28
 Have you tried c. Dorothy Parker 36
curious
 always very c.   Rey 1
 c. incident of the dog
  Arthur Conan Doyle 21
curiouser
 C. and c.   Carroll 4
curl
 who had a little c.   Longfellow 28
currency
 Debasing the Moral C. George Eliot 20
 debauch the c.   Keynes 3
 Europe to have one c.   Napoleon 2
current
 boats against the c.
  F. Scott Fitzgerald 35
curse
 c., bless me now Dylan Thomas 18
 c. of the drinking classes   Wilde 109
 c. the darkness   James Keller 1
 c. the darkness Adlai E. Stevenson 14
 C. you, Red Baron   Schulz 7
 public debt is a public c. Madison 11
cursed
 country c. with bigness   Brandeis 3
 c. the bread
  Edwin Arlington Robinson 2
 O c. spite   Shakespeare 173
curses
 C., foiled again   Sayings 8
 C. are like young chickens   Southey 6
curtain
 behind the "iron c." Ethel Snowden 1
 draw the c.   Rabelais 4
 iron c. has descended
  Winston Churchill 33
 iron c. of silence   Troubridge 1
 iron c. would at once   Goebbels 3
 man behind the c. Film Lines 195
 something behind a c. Thomas Paine 21
custard
 joke is ultimately a c. pie   Orwell 13

Daniel
D. come to judgment   Shakespeare 81
Godfrey D.   W. C. Fields 1
Danno
Book 'em, D.
        Television Catchphrases 27
Danny
Oh, D. boy   Weatherly 1
danse
l'on y d. Folk and Anonymous Songs 73
dapple
d.-dawn-drawn Falcon
        Gerard Manley Hopkins 5
dappled
Glory be to God for d. things
        Gerard Manley Hopkins 3
dare
Do I d. disturb the universe T. S. Eliot 5
Love that d. not speak its name
        Lord Alfred Douglas 1
Love that d. not speak its name
        Wilde 82
none d. call it treason   Harington 1
who d. do more   Shakespeare 346
dared
no mortal ever d. to dream   Poe 8
Darien
silent, upon a peak in D.   Keats 3
daring
d. young man   Leybourne 1
fails while d. greatly
        Theodore Roosevelt 18
dark
Afraid to Come Home in the D.
        Harry Williams 2
afraid to trust them in the d. Lincoln 68
All cats are gray in the d.   Proverbs 42
among these d. Satanic mills
        William Blake 19
"d. continent" for psychology
        Sigmund Freud 12
d. horse   Disraeli 5
D. night   St. John of the Cross 1
d. side which he never shows Twain 108
d. world is going to submit   Du Bois 10
d. world thinking   Du Bois 9
follow the talent to the d. place   Jong 1
go home in the d.   O. Henry 8
In a d., glassly   Spooner 1
In the nightmare of the d.   Auden 24
It was a d. and stormy night
        Bulwer-Lytton 1
it's too d. to read   "Groucho" Marx 49
leap into the d.   Hobbes 11
O d., d., d.   Milton 47
O d. d. d.   T. S. Eliot 104
real d. night of the soul
        F. Scott Fitzgerald 41
seduced by the d. side   George Lucas 3
These are not d. days
        Winston Churchill 23
We work in the d.   Henry James 12
what other dungeon is so d.
        Hawthorne 16
woods are lovely, d., and deep   Frost 16
darken
Never d. my Dior   Lillie 2
never d. my towels again
        "Groucho" Marx 23

darkest
d. hour is just before   Proverbs 61
darkling
we are here as on a d. plain
        Matthew Arnold 19
darkly
through a glass eye, d.   Twain 79
we see through a glass, d.   Bible 355
darkness
cast out into outer d.   Bible 231
curse the d.   James Keller 1
curse the d.   Adlai E. Stevenson 14
d. comprehended it not   Bible 309
d. is good   Bannon 1
encounter d. as a bride
        Shakespeare 256
heart of an immense d.   Conrad 18
Hello d. my old friend   Paul Simon 1
prince of d.   Shakespeare 299
rather d. visible   Milton 19
two eternities of d.   Nabokov 1
darling
Charlie he's my d.   Nairne 1
his mother's undisputed d.
        Sigmund Freud 10
Oh my d. Clementine   Montrose 2
darlings
Murder your d.   Quiller-Couch 1
We must march my d.   Whitman 17
Darwin
D.'s bulldog   Thomas Henry Huxley 9
Dasher
Now, D.! now, Dancer!
        Clement C. Moore 3
dashing
D. through the snow   Pierpont 1
dat
D. ole davil, sea   Eugene O'Neill 2
data
"hard" d. and "soft" d.
        Bertrand Russell 3
plural of anecdote is d.   Wolfinger 1
theorize before one has d.
        Arthur Conan Doyle 17
torture the d.   Coase 1
date
d. which will live in infamy
        Franklin D. Roosevelt 25
doubles your chances for a d.
        Woody Allen 39
dates
question of d.   Talleyrand 2
dating
saved in the world of d. Helen Fielding 2
daughter
As is the mother, so is the d.   Bible 186
coal miner's d.   Lynn 1
Like mother, like d.   Proverbs 201
London's d.   Dylan Thomas 16
marry the boss's d.
        Robert Emmons Rogers 1
My d.   Shakespeare 75
my d.'s my d. all her life   Craik 2
my d.'s my d. all the days of her life
        Proverbs 279
my sister and my d.   Film Lines 51
put your d. on the stage   Coward 12
daughters
even d. of the swan   Yeats 36

Words are men's d.   Samuel Madden 1
words are the d. of earth
        Samuel Johnson 5
dauphin
kingdom of daylight's d.
        Gerard Manley Hopkins 5
David
all that D. Copperfield   Salinger 1
dawn
Bliss was it in that d.
        William Wordsworth 23
by the d.'s early light Francis Scott Key 1
D., n. The time when men   Bierce 31
just before the d.   Proverbs 61
My regiment leaves at d.
        "Groucho" Marx 12
passionate as the d.   Yeats 20
Rosy-fingered d.   Homer 8
daws
for d. to peck at   Shakespeare 258
day
always a d. away   Charnin 2
Any d. above ground
        Modern Proverbs 22
apple a d.   Modern Proverbs 1
break of d. arising   Shakespeare 415
bright cold d. in April   Orwell 33
compare thee to a summer's d.
        Shakespeare 411
d. away from Tallulah   Dietz 3
d. is short   Talmud 5
d. I was meant not to see   Thatcher 7
d. of his death was a dark cold Auden 18
d. that I die   McLean 2
d. that reveals to him   Douglass 6
d. the music died   McLean 1
D.-o   Belafonte 1
dreamers of the d.   T. E. Lawrence 3
end of a perfect d. Carrie Jacobs Bond 1
Every d., in every way   Coué 1
Every dog has his d.   Proverbs 74
every dog his d.   Kingsley 2
first d. of Christmas Nursery Rhymes 10
follow as the night the d.
        Shakespeare 161
from this d. forward
        Book of Common Prayer 15
Go ahead, make my d.
        Ronald W. Reagan 9
He'd had a hard d.'s night   Lennon 2
It takes place every d.   Camus 8
It's been a hard d.'s night
        Lennon and McCartney 4
light of common d.
        William Wordsworth 15
Live every d. as if Modern Proverbs 53
live to fight another d.   Proverbs 102
longest d.   Rommel 1
make my d.   Film Lines 164
met them at close of d.   Yeats 26
Not a d. without a line   Apelles 1
rare as a d. in June
        James Russell Lowell 3
Rome was not built in a d. Proverbs 259
seize the d.   Horace 17
speak of the D. of Judgment   Kafka 7
Sufficient unto the d. is the evil
        Bible 220
That'll be the d.   Film Lines 151

day (cont.):
That'll be the d.   Holly 1
They who dream by d.   Poe 2
This is a good d. to die   Sayings 54
Today is the first d. of the rest
                              Abbie Hoffman 1
tomorrow is a new d.
                            Lucy Montgomery 2
Tomorrow is a new d.   Proverbs 302
tomorrow is another d.
                          Margaret Mitchell 8
what a wonderful d.   Wrubel 1
dayadhvam
D.: I have heard the key   T. S. Eliot 58
days
After three d. men grow weary
                          Benjamin Franklin 3
D. and months are travellers   Basho 1
d. of our years are threescore   Bible 117
d. of wine and roses   Dowson 3
forty d. and forty nights   Bible 63
forty d. and forty nights   Bible 28
golden d. of Saturn's reign   Virgil 15
halcyon d.   Aristophanes 4
Happy d. are here   Yellen 3
In olden d., a glimpse   Cole Porter 2
In the prison of his d.   Auden 25
MY D. ARE DARKER THAN YOUR NIGHTS
                                       Herr 3
My salad d.   Shakespeare 399
our dancing d.   Shakespeare 29
seen better d.   Shakespeare 407
shower of all my d.   Dylan Thomas 11
Ten D. That Shook the World
                                  John Reed 1
Thirty d. hath September
                            Nursery Rhymes 67
we have seen better d.   Shakespeare 87
dazzle
mine eyes d.   John Webster 3
de
D. minimus non curat lex
                         Anonymous (Latin) 5
dead
After I am d., the boy   George V 1
been d. many times   Pater 1
besides, the wench is d.   Marlowe 3
Better d. than Red   Political Slogans 6
Better Red than d.   Political Slogans 7
between the quick and the d.   Baruch 1
communication of the d.   T. S. Eliot 117
D. battles   Tuchman 1
d. don't stay interested
                            Thornton Wilder 2
d. for a ducat   Shakespeare 214
d. for several weeks   Tartt 1
d. man's town   Springsteen 4
D. men tell no tales   Proverbs 62
d. troublemakers   McLaughlin 2
Either he's d.   "Groucho" Marx 28
fallen cold and d.   Whitman 12
fell across the picture—d.   D'Arcy 2
Fifteen men on the d. man's
                     Robert Louis Stevenson 8
fool than to be d.
                     Robert Louis Stevenson 3
Ford to City: Drop D.   Anonymous 9
God is d.   Nerval 2
God is d.   Nietzsche 7

God is d.   Nietzsche 12
he had been d. for two years   Lehrer 7
healthy and wealthy and d.   Thurber 8
He's d., Jim   Star Trek 3
I see d. people   Film Lines 156
I'd rather be d. than cool   Cobain 3
I'll Sleep When I'm D.   Zevon 2
I'm not d.   Monty Python 8
In the long run we are all d.   Keynes 4
king is d.   Sayings 34
Laws are a d. letter
                        Alexander Hamilton 7
Let the d. bury their dead   Bible 233
Let the d. Past bury its dead
                               Longfellow 3
living will envy the d.   Khrushchev 7
Mistah Kurtz—he d.   Conrad 17
more to say when I am d.
                    Edwin Arlington Robinson 3
Never speak ill of the d.   Proverbs 281
not until long after I'm d.   Goldwyn 6
oats for a d. horse   Film Lines 105
one of two things, young or d.
                            Dorothy Parker 46
only good Indian is a d. Indian
                               Proverbs 126
Only the d. have seen   Santayana 9
only the d. smiled   Akhmatova 1
our d. bodies   Robert Falcon Scott 3
people my age are d.   Stengel 4
politician—who is d.   Thomas B. Reed 1
politician who's been d.   Truman 10
Pray for the d.   Mother Jones 1
pry it from my cold d. hand
                          Political Slogans 22
pure and very d.   Sinclair Lewis 4
Rosencrantz and Guildenstern are d.
                            Shakespeare 238
sex and the d.   Yeats 33
10,000 d. in one battle   Hussein 3
There are no d.   Maeterlinck 2
tuned to a d. channel   Gibson 2
wanted to make sure he was d.
                                  Goldwyn 5
Wanted, D. or Alive   George W. Bush 7
When I am d. and opened   Mary I 1
Why Aren't You D. Yet   Heimel 1
Wicked Witch is d.   Harburg 2
with soul so d.   Walter Scott 2
yellow stripes and d. armadillos
                                Hightower 2
deadlines
I love d.   Douglas Adams 12
deadly
female of the species is more d.
                                 Kipling 34
deaf
d., inexorable, inflexible
                          Algernon Sidney 1
d. adder that stoppeth   Bible 114
d. as an adder   John Adams 3
roomful of d. people   Paul H. O'Neill 1
deal
each is given a square d.
                        Theodore Roosevelt 12
from our Government a fair d.
                                  Truman 5
given a square d.   Theodore Roosevelt 11
needed was a new d.   Twain 40

new d. and a change Woodrow Wilson 4
new d. for the American
                       Franklin D. Roosevelt 4
Shut up and d.   Film Lines 12
deals
D. are my art form   Trump 1
dean
I think of D. Moriarty   Kerouac 2
To our queer old d.   Spooner 5
dear
D. 338171   Coward 7
Elementary, my d. Watson
                        Arthur Conan Doyle 39
Experience keeps a d. school
                        Benjamin Franklin 22
fault, d. Brutus   Shakespeare 98
My d., I don't give a damn
                          Margaret Mitchell 7
too d. for my possessing
                            Shakespeare 422
dearer
d. half   Milton 37
dearest
Mommie d.   Cristina Crawford 1
dearly
D. beloved   Book of Common Prayer 16
death
After the first d.   Dylan Thomas 16
be not told of my d.   Thomas Hardy 9
Because I could not stop for D.
                          Emily Dickinson 8
best cure for the fear of d.   Hazlitt 6
Birth, and copulation, and d.
                             T. S. Eliot 88
brought d. into the world   Milton 17
brought d. into the world   Twain 56
build the house of d.   Montaigne 6
come away d.   Shakespeare 243
covenant with d.   Garrison 4
day of his d. was a dark cold   Auden 18
D., old admiral   Baudelaire 5
d., where is thy sting   Bible 359
D., where is thy sting   W. C. Fields 17
D. and Taxes   Proverbs 63
D. and taxes and childbirth
                          Margaret Mitchell 6
D. be not proud   Donne 2
D. cancels all   Beerbohm 3
D. ends a life   Robert Anderson 3
d. had undone so many   T. S. Eliot 44
d. hath no more dominion   Bible 343
D. is a displaced name   De Man 1
D. is a master   Paul Celan 1
D. is always   Theodore Roosevelt 8
D. is going to be a great Virginia Woolf 7
D. is nothing at all
                       Henry Scott Holland 1
d. is one of the few things
                            Woody Allen 22
D. is the great leveller   Proverbs 64
d. lies dead   Swinburne 5
d. of a feeling   Nietzsche 5
d. of the Author   Barthes 2
d. of the poet was kept from   Auden 19
d. panel   Palin 4
d. penalty is to be abolished   Karr 1
D. shall be no more   Donne 3
d. shall have no dominion
                          Dylan Thomas 3

defending
make it worth d.   Robert Wilson 1
defense
best d. is a good offense
                        Modern Proverbs 23
Extremism in the d. of liberty
                        Goldwater 3
Millions for d. but not a cent
                        Robert Harper 1
deferred
What happens to a dream d.
                        Langston Hughes 8
defining
difficult and d. moment
                        George W. Bush 13
definite
a d. maybe   Goldwyn 2
deformity
Art is significant d.   Roger Fry 1
behold a Lump of D.   Jonathan Swift 17
defunct
slaves of some d. economist   Keynes 12
degenerates
everything d. in the hands   Rousseau 8
degeneration
from barbarism to d.   Clemenceau 6
degrading
All authority is quite d.   Wilde 48
degree
d. of civilization in a society
                        Dostoyevski 1
depends upon differences of d.
                Oliver Wendell Holmes, Jr. 23
degrees
Six d. of separation   Guare 1
dei
Agnus D.   Missal 6
Vox populi, vox D.   Alcuin 1
déjà vu
It's d. all over again   Berra 15
Delacroix
making a man like D.
                Pierre-Auguste Renoir 3
delay
D. is the deadliest form   Parkinson 13
law's d.   Shakespeare 190
deliberation
D., n. The act of examining   Bierce 32
delicate
expensive d. ship   Auden 30
delicious
Goodness, how d.
                Folk and Anonymous Songs 31
delight
begins in d. and ends in wisdom
                        Frost 20
Idiot's D.   Sherwood 2
lonely impulse of d.   Yeats 22
our capacity for d. and wonder   Conrad 3
delighted
You have d. us long enough   Austen 9
delights
Man d. not me   Shakespeare 181
dell
farmer in the d.   Nursery Rhymes 17
de-lovely
it's d.   Cole Porter 14
déluge
Après nous le d.   Pompadour 1

delusion
d., a mockery, and a snare   Denman 1
demagogue
D., n. A political opponent   Bierce 33
demand
concedes nothing without a d.
                        Douglass 8
I'd d. a recount   Buckley 3
demanded
age d. an image   Ezra Pound 12
must be d. by the oppressed
                Martin Luther King, Jr. 6
demands
public . . . d. certainties   Mencken 16
demarcations
ghostlier d., keener sounds
                Wallace Stevens 13
demi-monde
Le D.   Dumas the Younger 1
demi-vierges
Les D.   Prévost 1
democ'acy
D. gives every man
                James Russell Lowell 4
democracy
arsenal of d.   Franklin D. Roosevelt 22
cure for the ills of D.   Addams 1
death of d. is not likely   Hutchins 2
D., which shuts the past   Tocqueville 15
D. applied to love   Mencken 18
d. cannot exist   Tytler 1
D. dies in darkness   Bob Woodward 1
D. is based on the assumption
                        Heinlein 6
D. is grounded upon so childish
                        Mencken 26
D. is the recurrent suspicion
                        E. B. White 2
D. is the theory   Mencken 2
D. is the wholesome   Gorbachev 1
D. is the worst form of government
                        Briffault 1
d. is the worst form of Government
                Winston Churchill 34
D. means everybody but me
                Langston Hughes 7
D. substitutes election
                George Bernard Shaw 19
D. . . . would, it seems   Plato 9
expresses my idea of d.   Lincoln 13
in a functioning d.   Sen 1
made safe for d.   Woodrow Wilson 15
makes d. possible   Niebuhr 1
never has been a real d.   Rousseau 5
Not only does d. make every man forget
                        Tocqueville 16
test of a d.   Helen Keller 4
There never was a d. yet   John Adams 15
Two cheers for D.   Forster 7
United States to be a d.   Beard 2
democrat
boy of fifteen who is not a d.
                        John Adams 19
I am a D.   Will Rogers 15
demolish
d. everything completely   Descartes 5
demon
d.'s that is dreaming   Poe 13

demon-lover
woman wailing for her d.   Coleridge 20
demonstrandum
Quod erat d.   Euclid 1
den
beard the lion in his d.   Walter Scott 4
deniability
provide some future d.   Poindexter 1
denied
call that may not be d.   Masefield 2
denies
spirit that always d.   Goethe 12
Denmark
rotten in the state of D.   Shakespeare 165
denominations
d. of Protestant   Tone 1
dentist
d. to be drilling   Alan Jay Lerner 5
dentists
Four out of five d.
                Advertising Slogans 117
deny
D. thy father   Shakespeare 33
thou shalt d. me thrice   Bible 269
which nobody can d.
                Folk and Anonymous Songs 22
depart
after I d. this vale   Mencken 25
Wayward sisters, d. in peace
                Winfield Scott 1
department
fair sex is your d.
                Arthur Conan Doyle 31
dependence
women be educated for d.
                Wollstonecraft 7
dependent
she is d. on what happens
                George Eliot 9
depends
d. on what the meaning of "is" is
        William Jefferson "Bill" Clinton 9
progress d. on the unreasonable
                George Bernard Shaw 22
so much d. upon
                William Carlos Williams 2
deplorables
basket of b.   Hillary Clinton 10
deposit
d. of prejudices laid down   Einstein 26
making a large d. in my name
                Woody Allen 11
depravity
total d. of inanimate things
                Katherine Walker 1
depression
d. is when you lose your own   Beck 1
it's called a d.   Jesse Jackson 3
depths
Out of the d. have I cried   Bible 121
derangement
nice d. of epitaphs
                Richard Brinsley Sheridan 3
descend
Almost all people d. to meet
                Ralph Waldo Emerson 9
descended
d. from that heroic   Charles Darwin 12

descent
d. from a certain group of people Boas 3
describe
Can you d. this Akhmatova 2
description
it beggared all d. Shakespeare 401
desert
d. of the real itself Baudrillard 1
I never will d. Mr. Micawber Dickens 60
In the d. I saw a creature
  Stephen Crane 1
make a d. and call it peace Tacitus 1
Operation D. Storm
  George Herbert Walker Bush 11
deserts
d. of vast eternity Andrew Marvell 12
deserve
d. hanging ten times Montaigne 16
d. to get it good and hard Mencken 2
I don't d. all these kind words Benny 1
You d. a break today
  Advertising Slogans 80
deserved
no man d. less at her hands
  Edward Everett Hale 2
deserves
d. all the consequences Duncan 1
face he d. Orwell 51
government it d. Maistre 1
One good turn d. another Proverbs 127
design
I don't d. clothes Lauren 1
Luck is the residue of d. Rickey 1
no evidence of beneficent d.
  Charles Darwin 8
designed
d. by geniuses Wouk 1
d. for use rather than ostentation
  Gibbon 5
desire
D., d.! I have too dearly bought
  Philip Sidney 1
d. for desires Tolstoy 10
d. his father's death Dostoyevski 7
d. of the moth for the star
  Percy Shelley 18
d. should so many years
  Shakespeare 63
d. to be desired Naomi Wolf 4
From what I've tasted of d. Frost 11
horizontal d. George Bernard Shaw 59
in women, love begets d.
  Jonathan Swift 37
mixing memory and d. T. S. Eliot 39
provokes the d. Shakespeare 358
streetcar named D.
  Tennessee Williams 1
That Obscure Object of D. Buñuel 2
woman's d. is rarely other Coleridge 39
desires
doing what one d. Mill 13
desiring
D.'s this man's art Shakespeare 414
desks
Stick close to your d. W. S. Gilbert 10
desolation
Magnificent d. Aldrin 1
despair
beauty born out of its own d. Yeats 40

Never d. Horace 16
on the far side of d. Sartre 4
ye Mighty, and d. Percy Shelley 7
desperate
D. diseases must have d. remedies
  Proverbs 65
Diseases d. grown Shakespeare 219
desperation
lives of quiet d. Thoreau 18
despise
I work for a Government I d. Keynes 1
know whom to d. Thomas Hardy 4
some other Englishman d. him
  George Bernard Shaw 38
despised
old, mad, blind, d. Percy Shelley 8
despond
name of the slough was D. Bunyan 2
despondency
d. and madness William Wordsworth 19
despotism
d. tempered by epigrams
  Thomas Carlyle 4
destiny
Anatomy is d. Sigmund Freud 8
character is d. George Eliot 6
d. of the colored American Douglass 10
frame of our d. Hammarskjöld 1
no other d. Sartre 7
our manifest d. O'Sullivan 2
rendezvous with d.
  Franklin D. Roosevelt 9
tryst with d. Nehru 1
destroy
d. my beautiful wickedness
  Film Lines 193
d. the town to save it Anonymous 13
I am not come to d. Bible 208
I'd rather d. it Ibsen 18
involves the power to d. John Marshall 7
not the power to d.
  Oliver Wendell Holmes, Jr. 38
right to d. Daniel Webster 2
What does not d. me Nietzsche 25
Whom the gods wish to d.
  Cyril Connolly 2
Whom the gods would d. Proverbs 123
destroyed
d. but not defeated Hemingway 28
d. by madness Ginsberg 7
destroyer
death, the d. of worlds Oppenheimer 3
destruction
causes of its d. Rousseau 6
politics of personal d.
  William Jefferson "Bill" Clinton 13
prefer the d. David Hume 3
Pride goeth before d. Bible 133
that leadeth to d. Bible 226
to say that for d. ice Frost 12
urge for d. is also Bakunin 1
destructive
d. element submit yourself Conrad 10
details
devil is in the d. Modern Proverbs 24
God is in the d. Flaubert 3
God is in the D. Mies van der Rohe 2
God is in the d. Warburg 1

detection
D. is, or ought to be
  Arthur Conan Doyle 9
detective
d. only the critic Chesterton 20
d. story is about P. D. James 2
d.-story is the normal recreation
  Guedalla 2
only unofficial consulting d.
  Arthur Conan Doyle 8
detector
shock-proof shit d. Hemingway 35
détente
prepared to discuss a d.
  John F. Kennedy 28
deteriorate
d. the cat Twain 50
determined
Bin Laden D. to Attack
  Condoleezza Rice 1
D. to save succeeding generations
  Anonymous 35
detest
Englishmen detest a siesta Coward 8
deum
Te D. Niceta 1
Deutschland
D. über alles Hoffmann 1
development
course of human d. Sigmund Freud 7
What a revoltin' d. "Groucho" Marx 36
What a revolting d.
  Radio Catchphrases 14
deviates
Shadwell never d. into sense
  John Dryden 6
device
It was a miracle of rare d. Coleridge 22
devil
apology for the D.
  Samuel Butler (1835–1902) 12
Better the d. you know Proverbs 24
blue-eyed d. white man Fard 1
deny the being of a D. Mather 1
D. and the Deep Blue Sea Koehler 1
d. can cite Scripture Shakespeare 72
d. damn thee black Shakespeare 388
D. howling "Ho!" Squire 1
D. in human form Inge 2
d. is in the details Modern Proverbs 24
d. is not so black Proverbs 66
d. should have all the good tunes
  Rowland Hill 1
D. take the hindmost Proverbs 67
d. take you now Pushkin 1
D. turned round on you Bolt 2
d. would also build Luther 2
D.'s party without knowing it
  William Blake 8
finest trick of the d. Baudelaire 8
give the D. benefit of law Bolt 1
Give the d. his due Proverbs 119
given up believing in the d.
  Ronald Knox 1
However, the d., so far Kleist 1
idle brain is the D.'s workshop
  Proverbs 151
if bird or d. Poe 10

devil (cont.):
world, the flesh, and the d.
Book of Common Prayer 8
your adversary the d.   Bible 385
devils
poor d. are dying   Philip 1
devise
To lovers I d.   Fish 1
devote
he should d. his whole life   Joyce 26
devour
d. each of her children   Vergniaud 1
devourer
Time the d.   Ovid 5
devours
it d. its own children   Büchner 1
devoutly
consummation d. to be wish'd
Shakespeare 189
dew
debauchee of d.   Emily Dickinson 4
Dewey
D. Defeats Truman   Anonymous 5
deye
if thow d. a martyr   Chaucer 2
dì
Un bel d.   Giacosa 4
diadem
no adjunct to the Muses' d.
Ezra Pound 11
diagnosis
telling you the d.   Osler 4
dialect
language is a d. with an army
Weinreich 1
purify the d. of the tribe   T. S. Eliot 119
dialectical
d. materialism   Plekhanov 1
diamond
d. and safire bracelet lasts   Loos 2
d. is forever   Advertising Slogans 38
O D.! D.!   Isaac Newton 8
diamonds
d. are a girl's best friend   Robin 2
give him d. back   Gabor 1
Lucy in the Sky with D.
Lennon and McCartney 15
never seen a d.   Lorde 1
They bring d. and rust   Baez 2
diaper
threw his d. into the ring   Ickes 1
diapers
Politicians, like d.   Betty Carpenter 1
diary
keep a d.   Mae West 15
dice
He does not play d.   Einstein 8
he would choose to play d.   Einstein 16
Throw of the D.   Mallarmé 5
dictates
conform to the d. of reason
Alexander Hamilton 6
dictation
I merely did His d.   Stowe 6
dictatorship
d. as absolute   Franklin D. Roosevelt 19
d. of the proletariat   Lenin 2
d. of the proletariat   Karl Marx 6

dictatress
d. of the world   John Quincy Adams 1
dictionaries
D. are but the depositories   Jefferson 46
D. are like watches   Samuel Johnson 40
to make d. is dull work
Samuel Johnson 9
dictionary
borrowing a d.   Partridge 1
but a walking d.   George Chapman 3
D., *n.* A malevolent literary   Bierce 34
d. the most interesting book   Nock 1
English D. was written
Samuel Johnson 8
it isn't in the d.   Bierce 142
diddle
D., d., dumpling   Nursery Rhymes 31
Hey d. d.   Nursery Rhymes 22
die
better to d. on your feet   Ibarruri 1
cannot d. without them
Joseph H. Choate 1
Cowards d. many times
Shakespeare 102
day that I d.   McLean 2
Death thou shalt d.   Donne 3
d., and go we know not
Shakespeare 257
d. but once   Addison 3
d. in the last ditch   William III 1
d. is cast   Julius Caesar 5
d. of their remedies   Molière 13
Do or d.   Proverbs 72
dream shall never d.
Edward M. Kennedy 1
Eternal in man cannot d.   Upanishads 3
first you have to d.   Rushdie 2
for to morrow we shall d.   Bible 170
good Americans d.   Wilde 30
good d. young   Proverbs 124
good men d. like dogs
Hunter S. Thompson 7
Guns don't d., people d.
Political Slogans 17
he had to d. in my week   Joplin 4
He who would teach men to d.
Montaigne 7
Hope I d. before I get old   Townshend 1
how to d.   Porteus 2
I am prepared to d.   Nelson Mandela 1
I d. because I do not d.   Teresa of Ávila 1
I do not d.   Frye 2
I hope I would d. for it
Oliver Wendell Holmes, Jr. 30
I shall d. of having lived   Cather 8
I shall not altogether d.   Horace 23
I shall not d. of a cold   Cather 8
I'll d. young   Lenny Bruce 4
If I should d.   New England Primer 2
It's not that I'm afraid to d.
Woody Allen 19
it's the poor who d.   Sartre 9
it was sure to d.   Thomas Moore 4
last man to d. for a mistake   Kerry 1
Live and Let D.   Ian Fleming 2
Live fast, d. young   Willard Motley 1
live forever or d. in the attempt   Heller 2
Live free or d.   John Stark 1
Never say d.   Proverbs 207

Old habits d. hard   Proverbs 223
Old soldiers never d.   Foley 1
old soldiers never d.
Douglas MacArthur 2
only d. once   Proverbs 68
pie in the sky when you d.   Joe Hill 1
Root, hog, or d.   Proverbs 260
shall not d. because of them   Talmud 3
theirs but to do and d.   Tennyson 39
Them that d.'ll be the lucky
Robert Louis Stevenson 10
then you d.   Modern Proverbs 52
This is a good day to d.   Sayings 54
those who are about to d.
Anonymous (Latin) 2
To d. will be an awfully big adventure
Barrie 9
To go away is to d. a little   Haraucourt 1
We d. containing a richness   Ondaatje 2
We d. soon   Gwendolyn Brooks 2
We must love one another or d.
Auden 13
We shall d. alone   Pascal 6
we should d. of that roar   George Eliot 15
when I d.   Nyro 1
when they d., go to Paris
Oliver Wendell Holmes 4
when we d.   Twain 59
died
As estimated, you d.   Geoffrey Hill 3
as He d. to make men holy
Julia Ward Howe 3
before or after he d.   Lardner 3
day the music d.   McLean 1
d. as men before their bodies d.
Auden 35
d. in a hotel room   Eugene O'Neill 5
D. of a theory   Jefferson Davis 1
dog it was that d.   Oliver Goldsmith 4
he d. and the jury
Folk and Anonymous Songs 8
he d. on the cross   Nietzsche 21
He should have d.   Corneille 3
I d. for beauty   Emily Dickinson 11
lived well and d. poor
Daniel Webster 13
made that picture before he d.   Berra 18
Mithridates, he d. old   Housman 6
not have d. in vain   Lincoln 42
patient d.   Sayings 45
they suffered, they d.   France 2
too many people have d.   Dylan 3
when he d. the little children
John Motley 1
When I d. they washed me out   Jarrell 1
diem
Carpe d.   Horace 17
dies
d. harder than the desire   T. S. Eliot 72
d. the swan   Tennyson 43
happy before he d.   Solon 2
It matters not how a man d.
Samuel Johnson 64
little something in me d.   Vidal 4
man who d. rich   Andrew Carnegie 3
one either triumphs or d.   Guevara 2
What an artist d. with me   Nero 1
Whom the gods love d. young
Menander 1

differ
freedom to d. is not limited
Robert H. Jackson 4
difference
d. between a dog   Twain 69
d. of taste in jokes   George Eliot 17
d. of opinion   Twain 73
Distinction without a d.
Henry Fielding 5
more d. within the sexes
Compton-Burnett 1
that has made all the d.   Frost 9
There was a d.   Dorothy Baker 1
différence
Vive la d.   Sayings 57
differences
d. of degree
Oliver Wendell Holmes, Jr. 23
D. of habit and language   Rowling 6
different
but had thought they were d.
T. S. Eliot 69
d. from everyone else
David Foster Wallace 5
d. from you and me
F. Scott Fitzgerald 36
D. strokes   Modern Proverbs 25
hears a d. drummer   Thoreau 30
I was a d. person then   Carroll 22
moved to lead a d. life   Twain 66
only on d. subjects   Will Rogers 3
something completely d.
Monty Python 1
Think d.   Advertising Slogans 14
two d. oil companies   Shrum 1
wear d. coats   Trollope 4
Why is this night d.   Talmud 4
differently
one who thinks d.   Luxemburg 2
they do things d. there   Hartley 1
differs
One woman d. from another Mencken 1
difficult
D. is that which can be done
Santayana 14
d. is that which can be done Nansen 1
excellent are as d.   Spinoza 5
fascination of what's d.   Yeats 9
having a d. stool   Winston Churchill 52
If it is simply d.   Trollope 3
It has been found d.   Chesterton 17
more d. than physics   Einstein 28
must be d.   T. S. Eliot 35
that is most d.   Yeats 18
difficulties
D. are just things to   Shackleton 1
difficulty
crimes which present some d.
Arthur Conan Doyle 22
England's d. is Ireland's   O'Connell 1
diffidence
all in the d. that faltered   Ezra Pound 28
diffusion
increase and d. of knowledge
Smithson 1
dig
he'll d. them up again   John Webster 1
digestion
d. wait on appetite   Shakespeare 370

digging
in a hole, stop d.   Modern Proverbs 42
dignity
d. in tilling a field
Booker T. Washington 1
equal d. in the eyes   Anthony Kennedy 1
live out in d.   Ethel Rosenberg 1
Dilbert
D. Principle   Scott Adams 1
diller
d., a dollar   Nursery Rhymes 66
dim
I took a d. view   John Wayne 2
DiMaggio
take the great D. fishing   Hemingway 27
dime
Brother, Can You Spare a D.   Harburg 1
dimension
d. of sound   Serling 3
fifth d.   Serling 4
traveling through another d.   Serling 1
diminishes
every man's death d. me   Donne 5
dimmycratic
d. party ain't on speakin' terms
Dunne 10
Dinah
D., blow your horn
Folk and Anonymous Songs 38
kitchen with D.
Folk and Anonymous Songs 39
dine
jury-men may d.   Pope 6
dined
I have d. to-day   Sydney Smith 10
They d. on mince   Lear 7
ding
D., dong, bell   Nursery Rhymes 14
D. Dong! The Wicked Witch   Harburg 2
dingo
d.'s got my baby
Chamberlain-Creighton 1
dinner
don't call me late to d.   Sayings 19
Guess Who's Coming to D.
Stanley Kramer 1
having an old friend for d. Film Lines 155
ideal number for a d. party   Rombauer 2
Man Who Came to D.
George S. Kaufman 3
not a d. to ask a man to
Samuel Johnson 57
revolution is not a d. party
Mao Tse-tung 1
dinosauria
propose the name of D.   Richard Owen 1
Diogenes
If I were not Alexander, I would be D.
Alexander the Great 1
Dior
Never darken my D.   Lillie 2
diplomacy
D., *n.* The patriotic art   Bierce 35
D. is to do and say   Goldberg 1
direction
together in the same d.   Saint-Exupéry 2
directions
rode madly off in all d.   Leacock 1

directive
Prime D.   Star Trek 8
director
d. makes only one film   Jean Renoir 1
dirt
do d. on it   D. H. Lawrence 12
Stronger than d.   Advertising Slogans 3
Throw d. enough   Proverbs 69
dirty
think that sex is d.   Woody Allen 6
You d., double-crossing rat   Cagney 1
disadvantage
to his own d.   Samuel Johnson 83
disagree
when doctors d.   Pope 14
disagreeable
most d.-looking child ever seen
Frances Hodgson Burnett 2
disappear
it will d.   Trump 25
it will instantly d.   Douglas Adams 6
disappearing
d. railroad blues   Steve Goodman 2
disappointed
d. in the monkey   Twain 134
never be d.   Proverbs 29
disappointments
d. in American married life   Wilde 97
disapprove
I d. of what you say   Tallentyre 1
disarmament
d. of such nations
Roosevelt and Churchill 4
disaster
meet with Triumph and D.   Kipling 32
disavow
secretary will d.
Television Catchphrases 45
disbelief
d. in great men   Thomas Carlyle 13
willing suspension of d.   Coleridge 26
discharge
d. for loving one   Matlovich 1
discontent
winter of our d.   Shakespeare 1
discontents
Civilization and Its D.   Riviere 1
discord
hark what d. follows   Shakespeare 247
discordant
D. harmony   Horace 12
discouraging
seldom is heard a d. word   Higley 1
discover
d. I had no talent   Benchley 10
somebody who did not d. it Whitehead 2
discovered
A land may be said to be d.   Steffanson 1
everything has been d.   Ingres 1
poets and philosophers before me d.
Sigmund Freud 20
they themselves d. it   William James 19
discoverer
six thousand years for a d.   Kepler 2
discovery
d. of a new dish   Brillat-Savarin 2
portals of d.   Joyce 19
discreet
D. Charm of the Bourgeoisie   Buñuel 1

discrete
d. and insular minorities
      Harlan F. Stone 1
discretion
better part of valor is d. Shakespeare 60
discriminating
stop d. on the basis John Roberts 1
discrimination
all d. and selection Henry James 22
discuss
with myself I too much d. T. S. Eliot 77
disease
Cure the d. and kill Francis Bacon 11
D. is an experience   Eddy 6
d. of language   Müller 1
incurable d. of writing Juvenal 4
I've got Bright's D.   Perelman 1
Life is an incurable d.
      Abraham Cowley 1
remedy is worse than the d.
      Francis Bacon 19
this long d., my life   Pope 31
diseases
Desperate d. must have Proverbs 65
D. desperate grown Shakespeare 219
disfranchisement
in view of this entire d.
    Elizabeth Cady Stanton 3
disgrace
d. to our family name
     "Groucho" Marx 14
It's no d. t' be poor "Kin" Hubbard 1
disgraced
rich dies d.   Andrew Carnegie 3
disguise
naked is the best d. Congreve 2
disguised
d. as Clark Kent
   Television Catchphrases 6
dish
discovery of a new d. Brillat-Savarin 2
d. fit for the gods Shakespeare 100
d. ran away with the spoon
     Nursery Rhymes 22
dishes
end up with who does the d. French 1
dishonest
after one piece of d. writing
     Hemingway 26
low d. decade   Auden 10
disillusion
one d.—mankind Keynes 2
disinfectants
said to be the best of d. Brandeis 4
disinheriting
damned d. countenance
   Richard Brinsley Sheridan 6
disinterested
d. endeavor to learn and propagate
    Matthew Arnold 12
disloyalty
confuse dissent with d. Murrow 3
dismal
d. science Thomas Carlyle 18
dismantle
d. the arms Khrushchev 4
dismay
let nothing you d.
   Folk and Anonymous Songs 30

dismayed
Was there a man d. Tennyson 38
dismissed
immediately d. by the British
   Winston Churchill 36
dismount
afraid to d.   Proverbs 254
disobedience
Civil D. or Civil Resistance
    Mohandas Gandhi 1
Of man's first d. Milton 17
disorder
policeman is there to preserve d. Daley 1
sweet d. in the dress Herrick 1
violent order is d. Wallace Stevens 14
disposes
Man proposes and God d. Proverbs 186
man proposes, but God d.
    Thomas à Kempis 1
disposition
put an antic d. Shakespeare 171
disputes
Most of the d. Lord Mansfield 3
dissect
We murder to d. William Wordsworth 3
dissections
not from books but from d. Harvey 1
dissent
confuse d. with disloyalty Murrow 3
D. is the highest form Jefferson 56
in the West is called "d." Havel 1
dissenters
eliminating d. Robert H. Jackson 2
dissociation
d. of sensibility set in T. S. Eliot 34
dissolve
all which it inherit, shall d.
    Shakespeare 442
d. the people   Brecht 7
dissolved
ought to be totally d. Jefferson 7
distance
hit an elephant at this d. Sedgwick 1
Ships at a d. Hurston 2
'Tis d. lends enchantment to the view
    Thomas Campbell 1
distinction
D. without a difference Henry Fielding 5
no d. between terrorists
    George W. Bush 4
distinguished
at last, the d. thing Henry James 27
distinguishes
even a dog d. between being
  Oliver Wendell Holmes, Jr. 4
distraction
I will have less d. Euler 1
distress
D., n. A disease incurred Bierce 36
reality of d. touching Thomas Paine 16
distrust
Seek simplicity and d. it Whitehead 3
disturb
Do I dare d. the universe T. S. Eliot 5
disturbance
great d. in the Force George Lucas 5
ditch
die in the last d. William III 1
It is a mere d. Napoleon 1

dive
men d. for them Whately 1
diver
been a d. in deep seas Pater 1
diverged
Two roads d. in a yellow wood Frost 8
diversity
make the world safe for d.
    John F. Kennedy 30
diverting
d. myself in now and then
    Isaac Newton 7
dives
I sit in one of the d. Auden 10
literary German d. Twain 42
divide
D. and rule Anonymous (Latin) 6
D. and rule Proverbs 70
if you d. it into small jobs Henry Ford 3
those who constantly d. Benchley 1
divided
All Gaul is d. into three parts
    Julius Caesar 1
d. an inheritance with him Lavater 1
d. duty Shakespeare 265
house be d. against itself Bible 276
house d. against itself Lincoln 11
When they d. the Man Rig Veda 1
dividing
by d. we fall John Dickinson 1
divine
I myself am more d. Margaret Fuller 1
that the Emperor is d. Hirohito 3
to forgive, d. Pope 4
divinest
Much Madness is d. Sense
    Emily Dickinson 18
divinity
by a doctor of d. W. S. Gilbert 18
d. that shapes our ends
    Shakespeare 230
such d. doth hedge a king
    Shakespeare 223
divisions
How many d. has he got Stalin 4
divorce
d., the inquest Helen Rowland 5
d. is like an amputation Atwood 5
if you existed I'd d. you Albee 3
only good thing about d.
    Clare Boothe Luce 2
think d. a panacea for every ill Dix 1
D-I-V-O-R-C-E
Our D. becomes final today Wynette 1
divulge
I will never d. Hippocrates 5
Divus
Lie quiet D. Ezra Pound 15
Dixie
In D.'s land Emmett 2
Look away! D. Land Emmett 1
Night They Drove Old D.
    Robbie Robertson 2
DNA
D. just is Dawkins 5
do
damned if you d. Dow 1
d. anything about it Twain 145
D. as I say, not as I d. Proverbs 71

D. as you would be done by
                    Chesterfield 4
D. be d. be d.   Sinatra 1
d. it yourself   Proverbs 319
d. no harm   Hippocrates 2
D. not d. to others   Confucius 9
D. or die   Proverbs 72
D. Or d. not   George Lucas 14
D. other men   Dickens 51
D. what thou wilt   Crowley 1
D. what you like   Rabelais 3
d. ye even so them   Bible 225
d. your thing   Ralph Waldo Emerson 15
I d. my thing   Perls 1
Just d. it   Advertising Slogans 93
Monkey see, monkey d.
                 Modern Proverbs 62
so much to d.   Rhodes 2
so much to d.   Tennyson 31
that write what men d.   Francis Bacon 4
theirs but to d. and die   Tennyson 39
would that men should d. to you
                          Bible 225
you d. not want them to d. to you
                         Confucius 9
Doc
play cards with a man called D. Algren 2
What's up, D.   Avery 1
dock
sittin' on the d. of the bay   Redding 2
doctor
apple a day keeps the d.
                  Modern Proverbs 1
I'm not a d., but I play one on TV
              Advertising Slogans 127
You, D. Martin   Sexton 1
doctors
when d. disagree   Pope 14
doctrine
Augustinian d. of the damnation Lecky 1
dodger
artful D.   Dickens 16
doe
D.—a deer, a female deer
                  Hammerstein 24
doer
d., not the mere critic
             Theodore Roosevelt 1
d. of deeds   Theodore Roosevelt 2
does
D. she . . . or doesn't she
             Advertising Slogans 31
Easy d. it   Proverbs 83
genius d. what it must   Baring 1
He who can, d.   George Bernard Shaw 17
talent which d. what it can   Baring 1
dog
ain't nothin' but a hound d.
                    Jerry Leiber 1
between a d. and a man   Twain 69
Beware of the d.   Petronius 1
black d. I hope always
                Samuel Johnson 39
characteristic of a d. except loyalty
                  Sam Houston 1
curious incident of the d.
              Arthur Conan Doyle 21
d. is man's best friend   Proverbs 75
d. is turned to his own vomit Bible 386

d. it was that died   Oliver Goldsmith 4
d. returneth to his vomit   Bible 136
d. starv'd at his master's gate
                William Blake 16
door is what a d.   Nash 14
even a d. distinguishes
           Oliver Wendell Holmes, Jr. 4
Every d. has his day   Proverbs 74
every d. his day   Kingsley 2
fetch her poor d. a bone
                 Nursery Rhymes 45
I am his Highness' d. at Kew   Pope 36
Like a d.   Kafka 11
like all kids, loved the d.
                  Richard Nixon 1
Little Tom Tinker's d.
                 Nursery Rhymes 15
Love me, love my d.   Proverbs 180
man biting a d.   Dana 1
mine little d. gone   Winner 2
nobody knows you're a d. Peter Steiner 1
not been the same d.
            Franklin D. Roosevelt 28
Outside of a d.   "Groucho" Marx 49
pick up a starving d.   Twain 69
tail must wag the d.   Kipling 7
teach an old d. new tricks Proverbs 292
Thou art a beaten d.   Ezra Pound 27
We'll Kill This D.   Bluestone 1
When the d. bites   Hammerstein 26
Why should a d.   Shakespeare 318
doggie
How much is that d.   Bob Merrill 1
dogies
git along, little d.
         Folk and Anonymous Songs 83
dogmas
d. of the quiet past   Lincoln 36
dogs
All the d. of Europe bark   Auden 24
D., would you live forever
              Frederick the Great 3
d. and cats living together
                   Film Lines 86
Hark, hark, the d. do bark
                 Nursery Rhymes 20
I detest d.   Strindberg 2
Let sleeping d. lie   Proverbs 273
let slip the d. of war   Shakespeare 107
mad d. and Englishmen   Coward 9
more I like d.   Roland 2
more one values d.   Toussenel 1
No man who hates d. and children
                    Darnton 1
regard all things as straw d.   Lao Tzu 2
treats us all like d.   Henry Jordan 1
Who Let the D. Out   Anselm Douglas 1
d'oh
D.   Groening 5
d-ohhhh
D.!   Finlayson 1
doing
d. what one desires   Mill 13
He is d. his best   Wilde 96
If a thing is worth d.   Chesterton 18
Insanity is d. the same thing
                Rita Mae Brown 2
is worth d. well   Chesterton 2
It is if you're d. it right Woody Allen 6

Whatever is worth d. at all Chesterfield 2
dolce
D. Vita   Fellini 1
dole
Love on the D.   Greenwood 1
doleful
Knight of the D. Countenance
                   Cervantes 3
doll
d. in the d.'s house   Dickens 106
I have been your d. wife   Ibsen 5
only doing it for some d.   Loesser 5
dollar
almighty d.   Washington Irving 5
diller, a d.   Nursery Rhymes 66
Nothing that costs only a d.   Arden 1
One d. and eighty-seven cents
                  O. Henry 2
one eyed shrew of the heterosexual d.
                   Ginsberg 8
sixty-four thousand d. question
            Radio Catchphrases 23
tax d. will go farther   Braun 2
dolls
Valley of the D.   Susann 1
Dolly
Hello, D.   Herman 1
dolphin
d.-torn, that gong-tormented   Yeats 57
dolphins
all the d. had ever done
                Douglas Adams 2
dome
d. of atoms rose   Karl Jay Shapiro 3
domestic
distinguished in its d. virtues Austen 22
D. Goddess   Barr 2
domesticity
of unbounded d.   W. S. Gilbert 17
dominance
Pornography is about d.   Steinem 4
dominating
are termed d.   Mendel 2
three receive the d.   Mendel 1
domination
no Soviet d. of Eastern   Gerald R. Ford 5
dominion
death hath no more d.   Bible 343
death shall have no d.   Dylan Thomas 3
domino
"falling d." principle   Eisenhower 7
dominoes
You have a row of d. set up Eisenhower 7
don't
damned if you d.   Dow 1
D. ask, d. tell   Moskos 1
D. fire till you see   Putnam 1
D. get mad, get even
             Joseph P. Kennedy 1
D. give up the ship
             Oliver Hazard Perry 1
D. know much about history   Cooke 1
D. leave home without it
             Advertising Slogans 11
D. look back   Paige 6
D. PANIC   Douglas Adams 1
D. Sit Under the Apple Tree
                  Lew Brown 3
D. speak   Stefani 1

don't (cont.):
D. tread on me   Anonymous 6
d. trip over the furniture   Coward 14
D. worry, be happy   Baba 1
I d. know much about Art
                                  Gelett Burgess 6
done
be seen to be d.   Hewart 1
D. because we are too menny
                                  Thomas Hardy 19
he d. her wrong
              Folk and Anonymous Songs 23
he's d.   Jay Hanna "Dizzy" Dean 1
I have d. my duty   Horatio Nelson 9
I say let it be d.   John Brown 2
If it were d.   Shakespeare 340
If you want anything d.   Thatcher 1
Not my will, but thine, be d.   Bible 305
nothing d. while anything remained
                                  Lucan 2
Nothing to be d.   Beckett 1
So little d.   Rhodes 2
we ought not to have d.
              Book of Common Prayer 10
What have I d. for you   W. E. Henley 3
What's d. is d.   Proverbs 77
what's d. is d.   Shakespeare 365
woman's work is never d.   Proverbs 331
donkey
d. appears to me   Lichtenberg 4
donna
La d. è mobile   Piave 1
donuts
Time to make the d.
              Advertising Slogans 42
Doodle
Yankee D. came to town
              Folk and Anonymous Songs 84
Yankee D. dandy   Cohan 1
doodling
It's called d.   Film Lines 119
Dooley
Hang down your head, Tom D.
              Folk and Anonymous Songs 77
doom
abide the D. of Men   Tolkien 13
prepare to meet thy d.   Barrie 12
doomed
poet d. at last to wake Samuel Johnson 7
dooms
my father moved through d. of love
                              e.e. cummings 17
door
d. is what a dog   Nash 14
d. opens and lets the future in
                              Graham Greene 1
form from off my d.   Poe 11
hard going to the d.   Creeley 1
knockin' on heaven's d.   Dylan 23
lift my lamp beside the golden d.
                                  Lazarus 2
make a beaten path to his d.
              Ralph Waldo Emerson 51
Open the pod d., Hal   Film Lines 181
poverty comes in at the d.   Proverbs 240
through a d. with a gun
              Raymond Chandler 11
When one d. shuts   Proverbs 226

doorkeeper
I had rather be a d.   Bible 115
doormat
d. or a prostitute   Rebecca West 1
doors
d. of perception   William Blake 2
d. to rooms they will not be   Justice 1
taxi-cab with both d. open
                              Howard Hughes 1
dooth
d. with youre owene thyng   Chaucer 10
dope
D. will get you through times
                              Gilbert Shelton 1
Doris
D. Day before she was a virgin
                          "Groucho" Marx 43
dormez
d.-vous   Folk and Anonymous Songs 25
dormouse
Remember what the d. said   Slick 2
summer of a d.   Byron 3
Dorothy
credited to D. Parker
              George S. Kaufman 5
double
deep peace of the d.-bed
              Beatrice Campbell 1
D., d. toil and trouble   Shakespeare 375
D. your pleasure, d. your fun
              Advertising Slogans 140
You have a d.-o number   Ian Fleming 3
doubles
d. your chances for a date
              Woody Allen 39
doublethink
D. means the power   Orwell 44
doubt
beyond reasonable d.
              Robert Treat Paine 1
dogmas or goals are in d.   Pirsig 3
d. as a philosophy   Martel 2
d. everything or to believe   Poincaré 3
d. is what gets you an education
                                  Mizner 3
jurisprudence of d.
              Sandra Day O'Connor 1
Life is d.   Unamuno 1
Never d. that a small group
              Margaret Mead 10
To d. is intensely   Wilde 119
When in d., tell the truth   Twain 84
When in d., win the trick
                              Edmond Hoyle 1
When in d. have a man
              Raymond Chandler 11
doubts
he shall end in d.   Francis Bacon 3
I have such d.   Shanley 1
mystic does not bring d.   Chesterton 19
dove
wings of the d.   Byron 6
Dover
milestones on the D. Road   Dickens 94
We're the pros from D.
              Richard Hooker 1
white cliffs of D.   Nat Burton 1
down
Been D. So Long   Fariña 1

Blow the man d.
              Folk and Anonymous Songs 7
Come on d.   Television Catchphrases 50
D., wanton, d.   Graves 3
D. by the old mill stream   Tell Taylor 1
D. in the valley
              Folk and Anonymous Songs 18
D. on me   Joplin 1
D. these mean streets
              Raymond Chandler 8
Keep 'Em D. on the Farm
              Sam M. Lewis 1
must come d.   Proverbs 315
same people on the way d.   Mizner 1
sun go d. upon your wrath   Bible 366
Up the D. Staircase   Bel Kaufman 1
We live in fame or go d. in flame
              Robert Crawford 2
When You're D. and Out   Jimmy Cox 1
downstairs
Upstairs, D. Television Catchphrases 79
downtown
beautiful d. Burbank
              Television Catchphrases 58
Dr.
D. Jekyll and Mr. Hyde
              Robert Louis Stevenson 18
D. Livingstone, I presume
              Henry Morton Stanley 1
D. Strangelove   Kubrick 1
Dracula
I am D.   Stoker 1
draft
first d. of history   Fitch 1
drag
What a d. it is getting old
              Jagger and Richards 5
dragged
d. kicking and screaming
              Adlai E. Stevenson 13
dragon
d. lives forever   Yarrow 2
Puff, the magic d.   Yarrow 1
dragons
I am a brother to d.   Bible 103
I desired d.   Tolkien 3
Never laugh at live d.   Tolkien 2
dramatics
I studied d. under him Eisenhower 14
dramatist
d. only wants more liberties
              Henry James 21
drang
Sturm und D.   Klinger 1
drank
d. rapidly a glass of water
              e.e. cummings 10
draw
d. like these children   Picasso 2
I can d. for a thousand pounds
                                  Addison 6
drawer
leaves a pistol in the d. Richard Nixon 22
drawing
back to the old d. board   Arno 1
d. shows me at a glance   Turgenev 3
draws
d. necessary conclusions
              Benjamin Peirce 1

drown
D. in a vat of liquor   W. C. Fields 17
d. it in the bathtub   Norquist 1
I'll d. my book   Shakespeare 445
wake us, and we d.   T. S. Eliot 12
drowned
d. face always staring   Rich 6
drowning
d. man will clutch   Proverbs 78
not waving but d.   Stevie Smith 4
drudge
harmless d.   Samuel Johnson 13
drug
I am on a d.   Sheen 2
drugs
d. began to take hold
          Hunter S. Thompson 2
people who can't cope with d.
          Jane Wagner 1
Sex and D. and Rock 'n' Roll   Dury 1
your brain on d.   Advertising Slogans 98
drum
bang the d. slowly
          Folk and Anonymous Songs 14
I was a d. major for justice
          Martin Luther King, Jr. 19
melancholy as an unbraced d.
          Centlivre 3
drummer
hears a different d.   Thoreau 30
drunk
being d.   Stein 10
constantly d. on books   Mencken 44
d. deep of the Pierian spring   Drayton 2
d. only once in my life   W. C. Fields 28
D. on the wind   Dickey 1
long as it gets you d.   Musset 1
My mother, d. or sober   Chesterton 3
when d., one sees   Tynan 1
drunken
do with the d. sailor
          Folk and Anonymous Songs 19
than a d. Christian   Melville 3
Drury
who lives in D. Lane
          Folk and Anonymous Songs 53
dry
crawls between d. ribs   T. S. Eliot 20
gonna walk around, d. bones
          Folk and Anonymous Songs 20
into a d. Martini   Benchley 6
keep your powder d.   Cromwell 4
O ye d. bones   Bible 188
old man in a d. month   T. S. Eliot 21
thoughts of a d. brain   T. S. Eliot 24
Dublin
picture of D. so complete   Joyce 28
Dubuque
old lady from D.   Harold Ross 1
ducat
dead for a d.   Shakespeare 214
ducats
O my d.   Shakespeare 75
duchess
That's my last D.   Robert Browning 3
duck
I forgot to d.   Dempsey 1
quacks like a duck   Mazey 1
rolls off my back like a d.   Goldwyn 12

Why a d.   "Groucho" Marx 3
duckling
Ugly D.   Andersen 4
ducks
Always do that, wild d.   Ibsen 22
dude
The d. abides   Film Lines 22
due
d. process is a bullet   Film Lines 92
d. process of law   Anonymous 30
Give the devil his d.   Proverbs 119
without d. process of law   Constitution 14
without d. process of law   Constitution 21
dukedom
My library was d. large enough
          Shakespeare 438
dulce
D. et decorum est   Horace 20
D. et decorum est   Wilfred Owen 3
dull
He was d. in a new way
          Samuel Johnson 78
makes Jack a d. boy   Proverbs 334
not only d. himself   Foote 1
to make dictionaries is d. work
          Samuel Johnson 9
dullness
cause of d. in others   Foote 1
dulls
borrowing d. the edge   Shakespeare 160
dumb
D. as a drum with a hole   Dickens 6
d. enough to think   Eugene McCarthy 1
d. son of a bitch   Truman 13
poor d. mouths   Shakespeare 124
So d. he can't fart and chew gum
          Lyndon B. Johnson 14
dump
What a d.   Film Lines 20
Dumpty
Humpty D. sat on a wall
          Nursery Rhymes 24
Duncan
this D. hath borne   Shakespeare 342
dunces
D. are all in Confederacy
          Jonathan Swift 5
dung
sniff the French d.   Ho Chi Minh 3
dungeon
what other d. is so dark   Hawthorne 16
Dunsinane
to high D. hill   Shakespeare 381
dusky
rear my d. race   Tennyson 9
dust
as chimney-sweepers, come to d.
          Shakespeare 437
ashes to ashes, d. to d.
          Book of Common Prayer 4
d. of creeds outworn   Percy Shelley 12
d. thou art   Bible 22
Excuse My D.   Dorothy Parker 25
fear in a handful of d.   T. S. Eliot 43
great d.-heap called "history"   Birrell 1
Less than the d.   Laurence Hope 2
life in the handful of d.   Conrad 20
not without d. and heat   Milton 7
quintessence of d.   Shakespeare 181

rather be ashes than d.   London 2
shake off the d.   Bible 235
we have first raised a d.   Berkeley 1
what foul d. floated
          F. Scott Fitzgerald 12
dustbin
d. of history   Trotsky 2
Dutch
horse translated into D.   Lichtenberg 4
duty
constabulary d.'s to be done
          W. S. Gilbert 23
D., honor, country   Douglas MacArthur 4
d. to worship the sun   John Morley 1
every man will do his d.
          Horatio Nelson 7
found that life was D.   Hooper 1
I have done my d.   Horatio Nelson 9
My d. to myself   Ibsen 7
When D. whispers low
          Ralph Waldo Emerson 46
worst of doing one's d.   Wharton 8
dwarf
d. sees farther than the giant
          Coleridge 30
d. standing on the shoulders
          Robert Burton 1
dwarfs
d. on the shoulders of giants
          Bernard of Chartres 1
dwell
d. in the house of the Lord   Bible 109
I d. in Possibility   Emily Dickinson 12
Two souls d.   Goethe 13
dwelling
rich men d. at peace
          Winston Churchill 41
dwells
She d. with Beauty   Keats 17
dyer
like the d.'s hand   Shakespeare 428
dying
achieve it through not d.
          Woody Allen 40
despised, and d. king   Percy Shelley 8
d., as I have lived   Wilde 120
D. is an art   Plath 6
forgets the d. bird   Thomas Paine 16
get busy living or get busy d.
          Stephen King 3
going out and d. for his country   Patton 3
I am d., Egypt   Shakespeare 403
If this is d.   Strachey 4
is busy d.   Dylan 13
it had a d. fall   Shakespeare 239
it is not death, but d.   Henry Fielding 7
I was d. helplessly   Hamsun 2
man's d. is more   Thomas Mann 4
poor devils are d.   Philip 1
rage against the d.   Dylan Thomas 17
those d. generations   Yeats 46
those of the d.   Malcolm Lowry 1
time held me green and d.
          Dylan Thomas 7
unconscionable time d.   Charles II 2
We are continually d.   Petrarch 1
We are d., we are d.   D. H. Lawrence 11
When a man is d. of hunger
          Napoleon 12

ecdysiast
ecdysist and e.   Mencken 39
ech
e. man for hymself   Chaucer 12
echo
choice, not an e.   Goldwater 2
distant footsteps e.   Longfellow 12
e. beyond the Mexique Bay
                         Andrew Marvell 8
Footfalls e. in the memory   T. S. Eliot 95
eclipsed
e. the gaiety of nations
                        Samuel Johnson 34
economic
decided upon an e. theory
             Oliver Wendell Holmes, Jr. 18
e. freedom is an end   Milton Friedman 2
e. liberties   Kristol 1
e. royalists   Franklin D. Roosevelt 10
function of e. forecasting   Solomon 1
economical
e. with the truth   Robert Armstrong 1
economics
E. and art are strangers   Cather 10
E. is a study of mankind
                       Alfred Marshall 1
E. is all about   Duesenberry 1
E. limps along with one foot
                        Joan Robinson 5
e. of socialism   Joan Robinson 6
Everybody thinks of e.   Mises 3
it is bad e.   Franklin D. Roosevelt 14
master of e.
             Oliver Wendell Holmes, Jr. 13
orthodox traditional e.   Joan Robinson 2
thought of studying e.   Keynes 5
Voodoo e.
           George Herbert Walker Bush 1
economist
slaves of some defunct e.
                              Keynes 12
economists
avoid being deceived by e.
                         Joan Robinson 4
That of sophisters, e.   Edmund Burke 18
economize
Let us e. it   Twain 86
economy
e., stupid   Carville 1
In art e.   Henry James 19
People want e.   Iacocca 1
there is an e. of truth   Edmund Burke 25
ecstasy
Agony and the E.   Irving Stone 1
Eden
east of E.   Bible 25
edge
Come to the e.   Logue 1
e. of the precipice   F. Scott Fitzgerald 50
narrow as the e. of a razor
                            Upanishads 4
teeth are set on e.   Bible 184
edged
Science is an e. tool   Eddington 3
edited
His wife not only e. his works
                       Van Wyck Brooks 1
editing
We are the products of e.   Wald 2

edition
new & more perfect E.
                      Benjamin Franklin 1
editor
E.: a person employed
                         Elbert Hubbard 4
too much of a temptation to the e.
                               Lardner 2
educated
e. fleas do it   Cole Porter 25
education
doubt is what gets you an e.   Mizner 3
e., education   Blair 3
e. is a leading out   Spark 4
e. is always to be conceived Montessori 1
E. is what is left after all   Conant 1
If you think e. is expensive   Bok 2
interfere with my e.   Twain 151
love her is a liberal e.   Richard Steele 1
race between e.   H. G. Wells 7
Soap and e.   Twain 8
We don't need no e.   Roger Waters 2
with a college e.   Twain 58
eena
E., meena, mina, mo
                       Nursery Rhymes 16
effect
Butterfly E.   Gleick 1
chilling e. upon the exercise   Brennan 5
E., n. The second of two   Bierce 37
Matthew e.   Merton 4
effects
Consider what e.
                  Charles Sanders Peirce 1
effete
e. corps of impudent snobs   Agnew 2
efficiency
doing with great e.   Drucker 1
Northern charm and Southern e.
                         John F. Kennedy 22
effort
redoubling your e.   Santayana 1
What is written without e.
                      Samuel Johnson 108
egg
chicken or the e.   Sayings 62
hen is only an e.'s way
                Samuel Butler (1835–1902) 1
Wall St. Lays an E.   Silverman 1
eggs
all my e. in one bastard
                       Dorothy Parker 43
all your e. in one basket   Proverbs 84
e. in one basket   Carnegie 1
green e. and ham   Seuss 11
without breaking e.   Proverbs 224
ego
e. is not master in his own
                        Sigmund Freud 11
e.'s relation to the id   Sigmund Freud 14
poor e. . . . serves three severe
                        Sigmund Freud 15
Where id was, there e.
                        Sigmund Freud 16
egotist
E., n. A person of low taste   Bierce 38
egotistical
I make no apologies for being e.
                        Stella Franklin 1

Egypt
corn in E.   Bible 34
I am dying, E.   Shakespeare 403
eight
e. million stories   Film Lines 123
I don't think I can eat e.   Berra 11
Now I was e. and very small   Cullen 2
Pieces of e.   Robert Louis Stevenson 9
eightfold
Noble E. Path   Pali Tripitaka 4
80
Showing up is 80 percent of life
                          Woody Allen 41
would that I were only 80   Fontenelle 3
eighty
In a dream you are never e.   Sexton 2
ein
E. Reich, e. Volk   Political Slogans 13
Einstein
Let E. be   Squire 1
Eisenhower
E. was the best clerk I ever had
                      Douglas MacArthur 7
either
E. he's dead   "Groucho" Marx 28
e. part of the solution   Cleaver 2
élan
L'é. vital   Bergson 1
Elba
ere I saw E.   Napoleon 15
elder
e. man not at all   Francis Bacon 16
e. than herself   Shakespeare 242
Eleanor
E. Rigby died in the church
                   Lennon and McCartney 9
elected
E. silence, sing to me
                    Gerard Manley Hopkins 1
if unanimously e.
              William Tecumseh Sherman 3
More men have been e.   Will Rogers 5
will not serve if e.
              William Tecumseh Sherman 5
election
e. by the incompetent many
                   George Bernard Shaw 19
e. is coming   George Eliot 8
Free e. of masters   Marcuse 1
Supreme Coort follows th' e. returns
                               Dunne 11
elections
E. are won by men and women
                     Franklin P. Adams 3
had e. been held   Eisenhower 12
You won the e.   Somoza 1
elective
E. Affinities   Goethe 14
electric
e. and magnetic phenomena   Maxwell 1
I Sing the Body E.   Whitman 1
put a hog in the e. chair   Gaines 1
electricity
e. was dripping   Thurber 3
electrification
e. of the whole country   Lenin 5
electrified
e. particle passes   Rutherford 2

elegant
You e. fowl   Lear 6
elemental
e. experiences   Joyce Carol Oates 2
e. force freed from its bonds   Laurence 1
elementary
E., my dear Watson
                        Arthur Conan Doyle 39
"E.," said he   Arthur Conan Doyle 23
elements
e. so mixed in him   Shakespeare 131
elephant
couldn't hit an e.   Sedgwick 1
e.'s faithful   Seuss 1
herd of e.   Dinesen 3
high as an e.'s eye   Hammerstein 6
I shot an e. in my pajamas
                        "Groucho" Marx 7
Once there was an e.   Laura Richards 1
elephants
E. never forget   Modern Proverbs 26
eli
E., E., lama sabachthani   Bible 274
eliminated
you have e. the impossible
                        Arthur Conan Doyle 10
Eliot
How unpleasant to meet Mr. E.
                        T. S. Eliot 89
elite
corps of the e.   Dole 2
power e.   C. Wright Mills 1
where the e. meet   Radio Catchphrases 7
Eliza
E. made her desperate retreat   Stowe 1
ellipse
path of the planet is an e.   Kepler 1
elliptical
e. billiard balls   W. S. Gilbert 41
eloquence
Take e. and break its neck   Verlaine 5
eloquent
country to be too e.   Wilde 6
Elvis
E. has left the building   Horace Logan 1
Elysium
E., n. An imaginary   Bierce 39
emails
existence of e.   Comey 1
hearing about your damn e.
                        Bernie Sanders 2
emancipate
E. yourselves from mental   Marley 3
embalmer
triumph of the e.'s art   Vidal 7
embarrassment
E. of Riches   Allainval 1
embattled
here once the e. farmers stood
                        Ralph Waldo Emerson 6
ember
each separate dying e.   Poe 7
embittered
He was an e. atheist   Orwell 1
embodiment
Law is the true e.   W. S. Gilbert 26
embrace
E. me, my sweet embraceable you
                        Gershwin 4

e. your lordship's mistress   Foote 2
none, I think, do there e.
                        Andrew Marvell 14
embraceable
Embrace me, my sweet e. you
                        Gershwin 4
emerald
E. Isle   Drennan 1
going to the E. City   L. Frank Baum 2
emeralds
road to the City of E.   L. Frank Baum 1
emeritus
professor e.   Leacock 3
Emmas
If there were more E.   Horatio Nelson 5
emotion
as they occur is the e.   William James 23
e. recollected in tranquillity
                        William Wordsworth 6
escape from e.   T. S. Eliot 33
express the e. of all the ages
                        Thomas Hardy 30
formula of that particular e.
                        T. S. Eliot 27
I second that e.   "Smokey" Robinson 2
in the stress of some e.   Ezra Pound 3
produced the e.   Hemingway 14
tranquility remembered in e.
                        Dorothy Parker 24
undisciplined squads of e.
                        T. S. Eliot 108
emotional
e. intelligence   Goleman 1
emotions
refusal to admit our e.   Rattigan 1
run the gamut of e.   Dorothy Parker 29
emperor
dey makes you E.   Eugene O'Neill 1
e. has nothing at all on   Andersen 3
e. of ice-cream   Wallace Stevens 4
E.'s New Clothes   Andersen 2
that the E. is divine   Hirohito 3
empire
aggressive impulses of an evil e.
                        Ronald W. Reagan 6
Decline and Fall of the Roman E.
                        Gibbon 1
E. Strikes Back   George Lucas 10
evil Galactic E.   George Lucas 11
liquidation of the British E.
                        Winston Churchill 26
lost an e.   Acheson 1
nor an e.   Voltaire 5
poison into the vitals of the e.   Gibbon 3
thinking of an e. falling   Thackeray 13
Westward the course of e. takes
                        Berkeley 3
empires
e. of the future   Winston Churchill 30
employee
e. incompetent to execute   Peter 2
In a hierarchy, each e.   Peter 1
emptiness
Form is e.   Anonymous 10
empty
as e. experiences go   Woody Allen 16
half e.   Stamp 2
life is but an e. dream   Longfellow 1

emulation
propensity for e.   Veblen 4
enacted
e. on this same divan or bed
                        T. S. Eliot 53
enchanted
Enter these e. woods George Meredith 2
Some e. evening   Hammerstein 14
enchantment
'Tis distance lends e. to the view
                        Thomas Campbell 1
enchantments
last e. of the Middle Age
                        Matthew Arnold 8
enchilada
He's the Big E.   Ehrlichman 1
encounters
Close E. of the Third Kind   Spielberg 1
encourage
e. the others   Voltaire 9
encroachment
insidious e. by men of zeal   Brandeis 9
encroachments
e. of those in power   Madison 10
end
appointment at the e.   Dinesen 3
as e. and never merely as means Kant 5
beginning, middle, and e.   Aristotle 6
beginning of the e.   Talleyrand 3
commit adultery at one e.   Joyce Cary 1
e. as superstitions   T. H. Huxley 6
e. be clearly comprehended
                        Alexander Hamilton 11
e. cannot justify the means
                        Aldous Huxley 4
e. crowns all   Shakespeare 251
e. is where we start from   T. S. Eliot 122
e. justifies the means   Proverbs 85
e. of a perfect day   Carrie Jacobs Bond 1
e. of history   Fukuyama 1
e. of History   Sellar 3
e. of law   John Locke 6
e. of our foundation   Francis Bacon 25
e. of the beginning
                        Winston Churchill 27
E. of the World As We Know It   Stipe 1
e. to the beginnings
                        Franklin D. Roosevelt 29
get to the e. of your rope
                        Franklin D. Roosevelt 31
great e. of life   T. H. Huxley 5
I decline to accept the e. of man
                        Faulkner 10
In my beginning is my e.   T. S. Eliot 101
In my e. is my beginning   T. S. Eliot 112
In my e. is my beginning
                        Mary, Queen of Scots 1
is this the e. of Rico   W. R. Burnett 1
it will e. without him   Lévi-Strauss 1
just the e. of time   Hendrix 4
Let the e. be legitimate   John Marshall 6
Life is an e. in itself
                        Oliver Wendell Holmes, Jr. 16
light at the e. of a tunnel   Navarre 1
light at the e. of the tunnel   Alsop 1
light at the e. of the tunnel
                        Paul Dickson 1
must come to an e.   Proverbs 7
no e. to the laws   Twain 11

end (cont.):
not e. times   Jon Stewart 1
not the e. of the world
                          Modern Proverbs 27
palm at the e. of the mind
                          Wallace Stevens 15
seen the e. of war   Santayana 9
there was no e.   Patrick White 1
think that this is the e.
        This is the e.   Jim Morrison 1
till you come to the e.   Carroll 23
War That Will E. War   H. G. Wells 3
wept for the e. of innocence   Golding 1
where's it going to e.   Stoppard 1
world may e. tonight
                        Robert Browning 14
world without e., Amen
                  Book of Common Prayer 11

endearing
all those e. young charms
                          Thomas Moore 1

ended
Our revels now are e.   Shakespeare 442

ending
bread-sauce of the happy e.
                          Henry James 13

endow
e. a college, or a cat   Pope 15
I thee e.   Book of Common Prayer 18

endowed
e. by the ruined millionaire
                              T. S. Eliot 106
e. us with senses   Galileo 1

ends
All's well that e. well   Proverbs 326
begins in delight and e. in wisdom
                                  Frost 20
candle burns at both e.   Millay 4
divinity that shapes our e.
                          Shakespeare 230
this is the way the world e. T. S. Eliot 67

endurance
e. for one moment more
                          George Kennan 1

endure
man will not merely e.   Faulkner 11
No picture is made to e.   Ezra Pound 22

endures
Nothing e. but change   Heraclitus 5

enemies
Always forgive your e.
                       Robert F. Kennedy 1
choice of his e.   Wilde 24
crush your e.   Genghis Khan 1
E. in War, in Peace Friends   Jefferson 6
he has no e.   Wilde 104
hundred men his e.   John Adams 18
left me naked to mine e.
                          Shakespeare 452
make my e. ridiculous   Voltaire 16
They love him for the e.   Bragg 1
trying to live without e.   Babel 3
Whether we bring our e. to justice
                          George W. Bush 9
who have no e.   Wilde 39
You talk to your e.   Dayan 1
your e. closer   Puzo 5

your e. will not believe you
                        Elbert Hubbard 2
enemy
alongside that of an e.   Horatio Nelson 6
best is the e. of the good   Voltaire 2
better class of e.   Milligan 1
e. advances, we retreat   Mao Tse-tung 2
e. of my e. is my friend   Proverbs 86
e. of the people   Ibsen 12
great e. of clear language   Orwell 29
if he was indeed the e.   Knowles 2
If thine e. be hungry   Bible 135
last e. that shall be destroyed   Bible 357
met the e. and he is us   Walt Kelly 4
mine e.'s dog   Shakespeare 309
Nobody's e. but his own   Dickens 66
peace with one's e.   Rabin 2
third time it's e. action   Ian Fleming 7
We have met the e.
                     Oliver Hazard Perry 2
we shall meet the e.   Walt Kelly 3
your bitterest e. is dead   George IV 1
your e. and your friend   Twain 103
energize
E.   Star Trek 2
energy
e. of the universe is constant   Clausius 3
e. too cheap to meter   Strauss 1
I think the e. locked up   Friedan 3
enfants
Allons, e. de la patrie   Rouget de Lisle 1
E. Terribles   Gavarni 1
enforce
now let him e. it   Andrew Jackson 6
engage
E.   Star Trek 1
engenders
shudder in the loins e. there   Yeats 44
engine
Analytical E. has no pretensions
                      Countess of Lovelace 1
Analytical E. weaves algebraical
                      Countess of Lovelace 2
Little E. That Could   Watty Piper 1
engineering
e. of consent   Bernays 1
engineers
e. of human souls   Stalin 1
look out for e.   Pagnol 1
engines
Gentlemen—start your e.   Sayings 13
England
Be E. what she will   Charles Churchill 1
E., my E.   W. E. Henley 3
E., with all thy faults, I love
                      William Cowper 6
E. and America are two
                  George Bernard Shaw 58
E. expects that every man
                        Horatio Nelson 7
E. is a nation of shopkeepers Napoleon 5
E. is generally given to horses
                      Samuel Johnson 15
E. is the mother of parliaments   Bright 1
E.'s difficulty is Ireland's   O'Connell 1
E.'s green and pleasant land
                      William Blake 21
Goodbye E.'s rose   John and Taupin 2
Hating E. is a form   Mahfouz 2

high road that leads him to E.
                        Samuel Johnson 52
history is now and E.   T. S. Eliot 123
know of E.   Kipling 8
part of the law of E.   John Scott 1
Platonic E., house   Geoffrey Hill 4
shaking E. with the thunder
                  George Bernard Shaw 33
stately Homes of E.   Hemans 3
stately homos of E.   Crisp 2
that is for ever E.   Rupert Brooke 1
There'll always be an E.   Ross Parker 1
think of E.   Hillingdon 1
this E.   Shakespeare 17
to be in E.   Robert Browning 8
English
All my men wear E. Leather
                      Advertising Slogans 46
among the E. Poets   Keats 11
circle of the E. language
                        James Murray 1
E. mind is always in a rage   Wilde 17
E. scene   Orwell 14
E. seem to bid adieu   Sydney Smith 1
E. tongue I love   Walcott 1
E. winter   Byron 32
E.-speaking nations   Thatcher 11
God has for the E.   Joan of Arc 1
great principle of the E. law   Dickens 88
If E. was good enough   Sayings 21
made our E. tongue   Spenser 2
mobilized the E. language   Murrow 5
Queen's E.   Twain 96
This is my page for E. B.
                      Langston Hughes 9
well of E. undefiled   Spenser 6
wells of E. undefiled   Samuel Johnson 6
Why can't the E. teach
                      Alan Jay Lerner 9
Englishman
E. thinks he is moral
                  George Bernard Shaw 15
E. to open his mouth
                  George Bernard Shaw 38
Every E. is convinced   Nash 9
He is an E.   W. S. Gilbert 12
he remains an E.   W. S. Gilbert 13
heart of every E.   Robert Falcon Scott 3
last E. to rule in India   Nehru 3
not that the E. can't feel   Forster 5
you are an E.   Rhodes 3
Englishmen
E. detest a siesta   Coward 8
mad dogs and E.   Coward 9
enigma
mystery inside an e.
                      Winston Churchill 11
enjoy
e. both operations at once   Joyce Cary 1
E. every sandwich   Zevon 5
save to e. the interval   Santayana 10
seemed to e. the waking hours
                          Woody Allen 33
what I most e.   Shakespeare 414
enjoyment
capacity for e. so vast Dorothy Parker 19
enlisted
one for the e. men   Mauldin 5

enormous
E. Changes at the Last   Grace Paley 1
enough
E. is e.   Proverbs 87
e. of blood and tears   Rabin 1
just e. of learning to misquote   Byron 1
enquiring
E. minds want to know
        Advertising Slogans 90
entangling
e. alliances with none   Jefferson 30
entente
L.'e. cordiale   Louis Philippe 1
enter
E. these enchanted woods
        George Meredith 2
E. to grow in wisdom   Charles W. Eliot 1
fatal to e. any war   Douglas MacArthur 3
shall not e. into the kingdom   Bible 248
enterprise
e. employing more than 1000
        Parkinson 14
more e. in walking naked   Yeats 14
voyages of the starship E.
        Roddenberry 1
enterprises
e. that require new clothes   Thoreau 19
enters
He who e. a university   Conant 3
entertain
Here we are now, e. us   Cobain 1
entertained
Are you not e.   Film Lines 87
entertainer
only a public e.   Picasso 6
entertainment
e. branch of industry   Zappa 3
exotic and irrational e.
        Samuel Johnson 36
That's E.   Dietz 1
enthusiasm
ever achieved without e.
        Ralph Waldo Emerson 7
enthusiasts
how to deal with e.   Thomas Macaulay 10
entire
rescued the e. world   Talmud 8
entropy
e. of the universe tends   Clausius 3
envelope
e., please   Television Catchphrases 4
outside of the e.   Tom Wolfe 5
environment
I want my e.   Film Lines 61
subsidiary of the e.   Gaylord Nelson 1
envy
commit the sin of e.   Weil 5
e. of great Caesar   Shakespeare 130
E. was once considered   Sowell 1
living will e. the dead   Khrushchev 7
prisoners of e.   Illich 1
epic
some sort of e. grandeur
        F. Scott Fitzgerald 44
epicure
e. would say   Sydney Smith 10
epigram
all existence in an e.   Wilde 87
e. is a gag   Levant 1

impelled to try an e.   Dorothy Parker 13
epigrams
despotism tempered by e.
        Thomas Carlyle 4
epiphany
By an e. he meant   Joyce 25
epitaph
Let no man write my e.   Robert Emmet 1
epitaphs
nice derangement of e.
        Richard Brinsley Sheridan 3
equal
all men are created e.   Jefferson 2
all men are created e.   Lincoln 41
always opposed an e. reaction
        Isaac Newton 6
because my e. is here
        Charlotte Brontë 2
E., adj. As bad as something   Bierce 40
E. and exact justice   Jefferson 30
e. and permanent partnership
        Lucy Stone 2
E. Justice Under Law   Anonymous 8
E. Pay for E. Work   Susan B. Anthony 2
e. protection of the laws   Constitution 21
ivry man is th' e.   Dunne 18
love you take is e.
        Lennon and McCartney 24
men and women are created e.
        Elizabeth Cady Stanton 1
men are naturally e.
        Samuel Johnson 60
minority possess their e. rights
        Jefferson 29
more e. than others   Bierce 141
separate but e.   Earl Warren 1
separate but e. accommodations
        John. M. Harlan (1833–1911) 1
SOME ANIMALS ARE MORE E.   Orwell 25
We will be e. again   Schreiner 5
equality
E. of rights under the law   Anonymous 7
e. of the white and black   Lincoln 14
in a general state of e.
        Samuel Johnson 86
Liberty, E., Fraternity   Robespierre 1
majestic e. of the law   France 3
Negro e.   Lincoln 18
perfect e., social   Lincoln 15
society that puts e.   Milton Friedman 5
equally
I hate everyone e.   W. C. Fields 24
equals
e. and unequals alike   Plato 9
flourish amongst e.   Wollstonecraft 2
peace between e.   Woodrow Wilson 13
equation
e. has no meaning   Ramanujan 2
each e. I included   Hawking 1
equity
come into a court of e.   Eyre 1
He who will have e.
        William Cowper, First Earl Cowper 1
equivalent
moral e. of war   William James 13
era
e. of big government is over
        William Jefferson "Bill" Clinton 6
E. of Good Feelings   Benjamin Russell 1
E. of Wonderful Nonsense   Pegler 1

ere
Oon e. it herde   Chaucer 1
erected
I have e. a monument   Horace 22
Eros
Sad is E., builder of cities   Auden 8
erotica
E. is about mutuality   Steinem 4
err
E., v.i. To believe or act   Bierce 41
To e. is human   Pope 4
erroneous
All e. ideas   Mao Tse-tung 7
error
All men are liable to e.   John Locke 4
but for a typographical e.
        Dorothy Parker 41
Encyclopedia of E.   Acton 2
E. has never approached
        Klemens von Metternich 2
e. is all in the not done   Ezra Pound 28
e. of opinion may be tolerated
        Jefferson 28
eternal e. men make   Tolstoy 9
It is e. alone which needs   Jefferson 10
errors
E. are not in the art   Isaac Newton 3
e. in religion are dangerous
        David Hume 1
His e. are volitional   Joyce 19
my e. and wrecks   Ezra Pound 30
errs
Man e. as long   Goethe 10
Esau
E. selleth his birthright   Bible 400
escalier
L'esprit de l'e.   Diderot 3
escape
better 100 guilty Persons should e.
        Benjamin Franklin 37
e. calumny   Shakespeare 195
e. from personality   T. S. Eliot 33
Let no guilty man e.   Ulysses S. Grant 5
some criminals should e.
        Oliver Wendell Holmes, Jr. 37
we cannot e. history   Lincoln 37
escaped
I only am e. alone   Bible 96
E.S.P.
"Extra-Sensory Perception" or E. Rhine 1
esprit
L'e. de l'escalier   Diderot 3
essence
e. of all religion   Blavatsky 1
Existence precedes e.   Sartre 8
History is the e. of innumerable
        Thomas Carlyle 5
establishment
By the "E." I do not mean   Fairlie 1
E. and the Movement
        Ralph Waldo Emerson 44
e. of religion   Constitution 11
estate
fourth e. of the realm
        Thomas Macaulay 4
kind of fourth e.   Hazlitt 4
of the fourth e.   Thackeray 10
there sat a Fourth E.   Thomas Carlyle 14
Third E. contains   Sieyès 1

esteem
hold the e. of men   Veblen 1
E.T.
E. phone home   Film Lines 74
et
E. in Arcadia ego   Anonymous (Latin) 7
E. tu, Brute   Julius Caesar 7
E. tu, Brute   Shakespeare 104
état
L'É. c'est moi   Louis XIV 2
etcetera
eyes knees and of your E.
                                        e.e. cummings 11
etchings
some remarkably fine e.
                                        Dorothy Parker 22
eternal
e. error men make   Tolstoy 9
E. Feminine draws us on   Goethe 20
e. hostility against every form
                                        Jefferson 27
E. in man cannot die   Bhagavadgita 1
E. in man cannot kill   Upanishads 3
e. note of sadness   Matthew Arnold 16
E. sunshine   Pope 7
e. thing in man   Thomas Hardy 29
E. vigilance by the people
                                        Andrew Jackson 5
Hope springs e.   Pope 18
liberty to man is e. vigilance   Curran 1
nearest thing to e. life
                                        Ronald W. Reagan 1
swear an e. friendship   Molière 8
thy e. summer   Shakespeare 412
We have no e. allies   Palmerston 1
eternities
two e. of darkness   Nabokov 1
eternity
artifice of e.   Yeats 48
deserts of vast e.   Andrew Marvell 12
E. has changed him   Mallarmé 2
e. in an hour   William Blake 14
E. is a terrible thought   Stoppard 1
from here to E.   Kipling 9
great wink of e.   Hart Crane 1
teacher affects e.   Henry Adams 11
What? E.   Rimbaud 3
white radiance of E.   Percy Shelley 14
etherized
like a patient e. upon a table   T. S. Eliot 3
ethic
e. of justice proceeds from   Gilligan 1
Protestant E.   Max Weber 1
Ethiopian
Can the E. change his skin   Bible 183
ethos
e. of modern science   Merton 1
Eton
playing fields of E.   Wellington 8
Eucharist
E., *n.* A sacred feast   Bierce 42
Euclid
E. alone has looked   Millay 6
eugenics
word *e.*   Galton 2
eunuch
female e.   Greer 1
eureka
E.!   Archimedes 2

Europe
All the dogs of E. bark   Auden 24
Better fifty years of E.   Tennyson 12
E. to have one currency   Napoleon 2
going out all over E.   Edward Grey 1
I long for E.   Rimbaud 6
Leave this E. where they are never
                                        Fanon 2
specter is haunting E. Marx and Engels 1
technique and the style of E.   Fanon 3
that's old E.   Rumsfeld 2
United States of E.   Hugo 3
Whoever speaks of E. is wrong
                                        Bismarck 5
European
instruments of E. greatness
                                        Alexander Hamilton 4
Eustace
E. Clarence Scrubb   C. S. Lewis 5
even
Don't get mad, get e.
                                        Joseph P. Kennedy 1
mind to get e.   Twain 41
Never give a sucker an e. break
                                        W. C. Fields 19
evening
e. and the morning were the first day
                                        Bible 2
had a wonderful e.   "Groucho" Marx 47
Some enchanted e.   Hammerstein 14
when the e. is spread out   T. S. Eliot 3
winter e. settles down   T. S. Eliot 14
event
How much the greatest e.
                                        Charles James Fox 1
events
coming e. cast their shadows
                                        Thomas Campbell 3
E., dear boy, e.   Macmillan 3
In historic e.   Tolstoy 3
not to have controlled e.   Lincoln 45
When in the Course of human e.
                                        Jefferson 1
ever
Happy e. after   Sayings 17
everlasting
believeth on me hath e. life   Bible 317
but have e. life   Bible 315
every
Behind e. great man   Proverbs 129
England expects that e. man
                                        Horatio Nelson 7
E. breath you take   Sting 2
e. characteristic of a dog except
                                        Sam Houston 1
e. cop is a criminal
                                        Jagger and Richards 12
E. country has the government Maistre 1
E. day, in every way   Coué 1
E. dog has his day   Proverbs 74
e. dog his day   Kingsley 2
e. inch a king   Shakespeare 305
e. knee should bow   Bible 369
E. little helps   Proverbs 88
E. Man a King   Huey Long 1
e. man against e. man   Hobbes 7
E. man dies   Film Lines 29
E. Other Inch a Lady   Lillie 1
e. School-boy knows it   Jeremy Taylor 1

E. schoolboy knows who
                                        Thomas Macaulay 8
E. word she writes is a lie
                                        Mary McCarthy 6
To e. thing there is a season   Bible 143
two sides to e. question   Protagoras 1
want e. man, woman, and child
                                        Goldwyn 7
what e. schoolboy knows
                                        Jonathan Swift 23
When e. one is somebodee
                                        W. S. Gilbert 47
everybody
Always suspect e.   Dickens 37
Democracy means e. but me
                                        Langston Hughes 7
E. hurts sometimes   Stipe 3
E. is ignorant   Will Rogers 3
E. knows that the dice   Leonard Cohen 4
E. wants to get into da act
                                        Radio Catchphrases 13
e. will be world famous   Warhol 3
E.'s Doin' It Now   Irving Berlin 2
e.'s in movies   Ray Davies 3
everyone
You can't please e.   Proverbs 236
everything
e. goes and nothing matters   Roth 9
E. has been said before   Gide 1
E. has been written   Fernández 1
E. human is pathetic   Twain 88
e. in its place   Proverbs 234
E. in Rome has its price   Juvenal 1
E. that rises must converge
                                        Teilhard de Chardin 1
E. was twice repeated   Ewart 3
e. would be lawful   Dostoyevski 4
E. You Always Wanted to Know
                                        Reuben 1
E.'s Coming Up Roses   Sondheim 3
E.'s up to date   Hammerstein 5
except e., but just   Doris Lessing 2
first time for e.   Proverbs 107
knowledge of e. but power Herodotus 2
Money isn't e.   Proverbs 197
price of e.   Wilde 32
There is a time for e.   Proverbs 299
this gleam which is e.   Poincaré 1
time and place for e.   Proverbs 296
Timing is e.   Modern Proverbs 91
We can't all do e.   Virgil 16
Winning isn't e.   Lombardi 1
Winning isn't e.   Modern Proverbs 99
Winning isn't e.   "Red" Sanders 1
world is e. that is the case Wittgenstein 1
You can't have e.   Proverbs 138
you don't take e.   Solzhenitsyn 1
everywhere
bad girls go e.   Helen Gurley Brown 2
e. he is in chains   Rousseau 3
Water, water, e.   Coleridge 6
evidence
Absence of e.   Rees 1
circumstantial e. is very strong
                                        Thoreau 15
e. for God lies primarily
                                        William James 18
e. of things not seen   Bible 381
take everything on e.   Dickens 103

falling
Am I f.	Tolstoy 1
F. in love is the one	
	Robert Louis Stevenson 6
f. in love is wonderful	Irving Berlin 16
F. in love with love	Lorenz Hart 6
Go, and catch a f. star	Donne 11
like a f. star	Milton 25
sky is f.	Anonymous 27
thinking of an empire f.	Thackeray 13

falls
f. in love with Himself	
	Benjamin Franklin 15
f. the Shadow	T. S. Eliot 66
when our arrow f. to earth	
	Oliver Wendell Holmes, Jr. 41

false
bear f. witness	Bible 59
Beware of f. prophets	Bible 228
canst not then be f. to any man	
	Shakespeare 161
f. heart doth know	Shakespeare 349
F. ideas are those that we cannot	
	William James 20
F. views, if supported	
	Charles Darwin 10
f.-hearted lover's far worse	
	Folk and Anonymous Songs 15
no such thing as a f. idea	
	Lewis Powell 1
stifle is a f. opinion	Mill 8
True and F. are attributes of speech	
	Hobbes 2

falsehood
its f. would be more miraculous	
	David Hume 7
Let her and F. grapple	Milton 8

falsifiability
f. of a system	Popper 1

falter
we will not f.	George W. Bush 8

faltered
all in the diffidence that f.	
	Ezra Pound 28

fame
f. gives them some kind	
	Marilyn Monroe 7
F. is a potent aphrodisiac	
	Graham Greene 5
to fortune and to f. unknown	
	Thomas Gray 10
We live in f. or go down in flame	
	Robert Crawford 2

familiar
New things are made f.	
	Samuel Johnson 38
old f. faces	Charles Lamb 1

familiarity
F. breeds contempt	Proverbs 98
F. breeds contempt	Twain 51

families
F., I hate you	Gide 2
happy f. resemble	Tolstoy 8
there are no happy f.	Susan Cheever 1

family
disgrace to our f. name	
	"Groucho" Marx 14
F.! Home of all social evils	Strindberg 1

F. is a petty despotism	
	George Bernard Shaw 1
f. is a survival	
	Samuel Butler (1835–1902) 5
f. that prays together	Scalpone 1
I am the f. face	Thomas Hardy 28
if you have a f.	Morita 1
in a very large f.	
	Samuel Butler (1835–1902) 8
In our f., there was no	
	Norman Maclean 1
Insanity runs in my f.	Kesselring 1
running of a f.	Montaigne 9

famous
f. for fifteen minutes	Warhol 3
F. remarks are very seldom	Strunsky 1
f. too young	Ellington 3
found myself f.	Byron 35
I was too f.	Benchley 10
I'm world-f.	Richler 1
Let us now praise f. men	Bible 195
'twas a f. victory	Southey 5
Washington is full of f. men	
	Fanny Dixwell Holmes 1

fanatic
f. is a man	Dunne 3

fanaticism
F. consists in redoubling	Santayana 1

fancy
f. prose style	Nabokov 3
F. thinking the Beast	Golding 1
where is F. bred	Shakespeare 77
young man's f.	Tennyson 5

fantastic
light f. round	Milton 1
light f. toe	Milton 12

far
can Spring be f. behind	Percy Shelley 4
f., f. better thing	Dickens 99
F. from the madding crowd's	
	Thomas Gray 9
galaxy f., f. away	George Lucas 2
going a bridge too f.	
	Frederick Browning 1
So f. from God	Díaz 1
so near and yet so f.	Tennyson 32
To go too f.	Confucius 8
you seem f. away	Neruda 4

farce
f. is played	Rabelais 4
Prologue to a F.	Madison 14
second time as f.	Karl Marx 4

farcical
some f. aquatic ceremony	
	Monty Python 10

fare
f. forward, voyagers	T. S. Eliot 114

farewell
F. to Arms	Peele 1
f. to shining trifles	Philip Sidney 3
F. to thee	Liliuokalani 1

farm
I had a f. in Africa	Dinesen 2
Keep 'Em Down on the F.	
	Sam M. Lewis 1
Old MacDonald had a f.	
	Folk and Anonymous Songs 59

farmer
f. in the dell	Nursery Rhymes 17

farmers
here once the embattled f. stood	
	Ralph Waldo Emerson 6

fart
bear could not f.	Farmer 2
My Lord, I had forgot the f.	Elizabeth I 3
So dumb he can't f. and chew gum	
	Lyndon B. Johnson 14

farther
dwarf sees f. than the giant	
	Coleridge 30
tax dollar will go f.	Braun 2

fascinating
F.	Star Trek 5

fascination
f. of what's difficult	Yeats 9

fascism
first victims of American f.	
	Ethel Rosenberg 3

fascist
Every woman adores a F.	Plath 5
no f.-minded people like you	Robeson 3

fascists
This machine kills f.	"Woody" Guthrie 7

fashion
faithful to thee, Cynara! in my f.	
	Dowson 1
glass of f.	Shakespeare 198
in my f.	Cole Porter 20

fashions
fit this year's f.	Hellman 1

fast
Bad news travels f.	Proverbs 15
grew f. and furious	Robert Burns 7
You got a f. car	Tracy Chapman 1

fasten
F. your seat belts	Film Lines 6

fastened
f. about his own neck	Douglass 14

faster
F. than a speeding bullet	
	Radio Catchphrases 21
run f. than an express train	Siegel 1

fastidious
few f. people	Logan Smith 2

fat
F. Is a Feminist Issue	Orbach 1
f. lady sings	Ralph Carpenter 1
f. white woman	Frances Cornford 1
Imprisoned in every f. man	
	Cyril Connolly 3
Jack Sprat could eat no f.	
	Nursery Rhymes 30
no sex if you're f.	Giovanni 1
Seymour's F. Lady	Salinger 7
sweat less than any f. girl	Nash 15
take the f. with the lean	Dickens 73
thin man inside every f. man	Orwell 10
ye shall eat the f. of the land	Bible 37

fatal
f. futility of Fact	Henry James 23
f. to enter any war	Douglas MacArthur 3
Life is a f. complaint	
	Oliver Wendell Holmes 11
that's the most f. complaint	
	Hilton 2

fate
F. and character are the same	Novalis 2
F. chooses our relatives	Delille 1

F. is not an eagle   Elizabeth Bowen 2
F. is shaped half by   Tan 1
f. of a nation was riding   Longfellow 25
F. sits on these   Radcliffe 1
I am the master of my f.   W. E. Henley 2
man's character is his f.   Heraclitus 2
Politics is f.   Napoleon 13
revolt against man's f.   Malraux 2
take a bond of F.   Shakespeare 380
Though Justice against F.
        Andrew Marvell 3

fates
so many hostages to the f.   Lucan 3

father
being the f. of their son   Stein 10
Child is f. of the Man
        William Wordsworth 12
desire his f.'s death   Dostoyevski 7
F., forgive them   Bible 306
F., Son, and Holy Ghost   Ken 1
F. knows best   Proverbs 99
f. of many nations   Bible 342
F. of Waters again goes unvexed
        Lincoln 39
Honor thy f.   Bible 55
I am your f.   George Lucas 15
I bet your f. spent   "Groucho" Marx 35
I must be about my F.'s business
        Bible 291
In my F.'s house are many   Bible 324
In the Name of the F.   Missal 2
knows its own f.   Proverbs 328
Like f. like son   Proverbs 100
man first quarrels with his f.
        Samuel Butler (1835–1902) 9
man whose f.   Barack Obama 8
matter who my f. was   Sexton 7
my f. moved through dooms of love
        e.e. cummings 17
My f. thanks you   Cohan 7
my f. was so ignorant   Twain 149
neither f. nor lover   Roethke 1
nothing other than an exalted f.
        Sigmund Freud 9
Old f., old artificer   Joyce 12
Our F., who art in heaven   Missal 5
Our F. which art in heaven   Bible 215
Our F.-Mother God   Eddy 1
religion of the f.   Sigmund Freud 19
resembled my f. as he slept
        Shakespeare 353
rule the galaxy as f. and son
        George Lucas 16
There is a higher f.   George W. Bush 27
Thy wish was f.   Shakespeare 66
wise f. that knows his own
        Shakespeare 74
You are old, F. William   Carroll 9
You are old, F. William   Southey 2

fatherhood
f. of God   John D. Rockefeller, Jr. 1

fatherland
German's f.   Arndt 1

fathers
because our f. lied   Kipling 36
land of my f.   Evan James 1
our f. brought forth   Lincoln 41
Victory has a hundred f.   Ciano 1
victory has 100 f.   John F. Kennedy 18

fathom
Full f. five   Shakespeare 439

fatigue
f. of supporting it   Thomas Paine 11

fatted
Bring hither the f. calf   Bible 299

fattening
immoral, illegal, or f.   Woollcott 4

Faulkner
Poor F.   Hemingway 36
WILLIAM F., Sole Owner   Faulkner 6

fault
f., dear Brutus   Shakespeare 98
nothing is anybody's f.   O'Rourke 3

faults
Love to f. is always blind William Blake 1

faun
Afternoon of a F.   Mallarmé 1

Fauntleroy
Little Lord F.
        Frances Hodgson Burnett 1

Faustus
Backwardly tolerant, F.
        Karl Jay Shapiro 3
F. must be damned   Marlowe 11

fauves
Donatello chez les f.   Vauxcelles 2

fava
ate his liver with some f. beans
        Thomas Harris 1

favor
I would like you to do us a f.   Trump 24

favorite
F. . . . One chosen as a companion
        Samuel Johnson 11
few of my f. things   Hammerstein 25
my second f. organ   Woody Allen 13
That f. subject, Myself   Boswell 1

favors
chance f. only the prepared   Pasteur 1
Fortune, that f. fools   Jonson 4
Fortune f. the brave   Virgil 12

fear
afraid of is f.   Wellington 3
arousing pity and f.   Aristotle 5
best cure for the f. of death   Hazlitt 6
direction of our f.   John Berryman 1
Do right and f. no man   Proverbs 73
F. and Loathing in Las Vegas
        Hunter S. Thompson 1
F. God, and keep his commandments
        Bible 154
f. is f. itself   Franklin D. Roosevelt 6
F. is the mind-killer   Frank Herbert 1
F. of Flying   Jong 2
F. tastes like a rusty knife
        John Cheever 1
f. the most is f.   Montaigne 4
haunting f. that someone   Mencken 42
I f. Greeks   Virgil 4
I f. thee, ancient Mariner   Coleridge 9
I will f. no evil   Bible 109
is not the f. of death Samuel Johnson 62
never f. to negotiate John F. Kennedy 11
no Hope without F.   Spinoza 1
not absence of f.   Twain 65
Nothing is terrible except f. itself
        Francis Bacon 7
perfect love casteth out f.   Bible 389

salvation with f. and trembling
        Bible 370
show you f. in a handful   T. S. Eliot 43
so much to be feared as f.   Thoreau 16
We Germans f. God   Bismarck 8
where angels f. to tread   Pope 5

feared
more secure to be f.   Machiavelli 6

fearful
could frame thy f. symmetry
        William Blake 10
f. are caught as often   Helen Keller 6
f. of the night   Sarah Williams 1
upon a f. summons   Shakespeare 143

fears
Present f. are less   Shakespeare 329
sum of their f.   Winston Churchill 51
When I have f. that I may cease   Keats 7

feast
f. of reason   Pope 30
outcast from life's f.   Joyce 3
Paris is a moveable f.   Hemingway 30
perpetual f.   Logan Smith 1

feather
Birds of a f. flock together   Proverbs 27
despotism to liberty in a f. bed
        Jefferson 22
f. does not fly   Hildegard of Bingen 1
stuck a f. in his hat
        Folk and Anonymous Songs 84

feathered
f. glory   Yeats 43

feathers
Hope is not "the thing with f."
        Woody Allen 20
"Hope" is the thing with f.
        Emily Dickinson 10

feature
not a bug, that's a f.   Sayings 50

February
not Puritanism but F.   Krutch 1

federal
New F.   Richard Nixon 8

Federalists
we are all F.   Jefferson 31

federation
F. of the world   Tennyson 8

feed
F. the Birds   Travers 1
F. the world   Geldof 1
F. your head   Slick 2

feeds
bite the hand that f. us Edmund Burke 2

feel
did thee f. the earth move
        Hemingway 23
Do I f. lucky   Film Lines 63
Englishman can't f.   Forster 5
f. inferior without your consent
        Eleanor Roosevelt 6
f. sorry for the good Lord   Einstein 31
I f. your pain
        William Jefferson "Bill" Clinton 2
men who do not f. quite well
        Galbraith 4
moral is what you f. good
        Hemingway 13
smile I could f. in my hip pocket
        Raymond Chandler 6

feel (cont.):
some women may f.   Thomas Hardy 11
speak what we f.   Shakespeare 320
tragedy to those that f.   Walpole 3
When I f. like exercising   Terry 1
feeling
After great pain, a formal f.
Emily Dickinson 7
comfort of f. safe with a person   Craik 1
feelings
Era of Good F.   Benjamin Russell 1
feels
man is as old as he f.   Proverbs 185
old as the woman he f.
"Groucho" Marx 45
feet
better to die on your f.   Ibarruri 1
dust of your f.   Bible 235
fog comes on little cat f.   Sandburg 4
his f. part of iron   Bible 189
If her horny f. protrude
Wallace Stevens 5
man who had no f.   Sadi 1
patter of little f.   Longfellow 22
They hadn't any f.   Carroll 33
vote with their f.   Lenin 12
feets
F., don't fail me now   Moreland 1
feldes
out of olde f.   Chaucer 5
felicity
Human F. is produc'd
Benjamin Franklin 39
indulge in the f.   W. S. Gilbert 17
fell
f. among thieves   Bible 295
f. like a stick   Thomas Paine 20
f. likewise upon his sword   Bible 85
f. upon their knees   William Bradford 1
f. upon their knees   Evarts 1
From morn to noon he f.   Milton 25
it f. to earth   Longfellow 14
love f. out with me   Lorenz Hart 2
night the bed f.   Thurber 2
one f. swoop   Shakespeare 383
Some seeds f. by the wayside   Bible 239
wall f. down   Bible 74
fellow
f. of infinite jest   Shakespeare 226
"F. Travelers" of the Revolution   Trotsky 1
For he's a jolly good f.
Folk and Anonymous Songs 22
You shoot a f. down   Thomas Hardy 24
fellow-men
one that loves his f.   Leigh Hunt 3
felon
When a f.'s not engaged   W. S. Gilbert 22
female
being f. put many more   Chisholm 2
characterizes the f. mind
Wollstonecraft 15
civilization had been left in f.   Paglia 1
F. animals defending their young
Margaret Mead 4
f. eunuch   Greer 1
f. of the species   Kipling 34
f. worker is the slave   James Connolly 1
hearty f. stench   T. S. Eliot 38
no f. Mozart   Paglia 2

Patriotism in the f. sex   Abigail Adams 5
speak of a f. liver   Charlotte Gilman 4
There is no f. mind   Charlotte Gilman 4
feminine
Eternal F. draws us on   Goethe 20
Taste is the f. of genius
Edward FitzGerald 7
what f. intuition really is
Margaret Mead 8
feminism
F. is a theory   Atkinson 2
F. is the radical notion   Sayings 12
I hate discussions of f.   French 1
feminist
Fat Is a F. Issue   Orbach 1
people call me a F.   Rebecca West 1
femme
Cherchez la f.   Dumas the Elder 5
fence
don't f. me in   Cole Porter 17
f. around the Law   Talmud 6
only f. against the world   John Locke 12
fences
Good f. make good neighbors   Frost 3
Good f. make good neighbors
Proverbs 125
look after my f.   John Sherman 1
Fermat
F. theorem as an isolated   Gauss 1
fester
Lilies that f.   Shakespeare 425
fetch
f. a pail of water   Nursery Rhymes 26
fetishist
f. who yearns for a woman's shoe
Kraus 2
fetters
reason Milton wrote in f.
William Blake 8
fetus
laughed like an irresponsible f.
T. S. Eliot 13
fever
Stuff a cold and starve a f.   Proverbs 286
few
f. are chosen   Bible 254
f. good men
William Jones (1753–1822) 1
f. of my favorite things
Hammerstein 25
owed by so many to so f.
Winston Churchill 17
The F. The Proud
Advertising Slogans 121
We f., we happy f.   Shakespeare 138
win a f., you lose a f.
Modern Proverbs 97
fewer
f. and f. words   Orwell 39
women have f. teeth   Bertrand Russell 10
fewest
most words in the f. ideas   Lincoln 58
fez
abolish the f.   Atatürk 1
fiat
f. justitia, ruat caelum   Lord Mansfield 1
fickle
F. and changeable   Virgil 6

fiction
best thing in f.   Wilde 63
f. as though it were philosophy
Rebecca West 3
F. is obliged to stick   Twain 93
F. is Truth's elder sister   Kipling 37
house of f. has in short   Henry James 18
I write f.   Roth 6
if she is to write f.   Virginia Woolf 9
Poetry is the supreme f.
Wallace Stevens 6
Reality, as usual, beats f.   Conrad 27
science f.   Gernsback 1
Science-F.   William Wilson 1
stranger than f.   Byron 33
stranger than f.   Chesterton 6
That is what f. means   Wilde 81
fictitious
We live in f. times   Michael Moore 2
fiddle
beyond all this f.   Marianne Moore 1
fiddler
must pay the f.   Proverbs 60
fidelity
F., n. A virtue peculiar   Bierce 45
Your idea of f.   Film Lines 60
fie
F., foh, and fum   Shakespeare 301
field
color purple in a f.   Alice Walker 5
Consider the lilies of the f.   Bible 219
corner of a foreign f.   Rupert Brooke 1
Good f. No hit.
Miguel "Mike" Gonzalez 1
I am Goya of the bare f.   Voznesensky 1
Never in the f. of human conflict
Winston Churchill 17
fields
In Flanders f.   McCrae 1
playing f. of Eton   Wellington 8
fiercer
There is not a f. hell   Keats 8
Fife
Thane of F.   Shakespeare 386
fifteen
F. men on the dead man's
Robert Louis Stevenson 8
f.-year-old boy   Roth 2
famous for f. minutes   Warhol 3
fifth
F. column   Mola 1
f. dimension   Serling 4
Fifties
tranquilized F.   Robert Lowell 1
50
At 50, everyone has the face   Orwell 51
fifty
at f. you will be George Bernard Shaw 48
F. Million Frenchmen   Rose 2
f. ways to leave your lover
Paul Simon 10
fifty-four
F. Forty or Fight   Political Slogans 14
57
57 Channels (and Nothin' On)
Springsteen 7
fig
they sewed f. leaves together   Bible 17

fight

Fifty-four Forty or F.

  Political Slogans 14

F. fire with fire   Proverbs 101

f. for your right to party   Rubin 1

f. like hell for the living Mother Jones 1

F. the good f. of faith   Bible 378

F. the Power   Shocklee 1

f. to prove I'm right   Townshend 3

first rule about f. club   Palahniuk 1

hour of the honest f.   Trollope 1

I have fought a good f.   Bible 379

I have not yet begun to f.

  John Paul Jones 2

I went to a f. last night Dangerfield 2

I will f. no more   Chief Joseph 3

live to f. another day   Proverbs 102

man who runs may f. again

  Menander 2

propose to f. it out Ulysses S. Grant 2

Stay up and f.   Diller 1

those that I f.   Yeats 21

too proud to f.   Woodrow Wilson 10

We f., not to enslave Thomas Paine 12

We f., therefore we are   Begin 1

We shall f. on the beaches

  Winston Churchill 14

We will f. on the Loire Clemenceau 3

We'd rather f. than switch

  Advertising Slogans 115

You cannot f. against the future

  Gladstone 1

You can't f. City Hall

  Modern Proverbs 29

you can't f. in here   Film Lines 70

fighter

Am I no a bonny f.

  Robert Louis Stevenson 17

fighting

dying, but f. back   McKay 2

f. for this woman's honor

  "Groucho" Marx 26

I am tired of f.   Chief Joseph 2

no place for street f. man

  Jagger and Richards 8

upset many f. faiths

  Oliver Wendell Holmes, Jr. 28

what are we f. for

  "Country" Joe McDonald 1

without f. at all   Sun Tzu 4

worth the f. for   Hemingway 24

fights

He who f. and runs away Proverbs 102

married life is the f. Thornton Wilder 4

Whosoever f. in the way of God

  Koran 10

figure

f. a poem makes   Frost 20

f. in the carpet   Henry James 14

figures

good at f. myself   Mae West 17

prove anything by f. Thomas Carlyle 9

filled

can only be f. by an infinite Pascal 5

He hath f. the hungry   Bible 286

fin

F. de Siècle   Jouvenot 1

final

f. cause of the human nose

  Coleridge 36

f. proof of God's   De Vries 1

f. solution   Heydrich 1

f. solution of the Jewish Goering 2

Is that your f. answer

  Television Catchphrases 86

only because we are f.

  Robert H. Jackson 12

Space, the f. frontier Roddenberry 1

undaunted the f. sacrifice Spring-Rice 1

finale

Let be be f. of seem Wallace Stevens 4

finality

F. is not the language   Disraeli 20

financial

if only for f. reasons Woody Allen 23

find

f. a foe   Dorothy Parker 2

Good Man Is Hard to F. Eddie Green 1

I'll f. what I'm after

  Bricusse and Newley 3

if by chance we f. each other Perls 1

Love will f. a way   Proverbs 181

seek, and ye shall f.   Bible 224

strive, to seek, to f.   Tennyson 26

we can f. information

  Samuel Johnson 81

Where does she f. them

  Dorothy Parker 32

finders

F. keepers   Proverbs 103

fine

grave's a f. and private place

  Andrew Marvell 14

OLD CARY GRANT F.   Cary Grant 2

put too f. a point upon it Dickens 85

think is particularly f.

  Samuel Johnson 75

with so f. a brush   Austen 17

world is a f. place   Hemingway 24

finer

Nothing could be f.   Gus Kahn 2

finest

their f. hour   Winston Churchill 15

finger

f. lickin' good Advertising Slogans 68

moving f. writes Edward FitzGerald 3

to the scratching of my f. David Hume 3

fingered

Rosy-f. dawn   Homer 8

fingernails

paring his f.   Joyce 7

fingers

five sovereign f.   Dylan Thomas 4

four of his f. are pointing Nizer 1

Let your f. do the walking

  Advertising Slogans 19

my f. wandered idly   Procter 2

separate as the f.

  Booker T. Washington 3

terrified vague f.   Yeats 43

finish

didn't make it to the f. line Landers 2

Give us the tools, and we will f.

  Winston Churchill 19

finished

I've almost f.   Calvino 4

I've f. that chapel   Michelangelo 1

poem is never f.   Valéry 2

then he's f.   Gabor 2

until it is f. with you

  David Foster Wallace 6

finita

La commedia è f.   Leoncavallo 2

finned

giant f. car nose forward

  Robert Lowell 3

Finnigin

Gone agin.—F.   Gillilan 1

fire

baptism of f.   Napoleon 7

between the f. brigade

  Winston Churchill 5

bound upon a wheel of f.

  Shakespeare 310

Bring me my chariot of f.

  William Blake 20

burnt child dreads the f. Proverbs 37

consumed by either f. or f. T. S. Eliot 121

Don't f. till you see   Putnam 1

Don't f. unless fired upon John Parker 1

Fight f. with f.   Proverbs 101

f. and fury   Trump 17

f. and the rose are one T. S. Eliot 125

f. bell in the night   Jefferson 45

f. in which we burn   Schwartz 1

f. next time   James Baldwin 2

f. next time

  Folk and Anonymous Songs 36

f. of my loins   Nabokov 2

f. when you are ready George Dewey 1

glow from that f. John F. Kennedy 15

great balls of f.   Otis Blackwell 1

heart is an organ of f.   Ondaatje 1

I hold with those who favor f. Frost 11

If a house was on f.   Lincoln 21

If you play with f.   Proverbs 235

I've seen f.   James Taylor 2

light my f.   Jim Morrison 3

No smoke without f.   Proverbs 276

O for a muse of f.   Shakespeare 132

sacred f. of liberty George Washington 3

shouting f. in a theatre

  Oliver Wendell Holmes, Jr. 29

so cold no f. ever can warm me

  Emily Dickinson 29

Tell a man whose house is on f.

  Garrison 2

throw the book into the f. Sand 1

walk into the f.   Engels 4

We didn't start the f.   Joel 5

world will end in f.   Frost 10

fired

f. the shot heard round the world

  Ralph Waldo Emerson 6

I just f. the head   Trump 16

You're f. Television Catchphrases 8

fires

Only you can prevent forest f.

  Advertising Slogans 123

firing

no one is thinking of f. it Chekhov 3

firmament

brave o'erhanging f. Shakespeare 180

first

After the f. death Dylan Thomas 16

America f.   Woodrow Wilson 9

called is F. Lady

  Jacqueline Kennedy Onassis 3

flee
They f. from me   Wyatt 1
fleece
f. was white as snow   Sara Hale 1
fleeting
Time is f.   Longfellow 2
flesh
f. is heir to   Shakespeare 189
f. is weak   Bible 270
f. is weary   Mallarmé 4
f. of my f.   Bible 12
F. was the reason   de Kooning 1
he is merely f. and blood   T. S. Eliot 25
make your f. creep   Dickens 2
they shall be one f.   Bible 13
thorn in the f.   Bible 363
too too sullied f. would melt
                                     Shakespeare 149
when we sat by the f. pots   Bible 49
Word was made f.   Bible 311
world, the f., and the devil
                     Book of Common Prayer 8
wrestle not against f. and blood
                                             Bible 368

flew
he pushed and they f.   Logue 1
one f. over the cuckoo's nest
                  Folk and Anonymous Songs 52
flicker
moment of my greatness f.   T. S. Eliot 8
flies
As f. to wanton boys   Shakespeare 304
f. don't practice law   "Groucho" Marx 34
Honey catches more f.   Proverbs 145
love f. out of the window   Proverbs 240
may catch small F.   Jonathan Swift 3
Time f.   Proverbs 298
Time f.   Virgil 21
flights
f. of angels sing thee   Shakespeare 237
fling
I will f. myself   Virginia Woolf 15
float
F. like a butterfly   Ali 3
floated
what foul dust f.   F. Scott Fitzgerald 12
floating
f. bulwark of the island   Blackstone 5
f. opera   John Barth 1
floats
It f.   Advertising Slogans 63
flock
Birds of a feather f. together Proverbs 27
flood
taken at the f.   Shakespeare 128
ten years before the F.
                            Andrew Marvell 11
flooded
STREETS F.   Benchley 12
floor
upon the bar-room f.   D'Arcy 1
flour
f. goes into the making of bread
                                         Neruda 7
flow
Go with the f.   Modern Proverbs 34
flower
drives the f.   Dylan Thomas 1
f. in his hand when he awoke
                                      Coleridge 42

Let the black f. blossom   Hawthorne 8
meanest f. that blows
                         William Wordsworth 18
O F. of Scotland   Roy Williamson 1
When you take a f.   O'Keeffe 1
flowers
bring forth May f.   Proverbs 13
buy the f. herself   Virginia Woolf 6
f. of the forest   Jane Elliot 1
f. that bloom in the spring
                               W. S. Gilbert 44
I hate f.   O'Keeffe 2
Letting a hundred f. blossom
                              Mao Tse-tung 6
much to hope from the f.
                         Arthur Conan Doyle 27
nosegay of other men's f.   Montaigne 17
Say it with f.   Advertising Slogans 111
smell the f.   Hagen 1
Where have all the f. gone Pete Seeger 4
flowing
land f. with milk and honey   Bible 41
flown
all the birds are f.   Charles I 1
fluidity
terrible f. of self-revelation
                               Henry James 20
fluids
precious bodily f.   Film Lines 67
flung
f. himself upon his horse   Leacock 1
flux
All is f.   Heraclitus 4
fly
Angels can f.   Chesterton 12
birds got to f.   Hammerstein 1
don't kill that f.   Issa 1
f. away home   Nursery Rhymes 33
F. me   Advertising Slogans 88
F. me to the moon   Bart Howard 1
F. the friendly skies
                        Advertising Slogans 119
He'd f. through the air   Leybourne 1
It's the only way to f.
                        Advertising Slogans 133
My words f. up   Shakespeare 213
religion and f. fishing
                            Norman Maclean 1
said a spider to a f.   Howitt 1
she wouldn't even harm a f.
                               Robert Bloch 1
Shoo f., don't bother me   Reeves 1
show the f. the way out   Wittgenstein 4
Straighten Up and F. Right
                             Nat King Cole 1
verdict was the blue-tail f.
                  Folk and Anonymous Songs 8
way out of the f.-bottle   Wittgenstein 4
We have already begun to f. Fontenelle 1
wouldn't even harm a f.   Film Lines 141
flying
Fear of F.   Jong 2
make a f. Chariot   Wilkins 1
on the f. trapeze   Leybourne 1
fly-wheel
cosmos is a gigantic f.   Mencken 23
enormous f. of society   William James 4
foaming
Tiber f. with much blood   Virgil 7

focus
products by f. groups   Jobs 4
foe
find a f.   Dorothy Parker 2
His f. was folly   Anthony Hope 1
foeman
When the f. bares his steel
                               W. S. Gilbert 21
fog
f. comes on little cat feet   Sandburg 4
F. everywhere   Dickens 76
London particular . . . a f.   Dickens 82
Never can there come f.   Dickens 77
Night and f.   Richard Wagner 2
wrapped in a f. of greater   Clausewitz 1
foiled
Curses, f. again   Sayings 8
fold
Do not f., spindle   Sayings 9
f. their tents   Longfellow 13
know when to f. 'em   Schlitz 1
folk
All music is f. music Louis Armstrong 1
excepting incest and f.-dancing   Bax 1
F.-lore, the Lore of the People   Thoms 1
folks
Different strokes for different f.
                          Modern Proverbs 25
poor f. hate the rich f.   Lehrer 3
follow
f. as the night the day   Shakespeare 161
F. me around   Gary Hart 1
F. the money   Film Lines 8
F. the yellow brick road   Harburg 6
F. your bliss   Joseph Campbell 2
I f. the worse   Ovid 4
I really had to f. them   Ledru-Rollin 1
If thou f. thy star   Dante 8
follows
Form ever f. function Louis H. Sullivan 1
Lie f. by post   Beresford 1
Trade f. the flag   Proverbs 305
folly
having lived in f.   Cervantes 8
His foe was f.   Anthony Hope 1
lovely woman stoops to f.   T. S. Eliot 54
lovely woman stoops to f.
                          Oliver Goldsmith 6
'tis f. to be wise   Thomas Gray 1
weep at the f. of mankind   Gibbon 8
fond
grow too f. of it   Robert E. Lee 1
I am f. of children (except boys)
                                   Carroll 46
fonder
Absence makes the heart grow f.
                                 Propertius 1
Absence makes the heart grow f.
                                  Proverbs 1
food
f. and medicine   Lin Yutang 1
F. comes first   Brecht 2
He kills for f.   Woody Allen 21
If music be the f. of love
                             Shakespeare 239
live on f. and water   W. C. Fields 15
put f. on your family George W. Bush 24
struggle for room and f.   Malthus 2
What is f. to one   Lucretius 4
why the poor have no f.   Câmara 1

f. some sinner   Mencken 25
f. us our debts   Bible 215
f. us our trespasses
       Book of Common Prayer 12
sometimes they f. them   Wilde 36
to f., divine   Pope 4

forgiveness
After such knowledge, what f.
       T. S. Eliot 23
ask of thee f.   Shakespeare 313

forgives
f. everything except genius   Wilde 7

forgot
I f. to duck   Dempsey 1
Land That Time F.
       Edgar Rice Burroughs 2

forgotten
all that has been learnt has been f.
       Conant 1
F. Man   Sumner 3
f. man at the bottom
       Franklin D. Roosevelt 2
f. nothing and learnt nothing
       Dumouriez 1
He hath not f. my age   Southey 3
If you would not be f.
       Benjamin Franklin 16
injury is much sooner f.   Chesterfield 3
volume of f. lore   Poe 6
when you have f. your aim   Santayana 1

fork
come to a f. in the road   Berra 17
You can stick a f. in him
       Jay Hanna "Dizzy" Dean 1

form
Democracy is the worst f.   Briffault 1
democracy is the worst f.
       Winston Churchill 34
f. and not the message   McLuhan 1
F. ever follows function
       Louis H. Sullivan 1
F. is emptiness   Anonymous 10
my bodily f.   Yeats 49
Shape without f.   T. S. Eliot 64

formal
After great pain, a f. feeling
       Emily Dickinson 7

formed
f. for the ruin of our sex   Smollett 1
Man was f. for society   Blackstone 1
water never f. to mind
       Wallace Stevens 10

forms
f. of action we have buried   Maitland 2

formula
f. of that particular emotion
       T. S. Eliot 27

forsake
Do not f. me   Ned Washington 3

forsaken
why hast thou f. me   Bible 274

forsaking
f. all other   Book of Common Prayer 14

fort
Hold the f.   Bliss 1

fortissimo
F. at last   Gustav Mahler 1

fortunate
I ain't no f. one   Fogerty 1

fortune
Behind every great f.   Balzac 2
F., that favors fools   Jonson 4
f. and men's eyes   Shakespeare 413
F. favors the brave   Virgil 12
F. helps the brave   Terence 4
given hostages to f.   Francis Bacon 15
I am f.'s fool   Shakespeare 43
little value of f.   Richard Steele 2
moment of excessive good f.
       Lew Wallace 1
slings and arrows of outrageous f.
       Shakespeare 188
wheel of f. goes 'round
       Radio Catchphrases 19
youth to f. and to fame   Thomas Gray 10

fortunes
our Lives, our F.   Jefferson 8

forty
Every man over f.
       George Bernard Shaw 23
fool at f.   Edward Young 2
f. centuries look down   Napoleon 8
f. days and forty nights   Bible 28
f. days and forty nights   Bible 63
F. Second Street   Dubin 1
f. thousand men   Wellington 2
F. two   Douglas Adams 3
gave her mother f. whacks
       Anonymous 18
Life Begins at F.   Pitkin 1
Men at f.   Justice 1
wander in the wilderness f. years
       Bible 67
when you are f.
       George Bernard Shaw 48
work of the men above f.   Osler 2

forward
fare f., voyagers   T. S. Eliot 114
f. Youth that would appear
       Andrew Marvell 1
from this day f.
       Book of Common Prayer 15
One Step F.   Lenin 1

forwards
it must be lived—f.   Kierkegaard 1

Foster
behind those F. Grants
       Advertising Slogans 48

fought
I f. the law   Sonny Curtis 1
I have f. a good fight   Bible 379
what they f. each other for   Southey 4

foul
f. is fair   Shakespeare 322
Murder most f.   Shakespeare 167
what f. dust floated
       F. Scott Fitzgerald 12

found
art f. wanting   Bible 190
f. myself famous   Byron 35
I have f. you an argument
       Samuel Johnson 106
lack of what is f. there
       William Carlos Williams 6
tragedy of a man who has f.   Barrie 1
When f., make a note   Dickens 54

founder
by the F. of Christianity   Chesterton 15

four
find me a f.-year-old child
       "Groucho" Marx 21
F. be the things   Dorothy Parker 6
f. colors may be wanted
       Francis Guthrie 1
f. essential human freedoms
       Franklin D. Roosevelt 23
F. Horsemen of the Apocalypse
       Blasco-Ibáñez 1
F. Horsemen rode again
       Grantland Rice 2
F. LEGS GOOD   Orwell 24
f. little Rabbits   Beatrix Potter 1
F. out of five dentists
       Advertising Slogans 118
F. score and seven years ago   Lincoln 41
my f. little children
       Martin Luther King, Jr. 13
only use f.-letter words   Cole Porter 3
than you were f. years ago
       Ronald W. Reagan 4
There'll be f. of us in no time
       Woody Allen 36

400
only about 400 people   McAllister 1

fourteen
When I was a boy of f.   Twain 149

fourteenth
F. Amendment does not enact
       Oliver Wendell Holmes, Jr. 19

fourth
born on the F. of July   Cohan 1
f. estate   Thackeray 10
f. estate of the realm
       Thomas Macaulay 4
kind of f. estate   Hazlitt 4
there sat a F. Estate   Thomas Carlyle 14
they'll use in the f.—rocks   Einstein 18
This is the F.   Jefferson 55

fowl
You elegant f.   Lear 6

fox
choose the f. and the lion   Machiavelli 7
f. knows many things   Archilochus 1
f.'s nose touches   Ted Hughes 2
patch it out with the f.'s   Plutarch 3
sharp hot stink of f.   Ted Hughes 3

foxes
f. have a sincere interest   George Eliot 8
second to the f.   Isaiah Berlin 1

foxholes
f. or graveyards of battle
       John F. Kennedy 32
no atheists in f.   Modern Proverbs 3

frabjous
O f. day!   Carroll 29

fracture
f. of good order   Berrigan 1

fragment
moon rattles like a f.   e.e. cummings 8

fragments
f. I have shored against   T. S. Eliot 60

Fragonard
what sort of man was F.
       William Carlos Williams 4

frailty
F., thy name is woman   Shakespeare 152

frame
choose the f. of our destiny
                    Hammarskjöld 1
I f. no hypotheses   Isaac Newton 2
still bears in his bodily f.
                    Charles Darwin 13
This goodly f.   Shakespeare 180
France
better in F.   Sterne 5
certain idea of F.   de Gaulle 4
F., mother of arts   Joachim du Bellay 1
F. cannot be F.   de Gaulle 5
F. has lost a battle   de Gaulle 1
F. was long a despotism
                    Thomas Carlyle 4
F. will declare   Einstein 6
F. will say that I am a German
                    Einstein 6
He had one illusion—F.   Keynes 2
I now speak for F.   de Gaulle 2
franchise
right to the elective f.
                Elizabeth Cady Stanton 6
Frankenfood
If they want to sell us F.   Paul Lewis 1
Frankenstein
F.   Mary Shelley 1
Frankie
F. and Johnny
            Folk and Anonymous Songs 23
frankincense
gold, and, f., and myrrh   Bible 197
Franklin
body of B. F.   Benjamin Franklin 1
frankly
F., my dear   Margaret Mitchell 7
fraternity
Liberty, Equality, F.   Robespierre 1
fraud
Force, and, f., are in war   Hobbes 9
freaks
F. were born with their trauma
                    Diane Arbus 1
Fred
F.'s studies are not very deep
                    George Eliot 13
free
All human beings are born f.
                    Anonymous 2
believe in f. will Isaac Bashevis Singer 2
best things in life are f.   DeSylva 3
Best Things in Life Are F.
                Howard E. Johnson 2
butterflies are f.   Dickens 84
Comment is f.   C. P. Scott 1
expects to be ignorant and f. Jefferson 41
forever f.   Lincoln 34
f., equal, and independent John Locke 7
F. and Independent States   Jefferson 7
f. and independent states
                Richard Henry Lee 1
f. and open encounter   Milton 8
F. at last Folk and Anonymous Songs 24
F. at last   Martin Luther King, Jr. 14
F. election of masters   Marcuse 1
F.—Even from me
            Anne Morrow Lindbergh 5
f. exercise thereof   Constitution 11
f. for irreligion   Robert H. Jackson 11

f. love   Chesterton 4
f. lunch   Walter Morrow 1
f. play of the mind   Matthew Arnold 11
F. to Be . . . You and Me
                    Marlo Thomas 1
F. women are not women   Colette 1
F. Your Mind   George Clinton 1
Give a man a f. hand   Mae West 14
henceforward shall be f.   Lincoln 38
home of the f.   Cohan 3
hungry man is not a f. man
                Adlai E. Stevenson 4
I am a f. man   Lyndon B. Johnson 1
I am a f. man
            Television Catchphrases 51
I am condemned to be f.   Sartre 2
I am f. of all prejudice   W. C. Fields 24
I am truly f.   Bakunin 3
I was f.   Tubman 2
If a f. society   John F. Kennedy 9
in chains than to be f.   Kafka 10
Information wants to be f.   Brand 4
know how to be f.   Valéry 3
let it go f.   Lair 1
Live f. or die   John Stark 1
Man was born f.   Rousseau 3
My first act of f. will   William James 1
no such thing as a f. lunch
                    Commoner 1
no such thing as a f. lunch   Heinlein 3
No woman can call herself f.   Sanger 3
o'er the land of the f. Francis Scott Key 2
Only a f. society can produce Laumer 1
our will is f.   Samuel Johnson 61
rockin' in the f. world   Neil Young 5
security of all is in a f. press
                    Jefferson 51
such invasion of f. speech   Hand 7
Teach the f. man how to praise
                    Auden 25
tell them they are f.   Layton 1
This is a f. country   Proverbs 116
truth shall make you f.   Bible 319
Was he f.   Auden 16
Writing f. verse is like   Frost 18
freedom
abridging the f. of speech
                Constitution 11
another man's f. fighter   Sayings 44
battle cry of f. George Frederick Root 2
behavioristic f.   John B. Watson 4
better to die with f.   Haile Selassie 1
cause of f.   Anna Julia Cooper 2
condition for political f.
                Milton Friedman 1
development of the Idea of F.   Hegel 4
economic f. is an end
                Milton Friedman 2
fight for f. or slavery   Robeson 1
f. depends on being courageous
                Thucydides 2
f. for the one who thinks Luxemburg 2
f. for the thought that we hate
            Oliver Wendell Holmes, Jr. 39
f. from fear and want
            Roosevelt and Churchill 3
f. from the press   Navratilova 1
F. hath been hunted   Thomas Paine 5
F. in a commons   Hardin 3

F. is never voluntarily
            Martin Luther King, Jr. 6
F. IS SLAVERY   Orwell 35
f. of speech   Twain 95
F. of the press   Liebling 1
f. of the press   George Mason 3
f. of thinking   John Adams 2
F. of Writing   John Adams 16
f. to differ   Robert H. Jackson 4
f. to say that two plus two   Orwell 41
f. women were supposed to have
                    Burchill 1
F.'s just another word   Kristofferson 1
F.'s untidy   Rumsfeld 9
giving f. to the slave   Lincoln 37
illusions about f.   Martel 1
let f. ring   Martin Luther King, Jr. 14
let f. ring   Samuel Francis Smith 1
LET F. RING   Archibald Carey, Jr. 1
Long live f.   Scholl 1
love not f., but licence   Milton 14
new birth of f.   Lincoln 42
new f. for America   Woodrow Wilson 7
Of that f. one may say   Cardozo 4
preserve and enlarge f.   John Locke 6
really important kind of f.
                David Foster Wallace 9
so celestial an article as F.
                    Thomas Paine 9
that cure is f.   Thomas Macaulay 2
we call love of f.   Wheatley 4
freedoms
four essential human f.
            Franklin D. Roosevelt 23
freeing
save the Union without f.   Lincoln 32
freely
interpreted nature as f. as a lawyer
                    Giraudoux 1
freethinking
f. of one age is the common sense
                Matthew Arnold 29
French
believe only in F. culture   Nietzsche 24
F. are wiser than they seem
                Francis Bacon 20
finest F. novel in the English
                Ford Madox Ford 3
General F.'s contemptible   Wilhelm II 3
not clear is not F.   Rivarol 1
Odors, confected by the cunning F.
                    T. S. Eliot 38
Paris was F.   Tuchman 2
sniff the F. dung   Ho Chi Minh 3
that is not F.   Napoleon 3
We are not F.   Bernard Montgomery 2
Frenchmen
Fifty Million F.   Rose 2
frequencies
Hailing f. still open   Star Trek 4
on the lower f.   Ralph Ellison 3
frequency
What is the f., Kenneth   Tager 1
frère
F. Jacques Folk and Anonymous Songs 25
Fresca
F. slips softly   T. S. Eliot 37
fresh
f., green breast   F. Scott Fitzgerald 32

What f. hell is this   Dorothy Parker 44
freshmen
f. bring a little in   A. Lawrence Lowell 1
frets
struts and f. his hour   Shakespeare 394
Freud
ideas of F. were popularized
                              Whitehead 11
Freudian
analysis with a strict F.   Woody Allen 30
friction
cold f. of expiring sense   T. S. Eliot 120
Friday
my man F.   Defoe 4
My name's F.   Radio Catchphrases 4
Thank God It's F.   Sayings 49
we call this F. good   T. S. Eliot 107
fried
Avoid f. meats   Paige 1
friend
be a f. to man   Foss 1
betraying my f.   Forster 8
boy's best f.   Film Lines 140
Boy's Best F.   Henry Miller (f. 1883) 1
dog is man's best f.   Proverbs 75
diamonds are a girl's best f.   Robin 2
enemy is my f.   Proverbs 86
f. in need is a f. indeed   Proverbs 117
f. in power is a f. lost   Henry Adams 5
guide, philosopher, and f.   Pope 28
having an old f. for dinner
                            Film Lines 155
He was my f.   Shakespeare 114
I lose a f.   John Singer Sargent 1
lay down his wife for his f.   Joyce 21
One f. in a life-time   Henry Adams 12
one f. in an indifferent world   Jong 7
only way to have a f.
                    Ralph Waldo Emerson 10
Say hello to my little f.   Film Lines 150
true, wise f.   Golding 1
What is a f.   Aristotle 13
Whenever a f. succeeds   Vidal 4
you have a f.   Lucy Montgomery 1
You've got a f.   Carole King 2
your enemy and your f.   Twain 103
friendless
F., n. Having no favors   Bierce 48
friendly
Fly the f. skies   Advertising Slogans 119
friends
disliked by their f.   Wilde 39
F., Romans, countrymen
                          Shakespeare 111
F. are born, not made   Henry Adams 6
F. don't let f.   Advertising Slogans 1
I have lost f.   Virginia Woolf 14
If My F. Could See Me Now
                         Dorothy Fields 5
kind to your web-footed f.
                 Folk and Anonymous Songs 5
lay down his life for his f.   Bible 326
Men and women can't be f.
                            Film Lines 185
Money couldn't buy f.   Milligan 1
none of his f. like him   Wilde 104
Of two f.   Lermontov 2
stand up to our f.   Rowling 3
that we want f.   F. Scott Fitzgerald 51

three faithful f.   Benjamin Franklin 17
we choose our f.   Delille 1
What's the constitution between f.
                        Timothy J. Campbell 1
with a little help from my f.
                     Lennon and McCartney 18
your f. do not need it   Elbert Hubbard 2
friendship
beginning of a beautiful f.
                              Film Lines 50
F. Faded   Stein 3
f. in constant repair
                       Samuel Johnson 48
holy passion of f.   Twain 61
swear an eternal f.   Molière 8
frigate
no F. like a Book   Emily Dickinson 25
fright
formed in f.   Melville 8
frighten
f. the horses   Beatrice Campbell 2
fringe
lunatic f.   Theodore Roosevelt 24
surrey with the f. on top
                            Hammerstein 10
frog
f. tumbles in   Basho 2
frogs
f. don't die for "fun"   Bion 1
from
F. Russia with Love   Ian Fleming 4
front
All quiet on the Western F.   Remarque 1
frontal
f. lobotomy   Waits 1
frontier
edge of a new f.   John F. Kennedy 4
f. has gone   Frederick Jackson Turner 2
hardly be said to be a f.
                          Robert P. Porter 1
Space, the final f.   Roddenberry 1
frozen
Architecture in general is f. music
                               Schelling 1
f. sea within us   Kafka 1
virgin—a f. asset   Clare Boothe Luce 1
fruit
f. of that forbidden tree   Milton 17
over-ripe f. into our hands   Lenin 10
Southern trees bear a strange f.   Allan 1
fruitful
Be f., and multiply   Woody Allen 1
Be f., and multiply   Bible 6
fruits
By their f. ye shall know them   Bible 229
frying-pan
frizzled in my f.   Engels 4
fuck
because fish f. in it   W. C. Fields 26
They f. you up   Larkin 3
who do I have to f.   Southern 2
zipless f.   Jong 5
fucked
Peru f. itself up   Vargas Llosa 1
fucking
too f. busy   Dorothy Parker 38
fugitive
f. from th' law of averages   Mauldin 1

fulfill
not come to destroy, but to f.   Bible 208
full
F. Faith and Credit   Constitution 9
F. fathom five   Shakespeare 439
F. many a glorious morning
                          Shakespeare 418
F. may a gem of purest ray
                            Thomas Gray 7
f. of sound and fury   Shakespeare 394
half f.   Stamp 2
Her voice is f. of money
                    F. Scott Fitzgerald 24
it's f. of stars   Arthur C. Clarke 3
My schedule is already f.   Kissinger 2
Reading maketh a f. man
                          Francis Bacon 22
Show me someone not f. of herself
                               Giovanni 3
wheel is come f. circle   Shakespeare 315
woods are f. of them
                        Alexander Wilson 1
fullness
f. thereof   Bible 110
fulness
f. thereof   Bible 351
fun
ain't we got f.   Gus Kahn 1
Are we having f. yet   Griffith 1
blondes have more f.
                    Advertising Slogans 30
girls just want to have f.   Hazard 1
most f. I ever had   Woody Allen 28
most f. you can have   Mencken 41
she'll have f., f., f.   Brian Wilson 1
function
Form ever follows f.   Louis H. Sullivan 1
fundamental
f. things apply   Hupfeld 1
fundamentals
f. of America's economy   John McCain 1
funeral
f. was because they wanted   Goldwyn 5
funerals
don't go to other men's f.   Day 1
Funiculì
F.—Funiculà   Turco 1
funny
Everything is f. as long   Will Rogers 6
f. thing happened to me
                       Adlai E. Stevenson 8
have ceased to be f.   Orwell 4
[I'm] f. how   Film Lines 89
'Tain't f., McGee   Radio Catchphrases 9
fur
Oh my f. and whiskers   Carroll 8
furious
grew fast and f.   Robert Burns 7
furiously
Colorless green ideas sleep f.
                              Chomsky 1
furnish
f. you with argument
                        Oliver Goldsmith 5
I'll f. the war   Hearst 1
furnished
Cambridge ladies who live in f.
                           e.e. cummings 6

furniture
bumping into the f.   Fontanne 1
don't trip over the f.   Coward 14
No f. so charming as books
    Sydney Smith 7
rearrange the f.   Rogers Morton 1
further
F. sacrifice of life   de Valera 2
If I have seen f.   Isaac Newton 1
fury
full of sound and f.   Shakespeare 394
f., like a woman scorned   Congreve 6
fuse
through the green f.   Dylan Thomas 1
futile
Resistance is f.   Star Trek 10
futility
fatal f. of Fact   Henry James 23
future
Back to the F.   Zemeckis 1
best way to predict the f.   Kay 1
controls not only the f.   Orwell 19
controls the f.   Orwell 37
difficult to predict, especially the f.
    Bohr 2
door opens and lets the f. in
    Graham Greene 1
fight against the f.   Gladstone 1
f., like everything else   Valéry 5
F., n. That period of time   Bierce 49
f. has arrived   Gibson 4
f. shock   Toffler 1
F. . . . something which   C. S. Lewis 2
F.'s So Bright   Pat MacDonald 1
I am interested in the f.   Kettering 1
I dipp'd into the f.   Tennyson 6
I have seen the f.   Steffens 2
In the f. everybody will be   Warhol 3
no f. in England's dreaming   Rotten 2
once and f. king   Malory 3
picture of the f.   Orwell 46
pleading for the f.   Clarence S. Darrow 4
remember the f.   Namier 1
talk about the f.   Céline 1
Wave of the F.
    Anne Morrow Lindbergh 1
futurism
we establish F.   Marinetti 2
fuzzy
f. end of the lollipop   Film Lines 157
F. Wuzzy was a bear
    Folk and Anonymous Songs 26
fwowed
Tonstant Weader F. up
    Dorothy Parker 18
fy
F., fa, fum   Nashe 1

G

nuthin' but a G thang
    Snoop Doggy Dogg 1
Gabriel
If I were the Archangel G.   Menzies 1
gaffe
"g." is . . . when a   Kinsley 1
Gaia
G. as a complex entity   Lovelock 1

gaiety
eclipsed the g. of nations
    Samuel Johnson 34
gain
another man's g.   Proverbs 177
same Arts that did g.   Andrew Marvell 7
gained
Nothing ventured, nothing g.
    Proverbs 220
gaining
Something might be g. on you   Paige 6
gains
no g. without pains   Adlai E. Stevenson 2
No pains, no g.   Proverbs 212
gaiters
gas and g.   Dickens 30
gal
For me and my g.   Leslie 1
galaxy
in a g. far, far away   George Lucas 2
rule the g. as father and son
    George Lucas 16
gales
g. of November come early   Lightfoot 1
Galilean
You have won, G.   Julian the Apostate 1
galled
Let the g. jade wince   Shakespeare 205
galley
doing in that g.   Molière 10
gallop
G. apace   Shakespeare 44
galloped
I g., Dirck g.   Robert Browning 10
gallops
It practically g.   Kesselring 1
gals
Buffalo g., woncha come
    Folk and Anonymous Songs 12
gamble
Life is a g.   Stoppard 2
gambled
they g. for my clothes   Dylan 24
gambling
find that g. is going on   Film Lines 45
game
anybody here play this g.   Stengel 2
Beautiful G.   Pelé 1
g. is afoot   Arthur Conan Doyle 30
g. is up   Shakespeare 436
g.'s afoot   Shakespeare 134
get out of the g.   Sayings 67
how you played the G.   Grantland Rice 1
it is a g. of skill   Stengel 1
play the g.   Arthur Conan Doyle 34
play the g. of thrones
    George R. R. Martin 2
Take me out to the ball g.   Norworth 2
You play to win the g.
    Herman Edwards 1
games
Forbidden G.   François Boyer 1
G. in which all may win   Melville 19
G. People Play   Berne 1
Mind G.   Lennon 11
zero-sum g.   von Neumann 1
gamesmanship
What is g.   Stephen Potter 1

gammon
world of g. and spinnage   Dickens 65
gamut
g. of human potentialities
    Margaret Mead 2
run the g. of emotions
    Dorothy Parker 29
gander
sauce for the g.   Proverbs 265
gang
G. That Couldn't Shoot Straight
    Breslin 1
g.'s all here   Morse 1
gangsta
living in the g.'s paradise   Coolio 2
garage
Car in Every G.   Political Slogans 12
full g.   Herbert C. Hoover 3
garbage
G. in, g. out   Modern Proverbs 33
If you covered him with g.   Ray Davies 4
Garbo
G. talks   Advertising Slogans 12
one sees in G. sober   Tynan 1
Garcia
Carry a message to G.   Elbert Hubbard 1
garden
g. is a lovesome thing   T. E. Brown 1
go into Mr. McGregor's g.
    Beatrix Potter 2
God Almighty first planted a g.
    Francis Bacon 12
God the first G. made
    Abraham Cowley 2
how does your g. grow
    Nursery Rhymes 41
Lord God planted a g.   Bible 7
my mothers' g.   Alice Walker 1
nearer God's Heart in a g.   Gurney 1
Never Promised You a Rose G.
    Hannah Green 1
We must cultivate our g.   Voltaire 10
gardens
closing time in the g.   Cyril Connolly 4
imaginary g. with real toads
    Marianne Moore 2
garment
as in a strange g.   Merwin 2
Garp
world according to G.   John Irving 1
garret
Genius in a g. starving
    Mary Robinson 1
Gary
G. Cooper killing off   James Baldwin 5
gas
g. and gaiters   Dickens 30
g. smells awful   Dorothy Parker 9
Gascoyne
Cadets of G.   Edmond Rostand 1
gas-light
g. is found to be the best
    Ralph Waldo Emerson 42
Gaston
You first, my dear G.   Opper 1
gate
at the schoolhouse g.   Fortas 1
g. was made only for you   Kafka 3

It matters not how strait the g.
                     W. E. Henley 2
Strait is the g.   Bible 227
Wide is the g.   Bible 226
gates
  on the g. of Baghdad   Sahhaf 1
gather
  G. the roses of life   Ronsard 2
  G. ye rosebuds while ye may   Herrick 3
  we'll g. at the river   Robert Lowry 1
gathered
  we are g. together
        Book of Common Prayer 16
gathers
  rolling stone g. no moss   Proverbs 257
gaudeamus
  G. igitur   Anonymous (Latin) 8
gaudy
  rich, not g.   Shakespeare 159
Gaul
  All G. is divided   Julius Caesar 1
gave
  g. me a medal   Matlovich 1
  g. up the ghost   Bible 307
gay
  come out, they're g.   Benjamin Carson 1
  g. Lothario   Rowe 1
  g. marriage is something
        Schwarzenegger 1
  G. Nineties   Culter 1
  I'm a g. deceiver   Colman the Younger 1
  I've just gone g.   Film Lines 32
  regular in being g.   Stein 2
Gaza
  Eyeless in G.   Milton 46
gelida
  Che g. manina   Giacosa 1
gem
  Columbia the g. of the ocean
        David T. Shaw 1
gemlike
  hard, g. flame   Pater 3
gender
  G. is an identity   Judith Butler 1
gene
  "Das Gen" and "Die G."   Johannsen 1
general
  good for G. Motors   Charles E. Wilson 1
  law so g. a study   Edmund Burke 6
  snow was g.   Joyce 1
generalities
  glittering and sounding g.
        Rufus Choate 1
generalization
  No g. is wholly true
      Oliver Wendell Holmes, Jr. 42
generalize
  To g. is to be an idiot   William Blake 17
generals
  bite some of my g.   George II 1
  Russia has two g.   Nicholas 2
generation
  at ease in my g.   Zola 1
  beat g.   Kerouac 3
  best minds of my g.   Ginsberg 7
  Every g. revolts   Mumford 1
  g. of vipers   Bible 200
  G. X: Tales for an Accelerated
        Coupland 1

greatest g.   Brokaw 1
ills of an entire g.   Isherwood 2
lost g.   Stein 13
never been seen by this g.   Paige 10
nothing to do with his g.
      F. Scott Fitzgerald 37
Pepsi G.   Advertising Slogans 100
wrong-doing of one g.   Hawthorne 14
generations
  first Kinnock in a thousand g.   Kinnock 3
  in no two consecutive g.
        Frances Willard 1
  those dying g.   Yeats 46
  Three g. of imbeciles
      Oliver Wendell Holmes, Jr. 35
generous
  G., *adj.* Originally   Bierce 50
genes
  our own selfish g.   Dawkins 1
genetics
  "G." might do   William Bateson 1
Geneva
  G.'s strict limitations
      Alberto R. Gonzales 1
genius
  Eccentricities of g.   Dickens 7
  Everyone is a g.   Lichtenberg 3
  forgives everything except g.   Wilde 7
  "G." (which means transcendent
      Thomas Carlyle 19
  G. all over the world   Melville 1
  g. which does what it must   Baring 1
  G. does what it must   Owen Meredith 2
  G. in a garret starving   Mary Robinson 1
  G. . . . an infinite capacity
      Jane Hopkins 1
  G. is 1 per cent inspiration   Edison 2
  G. is only a greater aptitude   Buffon 2
  G. is the capacity to see   Ezra Pound 20
  happy g. of my household
      William Carlos Williams 1
  Hats off, gentlemen—a g.   Schumann 1
  Heartbreaking Work of Staggering G.
      Eggers 1
  I had g.   Wilde 86
  last thing required of g.   Goethe 17
  man of g. makes no mistakes   Joyce 19
  nature of g. is to provide idiots   Aragon 1
  nothing to declare but my g.   Wilde 108
  picking men of g.   Conant 2
  prays to the g. of the place   Virgil 10
  put my g. into my life   Wilde 103
  sang beyond the g.   Wallace Stevens 9
  talent instantly recognizes g.
      Arthur Conan Doyle 36
  Taste is the feminine of g.
      Edward FitzGerald 7
  true G. appears in the World
      Jonathan Swift 5
  unrewarded g. is a   Munger 1
  very stable g.   Trump 20
  what a g. I had   Jonathan Swift 38
geniuses
  designed by g.   Wouk 1
  hostile to g.   Ralph Waldo Emerson 38
  some g. were laughed at   Carl Sagan 1
  three originative g.   Stein 16
  two authentic g. in the world
      Bankhead 7

genocide
  By g. we mean   Lemkin 1
gentil
  verray, parfit g. knyght   Chaucer 8
gentle
  Do not go g.   Dylan Thomas 17
  droppeth as the g. rain   Shakespeare 79
  I am meek and g.   Shakespeare 106
  notion of some infinitely g.   T. S. Eliot 15
  sleep! it is a g. thing   Coleridge 11
gentleman
  every other inch a g.   Woollcott 5
  shew'd him the g. and scholar
      Robert Burns 4
gentlemen
  G. do not read each other's mail
      Stimson 1
  g. do read each other's mail
      Allen W. Dulles 1
  G. Prefer Blondes   Loos 1
  G.—start your engines   Sayings 13
  God rest you merry, g.
      Folk and Anonymous Songs 30
gentler
  kinder, g. nation
      George Herbert Walker Bush 5
gently
  g. down the stream
      Folk and Anonymous Songs 67
  while my guitar g. weeps
      George Harrison 1
genuflect
  g., g., g.   Lehrer 8
genuine
  G., *adj.* Real, veritable   Bierce 51
geographical
  g. concept   Bismarck 5
  Italy is a g. expression
      Klemens von Metternich 1
geography
  we have too much g.
      William Lyon Mackenzie King 1
geometrical
  increases in a g. ratio   Malthus 1
geometrizes
  God ever g.   Plato 11
geometry
  G. enlightens the intellect
      Ibn-Khaldūn 1
  no "royal road" to g.   Euclid 3
George
  G. Bush doesn't care   Kanye West 1
  G. Washington slept here   Moss Hart 2
  This is G.   Rey 1
Georgia
  G. on my mind   Gorrell 1
  on the red hills of G.
      Martin Luther King, Jr. 12
Georgie
  G. Porgie, pudding and pie
      Nursery Rhymes 18
German
  France will say that I am a G.   Einstein 6
  G.'s fatherland   Arndt 1
  I am called a G.   Einstein 4
  in the original G.   Ivins 1
  literary G. dives   Twain 42
  not to speak of G. culture   Nietzsche 24
  supremacy of G. music   Schoenberg 1

German (cont.):
to his horse he would speak G.
Charles V 1
unity of the G. nation   Hitler 5
Germans
G. bombed Pearl Harbor   Film Lines 9
We G. fear God   Bismarck 8
Germany
As far as G. extends   Nietzsche 23
Death is a master from G.   Paul Celan 1
G. was the cause of Hitler Woollcott 3
G. will declare that I am a Jew
Einstein 6
I love G. so dearly   Mauriac 1
put G. in the saddle   Bismarck 3
today G. hears us   Baumann 1
Where I am, there is G.
Thomas Mann 6
Geronimo
G. EKIA   McRaven 1
Gestapo
G. tactics in the streets   Ribicoff 1
gesture
warm personal g.   Galbraith 5
gestures
unbroken series of successful g.
F. Scott Fitzgerald 11
get
can we all g. along   Rodney King 1
Don't g. mad, g. even
Joseph P. Kennedy 1
G. a life   Sayings 14
g. it in writing   Gypsy Rose Lee 1
G. It While You Can   Joplin 3
g. me to the church   Alan Jay Lerner 2
g. out while we're young Springsteen 2
g. the trick   Twain 53
G. thee behind me   Bible 247
g. to the end of your rope
Franklin D. Roosevelt 31
G. up, stand up   Marley 1
g. with child a mandrake root Donne 11
I can't g. no satisfaction
Jagger and Richards 2
I don't g. no respect   Dangerfield 1
If you want to g. along   Rayburn 1
I'll g. you, my pretty   Film Lines 190
let's g. on with it   Sartre 6
mind to g. even   Twain 41
never know what you're goin' to g.
Film Lines 80
other is to g. it George Bernard Shaw 16
rich g. richer   Modern Proverbs 75
Stop the World, I Want to G. Off
Bricusse and Newley 2
write if you g. work
Radio Catchphrases 3
You can g. anything you want
Arlo Guthrie 1
gets
g. late early   Berra 8
lucky if he g. out of it alive
W. C. Fields 6
No one here g. out alive Jim Morrison 4
smoke g. in your eyes   Harbach 1
Whatever G. You Thru the Night
Lennon 12
getting
I am g. better and better   Coué 1

other is g. it   Wilde 56
ghetto
g. is to the Negro   Kenneth Clark 1
ghost
G. in the Machine   Ryle 1
G. of Christmas Past   Dickens 42
G. of Christmas Present   Dickens 43
G. of Christmas Yet to Come
Dickens 46
he gave up the g.   Bible 307
of the Holy G.   Missal 2
please my g.   Mencken 25
ghostbusters
Who you gonna call? G.   Ray Parker 1
ghostlier
g. demarcations   Wallace Stevens 13
ghosts
g. of the villages   Merwin 3
there must be g.   Ibsen 10
we are all g.   Ibsen 9
giant
awaken a sleeping g.   Film Lines 178
g. rat of Sumatra
Arthur Conan Doyle 38
g.'s shoulder to mount on
Coleridge 30
have a g.'s strength   Shakespeare 253
Not like the brazen g.   Lazarus 1
pitiful, helpless g.   Richard Nixon 11
standing on the shoulders of a g.
Robert Burton 1
giants
dwarfs on the shoulders of g.
Bernard of Chartres 1
G. win the pennant   Hodges 1
standing on the shoulders of g.
Isaac Newton 1
There were g. in the earth   Bible 26
gift
born with a g. of laughter Sabatini 1
g. of a nine-hundred-year-old name
Robert Browning 5
look a g. horse   Proverbs 118
make money is a g. from God
John D. Rockefeller 2
gifted
young, g., and black   Hansberry 2
gifts
even when they bring g.   Virgil 4
Greeks bearing g.   Proverbs 131
gigantic
but a g. mistake   Sigmund Freud 22
footprints of a g. hound
Arthur Conan Doyle 29
gild
g. refined gold   Shakespeare 70
Gilda
fall in love with G.   Hayworth 1
gilded
bird in a g. cage   Arthur J. Lamb 1
G. Age   Twain 13
Gilead
Is there no balm in G.   Bible 182
gilt
round its g. cage   Wollstonecraft 6
gimme
G. a whiskey   Film Lines 11
G. a whiskey   Eugene O'Neill 3

gin
G. was mother's milk
George Bernard Shaw 40
g.-soaked, bar-room queen
Jagger and Richards 14
Of all the g. joints   Film Lines 43
sippin' on g. and juice
Snoop Doggy Dogg 2
Ginger
G. Rogers did everything   Thaves 1
Gipper
win just one for the G.   Gipp 1
giraffe
shape and size of the g.   Lamarck 1
girded
He g. up his loins   Bible 93
girl
diamonds are a g.'s best friend   Robin 2
G. I Left Behind Me
Folk and Anonymous Songs 27
G. Interrupted at Her Music Kaysen 1
g. needs good parents   Sophie Tucker 1
Give me a g.   Spark 2
I am a material g.   Peter Brown 1
I want a g. just like the g.   Dillon 1
little g. like you   L. Frank Baum 5
little g. like you   Film Lines 193
man sits with a pretty g.   Einstein 29
only g. in the world   Clifford Grey 1
Poor little rich g.   Coward 2
Poor Little Rich G.   Eleanor Gates 1
pretty g. is like a melody
Irving Berlin 4
Protect the Working G.   Edgar Smith 1
sort of g. I like to see   Betjeman 2
sweetest g. I know   Judge 1
take the g.'s clothes off
Raymond Chandler 12
talkin' 'bout my g. "Smokey" Robinson 1
There was a little g.   Longfellow 28
Valley G.   Zappa 1
girls
bad g. go everywhere
Helen Gurley Brown 2
California g.   Brian Wilson 2
Catholic g. start much too late   Joel 3
g. just want to have fun   Hazard 1
g. who wear glasses Dorothy Parker 7
G. will be boys   Ray Davies 2
kissed the g.   Nursery Rhymes 18
rather have two g. at 21 each
W. C. Fields 11
Thank heaven for little g.
Alan Jay Lerner 15
Treaties, you see, are like g.   de Gaulle 7
twelve little g.   Bemelmans 1
with the g. be handy
Folk and Anonymous Songs 85
git
g. along, little dogies
Folk and Anonymous Songs 83
Gitche
By the shores of G. Gumee
Longfellow 17
give
Don't g. up the ship
Oliver Hazard Perry 1
G. 'em hell, Harry   Political Slogans 16
G. em hell, Harry   Truman 7

God

all o' G.'s chillun got-a wings
    Folk and Anonymous Songs 1
Any G. I ever felt   Alice Walker 4
arm's too short to box wid G.
    James Weldon Johnson 2
as G. is my witness Margaret Mitchell 5
baby is G.'s opinion   Sandburg 12
be a saint without G.   Camus 5
believe only in a G.   Nietzsche 15
But for the grace of G.   John Bradford 1
cannot serve G. and mammon Bible 218
charged with the grandeur of G.
    Gerard Manley Hopkins 2
Cocaine is G.'s way   Robin Williams 1
doing G.'s work   Blankfein 1
evidence for G.   William James 18
fatherhood of G.
    John D. Rockefeller, Jr. 1
final proof of G.'s omnipotence
    De Vries 1
For G., for Country, and for Yale
    Durand 1
for the grace of G., goes G.
    Mankiewicz 1
From G. and a woman   Truth 2
garden is a lovesome thing, G. wot
    T. E. Brown 1
give G. the glory
    Folk and Anonymous Songs 64
Glory be to G. for dappled
    Gerard Manley Hopkins 3
Glory to G. in the highest Bible 290
G., or Nature   Spinoza 3
G., to me, it seems
    R. Buckminster Fuller 1
G. bless America   Irving Berlin 8
G. bless America   Peeke 1
G. bless Captain Vere   Melville 20
G. bless the child   Holiday 1
G. bless us every one   Dickens 45
G. cannot be for and against Lincoln 33
G. caught his eye   McCord 1
G. commonly gives riches   Luther 3
G. could have commanded Pollitt 1
G. damn you all to hell Film Lines 136
G. disposes   Thomas à Kempis 1
G. does not take sides George Mitchell 1
G. ever geometrizes   Plato 11
G. forbid   Bible 36
g. from the machine   Menander 3
G. gave Noah the rainbow sign
    James Baldwin 2
G. gave Noah the rainbow sign
    Folk and Anonymous Songs 36
G. has written all the books
    Samuel Butler (1835–1902) 12
G. hates all the same people Lamott 1
G. helps them   Proverbs 122
G. is a concept   Lennon 3
G is a foreman   Heaney 3
G. is afraid to trust them Lincoln 68
G. is always with the strongest
    Frederick the Great 1
G. is dead   Nerval 2
G. is dead   Nietzsche 7
G. is dead   Nietzsche 3
G. is in the details   Flaubert 3
G. is in the Details Mies van der Rohe 2

G. is in the details   Warburg 1
G. is love   Bible 388
G. is Love Samuel Butler (1835–1902) 10
G. is love   Gypsy Rose Lee 1
G. is male   Daly 1
G. is no respecter of persons Bible 333
G. is not neutral   George W. Bush 11
G. is nothing other Sigmund Freud 9
G. is omnipotent, omniscient Heinlein 7
G. is really only another   Picasso 3
G. is responsible   Twain 137
G. is usually on the side Bussy-Rabutin 1
G. made idiots   Twain 48
G. made integers   Kronecker 1
G. made the country William Cowper 5
G. moves in a mysterious way
    William Cowper 1
G. must think it exceedingly odd
    Ronald Knox 3
g. of my idolatry   Shakespeare 36
G. of universal laws William James 14
G. reigns   Garfield 2
G. rest you merry, gentlemen
    Folk and Anonymous Songs 30
G. said, Let Newton be!   Pope 11
G. save the king   Bible 82
G. save the king   Henry Carey 2
G. saw that it was good   Bible 3
G. shall wipe away all tears Bible 394
G. shall wipe away all tears Bible 399
G. so loved the world   Bible 315
G. That Failed   Koestler 2
G. the first Garden made
    Abraham Cowley 2
G. waited six thousand years Kepler 2
G. wants to know if you'd sign Costas 1
G. will give him blood Hawthorne 15
G. will pardon me   Heine 5
G. will recognize his own
    Arnauld-Amaury 1
G. wrote it   Stowe 6
G.'s apology for relations Kingsmill 1
G.'s in his heaven Robert Browning 1
go one g. further   Dawkins 7
Had I but served my G.
    Shakespeare 452
Hard to grasp, the g.   Hölderlin 1
her seat is the bosom of G.
    Richard Hooker 1
here is G.'s plenty John Dryden 12
here on earth G.'s work
    John F. Kennedy 17
How odd of G. to choose the Jews
    Ewer 1
I am becoming a g.   Vespasian 1
I am the Lord thy G.   Bible 50
I believe in Spinoza's G. Einstein 23
I could prove G. statistically Gallup 1
I don't believe in G. because
    Clarence S. Darrow 7
I have sworn upon the altar of g.
    Jefferson 27
I never spoke with G.
    Emily Dickinson 21
I remembered my G.   Southey 3
If G. did not exist   Voltaire 18
if G. talks to you   Szasz 2
in apprehension how like a g.
    Shakespeare 181

In G. is our trust Francis Scott Key 3
In G. we trust   Salmon P. Chase 1
In G. we trust   Sayings 26
In the beginning G. created Bible 1
in the sight of G.
    Book of Common Prayer 16
it pisses G. off   Alice Walker 5
it's like kissing G.   Lenny Bruce 4
jealous G.   Bible 52
Just are the ways of G.   Milton 49
justify G.'s ways to man Housman 5
justify the ways of G. to men Milton 18
kills the image of G.   Milton 6
kingdom of G. is within you Bible 303
lend a myth to G.   Hart Crane 3
Lord G. is subtle   Einstein 24
Lord our G. is one Lord   Bible 69
Lowells speak only with G. Bossidy 1
man is a g. in ruins
    Ralph Waldo Emerson 3
Man proposes and G. disposes
    Proverbs 186
man with G. is always John Knox 1
Maybe G. is malicious   Einstein 34
mills of G. grind slowly   Logau 1
mills of G. grind slowly Proverbs 192
money is a gift from G.
    John D. Rockefeller 2
nearer G.'s Heart in a garden Gurney 1
next to of course g. america
    e.e. cummings 9
noblest work of G.   Pope 26
not believing in G.   Chesterton 25
Not only is there no G. Woody Allen 3
now G. alone knows   Klopstock 1
now there is a G. Fredric Brown 1
O G.! O Montreal!
    Samuel Butler (1835–1902) 2
only G. can make a tree   Kilmer 2
Our Father-Mother G.   Eddy 1
part and particle of G.
    Ralph Waldo Emerson 33
peacock is the glory of G.
    William Blake 6
Praise G., from whom   Ken 1
river is a strong brown g. T. S. Eliot 113
see the face of G.   Kretzmer 1
served G. as diligently   Wolsey 1
So far from G.   Díaz 1
some lesser g.   Tennyson 44
something beautiful for G.
    Mother Teresa 2
Spinoza is a G.-intoxicated man
    Novalis 1
Thank G. It's Friday   Sayings 49
Thanks be to G.   Buñuel 3
their eyes were watching G. Hurston 5
there is a G.   Woody Allen 18
There is no G.   Santayana 15
There is no g. but G.   Koran 7
there is no g. but He   Koran 4
there is still G.   Hansberry 1
to G. he would speak Spanish
    Charles V 1
TO THE UNKNOWN G.   Bible 335
touched the face of G.   Magee 2
triangles were to make a G.
    Montesquieu 3
Verb is G.   Hugo 5

walk humbly with thy G.   Bible 194
We Germans fear G.   Bismarck 8
we must obey G.   John XXIII 1
we would know the mind of G.
        Hawking 3
we're on G.'s side   Joe Louis 1
What g. would be hanging around
        Douglas Adams 10
what G. would have done
        Peter Fleming 1
What hath G. wrought   Bible 68
What therefore G. hath joined
        Bible 249
what we have instead of G.
        Hemingway 5
when G. and her were born   Dylan 25
when G. was tired   Twain 118
Where it will all end, knows G.   Gibbs 2
wife to believe in G.   Voltaire 17
With G. all things are possible   Bible 251
woman is the work of G.
        William Blake 6
Woman was G.'s second mistake
        Nietzsche 22

Goddamn
lhude sing G.   Ezra Pound 8
goddess
bitch-g. SUCCESS   William James 16
Domestic G.   Barr 2
Sing, g.   Homer 1
White G.   Graves 6
Godfrey
G. Daniel   W. C. Fields 1
Godhead
G. is broken like bread   Auden 5
godliness
next to g.   John Wesley 2
Godot
waiting for G.   Beckett 3
gods
after strange g.   Kipling 3
alien people clutching their g.
        T. S. Eliot 70
altars to unknown g.   William James 3
convenient that there are g.   Ovid 2
g. are on the side   Tacitus 4
G. do not answer letters   Updike 1
g. thought otherwise   Virgil 5
g. wish to punish us   Wilde 74
he creates g. by the dozens
        Montaigne 13
holy because the g. approve it   Plato 3
I do not know much about g.
        T. S. Eliot 113
making of g.   Bergson 3
men that strove with g.   Tennyson 23
no other g. before me   Bible 50
UNIVERSE BEGGING FOR G.   Farmer 1
Whom the g. love dies young
        Menander 1
Whom the g. wish to destroy
        Cyril Connolly 2
Whom the g. would destroy
        Proverbs 123
With stupidity the g. themselves
        Schiller 4
world of g. and monsters   Film Lines 30
ye shall be as g.   Bible 16

Godspeed
G., John Glenn   Scott Carpenter 1
goes
anything g.   Cole Porter 2
Music G. 'Round and Around
        "Red" Hodgson 1
so g. the nation   Political Slogans 4
What g. around, comes around
        Modern Proverbs 35
What g. up   Proverbs 315
goest
Whither g. thou   Bible 327
goeth
Pride g. before destruction   Bible 133
Gogol
come out of G.'s Overcoat.
        Dostoyevski 9
going
g. gets weird   Hunter S. Thompson 4
Hello, I must be g.   "Groucho" Marx 5
keeps g., and g.   Advertising Slogans 45
lamps are g. out   Edward Grey 1
my mind is g.   Film Lines 182
not worth g. to see   Samuel Johnson 96
order of your g.   Shakespeare 372
When the g. gets tough   Frank Leahy 1
You are g. to women   Nietzsche 16
gold
All that glitters is not g.   Proverbs 121
As good as g.   Dickens 44
crucify mankind upon a cross of g.
        William Jennings Bryan 3
G., n. A yellow metal   Bierce 14
her hair turned quite g.   Wilde 40
nor all that glisters, g.   Thomas Gray 2
Stay g., Ponyboy   Hinton 2
travelled in the realms of g.   Keats 1
wear the g. hat   F. Scott Fitzgerald 6
Whoever has the g.   Sayings 16
golden
beside the g. door   Lazarus 2
Dem G. Slippers   Bland 2
end of a g. string   William Blake 22
g. apples of the sun   Yeats 6
g. bowl be broken   Bible 152
g. daffodils   William Wordsworth 25
g. days of Saturn's reign   Virgil 15
g. opinions   Shakespeare 344
G. Road to Samarkand   Flecker 1
loves the g. mean   Horace 19
respected—the g. boy   Odets 1
Silence is g.   Proverbs 271
there are no g. rules
        George Bernard Shaw 18
We are g.   Joni Mitchell 3
goldfish
g. in a glass bowl   Saki 1
Goldsmith
To Oliver G.   Samuel Johnson 88
golf
G. is a good walk spoiled   Twain 152
g. links lie so near the mill   Cleghorn 1
thousand lost g. balls   T. S. Eliot 91
gone
g. in the wind   Mangan 1
g. with the wind   Dowson 2
g. with the wind   Margaret Mitchell 4
Here today and g. tomorrow
        Proverbs 140

my baby was g.   B. B. King 1
old massa's g. away
        Folk and Anonymous Songs 9
Where have all the flowers g.
        Pete Seeger 4
where no man has g. before
        Roddenberry 1
where no man has g. before
        Roddenberry 2
where no one has g. before   Killian 1
where no one has g. before
        Roddenberry 3
gong
g.-tormented sea   Yeats 57
gongs
struck regularly, like g.   Coward 6
gonzo
G. journalism   Hunter S. Thompson 6
goober
Eating g. peas
        Folk and Anonymous Songs 31
good
All g. books are alike   Hemingway 17
All g. things must come   Proverbs 7
All g. writing is swimming
        F. Scott Fitzgerald 52
All publicity is g. publicity
        Modern Proverbs 70
annoyance of a g. example   Twain 72
As g. as gold   Dickens 44
As g. luck would have it
        Shakespeare 68
bad things happen to g. people
        Harold S. Kushner 1
Be g., sweet maid   Kingsley 1
Be g. & you will be lonesome   Twain 83
Be of g. cheer   Bible 242
because America is g.   Tocqueville 24
best is the enemy of the g.   Voltaire 2
bring g. things to life
        Advertising Slogans 54
can't be a g. example   Aird 1
can't make people g.   Wilde 59
can't say something g.
        Alice Longworth 4
devil should have all the g. tunes
        Rowland Hill 1
Era of G. Feelings   Benjamin Russell 1
Evil, be thou my g.   Milton 32
Fight the g. fight   Bible 378
for a g. man's love   Shakespeare 93
For he's a jolly g. fellow
        Folk and Anonymous Songs 22
FOUR LEGS G.   Orwell 24
gentle into that g. night
        Dylan Thomas 17
Golf is a g. walk spoiled   Twain 152
G., but not religious-good
        Thomas Hardy 3
G., the Bad, and the Ugly   Leone 1
g. Americans die   Wilde 30
G. Americans, when they die
        Oliver Wendell Holmes 4
G. and evil   John Locke 10
g. Cigar is a Smoke   Kipling 1
g. die young   Proverbs 124
g. eater must be a g. man   Disraeli 4
g. ended happily   Wilde 81
G. fences make g. neighbors   Frost 3

gray (cont.):
Man in the G. Flannel Suit
    Sloan Wilson 1
old g. head   Whittier 3
old g. mare
    Folk and Anonymous Songs 58
grease
one that gets the g.   Billings 2
greasy
top of the g. pole   Disraeli 30
great
All creatures g. and small
    Cecil Alexander 1
all things both g. and small
    Coleridge 14
altitude of its "g. intellects"   Karl Marx 9
America is g.   Tocqueville 24
at least a g. poster   Margot Asquith 1
Behind every g. fortune   Balzac 2
Behind every g. man   Proverbs 129
biography of g. men   Thomas Carlyle 12
build a g. society   Lyndon B. Johnson 5
build the G. Society
    Lyndon B. Johnson 8
burden than a g. potential   Schulz 6
disbelief in g. men   Thomas Carlyle 13
do in the G. War, Daddy   Lumley 1
envy of g. Caesar   Shakespeare 130
failure in a g. object   Keats 8
G. American Novel   De Forest 1
g. artists of the world   Mencken 17
g. balls of fire   Otis Blackwell 1
G. cases like hard cases
    Oliver Wendell Holmes, Jr. 17
g. Cham of literature   Smollett 2
g. chess-player is not a g. man
    Hazlitt 5
g. end of life   T. H. Huxley 5
g. expectations   Dickens 101
G. Illusion   Angell 1
g. interest of man on earth
    Daniel Webster 12
g. is to be misunderstood
    Ralph Waldo Emerson 17
g. life if you don't weaken   Buchan 1
g. majority   Edward Young 1
g. man is the one   Mencius 1
G. men are simply men   Einstein 22
g. minds think alike   Proverbs 130
g. ocean of truth   Isaac Newton 7
g. ones eat up the little ones
    Shakespeare 408
g. poet, in writing himself   T. S. Eliot 71
g. shroud of the sea   Melville 13
G. Society   Wallas 1
G. Society created by steam
    John Dewey 1
G. things are done when men
    William Blake 18
g. wink of eternity   Hart Crane 1
G. wits are sure to madness near
    John Dryden 4
g. woman   Proverbs 129
I lived with a g. dream
    F. Scott Fitzgerald 43
If this is a G. Society   Hamer 1
Insanely g.   Jobs 1
Make America g. again
    Political Slogans 26

malefactors of g. wealth
    Theodore Roosevelt 17
my chance of being a g. man   Disraeli 2
never a g. man   Schreiner 3
No people can be g.   Samuel Johnson 19
Nothing g. was ever achieved
    Ralph Waldo Emerson 7
One g. society   William Wordsworth 30
pearl of g. price   Bible 240
[Richard Nixon] would have been a g.
    Kissinger 6
so-called g. men   Tolstoy 3
Some are born g.   Shakespeare 244
thrown with g. force   Dorothy Parker 40
tidings of g. joy   Bible 289
Time is the g. healer   Proverbs 300
To be a g. lawyer   Disraeli 2
upward to the G. Society
    Lyndon B. Johnson 6
when the One G. Scorer
    Grantland Rice 1
With g. power   Stan Lee 1
would make a g. book   Sydney Smith 11
your people is a g. beast
    Alexander Hamilton 12
greater
Al Jolson is g. than Jesus
    Zelda Fitzgerald 2
G. love hath no man   Bible 326
g. restrictions   Keillor 3
g. than the whole   Hesiod 1
no g. pain than to recall   Dante 7
nothing g. can be   Anselm 1
Thy necessity is yet g.   Philip Sidney 6
greatest
g. artists, saints   Muggeridge 1
g. generation   Brokaw 1
g. Happiness   Hutcheson 1
g. happiness of the g. number
    Bentham 1
g. happiness shared by the g. number
    Beccaria 1
g. invention of mankind   Einstein 37
g. number of the g.   Ruskin 1
g. poem   Whitman 2
G. Show on Earth
    Advertising Slogans 103
g. week in the history   Richard Nixon 7
How much the g. event
    Charles James Fox 1
I am the g.   Ali 1
with the g. of ease   Leybourne 1
greatness
France cannot be France without g.
    de Gaulle 5
G. no longer depends on rentals
    Disraeli 12
g. thrust upon 'em   Shakespeare 244
instruments of European g.
    Alexander Hamilton 4
seen the moment of my g.   T. S. Eliot 8
Greece
glory that was G.   Poe 1
greed
G., for lack of a better word
    Film Lines 184
G. is all right   Boesky 1
infectious g.   Greenspan 2
make g. into a science   Du Bois 11

Greek
Thou hadst small Latin, and less G.
    Jonson 9
Greeks
G. bearing gifts   Proverbs 131
G. Had a Word for It   Akins 1
fundamental fact about the G.
    Edith Hamilton 1
I fear G.   Virgil 4
When G. joined G.   Nathaniel Lee 1
green
Doesn't the sky look g.   Milne 3
drives my g. age   Dylan Thomas 1
fresh, g. breast   F. Scott Fitzgerald 32
Gatsby believed in the g. light
    F. Scott Fitzgerald 35
G., how much I want you g.
    García Lorca 1
g. casque has outdone   Ezra Pound 26
g. eggs and ham   Seuss 11
g. hunting cap   Toole 1
g. in judgement   Shakespeare 399
g. light at the end   F. Scott Fitzgerald 34
g. mantle of the standing
    Shakespeare 298
g. thought in a g. shade
    Andrew Marvell 9
g.-eyed monster   Shakespeare 270
How g. was my Valley   Llewellyn 1
in England's g. and pleasant land
    William Blake 21
laid him on the g.   Ballads 2
legends of the g. chapels
    Dylan Thomas 12
lie down in g. pastures   Bible 108
memory be g.   Shakespeare 146
time held me g. and dying
    Dylan Thomas 7
wearin' of the G.
    Folk and Anonymous Songs 78
greener
Grass Is Always G.   Bombeck 1
grass is always g.   Proverbs 128
greenery
There is no g.   Khrushchev 6
greening
g. of America   Reich 5
Greenland
G. and Australia   Dorothy Parker 42
Greensleeves
who but Lady G.
    Folk and Anonymous Songs 55
greenwood
Under the g. tree   Shakespeare 85
greetings
g. are intended for me   Beethoven 5
Gregor
As G. Samsa awoke one morning
    Kafka 4
grenades
horseshoes and g.   Frank Robinson 1
grenadier
single Pomeranian g.   Bismarck 6
Grendel
Poor G.'s had an accident
    John Gardner 1
Gresham
G.'s law of the currency
    Henry Dunning Macleod 1

grey
G. silent fragments   Ted Hughes 1
These little g. cells   Christie 2

Gridley
fire when you are ready, G.
                                     George Dewey 1

grief
Between g. and nothing   Faulkner 7
g. is the price we pay   Elizabeth II 3
Good g., Charlie Brown   Schulz 1

griefs
g. of the ages   Dylan Thomas 9

grievance
Scotsman with a g.   Wodehouse 6

grieve
I g. over them   Raymond Chandler 1

grievously
g. hath Caesar answered it
                                     Shakespeare 112

grin
g. without a cat   Carroll 13

Grinch
G., who lived just north   Seuss 7

grind
axe to g.   Miner 1
mills of God g. slowly   Logau 1
mills of God g. slowly   Proverbs 192

gripping
life g. a baseball   Bouton 1

Grishkin
G. is nice   T. S. Eliot 19

grits
Kiss my g.   Television Catchphrases 7

groans
g. of love   Malcolm Lowry 1

grooves
ringing g. of change   Tennyson 11

grotesque
called g. by the Northern reader
                                     Flannery O'Connor 2

ground
enough g. to bury them   Colin Powell 2
G. control to Major Tom   Bowie 1
g. opens up and envelops me   Baraka 3
sorrow there is holy g.   Wilde 85
whereon thou standest is holy g.
                                     Bible 40

group
Never doubt that a small g.
                                     Margaret Mead 10
one's own g. is the center   Sumner 7

grouse
g. against life   T. S. Eliot 127

grove
olive g. of Academe   Milton 44

groves
g. of Academe   Horace 14

grow
Absence makes the heart g. fonder
                                     Propertius 1
Absence makes the heart g. fonder
                                     Proverbs 1
All children, except one, g. up   Barrie 2
Blades of Grass to g.   Jonathan Swift 12
Enter to g. in wisdom   Charles W. Eliot 1
G. old along with me
                                     Robert Browning 19
I g. old   T. S. Eliot 10
Let knowledge g.   Tennyson 28

like hearing the grass g.   George Eliot 15
Money doesn't g. on trees
                                     Modern Proverbs 60

growed
I s'pect I g.   Stowe 2

grown
g. accustomed to her face
                                     Alan Jay Lerner 6

grown-up
Catholic & g.   Orwell 50

grown-ups
G. never understand anything
                                     Saint-Exupéry 3

grows
appetite g. by eating   Rabelais 2
That which is g.   Galen 1
tree that g. in Brooklyn   Betty Smith 1

growth
children of a larger g.   John Dryden 3
G. for the sake of g.   Abbey 1

gr-r-reat
They're g.   Advertising Slogans 66

Grubstreet
G. . . . . Originally the name
                                     Samuel Johnson 12

grudges
I don't hold no g.   William Kennedy 1

grumbling
just a piece of rhythmical g.
                                     T. S. Eliot 127

Grundy
What will Mrs. G. zay   Thomas Morton 1

gruntled
far from being g.   Wodehouse 2

guarantee
I g. it   Namath 1
I triple g. you   Sahhaf 2

guard
changing g. at Buckingham Palace
                                     Milne 1
g. I do not love   Yeats 21
g. you while you sleep   Kipling 5
to g. and feed them   Orwell 20
who is to g. the guards   Juvenal 3

guarded
find the streets are g.
                           Folk and Anonymous Songs 50

guards
G. die but do not surrender
                                     Cambronne 1
Up G. and at them   Wellington 1
who is to guard the g.   Juvenal 3

guerilla
g. army wins if he does not lose
                                     Kissinger 1
g. to exist long   Mao Tse-tung 3

guerre
ce n'est pas la g.   Bosquet 1

guess
g. what a man is going to do
                                     Christopher Morley 4
G. Who's Coming to Dinner
                                     Stanley Kramer 1
Your g. is as good as mine
                                     Modern Proverbs 37

guest
Earth, receive an honored g.   Auden 23
speed the parting g.   Pope 9
This g. of summer   Shakespeare 339

guide
conscience be your g.   Film Lines 132
g., philosopher, and friend   Pope 28

guided
We have g. missiles
                          Martin Luther King, Jr. 15

Guildenstern
Rosencrantz and G. are dead
                                     Shakespeare 238

guilt
assumption of g.   Heilbrun 1
g. of Stalin   Gorbachev 2
nearly all the g. of this world
                                     Hawthorne 17
whole earth one stain of g.   Hawthorne 1

guilty
better 100 g. Persons should escape
                                     Benjamin Franklin 37
find the defendants incredibly g.
                                     Mel Brooks 9
g. thing surprised
                                     William Wordsworth 16
I knew—he was g.   Christie 4
innocent until proved g.   Proverbs 156
Let no g. man escape   Ulysses S. Grant 5
100 percent not g.   O. J. Simpson 1
started like a g. thing   Shakespeare 143
ten g. persons escape   Blackstone 7
thousand g. persons   Maimonides 1
twenty g. men to escape death
                                     Fortescue 1
until he be found g.   Beccaria 2
Where all, or almost all, are g.   Arendt 7

guitar
he could play a g.   Chuck Berry 5
while my g. gently weeps
                                     George Harrison 1

Gulag
G. Archipelago   Solzhenitsyn 3

gulf
g. of mutual incomprehension   Snow 3

gum
chewing g. for the eyes
                                     John Mason Brown 1
G., n. A substance   Bierce 54
So dumb he can't fart and chew g.
                                     Lyndon B. Johnson 14

gun
further with a kind word and a g.
                                     Capone 3
I reach for my g.   Johst 1
I'll give up my g.   Political Slogans 22
Is that a g. in your pocket   Mae West 24
kind word and a g.   Corey 1
out of the barrel of a g.   Mao Tse-tung 4
persuade her with g.   Dorothy Parker 37
rob you with a six g.   "Woody" Guthrie 2
we will point the g.   Trumbo 1
with a g. in his hand
                                     Raymond Chandler 11

Gunga
better man than I am, G. Din   Kipling 11

gunpowder
G., Printing, and the Protestant
                                     Thomas Carlyle 7
Printing, g.   Francis Bacon 6

guns
cling to g. or religion   Barack Obama 3
G. aren't lawful   Dorothy Parker 9

guns (cont.):
G. don't die, people die
　　　　Political Slogans 17
G. don't kill people　Political Slogans 18
g. not with butter　　　　Goebbels 1
haven't found any smoking g.　　Blix 1
rather have butter or g.　　Goering 1
Send lawyers, g., and money　Zevon 3
When g. are outlawed
　　　　Political Slogans 36
gush
they're oil wells; they g.
　　　　Dorothy Parker 35
gut
my g. tells me more　　　Trump 23
Gutenberg
G. made everybody a reader
　　　　McLuhan 11
gutless
sort of g. Kipling　　　　Orwell 9
guts
g. of priests　　　　Meslier 1
g. of the last priest　　　Diderot 4
g. to betray my country　　Forster 8
No g., no glory　Modern Proverbs 38
War will be won by Blood and G.
　　　　Patton 1
You spill your g.　　　Connors 1
gutter
We are all in the g.　　　Wilde 55
guy
g. in the glass　　　Wimbrow 2
g.'s only doing it　　　Loesser 5
guys
nice g. are all over there　Durocher 2
Who are those g.　　Film Lines 38
wild and crazy g.
　　Television Catchphrases 65
gwine
G. to run all night　Stephen Foster 2
gyre
turning in the widening g.　Yeats 29

H

habeas
H. corpus　　Anonymous (Latin) 9
habit
Cocaine h.-forming　　Bankhead 1
Costly thy h.　　Shakespeare 159
H., *n*. A shackle　　　Bierce 55
H. is more dependable　Octavia Butler 1
H. is thus the enormous fly-wheel
　　　　William James 4
habits
H. form a second nature　Lamarck 4
Old h. die hard　　Proverbs 223
other people's h.　　　Twain 68
hacking
h. at the branches of evil　Thoreau 21
haddock
H. and sausage meat　Virginia Woolf 18
hags
midnight h.　　Shakespeare 378
hail
h. and farewell　　　Catullus 5
H. Caesar　　Anonymous (Latin) 2
H., Columbia　　Joseph Hopkinson 1

H., fellow, well met　Jonathan Swift 25
H., h. rock 'n' roll　　Chuck Berry 3
H.! H.! the gang's all here　　Morse 1
H. to the Chief　　Walter Scott 7
H. to thee, blithe Spirit　Percy Shelley 9
hailing
H. frequencies still open　Star Trek 4
hair
Blown h. is sweet　　T. S. Eliot 81
by the h. of my chiny chin　Halliwell 1
get our h. mussed　　Film Lines 68
h. across your cheek　Marian Anderson 1
her h. turned quite gold　　Wilde 40
I just washed my h.　　Film Lines 41
If a woman have long h.　　Bible 352
Jeanie with the light brown h.
　　　　Stephen Foster 6
let your h. down　Grimm and Grimm 1
Shall I part my h. behind　T. S. Eliot 11
vine leaves in his h.　　　Ibsen 24
Wash That Man Right Outa My H.
　　　　Hammerstein 13
weave the sunlight in your h.
　　　　T. S. Eliot 2
Who touches a h.　　　Whittier 4
hairdo
remembered as a h.　Angela Davis 2
hairdresser
Only her h. knows for sure
　　Advertising Slogans 31
Hal
Open the pod door, H.　Film Lines 181
halcyon
h. days　　Aristophanes 4
half
able to decide which h.　Wanamaker 1
dearer h.　　　Milton 37
game is h. mental　　Wohlford 1
H. a league　　Tennyson 37
h. grant what I wish　　Frost 6
h. is greater than the whole　Hesiod 1
h. slave and h. free　　Lincoln 11
h. was not told me　　Bible 91
how the other h. lives　Proverbs 132
just as proud for h. the money
　　　　Godfrey 1
make one h. the world fools
　　　　Jefferson 12
making love to the other h.　Film Lines
127
my better h.　　Philip Sidney 4
My son's only h. Jewish
　　"Groucho" Marx 44
not told h. of what I saw　　Polo 1
One h. of the world　　Austen 15
served my God with h. the zeal
　　Shakespeare 452
take h. my money from me　Filene 1
Too clever by h.　　Salisbury 1
half-truths
all truths are h.　　Whitehead 9
hall
Deck the h.
　　Folk and Anonymous Songs 17
You can't fight City H.
　　Modern Proverbs 29
hallelujah
Glory, Glory! H.!
　　Folk and Anonymous Songs 41

Glory! Glory! H.　Julia Ward Howe 2
king composing H.　Leonard Cohen 3
hallowed
H. be thy name　　Bible 215
h. be thy name　　　Missal 5
walks on h. ground　　Conant 3
halls
From the H. of Montezuma
　　Folk and Anonymous Songs 49
h. of justice　　Lenny Bruce 2
through Tara's h.　Thomas Moore 2
hallucination
consensual h. that was the Matrix
　　　　Gibson 3
halt
maimed, and the h.　　Bible 298
ham
green eggs and h.　　Seuss 11
indict a h. sandwich　　Puccio 1
hamburger
for a h. today　　Segar 3
go out for h.　　Paul Newman 1
Sacred cows make the tastiest h.
　　Abbie Hoffman 3
Hamilton
I leave Emma Lady H.　Horatio Nelson 2
Hamlet
H. is but a name　　Hazlitt 1
I am not Prince H.　　T. S. Eliot 9
It is we who are H.　　Hazlitt 1
rude forefathers of the h.
　　Thomas Gray 4
Hamlets
They have their H.　Dostoyevski 8
hammer
anvil or the h.　　　Goethe 4
anvil or the h.　　　Voltaire 2
I'd h. out danger　　Pete Seeger 2
If I had a h.　　Pete Seeger 1
only tool you have is a h.　Maslow 1
What the h.?　William Blake 11
Hampden
Some village-H.　Thomas Gray 8
Hampshire
In H., Hereford, and Hertford
　　George Bernard Shaw 50
hand
bird in the h.　　Proverbs 26
bite the h. that feeds us
　　Edmund Burke 2
by the h. of God　　Maradona 1
Give a man a free h.　Mae West 14
h. that cradles the rock
　　Clare Boothe Luce 5
h. that held the dagger
　　Franklin D. Roosevelt 20
h. that rocks the cradle　Proverbs 133
h. that signed the paper
　　Dylan Thomas 4
h. will be against every man　Bible 30
I have here in my h.　Joseph McCarthy 1
I want to hold your h.
　　Lennon and McCartney 1
if thy right h. offend thee　Bible 210
kingdom of heaven is at h.　Bible 198
led by an invisible h.　Adam Smith 6
led by an invisible h.　Adam Smith 1
let my right h. forget　　Bible 123
let not thy left h. know　　Bible 214

like the dyer's h.   Shakespeare 428
May I kiss the h. that wrote   Joyce 27
My own right h.   Walter Scott 15
one h. in my pocket   Morrissette 1
One h. washes the other   Proverbs 134
put his h. to the plough   Bible 293
Sound of the Single H.   Hakuin 1
This was the h. that wrote it   Cranmer 1
to lend a h.   Edward Everett Hale 3
Whatsoever thy h. findeth   Bible 148

handful
fear in a h. of dust   T. S. Eliot 43

handkerchief
conditions in the h. industry
                    Cyril Connolly 5

handle
You can't h. the truth   Sorkin 1

hands
bend steel in his bare h.
          Television Catchphrases 6
blood on their h.   Charles Spencer 3
court of equity with clean h.   Eyre 1
good h. with Allstate
            Advertising Slogans 8
h. in his own pockets   Twain 144
horny h. of toil   James Russell Lowell 1
idle H.   Watts 2
If you believe, clap your h.   Barrie 11
into thy h. I commend   Bible 307
over-ripe fruit into our h.   Lenin 10
pry it from my cold dead h.
            Political Slogans 22
union of h. and hearts   Jeremy Taylor 2
washed his h. before the multitude
                    Bible 272
whole world in his h.
        Folk and Anonymous Songs 34

handsome
H. is as h. does   Proverbs 135
I was strangely h.   Twain 153

handsomest
h., cleverest, and best man   Tolstoy 2

handy
with the girls be h.
        Folk and Anonymous Songs 85
which I also keep h.   W. C. Fields 25

hang
h. a man first   Molière 5
H. down your head
        Folk and Anonymous Songs 77
H. it all, Robert Browning
                  Ezra Pound 16
he will h. himself   Proverbs 261
I will not h. myself   Chesterton 23
more to h. for   John Brown 3
pegs to h. ideas on   Beecher 2
she would h. on him   Shakespeare 151
We must all h. together
          Benjamin Franklin 34
which will h. him   Richelieu 1
wretches h. that jury-men   Pope 6
You may h. these boys
          Clarence S. Darrow 3
You might as well h. a man
          Clarence S. Darrow 2

hanged
man knows he is to be h.
            Samuel Johnson 89
Men are not h. for stealing   Halifax 1

hangers
No wire h.   Joan Crawford 1

hangin'
they're h. men and women
        Folk and Anonymous Songs 79

hanging
deserve h. ten times   Montaigne 16
H. is too good for him   Bunyan 4
h. on as long as possible   Mencken 37

hangover
h. became a part of the day
            F. Scott Fitzgerald 38

hangs
h. upon the cheek of night
              Shakespeare 30
He h. around this one   Farmer 1
thereby h. a tale   Shakespeare 86

haply
H. I think on thee   Shakespeare 415

happen
Accidents will h.   Proverbs 2
It Can't H. Here   Sinclair Lewis 5

happened
All this has h. before   Film Lines 131
it never h.   Orwell 36
most of them never h.   Twain 148
things that never h.   Twain 123
too strange to have h.   Thomas Hardy 2

happening
keeps everything from h. at once
              Ray Cummings 1

happens
least expected generally h.   Disraeli 7
Life is what h. to us   Allen Saunders 1
Shit h.   Modern Proverbs 81
Stuff h.   Rumsfeld 3
Truth h. to an idea   William James 21
What h. to a dream deferred
            Langston Hughes 8

happier
could have been h.   Virginia Woolf 20
having had a h. childhood
        Samuel Butler (1835–1902) 6

happiest
h. women   George Eliot 4

happily
good ended h.   Wilde 81

happiness
definition of h. of the Greeks
            John F. Kennedy 36
greatest H. for the *greatest Numbers*
                Hutcheson 1
greatest h. of the greatest number
                Bentham 1
greatest h. shared by the greatest number
                Beccaria 1
H., *n.* An agreeable   Bierce 56
H. is a warm puppy   Schulz 2
H. is an imaginary condition   Szasz 1
H. lies in the consciousness   Sand 4
H. Makes Up in Height   Frost 24
here and now is h.   Kazantzakis 1
lifetime of h.   George Bernard Shaw 13
no moment to the h.
            Samuel Johnson 72
only one h. in life   Sand 2
pursuit of H.   Jefferson 2
result h.   Dickens 59
sound off about h.   I Ching 1

supply the materials for h.
            Thomas Hardy 10
thought myself out of h.   Foer 1

happy
as h. as kings Robert Louis Stevenson 13
Ask yourself whether you are h.   Mill 24
bread-sauce of the h. ending
              Henry James 13
Don't worry, be h.   Baba 1
h. as they make up their minds
                  Lincoln 61
h. before he dies   Solon 2
H. Birthday to You
        Folk and Anonymous Songs 33
H. days are here   Yellen 3
h. ending is our national
            Mary McCarthy 2
H. ever after   Sayings 17
h. families resemble   Tolstoy 8
h. genius of my household
        William Carlos Williams 1
H. is the country   Proverbs 54
H. the man, and h. he alone
              John Dryden 8
H. the people whose annals
            Montesquieu 6
H. trails to you   Dale Evans 1
H. Warrior of the political
          Franklin D. Roosevelt 1
I was quite h.   Giovanni 2
If you want to be h.   De Leon 1
instead of h. childhoods   Herr 2
Make someone h. Comden and Green 5
not to seem too h.   Robert Browning 18
Oh h. day   Hawkins 1
policeman's lot is not a h. one
              W. S. Gilbert 23
recall the h. time   Dante 7
somewhere, may be h.   Mencken 42
there are no h. families
            Susan Cheever 1
we shall touch the H. Isles Tennyson 25
whistle a h. tune   Hammerstein 21
Who is the h. Warrior
        William Wordsworth 7

harbor
ship in h. is safe   Shedd 1
those who h. them   George W. Bush 4

hard
Good Man Is H. to Find   Eddie Green 1
got rich through h. work   Marquis 2
h., gemlike flame   Pater 3
"H.," replied the Dodger   Dickens 17
H. cases make bad law   Proverbs 136
"h." data and "soft" data
            Bertrand Russell 3
h. rain's a-gonna fall   Dylan 5
h. to be a woman   Wynette 2
H. work never hurt anyone
            Modern Proverbs 39
H. work never killed anybody   Bergen 1
He's had a h. day's night   Lennon 2
hits the line h.   Theodore Roosevelt 4
It's been a h. day's night
        Lennon and McCartney 4
not as h. as playing comedy   Gwenn 1
Old habits die h.   Proverbs 223

hardball
I can play h.   Frist 1

You had me at "h."   Film Lines 103
helluva
New York, a h. town
            Comden and Green 1
helmet
football too long without a h.
            Lyndon B. Johnson 11
help
H. me   Film Lines 77
h. themselves   Proverbs 122
make him an h. meet   Bible 10
very present h.   Bible 113
with a little h. from my friends
            Lennon and McCartney 18
helper
mother's little h.   Jagger and Richards 4
helpless
h. and contemptible Woodrow Wilson 14
pitiful, h. giant   Richard Nixon 11
helps
Every little h.   Proverbs 88
God h. them   Proverbs 122
helter
H. Skelter   Lennon and McCartney 19
Hemingway
young man named Ernest H.
            F. Scott Fitzgerald 5
hemispheres
jars two h.   Thomas Hardy 26
hen
h. is only an egg's way
        Samuel Butler (1835–1902) 1
h. who has laid an egg   Twain 85
my black h.   Nursery Rhymes 21
Henry
John H. was just a li'l baby
        Folk and Anonymous Songs 42
Poor H.   Maugham 6
work of H. James   Guedalla 1
Hepburn
Miss H. runs the whole gamut
            Dorothy Parker 29
herald
remember me to H. Square   Cohan 3
herd
Morality is h.-instinct   Nietzsche 8
herds
think in h.   Mackay 1
here
Buck Stops H.   Truman 11
from h. to Eternity   Kipling 9
H. come de judge
        Television Catchphrases 59
H. I am, and h. I stay   MacMahon 1
H. I stand   Luther 1
H. men from the planet Earth
            Anonymous 12
h. on earth God's work
            John F. Kennedy 17
H. today and gone tomorrow
            Proverbs 140
H. we are now, entertain us   Cobain 1
H. we are, and h. we shall   Douglass 4
H.'s a how-de-do   W. S. Gilbert 38
H.'s looking at you, kid   Film Lines 44
H.'s richness   Dickens 22
I'll be right h.   Film Lines 75
it was h. first   Burdette 1
Lafayette, we are h.   Charles E. Stanton 1

hereditary
idea of h. legislators   Thomas Paine 17
heresies
begin as h.   T. H. Huxley 6
hero
conquering h. comes   Morell 1
h. of my own life   Dickens 55
No man is a h. to his valet   Cornuel 1
Show me a h.   F. Scott Fitzgerald 47
working class h.   Lennon 6
Herod
out-Herods H.   Shakespeare 201
heroes
h. don't appear on no stamps Shocklee 2
land that needs h.   Brecht 4
heroic
greatest obstacle to being h.
            Hawthorne 19
h. little monkey   Charles Darwin 12
h. poem of its sort   Thomas Carlyle 6
heroism
H. is endurance   George Kennan 1
heron
h. priested shore   Dylan Thomas 10
herself
isn't quite h. today   Film Lines 139
hesitate
leader who doesn't h.   Meir 5
hesitates
He who h. is lost   Proverbs 141
heterosexual
one eyed shrew of the h. dollar
            Ginsberg 8
hewers
H. of wood   Bible 75
hey
H., big spender   Dorothy Fields 4
H. ho, let's go   Tommy Ramone 1
h., ho, the wind   Shakespeare 246
H. diddle diddle   Nursery Rhymes 22
H. Joe   Hendrix 2
Say, h.   Mays 1
hickety
H., pickety, my black hen
            Nursery Rhymes 21
hickory
H., dickory, dock   Nursery Rhymes 23
hid
lay h. in night   Pope 11
hidden
Something deeply h.   Einstein 30
hide
death to h.   Milton 52
doing my best to h. it   Mae West 18
h. it from yourself   Orwell 47
run but he can't h.   Joe Louis 2
hiding
must have its h. places   Reich 3
hierarchy
In a h., each employee   Peter 1
high
backwards and in h. heels   Thaves 1
corn is as h.   Hammerstein 6
engaged in h. moral purpose
        George Herbert Walker Bush 6
h. as a flag on the Fourth
            Hammerstein 16
h. Crimes and Misdemeanors
            Constitution 7

h. on cocaine   Robert Hunter 2
h. road that leads him to England
            Samuel Johnson 52
retiring at h. speed   William F. Halsey 2
wickedness in h. places   Bible 368
ye'll tak' the h. road
        Folk and Anonymous Songs 10
higher
explain school to a h. intelligence
            Film Lines 73
h. law than the Constitution   Seward 1
There is a h. father   George W. Bush 27
we couldn't get much h.   Jim Morrison 2
highest
Glory to God in the h.   Bible 290
h. good   Cicero 7
highland
My heart's in the H.   Robert Burns 6
highness
I am his H.' dog at Kew   Pope 36
high-tech
h. lynching   Clarence Thomas 1
highwayman
h. came riding   Noyes 1
hill
amount to a h. of beans   Film Lines 48
city that is set on an h.   Bible 208
City upon a h.   Winthrop 1
H. House, not sane   Shirley Jackson 2
hunter home from the h.
        Robert Louis Stevenson 21
I saw Joe H. last night   Alfred Hayes 1
It should be of the h.
            Frank Lloyd Wright 1
Jack and Jill went up the h.
            Nursery Rhymes 26
Over h., over dale   Gruber 1
Over h., over dale   Shakespeare 53
hills
blue remembered h.   Housman 2
h. are alive   Hammerstein 27
over the h. and everywhere
        Folk and Anonymous Songs 32
hindmost
Devil take the h.   Proverbs 67
hindsight
H. is always twenty-twenty
            Billy Wilder 2
hip
I said a h. hop   Michael Wright 1
smile I could feel in my h. pocket
            Raymond Chandler 6
hippocampus
Indelible in the h.
            Christine Blasey Ford 1
hippopotamus
broad-backed h.   T. S. Eliot 25
hire
laborer is worthy of his h.   Bible 294
hired
They h. the money   Coolidge 7
Hiroshima
Where? H.?   Twiggy 1
You saw nothing in H.   Duras 1
his
H. Majesty's Government view
            Balfour 1
H. Master's Voice
        Advertising Slogans 128

H.'s a place   Marilyn Monroe 8
not have been invited to H.
     Raymond Chandler 9
phony tinsel of H.   Levant 2
Holmes
My name is Sherlock H.
     Arthur Conan Doyle 18
holy
He died to make men h.
     Julia Ward Howe 3
H., h., h., Lord God   Missal 4
H., h., h., is the Lord of hosts   Bible 163
h. because the gods approve it   Plato 3
H. night   Mohr 1
H. Russian land   Kurbsky 1
h. simplicity   Huss 1
h. simplicity   St. Jerome 1
in h. Matrimony
     Book of Common Prayer 16
joined together in h. Matrimony
     Book of Common Prayer 13
neither H., nor Roman   Voltaire 5
of the H. Ghost   Missal 2
sorrow there is h. ground   Wilde 85
whereon thou standest is h. ground
     Bible 40
home
all the way h. they walked   Agee 3
any more at h. like you   Owen Hall 1
birds came h. to roost   Arthur Miller 4
Charity begins at h.   Proverbs 45
come h. to roost   Southey 6
do not try this at h.
     Television Catchphrases 2
eaten me out of house and h.
     Shakespeare 62
E.T. phone h.   Film Lines 74
get h. from work   Rosa Parks 1
give me a h.   Higley 1
go h. in the dark   O. Henry 8
H., Sweet H.   Payne 1
h. again, h. again   Nursery Rhymes 40
h. his footsteps   Walter Scott 2
H. is the place where   Frost 1
H. is the sailor
     Robert Louis Stevenson 21
H. is where one starts from
     T. S. Eliot 110
H. is where the heart is   Proverbs 143
H. of lost causes   Matthew Arnold 8
h. of the brave   Francis Scott Key 2
h. of the free and brave   Cohan 3
House Is Not a H.   Polly Adler 1
hunter h. from the hill
     Robert Louis Stevenson 21
I tank I go h.   Garbo 3
Johnny comes marching h.
     Patrick S. Gilmore 1
make it h.   Guest 1
More at H. Like You   Boyd-Jones 1
nearer h. to-day   Phoebe Cary 1
no place like h.   L. Frank Baum 3
no place like h.   Hesiod 3
no place like h.   Payne 2
nobody at h.   Pope 13
old Kentucky h.   Stephen Foster 5
plagiarism begins at h.
     Zelda Fitzgerald 1
take us right h.   Film Lines 117

their h. in the sky   James Taylor 3
then I go h. alone   Joplin 5
till the cows come h.
     "Groucho" Marx 20
woman's place is in the h.   Proverbs 330
you can't go h. again   Winter 1
home-fires
Keep the H. burning   Lena Ford 1
Homer
Achilles exists only through H.
     Chateaubriand 2
excellent H. nods   Horace 8
Seven cities warred for H.   Heywood 2
single exception of H.
     George Bernard Shaw 7
you must not call it H.
     Richard Bentley 1
homes
In h., a haunted   Raine 2
stately H. of England   Hemans 3
stately h. of England   Virginia Woolf 4
homesick
H., *adj.* Dead broke   Bierce 62
hometown
Paris is my h.   Stein 7
homeward
Look h. angel   Milton 3
homos
stately h. of England   Crisp 2
homosexual
heterosexual and h.   Kinsey 2
h. was now a species   Foucault 3
prevalence of h. passions   Symonds 1
homosexuality
H. is assuredly no advantage
     Sigmund Freud 17
his latent h.   Mailer 2
homosexuals
removed all of the h.   Lebowitz 9
honest
brow is wet with h. sweat   Longfellow 8
cannot be both h. and intelligent
     Orwell 32
Can't Cheat an H. Man   W. C. Fields 8
h. and rich   Austen 14
h. broker   Bismarck 7
h. man's noblest work   Pope 26
Lawyer, an h. Man   Benjamin Franklin 4
looking for an h. man   Diogenes 1
May none but h. and wise Men
     John Adams 13
most h. of men   Richelieu 1
one of the few h. people
     F. Scott Fitzgerald 17
parents were h. but poor
     Bertrand Russell 9
poor, but h.   Shakespeare 252
write your h. opinions   Swinton 1
you must be h.   Dylan 20
honestly
If possible h.   Horace 10
honesty
H. is the best policy   Proverbs 144
main thing about acting is h.
     George Burns 2
honey
H. catches more flies   Proverbs 145
land flowing with milk and h.   Bible 41
Pedigree of H.   Emily Dickinson 26

speech sweeter than h.   Homer 3
honey-dew
for he on h. hath fed   Coleridge 23
honeydew
ten h. melons   Streisand 1
honor
Duty, h., country   Douglas MacArthur 4
h., and keep her
     Book of Common Prayer 14
h. among thieves   Proverbs 146
h. and life have been spared   Francis I 1
h. Christmas in my heart   Dickens 47
H. the lofty poet   Dante 5
H. thy father and thy mother   Bible 55
louder he talked of his h.
     Ralph Waldo Emerson 41
loved I not h. more   Richard Lovelace 2
our Fortunes and our sacred H.
     Jefferson 8
peace cannot be maintained with h.
     John Russell 1
peace I hope with h.   Disraeli 27
peace with h.   Chamberlain 2
prophet is not without h.   Bible 241
honorable
Brutus is an h. man   Shakespeare 113
your intentions are h.   Beaumarchais 2
honor'd
more h. in the breach   Shakespeare 163
honored
Earth, receive an h. guest   Auden 23
honors
h. its live conformists   McLaughlin 2
Hoover
right back of J. Edgar H.   Lenny Bruce 1
hope
ABANDON EVERY H.   Dante 3
abideth faith, h., charity   Bible 355
against h. believed in h.   Bible 342
audacity of h.   Barack Obama 2
h. and history rhyme   Heaney 8
H. deferred maketh the heart   Bible 130
H. for the best   Proverbs 147
H. I die before I get old   Townshend 1
h. is a good thing   Stephen King 2
H. is a song in a weary   Pauli Murray 2
H. is like a road   Lu Xun 1
H. is not "the thing with feathers"
     Woody Allen 20
H. is the feeling we have   McLaughlin 1
"H." is the thing with feathers
     Emily Dickinson 10
h. of the world   Muir 2
H. springs eternal   Pope 18
h. the Pacific is as blue   Stephen King 4
I do not h. to turn   T. S. Eliot 75
Land of H. and Glory   A. C. Benson 1
last best, h. of earth   Lincoln 37
no H. without Fear   Spinoza 1
still h. for America   Christopher Morley 1
there's life, there's h.   Proverbs 171
Things which you do not h.   Plautus 3
triumph of h.   Samuel Johnson 68
Wait and h.   Dumas the Elder 4
we sell h.   Revson 1
White H.   Sackler 1
hopefully
To travel h.   Robert Louis Stevenson 5

household
happy genius of my h.
William Carlos Williams 1
h. words Shakespeare 137
housekeeper
h. must consider Beeton 1
housekeeping
H. ain't no joke Louisa May Alcott 3
houses
Have nothing in your h.
William Morris 1
h. are all gone under the sea
T. S. Eliot 103
h. rise and fall T. S. Eliot 101
live in glass h. Proverbs 120
plague o'both your h. Shakespeare 42
selling h. for more Sinclair Lewis 2
housetops
proclaimed upon the h. Bible 296
housework
h., with its endless de Beauvoir 3
I hate h. Rivers 4
Houston
H., we've had a problem Lovell 1
how
h. are the mighty fallen Bible 86
H. beastly the bourgeois is
D. H. Lawrence 7
H. can they tell Dorothy Parker 30
H. cheerfully he seems to grin
Carroll 6
H. green was my Valley Llewellyn 1
H. had I come to be here
Elizabeth Bishop 3
h. little one knows oneself de Gaulle 9
H. Long Is the Coast of Britain
Mandelbrot 1
h. long must we sing Bono 1
H. many dawns Hart Crane 2
H. much is that doggie Bob Merrill 1
H. much justice can you afford
Handelsman 1
H. NOT TO DO IT Dickens 93
H. odd of God to choose the Jews Ewer 1
H. pleasant to know Mr. Lear Lear 3
H. sweet it is
Television Catchphrases 38
h. the other half lives Proverbs 132
h. to die Porteus 2
H. to Succeed in Business
Shepherd Mead 1
H. to Win Friends Dale Carnegie 1
H. unpleasant to meet Mr. Eliot
T. S. Eliot 89
H. YOU Cary Grant 2
H. YOU DOIN' Television Catchphrases 21
H.'m I doing Edward I. Koch 1
Lord, h. long Bible 164
how-de-do
Here's a h. W. S. Gilbert 38
Howdy
It's H. Doody Time
Television Catchphrases 33
howl
H., h., h., h. Shakespeare 316
make all hell h. Nation 1
hub
Boston State-House is the h.
Oliver Wendell Holmes 5

Hubbard
Old Mother H. Nursery Rhymes 45
Huckleberry
book by Mark Twain called *H. Finn*
Hemingway 18
huddled
h. masses yearning Lazarus 2
huelga
Viva la h. Cesar Chavez 1
huff
I'll h., and I'll puff Halliwell 1
leave in a h. "Groucho" Marx 17
hugging
h. the shore Updike 3
Hugo
H., hélas Gide 4
Victor H. was a madman Cocteau 2
humaine
Comedie h. Balzac 4
human
All h. beings are born free
Anonymous 2
all h. life is there Henry James 6
all that h. hearts endure
Samuel Johnson 26
arresting h. intelligence Leacock 2
burn h. beings Heine 1
Course of h. events Jefferson 1
engineers of h. souls Stalin 1
eternal in the h. breast Pope 18
Everything h. is pathetic Twain 88
existence of the h. species
Christa Wolf 1
field of h. conflict Winston Churchill 17
glimpses into the h. heart
F. Scott Fitzgerald 10
h. being should be able Heinlein 5
h. being was crushed by books Hersey 1
h. character changed Virginia Woolf 3
H. Condition Malraux 1
H. contact seemed to her Drabble 3
h. experience is the highest
William James 22
h. heart in conflict Faulkner 8
H. history becomes H. G. Wells 7
H. kind cannot bear T. S. Eliot 96
H. life begins Sartre 4
H. life is but a series Nabokov 7
H. life is everywhere
Samuel Johnson 23
h. mind to correlate Lovecraft 1
h. mind will contemplate Pavlov 1
h. nature is good Mencius 2
h. rights are women's Hillary Clinton 4
h. rights must have
Theodore Roosevelt 19
h. species was given Franzen 2
H. speech is like Flaubert 1
I am a h. being Film Lines 72
limited supply of H. Beings Berger 1
lose its h. face Dubček 1
loved the H. Race Raleigh 1
majesty of h. suffering Vigny 2
man is a h. being Twain 111
mathematics is not fully h. Heinlein 9
milk of h. kindness Shakespeare 333
naked h. soul Pasternak 3
no known h. society Margaret Mead 6
nothing h. is foreign Terence 3

Of H. Bondage Spinoza 2
stamp of the h. condition Montaigne 14
till h. voices wake us T. S. Eliot 12
To err is h. Pope 4
two or three h. stories Cather 2
universe and h. stupidity Einstein 38
unspectacular and always h. Auden 4
utmost bound of h. thought
Tennyson 20
when they espouse h. rights LaFollette 1
you've conquered h. natur Dickens 23
humanity
Ah, h. Melville 18
crooked timber of h. Kant 1
h. in the abstract
George Bernard Shaw 44
Oh, the h. Herbert Morrison 1
humans
h. should have Lagerlöf 1
made Women h. by Act of Congress
Will Rogers 9
humble
be it ever so h. Payne 2
Don't be so h. Meir 2
It's hard to be h. Ali 5
most h. day of my life Rupert Murdoch 1
humbling
No h. of reality Ammons 2
humbly
walk h. with thy God Bible 194
humbug
"Bah!" said Scrooge. "H.!" Dickens 39
humidity
isn't heat . . . as the h. Gelett Burgess 5
humiliate
defeat or h. the United States
Richard Nixon 9
humiliation
never experience the h. Black Hawk 1
humility
H. is the most difficult T. S. Eliot 72
humor
secret source of H. Twain 88
two kinds of h. Ivins 2
hump
whale's white h. Melville 7
without a positive h. Thackeray 3
Humpty
H. Dumpty sat Nursery Rhymes 24
Hun
H. is always either at your
Winston Churchill 29
hunch
collective h. Jane Wagner 2
hundred
all be the same a h. years hence
Dickens 25
all one a h. years hence
Ralph Waldo Emerson 35
first h. years Modern Proverbs 30
first one h. days John F. Kennedy 12
h. men his enemies John Adams 18
h. years to make a law Beecher 1
Letting a h. flowers blossom
Mao Tse-tung 6
one h. years of solitude
García Márquez 3
steal more than a h. men Puzo 1
Victory has a h. fathers Ciano 1
When nine h. years old George Lucas 17

hung
A man had never yet been h.
                    Grover Cleveland 1
Hungarian
not enough to be H.   Korda 1
hunger
No fear can stand up to h.   Conrad 14
When a man is dying of h.   Napoleon 12
When I write of h.   M. F. K. Fisher 1
hungry
eat when we were not h.
                    Jonathan Swift 16
h. man is not a free man
                    Adlai E. Stevenson 4
i'll show you a h. person   Giovanni 3
lean and h. look   Shakespeare 99
never going to be h. again
                    Margaret Mitchell 5
hunted
most h. person   Charles Spencer 1
hunter
Heart Is a Lonely H.   McCullers 1
heart is a lonely h.   Sharp 1
h. home from the hill
            Robert Louis Stevenson 21
hunting
a-h. we will go   Henry Fielding 1
Memories are h. horns   Apollinaire 1
passion for h. something   Dickens 18
huntress
Queen and h.   Jonson 1
hurdles
see the h.   Moses 1
hurrah
Last H.   Edwin O'Connor 1
hurricane
story of the H.   Dylan 26
hurricanes
some serious h.   Pat Robertson 1
hurries
h. to the main event   Horace 6
hurry
H. UP PLEASE ITS TIME   T. S. Eliot 49
no special h.   Hemingway 10
hurt
can't h. you   Proverbs 161
Hard work never h. anyone
            Modern Proverbs 39
H. the One You Love   Allan Roberts 1
I h. myself today   Reznor 1
know how to h. a guy
            Television Catchphrases 49
power to h.   Francis Beaumont 1
power to h.   Shakespeare 424
hurting
policy isn't h.   Major 1
hurts
h. a lot worse   Truman 7
h. me more   Sayings 53
h. so much   Kerrigan 1
truth h.   Modern Proverbs 93
husband
accept me as a h.   Charlotte Brontë 3
h. for a comfort   Stevie Smith 1
h. is always the last   Proverbs 150
h. is what is left   Helen Rowland 1
if I were your h.   Winston Churchill 55
My h. and I   Elizabeth II 1
that person is the h.   Mott 1

husbandry
dulls the edge of h.   Shakespeare 160
husbands
H. are like fires   Gabor 3
reasons for h. to stay at home
                    George Eliot 5
hush
H., little baby
            Folk and Anonymous Songs 35
H.-a-bye, baby   Nursery Rhymes 1
whispering "h."
            Margaret Wise Brown 2
huts
living in grass h.   Paglia 1
Hutton
When E. F. H. talks
            Advertising Slogans 44
Hyde
Dr. Jekyll and Mr. H.
            Robert Louis Stevenson 18
hygienist
"Dental H." has been added   Barr 1
hymself
ech man for h.   Chaucer 12
hyperion
H. to a satyr   Shakespeare 151
hypertext
introduce the word "h."   Ted Nelson 1
hyphenated
h. Americanism   Theodore Roosevelt 25
hypocrisy
base alloy of h.   Lincoln 9
H. is a tribute which vice
            la Rochefoucauld 5
organized h.   Disraeli 18
safe for h.   Thomas Wolfe 1
hypocrite
H. reader   Baudelaire 1
h.'s crime is that he bears   Arendt 8
hypocrites
other half h.   Jefferson 12
political h. before the world   Lincoln 6
hypotheses
I frame no h.   Isaac Newton 2
hypothesis
discard a pet h.   Konrad Lorenz 1
I have no need for this h.   Laplace 2
slaying of a beautiful h.   T. H. Huxley 3
hysterical
h. symptoms   Sigmund Freud 1

I

I AM THAT I AM   Bible 42
I am the greatest   Ali 1
I am the Lord thy God   Bible 50
I am the resurrection   Bible 321
I am what I am   Prévert 1
I do not love you, Dr. Fell
            Thomas Brown 1
I pledge allegiance to my Flag
            Francis Bellamy 1
I shall not want   Bible 108
There's no "I" in team
            Modern Proverbs 44
ice
All Scream for I. Cream   Moll 1
emperor of i.-cream   Wallace Stevens 4

his father took him to discover i.
                    García Márquez 1
for destruction i.   Frost 12
I. formed on the butler's   Wodehouse 4
i. was here, the i. was there   Coleridge 2
i. weasels come   Groening 9
rich man gets his i.   Lawler 1
skating over thin i.
            Ralph Waldo Emerson 14
some say in i.   Frost 10
ice-berg
dignity of movement of an i.
                    Hemingway 15
iceberg
grew the I. too   Thomas Hardy 25
ich
I. bin ein Berliner   John F. Kennedy 33
icumen
Sumer is i. in
            Folk and Anonymous Songs 16
Winter is i. in   Ezra Pound 8
id
ego's relation to the i.
            Sigmund Freud 14
PUT THE I. BACK IN YID   Roth 3
Where i. was, there ego
            Sigmund Freud 16
idea
Between the i. and the reality
            T. S. Eliot 66
Every i. is an incitement
            Oliver Wendell Holmes, Jr. 34
he had only one i.   Disraeli 17
He who receives an i.   Jefferson 36
i. of writing the decline   Gibbon 10
It would be a good i.
            Mohandas Gandhi 6
no such thing as a false i.   Lewis Powell 1
possess but one i.   Samuel Johnson 66
seemed like a good i.
            John Monk Saunders 1
teach the young i.   Thomson 2
Truth happens to an i.   William James 21
you have only one i.   Alain 1
ideal
i. for which I am prepared
            Nelson Mandela 1
in the service of an i.   Matthew Arnold 3
idealism
alcohol or morphine or i.   Jung 6
idealist
i. is one who   Mencken 3
people call me an i.   Woodrow Wilson 23
idealists
fate of i.   Bertrand Russell 7
ideals
tell the i. of a nation   Norman Douglas 1
ideas
brute force cannot kill i.   Weil 2
Colorless green i. sleep   Chomsky 1
I don't adopt any one's i.   Turgenev 2
I. Have Consequences   Weaver 1
most words in the fewest i.   Lincoln 58
no i. but in things
            William Carlos Williams 5
number of the greatest i.   Ruskin 1
one cannot resist the invasion of i.
                    Hugo 8
pegs to hang i. on   Beecher 2

ruling i. of each age
                    Marx and Engels 7
True i. are those that we can
                    William James 20
identity
i. crisis   Erikson 1
Ides
Beware the I. of March   Shakespeare 97
idiocy
i. of rural life   Marx and Engels 5
idiot
any i. can run   Lynch 1
from which comes i. children
                        Film Lines 1
He really is an i.   "Groucho" Marx 25
I.'s Delight   Sherwood 2
law is a ass—a i.   Dickens 20
possibly an i.   Dalí 2
Suppose you were an i.   Twain 140
tale told by an i.   Shakespeare 394
to be an i.   William Blake 17
idiots
for execution by i.   Wouk 1
God made i.   Twain 107
God made i.   Twain 48
produce bigger i.   Rick Cook 1
Useful i.   Lenin 11
idle
Be not solitary, be not i.
                    Robert Burton 8
i. brain is the Devil's workshop
                        Proverbs 151
i. Hands   Watts 2
i. king   Tennyson 14
If you are i., be not solitary
                    Samuel Johnson 97
We would all be i. if we could
                    Samuel Johnson 82
idleness
I. is the root of all evil   Proverbs 152
idol
of whom I had made an i.
                    Charlotte Brontë 4
idolator
I., n. One who   Bierce 63
idolatry
god of my i.   Shakespeare 36
idols
four classes of I.   Francis Bacon 5
if
I. anything can go wrong
                    Modern Proverbs 100
I. I am not for myself   Hillel 1
I. I did it   O. J. Simpson 2
I. I forget thee, O Jerusalem   Bible 123
I. it does not fit   Cochran 1
i. not now, when   Hillel 1
I. you build it, he will come Kinsella 1
I. you can keep your head   Kipling 31
I. you've seen one city slum   Agnew 1
ignis
i. fatuus of the mind   Rochester 1
ignoble
doctrine of i. ease Theodore Roosevelt 6
ignorance
complete i. of both life   Wilde 10
cult of i.   Asimov 4
fact of my i.   Socrates 2
I., Madam, pure i.   Samuel Johnson 47

I. is more costly
                Booker T. Washington 4
I. IS STRENGTH   Orwell 35
I. of the law excuses   Selden 1
I. of the law is no excuse Proverbs 153
no sin but i.   Marlowe 2
try i.   Bok 2
where i. is bliss   Thomas Gray 1
ignorant
conscious that you are i.   Disraeli 13
Everybody is i.   Will Rogers 3
expects to be i. and free   Jefferson 41
i. armies clash by night
                    Matthew Arnold 19
i. of one's ignorance
                Amos Bronson Alcott 1
Jane, you i. slut
            Television Catchphrases 64
most i. of what he's most
                    Shakespeare 254
ignored
because they are i.   Aldous Huxley 1
ignoring
politics consists in i.   Henry Adams 15
Ike
I like I.   Political Slogans 21
Ilium
topless towers of I.   Marlowe 8
I'll
I. be back   Film Lines 170
I. be there   Steinbeck 5
I. go on   Beckett 10
I. have what she's having
                    Film Lines 186
ill
i. met by moonlight   Shakespeare 54
i. wind that blows no good
                        Proverbs 154
impulses to men i. at ease
                      Hawthorne 18
Never speak i. of the dead   Proverbs 281
illegal
i., or fattening   Woollcott 4
i. we do immediately   Kissinger 4
it is not i.   Richard Nixon 18
it would be made i.   Sayings 24
never threw an i. pitch   Paige 10
Nothing is i. if   Andrew Young 1
illegitimate
only i. parents   Yankwich 1
illigitimi
Ni i. carborundum   Sayings 42
ill-favored
i. thing   Shakespeare 96
ill-housed
i., ill-clad   Franklin D. Roosevelt 13
illiterates
i. can read and write   Moravia 1
illness
I. is the night-side   Sontag 7
illnesses
not of their i.   Molière 13
illogical
i. belief in   Mencken 31
illusion
Certainty generally is i.
                Oliver Wendell Holmes, Jr. 12
Great I.   Angell 1
He had one i.   Keynes 2

i. that the times   Greeley 1
illusions
Don't part with your i.   Twain 106
im
in two words, "I. possible" Goldwyn 11
image
kills the i. of God   Milton 6
make man in our i.   Bible 4
make unto thee any graven i.   Bible 51
images
heap of broken i.   T. S. Eliot 42
No graven i.   Clough 3
nuns and mothers worship i.   Yeats 39
unpurged i. of day   Yeats 53
imaginaire
Malade I.   Molière 12
imaginary
i. gardens with real toads
                Marianne Moore 2
i. is what tends   Breton 3
imagination
I., not invention   Conrad 26
I.! who can sing   Wheatley 2
i. all compact   Shakespeare 56
i. enables us   C. Wright Mills 1
key of i.   Serling 3
primary i. I hold   Coleridge 25
imagine
i. the past   Namier 1
I. there's no countries   Lennon 9
I. there's no heaven   Lennon 8
imbeciles
Three generations of i.
            Oliver Wendell Holmes, Jr. 35
imitate
i. him if you can   Jonathan Swift 34
I. him if you dare   Yeats 58
i. the action of the tiger
                    Shakespeare 133
imitated
he who can be i.   Chateaubriand 1
imitates
Life i. Art   Wilde 19
imitation
also a form of i.   Lichtenberg 1
i. game   Turing 2
I. is the sincerest form   Proverbs 155
Immanuel
call his name I.   Bible 165
immature
I. poets imitate   T. S. Eliot 28
immediately
can be done i.   Santayana 14
illegal we do i.   Kissinger 4
immense
heart of an i. darkness   Conrad 18
i. pile of filth   Francis 2
immigrant
I., n. An unenlightened   Bierce 64
immigrants
descended from i.
            Franklin D. Roosevelt 17
I.: we get the job done   Miranda 5
immoral
art is i.   Wilde 13
books that the world calls i.   Wilde 44
i., illegal   Woollcott 4
moral or an i. book   Wilde 21

immorality
I. The morality of those Mencken 19
immortal
i. bird Keats 19
i. longings in me Shakespeare 405
lost the i. part Shakespeare 267
make me i. with a kiss Marlowe 9
no i. work behind me Keats 22
what i. hand or eye William Blake 10
immortality
achieve i. through my work
 Woody Allen 40
forget themselves into i.
 Wendell Phillips 4
Millions long for i. Ertz 1
only i. you and I Nabokov 5
organize her own i. Laski 1
immortals
President of the I. Thomas Hardy 13
impartial
i. as between the fire brigade
 Winston Churchill 5
impeachable
i. offense is whatever Gerald R. Ford 1
impediment
cause, or just i.
 Book of Common Prayer 13
impediments
true minds admit i. Shakespeare 429
imperative
This i. is categorical Kant 4
imperial
i. Presidency Schlesinger 2
imperialism
I. is the monopoly stage Lenin 3
imperious
I. Caesar Shakespeare 227
importance
redeeming social i. Brennan 1
important
anything so i. T. A. D. Jones 1
i. in the life of a boy Witcraft 1
think it's i. Eugene McCarthy 1
impossibility
likely i. is always Aristotle 7
impossible
i., it shall be done Calonne 1
because it is i. Tertullian 3
dream the i. dream Darion 1
eliminated the i.
 Arthur Conan Doyle 10
I wish it were i. Samuel Johnson 107
If it is i. Trollope 3
i. is that which takes a little Nansen 1
i. person so long Bakunin 1
I. that which takes Santayana 14
i. to carry Edward 1
i. to say which was which Orwell 26
i. to understand Freeman Dyson 1
part of the "i." must be possible
 Boucher 1
six i. things Carroll 38
impostors
treat those two i. just the same
 Kipling 32
impressionists
create the new term i. Castagnary 1

impressions
First i. Proverbs 105
imprisoned
I. in every fat man Cyril Connolly 3
improbable
occurrence of the i. Mencken 31
whatever remains, however i.
 Arthur Conan Doyle 10
improper
i. mind is a perpetual feast
 Logan Smith 1
improve
i. each shining Hour Watts 1
i. his shining tail Carroll 5
it would i. man Twain 50
improved
enormously i. by death Saki 4
improvement
human i. must end Ellsworth 1
Most schemes of political i.
 Samuel Johnson 63
improvements
delivering down those i.
 Erasmus Darwin 1
impudence
Cockney i. Ruskin 20
impudent
effete corps of i. snobs Agnew 2
impulse
lonely i. of delight Yeats 22
impunity
I., n. Wealth Bierce 65
in
I. God we trust Salmon P. Chase 1
I. my Father's house Bible 324
I. the beginning God created Bible 1
I. the beginning was the Word Bible 308
inability
i. of the human mind Lovecraft 1
inactivity
wise and masterly i. Mackintosh 1
inanimate
total depravity of i. things
 Katherine Walker 1
inarticulate
raid on the i. T. S. Eliot 108
inattention
i. of one Helen Rowland 8
incarnation
i. was complete F. Scott Fitzgerald 22
incest
i. and folk-dancing Bax 1
inch
every i. a king Shakespeare 305
every other i. a gentleman Woollcott 5
Every Other I. a Lady Lillie 1
inches
die by i. Matthew Henry 1
your nine i. Harriette Wilson 2
incident
curious i. of the dog
 Arthur Conan Doyle 21
incite
I i. this meeting Emmeline Pankhurst 1
incitement
Every idea is an i.
 Oliver Wendell Holmes, Jr. 34

include
i. me out Goldwyn 1
inclusion
Life being all i. Henry James 22
income
Annual i. twenty pounds Dickens 59
Expenditure rises to meet i. Parkinson 6
habits with my net i. Flynn 1
he has i. Nash 13
in favor of an i. tax
 William Jennings Bryan 1
I. Tax has made more Liars
 Will Rogers 4
understand is i. taxes Einstein 35
incommunicable
i. past Cather 6
what i. small terrors infants Drabble 2
incompatability
i. is the spice of life Nash 13
incompetence
rise to his level of i. Peter 1
their level of i. Peter 3
incompetent
election by the i. many
 George Bernard Shaw 19
employee i. to execute Peter 2
incomplete
male is an i. female Solanas 1
incomprehension
gulf of mutual i. Snow 3
inconvenience
amidst i. and distraction
 Samuel Johnson 8
inconveniences
All the modern i. Twain 27
inconvenient
lie even when it is i. Vidal 1
increase
as if i. of appetite Shakespeare 151
i. and diffusion of knowledge
 Smithson 1
may his tribe i. Leigh Hunt 2
incredibly
find the defendants i. guilty
 Mel Brooks 9
increment
Unearned i. of value Mill 26
incurable
i. disease of writing Juvenal 4
Life is an i. disease Abraham Cowley 1
indebted
one thing I'm i. to her for
 W. C. Fields 16
indecent
sent down for i. behavior Waugh 1
indefensible
defence of the i. Orwell 28
indelible
I. in the hippocampus
 Christine Blasey Ford 1
i. stamp of his lowly Charles Darwin 13
independence
i. and liberty Ho Chi Minh 4
I. now Daniel Webster 3
Those who won our i. Brandeis 5
independent
Free and I. States Jefferson 7
i. sovereign state Nkrumah 2
indestructible
looks to an i. Union Salmon P. Chase 2

injustice (cont.):
No i. is done to someone   Ulpian 1
so finely felt, as i.   Dickens 100
ink
buys i. by the barrel   Branigin 1
I. runs from the corners   Strand 2
i.-stained wretches   Woollcott 1
inmate
i. of a mental hospital   Grass 1
inn
gain the timely i.   Shakespeare 368
not an i., but a hospital
Thomas Browne 2
inner
i. personal experiences
William James 18
i. voice which warns us   Mencken 7
no such thing as i. peace   Lebowitz 4
Innisfree
go to I.   Yeats 2
innocence
badge of lost i.   Thomas Paine 3
wept for the end of i.   Golding 1
innocent
changed to protect the i.
Radio Catchphrases 6
i. man is sent t' th' legislature
"Kin" Hubbard 3
i. until proved guilty   Proverbs 156
one i. Person should suffer
Benjamin Franklin 37
source of i. merriment W. S. Gilbert 40
than one i. to be condemned
Fortescue 1
than that one i. suffer   Blackstone 7
virtuous and i.   Voltaire 3
innovate
To i. is not to reform Edmund Burke 24
innuendo
when money comes i.
"Groucho" Marx 11
inoperative
previous statements are i.   Ziegler 2
inquest
divorce, the i.   Helen Rowland 5
inquisition
expects the Spanish I.   Monty Python 6
insane
Man is quite i.   Montaigne 13
our adversaries are i.   Twain 122
insanely
I. great   Jobs 1
insanity
beneficent I. Plea   Twain 7
ground of i.   Tindal 1
I. is doing the same thing
Rita Mae Brown 2
I. is hereditary   Levenson 1
I. runs in my family   Kesselring 1
inscrutable
i. to the last   Thurber 10
insect
into a gigantic i.   Kafka 4
insects
Specialization is for i.   Heinlein 10
insensibility
stark i.   Samuel Johnson 43
inseparable
one and i.   Daniel Webster 7

inside
good for the i. of a man   Proverbs 218
i. the tent pissing out
Lyndon B. Johnson 12
those i. despair   Montaigne 15
what's i. that counts
Modern Proverbs 45
insignificant
how i. this will appear
Samuel Johnson 51
most i. Office   John Adams 12
insincere
being i.   Anne Morrow Lindbergh 3
insincerity
enemy of clear language is i.   Orwell 29
insolence
i. of office   Shakespeare 190
insoluble
disguised as i. problems
John W. Gardner 1
inspiration
Genius is 1 per cent i.   Edison 2
Wit invents, i. reveals   Paz 5
instead
what we have i. of God   Hemingway 5
instincts
for us no i.   John B. Watson 5
institution
Any i. which does not   Robespierre 3
I'm not ready for an i.   Mae West 9
i. is the lengthened shadow
Ralph Waldo Emerson 18
transformed into an i.   Sartre 10
institutions
Liberal i. straightway cease Nietzsche 27
instruction
Back to the i. manual   Ashbery 3
no i. book came with it
R. Buckminster Fuller 4
true histories contain i.   Anne Brontë 1
instructional
write the i. manual   Ashbery 1
instructions
try reading the i.   Sayings 61
instrument
i. plays itself Johann Sebastian Bach 1
make me an i.   St. Francis 2
instruments
i. of European greatness
Alexander Hamilton 4
i. to plague us   Shakespeare 314
What i. we have agree   Auden 18
insubstantial
i. pageant faded   Shakespeare 442
insult
adding i. to injuries   Edward Moore 1
sooner forgotten than an i.
Chesterfield 3
insulted
get i. in places   Sammy Davis, Jr. 1
insurgency
i. is in its last throes   Cheney 2
insurrectionary
Rape was an i. act   Cleaver 1
integers
God made i.   Kronecker 1
integrated
i. into a burning house James Baldwin 3
racially i. community   Alinsky 1

integrity
breaking of one's own i.
D. H. Lawrence 3
Intel
I. inside   Advertising Slogans 61
intellect
chastity of the i.   Santayana 11
no i. comparable to Margaret Fuller 2
revenge of the i.   Sontag 1
intellects
argument and i.   Oliver Goldsmith 5
intellectual
i. brothel   Tolstoy 7
I. freedom is essential   Sakharov 1
i. hatred is the worst   Yeats 24
i. on the winning side   Havel 2
i. prostitutes   Swinton 3
intellectuals
anti-Semitism of the i.   Viereck 1
I'm one of the i.   Sherwood 1
i. of this country deserve   Einstein 19
intelligence
arresting human i. long enough
Leacock 2
Artificial I.   John McCarthy 1
emotional i.   Goleman 1
explain school to a higher i.
Film Lines 73
i. which could comprehend   Laplace 1
Military i.   "Groucho" Marx 48
raises the i. quotient
Clare Boothe Luce 6
specimen of I., Military
Aldous Huxley 2
sum of i. on the planet   Arthur Bloch 1
test of a first-rate i.
F. Scott Fitzgerald 40
underestimating the i.   Mencken 35
utterly inadequate that i. is   Einstein 12
intelligent
highly i. beings   Wheelock 1
honest and i.   Orwell 32
i. life exists   Watterson 1
one i. man   Maimonides 3
intelligentsia
belong to the i.   Orwell 22
written for the i.   Coward 15
intensity
full of passionate i.   Yeats 29
intentions
Hell is full of good i.   St. Bernard 2
paved with good i.   Proverbs 255
your i. are honorable   Beaumarchais 2
intercourse
No woman needs i.   Dworkin 2
Sexual i. began   Larkin 2
interest
compound i.   Einstein 37
great i. of man   Daniel Webster 12
regard to their own i.   Adam Smith 2
interesting
it be i.   Henry James 8
live in i. times   Sayings 39
more i. to men   Virginia Woolf 10
most i. man in the world
Advertising Slogans 41
proposition be i.   Whitehead 8
Very i.   Television Catchphrases 56

Italian
I. navigator has landed
    Arthur H. Compton 1
Italy
I. is a geographical
    Klemens von Metternich 1
Paradise of exiles, I.   Percy Shelley 1
itches
scratch where it i.   Alice Longworth 5
itchez
When Ah i.   Nash 11
itching
have an i. palm   Shakespeare 127
Ithaka
set out for I.   Cavafy 3
itsy
i. bitsy teenie weenie   Paul J. Vance 1
Ivan
I. Ilych's life had been   Tolstoy 13
ivory
in his i. tower   Sainte-Beuve 1
i. on which I work   Austen 17
ivy
i. colleges   Stanley Woodward 1

J

jabberwock
Beware the J.   Carroll 28
hast thou slain the J.   Carroll 29
Jack
Hit the road J.   Mayfield 1
house that J. built   Nursery Rhymes 28
J. and Jill went up the hill
    Nursery Rhymes 26
J. be nimble   Nursery Rhymes 27
J. Frost nipping   Robert Wells 1
J. Sprat could eat no fat
    Nursery Rhymes 30
Little J. Horner   Nursery Rhymes 29
makes J. a dull boy   Proverbs 334
no female J. the Ripper   Paglia 2
you are no J. Kennedy   Bentsen 1
jackpot
you just hit the j.   Stan Lee 2
Jackson
J. standing like a stone wall   Bee 1
Jacqueline
man who accompanied J. Kennedy
    John F. Kennedy 20
Jacques
Frère J.   Folk and Anonymous Songs 25
jagged
j. little pill   Morrissette 3
jail
Go to j.   Charles B. Darrow 1
like living in j.   Richard Wright 1
ship is being in a j.   Samuel Johnson 50
They are in j.   Clarence S. Darrow 1
jailer
What j. so inexorable   Hawthorne 16
jails
J. and prisons   Angela Y. Davis 1
not enough j.   Humphrey 1
jam
j. to-morrow   Carroll 36
James
Bond—J. Bond   Ian Fleming 1

J. J. Morrison Morrison   Milne 2
work of Henry J.   Guedalla 1
Jane
J., J., tall as a crane   Sitwell 1
J., you ignorant slut
    Television Catchphrases 64
Me Tarzan, you J.   Weismuller 1
jangled
sweet bells j.   Shakespeare 199
jangling
j. around gently   Paige 3
Japan
not necessarily to J.'s advantage
    Hirohito 1
this island country of J.   Tojo 1
Japanese
If any J. returns   Tokugawa Iemitsu 3
J. ships are strictly   Tokugawa Iemitsu 1
No J. is permitted   Tokugawa Iemitsu 2
jar
on my desk, in a j.   Robert Bloch 2
person in the bell j.   Plath 4
placed a j. in Tennessee
    Wallace Stevens 1
Jarndyce
J. and J. drones on   Dickens 79
J. and J. still drags its   Dickens 81
Wards in J.   Dickens 89
jars
j. two hemispheres   Thomas Hardy 26
jaw
Meeting j. to j.   Winston Churchill 42
jawbone
j. of an ass   Bible 78
jaws
j. of death   Bartas 1
j. of Death   Tennyson 41
j. of power   John Adams 2
j. of victory   Sayings 18
j.' hooked clamp   Ted Hughes 7
jazz
J. was like the kind of man   Ellington 4
Tales of the J. Age   F. Scott Fitzgerald 4
je
J. pense, donc je suis   Descartes 4
jealous
j. God   Bible 52
j. mistress   Story 1
law is a j. science
    William Jones (1746–1794) 1
To j., nothing is   Françoise Sagan 1
to the j. confirmations   Shakespeare 273
jealousy
j. can no more bear   George Eliot 2
Jeanie
I dream of J.   Stephen Foster 6
jeepers
J. creepers   Johnny Mercer 1
Jefferson
Here was buried Thomas J.   Jefferson 53
J., YOKNAPATAWPHA CO.   Faulkner 6
Thomas J. dined alone
    John F. Kennedy 25
Thomas J. still survives   John Adams 21
Jehovah
name of the Lord J.   Ethan Allen 1
Jekyll
Dr. J. and Mr. Hyde
    Robert Louis Stevenson 18

jelly
like a bowlfull of j.   Clement C. Moore 4
secrete a j.   Virginia Woolf 17
Jenny
J. kissed me   Leigh Hunt 5
jeopardy
twice put in j.   Constitution 14
Jeremiah
J. was a bullfrog   Hoyt Axton 1
Jericho
Joshua fit the battle of J.
    Folk and Anonymous Songs 44
Jerusalem
If I forget thee, O J.   Bible 123
Next year in J.   Anonymous 20
Till we have built J.   William Blake 21
was J. builded here   William Blake 19
jest
fellow of infinite j.   Shakespeare 226
Life is a j.   Gay 2
spoken in j.   Proverbs 306
jesting
What is truth? said j. Pilate
    Francis Bacon 23
jests
He j. at scars   Shakespeare 32
Jesus
Al Jolson is greater than J.
    Zelda Fitzgerald 2
Either this man [J.]   C. S. Lewis 3
good enough for J.   Sayings 21
J. Christ Superstar   Tim Rice 2
J. Christ . . . who are you   Tim Rice 1
J. died for somebody's   Patti Smith 1
J. loves me   Anna Warner 1
J. of Nazareth was   Eddy 3
J. wept   Bible 322
J. wept   Hugo 9
just like J.'s son   Lou Reed 1
more important than J.   Lennon 13
never heard of J.   "Charlie" Chaplin 2
What would J. do   Sheldon 1
jet
leavin' on a j. plane   Denver 1
Jew
avoid the J.   Karl Jay Shapiro 4
Germany will declare that I am a J.
    Einstein 6
Hath not a J. eyes   Shakespeare 76
I shall become a Swiss J.   Einstein 4
important J. who died in exile   Auden 6
J. reading a Nazi manual   Steinem 1
neither J. nor Gentile   Frankfurter 2
not really a J.   Jonathan Miller 1
jewelry
just rattle your j.   Lennon 1
jewels
useless Fashion of wearing J.
    Benjamin Franklin 40
Jewish
first non-J. professor   Tillich 2
J. man with parents alive   Roth 2
J. nation remained   Ibsen 3
My son's only half J.   "Groucho" Marx 44
national home for the J. people
    Balfour 1
No J. blood   Yevtushenko 1
You don't have to be J.
    Advertising Slogans 72

Jews
born King of the J.   Bible 196
How odd of God to choose the J.   Ewer 1
J. are among the aristocracy
                                    George Eliot 18
J. have produced   Stein 16
thrown back at all J.   Anne Frank 2
till the Conversion of the J.
                                    Andrew Marvell 11
We J. walk closer   George Steiner 2
When Hitler attacked the J.   Niemöller 1

Jill
Jack and J. went up the hill
                                    Nursery Rhymes 26

Jim
He's dead, J.   Star Trek 3

jimmy
J., crack corn
                    Folk and Anonymous Songs 9

jingle
J. Bells   Pierpont 2

jingo
by j. if we do   G. W. Hunt 1

jitter
J. Bug   Swayzee 1

jivin'
she could be j.   B. B. King 2

job
Choose a j. you love
                        Modern Proverbs 46
Take This J. and Shove   Coe 1
we will finish the j.
                    Winston Churchill 19
when your neighbor loses his j.   Beck 1

jobs
There are very few j.
                    Florynce Kennedy 3

Joe
dreamed I saw J. Hill   Alfred Hayes 1
Hey J.   Hendrix 2
Say it ain't so, J.   Anonymous 26
Where have you gone, J. DiMaggio
                                Paul Simon 7

jog
J. on, j. on   Shakespeare 450

Johannesburg
No second J. is needed   Paton 3

John
J., why do you not speak   Alden 1
J. Brown's body
                Folk and Anonymous Songs 40
J. Henry was just a li'l baby
                Folk and Anonymous Songs 42
J. Thomas says good-night
                            D. H. Lawrence 6
my son J.   Nursery Rhymes 31
there goes J. Bradford   John Bradford 1

Johnny
Frankie and J.
                Folk and Anonymous Songs 23
Go J. go   Chuck Berry 4
He-e-ere's . . . J.
                Television Catchphrases 75
J., I hardly knew ye   Ballads 4
J. One Note   Lorenz Hart 4
J.'s so long at the fair
                Folk and Anonymous Songs 57
When J. comes marching home
                        Patrick S. Gilmore 1

Johnson
J. did when he should
                    George Bernard Shaw 33

join
J. me, and together   George Lucas 16
j. together this Man
                Book of Common Prayer 16
someday you'll j. us   Lennon 10
will you j. the dance   Carroll 21

joined
God hath j. together   Bible 249
God hath j. together
                Book of Common Prayer 19
should not be j. together
                Book of Common Prayer 13

joint
J. Is Jumpin'   Razaf 2
time is out of j.   Shakespeare 173

joints
Of all the gin j.   Film Lines 43

joke
every j. that's possible   W. S. Gilbert 48
Housekeeping ain't no j.
                    Louisa May Alcott 3
j. is ultimately a custard pie   Orwell 13
Life is a j.   W. S. Gilbert 35
something of a dirty j.   Steinem 2
That's a j., son   Fred Allen 1

joker
said the j. to the thief   Dylan 21

jokes
difference of taste in j.   George Eliot 17

jolly
he's a j. good fellow
                Folk and Anonymous Songs 22
season to be j.
                Folk and Anonymous Songs 17

Jolson
Al J. is greater   Zelda Fitzgerald 2

Joltin'
J. Joe has left   Paul Simon 7

Jones
This is the army, Mr. J.   Irving Berlin 9

Joneses
Keeping Up with the J.   Momand 1

Jordan
J. and the Ilyssus   Disraeli 19

Joseph
must have traduced J. K.   Kafka 8

Josephine
Not tonight, J.   Sayings 43

Joshua
J. fit the battle of Jericho
                Folk and Anonymous Songs 44

jostling
j. in the street   William Blake 18

jour
j. de gloire est arrivé   Rouget de Lisle 1

journalism
but why j.   Balfour 3
J. governs for ever   Wilde 50
J. is the ability to meet   Rebecca West 7
J. largely consists in saying
                            Chesterton 22
Rock j.   Zappa 2

journalist
British j.   Humbert Wolfe 1
business of the New York j.   Swinton 2

Every j. who is not too stupid
                                Malcolm 1

journey
Here is my j.'s end   Shakespeare 281
I prepare for a j.   Katherine Mansfield 2
j. of a thousand miles   Lao Tzu 9
Life is a j.   Modern Proverbs 49
long j. towards oblivion
                            D. H. Lawrence 9
Men Wanted for Hazardous J.
                                Shackleton 3
middle of the j. of our life   Dante 2

joy
J., beautiful radiance   Schiller 1
J., n. An emotion   Bierce 68
j. in labor   William Morris 2
J. of Cooking   Rombauer 1
j. of the working   Kipling 15
J. to the world   Hoyt Axton 2
J. to the world   Watts 3
let j. be unconfined   Byron 2
neither j., nor love   Matthew Arnold 18
no j. in Mudville   Ernest L. Thayer 4
politics of j.   Humphrey 2
possess the secret of j.   Ricciardi 1
possess the secret of j.   Alice Walker 8
Resistance is the secret of j.
                            Alice Walker 9
Strength through j.   Ley 1
Surprised by j.   William Wordsworth 27
thing of beauty is a j.   Keats 9
tidings of great j.   Bible 289
When J. and Duty clash
                                Wiggin 1

Judaism
Christianity is completed J.   Disraeli 15
J. had been a religion
                        Sigmund Freud 19

Judas
jealous J.   Graham Greene 3
J. Iscariot was nothing   Twain 12
J. who writes the biography   Wilde 3

judge
decision of no unjust j.
                        Daniel Webster 10
Here come de j.
                Television Catchphrases 59
I am as sober as a j.   Henry Fielding 2
j. a book by the cover   Proverbs 32
j. has had for breakfast   Hutchins 1
j. in his own cause   Proverbs 157
J. not, that ye be not judged   Bible 221
j. ourselves by our ideals   Nicolson 1
more difficult to j. oneself
                        Saint-Exupéry 4
never sleeps, the j.   Cormac McCarthy 1
own mouth will I j.   Bible 304
overspeaking j. is no well-tuned
                        Francis Bacon 14
who am I to j. him   Francis 1

judged
heart is not j.   Film Lines 197
j. as a captain   Columbus 1
j. by the color   Martin Luther King, Jr. 13
that ye be not j.   Bible 221

judges
as j. we are neither Jew   Frankfurter 2
lot of mediocre j.   Hruska 1
what the j. say   Charles Evans Hughes 1

k. thinking, Butch   Film Lines 37
K. up appearances   Dickens 50
K. your eye on the ball   Proverbs 158
K. your eyes wide open
                    Benjamin Franklin 18
k. your powder dry   Cromwell 4
K. Your Sunny Side Up   Lew Brown 1
K. yourself to yourself   Dickens 8
republic, if you can k. it
                    Benjamin Franklin 44
shop will k. you   Proverbs 159
someday it'll k. you   Mae West 15
Three may k. a secret   Proverbs 294
try to k. it all the year   Dickens 47
we are going to k. it   Richard Nixon 1
we k. a-comin'   Steinbeck 4
which I also k. handy   W. C. Fields 25
keeper
my brother's k.   Bible 23
keepers
Finders k.   Proverbs 103
keeping
K. Up with the Joneses   Momand 1
keeps
apple a day k. the doctor
                   Modern Proverbs 1
k. going, and going
                Advertising Slogans 44
known by the company he k.
                        Proverbs 50
Time is what k. everything
                    Ray Cummings 1
kemo
K. Sabe   Radio Catchphrases 17
Kennedy
Mrs. K. is going   Lady Bird Johnson 1
you are no Jack K.   Bentsen 1
Kennedys
Who killed the K.
                Jagger and Richards 11
Kenneth
What is the frequency, K.   Tager 1
Kenny
They killed K.
            Television Catchphrases 72
Kentucky
old K. home   Stephen Foster 5
kept
He k. us out of war   Glynn 1
I have k. the faith   Bible 379
I k. my word   de la Mare 2
kernel
k. of the brute   Goethe 11
Kerouac
K. opened a million coffee bars
                William S. Burroughs 4
kettle
Polly put the k. on   Nursery Rhymes 57
speech is like a cracked k.   Flaubert 1
Kew
his Highness' dog at K.   Pope 36
key
with this k. Shakespeare
              William Wordsworth 28
Keynesians
We are all K. now   Milton Friedman 6
keys
k. of the kingdom of heaven Bible 246

kick
first k. I took   Springsteen 4
I get a k. out of you   Cole Porter 5
k. against the pricks   Bible 332
make a bishop k. a hole
                Raymond Chandler 5
Nixon to k. around   Richard Nixon 3
tried to k. a little ass
          George Herbert Walker Bush 15
kicked
stumbled over and being k.
          Oliver Wendell Holmes, Jr. 4
kicking
dragged k. and screaming
                Adlai E. Stevenson 13
kid
Here's looking at you, k.   Film Lines 44
I k. you not   Wouk 2
There's one more k.   Neil Young 6
kidnapped
other k. grandchildren   Getty 2
kids
k. did you kill today Political Slogans 20
leave those k. alone   Roger Waters 2
kill
fall will probably k. you   Film Lines 40
forever bent upon the k.   Geoffrey Hill 1
go and k. the yellow man   Springsteen 5
Guns don't k. people
                 Political Slogans 18
he knows he shouldn't k. Sainte-Marie 2
I k. you   Chamfort 2
I'll k. you if you quote it
                   Gelett Burgess 8
I will k. you   Film Lines 168
kids did you k. today
                 Political Slogans 20
k. Americans   bin Laden 1
k. a wife with kindness   Shakespeare 9
k. an admiral   Voltaire 9
K. everyone, and you are a god
                     Jean Rostand 1
K. reverence   Rand 2
k. the patient   Francis Bacon 11
K. them all   Arnauld-Amaury 1
k. you in a new way   Will Rogers 14
let's k. all the lawyers   Shakespeare 6
licence to k.   Ian Fleming 1
nothing to k. or die for   Lennon 9
smile as you k.   Lennon 7
sure you shall k. him
                Ralph Waldo Emerson 21
They k. us for their sport
                    Shakespeare 304
Thou shalt not k.   Bible 56
Thou shalt not k.   Clough 4
to k. a mockingbird   Harper Lee 4
we are going to k. it   Colin Powell 1
What does not k. me   Nietzsche 25
When I k. a man   Akutagawa 1
Why do we k. people   Near 1
you can k. anyone   Puzo 3
killed
Curiosity k. the cat
               Modern Proverbs 20
Hard work never k. anybody   Bergen 1
I would have k. myself   Cioran 1
so I k. her   Dumas the Elder 1

They k. Kenny
            Television Catchphrases 72
When a man's partner is k.   Hammett 2
Who k. Cock Robin   Nursery Rhymes 12
Who k. the Kennedys
                Jagger and Richards 11
Woman K. with Kindness   Heywood 1
killeth
letter k.   Bible 360
killing
K. them, therefore   Peter Singer 1
medal for k. two men   Matlovich 1
killings
Outside of the k.   Barry 1
kills
k. its pupils   Berlioz 1
k. reason itself   Milton 6
k. the thing he loves   Wilde 92
those that will not break it k.
                    Hemingway 10
who k. a man   Milton 6
killy-loo
Law is the k. bird   Rodell 2
Kilmer
Surely the K. tongue Heywood Broun 2
Kilroy
K. was here   Faulkner 17
K. was here   Sayings 33
kin
makes the whole world k.
                   Shakespeare 250
more than k.   Shakespeare 147
kind
be k.   Robert Anderson 2
Be k. to your web-footed friends
              Folk and Anonymous Songs 5
cruel only to be k.   Shakespeare 217
K. hearts are more than coronets
                       Tennyson 4
k. of guy who would   McInerney 1
k. word and a gun   Corey 1
less than k.   Shakespeare 147
what k. of man   Thoreau 17
kinder
k., gentler nation
          George Herbert Walker Bush 5
make k. the face of the nation
          George Herbert Walker Bush 6
kindergarten
need to know in k.   Kaminer 1
kindle
k. a light in the darkness   Jung 5
kindly
Lead, k. Light   John Henry Newman 1
kindness
kill a wife with k.   Shakespeare 9
k. I've received   Maugham 8
k. of strangers   Tennessee Williams 5
milk of human k.   Shakespeare 333
RANDOM K. AND SENSELESS ACTS
                       Anne Herbert 1
Woman Killed with K.   Heywood 1
we need k.   Film Lines 91
We'll tak a cup o' k.   Robert Burns 9
king
all the k.'s horses   Nursery Rhymes 24
anointed k.   Shakespeare 19
born K. of the Jews   Bible 196

king (cont.):

catch the conscience of the K.
    Shakespeare 187
despised, and dying k. Percy Shelley 8
every inch a k. Shakespeare 305
Every Man a K. Huey Long 1
Glory to the new-born K.
    Charles Wesley 1
God save the k. Bible 82
God save the k. Henry Carey 2
heart and stomach of a k. Elizabeth I 2
history of the present K. Jefferson 4
I served my K. Shakespeare 452
I'm the k. of the world Film Lines 176
in America the law is k.
    Thomas Paine 4
It's good to be the k. Mel Brooks 1
k., moreover, is not only Blackstone 5
K. born of all England Malory 1
k. can do no wrong Blackstone 6
k. can do no wrong Proverbs 160
K. Charles's head Dickens 63
K. COTTON Christy 1
k. for a night Film Lines 108
k. is always a k. Wollstonecraft 9
k. is dead Sayings 34
k. is history's slave Tolstoy 4
K. of England cannot enter
    William Pitt, Earl of Chatham 2
k. of infinite space Shakespeare 179
k. of shreds and patches
    Shakespeare 215
k. of the road Roger Miller 2
k. sits in Dumferling toune Ballads 7
k. was pregnant Le Guin 4
k. will never leave
    Elizabeth the Queen Mother, 1
Never strike a k.
    Ralph Waldo Emerson 21
not offended the k. Thomas More 4
Old K. Cole Nursery Rhymes 13
once and future k. Malory 3
one-eyed man is k. Erasmus 1
Ozymandias, k. of kings Percy Shelley 7
singeing of the K. of Spain's
    Francis Drake 1
strangle the last k. Diderot 4
that an idle k. Tennyson 14
the K.'s our only lord Lope de Vega 2
to be a Pirate K. W. S. Gilbert 14
Your K. and Country
    Advertising Slogans 138

kingdom

enter into the k. of God Bible 250
enter into the k. of heaven Bible 248
keys of the k. of heaven Bible 246
k., and the power Bible 215
k. by the sea Poe 16
k. given them isn't worth
    Louisa May Alcott 6
k. of God is within you Bible 303
k. of heaven is at hand Bible 198
My k. for a horse Shakespeare 5
My mind to me a k. is Earl of Oxford 1
Obscenity is such a tiny k.
    Heywood Broun 3
theirs is the k. of heaven Bible 204
Thy k. come Bible 215
thy k. come Missal 5

to death's other K. T. S. Eliot 65

kingfish

call me the K. Huey Long 2

kingly

presented him a k. crown
    Shakespeare 116

kings

captains and the k. depart Kipling 22
change my state with k.
    Shakespeare 416
control even k. Molière 11
happy as k. Robert Louis Stevenson 13
k. is mostly rapscallions Twain 32
of cabbages—and k. Carroll 34
only five K. left Farouk 1
philosophers become k. Plato 7
politeness of k. Louis XVIII 2
sport of k. Somerville 1
stories of the death of k. Shakespeare 21
such is the breath of k. Shakespeare 13
walk with K. Kipling 33

Kingsley

Making Cocoa for K. Amis Cope 1

Kinnock

first K. in a thousand Kinnock 3

kinquering

K. congs Spooner 3

Kipling

Do you like K. McGill 1
Rudyards cease from k. J. K. Stephen 1
sort of gutless K. Orwell 9

kippled

I've never k. McGill 1

kiss

come let us k. and part Drayton 1
first k. is magic Raymond Chandler 12
I couldn't k. the girl James M. Cain 4
I want him to k. my ass
    Lyndon B. Johnson 13
I will not k. your f.ing flag
    e.e. cummings 13
I'd love to k. you Film Lines 41
immortal with a k. Marlowe 9
k. a lot of toads Modern Proverbs 69
k. is still a k. Hupfeld 1
K. K. Bang Bang Kael 1
K. me, Hardy Horatio Nelson 8
K. me, Kate Shakespeare 8
K. my grits Television Catchphrases 7
k. of death Alfred E. Smith 2
k. on the hand Robin 2
"k.-k." and "bang-bang" Powdermaker 1
May I k. the hand Joyce 27
must not k. and tell Congreve 3
When women k. Mencken 12
while I k. the sky Hendrix 3

kissed

Jenny k. me Leigh Hunt 5
k. the girls Nursery Rhymes 18
she wants to be k. Chanel 2

kissing

k. your hand Loos 2
like k. God Lenny Bruce 4
like k. Hitler Tony Curtis 1
like k. your sister Edgar E. Miller 1
when the k. had to stop
    Robert Browning 17

Kissinger

K. brought peace to Vietnam Heller 7

kit-bag

troubles in your old k. Asaf 1

kitchen

in the k. with Dinah
    Folk and Anonymous Songs 39
k. things Glaspell 1
sitting in the k. sink Dodie Smith 1
stay out of the k. Purcell 1

kitten

trouble with a k. Nash 12

kittens

Three little k. Nursery Rhymes 32

Klan

K. is actually Mencken 34

knave

supposed a k. David Hume 5

knee

banjo on my k. Stephen Foster 1
every k. should bow Bible 369

knees

fell upon their k. William Bradford 1
fell upon their k. Evarts 1
live on your k. Ibarruri 1
water up to his k. "Groucho" Marx 44

knell

curfew tolls the k. Thomas Gray 3

knew

builded better than he k.
    Ralph Waldo Emerson 32
he nothing k. Milton 45
I hardly k. ye Ballads 4
I k. him, Horatio Shakespeare 226
I k. nothing about it Brink 1
If men k. how women O. Henry 3
k. you had it in you Dorothy Parker 28

knife

Fear tastes like a rusty k. John Cheever 1
I am the k. and the wound Baudelaire 3
sharpening my oyster k. Hurston 1
when they take the k. Emily Dickinson 3

knight

K. of the Doleful Countenance
    Cervantes 3
like a plumed k. Ingersoll 1

knight-at-arms

what can ail thee k. Keats 13

knight-errantry

K. is religion Cervantes 4

knights

K. who say . . . NI! Monty Python 12

knits

k. up the ravell'd sleave Shakespeare 354

knives

night of the long k. Hitler 2

knocked

k. the bastard off Hillary 1

knockin'

k. on heaven's door Dylan 23

knocking

k. on the moonlit door de la Mare 1
k. the American system Capone 1

knocks

Opportunity never k. twice
    Proverbs 227

knot

tie a k. and hang on
    Franklin D. Roosevelt 31

know

Ah doan k. nuthin' Margaret Mitchell 3

lady (cont.):
fat l. sings   Ralph Carpenter 1
Give the l. what she wants
          Marshall Field 1
know at once she was a l.
          Flannery O'Connor 1
l., or the tiger   Stockton 1
L., three white leopards   T. S. Eliot 79
l. doth protest too much
          Shakespeare 204
l. is a tramp   Lorenz Hart 5
l. like a whore   Mizner 11
l. novelist   W. S. Gilbert 33
l. of Christ's College   Aubrey 1
L. of Shalott   Tennyson 1
L. with a Lamp   Longfellow 20
L.'s Not for Burning   Christopher Fry 1
l.'s not for turning   Thatcher 4
Luck Be a L. Tonight   Loesser 6
my fair l.   Nursery Rhymes 34
My L. Bountiful   Farquhar 1
Oh l., be good to me   Gershwin 1
Old L. of Threadneedle Street   Gillray 1
Seymour's Fat L.   Salinger 7
She ain't no l.   Joseph Weber 1
young l. of Niger   Monkhouse 1
ladybird
L., l., fly away home   Nursery Rhymes 33
Lafayette
L., we are here   Charles E. Stanton 1
laid
l. end to end   Dorothy Parker 47
lair
Rouse the lion from his l.
          Walter Scott 14
laisser
l. faire   Boisguilbert 1
L. faire   Quesnay 1
laissez
L. faire does not mean   Mises 2
laity
conspiracies against the l.
          George Bernard Shaw 28
lake
took the l. between my legs   Kumin 1
lamb
blood of the L.   Bible 393
dwell with the l.   Bible 167
goes out like a l.   Proverbs 188
he who made the L.   William Blake 12
L. of God   Bible 312
L. of God   Missal 6
l. to the slaughter   Bible 178
Mary had a little l.   Sara Hale 1
lambs
poor little l. who've lost our way
          Kipling 9
lame
Science without religion is l.   Einstein 15
Lamont
divinity of L. Cranston   Baraka 1
lamp
Lady with a L.   Longfellow 20
lift my l. beside the golden   Lazarus 2
lamppost
asking a l. what it feels   Osborne 2
lamps
l. are going out   Edward Grey 1
old l. for new ones   Arabian Nights 1

lance
keep a l. upon a rack   Cervantes 1
land
all over this l.   Pete Seeger 1
appeared the l.   Columbus 3
between the l. and the ship
          George Lucas 12
by sea as by l.   Humphrey Gilbert 1
fat of the l.   Bible 37
give me l.   Cole Porter 17
going to the L. of Nod   Jonathan Swift 33
I saw l.   Charles Lindbergh 2
I wish I was in de l.   Emmett 1
if by L., one   Revere 1
I've seen the promised l.
          Martin Luther King, Jr. 20
l. as a community   Leopold 1
l. flowing with milk and honey   Bible 41
l. is not to be sold   Pearl S. Buck 2
L. is the only thing   Margaret Mitchell 1
L. of Hope and Glory   A. C. Benson 1
l. of lost content   Housman 3
l. of my fathers   Evan James 1
L. of Unlimited Possibilities
          Goldberger 1
L. That Time Forgot
          Edgar Rice Burroughs 2
l. was ours before we were   Frost 21
liberty throughout all the l.   Bible 66
like a l. of dreams   Matthew Arnold 18
my own, my native l.   Walter Scott 2
o'er the l. of the free   Francis Scott Key 2
One if by l.   Longfellow 24
Plymouth Rock would l. on them
          Cole Porter 4
precious than a piece of l.   Sadat 1
private property in l.   Mill 1
raised on city l.
          Charles Dudley Warner 3
stranger in a strange l.   Bible 38
supreme Law of the L.   Constitution 10
There is a l. of the living
          Thornton Wilder 1
they had the l.   Dick Gregory 4
This l. is your l.   "Woody" Guthrie 6
unexploded l. mines   Mueller 1
landed
Eagle has l.   Neil A. Armstrong 2
Italian navigator has l.
          Arthur H. Compton 1
Plymouth Rock l. on us   Malcolm X 2
landing
l. a man on the moon
          John F. Kennedy 19
landmarks
great l. in man's struggle
          William O. Douglas 3
lands
shall I at least set my l.   T. S. Eliot 59
landscape
mute melancholy l.   Wharton 2
language
circle of the English l.   James Murray 1
disease of l.   Müller 1
dream of a common l.   Rich 8
except, of course, l.   Wilde 4
Finality is not the l.   Disraeli 20
great enemy of clear l.   Orwell 29
L. and our thought-grooves   Sapir 2

L. can . . . be compared   Saussure 4
l. charged with meaning   Ezra Pound 18
l. into its meaning   T. S. Eliot 35
l. is a dialect with an army   Weinreich 1
L. is the dress of thought
          Samuel Johnson 33
L. is the house of Being   Heidegger 1
l. of the heart   Pope 34
l. of the unheard
          Martin Luther King, Jr. 17
L. speaks   Heidegger 2
Life is a foreign l.   Christopher Morley 3
limits of my l.   Wittgenstein 2
mobilized the English l.   Murrow 5
My l. is understood   Haydn 2
mystery of l. was revealed
          Helen Keller 2
obscurity of a learned l.   Gibbon 11
Our l. lacks words   Primo Levi 1
Political l. . . . is designed   Orwell 31
separated by the same l.
          George Bernard Shaw 58
she speaks a various l.
          William Cullen Bryant 2
Slang is l. that takes off   Sandburg 13
unconscious is structured like a l.
          Lacan 1
what is l.   Saussure 1
languages
our native l.   Whorf 1
woman speaks eighteen l.
          Dorothy Parker 27
lap
I like to see it l.   Emily Dickinson 13
lies in the l.   Homer 6
lapel
plucked from my l.   O. Henry 7
Lara
One day L. went out   Pasternak 4
larceny
You sparkle with l.   Mizner 10
Laredo
in the streets of L.
          Folk and Anonymous Songs 13
large
hated by l. numbers of people   Orwell 5
I am l.   Whitman 8
l. as life, and twice as natural   Carroll 42
l. as life and twice as natural
          Haliburton 1
l. nose is the mark   Cyrano de Bergerac 1
L. party waiting   Taft 1
larger
children of a l. growth   John Dryden 3
Send up a l. room   "Groucho" Marx 33
largest
Shout with the l.   Dickens 3
lariat
with gun or l.   Dorothy Parker 37
lark
Hark, hark, the l.   Shakespeare 435
like to the l.   Shakespeare 415
larke
bisy l., messager of day   Chaucer 13
larks
What l.   Dickens 102
Las Vegas
Fear and Loathing in L.
          Hunter S. Thompson 1

lash
prayers, and the l.   Winston Churchill 45
lassie
I love a l.   Lauder 1
last
always the l. to know   Proverbs 150
Ambition is the l. refuge   Wilde 68
as if it were your l.   Modern Proverbs 53
best who laughs l.   Proverbs 164
Consistency is the l. refuge   Wilde 121
die in the l. ditch   William 1
Free at l.   Folk and Anonymous Songs 24
Good to the l. drop
    Advertising Slogans 78
He is the First and the L.   Koran 14
his l. breath   Twain 102
in its l. throes   Cheney 2
l. best, hope of earth   Lincoln 37
l. breath of, say, Julius Caesar   Jeans 2
l. chapter is wanting   Thomas Hardy 5
l. enchantments of the Middle Age
    Matthew Arnold 8
l. enemy that shall be destroyed
    Bible 357
l. Englishman to rule in India   Nehru 3
L. Hurrah   Edwin O'Connor 1
l. in the American League
    Charles Dryden 1
l. infirmity of noble mind   Milton 2
l. leaf upon the tree
    Oliver Wendell Holmes 1
l. man to die for a mistake   Kerry 1
L. night I dreamt   Du Maurier 1
l. of the Mohicans
    James Fenimore Cooper 1
L. of the Red-Hot Mamas   Yellen 2
l. refuge of a scoundrel
    Samuel Johnson 80
l. refuge of the complex   Wilde 28
l. romance   Wilde 62
l. shall be first   Bible 252
l. syllable of recorded time
    Shakespeare 393
l. territorial claim   Hitler 4
l. time I saw Paris   Hammerstein 4
l. time I see Paris   Elliot Paul 1
l. voice you hear   Sinatra 2
love would l. for ever   Auden 1
my l. Duchess   Robert Browning 3
my l. press conference   Richard Nixon 3
our l. dance   Bowie 4
prepare for the l. war   Tuchman 1
they l. while they last   de Gaulle 7
This is the l. of earth
    John Quincy Adams 3
wait for the L. Judgment   Camus 8
When Earth's l. picture   Kipling 14
will later be l.   Dylan 7
world's l. night   Donne 8
lasted
l. for twenty-five years   W. C. Fields 28
lasting
has more l. value   Pirsig 4
lasts
l. for a thousand years
    Winston Churchill 15
Nothing l. forever   Proverbs 217
late
Better l. than never   Proverbs 23

Catholic girls start much too l.   Joel 3
don't call me l. to dinner   Sayings 19
even that too l.   Nevins 1
gets l. early out there   Berra 8
I shall be too l.   Carroll 3
L. l. yestreen I saw   Ballads 8
l. onpleasantniss   Nasby 1
never too l.   Proverbs 208
rather l. for me   Larkin 2
latent
his l. homosexuality   Mailer 2
later
l. than you think   Service 4
See you l. alligator   Guidry 1
lateral
term "l. thinking"   De Bono 1
Latin
small L., and less Greek   Jonson 9
Latina
wise L. woman   Sotomayor 1
laugh
badly hurt to l.   Lincoln 53
I hasten to l.   Beaumarchais 1
if I l. at any mortal thing   Byron 25
L., and the world laughs   Wilcox 1
l. is proper to man   Rabelais 1
l. or weep at the folly   Gibbon 8
l. with the sinners   Joel 4
Make her l. at that   Shakespeare 226
you l. at him   Nathan 1
laughed
comedies are not to be l. at   Goldwyn 9
Howard Roark l.   Rand 1
l. all the way to the bank   Liberace 1
l. at Bozo the Clown   Carl Sagan 1
l. like an irresponsible fetus T. S. Eliot 13
They L. When I Sat Down
    Advertising Slogans 124
When he l.   Auden 17
when the first baby l.   Barrie 5
laughing
cannot be always l. at a man   Austen 11
fun you can have without l.   Mencken 41
Leave Them L.   Cohan 2
Little Nell without l.   Wilde 111
most fun I ever had without l.
    Woody Allen 28
penalty for l. in a courtroom   Mencken 8
laughs
He l. best who l. last   Proverbs 164
Man is the only animal that l.   Hazlitt 3
laughter
Against the assault of L.   Twain 125
born with a gift of l.   Sabatini 1
launched
face that l. a thousand ships   Marlowe 8
laundry
Give me a l. list   Rossini 2
law
administer the l.
    Oliver Wendell Holmes, Jr. 43
against the forces of l.
    Michael Harrington 2
Any l. which violates   Robespierre 2
as if it were a l. of nature   Orwell 17
break the l.   Thoreau 7
breaking the spirit of a l.
    Grover Cleveland 1
bred to the l.   Edmund Burke 4

built with stones of L.   William Blake 5
by the l. of the land   Magna Carta 1
care about the l.   Cornelius Vanderbilt 1
Christianity is part of the l.   John Scott 1
due process of l.   Anonymous 30
end of l.   John Locke 6
fence around the L.   Talmud 6
fugitive from th' l.   Mauldin 1
give the Devil benefit of l.   Bolt 1
great principle of the English l.
    Dickens 88
Hard cases make bad l.   Proverbs 136
head and the hoof of the L.   Kipling 19
higher l. than the Constitution   Seward 1
highest respect for l.
    Martin Luther King, Jr. 8
hundred years to make a l.   Beecher 1
I am the l.   Hague 1
I fought the l.   Sonny Curtis 1
Ignorance of the l.   Proverbs 153
Ignorance of the l.   Selden 1
in America the l. is king
    Thomas Paine 4
in the l., concealment   Twain 99
l., which is the perfection   Coke 5
l. embodies the story
    Oliver Wendell Holmes, Jr. 3
l. for those who can afford   Bok 1
l. is a ass   Dickens 20
l. is a jealous science
    William Jones (1746–1794) 1
L. is a science   Langdell 1
l. is a sort of hocus-pocus   Macklin 1
l. is above you   Thomas Fuller 1
l. is always too short
    Robert Penn Warren 1
l. is not concerned with trifles
    Anonymous (Latin) 5
l. is only a memorandum
    Ralph Waldo Emerson 26
l. is such an Ass   Glapthorne 1
L. is the intersection   Fred Shapiro 1
l. is the last result   Samuel Johnson 42
l. is the only profession
    Elliott Dunlap Smith 1
L. is the true embodiment
    W. S. Gilbert 26
l. is too slow   Cornelius Vanderbilt 2
L. is whatever is boldly   Burr 1
L. is where you buy it
    Raymond Chandler 7
L.: It has honored us   Daniel Webster 14
L. must be stable   Roscoe Pound 1
l. not supported by the people
    Humphrey 1
L. of Nations   Grotius 1
L. of the Jungle   Kipling 17
L. of the Jungle—as old and as true
    Kipling 18
l. of the Medes and Persians   Bible 191
l. school belongs   Veblen 6
l. sees and treats women   MacKinnon 1
l. so general a study   Edmund Burke 6
l. unto themselves   Bible 341
lawless science of our l.   Tennyson 42
l.'s delay   Shakespeare 190
lesser breeds without the L.   Kipling 23
letter of the l.   Solzhenitsyn 5

law (cont.):
life of the l.
    Oliver Wendell Holmes, Jr. 2
live outside the l.   Dylan 20
majestic equality of the l.   France 3
man's respect for l.
    Adam Clayton Powell, Jr. 2
may be very good l.   Walter Scott 9
moral l. within me   Kant 6
my maxim become a universal l. Kant 3
nine points of the l.
    Proverbs 239
No brilliance is needed in the l.
    Mortimer 1
no l. for anybody   Wilde 102
No man is above the l.
    Theodore Roosevelt 13
Of L. there can be no less
    Richard Hooker 1
One L. for the Lion & Ox
    William Blake 3
One l. for the rich   Proverbs 165
One with the l.   Coolidge 2
reason for a rule of l.
    Oliver Wendell Holmes, Jr. 14
Reason is the life of the l.   Coke 4
say what the l. is   John Marshall 3
strives to reach the L.   Kafka 2
supreme L. of the Land
    Constitution 10
there will be nothing but l.
    Grant Gilmore 1
this is the l. and the prophets
    Bible 225
truly the L. Giver   Hoadly 1
Wherever L. ends   John Locke 9
who breaks an unjust l.
    Martin Luther King, Jr. 7

lawbreaker
Government becomes a l.   Brandeis 10

lawful
everything would be l.   Dostoyevski 4
Guns aren't l.   Dorothy Parker 9
L., *adj.* Compatible with the   Bierce 2
l. rapes exceed   Sanger 5
this man's l. prey   Ruskin 23

lawless
l. science of our law   Tennyson 42

lawn
l. of life   Schulz 4
L. Tennyson   Joyce 18

laws
all l. which prevent women
    Elizabeth Cady Stanton 4
Bad l. are the worst sort of tyranny
    Edmund Burke 12
bad or obnoxious l.   Ulysses S. Grant 3
care not who makes th' l.   Dunne 4
country's planted thick with l.   Bolt 2
crack a few l.   Mae West 16
empire of l. and not of men
    James Harrington 1
examine the l. of heat   John Morley 1
Good l. lead to the making   Rousseau 7
government of l., and not of men
    John Adams 4
Government of l. and not of men
    Archibald Cox 1

government of l. and not of men
    Gerald R. Ford 3
In the new Code of L.   Abigail Adams 1
L., like sausages   Saxe 1
L. are a dead letter
    Alexander Hamilton 7
L. are like Cobwebs   Jonathan Swift 3
L. are sand   Twain 120
L. are silent in time of war   Cicero 11
l. be so voluminous   Madison 9
l. of death   Ruskin 10
l. of mathematics   Einstein 5
l. or kings can cause or cure
    Samuel Johnson 26
L. too gentle are seldom
    Benjamin Franklin 29
L. were made to be broken   North 2
make the l. of a nation
    Andrew Fletcher 1
more l. and orders   Lao Tzu 8
no end to the l.   Twain 11
not obey the l. too well
    Ralph Waldo Emerson 27
To abolish the fences of l.   Arendt 4
trample bad l.   Wendell Phillips 2
unequal l. unto a savage race
    Tennyson 14
We enact many l.   Benjamin R. Tucker 1
whatever the l. permit   Montesquieu 4
When you break the big l.   Chesterton 5
whether L. be right   Wilde 94
Written l. are like spiders' webs
    Anacharsis 1
you do not make the l.   Grimké 1

lawsuit
I should dread a l.   Hand 1
useless l. in every useless   Elihu Root 1

lawyer
against a l.   Twain 24
as a l. interprets the truth   Giraudoux 1
I'm here as the l.   Brendan Sullivan 1
L., an honest Man   Benjamin Franklin 4
l. has no business with the justice
    Samuel Johnson 41
l. is one who protects you   Mencken 5
l. should never ask   David Graham 1
l. tells me I may do   Edmund Burke 9
l. to tell me what I cannot J. P. Morgan 1
l. with his briefcase   Puzo 1
l. with his hands   Twain 144
l. without history or literature
    Walter Scott 10
l. writes something   Will Rogers 10
l.'s time and advice   Lincoln 69
l.'s truth is not Truth   Thoreau 12
leave l. enough   Film Lines 129
man who is his own l.   Proverbs 112
practice of a decent l.   Elihu Root 2
prairie-l., master of us all   Lindsay 1
To be a great l.   Disraeli 2
when a l. cashes in   Sandburg 9

lawyers
America, the paradise of l.
    Joseph H. Choate 2
cannot live without the l.
    Joseph H. Choate 1
good l.   Daniel Webster 13
heaviest concentration of l.
    "Jimmy" Carter 6

high opinion of l.   Tweed 1
I know you l. can   Gay 4
influence of l.   Tocqueville 8
L., I suppose, were children
    Charles Lamb 3
L., Preachers, and Tomtits
    Benjamin Franklin 7
l. as a body   Tocqueville 10
L. like to leave no stone   Rhode 1
L. should never marry other l.
    Film Lines 1
let's kill all the l.   Shakespeare 6
Maxim among these L.
    Jonathan Swift 15
One hires l.   Heilbrun 2
150. l. should do business   Jefferson 50
Send l., guns, and money   Zevon 3
they become l.   Woody Allen 15
They have no l. among them
    Thomas More 2

lay
l., lady, l.   Dylan 22
l. down his life   Bible 326
l. me down to sleep
    New England Primer 2
L. on, Macduff   Shakespeare 397
l. waste our powers
    William Wordsworth 21
L. your sleeping head   Auden 27
man l. down his wife   Joyce 21

lays
l. eggs for gentlemen
    Nursery Rhymes 21
Wall St. L. an Egg   Silverman 1

LBJ
All the way with L.   Political Slogans 2
Hey, hey, L.   Political Slogans 20

lead
All roads l. to Rome   Proverbs 256
blind l. the blind   Bible 244
don't l. 'em so much   Herr 1
L., kindly Light   John Henry Newman 1
l. a horse to water   Proverbs 148
l. a whore to culture   Dorothy Parker 39
l. us not into temptation   Bible 215
little child shall l. them   Bible 167
paths of glory l.   Thomas Gray 6

leader
I am their l.   Ledru-Rollin 1
l. who doesn't hesitate   Meir 5

leaders
Don't follow l.   Dylan 19

leadeth
he l. me beside the still   Bible 108
that l. to destruction   Bible 226

leaf
are you the l.   Yeats 41
last l. upon the tree
    Oliver Wendell Holmes 1
yellow l.   Shakespeare 389

league
form a l. of peace Theodore Roosevelt 20
Half a l.   Tennyson 37
president of was the American L.
    Giamatti 2

leak
All grammars l.   Sapir 1
prosperity will l. through
    William Jennings Bryan 2

lean
his wife could eat no l.
Nursery Rhymes 30
l. and hungry look   Shakespeare 99
take the fat with the l.   Dickens 73
you can always l.   Warner Anderson 1

leaning
person to make l. unnecessary
Dorothy Canfield Fisher 1

leap
grand L. of the Whale
Benjamin Franklin 32
l. into the dark   Hobbes 11
l. 1/8th of a mile   Siegel 1
l. tall buildings   Radio Catchphrases 21
Look before you l.   Proverbs 175

leapin'
L. lizards   Harold Gray 1

leaps
heart l. up   William Wordsworth 12

Lear
How pleasant to know Mr. L.   Lear 3

learn
cannot l. men from books   Disraeli 3
l. after we think   "Kin" Hubbard 2
l. everything all over   McInerney 2
L. to say, "I don't know"   Rumsfeld 7
live and l.   Pomfret 1
Live and l.   Proverbs 173
school in which we l.   Schwartz 1

learned
l. anything from history   Hegel 3
obscurity of a l. language   Gibbon 11

learning
advance L. and perpetuate it
Anonymous 1
ever l. many things   Solon 1
just enough of l. to misquote   Byron 1
little l. is a dangerous thing   Pope 1
l. doth make thee mad   Bible 339
L. Tree   Gordon Parks 1
love of l.   Longfellow 27

learnt
all that has been l. is forgotten   Conant 1
forgotten nothing and l. nothing
Dumouriez 1

least
best which governs l.   Thoreau 3
l. dangerous to the political rights
Alexander Hamilton 8
myself not l.   Tennyson 17
take the l. of the evils   Aristotle 3
that which governs l.   O'Sullivan 1
Time is the l. thing   Hemingway 33

leather
All my men wear English L.
Advertising Slogans 45
l. or prunella   Pope 25

leave
America: Love It or L. It
Political Slogans 3
Don't l. home without it
Advertising Slogans 11
if you must l. a place   Beryl Markham 1
it will l. without us   Joanne Harris 1
l. in a huff   "Groucho" Marx 17
l. it on the dresser   MacLaine 1
L. me, O Love   Philip Sidney 2
L. No One Behind   Bethune 1

l. off thinking about a thing   Mill 7
l. out the parts   Leonard 3
L. the driving to us
Advertising Slogans 57
l. theirs on the ground   Kinnock 1
L. Them Laughing   Cohan 2
L. well enough alone   Proverbs 166
Love Me or L. Me   Gus Kahn 6
Take me or l. me   Dorothy Parker 16
We'll l. a light on
Advertising Slogans 86

leaves
My regiment l. at dawn
"Groucho" Marx 12
they sewed fig l. together   Bible 17
Though l. are many   Yeats 8
vine l. in his hair   Ibsen 24

leavin'
l. on a jet plane   Denver 1

leaving
became him like the l. it
Shakespeare 331

lectured
I will not be l.   Gillard 1

led
Ben Adhem's name l.   Leigh Hunt 4
blind l. by the blind   Upanishads 2

Ledaean
I dream of a L. body   Yeats 35

lees
drink life to the l.   Tennyson 15

left
any wife has l. any husband
Anthony Powell 1
Education is what is l.   Conant 1
Elvis has l. the building   Horace Logan 1
Exit, stage l.   Television Catchphrases 88
Girl I L. Behind Me
Folk and Anonymous Songs 27
I l. my heart   Cross 1
l. any stone unturned   Euripides 1
let not thy l. hand know   Bible 214
nobody l. to be concerned   Niemöller 1
Thunder on the L.   Christopher Morley 2
to be l. to the politicians   de Gaulle 10
what is l. out of it   Twain 110

leg
calling the tail a l.   Lincoln 63

legal
almost all l. writing   Rodell 1
Hitler did in Germany was "l."
Martin Luther King, Jr. 9
no controlling l. authority   Gore 2
no other scale but the l. one
Solzhenitsyn 4
you have a l. mind
Thomas Reed Powell 1

legality
any taint of l.   Philander C. Knox 1

legalizer
Time is a great l.   Mencken 15

legend
I am l.   Matheson 1
l. is an old man   Miles Davis 1
more or less connected l.   Tolkien 5
Now he is a l.
Jacqueline Kennedy Onassis 2
When the l. becomes fact
Film Lines 113

your l. ever will   John and Taupin 2

legendary
L.   Television Catchphrases 34

legends
l. of the green chapels   Dylan Thomas 12

legion
My name is L.   Bible 277
soldier of the L. lay dying
Caroline Norton 1

legions
give me back my l.   Augustus 1

legislated
Morals cannot be l.
Martin Luther King, Jr. 2

legislative
l. and executive powers   Montesquieu 5

legislator
L., n. A person who goes   Bierce 71
l. of mankind   Samuel Johnson 22

legislators
unacknowledged l. of the world
Auden 39
unacknowledged l. of the world
Percy Shelley 15

legislature
innocent man is sent t' th' l.
"Kin" Hubbard 3
safe while the L. is in session
Gideon J. Tucker 1

legitimate
Let the end be l.   John Marshall 6

legs
FOUR L. GOOD   Orwell 24
lake between my l.   Kumin 1

leisure
amount of real l.   Schumacher 1
L. with dignity   Cicero 13
we may repent at l.   Congreve 1

lemon
If life hands you a l.
Modern Proverbs 48
You can squeeze my l.
Robert Johnson 4

lemonade
make l.   Modern Proverbs 48
starts a l.-stand   Elbert Hubbard 6

lemons
Oranges and l.   Nursery Rhymes 50
takes the l. that Fate hands him
Elbert Hubbard 6

lend
l. me your ears   Shakespeare 111
man who will l. you money
Joe E. Lewis 1
not asked to l. money   Twain 61
to l. a hand   Edward Everett Hale 3

lender
borrower nor a l. be   Shakespeare 160

lends
distance l. enchantment
Thomas Campbell 1

length
What It Lacks in L.   Frost 24
works of major l.   Stravinsky 1

lengthened
institution is the l. shadow
Ralph Waldo Emerson 18

lenient
hoped the court would be l.   Lincoln 64

life (cont.):
L. is pain   William Goldman 2
L. is painting a picture
·   Oliver Wendell Holmes, Jr. 21
L. is short, the art long   Hippocrates 1
l. is 6 to 5 against   Runyon 3
L. is so constructed   Charlotte Brontë 8
L. is the ensemble   Bichat 1
L. is too short   Conran 1
L. is unfair   John F. Kennedy 24
L. is washed in the speechless real
                              Barzun 2
L. is what happens to us
                        Allen Saunders 1
l. is worth living   Santayana 2
L. isn't all beer and skittles Proverbs 170
l. itself has become one
                  Theodore Roosevelt 8
L. itself still remains a very   Horney 1
l. may be much happier   Ewart 1
L. must be understood backwards
                        Kierkegaard 1
l. of significant soil   T. S. Eliot 116
l. of the law
            Oliver Wendell Holmes, Jr. 2
l. should go on   Sandburg 12
l. subdued to its instrument
                        Ted Hughes 7
L. was meant to be lived
                  Eleanor Roosevelt 5
l. we learn with   Malamud 2
l. which is unexamined   Plato 2
l. will break you   Erdrich 3
L. without industry   Ruskin 18
l. without theory   Disraeli 6
L.'s a bitch   Modern Proverbs 52
L.'s longing for itself   Gibran 2
Lolita, light of my l.   Nabokov 2
man's l. is cheap   Shakespeare 291
many things in l. that are not fair
                        "Jimmy" Carter 5
matter of l. and death   Shankly 1
My l. closed twice   Emily Dickinson 27
not l. alone   Malraux 3
Our common lust for l.   Ibsen 23
our little l. is rounded   Shakespeare 443
outcast from l.'s feast   Joyce 3
Poetry is at bottom a criticism of l.
                  Matthew Arnold 34
Reason is the l. of the law   Coke 4
Reverence for L.   Schweitzer 1
Secret L. of Walter Mitty   Thurber 9
see into the l. of things
                  William Wordsworth 2
seek out new l.-forms   Roddenberry 3
she is mine for l.   Spark 2
Showing up is 80 percent of l.
                  Woody Allen 41
stirs the Culprit—L.! Emily Dickinson 3
story of my l.   Dorothy Parker 41
Such is l.   Ned Kelly 1
sweet mystery of l.
            Rida Johnson Young 1
there's l., there's hope   Proverbs 171
this long disease, my l.   Pope 31
time of your l.   Saroyan 1
total reaction upon l.   William James 10
Trifles make the sum of l.   Dickens 74
two tragedies in l.
            George Bernard Shaw 16

Variety's the very spice of l.
                  William Cowper 7
weave the web of l.   Ted Perry 5
what to do with his l.   France 4
whoever rescues a single l.   Talmud 8
Your money or your l.   Thoreau 11
life-in-death
nightmare L. was she   Coleridge 8
lifestyle
just another "l. choice"   Quayle 4
lifetime
come once in a l.   Woody Allen 14
he will eat for a l.   Modern Proverbs 31
l. of happiness   George Bernard Shaw 13
lit again in our l.   Edward Grey 1
work of a l.   Whistler 2
lift
L. Ev'ry Voice and Sing
                James Weldon Johnson 1
l. my lamp beside the golden   Lazarus 2
l. of a driving dream   Richard Nixon 4
nation shall not l. up sword   Bible 161
lifts
rising tide l. all the boats
                  John F. Kennedy 26
light
afraid of the l.   Ibsen 10
all was l.   Pope 11
and there was l.   Bible 1
better to l. one candle   James Keller 1
certain Slant of l.   Emily Dickinson 6
dance by the l. of the moon
                Folk and Anonymous Songs 12
danced by the l. of the moon   Lear 7
dreams of those l. sleepers   Symons 1
dying of the l.   Dylan Thomas 17
fire can truly l. the world
                  John F. Kennedy 15
Forward the L. Brigade   Tennyson 37
Gatsby believed in the green l.
                  F. Scott Fitzgerald 35
gladsome l. of Jurisprudence   Coke 6
God is the L. of the heavens   Koran 12
green l. at the end of Daisy's dock
                  F. Scott Fitzgerald 34
He was not that L.   Bible 310
how my l. is spent   Milton 52
how the l. gets in   Leonard Cohen 5
in a l. fantastic round   Milton 1
Ironic points of l.   Auden 14
Jeanie with the l. brown hair
                  Stephen Foster 6
Lead, kindly L.   John Henry Newman 1
Let there be l.   Bible 1
l., not heat   Woodrow Wilson 11
l. at the end of a tunnel   Navarre 1
l. at the end of the tunnel   Alsop 1
l. at the end of the tunnel Paul Dickson 1
l. consists in the transverse undulations
                        Maxwell 1
l. has gone out of our lives   Nehru 2
l. my fire   Jim Morrison 3
l. of a whole life dies   Bourdillon 2
l. of common day
                William Wordsworth 15
l. out for the Territory   Twain 36
l. so dim   Chevalier 2
l. this candle   Shepard 1
Lolita, l. of my life   Nabokov 2

More l.   Goethe 21
Neither do men l. a candle   Bible 208
No l., but rather   Milton 19
not l. that is needed   Douglass 5
on the l. fantastic toe   Milton 1
out of hell leads up to l.   Milton 29
pursuit of sweetness and l.
                  Matthew Arnold 27
put on the red l.   Sting 1
Put out the l.   Shakespeare 280
Radiant l. consists   Thomas Young 1
rather l. a candle   Adlai E. Stevenson 14
soft, what l.   Shakespeare 32
Star l., star bright   Nursery Rhymes 70
sweetness and l.   Jonathan Swift 1
There wasn't a l. on   Hoyt A. Moore 1
They made l. of it   Bible 253
this day l. such a candle   Latimer 1
thousand points of l.
            George Herbert Walker Bush 3
two ways of spreading l.   Wharton 1
We'll leave a l. on
                Advertising Slogans 86
Yesterday a shaft of l.
                  John F. Kennedy 34
lighthouse
took the sitivation at the l.   Dickens 14
lighthouses
L. don't go running   Lamott 2
lightly
can take themselves l.   Chesterton 12
l. like a flower   Tennyson 34
tossed aside l.   Dorothy Parker 40
walk l. on the earth   Barbara Ward 1
lightness
unbearable l. of being   Kundera 3
lightning
flashes of l.   Coleridge 37
L. never strikes   Proverbs 172
l. that does the work   Twain 124
l.-bug & the l.   Twain 38
writing history with l.
                  Woodrow Wilson 26
lights
Hang on to your l.   Film Lines 79
L., camera, action   Sayings 36
l. his taper at mine   Jefferson 36
Turn up the l.   O. Henry 8
like
Do what you l.   Rabelais 3
I know what I l.   Gelett Burgess 6
I l. Ike   Political Slogans 21
I l. that in a man   Film Lines 27
I l. to watch   Kosinski 1
If you don't l. them   "Groucho" Marx 46
L. father l. son   Proverbs 100
L. love we don't know   Auden 9
look upon his l. again   Shakespeare 156
met a man that I didn't l.   Will Rogers 8
No time l. the present   Manley 1
People who l. this sort of thing
                        Lincoln 59
the more I l. dogs   Roland 2
You l. me   Sally Field 1
likely
Not bloody l.   George Bernard Shaw 41
likeness
after our l.   Bible 4
l. of a man   Rousseau 9

lockjaw
either stiff neck or l.   Bankhead 5
locomotive
more powerful than a l.
                    Radio Catchphrases 21
lodged
l. with me useless   Milton 52
log
L.-cabin to the White House
                William Roscoe Thayer 1
Take a l. cabin   Garfield 1
logic
danger does lie in l.   Chesterton 10
law has not been l.
            Oliver Wendell Holmes, Jr. 2
L. is l.   Oliver Wendell Holmes 8
That's l.   Carroll 31
logical
absurdity which is l.   Joyce 8
built in such a l. way
                Oliver Wendell Holmes 7
loins
fire of my l.   Nabokov 2
girded up his l.   Bible 93
shudder in the l.   Yeats 44
Lolita
L., light of my life   Nabokov 2
lollipop
fuzzy end of the l.   Film Lines 157
On the good ship L.   Clare 1
lollipops
reeking of popcorn and l. W. C. Fields 9
Loman
Willy L. never made a lot
                    Arthur Miller 3
London
been to L. to look at the queen
                    Nursery Rhymes 59
crowd flowed over L. Bridge
                    T. S. Eliot 44
L., that great cesspool
                    Arthur Conan Doyle 2
L. Bridge is broken down
                    Nursery Rhymes 34
L. is drowning   Strummer 1
L.'s daughter   Dylan Thomas 16
Lord Mayor of L.   Ballads 3
still 1938 in L.   Midler 1
This is a L. particular   Dickens 82
This is—L.   Radio Catchphrases 8
tired of L.   Samuel Johnson 90
way to L. town   Nursery Rhymes 35
werewolves of L.   Zevon 1
lone
I am a l. lorn creetur   Dickens 56
l. and level sands   Percy Shelley 7
L. Ranger rides again
                    Radio Catchphrases 15
loneliness
L. of the Long-Distance Runner
                    Sillitoe 1
poets would die of l.   Yeats 59
Well of L.   Radclyffe Hall 1
lonely
All the l. people
                Lennon and McCartney 8
Heart Is a L. Hunter   McCullers 1
heart is a l. hunter   Sharp 1
l. at the top   Modern Proverbs 55

L. Crowd   Riesman 1
love's austere and l. offices
                    Robert Hayden 1
None but the l. heart   Goethe 6
one l. reporter   Richard Nixon 20
Only the L.   Orbison 1
wandered l. as a cloud
                William Wordsworth 25
lonesome
I'm so l. I could cry Hank Williams 1
very l. at the summit Hawthorne 22
you will be l.   Twain 83
long
Art is l.   Longfellow 2
ask that your way be l. Cavafy 3
calamity of so l. life Shakespeare 189
craft so l. to lerne   Chaucer 4
going to live this l.   Sayings 23
How L. Is the Coast of Britain
                    Mandelbrot 1
how l. must we sing   Bono 1
In the l. run we are all dead Keynes 4
Life is short, the art l. Hippocrates 1
Live l. and prosper Star Trek 6
Loneliness of the L.-distance Runner
                    Sillitoe 1
L., l. ago   Bayly 1
l. arm of coincidence Chambers 1
L. Hot Summer   Faulkner 15
l. in city pent   Keats 4
l. live the king   Sayings 34
l. pull   Dickens 69
l. time ago in a galaxy George Lucas 2
l. time between drinks Sayings 27
l. time in politics Harold Wilson 3
l. way to Tipperary Judge 1
l. winter evenings Raymond Chandler 1
Never is a l. time Proverbs 206
night of the l. knives Hitler 2
sat too l. here   Cromwell 2
so l., it's been good "Woody" Guthrie 1
so l. as ye both shall live
                Book of Common Prayer 14
this l. disease, my life Pope 31
thou art l., and lank Coleridge 9
what a l., strange trip it's been
                    Robert Hunter 1
You have delighted us l. enough
                    Austen 9
You've come a l. way baby
                    Advertising Slogans 129
longer
it just seems l.   Clement Freud 1
None ever wished it l.
                    Samuel Johnson 37
takes a little l.   Santayana 14
that which takes a little l. Nansen 1
longest
l. day   Rommel 1
Longfellow
they believe in Christ and L.
                    e.e. cummings 7
longing
L., we say   Hass 3
longings
immortal l. in me Shakespeare 405
look
always l. for the silver lining DeSylva 1
come to l. for America Paul Simon 4

Don't l. back   Paige 6
Hey, l. me over   Carolyn Leigh 2
I can l. the East End
                Elizabeth the Queen Mother 2
I can sit and l. at it Jerome K. Jerome 1
I love the l. of you Cole Porter 24
lean and hungry l. Shakespeare 99
Let's l. at the record Alfred E. Smith 1
l. a gift horse   Proverbs 118
l. after our people Robert Falcon Scott 2
L. Back in Anger John Osborne 1
L. before you leap Proverbs 175
L. for the union label
                    Advertising Slogans 62
L. homeward angel Milton 3
L. Ma! No cavities
                    Advertising Slogans 37
l. not on his picture Jonson 8
l. on my works   Percy Shelley 7
never l. at any other horse
                    "Groucho" Marx 32
You Could L. It Up Thurber 13
You l. almost like a man Ferber 1
looked
I've l. at life   Joni Mitchell 1
looking
all night l. for them Stengel 6
avoid l. a fool   Orwell 6
Here's l. at you   Film Lines 44
l. at the stars   Wilde 55
l. for an honest man Diogenes 1
l. for loopholes   W. C. Fields 23
l. uncomfortably to the world
                    Tom Hayden 1
someone may be l. Mencken 7
you have been l. for them
                    Samuel Johnson 110
lookingglass
cracked l. of a servant Joyce 15
looking-glasses
l. possessing the magic
                    Virginia Woolf 11
looks
It L. Like Up   Fariña 1
woman as old as she l. Proverbs 185
looney
misfits, l. tunes Ronald W. Reagan 10
loop
We were not in the l.
                George Herbert Walker Bush 17
loopholes
looking for l.   W. C. Fields 23
loose
all hell broke l.   Milton 36
everything l. will land
                Frank Lloyd Wright 3
l. cannon   Richard Nixon 21
L. lips sink ships
                    Advertising Slogans 139
loosed
l. from its dream of life Jarrell 1
loosening
her l. thighs   Yeats 43
lopping
l. off our desires Jonathan Swift 6
loquacity
L., n. A disorder Bierce 76
loquendi
norma l.   Horace 2

lorax
I am the L.   Seuss 12
L. and all of his friends   Seuss 14
lord
doth magnify the L.   Bible 283
dwell in the house of the L.   Bible 109
earth is the L.'s   Bible 110
earth is the L.'s   Bible 351
except the L. keep the city   Bible 120
feel sorry for the good L.   Einstein 31
glory of the coming of the L.
                        Julia Ward Howe 1
good l. had only ten   Clemenceau 7
hear the word of the L.   Bible 188
hear the word of the L.
                  Folk and Anonymous Songs 20
holy, is the L. of hosts   Bible 163
I am the L. thy God   Bible 50
Little L. Fauntleroy
                  Frances Hodgson Burnett 1
L., make me an instrument St. Francis 2
L. be with thee   Bible 84
L. God made them all Cecil Alexander 1
L. High Executioner   W. S. Gilbert 30
L. is my shepherd   Bible 108
L. Mayor of London   Ballads 3
L. our God is one L.   Bible 69
may L. Christ enter in   Wilde 95
Praise the L. and pass   Forgy 1
where ha you been, L. Randal   Ballads 5
lords
he is only a wit among L.
                        Samuel Johnson 46
Los Angeles
land in L.   Frank Lloyd Wright 3
lose
I l. a friend   John Singer Sargent 1
l. his own soul   Bible 278
l. no time in reading it   Disraeli 34
l. the name of action   Shakespeare 192
l. what he never had   Proverbs 176
l. what he never had   Izaak Walton 1
nothin' left to l.   Kristofferson 1
nothing to l. but their chains
                        Marx and Engels 8
To l. one parent   Wilde 78
Use it or l. it   Modern Proverbs 94
waste it is to l. one's mind   Quayle 2
you look at it, you l.   Paul Simon 6
You l.   Coolidge 8
you l. a few   Modern Proverbs 97
You l. more of yourself   Heaney 7
loser
I'm a l. baby   Hansen 2
show me a good l.   Rockne 1
turned being a Big L.   Vidal 2
losers
l. weepers   Proverbs 103
loses
conventional army l.   Kissinger 1
losing
all around you are l. theirs   Beville 1
l. cause pleased Cato   Lucan 1
l. her figure or her face   Cartland 1
L. my timing so late   Sondheim 7
peace to Europe: by l.   Heller 7
loss
new thinking is about l.   Hass 1
One man's l.   Proverbs 177

lost
All is not l.   Milton 20
And the l. heart stiffens   T. S. Eliot 86
Are you l. daddy   Lardner 1
badge of l. innocence   Thomas Paine 3
better to have loved and l.   Tennyson 29
fighting for were the l. causes
                        Film Lines 122
France has l. a battle   de Gaulle 1
He who hesitates is l.   Proverbs 141
Home of l. causes   Matthew Arnold 8
I am not yet so l.   Samuel Johnson 5
I have l. a day   Titus 1
I have l. friends   Virginia Woolf 14
I once was l.   John Newton 1
land of l. content   Housman 3
l. a very important part   Brooke Shields 1
l. all contact   T'ao Ch'ien 1
l. an empire   Acheson 1
l. and gone for ever   Montrose 2
L. Cause   Pollard 1
L. Chord   Procter 1
l. generation   Stein 13
l. her sheep   Nursery Rhymes 6
l. money by underestimating
                        Mencken 35
l. on a coin toss   Cormac McCarthy 3
l. that lovin' feelin'   Spector 2
L. Weekend   Charles Jackson 1
men have l. their reason
                        Shakespeare 117
moments will be l. in time
                        Film Lines 24
Most ball games are l.   Stengel 10
never l. a passenger   Tubman 3
never l. a war   Will Rogers 12
no great l. without some   Laura Wilder 1
not l. but gone before
                        Caroline Norton 2
people on whom nothing is l.
                        Henry James 10
poor little lambs who've l. our way
                        Kipling 9
rider is l.   Proverbs 320
we are l.   Pyrrhus 1
We have l.   Film Lines 152
what is l. in translation   Frost 25
lot
on a Metro-Goldwyn-Mayer l.
                        Judy Garland 1
policeman's l. is not a happy one
                        W. S. Gilbert 23
Lothario
gay L.   Rowe 1
lottery
l. of life   Rhodes 3
louder
l. he talked of his honor
                  Ralph Waldo Emerson 41
l. than words   Proverbs 4
loudest
l. noise in this new Rolls-Royce
                  Advertising Slogans 108
l. yelps for liberty   Samuel Johnson 30
loud-speakers
spokesmen have all the l.
                        Paul Goodman 1
Louie
L., L.   Richard Berry 1

lousy
play l.   Dorothy Parker 21
unethical and l.   Arno 1
Louvre
You're the L. Museum   Cole Porter 6
love
all for l.   Spenser 5
All mankind l. a lover
                  Ralph Waldo Emerson 13
All You Need Is L.
                  Lennon and McCartney 11
all your l. to just one man   Wynette 2
All's fair in l. and war   Proverbs 96
almost like being in l.   Alan Jay Lerner 1
Black l. is Black wealth   Giovanni 2
but not for l.   Shakespeare 94
could not l. thee, Dear
                  Richard Lovelace 2
course of true l.   Shakespeare 51
Dallas doesn't l. you   Connally 1
Democracy applied to l.   Mencken 18
Do Not Trifle with L.   Musset 2
Do you know what l. is   le Carré 4
dooms of l.   e.e. cummings 17
Dost thou l. life   Benjamin Franklin 24
each day I l. you more   Gérard 1
energies of l.   Teilhard de Chardin 2
fall in l. with a rich girl   Howells 1
Falling in l. is the one
                  Robert Louis Stevenson 6
falling in l. is wonderful
                        Irving Berlin 16
Falling in l. with love   Lorenz Hart 6
falls in l. with Himself
                  Benjamin Franklin 15
for a good man's l.   Shakespeare 93
free l.   Chesterton 4
From Russia with L.   Ian Fleming 4
Give a little l. to a child   Ruskin 15
God is l.   Bible 388
God is L.   Samuel Butler (1835–1902) 10
God is l.   Gypsy Rose Lee 1
Greater l. hath no man   Bible 326
greater torment of l. satisfied
                        T. S. Eliot 80
groans of l.   Malcolm Lowry 1
guard I do not l.   Yeats 21
hate is conquered by l.   Pali Tripitaka 1
his or her l. affairs   Rebecca West 5
How do I l. thee
                  Elizabeth Barrett Browning 2
how to make l. stay   Robbins 1
I do not l. you, Dr. Fell   Thomas Brown 1
I don't l. you, Sabidius   Martial 1
I got to l. one man till I die
                        Hammerstein 1
I heartily l. John, Peter
                        Jonathan Swift 10
I l. a lassie   Lauder 1
I l. having written
                  Robert Louis Stevenson 23
I l. New York   Advertising Slogans 92
I l. Paris in the springtime
                        Cole Porter 23
I l. the look of you   Cole Porter 24
I l. the smell of napalm   Film Lines 14
I l. thee still   William Cowper 6
If it's what you say I l. it
                        Donald Trump, Jr. 1
If l. were what the rose   Swinburne 4

If music be the food of l.
Shakespeare 239
I'm in the mood for l.   Dorothy Fields 2
in l. with a cold climate   Southey 1
in women, l. begets desire
Jonathan Swift 37
know that l. is gone   Dietrich 1
labor of l.   Bible 373
lack of l.   Atwood 4
let's fall in l.   Cole Porter 25
Like l. we don't know   Auden 9
like nobody else since I l. you   Neruda 2
like the word l. in the mouth
Ralph Waldo Emerson 36
live with me, and be my l.   Marlowe 1
l., cherish, and to obey
Book of Common Prayer 15
l., let us be true   Matthew Arnold 18
L., thou art absolute   Crashaw 1
L. and a cottage   Colman the Elder 1
l. and be loved   Sand 2
l. and be loved by me   Poe 15
L. and marriage   Cahn 1
l. at first sight   Heller 1
L. bade me welcome   George Herbert 4
L. ceases to be a pleasure   Behn 3
L. conquers all things   Virgil 17
l. dares you to care   Bowie 4
l. does not consist in gazing
Saint-Exupéry 2
L. doesn't just sit there   Le Guin 6
l. fell out with me   Lorenz Hart 7
l. flies out of the window   Proverbs 240
l. foolishly   Thackeray 8
l. for mankind and hatred of sins
Augustine 5
L. has pitched his mansion   Yeats 52
L. in a Cold Climate   Mitford 2
l. is a banquet   Patti Smith 2
L. is a fire that burns   Camões 1
L. Is a Many-Splendored Thing   Suyin 1
L. is a snowmobile   Groening 9
L. is blind   Proverbs 178
l. is l. is l.   Miranda 7
L. is not all   Millay 8
l. is not madness   Calderón 2
L. is so short   Neruda 6
L. is strong as death   Bible 159
L. is the delusion   Mencken 1
L. is the extremely   Iris Murdoch 2
L. is the most fun   Mencken 41
L. is the victim's response   Atkinson 1
L. is the whole history   Staël 6
L. is three minutes   Rotten 4
L. It or Leave It   Political Slogans 3
L. looks not with the eyes
Shakespeare 52
L. loves to l. l.   Joyce 20
L. makes the world go round
Proverbs 179
L. Me or Leave Me   Gus Kahn 6
L. me, love my dog   Proverbs 180
L. me tender   Presley 1
L. means not ever having   Segal 2
l. of learning   Longfellow 27
l. of money has taken   Tocqueville 1
l. of money is the root   Bible 377
l. of property   Tocqueville 21
l. of wealth   Tocqueville 20

L. on the Dole   Greenwood 1
l. oneself   Wilde 71
l. prove likewise variable   Shakespeare 35
L. rules the court   Walter Scott 1
l. sometimes occurs   Proulx 2
L. that dare not speak its name
Lord Alfred Douglas 1
L. that dare not speak its name
Wilde 82
l. that makes undaunted   Spring-Rice 1
L. that moves the sun   Dante 14
l. thee better after death
Elizabeth Barrett Browning 3
l. thy neighbor as thyself   Bible 65
L. to faults is always blind
William Blake 1
L. was all they had   McEwan 3
l. were longer-lived   Millay 5
l. will find a way   Proverbs 181
l. with the whole world   Erdrich 1
L. wol nat been constreyned   Chaucer 11
l. would last for ever   Auden 2
l. you take is equal
Lennon and McCartney 24
l. you ten years   Andrew Marvell 11
l.'s austere and lonely offices
Robert Hayden 1
L.'s sorrow lasts   Florian 1
l.'s young dream   Thomas Moore 3
loving to l.   Augustine 2
Make l. not war   Legman 2
man may l. a paradox
Ralph Waldo Emerson 20
Man's l. is of man's life   Byron 20
money can't buy me l.
Lennon and McCartney 3
My only l. sprung   Shakespeare 31
my true l. sent to me
Nursery Rhymes 10
never l. a stranger   Stella Benson 1
not enough to make us l.
Jonathan Swift 4
not everybody deserves l.   Zadie Smith 1
Not universal l.   Auden 12
Once in l. with Amy   Loesser 3
opposite of l. is not hate   Wiesel 3
passing the l. of women   Bible 88
people will say we're in l.
Hammerstein 9
perfect l. casteth out fear   Bible 389
prettiest l. stories   Dorothy Parker 12
right to l. whom I may   Woodhull 1
save us any more than l. did
F. Scott Fitzgerald 51
search for l.   Walesa 1
sex to do the work of l.
Mary McCarthy 4
something to l.   George Eliot 1
support of the woman I l.   Edward VIII 1
symptom of true l.   Hugo 7
that doesn't l. a wall   Frost 4
there are those who l. it
Daniel Webster 1
They l. him for the enemies   Bragg 1
they still say, "I l. you"   Hupfeld 2
this blessing l. gives again   Kinnell 2
Thou shalt l. the Lord   Bible 256
Thou shalt l. thy neighbor   Bible 256
thy sweet l.   Shakespeare 416

To be wise and l.   Shakespeare 248
To Know Him Is to L. Him   Spector 1
to l. and to work   Sigmund Freud 23
To l. another person   Kretzmer 1
to l. her is a liberal education
Richard Steele 1
Tobacco is the tomb of l.   Disraeli 16
too much l. of living   Swinburne 3
tragedy of l. is indifference   Maugham 5
turns to thoughts of l.   Tennyson 5
Twenty l.-sick maidens we
W. S. Gilbert 25
unlucky in l.   Proverbs 182
way of truth and l.   Mohandas Gandhi 8
We must l. one another   Auden 13
What is l.   Shakespeare 240
What will survive of us is l.   Larkin 1
What's l. got to do   Britten 1
When I fall in l.   Heyman 2
When l. congeals   Lorenz Hart 3
where the l. of God goes   Lightfoot 2
Whom the gods l.   Menander 1
wilder shores of l.   Blanch 1
Will you l. me in December
James J. Walker 1
Wilt thou l. her
Book of Common Prayer 14
woman has got to l. a bad   Rawlings 1
Work is l. made visible   Gibran 4
world needs now is l.   Hal David 2
You Always Hurt the One You L.
Allan Roberts 1

loved
be feared than to be l.   Machiavelli 6
better to have l. and lost   Tennyson 29
God so l. the world   Bible 315
had somebody l. him   Kissinger 6
He l. Big Brother   Orwell 49
I have l. the principle of beauty   Keats 22
I l. Rome more   Shakespeare 101
I've l. another with all   Sparks 1
love and be l.   Sand 2
love and be l. by me   Poe 15
l. I not honor more   Richard Lovelace 2
l. not at first sight   Marlowe 5
l. not wisely, but too well
Shakespeare 282
never to have been l.   Congreve 7
Not that I l. Caesar less
Shakespeare 108

loveliest
L. of trees   Housman 1
loveliness
This Adonis in l.   Leigh Hunt 1
lovely
As you are woman, so be l.   Graves 1
billboard l. as a tree   Nash 7
faded but still l. woman
F. Scott Fitzgerald 42
Go, l. rose   Edmund Waller 1
He'd make a l. corpse   Dickens 52
keep that l. body   Glück 2
l., dark, and deep   Frost 16
l. bones   Sebold 2
l. woman stoops to folly   T. S. Eliot 54
l. woman stoops to folly
Oliver Goldsmith 6
l. wonderful thoughts   Barrie 8
poem l. as a tree   Kilmer 1

machines
Can m. think   Turing 1
make m. what they ought to be
    Havelock Ellis 2
speak of m. thinking   Turing 3
we are their survival m.   Dawkins 3
whether M. Can Think   Dijkstra 1
whether m. think   B. F. Skinner 1
mad
Don't get m., get even
    Joseph P. Kennedy 1
I am but m. north-north-west
    Shakespeare 182
I am going m. again   Virginia Woolf 19
I am not m.   Dalí 1
if he is m.   George II 1
I'm m. as hell   Film Lines 124
It's a m. world   Dickens 61
Men are m.   Twiggy 1
M., *adj.* Affected with   Bierce 77
M., bad, and dangerous   Caroline Lamb 1
m. and savage master   Sophocles 4
m. dogs and Englishmen   Coward 9
M. Ireland hurt you into poetry
    Auden 21
Never go to bed m.   Diller 1
old, m., blind, despised   Percy Shelley 8
people for me are the m. ones
    Kerouac 1
they first make m.   Proverbs 123
We are all born m.   Beckett 6
world was m.   Sabatini 1
madame
M. Bovary, *c'est moi*   Flaubert 2
madding
Far from the m. crowd's   Thomas Gray 9
made
dreams are m. on   Shakespeare 443
I never had it m.   Jackie Robinson 1
m. for you and me   "Woody" Guthrie 6
m. in heaven   Proverbs 189
m. to be broken   North 2
m. to be broken   Proverbs 245
Nature m. him   Ariosto 1
sabbath was m. for man   Bible 275
They m. light of it   Bible 253
What are little boys m. of   Southey 7
Word was m. flesh   Bible 311
world I never m.   Housman 7
madeleine
little piece of m.   Proust 3
mademoiselle
M. from Armentières
    Folk and Anonymous Songs 48
madman
between myself and a m.   Dalí 1
Victor Hugo was a m.   Cocteau 2
madmen
M. in authority   Keynes 12
madness
despondency and m.
    William Wordsworth 19
destroyed by m.   Ginsberg 7
M.! M.!   Film Lines 31
m. of an autumn   Franzen 1
m. on which the whole world
    George Bernard Shaw 37
Much M. is divinest Sense
    Emily Dickinson 18

rest is the m. of art   Henry James 12
that way m. lies   Shakespeare 295
Though this be m.   Shakespeare 177
to m. near allied   John Dryden 4
war is m.   Updike 4
magazine
m. which is not edited   Harold Ross 1
magic
as in a m. mirror
    Oliver Wendell Holmes, Jr. 8
I want m.   Tennessee Williams 4
If there is m. in this planet   Eiseley 1
indistinguishable from m.
    Arthur C. Clarke 5
m. deeper still   C. S. Lewis 4
mistake medicine for m.   Szasz 3
Puff, the m. dragon   Yarrow 1
That Old Black M.   Johnny Mercer 3
this rough m.   Shakespeare 444
magistrate
by the m., as equally useful   Gibbon 2
magna
M. Charta is such a fellow   Coke 7
magnificent
M. desolation   Aldrin 1
magnify
My soul doth m. the Lord   Bible 283
magpie
swollen m.   Ezra Pound 27
Mahatma
You're M. Gandhi   Cole Porter 9
Mahomet
M. must go to the mountain
    Proverbs 202
maid
m. in the living room   Jerry Hall 1
Yonder a m.   Thomas Hardy 27
maiden
m. of bashful fifteen
    Richard Brinsley Sheridan 5
my pretty m.   Nursery Rhymes 36
maids
old m. biking   Orwell 14
pretty m. all in a row
    Nursery Rhymes 41
Three little m. from school
    W. S. Gilbert 34
mail
check is in the m.   Sayings 4
read each other's m.   Allen W. Dulles 1
read each other's m.   Stimson 1
m. must go through   Joaquin Miller 1
mailed
your m. fist   Wilhelm II 2
maimed
poor, and the m.   Bible 298
main
M. Street   Sinclair Lewis 1
Maine
As M. goes, so goes   Farley 1
As M. goes, so goes   Political Slogans 4
M. and Texas   Thoreau 20
Princes of M.   John Irving 2
maintain
m. it before the whole world   Molière 9
majestic
m. equality of the law   France 3
m. though in ruin   Milton 28

majesty
m. of human suffering   Vigny 2
Major
Ground control to M. Tom   Bowie 1
M. combat operations in Iraq
    George W. Bush 16
M. Strasser has been shot
    Film Lines 49
model of a modern M.-General
    W. S. Gilbert 19
majority
abide by m. rule   Harper Lee 2
always in the m.   John Knox 1
as a rule the m. are wrong   Debs 1
big enough m.   Twain 33
compact m.   Ibsen 13
ever in a m.   Thoreau 35
gone to join the m.   Petronius 2
great m.   Edward Young 1
in which the m. was right   Heinlein 14
m. is never right   Ibsen 14
m. of one   Thoreau 9
m. rule is not a reliable   Guinier 1
makes a m.   Andrew Jackson 7
man who is right has a m.   Douglass 7
on the side of the m.   Twain 119
One on God's side is a m.
    Wendell Phillips 3
One with the law is a m.   Coolidge 2
silent m. of my fellow
    Richard Nixon 10
Tyranny of the M.   Tocqueville 6
make
can't m. him drink   Proverbs 148
Clothes m. the man   Proverbs 48
conscience does m. cowards
    Shakespeare 192
could not m. up his mind   Film Lines 93
Don't m. the same mistake
    Modern Proverbs 77
Don't m. waves   Modern Proverbs 56
easier to m. war   Clemenceau 2
He died to m. men holy
    Julia Ward Howe 3
I could not well m. out   Southey 4
I m. all things new   Bible 399
If I can m. it there   Ebb 6
I'll m. me a world
    James Weldon Johnson 4
M. America great again
    Political Slogans 26
m. believe I love you   Hammerstein 2
m. business for itself   Dickens 88
M. haste deliberately   Augustus 2
M. hay while the sun shines
    Proverbs 183
M. her laugh at that   Shakespeare 226
m. him an offer he can't refuse   Puzo 2
M. it so   Star Trek 9
M. it work   Television Catchphrases 53
M. love not war   Legman 2
m. me immortal with a kiss   Marlowe 9
m. money the old-fashioned way
    Advertising Slogans 109
m. my day   Film Lines 164
m. my day   Ronald W. Reagan 9
M. no little plans   Burnham 1
m. our sun stand still
    Andrew Marvell 15

make (cont.):
M. someone happy
    Comden and Green 5
m. the most of it   Patrick Henry 1
m. your bed   Proverbs 184
truth shall m. you free   Bible 319
Two wrongs will not m.   Proverbs 313
When found, m. a note of   Dickens 54
maker
prepared to meet my M.
    Winston Churchill 47
makes
gold m. the rules   Sayings 16
maketh
He m. me to lie down   Bible 108
making
after m. love   Kinnell 1
He's m. a list   Gillespie 2
m. good time   Berra 2
m. men talk   Film Lines 110
m. other plans   Allen Saunders 1
Of m. many books   Bible 153
malade
M. Imaginaire   Molière 12
malaise
energy and m.   "Jimmy" Carter 7
malcontents
make a hundred m.   Louis XIV 1
male
glory of m. domination   Alfred Adler 1
M. and female created he   Bible 5
m. is a biological accident   Solanas 1
m. of the species   D. H. Lawrence 7
more deadly than the m.   Kipling 34
malefactors
m. of great wealth
    Theodore Roosevelt 17
malfunction
wardrobe m.   Timberlake 1
Malherbe
At last came M.   Boileau 2
malice
bearing no m. or ill will
    John Quincy Adams 2
made with "actual m."   Brennan 4
With m. toward none   Lincoln 51
malicious
m. he is not   Einstein 24
Maybe God is m.   Einstein 34
malignant
that was not m.   Waugh 5
malignity
motiveless m.   Coleridge 41
malt
m. does more than Milton can
    Housman 5
mama
M. Mia, that's a spicy
    Advertising Slogans 6
m. of dada   Clifton Fadiman 2
mamas
Last of the Red-Hot M.   Yellen 2
mamma
M.'s little baby
    Folk and Anonymous Songs 71
mammas
M., Don't Let Your Babies   Ed Bruce 1
mammon
cannot serve God and m.   Bible 218

M., *n*. The god   Bierce 78
m. of unrighteousness   Bible 300
man
'A was a m.   Shakespeare 156
apparel oft proclaims the m.
    Shakespeare 159
Arms, and the m.   John Dryden 11
As a m. he was a failure
    Aldous Huxley 6
Behind every great m.   Proverbs 129
Behold the m.   Bible 329
Beware the m. of one book
    Anonymous (Latin) 4
Blessed is the m. who expects
    Proverbs 29
Blow the m. down
    Folk and Anonymous Songs 7
both m. and bird and beast   Coleridge 13
Brotherhood of m.
    John D. Rockefeller, Jr. 1
Brutus is an honorable m.
    Shakespeare 113
Child is father of the M.
    William Wordsworth 12
childhood shows the m.   Milton 43
Clothes make the m.   Proverbs 48
Desiring this m.'s art   Shakespeare 414
do a m.'s work   Modern Proverbs 9
dog is m.'s best friend   Proverbs 75
earth does not belong to m.   Ted Perry 4
ech m. for hymself   Chaucer 12
England expects that every m.
    Horatio Nelson 7
every m. against every m.   Hobbes 7
Every m. is like the company
    Euripides 3
fit night out for m. or beast
    W. C. Fields 4
Forgotten M.   Sumner 3
Go West, young m.   Greeley 2
Good M. Is Hard to Find   Eddie Green 1
Greater love hath no m.   Bible 326
guess what a m. is going
    Christopher Morley 4
he was her m.
    Folk and Anonymous Songs 23
Heavenly Father invented m.   Twain 134
honest m.'s the noblest work   Pope 26
How many roads must a m.   Dylan 1
How marvelous is M.   Gorky 1
I am a free m.
    Television Catchphrases 51
I decline to accept the end of m.
    Faulkner 10
I like that in a m.   Film Lines 27
I met a m. with seven wives
    Nursery Rhymes 65
I'm a m. of wealth and taste
    Jagger and Richards 9
I'm Gonna Wash That M.
    Hammerstein 13
In wit, a m.   Pope 17
incomprehensible machine is m.
    Jefferson 14
it would improve m.   Twain 50
join together this M.
    Book of Common Prayer 16
landing a m. on the moon
    John F. Kennedy 19

last m. to die for a mistake   Kerry 1
let no m. put asunder
    Book of Common Prayer 19
let not m. put asunder   Bible 249
Let us make m. in our image   Bible 4
Low M. on a Totem Pole
    H. Allen Smith 1
luckiest m.   Gehrig 1
m., a plan   Leigh Mercer 1
m. after his own heart   Bible 83
m. ain't nothin' but a m.
    Folk and Anonymous Songs 43
m. alone ain't got no bloody
    Hemingway 19
M. and Superman
    George Bernard Shaw 11
m. ask for advice   Steinem 5
m. behind the curtain   Film Lines 195
m. biting a dog   Dana 1
m. can be destroyed   Hemingway 28
M. delights not me   Shakespeare 181
M. did not weave the web   Ted Perry 5
M. errs as long   Goethe 10
m. for all seasons   Whittington 1
m. got to do   Steinbeck 1
m. in black   Stephen King 1
M. in the Brooks Brothers
    Mary McCarthy 1
M. in the Gray Flannel Suit
    Sloan Wilson 1
m. is a god in ruins
    Ralph Waldo Emerson 3
m. is a marvelously   Montaigne 3
M. is a tool-making animal
    Benjamin Franklin 43
M. is a useless passion   Sartre 3
m. is a wolf   Plautus 1
m. is an invention   Foucault 2
m. is as old as he feels   Proverbs 185
M. is born to live   Pasternak 1
m. is by nature a political animal
    Aristotle 8
m. is descended   Charles Darwin 11
m. is not enough   Matthew Arnold 9
m. is only as old   "Groucho" Marx 45
M. is quite insane   Montaigne 13
m. is richest   Thoreau 33
M. is the measure of all things
    Protagoras 2
m. is the only animal   Aristotle 9
M. is the only animal   Hazlitt 3
M. is the Only Animal   Twain 98
m. lay down his wife   Joyce 21
m. made the town   William Cowper 5
m. may love a paradox
    Ralph Waldo Emerson 20
m. may write at any time
    Samuel Johnson 44
m. of all hours   Erasmus 3
m. of genius makes no mistakes
    Joyce 19
m. of many resources   Homer 7
m. of many wiles   Pope 8
m. of my   David Foster Wallace 1
m. of two truths   Iris Murdoch 5
m. on horseback   Cushing 1
M. proposes   Proverbs 186
m. proposes   Thomas à Kempis 1
m. said to the universe Stephen Crane 4

m. shall not live by bread alone
    Bible 202
M. that is born of a woman
    Book of Common Prayer 2
M. wants but little here below
    Oliver Goldsmith 3
M. was born free   Rousseau 3
M. was formed for society   Blackstone 1
M. was made at the end   Twain 118
M. Who Broke the Bank   Fred Gilbert 1
M. Who Came to Dinner
    George S. Kaufman 3
m. who dies rich   Andrew Carnegie 3
m. who had no feet   Sadi 1
M. Who Mistook His Wife   Sacks 1
m. will not merely endure   Faulkner 11
M. with all his noble qualities
    Charles Darwin 13
m. with God is always   John Knox 1
m. without faith is like a fish
    Charles S. Harris 1
M. Without Qualities   Musil 2
m.'s a man for a' that   Robert Burns 5
m.'s character is his fate   Heraclitus 2
m.'s dying is more   Thomas Mann 4
m.'s house is his castle   Coke 8
M.'s inhumanity to m.   Robert Burns 1
m.'s life is cheap   Shakespeare 291
M.'s life is not a business   Bellow 2
M.'s love is of m.'s life   Byron 20
m.'s reach should exceed
    Robert Browning 13
m.'s unconquerable mind
    William Wordsworth 20
m.'s word is his bond   Proverbs 333
met a m. that I didn't like   Will Rogers 8
more wonderful than m.   Sophocles 2
my chance of being a great m.   Disraeli 2
my m. Friday   Defoe 4
never a great m.   Schreiner 3
no indispensable m.   Woodrow Wilson 5
No m. can do the work   Elbert Hubbard 3
No m. is a hero to his valet   Cornuel 1
No m. is above the law
    Theodore Roosevelt 13
No m. is an Island   Donne 5
no m.'s life, liberty   Gideon J. Tucker 1
Of arms and the m.   Virgil 1
Of m.'s first disobedience   Milton 17
Ol' M. River   Hammerstein 3
old m. was dreaming   Hemingway 29
One m., one vote   Cartwright 1
one m. one vote   Chesterton 16
One m. with courage   Andrew Jackson 7
one small step for a m.
    Neil A. Armstrong 3
one-eyed m. is king   Erasmus 1
organization m.   Whyte 2
pain of being a m.   Samuel Johnson 109
people arose as one m.   Bible 79
proper study of mankind is m.   Pope 21
Reading maketh a full m.
    Francis Bacon 22
relation between m. and woman
    Hawthorne 13
sabbath was made for m.   Bible 275
send your m. to my m.   J. P. Morgan 5
sit on a m.'s back   Tolstoy 12
slave was made a m.   Douglass 2

some kind of a m.   Film Lines 179
Stand by your m.   Wynette 3
Stand by your m.   Wynette 4
talked like a m.   Ray Davies 1
Teach a m. to fish   Modern Proverbs 31
that the m. should be alone   Bible 10
this was a m.   Shakespeare 131
Time and tide wait for no m.
    Proverbs 297
tragedy of a m. who could
    Film Lines 93
true study of m.   Charron 1
way to a m.'s heart   Proverbs 324
we find a m.   Pascal 10
What a piece of work is a m.
    Shakespeare 181
When a m. is tired of London
    Samuel Johnson 90
When a m.'s partner is killed
    Hammett 2
who kills a m.   Milton 6
Who was that masked m.
    Radio Catchphrases 18
woman without a m.   Dunn 1
world began without m.   Lévi-Strauss 1
You look almost like a m.   Ferber 1
you'll be a M., my son   Kipling 33
young m.'s fancy   Tennyson 5
manage
m. somehow to muddle through
    Bright 2
management
do the least damage: m.   Scott Adams 1
manchild
m. was born   Alex Haley 1
Mandalay
On the road to M.   Kipling 12
mandarin
christen this style the M.
    Cyril Connolly 1
Manderley
I dreamt I went to M.   Du Maurier 1
mandrake
get with child a m. root   Donne 11
Manhattan
We'll have M.   Lorenz Hart 1
manhood
m. thing with him   Pelosi 2
manifest
our m. destiny   O'Sullivan 2
manifestations
special m. of religion   William James 9
Manila
thriller in M.   Ali 7
mankind
All m. love a lover
    Ralph Waldo Emerson 13
all m. minus one   Mill 5
cause of all m.   Thomas Paine 2
crucify m. upon a cross
    William Jennings Bryan 3
history of m.   Elizabeth Cady Stanton 2
In charity to all m.
    John Quincy Adams 2
legislator of m.   Samuel Johnson 22
M. must put an end to war
    John F. Kennedy 21
one disillusion—m.   Keynes 2
one giant leap for m.
    Neil A. Armstrong 3

proper study of m.   Pope 21
ride m.   Ralph Waldo Emerson 31
willing to love all m.
    Samuel Johnson 93
manna
M., n. A food   Bierce 79
manner
to the m. born   Shakespeare 163
manners
if you don't like my m.
    Raymond Chandler 1
M. are of more importance
    Edmund Burke 26
m. of a dancing master
    Samuel Johnson 45
manpower
Adding m. to a late software
    Frederick P. Brooks 1
mansion
Love has pitched his m.   Yeats 52
mansions
are many m.   Bible 324
more stately m.
    Oliver Wendell Holmes 9
ride through m. of glory   Springsteen 1
mantle
cast his m. upon him   Bible 95
manure
its natural m.   Jefferson 17
manuscripts
M. don't burn   Bulgakov 1
many
after m. a summer   Tennyson 43
coat of m. colors   Bible 33
Cowards die m. times   Shakespeare 102
death had undone so m.   T. S. Eliot 44
fox knows m. things   Archilochus 1
Full m. a glorious morning
    Shakespeare 418
Lord makes so m. of them   Lincoln 54
m. a slip 'twixt cup   Proverbs 187
M. a true word   Proverbs 306
M. are called   Bible 254
M. brave men lived before
    Agamemnon's   Horace 25
M. rivers to cross   Cliff 1
M.-splendored Thing   Suyin 1
m.-splendored thing
    Francis Thompson 1
Of making m. books   Bible 153
people are a m.-headed beast   Horace 11
so much owed by so m.
    Winston Churchill 17
map
m. is not the territory   Korzybski 1
Roll up that m.   William Pitt 1
maps
edges of their m.   Plutarch 1
Marat
Assassination of Jean-Paul M.
    Peter Weiss 1
marble
left it m.   Augustus 3
m. index of a mind
    William Wordsworth 29
m. not yet carved   Michelangelo 2
Not m., nor the gilded   Shakespeare 419
Marcela
M. loved me   Machado de Assis 1

measured
amount can be m.   McCall 1
I have m. out my life   T. S. Eliot 6
She m. to the hour   Wallace Stevens 12
measurements
carry on these m.   Maxwell 2
measures
opposed m. not men   Chesterfield 1
There are few better m.   Ramsey Clark 1
Tory men and Whig m.   Disraeli 9
meat
Not much m. on her   Film Lines 130
One man's m.   Proverbs 190
meatloaf
mistaken for a m.   Kliban 1
meats
Avoid fried m.   Paige 1
mechanic
m., a mere working mason
                                 Walter Scott 9
mechanical
m. slavery   Wilde 49
medal
they gave me a m.   Matlovich 1
meddle
m. in the affairs of Wizards   Tolkien 8
Medes
given to the M. and Persians   Bible 190
law of the M. and Persians   Bible 191
media
cool m. are high   McLuhan 9
m. are not toys   McLuhan 2
m.'s the opposition   Bannon 2
medical
M. men all over the world   Jane Carlyle 2
medicine
desire to take m.   Osler 1
distinction between food and m.
                                 Lin Yutang 1
M. is my lawful wife   Chekhov 1
mistake m. for magic   Szasz 3
medieval
get m. on your ass   Film Lines 143
mediocre
lot of m. judges   Hruska 1
m. brain   Turing 4
m. writer   Maugham 11
Some men are born m.   Heller 4
mediocrities
M. everywhere   Shaffer 1
mediocrity
compliments that m. pays   Wilde 98
have m. thrust upon them   Heller 4
M. knows nothing higher
                          Arthur Conan Doyle 36
m. of the apparatus   Trotsky 3
Only m. can be trusted   Beerbohm 2
meditation
M. is not a means   Krishnamurti 1
medium
hot m. like radio   McLuhan 9
m. is the message   McLuhan 5
M. Is the Message   McLuhan 8
meek
Blessed are the m.   Bible 205
I am m. and gentle   Shakespeare 106
m. really will inherit the earth
                              John M. Henry 1
m. shall inherit the earth   Bible 112

m. shall inherit the earth   Getty 1
m. shall inherit the earth   Heinlein 16
meet
all people descend to m.
                       Ralph Waldo Emerson 9
If I should m. thee   Byron 11
May the road rise to m. you
                              Anonymous 19
M. me in St. Louis   Andrew B. Sterling 1
M. the new boss   Townshend 7
m. the same people   Mizner 1
m. with Triumph and Disaster
                                  Kipling 32
until we m. again   Liliuokalani 1
we m. with champagne
                           Mary Montagu 1
we shall m. the enemy   Walt Kelly 3
we three m. again   Shakespeare 321
We'll m. again   Ross Parker 2
where the elite m.   Radio Catchphrases 7
you m.—not really by chance
                             Hammerstein 20
meeting
as if I were a public m.   Victoria 5
meets
less in this than m. the eye   Bankhead 3
melancholy
chronic m. which is taking hold
                            Thomas Hardy 12
M. has ceased to be   Grass 4
melodies
Heard m. are sweet   Keats 15
melody
M. Lingers On   Irving Berlin 5
pretty girl is like a m.   Irving Berlin 4
melt
butter wouldn't m.   Lanchester 1
too too sullied flesh would m.
                             Shakespeare 149
melted
m. into a new race of men   Crèvecoeur 1
m. into air   Shakespeare 442
m. into spring   Emily Brontë 2
we haven't m.   Jesse Jackson 2
melting
great M.-Pot   Zangwill 2
I'm m.   Film Lines 194
m. pot   Baudouin 1
melts
m. in your mouth
                      Advertising Slogans 76
member
m. of any organized party
                              Will Rogers 15
m. of the Communist Party
                           J. Parnell Thomas 1
members
me as one of its m.   "Groucho" Marx 41
memorandum
law is only a m.
                      Ralph Waldo Emerson 26
make a m. of it   Carroll 27
m. is written not to inform   Acheson 2
Memorex
Is it live, or is it M.
                      Advertising Slogans 81
memorial
Vietnam Veterans M.   Lin 1

memoriam
In M.   Tennyson 27
memories
M. are hunting horns   Apollinaire 1
m. will be so thick   Kinsella 4
memory
all m. and fate driven deep   Dylan 9
good health and a bad m.   Schweitzer 2
hold the m. of a wrong
                       Ralph Waldo Emerson 47
liar ought to have a good m.
                              Proverbs 167
m. be green   Shakespeare 146
M. likes to play   Grass 5
m. of man runneth not   Blackstone 2
mixing m. and desire   T. S. Eliot 39
mystic chords of m.   Lincoln 30
not intellect but rather m.
                        Leonardo da Vinci 4
poor sort of m.   Carroll 37
Thanks for the M.   Robin 1
Memphis
M. Blues   Handy 1
men
all m. are created equal   Jefferson 2
all m. are rapists   French 2
all m. are strange as hell
                            Robin Morgan 1
all m. keep all women   Brownmiller 1
all m. would be tyrants   Defoe 2
all the king's m.   Nursery Rhymes 24
all the m. are good-looking   Keillor 1
all the President's m.   Kissinger 5
all things to all m.   Bible 350
Are we not M.   H. G. Wells 2
Bad m. need nothing more   Mill 18
becoming the m. we wanted   Steinem 3
brave m. lived before Agamemnon's
                                  Horace 25
Dead m. tell no tales   Proverbs 62
difference between m. and women
                           Margaret Mead 5
differences between m. and women
                      Oliver Wendell Holmes, Jr. 32
empire of laws and not of m.
                          James Harrington 1
Fifteen m. on the dead man's
                      Robert Louis Stevenson 8
fishers of m.   Bible 203
fortune and m.'s eyes   Shakespeare 413
good will toward m.   Bible 290
government of laws, and not of m.
                              John Adams 4
Government of laws and not of m.
                          Archibald Cox 1
government of laws and not of m.
                            Gerald R. Ford 3
He who would teach m. to die
                            Montaigne 7
Here m. from the planet Earth
                            Anonymous 12
Here's how m. think   Carrie Fisher 1
I eat m. like air   Plath 7
If m. could get pregnant
                       Florynce Kennedy 2
If m. knew how women   O. Henry 3
If m. were angels   Madison 8
impulses to m. ill at ease   Hawthorne 18
justify the ways of God to m.   Milton 18

life in my m.   Mae West 5
lurks in the hearts of m.
                    Radio Catchphrases 20
made by m.   Vico 1
make life easier for m.   Burchill 1
M., their rights   Susan B. Anthony 1
m. alone are quite capable   Conrad 24
M. and women, women and m.   Jong 8
m. and women are created equal
            Elizabeth Cady Stanton 1
M. and women can't be friends
                    Film Lines 185
m. and women really suit   Hepburn 1
M. are but children of a larger
                    John Dryden 3
m. are like bloody buses   Cope 2
m. are mad   Twiggy 1
m. are not hanged   Halifax 1
m. are the managers   Koran 8
M. are what their mothers
            Ralph Waldo Emerson 39
M. at forty   Justice 1
M. fight and lose   William Morris 3
m. go right after them   Mae West 11
m. have lost their reason
                    Shakespeare 117
m. know so little of m.   Du Bois 6
M. never do evil   Pascal 15
M. seldom make passes
                    Dorothy Parker 7
m. that strove with gods   Tennyson 23
m. were deceivers   Shakespeare 139
more I see of m.   Roland 2
more one gets to know of m.
                    Toussenel 1
Nine Old M.   Drew Pearson 1
opposed measures not m.
                    Chesterfield 1
Practical m., who believe   Keynes 12
same is true of m.
            George Bernard Shaw 25
schemes o' mice an' m.   Robert Burns 3
so-called great m.   Tolstoy 3
stupid white m.   Michael Moore 1
these m. saved the world
        William Jefferson "Bill" Clinton 5
tide in the affairs of m.
                    Shakespeare 128
times that try m.'s souls
                    Thomas Paine 8
Tory m. and Whig measures   Disraeli 9
War Between M. and Women
                    Thurber 4
watch the m. at play   Cleghorn 1
We are the hollow m.   T. S. Eliot 63
We cannot learn m. from books
                    Disraeli 3
we should be m. first   Thoreau 5
When bad m. combine
                    Edmund Burke 1
when m. and mountains meet
                    William Blake 18
White M. Can't Jump   Ron Shelton 1
you are m. of stones   Shakespeare 316
mendacities
Better m.   Ezra Pound 13
mene
M., MENE, TEKEL, UPHARSIN   Bible 190

menny
Done because we are too m.
                    Thomas Hardy 19
mental
cease from m. fight   William Blake 21
delight of m. superiority
                    Samuel Johnson 3
Emancipate yourselves from m.
                    Marley 3
game is half m.   Wohlford 1
m. masturbation   Byron 22
m. reservations   LaFollette 1
Mercedes
buy me a M.-Benz   Joplin 2
merchants
M. of Death   Englebrecht 1
merci
Belle Dame sans M.   Keats 14
mercies
tender m. of the wicked   Bible 128
merciful
be m. unto a broken reed
                    Francis Bacon 26
merciless
m. glare   Tennessee Williams 2
mercy
m. upon us miserable sinners
            Book of Common Prayer 7
quality of m. is not strain'd
                    Shakespeare 79
temper so justice with m.   Milton 41
'Twas m. brought me   Wheatley 1
merdre
M.!   Jarry 1
mere
M. alcohol doesn't thrill   Cole Porter 5
Meredith
M.'s a prose Browning   Wilde 8
merely
M. corroborative detail   W. S. Gilbert 43
meritocracy
m. of talent   Michael Young 1
mermaids
heard the m. singing   T. S. Eliot 11
merrier
more the m.   Proverbs 199
merrily
m., m., life is but a dream
            Folk and Anonymous Songs 67
M. We Roll Along   George S. Kaufman 2
merriment
source of innocent m.   W. S. Gilbert 40
merry
God rest you m.
            Folk and Anonymous Songs 30
May your days be m.   Irving Berlin 11
m. monarch   Rochester 3
to drink, and to be m.   Bible 147
mess
another nice m.   Laurel 1
birthright for a m.   Bible 400
Don't make a m. of it   Morant 1
do till a m. gets here Cormac McCarthy 5
message
Carry a m. to Garcia   Elbert Hubbard 1
form and not the m.   McLuhan 1
medium is the m.   McLuhan 5
Medium Is the M.   McLuhan 8
take a m. to Albert   Disraeli 35

messages
M. are for Western   Goldwyn 3
messenger
he was a m.   Joseph Smith 1
messiah
M. will come   Kafka 5
messing
m. about in boats   Grahame 1
met
all that I have m.   Tennyson 17
I m. a man with seven wives
                    Nursery Rhymes 65
I m. a traveller from an antique
                    Percy Shelley 5
I m. Murder on the way   Percy Shelley 2
ill m. by moonlight   Shakespeare 54
m. a man that I didn't like   Will Rogers 8
m. a man who wasn't there   Mearns 1
m. the enemy   Walt Kelly 4
m. the enemy   Oliver Hazard Perry 2
m. them at close of day   Yeats 26
metal
another Heavy M. Boy
            William S. Burroughs 3
Heavy m. thunder   Bonfire 1
metaphysical
termed the m. poets   Samuel Johnson 32
metaphysics
cheating on my m. final Woody Allen 29
more towards m. than Locke
                    Charles Darwin 1
meteor
shone like a m. streaming   Milton 23
meter
energy too cheap to m.   Strauss 1
method
I do not know the m.   Edmund Burke 8
there is m. in't   Shakespeare 177
With m. and logic   Christie 3
methods
You know my m., Watson
            Arthur Conan Doyle 24
Mets
last miracle I did was the 1969 M.
                    Corman 1
M. are gonna be amazin'   Stengel 5
Mexican
judge is of M. heritage   Trump 10
Mexico
Poor M.   Díaz 1
when M. sends its people   Trump 3
Mi
M. chiamano Mimi   Giacosa 2
miasmal
wrapt in the old m. mist   T. S. Eliot 26
Micawber
I never will desert Mr. M.   Dickens 60
mice
as long as it catches m. Deng Xiaoping 2
m. will play   Proverbs 41
schemes o' m. an' men   Robert Burns 3
Three blind m.   Nursery Rhymes 42
Michael
M., row the boat ashore
            Folk and Anonymous Songs 51
Michelangelo
regrets that M. died   Twain 70
talking of M.   T. S. Eliot 4

Michelle
M. ma belle   Lennon and McCartney 5
Mickey
I love M. Mouse   Disney 2
You're M. Mouse   Cole Porter 7
microcosm
m. of a public school   Disraeli 1
midday
go out in the m. sun   Coward 9
middle
beginning, m., and end   Aristotle 6
dead center of m. age
    Franklin P. Adams 2
In the m. of the journey   Dante 2
m. of the night   Carroll 32
m. station is most favorable   Goethe 22
M. Way is none at all   John Adams 6
nothing in the m. of the road
    Hightower 2
realized the M. Path   Pali Tripitaka 1
safely by the m. way   Ovid 3
stay in the m. of the road   Bevan 2
That's my M. West
    F. Scott Fitzgerald 28
we call the m. class   Matthew Arnold 31
middle-age
restraining reckless m.   Yeats 12
mid-life
m. crisis   Jaques 1
midnight
chimes at m.   Shakespeare 65
m. never come   Marlowe 10
m. ride of Paul Revere   Longfellow 23
Once upon a m. dreary   Poe 6
our m. oil   Quarles 1
stroke of the m. hour   Nehru 1
wisdom out of m. oil   Yeats 40
midst
In the m. of life
    Book of Common Prayer 3
might
It m. have been   Whittier 1
m., could, would   George Eliot 14
M. is right   Proverbs 191
right makes m.   Lincoln 22
mightier
m. than the sword   Bulwer-Lytton 3
mighty
He hath put down the m.   Bible 285
how are the m. fallen   Bible 86
look on my works, ye M.   Percy Shelley 7
m. Casey has struck out
    Ernest L. Thayer 4
then burst his m. heart   Shakespeare 120
mild-mannered
m. reporter   Television Catchphrases 6
mile
compel thee to go a m.   Bible 212
miss is as good as a m.   Proverbs 194
walk a m. for a Camel
    Advertising Slogans 25
walked a m.   Modern Proverbs 19
miles
journey of a thousand m.   Lao Tzu 9
m. to go before I sleep   Frost 16
see it lap the M.   Emily Dickinson 13
milestones
There's m. on the Dover Road
    Dickens 94

military
as m. music is to music   Clemenceau 8
conjunction of an immense m.
    Eisenhower 10
entrust to m. men   Clemenceau 4
M. intelligence   "Groucho" Marx 48
M. justice is to justice   Clemenceau 8
m. science seems a real   Rebecca West 6
m.-industrial complex   Eisenhower 11
overgrown M. establishments
    George Washington 6
professional m. mind   H. G. Wells 6
specimen of Intelligence, M.
    Aldous Huxley 2
too important to be left to m.   Briand 2
milk
crying over spilt m.   Proverbs 58
Gin was mother's m.
    George Bernard Shaw 40
Got m.   Advertising Slogans 10
incomparable m. of wonder
    F. Scott Fitzgerald 20
land flowing with m.   Bible 41
m. of human kindness   Shakespeare 333
m. the cow of the world   Wilbur 1
Money is the mother's m.   Unruh 1
skim m. masquerades   W. S. Gilbert 11
take my m. for gall   Shakespeare 336
trout in the m.   Thoreau 15
milkshake
drink your m.   Film Lines 172
mill
old m. stream   Tell Taylor 1
so near the m.   Cleghorn 1
Miller
It's M. time   Advertising Slogans 84
million
eight m. stories   Film Lines 123
Fifty M. Frenchmen   Rose 2
I've got a m. of 'em   Durante 1
m. deaths is a statistic   Stalin 5
m. men are wiser   Heinlein 6
m. monkeys banging   Wilensky 1
m. monkeys have been trained   Borel 1
one m. divided by one m.   Koestler 1
turn $100 m. into   Bronfman 1
millionaire
endowed by the ruined m.   T. S. Eliot 106
I am a M.   George Bernard Shaw 27
silk hat on a Bradford m.   T. S. Eliot 52
Who Wants to Be a M.   Cole Porter 26
millions
hundred and fifty m. of men
    Tocqueville 13
I had m. of them   Van Doren 1
I will be m.   Fast 1
M. a hero   Film Lines 118
m. a hero   Porteus 1
M. are to be grabbed   Mankiewicz 2
M. for defense   Robert Harper 1
M. long for immortality   Ertz 1
M. of spiritual creatures   Milton 35
mills
dark Satanic m.   William Blake 19
m. of God grind slowly   Logau 1
m. of God grind slowly   Proverbs 192
Milton
M.! thou shouldst be living
    William Wordsworth 11

malt does more than M.   Housman 5
mute inglorious M.   Thomas Gray 8
one sound test of a M.   Mencken 30
reason M. wrote in fetters
    William Blake 8
what M. saw   Marquis 3
mince
dined on m.   Lear 7
mind
Clear your m. of cant
    Samuel Johnson 103
could not make up his m.   Film Lines 93
did not have him in m.
    George Gaylor Simpson 1
empires of the m.   Winston Churchill 30
eternal sunshine of the spotless m.
    Pope 7
favors only the prepared m.   Pasteur 1
find the m.'s construction
    Shakespeare 332
free play of the m.   Matthew Arnold 11
Free Your M.   George Clinton 1
Georgia on my m.   Gorrell 1
give a sex to m.   Wollstonecraft 5
human m. to correlate   Lovecraft 1
improper m. is a perpetual
    Logan Smith 1
last infirmity of noble m.   Milton 2
Let us suppose the m.   John Locke 2
man's m. is stretched
    Oliver Wendell Holmes 6
man's unconquerable m.
    William Wordsworth 20
marble index of a m.
    William Wordsworth 29
m., that very fiery particle   Byron 31
M. Games   Lennon 11
M. in its purest play   Wilbur 3
m. is a terrible thing to waste
    Advertising Slogans 120
m. is its own place   Milton 21
m. is not sex-typed   Margaret Mead 7
m. of Ronald Reagan   Noonan 1
m. of the oppressed   Biko 1
m. the music and the step
    Folk and Anonymous Songs 85
minister to a m. diseas'd
    Shakespeare 390
more the m. takes in   Henry James 2
my m. is going   Film Lines 182
my m. is not on oath   Euripides 1
My m. to me a kingdom   Earl of Oxford 1
nobler in the m. to suffer
    Shakespeare 188
not changing one's m.   Maugham 1
O the m., m. has mountains
    Gerard Manley Hopkins 8
out of m.   Thomas à Kempis 2
Out of sight, out of m.   Proverbs 229
palm at the end of the m.
    Wallace Stevens 15
passing through the m.   Slosson 1
pleased to call your m.   Westbury 1
professional military m.   H. G. Wells 6
sound m. in a sound body   Juvenal 6
subsistence without a m.   Berkeley 2
There is no female m.
    Charlotte Gilman 4

Those who m. don't matter
                    Modern Proverbs 57
true peace of m.   W. S. Gilbert 16
until reeled the m.   Gibbs 1
waste it is to lose one's m.   Quayle 2
water never formed to m.
                    Wallace Stevens 10
we would know the the m. of God
                    Hawking 3
what a noble m.   Shakespeare 197
you have a legal m.
                    Thomas Reed Powell 1
Your m. and you are our Sargasso
                    Ezra Pound 7
minded
m. what they were about   Sterne 1
minding
Who's m. the store   Sayings 63
minds
corrupting the m. of the young   Plato 1
Enquiring m. want to know
                    Advertising Slogans 90
Great m. think alike   Proverbs 130
hearts and m. will follow
                    Modern Proverbs 36
hobgoblin of little m.
                    Ralph Waldo Emerson 16
I saw the best m.   Ginsberg 7
marriage of true m.   Shakespeare 429
master m. of all nations   Twain 43
m. and hearts of the people
                    John Adams 17
M. are like parachutes   Dewar 1
recreation of noble m.   Guedalla 2
mine
as good as m.   Modern Proverbs 37
but m. own   Shakespeare 96
M. eyes have seen the glory
                    Julia Ward Howe 1
m. hour is not yet come   Bible 313
necessity is yet greater than m.
                    Philip Sidney 6
she is m. for life   Spark 2
Vengeance is m.   Bible 346
world's m. oyster   Shakespeare 67
miner
coal m.'s daughter   Lynn 1
dwelt a m.   Montrose 1
mineral
not the m. rights   Getty 1
minerals
If poisonous m.   Donne 6
Minerva
owl of M.   Hegel 2
minimal
m. state   Nozick 2
m. state   Nozick 5
minimis
De m. non curat lex
                    Anonymous (Latin) 5
minimum
m.-wage law is   Milton Friedman 3
minister
Canst thou not m.   Shakespeare 390
ministering
m. angel   Walter Scott 6
minist'ring
m. angel   Shakespeare 228

Minnehaha
M., Laughing Water   Longfellow 18
minorities
discrete and insular m.
                    Harlan F. Stone 1
M. . . . are almost always
                    Sydney Smith 6
protect m. in its own   Charles Houston 1
minority
m. are right   Debs 1
m. is always right   Ibsen 16
m. possess their equal rights
                    Jefferson 29
minstrel
no M. raptures swell   Walter Scott 3
wandering m. I   W. S. Gilbert 28
minute
every, every m.   Thornton Wilder 3
fill the unforgiving m.   Kipling 33
it seems like a m.   Einstein 29
made up of m. fractions   Coleridge 34
sucker born every m.   Barnum 1
minutes
famous for fifteen m.   Warhol 3
Love is three m.   Rotten 4
our m. hasten to their end
                    Shakespeare 420
rate of sixty m. an hour   C. S. Lewis 2
wait a few m.   Twain 150
mio
O sole m.   Capurro 1
Mirabeau
Under M. Bridge   Apollinaire 2
miracle
It was a m.   Gordimer 1
last m. I did was the 1969 Mets
                    Corman 1
m., mystery, and authority
                    Dostoyevski 6
m. of rare device   Coleridge 22
sufficient to establish a m.
                    David Hume 7
that it is comprehensible is a m.
                    Einstein 13
miracles
attended with m.   David Hume 8
Do you believe in m.   Al Michaels 1
M. are instantaneous
                    Katherine Anne Porter 1
M. are propitious accidents
                    Santayana 6
must believe in m.   Ben-Gurion 1
mirage
this m. of social justice   Hayek 2
mirror
as in a magic m.
                    Oliver Wendell Holmes, Jr. 8
faithful m. of manners
                    Samuel Johnson 29
go to the m.   Wimbrow 1
live in front of a m.   Pirandello 2
M., m., on the wall
                    Grimm and Grimm 3
m. cracked   Tennyson 1
m. up to nature   Shakespeare 203
mirrors
M. and blue smoke   Breslin 2
misbehavin'
Ain't m.   Razaf 1

mischief
M., thou art afoot   Shakespeare 126
misdemeanors
high Crimes and M.   Constitution 7
miserable
make only two people m.
                    Samuel Butler (1835–1902) 3
making the last m.   la Bruyère 1
m. Irish childhood   McCourt 1
upon us m. sinners
                    Book of Common Prayer 7
misery
first is but a splendid m.   Jefferson 24
M. acquaints a man   Shakespeare 441
M. loves company   Proverbs 193
result m.   Dickens 59
misfortune
m. of our best friends
                    la Rochefoucauld 1
misfortunes
bear another's m.   Pope 10
bear the m. of others
                    la Rochefoucauld 3
tableau of crimes and m.   Voltaire 15
misgovernment
augur m. at a distance   Edmund Burke 7
misprint
die of a m.   Herz 1
mispronounce
all men m. it   Christopher Morley 3
misquotation
M. is, in fact, the pride
                    Hesketh Pearson 1
misquote
just enough of learning to m.   Byron 1
miss
Little M. Muffet   Nursery Rhymes 47
m. for pleasure   Gay 1
m. is as good as a mile   Proverbs 194
M. Twye was soaping   Ewart 2
We may not m. them
                    F. Scott Fitzgerald 39
missed
he m. the bus   Chamberlain 4
never m. a chance
                    George Bernard Shaw 56
never m. an opportunity   Eban 3
missiles
We have guided m.
                    Martin Luther King, Jr. 15
missing
after her m. children   Melville 14
m. link   Konrad Lorenz 2
mission
Its five-year m.   Roddenberry 1
M. Accomplished   Sforza 1
m. from God   Film Lines 26
Your m. . . . should you decide
                    Television Catchphrases 45
missionaries
eaten by m.   Spooner 2
missionary
m. position   Kinsey 1
Mississippi
M. Delta was shining   Paul Simon 12
mistake
but a gigantic m.   Sigmund Freud 22
Don't make the same m.
                    Modern Proverbs 77

mistake (cont.):

every time you make a m.	Plante 1
God's second m.	Nietzsche 22
it is seldom a m.	Mencken 10
last man to die for a m.	Kerry 1
When I make a m.	La Guardia 1

mistaken

m. for fair weather	Twain 153
ye may be m.	Hand 10
you may be m.	Cromwell 1

mistakes

do nothing that make no m.	Conrad 1
forgive others their m.	Jessamyn West 2
made my own m.	Kazuo Ishiguro 3
man of genius makes no m.	Joyce 19
m. were made	
	George Herbert Walker Bush 2
name men gave to their m.	Wilde 35
new day with no m.	Lucy Montgomery 2
records its m. carefully	
	Elliott Dunlap Smith 1
regrets are one's m.	Wilde 31

mistook

Man Who M. His Wife	Sacks 1

mistress

embrace your lordship's m.	Foote 2
great-great grandfather's m.	
	Parker Bowles 1
If you marry your m.	
	James Goldsmith 1
in ev'ry port a m.	Gay 3
jealous m.	Story 1
literature is my m.	Chekhov 1
m. of the Earl of Craven	
	Harriette Wilson 1
m. of the party	
	Timothy Michael Healy 1
music is my m.	Ellington 1

misunderstood

To be great is to be m.	
	Ralph Waldo Emerson 17

mite

how to create a m.	Montaigne 13

mittens

they lost their m.	Nursery Rhymes 32

mix

m. business with pleasure	
	Modern Proverbs 58
Oil and water don't m.	Proverbs 222

mixed

elements so m. in him	Shakespeare 131
It's a m. up muddled up	Ray Davies 2

mixing

m. memory and desire	T. S. Eliot 39

moans

deep m. round	Tennyson 24

mob

never saw a m. rush	Mizner 13
redress by m. law	Lincoln 1

mobile

La donna è m.	Piave 1

mobilized

m. the English language	Murrow 5

moccasins

walked a mile in his m.	
	Modern Proverbs 19

mockery

delusion, a m.	Denman 1
travesty of a m.	Woody Allen 8

mockingbird

buy you a m.	
	Folk and Anonymous Songs 35
Listen to the m.	Winner 1
to kill a m.	Harper Lee 1

model

very m. of a modern	W. S. Gilbert 19

moderation

astonished at my own m.	
	Clive of Plassey 1
M. in all things	Proverbs 195
m. in everything	Horace 26
M. in temper	Thomas Paine 24
M. in the pursuit	Goldwater 3
spirit of m. is gone	Hand 3
urge me not to use m.	Garrison 2
write, with m.	Garrison 3

modern

ethos of m. science	Merton 1
gives us m. art	Stoppard 3
making the m. world possible	
	T. S. Eliot 36
M. Art has become	Tom Wolfe 2
m. inconveniences	Twain 27
m. life out to be worse	Orwell 11
Much of m. art	Sontag 5
very model of a m.	W. S. Gilbert 19

modes

various m. of worship	Gibbon 2

modest

m. man who has a good deal	
	Winston Churchill 46
M. Proposal	Jonathan Swift 26

Mohicans

last of the M.	James Fenimore Cooper 1

moi

L'État c'est m.	Louis XIV 2

moider

I'll m. that bum	Galento 1

mojo

Got My M. Workin'	Muddy Waters 2

mold

then broke the m.	Ariosto 1

molehill

m. man is a pseudo-busy executive	
	Fred Allen 5

moment

decisive m.	Retz 1
m. of Zen	Television Catchphrases 15
not one m. longer	Du Bois 10
one brief shining m.	Alan Jay Lerner 17
possessions for a m.	Elizabeth I 5
seen the m. of my greatness	
	T. S. Eliot 8
without the m.	Matthew Arnold 9

momentary

Beauty is m.	Wallace Stevens 7
pleasure is m.	Chesterfield 7

moments

m. will be lost in time	Film Lines 24

mommie

M. dearest	Cristina Crawford 1

Mona

on the M. Lisa	Cole Porter 8

monarch

merry m.	Rochester 3
m. of all I survey	William Cowper 4

monarchy

M. is a strong government	Bagehot 3

Monday

M.'s child is fair	Nursery Rhymes 43

Monet

M. is only an eye	Cézanne 3

money

add up to real m.	Dirksen 1
all the m. in the world	
	Aristotle Onassis 1
always to worry for m.	Tillie Olsen 1
Bad m. drives out good	
	Henry Dunning Macleod 2
ever wrote, except for m.	
	Samuel Johnson 85
Follow the m.	Film Lines 8
fool and his m.	Proverbs 111
Her voice is full of m.	
	F. Scott Fitzgerald 24
if he'd had the m.	Peter Fleming 1
If you can count your m.	Getty 3
If You've Got the M.	Frizzell 1
It hain't th' m.	"Kin" Hubbard 4
it is m. they have	Kinsella 3
It's not the m.	Sayings 30
just as proud for half the m.	Godfrey 1
lawyers, guns, and m.	Zevon 3
long enough to get m.	Leacock 2
lost m. by underestimating	Mencken 35
love of m. as a possession	Keynes 10
love of m. has taken	Tocqueville 1
love of m. is the root	Bible 377
make m. the old-fashioned way	
	Advertising Slogans 109
M., it turned out	James Baldwin 1
M., which represents	
	Ralph Waldo Emerson 24
M. can't buy life	Marley 4
m. can't buy me love	
	Lennon and McCartney 3
m. cheerfully refunded	Selfridge 1
M. couldn't buy friends	Milligan 1
M. doesn't grow on trees	
	Modern Proverbs 60
M. doesn't talk	Dylan 15
M. for nothin'	Knopfler 1
M. . . . ? in a voice	Gaddis 2
m. is a distinctly male	Dworkin 3
M. is better than poverty	
	Woody Allen 23
m. is like muck	Francis Bacon 18
M. . . . is none of the wheels	
	David Hume 6
M. is the mother's milk	Unruh 1
M. isn't everything	Proverbs 197
M. makes the world go around	Ebb 2
M. talks	Proverbs 198
m. where your mouth	
	Modern Proverbs 61
no trick to make a lot of m.	
	Film Lines 54
not asked to lend m.	Twain 61
only interested in m.	
	George Bernard Shaw 54
other people's m.	Girardin 1
other people's m.	Thatcher 3
power to make m.	John D. Rockefeller 2
previntion of croolty to m.	Dunne 22
print your own m.	Roy Thomson 1
right to use m.	Leo XIII 1
rub up against m.	Runyon 1

Out of thine own m.   Bible 304
take it out of my m.   "Groucho" Marx 37
mouths
m. only and no hands   Lincoln 19
poor dumb m.   Shakespeare 124
move
did thee feel the earth m. Hemingway 23
Faith can m. mountains   Proverbs 97
I will m. the earth   Archimedes 1
Ladies don't m.   Curzon 1
m. immediately upon your works
    Ulysses S. Grant 1
yet it does m.   Galileo 4
moveable
Paris is a m. feast   Hemingway 30
moved
we shall not be m.
    Folk and Anonymous Songs 81
movement
Establishment and the M.
    Ralph Waldo Emerson 44
m. at the station   Banjo Paterson 1
mover
prime m.   Aquinas 1
movers
m. and shakers   O'Shaughnessy 1
moves
God m. in a mysterious way
    William Cowper 1
If it m., salute it   Sayings 22
If it m., tax it   Ronald W. Reagan 11
Love that m. the sun   Dante 14
whole creation m.   Tennyson 35
movie
mistake each other for m. stars
    Fred Allen 6
quite happy in a m.   Percy 1
movies
everybody's in m.   Ray Davies 3
It is at the m.   Breton 4
popularity of American m.
    Mary McCarthy 3
moving
m. finger writes   Edward FitzGerald 3
Mozart
en famille, they play M.   Karl Barth 1
no female M.   Paglia 2
sonatas of M. are unique   Schnabel 2
when M. was my age   Lehrer 7
Mr.
M. Gorbachev, tear down
    Ronald W. Reagan 14
M. President, you can't say Dallas
    Connally 1
M. Watson—come here
    Alexander Graham Bell 1
No more M. Nice Guy   Sayings 41
They call me M. Tibbs   Ball 1
This is the army, M. Jones
    Irving Berlin 9
Mrs.
This is M. Norman Maine
    Film Lines 162
What will M. Grundy zay
    Thomas Morton 1
MTV
I want my M.!   Advertising Slogans 87
much
M. have I seen and known   Tennyson 17

m. is required   John F. Kennedy 6
M. Madness is divinest Sense
    Emily Dickinson 18
M. may be made   Samuel Johnson 70
m. might be said   Addison 1
of him shall be m. required   Bible 297
so m. to do   Rhodes 2
so m. to do   Tennyson 31
Tho' m. is taken   Tennyson 26
to whom m. is given   John F. Kennedy 6
unto whomsoever m. is given   Bible 297
muck
money is like m.   Francis Bacon 18
Sing 'em m.   Melba 1
muckrake
with a m. in his hands   Bunyan 6
muck-rakes
men with the m.   Theodore Roosevelt 15
mud
the world is m.-lusciou
    e.e. cummings 4
muddle
manage somehow to m. through
    Bright 2
muddy
waist deep in the big m.   Pete Seeger 6
Mudville
M. nine   Ernest L. Thayer 1
no joy in M.   Ernest L. Thayer 4
Muffet
Little Miss M.   Nursery Rhymes 47
muffin
Do you know the m. man
    Folk and Anonymous Songs 53
mugged
m. by reality   Kristol 3
muggle
"M.," said Hagrid   Rowling 1
mulberry
round the m. bush
    Folk and Anonymous Songs 54
mule
de m. uh de world   Hurston 4
multiply
Be fruitful, and m.   Bible 6
multitude
cover the m. of sins   Bible 384
m. is always in the wrong
    Earl of Roscommon 1
m. of tongues   Hand 4
multitudes
I contain m.   Whitman 8
mum
your m. and dad   Larkin 3
mundi
Sic transit gloria m. Anonymous (Latin) 13
murder
I met M. on the way   Percy Shelley 2
man indulges himself in m.
    De Quincey 1
m. a man who is committing
    Woodrow Wilson 12
M. is a crime   Legman 1
m. men everywhere   Fanon 2
M. most foul   Shakespeare 167
m. thousands   Edward Young 3
M. your darlings   Quiller-Couch 1
One m. made a villain   Porteus 1
One m. makes a villain   Film Lines 118

order a public m.   Beccaria 3
scarlet thread of m.
    Arthur Conan Doyle 6
We m. to dissect   William Wordsworth 3
worse than m.   Irving R. Kaufman 1
murdered
I was m.   Sebold 1
murderer
count on a m.   Nabokov 3
murderers
m., do it first   Karr 1
We are all m. at heart
    Clarence S. Darrow 6
murderous
all the m. ideologies George W. Bush 10
Murgatroyd
Heavens to M.
    Television Catchphrases 89
murmuring
m. pines and the hemlocks
    Longfellow 15
murther
Macbeth does m. Sleep Shakespeare 354
muscular
His Christianity was m.   Disraeli 29
m. strength, which it gave   Carroll 10
muse
for a m. of fire   Shakespeare 132
Tell me, m.   Homer 7
Muses
adjunct to the M.'s diadem
    Ezra Pound 11
mush
head full of m.   Film Lines 129
mushroom
supramundane m.   Laurence 2
too short to stuff a m.   Conran 1
music
as military m. is to m.   Clemenceau 8
aspires towards the condition of m.
    Pater 2
day the m. died   McLean 1
frozen m.   Schelling 1
How sour sweet m. is Shakespeare 23
I don't like my m.   Loewe 1
I got m.   Gershwin 5
If m. be the food of love
    Shakespeare 239
meaning to m.   Copland 1
mind the m. and the step
    Folk and Anonymous Songs 85
m., even in the most   Mozart 4
M. above all   Verlaine 4
m. and women I cannot   Pepys 4
M. Goes 'Round and Around
    "Red" Hodgson 1
M. has charms to sooth   Congreve 5
M. heard so deeply   T. S. Eliot 115
m. in the air   Elgar 1
M. is my mistress   Ellington 1
m. is no different   Khomeini 1
m. is the brandy
    George Bernard Shaw 14
m. of a poem   Synge 1
My m. is best understood   Stravinsky 2
so much m. in my head   Ravel 1
supremacy of German m.   Schoenberg 1
Wagner's m.   Nye 1
What m. they make   Stoker 3

dull in a n. way   Samuel Johnson 78
edge of a n. frontier   John F. Kennedy 4
emergence of this N. Class   Galbraith 3
Emperor's N. Clothes   Andersen 2
fresh woods, and pastures n.   Milton 4
green breast of the n. world
                F. Scott Fitzgerald 32
house in N. Orleans
            Folk and Anonymous Songs 65
I called the N. World   Canning 1
I love N. York   Advertising Slogans 92
I make all things n.   Bible 399
If only the true were n.   Voss 1
If two N. Hampshiremen   Benét 3
It's up to you, N. York   Ebb 6
Live from N. York
            Television Catchphrases 68
Meet the n. boss   Townshend 7
needed was a n. deal   Twain 40
n. birth of freedom   Lincoln 42
n. broom sweeps clean   Proverbs 210
n. class   Djilas 1
n. deal and a change   Woodrow Wilson 4
n. deal for the American
            Franklin D. Roosevelt 4
N. England weather   Twain 18
N. Federalism   Richard Nixon 8
n. freedom   Woodrow Wilson 7
N. Jersey Turnpike   Paul Simon 4
N. Nationalism   Theodore Roosevelt 21
N. opinions   John Locke 1
n. terrors of Death   Arbuthnot 1
N. Testament, and to a very
            John Jay Chapman 1
n. theory is attacked   William James 19
N. things are made familiar
            Samuel Johnson 38
N. Way to Pay Old Debts   Massinger 1
n. wine into old bottles   Bible 234
n. world order, where diverse
        George Herbert Walker Bush 12
n. world order—a world where
        George Herbert Walker Bush 10
n. world order is being born
            Martin Luther King, Jr. 1
n. world order came about
        George Herbert Walker Bush 7
n. world order outlast   P. J. Bailey 1
N. York, a helluva town
            Comden and Green 1
N. York, N. York   Ebb 5
N. York is the greatest   Dick Gregory 3
N. York makes one think   Bellow 3
N. York state of mind   Joel 2
N. Yorker will be the magazine
            Harold Ross 1
no n. thing under the sun   Bible 141
nothing n. in the world   Truman 12
Of all targets, N. York   E. B. White 5
old lamps for n. ones   Arabian Nights 1
old N. York way   Wharton 7
require n. clothes   Thoreau 19
rightly call a N. World   Vespucci 1
ring in the n.   Tennyson 33
sidewalks of N. York   James W. Blake 1
something n. out of Africa   Pliny 1
teach an old dog n. tricks   Proverbs 292
tomorrow is a n. day Lucy Montgomery 2
Tomorrow is a n. day   Proverbs 302
weather in N. England   Twain 150

What good is a n.-born baby
            Benjamin Franklin 42
What is true is alas not n.   Ebbinghaus 1
yielding place to n.   Tennyson 45
newe
cometh al this n. corn   Chaucer 5
newer
seek a n. world   Tennyson 24
Newman
Hello, N.   Television Catchphrases 69
news
All the n. that's fit to print
                Adolph Ochs 1
Bad n. travels fast   Proverbs 15
I can't believe the n. today   Bono 1
man who brings bad n.   Sophocles 1
n. is history in its first   Twain 130
n. that STAYS news   Ezra Pound 19
No n. is good n.   Proverbs 211
President who never told bad n.
                Keillor 2
What n. on the Rialto   Shakespeare 71
newspaper
amounts to n. death   Henry Adams 14
n. is in all literalness   Lippmann 1
Once a n. touches a story   Mailer 3
newspapers
government without n.   Jefferson 15
Newspeak
whole aim of N.   Orwell 38
newt
Eye of n.   Shakespeare 376
Newton
Let N. be   Pope 11
Single vision and N.'s sleep
            William Blake 13
statue stood of N.
            William Wordsworth 29
Newtons
evolved a race of Isaac N.
            Aldous Huxley 6
next
fire n. time   James Baldwin 2
fire n. time
        Folk and Anonymous Songs 36
n. item on the agenda   Stalin 6
n. stop, the Twilight Zone   Serling 1
n. to godliness   John Wesley 2
n. to of course god america
                e.e. cummings 9
N. year in Jerusalem   Anonymous 20
slipped away into the n. room
            Henry Scott Holland 1
Wait till n. year   Sayings 58
nexus
sole n. of man to man Thomas Carlyle 11
Niagara
up the Fall of N.   Benjamin Franklin 32
nice
all things n.   Southey 8
n. guys are all over there   Durocher 2
n. place to visit   Sayings 28
N. work if you can get it   Gershwin 9
No more Mr. N. Guy   Sayings 41
not n. to fool Mother Nature
            Advertising Slogans 29
not very n. people   Frankfurter 3
someone wants to be n.   Puig 1
who's naughty and n.   Gillespie 2

niche
got your n. in creation   Radclyffe Hall 2
nick
N., nack, paddy whack
            Nursery Rhymes 38
nickel
if it doesn't make a n.   Goldwyn 7
n. in my pocket   "Groucho" Marx 1
Niger
young lady of N.   Monkhouse 1
nigger
called me, "N."   Cullen 2
ever called me "n."   Ali 9
Woman is the n.   Ono 1
niggers
Irish are the n. of Europe Roddy Doyle 1
night
ain't a fit n. out   W. C. Fields 4
children of the n.   Stoker 3
Come, seeing N.   Shakespeare 367
Come n., strike the hour   Apollinaire 3
Dark n.   St. John of the Cross 1
dark n. of the soul F. Scott Fitzgerald 41
fearful of the n.   Sarah Williams 1
follow as the n. the day Shakespeare 161
go bump in the n.   Anonymous 11
Good n., ladies   Shakespeare 221
Good n., sweet prince   Shakespeare 237
Gwine to run all n.   Stephen Foster 2
He'd had a hard day's n.   Lennon 2
I could have danced all n.
                Alan Jay Lerner 4
ignorant armies clash by n.   Matthew Arnold 19
Illness is the n.-side   Sontag 7
It was a dark and stormy n.
                Bulwer-Lytton 1
It's been a hard day's n.
            Lennon and McCartney 4
Last n. I dreamt   Du Maurier 1
lay hid in n.   Pope 11
midst of a long n.   Poincaré 1
moon at n.   Irving Berlin 13
N. and day   Cole Porter 1
N. and fog   Richard Wagner 2
n. before Christmas Clement C. Moore 1
n. has a thousand eyes   Bourdillon 1
N. hath a thousand eyes   Lyly 2
n. of the long knives   Hitler 2
n. the bed fell   Thurber 2
N. They Drove Old Dixie
            Robbie Robertson 2
N.'s candles are burnt out
                Shakespeare 47
one acquainted with the n.   Frost 17
Red sky at n.   Proverbs 251
Ships that pass in the n.   Longfellow 26
Silent n.! Holy n.!   Mohr 1
something of the n.   Widdecombe 1
Spirit of N.   Percy Shelley 17
staying up all n.   Stengel 6
tender is the n.   Keats 18
Tonight's the N.   Reubens 1
what of the n.   Bible 169
Whatever Gets You Thru the N.
                Lennon 12
Why is this n. different   Talmud 4
world's last n.   Donne 8

nightingales
n. are singing   T. S. Eliot 17
nightmare
long national n. is over   Gerald R. Ford 3
n. from which I am trying   Joyce 17
n. of real things   DeLillo 1
n. of the dark   Auden 24
your worst n.   Film Lines 145
nights
just one of those n.   Cole Porter 13
nightstick
at the end of a n.
            Alexander S. Williams 1
nihilist
n. is a man   Turgenev 1
Nijinsky
What mad N. wrote   Auden 12
Nile
old Father N.   Speke 1
sources of the N.   George Eliot 11
nimble
Jack be n.   Nursery Rhymes 27
nine
cat only has n. lives   Twain 60
her shoes were number n.   Montrose 3
n. cases out of ten   Austen 7
n. old men   Berle 1
N. Old Men   Drew Pearson 1
playing at n.-pins   Washington Irving 4
Possession is n. points   Proverbs 239
stitch in time saves n.   Proverbs 285
takes n. months   Frederick P. Brooks 2
When n. hundred years old
            George Lucas 17
your n. inches   Harriette Wilson 2
nineteen
party like it's n. ninety nine   Prince 1
nineteenth
N. Amendment   Will Rogers 9
nineties
Gay N.   Culter 1
ninety
n. miles from Cuba   Castro 4
N. percent of everything   Sturgeon 1
N. percent of this game   Wohlford 1
nix
Stix N. Hick Pix   Abel Green 1
Nixon
between N. and the White House
            John F. Kennedy 41
N. himself who represents
            Hunter S. Thompson 4
N. to kick around anymore
            Richard Nixon 3
N.'s the One   Political Slogans 27
one person who voted for N.   Kael 2
Tin soldiers and N. coming
            Neil Young 2
no
can't say N. in any of them
            Dorothy Parker 27
Good field. N. hit
            Miguel "Mike" Gonzalez 1
Just say n.   Advertising Slogans 2
n. fool like an old fool   Proverbs 113
N. good deed   Clare Boothe Luce 7
N. guts, n. glory   Modern Proverbs 38
n. joy in Mudville   Ernest L. Thayer 4
n. man cometh   Bible 325

N. man is a hero   Cornuel 1
N. man is above the law
            Theodore Roosevelt 13
N. man is an Island   Donne 5
n. man's life, liberty   Gideon J. Tucker 1
N. mas   Duran 1
"N." means no   Modern Proverbs 64
N. more Mr. Nice Guy   Sayings 41
N. news is good news   Proverbs 211
N. No. No.   Thatcher 10
n. pain, n. palm   William Penn 1
N. pains, n. gains   Proverbs 212
n. place like home   L. Frank Baum 1
n. place like home   Payne 2
N. sex, please   Marriott 1
N. Viet Cong ever called me   Ali 9
N. way?! Way!
            Television Catchphrases 67
problem that has n. name   Friedan 2
then n. one's anybody
            W. S. Gilbert 47
Noah
God gave N. the rainbow
        Folk and Anonymous Songs 36
Nobel
N. Peace Prize   Nobel 2
noble
how n. in reason   Shakespeare 181
last infirmity of n. mind   Milton 2
N. be man   Goethe 3
N. Eightfold Path   Pali Tripitaka 4
n. in motive   Herbert C. Hoover 1
n. savage   John Dryden 3
N. Truth of Suffering   Pali Tripitaka 3
Now cracks a n. heart   Shakespeare 237
recreation of n. minds   Guedalla 2
what a n. mind   Shakespeare 197
nobler
n. in the mind to suffer
            Shakespeare 188
noblesse
N. oblige   Lévis 1
noblest
honest man's the n. work   Pope 26
n. man that ever lived   Shakespeare 106
n. of causes   Mohandas Gandhi 4
n. prospect which a Scotchman
            Samuel Johnson 52
n. Roman of them all   Shakespeare 130
nobody
bureaucracy, the rule of n.   Arendt 2
I'm N.   Emily Dickinson 5
n. at home   Pope 13
N. ever lives their life   Hemingway 3
N. expects the Spanish   Monty Python 6
N. goes there anymore   McNulty 1
n. here but us chickens   Sayings 51
N. is perfect   Proverbs 214
n. knows anything   William Goldman 4
N. knows the trouble
        Folk and Anonymous Songs 56
n. knows you're a dog   Peter Steiner 1
n. left to be concerned   Niemöller 1
N. likes the man who brings
            Sophocles 1
N. tells me anything   Galsworthy 1
n. will come   Sandburg 10
N.'s enemy but his own   Dickens 66
n.'s perfect   Film Lines 158

space where n. is   Stein 8
which n. can deny
        Folk and Anonymous Songs 22
nocturnal
best n. police   Ralph Waldo Emerson 42
nod
Land of N.   Jonathan Swift 33
n. is as good as a wink   Proverbs 215
nods
excellent Homer n.   Horace 8
N., and becks   Milton 11
noise
Go placidly amid the n.   Ehrmann 1
noises
Goodnight n. everywhere
            Margaret Wise Brown 3
three minutes of squelching n.
            Rotten 4
nominated
if n. by either party
            William Tecumseh Sherman 3
will not accept if n.
            William Tecumseh Sherman 5
nomination
n. of my party   Lyndon B. Johnson 10
nonbelievers
Jews and Hindus, and n.   Obama 6
noncooperation
N. with evil   Mohandas Gandhi 3
none
n., I think, do there embrace
            Andrew Marvell 14
N. but the brave   John Dryden 10
N. but the lonely heart   Goethe 6
n. dare call it treason   Harington 1
n. ever returned alive   Dante 10
N. ever wished it longer
            Samuel Johnson 37
n. of woman born   Shakespeare 379
n. so poor to do him reverence
            Shakespeare 118
n. would be old   Benjamin Franklin 26
will do n.   Shakespeare 424
nonsense
Era of Wonderful N.   Pegler 1
non-violence
N. is the first article
            Mohandas Gandhi 2
nooks
sequestered n.   Longfellow 27
noon
From morn to n. he fell   Milton 25
nooses
n. give   Dorothy Parker 9
Nora
N.'s freezin'   Walt Kelly 1
Norfolk
Very flat, N.   Coward 5
norma
n. loquendi   Horace 2
normal
Is true of the n. heart   Auden 12
N. is the average   Rita Mae Brown 3
n. recreation of noble minds   Guedalla 2
N. science   Thomas Kuhn 1
normalcy
not nostrums but n.   Harding 1
Norman
This is Mrs. N. Maine   Film Lines 162

nut
Sometimes you feel like a n.
                    Advertising Slogans 9
nuts
N.!   McAuliffe 1
nymph
N., in thy orisons   Shakespeare 193
nymphets
propose to designate as "n."   Nabokov 4

O

O God! O Montreal!
            Samuel Butler (1835–1902) 2
O sole mio   Capurro 1
O tempora, O mores   Cicero 9
oak
Heart of o. are our ships   Garrick 1
oaks
Tall o. from little   Proverbs 291
oath
following O. of Affirmation
                        Constitution 4
O., *n.* In law   Bierce 82
oats
O. . . . A grain   Samuel Johnson 15
o. for a dead horse   Film Lines 105
season for wild o.   Wharton 6
obey
Good men must not o.
                    Ralph Waldo Emerson 27
obeyed
I o. as a son   Gibbon 9
She who must be o.   H. Rider Haggard 1
obituary
except an o. notice   Behan 4
I have often read an o. notice
                    Clarence S. Darrow 6
object
failure in a great o.   Keats 8
My o. all sublime   W. S. Gilbert 39
o. of power   Orwell 45
see the o. as it really is
                    Matthew Arnold 5
That Obscure O. of Desire   Buñuel 2
objectification
Art is the o.   Langer 1
objective
o. correlative   T. S. Eliot 27
O. evidence and certitude
                    William James 8
objectivity
some element of o.   Warnock 1
objects
All visible o.   Melville 6
obligation
sense of o.   Stephen Crane 4
oblige
Noblesse o.   Lévis 1
obliged
whatever a body is o.   Twain 16
oblivion
journey towards o.   D. H. Lawrence 9
Oblomovism
O.   Goncharov 1
obnoxious
o. to each carping tongue   Bradstreet 1

obscene
courage, or hallow were o.
                    Hemingway 9
Women should be o.   Heinlein 2
obscenity
O. is such a tiny kingdom
                    Heywood Broun 3
obscure
O. Object of Desire   Buñuel 2
obscurity
o. of a learned language   Gibbon 11
observance
breach than the o.   Shakespeare 163
observe
O. good faith and justice
                    George Washington 7
what we o. is not nature   Heisenberg 2
You can o. a lot by watchin'   Berra 9
you do not o.   Arthur Conan Doyle 16
obsolete
war is o. or men are
                    R. Buckminster Fuller 5
obstacles
throw o. in the way
                    Elizabeth Cady Stanton 12
obstinate
o. virtue   Molière 1
obstructed
o. interstate commerce
                    J. Edgar Hoover 1
occasions
all o. do inform against me
                    Shakespeare 220
Occident
O., *n.* The part   Bierce 83
occupation
Othello's o.'s gone   Shakespeare 276
occupy
We o. the same cage
                    Tennessee Williams 9
ocean
Columbia the gem of the o.
                    David T. Shaw 1
Columbus sailed the o. blue   Stoner 1
deep and dark blue O.   Byron 15
great o. of truth   Isaac Newton 7
it is clearly O.   Arthur C. Clarke 6
O., *n.* A body of water   Bierce 84
o. without its unnamed monsters
                    Steinbeck 6
o. without the awful   Douglass 9
oceanic
his own o. mind   Coleridge 40
October
blue-gray O. sky   Grantland Rice 2
odd
How o. of God   Ewer 1
o., because it was   Carroll 32
o., evening hour   John Hollander 1
O. Couple   Neil Simon 1
this was scarcely o.   Carroll 35
odds
May the o. be ever   Suzanne Collins 1
Never tell me the o. George Lucas 13
ode
O. on a Grecian Urn   Faulkner 16
odious
Comparisons are o.   Proverbs 51

Oedipus
legend of King O.   Sigmund Freud 4
off
caught you o. base   Hemingway 11
get o. the pot   Modern Proverbs 84
get o. this picture   Southern 2
O. agin, on agin   Gillilan 1
o. to see the wizard   Harburg 7
O. we go into the wild
                    Robert Crawford 1
O. with her head   Carroll 18
O. with his head   Cibber 1
o. with his head   Shakespeare 3
Voted o. the island
                    Television Catchphrases 74
offence
my o. is rank   Shakespeare 211
offend
thy right hand o. thee   Bible 210
offended
hath not o. the king Thomas More 4
offense
best defense is a good o.
                    Modern Proverbs 23
punishment match the o.   Cicero 5
offer
o. he can't refuse   Puzo 2
office
Every time I fill an o.   Louis XIV 1
for every o. he can bestow
                    John Adams 18
insolence of o.   Shakespeare 190
most insignificant O.   John Adams 12
o. boy to an Attorney's firm
                    W. S. Gilbert 8
second o. of this government
                    Jefferson 24
offices
love's austere and lonely o.
                    Robert Hayden 1
official
Where there is o. censorship
                    Paul Goodman 1
oh
O., to be in England   Robert Browning 8
O. wow   Jobs 5
O. You Beautiful Doll
                    A. Seymour Brown 1
Ohio
did I ever leave O.   Comden and Green 3
four dead in O.   Neil Young 2
oil
Middle East that has no o.   Meir 1
O. and water don't mix   Proverbs 222
o. painting was invented   de Kooning 1
o. which renders   David Hume 6
our midnight o.   Quarles 1
two different o. companies   Shrum 1
wisdom out of midnight o.   Yeats 40
oiseau
o. *rebelle*   Meilhac 1
OK
I'm O.—You're O.   Thomas A. Harris 1
Okie
O. from Muskogee   Merle Haggard 1
O. use' ta mean   Steinbeck 2
Oklahoma
O., where the wind   Hammerstein 8

ol'
O. Man River   Hammerstein 3
Olaf
i sing of O. glad and big
                            e.e. cummings 12
old
always the o. to lead us   Phil Ochs 2
at the o. ball game   Norworth 3
Down by the o. mill stream   Tell Taylor 1
far from the o. folks at home
                            Stephen Foster 4
fill o. bottles with banknotes   Keynes 11
Give me that o. time religion
            Folk and Anonymous Songs 28
good o. Cause   Milton 16
"good o. times"   Byron 27
Grow o. along with me
                        Robert Browning 19
having an o. friend for dinner
                            Film Lines 155
hell of women is o. age
                        la Rochefoucauld 8
Hope I die before I get o.   Townshend 1
hot time in the o. town   Joseph Hayden 1
How o. would you be   Paige 8
I grow o.   T. S. Eliot 10
I like the o. masters   Welles 5
I name thee O. Glory   Driver 1
in o. age one has   Goethe 15
in the o. Kentucky home
                        Stephen Foster 5
Ireland is the o. sow   Joyce 5
Little o. ladies in tennis shoes   Mosk 1
make me conservative when o.   Frost 19
man is as o. as he feels   Proverbs 185
man is only as o.   "Groucho" Marx 45
Mithridates, he died o.   Housman 6
Never too o.   Proverbs 209
new wine into o. bottles   Bible 234
Nine O. Men   Drew Pearson 1
nine o. men   Berle 1
no country for o. men   Yeats 46
no fool like an o. fool   Proverbs 113
no man would be o.   Jonathan Swift 24
none would be o.   Benjamin Franklin 26
o., unknown world
                    F. Scott Fitzgerald 34
o., mad, blind, despised   Percy Shelley 8
O. Age and Experience   Rochester 2
o. age is always fifteen years older
                                Baruch 4
o. age is a massacre   Roth 8
o. age isn't so bad   Chevalier 1
o. age should burn and rave
                        Dylan Thomas 17
o. believe everything   Wilde 70
O. Boys have their Playthings
                    Benjamin Franklin 27
O. CARY GRANT FINE   Cary Grant 2
o. familiar faces   Charles Lamb 1
make money the o.-fashioned way
                    Advertising Slogans 109
O. father, o. artificer   Joyce 12
o. gray mare
            Folk and Anonymous Songs 58
O. habits die hard   Proverbs 223
o. have rubbed it into the young
                            Maugham 7
O. King Cole   Nursery Rhymes 13

O. Lady of Threadneedle Street Gillray 1
o. lamps for new ones   Arabian Nights 1
O. MacDonald had a farm
            Folk and Anonymous Songs 59
o. maids biking   Orwell 14
o. man can't do nothin'   Mabley 1
o. man in a dry month   T. S. Eliot 21
o. man was dreaming about
                          Hemingway 29
O. Man with a beard   Lear 1
o. man with wrinkled dugs   T. S. Eliot 51
O. Masters: how well they understood
                                Auden 28
o. men know young men are fools
                        George Chapman 1
O. men ought to be explorers
                          T. S. Eliot 111
o. men shall dream dreams   Bible 193
O. Mother Hubbard Nursery Rhymes 45
o. order changeth   Tennyson 45
O. Pretender   Guedalla 1
O. soldiers never die   Foley 1
o. soldiers never die
                    Douglas MacArthur 2
o. woman tossed up Nursery Rhymes 76
o. woman who lived in a shoe
                      Nursery Rhymes 77
On top of O. Smokey
            Folk and Anonymous Songs 60
profane and o. wives' fables   Bible 374
putting o. heads   Spark 1
Ring out the o.   Tennyson 33
same as the o. boss   Townshend 7
so o. a head   Shakespeare 78
Something o., something new
                          Anonymous 28
teach an o. dog new tricks   Proverbs 292
That O. Black Magic   Johnny Mercer 3
that's o. Europe   Rumsfeld 2
They shall not grow o.   Binyon 1
this o. gray head   Whittier 3
This o. man he played one
                      Nursery Rhymes 38
thought the o. man   Shakespeare 385
very o. are the most selfish Thackeray 15
wars are planned by o. men
                      Grantland Rice 3
What a drag it is getting o.
                    Jagger and Richards 5
When I am an o. woman   Jenny Joseph 1
When you are o. and grey   Yeats 4
woman as o. as she looks   Proverbs 185
worth any number of o. ladies
                            Faulkner 16
You are o., Father William   Carroll 9
You are o., Father William   Southey 2
olde
out of o. feldes   Chaucer 5
olden
In o. days, a glimpse   Cole Porter 2
older
ask somebody o. than me   Eubie Blake 1
better humored as he grows o.
                        Samuel Johnson 77
I was so much o. then   Dylan 10
O. men declare war   Herbert C. Hoover 5
o. than the rocks   Pater 1
O. women are best   Ian Fleming 9

oldest
o. hath borne most   Shakespeare 320
second o. profession
                        Ronald W. Reagan 2
two o. professions   Woollcott 2
Oldsmobile
not your father's O.
                    Advertising Slogans 95
om
sound of Brahman is O.   Upanishads 5
omega
I am Alpha and O.   Bible 390
omelets
O. are not made   Proverbs 224
omit
but one art, to o.
                  Robert Louis Stevenson 11
O. needless words   Strunk 1
omnipotence
final proof of God's o.   De Vries 1
omnipresence
brooding o. in the sky
                Oliver Wendell Holmes, Jr. 24
omnis
O. cellula e cellula   Raspail 1
once
die but o.   Addison 3
o. and future king   Malory 3
O. bit twice shy   Proverbs 225
O. in love with Amy   Loesser 3
O. more unto the breach
                        Shakespeare 133
O. upon a midnight dreary   Poe 6
only die o.   Proverbs 68
taste of death but o.   Shakespeare 102
We're only young o.
                    Modern Proverbs 101
You only live o.   Modern Proverbs 54
one
All for o., o., for all Dumas the Elder 3
Beware the man of o. book
                      Anonymous (Latin) 4
Busy as a o.-armed man   O. Henry 5
he had only o. idea   Disraeli 17
heard o. side of the case
                      Samuel Butler (1835–1902) 12
I have only o. eye   Horatio Nelson 4
I see o.-third of a nation
                  Franklin D. Roosevelt 13
If it isn't o. thing   Modern Proverbs 65
Johnny O. Note   Lorenz Hart 4
just o. of those things   Cole Porter 12
live as cheap as o.   Proverbs 309
Lord our God is o. Lord   Bible 69
make o. man ungrateful   John Adams 18
never do merely o. thing   Hardin 1
O., two, buckle my shoe
                      Nursery Rhymes 49
O. COUNTRY   Daniel Webster 11
o. damn thing after another
                    Modern Proverbs 51
o. flew over the cuckoo's nest
            Folk and Anonymous Songs 52
O. foot already in   Cervantes 9
o. friend in an indifferent world   Jong 7
o. giant leap for mankind
                    Neil A. Armstrong 3
O. good turn deserves another
                          Proverbs 127

one (cont.):

O. half of the world   Austen 15
o. hand in my pocket   Morrissette 1
O. hand washes the other   Proverbs 134
o. hundred years of solitude
                              García Márquez 3
O. if by land   Longfellow 24
o. intelligent man   Maimonides 3
O. Law for the Lion & Ox
                                 William Blake 3
o. life to lose   Nathan Hale 1
O. life, with each   Bono 3
o. lonely reporter   Richard Nixon 20
O. man, one vote   Cartwright 1
o. man o. vote   Chesterton 16
O. man with courage   Andrew Jackson 7
O. man's ways may be as good
                                       Austen 20
O. more drink and I'd have
                               Dorothy Parker 31
O. murder made a villain   Porteus 1
O. murder makes a villain
                               Film Lines 118
o. Nation indivisible   Francis Bellamy 1
O. of these days, Alice
                    Television Catchphrases 29
o. of us will have to go   Wilde 123
o. of you is lying   Dorothy Parker 11
o. of you three
                     Edward H. "Bull" Warren 1
"o. percent," namely its Jews
                               Thomas Perkins 1
o. perfect rose   Dorothy Parker 8
o. person, o. vote   William O. Douglas 4
O. rational voice is dumb   Auden 8
O. Ring to rule them all   Tolkien 6
O. riot, o. Ranger
                          W. J. "Bill" McDonald 1
o. small step for a man
                           Neil A. Armstrong 3
O. soul occupying two bodies
                                    Aristotle 13
O. step at a time   Proverbs 282
O. Step Forward, Two Steps Back
                                        Lenin 1
o. talent which is death to hide
                                      Milton 52
O. to make ready   Nursery Rhymes 48
O. with the law   Coolidge 2
o.-eyed man is king   Erasmus 1
O.'s a born liar   Martin 1
people arose as o. man   Bible 79
possess but o. idea   Samuel Johnson 66
spell a word only o. way   Twain 147
Thing O. and Thing Two   Seuss 5
Two heads are better than o.
                               Proverbs 310
two hearts that beat as o.   Halm 1
We must love o. another   Auden 13
when the O. Great Scorer
                               Grantland Rice 1
where no o. has gone before
                               Roddenberry 2
win just o. for the Gipper   Gipp 1
wonderful o.-hoss shay
                      Oliver Wendell Holmes 7
you have only o. idea   Alain 1

100

100 per cent American
                      George Bernard Shaw 46

101

Room 101 is the worst thing   Orwell 48

1000

1000% for Tom Eagleton   McGovern 1

oneself

Hell is o.   T. S. Eliot 126
know how to be o.   Montaigne 10
love o.   Wilde 71

one-upmanship

O.   Stephen Potter 2

only

America is the o. nation   Clemenceau 6
he gave his o. begotten Son   Bible 315
If I o. had a brain   Harburg 3
It's the o. thing   "Red" Sanders 1
It's the o. way to fly
                       Advertising Slogans 133
Man is the o. animal that laughs
                                      Hazlitt 3
My o. love sprung   Shakespeare 31
o. begetter   Shakespeare 409
o. begotten of the Father   Bible 311
O. by love can men see me
                               Bhagavadgita 4
O. connect   Forster 3
o. girl in the world   Clifford Grey 1
o. good Indian is a dead Indian
                               Proverbs 126
O. make believe I love you
                               Hammerstein 2
o. people who count in any marriage
                               Hillary Clinton 5
O. the dead have seen   Santayana 9
O. the little people pay taxes   Helmsley 1
O. the Lonely   Orbison 1
o. thing I am afraid of   Wellington 3
o. thing that ever has   Margaret Mead 10
o. thing we have to fear
                        Franklin D. Roosevelt 6
o. way to have a friend
                         Ralph Waldo Emerson 10
O. you can prevent forest fires
                       Advertising Slogans 123
sprung from my o. hate   Shakespeare 31
We're o. young once
                         Modern Proverbs 101
You o. live once   Modern Proverbs 54
You O. Live Twice   Ian Fleming 8

ontogenesis

O., or the development   Haeckel 1

onward

O., Christian soldiers   Baring-Gould 1

oops

O.   "Rick" Perry 1

oozy

o. weeds about me twist   Melville 21

open

He has not left that o. to us   C. S. Lewis 3
Keep your eyes wide o.
                         Benjamin Franklin 18
O. covenants of peace
                          Woodrow Wilson 17
O. Sesame   Arabian Nights 2
O. the pod door, Hal   Film Lines 181
they function only when they are o.
                                      Dewar 1

opening

o. battles of all subsequent   Orwell 15

opens

another o.   Proverbs 226
before he o. his mouth   Nathan 1
door o. and lets the future in
                               Graham Greene 1

opera

floating o.   John Barth 1
Going to the o.   Hannah More 1
O., n. A play   Bierce 85
o. ain't over   Ralph Carpenter 1
o. is when a guy gets stabbed
                               Ed Gardner 1
o. isn't what it used to be   Coward 10
pretty air in an o.   Twain 21

operas

text of French o.   Wharton 5

operation

O. Desert Storm
                    George Herbert Walker Bush 11
o. was successful   Sayings 45

opinion

barriers to the liberty of o. Tocqueville 7
difference of o.   Twain 73
how to defy o.   Staël 2
In all matters of o.   Twain 122
more than a mere o.   Heine 4
o. has been widely held
                            Bertrand Russell 6
o. of the strongest   la Fontaine 2
o. that has survived   Wilde 15
public o. for law
                       James Fenimore Cooper 2
stifle is a false o.   Mill 8
whole climate of o.   Auden 7
worship of O.   Martineau 1

opinions

diverse Climates of O.   Glanvill 1
golden o.   Shakespeare 344
halt ye between two o.   Bible 92
Loyalty to petrified o.   Twain 37
O. in politics and religion
                            Bertrand Russell 11
There are as many o.   Terence 5
There's allays two o.   George Eliot 7
write your honest o.   Swinton 1

opium

o. of the Marxists   Joan Robinson 3
o. of the people   Karl Marx 2

opporchunity

This home iv o.   Dunne 18

opportunities

I seen my o.   Plunkitt 1

opportunity

commit when he had the o.
                             Helen Rowland 7
Here's a first-rate o.   W. S. Gilbert 17
Ireland's o.   O'Connell 1
maximum of o.
                       George Bernard Shaw 20
missing an o.   George Bernard Shaw 56
never missed an o.   Eban 3
O. is missed   Edison 3
O. is the great bawd
                         Benjamin Franklin 12
O. never knocks twice   Proverbs 227

opposed

o. an equal reaction   Isaac Newton 6

opposing
by o. end them   Shakespeare 188
not o. values
          William Jefferson "Bill" Clinton 12

opposite
do just the o.   Lichtenberg 1
giving them the o.   Kettle 1
I on the o. shore   Longfellow 24
o. also contains deep truth   Bohr 1
o. of love is not hate   Wiesel 3

opposites
O. attract   Modern Proverbs 66

oppressed
mind of the o.   Biko 1
O. people are frequently
          Florynce Kennedy 1

oppression
for the Lion & Ox is O.   William Blake 3
o. of one by another   Nelson Mandela 3

oppressor
right to be his own o.
          James Russell Lowell 4
weapon in the hands of the o.   Biko 1

optimism
o. of the will   Rolland 1

optimist
if he is an o. after it   Twain 116
o., who generally lives   Chesterton 1
o. is a guy   Marquis 1
o. looks at it   Stamp 2
o. proclaims that we live   Cabell 1

oral
fast word about o. contraception
          Woody Allen 2

orange
CLOCKWORK o.   Anthony Burgess 1
if you happen to be an o.   Fred Allen 3

oranges
O. and lemons   Nursery Rhymes 50

orator
o. with his flood   Benjamin Franklin 13

ordain
o. and establish this Constitution
          Constitution 1

order
all is in o.   Katherine Mansfield 2
All is o. there   Baudelaire 4
best words in the best o.   Coleridge 38
Blessed rage for o.   Wallace Stevens 13
construct the socialist o.   Lenin 4
new world o., where diverse
          George Herbert Walker Bush 12
new world o.—a world where
          George Herbert Walker Bush 10
new world o. came about
          George Herbert Walker Bush 7
new world o. is being born
          Martin Luther King, Jr. 1
new world o. outlast   P. J. Bailey 1
old o. changeth   Tennyson 45
o. of your going   Shakespeare 372
violent o. is disorder   Wallace Stevens 14

ordered
concept of o. liberty   Cardozo 3

ordering
better o. of the universe   Alfonso 1

ordinary
extraordinary man feel o.   Chesterton 7
o. business of life   Alfred Marshall 1

organ
brain is not an o. of sex
          Charlotte Gilman 4
heart is an o. of fire   Ondaatje 1
my second favorite o.   Woody Allen 13
Seated one day at the o.   Procter 2

organization
o. man   Whyte 2
systematic o. of hatreds   Henry Adams 1

organize
o. her own immortality   Laski 1
waste any time mourning—o.   Joe Hill 2

organized
member of any o. party   Will Rogers 15
o. hypocrisy   Disraeli 18
Science is o. knowledge
          Herbert Spencer 3

orgasm
gong of the o.   Nin 2
vaginal and the clitoral o.   Koedt 1

orgy
o. of self-sacrifing   Rand 4

Orientalism
O. can be discussed   Said 1

origin
o. of all poems   Whitman 4
O. of man now proved
          Charles Darwin 1
stamp of his lowly o.   Charles Darwin 13

original
all stain of o. sin   Pius 1
o. good time   Bette Davis 2
O. thought is like o. sin   Lebowitz 7
o. writer is not he who refrains
          Chateaubriand 1

originality
O., I fear, is too often   Inge 4
What is o.   Nietzsche 10

originative
three o. geniuses   Stein 16

originator
o. of a good sentence
          Ralph Waldo Emerson 45

orisons
Nymph, in thy o.   Shakespeare 193

ornament
respecting all o.   Ruskin 2
She's the o. of her sex   Dickens 34

orphan
because he was a poor o.   Lincoln 64
defeat is an o.   Ciano 1
defeat is an o.   John F. Kennedy 18
FEELINGS OF A POOR O.   Artemus Ward 1
found another o.   Melville 14
O., n. A living person   Bierce 86

Orpheus
O., with his lute   Shakespeare 451

Oscar
O. said it   Dorothy Parker 13
were an O. Mayer wiener
          Advertising Slogans 96
You will, O.   Whistler 5

ospreys
Merrily the o. cry   Shijing 1

ostentation
use rather than o.   Gibbon 5

other
Hear the o. side   Augustine 6
Hell is o. people   Sartre 5

how the o. half lives   Proverbs 132
making o. plans   Allen Saunders 1
One hand washes the o.   Proverbs 134
o. America   Michael Harrington 1
o. people are as real   McEwan 1
o. people's habits   Twain 68
o. people's money   Girardin 1
o. people's money   Thatcher 3
O. times, o. manners   Proverbs 228
o. voices, o. rooms   Capote 1
she is the O.   de Beauvoir 1
think like o. people   Mary Shelley 8
write the o. way   Jiménez 1

others
all o. pay cash   Sayings 26
as o. see us   Robert Burns 2
cause of dullness in o.   Foote 1
Do not do to o.   Confucius 9
encourage the o.   Voltaire 9
I have o.   "Groucho" Marx 46

otherwise
gods thought o.   Virgil 5

ought
not what they o. to do   Francis Bacon 4
not what we o. to say   Shakespeare 320

ounce
o. of prevention   Proverbs 243

our
o. country, right or wrong   Decatur 1
O. Father, who art in heaven   Missal 5
O. Father which art in heaven   Bible 215
O. revels now are ended
          Shakespeare 442
o. son of a bitch
          Franklin D. Roosevelt 30
O. Union: It must be preserved
          Andrew Jackson 1

ours
land was o. before we were   Frost 21
they are o.   Oliver Hazard Perry 2

ourselves
not in our stars but in o.
          Shakespeare 98
o. to know   Pope 29

out
at tother o. it wente   Chaucer 1
He kept us o. of war   Glynn 1
include me o.   Goldwyn 1
Mordre wol o.   Chaucer 15
nor am I o. of it   Marlowe 6
O., damned spot   Shakespeare 384
O., vile jelly   Shakespeare 302
o. of key with his time   Ezra Pound 9
O. of sight, o. of mind   Proverbs 229
o. of sight   Thomas à Kempis 2
O. of the cradle   Whitman 16
O. of the depths   Bible 121
O. of the mouth of babes   Bible 107
O. of thine own mouth   Bible 304
O. where the hand-clasp's
          Arthur Chapman 1
something new o. of Africa   Pliny 1
thought that I was o.   Puzo 6
Three strikes, you're o.
          Modern Proverbs 88
truth is o. there
          Television Catchphrases 87

outcast
my o. state   Shakespeare 413
o. from life's feast   Joyce 3

outdo
O., *v.t.* To make   Bierce 87
outer
cast out into o. darkness   Bible 231
out-groups
others-groups, o.   Sumner 6
outlandish
almost always o.   Taleb 2
outlawed
When guns are o.   Political Slogans 36
outlaws
legislation which o. Russia forever
                          Ronald W. Reagan 7
only o. will have guns
                         Political Slogans 36
outlined
O. against a blue-gray   Grantland Rice 2
outlive
o. this powerful rhyme   Shakespeare 419
outlook
o. wasn't brilliant   Ernest L. Thayer 1
outrageous
arrows of o. fortune   Shakespeare 188
outright
we gave ourselves o.   Frost 22
outside
birds who are o. despair   Montaigne 15
I am just going o.   Lawrence Oates 1
live o. the law   Dylan 20
nothing o. of the text   Derrida 1
O. of a dog   "Groucho" Marx 49
o. of a horse   Proverbs 218
o. of the envelope   Tom Wolfe 5
outspoken
O. by whom   Dorothy Parker 33
outstubborn
Never try to o. a cat   Heinlein 15
outworn
dust of creeds o.   Percy Shelley 12
over
It ain't o. 'til it's o.   Berra 14
My Life to Live O.   Herold 1
one damn thing o. and o.   Millay 7
O. hill, o. dale   Gruber 1
O. hill, o. dale   Shakespeare 53
O. the river and through
                          Lydia Maria Child 2
O. there, o. there   Cohan 5
o.-ripe fruit into our hands   Lenin 10
Party's O. Now   Coward 11
party's o.   Comden and Green 4
Somewhere o. the rainbow   Harburg 5
They think it's all o.   Wolstenholme 1
they're o. here   Sayings 52
They're o.-paid   Sayings 52
they're o.-sexed   Sayings 52
till it's o. o. there   Cohan 6
when the war is o.   Lehrer 6
overcoat
come out of Gogol's O.   Dostoyevski 9
overcome
I'll o. some day   Tindley 1
we shall o.   Pete Seeger 5
overestimate
People often o.   Bill Gates 1
overlooked
looked over than o.   Mae West 12
overman
I teach you the o.   Nietzsche 13

overnight
has to be there o.
                         Advertising Slogans 48
overthrowing
In o. me, you have
                       Toussaint-Louverture 2
owed
so much o. by so many
                        Winston Churchill 17
owene
dooth with youre o. thyng   Chaucer 10
owes
world o. me a living   Morey 1
world o. you a living   Burdette 1
owl
O. and the Pussy-Cat   Lear 4
o. of Minerva   Hegel 2
o. that shriek'd   Shakespeare 352
own
hoist with his o. petard   Shakespeare 218
man after his o. heart   Bible 83
me or your o. eyes   "Groucho" Marx 24
room of her o.   Virginia Woolf 9
To each his o.   Proverbs 79
turned to his o. vomit   Bible 386
Virtue is its o. reward   Proverbs 316
oxygen
o. of publicity   Thatcher 9
oyster
first eat an o.   Jonathan Swift 31
sharpening my o. knife   Hurston 1
try the patience of an o.   Carroll 7
world's mine o.   Shakespeare 67
Oz
ask the great O.   L. Frank Baum 2
I am O., the Great and Terrible
                           L. Frank Baum 4
Ozymandias
My name is O.   Percy Shelley 7

P

pa
Where's my p.   Political Slogans 25
Pablo
P. was waiting for me   Hesse 5
pace
creeps in this petty p.   Shakespeare 393
Requiescat in p.   Missal 1
Pacific
he stared at the P.   Keats 3
I hope the P. is as blue   Stephen King 4
pacification
P. of the Primitive Tribes   Achebe 2
pacify
p. it with cool thoughts   Paige 2
pack
nothing but a p. of cards   Carroll 25
P. up your troubles   Asaf 1
packages
come in small p.   Proverbs 20
pact
Bill of Rights into a suicide p.
                        Robert H. Jackson 8
paddy
Nick, nack, p. whack
                         Nursery Rhymes 38

pagan
P. suckled in a creed
                       William Wordsworth 21
page
tear out a single p.   Sand 1
pageant
insubstantial p. faded   Shakespeare 442
Pagliacci
Ridi, P.   Leoncavallo 1
paid
attention must be p.   Arthur Miller 3
He is well p.   Shakespeare 82
She P. the Bills   Gloria Swanson 1
pail
fetch a p. of water   Nursery Rhymes 26
pain
After great p.   Emily Dickinson 7
by which we measure of p.   Lennon 3
I feel your p.
             William Jefferson "Bill" Clinton 2
Life is p.   William Goldman 2
no greater p. than   Dante 7
no p., no palm   William Penn 1
P., *n.* An uncomfortable   Bierce 88
p. and pleasure   Bentham 3
P. is an event   Audre Lorde 2
p. of being a man   Samuel Johnson 109
with some p. is fraught   Percy Shelley 11
pains
infinite capacity for taking p.
                           Jane Hopkins 1
Marriage has many p.
                        Samuel Johnson 24
No p., no gains   Proverbs 212
paint
Every time I p. a portrait
                      John Singer Sargent 1
If you can p.   Film Lines 3
no reason to p.   Edward Hopper 1
p. the lily   Shakespeare 70
price of the p.   van Gogh 1
painted
Cupid p. blind   Shakespeare 52
Earth's last picture is p.   Kipling 14
idle as a p. ship   Coleridge 5
not so black as he is p.   Proverbs 66
seen your p. women   Sandburg 2
painter
I, too, am a p.   Correggio 1
one American p. after another
                        Harold Rosenberg 1
O wily p.   Gunn 3
p. saw what was   Gunn 4
subject is to the p.   Rivera 1
painters
P. had found it difficult
                      Benjamin Franklin 38
painting
How vain p. is   Pascal 3
Life is p. a picture
                  Oliver Wendell Holmes, Jr. 21
oil p. was invented   de Kooning 1
P., in fact, is nothing   Cellini 1
poem is like a p.   Horace 9
predilection for p.
                   Pierre-Auguste Renoir 2
pair
p. of ragged claws   T. S. Eliot 7

PAKSTAN
live in P.   Choudhry Rahmat Ali 1
Palace
changing guard at Buckingham P.
                              Milne 1
P., *n.* A fine   Bierce 89
pale
Behold a p. horse   Bible 392
p. cast of thought   Shakespeare 192
P. hands I loved   Laurence Hope 1
those p. and thin ones   Plutarch 2
Why so p. and wan   Suckling 1
Palestine
establishment in P.   Balfour 1
In P. we do not propose   Balfour 2
state of P.   Arafat 1
Palestinians
no such things as P.   Meir 3
1.5 million P.   Rabin 3
pallor
p. of girls' brows   Wilfred Owen 2
palm
have an itching p.   Shakespeare 127
hold infinity in the p. William Blake 14
p. at the end of the mind
                     Wallace Stevens 15
palmistry
P., *n.* The 947th method   Bierce 90
palpable
very p. hit   Shakespeare 232
Pan
great god P.
          Elizabeth Barrett Browning 5
Panama
canal—P.   Leigh Mercer 1
pancreas
adorable p.   Jean Kerr 1
Pandemonium
P., the high capital of Satan   Milton 26
panic
DON'T P.   Douglas Adams 1
panjandrum
grand P. himself   Foote 3
pap
suck on the p. of life
              F. Scott Fitzgerald 20
papa
P., potatoes, poultry   Dickens 96
P. don't preach   Madonna 1
P.'s Got a Brand New Bag
                    James Brown 1
paper
All reactionaries are p. tigers
                 Mao Tse-tung 5
hand that signed the p. Dylan Thomas 4
If they give you ruled p.   Jiménez 1
just for a scrap of p.
               Bethmann-Hollweg 1
P. Chase   Osborn 1
things in that p. that nobody knows
                Charlotte Gilman 1
white p., void of all   John Locke 2
worth the p. it's written on   Goldwyn 8
papers
more p. to pile   Du Fu 2
What I Read in the P.   Will Rogers 1
Paquin
P. pull down   Ezra Pound 26

parables
p. of sunlight   Dylan Thomas 12
parachutes
Minds are like p.   Dewar 1
parade
p. of riches   Adam Smith 4
paradigm
so in p. choice   Thomas Kuhn 2
paradigms
proponents of competing p.
                  Thomas Kuhn 3
paradise
academy is not p.   hooks 1
America, the p. of lawyers
              Joseph H. Choate 2
living in the gangsta's p.   Coolio 1
man could pass through P. Coleridge 42
P. in form and image   Borges 7
P. of exiles, Italy   Percy Shelley 1
They paved p.   Joni Mitchell 2
this side of P.   Rupert Brooke 2
paradox
man may love a p.
           Ralph Waldo Emerson 20
parallelogram
Who can tell whether the p.   Carroll 26
parallelograms
My Princess of P.   Byron 2
paranoid
Just because you're p.   Sayings 31
Only the p. survive   Grove 1
p. is someone who has
             William S. Burroughs 5
paranoids
P. are not paranoid   Pynchon 2
parapets
Europe of the ancient p.   Rimbaud 6
paraphrase
classics in p.   Ezra Pound 13
parcel
p. of vain strivings   Thoreau 1
parcelled
p. out unequally at birth
              F. Scott Fitzgerald 9
pardon
full, free, and absolute p.
                Gerald R. Ford 4
God will p. me   Heine 5
p. me, thou bleeding   Shakespeare 106
pardons
P. him for writing well   Auden 26
Paree
After They've Seen P.   Sam M. Lewis 1
parent
rather an indifferent p.   Dickens 83
To lose one p.   Wilde 78
parents
excessive regard of p.   Thomas Hardy 18
Jewish man with p. alive   Roth 2
only illegitimate p.   Yankwich 1
p., I fear, will still insist
               Wollstonecraft 14
p. are the very worst   William Morris 4
p. to inter their children   Herodotus 1
p. were honest but poor
              Bertrand Russell 9
parfit
verray, p. gentil knyght   Chaucer 8

paring
p. his fingernails   Joyce 7
Paris
I love P. in the springtime
                  Cole Porter 23
Is P. burning   Hitler 7
last time I saw P.   Hammerstein 4
last time I see P.   Elliot Paul 1
One half of P.   Film Lines 127
P. is a moveable feast   Hemingway 30
P. is my hometown   Stein 7
P. is well worth a mass   Henri 2
P. was French   Tuchman 2
they go to P.   Wilde 30
We'll always have P.   Film Lines 47
When P. sneezes
            Klemens von Metternich 3
when they die, go to P.
            Oliver Wendell Holmes 4
parish
all the world as my p.   John Wesley 1
park
come out to the p.   Berra 7
strolling through the p.   Ed Haley 1
parkin'
watch the p. meters   Dylan 19
parking
put up a p. lot   Joni Mitchell 2
parlez
hinky-dinky p.-vous
       Folk and Anonymous Songs 48
parliament
P. of man   Tennyson 8
p. of whores   O'Rourke 2
Scottish P., adjourned   Ewing 1
parliaments
England is the mother of p.   Bright 1
parlor
walk into my p.   Howitt 1
parochial
he was p.   Henry James 5
parole
Classical quotation is the p.
              Samuel Johnson 100
parrot
This p. is no more   Monty Python 3
parsley
depth to which the p. had sunk
             Arthur Conan Doyle 32
p., sage, rosemary   Nursery Rhymes 9
part
better p. of valor   Shakespeare 60
Don't p. with your illusions   Twain 106
either p. of the solution   Cleaver 2
I am a p. of all   Tennyson 17
I read p. of it   Goldwyn 10
p. as friends   Jinnah 1
p. never calls for it   Mirren 1
p. with their brightest hour   Hellman 2
Shall I p. my hair   T. S. Eliot 11
till death us do p.
         Book of Common Prayer 15
parted
money are soon p.   Proverbs 111
particle
mind, that very fiery p.   Byron 31
particles
names of all these p.   Fermi 3

particular
This is a London p.   Dickens 82
particulars
in minutely organized p.
                    William Blake 24
parties
I like large p.   F. Scott Fitzgerald 16
parting
no shadow of another p.   Dickens 105
P. is all we know of heaven
                    Emily Dickinson 28
P. is such sweet sorrow Shakespeare 39
p. of the way   Bible 187
speed the p. guest   Pope 9
partition
Even an iron p.   Talmud 2
partly
living and p. living   T. S. Eliot 92
partner
When a man's p. is killed   Hammett 2
partridge
p. in a pear tree   Nursery Rhymes 10
parts
All Gaul is divided into three p.
                    Julius Caesar 1
If p. allure thee   Pope 27
made a man of p.   Graves 4
naming of p.   Henry Reed 1
naming of p.   Henry Reed 3
no small p.   Stanislavsky 1
plays many p.   Shakespeare 88
something besides the p.   Aristotle 1
party
All the people at this p.   Joni Mitchell 5
come to the aid of the p. Anonymous 22
fight for your right to p.   Rubin 1
Large p. waiting   Taft 1
member of any organized p.
                    Will Rogers 15
member of the Communist P.
                    J. Parnell Thomas 1
mistress of the p.
                    Timothy Michael Healy 1
p. like it's nineteen ninety nine Prince 1
p. programs grab hold   Ibsen 20
p.'s over   Comden and Green 4
P.'s Over Now   Coward 11
revolution is not a dinner p.
                    Mao Tse-tung 1
Stick to your p.   Disraeli 38
you walked into the p.   Carly Simon 1
pass
Do not p. go   Charles B. Darrow 1
have to p. the bill   Pelosi 1
I shall not p. this way   Grellet 1
I won't p. the buck   Coolidge 5
p. over in silence   Wittgenstein 3
Praise the Lord and p. the ammunition
                    Forgy 1
Ships that p. in the night Longfellow 26
They shall not p.   Ibarruri 2
They shall not p.   Pétain 1
this, too, shall p. away   Lincoln 20
This also shall p. away
                    Edward FitzGerald 1
this also shall p. away   Walter Scott 8
passage
P. to India   Whitman 13
p. which you think   Samuel Johnson 75

rites of p.   Gennep 1
passages
many cunning p.   T. S. Eliot 23
passenger
never lost a p.   Tubman 3
passengers
p. on a little space ship
                    Adlai E. Stevenson 12
p. will ask the conductor Sandburg 8
passes
Men seldom make p.   Dorothy Parker 7
passeth
p. all understanding   Bible 371
passing
p. the love of women   Bible 88
passion
all p. spent   Milton 50
every artist's secret . . . p. Cather 5
Every true p.   Stendhal 2
life is action and p.
                    Oliver Wendell Holmes, Jr. 7
Man is a useless p.   Sartre 3
p. of revenge James Fitzjames Stephen 1
prose in us with the p.   Forster 2
ruling p.   Pope 16
utmost p. of her heart   Hawthorne 9
What p. cannot Music   John Dryden 9
passionate
cold and p. as the dawn   Yeats 20
full of p. intensity   Yeats 29
passions
p. of men will not conform
                    Alexander Hamilton 6
p. to prevail over reason
                    Jonathan Swift 35
slave of the p.   David Hume 2
Three p., simple   Bertrand Russell 13
well those p. read   Percy Shelley 6
passover
It is the Lord's p.   Bible 45
passport
Look Like Your P. Photo   Bombeck 3
My p.'s green   Heaney 6
past
ceaselessly into the p.
                    F. Scott Fitzgerald 35
Each had his p. shut   Virginia Woolf 1
Ghost of Christmas P.   Dickens 42
imagine the p.   Namier 1
It's not even p.   Faulkner 13
not only the future but the p. Orwell 19
P., n. That part   Bierce 91
p., or passing   Yeats 50
p. is a foreign country   Hartley 1
p. is always tense   Zadie Smith 2
p. is never dead   Faulkner 13
praiser of p. times   Horace 7
remembrance of things p.
                    Shakespeare 417
shut the door on the p.   Tutu 1
What's p. is prologue Shakespeare 440
who cannot remember the p.
                    Santayana 3
Who controls the p.   Orwell 37
pastures
fresh woods, and p. new   Milton 4
Green p. of plenty   "Woody" Guthrie 3
lie down in green p.   Bible 108

pat
We'll stand p.   Political Slogans 34
pat-a-cake
P., p., baker's man   Nursery Rhymes 52
patch
purple p. or two stitched on   Horace 1
patches
king of shreds and p.   Shakespeare 215
thing of shreds and p. W. S. Gilbert 28
patent
Could you p. the sun   Salk 1
pater
P. noster   Missal 5
path
make a beaten p.
                    Ralph Waldo Emerson 51
Noble Eightfold P.   Pali Tripitaka 4
primrose p. of dalliance
                    Shakespeare 158
realized the Middle P. Pali Tripitaka 2
where there is no p.   Strode 1
pathetic
Everything human is p.   Twain 88
P. Fallacy   Ruskin 5
pathology
p. of the skin   F. Scott Fitzgerald 39
paths
make his p. straight   Bible 199
p. of glory lead   Thomas Gray 6
patience
greater aptitude for p.   Buffon 2
P., n. A minor form   Bierce 92
P. has its limits   George Jackson 2
p. of an oyster   Carroll 7
patient
kill the p.   Francis Bacon 11
like a p. etherized   T. S. Eliot 3
successful, but the p. died   Sayings 45
patriarchy
p.'s greatest psychological weapon
                    Millett 2
patrie
Allons, enfants de la p.   Rouget de Lisle 1
patriot
duty of a true p.   Douglass 3
P., n. One to whom   Bierce 93
sunshine p.   Thomas Paine 8
patriotic
Avenge the p. gore
                    James Ryder Randall 1
patriotism
P., n. . . . In Dr.   Bierce 94
P. in the female sex   Abigail Adams 5
P. is, fundamentally
                    George Bernard Shaw 5
P. is often an arbitrary   Nathan 2
P. is the last refuge   Samuel Johnson 80
p. which consists in hating   Gaskell 4
Talking of p.   Twain 82
whole nation is roaring P.
                    Ralph Waldo Emerson 1
patron
Is not a P., my Lord Samuel Johnson 49
P. . . . Commonly a wretch
                    Samuel Johnson 16
patsy
I'm just a p.   Oswald 1
pattable
she is p.   Nash 13

patter
p. of little feet   Longfellow 22

patterns
Christ! what are p. for   Amy Lowell 2

Paul
midnight ride of P. Revere
                                    Longfellow 23
name is P. Revere   Loesser 4
P., thou art beside thyself   Bible 339
P. Newman and a ride home   Hinton 1

pause
eine kleine P.   Ferrier 1
p. for a reply   Shakespeare 110
p. that refreshes   Advertising Slogans 35

pauses
p. between the notes   Schnabel 1

pave
p. the whole country
                              Ronald W. Reagan 16

paved
road to hell is p.   Proverbs 255
They p. paradise   Joni Mitchell 2

paws
Take your stinking p. off me
                                    Film Lines 135

pay
all others p. cash   Sayings 26
Crime does not p.   Proverbs 56
Equal P. for Equal Work
                              Susan B. Anthony 2
gladly p. you Tuesday   Segar 3
If he'd just p. me   Film Lines 39
must p. the fiddler   Proverbs 60
P. no attention to that man
                                    Film Lines 195
Those who p. the piper   Proverbs 230

paycheck
size of his p.   Adam Clayton Powell, Jr. 2

paying
I'm p. for this broadcast   Film Lines 163

pea
small p. through twenty mattresses
                                    Andersen 1

peace
depart in p.   Winfield Scott 1
for ever hold his p.
                  Book of Common Prayer 17
forever in p. may you wave   Cohan 3
give p. a chance
                        Lennon and McCartney 25
If you want to make p.   Dayan 1
in His will is our p.   Dante 12
inglorious Arts of P.   Andrew Marvell 2
instrument of Your p.   St. Francis 2
Kissinger brought p. to Vietnam
                                    Heller 7
Let him who desires p.   Vegetius 1
make a desert and call it p.   Tacitus 1
May he rest in p.   Anonymous (Latin) 11
May they rest in p.   Missal 1
my soul may find her p.
                              D. H. Lawrence 8
never be at p.   Pearse 1
No justice, no p.   Sonny Carson 1
on earth p., good will   Bible 290
One does not make p.   Rabin 2
Open covenants of p.
                          Woodrow Wilson 17
or a bad P.   Benjamin Franklin 35

our p. in His will   T. S. Eliot 87
P., *n.* In international   Bierce 95
p. cannot be maintained   John Russell 1
p. for our time   Chamberlain 2
P. goes into the making   Neruda 7
p. has broken out   Brecht 5
P. hath her victories   Milton 15
p. I hope with honor   Disraeli 27
P. is indivisible   Litvinov 1
P. is much more precious   Sadat 1
P. is poor reading   Thomas Hardy 23
P. is the way   Muste 1
p.—lasting p.   Lula da Silva 1
p. of God, which passeth   Bible 371
P. on earth   Charles Wesley 1
p. they lack   Kinsella 3
p. with honor   Chamberlain 2
p. without victory   Woodrow Wilson 13
people want p. so much   Eisenhower 8
There is no p.   Bible 174
true p. of mind   W. S. Gilbert 16
War and P.   Proudhon 2
WAR IS P.   Orwell 35
we've made a separate p.   Hemingway 1

peacemaker
title of p.   Richard Nixon 6

peacemakers
Blessed are the p.   Bible 206

peacetime
where they're living it's p.
                              Larry Kramer 1

peacock
pride of the p.   William Blake 6

peacocks
p. and lilies   Ruskin 4

pear
partridge in a p. tree
                            Nursery Rhymes 10

pearl
Germans bombed P. Harbor
                                    Film Lines 9
one p. of great price   Bible 240
Remember P. Harbor   Anonymous 24
threw a p. away   Shakespeare 282

pearls
p. before swine   Bible 223
P. before swine   Dorothy Parker 49
p. that were his eyes   Shakespeare 439

peas
Eating goober p.
                  Folk and Anonymous Songs 31

peasant
thankful I am a p.   Stella Franklin 3
what a rogue and p. slave
                            Shakespeare 185

pease
P. porridge hot   Nursery Rhymes 53

pebble
only p. on the beach   Braisted 1

peck
for daws to p. at   Shakespeare 258

pecker
his p. in my pocket   Lyndon B. Johnson 13

pedigree
P. of Honey   Emily Dickinson 26

pee
p. stains on my underwear   Corso 3

peel
p. me a grape   Mae West 4

peepers
Where'd ya get those p.   Johnny Mercer 1

peerage
p., or Westminster Abbey
                              Horatio Nelson 3
Study the P.   Wilde 63

pegs
All words are p.   Beecher 2

peignoir
Complacencies of the p.
                          Wallace Stevens 8

pen
less brilliant p. than mine   Beerbohm 1
P. is certainly an excellent John Adams 1
p. is mightier than the sword
                              Bulwer-Lytton 3

penalty
death p. is to be abolished   Karr 1

pence
Take care of the p.   Chesterfield 5

pencil
p., sharpened by any women   Twain 74

Penelope
His true P. was Flaubert   Ezra Pound 10

penicillin
p. is certainly useful
                          Alexander Fleming 1

penis
require a p. or vagina
                          Florynce Kennedy 3

penitent
P., *adj.* Undergoing   Bierce 96

pennant
Giants win the p.   Hodges 1

pennies
p. from heaven   Johnny Burke 1

penny
bad p. is sure to return   Proverbs 16
p. saved is a p. earned   Proverbs 231
P. wise and pound foolish   Proverbs 232

pense
Je p., donc je suis   Descartes 4

pension
P. . . . In England   Samuel Johnson 17

pent
long in city p.   Keats 4
long in populous city p.   Milton 40

penumbra
First Amendment has a p.
                          William O. Douglas 5
p. between darkness and light
                        Oliver Wendell Holmes, Jr. 1

penumbras
Bill of Rights have p.
                          William O. Douglas 6

people
alien p. clutching their gods
                              T. S. Eliot 70
All the lonely p.
                        Lennon and McCartney 8
All the p. at this party   Joni Mitchell 5
bad things happen to good p.
                          Harold S. Kushner 1
business of the American p.   Coolidge 3
but the p. themselves   Jefferson 47
called the p.'s cudgel   Bakunin 4
common p. have scarcely   la Bruyère 3
enemy of the p.   Ibsen 12
few fastidious p.   Logan Smith 2

people (cont.):

fool all of the p.	Lincoln 66
Games P. Play	Berne 1
government of all the p.	
	Theodore Parker 3
government of the p.	Lincoln 42
Guns don't die, p. die	
	Political Slogans 17
hated by large numbers of p.	Orwell 5
Hell is other p.	Sartre 5
Here the p. rule	Gerald R. Ford 3
Here, sir, the p. govern	
	Alexander Hamilton 9
I am the p.	Sandburg 5
it's p. I can't stand	Schulz 3
Let my p. go	Bible 43
Let my p. go	
	Folk and Anonymous Songs 29
little p. pay taxes	Helmsley 1
made for the p.	Daniel Webster 5
No p. can be great	Samuel Johnson 19
no vision, the p. perish	Bible 137
not very nice p.	Frankfurter 3
only p. who count in any marriage	
	Hillary Clinton 5
opium of the p.	Karl Marx 2
over all the p.	Theodore Parker 3
p. are a many-headed beast	Horace 11
p. are really good at heart	Anne Frank 3
p. are the masters	Edmund Burke 11
p. can always be brought	Goering 3
P. don't do such things	Ibsen 25
p. have spoken	Tuck 1
p. just liked it better	Jimmy Kennedy 3
p. kill p.	Political Slogans 18
P. of the same trade	Adam Smith 3
p. on the edge of the night	Bowie 4
p. to be very agreeable	Austen 1
p. we used to be	Didion 4
P. who need p.	Bob Merrill 2
p. whose annals are blank	
	Montesquieu 6
p. will live on	Sandburg 11
p. will say we're in love	Hammerstein 9
"p.'s lawyer"	Brandeis 2
P.'s Princess	Blair 7
Power to the p.	Political Slogans 28
queen in p.'s hearts	
	Diana, Princess of Wales 1
right of the p. to keep	Constitution 12
special p. unto himself	Bible 71
too many p. have died	Dylan 3
We the P.	Constitution 1
We the P.	Barbara C. Jordan 1
we're the p.	Steinbeck 3
women are p.	Sayings 12
world is bereft of p.	Lamartine 1
your p. is a great beast	
	Alexander Hamilton 12

peoples

p. of the United Nations	Anonymous 35

Peoria

It'll play in P.	Ehrlichman 2

peppermint

sunny beach of P. Bay	Clare 1

Pepsi

Ain't singin' for P.	Neil Young 4
P. Generation	Advertising Slogans 100

percent

47 p. of the people	Mitt Romney 1
Ninety p. of everything	Sturgeon 1
Ninety p. of this game	Wohlford 1
99 P.	Grim 1
100 p. not guilty	O. J. Simpson 1
Showing up is 80 p. of life	
	Woody Allen 41

perception

doors of p.	William Blake 2

perdition

p. catch my soul	Shakespeare 268

perdu

Recherche du Temps P.	Proust 1

perestroika

idea of restructuring [p.]	Gorbachev 3

perfect

end of a p. day	Carrie Jacobs Bond 1
I'm p.	Crisp 3
It's such a p. day	Lou Reed 2
more p. the artist	T. S. Eliot 32
more p. Union	Constitution 1
Nobody is p.	Proverbs 214
nobody's p.	Film Lines 158
one p. rose	Dorothy Parker 8
p. love casteth out fear	Bible 389
Practice makes p.	Proverbs 241

perfection

it is a study of p.	Matthew Arnold 25
P. of planned layout	Parkinson 3
p. of reason	Coke 5
true p. of man	Wilde 46
very pink of p.	Oliver Goldsmith 9

perfectly

p. good or completely bad	
	Henry Fielding 8

perfidious

p. Albion	Ximénèz 1

perform

one cannot p.	Kinsey 4

performance

p. (the actual use	Chomsky 2
p. every four days	Pavarotti 1
so many years outlive p.	
	Shakespeare 63
takes away the p.	Shakespeare 358

performing

literature's p. flea	O'Casey 2

perfumes

All the p. of Arabia	Shakespeare 387

perhaps

seek a grand p.	Rabelais 4

period

p. at the right moment	Babel 1

periodic

p. repetition of properties	Mendeleev 1
p. table folded up	John Hollander 1
use of the p. sentence	
	Edmund Wilson 1

perish

people p.	Bible 137
P. the thought	Cibber 2
shall not p. from the earth	Lincoln 42
take the sword shall p.	Bible 271
though the world p.	Ferdinand 1
to p. twice	Frost 12

perishable

her p. breath	F. Scott Fitzgerald 21

permanent

ain't nohow p.	Walt Kelly 2
Nothing is so p.	Milton Friedman 8
something more p.	Rich 5
steer clear of p. Alliances	
	George Washington 9

permitted

all is p.	Megarry 1
everything is p.	Dostoyevski 4
not forbidden is p.	Schiller 3

pernicious

p. Race of little odious	Jonathan Swift 11

perpendicular

p. expression of a horizontal	
	George Bernard Shaw 59

perpetual

improper mind is a p. feast	
	Logan Smith 1
p. struggle for room and food	Malthus 2
summary court in p. session	Kafka 7

persecution

P. and Assassination	Peter Weiss 1
P. for the expression	
	Oliver Wendell Holmes, Jr. 27
P. is not an original feature	
	Thomas Paine 18
p. no assistance	George Washington 4

Persian

How can anyone be P.	Montesquieu 1

Persians

given to the Medes and P.	Bible 190
law of the Medes and P.	Bible 191

persisted

Nevertheless, she p.	McConnell 1

person

husband and wife one p.	Mott 1
No p. must have to	
	Gotthold Ephraim Lessing 2
no sich a p.	Dickens 53
one p., one vote	William O. Douglas 4
p. who agrees with me	Disraeli 25
To love another p.	Kretzmer 1

personal

P. Is Political	Hanisch 1
politics of p. destruction	
	William Jefferson "Bill" Clinton 13
This time . . . It's p.	
	Advertising Slogans 65
Up close and p.	
	Television Catchphrases 1
warm p. gesture	Galbraith 5

personality

continual extinction of p.	T. S. Eliot 31
escape from p.	T. S. Eliot 33
p. is an unbroken series	
	F. Scott Fitzgerald 11

personally

see it tried on him p.	Lincoln 52

personified

visibly p.	Melville 7

persons

God is no respecter of p.	Bible 333
P. attempting to find a motive	Twain 28

perspiration

99 per cent p.	Edison 2

persuadest

Almost thou p. me	Bible 340

perturbed

rest, p. spirit	Shakespeare 172

Peru
P. fucked itself up   Vargas Llosa 1
perverse
p. to withhold provisional
                          Stephen Jay Gould 2
perverted
Is she p. like me   Morrissette 4
pessimism
justified itself is p.   Orwell 12
P. (or rather what is called
                          Thomas Hardy 21
pessimist
p. before 48   Twain 116
p. fears this is true   Cabell 1
p. looks at his glass   Stamp 2
pet
discard a p. hypothesis   Konrad Lorenz 1
petals
p. on a wet, black bough   Ezra Pound 4
petard
hoist with his own p.   Shakespeare 218
Peter
P., P., pumpkin eater
                          Nursery Rhymes 54
P. Piper picked a peck
                          Nursery Rhymes 55
robs P. to pay Paul
                    George Bernard Shaw 53
petrified
Loyalty to p. opinions   Twain 37
petticoat
Realm in my p.   Elizabeth I 1
petty
creeps in this p. pace   Shakespeare 393
Peyton
P. Farquhar was dead   Bierce 1
P. Place   Metalious 1
Pharaoh
harden P.'s heart   Bible 44
phatic
p. communion   Malinowski 1
phenomenal
P. woman   Angelou 1
phenomenon
describe the infant p.   Dickens 27
Philadelphia
I went to P.   W. C. Fields 27
in P., Who were   Twain 80
rather be living in P.   W. C. Fields 18
Philistine
P. must have originally
                          Matthew Arnold 14
Philistines
Barbarians, P.   Matthew Arnold 23
Philistinism
P.!—We have not   Matthew Arnold 13
philologists
P., who chase   William Cowper 3
philosopher
greater p. a man is   Sienkiewicz 1
guide, p., and friend   Pope 28
p., according to his temper   Gibbon 8
profound p.   Coleridge 27
some p. has said it   Cicero 2
philosophers
p. become kings   Plato 7
p. have only interpreted   Karl Marx 3
poets and p. before me
                          Sigmund Freud 20

worldly p.   Heilbroner 1
philosophically
P., still trying   Jagger 1
philosophy
as though it were p.   Rebecca West 3
dreamt of in your p.   Shakespeare 170
little p. inclineth man's mind
                          Francis Bacon 9
system of p.   Santayana 12
those in p. only ridiculous
                          David Hume 1
phlegm
p. and tooth decay   Heller 5
phobias
Tell us your p.   Benchley 3
Phoenician
Phlebas the P.   T. S. Eliot 55
phoenix
p. does not die   May Sarton 2
wakes up the p. bird   Anne Baxter 1
phone
E.T. p. home   Film Lines 74
p. is for you   Lebowitz 8
why did you answer the p.   Thurber 6
phonetically
That's fine p.   Quayle 8
phonograph
vaccinated with a p. needle
                          "Groucho" Marx 18
phony
p. tinsel of Hollywood   Levant 2
p. war   Daladier 1
photograph
p. me through linoleum   Bankhead 6
P. of the Whole Earth   Brand 1
photographed
unless I p. them   Diane Arbus 2
photography
mission of p. is to explain   Steichen 1
phrase
p. is born into the world   Babel 2
phrases
army of pompous p.   McAdoo 1
physic
Take p., pomp   Shakespeare 296
Throw p. to the dogs   Shakespeare 391
physical
any mere p. experience   Film Lines 4
facts of p. science   Michelson 1
physician
P., heal thyself   Bible 292
physicists
p. have known sin   Oppenheimer 1
physics
cancels our p.   Karl Jay Shapiro 2
explain your p. to a barmaid
                          Rutherford 7
more difficult than p.   Einstein 28
no democracy in p.   Alvarez 1
p. and stamp-collecting   Rutherford 6
pianist
do not shoot the p.   Wilde 96
piano
Sat Down at the P.
                    Advertising Slogans 124
you're the p. man   Joel 1
Picasso
became P.   Picasso 5

pick
five, six, p. up sticks
                          Nursery Rhymes 49
I p. the round   Ali 2
I'd P. More Daisies   Herold 1
will p. my pocket   Dennis 1
picked
Peter Piper p. a peck
                          Nursery Rhymes 55
picking
p. men of genius   Conant 2
pickle
weaned on a p.   Alice Longworth 1
picks
It neither p. my pocket   Jefferson 11
Pickwickian
used the word in its P. sense   Dickens 1
picture
Do not attempt to adjust the p.
                    Television Catchphrases 47
Earth's last p. is painted   Kipling 14
envisage a p. as being other   Breton 2
Every p. tells a story
                    Advertising Slogans 40
get off this p.   Southern 2
Life is painting a p.
                    Oliver Wendell Holmes, Jr. 21
No p. is made to endure   Ezra Pound 22
not on his p., but his book   Jonson 8
p. is worth a thousand
                    Modern Proverbs 67
p. of the future   Orwell 46
p. that was to grow old   Wilde 27
pictures
p. that got small   Film Lines 165
without p. or conversations   Carroll 2
You furnish the p.   Hearst 1
You oughta be in p.   Heyman 1
piddling
exclusively with the p.   Thurber 14
pie
American as cherry p.   H. Rap Brown 1
baked in a p.   Nursery Rhymes 69
bye bye Miss American P.   McLean 2
joke is ultimately a custard p.   Orwell 13
Promises, like p.-crust   Proverbs 245
you'll get p. in the sky   Joe Hill 1
piece
best p. of poetry   Jonson 5
little p. of my heart   Berns 1
What a p. of work is a man
                          Shakespeare 181
pieces
P. of eight   Robert Louis Stevenson 9
thirty p. of silver   Bible 267
pierced
Men with p. ears   Rudner 1
Pierian
deep of the P. spring   Drayton 2
piety
P., n. Reverence   Bierce 97
pig
Little p., little p.   Halliwell 1
looked from p. to man   Orwell 26
Never wrestle with a p.
                    Modern Proverbs 68
p. satisfied   Mill 16
teach a p. to sing   Heinlein 13

poem (cont.):
heroic p. of its sort   Thomas Carlyle 6
It is a pretty p.   Richard Bentley 1
music of a p.   Synge 1
one p. maybe as cold   Yeats 20
p. is like a painting   Horace 9
p. is never finished   Valéry 2
p. lovely as a tree   Kilmer 1
p. points to nothing but itself   Forster 6
p. should not mean   MacLeish 2
when reading a p.   Auden 40

poems
get the news from p.
    William Carlos Williams 6
origin of all p.   Whitman 4
P. are made by fools   Kilmer 2
We all write p.   Fowles 2
We want "p. that kill"   Baraka 4

poet
common man and a recognized p.
    Thomas Hardy 1
death of the p. was kept   Auden 19
dreams of a p. doomed
    Samuel Johnson 7
ever yet a great p.   Coleridge 27
every fool is not a p.   Pope 12
Good Gray P.   William D. O'Connor 1
great p., in writing himself   T. S. Eliot 71
Honor the lofty p.   Dante 5
limbs of a dismembered p.   Horace 27
making of a p.   Neruda 7
No p. ever interpreted nature
    Giraudoux 1
P. in your Poket   John Adams 10
p. is a pretender   Pessoa 1
p. lies   Coleridge 35
p. should express the emotion
    Thomas Hardy 30
p.'s eye, in a fine frenzy   Shakespeare 57
p.'s voice need not   Faulkner 12
their sacred p.   Horace 25
to make a p. black   Cullen 4

poetic
hunting-grounds for the p. imagination
    George Eliot 11
P. Justice   Pope 37

poetry
best p. will be found   Matthew Arnold 32
difference between genuine p.
    Matthew Arnold 33
grand style arises in p.
    Matthew Arnold 7
his best piece of p.   Jonson 5
I have been eating p.   Strand 2
I know that is p.   Emily Dickinson 29
If p. comes not as naturally   Keats 10
line of p. strays   Housman 8
Mad Ireland hurt you into p.   Auden 21
no man ever talked p.   Dickens 9
p., prophecy, and religion   Ruskin 6
p. after Auschwitz   Adorno 1
p. almost necessarily declines
    Thomas Macaulay 1
P. fettered fetters the human race
    William Blake 23
P. is about as much   Ezra Pound 1
P. is at bottom a criticism
    Matthew Arnold 34
P. is not a turning loose   T. S. Eliot 33

P. is not the proper antithesis
    Coleridge 16
P. is the spontaneous
    William Wordsworth 6
P. is the supreme fiction
    Wallace Stevens 6
P. is what is lost   Frost 25
P. is what Milton saw   Marquis 3
p. makes nothing happen   Auden 22
P. must be as well written   Ezra Pound 2
p. reminds him   John F. Kennedy 35
receptive to p.   Dove 2
that is p.   Cage 1
We campaign in p.   Cuomo 1

poets
among the English P.   Keats 11
Immature p. imitate   T. S. Eliot 28
Irish p., learn your trade   Yeats 61
mature p. steal   T. S. Eliot 28
P., you know, are always   Wilde 99
p. and philosophers before me
    Sigmund Freud 20
P. are the unacknowledged
    Percy Shelley 15
P. in our civilization   T. S. Eliot 35
p. would die of loneliness   Yeats 59
p. would starve   Thomas Hardy 7
touchy breed of p.   Horace 15
we p. in our youth
    William Wordsworth 19

point
at the p. of death   Shakespeare 50
Don't p. that beard at me
    "Groucho" Marx 31
one fixed p.   Arthur Conan Doyle 37
put too fine a p. upon it   Dickens 85
we will p. the gun   Trumbo 1

pointless
it all seems p.   Steven Weinberg 1

points
Ironic p. of light   Auden 14
Possession is nine p.   Proverbs 239
thousand p. of light
    George Herbert Walker Bush 3

Poirot
P. was an extraordinary-looking
    Christie 1

poison
another man's p.   Proverbs 190
to others bitter p.   Lucretius 4

poisoned
p. chalice   Robert H. Jackson 6

poisonous
If p. minerals   Donne 6

poky
p. little puppy   Lowrey 2

pole
beloved from p. to p.   Coleridge 11
Low Man on a Totem P.
    H. Allen Smith 1
top of the greasy p.   Disraeli 30

police
best nocturnal p.
    Ralph Waldo Emerson 42
international p. power
    Theodore Roosevelt 14

policeman
p.'s lot is not a happy one
    W. S. Gilbert 23

terrorist and the p. both   Conrad 21
policy
Honesty is the best p.   Proverbs 144
Our p. is directed   George C. Marshall 1
polished
I p. up that handle   W. S. Gilbert 8
polite
P., *adj.* Skilled in   Bierce 105
You're exceedingly p.   W. S. Gilbert 5
politeness
Punctuality is the p. of kings
    Louis XVIII 2
very pineapple of p.
    Richard Brinsley Sheridan 2
politic
body p.   Rousseau 6
political
man is by nature a p. animal Aristotle 8
Most schemes of p. improvement
    Samuel Johnson 63
Personal Is P.   Hanisch 1
P. language . . . is designed   Orwell 31
p. speech and writing   Orwell 28
politically
Beware the p. obsessed   Noonan 2
p. correct   James Wilson 1
politician
like a scurvy p.   Shakespeare 307
P., *n.* An eel   Bierce 106
p. is an arse upon   e.e. cummings 18
p.—who is dead   Thomas B. Reed 1
statesman is a p.   Truman 10
Under every stone lurks a p.
    Aristophanes 6
politicians
left to the p.   de Gaulle 10
P., like diapers   Betty Carpenter 1
whole Race of P.   Jonathan Swift 12
politics
Academic p. is the most vicious Sayre 1
all p. is Apple Sauce   Will Rogers 2
All p. is local   "Tip" O'Neill 1
Being in p. is like   Eugene McCarthy 1
Finality is not the language of p.
    Disraeli 20
he saturates p. with thought
    Matthew Arnold 10
Modern p. is, at bottom
    Henry Adams 17
mother's milk of p.   Unruh 1
new p. of meaning   Hillary Clinton 3
not interested in p.   Gellhorn 1
playing p.   Herbert C. Hoover 4
P., as a practice   Henry Adams 1
"P.," he says, "ain't bean bag"   Dunne 1
P., *n.* A strife   Bierce 107
P. are too serious   de Gaulle 10
P. in the middle of things   Stendhal 4
P. is fate   Napoleon 13
p. is more difficult   Einstein 28
P. is not an exact science   Bismarck 1
P. is perhaps the only profession
    Robert Louis Stevenson 7
P. is show business   Bill Miller 1
P. is the art of looking   Benn 1
P. is the art of preventing   Valéry 7
P. is the art of the possible Bismarck 9
P. is the study   Lasswell 1

P. makes strange bed-fellows
                    Charles Dudley Warner 2
P. makes strange bedfellows
                    Proverbs 237
p. of joy   Humphrey 2
p. of personal destruction
        William Jefferson "Bill" Clinton 13
Practical p. consists   Henry Adams 15
religion and p.   Twain 136
Sexual P.   Millett 1
War is the continuation of p.
                    Clausewitz 2
pollution
80% of our air p.   Ronald W. Reagan 19
right amount of p.   Milton Friedman 4
Polly
P. put the kettle on   Nursery Rhymes 57
P. Wolly Doodle
        Folk and Anonymous Songs 61
polo
wherever people played p.
                    F. Scott Fitzgerald 14
Pollyanna
P.   Eleanor Porter 1
Pomeranian
single P. grenadier   Bismarck 6
pomp
Pride, p., and circumstance
                    Shakespeare 275
Take physic, p.   Shakespeare 296
pompous
army of p. phrases   McAdoo 1
pond
big fish in a small p.
                    Modern Proverbs 7
old p.   Basho 2
pont
Sur le p. d'Avignon
        Folk and Anonymous Songs 73
pony
riding on a p.
        Folk and Anonymous Songs 84
poor
Alas, p. Yorick   Shakespeare 226
annals of the p.   Thomas Gray 5
another for the p.   Proverbs 165
as easily as a p. one   Howells 1
desire a p. man has   Céline 2
Give me your tired, your p.   Lazarus 2
great men have their p. relations
                    Dickens 87
grind the faces of the p.   Bible 162
honest but p.   Bertrand Russell 9
I've been p. and I've been rich
                    Beatrice Kaufman 1
it's the p. who die   Sartre 9
keep the p. man just stout
                    Chesterton 24
lived well and died p.   Daniel Webster 13
makes me p. indeed   Shakespeare 269
no disgrace t' be p.   "Kin" Hubbard 1
none so p. to do him reverence
                    Shakespeare 118
p., but honest   Shakespeare 252
p. always ye have with you   Bible 323
p. and obscure   Charlotte Brontë 3
p., and the maimed   Bible 298
p. devils are dying   Philip 1
p. falls upon society   Spinoza 4

P. Faulkner   Hemingway 36
p. folks hate the rich folks   Lehrer 3
p. get children   Gus Kahn 1
p. get poorer   Modern Proverbs 75
p. little lambs   Kipling 3
P. little rich girl   Coward 2
P. Little Rich Girl   Eleanor Gates 1
p. man at his gate   Cecil Alexander 2
p. man's chanst   Dunne 23
P. Mexico   Díaz 1
p. race in a land of dollars   Du Bois 4
p. son-of-a-bitch   F. Scott Fitzgerald 27
P. Tom's a-cold   Shakespeare 300
P. wandering one   W. S. Gilbert 15
property of the p.   Ruskin 11
provision for the p.   Samuel Johnson 69
RICH AND THE P.   Disraeli 14
rich as well as the p.   France 3
scandalous and p.   Rochester 3
scandals iv th' p.   Dunne 8
why the p. have no food   Câmara 1
poorer
for richer for p.
        Book of Common Prayer 15
pop
fated soon to p.   Cole Porter 10
I don't p. my cork   Dorothy Fields 4
P. Goes the Weasel
        Folk and Anonymous Songs 62
popcorn
p. and lollipops   W. C. Fields 9
pope
I am the P.   John XXIII 3
P.? How many divisions   Stalin 4
Popeye
I'm P. the sailor man   Sammy Lerner 1
popular
more p. than Jesus   Lennon 13
p. prejudice runs in favor   Dickens 21
popularization
what p. is to science   Bergson 2
population
P., when unchecked   Malthus 1
populi
Vox p., vox Dei   Alcuin 1
populous
long in p. city pent   Milton 40
pore
I'm p., I'm black   Alice Walker 6
Porgie
Georgie P., pudding and pie
                    Nursery Rhymes 18
Porlock
on business from P.   Coleridge 18
pornographic
What p. literature does   Sontag 4
pornography
men believe what p. says   Dworkin 4
P. is about dominance   Steinem 4
P. is the attempt to insult sex
                    D. H. Lawrence 12
P. is the theory   Robin Morgan 2
What p. is really about   Sontag 3
porpoise
There's a p. close   Carroll 20
porridge
Pease p. hot   Nursery Rhymes 53
Somebody has been at my p.   Southey 9
Somebody has been at my p.   Southey 10

Porsches
My friends all drive P.   Joplin 2
port
Any p. in a storm   Proverbs 10
in ev'ry p. a mistress find   Gay 3
portals
p. of discovery   Joyce 19
portmanteau
it's like a p.   Carroll 41
portrait
Every time I paint a p.
                    John Singer Sargent 1
two styles of p. painting   Dickens 26
portraits
number of p. one saw   Musil 3
portray
myself that I p.   Montaigne 1
poses
animals strike curious p.   Prince 3
posies
pocket full of p.   Nursery Rhymes 62
position
her p. in the universe   Chopin 1
missionary p.   Kinsey 1
p. ridiculous   Chesterfield 7
positive
accent-tchu-ate the p.   Johnny Mercer 4
P., *adj.* Mistaken   Bierce 108
Power of P. Thinking   Peale 1
positronic
p. brains of all robots   Asimov 1
possess
He does not p. wealth
                    Benjamin Franklin 8
p. the secret of joy   Alice Walker 8
possessed
She is p. by time   Louise Bogan 1
possesses
confusing a man with what he p.
                    Wilde 45
possession
Every increased p.   Ruskin 19
P. is nine points of the law   Proverbs 239
possessions
All my p. for a moment   Elizabeth I 5
behind the great p.   Henry James 25
possibilities
Land of Unlimited P.   Goldberger 1
p. of defeat   Victoria 4
stick to p.   Twain 93
possibility
I dwell in P.   Emily Dickinson 12
possible
all things are p.   Bible 251
because it is p.   Freeman Dyson 1
best among all p. worlds   Leibniz 3
best of all p. worlds   Voltaire 8
best of p. worlds   Voltaire 7
if it is p.   Calonne 1
It is not p.   Napoleon 3
limits of the p.   Arthur C. Clarke 2
Politics is the art of the p.   Bismarck 9
those who are now p.   Bakunin 2
post
every p. tends to be occupied   Peter 2
P. coitum omne animal triste
                    Anonymous (Latin) 10
poster
at least a great p.   Margot Asquith 1

prevention
ounce of p.   Proverbs 243
prey
this man's lawful p.   Ruskin 23
price
buyers who consider p. only   Ruskin 23
even greater p. than life Saint-Exupéry 1
Every man has his p.   Proverbs 89
Everything in Rome has its p.   Juvenal 1
fetch a high p.   Whately 1
her p. is far above rubies   Bible 138
one pearl of great p.   Bible 240
p. of everything   Wilde 32
p. of liberty   Andrew Jackson 5
p. of wisdom   Bible 102
prick
if you p. us   Shakespeare 76
pricks
kick against the p.   Bible 332
pride
could not take your p.   Bono 2
P., pomp, and circumstance
                        Shakespeare 275
P. AND PREJUDICE   Burney 3
P. goeth before destruction   Bible 133
p. of the peacock   William Blake 6
smitten with P.   Jonathan Swift 17
priest
guts of the last p.   Diderot 4
P., the Lawyer, and Death
                    Benjamin Franklin 14
this turbulent p.   Henry II 1
prigs
slang of p.   George Eliot 12
primal
p. eldest curse   Shakespeare 211
prime
grow up to be P. Minister   Richler 3
One's p. is elusive   Spark 3
P. Directive   Star Trek 8
p. mover   Aquinas 1
P. numbers are what   Haddon 1
will be P. Minister   Thatcher 2
primeval
This is the forest p.   Longfellow 15
primrose
p. path of dalliance   Shakespeare 158
prince
black shining P.   Ossie Davis 1
Good night, sweet p.   Shakespeare 237
I am not P. Hamlet   T. S. Eliot 9
only one P. of Peace
                George Bernard Shaw 52
p. of darkness   Shakespeare 299
P. of Peace   Bible 166
Someday My P. Will Come   Morey 3
princes
thousands of p.   Beethoven 1
you P. of Maine   John Irving 2
princess
People's P.   Blair 7
P. of Parallelograms   Byron 2
P. of Wales was the queen   Dowd 1
was a real P.   Andersen 1
princesses
p. could never leave
            Elizabeth the Queen Mother 1

principle
does everything on p.
                George Bernard Shaw 10
great p. of the English law   Dickens 88
hain't th' money but th' p.
                        "Kin" Hubbard 3
It's the p.   Sayings 30
p. comes a moment of repose
                        John W. Davis 2
society can be p.-ridden   Bickel 1
principles
Damn your p.   Disraeli 38
These are my p.   "Groucho" Marx 46
Three P. of the People   Sun Yat-sen 2
your lordship's p.   Foote 2
print
All the news that's fit to p.
                        Adolph Ochs 1
p. the legend   Film Lines 113
p. your own money   Roy Thomson 1
printed
p. word expands to fill   Parkinson 10
printer
body of B. Franklin, P.
                    Benjamin Franklin 1
printing
Gunpowder, P., and the Protestant
                    Thomas Carlyle 7
P., gunpowder   Francis Bacon 6
prints
P. in the next Room   Centlivre 1
priorities
I had other p.   Cheney 3
prison
adorn its p.   Wollstonecraft 6
also a p.   Thoreau 10
at home in p.   Waugh 3
each in his p.   T. S. Eliot 58
I was prepared for p. George Jackson 1
p. of his days   Auden 25
Shades of the p.-house
                William Wordsworth 14
Stone walls do not a p. make
                    Richard Lovelace 1
What is a ship but a p. Robert Burton 6
prisoner
your being taken p.   Kitchener 1
prisoners
p. call the sky   Wilde 91
P. cannot enter into contracts
                    Nelson Mandela 2
p. of addiction   Illich 1
prisons
judged by entering its p. Dostoyevski 1
P. are built with stones William Blake 5
reform needed in our p.   Ruskin 9
privacy
create zones of p. William O. Douglas 6
glass bowl for all the p.   Saki 1
p. is protected   William O. Douglas 5
right of p.   Blackmun 1
right of p. means anything   Brennan 6
society of p.   Rand 3
You have zero p.   McNeely 1
private
Abolition of p. property
                    Marx and Engels 6
grave's a fine and p. place
                    Andrew Marvell 14

p. property in land   Mill 1
system of p. property   Hayek 1
trust p. people with theirs
                        Adam Smith 5
privatize
p. profits   Rickover 1
prize
Third p. is you're fired   Film Lines 88
prize-fighters
p. shaking hands   Mencken 12
prizes
distributed in the form of p.   Nobel 1
glittering p.   Frederick Edwin Smith 1
pro
weird turn p.   Hunter S. Thompson 5
probable
upon p. cause   Constitution 13
problem
Before the p. of the artist
                    Sigmund Freud 13
Houston, we've had a p.   Lovell 1
I've yet to see any p.   Poul Anderson 1
No p. is so big   Schulz 5
p. can be shown to exist   Rumsfeld 6
p. of the twentieth century   Du Bois 5
p. that has no name   Friedan 2
solution to every human p. Mencken 22
three-pipe p.   Arthur Conan Doyle 14
you're part of the p.   Cleaver 2
problems
disguised as insoluble p.
                    John W. Gardner 1
p. of three little people   Film Lines 48
procedural
observance of p. safeguards
                        Frankfurter 1
procedure
interstices of p.   Maine 2
process
due p. of law   Anonymous 30
due p. of law   Constitution 14
p. to be prolonged   Richard Nixon 15
without due p. of law   Constitution 21
proclaim
p. liberty throughout   Bible 66
proclaims
apparel oft p. the man Shakespeare 159
procrastinated
p. rape   Pritchett 1
procrastination
P. is the thief of time   Edward Young 4
product
p. is no sooner created   Say 1
profanity
p. furnishes a relief   Twain 139
profession
most ancient p.   Kipling 2
second oldest p.   Ronald W. Reagan 2
professions
p. are conspiracies
                George Bernard Shaw 28
two oldest p.   Woollcott 2
professor
p. is one who talks   Auden 43
profit
between the p. and the loss
                        T. S. Eliot 84
opposeth no man's p.   Hobbes 10
what should it p. a man   Bible 278

psychoanalysis
  father of p.   Greer 2
  pay for his or her own p.   Ephron 2
psychoanalysts
  p. on the Pan Am flight   Jong 4
psychobabble
  P. spoken here   Rosen 1
psychology
  P., as the behaviorist   John B. Watson 1
public
  aimed at the p.'s heart   Sinclair 1
  as if I were a p. meeting   Victoria 5
  British p. in one of its
                              Thomas Macaulay 6
  conspiracy against the p.   Adam Smith 3
  dressing a p. monument
                              Eleanor Roosevelt 3
  English p. school   Waugh 3
  intelligence of the American p.
                                      Mencken 35
  microcosm of a p. school   Disraeli 1
  Our researchers into P. Opinion
                                       Auden 15
  precedence over p. relations
                                      Feynman 3
  P., _n._ The negligible   Bierce 119
  p. and a private position
                              Hillary Clinton 11
  p. be damned   William H. Vanderbilt 2
  p. debt is a public curse   Madison 11
  p. . . . demands certainties   Mencken 16
  P. opinion is a permeating   Bagehot 1
  smiling p. man   Yeats 34
publications
  number of earlier p.   Hilbert 2
publicity
  All p. is good   Behan 4
  All p. is good p.   Modern Proverbs 70
  pitiless p.   Ralph Waldo Emerson 42
  P. is justly commended   Brandeis 4
publish
  P. or perish   Modern Proverbs 71
publisher
  Xerox makes everybody a p.
                                    McLuhan 11
puck
  where the p.'s going   Walter Gretzky 1
pudding
  proof of the p.   Proverbs 246
puddle
  world is p.-wonderful   e.e. cummings 5
puddy
  I tawt I taw a p. tat
                  Television Catchphrases 81
Puff
  I'll huff, and I'll p.   Halliwell 1
  P., the magic dragon   Yarrow 1
pull
  easier to p. down   Proverbs 247
  long p., and a strong p.   Dickens 69
  P. down thy vanity   Ezra Pound 25
  p. his weight   Theodore Roosevelt 10
pulpit
  bully p.   Theodore Roosevelt 27
pumpkin
  Peter, Peter, p. eater   Nursery Rhymes 54
pun
  such an execrable p.   Dennis 1

punched
  they get p. in the mouth   Tyson 1
punctuality
  P. is the politeness of kings
                                  Louis XVIII 2
punish
  few that p. them   Benjamin R. Tucker 1
  gods wish to p. us   Wilde 74
  if they must p. him   Sinclair 2
  life to p. ourselves   Kingsolver 1
punishment
  let the p. fit the crime   W. S. Gilbert 39
  p. match the offense   Cicero 5
  p. tames man   Nietzsche 20
punishments
  cruel and unusual p.   Constitution 17
punk
  exposition of p.-rock   Marsh 1
punk'd
  You've been p.
                  Television Catchphrases 54
puny
  p. and inexhaustible voice   Faulkner 14
puppets
  box and the p.   Thackeray 7
puppies
  Five little p. dug a hole   Lowrey 1
puppy
  Happiness is a warm p.   Schulz 2
  poky little p.   Lowrey 2
  snails and p.-dog tails   Southey 7
pure
  Blessed are the p. in heart   Bible 206
  breathe its p. serene   Keats 2
  England was too p. an Air
                                  Anonymous 14
  my heart is p.   Tennyson 13
  99–44/100% P.   Advertising Slogans 63
  p. as the driven slush   Bankhead 4
  P. mathematics   Henry Smith 1
  solidity to p. wind   Orwell 31
  truth is rarely p.   Wilde 76
  Unto the p. all things are p.   Bible 380
purely
  if you stated it p. enough Hemingway 14
purer
  day is not p.   Racine 5
  give a p. sense   Mallarmé 3
purest
  p. treasure   Shakespeare 11
purify
  p. the dialect   T. S. Eliot 119
Puritan
  P. hated bear-baiting
                              Thomas Macaulay 12
Puritanism
  P.—The haunting fear   Mencken 42
purple
  I never saw a P. Cow   Gelett Burgess 1
  I shall wear it   Jenny Joseph 1
  I wrote the "P. Cow"   Gelett Burgess 8
  p. patch or two   Horace 1
  p. rain   Prince 2
  walk by the color p.   Alice Walker 5
purpose
  being used for a p.
                          George Bernard Shaw 12
  P. Driven Life   Rick Warren 1
  time for every p.   Pete Seeger 3

  time to every p.   Bible 143
purse
  as thy p. can buy   Shakespeare 159
  silk p. out of a sow's ear   Proverbs 272
  Who steals my p.   Shakespeare 269
pursue
  p. Culture in bands   Wharton 4
pursued
  Exit, p. by a bear   Shakespeare 448
pursuit
  p. of Happiness   Jefferson 2
push
  big fool says to p. on   Pete Seeger 6
  total p. and pressure   William James 17
pushed
  I will not be p.
                  Television Catchphrases 52
  I'll be p. just so far   Harry L. Wilson 1
pushing
  p. the outside   Tom Wolfe 5
pussy
  Grab 'em by the p.   Trump 2
  I love little p.   Nursery Rhymes 58
  Owl and the P.-cat went to sea   Lear 4
  P. cat, p. cat   Nursery Rhymes 59
  what a beautiful P. you are   Lear 5
pussyfooting
  pusillanimous p.   Agnew 3
put
  just p. your lips together
                                  Film Lines 177
  Never p. off till tomorrow   Proverbs 248
  Polly p. the kettle on
                          Nursery Rhymes 57
  p. a bullet through his head
                          Edwin Arlington Robinson 2
  P. a tiger in your tank
                          Advertising Slogans 47
  p. away childish things   Bible 355
  p. off till to-morrow   Wilde 113
  p. on his knowledge   Yeats 45
  P. out the light   Shakespeare 280
  P. up or shut up   Proverbs 249
  P. your money where
                          Modern Proverbs 61
  shall never be p. out   Latimer 1
  up with which I will not p.
                          Winston Churchill 54
puttin'
  P. on the Ritz   Irving Berlin 6
putting
  p. all my eggs   Dorothy Parker 43
  p. my queer shoulder   Ginsberg 6
  p. old heads   Spark 1
  That was a way of p. it   T. S. Eliot 102
puzzling
  what's p. you   Jagger and Richards 10
pyjamas
  elephant in my p.   "Groucho" Marx 7
pyramids
  summit of these p.   Napoleon 8

Q

quagmires
  I don't do q.   Rumsfeld 4
quaint
  renders q.   Alberto R. Gonzales 1

racist
definition of a r. comment   Ryan 1
rack
leave not a r. behind   Shakespeare 442
r. of this tough world   Shakespeare 319
racket
Would I were her r. pressed   Betjeman 3
radiance
r. of a thousand suns   Bhagavadgita 2
radical
most r. revolutionary   Arendt 9
never dared be r.   Frost 19
perplexity of r. evil   Arendt 8
r. chic   Krim 1
R. Chic   Tom Wolfe 1
r. is a man with both feet
                    Franklin D. Roosevelt 18
radio
I had the r. on   Marilyn Monroe 3
make r. a "household utility"   Sarnoff 1
radioactivity
R. is shown   Rutherford 1
radium
give the name of r.   Curie 1
raft
no home like a r.   Twain 31
rag
I r. nobody   Mark Harris 1
r.-and-bone shop   Yeats 60
That Shakespearian r.   Gene Buck 1
that Shakespeherian R.   T. S. Eliot 48
rage
Blessed r. for order   Wallace Stevens 13
r. against the dying   Dylan Thomas 17
ragged
pair of r. claws   T. S. Eliot 7
ragtime
Alexander's R. Band   Irving Berlin 1
era of R. had run out   Doctorow 1
railroad
disappearing r. blues
                    Steve Goodman 2
I've been working on the r.
                    Folk and Anonymous Songs 37
way to run a r.   Ralph Fuller 1
We do not ride on the r.   Thoreau 25
railway
R. termini . . . are our gates   Forster 1
rain
droppeth as the gentle r.
                    Shakespeare 79
hard r.'s a-gonna fall   Dylan 5
into each life some r.   Longfellow 11
I've seen r.   James Taylor 2
left out in the r.   Auden 44
like the r. falling   Verlaine 2
Neither snow nor r.   Kendall 1
r., it raineth on the just   Lord Bowen 2
R., r., go away   Nursery Rhymes 61
R. falls into the open   Merwin 4
r. in Spain stays mainly
                    George Bernard Shaw 49
r. it raineth every day   Shakespeare 246
r. on the just   Bible 213
r. was upon the earth   Bible 28
Singin' in the r.   Arthur Freed 1
Still falls the R.   Sitwell 3
takes credit for the r.   Dwight Morrow 1
waiting for r.   T. S. Eliot 21

rainbow
God gave Noah the r. sign
                    James Baldwin 2
God gave Noah the r. sign
                    Folk and Anonymous Songs 36
our nation is a r.   Jesse Jackson 1
R. Is Enuf   Shange 1
reverent feeling for the r.   Twain 23
Somewhere over the r.   Harburg 5
raindrops
R. keep fallin'   Hal David 5
rains
Don't pray when it r.   Paige 12
never r. but it pours   Proverbs 250
rainy
lived in its r. arms   Erdrich 1
r. Sunday afternoon   Ertz 1
raise
make it r. your hair   Dorothy Parker 19
R. less corn   Lease 1
raised
r. on city land   Charles Dudley Warner 3
raisin
r. in the sun   Langston Hughes 8
rake
R.'s Progress   Hogarth 1
rally
R. round the flag   James T. Fields 1
r. round the flag
                    George Frederick Root 2
Ralph
R. wept for the end   Golding 1
ram
old black r.   Shakespeare 259
Ramadan
month of R.   Koran 3
ramble
social r. ain't restful   Paige 4
ranch
back at the r.   Sayings 40
Randal
where ha you been, Lord R.   Ballads 5
random
R. KINDNESS AND SENSELESS ACTS
                    Anne Herbert 1
rang
You r.   Television Catchphrases 42
ranger
Lone R. rides again
                    Radio Catchphrases 15
One riot, one R.   W. J. "Bill" McDonald 1
rank
my offence is r.   Shakespeare 211
ransom
Alimony is the r.   Mencken 13
R. notes   Leonard 2
rape
give r. its history   Brownmiller 2
legitimate r.   Akin 1
procrastinated r.   Pritchett 1
r. has played a critical   Brownmiller 1
r. law affirmatively rewards MacKinnon 3
r. the practice   Robin Morgan 2
r. us with their eyes   French 2
R. was an insurrectionary act   Cleaver 1
you r. it   Degas 1
raped
Dukakis were r. and murdered
                    Bernard Shaw 1

rapes
lawful r. exceed   Sanger 5
raping
Who's doing the r.   Trump 5
rapist
r. bothers to buy   Dworkin 1
victim's response to the r.   Atkinson 1
rapists
all men are r.   French 2
rapscallions
kings is mostly r.   Twain 32
rapture
first fine careless r.   Robert Browning 9
r. of the deep   Cousteau 1
raptures
no Minstrel r. swell   Walter Scott 3
Rapunzel
R., R., let down   Grimm and Grimm 1
rara
R. avis   Juvenal 2
rare
miracle of r. device   Coleridge 22
r. as a day in June
                    James Russell Lowell 3
r. bird   Juvenal 2
rarer
r. than the unicorn   Jong 5
rarity
thought a r.   Robert Browning 7
rascals
Turn the r. out   Political Slogans 33
rash
It is too r.   Shakespeare 37
R., *adj.* Insensible   Bierce 121
rat
dirty, double-crossing r.   Cagney 1
field r., startled   Toomer 1
giant r. of Sumatra
                    Arthur Conan Doyle 38
studying to be a r.   Mizner 9
win a r. race   Coffin 1
rate
r. can be expected   Gordon E. Moore 1
rather
r. be dead than cool   Cobain 3
r. be living in Philadelphia
                    W. C. Fields 18
r. be right than be President   Clay 1
ration
Thou shalt not r. justice   Hand 9
rational
man as a r. animal   Wilde 29
One r. voice is dumb   Auden 8
What is r. is actual   Hegel 1
rationed
it must be r.   Lenin 9
rattle
just r. your jewelry   Lennon 1
rattles
moon r. likes a fragment
                    e.e. cummings 8
rattlesnake
r. poised to strike
                    Franklin D. Roosevelt 24
r. that doesn't bite   Jessamyn West 4
raven
Quoth the R., "Nevermore"   Poe 9
r. himself is hoarse   Shakespeare 334
r. like a writing-desk   Carroll 14

No compulsion is there in r.   Koran 5
old time r.
                    Folk and Anonymous Songs 28
R., *n.* A daughter   Bierce 125
r. and fly fishing   Norman Maclean 1
r. and politics   Twain 136
R. enough to make us hate
                              Jonathan Swift 4
R. . . . is a man's total reaction
                              William James 10
R. is love   Beatrice Potter Webb 1
R. is the sigh   Karl Marx 2
R. is the theory   Mencken 23
r. is the thing   Chesterton 7
R. is to mysticism   Bergson 2
r. makes men virtuous
                          Bertrand Russell 4
r. of pomp   Thomas Paine 28
r. of the father   Sigmund Freud 19
r. that has any thing in it
                          Thomas Paine 29
R.; which by reason   Hobbes 6
respect the other fellow's r.   Mencken 45
Science without r.   Einstein 15
special manifestations of r.
                          William James 9
substitute for r.   T. S. Eliot 73
Superstition is the r.   Edmund Burke 21
That is my r.   George Bernard Shaw 27
that takes r.   Steven Weinberg 2
To die for a r.   Borges 4
True R.   Twain 133
What r. a man shall have   Santayana 5
wrong could r. induce   Lucretius 1

religions
sixty different r.   Caracciolo 1

religious
do it from r. conviction   Pascal 15
finding a r. outlook   Jung 2
first-hand r. experience
                          William James 12
Good, but not r.-good   Thomas Hardy 3
r. vision   Whitehead 6
We are a r. people
                        William O. Douglas 2

reload
Don't retreat, r.   Palin 5

remain
right to r. silent   Earl Warren 3
they r. the same   Karr 2

remained
nothing done while anything r.   Lucan 2

remains
he r. an Englishman   W. S. Gilbert 13
What thou lovest well r.   Ezra Pound 24

remake
myself that I r.   Yeats 7

remarks
R. are not literature   Stein 4

remedies
desperate r.   Proverbs 65
die of their r.   Molière 13

remedy
r. is worse than the disease
                          Francis Bacon 19

remember
I cannot r. things   Snyder 1
If you r. the '60s   Fleischer 1
must I r.   Shakespeare 151

r. any but the things   Twain 123
r. even these things   Virgil 2
r. me to Herald Square   Cohan 3
R. Pearl Harbor   Anonymous 24
R. the Alamo   Sidney Sherman 1
r. the future   Namier 1
R. the Ladies   Abigail Adams 1
r. the Red River Valley
                    Folk and Anonymous Songs 63
that no man r. me   Thomas Hardy 9
that's all that I r.   Cullen 3
Those who cannot r. the past
                              Santayana 3
Try to r.   Tom Jones 1
You must r. this   Hupfeld 1
you should r. and be sad   Rossetti 2

remembered
blue r. hills   Housman 2
I r. my God   Southey 3
made myself r.   Keats 22
sweet love r.   Shakespeare 416
tranquility r. in emotion
                          Dorothy Parker 24

remembers
who r. that famous day   Longfellow 23

remembrance
R. of Things Past   Proust 1
r. of things past   Shakespeare 417
writ in r.   Shakespeare 15

remind
foolish things r. me of you
                            Holt Marvell 1

remove
so that I could r. mountains   Bible 353

removes
Three r. is as bad as a fire
                        Benjamin Franklin 31

render
R. therefore unto Caesar   Bible 255

rendezvous
I have a r. with Death   Alan Seeger 1
I shall not fail that r.   Alan Seeger 2
r. with destiny   Franklin D. Roosevelt 9

renowned
no less r. than war   Milton 15

rent
that has not been r.   Yeats 52

rental
washed a r. car   Peters 1

repair
friendship in constant r.
                          Samuel Johnson 48

repeat
But I r. myself   Twain 140
condemned to r. it   Santayana 3

repeats
History r. itself   Proverbs 142

repent
Married in haste, we may r.   Congreve 1
R. ye: for the kingdom   Bible 198

repetition
By r. that which at first   Hegel 5
housework, with its endless r.
                          de Beauvoir 3

replaced
r. by something even more
                          Douglas Adams 6

report
r. of my death   Twain 138

reporter
mild-mannered r.
                    Television Catchphrases 6
one lonely r.   Richard Nixon 20

repose
moment of r.   John W. Davis 2
r. is not the destiny
                    Oliver Wendell Holmes, Jr. 12

representation
Taxation without r.   Otis 6

representative
office of a r. assembly   Mill 14
Your r. owes you   Edmund Burke 5

representatives
Women ought to have r.
                        Wollstonecraft 13

repressed
r. desire for aesthetic   Waugh 2

repression
STOP THE R.   Romero 1

republic
banana r.   O. Henry 1
r., if you can keep it
                    Benjamin Franklin 44

republican
He who is not a r.   Batbie 1
R. cloth coat   Richard Nixon 2

Republicans
Please tell me you're R.
                    Ronald W. Reagan 20
We are all R.   Jefferson 31

reputation
I have lost my r.   Shakespeare 267
seeking the bubble r.   Shakespeare 90
sold my R. for a Song
                    Edward FitzGerald 6
spotless r.   Shakespeare 11

requiescat
R. *in pace*   Anonymous (Latin) 11
R. *in pace*   Missal 1

required
much is r.   John F. Kennedy 6
of him shall be much r.   Bible 297

rerun
r. of a bad movie   George W. Bush 26

research
it's called r.   Mizner 6
Successful r. attracts   Parkinson 8

researches
r. in original sin   Plomer 1

resemblances
far more sensitive to r.   William James 7

resembled
Had he not r. my father
                          Shakespeare 353

reservations
make their own mental r.   LaFollette 1

reserved
r. to the States   Constitution 19

reserving
R. judgments is a matter
                    F. Scott Fitzgerald 8

resident
R., *adj.* Unable to leave   Bierce 126

residue
Luck is the r. of design   Rickey 1

resign
I shall r. the presidency
                    Richard Nixon 16

resignation
by r. none   Jefferson 32
resist
functions that r. death   Bichat 1
one cannot r. the invasion   Hugo 8
r. everything except temptation
                                                 Wilde 53
r. him that is set   Ptahhotep 1
resistance
R. is futile   Star Trek 10
R. is the secret of joy   Alice Walker 9
resisted
She r. me   Dumas the Elder 1
resistible
R. Rise of Arturo Ui   Brecht 6
resolute
R., *adj.* Obstinate   Bierce 127
resolution
In war: r.   Winston Churchill 35
native hue of r.   Shakespeare 192
respect
askin' for is a little r.   Redding 1
highest r. for law
                         Martin Luther King, Jr. 8
I don't get no r.   Dangerfield 1
more properly r. it   Chesterton 9
r. for the rights   Juarez 1
r. me in the morning   Sayings 64
white man was bound to r.   Taney 2
R-E-S-P-E-C-T
R.   Aretha Franklin 1
respecter
God is no r. of persons   Bible 333
response
stimulus and r.   John B. Watson 2
responsibility
great r.   Stan Lee 1
I do not shrink from this r.
                                  John F. Kennedy 14
In dreams begins r.   Yeats 16
individual r.   Elizabeth Cady Stanton 13
Power without r.   Kipling 39
R., *n.* A detachable   Bierce 128
rest
Ben Adhem's name led all the r.
                                           Leigh Hunt 4
continues in its state of r.
                                       Isaac Newton 4
crazy the r. of your life   W. C. Fields 5
f., far better r.   Dickens 99
first day of the r. of your life
                                      Abbie Hoffman 1
for the r. of your life   Film Lines 46
God r. you merry
                      Folk and Anonymous Songs 30
I cannot r. from travel   Tennyson 15
May he r. in peace
                               Anonymous (Latin) 11
May they r. in peace   Missal 1
No r. for the weary   Proverbs 213
r., perturbed spirit   Shakespeare 172
r. as long as I am living   Emily Brontë 5
r. is commentary   Hillel 2
r. is dross   Ezra Pound 24
r. is literature   Verlaine 3
r. is not our business   T. S. Eliot 109
r. is silence   Shakespeare 236
r. under the trees   "Stonewall" Jackson 1
Where's the r. of me   Bellamann 1

restaurant
at Alice's R.   Arlo Guthrie 1
restful
social ramble ain't r.   Paige 4
restless
They are r. tonight   Film Lines 97
restraining
r. reckless middle-age   Yeats 12
restraint
Moral r.   Malthus 4
wholesome r.   Daniel Webster 15
restrictions
greater r.   Keillor 3
result
firm ground of R.   Winston Churchill 1
resurrection
I am the r.   Bible 321
retaliatory
massive r. power   John Foster Dulles 2
retreat
In case of a forced r.   Stalin 3
no r., baby   Springsteen 6
retreating
seen yourself r.   Nash 6
retribution
exacting an awful r. Patrick J. Buchanan 1
return
I shall r.   Douglas MacArthur 6
I will r.   Fast 1
to r. the compliment   W. S. Gilbert 5
unto dust shalt thou r.   Bible 22
returned
His Grace r. from the wars
                                         Marlborough 1
I have r.   Douglas MacArthur 1
returneth
dog r. to his vomit   Bible 136
returns
criminal always r.   Modern Proverbs 18
reveals
sports r. character
                             Heywood Hale Broun 1
revelation
appetite for bogus r.   Mencken 14
revelry
sound of r. by night   Byron 8
revels
Our r. now are ended   Shakespeare 442
reveng'd
so am I r.   Shakespeare 212
revenge
passion of r.   James Fitzjames Stephen 1
R. can be eaten cold   Proverbs 252
R. is a kind of wild justice
                                       Francis Bacon 17
R. is sweet   Proverbs 253
R. me if I die   Diem 1
r. of the intellect   Sontag 1
r. on behalf of the Clintons Kavanaugh 1
shall we not r.   Shakespeare 76
Revere
midnight ride of Paul R.   Longfellow 23
reverence
How much r.   Heller 5
Kill r.   Rand 2
R. for Life   Schweitzer 1
to do him r.   Shakespeare 118
reviewers
R. are usually people   Coleridge 17

reviewing
read a book before r.   Sydney Smith 13
revolt
Art is a r.   Malraux 2
revoltin'
What a r. development
                                   "Groucho" Marx 36
What a r. development
                          Radio Catchphrases 14
revolting
r. to have no better reason
                         Oliver Wendell Holmes, Jr. 14
revolution
Every successful r.   Tuchman 4
In a r., one either   Guevara 2
it is a big r.
                       la Rochefoucauld-Liancourt 1
justify r.   Lincoln 27
make peaceful r. impossible
                                  John F. Kennedy 23
not the leaders of a r.   Conrad 23
pregnant with r.   Cézanne 2
R., *n.* In politics   Bierce 129
R. is like Saturn   Büchner 1
r. is not a dinner party   Mao Tse-tung 1
R. may, like Saturn   Vergniaud 1
R. of Rising Expectations
                                   Harlan Cleveland 1
R. that does not constantly   Guevara 1
R. was in the minds   John Adams 17
R. Will Not Be Televised   Scott-Heron 1
There is a r. coming   Reich 4
time to stop a r.   Adlai E. Stevenson 5
You say you want a r.
                          Lennon and McCartney 20
revolutionary
r. right to dismember   Lincoln 29
true r. is guided   Guevara 4
truth is a r. act   Orwell 52
revolutionist
r. at the age of twenty
                             George Bernard Shaw 48
revolutions
share in two r.   Thomas Paine 15
revolve
worlds r. like ancient women
                                           T. S. Eliot 16
reward
not be working for a r.   Kālidāsa 1
nothing for r.   Spenser 5
receive his r. in this world
                                      Henry Fielding 9
r. of a thing well done
                             Ralph Waldo Emerson 23
Virtue is its own r.   Proverbs 316
rhetorician
sophistical r.   Disraeli 28
Rhine
watch along the R.   Schneckenburger 1
rhyme
hope and history r.   Heaney 8
I r. to see myself   Heaney 1
outlive this powerful r.
                                      Shakespeare 419
rhymed
r. out in love's despair   Yeats 19
rhymes
but it r.   Twain 154
it r. with rich   Barbara Bush 1

r. of iron   Bible 106
Spare the r. and spoil   Proverbs 280
thy r. and thy staff   Bible 109
rode
Four Horsemen r. again
                          Grantland Rice 2
r. madly off   Leacock 1
r. the six hundred   Tennyson 37
rogue
r. and peasant slave   Shakespeare 185
roll
Let us r. all our strength
                          Andrew Marvell 15
Let's r.   Beamer 1
Merrily We R. Along
                          George S. Kaufman 2
R. on, Columbia   "Woody" Guthrie 4
R. on, thou deep   Byron 15
R. over Beethoven   Chuck Berry 1
R. up that map   Pitt 1
roller
r. of big cigars   Wallace Stevens 3
rolling
caissons go r. along   Gruber 1
Gonna be a r. stone   Muddy Waters 1
like a r. stone   Dylan 17
r. stone gathers   Proverbs 257
rolls
r. off my back like a duck   Goldwyn 12
Roman
butchered to make a R. holiday   Byron 14
Decline and Fall of the R. Empire
                               Gibbon 1
I am a R. citizen   Cicero 10
more an antique R.   Shakespeare 234
neither Holy, nor R.   Voltaire 5
noblest R. of them all   Shakespeare 130
romance
last r.   Wilde 62
romances
need never try to write r.   Hawthorne 4
Romans
do as the R. do   Proverbs 258
Friends, R., countrymen
                          Shakespeare 111
what have the R.   Monty Python 13
romantic
R. Ireland's dead   Yeats 17
romanticism
r. is disease   Goethe 24
Rome
All roads lead to R.   Proverbs 256
Everything in R. has its price   Juvenal 1
grandeur that was R.   Poe 1
I loved R. more   Shakespeare 108
It was at R.   Gibbon 10
Let R. in Tiber melt   Shakespeare 398
man I loved in R.   Millay 3
R. has spoken   Augustine 7
R. was not built in a day   Proverbs 259
R.-Berlin axis   Mussolini 2
second man in R.   Julius Caesar 4
stones of R. to rise   Shakespeare 124
when I go to R.   Ambrose 1
When in R.   Proverbs 258
Romeo
wherefore art thou R.   Shakespeare 33
Ronsard
R. sang of me   Ronsard 3

roof
cat on a hot tin r.   Tennessee Williams 8
tongue cleave to the r.   Bible 123
room
boys in the back r.   Dorgan 2
died in a hotel r.   Eugene O'Neill 5
in a smoke-filled r.
                       Harry M. Daugherty 1
In the r. the women come   T. S. Eliot 4
in the r. where it happens   Miranda 6
into the next r.   Henry Scott Holland 1
no r. in it   Ralph Waldo Emerson 47
r. at the top   Lennon 3
r. enough at the top   Daniel Webster 17
r. enough to swing a cat   Smollett 3
r. of her own   Virginia Woolf 9
R. 101 is the worst   Orwell 48
Send up a larger r.   "Groucho" Marx 33
smallest r. of my house   Reger 1
struggle for r. and food   Malthus 2
roomful
r. of deaf people   Paul H. O'Neill 1
rooms
r. to let   Roger Miller 1
Roosevelt
R. is no crusader   Lippmann 3
Roosian
he might have been a R.   W. S. Gilbert 13
roost
birds came home to r.   Arthur Miller 4
chickens coming home to r.
                               Malcolm X 3
come home to r.   Southey 6
root
Idleness is the r. of all evil   Proverbs 152
money is the r. of all evil   Bible 377
R., hog, or die   Proverbs 260
r. for the home team   Norworth 3
r. is one   Yeats 8
r. of the matter   Bible 101
Split at the r.   Rich 1
striking at the r.   Thoreau 21
rooting
R. for the Yankees   Joe E. Lewis 2
roots
dull r. with spring rain   T. S. Eliot 39
rope
end of your r.   Franklin D. Roosevelt 31
Give a man r. enough   Proverbs 261
r. and the hanged man   Castro 3
R.-A-Dope   Ali 6
rose
fire and the r. are one   T. S. Eliot 125
Go, lovely r.   Edmund Waller 1
Goodbye England's r.
                           John and Taupin 2
I am the r. of Sharon   Bible 157
my Luve's like a red, red r.
                           Robert Burns 11
Never Promised You a R. Garden
                           Hannah Green 1
No r. without a thorn   Proverbs 262
one perfect r.   Dorothy Parker 8
R., thou art sick   William Blake 9
R. is a r. is a r.   Stein 1
r. is red   Nursery Rhymes 63
r. like a rocket   Thomas Paine 20
r. smells better   Mencken 3
second hand R.   Grant Clarke 1

That which we call a r.   Shakespeare 34
yellow r. in Texas
                    Folk and Anonymous Songs 86
young woman to a r.   Dalí 2
rosebud
R.   Film Lines 53
R. was something   Film Lines 55
rosebuds
Gather ye r.   Herrick 3
rosemary
There's r.   Shakespeare 224
Rosenbergs
dictate terms to the R.
                          Ethel Rosenberg 2
executed the R.   Plath 2
Rosencrantz
R. and Guildenstern are dead
                          Shakespeare 238
roses
days of wine and r.   Dowson 3
Everything's Coming Up R.
                          Sondheim 3
Gather the r. of life   Ronsard 2
lived as r. do   François de Malherbe 1
Ring-a-ring o' r.   Nursery Rhymes 62
r., r., all the way   Robert Browning 16
rosy
R.-fingered dawn   Homer 8
rotten
r. in the state of Denmark
                          Shakespeare 165
rotting
thousand r. buffalos   Ted Perry 3
rough
These r. notes   Robert Falcon Scott 3
r.-hew how we will   Shakespeare 230
this r. magic   Shakespeare 444
what r. beast   Yeats 30
round
comin' r. the mountain
                    Folk and Anonymous Songs 69
I pick the r.   Ali 2
If we went r. the moon
                       Arthur Conan Doyle 4
lie will go r. the world   Proverbs 168
Love makes the world go r.
                          Proverbs 179
Music Goes 'R. and Around
                          "Red" Hodgson 1
Rally r. the flag   James T. Fields 1
r. hole   Sydney Smith 5
r. the mulberry bush
                    Folk and Anonymous Songs 54
R. up the usual suspects   Film Lines 49
trivial r.   Keble 1
rounded
our little life is r.   Shakespeare 443
rounds
their appointed r.   Kendall 1
rouse
R. the lion   Walter Scott 14
roving
go no more a-r.   Byron 12
row
R., r., r. your boat
                    Folk and Anonymous Songs 67
r. the boat ashore
                    Folk and Anonymous Songs 51

royal
dreams is the r. road   Sigmund Freud 6
no "r. road" to geometry   Euclid 3
r. throne of kings   Shakespeare 16
royalist
r. in politics   T. S. Eliot 74
royalists
economic r.   Franklin D. Roosevelt 10
royalty
Our r. is to be reverenced   Bagehot 4
rub
ay, there's the r.   Shakespeare 189
r. off on you   Runyon 1
R.-a-dub-dub   Nursery Rhymes 64
rubbish
What r.   Blücher 1
rubble
more offensive than r.
    Charles, Prince of Wales 4
rubies
price is far above r.   Bible 138
price of wisdom is above r.   Bible 102
ruby
Goodbye, R. Tuesday
    Jagger and Richards 6
rude
By the r. bridge Ralph Waldo Emerson 6
Rudolph
R., the Red-Nosed Reindeer
    Johnny Marks 1
rug
r. really tied the room   Film Lines 21
rugged
r. individualism   Herbert C. Hoover 2
harsh cadence of a r. line John Dryden 7
ruin
boy will r. himself   George V 1
I will r. you   Cornelius Vanderbilt 1
majestic though in r.   Milton 28
resolved to r.   John Dryden 5
r. of many poor girls
    Folk and Anonymous Songs 65
r. of our sex   Smollett 1
sooner learns r.   Machiavelli 5
ruined
bare r. choirs   Shakespeare 421
r. by amateurs   Woollcott 2
ruins
man is a god in r.
    Ralph Waldo Emerson 3
r. of St. Paul's   Thomas Macaulay 9
r. of St. Paul's   Walpole 2
shored against my r.   T. S. Eliot 60
Thou art the r.   Shakespeare 106
rule
Divide and r.   Proverbs 70
exception proves the r.   Proverbs 91
exception to every r.   Proverbs 92
first r. about fight club   Palahniuk 1
Here the people r.   Gerald R. Ford 3
R., Britannia   James Thomson 1
r. us from their graves   Maitland 2
together we can r.   George Lucas 16
ruled
they give you r. paper   Jiménez 1
ruler
R. of the Queen's Navee W. S. Gilbert 8
r. of her own spirit
    John Quincy Adams 1

rulers
best [r.] are those   Lao Tzu 3
you all may be R.   W. S. Gilbert 10
rules
gold makes the r.   Sayings 16
no golden r.   George Bernard Shaw 18
R. are made to be broken   Proverbs 263
r. the world   Proverbs 133
Who r. East Europe   Mackinder 1
ruling
r. ideas of each age   Marx and Engels 7
r. passion   Pope 16
rum
bottle of r.   Robert Louis Stevenson 8
r., Romanism, and rebellion Burchard 1
r., sodomy, prayers
    Winston Churchill 45
rumble
get ready to r.   Buffer 1
rumors
r. of wars   Bible 259
rumpus
Let the wild r. start   Sendak 3
run
born to r.   Springsteen 2
can't be r. away from   Schulz 5
Gwine to r. all night   Stephen Foster 2
I do not choose to r.   Coolidge 4
In the long r.   Keynes 4
know how to r.   George Burns 1
lady, better r.   Dorothy Parker 10
never did r. smooth   Shakespeare 51
r. but he can't hide   Joe Louis 2
r. it up the flagpole   Sayings 35
Still waters r. deep   Proverbs 284
Sweet Thames, r. softly   Spenser 7
They get r. over   Bevan 2
walk before we r.   Proverbs 317
What Makes Sammy R.   Schulberg 1
we will make him r.   Andrew Marvell 15
runcible
ate with a r. spoon   Lear 7
Runic
in a sort of R. rhyme   Poe 18
runner
Loneliness of the Long-Distance R.
    Sillitoe 1
runners
like r. relay the torch   Lucretius 3
runneth
my cup r. over   Bible 109
running
all the r. you can do   Carroll 30
Avoid r. at all times   Paige 5
blood is r. in the streets   Rothschild 1
r. people is considered   Vince Foster 1
runs
fights and r. away   Proverbs 102
Insanity r. in my family   Kesselring 1
man who r. may fight   Menander 2
river r. through it   Norman Maclean 2
rural
idiocy of r. life   Marx and Engels 5
rus
R. in urbe   Martial 3
rush
Fools r. in where angels   Pope 5
R. Limbaugh Is a Big Fat Idiot
    Franken 1

r. to judgment   Erskine 1
Russia
action of R.   Winston Churchill 11
From R. with Love   Ian Fleming 4
outlaws R. forever   Ronald W. Reagan 7
R., if you're listening   Trump 12
R., speeding along   Gogol 1
R. has two generals   Nicholas 2
see R.   Palin 2
they think it's R.   Trump 22
Russian
Holy R. land   Kurbsky 1
Russians
fewer but better R.   Film Lines 126
R. and the Americans   Tocqueville 14
rust
diamonds and r.   Baez 2
r. unburnish'd   Tennyson 19
wear out, than r. out
    Richard Cumberland 1
rustling
r. of each purple curtain   Poe 7
rusty
tastes like a r. knife   John Cheever 1
rye
catcher in the r.   Salinger 4
Comin thro' the r.   Robert Burns 10
Levy's R. Bread   Advertising Slogans 71
pocket full of r.   Nursery Rhymes 69

S

sabbath
Remember the s. day   Bible 54
s. was made for man   Bible 275
sabe
Kemo S.   Radio Catchphrases 17
sabotage
no s. has taken   DeWitt 1
Sacco
S.'s name will live   Vanzetti 1
sack
Sad S.   George Baker 1
sacking
This is the s. of cities   Jane Jacobs 1
sacrament
abortion would be a s.
    Florynce Kennedy 2
sacred
facts are s.   C. P. Scott 1
our s. Honor   Jefferson 8
S. cows make the tastiest
    Abbie Hoffman 3
s. fire of liberty George Washington 3
s. rights of mankind
    Alexander Hamilton 1
seen nothing s.   Hemingway 9
sacrifice
painful and absolute s.   Maeterlinck 1
refused a lesser s.   Queen Mary 1
so costly a s.   Lincoln 48
Too long a s.   Yeats 28
undaunted the final s.   Spring-Rice 1
sacrificed
I have s. everything   Pat Nixon 1
What have you s.   Tim Rice 1
would have s. his life   Renan 2
You have s. nothing   Khan 1

sad
all s. words — Whittier 1
remember and be s. — Rossetti 2
S. is Eros — Auden 8
s. is the sound — Vigny 1
S. Sack — George Baker 1
tell s. stories — Shakespeare 21
weight of this s. time — Shakespeare 320
world is s. and dreary — Stephen Foster 4
Saddam
I am S. Hussein — Hussein 2
sadder
s. and a wiser man — Coleridge 15
saddest
I can write the s. lines — Neruda 5
s. are these — Whittier 1
s. of possible words — Franklin P. Adams 1
s. story — Ford Madox Ford 1
saddle
Back in the S. Again — Autry 1
Germany in the s. — Bismarck 3
sounds like a s. horse
— Jacqueline Kennedy Onassis 3
Things are in the s.
— Ralph Waldo Emerson 31
saddles
s. on their backs — Jefferson 54
Sade
Direction of the Marquis de S.
— Peter Weiss 1
safe
be on the s. side — Proverbs 21
Better be s. than sorry — Proverbs 22
feeling s. with a person — Craik 1
He wants to be s. — Mencken 36
Is it s. — William Goldman 3
persons nor property will be s.
— Douglass 16
s., polite, obedient — Sinclair Lewis 3
s. for children to grow up — Le Guin 5
s. for democracy — Woodrow Wilson 15
s. for hypocrisy — Thomas Wolfe 1
s. while the Legislature
— Gideon J. Tucker 1
ship in harbor is s. — Shedd 1
you thought it was s.
— Advertising Slogans 64
safeguards
s. of liberty — Frankfurter 3
safely
sleep s. in their beds — le Carré 3
safest
s. road to Hell — C. S. Lewis 1
safety
neither Liberty nor S.
— Benjamin Franklin 28
our s. and our ideals — Obama 5
S. first — Modern Proverbs 76
s. in numbers — Proverbs 264
s. is in our speed
— Ralph Waldo Emerson 14
s. valve of our system — Bancroft 1
sage
s. does not accumulate — Lao Tzu 12
said
if you want anything s. — Thatcher 1
never s. a foolish Thing — Rochester 4
not been s. before — Terence 2
some philosopher has s. it — Cicero 2

sail
constitution is all s. — Thomas Macaulay 13
s. beyond the sunset — Tennyson 25
sailed
Columbus s. the ocean blue — Stoner 1
sailor
do with the drunken s.
— Folk and Anonymous Songs 19
Home is the s.
— Robert Louis Stevenson 21
Popeye the s. man — Sammy Lerner 1
sailors
s., when away — Gay 3
s. won't believe it — Walter Scott 12
saint
S., n. A dead sinner — Bierce 131
s. without God — Camus 5
saintliness
S. is a temptation — Anouilh 1
saints
all the sinners s. — Jagger and Richards 12
s. were rarely married women
— Anne Morrow Lindbergh 2
when the s. come marchin' in
— Folk and Anonymous Songs 82
sake
Art for art's s. — Constant de Rebecque 1
art for art's s. — Cousin 1
salad
crazy s. — Yeats 23
My s. days — Shakespeare 399
salary
his s. depends — Sinclair 4
keep it s. — "Lefty" Gomez 1
S. is no object — Dorothy Parker 15
salesman
For a s. — Arthur Miller 1
s. is got to dream — Arthur Miller 2
sallies
s. out of the race — Milton 7
salt
grain of s. — Pliny 2
how s. is the taste — Dante 13
Not worth his s. — Petronius 3
pillar of s. — Bible 31
s. of the earth — Bible 207
s. wind from the sea — du Maurier 3
seasoned with s. — Bible 372
salute
about to die s. you — Anonymous (Latin) 2
If it moves, s. it — Sayings 22
salutes
see if anyone s. — Sayings 35
salvaged
ships have been s. — William F. Halsey 2
Sam
I am S. — Seuss 10
I cremated S. McGee — Service 1
Play it again, S. — Woody Allen 4
Play it, S. — Film Lines 42
Samarra
tonight in S. — Maugham 9
same
fart and chew gum at the s. time
— Lyndon B. Johnson 14
in the s. boat — Cicero 1
keep in the s. place — Carroll 30
more they remain the s. — Karr 2

not been the s. dog
— Franklin D. Roosevelt 28
People of the s. trade — Adam Smith 3
s. a hundred years hence — Dickens 25
s. as the old boss — Townshend 7
s. mistake twice — Modern Proverbs 77
separated by the s. language
— George Bernard Shaw 58
together in the s. direction
— Saint-Exupéry 2
twice into the s. river — Heraclitus 3
We occupy the s. cage
— Tennessee Williams 9
Sammy
What Makes S. Run — Schulberg 1
San
heart in S. Francisco — Cross 1
in S. Francisco in the rainy — Twain 153
S. Quentin, I hate — Johnny Cash 3
sanction
attended by a s. — Alexander Hamilton 5
sanctuary
S.! — Hugo 1
sand
face drawn in s. — Foucault 2
heap of loose s. — Sun Yat-sen 1
house upon the s. — Bible 230
Laws are s. — Twain 120
line has been drawn in the s.
— George Herbert Walker Bush 9
world in a grain of s. — William Blake 14
sands
footprints on the s. of time — Longfellow 4
lone and level s. — Percy Shelley 7
sandwich
Enjoy every s. — Zevon 5
sanest
s. man in this entire jurisdiction
— Irvin S. Cobb 1
s. man that ever walked — Film Lines 121
sang
s. beyond the genius — Wallace Stevens 9
s. in my chains — Dylan Thomas 7
s. within the bloody wood — T. S. Eliot 17
sanitary
s. and mechanical age — Havelock Ellis 1
sanity
ain't no S. Claus — "Groucho" Marx 27
s. is, in the last analysis
— George Bernard Shaw 37
sank
s. beneath your wisdom
— Leonard Cohen 1
S. same — Donald F. Mason 1
They s. my boat — John F. Kennedy 40
sans
s. teeth, s. eyes — Shakespeare 91
Santa Claus
No S. — Church 1
one and only S. — Film Lines 116
S. is comin' — Gillespie 1
shoot S. — Alfred E. Smith 3
stopped believing in S. — Temple Black 1
there is a S. — Church 2
sap
won't play the s. for you — Hammett 1
Sargasso
our S. Sea — Ezra Pound 7

sat
difficult to be s. on   Douglas Adams 8
everyone has s. except e.e. cummings 18
Humpty Dumpty s. on a wall
    Nursery Rhymes 24
I s. upon the shore   T. S. Eliot 59
They Laughed When I S.
    Advertising Slogans 124
we s. in the house   Seuss 3
Satan
Get thee behind me, S.   Bible 247
Satanic
S. Verses   Khomeini 2
these dark S. mills   William Blake 19
satire
S. is something   George S. Kaufman 4
satisfaction
can't get no s.   Jagger and Richards 2
Complete s.   Selfridge 1
sing "S." when I'm 45   Jagger 2
satisfied
I can never be s.   Lincoln 2
torment of love s.   T. S. Eliot 80
Saturday
close on S.   Coward 15
closes on S.   George S. Kaufman 4
it's S. Night Television Catchphrases 68
Saturn
Revolution is like S.   Büchner 1
Revolution may, like S.   Vergniaud 1
satyr
Hyperion to a s.   Shakespeare 151
sauce
only one s.   Caracciolo 1
s. for the goose   Proverbs 265
saucy
s. doubts and fears   Shakespeare 369
Saul
S., S., why persecutest   Bible 331
sausage
hold on s. and haddock
    Virginia Woolf 18
sausages
Laws, like s.   Saxe 1
savage
charms to sooth a s. breast   Congreve 5
noble s. ran   John Dryden 2
old-stone s. armed   Frost 5
s. indignation can no longer
    Jonathan Swift 34
s. indignation there   Yeats 58
take some s. woman   Tennyson 9
unto a s. race   Tennyson 14
we all resemble this s.   Nietzsche 1
save
destroy the town to s. it   Anonymous 13
God s. the king   Bible 82
God s. the king   Henry Carey 2
s. the Union   Lincoln 32
S. the Whales   Political Slogans 30
s. you 15 percent or more
    Advertising Slogans 52
they won't s. us   F. Scott Fitzgerald 51
saved
No one was s. Lennon and McCartney 9
penny s. is a penny earned Proverbs 231
s. a wretch like me   John Newton 1
these men s. the world
    William Jefferson "Bill" Clinton 5

we are not s.   Bible 181
Whosoever shall be s.
    Book of Common Prayer 1
world will be s.   Dostoyevski 3
saves
stitch in time s. nine   Proverbs 285
savior
remember Christ our S.
    Folk and Anonymous Songs 30
saw
first time ever I s. your face   MacColl 1
I came, I s., I conquered Julius Caesar 6
I never s. a Moor   Emily Dickinson 20
I s. him, I blushed   Racine 3
I s. the best minds   Ginsberg 7
I s. the whole of Baltimore   Cullen 3
just s. off the Eastern Seaboard
    Goldwater 1
last time I s. Paris   Hammerstein 4
say
can't s. something good
    Alice Longworth 4
care what you s. about me   Cohan 9
didn't s. everything I said   Berra 16
Ev'ry time we s. goodbye Cole Porter 19
having nothing to s.   George Eliot 19
having to s. you're sorry   Segal 2
I s. "Why not?"
    George Bernard Shaw 45
I s. a little prayer   Hal David 4
If you can't s. anything good
    Modern Proverbs 78
it's how you s. it   Modern Proverbs 79
Just s.   Advertising Slogans 2
Just s. the lines   Coward 14
more to s. when I am dead
    Edwin Arlington Robinson 3
Never s. die   Proverbs 207
Never s. never   Modern Proverbs 63
people will s. we're in love
    Hammerstein 9
S., hey   Mays 1
s. good night   Shakespeare 39
S. goodnight, Gracie
    Television Catchphrases 23
S. hello to my little friend
    Film Lines 150
S. it ain't so, Joe   Anonymous 26
S. It Loud—I'm Black James Brown 2
S. it with flowers
    Advertising Slogans 111
S. not the struggle   Clough 1
sure as hell can't s. it Harrison Ford 1
What can you s. about   Segal 1
what others s. of them   Pascal 11
what would they s.   Yeats 25
whatever you s., you s. nothing
    Heaney 4
your right to s. it   Tallentyre 1
saying
s. good-bye to a statue Hemingway 12
We were s. yesterday Luis de León 1
says
who s. it best James Russell Lowell 5
scaffold
Truth forever on the s.
    James Russell Lowell 2
scandal
most conspicuous s.   Myrdal 1

scandalous
s. and poor   Rochester 3
scape
who shall s. whipping Shakespeare 184
scapegoat
Let him go for a s.   Bible 64
scar
s. had not pained Harry   Rowling 8
Scarborough
To S. Fair
    Folk and Anonymous Songs 68
scarcely
S. any question   Tocqueville 11
scarecrow
kind of old s.   Yeats 37
scares
that s. you   Schmich 2
scarlet
S. Letter   Hawthorne 3
s. letter was her passport
    Hawthorne 11
s. thread of murder
    Arthur Conan Doyle 6
though your sins be as s.   Bible 160
scarred
s. by the war   Coward 13
scars
He jests at s.   Shakespeare 32
One writes of s. healed
    F. Scott Fitzgerald 39
S. have the strange power
    Cormac McCarthy 2
scene
returns to the s. of the crime
    Modern Proverbs 18
This is not the s.   Coetzee 2
scenery
ever spoke of s.
    Robert Louis Stevenson 20
scepticism
S. is the chastity   Santayana 11
schedule
My s. is already full   Kissinger 2
schemes
s. of political improvement
    Samuel Johnson 63
s. o' mice an' men   Robert Burns 3
schizophrenia
you have s.   Szasz 2
schlemiel
woman s.   Abzug 1
scholar
gentleman and s.   Robert Burns 4
school
Experience keeps a dear s.
    Benjamin Franklin 22
He made S. Boards   Twain 107
How do you explain s.   Film Lines 73
microcosm of a public s.   Disraeli 1
Never tell tales out of s. Proverbs 289
s. to learn art in   Wilde 18
s.-days, dear old golden rule
    Will D. Cobb 1
Thirty-one s. shootings John Oliver 1
Three little maids from s.
    W. S. Gilbert 34
time is the s.   Schwartz 1
school-boy
every S. knows   Jeremy Taylor 1

seizures
unreasonable searches and s.
Constitution 13
seldom
it is s. a mistake   Mencken 10
Men s. make passes   Dorothy Parker 7
s. what they seem   W. S. Gilbert 11
where s. is heard   Higley 1
select
recommend him by s. quotations
Samuel Johnson 27
selection
by the term of Natural S.
Charles Darwin 4
selects
Soul s. her own Society
Emily Dickinson 14
self
fluidity of s.-revelation   Henry James 20
luxury in s.-reproach   Wilde 38
man's S. is the sum total
William James 6
naked s.-interest   Marx and Engels 4
orgy of s.-sacrificing   Rand 4
profits more than s.-esteem   Milton 38
reaction is s.-sustaining   Fermi 1
s. made man   Clapp 1
S.-Esteem, n. An erroneous   Bierce 133
S.-Evident, adj. Evident   Bierce 134
s.-fulfilling prophecy   Merton 1
S.-love is the greatest
la Rochefoucauld 2
s.-made man is one   Stead 1
S.-preservation is the first law
Proverbs 268
strike at his s.-love   Lew Wallace 2
This tape will s.-destruct
Television Catchphrases 45
to thine own s. be true   Shakespeare 161
truths to be s.-evident   Jefferson 2
We prefer s. government   Nkrumah 1
selfish
our own s. genes   Dawkins 1
S., adj. Devoid   Bierce 135
sell
Don't s. America short   J. P. Morgan 2
Don't S. the Steak   Elmer Wheeler 1
s. no wine before its time
Advertising Slogans 99
S. the Sizzle   Elmer Wheeler 1
we s. hope   Revson 1
Why not s. the air   Tecumseh 1
selling
always s. someone out   Didion 2
seminary
come from a ladies' s.   W. S. Gilbert 36
semiology
I shall call it s.   Saussure 2
senate
House, and the S., too   Sayings 65
senators
Come s., congressmen   Dylan 6
send
Never s. a boy   Modern Proverbs 9
s. American boys   Lyndon B. Johnson 9
s. him to the cemetery   Malcolm X 1
S. in the clowns   Sondheim 6
S. lawyers, guns   Zevon 3

seniors
s. take none out   A. Lawrence Lowell 1
sense
Common s. is not so common
Voltaire 14
Common s. is nothing more Einstein 26
divinest S.   Emily Dickinson 18
Good s. is the best   Descartes 1
never deviates into s.   John Dryden 6
seem an echo to the s.   Pope 3
s. of obligation   Stephen Crane 4
talk s. to the American
Adlai E. Stevenson 2
senseless
RANDOM KINDNESS AND S. ACTS
Anne Herbert 1
senses
Five and Country S.   Dylan Thomas 5
till I lose my s.   Cole Porter 18
sensibility
dissociation of s. set in
T. S. Eliot 34
sent
innocent man is s.   "Kin" Hubbard 3
s. it into battle   Murrow 5
sentence
dives into a s.   Twain 42
it's a s.   Cantor 1
it's a s.   Film Lines 57
ordinary British s.   Winston Churchill 6
S. first—verdict afterwards   Carroll 24
s. me to hell   Mill 17
use of the periodic s.   Edmund Wilson 1
what can be said in a s.
Oliver Wendell Holmes, Jr. 25
sentenced
s. to solitary confinement
Tennessee Williams 10
sentences
Backward ran s.   Gibbs 1
sentiments
Them's my s.   Thackeray 4
separate
s. and unequal   Kerner 1
s. but equal   Earl Warren 1
s. but equal accommodations
John M. Harlan (1833–1911) 1
s. peace   Hemingway 1
we cannot s.   Lincoln 28
separated
two countries s.
George Bernard Shaw 58
separately
we shall all hang s.
Benjamin Franklin 34
separation
Six degrees of s.   Guare 1
wall of s.   Jefferson 33
September
Thirty days hath S.   Nursery Rhymes 67
septic
Greener Over the S. Tank   Bombeck 1
sepulchre
her s. there by the sea   Poe 17
sepulchres
Whited s.   Bible 258
sequestered
Each s. in its hate   Auden 24
s. nooks   Longfellow 27

sera
Que s., s.   Jay Livingston 1
serendipity
S. . . . you will understand   Walpole 1
serene
breathe its pure s.   Keats 2
s. confidence   Twain 2
serenity
s. to accept   Wygal 1
serfdom
Better to abolish s.   Alexander II 1
series
victim of a s. of accidents   Vonnegut 2
serious
I can be as s. as anyone   Mozart 2
much more s. than that   Shankly 1
nothing s. in mortality   Shakespeare 362
Politics are too s. a matter   de Gaulle 10
War is too s. a matter   Clemenceau 4
Why so s.   Film Lines 58
You can't be s.   McEnroe 1
seriously
take anything s.   Coward 1
serpent
be the s. under't   Shakespeare 338
not forbidding the s.   Twain 55
s. beguiled me   Bible 19
s. subtlest beast   Milton 39
s. was more subtil   Bible 15
sharper than a s.'s tooth
Shakespeare 289
servant
good and faithful s.   Bible 262
s. in the House of the Lord   Barkley 1
servants
conversation with one of his s.
Samuel Johnson 1
serve
cannot s. God and mammon   Bible 218
I should decline to s.
William Tecumseh Sherman 3
No man can s. two masters   Bible 218
not yet able to s. man   Confucius 7
s. in heaven   Milton 22
They also s.   Milton 53
will not s. if elected
William Tecumseh Sherman 5
served
Had I but s. my God   Shakespeare 452
he s. human liberty   Yeats 58
s. God as diligently   Wolsey 1
When I was a lad I s. a term
W. S. Gilbert 8
Youth must be s.   Proverbs 336
service
done the state some s.   Shakespeare 282
serving-men
I keep six honest s.   Kipling 27
servitude
badge of s.
John M. Harlan (1833–1911) 3
sesame
Open S.   Arabian Nights 2
session
while the Legislature is in s.
Gideon J. Tucker 1
sessions
s. of sweet silent thought
Shakespeare 417

s. tongue is the only
                    Washington Irving 3
sharpening
s. my oyster knife   Hurston 1
sharper
s. than a serpent's tooth
                    Shakespeare 289
shattered
air is s.   Ernest L. Thayer 3
s. visage lies   Percy Shelley 6
shay
wonderful one-hoss s.
                    Oliver Wendell Holmes 7
she
Loves of a S.-Devil   Weldon 1
S. loves you   Lennon and McCartney 2
S. walks in beauty   Byron 7
S. who must be obeyed
                    H. Rider Haggard 1
she'd
s. better   Thomas Carlyle 20
shears
resembles a pair of s.   Sydney Smith 9
shed
prepare to s. them   Shakespeare 119
sheep
Baa, baa, black s.   Nursery Rhymes 5
Bo-Peep has lost her s.
                    Nursery Rhymes 6
come to you in s.'s clothing   Bible 228
s. and the wolf are not agreed
                    Lincoln 46
s. from the goats   Bible 265
s. in s.'s clothing   Winston Churchill 48
s. in s.'s clothing   Gosse 1
s. to pass resolutions   Inge 1
to add the s. was tautology   Twain 117
Wolf in S.'s Clothing   Aesop 3
Shelley
once see S. plain   Robert Browning 15
shelter
s. from the storm   Dylan 25
sheltering
talk of s. woman
                    Elizabeth Cady Stanton 14
shepherd
good s. giveth his life   Bible 320
Lord is my s.   Bible 108
sheriff
I shot the s.   Marley 2
Sherlock
My name is S. Holmes
                    Arthur Conan Doyle 18
shew
re-e-eally big s.
                    Television Catchphrases 17
shibboleth
Say now S.   Bible 76
shift
let me s. for myself   Thomas More 3
shine
Arise, s.   Bible 179
not to s. in use   Tennyson 19
Rise and s.
                    Folk and Anonymous Songs 64
s. on, harvest moon   Norworth 1
shines
Make hay while the sun s.   Proverbs 183
sun s. bright   Stephen Foster 5

shining
farewell to s. trifles   Philip Sidney 3
From sea to s. sea   Bates 1
one brief s. moment   Alan Jay Lerner 17
s. on the broken   Daniel Webster 6
sun is s. bright   Ernest L. Thayer 4
shiny
had a very s. nose   Johnny Marks 1
ship
As idle as a painted s.   Coleridge 5
as the smart s. grew   Thomas Hardy 25
being in a s.   Samuel Johnson 50
built your s. of death
                    D. H. Lawrence 10
Don't give up the s.
                    Oliver Hazard Perry 1
expensive delicate s.   Auden 30
good s. Lollipop   Clare 1
how to sail my s.   Louisa May Alcott 4
places his s. alongside
                    Horatio Nelson 6
s. has weather'd   Whitman 11
s. in harbor is safe   Shedd 1
s. is anchor'd   Whitman 12
S. of Fools   Brant 1
S. of State   Longfellow 16
tall s. and a star   Masefield 1
We (that's my s. and I)
                    Charles Lindbergh 1
What is a s. but a prison
                    Robert Burton 6
shipped
what ye have s. for   Melville 5
ships
all the s. at sea   Radio Catchphrases 24
go down to the sea in s.   Bible 118
launched a thousand s.   Marlowe 8
Loose lips sink s.
                    Advertising Slogans 139
S. at a distance   Hurston 2
S. that pass in the night   Longfellow 26
shirt
Brooks Brothers S.   Mary McCarthy 1
shit
hasn't got s. all over him
                    Monty Python 9
S. happens   Modern Proverbs 81
S. or get off the pot
                    Modern Proverbs 82
shock-proof s. detector   Hemingway 35
you can type this s.   Harrison Ford 1
you do when you s.   Caruso 1
shithole
people from s. countries   Trump 29
shock
future s.   Toffler 1
S. and Awe   Ullman 1
s. of recognition   Melville 1
shocked
I'm s., s.   Film Lines 45
shocks
s. the conscience   Frankfurter 5
s. the mind of a child   Thomas Paine 29
shoe
If the s. fits   Proverbs 269
One, two, buckle my s.
                    Nursery Rhymes 49
woman who lived in a s.
                    Nursery Rhymes 77

shoes
Goody Two-S.   Oliver Goldsmith 2
heard s. described   Margaret Halsey 1
her s. were number nine   Montrose 3
ladies in tennis s.   Mosk 1
my blue suede s.   Carl Perkins 1
of s.—and ships   Carroll 34
shoo
S. fly, don't bother me   Reeves 1
shook
Ten Days That S. the World   John Reed 1
shoot
do not s. the pianist   Wilde 96
Gang That Couldn't S. Straight
                    Breslin 1
How can you s. women   Herr 1
S., if you must   Whittier 3
s. a fellow down   Thomas Hardy 24
S. first and ask questions
                    Modern Proverbs 83
s. me in my absence   Behan 2
s. Santa Claus   Alfred E. Smith 3
s. somebody   Trump 9
S. straight you bastards   Morant 1
s. your murderer in the chest Achebe 3
they s. horses   McCoy 1
They s. the white girl   Toni Morrison 7
shoots
He s.! He scores!   Hewitt 1
shop
Nation of s. keepers   Samuel Adams 1
s. will keep you   Proverbs 159
shop-keeping
S. Nation   Josiah Tucker 1
shopkeepers
England is a nation of s.   Napoleon 5
for a nation of s.   Adam Smith 7
shore
boy playing on the s.   Isaac Newton 7
hugging the s.   Updike 3
I on the opposite s. will be
                    Longfellow 24
I sat upon the s.   T. S. Eliot 59
shored
fragments I have s. against
                    T. S. Eliot 60
shores
By the s. of Gitche Gumee
                    Longfellow 17
to the s. of Tripoli
                    Folk and Anonymous Songs 49
wilder s. of love   Blanch 1
short
day is s.   Talmud 5
Don't sell America s.   J. P. Morgan 2
Life is s.   Hippocrates 1
long while to make it s.   Thoreau 34
nasty, brutish, and s.   Hobbes 8
s.-fingered vulgarian   Graydon Carter 1
s., sharp shock   W. S. Gilbert 37
s. and simple annals   Thomas Gray 5
That lyf so s.   Chaucer 4
too s. to box wid God
                    James Weldon Johnson 2
shortcomings
showing his s.   Niven 1
shorter
had it been s.   Pascal 2
time to make it s.   Pascal 1

shortnin'
Mamma's little baby loves s.
Folk and Anonymous Songs 71
shorts
Eat my s.   Groening 6
shot
I s. a man in Reno   Johnny Cash 1
I s. an arrow into the air   Longfellow 14
I s. the Albatross   Coleridge 3
I s. the sheriff   Marley 2
it's just a s. away Jagger and Richards 13
Major Strasser has been s.
Film Lines 49
plot in it will be s.   Twain 28
s. at without result Winston Churchill 2
s. heard round the world
Ralph Waldo Emerson 6
shots
s. you don't take   Wayne Gretzky 1
throwing away my s.   Miranda 3
should
I s. have stood in bed   Joe Jacobs 2
S. auld acquaintance   Robert Burns 8
shoulder
giant's s. to mount on   Coleridge 30
I have a left s.-blade   W. S. Gilbert 42
queer s. to the wheel   Ginsberg 6
stand s. to s.   Blair 6
shoulders
city of the big s.   Sandburg 1
dwarf standing on the s.
Robert Burton 1
dwarfs on the s.   Bernard of Chartres 1
standing on the s.   Isaac Newton 1
young s.   Spark 1
shout
S. with the largest   Dickens 3
shouted
I s. out   Jagger and Richards 11
shouting
s. fire in a theatre
Oliver Wendell Holmes, Jr. 29
shovel
S. them under   Sandburg 7
show
Greatest S. on Earth
Advertising Slogans 103
no bus'ness like s. bus'ness
Irving Berlin 14
s. business for ugly people Bill Miller 1
S. me a hero   F. Scott Fitzgerald 47
S. me someone not full   Giovanni 3
s. me the money   Film Lines 102
s. must go on   Proverbs 270
s. you fear in a handful   T. S. Eliot 43
until you s. it to them   Jobs 4
shower
abundant s. of curates
Charlotte Brontë 7
s. of all my days   Dylan Thomas 11
showers
April s. bring forth   Proverbs 13
April s. may come   DeSylva 2
showing
it is worth s.   Danton 2
S. up is 80 percent   Woody Allen 41
shows
childhood s. the man   Milton 43

shreds
king of s. and patches   Shakespeare 215
thing of s. and patches   W. S. Gilbert 28
shrimp
s. learns to whistle   Khrushchev 1
shrink
discussed it with his s.   Mia Farrow 1
do not s. from this responsibility
John F. Kennedy 14
shrinks
never s. back to its
Oliver Wendell Holmes 6
shroud
great s. of the sea   Melville 13
stiff dishonored s.   T. S. Eliot 17
shrunken
like a race with s. muscles
Henry James 3
shudder
s. in the loins   Yeats 44
shuffle
patience, and s. the cards   Cervantes 7
S. Off to Buffalo   Dubin 2
shuffled
s. off this mortal coil   Shakespeare 189
shut
I am now going to s. it   Kafka 3
Put up or s. up   Proverbs 249
S. up and deal   Film Lines 1
S. up he explained   Lardner 1
s. up the box   Thackeray 7
They s. me up in Prose
Emily Dickinson 15
shuts
When one door s.   Proverbs 226
shuttlecock
vhen you an't the s.   Dickens 4
shy
Once bit twice s.   Proverbs 225
shyster
I'm a s. lawyer   "Groucho" Marx 9
siècle
Fin de S.   Jouvenot 1
sic
S. semper tyrannis
Anonymous (Latin) 12
S. semper tyrannis
John Wilkes Booth 1
S. transit gloria mundi
Anonymous (Latin) 13
sick
between the s. and the well
F. Scott Fitzgerald 25
help the s.   Hippocrates 4
never, never s. at sea   W. S. Gilbert 3
Rose, thou art s.   William Blake 9
s. at heart   Shakespeare 140
s. of both   Samuel Johnson 87
were you not extremely s.   Prior 1
when the s. man dies   Nicholas 1
sickness
in s. and in health
Book of Common Prayer 14
in s. and in health
Book of Common Prayer 15
side
by the s. of the road   Foss 1
dark s.   Twain 108
East S., West S.   James W. Blake 1

God is usually on the s. Bussy-Rabutin 1
Hear the other s.   Augustine 6
history is on our s.   Khrushchev 3
on God's s.   Joe Louis 1
on the safe s.   Proverbs 21
on the s. of the angels   Disraeli 21
on the s. of the stronger   Tacitus 4
on the wrong s.   Nash 14
only heard one s. of the case
Samuel Butler (1835–1902) 12
only his own s. of the case Mill 6
seduced by the dark s.   George Lucas 3
sunny s. of the street   Dorothy Fields 1
this s. of Paradise   Rupert Brooke 2
Time is on my s. Jagger and Richards 1
Time is on our s.   Gladstone 1
Which s. are you on   Reece 1
Walk on the Wild S.   Algren 1
walk on the wild s.   Lou Reed 3
sides
from both s. now   Joni Mitchell 1
give him three s.   Montesquieu 3
God does not take s.   George Mitchell 1
two s. to every question   Protagoras 1
two s. to every question   Proverbs 312
sidewalks
s. of New York   James W. Blake 1
siesta
as the Spanish s.   F. Scott Fitzgerald 38
Englishmen detest a s.   Coward 8
sighed
I s. as a lover   Gibbon 9
sighs
Bridge of S.   Byron 13
sight
add radio s. to sound   Sarnoff 2
in the s. of God
Book of Common Prayer 16
loved not at first s.   Marlowe 5
Out of s., out of mind   Proverbs 229
out of s.   Thomas à Kempis 2
S. of you is good   Jonathan Swift 30
thousand years in thy s.
Bible 116
sighted
S. sub   Donald F. Mason 1
sign
God gave Noah the rainbow s.
Folk and Anonymous Songs 36
I define a S. as anything
Charles Sanders Peirce 3
retain the word s.   Saussure 3
signal
do not see the s.   Horatio Nelson 4
signed
hand that s. the paper   Dylan Thomas 4
significance
s. of man   Becker 1
significant
Art is s. deformity   Roger Fry 1
life of s. soil   T. S. Eliot 116
signifier
s. and the signified   Saussure 3
signifying
s. nothing   Shakespeare 394
signs
S. are taken for wonders   T. S. Eliot 22
s. of the times   Bible 245
truth of s.   Eco 1

silence
Conspiracy of s.   Comte 2
eternal s. of these infinite   Pascal 9
Go to where the s. is   Amy Goodman 1
left a stain upon the s.   Beckett 11
loves s.   Mazzini 1
occasional flashes of s.   Sydney Smith 12
other side of s.   George Eliot 15
pass over in s.   Wittgenstein 3
rest is s.   Shakespeare 236
s., exile, and cunning   Joyce 9
S. is death   Djaout 1
S. is golden   Proverbs 271
S. is so accurate   Rothko 2
S. is the real crime
                    Nadezhda Mandelstam 1
S. more musical   Rossetti 3
sounds of s.   Paul Simon 2
There is a s.   Hood 1
they walked in s.   Agee 3
silenced
you have s. him   John Morley 2
silencing
s. that one person   Mill 5
silent
better to remain s.   Lincoln 67
into that s. sea   Coleridge 4
Laws are s.   Cicero 11
right to remain s.   Earl Warren 3
s., unlike your family   Margot Asquith 3
s., upon a peak   Keats 3
s. majority of my fellow
                         Richard Nixon 10
S. night   Mohr 1
sweet s. thought   Shakespeare 417
three s. things   Crapsey 1
silicon
Had s. been a gas   Whistler 6
S. Valley   Hoefler 1
silk
s. hat on a Bradford millionaire
                            T. S. Eliot 52
s. purse out of a sow's ear   Proverbs 272
silly
holy litany in your s. mood   Ginsberg 5
S. rabbit   Advertising Slogans 118
You were s. like us   Auden 21
silver
Every cloud has a s. lining   Proverbs 49
Hi-yo S.   Radio Catchphrases 16
look for the s. lining   DeSylva 1
no s. bullet   Condoleezza Rice 2
s. apples of the moon   Yeats 6
There's a s. lining   Lena Guilbert Ford 1
thirty pieces of s.   Bible 267
simians
true fairy tale of s.   Day 3
Simon
real S. Pure   Centlivre 2
Simple S. met a pieman
                     Nursery Rhymes 68
simple
I adore s. pleasures   Wilde 28
Keep it s., stupid   Sayings 32
never s.   Wilde 76
s. as possible, but not simpler
                            Einstein 36
S. Simon met a pieman
                     Nursery Rhymes 68

simpler
simple as possible, but not s.
                            Einstein 36
simplicity
holy s.   St. Jerome 1
O holy s.   Hus 1
Seek s.   Whitehead 3
s., a child   Pope 17
thing seemed s. itself
                    Arthur Conan Doyle 28
simplify
S., s.   Thoreau 24
sin
all stain of original s.   Pius 1
Hate the s. and not the sinner
                      Mohandas Gandhi 5
He that is without s.   Bible 318
no s. but ignorance   Marlowe 2
physicists have known s.
                        Oppenheimer 1
S. is a queer thing   D. H. Lawrence 3
s. to believe evil   Mencken 10
taketh away the s. of the world   Bible 312
those who s.
            Samuel Butler (1835–1902) 7
wages of s. is death   Bible 344
Sinatra
Frank S.'s son   Ronan Farrow 1
sincerest
s. form of criticism   Sheed 1
s. form of flattery   Proverbs 155
sincerity
All the s. in Hollywood   Fred Allen 8
sinews
s. of war   Cicero 8
sing
Arms, and the man I s.   John Dryden 11
arms and the man I s.   Virgil 1
bid him s.   Cullen 4
caged birds s.   John Webster 2
can s. openly   Charles Spencer 2
how long must we s.   Bono 1
I too, s. America   Langston Hughes 2
lhude s. cuccu
            Folk and Anonymous Songs 16
Lift Ev'ry Voice and S.
                  James Weldon Johnson 1
of thee I s.   Samuel Francis Smith 1
S., goddess   Homer 1
S. a song of sixpence
                     Nursery Rhymes 69
S. 'em muck   Melba 1
s. of Olaf glad and big
                        e.e. cummings 12
S. the Body Electric   Whitman 1
s. the same song   Holiday 2
s. whatever is well made   Yeats 61
teach a pig to s.   Heinlein 13
they will s. to me   T. S. Eliot 11
singeing
s. of the King   Francis Drake 1
singin'
S. in the rain   Arthur Freed 1
singing
heard the mermaids s.   T. S. Eliot 11
I hear America s.   Whitman 10
S., it's the same thing   Caruso 1
s. still dost soar   Percy Shelley 10
s. works just fine   James Taylor 3

single
begin with a s. step   Lao Tzu 9
s. death is a tragedy   Stalin 5
s. man in possession   Austen 6
S. vision and Newton's sleep
                     William Blake 13
whoever rescues a s. life   Talmud 8
sings
caged bird s.   Dunbar 2
fat lady s.   Ralph Carpenter 1
instead of bleeding, he s.   Ed Gardner 1
s. for his supper   Nursery Rhymes 74
singularity
S. is almost invariably
                    Arthur Conan Doyle 12
sink
Loose lips s. ships
                  Advertising Slogans 139
S. or swim   John Adams 20
sinned
more s. against   Shakespeare 294
sinner
forgive some s.   Mencken 25
Hate the sin and not the s.
                      Mohandas Gandhi 5
Love the s. but hate the sin   Augustine 5
sinners
all the s. saints   Jagger and Richards 12
laugh with the s.   Joel 4
mercy upon us miserable s.
                  Book of Common Prayer 7
sinning
sinned against than s.   Shakespeare 294
sins
All s. are attempts   Weil 4
be all my s. remember'd
                       Shakespeare 193
cover the multitude of s.   Bible 384
His s. were scarlet   Belloc 3
love for mankind and hatred of s.
                         Augustine 5
somebody's s. but not mine
                        Patti Smith 1
though your s. be as scarlet   Bible 160
sip
it can't be tasted in a s.   Dickens 36
sister
Fiction is Truth's elder s.   Kipling 37
Go tell my baby s.
            Folk and Anonymous Songs 66
like kissing your s.   Edgar E. Miller 1
my s. and my daughter   Film Lines 51
sisterhood
S. is powerful   Amatniek 1
sisters
Big s. are the crab grass   Schulz 4
his s., and his cousins   W. S. Gilbert 7
S. Are Doin' It   Lennox 2
s. under their skins   Kipling 20
Wayward s.   Winfield Scott 1
Weird S.   Shakespeare 325
Sisyphus
imagine that S. is happy   Camus 4
more like the torture of S.   de Beauvoir 3
sit
Don't S. Under the Apple Tree
                        Lew Brown 3
except s. on them   Talleyrand 1

s. upon his hill — Lindsay 2
s. with the river — Silko 1
s. with your mother — Clare Boothe Luce 2
sleeping the big s. — Raymond Chandler 2
talks in someone else's s. — Auden 43
we shall not s. — McCrae 3

sleepers
dreams of those light s. — Symons 1
s. in that quiet earth — Emily Brontë 6

sleeping
awaken a s. giant — Film Lines 178
Let s. dogs lie — Proverbs 273

sleeps
city that never s. — Ebb 5
s. with the fishes — Puzo 2
She s. alone at last — Benchley 8
thinking woman s. with monsters — Rich 2

sleepwalker
assurance of a s. — Hitler 3

sleepy
name of S. Hollow — Washington Irving 2
you s.-head — Robert Louis Stevenson 15

sleeve
heart upon my s. — Shakespeare 258

sleigh
one-horse open s. — Pierpont 1

slept
George Washington s. here — Moss Hart 2
my father as he s. — Shakespeare 353

slices
It s.! It dices — Advertising Slogans 125

sliding
s. down a barrister — Dorothy Parker 48

slim
I'm S. Shady — Eminem 2

slimy
s. things did crawl — Coleridge 7

slings
s. and arrows of outrageous fortune — Shakespeare 188

slip
Cry havoc and let s. — Shakespeare 107
many a s. 'twixt cup — Proverbs 187
S. slidin' away — Paul Simon 11

slipped
s. away into the next room — Henry Scott Holland 1
s. the surly bonds — Magee 1

slipper
Watteau hung a lady's s. — William Carlos Williams 3

slippers
Dem Golden S. — Bland 2
Where the devil are my s. — George Bernard Shaw 51

slippery
words are s. — Henry Adams 18

slithy
'Twas brillig, and the s. toves — Carroll 28

slopes
butler's upper s. — Wodehouse 4

slouches
s. towards Bethlehem — Yeats 30

slough
name of the s. was Despond — Bunyan 2

slow
S. and steady wins the race — Proverbs 274

s. boat to China — Loesser 2
s. the car down — Howar 1
telling you to s. down — Sayings 29

slowly
bang the drum s. — Folk and Anonymous Songs 14
mills of God grind s. — Logau 1
mills of God grind s. — Proverbs 192

sluggard
Go to the ant, thou s. — Bible 124

slum
If you've seen one city s. — Agnew 1

slump
I ain't in no s. — Berra 13

slush
pure as the driven s. — Bankhead 4

slut
Jane, you ignorant s. — Television Catchphrases 64

small
All creatures great and s. — Cecil Alexander 1
all things both great and s. — Coleridge 14
best things come in s. — Proverbs 20
big fish in a s. pond — Modern Proverbs 7
chronicle s. beer — Shakespeare 266
divide it into s. jobs — Henry Ford 3
Don't sweat the s. stuff — Sayings 11
It's a s. world — Proverbs 275
Never doubt that a s. group — Margaret Mead 10
no s. parts — Stanislavsky 1
one s. step for a man — Neil A. Armstrong 3
pictures that got s. — Film Lines 165
s. college — Daniel Webster 1
s. is beautiful — Schumacher 1
s. Latin, and less Greek — Jonson 9
s. loan of a million dollars — Trump 8
s. things with great love — Mother Teresa 1
still s. voice — Bible 94
still s. voice of gratitude — Thomas Gray 11
they grind exceeding s. — Proverbs 192
very s. portion of their possible — William James 15
What s. potatoes — Charles Dudley Warner 1

smallest
s. fact is a window — T. H. Huxley 2
s. room of my house — Reger 1

smart
For years I was s. — Mary Chase 2
s. enough to understand — Eugene McCarthy 1
That makes me s. — Trump 13
To be s. enough — Chesterton 21

smarter
S. than the average bear — Television Catchphrases 90

smash
English never s. in a face — Margaret Halsey 2
s. and grab — Adlai E. Stevenson 10

smattering
s. of everything — Dickens 32

smell
I love the s. of napalm — Film Lines 14
s. far worse than weeds — Shakespeare 425

s. the blood — Shakespeare 301
s. the coffee — Landers 1
s. the flowers — Hagen 1
sweet s. of success — Lehman 1
would s. as sweet — Shakespeare 34

smells
it s. to heaven — Shakespeare 211

smile
call me that, s. — Wister 2
one may s. — Shakespeare 169
s. as you kill — Lennon 7
s. I could feel in my hip pocket — Raymond Chandler 6
s. is the chosen vehicle — Melville 16
s. when you call me that — Wister 1
S.! You're on Candid Camera — Television Catchphrases 12

smiles
then all s. stopped — Robert Browning 6
whole world s. with you — Goodwin 1

smiling
s. and beautiful countryside — Arthur Conan Doyle 19
s. damned villain — Shakespeare 169
s. public man — Yeats 34
S. through her tears — Homer 4
they start not s. back — Arthur Miller 1
When Irish eyes are s. — Olcott 1
when you're s., the whole world — Goodwin 1

smite
will s. all the firstborn — Bible 46

Smithsonian
S. Institution — Smithson 1

smithy
s. of my soul — Joyce 11
village s. stands — Longfellow 7

smoke
good Cigar is a S. — Kipling 1
he doesn't s. the same cigarettes — Jagger and Richards 3
Mirrors and blue s. — Breslin 2
No s. without fire — Proverbs 276
in a s.-filled room — Harry M. Daugherty 1
s. gets in your eyes — Harbach 1
s. more than one cigar — Twain 146

Smokey
On top of Old S. — Folk and Anonymous Songs 60

smoking
haven't found any s. guns — Blix 1
S. . . . kills you — Brooke Shields 1
s. pistol in his hand — Arthur Conan Doyle 26

Smoot
S. is an institute — Nash 3

smooth
never did run s. — Shakespeare 51

smote
s. the rock — Daniel Webster 9
s. them hip and thigh — Bible 77

Smuckers
name like S. — Advertising Slogans 110

smylere
s. with the knyf — Chaucer 14

snake
in case I see a s. — W. C. Fields 25
s. hidden in the grass — Virgil 14
S. Pit — Mary Jane Ward 1

soul (cont.):
smithy of my s.   Joyce 11
s. in bliss   Shakespeare 310
s. of man   John Jay Chapman 1
s. of man is unknowable   Wilde 90
s. power   James Brown 3
S. selects her own Society
                        Emily Dickinson 14
vale of s.-making   Keats 12
windows of the s.   Proverbs 94
with s. so dead   Walter Scott 2
souls
engineers of human s.   Stalin 1
some s. so compressed   Schreiner 4
Two s. dwell   Goethe 13
they have no s.   Coke 9
times that try men's s.   Thomas Paine 8
Two s. with but a single   Halm 1
sound
full of s. and fury   Shakespeare 394
giant sucking s. going south   Perot 1
how sweet the s.   John Newton 1
no other s.   Gibran 1
s. mind in a s. body   Juvenal 6
s. of music   Hammerstein 27
s. must seem an echo   Pope 3
s. of revelry by night   Byron 8
s. of the horn   Vigny 1
S. of the Single Hand   Hakuin 1
s. of tireless voices Adlai E. Stevenson 3
S. off your numbers   Gruber 2
sounds
better than it s.   Nye 1
s., the scents   Baudelaire 2
s. of silence   Paul Simon 2
soup
chicken s. with rice   Sendak 1
sour
eaten a s. grape   Bible 184
s. grapes   Aesop 2
source
secret s. of Humor   Twain 88
sprung from some common s.
           William Jones (1746–1794) 2
sources
not to know the s. of the Nile
                        George Eliot 11
south
away down S. in Dixie   Emmett 2
I go to the s.   Pizarro 1
S. will rise again   Sayings 48
S.'s preoccupation C. Vann Woodward 1
Why do you hate the S.   Faulkner 4
Southern
S. efficiency   John F. Kennedy 22
souvenirs
S.? More than if I   Baudelaire 7
sovereign
five s. fingers   Dylan Thomas 4
he will no s.   Coke 7
S. has, under a constitutional Bagehot 5
S. is he who decides   Schmitt 1
Soviet
collapse of the S. Union   Putin 1
no S. domination of Eastern
                    Gerald R. Ford 5
S. power plus the electrification Lenin 5
S. Union, as everybody
                Franklin D. Roosevelt 19

under S. substantive law
                    Robert H. Jackson 13
Soviets
All power to the S.   Political Slogans 1
sow
Ireland is the old s.   Joyce 5
out of a s.'s ear   Proverbs 272
soweth
whatsoever a man s.   Bible 365
sown
where thou hast not s.   Bible 263
Soylent
S. Green is people   Film Lines 160
space
how to waste s.   Philip C. Johnson 2
In s. no one can hear
                 Advertising Slogans 4
king of infinite s.   Shakespeare 179
more s. where nobody is   Stein 8
outer-s. program   Braun 2
shining isles of s.   Thoreau 2
S., the final frontier   Roddenberry 1
S. is almost infinite   Quayle 6
spaces
s. in your togetherness   Gibran 3
spaceship
s. called earth R. Buckminster Fuller 2
S. Earth   R. Buckminster Fuller 4
spade
figs figs and a s. a s.   Erasmus 4
spaghetti
I owe to s.   Loren 2
Spahn
S. and Sain   Hern 1
Spain
rain in S.   George Bernard Shaw 49
spam
S., s., s., s.   Monty Python 7
span
s. of a man's   Leonardo da Vinci 1
Spaniards
S. seem wiser   Francis Bacon 20
Spanish
expects the S. Inquisition
                      Monty Python 6
to God he would speak S.   Charles V 1
spare
Can You S. a Dime   Harburg 1
S., woodman, s.   Thomas Campbell 2
S. the rod and spoil   Proverbs 280
s. your country's flag   Whittier 3
Woodman, s. that tree
                  George Pope Morris 1
spared
honor and life have been s.   Francis I 1
spareth
He that s. his rod   Bible 131
sparkle
When did your s. turn to fire
                    Alan Jay Lerner 14
You s. with larceny   Mizner 10
sparrow
My lady's s. is dead   Catullus 1
Sparta
This is S.   Film Lines 175
Spartacus
I'm S.   Film Lines 161
Spartans
Go tell the S.   Simonides 1

spatters
s. all we knew   Karl Jay Shapiro 2
Spayne
castels thanne in S.   Meun 1
speak
Actions s. louder   Proverbs 4
dare not s. its name
                  Lord Alfred Douglas 1
dare not s. its name   Wilde 82
Don't s.   Stefani 1
He who knows does not s.   Lao Tzu 7
I began to s. fairly late   Einstein 20
I now s. for France   de Gaulle 2
I s. for the trees   Seuss 12
let him now s.
              Book of Common Prayer 17
Never s. ill of the dead   Proverbs 281
one to s.   Thoreau 14
s. and purpose not   Shakespeare 285
s. for yourself   Alden 1
s. no evil   Modern Proverbs 80
S. roughly to your little boy   Carroll 12
S. softly and carry Theodore Roosevelt 7
S. the speech   Shakespeare 200
S. Truth to Power   Anonymous 29
s. what we feel   Shakespeare 320
s. your mind   Maggie Kuhn 1
to God he would s. Spanish Charles V 1
What we cannot s. about Wittgenstein 3
speakin'
ain't on s. terms   Dunne 10
speaking
s. and writing Truth
                  Andrew Hamilton 2
S. is difficult   Giffords 1
s. more clearly than you think
                    Howard Baker 1
s. prose without knowing it   Molière 7
speaks
woman s. eighteen languages
                  Dorothy Parker 27
spears
s. into pruninghooks   Bible 161
special
our s. relationship Winston Churchill 32
without any s. attachment   Einstein 3
specialist
s. is one who knows   Mayo 1
specialization
S. is for insects   Heinlein 10
species
female of the s.   Kipling 34
preservation of the s. Wollstonecraft 18
speciesism
I use the word "s."   Ryder 1
specific
should have been more s.
                    Jane Wagner 3
specter
s. is haunting eastern Europe   Havel 1
s. is haunting Europe
                Marx and Engels 1
speculate
he should not s.   Twain 105
s. in stocks   Twain 67
speech
abridging the freedom of s.
                    Constitution 11
attributes of s.   Hobbes 2

freedom of s.   Twain 95
more s., not enforced silence
                            Brandeis 6
our concern was s.   T. S. Eliot 119
political s. and writing   Orwell 28
Speak the s.   Shakespeare 200
S. is civilization itself   Thomas Mann 3
s. is like a cracked kettle   Flaubert 1
strange power of s.   Coleridge 12
such invasion of free s.   Hand 7

speeches
S. measured by the hour   Jefferson 52

speechless
washed in the s. real   Barzun 2

speed
beauty of s.   Marinetti 1
our safety is in our s.
            Ralph Waldo Emerson 14
retiring at high s.   William F. Halsey 2
s. the parting guest   Pope 9
Unsafe at Any S.   Nader 1
whose s. was far faster   Buller 1

speeding
Faster than a s. bullet
            Radio Catchphrases 21

speedy
s. and public trial   Constitution 15

spell
foreigners always s. better   Twain 5
s. a word only one way   Twain 147
s. my name right   Cohan 9

spend
s. a little time with me Dorothy Fields 4
s. less   Samuel Johnson 101
s. the rest of my life   Kettering 1

spender
Hey! big s.   Dorothy Fields 3

spent
all passion s.   Milton 50
Hours s. fishing   Sayings 55
how my light is s.   Milton 52

spice
s. of life   Nash 13
Sugar and s.   Southey 8
very s. of life   William Cowper 7

spicy
that's a s. meatball
            Advertising Slogans 6

spider
as one holds a s.   Jonathan Edwards 1
noiseless patient s.   Whitman 15
said a s. to a fly   Howitt 1
there came a big s.   Nursery Rhymes 47

spilt
crying over s. milk   Proverbs 58

spin
neither do they s.   Bible 219

spinach
I eats me s.   Sammy Lerner 1
I say it's s.   E. B. White 1

spindle
fold, s., or mutilate   Sayings 9

spinnage
gammon and s.   Dickens 65

spinner
S. of the Years   Thomas Hardy 26

spinning-jenny
God took the s.   Yeats 51

Spinoza
I believe in S.'s God   Einstein 23
S. is a God-intoxicated man   Novalis 1

spires
City with her dreaming s.
            Matthew Arnold 15

spirit
Hail to thee, blithe S.   Percy Shelley 9
hung for breaking the s.
            Grover Cleveland 1
I commend my s.   Bible 111
present in s.   Bible 348
rest, perturbed s.   Shakespeare 172
s. giveth life   Bible 360
s. indeed is willing   Bible 270
S. is the real and eternal   Eddy 4
S. of Capitalism   Max Weber 1
s. of liberty   Hand 6
s. of moderation is gone   Hand 3
S. of Night   Percy Shelley 17
s. that always denies   Goethe 12
Th'expense of s.   Shakespeare 431
thunder of his s.
            George Bernard Shaw 33
Thy s. walks abroad   Shakespeare 129

spirits
choice and master s.   Shakespeare 105

spiritual
Millions of s. creatures   Milton 35

spit
I have no gun, but I can s.   Auden 41
I s. my last breath at thee   Melville 12
pitcher of warm s.   John Nance Garner 1

spite
in s. of all temptations   W. S. Gilbert 13
O cursed s.   Shakespeare 173
s. your face   Proverbs 59

splendid
first is but a s. misery   Jefferson 24
s. little war   John Hay 2

splendor
s. in the grass   William Wordsworth 17

split
S. at the root   Rich 1
what a s. infinitive is   H. W. Fowler 1
when I s. an infinitive
            Raymond Chandler 10
world would s. open   Rukeyser 2

spoil
Spare the rod and s.   Proverbs 280
Too many cooks s.   Proverbs 303

spoiled
Golf is a good walk s.   Twain 152

spoils
victor belong the s.   Marcy 1
victor belongs to the s.
            F. Scott Fitzgerald 3

spoke
I never s. with God   Emily Dickinson 21
s. in the wheel   Bonhoeffer 1

spoken
people have s.   Tuck 1
s. in jest   Proverbs 306

sponge
Moscow will be the s.   Kutuzov 1

spoon
ate with a runcible s.   Lear 7

spoons
faster we counted our s.
            Ralph Waldo Emerson 41
let us count our s.   Samuel Johnson 54
my life with coffee s.   T. S. Eliot 6

sport
considered a s.   Vince Foster 1
Football is not a contact s.
            Hugh "Duffy" Daugherty 1
I owe to s.   Camus 10
kill us for their s.   Shakespeare 304
make s. for our neighbors   Austen 13
Serious s. has nothing   Orwell 23
s. of it, not the inhumanity
            David Hume 11
s. of kings   Somerville 1

sports
S. doesn't build character
            Heywood Hale Broun 1
s. section records man's   Earl Warren 4

spot
Out, damned s.   Shakespeare 384
See S. run   Clara Murray 1
s. where some great   Hawthorne 7

spotless
s. mind   Pope 7

spots
or the leopard his s.   Bible 183

sprang
s. from his Platonic
            F. Scott Fitzgerald 19

spread
when the evening is s. out   T. S. Eliot 3

spreading
two ways of s. light   Wharton 1
Under a s. chestnut tree   Longfellow 7
Under the s. chestnut tree   Orwell 40

spring
can S. be far behind   Percy Shelley 4
easing the s.   Henry Reed 2
flowers that bloom in the s.
            W. S. Gilbert 44
in Just-s.   e.e. cummings 4
In the s. a young man's   Tennyson 5
Pierian s.   Drayton 2
s. does with the cherry trees   Neruda 3
s. ev'ry year   Alan Jay Lerner 12
s. now comes unheralded
            Rachel Carson 1
Sweet s.   George Herbert 6
we force the s.
            William Jefferson "Bill" Clinton 4
whenever S. breaks through   Coward 4
Where are the songs of S.   Keats 21
woman only has the right to s.   Fonda 1

springs
Hope s. eternal   Pope 18

springtime
I love Paris in the s.   Cole Porter 23
S. for Hitler   Mel Brooks 6
Younger than s.   Hammerstein 17

sprung
My only love s.   Shakespeare 31

spur
I have no s.   Shakespeare 343
s. of all great minds   George Chapman 4

spurred
booted and s. to ride
            Thomas Macaulay 11

spy
S. Who Came in   le Carré 1

squads
undisciplined s. of emotion
                         T. S. Eliot 108

squander
do not s. time   Benjamin Franklin 24

square
each is given a s. deal
                   Theodore Roosevelt 12
given a s. deal   Theodore Roosevelt 11
s. on the side   Euclid 2
s. person has squeezed   Sydney Smith 5

squat
s. pen rests   Heaney 2

squeak
until the pips s.   Geddes 1

squeaking
some s. Cleopatra   Shakespeare 404

squeaky
s. wheel gets the grease   Billings 2

squeeze
s. my lemon   Robert Johnson 4

squelching
three minutes of s. noises   Rotten 4

squirrel
s.'s heart beat   George Eliot 15

St.
Got de S. Louis Blues   Handy 4
Meet me in S. Louis
                   Andrew B. Sterling 1
S. Louis woman   Handy 3

stab
I s. at thee   Melville 12

stabbed
s. in the back   Ed Gardner 1
s. in the back   Hindenburg 1

stable
very s. genius   Trump 20

stage
All the world's a s.   Shakespeare 88
Exit, s. left Television Catchphrases 88
loaded rifle on the s.   Chekhov 3

stages
Five s. in the life   Mary Astor 1

stagflation
"s." situation   Iain Macleod 2

staggering
Heartbreaking Work of S. Genius
                               Eggers 1

stain
one s. of guilt   Hawthorne 1
s. the stiff dishonored shroud
                           T. S. Eliot 17
s. upon the silence   Beckett 11

stained
hole in a s. glass window
                   Raymond Chandler 5

staircase
S. wit   Diderot 3
Up the Down S.   Bel Kaufman 1

stairs
another man's s.   Dante 13

stakeholder
S. Economy   Blair 2

stakes
s. are so low   Sayre 1

stale
How weary, s., flat   Shakespeare 150

nor custom s. her infinite
                        Shakespeare 402

stalemate
mired in s.   Cronkite 1

Stalin
guilt of S.   Gorbachev 2
S. himself rose   Trotsky 3
S. rather than Hitler   Robert Harris 1

stamp
indelible s.   Charles Darwin 13
physics and s.-collecting   Rutherford 6
s. of the human condition
                           Montaigne 14

stamping
boot s. on a human face   Orwell 46

stamps
heroes don't appear on no s. Shocklee 2

stand
by uniting we s.   John Dickinson 1
can s. prosperity   Twain 101
divided against itself cannot s.
                            Lincoln 11
Do not s. at my grave and cry   Frye 2
Do not s. at my grave and weep   Frye 1
Every tub must s.   Proverbs 307
firm spot on which to s.   Archimedes 1
Get up, s. up   Marley 1
Here I s.   Luther 1
it cannot s. still   Roscoe Pound 1
learn to s. alone   Ibsen 6
make our sun s. still Andrew Marvell 15
nature might s. up   Shakespeare 131
no time to s. and stare   W. H. Davies 1
S. by your man   Wynette 4
S. by your man   Wynette 3
s. me now and ever   Joyce 12
S. not upon the order   Shakespeare 372
s. out of my sun   Diogenes 2
s. up to show pride   Kaepernick 1
This will not s.
             George Herbert Walker Bush 8
We'll s. pat   Political Slogans 34
who only s. and wait   Milton 53

standard
any s. against which   Orwell 42
s. to which the wise
                 George Washington 10

standing
s. government   Thoreau 4
s. here today   Lyndon B. Johnson 2
s. in the breadline   Lenny Bruce 1
s. on the shoulders of giants
                         Isaac Newton 1
woman s. by my man   Hillary Clinton 1
your s. in the community
                      Edgar W. Howe 1

stands
man who s. alone   Ibsen 21
sun now s.   Chief Joseph 3

star
Being a s. has made it
                   Sammy Davis, Jr. 1
catch a falling s.   Donne 11
come back a s.   Film Lines 82
constant as the northern s.
                        Shakespeare 103
give birth to a dancing s.   Nietzsche 14
Hitch your wagon to a s.
               Ralph Waldo Emerson 50

If there is any fixed s.
                    Robert H. Jackson 4
If thou follow thy s.   Dante 8
like a falling s.   Milton 25
like the north polar s.   Confucius 2
my gracious evening s. Richard Wagner 1
new and unusual s.   Brahe 1
No s. is ever lost   Procter 4
S. light, s. bright   Nursery Rhymes 70
s. to steer her by   Masefield 1
S. Wars   George Lucas 1
s.-crossed lovers   Shakespeare 27
s.-spangled banner Francis Scott Key 2
sun is but a morning s.   Thoreau 31
Twinkle, twinkle, little s. Ann Taylor 2
we have seen his s.   Bible 196
When you wish upon a s.
                    Ned Washington 2

stardust
We are s.   Joni Mitchell 3

stark
Molly S. is a widow   John Stark 2
s. insensibility   Samuel Johnson 43

starry
under s. skies above   Cole Porter 17
Under the wide and s. sky
              Robert Louis Stevenson 21

stars
build beneath the s.   Edward Young 5
cut him out in little s. Shakespeare 45
I am tasting s.   Perignon 1
it's full of s.   Arthur C. Clarke 3
like the moon, the s.   Truman 1
looking at the s.   Wilde 55
loved the s. too truly   Sarah Williams 1
not in our s.   Shakespeare 98
play among the s.   Bart Howard 1
see again the s.   Dante 11
s. were going out   Arthur C. Clarke 1
s. will be as familiar Beryl Markham 2
strives to touch the s.   Spenser 1
sun and the other s.   Dante 14
teach ten thousand s. e.e. cummings 16
way to the s.   Virgil 11
We have the s.   Prouty 1

starship
voyages of the s. *Enterprise*
                         Roddenberry 1

start
Catholic girls s. much too late   Joel 3
Gentlemen—s. your engines   Sayings 13
s. quoting him now   Cole Porter 22
We didn't s. the fire   Joel 5
where we s. from   T. S. Eliot 122

started
s. at the top   Welles 4
s. like a guilty thing Shakespeare 143
s. out very quiet   Hemingway 34

starting-point
s. for a new creation   Wilde 12

starts
where one s. from   T. S. Eliot 110

starve
Let not poor Nelly s.   Charles II 1
s. a fever   Proverbs 286

starved
s. in Christiana   Hamsun 1

starving
Genius in a garret s. Mary Robinson 1

pick up a s. dog   Twain 69
s. to death   Jerome Lawrence 1

state
done the s. some service   Shakespeare 282
first duty of a S.   Ruskin 17
man is necessary to the S.   Thomas Macaulay 7
minimal s.   Nozick 2
New York s. of mind   Joel 2
no s. more extensive   Nozick 5
rotten in the s. of Denmark   Shakespeare 165
separation between church and s.   Jefferson 33
Ship of S.   Longfellow 16
S. Farm is there   Advertising Slogans 112
S. has no business   Thurgood Marshall 1
S. has provided   Thoreau 8
S. is not "abolished"   Engels 1
S. may be given up   Rousseau 7
s. of a man's mind   Lord Bowen 1
S. of the Union   Constitution 6
s. without the means   Edmund Burke 13

stately
more s. mansions   Oliver Wendell Holmes 9
S., plump Buck Mulligan   Joyce 13
s. Homes of England   Hemans 3
s. homes of England   Virginia Woolf 4
s. homos of England   Crisp 2
s. pleasure dome decree   Coleridge 19

states
God in the blue s.   Barack Obama 1

statesman
s. is a successful politician   Thomas B. Reed 1
s. is a politician   Truman 10

statistic
million deaths is a s.   Stalin 5

statistically
I could prove God s.   Gallup 1

statistics
He uses s. as a drunken man   Lang 1
Lies, damned lies, and s.   Anonymous 15
Proved by s.   Auden 33
unless s. lie   e.e. cummings 15

statue
ask why I have no s.   Cato 3
S. of Liberty is situated   Dorothy Parker 17
saying good-bye to a s.   Hemingway 12

status
movement from S. to Contract   Maine 1

statute
pages of your s. books   Elizabeth Cady Stanton 7

stay
s. bought   Twain 47
S. gold, Ponyboy   Hinton 2

staying
s. up all night   Stengel 6

stays
nothing s. still   Heraclitus 4

steady
Slow and s.   Proverbs 274
S.-State Theory   Bondi 1

steak
Don't Sell the S.   Elmer Wheeler 1
I have s. at home   Paul Newman 1
smell of s. in passageways   T. S. Eliot 14

steal
he cannot s. from you   Saroyan 2
mature poets s.   T. S. Eliot 28
s. more than a hundred men   Puzo 1
s. my thunder   Dennis 2
S. This Book   Abbie Hoffman 2
Thou shalt not s.   Bible 58
Thou shalt not s.   Clough 5

stealin'
For de big s.   Eugene O'Neill 1

stealing
S. too fast   Trillin 1

steals
Who s. my purse   Shakespeare 269

steam
All the s. in the world   Henry Adams 16
s.-engine in trousers   Sydney Smith 8

steamroller
not part of the s.   Brand 2

steel
bend s. in his bare hands   Television Catchphrases 6
like rooting for U. S. S.   Joe E. Lewis 2
topped with a line of s.   William Howard Russell 1
We're bigger than U.S. S.   Lansky 1
When the foeman bares his s.   W. S. Gilbert 21

steeple
here is the s.   Nursery Rhymes 11

steer
star to s. her by   Masefield 1

Stell-lahhhhh
S.!   Tennessee Williams 3

step
begin with a single s.   Lao Tzu 9
can't s. twice   Heraclitus 3
One s. at a time   Proverbs 282
One S. Forward   Lenin 1
one small s. for a man   Neil A. Armstrong 3
only the first s. that is difficult   Du Deffand 1
s. to the music   Thoreau 30
Trying is the first s.   Groening 8

steps
Two S. Back   Lenin 1

stereotypes
repertory of s.   Lippmann 2

sterilized
s. woman with two   Ehrlich 1

sterner
made of s. stuff   Shakespeare 115

stick
carry a big s.   Theodore Roosevelt 7
fell like a s.   Thomas Paine 20
some will s.   Proverbs 69
s. a fork in him   Jay Hanna "Dizzy" Dean 1
S. close to your desks   W. S. Gilbert 10
s. your neck out   Modern Proverbs 85

sticking
s. to the union   "Woody" Guthrie 5

sticks
pick up s.   Nursery Rhymes 49

S. and stones   Proverbs 283
S. Nix Hick Pix   Abel Green 1

stiffens
lost heart s.   T. S. Eliot 86

stiffnecked
s. people   Bible 62

stifle
universities s. writers   Flannery O'Connor 4

stifling
s. it would be an evil   Mill 8

still
I s. exist   Film Lines 95
I'm s. doing it   Miles Davis 1
make our sun stand s.   Andrew Marvell 15
nothing stays s.   Heraclitus 4
Philosophically, s. trying   Jagger 1
s. point of the turning world   T. S. Eliot 97
s. small voice   Bible 94
s. small voice of gratitude   Thomas Gray 11
S. to be neat   Jonson 2
S. waters run deep   Proverbs 284
S. we do it   McCullough 2

stimulating
physical experience could be so s.   Film Lines 4

stimulus
s. and response   John B. Watson 2

sting
death, where is thy s.   Bible 359
Death, where is thy s.   W. C. Fields 17
s. like a bee   Ali 3

stings
when the bee s.   Hammerstein 26

stingy
don't be s.   Film Lines 11
don't be s.   Eugene O'Neill 3

stinking
show you any s. badges   Traven 1
Take your s. paws off me   Film Lines 135

stinks
Fish always s.   Proverbs 108

stir
s. men's blood   Shakespeare 123

stirred
Shaken and not s.   Ian Fleming 6
s. the heart   Robert Falcon Scott 3

stirring
Not a mouse s.   Shakespeare 141

stirrup
foot already in the s.   Cervantes 9

stirs
straw that s. the drink   Reggie Jackson 3

stitch
s. in time   Proverbs 285

stock
his s. in trade   Lincoln 69

stocking
glimpse of s.   Cole Porter 2

stocks
speculate in s.   Twain 67

stockyards
s. at Chicago   Hemingway 9

stole
s. it fair and square   Hayakawa 1
son of a bitch s. my watch   Hecht 1

stolen
horses may not be s.   Halifax 1
S. waters are sweet   Bible 126
stomach
army marches on its s.
                    Frederick the Great 2
hit it in the s.   Sinclair 1
If your s. disputes you   Paige 2
through his s.   Proverbs 324
stone
back into the S. Age   LeMay 1
left any s. unturned   Euripides 1
let him first cast a s.   Bible 318
like a rolling s.   Dylan 17
rolling s. gathers   Proverbs 257
standing like a s. wall   Bee 1
S. walls do not a prison make
                     Richard Lovelace 1
sword of this s.   Malory 1
Third S. from the Sun   Hendrix 5
Under every s.   Aristophanes 6
why am I not of s.   Hugo 2
stones
men of s.   Shakespeare 316
shouldn't throw s.   Proverbs 120
Sticks and s.   Proverbs 283
s. of Rome to rise   Shakespeare 124
stonewall
s. it   Richard Nixon 12
stood
I should have s. in bed   Joe Jacobs 2
s. against the world   Shakespeare 118
stool
as when they are at S.   Jonathan Swift 19
having a difficult s.
                  Winston Churchill 52
stoop
nearer when we s.
               William Wordsworth 24
stoops
lovely woman s. to folly   T. S. Eliot 54
lovely woman s. to folly
                 Oliver Goldsmith 6
stop
I could not s. for Death
                  Emily Dickinson 8
I'll s. here   Wiles 1
next s., the Twilight Zone   Serling 1
S. all the clocks   Auden 1
s. one Heart from breaking
                  Emily Dickinson 23
S. the World   Bricusse and Newley 2
when the kissing had to s.
                 Robert Browning 17
when you s. believing in it   Dick 1
will you s., s., s.   Nursery Rhymes 4
stopped
Christ s. at Eboli   Carlo Levi 1
little heart, dispossessed, had s.
                   Henry James 15
my watch has s.   "Groucho" Marx 28
stoppeth
he s. one of three   Coleridge 1
stops
Buck S. Here   Truman 11
where she s. nobody knows
               Radio Catchphrases 19
store
doesn't come from a s.   Seuss 9

Who's minding the s.   Sayings 63
stories
eight million s.   Film Lines 123
only two or three human s.   Cather 2
secret of the Great S.   Roy 1
tell sad s.   Shakespeare 21
We tell ourselves s.   Didion 5
stork
throwing rocks at the s.
                   "Groucho" Marx 35
storm
After a s. comes a calm   Proverbs 5
Any port in a s.   Proverbs 10
Operation Desert S.
           George Herbert Walker Bush 11
quiet of a s. centre
           Oliver Wendell Holmes, Jr. 22
raise a s. in a teapot   Cicero 4
Riders on the s.   Jim Morrison 5
shelter from the s.   Dylan 25
s. of thoughts   Twain 129
stormy
dark and s. night   Bulwer-Lytton 1
S. weather   Koehler 2
story
ere their s. die   Thomas Hardy 27
I'll tell you a s.   F. Scott Fitzgerald 50
not the s. of the wreck   Rich 6
s. of my life   Dorothy Parker 41
s. you have just heard
               Radio Catchphrases 6
That's another s.   Sterne 3
This is not a s.   Toni Morrison 5
This is the saddest s.
                 Ford Madox Ford 1
stove
sit on a hot s.   Einstein 29
straight
crooked shall be made s.   Bible 173
Shoot s. you bastards   Morant 1
s. on till morning   Barrie 4
s. sort of guy   Blair 4
straighten
S. Up and Fly Right   Nat King Cole 1
strain
s. at a gnat   Bible 257
straining
without s. or artifice   Montaigne 1
strait
how s. the gate   W. E. Henley 2
S. is the gate   Bible 227
stranded
s. out in the cold   Irving Berlin 15
strands
woven of many s.   Ralph Ellison 2
strange
after s. gods   Kipling 3
cannot dream s. things   Hawthorne 4
men are s. as hell   Robin Morgan 1
nothing is too s.   Thomas Hardy 2
Politics makes s. bed-fellows
            Charles Dudley Warner 2
Politics makes s. bedfellows
                       Proverbs 237
s. bedfellows   Shakespeare 441
s. fruit   Allan 1
S. interlude   Eugene O'Neill 4
s. power of speech   Coleridge 12

s. visitor from another planet
               Radio Catchphrases 21
s. visitor from another planet
          Television Catchphrases 6
stranger in a s. land   Bible 38
what a long, s. trip   Robert Hunter 1
Strangelove
Dr. S.   Kubrick 1
strangely
I was s. handsome   Twain 153
stranger
I was a s.   Bible 266
I'm a S. Here Myself   Nash 10
never love a s.   Stella Benson 1
s. and afraid   Housman 7
s. in a strange land   Bible 38
s. than fiction   Byron 33
s. than fiction   Chesterton 6
you may see a s.   Hammerstein 14
strangers
at the hands of perfect s.   Maugham 8
kindness of s.   Tennessee Williams 5
strangle
s. his father   Diderot 2
s. the last king   Diderot 4
strategery
S.   Ferrell 1
straw
clutch at a s.   Proverbs 78
make bricks without s.   Proverbs 35
s. breaks the camel's back   Proverbs 163
s. dogs   Lao Tzu 2
s. that stirs the drink   Reggie Jackson 3
Take a s. and throw it up   Selden 2
streak
thin red s.   William Howard Russell 1
stream
old mill s.   Tell Taylor 1
s. of thought   William James 5
streams
when crossing s.   Lincoln 47
street
eyes upon the s.   Jane Jacobs 2
great s. sweeper
            Martin Luther King, Jr. 18
inability to cross the s.   Virginia Woolf 14
Main S.   Sinclair Lewis 1
s. fighting man   Jagger and Richards 8
s. where you live   Alan Jay Lerner 8
sunny side of the s.   Dorothy Fields 1
streetcar
s. named Desire   Tennessee Williams 1
streets
children cried in the s.   John Motley 1
Down these mean s.
               Raymond Chandler 8
find the s. are guarded
           Folk and Anonymous Songs 50
s. FLOODED   Benchley 12
s. of Laredo
           Folk and Anonymous Songs 13
s. of our country   Hitler 9
sweat it out in the s.   Springsteen 1
Tales of Mean S.   Arthur Morrison 1
strength
My s. is as the s.   Tennyson 13
roll all our s.   Andrew Marvell 15
S. and wisdom
        William Jefferson "Bill" Clinton 12

subtle
Lord God is s.   Einstein 24
s. thief of youth   Milton 9
subtlest
serpent s. beast   Milton 39
subtracting
s. from the sum   Thomas B. Reed 2
subway
Bagdad-on-the-S.   O. Henry 4
written on s. walls   Paul Simon 2
succeed
How to S. in Business
                           Shepherd Mead 1
If at first you don't s.   W. C. Fields 20
succeeds
Nothing s. like success   Proverbs 219
Whenever a friend s.   Vidal 4
success
bitch-goddess S.   William James 16
can't argue with s.   Modern Proverbs 2
eternal condition of s.   Munger 1
He has achieved s.   Bessie A. Stanley 1
I dread s.   George Bernard Shaw 6
If A is a s. in life   Einstein 25
meet with a s.   Thoreau 28
Nothing succeeds like s.   Proverbs 219
S. Four flights   Wright and Wright 1
S. is counted sweetest
                         Emily Dickinson 1
S. to me is having   Streisand 1
sweet smell of s.   Lehman 1
successful
operation was s.   Sayings 45
such
People don't do s. things   Ibsen 25
S. is life   Ned Kelly 1
suck
I have given s.   Shakespeare 347
s. on the pap of life
                     F. Scott Fitzgerald 20
sucker
Hello, s.   Mizner 2
Hello s.   Guinan 1
Never give a s.   W. C. Fields 19
s. born every minute   Barnum 1
sucking
giant s. sound going south   Perot 1
suckled
Pagan s. in a creed
                   William Wordsworth 21
Sue
Boy Named S.   Silverstein 1
not born to s.   Shakespeare 12
S. me   Jessel 1
S. the bastards   Yannacone 1
suede
blue s. shoes   Carl Perkins 1
Suez
east of S.   Kipling 13
S. Canal was flowing   Eden 1
suffer
Can they s.   Bentham 4
nobler in the mind to s.
                         Shakespeare 188
S. any wrong   Dickens 78
s. fools gladly   Bible 362
S. the little children   Bible 280
suffered
They were born, they s.   France 2

suffering
About s. they were never wrong
                               Auden 28
Birth is s.   Pali Tripitaka 3
majesty of human s.   Vigny 2
world is full of s.   Helen Keller 3
suffers
man who s.   T. S. Eliot 32
sufficient
drawing s. conclusions
              Samuel Butler (1835–1902) 11
S. unto the day   Bible 220
sufficiently
s. advanced technology
                       Arthur C. Clarke 5
sugar
S. and spice   Southey 8
visions of s.-plums   Clement C. Moore 2
we are made of s. candy
                     Winston Churchill 25
sugared
selling s. water   Jobs 2
suggested
s. the research project   Parkinson 9
suicide
alone in s.   Eugenides 1
Bill of Rights into a s. pact
                     Robert H. Jackson 8
commit s.   Mishima 1
commit s. to avoid   Truman 8
Considered S.   Shange 1
did not commit s.   John Adams 15
if you have to die, commit s.   Le Guin 8
infidels are committing s.   Sahhaf 1
man who is committing s.
                     Woodrow Wilson 12
possibility of s.   Cioran 1
problem and that is s.   Camus 3
S.: a belated acquiescence   Mencken 11
S. . . . is about life   Sheed 1
s. is confession   Daniel Webster 8
s. kills two people   Arthur Miller 5
their own s.   Lenin 7
tolerance with regard to s.   Durkheim 1
suicides
s. have a special language   Sexton 3
suit
Gray Flannel S.   Sloan Wilson 1
S. the action   Shakespeare 202
S. up   Television Catchphrases 35
sullen
craft or s. art   Dylan Thomas 8
sum
s. of human knowledge
                        Thomas B. Reed 2
s. of their fears   Winston Churchill 51
Trifles make the s. of life   Dickens 74
Sumatra
giant rat of S.   Arthur Conan Doyle 38
sumer
S. is icumen in
              Folk and Anonymous Songs 16
summary
s. court in perpetual session   Kafka 7
summer
after many a s.   Tennyson 43
boys of s.   Dylan Thomas 2
compare thee to a s.'s day
                        Shakespeare 411

if it takes all S.   Ulysses S. Grant 2
invincible s.   Camus 7
Long Hot S.   Faulkner 15
made glorious s.   Shakespeare 1
spent his s. in Paris   Twain 20
S. afternoon   Henry James 28
s. evenings in Knoxville   Agee 1
s. grasses   Basho 5
s. of a dormouse   Byron 3
s. soldier   Thomas Paine 8
s. they executed   Plath 2
thy eternal s.   Shakespeare 412
summertime
S. and the livin' is easy   Heyward 1
summit
lonesome at the s.   Hawthorne 22
parley at the s.   Winston Churchill 44
s. of these pyramids   Napoleon 8
summits
Nations touch at their s.   Bagehot 2
summon
s. up remembrance   Shakespeare 417
summons
s. thee to Heaven   Shakespeare 351
trumpet s. us again   John F. Kennedy 13
upon a fearful s.   Shakespeare 143
sun
against a setting s.   Shakespeare 406
Falter! When the S.   Emily Dickinson 17
From where the s.   Chief Joseph 3
go out in the midday s.   Coward 9
golden apples of the s.   Yeats 6
I got the s. in the morning
                          Irving Berlin 13
Love that moves the s.   Dante 14
Make hay while the s.   Proverbs 183
make our s. stand still
                      Andrew Marvell 15
Mother, give me the s.   Ibsen 11
no new thing under the s.   Bible 141
nothing like the s.   Shakespeare 432
old fool, unruly s.   Donne 12
patent the s.   Salk 1
place in the s.   Bülow 1
place in the s.   Pascal 4
place in the s.   Wilhelm II 1
raisin in the s.   Langston Hughes 8
red s. was pasted   Stephen Crane 3
rising and not a setting S.
                     Benjamin Franklin 38
set a candle in the s.   Robert Burton 7
Sir Brother S.   St. Francis 1
stand out of my s. a little   Diogenes 2
s. also ariseth   Bible 140
s. go down upon your wrath   Bible 366
s. is but a morning star   Thoreau 31
S. is God   J. M. W. Turner 2
s. is shining bright   Ernest L. Thayer 4
s. is the center   Copernicus 1
s. never sets   North 1
s. shines bright   Stephen Foster 5
s. shone, having no   Beckett 1
S.-Beams out of Cucumbers
                        Jonathan Swift 18
they call the Rising S.
              Folk and Anonymous Songs 65
Third Stone from the S.   Hendrix 5
this s. of York   Shakespeare 1
too much in the s.   Shakespeare 148

worship the s.   John Morley 1

Sunday
Never on S.   Dassin 1
on a rainy S.   Ertz 1
S. Bloody S.   Gilliatt 1
sundered
S. by peaks   Du Fu 3
sundown
between s. and sunup   Will Rogers 5
sunless
Down to a s. sea   Coleridge 19
sunlight
parables of s.   Dylan Thomas 12
S. is said to be   Brandeis 4
Weave, weave the s.   T. S. Eliot 2
sunny
Keep Your S. Side Up   Lew Brown 1
s. side of the street   Dorothy Fields 1
suns
radiance of a thousand s.
                              Bhagavadgita 2
sunscreen
s. would be it   Schmich 1
sunset
sail beyond the s.   Tennyson 25
sunshine
Eternal s.   Pope 7
ray of s.   Wodehouse 6
s. of my life   Wonder 1
s. patriot   Thomas Paine 8
You are my s.   Jimmie Davis 1
superb
as a monster he was s.   Aldous Huxley 6
supercalifragilisticexpialidocious
S.   Robert B. Sherman 1
superficial
I'm pretty s.   Ava Gardner 1
superfluous
earlier publications rendered s.
                              Hilbert 2
poorest things s.   Shakespeare 291
s. in me to point out
                  Charles Francis Adams 1
superhighways
information s.   Gore 1
superhuman
S. effort isn't worth   Shackleton 2
superior
S. people never   Marianne Moore 3
superiority
acquire an evident s.
                              Samuel Johnson 60
delight of mental s.   Samuel Johnson 3
s. as a painter   Wilde 101
s. of their women   Tocqueville 19
Superman
Clark Kent is S.'s critique
                              Film Lines 106
I teach you the s.   Nietzsche 13
It's S.   Radio Catchphrases 21
Man and S.   George Bernard Shaw 11
tug on S.'s cape   Croce 1
supernatural
belief in a s. source   Conrad 24
existence of the s.   Santayana 13
superstar
Jesus Christ S.   Tim Rice 2
superstition
S. is the religion   Edmund Burke 21

superstitions
end as s.   T. H. Huxley 6
s. of a nation   Twain 104
supped
s. with their ancestors   Boccaccio 1
supper
sings for his s.   Nursery Rhymes 74
supplies
bought some new s.   Brecht 5
supply
s. has always been   Billings 4
support
invisible means of s.   Buchan 2
s. free peoples   Truman 3
suppose
S. you were an idiot   Twain 140
supposes
Moses s. his toeses
                  Comden and Green 2
Supreme
old men of the S. Court   Berle 1
Poetry is the s. fiction   Wallace Stevens 6
sitting on the S. Court   Eisenhower 15
s. beauty   Bertrand Russell 2
S. Coort follows th' election   Dunne 11
s. Law of the Land   Constitution 10
wield s. executive power
                              Monty Python 11
sur
S. le pont d'Avignon
              Folk and Anonymous Songs 73
sure
make s. he was dead   Goldwyn 5
wrested from a s. defeat
                              T. E. Lawrence 4
surely
s. goodness and mercy   Bible 109
surface
look at the s.   Warhol 2
surfaces
queen of s.   Dowd 1
surf-boarding
s. along the new electronic   McLuhan 7
surfing
s. the Net   Elizabeth II 4
surgeon
Warning: The S. General
                              Anonymous 32
surgeons
S. must be very careful
                              Emily Dickinson 3
surly
slipped the s. bonds   Magee 1
surmise
with a wild s.   Keats 3
surplus
S. wealth is a sacred trust
                              Andrew Carnegie 2
surprise
going to get a big s.
                  Diana, Princess of Wales 3
surprised
guilty thing s.   William Wordsworth 16
S. by joy   William Wordsworth 27
sur-realisme
kind of "s."   Apollinaire 4
surrender
daring of a moment's s.   T. S. Eliot 57
Cheese-eating s. monkeys   Groening 7

no retreat, baby, no s.   Springsteen 6
to Him we s.   Koran 2
unconditional and immediate s.
                       Ulysses S. Grant 1
surrey
s. with the fringe on top
                              Hammerstein 10
surroundings
I am I plus my s.   Ortega y Gasset 1
survey
monarch of all I s.   William Cowper 4
survival
s. machines   Dawkins 3
s. of the fittest   Philander C. Johnson 1
s. of the fittest   Herbert Spencer 6
s. of the fittest   Herbert Spencer 5
S. of the Fittest   Charles Darwin 7
survive
I will s.   Perren 1
not merely s.   Walter Marks 1
Only the paranoid s.   Grove 1
What will s. of us   Larkin 1
survived
I s.   Sieyès 2
survivors
written by the s.   Modern Proverbs 41
more the s.' affair   Thomas Mann 4
Susanna
O, S.   Stephen Foster 1
suspect
Always s. everybody   Dickens 37
suspects
Every one s. himself
                   F. Scott Fitzgerald 17
Round up the usual s.   Film Lines 49
suspend
s. the functioning   Hemingway 25
suspension
willing s. of disbelief   Coleridge 26
suspicion
Caesar's wife must be above s.
                              Julius Caesar 3
suspicions
usually has his s.   Mizner 4
suspire
only live, only s.   T. S. Eliot 121
swaddling
wrapped him in s. clothes   Bible 287
swagman
Once a jolly s.   Paterson 2
swallow
One s. does not make   Aristotle 2
s. a camel   Bible 257
swallows
s. build in the eaves   Barrie 7
swan
beautiful and graceful s.   Andersen 5
dies the s.   Tennyson 43
even daughters of the s.   Yeats 36
Sweet S. of Avon   Jonson 11
Swanee
upon the S. River   Stephen Foster 3
swap
s. horses when crossing   Lincoln 47
swarms
sent hither s. of Officers   Jefferson 5
sway
s. in the wind   T. S. Eliot 1

tactical
made a t. error   Zevon 4
tactics
Gestapo t.   Ribicoff 1
tail
calling the t. a leg   Lincoln 63
he's treading on my t. Carroll 20
t. must wag the dog   Kipling 7
tailor
Tinker, t.   Nursery Rhymes 71
tails
cut off their t.   Nursery Rhymes 42
taint
any t. of legality Philander C. Knox 1
take
big enough to t. away Gerald R. Ford 6
can t. themselves lightly Chesterton 12
can't t. it with you Proverbs 288
God does not t. sides George Mitchell 1
not going to t. this anymore
     Film Lines 124
Precious Lord, t. my hand
    Thomas A. Dorsey 1
T. another little piece   Berns 1
t. arms against a sea Shakespeare 188
t. away all he's got Film Lines 183
t. care of the pence Chesterfield 5
t. care of themselves Chesterfield 5
T. it off, take it all off
   Advertising Slogans 94
T. me or leave me Dorothy Parker 16
T. me out to the ball game Norworth 2
T. my wife . . . please Youngman 1
t. the bad with the good
    Modern Proverbs 4
t. the fat with the lean Dickens 73
t. the name of the Lord Bible 53
T. This Job and Shove   Coe 1
t. thou what course Shakespeare 126
T. up and read   Augustine 4
t. us to your President Alex Graham 1
t. you in   Frost 1
taken
I have t. all knowledge Francis Bacon 1
t. at the flood Shakespeare 128
t. better care of myself Sayings 23
takes
It t. a village Modern Proverbs 95
t. all sorts   Proverbs 8
t. place every day   Camus 8
T. Two to Tango Al Hoffman 1
taking
capacity for t. pains Jane Hopkins 1
tale
I could a t. unfold Shakespeare 166
I should have had a t.
   Robert Falcon Scott 3
round unvarnished t. Shakespeare 262
T. as old as time   Ashman 2
t. told by an idiot Shakespeare 394
thereby hangs a t. Shakespeare 86
talent
Everybody has t.   Degas 2
extraordinary collection of t.
   John F. Kennedy 25
follow the t. to the dark place Jong 1
hid thy t. in the earth Bible 263
His t. was as natural Hemingway 31
If he has a t. Thomas Wolfe 3

if you like t.   Merman 1
must have t. too   Korda 1
no t. for writing   Benchley 10
one t. which is death Milton 52
T. does what it can Owen Meredith 2
t. in privacy Marilyn Monroe 6
t. instantly recognizes
   Arthur Conan Doyle 36
t. to amuse   Coward 3
t. which does what it can Baring 1
talented
T. Tenth   Du Bois 3
talents
career open to the t. Napoleon 6
I'm taking my t. LeBron James 1
tales
Dead men tell no t. Proverbs 62
Never tell t.   Proverbs 289
talk
Can we t.   Rivers 2
Let us not t. of them   Dante 4
Let's t. of graves Shakespeare 20
Money doesn't t.   Dylan 15
t. about the past   McGwire 1
T. is cheap   Proverbs 290
t. sense to the American
   Adlai E. Stevenson 2
ways of making men t. Film Lines 110
We must not always t. Hawthorne 12
You t., you t.   Queneau 1
talked
he t. of his honor
   Ralph Waldo Emerson 41
not being t. about   Wilde 22
t. about the weather Twain 145
t. like a man   Ray Davies 1
We have t. long enough
   Lyndon B. Johnson 3
talkers
greatest t. since the Greeks Wilde 112
talkin'
You t. to me Film Lines 169
talking
I've been t. to your boss Mizner 5
t. at street corners Vanzetti 2
t. bad grammar   Disraeli 36
t. of Michelangelo T. S. Eliot 4
talks
He t. to me   Victoria 5
if God t. to you   Szasz 2
Money t.   Proverbs 198
professor is one who t. Auden 43
tall
t. as a crane   Sitwell 1
T. oaks from little Proverbs 291
t. ship and a star Masefield 1
taller
make you grow t.   Carroll 11
tambourine
Hey! Mr. T. Man   Dylan 8
Tampax
Or, God forbid, a T.
  Charles, Prince of Wales 5
tan
cheek of t.   Whittier 2
I don't t.—I stroke Woody Allen 10
tangled
t. web we weave Walter Scott 5

tango
Takes Two to T. Al Hoffman 1
tank
I t. I go home   Garbo 3
tiger in your t. Advertising Slogans 47
tanstaafl
Oh, "t."   Heinlein 3
Tao
action of the T. Lao Tzu 5
T. that can be told Lao Tzu 1
tape
men with a t. worm Conkling 1
t. will self-destruct
  Television Catchphrases 45
Tara
through T.'s halls Thomas Moore 2
tarantara
T.! t!   W. S. Gilbert 21
ta-ra-ra-boom-de-ay
T.   Henry J. Sayers 1
tar-baby
T. ain't sayin' nuthin'
   Joel Chandler Harris 1
targets
good t. in Iraq   Rumsfeld 10
tart
some watery t. Monty Python 11
Tarzan
we would each like to be T.
   Edgar Rice Burroughs 3
Me T., you Jane Weismuller 1
tase
Don't T. me, bro   Meyer 1
task
common t.   Keble 1
hardest t. in the world
   Ralph Waldo Emerson 12
taste
arbiter of t.   Tacitus 2
Bad t. is simply saying Mel Brooks 15
difference of t. in jokes George Eliot 17
Every man to his own t. Proverbs 90
himself create the t.
   William Wordsworth 10
how salt is the t.   Dante 13
T. is the feminine of genius
   Edward FitzGerald 7
t. my meat George Herbert 5
valiant never t. of death
   Shakespeare 102
tasted
it can't be t. in a sip Dickens 36
what I've t. of desire Frost 11
You have t. your worm Spooner 4
tastes
no accounting for t. Proverbs 3
T. great, less filling
  Advertising Slogans 85
Winston t. good
  Advertising Slogans 135
tasting
I am t. stars   Perignon 1
taught
got to be carefully t. Hammerstein 18
knowing can be t.   Wilde 9
tautology
add the sheep was t. Twain 117

tavern
 t. in the town
  Folk and Anonymous Songs 75
taverns
 fools in t.   George Bernard Shaw 33
tawt
 I t. I taw a puddy tat
  Television Catchphrases 81
tax
 I t. not you   Shakespeare 293
 If it moves, t. it   Ronald W. Reagan 11
 in favor of an income t.
  William Jennings Bryan 1
 Income T. has made   Will Rogers 4
 power to t. involves   John Marshall 7
 power to t. is not the power
  Oliver Wendell Holmes, Jr. 38
 right to t.   Daniel Webster 2
 soon be able to t. it   Faraday 2
 t. and tax and tax   Harry Hopkins 1
 t. and to please   Edmund Burke 3
 taxidermist and a t. collector   Twain 115
taxation
 system of t.   Andrew Jackson 4
 T. without representation   Otis 6
taxes
 Death and T.   Proverbs 63
 Death and t. and childbirth
  Margaret Mitchell 6
 duty to increase one's t.   Hand 2
 except death and t.
  Benjamin Franklin 41
 good enough to pay t.   Will Rogers 7
 little people pay t.   Helmsley 1
 no new t.
  George Herbert Walker Bush 4
 raised on city land is t.
  Charles Dudley Warner 3
 T. are what we pay
  Oliver Wendell Holmes, Jr. 36
 that is to increase t.   Thomas Paine 14
 understand is income t.   Einstein 35
taxi-cab
 t. with both doors open
  Howard Hughes 1
taxidermist
 t. takes only your skin   Twain 115
T-bird
 daddy takes the T. away   Brian Wilson 1
te
 T. Deum   Niceta 1
tea
 like a t.-tray in the sky   Carroll 16
 t. and sympathy   Robert Anderson 1
 t. for two   Irving Caesar 1
 we'll all have t.   Nursery Rhymes 57
 woman is like a t. bag   Nancy Reagan 1
teach
 qualified to t. others   Confucius 3
 T. a man to fish   Modern Proverbs 31
 t. a pig to sing   Heinlein 13
 t. an old dog new tricks   Proverbs 292
 t. him rather to think   Mary Shelley 8
 t. men to die   Montaigne 7
 t. only what is not worth   Austen 12
 T. the free man   Auden 25
 t. the world to sing
  Advertising Slogans 33
 t. us to care   T. S. Eliot 78

Why can't the English t.
  Alan Jay Lerner 9
teacher
 Experience is the best t.   Proverbs 93
 omnipresent t.   Brandeis 10
 sign of success for a t.   Montessori 2
 t. affects eternity   Henry Adams 11
teaches
 He who cannot, t.
  George Bernard Shaw 17
team
 There's no "I" in t.   Modern Proverbs 44
teapot
 raise a storm in a t.   Cicero 4
tear
 no longer t. his heart   Jonathan Swift 34
 t. down this wall   Ronald W. Reagan 14
 t.-wrung millions   Byron 28
tears
 blood, toil, t., and sweat
  Winston Churchill 12
 blood and sweat and t.
  Theodore Roosevelt 3
 God shall wipe away all t.   Bible 394
 God shall wipe away all t.   Bible 399
 Hence those t.   Terence 1
 I ain't got no t.   August Wilson 2
 If you have t.   Shakespeare 119
 shed t. when they would devour
  Francis Bacon 24
 Smiling through her t.   Homer 4
 sweat, their t., their blood
  Winston Churchill 9
 t., or sweat, or blood   Donne 4
 t. in my heart   Verlaine 2
 t. in rain   Film Lines 24
 t. of the crocodile   George Chapman 2
 t. shed for things   Virgil 3
 tracks of my t.   "Smokey" Robinson 3
teche
 gladly t.   Chaucer 9
technically
 t. sweet   Oppenheimer 2
technocratic
 t. imperative   Roszak 1
technology
 Any sufficiently advanced t.
  Arthur C. Clarke 5
 For a successful t.   Feynman 3
 t. that makes tyranny   Laumer 1
 T. . . . the knack of   Frisch 1
Ted
 There goes T. Williams
  Theodore S. "Ted" Williams 2
teddy
 t. bears have their picnic
  Jimmy Kennedy 1
tedious
 charming or t.   Wilde 52
teenage
 t. wasteland   Townshend 3
teeth
 did it with her t.   Twain 74
 gnashing of t.   Bible 231
 gone in the t.   Ezra Pound 14
 iron t.   Gromyko 1
 skin of my t.   Bible 100
 t. are set on edge   Bible 184

women have fewer t.
  Bertrand Russell 10
teething
 they escaped t.   Twain 57
Teflon
 T.-coated Presidency   Schroeder 1
Telemachus
 mine own T.   Tennyson 21
telephone
 Boston t. directory   Buckley 2
 cut off the t.   Auden 1
 effectiveness of a t. conversation
  Parkinson 11
 T., *n.* An invention   Bierce 136
 tried to use the t.   Laura Richards 1
telescope
 T., *n.* A device   Bierce 137
televised
 Revolution Will Not Be T.   Scott-Heron 1
television
 I find t. very educating
  "Groucho" Marx 42
 see bad t.   Goldwyn 4
 t., tuned to a dead   Gibson 2
 T. has proved   Landers 3
tell
 Dead men t. no tales   Proverbs 62
 did you t. me   Dillard 1
 Don't ask, don't t.   Moskos 1
 Don't ever t. anybody   Salinger 5
 Go t. the Spartans   Simonides 1
 How can they t.   Dorothy Parker 30
 I can't t. a lie   Weems 1
 Let me t. the world   Shakespeare 59
 must not kiss and t.   Congreve 3
 Never t. me the odds   George Lucas 13
 Never t. tales   Proverbs 289
 right to t. people   Orwell 21
 t. it on the mountain
  Folk and Anonymous Songs 32
 T. me, muse   Homer 7
 T. me the tales   Bayly 1
 T. me what you eat   Brillat-Savarin 1
 T. me what you know
  Ralph Waldo Emerson 34
 t. sad stories   Shakespeare 21
 T. that to the marines   Walter Scott 13
 t. the truth   Twain 84
 T. the truth or trump   Twain 53
 t. them im a man   Gaines 2
 t. you what you are   Ruskin 16
 Time will t.   Proverbs 301
 will not ever t. me   Agee 2
telling
 I am t. you   Whistler 4
 nature's way of t. you   Sayings 29
 no business t. a man
  Thurgood Marshall 1
 stop t. lies   Adlai E. Stevenson 6
tells
 Bible t. me so   Anna Warner 1
 Nobody t. me anything   Galsworthy 1
temper
 t. so justice with mercy   Milton 41
temperament
 creation seen through a t.   Zola 2
 first-class t.
  Oliver Wendell Holmes, Jr. 44

tempered
despotism t. by epigrams
                    Thomas Carlyle 4
monarchy t. by assassination   Custine 1
tempest-tost
it shall be t.   Shakespeare 324
tempora
O t., O mores   Cicero 9
temporary
t. government program
                    Milton Friedman 8
temps
Recherche du T. Perdu   Proust 1
tempt
T. not a desperate man   Shakespeare 49
temptation
get rid of a t.   Wilde 25
I generally avoid t.   Mae West 19
lead us not into t.   Bible 215
maximum of t.
                George Bernard Shaw 20
resist everything except t.   Wilde 53
taking away the t.   Mencken 5
t. is just to yield   Clementina Graham 1
t. to the editor   Lardner 2
temptations
in spite of all t.   W. S. Gilbert 13
ten
as the strength of t.   Tennyson 13
good lord had only t.   Clemenceau 7
t. commandments   Bible 63
T. Days That Shook   John Reed 1
t. guilty persons   Blackstone 7
t. thousand swords   Edmund Burke 17
tenants
T. of the house   T. S. Eliot 24
tender
how it. can we bear   Rebecca Wells 1
Love me t.   Presley 1
t. is the night   Keats 18
t. mercies   Bible 128
Tennessee
nothing else in T.   Wallace Stevens 2
placed a jar in T.   Wallace Stevens 1
tennis
game of t.   George Bernard Shaw 35
ladies in t. shoes   Mosk 1
shouldn't play t.   Black 3
t. with the net down   Frost 18
Tennyson
Lawn T.   Joyce 18
tent
If a man have a t.   Leonardo da Vinci 3
inside the t. pissing out
                    Lyndon B. Johnson 12
nose into the t.   Modern Proverbs 12
Strike the t.   Robert E. Lee 2
tenth
submerged t.   William Booth 1
Talented T.   Du Bois 3
tenting
t. on the old campground   Kittredge 1
tents
fold their t.   Longfellow 13
tenure
like getting t.   Dennett 1
Terence
T., this is stupid stuff   Housman 4

terminal
all t. cases   John Irving 1
termination
for its own t.   Lincoln 26
terminological
risk of t. inexactitude
                    Winston Churchill 3
terrible
lend the eye a t. aspect   Shakespeare 133
t. beauty is born   Yeats 27
t. swift sword   Julia Ward Howe 1
t. thing to waste
              Advertising Slogans 120
terribles
Enfants T.   Gavarni 1
terrified
t. vague fingers   Yeats 43
territorial
last t. claim   Hitler 4
no t. changes   Roosevelt and Churchill 2
territory
comes with the t.   Arthur Miller 2
light out for the T.   Twain 36
map is not the t.   Korzybski 1
terror
carry t. and devastation   Nat Turner 1
t. of knowing   Bowie 3
terrorism
democratic world and t.   Blair 6
denounce a t.   Camus 9
Fighting t. is like   Wilkinson 1
trying to suppress t.   Schumacher 3
terrorist
One man's t.   Sayings 44
t. and the policeman   Conrad 21
terrorists
no distinction between t.
                    George W. Bush 4
terrors
Annihilation has no t.   Twain 135
incommunicable small t.   Drabble 2
new t. of Death   Arbuthnot 1
test
moral t. of government   Humphrey 3
t. of a civilization   Pearl S. Buck 3
t. of a democracy   Helen Keller 4
t. of a first-rate intelligence
                F. Scott Fitzgerald 40
t. of civilisation   Samuel Johnson 69
Texas
Deep in the Heart of T.   Hershey 1
If I owned T. and Hell
                    Philip Henry Sheridan 1
is from T.   Maines 1
Maine and T.   Thoreau 20
yellow rose in T.
              Folk and Anonymous Songs 86
text
outside of the t.   Derrida 1
Thames
Sweet T., run softly   Spenser 7
Thane
T. of Fife   Shakespeare 386
thank
t. everyone who made   Berra 5
T. God It's Friday   Sayings 49
T. heaven for little girls
                    Alan Jay Lerner 15
T. me no thankings   Shakespeare 48

t. you, ma'am   Sayings 59
thanks
For this relief much t.   Shakespeare 140
T. for the Memory   Robin 1
T. . . . I needed that
              Television Catchphrases 48
thanksgiving
day of t. and praise   Lincoln 40
that
T. ART THOU   Upanishads 1
T. Was the Week   Bird 1
T.'ll be the day   Film Lines 151
T.'ll be the day   Holly 1
T.'s Entertainment   Dietz 1
Thatcher
If Margaret T. wins   Kinnock 2
theater
When you leave the t.   Edith Evans 1
theatre
shouting fire in a t.
                Oliver Wendell Holmes, Jr. 29
theft
Property is t.   Proudhon 1
t. from those who hunger   Eisenhower 5
theirs
t. not to reason why   Tennyson 39
them
T. that die'll be
                Robert Louis Stevenson 10
themselves
help t.   Proverbs 122
law unto t.   Bible 341
thenne
thikke and thurgh t.   Chaucer 16
theologians
greeted by a band of t.   Jastrow 1
theology
if his t. isn't straight   Twain 81
theorems
turning coffee into t.   Erdős 1
theorize
t. before one has data
                Arthur Conan Doyle 17
theory
decided upon an economic t.
                Oliver Wendell Holmes, Jr. 18
Died of a t.   Jefferson Davis 1
Feminism is a t.   Atkinson 2
If my t. of relativity   Einstein 6
life without t.   Disraeli 6
new t. is attacked   William James 19
Pornography is the t.   Robin Morgan 2
t. is correct anyway   Einstein 31
theosophy
[T.] is the essence   Blavatsky 1
therapist
very effective t.   Horney 1
there
Because it's t.   Mallory 1
I'll be t.   Steinbeck 5
I simply am not t.   Bret Easton Ellis 2
Over t.   Cohan 4
t. goes Roy Hobbs   Malamud 1
T. goes Ted Williams
              Theodore S. "Ted" Williams 2
T. is no god but God   Koran 7
T. is no place like home
                    L. Frank Baum 3
t. is no t. t.   Stein 12

traveller

no t. returns   Shakespeare 191
t. from an antique land   Percy Shelley 5

travelling

T. is the ruin   Burney 2

travels

Bad news t. fast   Proverbs 15

travesty

t. of a mockery of a sham   Woody Allen 8

treachery

Age and t. will overcome   Sayings 1

tread

Don't t. on me   Anonymous 6
where angels fear to t.   Pope 5
you t. on my dreams   Yeats 5

treading

he's t. on my tail   Carroll 20

treason

If this be t.   Patrick Henry 1
none dare call it t.   Harington 1
T. doth never prosper   Harington 1
t. of the intellectuals   Benda 1

treasure

purest t.   Shakespeare 11
Where your t. is   Bible 217

treasures

t. in heaven   Bible 216

treated

first time he is t. unfairly   Barrie 3
t. as he would wish   John F. Kennedy 31
t. by at least six   Jong 4

treaties

T., you see, are like girls   de Gaulle 7

treats

t. us all like dogs   Henry Jordan 1

treaty

not a peace t.   Foch 1

tree

billboard lovely as a t.   Nash 7
fall far from the t.   Proverbs 12
If a t. falls in a forest   Sayings 20
on the t. top   Nursery Rhymes 1
only God can make a t.   Kilmer 2
poem lovely as a t.   Kilmer 1
spare that t.   George Pope Morris 1
spare the beechen t.
      Thomas Campbell 2
spreading chestnut t.   Longfellow 7
t. of knowledge   Bible 8
t. of liberty   Jefferson 17
t. that grows in Brooklyn   Betty Smith 1
t.'s a t.   Ronald W. Reagan 18
t.'s inclined   Pope 24

trees

I cut down t.   Monty Python 5
I like t. because   Cather 3
I speak for the t.   Seuss 12
If t. could scream   Handey 1
Money doesn't grow on t.
      Modern Proverbs 60
rest under the t.   "Stonewall" Jackson 1

tremble

t. for my country   Jefferson 13
t. like a guilty thing
      William Wordsworth 16

trembling

salvation with fear and t.   Bible 370

trenches

hundreds in vast t.   Boccaccio 2

trespasses

forgive us our t.
      Book of Common Prayer 12

trial

fair t. anywhere   Brewster 1
man is never so on t.   Lew Wallace 1
only a t. if I recognize it   Kafka 9
right of t. by jury   Constitution 16
speedy and public t.   Constitution 15
T. by jury   Denman 1
t. of the century   Frances Noyes Hart 1

triangles

t. were to make a God   Montesquieu 3

tribe

may his t. increase   Leigh Hunt 2
dialect of the t.   T. S. Eliot 119
t. has spoken
      Television Catchphrases 73
words of the t.   Mallarmé 3

tribute

Hypocrisy is a t.   la Rochefoucauld 5
not a cent for t.   Robert Harper 1

tributes

t. that Power ever has paid
      Robert H. Jackson 5

trick

get the t.   Twain 53
win the t.   Edmond Hoyle 1

trickle

t. down to the rest of us
      Franklin D. Roosevelt 5
T.-down theory   Galbraith 6

tricks

old dog new t.   Proverbs 292

trickster

she is a t.   Einstein 10

tried

one I never t. before   Mae West 13
proved it correct, not t. it   Knuth 1

trifle

Do Not T. with Love   Musset 2

trifles

farewell to shining t.   Philip Sidney 3
law is not concerned with t.
      Anonymous (Latin) 5
t. make the sum of human things
      Hannah More 2
T. make the sum of life   Dickens 74

trifling

t. investment of fact   Twain 26
t. with literary fools
      George Bernard Shaw 33

trilobite

eye of the t. tells us   Agassiz 1

trip

don't t. over the furniture   Coward 14
long, strange t. it's been
      Robert Hunter 1
t. through a sewer   Mizner 12
t. to the moon   Cole Porter 13

triple

I t. guarantee you   Sahhaf 2
thinks he hit a t.   Hightower 1

Tripoli

to the shores of T.
      Folk and Anonymous Songs 49

trippingly

t. on the tongue   Shakespeare 200

triste

omne animal t.   Anonymous (Latin) 10

tristesse

Bonjour t.   Éluard 2

triumph

T. and Disaster   Kipling 32
t. of evil   Edmund Burke 28
t. of hope   Samuel Johnson 68
t. of the embalmer's art   Vidal 7

triumphs

one either t. or dies   Guevara 2

trivial

t. round   Keble 1
t. skirmish   Graves 5

troika

like a spirited t.   Gogol 1

Trojan

since the T. war   Byron 21

trombones

Seventy-six t.   Willson 1

Trotskyites

worthy of your million T.   Ginsberg 2

trotted

t. away into the other world   Dickens 80

trouble

Life is t.   Kazantzakis 2
man in very great t.   John W. Sterling 1
Nobody knows the t. I see
      Folk and Anonymous Songs 56
saves me the t.   Austen 1
toil and t.   Shakespeare 375
t. deaf heav'n   Shakespeare 413
T. Is My Business   Raymond Chandler 4
Ya got t.   Willson 2

troubled

bridge over t. water   Paul Simon 8

troublemakers

dead t.   McLaughlin 2

troubles

against a sea of t.   Shakespeare 188
known a great many t.   Twain 148
Pack up your t.   Asaf 1
woman whose t. are greater   Algren 2

troubleth

t. his own house   Bible 127

trousers

best t. on   Ibsen 19
bottoms of my t. rolled   T. S. Eliot 10
cloud in t.   Mayakovski 1
steam-engine in t.   Sydney Smith 8

trout

t. in the milk   Thoreau 15

trowel

lay it on with a t.   Disraeli 31

Troy

another T. for her   Yeats 11

truck

t. passing by a factory   Cage 2

truckin'

Keep on t.   "Blind Boy" Fuller 1

true

always t. to you   Cole Porter 20
course of t. love   Shakespeare 51
Every t. passion   Stendhal 2
His t. Penelope   Ezra Pound 10
If only the t. were new   Voss 1
love, let us be t.   Matthew Arnold 18
Many a t. word   Proverbs 306
marriage of t. minds   Shakespeare 429

uglier
woman u. than you   De Leon 2
uglification
U., and Derision   Carroll 19
ugly
by an u. fact   T. H. Huxley 3
Good, the Bad, and the U.   Leone 1
pretty u. feet   David Foster Wallace 1
subhumanly u. mate   Greer 3
There is nothing u.   Constable 1
U. American   Lederer 1
U. Duckling   Andersen 4
u. duckling girls like me   Ian 2
u. mathematics   G. H. Hardy 2
ulcer
eight u. man   Truman 6
ulcers
I don't get u.   Selznick 1
Ulster
U. will fight   Randolph Churchill 2
ultimate
u. driving machine
    Advertising Slogans 20
ultimatum
U., n. In diplomacy   Bierce 139
Ulysses
he who like U.   Joachim du Bellay 2
U. may, therefore   Woolsey 2
umble
very u. person   Dickens 62
umbrella
steals the just's u.   Lord Bowen 2
umpire
Chaos u. sits   Milton 30
integrity of an u.   Durocher 1
unacknowledged
u. legislators of the world   Auden 39
u. legislators of the world
    Percy Shelley 15
unadorned
Beauty u.   Behn 2
un-Americans
You are the u.   Robeson 4
unbearable
in victory u.   Winston Churchill 49
u. lightness of being   Kundera 3
unbelief
help thou mine u.   Bible 279
un-birthday
u. present   Carroll 39
unblack
not u. dog   Orwell 30
unbought
U. and Unbossed   Chisholm 1
unbowed
bloody, but u.   W. E. Henley 1
unbroken
Can the circle be u.   A. P. Carter 1
u. wings   T. S. Eliot 85
uncertain
u. hour before the morning
    T. S. Eliot 118
uncertainty
permanent, intolerable u.   Le Guin 3
Uncle
nephew of my U. Sam's   Cohan 1
unclench
u. your fist   Barack Obama 7

unclubable
very u. man   Samuel Johnson 59
uncomfortably
looking u. to the world   Tom Hayden 1
uncommon
U. valor   Nimitz 1
unconditional
u. and immediate surrender
    Ulysses S. Grant 1
unconfined
let joy be u.   Byron 9
unconquerable
man's u. mind   William Wordsworth 20
unconscionable
u. time dying   Charles II 2
unconscious
collective u.   Jung 1
discovered the u.   Sigmund Freud 20
region of the u.   Carus 1
u. is structured   Lacan 1
u. is the ocean   Calvino 1
unconstitutional
statute to be u.   Tocqueville 2
u. takes a little longer   Kissinger 4
unconventional
not difficult to be u.   Maugham 4
uncorseted
U., her friendly bust   T. S. Eliot 19
uncreated
u. conscience of my race   Joyce 11
undecided
five who are u.   Stengel 9
undefiled
well of English u.   Spenser 6
wells of English u.   Samuel Johnson 6
under
no new thing u. the sun   Bible 141
U. a spreading chestnut tree
    Longfellow 7
U. bare Ben Bulben's head   Yeats 63
u. dog in the fight   Barker 1
u. my skin   Cole Porter 15
u. pressure   Bowie 4
U. the greenwood tree   Shakespeare 85
u. the knot   Dorothy Parker 31
underachiever
he's an u.   Woody Allen 18
underbelly
u. of the Axis   Winston Churchill 28
underclass
"u." of unemployed   Myrdal 2
underestimate
Never u. the power
    Advertising Slogans 69
u. what will happen   Bill Gates 1
underestimating
lost money by u.   Mencken 35
undergraduates
met are college u.   Woodrow Wilson 1
underground
U. Railroad   Tubman 3
understand
can really u. another   Graham Greene 2
I do not u.   Feynman 4
u. a little less   Major 2
u. everything   Staël 3
u. others   Fuentes 1
u. the problem   Beville 1
u. the situation   Murrow 6

u. them   Spinoza 6
understanding
find you an u.   Samuel Johnson 106
u. of life   Anne Morrow Lindbergh 6
which passeth all u.   Bible 371
understands
He who u. baboon   Charles Darwin 1
u. what no other church
    Thomas Macaulay 10
understood
had ever u.   Palmerston 2
I have u. you   de Gaulle 6
If you u. everything   Miles Davis 2
My language is u.   Haydn 2
who has u. his time   Picasso 6
undertaker
u. will be sorry   Twain 59
underworld
way down to the U.   Virgil 8
undetected
u. plagiarism   Herbert Paul 1
undigested
u. bit of beef   Dickens 40
undisciplined
u. squads of emotion   T. S. Eliot 108
undiscover'd
u. country   Shakespeare 191
undiscovered
lay all u. before me   Isaac Newton 7
undisputed
mother's u. darling   Sigmund Freud 10
un-done
John Donne, Anne Donne, U.   Donne 14
undone
death had u. so many   T. S. Eliot 44
left u. those things
    Book of Common Prayer 10
unearned
U. increment of value   Mill 26
uneasy
U. lies the head   Shakespeare 64
uneatable
in pursuit of the u.   Wilde 60
uneducated
good thing for an u. man
    Winston Churchill 7
unemployed
When we're u.   Jesse Jackson 3
unemployment
u. results   Coolidge 9
unequal
inherently u.   Earl Warren 1
separate and u.   Kerner 1
u. laws unto a savage race   Tennyson 14
unequals
equals and u. alike   Plato 9
unethical
conduct u. and lousy   Arno 1
unexamined
life which is u.   Plato 2
unfair
Life is u.   John F. Kennedy 24
unfairly
first time he is treated u.   Barrie 3
unfairness
life's essential u.   Mitford 1
unfit
u. to go there   Twain 14

unforgiving
fill the u. minute   Kipling 33
unfree
Ireland u. shall never   Pearse 1
unfriendly
u. disposition   James Monroe 4
unhappy
each u. family   Tolstoy 8
some should be u.   Samuel Johnson 86
u. sort of unfortunate man   Boethius 1
U. the land   Brecht 4
unhealthy
u. excitement   Arthur Conan Doyle 35
unheard
language of the u.
     Martin Luther King, Jr. 17
those u. are sweeter   Keats 15
unhistoric
dependent on u. acts   George Eliot 16
unicorn
rarer than the u.   Jong 5
unimportant
completely u.   Christie 5
uninhibited
u., robust, and wide-open   Brennan 3
unintended
u. consequences   Merton 3
union
form a more perfect U.   Constitution 1
Liberty and U.   Daniel Webster 7
Look for the u. label
     Advertising Slogans 62
Our U.: It must be preserved
     Andrew Jackson 1
save the U. without freeing   Lincoln 32
State of the U.   Constitution 6
sticking to the u.   "Woody" Guthrie 5
U. forever   George Frederick Root 2
U. is strength   Proverbs 314
u. makes us strong   Ralph Chaplin 1
u. of English-speaking   Rhodes 1
u. of hands and hearts   Jeremy Taylor 2
unite
Workers of the world, u.
     Marx and Engels 8
united
by U. States Marines
     Folk and Anonymous Songs 50
friendly skies of U.
     Advertising Slogans 119
from the U. States of America to Spain
     Moylan 1
It was the U. States   Didion 3
never hear of the U. States
     Edward Everett Hale 1
provided by the U. Nations   Annan 1
so close to the U. States   Díaz 1
sword u. nations drew   Byron 10
U. Nations   Minor 1
U. Nations a difficult   George W. Bush 13
U. States can find time   James Jones 1
U. States of Europe   Hugo 3
U. States themselves   Whitman 2
We, the peoples of the U. Nations
     Anonymous 35
We the People of the U. States
     Constitution 1
unities
Three U.   John Dryden 1

u., sir   Dickens 28
uniting
by u. we stand   John Dickinson 1
universal
become a u. law   Kant 3
books are of u. appeal
     Ford Madox Ford 2
hint of the u. law
     Oliver Wendell Holmes, Jr. 15
Not u. love   Auden 12
U. peace is declared   George Eliot 8
universally
u. recognized   Stoppard 1
universe
all the u. conspires   Coelho 1
benign indifference of the u.   Camus 3
better ordering of the u.   Alfonso 1
center of the u.   Copernicus 1
child of the u.   Ehrmann 2
Do I dare disturb the u.   T. S. Eliot 5
entire weight of the u.   Le Guin 7
everything in the u.   Muir 1
fate of the u.   Kurzweil 1
first invent the u.   Carl Sagan 3
I accept the u.   Margaret Fuller 3
man said to the u.   Stephen Crane 4
Masters of the U.   Tom Wolfe 8
This u. is not hostile   John H. Holmes 1
u. as a clockwork   Dillard 2
u. go to all the bother   Hawking 4
u. is not only queerer   Haldane 1
u. is unfolding   Ehrmann 2
U. is winning   Rick Cook 1
u. makes rather an indifferent
     Dickens 83
u. seems comprehensible
     Steven Weinberg 1
u. wants to be noticed   John Green 1
U. was created   Douglas Adams 4
we are alone in the U.
     Arthur C. Clarke 7
universes
U. BEGGING FOR GODS   Farmer 1
universities
U. are, of course, hostile
     Ralph Waldo Emerson 38
u. stifle writers   Flannery O'Connor 4
university
able to get to a u.   Kinnock 3
true U. of these days   Thomas Carlyle 15
who enters a u. walks   Conant 3
unjust
decision of no u. judge
     Daniel Webster 10
One who breaks an u. law
     Martin Luther King, Jr. 7
unkindest
most u. cut of all   Shakespeare 120
unknown
altars to u. gods   William James 3
old, u. world   F. Scott Fitzgerald 34
there are also u. unknowns   Rumsfeld 1
to fortune and to fame u.
     Thomas Gray 10
TO THE U. GOD   Bible 335
unleashed
u. power of the atom   Einstein 17
unleavened
eat u. bread   Bible 47

unless
U. someone like you   Seuss 13
unlimited
Land of U. Possibilities   Goldberger 1
U. power is apt to corrupt
     William Pitt, Earl of Chatham 3
unlocked
Shakespeare u. his heart
     William Wordsworth 28
unlucky
u. in love   Proverbs 182
unmanageable
u. realm   Decter 1
unmarked
history's u. grave   George W. Bush 10
unnatural
naturally appears u.   Mill 20
only u. sex act   Kinsey 4
unnecessary
one of them is u.   Wrigley 1
unpleasant
How u. to meet Mr. Eliot   T. S. Eliot 89
unplumbed
u., salt, estranging sea
     Matthew Arnold 1
unprofitable
stale, flat, and u.   Shakespeare 150
unpunished
No good deed goes u.
     Clare Boothe Luce 7
unpurged
u. images of day   Yeats 53
unquiet
u. slumbers   Emily Brontë 6
unreal
U. City   T. S. Eliot 44
unreality
u. that he cannot bear   Le Guin 7
unreasonable
progress depends on the u. man
     George Bernard Shaw 22
unrighteousness
mammon of u.   Bible 300
unsafe
U. at Any Speed   Nader 1
unsatisfactory
realistic, yet u., conclusion   Cronkite 1
unsealed
lips are not yet u.   Stanley Baldwin 2
unsettled
in their adolescence u.   John Morley 3
unsex
U. me here   Shakespeare 335
unspeakable
u. in pursuit of the uneatable   Wilde 60
unspoken
u. contract of a wife   Hardwick 1
unstoried
still u., artless   Frost 22
unstuck
u. in time   Vonnegut 6
unthought
can never be u.   Dürrenmatt 1
untidy
Freedom's u.   Rumsfeld 9
until
u. we meet again   Liliuokalani 1
untimely
u. ripp'd   Shakespeare 396

variety
her infinite v.   Shakespeare 402
V. is the soul of pleasure   Behn 1
V.'s the very spice of life
                William Cowper 7
various
as you are lovely, so be v.   Graves 1
speaks a v. language
            William Cullen Bryant 2
v. modes of worship   Gibbon 2
vas
V. you dere, Sharlie
            Radio Catchphrases 12
Vassar
reading their poems to V. girls
                Louis Simpson 1
vast
deserts of v. eternity
                Andrew Marvell 12
footnotes to a v. obscure   Nabokov 7
V. chain of Being   Pope 19
v. right-wing conspiracy
                Hillary Clinton 6
v. wasteland   Minow 1
vault
heaven's v. should crack
                Shakespeare 316
vaulting
v. ambition   Shakespeare 343
Vegas
What happens in V.
            Advertising Slogans 70
vegetable
v. love should grow   Andrew Marvell 11
vegetarianism
resolutions in favor of v.   Inge 1
vegetarians
Most v. I ever see   Dunne 7
veil
v. of ignorance   Rawls 3
veiled
So v. and subtle   Sun Tzu 7
vein
not in the giving v.   Shakespeare 4
Velasquez
Why drag in V.   Whistler 7
venal
v. city ripe to perish   Sallust 1
vengeance
V. is mine   Bible 346
veni
V., *vidi, vici*   Julius Caesar 6
venom
Full of a baby's v.   Toni Morrison 4
ventured
Nothing v.   Proverbs 220
Venus
v. entire latched   Racine 4
verb
I am a v.   Ulysses S. Grant 6
v. in his mouth   Twain 42
V. is God   Hugo 5
v. not a noun   R. Buckminster Fuller 1
verbal
v. contract isn't worth   Goldwyn 8
verdict
Sentence first—v. afterwards   Carroll 24
v. was the blue-tail fly
            Folk and Anonymous Songs 8

Vere
God bless Captain V.   Melville 20
verge
v. of her confine   Shakespeare 290
Women on the V.   Almodóvar 1
verify
trust, but v.   Ronald W. Reagan 12
Trust but v.   Modern Proverbs 92
verifying
v. your references   Routh 1
verities
v. and truths   Faulkner 9
Verlaine
I get a little V.   Frank O'Hara 1
vermin
little odious V.   Jonathan Swift 11
Vermont
As Maine goes, so goes V.   Farley 1
verse
All that is not prose is v.   Molière 6
if my V. is alive   Emily Dickinson 16
Writing free v. is like   Frost 18
very
Be afraid. Be v. afraid   Film Lines 78
Bear of V. Little Brain   Milne 5
she was v., v. good   Longfellow 28
tell you about the v. rich
            F. Scott Fitzgerald 36
V. flat, Norfolk   Coward 5
v. model of a modern   W. S. Gilbert 19
v. pink of perfection
                Oliver Goldsmith 9
v. stable genius   Trump 20
V. well, alone   Low 1
vessel
Let the Irish v. lie   Auden 23
unto the weaker v.   Bible 383
vet
if a v. can't catch   Herriot 1
vice
Art is v.   Degas 1
defense of liberty is no v.   Goldwater 3
in principle is always a v.
                Thomas Paine 24
prefer an accommodating v.   Molière 1
too fucking busy and v. versa
                Dorothy Parker 38
tribute which v. pays
            la Rochefoucauld 5
V. and virtue are products   Taine 3
vice-president
never wanted to be v.
                Nelson Rockefeller 1
vice-prisidincy
v. is th' nex' highest   Dunne 16
vices
Never practice two v. at once
                Bankhead 2
v. are v. aped from white   Faulkner 2
victim
Love is the v.'s response   Atkinson 1
refuse to be a v.   Atwood 1
v. of a series of accidents   Vonnegut 2
victims
there were only v.   Trumbo 2
They are its v.   Conrad 23
v. of American fascism
                Ethel Rosenberg 3

victor
No v. believes in chance   Nietzsche 9
v. belong the spoils   Marcy 1
v. belongs to the spoils
            F. Scott Fitzgerald 3
V. Hugo was a madman   Cocteau 2
Victoria
monstrous dwarf Queen V.   Fowles 1
victories
Peace hath her v.   Milton 15
victorious
v. army only enters   Sun Tzu 6
victory
defeat from the jaws of v.   Sayings 18
grave, where is thy v.   Bible 359
in v. unbearable   Winston Churchill 49
knows not v. or defeat
            Theodore Roosevelt 5
no substitute for v.   Eisenhower 3
not the v. but the contest   Coubertin 1
One more such v.   Pyrrhus 1
peace without v.   Woodrow Wilson 13
thrill of v.   Television Catchphrases 3
'twas a famous v.   Southey 5
v. at all costs   Winston Churchill 13
v. has 100 fathers   John F. Kennedy 18
V. has a hundred fathers   Ciano 1
V. or Death   William B. Travis 1
videos
best v. of all time   Kanye West 2
videotapes
gotta return some v.   Brett Easton Ellis 1
Viet Cong
no quarrel with them V.   Ali 4
No V. ever called me "nigger"   Ali 9
Vietnam
avoided serving in V.   Dowd 2
Kissinger brought peace to V.   Heller 7
V. syndrome
            George Herbert Walker Bush 20
V. was lost in the living rooms
                McLuhan 10
V. was the first war   Westmoreland 1
V. was what we had   Herr 2
Vietnams
two, three . . . many V.   Guevara 3
view
motley to the v.   Shakespeare 427
this v. of life   Charles Darwin 6
views
False v., if supported   Charles Darwin 10
vigilance
Eternal v. by the people
                Andrew Jackson 5
liberty to man is eternal v.   Curran 1
vigorous
V. writing is concise   Strunk 1
vilified
most v. and persecuted   Frankfurter 2
village
events in the global v.   McLuhan 4
Global V.   McLuhan 5
image of a global v.   McLuhan 6
It takes a v.   Modern Proverbs 95
one big v.   Wyndham Lewis 1
place for a V.   Batman 1
Some v.-Hampden   Thomas Gray 8
v. explainer   Stein 5
v. smithy stands   Longfellow 7

vulgar
it's v.   Punch 2
vulgarity
One man's v.
    John M. Harlan (1899–1971) 1
vultures
v. got into the presidential palace
                    García Márquez 4

W

Wabash
on the banks of the W.   Dreiser 1
wafer
pasted in the sky like a w.
                    Stephen Crane 3
wag
tail must w. the dog   Kipling 7
wage
give themselves for w.   Yeats 12
I w. war   Clemenceau 1
wager
W. then without hesitation   Pascal 13
what will you w.   Pascal 12
wages
law that governs w.   Lassalle 1
w. is just the same   Twain 30
w. of sin is death   Bible 344
Wagner
W. has lovely moments   Rossini 1
W.'s music   Nye 1
wagon
Hitch your w. to a star
                Ralph Waldo Emerson 50
wags
why the world w.   T. H. White 1
waist
w. deep in the big muddy   Pete Seeger 6
wait
come to those who w.   Proverbs 9
I almost had to w.   Louis XIV 3
I can w.   Franz Liszt 1
learn to labor and to w.   Longfellow 5
Time and tide w.   Proverbs 297
w., there's more   Advertising Slogans 39
w. a few minutes   Twain 150
W. and hope   Dumas the Elder 4
W. till next year   Sayings 58
w. until he has struck
                Franklin D. Roosevelt 24
We shall w. and see   Herbert Asquith 1
who only stand and w.   Milton 53
waited
God w. six thousand years   Kepler 2
waiting
w. for Godot   Beckett 3
w. for rain   T. S. Eliot 21
w. seven hundred years
                    Michael Collins 2
watchful w.   Woodrow Wilson 8
wake
better to w. up   Chopin 2
doomed at last to w.   Samuel Johnson 7
moment I w. up   Hal David 4
till human voices w. us   T. S. Eliot 12
W. up and smell the coffee   Landers 1
w. up for less   Evangelista 1
wakes
w. up the phoenix bird   Anne Baxter 1

waketh
watchman w. but in vain   Bible 120
waking
w. from a troubled dream   Hawthorne 2
Waldo
W. is one of those people   Saki 4
Wales
But for W.   Bolt 3
walk
Catullus w. that way   Yeats 25
Golf is a good w. spoiled   Twain 152
I can w.   Film Lines 3
I can w.!   Film Lines 71
I w. the line   Johnny Cash 2
no possibility of taking a w.
                    Charlotte Brontë 1
roads must a man w. down   Dylan 1
w. a mile for a Camel
                Advertising Slogans 25
w. before we run   Proverbs 317
w. humbly with thy God   Bible 194
w. in the wide, wide world   Lowrey 1
w. lightly on the earth   Barbara Ward 1
W.! Not bloody likely
                George Bernard Shaw 41
W. on the Wild Side   Algren 1
w. on the wild side   Lou Reed 3
w. over my grandmother   Colson 1
w. the deck my Captain lies   Whitman 12
w. through the valley   Bible 109
w. with Kings   Kipling 33
Will you w. into my parlor   Howitt 1
you'll never w. alone   Hammerstein 12
walked
all the way home they w.   Agee 3
Cat That W. by Himself   Kipling 26
she w. like a woman   Ray Davies 1
w. a mile   Modern Proverbs 19
w. among the lowest   T. S. Eliot 53
w. out in the streets of Laredo
                Folk and Anonymous Songs 13
w. through the wilderness   Bunyan 1
walkin'
These boots are made for w.
                    Hazlewood 1
walking
I'm w. here   Film Lines 115
Let your fingers do the w.
                Advertising Slogans 19
more enterprise in w. naked   Yeats 14
w. dictionary   George Chapman 3
walks
She w. in beauty   Byron 7
she w. into mine   Film Lines 43
w. on hallowed ground   Conant 3
wall
backs to the w.   Haig 1
Humpty Dumpty sat on a w.
                    Nursery Rhymes 24
joyousness to a w.
                Pierre-Auguste Renoir 2
Mexico pay for that w.   Trump 4
scratch on that w.   Faulkner 17
show me a 50-foot w.   Napolitano 1
standing like a stone w.   Bee 1
tear down this w.   Ronald W. Reagan 14
that doesn't love a w.   Frost 4
that doesn't love a w.   Frost 2
w. fell down   Bible 74

w. of separation   Jefferson 33
W. St. Lays an Egg   Silverman 1
W. Street indexes predicted
                    Samuelson 1
wallet
What's in your w.
                Advertising Slogans 27
walling
w. in or w. out   Frost 4
walls
Stone w. do not a prison make
                Richard Lovelace 1
w. came tumbling down
            Folk and Anonymous Songs 44
W. have ears   Proverbs 318
world that has w.   Sorkin 2
walrus
I Am the W.   Lennon and McCartney 14
"time has come," the W. said   Carroll 34
Walt
pact with you, W. Whitman
                    Ezra Pound 5
Walter
Secret Life of W. Mitty   Thurber 9
W. Mitty, the undefeated   Thurber 10
waltzing
You'll come a-w., Matilda   Paterson 2
wander
Not all those who w.   Tolkien 9
w. in the wilderness   Bible 67
wandered
w. lonely as a cloud
            William Wordsworth 25
wandering
Poor w. one   W. S. Gilbert 15
W. between two worlds
                Matthew Arnold 2
w. minstrel I   W. S. Gilbert 28
w. on a foreign strand   Walter Scott 2
wanna
If you w. be my lover   Rowbottom 1
want
change you w. to see
                Mohandas Gandhi 7
find out what they w.   Truman 9
For w. of a nail   Proverbs 320
girls just w. to have fun   Hazard 1
I shall not w.   Bible 108
I w. a girl just like the girl Dillon 1
I w. to be alone   Garbo 1
I w. to see you Alexander Graham Bell 1
I W. What I W.   Blossom 1
If you w. anything done   Thatcher 1
If you w. something   Lair 1
If you w. to be happy   De Leon 1
must be in w. of a wife   Austen 6
never w. advocates   Richardson 1
Please, sir, I w. some more   Dickens 15
Waste not, w. not   Proverbs 322
What does a woman w.
                Sigmund Freud 21
You can get anything you w.
                    Arlo Guthrie 1
wanted
I w. simply you   Héloïse 1
W., Dead or Alive   George W. Bush 7
where I w. to go today   Milne 4
wanting
art found w.   Bible 190

wanton
As flies to w. boys   Shakespeare 304
Down, w., down   Graves 3
wants
heart w. what it w.   Woody Allen 42
Man w. but little here below
        Oliver Goldsmith 3
Who W. to Be a Millionaire
        Cole Porter 26
war
All's fair in love and w.   Proverbs 96
Among the calamities of w.
        Samuel Johnson 21
ancestral voices prophesying w.
        Coleridge 21
anyone who wasn't against w.   Low 2
art of w. and its ordering   Machiavelli 4
"cold w." with its neighbors   Orwell 27
country is at w. with Germany
        Chamberlain 3
Dakotas, I am for w.   Red Cloud 1
declared w. upon nature
        Patrick J. Buchanan 1
do in the Great W., Daddy   Lumley 1
Do you want total w.   Goebbels 2
easier to make w.   Clemenceau 2
Either w. is obsolete
        R. Buckminster Fuller 5
enable it to make w.   Weil 1
ever was a just w.   Thomas Paine 13
every morning w. is declared   Proust 8
fatal to enter any w.
        Douglas MacArthur 3
First in w.   "Light-Horse Harry" Lee 1
first w. of the 21st century
        George W. Bush 6
first world w.   Haeckel 2
First World W.   Repington 1
fought a w. against each other
        Thomas L. Friedman 1
France has lost the w.   de Gaulle 1
from an extended w.   Sun Tzu 3
from the w. of nature   Charles Darwin 6
go to w. on behalf   Robeson 2
He kept us out of w.   Glynn 1
I can't go to w.   Rankin 2
I hate w.   Franklin D. Roosevelt 11
I wage w.   Clemenceau 1
I'll furnish the w.   Hearst 1
in every w. they kill you   Will Rogers 14
in the midst of a cold w.   Baruch 2
in w. and in peace   David Davis 1
In w. there is no substitute
        Eisenhower 3
Laws are silent in time of w.   Cicero 11
lead this people into w.
        Woodrow Wilson 24
learn w. any more   Bible 161
let slip the dogs of w.   Shakespeare 107
lives in a state of w.   Jonathan Swift 28
looks on w. as all glory
        William Tecumseh Sherman 4
made this great w.   Lincoln 60
magnificent, but it is not w.   Bosquet 1
Make love not w.   Legman 2
moral equivalent of w.
        William James 13
more than I hate w.   Eisenhower 1
My w. ended   Knowles 1

nation has its w. party
        Robert La Follette 1
never lost a w.   Will Rogers 12
never was a good W.
        Benjamin Franklin 35
no dumb bastard ever won a w.   Patton 3
no less renowned than w.   Milton 15
no more win a w.   Rankin 3
not a w. hero   Trump 6
pattern called a w.   Amy Lowell 2
peaceful people into w.
        Woodrow Wilson 16
prepare for the last w.   Tuchman 1
prepare for w.   Lester Pearson 1
prepare for w.   Vegetius 1
quaint and curious w.
        Thomas Hardy 24
Real W. Will Never Get   Whitman 19
say there has been no w.
        Robert H. Jackson 7
seen the end of w.   Santayana 9
sinews of w.   Cicero 8
splendid little w.   John Hay 2
subject of it is W.   Wilfred Owen 4
such a w. as is of every man   Hobbes 7
they condemn recourse to w.   Briand 1
they'll give a w.   Sandburg 10
This is a phony w.   Daladier 1
This is the W. Room   Film Lines 70
this is w.   Charles Francis Adams 1
This means w.   "Groucho" Marx 22
true w. story   Tim O'Brien 2
tug of w.   Nathaniel Lee 1
W., children, it's just a shot
        Jagger and Richards 13
W. alone brings up   Mussolini 1
W. and Peace   Proudhon 2
W. Between Men and Women
        Thurber 4
w. has used up words   Henry James 26
W. involves in its progress
        Thomas Paine 14
W. is a condition of progress   Renan 1
w. is a necessary part   Moltke 2
W. is a vital matter   Sun Tzu 1
W. is cruelty
        William Tecumseh Sherman 1
W. is hell   Napoleon 11
w. is madness   Updike 4
W. is not healthy   Lorraine Schneider 1
W. IS PEACE   Orwell 35
W. is regarded as nothing   Clausewitz 2
w. is regarded as wicked   Wilde 4
[w.] is so terrible   Robert E. Lee 1
W. is the greatest of all   Orwell 16
W. is the health   Bourne 1
W. is the realm of uncertainty
        Clausewitz 1
w. is the surest   Tocqueville 23
w. is too important   Briand 2
W. is too serious a matter   Clemenceau 4
W. makes rattling good history
        Thomas Hardy 23
w. on poverty   Lyndon B. Johnson 4
W. on the palaces   Chamfort 1
w. situation has developed   Hirohito 1
W. That Will End W.   H. G. Wells 3
w. violates the order   Herodotus 1
w. was always there   Hemingway 7

W. will be won by Blood and Guts
        Patton 1
w. will put an end to mankind
        John F. Kennedy 21
w.'s annals will cloud   Thomas Hardy 27
We . . . make w. that we may live
        Aristotle 4
We still seek no wider w.
        Lyndon B. Johnson 7
when the w. is over   Lehrer 6
worst barbarity of w.   Ellen Key 2
wrong w., at the wrong place
        Omar Bradley 2
wardrobe
w. malfunction   Timberlake 1
wards
W. in Jarndyce   Dickens 89
warfare
W. . . . . is just an invention
        Margaret Mead 3
W. is the art of deceit   Sun Tzu 2
warlike
just w. leaders   Bunche 1
warm
Happiness is a w. puppy   Schulz 2
it was still w.   Sendak 5
pitcher of w. spit   John Nance Garner 1
w. personal gesture   Galbraith 5
Winter kept us w.   T. S. Eliot 40
warmed
glow has w. the world
        Adlai E. Stevenson 14
They w. me twice   Thoreau 27
warn
I w. you not to be ordinary   Kinnock 2
warned
our mothers w. us   Behan 3
Warner
especially Jack W.   Andrews 1
warning
have to be a horrible w.   Aird 1
W.: The Surgeon General
        Anonymous 32
warrant
I signed my death w.   Michael Collins 1
warrior
Happy W. of the political
        Franklin D. Roosevelt 1
Who is the happy W.
        William Wordsworth 7
wars
beginnings of all w.
        Franklin D. Roosevelt 29
diminishing the number of w.   Lecky 2
His Grace returned from the w.
        Marlborough 1
my w. were global   Henry Reed 4
sent into any foreign w.
        Franklin D. Roosevelt 21
Star W.   George Lucas 1
w. and rumors of w.   Bible 259
w. are planned by old men
        Grantland Rice 3
W. of extermination   Ulysses S. Grant 4
w. of the European powers
        James Monroe 1
You plan the w.   Trumbo 1
warts
roughnesses, pimples, w.   Cromwell 3

wash

all come out in the w.	Proverbs 321
Gonna W. That Man	Hammerstein 13
I w. off	Sexton 6
w. the balm off	Shakespeare 19
w. this blood clean	Shakespeare 357

washed

I just w. my hair	Film Lines 41
Life is w.	Barzun 2
they w. me out of the turret	Jarrell 1
w. a rental car	Peters 1
w. his hands	Bible 272

washes

One hand w. the other	Proverbs 134

Washington

George W. slept here	Moss Hart 2
Government at W. still lives	Garfield 2
W.—First in war	Charles Dryden 1
W. is full of famous men	
	Fanny Dixwell Holmes 1
W. was a city of Northern	
	John F. Kennedy 22

waste

Don't w. any time mourning	Joe Hill 2
doth time w. me	Shakespeare 24
Haste makes w.	Proverbs 137
how to w. space	Philip C. Johnson 2
lay w. our powers	
	William Wordsworth 21
mind is a terrible thing to w.	
	Advertising Slogans 120
W. not, want not	Proverbs 322
w. that is commmon	Veblen 3
What a w. it is	Quayle 2

wasted

chronicle of w. time	Shakespeare 426
I have w. my life	James Wright 1

wasteland

teenage w.	Townshend 3
vast w.	Minow 1

watch

ef you don't w. out	Riley 1
I like to w.	Kosinski 1
Just w. me	Trudeau 2
my w. has stopped	"Groucho" Marx 28
son of a bitch stole my w.	Hecht 1
w. along the Rhine	Schneckenburger 1
w. must have had a maker	Paley 3
w. the men at play	Cleghorn 1
W. the skies	Film Lines 173
w. the world burn	Film Lines 59
W. what we do	John N. Mitchell 1
why not carry a w.	Tree 1
You better w. out	Gillespie 1

watched

w. pot never boils	Proverbs 323

watcher

posted presence of the w.	
	Henry James 18
until the W. turns his eyes	Hurston 2
w. of the skies	Keats 3

watches

Dictionaries are like w.	
	Samuel Johnson 40

watchful

w. waiting	Woodrow Wilson 8

watching

BIG BROTHER IS W. YOU	Orwell 34
I'll be w. you	Sting 3

their eyes were w. God	Hurston 5
whole world is w.	Political Slogans 37

watchmaker

blind w.	Dawkins 4

watchman

W., what of the night	Bible 169
w. waketh but in vain	Bible 120

water

Blood's thicker than w.	Proverbs 31
bridge over troubled w.	Paul Simon 8
don't drink the w.	Lehrer 4
don't go near the w.	Nursery Rhymes 46
fetch a pail of w.	Nursery Rhymes 26
I don't drink w.	W. C. Fields 26
it is contained in w.	Eiseley 1
lead a horse to w.	Proverbs 148
live on food and w.	W. C. Fields 15
name was writ in w.	Keats 24
no w. but only rock	T. S. Eliot 56
Oil and w. don't mix	Proverbs 222
reached the calm of w.	Henry Adams 7
safe to go back in the w.	
	Advertising Slogans 64
softer and weaker than w.	Lao Tzu 11
swimming under w.	
	F. Scott Fitzgerald 52
This is w.	David Foster Wallace 10
virtues we write in w.	Shakespeare 453
W., w., everywhere	Coleridge 6
w. never formed to mind	
	Wallace Stevens 10
w. up to his knees	"Groucho" Marx 44
w. was clear and swiftly moving	
	Hemingway 8

waterbeetle

w. here shall teach	Belloc 2

waterfalls

Don't go chasing w.	Lopes 1

waterfront

I Cover the W.	Max Miller 1

Watergate

President know about W.	
	Howard Baker 2

Waterloo

Battle of W. was won	Wellington 8
W.! W.!	Hugo 4

waters

Cast thy bread upon the w.	Bible 151
Father of W.	Lincoln 39
Still w. run deep	Proverbs 284
Stolen w. are sweet	Bible 126

watery

some w. tart	Monty Python 11

Watson

Elementary, my dear W.	
	Arthur Conan Doyle 39
Good old W.	Arthur Conan Doyle 37
Mr. W.—come here	
	Alexander Graham Bell 1
You know my methods, W.	
	Arthur Conan Doyle 24

Watteau

sky where W. hung	
	William Carlos Williams 3

wave

as w. follows upon w.	H. A. L. Fisher 1
I made the w.	Rutherford 5
in peace may you w.	Cohan 3

W. of the Future	
	Anne Morrow Lindbergh 1

wavering

W. between the profit	T. S. Eliot 84

waves

Don't make w.	Modern Proverbs 56
rule the w.	James Thomson 1

waving

not w. but drowning	Stevie Smith 4

way

All the w. with LBJ	Political Slogans 2
ask that your w. be long	Cavafy 3
broad is the w.	Bible 226
cried all the w. to the bank	Liberace 2
I am the w.	Bible 325
I did it my w.	Anka 1
in harm's w.	John Paul Jones 1
It's a long w. to Tipperary	Judge 1
kind to everyone on the w. up	Mizner 1
lambs who've lost our w.	Kipling 9
laughed all the w.	Liberace 1
Love will find a w.	Proverbs 181
Middle W. is none at all	John Adams 6
narrow is the w.	Bible 227
No w.?! W.!	Television Catchphrases 67
Not the w. I play it	W. C. Fields 13
on the w. to the White House	
	Adlai E. Stevenson 8
only w. to have a friend	
	Ralph Waldo Emerson 10
parting of the w.	Bible 187
Peace is the w.	Muste 1
same people on the w. down	Mizner 1
shall not pass this w.	Grellet 1
that w. madness lies	Shakespeare 295
that's the w. it is	
	Television Catchphrases 13
there's a w.	Proverbs 327
W. down upon the Swanee River	
	Stephen Foster 3
W. of our Master	Confucius 5
w. of truth and love	Mohandas Gandhi 8
w. the ball bounces	Modern Proverbs 5
w. to a man's heart	Proverbs 324
w. to London town	Nursery Rhymes 35
w. to skin a cat	Proverbs 325
w. to the stars	Virgil 11

ways

can't have it both w.	Modern Proverbs 8
Just are the w. of God	Milton 49
justify the w. of God	Milton 18
Let me count the w.	
	Elizabeth Barrett Browning 2
w. of making men talk	Film Lines 110

wayside

seeds fell by the w.	Bible 239

wayward

W. sisters, depart in peace	
	Winfield Scott 1

we

W. (that's my ship and I)	
	Charles Lindbergh 1
W., the peoples	Anonymous 35
W. are all Republicans	Jefferson 31
w. are here as on a darkling plain	
	Matthew Arnold 19
W. are not amused	Victoria 3
W. few, w. happy few	Shakespeare 138
w. got him	Bremer 1

we (cont.):
W. hold these truths   Jefferson 2
W. must love one another   Auden 13
w. shall not be moved
          Folk and Anonymous Songs 81
w. shall overcome   Pete Seeger 5
W. the People   Constitution 1
W. the people   Barbara C. Jordan 1
W. will not tire   George W. Bush 8
we're
W. here because w. here
          Folk and Anonymous Songs 80
W. in the money   Dubin 3
W. on a mission from God
                              Film Lines 26
weader
Tonstant W. Fwowed up
                        Dorothy Parker 18
weak
body of a w. and feeble   Elizabeth I 2
courage is w.   Benjamin Franklin 5
flesh is w.   Bible 270
w. minds be carried   Coleridge 24
w. piping time of peace   Shakespeare 2
weaken
great life if you don't w.   Buchan 1
weaker
unto the w. vessel   Bible 383
w. side inclined
          Samuel Butler (1612–1680) 1
weakest
w. link   Proverbs 43
You are the w. link
          Television Catchphrases 84
wealth
He does not possess w.
                       Benjamin Franklin 8
I'm a man of w. and taste
                   Jagger and Richards 9
love of w.   Tocqueville 20
malefactors of great w.
                    Theodore Roosevelt 17
private w. I should decline   Santayana 7
Surplus w. is a sacred trust
                        Andrew Carnegie 2
w. accumulates   Oliver Goldsmith 7
w. concentrated in the hands
                             Brandeis 12
wealthiest
w. man in the cemetery   Wynn 1
wealthy
healthy, w., and wise   Proverbs 81
very w. man   John W. Sterling 1
weaned
w. on a pickle   Alice Longworth 1
weapon
As crude a w.   Rachel Carson 2
his w. wit   Anthony Hope 1
most potent w.   Biko 1
weapons
books are w.   Franklin D. Roosevelt 26
wear
better w. out   Richard Cumberland 1
girls who w. glasses   Dorothy Parker 7
I shall w. purple   Jenny Joseph 1
I w. the chain I forged   Dickens 41
If the shoe fits, w. it   Proverbs 269
w. nothing at all   Advertising Slogans 46

w. my heart upon my sleeve
                           Shakespeare 258
w. the bottoms of my trousers
                             T. S. Eliot 10
w. the gold hat   F. Scott Fitzgerald 6
w. the mask   Dunbar 1
wearin'
w. of the Green
          Folk and Anonymous Songs 78
wearing
W. all that weight   Tennyson 34
wears
head that w. a crown   Shakespeare 64
weary
flesh is w.   Mallarmé 4
Got the W. Blues   Langston Hughes 4
How w., stale, flat   Shakespeare 150
men grow w.   Benjamin Franklin 3
No rest for the w.   Proverbs 213
w. of the existing government
                             Lincoln 29
weasel
Pop Goes the W.
          Folk and Anonymous Songs 62
w. under the cocktail   Pinter 1
w. words   Theodore Roosevelt 26
weasels
ice w. come   Groening 9
weather
Grant us fair w.   James O'Neill 1
If you don't like the w.   Twain 150
It's always fair w.   Hovey 1
mistaken for fair w.   Twain 153
New England w.   Twain 18
Stormy w.   Koehler 2
talked about the w.   Twain 145
w. turned around   Dylan Thomas 13
You don't need a w. man   Dylan 18
weave
W., w. the sunlight   T. S. Eliot 2
w. the web of life   Ted Perry 1
what a tangled web we w.   Walter Scott 5
weaves
Analytical Engine w.
                 Countess of Lovelace 2
web
Caught in the W. of Words
                   K. M. Elisabeth Murray 1
kind to your w.-footed friends
          Folk and Anonymous Songs 5
tears a seamless w.   Maitland 1
weave the w. of life   Ted Perry 5
what a tangled w.   Walter Scott 5
Webster
Daniel W. struck me   Sydney Smith 8
in the mouth of Mr. W.
                    Ralph Waldo Emerson 36
W. was much possessed   T. S. Eliot 18
wed
I thee w.   Book of Common Prayer 18
wedded
that I have w. fyve   Chaucer 17
wedding
bridegroom on a w. cake
                       Alice Longworth 2
w.-cake left out in the rain   Auden 44
wee
W. Willie Winkie   Nursery Rhymes 75

weeds
oozy w. about me twist   Melville 21
smell far worse than w.
                           Shakespeare 425
week
greatest w. in the history
                          Richard Nixon 7
he had to die in my w.   Joplin 4
If you give me a w.   Eisenhower 9
That Was the W. That Was   Bird 1
w. is a long time   Harold Wilson 3
weekend
Lost W.   Charles Jackson 1
weekends
try getting a plumber on w.
                            Woody Allen 3
weep
Do not stand at my grave and w.   Frye 1
he should w. for her   Shakespeare 186
I w. for Adonais   Percy Shelley 13
laugh or w. at the folly   Gibbon 8
weepers
losers w.   Proverbs 103
weeping
I seem to hear a child w.   Will Dyson 1
w. and gnashing of teeth   Bible 231
weeps
only animal that laughs and w.   Hazlitt 3
w. at a nude by Michael Angelo
                             MacLeish 1
while my guitar gently w.
                      George Harrison 1
weigh
If you cannot w., measure   Fleay 1
weighed
could not be w., measured   Dickens 92
Thou art w. in the balances   Bible 190
weight
entire w. of the universe   Le Guin 7
pull his w.   Theodore Roosevelt 10
w. of this sad time   Shakespeare 320
weird
W. Sisters   Shakespeare 325
w. turn pro   Hunter S. Thompson 5
welcome
I bid you w.   Stoker 1
Love bade me w.   George Herbert 4
they're not w.   Maxine Waters 1
w. the coming   Pope 9
well
All's w. that ends w.   Proverbs 326
between the sick and the w.
                     F. Scott Fitzgerald 25
foolish thing w. done
                      Samuel Johnson 73
He is w. paid   Shakespeare 82
in whom I am w. pleased   Bible 201
is worth doing w.   Chesterfield 2
Leave w. enough alone   Proverbs 166
loved not wisely, but too w.
                           Shakespeare 282
pitcher will go to the w.   Proverbs 233
W. done, thou good and faithful
                              Bible 262
w. of English undefiled   Spenser 6
W. of Loneliness   Radclyffe Hall 1
"w.-rounded man"   F. Scott Fitzgerald 13
w.-written Life   Thomas Carlyle 1
worth doing w.   Proverbs 76

well-behaved
W. women seldom make   Ulrich 1
wells
w. of English undefiled
                    Samuel Johnson 6
Weltschmerz
W.   Jean Paul 1
wench
besides, the w. is dead   Marlowe 3
went
as cooks go, she w.   Saki 2
wept
Caesar hath w.   Shakespeare 115
Jesus w.   Bible 322
Ralph w. for the end   Golding 1
we w., when we remembered   Bible 122
werewolves
w. of London   Zevon 1
West
decline of the W.   Spengler 1
gardens of the W.   Cyril Connolly 4
Go W., young man   Greeley 2
story of the W.   F. Scott Fitzgerald 29
W. is W.   Kipling 6
where the W. begins   Arthur Chapman 1
where the W. commences
                       Cole Porter 18
western
All quiet on the W. Front   Remarque 1
great w. myth   Robert Harris 2
Playboy of the W. World   Synge 2
W. wind, when will thou blow
                       Anonymous 33
Westminster
peerage, or W. Abbey   Horatio Nelson 3
westward
But w., look, the land   Clough 2
W. the course of empire   Berkeley 3
wet
out of this w. suit   Benchley 6
petals on a w., black bough
                       Ezra Pound 4
we were w.   McCourt 2
whacks
gave her mother forty w.   Anonymous 18
whale
chase that white w.   Melville 5
grand Leap of the W.
                    Benjamin Franklin 32
very like a w.   Shakespeare 208
whales
Save the W.   Political Slogans 30
whaleship
w. was my Yale College   Melville 4
wham
W. bam thank you   Sayings 59
whan
W. that Aprill   Chaucer 6
whassup
W.   Advertising Slogans 22
what
lack of w. is found
                 William Carlos Williams 6
not w. you know   Modern Proverbs 47
W. a drag it is getting old
                  Jagger and Richards 5
W. a dump   Film Lines 20
W. a glorious morning
                    Samuel Adams 2

W. are little boys made of   Southey 7
w. big ears you have
                    Grimm and Grimm 2
w. can I do for her   Briggs 1
w. can the matter be
                Folk and Anonymous Songs 57
W. did the President know
                      Howard Baker 2
W. does a woman want
                     Sigmund Freud 21
W. goes around   Modern Proverbs 35
W. good is a new-born baby
                   Benjamin Franklin 42
W. happens to a dream deferred
                     Langston Hughes 8
W. hath God wrought   Bible 68
W. HAVE I DONE   Byrne 2
w. immortal hand or eye
                     William Blake 10
W. instruments we have   Auden 18
W. Is to Be Done   Chernyshevsky 1
W. kind of fool am I
                 Bricusse and Newley 1
W. larks   Dickens 102
W. Makes Sammy Run   Schulberg 1
W.—me worry   Kurtzman 1
w. price glory   Maxwell Anderson 1
w. shall it profit a man   Bible 278
W. the world needs now   Hal David 2
w. they fought each other for   Southey 4
W. thou lovest well remains
                      Ezra Pound 24
w.'s a heaven for   Robert Browning 13
w.'s done is done   Shakespeare 365
W.'s it all about Alfie   Hal David 3
W.'s love got to do   Britten 1
W.'s up, Doc   Avery 1
W.'ve you got   Film Lines 188
whatever
W. Gets You Thru the Night   Lennon 12
W. is, is right   Bentham 9
W. is worth doing   Chesterfield 2
w. that may mean
                Charles, Prince of Wales 1
wheel
bound upon a w. of fire
                    Shakespeare 310
breaks a butterfly upon a w.   Pope 33
my queer shoulder to the w.   Ginsberg 6
red w. barrow
                 William Carlos Williams 2
squeaky w. gets the grease   Billings 2
w. in the middle of a w.   Bible 185
w. is come full circle   Shakespeare 315
w. of fortune goes 'round
                  Radio Catchphrases 19
w. that does the squeaking   Billings 2
wheels
Money . . . is none of the w.
                      David Hume 6
wheelwork
very w. of nature   Tesla 1
when
if not now, w.   Hillel 1
W. angry, count four   Twain 64
W. Earth's last picture is painted
                       Kipling 14
W. I am dead, my dearest   Rossetti 5
W. I am dead and opened   Mary I 1

w. I die   Nyro 1
W. I fall in love   Heyman 2
W. I have fears   Keats 7
W. I hear the word "culture"   Johst 1
W. I was a lad   W. S. Gilbert 8
W. in doubt, win the trick
                     Edmond Hoyle 1
W. in doubt have a man
                   Raymond Chandler 11
W. in Rome   Proverbs 258
W. in the Course   Jefferson 3
W. Irish eyes are smiling   Olcott 1
W. Johnny comes marching home
                   Patrick S. Gilmore 1
W. lilacs last   Whitman 18
W. lovely woman stoops to folly
                   Oliver Goldsmith 6
W. the first baby laughed   Barrie 5
W. the foeman bares his steel
                      W. S. Gilbert 21
w. the kissing had to stop
                   Robert Browning 17
w. the saints come marchin' in
                Folk and Anonymous Songs 82
w. the wind blows   Nursery Rhymes 1
W. you call me that   Wister 2
W. you care enough to send
                  Advertising Slogans 58
W. you're hot, you're hot
                   Modern Proverbs 43
w. you're smiling   Goodwin 1
where
W. are the snows   Villon 1
W. did I go right   Mel Brooks 8
W. do the noses go   Hemingway 22
W. does she find them
                    Dorothy Parker 32
W. have all the cowboys gone
                       Paula Cole 1
W. have all the flowers gone
                      Pete Seeger 4
W. have you gone, Joe DiMaggio
                      Paul Simon 7
w. ignorance is bliss   Thomas Gray 1
W. is everybody   Fermi 2
W. is that coming from   Berra 1
w. no one has gone before   Killian 1
w. the money is   Sutton 1
W. there is no vision   Bible 137
W.'s the beef   Advertising Slogans 132
W.'s the beef   Mondale 1
W.'s the rest of me   Bellamann 1
wherefore
w. art thou Romeo   Shakespeare 33
wherever
W. Macdonald sits
                 Ralph Waldo Emerson 5
which
w. way the wind is   Selden 2
whiff
w. of grapeshot   Thomas Carlyle 3
Whig
Tory men and W. men   Disraeli 9
while
rosebuds w. ye may   Herrick 3
w. my guitar gently weeps
                    George Harrison 1
whimper
not with a bang but a w.   T. S. Eliot 67

whip
Do not forget the w.   Nietzsche 16
whipping
W. and abuse are like   Stowe 3
who shall scape w.   Shakespeare 184
whips
w. and scorns of time   Shakespeare 190
whipstock
w. on the dashboard   Robert S. Lynd 1
whirligig
w. of time   Shakespeare 245
whirlwind
they shall reap the w.   Bible 192
whiskers
if you let your w. grow   Bedell 1
whiskey
Gimme a w.   Film Lines 11
Gimme a w.   Eugene O'Neill 3
whiskies
eighteen straight w.   Dylan Thomas 22
whisky
where he gets his w.   Lincoln 65
whispering
w. of the dream   Gibran 1
whispers
When Duty w. low
                       Ralph Waldo Emerson 46
whistle
shrimp learns to w.   Khrushchev 1
w. a happy tune   Hammerstein 21
W. While You Work   Morey 4
You know how to w.   Film Lines 177
Whistler
W. always spelt art   Wilde 122
W. himself entirely concurs   Wilde 2
W.'s ideas about art   Wilde 101
white
blue-eyed devil w. man   Fard 1
chase that w. whale   Melville 5
considered a W. Negro   Mailer 1
dreaming of a w. Christmas
                              Irving Berlin 10
eaten by those w. men   Equiano 1
fat w. woman   Frances Cornford 1
fleece was w. as snow   Sara Hale 1
forged in the w. heat   Harold Wilson 2
gotta say this for the w. race
                            Dick Gregory 2
life of w. men is slavery   Sitting Bull 1
may all your Christmases be w.
                              Irving Berlin 11
no rights which the w. man   Taney 2
no whitewash at the W. House
                            Richard Nixon 13
on the way to the W. House
                         Adlai E. Stevenson 8
so-called w. races   Forster 4
So the w. people did   Rhys 1
stupid w. men   Michael Moore 1
take back the W. House   Howard Dean 1
There was a w. horse   Helprin 1
whale's w. hump   Melville 7
w., clear w.   Kipling 10
w. cliffs of Dover   Nat Burton 1
W. Goddess   Graves 6
W. Hope   Sackler 1
w. in the blood of the Lamb   Bible 393
w. intruders become more   Tecumseh 2
w. is black   Ignatius 1

W. is Black   Jonathan Swift 14
W. Man's burden   Kipling 25
W. Men Can't Jump   Ron Shelton 1
w. men cheat black men   Harper Lee 5
w. paper, void of all   John Locke 2
w. race is the cancer   Sontag 2
whited
W. sepulchres   Bible 258
whites
w. of their eyes   Putnam 1
whitewash
bucket of w.   Twain 15
no w. at the White House
                            Richard Nixon 13
whither
W. goest thou   Bible 327
W. thou goest   Bible 81
Whitman
pact with you, Walt W.   Ezra Pound 5
Whittington
Turn again, W.   Ballads 3
whiz
w. of a Wiz   Harburg 7
who
It's w. you know   Woody Allen 7
I've been in W.'s W.   Mae West 21
then again, w. does   Film Lines 25
W. am I   Stockdale 1
w. am I to judge him   Francis 1
W. are those guys   Film Lines 38
w. gets what   Lasswell 1
W. is John Galt   Rand 5
w. is to guard the guards   Juvenal 3
W. killed Cock Robin
                          Nursery Rhymes 12
W. knows what evil lurks
                        Radio Catchphrases 20
W. Let the Dogs Out   Anselm Douglas 1
W. loves ya, baby
                   Television Catchphrases 39
W. masters whom   Lenin 8
W. sent you to me   Puccini 1
W. the hell are you   Groening 4
W. Wants to Be a Millionaire
                             Cole Porter 26
W. was that masked man
                        Radio Catchphrases 18
w. you know   Modern Proverbs 47
W.'s Afraid of the Big Bad Wolf
                          Frank E. Churchill 1
W.'s afraid of Virginia Woolf   Albee 2
W.'s on first   Abbott and Costello 1
whole
before the w. world   Molière 9
half is greater than the w.   Hesiod 1
light of a w. life   Bourdillon 2
Photograph of the W. Earth   Brand 1
That is the w. Torah   Hillel 2
'Tis woman's w. existence   Byron 20
w. against the sky   Rilke 1
w. earth one stain of guilt   Hawthorne 1
w. is not, as it were, a mere   Aristotle 1
w. is that which has beginning
                            Aristotle 6
w. world in his hands
                Folk and Anonymous Songs 34
w. world is watching Political Slogans 37
w. world smiles with you   Goodwin 1
w. world stills to listen   McCullough 1

wholesale
w. libel on a Yale prom
                            Dorothy Parker 47
whom
for w. the bell tolls   Donne 5
"W. are you?" he asked   Ade 1
W. the gods wish   Cyril Connolly 2
whoopee
Makin' W.   Gus Kahn 7
whooshing
I like the w. sound   Douglas Adams 12
whopper
give birth to a w.   Grass 2
whore
lead a w. to culture   Dorothy Parker 39
morals of a w.   Samuel Johnson 45
Protestant w.   Gwyn 1
'tis pity she's a w.   John Ford 1
Treat a w. like a lady   Mizner 11
woman's a w.   Samuel Johnson 76
whorehouses
territory out here for w.   Capone 2
whores
parliament of w.   O'Rourke 2
w. in everything but name   Polly Adler 2
why
I say "W. not?" George Bernard Shaw 45
theirs not to reason w.   Tennyson 39
W., O w., O w.-o   Comden and Green 3
W. a duck   "Groucho" Marx 3
W. am I here   Stockdale 1
W. are you not here   Thoreau 39
w. hast thou forsaken me   Bible 274
W. is this night different   Talmud 4
w. not the best   "Jimmy" Carter 1
w. then oh w. can't I   Harburg 5
wicked
end my w. deeds   L. Frank Baum 5
something w. this way   Shakespeare 377
unto the w.   Bible 174
W. Witch is dead   Harburg 2
worse than w.   Punch 2
wickedness
destroy my beautiful w.   Film Lines 193
dwell in the tents of w.   Bible 115
quite capable of every w.   Conrad 24
spiritual w. in high places   Bible 368
W. is a myth   Wilde 65
wicket
flannelled fools at the w.   Kipling 29
wide
Alone on a w. w. sea   Coleridge 10
eyes w. open   Benjamin Franklin 18
I am very w.   Balzac 3
w. and starry sky
                    Robert Louis Stevenson 21
W. is the gate   Bible 226
walk in the w., w. world   Lowrey 1
widening
turning in the w. gyre   Yeats 29
wider
We still seek no w. war
                        Lyndon B. Johnson 7
widget
We're in the w. business
                       George S. Kaufman 1
widow
Molly Stark is a w.   John Stark 2

wiener
I wish I were an Oscar Mayer w.
    Advertising Slogans 96

wife
all the World, and his W.
    Jonathan Swift 32
any w. has left any husband
    Anthony Powell 1
as a w. is   Mill 22
Caesar's w. must be above suspicion
    Julius Caesar 3
Come, be my w.   Schreiner 2
his w. could eat no lean
    Nursery Rhymes 30
his w. is beautiful   Mencken 45
I have a w.   Lucan 3
I have been your doll w.   Ibsen 5
If ever w. was happy   Bradstreet 2
if Laura had been Petrarch's w. Byron 24
kill a w. with kindness   Shakespeare 9
man lay down his w.   Joyce 21
Medicine is my lawful w.   Chekhov 1
Mistook His W. for a Hat   Sacks 1
must be in want of a w.   Austen 6
my w.'s bottom   Nicholas Longworth 1
never make a pretty woman your w.
    De Leon 1
she's my w.   Joseph Weber 1
Take my w. . . . please   Youngman 1
Thane of Fife had a w. Shakespeare 386
till he gets him a w.   Craik 2
unspoken contract of a w.   Hardwick 1
w., as unto the weaker vessel Bible 383
W. and Servant are the same
    Chudleigh 2
w. for breed   Gay 1
w. represents the proletariat Engels 3

wild
Always do that, w. ducks   Ibsen 22
born to be w.   Bonfire 2
Born to Be W.   Edmonton 1
Call of the W.   London 1
How w. it was   Strayed 1
into the w. blue yonder
    Robert Crawford 1
just w. about Harry   Sissle 1
Let the w. rumpus start   Sendak 3
Making contact with this W. Man Bly 2
season for w. oats   Wharton 6
Walk on the W. Side   Algren 1
walk on the w. side   Lou Reed 3
Where the W. Things Are   Sendak 2
w. and crazy guys
    Television Catchphrases 65
W. horses couldn't drag me
    Jagger and Richards 16
w. justice   Francis Bacon 17
with a w. surmise   Keats 3

Wilde
Oscar W. posing as Somdomite
    Marquess of Queensberry 1

wilder
w. shores of love   Blanch 1

wilderness
As I walked through the w. Bunyan 1
crying in the w.   Bible 199
him that crieth in the w.   Bible 172
unredeemed w.   Muir 2
wander in the w.   Bible 67

wildness
W. is the preservation   Thoreau 37

wiles
man of many w.   Pope 8

wilkommen
W.! Bienvenue! Welcome!   Ebb 3

will
Danger, W. Robinson
    Television Catchphrases 41
good w.   Kant 2
His w. is our peace   Dante 12
Man cannot w.   Sartre 7
Not my w., but thine   Bible 305
optimism of the w.   Rolland 1
our peace in His w.   T. S. Eliot 87
peace, good w. toward men Bible 290
Thy w. be done   Bible 215
thy w. be done   Missal 5
we know our w. is free
    Samuel Johnson 61
Where there's a w.   Proverbs 327
W. to Power   Nietzsche 28
without the w. to win it
    Douglas MacArthur 3

willful
little group of w. men
    Woodrow Wilson 14

William
You are old, Father W.   Carroll 9
You are old, Father W.   Southey 2

Willie
W. Mays and W. Shakespeare
    Bankhead 7
Wee W. Winkie   Nursery Rhymes 75

willin'
Barkis is w.   Dickens 57

willing
Coalitions of the w. Harlan Cleveland 2
spirit indeed is w.   Bible 270
w. to believe   Julius Caesar 2

Willis
What'chu talkin' 'bout, W.
    Television Catchphrases 16

willow
sang "W., titwillow"   W. S. Gilbert 45
sing w., w., w.   Shakespeare 279

win
do we get to w. this time Film Lines 144
Games in which all may w. Melville 19
Giants w. the pennant   Hodges 1
Joy, we w.   Pheidippides 1
no more w. a war   Rankin 3
play to w. the game Herman Edwards 1
Those who hate you don't w.
    Richard Nixon 17
unless they w. along with it
    Hawthorne 9
w. a few, you lose a few
    Modern Proverbs 97
w. just one for the Gipper   Gipp 1
w. the trick   Edmond Hoyle 1
without the will to w. it
    Douglas MacArthur 3
You can't w.   Sayings 67
You can't w. them all
    Modern Proverbs 98

wind
agitate a bag of w. Andrew D. White 1
blow, thou winter w.   Shakespeare 92

blowin' in the w.   Dylan 2
chill w. blows   Blackmun 3
gone in the w.   Mangan 1
gone with the w.   Dowson 2
gone with the w. Margaret Mitchell 4
ill w. that blows   Proverbs 154
inherit the w.   Bible 127
like a candle in the w.
    John and Taupin 1
moved about like the w. Geronimo 1
solidity to pure w.   Orwell 31
twist slowly, slowly in the w.
    Ehrlichman 3
Western w., when will Anonymous 33
when the w. blows Nursery Rhymes 1
which way the w. blows   Dylan 18
which way the w. is   Selden 2
w. and the rain   Shakespeare 246
w. be ever at your back Anonymous 19
w. of change is blowing Macmillan 2
w. that blows through me
    D. H. Lawrence 1

windmills
tilt against w.   Cervantes 2

window
broken w. pane Emmeline Pankhurst 3
love flies out of the w.   Proverbs 240
smallest fact is a w.   T. H. Huxley 2
that doggie in the w.   Bob Merrill 1
through yonder w.   Shakespeare 32

windows
library doesn't need w.   Brand 3
w. of the soul   Proverbs 94

winds
Blow w.   Shakespeare 292
w. that would blow   Bolt 2

wine
days of w. and roses   Dowson 3
I never drink . . . w.   Film Lines 66
Jug of W.   Edward FitzGerald 8
new w. into old bottles   Bible 234
red w. of Shiraz   Dinesen 1
sell no w. before its time
    Advertising Slogans 99
Use a little w.   Bible 375
W., dear boy, and truth   Alcaeus 1
w., woman, and song   Luther 4
w.-dark sea   Homer 9
W. maketh merry   Bible 150

wing
Bird is on the W. Edward FitzGerald 2
on a W. and a Pray'r   Adamson 1
word takes w. beyond recall Horace 13

winged
he addressed her w. words Homer 2
time's w. chariot Andrew Marvell 12

wings
angel gets his w.   Film Lines 98
God's chillun got-a w.
    Folk and Anonymous Songs 1
great w. beating still   Yeats 42
On W. of Song   Heine 2
w. are no longer w. to fly T. S. Eliot 78
w. of the dove   Byron 6

wink
as good as a w.   Proverbs 215
great w. of eternity   Hart Crane 1
w., w.   Monty Python 2

winner
And the w. is   Television Catchphrases 5
w. never quits   Modern Proverbs 72
winning
intellectual on the w. side   Havel 2
w. every second   Sheen 1
W. isn't everything   Lombardi 1
W. isn't everything
    Modern Proverbs 99
W. isn't everything   "Red" Sanders 1
wins
quitter never w.   Modern Proverbs 72
steady w. the race   Proverbs 274
Winston
W. tastes good   Advertising Slogans 135
winter
blow, thou w. wind   Shakespeare 92
English w.   Byron 32
hazy shade of w.   Paul Simon 3
If W. comes   Percy Shelley 4
In the midst of w.   Camus 7
In w. I get up
    Robert Louis Stevenson 12
long w. evenings   Raymond Chandler 1
such a w. in all your life   Twain 20
W., spring, summer, or fall
    Carole King 2
w. evening settles down   T. S. Eliot 14
W. is coming   George R. R. Martin 1
w. is forbidden till December
    Alan Jay Lerner 16
W. is icumen in   Ezra Pound 8
W. kept us warm   T. S. Eliot 40
w. of our discontent   Shakespeare 1
w.'s rains and ruins   Swinburne 2
winters
sixty or more w.   Yeats 38
wipe
God shall w. away all tears   Bible 394
God shall w. away all tears   Bible 399
wire
No w. hangers   Joan Crawford 1
wireless
When w. is perfectly applied   Tesla 3
wire-tapping
when compared with w.   Brandeis 7
wisdom
all men's w.   John Russell 3
beginning of w.   Bible 119
conventional w.   Galbraith 2
ends in w.   Frost 20
knowledge becomes w.   Stoll 1
little w. the world is governed
    Oxenstierna 1
more than one kind of w.   Yourcenar 2
price of w. is above rubies   Bible 102
Strength and w. are not opposing
    William Jefferson "Bill" Clinton 12
to grow in w.   Charles W. Eliot 1
W. cannot be passed on   Hesse 3
W. hath builded her house   Bible 125
W. is higher than a fool   Wheatley 3
W. is oft-times nearer
    William Wordsworth 24
w. of the head   Dickens 91
w. to choose correctly   Woody Allen 34
w. we have lost in knowledge
    T. S. Eliot 90

wise
healthy, wealthy, and w.   Proverbs 81
nor ever did a w. one   Rochester 4
Penny w. and pound foolish
    Proverbs 232
'tis folly to be w.   Thomas Gray 1
To be w. and love   Shakespeare 248
w. and good in slavery
    Thomas Macaulay 3
w. and the honest can repair
    George Washington 10
w. as serpents   Bible 236
w. child that knows   Proverbs 328
w. father that knows his own
    Shakespeare 74
w. Latina woman   Sotomayor 1
W. men fish here   Steloff 1
w. men from the east   Bible 196
w.-cracking is simply calisthenics
    Dorothy Parker 34
word is enough for the w.   Plautus 4
wisely
loved not w., but too well
    Shakespeare 282
Nations do behave w.   Eban 1
wiser
French are w. than they seem
    Francis Bacon 20
not the w. grow   Pomfret 1
sadder and a w. man   Coleridge 15
Spaniards seem w.   Francis Bacon 20
things I am w. to know   Dorothy Parker 5
wisest
w., brightest, meanest   Pope 27
w. and most upright man   Plato 4
wish
as we would w. our friends   Aristotle 12
Be careful what you w. for
    Modern Proverbs 14
believe what they w.   Julius Caesar 2
I w. I was in de land   Emmett 1
I w. I were an Oscar Mayer wiener
    Advertising Slogans 96
I w. it were impossible
    Samuel Johnson 107
Thy w. was father   Shakespeare 66
When you w. upon a star
    Ned Washington 2
wished
Much w., hoped little   Tartt 1
None ever w. it longer
    Samuel Johnson 37
w. for in youth   Goethe 15
wishes
all your saved-up w.   Elizabeth Bowen 4
If w. were horses   Proverbs 329
wit
Brevity is the soul of w.   Shakespeare 174
cause that w. is   Shakespeare 61
his weapon w.   Anthony Hope 1
In w., a man   Pope 17
One man's w.   John Russell 3
only a w. among Lords
    Samuel Johnson 46
Staircase w.   Diderot 3
W. has truth in it   Dorothy Parker 34
W. will shine   John Dryden 7
witch
Aroynt thee, w.   Shakespeare 323

I'm not a w.   Christine O'Donnell 1
Wicked W. is dead   Harburg 2
witching
very w. time of night   Shakespeare 210
with
He that is not w. me   Bible 238
w. you—or without you   Martial 2
wither
Age cannot w. her   Shakespeare 402
w. into the truth   Yeats 8
withered
they w. all   Shakespeare 225
withers
it w. away   Engels 1
within
kingdom of God is w. you   Bible 303
witness
as God is my w.   Margaret Mitchell 5
bear false w.   Bible 59
bear w. of that Light   Bible 310
never ask a w.   David Graham 1
wits
w. are sure to madness near
    John Dryden 4
witticism
w. is an epigram   Nietzsche 5
witty
not w. in myself   Shakespeare 61
wives
absolute power over W.   Abigail Adams 2
changes when they are w.
    Shakespeare 95
man with seven w.   Nursery Rhymes 65
profane and old w.' fables   Bible 374
w. and mothers   Grimké 1
wizard
I'm a very bad W.   L. Frank Baum 6
We're off to see the w.   Harburg 7
wizards
meddle in the affairs of W.   Tolkien 8
woe
all our w.   Milton 17
woke
I w. up this morning   B. B. King 1
wolf
along came a w.   Halliwell 1
Big Bad W.   Frank E. Churchill 1
may become a w.   Film Lines 199
no w. behind him   Nabokov 10
spotted w. of sameness   Soyinka 1
there really was a w.   Aesop 1
W. in Sheep's Clothing   Aesop 3
w. is at the door   Charlotte Gilman 2
w. of the Steppes   Hesse 3
w. on the fold   Byron 5
w. rather than a man   Plautus 1
w. remains of a different   Inge 1
woman
ain't I a w.   Truth 1
as a w., I have no country
    Virginia Woolf 16
As you are w.   Graves 1
ask a w.   Thatcher 1
ask for w. voice
    Elizabeth Cady Stanton 11
been born a beautiful w.   Mauldin 3
being a w. is like being Irish
    Iris Murdoch 4

Being a w. is of special interest
    Lebowitz 2
body of a weak and feeble w.
    Elizabeth I 2
born of a w. Book of Common Prayer 2
But what is w.? Hannah Cowley 1
Catholic w. to avoid pregnancy
    Mencken 43
changeable always is w. Virgil 6
easy to marry a rich w. Thackeray 9
ever let a w. in my life Alan Jay Lerner 5
excellent thing in w. Shakespeare 317
feel like a natural w. Carole King 1
fighting for this w.'s honor
    "Groucho" Marx 26
folly of W.'s Rights Victoria 1
found a w. in bed with him Mizner 14
Frailty, thy name is w. Shakespeare 152
From God and a w. Truth 2
Funny business, a w.'s career
    Film Lines 7
giving w. all the opportunities
    Elizabeth Cady Stanton 10
good w. appeared to me Piercy 2
great w. Proverbs 129
hard to be a w. Wynette 2
I am w. hear me roar Reddy 1
I could be a good w. Thackeray 6
I saw a w. flayed Jonathan Swift 2
If a w. have long hair Bible 352
laid the blame on w. Nancy Astor 1
like a w. scorned Congreve 6
little w. standing by my man
    Hillary Clinton 1
lovely w. stoops to folly T. S. Eliot 54
lovely w. stoops to folly
    Oliver Goldsmith 6
never make a pretty w. your wife
    De Leon 1
No w. can call herself free Sanger 4
No w. can call herself free Sanger 3
No w. in my time Thatcher 2
no w. in the world Hawthorne 20
No w. needs intercourse Dworkin 2
none of w. born Shakespeare 379
nor w. either Shakespeare 181
not permitted to kill a w. Bierce 143
old as the w. he feels
    "Groucho" Marx 45
old w. tossed up Nursery Rhymes 76
old w. who lived in a shoe
    Nursery Rhymes 77
One is not born a w. de Beauvoir 2
one w. differs from another Mencken 1
one w. told the truth Rukeyser 2
Phenomenal w. Angelou 1
put an end to a w.'s liberty Burney 1
relation between man and w.
    Hawthorne 13
rights of w. Elizabeth Cady Stanton 9
she is always the w.
    Arthur Conan Doyle 15
she shall be called W. Bible 12
she walked like a w. Ray Davies 1
So you're the little w. Lincoln 60
support of the w. I love Edward 3
take some savage w. Tennyson 9
takes one w. twenty years
    Helen Rowland 3

talk of sheltering w.
    Elizabeth Cady Stanton 14
things to be done with a w. Durrell 1
thinking w. sleeps with monsters
    Rich 2
'Tis w.'s whole existence Byron 20
underestimate the power of a w.
    Advertising Slogans 69
very clever w. Kipling 4
was often a w. Virginia Woolf 12
What does a w. want Sigmund Freud 1
what every w. says Thomas Hardy 11
When a w. goes out Munro 1
Who can find a virtuous w. Bible 138
Why can't a w. Alan Jay Lerner 3
will raise w. Tocqueville 18
wine, w., and song Luther 4
w. always a w. Wollstonecraft 9
w. as old as she looks Proverbs 185
w. can hardly ever choose
    George Eliot 9
w. can make 19 or 20 Rivers 3
w. had better show more affection
    Austen 7
w. has got to love Rawlings 1
w. has to be twice as good Hurst 1
w. is like a tea bag Nancy Reagan 1
w. is only a w. Kipling 1
w. is perfected Plath 8
W. is the nigger of the world Ono 1
W. Killed with Kindness Heywood 1
w. loves her lover Byron 23
w. mov'd Shakespeare 10
w. must have money Virginia Woolf 9
w. only has the right Fonda 1
w. possessed of a common share
    Abigail Adams 3
w. schlemiel Abzug 1
w. the happiness she gives Laclos 1
W. was and is condemned Sanger 5
W. was God's second mistake
    Nietzsche 22
w. which is in every man's
    Faulkner 18
w. who shows genius Maria Mitchell 1
w. will always have to be better
    Eleanor Roosevelt 2
w. with fair opportunities Thackeray 3
w. without a man Dunn 1
w.'s desire is rarely other Coleridge 39
w.'s physical structure Brewer 1
w.'s place is in the home Proverbs 330
w.'s place is in the House Sayings 65
w.'s preaching is like
    Samuel Johnson 56
w.'s protector and defender
    Joseph P. Bradley 1
W.'s role has been that Sanger 6
W.'s virtue is man's
    Cornelia Otis Skinner 1
w.'s work is never done Proverbs 331
wrapped in a w.'s hide Shakespeare 7
womanhood
make an issue of my w. Film Lines 125
womanist
W. is to feminist Alice Walker 7
womb
from his mother's w. Shakespeare 396

wombs
think just with our w.
    Clare Boothe Luce 4
women
all men keep all w. Brownmiller 1
all the w. are strong Keillor 1
all W. are born Slaves Astell 1
binders full of w. Mitt Romney 2
blessed art thou among w. Bible 282
Certain w. should be struck Coward 6
d——d mob of scribbling w.
    Hawthorne 21
die of loneliness but for w. Yeats 59
difference between men and w.
    Margaret Mead 5
differences between men and w.
    Oliver Wendell Holmes, Jr. 32
emancipation of w. Ellen Key 1
extension of w.'s rights Fourier 1
Free w. are not w. Colette 1
freedom w. were supposed Burchill 1
happiest w. George Eliot 4
hell of w. is old age la Rochefoucauld 8
How can you shoot w. Herr 1
how w. pass the time O. Henry 3
how w. think Carrie Fisher 1
Human rights are w.'s Hillary Clinton 4
If w. didn't exist Aristotle Onassis 1
In the room the w. come and go
    T. S. Eliot 4
in w., love begets desire
    Jonathan Swift 37
infernal constancy of the w.
    George Bernard Shaw 4
law sees and treats w. MacKinnon 1
made W. humans Will Rogers 9
making w. artificially
    Janet Radcliffe Richards 1
man who doesn't know w. Chanel 3
managers of the affairs of w. Koran 8
married beneath me, all w. do
    Nancy Astor 4
Men and w., w. and men Jong 8
men and w. are created equal
    Elizabeth Cady Stanton 1
music and w. I cannot Pepys 4
Nature has given w. Samuel Johnson 25
nature of w. Mill 21
no matter how many w. Brooks 2
passing the love of w. Bible 88
proper function of w. George Eliot 5
respond to w. as well as men
    MacKinnon 2
saints were rarely married w.
    Anne Morrow Lindbergh 2
sexual life of adult w. Sigmund Freud 12
subjection of w. to men Mill 20
superiority of their w. Tocqueville 19
These impossible w. Aristophanes 5
twisted and pruned w. Janet Richards 2
Very learned w. Voltaire 12
War Between Men and W. Thurber 4
Well-behaved w. seldom Ulrich 1
When w. kiss Mencken 12
whole people—w. as well as men
    Susan B. Anthony 3
w., their rights and nothing less
    Susan B. Anthony 1

wore

she w. a yellow ribbon
Folk and Anonymous Songs 70

work

All w. and no play   Proverbs 334
do a man's w.   Modern Proverbs 9
Equal Pay for Equal W.
Susan B. Anthony 2
get from his w.   Gaddis 1
got rich through hard w.   Marquis 2
Hard w. never hurt anyone
Modern Proverbs 39
Hard w. never killed anybody   Bergen 1
harder you w. the more
Esther Eberstadt Brooke 1
hate to w. for a living   Helen Rowland 1
honest man's the noblest w.   Pope 26
I like w.   Jerome K. Jerome 1
I like what is in w.   Conrad 13
I w. for a Government I despise
Keynes 1
If w. was a good thing   Leonard 1
It will never w.   Jong 8
Let's go to w.   Film Lines 146
most of my w. sitting down   Benchley 7
Nice w. if you can get it   Gershwin 9
off to w. we go   Morey 2
piece of w. to perform   Twain 1
rid a great deal of w.   Pepys 3
sex to do the w. of love
Mary McCarthy 4
to love and to w.   Sigmund Freud 23
We w. in the dark   Henry James 12
What a piece of w. is a man
Shakespeare 181
Whistle While You W.   Morey 4
woman's w. is never done   Proverbs 331
W.!   Television Catchphrases 43
W. as if you were to live
Benjamin Franklin 30
W. before play   Proverbs 335
W. consists of whatever   Twain 16
W. expands so as to fill   Parkinson 1
w. goes on   Edward M. Kennedy 1
w. he is supposed to be doing
Benchley 13
w. is done by people   Peter 3
W. is love made visible   Gibran 4
W. is the curse   Wilde 109
w. of God   William Blake 6
w. of the world   Sandburg 5
w. that aspires   Conrad 2
write if you get w.
Radio Catchphrases 3

worked

they've always w. for me
Hunter S. Thompson 9
w. my way down   Welles 4
w. myself up   "Groucho" Marx 10

worker

distort the w.   Karl Marx 10
w. in the vineyard   Benedict XVI 1

workers

W. of the world   Marx and Engels 8

working

end up w. for them   Sykes 1
it isn't w.   Major 1
Protect the W. Girl   Edgar Smith 1
this w.-day world   Shakespeare 83

w. class hero   Lennon 6
w. on the railroad
Folk and Anonymous Songs 37

workman

poor w. blames his tools   Proverbs 238

works

He w. his work   Tennyson 22
memory that only w.   Carroll 37
seen the future; and it w.   Steffens 2

workshop

idle brain is the Devil's w.   Proverbs 151

world

all the W., and his Wife
Jonathan Swift 32
All the w.'s a stage   Shakespeare 88
all's right with the w.   Robert Browning 1
appointment at the end of the w.
Dinesen 3
before the whole w.   Molière 9
begin the w. over again   Thomas Paine 7
brave new w.   Shakespeare 447
breast of the new w.
F. Scott Fitzgerald 32
Bring me back the w.   Film Lines 200
can change the w.   Margaret Mead 10
dark w. is going to submit   Du Bois 10
destruction of the whole w.
David Hume 3
End of the W.   Stipe 1
Feed the w.   Geldof 1
first w. war   Haeckel 2
First W. War   Repington 1
for the w., which seems
Matthew Arnold 18
God so loved the w.   Bible 315
government of the w.
Winston Churchill 41
Had we but w. enough
Andrew Marvell 10
Hog Butcher for the W.   Sandburg 1
I am not in this w.   Perls 1
I'll make me a w.
James Weldon Johnson 4
I'm the king of the w.   Film Lines 176
I'm w.-famous   Richler 1
in a w. I never made   Housman 7
In the beginning all the W.
John Locke 5
indifferent w.   Jong 7
interpreted the w.   Karl Marx 3
It's a mad w.   Dickens 61
It's a small w.   Proverbs 275
Joy to the w.   Watts 3
Laugh, and the w. laughs   Wilcox 1
letter to the W.   Emily Dickinson 19
lie will go round the w.   Proverbs 168
light the w.   John F. Kennedy 15
limits of my w.   Wittgenstein 2
little wisdom the w. is governed
Oxenstierna 1
looking uncomfortably to the w.
Tom Hayden 1
Love makes the w. go round
Proverbs 179
love with the whole w.   Erdrich 1
lover's quarrel with the w.   Frost 23
make such a w.   Byron 4
Make the W. Over   Sumner 4

makes the whole w. kin
Shakespeare 250
Money makes the w. go around   Ebb 2
My country is the w.   Thomas Paine 23
new w. order
George Herbert Walker Bush 7
new w. order
George Herbert Walker Bush 12
new w. order
George Herbert Walker Bush 10
new w. order   Martin Luther King, Jr. 1
not the end of the w.
Modern Proverbs 27
old, unknown w.   F. Scott Fitzgerald 34
one-third of the w. is asleep   Rusk 1
Playboy of the Western W.   Synge 2
preservation of the W.   Thoreau 37
rescued the entire w.   Talmud 8
rightly call a New W.   Vespucci 1
rules the w.   Proverbs 133
saw the vision of the w.   Tennyson 6
say to all the w.   Shakespeare 131
see in the w.   Mohandas Gandhi 7
shot heard round the w.
Ralph Waldo Emerson 6
stood against the w.   Shakespeare 118
Stop the W.   Bricusse and Newley 2
submitted to a candid w.   Jefferson 4
such a lot of w. to see   Johnny Mercer 6
teach the w. to sing
Advertising Slogans 33
Ten Days That Shook the W.
John Reed 1
these men saved the w.
William Jefferson "Bill" Clinton 5
Third W.   Sauvy 1
this new w. order outlast   P. J. Bailey 1
this working-day w.   Shakespeare 83
though the w. perish   Ferdinand 1
Top of the w.   Film Lines 187
understood all over the w.   Haydn 2
uses of this w.   Shakespeare 150
watch the w. burn   Film Lines 59
way the w. ends   T. S. Eliot 67
We are the w.   Michael Jackson 1
we have the W. Wide Web
Douglas Adams 11
What the w. needs now   Hal David 2
whole w. in his hands
Folk and Anonymous Songs 34
whole w. is watching
Political Slogans 37
whole w. smiles with you   Goodwin 1
whole w. stills to listen   McCullough 1
why the w. wags   T. H. White 1
Woman is the nigger of the w.   Ono 1
Workers of the w.   Marx and Engels 8
w., the flesh   Book of Common Prayer 8
w. according to Garp   John Irving 1
w. as my parish   John Wesley 1
w. began without man   Lévi-Strauss 1
w. breaks everyone   Hemingway 10
w. in a grain of sand   William Blake 14
w. is a fine place   Hemingway 24
w. is charged with the grandeur
Gerard Manley Hopkins 2
w. is everything   Wittgenstein 1
w. is going crazy   Rock 1
w. is puddle-wonderful e.e. cummings 5

world (cont.):
w. is sad and dreary   Stephen Foster 4
w. is too much with us
    William Wordsworth 21
w. itself was going to last
    George Bernard Shaw 30
w. loves a clown   Cole Porter 21
w. market for about five
    Thomas J. Watson, Jr. 1
w. may end tonight   Robert Browning 14
w. must be made safe
    Woodrow Wilson 15
w. owes me a living   Morey 1
w. owes you a living   Burdette 1
W. peace cannot be safeguarded
    Schuman 1
w. was all before them   Milton 42
w. was mad   Sabatini 1
w. will be as one   Lennon 10
w. will end in fire   Frost 10
w. will little note   Lincoln 42
w. will make a beaten path
    Ralph Waldo Emerson 51
w. without end
    Book of Common Prayer 11
w. without war   Handey 2
w. would have been changed   Pascal 2
w. would split open   Rukeyser 2
w.-destroying Time   Bhagavadgita 3
w.'s best pitcher   Ruth 1
w.'s history is the w.'s   Schiller 2
w.'s last night   Donne 8
w.'s mine oyster   Shakespeare 67
yourself and the w.   Kafka 6
worldly
all my w. goods
    Book of Common Prayer 18
w. philosophers   Heilbroner 1
worlds
best among all possible w.   Leibniz 3
best of all possible w.   Voltaire 8
best of possible w.   Voltaire 7
between two w.   Matthew Arnold 2
destroyer of w.   Oppenheimer 3
infinity of w.   Bruno 1
w. revolve like ancient women
    T. S. Eliot 16
WorldWideWeb
W.: Proposal   Berners-Lee 1
worm
early bird catches the w.   Proverbs 80
rather tough w.   W. S. Gilbert 46
You have tasted your w.   Spooner 4
worms
Then w. shall try   Andrew Marvell 13
w. have eaten them   Shakespeare 94
worry
Don't w., be happy   Baba 1
What—me w.   Kurtzman 1
you need never w. about   Film Lines 62
worse
altered her person for the w.
    Jonathan Swift 2
books had been any w.
    Raymond Chandler 9
crime is w. than murder
    Irving R. Kaufman 1
for better for w.
    Book of Common Prayer 15

I follow the w.   Ovid 4
modern life out to be w.   Orwell 11
smell far w. than weeds
    Shakespeare 425
w. appear the better reason
    Aristophanes 1
w. appear the better reason   Milton 27
w. than provincial   Henry James 5
w. than the disease   Francis Bacon 19
w. than wicked   Punch 2
worship
duty to w. the sun   John Morley 1
nuns and mothers w. images   Yeats 39
various modes of w.   Gibbon 2
worships
Everybody w.   David Foster Wallace 8
worst
Democracy is the w. form   Briffault 1
democracy is the w. form
    Winston Churchill 34
it was the w. of times   Dickens 97
one's w. moments   Donleavy 2
prepare for the w.   Proverbs 147
so much good in the w.
    Edward W. Hoch 1
This is the w.   Shakespeare 303
tomorrow do thy w.   John Dryden 8
w. are full of passionate   Yeats 29
w. is yet to come   Twain 49
w. sort of tyranny   Edmund Burke 12
w. thing they have ever done   Prejean 1
w. things   F. Scott Fitzgerald 49
w. time of the year   Andrewes 1
You do your w.   Winston Churchill 20
your w. nightmare   Film Lines 145
worth
Because I'm w. it
    Advertising Slogans 74
do things w. the writing
    Benjamin Franklin 16
If a thing is w. doing   Chesterton 18
is w. doing well   Chesterfield 2
life is w. living   Santayana 2
not w. going to see   Samuel Johnson 96
Not w. his salt   Petronius 3
not w. living   Plato 1
Nothing that is w. knowing   Wilde 9
Paris is well w. a mass   Henri 2
what is w. knowing   Wilde 51
w. any number of old ladies   Faulkner 16
w. a pitcher of warm spit
    John Nance Garner 1
w. cheating for   W. C. Fields 14
w. doing at all   Chesterfield 2
w. doing well   Proverbs 76
w. the fighting for   Hemingway 24
worthy
laborer is w. of his hire   Bible 294
We're not w.
    Television Catchphrases 62
w. of your million Trotskyites
    Ginsberg 2
wot
God w.   T. E. Brown 1
She knows w.'s w.   Dickens 12
would
He w., wouldn't he   Rice-Davies 1
wound
never felt a w.   Shakespeare 32

wounded
Bury my heart at W. Knee   Benét 2
charge when they're w.   Mauldin 4
wounds
Time w. all heels   Case 1
woven
w. of many strands   Ralph Ellison 2
wrath
grapes of w.   Julia Ward Howe 1
soft answer turneth away w.   Bible 132
sun go down upon your w.   Bible 366
tygers of w. are wiser   William Blake 7
wreck
I came to explore the w.   Rich 4
wreckage
w. of a civilization   Margaret Mitchell 2
wrecks
my errors and w.   Ezra Pound 30
wrestle
intolerable w. with words   T. S. Eliot 102
Never w. with a pig
    Modern Proverbs 68
wrestled
I w. with reality   Mary Chase 1
w. with his conscience   Eban 2
wrestles
He that w. with us   Edmund Burke 22
wretch
I beheld the w.   Mary Shelley 3
wretched
w. hive of scum and villainy
    George Lucas 4
w. refuse of your teeming   Lazarus 2
wretches
w. hang   Pope 6
w. hired by those   Samuel Johnson 10
Wrigley
historic W. Field   Ernie Banks 1
wringer
caught in a big fat w.   John N. Mitchell 2
wrinkle
W. in Time   L'Engle 1
wrinkled
old man with w. dugs   T. S. Eliot 51
writ
I never w.   Shakespeare 430
name was w. in water   Keats 24
write
difficult to w. a good life   Strachey 2
great man can w. it   Wilde 11
I don't like to w.   Norris 1
I shall w. bad if   Françoise Sagan 2
if she is to w. fiction   Virginia Woolf 9
man may w. at any time
    Samuel Johnson 44
never try to w. romances   Hawthorne 4
That is why I w.   Head 1
to read a novel, I w. one   Disraeli 33
virtues we w. in water   Shakespeare 453
w. against your name   Grantland Rice 1
w. faster than anyone   Liebling 2
w. for the youth   F. Scott Fitzgerald 2
w. if you get work   Radio Catchphrases 3
W. me as one that loves   Leigh Hunt 3
w. that history myself
    Winston Churchill 38
w. the other way   Jiménez 1
w. the saddest lines   Neruda 5

w. things worth reading
Benjamin Franklin 16

writer
chase the w.   Julian Barnes 1
no eminent w.   George Bernard Shaw 7
Only a mediocre w.   Maugham 11
original w. is not he   Chateaubriand 1
true friend and a good w.   E. B. White 8
w. creates his own precursors   Borges 6
w. should be   Hemingway 26
w.'s only responsibility   Faulkner 16

writerly
Opposite the w. text   Barthes 3

writers
put upon w.   Sinclair Lewis 3
universities stifle w.
Flannery O'Connor 4
W. are always selling   Didion 2

writes
moving finger w.   Edward FitzGerald 3
w. his time   T. S. Eliot 71

writing
almost all legal w.   Rodell 1
easy w.'s vile hard
Richard Brinsley Sheridan 1
get it in w.   Gypsy Rose Lee 1
good w. is swimming
F. Scott Fitzgerald 52
idea of w. the decline   Gibbon 10
incurable disease of w.   Juvenal 4
no talent for w.   Benchley 10
raven like a w.-desk   Carroll 14
rid of many things by w. them
Hemingway 16
Take away the art of w.
Chateaubriand 2
this is the w.   Bible 190
Vigorous w. is concise   Strunk 1
W. about music   Mull 1
W. free verse is like   Frost 18
w. history with lightning
Woodrow Wilson 26
W. is so difficult   Jessamyn West 1
W. is turning one's worst   Donleavy 2

writings
w. of the Greeks   Omar 1

written
History is w. by the survivors
Modern Proverbs 41
I have w. only five   Wilde 118
I love having w.
Robert Louis Stevenson 23
like having w.   Norris 1
paper it's w. on   Goldwyn 8
Philosophy is w.   Galileo 1
power of the w. word   Conrad 4
w. by the hand of   Richelieu 1
w. on subway walls   Paul Simon 2
w. without effort   Samuel Johnson 108

wrong
asking the w. questions   Pynchon 3
atone for the w.
John M. Harlan (1833–1911) 3
customer is never w.   Ritz 1
do a little w.   Shakespeare 80
doing what was w.   Tindal 1
Frenchmen Can't Be W.   Rose 2
he done her w.
Folk and Anonymous Songs 23

I must be w.   Wilde 54
I was w. to have thought
John Foster Dulles 4
If anything can go w.
Modern Proverbs 100
if I called the w. number   Thurber 6
If slavery is not w.   Lincoln 43
If there is a w. thing to do   Orwell 17
if you w. us   Shakespeare 76
In fact, it was w.
William Jefferson "Bill" Clinton 10
It is not even w.   Pauli 1
It was a w. number   Auster 1
king can do no w.   Blackstone 6
King can do no w.   Proverbs 160
multitude is always in the w.
Earl of Roscommon 1
neat, plausible, and w.   Mencken 22
not present are always w.   Destouches 1
Not that there's anything w.
Larry Charles 1
nothing w. with America
William Jefferson "Bill" Clinton 3
nothing w. with your television
Television Catchphrases 47
on the w. side of   Nash 14
rather be w., by God, with Plato
Cicero 14
rather be w. with Dante   Muggeridge 1
right deed for the w. reason
T. S. Eliot 93
that is a w. one   Samuel Johnson 66
that was w.   Disraeli 5
turned into the w. person   Tyler 2
When women go w.   Mae West 11
W. forever on the throne
James Russell Lowell 2
w. war, at the w. place   Omar Bradley 2

wrong-doing
w. of one generation   Hawthorne 14

wrongs
Two w. will not make   Proverbs 313

wrote
God w. it   Stowe 6
No man but a blockhead ever w.
Samuel Johnson 85
when I w. that book   Jonathan Swift 38
w. my will across the sky
T. E. Lawrence 1

wrought
What hath God w.   Bible 68

wunnerful
W., w.   Television Catchphrases 40

Wynken
W., Blynken, and Nod   Eugene Field 1
W. and Blynken are two   Eugene Field 2

X

Xanadu
In X. did Kubla Khan   Coleridge 19

Xerox
X. makes everybody a publisher
McLuhan 11

X-rays
I shall call them "X."   Roentgen 1

Y

yabba
Y., Dabba Do
Television Catchphrases 19

yacht
walking onto a y.   Carly Simon 1

Yale
for Country, and for Y.   Durand 1
whaleship was my Y. College   Melville 4
wholesale libel on a Y. prom
Dorothy Parker 47

yam
I y. what I y.   Segar 2

Yankee
One is Y. Doodle   Ulysses S. Grant 7
Y. Doodle came to town
Folk and Anonymous Songs 84
Y. Doodle dandy   Cohan 1

Yankees
Rooting for the Y.   Joe E. Lewis 2

Yanks
Y. are coming   Cohan 5

yawning
one man's y.   Robert Burton 2

yawp
barbaric y.   Whitman 9

yeah
She loves you y., y., y.
Lennon and McCartney 2
Y., baby   Film Lines 18
Y., y.   Morgenbesser 1

year
better y. than he did   Ruth 1
my thirtieth y. to heaven
Dylan Thomas 10
Next y. in Jerusalem   Anonymous 20
on nothing a y.   Thackeray 5
That time of y.   Shakespeare 421
try to keep it all the y.   Dickens 47
Wait till next y.   Sayings 58
Y., n. A period of three   Bierce 140

years
At 20 y. of age   Benjamin Franklin 20
first hundred y.   Modern Proverbs 30
For three y., out of key   Ezra Pound 9
Four score and seven y. ago   Lincoln 41
good to eat a thousand y.   Ginsberg 9
hundred y. hence
Ralph Waldo Emerson 35
lasts for a thousand y.
Winston Churchill 15
next thirty y.   F. Scott Fitzgerald 23
one hundred y. of solitude
García Márquez 3
second and third y.   Yamamoto 2
Spent twenty y. there one night
Dick Gregory 1
Spinner of the Y.   Thomas Hardy 26
than you were four y. ago
Ronald W. Reagan 4
thousand y. in thy sight   Bible 116
When nine hundred y. old
George Lucas 17
Y. from now   Robert Anderson 2
y. of praise   May Sarton 1

Yeats
Y. is laid   Yeats 63
Y. is laid to rest   Auden 23

yellow
diverged in a y. wood   Frost 8
He put down *The Y. Book*   Betjeman 1
kill the y. man   Springsteen 5
paved with y. brick   L. Frank Baum 1
she wore a y. ribbon
            Folk and Anonymous Songs 70
tie a y. ribbon   Levine 1
We all live in a y. submarine
            Lennon and McCartney 10
y. brick road   Harburg 6
y. leaf   Shakespeare 389
y. polkadot bikini   Paul J. Vance 1
y. rose in Texas
            Folk and Anonymous Songs 86
y. stripes and dead armadillos
                                            Hightower 2
yelps
loudest y. for liberty   Samuel Johnson 30
yes
Y., I have   DiMaggio 1
Y., Virginia   Church 2
Y., we can   Political Slogans 39
y. I said y.   Joyce 22
Y. we can   Toussaint 1
yesterday
maybe it was y.   Camus 1
today more than y.   Gérard 1
We were saying y.
Y., all my troubles
            Lennon and McCartney 7
Y., December 7, 1941
            Franklin D. Roosevelt 25
yesteryear
snows of y.   Villon 1
yet
but not y.   Augustine 3
Christmas Y. to Come   Dickens 46
so near and y. so far   Tennyson 32
yew
too far from the y.-tree   T. S. Eliot 116
Yid
PUT THE ID BACK IN Y.   Roth 3
yield
find, and not to y.   Tennyson 26
to y. to it   Clementina Stirling Graham 1
y. to it   Wilde 25
yo
Y., Adrian   Film Lines 148
yo-ho-ho
Y., and a bottle of rum
            Robert Louis Stevenson 8
Yoknapatawpha
JEFFERSON, Y. CO.   Faulkner 6
YOLO
MOTTO NIGGA Y.   Drake 1
yond
Y. Cassius has a lean   Shakespeare 99
yonder
into the wild blue y.   Robert Crawford 1
through y. window   Shakespeare 32
Y. a maid   Thomas Hardy 27
Yorick
Alas, poor Y.   Shakespeare 226
York
this sun of Y.   Shakespeare 1
you
Y. ain't heard nothin' yet   Jolson 2
y. are the music   T. S. Eliot 115

Y. can trust your car
            Advertising Slogans 116
Y. deserve a break today
            Advertising Slogans 80
Y. have delighted us   Austen 9
Y. lose   Coolidge 8
Y. were silly like us   Auden 21
young
always the y. to fall   Phil Ochs 1
Angry Y. Man   Leslie Paul 1
Conservatives are y. people   Tolstoy 14
corrupting the minds of the y.   Plato 1
crime of being a y. man
            William Pitt, Earl of Chatham 1
daring y. man   Leybourne 1
endearing y. charms   Thomas Moore 1
get out while we're y.   Springsteen 2
give me the y. man
            Robert Louis Stevenson 4
Go West, y. man   Greeley 2
good die y.   Proverbs 124
Hello, y. lovers   Hammerstein 19
if he be caught y.   Samuel Johnson 70
if you're y. at heart   Carolyn Leigh 1
I'll die y.   Lenny Bruce 4
Live fast, die y.   Willard Motley 1
love's y. dream   Thomas Moore 3
married when they were y.
            Fanny Dixwell Holmes 1
one of two things, y. or dead
                                    Dorothy Parker 46
only y. men in libraries
            Ralph Waldo Emerson 4
radical when y.   Frost 19
rubbed it into the y.   Maugham 7
she is a y. thing   Nursery Rhymes 3
So y., my lord, and true
                                    Shakespeare 284
so y. a body   Shakespeare 78
teach the y. idea   Thomson 2
to be y. was very heaven
            William Wordsworth 23
too y. to take up golf
            Franklin P. Adams 2
we that are y.   Shakespeare 320
We're only y. once   Modern Proverbs 101
when they were y.
            William Jefferson "Bill" Clinton 5
Whom the gods love dies y.   Menander 1
y., gifted, and black   Hansberry 2
y. always have   Crisp 1
y. and easy   Dylan Thomas 6
y. and irresponsible   George W. Bush 23
y. know everything   Wilde 70
y. lady named Bright   Buller 1
y. lady of Niger   Monkhouse 1
y. man yet   Francis Bacon 16
y. man's fancy   Tennyson 5
y. men shall see visions   Bible 193
Y. men think old men
                                    George Chapman 1
y. men tossing   Yeats 19
y. shoulders   Spark 1
younger
y. man has all the joy   Wilde 83
Y. than springtime   Hammerstein 17
y. than that now   Dylan 10
your
Y. mind and you   Ezra Pound 7

yours
y. is the Earth   Kipling 33
yourself
do it y.   Proverbs 319
hide it from y.   Orwell 47
Keep y. to y.   Dickens 8
speak for y.   Alden 1
youth
forward Y. that would appear
                                    Andrew Marvell 1
I remember my y.   Conrad 20
If y. knew; if age could   Estienne 1
I'm y., I'm joy   Barrie 13
my opponent's y.   Ronald W. Reagan 8
of glamour—of y.   Conrad 19
overcome y. and skill   Sayings 1
poets in our y.   William Wordsworth 19
Proud and insolent y.   Barrie 12
subtle thief of y.   Milton 9
Thou hast nor y., nor age
                                    Shakespeare 255
To get back my y.   Wilde 43
wished for in y.   Goethe 15
Y. . . . is wasted
            George Bernard Shaw 57
Y. must be served   Proverbs 336
y. replies, I can
            Ralph Waldo Emerson 46
y. restraining reckless   Yeats 12
y. that must fight   Herbert C. Hoover 5
y. to fortune   Thomas Gray 10
yuppie
Exercise is the y. version   Ehrenreich 1

Z

zeal
half the z.   Shakespeare 452
men of z.   Brandeis 9
Zen
moment of Z.
            Television Catchphrases 15
Z. and the Art   Pirsig 1
zenith
dropped from the z.   Milton 25
zero
z. at the bone   Emily Dickinson 24
z.-sum games   von Neumann 1
Zion
when we remembered Z.   Bible 122
zip
Z. a dee doo dah   Wrubel 1
zip-a-dee-doo-dah
Z.   Ray Gilbert 1
zipless
z. fuck   Jong 5
zombie
in your head, Z.   O'Riordan 1
zone
He who, from z. to z.
            William Cullen Bryant 1
into the Twilight Z.   Serling 3
next stop, the Twilight Z.   Serling 1
we call the Twilight Z.   Serling 4
Zurich
gnomes in Z.   Harold Wilson 1
specialist in Z.   Woody Allen 20

CREDITS